D0138570

The Hornbook

Dr. Johnson described the hornbook as "the first book of children, covered with horn to keep it unsoiled." Pardon's New General English Dictionary (1758) defined it as "A leaf of written or printed paper pasted on a board, and covered with horn, for children to learn their letters by, and to prevent their being torn and daubed."

It was used throughout Europe and America between the late 1400s and the middle 1700s.

Shaped like an old-fashioned butter paddle, the first hornbooks were made of wood. The paper lesson the child was to learn was fastened to the wooden paddle and covered with a piece of horn. The transparent strip of horn was made by soaking a cow's horn in hot water and peeling it away at the thickness of a piece of celluloid. The horn was necessary to protect the lesson from the damp and perhaps grubby hands of the child. Hornbooks commonly contained the alphabet, the vowels, and the Lord's Prayer. Later hornbooks were made of various materials: brass, copper, silver, ivory, bronze, leather, and stone.

As the art of printing advanced, the hornbook was supplanted by the primer in the book form we know today. Subsequently West Publishing Company developed its "Hornbook Series", a series of scholarly and well-respected one volume treatises on particular areas of law. Today they are widely used by law students, lawyers and judges.

WEST'S LAW SCHOOL
ADVISORY BOARD

JESSE H. CHOPER
Professor of Law,
University of California, Berkeley

DAVID P. CURRIE
Professor of Law, University of Chicago

YALE KAMISAR
Professor of Law, University of Michigan

MARY KAY KANE
Dean and Professor of Law, University of California,
Hastings College of the Law

WAYNE R. LaFAVE
Professor of Law, University of Illinois

ARTHUR R. MILLER
Professor of Law, Harvard University

GRANT S. NELSON
Professor of Law, University of California, Los Angeles

JAMES J. WHITE
Professor of Law, University of Michigan

CHARLES ALAN WRIGHT
Charles Alan Wright Chair in Federal Courts
The University of Texas

MODERN COMMUNICATION LAW

By

Harvey L. Zuckman
*Ordinary Professor of Law and
Director, Institute for Communications Law Studies
The Catholic University of America*

Robert L. Corn-Revere
*Member Adjunct Law Faculty
The Catholic University of America and
Member, Hogan & Hartson,
Washington, D.C.*

Robert M. Frieden
*Professor of Telecommunications
College of Communications
Pennsylvania State University*

Charles H. Kennedy
*Member Adjunct Law Faculty
The Catholic University of America and
Of Counsel, Morrison & Foersier,
Washington, D.C.*

**General Editor
Harvey L. Zuckman**

**HORNBOOK SERIES®
STUDENT EDITION**

Hornbook Series, *WESTLAW,* and the West Group symbol
are registered trademarks used herein under license.

COPYRIGHT © 1999 By WEST GROUP
           610 Opperman Drive
           P.O. Box 64526
           St. Paul, MN 55164–0526
           1–800–328–9352

All rights reserved
Printed in the United States of America

ISBN 0–314–21176–4

 TEXT IS PRINTED ON 10% POST
CONSUMER RECYCLED PAPER

For George Zuckman who wanted to be a journalist
but was never given the opportunity and for his
granddaughter Jill Zuckman who was.

————————

For Sigrid Fry-Revere, whose love, inspiration and,
above all, patience, made this book possible. And
for Nathan, Ian, Jackson and Lauren, because
children deserve a strong First Amendment too.

————————

For Alex and Elizabeth Frieden
with the hope they pursue life-long projects

————————

For Marney, who has endured the writing
of three books with loyalty, patience
and good humor.

*

Using This Hornbook

This Hornbook is an abridgement. The full text is found in the three-volume Practitioner Treatise edition. Sections and parts of sections that appear in the three-volume work have been omitted here. Footnotes have also been omitted.

In most instances the reader will be able to determine whether additional material can be found in the Practitioner's Edition. However, to avoid clutter, many shorter omissions are not designated.

To acquire more detailed information concerning omissions and how to best utilize the material found in this abridged edition, read the material below.

Text Omissions and Footnotes

1. When entire sections or chapters are omitted from this edition, their titles are retained in this Hornbook without accompanying text. Many omitted subsections are shown in the same way. All chapter, section and subsection headings are retained in the Table of Contents with asterisks denoting their omissions.

2. When the omission of textual material is shorter in length than a section or subsection, no direct indication of the omission is given. This very occasional inconvenience is preferable to repeated and intrusive indications that something has been deleted.

3. When short textual passages containing footnote references are omitted, the text superior numbers will not be consecutive. This alerts the reader to such omissions. Omissions of text not containing footnote references are not indicated, but they are few in number and should have little impact on the usefulness of this work.

4. Cross-references to text and footnotes are keyed to the Practitioner's Edition only.

Preface to Hornbook Edition

Every effort has been made to make this edition of *Modern Communication Law* a worthy and economical tool for busy law students, instructors and lawyers. While considerably shorter in length than the three-volume Practitioner's Edition, deletions were made only after careful consideration and then only if the material omitted was determined not to be central to legal education in communication law. Of course, the extended edition is always available for detailed reference when this abridgement is silent on a topic.

Most omissions in this Hornbook are clearly deliberated in the table of cases and in the text itself by asterisks after section headings, facilitating cross-reference to the larger work.

It is the co-authors' and editor's hope that this one-volume treatise will encourage greater interest, study and research in the important area of communication law.

HARVEY L. ZUCKMAN
ROBERT CORN-REVERE
ROBERT M. FRIEDEN
CHARLES H. KENNEDY

Washington, D.C.
March, 1999

Preface to Practitioner's Edition

We like to think of this work as the first comprehensive communication law treatise of the Information Age. As we prepare to cross the invisible border into the next millennium, it is important to understand that the once separate media technologies and the disciplines of media law, common carrier law, cable and broadcasting law, computer law and the overarching principles of the First Amendment governing the technologies are all interrelated as never before. This coming together of technology and law is a major feature of the Information Age. As Mr. Robinson might have said to young Benjamin in the classic motion picture "The Graduate" had it been filmed today, "Ben, I have one word for you and that word is "convergence."

Telephone companies provide cable television and high speed data transmission; cable television systems provide telephone service; and the Internet provides a common medium for what we once considered separate radio, television, telephone and publishing media. With such convergence comes a necessary mandate for change in the way legislators, regulators and judges view telecommunications and information technology and the law that affects them.

In addition to convergence, volatility in the law has been fostered by the emergence in recent years of dynamic new media of communication and information. Since this book project began, the Internet became a mainstream medium of communication and the World Wide Web emerged; a domestic Direct Broadcasting Satellite ("DBS") industry came into being; a plan to move the television signal from the longstanding NTSC analog standard to digital transmission was adopted; long imposed restrictions that prevented common carriers from providing video service were eliminated, new forms of wireless communications were authorized and competition came to long distance and even local telephony, a field historically characterized and regulated as a natural monopoly. During this same time, the basic statutory charter governing electronic media, the Communications Act of 1934, was broadly revamped through the enactment of the Telecommunications Act of 1996. Quite literally, there has been more change in communication law in the span it took to produce this treatise than in all the years from the point of commencement of our work back to the passage of the Radio Act of 1927.

This work has the ambitious goal of tracking and analyzing the converging bodies of law that have developed for both print and electronic media of communication and information. It is our hope that we accomplish that goal and by doing so provide, for the first time, a comprehensive reference tool for the benefit of the practitioners and students who will be confronting the new Information Age.

HARVEY L. ZUCKMAN
ROBERT L. CORN-REVERE
ROBERT M. FRIEDEN
CHARLES H. KENNEDY

Washington, D.C.
December 1998

WESTLAW® Overview

Modern Communications Law by Harvey L. Zuckman, Robert L. Corn Revere, Robert M. Frieden and Charles H. Kennedy, offers a detailed and comprehensive treatment of basic rules, principles and issues relating to communications law. To supplement the information contained in this book, you can access Westlaw, a computer-assisted legal research service of West Group. Westlaw contains a broad array of legal resources, including case law, statutes, expert commentary, current developments and various other types of information.

Learning how to use these materials effectively will enhance your legal research abilities. To help you coordinate the information in the book with your Westlaw research, this volume contains an appendix listing Westlaw databases, search techniques and sample problems.

THE PUBLISHER

*

Acknowledgments

Harvey L. Zuckman acknowledges with appreciation the assistance of Professor Clifford S. Fishman who reviewed the portion of the manuscript discussing search and seizure of obscene materials, Howard Kolodny, Esquire, who reviewed the portion of the manuscript discussing the history of motion picture censorship and Charlotte S. Zuckman, who endured with patience and considerable tolerance the preparation of this work for more than a decade even when it threatened physically to take over our home. Professor Zuckman expresses appreciation to the staff of the Columbus School of Law Library, including Patrick Petit, Diana Botluk, Yvett Brown, Frances M. Brillantine and Matthew Mahaffie, whose assistance added greatly to the depth and breadth of the research. He also expresses appreciation to Professor Dan B. Dobbs of the University of Arizona College of Law for his encouragement and advice in the abridgement process, and to the many students who served as his research assistants over the years, including Michael Donahue, Jennifer Nix, Allyn Engelstein, Kate Reese, Paula Cagnacci, Paul Nagle, Theresa McClendon, Mike Zuckman, Steve Harris and Gie Kim. He also owes very great thanks to deans of the Columbus School of Law, including Ralph J. Rohner, Bernard Dobranski and George E. Garvey, for their continuing support and encouragement. Appreciation is expressed to Herman B. Siegel, M.D., and Hubert J. Alpert, M.D., whose medical skill and dedication kept the author going through some difficult times. But the greatest thanks is owed to Arthienyer Laurie Fraser, secretary and wordprocessor par excellence, for the efficiency, dispatch and accuracy with which she prepared the manuscript for this work and archived the many drafts. Truly, without Laurie this work would never have made it to the press.

Further appreciation is expressed to the many publishers and authors who gave permission to reprint their copyrighted material. In chapter three (The Commercial Speech Doctrine and Control of Advertising by Private Civil Actions and Public Regulation): Bruce P. Keller, Esquire for material from his discussion of the Lanham Act in New York University School of Law's 1985 Annual Survey of American Law at pp. 576-577. In chapter four (Privacy and the Media): Professor Dan B. Dobbs and West Publishing Company for material in REMEDIES 537 (West 1973) and REMEDIES § 7.3 (5) (West 2d ed. 1993); The University of California Press Journals for material from William L. Prosser, *Privacy*, 48 Cal. L. Rev. at 389 (1960); Professor Diane L. Zimmerman for material from her article *Requiem for a Heavyweight: A Farewell to Warren and Brandeis's Privacy Tort*, 68 Cornell L. Rev. at 341 (1983); Clark Boardman Callaghan Publishers for material originally published in J. THOMAS MCCARTHY, THE RIGHTS OF PUBLICITY AND PRIVACY § 11.8 [B] (1987). (This material is available from Clark Boardman Callaghan, 155 Pfingsten Road, Dearfield, IL (1-

800-323-1336)); the Harvard Law Review Association for material in Samuel D. Warren and Louis D. Brandeis, *The Right to Privacy*, 4 Harv. L. Rev. at 213-214 (1890); The American Law Institute for permission to quote from or paraphrase sections 652A, 652C and Comment *d* thereto and section 652D and Comment *a* thereto (copyright 1977 by the American Law Institute and reprinted with permission); the Kentucky Law Journal for material from Dean John Henry Wigmore, *The Right Against False Attribution of Belief or Utterance*, 4 Ky. L. J. No. 8, p. 7 (1916). In chapter five (The New Media Law of Defamation): Martin J. Gaynes, T. Barton Carter, Juliet Dee and West Publishing Company for permission to use material from chapter two of MASS COMMUNICATION LAW pp. 44-111 (West 4th ed. 1994); Aspen Law & Business/Panel Publishers, a division of Aspen Publishers, Inc. for material in JOHN HENRY WIGMORE, EVIDENCE 14-16 (Chadbourne rev. ed. 1978); Dan B. Dobbs and West Publishing Company for material in REMEDIES 514-519 (West 1973); the University of North Carolina Law Review for material in Robert M. Ackerman, *Bringing Coherence to Defamation Law*, 72 N.C.L. Rev. at 302 (1994); the Virginia Environment Law Journal for material in Megan W. Semple, *Veggie Libel Meets Free Speech: A Constitutional Analysis of Agricultural Disparagement Laws*, 15 Virginia Environmental L. J. at 413-415 (1995-96). In chapter seven (Newspersons' Privileges, Rights and Responsibilities): Detroit College of Law at Michigan State University Law Review for material in Mark Fink, Note, *The Newspaper Preservation Act of 1970: Help for the Needy or the Greedy?*, 1990 Detroit C. L. Rev. at 116 (1990); the Trustees of Indiana University for material in John H. Carlson, Note, *Newspaper Preservation Act*, 46 Ind. L. J. at 411, 412 (1971) (copyright 1971 by the Trustees of Indiana University and reprinted by permission); the Missouri Law Review for material in Tom A. Collins, *The Press Clause Construed in Context*, 52 Mo. L. Rev. at 791, 793, 801 (1987); the University of Pennsylvania Law Review for material in Robbie Steel, *Joint Operating Agreements in the Newspaper Industry: A Threat to First Amendment Freedoms*, 138 U. Pa. L. Rev. at 299-315 (1989) (copyright 1989 by the University of Pennsylvania Law Review). In chapter eight (Free Press and Fair Trial): the American Bar Association for permission to quote or paraphrase the ABA STANDARDS FOR CRIMINAL JUSTICE: FAIR TRIAL AND FREE PRESS (Third ed.) sections 8-1.1, 8-2.2, 8-7.1 (copyright 1981 by the American Bar Association); ABA MODEL CODE OF PROFESSIONAL RESPONSIBILITY rules DR 2-101 (B), DR 7-107 (copyright 1981 by the American Bar Association); ABA MODEL RULES OF PROFESSIONAL CONDUCT rules 7.1, 7.2, 7.3 (copyright 1981 by the American Bar Association; reprinted by permission of the American Bar Association); ABA Code of Judicial Conduct canon 3A7 (1972) (copyright 1972 by the American Bar Association; reprinted by permission of the American Bar Association); the Institute of Government of the University of North Carolina for permission to quote and paraphrase material from THE NEWS MEDIA AND THE COURTS (Free Press—Fair Trial Guidelines) at 34-37 (3d ed.); Duke University Law School's Law and Contemporary Problems for material in Thomas I. Emerson, *The Doctrine of Prior Restraint*, 20 Law and Contemp. Probs. at 656-660 (1955); The

Southern California Law Review for material in Charles H. Whitebread and Darrell W. Contreros, *Free Press v. Fair Trial: Protecting the Criminal Defendant's Rights in a Highly Publicized Trial by Applying the Sheppard-Mu' Min Remedy*, 69 S. Cal. L. Rev. at 1619-20 (1996).

Robert L. Corn-Revere acknowledges with thanks his friend and colleague Mace Rosenstein for his thoughtful assistance and sound advice. He also thanks Paul Rusinoff, Linda Bloss-Baum and Julie Raines for their research assistance as well as that of Eric Loeb, Maureen Cafferty, Christine L. Kurek and Amber Cottle and owes a debt of gratitude to his assistant, Rose Ball, whose tireless and dedicated work on this book went far beyond the call of duty. And finally he thanks Ronald K. L. Collins & David M. Skover for permission to quote or paraphrase material in their works *The First Amendment in an Age of Paratroopers*, 68 Tex. L. Rev. 1087, 1088, 1096, 1097-1099, 1116 (1990); and *The Pornographic State*, 107 Harv. L. Rev. 1374, 1375, 1381 1116-24, 1396, 1398-99 (1994).

Robert M. Frieden acknowledges with appreciation Dr. Eli M. Noam for permission to paraphrase material from articles that were published in the Journal Telecommunications Policy, the Rutgers Computer and Technology Law Journal and Rutgers University School of Law for permission to paraphrase material from Jerome A. Barron, *The Telcos, the Common Carrier Model and the First Amendment—The "Dial-A-Porn"* Precedent in 19 Rutgers Computer & Tech. L. J. at 386 (1993); the Federal Communications Law Journal and Indiana University School of Law for permission to paraphrase material from Michael J. Zpevak, *FCC Preemption After Louisiana PSC* in 45 Fed. Comm. L.J. at 206 (1993).

Charles H. Kennedy wishes to thank Daniel J. Smith, Kathryn M. Stasko and Pilar E. Rivera for their valuable assistance in the preparation of his chapter Computer Communications Law (chapter eleven).

*

Summary of Contents

Table of Contents

MODERN
COMMUNICATION
LAW

*

Chapter One

FIRST AMENDMENT HISTORY, THEORY AND APPLICATION

Analysis

1.1 Communications Law and the First Amendment

Communications law covers everything from megaphones to satellites. The First Amendment to the United States Constitution[1] is the basic charter defining the government's permissible role in regulating speech and the press—the available means of communication when the document was drafted. As such, the First Amendment is the beginning, and at times, the end, of many problems of communications law. Yet most regulatory matters do not raise constitutional questions, and few communications lawyers routinely practice First Amendment law. For that reason, commentators describing the nature of communications law practice often overlook its inherent First Amendment dimension.[2] For the same reason, it may be reasonable to ask why the first chapter of a treatise on communications law should be devoted to the general history, theory and application of the First Amendment.

The answer lies in the changing nature of the communications marketplace, and, as a result, the types of problems addressed by regulators and communications lawyers. A proliferation of new technologies and communications services and the emergence of the so-called

---

1. U.S. Const. Amend. I. All references to the First Amendment throughout this treatise will be capitalized.

2. *See, e.g.,* Stuart N. Brotman, *The Changing Nature of Communications Law Practice*, 9 Comm/Ent L.J. 179 (1987); Henry Geller, *Communications Law—A Half Century Later*, 37 Fed. Comm. L.J. 73 (1985). *But see* Monroe E. Price, *Congress, Free Speech, and Cable Legislation: An Introduction*, 8 Card. Arts & Ent. L.J. 225, 226 (1990) ("'Free speech' is becoming a controlling force in federal communications antitrust law.").

"Information Superhighway" has blurred the conventional regulatory lines separating the traditional media from broadcasters, private network operators and common carriers.[3] The same factors radically shifted the economic balance among various players in the information marketplace.[4] First Amendment decisions began to determine the extent to which telephone companies could participate in the business of video delivery,[5] while at the same time such decisions determined the extent to which the government could intrude on the business decisions of existing video providers.[6] Consequently, some service providers, who for years comfortably accepted the yoke of governmental restrictions borne of technology-specific regulatory classifications[7], began to challenge their second-class constitutional status. With increasing frequency, First Amendment questions arose in virtually every branch of communications law, involving broadcasting, cable television service, common carrier service, satellites and other new delivery systems, such as the Internet.[8]

Broadcasting, the first mass medium subjected to comprehensive federal regulation,[9] was also the focus of efforts to extend comprehensive First Amendment protections to electronic media. In 1984, the Supreme Court held that restrictions on editorializing by public broadcast stations were unconstitutional.[10] It was the first time the Supreme Court invali-

3. Traditional print media are outside the scope of regulation by the Federal Communications Commission to the extent they are not transmitted by "wire or radio." 47 U.S.C.A. § 151 (West Supp.1997). The Communications Act of 1934, as amended, sets out separate regulatory schemes for radio broadcasters (47 U.S.C.A. §§ 301–331), common carriers (47 U.S.C.A. §§ 201–276), cable television operators (47 U.S.C.A. §§ 521–561), and non-broadcast users of the radio spectrum (47 U.S.C.A. §§ 351–386). The Telecommunications Act of 1996 began to blur these clear lines by authorizing hybird services such as Open Video Systems (47 U.S.C.A. §§ 571, 573), and by establishing flexible licensing policies for the use of advanced television spectrum (47 U.S.C.A. § 336).

4. *See generally* H. Rep. 104–204, 104th Cong., 1st Sess. 47–55 (July 24, 1995); S. Rep. 104–23, 104th Cong., 1st Sess. 2–10 (Mar. 30, 1995); Television For The 21st Century: The Next Wave (Charles Firestone, Ed., Media Institute 1993); *Competition, Rate Deregulation and the Commission's Policies Relating to the Provision of Cable Television Service*, 5 F.C.C.R. 4962, 5012–27 (1990).

5. Chesapeake and Potomac Telephone Co. v. United States, 830 F.Supp. 909 (E.D.Va.1993), *aff'd*, 42 F.3d 181 (4th Cir. 1994), *vacated*, 516 U.S. 415, 116 S.Ct. 1036, 134 L.Ed.2d 46 (1996); U.S. West, Inc. v. United States, 855 F.Supp. 1184 (W.D.Wash.1994), *aff'd*, 48 F.3d 1092 (9th Cir.1994), *vacated*, 516 U.S. 1155 116 S.Ct. 1037, 134 L.Ed.2d 186 (1996).

6. *E.g.*, Turner Broadcasting System, Inc. v. FCC, 520 U.S. 180, 117 S.Ct. 1174, 137 L.Ed.2d 369 (1997) ("Turner II"); Turner Broadcasting System, Inc. v. FCC ("Turner I"), 512 U.S. 622, 114 S.Ct. 2445, 129 L.Ed.2d 497 (1994).

7. *See* Price, *supra* note 2, at 227–28 ("One can look back at the history of radio and television regulation prior to the mid–1970's, virtually in vain, for a decision in which the constitution limited congressional or [Federal Communications] Commission decisions as to structure.")

8. See Reno v. ACLU, 521 U.S. 844, 117 S.Ct. 2329, 138 L.Ed.2d 874 (1997); Shea v. Reno, 930 F.Supp. 916 (S.D.N.Y.1996).

9. Radio Act of 1927, Ch. 169, 44 Stat. 1162, 47 U.S.C.A. § 81 (1927), repealed and superceded by the Communications Act of 1934, 47 U.S.C.A. §§ 151–158, amended by the Telecommunications Act of 1996, P.L. 104–104, 110 Stat. 56 (1996).

10. FCC v. League of Women Voters of Cal., 468 U.S. 364, 104 S.Ct. 3106, 82 L.Ed.2d 278 (1984). Public broadcasting stations, as distinguished from commercial stations, receive government funding, 47 U.S.C.A. §§ 390–399, and are subject to certain programming restrictions not imposed on commercial licensees. *E.g.*, 47 U.S.C.A. § 399b(b)(2) (West Supp. 1997) (advertising on public broadcasting stations prohibited).

dated any aspect of broadcast regulation on First Amendment grounds.[11] In the wake of that decision, the courts and the FCC addressed various constitutional challenges based on broadcasters' obligation to air controversial issues of public importance (the so-called "fairness doctrine"),[12] political broadcasting requirements,[13] prohibitions on indecent or obscene programming,[14] and ownership restrictions.[15]

First Amendment issues also began to figure prominently in litigation involving cable television systems. Cable operators challenged the constitutionality of various local franchise requirements, including access channel requirements,[16] local programming origination requirements,[17] franchise fees,[18] exclusive franchising arrangements[19] and numerous oth-

---

11. Lower courts, however, had previously invalidated some regulations on First Amendment grounds. *See, e.g.,* Community–Service Broadcasting of Mid–America, Inc. v. FCC, 593 F.2d 1102, 192 U.S. App. D.C. 448 (D.C.Cir.1978) (en banc).

12. Arkansas AFL–CIO v. FCC, 11 F.3d 1430 (8th Cir.1993) (en banc); Syracuse Peace Council, 2 F.C.C.R. 5043 (1987), *aff'd on nonconstitutional grounds,* Syracuse Peace Council v. FCC, 867 F.2d 654, 276 U.S.App.D.C. 38 (D.C.Cir.1989), cert. denied, 493 U.S. 1019, 110 S.Ct. 717, 107 L.Ed.2d 737 (1990). *See generally* Inquiry into Section 73.1910 of the Commission's Rules and Regulations Concerning the General Fairness Doctrine Obligations of Broadcast Licensees, 102 F.C.C.2d 142, 145 (1985); Inquiry Into Section 73.1910 of the Commission's Rules and Regulations Concerning Alternatives to the General Fairness Doctrine Obligations of Broadcast Licensees, 2 FCC Rcd. 5272 (1987).

13. Branch v. FCC, 824 F.2d 37, 262 U.S. App. D.C. 310 (D.C.Cir.1987), cert. denied, 485 U.S. 959, 108 S.Ct. 1220, 99 L.Ed.2d 421 (1988).

14. Action for Children's Television v. FCC, 59 F.3d 1249, 313 U.S.App.D.C. 261 (D.C.Cir.1995) cert. denied, 516 U.S. 1072, 116 S.Ct. 773, 133 L.Ed.2d 726 (1996); Action for Children's Television v. FCC, 58 F.3d 654, 313 U.S.App.D.C. 94 (D.C.Cir. 1995) (en banc), cert. denied, 516 U.S. 1043, 116 S.Ct. 701, 133 L.Ed.2d 658 (1996); United States v. Evergreen Media Corp., 832 F.Supp. 1183 (N.D.Ill.1993); Action for Children's Television v. FCC, 932 F.2d 1504, 290 U.S.App.D.C. 4 (D.C.Cir.1991); Action for Children's Television v. FCC, 852 F.2d 1332, 271 U.S. App. D.C. 365 (D.C.Cir. 1988). *See also* New Indecency Enforcement Standards to be Applied to All Broadcast and Amateur Radio Licensees, 2 FCC Rcd. 2726 (1987); In re Pacifica Found., Inc., 2 F.C.C. Rcd. 2698 (1987); In re Infinity Broadcasting Corp. of Pa., 2 F.C.C. Rcd.

2705 (1987); In re The Regents of the Univ. of Cal., 2 FCC Rcd. 2703 (1987).

15. News America Publishing, Inc. v. FCC, 844 F.2d 800, 269 U.S. App. D.C. 182 (D.C.Cir.1988). *Compare* FCC v. National Citizens Committee for Broadcasting, 436 U.S. 775, 98 S.Ct. 2096, 56 L.Ed.2d 697 (1978).

16. *E.g.,* Group W Cable, Inc. v. City of Santa Cruz, 669 F.Supp. 954 (N.D.Cal. 1987); Erie Telecommunications, Inc. v. City of Erie, 659 F.Supp. 580 (W.D.Pa. 1987), *aff'd on other grounds,* 853 F.2d 1084 (3d Cir.1988); Berkshire Cablevision of Rhode Island, Inc. v. Burke, 571 F.Supp. 976 (D.R.I.1983), *vacated as moot,* 773 F.2d 382 (1st Cir.1985). *See* Missouri Knights of the Ku Klux Klan v. Kansas City, Missouri, 723 F.Supp. 1347 (W.D.Mo.1989)

17. Chicago Cable Communications v. Chicago Cable Commission, 678 F.Supp. 734 (N.D.Ill.1988), *aff'd,* 879 F.2d 1540 (7th Cir.1989), cert. denied, 493 U.S. 1044, 110 S.Ct. 839, 107 L.Ed.2d 835 (1990).

18. *E.g.,* Erie Telecommunications, Inc. v. City of Erie, 659 F.Supp. 580 (W.D.Pa. 1987), *aff'd on other grounds,* 853 F.2d 1084 (3d Cir.1988); Group W Cable, Inc. v. City of Santa Cruz, 679 F.Supp. 977 (N.D.Cal.1988). *See generally* David Saylor, *Municipal Ripoff: The Unconstitutionality of Cable Television Franchise Fees and Access Support Payments,* 35 Cath. U. L. Rev. 671 (1986); Peter Krug, *Cable Television Franchise Fees for General Revenue: The 1984 Cable Act, Wisconsin Law, and the First Amendment,* 1985 Wis. L. Rev. 1273.

19. Preferred Communications, Inc. v. City of Los Angeles, 13 F.3d 1327 (9th Cir.1994), cert. denied, 512 U.S. 1235, 114 S.Ct. 2738, 129 L.Ed.2d 859 (1994); Pacific West Cable Co. v. City of Sacramento, 672 F.Supp. 1322 (E.D.Cal.1987); Group W Cable, Inc. v. City of Santa Cruz, 669 F.Supp. 954 (N.D.Cal.1987); Century Federal, Inc. v. City of Palo Alto, 648 F.Supp. 1465

er conditions of doing business. Successful First Amendment challenges were mounted against local laws attempting to regulate "indecent" cable programming[20] and against federal signal carriage requirements.[21] Passage of the Cable Television Consumer Protection and Competition Act of 1992[22] further highlighted questions about the constitutional status of cable operators, and led to additional First Amendment litigation.[23]

Even common carriers were engulfed in the trend toward First Amendment litigation. A series of federal court decisions invalidated on First Amendment grounds the prohibition against video programming delivery by telephone companies. These decisions generally were rendered moot by passage of the Telecommunications Act of 1996, which permits telephone companies to provide video services.[24] This ended a period of judicial reluctance to address the constitutional ability of common carriers to act as electronic speakers.[25] Still, even as some courts

(N.D.Cal.1986); Nor–West Cable Communications Partnership v. City of St. Paul, 924 F.2d 741 (8th Cir.), cert. denied, 501 U.S. 1231, 111 S.Ct. 2853, 115 L.Ed.2d 1021 (1991); Omega Satellite Prods. Co. v. City of Indianapolis, 694 F.2d 119 (7th Cir.1982).

20. Wilkinson v. Jones, 480 U.S. 926, 107 S.Ct. 1559, 94 L.Ed.2d 753 (1987), *aff'ing mem.* 800 F.2d 989 (10th Cir.1986); Cruz v. Ferre, 755 F.2d 1415 (11th Cir. 1985); Altmann v. Television Signal Corp. 849 F.Supp. 1335 (N.D.Cal.1994); Community Television of Utah, Inc. v. Roy City, 555 F.Supp. 1164 (D.Utah 1982); Home Box Office, Inc. v. Wilkinson, 531 F.Supp. 987 (D.Utah 1982).

21. Century Communications Corp. v. FCC, 835 F.2d 292, 266 U.S. App. D.C. 228 (D.C.Cir.1987), *clarified,* 837 F.2d 517, 267 U.S. App. D.C. 94 (D.C.Cir.), cert. denied, 486 U.S. 1032, 108 S. Ct. 2014, 100 L. Ed. 2d 602 (1988); Quincy Cable TV, Inc. v. FCC, 768 F.2d 1434, 248 U.S. App. D.C. 1 (D.C.Cir.1985), *cert. denied sub nom.* National Ass'n of Broadcasters v. Quincy Cable TV, Inc., 476 U.S. 1169, 106 S.Ct. 2889, 90 L.Ed.2d 977 (1986).

22. Pub. L. No. 102–385, 106 Stat. 1460 (1992).

23. *E.g.,* Turner Broadcasting System, Inc. v. FCC, 520 U.S. 180, 117 S.Ct. 1174, 137 L.Ed.2d 369 (1997) ("Turner II"); Turner Broadcasting System, Inc. v. FCC ("Turner I"), 512 U.S. 622, 114 S.Ct. 2445, 129 L.Ed.2d 497 (1994); Time Warner Entertainment Co., L.P. v. FCC, 93 F.3d 957, 320 U.S.App.D.C. 294 (D.C.Cir.1996).

24. *See* U.S. West, Inc. v. United States, 855 F.Supp. 1184 (W.D.Wash.1994) *aff'd,* 48 F.3d 1092 (9th Cir.1994), *vacated,* 516 U.S. 1155, 116 S.Ct. 1037, 134 L.Ed.2d 186 (1996). Southern New England Telephone

Co. v. United States, 886 F.Supp. 211 (D.Conn.1995); Ameritech Corp. v. United States, 867 F.Supp. 721 (N.D.Ill.1994); BellSouth Corp. v. United States, 868 F.Supp. 1335 (N.D.Ala.1994). *But see* BellSouth Corp. v. FCC, 144 F.3d 58, 330 U.S.App. D.C. 109 (D.C.Cir.1998); SBC Communications, Inc. v. FCC, 981 F.Supp. 996 (N.D.Tex.1997).

25. In the settlement that led to the breakup of AT & T, the Modified Final Judgment ("MFJ") prohibited the divested Bell Operating Companies ("BOCs"), which operate local telephone systems, from providing information services, which includes video programming. United States v. American Tel. and Tel. Co., 552 F.Supp. 131, 189–90 (D.D.C.1982), *aff'd sub nom.* Maryland v. United States, 460 U.S. 1001, 103 S.Ct. 1240, 75 L.Ed.2d 472 (1983). AT & T, which provides long-distance telephone service, was barred from engaging in "electronic publishing," but this restriction expired in 1989. United States v. Western Elec. Co., Inc., 1989 WL 108310 (D.D.C.) (unpublished memorandum). The BOC's challenged the prohibition as a violation of their First Amendment rights in the first periodic review of the MFJ. But while the antitrust settlement in which the restriction was imposed, the District Court rejected these claims. United States v. Western Elec. Co., Inc., 673 F.Supp. 525, 586 n. 273 (D.D.C.1987). The Court of Appeals reversed the District Court, thus allowing the BOCs to enter the information services market. But it did so without discussing the First Amendment issue. United States v. Western Elec. Co., 283 U.S. App. D.C. 299, 900 F.2d 283 (D.C.Cir.1990), *cert. denied sub nom.* MCI Communications Corp. v. United States, 498 U.S. 911, 111 S.Ct. 283, 112 L.Ed.2d 238 (1990).

had hesitated to define telephone companies' rights as speakers, others upheld common carriers' ability to exclude certain other information services from their systems. In *Carlin Communication v. Southern Bell Telephone and Telegraph Co.*,[26] the court held that telephone companies have a right not to be associated with so-called dial-a-porn services that would conflict with the carriers' corporate image and that such exclusion does not violate the First Amendment rights of the service providers.[27] Additionally, Congress and the FCC engaged in successive efforts to fashion dial-a-porn restrictions that would survive judicial review.[28]

Not all commentators have welcomed the growing influence of the First Amendment on communications policy. One consequence of this emerging area of jurisprudence, according to some, is that "courts, not the [Federal Communications] Commission or Congress, make telecommunications policy."[29] In this view, First Amendment positions are being advocated not to promote legitimate interests in free speech, but to limit the government's regulatory power to the advantage of big business. Thus, "[t]he soapbox is being replaced with the [shopping] mall" and "[w]e become flooded with images, but poorer in public debate."[30] This analysis assumes that government is both inclined and well-suited to guarantee wide-open public debate. It is predicated on the proposition that public policy, however it may be defined, should take precedence over First Amendment considerations. Such views, however, are unlikely to slow the trend toward an expanding First Amendment jurisprudence.

The debate over the proper role of government in regulating the mass media versus the First Amendment rights of speakers may be just getting started. Even as court decisions begin to recognize greater rights

---

26. 802 F.2d 1352 (11th Cir.1986).

27. *Id.* at 1361. *See also* Carlin Communications, Inc. v. Mountain States Telephone and Telegraph Co., 827 F.2d 1291 (9th Cir.1987), cert. denied, 485 U.S. 1029, 108 S.Ct. 1586, 99 L.Ed.2d 901 (1988).

28. Congress adopted Section 223 of the Communications Act which required the Commission to enact regulations restricting adult telephone services. 47 U.S.C.A. § 223 (West Supp. 1998). After the regulations were twice struck down as being too restrictive of adults' rights to receive sexually-oriented telephone messages, Carlin Communications, Inc. v. FCC, 749 F.2d 113 (2d Cir.1984) (*Carlin I*); Carlin Communications, Inc. v. FCC, 787 F.2d 846 (2d Cir. 1986) (*Carlin II*), the FCC fashioned judicially-acceptable regulations. Carlin Communications, Inc. v. FCC, 837 F.2d 546 (2d Cir.1988), *cert. denied*, 488 U.S. 924 109 S.Ct. 305, 102 L.Ed.2d 324 (1988) (*Carlin III*). *See also* Information Providers' Coalition For Defense of the First Amendment v. FCC, 928 F.2d 866 (9th Cir.1991); Dial Information Services Corp. v. Thornburgh, 938 F.2d 1535 (2d Cir.1991), *cert. denied*, 502 U.S. 1072, 112 S.Ct. 966, 117 L.Ed.2d

132 (1992). Congress also banned all interstate dial-a-porn calls, including calls that were indecent but not obscene, but this measure was invalidated. Sable Communications of California, Inc. v. FCC, 492 U.S. 115, 109 S.Ct. 2829, 106 L.Ed.2d 93 (1989).

29. Price, *supra*, note 2, at 227; Jerome A. Barron, *On Understanding the First Amendment Status of Cable: Some Obstacles in the Way*, 57 Geo. Wash. L. Rev. 1495 (1989) ("Too many cable regulatory issues are treated as if they necessarily present First Amendment problems when in fact they do not."); Kenneth Robinson, *Implications of the Court's Video Programming Decision: Telcos Will Enter the Cable Industry in a Big Way*, The Cable–Telco Report, September 13, 1993 at 13 ("the U.S. Supreme Court [has] recognize[d] yet another First Amendment right: the right to string wires on poles").

30. Price, *supra*. note 2, at 226. *See generally* Ronald K. L. Collins & David M. Skover, *The First Amendment in an Age of Paratroopers*, 68 Tex. L. Rev. 1087 (1990).

for the electronic media, Congress and the Federal Communications Commission have pursued a more aggressive regulatory agenda. The Telecommunications Act of 1996, generally considered a deregulatory law, contained several provisions that expanded content control over the media. Title V of the Act contains a number of speech regulations, including requirements that V-chip screening technology be included in television circuitry and rating systems be developed for television programming;[31] that adult programming services on cable television and other subscription video systems be "fully scrambled" as to non-subscribers or time channeled to late night hours;[32] and a prohibition on transmitting or displaying "indecent communications to minors using on-line media."[33]

At the same time, the FCC strengthened its requirements that television licensees broadcast more educational and informational programming pursuant to the Children's Television Act of 1990.[34] This action came amid calls to impose specific content requirements on broadcasters for use of digital spectrum, as well as demands that free broadcast time be provided to presidential candidates.[35]

The growing number of new and proposed speech regulations guarantees that the First Amendment debate will continue into the future. On the one hand, in *ACLU v. Reno* Judge Stuart Dalzell wrote that in regulating new technologies such as the Internet, courts must first determine "whether the Government has the power to regulate protected speech at all."[36] On the other, a plurality of the Supreme Court showed great reluctance to "impose judicial formulae so rigid that they become a straightjacket" in dealing with new technologies.[37] In particular, Justice Souter cautioned that "we should be shy about saying the final word today about what will be accepted as reasonable tomorrow."[38]

The first two chapters of this treatise address the emerging First Amendment problems of the Information Age. Chapter One provides a background for these issues by exploring the First Amendment's history, theory and application. Chapter Two examines some of the conceptual difficulties faced by courts and policymakers in applying the First Amendment to new technologies, and concludes that traditional First Amendment theory can and should be applied to cope with media convergence.

31. 47 U.S.C.A. §§ 303(w), (West Supp. 1997).

32. 47 U.S.C.A. § 561.

33. 47 U.S.C.A. § 223. *But see* Reno v. ACLU, 521 U.S. 844, 117 S.Ct. 2329, 138 L.Ed.2d 874 (1997).

34. Policies and Rules Concerning Children's Television Programming, 11 FCC Rcd. 10660 (1996).

35. See e.g., Reed Hundt and Karen Kornbluh, *Renewing the Deal between Broadcasters and the Public: Requiring Clear Rules for Children's' Educational Television,* 9 Harv. J. L. & Tech. 11, 16–19 (Winter 1996).

36. 929 F.Supp. 824, 877 (E.D.Pa.1996).

37. Denver Area Educational Telecommunications Consortium, Inc. v. FCC, 518 U.S. 727, 116 S.Ct. 2374, 2385, 135 L.Ed.2d 888, 901 (1996).

38. Id. at 777, 116 S.Ct. at 2402, 135 L.Ed.2d at 924 (Souter, J., concurring).

1.2 Interpreting the First Amendment

> Congress shall make no law ... abridging the freedom of speech, or of the press; or the right of the people peaceably to assemble, and to petition the Government for redress of grievances.[1]

At first blush, the First Amendment appears to present little problem of interpretation. But in the more than two centuries since it was written, there has been wide disagreement about its meaning among both judges and scholars.[2] The difficulty depends, in part, on whether one seeks meaning in the words of the Amendment, the intentions of its Framers or in some set of values that evolves with society.[3] Of course, the ultimate answer may reside, in varying degrees, in all three methods of interpretation, a fact that only increases the complexity of the inquiry.[4] Nevertheless, the language of the First Amendment necessarily is the starting point of any analysis.

Justice Hugo Black, the Supreme Court's primary proponent of an absolutist interpretation of the Constitution, noted that "[t]he phrase 'Congress shall make no law' is composed of plain words, easily understood"[5] and that no law means no law "without any 'ifs' or 'buts', or 'whereases'."[6] The seeming clarity of such literalism obscures a great deal of ambiguity as to the First Amendment's scope. But advocates of the absolutist position have never shied away from acknowledging the difficulty of interpreting the First Amendment. Alexander Meiklejohn, for example, wrote that "even if we are convinced that ... the First Amendment admits of no exceptions, we are ... plunged at once into a multitude of bewildering questions."[7]

---

1. U.S. Const. Amend. I.

2. *E.g.*, Eric M. Barendt, Freedom of Speech 31 (1985) ("Rarely has such an apparently simple legal text produced so many problems of interpretation.").

3. Jonathan W. Emord has described the three principle theories of First Amendment construction as the "literalist perspective," the "narrow intentionalist" perspective and "relativist" perspective. Jonathan W. Emord, Freedom, Technology, and the First Amendment 101–18 (1991).

4. *See* Kent Greenawalt, *Speech and Crime*, 1980 Am. B. Found. Res. J. 645, 729 ("Judges in constitutional cases are properly guided by a number of criteria, including constitutional language, historical background shedding light on the framers' intent, precedent and other relevant law at the time of decision, the relationship of the particular issue to the structure of constitutional government, deference to the views of other branches of the government, and considerations of justice and social welfare.").

5. Hugo L. Black, *The Bill of Rights*, 35 N.Y.U. L. Rev. 865, 874 (1960).

6. Beauharnais v. Illinois, 343 U.S. 250, 275, 72 S.Ct. 725, 740, 96 L.Ed. 919, 937, (1952) (Black, J., dissenting). *See* Edmond N. Cahn, *Justice Black and First Amendment 'Absolutes': A Public Interview*, 37 N.Y.U. L. Rev. 549, 553 (1962).

7. Alexander Meiklejohn, Free Speech and its Relation to Self-Government 92 (1948); Meiklejohn, *The First Amendment is an Absolute*, 1961 Sup. Ct. Rev. 245, 246 n.4. One significant question is how the First Amendment has been interpreted as a limitation on all branches of government despite its literal fixation on the legislative branch acting in its lawmaking capacity. One view is that the Framers specifically intended to limit the Amendment's scope to congressional abridgments. *See* Mark P. Denbeaux, *The First Word of the First Amendment*, 80 Nw. U. L. Rev. 1156 (1986). In practice, however, the courts have protected against infringements by all branches of government. *E.g.*, Organization for a Better Austin v. Keefe, 402 U.S. 415, 91 S.Ct. 1575, 29 L.Ed.2d 1 (1971) (judicial prior restraint); Carroll v. President Comm'rs of Princess Anne, 393 U.S. 175, 89 S.Ct. 347, 21 L.Ed.2d 325 (1968) (prior re-

Under a literal interpretation of the First Amendment, difficult questions arise from the fact that the Amendment's absolute commands relate to ambiguous concepts. Assuming "no law" means just that, what types of expression are considered to be "speech" under the First Amendment? And what does it mean to "abridge" the freedom of speech? In contrast to Justice Black's reference to the clarity of First Amendment restrictions on Congress, Meiklejohn noted that "the words 'abridging the freedom of speech' ... are not 'plain words, easily understood.' "[8] Nor are they "self-defining."[9] He did agree with Justice Black that the meaning of these concepts must be "determined by the courts."[10]

The combination in the First Amendment of literal, absolute commands with more general substantive requirements thus explains the apparent paradox of self-described "absolutists" admitting of exceptions to freedom of expression. Justice Black, for example, argued that freedom of speech does not include such activities as picketing or wearing a jacket emblazoned with offensive words.[11] Meiklejohn suggested that the First Amendment's protection was limited to speech necessary for self-government and that defamation, incitement to crime and treason could be suppressed.[12] Similarly, Professor Thomas Emerson proposed that the First Amendment entitles speech to "full protection," yet drew a line between "expression" and "action."[13]

Properly understood, an absolutist view of the First Amendment is not an endorsement of "an unlimited license to talk," as some critics assert.[14] "The absolutist interpretation, when it is thus misstated, is, of course, easily destroyed."[15] Rather than to suggest that the First Amend-

straint initiated by executive branch). *See* David A. Anderson, *The Origins of the Press Clause,* 30 UCLA L. Rev. 455, 501 (1983).

8. Meiklejohn, *The First Amendment is an Absolute, supra* note 7, at 247.

9. *Id.* at 250.

10. *Id.,* quoting Black, *The Bill of Rights,* 35 N.Y.U. L. Rev. at 871. Of course, there remains the problem of determining the substantive purpose of the First Amendment. *See* Emord, *supra* note 3, at 111–12 ("Without knowing *why* the amendment is necessary we cannot know *which* definition best fits the constitutional crisis confronting us at any moment.")

11. Cox v. Louisiana, 379 U.S. 536, 85 S.Ct. 453, 13 L.Ed.2d 471, 500 (1965) (Black, J., concurring). Cohen v. California, 403 U.S. 15, 27, 91 S.Ct. 1780, 1789, 29 L.Ed.2d 284, 295 (1971) (Blackmun, J., dissenting, joined by Justice Black). *See also* Adderley v. Florida, 385 U.S. 39, 47–48, 87 S.Ct. 242, 247, 17 L.Ed.2d 149, 156 (1966), where Justice Black wrote for the Court that the First Amendment does not allow demonstrators to protest "whenever and however and wherever they please."

12. ALEXANDER MEIKLEJOHN, FREE SPEECH AND ITS RELATION TO SELF-GOVERNMENT at 17–19. *See* Meiklejohn, *The First Amendment is an Absolute, supra* note 7; MEIKLEJOHN, POLITICAL FREEDOM: THE CONSTITUTIONAL POWERS OF THE PEOPLE (1965). *See also* Robert H. Bork, *Neutral Principles and Some First Amendment Problems,* 47 Ind. L.J. 1 (1971).

13. THOMAS I. EMERSON, THE SYSTEM OF FREEDOM OF EXPRESSION 17 (1970).

14. Konigsberg v. State Bar, 366 U.S. 36, 49–50, 81 S.Ct. 997, 1006, 6 L.Ed.2d 105, 116 (1961). *See also* MELVILLE B. NIMMER, FREEDOM OF SPEECH § 2.01 (1984) ("no one can responsibly hold the position that the First Amendment is an absolute in the sense that it literally protects all speech").

15. Meiklejohn, *The First Amendment is an Absolute, supra* note 7, at 249. Meiklejohn complained that to frame the absolutist position in such a way was to "substitute caricature for refutation." *Id.* at 248. His concern that the mischaracterization of the absolutist position would undermine it has been borne out in the dismissive attitudes of other commentators. *See, e.g.,* NIM-

ment prohibits regulation of any or all speech activity, advocates of the absolutist position generally argue that the government is absolutely prohibited only from engaging in what the courts determine to be an abridgment of speech or of the press.[16] Thus, the guiding principle in a literal approach to the First Amendment is its rejection of ad hoc balancing as a means of constitutional adjudication.[17] The absolutist interpretation espoused by Black and Meiklejohn is more compatible with so-called "definitional balancing" in which certain categories of communicative acts are considered to be beyond the reach of the First Amendment.[18]

Regardless of whether one chooses ad hoc balancing as a means of constitutional interpretation or takes a more literalist approach, it is necessary to determine the scope of the First Amendment, either by reference to the Framers' intent or by some other means. This task is made more difficult by the First Amendment's limited legislative history.

MER, *supra* note 14 at § 2.01 ("But if the civil libertarian heart would accept it, the mind will not. Absolutism simply will not wash."); C. EDWIN BAKER, HUMAN LIBERTY AND FREEDOM OF SPEECH 272 (1989) (literal interpretations of the First Amendment "can be quickly put aside" for the same reason that the Constitution's prescription that the President must be a "natural born citizen" does not disqualify persons delivered by Cesarean section); Bork, *supra* note 12, at 21. ("Those who take [the First Amendment] as an absolute must be reading 'speech' to mean any form of verbal communication and 'freedom' to mean total absence of governmental restraint. Any such reading is, of course, impossible."); Emord, *supra* note 3, at 110–12. Even when the absolutist position is not misstated, however, it does not necessarily evoke agreement among commentators. *E.g.*, E. BARENDT, *supra* note 2, at 32 ("Absolutists can try to defend their corner by asserting that 'abridging' does not cover all forms of regulation and that 'the freedom of speech' is not the same as 'speech', so that rightly understood the term does not include restrictions on some modes of expression. But really the game is up, the poverty of literalism laid bare.").

16. Meiklejohn, *The First Amendment is an Absolute, supra* note 7, at 246–47; Black, *supra* note 5, at 871–74. This analysis applies generally to the Bill of Rights. As Justice Black wrote, "[t]here may be much difference of opinion about whether a particular search or seizure is unreasonable and therefore forbidden by [the Fourth] Amendment. But if it *is* unreasonable, it is absolutely prohibited." *Id.* at 873.

17. *See, e.g.*, EMERSON, *supra* note 13, at 17; Meiklejohn, *The First Amendment is an*

Absolute, supra note 7, at 251–54. However, on a number of occasions the Supreme Court has expressly rejected the absolutist position and endorsed the ad hoc view that the judiciary must "determine which of these two conflicting interests demands the greater protection under the particular circumstances presented." American Communications Assn. v. Douds, 339 U.S. 382, 399, 70 S.Ct. 674, 684, 94 L.Ed. 925, 944 (1950). *See also* Smith v. Daily Mail Publishing Co., 443 U.S. 97, 106, 99 S.Ct. 2667, 2672, 61 L.Ed.2d 399, 407 (1979); Gannett Co. Inc., v. DePasquale, 443 U.S. 368, 393, 99 S.Ct. 2898, 2912, 61 L.Ed.2d 608, 629 (1979); Saxbe v. Washington Post Co., 417 U.S. 843, 94 S.Ct. 2811, 41 L.Ed.2d 514 (1974); Konigsberg v. State Bar, 366 U.S. 36, 49–51, 81 S.Ct. 997, 1007, 6 L.Ed.2d 105, 116–117 (1961); Barenblatt v. United States, 360 U.S. 109, 126, 79 S.Ct. 1081, 1093, 3 L.Ed.2d 1115, 1129 (1959); Dennis v. United States, 341 U.S. 494, 540–541, 71 S.Ct. 857, 883, 95 L.Ed. 1137, 1169 (1951).

18. "Definitional balancing," as such, appears to assume that certain categories of expression are not protected because the regulatory interests involved outweigh the First Amendment values at issue. *See, e.g.*, William T. Mayton, *From a Legacy of Suppression to the "Metaphor of the Fourth Estate,"* 39 Stan. L. Rev. 139, 140 n.9 (1986); Frederick F. Schauer, *The Aim and the Target in Free Speech Methodology*, 83 NW. U. L. Rev. 562, 562 n.4 (1989). As a practical matter, definitional balancing seems little different from saying—without any reference to the weighing of interests—that there are "many forms of communication which ... are wholly outside the scope of the First Amendment." Meiklejohn, *The First Amendment is an Absolute, supra* note 7, at 258.

A common approach has been to define the purposes that the First Amendment was designed to serve and to tailor the Amendment's reach to promote the chosen goals. This methodology has been described as "more akin to philosophical reasoning than to conventional legal techniques such as the drawing of inferences from precedents."[19] Such analyses have resulted in some limited agreement about certain "core values" that inhere in the Amendment based on the historical context in which it was written,[20] but there remains a wide range of dispute over how far free speech guarantees should extend.

A. The Fragmentary Legislative History

The debate over the First Amendment's meaning and scope cannot be resolved by reference to the history of its adoption. The principal evidence of the Amendment's meaning is the language employed in the successive drafts, ranging from Madison's first proposal, introduced in Congress on June 8, 1789, through the final version ratified by the states in 1791.[21] Records of the legislative proceedings are scant, and there is little to suggest that the Framers debated the meaning or importance of freedom of speech and press.[22] Outside the official record, the writings contained in private correspondence, newspapers and tracts between 1787 and 1791 did not clarify the meaning of this fundamental right.[23] Indeed, noted constitutional historian Leonard Levy has suggested that "[i]t is not even certain that the Framers themselves knew what they had in mind" when they drafted the First Amendment or that they "represented a consensus."[24]

Before the Bill of Rights was introduced, the controversy centered on whether a declaration of rights was needed or would be helpful. At the constitutional convention a statement preserving "the liberty of the Press" was voted down on the theory that "[t]he power of Congress does not extend to the press."[25] Federalists also argued that a delineation of rights would imply that greater powers had been delegated to the federal government than had been intended.[26] But the absence of a bill of rights threatened to prevent ratification of the Constitution, and various states

---

19. Barendt, *supra* note 2, at 4.

20. *See, e.g.*, Kent Greenawalt, *Free Speech Justifications*, 89 Colum. L. Rev. 119 (1989).

21. The exact date of ratification is subject to dispute. *See, e.g.*, Anderson, *supra* note 7, at 485, n.187.

22. JOHN HART ELY, DEMOCRACY AND DISTRUST: A Theory Of Judicial Review 17 (1980) LEONARD W. LEVY, LEGACY OF SUPPRESSION: FREEDOM OF SPEECH AND PRESS IN EARLY AMERICAN HISTORY 221 (1960); Anderson, *supra* note 7 at 485.

23. LEONARD W. LEVY, LEGACY OF SUPPRESSION 5, 225 (1960).

24. *Id.* at 236.

25. "For why declare that things shall not be done which there is no power to do? Why for instance, should it be said, that the liberty of the press shall not be restrained, when no power is given by which restrictions may be imposed?" THE FEDERALIST No. 84 (A. Hamilton). *See* Mayton, *supra* note 18, at 143; 2 THE RECORDS OF THE FEDERAL CONVENTION OF 1787, 617–18 (Max Farrand, ed. 1911).

26. Leonard W. Levy, *The Legacy Reexamined*, 37 Stan. L. Rev. 767, 773 (1985); Mayton, *supra* note 18, at 143; Mark P. Denbeaux, *The First Word of the First Amendment*, 80 Nw. U. L. Rev. 1156, 1162–63 (1986).

included suggestions for amendments in their documents of ratification.[27] The politically charged environment surrounding the debate is exemplified by James Madison's conversion from opposing a bill of rights to becoming its principal draftsman. James Monroe, who ran against Madison for election to the first Congress, lost by 336 votes but only after Madison switched his position in support of a bill of rights.[28]

It is an exaggeration to suggest that there "was no record of legislative intent" underlying the First Amendment.[29] The process of draftsmanship yields some clues as to the Amendment's meaning, although these hints are far from conclusive. Given the environment in which the drafting took place, Professor David Anderson wrote that "it is important to remember that the Bill of Rights was written in essentially the same way as any other enactment of Congress—by politicians, through the deliberately inefficient legislative process."[30] After its introduction by Madison, the language of the First Amendment was modified by three committees and several floor amendments. The fifth and final version was necessarily a compromise.[31]

Nevertheless, it is significant to note that Madison originally introduced two amendments that touched on freedom of the press. The second would have limited state power to control the press—the only proposed amendment to touch on non-federal authority.[32] The House approved the second press amendment, but the Senate deleted it from the list.[33] Thus, this procedural history suggests that the First Amendment's reach was intentionally limited to restricting federal power, until the adoption of the Fourteenth Amendment.

Legislative compromise also transformed the First Amendment's command from a more positive guarantee of rights to speak and publish to a negative shield to protect against encroachments of federal power. As initially proposed by Madison, the amendment read: "The people shall not be deprived or abridged in their right to speak, to write, or to publish their sentiments; and the freedom of the press, as one of the great bulwarks of liberty, shall be inviolable."[34] Although the language was modified by a House Committee, it retained the form of a positive

---

27. Some argue that the Anti–Federalists used the question of a bill of rights merely to foment opposition to the Constitution, but that the Federalists diffused this effort by agreeing to the amendments. *See* Levy, *supra* note 22, at 226–31; Denbeaux, *supra* note 26 at 1162–63. *But see* Anderson, *supra* note 7, at 477, 497–98.

28. Anderson, *supra* note 7, at 476.

29. MELVILLE B. NIMMER, FREEDOM OF SPEECH § 1.01 at 1–3 (1984). It is true that the Senate at the time operated in secrecy and did not keep records of its debates. Denbeaux, *supra* note 26 at 1164–65. Nor are records available from the committees that shaped the First Amendment. *Id.* at 1170; Anderson, *supra* note 7, at 478.

30. Anderson, *supra* note 7, at 475.

31. *Id.* at 476.

32. The proposed amendment read: "No State shall violate the equal rights of conscience, or the freedom of the press, or the trial by jury in criminal cases." 1 THE DEBATES AND PROCEEDINGS IN THE CONGRESS OF THE UNITED STATES 452 (1789) (Joseph Gales, ed. 1789).

33. There is no record of the Senate's reason for rejecting the proposed amendment. *See* Anderson, *supra* note 7, at 483–84.

34. 1 ANNALS OF CONG. 452.

guarantee until it reached the Senate. There, it took on the current formulation that "Congress shall make no law, abridging the freedom of speech, or of the press...."[35] After final Senate debate, during which the religion clauses were added, and deliberations by a conference committee, the final version of the First Amendment emerged. There is no indication as to why the language was changed. Professor Anderson has suggested that it "may have been merely editorial, reflecting a desire to state the amendment in active rather than passive voice."[36]

Some have suggested that the deliberate use of the term "Congress" in the Amendment's final version is evidence that the Framers intended to leave the executive and federal courts free to punish seditious libel and that the First Amendment embraced the Blackstonian concept of censorship as the absence of prior restraint.[37] Others, however, have argued that federal authority emanated from Congress and that "[t]he legislature, rather than the executive or the courts, was the source of federal power that required limitation."[38] Viewed from this perspective, it is possible that "the reference to Congress had no significance whatsoever."[39] In any event, this academic debate has been rendered moot by experience.[40]

Other evidence from the legislative history provides some insight as to whether the Framers sought to incorporate Blackstonian concepts into the First Amendment. An unsuccessful Senate proposal would have modified the amendment to protect speech and press "in as ample a manner as hath at any time been secured by the common law."[41] Although there is no record of the reason the Senate rejected this language, this event has been described as "probably the most significant event in the entire formulation of the first amendment."[42] Professor Anderson noted that "had it passed, Blackstone's crabbed view of press freedom would have been frozen into our Constitution."[43]

B. Purposes of the First Amendment

Absent a decisive indication of the Framers' intentions, both judges and academics have sought to find meaning by identifying the First Amendment's purpose or function.[44] As a matter of philosophical inquiry,

---

35. JOURNAL OF THE FIRST SESSION OF THE SENATE 70–71 (1789) (Joseph Gales & William W. Seaton, printers 1820).

36. Anderson, *supra* note 7, at 481.

37. LEONARD W. LEVY, INTRODUCTION TO FREEDOM OF THE PRESS FROM ZENGER TO JEFFERSON lvi-lix (Leonard W. Levy ed. 1966); Denbeaux, *supra* note 26 at 1168–71.

38. Anderson, *supra* note 7, at 501. *See* RODNEY A. SMOLLA AND MELVILLE B. NIMMER, THE FIRST AMENDMENT, § 1:9 (3d ed. 1997); William Van Alstyne, *A Graphic Review of the Free Speech Clause*, 70 Cal. L. Rev. 107, 111 n.11 (1982).

39. Anderson, *supra* note 7, at 501.

40. Denbeaux, *supra* note 26 at 1158–59 ("Today the word 'Congress' is not considered to limit the scope of the first amendment to the legislative branch of government. No one even argues that judicial prior restraints, not expressly based on statutes, are outside the first amendment.").

41. Journal of the First Session of the Senate 70.

42. Anderson, *supra* note 7, at 481.

43. *Id.*

44. *See, e.g.*, Frederick F. Schauer, *Categories and the First Amendment: A Play in Three Acts*, 34 Vand. L. Rev. 265, 291 n.124

such discourse is necessary for determining whether or to what extent freedom of speech is a good.[45] In judicial practice, the articulation of First Amendment purposes often facilitates a balancing process, through which the free speech purpose at issue is weighed against some other competing social value.[46] Such analyses also are employed to give meaning to the First Amendment concepts of freedom of speech and press.

Perhaps the most stirring and comprehensive judicial statement of First Amendment values is contained in Justice Brandeis' concurring opinion in *Whitney v. California*:[47]

> Those who won our independence believed that the final end of the state was to make men free to develop their faculties; and that in its government the deliberative forces should prevail over the arbitrary. They valued liberty both as an end and as a means. They believed liberty to be the secret of happiness and courage to be the secret of liberty. They believed that freedom to think as you will and to speak as you think are means indispensable to the discovery and spread of political truth; that without free speech and assembly discussion would be futile; that with them, discussion affords ordinarily adequate protection against the dissemination of noxious doctrine; that the greatest menace to freedom is an inert people; that public discussion is a political duty; and that this should be a fundamental principle of the American government. They recognized the risks to which all human institutions are subject. But they knew that order cannot be secured merely through fear of punishment for its infraction; that it is hazardous to discourage thought, hope and imagination; that fear breeds repression; that repression breeds hate; that hate menaces stable government; that the path of safety lies in the opportunity to discuss freely supposed grievances and proposed remedies; and that the fitting remedy for evil counsels is good ones. Believing in the power of reason as applied through public discussion, they eschewed silence coerced by law—the argument of force in its worst form. Recognizing the occasional tyrannies of governing majorities, they amended the Constitution so that free speech and assembly should be guaranteed.

Thus, in a single statement, Justice Brandeis touched on virtually all the purposes that have been proposed as components of the First Amendment. Freedom of speech and the press, in his view, enables citizens to become enlightened, to be self-fulfilled, to govern themselves, to exert a check on arbitrary power and protects the government from

---

(1981) ("It is important that we recognize just how much of the legal structure of first amendment doctrine is determined by the first amendment's substantive philosophical foundations. We may choose to draw these philosophical foundations from the Framers' view of them, or we may ... choose to construct a theory of free speech not constrained by the views of those long dead. In any event, we must do something.").

45. *E.g.*, J.S. Mill, On Liberty (1859).

46. *See* Melville B. Nimmer, Freedom of Speech § 2.05[A] (1984). *See also* Smolla, *supra*, n. 38 at §§ 2:1–2:39; 2:12 n. 1 (questioning utility of term "definitional balancing").

47. 274 U.S. 357, 375–76, 47 S.Ct. 641, 648, 71 L.Ed. 1095, 1105–06 (1927).

the inevitable political reprisals caused by censorship. Although this impassioned statement did not help the defendant in *Whitney*, who was convicted for her activities in helping to organize the Communist Labor Party of California, the various values it recognized have provided a foundation for subsequent protections of free speech.

1. Free Speech as a Source of The Enlightenment Function

The First Amendment is rooted in the philosophy that free discussion is an essential precondition of the search for truth. It is based on John Milton's poetic notion that where "[Truth] and Falsehood grapple; who ever knew Truth put to the worse, in a free and open encounter?"[48] But where Milton's imagery may conjure a vision of *Godzilla vs. King Kong*, and along with it some doubt about truth's ultimate victory, John Stuart Mill's penetrating logic provides more assurance. Mill wrote that "the dictum that truth always triumphs over persecution" was "a pleasant falsehood ... which all experience refutes." But he concluded:

> The real advantage that truth has consists in this, that when an opinion is true, it may be extinguished once, twice or many times, but in the course of ages there will generally be found persons to rediscover it, until some one of its reappearances falls on a time when from favourable circumstances it escapes persecution until it has made such head as to withstand all subsequent attempts to suppress it.[49]

For those disinclined to await "the course of ages" for the discovery of truth, Mill argued that the only hope of attaining such knowledge was through the pursuit of open discussion. To permit the authorities to suppress an opinion, wrote Mill, is to presume their infallibility—a presumption not vindicated by history. Moreover, even where authorities may hold the key to truth, they deprive truth of its vitality by precluding open debate. "Truth, thus held [by official fiat], is but one superstition the more, accidentally clinging to the words which enunciate a truth."[50]

Such thinking was the basis for the "marketplace of ideas" metaphor in Justice Oliver Wendell Holmes' dissent in *Abrams v. United States*. Holmes wrote that "when men have realized that time has upset many fighting faiths, they may come to believe even more than they believe the very foundations of their own conduct that the ultimate good desired is better reached by free trade in ideas—that the best test of truth is the power of the thought to get itself accepted in the competition of the market. . . . That, at any rate, is the theory of our Constitution."[51] This metaphor has been criticized because of "distortions" in the marketplace (*e.g.*, media monopolies) or because of the inability of the market to produce truth,[52] but it has been defended as providing the

48. John Milton, Areopagitica.

49. J.S. Mill, On Liberty, Ch. II (1859).

50. *Id.*

51. 250 U.S. 616, 630, 40 S.Ct. 17, 22, 63 L.Ed. 1173, 1180 (1919) (Holmes, J., dissenting).

52. *E.g.*, C. Edwin Baker, Human Liberty and Freedom of Speech at 12–17 ("At least

"best test" of truth.[53] Noting the various purposes of free speech, Professor Blasi has suggested that Justice Holmes' metaphor "may have continuing force if a marketplace is thought of not so much as a site where prices are determined and purchases made but rather as a place where people gather to browse, to taste, and to commingle aimlessly."[54]

Whatever may be the status of the academic debate, the "enlightenment function" is well-entrenched in judicial decisions as a primary purpose of the First Amendment.[55] As the Supreme Court explained in *Milk Wagon Drivers Union v. Meadowmoor Dairies, Inc.*, "the Bill of Rights was the child of the Enlightenment. Back of the guaranty of free speech lay faith in the power of an appeal to reason by all the peaceful means for gaining access to the mind."[56] In *Red Lion Broadcasting Co. v. FCC*, the Court repeated Holmes' notion that "the purpose of the First Amendment [is] to preserve an uninhibited marketplace of ideas in which truth will ultimately prevail."[57] This view considers freedom of speech to be valuable both for the individual and society. As the Court noted in *Bose Corp. v. Consumers Union of United States Inc.*, "[t]he First Amendment presupposes that the freedom to speak one's mind is not only an aspect of individual liberty—and thus a good unto itself—but also is essential to the common quest for truth and the vitality of society as a whole."[58] These multiple benefits of free expression have led commenters to postulate subsets to the enlightenment function.

a. *Free Speech and Self-Governance*

The self-governance function of the First Amendment may be a subset of the enlightenment function, but it should not be considered to be a subordinate purpose. Some theorists have suggested that facilitating self-government is the First Amendment's only function, and the Supreme Court has noted that whatever else may be in dispute, "there is practically universal agreement that a major purpose of that Amendment was to protect the free discussion of governmental affairs."[59] Indeed, the

within the academic world, the assumptions on which the classic marketplace of ideas theory rests are almost universally rejected."); C. Edwin Baker, *Scope of the First Amendment Freedom of Speech*, 25 UCLA L. Rev. 964, 967–81 (1978); Kent Greenawalt, *Free Speech Justifications*, 89 Colum. L. Rev. 119, 132–41 (1989); Jerome A. Barron, *Access to the Press—A New First Amendment Right*, 80 Harv. L. Rev. 1641, 1647–48 (1967).

53. *See generally* MELVILLE B. NIMMER, FREEDOM OF SPEECH § 1.02 (1984).

54. Vincent Blasi, *The Checking Value in First Amendment Theory*, 1977 Am. B. Found. Res. J. 521, 551.

55. *See* ERIC M. BARENDT, FREEDOM OF SPEECH 8 (1985) ("Historically the most du-

rable argument for a free speech principle has been based on the importance of open discussion to the discovery of truth.").

56. 312 U.S. 287, 293, 61 S.Ct. 552, 555, 85 L.Ed. 836, 841 (1941).

57. 395 U.S. 367, 390, 89 S.Ct. 1794, 1806, 23 L.Ed.2d 371, 389 (1969).

58. 466 U.S. 485, 503, 104 S.Ct. 1949, 1961, 80 L.Ed.2d 502, 518 (1984).

59. Landmark Communications, Inc. v. Virginia, 435 U.S. 829, 838, 98 S.Ct. 1535, 1541, 56 L.Ed.2d 1, 10 (1978). *See* BARENDT, *supra* note 55 at 23 ("the argument from democracy has been the most influential theory in the development of twentieth-century free speech law").

Court has shown special sensitivity to the importance of political speech, and generally protects such expression with heightened scrutiny.[60]

It is not clear the extent to which the self-governance purpose is narrower than the general enlightenment function. Although speech that relates to the process of government would seem to be a less expansive category than all speech that relates to learning or education, the actual difference between the two is not readily apparent. Meiklejohn, for example, rejected the idea that the First Amendment protects a "freedom to speak." Rather, he concluded, it protects "the freedom of those activities of thought and communication by which we 'govern.' "[61] Meiklejohn did not intend by this that the First Amendment protects only campaign speeches and civics lessons. To the contrary, his theory of self-governance would extend protection to all expression that enables voters to develop "knowledge, intelligence [and] sensitivity to human values." This broad category would include "[e]ducation, in all its phases," the "achievements of philosophy and the sciences," "literature and the arts," and finally, "[p]ublic discussions of public issues."[62]

While Meiklejohn over the years expanded his concept of protected speech that promotes self government, the Court reached the same result, but by expressing the idea differently. Rather than describing political speech as an all-encompassing category, the Court found that First Amendment protections do not exclude non-political speech. Thus, the Court has stated that guarantees for speech and press are not the exclusive preserve of political expression,[63] but that the First Amendment creates a "right of the public to receive suitable access to social, political, esthetic, moral, and other ideas and experiences."[64] Indeed, the Court has made clear that the "First Amendment does not protect speech and assembly only to the extent it can be characterized as political.... 'free speech and a free press are not confined to any field of human interest.' "[65]

60. *E.g.*, Brown v. Hartlage, 456 U.S. 45, 52–53, 102 S.Ct. 1523, 1528–29, 71 L.Ed.2d 732, 740–741 (1982); In re Primus, 436 U.S. 412, 437–38, 98 S.Ct. 1893, 1908, 56 L.Ed.2d 417, 438–39 (1978); First National Bank of Boston v. Bellotti, 435 U.S. 765, 786, 98 S.Ct. 1407, 1421, 55 L.Ed.2d 707, 724 (1978); Buckley v. Valeo, 424 U.S. 1, 14, 96 S.Ct. 612, 632, 46 L.Ed.2d 659, 685 (1976).

61. Meiklejohn, *The First Amendment is an Absolute*, 1961 Sup. Ct. Rev. at 255.

62. *Id.* at 257. Judge Robert Bork has taken the position that the First Amendment protects only speech that is "explicitly political." Robert H. Bork, *Neutral Principles and Some First Amendment Problems*, 47 Ind. L.J. 20 (1971). However, he subsequently revised his view to include within the First Amendment "many forms of speech and writing that are not explicitly political." ROBERT H. BORK, THE TEMPTING OF AMERICA 333 (1990). Such an "obligingly expand[ed]" concept of political speech has been criticized as "tell[ing] us disappointingly little," for it "takes for granted the *virtues* of the self-governance to which it argues that free speech is so necessary." LAURENCE H. TRIBE, AMERICAN CONSTITUTIONAL LAW 787 (2d ed. 1988).

63. Time, Inc. v. Hill, 385 U.S. 374, 87 S.Ct. 534, 17 L.Ed.2d 456 (1967).

64. Red Lion Broadcasting Co., 395 U.S. at 390, 89 S.Ct. at 1807, 23 L.Ed.2d at 389. *See also* United Mine Workers v. Illinois State Bar Ass'n, 389 U.S. 217, 223, 88 S.Ct. 353, 356, 19 L.Ed.2d 426, 431 (1967); NAACP v. Alabama, 357 U.S. 449, 460–61, 78 S.Ct. 1163, 1171, 2 L.Ed.2d 1488, 1498–99 (1958).

65. United Mine Workers, 389 U.S. at 223, 88 S.Ct. at 356–57, 19 L.Ed.2d at 431. The Court also has noted that "full First

b.   *Free Speech and Self-Realization*

Another aspect of the enlightenment purpose values freedom of speech for its role in promoting individual development and fulfillment. As opposed to the social value of free expression represented by the self-governance model, self-realization is predicated on the idea that free speech is an end it itself because of its benefit to the individual.[66] Thus, "[t]he First Amendment serves not only the needs of the polity but also those of the human spirit—a spirit that demands self-expression."[67] This interest relates to the individual both as speaker and listener. By speaking, the person engages in self-expression, and by listening to others' ideas, the individual obtains the raw materials for personal development.

The Supreme Court has endorsed the self-realization purpose of the First Amendment in various ways. It has described free expression as "an integral part of the development of ideas and a sense of identity. . . . [underlying] the individual's worth and dignity;"[68] as promoting "self-fulfillment";[69] and as being a necessary precondition of "individual dignity and choice upon which our political system rests."[70] Accordingly, the Court has extended First Amendment protection to such presumably non-political subjects as "[s]exual expression which is indecent but not obscene";[71] "[m]usic, as a form of expression and communication";[72] and nude dancing.[73]

2.   *Free Speech as a "Check" on Official Abuse*

Another important purpose of free speech is its ability to serve as a check on the abuse of power by the government. This quality of free expression was described in an important article by Professor Vincent Blasi as the First Amendment's "checking value."[74] Although the checking value has been described alternately as a subset of the enlightenment

Amendment protection" extends to "expression about philosophical, social, artistic, economic, literary, or ethical matters." Abood v. Detroit Bd. of Educ., 431 U.S. 209, 231, 97 S.Ct. 1782, 1797, 52 L.Ed.2d 261, 281–82 (1977).

66. Meiklejohn's concept of self-governance relies on individual enlightenment, but for a utilitarian end. Meiklejohn, *The First Amendment is an Absolute*, 1961 Sup. Ct. Rev. at 263 ("I believe, as a teacher, that the people do need novels and dramas and paintings and poems, 'because they will be called upon to vote.'").

67. Procunier v. Martinez, 416 U.S. 396, 427, 94 S.Ct. 1800, 1818 40 L.Ed.2d 224, 248 (1974).

68. *Id.*

69. Police Dep't of Chicago v. Mosley, 408 U.S. 92, 96, 92 S.Ct. 2286, 2290, 33 L.Ed.2d 212, 216 (1972).

70. Cohen v. California, 403 U.S. 15, 24, 91 S.Ct. 1780, 1788, 29 L.Ed.2d 284, 293 (1971).

71. Sable Communications of California, Inc. v. FCC, 492 U.S. 115, 126, 109 S.Ct. 2829, 2836, 106 L.Ed.2d 93, 105 (1989).

72. Ward v. Rock Against Racism, 491 U.S. 781, 790, 109 S.Ct. 2746, 2753, 105 L.Ed.2d 661, 674 (1989).

73. Schad v. Mount Ephraim, 452 U.S. 61, 101 S.Ct. 2176, 68 L.Ed.2d 671 (1981). *But see* Barnes v. Glen Theatre, Inc., 501 U.S. 560, 111 S.Ct. 2456, 115 L.Ed.2d 504 (1991) (nude dancing may be banned where state's purpose is not to suppress communicative impact).

74. Blasi, *supra* note 54, at 527.

or self-governance functions,[75] its significance is independent of education or democratic theory. Free speech limits abusive government regardless whether citizens gain useful knowledge from exposés or have an active role in governmental affairs.

Even before the First Amendment institutionalized free speech, eighteenth century political writer John Wilkes commented that the press in colonial America was "the terror of all bad ministers; for their dark and dangerous designs, or their weakness, inability and duplicity, have thus been detected and shewn to the public, generally in too strong and just colours for them long to bear up against the odium of mankind."[76] Expanding on this sentiment, Blasi concluded that "the role of the ordinary citizen is not so much to contribute on a continuing basis to the formation of public policy as to retain a veto power to be employed when the decisions of officials pass certain bounds."[77] Thus, a free press acts as a check on government whether or not the public participates in governmental affairs.

The late Professor Melville Nimmer has suggested that the checking value should be considered a part of the enlightenment function because exposing malfeasance "provides a ground for public opposition to official action."[78] But this analysis may assume that the public takes more of an active role than is necessary. Organizations such as Amnesty International seek to reduce human rights violations around the world by focusing world opinion on such abuses. These tactics often have an effect even though the governments involved usually are not democratic and where there is no formal opposition by their citizens. Although the 1989 massacre in Tiennamen Square, which took place in full view of CNN, provides a counter example, one can only speculate whether the Chinese government's actions would have been more swift or harsh absent the glare of publicity.

3. Free Speech as a Safety Valve Function

Another related purpose of free speech is its capacity to reduce social unrest by allowing citizens to voice their concerns. In this regard, what has been called the "safety valve" function is the benign flip side of clear and present danger.[79] Rather than representing an incitement, the ability to give voice to deep social resentments may dissipate the pressures that otherwise would lead to violence or revolt.[80] This function of the First

---

75. MELVILLE B. NIMMER, FREEDOM OF SPEECH § 1.02[I] at 1–47 through 1–48 (1984) (enlightenment function); Herbert v. Lando, 441 U.S. 153, 185, 99 S.Ct. 1635, 1653, 60 L.Ed.2d 115, 139 (1979) (Brennan, J., dissenting in part) (self-governance function).

76. John Wilkes, The North Briton, No. 1, June 5, 1762, at 1–2, *quoted in* Blasi, *supra* note 54, at 531.

77. *Id.* at 542.

78. NIMMER, § 1.02[I] at 1–48.

79. *Id.* at § 1.04; Kenneth L. Karst, *Equality as a Central Principle in the First Amendment*, 43 U. Chi. L. Rev. 20, 23 n.18 (1975). *See also* Blasi, *supra* note 54, at 550 (describing safety valve as a positive aspect of a marketplace of ideas approach).

80. *See* Kent Greenawalt, *Speech and Crime*, 1980 Am. B. Found. Res. J. at 672–73. *See also* Thomas I. Emerson, *First Amendment Doctrine and the Burger Court*, 68 Cal. L. Rev. 422, 428 (1980) (free speech promotes "orderly social change").

Amendment was summed up in Justice Brandeis' statement that "it is hazardous to discourage thought, hope and imagination" and "the path of safety lies in the opportunity to discuss freely supposed grievances."[81] Not all would agree that this is beneficial. Herbert Marcuse, for example, complained that the safety valve function prevents revolution and thereby represents "repressive tolerance."[82]

The Supreme Court has recognized the importance of free expression as a means of forestalling social unrest but has not promoted the "safety valve" concept as a principal First Amendment justification. In cases involving labor unrest, for example, the Court has acknowledged the need for a safety valve but nevertheless upheld speech restrictions. Thus, in *Milk Wagon Drivers Union v. Meadowmoor Dairies, Inc.*, the Court noted that the First Amendment was given "generous scope" in order "to avert force and explosions due to restrictions upon rational modes of communication" but upheld an injunction against labor picketing in order to prevent violence.[83] Similarly, the Court upheld the right of a plant manager to bring a libel claim against a union and some of its members for defamatory statements made during a labor organizing campaign in *Linn v. United Plant Guard Workers, Local 114*.[84] Justice Fortas complained in dissent that "lusty speech provides a useful safety valve for the tensions which often accompany these controversies."[85]

This is not to suggest, however, that the Court has never found significant interpretive value in the First Amendment's safety valve effect. In the context of allowing access to criminal trials, the Supreme Court noted that denying citizens knowledge of "society's responses to criminal conduct" could result in "outrage and protest" that in turn could lead to "vengeful 'self-help.' "[86] The threat of violence, however, was substantiated by historical reference to "the activities of vigilante 'committees' on our frontiers."[87] This suggests that as the threat of violence becomes more immediate, the Court may have a tendency to favor the "clear and present danger" side of the equation, as it did in the labor cases, as opposed to exalting the First Amendment's "safety valve" effect.

4. *The Diversity Principle*

Another widely accepted purpose of the First Amendment is to promote "the widest possible dissemination of information from diverse and antagonistic sources."[88] This goal has been used as a rationale in

81. Whitney, 274 U.S. at 375, 47 S.Ct. at 648, 71 L.Ed. at 1106 (Brandeis, J. concurring).

82. *See, e.g.*, HERBERT MARCUSE, REPRESSIVE TOLERANCE IN WOLFF, MOORE JR. & MARCUSE, A CRITIQUE OF PURE TOLERANCE 81 (1965).

83. 312 U.S. 287, 293, 61 S.Ct. 552, 555, 85 L.Ed. 836, 841 (1941).

84. 383 U.S. 53, 86 S.Ct. 657, 15 L.Ed.2d 582 (1966).

85. *Id.* at 73, 86 S.Ct. at 668, 15 L.Ed.2d at 596.

86. Richmond Newspapers, Inc. v. Virginia, 448 U.S. 555, 571, 100 S.Ct. 2814, 2824, 65 L.Ed.2d 973, 986 (1980) (plurality opinion).

87. *Id.*

88. Associated Press v. United States, 326 U.S. 1, 20, 65 S.Ct. 1416, 1424–25, 89 L.Ed. 2013, 2030 (1945).

certain cases to permit the government to intervene in the media marketplace in order affirmatively to promote information diversity. Some theorists have taken this to be the "aim of the Amendment, its 'underlying premise.' "[89] This "diversity principle" differs from the other First Amendment functions that have been postulated in that it presupposes the value and purpose of free speech.[90] But whatever value one chooses, according to this theory, more of it will result from diverse and antagonistic sources.

The diversity principle emerged from a controversy over the extent to which the First Amendment immunized newspapers from the antitrust laws. In *Associated Press v. United States*, the Supreme Court upheld a Sherman Act claim against the news wire service that arose from AP's restrictive bylaws. Under the bylaws, AP could fine or suspend any member newspaper that failed to publish AP news regularly or that did not provide news from its region to the wire service. The bylaws also prohibited members from selling news to nonmembers or otherwise making AP stories available to nonmembers in advance of publication. Although a nonmember publication could easily join AP if it did not compete with an existing member, competing nonmembers had to overcome significant restrictions to obtain membership.

The Court made short shrift of AP's argument that its business practices were protected by the First Amendment. "It would be strange indeed," Justice Black wrote for the Court, "if the grave concern for freedom of the press which prompted adoption of the First Amendment should be read as a command that the government was without power to protect that freedom."[91] He explained:

> Surely a command that the government itself shall not impede the free flow of ideas does not afford non-governmental combinations a refuge if they impose restraints upon that constitutionally guaranteed freedom. Freedom to publish means freedom for all and not for some. Freedom to publish is guaranteed by the Constitution, but freedom to combine to keep others from publishing is not. Freedom of the press from governmental interference under the First Amendment does not sanction repression of that freedom by private interests.[92]

89. Henry Geller, Fiber Optics: An Opportunity for a New Policy? 11 (1991).

90. Although the "diversity principle" generally is used to describe the government's authority to promote First Amendment values affirmatively, some scholars have referred to the "diversity value" of free speech as a synonym for the marketplace of ideas concept. *E.g.*, Blasi, *supra* note 54, at 548–54.

91. 326 U.S. at 20, 65 S.Ct. at 1424, 89 L.Ed. at 2030.

92. *Id.*, 65 S.Ct. at 1425, 89 L.Ed. at 2030–31. Justice Roberts and Murphy argued in dissent that the record did not support a finding that the AP actually restrained the distribution of news. Justice Roberts pointed to the existence of 20 to 30 competing wire services and quoted the District Court's finding that "AP does not prevent or hinder nonmember newspapers from obtaining access to domestic and foreign happenings and events." *Id.* at 39, 65 S.Ct. at 1433, 89 L.Ed. at 2041 (Roberts, J., dissenting). Due to access to other wire services, Justice Roberts found no evidence that AP's bylaws "work any hindrance or restraint of competition as between agencies or newspapers." *Id.* at 41, 65 S.Ct. at 1434, 89 L.Ed. at 2041. Justice Murphy

Associated Press was not the first case to uphold the use of antitrust law against the press or other mass media businesses,[93] but it was the Court's first foray into the First Amendment implications of such intervention. Its conclusion that the government could restrain a speaker in order to promote the value of speech presented a novel conception of constitutional rights.

The Court, recognizing that "using law affirmatively to promote more effective functioning of the system of freedom of expression" is inherently "a risky enterprise"[94] has limited its use of the diversity principle. Thus, it has permitted only limited intervention into the publishing industry in the name of promoting competition among newspapers or expanding the marketplace of ideas.[95] On the other hand, the Court has endorsed more liberal use of the principle in regulating newer forms of communication. Broadcasting, for example, has been subjected to more extensive content regulation, as well as rules requiring diversification of ownership.[96] Similarly, telephone companies—most notably AT & T and the local Bell Operating Companies—for years were prevented from providing information services, including cable television.[97] Restrictions on the Bell companies were expressly predicated on the diversity principle enunciated in *Associated Press*. Finally, Congress extended the diversity principle to cable television by authorizing local franchising authorities to require public, educational and governmental access channels as a condition for obtaining a cable franchise.[98] These applications of

argued that the Court should have required "clear and unmistakable proof" of an antitrust violation in order to prevent "unjustified governmental interference" with the distribution of information. *Id.* at 52–53, 65 S.Ct. at 1439, 89 L.Ed. at 2047–48 (Murphy, J., dissenting).

93. Associated Press v. NLRB, 301 U.S. 103, 57 S.Ct. 650, 81 L.Ed. 953 (1937); Indiana Farmer's Guide Publishing Co. v. Prairie Farmer Publishing Co., 293 U.S. 268, 55 S.Ct. 182, 79 L.Ed. 356 (1934); Paramount Famous Lasky Corp. v. United States, 282 U.S. 30, 51 S.Ct. 42, 75 L.Ed. 145 (1930); United States v. First National Pictures, 282 U.S. 44, 51 S.Ct. 45, 75 L.Ed. 151 (1930); Binderup v. Pathe Exchange, Inc., 263 U.S. 291, 44 S.Ct. 96, 68 L.Ed. 308 (1923) (motion pictures).

94. Thomas I. Emerson, The System of Freedom of Expression at 627, 630.

95. *E.g.,* Miami Herald Publishing Co. v. Tornillo, 418 U.S. 241, 94 S.Ct. 2831, 41 L.Ed.2d 730 (1974) (state cannot impose right of reply obligation on press despite economic concentration in industry); Times–Picayune Publishing Co. v. United States, 345 U.S. 594, 73 S.Ct. 872, 97 L.Ed. 1277 (1953) (unit plan requiring purchase of advertising in co-owned newspapers not an illegal tying arrangement).

96. Red Lion Broadcasting Co. v. FCC, 395 U.S. 367, 390, 89 S.Ct. 1794, 1806, 23

L.Ed.2d 371, 389 (1969) (personal attack rules upheld on the theory that "[i]t is the purpose of the First Amendment to preserve an uninhibited marketplace of ideas in which truth will ultimately prevail, rather than to countenance monopolization of that market."); FCC v. National Citizens Committee for Broadcasting, 436 U.S. 775, 98 S.Ct. 2096, 56 L.Ed.2d 697 (1978) (newspaper-broadcast cross-ownership restrictions upheld).

97. Virtually all telephone companies were prevented from providing local cable television service within their local service areas by Section 611 of the Cable Communications Policy Act of 1984, 47 U.S.C.A. § 531 (West 1991). AT & T and the BOCs were precluded from involvement—both inside and outside their service areas—by the terms of the Modification of Final Judgment. United States v. American Tel. and Tel. Co., 552 F.Supp. 131, 180–86, 189–90 (D.D.C.1982), *aff'd sub nom.* Maryland v. United States, 460 U.S. 1001, 103 S.Ct. 1240, 75 L.Ed.2d 472 (1983). These restrictions were eliminated by the Telecommunications Act of 1996.

98. Cable Communications Policy Act of 1984, 47 U.S.C.A. § 531 (West 1991).

the diversity principle were far more expansive than *Associated Press*, for they were not limited responses to specific antitrust violations. Instead, they for the most part were prophylactic regulations of economic markets that were directed toward the same ultimate goal of promoting speech.[99] Proponents of the diversity principle argue that it creates an affirmative right of access to the mass media.[100]

Opponents, on the other hand, argue that the theory vests too much control in the government and thereby acts as a limitation on speech.[1] In court, telephone companies challenged the information services restrictions in the MFJ as violating their First Amendment rights. They suggested that by prohibiting market entry by a potential provider of information services, the restrictions only hampered the marketplace of ideas for all participants. The District Court rejected these arguments, again citing the diversity principle.[2] On appeal, however, the District of Columbia Circuit reversed the lower court, but without discussing the constitutional issue.[3] The United States Court of Appeals for the District of Columbia Circuit subsequently upheld against a First Amendment challenge a provision of the Telecommunications Act of 1996 that prevented BOCs from engaging in electronic publishing except through a separate subsidiary or joint venture. The court held that the provision addressed Congress' concern about potential anticompetitive abuses, and that, in any event, the affected companies "are free to use whatever portion of their pooled resources they wish for electronic publishing, subject only to the need for structural separation."[4]

---

99. The MFJ restrictions on AT & T and the BOCs were based on antitrust claims, but nevertheless were prospective in nature. There was no record of past anticompetitive activity in the information services industry because, for the most part, there was no information services industry. Judge Greene imposed the MFJ restrictions in the hope that the limitations would encourage the development of a competitive industry. United States v. American Tel. and Tel. Co., 552 F.Supp. at 189–90.

100. *E.g.*, Geller, *supra* note 88, at 11.

1. *E.g.*, THE DIVERSITY PRINCIPLE 47–53 (The Media Institute 1989); Jonathan W. Emord, *The First Amendment Invalidity of FCC Ownership Regulations,* 38 Cath. U. L. Rev. 401 (1989).

2. United States v. Western Elec. Co. Inc., 673 F.Supp. 525, 585–86 (D.D.C.1987), *rev'd*, 283 U.S.App.D.C. 299, 900 F.2d 283 (D.C.Cir.), cert. denied *sub nom*. MCI Communications Corp. v. United States, 498 U.S. 911, 111 S.Ct. 283, 112 L.Ed.2d 238 (1990). *See also* United States v. Western Elec. Co. Inc., 714 F.Supp. 1, 4 (D.D.C. 1988), *rev'd*, 900 F.2d 283, 283 U.S.App. D.C. 299 (D.C.Cir.), cert. denied *sub nom.*

MCI Communications Corp. v. United States, 498 U.S. 911, 111 S.Ct. 283, 112 L.Ed.2d 238 (1990).

3. 900 F.2d at 289, 283 U.S. App. D.C. at 305. The court noted that "relatively few information services were provided to the public" before the MFJ and that the parties agreed to the restriction "as a precautionary measure in light of uncertainty about how divestiture of AT&T would affect the development of this embryonic market." It remanded the question to the District Court with directions to lift the information services restriction unless it found, under current market conditions, that "the proposed modification would be certain to lessen competition in the relevant market." *Id.* at 323–24, 900 F. 2d at 307. Based on this mandate, the District Court reluctantly agreed to lift the information services restrictions. United States v. Western Elec. Co. Inc., 767 F.Supp. 308 (D.D.C.1991), *aff'd*, 993 F.2d 1572, 301 U.S. App. D.C. 268 (D.C.Cir.), cert denied, *sub. nom.* Consumer Fed'n of Am. v. United States, 510 U.S. 984, 114 S.Ct. 487, 126 L.Ed.2d 438 (1993).

4. BellSouth Corp. v. FCC, 144 F.3d 58, 71, 330 U.S.App.D.C. 109 (1998).

1.3 *Early First Amendment Experience

1.4 The State Action Requirement

"That 'Congress shall make no law ... abridging the freedom of speech, or of the press' is a restraint on government action, not that of private persons."[1] Although the First Amendment's express terms appear to restrict only federal lawmaking powers,[2] it has been construed to limit federal executive and judicial power as well as state and local government action.[3] Thus, while governmental actions at all levels clearly are covered by the First Amendment, it is not always a simple matter to separate private from government behavior. This is particularly true where certain speakers are subjected to extensive regulation.

In certain cases, private actions will be subject to constitutional scrutiny when those acts are facilitated by or enforced by the state.[4] For example, in *NAACP v. Alabama*,[5] the Supreme Court struck down a state law that compelled the NAACP to disclose its membership lists as a condition of doing business in the state. The state law was not considered an abridgment of speech *per se*, but disclosure of the membership information exposed the organization's members to reprisals by private parties that included economic sanctions, loss of jobs, threat of physical violence and "other manifestations of public hostility."[6] Similarly, in *Bates v. City of Little Rock*,[7] the Court held that the government could not compel NAACP to disclose its membership lists so that the city could enforce its occupational license tax. The Court acknowledged that the "repressive effect" of disclosure was due "in part" to "private attitudes and pressures," but concluded that the problem arose "only after the exercise of governmental power had threatened to force disclosure of the members' names."[8]

---

* Published in Practitioners Edition only.

1. Columbia Broadcasting Sys., Inc. v. Democratic Nat'l Comm., 412 U.S. 94, 114, 93 S.Ct. 2080, 2092, 36 L.Ed.2d 772, 790 (1973). *See* Hudgens v. NLRB, 424 U.S. 507, 513, 96 S.Ct. 1029, 1033, 47 L.Ed.2d 196, 202–203 (1976); Public Utilities Comm'n v. Pollak, 343 U.S. 451, 461, 72 S.Ct. 813, 820, 96 L.Ed. 1068, 1077 (1952).

2. Leonard B. Levy, Legacy of Suppression: Freedom of Speech and Press in Early American History 221–24 (1960); Phillip B. Kurland, *The Irrelevance of the Constitution: The First Amendment's Freedom of Speech and Freedom of Press Clauses*, 29 Drake L. Rev. 1, 2 (1979–80).

3. *E.g.,* Organization for a Better Austin v. Keefe, 402 U.S. 415, 91 S.Ct. 1575, 29 L.Ed.2d 1 (1971) (judicial prior restraint); Carroll v. President and Comm'r of Princess Anne, 393 U.S. 175, 89 S.Ct. 347, 21 L.Ed.2d 325 (1968) (prior restraint initi-

ated by executive branch); Gitlow v. New York, 268 U.S. 652, 45 S.Ct. 625, 69 L.Ed. 1138 (1925) (First Amendment applies to state government actions through the Fourteenth Amendment).

4. *E.g.,* Shelley v. Kraemer, 334 U.S. 1, 68 S.Ct. 836, 92 L.Ed. 1161 (1948); Marsh v. Alabama, 326 U.S. 501, 66 S.Ct. 276, 90 L.Ed. 265 (1946) (company town had characteristics of municipality and could be analogized to public property).

5. 357 U.S. 449, 78 S.Ct. 1163, 2 L.Ed.2d 1488 (1958).

6. *Id.* at 462, 78 S.Ct. at 1172, 2 L.Ed.2d at 1500.

7. 361 U.S. 516, 80 S.Ct. 412, 4 L.Ed.2d 480 (1960).

8. *Id.* at 524, 80 S.Ct. at 417, 4 L.Ed.2d at 486. *See also* Reitman v. Mulkey, 387 U.S. 369, 87 S.Ct. 1627, 18 L.Ed.2d 830 (1967).

Generally, reviewing courts will seek to determine if there is "a sufficiently close nexus" between the government and the private entity "so that the action of the latter may be fairly treated as that of the State itself."[9] The determination of whether state action exists in such cases generally is the result of a complicated and fact-specific inquiry. "Only by sifting facts and weighing circumstances can the nonobvious involvement of the State in private conduct be attributed its true significance."[10]

Such analysis does not normally result in a finding of state action. Thus, corporate policies generally are not considered to be actions of the state, even when implemented by highly regulated industries. The Supreme Court has ruled that the monopoly status granted public utilities, government licensing of business operations, and regulation of corporate activities are insufficient to convert private action to state action. For example, in *Jackson v. Metropolitan Edison Co.*, the Court held that termination of a customer's service by a public utility was not subject to constitutional review because it did not involve government action.[11] The Court held that the fact that disconnection was accomplished via a tariff filed with the state did not convert private action to state action.[12] It made clear that a service disconnection is not state action "where the initiative comes from [the utility] and not from the State."[13]

Under this analysis, the fact that certain communications media are licensed does not transform them into government agents. In *Columbia Broadcasting System v. Democratic National Committee*, the Supreme Court held that broadcast station operators are not engaged in state action despite being licensed by the federal government.[14] The Court acknowledged that the federal government subjects broadcasters to extensive regulation and that licensees operate as "public trustees." Nevertheless, it did not find that the government could be considered a "partner" in making editorial decisions or that the FCC and its licensees are engaged in a "symbiotic relationship" such as to create state action.[15]

The same cannot be said, however, when the licensee is itself a governmental body. Public television stations that are operated by state agencies are engaged in state action and may be subjected to First Amendment claims. In *Forbes v. Arkansas Educational Television Communication Network Foundation*, for example, the United States Court of Appeals for the Eighth Circuit held that the plaintiff had made out a

9. Jackson v. Metropolitan Edison Co., 419 U.S. 345, 351, 95 S.Ct. 449, 453, 42 L.Ed.2d 477, 484 (1974) (citation omitted).

10. Burton v. Wilmington Parking Auth., 365 U.S. 715, 722, 81 S.Ct. 856, 860, 6 L.Ed.2d 45, 50 (1961).

11. 419 U.S. 345, 95 S.Ct. 449, 42 L.Ed.2d 477 (1974).

12. *Id.* at 354–55, 95 S.Ct. at 455–56, 42 L.Ed.2d at 485–86.

13. *Id.* at 357, 95 S.Ct. at 457, 42 L.Ed.2d at 487. *See also* Blum v. Yaretsky, 457 U.S. 991, 1004, 102 S.Ct. 2777, 2786 73

L.Ed.2d 534, 546 (1982) ("a State normally can be held responsible for a private decision only when it has exercised coercive power or has provided such significant encouragement, either overt or covert, that the choice must in law be deemed to be that of the State.").

14. 412 U.S. 94, 114–121, 93 S.Ct. 2080, 2092–99, 36 L.Ed.2d 772, 790–794 (1973).

15. *Id.* at 119, 93 S.Ct. at 2094, 36 L.Ed.2d at 793.

First Amendment claim after being excluded from a candidates' debate hosted by a public television station. Unlike commercial stations, the court reasoned, public television licensees are "faced with constraints not shared by other television stations."[16] Accordingly, the licensee's decision to host a debate was treated as a public forum question. The Supreme Court reversed the Eighth Circuit's conclusion that the debate in question was a designated public forum but acknowledged that candidate debates on public broadcasting stations should be considered "a forum of some type."[16A]

This is not to suggest that public ownership of the means of communication is a necessary precondition to a finding of state action. Rather, a coercive relationship or coordinated action between the government and a regulated communications business may be sufficient. This question has arisen in cases involving public and leased access channels on cable television systems, which set aside channels for commercial, public and designated community groups. Although cable operators are private entities that, for the most part, exercise independent editorial control over their channels of communication, they are subject to both local and federal regulations. Local franchising ordinances determine the extent to which cable operators will provide public access channels, while federal law establishes a channel set-aside for unaffiliated commercial channels.[17] In this circumstance, changes in regulations that affect the terms of channel access present state action issues.

The Cable Television Consumer Protection and Competition Act of 1992 modified access requirements for sexually-oriented programming on these channels.[18] Whereas cable operators generally were precluded from exercising editorial control over access channels, the 1992 Act permitted them to ban "indecent" programming from leased or public access channels.[19] Cable operators who chose to permit such programming on leased channels were required to segregate indecent programming onto a separate channel and block subscriber access until a customer requested access in writing.[20] The Act also eliminated cable operators' immunity from criminal and civil liability for obscene programming shown on access channels.[21]

On review, a panel of the United States Court of Appeals for the District of Columbia Circuit invalidated the changes, finding state action.[22] Sitting en banc, however, the court reversed this holding, reasoning that cable operators were simply being given discretion as private

---

16. 93 F.3d 497, 505 (8th Cir.1996) (en banc). *See also* DeYoung v. Patten, 898 F.2d 628, 631–32 (8th Cir.1990) (public television licensee is a state actor).

16A. Arkansas Educational Television Comm'n v. Forbes, 523 U.S. 666, 118 S.Ct. 1633, 1641, 140 L.Ed.2d 875, 886 (1998).

17. 47 U.S.C.A. §§ 531–532 (West 1991).

18. Pub. L. No. 102–385, 106 Stat. 1460, 1486 (1992).

19. 47 U.S.C.A. §§ 531, 532(h) (West Supp. 1997).

20. *Id.* § 532(j).

21. *Id.* § 558.

22. Alliance for Community Media v. FCC, 10 F.3d 812, 304 U.S. App. D.C. 37 (D.C.Cir.1993), *vacated*, 15 F.3d 186, 304 U.S. App. D.C. 367 (D.C.Cir.1994).

actors to exercise their editorial prerogatives.[23] Noting that the case "turns on the presence or absence of 'state action,' "[24] the en banc court held that the prohibition on indecent speech was "voluntary, not mandatory," and that cable operators were not being deputized as "involuntary government surrogates."[25] The court's extended analysis of the state action questions concluded that cable operators were not being coerced into making programming choices favored by the government, but that if they were, the United States "would be hard put to defend the constitutionality of these provisions."[26]

In *Denver Area Educational Telecommunications Consortium* v. *FCC*[27], the Supreme Court reversed this decision, in substantial part. In a long and fragmented decision, the Court barely mentioned the state action issue, focusing instead upon the burdens the various sections of the Act imposed on constitutionally protected speech. It gave little weight to the District of Columbia Circuit's en banc ruling on this question, noting that "[a]lthough the court said that it found no 'state action,' . . . it could not have meant that phrase literally, for, of course, petitioners attack (as 'abridg[ing] . . . speech') a congressional statute—which, by definition, is an Act of 'Congress.' "[28] The Court upheld the section of the 1992 Cable act that permitted cable operators to refuse carriage of indecent programming on leased access channels, but subjected the law to close First Amendment scrutiny. It invalidated the other provisions that required segregation and blocking of indecent programming, and that permitted deletion of indecent programming on public access channels.[29]

Another scenario involving cable television access channels was presented in *Missouri Knights of the Ku Klux Klan v. Kansas City*.[30] The case involved a public access channel established by Kansas City through its franchise with the cable television operator. The arrangement provided a channel for general public use, and the cable operator also made available production facilities and staff assistance free of charge. Access to the channel was guaranteed to the public on a first-come, first-served basis and could not be denied based on the access viewpoints expressed.

This open policy was revised after the cable operator received an access request from the Missouri Knights of the Ku Klux Klan to transmit a series of 45 programs entitled "Race and Reason." After several pretextual attempts to deny access, the city and the cable operator devised a plan by which the access channel would be eliminated

---

23. Alliance for Community Media v. FCC, 56 F.3d, 105, 312 U.S. App. D.C. 141 (D.C.Cir.1995), *rev'd in part sub nom.* Denver Area Educational Telecommunications Consortium v. FCC, 518 U.S. 727, 116 S.Ct. 2374, 135 L.Ed.2d 888 (1996).

24. *Id.* at 113, 312 U.S. App. D.C. at 149.

25. *Id.* at 116, 312 U.S. App. D.C. at 152 (citation omitted).

26. *Id.* at 113, 312 U.S. App. D.C. at 149.

27. 518 U.S. 727, 116 S.Ct. 2374, 135 L.Ed.2d 888 (1996).

28. *Id.* at 735, 116 S.Ct. at 2382, 135 L.Ed.2d at 898.

29. *Id.* at 760, 116 S.Ct. at 2394, 135 L.Ed.2d at 913.

30. 723 F.Supp. 1347 (W.D.Mo.1989).

and a new channel created under the cable operator's editorial control. The new channel was to continue transmitting programs previously aired on the city's access channel without editorial interference, but with one exception. The cable operator would reserve its editorial powers for "extremist groups," including the Klan.

In the litigation that followed, Kansas City moved to dismiss the First Amendment claim for a lack of state action on grounds that the new channel was privately owned and controlled. The District Court declined to dismiss the suit, finding that the private ownership of the channel was less relevant than the fact that the city had worked together with the cable operator to restrict access by the Klan to what previously had been a public forum. The court noted that where a private channel of communication is "within the sphere of government control," then "any restriction of speech in that forum [must be] subjected to First Amendment analysis."[31]

Such coordination between the government and regulated communication industry also has occurred in the telephone context. Common carriers are highly regulated by state governments in such matters as rates and service. However, as certain information services became available by telephone, some states were tempted to use their regulatory powers to influence carriers' decisions to permit "objectionable" content. This occurred most frequently with telephone sex services, or "dial-a-porn." Courts have reached differing results on whether a local telephone company's decision to discriminate between "Dial–It" customers on the basis of content raises a constitutional question.

In *Carlin Communications, Inc. v. South Central Bell Telephone Co.*, for example, the Louisiana Court of Appeals held that a tariff authorizing disconnection of "dial-a-porn" service constituted state action under *Jackson* because it was adopted "to protect the public interest" as opposed to the company's "private economic interest."[32] Despite its holding on the state action issue, the court approved the carrier's decision to disconnect "dial-a-porn" operators. The tariff provision prohibited the transmission of obscene messages, and another state court had ruled that the messages in questions were "patently obscene."[33]

At least one federal court employed similar reasoning, but was reversed on appeal. Mountain States Telephone and Telegraph Company was permanently enjoined from terminating service to a "dial-a-porn" provider on First Amendment grounds. The district court considered the termination to be state action because the telephone company "assumed a public function ... of protecting the public from sexually suggestive

31. *Id*. at 1351.

32. 461 So.2d 1208, 1212 (La.App.1984). *Cf.* Cahill v. Public Service Comm'n, 113 A.D.2d 603, 498 N.Y.S.2d 499 (1986), *aff'd* 69 N.Y.2d 265, 513 N.Y.S.2d 656, 506 N.E.2d 187 (1986). (telephone rates adopted pursuant to PSC regulations which allowed the telephone company to pass to customers

the cost of charitable donations held to be state action); Figari v. New York Telephone Co., 32 A.D.2d 434, 303 N.Y.S.2d 245 (1969) (telephone service tariffs considered synonymous with state regulations).

33. 461 So.2d at 1210.

messages."[34] Although the court of appeals agreed that the initial decision to terminate service constituted state action, it reversed the district court with respect to a total ban on adult entertainment services, holding that telephone company policies did not constitute state action. The court found that Mountain Bell policies against dial-a-porn resulted from the company's "independent business judgment."[35]

Another circuit court used the same theory to uphold a telephone company tariff that all but banned "dial-a-porn" services. In *Carlin Communication, Inc. v. Southern Bell Telephone & Telegraph Co.*, the United States Court of Appeals for the Eleventh Circuit concluded that "[a] private business is free to choose the content of messages with which its name and reputation will be associated and such a choice is not the exercise of a public function."[36] Citing *Jackson*, the Eleventh Circuit disagreed with the reasoning of *South Central Bell Telephone Co.* The court stressed that "mere approval by the PSC of a business practice of the regulated utility does not 'transmute a practice initiated by the utility' into state action."[37]

The court also distinguished *South Central Bell Telephone Co.* factually, pointing out that the tariff in that case had been motivated by a desire to protect "the general public, including minors."[38] It found no such public policy intent underlying the "dial-a-porn" ban it upheld, but instead found as its purpose a desire by Southern Bell to "protect its own corporate image."[39] Moreover, the court noted that Southern Bell chose its tariff language specifically to divorce its message content requirement from the legal definition of obscenity.

In another case, however, the Ninth Circuit found state action in telephone company efforts to disconnect dial-a-porn services, where the carrier actively petitioned law enforcement agencies to take action against the adult information services.[40] The court noted that the state action requirement is satisfied where a private party becomes a "willful participant in joint activity with the State or its agents,"[41] and found that the telephone company's conduct "of 'repeatedly request[ing]' law enforcement agents to undertake action that would trigger a procedure that would violate [the message service provider's] first amendment rights satisfies the joint participation requirement."[42]

As these cases demonstrate, there is no clear answer to when public control over a regulated communications business may be considered

34. Hearing transcript, Aug. 2, 1985 at 107, Carlin Communications, Inc. v. Mountain States Telephone & Telegraph Co., No. CIV–85–1420–PHX–CLH (D. Ariz. 1985).

35. Carlin Communications v. Mountain States Tel. & Tel. Co., 827 F.2d 1291, 1297 (9th Cir.1987).

36. 802 F.2d 1352, 1361 (11th Cir.1986)

37. *Id.* at 1361, (*quoting* Jackson, 419 U.S. 345, 351, 95 S.Ct. 449, 454, 42 L.Ed.2d 477, 487).

38. *Id.* at 1361 n.4.

39. *Id.* at 1361.

40. Sable Communications of California, Inc. v. Pacific Telephone & Telegraph Co., 890 F.2d 184 (9th Cir.1989).

41. *Id.* at 189, (*quoting* Adickes v. S.H. Kress & Co., 398 U.S. 144, 152, 90 S.Ct. 1598, 1605, 26 L.Ed.2d 142, 151 (1970)).

42. *Id.* at 189.

"state action" for purposes of a First Amendment inquiry. However, the Supreme Court's decision in *Denver Area Educational Telecommunications Consortium* appears to exhibit growing judicial skepticism about the truly private nature of laws that are designed to structure "voluntary" editorial judgments. Assuming this trend continues, it may foreshadow significant disputes over such regulatory initiatives as the V-chip, adopted as part of the Telecommunications Act of 1996. The law authorizes the Federal Communications Commission, through an advisory committee, to recommend a ratings system for television programming if the industry fails within a specified time to establish "voluntary rules for rating video programming that contain violent, sexual, or other indecent material" and agree "voluntarily to broadcast signals that contain ratings of such programming."[43] Such convoluted statutory schemes tend to implicate the constitutional command that the government cannot employ indirect means to "produce a result which [it] could not command directly."[44]

1.5 Defining Protected Expression

By its terms, the First Amendment protects "speech" and "the press," but what does this encompass? It is well-settled that the First Amendment protects expression and not merely the vocalization or printing of words.[1] Thus, "communicative conduct" normally is considered to be constitutionally protected. But to say that this concept is firmly established is not to say that it is well understood or easily applied. One of the most troublesome and persistent problems of First Amendment analysis is determining when conduct is " 'sufficiently imbued with elements of communication' to implicate the First Amendment."[2] As Justice Harlan said in his concurring opinion in *Cowgill v. California*, "The Court has, as yet, not established a test for determining at what point conduct becomes so intertwined with expression that it becomes necessary to weigh the State's interest in proscribing conduct

43. Telecommunications Act of 1996, P. L. No. 104–104, § 551, 110 Stat. 56, 78 (1996). *See* H.R. Conf. Rep. 104–458, 104th Cong., 2d Sess. 90 (1996)

44. Speiser v. Randall, 357 U.S. 513, 526, 78 S.Ct. 1332, 1342, 2 L.Ed.2d 1460, 1473 (1958).

1. Dallas v. Stanglin, 490 U.S. 19, 25, 109 S.Ct. 1591, 1595, 104 L.Ed.2d 18, 25 (1989) (" 'freedom of speech' means more than simply the right to talk and to write"). *See also* Hurley v. Irish–American Gay, Lesbian and Bisexual Group of Boston, 515 U.S. 557, 115 S.Ct. 2338, 132 L.Ed.2d 487 (1995) (organization of a parade is expressive); United States v. Eichman, 496 U.S. 310, 110 S.Ct. 2404, 110 L.Ed.2d 287 (1990) (flag burning); Texas v. Johnson, 491 U.S. 397, 109 S.Ct. 2533, 105 L.Ed.2d 342 (1989) (flag burning); Ward v. Rock Against Racism, 491 U.S. 781, 790, 109 S.Ct. 2746, 2753, 105 L.Ed.2d 661, 674 (1989) (music);

Boos v. Barry, 485 U.S. 312, 108 S.Ct. 1157, 99 L.Ed.2d 333 (1988) (picketing at foreign embassies); Doran v. Salem Inn, Inc., 422 U.S. 922, 95 S.Ct. 2561, 45 L.Ed.2d 648 (1975) (topless dancing); Spence v. Washington, 418 U.S. 405, 94 S.Ct. 2727, 41 L.Ed.2d 842 (1974) (affixing peace symbol to American flag); Tinker v. Des Moines Independent Community School District, 393 U.S. 503, 89 S.Ct. 733, 21 L.Ed.2d 731 (1969) (black armbands to protest Vietnam War); Brown v. Louisiana, 383 U.S. 131, 86 S.Ct. 719, 15 L.Ed.2d 637 (1966) (library sit-in); Stromberg v. California, 283 U.S. 359, 51 S.Ct. 532, 75 L.Ed. 1117 (1931) (flying flag as means of protest).

2. United States v. Eichman, 496 U.S. at 313, 110 S.Ct. at 2407, 110 L.Ed.2d at 293 (*quoting* Texas v. Johnson, 491 U.S. at 406, 109 S.Ct. at 2533, 105 L.Ed.2d at 426).

against the constitutionally protected interest in freedom of expression."[3]

Almost thirty years later, Justice Harlan's observation holds true. No bright line rule exists for pigeonholing speech and conduct, and such questions often are the occasion for deep divisions on the Court.[4] Analysis of the problem is obscured by the fact that all expression requires conduct. Certainly use of a printing press entails a great deal of physical activity, and, as more than one commentator has noted, the same can be said of speech "even if it only be the use of one's vocal cords."[5]

As the United States Court of Appeals for the Ninth Circuit pointed out, "speech in any language consists of the 'expressive conduct' of vibrating one's vocal chords, moving one's mouth and thereby making sounds, or of putting pen to paper, or hand to keyboard."[6] The difficulty of drawing lines between speech and conduct does not excuse courts

3. 396 U.S. 371, 372, 90 S.Ct. 613, 614, 24 L.Ed.2d 590, 590–591 (1970) (Harlan, J. concurring). Professor Laurence Tribe has taken the position that no satisfactory test could be developed, and that "any particular course of conduct may be hung almost randomly on the 'speech' peg or the 'conduct' peg as one sees fit." Laurence H. Tribe, American Constitutional Law 827 (2d ed. 1988). *See also* Melville B. Nimmer, Freedom of Speech § 3.06[B] (1984) ("Any attempt to disentangle 'speech' from conduct which is itself communicative will not withstand analysis."); Harry Kalven, Jr., *The Concept of the Public Forum: Cox v. Louisiana*, 1965 Sup. Ct. Rev. 1, 23 ("The Court's neat dichotomy of 'speech pure' and 'speech plus' will not work. For it leaves us without an intelligible rationale."). *But see* Lawrence B. Solum, *Freedom of Communicative Action: A Theory of the First Amendment Freedom of Speech*, 83 Nw. U. L. Rev. 54 (1989) (distinguishing between "communicative action" and "strategic action" for purposes of First Amendment analysis).

4. *Compare, e.g.,* Justice Brennan's majority opinion in Texas v. Johnson, 491 U.S. at 406, 109 S. Ct. at 2540, 105 L. Ed. 2d at 354 (the "expressive, overtly political nature of this conduct [flag burning] was both intentional and overwhelmingly apparent"), *with* Justice Rehnquist's dissent. *Id.* at 432, 109 S. Ct. at 2554, 105 L. Ed. 2d at 371, ("flag burning is the equivalent of an inarticulate grunt or roar that, it seems fair to say, is most likely to be indulged in not to express any particular idea, but to antagonize others."). *Compare also* Clark v. Community for Creative Non–Violence, 468 U.S. 288, 300–301, 104 S.Ct. 3065, 3072–73, 82 L.Ed.2d 221, 231 (1984) (Burger, C.J. con-

curring) ("Respondents' attempt at camping in the park is a form of 'picketing'; it is conduct, not speech" . . . that "trivializes the First Amendment"), *with id.* at 306, 104 S. Ct. at 3075, 82 L. Ed. 2d at 235 (Marshall, J., dissenting) (by erecting tent city in Lafayette Park, protesters "can physically demonstrate the neglect from which they suffer with an articulateness even Dickens could not match.")

5. Nimmer, *supra* note 3, at § 3.06[B] n.15; *See* Kalven, *supra* note 3, at 23 ("[A]ll speech is necessarily 'speech plus.' If it is oral, it is noise and may interrupt someone else; if it is written, it may be litter."); L. Tribe, *supra* note 3, at 827 ("[a]ll communication except perhaps that of the extrasensory variety involves conduct."); John H. Ely, *Flag Desecration: A Case Study in the Roles of Categorization and Balancing in First Amendment Analysis*, 88 Harv. L. Rev. 1482, 1495–96 (1975) (communicative behavior is "100% action and 100% expression"); Alexander Meiklejohn, *The First Amendment is an Absolute*, 1961 Sup. Ct. Rev. 245, 252 ("Speech [is] a form of human action"). Conversely, the Supreme Court has noted that "[i]t is possible to find some kernel of expression in almost every activity a person undertakes—for example, walking down the street or meeting one's friends at a shopping mall—but such a kernel is not sufficient to bring the activity within the protection of the First Amendment." Dallas v. Stanglin, 490 U.S. at 25, 109 S. Ct. at 1595, 104 L. Ed. 2d at 25–26.

6. Yniguez v. Arizonans for Official English, 69 F.3d 920, 934 (9th Cir.1995) (en banc), *vacated as moot*, 520 U.S. 43, 117 S.Ct. 1055, 137 L.Ed.2d 170 (1997).

from making the attempt, and over time decisions have shaped something of a hierarchy of protected communicative conduct.

A. *The Speech/Action Continuum*

In the absence of a formula for separating speech from conduct, courts have addressed the issue on an ad hoc basis. The resulting body of law has placed various communicative acts into specified categories along a "speech/action continuum" that, to a certain extent, determines the level of First Amendment protection. Behavior classified as "pure speech" generally is accorded full constitutional immunity, and the level of protection declines to a certain extent as the communicative act is considered more action than speech.[7] Once the "pure conduct" end of the continuum is reached the First Amendment no longer applies.[8]

1. *Pure Speech*

Because the question whether a given act is or is not speech generally arises only where there is some doubt, few cases articulate what factors are associated with "pure speech." Courts normally assume without discussion that controversies centered on "the written or spoken word"[9] implicate pure speech. But the underlying assumption of this practice is that "pure speech" involves the use of words. Communication that is accomplished through the use of banners, pantomime, dancing or some other physical manifestation, while protected by the First Amendment, may not receive the same treatment.[10]

But even the use of language is not an absolute litmus test for protection as pure speech. Certain types of speech, such as extortion, perjury, bomb threats, price fixing agreements or publication of state secrets, would not be so protected.[11] Also, where words are conveyed by

7. Texas v. Johnson, 491 U.S. at 406, 109 S. Ct. at 2540, 105 L.Ed.2d at 354–355 ("[t]he government generally has a freer hand in restricting expressive conduct than it has in restricting the written or spoken word.").

8. *E.g.,* Arcara v. Cloud Books, Inc., 478 U.S. 697, 705, 106 S.Ct. 3172, 3176–77, 92 L.Ed.2d 568, 577 (1986) (closure of bookstore at which prostitution was occurring upheld because the prostitution "manifests absolutely no element of protected expression.").

9. Texas v. Johnson, 491 U.S. at 406, 109 S.Ct. at 2540, 105 L.Ed.2d at 354–55. *See* Cox v. Louisiana, 379 U.S. 559, 564, 85 S.Ct. 476, 480, 13 L.Ed.2d 487, 492 (1965) ("pure form[s] of expression" include such things as a "newspaper comment or a telegram by a citizen to a public official.").

10. *But see* Hurley v. Irish–American Gay, Lesbian and Bisexual Group of Boston, 515 U.S. 557, 115 S.Ct. 2338, 2340, 132 L.Ed.2d 487, 494 (1995) ("a private speaker does not forfeit constitutional protection simply by combining multifarious voices, [or] by failing to edit their themes to isolate a specific message as the exclusive subject matter of the speech."). Courts have also distinguished pure speech from commercial speech, but have declined to attempt separating the various components of a given speech act that fit into each category. Riley v. National Federation of the Blind of North Carolina, Inc., 487 U.S. 781, 796, 108 S.Ct. 2667, 2677, 101 L.Ed.2d 669, 689 (1988); Gaudiya Vaishnava Society v. San Francisco, 952 F.2d 1059 (9th Cir.1990).

11. *See, e.g.,* Frederick F. Schauer, *The Aim and the Target in Free Speech Methodology,* 83 N.W. U. L. Rev. 562, 563 (1989); C. Edwin Baker, *Scope of the First Amendment Freedom of Speech,* 25 UCLA L. Rev. 964 (1978); Thomas I. Emerson, *First Amendment Doctrine and the Burger Court,* 68 Cal. L. Rev. 422, 474–77 (1980). Professor Emerson would classify wartime

unconventional means, judges do not always agree that the communication is more speech than action. Such disagreements provide some insight as to the scope of the pure speech concept.

In *Cohen v. California*,[12] the Supreme Court reversed the conviction for "disturb[ing] the peace ... by ... offensive conduct" of an individual who wore a jacket bearing the slogan, "Fuck the Draft." The California Court of Appeals had upheld the conviction because the defendant's conduct (wearing the jacket) "might cause others to rise up to commit a violent act against the person of the defendant or attempt to forcibly remove his jacket." Justices Blackmun, Burger and Black agreed with the lower court's conclusion, writing in dissent that "Cohen's absurd and immature antic ... was mainly conduct and little speech."[13] But Justice Harlan, writing for the majority, emphasized that "[t]he only 'conduct' which the State sought to punish is the fact of communication." The opinion concluded that Cohen's conviction "rest[ed] solely upon 'speech'" because there was no "separately identifiable conduct" that "could be regulated without effectively repressing Cohen's ability to express himself."[14] Similarly, in *Wooley v. Maynard*, the Court held that the defendant's act of covering up the state motto ("Live Free or Die") on his license plates was speech protected by the First Amendment.[15] Thus, as a general principle, the ability to disseminate or display words or ideas of one's choosing, or to refrain from doing so, raises questions of pure speech.

2. Speech "Plus"

Speech "plus" is a concept for distinguishing between communication and conduct that grew out of labor and civil rights picketing cases. It relates to a situation in which speech or other communication takes place in the context of action that may not be itself communicative. Thus, according to the Court, the "plus" can be regulated without infringing on the protected interest in speech. Given its origin in the labor and civil rights contexts, speech "plus" is most often applied to

---

broadcasts made from enemy territory as "action" rather than "speech." THOMAS I. EMERSON, THE SYSTEM OF FREEDOM OF EXPRESSION 61, 80 (1970). However, it may be more analytically consistent to classify such speech—as well as that listed in the text—as unprotected speech, rather than as action.

12. 403 U.S. 15, 91 S.Ct. 1780, 29 L.Ed.2d 284 (1971).

13. *Id.* at 17 and 27, 91 S.Ct. at 1781 and 1789, 29 L.Ed.2d at 289 and 295. Criticizing this language in the dissent, Professor Nimmer noted that "'conduct' becomes a code word for that speech which for unarticulated reasons is thought to be undeserving of First Amendment protection." NIMMER, *supra* note 3, at 2–7.

14. 403 U.S. at 18, 91 S.Ct. at 1784, 29 L.Ed.2d at 290. The Court distinguished its decision from *United States v. O'Brien*, 391 U.S. 367, 88 S.Ct. 1673, 20 L.Ed.2d 672 (1968) which upheld Selective Service restrictions on draft card burning.

15. 430 U.S. 705, 97 S.Ct. 1428, 51 L.Ed.2d 752 (1977). The Court found it unnecessary to address the symbolic speech issue raised in *Wooley*, but treated it purely as a question of "freedom of thought protected by the First Amendment." *Id.* at 713 n.10, 714, 97 S.Ct. at 1435 n.10, 51 L.Ed.2d at 762, n.10. However, dissenting Justices Rehnquist and Blackmun disagreed "that there is any 'speech' or 'speaking' in the context of this case." *Id.* at 720, 97 S.Ct. at 1438, 51 L.Ed.2d at 766.

activity such as picketing or parading.[16] But the Court has also used the concept of speech "plus" to describe political campaign activity,[17] and various Justices have further suggested it encompasses litigation,[18] dissemination of foreign propaganda,[19] political sabotage,[20] and racially divisive campaigns.[21]

The concept was formulated originally to allow the Court to distinguish between peaceful labor picketing, which is constitutionally protected,[22] from advocacy of illegal labor actions, which is not.[23] In the civil rights context, the Court made clear that a societal interest in freedom of

16. *See* American Radio Ass'n, AFL–CIO v. Mobile S.S. Ass'n, 419 U.S. 215, 229, 95 S.Ct. 409, 418, 42 L.Ed.2d 399, 410 (1974); Teamsters Local 695 v. Vogt, Inc., 354 U.S. 284, 289, 77 S.Ct. 1166, 1169, 1 L.Ed.2d 1347, 1351 (1957); Bakery and Pastry Drivers and Helpers Local 802 v. Wohl, 315 U.S. 769, 776–777, 62 S.Ct. 816, 819–820, 86 L.Ed. 1178, 1184 (1942) (Douglas, J., concurring); Giboney v. Empire Storage & Ice Co., 336 U.S. 490, 501, 69 S.Ct. 684, 690, 93 L.Ed. 834, 843 (1949); Building Service Employees Int'l Union, Local 262 v. Gazzam, 339 U.S. 532, 536–37, 70 S.Ct. 784, 787, 94 L.Ed. 1045, 1050 (1950); Hughes v. Superior Court, 339 U.S. 460, 465, 70 S.Ct. 718, 721, 94 L.Ed. 985, 992 (1950); National Labor Relations Board v. Fruit & Vegetable Packers & Warehousemen, Local 760, 377 U.S. 58, 77, 84 S.Ct. 1063, 1073, 12 L.Ed.2d 129, 141 (1964) (Black, J., concurring), *id.*, at 93, 84 S.Ct. at 1081–82, 12 L.Ed.2d at 150 (Harlan, J., dissenting); Cox v. Louisiana, 379 U.S. 536, 578, 85 S.Ct. 466, 468, 13 L.Ed.2d 487, 499 (1965) ("Cox I") (opinion of Black, J.); Amalgamated Food Employees Union, Local 590 v. Logan Valley Plaza, Inc., 391 U.S. 308, 326, 88 S.Ct. 1601, 1612, 20 L.Ed.2d 603, 616 (1968) (Douglas, J., concurring). *But see* Hurley v. Irish–American Gay, Lesbian and Bisexual Group of Boston, 515 U.S. 557, 115 S.Ct. 2338, 132 L.Ed.2d 487 (1995).

17. Broadrick v. Oklahoma, 413 U.S. 601, 617, 93 S.Ct. 2908, 2918, 37 L.Ed.2d 830, 843 (1973); Thomas v. Collins, 323 U.S. 516, 535, 65 S.Ct. 315, 325, 89 L.Ed. 430, 443 (1945). *But see* Buckley v. Valeo, 424 U.S. 1, 16, 96 S.Ct. 612, 633, 46 L.Ed.2d 659, 686 (1976) (per curiam) (limiting contributions of money to a political campaign is not "comparable to . . . restrictions on conduct").

18. *See* NAACP v. Button, 371 U.S. 415, 83 S.Ct. 328, 9 L.Ed.2d 405 (1963). Writing for the majority, Justice Brennan described civil rights litigation as "a form of political expression." *Id.* at 429, 83 S.Ct. at 336, 9 L.Ed.2d at 416. But in dissent Justice Harlan noted that "litigation, whether or not associated with the attempt to vindicate constitutional rights, is conduct; it is speech plus." *Id.* at 455, 83 S.Ct. at 349, 9 L.Ed.2d at 431.

19. *See* Communist Party of the United States v. Subversive Activities Control Board, 367 U.S. 1, 173, 81 S.Ct. 1357, 1450–51, 6 L.Ed.2d 625, 733 (1961) (Douglas, J., dissenting) ("[r]egistration of those who disseminate propaganda of foreign origin . . .has been thought to fall in the same category as barring speech in places that will create traffic conditions"); Viereck v. United States, 318 U.S. 236, 251, 63 S.Ct. 561, 568, 87 L.Ed. 734, 743 (1943) (Black, J. and Douglas, J., dissenting).

20. Dennis v. United States, 341 U.S. 494, 584, 71 S.Ct. 857, 904, 95 L.Ed. 1137, 1191 (1951) (Douglas, J., dissenting) ("speech *plus* [includes] acts of sabotage or unlawful conduct.").

21. Beauharnais v. Illinois, 343 U.S. 250, 72 S.Ct. 725, 96 L.Ed. 919 (1952) (upholding statute forbidding any person from exhibiting any lithograph which portrayed lack of virtue of a class of citizens). The Court held that the criminal libel at issue—like all libel—was beyond First Amendment protection. *Id.* at 255–57, 72 S.Ct. at 729–731, 96 L.Ed. at 926–27. But Justice Douglas wrote that a conspiracy "which was aimed at destroying a race by exposing it to contempt, derision, and obloquy. . . . would be more than the exercise of free speech. Like picketing, it would be free speech plus." *Id.* at 284, 72 S.Ct. at 744, 96 L.Ed. at 943 (Douglas, J., dissenting).

22. Thornhill v. Alabama, 310 U.S. 88, 60 S.Ct. 736, 84 L.Ed. 1093 (1940) (state law prohibiting all labor picketing held facially invalid).

23. *E.g.,* Teamsters Local 695 v. Vogt, Inc., 354 U.S. 284, 77 S.Ct. 1166, 1 L.Ed.2d 1347 (1957) (state prohibition of picketing in support of "union shop" upheld); Giboney v. Empire Storage & Ice Co., 336 U.S. 490, 69 S.Ct. 684, 93 L.Ed. 834 (1949) (ban on picketing in support of secondary boycott upheld).

expression did not divest the government of its authority to prevent "mob law."[24] It explained that "placards used as an essential and inseparable part of a grave offense against an important public law cannot immunize that unlawful conduct from state control."[25] Therefore, as a general proposition, communication accomplished by means of speech "plus" is subject to a lower level of constitutional protection. As Justice Goldberg concluded in *Cox v. Louisiana,* "the First and Fourteenth Amendments [do not] afford the same kind of freedom to those who would communicate ideas by conduct such as patrolling, marching, and picketing on streets and highways, as these amendments afford to those who communicate ideas by pure speech."[26] But the Court never articulated the extent to which the presence of speech "plus" diminishes First Amendment protection.

Moreover, the Court has not been particularly consistent in distinguishing speech from whatever it is that constitutes a "plus." For example, in *Edwards v. South Carolina,* the Court described a mass demonstration at the State House as "an exercise of [free speech] rights in their most pristine and classic form."[27] Yet a mere two years later, the Court emphasized in *Cox I* that such conduct does not enjoy "the same kind of freedom" as those who communicate using "pure speech."[28] Moreover, the logic underlying the Court's characterization of picketing as speech "plus" is difficult to reconcile with its treatment of other communicative acts. For example, the Court traditionally has treated the distribution of leaflets and handbills as pure speech even though such activity poses much the same threat of disrupting public rights of way as picketing.[29]

The confusion is particularly striking in the Court's treatment of political activities, which it occasionally characterizes as speech "plus." The Court in *Broadrick v. Oklahoma* held that such political activities as soliciting contributions, working for a political party or running for office are akin to "conduct in the shadow of the First Amendment" and therefore subject to a less exacting test for facial overbreadth.[30] Yet in *Buckley v. Valeo,* the Court, in a *per curiam* opinion, stated that "[t]he expenditure of money [in a political campaign] simply cannot be equated with such conduct as destruction of a draft card."[31] It added that "this Court has never suggested that the dependence of a communication on

---

24. Cox v. Louisiana, 379 U.S. 559, 562, 85 S.Ct. 476, 480, 13 L.Ed.2d 487, 491 (1965) ("Cox II").

25. *Id.* at 564, 85 S.Ct. at 480.

26. Cox I, 379 U.S. at 555, 85 S.Ct. at 464–465, 13 L.Ed.2d at 484.

27. 372 U.S. 229, 235, 83 S.Ct. 680, 683, 9 L.Ed.2d 697, 702 (1963).

28. 379 U.S. at 555, 85 S.Ct. at 464–465, 13 L.Ed.2d at 484.

29. Kalven, *supra* note 3, at 22. *See, e.g.,* Talley v. California, 362 U.S. 60, 80 S.Ct. 536, 4 L.Ed.2d 559 (1960); Jamison v.

Texas, 318 U.S. 413, 63 S.Ct. 669, 87 L.Ed. 869 (1943); Schneider v. State, 308 U.S. 147, 60 S.Ct. 146, 84 L.Ed. 155 (1939).

30. 413 U.S. at 614, 93 S.Ct. at 2917, 37 L.Ed.2d at 841.

31. 424 U.S. 1, 16, 96 S.Ct. 612, 633, 46 L.Ed.2d 659, 686 (1976). The Court was distinguishing the campaign speech at issue from the symbolic speech analyzed in United States v. O'Brien, 391 U.S. 367, 88 S.Ct. 1673, 20 L.Ed.2d 672 (1968). The Court expressly declined to use the *O'Brien* test.

the expenditure of money operates itself to introduce a nonspeech element or to reduce the exacting scrutiny required by the First Amendment."[32] Similarly, in *First National Bank of Boston v. Bellotti*, the Court struck down a state prohibition on corporate political expenditures as an unconstitutional restriction on "speech ... at the heart of the First Amendment's protection."[33] More recently, in *Colorado Republican Federal Campaign Committee v. FEC*, the Supreme Court confirmed that political expenditures are fully protected as pure speech.[34]

Perhaps because it lacked a sustainable conceptual basis for distinguishing pure speech from speech "plus," or because it developed more useful analytic tests for dealing with communicative action, the Court has moved away from discussions of speech "plus." Whatever the reason, the concept has declined almost simultaneously with the ascension of the public forum doctrine, symbolic speech analysis and other doctrinal developments.[35] For example, in *Boos v. Barry*, the Court invalidated a District of Columbia ordinance that prohibited picketing within 500 feet of an embassy that was intended to "intimidate" or subject to "public odium" any foreign government. In sharp contrast with *Cox v. Louisiana*, the decision described the proscribed picketing as "classically political speech" at the "core of the First Amendment."[36] In *FTC v. Superior*

---

32. 424 U.S. at 16, 96 S.Ct. at 633, 46 L.Ed.2d at 686. The Court apparently placed different types of campaign expenditures on different points on the speech/action continuum. It invalidated restrictions upon a candidates use of his own funds during a campaign as being a "substantial restraint" upon "protected First Amendment expression." *Id*. at 52, 96 S.Ct. at 651, 46 L.Ed.2d at 707. It similarly struck down limits on independent expenditures as excessively burdensome to "core First Amendment rights of political expression." *Id*. at 45, 96 S.Ct. at 647, 46 L.Ed.2d at 702. But it upheld certain contribution limits on the theory that giving money to a candidate was not direct speech, but was a "symbolic act" or "symbolic expression." *Id*. at 21, 96 S.Ct. at 635–636, 46 L. Ed. 2d at 689.

33. 435 U.S. 765, 776, 98 S.Ct. 1407, 1415, 55 L.Ed.2d 707, 717 (1978). Citing *Buckley*, the Court emphasized that it is "too late to suggest" that political expenditures "introduce a nonspeech element" that would allow greater government intervention. *Id*. at 786 n.23, 98 S.Ct. at 1421 n. 23, 55 L.Ed.2d at 724 n.23.

34. 518 U.S. 604, 116 S.Ct. 2309, 135 L.Ed.2d 795 (1996).

35. Speech "plus" has been described as a discredited doctrine. *See* Susan H. Williams, *Content Discrimination and the First Amendment*, 139 U. Pa. L. Rev. 615, 638 n.100 (1991).

36. Boos v. Barry, 485 U.S. at 318, 108 S.Ct. at 1162, 99 L.Ed.2d at 343. The Court

focused on public forum analysis and on the content-based nature of the ordinance without regard to any speech/action distinctions. *See also* Frisby v. Schultz, 487 U.S. 474, 479, 108 S.Ct. 2495, 2499, 101 L.Ed.2d 420, 428 (1988) (under public forum analysis "we have traditionally subjected restrictions on public issue picketing to careful scrutiny."). Indeed, the Court's conviction that picketing is more like pure speech apparently evolved over time, along with the growth of the public forum doctrine. *Compare, e.g.,* Gregory v. City of Chicago, 394 U.S. 111, 112, 89 S.Ct. 946, 947, 22 L.Ed.2d 134, 136 (1969) (a peaceful and orderly march "falls well within the sphere of conduct protected by the First Amendment."), and Shuttlesworth v. Birmingham, 394 U.S. 147, 152, 89 S.Ct. 935, 939, 22 L.Ed.2d 162, 168 (1969) ("picketing and parading may ... constitute methods of expression, entitled to First Amendment protection."), *with* Carey v. Brown, 447 U.S. 455, 460, 100 S.Ct. 2286, 2290, 65 L.Ed.2d 263, 269 (1980) ("[t]here can be no doubt that.... peaceful picketing [is] expressive conduct that falls within the First Amendment's preserve") and United States v. Grace, 461 U.S. 171, 176, 103 S.Ct. 1702, 1706, 75 L.Ed.2d 736, 743 (1983)("peaceful picketing and leafleting are expressive activities involving 'speech' protected by the First Amendment."); Hurley v. Irish–American Gay, Lesbian and Bisexual Group of Boston, 515 U.S. 557, 115 S.Ct. 2338, 132 L.Ed.2d 487 (1995) (parade is fully protected act of expression).

Court Trial Lawyers Ass'n,[37] in denying First Amendment immunity for an economic boycott, the Court avoided any direct reference to speech "plus."[38] And in *City of Lakewood v. Plain Dealer Publishing Co.*, the Court applied full First Amendment protection to the distribution of newspapers via mechanical newsboxes, describing the practice as "conduct commonly associated with expression."[39]

While the speech "plus" concept has not been satisfactorily defined or consistently applied, and its usage appears to be in decline, the Court is still faced with distinguishing between speech that is protected and associated conduct that is not. It had no trouble making such a distinction in *Arcara v. Cloud Books, Inc.*, in which the Court upheld closure of adult bookstore at which prostitution was occurring. The state's order did not conflict with the First Amendment, according to the Court, because it was directed only at the illegal conduct "which manifests absolutely no element of protected expression."[40] Other cases present a somewhat more difficult problem where the illegal conduct itself has expressive elements, such as the boycott in *FTC v. Superior Court Trial Lawyers Ass'n*.[41] Many cases fall in this more problematic category since, as previously observed, all speech involves some degree of conduct. The difficulty of separating a communicative act into discrete components made up of speech and action, as the speech "plus" approach seems to require, no doubt prompted the Court to find more useful analytic concepts. But this development does not diminish the importance of the speech "plus" concept as subtext. The Court, through various means, continues to allow more government intervention where a "plus" can be identified.

3. Symbolic Speech

The Court extended First Amendment protection to acts that are inherently communicative even before it came up with the label "symbolic speech."[42] In *Brown v. Louisiana*, for example, the Court held that

---

37. 493 U.S. 411, 110 S.Ct. 768, 107 L.Ed.2d 851 (1990).

38. However, the Court cited the speech "plus" labor picketing cases. *Id.* at 428 & n.12, 110 S.Ct. at 778 & n.12, 107 L.Ed.2d at 869 & n.12. Consistent with those cases, the Court reasoned that application of the antitrust laws to the boycott would not curtail expressive activities ancillary to the labor action, such as publicizing the cause, talking to government officials and espousing a position. *Id.* at 426, 110 S.Ct. at 777, 107 L.Ed.2d at 868. The Court also distinguished *NAACP v. Claiborne Hardware Co.*, 458 U.S. 886, 102 S.Ct. 3409, 73 L.Ed.2d 1215 (1982), which had extended First Amendment protection to "a nonviolent, politically motivated boycott designed to force governmental and economic change." *Id.* 110 S.Ct. at 776, 107 L.Ed.2d at 868. In contrast with the *Claiborne Hardware* boy-

cott which sought social change, the trial attorneys sought to "increase the price that they would be paid for their services," a classic restraint of trade. *Id.* at 427, 110 S.Ct. at 777, 107 L.Ed.2d at 869.

39. 486 U.S. 750, 760, 108 S.Ct. 2138, 2145, 100 L.Ed.2d 771, 784 (1988).

40. 478 U.S. 697, 705, 106 S.Ct. 3172, 3176, 92 L.Ed.2d 568, 577 (1986).

41. 493 U.S. at 431, 110 S.Ct. at 779, 107 L.Ed.2d at 871. ("Every concerted refusal to do business with a potential customer or supplier has an expressive component.").

42. Indeed, the first case in which the Supreme Court upheld a First Amendment interest entailed symbolic speech, although it was not labeled as such. Stromberg v. California, 283 U.S. 359, 51 S.Ct. 532, 75 L.Ed. 1117 (1931). Although there may be

a silent sit-in at a public library was protected speech.[43] It noted that First Amendment rights "are not confined to verbal expression;" they "embrace appropriate types of action which certainly include[s] the right in a peaceable and orderly manner to protest by silent and reproachful presence."[44] As in previous sit-in cases, the Court apparently believed that the intended message was too evident to warrant much discussion.[45] It merely noted that the demonstrators "sat and stood in the room, quietly, as monuments of protest against the segregation of the library."[46] Although this early statement of the premises underlying symbolic speech did not gain the endorsement of the Court's majority,[47] it did lay the groundwork for later development.[48]

The quintessential symbolic speech case involves the use of flags or banners as a means of communication. The Supreme Court recognized the First Amendment dimension of such activity in one of its early free speech cases;[49] it defined the concept of symbolic speech in a case involving "misuse" of the American flag;[50] and, more recently, reaffirmed the concept in two divisive flag desecration cases.[51] Much scholarly writing has been focused on this peculiar free speech problem[52] and, on a

little practical effect to the distinction, symbolic speech differs from speech "plus" in that a symbolic act (e.g., waving good-bye) is inherently communicative, while speech "plus" entails pure speech combined with some action (e.g., marching) that is not in itself communicative.

43. 383 U.S. 131, 86 S.Ct. 719, 15 L.Ed.2d 637 (1966).

44. Id. at 142, 86 S.Ct. at 724, 15 L.Ed.2d at 645.

45. E.g., Garner v. Louisiana, 368 U.S. 157, 201–202, 82 S.Ct. 248, 271, 7 L.Ed.2d 207, 235–36 (1961) ("We would surely have to be blind not to recognize that petitioners were sitting at these [lunch] counters, where they knew they would not be served, in order to demonstrate that their race was being segregated in dining facilities in this part of the country."). See Taylor v. Louisiana, 370 U.S. 154, 82 S.Ct. 1188, 8 L.Ed.2d 395 (1962) (bus station sit-in).

46. Brown, 383 U.S. at 139, 86 S.Ct. at 722, 15 L.Ed.2d at 644.

47. Justice White concurred because the demonstrators' arrests violated the Fourteenth Amendment Equal Protection Clause. Id. at 150–51, 86 S.Ct. at 726–27, 15 L.Ed.2d at 650. Justice Black, joined by Justices Clark, Harlan and Stewart, dissented, stating that the First Amendment protects "speech, writings, and expression of views in any manner in which they can be legitimately and validly communicated" but does not give "any person or group of persons the constitutional right to go wher-

ever they want, whenever they please, without regard to the rights of private or public property or to state law." Id. at 166, 86 S.Ct. at 736, 15 L.Ed.2d at 659.

48. Other early symbolic speech cases include Schacht v. United States, 398 U.S. 58, 60–61, 90 S.Ct. 1555, 1157–58, 26 L.Ed.2d 44 (1970) (wearing military uniforms in dramatic presentation criticizing U.S. involvement in Vietnam), and Tinker v. Des Moines Independent Community School Dist., 393 U.S. 503, 505, 89 S.Ct. 733, 735, 21 L.Ed.2d 731, 736 (1969) (wearing black arm bands to protest involvement in Vietnam).

49. Stromberg v. California, 283 U.S. 359, 51 S.Ct. 532, 75 L.Ed. 1117 (1931) (flying flag as means of protest). See also West Virginia State Bd. of Educ. v. Barnette, 319 U.S. 624, 632, 63 S.Ct. 1178, 1182, 87 L.Ed. 1628, 1634 (1943) (flying of a flag is a "primitive but effective way of communicating ideas" that represents "a short cut from mind to mind"). See discussion in Texas v. Johnson, 491 U.S. at 404–06, 109 S.Ct. at 2538–42, 105 L.Ed.2d at 355–57.

50. Spence v. Washington, 418 U.S. 405, 94 S.Ct. 2727, 41 L.Ed.2d 842 (1974) (per curiam).

51. United States v. Eichman, 496 U.S. 310, 110 S.Ct. 2404, 110 L.Ed.2d 287 (1990); Texas v. Johnson, 491 U.S. 397, 109 S.Ct. 2533, 105 L.Ed.2d 342 (1989).

52. E.g., LAURENCE H. TRIBE, AMERICAN CONSTITUTIONAL LAW 799–808 (2d ed. 1988);

less intellectual level, questions involving the United States flag periodi-cally inflame public passions.[53] It is therefore fitting that the Court set out its test for symbolic speech in *Spence v. Washington*, a case involving the conviction of a college student for improper use of the flag. To protest the death of students at Kent State University and the American invasion of Cambodia, a student had hung an American flag from his apartment window. The flag was upside down and had a peace symbol, fashioned from removable black tape, affixed to both its front and back. The Court, in a per curiam opinion, reversed the conviction for violation of the Washington statute against improper use of the flag.[54] It found the defendant's use of the flag to be symbolic speech, protected by the First Amendment, because (1) there was an intent to convey a message via conduct; (2) the conduct could be perceived as communication because of the use of recognizable symbols; and (3) the intended message was understandable in context.[55]

Since *Spence*, the Court declined to uphold symbolic speech claims until the flag desecration cases of *Texas v. Johnson* and *United States v. Eichman*. In *Village of Hoffman Estates v. Flipside, Hoffman Estates, Inc.*, the Court upheld a local ordinance restricting the sale of drug

Melville B. Nimmer, Freedom of Speech § 3.06[E] [1](1984); Leora Harpaz, *Justice Jackson's Flag Salute Legacy: The Supreme Court Struggles to Protect Intellectual Individualism*, 64 Tex. L. Rev. 817 (1986); John H. Ely, *Flag Desecration: A Case Study in the Roles of Categorization and Balancing in First Amendment Analysis*, 88 Harv. L. Rev. 1482 (1975).

53. In the 1940s, Jehovah's Witnesses who refused to salute the flag were impris-oned, beaten and, in some cases, castrated. In Kennebunk, Maine a Jehovah's Witness meeting hall was burned. *See* Nat Hentoff, *A Frenzy of Flag Waving*, Wash. Post, July 1, 1989 at A17. *See also* Leora Harpaz, *Justice Jackson's Flag Salute Legacy: The Supreme Court Struggles to Protect Intellec-tual Individualism*, 64 Tex. L. Rev. 817, 830 (1986). In Litchfield, Illinois, during this period, a riot erupted resulting in the destruction of a dozen automobiles and 65 Jehovah's Witnesses were incarcerated. *See* T. Lavin, *The Litchfield Riot*, The (IL) State Journal–Register, June 24, 1990 at 33. Following the 1990 Supreme Court deci-sion in *United States v. Eichman*, the Loui-siana legislature considered a proposal to lower the fine to $25 for beating any person engaged in the act of flag burning. *Beating Flag Burner to Cost $25 Under Louisiana Bill*, Wash. Post, June 13, 1990 at A9 col. 4. In response, the State Senate adopted a resolution declaring that "the red, white, and blue of the flag are symbolic of the highest ideals of democratic government."

But the Senate resolution went on to state that "legislation which encourages any per-son to unlawfully interfere with a citizen's lawful expression of his First Amendment rights is also repugnant to the fundamental tenets of this nation ... and that any legis-lation which encourages that unlawful in-terference of such expression is unconscio-nable." 1990 La. Sess. Law Serv. Sen. Res. 35 (West).

54. 418 U.S. 405, 94 S.Ct. 2727, 41 L.Ed.2d 842. In doing so the Court distin-guished desecration, which entails casting contempt on the flag, from improper use, which in the Washington statute involved display of a flag upon which "any word, figure, mark, picture, design, drawing or advertisement of any nature" had been placed. *Id*. at 407, 94 S.Ct. at 2728, 41 L.Ed.2d at 845.

55. *Id*. at 410–411, 94 S.Ct. at 2730, 41 L.Ed.2d at 847. The Court backed away from a requirement for the speaker to show an intent to convey "a narrow succinctly articulable message" in Hurley v. Irish–American Gay, Lesbian and Bisexual Group of Boston, 515 U.S. 557, 569, 115 S.Ct. 2338, 2345, 132 L.Ed.2d 487, 501 (1995). One difference between symbolic speech and pure speech is that the initial burden is not on the government to justify its actions, as it is in a typical free speech case. Rather, those who wish to convey an idea through expressive conduct must first "demonstrate that the First Amendment even applies."

paraphernalia against the assertion that it infringed against symbolic speech interests.[56] It noted that "[a]lthough drug-related designs or names on cigarette papers may subject those items to regulation, the village does not restrict speech as such, but simply regulates the commercial marketing of items that the labels reveal may be used for an illicit purpose."[57] In *Clark v. Community for Creative Non–Violence*, the Court did not dispute that erection of a tent city in Lafayette Park near the White House and that overnight sleeping at the site could be considered expressive conduct.[58] But it upheld a Park Service ban on camping as a reasonable time, place or manner restriction.[59] In both cases the expression was, to some extent, segregable from the conduct that could be legitimately restricted.[60] However, when confronted with situations in which conduct was being regulated *because* of its expressive component, as in the flag cases, the Court reaffirmed the protected status of symbolic speech.[61]

In *Texas v. Johnson*, the Court held that the act of burning an American flag, in the context of a political protest, was "conduct 'sufficiently imbued with elements of communication' ... to implicate the

Clark v. Community for Creative Non–Violence, 468 U.S. 288, 293 n.5, 104 S.Ct. 3065, 3069 n.5, 82 L.Ed.2d 221, 227 n.5 (1984).

56. 455 U.S. 489, 102 S.Ct. 1186, 71 L.Ed.2d 362 (1982).

57. *Id.* at 496, 102 S. Ct. at 1192, 71 L.Ed.2d at 370.

58. 468 U.S. 288, 293, 104 S.Ct. 3065, 3071, 82 L.Ed.2d 221, 229 (1984). The Court declined to take issue with the D.C. Circuit's holding that sleeping in the tent city is symbolic speech. Rather, it "assume[d] for present purposes, but [did] not decide, that such is the case." In dissent, Justice Marshall argued that the majority failed to "examin[e] closely the reality of respondents' planned expression" and thereby "denatur[ing] respondents' asserted right." *Id.* at 302, 104 S.Ct. at 3073, 82 L.Ed.2d at 232

59. The Court has generally equated time, place or manner restrictions appropriate to the public forum, with the test articulated for symbolic speech in *United States v. O'Brien. See id.* at 298, 102 S. Ct. at 3069, 82 L. Ed. 2d at 230; Rock Against Racism, 491 U.S. at 797–98, 109 S.Ct. at 2757, 105 L.Ed.2d at 679–680. This approach has been criticized for creating an overly lenient First Amendment standard. *See* discussion in Century Federal, Inc. v. City of Palo Alto, 710 F.Supp. 1559 (N.D.Cal.1988); Susan H. Williams, *Content Discrimination and the First Amendment*, 139 U. Pa. L. Rev. 615; Keith Werhan, *The*

O'Briening of Free Speech Methodology, 19 Ariz. St. L.J. 635 (1987).

60. The Court's approach in *Clark* was similar to the speech "plus" analysis in public forum picketing cases. And it's treatment of the sale of drug paraphernalia in *Village of Hoffman Estates* is analogous to its holding in *FTC v. Superior Court Trial Lawyers Ass'n*, in which it held that the First Amendment does not immunize a crime—an economic boycott—merely because the conduct had an "expressive component." Moreover, the Court apparently applied the less restrictive test for commercial speech because the expressive component in *Village of Hoffman Estates* generally was the labeling of commercial products. 455 U.S. at 496, 102 S. Ct. at 1192, 71 L.Ed.2d at 370. *Compare* Street v. New York, 394 U.S. 576, 89 S.Ct. 1354, 22 L.Ed.2d 572 (1969) (flag burning conviction overturned where prosecution hinged on speech uttered at time of act), *with* Young v. New York City Transit Authority, 903 F.2d 146 (2d Cir.) (panhandling in subway is not symbolic speech; action can be distinguished from speech elements), cert. denied, 498 U.S. 984, 111 S.Ct. 516, 112 L.Ed.2d 528 (1990).

61. *But see* Barnes v. Glen Theatre, Inc., 501 U.S. 560, 111 S.Ct. 2456, 115 L.Ed.2d 504 (1991) (allowing regulation of nude dancing under general prohibition of public nudity). *But see also id.* at 587, 111 S. Ct. at 2471, 115 L.Ed.2d at 525 ("dancing is an ancient art form and 'inherently embodies the expression and communica-

First Amendment.''[62] It affirmed the decision of the Texas Court of Criminal Appeals which invalidated the conviction of an individual for violating the state flag desecration statute.[63] In doing so, the Court found that the government did not have a content-neutral interest in regulating the act of flag burning. The asserted state interests were analyzed in light of the statutory language,[64] and the Court concluded that the defendant was prosecuted "because of the content of the message he conveyed."[65] It noted that political expression of the type engaged in by the defendant is "situated at the core of our First Amendment values" and that government restrictions on such conduct are subject to "the most exacting scrutiny" regardless of the degree of conduct involved.[66] In short, symbolic speech is constitutionally protected to the same degree as "pure speech" where government restrictions target expressive content.[67]

The Court in *Johnson* was deeply divided, with four Justices, lead by Chief Justice Rehnquist, issuing a strong dissent. After quoting the *Star Spangled Banner* and the full text of the John Greenleaf Whittier poem *Barbara Frietchie*, the dissent stressed the "mystical reverence" Americans have for the flag, and concluded that the government has a strong interest in preserving its symbolic value.[68] The *Johnson* decision also ignited a political firestorm in which the President and a seeming majority of Congress advocated adopting a constitutional amendment to ban flag desecration. This movement was blunted, at least for a time, by passage of the federal Flag Protection Act of 1989, ostensibly designed to

tion of ideas and emotions.' '') (White, J. dissenting) (citation omitted).

62. 491 U.S. at 406, 109 S.Ct. at 2540, 105 L.Ed.2d at 354 (quoting *Spence v. Washington*, 418 U.S. at 409, 94 S. Ct. at 2727, 41 L.Ed.2d at 846). Although the Court noted that flags are "[p]regnant with expressive content," it emphasized that not all "action taken with respect to our flag is expressive." Rather, such a determination depends on the context in which the activity occurred. *Id.* at 405, 109 S. Ct. at 2540, 105 L. Ed. 2d at 354.

63. Johnson v. State, 755 S.W.2d 92 (Tex.Crim.App.1988), *aff'd*, 491 U.S. 397, 109 S.Ct. 2533, 105 L.Ed.2d 342 (1989).

64. The Texas law provided criminal penalties for anyone who "intentionally or knowingly" engages in conduct to "deface, damage, or otherwise physically mistreat [a state or national flag] in a way that the actor knows will seriously offend one or more persons likely to observe or discover his action." Tex. Penal Code Ann. § 42.09 (Vernon 1989). The state claimed interests in preventing breach of the peace and in preserving the flag as a symbol of national unity as support of the law.

65. 491 U.S. at 412, 109 S. Ct. at 2544, 105 L.Ed.2d at 359. The Court found that

no potential breach of the peace was implicated by the facts of the case, and the state's interest in preserving the symbolic value of the flag was content-based.

66. *Id.* at 411, 412, 109 S. Ct. at 2544, 2543, 105 L.Ed.2d at 358–59.

67. *But see* Barnes v. Glen Theatre, Inc., 501 U.S., 560, 565–66, 111 S.Ct. at 2456, 2460, 115 L.Ed.2d 504, 511 (1991) (certain types of expressive conduct, such as nude barroom dancing, receive only marginal First Amendment protection).

68. 491 U.S. at 429, 109 S. Ct. at 2552, 105 L.Ed.2d at 369 (Rehnquist, J., dissenting). The dissent also disputed the communicative aspect of flag burning, noting that such action "is most likely to be indulged in not to express any particular idea, but to antagonize others." Id. at 432, 109 S. Ct. at 2554, 105 L.Ed.2d at 371. *But see* United States v. Eichman, 496 U.S. at 320, 110 S. Ct. at 2410–11, 110 L.Ed.2d at 297–98, where dissenting Justice Stevens, joined by Justice Rehnquist, stated that "[a] flag burner might intend various messages" and "[t]he idea expressed by a particular act of flag burning is necessarily dependent on the temporal and political context in which it occurs."

be content neutral.[69] The Court invalidated the law in *United States v. Eichman*, which found that although the Act "contains no explicit content-based limitation on the scope of prohibited conduct, it is nevertheless clear that the Government's asserted *interest* is 'related to the suppression of free expression,' ... and concerned with the content of such expression."[70] The Court reaffirmed the holding in *Johnson* that symbolic speech receives the same degree of First Amendment protection as pure speech. *Eichman* also prompted demands to amend the Bill of Rights, but amendment proposals were promptly defeated in both the House and the Senate.[71]

In contrast with the situations addressed in *Johnson* and *Eichman*, the government is allowed greater latitude in regulating expressive conduct where the restriction is unrelated to the content of the communication. In *United States v. O'Brien*, the first Supreme Court case to use the term "symbolic speech," the Court upheld the conviction of an individual who burned his draft card to protest the Vietnam War. Chief Justice Earl Warren's opinion for the Court did not dispute that the defendant was engaged in expressive conduct, but said "[w]e cannot accept the view that an apparently limitless variety of conduct can be labeled 'speech' whenever the person engaging in the conduct intends thereby to express an idea."[72] The Court then gave life to the assumptions underlying its former speech "plus" cases, stating that "when 'speech' and 'nonspeech' elements are combined in the same course of conduct, a sufficiently important governmental interest in regulating the nonspeech element can justify incidental limitations on First Amendment freedoms."[73] Thus, a regulation will be upheld where: (1) "it is

---

69. 103 Stat. 777, 18 U.S.C.A. § 700 (Supp. 1990). The law imposed criminal penalties on anyone who "knowingly mutilates, defaces, physically defiles, burns, maintains on the floor or ground, or tramples upon any flag of the United States." However, it excepted from coverage "any conduct consisting of the disposal of a flag when it has become worn or soiled." The law also provided for expedited Supreme Court review. For an account of the legislative debates that led to passage of the Flag Protection Act, *See* Roger Parloff, *The Circus Leaves Town*, Legal Times, July 23, 990 at S29.

70. 496 U.S. 310, 315, 110 S.Ct. 2404, 2408, 110 L.Ed.2d 287, 294.(1990). *Eichman* was divided 5–4, with the same Justices as in *Johnson* dissenting. However, none of the dissenters suggested that the Flag Protection Act was content-neutral.

71. The House rejected a proposed constitutional amendment by a vote of 236 to 179 in favor, 38 votes short (including seventeen not voting) of the required 2/3 majority. 136 Cong. Rec. H4088, 4094 (daily ed. June 21, 1990). The Senate rejected a

proposed amendment 58 in favor to 42 opposed, nine votes short of the 2/3 majority. 136 Cong. Rec. S8736, 8737 (daily ed. June 26, 1990). Although the amendment was not adopted, the issue of flag desecration continued to generate controversy. *See, e.g., Man With Flag Stuffed in Pocket Guilty of Flag Desecration in Alabama*, Wash. Post, February 13, 1991 at A9, col. 1.

Another proposed constitutional amendment was narrowly defeated in 1996. *See* H.R.J. Res. 79, 104th Cong., 1st Sess. (1995), S.J. Res. 31, 104th Cong., 1st Sess (1995). As this treatise was being prepared for publication, passage of H.J.Res. 54 a proposed constitutional amendment to ban flag desecration was being considered by the 105th Congress. The Amendment stated: "The Congress shall have the power to prohibit the physical desecration of the flag of the United States." The resolution, however, was not voted on by the Senate before the end of the session.

72. 391 U.S. 367, 376, 88 S.Ct. 1673, 1678, 20 L.Ed.2d 672, 679 (1968).

73. *Id.*, 88 S. Ct. at 1678–79, 20 L.Ed.2d at 679–80.

within the constitutional power of government;" (2) "it furthers an important or substantial government interest;" (3) "the interest is unrelated to the suppression of free expression;" and (4) "the incidental restriction on First Amendment freedoms is no greater than essential" to further the governmental interest.[74]

The *O'Brien* standard has proven to be a remarkably flexible and useful test for situations in which speech and action are combined. But it must be applied with caution, since courts have described it as a "relatively lenient standard"[75] that is more forgiving of government intervention.[76] Courts must determine when the conduct element inherent in all speech acts triggers this less exacting test. And, as noted previously, there is no logical method "for determining at what point conduct becomes so intertwined with expression that it becomes necessary to weigh the State's interest in proscribing conduct."[77] Without such a guidepost, the Court has been left to grapple with this issue case by case in response to such issues as sleep as symbolic expression,[78] political contributions,[79] flag burning[80] and nude dancing.[81] The resolution of these matters provides scant guidance for how the Court may treat future questions with which it may be presented.[82]

74. *Id.* at 377, 88 S. Ct. at 1679, 20 L.Ed.2d at 680.

75. Texas v. Johnson, 491 U.S. at 407, 109 S.Ct. at 2541, 105 L.Ed.2d at 355.

76. It is instructive to note that application of the *O'Brien* test to prior symbolic speech cases might have reversed the original holdings. For example, the library sit-in in *Brown v. Louisiana*, 383 U.S. 131, 86 S.Ct. 719, 15 L.Ed.2d 637 (1966) might have been properly sanctioned under the state breach of peace law to the extent the Court found that the statute served an important interest unrelated to speech and did not unduly restrict expression. Various commenters have criticized the *O'Brien* test, suggesting that in its application it has become virtually a rational basis test. *See* Williams, *supra* note 35. Werhan, *supra* note 59.

77. Cowgill v. California, 396 U.S. at 372, 90 S. Ct. at 614, 24 L.Ed.2d at 590 (Harlan, J. concurring).

78. Clark v. Community for Creative Non–Violence, 468 U.S. at 294–95, 104 S. Ct. at 3071, 82 L. Ed. 2d at 227–28 (1984) and *id.* at 304–08, 104 S. Ct. at 3074, 82 L. Ed. 2d at 233–36 (Marshall, J., dissenting).

79. Buckley v. Valeo, 424 U.S. at 16, 96 S. Ct. at 633, 46 L.Ed.2d at 686.

80. United States v. Eichman, 496 U.S. 310, 110 S.Ct. 2404, 110 L.Ed.2d 287; Texas v. Johnson, 491 U.S. 397, 109 S.Ct. 2533, 105 L.Ed.2d 342 (1989).

81. Barnes v. Glen Theatre, Inc., 501 U.S. 560, 111 S.Ct. 2456, 115 L.Ed.2d 504 (1991).

82. The Court has not been entirely consistent in distinguishing pure speech from that speech "plus" action. Moreover, the Court's continuing quest to apply a different standard to speech that includes some action component sits uneasily next to its precedents involving charitable solicitations. Such solicitations obviously involve conduct and have as a principal object the transfer of money. But because such action is "characteristically intertwined with informative and perhaps persuasive speech seeking support for particular causes or for particular views on economic, political, or social issues," it is treated as a fully protected activity under the First Amendment. Village of Schaumburg v. Citizens for a Better Environment, 444 U.S. 620, 632, 100 S.Ct. 826, 834, 63 L.Ed.2d 73, 84 (1980). *See* Secretary of State of Maryland v. Joseph H. Munson Co. Inc., 467 U.S. 947, 104 S.Ct. 2839, 81 L.Ed.2d 786 (1984). Moreover, the Court has expressly eschewed any attempt to distinguish protected expression from less-protected expression, holding that "where ... the component parts of a single speech are inextricably intertwined, we cannot parcel out the speech, applying one test to one phrase and another test to another phrase." Riley v. National Federation of the Blind of North Carolina, Inc., 487 U.S. 781, 796, 108 S.Ct. 2667, 2677, 101 L.Ed.2d 669, 689 (1988); *See also* Gaudiya Vaishnava Society v. City and County of San Francisco,

The absence of an analytic framework also tends to polarize the Court. For example, in *Barnes v. Glen Theatre, Inc.*, the Court upheld an Indiana prohibition on nude barroom dancing.[83] Although such activity would seem to be such that the conduct and communicative content are inextricably related, the decision produced four opinions and some sharp disagreements. In a plurality opinion, Chief Justice Rehnquist, joined by Justices O'Connor and Kennedy, argued that the state's general ban on public nudity was not directed at suppressing the erotic message of the dancing and that the law could be enforced with only incidental effects on the message.[84] Justice Souter declined to separate conduct from expression, finding that "when nudity is combined with expressive activity, its stimulative and attractive value certainly can enhance the force of expression."[85] But he voted to uphold the law because of the importance of the asserted state interest in combating secondary effects associated with adult entertainment, such as crime and prostitution. Justice Scalia considered nude dancing to be pure conduct and "not subject to First Amendment scrutiny at all."[86] In sharp contrast, Justice White, along with Justices Marshall, Blackmun and Stevens argued that dance inherently "is the communication of emotion or ideas," and that the state's purpose was "to protect the viewers from what the State believes is the harmful message that nude dancing communicates."[87]

The multiple opinions in *Barnes* highlight the difficulty of separating conduct from content in symbolic speech cases. But they also suggest that it is not entirely clear when the government's interest is unrelated to the suppression of free expression. In *O'Brien*, for example, there was strong evidence that Congress amended the Selective Service Act to prohibit draft card burning solely to stop what had become a powerful method of protesting the Vietnam War.[88] Nevertheless, the Court con-

952 F.2d 1059, 1064 (9th Cir.1990) ("[w]here the pure speech and commercial speech [are] inextricably intertwined, the entirety must be classified as noncommercial and we must apply the test for fully protected speech."). *But see* Valentine v. Chrestensen, 316 U.S. 52, 62 S.Ct. 920, 86 L.Ed. 1262 (1942) (regulation of speech is permissible where primary purpose is commercial).

83. 501 U.S. 560, 111 S.Ct. 2456, 115 L.Ed.2d 504 (1991).

84. *Id.* at 571, 111 S.Ct. at 2463, 115 L.Ed.2d at 514. This was a straightforward application of the *O'Brien* test. However, it is based on the dubious assumption that the message is not fundamentally altered by enforcing the ban on total nudity. *See, e.g.,* *Cohen*, 403 U.S. at 18, 91 S. Ct. at 1784, 29 L. Ed. 2d at 290 (Cohen's conviction "rest[ed] solely upon 'speech'" because there was no "separately identifiable conduct" that "could be regulated without effectively repressing Cohen's ability to express himself").

85. 501 U.S. at 581, 111 S. Ct. at 2468, 115 L.Ed.2d at 521 (Souter, J., concurring).

86. *Id.* 572, 111 S. Ct. at 2463, 115 L.Ed.2d at 515 (Scalia, J., concurring).

87. *Id.* at 591 & n.1, 111 S. Ct. at 2471 & n.1, 2473, 115 L. Ed. 2d at 525 n.1, 527 (White, J., dissenting).

88. For a description of events leading up to passage of the Selective Service Act amendment, see Dean Alfange, Jr., *Free Speech and Symbolic Conduct: The Draft-Card Burning Case,* 1968 Sup. Ct. Rev. 1. Professor Tribe suggests that *"United States v. O'Brien* appears to have been wrongly decided since the showing of illicit motive should have triggered the more demanding requirements" reserved for content-based restrictions. LAURENCE H. TRIBE, *supra* note 3, at 825. Professor Nimmer, on the other hand, declined to engage in the "slippery undertaking" of assessing legislative motives, and concluded that the restrictions at issue in *O'Brien* were invalid because they were "overnarrow." Melville B.

cluded that congressional motive does not determine the constitutionality of an enactment, and, in any event, the petitioner failed to prove that Congress acted for an impermissible purpose.[89] The Court showed no such hesitancy in *Grosjean v. American Press Co.*, in which it invalidated a two percent gross receipts tax on large circulation newspapers on the assumption that the tax was motivated by a desire to censor a critical press.[90] And lower courts have at times followed suit. In *News America Publishing, Inc. v. FCC*, for example, the United States Court of Appeals for the District of Columbia Circuit invalidated a congressional budget amendment after finding that the amendment was narrowly crafted so as to burden the First Amendment rights of a targeted individual.[91] But in general, courts avoid inquiring into congressional motivations, and they are even more reluctant to disturb congressional findings.[92] Consequently, the most telling evidence that a particular law suppresses expression is a demonstration showing that the law or regulation at issue is viewpoint-based.

4. *Pure Conduct*

Some actions—including some that are inherently communicative—fall outside the scope of the First Amendment. Because speech activities are "100% action and 100% expression" and "[i]t is possible to find some kernel of expression in almost every activity,"[93] the label "pure conduct" is somewhat misleading. However, for lack of a more precise label, the term "pure conduct" applies to situations in which (1) communication is an integral part of criminal conduct and protecting the speech would immunize the conduct from prosecution; or (2) conduct is not inherently communicative or is not sufficiently intertwined with expression so as to warrant application of the *O'Brien* test.[94] Such activity is beyond the reach of the First Amendment.

Nimmer, *The Meaning of Symbolic Speech Under the First Amendment*, 21 UCLA L. Rev. 29, 41 (1973).

89. 391 U.S. at 383, 385–86, 88 S. Ct. at 1682, 1683–84, 20 L. Ed. 2d at 683, 684–85. The *O'Brien* holding that the governmental interest must be unrelated to the suppression of speech does not necessarily conflict with its conclusion that the motive behind a congressional enactment is not germane to constitutional analysis. In *Eichman*, for example, the Court found no illicit motive but concluded that the governmental interest in preserving the symbolic value of the flag was content-related. The analysis centers on the character of a legislative measure, not the possible motivations leading to its enactment.

90. 297 U.S. 233, 56 S.Ct. 444, 80 L.Ed. 660 (1936). The Court's perception was aided by Governor Huey Long's campaign for the tax in which he called on the legislature to impose a "tax on lying." *See* Minneapolis Star and Tribune Co. v. Minnesota Comm'r of Revenue, 460 U.S. 575, 579–80, 103 S.Ct. 1365, 1369, 75 L.Ed.2d 295, 301 (1983).

91. 844 F.2d 800, 269 U.S. App. D.C. 182 (D.C.Cir.1988). After an extensive review of congressional motivations underlying the enactment, the court expressly declined to decide whether there was illicit legislative purpose. Rather, it held that the budget amendment was too underinclusive to survive constitutional scrutiny. *See also* Hentoff v. Ichord, 318 F.Supp. 1175 (D.D.C. 1970).

92. *E.g.,* Columbia Broadcasting Sys., Inc. v. Democratic National Comm. 412 U.S. 94, 103, 93 S.Ct. 2080, 2087, 36 L.Ed.2d 772, 784 (1973). *But see* Sable Communications of California, Inc. v. FCC, 492 U.S. 115, 109 S.Ct. 2829, 106 L.Ed.2d 93 (1989) (explaining level of deference due to congressional findings).

93. *See supra* note 5 and authorities cited therein.

94. Some cases may straddle these two categories. For example, in Haig v. Agee, 453 U.S. 280, 101 S.Ct. 2766, 69 L.Ed.2d 640 (1981), the Court upheld the Secretary

Certain conduct is illegal regardless of communicative intent. For example, "the communicative value of a well-placed bomb in the Capitol does not entitle it to the protection of the First Amendment."[95] Similarly, the act of assassination, though fraught with political meaning, obviously would not be protected.[96] Consistent with this premise, the Court has upheld government actions to control certain types of illegal behavior—such as restraints of trade—even though expression was an integral part of the regulated conduct.[97] In such cases, the importance of the governmental interest in regulating the conduct outweighs whatever residual speech interest is involved.[98] For example, in *Barnes v. Glen Theatre, Inc.*, three members of the Court reasoned that the "substantial government interest in protecting order and morality" justified a ban on nude barroom dancing, which they considered to be expressive conduct "within the outer perimeters of the First Amendment."[99]

In other cases, the legitimacy of governmental regulation hinges not on the seriousness of the offense involved, but on the fact that the conduct subject to regulation simply is not expressive. For example, in *Heimbaugh v. City and County of San Francisco*, a recent law school graduate was cited for a violation of the Golden Gate Park code for playing softball in an area reserved for other activities. After demanding that police officers ticket him, the defendant claimed immunity from prosecution on the theory that he and his friends were engaged in symbolic speech. He asserted that by playing softball, he was making a statement about "the right to democracy in recreation as opposed to

of State's denial of a passport to a former CIA agent who was attempting to expose CIA agents abroad on the grounds that the Secretary's decision affected only Agee's "*action*", not his "speech." *Id.* at 309, 101 S. Ct. at 2783, 69 L.Ed.2d at 663 (emphasis in original). However, travel is not illegal per se, and when undertaken for the express purpose of conveying a message, travel arguably is intertwined with expression. Since the Court in *Haig* was concerned that Agee's message had "the declared purpose of obstructing intelligence operations and the recruiting of intelligence personnel," *id.* at 308–09, 101 S. Ct. at 2783, 69 L.Ed.2d at 663 it might have more properly confined its inquiry to whether Agee's speech was protected rather than getting into a speech versus action analysis.

95. Eichman, 496 U.S. at 322, 110 S. Ct. at 2412, 110 L.Ed.2d at 299. (Stevens, J., dissenting).

96. *See* Rodney A. Smolla, Smolla and Nimmer, Freedom of Speech § 2:51 (3d ed. 1997). Tribe, *supra* note 3, at 828 n.18. *Cf.* People v. Rubin, 158 Cal.Rptr. 488, 96 Cal. App.3d 968 (1979) (hyperbolic offer of reward for the killing or maiming of members of the American Nazi Party who march in

Skokie, Illinois not protected by the First Amendment), *cert. denied*, 449 U.S. 821, 101 S.Ct. 80, 66 L.Ed.2d 24 (1980).

97. Federal Trade Commission v. Superior Court Trial Lawyers Ass'n, 493 U.S. 411, 429–30, 110 S.Ct. 768–69, 107 L.Ed.2d 851, 870–71 (1990). *See generally* National Society of Professional Engineers v. United States, 435 U.S. 679, 694, 98 S.Ct. 1355, 1367, 55 L.Ed.2d 637 (1978); Giboney v. Empire Storage & Ice Co., 336 U.S. 490, 502, 69 S.Ct. 684, 691, 93 L.Ed. 834, 844 (1949); Associated Press v. United States, 326 U.S. 1, 65 S.Ct. 1416, 89 L.Ed. 2013 (1945).

98. Although this statement is beyond question for such acts as political bombings and assassinations, there may be some doubt about its general applicability to lesser offenses for which speech is an integral element. *See* Stephen G. Thompson, *Antitrust, the First Amendment, and the Communication of Price Information*, 56 Temple L.Q. 939 (1983).

99. 501 U.S. at 566, 569, 111 S. Ct. at 2460, 2462, 115 L. Ed. 2d at 511, 513 (1991), Justices Scalia and Souter concurred on separate grounds.

elitism.''[100] The court rejected this argument and fined the defendant for raising a frivolous defense.[1] Not only did the defendant in *Heimbaugh* lack an evident intent to convey a message, the act of playing softball could not be considered, in itself, communicative.

A more plausible, although equally unsuccessful, claim of First Amendment protection was made in *Young v. New York City Transit Authority*.[2] There, an organization representing the homeless brought a class action against New York Transit Authority regulations that prohibited panhandling in the subway. The central focus of the claim was that begging is an act of charitable solicitation that is fully protected by the First Amendment.[3] But the Second Circuit found that "begging is much more 'conduct' than it is 'speech' " and that communication "simply is not inherent to the act" of panhandling.[4] Additionally, the court doubted that such activity conveyed any particularized viewpoint. Rather, it found that "[t]he only message that we are able to espy as common to all acts of begging is that beggars want to exact money from those whom they accost.''[5] In a vigorous dissent, Judge Meskill argued that it was impossible to distinguish, for First Amendment purposes, between charitable solicitation by an organization—which is fully protected—and solicitation by an individual on his own behalf, which the majority viewed as pure conduct.[6] But the majority found that the lack of a particularized message distinguished begging from organized solicitations and held, as a matter of "common sense" that panhandling is more akin to conduct than speech.[7]

Although *Young* raised some troubling issues regarding the distinction between pure speech and pure conduct, the Second Circuit sharply limited its scope in a subsequent decision. In *Loper v. New York City Police Department*, the court invalidated a statute that prohibited loitering in public places for purposes of begging.[8] The court distinguished Young by noting that subway platforms are not an unlimited public forum, and to ban panhandling on the streets would "leave individual beggars without the means to communicate their individual wants and

---

100. 591 F.Supp. 1573, 1574 (N.D.Cal. 1984).

1. *Id. See* Rule 11 Fed. R. Civ. P. *See also* Friedman v. Village of Skokie, 763 F.2d 236, 239 (7th Cir.1985) ("Friedman does not cite, nor has this court found, any authority for the proposition that the first amendment to the United States Constitution protects his right to kick and rock a video game to retrieve fifty cents."). These cases notwithstanding, charge of frivolity should be used advisedly in the symbolic speech context given the level of judicial dispute in this area.

2. 903 F.2d 146 (2d Cir.1990).

3. *See* cases cited at *supra*, note 82.

4. 903 F.2d at 153, 154.

5. *Id.* at 154.

6. *Id.* at 164 (Meskill, J., dissenting in part).

7. *But see* United States v. Kokinda, 497 U.S. 720, 110 S.Ct. 3115, 111 L.Ed.2d 571 (1990), in which the Supreme Court upheld a ban on organized solicitations on a sidewalk which connected a Post Office to its parking lot. The restriction prohibited solicitation but not political dialogue. However, *Kokinda* was decided as a public forum case, and not on a speech/action distinction. *See id.* at 733, 110 S. Ct. at 3123, 111 L.Ed.2d at 586 (solicitation is "a particular form of speech").

8. 999 F.2d 699 (2d Cir.1993).

needs."[9] In sharp contrast to *Young*, the panel in *Loper* stressed that "[i]t cannot be gainsaid that begging implicates expressive conduct or communicative activity."[10] The court elaborated on this concept: "Even without particularized speech ... the presence of an unkempt and disheveled person holding out his or her hand or a cup to receive a donation itself conveys a message of need for support and assistance."[11] The Supreme Court subsequently confirmed that "the Constitution looks beyond written or spoken words" and "a narrow, succinctly articulable message is not a condition of constitutional protection."[12] These subsequent decisions are more consistent with a broad view of the First Amendment that does not limit protection based on subject matter or mode of expression.[13]

B. Silence as Protected Expression

Not only does the First Amendment encompass affirmative efforts to communicate, either by word or deed, it also protects the decision to be silent.[14] The Supreme Court held explicitly in *Wooley v. Maynard* that the Constitution protects "both the right to speak freely and the right to refrain from speaking at all."[15] Generally, both individuals and corporations enjoy this right, although the exact contours of the "freedom of silence" have not been fully—or consistently—defined.[16]

The cases suggest that individuals may not be compelled to salute the flag,[17] disseminate state-mandated messages,[18] support political activities of labor unions[19] or swear allegiance to the nation in terms that are

9. *Id.* at 702.

10. *Id.* at 704.

11. *Id.*

12. Hurley v. Irish–American Gay, Lesbian and Bisexual Group of Boston, 515 U.S. 557, 115 S.Ct. 2338, 2345, 132 L.Ed.2d 487, 500–01 (1995).

13. It is undeniable that the First Amendment's protections extend beyond speech that is explicitly political. *See, e.g.,* Sable Communications of California, Inc, 492 U.S. at 126, 109 S. Ct. at 2836, 106 L.Ed.2d at 105 ("'[s]exual expression which is indecent but not obscene is protected by the First Amendment."); Ward v. Rock Against Racism, 491 U.S. 790, 491 U.S. 781, 109 S.Ct. 2746, 2753, 105 L.Ed.2d 661, 674 ("Music, as a form of expression and communication, is protected under the First Amendment."); Schad v. Mount Ephraim, 452 U.S. 61, 101 S.Ct. 2176, 68 L.Ed.2d 671 (1981) (nude dancing protected by the First Amendment); Abood v. Detroit Board of Education, 431 U.S. 209, 232, 97 S.Ct. 1782, 1798, 52 L.Ed.2d 261, 282 (1977) (whether or not speech is "political" is not a relevant constitutional inquiry); United Mine Workers v. Illinois Bar Ass'n, 389 U.S. 217, 223, 88 S.Ct. 353, 356–57, 19 L.Ed.2d 426, 431

(1967) ("First Amendment does not protect speech and assembly only to the extent it can be characterized as political.... 'free speech and free press are not confined to any field of human interest.' ").

14. This does not relate to silence as a communicative act, which is analyzed as symbolic speech. *See e.g.,* Brown v. Louisiana, 383 U.S. 131, 86 S.Ct. 719, 15 L.Ed.2d 637 (library sit-in). Rather, it refers to the First Amendment right to convey no message whatsoever.

15. 430 U.S. 705, 714, 97 S.Ct. 1428, 1435, 51 L.Ed.2d 752, 762 (1977).

16. *See generally* NIMMER, *supra* note 3, at § 4.10. Leora Harpaz, *Justice Jackson's Flag Salute Legacy: The Supreme Court Struggles to Protect Intellectual Individualism,* 64 Tex.L.Rev. 817 (1986).

17. West Virginia State Bd. of Educ. v. Barnette, 319 U.S. 624, 63 S.Ct. 1178, 87 L.Ed. 1628 (1943).

18. Wooley v. Maynard, 430 U.S. 705, 97 S.Ct. 1428, 51 L.Ed.2d 752 (1977).

19. Abood v. Detroit Bd. of Educ., 431 U.S. 209, 97 S.Ct. 1782, 52 L.Ed.2d 261 (1977).

vague or that penalize disfavored political beliefs or associations.[20] Similarly, corporate entities may not be required to publish responses to news stories,[21] disseminate the political statements of their adversaries [22] or include disfavored groups in an organized parade.[22A] On the other hand, the owner of a shopping center may be required to allow access to his facilities by persons engaging in speech.[23] For a more thorough discussion of the freedom of silence, see section 1.7[G], *infra*.

1.6 "Free" Versus "Unfree" Speech

In the words of Professor Alexander Meiklejohn, the eminent First Amendment theorist, the First Amendment "does not forbid the abridging of speech ... it does forbid the abridging of freedom of speech."[1] Although this statement has been criticized as an example of "Talmudic (or Thomistic) reasoning,"[2] it accurately characterizes the operation of First Amendment law.[3] In short, not all speech is created equal under the Constitution. Certain categories of speech have long been considered outside the range of interests protected by the First Amendment.[4] Once a particular type of speech act was so defined, it tended to fall off the edge of the First Amendment earth for purposes of constitutional analysis. It traditionally was accorded the same level of First Amend-

20. Communist Party of Indiana v. Whitcomb, 414 U.S. 441, 94 S.Ct. 656, 38 L.Ed.2d 635 (1974); Cole v. Richardson, 405 U.S. 676, 679–80, 92 S.Ct. 1332, 1334–1335, 31 L.Ed.2d 593, 599 (1972).

21. Miami Herald Publishing Co. v. Tornillo, 418 U.S. 241, 94 S.Ct. 2831, 41 L.Ed.2d 730 (1974).

22. Pacific Gas & Electric Co. v. Public Utilities Commission of Cal., 475 U.S. 1, 106 S.Ct. 903, 89 L.Ed.2d 1 (1986).

22A. Hurley v. Irish–American Gay, Lesbian and Bisexual Group of Boston, 515 U.S. 557, 115 S.Ct. 2338, 132 L.Ed.2d 487 (1995).

23. PruneYard Shopping Center v. Robins, 447 U.S. 74, 100 S.Ct. 2035, 64 L.Ed.2d 741 (1980).

1. ALEXANDER MEIKLEJOHN, FREE SPEECH AND ITS RELATION TO GOOD GOVERNMENT 19 (1948).

2. MELVILLE B. NIMMER, FREEDOM OF SPEECH § 2.01 at 2–6 (1984). It also has been criticized as "sophistry" that "too patently begs the question." Hans A. Linde, *Courts and Censorship*, 66 Minn. L. Rev. 171, 195 (1981).

3. *See e.g.*, American Communications Ass'n v. Douds, 339 U.S. 382, 394, 70 S.Ct., 674, 682, 94 L.Ed. 925, 941 (1950) ("Freedom of speech ... does not comprehend the right to speak on any subject at any time.").

4. The "non-free" speech categories have evolved from a balancing process in which certain social interests were weighed against the competing interest in free expression. Courts have tended to deny First Amendment protection to the extent the social cost of the speech in question is considered excessive, or the communicative value of the speech is considered minimal, or a combination of both factors. *See* New York v. Ferber, 458 U.S. 747, 763–64, 102 S.Ct. 3348, 3358 73 L.Ed.2d 1113, 1127 (1982) ("Thus, it is not rare that a content-based classification of speech has been accepted because it may be appropriately generalized that within the confines of the given classification, the evil to be restricted so overwhelmingly outweighs the expressive interests, if any, at stake, that no process of case-by-case adjudication is required."). But certain Justices have expressed a preference for ad hoc balancing. *E.g.*, Smith v. Daily Mail Publishing Co., 443 U.S. 97, 106, 99 S.Ct. 2667, 2672, 61 L.Ed.2d 399, 407 (1979) (Rehnquist, J., concurring) ("[W]e have eschewed absolutes in favor of a more delicate calculus that carefully weighs the conflicting interests to determine which demands the greater protection under the particular circumstances presented."); Herbert v. Lando, 441 U.S. 153, 196, 99 S.Ct. 1635, 1659, 60 L.Ed.2d 115, 146–47 (1979) (Brennan, J., dissenting) ("In my view this tension is too fine to be resolved in the abstract ... there must be a more specific balancing of the particular interests asserted in a given lawsuit.").

ment protection as pure conduct—that is, none. Such speech has been described as being "beneath the dignity of the first amendment."[5] However, the Supreme Court more recently has begun to extend First Amendment protection to speech even when it falls within a typically "unprotected" class.[6] This Section outlines the traditionally accepted categories of "non-free" speech, as well as some categories for which the law is not entirely settled.

A. *Fighting Words*

Words whose utterance tend only to injure or to cause an immediate breach of the peace are generally excluded from constitutional protection. The Supreme Court first articulated this "fighting words" doctrine in *Chaplinsky v. New Hampshire*, a case involving potential religious brawls in the streets.[7] Chaplinsky, a Jehovah's Witness, gave speeches on the streets of Rochester, New York, in which he denounced other religions as rackets, among other things. Following a commotion among passers-by, Chaplinsky was warned by police that he was causing a disturbance and escorted to City Hall (although he was not arrested). Upon receiving the warning, Chaplinsky replied to the police officer, "You are a god damned racketeer; The whole government of Rochester are Fascists or agents of Fascists." Chaplinsky was then arrested. The incident resulted in Chaplinsky's conviction under a law that prohibited use of offensive, derisive or annoying words to another person with the intent to deride, offend or annoy.

In upholding Chaplinsky's conviction, the Court noted that "[t]here are certain well-defined and narrowly limited classes of speech, the prevention and punishment of which have never been thought to raise any Constitutional problem. These include the lewd and obscene, the profane, the libelous and the insulting or 'fighting' words."[8] The Court made clear that in weighing the social utility of such expression against the probable social costs, the balance did not favor free speech: "such utterances are no essential part of any exposition of ideas, and are of such slight social value as a step to truth that any benefit that may be derived from them is clearly outweighed by the social interest in order and morality."[9]

This First Amendment exception is confined to words whose "very utterance inflict[s] injury or tend to incite an immediate breach of the peace."[10] Thus, the fighting words doctrine generally applies only where (1) there is face to face communication;[11] (2) there is a direct tendency

---

5. Rodney A. Smolla, Law of Defamation § 4.10[4][c][i] (1991).

6. *See* R.A.V. v. City of St. Paul, 505 U.S. 377, 112 S.Ct. 2538, 120 L.Ed.2d 305 (1992). Such developments have led some scholars to describe the categorical approach as "outdated." *See, e.g.,* Smolla *supra,* n. 96 at § 2:67.

7. 315 U.S. 568, 62 S.Ct. 766, 86 L.Ed. 1031 (1942).

8. *Id.* at 571–572, 62 S. Ct. at 769, 86 L. Ed. at 1035.

9. *Id.* at 572, 62 S. Ct. at 769, 86 L. Ed. at 1035.

10. *Id.*

11. A related line of cases pertains to situations in which a speaker's remarks addressed to a general audience may provoke violence. In Terminiello v. Chicago, 337

under the circumstances for the words to cause the addressee to react violently; and (3) the words are objectively offensive.[12] Under this test, the Court found it unnecessary to discuss whether the expressions "damned racketeer" or "damned fascist," when addressed to a peace officer, were likely to provoke a fight. Such "epithets," the Court concluded, are "likely to provoke the average person to retaliation, and thereby cause a breach of the peace."[13]

Since *Chaplinsky*, the fighting words doctrine has been something of a moving target. Times change, and with them society's notions of what may be considered "classically" offensive. Moreover, the Supreme Court increasingly has focused on the context in which words are spoken, and has required that the confrontations must be likely to cause an immediate breach of the peace. In *Gooding v. Wilson*, for example, the Court invalidated the conviction of an anti-war protester who scuffled with police while uttering the words: "White son of a bitch. I'll kill you. You son of a bitch—I'll choke you to death. If you ever put your hands on me again, I'll cut you all to pieces."[14] The words and the setting appeared to be extremely provocative. But the Court in that case held that the Georgia statute prohibiting use of "opprobrious words or abusive language" was vague and overbroad.[15] The Court reached an identical result in *Lewis v. New Orleans*, where the defendant had said "you goddamn motherfucking police."[16] Although the decisions are couched more as due process holdings, the Court has indicated its intent to scrutinize careful-

U.S. 1, 3, 69 S.Ct. 894, 895, 93 L.Ed. 1131, 1134 (1949), the Court overturned a municipal ordinance prohibiting breaches of the peace that had been applied against speech that "stirs the public to anger, invites dispute, brings about a condition of unrest, or creates a disturbance." Writing for the majority, Justice Douglas explained that the First Amendment "may indeed best serve its high purpose when it induces a condition of unrest, creates dissatisfaction with conditions as they are, or even stirs people to anger." *Id*. at 4, 69 S. Ct. at 896, 93 L. Ed. at 1134. By contrast, in *Feiner v. New York*, 340 U.S. 315, 71 S.Ct. 303, 95 L.Ed. 295 (1951), the Court upheld a conviction under a state disorderly conduct statute of a speaker who had provoked at least one member of his audience to threaten violence. Since then, the Court has shown more fidelity to its reasoning in *Terminiello* than that in *Feiner*. *See, e.g.,* Cohen v. California, 403 U.S. 15, 20, 91 S.Ct. 1780, 1786, 29 L.Ed.2d 284 291 (1971); Cox v. Louisiana, 379 U.S. 536, 549, 85 S.Ct. 453, 462–63, 13 L.Ed.2d 471, 82 (1965); Edwards v. South Carolina, 372 U.S. 229, 236, 83 S.Ct. 680, 684, 9 L.Ed.2d 697, 702 (1963).

12. Relying on the bad tendency of certain speech, but without giving examples, the Court described fighting words as those which "men of common intelligence would understand would be words likely to cause an average addressee to fight." 315 U.S. at 573, 62 S. Ct. at 770, 86 L. Ed. at 1036. It subdivided the genre into "classical fighting words," which, "as ordinary men know, are likely to cause a fight ... when said without a disarming smile;" contemporary fighting words ("words in current use less 'classical' but equally likely to cause violence"); and "other disorderly words, including profanity, obscenity and threats." *Id*, 62 S. Ct. at 770, 86 L. Ed. at 1036.

13. *Id*. at 574, 62 S. Ct. at 770, 86 L. Ed. at 1036. Some suggest that the *Chaplinsky* language was mere dictum. *See* Stephen W. Gard, *Fighting Words as Free Speech*, 58 Wash. U.L.Q. 531, 534 (1980).

14. 405 U.S. 518, 520 n. 1, 92 S.Ct. 1103, 1105 n. 1, 31 L.Ed.2d 408, 412 n. 1 (1972).

15. It is difficult to reconcile this holding with the *Chaplinsky* Court's decision upholding against vagueness challenge the New Hampshire law that prohibited use of offensive, derisive or annoying words to another person with the intent to deride, offend or annoy.

16. 415 U.S. 130, 131, 94 S.Ct. 970, 971 n. 1, 39 L.Ed.2d 214, 218 n. 1 (1974).

ly any limitation on speech supported by the fighting words doctrine.[17] In any event, it is clear that calling a police officer a "god damned racketeer" would hardly suffice as a contemporary manifestation of fighting words.

Despite significant changes in both society and the state of the law, the fighting words doctrine still exhibits some vital signs in various state court decisions.[18] In *City of Billings v. Batten*, for example, the Montana Supreme Court upheld a breach of peace conviction when an altercation between neighbors resulted in the following diatribe: "[You are] a communist government worker, [a] no-good son of a bitch, [a] chicken-shit and [a] motherfucker. Fight me. Hit me. You have a golf club. Come on. I want to fight you."[19] The outburst touched on all three categories of fighting words described in *Chaplinsky*, and probably would have been considered to be such even if uttered with "a disarming smile." Similarly, the Indiana Court of Appeals relied on the fighting words doctrine in affirming the disorderly conduct conviction of a street preacher. The defendant had reviled his audience as "fuckers," "whores," "queers," and "AIDS people," and also claimed that the crowd was "condemned to Hell."[20] On the other hand, the Washington Supreme Court found no fighting words where, upon being asked to leave, a disgruntled patron of a restaurant told the host-doorman: "[C]ome outside so I can kick your fucking ass. I'll either get [you] tonight or later."[21] The court found that in the specific context presented, there was little likelihood of violence. Consequently, courts may be moving away from a broad doctrine in which certain expressions are considered "classic" or per se fighting words.[22]

17. The decisions indicate the Court's increasing discomfort with the fighting words doctrine. In *Lewis*, the Court noted that expressions conveying or intending to convey disgrace are not fighting words. *Id.* at 133, 94 S. Ct. at 972, 39 L. Ed. 2d at 219. *See also* Norwell v. City of Cincinnati, 414 U.S. 14, 94 S.Ct. 187, 38 L.Ed.2d 170 (1973) (no fighting words found where a person "verbally and negatively" protested his arrest); Hess v. Indiana, 414 U.S. 105, 94 S.Ct. 326, 38 L.Ed.2d 303 (1973) (statement during antiwar protest that "we'll take the fucking street later" not considered to be fighting words); Rosenfeld v. New Jersey, 408 U.S. 901, 92 S.Ct. 2479, 33 L.Ed.2d 321 (1972); Brown v. Oklahoma, 408 U.S. 914, 92 S.Ct. 2507, 33 L.Ed.2d 326 (1972). In his dissent in *Gooding*, Justice Blackmun complained that the Court was "merely paying lip service to *Chaplinsky*." 405 U.S. at 537, 92 S. Ct. at 1113, 31 L. Ed. 2d at 422.

18. The fighting words doctrine has not fared as well in the Supreme Court. Despite frequent citations of the *Chaplinsky* dictum, the Court has not found a single instance in which fights words were unprotected since 1942. *See* Nadine Strossen,

Regulating Racist Speech on Campus: A Modest Proposal? 1990 Duke L. J. 484, 510–11 n. 130.

19. 218 Mont. 64, 705 P.2d 1120, 1122 (1985).

20. Gilles v. State, 531 N.E.2d 220, 223 (Ind.App.1988), cert denied, 493 U.S. 939, 110 S.Ct. 337, 107 L.Ed.2d 325 (1989) ("In terms generally considered some of the most offensive in our culture, Gilles placed his listeners in categories defined by sexual activity, sexual orientation, and sexually transmitted disease."). *But see id.* at 225–26 (Miller, J., dissenting) (insults directed at crowd were protected speech because they were part of an exposition of ideas; fighting words doctrine is inapplicable because insults were not expressed face to face).

21. City of Seattle v. Camby, 104 Wash.2d 49, 701 P.2d 499, 500 (Wash. 1985).

22. Some state court decisions continue to emphasize the offensive nature of the speech at issue. *See, e.g.*, People v. Dietze, 75 N.Y.2d 47, 58, 550 N.Y.S.2d 595, 549 N.E.2d 1166 (1989); Estes v. State, 660

The Supreme Court reaffirmed the fighting words doctrine in *R.A.V. v. City of St. Paul*, yet it also held that such offensive words have a certain measure of First Amendment protection. The case involved the prosecution of a minor for violating the St. Paul, Minnesota Bias Motivated Crime Ordinance. The defendant and five other young men had burned a cross in the yard of a black family. After the trial court dismissed the charges on grounds that the law was overly broad and impermissibly content-based, the state Supreme Court reversed, and narrowed the ordinance to cover only fighting words.[23] Accepting this construction of the law, limiting its reach to expression "proscribable under the 'fighting words' doctrine," the United States Supreme Court struck down the ordinance as facially unconstitutional "in that it prohibits otherwise permitted speech solely on the basis of the subjects the speech addresses."[24]

In reaching this conclusion, the Court clarified its approach toward "unfree speech"—expression normally considered to be outside the First Amendment's protection. Acknowledging that it has noted repeatedly that certain categories of speech are "not within the area of constitutionally protected speech," or that the "protection of the First Amendment does not extend" to various categories of expression, the Court emphasized that such statements "must be taken in context."[25] The majority opinion rejected the view that such expression should be considered "as not being speech at all,"[26] and concluded that the traditional categories of unprotected speech are not "entirely invisible to the Constitution."[27] These categories of speech—obscenity, defamation, fighting words—can be regulated *because of their constitutionally proscribable content*" but cannot become "the vehicles for content discrimination."[28] Thus, the government may be able to prohibit defamation or obscenity, but it may not proscribe only those obscene or libelous messages that contain criticism of the city.

The St. Paul ordinance, according to the Court, was invalid because it engaged in both content and viewpoint discrimination. It applied only to fighting words that insult or provoke violence "on the basis of race, color, creed, religion or gender."[29] Justice Scalia's majority opinion pointed out that other examples of abusive invective, no matter how vicious or severe, were left alone by the ordinance "unless they are addressed to one of the specified disfavored topics." For example, fighting words used to express hostility "on the basis of political affiliation,

S.W.2d 873, 875 (Tex.App.1983). Other decisions focus on the context and the likelihood of provoking unrest. *See, e.g.,* State v. Fratzke, 446 N.W.2d 781, 785 (Iowa 1989); City of Maryville v. Costin, 805 S.W.2d 331, 332 (Mo.Ct.App.1991).

23. In the Matter of the Welfare of R.A.V., 464 N.W.2d 507, 510–11 (Minn. 1991).

24. R.A.V. v. City of St. Paul, 505 U.S. 377, 381, 112 S.Ct. 2538, 2542, 120 L.Ed.2d at 305, 316 (1992).

25. *Id.* at 383, 112 S. Ct. at 2543, 120 L. Ed. 2d at 317–18 (citations omitted).

26. Cass R. Sunstein, *Pornography and the First Amendment*, 1986 Duke L.J. 589, 615, n. 146.

27. R.A.V., 505 U.S. at 383, 112 S.Ct. at 2543, 120 L.Ed.2d at 318.

28. *Id.* 383–384, 112 S.Ct. at 2543, 120 L.Ed.2d at 318 (emphasis in original).

29. *Id.* at. 391, 112 S. Ct. at 2547, 120 L. Ed. 2d at 323.

union membership, or homosexuality" were not covered.[30] The Court found that such selectivity created the possibility that the city was seeking to handicap the expression of particular ideas and that such discrimination was unnecessary to the fulfillment of the government's compelling interests.[31]

In a concurring opinion, Justice White, joined by Justices Blackmun, O'Connor and Stevens, agreed with the result but argued that the majority was "inventing [a] brand of First Amendment underinclusiveness."[32] Applying the logic of the majority opinion, Justice White suggested that the law making it a crime to threaten the President's life, title 18 United States Code, section 871, would similarly violate the First Amendment. The statute, he explained, "incorporates a content-based distinction; it indicates that the Government especially disfavors threats against the President as opposed to threats against all others."[33] In response, Justice Scalia noted that such exclusions were constitutionally permissible "[w]hen the basis for the content discrimination consists entirely of the very reason the entire class of speech at issue is proscribable."[34] Thus, threats against the President may be outlawed because "the reasons why threats of violence are outside the First Amendment . . . have special force when applied to the person of the President." On the other hand, the government could not legitimately outlaw "only those threats against the President that mention his policy on aid to inner cities."[35]

30. *Id.*

31. *Id.* at 394–96, 112 S. Ct. at 2549–50, 120 L. Ed. 2d at 325–26. The Court disagreed with the city's contention that it could regulate the speech in question because of its "secondary effects" of victimizing particular groups. It noted that listeners' reactions to speech are not the type of secondary effects that legitimately may be regulated consistently with the First Amendment. Similarly, although the Court agreed that the government's goal of combating discrimination is compelling, it concluded that the law's content discrimination was not necessary to serve the city's interest. *Id.*

32. *Id.* at 402, 112 S. Ct. at 2553, 120 L. Ed. 2d at 330. Additional concurring statements were written by Justice Blackmun as well as by Justice Stevens, joined in part by Justices White and Blackmun. *But see* City of Ladue v. Gilleo, 512 U.S. 43, 45, 114 S.Ct. 2038, 2043, 129 L.Ed.2d 36, 45 (1994) ("the notion that a regulation of speech may be impermissibly *under-inclusive* is firmly grounded in basic First Amendment principles.").

33. 505 U.S. at 407, 112 S. Ct. at 2556, 120 L. Ed. 2d at 334. This concern aside, Justice White agreed that the St. Paul ordinance was overly broad because it criminalized "expressive conduct that causes only hurt feelings, offense, or resentment" in addition to unprotected fighting words. *Id.* at 414, 112 S. Ct. at 2559, 120 L. Ed. 2d at 338.

34. *Id.* at 388, 112 S.Ct. at 2545, 120 L. Ed. 2d at 320–21.

35. *Id.* at 388, 112 S.Ct. at 2546, 120 L. Ed. 2d at 321. Although *R.A.V. v. St. Paul* barred prosecution under a hate crimes ordinance, the case does not preclude the enhancement of criminal penalties where, for example, a person commits assault and intentionally selects the victim on the basis of "race, religion, color, disability, sexual orientation, national origin or ancestry." Wisconsin v. Mitchell, 508 U.S. 476, 481, 113 S.Ct. 2194, 2197, 124 L.Ed.2d 436, 442 (1993). The Court found that the motive for committing a crime is a traditional factor considered by sentencing judges and that doing so does not abridge the First Amendment. However, introducing evidence of a criminal defendant's abstract beliefs involving racial animus at a sentencing hearing may violate the First Amendment. Dawson v. Delaware, 503 U.S. 159, 112 S.Ct. 1093, 117 L.Ed.2d 309 (1992). *But see* Barclay v. Florida, 463 U.S. 939, 103 S.Ct. 3418, 77 L.Ed.2d 1134 (1983).

B. *Obscenity*

Like fighting words, obscenity represents another category of speech that courts have ruled provides "no essential part of any exposition of ideas. [It has] such slight social value as a step to truth that any benefit that may be derived from [it] is clearly outweighed by the social interest in order and morality."[36] Indeed, the Supreme Court, in holding that obscenity "is not within the area of constitutionally protected speech or press" expressly relied on the rationale of *Chaplinsky*, that speech of slight social value can be suppressed to further compelling social goals.[37] In *Roth v. United States*, the Supreme Court held that obscene speech is unprotected by the First Amendment, but found that utterances do not fall from constitutional grace unless they are "utterly without redeeming social importance."[38] Under current law, to exclude sexual speech from constitutional protection, the government must demonstrate: (1) that the average person, applying contemporary community standards, would find that the work, taken as a whole, appeals to the prurient interest; (2) that the work depicts or describe, in a patently offensive way as measured by contemporary community standards, sexual conduct specifically defined by applicable state law; and (3) that the work, taken as a whole, lacks serious literary, artistic, political, or scientific value.[39]

The law relating to the regulation of obscene and indecent speech, which has been described as a "tragicomic story of [a] luxuriant specialty of constitutional law,"[40] is considered in greater detail in chapter six.

C. *Publication of State Secrets*

The Supreme Court pointed out in *Near v. Minnesota* that "[n]o one would question but that a government might prevent actual obstruction to its recruiting service or the publication of the sailing dates of transports or the number and location of troops."[41] Although this dictum tended to establish the proposition that the First Amendment does not protect disclosure of national security information, its reach has re-

---

36. Chaplinsky, 315 U.S. at 571, 62 S. Ct. at 769, 86 L. Ed. at 1035.

37. Roth v. United States, 354 U.S. 476, 485, 77 S.Ct. 1304, 1309, 1 L.Ed.2d 1498, 1507 (1957). This approach prevailed over the contrary view, stated by Justice Douglas in dissent, that society's goals are not furthered by restrictions that punish the mere arousal of sexual thoughts. Rather, he would require a demonstration that the speech in question "have some relation to action which could be penalized by government." *Id*. at 509, 77 S. Ct. at 1321, 1 L. Ed. 2d at 1520 (Douglas, J., dissenting).

38. *Id*. at 484–485, 77 S. Ct. at 1309, 1 L. Ed. 2d at 1507. Sixteen years later, the Court refined this requirement to a showing that the material, taken as a whole, lacks serious literary, artistic, political or

scientific value. Miller v. California, 413 U.S. 15, 24, 93 S.Ct. 2607, 2617, 37 L.Ed.2d 419, 431 (1973). *See* Pope v. Illinois, 481 U.S. 497, 500–01, 107 S.Ct. 1918, 1921 95 L.Ed.2d 439, 443 (1987).

39. Miller, 413 U.S. at 24, 93 S. Ct. at 2615, 37 L. Ed. 2d at 431.

40. Linde, *supra* note 2, at 192.

41. 283 U.S. 697, 716, 51 S.Ct. 625, 631, 75 L.Ed. 1357, 1367 (1931). In questioning this premise, however, Associate Justice Hans A. Linde of the Oregon Supreme Court noted that "a phrase like 'no one would question' ... typically introduces an assertion without citation of legal or empirical support." Linde, *supra* note 2, at 192.

mained unclear. The Court finally was presented squarely with the issue in *New York Times v. United States*, the Pentagon Papers case.[42]

In *New York Times*, a fragmented Court held that the United States could not enjoin publication of a classified Pentagon-commissioned history of American involvement in Vietnam.[43] The decision produced nine separate opinions and no clear standard on how the Court should weigh national security versus First Amendment interests. In a three paragraph *per curiam* opinion, the Court, by a 6–3 vote, held only that the government had not met the heavy burden required to sustain a prior restraint.[44] Three Justices—Black, Douglas and Brennan—took the position that the First Amendment imposes an absolute (or near absolute) ban on prior restraints of news reports.[45] Justices White and Stewart argued that the Government had not met its burden of proof to sustain a prior restraint, a particularly heavy burden in the absence of statutory authorization for an injunction.[46] Justice Marshall argued that it was a legislative function to pass laws to protect national security and declined to use the Court's power of contempt "to prevent behavior that Congress has specifically declined to prohibit."[47] Chief Justice Burger, along with Justices Harlan and Blackmun, dissented, arguing that it was a matter for the Executive, and not the Judiciary, to determine the impact of information disclosure on national security.[48]

Although most of the Justices agreed with the government's emphatic position that disclosure of the Pentagon Papers would damage national interests, this was not considered sufficient to support a prior restraint on speech.[49] Still, there were skeptics on the Court regarding the government's claim that publication would cause "grave and irrepa-

---

42. 403 U.S. 713, 91 S.Ct. 2140, 29 L.Ed.2d 822 (1971) (per curiam). As Justice Brennan noted in his concurring opinion, "there is no question but that the material sought to be suppressed is within the protection of the First Amendment." *Id.* at 727, n. *, 91 S. Ct. at 2140, n. *, 29 L. Ed. 2d at 831, n. * (Brennan, J., concurring). The question, then, is the point at which the anticipated damage to national security outweighs the First Amendment interest in free discussion of public affairs. Without some type of balancing test, it is exceedingly difficult to separate protected from unprotected speech in this area.

43. The study, entitled "History of U.S. Decision–Making Process on Viet Nam Policy," became known popularly as the Pentagon Papers.

44. 403 U.S. at 714, 91 S. Ct. at 2141, 29 L. Ed. 2d at 824–825.

45. *Id.* at 715, 91 S. Ct. at 2142, 29 L. Ed. 2d at 825 (Black, J., concurring); *id.* at 720, 91 S. Ct. at 2144, 29 L. Ed. at 828 (Douglas, J., concurring); *id.* at 726, 91 S. Ct. at 2147, 29 L. Ed. 2d at 831 (Brennan, J., concurring) (recognizing "single, ex-

tremely narrow class of cases" in which First Amendment ban on prior restraints may be overridden).

46. *Id.* at 731, 91 S. Ct. at 2150, 29 L. Ed. 2d at 835 (White, J., concurring); *id.* at 730, 91 S. Ct. at 2149, 29 L. Ed. 2d at 834 (Stewart, J., concurring).

47. *Id.* at 742, 91 S. Ct. at 2155, 29 L. Ed. 2d at 840 (Marshall, J., concurring).

48. *Id.* at 757–58, 91 S. Ct. at 2163, 29 L. Ed. 2d at 849–50 (Harlan, J., dissenting).

49. However, a majority of the Justices suggested that they would uphold a statute establishing criminal penalties for disclosing national security information. Indeed, the government subsequently sought to prosecute Daniel Ellsberg and Anthony Russo for their role in the Pentagon Papers affair. The charges ultimately were dismissed because of governmental misconduct. Russo v. United States, No. 9373—(WMB)—CD (1971), *dismissed* (C.D. Cal. May 11, 1973). *See* Melville B. Nimmer, *National Security Secrets v. Free Speech: The Issues Left Undecided in the Ellsberg Case,* 26 Stan. L. Rev. 311 (1974).

rable danger" to the national security. After pointing out that the papers were solely historical, "[n]one ... more recent than 1968," Justice Douglas noted that "[t]he dominant purpose of the First Amendment was to prohibit the widespread practice of governmental suppression of embarrassing information."[50] Justice Brennan characterized the government's case as "surmise or conjecture that untoward consequences may result."[51]

Doubts about the Government's showing were corroborated almost two decades after the fact by Erwin N. Griswold, former Dean of the Yale Law School who, as Solicitor General, had argued the case. At the time the government was urging that publication would cause "grave and irreparable danger," Dean Griswold said that his review of the papers convinced him "that most of them presented no serious threat to national security."[52] In the years since the Supreme Court decision allowing publication, he wrote, "I have never seen any trace of a threat to the national security from the publication" and that no one else has suggested there was an "actual threat."[53] Dean Griswold concluded that the "lesson of the Pentagon Papers experience" is that there is "massive overclassification" of government information and that "the principal concern of the classifiers is not with national security, but rather with governmental embarrassment of one sort or another."[54]

The problem of assessing the validity of a perceived risk, or, for that matter the governmental motivation, is compounded by the lack of an analytical framework for comparing national security claims to speech interests. As Justice Blackmun pointed out in his *New York Times* dissent: "What is needed here is a weighing, upon properly developed standards, of the broad right of the press to print and the very narrow right of the Government to prevent. Such standards are not yet developed."[55] Nor did this case aid in their development. At one extreme, Justice Brennan suggested that an interim restraining order could be justified only upon "governmental allegation and proof that publication

---

50.   403 U.S. at 722 n.3, 723–24, 91 S. Ct. at 2146, 29 L. Ed. 2d at 829 (Douglas, J., concurring). Nevertheless, Justice Douglas agreed that the disclosures "may have a serious impact." *Id.* at 722, 91 S. Ct. at 2145, 29 L. Ed. 2d at 829.

51.   *Id.* at 725–26, 91 S. Ct. at 2147, 29 L. Ed. 2d at 831 (Brennan, J., concurring).

52.   Erwin N. Griswold, *Secrets Not Worth Keeping*, Wash. Post, February 15, 1989 p. A25.

53.   *Id.*

54.   *Id.* Griswold also has written that neither he nor counsel for the newspapers had seen the Pentagon Papers when he was directed to brief the case in the Court of Appeals. "And so the real objective of starting the suit," he concluded, "was simply to say, 'For Gods sake, give us time to find out what this is all about.'" Erwin N. Gris-

wold, *Teaching Alone is Not Enough*, 25 J. Legal Educ. 251, 257 (1973). *But see* DAVID RUDENSTINE, THE DAY THE PRESSES STOPPED 8–9 (1996) (suggesting that the government brought the case out of an honest belief that publication would damage rational security-not to prevent political embarrassment).

55.   403 U.S. at 761, 91 S. Ct. at 2165, 29 L. Ed. 2d at 851 (Blackmun, J., dissenting). *See also* Melville B. Nimmer, *National Security Secrets v. Free Speech: The Issues Left Undecided in the Ellsberg Case*, 26 Stan. L. Rev. 311, 328–29 (1974) (Courts must establish a standard to distinguish protected speech on matters of national security from unprotected speech on such matters. "This is precisely what the Supreme Court did in the area of libel in *New York Times Co. v. Sullivan* and its progeny.").

must inevitably, directly, and immediately cause the occurrence of an event kindred to imperiling the safety of a transport already at sea."[56] At the other end of the spectrum, Justices Harlan, Burger and Blackmun asserted that in overriding executive secrecy determinations, "the scope of [judicial] review must be exceedingly narrow."[57] Lacking guidance from the Court, lower courts have resorted to ad hoc balancing in resolving conflicts between national security and free speech interests.

The most notable case—and the only one in which a court has upheld an injunction barring publication for national security reasons—is *United States v. The Progressive, Inc.*[58] There, the United States District Court for the Western District of Wisconsin was asked to impose a preliminary injunction to prevent publication of the article "The H–Bomb Secret: How We Got It, Why We're Telling It" in *The Progressive* magazine.[59] At three different places in the opinion, the court described the issue before it as "a basic confrontation between the First Amendment right to freedom of the press and national security."[60] The court distinguished *New York Times*, but then applied the standard advocated by Justices White and Stewart—that a prior restraint may be upheld if the government can demonstrate "grave, direct, immediate and irreparable harm to the United States."[61]

But the court's statement of the question presented and its selection of a balancing test appear to have been more straightforward than its application of the test. Having framed the question on national security grounds, the court then reformulated the choice as being between

---

56. 403 U.S. at 726–27, 91 S. Ct. at 2148, 29 L. Ed. 2d at 832 (Brennan, J., concurring); *see also id.* at 730, 91 S. Ct. at 2149, 29 L. Ed. 2d at 834 (Stewart, J., joined by White, J., concurring) ("I cannot say that disclosure ... will surely result in direct, immediate, and irreparable damage to our Nation or its people.").

57. *Id.* at 758, 91 S. Ct. at 2163, 29 L. Ed. 2d at 850.

58. 467 F.Supp. 990 (W.D.Wis.1979), *request for writ of mandamus denied sub nom.* Morland v. Sprecher, 443 U.S. 709, 99 S.Ct. 3086, 61 L.Ed.2d 860 (1979), *dismissed as moot mem.* 610 F.2d 819 (7th Cir.1979). The injunction remained in place for almost seven months.

59. The article contained technical information on the construction of the hydrogen bomb, which the author claimed had been gleaned from declassified and public domain sources. It was being published, according to the magazine, to alert the public to the false illusion of security created by the government's classification system. The government disputed the assertion that the article was derived solely from declassified material, but claimed it had the constitutional authority to censor

public domain material "if when drawn together, synthesized and collated, such information acquires the character of presenting immediate, direct and irreparable harm to the interests of the United States." 467 F.Supp. at 991.

60. *Id.* at 995. *See also id.* at 991 ("the question before this Court involves a clash between allegedly vital security interests of the United States and the competing constitutional doctrine against prior restraint in publication"); *id.* at 996 (case "does present so starkly the clash between freedom of press and national security").

61. *Id.* at 996. *Compare* New York Times, 403 U.S. at 730, 91 S. Ct. at 2149, 29 L. Ed. at 834 (Stewart, J., joined by White, J., concurring) ("I cannot say that disclosure ... will surely result in direct, immediate, and irreparable damage to our Nation or its people."). The court distinguished *New York Times* by pointing out that (1) the Pentagon Papers involved the release of historical data only, (2) that the government advanced no interest stronger than avoiding embarrassment to the United States and (3) the current injunction was expressly authorized by the Atomic Energy Act. 467 F.Supp. at 994.

"freedom of the press" and "the right to continued life."[62] It acknowledged that the *Progressive* article was not "a 'do-it yourself' guide for the hydrogen bomb" and that it "*could possibly* provide sufficient information to allow a medium size nation to move faster in developing a hydrogen weapon,"[63] but ultimately concluded that "[a] mistake in ruling against the United States could pave the way for thermonuclear annihilation for us all."[64] In short, the court focused far more on the gravity of the potential national security problem than on whether the threat expected from the publication was direct, immediate or irreparable. As Professor Laurence Tribe cheekily observed after noting that the case was mooted by publication of the article in another magazine, "[a]t least as of this writing, the world has not ended."[65]

The decision in *The Progressive* suggests that it may be difficult for courts to give much weight to First Amendment values even when they have selected a formula for weighing competing interests. The court gave no weight to the magazine's claim that the article would demonstrate that the government's secrecy program was a charade and would "provide the people with needed information to make informed decisions on an urgent issue of public concern."[66] Instead, the court rather imperiously stated that it could find "no plausible reason why the public needs to know the technical details about hydrogen bomb construction to carry on an informed debate on this issue."[67] This view ignores the fact that public debate on the wisdom of nuclear proliferation could well be stimulated by the revelation that nuclear "secrets" are available in unclassified and other public documents.[68] It is important to note that "to suppress public reporting of government acts and policies in the name of security also means suppressing the political means of affecting those acts and policies."[69] Contrary to the dictum in *Near* regarding national security issues that "no one would question", the First Amendment perhaps should protect reporting on troop movements where "[t]he ships that are about to sail [are] headed for the Bay of Pigs" or "[t]he troops may secretly have been sent to Cambodia, in numbers and locations wholly unknown to and unapproved by the Congress."[70] This

---

62. *Id.* at 995.

63. *Id.* at 993 (emphasis added). District Judge Robert Warren was quoted widely as saying "I want to think a long, hard time before I'd give a hydrogen bomb to Idi Amin," but from the bench acknowledged that the suppressed article could have no such effect. *See* Erwin Knoll, *National Security: The Ultimate Threat to the First Amendment,* 66 Minn. L. Rev. 161, 164–65 (1981).

64. 467 F. Supp. at 996.

65. Laurence H. Tribe, American Constitutional Law 1054 n.53 (2d ed. 1988).

66. 467 F. Supp. at 994. Erwin Knoll, editor of *The Progressive,* wrote subsequently that "[a]ny case that pits the first

amendment against official assertions of national security is likely to turn out 'a real First Amendment loser.'" He added, "The logic is irresistible: who would not gladly permit a trivial and temporary incursion against the Bill of Rights when the alternative might be military defeat or even a nuclear holocaust?" Knoll, *supra* note 63, at 164–65.

67. 467 F. Supp. at 994.

68. *See* Tribe, *supra* note 65, at 1054 ("The world may be more likely to face a nuclear apocalypse if its leaders are not compelled to answer to an educated, and worried, public.").

69. Linde, *supra* note 2, at 197.

70. *Id.*

view was most forcefully stated by Justice Black, in his concurring statement in *New York Times*: "[P]aramount among the responsibilities of a free press is the duty to prevent any part of the government from deceiving the people and sending them off to distant lands to die of foreign fevers and foreign shot and shell. In my view, far from deserving condemnation for their courageous reporting, the New York Times, the Washington Post, and other newspapers should be commended for serving the purpose that the Founding Fathers saw so clearly."[71]

Rather than tackle head-on the problem of weighing speech versus national security interests as did the court in *The Progressive*, it is more typical for courts to seek ways to avoid balancing two vital interests. A court can more easily uphold a government measure in the name of national security where it can be said to impose only an incidental restriction on speech. For example, in *Haig v. Agee* the Supreme Court held that the Secretary of State could revoke the passport of a former CIA agent who had disclosed the names and addresses of field agents.[72] The Court found that by limiting Agee's travel, it was restricting his freedom of movement but not his freedom of speech. Similarly, courts have enforced secrecy agreements between the CIA and former agents in order to limit the disclosure of sensitive information.[73] One court has held that a prosecution for the unauthorized release of classified information does not implicate First Amendment rights at all, much less necessitate balancing. In *United States v. Morison*, the Fourth Circuit upheld the conviction of a civilian defense analyst who had procured and disseminated secret satellite photographs.[74] The court treated the matter as a straightforward application of a criminal statute, and not as a First Amendment case.

D. Incitement to Crime

As the early First Amendment cases made clear, the First Amendment does not immunize incitement to criminal activity. The World War I era cases, such as *Schenck v. United States*, established that speech may be proscribed where it creates a "clear and present danger" of causing "the substantive evils that Congress has a right to prevent," *i.e.,*

71. 403 U.S. at 717, 91 S. Ct. at 2143, 29 L. Ed. 2d at 826–27 (Black, J., concurring).

72. 453 U.S. 280, 101 S.Ct. 2766, 69 L.Ed.2d 640 (1981).

73. Snepp v. United States, 444 U.S. 507, 100 S.Ct. 763, 62 L.Ed.2d 704 (1980) (per curiam) (profits from book with unauthorized disclosures placed in constructive trust); United States v. Marchetti, 466 F.2d 1309 (4th Cir.1972), cert. denied, 409 U.S. 1063, 93 S.Ct. 553, 34 L.Ed.2d 516 (1972) (publication of book in violation of secrecy agreement enjoined). Courts give broad deference to the CIA's assessment of national security risks under such agreements.

McGehee v. Casey, 718 F.2d 1137, 231 U.S. App. D.C. 99 (D.C.Cir.1983). However, courts will not uphold secrecy agreements that do not provide for timely review or specify the type of information that would violate the agreement. Penguin Books USA, Inc. v. Walsh, 756 F.Supp. 770, 787–88 (S.D.N.Y.1991), *judgment vacated and appeal dismissed*, 929 F.2d 69 (2d Cir.1991). (there is no governmental interest in suppressing unclassified information or data obtained from public sources).

74. 844 F.2d 1057 (4th Cir.1988), cert. denied, 488 U.S. 908, 109 S.Ct. 259, 102 L.Ed.2d 247 (1988).

crime.[75] The standard evolved during the 1950s in a series of McCarthy era cases, and has since emerged as a speech protective formulation. Under the current approach, the Supreme Court has established a high threshold for drawing the line between protected advocacy and illegal incitement.

The leading case in this area is *Brandenburg v. Ohio*, in which the Court struck down the Ohio criminal syndicalism statute.[76] The case arose when a Cincinnati television station taped a Ku Klux Klan rally. Portions of the tape, that were broadcast both locally and nationally, depicted a number of hooded figures brandishing weapons in front of a burning cross. Racial and religious epithets punctuated a speech in which the speaker warned, "We're not a revengent organization, but if our President, our Congress, our Supreme Court, continues to suppress the white, Caucasian race, it's possible that there might have to be some revengence taken."[77] The speaker was convicted under the state law which made it a crime to advocate "the duty, necessity, or propriety of crime, sabotage, violence, or unlawful methods of terrorism as a means of accomplishing industrial or political reform."[78]

The Supreme Court invalidated the law because it sought to punish "mere advocacy" and was not directed toward "incitement to imminent lawless action."[79] The decision repudiated the earlier leniency of the "clear and present danger" test, and expressly overruled *Whitney v. California*.[80] The Court held that the First Amendment prohibits restrictions on advocacy unless the speech (1) is directed to inciting or producing imminent lawless action, and (2) is likely to produce such action.[81] Without discussing how the videotape of weapons-toting Klansmen fit into this construct, the Court held that the statute was void because the law "by its own words and as applied, purports to punish mere advocacy."[82]

Brandenburg was the culmination of decades of doctrinal development that increasingly emphasized the immediacy of the evil that justified restrictions on speech. At one end of the scale, were cases in which speech could be punished if only it had a "bad tendency" to produce lawless action. Under this approach, the legislature was permit-

---

75. 249 U.S. 47, 52, 39 S.Ct. 247, 249, 63 L.Ed. 470, 473–74 (1919).

76. 395 U.S. 444, 89 S.Ct. 1827, 23 L.Ed.2d 430 (1969) (per curiam).

77. *Id.* at 446, 89 S. Ct. at 1829, 23 L. Ed. 2d at 433.

78. *Id.* at 444–45, 89 S. Ct. at 1828, 23 L. Ed. 2d at 432. The law also prohibited assembly for the purpose of teaching or advocating "the doctrines of criminal syndicalism." *Id.* at 445, 89 S. Ct. at 1828, 23 L. Ed. 2d at 432. The ban on assembly was an additional ground for the Court's decision.

79. *Id.* at 449, 89 S. Ct. at 1830, 23 L. Ed. 2d at 434.

80. *Id.* at 449, 89 S. Ct. at 1831, 23 L. Ed. 2d at 435. In *Whitney*, the Court upheld the convictions of a communist party organizer under the California Criminal Syndicalism Act Justice Brandeis, joined by Justice Holmes, stressed the "wide difference between advocacy and incitement" and concluded that "it must be shown either that immediate serious violence was to be expected or was advocated." 274 U.S. 357, 376, 47 S.Ct. 641, 648, 71 L.Ed. 1095, 1106 (1927).

81. 395 U.S. at 447, 89 S. Ct. at 1829, 23 L. Ed. 2d at 434.

82. *Id.* at 449, 89 S. Ct. at 1830, 23 L. Ed. 2d at 435.

ted to proscribe certain "dangerous" categories of speech without reference to the factual setting. In other words, mere advocacy, without more, was sufficient to sustain a conviction.[83] In *Dennis v. United States*, the Court acknowledged the line between protected advocacy and prohibited incitement.[84] Nevertheless, it found that teaching communist doctrine was a sufficient incitement and that the government need not "wait until the putsch is about to be executed."[85] The immediacy, according to the plurality opinion, was caused by the "inflammable nature of world conditions."[86] Over the next decade, the Court gave more substance to the distinction between advocacy and incitement. In *Yates v. United States*, the Court drew the line between "advocacy ... to *do* something" and advocacy "to *believe* in something," and invalidated the convictions of several "lower echelon" communist organizers.[87] Similarly in *Scales v. United States*[88] and *Noto v. United States*,[89] the Court stressed the distinction between abstract advocacy and incitement, and refined the relevant evidentiary standards. *Brandenburg* drew on this line of authority, and added the requirement that proscribed advocacy be directed at producing imminent lawless activity.[90] The Court again applied this immediacy requirement in *Hess v. Indiana*, in the context of anti-war demonstrations.[91]

An interesting though seldom raised question arises when an incitement is transmitted by the mass media. That question was at the heart of *People v. Rubin*, in which a national director of the Jewish Defense League was charged with solicitation of murder.[92] The case arose when Irving Rubin held a press conference to protest the impending march of the American Nazi Party in Skokie, Illinois. After announcing a counter-demonstration at the televised conference, Rubin held up five one hundred dollar bills and stated:

> We are offering five hundred dollars, that I have in my hand, to any member of the community, be he Gentile or Jewish, who kills,

83. *E.g.*, Whitney v. California, 274 U.S. 357, 47 S.Ct. 641, 71 L.Ed. 1095 (1927); Gitlow v. New York, 268 U.S. 652, 671–72, 45 S.Ct. 625, 631–32, 69 L.Ed. 1138, 1147 (1925).

84. 341 U.S. 494, 502, 71 S.Ct. 857, 865, 95 L.Ed. 1137, 1150 (1951).

85. Id. at 509, 71 S. Ct. at 867, 95 L. Ed. at 1152. In his dissenting opinion, Justice Douglas pointed out that "[s]o far as the present record is concerned, what petitioners did was to organize people to teach and themselves teach the Marxist–Leninist doctrine contained chiefly in four books.... " *Id*. at 582, 71 S. Ct. at 904, 95 L. Ed. at 1190 (Douglas, J., dissenting).

86. *Id*. at 511, 71 S. Ct. at 868, 95 L. Ed. at 1153.

87. 354 U.S. 298, 325, 345, 77 S.Ct. 1064, 1080, 1090, 1 L.Ed.2d 1356, 1378; 1390 (1957).

88. 367 U.S. 203, 81 S.Ct. 1469, 6 L.Ed.2d 782 (1961).

89. 367 U.S. 290, 81 S.Ct. 1517, 6 L.Ed.2d 836 (1961).

90. 395 U.S. at 447, 89 S. Ct. at 1829, 23 L. Ed. 2d at 434.

91. 414 U.S. 105, 107–09, 94 S.Ct. 326, 328–29, 38 L.Ed.2d 303, 307 (1973) (per curiam). *But see* Rice v. Paladin Enterprises, Inc., 128 F.3d 233 (4th Cir.1997), cert. denied __ U.S. __, 118 S.Ct. 1515, 140 L.Ed.2d 668 (1998) (holding that "Hit Man" manual providing instruction on committing murders for hire constitutes incitement and not advocacy).

92. 96 Cal.App.3d 968, 158 Cal.Rptr. 488 (1979), cert. denied *sub nom.* Rubin v. California, 449 U.S. 821, 101 S.Ct. 80, 66 L.Ed.2d 24 (1980).

maims, or seriously injures a member of the American Nazi Party. This offer is being made on the East Coast, on the West Coast. And if they bring us the ears, we'll make it a thousand dollars. The fact of the matter is, that we're deadly serious. This is not said in jest, we are deadly serious.[93]

Rubin was charged with soliciting murder in violation of the California Penal Code, but the trial court set aside the information, finding that the comments were protected speech. The state court of appeals reinstated the information, finding that the comments could not be characterized as abstract advocacy.

The fact that the press conference had been televised led the court to apply a test more akin to *Schenck* than *Brandenburg*. It found that "in these days of the global village and the big trumpet ... the critical distinction between abstract advocacy of crime in general and concrete solicitation of crime in particular breaks down." The danger, according to the court, lay in the potential reaction to the words by the "unseen audience of unknown listeners," which may contain "another Oswald, or Ruby, or Sirhan, or Ray, or Bremer, or Moore, or Fromm, who may respond literally to the invitation of the speaker."[94] Although the court cited *Brandenburg*, it equated the standard articulated there with the "clear and present danger" test in *Schenck*, and said it could find incitement on the facts before it "regardless of the speaker's true intent."[95]

The decision is somewhat puzzling, in that *Brandenburg* also involved televised advocacy.[96] Yet the Supreme Court found it unnecessary to discuss any special impact of the mass media. Perhaps the different treatment can be explained, in part, by the fact that *Brandenburg* involved a criminal syndicalism law, which is historically associated with political suppression, while *Rubin* involved the state's general criminal law. On the other hand, at least one other court has held that a televised murder threat is unprotected by the First Amendment, even when made in a political context. In *United States v. Kelner*, the Second Circuit upheld the conviction of a member of the Jewish Defense League who during a press conference threatened to assassinate Yasser Arafat.[97] There, the court made no reference to the special impact of the mass media. Rather, it upheld the conviction based on the content of the speech and the circumstances that indicated it was a "true threat" and not "political hyperbole."

The approach taken in *Rubin* is similar to the Espionage Act and McCarthy era cases in that it focuses on the heightened risk of danger presented by social conditions. In *Frohwerk v. United States*, for example, the Court upheld convictions based on the publication of newspapers

93. Rubin, 158 Cal. Rptr. at 488–89.

94. *Id*. at 491.

95. *Id*. at 491–92.

96. Brandenburg, 395 U.S. at 445, 89 S. Ct. at 1828, 23 L. Ed. 2d at 432 ("Portions of the films were later broadcast on the local station and on a national network.").

97. 534 F.2d 1020 (2d Cir.), cert. denied, 429 U.S. 1022, 97 S.Ct. 639, 50 L.Ed.2d 623 (1976).

because they might be distributed to "quarters where a little breath would be enough to kindle a flame."[98] The convictions in *Dennis* for teaching communist doctrine were predicated on the "inflammable nature of world conditions."[99] In *Rubin*, the court assumed that "in these days of the global village . . . the staging of a media event . . . possess[es] a far greater capacity for civil disruption."[100]

Such facile assumptions should be more carefully examined. To apply a lower level of First Amendment scrutiny because we live in a "global village" provides no guidance for how the actual danger of civil disruption should be assessed. For example, would the same words and images present a danger if presented on a public television station that typically has a smaller and better educated audience? Would the same acts merit prosecution if the news conference was carried only on radio? Or does the worldwide reach of the Internet render more dangerous the availability of the same bombmaking information that is also published in books and encyclopedias?[1] Such questions must be addressed, for to simply apply the reasoning of *Rubin* generally to the mass media would undermine much of the doctrinal development since *Schenck*.

E. *Defamation*

It is well-established that libel is not "within the area of constitutionally protected speech."[2] In *Beauharnais v. Illinois,* the Supreme Court confirmed that false statements of fact that tend to damage the reputation of a person or group constitute "nonfree speech" for the same reasons as articulated in *Chaplinsky v. New Hampshire*: defamation is not "part of any exposition of ideas" and whatever value it may have "is clearly outweighed by the social interest in order and morality."[3] But speech is not rendered unprotected merely because it has been called libelous. As the Court made clear in the landmark case of *New York Times v. Sullivan,* "libel can claim no talismanic immunity from constitutional limitations. It must be measured by standards that satisfy the First Amendment."[4] Thus, with the "constitutionalization" of defama-

---

98. 249 U.S. 204, 209, 39 S.Ct. 249, 251, 63 L.Ed. 561, 565 (1919).

99. 341 U.S. at 511, 71 S. Ct. at 868, 95 L. Ed. at 1153.

100. 96 Cal. App. 3d at 975, 158 Cal. Rptr. at 490–91.

1. In 1996, legislation was introduced to outlaw the posting of bombmaking information on-line. 142 Cong. Rec. S7788–801 (July 11, 1996). The same information is readily available in print. *Mayhem Manuels and the Internet, Hearings before the Subcommittee on Terrorism, Technology, and Government Information of the Senate Judiciary Committee.* 1995 WL 283329 (May 11, 1995) (testimony of Professor Frank Tuerkheimer, University of Wisconsin Law School). *See also* 21 ENCYCLOPEDIA BRITANICA at 275–82 (1986 ed.) (describing manufac-

ture of ammonium nitrate an fuel oil bomb like that used in 1995 Oklahoma City bombing of federal office building); U.S. Forest Service, United States Department of Agriculture, BLASTER'S HANDBOOK (1980) (describing ammonium nitrate/fuel oil explosives).

2. Beauharnais v. Illinois, 343 U.S. 250, 266, 72 S.Ct. 725, 735, 96 L.Ed. 919, 932 (1952).

3. *Id.* at 257, 72 S. Ct. at 731, 96 L. Ed. at 927 (quoting Chaplinsky v. New Hampshire, 315 U.S. at 571–72, 62 S. Ct. at 769, 86 L. Ed. at 1035).

4. 376 U.S. 254, 269, 84 S.Ct. 710, 720, 11 L.Ed.2d 686, 700 (1964). *See also* NAACP v. Button, 371 U.S. 415, 429, 83 S.Ct. 328, 336, 9 L.Ed.2d 405, 416 (1963)

tion law, it may be more accurate to say that libel is unprotected by the First Amendment only under certain conditions.[5]

In *Sullivan* and in the cases that followed it, the Court defined the First Amendment values that circumscribed the tort of defamation. Although the Court in *Sullivan* accepted the premise that libel is unprotected speech, it found that "erroneous statement is inevitable in free debate, and. . . . must be protected if the freedoms of expression are to have the 'breathing space' that they 'need . . . to survive.' "[6] Thus, it held that a public official cannot recover damages for defamatory statements relating to his official conduct absent proof that the statements were made with "actual malice"—knowledge of the falsity or reckless disregard of the truth.[7] After *Sullivan*, the Court extended its principles to cover criminal libel[8] and defamation against public figures.[9] In addition, *Sullivan*'s rationale has been extended to cover common law and statutory privacy claims[10] as well as intentional infliction of emotional distress.[11]

Contrary to the description of libel in *Beauharnais*, that such speech is "not part of any exposition of ideas," the Court has sought to protect defamatory statements that have some redeeming First Amendment value. In *Sullivan*, for example, the Court created First Amendment immunity for statements critical of government officials—a well-established purpose of free speech—and for statements that are true.[12] Similarly, the Court has limited the scope of defamation law to statements of

("a State cannot foreclose the exercise of constitutional rights by mere labels").

5. *See* RODNEY A. SMOLLA, LAW OF DEFAMATION § 4.10[4][c][i] (1991) ("libelous speech is no longer outside of first amendment protection.").

6. 376 U.S. at 271–272, 84 S. Ct at 721, 11 L. Ed. 2d at 701 (quoting NAACP v. Button, 371 U.S. 415, 433, 83 S.Ct. 328, 338, 9 L.Ed.2d 405, 418 (1963)).

7. 376 U.S. at 279–80, 84 S. Ct. at 726, 11 L. Ed. 2d at 706.

8. Garrison v. Louisiana, 379 U.S. 64, 85 S.Ct. 209, 13 L.Ed.2d 125 (1964).

9. Public figures are persons who are not government officials but who are involved in a public controversy. *See* Curtis Publishing Co. v. Butts, 388 U.S. 130, 87 S.Ct. 1975, 18 L.Ed.2d 1094 (1967); Associated Press v. Walker, 388 U.S. 130, 87 S.Ct. 1975, 18 L.Ed.2d 1094 (1967); Rosenbloom v. Metromedia, Inc., 403 U.S. 29, 91 S.Ct. 1811, 29 L.Ed.2d 296 (1971). The Court has tended over the years to restrict the concept of public figure. *See, e.g.*, Hutchinson v. Proxmire, 443 U.S. 111, 99 S.Ct. 2675, 61 L.Ed.2d 411 (1979); Wolston v. Reader's Digest Ass'n, Inc., 443 U.S. 157, 99 S.Ct. 2701, 61 L.Ed.2d 450 (1979); Time, Inc. v.

Firestone, 424 U.S. 448, 96 S.Ct. 958, 47 L.Ed.2d 154 (1976); Gertz v. Robert Welch, Inc., 418 U.S. 323, 94 S.Ct. 2997, 41 L.Ed.2d 789 (1974).

10. The Florida Star v. B.J.F., 491 U.S. 524, 109 S.Ct. 2603, 105 L.Ed.2d 443 (1989); Smith v. Daily Mail Publishing Co., 443 U.S. 97, 99 S.Ct. 2667, 61 L.Ed.2d 399 (1979); Landmark Communications, Inc. v. Virginia, 435 U.S. 829, 98 S.Ct. 1535, 56 L.Ed.2d 1 (1978); Oklahoma Publishing Co. v. District Court, 430 U.S. 308, 97 S.Ct. 1045, 51 L.Ed.2d 355 (1977); Cox Broadcasting Corp. v. Cohn, 420 U.S. 469, 95 S.Ct. 1029, 43 L.Ed.2d 328 (1975); Time, Inc. v. Hill, 385 U.S. 374, 87 S.Ct. 534, 17 L.Ed.2d 456 (1967).

11. Hustler Magazine v. Falwell, 485 U.S. 46, 108 S.Ct. 876, 99 L.Ed.2d 41 (1988).

12. Sullivan, 376 U.S. at 279–80, 84 S. Ct. at 726, 11 L. Ed. 2d at 706. *See also* Garrison v. Louisiana, 379 U.S. at 74, 85 S. Ct. at 216, 13 L. Ed. 2d at 133 ("Truth may not be the subject of either civil or criminal sanctions where discussion of public affairs is concerned."); Philadelphia Newspapers, Inc. v. Hepps, 475 U.S. 767, 106 S.Ct. 1558, 89 L.Ed.2d 783 (1986).

fact, as opposed to rhetorical hyperbole or opinion.[13] However, the Court has made clear that "there is no constitutional value in false statements of fact."[14] It has therefore denied special protection for fabricated quotations ascribed to an interviewee[15] and for false statements of fact couched as opinion.[16] The Court also has attempted to focus constitutional protections for defamatory speech on matters that affect "political and social change." Thus, it held that there is no heightened scrutiny for defamatory statements that "involve no issue of public concern" where the plaintiff is a private person.[17]

Chapter five contains a more detailed examination of the law of defamation.

F. *Subliminal Communications*

A potential nonspeech category is the area of subliminal communications. Generally, subliminal communication involves the projection of messages by light or sound so quickly or faintly that they are received below the conscious awareness of the audience.[18] Perhaps the most famous example of subliminal persuasion is perhaps the first documented use of such communication techniques. In 1957, a marketing and motivational research specialist named James Vicary announced that he had increased cinema concession sales between 18 and 58 percent by flashing on the screen (for 1/3,000 of a second every five seconds) the messages "Drink Coca Cola" and "Hungry? Eat Popcorn." Although the effectiveness of subliminal techniques is disputed, subconscious communications are being used in a variety of commercial settings to: combat shoplifting, reduce stress, control weight gains, treat compulsive behavior, reduce employee turnover, increase real estate sales and encourage persons to quit smoking.[19]

Concern over the potential effects of subliminal communications has led federal agencies to incorporate in their regulations methods to

---

13. Milkovich v. Lorain Journal Co., 497 U.S. 1, 110 S.Ct. 2695, 111 L.Ed.2d 1 (1990). *See* Hustler Magazine v. Falwell, 485 U.S. at 50, 108 S. Ct. at 879, 99 L. Ed. 2d at 49 ("At the heart of the First Amendment is the recognition of the fundamental importance of the free flow of ideas and opinions on matters of public interest and concern."); Gertz, 418 U.S. at 339, 94 S. Ct. at 3007, 41 L. Ed. 2d at 805 ("Under the First Amendment there is no such thing as a false idea."); Greenbelt Cooperative Publishing Ass'n v. Bresler, 398 U.S. 6, 90 S.Ct. 1537, 26 L.Ed.2d 6 (1970).

14. Gertz, 418 U.S. at 340, 94 S. Ct. at 3007, 41 L. Ed. 2d at 805. *See* Milkovich, 497 U.S. at 2, 110 S. Ct. at 2706, 111 L. Ed. 2d at 17.

15. Masson v. The New Yorker Magazine, Inc., 501 U.S. 496, 111 S.Ct. 2419, 115 L.Ed.2d 447 (1991).

16. Milkovich, 497 U.S. at 2, 110 S. Ct. at 2706, 111 L. Ed. 2d at 17.

17. Dun & Bradstreet, Inc. v. Greenmoss Builders, Inc., 472 U.S. 749, 757 105 S.Ct. 2939, 2944, 86 L.Ed.2d 593, 601 (1985).

18. *See* Thomas A. Bliss, *Subliminal Projection: History and Analysis,* 5 Comm/Ent 419, 422 (1983); Olivia Goodkin and Maureen A. Phillips, Note, *The Subconscious Taken Captive: A Social, Ethical and Legal Analysis of Subliminal Communication Technology,* 54 S. Cal. L. Rev. 1077, 1080 (1981); Harry Schiller, Note, *First Amendment Dialogue and Subliminal Messages,* 11 N.Y.U. Rev. L. & Soc. Change 331 (1983).

19. *See* Vance v. Judas Priest, 1990 WL 130920, 16 Media L. Rptr. 2241, 2245 (Nev. Dist. Ct. 1989); Diane Kiesel, *Subliminal Seduction,* 70 A.B.A.J. 25, 26 (July 1984).

control its use. Following some product advertising complaints, the Federal Communications Commission announced in 1974 that "the use of subliminal perception is inconsistent with the obligations of a licensee" and "broadcasters employing such techniques are [airing programming] contrary to the public interest."[20] The FCC found that such broadcasts are inherently deceptive. For the same reason, the Bureau of Alcohol, Tobacco and Firearms adopted regulations banning alcohol advertisements employing subliminal methods.[21] Congress has considered banning subliminal communications but has not passed legislation on the subject.[22]

Those few courts that have considered both subliminal communications and communications with subconscious effects have concluded that such messages are entitled to no First Amendment protection, or to receive only diminished protection. Several cases involved allegations that subliminal messages in rock music induced troubled teenagers to commit suicide. In *Vance v. Judas Priest*, for example, the District Court of Washoe County, Nevada, held that subliminal commands purportedly inserted into the background of a heavy metal rock recording are nonfree speech under the First Amendment.[23] The issue was part of a tort claim against the rock band *Judas Priest*, brought by the families of two young men who committed suicide, in part, the families claimed, because of subliminal messages embedded in the music. The plaintiffs claimed that one song gave the subliminal command "Do it," and that others contained hidden messages such as "Fuck the Lord; fuck all of you" and "Sing my evil spirit."[24]

The court ultimately concluded that the plaintiffs failed to prove causation; that there was no evidence that subliminal commands were placed intentionally on the album or that such commands, if placed, could cause a person to perceive the message and act on it.[25] Nevertheless, in a carefully reasoned analysis, the court concluded that subliminal communications are not entitled to First Amendment protection. It found that subliminal communication does not advance any of the purposes of free speech (dissemination of ideas, self-governance or self-realization); that such messages do not permit a person to be free from unwanted communications; and that a person's right of privacy outweighs whatever speech interest may exist.[26] The court held that "[s]ince subliminal communication does not contribute to dialogue, truth, the free market of ideas, democracy or personal autonomy, it is not really 'speech.' "[27]

20. FCC Public Notice, Broadcast of Information by Means of "Subliminal Perception" Techniques, FCC 74–78, 2 (Jan. 24, 1974), 39 Fed. Reg. 3714 (1974).

21. 27 C.F.R. § 5.65(h) (1995).

22. *See* Bliss, *supra* note 18 at 426.

23. 1990 WL 130920, *25, 16 Media L. Rptr. 2241, 2248 (Nev. Dist. Ct. 1989).

24. *Id.* at *19, 16 Media L. Rptr. at 2244.

25. *Id.*

26. *See* 1990 WL 130920 at *23–32, 16 Med. L. Rptr. at 2247–54.

27. 1990 WL 130920 at *25, 16 Med. L. Rptr. at 2248–49. In Gilmer v. Buena Vista Home Video Inc., 939 F.Supp. 665 (W.D.Ark.1996), the court declined to dis-

In *Waller v. Osbourne*, the U.S. District Court for the Middle District of Georgia held that subliminal speech is "more akin to false and misleading commercial speech" and "would relegate the music containing such to a class worthy of little, if any, first amendment constitutional protection."[28] Nevertheless it granted summary judgment for the defendant in a claim almost identical to the one in *Vance*, holding that the Ozzy Osbourne song, *Suicide Solution* did not "incite" a teen suicide. The Court in *Waller* found no subliminal content in the song, but only audible lyrics that were "garbled and unintelligible."[29] As a result, it subjected the music to traditional First Amendment analysis, and found that the contested song did not constitute incitement to lawless action under the rigorous standard of *Brandenburg v. Ohio* and *Hess v. Indiana*.[30]

Other cases in this area have been concerned no so much with subliminal communications but with the subconscious effects of communications. That is, the message itself is not hidden, but the meaning derived by an audience may have little to do with the actual words used by the speaker. One such case is *United States v. Northrop Corp.*, in which the United States District Court for the Central District of California granted an order to restrain the defendant from showing certain institutional advertisements on television because of the potential subliminal impact on jurors.[31]

In *Northrop*, the federal government had brought criminal charges against Northrop Corporation and several former employees of its Western Services Department with conspiracy to defraud the United States by supplying untested and out-of specification flight stabilization and control packages and to make false and fraudulent statements to the United States. At about the time jury selection began, the defendant ran

---

miss a claim alleging that certain animated Disney features, as well as associated packaging, contained subliminal sexually oriented messages and imagery. The court agreed that such subliminal messages, if present, would receive diminished First Amendment protection, and found that it could not decide the factual questions presented in a motion to dismiss the case.

28. 763 F.Supp. 1144, 1148 (M.D.Ga. 1991), *aff'd mem.*, 958 F.2d 1084, cert. denied, 506 U.S. 916, 113 S.Ct. 325, 121 L.Ed.2d 245 (1992).

29. *Id.* at 1149 ("The most important character of a subliminal message is that it sneaks into the brain while the listener is completely unaware that he has heard anything at all. If the message is heard to any extent, even if garbled and unintelligible, the listener consciously attempts to discern a meaning from that which he hears. One is then dealing, not with a subliminal message, but rather the interpretation of an abstract medium which is akin to spotting objects in cloud formations.") (footnote omitted).

30. *Id.* at 1150–51. The California Court of Appeals reached the same conclusion in *McCollum v. CBS, Inc.*, 202 Cal.App.3d 989, 249 Cal.Rptr. 187 (1988), which also involved the allegation that Ozzy Osbourne's *Suicide Solution* incited a teen to kill himself. Although there was no claim that the song contained subliminal messages, plaintiffs alleged that the call to suicide was made with "masked" lyrics that were "not immediately intelligible." The court applied a straightforward First Amendment analysis and held that the test for incitement in *Brandenburg v. Ohio* had not been met.

31. 1990 WL 71352 (C.D.Cal.) (not otherwise reported). *See also* American Home Prods. Corp. v. Johnson & Johnson, 577 F.2d 160, 168 (2d Cir.1978) (advertisements for pain reliever Anacin enjoined because the "powerful 'subliminal' influence of modern advertisements" rendered certain claims false under Lanham Act).

on local television stations a number of institutional advertisements designed to enhance its corporate image.[32] The advertisements, which featured legendary pilot Chuck Yeager, focused on Northrop's commitment to quality. The court granted the government's motion to restrain the showing of the advertisements before or during the trial because of the message's "calculated but subliminal influence on prospective or impaneled jurors' perception of the character, reputation and state of mind of Northrop and its employees, as well as the public's perception of the fairness of the Northrop trial and the impartiality of the trial proceedings."[33]

Although the court in *Northrop* did not hold that defendant's advertisements were unprotected by the First Amendment, it concluded that the spots were entitled only to the diminished protection that is accorded commercial speech.[34] The court acknowledged that the advertisements "are not designed to induce consumers to purchase a specific product or service," but found that the messages "benefit the corporation economically" by "enhancing Northrop's public image."[35] Other

32. United States v. Northrop Corp., 1990 WL 71352. Northrop aired approximately 132 advertisements in the Los Angeles market in a ten week period.

33. *Id.* The court was not concerned with the actual content of the advertisements. Rather, it focused on the possible perceptions of the potential jurors:

The fact that these commercials do not make direct and specific statements about the case does not negate their effect on potential jurors or on the perceived or actual impartiality of the process. These spots are particularly sophisticated and, like all advertisements, have the ability to influence on a subconscious level and to plant in the minds of the jurors, before they have heard any evidence at all, the idea of how Northrop people think. This form of partiality or prejudice is much more difficult to uncover in voir dire, and is therefore more insidious than, for example, press releases by Northrop representatives proclaiming the defendants' innocence. *Id* at 4.

34. The court chose from two competing lines of authority, one involving prior restraints to further a fair trial under *Nebraska Press Ass'n v. Stuart*, 427 U.S. 539, 96 S.Ct. 2791, 49 L.Ed.2d 683 (1976), and the other relating to restrictions on commercial speech under Central Hudson Gas & Elec. Corp. v. Public Serv. Comm'n, 447 U.S. 557, 100 S.Ct. 2343, 65 L.Ed.2d 341 (1980). The court employed the less speech-protective *Central Hudson* test, but concluded it could have reached the same result under the more restrictive *Nebraska Press Ass'n* test. United States v. Northrop Corp., 1990 WL 71352 at *6.

35. *Id.* at 3. This analysis stretches the traditional definition of "commercial speech." *See generally* First Nat'l Bank of Boston v. Bellotti, 435 U.S. 765, 98 S.Ct. 1407, 55 L.Ed.2d 707 (1978); Consolidated Edison Co. of New York, Inc. v. Public Service Comm'n, 447 U.S. 530, 100 S.Ct. 2326, 65 L.Ed.2d 319 (1980). It also conflicts with the reasoning used by the FCC in determining whether to apply the broadcast fairness doctrine to product advertising. The Commission for a time applied the fairness doctrine to product advertising, in part because of its subliminal effects. *See* Friends of the Earth v. FCC, 449 F.2d 1164, 1170, 146 U.S. App. D.C. 88, 94 (D.C.Cir. 1971); Banzhaf v. FCC, 405 F.2d 1082, 132 U.S. App. D.C. 14, (D.C.Cir.1968), cert. denied, 396 U.S. 842, 90 S. Ct. 50, 24 L. Ed. 2d 93 (1969). However, having found that this approach opened a "Pandora's Box" because it applied the fairness doctrine to all advertising, the Commission changed its policy to cover only institutional or editorial advertising—announcements that present "a meaningful statement which obviously addresses and advocates a point of view on, a controversial issue of public importance." *The Handling of Public Issues Under the Fairness Doctrine and Public Interest Standards of the Communications Act*, 48 F.C.C. 1, 23 (1974). Thus, the FCC's view that institutional advertising presents a forum for controversial issues of public importance conflicts with the holding in *Northrop* that such advertising is commercial speech aimed only to "benefit the corporation economically." *But see* Public Interest Research Group v. FCC, 522 F.2d 1060, 1064 n. 4 (1st Cir.1975), ("institutional adver-

courts have applied diminished constitutional protection to advertisements that they perceived had a subliminal effect on viewers. In *Banzhaf v. FCC*, for example, the District of Columbia Circuit cited *Chaplinsky v. New Hampshire* to support the proposition that cigarette advertising "barely qualifies as constitutionally protected 'speech'" because "it does not affect the political process, does not contribute to the exchange of ideas, does not provide information on matters of public importance, and is not, except perhaps for the ad-men, a form of individual self-expression."[36]

This emerging "nonfree speech" category presents courts with ample reason to exercise caution, for it potentially would apply reduced—or nonexistent—First Amendment protection to at least three types of communications: (1) hidden messages; (2) hidden persuasion; or (3) messages transmitted on any electronic medium. The first potential subcategory presents little cause for concern. To hold that hidden messages are not protected by the First Amendment would be unlikely to have a major social impact and, as the court demonstrated in *Vance v. Judas Priest*, such a question, even though novel, is susceptible to traditional constitutional analysis. The second subcategory is more problematic. To conclude that "hidden persuasion," however that may be defined, receives diminished First Amendment protection, could redefine

---

tisements of a subliminal type . . . appear to discuss public issues but may not do so explicitly"), cert. denied, 424 U.S. 965, 96 S.Ct. 1458, 47 L.Ed.2d 731 (1976).

36. 405 F.2d at 1101–02. The court suggested that the video medium itself may be entitled to less constitutional protection because of its subliminal influence:

[T]he broadcasting medium may be different in kind from publishing in a way which has particular relevance to the case at hand. Written messages are not communicated unless they are read, and reading requires an affirmative act. Broadcast messages, in contrast, are 'in the air.' In an age of omnipresent radio, there scarcely breathes a citizen who does not know some part of a leading cigarette jingle by heart. Similarly, an ordinary habitual television watcher can *avoid* these commercials only by frequently leaving the room, changing the channel, or doing some other such affirmative act. It is difficult to calculate the subliminal impact of this pervasive propaganda, which may be heard even if not listened to, but it may reasonably be thought greater than the impact of the written word. *Id.* at 1100–01.

See also CBS, Inc. v. Democratic Nat'l Comm., 412 U.S. 94, 128, 93 S.Ct. 2080, 2099, 36 L.Ed.2d 772, 798 (1973); Robinson v. American Broadcasting Cos., 441 F.2d

1396, 1399 (6th Cir.1971); Capital Broadcasting Co. v. Mitchell, 333 F.Supp. 582, 586 (D.D.C.1971), *aff'd without opinion sub nom.* Capital Broadcasting Co. v. Acting Attorney General Kleindienst, 405 U.S. 1000, 92 S.Ct. 1289, 31 L.Ed.2d 472 (1972); Marc L. Sherman, Note, *We Can Share the Women, We Can Share the Wine: The Regulation of Alcohol Advertising on Television*, 58 S. Cal L. Rev. 1107 (1985). For a precursor to this analysis, *see* Mutual Film Corp. v. Industrial Comm'n of Ohio, 236 U.S. 230, 242, 35 S.Ct. 387, 390, 59 L.Ed. 552, 559 (1915) (film is "insidious" because "a prurient interest may be excited and appealed to"). *But see* Zamora v. Columbia Broadcasting System, 480 F.Supp. 199 (S.D.Fla. 1979), in which plaintiffs urged the court to impose tort liability on the defendants for their negligent broadcast of violent shows which allegedly caused a susceptible minor to engage in unlawful conduct. In noting that the broadcasts represented speech which did not incite nor in any other way qualify for less than full constitutional protection, the court determined that plaintiffs were in essence asking the court to fashion a new cause of action for the dissemination of protected speech which caused "an untoward reaction on the part of any 'susceptible' person." *Id.* at 206. The court in *Zamora* declined to take such a step asserting that it would be an unconstitutional imposition of a generally undefined and undefinable duty. *Id.*

the government's ability to inquire into the content of expression. Under such a theory, speech could be subjected to additional control to the extent it is too "persuasive."[37] Although the cases such as *Northrop* have applied only to commercial speech, it would not be difficult to extend their logic to other areas.[38] The third subcategory—electronic communications—is the most difficult. To suggest, as the *Banzhaf* court did, that television should receive less constitutional protection because it is a "passive medium," creates an entirely different framework for analyzing First Amendment questions for new technologies. It would apply a lower standard for all electronic forms of communications, independent of such factors as spectrum scarcity or use of public resources. Although the Supreme Court has flirted with some variations of this argument with respect to broadcasting, it has not shown a tendency toward applying it to newer video technologies.[39]

G. *Commercial Speech*

Commercial speech is the sole graduate from the category of non-free speech. Initially considered to be devoid of constitutional protection, courts over time came to recognize the First Amendment value of commercial speech. It still enjoys somewhat less protection than other forms of expression, and courts are struggling to draw the line between the protected and the unprotected in the commercial setting.

37. This theory conceivably could allow greater regulation of Mark Antony's funeral speech in Shakespeare's *Julius Ceasar* than it would the utterances of a less clever or articulate politician.

38. *E.g.,* Herceg v. Hustler Magazine, Inc., 814 F.2d 1017, 1026–27 (5th Cir.1987), cert denied 485 U.S. 959, 108 S.Ct. 1219, 99 L.Ed.2d 420 (1988) (Jones, J., dissenting) ("[P]ornography's appeal is ... non-cognitive and unrelated to, in fact exactly the opposite of, the transmission of ideas.... The warnings and cautionary comments in the article could be seen by a jury to conflict with both the explicit and subliminal message of Hustler, which is to tear down custom, explode myths and banish taboos about sexual matters."); Skyywalker Records, Inc. v. Navarro, 739 F.Supp. 578 591 (S.D.Fla.1990) (2 Live Crew lyrics "appeal ... to 'dirty' thoughts and the loins, not to the intellect and the mind"), *rev'd,* Luke Records, Inc. v. Navarro, 960 F.2d 134 (11th Cir.), cert. denied, 506 U.S. 1022, 113 S.Ct. 659, 121 L.Ed.2d 585 (1992).

It should be kept in mind that in *Northrop,* the court treated as commercial speech advertisements that were not designed to sell products. The same logic could be applied to advertisements that stated a corporate position on controversial public issues. Indeed, in Friends of the Earth v. FCC, 449 F.2d 1164, 146 U.S. App. D.C. 88 (D.C.Cir.1971) and Banzhaf v. FCC, 405 F.2d 1082, 132 U.S. App. D.C. 14 (D.C.Cir.1968), cert. denied, 396 U.S. 842, 90 S. Ct. 50, 24 L. Ed. 2d 93 (1969), product advertisements were regulated because they were presumed to have some impact on public debate over health issues. Thus, some nexus, real or imagined, between persuasive communications and traditionally protected political speech, would not necessarily be sufficient to prevent a "subliminal communications exception" to the First Amendment from spreading beyond the context of advertising.

39. *Compare* FCC v. Pacifica Found., 438 U.S. 726, 748, 98 S.Ct. 3026, 3040, 57 L.Ed.2d 1073, 1093 (1978) (plurality finds justification for reduced constitutional protection for broadcasting in its "pervasive presence") *with* City of Los Angeles v. Preferred Communications, Inc., 476 U.S. 488, 494, 106 S.Ct. 2034, 2038, 90 L.Ed.2d 480, 487 (1986) ("Cable television partakes of some of the aspects of speech and the communication of ideas as do the traditional enterprises of newspaper and book publishers, public speakers and pamphleteers."). Turner Broadcasting Sys. v. FCC, 512 U.S. 622, 114 S.Ct. 2445, 129 L.Ed.2d 497 (1994) ("Turner I").

The Supreme Court first articulated its "commercial speech doctrine" in *Valentine v. Chrestensen*.[40] The Court upheld the conviction of a businessman for violating a local sanitary code provision that prohibited the dissemination of advertising material in the streets. The defendant had distributed a handbill that, on one side, advertised an exhibition of a former Navy submarine, and on the other, protested local authorities' official actions regarding the commercial exhibition. The Court eschewed any attempt to distinguish the handbill's commercial and political messages, and held that the defendant's purpose was purely commercial.[41] Such activity, the Court reasoned, was entirely a matter for legislative judgment. In other words, local authorities were given carte blanche to prohibit business activities on public rights-of-way that might invade or interfere with "the public use to which streets are dedicated."[42] In short, the First Amendment was held not to apply "as respects purely commercial advertising."[43]

The Court's approach in *Chrestensen*, subsequently criticized as "casual" or "offhand,"[44] differed fundamentally from the analysis applied to other "nonfree speech" categories. Whereas definitional or categorical balancing normally obliges the Court to identify some social evil flowing from the speech under consideration and to weigh it against whatever communicative value pertains,[45] there was no attempt to do so in *Chrestensen*. The Court merely held that governments could control commercial speech just as they would any other commercial activity. Because of the nonprincipled nature of this analysis, the Court gradually

40. 316 U.S. 52, 62 S.Ct. 920, 86 L.Ed. 1262 (1942).

41. In the Court's view, the protest message was added to the handbill only to "evad[e] the prohibition of the ordinance." *Id.* at 55, 62 S. Ct. at 922, 86 L. Ed. at 1266.

42. *Id.* at 55, 62 S. Ct. at 921, 86 L. Ed. at 1265. Ironically, Justice Roberts, who wrote for a unanimous Court in *Chrestensen*, three years earlier had written that streets and parks "have immemorially been held in trust for the use of the public and, time out of mind, have been used for purposes of assembly, communicating thoughts between citizens, and discussing public questions." Hague v. CIO, 307 U.S. 496, 516, 59 S.Ct. 954, 964, 83 L.Ed. 1423, 1437 (1939) (Roberts, J., concurring). Presumably, neither Justice Roberts nor Justice Black (normally an absolutist in such matters), felt that a commercial message communicated any thoughts between citizens.

43. *Id. Accord* Halter v. Nebraska, 205 U.S. 34, 27 S.Ct. 419, 51 L.Ed. 696 (1907).

44. Cammarano v. United States, 358 U.S. 498, 514, 79 S.Ct. 524, 534, 3 L.Ed.2d 462, 472 (1959) (Douglas, J., concurring). *See* Lehman v. Shaker Heights, 418 U.S. 298, 314–15, 94 S.Ct. 2714, 2723, 41 L.Ed.2d 770, 784 (1974) (Brennan, J., dissenting); Pittsburgh Press Co. v. Pittsburgh Comm'n on Human Relations, 413 U.S. 376, 398, 93 S.Ct. 2553, 2565, 37 L.Ed.2d 669, 684 (1973) (Douglas, J., dissenting); *Id.* at 401 & n.6, 93 S. Ct. at 2566 & n.6, 37 L.Ed.2d at 686 & n.6 (Stewart, J., dissenting); Dun & Bradstreet, Inc. v. Grove, 404 U.S. 898, 904–06, 92 S.Ct. 204, 207–09, 30 L.Ed.2d 175, 178 (1971) (Douglas, J., dissenting from denial of certiorari). *See also* Ronald D. Rotunda, *The Commercial Speech Doctrine in the Supreme Court*, 1976 U. Ill. L. Forum 1080; Martin H. Redish, *The First Amendment in the Marketplace: Commercial Speech and the Values of Free Expression*, 39 Geo. Wash. L. Rev. 429, 450 (1971) (the *Chrestensen* Court effectively eliminated First Amendment protection for advertising "without citing precedent, historical evidence, or policy considerations").

45. *See, e.g.,* New York v. Ferber, 458 U.S. 747, 763–64, 102 S.Ct. 3348, 3358, 73 L.Ed.2d 1113, 1127 (1982) (In the case of child pornography, "the evil to be restricted so overwhelmingly outweighs the expressive interests, if any, at stake, that no process of case-by-case adjudication is required.").

accorded commercial communications greater constitutional status as it began to recognize greater value in such speech.[46]

More importantly, by the mid–1970s, the Court expressly adopted a categorical balancing approach for resolving commercial speech questions. In *Bigelow v. Virginia*, the Court reversed the conviction of a newspaper editor who ran advertisements for a New York abortion clinic in violation of a state antiabortion statute. The Court noted that "speech is not stripped of First Amendment protection merely because it appears in [commercial] form" and claimed as its task "assessing the First Amendment interest at stake and weighing it against the public interest allegedly served by the regulation." This breakthrough in the commercial speech doctrine was followed closely by the Court's decision in *Virginia State Board of Pharmacy v. Virginia Citizens Consumer Council Inc.*, in which the rule of *Chrestensen* finally was repudiated. There, the Court invalidated Virginia's ban on the advertising of prescription drug prices, thus rejecting the premise that commercial speech "is wholly outside the protection of the First Amendment."[47] Although these holdings ended the commercial speech doctrine as such, both *Bigelow* and *Virginia State Board of Pharmacy* stand for the proposition that the government is empowered to regulate commercial speech.

Since the demise of *Chrestensen*, the Court has struggled with defining commercial speech and determining the extent to which regulation is permissible. In *Central Hudson Gas & Electric Corp. v. Public Service Commission*, the Court characterized commercial speech as "expression related solely to the economic interests of the speaker and its audience," and set out a four-part test for approving government regulations: (1) speech is entitled to protection if it concerns lawful activity and is not misleading; but even if protected, regulation is allowable where (2) an asserted governmental interest is substantial, (3) the regulation directly advances the interest, and (4) the regulation is no more extensive than is necessary to achieve the asserted interest.[48]

The Court's more recent decisions have reintroduced a degree of confusion about the extent to which commercial speech may be regulated free of constitutional restraints, although the current trend is to apply greater constitutional protection.[49] A detailed discussion of commercial speech and the First Amendment is presented in chapter three.

1.7 The Concept of "Abridgment"

A familiar precept of constitutional jurisprudence is that the "main purpose" of the First Amendment "is 'to prevent all such previous restraints upon publications as had been practiced by other govern-

46. *See* CRAIG R. SMITH, ALL SPEECH IS CREATED EQUAL 13 (2d ed. 1990).

47. 425 U.S. 748, 761, 96 S.Ct. 1817, 1825, 48 L.Ed.2d 346, 358 (1976).

48. 447 U.S. 557, 561, 566, 100 S.Ct. 2343, 2349, 2351, 65 L.Ed.2d 341, 348, 351 (1980).

49. *E.g.*, 44 Liquormart, Inc. v. Rhode Island, 517 U.S. 484, 116 S.Ct. 1495, 134 L.Ed.2d 711 (1996); Rubin v. Coors Brewing Co., 514 U.S. 476, 115 S.Ct. 1585, 131 L.Ed.2d 532 (1995).

ments.' "[1] But this main purpose is not the exclusive purpose. "To 'abridge' means not merely to forbid altogether, but to curtail or to lessen."[2] The Supreme Court has noted that in some circumstances, "indirect 'discouragements' . . . have the same coercive effect upon the exercise of First Amendment rights as imprisonment, fines, injunctions or taxes."[3] Thus, the First Amendment protects against "inhibition as well as prohibition."[4] By the same token, not all restrictions on speech constitute "abridgments." Professor Alexander Meiklejohn noted that "a man may be denied the privilege of speaking at a meeting because someone else 'has the floor.' But the freedom of discussion is not thereby abridged."[5] This section discusses various ways in which governmental actions may abridge freedom of speech or of the press.

A. *Prior Restraint*

Ever since the Supreme Court's landmark decision in *Near v. Minnesota*, there has been a "heavy presumption" against prior restraints. Such restrictions on speech are considered "the most serious and the least tolerable infringement on First Amendment rights[;] . . . one of the most extraordinary remedies known to our jurisprudence."[6] But what is a prior restraint? Generally, it is a directive that proscribes a given speech activity in advance of the time the speech is to occur. Historically, the classic example of a prior restraint is an administrative licensing system.[7] In *Near*, the Court broadened the concept to include injunctions against a publication found to have engaged in "scandalous" and defamatory conduct, and not just press licensing systems.[8] The concept is not without ambiguity, as academic debate regarding the scope of the term "prior restraint" attests.[9] In general, however, the

---

1. Patterson v. Colorado, 205 U.S. 454, 462, 27 S.Ct. 556, 558, 51 L.Ed. 879, 881 (1907) (citations omitted).

2. William Van Alstyne, *A Graphic Review of the Free Speech Clause*, 70 Cal. L. Rev. 107, 111 (1982).

3. American Communications Ass'n v. Douds, 339 U.S. 382, 402, 70 S.Ct. 674, 686, 94 L.Ed. 925, 946 (1950).

4. Lamont v. Postmaster Gen., 381 U.S. 301, 309, 85 S.Ct. 1493, 1497, 14 L.Ed.2d 398, 403 (1965) (Brennan, J., concurring).

5. Alexander Meiklejohn, *The First Amendment is an Absolute*, 1961 Sup. Ct. Rev. 245, 252.

6. Nebraska Press Ass'n v. Stuart, 427 U.S. 539, 559, 562, 96 S.Ct. 2791, 2803, 2804, 49 L.Ed.2d 683, 697, 699 (1976).

7. *See, e.g.,* Staub v. City of Baxley, 355 U.S. 313, 322, 78 S.Ct. 277, 282, 2 L.Ed.2d 302, 311 (1958).

8. 283 U.S. 697, 51 S.Ct. 625, 75 L.Ed. 1357 (1931). In *Near*, the prior restraint was authorized by statute and enforced by judicial decree. The Court for the first time

dealt with a purely judicial prior restraint in Carroll v. President and Comm'rs of Princess Anne, 393 U.S. 175, 89 S.Ct. 347, 21 L.Ed.2d 325 (1968). *See generally* Mark Denbeaux, *The First Word of the First Amendment*, 80 Nw. U. L. Rev. 1156, 1202, 1217 (1986).

9. *E.g.*, OWEN FISS, THE CIVIL RIGHTS IN-JUNCTION (1978); LAURENCE H. TRIBE, AMERI-CAN CONSTITUTIONAL LAW 1039–42 (2d Ed. 1988); John Calvin Jeffries Jr., *Rethinking Prior Restraint*, 92 Yale L.J. 409 (1983); Vincent Blasi, *Toward a Theory of Prior Restraint: The Central Linkage*, 66 Minn. L. Rev. 11 (1981); Frederick F. Schauer, *Fear, Risk, and the First Amendment: Unraveling the "Chilling Effect,"* 58 B.U. L. Rev. 685 (1978); Thomas R. Litwack, *The Doctrine of Prior Restraint*, 12 Harv. C.R.-C.L. L. Rev. 519 (1977); Stephen R. Barnett, *The Puzzle of Prior Restraint*, 29 Stan. L. Rev. 539 (1977); William P. Murphy, *The Prior Restraint Doctrine in the Supreme Court: A Reevaluation*, 51 Notre Dame Law. 898 (1976); Thomas I. Emerson, *The Doctrine of Prior Restraint*, 20 Law & Contemp. Probs. 648 (1955).

Supreme Court since *Near* has regarded administrative licensing schemes and anti-speech injunctions as the main examples of prior restraints.[10]

Although *Near* generally is regarded as having expanded the prior restraint concept, and thereby fostered greater First Amendment protections, it is not certain that bringing injunctions within the prior restraint rules necessarily advanced free speech goals.[11] Like an administrative licensing scheme, the judicial process generally requires prior review of the material in question to determine whether it falls into one of the "exceptional cases" in which courts have permitted prior restraints.[12] Thus, before the Supreme Court held that publication of the Pentagon Papers could not be enjoined, a district court already had stopped the New York Times from printing stories as the case worked its way through the process.[13] Similarly, the district court in *United States v. The Progressive, Inc.* issued a temporary restraining order that lasted for nineteen days until eventually imposing a preliminary injunction preventing publication.[14] Although this practice is necessary to preserve the status quo as the courts rule on the legality of a proposed injunction, it operates "to forbid publication while a hierarchy of courts, on the basis of a secret record presented in secret proceedings, speculates on the likelihood of adverse effects from publication and their magnitude."[15] In

---

10. *E.g.*, City of Lakewood v. Plain Dealer Publishing Co., 486 U.S. 750, 108 S.Ct. 2138, 100 L.Ed.2d 771 (1988) (licensing regulations governing placement of newsboxes); Shuttlesworth v. City of Birmingham, 394 U.S. 147, 89 S.Ct. 935, 22 L.Ed.2d 162 (1969) (parade permit); Freedman v. Maryland, 380 U.S. 51, 85 S.Ct. 734, 13 L.Ed.2d 649 (1965) (film censorship board); New York Times Co. v. United States, 403 U.S. 713, 91 S.Ct. 2140, 29 L.Ed.2d 822 (1971) (injunction relating to national security); Nebraska Press Ass'n v. Stuart, 427 U.S. 539, 96 S.Ct. 2791, 49 L.Ed.2d 683 (1976) (judicial "gag" order).

The term "prior restraint" can apply to a broad array of regulatory mechanisms, and the Court has done so in various contexts. *E.g.*, Minneapolis Star & Tribune Co. v. Minnesota Comm'r of Revenue, 460 U.S. 575, 587 n. 9, 103 S.Ct. 1365, 1373 n. 9, 75 L.Ed.2d 295, 306 n. 9 (1983) (special taxation of the press is "a form of prior restraint on speech"); Southeastern Promotions, Ltd. v. Conrad, 420 U.S. 546, 95 S.Ct. 1239, 43 L.Ed.2d 448 (1975) (denial of permit to use municipal auditorium considered to be prior restraint). However, absent some limiting principle, the list of government actions that could be deemed prior restraints "could be extended almost infinitely." Blasi, *supra* note 9 at 15 n.17. For that reason, most commentators focus on

injunctions and licensing systems as examples of prior restraints. *See id.* at 14–15.

11. *See* Hans A. Linde, *Courts and Censorship*, 66 Minn. L. Rev. 171, 183–84 (1981) ("Enthusiasm for *Near* v. *Minnesota* as a landmark of liberty is sobered by how much was conceded on the way to achieving its formal establishment of liberty of speech and of the press under the fourteenth amendment and the doctrine against previous restraints. Near added nothing to the substance of free expression; if anything, it sacrificed some substance to gain its major goal.").

12. *See Near*, 283 U.S. at 716, 51 S. Ct. at 631, 75 L. Ed. at 1367. Dictum in Near suggested that these exceptions include obstruction of national defense in time of war, obscenity and incitement to acts of violence and forcible overthrow of the government. *Id.*

13. United States v. New York Times Co., 328 F.Supp. 324 (S.D.N.Y.1971) (the injunction continued for four days).

14. 467 F.Supp. 990, 991 (W.D.Wis.), *request for writ of mandamus denied sub nom.*, Morland v. Sprecher, 443 U.S. 709, 99 S.Ct. 3086, 61 L.Ed.2d 860 (1979), *dismissed as moot mem.* 610 F.2d 819 (7th Cir. 1979).

15. Linde, *supra* note 11 at 201.

short, "[i]t means [imposing] a prior restraint in order to decide that a prior restraint is unconstitutional" or not.[16]

Another aspect of judicial orders not necessarily shared by administrative procedures is the application of the collateral bar rule. Under this rule a speaker cannot violate a court order—as opposed to a facially defective licensing scheme—as a means of testing its constitutionality.[17] Thus, even where an injunction subsequently is determined to be unconstitutional, ignoring the order will subject the speaker to contempt of court. In this respect, judicially-imposed prior restraints may be far more burdensome than an administrative procedure.[18] This distinction may be mitigated by the uncertain scope of the collateral bar rule[19] and by the requirement that judicial challenge may be necessary to protect a speaker who would violate a narrowly-drawn licensing law.[20] However, as a practical matter, it may be more difficult to challenge an injunction than an administrative order limiting speech.[21]

These two troubling features of judicial orders undergirded the grant and subsequent affirmance of a temporary restraining order against Cable News Network (CNN) in *United States v. Noriega*.[22] In that case, CNN sought to broadcast tape recordings, secretly made by the government, of conversations between deposed Panamanian leader Manuel Noriega and his attorneys. Noriega, who was incarcerated in the United States awaiting trial on drug charges, sought to have the broadcasts enjoined to preserve his Sixth Amendment right to a fair trial.

The United States District Court for the Southern District of Florida granted a temporary restraining order to prevent further broadcasts and ordered CNN to produce the tapes for *in camera* review. In doing so, the

---

16. *Id.* This paradox formed part of the absolutist position taken by Justices Black and Douglas in the Pentagon Papers case: "I adhere to the view that the Government's case against the Washington Post should have been dismissed and that the injunction against the New York Times should have been vacated without oral argument when the cases were first presented to this Court. I believe that every moment's continuance of the injunctions against these newspapers amounts to a flagrant, indefensible, and continuing violation of the First Amendment." New York Times Co. v. United States, 403 U.S. at 714–15, 91 S. Ct. at 2142, 29 L. Ed. 2d at 825 (Black, J., joined by Douglas, J., concurring).

17. Walker v. City of Birmingham, 388 U.S. 307, 87 S.Ct. 1824, 18 L.Ed.2d 1210 (1967); United States v. Dickinson, 465 F.2d 496 (5th Cir.1972), cert. denied 414 U.S. 979, 94 S.Ct. 270, 38 L.Ed.2d 223 (1973). *But see* Shuttlesworth v. Birmingham, 394 U.S. 147, 151, 89 S.Ct. 935, 939, 22 L.Ed.2d 162, 167 (1969) ("a person faced with ... an unconstitutional licensing law may ignore it and engage with impunity in

the exercise of the right of free expression for which the law purports to require a license.").

18. *See* United States v. Dickinson 465 F.2d 496 (5th Cir.1972), cert. denied 414 U.S. 979, 94 S.Ct. 270, 38 L.Ed.2d 223 (1973). This has led some to conclude that injunctions merit greater judicial scrutiny than licensing systems. *See* Barnett, *supra* note 9 at 553; Fiss, *supra* note 9 at 30.

19. *See* Blasi, *supra* note 9, at 21–22; *See* TRIBE, *supra* note 9, at 1043 ("continued vitality of the collateral bar rule is in doubt").

20. Poulos v. New Hampshire, 345 U.S. 395, 73 S.Ct. 760, 97 L.Ed. 1105 (1953) (validity of license denial must first be tested in court where licensing ordinance is presumed to be constitutional on its face).

21. *See* TRIBE, *supra* note 9, at 1044.

22. 752 F.Supp. 1032 (S.D.Fla.), *aff'd*, 917 F.2d 1543 (11th Cir.) (per curiam), cert. denied *sub nom.* Cable News Network, Inc. v. Noriega, 498 U.S. 976, 111 S.Ct. 451, 112 L.Ed.2d 432 (1990).

court emphasized that "its Order was not a decision on the merits of the request for injunction, but rather a temporary restraint until such time as the Magistrate could review the tapes and permit this court to make a determination based on the merits."[23] Although the court acknowledged the irony of granting a TRO in order to reach the question of whether or not publication should be enjoined, it concluded that the "unique nature of the problem" was that "no such determination was nor is possible without knowing the precise contents of the speech sought to be restrained."[24] In fact, the problem identified by the court is not so "unique," but inheres in almost all cases involving prior restraints. To the extent it is permissible for a court to examine the underlying speech and weigh its relative value against some countervailing interest, it usually must restrain publication pending a final decision—just as did the courts in *The Progressive* and Pentagon Papers cases.

The *Noriega* case leaves open the question of the evidentiary threshold needed to restrain publication pending a decision on the merits. The district court relied on *Nebraska Press Ass'n v. Stuart* for the proposition that a criminal defendant's right to a fair trial might justify a prior restraint, but because of the posture of the case did not apply the *Nebraska Press Ass'n* safeguards.[25] The court did not comment on the type of showing necessary to obtain a "pre-merits" restraining order, and the facts of *Noriega* suggest that the proof required may be minimal. Since the court did not have access to the tapes, it relied on defense counsel's representation that the material included discussions of witnesses, defense investigation, and trial strategy.[26] There was no showing that CNN posed an imminent or substantial threat to Noriega's Sixth Amendment rights, nor was it evident that an injunction would restore the privacy of Noriega's attorney-client communications.[27] Thus, the court found that "the possibility of prejudicial disclosure" of attorney-client communications justified the TRO without regard to the immediacy or probability that the interest would be impaired.[28]

23. 752 F. Supp. at 1036.

24. *Id.*

25. *Id.* at 1035. In *Nebraska Press Ass'n* the Supreme Court established that the test for determining whether a prior restraint can issue where the right to a fair trial is at stake requires conclusions as to 1) whether the right to a fair trial would be impaired, 2) whether less restrictive alternative measures short of prior restraint are sufficient, and 3) whether a prior restraint would effectively prevent the harm. 427 U.S. at 562–68, 96 S. Ct. at 2804–07, 49 L. Ed. 2d at 699–702.

26. 752 F. Supp. at 1034.

27. It is important to note that the invasion of Noriega's attorney-client relationship was caused by the government's taping of telephone conversations, not by CNN's broadcasts. The court acknowledged this fact by noting that "[a]n injunction prohibiting CNN from broadcasting the tapes would go nowhere toward preventing the harm which has already occurred." 752 F. Supp. at 1033. Such a remedy, according to the court, would be only "symbolic and prophylactic" as far as this aspect of the attorney-client privilege is concerned. *Id.*

28. 752 F. Supp. at 1049. Upon review of the taped conversations, Noriega's attorneys withdrew their objections to the CNN broadcasts. Laura Parker, *Judge Lifts Noriega Tapes Broadcast Ban*, Wash. Post, Nov. 29, 1990, p. A1 col. 1. The district court also held that the showing was insufficient to support an injunction. United States v. Noriega, 752 F.Supp. 1045 (S.D.Fla.1990). The entire process, from the first judicial hearing, through the appeal and final resolution, lasted three weeks. Thus, the Noriega case was a classic example of the imposition of a prior restraint "in

The Eleventh Circuit denied an emergency appeal and the Supreme Court denied CNN's application for stay of the TRO as well as its Petition for Writ of Certiorari. The Court of Appeals held that a temporary restraint pending a decision on the merits was necessary, concluding that "the First Amendment interests of the press and the public will be best served by immediate production of the tapes held by CNN so that the District Court can conduct the difficult balancing of constitutional rights required under these circumstances."[29] Justice Marshall, joined by Justice O'Connor, dissented from the Supreme Court's decision to deny review, arguing that "if the lower courts in this case are correct in their remarkable conclusion that publication can be *automatically* restrained pending application of the demanding test established by Nebraska Press [Ass'n v. Stuart], then I think it is imperative that we re-examine the premises and operation of *Nebraska Press* itself."[30]

The Eleventh Circuit was concerned as much with the fact that CNN ignored the lower court's orders as with the other issues before it. Thus, the collateral bar rule was a significant factor in the outcome. The court noted that the required tapes had not been produced and that CNN, "in disregard and defiance of the District Court's explicit restraining order, broadcast portions of some of the purported attorney-client communications."[31] It concluded that "[n]o litigant should continue to violate a district court's order and attempt to have that district court's order reviewed at the same time."[32] Similarly, when the District Court finally ruled that there were "no factual basis for entering a permanent stay order," it appeared that the collateral bar issue may have been more dispositive than a ruling on the merits.[33]

The court downplayed the "potential precedent in First Amendment law" resulting from the TRO and emphasized that the temporary restraint was required only to perform the balancing of First and Sixth Amendment rights required by *Nebraska Press Ass'n.*[34] Yet its analysis of the merits suggested that the court could have reached the same conclusion without resort to prior restraint.[35] It by no means is certain that the court necessarily needed to review the contents of the tapes in order to find that a prior restraint would not materially preserve Noriega's Sixth Amendment interests. For example, the court perhaps

---

order to decide that a prior restraint is unconstitutional." Linde, *supra* note 11 at 201.

29. 917 F.2d at 1552.

30. Cable News Network, Inc. v. Noriega, 498 U.S. 976, 977, 111 S.Ct. 451, 451, 112 L.Ed.2d 432, 433 (1990) (Marshall, J. dissenting).

31. 917 F.2d 1543, 1546 n. 5 ("We are troubled by CNN's refusal to obey the District Court's order to release the tapes in question to the court for review."). *Id.* at 1550.

32. *Id.* at 1552. *But see* Walker v. City of Birmingham, 388 U.S. 307, 315, 87 S.Ct. 1824, 1829, 18 L.Ed.2d at 1210, 1217 (col-

lateral bar rule does not apply "where the injunction was transparently invalid or had only a frivolous pretense to validity").

33. 752 F. Supp. at 1049–50, 1054.

34. *Id.* at 1049.

35. The District Court maintained that review of the disputed tapes was required to allow it to assess the danger that prejudicial pre-trial publicity might preclude impaneling an impartial jury. It also required access to the tapes to ensure that Noriega's right to effective assistance of counsel would not be compromised.

should have analyzed whether it is reasonable to believe that a jury could be further prejudiced by CNN news reports given the context of the *Noriega* case. In that regard, the court acknowledged that nothing contained in the tapes "even approaches the prejudicial nature of the publicity which attended Noriega's apprehension by American military forces in Panama."[36] Similarly, the court never made clear how CNN's possession and possible disclosure of the tapes would harm Noriega's attorney-client relationship where the government created the tapes in the first instance and necessarily had access to their content.

The long term implication of *Noriega* is uncertain since the Supreme Court declined to review the case. However, it raised the concern, expressed by Justice Brennan in *Nebraska Press Ass'n*, that allowing prior restraints to vindicate Sixth Amendment rights would "entail the possibility of restraint proceedings collateral to every criminal case before the courts."[37] While this may overstate the case, the possibility is likely to arise in cases involving extensive press coverage. *Noriega* may well encourage such proceedings to the extent it can be read to suggest that a "pre-merits" TRO may issue where there is a credible assertion that prejudicial publicity may preclude a fair trial.

1.   *Substantive Requirements*

Threshold questions aside, prior restraints are permissible only in a relatively narrow range of "exceptional" cases.[38] The Supreme Court in *Near* specified the subject matter upon which prior restraints may be imposed: national security issues (*e.g.,* "publication of the sailing dates of transports or the number and location of troops" when the nation is at war), incitement to acts of violence and the forcible overthrow of the government, and obscene publications.[39] The Court in *Nebraska Press Ass'n* extended the prior restraint doctrine to include court orders protecting Sixth Amendment rights, an extension that three Justices opposed.[40] Justice Brennan worried that "creation of a second 'narrow' category of exceptions to the rule against prior restraints would be interpreted as a license to create further 'narrow' exceptions."[41] Whether or not new "exceptions" have officially been recognized, the Court has shown an increasing willingness to approve prior restraints under a far

---

36. *Id.* at 1053.

37. 427 U.S. at 608, 96 S. Ct. at 2826, 49 L. Ed. 2d at 726.

38. Near, 283 U.S. at 716, 51 S. Ct. at 631, 75 L. Ed. at 1367.

39. *Id.* It is interesting to note that the speech categories identified in *Near* involve unprotected speech. Nebraska Press Ass'n v. Stuart, 427 U.S. 539, 590, 96 S.Ct. 2791, 2818, 49 L.Ed.2d 683, 716 (1976) (Brennan, J., concurring) ("These exceptions [in *Near*] have since come to be interpreted as situations in which the 'speech' involved is not encompassed within the meaning of the First Amendment.").

40. Nebraska Press Ass'n v. Stuart, 427 U.S. 539, 561, 96 S.Ct. at 2804–07, 49 L.Ed.2d 683. *See id.* at 604, 96 S. Ct. at 2824, 49 L. Ed. 2d at 724. (Brennan, J., joined by Stewart, J., and Marshall, J., concurring) ("Damage to that Sixth Amendment right could never be considered so direct, immediate and irreparable, and based on such proof rather than speculation, that prior restraints on the press could be justified on this basis.")

41. Id. at 611 n.41, 96 S. Ct. at 2828 n. 41, 49 L. Ed. 2d at 728 n. 41.

more lenient standard in such areas as enforcement of antitrust laws,[42] restraints on commercial advertising,[43] protective orders regarding discovery material[44] and intellectual property matters.[45]

Except in these latter categories, once a restriction is considered to be a prior restraint, there is "a heavy presumption against its constitutional validity."[46] In *New York Times Co. v. United States*, the Pentagon Papers case, the Court denied the government's request for an injunction on national security grounds because it held that "the Government had not met that burden."[47] As a *per curiam* decision, with nine separate opinions, the Court did not articulate a substantive standard for evaluating the government's burden. Taken as a whole, the Court held that the government's showing was insufficient to justify an injunction even though most Justices apparently agreed that publication of the Pentagon Papers would damage national security interests.[48] The question was one of immediacy and degree.[49]

42. FTC v. Superior Court Trial Lawyers Ass'n, 493 U.S. 411, 110 S.Ct. 768, 107 L.Ed.2d 851 (1990) (FTC-mandated ban on future boycotts upheld under lenient application of *O'Brien* test); National Society of Professional Eng'rs v. United States, 435 U.S. 679, 98 S.Ct. 1355, 55 L.Ed.2d 637 (1978) (order suppressing speech to prevent further Sherman Act violations is valid so long as it is "a reasonable method of eliminating the consequences of illegal conduct);" Lorain Journal Co. v. United States, 342 U.S. 143, 155–56, 72 S.Ct. 181, 187–188, 96 L.Ed. 162, 172–173 (1951).

43. Pittsburgh Press Co. v. Pittsburgh Comm'n on Human Relations, 413 U.S. 376, 93 S.Ct. 2553, 37 L.Ed.2d 669 (1973).

44. Seattle Times Co. v. Rhinehart, 467 U.S. 20, 36–37, 104 S.Ct. 2199, 2209, 81 L.Ed.2d 17, 29 (1984), cert. denied, 467 U.S. 1230, 104 S.Ct. 2690, 81 L.Ed.2d 884 (1984) (protective order upheld under *O'Brien*-type test). *But see* Procter & Gamble Co. v. Bankers Trust Co., 78 F.3d 219 (6th Cir. 1996).

45. San Francisco Arts & Athletics, Inc. v. U.S. Olympic Comm., 483 U.S. 522, 107 S.Ct. 2971, 97 L.Ed.2d 427 (1987); *see* Zacchini v. Scripps–Howard Broadcasting Co., 433 U.S. 562, 576, 97 S.Ct. 2849, 2858–59, 53 L.Ed.2d 965, 977–78 (1977); International News Serv. v. Associated Press, 248 U.S. 215, 39 S.Ct. 68, 63 L.Ed. 211 (1918). *See* Salinger v. Random House, Inc., 811 F.2d 90, *reh'g denied*, 818 F.2d 252 (2d Cir. 1987). Prior restraints to prevent copyright infringement are supported by statutory authorization for injunctive relief in the Copyright Act. 17 U.S.C.A. § 502(a) (1976). *But see* Belushi v. Woodward, 598 F.Supp. 36 (D.D.C.1984).

46. New York Times Co. v. United States, 403 U.S. 713, 714, 91 S.Ct. 2140, 2141, 29 L.Ed.2d 822, 824 (1971) (per curiam), *quoting* Bantam Books, Inc. v. Sullivan, 372 U.S. 58, 70, 83 S.Ct. 631, 639, 9 L.Ed.2d 584, 593 (1963). This "heavy presumption" and related safeguards apparently is lost where the speech itself is an integral part of the offense or violation. Thus, the regulated behavior is considered more akin to "action" than to "speech." *E.g.*, FTC v. Superior Court Trial Lawyers Ass'n, 493 U.S. 411, 110 S.Ct. 768, 107 L.Ed.2d 851 (1990) (antitrust violation); Arcara v. Cloud Books, Inc., 478 U.S. 697, 106 S.Ct. 3172, 92 L.Ed.2d 568 (1986) (closing adult book store that was location of prostitution); San Francisco Arts & Athletics, Inc. v. U.S. Olympic Comm., 483 U.S. 522, 107 S.Ct. 2971, 97 L.Ed.2d 427 (1987) (trademark infringement). Similarly, there is no special protection where the restraints are considered to have an "incidental" impact on speech. Seattle Times Co. v. Rhinehart, 467 U.S. 20, 31–34, 104 S.Ct. 2199, 2207–08, 81 L.Ed.2d 17, 26–28 (protective order barring release of discovery material considered a limited invasion of speech interest).

47. New York Times Co., 403 U.S. at 714, 91 S. Ct. at 2141, 29 L. Ed. 2d at 824.

48. Nebraska Press Ass'n, 427 U.S. at 591–92, 96 S. Ct. at 2818–19, 49 L. Ed. 2d at 716 (Brennan, J., concurring).

49. A majority of Justices agreed that, at a minimum, the government must demonstrate that a publication would cause direct, immediate and irreparable harm to the nation. New York Times Co., 403 U.S. at 730, 91 S. Ct. at 2149, 29 L. Ed. 2d at 834 (Stewart, J., joined by White, J., concurring). *See also id.* at 724–27, 91 S. Ct. at

The Court adopted a similar approach toward prior restraints in *Nebraska Press Ass'n v. Stuart*. There, a unanimous Court invalidated a restraint on publication of pretrial information prejudicial to a confessed mass murderer. Although the Court was convinced that sensational pretrial news accounts of a murder in a small town created the risk of "some adverse impact on the attitudes of those who might be called as jurors,"[50] it nevertheless adopted a test for prior restraint that preserved the "heavy presumption" against validity. Before a prior restraint could be issued, according to the Court, there must be analysis of (1) the nature and extent of pretrial coverage, (2) whether other measures short of censorship would mitigate adverse effects and (3) whether a restraining order would be an effective remedy.[51] As in *New York Times Co.*, and in other cases,[52] the Court in *Stuart* held that the government had not met its heavy burden.

2. *Procedural Requirements*

The seriousness with which courts normally view prior restraints is summed up in Professor Bickel's oft-quoted statement that "[a] criminal statute chills, prior restraint freezes."[53] As a result, courts impose special burdens on most attempts to impose a prior restraint. First, the speech in question must fall into one of the "exceptional cases" recognized by the courts. Second, the government must meet the heavy burden of justification to support the extraordinary restriction on free expression. Third, the restraint must be accomplished "with procedural safeguards that reduce the danger of suppressing constitutionally protected speech."[54]

Procedural requirements necessary to sustain a prior restraint generally are focused on the existence and timing of judicial review. To the extent the government assumes the authority to permit or deny the ability to speak or publish, the relevant law must specify a set time within which authorities "will ... either issue a license or go to court to restrain" the expressive activity.[55] The government is permitted to

---

2146, 29 L. Ed. 2d at 831–32 (Brennan, J., concurring); *id.* at 714–20, 91 S. Ct. at 2142–44, 29 L. Ed. 2d at 825–28 (Black, J., concurring); *id.* at 720–24, 91 S. Ct. at 2144–46, 29 L. Ed. 2d at 828–32 (Douglas, J., concurring). The U.S. District Court for the Western District of Wisconsin held that this demanding test was met in *United States v. The Progressive, Inc.*, 467 F.Supp. 990 (W.D.Wis.1979), *request for writ of mandamus denied sub nom.* Morland v. Sprecher, 443 U.S. 709, 99 S.Ct. 3086, 61 L.Ed.2d 860 (1979), *dismissed as moot mem.* 610 F.2d 819 (7th Cir. 1979).

50. 427 U.S. at 568, 96 S. Ct. at 2807, 49 L. Ed. 2d at 703.

51. *Id.* at 562, 96 S. Ct. at 2804, 49 L. Ed. 2d at 699.

52. *E.g.*, National Socialist Party v. Village of Skokie, 432 U.S. 43, 97 S.Ct. 2205, 53 L.Ed.2d 96 (1977) (prohibition on display of Nazi symbols rejected); Organization for a Better Austin v. Keefe, 402 U.S. 415, 91 S.Ct. 1575, 29 L.Ed.2d 1 (1971) (injunction against leafleting invalidated).

53. ALEXANDER M. BICKEL, THE MORALITY OF CONSENT 61 (1975). *See* Nebraska Press Ass'n, 427 U.S. at 559, 96 S. Ct. at 2803, 49 L. Ed. 2d at 698.

54. Southeastern Promotions, Ltd. v. Conrad, 420 U.S. 546, 559, 95 S.Ct. 1239, 1247, 43 L.Ed.2d 448, 459 (1975). *But see* Brown v. Glines, 444 U.S. 348, 100 S.Ct. 594, 62 L.Ed.2d 540 (1980) (procedural safeguards may not be required in military setting).

55. Freedman v. Maryland, 380 U.S. 51, 59, 85 S.Ct. 734, 739, 13 L.Ed.2d 649, 655 (1965).

impose a temporary restraint before a final decision is rendered. However, "[a]ny restraint imposed in advance of a final judicial determination on the merits must ... be limited to preservation of the status quo for the shortest fixed period compatible with sound judicial resolution."[56] It is the government's burden—not the speaker's—to initiate the judicial process and to prove that the need for the restraint outweighs the First Amendment interest involved.[57] Moreover, ex parte proceedings normally are impermissible; the government must allow the presentation of evidence and argument in opposition to the proposed restraint.[58]

The requirement that judicial proceedings take place within "a set time" compels the government to provide expedited judicial review, from the initiation of proceedings through a final decision.[59] The law, for example, must specify the time within which judicial proceedings must be started.[60] It also must provide for a reasonably quick judicial proceeding.[61] Once an initial decision is rendered, either the restraint order must be stayed or be subject to immediate appellate review.[62]

B.   *The Requirement of Content Neutrality*

Just as prior restraints are presumptively invalid, the First Amendment presumes that the government has no power to discriminate against speech based on its content. The Supreme Court has called the content neutrality requirement so "obvious" that it does "not require

56. *Id. See* Capital Cities Media, Inc. v. Toole, 463 U.S. 1303, 1304, 103 S.Ct. 3524, 3525–26, 77 L.Ed.2d 1284, 1287 (1983).

57. 380 U.S. at 58, 85 S. Ct. at 739, 13 L.Ed.2d at 654. *See* Marcus v. Search Warrant, 367 U.S. 717, 81 S.Ct. 1708, 6 L.Ed.2d 1127 (1961).

58. Carroll v. President of Princess Anne, 393 U.S. 175, 180, 184, 89 S.Ct. 347, 351–53, 21 L.Ed.2d 325, 330–31 (1968); Marcus v. Search Warrant, 367 U.S. at 720–21, 81 S. Ct. at 1710, 6 L. Ed. at 1129–30.

59. This requirement can create tensions among those called upon to render a decision. In *New York Times Co.*, Justice Black complained that "every moment's continuance of the injunctions against these newspapers amounts to a flagrant, indefensible, and continuing violation of the First Amendment." 403 U.S. at 715, 91 S. Ct. at 2142, 29 L. Ed. 2d at 825 (Black, J., concurring). On the other hand, Justice Burger wrote that "these cases have been conducted in unseemly haste," *Id.* at 753, 91 S. Ct. at 2159, 29 L. Ed. 2d at 847 (Harlan, J., dissenting).

60. It is insufficient for the law to state that judicial proceedings will begin "forthwith." United States v. Thirty–Seven Photographs, 402 U.S. 363, 91 S.Ct. 1400, 28 L.Ed.2d 822 (1971). In Kingsley Books, Inc. v. Brown, 354 U.S. 436, 77 S.Ct. 1325, 1 L.Ed.2d 1469 (1957), for example, the Court

approved a procedure that required a trial within one day of the filing of a request for an injunction. *See also* Marcus v. Search Warrant, 367 U.S. at 737–38, 81 S. Ct. at 1719 6 L. Ed. at 1139. The Court has rejected a procedure that allowed the passage of 50 to 57 days prior to judicial review, Teitel Film Corp. v. Cusack, 390 U.S. 139, 88 S.Ct. 754, 19 L.Ed.2d 966 (1968), but approved one that allowed ten days between administrative denial and judicial review. Interstate Circuit, Inc. v. Dallas, 390 U.S. 676, 88 S.Ct. 1298, 20 L.Ed.2d 225 (1968).

61. Generally, it is not possible to set a time limit on the duration of judicial proceedings. *But see* Marcus v. Search Warrant, 367 U.S. at 737–38; 81 S. Ct. at 1719, 6 L. Ed. 2d at 1139; Kingsley Books, Inc. v. Brown, 354 U.S. at 439, 77 S Ct at 1327, 1 L. Ed. 2d at 1472–73 (upholding law that required judicial decision to be rendered within two days of trial).

62. *See* M.I.C., Ltd. v. Bedford Township, 463 U.S. 1341, 1342, 104 S.Ct. 17, 18, 77 L.Ed.2d 1442, 1444 (1983); National Socialist Party v. Village of Skokie, 432 U.S. 43, 97 S.Ct. 2205, 53 L.Ed.2d 96 (1977); Southeastern Promotions, Ltd. v. Conrad, 420 U.S. 546, 560, 95 S.Ct. 1239, 1247, 43 L.Ed.2d 448, 460 (1975); Bantam Books, Inc. v. Sullivan, 372 U.S. 58, 70, 83 S.Ct. 631, 639, 9 L.Ed.2d 584, 593 (1963).

explanation."[63] The inhibition on content controls stems from the fear that "the Government's ability to impose content-based burdens on speech ... may effectively drive certain ideas or viewpoints from the marketplace."[64] This "First Amendment['s] hostility" to content discrimination "extends not only to a restriction on a particular viewpoint, but also to a prohibition of public discussion of an entire topic."[65] Justice Thurgood Marshall penned perhaps the most expansive statement of this principle in *Police Department of Chicago v. Mosley*: "[A]bove all else, the First Amendment means that government has no power to restrict expression because of its message, its ideas, its subject matter, or its content."[66]

But just as not all prior restraints are invalid, neither are all content-based restrictions. Quite to the contrary, much of First Amendment jurisprudence is predicated on setting the boundaries for permissible content discrimination. Thus, defamation,[67] obscenity,[68] incitement to crime,[69] and fighting words[70] have been held to be beyond First Amendment protection. Such categorical exclusions from First Amendment protection are expressly content-based.[71] As the Court pointed out in *R.A.V. v. City of St. Paul*, the First Amendment permits regulation of these categories *"because of their constitutionally proscribable content."*[72] The Court reconciled this emphasis on speech content with protections for free expression by pointing out that it relates to "a few limited areas" involving content of "slight social value."[73] Although court decisions have narrowed the scope of these excluded content categories, "a limited categorical approach has remained an important part of ... First

---

63. Simon & Schuster, Inc. v. Members of N.Y. State Crime Victims Bd., 502 U.S. 105, 115–16, 112 S.Ct. 501, 508, 116 L.Ed.2d 476, 487 (1991); Leathers v. Medlock, 499 U.S. 439, 111 S.Ct. 1438, 113 L.Ed.2d 494 (1991).

64. Simon & Schuster, 502 U.S. at 116, 112 S. Ct. at 508, 116 L. Ed. 2d at 487.

65. Burson v. Freeman, 504 U.S. 191, 197, 112 S.Ct. 1846, 1850, 119 L.Ed.2d 5, 13 (1992).

66. 408 U.S. 92, 95, 92 S.Ct. 2286, 2290, 33 L.Ed.2d 212, 216 (1972). Cases involving content discrimination by the government are often analyzed as Fourteenth Amendment equal protection issues. In this regard, the Court has confirmed that "[t]here is an 'equality of status in the field of ideas,' and government must afford all points of view an equal opportunity to be heard" in the public forum. Id. at 96, 92 S. Ct. at 2290, 33 L. Ed. 2d. at 217. It has further noted that, while certain cases have "fused the First Amendment into the Equal Protection Clause in this fashion," this occurs only because "the First Amendment underlies [the] analysis." R.A.V. v. City of

St. Paul, 505 U.S. 377, 384 n. 4, 112 S.Ct. 2538, 2544 n. 4, 120 L.Ed.2d 305, 318 n. 4 (1992).

67. Beauharnais v. Illinois, 343 U.S. 250, 72 S.Ct. 725, 96 L.Ed. 919 (1952).

68. Miller v. California, 413 U.S. 15, 93 S.Ct. 2607, 37 L.Ed.2d 419 (1973).

69. Brandenburg v. Ohio, 395 U.S. 444, 89 S.Ct. 1827, 23 L.Ed.2d 430 (1969).

70. Chaplinsky v. New Hampshire, 315 U.S. 568, 62 S.Ct. 766, 86 L.Ed. 1031 (1942).

71. *See supra* Section 1.6.

72. 505 U.S. at 383, 112 S. Ct. at 2543, 120 L. Ed. 2d at 318 (emphasis in original). *See also id.* at 400, 112 S. Ct. at 2552, 120 L. Ed. 2d at 328 (White, J., concurring) ("All of these categories are content based."); *id.* at 420, 112 S. Ct. at 2563, 120 L. Ed. 2d at 342 (Stevens, J., concurring) ("our entire First Amendment jurisprudence creates a regime based on the content of speech").

73. *Id.* at, 383, 112 S. Ct. at 2543, 120 L. Ed. 2d at 317.

Amendment jurisprudence."[74]

Outside the content-based exclusions from constitutional protection, the government must advance either a compelling interest or a plausible rationale for regulation based on some interest other than content control. The history of First Amendment jurisprudence is littered with discarded government policies for which an excessive focus on speech content was fatal. For example, a requirement that a newspaper publish a reply to an article critical of a political candidate was considered an excessive intrusion into editorial autonomy.[75] The Supreme Court invalidated a New York victims' compensation law that confiscated the proceeds from book or movie contracts based on crime because it imposed "a financial disincentive . . . on speech of a particular content."[76] The Court also has struck down content-based magazine taxes because "official scrutiny of the content of publications as the basis for imposing a tax is entirely incompatible with the First Amendment."[77] And it voided state restrictions that barred an electric utility from distributing "opinions or viewpoints on controversial issues of public policy" in the monthly billing envelopes.[78]

Courts also strictly scrutinize any content-based regulation of speech in the public forum. As with other protected speech, the government must show that regulation of content is necessary to serve a compelling state interest and that it is narrowly drawn to achieve that end.[79] Under this strict standard the Court has invalidated restrictions on public issue picketing that discriminated against certain subjects by exempting peaceful labor picketing,[80] a ban on demonstrations critical of foreign governments in the proximity of their embassies,[81] and a parade permit fee that local authorities could vary depending on the expected level of controversy.[82] But while the presumption against content-based regulation is

---

74. *Id.* The Court noted that decisions have increased the level of First Amendment protection for defamation and obscenity. Although this conclusion regarding obscenity is debatable, the decision in *R.A.V. v. City of St. Paul* clearly limited the government's ability to penalize fighting words. *See, e.g.,* New York v. Ferber, 458 U.S. 747, 102 S.Ct. 3348, 73 L.Ed.2d 1113 (1982). *See generally* Frederick F. Shauer, *Categories and the First Amendment: A Play in Three Acts*, 34 Vand. L. Rev. 265 (1981).

75. Miami Herald Publishing Co. v. Tornillo, 418 U.S. 241, 94 S.Ct. 2831, 41 L.Ed.2d 730 (1974). *See* Pacific Gas & Elec. Co. v. Public Utilities Comm'n of California, 475 U.S. 1, 106 S.Ct. 903, 89 L.Ed.2d 1 (1986).

76. Simon & Schuster, 502 U.S. at 116, 112 S. Ct. at 508, 116 L. Ed. 2d at 487.

77. Arkansas Writers' Project, Inc. v. Ragland, 481 U.S. 221, 230, 107 S.Ct. 1722, 1728, 95 L.Ed.2d 209, 220 (1987). *See also* Texas Monthly, Inc. v. Bullock, 489 U.S. 1,

109 S.Ct. 890, 103 L.Ed.2d 1 (1989) (state sales tax exemption for religious publications violates Establishment Clause).

78. Consolidated Edison Co. v. Public Service Comm'n, 447 U.S. 530, 533 100 S.Ct. 2326, 2333, 65 L.Ed.2d 319, 325 (1980).

79. Rosenberger v. Rector and Visitors of Univ. of Virginia, 515 U.S. 819, 115 S.Ct. 2510, 132 L.Ed.2d 700 (1995); Perry Education Ass'n v. Perry Local Educators' Ass'n, 460 U.S. 37, 45, 103 S.Ct. 948, 955, 74 L.Ed.2d 794, 804 (1983).

80. *E.g.,* Carey v. Brown, 447 U.S. 455, 461–62, 100 S.Ct. 2286, 2290–91, 65 L.Ed.2d 263, 270 (1980); Police Dept of Chicago v. Mosley, 408 U.S. at 95, 92 S. Ct. at 2290, 33 L. Ed. 2d at 216.

81. Boos v. Barry, 485 U.S. 312, 108 S.Ct. 1157, 99 L.Ed.2d 333 (1988).

82. Forsyth County, Ga. v. Nationalist Movement, 505 U.S. 123, 134–35, 112 S.Ct. 2395, 2403–04, 120 L.Ed.2d 101, 114–15 (1992).

strong, it is not insurmountable. Thus, in *Burson v. Freeman*, a divided Supreme Court upheld a ban on political campaigning within 100 feet of polling places. The Court acknowledged that the restriction was a content-based limit on political speech in the public forum, but balanced the interest in free speech with "the right to vote in an election conducted with integrity and reliability."[83] The Court emphasized that it was "the rare case" that "survives strict scrutiny," but found the "minor geographic limitation" on speech was warranted given the compelling state interest in fair elections.[84]

Because there is such a high hurdle for such regulation, governments often seek to argue that certain regulatory distinctions that relate to content are not "content-based" for the purposes of First Amendment analysis.[85] The Supreme Court approved this use of speech content as an analytic device for drawing regulatory lines in *Young v. American Mini Theatres*, by approving a zoning ordinance requiring the dispersal of "adult" movie theaters.[86] The Court reasoned that a content-based classification was valid so long as it was not motivated by "sympathy or hostility for the point of view being expressed" and that the ordinance could be upheld as a means of preserving "the character" of the city's neighborhoods.[87] Four Justices characterized their approach as a time, place, or manner restriction.

The Court refined this approach in *City of Renton v. Playtime Theatres, Inc.*, another zoning case.[88] Although the operation of the ordinance was triggered exclusively by reference to the subject matter of the movies being shown, it was characterized by the Court as a content-neutral restriction. This was so, according to the Court, because "the Renton ordinance is aimed not at the *content* of the films shown at 'adult motion picture theatres,' but rather at the *secondary effects* of such

83. 504 U.S. 191, 199, 112 S.Ct. 1846, 1851, 119 L.Ed.2d 5, 14 (1992). For cases in which the Court invalidated content-based restructions, *see* City of Ladue v. Gilleo, 512 U.S. 43, 114 S.Ct. 2038, 129 L.Ed.2d 36 (1994); Linmark Associates, Inc. v. Willingboro, 431 U.S. 85, 97 S.Ct. 1614, 52 L.Ed.2d 155 (1977).

84. Burson, 504 U.S. at 210–11, 112 S. Ct. at 1857, 119 L. Ed. 2d at 21–22. Four Justices accepted this balancing formulation. In concurring opinions, Justice Kennedy argued that the state law was not intended "to suppress legitimate expression," *id.* at 214, 112 S. Ct. at 1859, 119 L. Ed. 2d at 24. (Kennedy, J., concurring), and Justice Scalia concluded that the restricted area was not included within the public forum. *Id.* at 216, 112 S. Ct. at 1860, 119 L. Ed. 2d at 25 (Scalia, J., concurring).

85. *Id.* at 213, 112 S. Ct. at 1858–59, 119 L. Ed. 2d at 23 (Kennedy, J., concurring) ("In some cases, a censorial justifica-

tion will not be apparent from the face of a regulation which draws distinctions based on content, and the government will tender a plausible justification unrelated to the suppression of speech or ideas.").

86. 427 U.S. 50, 52, 96 S.Ct. 2440–2444, 49 L.Ed.2d 310, 315 (1976). The ordinance prohibited locating an adult theatre within 1,000 feet of any two other "regulated uses" or within 500 feet of a residential zone.

87. *Id.* at 67, 71, 96 S. Ct. at 2451–52, 49 L. Ed. 2d at 324, 326. Only four Justices expressly adopted this rationale, but in his concurring opinion, Justice Powell supported such regulation of "different types of speech." *Id.* at 82 n.6, 96 S. Ct. at 2458 n. 6, 49 L. Ed. 2d at 333 n.6.

88. 475 U.S. 41, 106 S.Ct. 925, 89 L.Ed.2d 29 (1986). The ordinance prohibited adult motion picture theatres from locating within 1,000 feet of any residential zone, dwelling, church, park or school.

theatres on the surrounding community."[89] In other words, where the predominant intent of the ordinance was to combat crime and neighborhood blight, the city could impose certain incidental burdens on speech.[90] While the regulatory classifications in the ordinance were defined by speech content, the law was *"justified* without reference to the content of the . . . speech."[91]

The scope of *Renton* was limited somewhat in subsequent cases. In *Boos v. Barry*,[92] the Court invalidated a provision of the District of Columbia code that banned displaying any sign within 500 feet of a foreign embassy that tends to bring that foreign government into "public odium" or "public disrepute." In doing so, a majority of the Court rejected the argument that the D.C. ordinance was directed only at preventing "secondary effects."[93] They found that the "emotive impact of speech on its audience is not a 'secondary effect' " as contemplated in *Renton*, confining such effects to adverse social consequences that "happen to be associated with"—but not caused by—a specified type of communication.[94]

Although this analysis limited the concept of content neutrality as applied in *Renton*, it left open certain questions regarding the reach of the "secondary effects" approach. As Justice Brennan noted in his *Boos v. Barry* dissent, "[n]o doubt a plausible argument could be made that the political gatherings of some parties are more likely than others to attract large crowds causing congestion, that picketing for certain causes is more likely than other picketing to cause visual clutter, or that speakers delivering a particular message are more likely than others to attract an unruly audience."[95] To the extent the government can advance a colorable claim that a given speaker or a type of expression can be found to produce adverse social consequences, this argument suggests, it would be possible to justify regulations under a more lenient constitutional standard. It is not difficult to anticipate the possible candidates for

89. 475 U.S. at 47, 106 S. Ct. at 929, 89 L, Ed. 2d at 37 (emphasis in original).

90. *Id.* at 48, 106 S. Ct. at 929, 89 L. Ed. 2d at 38.

91. *Id., quoting, with emphasis,* Virginia Pharmacy Bd. v. Virginia Citizens Consumer Council, Inc., 425 U.S. 748, 771, 96 S.Ct. 1817, 1830, 48 L.Ed.2d 346, 364 (1976).

92. 485 U.S. 312, 108 S.Ct. 1157, 99 L.Ed.2d 333 (1988).

93. Justice O'Connor, joined by Justices Stevens and Scalia, concluded that the prohibition on displaying banners was content-based and subject to strict scrutiny. *Id.* at 318–21, 108 S. Ct. at 1162–64, 99 L. Ed. 2d at 343–45. Justice Brennan, joined by Justice Marshall, agreed with this assessment, but concluded further that the *Renton* "secondary effects" analysis is illegitimate. Id. at 334–38, 108 S. Ct. at 1171–73, 99 L. Ed. 2d at 353–56.

94. *Id.* at 320–21, 108 S. Ct. at 1163–64, 99 L. Ed. 2d at 344–45. The Court suggested that "[r]egulations that focus on the direct impact of speech on its audience present a different situation." *Id.* at 321, 108 S. Ct. at 1163, 99 L.Ed.2d at 344. Justice O'Connor explained that "[l]isteners' reactions to speech are not the type of 'secondary effects' we referred to in Renton. To take an example factually close to Renton, if the ordinance there was justified by the city's desire to prevent the psychological damage it felt was associated with viewing adult movies, then analysis of the measure as a content-based statute would have been appropriate." *Id.* at 321, 108 S. Ct. at 1163–64, 99 L.Ed.2d at 344–45.

95. *Id.* at 335, 108 S. Ct. at 1171, 99 L.Ed.2d at 354 (Brennan, J., dissenting).

such treatment: marches by the Nazis or Ku Klux Klan, hate speech on campus, political demonstrations by the homeless or perhaps rock concerts.

The Court addressed this concern in *Forsyth County, Ga. v. The Nationalist Movement* by striking down a parade permit fee that was based on "the administrator's measure of the amount of hostility likely to be created by the speech based on its content."[96] Expressly rejecting a *Renton*-type "secondary effects" analysis, the Court found that under the permit scheme "[t]hose wishing to express views unpopular with bottle-throwers ... may have to pay more for their permit."[97] It cited *Boos v. Barry* for the proposition that "[l]isteners' reaction to speech is not a content-neutral basis for regulation."[98] The Court was further troubled by the fact that the ordinance set no guidelines to limit the administrator's discretion to set a fee (other than a $1,000 upper limit) and by evidence that the law had been applied in a discriminatory fashion.[99]

In other cases, the Court has avoided content analysis by focusing on some attribute other than speech that permits government intervention. In *Barnes v. Glen Theatre, Inc.*, a divided Court upheld an Indiana ban on nude barroom dancing.[100] Although only one Justice expressly endorsed the *Renton* approach, a majority agreed that the state's independent interest in proscribing public nudity was sufficient to outweigh what they saw as the ban's minimal burden on the First Amendment. Similarly, in *Arcara v. Cloud Books, Inc.*, the Court held that closure of adult bookstore at which prostitution was occurring did not conflict with the First Amendment because it was directed only at the illegal conduct which "manifests ... no element of protected expression."[1]

The content neutrality requirement has a special application in the context of court orders as opposed to general laws. Thus, in *Madsen v. Women's Health Center, Inc.*, the Supreme Court upheld as content neutral an injunction barring certain protest activities that affected "only the speech of antiabortion protesters."[2] The protesters, associated with Operation Rescue, had engaged in protracted demonstrations, picketing at an abortion clinic and at the homes of its staff members. A Florida state court permanently enjoined the protesters from engaging in certain activities, such as obstructing access to the clinic; picketing, patrolling, demonstrating or entering that portion of the public right-of-

96. 505 U.S. 123, 134, 112 S.Ct. 2395, 2403, 120 L.Ed.2d 101, 113 (1992).

97. *Id.* at 134, 112 S. Ct. at 2403, 120 L.Ed.2d at 113–14.

98. *Id.* at 134, 112 S. Ct. at 2403, 120 L.Ed.2d at 114.

99. *Id.* at 135 n.12, Ct. at 2404 n.12, 120 L. Ed. 2d at 114 n.12. The Court noted that the county charged no fee for police protection for 4th of July parades "although they were substantial parades,

which required the closing of streets and drew large crowds."

100. 501 U.S. 560, 111 S.Ct. 2456, 115 L.Ed.2d 504 (1991).

1. 478 U.S. 697, 705, 106 S.Ct. 3172, 3176, 92 L.Ed.2d 568, 577 (1986).

2. 512 U.S. 753, 114 S.Ct. 2516, 129 L.Ed.2d 593 (1994). A similar injunction was upheld in *Schenck v. Pro–Choice Network of Western New York*, 519 U.S. 357, 117 S.Ct. 855, 137 L.Ed.2d 1 (1997).

way or private property within 36 feet of the clinic; singing, chanting or using bullhorns or other sound amplification equipment from 7:30 a.m. until noon on Mondays through Saturdays during surgical procedures and recovery periods or displaying images observable to persons within the clinic during the designated times; physically approaching any person within 300 feet of the clinic unless that person indicated a desire to communicate; among other restrictions.[3]

The Court found that "none of the restrictions imposed by the court were directed at the contents of petitioner's message." It suggested that Florida law would apply equally to restrain similar conduct in demonstrations unrelated to abortion. The Court rejected the argument that the injunction was content based because it targeted only antiabortion protesters, noting that an injunction, "by its very nature, applies only to a particular group ... and regulates the activities, and perhaps the speech, of that group." Unlike a general law, an injunction controls the actions of the group "because of the group's past actions in the context of a specific dispute between real parties."[4] The Court acknowledged that injunctions carry a greater risk of censorship and discriminatory application than do general laws. Accordingly, it concluded that cases involving such content neutral injunctions "require a somewhat more stringent application of general First Amendment principles."[5]

C. *Unconstitutional Conditions*

While there is a heavy presumption against government imposing direct restraints on speech, the First Amendment also ensures that the state cannot employ indirect means to "produce a result which [it] could not command directly."[6] Thus, the government generally cannot condition the distribution of government benefit upon the relinquishment of a free speech right, even though the recipient does not have a "right" to receive the benefit. For many years, this requirement was not observed under what came to be known as the "right-privilege" distinction. As then state-Justice Holmes wrote in *McAuliffe v. Mayor of New Bedford*, "[t]he petitioner may have a ... right to talk politics, but he has no

---

3. Operation Rescue v. Women's Health Center, Inc., 626 So.2d 664, 679–80 (Fla. 1993).

4. Madsen, 512 U.S. at 762, 114 S. Ct. at 2523, 129 L.Ed.2d at 606.

5. *Id.* at 264, 114 S. Ct. at 2524 129 L.Ed.2d at 607. The Court engaged in a review of the injunction that was more rigorous than that applied to time, place or manner restrictions, but less than strict scrutiny. Under this middle tier approach, the Court struck down the prohibitions on approaching individuals within 300 feet of the Clinic, displaying "images observable" within the clinic, picketing within 300 feet of staff residences, and a limited buffer zone relating to nearby private property. The Court upheld the injunction insofar as

it prohibited picketing within 36 feet of clinic entrances and driveways and limited noise during periods of surgery and recovery. Justice Scalia, in dissent, described the Court's approach as "intermediate-intermediate scrutiny" and commented that the "difference between it and intermediate scrutiny ... is frankly too subtle for me to describe." *Id.* at 791, 114 S. Ct. at 2538, 129 L.Ed.2d at 623–24 (Scalia, J., dissenting in part).

6. Speiser v. Randall, 357 U.S. 513, 526, 78 S.Ct. 1332, 1342, 2 L.Ed.2d 1460, 1473 (1958); Perry v. Sindermann, 408 U.S. 593, 597, 92 S.Ct. 2694, 2697, 33 L.Ed.2d 570, 577 (1972).

constitutional right to be a policeman."[7] More recently, the "right-privilege" distinction has been eclipsed, particularly in matters concerning freedom of speech.[8] Nevertheless, under "the unruly law of unconstitutional conditions,"[9] it is by no means certain that all expressions of government largess must be unconditional. A growing line of cases holds that the government is not required to subsidize the exercise of fundamental rights, and refusal to do so is not an unconstitutional condition.[10] As opposed to a "right-privilege" distinction, litigants must now navigate the uncertain waters of what might be called a "burden-subsidy" distinction. Nevertheless, where the Court perceives that a governmentally-imposed condition is unduly burdensome, it does not hesitate to invalidate the conditions.[11]

The unconstitutional conditions doctrine evolved from cases involving economic regulation. In *Frost v. Railroad Commission of California,* the Supreme Court struck down a state requirement that conditioned use of the public highways on a private carrier's agreement to operate as a common carrier. The Court did not question the state's authority (for the proper health, safety or other reasons) to withhold from the carrier the valuable right to operate on the highways. But it could not make the benefit contingent upon the carrier's willingness to accept special regulatory obligations, because the Court held that "one of the limitations [on any government's power to grant benefits] is that it may not impose conditions which require the relinquishment of constitutional rights."[12] Such a choice, according to the Court, is "a choice between the rock and

---

7. 155 Mass. 216, 220, 29 N.E. 517 (1892). Similarly, in Commonwealth v. Davis, 162 Mass. 510, 511, 39 N.E. 113, 113 (1895), *aff'd,* 167 U.S. 43, 47, 17 S.Ct. 731, 733, 42 L.Ed. 71, 72 (1897), Justice Holmes wrote that "absolutely or conditionally to forbid public speaking in a highway or public park is no more an infringement of the rights of a member of the public than for the owner of a private house to forbid it in his house."

8. *See* William Van Alstyne, *The Demise of the Right–Privilege Distinction in Constitutional Law,* 81 Harv. L. Rev. 1439 (1968); Speiser v. Randall, 357 U.S. 513, 518, 78 S.Ct. 1332, 1338, 2 L.Ed.2d 1460, 1468 (1958) ("The appellees are plainly mistaken in their argument that, because a tax exemption is a 'privilege' or 'bounty,' its denial may not infringe speech."). *But see* Rust v. Sullivan 500 U.S. 173, 111 S.Ct. 1759, 114 L.Ed.2d 233 (1991); Regan v. Taxation With Representation of Washington, 461 U.S. 540, 103 S.Ct. 1997, 76 L.Ed.2d 129 (1983); Cammarano v. United States, 358 U.S. 498, 515, 79 S.Ct. 524, 534, 3 L.Ed.2d 462, 473 (1959) (Douglas, J., concurring) ("Deductions are a matter of grace, not of right.").

9. Richard A. Epstein, *Unconstitutional Conditions, State Power, and the Limits of Consent,* 102 Harv. L. Rev. 4, 13 (1988) (this issue "for over a hundred years has bedeviled courts and commentators alike" *Id.* at 6); Kathleen M. Sullivan, *Unconstitutional Conditions,* 102 Harv. L. Rev. 1413, 1415–16 (1989) (unconstitutional conditions cases "seem a minefield to be traversed gingerly").

10. National Endowment for the Arts v. Finley, 524 U.S. 569, 118 S.Ct. 2168, 141 L.Ed.2d 500 (1998); Rust v. Sullivan, 500 U.S. 173, 111 S.Ct. 1759, 114 L.Ed.2d 233 (1991). *See* Planned Parenthood Fed'n of America, Inc. v. AID, 915 F.2d 59, 63 (2d Cir.1990), cert. denied, 500 U.S. 952, 111 S.Ct. 2257, 114 L.Ed.2d 709 (1991).

11. O'Hare Truck Service, Inc. v. City of Northlake, 518 U.S. 712, 116 S.Ct. 2353, 135 L.Ed.2d 874 (1996); Board of County Comm'rs Wabaunsee County v. Umbehr, 518 U.S. 668, 116 S.Ct. 2342, 135 L.Ed.2d 843 (1996); 44 Liquormart, Inc. v. Rhode Island, 517 U.S. 484, 116 S.Ct. 1495, 1513, 134 L.Ed.2d 711, 734 (1996).

12. 271 U.S. 583, 594, 46 S.Ct. 605, 607, 70 L.Ed. 1101, 1105 (1926).

the whirlpool."[13] A more modern expression of this principle came in *Nollan v. California Coastal Commission.*[14] There, the Court invalidated a demand that a property owner grant a public easement to its land in exchange for the issuance of a building permit. Writing for the Court, Justice Scalia highlighted the constitutional infirmity of such a condition in free speech terms. The state could forbid "shouting fire in a crowded theatre," he wrote, but it could not grant "dispensations to those willing to contribute $100 to the state treasury."[15]

Consistent with this reasoning, the Court over the years has made clear that the government "may not deny a benefit to a person on a basis that infringes his constitutionally protected interests—especially, his interest in freedom of speech."[16] Thus, courts have invalidated government conditions that limited freedom of expression in exchange for public employment,[17] tax benefits,[18] and monetary grants for public broadcasting.[19] This protection is not unlimited, however. The government may impose some conditions on the benefits it confers where it can provide "an appropriate justification."[20] For example, the Court held that to protect national security, the CIA could require its employees to sign confidentiality agreements as a condition of employment.[21] Similarly, it is permissible for Congress to condition public financing of campaigns on candidates' agreement to limit campaign spending to help protect the integrity of the electoral process.[22] The state may withhold liquor licenses from nightclubs that feature nude dancing to protect public morals.[23] In other words, a condition may be permitted where

---

13. *Id.* at 593, 46 S. Ct. at 607, 70 L. Ed. at 1104.

14. 483 U.S. 825, 107 S.Ct. 3141, 97 L.Ed.2d 677 (1987).

15. *Id.* at 837, 107 S. Ct. at 3148, 97 L. Ed. 2d at 689. The Court concluded that there must be some "essential nexus" between a legitimate regulatory interest and the condition imposed. *See* Dolan v. City of Tigard, 512 U.S. 374, 114 S.Ct. 2309, 129 L.Ed.2d 304 (1994).

16. Perry v. Sindermann, 408 U.S. 593, 597, 92 S.Ct. 2694, 33 L.Ed.2d 570, 577 (1972).

17. Rutan v. Republican Party of Illinois, 497 U.S. 62, 110 S.Ct. 2729, 111 L.Ed.2d 52 (1990); Rankin v. McPherson, 483 U.S. 378, 107 S.Ct. 2891, 97 L.Ed.2d 315 (1987); Branti v. Finkel, 445 U.S. 507, 100 S.Ct. 1287, 63 L.Ed.2d 574 (1980); Abood v. Detroit Bd. of Educ., 431 U.S. 209, 97 S.Ct. 1782, 52 L.Ed.2d 261 (1977); Elrod v. Burns, 427 U.S. 347, 96 S.Ct. 2673, 49 L.Ed.2d 547 (1976); Perry v. Sindermann, 408 U.S. at 597, 92 S. Ct. at 2697, 33 L. Ed. 2d at 577; Pickering v. Bd. of Educ., 391 U.S. 563, 88 S.Ct. 1731, 20 L.Ed.2d 811 (1968).

18. Speiser v. Randall, 357 U.S. 513, 518, 78 S.Ct. at 1332, 1338, 2 L.Ed.2d 1460, 1468 (tax exemption for veterans conditioned on oath that recipient does not advocate unlawful overthrow of the government invalidated).

19. FCC v. League of Women Voters of Cal., 468 U.S. 364, 104 S.Ct. 3106, 82 L.Ed.2d 278 (1984) (Section of Public Broadcasting Act that conditioned federal funding on a ban on editorializing invalidated).

20. Elrod, 427 U.S. at 359–360 n.13, 96 S. Ct. at 2683, 49 L.Ed.2d at 557 n.13.

21. Snepp v. United States, 444 U.S. 507, 509 n. 3, 100 S.Ct. 763, 765 n. 3, 62 L.Ed.2d 704, 708 n. 3 (1980) (agreement that employee not publish job-related material without prior agency review found to be "entirely appropriate").

22. Buckley v. Valeo, 424 U.S. 1, 96 S.Ct. 612, 46 L.Ed.2d 659 (1976) (per curiam).

23. California v. LaRue, 409 U.S. 109, 93 S.Ct. 390, 34 L.Ed.2d 342 (1972). However, the Court has said that such licenses do not convey excessive power to the government over licensees' speech. 44 Liquormart, Inc. v. Rhode Island, 517 U.S. 484, 116 S.Ct. 1495, 1513, 134 L.Ed.2d 711, 733–34 (1996).

there is an "essential nexus" between it and the state interest, so long as free speech interests are not excessively burdened.[24]

Another line of cases represents a more direct challenge to the unconstitutional conditions doctrine. The Supreme Court on various occasions has held that the government may appropriately limit the expenditure of public funds, and is not required to subsidize the exercise of fundamental rights.[25] One of the most controversial applications of this reasoning came in *Rust v. Sullivan*, where the Court upheld grant conditions under Title X of the Public Health Service Act. The conditions precluded any recipient of Title X funds from providing "counseling concerning the use of abortion as a method of family planning or provid[ing] referral for abortion as a method of family planning."[26] In other words, to receive a Title X grant, a recipient had to agree to forego abortion advocacy and counseling and to separate its project from any abortion-related activities.

A divided Court found that these conditions that directly targeted a specific viewpoint did not implicate the First Amendment. "[T]he government is not denying a benefit to anyone," according to the Court, "but is instead simply insisting that public funds be spent for the purposes for which they were authorized."[27] The Court found that the conditions did not restrict the recipients' rights because the grantee organization and its employees "remain free . . . to pursue abortion-related activities when they are not acting under the auspices of the Title X project."[28] Three of the four dissenting Justices strongly disagreed, and wrote that Title X regulations imposed an unconstitutional condition.[29] The dissenters argued that the Court has never held that "the First Amendment could be read to tolerate *any* governmental restriction upon . . . speech so long as that restriction is limited to the funded workplace."[30] They found the regulations to be an "intrusive,

---

24. *Cf.* Nollan v. California Coastal Comm'n, 483 U.S. 825, 837, 107 S.Ct. 3141, 3148, 97 L.Ed.2d 677, 689 (1987).

25. *E.g.*, National Endowment for the Arts v. Finley, 524 U.S. 569, 118 S.Ct. 2168, 141 L.Ed.2d 500 (1998) (NEA grants); Lyng v. International Union, United Auto. Workers, 485 U.S. 360, 108 S.Ct. 1184, 99 L.Ed.2d 380 (1988) (government may deny food stamps to a household because one of its members is participating in a labor strike); Regan v. Taxation With Representation of Washington, 461 U.S. 540, 103 S.Ct. 1997, 76 L.Ed.2d 129 (1983) (government may deny tax-exempt status to an organization because it engages in lobbying); Cammarano v. United States, 358 U.S. 498, 79 S.Ct. 524, 3 L.Ed.2d 462 (1959) (government may deny tax deductions for amounts expended for the promotion or defeat of legislation and initiative measures).

26. 500 U.S. 173, 179–80, 111 S.Ct. 1759, 1765–66, 114 L.Ed.2d 233, 246–47

(1991). The regulations also prohibited Title X grant recipients from encouraging, promoting or advocating abortion as a method of family planning. Finally, the conditions required Title X projects to be "physically and financially separate" from prohibited abortion activities.

27. *Id.* at 193, 194, 111 S. Ct. at 1772, 1774, 114 L. Ed. 2d at 255, 256. Title X was intended to subsidize family planning services "which will lead to conception and child birth." Additionally, the program did not fund post-conception medical care.

28. *Id.* at 198, 111 S. Ct. at 1775, 114 L. Ed. 2d at 259.

29. Justice Blackmun, joined by Justices Marshall, Stevens and O'Connor dissented. However, Justice O'Connor joined only part of the dissent and urged that the question be decided on nonconstitutional grounds.

30. *Id.* at 213, 111 S. Ct. at 1783, 114 L. Ed 2d at 268.

ideologically based regulation of speech" that "intrude[s] upon a wide range of communicative conduct, including the very words spoken to a woman by her physician."[31]

The core distinction recognized by the majority between the Title X restrictions and other cases involving unconstitutional conditions, other than characterizing the government action as a "subsidy," was that the limitations applied to the grant, and not to the recipient organization or its employees *per se*. Either are free to engage "in the protected conduct outside the scope of the federally funded program."[32] The majority illustrated the point by comparing two cases. In *FCC v. League of Women Voters of California*, the Supreme Court found an unconstitutional condition where a public broadcasting station that received only one percent of its overall funding was barred absolutely from editorializing.[33] On the other hand, the Court found no such infirmity in *Regan v. Taxation With Representation of Washington*, where the government denied tax-exempt status to an organization that engaged in lobbying. It noted that the organization would be free to conduct its political activities through an affiliate organization established under a different section of the tax code.[34] By the same logic, the Court concluded that Title X grantees and employees were unimpaired in their ability to engage in abortion related activities conducted separately from the grant.

In a subsequent case the Supreme Court was far less deferential to governmental discretion in distributing grants. In *Rosenberger v. Rector and Visitors of the University of Virginia*, the Court invalidated a restriction on a student activity fund that excluded support for religious publications, concluding that the limitation represented "viewpoint discrimination" in a limited public forum.[35] It distinguished *Rust*, claiming that the government in that situation had "used private speakers to transmit specific information pertaining to its own program," whereas in *Rosenberger*, the university had created "a program to encourage private speech."[36]

The *Rust* Court's distinction between conditions on the grant and conditions on the grantee appears to be more semantic than real. While it is true that the grantee is free to advocate abortion if it relinquishes the Title X grant, and its employees may provide abortion counseling if they get a different job, the result is precisely the same as where the conditions apply directly to the organizations and individuals involved. A condition may always be avoided through non-participation. In that regard, the majority's reference to *FCC v. League of Women Voters of California* may have been misplaced. In that case, the Court made clear that it would have approved the funding restriction if a public broadcast-

---

31. *Id.* at 211, 111 S. Ct. at 1782, 114 L. Ed. 2d at 267.

32. *Id.* at 197, 111 S. Ct. at 1774, 114 L. Ed. 2d at 258.

33. *Id.*

34. *Id.* at 197–98, 111 S. Ct. at 1774–75, 114 L. Ed. 2d at 258.

35. 515 U.S. 819, 115 S.Ct. 2510, 132 L.Ed.2d 700 (1995).

36. *Id.* at 834, 115 S. Ct. at 2519, 132 L. Ed. 2d at 718.

er "could ... use the station's facilities to editorialize with nonfederal funds" through an affiliate organization.[37] In *Rust*, however, Title X regulations required that funded programs be "physically and financially separate" from abortion related activities.[38] Had such a condition applied in *League of Women Voters*, public broadcasters would have been barred from using the same facilities to transmit editorials to the extent they were federally funded.

Although *Rust v. Sullivan* represented a low point for the doctrine of unconstitutional conditions, the Supreme Court subsequently expanded its scope. In a pair of cases decided at the close of the 1995 Term, the Supreme Court extended the unconstitutional conditions doctrine to independent government contractors. In *O'Hare Truck Service, Inc. v. City of Northlake*[39] and *Board of County Commissioners, Wabaunsee County v. Umbehr*,[40] the Court held that local governments could not cancel contracts in retaliation for the exercise of First Amendment rights. In *O'Hare*, a private towing service had been dropped from a government rotation list of available firms after the company's owner refused to contribute to the incumbent mayor's reelection campaign, and instead publicly supported the mayor's opponent. In *Umbehr*, a private at-will contractor for trash hauling service was denied renewal of his contract after publicly criticizing the county board. The principal question in both cases was whether private contractors should be treated differently than government employees who are punished after speaking out on a matter of public concern. The Court held that they should not, and that there is no material difference between the threat of job loss to an employee and the threat of loss of a contract to a contractor.[41]

Although *O'Hare* and *Umbehr* revitalized the unconstitutional conditions doctrine, neither case addressed the issue presented in *Rust v. Sullivan* regarding the extent to which speech-related conditions may be imposed on government subsidies. *Rosenberger* suggests that the government cannot discriminate when the subsidy relates to a forum that was created for expressive activities. But in *NEA v. Finley*, the Court held that competitive grants to subsidize artistic expression could include certain non-dispositive conditions (*e.g.*, a requirement to take into account "decency" and "respect for the diverse beliefs and values of the American public") so long as they did not impose a disproportionate burden on particular ideas or view points.[42] These decisions suggest that the debate over the murky doctrine of unconstitutional conditions will continue.

37. 468 U.S. at 400, 104 S. Ct. at 3128, 82 L. Ed. 2d at 304.

38. 500 U.S. at 180, 111 S. Ct. at 1766, 114 L. Ed. 2d at 247.

39. 518 U.S. 712, 116 S.Ct. 2353, 135 L.Ed.2d 874 (1996).

40. 518 U.S. 668, 116 S.Ct. 2342, 135 L.Ed.2d 843 (1996).

41. O'Hare, 518 U.S. at 720–21, 116 S. Ct. at 2358–2359, L.Ed.2d at 883. Umbehr, 518 U.S. at 678, 116 S. Ct. at 2349, 135 L. Ed.2d at 853–54.

42. 524 U.S. 569, 118 S.Ct. 2168, 141 L.Ed.2d 500 (1998).

D.　*Taxation and Other Financial Disincentives for Speech*

Just as "the power to tax involves the power to destroy,"[43] courts have long recognized that the power to tax also involves the power to censor. In fact, the Supreme Court has characterized special taxation of the press as "a form of prior restraint on speech"[44] and has regarded such assessments as inherently suspect in recognition of the fact that "obnoxious" taxes led directly to passage of constitutional safeguards for expression.[45] Differential taxation of different members of the press is especially disfavored.[46] Nevertheless, individuals and members of the institutional press are not exempt from generally applicable taxes, including those that may have a somewhat differential effect on the various taxpayers. For purposes of constitutional adjudication, the challenge is to determine the point at which differential tax treatment imposes too great a burden to survive First Amendment scrutiny.

1.　*Taxation of Speech*

The Supreme Court first articulated its aversion to special taxes on the press in *Grosjean v. American Press Co.* In that case, the Court invalidated a Louisiana special license tax of two percent on gross receipts of any advertiser-supported publication with a circulation of over 20,000 per week. It compared the tax to the Stamp Act and other "obnoxious" taxes imposed on the Colonies before the Revolution, and concluded that the First Amendment was intended to prohibit taxes that targeted the press generally or selected specific publications for adverse treatment.[47] The Court treated as irrelevant that the tax was facially viewpoint neutral or that the tax was paid after, rather than before, publication. Unlike the "ordinary form of tax" applied to all businesses generally, this tax was "single in kind" and necessarily had the effect and "plain purpose of penalizing the publishers and curtailing the circulation of a selected group of newspapers."[48]

43. M'Culloch v. Maryland, 17 U.S. (4 Wheat.) 316, 431, 4 L.Ed. 579 (1819).

44. Minneapolis Star & Tribune Co. v. Minnesota Comm'r of Revenue, 460 U.S. 575, 587 n. 9, 103 S.Ct. 1365, 1372 n. 9, 75 L.Ed.2d 295, 306 n. 9 (1983). In this view, speech is suppressed until the tax is paid. *E.g.*, Follett v. McCormick, 321 U.S. 573, 577, 64 S.Ct. 717, 719, 88 L.Ed. 938, 941 (1944); Murdock v. Pennsylvania, 319 U.S. 105, 112, 63 S.Ct. 870, 874, 87 L.Ed. 1292, 1298 (1943) ("[t]he power to tax the exercise of a privilege is the power to control or suppress its enjoyment"). Also, to the extent free speech is contingent on the payment of a tax, the revenue measure also may be characterized as an unconstitutional condition. *See* Jimmy Swaggart Ministries v. Board of Equalization of California, 493 U.S. 378, 110 S.Ct. 688, 107 L.Ed.2d 796 (1990); Minneapolis Star, 460 U.S. at 587 n.9, 103 S. Ct. at 1372 n. 9, 75 L. Ed. 2d at 305–06 n. 9.

45. Minneapolis Star, 460 U.S. at 583–84 & n.6; 103 S. Ct. at 1371 & n. 6, 75 L. Ed. 2d at 303–04 & n. 6. Grosjean v. American Press Co., 297 U.S. 233, 248, 56 S.Ct. 444, 448, 80 L.Ed. 660, 667 (1936).

46. Arkansas Writers' Project, Inc. v. Ragland, 481 U.S. 221, 229, 107 S.Ct. 1722, 1727, 95 L.Ed.2d 209, 219 (1987); Minneapolis Star, 460 U.S. at 585, 103 S. Ct. at 1371, 75 L. Ed. 2d at 305. *See* Texas Monthly, Inc. v. Bullock, 489 U.S. 1, 109 S.Ct. 890, 103 L.Ed.2d 1 (1989) (state sales tax exemption for religious publications violates Establishment Clause).

47. 297 U.S. 233, 248, 56 S.Ct. 444, 448, 80 L.Ed. 660, 667–68 (1936).

48. *Id.* at 250, 251, 56 S. Ct. at 449, 80 L. Ed. at 668–69. The opinion in Grosjean did not describe the political context of the Louisiana tax. The tax was explicitly designed to apply to large newspapers, most of

Taxes, or other tax-like burdens, are especially pernicious when linked to the content of a publication. A unanimous Supreme Court struck down New York's "Son of Sam" law, which required that "an accused or convicted criminal's income from works describing his crime be deposited in an escrow account" to be used to compensate the victims.[49] Such an encumbrance on the proceeds of a publication, according to the Court, "plainly imposes a financial disincentive only on speech of a particular content."[50] The Court saw no constitutional distinction between a discriminatory tax and the remedy prescribed in the victims' compensation law, that escrowed all of the speaker's speech-derived income for at least five years. It noted that "[b]oth forms of financial burden operate as disincentives to speak; indeed, in many cases it will be impossible to discern in advance which type of regulation will be more costly to the speaker."[51] The decision emphasized that the state has no legitimate power to use financial penalties to "suppress[] descriptions of crime out of solicitude for the sensibilities of readers."[52]

But a special tax on the press is invalid even where there is no apparent "impermissible or censorial motive" underlying its adoption, as there was in *Grosjean*. The Court in *Minneapolis Star & Tribune Co. v. Minnesota Commissioner of Revenue* struck down a state "special use" tax on the cost of paper and ink products consumed in newspaper production.[53] The Court noted that the statute, being limited to users of paper and ink, was "facially discriminatory, singling out publications for treatment that is … unique in Minnesota tax law."[54] The tax also impermissibly discriminated between newspapers of various sizes by exempting from its coverage the first $100,000 worth of paper and ink consumed in any calendar year.[55] Because "delicate and cherished First Amendment rights [we]re at stake,"[56] and because the Framers deemed special taxes on the press as "particularly suspect,"[57] the Court said the

which in the state had "ganged up" on Senator Huey Long. Long and the Governor campaigned for the newspaper tax, which they described to members of the legislature as "a tax on lying." Upon reviewing this history in Minneapolis Star, the Court concluded that legislature's censorial motivation "may have been significant." 460 U.S. at 579–80, 103 S. Ct. at 1369, 75 L. Ed. 2d at 301.

49. Simon & Schuster, Inc. v. New York Crime Victims Bd., 502 U.S. 105, 108, 112 S.Ct. 501, 504, 116 L.Ed.2d 476, 482 (1991).

50. *Id.* at 116, 112 S. Ct. at 508, 116 L.Ed.2d at 487.

51. *Id.* at 117, 112 S. Ct. at 508–9, 116 L.Ed.2d at 487.

52. *Id.* at 118, 112 S. Ct. at 509, 116 L.Ed.2d at 488. The Court noted that the Victims Compensation Board denied any intent to restrict speech involving crime, and

expressly declined to reach the question of whether the law was content-based. It focused, instead, on the overbreadth of the statute. *Id.* at 118–19, 112 S. Ct. at 509–10, 116 L.Ed.2d at 488–89.

53. 460 U.S. 575, 103 S.Ct. 1365, 75 L.Ed.2d 295 (1983).

54. *Id.* at 581, 103 S. Ct. at 1370, 75 L.Ed.2d at 302.

55. *Id.* at 591–92, 103 S. Ct. at 1375, 75 L.Ed.2d at 308–09. As a result of the exemption, only about two dozen publishers paid any tax out of nearly 400 publishers in the state. The Minneapolis Star paid over two-thirds of the total receipts collected. *Id.* at 591 n.15, 103 S. Ct. at 1375 n. 15, 75 L.Ed.2d at 309 n. 15.

56. *Id.* at 589–90 n.12, 103 S. Ct. at 1374 n. 12, 75 L.Ed.2d at 308 n. 12.

57. *Id.* at 583–84 n.6, 103 S. Ct. at 1371 n. 6, 75 L.Ed.2d at 303–04 n. 6.

government faced "a heavier burden of justification" than was normal.[58] Given the differential impact of the tax, the Court found it unnecessary to examine legislative motivations, and concluded that "[i]llicit legislative intent is not the *sine qua non* of a violation of the First Amendment."[59]

In the years following *Minneapolis Star*, the Court had various occasions to clarify its holding. It reaffirmed the prohibition against selective taxation of the press in *Arkansas Writers' Project, Inc. v. Ragland*, striking down a sales tax exemption that was based on a publication's content.[60] The exemption at issue, which precluded taxes on sales of religious, professional, trade and sports magazines, resulted in only "a few Arkansas magazines pay[ing] any sales tax."[61] The Court compared the Arkansas tax scheme to the exemption invalidated in *Minneapolis Star*, and found it to be an impermissible content-based tax differential. Similarly, in *Texas Monthly, Inc. v. Bullock*, the Court invalidated a sales tax exemption for religious publications.[62]

The Court articulated the first significant limitation on this line of authority in *Leathers v. Medlock*.[63] Although it previously had invalidated differential taxes as applied to different sized publications and to those with different content, in *Leathers* the Court approved differential taxation of different media of communication. At bar was an Arkansas gross receipts tax that applied to cable television and satellite video services but not to newspapers and magazines. Justice O'Connor, writing for a seven-Justice majority, found that "differential taxation of speakers, even members of the press, does not implicate the First Amendment unless the tax is directed at, or presents the danger of suppressing, particular ideas."[64] Consequently, the Court held that the First Amendment did not prevent the Arkansas legislature from deciding "simply to

---

58. *Id.* at 583, 103 S. Ct. at 1371, 75 L.Ed.2d at 303. Eight members of the *Minneapolis Star* Court viewed the problem as arising directly under the First Amendment and did not reach the Fourteenth Amendment equal protection argument. *Id.* at 585–86 n.7, 103 S. Ct. at 1372 n. 7, 75 L.Ed.2d at 305 n. 7. *See also id.* at 593, 103 S. Ct. at 1376, 75 L.Ed.2d at 310 (White, J., concurring).

59. *Id.* at 592. 103 S. Ct. at 1376, 75 L.Ed.2d at 309.

60. 481 U.S. 221, 107 S.Ct. 1722, 95 L.Ed.2d 209 (1987).

61. *Id.* at 229, 107 S. Ct. at 1727, 95 L.Ed.2d at 219.

62. 489 U.S. 1, 109 S.Ct. 890, 103 L.Ed.2d 1 (1989). *But see* Jimmy Swaggart Ministries v. Board of Equalization of California, 493 U.S. 378, 110 S.Ct. 688, 107 L.Ed.2d 796 (1990) (generally applicable

sales tax may encompass commercial sales of religious items).

63. 499 U.S. 439, 111 S.Ct. 1438, 113 L.Ed.2d 494 (1991).

64. *Id.* at 453, 111 S.Ct. at 1447, 113 L.Ed.2d at 507–08. The Court cited *Regan v. Taxation With Representation for Washington* for the proposition that "[i]nherent in the power to tax is the power to discriminate in taxation." *Id.* at 451, 111 S.Ct. at 1446, 113 L.Ed.2d at 506, *quoting* Regan v. Taxation With Representation of Washington, 461 U.S. 540, 547, 103 S.Ct. 1997, 2002, 76 L.Ed.2d 129, 138 (1983). It also relied heavily on *Cammarano v. United States*, 358 U.S. 498, 79 S.Ct. 524, 3 L.Ed.2d 462 (1959). *Id.* at 450–53, 111 S.Ct. at 1445–47, 113 L.Ed.2d at 506–07. Both cases also were critical to the Court's holding in *Rust* v. *Sullivan*, decided about a month later. This common line of authority underscores the interrelationship of the

exclude or exempt certain media from a generally applicable tax."[65]

A primary distinction between *Leathers* and *Minneapolis Star*, according to the Court, lay in the number of affected parties. It noted that the Arkansas sales tax was one of general applicability, listing over twenty different businesses or activities subject to its reach. The Court pointed out that "the tax affected approximately 100 suppliers of cable television services," so that the tax did not resemble "a penalty for particular speakers or particular ideas."[66] It contrasted the tax scheme with those invalidated in *Grosjean*, *Minneapolis Star* and *Arkansas Writers' Project*, where only "a narrow group [bore] fully the burden of the tax."[67] With the tax being applied to greater numbers, according to the Court, "the Arkansas sales tax presents none of the First Amendment difficulties that have led us to strike down differential taxation in the past."[68]

Justice Marshall, joined by Justice Blackmun, disputed the majority's conclusion that applying the tax to comparatively larger numbers diminished its censorial effect. He pointed out that there is only one cable operator in most communities and that "in any given locale, Arkansas' discriminatory tax may disadvantage a *single* actor, a 'small' number even under the majority's calculus."[69] The dissent also was skeptical that discriminating between different media was a content-free decision. Finding that "cable operators make unique contributions to the information market," Justice Marshall noted that the discriminatory tax "may well 'distort the market for ideas' in a manner akin to direct 'content-based regulation.' "[70] The majority's willingness to allow differential taxation, according to the dissent, "essentially annihilate[s] the nondiscrimination principle" established in *Minneapolis Star*, *Arkansas Writers' Project* and *Grosjean*.[71]

Although the scope of *Leathers* is not yet certain, the case clearly broadens the government's power to discriminate in taxing the media. The Court's decision to permit intermedia discrimination could allow local governments to favor or disfavor a given medium simply by adjusting tax rates or exemptions. Absent some proof of illegitimate

Court's analyses of taxes, subsidies and unconstitutional conditions.

65. *Id.* at 453, 111 S.Ct. at 1447, 113 L.Ed.2d at 508. The tone in *Leathers* sounded markedly different from Justice O'Connor's majority opinion in *Minneapolis Star*, in which she wrote: "Whatever the motive of the legislature in this case, we think that recognizing a power in the State not only to single out the press but also to tailor the tax so that it singles out a few members of the press presents such a potential for abuse that no interest suggested by Minnesota can justify the scheme." 460 U.S. at 591–92, 103 S.Ct. at 1375, 75 L.Ed.2d at 309.

66. 499 U.S. at 449, 111 S.Ct. at 1445, 113 L.Ed.2d at 505.

67. *Id.* at 448, 111 S.Ct. at 1444, 113 L.Ed.2d at 504.

68. *Id.* at 449, 111 S.Ct. at 1445, 113 L.Ed.2d at 505.

69. *Id.* at 462, 111 S.Ct. at 1452, 113 L.Ed.2d at 513. (Marshall, J., dissenting) (emphasis in original). Justice Marshall also noted that the majority opinion articulated no principle determining when a number of taxpayers is sufficiently "small" to warrant constitutional concern. *Id.* at 461, 111 S.Ct. at 1451, 113 L.Ed.2d at 513 ("the majority fails to pinpoint the magic number").

70. *Id.* at 462, 111 S.Ct. at 1451, 113 L.Ed.2d at 513 (Marshall, J. dissenting).

71. *Id.* at 464, 111 S.Ct. at 1452, 113 L.Ed.2d at 515 (Marshall, J. dissenting).

purpose, such manipulation will be difficult for a court to detect. Additionally, the Court's limiting reading of *Minneapolis Star* may give government greater latitude in taxing the traditional press. To the extent the number of taxpayers is not "limited" and there is no evidence of legislative intent to silence a particular viewpoint, the logic of *Leathers* would allow discriminatory treatment.

2. *Other Financial Disincentives*

Financial disincentives may also be unconstitutional if they impose too great a burden on speech even when they are entirely nondiscriminatory. Just as a tax or an escrow requirement can impose an unconstitutional burden on speech, the Supreme Court has held that preventing a speaker from receiving payment for speech is an infringement. In *United States* v. *National Treasury Employees Union*, the Court invalidated a federal ban on government workers receiving honoraria for writing and speaking.[72] Finding that the provision of the Ethics in Government Act "neither prohibits any speech nor discriminates among speakers," the Court still concluded that the law "imposes a significant burden on expressive activity."[73] It regarded as "self evident" the proposition that "compensation provides a significant incentive toward more expression," and found the limitation on such an incentive to be "the kind of burden that abridges speech under the First Amendment."[74] Like the escrow requirement struck down in *Simon & Schuster, Inc.*, the honoraria ban was found to be unconstitutional because it deprived authors of financial rewards for their work.[75] Blanket bans of this sort are particularly suspect. However, in a particular case where the government can demonstrate a sufficient interest in depriving an author of the profits derived from a book or speech, the measure may be upheld.[76]

E. *General Regulations as Abridgments*

Many governmental measures may have the effect of abridging speech. Professor Nimmer has pointed out that "[t]he applicable speed limit plus a series of red traffic lights may result in a speaker arriving at an auditorium too late to deliver his speech." In this case the traffic regulations "literally result in an abridgment of speech," but the example does not raise a First Amendment concern.[77] On the other hand, in certain circumstances the Supreme Court has held that generally applicable regulations can create an excessive burden on freedom of expression. This subsection explores some First Amendment ramifications of general purpose regulations.

---

72. 513 U.S. 454, 115 S.Ct. 1003, 130 L.Ed.2d 964 (1995).

73. *Id.* at 468, 115 S.Ct. at 1014, 130 L.Ed.2d at 981.

74. *Id.* at 468–469, 115 S.Ct. at 1014–1015, 130 L.Ed.2d at 981–982.

75. *Id.*; Simon & Schuster, Inc., 502 U.S. at 122, 112 S. Ct. at 511, 116 L.Ed.2d at 491.

76. *E.g.*, Snepp v. United States, 444 U.S. 507, 100 S.Ct. 763, 62 L.Ed.2d 704 (1980).

77. MELVILLE B. NIMMER, FREEDOM OF SPEECH § 2.06 (1984).

1. Burdensome Regulation

Courts normally defer to legislative choices for how best to achieve the government's policy objectives. However, this deference is not unlimited where the governmental actions affect adversely the exercise of fundamental rights. It is well settled that "legislation that regulates conduct but incidentally affects freedom of expression may, although it is a rational choice to effectuate a legitimate legislative purpose, be invalid because it imposes a burden on that right, or because other means, entailing less imposition, may exist."[78] The more difficult questions arise through application of this settled principle.[79] At what point does the practical effect of an otherwise valid enactment tread too heavily on speech?

There are no ready formulas to answer this question, although the Court from time to time has known the answer when it saw it. In *NAACP v. Alabama*, the Supreme Court held that the state could not compel NAACP to disclose its membership lists in order to qualify to do business.[80] The law in question was scrupulously neutral. It required only that to qualify to do business in the state, a foreign corporation had to file its charter with the Secretary of State and designate a place of business and an agent to receive service of process. In a state court action challenging NAACP's compliance with this statute, the local court ordered NAACP to produce its membership lists. NAACP challenged the order, arguing that governmental actions that indirectly burden speech must be justified by an overriding state interest.[81] The Supreme Court agreed, even though the burdens on speech and association resulted entirely from the actions of non-governmental third parties.[82] The Court noted that "revelation of the identity of [NAACP's] rank-and-file members has exposed these members to economic reprisal, loss of employment, threat of physical coercion, and other manifestations of public hostility."[83] The practical consequence of disclosure, according to the Court, was that "it may induce members to withdraw from the Association and dissuade others from joining it."[84] Accordingly, it held that the state interest in disclosure of the membership lists was insufficient to outweigh the First Amendment values at stake.[85]

78. Williams v. Illinois, 399 U.S. 235, 263, 90 S.Ct. 2018, 2033, 26 L.Ed.2d 586, 605 (1970) (Harlan, J., concurring).

79. As many First Amendment problems illustrate, "[t]he test of a test is not its formulation, but its application." Geoffrey R. Stone, *Content-Neutral Restrictions*, 54 U. Chi. L. Rev. 46, 52 (1987).

80. 357 U.S. 449, 78 S.Ct. 1163, 2 L.Ed.2d 1488 (1958).

81. *Id.* at 460, 78 S. Ct. at 1171, 2 L. Ed. 2d at 1498.

82. In *Bates v. City of Little Rock*, 361 U.S. 516, 80 S.Ct. 412, 4 L.Ed.2d 480 (1960), the Court held that the government could not compel NAACP to disclose its membership lists so that the city could en-force its occupational license tax. The Court acknowledged that the "repressive effect" of disclosure was due "in part" to "private attitudes and pressures," but concluded that the problem arose "only after the exercise of governmental power had threatened to force disclosure of the members' names." *Id.* at 524, 80 S. Ct. at 417, 4 L. Ed. 2d at 486.

83. 357 U.S. at 462, 78 S.Ct. at 1172, 2 L.Ed.2d at 1500.

84. *Id.* at 463, 78 S.Ct. at 1172, 2 L.Ed.2d at 1500.

85. 361 U.S. at 527, 80 S.Ct. at 419, 4 L.Ed.2d at 488.

Over time, the Court's *ad hoc* balancing approach represented by *NAACP v. Alabama* was supplanted by a more systematic approach for analyzing incidental burdens on expression. In *United States v. O'Brien*, the Court articulated a four part test for the validity of indirect abridgments. An incidental burden on speech is allowable, according to this analysis, when (1) the regulation is within the constitutional power of government, (2) it furthers a substantial or important governmental interest, (3) the interest is unrelated to the suppression of ideas, and (4) the incidental burden on expression is no greater than essential to further the government's interest.[86] This test was applied in *O'Brien* to uphold the conviction of a Vietnam War protester who burned his draft card.

Although originally conceived in the symbolic speech context, the *O'Brien* test has proven to be adaptable to a variety of other First Amendment issues. By its terms, it relates to government measures "unrelated to the suppression of free expression" that nonetheless impose an incidental burden on speech. Such an analytic framework easily encompasses the corporate registration law at issue in *NAACP v. Alabama*. However, the *O'Brien* test has been criticized for condoning excessive intrusion into First Amendment interests.[87] Indeed, if applied to the facts of *NAACP v. Alabama*, the *O'Brien* formulation would likely have led to a different result.

This conclusion is supported by the Court's application of *O'Brien* principles in *Clark v. Community for Creative Non–Violence*.[88] *Clark* involved the application of U.S. Park Service regulations prohibiting camping in national parks to deny a permit for a "tent city" demonstration in Lafayette Park, across from the White House. The majority held that the Park Service rules were a legitimate measure, unrelated to the suppression of speech, as contemplated by *O'Brien*. The regulations controlled only the time, place and manner of the demonstration, and thus were no more restrictive than necessary to serve the government's interest.[89] Missing from this analysis was any discussion of the practical effect of the regulations. Justice Marshall noted in dissent that one purpose for making sleep part of the demonstration "was to enable participants to weather the rigors of the round-the-clock vigil and to encourage other homeless persons to participate in the demonstration."[90]

---

86. 391 U.S. 367, 377, 88 S.Ct. 1673, 1679, 20 L.Ed.2d 672, 680 (1968).

87. *See, e.g.*, Keith Werhan, *The O'Briening of Free Speech Methodology*, 19 Ariz. St. L.J. 635, 641 (1987) ("The 'marginal first amendment protection' afforded by *O'Brien* flows from its refusal to allow 'serious balancing' of free speech interests against countervailing regulatory concerns. There is no speech side to the Court's balance.") (citations omitted); Frederick F. Schauer, *Cuban Cigars, Cuban Books, and the Problem of Incidental Restrictions on Communications*, 26 Wm. & Mary L. Rev.

779, 787–88 (1985) (describing *O'Brien* as a toothless standard); John Hart Ely, *Flag Desecration: A Case Study in the Roles of Categorization and Balancing in First Amendment Analysis*, 88 Harv. L. Rev. 1482, 1495 (1975).

88. 468 U.S. 288, 104 S.Ct. 3065, 82 L.Ed.2d 221 (1984).

89. *Id.* at 294–95, 104 S. Ct. at 3069–70, 82 L. Ed. 2d at 227–28.

90. *Id.* at 303 n.3, 104 S. Ct. at 3074 n. 3, 82 L. Ed. 2d at 233 n. 3. (Marshall, J., dissenting). The record indicated that

If the practical consequences of state regulation had been divorced from the Court's opinion in *NAACP v. Alabama* and *O'Brien* methodology applied, the case almost certainly would have been decided differently.

The current vitality of the doctrine that generally applicable regulations can abridge speech is uncertain after what has been described as the "O'Briening" of free speech methodology.[91] As described in the next subsection, those who challenge a generally applicable regulation will have greater success if they can demonstrate censorial intent by the government or some other structural flaw in the enactment.[92]

2. Non-Abridging Regulatory Burdens

a. general economic regulation

It is well established that the press and other speakers are subject to generally applicable economic regulations. For example, the Supreme Court has held that the First Amendment does not preclude applying wage and hour laws[93] or the National Labor Relations Act[94] to members of the press. By the same token, the First Amendment is no bar to enforcing the antitrust laws. As Justice Black wrote in *Associated Press v. United States*: "Freedom to publish is guaranteed by the Constitution, but freedom to combine to keep others from publishing is not.... The First Amendment affords not the slightest support for the contention that a combination to restrain trade in news and views has any constitutional immunity."[95]

The government's ability to enforce economic regulations is enhanced when the medium being regulated receives less than complete constitutional protection. For example, in *FCC v. National Citizens Committee for Broadcasting*, the Supreme Court upheld an FCC rule that prohibited broadcast-newspaper cross-ownership in the same com-

---

homeless people participated in the demonstration only when sleeping was permitted. *Id.*

91. Keith Werhan *supra* note 87, at 635.

92. *But see* Federal Election Comm'n v. Massachusetts Citizens for Life, 479 U.S. 238, 255, 107 S.Ct. 616, 626, 93 L.Ed.2d 539, 555 (1986), in which the plurality concluded that a statute's "practical effect may be to discourage protected speech is sufficient to characterize [it] as an infringement on First Amendment activities." *See also* Austin v. Michigan Chamber of Commerce, 494 U.S. 652, 668, 110 S.Ct. 1391, 1402, 108 L.Ed.2d 652, 670 (1990), in which the Court upheld an exemption for media corporations from a generally applicable law restricting use of a corporation's "general treasury funds" for expenditures in connection with state candidate elections. The Court noted that the law's restrictions on independent expenditures "might discourage incorporated news broadcasters or pub-

lishers ... from reporting on, and publishing editorials about, newsworthy events."

93. Oklahoma Press Publishing Co. v. Walling, 327 U.S. 186, 66 S.Ct. 494, 90 L.Ed. 614 (1946).

94. Associated Press v. NLRB, 301 U.S. 103, 57 S.Ct. 650, 81 L.Ed. 953 (1937).

95. 326 U.S. 1, 20, 65 S.Ct. 1416, 1425, 89 L.Ed. 2013, 2030–31 (1945). *See also* Citizen Publishing Co. v. United States, 394 U.S. 131, 89 S.Ct. 927, 22 L.Ed.2d 148 (1969); Lorain Journal Co. v. United States, 342 U.S. 143, 72 S.Ct. 181, 96 L.Ed. 162 (1951); United States v. Radio Corp. of America, 358 U.S. 334, 79 S.Ct. 457, 3 L.Ed.2d 354 (1959). For application of this principle in a non-media context, *see* FTC v. Superior Court Trial Lawyers Ass'n, 493 U.S. 411, 110 S.Ct. 768, 107 L.Ed.2d 851 (1990); National Society of Professional Eng'rs v. United States, 435 U.S. 679, 98 S.Ct. 1355, 55 L.Ed.2d 637 (1978).

munity.[96] Newspapers and broadcasters characterized the regulation as an unconstitutional condition, asserting that it conditioned the receipt of a broadcast license on relinquishment of the right to publish.[97] The Court rejected this analysis, in large part because of the "unique and special problems" inherent in broadcasting.[98] It described the goal of the FCC's rules as being "to promote free speech, not to restrict it," and pointed out that the ownership restriction was not content-based.[99] In this regard it is worth noting that the Commission expressly disclaimed any knowledge of whether the rules would promote free speech or not.[100] Nevertheless, the Court upheld the cross-ownership ban as "not an unreasonable means for seeking to achieve these [diversity] goals."

Similarly, in *United States v. AT & T Co.*, the U.S. District Court for the District of Columbia, in implementing a modification of the consent decree that led to the Bell System breakup, imposed a blanket ban on telephone company provision of information services.[1] The district court rejected a First Amendment challenge to the restriction, pointing out that, among other things, "common carriers are quite properly treated differently for First Amendment purposes than traditional news media."[2] The Court of Appeals reversed the district court's retention of the information services ban, but without reference to the constitutional issue.[3] More recently, however, lower courts subjected such restrictions to First Amendment scrutiny.[4]

96. 436 U.S. 775, 98 S.Ct. 2096, 56 L.Ed.2d 697 (1978).

97. *Id.* at 800, 98 S.Ct. at 2115, 56 L.Ed.2d at 717.

98. *Id.* at 799, 98 S.Ct. at 2114, 56 L.Ed.2d at 717.

99. *Id.* at 801, 98 S.Ct. at 2115, 56 L.Ed.2d at 718.

100. The FCC:

did not find that existing co-located newspaper-broadcast combinations had not served the public interest, or that such combinations necessarily "spea[k] with one voice" or are harmful to competition. In the Commission's view, the conflicting studies submitted by the parties concerning the effects of newspaper ownership on competition and station performance were inconclusive, and no pattern of specific abuses by existing cross-owners was demonstrated. The prospective rules were justified, instead, by reference to the Commission's policy of promoting diversification of ownership. Increases in diversification of ownership would possibly result in enhanced diversity of viewpoints, and, given the absence of persuasive countervailing considerations, "even a small gain in diversity" was "worth pursuing."

Id. at 786, 98 S. Ct. at 2107, 56 L. Ed. 2d at 708–09 (citations omitted).

1. 552 F.Supp. 131 (D.D.C.1982), *aff'd sub nom.* Maryland v. United States, 460 U.S. 1001, 103 S.Ct. 1240, 75 L.Ed.2d 472 (1983). AT & T, the surviving long-distance carrier, was barred for a period of seven years from engaging in electronic publishing. This restriction was lifted in 1989. United States v. Western Elec. Co. Inc., 1989 WL 108310 (D.D.C.) (unpublished memorandum). The divested Regional Holding Companies were prohibited from providing information services. This ban was dissolved in 1991 United States v. Western Elec. Co. Inc., 767 F.Supp. 308 (D.D.C.1991).

2. United States v. Western Elec. Co. Inc., 673 F.Supp. 525, 586 n. 273 (D.D.C. 1987), *rev'd on non-constitutional grounds*, 900 F.2d 283, 283 U.S. App. D.C. 299 (D.C.Cir.), *cert. denied sub nom.* MCI Communications Corp. v. United States, 498 U.S. 911, 111 S.Ct. 283, 112 L.Ed.2d 238 (1990).

3. United States v. Western Elec. Co. Inc., 900 F.2d 283, 283 U.S. App. D.C. 299 (D.C.Cir.), *cert. denied sub nom.* MCI Communications Corp. v. United States, 498 U.S. 911 111 S.Ct. 283, 112 L.Ed.2d 238 (1990).

4. U.S. West, Inc. v. United States, 855 F.Supp. 1184 (W.D.Wash.1994) *aff'd* 48 F.3d 1092 (9th Cir.1994), *vacated*, 516 U.S.

It also is clear, however, that the validity of general economic regulations depends on their neutral enforcement. As in the case of discriminatory taxation, courts will not permit the government to apply facially-neutral regulations in ways that target disfavored members of the press. In *News America Publishing, Inc. v. FCC*, for example, the District of Columbia Circuit reversed an FCC order that denied a temporary waiver of the newspaper-broadcast cross ownership rules.[5] The Commission decision was dictated by a facially-neutral congressional directive in an appropriations resolution that prohibited use of any funds "to extend the time period of current grants of temporary waivers" of the cross ownership rules.[6] The court of appeals found the legislation to be "general in form but not in reality" for it "burden[ed] a single publisher/broadcaster."[7] The court concluded that the provision was unconstitutional without regard to improper congressional motives in its enactment, yet it noted "the post-enactment debate's exclusive focus on Murdoch" arising from "heated criticism of several senators by Murdoch's papers."[8] The court held that the lower level of First Amendment protection normally accorded to broadcasters was not sufficiently lenient to support a measure that was "astonishingly underinclusive."[9] Consequently, economic or structural regulations that are neutral on their face but have a disproportionately burdensome effect may be subject to First Amendment challenge.[10]

b.   zoning or nuisance laws

The Supreme Court has approved another category of general regulations that affect speech by focusing on the governmental motivation underlying adopting the restriction.   Local control over land use provides a means of regulating speech-related businesses or activities.   To the extent such restrictions can be justified by reference to some public need that is separate from its effect on expression, the Court is likely to

---

1155, 116 S.Ct. 1037, 134 L.Ed.2d 186 (1996); Chesapeake and Potomac Telephone Co. v. United States, 830 F.Supp. 909 (E.D.Va.1993), *aff'd*, 42 F.3d 181 (4th Cir. 1994), *vacated* 516 U.S. 415, 116 S.Ct. 1036, 134 L.Ed.2d 46 (1996). *But see* BellSouth Corp. v. FCC, 144 F.3d 58, 330 U.S.App. D.C. 109 (D.C.Cir.1998).

5.   844 F.2d 800, 269 U.S. App. D.C. 182 (D.C.Cir.1988). The decision involved the same FCC regulations that were upheld in FCC v. National Citizens Committee for Broadcasting.

6.   *Id.* at 802, 269 U.S. App. D.C. at 184.

7.   *Id.* The affected party was Rupert Murdoch, a recently naturalized American citizen who had purchased a number of television stations in the U.S. and formed the Fox Broadcasting Network. In acquiring television stations in New York and Boston, Murdoch, through News America Publishing, Inc., had obtained temporary waivers of the FCC's newspaper-broadcast cross-ownership rules. News America was the only entity with outstanding temporary waivers of the rule when Congress enacted the appropriations restriction. Despite the general language of the enactment, the court found that the provision "strikes at Murdoch with the precision of a laser beam." *Id.* at 814, 269 U.S. App. D.C. at 184.

8.   *Id.* at 810, 269 U.S. App. D.C. at 192.

9.   *Id.* at 814, 269 U.S.App.D.C. at 195.

10.   *But see* Mabee v. White Plains Pub. Co., 327 U.S. 178, 184, 66 S.Ct. 511, 514, 90 L.Ed. 607, 613 (1946) and Oklahoma Press Pub. Co. v. Walling, 327 U.S. 186, 194, 66 S.Ct. 494, 498, 90 L.Ed. 614, 621 (1946), which held that small newspaper exemptions of the Fair Labor Standards Act of 1938 were permissible. *See also* Leathers v. Medlock, 499 U.S. at 453, 111 S.Ct. at 1447, 113 L. Ed. 2d at 507–08 (dictum approving differential regulation).

uphold the law regardless of its practical effect on speech. This approach has been used most often to uphold restrictions on sexually explicit speech, some Justices have hinted that it can be applied beyond that limited area.[11]

The first case in which a majority of the Court approved the "motivation" analysis was *City of Renton v. Playtime Theatres, Inc.*[12] In *Renton*, the Court upheld a zoning ordinance that prohibited adult motion picture theatres from locating within 1,000 feet of any residential zone, dwelling, church, park or school. The ordinance was justified, according to the Court, not because of the content of the films but because of "the *secondary effects* of such theatres on the surrounding community."[13] Such regulable "nuisance" effects included crime and neighborhood blight.[14]

The Court approved the restrictions without much regard for their practical effects on speech. Although it stressed that the existence of "reasonable alternative channels" for adult movie theatres in Renton was important to its analysis, the Court was not troubled by the fact that, as a practical matter, virtually no land was left available for such use. It noted that the ordinance left "some 520 acres, or more than five percent of the entire land area of Renton, open to use as adult theatre sites" and discounted claims that "practically none" of the undeveloped land was available for sale or lease or included "commercially viable" adult theatre sites.[15] The majority said that theatre owners "must fend for themselves in the real estate market" and concluded that the First Amendment contains no guarantee that speech-related businesses "will be able to obtain sites at bargain prices."[16] To the dissenters, however, the issue was not whether the theatre owners might not get a good deal, but whether they were being denied a reasonable opportunity to operate in Renton.[17]

11. *See* Boos v. Barry, 485 U.S. 312, 320–21, 108 S.Ct. 1157, 1163, 99 L.Ed.2d 333, 344 (1988) (plurality opinion analyzing restriction on political speech under "secondary effects" analysis of *City of Renton v. Playtime Theatres, Inc.*). *See* Note, *The Content Distinction in Free Speech Analysis After Renton*, 102 Harv. L. Rev. 1904 (1989). *But see* Forsyth County v. The Nationalist Movement, 505 U.S. 123, 134, 112 S.Ct. 2395, 2403, 120 L.Ed.2d 101, 114 (1992).

12. 475 U.S. 41, 106 S.Ct. 925, 89 L.Ed.2d 29 (1986). Four members of the Court adopted this approach in *Young v. American Mini Theatres, Inc.*, 427 U.S. 50, 96 S.Ct. 2440, 49 L.Ed.2d 310 (1976). There, the Court approved a Detroit zoning ordinance that prohibited locating an adult theatre within 1,000 feet of any two other "regulated uses" or within 500 feet of a residential zone. The ordinance was analyzed as a time, place or manner regulation.

13. 475 U.S. at 47, 106 S. Ct. at 929, 89 L. Ed. 2d at 37 (emphasis in original).

14. *Id.* at 48, 106 S. Ct. at 929, 89 L. Ed. 2d at 38.

15. *Id.* at 53, 106 S. Ct. at 932, 89 L. Ed. 2d at 41. Put another way, the zoning ordinance banned adult movie theatres from approximately 95 percent of Renton's land area. However, the Court viewed the issue as the theatre owners' glass being five percent full, rather than 95 percent empty.

16. *Id.* at 54, 106 S.Ct. at 932, 89 L.Ed.2d at 42.

17. *Id.* at 65, 106 S.Ct. at 938, 89 L.Ed.2d at 49. (Brennan, J., joined by Marshall, J., dissenting). *See also* American Mini Theatres, 427 U.S. at 71 n.35, 96 S.Ct. at 2453 n. 35, 49 L.Ed.2d at 327 n. 35 (plurality opinion) ("The situation would be quite different if the ordinance had the effect of ... greatly restricting access to, lawful speech.").

In other cases, the Court has approved restrictions on other public nuisances without resort to the "secondary effects" rationale of *Renton*. For example, in *Members of the City Council of the City of Los Angeles v. Taxpayers for Vincent*, the Court upheld a ban on posting signs on public property.[18] It found the ban to be a narrowly tailored means of eliminating clutter and visual blight. The Court found the government's interest in "proscribing intrusive and unpleasant formats for expression" to be "weighty" and concluded that "the City did no more than eliminate the exact source of the evil it sought to remedy."[19]

As the language of *Vincent* suggests, the Court's more recent cases evince a declining tolerance for speech that may be characterized as a nuisance. The more traditional approach is represented by *Schneider v. State*, in which the Court invalidated four city ordinances forbidding or regulating the distribution of literature along public streets and sidewalks.[20] The government had justified the anti-leafleting ordinances on the basis of aesthetics, that is, to prevent littering. But the Court was unimpressed with the proffered justification, finding that "the purpose to keep the streets clean and of good appearance is insufficient to justify an ordinance which prohibits a person rightfully on a public street from handing literature to one willing to receive it."[21] To the extent the government's interest was significant, the Court concluded that it could be served adequately by the less restrictive alternative of punishing those who actually litter.[22] This presumption toward preserving free speech appears to have been reversed in cases such as *Vincent*, in which the city's interest in avoiding "intrusive and unpleasant formats for expression" prevailed.[23]

F. Informal Censorship

Abridgment does not always depend on an official government decree, injunction or licensing decision. Less formal governmental actions also can have the effect of burdening or otherwise limiting speech. Such actions manifest themselves in a wide variety of contexts. This subsection examines various forms of informal censorship.

The facts of *Bantam Books, Inc. v. Sullivan* provide the classic example of informal censorship. In that case, the Rhode Island legislature established an advisory committee, the Rhode Island Commission to

18. 466 U.S. 789, 104 S.Ct. 2118, 80 L.Ed.2d 772 (1984).

19. *Id.* at 806, 808, 104 S.Ct. at 2129–30, 80 L.Ed.2d at 788, 789. *See also* Barnes v. Glen Theatre, Inc., 501 U.S. 560, 111 S.Ct. 2456, 115 L.Ed.2d 504 (1991); Arcara v. Cloud Books, Inc., 478 U.S. 697, 706–07, 106 S.Ct. 3172, 3177, 92 L.Ed.2d 568, 577–78 (1986).

20. 308 U.S. 147, 153–59, 60 S.Ct. 146, 147–150, 84 L.Ed. 155, 161–64 (1939).

21. *Id.* at 162, 60 S. Ct. at 151, 84 L. Ed. at 165. *See also id.* at 163, 60 S Ct. at

151, 84 L. Ed. at 165–66 ("the public convenience in respect of cleanliness of the streets does not justify an exertion of the police power which invades the free communication of information and opinion secured by the Constitution").

22. *Id.* at 160–61, 60 S. Ct. at 150, 84 L. Ed. at 164.

23. 466 U.S. at 806, 104 S.Ct. at 2129, 80 L.Ed.2d at 788. *See also* Clark v. Community for Creative Non–Violence, 468 U.S. 288, 104 S.Ct. 3065, 82 L.Ed.2d 221 (1984).

Encourage Morality in Youth. Members of the Commission would notify bookstores that certain books and magazines were considered "objectionable" for sale or display to youths under the age of 18. The written notice included a reminder that the Commission also had a mandate to recommend prosecution for purveyors of obscenity. Soon after the Commission's notice was sent, a local policeman would visit bookstores to determine what action they took in response, if any. The Supreme Court described the Commission's practice as a "blacklist," and found that "informal censorship may sufficiently inhibit the circulation of publications to warrant injunctive relief."[24] The Court discounted the Commission's claim that it was only providing legal advice, concluding that "the Commission deliberately set about to achieve the suppression of publications deemed 'objectionable' and succeeded in its aim."[25]

Despite *Bantam Books*, the government is not necessarily precluded from denouncing a given publication, even when the its purpose is to discourage certain views. In *Penthouse International, Ltd. v. Meese*, the District of Columbia Circuit rejected a claim requesting damages and a declaratory ruling arising from actions taken by the Attorney General's Commission on Pornography.[26] During the Commission's investigation, its executive director sent a letter to twenty-three corporations, including Southland Corporation, owner of 7–Eleven, a nationwide chain of convenience stores, noting that testimony before the Commission indicated "that your company is involved in the sale or distribution of pornography."[27] The letter offered the recipients "an opportunity to respond to the allegations" and said that "[f]ailure to respond will necessarily be accepted as indication of no objection" to being listed in the Commission's final report as an "identified distributor" of pornography.[28] In response to the letter, many stores stopped selling the offending magazines.[29]

24. 372 U.S. 58, 67–68, 83 S.Ct. 631, 637, 9 L.Ed.2d 584, 591–92 (1963).

25. *Id.* at 67, 83 S. Ct. at 637, 9 L. Ed. 2d at 591. The Court found that the Commission's practices "plainly serve as instruments of regulation independent of the law against obscenity." *Id.* at 68–69, 83 S. Ct. at 638, 9 L. Ed. 2d at 592.

26. 939 F.2d 1011, 291 U.S. App. D.C. 183 (D.C.Cir.1991), cert. denied, 503 U.S. 950, 112 S.Ct. 1513, 117 L.Ed.2d 650 (1992).

27. *Id.* at 1013, 291 U.S. App. D.C. at 185. Specifically, the allegation was made by one witness, Reverend Donald Wildmon, Executive Director of the National Federation of Decency, that convenience stores routinely sold "porn magazines," which in his view included Playboy and Penthouse magazines.

28. *Id.* A Commission member allegedly followed up the letter with a telephone call to the General Counsel of Southland Corporation with the message "that the Commission believed that Playboy and similar magazines were linked to child abuse and the Commission intended to publish this finding in its report." Since Southland had been leading a national campaign to fight child abuse, the resulting publicity would be embarrassing to Southland, whether or not there was in fact such a link. *Id.*

29. 7–Eleven stopped selling Playboy and Penthouse, and the two magazines were dropped by approximately 14,000 stores nationwide. As a result, Playboy's newsstand circulation reportedly declined by 700,000 copies. Robert Yoakum, *The Great Smut Hunt*, Columbia Journ. Rev., September/October, 1986 p. 24. Southland Corporation responded that it decided to stop selling adult magazines because of "growing public consciousness," but acknowledged that it "had been following the work of the Commission" and "had sent observers to the hearings." Southland also expressly denied that there was "conclusive

The United States District Court for the District of Columbia issued a preliminary injunction to stop the Commission's use of the letter to exert informal pressure on retailers.[30] However, in subsequent litigation on the merits, the District of Columbia Circuit held that the Commission's actions did not violate any "clearly established constitutional right[s]."[31] It characterized as a question of first impression "the scope of the government's right to speak where the government's speech discourages the constitutionally-protected speech of private citizens."[32] Although the court said it should "wait to decide this issue until it is squarely presented," it nevertheless proclaimed that "[a]t least when the government threatens no sanction—criminal or otherwise—we very much doubt that the government's criticism or effort to embarrass the distributor threatens anyone's First Amendment rights."[33] Thus, under this decision, the government may exert "deliberate and calculated pressure" to discourage the distribution of a specific magazine so long as there is no direct threat of prosecution.[34]

The facts of *Penthouse International, Ltd. v. Meese* test the limits of the Supreme Court's tolerance for informal tactics to suppress speech, although, as the District of Columbia Circuit pointed out, the Court has "signaled its reluctance to decide this very question."[35] However, In *Meese v. Keene*, the Court by a 5–3 vote upheld the government's authority to label films as "political propaganda" under the Foreign Agents Registration Act of 1938.[36] The Court, in assessing the claim of a California state legislator that the official designation impeded his ability to exhibit three Canadian films dealing with environmental issues and

evidence actually linking adult magazines to crime, violence and child abuse." Playboy Enterprises, Inc. v. Meese, 639 F.Supp. 581, 583–84 (D.D.C.1986).

30. Playboy Enterprises, Inc., 639 F. Supp. at 587–88. The District Court directed the Commission to retract the letter.

31. Penthouse Int'l, Ltd. v. Meese, 939 F.2d at 1017, 291 U.S. App. D.C. at 189.

32. 939 F.2d at 1020, 291 U.S.App.D.C. at 792.

33. *Id.* at 1016, 1020, 291 U.S. App. D.C. at 188, 192. The court distinguished Bantam Books by characterizing it as a case in which there was a genuine threat of prosecution, whereas the Pornography Commission's letter contained no such direct threat. *Id.* at 1014–1015, 291 U.S. App. D.C. at 186–187.

34. *Id.* at 1017, 291 U.S. App. D.C. at 189. *But see* Hentoff v. Ichord, 318 F.Supp. 1175 (D.D.C.1970) in which the district court enjoined publication of a committee report intended to discourage public speaking by "radicals" on college campuses. Without any legislative purpose, the report listed a number of " 'Pied Pipers of pernicious propaganda' … with the hope and

expectation that college officials, alumni and parents would bring social and economic pressures upon the institutions that had permitted these speeches in order to ostracize the speakers and stultify further campus discussion." *Id.* at 1178. The court noted:

It is alien to any legitimate congressional function, as well as contrary to our most established traditions, for any Committee of the Congress to disseminate lists designed to suppress speech. Members of the Committee may speak their minds, and their words will carry added weight because of the great prestige of their high office. They cannot, however, by the mere process of filing a report devoid of legislative purpose, transform these views into official action by the Congress and have them published and widely distributed at public expense.

Id. at 1182.

35. *See* 939 F.2d at 1020, 291 U.S.App. D.C. at 192.

36. 481 U.S. 465, 107 S.Ct. 1862, 95 L.Ed.2d 415 (1987). Justice Scalia took no part in the consideration or decision of the case.

with nuclear war, found that use of the term "political propaganda" threatened the appellee with "cognizable injury" and not just a "subjective chill."[37] But while this finding was sufficient to confer standing, the Court said it was "a separate matter" whether it rose to the level of a constitutional infirmity.[38] The Court held that there was no First Amendment violation on the facts presented because the term "propaganda" was used in a neutral sense in the statute and because there was no demonstration that the designation had any actual adverse impact on the distribution of foreign advocacy materials.[39] This holding, however, falls far short of approving governmental actions undertaken with the express intent, and having the effect, of substantially curtailing a publication's circulation.[40]

Nevertheless, the facts of *Keene* suggest that the government may employ a wide variety of tactics that can have the effect of discouraging speech. In this regard, official investigations historically have served as an effective means of "off the books" censorship. Although the courts generally accord broad deference to such investigations, there are constitutional limits to government inquiries. The issue typically arose in cases involving investigations of subversive activities in which the government's investigative power was upheld. In *Barenblatt v. United States*, for example, the Supreme Court held that there was no First Amendment right to refuse to testify before the House Committee on Un–American Activities.[41] In the circumstances presented in that case, the Court held that the legitimate congressional inquiry outweighed the free speech interest involved.[42]

Although the Court typically has upheld the ability to investigate, it also has made clear that "[n]o inquiry is an end in itself; it must be related to, and in furtherance of, a legitimate task of the Congress." Moreover, "[i]nvestigations conducted solely for the personal aggrandizement of the investigators or to 'punish' those investigated are indefensible."[43] Thus, the Court generally requires that investigations be conducted in pursuit of a legitimate legislative objective and within the scope of a valid authorizing resolution.[44] There must be a substantial relation between the governmental interest and the inquiry and the interest must outweigh the First Amendment interests involved. In *Watkins v. United States*, for example, the Court struck down a contempt of

37. *Id.* at 473, 107 S.Ct. at 1867, 95 L.Ed.2d at 424.

38. *Id.* at 479 n. 14, 107 S.Ct. at 1870 n. 14, 95 L.Ed.2d at 428 n. 14.

39. *Id.* at 484, 107 S.Ct. at 1873, 95 L.Ed.2d at 431. The Court expressly disavowed any decision on "the permissible scope of Congress' right to speak.'"

40. *E.g.,* Bullfrog Films, Inc. v. Wick, 847 F.2d 502, 509–514 (9th Cir.1988) (USIA procedures are constitutionally infirm when administered so as to suppress speech).

41. 360 U.S. 109, 79 S.Ct. 1081, 3 L.Ed.2d 1115 (1959).

42. *Id.* at 126–28, 79 S. Ct. at 1092–94, 3 L. Ed. 2d at 1128–30. *See also* Uphaus v. Wyman, 360 U.S. 72, 79 S.Ct. 1040, 3 L.Ed.2d 1090 (1959).

43. Watkins v. United States, 354 U.S. 178, 187, 77 S.Ct. 1173, 1179, 1 L.Ed.2d 1273, 1284 (1957).

44. *See* Hentoff v. Ichord, 318 F. Supp. at 1182 ("If a report has no relationship to any existing or future proper legislative purpose and is issued solely for sake of exposure or intimidation, then it exceeds the legislative function of Congress.").

Congress conviction on the argument that a vague authorizing resolution deprived Watkins of due process.[45] The Court has also stressed that "an essential prerequisite to the validity of an investigation which intrudes into the area of constitutionally protected rights of speech, press, association and petition [is] that the State convincingly show a substantial relation between the information sought and a subject of overriding and compelling state interest."[46] Under this requirement, the Court invalidated a state legislative committee's attempts to inquire into NAACP membership lists in order to ferret out suspected communists.[47]

To whatever extent such constitutional safeguards have been speech-protective, their effectiveness has depended on the scope of appropriate congressional concern. Where legislative power is more expansive, the ability to conduct investigations similarly is enlarged. Consequently, Congress has greater power to inquire into the content of the electronic media, which are subject to more intrusive regulations than traditional publishers.

Like the congressional concern with subversive speech in the 1950s and early 60s, legislative interest in broadcast programming has generated a number of hearings over the years. Through its power to investigate purported abuses, Congress has examined numerous broadcast practices including the content of various network documentaries, news coverage of the 1968 Democratic National Convention, violent and sexually-oriented programs, coverage of Olympic games and the broadcast of election projections.[48] Such investigations often have taken place without regard to any apparent connection to legislative action. In fact, "congressional committees have often investigated individual programs with the apparent purpose of publicly castigating broadcasters rather than to enact legislation."[49] Given the extent of government control over broadcast licensing, such inquiries have led broadcasters to alter their programming.[50] Consequently, "few doubt that congressional investigations

45. Watkins v. United States, 354 U.S. at 209, 77 S. Ct. at 1190, 1 L. Ed. 2d at 1296.

46. Gibson v. Florida Legislative Investigation Comm., 372 U.S. 539, 546, 83 S.Ct. 889, 893–94, 9 L.Ed.2d 929, 935 (1963). *Cf.* Deutch v. United States, 367 U.S. 456, 467–68, 81 S.Ct. 1587, 1593, 6 L.Ed.2d 963, 971–72 (1961) (inquiry must also be "pertinent" to statutory mandate).

47. 372 U.S. at 557–58, 83 S.Ct. at 899–900, 9 L.Ed.2d at 942.

48. *See generally* Timothy B. Dyk and Ralph E. Goldberg, *The First Amendment and Congressional Investigations of Broadcast Programming*, 111 J. Law & Politics, 625, 630–31 (1987).

49. *Id.*

50. The so-called "family viewing policy," which ultimately was invalidated in court, arose from a report of the House Appropriations Committee that required the FCC to outline the ways in which it would deal with violent and sexually-oriented programming. *Id.* at 636. *See* Writers Guild of America West, Inc. v. FCC, 423 F.Supp. 1064 (C.D.Cal.1976), *rev'd on other grounds sub nom.* Writers Guild of America West, Inc. v. ABC, Inc., 609 F.2d 355 (9th Cir.1979), cert. denied, 449 U.S. 824, 101 S.Ct. 85, 66 L.Ed.2d 27 (1980). Curiously, the District Court was more concerned about FCC than congressional pressure to adopt the policy. 423 F. Supp. at 1145 n.136.

The major networks also limited their use of exit polling during election news reports to accommodate congressional concerns. Dyk and Goldberg, *supra* note 49, at 635–36 n.48.

have a significant impact on broadcasters."[51]

In addition to the "stick" of occasional investigations, government may also hold out the "carrot" of various benefits to keep regulated industries in line. In 1994, Congressman Edward Markey informed industry witnesses at congressional hearings that broadcasters would be unlikely to receive favorable consideration in legislation to reform communications infrastructure unless the industry supported his "V-chip" proposal.[52] He has described broadcasting regulation as a "social compact" based on an explicit "quid pro quo."[53] As the Telecommunications Act of 1996 was being formulated, Congressman Markey emphasized that any effort to review restrictions on broadcast ownership must "affirmatively address both halves of the social compact" and include a strengthening of children's TV programming rules, violence limits and a greater commitment to minority programming.[54]

G. Abridging the Freedom of Silence

The Supreme Court first expressly recognized a First Amendment freedom from compelled expression in *West Virginia State Board of Education v. Barnette*, holding that school children could not be forced to salute the flag and recite the pledge of allegiance.[55] Justice Jackson's plurality opinion contained the quintessential statement of this right:

> If there is any fixed star in our constitutional constellation, it is that no official, high or petty, can prescribe what shall be orthodox in politics, nationalism, religion, or other matters of opinion or force citizens to confess by word or act their faith therein. If there are any circumstances which permit an exception, they do not now occur to us.[56]

51. Dyk and Goldberg, *supra* note 49 at 638. *See also* David L. Bazelon, *FCC Regulation of the Telecommunications Press*, 1975 Duke L. J. 213, 215–17 (detailing the effectiveness of informal content controls in the case of broadcasting).

52. *See* Communications Daily, Feb. 3, 1994 at 1–2 (Congressman Markey reportedly told McGraw–Hill Broadcasting President Edward Reilly that it is "difficult for broadcasters to claim that they will use the new spectrum for the public interest when they are unwilling to use a scintilla of spectrum for V-chips.")

53. Remarks of Rep. Edward Markey, Chairman, Subcommittee on Telecommunications and Finance, Broadcasting/Cable Interface VIII (Omni Shoreham Hote, Washington, D.C., October 4, 1994)

54. *Id.*

55. 319 U.S. 624, 63 S.Ct. 1178, 87 L.Ed. 1628 (1943). The Court previously had invalidated certain compulsory oaths on other grounds. *E.g.*, Ex Parte Garland, 71 U.S. (4 Wall) 333, 18 L. Ed. 366 (1866); Cummings v. Missouri, 71 U.S. (4 Wall)

277, 18 L.Ed. 356 (1866). But the Court on several occasions upheld flag salute laws, including a decision only three years before *Barnette*. *See* Minersville School Dist. v. Gobitis, 310 U.S. 586, 60 S.Ct. 1010, 84 L.Ed. 1375 (1940). *See also* Gabrielli v. Knickerbocker, 306 U.S. 621, 59 S.Ct. 786, 83 L.Ed. 1026 (1939) (per curiam); Johnson v. Deerfield, 306 U.S. 621, 59 S.Ct. 791, 83 L.Ed. 1027 (1939) (per curiam); Hering v. State Bd. of Educ., 303 U.S. 624, 58 S.Ct. 752, 82 L.Ed. 1087 (1938) (per curiam); Leoles v. Landers, 302 U.S. 656, 58 S.Ct. 364, 82 L.Ed. 507 (1937) (per curiam).

56. Barnette, 319 U.S. at 642, 63 S. Ct. at 1187, 87 L. Ed .. at 1639. In his concurring opinion, Justice Murphy acknowledged that individuals may be forced to speak "in so far as essential operations of government may require it for the preservation of an orderly society,—as in the case of compulsion to give evidence in court." *Id.* at 645, 63 S. Ct. at 1189, 87 L. Ed. at 1641. *Accord:* Branzburg v. Hayes, 408 U.S. 665, 92 S.Ct. 2646, 33 L.Ed.2d 626 (1972). Also, in the context of commercial speech, the govern-

The twin values underlying this statement of constitutional law include a tolerance for dissent as a means of promoting democracy and an interest in individual self-realization.

Since *Barnette*, the prohibition of compelled speech has become an established aspect of First Amendment jurisprudence in various contexts. The clearest statement of the principle in a case involving individual speech came in *Wooley v. Maynard*, in which the Court held that the State of New Hampshire could not compel a person to display the state motto on his automobile license plates.[57] In *Wooley*, a Jehovah's Witness who argued that the state motto, "Live Free or Die," was repugnant to his religious beliefs was arrested and jailed for covering the slogan on his license plates. The Supreme Court invalidated the conviction on the theory that "[t]he right to speak and the right to refrain from speaking are complementary components of the broader concept of 'individual freedom of mind.' "[58] As the Court viewed the issue, the government had not advanced an interest sufficient to justify compelling an individual to use his private property "as a 'mobile billboard' for the State's ideological message."[59] The asserted interest of promoting "appreciation of history, individualism, and state pride" was not "ideologically neutral," according to the Court, and the law was too broad to serve the interest in facilitating the identification of automobiles.[60] Accordingly, the Court found that the state law "invades the sphere of intellect and spirit which it is the purpose of the First Amendment to our Constitution to reserve from all official control."[61]

H. *Abridging Privacy and Anonymity of Speech*

A closely related concept to the right to refrain from speaking is the freedom to engage in private or anonymous speech. This constitutional protection stems from the nexus of free speech rights and the right of individual privacy. The First, Fourth and Fifth Amendments to the United States Constitution to a certain degree are all predicated on protecting individual privacy from governmental intrusion. The First Amendment guarantees that the government may not abridge freedom of speech, or of the press; the Fourth Amendment prohibits unreasonable searches or seizures, including those relating to a person's papers;[62]

---

ment can require the disclosure of factual information. *E.g.*, Zauderer v. Disciplinary Council, 471 U.S. 626, 105 S.Ct. 2265, 85 L.Ed.2d 652 (1985). *See also* Glickman v. Wileman Bros. & Elliott, Inc., 521 U.S. 457, 117 S.Ct. 2130, 138 L.Ed.2d 585 (1997) (fruit growers may be required to contribute to generic advertising programs as part of USDA marketing order).

57. 430 U.S. 705, 716, 97 S.Ct. 1428, 1436, 51 L.Ed.2d 752, 763–64 (1977).

58. *Id.* at 714, 97 S.Ct. at 1435, 51 L.Ed.2d at 762, (*quoting Barnette*, 319 U.S. at 637, 63 S.Ct. at 1185, 87 L.Ed. at 1637).

59. *Id.* at 715, 97 S.Ct. at 1435, 51 L.Ed.2d at 763.

60. *Id.* at 716–17, 97 S.Ct. at 1436, 51 L.Ed.2d at 763–64.

61. *Id.* at 715, 97 S.Ct. at 1435, 51 L.Ed.2d at 762–763, (*quoting Barnette*, 319 U.S. at 642, 63 S.Ct. at 1187, 87 L. Ed at 1640).

62. The Fourth Amendment provides: "The right of the people to be secure in their persons, houses, papers, and effects, against unreasonable searches and seizures, shall not be violated, and no Warrants shall issue, but upon probable cause, supported by Oath or affirmation, and particularly describing the place to be searched, and the persons or things to be seized." U.S. Const., amend. IV.

and the Fifth Amendment protects individuals against government-coerced self-incrimination.[63]

Early Fourth Amendment cases emphasized the conceptual connection between the amendments. In *Boyd v. United States*, for example, the Supreme Court struck down a U.S. customs law that required a person to produce in court his private books, papers or invoices or else government allegations would be taken as confessed.[64] In a thoughtful historical review, the Court traced the practice of issuing general warrants to the Star Chamber, which would search a suspects' papers for evidence of seditious libel. It discussed the case of John Wilkes, publisher of the North Briton, whose house was searched pursuant to a general warrant, and his books and papers indiscriminately seized to support a libel allegation. Such events "were fresh in the memories of those who achieved our independence and established our form of government."[65] Indeed, the Court found that the prohibition of such "grievous abuses" and "outrage[s]" provided by the Bill of Rights represented "the true and ultimate expression of constitutional law" and constituted "the very essence of constitutional liberty and security."[66] It stressed that "extorting the party's oath, or compelling the production of his private books and papers, to convict him of crime ... is contrary to the principles of a free government. It is abhorrent to the instincts of an ... American. It may suit the purposes of despotic power, but it cannot abide the pure atmosphere of political liberty and personal freedom."[67] In protecting such interests, the Court found that "the fourth and fifth amendments run almost into each other."[68]

Another early case, *Ex Parte Jackson*, established the principle that the Fourth Amendment protection for papers did not require that they be physically located in a person's home. Rather, "[t]he constitutional guaranty of the right of people to be secure in their papers against unreasonable searches and seizures extends to their papers, thus closed against inspection, wherever they may be" such as "in the mail."[69] As in *Boyd*, the connection to First Amendment concerns was close to the surface. The Court discussed the attempt by President Andrew Jackson to exclude from the mails "incendiary publications" in the southern states, and concluded in dictum that such a measure would "more effectively control the freedom of the press than any sedition law,

63. The Fifth Amendment provides, in relevant part, that "No person ... shall be compelled in a criminal case to be a witness against himself...." U.S. Const., amend. V.

64. 116 U.S. 616, 6 S.Ct. 524, 29 L.Ed. 746 (1886).

65. *Id.* at 625, 6 S. Ct. at 529, 29 L. Ed. at 749.

66. *Id.* at 625–26, 630, 6 S. Ct. at 530–32, 29 L. Ed. at 749.

67. *Id.* at 631–32, 6 S. Ct. at 533, 29 L. Ed. at 749.

68. *Id.* at 630, 6 S.Ct. at 532, 29 L. Ed. at 751. *See* Marcus v. Search Warrant, 367 U.S. 717, 81 S.Ct. 1708, 6 L.Ed.2d 1127 (1961) (describing historical connections between First, Fourth and Fifth Amendments).

69. 96 U.S. 727, 733, 6 Otto 727, 24 L.Ed. 877, 879 (1877). In this case, however, the Court, upheld a prohibition on mailing lottery advertisements.

however severe its penalties.''[70]

The Constitution's framers well understood the connection between privacy and freedom of speech, for it was a part of their day to day routine. Thomas Jefferson and James Madison corresponded with one another over a sixty-year period, exchanging views on politics, philosophy and constitutional theory. "Sometimes they wrote in code (later deciphered) so thoughts they exchanged would not fall into the hands of political foes."[71] Benjamin Franklin wrote under a variety of different pseudonyms.[72] Before the American Revolution, colonial patriots frequently concealed their authorship or circulation of literature to avoid reprisals by English-controlled courts.[73] The Letters of Junius, opposing the tea tax and other oppressive measures, were written anonymously "and the identity of their author is unknown to this day."[74] Similarly, some of Thomas Paine's pamphlets were written under pseudonyms.[75] After the Revolution, the Federalist Papers, debating the merits of the Constitution, were published pseudonymously,[76] as were many of the important political documents of that period.

Far from representing an abuse of freedom of speech, anonymity is part of "an honorable tradition of advocacy and dissent" that "exemplifies the purpose behind the Bill of Rights and the First Amendment in particular."[77] Indeed, the Court has pointed out that anonymous speech is part of a "respected tradition" in our political history, with a notable example being the right to cast secret ballots in elections.[78] The First Amendment interest in anonymous speech is not restricted to the political context, however, and the Court has noted that an author may wish to conceal his or her identity for various reasons, such as avoiding social ostracism, economic or official retaliation, or by a simple desire to maintain privacy. Or an author may believe that writings are more persuasive when readers are unaware of the writer's identity.[79] The Court added that "[g]reat works of literature have frequently been produced by authors writing under assumed names."[80] The Supreme Court has long considered individual privacy to be a core element of freedom of speech.

70. *Id.* at 734, 24 L. Ed. at 879–80 (*quoting* Senator Calhoun).

71. Alan Pell Crawford, *Founding Fathers' Forum*, Wall Street Journal, Feb. 2, 1995 at A16. *See generally,* John A. Fraser, III, The Use of Encrypted, Coded and Secret Communications is an "Ancient Liberty" protected by the United States Constitution, 2 Va.J.L. & Tech 2 (1997).

72. McIntyre v. Ohio Elections Comm'n, 514 U.S. 334, 341, 115 S.Ct. 1511, 1516 n. 4, 131 L.Ed.2d 426, 436, n. 4 (1995).

73. Talley v. California, 362 U.S. 60, 65, 80 S.Ct. 536, 539, 4 L.Ed.2d 559, 562 (1960).

74. *Id.*

75. *Id.* at 63 n.3, 80 S.Ct. at 538, 4 L.Ed.2d at 562 n.3.

76. *Id.* at 65, 80 S.Ct. at 539, 4 L.Ed.2d at 563. *See also* McIntyre, 514 U.S. at 334, 115 S.Ct. at 1517 n.6, 131 L.Ed.2d at 437 n.6 (citing additional examples).

77. McIntyre, 514 U.S. at 357, 115 S.Ct. at 1524, 131 L.Ed.2d at 446.

78. *Id.* at 343, 115 S.Ct. at 1517, 131 L.Ed.2d at 437.

79. *Id.*

80. *Id.* at 341, 115 S.Ct. at 1516, 131 L.Ed.2d at 436.

Accordingly, it has expressly upheld a First Amendment right to engage in anonymous speech. In *McIntyre v. Ohio Elections Commission*, the Court invalidated a state campaign law that prohibited the distribution of anonymous campaign literature.[81] The petitioner had been fined $100 for distributing unsigned pamphlets opposing a school tax referendum, and the Ohio Supreme Court upheld the sanction, reasoning that the law was intended to deter false statements made during elections.[82] The United States Supreme Court, however, found that neither the state's interest in providing voters with additional information, nor its concern about preventing libel of false statements justified compelling a writer to make "disclosures she would otherwise omit."[83] Similarly, in *Talley v. California*, the Court held that the First Amendment protects the distribution of unsigned handbills urging a boycott of specified merchants who were allegedly engaging in discriminatory employment practices.[84] The Court pointed out that "[p]ersecuted groups and sects from time to time throughout history have been able to criticize oppressive practices and laws either anonymously or not at all."[85]

A related line of cases holds that the First Amendment bars the government from prescribing an official language. The Ninth Circuit invalidated a provision of the Arizona Constitution that declared English to be the official state language and which required state employees to use English on the job, although the Supreme Court vacated this decision for mootness after the plaintiff left her state employment.[86] The Ninth Circuit ruling was consistent with Supreme Court precedent from the 1920s in which state statutes prohibiting the teaching or use of foreign languages were struck down. In *Meyer v. Nebraska*[87] and *Bartels v. State of Iowa*,[88] among other cases,[89] the Court held that under constitutional guarantees, use of a common language "cannot be coerced."[90] In particular, the language prohibitions in *Meyer* and *Bartels* had been prompted by the hostilities with Germany in World War I. But the Court held that, despite the "[u]nfortunate experiences during the late war," the asserted state interest in domestic security could not

81. *Id.* at 356–57, 115 S.Ct. at 1523–24, 131 L.Ed.2d at 445–46.

82. *Id.* at 339, 115 S.Ct. at 1514–15, 131 L.Ed.2d at 434–35.

83. *Id.* at 348, 115 S.Ct. at 1520, 131 L.Ed.2d at 441.

84. 362 U.S. 60, 80 S.Ct. 536, 4 L.Ed.2d 559 (1960).

85. *Id.* at 64, 80 S.Ct. at 538, 4 L.Ed.2d at 563.

86. Yniguez v. Arizonans for Official English, 69 F.3d 920 (9th Cir.1995) (en banc), *vacated as moot*, 520 U.S. 43, 117 S.Ct. 1055, 137 L.Ed.2d 170 (1997).

87. 262 U.S. 390, 43 S.Ct. 625, 67 L.Ed. 1042 (1923).

88. 262 U.S. 404, 43 S.Ct. 628, 67 L.Ed. 1047 (1923).

89. Farrington v. Tokushige, 273 U.S. 284, 47 S.Ct. 406, 71 L.Ed. 646 (1927) (restrictive permit requirements for foreign language schools invalidated); Eng v. Trinidad, 271 U.S. 500, 46 S.Ct. 619, 70 L.Ed. 1059 (1926) (prohibition on bookkeeping in Chinese language invalidated).

90. Meyer, 262 U.S. at 401, 43 S. Ct. at 627, 67 L. Ed. at 1046. The Court in *Meyer* and *Tokushige* based their decisions on substantive due process. However, these cases were decided before the development of First Amendment doctrine, and their holdings have since been construed as First Amendment precedent. Yniguez, 69 F.3d at 923, 937.

justify encroachment on fundamental rights.[91]

Following the same principles, the Court has struck down state laws that required members of groups to reveal their identities.[92] The holdings flow from the conclusion that identification of group members and their fear of reprisals might deter discussions of matters of public importance. Such laws, given their inhibitory effect on speech, are generally found to be facially invalid.[93] Similarly, the Court has invalidated the conviction of a labor leader who engaged in organizing activities without first registering and revealing his identity to state authorities;[94] a requirement that teachers file affidavits revealing the organizations to which they belong or contribute;[95] and a requirement that postal patrons reveal their identities in order to receive foreign political propaganda.[96]

I. *Restricting Transmission or Distribution of Speech*

The First Amendment applies not only to the expressive activity of originating a message but also to the circulation and distribution of that communication. Thus, freedom of the press extends beyond the printing press to include distribution along the streets and public ways.[97] In the case of newspapers, courts have held that freedom of the press encompasses distribution by newsboys,[98] delivery vans, and vending machines on public sidewalks.[99] The Supreme Court has noted that " '[l]iberty of circulating is as essential to th[e] freedom [of the press] as liberty of publishing; indeed, without the circulation, the publication would be of little value.' "[100] However, significant questions regarding this "freedom of circulation" relate to its scope and the extent to which it applies to non-print means of distribution.

The basic contours of the right were established in a series of cases involving restrictions on the circulation of leaflets. They established that

91. Meyer, 262 U.S. at 402, 43 S. Ct. at 627, 57 L. Ed. at 1046.

92. Bates v. City of Little Rock, 361 U.S. 516, 80 S.Ct. 412, 4 L.Ed.2d 480 (1960); NAACP v. State of Alabama, 357 U.S. 449, 78 S.Ct. 1163, 2 L.Ed.2d 1488 (1958).

93. Talley, 362 U.S. at 65, 80 S. Ct. at 539, 4 L. Ed. at 563; Lovell v. City of Griffin, 303 U.S. 444, 58 S.Ct. 666, 82 L.Ed. 949 (1938).

94. Thomas v. Collins, 323 U.S. 516, 65 S.Ct. 315, 89 L.Ed. 430 (1945).

95. Shelton v. Tucker, 364 U.S. 479, 81 S.Ct. 247 5 L.Ed.2d 231 (1960).

96. Lamont v. Postmaster General, 381 U.S. 301, 85 S.Ct. 1493, 14 L.Ed.2d 398 (1965).

97. *E.g.*, Martin v. City of Struthers, Ohio, 319 U.S. 141, 146–49, 63 S.Ct. 862, 865–66, 87 L.Ed. 1313, 1318–20 (1943); Ja-

mison v. Texas, 318 U.S. 413, 416, 63 S.Ct. 669, 672, 87 L.Ed. 869, 872–73 (1943); Schneider v. State, 308 U.S. 147, 162–63, 60 S.Ct. 146, 151–52, 84 L.Ed. 155, 164–65 (1939); Lovell v. City of Griffin, 303 U.S. 444, 58 S.Ct. 666, 82 L.Ed. 949 (1938).

98. Ad World, Inc. v. Township of Doylestown, 672 F.2d 1136, 1137–38 (3d Cir.), cert. denied, 456 U.S. 975, 102 S.Ct. 2240, 72 L.Ed.2d 850 (1982); Wulp v. Corcoran, 454 F.2d 826, 834–35 (1st Cir.1972); Strasser v. Doorley, 432 F.2d 567 (1st Cir. 1970).

99. Cincinnati v. Discovery Network, Inc., 507 U.S. 410, 113 S.Ct. 1505, 123 L.Ed.2d 99 (1993); City of Lakewood v. Plain Dealer Publishing Co., 486 U.S. 750, 108 S.Ct. 2138, 100 L.Ed.2d 771 (1988).

100. Lovell v. City of Griffin, 303 U.S. at 452, 58 S. Ct. at 669, 82 L. Ed. at 954, (quoting Ex Parte Jackson, 96 U.S. 727, 733, 6 Otto 727, 24 L.Ed. 877 (1877)).

the government cannot ban the distribution of leaflets,[1] nor subject such activities to permit requirements that leave unfettered discretion in the hands of local officials.[2] Additionally, the right to circulate information cannot by burdened by requiring disclosure of the identity of its author or distributor.[3] Even when the distribution of leaflets may conflict with an individual's interest in privacy, the government may not enjoin the distribution.[4]

Naturally, the freedom to circulate also applies to more traditional members of the press. Courts consider pamphlets and newspapers to be functionally equivalent.[5] Although the Supreme Court has not ruled on whether the First Amendment compels cities to permit distribution of newspapers by newsboxes, it has held that circulation of newspapers is constitutionally protected and that placement of newsboxes cannot be abridged by administratively lax permit schemes.[6] Nor can the government discriminate between newspapers and commercial matter in adopting rules governing newspapers.[7] The Court also has held that booksellers, who do no more than disseminate the speech of others, similarly are protected. In *Smith v. California*, the Court invalidated the obscenity prosecution of a bookseller because the state imposed a burden on the store owner to have affirmative knowledge of every book in his store.[8]

It took longer for the Court to apply the same principles to circulation of information via the United States Mail. The Court initially held that restricting mailing privileges posed no First Amendment problem.[9] It went so far as to uphold mailing restrictions that were directed at suppressing unpopular political opinions and doctrines. In 1921, the Court approved the Postmaster General's discretion to deny second class mailing rates to organizations that violated the espionage laws.[10] In dissent, however, Justice Holmes articulated what eventually became the

---

1. Jamison v. Texas, 318 U.S. 413, 63 S.Ct. 669, 87 L.Ed. 869 (1943); Kim Young v. California, 308 U.S. 147, 60 S.Ct. 146, 84 L.Ed. 155 (1939).

2. Lovell, 303 U.S. at 452; 58 S. Ct. at 669, 82 L. Ed. at 954; Schneider, 308 U.S. at 162–63, 60 S. Ct. at 151–52, 84 L. Ed. at 165–66.

3. Talley v. California, 362 U.S. 60, 64, 80 S.Ct. 536, 538, 4 L.Ed.2d 559, 563 (1960).

4. Organization for a Better Austin v. Keefe, 402 U.S. 415, 418–20, 91 S.Ct. 1575, 1577–78, 29 L.Ed.2d 1, 4–6 (1971).

5. City of Lakewood, 486 U.S. at 761, 108 S.Ct. at 2146, 100 L.Ed.2d at 785–86. *See also* Organization for a Better Austin v. Keefe, 402 U.S. at 419, 91 S.Ct. at 1578, 29 L.Ed.2d at 5.

6. City of Lakewood, 486 U.S. at 762 & n.7, 108 S.Ct. at 2147 & n.7, 100 L.Ed.2d at 786 & n.7. However, the Court noted that "[t]he effectiveness of the newsrack as a means of distribution, especially for low-budget, controversial neighborhood newspapers, means that the twin threats of self-censorship and undetectable censorship are, if anything, greater for newsracks than for pamphleteers." *Id.* at 762, 108 S.Ct. at 2146, 100 L.Ed.2d at 786.

7. City of Cincinnati v. Discovery Network, Inc., 507 U.S. 410, 113 S.Ct. 1505, 123 L.Ed.2d 99 (1993).

8. 361 U.S. 147, 80 S.Ct. 215, 4 L.Ed.2d 205 (1959).

9. In re Rapier, 143 U.S. 110, 12 S.Ct. 374, 36 L.Ed. 93 (1892); Ex parte Jackson, 96 U.S. 727, 6 Otto 727, 24 L.Ed. 877 (1877). *See also* Lewis Publishing Co. v. Morgan, 229 U.S. 288, 33 S.Ct. 867, 57 L.Ed. 1190 (1913) (government may condition lower postal rates for newspapers and magazines on publication of specified information).

10. Milwaukee Social Democratic Pub. Co. v. Burleson, 255 U.S. 407, 41 S.Ct. 352, 65 L.Ed. 704 (1921).

law, urging that "[t]he United States may give up the post office when it sees fit, but while it carries it on the use of the mails is almost as much a part of free speech as the right to use our tongues."[11] The Court gradually moved away from its restrictive position, first by restricting the Postmaster General's discretion to deny special mailing rates.[12] It also invalidated a 1962 law that permitted the mailing of "communist political propaganda" only upon written request by the recipient.[13] The decisions also extended traditional First Amendment procedural protections. Thus, although the government may proscribe the mailing of obscene materials,[14] it may not do so without proper constitutional safeguards.[15]

Not yet settled is the extent to which "freedom of circulation" applies to electronic means of communication. The regulated nature of electronic mass media generally restricts the application of these principles. Thus, there is no unqualified right to circulate speech by means of broadcasting—those who seek to use that medium must first obtain a government license.[16] Similarly, local governments generally require cable television operators to obtain a franchise.[17] In addition to restrictions on entry, the scope of the freedom to circulate appears to be more limited for the electronic media. Broadcasters are held more accountable for the programming they transmit than are booksellers for the books they sell.[18] Moreover, the government has greater latitude to control the dissemination of "offensive" speech transmitted by broadcasting compared to print.[19] On the other hand, courts have found a right to distribute offensive speech by cable television and telephones more comparable to that exercised by traditional publishers.[20] To the extent

---

11. *Id.* at 437, 41 S.Ct. at 363, 65 L. Ed. at 720 (Holmes, J., dissenting). *See* Bolger v. Youngs Drug Products Corp., 463 U.S. 60, 69 n. 18, 103 S.Ct. 2875, 2882 n. 18, 77 L.Ed.2d 469, 479 n. 18 (1983); Blount v. Rizzi, 400 U.S. 410, 416, 91 S.Ct. 423, 428, 27 L.Ed.2d 498, 503 (1971).

12. Hannegan v. Esquire, 327 U.S. 146, 158–59, 66 S.Ct. 456, 463, 90 L.Ed. 586, 593–94 (1946) (Postmaster General denied discretion to determine whether a publication's content meets "standard of the public good or welfare").

13. Lamont v. Postmaster General, 381 U.S. 301, 85 S.Ct. 1493, 14 L.Ed.2d 398 (1965).

14. Roth v. United States, 354 U.S. 476, 77 S.Ct. 1304, 1 L.Ed.2d 1498 (1957).

15. Blount v. Rizzi, 400 U.S. 410 91 S.Ct. 423, 27 L.Ed.2d 498 (1971).

16. NBC v. United States, 319 U.S. 190, 226–27, 63 S.Ct. 997, 1014, 87 L.Ed. 1344, 1368 (1943) ("Unlike other modes of expression, radio inherently is not available to all. That is its unique characteristic, and that is why, unlike other modes of expression, it is subject to governmental regulation. Because it cannot be used by all, some

who wish to use it must be denied. . . . The right of free speech does not include . . . the right to use the facilities of radio without a license."); United States v. Dunifer, 997 F.Supp. 1235 (N.D.Cal.1998).

17. City of Los Angeles v. Preferred Communications, Inc., 476 U.S. 488, 106 S.Ct. 2034, 90 L.Ed.2d 480 (1986); Cable Communications Policy Act of 1984, 47 U.S.C. §§ 521–556 (West 1991).

18. *Compare* Smith v. California, 361 U.S. 147, 80 S.Ct. 215, 4 L.Ed.2d 205 (1959) *with* Yale Broadcasting Co. v. FCC, 478 F.2d 594, 155 U.S. App. D.C. 390 (D.C.Cir.), cert. denied, 414 U.S. 914, 94 S.Ct. 211, 38 L.Ed.2d 152 (1973). The comparison may not be entirely fair, since broadcasters typically perform a more active editorial function than booksellers.

19. *Compare* Bolger v. Youngs Drug Products Corp., 463 U.S. at 74, 103 S. Ct. at 2884, 77 L. Ed. 2d at 482 *with* FCC v. Pacifica Foundation, 438 U.S. 726, 98 S.Ct. 3026, 57 L.Ed.2d 1073 (1978).

20. *See, e.g.,* Sable Communications of California, Inc. v. FCC, 492 U.S. 115, 109 S.Ct. 2829, 106 L.Ed.2d 93 (1989) (ban on

courts persist in applying different First Amendment standards to the various media because of the differing means of transmission, there will continue to be dissonance regarding the scope of the freedom to circulate speech and other information.

1.8   Access to the Channels of Communication

Freedom to circulate information under the First Amendment does not necessarily guarantee access to the channels of communication, whether privately or publicly owned. The problem of access also has led to the emergence of separate bodies of law regarding the government's duty to make public property available for speech activities and its power to compel private parties to do the same with their own property. In general, the government is required to facilitate speech on public land that is considered a public forum, either by tradition or designation. By contrast, private property normally is protected from the demands of third parties who wish to engage in expressive activities, except in a few situations. One such exception involves electronic media, where courts have recognized a limited right of access. This section examines the disparate rules relating to access to the channels of communication.

A.   The Elusive Concept of the Public Forum

Unlike the typical free speech question, the main focus of most public forum issues is not whether speech may take place, but where. Although the doctrine has fluctuated over time, the government's greater degree of control over its property often gives it more power to control speech activities that take place on public land, often via laws against trespassing or breach of the peace. Government power is most circumscribed in the traditional public forum—those streets, parks and sidewalks that "have immemorially been held in trust for the use of the public and, time out of mind, have been used for purposes of assembly, communicating thoughts between citizens, and discussing public questions."[1] Where the government creates a forum, it has greater latitude in establishing its scope, including the power to discontinue use of the property for communication. Finally, in non-forum property, the government may adopt any "reasonable" regulation of speech or forbid it altogether.

1.   Evolution of the Public Forum Concept

The complex and often confusing public forum doctrine began with *Hague v. CIO*, in which the Supreme Court struck down a municipal

transmission of indecent speech invalidated); Wilkinson v. Jones, 480 U.S. 926, 107 S.Ct. 1559, 94 L.Ed.2d 753 (1987), *aff'ing mem.* 800 F.2d 989 (10th Cir.1986) (regulation of indecent cable programming invalidated). However, courts have not fully applied the protections available to print media to other technologies. *See* Denver Area Educational Telecommunications Consortium v. FCC, 518 U.S. 727, 116 S.Ct. 2374, 135 L.Ed.2d 888 (1996); Infor-mation Providers' Coalition For the Defense of the First Amendment v. FCC, 928 F.2d 866 (9th Cir.1991); Dial Information Services Corp. v. Thornburgh, 938 F.2d 1535 (2d Cir.1991), cert. denied 502 U.S. 1072, 112 S.Ct. 966, 117 L.Ed.2d 132 (1992).

1.   Hague v. CIO, 307 U.S. 496, 515, 59 S.Ct. 954, 964, 83 L.Ed. 1423, 1436 (1939).

ordinance that banned meetings on public property without a permit.[2] The decision discarded the previous view, that permitted the government to exclude speech from public land the same way "the owner of a private house [may] forbid it in his house."[3] The new doctrine established what might be called a "free speech easement" by which members of the public could demand access to certain public property to exercise their First Amendment rights even though the government exerted ultimate control over the property.[4]

Driven by the civil rights and the anti-Vietnam War movements, the public forum doctrine was at its most expansive in the 1960s and 70s. In *Brown v. Louisiana*, the Supreme Court had to decide whether the public forum doctrine extended to government property that—unlike streets and parks—had not been used "time out of mind" for purposes of speech-making.[5] The case involved a silent protest in the reading room of a segregated public library. Five black men stood and sat as "monuments of protest" until they were arrested, and ultimately convicted, for violating the state's breach-of-the-peace statute. The Court struck down the convictions for being outside the scope of the law. In addition, Justice Fortas, joined by Chief Justice Warren and Justice Douglas, suggested that the statute could not constitutionally punish a "peaceable and orderly ... protest ... in a place where the protestant has every right to be."[6] The analysis did not gain majority support, but nevertheless was an "important first step" toward recognition that the public forum doctrine could extend to public property that was not historically associated with this type of First Amendment activity.[7]

The majority view of the public forum issue prevailed in *Adderley v. Florida*, in which the Court upheld the trespass convictions of students who had conducted a peaceful demonstration on the grounds of a county jail.[8] Writing for the 5–4 majority, Justice Black pointed out that "[t]he State, no less than a private owner of property, has power to preserve the property under its control for the use to which it is lawfully dedicated."[9] The opinion harkened back to the pre-*Hague* notion that permitted the government to curtail speech on public property the same way "the owner of a private house [may] forbid it in his house."[10] In this

---

2. *Id*. The plurality "public forum" dictum in *Hague* was affirmed by the Court in subsequent cases. *See* Jamison v. Texas, 318 U.S. 413, 63 S.Ct. 669, 87 L.Ed. 869 (1943); Cox v. New Hampshire, 312 U.S. 569, 61 S.Ct. 762, 85 L.Ed. 1049 (1941); Schneider v. New Jersey, 308 U.S. 147, 60 S.Ct. 146, 84 L.Ed. 155 (1939). This area of law was first labeled the public forum doctrine in Harry Kalven Jr., *The Concept of the Public Forum: Cox v. Louisiana*, 1965 Sup. Ct. Rev. 1.

3. Commonwealth v. Davis, 162 Mass. 510, 511, 39 N.E. 113 (1895) (Holmes, J.), *aff'd sub nom*. Davis v. Massachusetts, 167 U.S. 43, 17 S.Ct. 731, 42 L.Ed. 71 (1897).

4. *See* Kalven, *supra* n.2, at 13.

5. 383 U.S. 131, 86 S.Ct. 719, 15 L.Ed.2d 637 (1966).

6. *Id*. at 142, 86 S. Ct. at 724, 15 L. Ed. 2d at 645.

7. Geoffrey R. Stone, *Fora Americana: Speech in Public Places*, 1974 Sup. Ct. Rev. 233, 247.

8. 385 U.S. 39, 87 S.Ct. 242, 17 L.Ed.2d 149 (1966).

9. *Id*. at 47, 87 S. Ct. at 247, 17 L. Ed. 2d at 156.

10. Commonwealth v. Davis, 162 Mass. 510, 511, 39 N.E. 113 (1895) (Holmes, J.), *aff'd sub nom*. Davis v. Massachusetts, 167 U.S. 43, 17 S.Ct. 731, 42 L.Ed. 71 (1897).

view, only historic usage of public property for speech purposes would create a limited exception to the state's common law property rights.

The four *Adderley* dissenters adopted a far different view of the public forum. In their view, public property should be accessible for speech purposes unless such use interferes with "the uses to which the public property is normally put." Justice Douglas wrote that "[a] noisy meeting may be out of keeping with the serenity of the statehouse or the quiet of the courthouse" and that "[n]o one ... would suggest that the Senate gallery is the proper place for a vociferous protest rally."[11] But where the proposed communicative activity and the public property were not essentially incompatible, the dissenters would have permitted access.[12]

This minority position gained increasing acceptance in a line of cases beginning with *Tinker v. Des Moines Independent Community School District*.[13] By a 7–2 vote, the Court in *Tinker* upheld students' rights to engage in an unobtrusive antiwar protest inside a public high school. Justice Fortas' majority opinion noted that students did not "shed their constitutional rights to freedom of speech or expression at the schoolhouse gate"[14] and that the wearing of black armbands would not interfere with normal school activities. Although the decision was limited to "the special characteristics of the school environment,"[15] it provided substantial support for the "incompatibility theory" of the public forum articulated by Justice Fortas in *Brown* and in the *Adderley* dissent.[16]

The Court more directly embraced the incompatibility approach in *Grayned v. City of Rockford*.[17] There, the Court upheld a municipal ordinance that prohibited making "any noise or diversion" that would tend to disrupt educational activities "while on public or private grounds adjacent to any building in which a school or any class thereof is in session." It found the ordinance to be a reasonable time, place or manner restriction given the nature of the property involved and the type of speech that was restricted, and that "[t]he crucial question is whether the manner of expression is basically incompatible with the normal activity of a particular place at a particular time."[18] "In this passage," according to Professor Geoffrey Stone, "the right to a public forum came of age."[19]

---

11. 385 U.S. at 54, 87 S. Ct. at 250–251, 17 L. Ed. 2d at 159–160 (Douglas, J., dissenting).

12. Justice Douglas was joined by Justices Brennan, Fortas and Chief Justice Warren.

13. 393 U.S. 503, 89 S.Ct. 733, 21 L.Ed.2d 731 (1969).

14. *Id.* at 506, 89 S.Ct. at 736, 21 L.Ed.2d at 737.

15. *Id.*

16. *See* Stone, *supra* note 7, at 250. *See also* Greer v. Spock, 424 U.S. 828, 843, 96

S.Ct. 1211, 1219–1220, 47 L.Ed.2d 505, 517–518 (1976) (Powell, J., concurring).

17. 408 U.S. 104, 92 S.Ct. 2294, 33 L.Ed.2d 222 (1972).

18. *Id.* at 107–108, 116, 92 S.Ct. at 2298, 2303, 33 L.Ed.2d at 227, 232.

19. *See* Stone, *supra* note 7, at 251, 253 ("After years of focusing on the common law property rights of the state, the Court seems finally to have endorsed a comprehensive, intelligible approach to the problem."). *See also* MELVILLE B. NIMMER, FREEDOM OF SPEECH § 4.09[D] (1984) ("It is obvious that the incompatibility standard is more speech-protective.").

But while the *Grayned* approach became the prevailing analysis in public forum cases for a time, it did not lead to a significant expansion of First Amendment access to public property, as some had expected.[20] In the first decision on the subject following *Grayned*, the Court held that advertising space inside municipal buses did not constitute a public forum.[21] In *Lehman v. City of Shaker Heights*, a plurality decided that "[n]o First Amendment forum is here to be found" after examining "the nature of the forum and the conflicting interests involved."[22] In subsequent cases, the Court examined the character of the government property at issue and found that prisons,[23] military bases[24] and residential mail boxes[25] were not public forums. Where it did find a public forum, the Court did not take an expansive view of free speech rights. For example, in *Heffron v. International Society For Krishna Consciousness*, the Court upheld limitations on the distribution or sale of written materials and solicitation of funds at a state fairground as reasonable time, place or manner restrictions.[26] Justice Brennan, however, joined by

---

20. However, some lower courts applied *Grayned* so as to expand public forum access rights. *E.g.*, Chicago Area Military Project v. Chicago, 508 F.2d 921 (7th Cir.), cert. denied, 421 U.S. 992, 95 S.Ct. 1999, 44 L.Ed.2d 483 (1975) (city airport); Albany Welfare Rights Org. v. Wyman, 493 F.2d 1319 (2d Cir.), cert. denied *sub nom.* Lavine v. Albany Welfare Rights Org., 419 U.S. 838, 95 S.Ct. 66, 42 L.Ed.2d 64 (1974) (waiting room of welfare office is public forum for distribution of leaflets); Jeannette Rankin Brigade v. Chief of Capitol Police, 342 F.Supp. 575 (D.D.C.), *summarily aff'd*, 409 U.S. 972, 93 S.Ct. 311, 34 L.Ed.2d 236 (1972) (United States Capitol grounds); Reilly v. Noel, 384 F.Supp. 741 (D.R.I.1974) (courthouse rotunda).

21. Lehman v. City of Shaker Heights, 418 U.S. 298, 94 S.Ct. 2714, 41 L.Ed.2d 770 (1974).

22. *Id.* at 302–304, 94 S.Ct. at 2717–2718, 41 L.Ed.2d at 777–778. The Court found that the predominantly commercial nature of the transit system, plus the fact that passengers were a captive audience, militated against finding that the advertising space in the buses constituted a public forum.

23. Jones v. North Carolina Prisoners' Labor Union, 433 U.S. 119, 97 S.Ct. 2532, 53 L.Ed.2d 629 (1977).

24. Greer v. Spock, 424 U.S. 828, 96 S.Ct. 1211, 47 L.Ed.2d 505. The Court found that "it is ... the business of a military installation like Fort Dix to train soldiers, not to provide a public forum." *Id.* at 838, 96 S.Ct. at 1217, 47 L. Ed. 2d at 514. But while the Court examined the nature of the government property at issue, it did so more from the perspective of the

common law property approach of *Adderley* than the incompatibility analysis of *Grayned. Id.* at 836–38, 96 S.Ct. at 1216–17, 47 L.Ed.2d at 513–14. *But see id.* at 843, 96 S.Ct. at 1220, 47 L.Ed.2d at 517 (Powell, J., concurring) ("Some basic incompatibility must be discerned between the communication and the primary activity of an area."). *Compare with* Flower v. United States, 407 U.S. 197, 198, 92 S.Ct. 1842, 1843, 32 L.Ed.2d 653, 655–56 (1972) (per curiam) (First Amendment supports distribution of leaflets on military base where "the military has abandoned any claim that it has special interests in who walks, talks, or distributes leaflets on the avenue.").

25. United States Postal Service v. Council of Greenburgh Civic Ass'ns, 453 U.S. 114, 131 n. 7, 101 S.Ct. 2676, 2686 n. 7, 69 L.Ed.2d 517, 531 n. 7 (1981) ("What we hold is the principle reiterated by cases such as *Adderley v. Florida* ... and *Greer v. Spock* ... that property owned or controlled by the government which is *not* a public forum may be subject to a prohibition of speech, leafleting, picketing, or other forms of communication without running afoul of the First Amendment.") (citations omitted, emphasis in original).

26. 452 U.S. 640, 101 S.Ct. 2559, 69 L.Ed.2d 298 (1981). The Court distinguished the open space on a street from the more congested situation on a fairground and found that a rule confining leafleting and solicitation to a designated booth served the government's interest in safety and crowd control. The Court expressly relied on *Grayned* in its analysis. *Id.* at 650–51, 101 S.Ct. at 2565–66, 69 L.Ed.2d at 307–08.

Justices Marshall, Stevens and Blackmun, would have allowed the unrestricted distribution of literature, and disputed the majority's contention that respondents' desired " 'manner of expression is basically incompatible with the normal activity' of the fair."[27]

United States v. Grace[28] is another example of the Court's inclination to limit sharply its public forum analysis. There, the Court allowed a facial challenge to a federal statute that prohibited the display of "any flag, banner or device designed or adapted to bring into public notice any party, organization, or movement" in the United States Supreme Court building or on its grounds.[29] Generally considered to be a speech-protective decision, *Grace* invalidated the provision as it related to the sidewalks surrounding the Court. It found that sidewalks are part of the traditional public forum and could "discern no reason why [those adjacent to the Court] should be treated any differently . . . from any other sidewalks in Washington, D.C."[30] But the decision left intact the government's authority to arrest any speaker who took one step from the sidewalk onto the Court's "plaza and surrounding promenade, lawn area and steps." In a partial dissent, Justice Marshall criticized the Court's "piecemeal" approach, noting that the law "proscribes even the handing out of a leaflet and, presumably, the wearing of a campaign button" anywhere on the Court grounds. Such an expansive prohibition, he wrote, goes beyond "conduct that is incompatible with the primary activity being carried out in this Court." Accordingly, Justice Marshall would have invalidated the entire provision.[31]

As decisions such as *Grace* and *Heffron* suggest, the Court was uncomfortable with the "incompatibility" theory articulated in *Grayned*. Although *Grayned* remains good law, the view that First Amendment presumptively accords access to government-controlled property absent a showing of incompatibility did not command majority support. The Court has made clear in various opinions that it could not accept the logical extension of the incompatibility theory—that "display cases in public hospitals, libraries, office buildings, military compounds, and other public facilities immediately would become Hyde Parks open to every would-be pamphleteer and politician."[32] At the same time, the

---

27. *Id.* at 658 n.2, 101 S.Ct. at 2569 n.2, 69 L.Ed.2d at 313 n.2 (Brennan, J., dissenting in part) ("Despite the Court's suggestion to the contrary . . . a fair is surely a 'natural and proper plac[e] for the dissemination of information and opinion.' ") (citations omitted). *See id.* at 664, 101 S.Ct. at 2572–73 69 L.Ed.2d at 317 (Blackmun, J., dissenting in part).

28. 461 U.S. 171, 103 S.Ct. 1702, 75 L.Ed.2d 736 (1983).

29. *Id.* at 173, 103 S.Ct. at 1703, 75 L.Ed.2d at 741.

30. *Id.* at 179, 103 S.Ct. at 1708, 75 L.Ed.2d at 745.

31. *Id.* at 179, 186, 103 S.Ct. at 1708, 1711, 75 L.Ed.2d at 745, 749. (Marshall, J., dissenting in part). Justice Stevens concurred in part and dissented in part because he believed that neither of the appellees violated the statute. *Id.* at 188–89, 103 S.Ct. at 1713, 75 L.Ed.2d at 751.

32. Lehman, 418 U.S. at 304, 94 S.Ct. at 2718, 41 L.Ed.2d at 778; Perry Education Ass'n v. Perry Local Educators' Ass'n, 460 U.S. 37, 49–52 n. 9, 103 S.Ct. 948, 957–58 n. 9, 74 L.Ed.2d 794, 807–08 n. 9 (1983); United States Postal Service v. Council of Greenburgh Civic Ass'ns, 453 U.S. at 130 n.6, 101 S.Ct. at 2685–86 n.6, 69 L.Ed.2d at 530 n.6.

Court was reluctant to re-impose a rigid common law property rights approach, where the only property to which access was guaranteed was streets, sidewalks and parks. This tension led the Court to rethink its approach to the public forum.

Consequently, in *Perry Education Association v. Perry Local Educators' Association*,[33] the Court developed a new analytic framework by which to examine public forum issues. *Perry* involved the question of differential access by rival teachers' unions to a school system's internal mail system. The designated bargaining agent, Perry Education Association, was granted exclusive access to the mail system as part of its collective bargaining agreement. The challenger, Perry Local Educators' Association, previously had access to the mail system but was cut off when PEA was chosen as the exclusive bargaining agent. The situation made it impossible for the Court to conclude that the school mail system was "basically incompatible" with the intended communication. Not only had PLEA had access to the system before the union election, but teachers were allowed to send personal messages and certain outside groups, including parochial schools, church groups, YMCAs and scout units had been allowed access by various school principals.[34] Despite the character of the property involved, the Court upheld the denial of access to PLEA by establishing a new approach to analyzing public forum questions.

Upon review of earlier cases, the Court found that government property falls into one of three forum categories: "quintessential" or traditional public forums, designated public forums, and nonpublic forums.[35] The category applied to the property in question determines the level of access that the government must permit as well as its ability to restrict speech. Thus, in *Perry*, the Court found that the interschool mail system was a nonpublic forum, and that the school district could "without further justification—restrict use to those who participate in the forum's official business."[36] Such limitations were permissible, according to the Court, so long as they were "reasonable and not an effort to suppress expression merely because public officials oppose the speaker's view."[37]

The three forum categories articulated in *Perry* have become the prevailing constructs for analyzing First Amendment cases involving access to government property. Indeed, the Court has even revised its view of earlier public forum cases to comport with the analysis first set

---

33. 460 U.S. 37, 103 S.Ct. 948, 74 L.Ed.2d 794 (1983).

34. *See id.* at 39 n.2, 103 S.Ct. at 952 n.2, 74 L.Ed.2d at 801 n.2.

35. *Id.* at 45–47, 103 S. Ct. at 954–55, 74 L. Ed. 2d at 804–05.

36. *Id.* at 53, 103 S.Ct. at 959, 74 L.Ed.2d at 809. The Court held that selective access to the mail system by outside groups, such as civic or church organizations, did not transform the property into a public forum because access was not granted "as a matter of course to all who [sought] to distribute material." *Id.* at 47, 103 S. Ct. at 956, 74 L. Ed. 2d at 806. Moreover, PLEA's previous right of access was not dispositive because PLEA's status changed once it no longer was a designated collective bargaining agent. *Id.* at 48, 103 S.Ct. at 956–57, 74 L.Ed.2d at 807.

37. *Id.* at 46, 103 S. Ct. at 955, 74 L. Ed. 2d at 805.

out in *Perry*.[38] But while this approach repudiates the Court's more liberal "incompatibility" analysis, it does not mark a return to the pre-public forum common law concept. Dictum in current public forum cases suggests that the government may restrict the use of property under its control "no less than a private owner of property."[39] Yet even in the nonpublic forum, denial of access implicates constitutional interests and certain conditions restrict governmental authority that do not similarly bind a private landowner. For example, speech restrictions must be "reasonable," as evidenced by ample alternative channels of communication, and cannot be intended to suppress a particular speaker's viewpoint.[40] Moreover, there must be a substantial governmental interest to support speech limits.[41] In contrast, a private landowner need not demonstrate a significant private interest in order to eject a speaker, nor need his actions be reasonable or non-discriminatory.[42]

Nevertheless, the current manifestation of the public forum doctrine is less speech-protective than it was when it took root. It may be doubtful, for example, that the Court would now permit a silent protest in a public library, as it did in *Brown v. Louisiana*. Indeed, the United States Court of Appeals for the Third Circuit used a *Perry*-type analysis to uphold library regulations that authorized expulsion of troublesome patrons.[43] The library had expelled a homeless man, who was a frequent visitor, for violating newly-adopted guidelines regarding loitering, annoying behavior, such as staring at other patrons and requirements regarding personal hygiene.[44] The court found that the library was a designated public forum for limited purposes, but upheld the user guidelines as

38. *See* Kreimer v. Bureau of Police for the Town of Morristown, 958 F.2d 1242, 1256 n. 10 (3d Cir.1992) ("To place its jurisprudence within a consistent frame, the Court in its later decisions has placed its pre-*Perry* decisions within *Perry*'s framework.").

39. Perry, 460 U.S. at 46, 103 S.Ct. at 955, 74 L.Ed.2d at 805 (citations omitted).

40. *Id.* at 46, 53, 103 S.Ct. at 955, 74 L.Ed.2d at 805.

41. *Id.* at 50–55, 103 S.Ct. at 958–960, 74 L.Ed.2d at 808–811.

42. *See* United States v. Kokinda, 497 U.S. 720, 725–26, 110 S.Ct. 3115, 3119, 111 L.Ed.2d 571, 581 (1990) ("The Government, even when acting in its proprietary capacity, does not enjoy absolute freedom from First Amendment constraints, as does a private business, but its action is valid ... unless it is unreasonable, or ... arbitrary, capricious, or invidious.") (citation omitted). *See also* Board of Airport Comm'rs v. Jews for Jesus, Inc., 482 U.S. 569, 107 S.Ct. 2568, 96 L.Ed.2d 500 (1987) (rule prohibiting "all First Amendment activities" in airport terminal invalidated).

43. Kreimer v. Bureau of Police for the Town of Morristown, 958 F.2d 1242 (3d

Cir.1992). The Supreme Court confirmed its less expensive approach to public forum analysis in *International Society for Krishna Consciousness v. Lee*, 505 U.S. 672, 112 S.Ct. 2711, 120 L.Ed.2d 541 (1992). However, the divergent opinions also indicated that the "incompatibility analysis" in public forum cases still finds support among a substantial minority of Justices. *See id.* at 697–98, 112 S.Ct. at 2717–18, 120 L.Ed.2d at 562–63 (Kennedy, J., joined by Justices Blackmun, Stevens and Souter, concurring) ("[T]he policies underlying the doctrine cannot be given effect unless we recognize that open, public spaces and thoroughfares which are suitable for discourse may be public forums, whatever their historical pedigree and without concern for a precise classification of the property.... If the objective, physical characteristics of the property at issue and the actual public access and uses which have been permitted by the government indicate that expressive activity would be appropriate and compatible with those uses, the property is a public forum.").

44. Kreimer, 958 F.2d at 1247.

reasonable rules governing the manner of its use. In doing so, it rejected an overbreadth challenge concluding that the rules "do not reach a substantial amount of activity which would be constitutionally protected in the Library." Yet the court acknowledged that "[i]t is conceivable that one engaged in silent protest, an activity protected under the First Amendment, could be required to cease protesting or leave the Library."[45]

The public forum doctrine has not come full circle to its common law origins, but the pendulum has swung back toward greater limits on access to government property. Except in the traditional public forum, governmental restrictions on access are presumptively valid, unless the government has acted affirmatively to designate the property for expressive purposes. Even if it has done so, the analysis set out in *Perry*, and extended in subsequent cases, will tolerate more restrictions on regulation of speech. The following subsection examines the three forum categories and describes the substantive constitutional standard governing each.

2. *Public Forum Categories*

a. *The traditional forum*

The "quintessential" public forum, as designated by the Court in *Perry*, appears to comprise those streets and parks (and sidewalks) that "have immemorially been held in trust ... for purposes of assembly, communicating thoughts between citizens, and discussing public questions."[46] Such places occupy a "special position in terms of First Amendment protection" in which the government's ability to restrict expressive activity "is very limited."[47] Also limited, however, are the types of property accorded such status.

The Supreme Court has restricted the traditional forum designation to public property that has as "a principal purpose ... the free exchange of ideas" as shown by a long-standing historical practice of permitting speech.[48] The Court has expressly found that public streets,[49] sidewalks[50] and parks[51] are traditional fora, but it is not certain that any other types

---

45. *Id*. at 1265–66 & n.30. The court also attempted to distinguish *Brown v. Louisiana* on its facts.

46. Perry, 460 U.S. at 45, 103 S.Ct. at 954–55, 74 L.Ed.2d at 804, (*quoting* Hague v. CIO, 307 U.S. 496, 515, 59 S.Ct. 954, 964, 83 L.Ed. 1423, 1437 (1939)).

47. Grace, 461 U.S. at 177, 180, 103 S.Ct. at 1707–08, 75 L.Ed.2d at 743, 745.

48. International Society for Krishna Consciousness v. Lee, 505 U.S. 672, 679, 112 S.Ct. 2701, 2706, 120 L.Ed.2d 541, 550 (1992) (*quoting* Cornelius v. NAACP Legal Defense and Educ. Fund, Inc., 473 U.S. 788, 800, 105 S.Ct. 3439, 3448, 87 L.Ed.2d 567, 578 (1985)).

49. *E.g.*, Frisby v. Schultz, 487 U.S. 474, 108 S.Ct. 2495, 101 L.Ed.2d 420 (1988); Boos v. Barry, 485 U.S. 312, 108 S.Ct. 1157, 99 L.Ed.2d 333 (1988); Carey v. Brown, 447 U.S. 455, 460, 100 S.Ct. 2286, 2290, 65 L.Ed.2d 263, 269 (1980).

50. Grace, 461 U.S. at 179, 103 S.Ct. at 1708, 75 L.Ed.2d at 745.

51. Ward v. Rock Against Racism, 491 U.S. 781, 798, 109 S.Ct. 2746, 2757, 105 L.Ed.2d 661, 680 (1989); Clark v. Community for Creative Non-Violence, 468 U.S. 288, 104 S.Ct. 3065, 82 L.Ed.2d 221 (1984). *See also* Naturist Society, Inc. v. Fillyaw, 958 F.2d 1515, 1522 (11th Cir.1992); Central Florida Nuclear Freeze Campaign v. Walsh, 774 F.2d 1515, 1523 (11th Cir.1985).

of property would qualify. "If the category of 'traditional public forum' is to be a tool of analysis rather than a conclusory label," according to Justice Scalia, "it must remain faithful to its name and derive its content from *tradition*."[52] Accordingly, the Court held that public airport terminals are not a traditional forum, in part, because of "the lateness with which the modern air terminal has made its appearance."[53] This approach appears to foreclose any expansion of the category.[54]

This does not mean, however, that all streets, all sidewalks or all parks necessarily are public fora. Although it would be difficult to find a park that does not qualify as a traditional forum,[55] some streets and sidewalks are nonpublic fora, since "[t]he mere physical characteristics of the property cannot dictate forum analysis."[56] For example, the Court has held that the streets and sidewalks on a military base are not public fora because they have not "traditionally served as a place for free public assembly and communication of thoughts."[57] Similarly, a substantial minority of the Court held that the sidewalks adjacent to a post office were not a public forum because they did not have "the characteristics of public sidewalks traditionally open to expressive activity."[58] In short, the

52. Burson v. Freeman, 504 U.S. 191, 214, 112 S.Ct. 1846, 1859, 119 L.Ed.2d 5, 24 (1992) (Scalia, J., concurring) (emphasis in original). Ironically, by anchoring the traditional public forum to specific sites historically associated with speech, the Court's approach becomes less analytic and more conclusory. *See* International Society for Krishna Consciousness v. Lee, 505 U.S. 672, 112 S.Ct. 2711, 120 L.Ed.2d 541 (1992) (Kennedy, J., concurring, joined by Blackmun, Stevens and Souter, JJ).

53. International Society for Krishna Consciousness v. Lee, 505 U.S. 672, 680, 112 S.Ct. 2701, 2706, 120 L.Ed.2d 541, 551 (1992). The Court noted as well that airports do not have as their "principal purpose 'promoting the free exchange of ideas.' " But as noted in Justice Kennedy's concurring opinion, "even the quintessential public forums would appear to lack the necessary elements of what the Court defines as a public forum [since] ... 'the principal purpose of streets and sidewalks, like airports, is to facilitate transportation, not public discourse.' " *Id.* at 682, 696–697, 112 S. Ct. at 2707, 2719, 120 L.Ed.2d at 552, 562 (1992) (Kennedy, J., concurring).

54. *Id.* at 695, 112 S. Ct. at 2716, 120 L.Ed.2d at 561 (Kennedy, J., concurring) (The Court's analysis "leaves almost no scope for the development of new public forums.").

55. *E.g.*, Naturist Society, Inc. v. Fillyaw, 958 F.2d at 1522–23 (park, including public beach, is a traditional public forum).

56. United States v. Kokinda, 497 U.S. 720, 727, 110 S.Ct. 3115, 3120, 111 L.Ed.2d 571, 581 (1990).

57. Greer v. Spock, 424 U.S. 828, 838, 96 S.Ct. 1211, 1217, 47 L.Ed.2d 505, 514 (1976). *See also* United States v. Albertini, 472 U.S. 675, 686. 105 S.Ct. 2897, 2905, 86 L.Ed.2d 536, 546 (1985) ("'[m]ilitary bases generally are not public fora"); Brown v. Palmer, 944 F.2d 732 (10th Cir.) (en banc) (military base is not a public forum). *But see* Flower v. United States, 407 U.S. 197, 92 S.Ct. 1842, 32 L.Ed.2d 653 (1972) (per curiam) (portion of military base is public forum where military has abandoned right to exclude public traffic).

58. United States v. Kokinda, 497 U.S. at 727, 110 S.Ct. at 3120, 111 L.Ed.2d at 582. Lower courts have reached similar conclusions. *See* Longo v. United States Postal Service, 953 F.2d 790 (2d Cir.1992), *cert. granted judgment vac'd*, 506 U.S. 802, 113 S.Ct. 31, 121 L.Ed.2d 5 (1992); Monterey County Democratic Central Committee v. United States Postal Service, 812 F.2d 1194 (9th Cir.1987); U.S. v. Bjerke, 796 F.2d 643 (3d Cir.1986); National Anti-Drug Coalition, Inc. v. Bolger, 737 F.2d 717 (7th Cir. 1984). In *Kokinda*, Justices O'Connor, Rehnquist, White and Scalia held that the postal sidewalks were nonpublic fora. Justice Kennedy concurred in the result, finding only that the regulations at issue were reasonable time, place or manner restrictions. In International Society for Krishna Consciousness v. Lee, 505 U.S. 672, 112 S.Ct. 2701, 120 L.Ed.2d 541 (1992), the four Justices, however, were joined in the nonforum analysis by Justice Thomas. The five Justice majority in *Lee* held that airport terminals are not traditional public fora.

historical and current uses of property determine its status as a traditional forum. The Court, however, has confined this limiting analysis to streets or sidewalks that are in some ways separate from open public thoroughfares.[59] It has stopped short of holding that traditional public fora can lose their character via government regulation.[60]

Speech in a traditional forum is accorded the highest level of First Amendment protection. Content based restrictions will be upheld only when they are narrowly drawn to serve a compelling state interest.[61] The Court has emphasized that under strict scrutiny, the government "must do more than assert a compelling state interest—it must demonstrate that its law is necessary to serve the asserted interest." For this reason, "a law rarely survives such scrutiny."[62] One such rare case is *Burson v. Freeman*, in which a divided Court upheld campaign restrictions within 100 feet of polling places. It viewed the limits as a narrow incursion on public forum speech in order to serve the compelling interest in combating voter fraud and intimidation.[63] Similarly in *Madsen v. Women's Health Center, Inc.*, the Court upheld portions of an injunction barring certain types of conduct in the public forum near an abortion clinic. Because the Court said that the injunction was targeted at conduct and not speech content, it held that strict scrutiny was not required and instead applied intermediate scrutiny.[64]

Four Justices in *Lee*, in an opinion written by Justice Kennedy, called the majority analysis "inconsistent with the values underlying ... the First Amendment." *Id.* at 694, 112 S. Ct. at 2715, 120 L. Ed. 2d at 560 (Kennedy, J., concurring). The sharp doctrinal division on the Court may foreshadow the type of theoretical shift in public forum analysis that occurred in Grayned v. City of Rockford, 408 U.S. 104, 92 S.Ct. 2294, 33 L.Ed.2d 222 (1972).

59. *See, e.g.*, Kokinda, 497 U.S. at 727, 110 S. Ct. at 3120, 111 L. Ed. 2d at 582 ("The municipal sidewalk that runs parallel to the road in this case is a public passageway. The Postal Service's sidewalk is not such a thoroughfare.").

60. United States Postal Service v. Greenburgh Civic Ass'ns, 453 U.S. 114, 133, 101 S.Ct. 2676, 2687, 69 L.Ed.2d 517, 533 (1981) (government "may not by its own ipse dixit destroy the 'public forum' status of streets and parks which have historically been public forums"); Grace, 461 U.S. at 180, 103 S. Ct. at 1708, 75 L. Ed. 2d at 745–46 ("Nor may the government transform the character of the property by the expedient of including it within the statutory definition of what might be considered a nonpublic forum parcel of property."); Thomason v. Jernigan, 770 F.Supp. 1195 (E.D.Mich.) (city cannot vacate public forum by ordinance). *See* Henderson v. Lujan, 964 F.2d 1179, 296 U.S. App. D.C. 58 (D.C.Cir.1992). *See also* Burson v. Freeman,

504 U.S. 191, 112 S.Ct. 1846, 119 L.Ed.2d 5 (1992), in which the Court upheld a restriction on political campaigning on sidewalks and streets within 100 feet of a polling place on the basis that it was a narrowly drawn means of serving a compelling state interest. Only Justice Scalia concluded that the areas near polling places were converted to nonpublic fora by a history of governmental restrictions. *Id.* at 216, 112 S. Ct. at 1860, 119 L. Ed. 2d at 25 (Scalia, J., concurring).

61. Burson v. Freeman, 504 U.S. at 210–11, 112 S.Ct. at 1857, 119 L. Ed. 2d at 22; Boos v. Barry, 485 U.S. at 321, 108 S. Ct.at 1164, 99 L.Ed.2d at 345; Perry Education Ass'n v. Perry Local Educators' Ass'n, 460 U.S. at 45, 103 S.Ct. at 955, 74 L.Ed.2d at 804. *See also* Board of Airport Comm'rs v. Jews for Jesus, Inc., 482 U.S. 569, 573, 107 S.Ct. 2568, 2571, 96 L.Ed.2d 500, 506 (1987); Cornelius v. NAACP Legal Defense and Educ. Fund, Inc., 473 U.S. at 800, 105 S.Ct. at 3448, 87 L.Ed.2d at 579; United States v. Grace, 461 U.S. 171, 177, 103 S.Ct. 1702, 1707, 75 L.Ed.2d 736, 743–45 (1983).

62. Burson v. Freeman, 504 U.S. at 211, 112 S.Ct. at 1857, 119 L.Ed.2d at 22.

63. *Id.*

64. 512 U.S. 753, 764–65, 114 S.Ct. 2516, 2524, 129 L.Ed.2d 593, 606 (1994). Applying this holding in a subsequent case,

Given the rigors of strict scrutiny, content-based restrictions on speech in the public forum are seldom sustained. This does not mean, however, that the government lacks the ability to base certain regulations on the subject matter of speech. For example, in *Renton v. Playtime Theatres, Inc.*, the Court upheld zoning restrictions on adult bookstores that were designed to curb "secondary effects," such as crime, associated with such businesses.[65] Thus, a restriction on speech is content-neutral if it is *"justified* without reference to the content of the regulated speech."[66] But not every justification that purports to be neutral is acceptable. Speech restrictions that are justified by an interest in curbing hostile audience reactions are not content neutral.[67]

Lesser restrictions, such as those regulating the time, place or manner of speech, will be sustained only when narrowly tailored to serve a significant governmental interest and when there remains ample alternative channels of communication.[68] Time, place or manner restrictions, which permit the government to "channel" speech to accommodate conflicting interests, have been compared by the Court to the "incidental" limits on speech upheld in *O'Brien v. United States.*[69] This comparison has been criticized, however, as being insensitive to the speech interests at issue.[70] In this view, the *O'Brien* approach "lacks a

---

the Court upheld an injunction that imposed a fixed "buffer zone" to prevent protesters from blocking access to an abortion clinic, but struck down "floating buffer zones" around people entering the clinic as being too restrictive of speech. Schenck v. Pro–Choice Network of Western New York, 519 U.S. 357, 117 S.Ct. 855, 137 L.Ed.2d 1 (1997).

65. 475 U.S. 41, 106 S.Ct. 925, 89 L.Ed.2d 29 (1986).

66. Ward v. Rock Against Racism, 491 U.S. at 791, 109 S. Ct. at 2753, 105 L. Ed. 2d at 675 (quoting *Clark v. Community for Creative Non–Violence*, 468 U.S. at 293, 104 S. Ct. at 3069, 82 L. Ed. 2d at 2270) (emphasis added in *Ward*).

67. R.A.V. v. City of St. Paul, 505 U.S. 377, 112 S.Ct. 2538, 120 L.Ed.2d 305 (1992); Forsyth County, Georgia v. The Nationalist Movement, 505 U.S. 123, 135–36, 112 S.Ct. 2395, 2404, 120 L.Ed.2d 101, 114–15 (1992); Boos v. Barry, 485 U.S. at 321, 108 S.Ct. at 1163–64, 99 L.Ed.2d at 344–45. *But see* Madsen, 512 U.S. 753, 762–63, 114 S.Ct. 2516, 2523, 129 L.Ed.2d 593, 606 (1994) (hostile actions may provide the basis for injunction against a demonstration).

68. Forsyth County, Georgia v. The Nationalist Movement, 505 U.S. 123, 112 S.Ct. 2395, 120 L.Ed.2d 101 (1992); Ward v. Rock Against Racism, 491 U.S. at 791, 109 S.Ct. at 2753, 105 L.Ed.2d at 675; Clark v. Community for Creative Non–Violence, 468 U.S.

at 293, 104 S.Ct. at 3069, 82 L.Ed.2d at 227; Heffron v. International Society for Krishna Consciousness, 452 U.S. at 649, 101 S.Ct. at 2565, 69 L.Ed.2d at 307.

69. *See* International Society for Krishna Consciousness v. Lee, 505 U.S. 672, 703, 112 S.Ct. 2711, 2720, 120 L.Ed.2d 541, 566 (Kennedy, J., concurring). *See also* Clark v. Community for Creative Non–Violence, 468 U.S. at 298 & n.8, 104 S.Ct. at 3071 & n. 8, 82 L.Ed.2d at 230 & n.8; Members of the City Council of Los Angeles v. Taxpayers for Vincent, 466 U.S. 789, 804–05, 104 S.Ct. 2118, 2128–29, 80 L.Ed.2d 772, 787 (1984); Ward v. Rock Against Racism, 491 U.S. at 798, 109 S.Ct. at 2757, 105 L.Ed.2d at 680; Barnes v. Glen Theatre, Inc., 501 U.S. 560, 567, 111 S.Ct. 2456, 2461, 115 L.Ed.2d 504, 512 (1991).

70. *Compare, e.g.,* Schneider v. New Jersey, 308 U.S. at 164–65, 60 S. Ct. at 152, 84 L. Ed. at 166–67 (anti leafleting law struck down despite governmental objective to prevent littering) *with* Vincent, 466 U.S. at 804–05, 104 S. Ct. at 2128–29, 80 L. Ed. 2d at 786–87 (anti sign posting ordinance upheld as content-neutral means of preventing visual blight). The difference in the outcomes of these cases has been explained by the Court's reliance on *O'Brien* methodology in *Vincent* as opposed to a time, place or manner analysis. *See* Keith Werhan, *The O'Briening of Free Speech Methodology*, 19 Ariz. St. L.J. 635, 653–55 (1987). *See also and compare* Century Federal, Inc. v. City

speech side to its balance" and therefore "tilts in favor of government regulation."[71] Thus, to the extent *O'Brien* becomes the prevailing mode of analysis, the Court may be more lenient toward government restrictions even in the traditional public forum.

Finally, regulations that limit access to a public forum are invalid if they allow excessive administrative discretion.[72] The Court reaffirmed this principle in *Forsyth County, Georgia v. The Nationalist Movement*, in which it struck down parade permit fee scheme that vested excessive power in local officials.[73] There, the county administrator was given sole authority to determine whether to charge the permittee the administrative and police-protection costs associated with a parade. Additionally, the administrator was authorized to examine the content of the proposed message, estimate the public response to the message, gauge the necessary police presence, and assign costs accordingly (up to $1,000). The Court found that such "unbridled discretion" permitted the government to encourage some views while discouraging others through the arbitrary application of fees.[74] Generally, "a law subjecting the exercise of First Amendment freedoms to the prior restraint of a license" must contain "narrow, objective, and definite standards to guide the licensing authority."[75]

b. The designated forum

Public property that does not fall into the traditional category, but that is treated by the government as a site suitable for communications, is considered a public forum by designation. When the government opens non-traditional property for expressive purposes, the site is subject to the same First Amendment obligations as a quintessential public forum, with certain limitations. First, the government is not obligated to open the forum in the first place and may, at its discretion, discontinue use of the property for public expression. Second, the forum may be opened for only certain members of the public or for certain types of expression, depending on the character of the property.

The courts are not entirely clear on what constitutes "designating" a public forum. Perhaps this is because most cases focus on the reasons why property otherwise open to the public is not a designated forum. Thus, much of the dictum on the subject is framed in the negative. As

---

of Palo Alto, 710 F.Supp. 1559, 1570–78 (N.D.Cal.1988) (cable television franchise fee for use of designated public forum invalid under time, place or manner analysis) with Group W Cable, Inc. v. City of Santa Cruz, 669 F.Supp. 954, 972–75 (N.D.Cal. 1987), *further proceeding*, 679 F.Supp. 977, 979–80 (N.D.Cal.1988) (franchise fee upheld using the four-part *O'Brien* analysis rather than the three-part time, place, and manner test).

71. Werhan, *supra*, note 70 at 654–55.

72. Forsyth County, Georgia v. The Nationalist Movement, 505 U.S. at 123, 132–

33, 112 S. Ct. at 2402–03, 120 L. Ed. 2d at 112–13 (1992); City of Lakewood v. Plain Dealer Publishing Co., 486 U.S. 750, 108 S.Ct. 2138, 100 L.Ed.2d 771 (1988).

73. 505 U.S. at 132–33, 112 S.Ct. at 2402–03, 120 L.Ed.2d at 112–13.

74. *Id.* at 133, 112 S. Ct. at 2403, 120 L. Ed. 2d at 113.

75. Shuttlesworth v. Birmingham, 394 U.S. 147, 150–51, 89 S.Ct. 935, 938, 22 L.Ed.2d 162, 167 (1969). *See* Niemotko v. Maryland, 340 U.S. 268, 271, 71 S.Ct. 325, 327, 95 L.Ed. 267, 270 (1951).

the Supreme Court has noted, "[t]he government does not create a public forum by inaction or by permitting limited discourse, but only by intentionally opening a nontraditional forum for public discourse."[76] The analysis turns on a number of factors, including a history of allowing speech at a given location, the characteristics of the property and, perhaps most importantly, the government's intent.[77]

Under these guidelines, the Court has found university meeting rooms,[78] public school board meetings[79] and civic auditoriums[80] to be public forums by designation. On the other hand, it has denied forum status to various government-controlled locations despite their use for various types of communication. In *Perry Education Association*, for example, the Court held that a school mail system for teachers was a nonpublic forum even though selective access had been granted to outside groups, such as civic and church organizations.[81] Similarly, controlled access by certain charitable organizations to a federal fund-raising campaign was held insufficient to create a forum,[82] as was an open house at a military base which allowed free access by members of the public.[83] In *International Society for Krishna Consciousness v. Lee*, the Court majority brushed aside arguments that airport terminals had been opened as a forum by noting, "the frequent and continuing litigation evidencing the operators' objections belies any such claim."[84] And in *Arkansas Educational Television Commission v. Forbes*, the Court held that a candidate debate sponsored by a public broadcasting station was not a designated public forum because participation was determined by

76. Cornelius v. NAACP Legal Defense and Educ. Fund, Inc., 473 U.S. at 802, 105 S. Ct. at 3449, 87 L. Ed. 2d at 580. *See* International Society for Krishna Consciousness v. Lee, 505 U.S. at 679–80, 112 S. Ct. at 2706, 120 L.Ed.2d 541, 550–51. In *Cornelius,* the Court applied the *Perry* analysis to the facts of earlier cases and concluded that the government had created designated fora in certain instances. *See* 473 U.S. at 799–806, 105 S.Ct. at 3447–51, 87 L.Ed.2d at 578–82.

77. *See* Cornelius, 473 U.S. at 802–803, 105 S. Ct.at 3449, 87 L.Ed.2d at 580. The physical characteristics of certain property provides the key to understanding the government's intent, such as an auditorium built as a means of exhibiting expression. *But see* Arkansas Educational Television Comm'n v. Forbes, 523 U.S. 666, 118 S.Ct. 1633, 140 L.Ed.2d 875 (1998) (candidate debate on public television station held not to be a designated public forum).

78. Widmar v. Vincent, 454 U.S. 263, 102 S.Ct. 269, 70 L.Ed.2d 440 (1981).

79. Madison Joint School Dist. v. Wisconsin Employment Relations Comm'n, 429 U.S. 167, 97 S.Ct. 421, 50 L.Ed.2d 376 (1976).

80. Southeastern Promotions, Ltd. v. Conrad, 420 U.S. 546, 95 S.Ct. 1239, 43 L.Ed.2d 448 (1975). Lower courts have not been able to agree that civic auditoriums are designated forums. *Compare, e.g.,* Calash v. City of Bridgeport, 788 F.2d 80 (2d Cir.1986) (municipal stadium was a category-three nonpublic forum even though expressive activity had frequently been officially allowed there), *with* Cinevision Corp. v. City of Burbank, 745 F.2d 560, 570 (9th Cir.1984), cert. denied, 471 U.S. 1054, 105 S.Ct. 2115, 85 L.Ed.2d 480 (1985) (outdoor amphitheater held to be a category-two public forum).

81. 460 U.S. at 47, 103 S. Ct. at 956, 74 L. Ed. 2d at 806. The Court explained that there was no finding or evidence that "permission has been granted as a matter of course to all who seek to distribute material."

82. Cornelius, 473 U.S. at 805, 105 S. Ct. at 3450, 87 L. Ed. 2d at 581–82.

83. Albertini, 472 U.S. at 686. 105 S.Ct. at 2905, 86 L.Ed.2d at 546 (1985).

84. 505 U.S. 672, 680–81, 112 S.Ct. 2701, 2706–07, 120 L.Ed.2d 541, 551 (1992).

the station's news judgment, and it was not intended as an "open microphone" for all candidates.[85]

If as suggested in *Lee,* the government's intent is the principal factor that determines whether a forum has been created, its opposition in court to the intended speakers may be dispositive. If this fairly represents the Court's ruling, it means that courts would be unable to find a designated forum in contested cases except in the event of obvious viewpoint discrimination. Such a rule might blur the distinction between the designated forum and the nonforum.[86] This prompted four Justices in *Lee* to note that the Court's position "leaves almost no scope for the development of new public forums absent the rare approval of the government" and to wonder whether the designated forum category "has any content left at all."[87]

Although the dictum in the *Lee* opinions suggested that the designated forum category is quite limited, the result in that case appeared to be somewhat less restrictive. The divided Court upheld the New York and New Jersey Port Authority's ban on solicitation of money inside airport terminals. But at the same time, it struck down as unreasonable the Authority's prohibition on literature distribution.[88] As Justice O'Connor noted in a concurring opinion, the reasonableness of the distribution ban "must be assessed in light of the characteristic nature and function of the particular forum involved." Thus, the government may not create a forum by inaction, but the reasonableness of restrictions in a nonpublic forum hinges on the fact that the government has "chosen not to limit access to the airports under its control." Noting that the airports "house restaurants, cafeterias, snack bars, coffee shops, cocktail lounges, post offices, banks, telegraph offices, clothing shops, drug stores, food stores, nurseries, barber shops, currency exchanges, art exhibits, commercial advertising displays, bookstores, newsstands, dental offices and private clubs," Justice O'Connor concluded that "the Port Authority is operating a shopping mall as well as an airport" and that the ban on

---

85. ___ U.S. at ___, 118 S.Ct. at 1642, 140 L.Ed.2d at 888. The Court also stated that public broadcast stations in general should not be considered public fora. *Id.* at ___, 118 S.Ct. at 1639–40, 140 L.Ed.2d at 885–886.

86. In the non-public the government is barred, for example, from permitting access by Republican speakers while denying access to Democratic speakers. *See* Cornelius, 473 U.S. at 800; Perry Educ. Ass'n, 460 U.S. at 49–50, 103 S. Ct. at 957–58, 74 L. Ed. 2d at 807–08.

87. International Society for Krishna Consciousness v. Lee, 505 U.S. at 695, 697, 112 S. Ct. at 2709, 120 L.Ed.2d 541, 561, 562 (Kennedy, J., concurring). Justice Kennedy, joined by Justices Blackmun, Stevens and Souter, embraced a new formulation of the incompatibility theory first articulated

in Grayned v. City of Rockford. *See id.* at 698, 112 S. Ct. at 2709, 120 L.Ed.2d at 563 ("If the objective, physical characteristics of the property at issue and the actual public access and uses which have been permitted by the government indicate that expressive activity would be appropriate and compatible with those uses, the property is a public forum.").

88. The two decisions were announced as companion cases. In *International Society for Krishna Consciousness v. Lee*, 505 U.S. 672, 112 S.Ct. 2701, 120 L.Ed.2d 541 (1992), the Court upheld the ban on solicitation. But in *Lee v. International Society for Krishna Consciousness*, 505 U.S. 830, 112 S.Ct. 2709, 120 L.Ed.2d 669 (1992), the Court voided the ban on distribution of literature.

distributing literature could not be upheld.[89] The net effect of the decision, then, may have been to broaden somewhat the protection of speech in the nonpublic forum category while restricting the scope of the designated public forum.

The final characteristic of the designated public forum is that the identity of the speakers and the subject matter of the speech may be restricted to those compatible with the purpose of the forum. Such limitations are based on the purposes for which the forum was designated. Thus, a building designated for school board meetings may be restricted to allow only speakers who wish to discuss school-related business.[90] Similarly, access to university meeting rooms may be limited to campus groups.[91] Any analysis of such limitations is necessarily fact-specific. Whether a government entity has created a limited forum that is accessible to a particular group will depend on the character of the property, the government's policies and the type of access previously allowed.

The Supreme Court first applied these principles in cases involving access by religious groups to school facilities and financial support. In *Lamb's Chapel v. Center Moriches Union Free School District*,[92] the Court dealt with a school district's refusal to allow its facilities to be used for after school meetings in which a church group wanted to present a six-part film series on family-related issues. The facilities generally were open to social, civic and recreational meetings so long was they were non-exclusive and open to the general public. However, school facilities had not been opened for "religious purposes." Thus, the district denied access on grounds that the film series was "church related," and the lower courts upheld this decision.[93]

The Supreme Court reversed, although it sidestepped the issue of whether the school district had created a limited public forum. While it acknowledged that the church's argument regarding creation of a forum "has considerable force," it held that the school district's decision to exclude the group was unconstitutional because it was based on viewpoint discrimination.[94] The Court noted that the school property "had repeatedly been used by a wide variety of private organizations," and that there had never been any suggestion that the subjects of child-rearing or family values had been "placed off limits to any and all speakers." It found that the access request was denied "solely because

89. International Society for Krishna Consciousness, 505 U.S. at 687–89, 112 S.Ct. at 2709, 120 L.Ed.2d at 557–70 (O'Connor, J., concurring).

90. Madison Joint School Dist. v. Wisconsin Employment Relations Comm'n, 429 U.S. 167, 97 S.Ct. 421, 50 L.Ed.2d 376 (1976).

91. Widmar v. Vincent, 454 U.S. 263, 102 S.Ct. 269, 70 L.Ed.2d 440 (1981).

92. 508 U.S. 384, 113 S.Ct. 2141, 124 L.Ed.2d 352 (1993).

93. *Id.* at 389, 113 S. Ct. at 2145, 124 L. Ed. 2d at 359. *See* Lamb's Chapel v. Center Moriches Union Free School Dist., 770 F.Supp. 91 (E.D.N.Y.1991), *aff'd*, 959 F.2d 381 (2d Cir.1992) (school is limited public forum but Board may deny access to church group seeking to show religious film because there was no history of allowing access by religious groups).

94. 508 U.S. at 391–392, 113 S.Ct. at 2146–2147, 124 L.Ed.2d at 361.

the film dealt with the subject from a religious standpoint," and that this constituted viewpoint discrimination that is unconstitutional even in a nonforum.[95] In hindsight, the Court apparently concluded that the Center Moriches School District had in fact created a public forum by designation, and it extended that concept to forums that are more "metaphysical than . . . spatial or geographic."[96]

In *Rosenberger v. Rector and Visitors of the University of Virginia*, the Supreme Court held that a fund for student organizations at the University of Virginia could not be administered so as to exclude funding for a student publication because it was written from a Christian perspective. As in *Lamb's Chapel*, the Court found the exclusion constituted viewpoint discrimination and was therefore unconstitutional.[97] It found that such discrimination violates the First Amendment "even when the limited public forum is one of [the government's] own creation."[98] The Court distinguished funding for the practice of religion, which would violate the Establishment Clause of the First Amendment, and funding on a neutral basis for qualifying student organizations, including those with a religious orientation.

The Court pointed out that viewpoint discrimination "is but a subset or particular instance of the more general phenomenon of content discrimination."[99] However, it acknowledged that the distinction between content and viewpoint discrimination "is not a precise one," particularly where subjects of universal philosophic inquiry such as "the nature of our origins and destiny and their dependence upon the existence of a divine being" is characterized, for purposes of legal analysis, as a "viewpoint."[100] But the Supreme Court concluded that "[t]he first danger to liberty lies in granting the State the power to examine publications to determine whether or not they are based on some ultimate idea and if so for the State to classify them."[1] Not only does this holding suggest a broadening of the concept of viewpoint discrimination, it also appears to expand what government actions may open a limited public forum.

95. *Id.* at 393–394, 113 S.Ct. at 2147–2148, 124 L.Ed.2d at 362–63.

96. Rosenberger v. Rector and Visitors of the University of Virginia, 515 U.S. 819, 829, 115 S.Ct. 2510, 2517, 132 L.Ed.2d 700, 716 (1995). In *Denver Area Educational Telecommunications Consortium v. FCC*, 518 U.S. 727, 116 S.Ct. 2374, 135 L.Ed.2d 888 (1996), Justices Kennedy and Ginsburg found that cable television public access channels, created by local franchising requirements, constituted public forums. *Id.* at 791–794, 116 S. Ct. at 2409–2410, 135 L. Ed. 2d at 934 (Kennedy, J., concurring in part and dissenting in part). However, a plurality of the Court declined to decide "the extent to which private property can be designated as a public forum." *Id.* at 741, 116 S. Ct. at 2385, 135 L. Ed. 2d at 902.

97. Rosenberger, 515 U.S. at 830, 115 S. Ct. at 2517, 132 L. Ed. 2d at 716. The Court described *Lamb's Chapel* as "[t]he most recent and the most apposite case."

98. *Id.* at 829, 115 S. Ct. at 2516, 132 L. Ed. 2d at 715.

99. *Id.* at 830–831, 115 S. Ct. at 2517, 132 L. Ed. 2d at 716.

100. *Id.* at 831, 115 S. Ct. at 2517, 132 L. Ed. 2d at 716.

1. *Id.* at 835, 115 S. Ct. at 2520, 132 L. Ed. 2d at 719. *But see* Arkansas Educational Television Comm'n v. Forbes, 523 U.S. 666, 118 S.Ct. 1633, 140 L.Ed.2d 875 (1998) (public broadcasters' sponsorship of candidate debate does not constitute opening a designated public forum).

c. The nonpublic forum

To the extent the traditional public forum is confined by tradition to streets, parks and sidewalks, and the designated forum to property affirmatively opened by government, then the final category—the non-public forum—necessarily encompasses "all remaining public property."[2] Under this analysis, government property is considered a nonpublic forum even though members of the public may come and go at will. The Supreme Court has held that airport terminals, military bases, and Post Office sidewalks all fall into this category.

Government restrictions on speech in the nonpublic forum need only be "reasonable" and otherwise viewpoint neutral. The reasonableness of any restrictions in a nonpublic forum "must be assessed in the light of the purpose of the forum and all the surrounding circumstances."[3] Until recently, the Court appeared willing to accept rather stringent restrictions on speech in a nonpublic forum, provided the limits were viewpoint-neutral. Various decisions stressed that a restriction on speech " 'need only be *reasonable*; it need not be the most reasonable or the only reasonable limitation.' "[4] In *United States v. Grace*, for example, the Court left undisturbed a federal law that prohibited the display of "any flag, banner, or device designed or adapted to bring into public notice any party, organization, or movement" in the United States Supreme Court building or on its grounds.[5] The Court invalidated speech restrictions that applied to the sidewalks surrounding the Court, but not other parts of the grounds, which prompted Justice Marshall to warn that a person still could be arrested merely for "handing out of a leaflet" or "the wearing of a campaign button."[6]

This concern may be less pressing after *Lee*, however, where a majority struck down anti-leafleting rules in municipal airports. Justice O'Connor concluded in her concurring opinion that a ban on literature distribution "cannot be upheld as reasonable" in "the multipurpose environment that the Port Authority has deliberately created."[7] Thus, even where the government has not affirmatively created a forum for speech, denial of access to speakers may be unreasonable to the extent the public is otherwise admitted to the property. This analysis was

2. International Society for Krishna Consciousness, 505 U.S. at 678–79, 112 S. Ct. at 2705, 120 L. Ed. 2d at 550.

3. Cornelius, 473 U.S. at 809, 105 S. Ct. at 3453, 87 L. Ed. 2d at 584.

4. International Society for Krishna Consciousness, 505 U.S. at 683, 112 S. Ct. at 2708, 120 L.Ed.2d at 553 (quoting *Kokinda*, 497 U.S. at 730, 110 S. Ct. at 3122, 111 L.Ed.2d at 584) (plurality opinion) (quoting in turn *Cornelius*, 473 U.S. at 808, 105 S. Ct. at 3452, 87 L. Ed. 2d at 584) (emphasis in original). The popularity of this expression masks its incoherence. That a limit need not be the *most* reasonable one means only that government is not limited to the least restrictive alternative—something that has never been a requirement in the nonpublic forum. On the other hand, if a limit is, in fact, "the only reasonable limitation" available, one must presume that it would be required since even in the nonforum speech restrictions must at least be *"reasonable."*

5. 461 U.S. 171, 175, 103 S.Ct. 1702, 1706, 75 L.Ed.2d 736, 742 (1983).

6. *Id.* at 186, 103 S. Ct. at 1711, 75 L. Ed. 2d at 749 (Marshall, J., dissenting in part).

7. 505 U.S. at 689–90, 112 S. Ct. at 2709, 120 L. Ed. 2d at 557.

foreshadowed in *Greer v. Spock*, where the Court emphasized that it would be unreasonable to ban the distribution of conventional political campaign literature at Fort Dix, a nonpublic forum. Rather, the military commander was authorized to ban the distribution of publications that posed "a clear danger to loyalty, discipline, or morale."[8] However, where the proposed speech contains elements of action (*e.g.*, solicitation of funds), the Court has been more willing to uphold denial of access to a nonpublic forum.[9]

B. Access to Private Channels of Communication

1. Access to the Private Forum

Decisions that limit access to the public forum often start from the premise that "[t]he State, no less than a private owner of property, has power to preserve the property under its control for the use to which it is lawfully dedicated."[10] Although this statement fails to reflect the government's First Amendment obligations in the nonpublic forum, it is generally accurate regarding private property owners. That is, private owners typically have no obligation to make their property available for the speech of others. This is true for two reasons. First, unless the property owner resorts to some legal process to silence the speech, no state action is involved. Second, forcing property owners to accommodate speech with which they may disagree violates their First Amendment rights.

Generally, the Court has upheld the right of private property owners to avoid having their property used as a forum for speech. Such rights do not always prevail, however, particularly when the property involved shares all or some of the attributes of the traditional public forum. For example, in *Marsh v. Alabama*,[11] the Court struck down the trespass conviction of a Jehovah's Witnesses who had distributed literature without a license in the business district of a company town. In doing so, the Court denied that "the corporation's right to control the inhabitants of [the town] is coextensive with the right of a homeowner to regulate the conduct of his guests." It added that "[t]he more an owner, for his advantage, opens up his property for use by the public in general, the more do his rights become circumscribed by the statutory and constitutional rights of those who use it."[12]

The Court subsequently limited the implications of *Marsh* by confining the holding to "an economic anomaly of the past, 'the company town,'" in which "a private enterprise [assumed] all of the attributes of

---

8. 424 U.S. 828, 840, 96 S.Ct. 1211, 1218, 47 L.Ed.2d 505, 515 (1976).

9. *E.g.*, International Society for Krishna Consciousness v. Lee, 505 U.S. at 683, 112 S.Ct. at 2708, 120 L.Ed.2d at 553; Kokinda, 497 U.S. at 731, 110 S.Ct. at 3122, 111 L.Ed.2d at 584.

10. Adderley v. Florida, 385 U.S. at 47, 87 S.Ct. at 247, 17 L.Ed.2d at 156. *See also* International Society for Krishna Con-

sciousness, 505 U.S. at 677–78, 112 S.Ct. at 2705, 120 L.Ed.2d at 549.

11. 326 U.S. 501, 66 S.Ct. 276, 90 L.Ed. 265 (1946). The entire town, including streets and sidewalks, was owned by the Gulf Shipbuilding Corp.

12. *Id.* at 506, 66 S. Ct. at 278, 90 L. Ed. at 268.

a state-created municipality and ... exercise[d] ... semi-official municipal functions as a delegate of the State."[13] The question remains, however, as to the extent private property may be imbued with public forum obligations in situations that fall short of the company town. The Court has addressed this issue most often in cases involving the modern counterpart of the town square—the shopping mall. Although a mall owner certainly "opens up his property for use by the public in general," it is not entirely certain how this limits the owner's First Amendment rights.

2. Access to the Private Press

Whatever may be the state of the law regarding access to private property for the purpose of engaging in speech, the issue becomes quite clear when the property in question is a privately owned press. Courts have been consistent in holding that there is no right of access to newspapers or other publications. Such access is considered to be compelled speech, and is the equivalent of censorship under the First Amendment.

As discussed more fully in Section 1.7[G], the leading cases in this area are *Miami Herald Publishing Co. v. Tornillo*[14] and *Pacific Gas & Elec. Co. v. Public Utilities Commission of California*.[15] In *Tornillo*, the Court invalidated a Florida "right of reply" statute that required newspapers to print responses from political candidates that had been attacked in print. *Pacific Gas and Electric* extended *Tornillo* principles beyond "the institutional press" to strike down a state public utilities commission order that gave a consumer group access to a utility's billing envelopes so that the group could respond to the company newsletter. Viewed in these terms, the Court appears to treat compelled access to a publication as inherently intrusive since the access necessarily conflicts with the purposes of the publisher. Access to business property to engage in speech, on the other hand, may not be viewed as a significant conflict.

C. Access Concepts and New Media

With new communications technologies, the courts take the opposite approach from that in cases involving traditional media. Beginning with broadcasting, and continuing with newer electronic media, courts generally have approved a limited right of access for purposes of speech by certain members of the public. In other contexts, courts generally have recognized property owners' right to prevent access by those who would use it to engage in speech by electronic means. Professor Laurence Tribe has described the difference in treatment of the electronic media as "a chain-breaking departure from the constitutional approach to newspapers and magazines" and that the First Amendment is "most compro-

13. Lloyd Corp. v. Tanner, 407 U.S. 551, 561, 569, 92 S.Ct. 2219, 2225, 2229, 33 L.Ed.2d 131, 138, 143 (1972).

14. 418 U.S. 241, 94 S.Ct. 2831, 41 L.Ed.2d 730 (1974).

15. 475 U.S. 1, 106 S.Ct. 903, 89 L.Ed.2d 1 (1986).

mised in the realm of the most modern medium: electronic broadcasting."[16] Particularly when licensed by the government, media have been infused with certain public responsibilities, chief among them being some kind of access requirement. Current distinctions regarding different treatment of the media may be unlikely to persist, however, since the law is evolving. See Chapter Two for further discussion of this issue.

1. Electronic Speakers' Access to Private Property

The Supreme Court has upheld the right of private property owners to exclude electronic speakers from their property. It found the property interest to be inviolate without regard to the degree of intrusion by the purported speaker. In *Loretto v. Teleprompter Manhattan CATV Corp.*,[17] the Court invalidated a New York law that required the owners of apartment buildings to allow access by cable television operators. It held that the law amounted to a taking of the landlord's property without compensation in violation of the Fifth Amendment. The Court found it immaterial that the physical occupation by the cable attachments constituted about one and a half cubic feet, noting that "whether the installation is a taking does not depend on whether the volume of space it occupies is bigger than a breadbox."[18]

After *Loretto*, Congress decreed that a cable franchise includes authorization to construct "over public rights-of-way, and through easements...which have been dedicated for compatible uses."[19] It was assumed that access to easements was different from requiring access to an apartment building, since "most developers voluntarily grant easements for use by utilities."[20] Courts later confronted the question of whether the Cable Act conferred access to private apartment buildings, as well as easements. Generally, they held that Congress did not intend to create such a right of access, and to do so would conflict with *Loretto*.[21]

Private covenants also have been upheld as restrictions on access to electronic speech. In *Ross v. Hatfield*, for example, a federal district court refused to entertain a suit against a homeowner's association that by covenant banned satellite dishes within the development.[22] The court

---

16. Laurence H. Tribe, American Constitutional Law 1003–04 (2d Ed. 1988).

17. 458 U.S. 419, 102 S.Ct. 3164, 73 L.Ed.2d 868 (1982).

18. *Id.* at 438 n.16, 102 S.Ct. at 3177 n.16, 73 L.Ed.2d at 884 n.16. The Court focused on the fact that the cable facilities involved a permanent physical occupation of private property. It distinguished *PruneYard* by noting that the property invasion there "was temporary and limited in nature," the owner had otherwise permitted public access to the shopping center and had the additional option of imposing reasonable time, place and manner restrictions on speech. *Id.* at 434, 102 S.Ct. at 3175, 73 L.Ed.2d at 881.

19. 47 U.S.C.A. § 541(a)(2) (West 1991 & Supp. 1997).

20. Centel Cable Tel. Co. of Florida v. Admiral's Cove Assocs., 835 F.2d 1359, 1363 n. 7 (11th Cir.1988). The analysis is analogous to that used in *PruneYard*, where the shopping center owner's decision to allow general public access diminished his authority to exclude speakers.

21. *See* Cable Holdings of Georgia, Inc. v. McNeil Real Estate Fund VI, Ltd., 953 F.2d 600, 604–05 (11th Cir.) *cert denied*, 506 U.S. 862, 113 S.Ct. 182, 121 L.Ed.2d 127 (1992); Cable Investments, Inc. v. Woolley, 867 F.2d 151, 159–60 (3d Cir.1989).

22. 640 F.Supp. 708 (D.Kan.1986).

held that the covenant did not constitute state action and that the residential development was distinguishable from the company town in *Marsh v. Alabama.* Thus, the First Amendment right of a given homeowner to receive information did not outweigh the property interests controlled by the association. Courts generally reach a different conclusion, however, when satellite dishes are restricted by local ordinance rather than by private agreement.[23] Both types of local restrictions on access, however, were preempted by the Telecommunications Act of 1996.[24]

2. *Access to the Electronic Press*

In the Communications Act of 1934, Congress decreed that broadcasters would act as "public trustees" of the electromagnetic spectrum. As part of this obligation, radio and television licensees were required to make their facilities available for the speech of certain members of the public. For example, candidates for federal office have a right of "reasonable access" to purchase "reasonable amounts of time."[25] Similarly, political candidates at all levels have a right to "equal opportunities" to purchase broadcast time after an opponent has used a broadcast facility.[26] In addition to candidates, anyone subject to a "personal attack" in a broadcast has a right to reply on the air.[27] And prior to 1987, the "fairness doctrine" required broadcasters to provide "balanced" presentations of controversial issues of public concern, and this obligation could be triggered by citizen petitions.[28]

Despite these regulatory rights of access to broadcast facilities, courts have hesitated to define their scope and have sometimes applied them narrowly. In *CBS, Inc. v. Democratic National Committee,* the Supreme Court noted that "the 'public interest' standard necessarily invites reference to First Amendment principles," and that "maintenance of this balance [between free speech principles and public obli-

---

23. *See* Hunter v. City of Whittier, 209 Cal.App.3d 588, 257 Cal.Rptr. 559 (1989) (First Amendment interest in receiving satellite transmissions imposes greater burden of justification on local zoning regulations); Conrad v. Dunn, 92 Cal.App.3d 236, 238, 154 Cal.Rptr. 726 (1979). *But see* Johnson v. City of Pleasanton, 781 F.Supp. 632, 635–640 (N.D.Cal.1991) (property owner has no inherent First Amendment right to receive satellite signals; court must balance community's interest against that of individual antenna owner). Local regulation of satellite dishes was initially restricted by a Federal Communications Commission decision to preempt local zoning ordinances that lack a clearly articulated regulatory purpose. 47 C.F.R. § 25.104 (1996). *See* Kessler v. Town of Niskayuna, 774 F.Supp. 711 (N.D.N.Y.1991); Cawley v. City of Port Jervis, 753 F.Supp. 128 (S.D.N.Y.1990); Village of Elm Grove v. Py, 724 F.Supp. 612 (E.D.Wis.1989).

24. 47 U.S.C.A. § 541(b) (West 1991 & Supp. 1997).

25. *Id.* at § 312(a)(7).

26. *Id.* at § 315(a).

27. *See, e.g.,* Red Lion Broadcasting Co. v. FCC, 395 U.S. 367, 89 S.Ct. 1794, 23 L.Ed.2d 371 (1969). *But see* In re Radio–Television News Directors Assoc., No. 97–1528, 1998 WL 388796 (D.C.Cir.1998) (directing FCC to issue final ruling on 18–year–old petition challenging constitutionality of personal attack and political editorial rules).

28. Syracuse Peace Council, 809 F.2d 863, 258 U.S.App.D.C. 22 (1987), *aff'd sub nom.* Syracuse Peace Council v. FCC, 867 F.2d 654, 659 (D.C.Cir.1989), cert. denied, 493 U.S. 1019, 110 S.Ct. 717, 107 L.Ed.2d 737 (1990); Arkansas AFL–CIO v. FCC, 11 F.3d 1430 (8th Cir.1993) (en banc).

gations] has called on both the regulators and the licensees to walk a 'tightrope.' "[29] Thus, while broadcasters may be required to provide balanced presentations of controversial issues, they may not be compelled to provide a generalized right of access *by others* to discuss such issues.[30] Similarly, the Communications Act may require stations to provide "equal opportunities" for candidates to use their facilities and the First Amendment may permit a "limited right to 'reasonable' access that pertains only to legally qualified federal candidates ... for the purpose of advancing their candidacies," but this does not mean that all candidates necessarily have a right to participate in televised debates.[31] To the extent the exact contours of the right of access to broadcast facilities may be unclear, it is also uncertain whether such a right will continue to be upheld by the courts.[32]

With newer technologies, Congress has been more definite about the extent of required access for purposes of speech. In the Cable Communications Policy Act of 1984, Congress empowered local cable television franchising authorities to designate channel capacity for "public, educational, or governmental use" and decreed that cable operators "shall not exercise any editorial control" over any such channels.[33] Additionally, the Act required cable operators to set aside a certain percentage of channel capacity for lease to third parties subject to the requirement

29. 412 U.S. 94, 117, 122, 93 S.Ct. 2080, 2094, 2096, 36 L.Ed.2d 772, 792, 794 (1973).

30. *Compare* Red Lion Broadcasting Co. v. FCC, 395 U.S. 367, 89 S.Ct. 1794, 23 L.Ed.2d 371, *with* CBS, Inc. v. Democratic Nat'l Comm., 412 U.S. 94, 93 S.Ct. 2080, 36 L.Ed.2d 772 (1973). Although the FCC eliminated the fairness doctrine in 1987, courts have not yet held that its requirements are unconstitutional as applied to broadcasters. *But see* FCC v. League of Women Voters of California, 468 U.S. 364, 376–77 n. 11, 104 S.Ct. 3106, 3115 n. 11, 82 L.Ed.2d 278, 289, n. 11 (1984); News America Publishing, Inc v. FCC, 844 F.2d 800, 811, 269 U.S.App. D.C. 182, 193 (D.C.Cir.1988) ("The Supreme Court ... has recognized that new technology may render the [scarcity] doctrine obsolete—indeed, may have already done so."); Telecommunications Research and Action Center v. FCC, 801 F.2d 501, 506–09, 255 U.S.App.D.C. 287, 292–295 (D.C.Cir.1986), cert. denied, 482 U.S. 919, 107 S.Ct. 3196, 96 L.Ed.2d 684 (1987); Loveday v. FCC, 707 F.2d 1443, 1459, 228 U.S.App.D.C. 38, 54 (D.C.Cir.1983), cert. denied, 464 U.S. 1008, 104 S.Ct. 525, 78 L.Ed.2d 709 (1983).

31. *Compare* CBS, Inc. v. FCC, 453 U.S. 367, 396, 101 S.Ct. 2813, 2830, 69 L.Ed.2d 706, 729 (1981) and Branch v. FCC, 824 F.2d 37, 262 U.S. App. D.C. 310 (D.C.Cir. 1987), cert. denied, 485 U.S. 959, 108 S.Ct.

1220, 99 L.Ed.2d 421 (1988) *with* Johnson v. FCC, 829 F.2d 157, 264 U.S. App. D.C. 372, (D.C.Cir.1987) (candidates do not have a right of access to televised debates). *See also* Arkansas Educational Television Comm'n v. Forbes, 523 U.S. 666, 118 S.Ct. 1633, 140 L.Ed.2d 875 (1998) (sponsorship of debate by public television station does not create a public forum); Chandler v. Georgia Public Telecommunications Comm'n, 917 F.2d 486 (11th Cir.1990), cert. denied, 502 U.S. 816, 112 S.Ct. 71, 116 L.Ed.2d 45 (1991) (denial of access to candidate debate does not violate equal protection guarantee).

32. The constitutionality of broadcast regulation is not an immutable fact; it is based on " 'the present state of commercially acceptable technology' as of 1969." News America Publishing, Inc., 269 U.S.App.D.C. at 193, 844 F.2d at 811 (quoting Red Lion, 395 U.S. at 389–90, 89 S.Ct. at 1806–07, 23 L.Ed.2d at 388–89); Meredith Corp. v. FCC, 809 F.2d 863, 867 258 U.S. App. D.C. 22, 26 (D.C.Cir.1987). The Supreme Court has noted that "because the broadcast industry is dynamic in terms of technological change[,] solutions adequate a decade ago are not necessarily so now, and those acceptable today may well be outmoded 10 years hence." CBS, Inc., 412 U.S. at 102, 93 S. Ct. at 2086, 36 L.Ed.2d at 783.

33. 47 U.S.C.A. § 531(a), (e) (West 1991 & Supp. 1997).

that such access be provided under reasonable terms and conditions. As with the required public channels, cable operators are barred from exercising editorial control over leased access channels.[34]

These requirements were expanded in the Cable Television Consumer Protection and Competition Act of 1992. For example, with respect to leased access channels, the Act empowered the FCC to "establish reasonable terms and conditions" for the use of such channels by unaffiliated programmers.[35] The Act further provided that one-third of the required leased access channels could be designated for "qualified" minority or educational programming sources.[36] The Act imposed similar preferential access rights for operators of Direct Broadcast Satellite ("DBS") service. It required DBS licensees to reserve four to seven percent of their channel capacity "exclusively for noncommercial programming of an educational or informational nature."[37] Additionally, the Act imposed "must carry" requirements on cable operators, thus giving local broadcast stations a right of access to the cable facilities—a requirement that prior to 1985 had been imposed by FCC rule.[38]

Judicial response to such access requirements has been mixed. The United States Court of Appeals for the District of Columbia Circuit previously had twice struck down the FCC must carry rules,[39] and the Supreme Court in *Turner Broadcasting Sys., Inc. v. Federal Communications Commission*[40] initially declined to uphold the 1992 Cable Act's renewed broadcast carriage requirements. A divided Court found that the must carry rules were content neutral, and that the government had a legitimate role in requiring access because of the cable operator's "bottleneck, or gatekeeper, control over most (if not all) of the television programming that is channeled into the subscriber's home." The majority further concluded that must carry requirements may be needed "to preserve access to free television programming for the forty percent of Americans without cable." The decision hinged on Congress' determination that a lack of cable carriage would undermine the "survival of a

34. *Id.* § 532. The 1992 Cable Act, however, restored a limited measure of editorial control. With respect to leased access channels, the Act empowered cable operators to enforce a "prospectively written and published policy of prohibiting programming that the cable operator reasonably believes describes or depicts sexual or excretory activities or organs in a patently offensive manner as measured by contemporary community standards." *Id.* at § 532(h). A similar provision applied to indecent programming on public, educational or governmental access channels. *Id.* at § 531. The Supreme Court invalidated the provision relating to indecent speech on public access channels, while upholding the similar policy with respect to leased access channels. Denver Area Educational Telecommunications Consortium, Inc. v. FCC, 518 U.S. 727, 116 S.Ct. 2374, 135 L.Ed.2d 888 (1996).

35. 47 U.S.C.A. § 532(c)(4)(A)(ii) (West 1991 & Supp. 1997).

36. *Id.* at § 532(i)(1).

37. *Id.* at § 335(b)(1).

38. *Id.* §§ 534–35.

39. Century Communications, Corp. v. FCC, 835 F.2d 292, 266 U.S. App. D.C. 228 (D.C.Cir.1987), *clarified,* 837 F.2d 517, 267 U.S. App. D.C. 94 (D.C.Cir.), cert. denied, 486 U.S. 1032, 108 S.Ct. 2014, 100 L.Ed.2d 602 (1988); Quincy Cable TV, Inc. v. FCC, 768 F.2d 1434, 248 U.S.App.D.C. 1 (D.C.Cir. 1985), cert. denied *sub nom.* National Ass'n of Broadcasters v. Quincy Cable TV, Inc., 476 U.S. 1169, 106 S.Ct. 2889, 90 L.Ed.2d 977 (1986).

40. 512 U.S. 622, 114 S.Ct. 2445, 129 L.Ed.2d 497 (1994).

medium that has become a vital part of the Nation's communication system."[41] However, despite "unusually detailed statutory findings," the Court disagreed that the government had demonstrated that "the economic health of local broadcasting is in genuine jeopardy and in need of the protections afforded by must carry, and it remanded the case for further factual findings."[42] On further review, the Supreme Court upheld the must carry rules. A divided Court found that the record before Congress and on remand established a need for the rules.[43]

As with must carry, courts have reached disparate results in their review of other access requirements. For example, in reviewing the 1992 Cable Act, the United States Court of Appeals for the District of Columbia Circuit upheld local PEG and leased access requirements as content-neutral regulatory measures designed to correct a market to which access was controlled by those who own the technology as well as DBS public interest access requirements.[44] Similarly, other courts have reached opposite conclusions about the constitutionality of local access channel requirements,[45] and local programming origination requirements.[46]

The disparate conclusions reached by lower courts can be traced to the Supreme Court's reluctance to articulate a First Amendment standard for cable television.[47] As the Court noted in *Turner Broadcasting System*:

> Given the pace of technological advancement and the increasing convergence between cable and other electronic media, the cable industry today stands at the center of an ongoing telecommunications revolution with still undefined potential to affect the way we communicate and develop our intellectual resources.[48]

41. *Id.* at 646, 647, 656, 114 S. Ct. at 2461, 2466, 129 L. Ed. 2d at 520, 526.

42. *Id.* at 646, 664–665, 114 S. Ct. at 2461, 2470, 129 L. Ed. 2d at 520, 532.

43. Turner Broadcasting Sys., Inc. v. FCC, 520 U.S. 180, 117 S.Ct. 1174, 137 L.Ed.2d 369 (1997) ("Turner II").

44. Time Warner Entertainment Co., L.P. v. FCC, 93 F.3d 957, 320 U.S.App.D.C. 294 (D.C.Cir.1996). The district court had struck down the DBS requirements because it found "absolutely no evidence in the record upon which the Court could conclude that regulation of DBS service providers is necessary to serve any significant regulatory or market-balancing interest." Daniels Cablevision, Inc. v. United States, 835 F.Supp. 1, 7–8 (D.D.C.1993).

45. *E.g.*, Telesat Cablevision, Inc. v. City of Riviera Beach, 773 F.Supp. 383 (S.D.Fla.1991) (access requirements are constitutional); Century Federal, Inc. v. City of Palo Alto, 710 F.Supp. 1552 (N.D.Cal.1987) (access requirements are unconstitutional); Group W Cable, Inc. v. City of Santa Cruz, 669 F.Supp. 954 (N.D.Cal.1987) (access requirements are unconstitutional); Erie Telecommunications, Inc. v. City of Erie, 659 F.Supp. 580 (W.D.Pa.1987), *aff'd on other grounds*, 853 F.2d 1084, (3d Cir.1988) (access fee payments not unconstitutional); Berkshire Cablevision of Rhode Island, Inc. v. Burke, 571 F.Supp. 976 (D.R.I.1983), *vacated as moot*, 773 F.2d 382 (1st Cir.1985) (access requirements are constitutional).

46. Chicago Cable Communications, Inc. v. Chicago Cable Comm'n, 678 F.Supp. 734 (N.D.Ill.1988), *aff'd*, 879 F.2d 1540 (7th Cir. 1989), cert. denied, 493 U.S. 1044, 110 S.Ct. 839, 107 L.Ed.2d 835 (1990).

47. City of Los Angeles v. Preferred Communications, Inc., 476 U.S. 488, 494–95, 106 S.Ct. 2034, 2037–38, 90 L.Ed.2d 480, 487–88 (1986).

48. Turner I, 512 U.S. at 627, 114 S. Ct. at 2451, 129 L. Ed. 2d at 508.

Perhaps out of an awareness of these technological developments, the Court declined the government's invitation in *Turner I* to impose the lower level of First Amendment protection accorded broadcasters on cable operators. It found the First Amendment conclusions in *Red Lion* to be "inapt" when applied to cable television. Although it found the physical characteristics of cable transmission to be a relevant consideration, the Court concluded that such facts "do not require the alteration of settled principles of our First Amendment jurisprudence."[49]

At the same time, a significant block on the Court has been reluctant to declare that cable television and other electronic technologies are entitled to full First Amendment protection. In a fragmented decision in *Denver Area Educational Telecommunications Consortium v. FCC*, a plurality noted the "changes taking place in the law, the technology, and the industrial structure, related to telecommunications" and for that reason declined to "declare a rigid single [First Amendment] standard, good for now and for all future media and purposes."[50] A majority of the Court in *Denver* adopted a form of heightened scrutiny to the access questions presented in that case, but the Justices could not agree on how the standard should be applied.[51]

Although the issue was not presented in *Denver,* various opinions questioned the constitutional soundness of requiring cable operators to provide compelled access to third parties. Justice Thomas, joined by Chief Justice Rehnquist and Justice Scalia, declared categorically that "[t]here is no getting around the fact that leased and public access are a type of forced speech." Requiring such access, according to these Justices, "is directly contrary to *Turner* and our established precedents."[52] Similarly, Justice Kennedy, joined by Justice Ginsburg, noted that leased access requirements " 'interfere with [cable operators'] determinations regarding the total service offering to be extended to subscribers,' " but expressly declined to address the constitutionality of such measures under *Turner Broadcasting*.[53] For purposes of the *Denver* decision, the two Justices focused on the precise issue presented by the petitioners and assumed that "the cable operator's rights in these channels as extinguished."[54] It is conceivable that in another case, the Court would strike down access channel requirements. But until the Court directly

---

49. *Id.* at 639, 114 S. Ct. at 2457, 129 L. Ed. 2d at 516.

50. 518 U.S. at 742, 116 S. Ct. at 2385, 135 L. Ed. 2d at 901–02. *See also id.* at 776–777, 116 S. Ct. at 2402 135 L. Ed. 2d at 924 (Souter, J., concurring) ("[A]s broadcast, cable, and the cyber-technology of the Internet and the World Wide Web approach the day of using a common receiver, we can hardly assume that standards for judging the regulation of one of them will not have immense, but now unknown and unknowable, effects on the others").

51. *See id.* at 782–786, 116 S. Ct. at 2405–2406, 135 L. Ed. 2d at 928–29 (Kenne-

dy, J., concurring in part and dissenting in part); *id.* at 812–819, 116 S. Ct. at 2419–2422, 135 L. Ed. 2d at 947–951 (Thomas, J., concurring in part and dissenting in part).

52. *Id.* at 820, 822, 116 S. Ct. at 2423, 2424, 135 L. Ed. 2d at 952, 953 (Thomas, J., concurring in part and dissenting in part).

53. *Id.* at 796, 116 S. Ct. at 2411, 135 L. Ed. 2d at 936 (Kennedy, J., concurring in part and dissenting in part) (citation omitted).

54. *Id.,* 116 S. Ct. at 2411, 135 L.Ed.2d at 936 (Kennedy, J., concurring in part and dissenting in part).

addresses this issue, confusion regarding rights of access to new technologies is likely to continue. Chapter Two examines the issue of the appropriate First Amendment standard for new technologies.

1.9   First Amendment Procedural Approaches

In addition to the substantive standards articulated in previous sections, courts have developed due process requirements to act as First Amendment safeguards. The procedural requirements provide guidelines for judicial review in First Amendment cases and help ensure that courts show sufficient deference to the constitutional interest in free speech. Additionally, this approach can give judges an analytical framework to help resolve novel First Amendment issues where the courts have not yet articulated a substantive standard. The procedural requirements take several forms: (1) First Amendment due process, including procedures relevant to prior restraints; (2) the overbreadth doctrine; (3) First Amendment underinclusiveness; and (4) the void for vagueness doctrine. The following subsections analyze the various procedural approaches.

A. *First Amendment Due Process*

A central tenet of First Amendment doctrine is that ultimate authority resides in the judiciary. Generally, any final decision as to suppression of speech must be made by a court. An administrative decision to restrict speech must be presented to a court either before, or very soon after implementation, and the burden of proof is on the government to justify the suppression. As the Supreme Court noted in *Freedman v. Maryland*, such protections are necessary "[b]ecause the censor's business is to censor." As a consequence, "there inheres the danger that [the executive] may well be less responsive than a court . . . to the constitutionally protected interests in free expression."[1] First Amendment due process is based on these principles.[2]

An essential requirement of due process is a limitation on the executive's unbridled discretion to restrict speech. The Supreme Court has long held that standardless licensing schemes governing speech constitutes prior restraint.[3] By the same reasoning, any other administrative arrangement that empowers an executive officer to suppress expression unilaterally is suspect. Consequently, the Court has invalidated ordinances that establish no criteria for deciding whether certain

---

1. 380 U.S. 51, 57–58, 85 S.Ct. 734, 738, 13 L.Ed.2d 649, 654 (1965).

2. *See* Henry P. Monaghan, *First Amendment "Due Process,"* 83 Harv. L. Rev. 518 (1970); Thomas I. Emerson, *The Doctrine of Prior Restraint*, 20 Law & Contemp. Probs. 648, 658–59 & n.34 (1955).

3. City of Lakewood v. Plain Dealer Publishing Co., 486 U.S. 750, 757, 108 S.Ct. 2138, 2144, 100 L.Ed.2d 771, 782 (1988); Shuttlesworth v. City of Birmingham, 394 U.S. 147, 151, 89 S.Ct. 935, 938–39, 22 L.Ed.2d 162, 167 (1969); Cox v. Louisiana, 379 U.S. 536, 557, 85 S.Ct. 453, 465–66, 13 L.Ed.2d 471, 485–86 (1965); Staub v. City of Baxley, 355 U.S. 313, 321–22, 78 S.Ct. 277, 281–82, 2 L.Ed.2d 302, 310–11 (1958); Kunz v. New York, 340 U.S. 290, 294, 71 S.Ct. 312, 315, 95 L.Ed. 280, 284 (1951); Saia v. New York, 334 U.S. 558, 560, 68 S.Ct. 1148, 1149, 92 L.Ed. 1574, 1577 (1948).

actions constitute "First Amendment activities;"[4] when to issue a parade permit;[5] whether to authorize charitable solicitations;[6] whether to permit the placement of news boxes on city streets;[7] or that authorize the police to arrest those who "interrupt" them.[8]

As described in Section 1.7[A], procedural requirements necessary to sustain a prior restraint generally are focused on the existence and timing of judicial review. The relevant law must specify a set time for action by public authorities.[9] This compels the government to provide expedited judicial review, from the initiation of proceedings through a final decision. The law must specify the time within which judicial proceedings must be started[10] and provide for a reasonably quick judicial proceeding.[11] Once an initial decision is rendered, either the restraint order must be stayed or be subject to immediate appellate review.

During these proceedings the government may temporarily bar publication, but "[a]ny restraint imposed in advance of a final judicial determination on the merits must ... be limited to preservation of the status quo for the shortest fixed period compatible with sound judicial resolution."[12] While this rule ensures expedited consideration, the practical effect is to delay publication until the courts complete their review. For example, three weeks passed before federal courts held that CNN could transmit the contents of taped conversations between General

---

4. In *Board of Airport Commissioners of Los Angeles v. Jews for Jesus, Inc.*, 482 U.S. 569, 576, 107 S.Ct. 2568, 2573, 96 L.Ed.2d 500, 508–09 (1987), a rule banning all "First Amendment activities" in an airport terminal was invalidated where administrative officials had unlimited authority to decide what activities fell within the prohibition.

5. Shuttlesworth v. Birmingham, 394 U.S. at 151, 89 S.Ct. at 938, 22 L.Ed.2d at 167; Cox v. Louisiana, 379 U.S. at 557, 85 S.Ct. at 465–66, 13 L.Ed.2d at 485–86.

6. Secretary of State of Maryland v. Joseph H. Munson Co., 467 U.S. 947, 964 n. 12, 104 S.Ct. 2839, 2850–51 n. 12, 81 L.Ed.2d 786, 800–801 n. 12 (1984); Cantwell v. Connecticut, 310 U.S. 296, 305–07, 60 S.Ct. 900, 904–05, 84 L.Ed. 1213, 1218–20 (1940); Lovell v. City of Griffin, 303 U.S. 444, 450–53, 58 S.Ct. 666, 668–69, 82 L.Ed. 949, 952–54 (1938).

7. City of Lakewood v. Plain Dealer Publishing Co., 486 U.S. at 755–762, 108 S.Ct. at 2142–46, 100 L.Ed.2d at 781–86.

8. City of Houston v. Hill, 482 U.S. 451, 107 S.Ct. 2502, 96 L.Ed.2d 398 (1987).

9. Freedman v. Maryland, 380 U.S. at 59, 85 S. Ct. at 739, 13 L.Ed.2d at 654–55.

10. It is insufficient for the law to state that judicial proceedings will begin "forthwith." United States v. Thirty-Seven Photo-graphs, 402 U.S. 363, 91 S.Ct. 1400, 28 L.Ed.2d 822 (1971). In *Kingsley Books, Inc. v. Brown*, 354 U.S. 436, 77 S.Ct. 1325, 1 L.Ed.2d 1469 (1957), for example, the Court approved a procedure that required a trial within one day of the filing of a request for an injunction. *See also* Marcus v. Search Warrant, 367 U.S. 717, 718, 81 S.Ct. 1708, 1709, 6 L.Ed.2d 1127, 1129 (1961). The Court has rejected a procedure that allowed the passage of 50 to 57 days prior to judicial review, Teitel Film Corp. v. Cusack, 390 U.S. 139, 88 S.Ct. 754, 19 L.Ed.2d 966 (1968), but approved one that allowed ten days between administrative denial and judicial review. Interstate Circuit, Inc. v. City of Dallas, 390 U.S. 676, 88 S.Ct. 1298, 20 L.Ed.2d 225 (1968).

11. Generally, it is not possible to set a time limit on the duration of judicial proceedings. *But see* Marcus v. Search Warrant, 367 U.S. at 737, 81 S.Ct. at 1719, 6 L.Ed.2d at 1139; Kingsley Books, Inc. v. Brown, 354 U.S. at 437–38 n.1, 77 S.Ct. at 1326 n.1, 1 L.Ed.2d at 1472 n.1 (upholding law that required judicial decision to be rendered within two days of trial).

12. Freedman, 380 U.S. at 59, 85 S.Ct. at 739, 13 L.Ed.2d at 655; *see* Capital Cities Media, Inc. v. Toole, 463 U.S. 1303, 1304, 103 S.Ct. 3524, 3526, 77 L.Ed.2d 1284, 1287 (1983).

Manuel Noriega and his lawyers.[13] Such restraints on publication pending review have been criticized as imposing a prior restraint "in order to decide that a prior restraint is unconstitutional."[14]

Once judicial proceedings commence, the government has the burden to prove that the need for the restraint outweighs the First Amendment interest involved.[15] In addition to shouldering the burden of proof, the government normally must give the affected party the opportunity to present evidence and argument in opposition to the proposed restraint.[16] The absence of adversary proceedings presumably would limit the decisionmaker's ability to engage in "balanced analysis and [reach] careful conclusions" required in the sensitive area of First Amendment adjudication. Moreover, participation by both sides is considered essential to help ensure that any resulting remedies are sufficiently narrow.[17]

One exception to the requirement of an adversary proceeding involves the use of search warrants directed at members of the press, when the government is seeking the "fruits, instrumentalities, or evidence of crime." Thus, in *Zurcher v. Stanford Daily*, the Court upheld a search of the Stanford University student newspaper offices to obtain photographs of or other evidence of implicating student demonstrators who had assaulted police officers.[18] The Court overturned lower court orders that would have allowed adversary proceedings except where there was a clear showing that "important materials will be destroyed or removed from the jurisdiction" and where "a restraining order would be futile."[19] The plurality opinion discounted the dangers of allowing such searches and noted that "presumptively protected materials are not necessarily immune from seizure under warrant for use at a criminal trial."[20] But the Court acknowledged that where search warrants are issued for First Amendment materials, the Fourth Amendment must be applied with "scrupulous exactitude."[21] In this regard, "special Fourth Amendment

13. *See* United States v. Noriega, 752 F.Supp. 1045, 1049 (S.D.Fla.1990); Laura Parker, *Judge Lifts Noriega Tapes Broadcast Ban*, Wash. Post, November 29, 1990 p. A1 col. 1. The district also held that the showing was insufficient to support an injunction. United States v. Noriega, 752 F.Supp. 1045 (S.D.Fla.1990). The entire process, from the first judicial hearing, through the appeal and final resolution, lasted three weeks.

14. Hans A. Linde, *Courts and Censorship*, 66 Minn. L. Rev. 171, 201 (1981).

15. *Freedman,* 380 U.S. at 58, 85 S. Ct. at 739, 13 L.Ed.2d at 654. *See* Marcus v. Search Warrant, 367 U.S. 717, 81 S.Ct. 1708, 6 L.Ed.2d 1127 (1961).

16. Carroll v. President and Commissioners of Princess Anne, 393 U.S. 175, 180, 184, 89 S.Ct. 347, 351, 353, 21 L.Ed.2d 325, 331, 333 (1968); Marcus, 367 U.S. at 720–21, 81 S. Ct. at 1710, 6 L.Ed.2d at 1129–30.

17. Carroll, 393 U.S. at 180, 183, 89 S. Ct. at 351, 353, 21 L.Ed.2d at 330, 332.

18. 436 U.S. 547, 550, 98 S.Ct. 1970, 1973, 56 L.Ed.2d 525, 531 (1978).

19. *Id*. at 552, 98 S. Ct. at 1975, 56 L. Ed. 2d at 533. Absent proof that such methods would be ineffectual, the district court and court of appeals held that the government must proceed via a subpoena *duces tecum* rather than by search warrant. Such procedure would permit the newspaper to move to quash the subpoena. *See* Stanford Daily v. Zurcher, 353 F.Supp. 124 (N.D.Cal. 1972), *aff'd*, 550 F.2d 464 (9th Cir.1977).

20. 436 U.S. at 567, 98 S.Ct. at 1982, 56 L.Ed.2d at 542.

21. *Id*. at 564, 98 S. Ct. at 1981, 56 L. Ed. 2d at 541. Justice Powell, who supplied the fifth vote, wrote in his concurring opinion that "a magistrate asked to issue a warrant for the search of press offices can and should take cognizance of the indepen-

protections [are] accorded searches for and seizure of First Amendment materials.''[22]

Given this caveat, the government's ability to seize First Amendment materials without an adversary hearing is limited. Where "things" to be seized include papers, books, photos or other expressive materials, a warrant will be considered to be excessively general unless the relevant materials are specifically described in the warrant.[23] Generally, where presumptively protected material "is not described in the warrant, it [is] not subject to seizure."[24] And it is insufficient to lump protected items into the warrant's scope by general reference to "other materials" that may be seized.[25] Similarly, the scope of the seizure is limited. Until there is an adversary hearing, the government is barred from seizing copies of a specified publication and thereby keeping it out of circulation. Instead, the government may seize a single copy for evidentiary purposes until the hearing.[26]

For the same reasons the government may not stage preemptive seizures in an effort to combat racketeering activity. Thus, while it may seize "all contraband, instrumentalities, and evidence of crimes" based on a probable cause showing, the risk of prior restraint dictates greater procedural protection when the contraband includes expressive materials. This rule usually applies in obscenity prosecutions. In *Fort Wayne Books, Inc. v. Indiana*,[27] the Supreme Court invalidated part of a state Racketeer Influenced and Corrupt Organizations ("RICO") statute that authorized pretrial seizure of all property "used in the course of, intended for use in the course of, derived from, or realized through" defendant's "racketeering activity" of running an adult book store. Noting that "there was not—and has not been—any determination that the seized items were 'obscene' or that a RICO violation has occurred,"[28] the Court was concerned that due to a pretrial order "literally thousands of books and films were carried away and taken out of circulation."[29] Consequently, it held that the First Amendment will not tolerate such seizures until the government's reasons for seizure weather the crucible

dent values protected by the First Amendment." *Id*. at 570, 98 S. Ct. at 1984, 56 L.Ed.2d at 544 (Powell, J., concurring).

22. Maryland v. Macon, 472 U.S. 463, 470, 105 S.Ct. 2778, 2782, 86 L.Ed.2d 370, 377 (1985).

23. Stanford v. Texas, 379 U.S. 476, 85 S.Ct. 506, 13 L.Ed.2d 431 (1965) (warrant issued to seize books, papers or other proof of membership in the Communist Part invalid as a general warrant).

24. United States v. Premises Known as 1007 Morningside Ave., 625 F.Supp. 1343, 1350 (N.D.Iowa 1985).

25. United States v. Apker, 705 F.2d 293, 301 (8th Cir.1983), *cert. denied*, 465 U.S. 1005, 104 S.Ct. 996, 79 L.Ed.2d 229 (1984).

26. Fort Wayne Books, Inc. v. Indiana, 489 U.S. 46, 63, 109 S.Ct. 916, 927, 103 L.Ed.2d 34, 51–52 (1989); New York v. P.J. Video, Inc., 475 U.S. 868, 874–76, 106 S.Ct. 1610, 1614–15, 89 L.Ed.2d 871, 880–81 (1986); Lo–Ji Sales, Inc. v. New York, 442 U.S. 319, 326 n. 5, 99 S.Ct. 2319, 2324 n. 5, 60 L.Ed.2d 920, 928 n. 5 (1979); Heller v. New York, 413 U.S. 483, 492, 93 S.Ct. 2789, 2794–95, 37 L.Ed.2d 745, 754 (1973).

27. 489 U.S. 46, 109 S.Ct. 916, 103 L.Ed.2d 34 (1989).

28. *Id*. at 66, 109 S.Ct. at 929, 103 L.Ed.2d at 53.

29. *Id*. at 66, 109 S.Ct. at 930, 103 L.Ed.2d at 54.

of an adversary hearing.[30] The Court's primary concern has been to prevent the government from seizing materials or otherwise halting speech prior to a determination that the speech is actually harmful.[31]

B. The Overbreadth Doctrine

An overly broad law may be considered an "abridgment" of speech even if properly and narrowly applied in a given case. This overbreadth doctrine permits parties to challenge governmental regulations that create a risk of suppressing the speech of others who are not involved in the case at issue. In this regard, the doctrine is an exception to traditional standing rules. Overbreadth analysis assumes that "the very existence of some broadly written laws has the potential to chill the expressive activity of others not before the court."[32] Accordingly, in certain cases courts will entertain facial challenges to laws and regulations considered overly broad.[33]

A law may be overly broad either by its terms or by its lack thereof. That is, a law may expressly restrict speech that otherwise is protected by the First Amendment.[34] Or, by failing to delineate its scope, a law may give government authorities too much latitude to infringe on speech.[35] In

---

30. *Id.* at 67, 109 S.Ct. at 930, 103 L.Ed.2d at 54.

31. *See, e.g.,* Fort Wayne Books, 489 U.S. at 65–66, 109 S. Ct. at 929, 103 L. Ed. 2d at 53 (seizure inappropriate because effected prior to a judicial determination of obscenity); Vance v. Universal Amusement Co., 445 U.S. 308, 316–17, 100 S.Ct. 1156, 1161–62, 63 L.Ed.2d 413, 420–21 (1980) (per curiam) (prior restraint unconstitutional because speech not yet adjudged unlawful); Quantity of Copies of Books v. Kansas, 378 U.S. 205, 210, 84 S.Ct. 1723, 1725, 12 L.Ed.2d 809, 812–13 (1964) (warrant for seizure unconstitutional because not preceded by a hearing on obscenity); Marcus v. Search Warrant, 367 U.S. at 731, 81 S. Ct. at 1716, 6 L.Ed.2d at 1135–36 (warrants to seize alleged obscenity unconstitutional because of inadequate procedural safeguards); *cf.* Kingsley Books, Inc. v. Brown, 354 U.S. 436, 444–45, 77 S.Ct. 1325, 1329–30, 1 L.Ed.2d 1469, 1475–76 (1957) (seizure after determination of obscenity in a criminal trial does not violate the First Amendment).

32. Forsyth County, Ga. v. The Nationalist Movement, 505 U.S. 123, 129–130, 112 S.Ct. 2395, 2401, 120 L.Ed.2d 101, 110 (1992); Brockett v. Spokane Arcades, Inc., 472 U.S. 491, 503, 105 S.Ct. 2794, 2801–02, 86 L.Ed.2d 394, 405–06 (1985); New York v. Ferber, 458 U.S. 747, 772, 102 S.Ct. 3348, 3362–63, 73 L.Ed.2d 1113, 1132 (1982); Keyishian v. Board of Regents, 385 U.S. 589, 609, 87 S.Ct. 675, 687, 17 L.Ed.2d 629, 644 (1967).

33. Forsyth County, 505 U.S. at 129, 112 S. Ct. at 2400–01, 120 L.Ed.2d at 110; City of Lakewood v. Plain Dealer Publishing Co., 486 U.S. 750, 108 S.Ct. 2138, 100 L.Ed.2d 771 (1988); City Council of Los Angeles v. Taxpayers for Vincent, 466 U.S. 789, 798–99 & n. 15, 104 S.Ct. 2118, 2125–26 & n. 15, 80 L.Ed.2d 772, 782–83 & n. 15 (1984). A law will be invalidated on its face only where the overbreadth is substantial. City of Houston v. Hill, 482 U.S. 451, 458–60, 107 S.Ct. 2502, 2508–09, 96 L.Ed.2d 398, 410–11 (1987).

34. *See, e.g.,* Erznoznik v. City of Jacksonville, 422 U.S. 205, 95 S.Ct. 2268, 45 L.Ed.2d 125 (1975) (invalidating prohibition on exhibiting films at drive-in theaters so that nude portions of the human anatomy were visible from the street); Lewis v. City of New Orleans, 415 U.S. 130, 94 S.Ct. 970, 39 L.Ed.2d 214 (1974) (invalidating as overbroad ordinance making it illegal "wantonly to curse or revile or to use obscene or opprobrious language"); Gooding v. Wilson, 405 U.S. 518, 92 S.Ct. 1103, 31 L.Ed.2d 408 (1972) (invalidating as overbroad prohibition of "opprobrious words or abusive language, tending to cause a breach of the peace").

35. *E.g.,* Forsyth County, 505 U.S. at 131–32, 112 S. Ct. at 2401–02, 120 L.Ed.2d at 111–12; Taxpayers for Vincent, 466 U.S. at 798 n.15, 104 S. Ct. at 2125 n.15, 80 L.Ed.2d at 782 n.15; Freedman v. Maryland, 380 U.S. at 56, 85 S. Ct. at 737–38, 13 L.Ed.2d at 653; Thornhill v. Alabama, 310

rare cases, a law may suffer from both infirmities. In *Board of Airport Commissioners v. Jews for Jesus, Inc.,*[36] the Court invalidated on overbreadth grounds a rule prohibiting "all First Amendment activities" in the Los Angeles airport terminal. The Court found that the sweeping language of the rule created "a virtual 'First Amendment Free Zone' at LAX."[37] At the same time, the open ended terms of the rule gave "LAX officials alone the power to decide in the first instance whether a given activity" is prohibited.[38] The Court found that the "opportunity for abuse" inherent with unrestricted discretion was "self-evident."[39]

The government may avoid invalidation on overbreadth grounds by adopting a narrowing construction of the law. Local authorities are free to interpret a law so as to avoid a constitutional conflict, and federal reviewing courts normally will defer to the interpretation.[40] Similarly, federal courts generally will attempt to construe statutes in ways that minimize constitutional problems.[41] Of course, the law must be fairly susceptible to a limiting construction.[42] The courts "will not rewrite a state law to conform it to constitutional requirements."[43] Additionally, a narrow reading of a law may not be sufficient to prevent a First Amendment problem if the resulting construction is vague or otherwise fails to cure the overbreadth.[44] Finally, if an overly broad statute is amended to cure its excessive sweep, challenges to the law based on the overbreadth of its original formulation are moot.[45]

The level of scrutiny a court will apply in an overbreadth inquiry will depend primarily on the extent to which the law at issue touches on protected speech. Where the threatened speech lies "in the shadow of the First Amendment," either because it is mixed with proscribable conduct or because it involves low value speech, then the asserted overbreadth "must not only be real, but substantial as well."[46] The courts must be

U.S. 88, 97, 60 S.Ct. 736, 741–42, 84 L.Ed. 1093, 1099–1100 (1940).

36. 482 U.S. 569, 107 S.Ct. 2568, 96 L.Ed.2d 500 (1987).

37. *Id.* at 574, 107 S.Ct. at 2572, 96 L.Ed.2d at 507.

38. *Id.* at 576, 107 S.Ct. at 2573, 96 L.Ed.2d at 509.

39. *Id.* (quoting Lewis v. City of New Orleans, 415 U.S. at 135–36, 94 S. Ct. at 974, 39 L.Ed.2d at 221) (Powell, J., concurring).

40. Osborne v. Ohio, 495 U.S. 103, 113–14, 110 S.Ct. 1691, 1698, 109 L.Ed.2d 98, 111–12 (1990); Village of Hoffman Estates v. Flipside, Hoffman Estates, Inc., 455 U.S. 489, 494 n. 5, 102 S.Ct. 1186, 1191, n. 5, 71 L.Ed.2d 362, 369 n. 5 (1982); Broadrick v. Oklahoma, 413 U.S. 601, 613, 93 S.Ct. 2908, 2916, 37 L.Ed.2d 830, 840–41 (1973).

41. New York v. Ferber, 458 U.S. 747, 769 n. 24, 102 S.Ct. 3348, 3361 n. 24, 73 L.Ed.2d 1113, 1130–31 n. 24 (1982).

42. Ferber, 458 U.S. at 769 n.24, 102 S. Ct. at 3361 n.24, 73 L.Ed.2d at 1130–31 n.24; Erznoznik, 422 U.S. at 216, 95 S. Ct. at 2276, 45 L.Ed.2d at 135; Broadrick, 413 U.S. at 613, 93 S. Ct. at 2916, 37 L.Ed.2d at 841.

43. Virginia v. American Booksellers Ass'n, 484 U.S. 383, 397, 108 S.Ct. 636, 645, 98 L.Ed.2d 782, 796 (1988).

44. R.A.V. v. City of St. Paul, 505 U.S. 377, 381 & n. 3, 112 S.Ct. 2538, 2542 & n. 3, 120 L.Ed.2d 305, 316–17 & n. 3 (1992); Jews for Jesus, Inc., 482 U.S. at 575–76, 107 S. Ct. at 2573, 96 L. Ed. 2d at 508.

45. Massachusetts v. Oakes, 491 U.S. 576, 109 S.Ct. 2633, 105 L.Ed.2d 493 (1989); Bigelow v. Virginia, 421 U.S. 809, 817–18, 95 S.Ct. 2222, 2230, 44 L.Ed.2d 600, 609 (1975).

46. Broadrick, 413 U.S. at 614, 615, 93 S. Ct. at 2917–18, 37 L. Ed. 2d at 841–42.

convinced of "a realistic danger that the statute ... will significantly compromise recognized First Amendment protections of parties not before the Court" before overbreadth will be considered substantial.[47] The "substantial overbreadth" requirement was articulated in *Broadrick v. Oklahoma*, in which the Court upheld state restrictions on political activity by public workers. In approving bans on state employees' soliciting contributions, running for office, managing campaigns or being an officer in a political party, the Court noted that overbreadth analysis attenuates "as the otherwise unprotected behavior that it forbids the State to sanction moves from 'pure speech' toward conduct."[48]

The Court extended the substantiality requirement to matters clearly involving "speech" in *New York v. Ferber*, where it upheld a state law prohibiting depictions of children engaged in sexual conduct. It held that any overbreadth was not substantial since only "a tiny fraction" of the prohibited depictions would not be considered obscene.[49] Similarly, the Court is reluctant to engage in overbreadth analysis in cases involving commercial speech. Although it receives First Amendment protection, the Court has held that commercial speech is entitled to a lower level of protection than speech on other matters.[50] Citing the different characteristics of commercial speech, the Court said that it "is not as likely to be deterred as noncommercial speech, and therefore does not require the added protection afforded by the overbreadth approach."[51]

C. First Amendment Underinclusiveness

Another doctrine that is "firmly grounded in basic First Amendment principles" is the concept that a regulation of speech may be impermissibly underinclusive.[52] This is similar, but different from the concept that regulatory distinctions among different types of speech, or between different media, may violate the Equal Protection Clause.[53] Rather than

47. Taxpayers for Vincent, 466 U.S. at 801, 104 S. Ct. at 2126, 80 L.Ed.2d at 784.

48. 413 U.S. at 615, 93 S. Ct. at 2917, 37 L.Ed.2d at 842. Broadrick raises some difficult questions regarding treatment of political activity as something less than "pure speech." *Compare with* Burson v. Freeman, 504 U.S. 191, 196, 112 S.Ct. 1846, 1850, 119 L.Ed.2d 5, 12–13 (1992); Monitor Patriot Co. v. Roy, 401 U.S. 265, 272, 91 S.Ct. 621, 625, 28 L.Ed.2d 35, 41 (1971) ("the constitutional guarantee has its fullest and most urgent application precisely to the conduct of campaigns for political office").

49. 458 U.S. at 773, 102 S. Ct. at 3363, 73 L.Ed.2d at 1133. *See also* Massachusetts v. Oakes, 491 U.S. at 589, 109 S. Ct. at 2641, 105 L.Ed.2d at 505 (Scalia, J., concurring) (legitimate photographs of nude children are not so common as to make a law prohibiting such photography substantially overbroad).

50. *See supra* section 1.7.

51. Ohralik v. Ohio State Bar Ass'n, 436 U.S. 447, 462 n. 20, 98 S.Ct. 1912, 1922 n. 20, 56 L.Ed.2d 444, 457–58 n. 20 (1978); Board of Trustees of the State University of New York v. Fox, 492 U.S. 469, 475–76, 109 S.Ct. 3028, 3032, 106 L.Ed.2d 388, 400–401 (1989); Bates v. State Bar of Arizona, 433 U.S. 350, 380, 51 Ohio Misc. 1, 97 S.Ct. 2691, 2707, 53 L.Ed.2d 810, 833–34 (1977).

52. City of Ladue v. Gilleo, 512 U.S. 43, 49, 114 S.Ct. 2038, 2043, 129 L.Ed.2d 36, 50 (1994).

53. *Id.* at 51 n.9, 114 S. Ct. at 2043 n.9, 129 L.Ed.2d at 45 n.9. *See* Leathers v. Medlock, 499 U.S. 439, 111 S.Ct. 1438, 113 L.Ed.2d 494 (1991); Carey v. Brown, 447 U.S. 455, 459–471, 100 S.Ct. 2286, 2289–2296, 65 L.Ed.2d 263, 268–276 (1980); Police Dept. of Chicago v. Mosley, 408 U.S. 92, 98–102, 92 S.Ct. 2286, 2291–2294, 33 L.Ed.2d 212, 218–220 (1972). *See supra* section 1.7[B].

focusing on the existence of viewpoint or content discrimination, such an underinclusiveness analysis examines whether or not a governmental restriction solves a sufficient amount of a targeted problem to justify the restriction on speech. Failure to address a sufficient amount of the problem "may diminish the credibility of the government's rationale for restricting speech in the first place."[54]

Courts have held that such incomplete solutions cannot justify the resulting intrusions on speech. In *Erznoznik v. City of Jacksonville*,[55] for example, the government had sought to justify regulating of public displays of movies containing nudity that were visible from a drive-in theater on the theory that such displays created a traffic hazard. The Court rejected this rationale as being "strikingly underinclusive."[56] It held that the First Amendment prohibited "singling out" such films based on their content where "a wide variety of other scenes in the customary screen diet" would create the same problem.[57] Some burden on speech might be permitted where no content distinctions are made, perhaps by requiring drive-in movie theaters to block the view from surrounding streets for all films, regardless of subject matter.[58] But where content discrimination appears to be gratuitous, and does not further the governmental purpose, the underinclusiveness may be fatal.

Typically, governments are permitted to address problems one step at a time.[59] And, in cases involving regulation of speech, courts are more likely to permit a one-step-at-a-time approach in matters in which constitutional scrutiny is not strict. In *United States v. Edge Broadcasting Company*,[60] for example, the Supreme Court upheld against First Amendment challenge a federal law that prohibited broadcasting of lottery advertisements in states in which lotteries are illegal. The law was challenged by a North Carolina radio station that wanted to air advertisements for the Virginia state lottery. Although it was licensed to broadcast in a state that prohibited lotteries, over 92 percent of the station's audience, and 95 percent of its advertising revenue, came from Virginia, a state which permitted lotteries. The Court nevertheless upheld the restriction under the commercial speech doctrine, finding

---

54. Gilleo, 512 U.S. at 52, 114 S. Ct. at 2044, 129 L.Ed.2d at 45.

55. 422 U.S. 205, 95 S.Ct. 2268, 45 L.Ed.2d 125 (1975).

56. *Id.* at 214, 95 S. Ct. at 2275, 45 L.Ed.2d at 131.

57. *Id.* at 214–215, 95 S. Ct. at 2275, 45 L. Ed. 2d at 134. *See also* FCC v. League of Women Voters of Cal., 468 U.S. 364, 396, 104 S.Ct. 3106, 3126, 82 L.Ed.2d 278, 301–02 (1984) (underinclusive regulation of speech provides ineffective or remote support for the government's purpose); Community–Service Broadcasting v. FCC, 593 F.2d 1102, 1122–1123, 192 U.S. App. D.C.

448, 468 (D.C.Cir.1978) (en banc) (recording requirement imposed on noncommercial stations but not on commercial stations is underinclusive); Carlin Communications, Inc. v. FCC, 749 F.2d 113, 121 (2d Cir.1984) (striking down safe harbor hours for dial-a-porn operations because of underinclusiveness).

58. Erznoznik, 422 U.S. at 215 n.13, 95 S. Ct. at 2276 n.13, 45 L.Ed.2d at 134 n.13.

59. Williamson v. Lee Optical, Inc., 348 U.S. 483, 488–489, 75 S.Ct. 461, 465, 99 L.Ed. 563, 572–573 (1955).

60. 509 U.S. 418, 113 S.Ct. 2696, 125 L.Ed.2d 345 (1993).

that the limited solution "would directly serve the statutory purpose of supporting North Carolina's antigambling policy."[61]

D. The Void for Vagueness Doctrine

A distinct but similar rule to the overbreadth doctrine holds that a law may abridge speech if it is impermissibly vague. This springs from the basic tenet of due process that a law is invalid if "men of common intelligence must necessarily guess at its meaning and differ as to its application."[62] Vagueness is especially pernicious in the First Amendment context, however. Not only do vague laws fail to put citizens sufficiently on notice that they may be violating the law, such enactments chill the exercise of free speech.[63] "[V]ague laws ... operate to inhibit protected expression by inducing 'citizens to steer far wider of the unlawful zone ... than if the boundaries of the forbidden areas were clearly marked.' "[64] Moreover, vague statutes have the same defect as overbroad ones: they allow excessive discretion to government officials to regulate speech.

A law is impermissibly vague if compliance depends entirely upon the subjective judgments of authorities. Thus, in *Smith v. Goguen*, the Supreme Court struck down a Massachusetts law making it a crime to "publicly ... treat[] contemptuously the flag of the United States."[65] The Court found no guidance in the law for what may or may not be "contemptuous" and concluded that enforcement was a matter of personal preference.[66] It is incumbent upon lawmakers to provide at least some enforcement criteria. "Where the legislature fails to provide such minimal guidelines, a criminal statute may permit 'a standardless sweep [that] allows policemen, prosecutors, and juries to pursue their personal predilections.' "[67] A law must contain some ascertainable standard for inclusion or exclusion to avoid being considered perfectly vague in all possible applications.[68]

---

61. *Id.* at 432, 113 S. Ct. at 2706, 125 L. Ed. 2d at 358. *But see* 44 Liquormart, Inc. v. Rhode Island, 517 U.S. 484, 116 S.Ct. 1495, 134 L.Ed.2d 711 (1996) (commercial speech restriction will not be upheld if it provides only remote support for government's purpose); Rubin v. Coors Brewing Co., 514 U.S. 476, 115 S.Ct. 1585, 131 L.Ed.2d 532 (1995) (same).

62. Zwickler v. Koota, 389 U.S. 241, 249, 88 S.Ct. 391, 396, 19 L.Ed.2d 444, 451 (1967), (*quoting* Connally v. General Construction Co., 269 U.S. 385, 391, 46 S.Ct. 126, 127, 70 L.Ed. 322, 328 (1926)). *See* Reno v. ACLU, 521 U.S. 844, 117 S.Ct. 2329, 138 L.Ed.2d 874 (1997).

63. NAACP v. Button, 371 U.S. 415, 433, 83 S.Ct. 328, 338, 9 L.Ed.2d 405, 418 (1963) ("The threat of sanctions may deter [speech] almost as patently as the actual application of sanctions.").

64. Buckley v. Valeo, 424 U.S. 1, 41 n. 48, 96 S.Ct. 612, 645 n. 48, 46 L.Ed.2d 659, 700 n. 48 (1976).

65. 415 U.S. 566, 568–69, 94 S.Ct. 1242, 1245, 39 L.Ed.2d 605, 609 (1974).

66. *Id.* at 575, 94 S. Ct. at 1248, 39 L.Ed.2d at 613.

67. Kolender v. Lawson, 461 U.S. 352, 358, 103 S.Ct. 1855, 1858, 75 L.Ed.2d 903, 909 (1983), (*quoting* Smith v. Goguen, 415 U.S. at 575, 94 S. Ct. at 1248, 39 L.Ed.2d at 613.)

68. *See* Gentile v. State Bar of Nevada, 501 U.S. 1030, 111 S.Ct. 2720, 115 L.Ed.2d 888 (1991) (invalidating Bar rule regulating extra judicial statements by lawyers); Coates v. City of Cincinnati, 402 U.S. 611, 611, 91 S.Ct. 1686, 1687, 29 L.Ed.2d 214, 216 (1971) (invalidating ordinance making it illegal for three or more persons to assemble on a sidewalk and conduct them-

Nevertheless, some vagueness is inherent in all legislation. Too much specificity renders a law incapable of general application and makes evasion easy by those not covered by the statutory terms. To strike the required balance between necessary generality and undue vagueness, the Court normally applies an objective test. Thus, in *Village of Hoffman Estates v. Flipside, Hoffman Estates, Inc.*, the Court found that a "business person of ordinary intelligence" would understand the terms of a local ordinance that regulated the sale of products "designed or marketed for use" with illegal drugs.[69] Additionally, the Court will not impose an impractical burden of precision on lawmakers. A law generally will not be considered unduly vague where it could not have realistically been made more specific.[70] As with overbreadth, however, the vagueness doctrine is more strictly applied to laws that directly affect First Amendment interests.[71] The Court has held that in such circumstances a "greater degree of specificity" is demanded than in other contexts to prevent arbitrary enforcement and the resulting chill of fundamental rights.[72]

The courts traditionally have treated vagueness and overbreadth "as logically related and similar doctrines."[73] Despite their similarities, how-

---

selves in a manner "annoying to persons passing by"); Baggett v. Bullitt, 377 U.S. 360, 371, 84 S.Ct. 1316, 1322, 12 L.Ed.2d 377, 384–85 (1964) (invalidating loyalty oath requiring teachers to swear that "by precept and example" the affiant will "promote respect for the flag" and "undivided allegiance" to the federal government).

69. 455 U.S. at 500, 501, 102 S. Ct. at 1194–95, 71 L.Ed.2d at 373. *See also* Young v. American Mini Theatres, Inc., 427 U.S. 50, 51, 96 S.Ct. 2440, 2444, 49 L.Ed.2d 310, 316 (1976) (zoning ordinance regulating "adult" movie theaters "characterized by an emphasis" on sexual themes upheld against vagueness challenge).

70. United States v. Petrillo, 332 U.S. 1, 7–8, 67 S.Ct. 1538, 1541–42, 91 L.Ed. 1877, 1882–83 (1947) ("Clearer and more precise language might have been framed by Congress to express what it meant by 'number of employees needed.' But none occurs to us, nor has any better language been suggested, effectively to carry out what appears to have been the Congressional purpose."); Broadrick, 413 U.S. at 608, 93 S. Ct. at 2913–14, 37 L. Ed. 2d at 837 ("there are limitations in the English language with respect to being both specific and manageably brief") (citation omitted). *See* NBC v. United States, 319 U.S. 190, 216, 63 S.Ct. 997, 1009, 87 L.Ed. 1344, 1362 (1943) (the public interest standard for regulating broadcasting "is as concrete as the complicated factors for judgment in such a field of delegated authority permit").

71. *But see* Village of Hoffman Estates v. Flipside, Hoffman Estates, Inc., 455 U.S. 489, 498–99, 102 S.Ct. 1186, 1193–1194, 71 L.Ed.2d 362, 371–72 (1982). Although the Hoffman Estates ordinance regulating "head" shops was challenged, *inter alia*, on First Amendment grounds, the Court emphasized that the ordinance "simply regulates business behavior" and that "economic regulation is subject to a less strict vagueness test because its subject matter is often more narrow."

72. *Id.*; Smith v. Goguen, 415 U.S. 566, 573, 94 S.Ct. 1242, 1247, 39 L.Ed.2d 605, 612 (1974). On the other hand, the Court may be more lenient when the vagueness in a law is not dispositive of its violation. For example, the Court has approved an ordinance relating to the issuance of business licenses for video arcades that directed the police chief to consider whether the applicant had "connections with criminal elements." City of Mesquite v. Aladdin's Castle, Inc., 455 U.S. 283, 291, 102 S.Ct. 1070, 1075, 71 L.Ed.2d 152, 160–61 (1982). The distinction, according to the Court, was that the vagueness related to the standard for investigating applicants, and did not control the final licensing decision by the city manager.

73. Kolender v. Lawson, 461 U.S. at 358 n.8, 103 S. Ct. at 1859 n.8, 75 L.Ed.2d at 910 n.8. The Supreme Court often refers to the two doctrines in tandem. *E.g.*, Keyishian v. Board of Regents, 385 U.S. 589, 609, 87 S.Ct. 675, 687, 17 L.Ed.2d 629, 644 (1967); Dombrowski v. Pfister, 380 U.S.

ever, the two doctrines are not identical. All vague statutes are potentially overbroad, since a lack of specificity empowers administrators with excessive discretion. This does not mean, however, that overbroad statutes are imprecise. A law prohibiting any public display of nudity might not be considered vague, but it may be overbroad.[74] Similarly, a regulation prescribing a specific decibel level for noise made at a public demonstration may be the model of precision, but it is overbroad to the extent it requires demonstrators to be too quiet.[75]

Another difference between the two doctrines is the extent to which they permit third party standing. A person who falls within the proscription of an overly broad law may nonetheless challenge the law's legality on behalf of those who may be chilled by the enactment.[76] However, the Court appears to be more reserved about allowing vicarious standing where a law is being challenged as being facially vague. For example, a person whose actions fall within the "hard core" of conduct prohibited by a law normally will not be allowed to assert that the law is possibly vague as applied to others.[77] The same is true where a law legitimately applies to nonspeech activities but arguably may extend to some protected speech. The Court thus rejected a vagueness challenge to the economic regulation in *Village of Hoffman Estates*.[78] Standing to assert a vagueness challenge is most likely to be permitted when the law at issue is "perfectly vague" as to all possible applications.

479, 486, 85 S.Ct. 1116, 1120–21, 14 L.Ed.2d 22, 28 (1965); NAACP v. Button, 371 U.S. at 433, 83 S. Ct. at 338, 9 L. Ed. 2d at 418. *But see* Zwickler v. Koota, 389 U.S. at 249–50, 88 S. Ct. at 396–97, 19 L.Ed.2d at 450–51 (explaining the difference between vagueness and overbreadth).

74. *See* Erznoznick, 422 U.S. at 213, 95 S. Ct. at 2274–75, 45 L.Ed.2d at 133.

75. United States v. Doe, 296 U.S. App. D.C. 350, 968 F.2d 86 (D.C.Cir.1992) (Park Service regulation limiting noise at demonstrations to 60 decibels held to be too restrictive).

76. *E.g.*, Keyishian v. Board of Regents, 385 U.S. at 609, 87 S. Ct. at 687, 17 L. Ed. 2d at 644.

77. Broadrick, 413 U.S. at 608–610, 93 S. Ct. at 2914–2915, 37 L. Ed. 2d at 838–39; Parker v. Levy, 417 U.S. 733, 748, 94 S.Ct. 2547, 2558, 41 L.Ed.2d 439, 453 (1974) (court martial for "conduct unbecoming an officer and a gentleman" and actions that "prejudice ... good order and military discipline" upheld where officer advised troops to defy orders to go to Vietnam). The Court in Parker also emphasized the "factors differentiating military society from civilian society" in evaluating the vagueness of the Uniform Code of Military Justice. *Id.* at 756, 94 S. Ct. at 2562, 41 L.Ed.2d at 458.

78. 455 U.S. at 498–99, 102 S.Ct. at 1193–94, 71 L.Ed.2d at 371–72.

Chapter Two

FIRST AMENDMENT TRADITIONS AND NEW COMMUNICATION TECHNOLOGY

Analysis

2.1 New Media and the Variable First Amendment

Consider the following scenario:

A federal regulator walks into a room and is confronted with six television sets, each displaying the same program. The show features a steamy sex scene between a man and a woman, complete with nudity, adult language and lots of sweat. Although transparent to the viewer, each TV is fed via a different transmission source. The first television is receiving a terrestrial broadcast transmission, the second obtains the images by coaxial cable, the third is connected to a fiber optic common carrier network, the fourth is hooked to a VCR or video disc player, the fifth is receiving a direct broadcast satellite ("DBS") feed and the sixth is receiving the transmission via the Internet. Leaving aside any questions of federal versus local jurisdiction, and assuming that the images are not obscene, what is the regulator's constitutional authority to control these images?

The answer is—it depends.

For the broadcast transmission, the answer depends upon whether the images are sufficiently salacious to be considered "patently offensive" based on "contemporary community standards for the broadcast medium."[1] It also depends on whether the telecast is post 10 p.m., after which time current law assumes there is no longer a "reasonable risk

---

1. Citizens complaint against Pacifica Foundation, 56 F.C.C.2d 94, 98 (1975), *quoted in* FCC v. Pacifica Foundation, 438 U.S. 726, 731–32, 98 S.Ct. 3026, 3031, 57 L.Ed.2d 1073, 1082 (1978).

153

that children may be in the audience."[2] Assuming these conditions are met, the government may require that the telecast be restricted to the appropriate time of day.

With respect to the cable connection the government's ability to regulate is more limited than in the case of broadcasting. Various courts have held that indecency regulations are invalid when applied to cable television,[3] although the Supreme Court has indicated that there is some limited ability for the government to authorize cable operators to restrict indecent leased access programming.[4] As with broadcast television, however, the law remains a work in progress.

With respect to the third television, the transmission source for which is a fiber optic common carrier network, a court might apply the cases relating to the regulation of "dial-a-porn." Although Congress would be permitted to regulate indecent transmissions in this situation, any regulations would be subjected to strict constitutional scrutiny and would be invalidated if the government failed to employ the least restrictive means of control.[5]

The answer is not entirely certain with respect to television set number four. There is much logic and some case law to suggest that the VCR or video disc-originated images would receive the same constitutional protection as the print media. None of the "special justifications"

2. Action for Children's Television v. FCC, 58 F.3d 654, 657, 313 U.S.App.D.C. 94 (D.C.Cir.1995) ("Act III"), cert. denied, 516 U.S. 1043, 116 S. Ct. 701, 133 L.Ed.2d 658 (1996). This "safe harbor" period has passed through various incarnations. Before finally approving the FCC's rules in 1995, the United States Court of Appeals for the District of Columbia Circuit previously rejected a 24–hour ban on indecent broadcasts and a 12 a.m. to 6 a.m. "safe harbor" period. *See* Action for Children's Television v. FCC, 932 F.2d 1504, 290 U.S. App. D.C. 4 (D.C.Cir.1991), cert. denied, 503 U.S. 913, 112 S.Ct. 1281 117 L.Ed.2d 507 (1992) ("ACT II") (24–hour indecency ban rejected); Action for Children's Television v. FCC, 852 F.2d 1332, 271 U.S. App. D.C. 365 (D.C.Cir.1988) ("ACT I") (12 a.m. to 6 a.m. "safe harbor" period rejected).

3. Community Television of Utah, Inc. v. Wilkinson, 611 F.Supp. 1099 (D.Utah 1985), *aff'd sub nom.* Jones v. Wilkinson, 800 F.2d 989 (10th Cir.1986), *aff'd mem.* 480 U.S. 926, 107 S.Ct. 1559, 94 L.Ed.2d 753 (1987); Cruz v. Ferre, 755 F.2d 1415 (11th Cir.1985); Daniels Cablevision, Inc. v. United States, 835 F.Supp. 1, 9–10 (D.D.C. 1993); Community Television of Utah, Inc. v. Roy City, 555 F.Supp. 1164 (D.Utah 1982); Home Box Office, Inc. v. Wilkinson, 531 F.Supp. 987 (D.Utah 1982).

4. *See* Denver Area Educational Telecommunications Consortium v. FCC, 518 U.S. 727, 116 S.Ct. 2374, 135 L.Ed.2d 888 (1996) (cable operator may exercise editorial discretion to ban indecent leased access programming from its system, but government may not require that such programming, if carried, be segregated to a separate channel and subjected to a presubscription requirement).

5. After dial-a-porn regulations were twice struck down as being too restrictive of adults' rights to receive sexually-oriented telephone messages, Carlin Communications, Inc. v. FCC, 749 F.2d 113 (2d Cir. 1984) (Carlin I); (Carlin Communications, Inc. v. FCC, 787 F.2d 846 (2d Cir.1986) (Carlin II), the FCC fashioned judicially-acceptable regulations. Carlin Communications, Inc. v. FCC, 837 F.2d 546 (2d Cir. 1988), cert. denied, 488 U.S. 924, 109 S.Ct. 305, 102 L.Ed.2d 324 (1988) (Carlin III). *See also* Information Providers' Coalition For Defense of the First Amendment v. FCC, 928 F.2d 866 (9th Cir.1991); Dial Information Services Corp. of New York v. Thornburgh, 938 F.2d 1535 (2d Cir.1991), cert. denied, 502 U.S. 1072, 112 S.Ct. 966, 117 L.Ed.2d 132 (1992). Congress attempted to ban all interstate dial-a-porn calls, including calls that were indecent but not obscene, but this measure was invalidated as a First Amendment infringement. Sable Communications of California, Inc. v. FCC, 492 U.S. 115, 109 S.Ct. 2829, 106 L.Ed.2d 93 (1989).

used to support the regulation of indecent broadcasting apply since there is no use of the radio spectrum, and, presumably, video material would not enter the home uninvited.[6] Accordingly, in *Video Software Dealers Ass'n. v. Webster*, the United States Court of Appeals for the Eighth Circuit invalidated a state law that prohibited the rental of "violent" videotapes to minors.[7] However, the issue has never been formally resolved by the Supreme Court.[8]

The appropriate First Amendment standard for the DBS transmissions received on set number five is even more confused. To the extent satellite programmers operate as broadcasters, making their transmissions freely available to all receivers, they would be subject to much the same statutory requirements as terrestrial TV stations.[9] In this regard, Congress determined that DBS operators must set aside four to seven percent of channel capacity for "public interest" programming,[10] and the United States Court of Appeals for the District of Columbia Circuit so far has upheld the requirement under the same rationale used to support traditional broadcast controls.[11] Notwithstanding the holding of the Court of Appeals, it is not entirely clear that the spectrum scarcity that has served to justify less First Amendment protection for terrestrial broadcasters realistically applies to DBS operators. In a dissent from a denial of rehearing, five judges of the Circuit pointed out that "DBS is more than an order of magnitude less scarce than traditional broadcasting" and concluded that the "factual predicate" of broadcast regulation—"scarcity of channels—is absent here."[12] In any event, the type of regulation relevant to the hypothetical situation raised here—indecency restrictions—has not been applied to DBS. In this respect, DBS operates more like cable television and would most likely be subject to the same First Amendment standard. There is no word yet on this from the Supreme Court.

Ironically, the greatest constitutional guidance regarding the appropriate First Amendment standard for new technologies has been given with regard to the Internet, which has not yet become a significant source of video programming. The FCC's annual report on the state of video competition has begun to list "Internet Video" among the competitors, but with the caveat that "it is premature to assess the impact of the

---

6. Similarly, private viewing of videotapes in the home "affects the community interest to a lesser degree" than the public exhibition of adult films. Gascoe, Ltd. v. Newtown Township, Bucks County, 699 F.Supp. 1092, 1098 (E.D.Pa.1988).

7. 968 F.2d 684 (8th Cir.1992).

8. *See* Karl A. Groskaufmanis, *What Films We May Watch: Videotape Distribution and the First Amendment*, 136 U. Pa. L. Rev. 1263, 1284 (1988).

9. 18 U.S.C.A. § 1464 (West Supp. 1997) provides: "Whoever utters any obscene, indecent, or profane language by means of radio communication shall be

fined [under this title not more than $10,000] or imprisoned not more than two years, or both."

10. Section 25, Cable Television Consumer Protection and Competition Act of 1992, Pub. L. No. 102–385, 106 Stat. 1460 ("1992 Cable Act") (codified at 47 U.S.C.A. § 335(b)(1)) (West Supp. 1997).

11. Time Warner Entertainment Co., L.P. v. FCC, 93 F.3d 957, 974–977, 320 U.S. App. D.C. 294, 311–14 (D.C.Cir.1996).

12. Time Warner Entertainment Co., L.P. v. FCC, 105 F.3d 723, 725, 323 U.S. App. D.C. 109, 111 (D.C.Cir.1997).

Internet on the video marketplace."[13] Nevertheless, in *Reno v. ACLU* the Supreme Court invalidated federal regulation of indecent speech on the Internet.[14] The Court contrasted the Internet with broadcasting with respect to its scarcity, invasiveness and regulatory history, finding that "[t]hose factors are not present in cyberspace."[15] It therefore held that prior cases "provide no basis for qualifying the level of First Amendment scrutiny that should be applied to this medium."[16] Other judges have been even more emphatic. One of the lower court judges who reviewed the law concluded that "Congress may not regulate indecency on the Internet at all."[17]

Given these myriad approaches to technology and its effect on the First Amendment, it is likely to take years for our hypothetical federal regulator to know the constitutional limits of his authority with respect to the six televisions. And if case law develops as it has in the past, it is entirely possible that the six transmissions could be governed by entirely distinct First Amendment standards. Moreover, by the time those legal standards are in place (perhaps an overly optimistic assumption), there will no doubt be additional technologies to further complicate the analysis. For example, what potential constitutional implications flow from interactivity of a particular medium? Or, what will courts do if or when new media no longer confine themselves to transmitting images and information but begin to transmit physical sensations?[18] Should there be a separate First Amendment test for virtual reality?[19]

The distinct First Amendment standards applicable to different technologies have been attributed to differences in the characteristics of the various media. Certainly such differences exist: Broadcast signals come to the home free of charge and can be received by any television within range of the transmission; cable television and common carrier fiber optic links requires a physical connection and are provided to customers by subscription; video tapes or discs generally are obtained from an external source and require additional hardware for playback; DBS requires specialized receiving equipment and is provided, for the

---

13. *See* Annual Assessment of the Status of Competition in the Market for the Delivery of Video Programming, Third Annual Report, 12 FCC Rcd. 4358, 4413–4417 (1997).

14. 521 U.S. 844, 117 S.Ct. 2329, 138 L.Ed.2d 874 (1997).

15. *Id.* at 868, 117 S. Ct. at 2343, 138 L. Ed. 2d at 895.

16. *Id.* at 870, 117 S. Ct. at 2344, 138 L. Ed. 2d at 897.

17. ACLU v. Reno, 929 F.Supp. 824, 877 (E.D.Pa.1996) (Dalzell J.).

18. *See, e.g.,* Vic Sussman, *Small Operators Can Make Big Killings on the Web*, USA Today, Aug. 20, 1997 at 2A (Penthouse magazine is exploring the use of "neural and sensory interfaces" to provide new services over the Internet, proposing to

"transmit not just audio and video but actual sensations").

19. As the United States Court of Appeals for the Fifth Circuit pointed out in the somewhat different context of intellectual property: "In some computer programs, the user interface may merge almost wholly with the expression, processes or ideas embodied in the program—voice-activated or virtual reality programs or those attuned to the human heartbeat furnish some examples that may trouble courts in the future. We do not presume to anticipate the legal consequences of such technological developments." Engineering Dynamics, Inc. v. Structural Software, Inc., 26 F.3d 1335, 1342 (5th Cir.1994), *supplemented on denial of reh'g* 46 F.3d 408 (5th Cir.1995).

most part, by subscription; the Internet requires a connection to an Internet Service Provider or other online service, but provides access to a wide array of information that, like broadcast television, is advertiser-supported and free to the consumer. The relevant question is not whether such differences exist—it is whether these differences justify constitutional distinctions between the various media.

After all, the different First Amendment standards that have been applied to electronic communication usually are contrasted with the "full" First Amendment protection provided under the "print model." Yet different "characteristics" typify the world of printed communication that are at least as significant as the distinctions attributable to electronic speech. Printed material comes in many forms and is distributed in a wide variety of economic arrangements. Leaflets, handbills and some newspapers often are distributed without charge and are made available to all within the range of the publisher. In addition to such free distribution, newspapers are sent through the government mail system and sold on public rights of way. The same can be said of magazines. Some such distribution is favored with preferential mail rates. Some printed material can be read only with the aid of specialized equipment, such as a microfilm or microfiche reader. Despite these differences, all print media generally receive the same (and the strongest) First Amendment protections.

The conceptual problem inherent in drawing doctrinal lines in this way was underscored in a lower court case that enjoined federal government export controls on encryption software as an unconstitutional prior restraint. Federal law required a license from the Department of Commerce (and previously, from the Department of State) because of the national security implications of computer code and software that could be used to encode speech to make it unreadable without decryption. The regulations prohibited unlicensed electronic transmissions of encryption software (either by computer disk or by Internet posting), but did not preclude export of identical source code or information in printed form. In *Bernstein v. Department of State*, Judge Marilyn Hall Patel of the United States District Court for the Northern District of California found this "distinction between print and electronic media increasingly untenable."[20] Citing the Supreme Court's opinion in *Reno v. ACLU*, Judge Patel found that "the dramatically different treatment of the same materials depending on the medium by which they are conveyed is not only irrational, it may be impermissible under traditional First Amendment analysis."[21]

This Chapter examines the treatment of new communications technologies and assesses various theoretical approaches that have been formulated to explain such treatment. While there are many different

20. 974 F.Supp. 1288, 1306 (N.D.Cal. 1997). *See also* Bernstein v. Department of State, 945 F.Supp. 1279 (N.D.Cal.1996); Bernstein v. Department of State, 922 F.Supp. 1426 (N.D.Cal.1996).

21. *Id.* at 1307. *But see* Junger v. Daley, 8 F.Supp.2d. 708, (N.D.Ohio 1998) (reaching opposite conclusion).

views on this subject, this Chapter separates the theories into three categories: the Incrementalist Perspective, the Revisionist Perspective and the Traditionalist Perspective.[22]

Incrementalism defends the existing method of gradual application of free speech rights to new media. Proponents of this approach support having different levels of protection for different media, reserving full protection only for print, and concluding that freedom of expression is maximized in the system as a whole. Revisionism generally supports the expanded use of regulatory power over new media based on a similar utilitarian balancing approach. Government intervention is justified under Revisionist theory to the extent it is intended to produce more speech, thereby serving First Amendment values. Finally, the Traditionalist Perspective maintains that the First Amendment's principal command is the separation of press and state. It rejects the idea that government may obtain some optimal level of public discourse by intervening in the choices of private speakers. Under this approach, traditional understandings of First Amendment law would be applied to all media.

The Chapter concludes that the Traditionalist Perspective provides the most reliable method of analyzing new media under the First Amendment. The Incrementalist approach has brought us to where we are today, with different standards for different media and no clear guidelines for the future. The constitutional foundations upon which existing regulations are based (such as radio spectrum scarcity) are eroding away, while the underlying premise of Incrementalism—that each medium is a law unto itself—loses meaning as the various media converge. Revisionism, by contrast, tends to elevate policy preferences over constitutional principle. Common among Revisionist theories is the selection of a transcendent First Amendment "value" that overrides the command that "Congress shall make no law ...," quite often to the exclusion of other First Amendment values. Such theories tend to overestimate the government's ability to correct perceived deficiencies in the marketplace of ideas and underestimate the dangers of making the attempt. Moreover, when Revisionist theory proposes different First Amendment treatment based on the medium of communication, it suffers from the same problem that plagues Incrementalism: technology evolves faster than the law can change, thus undercutting the factual predicates of regulation.

The Traditionalist Perspective, on the other hand, helps simplify First Amendment adjudication by foregoing the seemingly endless search for the appropriate standard for each medium. Instead, well-tested

22. The concepts in this Chapter have been explored previously in Robert Corn–Revere, Paper, *Fear and Loathing in Cyberspace*, (Presentation to the Library of Congress Network Advisory Committee Meeting, Legal Issues Surrounding the Digital Library, December 4–5, 1995); Robert Corn–Revere, *Lost on the Infobahn Without* a Map: The Need for a Coherent First Amendment Approach, in TOWARD A COMPETITIVE TELECOMMUNICATION INDUSTRY 331–366 (Gerald W. Brock, ed. 1995); Robert Corn–Revere, *New Technology and the First Amendment: Breaking the Cycle of Repression*, 17 Comm./Ent. L.J. 247 (1994).

analytic approaches can be applied in each case, such as whether the government's interest is compelling, the regulatory means chosen sufficiently narrow and whether the government's interest is, in fact, served. These and other traditional First Amendment inquiries may be readily applied without regard to the medium of transmission. Doing so avoids the confusion of multiple standards and ends the need to constantly reassess the First Amendment as new media emerge. It also allows the law to adapt more quickly to new factual developments, and thus provides more stable and predictable protection for new forms of expression. Different characteristics of the various media forms are not left out of the calculus, but they would not be the basis for wholly different constitutional standards.

Some may characterize the Traditionalist Perspective as simply applying the "print model" of the First Amendment to all electronic media. While it has this effect, a Traditionalist understanding of the First Amendment goes further. It suggests that the search for different models, whether the "print model," or the "broadcast model" or something else, such as a "cyberspace model,"is inherently futile. Any model that is based on the particular characteristics of a given medium becomes obsolete as technology evolves. Moreover, the typically long periods in which courts and policymakers grope for new models lead to confusion as well as the use of interim standards that often undermine free speech values.

2.2 Technology, Regulation and the First Amendment

In January 1829, Martin Van Buren, then Governor of New York, wrote to President Andrew Jackson, urging him to forestall the development of "a new form of transportation"—the railroad. If railroads were to supplant canal boats, he warned, serious unemployment would result. "Captains, cooks, drivers, hostlers, repairmen, and lock tenders will be left without means of livelihood, not to mention the numerous farmers now employed in growing hay for horses. Boat builders would suffer and towline, whip and harness makers would be left destitute." Van Buren added that railroads posed a threat to national security. "In the event of unexpected trouble with England, the Erie Canal would be the only means by which we could ever move the supplies so vital to waging modern war."[1]

Finally, he warned of the dangers of the technology itself: "As you may well know, Mr. President, 'railroad' carriages are pulled at the enormous speed of 15 miles per hour by 'engines' which, in addition to endangering life and limb of passengers, roar and snort their way through the countryside, setting fire to crops, scaring the livestock and frightening women and children. The Almighty certainly never intended that people should travel at such breakneck speed."[2]

1. Letter from Gov. Martin Van Buren to President Andrew Jackson, January 31, 1829, *reprinted in* Hagerstown (MD) Morning Herald, June 29, 1990, p. A4.

2. *Id.*

It is likely that Van Buren's concern had more to do with preserving the economic superiority of his state's canal industry than it did with genuine fears about the rate of human travel and its relationship to a supreme being. But whatever may have been his motivation, he employed a technique that has been used countless times in the history of lobbying—exploiting fear of technology to drive social policy.

The comparison between advances in transportation and communications technologies is apt, but not at all because of the unfortunate "Information Superhighway" metaphor.[3] Rather, it is because the regulatory structure created for one technology was used as the model to control the other. The Interstate Commerce Commission—the first independent regulatory agency—was used as the form for the creation of the Federal Communications Commission. And, as described more fully below, the choice of how to regulate communications media helps to define each medium's status under the First Amendment.

Another important insight is that new media have always generated fear among policymakers, and fear leads to regulation. As Professor Donald E. Lively has written,

> [s]ince early in the twentieth century, an undifferentiated phobia of a potential for some evil, rather than a palpable fear of demonstrable social harm, has been the initial response to the emergence of each major new medium. Anxiety has been consistently translated into an identification of certain "peculiar characteristics," which purportedly offer a principled ground for exclusion of the medium from the full sweep of the first amendment.[4]

This trend has led to greater regulation of electronic media which "has yielded an increasingly narrower ambit of press freedom overall."[5]

A. *Fear and Loathing in Cyberspace*

Nowhere is this trend more evident than in the drive to regulate the newest of the new media—cyberspace. On the one hand, the technology

---

3. "Information Superhighway" is a particularly inapt term, and not just because it compares unprecedented developments in the history of human communication to a public works project. A technology supplement to the WASHINGTON POST launched a contest to search for a better term. *See* Craig Stolz, *Giving the Information Superhighway a Good Name*, Wash. Post Fast Forward, September 1994 at p. 4 ("Bad enough the phrase resonates with the oaken earnestness of Vice President Al Gore, the guy responsible for introducing it to the public. Far worse are the dozens of winky 'highway' metaphors, all too cute by half, that have thumbed a ride: 'Toll booth.' 'Traffic cops.' 'Road kill.'"). Such a reaction is understandable in light of the following metaphorical hash used to describe new infrastructure investments designed to

"create as much infobahn spaghetti with cybersauce as we can cook up to throw on the wall and see what sticks with our customers." Multichannel News, Oct. 3, 1994, p. 100. On the legislative front, one bill was introduced just before April 1, 1994 to make it a crime "to use a computer network while intoxicated;" that is, banning drunk driving on the Information Superhighway. *See April Fools Day on the Data Superhighway; Prankster Reports Bill Would Ban Drunk Driving on Networks*, Wash. Post, Mar. 30, 1994 p. C3.

4. Donald E. Lively, *Fear and the Media: A First Amendment Horror Show*, 69 Minn. L. Rev. 1071, 1076 (1985) (citations omitted).

5. *Id.* at 1074.

of interconnected computer networks has been lauded as "a never-ending worldwide conversation" and "the most participatory form of mass speech yet developed."[6] The United States Supreme Court similarly proclaimed that the information available on the Internet is as "diverse as human thought" with the capability of providing instant access on topics ranging from "the music of Wagner to Balkan politics to AIDS prevention to the Chicago Bulls."[7] The Court compared the World Wide Web, which allows Internet users to search for and retrieve information from remote computers using a graphical interface, to "both a vast library including millions of readily available and indexed publications and a sprawling mall offering goods and services."[8] But in a bizarre twist, the good news about cyberspace *is* the bad news. That is, the very capabilities of the technology that spark Utopian dreams also lead to demands in some quarters for regulation. Senator James Exon of Nebraska, author of the ill-fated Communications Decency Act ("CDA"), summed this up succinctly:

> The information superhighway is . . . a revolution that in years to come will transcend newspapers, radio and television as an information source. Therefore, I think this is the time to put some restrictions or guidelines on it.[9]

Judge Stuart Dalzell, a member of the first panel of judges to evaluate and invalidate two sections of the CDA, wrote that the law was premised on the assumption "that too much speech occurs in that medium, and that speech there is too available to the participants"—a premise he described as "profoundly repugnant to First Amendment principles."[10]

Repugnant or not, such concerns have always contributed to the fear of new media and have led to proposals for regulation. After the bombing of a federal office building in Oklahoma City in 1995, for example, federal legislators began to focus on the idea that new communications technologies could be used to transmit dangerous information. Although no such transmissions were connected to the Oklahoma City bombing, the incident heightened concerns that electronic communications could be used to promote domestic terrorism. The subsequent inquiry focused attention on whether the constitutional standard for restricting incitement should be relaxed when the information is transmitted electronically.

In May 1995, the Senate Judiciary Committee's Subcommittee on Terrorism, Technology and Government Information held hearings on "The Availability of Bomb Making Information on the Internet." Testimony at the hearing revealed that "recipes" for building bombs were

---

6. American Civil Liberties Union v. Reno, 929 F.Supp. 824, 883 (E.D.Pa.1996) (Dalzell J.), *aff'd* 521 U.S. 844, 117 S.Ct. 2329, 138 L.Ed.2d 874 (1997).

7. Reno v. ACLU, 521 U.S. 844, 851, 117 S.Ct. 2329, 2335, 138 L.Ed.2d 874 (1997).

8. Id. at 853, 117 S. Ct. at 2335, 138 L. Ed. 2d at 886.

9. Quoted in Peter H. Lewis, *Cybersex Stays Hot, Despite a Plan for Cooling it Off*, N. Y. Times, Mar. 26, 1995, p. 1.

10. American Civil Liberties Union v. Reno, 929 F. Supp. at 881 (Dalzell, J.).

available on the Internet, and that "information once in a few counter-culture bookstores is now daily promoted into millions of American homes."[11] The Department of Justice provided testimony that information on how to construct bombs "is freely available on the Internet" and "computer bulletin boards" and that "acts of violence like the Oklahoma City bombing are facilitated by the free flow of information on how to construct destructive weapons."[12] Senator Edward Kennedy of Massachusetts concluded that "we should do something about this terrorist information," noting that his staff had downloaded from the Internet a 76–page document called the *Terrorist's Handbook*. It contained instructions for building different types of bombs, including the ammonium nitrate bomb used in Oklahoma City.[13] Senator Diane Feinstein stated flatly: "First Amendment rights don't extend to [bomb recipes on] the Internet."[14]

The underlying premise of these concerns is the same as in the CDA—the information is rendered more dangerous because it is too available online. There is no question but that bombmaking information is widely available in, among other publications, the ENCYCLOPEDIA BRITANNICA and books published by the United States Department of Agriculture (not to mention the transcript of the Hearing).[15] An analysis by the Department of Justice revealed that even a "cursory search of the Library of Congress located at least 50 publications substantially devoted to [bombmaking] information, all readily available to any member of the public interested in reading them and copying their contents."[16] The FBI Explosives Unit has collected for its library approximately 48 "underground publications" dealing with bombmaking that the Justice Department has characterized as "easily obtainable from commercial sources." Even popular literature and magazines—including such periodicals as

---

11. *See The Availability of Bomb Making Information on the Internet,* Hearings before the Subcommittee on Terrorism, Technology and Government Information, Senate Judiciary Committee, 104th Cong., 1st Sess. (May 11, 1995) (testimony of Rabbi Marvin Hier, The Simon Wiesenthal Center) ("Internet Terrorism Hearings").

12. *Id.* (testimony of Robert S. Litt, Deputy Assistant Attorney General, Criminal Division, United States Department of Justice).

13. Brock N. Meeks, *Will the Net Be the Next Bomb "Victim"?*, Interactive Week, May 8, 1995, p. 42.

14. Brock N. Meeks, *Controlling Online Content for Kids: Why Johnny Can't Surf,* Interactive Week, May 8, 1995, p. 43.

15. *See* 21 Encyclopedia Britannica at 275–82 (1986 ed.). The entry describes manufacture of the ammonium nitrate and fuel oil bomb used in Oklahoma City. *Id.* at 279. *See also* U.S. Forest Service, United States Department of Agriculture, BLASTER'S

HANDBOOK (1980) (describes ammonium nitrate/fuel oil explosives). *See Internet Terrorism Hearings, supra, note* 11 (testimony of Professor Frank Tuerkheimer, University of Wisconsin Law School). The widespread availability of the same books in print form as may be found online distinguishes this case from United States v. Progressive, Inc., 467 F.Supp. 990 (W.D.Wis. 1979), in which publication of "the H Bomb secret" was initially enjoined. However, the injunction in that was lifted after the same article appeared in another publication.

16. U.S. DEPARTMENT OF JUSTICE, REPORT ON THE AVAILABILITY OF BOMBMAKING INFORMATION, THE EXTENT TO WHICH ITS DISSEMINATION IS CONTROLLED BY FEDERAL LAW, AND THE EXTENT TO WHICH SUCH DISSEMINATION MAY BE SUBJECT TO REGULATION CONSISTENT WITH THE FIRST AMENDMENT TO THE UNITED STATES CONSTITUTION 5 (April 1997) ("DOJ Bombmaking Report").

Reader's Digest—were found to constitute "a rich source of bombmaking information."[17]

Although witnesses at the Hearing acknowledged that "similar guides have been available in bookstores and public libraries for years," there was concern that "the Internet has … increased the flow of this information; it is now easily available to millions of people."[18] Such easy access may increase terrorism, according to some witnesses, by removing "the constraints [the terrorist] might normally feel about purchasing a bomb cookbook at the local bookstore."[19] Others suggest, on the other hand, that "shouting fire in cyberspace is actually *far less threatening*, and thus less deserving of censure, than the equivalent act in the physical world."[20]

There is little doubt that the government can investigate and prosecute those who disseminate bombmaking information as part of a plan to commit a crime.[21] But legislative inquiries about proscribing bombmaking information on the Internet raised a more basic constitutional question. Can the government prohibit "the widespread distribution of information about making a bomb" without a showing of intent to cause harm, or the imminent risk that violence will occur?[22] A 1997 report to Congress by the Department of Justice concluded that such a broad prohibition would be constitutionally suspect, because it would "deter altogether the dissemination of information." The report applied the same First Amendment standards to the Internet as are appropriate for printed materials and concluded that any proposed law must be tailored to restrict particular persons about whom the sender of information knows that criminal use of bombmaking information is likely.[23] Under this analysis, the government could not simply ban the publication of bombmaking materials on the Internet.[24]

---

17. *Id.* at 5–6.

18. *Internet Terrorism Hearings, supra, note* 11 (testimony of Robert S. Litt, Deputy Assistant Attorney General, Criminal Division, United States Department of Justice).

19. *Id.*

20. *Id.* (testimony of Jerry Berman, Executive Director, Center for Democracy and Technology) (emphasis in original). *See also id.* (testimony of Professor Frank Tuerkheimer, University of Wisconsin Law School: "If we are concerned with a particular item being communicated, in addition to the purpose of the communication, we ought to focus on what it is that is being communicated, rather than the form of [the] communication.").

21. *Id.* ("[W]e can prosecute individuals under 18 U.S.C. § 231 for showing how to make a bomb if they know it will be used in a civil disorder") (testimony of Professor Frank Tuerkheimer, University of Wisconsin Law School giving examples from the United States Criminal Code).

22. *Id.* (testimony of Robert S. Litt, Deputy Assistant Attorney General, Criminal Division, United States Department of Justice).

23. DOJ Bombmaking Report at 49–50.

24. In 1995 and 1996 Senator Dianne Feinstein sponsored legislation designed to address the issue of bombmaking information on the Internet. Although the Senate adopted the proposals as part of larger bills, the Feinstein amendments were deleted in Conference both times. *Id.* at 4. Instead, Congress directed the Attorney General to study the availability of bombmaking information in any medium (including print electronic, or film) and to report on the need for new legislation. Section 709(a), Antiterrorism and Effective Death Penalty Act of 1996, Pub. L. 104–132, 110 Stat. 1214, 1297 (1996). Based on the resulting DOJ Bombmaking Report, Senator Feinstein proposed a narrower version of the legislation that was restricted to dissemination of bombmaking information "by any means" with

Despite these basic constitutional considerations, online bulletin board operators have been arrested merely for possessing "dangerous" information. In 1993 a Connecticut system operator was jailed and held on $500,000 bail for maintaining a text file that contained bomb making information.[25] The judge who presided over the bail hearing for the 21–year-old operator refused to lower the amount, claiming that the bulletin board was a "bomb-making factory" and that the defendant was "just as dangerous as the bomber who blew up the World Trade Center."[26] The text file in question was not written by the defendant, but had been uploaded by one of the board's users and was widely available on other systems.[27] The initial assessments of the danger posed by the BBS operator and the text file were never presented in court because the charges were dropped.

The government similarly has acted in a preemptory fashion in other cases involving less serious potential crimes. In 1990, the Secret Service raided Steve Jackson Games, a Texas computer game and publishing company, to uncover evidence of illegal hacking, and seized the company's computer equipment, its BBS system, 300 computer disks and software.[28] Although no arrests were made and no criminal charges ever filed, the Secret Service retained the seized items for four months. Agents also read private e-mail and deleted certain files.[29] The company sued the Secret Service for violating its privacy under various federal statutes and won a judgment against the government.[30]

Allegations of electronic "stalking" have also prompted governmental overreactions. A notorious example involved the prosecution and incarceration of a University of Michigan student who posted to a newsgroup disturbing and distasteful stories about rape and abduction and who described his interest in such things to an unidentified correspondent via e-mail. The defendant, Jacob Alkhabaz (aka Jake Baker), had graphically described the torture, rape and murder of a woman in postings on the "alt.sex.stories" Usenet newsgroup. Although the posting was a work of fiction, Baker used the actual name of a fellow student for that of his story's victim. Baker also corresponded with an anonymous e-mail recipient in Canada to whom he communicated his fascina-

---

the intention, or knowing that the information will be used to commit a crime. [Feinstein Amendment No. 419] This proposal adds little to pre-existing federal law. *See, e.g.,* 18 U.S.C.A. § 231(a)(1) and 373 (West 1968 and Supp. 1997).

25. Lance Rose, *Michael Elansky & His Connecticut BBS Bomb Factory*, Boardwatch Magazine (Oct. 1993).

26. *Id.*

27. *Id.*

28. Steve Jackson Games, Inc. v. United States Secret Service, 816 F.Supp. 432 (W.D.Tex.1993), *aff'd*, 36 F.3d 457 (5th Cir. 1994). A "hacker" is an individual who

accesses another's computer system without authority.

29. 816 F. Supp. at 437–38.

30. *See id.* at 434 n.1. At the same time, the court rejected claims that seizure of email constituted an "interception" in violation of the Electronic Communication Privacy Act of 1986 because the messages had not been transmitted. *Id.* at 441–43. *See* Nicole Giallonardo, *Steve Jackson Games v. United States Secret Service: The Government's Unauthorized Seizure of Private E-Mail Warrants More Than the Fifth Circuit's Slap on the Wrist*, 14 J. Comp. & Info. L. 179 (1995).

tion with abduction and rape. The episode led to a highly publicized FBI investigation, Baker's arrest and his incarceration.[31]

Although Baker never communicated with the person named in his Usenet posting, he was prosecuted for transmitting a threat to kidnap or injure another by means of interstate or foreign commerce.[32] Additionally, Baker was incarcerated for a month despite the fact that three separate psychological evaluations found that he posed no threat to any other person.[33] A federal court eventually quashed the indictment upon finding that the postings contained no actual threat to another individual. The court found the government's justifications for its actions to be "farfetched" and described as "inexplicable" the fact that Baker was taken into custody.[34] The court found that none of the transmissions amounted to a threat, but were merely "a rather savage and tasteless piece of fiction."[35]

The court also analyzed the government's case under the First Amendment, and found that Baker's communications were constitutionally protected. In reaching this conclusion, the court was undaunted by the technical issues. "While new technology such as the Internet may complicate analysis and may sometimes require new or modified laws," the court noted, "it does not in this instance qualitatively change the analysis under the statute or under the First Amendment."[36] The decision was upheld by the United States Court of Appeals for the Sixth Circuit without reaching the constitutional issue.[37]

Other examples suggest that the problem of electronic "stalking" or other such behavior may be addressed more effectively by improved investigative techniques that use the attributes of the communications technology in question. In September 1995, the FBI arrested a number of people as part of nationwide investigation of child pornography. Some of those who were apprehended had used online services to communicate with minors to arrange meetings.[38] The FBI apprehended these individuals as part of a sting operation, with agents posing as children online.[39] This example suggests that public safety may be protected without reflexively seeking to diminish the constitutional standard applicable to new communications technologies.

B. New Technologies and Cycles of Regulation

As experience with the Internet attests, censorship can be the bastard child of technology. But this is hardly a new phenomenon.

31. United States v. Baker, 890 F.Supp. 1375, 1378 (E.D.Mich.1995), *aff'd sub nom.* United States v. Alkhabaz, 104 F.3d 1492 (6th Cir.1997).

32. 18 U.S.C.A. § 875(c) (West 1976 and Supp. 1997).

33. Baker, 890 F.Supp. at 1379.

34. *Id.* at 1379 n.5.

35. *Id.* at 1390.

36. *Id.*

37. United States v. Alkhabaz, 104 F.3d 1492 (6th Cir.1997).

38. Jared Sandberg and Glenn R. Simpson, *FBI Crackdown on Computer Child Pornography Opens Hornets Nest, Stinging America Online*, Wall Street Journal, September 15, 1995 p. 16.

39. *See, e.g., The Child Porn Bust,* Wash. Post, Sept. 17, 1995 at A24 (editorial).

Before the printing press, government suppression of expression was largely unnecessary and seldom practiced. There was no central authority over scribes, nor was there any need for one. They worked in isolation on individual manuscripts which largely were incapable of causing a major controversy.[40] But the advent of the printing press changed all of that.

Commonly cited examples of censorship of the sixteenth and seventeenth centuries were direct reactions to "a new communications environment in which dissatisfied individuals possessed a capacity for finding allies or reaching others in ways that had not existed previously."[41] Accordingly, it "is no accident that shortly after Gutenberg invented the printing press, official authorities invented the first censorship bureau."[42] As M. Ethan Katsh has explained:

> The spread of printing in the last half of the 15th century created a new communications environment that undermined the authority of powerful institutions. Those whose power derived from their ability to control the written word were threatened by a reduced ability to control the new medium of print. As a result, many censorship laws were enacted, trials held, and punishments meted out. By the late 16th century, "censorship of the printed word had become the universal practice of the lay and church authorities throughout Europe."[43]

Thus, governments employed censorship because of an acute awareness that the authority of the state waned as the power of the press ascended. In particular, press licensing laws were "an attempt to foster only books that promoted the values or interests of the authorities, something the scribal system did automatically."[44]

Yet even as the new technology of print increased the government's need to censor, it thwarted the accomplishment of this state objective. The ability of the press to mass produce books and other works negated most efforts to exert control.[45] In Britain, for example, the government

---

40. Ithiel de Sola Pool, Technologies of Freedom 14–15 (Harvard Univ. Press 1983). *See also* M. Ethan Katsh, The Electronic Media and the Transformation of Law 136 (Oxford University Press, 1989) ("Writing itself was mainly a means of acquiring and exercising power but was not a threat to power. Those in power did not worry about it or have to censor it.").

41. Pool, *supra* note 40 at 15–16; M. Ethan Katsh, *The First Amendment and Technological Change: The New Media Have a Message*, 57 Geo. Wash. L. Rev. 1459, 1467 (1989); *See* Rodney A. Smolla, Free Speech in an Open Society 337–338 (New York: Alfred A. Knopf, 1992); L.R. Sussman, Power, The Press and the Technology of Freedom 10–12 (New York: Freedom House, 1989); The First Amendment—The Challenge of New Technology 9–11 (Sig

Mickelson and E. Mier Y. Teran, eds., 1989).

42. Smolla, *supra* note 41 at 338.

43. M. Ethan Katsh, The Electronic Media and the Transformation of Law 136, *quoting* S.H. Steinberg, 500 Years of Printing 260 (3d ed. 1974). *See also* Pool, *supra* Note 40 at 14–15; Lee Loevinger, *Earl F. Nelson Lecture: Law, Technology and Liberty*, 49 Mo. L. Rev. 767, 777 (1984).

44. Katsh, *supra* note 43 at 142; Pool, *supra* note 40 at 15–16.

45. Katsh, *supra* note 41 at 1469–70. It has been suggested that as new electronic communications technologies become universal, "censors will be overwhelmed, and finally made superfluous." Sussman, *supra* note 41 at 12.

successively attempted the creation of state monopolies, press licensing, taxation and criminal libel as methods of restricting the press.[46] In the end, however, such attempts at control were abandoned, not "due to any philosophical conclusion concerning the advisability of a free press but primarily to an inability to devise an enforceable system of regulation capable of achieving the results desired."[47]

Consequently, the rise and fall of government regulation over the press tends to be cyclical. New technologies increase the demand for government control by challenging established state policies and by threatening to undermine official authority. Governments respond by enacting measures to reassert their authority and to otherwise regulate the press. Such efforts ultimately fail, however, because of the power of a given technology or because of technological expansion of the means of communication. Although this evolutionary process can result in movement toward a system of free expression, it typically leads to an initial period of overreaction to new technology and repression.

The United States established the first political system that promised to break this cycle. By adopting the First Amendment, this nation embraced the new technology of the printing press as an essential component of its political system. This choice evolved not only from the colonists' experience with suppression but from the Framers' appreciation for "the highly active and uninhibited communications environment" that print made possible.[48] It has been suggested that the nature of the technology and the actual practices of publishers of the period may be a better guide to understanding the First Amendment than attempts to divine the intentions of the Framers by dissecting their words or reading contemporary common law. Thus, while "[t]he particular words chosen for the First Amendment may have been fortuitous or accidental, . . . the evolution of a law that was more protective of expression than anything that existed pre-Gutenberg was not."[49]

Although the new technology of the printing press was "born free" in the United States, this break with tradition was not sufficient to end the cycle of repression. As newer technologies have been introduced, courts and other policymakers have been slow to recognize their First Amendment status. Professor Laurence Tribe has noted that the decisions "reveal a curious judicial blindness, as if the Constitution had to be reinvented with the birth of each new technology."[50] Thus, contrary to the First Amendment tradition, and particularly with the rise of the regulatory state, new technologies now are born in captivity.[51]

---

46. Pool, *supra* note 40 at 15–16.

47. KATSH, *supra* note 43 at 145 (citation omitted). *See also id.* at 146–65.

48. KATSH, *supra* note 41 at 1470.

49. KATSH, *supra* note 43 at 148. *See generally*, LEONARD LEVY, EMERGENCE OF A FREE PRESS (Oxford University Press, 1985).

50. Laurence H. Tribe, *The Constitution in Cyberspace: Law and Liberty Beyond the Electronic Frontier*, Keynote Address at the First Conference on Computers, Freedom & Privacy (San Diego, California, March 26, 1991).

51. *See generally* Donald E. Lively, *Fear and the Media: A First Amendment Horror Show*, 69 Minn. L. Rev. 1071 (1985). *See also* Karl A. Groskaufmanis, *What Films We May Watch: Videotape Distribution and*

Examples are not hard to find. In 1915, film was too new a medium to qualify for constitutional protection as "speech." The Supreme Court in a trilogy of cases involving the Mutual Film Corporation[52] upheld the authority of state censorship boards to subject moving pictures to prior restraint. Analyzing the regulatory scheme in terms of state constitutional protections for freedom of speech, the Court found, as a matter of "common sense," that the constitution was inapplicable to cinema.[53] The Court said that the technology of film poses a special danger that "a prurient interest may be excited and appealed to," and noted that "there are some things which should not have pictorial representation in public places and to all audiences."[54] It concluded that "the exhibition of moving pictures is a business, pure and simple, originated and conducted for profit, like other spectacles, and not to be regarded as part of the press of the country or as organs of public opinion."[55]

Courts first confronted the First Amendment status of broadcasting in 1932 and again were reluctant to extend constitutional protection to a new medium of expression. In *Trinity Methodist Church, South v. Federal Radio Comm'n*,[56] the United States Court of Appeals for the District of Columbia Circuit upheld against constitutional attack a Federal Radio Commission decision to revoke a radio station license.[57] The FRC argued in its brief to the court that broadcasting is not protected speech under the First Amendment.[58] Although the court did not exclude radio from constitutional protection in the same stark terms used by the Supreme Court in reference to film seventeen years earlier, the result was the same. It described radio as a mere "instrumentality of commerce," and upheld the license revocation as simply "application of the regulatory power of Congress in a field within the scope of its legislative authority."[59]

The "application of regulatory power" at issue was the denial of a license renewal because of a licensee's intemperate attacks on public officials and for broadcasts that were "sensational rather than instruc-

---

the *First Amendment*, 136 U. Pa. L. Rev. 1263, 1284 (1988).

52. Mutual Film Corp. v. Industrial Comm'n of Ohio, 236 U.S. 230, 35 S.Ct. 387, 59 L.Ed. 552 (1915); Mutual Film Co. v. Industrial Comm'n of Ohio, 236 U.S. 247, 35 S.Ct. 393, 59 L.Ed. 561 (1915); Mutual Film Corp. of Missouri v. Hodges, 236 U.S. 248, 35 S.Ct. 393, 59 L.Ed. 561 (1915).

53. Mutual Film Corp. v. Industrial Comm'n of Ohio, 236 U.S. at 244, 35 S. Ct. at 391, 591 L. Ed. at 559.

54. *Id.* at 242, 35 S. Ct. at 390, 59 L. Ed. at 559.

55. *Id.* at 244, 35 S. Ct. at 391, 59 L. Ed. at 560.

56. 62 F.2d 850, 61 App. D.C. 311 (D.C.Cir.1932), cert. denied, 288 U.S. 599, 53 S.Ct. 317, 77 L.Ed. 975 (1933).

57. The FRC was the predecessor agency to the Federal Communications Commission.

58. *See* Lucas A. Powe, Jr., American Broadcasting and the First Amendment 16 (1987). When placed in historical context, the FRC's position may not seem so extreme. *See* Monroe E. Price, *Congress, Free Speech, and Cable Legislation: An Introduction*, 8 Card. Arts & Ent. L. J. 225, 230 (1990)("At the outset, radio was perceived primarily not as a medium for speech, but as a device to aid ships at sea.... No substantial body of thought conceived of radio or television in their infancy, as a new form of newspaper.").

59. Trinity Methodist Church, South, 62 F.2d at 51–53, 61 U.S. App. D.C. at 312–314.

tive."[60] The Supreme Court declined to review the holding, even though it had struck down a Minnesota press law a year earlier in *Near v. Minnesota* on strikingly similar facts.[61] When the Court finally did consider the First Amendment rights of broadcasters, it recognized some application of constitutional protections, but at a lower level than to "traditional" media.[62]

This practice of extending First Amendment rights incrementally has been supported rhetorically by treating different communications delivery methods as being constitutionally distinct. As Justice Robert Jackson wrote in his concurring opinion in *Kovacs v. Cooper*:

> The moving picture screen, the radio, the newspaper, the handbill, the sound truck and the street corner orator have differing natures, values, abuses and dangers. Each ... is a law unto itself.... [63]

This dictum has been elevated to a defining principle of constitutional interpretation seemingly through sheer repetition. While there is no serious question about its persuasive force to courts when they confront new communications technologies, the dictum's superficial appeal fails to explain why it is necessary to establish distinct constitutional standards. Nor does it account for the cyclical nature of constitutional protection, whereby new media eventually may acquire full First Amendment protection.

It is true that the various media may have different physical characteristics and that these characteristics can be relevant to the government's regulatory interest. For example, amplified sound can cause excessive noise and may be regulated accordingly,[64] whereas print provides no similar basis for government intervention. Printed matter, on the other hand, unlike aural communications, may cause litter or be distributed via physical means such as newsboxes that may be regulated.[65] Face-to-face communications, compared to the other methods of spreading ideas, can tie up traffic, cause fights or lead to other problems that require some type of control.[66] These considerations may result in a somewhat different First Amendment *analysis* for each medium of

---

60. *Id.* at 851, 61 U.S. App. D.C. at 312.

61. 288 U.S. 599, 53 S.Ct. 316, 77 L.Ed. 975 (1933). *Compare* Near v. Minnesota, 283 U.S. 697, 51 S.Ct. 625, 75 L.Ed. 1357 (1931) (scandalous attacks on public officials by newspaper protected from prior restraint). For an insightful comparison of the two cases, *see* Powe, *supra* note 58 at 13–21.

62. *See, e.g.*, NBC v. United States, 319 U.S. 190, 63 S.Ct. 997, 87 L.Ed. 1344 (1943); Red Lion Broadcasting Co. v. FCC, 395 U.S. 367, 89 S.Ct. 1794, 23 L.Ed.2d 371 (1969).

63. 336 U.S. 77, 97, 69 S.Ct. 448, 459, 93 L.Ed. 513, 528 (1949) (Jackson, J., concurring).

64. Ward v. Rock Against Racism, 491 U.S. 781, 109 S.Ct. 2746, 105 L.Ed.2d 661 (1989); Kovacs v. Cooper, 336 U.S. 77, 69 S.Ct. 448, 93 L.Ed. 513 (1949).

65. City of Lakewood v. Plain Dealer Publishing Co., 486 U.S. 750, 108 S.Ct. 2138, 100 L.Ed.2d 771 (1988).

66. Chaplinsky v. New Hampshire, 315 U.S. 568, 62 S.Ct. 766, 86 L.Ed. 1031(1942); R.A.V. v. City of St. Paul, MN. 505 U.S. 377, 112 S.Ct. 2538, 120 L.Ed.2d 305 (1992); Madsen v. Women's Health Center, Inc.., 512 U.S. 753, 114 S.Ct. 2516, 129 L.Ed.2d 593 (1994); Frisby v. Schultz, 487 U.S. 474, 108 S.Ct. 2495, 101 L.Ed.2d 420 (1988).

communication, such as determining what measures may constitute the least restrictive means of control in a given situation. But it is not evident that such differences in characteristics require different First Amendment *standards*.

Notwithstanding the popularity of Justice Jackson's quotable dictum, some courts have seemed somewhat uneasy about the "law unto itself" approach to First Amendment analysis. Perhaps for that reason, once a communication technology is no longer novel courts have honored that dictum more in the breach than in the observance. Just as precolonial regulatory schemes faded as it became evident that they were no match for the technology they attempted to control, regulation of new media forms in the United States tends to relax over time.

Courts' ambivalence toward the command to treat each medium differently has been underscored by their recognition of traditional First Amendment values. For example, thirty-seven years after the Supreme Court held that cinema was not "speech" in *Mutual Film Corp. v. Industrial Comm'n of Ohio,* it expressly overruled that decision and found that "expression by means of motion pictures is included within the free speech and free press guaranty of the First and Fourteenth Amendments."[67] Although the Court felt compelled to observe that "[e]ach method [of communication] tends to present its own peculiar problems," it more importantly found that "the basic principles of freedom of speech and the press, like the First Amendment's command, do not vary. Those principles, as they have frequently been enunciated by this Court, make freedom of expression the rule."[68]

Thus, as a particular medium becomes more commonplace, the recognition of "basic principles" tends to outweigh the rhetoric regarding its "peculiar problems." At the same time, however, dictum about the uniqueness of each communications medium lives on long after courts have chosen to apply traditional First Amendment doctrine. The Court's rejection in *Joseph Burstyn, Inc. v. Wilson,* of an almost four-decades'-old precedent that excluded film from constitutional protection is a clear example of this phenomenon. Rather than create a new First Amendment theory tailored to the medium, it relied on established First Amendment prohibitions against prior restraint and discriminatory taxation of the traditional press.[69] Although the Court suggested that the constitution does not necessarily require "absolute freedom to exhibit every motion picture of every kind at all times and all places," the

67. Joseph Burstyn, Inc. v. Wilson, 343 U.S. 495, 502, 72 S.Ct. 777, 780, 96 L.Ed. 1098, 1106 (1952). *See also* United States v. Paramount Pictures, Inc., 334 U.S. 131, 166, 68 S.Ct. 915, 933, 92 L.Ed. 1260, 1297 (1948) ("We have no doubt that moving pictures, like newspapers and radio, are included in the press whose freedom is guaranteed by the First Amendment.").

68. Joseph Burstyn, Inc., 343 U.S. at 503, 72 S. Ct. at 781, 96 L. Ed. at 1106.

69. The Court expressly relied on *Near v. Minnesota,* 283 U.S. 697, 51 S.Ct. 625, 75 L.Ed. 1357 (1931) and *Grosjean v. American Press Co., Inc.,* 297 U.S. 233, 56 S.Ct. 444, 80 L.Ed. 660 (1936). *See* Joseph Burstyn, Inc., 343 U.S. at 503 n.14, 72 S. Ct. at 381 n. 14, 96 L. Ed. at 1107 n. 14.

exceptions it recognized to First Amendment protection were well-settled at the time for established media.[70]

Even though subsequent decisions suggested that requiring pre-distribution submission of films to "censorship boards" is not necessarily unconstitutional, closer examination belies the notion that films were accorded lesser protection than "traditional media." In *Freedman v. Maryland*, for example, the Court struck down a Maryland film censorship statute as providing inadequate procedural safeguards.[71] In doing so, the Court applied "the settled rule of our cases" and suggested as a model "a New York injunctive procedure designed to prevent the sale of obscene books."[72] In short, the Court removed any basis for treating films differently from print media.[73] It also repudiated precedent that suggested otherwise.[74] Accordingly, the Maryland legislature disbanded the state film licensing board in 1981 after 65 years of operation. Censorship boards in all other states had been abandoned by the mid–1960s.[75] By 1982, the Court was willing to describe film (at least in

70. *Id.* at 502–03 & n.13. 72 S. Ct. at 181 & n.13, 96 L. Ed. at 1106 & n.13. The Court cited Feiner v. New York, 340 U.S. 315, 71 S.Ct. 303, 95 L.Ed. 295 (1951) (threat of violent crowd reaction may justify restricting speech); Kovacs v. Cooper, 336 U.S. 77, 69 S.Ct. 448, 93 L.Ed. 513 (1949) (government may regulate decibel level of sound amplification devices); Chaplinsky v. New Hampshire, 315 U.S. 568, 62 S.Ct. 766, 86 L.Ed. 1031 (1942) ("fighting words" not constitutionally protected); and Cox v. New Hampshire, 312 U.S. 569, 61 S.Ct. 762, 85 L.Ed. 1049 (1941) (government may require parade permits).

71. 380 U.S. 51, 85 S.Ct. 734, 13 L.Ed.2d 649 (1965). The Court held that certain procedures must be followed where the government seeks to halt distribution of a film. First, the government bears the burden of instituting judicial proceedings and proving that the material is unprotected. Second, any restraint prior to court proceedings is strictly limited to a brief, specified period solely in order to maintain the status quo. Third, rapid judicial determination must be guaranteed. *Id.* at 59–60, 85 S. Ct. at 739, 13 L. Ed. 2d at 654–55.

72. *Id.* at 58, 60, 85 S. Ct. at 738, 740, 13 L. Ed. 2d at 654, 655. Virtually all of the precedent cited in *Freedman* related to traditional media.

73. The one exception the Court allowed was in the time limits prescribed for review of films as contrasted with that for books. It found that the long lead times generally associated with film exhibition may lead to a different standard for what constitutes "prompt judicial determination" of the status of a film as compared to a book. But the Court laid down no "rigid

time limits or procedures" and made no concrete findings other than "the statute would have to require adjudication considerably more prompt than has been the case under the Maryland statute." *Id.* at 60–61, 85 S. Ct. at 740, 13 L. Ed.2d at 656.

74. An earlier case, *Times Film Corp. v. City of Chicago*, 365 U.S. 43, 81 S.Ct. 391, 5 L.Ed.2d 403 (1961) had suggested that the government might require submission of motion pictures in advance of exhibition. But in *Freedman*, the Court limited the holding in *Times Film* to the narrow and very abstract proposition that "a prior restraint was [not] necessarily unconstitutional *under all circumstances*." 380 U.S. at 53–54, 85 S. Ct. at 736, 13 L. Ed. 2d at 652 (emphasis in original).

Indeed, the Court disavowed the notion that *Times Film* had upheld "the specific features of the Chicago censorship ordinance." *Id.* at 54, 85 S. Ct. at 737, 13 L. Ed. 2d at 652. As Justice Douglas pointed out in his concurring opinion, "the Chicago censorship system, upheld by the narrowest of margins in *Times Film Corp. v. Chicago*, 365 U.S. 43, 81 S.Ct. 391, 5 L.Ed.2d 403, could not survive under today's standards." *Id.* at 62, n.1, 85 S. Ct. at 740 n.1, 13 L. Ed. 2d at 651 n.1.

75. EDWARD DEGRAZIA AND ROGER NEWMAN, BANNED FILMS 147 (1982). By 1992, Dallas, Texas was the only city in the United States that continued to have a film review board, and it was eliminated the following year. *See* Elizabeth Kastor, *It's a Wrap: Dallas Kills Film Board*, Wash. Post, Aug. 13, 1993, p. D1; David Landis, *'Kuffs' Compromise*, USA Today, Jan. 8, 1992, p. D1 col.1. It is interesting to note that main-

dictum) as "one of the traditional forms of expression such as books" that are protected as "pure speech."[76]

The procedural safeguards articulated in *Freedman* have been used interchangeably among various media ever since. The Court has required the same protections in cases involving censorship of mail[77] and seizure of imported material by United States customs agents.[78] In *Southeastern Promotions, Ltd. v. Conrad*, the Court applied the same procedural requirements to theatrical performances.[79] Despite the application of traditional First Amendment doctrine, the Court nevertheless repeated dictum that "[e]ach medium of expression ... must be assessed ... by standards suited to it, for each may present its own problems."[80] But it reasoned that theater generally involves the acting or singing out of the written word and found "no reason to hold theater subject to a drastically different standard."[81] In short, the rhetoric regarding "peculiar problems" has little effect on the result.

The Internet appears to have broken free of this cycle of regulation, at least in its initial brush with federal regulation. It has managed to do this despite the fact that policymakers greeted its emergence as a medium of mass communication with the same apprehension that accompanies almost all powerful new technologies, and in the face of efforts to treat it as a "law unto itself." The Supreme Court struck down two key sections of the Communications Decency Act and found that full, traditional First Amendment protections apply to cyberspace *because of* the technology's peculiar characteristics, not in spite of them. The Court in *Reno v. ACLU* pointed out that:

> Through the use of chat rooms, any person with a phone line can become a town crier with a voice that resonates farther than it could from any soapbox. Through the use of Web pages, mail exploders and newsgroups, the same individual can become a pamphleteer. As the District Court found, "the content of the Internet is as diverse as human thought." We agree with its conclusion that our cases

stream films began to include more realistic depictions of reality—particularly sexual relations—after the demise of licensing boards. To respond to this trend, the film industry in 1968 established a voluntary rating system (on a scale of G to X and later to NC–17) to provide guidance to prospective audience members. *See* Hal Hinson, *The 20–Year Rating Game*, Wash. Post, p. G1, col. 4, Nov. 6, 1988. Although the rating system does not necessarily pose a First Amendment problem, it has been subject to criticism. *See* Miramax Films, Corp. v. Motion Picture Ass'n of America, Inc., 148 Misc.2d 1, 560 N.Y.S.2d 730 (N.Y.Sup.1990) (rating system is "an effective form of censorship"); Kim Masters, *Judge Blasts Movie Rating System*, Wash. Post., July 20, 1990, p. A1 col. 2.

76. *See* New York v. Ferber, 458 U.S. 747, 771, 102 S.Ct. 3348, 3362, 73 L.Ed.2d 1113, 1131 (1982).

77. Blount v. Rizzi, 400 U.S. 410, 419–21, 91 S.Ct. 423, 430, 27 L.Ed.2d 498, 505 (1971).

78. United States v. Thirty–Seven Photographs, 402 U.S. 363, 367, 91 S.Ct. 1400, 1403, 28 L.Ed.2d 822, 828 (1971).

79. 420 U.S. 546, 559–60, 95 S.Ct. 1239, 1247, 43 L.Ed.2d 448, 459–60 (1975).

80. *Id.* at 557, 95 S. Ct. at 1246, 43 L. Ed. 2d at 458.

81. *Id.* at 557–58, 95 S. Ct. at 1246, 43 L.Ed.2d at 458–59.

provide no basis for qualifying the level of First Amendment scrutiny that should be applied to this medium.[82]

In short, the Internet technology won Round One. Some observers have suggested that *Reno v. ACLU* "made no fundamental rulings on free speech on the Internet," but only held that the Court "merely decided that a few words in the CDA were imprecisely drafted."[83] Such an exceedingly narrow reading of this landmark case fails to grasp the significance of *Reno* to the cycles of regulation that historically have plagued new communications technologies. For the first time in United States history, the courts accorded a new communications technology full First Amendment rights in the initial judicial test. Nevertheless, it remains to be seen whether full protection for new media will continue to prevail against the formidable pressures of the regulatory state.

2.3 Freedom of Expression in the Regulatory State

When different methods of electronic communication are created and put to commercial use, the government typically classifies the media according to the types of services provided and subjects them to various levels of regulation. The Communications Act of 1934 set out the basic regulatory models: broadcasting, common carrier and private radio. These basic categories were later augmented by the Cable Communications Act of 1984 and the Telecommunications Act of 1996. The different categories are not dictated "by technology or economics, but by regulators pursuing a variety of social goals."[1]

The category assigned to a particular medium often has profound constitutional implications. In the modern administrative state, the oft-repeated maxim of First Amendment jurisprudence that "differences in the characteristics of new media justify differences in the First Amendment standards applied to them"[2] has been institutionalized through the use of regulatory classifications. Differences in the characteristics of new media first result in some type of categorization and each category is accorded different treatment in constitutional inquiries. Or, as the FCC's Office of Plans and Policy noted, "[t]he regulatory/legal world is ruled by definitions."[3] These definitions can overshadow reality when courts evaluate the attributes of a given medium, thus confusing its constitutional status, particularly as media and society change. Additionally,

82. Reno v. ACLU, 521 U.S. 844, 870, 117 S.Ct. 2329, 2344, 138 L.Ed.2d 874, 896–897 (1997), quoting ACLU v. Reno, 929 F.Supp. 824, 842 (E.D.Pa.1996).

83. *See* Lance Rose, *The U.S. Supreme Court's Indecency Decision: A Minor Ruling for the Multiple Media Internet*, Electronic Information Policy & Law Report, 890 (Aug. 22, 1997).

1. Symposium: *Telecommunications Law: Unscrambling the Signals, Unbundling the Law*: Howard A. Shelanski, *The Bending Line Between Conventional* *"Broadcast" and Wireless "Carriage,"* 97 Colum. L. Rev. 819, 1048 (1997).

2. Red Lion Broadcasting Co. Inc. v. FCC, 395 U.S. 367, 386, 89 S.Ct. 1794, 1805, 23 L.Ed.2d 371, 387 (1969), quoting Joseph Burstyn, Inc. v. Wilson, 343 U.S. 495, 503, 72 S.Ct. 777, 781, 96 L.Ed. 1098, 1106 (1952).

3. *See* Federal Communications Commission, *Through The Looking Glass: Integrated Broadband Networks, Regulatory Policies, and Institutional Change* 21 (OPP Working Paper No. 24, November 1988).

statutory and administrative classification schemes tend to maintain a medium's regulated status thereby retarding evolution toward greater protection.

A. First Amendment Implications of Regulatory Classifications Under the Communications Act

1. Broadcasting

Broadcasting, typified by over-the-air radio or television, is defined as "the dissemination of radio communications intended to be received by the public" and broadcast licensees are charged with certain "public trustee" obligations.[4] These public trustee obligations include both affirmative and negative requirements. That is, by virtue of the federal licensing requirement, broadcasters historically have been required to air some types or programming and barred from transmitting other types, than if left to their own editorial choices.

Affirmative obligations include requirements that all licensees serve their community needs and interests,[5] provide reasonable amounts of air time to candidates for federal elective office,[6] accord "equal opportunities" to political candidates at all levels to appear on the airwaves when their opponents have appeared,[7] and that television licensees provide sufficient amounts of educational programs for children.[8] Negative requirements include licensees not transmitting "indecent" programming,[9] advertisements for tobacco products or casinos,[10] or "false information concerning a crime or catastrophe."[11] Thus, although the Supreme Court has described broadcasting as "a medium affected by a First Amendment interest,"[12] it also has proclaimed that "of all [the] forms of communication, it is broadcasting that has received the most limited First Amendment protection."[13]

These constitutional limits historically have been justified by reference to the special characteristics of the medium. Affirmative public interest mandates have been upheld on the basis of "scarcity of the broadcast spectrum." The Supreme Court explained in *NBC v. United States* that radio is subject to government regulation because, "[u]nlike

4. 47 U.S.C.A. § 153(b) (West Supp. 1997).

5. *Id.* § 307(b); United States v. Southwestern Cable Co., 392 U.S. 157, 174, 88 S.Ct. 1994, 2003, 20 L.Ed.2d 1001, 1014 (1968); Malrite TV of New York v. FCC, 652 F.2d 1140, 1144 (2d Cir.1981).

6. 47 U.S.C.A. § 312(a)(7) (West 1991).

7. *Id.* § 315(a).

8. *Id.* § 303b.

9. 18 U.S.C.A. § 1464 (West Supp. 1997).

10. 18 U.S.C.A. § 1304 (West Supp. 1997); 15 U.S.C.A. § 1335 (West 1991).

11. 47 C.F.R. § 73.1217 (1997).

12. Red Lion Broadcasting Co., 395 U.S. at 386, 89 S. Ct. at 1805, 23 L.Ed.2d at 387.

13. FCC v. Pacifica Foundation, 438 U.S. 726, 748, 98 S.Ct. 3026, 3039, 57 L.Ed.2d 1073, 1092 (1978). *See also* Action for Children's Television v. FCC, 827 F.Supp. 4, 17–18 (D.D.C.1993), *aff'd*, 59 F.3d 1249, 313 U.S. App. D.C. 261 (D.C.Cir. 1995), cert. denied, 516 U.S. 1072, 116 S.Ct. 773, 133 L.Ed.2d 726 (1996) ("ACT IV") ([B]roadcasting is a medium "that the Supreme Court places at the bottom of the protection spectrum ... a medium of expression that is so much more limited in the First Amendment protection it receives").

other modes of expression, radio inherently is not available to all. That is its unique characteristic. . . ."[14] Similarly, in *Red Lion Broadcasting Co. v. FCC*, the Court stated that "[b]ecause of the scarcity of radio frequencies, the Government is permitted to put restraints on licensees in favor of others whose views should be expressed on this unique medium."[15] The Court asserted that the public has a "collective right to have the medium function consistently with the ends and purposes of the First Amendment," and concluded: "It is the right of viewers and listeners, not the right of the broadcasters, which is paramount."[16]

Negative public interest requirements have been based on different attributes ascribed to broadcasting. As the Supreme Court explained in *FCC v. Pacifica Foundation,* the case in which FCC "indecency" restrictions were upheld: (1) broadcasters historically have received less constitutional protection than the traditional press; (2) "the broadcast media have established a uniquely pervasive presence in the lives of all Americans;" (3) the medium is "uniquely accessible to children, even those too young to read;" and (4) a broadcast station's prior warnings about a program could not protect the public because the broadcast audience "is constantly tuning in and out."[17] This holding spawned over a decade of litigation over the scope of permissible indecency restrictions,[18] after which the courts upheld a rule that prohibited indecent broadcasts "only . . . for two-thirds of the broadcast day,"[19] from 6 a.m. to 10 p.m., based on the conclusion that "radio and television broadcasts may properly be subject to different—and often more restrictive—regulation than is permissible for other media under the First Amendment."[20]

The broadcasting classification, and resulting constitutional treatment has been put to the test by the development of new forms of broadcasting, such as Direct Broadcast Satellites ("DBS"). Although DBS has the same general characteristics as terrestrial broadcasting—"the dissemination of radio communications intended to be received by the public"—the FCC has grappled with establishing the appropriate regulatory category for this service. It first groped for new ways to classify such video services in its 1982 order authorizing DBS service.[21]

14. National Broadcasting Co., Inc. v. United States, 319 U.S. 190, 226, 63 S.Ct. 997, 1014, 87 L.Ed. 1344, 1368 (1943).

15. Red Lion Broadcasting Co., 395 U.S. at 390, 89 S. Ct. at 1806, 23 L. Ed. 2d at 389.

16. *Id.*

17. Pacifica Foundation, 438 U.S. at 748–49, 98 S. Ct. at 3040, 57 L.Ed.2d at 1093.

18. Action for Children's Television v. FCC, 58 F.3d 654, 313 U.S. App. D.C. 94 (D.C.Cir.1995) (approving safe harbor requirements specified in 1992 Cable Act) ("Act III"); Action for Children's Television v. FCC, 59 F.3d 1249, 313 U.S. App. D.C. 261 (D.C.Cir.1995)(Act IV) (approving FCC

forfeiture procedures); Action for Children's Television v. FCC, 932 F.2d 1504, 1509, 290 U.S.App.D.C. 4, 9 (D.C.Cir.1991) ("Act II") (striking down 24–hour indecency ban); Action for Children's Television v. FCC, 852 F.2d 1332, 271 U.S. App. D.C. 365 (D.C.Cir. 1988) ("ACT I") (striking down FCC safe harbor ruling).

19. Act IV, 827 F. Supp. at 19.

20. Act III, 58 F.3d at 660, 313 U.S. App. D.C. at 100.

21. DBS Report and Order, Development of Regulatory Policy in Regard to Direct Broadcast Satellites for the period following the 1983 Regional Administrative Radio Conference Report and Order, 90 F.C.C.2d 676, 709 (1982), *aff'd in part, va-*

The agency adopted what it called a "flexible regulatory approach," wherein the service could be regulated either as broadcasting or common carriage. An operator that retained control over the content of his transmissions and provided service directly to homes was treated as a broadcaster; an operator that leased transponder capacity on a first-come, first-served basis and relinquished editorial control was treated as a common carrier. "Customer-programmers" who leased satellite capacity were essentially unregulated. The United States Court of Appeals for the District of Columbia Circuit rejected this approach and held that the Communications Act definition of broadcasting encompasses most DBS applications.[22]

In response, the FCC initiated a proceeding "to determine what criteria may be used by the Commission to determine whether a communications service should be treated as 'broadcasting' under the Communications Act."[23] The Commission determined that subscription video services should be classified as "non-broadcast" services and freed from broadcast regulation. The appropriate classification hinged on the operator's intent: the service is not broadcasting if the licensee does not intend to serve the public generally.[24] Based on the *Subscription Video* rules, a DBS operator could opt for regulatory treatment as a broadcaster, a non-broadcaster or a common carrier. The District of Columbia Circuit affirmed.[25]

Congress subsequently weighed in with its judgment of the appropriate regulatory status when it required as part of the 1992 Cable Act that DBS operators must set aside four to seven percent of channel capacity for "public interest" programming.[26] The United States Court of Appeals for the District of Columbia Circuit upheld the requirement using the traditional scarcity rationale for broadcast content controls.[27] However, in a thoughtful dissent from a denial of rehearing of this decision, five judges of the Circuit pointed out that "DBS is ... an order of magnitude less scarce than traditional broadcasting" and concluded that the "factual predicate" of broadcast regulation—"scarcity of channels"—is absent here.[28] The dissenters noted that the *Red Lion* Court suggested that the

cated in part sub nom. National Ass'n of Broadcasters v. FCC, 740 F.2d 1190, 239 U.S. App. D.C., 87 (D.C.Cir.1984).

22. National Ass'n of Broadcasters v. FCC, 740 F.2d 1190, 1205, 239 U.S. App. D.C. 87, 102 (D.C.Cir.1984). *See also* Telecommunications Research and Action Center v. FCC, 836 F.2d 1349, 267 U.S. App. D.C. 1 (D.C.Cir.1988) (remanding FCC decision to classify nonsubscription use of ITFS capacity as nonbroadcasting).

23. Subscription Video, Report and Order, 2 FCC Rcd 1001, 1003 (1987).

24. *Id.* at 1006. As indicia of intent, the Commission focused on whether the customer needs a special encoder to receive the transmission, the information is encrypted

and the operator and subscriber are in a contractual relationship.

25. National Ass'n For Better Broadcasting v. FCC, 849 F.2d 665, 270 U.S. App. D.C. 334 (D.C.Cir.1988).

26. Section 25, Cable Television Consumer Protection and Competition Act of 1992, Pub. L. 102–385, 106 Stat. 1460 (1992) ("1992 Cable Act"), *codified at* 47 U.S.C.A. § 335(b)(1) (West Supp. 1997).

27. Time Warner Entertainment Co., L.P. v. FCC, 93 F.3d 957, 974–977, 320 U.S. App. D.C. 294, 311 (D.C.Cir.1996).

28. Time Warner Entertainment Co., L.P. v. FCC, 105 F.3d 723, 725, 323 U.S. App. D.C. 109 (D.C.Cir.1997).

reason for relaxed constitutional treatment of broadcasting would vanish along with the end of scarcity, and pointed out that, even in its nascent state, "[t]he new DBS technology already offers more channel capacity than the cable industry, and far more than traditional broadcasting."[29] It further noted that DBS compression is expected to increase the number of channels five-fold by the year 2000.

The analysis is complicated somewhat by the fact that the "negative" public interest obligations associated with broadcasting generally have not been applied to DBS. Thus, the FCC does not restrict indecency on DBS service as it does on other broadcast services. In this respect, DBS operates like a cable television service, offering subscription video service to customers, including services featuring uncut films, that would not be permitted on broadcast television during prime time.

While anomalies remain—such as the status of DBS within the broadcasting classification—the difference in constitutional treatment for entities classified as broadcasters is highly significant. As Dean Lee Bollinger has noted, the Supreme Court decisions regarding broadcasting and the First Amendment amount to a "virtual celebration of public regulation" representing "[n]othing less ... than a complete conceptual reordering of the relationships between the government, the press and the public that was established with *New York Times v. Sullivan.*"[30] To read cases like *Red Lion Broadcasting* is to "step into another world," where the press itself represents the greatest threat to First Amendment values, and government intervention in editorial choices is the preferred method of salvation.[31] It is a vision of the First Amendment, in the words of the late Supreme Court Justice William O. Douglas, "that is agreeable to the traditions of nations that never have known freedom of [the] press." [32]

2. Cable Television

Cable television initially defied classification as either broadcasting or common carriage. To resolve this confusion, Congress created a new but complex regulatory definition in the Cable Communications Policy Act of 1984, defining a "cable system" as:

> a facility, consisting of a set of closed transmission paths and associated signal generation, reception, and control equipment that is designed to provide cable service which includes video programming and which is provided to multiple subscribers within a community.... [33]

29. *Id.*

30. Lee C. Bollinger, Images of a Free Press, 66, 71 (University of Chicago Press, 1991).

31. *Id.* at 72.

32. Columbia Broadcasting System Inc. v. Democratic National Committee, 412 U.S. 94, 163, 93 S.Ct. 2080, 2116, 36 L.Ed.2d 772, 818 (1973)(Douglas, J. concurring).

33. 47 U.S.C.A. § 522(7) (West Supp. 1997). The Cable Act expressly excludes from the definition (1) a facility that serves only to transmit the signals of one or more television stations; (2) a facility that serves subscribers without using any public rights-of-way; (3) common carrier facilities regu-

The Cable Act provides guidelines for cable regulation through local franchising, with the proviso that cable systems "shall not be subject to regulation as a common carrier or utility."[34] But it is not entirely clear what this statement means. Although the Act avoids imposing certain indicia of common carrier status it treats cable operators as common carriers in other respects. For example, operators are required to set aside channel capacity under reasonable price, terms and conditions for "leased access" by unaffiliated entities, rates in most communities have been regulated according to complex formulas and operators are prohibited from exerting any editorial control over the leased access programming.[35] The Supreme Court has referred to such obligations as common carrier-type requirements.[36]

The Cable Communications and Consumer Protection Act of 1992 added further regulatory obligations to entities classified as cable operators, including must-carry requirements for commercial and non-commercial broadcasters,[37] retransmission consent,[38] leased-access channel rate regulations,[39] indecency restrictions on both leased-access and public access channels,[40] notice requirements for previews of unsolicited R-rated movies on premium channels,[41] and vertical and horizontal ownership limits.[42]

First Amendment claims were filed challenging the must-carry requirements, as well as against many other provisions of the Act.[43] In these cases the threshold question involved the selection of a First Amendment standard for cable television. In *Turner Broadcasting System v. FCC*, the government argued that must carry rules trigger only minimal scrutiny as "a reasonable attempt to correct ... market dysfunction" that restricts the transmission of broadcast signals.[44] While acknowledging that "cable television is not affected by the scarcity of the

lated under Title II of the Communications Act unless video programming is transmitted directly to subscribers; (4) an Open Video System as defined by the Act; and (5) facilities of electric utilities when used solely for operating utility systems. *Id.* The definition was modified slightly by the Telecommunications Act of 1996.

34. 47 U.S.C.A. § 541(c) (West 1991).

35. 47 U.S.C.A. § 532 (West 1991 & Supp. 1997). *See generally* Cable Communications Consumer Protection and Competition Act of 1992, 47 U.S.C.A. §§ 532(c) (West Supp. 1997).

36. *See* Denver Area Educational Telecommunications Consortium v. FCC, 518 U.S. 727, 738–740, 116 S.Ct. 2374, 2384, 135 L.Ed.2d 888, 900–901 (1996) ("in respect to leased channels [cable operators] act less like editors ... than like common carriers, such as telephone companies").

37. 47 U.S.C.A. §§ 534, 535 (West Supp. 1997).

38. 47 U.S.C.A. § 325(b) (West Supp. 1997).

39. 47 U.S.C.A. § 532(c) (West 1991 & Supp. 1997).

40. 47 U.S.C.A. §§ 531, 532(h) (West 1991 & Supp. 1997)

41. 47 U.S.C.A. § 544(d) (West 1991 & Supp. 1997)

42. 47 U.S.C.A. § 533(f) (West Supp. 1997).

43. Turner Broadcasting System v. FCC, 819 F.Supp. 32, 37 (D.D.C.1993) *remanded,* 512 U.S. 622, 114 S.Ct. 2445, 129 L.Ed.2d 497 (1994); Daniels Cablevision, Inc. v. United States, 835 F.Supp. 1 (D.D.C. 1993), *aff'd in part, rev'd in part,* Time Warner Entertainment Co., L.P. v. FCC, 93 F.3d 957, 320 U.S.App.D.C. 294 (D.C.Cir. 1996).

44. Brief for the Federal Appellees in Turner Broadcasting System v. FCC, No. 93–44, at 13.

broadcast spectrum," the government asserted that cable should be governed by a constitutional standard "comparable" to that applied to broadcasting.[45] Alternatively, the government argued that must carry rules could be upheld under what it described as the "more exacting standard" of *United States v. O'Brien* which is applicable to content-neutral regulations that have incidental effects on speech.[46]

The cable industry, in sharp contrast, argued that First Amendment "strict scrutiny," the standard applicable to printed communications, should be used to analyze the must carry rules. The rules, according to the industry briefs, are content-based because they compel carriage on the grounds that local broadcast signals convey information important to the public interest.[47] On a more general level, however, the industry argued that none of the particular characteristics of cable communications justified a lower level of constitutional scrutiny. Cable television operators do not have power to distort the market for television signals, according to the industry, and such economic power does not justify a different constitutional approach in any event.[48] Nor do such purported factors as a scarcity of physical space to place cables or the receipt of a government benefit via franchise rights support a lower First Amendment standard.[49]

The debate in *Turner Broadcasting System* regarding the applicable First Amendment standard for cable television brought to a head an ongoing dispute of at least two decades duration. While the Supreme Court in 1979 described First Amendment concerns about cable access programming requirements as "not frivolous" it did not take a position on the correct approach.[50] In the ensuing years the Court expressly avoided articulating a First Amendment standard for cable television.[51] Given this void, lower courts have been forced to find their way as best they can in the constitutional thicket. This led litigants to propose

---

45. *Id.* at 14, 32–36.

46. *Id.* at 37–47. The District Court upheld the must carry rules using this constitutional standard. Turner Broadcasting System, 819 F. Supp. at 41.

47. *See e.g.,* Brief for Appellant National Cable Television Association, Inc., in Turner Broadcasting System v. FCC, No. 93–44, at 16–23; Brief for Appellant Time Warner Entertainment Company, L.P., in Turner Broadcasting System v. FCC, No. 93–44, at 14–21.

48. Brief for Appellant Time Warner Entertainment Company, L.P., in Turner Broadcasting System v. FCC, No. 93–44, at 33–36.

49. *Id.* at 32–33, 36–38.

50. FCC v. Midwest Video Corp., 440 U.S. 689, 709 n. 19, 99 S.Ct. 1435, 1446, n.19, 59 L.Ed.2d 692, 707 n.19 (1979). The dispute regarding the First Amendment status of cable goes back even further if one

includes those cases in which free speech claims were summarily rejected. *See e.g.,* Black Hills Video Corp. v. FCC, 399 F.2d 65 (8th Cir.1968); Buckeye Cablevision, Inc. v. FCC, 387 F.2d 220, 225, 128 U.S. App. D.C. 262, 267 (D.C.Cir.1967); Idaho Microwave, Inc. v. FCC, 352 F.2d 729, 122 U.S. App. D.C. 253 (D.C.Cir.1965); Carter Mountain Transmission Corp. v. FCC, 321 F.2d 359, 116 U.S. App. D.C. 93 (D.C.Cir.1963), cert. denied, 375 U.S. 951, 84 S.Ct. 439, 11 L.Ed.2d 312 (1963).

51. Leathers v. Medlock, 499 U.S. 439, 111 S.Ct. 1438, 113 L.Ed.2d 494 (1991); City of Los Angeles v. Preferred Communications, Inc., 476 U.S. 488, 494–95, 106 S.Ct. 2034, 2037–38, 90 L.Ed.2d 480, 487 (1986). *See also* Turner Broadcasting System, Inc. v. FCC, 507 U.S. 1301, 113 S.Ct. 1806, 123 L.Ed.2d 642 (1993) (denial of application for injunction) ("We have not decided whether the activities of cable operators are more akin to that of newspapers or wireless broadcasters").

"clever and flavorful analogies to other corners of first amendment law on which more light has been shed," to help courts decide the necessary threshold question of what law to apply.[52]

Most courts that addressed the question concluded that the First Amendment standard for broadcasting was inapplicable to cable television,[53] but they could not agree on a uniform constitutional approach.[54] Some courts justified even greater regulation of cable television on the theory it is a natural monopoly,[55] while others rejected this proposition.[56] The debate outside the courtroom has been no less intense. Some have argued that cable television systems are like newspapers, and should be accorded full First Amendment status.[57] Others have focused on some of the particular characteristics of cable technology, or on various public policy goals, and have argued that cable television should be subject to a

52. Century Communications Corp. v. FCC, 835 F.2d 292, 298, 266 U.S. App. D.C. 228, 234 (D.C.Cir.1987), *clarified*, 837 F.2d 517, 267 U.S. App. D.C. 94 (D.C.Cir.), cert. denied, 486 U.S. 1032, 108 S. Ct. 2014, 100 L.Ed.2d 602 (1988).

53. Home Box Office, Inc. v. FCC, 567 F.2d 9, 44–45, 185 U.S. App. D.C. 142, 177–78 (D.C.Cir.), cert. denied, 434 U.S. 829, 98 S. Ct. 111, 54 L. Ed. 2d 89 (1977) ("the First Amendment theory espoused in *National Broadcasting Co.* and reaffirmed in *Red Lion Broadcasting Co.* cannot be directly applied to cable television since an essential precondition of that theory, physical interference and scarcity requiring an umpiring role for government, is absent"). *See also* Preferred Communications, Inc. v. City of Los Angeles, 754 F.2d 1396, 1404 (9th Cir.1985), *aff'd on narrower grounds*, 476 U.S. 488, 106 S.Ct. 2034, 90 L.Ed.2d 480 (1986); Omega Satellite Prods. Co. v. City of Indianapolis, 694 F.2d 119, 127 (7th Cir.1982); Cruz v. Ferre, 571 F.Supp. 125, 131 (S.D.Fla.1983); Community Television, Inc. v. Roy City, 555 F.Supp. 1164, 1168–69 (D.Utah 1982). However, early cases, decided before the cable industry developed as a serious competitor to broadcasting, treated the two technologies as constitutionally indistinguishable. Black Hills Video Corp. v. FCC, 399 F.2d 65, 69 (8th Cir.1968). *See* Quincy Cable TV, Inc. v. FCC, 768 F.2d 1434, 1443–44, 248 U.S. App. D.C. 1, 9–10 (D.C.Cir.1985).

54. *See* U.S. Department of Commerce, Video Program Distribution and Cable Television: Current Policy Issues and Recommendations, NTIA Report 88–233, Appendix C (June 1988). Various courts expressly eschewed any attempt to set a standard for cable. *See e.g.*, Century Communications, Corp. v. FCC, 835 F.2d at 298; Quincy Cable TV, Inc., 768 F.2d at 1454, 248 U.S. App. D.C. at 21, cert. de-

nied, *sub nom.* National Ass'n. of Broadcasters v. Quincy Cable TV, Inc., 476 U.S. 1169, 106 S.Ct. 2889, 90 L.Ed.2d 977 (1986); Pacific West Cable Co. v. City of Sacramento, 672 F.Supp. 1322, 1327 (N.D.Cal.1987).

55. Central Telecommunications, Inc. v. TCI Cablevision, Inc., 800 F.2d 711 (8th Cir.1986); Omega Satellite Prods., 694 F.2d at 128; Community Communications Co. Inc. v. City of Boulder, 660 F.2d 1370 (10th Cir.1981), cert. denied, 456 U.S. 1001, 102 S.Ct. 2287, 73 L.Ed.2d 1296 (1982); Berkshire Cablevision of Rhode Island, Inc. v. Burke, 571 F.Supp. 976 (D.R.I.1983), *vacated as moot*, 773 F.2d 382 (1st Cir.1985).

56. Preferred Communications, Inc. v. City of Los Angeles, 13 F.3d 1327 (9th Cir.1994); Preferred Communications, Inc. v. City of Los Angeles, 754 F.2d 1396 (9th Cir.1985), *aff'd* 476 U.S. 488, 106 S.Ct. 2034, 90 L.Ed.2d 480 (1986); Quincy Cable TV, Inc., 768 F.2d at 1449–50; Pacific West Cable Co. v. City of Sacramento, California, 672 F.Supp. 1322 (E.D.Cal.1987); Century Federal, Inc. v. City of Palo Alto, 648 F.Supp. 1465 (N.D.Cal.1986).

57. *See e.g.*, Jonathan Emord, Freedom, Technology, and the First Amendment (1991); Lucas Powe, American Broadcasting and the First Amendment 216–47 (1987); George Shapiro, Philip Kurland & James Mercurio, Cablespeech (1983); John P. Cole, *The Cable Television "Press" and the Protection of the First Amendment—A Not So "Vexing Question"*, 28 Cal. Western L. Rev. 347 (1991–92); David J. Saylor, *Municipal Ripoff: The Unconstitutionality of Cable Television Franchise Fees and Access Support Payments*, 35 Cath. U. L. Rev. 671 (1986); William E. Lee, *Cable Franchising and the First Amendment*, 36 Vand. L. Rev. 867 (1983).

less demanding constitutional regime.[58]

The Supreme Court in its initial decision *Turner Broadcasting System* (*"Turner I"*) stopped short of resolving this dispute. Although the Court emphasized that "[t]here can be no disagreement" that "[c]able programmers and cable operators engage in and transmit speech, and they are entitled to the protection of the speech and press provisions of the First Amendment," it did not articulate a standard for evaluating these rights.[59] It agreed with the cable industry that the less rigorous scrutiny applicable to broadcasting "does not apply in the context of cable regulation" because of "fundamental technological differences."[60] It also rejected the government's assertion that market dysfunction justified "industry-specific antitrust legislation" in the form of must carry rules, subject only to rational basis scrutiny.[61] Accordingly, the Court found that "at least some degree of heightened First Amendment scrutiny [is demanded.]"[62]

At the same time, the Court did not accept industry arguments that strict scrutiny must be applied to must carry rules. It rejected the notion that broadcast carriage obligations are content-based, either in purpose or effect, and concluded that burdens were imposed on cable operators "only because they control access to the cable conduit."[63] As with constitutional questions relating to other technologies, the Court predicated its findings upon "the unique physical characteristics of cable transmission" but foreshadowed the time when such characteristics may be less pivotal. Indeed, the majority noted that "given the rapid advances in fiber optics and digital compression technology, soon there may be no practical limitation on the number of speakers who may use the cable medium."[64]

After establishing an intermediate level of scrutiny, the Court remanded the case to determine whether the economic health of broadcasters actually was at risk and whether the must carry rules are an appropriately tailored means of addressing the problem. In particular—and despite "unusually detailed statutory findings"—the Court found

58. *See e.g.*, Monroe Price, *Congress, Free Speech, and Cable Legislation: An Introduction*, 8 Cardozo Arts & Ent. L. J. 225 (1990); Jerome Barron, *On Understanding the First Amendment Status of Cable: Some Obstacles in the Way*, 57 Geo. Wash. L. Rev. 1495 (1989); Daniel Brenner, *Cable Television and the Freedom of Expression*, 1988 Duke L.J. 329; Nicholas Miller and Alan Beals, *Regulating Cable Television*, 57 Wash. L. Rev. 85 (1981).

59. Turner Broadcasting System, Inc. v. FCC, 512 U.S. 622, 114 S.Ct. 2445, 129 L.Ed.2d 497 (1994) ("Turner I").

60. *Id*. at 637–8, 114 S. Ct. at 2456–57, 129 L. Ed. 2d at 514–15.

61. *Id*. at 640, 114 S. Ct. at 2458, 129, L.Ed.2d at 516.

62. *Id*. at 641, 114 S. Ct. at 2458, 129 L.Ed.2d at 516–17.

63. *Id*. The Court also pointed to "an important technological difference between newspapers and cable television.... [T]he cable network gives the cable operator bottleneck, or gatekeeper, control over most (if not all) of the television programming that is channeled into the subscriber's home." *Id*. at 645, 656, 114 S. Ct. at 2460, 2466, 129 L.Ed.2d at 519, 526.

64. *Id*. at 639, 114 S. Ct. at 2457, 129 L.Ed.2d at 516. *See also* Nat'l Cable Television Ass'n, Inc. v. FCC, 33 F.3d 66, 308 U.S. App. D.C. 221 (D.C.Cir.1994).

insufficient evidence that broadcast stations had been harmed by cable operators, no findings regarding the adverse effects of must carry on cable programming services, and no judicial findings on less restrictive measures that might be available.[65]

Following remand, the Court voted 5 to 4 to uphold the must carry requirements in *Turner II*.[66] The majority opinion, written by Justice Kennedy, began where *Turner I* left off, with the assumption that intermediate constitutional scrutiny was appropriate because the must carry rules are content-neutral.[67] As Justice Stevens wrote in a concurring opinion, "[i]f this statute regulated the content of speech rather than the structure of the market, our task would be quite different."[68] The balance of the opinion was devoted to finding that the record, both before Congress and as established in the litigation, supported the government's interest in must carry rules and that the obligation burdened no more speech than necessary. The four dissenting Justices, in an opinion written by Justice O'Connor, disputed the contention that must carry rules are content neutral or narrowly tailored, or that the government had proven the need for the carriage requirement.[69] By treating the must carry rules as a specialized form of antitrust law, the *Turner II* decision broke no new ground in defining the First Amendment standard applicable to cable television.

The Court provided far more analysis of the constitutional standard in a decision from the previous term, although it reached no firmer conclusions. In *Denver Area Educational Telecommunications Consortium, Inc. v. FCC*, a plurality of the Court expressly declined to make "a definitive choice among competing analogies (broadcast, common carrier, bookstore)" or "to declare a rigid single standard, good for now and for all future media and purposes."[70] Justices Breyer, Stevens, O'Connor and Souter joined in an opinion stating that it would be "unwise and unnecessary definitively to pick one analogy or one specific set of words now."[71] In a concurring opinion, Justice Stevens reinforced the conclusion that "it would be unwise to take a categorical approach to the resolution of novel First Amendment questions arising in an industry as dynamic as this."[72] Similarly, Justice Souter wrote that the Court should be "shy about saying the final word today about what will be accepted as reasonable tomorrow."[73]

---

65. Turner I, 512 U.S. at 646, 114 S. Ct. at 2461,129 L. Ed. 2d at 520.

66. Turner Broadcasting System, Inc. v. FCC, 520 U.S. 180, 117 S.Ct. 1174, 137 L.Ed.2d 369 (1997) ("Turner II").

67. *Id.* at 189, 117 S. Ct. at 1186, 137 L.Ed.2d at 385.

68. *Id.* at 225, 117 S.Ct. at 1203, 137 L.Ed.2d at 410 (Stevens, J., concurring).

69. *Id.* at 230–258, 117 S.Ct. at 1206–1219, 137 L.Ed.2d at 412–31.

70. 518 U.S. 727, 742, 116 S.Ct. 2374, 2385, 135 L.Ed.2d 888, 901 (1996) (plurality opinion).

71. *Id.*, 116 S.Ct. at 2385, 135 L.Ed.2d at 902.

72. *Id.* at 768, 116 S.Ct. at 2398, 135 L.Ed.2d at 919 (Stevens, J., concurring).

73. *Id.* at 777, 116 S.Ct. at 2402, 135 L.Ed.2d at 924 (Souter, J., concurring).

In sharp contrast, Justice Thomas, joined by Chief Justice Rehnquist and Justice Scalia, wrote that the Court's "First Amendment distinctions between media, dubious from their infancy, placed cable in a doctrinal wasteland in which regulators and cable operators alike could not be sure whether cable was entitled to the substantial First Amendment protections afforded the print media or was subject to the more onerous obligations shouldered by the broadcast media."[74] The opinion traced the development of First Amendment doctrine applicable to cable television, and found that "[o]ver time ... we have drawn closer to recognizing that cable operators should enjoy the same First Amendment rights as the nonbroadcast media."[75] Justices Kennedy and Ginsburg also faulted the plurality for declining to adopt a definitive constitutional standard by which to evaluate cable regulation. They noted that the plurality "applie[d] no standard, and by this omission [lost] sight of existing First Amendment doctrine." The Court, Justice Kennedy wrote, "ought to have the discipline to analyze the case by reference to existing elaborations of constant First Amendment principles."[76]

Denver is an extremely complicated decision, not only because it resulted in six opinions and adopted no clear First Amendment standard for cable television. A majority of the Justices, writing separately, agreed that a standard should be established and that certain cable television regulations should be subjected to strict constitutional review, but they could not agree on a consistent result. In addition, Justices Kennedy and Rehnquist, who both opined that strict scrutiny should be the norm, one year later applied intermediate review to uphold must carry requirements in *Turner II*.[77] Perhaps more notable is that the choice of standards by the Justices in *Denver* did little to clarify the outcome of their respective constitutional analyses. Justices who embraced a less protective First Amendment standard on the theory that they should not impose a "straightjacket that disables Government from responding to serious problems"[78] nevertheless voted to strike down most of the regulations at issue. At the same time, Justices who opposed differential constitutional treatment for cable television, and who insisted "that cable operators should enjoy the same First Amendment rights as the nonbroadcast media"[79] would have upheld the regulations completely.

---

74. *Id*. at 813–814, 116 S. Ct. at 2420, 135 L. Ed. 2d at 947 (Thomas, J., concurring in the judgment in part, and dissenting in part). *See also id*. at 818 n.3, 116 S. Ct. at 2422 n.3, 135 L. Ed. 2d at 950 n.3 (noting that changes in technology are "negating the primary justifications for treating cable operators differently from other First Amendment speakers").

75. *Id*. at 814, 116 S. Ct. at 2420, 135 L. Ed. 2d at 948.

76. *Id*. at 781, 116 S. Ct. at 2404, 135 L. Ed. 2d at 926 (Kennedy, J., concurring in part, concurring in the judgment in part, and dissenting in part).

77. Turner II, 520 U.S. at 186, 117 S. Ct. at 1184–85, 137 L. Ed. 2d at 385–386. The level of scrutiny was determined by the majority's conclusion that the regulations were content-neutral, a point strongly disputed by the dissenters.

78. Denver, 518 U.S. at 741, 116 S. Ct. at 2385, 135 L. Ed. 2d at 901 (plurality opinion).

79. *Id*. at 814, 116 S. Ct. at 2420, 135 L. Ed. 2d at 948 (Thomas, J., concurring in the judgment in part, and dissenting in part).

Although the *Denver* plurality refused to make a definitive choice among competing analogies, it appeared to adopt much of the *Pacifica* approach for regulating "indecent" broadcasts as the standard by which to judge regulation of indecency on cable access channels. The plurality found that cable television has "established a uniquely pervasive presence in the lives of all Americans," that cable television "is as 'accessible to children' as over-the-air broadcasting, if not more so," and that patently offensive material "can 'confron[t] the citizen' in the 'privacy of the home.' "[80] Despite these findings, it cannot be said that *Denver* upheld a regulatory regime for "indecent" programming on cable television comparable to that for broadcasting. The Court invalidated requirements that indecent leased access programming be segregated on a separate channel and access permitted only after a written request, as well as rules that would permit cable operators to ban indecent programming from public access channels.

The only aspect of the leased access rules upheld in *Denver* involved a provision the Court characterized as "permissive." That is, cable operators were permitted—but not required—to ban indecent programming on leased access channels. The Court subjected even this voluntary policy to First Amendment review, and concluded it was constitutionally acceptable to the extent "it permits cable operators to screen programs only pursuant to a 'written and published policy,' " and it requires the cable operators' decisions to be consistent with respect to "substantially similar programming."[81] The decision made clear that cable operators could choose to carry indecent programing on leased access channels, including material generally considered far more explicit than on broadcast television or even on other cable networks.[82] The Court's references to *Pacifica* notwithstanding, the fact remains that over-the-air broadcasters are barred from transmitting programming before 10 p.m. that includes brief scenes of indecency and/or profane language,[83] while cable operators face no such restriction.[84]

80. Denver, 518 U.S. at 744, 116 S. Ct. at 2386, 135 L. Ed. 2d at 903–04 (Plurality opinion), quoting FCC v. Pacifica Found., 438 U.S. 726, 748, 98 S.Ct. 3026, 3039–40, 57 L.Ed.2d 1073, 1092–93.

81. Denver, 518 U.S. at 752, 116 S. Ct. at 2390, 135 L. Ed. 2d at 909 (plurality opinion).

82. *See id.*, 116 S. Ct. at 2390, 135 L. Ed. 2d at 908 (leased access programming may contain "pictures of oral sex, bestiality, and rape"); Goldstein v. Manhattan Cable Television, 916 F.Supp. 262, 267 (S.D.N.Y. 1995) (leased access program "Midnight Blue" described as "outrageous, indecent programming"); Altmann v. Television Signal Corp., 849 F.Supp. 1335, 1339 (N.D.Cal. 1994) (leased access program described as " 'hardcore pornography' containing 'indecent' (and possibly 'obscene') scenes depicting nudity and explicit sex acts"); Rees v.

Texas, 909 S.W.2d 264 (Tex.App.1995), cert. denied, 519 U.S. 863, 117 S.Ct. 169, 136 L.Ed.2d 111 (1996) (obscenity conviction for leased access program depicting scenes of homosexual sodomy).

83. *See* Letter to Grant Broadcasting System II, Inc., DA 97–1287 (Mass Media Bureau, released June 24, 1997) (imposing a fine for prime time broadcast of science fiction movie "Deepstar Six," which contained harsh language but no depictions of sexual activity); Kansas City Television, Ltd., Order, 4 FCC Rcd. 6706 (1989) (finding broadcast of teen sex comedy "Private Lessons" violates indecency rule).

84. Community Television of Utah, Inc. v. Wilkinson, 611 F.Supp. 1099 (D.C.Utah 1985), *aff'd sub nom.* Jones v. Wilkinson, 800 F.2d 989 (10th Cir.1986), *aff'd mem.* 480 U.S. 926, 107 S.Ct. 1559, 94 L.Ed.2d 753 (1987); Cruz v. Ferre, 755 F.2d 1415

In sharp contrast, Justices Thomas, Scalia and Chief Justice Rehnquist would have upheld all of the access channel restrictions at issue in *Denver* even though they advocated extending full First Amendment rights to cable television.[85] They reasoned that the requirement that indecent leased access programming be segregated on a separate channel and blocked until a subscriber submitted a written request for the channel served a compelling interest and that the regulation at issue was the least restrictive means of serving the interest.[86] In contrast to the material made available on access channels, they noted that "[m]ost sexually oriented programming appears on premium or pay-per-view channels that are naturally blocked from nonpaying customers by market forces." The regulation merely "emulate[s] market forces," because "it is only governmental intervention in the first instance that requires access channels, on which indecent programming may appear, to be made part of the basic cable package."[87]

In the wake of *Denver* and *Turner II*, all that can be said with certainty is that cable television regulations that are characterized as content neutral will receive "intermediate" constitutional scrutiny, while those characterized as content based will receive "strict" scrutiny. But it is not entirely clear what this means. The "intermediate scrutiny" contemplated in *Turner I* seemed closer to strict scrutiny,[88] at least until *Turner II*. Similarly, the strict scrutiny proposed by some Justices in *Denver* seems fairly intermediate, while the intermediate scrutiny proposed by others seems fairly strict. Such indeterminacy suggests that the level of constitutional protection will continue to be decided on an ad hoc basis.

3. Common Carriers

Common carriers, typified at least originally by standard telephone service providers, are defined as "any person engaged as a common carrier for hire, in interstate or foreign communication by wire or radio or in interstate or foreign radio transmission of energy."[89] The Act's definition also stresses that "a person engaged in radio broadcasting shall not ... be deemed a common carrier."[90] Title II of the Communications Act requires carriers to provide service upon reasonable request therefor, at reasonable rates and without discrimination between cus-

(11th Cir.1985); Community Television of Utah, Inc. v. Roy City, 555 F.Supp. 1164 (D.Utah 1982); Home Box Office, Inc. v. Wilkinson, 531 F.Supp. 987 (D.Utah 1982).

85.   Denver Area, 518 U.S. at 813, 116 S. Ct. at 2420, 135 L. Ed. 2d at 946 (Thomas, J., concurring in the judgment in part, and dissenting in part). *See also* Playboy Entertainment Group, Inc. v. United States, 945 F.Supp. 772, 784–785 (D.Del.1996) (upholding content-based restriction on cable television programming despite concluding that "we should apply either strict scrutiny or something very close to strict scrutiny").

86.   Denver Area, 518 U.S. at 832, 116 S. Ct. at 2429, 135 L. Ed. 2d at 961 (Thomas, J., concurring in the judgment in part, and dissenting in part).

87.   *Id.* at 831, 116 S. Ct. at 2428, 135 L. Ed. 2d at 958–59 (Thomas, J., concurring in the judgment in part, and dissenting in part).

88.   *Id.* at 816, 116 S. Ct. at 2420, 135 L. Ed. 2d at 948–49 ("*Turner* ... adopt[ed] much of the print paradigm").

89.   47 U.S.C.A. § 153(h) (West 1991 & Supp. 1997).

90.   *Id.*

tomers.[91] Also, unlike broadcasters, common carriers generally have no editorial control over communications, but rather, transmit intelligence of a customer's design and choosing.[92] Although the regulatory classification of common carriers has become more complex with the advent of enhanced services and with the regulatory categories of "telecommunications," "telecommunications services," "telecommunications carrier," "information service," "telephone exchange service" and "local exchange carrier" in the 1996 Telecommunications Act, the essential nature of common carriage as a conduit has persisted.[93]

For many years, any First Amendment analysis was considered inapplicable to common carriers because of their nature as conduits for the speech of others. Since common carriers are defined by their purpose of indiscriminately relaying the messages of others, and by the absence of editorial control, the constitutional status of common carriers did not normally arise. When courts discussed such matters, it generally was to contrast common carriers with speakers who are protected by the First Amendment.

This approach was central to the Supreme Court's opinion in *Columbia Broadcasting System, Inc. v. Democratic National Committee.*[94] The Court held that a broadcast licensee could have a blanket policy of refusing to air paid editorial announcements without running afoul of the public interest mandate of the Communications Act. In reaching this conclusion, the Court examined the legislative history of the Radio Act of 1927 and the Communications Act of 1934 and found that Congress considered and "firmly ... rejected the argument that the broadcast facilities should be open on a nonselective basis to all persons wishing to talk about public issues."[95] After all, the Court reasoned, the Communications Act specifies that a person "engaged in radio broadcasting shall not ... be deemed a common carrier."[96]

---

91. *Id.* §§ 201–202. *See* National Ass'n of Regulatory Utility Commissioners v. FCC, 525 F.2d 630, 640–42, 173 U.S. App. D.C. 413, 423–25 (D.C.Cir.), cert. denied, 425 U.S. 992, 96 S.Ct. 2203, 48 L.Ed.2d 816 (1976) ("NARUC I").

92. National Ass'n of Broadcasters v. FCC, 740 F.2d 1190, 1203, 239 U.S. App. D.C. 87, 100 (D.C.Cir.1984) ("the sine qua non of a common carrier is the obligation to accept applicants on a non-content oriented basis"); Frontier Broadcasting Co., 24 F.C.C. 251, 253–55 (1958). *See* Mark A. Hall, Note, *Common Carriers Under the Communications Act*, 48 U. Chi. L. Rev. 409, 428 (1981). *But see* Carlin Communication, Inc. v. Southern Bell Telephone & Telegraph Co., 802 F.2d 1352 (11th Cir. 1986); Carlin Communications, Inc. v. The Mountain States Telephone and Telegraph Co., 827 F.2d 1291 (9th Cir.1987).

93. 47 U.S.C.A. § 153 (West 1991). The Act generally treats electronic publishing as

an information service and telecommunications as common carriage. More complex issues of classification arise with the emergence of "hybrid services" such as Internet telephony. *See* In the Matter of Federal–State Joint Board on Universal Service, FCC 98–67 (released Apr. 10, 1998). The Commission noted that such hybrid services should not be subject to common carrier regulation "simply by virtue of the fact that it involves telecommunications components." *Id.* at ¶ 58. Rather, regulatory classification depends on "the fundamental nature of the end-user offering." *Id.* at § 86.

94. 412 U.S. 94, 105–14, 93 S.Ct. 2080, 2087–92, 36 L.Ed.2d 772, 785–90 (1973).

95. *Id.* at 105–08, 93 S. Ct. at 2088–89, 36 L. Ed. 2d at 785–87.

96. *Id.* at 108–09, 93 S.Ct. at 2089, 36 L.Ed.2d at 787 (quoting 47 U.S.C.A. § 153(h)).

Such analysis raises questions about the dictum that "of all the forms of communication, it is broadcasting that has received the most limited First Amendment protection."[97] Common carriers appear to receive the lowest level of First Amendment protection by definition, for they do not have a recognized right to speak on their own and are denied editorial control over their communication traffic.[98]

This placement on the lowest rung of the First Amendment ladder began to change in the mid–1990s as a number of courts began to hold that telephone companies have a First Amendment right to enter the cable television business.[99] The uniformity of the decisions was remarkable since common carriers historically were denied editorial control over their communication traffic.[100] Indeed, the Fourth Circuit noted that "common carriers are not members of 'the press' insofar as the [Communications Act] precludes them from exercising editorial control over the communications they transmit."[1] But the decisions affirmed the telephone companies' constitutional right to devote a portion of their facilities to non-common carrier purposes in which they would exercise editorial control—the provision of entertainment programming.

In reaching this conclusion, the courts uniformly rejected the notion that the First Amendment standard applicable to broadcasting was appropriate.[2] Rather, they employed the same constitutional analysis adopted in *Turner I*: that the government must show that the law serves an important governmental interest and that it is narrowly tailored to avoid excessive infringement of speech.[3] The courts employed an intermediate standard of review after concluding that the cross-ownership restriction at issue was not content-based or otherwise discriminatory.[4] If the law in question had been deemed to be a direct infringement of speech (*e.g.*, a prior restraint), then strict scrutiny would have applied,

97. FCC v. Pacifica Foundation, 438 U.S. 726, 748, 98 S.Ct. 3026, 3040, 57 L.Ed.2d 1073, 1092 (1978).

98. *See* United States v. Western Elec. Co. Inc., 552 F.Supp. 131, 189–90 (D.D.C. 1982), *aff'd sub nom.* Maryland v. United States, 460 U.S. 1001, 103 S.Ct. 1240, 75 L.Ed.2d 472 (1983); United States v. Western Elec. Co., Inc., 673 F.Supp. 525, 586 n. 273 (D.D.C.1987). *But see* Carlin Communication, Inc. v. Southern Bell Telephone & Telegraph Co., 802 F.2d 1352 (11th Cir. 1986); Carlin Communications, Inc. v. Mountain States Telephone and Telegraph Co., 827 F.2d 1291 (9th Cir.1987).

99. *See* Chesapeake & Potomac Tel. Co. of Virginia v. United States, 42 F.3d 181 (4th Cir.1994), *cert. granted, judgment vacated following passage of 1996 Telecommunications Act,* 516 U.S. 415, 116 S.Ct. 1036, 134 L.Ed.2d 46 (1996); US West, Inc. v. United States, 48 F.3d 1092 (9th Cir.1994), *cert. granted, judgment vacated following*

passage of 1996 Telecommunications Act, 516 U.S. 1155, 116 S.Ct. 1037, 134 L.Ed.2d 186 (1996); United States Telephone Assn. v. United States, CA No. 94–1961 (D.D.C. Jan. 27, 1995) (Transcript of proceedings); NYNEX Corp. v. United States, No. 92–323–P–C (D. Maine, 1994); Ameritech Corp. v. United States, 867 F.Supp. 721 (N.D.Ill. 1994); BellSouth Corp. v. United States, 868 F.Supp. 1335 (N.D.Ala.1994).

100. *See* Western Elec. Co., Inc., 552 F. Supp. at 189–90, *aff'd sub nom.* Maryland v. United States, 460 U.S. 1001, 103 S.Ct. 1240, 75 L.Ed.2d 472 (1983); Western Elec. Co. Inc., 673 F. Supp. at 586 n.273.

1. *See e.g.*, Chesapeake & Potomac Telephone Co. v. United States, 42 F.3d 181, 196 (4th Cir.1994).

2. *Id.*; US West, Inc., 48 F. 3d at 1092.

3. *Id.*

4. *Id.*

the same as in any traditional First Amendment case.[5]

Even though the relevant test for the structural regulation at issue was characterized as "intermediate review," the courts made clear that the "heightened scrutiny" required the government to "demonstrate that the recited harms are real, not merely conjectural, and that the regulation will in fact alleviate these harms in a direct and material way."[6] In each case, the courts held that the government had not met its burden. Indeed, the constitutional issues were considered so plain that in January 1995, a Judge of the United States District Court for the District of Columbia ruled from the bench that the cable-telco cross-ownership ban violates the First Amendment.[7]

These conclusions have not been tested in the Supreme Court. Although the Court granted certiorari in *C&P Telephone Company of Virginia*, and received briefs and heard oral argument in the case,[8] the question was mooted by passage of the Telecommunications Act of 1996, which eliminated the statutory ban on cable-telephone company cross-ownership. Accordingly, the Supreme Court terminated the proceeding and vacated the lower court rulings.[9]

The constitutional status of common carriers is further complicated by the development of hybrid regulatory classifications. As in the case of Direct Broadcast Satellites, the FCC has attempted to develop regulatory classifications for common carrier-based video services that do not fit cleanly within a particular category. The first of these attempts was with a proposed service called Video Dial Tone ("VDT"). This was a regulatory category conceived to provide a competitive alternative to traditional cable television service.[10] However, the conditions for providing such service were crafted carefully to avoid the statutory definition of "cable service," thus avoiding the regulatory requirements of cable, even though the service was intended to be virtually indistinguishable to the consumer.[11]

Video Dial Tone raised a number of questions regarding the appropriate regulatory classification as telephone company programmers sought to emulate the type of existing video services provided by cable television systems, and, in 1995, the FCC initiated an inquiry to confront

5. *See* Sable Comms. of Cal., Inc. v. FCC, 492 U.S. 115, 126, 109 S.Ct. 2829, 2836, 106 L.Ed.2d 93, 105 (1989).

6. Chesapeake & Potomac Telephone Co., 42 F. 3d at 202, (quoting Turner Broadcasting System, 512 U.S. at 664, 114 S. Ct. at 2470, 129 L. Ed. 2d at 531).

7. United States Telephone Assn. v. United States, CA No. 94–1961 (D.D.C., Transcript of Proceedings, Jan. 27, 1995).

8. United States v. C&P Telephone Company of Virginia, 515 U.S. 1157, 115 S. Ct. 2608, 132 L.Ed. 2d 852 (1995).

9. 516 U.S. 415, 116 S.Ct. 1036, 134 L.Ed.2d 46 (1996).

10. Telephone Company–Cable Television Cross–Ownership Rules, Sections 63.54–63.58, Second Report and Order, Recommendation to Congress, and Second Further Notice of Proposed Rulemaking, 7 FCC Rcd. 5781, 5794 (1992), *aff'd*, Nat'l Cable Television Ass'n, Inc. v. FCC, 33 F.3d 66, 308 U.S. App. D.C. 221 (D.C.Cir.1994).

11. National Cable Television Assn. v. FCC, 33 F.3d 66, 75, 308 U.S. App. D.C. 221, 230 (D.C.Cir.1994) ("study of the statutory scheme makes it quite clear that video dialtone service and cable service are very different creatures").

this issue.[12] Notwithstanding court decisions invalidating the cable-telephone company cross-ownership ban, the Commission sought comment on whether it had authority to require telephone companies to provide video services on a common carrier basis only, and not as a cable system. [13] It also sought comment on the extent to which cable television rules should be applied to VDT operations.[14] The FCC also sought to determine the extent to which some hybrid classification—somewhere between cable television and common carriage—might be applied. It also sought to examine the constitutionality of its proposed classifications.[15]

As in the case of litigation challenging the cable-telco cross ownership rules, the Telecommunications Act cut short the FCC's analysis of VDT. The 1996 Act expressly eliminated VDT and in its place established a new concept called Open Video Systems ("OVS").[16] The term "new concept" perhaps should be used advisedly, for as Professor (and former FCC Commissioner) Glen Robinson pointed out, the OVS classification consists of "old, new, and borrowed pieces from the hope chests of Congress and the FCC" and that the "[o]ld and borrowed parts predominate."[17]

In this new regulatory category, OVS operators bear some of the obligations of common carriers and some of the obligations of traditional cable operators. Although OVS providers are not subject to most local franchising requirements, they must comply with must carry, retransmission consent, network nonduplication, sports exclusivity and syndicated exclusivity requirements.[18] Like a traditional cable operator, however, an OVS provider must pay a fee based on gross revenues to the local government and must negotiate regarding the provision of public, educational and government ("PEG") Access channels. In the absence of an agreement between local authorities and the provider, the OVS operator is required to provide the same PEG capacity as the franchised cable operator in the community.[19] In addition, the OVS provider must generally devote two-thirds of activated channel capacity to independent programmers on a common carriage basis.[20] The merger of cable and common carrier obligations is certain to complicate any resulting constitutional analysis of this service.

B. *Classification and the Cycle of Regulation*

The constitutional implications of regulatory classifications extend beyond the selection of a particular First Amendment standard for a

12. *See* Telephone Company–Cable Television Cross–Ownership Rules, Sections 63.54–63.58, Fourth Further Notice of Proposed Rulemaking, 10 FCC Rcd 4617 (1995).

13. *Id.* at 4626–27 ¶ 13.

14. *Id.* at 4627–29 ¶¶ 14–17.

15. *Id.* at 4643–44 ¶¶ 46–48.

16. 47 U.S.C.A. §§ 571–573 (West Supp. 1997).

17. Glen O. Robinson, *The New Video Competition: Dances With Regulators*, 97 Colum. L. Rev. 1016, 1024 (1997).

18. Open Video Systems, Second Report and Order, 11 FCC Rcd. 18223, 18327 (1996).

19. 47 U.S.C.A. § 573(c)(2) (West Supp. 1997).

20. Open Video Systems, Second Report and Order at 11 FCC Rcd. at 18248, 18267–18284.

given medium. The process of administrative definition also affects the cycles of regulation that historically govern analysis of new technologies. This phenomenon determines the constitutional status of new technologies at birth, as well as judicial analysis as the technologies mature. Thus, the administrative state tends to capture new technologies at the outset and to prolong separate constitutional treatment beyond the usefulness of the original classification.

1. Classification at the Beginning of the Cycle

One consequence of assigning regulatory classifications to different transmission media is that courts must determine the correct category *before* addressing the substance of First Amendment claims where the government imposes regulations. Thus, as in the hypothetical situation set out at the beginning of this Chapter, our regulator may seek to impose different obligations to media forms that are indistinguishable to the consumer. A good example is a comparison of cable television and satellite master antenna television ("SMATV"), a form of "private cable" generally provided to apartment buildings and condominiums.

In *City of Chicago v. Day*,[21] for example, the Circuit Court of Cook County Illinois was asked to decide whether a SMATV system, should be classified as a cable television system and subjected to franchising requirements under the federal Cable Act. The court refused to consider First Amendment defenses, saying that "[f]or [defendant's] argument to have any legal merit, it would have to prove that it is a SMATV system. However, this it has failed to do."[22] The court reasoned that the defendant would first be required to submit to regulations appropriate to its regulatory category before sorting out its constitutional status.

Given the overriding importance of regulatory classification to the constitutional analysis, the question necessarily arises as to the level of scrutiny courts should bring to the government's classifications. The Supreme Court addressed this question, although not on First Amendment grounds, in *FCC v. Beach Communications, Inc.*[23] The case involved the same basic question as *City of Chicago v. Day*: whether a SMATV system could be subjected to franchising requirements under the Cable Act. The United States Court of Appeals for the District of Columbia Circuit had struck down a statutory distinction that exempted SMATV systems from franchising requirements where such systems connected commonly owned or managed buildings (and to the extent no public rights of way were crossed) while subjecting to regulation identical SMATV systems that connected buildings not commonly owned or managed.[24] The court held that the statutory definition violated equal

---

21. No. 88–MC–313994 (Circuit Ct., Cook Co., IL, May 21, 1990).

22. *Id.*, slip op. at 8.

23. 508 U.S. 307, 113 S.Ct. 2096, 124 L.Ed.2d 211 (1993).

24. Beach Communications, Inc. v. FCC, 959 F.2d 975, 294 U.S. App. D.C. 377 (D.C.Cir.1992), *aff'd following remand*, 965 F.2d 1103, 296 U.S. App. D.C. 141 (D.C.Cir. 1992), *reversed*, 508 U.S. 307, 113 S.Ct. 2096, 124 L.Ed.2d 211 (1993).

protection because it was "unable to imagine" any conceivable basis for the regulatory distinction.[25]

The Supreme Court reversed the District of Columbia Circuit, holding that the Cable Act's definition of a cable system that excluded certain SMATV systems while including others, was entitled to the presumption of having a rational basis. "In establishing the franchise requirement," the Court noted, "Congress had to draw the line somewhere; it had to choose which facilities to franchise. This necessity renders the precise coordinates of the resulting legislative judgment virtually unreviewable, since the legislature must be allowed leeway to approach a perceived problem incrementally."[26] Like the District of Columbia Circuit, however, the Court emphasized that it was limiting its review to "the question presented" of whether the regulatory classification is "rationally related to a legitimate government purpose under the Due Process Clause." Whether heightened First Amendment scrutiny should apply—particularly in light of the "burdens imposed on franchised cable systems under the newly enacted [Cable Act of 1992]"—was a question left open for the Court of Appeals to decide on remand.[27] That court summarily dismissed the appeal, finding "no basis for the application of a heightened scrutiny standard."[28]

The specific issue raised in *Beach Communications* was ultimately resolved by the Telecommunications Act of 1996, in which Congress changed the definition of cable system to exclude all SMATV systems that do not use public rights of way.[29] These cases highlight the extraordinary importance of regulatory classifications in the current system. Such classifications may determine the outcome in the event of a constitutional challenge, by establishing the applicable standard of review.

2. The Role of Classification in Prolonging the Cycle

To the extent new communications technologies are born in captivity, they also tend to evolve toward greater protection. As described in Section 2.2[B] *supra*, courts tend to increase the level of constitutional protection for new technologies after they attain significant penetration and become more mainstream. However, the correlation between traditional First Amendment protection and cultural penetration of a given

---

25. 959 F. 2d at 987, 294 U.S. App. D.C. at 389. The court expressly declined to address the SMATV operators' First Amendment claims, holding them to be "unripe." *Id.* at 984–85, 294 U.S. App. D.C. at 386–87.

26. Beach Communications, Inc., 508 U.S. at 316, 113 S. Ct. at 2102, 124 L. Ed. 2d at 223.

27. *Id.* at 314 n.6, 113 S. Ct. at 2101 n.6, 1241 Ed.2d at 221 n.6.

28. Beach Communications, Inc. v. FCC, 10 F.3d 811, 304 U.S. App. D.C. 36 (D.C.Cir.1993).

29. *See* Section 301(a)(2), Telecommunications Act of 1996, *codified* at 47 U.S.C.A. § 522(7) (West Supp. 1997). In Entertainment Corrections, Inc., FCC 98–111 (released June 30, 1998), the FCC ruled that a SMATV system could not be regulated as a cable system where the operator connected separate buildings across public rights-of-way by using a tariffed common carrier service.

medium can be disrupted by the process of administrative categorization that is an inherent aspect of regulation. The classification of new media for regulatory purposes tends to institutionalize, and thereby prolong, distinct constitutional treatment.

Government control over broadcasting is the clearest example of this. Commercial television existed for more than forty years and had long become a dominant social force before courts began to reconsider their constitutional approach. Many observers have concluded that the original justification for different treatment of broadcasting—the purported scarcity of frequencies—has for years been nothing more than a legal fiction.[30]

President Bill Clinton underscored this point when he described the differences between the constitutional treatment of broadcasting and the print media in 1996:

> As you know, the distinction between broadcasting and publishing in terms of the First Amendment is based on the scarcity principle. Free over-the-air broadcasting will continue to be a vital part of our media, and availability of licenses will continue to be limited. When that changes, the distinction between broadcasting and print will change too.[31]

Passage of the Telecommunications Act of 1996 promised to eliminate this constitutional anomaly and apply more traditional First Amendment understandings to broadcasting. As the first comprehensive rewrite of communications law in over six decades, the Act was intended to remove regulation and stimulate competition. The Senate Report on the legislation noted that "[c]hanges in technology and consumer preferences have made the 1934 [Communications] Act a historical anachronism." It noted that "the Act was not prepared to handle the growth of cable television" and that "[t]he growth of cable programming has raised questions about the rules that govern broadcasters" among others.[32]

The House of Representatives' legislative findings were even more emphatic. The House Commerce Committee pointed out that the audio and video marketplace has undergone significant changes over the past 50 years "and the scarcity rationale for government regulation no longer applies."[33] The Committee Report noted that there are more than 11,000

---

30. *See, e.g.*, HENRY GELLER, FIBER OPTICS: AN OPPORTUNITY FOR A NEW POLICY? 15 (1991) ("the broadcast regulatory model is a failed concept" and "the public trustee scheme . . . is a joke"); LEE BOLLINGER, IMAGES OF A FREE PRESS 88–90 (University of Chicago Press, 1991) (describing the rationale of *Red Lion* as having "devastating—even embarrassing—deficienc[ies]," as "illogical," and as being based on the "simple-minded and erroneous assertion that public regulation is the only allocation scheme that can avoid chaos in broadcasting"); Donald E. Lively, *Fear and the Media: A First Amendment Horror Show,* 69 Minn.L.Rev. 1071,

1085 (1985); Mark Fowler and Daniel Brenner, *A Marketplace Approach to Broadcast Regulation,* 60 Texas L. Rev. 207, 221–226 (1982).

31. *Clinton on Communications,* Broadcasting & Cable, Sept. 23, 1996, p. 22.

32. Telecommunications Competition and Deregulation Act of 1995, S. Rep. 104–23, 104th Cong. 1st Sess. 2–3 (Mar. 30, 1995).

33. Communications Act of 1995, H. Rep. 104–204, 104th Cong. 1st Sess. 54 (July 24, 1995).

radio stations and 1,100 commercial television stations—a 30 percent increase over the past decade. During this time, a fourth broadcast network came into existence and two other networks were emerging. The Report also pointed to additional competition from cable television. It stated that cable systems passed more than 95 percent of television households and that 63 percent subscribe to cable. In addition, it pointed to other technologies such as wireless cable, low-power television, backyard satellite dishes, satellite master antenna television service and VCRs, all of which "provide customers with additional program distribution outlets that compete with broadcast stations."[34] Finally, the Report pointed to the strong interest by telephone companies in providing video programming. "This explosion of programming distribution sources," the House Report found, "calls for a substantial reform of Congressional and Commission oversight of the way the broadcasting industry develops and competes."[35]

Over time increasing tensions between the media marketplace and the theories upon which regulation of broadcasting is based persuaded a number of courts to focus more on the First Amendment concerns inherent in regulation. Accordingly, some courts began to analyze free speech claims of broadcasters by giving less weight to—or by not relying at all on—the "special" nature of the medium.

In *FCC v. League of Women Voters of California*, for example, the Supreme Court invalidated a statutory prohibition on editorializing by public broadcasting stations that received funds from the Corporation for Public Broadcasting.[36] Although the Court expressly upheld the "public trustee" concept and declined to apply strict scrutiny, it nevertheless subjected the government's asserted interests to a far more rigorous analysis than ever before and questioned the continuing validity of the scarcity rationale.[37] The Court conducted a thorough review of the purposes of public broadcasting and the legislative objectives and found that the ban on editorializing was not narrowly tailored and did not serve the asserted governmental interests.[38] As in other cases of the "law unto itself" genre, the Court continued to pay lip service to the "public trustee" concept, but it also emphasized that "the broadcasting industry is indisputably a part [of the press]", and the decision relied primarily on precedents involving traditional media.[39]

---

34. *Id.* at 55.

35. *Id.*

36. 468 U.S. 364, 104 S.Ct. 3106, 82 L.Ed.2d 278 (1984).

37. *Id.* at 374–381, 104 S. Ct. at 3113–18, 82 L.Ed.2d at 287–92. *See also id.* at 377 n.11 104 S. Ct. at 3115 n.11, 82 L.Ed.2d at 289, n.11. (Noting criticisms of scarcity rationale, the Court indicated that it would be willing "to reconsider our longstanding approach" if given "some signal from Congress or the FCC that technological developments have advanced so far that some revi-

sion of the system of broadcast regulation may be required."); *id.* at 376 n.12, 104 S. Ct. at 3115, n.12, 82 L.Ed.2d at 289 n.12 ("were it to be shown by the Commission that the fairness doctrine '[has] the net effect of reducing rather than enhancing' speech, we would then be forced to reconsider the constitutional basis of our decision in [*Red Lion*]").

38. *Id.* at 384–399, 104 S. Ct. at 3119–27, 82 L.Ed.2d at 294–303.

39. *Id.* at 382, 104 S. Ct. at 3118–19, 82 L.Ed.2d at 290 *citing* United States v. Paramount Pictures, Inc., 334 U.S. 131, 166, 68

In *Turner Broadcasting System v. FCC*, a case analyzing the First Amendment rights of cable television operators, the Court again declined to question the scarcity rationale,[40] but limited its importance as a justification for broadcast content controls. To support its conclusion that compelling cable operators to carry local broadcast signals is content neutral, the majority emphasized "the limited nature of [the FCC's] jurisdiction" over the content of television programming.[41] In particular, the Court noted that "the FCC's oversight responsibilities do not grant it the power to ordain any particular type of programming that must be offered by broadcast stations; for although 'the Commission may inquire of licensees what they have done to determine the needs of the community they propose to serve, the Commission may not impose upon them its private notions of what the public ought to hear.' "[42]

Lower courts have been more willing to question the public trustee doctrine or to apply its First Amendment precepts in a far stricter way. In *Community–Service Broadcasting of Mid–America, Inc. v. FCC*, the United States Court of Appeals for the District of Columbia Circuit, sitting *en banc*, noted that "spectrum scarcity cannot be invoked to support a government attempt to penalize or suppress speech, based on its general content, by some, but not all, broadcast licensees."[43] The court's plurality opinion stated that under either strict scrutiny or the *O'Brien* test for incidental speech restrictions, a requirement that public broadcast stations make and retain recordings of programs "in which any issue of public importance is discussed, violated the First Amendment."[44] Similarly, in *News America Publishing Inc. v. FCC*, the District of Columbia Circuit demanded "a better fit between the law and its asserted legitimate purposes" than was evident in a congressional re-

S.Ct. 915, 933, 92 L.Ed. 1260, 1297 (1948), in which the Court for the first time stated that "[w]e have no doubt that moving pictures, like newspapers and radio, are included in the press whose freedom is guaranteed by the First Amendment." *See also id.* at 382–399, 104 S. Ct. at 3118–27, 82 L. Ed.2d at 293–303 citing, *inter alia*, Bolger v. Youngs Drug Products Corp., 463 U.S. 60, 103 S.Ct. 2875, 77 L.Ed.2d 469 (1983); Carey v. Brown, 447 U.S. 455, 100 S.Ct. 2286, 65 L.Ed.2d 263 (1980); First National Bank of Boston v. Bellotti, 435 U.S. 765, 98 S.Ct. 1407, 55 L.Ed.2d 707 (1978); Wooley v. Maynard, 430 U.S. 705, 97 S.Ct. 1428, 51 L.Ed.2d 752 (1977); Buckley v. Valeo, 424 U.S. 1, 96 S.Ct. 612, 46 L.Ed.2d 659 (1976) (per curiam); and New York Times v. Sullivan, 376 U.S. 254, 84 S.Ct. 710, 11 L.Ed.2d 686 (1964).

40. Turner Broadcasting Sys., 512 U.S. at 622, 114 S. Ct. at 2445, 129 L.Ed.2d at 497. The Court found the scarcity analysis to be "inapposite" in the context of cable television.

41. *Id.* at 638, 114 S. Ct. at 2457, 129, L.Ed.2d at 522.

42. *Id.* at 650, 114 S. Ct. at 2563, 129 L.Ed.2d at 522 quoting *En Banc Programming Inquiry*, 44 F.C.C.2d 2303, 2312 (1960). Of special relevance to the congressional mandate regarding children's programming, (47 U.S.C.A. § 303b (West 1991)), the Court noted that noncommercial broadcasters—and by implication their commercial counterparts—"are not required by statute or regulation to carry any specific quantity of 'educational' programming or any particular 'educational' programs." 512 U.S. at 650, 114 S. Ct. at 2465, 129 L. Ed. 2d at 523.

43. 593 F.2d 1102, 1111 n. 21, 192 U.S. App. D.C. 448, 457 n. 21 (D.C.Cir.1978) (en banc).

44. *Id.* at 1111–22, 192 U.S. App. D.C. at 457–468. Only four judges (Wright, Bazelon, McGowan and Wilkey) endorsed this section of the opinion. Judge Robinson found that the regulation could not survive even minimal scrutiny, and found it unnecessary to apply a stricter test. *Id.* at 1127, 192 U.S. App. D.C. at 473 (Robinson, J., concurring in part and concurring in the judgment).

striction on the FCC's ability to grant waivers of the newspaper-television cross-ownership rule.[45] The court pointedly outlined the weakness of separate constitutional treatment based on spectrum scarcity, but noted that even under the public trustee doctrine, regulations must be narrowly tailored to further a substantial government interest.[46] It found the cross-ownership limit at issue to be "astonishingly underinclusive," and therefore unconstitutional.[47]

Some courts that rejected First Amendment challenges broadcasting regulations began to do so without reference to spectrum scarcity. In *United States v. Edge Broadcasting Co.*, for example, the Supreme Court upheld against a First Amendment challenge a prohibition on the broadcast of lottery advertisements in states that did not have a government lottery. Although the decision is a highly fragmented one in which seven Justices supported the outcome for various reasons, not a single one relied on the rationale of *Red Lion*. Indeed, none even cited it.[48] The Court's decision ultimately rested on the commercial speech doctrine as articulated in *Central Hudson Gas & Electric Corp. v. Public Service Commission of New York*.[49]

Another indication of a change in judicial attitudes toward broadcasting is the language courts have begun to use in framing their constitutional analyses. As Dean Bollinger has observed, the *Red Lion* Court "never referred to the broadcast media as the press nor to broadcasters as editors or journalists; they were consistently described as licensees and fiduciaries."[50] But a different view has begun to emerge in some later cases. The Supreme Court has stated that "broadcasters are engaged in a vital and independent form of communicative activity" and that "the First Amendment must inform and give shape to the manner in which Congress exercises its regulatory [authority] in this area."[51] The recognition of broadcasters as being an important segment of the press has been even more direct among the lower courts. As the District of Columbia Circuit noted in *Community–Service Broadcasting of Mid–America, Inc.*, public affairs programming on broadcast stations "lies at

45. 844 F.2d 800, 805, 269 U.S. App. D.C. 182, 187 (D.C.Cir.1988).

46. *Id.* at 810–12, 269 U.S. App. D.C. at 192–94.

47. *Id.* at 814, 269 U.S. App. D.C. at 196.

48. 509 U.S. 418, 113 S.Ct. 2696, 125 L.Ed.2d 345 (1993). *See also* Valley Broadcasting Co. v. United States, 820 F.Supp. 519 (D.Nev.1993), *aff'd,* 107 F.3d 1328 (9th Cir.1997), *cert. denied,* ___ U.S. ___, 118 S.Ct. 1050, 140 L.Ed.2d 114 (1998), in which the court invalidated a prohibition of broadcast advertising of casino gambling using the *Central Hudson* test. The court did not mention *Red Lion* or the public trustee standard. *See also* Players International, Inc. v. United States, 988 F.Supp.

497 (D.N.J.1997). *But see* Greater New Orleans Broad. Ass'n. v. United States, 69 F.3d 1296 (5th Cir.1995).

49. 447 U.S. 557, 566, 100 S.Ct. 2343, 2351, 65 L.Ed.2d 341, 350 (1980).

50. Bollinger, *supra* note 30 at 91.

51. League of Women Voters of California, 468 U.S. at 378, 104 S. Ct. at 3116, 82 L. Ed.2d at 290. *See also* CBS, Inc. v. FCC, 453 U.S. 367, 395, 101 S.Ct. 2813, 2829, 69 L.Ed.2d 706, 728 (1981) (broadcasters are "entitled under the First Amendment to exercise 'the widest journalistic freedom consistent with [their] public [duties]'"). *See also* Arkansas Educational Television Commission v. Forbes, 523 U.S. 666, 118 S.Ct. 1633, 1639, 140 L.Ed.2d875, 140 L.Ed. 875, 885 (1998).

the core of the First Amendment's protections."[52] This rhetorical shift is significant. As they did with film a generation ago, courts appear to be distancing themselves from the historic justifications for separate constitutional treatment of broadcasting.

However, despite the growing unease with which courts have confronted the scarcity doctrine, they have declined to take the final step of overruling the prior precedent. Professor Donald Lively has suggested that courts will refuse to take this step until they have devised a new theory that would continue to permit government control of the media.[53] And indeed, there has been a recent resurgence of interest in broadcast regulation, along with the promotion of new theories of regulation as a means of perpetuating government control and subordinating constitutional considerations.[54]

This phenomenon was most evident in the FCC's failure in 1997 and 1998 to eliminate the personal attack and political editorial rules—two fairness doctrine corollaries—that had survived for ten years past the demise of the doctrine upon which they are premised.[55] Indeed, the Commission was deadlocked on whether to repeal the rules despite the fact that it had opened a docket to study the issue fourteen years earlier[56] and in 1988 had found that the factual and constitutional underpinnings of the fairness doctrine were no longer valid. Following a thorough review of the evolving media marketplace, the FCC found that spectrum scarcity no longer supported enforcement of the fairness doctrine.[57] Importantly, the Commission found that "the overall net effect of the doctrine is to reduce the coverage of controversial issues of public importance, in contravention of the standard announced in *Red Lion*."[58] The FCC subsequently extended this analysis and repealed another fairness doctrine corollary that applied to broadcasts relating to ballot issues. [59]

---

52. 593 F.2d at 1110 ("noncommercial licensees are fully protected by the First Amendment"). *See also* Syracuse Peace Council v. FCC, 867 F.2d 654, 276 U.S. App. D.C. 38 (D.C.Cir.1989) cert. denied, 493 U.S. 1019, 110 S.Ct. 717, 107 L.Ed.2d 737 (1990); News America Pub., Inc., 844 F.2d at 812–813, 269 U.S.App.D.C. at 194–195; Johnson v. FCC, 829 F.2d 157, 161–63, 264 U.S. App. D.C. 372, 376–78 (D.C.Cir.1987).

53. *See, e.g.*, Lively, *supra* n. 30 at 1085 ("What may be evinced is a long-standing mind-set, traceable to *Mutual Film*, that the risk of abandoning control premises, no matter how unpersuasive or irreconcilable with the first amendment, is unacceptable."); Robert M. O'Neil, *Dead or Alive: How Long Will the Red Lion Specter Haunt Free Speech and Broadcasting?* in RATIONALES & RATIONALIZATIONS 19–41 (Robert Corn–Revere, ed., Media Institute 1997).

54. *See generally* RATIONALES & RATIONALIZATIONS (Robert Corn–Revere, ed., Media Institute 1997).

55. The personal attack and political editorial rules were formulated by the FCC in 1967 "to effectuate important aspects of the well-established Fairness Doctrine." Personal Attacks; Political Editorials, 8 F.C.C. 2d 721, 722 (1967).

56. *See* Repeal or Modification of the Personal Attack and Political Editorial Rules, Notice of Proposed Rulemaking, 48 Fed. Reg. 28295 (June 21, 1983).

57. In re Complaint of Syracuse Peace Council Against Television Station WTVH, 2 FCC Rcd. 5043 (1987), *aff'd sub nom.* Syracuse Peace Council v. FCC, 867 F.2d 654 (D.C.Cir.1989), cert. denied, 493 U.S. 1019, 110 S.Ct. 717, 107 L.Ed.2d 737 (1990).

58. *Id.* at 5050.

59. *In re* Complaint of The Arkansas AFL–CIO, 7 FCC Rcd. 541 (1992), *aff'd sub nom.* Arkansas AFL–CIO v. FCC, 11 F.3d 1430 (8th Cir.1993) (en banc).

Following these decisions, however, the political makeup of the FCC changed, and with it the institutional momentum to apply the agency's previous findings regarding spectrum scarcity and content control. After the District of Columbia Circuit prompted the FCC to consider a long-pending petition for rulemaking on the personal attack and political editorial rules,[60] the Commission, in a 2–2 vote, was unable to resolve the issue. Then–Chairman Reed Hundt, who opposed repeal, suggested that the FCC had retreated from its findings in *Syracuse Peace Council,* and that spectrum scarcity persisted because "[m]any more people continue to seek to acquire broadcast licenses, and the right to broadcast, than do obtain them."[61] He added that "[s]carcity is not the only justification on which we can appropriately base minimal, nonburdensome requirements for broadcast licensees to serve the public interest, such as the requirements imposed by Congress on cable (*e.g.,* must-carry and 'PEG' requirements) or on direct-to-home satellites."[62] He invoked other First Amendment theories to support continuing content regulation, such as the public forum doctrine and "a quid-pro-quo approach or conditional license approach."[63] One year later, the FCC was still deadlocked 2–2.[64] Two Commissioners strongly supported the continuing validity of the scarcity doctrine, while two other Commissioners argued that the scarcity doctrine is obsolete and had already been repudiated by the FCC.[65]

Former FCC Commissioner Glen O. Robinson has written that regulation persists among electronic media such as cable television because both business and government actors play the game of "strategic regulation." Incumbent industries seek to forestall competition and increase certainty, while "bureaucrats play to gain power, position, post-government employment and who knows what else."[66] Thus, although there have been changes in the details of regulation over the years, Professor Robinson noted that "the most remarkable thing about [such] regulation has been its constancy." He concluded that "the regulation game has an equilibrium strategy that no combination of players can defeat: it is nothing less than the game itself, regulation."[67] As such regulation persists, so does separate constitutional treatment.

60. *In re* Radio–Television News Directors Ass'n., Case No. 96–1338 (D.C.Cir., 1997).

61. FCC Release, In the Matter of the Repeal or Modification of the Personal Attack and Political Editorial Rules (Aug. 11, 1997) (Statement of Chairman Hundt) at 2.

62. *Id.*

63. *Id.* at 2–3. For an analysis of these theories of regulation, *See* RATIONALES & RATIONALIZATIONS (Robert Corn–Revere, ed., Media Institute 1997).

64. In re Radio–Television News Directors Assn. and National Assn. of Broadcasters, FCC 98–126 (released June 22, 1998).

65. *See* Joint Statement of Commissioner Susan Ness and Commissioner Gloria Tristani concerning the Political Editorial and Personal Attack Rules, Gen. Docket No. 83–84 (Junes 22, 1998) (supporting scarcity doctrine); Joint Statement of Commissioners Powell and Furchgott–Roth, Gen.Docket 83–84 (June 22, 1998) (opposing scarcity doctrine). The Chairman, William Kennard, was recused from the proceeding because he had participated in an earlier stage of the matter as a lawyer in the 1980s.

66. Glen O. Robinson, *The New Video Competition: Dances With Regulators,* 97 Colum. L. Rev. 1016, 1045 (1997).

67. *Id.* at 1046.

2.4 Breakdown of the Categorical Approach to the First Amendment

Whatever other implications may flow from basing First Amendment analysis on regulatory classifications, the doctrine that "each [communications medium] is a law unto itself"[1] makes constitutional analysis exceedingly complex in a world of burgeoning technology and proliferating, and nonexclusive, administrative categories. Courts, policymakers and legal scholars simultaneously are being presented with an expansion and contraction of regulatory options. In the first instance, the variety of delivery systems and media services has multiplied, as have the number of regulatory classifications. This raises the possibility that a separate First Amendment test must be applied to each medium and a new standard developed with each technical innovation.[2] Secondly, with convergence, the once discrete functions of the various media are coming together. The synthesis of form and function vastly complicates segregating the different media for separate constitutional treatment. But if history can teach, the lesson should be this: the gradual evolution of constitutional rights based on regulatory classifications is unsuited to the new media environment.

A. The Rapid Pace of Technology Versus the Glacial Pace of Doctrinal Change

There is a wide and growing chasm between the rate of technological change and that of legal development. The case-by-case legal process by which courts seek to define the appropriate constitutional standard for a given medium typically takes decades, while the communications industry is evolving far more quickly. If anything, the disparity between the two is growing as the nation moves steadily toward creation of broadband, digital, interactive networks while courts and policymakers continue to debate the constitutionality of the fairness doctrine and other content regulations.[3] As Professor Rodney Smolla has perceptively pointed out, "[s]cientists move more quickly than lawyers."[4]

This is especially true when the lawyers are judges. The fact that courts are reluctant to resolve the difficult questions raised by new technologies is not a new phenomenon. The Supreme Court in the 1930s delayed taking up cases on the constitutional status of radio, perhaps

---

1. Kovacs v. Cooper, 336 U.S. 77, 97, 69 S.Ct. 448, 459, 93 L.Ed. 513, 528 (1949) (Jackson J., concurring).

2. See Lance Rose, *The U.S. Supreme Court's Indecency Decision: A Minor Ruling for the Multiple Media Internet,* Electronic Information Policy and Law Report, p. 890, Aug. 22, 1997.

3. See ITHIEL DESOLA POOL, TECHNOLOGIES OF FREEDOM 7 (1983); LAURENCE H. TRIBE, AMERICAN CONSTITUTIONAL LAW 1007 (2d ed. 1988); M. Ethan Katsh, The First Amendment and Technological Change: The New

Media Have a Message, 57 Geo. Wash. L. Rev. 1459, 1493 (1989). *See also* Richard L. Wiley, *"Fairness" in Our Future?* Quill, Mar. 1994 p. 36; Gigi B. Sohn, *Pro: Fairness Doctrine—A Practical Solution for Handling Irresponsibility,* Quill, Mar. 1994 p. 38; Robert L. Corn–Revere, *Con: Fairness Doctrine—A Bad Idea Just Keeps Going, Going—Wrong,* Quill, Mar. 1994 p. 39.

4. RODNEY A. SMOLLA, FREE SPEECH IN AN OPEN SOCIETY 321 (1992).

because it found the new medium too intimidating. Chief Justice Taft is reported to have explained his lack of eagerness as follows:

> [I]nterpreting the law on this subject is something like trying to interpret the law of the occult. It seems like dealing with something supernatural. I want to put it off as long as possible in the hope that it becomes more understandable before the court passes on the questions involved.[5]

Many of these feelings appear to be shared by members of the modern judiciary as they seek to cope with newer electronic forms of communication, such as computers. Justice David Souter has pointed out that "as broadcast, cable and the cyber-technology of the Internet and World Wide Web approach the day of using a common receiver, we can hardly assume that standards for judging the regulation of one of them will not have immense, but now unknown and unknowable effects on the others." Such considerations, he wrote, "demand a subtlety tantamount to prescience."[6]

The problem of adjusting legal standards to accommodate evolving technology is well illustrated by the shifting legal status of electronic eavesdropping under both constitutional and statutory law. In 1928 the Supreme Court considered whether warrantless wiretapping violated the Fourth Amendment prohibition against unreasonable searches and seizures. The Court found no constitutional violation because the surveillance was accomplished without intruding on the physical property of the defendant.[7] By failing to acknowledge that technology permitted the government to intrude on communications in a way that previously was impossible, Chief Justice Taft (still no futurist) was able to conclude that "[t]here was no searching [and there] was no seizure."[8] The Fourth Amendment "does not forbid what was done here" because "[t]he United States takes no such care of telegraph or telephone messages as of mailed sealed letters."[9]

Justice Brandeis, whose views ultimately prevailed, argued in dissent that constitutional principles were undermined to the extent the Court focused excessively on the medium of communication. He argued forcefully that constitutions must be interpreted with technological advancements in mind to preserve fundamental rights. In particular, Justice Brandeis wrote, constitutions must be designed "to approach immortality" and "our contemplation cannot only be what has been but of what may be."[10] Anticipating the rise of a computer-based society, he warned that:

---

5. Ronald Coase, *The Federal Communications Commission*, 2 J. Law & Econ. 1, 40 (1959), *quoting* C.C. DILL, RADIO LAW 1–2 (1938).

6. Denver Area Educational Telecommunications Consortium v. FCC, 518 U.S. 727, 776–777, 116 S.Ct. 2374, 2402, 135 L.Ed.2d 888, 923 (1996) (Souter, J., concurring).

7. Olmstead v. United States, 277 U.S. 438, 464, 48 S.Ct. 564, 568, 72 L.Ed. 944, 950 (1928).

8. *Id.*

9. *Id.*

10. *Id.* at 473, 48 S. Ct. at 570, 72 L. Ed. at 954 (Brandeis, J., dissenting).

Discovery and invention have made it possible for the Government, by means far more effective than stretching upon the rack, to obtain disclosure in court of what is whispered in the closet.

* * *

The progress of science in furnishing the Government with means of espionage is not likely to stop with wire-tapping. Ways may some day be developed by which the Government, without removing papers from secret drawers, can reproduce them in court, and by which it will be enabled to expose to a jury the most intimate occurrences of the home. Advances in the psychic and related sciences may bring means of exploring unexpressed beliefs, thoughts and emotions.

* * *

Can it be that the Constitution affords no protection against such invasions of individual security?

Justice Brandeis concluded that if the courts did not adapt to new realities, then constitutional principles would be "converted by precedent into impotent and lifeless formulas" and that "[r]ights declared in words might be lost in reality."[11] The Court eventually adopted Brandeis' analysis toward wiretapping as a search, but it took nearly forty years to do so. In *Katz v. United States*, the Court declared that the Fourth Amendment "protects people, not places" and held that wiretapping is allowable only after a valid warrant is issued—the same as for any other search.[12]

The very nature of law, with its emphasis for creating certainty, makes keeping up with rapid technological development difficult if not impossible. Even Justice Brandeis, the champion of a dynamic constitution in *Olmstead*, wrote that "in most matters it is more important that the applicable rule of law be settled, than that it be settled right."[13] Consequently, the nature of constitutional adjudication makes it easy to understand why it took 37 years for the Supreme Court to change its First Amendment approach to cinema, and why it has continued to spend decades debating the appropriate standards for broadcasting and cable television.

This time-consuming quest for a stable legal standard creates a special dissonance in the dynamic field of electronic communications. Congress created the Federal Communications Commission precisely because the field is rapidly changing; it recognized that legislative changes could not keep up with advancements in radio communication. The Communications Act of 1934 was envisioned as a flexible regulatory system "because the broadcast industry is dynamic in terms of techno-

---

11. *Id.* (internal quotations omitted).

12. 389 U.S. 347, 88 S.Ct. 507, 19 L.Ed.2d 576 (1967).

13. Burnet v. Coronado Oil and Gas Co., 285 U.S. 393, 406, 52 S.Ct. 443, 447, 76 L.Ed. 815, 823 (1932).

logical change."[14] The administrative approach it created is predicated on the assumption that "solutions adequate a decade ago are not necessarily so now, and those acceptable today may well be outmoded 10 years hence."[15] Yet even in a regulatory system based on this premise, it is difficult for the administrative agency to keep up with changes and adjust its rules accordingly. Consequently, burdensome regulations may live on long after their reason for existence has vanished.[16]

So we are left with an evident paradox. On one hand, the law is criticized for failing to keep up with innovations. On the other, it seems that the purpose of the law is undermined if it changes too quickly.[17] The dilemma is magnified to the extent that the rate of innovation is accelerating.

But this is a false paradox. It exists only to the extent a new legal standard is expected to spring into place with each new medium. Where First Amendment principles are not dependent on the specific communications technology, there will be a greatly diminished perception that the law has failed to keep pace, for there will be no expectation of a major doctrinal shift with each new invention. Such an approach also preserves the law's function of promoting certainty. Conflicts about the appropriate First Amendment standard for broadcasting, cable television, and other new media have done more to create instability from both the perspective of the regulator and that of the regulated industries than perhaps any other single factor in the law.

B.   Convergence and the Problem of Regulatory Classification

Courts and legislators generally attempt to fill gaps in legal doctrine by analogy rather than by developing new concepts.[18] Just as notions of

14. CBS, Inc. v. Democratic National Committee, 412 U.S. 94, 102, 93 S.Ct. 2080, 2086, 36 L.Ed.2d 772, 783 (1973).

15. *Id.*.

16. *See, e.g.*, Capital Cities/ABC, Inc. v. FCC, 29 F.3d 309 (7th Cir.1994), *affirming*, In re Evaluation of the Syndication and Financial Interest Rules, Second Report and Order, 8 FCC Rcd. 3282 (1993) and Memorandum Opinion on Recon., 8 FCC Rcd. 8270 (1993). *See also* Evaluation of the Syndication and Financial Interest Rules (Report and Order), 6 FCC Rcd. 3094 (1991), *rev'd and remanded,* Schurz Communications v. FCC, 982 F.2d 1043 (7th Cir.1992). *See also* Quincy Cable TV, Inc. v. FCC, 768 F.2d 1434, 1455–57, 248 U.S. App. D.C. 1, 22–24 (D.C.Cir.1985) cert. denied, 476 U.S. 1169, 106 S.Ct. 2889, 90 L.Ed.2d 977 (1986).

17. M. Ethan Katsh, The Electronic Media and the Transformation of Law 17–19 (Oxford University Press 1989).

18. *See e.g.*, Harry Kalven, Jr., *Broadcasting, Public Policy and the First Amendment*, 10 J. Law & Econ. 15, 38 (1967) ("Law, it has been said, is determined by a choice between competing analogies."). Policymakers have been forced to develop new analogies as technology and the communications marketplace have evolved. Former FCC Commissioner Patricia Diaz Dennis half facetiously suggested that broadcasters should be regulated as if they were in a "game preserve," as opposed to the unregulated "jungle" advocated by opponents of government control or the paternalistic "zoo" favored by proponents of public intervention. Speech of Patricia Diaz Dennis before the Broadcast Financial Management Association (April 18, 1988). *See Trying a New Policy On For Size*, Broadcasting, April 25, 1988, p. 41. Coming up with new concepts to accommodate the rapidly changing communications landscape is no easy task, and Commissioner Dennis was forced to admit, "I am no closer to solving this problem than scientists are to coming

"common carriage" and "public interest, convenience and necessity" in the Communications Act were drawn from 19th century concepts of transportation law,[19] courts usually have borrowed the constitutional analysis articulated for established media and applied it to new technologies. Many scholars such as Ithiel de Sola Pool have criticized the weakness of this approach. Pool explained that "[a] long series of precedents, each based on the last and treating clumsy new technologies in their early forms as specialized business machines, has led to a scholastic set of distinctions that no longer correspond to reality. As new technologies have acquired the functions of the press, they have not acquired the rights of the press."[20]

Courts did create a genuinely new (if not well defined) First Amendment standard for broadcasting, but they have failed so far to do the same for cable television or other new video delivery systems. In the search for a new standard, the debate in most cases comes down to a battle of competing analogies—whether the new technology has more characteristics in common with broadcasting than with print. If the medium is deemed more like over-the-air television, a standard more forgiving of government intrusion is applied; if it is considered more akin to traditional publishing, full First Amendment rights attach. The Supreme Court, recognizing the complexity of this analysis, thus far has declined to make a "definitive choice among competing analogies (broadcast, common carrier, bookstore) [that] allows us to declare a rigid single standard, good for now and for all future media and purposes."[21]

A basic problem with this categorical approach is that it lacks a principled or consistent method of application. The similarities among media are in the eye of the beholder, and the resulting judicial approaches have been mixed. Another problem is this: what if the real answer to the question of whether a new medium is "like" one technology or another is "all of the above?" Multimedia, for example, is "like" newspapers because it transmits text; it is "like" books when presented over a personal player on CD–ROM. But it is also "like" broadcasting or cable because it may transmit video. And it may be "like" common carriers when transmitted over the telephone network or when used for point-to-point communication. The philosophy that "differences in the characteristics of new media justify differences in the First Amendment standards applied to them" is illogical in the case of multimedia.[22]

up with a unified theory to explain how the universe operates." *Id.*

19. *See* Pensacola Tel. Co. v. Western Union Tel. Co., 96 U.S. 1, 8–9, 24 L.Ed. 708, 710 (1877); National Ass'n of Regulatory Utility Commissioners v. FCC, 525 F.2d 630, 640–42, 173 U.S. App. D.C. 413, 423–25 (D.C.Cir.1976) (D.C. Cir.), cert. denied, 425 U.S. 992, 96 S.Ct. 2203, 48 L.Ed.2d 816 (1976); Mickelson, Offer & Whalen, The Common Carrier Principle 3–5 (1989); Richard A. Hindman, Comment, *The Diversity Principle and the MFJ Information Services Restriction: Applying Time–Worn First Amendment Assumptions to New Technologies*, 38 Cath. U. L. Rev. 471, 496–97 (1989); Mark A. Hall, Note, *Common Carriers Under the Communications Act*, 48 U. Chi. L. Rev. 409 (1981).

20. Pool, *supra* note 3 at 250.

21. Denver Area, 518 U.S. at 742, 116 S. Ct. at 2385, 135 L. Ed. 2d at 901 (plurality opinion).

22. Robert Corn–Revere, *Multimedia and the Future of the First Amendment*, Quick–Time Forum, Sept./Oct. 1993 at 22.

The Supreme Court addressed this problem in *Reno v. ACLU*.[23] The Court for the first time considered the Internet and World Wide Web and noted that "[t]his dynamic, multifaceted category of communication includes not only traditional print and news services, but also audio, video, and still images, as well as interactive, real-time dialogue."[24] It found that the Internet is "a unique and wholly new medium of worldwide communication," the content on which is "as diverse as human thought."[25] The Internet, in short, is a medium characterized by convergence.

But this phenomenon is by no means limited to the Internet. In early 1994, Vice President Gore proclaimed that, like our Universe,

> current communications industries—cable, local telephone, long distance telephone, television, film, computers, and others—seem to be headed for a Big Crunch/Big Bang of their own. The space between these diverse functions is rapidly shrinking—between computers and televisions, for example, or inter-active communication and video. But after the next Big Bang, in the ensuing expansion of the information business, the new marketplace will no longer be divided along current sectoral lines. There may not be cable companies or phone companies or computer companies, as such. Everyone will be in the *bit* business. The *functions* provided will define the marketplace.[26]

This is not a new insight, but it is an especially important point. In the early 1980s Ithiel de Sola Pool described the "convergence of modes" that is "blurring the lines between media." He noted that "[a] single physical means—be it wires, cables, or airwaves—may carry services that in the past were provided in separate ways. Conversely, a service that was provided in the past by any one medium—be it broadcasting, the press, or telephony—can now be provided in several different physical ways."[27] The Congressional Office of Technology Assessment similarly found that "technology is ushering in a convergence of forms of press publishing that were once partitioned by technology: print publishing, mail, broadcasting, and telephone."[28] This change in the media environment has seriously complicated the once-simple task of regulatory classification.[29]

23. 521 U.S. 844, 117 S.Ct. 2329, 138 L.Ed.2d 874 (1997).

24. *Id.* at 870, 117 S. Ct. at 2344, 138 L. Ed. 2d at 897.

25. *Id.* at 851, 117 S. Ct. at 2334–35, 138 L. Ed. 2d at 884.

26. Speech of Vice President Albert Gore at UCLA, Los Angeles, California, January 11, 1994.

27. POOL, *supra* note 3 at 23. *See also* Mark S. Nadel, *A Unified Theory of the First Amendment: Divorcing the Medium From the Message*, 11 Ford. Urban L. J. 163, 166 (1982).

28. U.S. Congress, Office of Technology Assessment, SCIENCE, TECHNOLOGY AND THE FIRST AMENDMENT, OTA–CIT–369 at 27. (Gov't Printing Office, January 1988).

29. *See generally* Jill Abeshouse Stern, Erwin G. Krasnow, R. Michael Senkowski, *The New Video Marketplace and the Search for a Coherent Regulatory Philosophy*, 32 Cath. U. L. Rev. 529, 571–76 (1983).

This phenomenon is causing extensive changes in communications networks, with trends toward reduced costs, declining sensitivity to distance, faster communications, increasing information traffic, greater channel diversity, increasing interactivity, increasing flexibility and expandability and increasing interconnectivity.[30] Former FCC Commissioner Andrew Barrett similarly pointed out that "to pursue the multimedia future, cable companies must replace their existing one-way, coaxial-based networks with optic-fiber based interactive information superhighways."[31] Traditional broadcasters are in the process of converting to digital transmission and eventually will offer a range of new services.

The changes affecting one sector of the industry are not occurring in a vacuum. Technology is evolving along various lines, each of which promises to expand individual citizens' access to information. Thus, in addition to the technical advancements in the cable industry, telephone companies are aggressively developing advanced video and data networks, both with cable partners and independently; high-powered DBS service has emerged, providing an alternative, opening method of digital video delivery;[32] and the various information service providers all are beginning to offer increasing amounts of interactivity to the consumer.

These developments are quite unlike previous transformations of media technology. For example, the introduction of steam-powered presses and inexpensive pulp paper in the mid-nineteenth century made possible book and newspaper publication on a mass scale, but it was essentially an enhancement of an existing method of communication.[33] The second major transformation, brought about by the introduction of broadcasting, introduced a totally new means of conveying information.[34] But this new means of communication was not a complete substitute for print or for face-to-face speech. Each medium continued to play a fairly distinct role in the information marketplace. The current transformation of the media, however, is of a distinctly different nature. Multiple methods of delivering video images have emerged, including multimedia forms that combine video and print. Print can be delivered electronically, and, with interactive capability, may assume some attributes of speech. Many examples of convergence can be described, but the point is, the current transformation is not conducive to analyzing new media forms in terms of their particular characteristics.[35]

30. W. R. Neuman, *The Technological Convergence: Television Networks and Telephone Networks*, in TELEVISION FOR THE 21ST CENTURY: THE NEXT WAVE 3–17 (C. Firestone, ed. 1993). *See also* WILSON P. DIZARD, OLD MEDIA/NEW MEDIA 38–56 (1993); GEORGE GILDER, LIFE AFTER TELEVISION (1992).

31. Andrew Barrett, *Shifting Foundations: The Regulation of Telecommunications in an Era of Change*, 46 Fed. Comm. L.J. 39, 49 (1993).

32. Kent Gibbons and Linda Haugsted, *DSS Reaches 100K Subs, Goes National*, MULTICHANNEL NEWS, October 10, 1994, p. 1.

See also Prices for DBS Programming Launched, Broadcasting & Cable, Jan. 3, 1994, p. 47. By 1997, high-power DBS service had more than five million subscribers. Annual assessment of the status of competition in the Markets for the Delivery of Video Programming, 13 FCC Rcd. 1034 (1998).

33. Dizard, *supra* note 30 at 19.

34. *Id.*

35. *See, e.g.,* Corn–Revere, *supra*, note 22.

C. Convergence and the Erosion of First Amendment Traditions

The conceptual difficulties presented by convergence have not been lost on the courts, but this has not solved the problem of the categorical approach to First Amendment analysis. In many ways, it has made the problem worse. In *Denver Area Educational Telecommunications Consortium v. FCC*, for example, the Court simply refused to choose among the "competing analogies" as they relate to cable television because of the "changes taking place in the law, the technology, and the industrial structure, related to telecommunications."[36] In a concurring opinion endorsing this approach, Justice David Souter pointed to the convergence taking place and wrote that "we have to accept the likelihood that the media of communication will become less categorical and more protean."[37] Accordingly, he added, "we cannot be confident that for purposes of judging speech restrictions it will continue to make sense to distinguish cable from other technologies."[38] He extended this reasoning to the "cyber-technology of the Internet and the World Wide Web," concluding that " 'if we had to decide today . . . just what the First Amendment should mean in cyberspace, . . . we would get it fundamentally wrong.' "[39] Justice Souter advised the Court to approach the selection of a First Amendment standard with a sort of judicial Hippocratic Oath: "First, do no harm."[40]

However, it is by no means clear that the Court's decision in *Denver* met the test of Hippocrates. The result of the decision was to extend the regime of broadcast indecency law—however incrementally—to the field of cable television.[41] The Court's refusal to choose an "analogy" did not preclude it from applying to a newer technology a form of regulation that primarily had been confined, among video delivery media, to broadcasting. Thus, the justification that led to heightened regulation and diminished constitutional protection for one medium began to affect another— in part *because* of convergence. By the same reasoning, Congress attempted to apply the same body of law—and attenuated First Amendment rights—to the Internet in the Communications Decency Act.[42]

These developments underscore the fact that convergence of the media has significant implications far beyond its effect on the integrity

---

36. 518 U.S. 727, 741, 116 S.Ct. 2374, 2385, 135 L.Ed.2d 888, 901–02 (1996) (plurality opinion).

37. *Id.* at 777, 116 S. Ct. at 2402, 135 L. Ed. 2d at 924.

38. *Id.*, 116 S. Ct. at 2402, 135 L. Ed. 2d at 924 (Souter, J., concurring).

39. *Id.*, 116 S. Ct. at 2402, 135 L. Ed. 2d at 924, *quoting* Lawrence Lessig, *The Path of Cyberlaw*, 104 Yale L.J. 1743, 1745 (1995).

40. Denver Area, 518 U.S. at 778, 116 S. Ct. at 2403, 135 L. Ed. 2d at 925.

41. The Court struck down regulation of leased and public access channels in *Den-*

ver, but upheld a "permissive" rule that allowed cable operators to reject carriage of "indecent" leased access programming. Nevertheless, a plurality expressly extended the reasoning of *FCC v. Pacifica Foundation*, 438 U.S. 726, 98 S.Ct. 3026, 57 L.Ed.2d 1073 (1978) beyond the broadcasting context to cable. 518 U.S. at 744, 116 S. Ct. at 2386, 135 L. Ed. 2d at 904–05. *See* Playboy Entertainment Group v. United States, 945 F.Supp. 772 (D.Del.1996).

42. Reno v. ACLU, 521 U.S. 844, 117 S.Ct. 2329, 2343, 138 L.Ed.2d 874 (1997).

of existing regulatory classifications. Justifications to apply a lower level of constitutional protection for one medium may well be communicable as traditional media move toward new means of delivery. The jurisdictional "hook" from one regulatory category can be used to create a justification for control over another.

It is significant, in this regard, that traditional publications typically use electronic production methods, including computers and local area networks to support writing, editing and production as well as satellite links to transmit copy between remote plants.[43] Because such new technologies have become the predominant forms of communication and distribution of ideas, the overall level of First Amendment protection in society may be diminished, even among traditionally protected media.[44]

This issue was presented squarely in *Telecommunications Research and Action Center and Media Access Project v. FCC*,[45] ("*TRAC*"), in which the United States Court of Appeals for the District of Columbia Circuit held that broadcast content controls apply to teletext transmissions. Teletext was developed as a means of transmitting textual and graphic material to television screens of home viewers, using an otherwise unused portion of the broadcast signal.[46] In its *Report and Order* authorizing teletext service, the FCC declined to apply political broadcasting controls "primarily [because of] a recognition that teletext's unique blending of the print medium with radio technology fundamentally distinguishes it from traditional broadcast programming."[47] The Court of Appeals reversed the Commission's decision, focusing on the means of *delivering* the printed word. "The dispositive fact is that teletext is transmitted over broadcast frequencies that the Supreme Court has ruled scarce and this makes teletext's content regulable,"[48] the Court reasoned. "Teletext, whatever its similarities to the print media, uses broadcast frequencies, and that, given *Red Lion*, would seem to be that."[49]

TRAC suggests that newspapers delivered by electronic means have less constitutional protection than when the exact same stories written by the exact same reporters and edited by the same editors are delivered on paper. Consistent with this reasoning, there have been proposals to apply political broadcasting regulations to online computer services such

---

43. Lee Loevinger, *Earl F. Nelson Lecture: Law, Technology and Liberty*, 49 Mo. L.Rev. 767, 776 (1984).

44. *See* Donald E. Lively, *Fear and the Media: A First Amendment Horror Show*, 69 Minn.L.Rev. 1071, 1074 (1985).

45. 801 F.2d 501, 255 U.S. App. D.C. 287 (D.C.Cir.), *reh'g en banc denied*, 806 F.2d 1115, 257 U.S. App. D.C. 23 (D.C.Cir. 1986), cert. denied, 482 U.S. 919, 107 S.Ct. 3196, 96 L.Ed.2d 684 (1987).

46. *Id*. at 503. Teletext or videotext may also be transmitted by way of cable or telephone, but the *Telecommunications Re-*

search and Action Center decision dealt only with over-the-air teletext transmissions. However, teletext never caught on with American consumers.

47. 53 Rad. Reg. (P&F) 2d 1309 (1983).

48. 801 F. 2d at 508, 255 U.S. App. D.C. at 294.

49. 801 F.2d at 508–509, 255 U.S. App. D.C. at 294. Nevertheless, the court ruled that the FCC could refrain from enforcing the fairness doctrine for teletext transmissions since the doctrine was an FCC policy and not a statutory requirement. *Id*. at 516–18, 255 U.S. App. D.C. at 302–303.

as *Prodigy*, *CompuServe* and *America Online*.[50] To avoid the risk that online services might discriminate between candidates, Congress could require such services to provide "reasonable access" to candidates, "equal time" in the event an opponent uses the service and limit prices to the "lowest unit charge." This could be accomplished constitutionally, according to this argument, by assuming that broadcasting provides the appropriate regulatory and constitutional metaphor.[51]

Such a theoretical approach poses an interesting logical question. If traditional media are properly subject to a different constitutional standard when the link between the publisher and the reader is electronic, what is the appropriate standard when the electronic link is between the writer and the publisher? In other words, so long as electronic methods are used *at some stage* in the production process, does the government have jurisdiction to regulate the content of the publication, just as with broadcasting?

In a 1987 Senate hearing on the fairness doctrine, Professor Robert Shayon of the Annenberg School of Communications appeared to suggest that any use of spectrum in the production process would justify content regulation of the press. Shayon asserted that content controls might constitutionally be imposed on the *New York Times* or the *Wall Street Journal* because they transmit their copy via satellite to printing plants across the country. "I think that the spectrum is limited," Shayon observed, "And if the big users shut out the small users, then the government should act to make fairness the ruling guideline.... The government is not only a repressive factor, it represents the total community and sometimes can be used constructively."[52] In other words, based on the choice of distribution media, the "total community" may gain the ability to tell the *New York Times* and the *Wall Street Journal* what is "fair" and to enforce any such determination. In short, the choice of a First Amendment standard for one regulated medium does not have an isolated effect. Because the media are converging, the constitutional approach selected for one could well determine the nature of the First Amendment for all regulated media.

The FCC has articulated the constitutional risks of medium-specific constitutional analyses. As the Commission noted when it eliminated the broadcast fairness doctrine:

> Terrestrial broadcasters are not the only journalistic entities whose
> First Amendment rights are endangered by theories of government

---

50. Angela J. Campbell, *Political Campaigning in the Information Age: A Proposal for Protecting Political Candidates' Use of On–Line Computer Services*, 38 Vill. L. Rev. 517 (1993).

51. *Id.* at 519 and n.9, 521, 542–45 ("The assimilation of computer-based communications is [remarkably] similar to the process by which radio became an accepted medium for communication."). *See also* SERVING THE COMMUNITY: A PUBLIC INTEREST VISION OF THE NATIONAL INFORMATION INFRA- STRUCTURE 22–23 (1993) (wherein Computer Professionals for Social Responsibility advocate government policies to promote diversity in content markets).

52. *Fairness in Broadcasting Act of 1987*, Sen. Hearing 100–48, 100th Cong. 1st Sess. 73–74 (March 18, 1987). *See Licensing Broadcasters: Just What the Framers Feared?*, Cato Policy Report 6, 8–9 (January/February 1988).

power to regulate program content based on the FCC's licensing function. Other mass-media entities, including cable television systems, DBS systems, newspaper companies, and program networks and syndicators use—and soon telephone companies will use—licensed radio spectrum as part of the chain of distribution of informational material to the public.[53]

As the FCC previously acknowledged, the choice of a First Amendment approach for one medium might represent a fundamental shift in the relationship between the government and the press for all media.

The Telecommunications Act of 1996 in many ways embodies this approach by extending content regulation of electronic media beyond the traditional regulatory categories. The 1996 Act was largely deregulatory and was premised on congressional awareness of media convergence. The legislative history included a detailed review of the emerging video competition between media that previously had been confined to providing different service. The House Commerce Committee pointed out that there had been significant changes in the marketplace, that "the scarcity rationale for government regulation no longer applies," and that the "explosion of programming distribution sources calls for a substantial reform of Congressional and Commission oversight of the way the broadcasting industry develops and competes."[54] Despite these findings, every provision of the Telecommunications Act relating to speech content was expressly re-regulatory. In addition, the law was indifferent to the constitutional boundaries that previously limited government incursions outside a particular medium. As a result, convergence led to a general expansion of government control.

Key regulatory provisions of the Telecommunications Act imposed content controls on all video distribution media without respect to their different characteristics. Title V of the Act, the so-called Communications Decency Act, included the V-chip regime governing video programming on all television distribution media,[55] scrambling and time-shifting requirements on "adult" video services,[56] as well as the Exon amendment, which sought to regulate "indecent" speech on the Internet. In addition, Section 713 of the Act required the FCC to establish regulations and implementation schedules requiring closed captioning for "all types of video programming delivered electronically to consumers, regardless of the entity that provides the programming or the category of programming."[57] Thus, Congress expanded the reach of broadcast-type

53. *In re* Complaint of Syracuse Peace Council Against Television Station WTVH, 2 FCC Rcd. 5043, 5055 (1987), *aff'd sub nom.* Syracuse Peace Council v. FCC, 867 F.2d 654 (D.C.Cir.1989), cert. denied, 493 U.S. 1019, 110 S.Ct. 717, 107 L.Ed.2d 737 (1990).

54. Communications Act of 1995, H. Rep. 204, 104th Cong. 1st Sess. 54 (July 24, 1995).

55. Telecommunications Act of 1996, § 551(c)-(d), codified at 47 U.S.C.A. § 330(c)-(d) (West Supp. 1997).

56. *Id.* § 505.

57. Closed Captioning and Video Description of Video Programming, FCC 97–279 at & § 6 (rel. Aug. 22, 1997). *See* H. Rep. 458, 104th Cong., 2d Sess. 183 (1996). *See generally* Telecommunications Act of 1996, Pub. L. 104–104, 110 Stat. 56 (1996).

speech regulations that represent "a complete conceptual reordering" between the government and the press and a "virtual celebration of public regulation"[58] to all electronic media.

In sharp contrast to the FCC's previous warnings about the expansion of broadcast-type content controls, the Commission in more recent years has embraced the possibility of expanded authority over speech. In particular, former FCC Chairman Reed Hundt strongly advocated such an expanded governmental role with respect to regulated media. He argued that it is "reasonable to put all media under some obligation to serve the public interest. Indeed, all media have typically been party to some sort of social compact."[59] He suggested that "[i]t isn't fair or sustainable to put obligations on broadcast and cable that cannot be sustained amid the increasing competition among broadcast, cable, DBS, LMDS, [and] wireless cable." Consequently, government control should apply to all, and "it is going to be necessary to quantify public interest obligations."[60]

In this view, such obligations also should extend to the Internet. Former Chairman Hundt cited the children's television precedent and free time offers for political broadcasting and called upon Internet access providers to "give some thought to their abilities to contribute to the public good." Pointing to an estimated $10 billion price tag associated with wiring the schools for Internet access, he said it "may seem like a big number but it's actually less than two tenths of one percent of the revenues of the information technology industry." Hundt concluded: "[T]here is no more appropriate time ... to think about renewing the social compact between the communications industries and the public."[61] Similarly, some influential members of congress have suggested that services provided over the Internet should be regulated in the same manner, and to the same degree, as services offered by other media. Citing the potential for "cable programming over the Internet," they have opposed measures that would "preclude the FCC from applying local franchising requirements to the Internet."[62]

D. Reno v. ACLU: Breaking the Cycle of Regulation

The Supreme Court in *Reno v. ACLU* cut the gordian knot created by categorical analysis of the First Amendment rights of new media by

58. LEE C. BOLLINGER, IMAGES OF A FREE PRESS 71 (1991).

59. Speech of FCC Chairman Reed Hundt, *Reinventing the Social Compact*, Broadcasting & Cable Interface Conference (Washington, D.C. Sept. 24, 1996).

60. *Id.*

61. Speech of FCC Chairman Reed E. Hundt, *Children and the Information Superhighway: Directions for the Future*, Children's Now Conference, Menlo Park, California, Sept. 27, 1996. *See also* Angela J. Campbell, *Political Campaigning in the In-* *formation Age: A Proposal for Protecting Candidates' Use of On–Line Computer Services*, 38 Vill. L. Rev. 517 (1993).

62. Ted Hearn, *Internet Regulation in On Hill Agenda*, MultiChannel News, Sept. 23, 1996, p. 80. The House Subcommittee on Telecommunications and Finance voted 13–6 to support the FCC reform bill that would have restricted FCC regulatory authority. However, the bill died with the end of the 104th Congress. In any event, the bill was notable because of the views—and prominence—of its opponents.

holding that the Internet is entitled to the highest level of constitutional protection. The "converged" nature of the medium did not prevent this conclusion, and, in fact, was integral to the Court's reasoning. After noting that online communication "includes not only traditional print and news services, but also audio, video and still images, as well as interactive real-time dialogue" the Court held that "our cases provide no basis for qualifying the level of First Amendment scrutiny that should be applied to this medium".[63]

The government had argued that the Internet could be compared to broadcasting and regulated in the same way. The Court, however, expressly rejected this approach, indicating that it raised more questions than it answered. It expressly distinguished the Internet from other technologies, such as broadcasting, by noting that "the Internet can hardly be considered a 'scarce' expressive commodity." It added that the Internet is not as "invasive" as radio or television, and that "[n]either before nor after the enactment of the CDA have the vast democratic fora of the Internet been subject to the type of government supervision and regulation that has attended the broadcast industry."[64] In other words, the fact that the Internet had never been classified and regulated was highly significant to the Court's decision to accord the medium full constitutional protection.

Most importantly, the Court's opinion represents a significant departure from the usual way in which new communications media are treated. New media are usually born in captivity, and the Court takes a great deal of time—usually decades—before recognizing that the First Amendment applies, much less that full protection is appropriate. Here, rather than presuming that the Internet should receive less protection, the Court held that full First Amendment protection applies unless the government can prove otherwise. The lasting importance of this decision will depend on whether it is read narrowly, as a simple decision that the Internet is "not broadcasting," or whether it means that new media are presumed to receive full protection until the government proves they should get less.

With such a beginning, it is possible that we are not condemned to repeat past mistakes. In the wake of *Reno*, the government espoused a hands-off approach to Internet regulation. In a July 1997 policy statement the Clinton Administration announced that any attempts at regulation should be predicated on five principles: (1) Expansion of the Internet "has been driven primarily by the private sector" and for electronic commerce to flourish, "the private sector must continue to lead;" (2) There should be "minimal government involvement or intervention;" (3) Governments should establish a predictable and simple legal environment based on "a decentralized, contractual model or law rather than one based on top-down regulation;" (4) The success of the Internet as a new medium stems, in part, from "its decentralized nature

63. 521 U.S. 844, 870, 117 S.Ct. 2329,   **64.** *Id.*
2344, 138 L.Ed.2d 874, 897, (1997).

and ... its tradition of bottom-up governance;" and (5) National governments must recognize that the Internet is a global medium.[65] Similar recommendations to limit government intervention and control of Internet content emerged in Europe.[66]

Specifically with respect to content regulation such as the CDA, the Clinton Administration's policy statement concluded that "content regulations traditionally imposed on radio and television would not need to be applied to the Internet. In fact, unnecessary regulation could cripple the growth and diversity of the Internet."[67] Among other reasons, the Administration based its conclusions on the rapid pace of technological development and the phenomenon of convergence. The report concluded that "government attempts to regulate are likely to be outmoded by the time they are finally enacted, especially to the extent such regulations are technology-specific."[68] Only time will tell whether such sound reasoning can forestall the inherent gravitational pull of government toward regulation.[69]

2.5   *Alternative Visions of the First Amendment for the Digital Age

"What kind of First Amendment would best serve our needs as we approach the twenty-first century?," may be an open question.[1] Most theorists agree that a different analytical approach is needed to cope with changes in the media marketplace and to replace judicial doctrines with increasingly obvious deficiencies. But there is little agreement about what that approach should be. The debate on this issue in the courts typically has pitted advocates from each side of the dispute proposing competing analogies for how the technology at issue should be treated; whether it should be analyzed under a "print model of the First Amendment," a "broadcast model" or some entirely new model for cyberspace.

Although technology has become the focal point for this debate, the real disagreement is part of the larger issue of defining the appropriate relationship between government and the press. The principal ap-

---

65. A Framework for Global Electronic Commerce at 4–5 (The White House, July 1, 1997). *See also* Kevin Werbach, Digital Tornado: The Internet and Telecommunications Policy at ii (FCC Office of Plans & Policy, Working Paper #29, March 1997) ("Government policy approaches toward the Internet should ... start from two basic principles: avoid unnecessary regulation, and question the applicability of traditional rules.").

66. Commission of the European Communities, Illegal and Harmful Content on the Internet (1996).

67. A Framework for Global Electronic Commerce, *supra*, note 65 at 25.

68. *Id.* at 4.

69. *See* Declan McCullagh, *Framework for Redemption?*, Wired, April 1997 at 88 ("Any harm will come not from what the [White House policy statement] says, but from what those agencies actually do. For that, netizens will have to wait and see.").

* Extended text published in Practitioners Edition, Vol. 1.

1. Columbia Broadcasting System, Inc. v. Democratic National Committee, 412 U.S. 94, 160, 93 S.Ct. 2080, 2115, 36 L.Ed.2d 772, 817 (1973) (Douglas, J., concurring).

proaches to this question fall generally into three categories: that the First Amendment is best served by allowing regulation of new media as constitutional protections slowly evolve (Incrementalism); that government intervention is necessary to promote First Amendment "values" (Revisionism); that the First Amendment requires a separation between press and state (Traditionalism).

Chapter Three

THE COMMERCIAL SPEECH DOCTRINE AND CONTROL OF ADVERTISING BY PRIVATE CIVIL ACTIONS AND PUBLIC REGULATION

Analysis

3.1 Introduction to the Doctrine

The commercial speech doctrine briefly stated holds that expression proposing a commercial transaction is protected by the First Amendment so long as it is not false, misleading, potentially misleading, coercive or encouraging of illegal products and services.[1] Under the doctrine the

---

1. *See* Board of Trustees of the State University of New York v. Fox, 492 U.S. 469, 475, 109 S.Ct. 3028, 3032, 106 L.Ed.2d 388, 400 (1989); Central Hudson Gas & Elec. Corp. v. Public Service Comm'n, 447 U.S. 557, 566, 100 S.Ct. 2343, 2351, 65 L.Ed.2d 341, 351 (1980); Virginia State Bd. of Pharmacy v. Virginia Citizens Consumer Council, Inc., 425 U.S. 748, 762, 771–773, 96 S.Ct. 1817, 1825–1826, 1830–1831, 48 L.Ed.2d 346, 358, 364–365 (1976).

213

extent of constitutional protection afforded commercial speech by the United States Supreme Court is of lesser degree than that given political expression.[2] The present Court's practice of attaching hierarchical value to particular speech and its consequent unwillingness to accord full constitutional protection to less "worthy" speech such as that involved in commerce has been condemned by some.[3] But this limitation on First Amendment protection for commercial speech, whatever its exact parameters, should be contrasted with the lack of recognition of *any* such protection until relatively recently.

3.2 Doctrinal Development

The Supreme Court first confronted the question whether commercial speech was protected from suppression or unrestrained regulation in *Valentine v. Chrestensen*, decided in 1942.[1] There, the owner of an old Navy submarine moored the vessel at a pier in the East River of New York City preparatory to exhibiting it commercially. He had printed handbills advertising the boat and encouraging visitors to board it for a stated admission fee. When advised by the police commissioner that, consistent with a city ordinance, only handbills devoted to information or a public protest might be distributed on the streets of New York, the vessel owner reprinted the handbills but this time deleted the statement as to the admission fee and added a message on the back side protesting the action of the City Dock Department refusing him wharfage facilities for the exhibition of the submarine. When he attempted to distribute the new handbills he was prevented by the police from doing so. He then brought suit to enjoin the police from interfering with the distribution. He obtained a permanent injunction and the United States Court of Appeals affirmed. On certiorari the Supreme Court stated the question to be "whether the application of the ordinance to the respondent's activity was, in the circumstances, an unconstitutional abridgement of the freedom of the press and of speech."[2] In answering the question in the negative the Court held that the Constitution imposed no restraint on government in controlling purely commercial advertising on public thoroughfares. In response to the submarine owner's contention that he was engaged in disseminating a political protest along with the commercial advertising, the Court said that his intent was to circumvent the ordinance and could not be permitted.

2. *See* Posadas de Puerto Rico Associates v. Tourism Company of Puerto Rico, 478 U.S. 328, 340, 106 S.Ct. 2968, 2976, 92 L.Ed.2d 266, 279–280 (1986); Bolger v. Youngs Drug Products Corp., 463 U.S. 60, 64–65, 103 S.Ct. 2875, 2879, 77 L.Ed.2d 469, 476 (1983); Central Hudson Gas & Elec. Corp. v. Public Service Comm'n, 447 U.S. 557, 562–563, 100 S.Ct. 2343, 2349–2350, 65 L.Ed.2d 341, 348–349 (1980); Virginia Pharmacy Bd. v. Virginia Citizens Consumer Council, Inc. 425 U.S. 748, 771– 772 n. 24, 96 S.Ct. 1817, 1830–1831 n. 24, 48 L.Ed.2d 346, 364 n. 24 (1976).

3. *See, e.g.*, Patrick Maines, *Preface* to RICHARD KAPLAR, ADVERTISING RIGHTS THE NEGLECTED FREEDOM vii—ix (Media Institute 1991).

1. 316 U.S. 52, 62 S.Ct. 920, 86 L.Ed. 1262 (1942).

2. *Id.* at 54, 62 S. Ct. at 921, 86 L. Ed. at 1265.

The absence of protection for commercial expression continued through the 1960s.[3] Then in the 1970s the Supreme Court began to rethink its position. In *Bigelow v. Virginia*,[4] the managing editor of the *Virginia Weekly*, a newspaper published in the college town of Charlottesville, ran an advertisement for a New York City organization that arranged for low cost abortions in accredited hospitals and clinics in New York where abortions were legal even for non-residents. The editor was convicted of violating a statute making it a misdemeanor to circulate any publication encouraging or prompting the procuring of an abortion. The trial court rejected the editor's contention that the statute was unconstitutional under the First and Fourteenth Amendments. The Virginia Supreme Court affirmed the conviction holding that the advertisement was commercial speech not entitled to constitutional protection.

On appeal, the United States Supreme Court reversed, holding that the state was not free of all constitutional restraints in regulating advertising because it involved the encouragement of sales of goods or the solicitation of services or because it was published for financial gain. Virginia's regulation of the advertising in question went too far because it suppressed speech that did not fall into any of the very few categories that are unprotected by the First Amendment, such as "fighting words," immediate incitement to violent acts and obscenity.

The Court, speaking through Justice Blackmun, distinguished *Valentine v. Chrestensen* into oblivion when it said, "[T]he holding is distinctly a limited one: the ordinance was upheld as a reasonable regulation of the manner in which commercial advertising could be distributed. The fact that it had the effect of banning a particular handbill does not mean that *Chrestensen* is authority for the proposition that all statutes regulating commercial advertising are immune from constitutional challenge."[5]

Though Justice Blackmun's explanation of *Valentine* as merely an example of time, place and manner regulation of otherwise protected speech is of dubious merit because non-commercial handbills distributed in the very same manner were not suppressed under the New York City ordinance, the *Bigelow* decision resulted in the Court repositioning itself on the issue of protection for commercial speech.

The broadest and most unequivocal statement protective of commercial speech came from the Court in *Virginia State Bd. of Pharmacy* v. *Virginia Citizens Consumer Council, Inc.*,[6] decided within a year of *Bigelow*. In this case a consumers group went into federal court for a

---

3. *See* New York Times v. Sullivan, 376 U.S. 254, 266, 84 S.Ct. 710, 718, 11 L.Ed.2d 686, 698 (1964).

4. 421 U.S. 809, 95 S.Ct. 2222, 44 L.Ed.2d 600 (1975).

5. *Id.* at 819–820, 95 S. Ct. at 2231, 44 L. Ed. 2d at 610; *see* Cammarano v. United States, 358 U.S. 498, 514, 79 S.Ct. 524, 534, 3 L.Ed.2d 462, 472–473 (1959) (Douglas, J. concurring); Lehman v. City of Shaker Heights, 418 U.S. 298, 314 n. 6, 94 S.Ct. 2714, 2723 n. 6, 41 L.Ed.2d 770, 784 n. 6 (1974) (dissenting opinion); *see also* Pittsburgh Press Co. v. Pittsburgh Human Rel. Comm'n, 413 U.S. 376, 393, 93 S.Ct. 2553, 2562, 37 L.Ed.2d 669, 681 (1973) (Burger, C.J. dissenting).

6. 425 U.S. 748, 96 S.Ct. 1817, 48 L.Ed.2d 346 (1976).

declaration that a Virginia statute prohibiting advertising of the price of prescription drugs and an injunction to prevent its enforcement. A three-judge court declared the statutory prohibition void and enjoined the Virginia State Board of Pharmacy and its individual members from enforcing it. The Board and its members appealed and the Supreme Court affirmed the judgment. Again speaking for the Court, Justice Blackmun recognized the case as presenting the purest form of commercial speech for constitutional protection—speech which did no more than propose a lawful commercial transaction at a truthful price. Justice Blackmun had no trouble concluding that such pure commercial speech was protected by the First Amendment. Repeating what he had written in *Bigelow*, the justice asserted that merely because an advertiser's interest was purely economic did not disqualify his expression from First Amendment protection.

He then broke new ground in the commercial speech debate by referring to the *consumer's* interest in the free flow of commercial information. He argued that the suppression of prescription drug price information had a direct impact on the consumer's pocketbook and held that the members of the consuming public had a First Amendment right to receive such economic information from willing sellers even if the state thought their best interest lay in its suppression. "It is a matter of public interest that those economic decisions, in the aggregate, be intelligent and well informed. To this end, the free flow of commercial information is indispensable.... And if it is indispensable to the proper allocation of resources in a free enterprise system, it is also indispensable to the formation of intelligent opinions as to how that system ought to be regulated or altered."[7]

Justice Blackmun's analysis involved no balancing of interests. If the commercial speech was truthful and neither misleading nor deceptive it was entitled to First Amendment protection though subject to reasonable time, place and manner restriction like any other speech.[8] In addition, he said, "[t]he First Amendment ... does not prohibit the state from insuring that the stream of commercial information flow cleanly as well as freely."[9]

The Court's opinion in *Virginia State Bd. of Pharmacy* proved to be the high water mark for the protection of commercial speech. The gradual erosion of the doctrine developed in *Bigelow* and *Virginia State Bd. of Pharmacy* was foreshadowed by the dissent of then Associate Justice Rehnquist in the latter case.[10]

Justice Rehnquist was disturbed by the extension of substantial constitutional protection to commercial expression because, in his view, it opened the way for the active promotion of prescription drugs and

---

7. *Id.* at 765, 96 S. Ct. at 1827, 48 L. Ed. 2d at 360.

8. *Id.* at 771, 96 S. Ct. at 1830, 48 L. Ed. 2d at 364.

9. *Id.* at 772, 96 S. Ct. at 1831, 48 L. Ed. 2d at 364–365.

10. *Id.* at 781, 96 S. Ct. at 1835, 48 L. Ed. 2d at 370.

liquor, cigarettes and other undesirable products.[11] He also argued that the commercial speech doctrine trivialized the First Amendment by allowing its application to the choice of shampoos as well as the choice of public officials.[12] While it is somewhat difficult to discern his constitutional theory for denying protection for purely commercial speech, it appears that his opposition is based on the belief that the police powers of the state should be left unhindered in suppressing the promotion of goods and services believed to be harmful to the public though not illegal.[13] Justice Rehnquist's views in this area took on added weight when he was elevated to Chief Justice and a number of like-minded associate justices were appointed to the Court in the 1980s.

Virginia State Bd. of Pharmacy was followed in quick succession by *Linmark Associates, Inc. v. Township of Willingboro*[14] and *Carey v. Population Services, International.*[15] In the former case the Court held that a township ordinance prohibiting the posting of real estate "For Sale" and "sold" signs in order to stem what the township perceived as the flight of white homeowners from a racially integrated community was unconstitutional. No matter how praiseworthy the goal of preserving an integrated community, the township could not achieve it by denying to its residents supposedly for their own good the substance of the information communicated by the signs. As in *Virginia State Bd. of Pharmacy*, this highly paternalistic approach did not pass muster.

Carey involved, among other things, a New York statute totally outlawing the advertising or display of contraceptives in the state. The Court struck down the New York statute because it raised the very same questions disposed of in *Virginia State Bd. of Pharmacy*. It rejected the argument of the statute's defenders that such advertising would be offensive to many of those exposed thereto and would legitimize sexual activity by young people. "At least where obscenity is not involved, we have consistently held that the fact that protected speech may be offensive to some does not justify its suppression."[16] As for the possible legitimization of illicit sexual activity, the Court noted that the ads in question did not advocate or likely incite imminent lawless behavior but "merely state the availability of products and services that are not only legal ... but constitutionally protected.... These arguments therefore do not justify the total suppression of advertising concerning contraceptives."[17]

Reading *Virginia State Bd. of Pharmacy*, *Linmark Associates, Inc.* and *Carey* together, it can be concluded that while commercial speech

11. *Id.*

12. *Id.* at 787–788, 96 S. Ct. at 1838–1839, 48 L. Ed. 2d at 374.

13. Compare his dissenting opinion in Carey v. Population Services, Int'l., 431 U.S. 678, 719, 97 S.Ct. 2010, 2033, 52 L.Ed.2d 675, 706 (1977).

14. 431 U.S. 85, 97 S.Ct. 1614, 52 L.Ed.2d 155 (1977).

15. 431 U.S. 678, 97 S.Ct. 2010, 52 L.Ed.2d 675 (1977).

16. *Id.* at 701, 97 S. Ct. at 2024, 52 L. Ed. 2d at 695; *see* Bolger v. Youngs Drug Products Corp., 463 U.S. 60, 71, 103 S.Ct. 2875, 2883, 77 L.Ed.2d 469, 480 (1983).

17. *Id.* at 701–702, 97 S. Ct. at 2024–2025, 52 L. Ed. 2d at 695.

was entitled to considerable protection, it would be less than that afforded political speech. But the limitations on protection were not made precise. This uncertainty provided a vehicle for a changing Court majority to erode the doctrine by applying an ad hoc balancing approach or by simply taking the more doctrinaire approach championed by now Chief Justice Rehnquist.

3.3 Ad Hoc Balancing and the Decline of the Doctrine

A. The Central Hudson Test

In *Central Hudson Gas & Elec. Corp. v. Public Service Comm'n*[1] a New York state regulatory body ordered electric utilities in New York to stop all advertising that promoted the use of electricity. The order was driven by the agency's finding that New York's electrical system did not have sufficient fuel stocks or sources of supply to meet consumer demands for electricity for the winter of 1973–1974. Three years later the advertising ban was still in effect though the fuel shortage had eased. In response to a request by the agency for comments on whether to continue the ban, Central Hudson Gas & Electric Corporation opposed its continuation on First Amendment grounds. Finding that such promotional advertising encouraging consumption of electricity was contrary to the national policy of conserving energy and its prohibition likely to result in some dampening of unnecessary growth in energy use, the state agency ordered the ban continued.

Following the Public Service Commission's denial of requests for rehearing, Central Hudson challenged the order in state court as a violation of the First and Fourteenth Amendments. The utility was unsuccessful at every level of the state court system. It then appealed to the Supreme Court where it finally met with success.

In his opinion for the majority Justice Powell began his analysis by noting that the Constitution accorded lesser protection to commercial speech than to other constitutionally safeguarded expression. The rationale he presented for such lesser protection was first, that commercial speakers have extensive knowledge of both the market and their product and are thus well situated to evaluate the accuracy of their messages and the lawfulness of the underlying activity; and second, that commercial expression is a hardy breed that is not particularly susceptible to being crushed by overbroad regulation.[2] Justice Powell then went on to add that the protection available for advertising turned on both the nature of the commercial expression involved and the governmental interest served by its regulation.[3] The latter qualification on constitutional protection had not been imposed in the previous cases, as Justice Blackmun's concurring opinion pointed out.[4]

1. 447 U.S. 557, 100 S.Ct. 2343, 65 L.Ed.2d 341 (1980).

2. *Id.* at 564 n.6, 100 S. Ct. at 2350 n.6, 65 L. Ed. 2d at 349 n.6.

3. *Id.* at 563, 100 S. Ct. at 2350, 65 L. Ed. 2d at 349.

4. *Id.* at 576–578, 100 S. Ct. at 2356–2358, 65 L. Ed. 2d at 357–358.

Following his premise that governmental interests must be taken into consideration, Justice Powell applied a four-part ad hoc balancing test for determining whether the particular commercial speech was constitutionally protected. The first prong requires a determination whether the expression is at all protected by the First Amendment.[5] Commercial speech which promotes illegal products, services or activities or is false or misleading is not protected.[6] Then, assuming the legality of what is advertised and the truthfulness of the expression, the second prong addresses whether the government's asserted interest in prohibition or limitation of the commercial speech is substantial and, if substantial, whether the regulation involved is proportional to the substantiality of the interest.

The third and fourth prongs of the test are designed to measure the appropriateness of the particular regulation in relation to the government's substantial interest. The third prong tests whether the restriction on expression directly advances the state interest involved. If the restriction provides only ineffective or remote support for the interest asserted, it fails the test and must be struck down. But even if it advances the state's interest, the regulation will not be upheld unless it meets the fourth prong.

This final prong of the test requires that the advertising regulation be only as broad as necessary to advance the state's interest. If the interest could be as well served by a more limited restriction, the excessive regulation will be struck down. It was the failure to meet this fourth requirement that resulted in the voiding of the New York Public Service Commission's order. The majority in *Central Hudson* was not persuaded that the Commission's *total* ban on promotional advertising by New York electric power utilities was necessary to further the state's interest in energy conservation. The Court noted that the Commission had made no showing that a more limited restriction would not have been effective.[7]

While concurring in the judgment, Justice Blackmun protested that the Court's new test did not provide adequate protection for truthful, non-misleading, non-coercive commercial speech.[8] Conceding that a lower level of protection from regulation was provided by the First Amendment for commercial expression, this was so to safeguard consumers against fraudulent, misleading or coercive speech and not to further a

---

5. *Id.* at 564, 566, 100 S. Ct. at 2350, 2351 65 L. Ed. 2d at 349–351.

6. *See, e.g.,* Friedman v. Rogers, 440 U.S. 1, 99 S.Ct. 887, 59 L.Ed.2d 100 (1979) (statute prohibiting practice of optometry under a trade name upheld because ill-defined association of trade name with price and quality could be manipulated by the user of the name to mislead the public); Pittsburgh Press Co. v. Pittsburgh Comm'n on Human Relations, 413 U.S. 376, 93 S.Ct. 2553, 37 L.Ed.2d 669 (1973) (ordinance prohibiting newspapers from carrying help wanted ads categorized by gender upheld); Princess Sea Industries, Inc. v. Nevada, 97 Nev. 534, 635 P.2d 281 (1981), cert. denied, 456 U.S. 926, 102 S.Ct. 1972, 72 L.Ed.2d 441 (1982) (statute prohibiting advertising of prostitution service in those counties of Nevada in which such service is illegal upheld).

7. 447 U.S. at 569–572, 100 S. Ct. at 2353–2354, 65 L. Ed. 2d at 353–355.

8. *Id.* at 573, 100 S. Ct. at 2355, 65 L.Ed 2d at 355.

state interest in discouraging the sale or consumption of some advertised legal product or service. "Virginia Pharmacy Board did not analyze the State's interest to determine whether they were 'substantial.' ... We also did not inquire whether a 'more limited regulation of ... commercial expression ... would adequately serve the state's interests. Rather, we held that the State 'may not [pursue its goals] by keeping the public in ignorance.' "[9]

The four-part test of *Central Hudson* is subject to the criticism that it requires highly subjective judgments by judges as to the substantiality of state's interest in regulation, the efficacy of the particular regulation involved and the permissible breadth of the regulation. Because the test leaves the judges administering it great latitude to insert their own subjective views as to the extent of protection which should be accorded specific commercial expression, subsequent decisions have not followed a clear direction or rationale. For example, in *Metromedia, Inc. v. San Diego*,[10] the Court struck down a city ordinance banning nearly all offsite billboards. In attempting to deal with the test of *Central Hudson* and time, place and manner regulation, the justice produced five separate and, for the most part, difficult to follow opinions, leading then Justice Rehnquist, in dissent, to term the Court's decision "a virtual tower of Babel."[11]

Later, in *City Council v. Taxpayers for Vincent*,[12] the Court, reaffirming the plurality opinion of Justice White in *Metromedia*,[13] upheld an ordinance prohibiting the posting of political, commercial and other signs on public property in order to protect the local citizenry from visual assault. The Court held that protection from such assault constituted a substantial evil within the City's power to prohibit. But while protecting citizens from visual clutter and blight was found to be a substantial interest of the state justifying the restriction of commercial speech, protecting citizens from advertisements for products which some find offensive is not. In *Bolger v. Youngs Drug Products Corp.*,[14] a unanimous Supreme Court, directly applying the *Central Hudson* test, held that offensiveness was not a valid justification for government suppression of commercial advertising and struck down a postal regulation prohibiting the mailing of unsolicited advertisements for contraceptive devices.

The difference in the substantiality of the governmental interest in *Taxpayers for Vincent* and *Bolger* is difficult to discern and may only be in the mind of the beholders—normally federal judges. The above comparison illustrates the highly subjective nature of the *Central Hudson* test.

9. *Id.* at 576, 100 S. Ct. at 2356, 65 L.Ed 2d at 357.

10. 453 U.S. 490, 101 S.Ct. 2882, 69 L.Ed.2d 800 (1981).

11. *Id.* at 569, 101 S. Ct. at 2924, 69 L.Ed 2d at 854.

12. 466 U.S. 789, 104 S.Ct. 2118, 80 L.Ed.2d 772 (1984).

13. 453 U.S. at 493, 101 S. Ct. at 2885, 69 L. Ed. 2d at 805.

14. 463 U.S. 60, 103 S.Ct. 2875, 77 L.Ed.2d 469 (1983).

B. *Distortion of the Central Hudson Test*

While adoption in *Central Hudson* of the four-part ad hoc balancing test clearly weakened the safeguards for commercial speech earlier afforded by the Court, the test, conscientiously applied, still provided a degree of protection.[15] But in *Posadas de Puerto Rico Associates v. Tourism Company of Puerto Rico*,[16] the Court's simplistic application of the test further eroded constitutional protection for commercial speech. There, the legislature of Puerto Rico, while permitting casino gambling on its island, prohibited casino operators from directing their advertising to the local residents. As interpreted by the Puerto Rican courts, on and off island advertising to be lawful might only be directed to tourists and prospective tourists. The plaintiff casino operation, which had previously paid fines for violations of the tourism agency's advertising regulation, filed a declaratory judgment action seeking a declaration that Puerto Rico's gaming statute and the regulations promulgated thereunder banning advertising to residents violated the First Amendment. After narrowing construction of the statute and regulations, the trial court upheld their constitutionality. The Puerto Rico Supreme Court then dismissed the casino operator's appeal on the ground that it did not present a substantial constitutional question.

On the appeal the Supreme Court held that regulating advertising to local residents by the casinos was constitutionally permissible. Then Associate Justice Rehnquist, writing for a five member majority, was guided by the belief that the Puerto Rico legislature could ban completely casino gambling and that the power to ban necessarily included the lesser power to prohibit casino advertising.[17] Starting from that premise, unsupported by any cited authority, it was relatively easy for the justice to conclude that the regulation of commercial speech here comported with the *Central Hudson* four-prong test.

Conceding that what was being advertised was legal and that therefore further scrutiny of the regulation was necessary, Justice Rehnquist had no trouble deeming Puerto Rico's governmental interest to be substantial. He accepted at face value the assertions of the Tourism Company that excessive casino gambling among local residents would produce serious harmful effects such as increase in crime, prostitution and public corruption and the infiltration of organized crime but ignored the fact that legal advertising encouraging the local population to bet on horse racing and cockfighting and to play the Puerto Rico lottery could arguably lead to the same harmful affects.

15. *See, e.g.*, Zauderer v. Office of Disciplinary Counsel, 471 U.S. 626, 637–651, 105 S.Ct. 2265, 2274–2282, 85 L.Ed.2d 652, 633–673 (1985); Bolger v. Youngs Drug Products Corp., 463 U.S. 60, 103 S.Ct. 2875, 77 L.Ed.2d 469 (1983).

16. 478 U.S. 328, 106 S.Ct. 2968, 92 L.Ed.2d 266 (1986).

17. "[I]t is precisely *because* the government could have enacted a wholesale prohibition of the underlying conduct that it is permissible for the government to take the less intrusive step of allowing the conduct, but reducing the demand through restrictions on advertising." Id. at 346, 106 S. Ct. at 2979, 92 L. Ed. 2d at 784.

Finding that the governmental interest was substantial, Justice Rehnquist addressed prong three and, without requiring proof by the Tourism Company that the suppression of advertising would truly further Puerto Rico's interest in preventing harmful effects from residents frequenting the casinos, simply concluded that there was a direct connection to the reduction of demand by local residents for casino gaming.

Finally, without considering alternative efforts available to Puerto Rico to prevent the harmful effects perceived from casino gambling other than counter advertising, which he dismissed as being for the legislature to consider, Justice Rehnquist held that the complete ban on advertising to the local residents was no broader than necessary to serve the government's substantial interest.

Needless to say there was a vigorous dissent by Justice Blackmun. Referring to what he believed was a misguided and superficial application of the *Central Hudson* four-part test, Justice Blackmun wrote, "While tipping its hat to these standards, the Court does little more than defer to what it perceives to be the determination by Puerto Rico's Legislature that a ban on casino advertising aimed at residents is reasonable. The Court totally ignores the fact that commercial speech is entitled to substantial First Amendment protection, giving the government unprecedented authority to eviscerate constitutionally protected expression."[18] He then went on to criticize the statute and regulation for the same kind of paternalism that the Court had previously rejected in *Virginia State Bd. of Pharmacy* and *Linmark Associates, Inc.* "The First Amendment presupposes that 'people will perceive their own best interests if only they are well enough informed, and . . . the best means to that end is to open the channels of communication, rather than to close them.' "[19]

C. Conscious Erosion of the Central Hudson Test and Protection of Commercial Speech by the Court

Despite Justice Blackmun's best efforts the erosion of the commercial speech doctrine continued. While *Posadas* might be viewed simply as an aberrational application of the *Central Hudson* test, the next major commercial speech case to come before the Court resulted in a weakening of the test itself. In *Board of Trustees of the State University of New York v. Fox*,[20] what amounted to a Tupperware party in a university dorm was broken up by campus police and the housewares demonstrator was arrested when she refused to leave the premises. The police had acted under the State University of New York's (SUNY) regulation banning most commercial enterprises from operating on its campuses. Thereafter, several students went into the United States District Court seeking a declaratory judgment that the prohibition against hosting and attending such houseware parties and having commercial discussions

---

18. *Id.* at 352, 106 S. Ct. at 2982, 92 L. Ed. 2d at 288.

19. *Id.* at 358, 106 S. Ct. at 2986, 92 L. Ed. 2d at 291–292.

20. 492 U.S. 469, 109 S.Ct. 3028, 106 L.Ed.2d 388 (1989).

with other invitees in their own rooms violated the First Amendment. The district court eventually found for the University. A divided panel of the second Circuit reversed and remanded. Viewing the SUNY regulation as a restriction on commercial speech requiring the application of the *Central Hudson* test, the appeals court found it unclear, inter alia, whether the regulation involved employed the least restrictive means in advancing the government's asserted interests.

Before reaching the Court of Appeals' application of the *Central Hudson* test, the Supreme Court, on certiorari, was confronted with the argument of the students that the expression prohibited should not be classified as commercial speech because it was inextricably intertwined with protected noncommercial speech.[21] Detained only briefly by this contention the majority held that any noncommercial speech involved such as teaching home economics during the sales party was not "inextricably intertwined" with the commercial speech and could be separated out.[22]

Turning to the main issue, that of the Second Circuit's handing of the *Central Hudson* test and the consequent reversal and remand, the Court took issue with the appeals court's formulation of the fourth prong of the test to be followed by the district court on remand. The Second Circuit had in effect, instructed the trial court that it could find the SUNY regulation "not more extensive than is necessary" only if it is the "least restrictive measure" that could effectively protect the state's interests.

While conceding that was essentially the formulation in *Central Hudson* itself, Justice Scalia writing for the majority believed that the word "necessary" did not require such a strict requirement, dismissed a similar formulation in one other case as dictum[23] and found formulations in other commercial speech cases, particularly *Posadas*, supporting "a more flexible meaning" for the fourth prong. After parsing these latter cases, Justice Scalia concluded that what is required is only "a 'fit' between the legislature's ends and the means chosen to accomplish those ends '... a fit that is not necessarily perfect, but reasonable;' that represents not necessarily the single best disposition but one whose scope is 'in proportion to the interest served....' "[24] Elaborating further, Justice Scalia wrote that regulation on commercial speech would pass muster regarding the fourth prong if it employed "not necessarily the least restrictive means but ... a means narrowly tailored to achieve the desired objective. Within those bounds we leave it to governmental

---

21. *Compare* Riley v. National Federation of the Blind of North Carolina, Inc., 487 U.S. 781, 796, 108 S.Ct. 2667, 2677, 101 L.Ed.2d 669, 689 (1988).

22. Board of Trustees (SUNY), 492 U.S. at 474, 109 S. Ct. at 3031–3032, 106 L. Ed. 2d at 399; *see* Bolger v. Youngs Drug Products Corp., 463 U.S. 60, 67–68, 103 S.Ct. 2875, 2880–2881, 77 L.Ed.2d 469, 477–478 (1983).

23. Zauderer v. Office of Disciplinary Counsel, 471 U.S. 626, 644, 651 n. 14, 105 S.Ct. 2265, 2278, 2282 n. 14, 85 L.Ed.2d 652, 668, 673 n. 14 (1985).

24. Board of Trustees (SUNY), 492 U.S. at 480, 109 S. Ct. at 3035, 106 L. Ed. 2d at 403–404 (1989).

decisionmakers to judge what manner of regulation may best be employed."[25]

Thus, the majority reformulated the fourth requirement of *Central Hudson* to give the regulators more leeway to suppress commercial speech,[26] and though he denied the new test was the old "rational basis" test in disguise,[27] Justice Scalia's reliance on the language in *Posadas* that it was up to the legislature to decide what mode of regulation would be effective[28] casts doubt on his denial.

Justice Blackmun limited his dissent to the majority's reformulation of *Central Hudson* to a footnote underscoring the majority's repudiation of Central Hudson's fourth requirement and taking issue with Justice Scalia's assertion that the "least restrictive means" formulation in *Zauderer v. Office of Disciplinary Counsel*[29] was mere dictum.

3.4 Present Status of the Commercial Speech Doctrine

A. *Decreasing Constitutional Protection—Comparative Case Analysis*

The weakening of the commercial speech doctrine has taken its toll in the real world. In *Linmark Associates, Inc. v. Township of Willingboro*,[1] decided on the heels of *Virginia State Bd. of Pharmacy v. Virginia Citizens Consumer Council, Inc.*,[2] no consideration was given by the Court to the government's interest in stabilizing multi-racial neighborhoods through an ordinance banning "For Sale" and "Sold" signs from residential property. When the township sought to justify the ordinance by relying on the goal of the ordinance, *i.e.*, promotion of stable, racially integrated housing, the Court conceded the substantial governmental interest but declared the legislation violative of the First Amendment because it attempted to protect its interest by restricting the free flow of truthful information.[3]

In contrast, following the weakening of the commercial speech doctrine in *Central Hudson* and *Posadas*, the United States Court of Appeals upheld an Illinois statute in *Curtis v. Thompson*[4] prohibiting the

---

25. *Id.*

26. *See* Mark A. Conrad, Board of Trustees of the State University of New York v. Fox: *The Dawn of a New Age of Commercial Speech Regulation of Tobacco and Alcohol*, 9 Cardozo Arts & Ent. Law Rev. 61, 88 (1990) ("Fox's weakening of the constitutional protection accorded commercial speech is unmistakable."); Howell A. Burkhalter, Comment, *Advertorial Advertising and the Commercial Speech Doctrine*, 25 Wake Forest L. Rev. 861, 866–867 (1990).

27. Board of Trustees (SUNY), 492 U.S. at 480, 109 S. Ct. at 3035, 106 L. Ed. 2d at 404.

28. Posadas, 478 U.S. at 344, 106 S. Ct. at 2978, 92 L. Ed. 2d at 282.

29. 471 U.S. 626, 644, 105 S.Ct. 2265, 2278, 85 L.Ed.2d 652, 668 (1985).

1. 431 U.S. 85, 97 S.Ct. 1614, 52 L.Ed.2d 155 (1977).

2. 425 U.S. 748, 96 S.Ct. 1817, 48 L.Ed.2d 346 (1976).

3. Linmark Associates, Inc., 431 U.S. at 94–95, 97 S. Ct. at 1619–1620, 52 L. Ed. 2d at 163.

4. 840 F.2d 1291 (7th Cir.1988), *cert. granted, vac'd* 507 U.S. 1015, 113 S.Ct. 1809, 123 L.Ed.2d 441 (1993).

solicitation of any home owner of residential property to sell or list such property after the owner gives notice that he does not wish to sell his property. The legislature's stated purpose for the statute was to prevent "blockbusting" or "panic selling" based on racial concerns.

While the legislative interest would previously have been disregarded pursuant to *Virginia State Bd. of Pharmacy* and *Linmark*, it became central to the Seventh Circuit's analysis in affirming the trial court's refusal to enjoin the enforcement of the criminal statute. Focusing on the substantial governmental interest and advancement prongs of the four-part *Central Hudson* test, the appeals court held that even if the anti-blockbusting interest of the state was not advanced by the statute, the state's less obvious interest in insuring the privacy of homeowners was.[5]

Clearly the Seventh Circuit's analysis would have been different in *Thompson v. Curtis* if the state's interests had not been considered since the appeals court held that as in *Linmark* the commercial real estate speech involved concerned lawful activity (the purchase and sale of residential property) and was not misleading.[6]

B. Is There Yet Another Twist in the Road?

While decisions such as *Central Hudson*, *Posadas* and *SUNY* have clearly eroded constitutional protection for commercial speech, which erosion has already impacted the freedom of advertisers of legal goods and services, another twist in the doctrine seems to be at hand. Hard on the heels of *Peel v. Attorney Registration and Disciplinary Commission*,[7] a lawyer advertising case suggesting a disposition of a plurality of the Supreme Court to recognize the need for a vital commercial speech doctrine,[8] the Court decided *City of Cincinnati v. Discovery Network, Inc.*.[9] In this case the Discovery Network, which is in the business of providing adult educational, recreational and social programs to individuals in the Cincinnati area, advertised these programs in a free magazine published several times a year and distributed in part through a number of newsracks placed on public property with the city's permission.[10] Within a year of giving its permission, the city, through its director of public works, notified the Discovery Network that its permit to use newsracks on public property was revoked and ordered the newsracks removed. The notice explained that the private company's publication was a "commercial handbill" and, as such, a city ordinance prohibited its

---

5. *Id.* at 1298–1302.

6. *Id.* at 1298.

7. 496 U.S. 91, 110 S.Ct. 2281, 110 L.Ed.2d 83 (1990).

8. "The Commission's authority is necessarily constrained by the First Amendment to the Federal Constitution, and specifically by the principle that disclosure of truthful, relevant information is more likely to make a positive contribution to decisionmaking [by the public] than is concealment

of such information." Id. at 108, 110 S. Ct. at 2292, 110 L. Ed. 2d at 99 (1990).

9. 507 U.S. 410, 113 S.Ct. 1505, 123 L.Ed.2d 99 (1993).

10. Another publisher of free magazines in newsracks advertising real estate for sale, Harmon Publishing Company, was also involved in this litigation in essentially the same position as Discovery Network.

distribution on public property. After administrative hearings and review that upheld the city's position, the company sought relief in the United States District Court.

Following an evidentiary hearing, the trial court found that "the regulatory scheme advanced by the City of Cincinnati completely prohibiting the distribution of commercial handbills on the public right of way violates the First Amendment."[11] Recognizing that the city had the burden of establishing only a reasonable fit between the legislative purpose and the means chosen to achieve that purpose under *SUNY*, it found the fit unreasonable because the number of commercial newsracks involved was minute compared to the total number of newsracks on public property; because the newsracks in issue affected the public safety in only a marginal way; and because practices elsewhere indicated that Cincinnati's safety and esthetic interests could be "adequately protected by regulating the size, shape, number or placement of such devices."[12] On appeal the United States Court of Appeals for the Sixth Circuit affirmed, holding that the burden placed on commercial speech could not be "justified by the paltry gains in safety and beauty achieved by the ordinance."[13]

On certiorari the Supreme Court affirmed the judgment below, sharing the lower courts' evaluation that the fit between the city's goal and its method of achieving it was unreasonable because the benefit to be derived by the ban on the commercial newsracks was "minute" or "paltry."[14] In concluding that the commercial speech was entitled to First Amendment protection here, the Court quoted approvingly and at length from Justice Blackmun's opinion in *Virginia Pharmacy Bd.* representing the anti-paternalistic view of commercial speech protection that a majority of the Court, particularly Chief Justice Rehnquist, had previously attempted to discredit in *Posadas*.[15]

Though not fully repudiating *Posadas* and *SUNY*, the majority in *Discovery Network*, speaking through Justice Stevens, made clear that commercial advertising of legal products and services was to be given considerable protection and the benefit to the government in suppressing it, as part of the reasonable fit requirement of *SUNY*, had better be substantial. Along this line the Court rejected Cincinnati's assertion that the "low value" of commercial speech was in itself sufficient justification for its selective and categorical ban on a small member of newsracks dispensing commercial handbills.[16]

11. 507 U.S. at 414, 113 S. Ct. at 1508, 123 L. Ed. 2d at 106.

12. *Id.*, 113 S. Ct. at 1509, 123 L. Ed. 2d at 107.

13. *Id.* at 415, 113 S. Ct. at 1509, 123 L. Ed. 2d at 107.

14. *Id.* at 418, 113 S. Ct. at 1510, 123 L. Ed. 2d at 108–109. *See* Rubin v. Coors Brewing Co., 514 U.S. 476, 115 S.Ct. 1585, 131 L.Ed.2d 532 (1995); Edenfield v. Fane,

507 U.S. 761, 113 S.Ct. 1792, 123 L.Ed.2d 543 (1993).

15. City of Cincinnati, 507 U.S. at 420, 113 S. Ct. at 1512, 123 L. Ed. 2d at 110–111.

16. *Id.* at 429–430, 113 S. Ct. at 1517, 123 L. Ed. 2d at 116. *See* Edward J. McAndrew, Note, City of Cincinnati v. Discovery Network, Inc.: *Elevating the Value of Commercial Speech?*, 43 Cath. U. L. Rev. 1247, 1281, 1287 (1994).

As to the city's alternative argument that its ordinance involved reasonable time, place and manner restrictions on commercial speech, the Court seized on the obvious fact that the very basis for regulation here was the difference in content between ordinary newspapers dispensed from newsracks and so-called commercial handbills, saying, "[B]y any common sense understanding of the term, the ban in this case is 'content based.' "[17] The majority added that "regardless of whether or not ... [the ordinance] leaves open ample alternative channels of communication, it cannot be justified as a legitimate time, place, or manner restriction on protected speech."[18] This idea of availability of alternative means of commercial communication as justifying regulation had been previously embraced by the Court as justifying a time, place and manner restriction on commercial speech.[19]

If the importance of a judicial decision is measured by the vigorousness of the arguments of those who dissent from it, *Discovery Network* is a very important precedent. Chief Justice Rehnquist, who had written the opinion in *Posadas* and who voted with the majority in *Central Hudson* and *SUNY*, wrote a dissent joined by Justices White and Thomas setting out a jurisprudential philosophy of the First Amendment that accords a very low priority to the protection of commercial speech. He took the majority to task for really ignoring the doctrine of *SUNY* and following what he believed to be "the discredited notion that the availability of 'less restrictive means' to accomplish the city's objectives renders its regulation of commercial speech unconstitutional."[20] Consistent with his philosophy expressed in *Posadas*, he laments the majority's position refusing to permit Cincinnati's suppression of the newsracks based on the city's "bare assertion that the 'low value' of commercial speech is a sufficient justification for its selective and categorical ban on newsracks dispensing 'commercial handbills'."[21] The general tenor of his dissent suggests that the Chief Justice is fully aware that the majority is pulling back from the full implications permitting suppression of commercial speech emanating from *Posadas* and *SUNY*.[22]

And the pullback continued in *44 Liquormart, Inc. and Peoples Super Liquor Stores, Inc. v. Rhode Island and Rhode Island Liquor Stores Ass'n.*[23] in which the Court unanimously struck down Rhode Island statutes that prohibited vendors licensed in Rhode Island as well

---

17. City of Cincinnati, 507 U.S. at 429, 113 S. Ct. at 1516–1517, 123 L. Ed. 2d at 116.

18. *Id.* at 430, 113 S. Ct. at 1517, 123 L. Ed. 2d at 117.

19. *See* Virginia State Bd. of Pharmacy v. Virginia Citizens Consumer Council, Inc., 425 U.S. 748, 771, 96 S.Ct. 1817, 1830, 48 L.Ed.2d 346, 363–364 (1976).

20. City of Cincinnati, 507 U.S. at 441, 113 S. Ct. at 1523, 123 L. Ed. 2d at 124.

21. *Id.* at 443, 113 S. Ct. at 1524, 123 L. Ed. 2d at 125.

22. Justice Blackmun filed a concurring opinion applauding the Court's decision rejecting "the extreme extension of *Central Hudson's* logic" and expressing the hope that the court would ultimately abandon *Central Hudson* and presumably *Posadas* and *SUNY*. *Id.* at 431–438, 113 S. Ct. at 1517, 1521, 123 L. Ed. 2d at 117, 122.

23. 517 U.S. 484, 116 S.Ct. 1495, 134 L.Ed.2d 711 (1996).

as out-of-state manufacturers, wholesalers and shippers from "advertising in any manner whatsoever" the price of any alcoholic beverage offered for sale in the state[24] and prohibited news media in the state from publishing or broadcasting such price advertising.[25] Unfortunately, the Court was badly split over the rationale for its holding except to agree that the twenty-first amendment repealing the prohibition on manufacture, transportation and sale of alcoholic beverages gave the states no authority to impinge on protection of commercial speech provided by the First Amendment and that the state had otherwise failed to carry its heavy constitutional burden of justifying the complete ban on price advertising of alcoholic beverages.[26]

C. Assessment and Prognosis

There is no doubt that following *Central Hudson*, *Posadas* and *SUNY* the commercial speech doctrine had been seriously weakened at that time, leaving much, though by no means all,[27] commercial speech vulnerable to governmental regulation. The only doubt seems to have been whether the Court would apply the *Central Hudson* test in a conscientious manner or would continue to erode even further its limited protection in order to permit government to regulate commercial expression concerning admittedly legal products, services and activities which legislatures, administrative agencies and a majority of the justices feel are harmful to the public good.

But then a ray of hope for proponents of broad constitutional protection for commercial speech penetrated the gloom when a majority of the Court expressed continued support for lawyer advertising and a four member plurality cited *Virginia Pharmacy Bd.* approvingly in rejecting an administrative agency's paternalistic approach to protecting the public.[28]

Much of the gloom itself has now been dissipated by the clear cut support for a substantial commercial speech doctrine in *Discovery Network*. This decision together with the departure from the Court of Justice White, who generally cast votes to cut back on protection for commercial speech, suggests that the doctrine may very well take on new vitality in the coming years. Such a change of direction would be nothing

---

24. R.I. Gen. L. § 3–8–7 (1987).

25. R.I. Gen. L. § 3–8–8.1 (1987).

26. 44 Liquormart, Inc., 517 U.S. 484, 514–515, 116 S.Ct. 1495, 1514–1515, 134 L.Ed.2d 711, 735–736 (1996).

27. *See, e.g.,* Project 80's, Inc. v. City of Pocatello, 942 F.2d 635 (9th Cir.1991) (city ordinances banning door to door commercial solicitation held violative of the First Amendment); Abramson v. Gonzalez, 949 F.2d 1567, 1575–1578 (11th Cir.1992) (state statute prohibiting unlicensed practitioners of psychology from holding themselves out

as psychologists held to place an unconstitutional burden on commercial speech); Lueth v. St. Clair County Community College, 732 F.Supp. 1410, 1413–1416 (E.D.Mich.1990) (community college's prohibition of advertising of a nude dancing club in its student-run newspaper held unconstitutional as not sufficiently narrowly tailored to serve the college's interests).

28. Peel v. Attorney Registration and Disciplinary Comm'n, 496 U.S. 91, 110 S.Ct. 2281, 110 L.Ed.2d 83 (1990).

new for a court which has waxed and waned regarding constitutional safeguards for this category of speech for more than fifty years. However, given the centrist nature of the present court it seems unlikely that in the near term, it will fulfill the hope of Justice Blackmun for a return to the very broad protection of commercial speech he espoused and the Court had accepted in *Virginia Pharmacy Bd.*.

But in the long term, more protection for commercial speech could be achieved if the Court were to abandon the categorical approach to speech issues championed by the now retired Justice White and choose instead to embrace a structural approach, which takes into consideration the context of the speech clause within the entire Constitution and questions the source of the Court's power to rank the types of speech and provide them with differing levels of First Amendment protection. Article III simply provides for judicial review by the Court—it says nothing about categorizing free speech according to its nature, content or function. And nowhere else in the Constitution is there any suggestion that the Court has this power. In other words, "speech is speech" under the First Amendment. If the Court were to accept this structural approach, it could focus on the proper question to be addressed: whether, in the given case, the government's interest in regulating speech outweighs the interest in protecting the speech, whatever its type.

Moreover, by taking a structural approach, the Court might recognize that the Constitution taken as a whole, provides as much a mandate for the protection of commercial speech as it does for political speech. The Commerce Clause,[29] the most potent source of power for the federal government, was designed to insure commercial intercourse among the citizenry[30] free from interference from the states. In turn, this commerce would insure an economically viable United States.[31] How better to promote commercial intercourse than to permit those in commerce to speak freely concerning commercial matters.[32] In fact, Justices Holmes and Brandeis borrowed from the commercial world in justifying First Amendment protection for political speech when they spoke of the marketplace of ideas.[33]

---

29. U.S. Const. art. I, § 8, cl. 3.

30. *See generally* WILLIAM W. CROSSKEY, POLITICS AND THE CONSTITUTION IN THE HISTORY OF THE UNITED STATES, Chapter 3 (1953); Symposium on the work of William W. Crosskey, 21 U. Chi. L. Rev. 1–92 (1953); Malcolm Sharp, Book Review, 54 Col. Rev. 438 (1954).

31. *Cf.* CHARLES A. BEARD, AN ECONOMIC INTERPRETATION OF THE CONSTITUTION OF THE UNITED STATES (Free Press Ed. 1986).

32. The author wishes he could take credit for this structural analysis of the Speech Clause of the First Amendment but the idea was developed and shared by his colleague, Ordinary Professor Robert A. Destro of the Columbus School of Law of the Catholic University of America.

33. *See, e.g.*, Abrams v. United States, 250 U.S. 616, 630, 40 S.Ct. 17, 22, 63 L.Ed. 1173, 1180 (1919) (dissenting opinion).

3.5 *Private Actions to Control Advertising Under Section 43(a) of the Lanham Act

3.6 *Standing to Bring a Private Action for False, Deceptive or Misleading Advertising Under Section 43(a)

3.7 *Remedies Available Under Section 43(a)

3.8 *The Role of the Federal Trade Commission in the Control of Deceptive or Unfair Advertising

3.9 *The Commission's Trade Regulation Rules and Industry Guides Contrasted

3.10 *The Commission's "Deception" Policy

3.11 *The Commission's Substantiation Policy

3.12 *The Commission's Consumer Unfairness Policy

3.13 *Administrative Remedies of the Commission

3.14 *Judicial Remedies Available to the Commission

3.15 Special Legal Issues in Advertising

A. Tort Liability for Commercial Communications

On principle there is no reason at common law why a publisher of advertising messages should not be held liable for tortious injury inflicted as a result of the publication of his messages. Liability for the commission of the communicative torts of libel and invasion of privacy through advertising have never been questioned on purely common law grounds.[1] Nor on principle is there any reason to reject liability of advertisers for their messages.[2] In determining such liability traditional

---

* Published in Practitioners Edition, Vol. 1.

1. *See, e.g.*, New York Times Co. v. Sullivan, 273 Ala. 656, 144 So.2d 25 (1962), *rev'd and rem.*, 376 U.S. 254, 84 S.Ct. 710, 11 L.Ed.2d 686 (1964) (libel in a newspaper "advertorial"); Braun v. Armour & Co., 254 N.Y. 514, 173 N.E. 845 (1930) (business libel in an ad of a meat packer suggesting that a kosher butcher sold bacon); Midler v. Ford Motor Co., 849 F.2d 460 (9th Cir. 1988), *aff'd on appeal after remand* 944 F.2d 909 (9th Cir.1991), cert. denied *sub. nom.* Young & Rubicam, Inc. v. Midler, 503 U.S. 951, 112 S.Ct. 1513–1514, 117 L.Ed.2d 650 (1992) (appropriation of famous female pop singer's voice for an automobile commercial); Allen v. Men's World Outlet, 679 F.Supp. 360 (S.D.N.Y.1988) (appropriation of famous motion picture actor's image and persona for a men's clothing commercial);

Kerby v. Hal Roach Studios, 53 Cal.App.2d 207, 127 P.2d 577 (1942) (false light invasion of privacy by suggesting in an advertisement for a motion picture that the plaintiff was a woman of loose morals).

2. *See, e.g.*, Braun v. Soldier of Fortune Magazine, Inc., 968 F.2d 1110, 1113–1116 (11th Cir.1992), cert. denied, 506 U.S. 1071 , 113 S.Ct. 1028, 122 L.Ed.2d 173 (1993); Norwood v. Soldier of Fortune Magazine, Inc., 651 F.Supp. 1397 (W.D.Ark. 1987); *see also* Michael I. Meyerson, *This Gun for Hire: Dancing in the Dark of the First Amendment*, 47 Wash. & Lee L. Rev. 267, 268–274 (1990); *but see, e.g.*, Walters v. Seventeen Magazine, 195 Cal.App.3d 1119, 241 Cal.Rptr. 101 (1987) (advertisement for a tampon causing toxic shock syndrome) *and* Yuhas v. Mudge, 129 N.J.Super. 207, 322 A.2d 824 (App.Div.1974) (advertise-

tort concepts of duty, foreseeability, breach of duty, weighing of costs and benefits, causation in fact and proximate cause are employed.[3]

The main sticking points in imposing tort liability for negligent injurious advertising are first finding a duty on the part of the publisher to investigate the advertiser's claims[4] and then finding that the risk from not investigating the claims before publication outweighs the burden imposed by such investigation.[5] If every advertising claim that had any potential for causing harm had to be checked out before it could reasonably be published, the financial and editorial burdens on the publisher would be unacceptably large in relation to the risk.[6]

But if the duty to investigate extends only to those claims that on their face pose an obvious risk to life, liberty or property, as viewed by a reasonable publisher, the burden is substantially lessened while the probability of injury from the particular advertising is that much greater. Under this narrower view of the duty involved in advertising cases, the cost of failing to investigate and, if necessary, refusing to run the ad may not be so large as to negate negligence.[7]

Whether the tort found to have been committed by the publisher is a peculiarly communicative one *i.e.*, libel or invasion of privacy, or is the more general one of negligent infliction of injury to person or property, the tort involves media of expression and implicates the First Amendment now that the Supreme Court has recognized constitutional protection for commercial speech.[8] Therefore, even when an advertising tort is found, liability for the injury caused can only be imposed if First Amendment concerns are satisfied.

The constitutionalization of the communicative torts is considered in the chapters on defamation and invasion of privacy.[9] The main concern of this section is the interrelationship of the First Amendment and the tort of negligent infliction of injury to persons and property. And here the tort duty and breach requirements parallel the First Amendment interest in preventing serious encroachment on the freedom of commercial speech.[10]

ment for fireworks causing injury because of defective condition), in which intermediate appellate courts of California and New Jersey refused to recognize a legal duty owing from the publishers of the advertisements to the injury victims in the absence of some guarantee or endorsement by the publishers.

3. *See* Braun, 968 F.2d at 1113–1116; Norwood, 651 F. Supp. at 1402–1403.

4. *See* Walters v. Seventeen Magazine, 195 Cal.App.3d 1119, 241 Cal.Rptr. 101 (1987); Yuhas v. Mudge, 129 N.J.Super. 207, 322 A.2d 824 (App.Div.1974).

5. *See* Eimann v. Soldier of Fortune Magazine, Inc., 880 F.2d 830, 835–838 (5th Cir.1989), cert. denied, 493 U.S. 1024, 110 S.Ct. 729, 107 L.Ed.2d 748 (1990).

6. *Id.* at 837–838.

7. *See* Braun, 968 F.2d at 1114–1116.

8. *See, e.g.*, City of Cincinnati v. Discovery Network, Inc., 507 U.S. 410, 113 S.Ct. 1505, 123 L.Ed.2d 99 (1993); Central Hudson Gas and Elec. Corp. v. Public Service Comm'n, 447 U.S. 557, 100 S.Ct. 2343, 65 L.Ed.2d 341 (1980); Virginia State Board of Pharmacy v. Virginia Citizens Consumer Council, Inc., 425 U.S. 748, 96 S.Ct. 1817, 48 L.Ed.2d 346 (1976).

9. Chapters 5 and 4 respectively, *infra*.

10. *See* Michael I. Meyerson, *This Gun for Hire: Dancing in the Dark of the First Amendment*, 47 Wash. & Lee L. Rev. 267, 268–269 (1990); *cf*. Rice v. Paladin Enterprises, Inc., 128 F.3d 233, 247 (4th Cir. 1997).

If the tort duty imposed on a publisher to police advertising placed by others is too demanding, the First Amendment would surely prevent tort liability.[11] Thus, a requirement that all advertising copy or even all suspicious or ambiguous advertising copy be investigated to reduce or eliminate risk of injury to the public could be so burdensome financially that it might threaten the very existence of publications. The First Amendment stands as a protection against such a threat to a free press and commercial speech.

If, however, the tort duty is narrowed to require investigation of and, if necessary, refusal to publish ads posing *on their face* physical or financial risk to members of the public, the burden on publishers is substantially minimized and the chill of protected commercial speech reduced. The question then becomes whether the First Amendment provides virtually absolute protection against tort liability for breaches of even this narrow duty. There is little authority supporting an absolutist approach to protection of publishers of advertising,[12] but, until recently,[13] there was no authority permitting the imposition of liability.

The cross currents of tort liability for negligent advertising and First Amendment protection for commercial speech finally met with full force in *Braun* v. *Soldier of Fortune Magazine, Inc.*[14] There, the magazine (SOF) ran a classified ad placed by one Michael Savage which read "GUN FOR HIRE: 37 year old professional mercenary desires jobs. Vietnam Veteran. Discrete [sic] and very private. Body guard, courier, and other special skills. All jobs considered." Day and evening phone numbers and an address for correspondence were included in the ad. The overwhelming majority of responses received by Savage sought his participation in serious criminal activity including murder, assault and kidnapping. Eventually Savage was retained by a business man to murder his partner, Richard Braun. Savage and two others went to Braun's suburban Atlanta home. As Braun and his sixteen year-old son Michael were driving down the driveway, one of Savage's confederates fired several shots into the car with a MAC II automatic pistol wounding both Braun and his son. Braun managed to roll out of the car onto the driveway where the confederate cooly finished the job by firing two more shots into the back of Braun's head.

Later Michael and another son, Ian, sued the magazine and its parent company in the United States District Court for Northern Geor-

---

11. *See* Braun, 968 F.2d at 1114–1115.

12. *But see* Note, *Thick Veils and Undrawn Lines: Eimann v. Soldier of Fortune and the Demise of the Negligent Advertising Cause of Action*, 23 Comm. L. Rev. 451, 453–456 (1991); Pittman v. Dow Jones & Co., 662 F.Supp. 921, 923 (E.D.La.1987) (semble), *aff'd*, 834 F.2d 1171 (5th Cir. 1987); Walters, 195 Cal. App. at 1122–1123.

13. *See* Braun, 968 F.2d at 1118–1120; Norwood Fortune Magazine, Inc., 651 F. Supp. at 1399–1400 ("Defendant contends that its 'gun for hire' advertisements are absolutely privileged [under the First Amendment].... That simply cannot be the law....);" *cf.* Weirum v. RKO General, Inc., 15 Cal.3d 40, 48, 539 P.2d 36, 40, 123 Cal.Rptr. 468, 472 (1975) (liability for personal injury from negligently produced radio promotional contest not barred by First Amendment).

14. 968 F.2d 1110 (11th Cir.1992), cert. denied, 506 U.S. 1071, 113 S.Ct. 1028, 122 L.Ed.2d 173 (1993).

gia for the wrongful death of their father. Michael also sued the companies for the personal injuries he received. At trial, the sons introduced evidence to show that SOF knew of the likelihood that criminal activity would result from placing an ad worded like Savage's. This included newspaper and magazine articles published prior to Braun's murder which described connections between SOF personal service ads and a number of criminal convictions for, among other things, murder. Also included was testimony that, prior to SOF's acceptance of Savage's ad, law enforcement officials had contacted SOF staff employees regarding such ads on two separate occasions in connection with criminal investigations of a solicitation to commit murder in Texas and a kidnaping in New Jersey. In response, SOF's president, a former managing editor and the advertising manager all denied knowledge of information linking its ads with criminal activity. The advertising manager further testified that she had understood the term "Gun for Hire" in the Savage ad to refer to a "bodyguard or protection service-type thing" rather than to any illegal activity.

At the end of the trial, the district judge gave the following instructions: "In order to prevail in this case Plaintiffs must prove to your reasonable satisfaction by a preponderance of the evidence that a reasonable reading of the advertisement in this case would have conveyed to a magazine publisher, such as Soldier of Fortune, that this ad presented the clear and present danger of causing serious harm to the public from violent criminal activity. The Plaintiffs must prove that the ad in question contained a clearly identifiable unreasonable risk, that the offer in the ad is one to commit a serious violent crime, including murder. Now, while Defendants owe a duty of reasonable care to the public, the magazine publisher does not have a duty to investigate every ad it publishes. Defendants owe no duty to the Plaintiffs for publishing an ad if the ad's language on its face would not convey to the reader that it created an unreasonable risk that the advertiser was available to commit such violent crimes as murder. Now, of course, the tendency to read the advertisement in question in hindsight is hard to avoid, but it must be avoided. The test for you is not how the advertisement in question reads now in light of subsequent events, but rather how the advertisement read to a reasonable publisher at the time of publication. You should view the facts and these instructions with particular care in this case, in view of the First Amendment to the Constitution, which protects the free flow of truthful and legitimate information even when it is of a commercial rather than a political nature."

The district court further instructed that, if the jury found that SOF was negligent and that this negligence was the proximate cause of appellee's father's death, it could "award damages for the value of the life of Richard Braun," but not for mental anguish, emotional distress, or the family's loss of companionship. The court also stated that, if the jury found that SOF was negligent and that this negligence was the proximate cause of appellee Michael Braun's injuries, it could award full compensation, including recovery for both physical pain and mental anguish. The district court also noted that Georgia law permitted punitive damages for appellee Michael Braun's personal injury claim but that, to award punitive damages, the jury must first find that SOF "acted maliciously or with an entire want of care which constitutes conscious indifference to the consequences."[15]

The jury returned a verdict in favor of the Braun's, awarding compensatory damages on the wrongful death claim in the amount of $2,000,000 and $375,000 for Michael's injuries. A punitive damages award of $10,000,000 was also made but was later reduced on remittitur to $2,000,000.

On appeal the United States Court of Appeals for the Eleventh Circuit determined under Georgia law that a duty not to print ads dangerous on their face exists, in this case ads that openly solicit criminal activity.[16] The question then for the appeals court was whether the district court's instructions on negligence were correct.

The appeals court agreed with the trial court's instruction that under Georgia law "Defendants owe no duty to the Plaintiffs for publishing an ad if the ad's language on its face would not convey to the reader that it created an unreasonable risk that the advertiser was available to commit such violent crimes as murder." Obversely, the court upheld this instruction because it recognized the narrow duty to refuse to run only ads highly dangerous on their face.

At this point the Eleventh Circuit's review was limited to insuring that the trial court's instruction on determining breach of that narrow duty was correct. In making this determination, the federal district court, of course, was bound to follow Georgia law which requires a weighing of the burden on the defendant of adopting adequate precautions to eliminate the risk posed against the probability of harm from the defendant's unmodified conduct (running the ad as received) multiplied by the gravity of the injury that might result from the unmodified conduct (personal injury up to and including murder).[17] The appeals court found that the district court's instruction that the jury could only find a breach (negligence) if the ad on its face would have alerted a reasonably prudent publisher to the clearly identifiable and unreasonable risk of harm to members of the public that the ad posed did meet the Georgia standard.[18]

The appeals court then confronted the question whether Georgia tort law applied by the district court met federal constitutional standards. The court began its constitutional analysis by recognizing the First Amendment's protection of speech that does no more than propose a commercial transaction and acknowledging that imposition of tort

---

15. *Id.* at 1113–1115.

16. *Id.* at 1114–1115.

17. *Id.* at 1115. This is a restatement of Judge Learned Hand's classic formulation for determining breach of duty set out in

United States v. *Carroll Towing Co.*, 159 F.2d 169, 173 (2d Cir.1947).

18. The trial court's instruction could certainly have been clearer on Hand's cost-benefit balance but the Eleventh Circuit obviously felt that it was clear enough.

liability for publishing advertisements that result in injury implicates First Amendment interests.[19] But the appeals court also recognized that the First Amendment does not protect commercial speech related to illegal activity.[20] However, the court went on to state that if the burden placed on publishers of advertising is too great in preventing illegal activity and injury to members of the public, then self censorship, loss of revenue needed to continue publication and the consequent chill on legitimate commercial speech may be the end products.

In *Braun*, however, the appeals court held that the burden imposed by the district court's instructions on publishers did not create these problems and therefore did not run afoul of the First Amendment. By limiting the burden to rejecting ads that on their face would alert reasonably prudent publishers that the ads posed a clearly identifiable risk to members of the public, the tort liability here comported with the requirements of the First Amendment.[21]

Braun is significant because it is the first decision of an influential appellate court rejecting the idea of absolute First Amendment protection of communications media from tort liability for negligently published advertising that results in physical harm to members of the public. Moreover, the decision could signal a reevaluation of those decisions rejecting tort liability for injury resulting from negligently produced entertainment programming though First Amendment protection is, of course, broader there than for purely commercial speech.[22]

---

19. *Id.* at 1117.

20. *Id*; *see* Central Hudson Gas & Elec. Corp. v. Public Service Comm'n, 447 U.S. 557, 564, 100 S.Ct. 2343, 2350, 65 L.Ed.2d 341, 349–350 (1980) (dictum); Pittsburgh Press Co. v. Pittsburgh Comm'n, on Human Relations, 413 U.S. 376, 388, 93 S.Ct. 2553, 2560, 37 L.Ed.2d 669, 678–679 (1973); Princess Sea Industries, Inc. v. Nevada, 97 Nev. 534, 635 P.2d 281 (Nev. 1981), cert. denied, 456 U.S. 926, 102 S.Ct. 1972, 72 L.Ed.2d 441 (1982).

21. Braun, 968 F.2d at 1118. For critical analyses, *see* Brian J. Cullen, Note, *Putting a 'Chill' on Contract Murder*: Braun v. Soldier of Fortune *and Tort Liability for Negligent Publishing*, 38 Vill. L. Rev. 625, 643–646 (1993); Stephen T. Rafotis, Note, *Guns for Hire, Commercial Speech and Tort Liability: Making a Case for Preserving First Amendment Free Speech Rights*, 97 W. Va. L. Rev. 215, 241–247 (1994).

22. *See, e.g.*, Olivia N. v. NBC, 126 Cal. App.3d 488, 178 Cal.Rptr. 888 (1981); De Filippo v. NBC, 446 A.2d 1036 (R.I.1982); *see also* Herceg v. Hustler Magazine, 814 F.2d 1017 (5th Cir.1987), cert. denied, 485 U.S. 959, 108 S.Ct. 1219, 99 L.Ed.2d 420 (1988); Juliet L. Dee, *From "Pure Speech" to Dial–A–Porn: Negligence, First Amendment Law and the Hierarchy of Protected*

Speech, 13 Comm. & Law 27 (No. 4, 1991) (exhaustive collection of reported and unreported cases involving the intersection of negligence law and the First Amendment). The rationale of the cases denying liability in tort appears to be that short of incitement to immediate violence the First Amendment protects artistic expression.

One analogous case utilizing this rationale was recently reversed. In *Rice v. Paladin Enterprises, Inc.*, plaintiffs filed wrongful death and survival actions against the publisher of "Hitman: A Technical Manual for Independent Contractors" and "How to Make a Disposable Silencer, Vol. II," which works were consulted by a hired killer who murdered three members of a Maryland family under a contract with the estranged husband and father. The United States District Court granted the defendant publisher's motion for summary judgment, distinguishing *Braun* as involving "commercial speech that is afforded limited First Amendment protection." 940 F.Supp. 836, 848 (D.Md.1996), *rev'd*, 128 F.3d 233 (4th Cir.1997), cert. denied __ U.S. __, 118 S.Ct. 1515, 140 L.Ed.2d 668 (1998). In reversing the judgment of the District Court, the Fourth Circuit held that the First Amendment does not protect against civil liability of publishers who by the clearest of

B. Control of Advertising of Potentially Dangerous But Legal Products

Unlike the control of advertising that plainly proclaims that someone is available to engage in illegal acts such as contract killing[23] or providing sexual services for a price[24] or advertising that is itself unlawful because it discriminates on the basis of gender in providing employment opportunities,[25] the regulation of advertising of potentially dangerous products that are nevertheless legal poses difficult legal questions. Not the least of these questions is whether the costs to society engendered by consumption of such goods justifies the denial of constitutional protection to commercial speech promoting the consumption.

1. Tobacco Products

It has been estimated that in excess of 300,000 Americans die every year from tobacco related diseases and the cost to society of lost productivity and additional health care is at least 65 billion dollars.[26] While a complete ban on the manufacture, sale and consumption of these products seems politically and practically infeasible,[27] attempts by the federal and state legislatures have been made to regulate tobacco advertising in an effort to reduce consumption, particularly by the young. Much of this existing regulation was negotiated with the tobacco industry and has not been challenged by tobacco interests.

communications intend to and do actually aid and abet criminal enterprises.

The flavor of this chilling case can be extracted from the deposition of Paladin Press Publisher Peder C. Lund, taken before trial. At one point in the deposition the lawyers for the victims' relatives asked Mr. Lund whether it mattered to him for what purpose his books are being ordered . . . ? "No" replied the publisher. Counsel then asked "Do you care?" The response again was "No". When the plaintiffs' counsel asked Lund whether killers might be interested in a Paladin book on disposing of dead bodies, he said "Possibly" and added that he would sell books on explosives to people around the world linked to terrorism, provided that doing so was legal. *See* Ruben Castenada *"Hit Man" Publisher Doesn't Care Why It Sells,* Wash. Post, June 25, 1998, p. D1, col. 1, D7, cols. 3-6. *See also* David Montgomery, *If Books Could Kill; This Publisher Offers Lessons in Murder, Now He's a Target Himself,* Wash. Post, July 26, 1998, pp. F1, F5 for a fairly objective profile of Peder C. Lund and his sensational case. Lund later settled the case.

23. *See* Braun v. Soldier of Fortune Magazine, Inc., 968 F.2d 1110 (11th Cir.

1992), cert. denied, 506 U.S. 1071, 113 S.Ct. 1028, 122 L.Ed.2d 173 (1993); Norwood v. Soldier of Fortune Magazine, Inc. 651 F.Supp. 1397 (W.D.Ark.1987).

24. Princess Sea Industries, Inc. v. Nevada, 97 Nev. 534, 635 P.2d 281 (Nev. 1981), cert. denied, 456 U.S. 926, 102 S.Ct. 1972, 72 L.Ed.2d 441 (1982).

25. Pittsburgh Press Co. v. Pittsburgh Comm'n on Human Relations, 413 U.S. 376, 93 S.Ct. 2553, 37 L.Ed.2d 669 (1973).

26. Vincent Blasi & Henry P. Monaghan, *The First Amendment and Cigarette Advertising,* 256 J.A.M.A. 502, 502 (1986).

27. The combined tobacco farming and manufacturing economy of the country employed approximately 2.3 million full-time and part-time workers in 1978. *See* Monograph, *The Economic Importance of the U.S. Tobacco Industry, reprinted in* 124 Cong. Rec. 15554, 15556 (1978). With tobacco farming and manufacture spread over at least a dozen states, enactment of a tobacco ban by Congress would be practically impossible. Moreover, the legislators know as well as anyone the disastrous consequences of the Eighteenth Amendment to the Constitution ("Prohibition").

a. Warning labels

Following the Surgeon General's 1964 report demonstrating a strong statistical correlation between cigarette smoking and lung cancer and heart disease,[28] the Congress enacted the Federal Cigarette Labeling and Advertising Act[29] in part to educate the public as to the danger of cigarette smoking.[30] Regarding labeling, the act required anyone manufacturing, importing, packaging for sale or distributing within the United States cigarettes to include in a conspicuous place and in conspicuous type on the packages thereof the following statement: "Warning: The Surgeon General Has Determined That Cigarette Smoking is Dangerous to Your Health."[31] The warning was later made more detailed,[32] and extended to advertising of cigarettes.[33] Similar packaging and advertising warnings were imposed on smokeless tobacco products in the "Comprehensive Smokeless Tobacco Health Education Act of 1986."[34]

Violation of these warning requirements is a misdemeanor punishable by a fine of not more than $10,000.[35] The Attorney General of the United States besides prosecuting violators is also authorized to seek injunctions in the district courts of the United States to prevent and restrain violations of the cigarette and smokeless tobacco acts.[36]

The constitutionality of these acts and their enforcement has not been definitively decided. But by analogizing the required warnings to longstanding practice of the FTC to require in certain cases corrective or affirmative advertising to prevent deception of or unfairness to the public,[37] a strong case can be made that statutorily mandated warnings

28. Report of the Surgeon General's Advisory Commission on Smoking and Health, 29–32 (1964).

29. P.L. 89–92, 79 Stat. 282 (1965), *codified at* 15 U.S.C.A. §§ 1331–1340 (West 1982).

30. 15 U.S.C.A. § 1331(1) (West 1982). Congress' other purpose was to preempt the authority of the states and federal agencies to regulate by statute or common law decision cigarette labeling and advertising. *Id.* § 1331(2); *see* Cipollone v. Liggett Group, Inc., 505 U.S. 504, 517–526, 112 S.Ct. 2608, 2618–2622, 120 L.Ed.2d 407, 420–422 (1992); Pennington v. Vistron Corp., 876 F.2d 414, 418–421 (5th Cir.1989).

31. 15 U.S.C.A. § 1333 (West 1982).

32. "SURGEON GENERAL'S WARNING: Smoking Causes Lung Cancer, Heart Disease, Emphysema, and May Complicate Pregnancy."

SURGEON GENERAL'S WARNING: Quitting Smoking Now Greatly Reduces Serious Risks to Your Health.

SURGEON GENERAL'S WARNING: Smoking By Pregnant Women May Result in Fetal Injury, Premature Birth, and Low Birth Weight.

"SURGEON GENERAL'S WARNING: Cigarette Smoke Contains Carbon Monoxide." 15 U.S.C.A. § 1333 (a)(1)-(2) (West Supp. 1993). The above warnings are to be rotated on tobacco product packages and advertising other than billboards on the basis of plans prepared by the manufacturers or importers and approved by the Federal Trade Commission. *Id.* § 1333(c)(1). Slightly different rotating warnings are to be used in billboard advertising. *Id.* § 1333(a)(3)."

33. *Id.* § 1333(a)(2).

34. Pub. L. 99–252, § 3, 100 Stat. 30 (1986), *codified at* § 15 U.S.C.A. § 4402 (West Pam.1993).

35. 15 U.S.C.A. § 1338 (West 1982); 15 U.S.C.A. § 4404(2) (West Pam.1993).

36. 15 U.S.C.A. § 1339 (West 1982); 15 U.S.C.A. § 4405 (West Pam.1993).

37. *See, e.g.,* Porter & Dietsch, Inc. v. Federal Trade Comm'n, 605 F.2d 294, 306–308 (7th Cir.1979), cert. denied, 445 U.S. 950, 100 S. Ct. 1597, 63 L. Ed. 2d 784 (1980); Grolier, Inc. v. Federal Trade Comm'n, 699 F.2d 983 (9th Cir.1983), cert. denied, 464 U.S. 891, 104 S.Ct. 235, 78 L.Ed.2d 227 (1983); Warner–Lambert Co. v.

on tobacco packages and in advertising messages would pass constitutional muster. After all, there is at least unfairness in not informing the public of the risks involved in consuming cigarettes and smokeless tobacco. But it must be remembered that while a number of courts of appeal have ruled in favor of the constitutionality of FTC mandated corrective and affirmative advertising,[38] the Supreme Court has not yet ruled decisively. However, the Court did say, by way of dictum, in *Virginia State Bd. of Pharmacy v. Virginia Citizens Consumer Council, Inc.* that the greater objectivity and hardiness of commercial speech "may also make it appropriate to require that a commercial message appear in such a form, or include such additional information, warnings and disclaimers, as are necessary to prevent its being deceptive."[39]

b. Banning Advertising on Electronic Media

It is one thing to require warning labels and affirmative warnings in advertising messages, it is something else again to prohibit advertising through specific media of communications. In both the "Federal Cigarette Labeling and Advertising Act" and the "Comprehensive Smokeless Tobacco Health Education Act" Congress imposed a complete ban on the advertising of cigarettes, little cigars and smokeless tobacco products "on any medium of electronic communications subject to the jurisdiction of the Federal Communications Commission."[40]

Such *total* prohibition of commercial speech with criminal punishment for violation immediately raises the specter of censorship and some commentators have argued that complete advertising bans run afoul of the First Amendment.[41] But not all bans on publication violate the First Amendment[42] and, indeed, the constitutionality of the ban on cigarette advertising over the electronic media was summarily upheld by the

Federal Trade Comm'n, 562 F.2d 749, 756–764, 183 U.S. App. D.C. 230, 234–242 (D.C.Cir.1977), cert. denied, 435 U.S. 950, 98 S. Ct. 1575, 55 L. Ed. 2d 800 (1978).

38. *See* Porter & Dietsch, 605 F.2d at 304–307 (citing *Virginia State Bd. of Pharmacy v. Virginia Citizens Consumer Council, Inc.*, 425 U.S. 748, 96 S.Ct. 1817, 48 L.Ed.2d 346 (1976)); Grolier, Inc., 699 F.2d at 988; Warner–Lambert Co., 562 F.2d at 758–759 (also citing *Virginia State Bd. of Pharmacy*).

39. 425 U.S. 748, 772 n. 24, 96 S.Ct. 1817, 1830 n. 24, 48 L.Ed.2d 346, 364 n. 24 (1976).

40. 15 U.S.C.A. § 1335 (West 1982); 15 U.S.C.A. § 4402(f) (West Supp. Pam. 1993).

41. *See* David S. Welkowitz, *Smoke in the Air: Commercial Speech and Broadcasting*, 7 Cardozo L. Rev. 47, 91 (1985) ("[N]o less drastic alternative has been seriously attempted. Thus, the ban is constitutionally suspect.") Gregory T. Wuliger, *The Constitutional Rights of Puffery: Commercial*

Speech and the Cigarette Broadcast Advertising Ban, 36 Fed. Com. L.J. 1, 2 (1984) ("[I]f *Virginia Pharmacy* and its progeny are applied to cigarette broadcast advertising, the ban must be regarded as unconstitutional.") Matthew L. Miller, Note, *The First Amendment and Legislative Bans of Liquor and Cigarette Advertisements*, 85 Colum. L. Rev. 632, 633 (1985) ("[B]ans on the advertising of potentially harmful substances such as liquor and cigarettes are unconstitutional because they violate the first amendment rights of those who receive commercial messages."); *see also* Clara S. Ross, Note, *Judicial and Legislative Control of the Tobacco Industry: Toward a Smoke Free Society?* 56 U. Cinn. L. Rev. 317, 327–328 (1987).

42. *See, e.g.,* New York Times Co. v. United States, 403 U.S. 713, 733–740, 91 S.Ct. 2140, 2151–2153 29 L.Ed.2d 822, 835–840 (1971) (White, J. concurring); Near v. Minnesota ex rel. Olson, 283 U.S. 697, 713–717, 51 S.Ct. 625, 630–631, 75 L.Ed. 1357, 1366–1368 (1931).

Supreme Court in *Capital Broadcasting Co.* v. *Acting Attorney General Kleindienst.*[43] There, a group of broadcasting licensees and the National Association of Broadcasters sought to enjoin the enforcement of the cigarette advertising ban as violative of the First and Fifth Amendments. Relying on precedents and assumptions that commercial speech and electronic media were much less protected by the First Amendment than other types of expression and other media, a three-judge United States District Court for the District of Columbia upheld the advertising ban as a proper exercise of the commerce clause not in conflict with the First Amendment.[44]

The fifth amendment argument of the broadcasters was that the statute involved violated due process because it created arbitrary and invidious discrimination between electronic media subject to Federal Communications Commission regulation and all other advertising media. The district court rejected the argument of invidious discrimination because in its view there was a significant difference between media, with the electronic media having by far the most impact on young people, an audience the Congress particularly wanted to protect from risks of cigarette smoking.[45] As noted above, the Supreme Court summarily affirmed the three-judge district court's judgment that the statutory ban on cigarette advertising was constitutional without saying anything substantive concerning the merits of the issues presented.

Critics of the precedent[46] are quick to note that *Capital Broadcasting* was decided prior to the Court's change of direction toward greater protection for commercial speech and rejection of state paternalism beginning in the mid 1970s.[47] These critics argue that application of principles set down in *Virginia State Bd. of Pharmacy* v. *Virginia Citizens Consumer Council, Inc.*[48] striking down prohibitions on the advertising of prices for prescription drugs and *Central Hudson Gas and Electric Corp.* v. *Public Service Commission*[49] modifying *Virginia Pharmacy Bd.* with a four-part test for the protection of commercial speech[50] would today likely yield a determination by the courts of unconstitutionality of tobacco products advertising bans[51] or at least a high degree of

43. 405 U.S. 1000, 92 S.Ct. 1289, 31 L.Ed.2d 472 (1972), *aff'g mem.*, Capital Broadcasting Co. v. Mitchell, 333 F.Supp. 582 (D.D.C.1971).

44. Capital Broadcasting Co., 333 F. Supp. at 584.

45. *Id.* at 585–586.

46. *See* David A. Welkowitz, *Smoke in the Air: Commercial Speech and Broadcasting* 7 Cardozo L. Rev. 47, 48 (1985); Matthew L. Miller, Note, *The First Amendment and Legislative Bans of Liquor and Cigarette Advertisements*, 85 Colum. L. Rev. 632, 632–633 (1985); *see also* Dunagin v. City of Oxford, Miss., 718 F.2d 738, 746 (5th Cir. 1983) (en banc).

47. *See* Linmark Associates, Inc. v. Township of Willingboro, 431 U.S. 85, 97

S.Ct. 1614, 52 L.Ed.2d 155 (1977); Virginia State Board of Pharmacy v. Virginia Citizens Consumer Council, Inc., 425 U.S. 748, 96 S.Ct. 1817, 48 L.Ed.2d 346 (1976); Bigelow v. Virginia, 421 U.S. 809, 95 S.Ct. 2222, 44 L.Ed.2d 600 (1975).

48. 425 U.S. 748, 96 S.Ct. 1817, 48 L.Ed.2d 346 (1976).

49. 447 U.S. 557, 100 S.Ct. 2343, 65 L.Ed.2d 341 (1980).

50. *See supra* section 3.3. A. at pp. 287–289 in Practitioners Edition Vol. 1.

51. *See* Matthew L. Miller, Note, *The First Amendment and Legislative Bans of Liquor and Cigarette Advertisements*, 85 Colum. L. Rev. 632 (1985); *see also* Cherie A. Binger, *Up in Smoke: Commercial*

skepticism as to their constitutionality.[52] Adding to this skepticism is the increasing questioning in recent years of the assumption that the broadcasting media are entitled to less First Amendment protection than are the print media.[53]

Countering this revisionary movement are two more recent decisions of the Supreme Court cutting back on constitutional support for commercial speech,[54] leading other commentators to suggest that bans on some or all aspects of tobacco and alcohol advertising would be constitutional.[55] In *Posadas de Puerto Rico Associates* v. *Tourism Company of Puerto Rico*,[56] a five-member majority upheld a complete ban on casino advertising directed to local residents although casino gambling itself was legal in Puerto Rico. Then Associate Justice Rehnquist writing for the majority accepted at face value the assertions of the tourism company that excessive casino gambling among local residents would produce serious harmful effects which the government had a substantial interest in preventing. He also accepted uncritically the idea that there was a direct connection between a total ban on such advertising and the reduction of demand by local residents for such gaming. And finally, without considering alternative means to reduce gambling by local residents, Justice Rehnquist held that the complete ban was no broader than necessary to serve the government's substantial interest. He then concluded that this ban on advertising met the test for constitutionality laid down earlier by the Court in *Central Hudson Gas & Elec. Corp.* v. *Public Service Comm'n.*[57]

Much the same uncritical and paternalistic analysis by the majority in *Posadas* can be overlaid on the electronic media advertising ban for tobacco products. Tobacco products are legal; the harm they cause, according to the Surgeon General and other medical experts, is immense and therefore the government has a substantial interest in preventing there consumption; common sense tells us that advertising must increase demand for tobacco products particularly among the young; and a

Speech and a Tobacco Products Advertising Ban, 54 Tenn. L. Rev. 703 (1987).

52. *See* David S. Welkowitz, *Smoke in the Air: Commercial Speech and Broadcasting*, 7 Cardozo L. Rev. 47 (1985).

53. *See, e.g.*, Jonathan W. Emord, *The First Amendment Invalidity of FCC Ownership Regulations*, 38 Cath. L. Rev. 401, 402–403 (1989); Matthew L. Spitzer, *Controlling the Content of Print and Broadcast*, 58 So. Calif. L. Rev. 1349 (1985) (economic analysis); Mark S. Fowler & Daniel L. Brenner, *A Marketplace Approach to Broadcast Regulation*, 60 Tex. L. Rev. 207, 218–219 (1982).

54. Posadas de Puerto Rico Associates v. Tourism Co. of Puerto Rico, 478 U.S. 328, 106 S.Ct. 2968, 92 L.Ed.2d 266 (1986); Central Hudson Gas & Elec. Corp. v. Public Service Comm'n, 447 U.S. 557, 100 S.Ct. 2343, 65 L.Ed.2d 341, (1980). For a detailed

analysis of *Central Hudson* and *Posadas*, see *supra*, pp. 286-291.

55. *See* Vincent Blasi & Henry P. Monaghan, *The First Amendment and Cigarette Advertising*, 256 J.A.M.A. 502 (1986); (arguing for the constitutionality of a complete ban on all cigarette advertising even before the Supreme had decided cases more favorable to the authors' position); Mark A. Conrad, *Board of Trustees of the State University of New York v. Fox—The Dawn of a New Age of Commercial Speech Regulation of Tobacco and Alcohol*, 9 Cardozo A. & E. L. Rev. 61, 92–98 (1990).

56. 478 U.S. 328, 348, 106 S.Ct. 2968, 2980 92 L.Ed.2d 266, 285 (1986).

57. *Id.* at 344, 106 S. Ct. at 2978, 92 L. Ed. 2d at 283.

complete ban of tobacco product advertising over the powerful electronic media is no broader than necessary to reduce consumption, particularly among impressionable young people.

This *Posadas*-type analysis favoring the constitutionality of tobacco advertising bans is strengthened by the holding in the subsequent case of *Board of Trustees of the State University of New York* v. *Fox* modifying the fourth prong of the *Central Hudson* test by eliminating the requirement that control of advertising involve the "least restrictive measure" effective to safeguard the state's substantial interest and substituting therefor the requirement of only a reasonable fit between the legislature's ends and the means chosen by it to accomplish those ends.[58] After *SUNY* it need only be shown that a total ban on electronic media advertising of tobacco products is reasonably related to the government's substantial interest in reducing consumption to protect the public health.[59]

While it is difficult to predict what the Court would do if confronted with a new challenge to the electronic media ban, a strong case for constitutionality based on *Posadas* and *SUNY* could be made. However, the continuing strength of these two cases, particularly *Posadas*, has been put in question by the Court's recent decision in *City of Cincinnati* v. *Discovery Network, Inc.*[60] questioning the "fit" between a complete ban on certain periodical distribution boxes on the streets of Cincinnati and the interest in public safety and esthetics as not being reasonable because the benefits to be derived were "minute" or "paltry" and *44 Liquormart, Inc.* v. *Rhode Island*[61] in which a plurality of the Court rejected the rationale of *Posadas*. While the benefits obtained from a total ban on tobacco advertising or even the limited ban on electronic media advertising may, in contrast to *Discovery Network*, be great, that case could signal a retreat by the Court from its earlier anti-commercial speech approach in *Posadas* and *SUNY* and ultimately resulting in the disapproval of such bans.

Perhaps more important is the change of personnel on the Court. Justice White who retired was a member of the majority in both *Posadas* and *SUNY*. His replacement, Justice Ruth Bader Ginsburg, may have a different view of the scope of constitutional protection of commercial speech. But, in sum, *Capital Broadcasting Co.*, shaky though it may be as precedent for the constitutionality of the electronic media ban, is still in place.

c. *Restricting Tobacco Advertising Directed to Minors*

After considerable study and gathering much evidence on the harm done to the public health by minors taking up the smoking of cigarettes

---

58. 492 U.S. 469, 109 S.Ct. 3028, 106 L.Ed.2d 388 (1989).

59. *See* Mark A. Conrad, Board of Trustees of the State University of New York v. Fox—*The Dawn of a New Age of Commercial Speech Regulation of Tobacco and Alcohol,* 9 Cardozo A. & E. L. Rev. 61, 96–97 (1990).

60. 507 U.S. 410, 113 S.Ct. 1505, 123 L.Ed.2d 99 (1993).

61. 517 U.S. 484, 116 S.Ct. 1495, 134 L.Ed.2d 711 (1996).

chewing of smokeless tobacco and snorting of snuff, the Food and Drug Administration promulgated final regulations in 1996 sharply curtailing the freedom of manufacturers of such tobacco products to advertise their wares.[62] Sections 897.24 and 897.25 deal with the labeling of cigarette smokeless tobacco and snuff packages and require them to identify the precise tobacco product contained within and bear the language "Nicotine—Delivery Device for Persons 18 or Older."[63]

The advertising restrictions are found in sections 897.30 and 897.32.[64] Section 897.30 begins permissively in paragraph (a)(1) by allowing manufacturers, distributors and retailers to advertise their tobacco product brand names in nonprofit of sale nonelectronic media, in point of sale promotional material including audio and video formats.[65] If a manufacturer, distributor or retailer intends to advertise their products in a medium other than those listed in paragraph (a)(1), it must notify the FDA 30 days before the advertising appears of the medium it will use and discuss the extent to which the advertising may be seen by persons under the age of eighteen.[66]

Paragraph (b) prohibits outdoor advertising of cigarettes or smokeless tobacco within 1,000 feet of the perimeter of any public playground or playground area in a public park, elementary school or secondary school.[67]

Section 897.32(a) limits advertising and labeling of cigarettes or smokeless tobacco to black text on a white background. There are two exceptions to this proscription. The first encompasses the situation where labeling or advertising is indoors and affixed to a wall or fixture at the point of vending machine sales and cannot be viewed from outside the facility.[68] The second exception covers advertising appearing in any publication that the manufacturer, distributor, or retailer demonstrates is an adult publication.[69] An adult publication is defined as one whose readers include those younger than eighteen years of age, those readers constitute no more than fifteen percent of the total readership and the publication is read by fewer than two million persons younger than eighteen years of age, as measured by competent and reliable survey evidence.[70]

Labeling and advertising in an audio format is limited to words only with no music or sound effects.[71] Labeling and advertising in a video format is limited to static black text on a white background.[72]

Finally, all permitted advertising is required to include the product's established name and a statement of its intended use. The required

62. 61 Fed. Reg. 44617–618 (Aug. 28, 1996), *codified at* 21 C.F.R. §§ 897.24 and 897.25, 897.30 and 897.32 (1997).

63. 61 Fed. Reg. 44617 (Aug. 28, 1996), *codified at* 21 C.F.R. §§ 897.24 and 897.25 (1997).

64. *Id.* at §§ 897.30, 897.32.

65. *Id.* at § 897.30 (a)(1).

66. *Id.* at § 897.30 (a)(2).

67. *Id.* at § 897.30(b).

68. *Id.* at § 897.32(a)(1).

69. *Id.* at § 897.32(a)(2).

70. *Id.*

71. *Id.* at § 897.32(b)(1).

72. *Id.* at § 897.32(b)(2).

statement concludes with the words "A Nicotine–Delivery Device for Persons 18 or Older."[73]

On its face this regulatory labeling and advertising scheme appears to conflict with commercial speech protections of the First Amendment because of its breadth and total elimination of many traditional forms of tobacco advertising. But because the regulations are directed to the protection of the health and welfare of children[74] and First Amendment safeguards for commercial advertising are weaker than for political expression,[75] a case can certainly be made for their constitutionality.

However, it was not on constitutional grounds that this regulatory scheme was struck down. In *Coyne Beahm, Inc. v. United States Food & Drug Administration*[76] the United States District Court for the Middle District of North Carolina held that the Food and Drug Administration had no statutory authority to promulgate regulations limiting the advertising of tobacco products[77] but did uphold the FDA's statutory authority to require tobacco products to bear the product's established name and a statement of its intended use as a nicotine delivery device.[78] Both sides to the tobacco regulation dispute have noted an appeal to the United States Court of Appeals for the Fourth Circuit sitting in Richmond, Virginia.

2. Alcoholic Beverages

Many of the same considerations regarding the constitutionality of the federal ban on tobacco product advertising discussed above may be relevant to state bans on the advertising of alcoholic beverages over the electronic media, especially the *Central Hudson* analysis. But the analysis here is made more concrete by the presence of several precedents regarding alcohol advertising and, at the same time, made more complex by the presence of the twenty-first amendment to the United States Constitution.[79]

---

73. *Id.* at § 897.32(c).

74. *See* Penn Advertising of Baltimore, Inc. v. Mayor and City Council of Baltimore, 101 F.3d 332 (4th Cir.1996), *reaffirming* 63 F.3d 1318 (4th Cir.1995) *on remand from the Supreme Court*, 518 U.S. 1030, 116 S.Ct. 2575, 135 L.Ed.2d 1090 (1996), cert. denied 520 U.S. 1204, 117 S.Ct. 1569, 137 L.Ed.2d 715 (remand based on 44 Liquormart, Inc. v. Rhode Island, 517 U.S. 484, 116 S.Ct. 1495, 134 L.Ed.2d 711 (1996)); *cf.* New York v. Ferber, 458 U.S. 747, 102 S.Ct. 3348, 73 L.Ed.2d 1113 (1982); Ginsberg v. New York, 390 U.S. 629, 88 S.Ct. 1274, 20 L.Ed.2d 195 (1968); Prince v. Massachusetts, 321 U.S. 158, 64 S.Ct. 438, 88 L.Ed. 645, (1944).

75. *See, e.g.,* Central Hudson Gas & Elec. Corp. v. Public Service Comm'n, 447 U.S. 557, 100 S.Ct. 2343, 65 L.Ed.2d 341 (1980); JOHN E. NOWAK & RONALD D. ROTUNDA, CONSTITUTIONAL LAW 1062 (5th ed. 1995); Jef I. Richards, *Politicizing Cigarette Advertising*, 45 Cath. U. L. Rev. 1147, 1162–1163 (1996) (the author decries the weakness of First Amendment protection for tobacco advertising and suggests that the politicizing of the issue transforms "Joe Camel" into a political figure entitled to political speech protection.). *See also* Howard K. Jeruchimowitz, Note, *Tobacco Advertisements and Commercial Speech Balancing: A Potential Cancer to Truthful, Nonmisleading Advertisements of Lawful Products*, 82 Corn. L. Rev. 432 (1997).

76. 966 F.Supp. 1374 (M.D.N.C.1997).

77. *Id.* at 1083–1086.

78. *Id.* at 1086.

79. U.S. Const. amend. XXI, repealing U.S. Const. amend. XVIII (1933).

That amendment provides a unique delegation of specific authority to the states, territories or possessions of the United States to regulate the transportation, or importation for delivery or use therein of intoxicating liquors and makes the control of advertising of these products *sui generis*.[80] The power to control alcoholic products in interstate commerce would seem to include regulation of advertising to stimulate consumption of those products.[81] But that power of the states over interstate and foreign commerce in alcohol is not dispositive of the issue of the constitutionality of advertising restrictions under the First and Fourteenth Amendments.[82]

The precise relationship between the twenty-first amendment and First Amendment had not for a considerable time been explicated clearly. This lack of a clear explanation of the interface between the two amendments can be explained by the fact that state and lower federal courts dealing with challenges to the constitutionality of state regulation of advertising of alcoholic beverages tended, in the first instance, to find no violation of the First Amendment under the four-part test set down in *Central Hudson* and thus detailed discussion of that interface was considered unnecessary.[83] In these cases the twenty-first amendment was used simply as a make-weight to bolster the determination, pursuant to the second prong of *Central Hudson*, that the state has a substantial interest in regulating the advertising of alcoholic beverages, or as a questionable justification for shifting the burden of proof on the issue of the constitutionality of regulation from the state to the challenger[84] or

80. *See* Dunagin v. City of Oxford Miss., 718 F.2d 738, 743–745 (5th Cir.1983), *cert. denied*, 467 U.S. 1259, 104 S.Ct. 3553–3554, 82 L.Ed.2d 855 (1984); Oklahoma Telecasters Ass'n. v. Crisp, 699 F.2d 490, 498 (10th Cir.1983), *rev'd on other grounds sub nom.*Capital Cities Cable, Inc. v. Crisp, 467 U.S. 691, 104 S.Ct. 2694, 81 L.Ed.2d 580 (1984); Queensgate Investment Co. v. Liquor Control Commission, 69 Ohio St.2d 361, 366, 433 N.E.2d 138, 141–142 (1982), *appeal dismissed for want of a substantial federal question* 459 U.S. 807, 103 S.Ct. 31, 74 L.Ed.2d 45 (1982); *see also* S & S Liquor Mart, Inc. v. Pastore, 497 A.2d 729, 732 (1985).

81. *See* Oklahoma Telecasters Ass'n., 699 F.2d at 498–499 ("In this case . . . we must consider the Twenty-first Amendment in the light of the First Amendment."); Queensgate Investment Co., 69 Ohio St. 2d at 366, 433 N.E.2d at 141–142; *cf.* Craig v. Boren, 429 U.S. 190, 206–09, 97 S.Ct. 451, 461–63, 50 L.Ed.2d 397, 412–414 (1976); Wisconsin v. Constantineau, 400 U.S. 433, 436, 91 S.Ct. 507, 509, 27 L.Ed.2d 515, 518 (1971).

82. *See, e.g.* Oklahoma Telecasters Ass'n, 699 F.2d 490; Queensgate Investment Co., 69 Ohio St.2d 361, 433 N.E.2d 138; Rhode Island Liquor Stores Ass'n v. Evening Call Pub. Co., 497 A.2d 331 (R.I. 1985).

83. *See* 44 Liquormart Inc. v. Rhode Island, 39 F.3d 5, 6–8 (1st Cir.1994), *rev'd* 517 U.S. 484, 116 S.Ct. 1495, 134 L.Ed.2d 711 (1996); Oklahoma Telecasters Ass'n., 699 F.2d at 500; Queensgate Investment Co., 69 Ohio St. at 366, 433 N.E. 2d at 141–142; S & S Liquor Mart, Inc., 497 A.2d at 732.

84. *See* Rhode Island Liquor Stores Ass'n., 497 A.2d at 337 n.7. The Rhode Island Supreme Court's placement of the burden of proof on the First Amendment challenger of alcohol advertising regulation flies in the face of the United States Supreme Court's footnote in *Bolger v. Youngs Drug Prods. Corp.*, 463 U.S. 60, 71 n. 20, 103 S.Ct. 2875, 2882 n. 20, 77 L.Ed.2d 469, 480 n. 20 (1983) wherein the Court said, "The party seeking to uphold a restriction on commercial speech carries the burden of justifying it." The Rhode Island court gives no reason why an evidentiary rule of First Amendment jurisprudence should be turned inside out merely because the twenty-first amendment provides authority to regulate the advertising of intoxicating liquids other than that the amendment strengthens the presumption of constitutionality of that reg-

simply increasing the challenger's burden by strengthening the normal presumption of constitutionality of legislative actions.[85]

Recently, the Supreme Court thought it necessary to consider the relationship between the amendments. In *44 Liquormart, Inc.* v. *Rhode Island*[86] a six-member majority held that the twenty-first amendment plays no part in determining the constitutionality of government regulation of alcoholic beverage advertising. Justice Stevens, writing for the Court, echoed the words of an earlier decision saying, " 'the [twenty-first] Amendment does not license the States to ignore their obligations under other provisions of the Constitution,' "[87] one of those provisions being the First Amendment. Thus, government regulators are left to defend limitations on and prohibitions of alcohol advertising by meeting the requirements of *Central Hudson*.[88]

In the past the regulators have had no problem regarding the first requirement that what is advertised must be legal and the advertising not be misleading. In all of the states involved in this type of litigation the sale and consumption of alcoholic beverages is legal and the veracity of the proposed or actual advertising is not in issue.

Nor regarding the second requirement has there been any problem for proponents of regulation establishing a substantial governmental interest in controlling the consumption of alcohol. When the force of the twenty-first amendment is added to realistic governmental concerns about the threat to the public health and safety engendered by over-consumption of alcoholic beverages, the conclusion that the second test of *Central Hudson* is met in these cases has been easily reached.[89]

The question raised by the third prong of the *Central Hudson* test is more problematic. Does regulation of alcohol advertising reduce demand for and consumption of intoxicating beverages? Most courts make the *a priori* assumption that it does, often supporting their conclusions by appeals to common sense and, in essence, asking why the liquor industry

ulation. But strength of presumptions and burden of proof are two very different aspects of evidence, and it does not follow that a strengthened presumption results in a shift of the burden of proof.

85. *See* 44 Liquormart Inc. v. Rhode Island, 39 F.3d 5, 7–8 (1st Cir.1994), *rev'd*, 517 U.S. 484, 116 S.Ct. 1495, 134 L.Ed.2d 711 (1996); Dunagin v. City of Oxford, Miss., 718 F.2d 738, 745 (5th Cir.1983), cert. denied, 467 U.S. 1259, 104 S. Ct. 3553–3554, 82 L. Ed. 2d 855 (1984); S & S Liquor Mart, Inc. v. Pastore, 497 A.2d 729, 732 (R.I.1985).

86. 517 U.S. 484, 116 S.Ct. 1495, 134 L.Ed.2d 711 (1996).

87. *Id.* at 514, 116 S. Ct. at 1514, 134 L. Ed. 2d at 736.

88. *See* Rubin v. Coors Brewing Co., 514 U.S. 476, 115 S.Ct. 1585, 131 L.Ed.2d 532 (1995) (striking down a *federal* prohibition of labeling malt beverages for alcoholic strength because it did not comply with certain of *Central Hudson's* requirements).

89. Indeed, this conclusion is normally not challenged. *See*, *e.g.*, Dunagin v. City of Oxford, Miss., 718 F.2d 738, 747 (5th Cir. 1983), cert. denied, 467 U.S. 1259, 104 S. Ct. 3553–3554, 82 L.Ed.2d 855 (1984); Oklahoma Telecasters Ass'n v. Crisp, 699 F.2d 490, 500 (10th Cir.1983), *rev'd on grounds not directly involving regulation of advertising sub nom.* Capital Cities Cable Inc. v. Crisp, 467 U.S. 691, 104 S.Ct. 2694, 81 L.Ed.2d 580 (1984); Michigan Beer & Wine Wholesalers Ass'n. v. Attorney General, 142 Mich.App. 294, 307–309, 370 N.W.2d 328, 333 (1985); S & S Liquor Mart, Inc. v. Pastore, 497 A.2d 729, 732 (R.I.1985).

interests would spend money for advertising their products if not to sell more of them.[90]

The cases are singularly devoid of studies supporting the conclusion that advertising increases consumption. Indeed, what studies there are seem rather to support the conclusion that regulation of price advertising has no effect on consumption.[91] In *Michigan Beer & Wine Wholesalers Association* v. *Attorney General*,[92] the Michigan Court of Appeals struck down a state regulation restricting the advertising of prices and brands of liquor, wine and beer because the state could not establish that its restrictions directly advanced its interest in promoting temperance. This appellate court emphasized that the burden of proof was on the proponents of state regulation to justify restrictions on commercial speech and that *a priori* assumptions and irrelevant studies are not sufficient for that purpose.[93] If the Michigan appeals court is correct in its allocation of the burden of proof,[94] it would be difficult, indeed, for proponents of alcohol advertising restrictions to satisfy the constitutional requirements of the third prong of *Central Hudson*.

If the proponents are successful they must then satisfy the fourth and final prong by establishing that the restrictions on advertising are a reasonable means to achieving the governmental end of controlling consumption.[95] In cases of price or brand advertising regulation, the regulators make the argument that other types of alcohol advertising are permitted, making price and brand regulation limited enough to meet constitutional requirements.[96] But the very narrowness or alleged reasonable fit of these restrictions brings into question whether a ban simply on price and brand advertising really advances the state's sub-

90. *See* Dunagin, 718 F.2d at 747–750; Oklahoma Telecasters Ass'n, 699 F.2d at 500–501; Queensgate Investment Co., 69 Ohio St. 2d at 366, 433 N.E.2d at 142.

91. *See* Seagram & Sons v. Hostetter, 16 N.Y.2d 47, 53–54, 262 N.Y.S.2d 75, 77, 209 N.E.2d 701, 702–703 (1965); *see also* *Michigan Beer & Wine Wholesalers Ass'n.* v. *Attorney General*, 142 Mich.App. 294, 309–310, 370 N.W.2d 328, 336 (1985).

92. 142 Mich.App. 294, 370 N.W.2d 328 (1985).

93. *Id.* at 309, 370 N.W.2d at 335–336. The court cited footnote 20 in *Bolger* v. *Youngs Drug Prods. Corp.*, 463 U.S. 60, 71, 103 S.Ct. 2875, 2882, 77 L.Ed.2d 469, 480 (1983) in support of its allocation of the burden of proof. That footnote as part of the opinion of the court in *Bolger* states, "The party seeking to uphold a restriction on commercial speech carries the burden of justifying it." The burden of proof issue stands out in *Michigan Beer & Wine Wholesalers* because, in a reversal of the normal position of the parties, it was the state attorney general who was challenging the

constitutionality of the advertising regulations of the Liquor Control Commission and it was private interests who were defending their constitutionality.

94. One court has disputed this allocation holding that the twenty-first amendment justifies the imposition of the burden of proof on the challenger of state regulation. *See* Rhode Island Liquor Stores Ass'n v. Evening Call Pub. Co., 497 A.2d 331, 337 n. 7 (1985).

95. This is the fourth prong of *Central Hudson* as modified in Board of Trustees of the State University of New York v. Fox, 492 U.S. 469, 480, 109 S.Ct. 3028, 3035, 106 L.Ed.2d 388, 403–404 (1989).

96. *See* S & S Liquor Mart, Inc. v. Pastore, 497 A.2d 729, 735 (R.I.1985). *See also* Queensgate Investment Co., 69 Ohio St.2d 361, 366, 433 N.E.2d 138, 142, *appeal dismissed for want of a substantial federal question* 459 U.S. 807, 103 S.Ct. 31, 74 L.Ed.2d 45 (1982).

stantial interest in reducing alcohol consumption as required by the third prong of *Central Hudson*.[97]

If regulation is broadened to restrict all or most alcohol advertising over specified media of communications in an attempt to assure advancement of the governmental interest in depressing consumption, the argument has been made that such restrictions are too broad, violating the fourth prong and thereby trenching on protected First Amendment interests. The rejoinder provided by the United States Courts of Appeal for the Fifth and Tenth Circuits in upholding restrictions on electronic media advertising imposed by Mississippi and Oklahoma is first that total bans on advertising through particular media of communications were approved by a plurality of Supreme Court justices in *Metromedia, Inc.* v. *City of San Diego*,[98] second, and more substantively, that less restrictive alternatives such as tobacco-like warnings in advertising of the dangers of alcohol would not be effective and third that certain alternative means of advertising are available.[99]

It must be pointed out that this rejoinder is weak because only a plurality of the Supreme Court, none of whose members remain on the Court,[100] held that a near total ban on billboard advertising in San Diego was constitutionally permissible. Moreover, dismissing alternatives such as danger warnings in advertising as unlikely to be effective without first trying them smacks of suspect *a priori* reasoning and, finally, if alternative means of communication of alcohol advertising are available, the question of the effectiveness of the electronic media ban in reducing consumption is raised, just as it is with bans on price and brand advertising.

That state restrictions will not be upheld if they do not comport with all of the requirements imposed by *Central Hudson* was made abundantly clear by the Supreme Court in a recent case involving analogous *federal* regulation. In *Rubin v. Coors Brewing Co.*,[1] the Supreme Court struck down as violative of the First Amendment a federal

97. *Cf.* Michigan Beer & Wine Wholesalers Ass'n v. Attorney General, 142 Mich. App. 294, 311–312, 370 N.W.2d 328, 336 (1985); Seagram & Sons v. Hostetter, 16 N.Y.2d 47, 53–54, 262 N.Y.S.2d 75, 77, 209 N.E.2d 701, 702–703 (1965); Rhode Island Liquor Stores Ass'n v. Evening Call Pub. Co., 497 A.2d 331, 336 (R.I.1985)(stating the obverse proposition "that a more restrictive statutory scheme for reducing alcoholic consumption, such as a total ban on liquor advertising, would increase the risk that the statute violated the fourth facet of the Central Hudson analysis, relating to the extensiveness of the regulation.").

98. 453 U.S. 490, 507–09, 512 101 S.Ct. 2882, 2892–93, 2895, 69 L.Ed.2d 800, 814–816 (1981). And a partial ban on billboard advertising of alcoholic beverages by the city of Baltimore in places where children are expected to walk to school or engage in

play was upheld on remand from the Supreme Court following its decision in *44 Liquormart, Inc.* v. *Rhode Island*. Anheuser–Busch, Inc. v. Schmoke, 101 F.3d 325 (4th Cir.1996), cert. denied 520 U.S. 1204, 117 S.Ct. 1569, 137 L.Ed.2d 715 (1997).

99. *See* Dunagin v. City of Oxford, Miss., 718 F.2d 738, 751 (5th Cir.1983), cert. denied, 467 U.S. 1259, 104 S.Ct. 3553–3554, 82 L.Ed.2d 855 (1984); Oklahoma Telecasters Ass'n. v. Crisp, 699 F.2d 490, 501–502 (10th Cir.1983), *rev'd on other grounds sub nom.* Capital Cities Cable, Inc. v. Crisp, 467 U.S. 691, 104 S.Ct. 2694, 81 L.Ed.2d 580 (1984).

100. White, Stewart, Marshall and Powell, JJ.

1. 514 U.S. 476, 115 S.Ct. 1585, 131 L.Ed.2d 532 (1995).

statute prohibiting statements on malt beverage container labels as to "alcoholic content ... unless required by State law.... "[2] Because only 18 states affirmatively prohibit "strength" advertising of malt beverages beyond the labels themselves, brewers are free to advertise broadly the alcoholic strength of their products in much of the country if not on their labels. As the Court noted, "The failure to prohibit the disclosure of alcohol content in advertising which would seem to constitute a more influential weapon in any strength war than labels, makes no rational sense if the government's true aim is to suppress strength wars."[3] Thus, it was clear to the Court that the legislation failed the third prong of the *Central Hudson* test requiring that governmental restrictions on commercial speech advance the interest asserted "in a direct and material way."[4] The legislation in *Rubin* also failed the fourth prong of the *Central Hudson* test according to the Court because it was not sufficiently tailored in achieving the goal of preventing strength wars. As the respondent brewing company pointed out in the course of the litigation, there were alternatives less intrusive on First Amendment interests such as directly limiting the alcohol content of malt beverages.[5]

3. Fourteenth Amendment Equal Protection and Due Process

Certain other challenges to the validity of state restrictions on alcohol advertising have been made over the years. In *Dunagin* v. *City of Oxford, Mississippi*,[6] certain media attacked a regulation prohibiting anyone in the state of Mississippi from originating all but an extremely narrow range of advertising. Members of the print and electronic advertising media affected by the ban argued that such regulation improperly discriminated against local media because it allowed alcohol advertising to enter Mississippi from out-of-state media.[7] Since it had earlier ruled that no First Amendment rights of advertisers were implicated by the regulation, the appeals court held that strict scrutiny of the ban was not justified. Under the more relaxed test that classification not involving fundamental rights need only be rationally related to a state interest, here the control of alcohol consumption, the court found a rational basis for discrimination simply in the state's ability to regulate local media and its inability to control out of state media whose commercial messages cross the state's boundaries. According to the court, "The Equal Protection Clause does not require 'a legislature to enact a statute so broad that it may well be incapable of enforcement.' "[8]

---

2. 27 U.S.C.A. § 205(e)(2) (West Supp. 1996).

3. Rubin v. Coors Brewing Co., 514 U.S. 476, 488, 115 S.Ct. 1585, 1592, 131 L.Ed.2d 532, 542 (1995). Moreover, manufacturers are free to distinguish on their labels a class of stronger malt beverages by identifying them as "malt liquors." *Id.* at 488–489, 115 S. Ct. at 1592, 131 L.Ed.2d at 543.

4. *Id.* at 487, 115 S. Ct. at 1592, 131 L.Ed.2d at 541 (quoting Edenfield v. Fane, 507 U.S. 761, 767, 113 S.Ct. 1792, 1800, 123 L.Ed.2d 543, 555 (1993)).

5. *Id.* at 490–491, 115 S. Ct. at 1593, 131 L.Ed.2d at 544.

6. 718 F.2d 738 (5th Cir.1983), cert. denied 467 U.S. 1259, 104 S. Ct. 3553–3554, 82 L.Ed.2d 855 (1984).

7. *Id.* at 752.

8. *Id.* at 753; *see* Michael M. v. Superior Court, 450 U.S. 464, 474, 101 S.Ct. 1200, 1207, 67 L.Ed.2d 437 (1981).

Accepting *arguendo* the court's determination in *Dunagin* that First Amendments rights of local media were not violated, its ruling on the equal protection challenge seems correct. Under the relaxed test a rational basis can almost always be found for state regulation of alcohol advertising given the broad governmental interest involved.[9]

Due process challenges have also been mounted to the imposition of alcohol advertising restrictions. In *S & S Liquor Mart, Inc.* v. *Pastore*,[10] a liquor retailer argued that a Rhode Island statute prohibiting price advertising except within licensed premises violated the due process clause in that it constituted an arbitrary and unreasonable restriction on its liberty of contract and a taking of its property without due process of law.[11]

In upholding the statute (later struck down in *44 Liquormart*) the Rhode Island Supreme Court merely said that the prohibition on price advertising represented a reasonable means of furthering the state's significant interest in promoting temperance. This seems a rather cursory rationale for upholding the statute since state interests may be furthered even when regulation improperly restricts freedom of contract or involves an unjustified taking of property.[12]

4. Assessment and Prognosis

Until recently, it seemed very clear from the march of the appellate decisions that the judiciary, particularly the federal judiciary, was likely to give the benefit of the constitutional doubt to those favoring regulation of the advertising of alcoholic beverages. But that may no longer be the case. In the two recent cases of *Rubin* and *44 Liquormart*, the Supreme Court first struck down a federal prohibition of alcohol strength labeling as not comporting with the third and fourth requirements of *Central Hudson* and then struck down a state ban on price advertising and, at the same time, took away from state regulators the make-weight argument of the Twenty-first Amendment.

While it is too early to draw hard and fast conclusions from the Supreme Court's actions, it is safe to say that the federal courts, at least, will scrutinize liquor advertising regulations by the states more closely than in the past and will engage in more rigorous analysis pursuant to the *Central Hudson* standard.

9. *See* Boscia v. Warren, 359 F.Supp. 900 (E.D.Wis.1973); *cf.* S & S Liquor Mart, Inc. v. Pastore, 497 A.2d 729, 736 (R.I. 1985); *but see* Portwood v. Falls City Brewing Co., 318 S.W.2d 535, 536 (Ky.1958) (prohibition of illuminated alcohol advertising signs which could not be seen by patrons until they had entered retail liquor establishment bears little rational relationship to the control of alcoholic beverages).

10. 497 A.2d 729 (R.I.1985).

11. *Id.* at 736.

12. The modern due process analysis involving fundamental rights balanced against competing state interests does not appear applicable to this very old problem of regulating alcohol consumption. Other bases for challenging the validity of alcohol advertising restrictions beyond the scope of this chapter are treated in an annotation in American Law Reports. *See* M. David LeBrun, Annot., *Validity, Construction, and Effect of Statutes, Ordinances, or Regulations Prohibiting or Regulating Advertising of Intoxicating Liquors*, 20 A.L.R. 4th 600 (1983).

5. Lotteries and Casino Gambling

a. History

While lotteries have been present in the United States since the country's founding, most states until recently considered them a trap for their unwary citizens and sought to restrict them.[13] Congress has lent the states a hand by enacting, among other legislation,[14] the Anti–Lottery Act of 1890 which banned, under criminal penalty, the advertising of lotteries in newspapers and other printed matter deposited in the United States mail.[15] The Supreme Court quickly upheld this act under the First Amendment.[16] After the coming of broadcasting in the twentieth century, Congress passed parallel legislation, as part of the Federal Communications Act of 1934, making it a crime knowingly to broadcast "any advertisement of or information concerning any lottery, gift, enterprise or similar scheme, offering prizes dependent in whole or in part upon lot or chance.... "[17]

With the coming of the epidemic of state run lotteries beginning in the 1970's, Congress was forced to loosen the prohibition on the advertising of lotteries. In 1975 Congress added Section 1307 to the United States Criminal Code.[18] This section provides that other sections of the criminal code dealing with lotteries will not apply to advertisements, lists of prizes or other information concerning lotteries conducted by a state, lotteries authorized by a state and conducted by not-for-profit or governmental organizations and lotteries conducted occasionally by a commercial organization as a promotional activity "(A) contained in a publication published in that state or in a state which conducts such a lottery; or (B) broadcast by a radio or television station licensed to a location in that state or a state which conducts such a lottery.... "[19]

---

13. *See* United States v. Edge Broadcasting Co., 509 U.S. 418, 421, 113 S.Ct. 2696, 2700, 125 L.Ed.2d 345, 352 (1993).

14. *Id.*, 113 S. Ct. at 2700, 125 L.Ed.2d at 352.

15. 26 Stat. 465, *codified at* Rev. Stat. § 3894 (Supp. 2d ed. 1891).

16. Ex parte Rapier, 143 U.S. 110, 134–135, 12 S.Ct. 374, 374–375 36 L.Ed. 93, 102–103 (1892); *see* United States v. Edge Broadcasting Co., 509 U.S. at 421, 113 S. Ct. at 2701, 125 L.Ed.2d at 352.

17. 48 Stat. 1064, 1088–1089 (1934), *codified at* 18 U.S.C.A. § 1304, as amended (West Supp. 1993). The constitutionality of Section 316 of the Federal Communications Act was upheld in American Broadcasting Co. v. United States, 110 F.Supp. 374, 389, *aff'd* 347 U.S. 284, 74 S.Ct. 593, 98 L.Ed. 699 (1954).

18. Pub. L. 93–583 § 1, 88 Stat. 1916 (1975), *codified at* 18 U.S.C.A. § 1307 (West 1984 and Supp. 1996).

19. *Id.* § 1307(a), *as amended* (West Supp. 1993). The exact provisions of § 1307(a) are as follows:

(a) The provisions of sections 1301, 1302, 1303, and 1304 shall not apply to—

(1) an advertisement, list of prizes, or other information concerning a lottery conducted by a State acting under the authority of State law which is—

(A) contained in a publication published in that State or in a State which conducts such a lottery; or

(B) broadcast by a radio or television station licensed to a location in that State or a State which conducts such a lottery; or

(2) an advertisement, list of prizes, or other information concerning a lottery, gift enterprise, or similar scheme, other than one described in paragraph (1), that is authorized or not otherwise prohibited by the State in which it is conducted and which is—

The import of this statute is to leave in place all existing criminal prohibitions on advertising of lotteries and other games of chance not falling within the three classes of lottery sponsorship designated therein and on advertising of even the designated categories of lotteries through media not specifically exempted by the statute. The issue raised by this act is whether application of federal criminal statutes to non-exempt lotteries and media is constitutional in light of the recognition of First Amendment protection for commercial speech made subsequent to the enactment of the criminal prohibitions involved and in light, as well, of the equal protection clause of the Fourteenth Amendment.

b. The Constitutionality of Sections 1304 and 1307 of Title 18, United States Code

(1) Edge Broadcasting and lottery advertising

These constitutional questions were presented to the Supreme Court in *United States* v. *Edge Broadcasting Co.*[20] In that case Edge Broadcasting Company was the owner of an FM station licensed by the Federal Communications Commission (FCC) to Elizabeth City, North Carolina. The station, known by the catch phrase "Power 94" and broadcasting from Moyock, North Carolina, is literally at the northeastern edge of North Carolina and draws 92.2 percent of its listening audience and 95 percent of its advertising revenue from the state of Virginia.[21] Because Edge is licensed to serve a North Carolina city, and North Carolina had no state-conducted or authorized lottery, the broadcaster is prohibited by the plain words of Section 1304 of Title 18 of the United States Code from broadcasting advertisements for Virginia's state run lottery.[22] Motivated by a serious loss of revenue from its inability to accept advertising from the Virginia lottery, Edge filed suit against the United States and the Federal Communications Commission whose concurrent duty it is to enforce the section.[23] Edge sought a declaratory judgment that Section 1304 together with the exemption statute, Section 1307, and FCC regulations issued thereunder, violated the First and Fourteenth Amend-

---

(A) conducted by a not-for-profit organization or a governmental organization; or

(B) conducted as a promotional activity by a commercial organization and is clearly occasional and ancillary to the primary business of that organization.

20. 509 U.S. 418, 113 S.Ct. 2696, 125 L.Ed.2d 345 (1993).

21. *Id.* at 423–424, 113 S. Ct. at 2702, 125 L. Ed. 2d at 353.

22. 18 U.S.C.A. § 1304, as amended (West Supp. 1993) provides:

Whoever broadcasts by means of any radio or television station for which a license is required by any law of the Unit-

ed States, or whoever, operating any such station, knowingly permits the broadcasting of, any advertisement of or information concerning any lottery, gift enterprise, or similar scheme, offering prizes dependent in whole or in part upon lot or chance, or any list of the prizes drawn or awarded by means of any such lottery, gift enterprise, or scheme, whether said list contains any part or all of such prizes, shall be fined not more than $1,000 or imprisoned not more than one year, or both. Each day's broadcasting shall constitute a separate offense.

23. *See* Federal Communications Comm'n v. American Broadcasting Co., 347 U.S. 284, 289, 74 S.Ct. 593, 597, 98 L.Ed. 699, 705 (1954).

ments. Injunctive relief was sought as well to prevent enforcement of these statutes and regulations.

The United States District Court for the Eastern District of Virginia, after construing the statutes not to cover the broadcast of noncommercial information about lotteries, held that even as to commercial messages the statutes violated the First Amendment as applied to Edge under the *Central Hudson* four-part test. The trial court concluded that the statutes failed the third requirement because they did not directly advance North Carolina's interest in reducing or eliminating gambling on lotteries by its citizens. The ban on lottery advertising by the licensee's radio station was ineffective in furthering this interest given the small number of listeners in North Carolina and given the alternative Virginia based media's messages about the Virginia lottery flowing into the state.

A divided Fourth Circuit, in an unpublished per curiam opinion, affirmed, rejecting the government's claim that the trial court had erred in judging the validity of the statutes on an "as applied" standard looking at their effect on Edge's situation alone. The Supreme Court granted certiorari and reversed in an opinion by Justice White.

Cutting to the heart of the case, Justice White proclaimed, "We have no doubt that the statutes directly advanced the governmental interest at stake in this case."[24] Taking issue with the lower courts' view of the governmental interest involved, Justice White found it to be *Congress'* concern to balance the interests of lottery and non-lottery states and that interest was directly served by applying the statutory restriction on advertising to *all* stations in North Carolina, regardless of whether the restriction had only marginal effect as applied to any one station.[25] "The statutes were not 'adopted to keep North Carolina residents ignorant of the Virginia Lottery for ignorance's sake,' " according to Justice White, "but to accommodate non-lottery states' interest in discouraging public participation in lotteries."[26]

Justice White also took issue with the lower courts' conclusion that prohibiting Virginia lottery commercial messages over the facilities of Edge's station would have, at best, marginal effect, pointing out that the percentage of radio listening time to the commercials would increase by 11 percent, given the numbers in the record, if "Power 94" were allowed to carry the lottery advertising.[27] "If there is an immediate connection between advertising and demand, and the federal regulation decreases advertising, it stands to reason that the policy of decreasing demand for gambling is correspondingly advanced. Accordingly, the Government may be said to advance its purpose by substantially reducing lottery advertising, even where it is not wholly eradicated."[28]

24. United States v. Edge Broadcasting Co., 509 U.S. at 428, 113 S. Ct. at 2704, 125 L. Ed. 2d at 356.

25. *Id.*

26. *Id.* at 433–434, 113 S. Ct. at 2707, 125 L. Ed. 2d at 360.

27. *Id.* at 431–432, 113 S. Ct. at 2706, 125 L. Ed. 2d at 358.

28. *Id.* at 434, 113 S. Ct. at 2707, 125 L. Ed. 2d at 360.

Justice White did not directly address Edge's equal protection claim but implicit in the opinion is the idea that statutes treating similar media of communications licensed to different states differently do not create invidious discrimination when the states have different policies directly relevant to the different treatment.

Taking issues with Justice White's First Amendment analysis, Justice Stevens, in a dissenting opinion joined by Justice Blackmun,[29] asserted that Congress' interest in enacting the two statutes was entirely derivative from the interest of the non-lottery states' in discouraging public participation in lotteries and that the suppression of truthful advertising regarding a neighboring state's legal lottery is a patently unconstitutional means of effectuating the federal government's asserted interest in protecting the policies of non-lottery states.[30] Justice Stevens also disagreed with the majority's conclusion that a state's interest in discouraging lottery participation by its citizens is substantial enough to justify the ban on advertising by local media, pointing to the sea change in public attitudes and the acceptance of state run lotteries in recent years.[31]

Justice White's valedictory First Amendment analysis here is open to question at least insofar as it holds that the third prong of the *Central Hudson* test permits a level of generality as to a statute's advancement of a governmental interest going beyond the statute's application to the case immediately at hand. In the *Central Hudson* case itself the Court discussed the directness of the link between Central Hudson Gas & Electric Corporation's own rate structure as affected by proposed promotional advertising and the demand for power that the New York Public Service Commission was trying to reduce by its ban on such advertising.[32] While no discussion was directed to the question of the level of generality required by the third prong, the Court seemed to be focusing on the impact of the advertising ban on the particular electric utility involved as its rate structure effected the state's interest in a reduced demand for electrical energy. None of the Court's commercial speech decisions following *Central Hudson* which actively focus on the third requirement of the test suggest a broader reach than that of measuring the impact of the facts directly at hand on the governmental interest involved.[33] Of course, the Court has the power to elaborate upon

29. *Id.* at 436, 113 S. Ct. at 2708, 125 L. Ed. 2d at 361.

30. *Id.* at 436–438, 113 S. Ct. at 2709, 125 L. Ed. 2d at 362. Justice Stevens supported his second proposition that the statutory means chosen to effectuate the derived interest were unconstitutional by citing *Bigelow v. Virginia*, 421 U.S. 809, 95 S.Ct. 2222, 44 L.Ed.2d 600 (1975) in which the Court held unconstitutional as applied a Virginia criminal statute utilized to convict a Virginia newspaper publisher for publishing an ad for abortion services in New York where such services were legal though they were not legal in Virginia.

31. *Id.* at 440, 113 S. Ct. at 2710–2711, 125 L. Ed. 2d at 364–365.

32. Central Hudson Gas & Elec. Corp. v. Public Service Comm'n, 447 U.S. 557, 568–570, 100 S.Ct. 2343, 2352–2353, 65 L.Ed.2d 341, 352–354 (1980).

33. *See* Posadas de Puerto Rico Associates v. Tourism Co. of Puerto Rico, 478 U.S. 328, 341–343, 106 S.Ct. 2968, 2977–2978, 92 L.Ed.2d 266 (1986); Bolger v. Youngs Drug Products Corp., 463 U.S. 60, 73, 103

or modify its own rules as it did in *Board of Trustees of the State University of New York v. Fox* in relaxing the fourth requirement of *Central Hudson* from a least restrictive effective alternative test to a "reasonable fit" test.[34] But a decent respect for the development of First Amendment doctrine requires, at the very least, a principled justification for such changes. Justice White's opinion is devoid of such justification and seems to be an *ad hoc* rationalization designed to save the constitutionality of two federal statutes.

c. Casino Advertising and the Constitutionality of Section 1304.

Section 1304 of title 18 of the United States Code was challenged anew in *Greater New Orleans Broadcasting Ass'n v. United States.*[35] Again, it was broadcast interests seeking the freedom to broadcast commercials explicitly referring to gaming activities but this time on behalf of casinos legally operating in Louisiana and Mississippi. These interests could not, of course, find comfort in the *lottery* exemption of section 1307 and had to make a frontal assault on section 1304 as violative of the First Amendment under the *Central Hudson* four-prong test. A panel of the United States Court of Appeals for the Fifth Circuit rejected the broadcasters' challenge to the statute and upheld its validity by a split vote.[36]

After noting that there was no dispute that the proposed commercial messages regarded activities legal in Louisiana and Mississippi, and would not be misleading,[37] the appeals court held that the government's interests in protecting states that did not countenance casino gambling from interstate broadcast messages promoting it and in discouraging the participation of its citizens in casino gambling with all of the attendant evils that such participation creates were substantial.[38]

S.Ct. 2875, 2884, 77 L.Ed.2d 469, 481–482 (1983); Metromedia Inc. v. City of San Diego, 453 U.S. 490, 508–512, 101 S.Ct. 2882, 2893–2895, 69 L.Ed.2d 800 815–818 (1981) (plurality opinion by Justice White); *see also* City of Cincinnati v. Discovery Network, Inc., 507 U.S. 410, 417–418, 113 S.Ct. 1505, 1510–1511, 123 L.Ed.2d 99, 108–109 (1993) (though concentrating on the fourth prong of *Central Hudson*, the Court shared the lower courts' view that the city's ban of respondent's 62 commercial periodical newsracks from the sidewalks out of more than 1500 remaining resulted in only a "minute" or "paltry" benefit to the city).

34. 492 U.S. 469, 475–481, 109 S.Ct. 3028, 3032–3035, 106 L.Ed.2d 388, 400–408 (1989).

35. 69 F.3d 1296 (5th Cir.1995), cert. granted, vacated and remanded 519 U.S. 801, 117 S.Ct. 39, 136 L.Ed.2d 3 (1996), *reaff'd* 149 F.3d 334 (5th Cir.1998), cert. granted ___ U.S. ___, 119 S.Ct. 863, 142 L.Ed.2d 716 (1999) (distinguishing *44 Li-*

quormart and *Rubin v. Coors*). *See* Dana M. Shelton, Greater New Orleans Broadcasting Ass'n v. United States, *The Fifth Circuit Upholds the Federal Ban on Casino Gambling Advertising against a First Amendment Challenge*, 70 Tul. L. Rev. 1725 (1996).

36. The broadcasters first had a threshold argument that 18 U.S.C.A. § 1304 did not cover commercials for casino gambling because casino games cannot be considered a "lottery, gift enterprises or similar scheme." The Fifth Circuit found this contention foreclosed by the Supreme Court's decision in *FCC v. American Broadcasting Co.*, 347 U.S. 284, 74 S.Ct. 593, 98 L.Ed. 699 (1954).

37. 69 F.3d at 1298–1299.

38. The court relied heavily on *Posadas de Puerto Rico Assoc. v. Tourism Co. of Puerto Rico*, 478 U.S. 328, 106 S.Ct. 2968, 92 L.Ed.2d 266 (1986) to support this conclusion.

As to the third test of *Central Hudson*, the appeals court held that the "fit" between the statutory means chosen and the government's interests was a proper one. Relying on *Posadas de Puerto Rico Assoc.* v. *Tourism Co. Of Puerto Rico*,[39] the Court said that "[i]t is axiomatic that the purpose and effect of advertising is to increase consumer demand."[40] Therefore, the suppression of casino advertising would reduce demand and further the government's legitimate interests.

As for the fourth prong of *Central Hudson* that the restriction on commercial speech be no more extensive than necessary to further the governments' interest or interests, the court held that the statutory restriction on casino advertising was narrowly tailored because limited to broadcast advertising. "No less restrictive alternative seems viable in view of the ability of broadcast signals to cross state borders."[41]

Chief Judge Politz dissented from the upholding of the statute and suggested a misapplication of *Central Hudson* by the majority by saying that "[w]hen the government would forbid dissemination of information about things which legally may be done, the *Central Hudson* test ought to be carefully conducted in order to protect ... core first amendment values."[42] He pointed out that the broadcast ban of casino advertising was now riddled with exceptions and in conflict with the policies of the many states which have legalized gambling.[43] Licensed casinos are, according to the Chief Judge, allowed to advertise their existence, to air the word "casino" as part of their business name and to refer to the non-gambling amenities and the "excitement" offered within. Moreover, state-licensed casino gambling is advertised on billboards and in newspapers.[44]

Because the statute is so riddled with exceptions and ineffectual in reducing consumer demand, it does not satisfy the third prong of *Central Hudson* test. "[F]aithful application of *Central Hudson* compels the conclusion that the residual ban on broadcasting direct references to the games played in the casinos amounts to little more than a gratuitous suppression of expression."[45]

Given the majority's reliance upon *Posadas*, whose precedential value has been seriously eroded by the majority opinion in *Discovery Network*[46] and the plurality opinion in *44 Liquor Mart*,[47] its supporting citation[48] to the trial court decision and opinion in *Valley Broadcasting*

---

39. *Id.* at 342, 106 S. Ct. at 2977, 92 L. Ed. 2d at 281.

40. Greater New Orleans Broadcasting Ass'n, 69 F.3d at 1301.

41. *Id.* at 1302.

42. *Id.* at 1303 (position reaffirmed on basis of *44 Liquormart*, 149 F.3d at 341), certiorari was granted a second time, ___ U.S. ___, 119 S.Ct. 863, 142 L.Ed.2d 716 (1999).

43. *Id.* The Chief Judge's unofficial count put the number of states with licensed casinos at 21. *Id.* at 1303 n.6.

44. *Id.* at 1303.

45. *Id.* at 1304.

46. 507 U.S. 410, 113 S.Ct. 1505, 123 L.Ed.2d 99 (1993).

47. 517 U.S. 484, 116 S.Ct. 1495, 134 L.Ed.2d 711 (1996).

48. Greater New Orleans Broadcasting Ass'n, 69 F.3d at 1299.

Co. v. United States[49] later reversed by the United States Court of Appeals for the Ninth Circuit[50] and the strong dissent of Chief Judge Politz, there is some reason to believe that section 1304 will eventually be struck down as an unconstitutional anachronism.[51]

C.* Electronic Advertising Directed To Children

D.* Regulation of Advertising by Telephone and Facsimile Transmission

E. Advertising By Professionals

1. Historical Background of Lawyer Advertising

Given the nineteenth and early twentieth century view of the legal profession as one in which selfless service was paramount and pursuit of commercial gain was, at least publicly, to be frowned upon,[52] it is not surprising that soon after the rise in the late nineteenth century of modern bar associations in the United States[53] whose membership consisted initially of only elite practitioners,[54] the organized bar would seek to suppress advertising by lesser lawyers. It did so through ethical codes, the most influential, of course, being that of the American Bar Association which adopted its first Canons of Ethics in 1908 and its first anti-advertising opinion under the Canons in 1922.[55] Thereafter, the curtain rang down on such commercialism across the country as state and local

---

49. 820 F.Supp. 519, 524 (D.Nev.1993).

50. 107 F.3d 1328 (9th Cir.1997).

51. The Ninth Circuit struck down section 1304 as violative of the First Amendment rights of broadcasters because, given the exceptions for not for profit and Indian reservation casino operations, the statute did not adequately advance the government's recognized interest in protecting non-casino states from having their citizens receive gambling advertisements from sister casino states. Valley Broadcasting Co. v. United States, 107 F.3d 1328, 1335 (9th Cir.1997), petition for rehearing and rehearing in banc filed (April 11, 1997). The appeals court took guidance from *Rubin v. Coors Brewing Co.*, 514 U.S. 476, 115 S.Ct. 1585, 131 L.Ed.2d 532 (1995) which struck down an analogous statute (27 U.S.C.A. § 205)(e)(2) (West Supp. 1996) prohibiting brewers from disclosing on their labels the alcohol content of their products, because of numerous exceptions allowing disclosure elsewhere and allowing distillers to place such information on the labels of distilled spirits. *But compare* Greater New Orleans Broadcasting Assn. *on remand* at 149 F.3d 334.

* Published in Practitioners Edition, Vol. 1.

52. *See* Roscoe Pound, The Lawyer From Antiquity to Modern Times 5 (1953); Whitney Thier, Comment, *In a Dignified Manner: The Bar, the Court, and Lawyer Advertising*, 66 Tul. L. Rev. 527, 529–531 (1991) (an extraordinarily insightful essay on the mindset of the organized bar in relation to modern advertising); *see also* Tiffany S. Meyer and Robert E. Smith, *Attorney Advertising: Bates and a Beginning*, 20 Ariz. L. Rev. 427, 429–430 (1978).

53. Historically, the first modern bar association was the Association of the Bar of the City of New York, founded in 1870. *See* Roscoe Pound, the Lawyer From Antiquity to Modern Times 254 (1953). The American Bar Association was founded shortly after, in 1878, also in New York state. *Id.* at 255–58.

54. *See* Lloyd B. Snyder, *Rhetoric, Evidence, and Bar Agency Restrictions on Speech By Attorneys*, 28 Creighton L. Rev. 357, 360–364 (1995) (detailed historical review); Whitney Thier, Comment, *In a Dignified Manner: The Bar, The Court and Lawyer Advertising*, 66 Tul. L. Rev. 527, 531–533 (1991).

55. *Id.* at 532, 543 n.63.

bar associations adopted similar prohibitions and state courts issued disciplinary rules condemning advertising by members of the bar.

The medical profession was a bit slower to recognize the "evil" of informing the public about professional services, adopting a prohibition against this commercial activity in the American Medical Association's 1957 revision of its Principles of Medical Ethics. Section 5 prohibited the solicitation of patients and that section was interpreted to preclude advertising.[56] According to knowledgeable commentators, policing of the solicitation and advertising prohibitions by the local medical societies and bar associations was very effective.[57] But in the mid to late 1970s, tears began to appear in the shroud muffling commercial advertising by professionals and by the 1990s the shroud was very much tattered.

2.   The Sherman and Clayton Acts Get into the Act

When private organizations such as bar associations and medical societies act to suppress advertising and solicitation regarding professional services the inescapable result is a reduction in competition to provide these services to the public and a negative effect on price. This in turn raises questions as to whether the antitrust laws of the United States are being violated by this suppression.

In *Goldfarb v. Virginia State Bar*,[58] the Fairfax County Bar Association set minimum fees for legal services to which its members were to adhere. Enforcement of the fee schedule was left to the Virginia State Bar and its disciplinary committee. When a married couple, in the process of buying a home in Fairfax County, sought the necessary title examination they discovered that only members of the Virginia State Bar could legally perform that service and that they all had to charge at least the minimum fee set by the county bar. The couple contracted for the service at the minimum fee and then brought a class action in the United States District Court for the Eastern District of Virginia seeking injunctive relief and damages and alleging that the minimum fee schedule as it applied to legal services relating to real estate transactions and enforced by the state bar constituted price fixing in violation of Section 1 of the Sherman Act.[59]

The trial court found a violation of Section 1 by the private county bar association and enjoined enforcement of the fee schedule. The United States Court of Appeals for the Fourth Circuit reversed, holding that the local bar association was not in interstate trade and commerce as required by the Sherman Act and the state bar, as an agency of the state, was immune from liability under the act. On certiorari the Supreme

---

56. *See* American Medical Ass'n v. Federal Trade Comm'n, 638 F.2d 443, 446 (2d Cir.1980), *aff'd per curiam by an equally divided court*, 455 U.S. 676, 102 S.Ct. 1744, 71 L.Ed.2d 546 (1982); William C. Canby, Jr. & Ernest Gellhorn, *Physician Advertising: The First Amendment and the Sherman Act*, 1978 Duke L.J. 543, 546–547.

Enforcement was effectuated by the local medical societies. *Id.*

57. *Id.* at 547.

58. 421 U.S. 773, 95 S.Ct. 2004, 44 L.Ed.2d 572 (1975).

59. 15 U.S.C.A. § 1, as amended (West 1992).

Court reversed the appeals court judgment. It found that price fixing was present and competition suppressed; that the activities of the two bars sufficiently effected interstate commerce; and that neither were exempt from liability for their price fixing activities.[60]

Shortly after *Goldfarb*, the Court, by an equally divided vote, upheld, in a one sentence per curiam opinion,[61] a Second Circuit ruling that the American Medical Association's restrictions on advertising of prices and availability of individual and group medical services imposed by Section 5 of its Principles of Medical Ethics[62] violated Section 5 of the Federal Trade Commission (Clayton) Act.[63] The Second Circuit held that the AMA engaged in concerted actions with local and state medical societies to effectuate restraints on advertising and solicitation that prevented individual physicians from pursuing commercial activities protected by the act.[64]

Between the above two antitrust cases, the Supreme Court had a change of heart about the reach of the First Amendment in relation to commercial speech. Hard on the heels of the *Goldfarb* case from Virginia, the Court extended constitutional protection to commercial speech in *Bigelow v. Virginia,* involving suppression of advertising of medical abortion services[65] and *Virginia State Bd. of Pharmacy v. Virginia Citizens Consumer Council, Inc.* involving suppression of price advertising by pharmacists.[66]

Virginia's attempts to prohibit competition within the professions operating inside its borders through the suppression of advertising and price competition was leading inexorably toward a meeting of First

---

60. 421 U.S. at 781–792, 95 S. Ct. at 2010–2016, 44 L. Ed. 2d at 581–588.

61. American Medical Ass'n v. Federal Trade Comm'n, 455 U.S. 676, 102 S.Ct. 1744, 71 L.Ed.2d 546 (1982).

62. Section 5 of the Principles provided:

"A physician may choose whom he will serve. In an emergency, however, he should render service to the best of his ability. Having undertaken the care of a patient, he may not neglect him; and unless he has been discharged he may discontinue his services only after giving adequate notice. *He should not solicit patients*" (italics the authors').

63. American Medical Ass'n v. Federal Trade Comm'n, 638 F.2d 443 (2d Cir.1980). As a direct result of this ruling the American Dental Association entered into a consent agreement with the FTC not to engage in unfair competition by unduly restricting the advertising of its members.

64. *Id.* at 450. Interestingly, in attempting to fend off injunctive relief, the AMA invoked the protection of the First Amendment, claiming that the FTC's cease and desist order constituted a prior restraint on the AMA's speech and an impermissible interference with the right of free association with its membership. *Id.* at 451–452. In rejecting this dubious argument the Second Circuit quoted another case striking down restrictions on competition imposed by a professional society, *National Society of Professional Engineers v. United States,* 435 U.S. 679, 98 S.Ct. 1355, 55 L.Ed.2d 637 (1978) which prohibited competitive bidding for engineering services. "Just as an injunction against price fixing abridges the freedom of businessmen to talk to one another about prices, so too the injunction in this case must restrict the Society's range of expression on the ethics of competitive bidding." *Id.* at 697, 98 S. Ct. at 1367, 55 L. Ed. 2d at 654. The Second Circuit substituted "AMA" for the engineering society and the words "contract practices of physicians" for "competitive bidding." 638 F.2d at 452.

65. 421 U.S. 809, 95 S.Ct. 2222, 44 L.Ed.2d 600 (1975).

66. 425 U.S. 748, 96 S.Ct. 1817, 48 L.Ed.2d 346 (1976).

Amendment and antitrust doctrine and the substantial liberation of the learned professions to advertise.

3. And Then Came Bates

Particularly given the Supreme Court's endorsement of protection of commercial speech in *Virginia State Bd. of Pharmacy*, it was only a matter of time before some brave (or foolhardy) lawyer would advertise his services and fees in defiance of the organized bar and be disciplined by the legal establishment. That time came in *Bates v. State Bar of Arizona*.[67] There, at a period when the legal profession was in ferment over how best to make legal services available to poor and moderate income individuals, two lawyers, Bates and O'Steen, who had founded a legal clinic (then a new concept in legal services delivery), placed an advertisement in the Arizona Republic, a daily newspaper of general circulation in the Phoenix area, announcing the legal services the clinic provided and the fees charge for these services.[68] The ad constituted a clear violation of then existing ABA Disciplinary Rule 2–101(B) which was incorporated in Rule 29(a) of the Arizona Supreme Court's rules.[69] The two attorneys were recommended for one-week suspensions from the practice of law from the state bar. On appeal to the very same court whose rule they had recently breached, Bates and O'Steen argued that the court's rule violated the Sherman Act and the First Amendment. Not surprisingly the Arizona Supreme Court did not see it their way and imposed the recommended discipline.

On appeal the United States Supreme Court in an opinion by Justice Blackmun held first that unlike *Goldfarb* where the state of Virginia did not require adoption and enforcement of the bar's anticompetitive rule, it was an anticompetitive rule of a *state* governmental body that was involved in *Bates* and therefore the rule was immune from attack on antitrust grounds under the state action exemption.[70]

But second, the Court held that the Arizona Supreme Court rule under which the lawyers were disciplined did run afoul of the First and Fourteenth Amendments. Recognizing that it had specifically reserved the issue of advertising by professionals other than pharmacists in its *Virginia Pharmacy* opinion[71] because of perceived differences in the professions, the Court could not dispose of *Bates* by mere citation to the Virginia case. It therefore launched a full-scale First Amendment analy-

---

67. 433 U.S. 350, 51 Ohio Misc. 1, 97 S.Ct. 2691, 53 L.Ed.2d 810 (1977).

68. The ad is reproduced in the appendix to the Court's opinion. *Id.* at 385, 97 S. Ct. at 2710, 53 L. Ed. 2d at 837.

69. The disciplinary rule provided in part:

"(B) A lawyer shall not publicize himself, or his partner, or associate, or any other lawyer affiliated with him or his firm, as a lawyer through newspaper or magazine advertisements, radio or television announcements, display advertisements in

the city or telephone directories or other means of commercial publicity, nor shall he authorize or permit others to do so in his behalf."

70. 433 U.S. at 359–363, 97 S. Ct. at 2696–2698, 53 L. Ed. 2d at 820–823; *see* Parker v. Brown, 317 U.S. 341, 63 S.Ct. 307, 87 L.Ed. 315 (1943).

71. 425 U.S. 748, 773 n. 25, 96 S.Ct. 1817, 1831 n. 25, 48 L.Ed.2d 346, 365 n. 25 (1976).

sis, beginning with the question whether price advertising by lawyers was generally protected by the First Amendment.

Justice Blackmun considered six defenses of the Arizona rule proscribing advertising of fees and rejected every one. He was not impressed by the first claim of adverse effect on professionalism (the dignity argument), writing, "Since the belief that lawyers are somehow 'above' trade has become an anachronism, the historical foundation for the advertising restraint has crumbled."[72] Nor was he persuaded by the claim that advertising by attorneys was inherently misleading. He noted that even though services from attorney to attorney may vary slightly and legal services are not fungible, "these facts do not make advertising misleading so long as the attorney does the necessary work at the advertised price."[73] And though conceding that advertising does not provide a complete foundation on which to select an attorney, Justice Blackmun found it peculiar to deny the consumer some information by which to make a choice simply because all desirable information is not provided.[74]

The third argument advanced by the Arizona bar was that advertising would have the undesirable effect of stirring up litigation. Justice Blackmun's short answer to this rather strange assertion was that advertising by attorneys is not an unmitigated source of harm to the administration of justice and may even be beneficial. "Although advertising might increase the use of the judicial machinery, we cannot accept the notion that it is always better for a person to suffer a wrong silently than to redress it by legal action. As the bar acknowledges, 'the middle 70% of our population is not being reached or served by the legal profession'. . . .Advertising can help solve this acknowledged problem."[75]

The bar's fourth argument was the economic one that advertising would (1) increase overhead costs which would then be passed on to consumers in the form of higher fees and (2) create a higher entry barrier for young attorneys. These claims were labeled questionable and irrelevant to the question of First Amendment protection.[76]

The bar then made its fifth contention that advertising would have an adverse effect on the quality of legal services. The bar suggested that attorneys might advertise standard packages of services at set fees and would be inclined to provide only the standard packages regardless of whether they fit their clients' needs. Justice Blackmun's powerful response to this contention was two fold. First, restraints on advertising are an ineffective way of preventing shoddy professional work. "An attorney who is inclined to cut quality will do so regardless of the rule on advertising."[77] Second, even if advertising leads to the creation of legal

72. Bates, 433 U.S. at 371–372, 97 S. Ct. at 2703, 53 L. Ed. 2d at 828.

73. *Id.* at 372–373, 97 S. Ct. at 2703, 53 L. Ed. 2d at 829.

74. *Id.* at 374–375, 97 S. Ct. at 2704, 53 L. Ed. 2d at 829–830.

75. *Id.* at 376, 97 S. Ct. at 2705, 53 L. Ed. 2d at 831.

76. *Id.* at 377–378, 97 S. Ct. at 2706, 53 L. Ed. 2d at 831–832.

77. *Id.* at 378, 97 S. Ct. at 2706, 53 L. Ed. 2d at 832.

clinics emphasizing standardized procedures for the routine problems brought to them by persons of modest means, "it is possible that such clinics will improve service by reducing the likelihood of error" in these matters.[78]

The sixth contention generally questioning lawyer advertising was that it would make enforcement of ethical standards and protection of the public very difficult. Justice Blackmun's response here was like that of a fencer making contact with his rapier ("touché"). "It is at least somewhat incongruous for the opponents of advertising to extol the virtues and altruism of the legal profession at one point, and, at another, to assert that its members will seize the opportunity to mislead and distort. We suspect that, with advertising, most lawyers will behave as they always have: They will abide by their solemn oaths to uphold the integrity and honor of their profession and of the legal system."[79]

Justice Blackmun stated in summary that the Court was not persuaded that any of the bar's proffered justifications rose to the level of a sufficient reason to permit the general suppression of advertising by attorneys. He then turned to the question whether the First Amendment overbreadth doctrine was applicable to regulatory bans on professional advertising. Determining that it was not because of the hardiness of the commercial speech involved,[80] he reached the question whether Bates and O'Steen's specific ad was beyond the protection of the First Amendment.

The bar made three points in defense of its sanctioning the two attorneys: (1) the advertisement made reference to a "legal clinic," an undefined term; (2) the ad claimed that the clinic offered services at "very reasonable" prices but at least with regard to uncontested divorce services the fee advertising was no bargain; and (3) the ad did not inform the consumer that he could obtain a name change without the aid of an attorney.

Again, Justice Blackmun found the bar's arguments unpersuasive and he dismissed them in summary fashion. He was of the belief that the public would understand the nature of legal clinics as providing standardized and multiple services. As to the charge for an uncontested divorce, he noted that it was lower than that charged by the Arizona Bar's own Legal Services Program. And as to the bar's final point, the failure to disclose that a name change might be obtained from the courts without the aid of an attorney, Justice Blackmun pointed out that *most* legal services may be performed *pro se*.[81]

78. *Id.* at 378–379, 97 S. Ct. at 2706, 53 L. Ed. 2d at 832.

79. *Id.* at 379, 97 S. Ct. at 2707, 53 L. Ed. 2d at 833.

80. *Id.* at 380–381, 97 S. Ct. at 2707–2708, 53 L. Ed. 2d at 834.

81. *Id.* at 381–382, 97 S. Ct. at 2708, 53 L. Ed. 2d at 834–835. Given the weakness of the Arizona Bar's arguments it seems fair to observe that not all legal wisdom is reposed in practicing lawyers either individually or in combination, particularly when they are defending the legal establishment status quo. *See* Lloyd B. Snyder, *Rhetoric, Evidence and Bar Agency Restrictions on Speech By Attorneys*, 28 Creighton L. Rev. 357, 365 (1995) ("The organized bar has been singularly unsuccessful in defending

The opinion in *Bates* is defensive in nature, fending off arguments by the legal establishment that the protection of commercial speech recognized in *Virginia State Bd. of Pharmacy* should not be extended to advertising by lawyers and is therefore hardly a strong affirmation of the commercial speech rights of professional persons. Perhaps the defensive nature of the opinion can be explained by the fact that Justice Blackmun had given a strong endorsement to constitutional protection for commercial speech in the *Virginia Pharmacy* case just a year before.

The ruling is further weakened by Justice Blackmun's conciliatory words to the organized bar at the end of the opinion emphasizing the important role it had to play in insuring the prevention of false, deceptive or misleading commercial advertising and further emphasizing the sensitive nature of such advertising because of the general public's lack of sophistication concerning legal services. "[M]isstatements that might be overlooked or deemed unimportant in other advertising may be found quite inappropriate in legal advertising."[82] This proposition had the following footnote attached to it. "The determination whether an advertisement is misleading requires consideration of the legal sophistication of its audience. Cf. *Feil v. FTC*, 285 F.2d 879, 897 (C.A.9 1960). Thus, different degrees of regulation may be appropriate in different areas."[83] This footnote, combined with the Justice's rather cryptic statement that " ... the special problems of advertising on the electronic broadcast media will warrant special consideration," presented, surely inadvertently, an invitation to the organized bar to limit or undermine the just recognized freedom of commercial speech of lawyers and other professionals.[84] These words would haunt the Court as continued litigation over nearly two decades from the date of *Bates* would expend the Court's time, energy and resources.

Also contributing to this large volume of lawyer advertising litigation is the narrow thrust of the decision in *Bates*. As Justice Blackmun put it, "The constitutional issue in this case is only whether the State may prevent the publication in a newspaper of appellants' truthful advertisement concerning the availability and terms of routine legal services. We rule simply that the flow of such information may not be restrained ..."[85] The Court did not decide what, if any, protection extended to advertising claims as to *quality* of services. Nor did the Court confront the issues associated with in-person and more indirect

First Amendment challenges brought by attorneys."); *but see* Florida Bar v. Went for It, Inc., 515 U.S. 618 , 115 S.Ct. 2371, 132 L.Ed.2d 541 (1995) (temporal restriction as to when solicitation letters may be sent in personal injury and wrongful death cases upheld).

82. *Id.* at 383, 97 S. Ct. at 2709, 53 L. Ed. 2d at 835.

83. *Id.* at 384, 97 S. Ct. at 2709, 53 L. Ed. 2d at 835.

84. There is striking similarity between the issues raised by lawyer advertising and physician advertising, though the issues may diverge regarding face to face or more indirect solicitation. *See* William C. Canby, Jr. & Ernest Gellhorn, *Physician Advertising: The First Amendment and the Sherman Act*, 1978 Duke L.J. 543; *see also* Desnick v. Illinois Dep't of Professional Regulation, 171 Ill.2d 510, 216 Ill.Dec. 789, 665 N.E.2d 1346, cert. denied 519 U.S. 965, 117 S.Ct. 390, 136 L.Ed.2d 306 (1996).

85. Bates, 433 U.S. at 384, 97 S. Ct. at 2709, 53 L. Ed. 2d at 836.

solicitation of specific clients. These issues would be addressed in future litigation.

4. The Organized Bar's Response to Bates

Shortly after *Bates* was decided the American Bar Association promulgated two alternative plans to deal with lawyer advertising. Plan "A", the then preferred alternative, listed 25 categories of information that a lawyer could include in his advertising copy. Nothing more could be communicated. The approved "laundry list" included the attorney's name, address and telephone number; date and place of birth, schools attended; office hours; areas of practice; fee to be charged for an initial consultation; fixed fees to be charged for certain routine legal services; availability of a fee schedule; and credit arrangements.[86] Further, whatever advertising was to be done was to be done in a dignified manner. Plan A was later incorporated in DR 2–101 of the now superseded ABA Model Code of Professional Responsibility.[87]

Plan "B", which is essentially incorporated as Rule 7.1 in the present Model Rules of Professional Conduct, has now been adopted by a substantial majority of states.[88] It declares that "[a] lawyer shall not make a false or misleading communication about the lawyer or the lawyer's services." It then goes on to define what is false or misleading.[89] Plainly, Plan B reflects much more closely the spirit of *Bates* than does

---

86. *See* In re R.MJ., 455 U.S. 191, 194–195, 102 S.Ct. 929, 932–933, 71 L.Ed.2d 64, 68–69 (1982); Charles W. Wolfram, Modern Legal Ethics 1147 (1986).

87. The code was repealed in 1983 in favor of the ABA's Model Rules of Professional Conduct. *See* Charles W. Wolfram, Modern Legal Ethics 1021 (1986).

88. *See* Bernadette Miraglia, Note, *First Amendment: The Special Treatment of Legal Advertising*, 1990 Ann. Surv. Am. L. 597, 602 at n.44 (1991) (listing 33 states and the District of Columbia).

89. RULE 7.1 provides in its entirety:

"A lawyer shall not make a false or misleading communication about the lawyer or the lawyer's services. A communication is false or misleading of it:

(a) contains a material misrepresentation of fact or law, or omits a fact necessary to make the statement considered as a whole not materially misleading;

(b) is likely to create an unjustified expectation about results the lawyer can achieve, or states or implies that the lawyer can achieve results by means that violate the rules of professional conduct or other law; or

(c) compares the lawyer's services with other lawyers' services, unless the comparison can be factually substantiated.

ABA Model Rules of Professional Conduct (1983), as amended to February 1993."

Further strictures for attorneys who advertise are found in Rule 7.2, as amended to February 1993:

"(a) Subject to the requirements of rule 7.1 and 7.3, a lawyer may advertise services through public media, such as a telephone directory, legal directory, newspaper or other periodical, outdoor advertising, radio or television, or through written or recorded communication.

(b) A copy or recording of an advertisement or written communication shall be kept for two years after its last dissemination along with a record of when and where it was used.

(c) A lawyer shall not give anything of value to a person for recommending the lawyer's services, except that a lawyer may

(1) pay the reasonable costs of advertisements or communications permitted by this Rule;

(2) pay the usual charges of a not-for-profit lawyer referral service or legal service organization; and

(3) pay for a law practice in accordance with Rule 1.17.

Plan A, which is now relegated to decidedly minority status among the state jurisdictions.

But whichever plan is adopted, bar rules on lawyer advertising are not window dressing. There have been numerous admonitions by bar leaders to attorneys to toe the line or, better yet, stay well behind it when choosing to advertise.[90] Obey the rules or face disciplinary action, injunctions, ostracism and perhaps exhausting and expensive litigation.[91] In short, the legal establishment's reaction to the supposed "brave new world" of lawyer commercial speech has been a mixed bag of either enthusiastic response, grudging acceptance or guerilla warfare, with some luckless attorneys caught in the crossfire.[92] And this mixed bag reaction has spawned continuing litigation.

5. *The Development of Constitutional Doctrine Since Bates*

a. *Mass advertising*

Justice Blackmun rightly recognized that professional commercial speech has two major divisions: general advertising and solicitation of specific clients. Regarding advertising, the question since *Bates* has been what specifically may an attorney say or not say in his advertising. While the question of quality claims was reserved in *Bates*,[93] the consensus

(d) Any communication made pursuant to this rule shall include the name of at least one lawyer responsible for its content."

90. See, *e.g.*, Whitney Thier, Comment, *In a Dignified Manner: The Bar, the Court, and Lawyer Advertising*, 66 Tul. L. Rev. 527, 546–548 (1991) (discussing the warnings of bar leaders A.L. Moses and Harry Haynsworth that local bar rules had better be observed even if constitutionally suspect). In his forward to an ABA publication on marketing of services and legal ethics, Moses makes the rather chilling statement, "Lawyers who want to test unduly restrictive local rules should remember the definition of a pioneer as the person lying beside the trail with an arrow in his back." *Forward to* HARRY J. HAYNSWORTH, MARKETING AND LEGAL ETHICS: THE RULES AND THE RISKS ix-x (1990). *See also* Lloyd B. Snyder, *Rhetoric, Evidence, and Bar Agency Restrictions on Speech by Attorneys*, 28 Creighton L. Rev. 357, 385–386 (1995) for a major reason why organized bars often oppose lawyer advertising.

91. *See, e.g,* Ex parte Howell, 487 So.2d 848 (Ala.1986) (Alabama Supreme Court declared that the state bar's assertion of deception from specialization claims to be extreme and ordered the bar to sharpen its rules); Mezrano v. Alabama State Bar, 434 So.2d 732 (Ala.1983) (120 day suspension for advertising in violation of rules upheld);

In re Petition of Felmeister & Isaacs, 104 N.J. 515, 518 A.2d 188 (1986) and *related case* of In re Felmeister, 95 N.J. 431, 471 A.2d 775 (1984) (bar claim of unethical radio advertising leads to extended litigation and eventually a change in rules); Committee of Professional Ethics v. Humphrey, 355 N.W.2d 565 (Iowa 1984), *vacated and remanded* 472 U.S. 1004, 105 S.Ct. 2693, 86 L.Ed.2d 710 (1985), *on remand* 377 N.W.2d 643 (Iowa 1985), *appeal dismissed* 475 U.S. 1114, 106 S.Ct. 1626, 90 L.Ed.2d 174 (1986) (attorneys enjoined from continuing television advertising violative of very strict bar rules regarding visual presentation); *see also* Bernadette Miraglia, Note, *First Amendment: The Special Treatment of Legal Advertising*, 1990 Ann. Surv. Am. L. 597, 610–627.

92. The optimist sees the professional advertising glass as half full (*see* Bernadette Miraglia, Note, *First Amendment: The Special Treatment of Legal Advertising*, 1990 Ann. Surv. Am. L. at 598–599) and the pessimist sees it as half empty (*see* Whitney Thier, Comment, *In a Dignified Manner: The Bar, The Court and Lawyer Advertising*, 66 Tul. L. Rev. at 546–550). The two cited law review articles are examples of outstanding student commentary on a difficult, multifaceted subject.

93. Bates v. State Bar, 433 U.S. 350, 384, 51 Ohio Misc. 1, 97 S.Ct. 2691, 2709, 53 L.Ed.2d 810, 836 (1977).

today is that claims as to the quality of one's services are necessarily subjective and not susceptible to being proved and are thus inherently deceptive.[94] Testimonials by "satisfied" clients would also seem to fall into the category of misleading or deceptive advertising subject to regulation because they, too, are subjective and may reflect the lack of sophistication of the lay testimonial givers as to the value of the legal services rendered them.

Holding oneself out as a specialist or as certified in a particular field of law has also created problems, or at least litigation. In *In re R.M.J.*[95] a lawyer advertised the areas of his practice in language not permitted by Missouri's very restrictive "Plan A" rule and he received a private reprimand which sanction he appealed. The Missouri Supreme Court judgment upholding the constitutionality of the rule and the discipline imposed thereunder was reversed by the Supreme Court. The Court held that since listing "real estate" rather than "property law" practice was not demonstrated to be misleading nor was any substantial state interest shown to be involved in dictating such choice of words, the portion of the Missouri rule dictating the exact way in which areas of practice must be stated was unconstitutional.

In *Peel v. Attorney Registration & Disciplinary Commission*,[96] an Illinois attorney received a "certificate in Civil Trial Advocacy" from the National Board of Trial Advocacy (NBTA) and announced this fact on his professional letterhead. The Administrator of the Illinois Attorney Registration and Disciplinary Commission filed a complaint alleging that the attorney had violated a rule of the Illinois Code of Professional Responsibility prohibiting practitioners from holding themselves out as "certified" or "specialist[s]". The attorney was subsequently censured and this disciplinary measure was upheld by the Illinois Supreme Court.

The Illinois judgment was reversed, the Supreme Court stating that "[a] claim of certification is not an unverifiable opinion of the ultimate quality of a lawyer's work or a promise of success, ... but is simply a fact, albeit one with multiple predicates, from which a consumer may or may not draw an influence of the likely quality of an attorney's work in a given area of practice."[97] The fact of certification was objectively verifiable and therefore was not inherently deceptive or misleading.

In response to the Commission's claim that the words "certified" or "specialist" were potentially misleading because members of the general public might not understand them, the Court stated that a total ban on such advertising is broader than reasonably necessary to prevent the

94. *See Id.* (dictum); Lyon v. Alabama State Bar, 451 So.2d 1367, 1372–1373 (Ala. 1984), cert. denied, 469 U.S. 981, 105 S.Ct. 385, 83 L.Ed.2d 320 (1984) (requirement that advertising carry a disclaimer that no representation is made concerning quality of advertiser's legal services upheld); Charles W. Wolfram, Modern Legal Ethics 782 (1986); *see also* Board of Dental Examiners v. Franks, 507 So.2d 517 (Ala.Civ.App. 1986) (necessary disclaimer of quality of dental services upheld).

95. 455 U.S. 191, 102 S.Ct. 929, 71 L.Ed.2d 64 (1982).

96. 496 U.S. 91, 110 S.Ct. 2281, 110 L.Ed.2d 83 (1990).

97. *Id.* at 101, 110 S. Ct. at 2288, 110 L. Ed. 2d at 95.

perceived evil of public misunderstanding.[98] In short, "A State may not ... completely ban statements that are not actually or inherently misleading, such as certification as a specialist by bona fide organizations such as NBTA."[99]

The teachings of the above decisions and concordant state court rulings are that

(1) false, misleading or deceptive advertising by professionals may be banned and disciplinary sanctions, perhaps severe in nature, imposed;

(2) advertising messages that are neither actually nor inherently misleading or deceptive may not be totally prohibited but may be regulated to avoid misunderstanding by requiring explanations or disclaimers; and

(3) professional advertising not otherwise subject to regulation may be restricted only if the bar can demonstrate a compelling state interest clearly furthered by such regulation.[100]

b. Solicitation of specific clients

Even more sensitive than general advertising of professional services is the solicitation of specific clients or patients. Many professional codes of ethics prohibit one-to-one solicitations.[1] This prohibition appeared to be strengthened in one of the first cases decided by the Supreme Court following *Bates*. In *Ohralik v. Ohio State Bar Association*,[2] a member of the Ohio bar, went to a eighteen-year-old victim's hospital soon where he found her lying in traction. After a brief conversation about her condition, the lawyer told the victim he would represent her and asked her to sign a contingent fee agreement. She said she would have to discuss the matter with her parents before signing anything. Eventually, this victim signed the agreement. The attorney also sought out a second victim, also

---

98. *Id.* at 106–111, 110 S. Ct. at 2290–2292, 110 L. Ed. 2d at 98–101. For the Court's rejection of the parallel claim that a Certified Public Accountant's use of the designation "Certified Financial Planner" in advertising and other communications with the public was "false, deceptive, and misleading" *see* Ibanez v. Florida Dept. of Bus. and Prof. Regulation, Bd. of Accountancy, 512 U.S. 136, 114 S.Ct. 2084, 129 L.Ed.2d 118 (1994).

99. *Id.* at 110–111, 110 S. Ct. at 2292–2293, 110 L. Ed. 2d at 100–101; *accord* Ex Parte Howell, 487 So.2d 848 (Ala.1986); In re Johnson, 341 N.W.2d 282 (Minn.1983). In light of the protection afforded advertising of national board certifications in *Peel*, one commentator suggested that 1983 ABA Model Rule of Professional Conduct 7.4 prohibiting claims of specialization beyond those authorized by state sponsored programs was constitutionally suspect. *See* Bernadette Miraglia, Note, *First Amend-*

ment: The Special Treatment of Legal Advertising, 1990 Ann. Surv. Am. L. 597, 620–621. The rule was amended by the ABA in 1992 to permit advertising of national board certifications provided that the advertising state that there is no procedure in the attorney's jurisdiction for approving the certifying organization. And in 1993 the ABA, for the first time, accredited private organizations including the NBTA for the purpose of certifying lawyers as specialists in certain areas of practice. *See* 62 U.S.L.W. 2095 (Aug. 17, 1993).

100. *Compare* Ex parte Howell, 487 So.2d 848, 850 (Ala.1986).

1. *See, e.g.*, ABA Model Rule of Professional Conduct 7.3 (1983), as amended to February 1993; AMA Principle of Medical Ethics § 5 (1957).

2. 436 U.S. 447, 98 S.Ct. 1912, 56 L.Ed.2d 444 (1978).

eighteen, and visited her at her home without being invited to do so just after her hospital discharge. After informing her of the status of insurance coverage regarding the accident and hearing her say that she really did not understand what was going on, she orally agreed to the contingent fee agreement providing the lawyer with one-third of any recovery. Eventually both young women repudiated the agreement and the lawyer sued the first victim who had actually signed the agreement, receiving in settlement one third of the first victim's recovery from her uninsured motorist claim against her own insurance company. The young women filed complaints against the lawyer with the grievance committee of the local county bar association. Eventually the complaint made its way to the Ohio Supreme Court's Board of Commissioners on Grievances and Discipline which, after rejecting the lawyer's claim that his conduct was constitutionally protected, recommended a public reprimand. The Ohio Supreme Court adopted the board's findings increased the punishment to indefinite suspension from the practice of law. An appeal was filed with the Supreme Court which had decided *Bates* after the Ohio Supreme Court's disciplinary order had been entered.

The High Court heard the appeal and affirmed the judgment of the Ohio court. Mr. Justice Powell, a former president of the American Bar Association, speaking for the Court began the constitutional analysis by contrasting in-person solicitation of clients from general advertising of services and fees approved in *Bates*. In-person solicitation, according to Justice Powell, involves the conduct of a business transaction in which speech is an essential but subordinate component subject to a lesser level of judicial scrutiny.[3] Here, the speech employed to drum up business did not rise to the level of compelling First Amendment protection but fell within the state's proper sphere of economic and professional regulation in furtherance of important state interests.[4]

The state interests involved in *Ohralik* were found by Justice Powell to be particularly strong. The antisolicitation rules are prophylactic measures designed to prevent overreaching and imposition harmful to the public. "[T]he potential for overreaching is significantly greater when a lawyer, a professional trained in the art of persuasion, personally solicits an unsophisticated, injured, or distressed by person. Such an individual may place his trust in a lawyer, regardless of the latter's qualifications or the individual's actual need for legal representation, simply in response to persuasion under circumstances conducive to uninformed acquiescence."[5] Justice Powell then added, "Under such circumstances, it is not unreasonable for the State to presume that in-

---

3. *Id.* at 457, 98 S. Ct. at 1919, 56 L. Ed. 2d at 454.

4. *Id.* at 459, 98 S. Ct. at 1920, 56 L. Ed. 2d at 455–456.

5. *Id.* at 464–465, 98 S. Ct. at 1923, 56 L. Ed. 2d at 458–459. *Cf.* Desnick v. Illinois Dep't of Professional Regulation, 171 Ill.2d 510, 528, 216 Ill.Dec. 789, 799, 665 N.E.2d 1346, 1356, cert. denied, 519 U.S. 965, 117 S.Ct. 390, 136 L. Ed. 2d 306 (1996) (stating that regarding physician solicitations, "[i]t is also recognized that the State has substantial interest in maintaining professional standards and preventing undue influence, over-reaching and the invasion of its citizens privacy.")

person solicitation by lawyers more often than not will be injurious to the person solicited."[6]

Ohralik left unanswered the question whether solicitation by lawyers beyond straight person-to-person might also be prohibited and whether such prohibition might be imposed on other professionals not so schooled in the art of persuasion. Answers were not long in coming. First, in *Zauderer v. Office of Disciplinary Counsel,* another Ohio attorney placed an ad in 36 Ohio newspapers announcing his willingness to represent women who had been injured as a result of using the Dalkon Shield intrauterine contraceptive device.[7] The ad repeated allegations as to the types of injury women had sustained using the device and included a line drawing of the device accompanied by the question, "Did you use this IUD?" The ad continued with the statements that the lawyer's firm was presently representing women in Dalkon Shield cases and that they were being handled on a contingent fee basis. It concluded with the firm name, address and a phone number that interested persons might call for free information.

The ad was effective in attracting more than 100 new clients on whose behalf law suits were filed. It also attracted the attention of the Ohio bar's Office of Disciplinary Counsel which had previously warned the lawyer that a smaller ad promising a full refund of attorney fees in drunk driving cases if the client is convicted appeared to violate a disciplinary rule prohibiting contingent fees in such cases. The office filed a complaint charging the attorney with numerous disciplinary rules violations arising out of the drunk driving and Dalkon Shield ads.

One count alleged that the drunk driving ad violated the rule banning ads that were "false, fraudulent, misleading, and deceptive to the public" in that it offered representation on a contingent fee basis which could not legally be carried out. As for the Dalkon Shield ad the complaint alleged violation of disciplinary rules that (1) prohibited use of illustrations in attorney advertising; (2) required that ads be "dignified"; (3) limited the information in ads by attorneys to a list of 20 items (essentially ABA Plan "A"); (4) prohibited lawyers from recommending themselves or their associates to non-lawyers who had not sought such recommendation; (5) prohibited lawyers from accepting employment from such solicited persons; (6) required disclosure of how contingent fees rates are to be determined; and (7) required disclosure that clients would be responsible for costs as opposed to fees even if their claims were unsuccessful.

6. *Id.* at 466, 98 S. Ct. at 1923, 56 L. Ed. 2d at 460. In contrast to *Ohralik,* in *In re Primus,* 436 U.S. 412, 98 S.Ct. 1893, 56 L.Ed.2d 417 (1978), the Court, per Justice Powell, held that the solicitation of a client solely to further political and ideological goals through associational activity, including litigation, the giving of advice as to the solicited person's legal rights and the disclo-sure in a follow-up letter that free legal assistance would be available to her from a non-profit organization with which the lawyer was affiliated were all protected by the First and Fourteenth Amendments.

7. Zauderer v. Office of Disciplinary Counsel, 471 U.S. 626, 105 S.Ct. 2265, 85 L.Ed.2d 652 (1985).

The attorney's primary defense to the charges against him was that Ohio's rules restricting the content of advertising by members of the bar violated the First and Fourteenth Amendments as construed in *Bates* v. *State Bar of Arizona*[8] and *In re R.M.J.*[9] A panel of the Board of Commissioner on Grievances and Discipline of the Supreme Court of Ohio rejected the constitutional defense noting that neither *Bates* nor *R.M.J.* had forbidden all regulation of attorney advertising, that those cases involved more restrictive rules on advertising and that *Ohralik* justified the application of the antisolicitation rules in *Zauderer*. Ultimately discipline in the form of a public reprimand was imposed by the Ohio Supreme Court.

On appeal the Supreme Court reversed in major part. Justice White, speaking for the Court, began with the proposition that advertising geared to persons with specific legal problems cannot be barred by antisolicitation rules. Because, with one minor exception, the contents of the Dalkon Shield ad were neither false nor deceptive, such advertising could not be barred unless the prohibition directly advanced a substantial state interest. But Ohio's embrace of *Ohralik* was misguided. In-person solicitation is one thing and solicitation by targeted advertising is another. While some may have found the attorney's ad to be in bad taste and undignified, it could not invade anyone's privacy. And "[m]ore significantly appellant's advertisement—and print advertising generally—poses much less risk of overreaching or undue influence. Print advertising may convey information and ideas more or less effectively, but in most cases, it will lack the coercive force of the personal presence of a trained advocate. In addition, a printed advertisement, unlike a personal encounter initiated by an attorney, is not likely to involve pressure on the potential client for an immediate yes-or-no answer to the offer of representation."[10]

The state claimed that aside from the rather egregious situation in *Ohralik* its substantial interest was that of prophylaxis. The antisolicitation rule was needed to ensure that attorneys do not use false or misleading advertising to stir up meritless litigation. But in justifying the rule on a prophylactic basis, the Ohio bar undermined its case because of the virtual absence in the ad in question of false or deceptive material.

And its related argument that the state, in seeking to protect the public, had the right to ban all solicitation because of the difficulty of distinguishing between advice that is truthful and helpful and that which is false or deceptive fell on deaf ears since in the case at bar virtually all the statements in the Dalkon Shield ad were in fact easily verifiable and completely accurate. According to Justice White, "Were we to accept the State's argument in this case, we would have little basis for

8. 433 U.S. 350, 51 Ohio Misc. 1, 97 S.Ct. 2691, 53 L.Ed.2d 810 (1977).

9. 455 U.S. 191, 102 S.Ct. 929, 71 L.Ed.2d 64 (1982).

10. Zauderer, 471 U.S. at 642, 105 S. Ct. at 2277, 85 L. Ed. 2d at 666–667.

preventing the government from suppressing other forms of truthful and non-deceptive advertising simply to spare itself the trouble of distinguishing such advertising from false or deceptive advertising. The First Amendment protection afforded commercial speech would mean little indeed if such arguments were allowed to prevail."[11]

Thus an attorney may not be disciplined for soliciting legal business through printed advertising containing truthful and nondeceptive information and advice regarding the legal rights of potential clients.[12] And in *Shapero v. Kentucky Bar Association*,[13] the Court took the next logical step and held that organized bars may not, consistent with the First and Fourteenth Amendments, prohibit lawyers from soliciting business through the employment of truthful letters addressed to persons known to have specific legal problems.

In *Shapero*, a member of the Kentucky bar, applied to the Kentucky Attorneys Advertising Commission for approval of a letter that he proposed to mail to persons who have had foreclosure actions filed against them telling them of their legal rights and urging them to call him for free information on how they might be able to keep their homes.[14] While the Commission did not find the letter false or misleading, it declined to approve its mailing on the ground of a Kentucky Supreme Court anti-solicitation rule prohibiting the mailing or delivery of written advertisements precipitated by a specific event or occurrence involving or relating to the addressee or addressees. The Commission did recognize that this rule obviously ran afoul of the Supreme Court's construction of the First Amendment in *Zauderer* and recommended that the Kentucky Supreme Court amend its rule. However, the Committee on Legal Ethics of the Kentucky Bar, in an advisory opinion, upheld the mail ban on the ground that the rule was consistent with Rule 7.3 of the American Bar Association's Model Rules of Professional

---

11. *Id.* at 646, 105 S. Ct. at 2279, 85 L. Ed. 2d at 669.

12. *Id.* at 647, 105 S. Ct. at 2279, 85 L. Ed. 2d at 670. The imposition of discipline for including in the Dalkon Shield ad truthful matter not permitted by Ohio's disciplinary rules was held improper for much the same reasons the barring print solicitation of clients was improper here. And protection of dignity of the bar is no justification for disciplining lawyers who have the temerity to use illustrations in their advertising. *Id.* at 647–648, 105 S. Ct. at 2280, 85 L. Ed. 2d at 670. The one point won by the Ohio bar was its argument that it could require attorneys who advertise to disclose that clients will be responsible for costs even if they are unsuccessful. *Id.* at 650–653, 105 S. Ct. at 2281–2283, 85 L. Ed. 2d at 671–673.

13. 486 U.S. 466, 108 S.Ct. 1916, 100 L.Ed.2d 475 (1988).

14. The letter in its entirety read as follows:

"It has come to my attention that your home is being foreclosed on. If this is true, you may be about to lose your home. Federal law may allow you to keep your home by ORDERING your creditor [sic] to STOP and give you more time to pay them.

"You may call my office anytime from 8:30 a.m. to 5:00 p.m. for FREE information on how you can keep your home.

"Call NOW, don't wait. It may surprise you what I may be able to do for you. Just call and tell me that you got this letter. Remember it is FREE, there is NO charge for calling."

Id. at 469, 108 S. Ct. at 1919, 100 L. Ed. 2d at 482.

Conduct.[15] On review the Kentucky Supreme Court felt compelled by the decision in *Zauderer* to substitute the ABA rule for its own rule. Like its local predecessor, then ABA Rule 7.3 prohibited attorneys from employing targeted, direct-mail solicitation regardless of the truthfulness of the material, thus preventing the mailing here.[16]

The Supreme Court granted certiorari and reversed the judgment of the Kentucky Supreme Court which had blocked the mailing on the authority of *Zauderer*, pointing out that its cases have never distinguished between the various modes of printed advertising. Like general print advertising, targeted mail solicitation poses much less risk of overreaching, undue influence or invasion of privacy than does in-person solicitation. "A letter, like a printed advertisement (but unlike a lawyer), can readily be put in a drawer to be considered later, ignored, or discarded. In short, both types of written solicitation 'conve[y] information about legal services [by means] that [are] more conducive to reflection and the exercise of choice on the part of the consumer than is personal solicitation by an attorney.' "[17] Clearly then ABA Rule 7.3 adopted by Kentucky was found by the Court to be unconstitutionally broad in not accounting for the different methods of solicitation and the truthfulness of the content.

A rather serious breach was driven in the First Amendment's wall of protection for direct mail lawyer advertising in *Florida Bar v. Went For It, Inc.*[18] At least since *Bates v. State Bar of Arizona*, Justice Sandra Day O'Connor, who wrote the opinion for the Court in *Florida Bar*, has been an implacable foe of lawyer advertising[19] but until this case had always been outvoted by a bloc led by the Court's premier champion of commercial speech protection—Harry A. Blackmun.[20] Upon his retirement Black-

---

15. Apparently the Kentucky Bar's ethics committee never explained how consistency of the local rule with the ABA rule made the local rule valid under the United States Constitution.

16. ABA MODEL RULE OF PROFESSIONAL CONDUCT § 7.3 provides: [text in Practitioner's Edition only].

17. Shapero, 486 U.S. at 475–476, 108 S. Ct. at 1923, 100 L. Ed. 2d at 486 (quoting *Zauderer*, 471 U.S. at 642, 105 S.Ct. at 2277, 85 L.Ed.2d at 652); *see also* Adams v. Attorney Regis. & Discip. Comm'n, 617 F.Supp. 449 (N.D.Ill.1985); In re Von Wiegen, 63 N.Y.2d 163, 481 N.Y.S.2d 40, 470 N.E.2d 838 (1984).

18. 515 U.S. 618, 115 S.Ct. 2371, 132 L.Ed.2d 541 (1995). For contemporary commentary on *Florida Bar*, *see* Marcia Coyle, *Ad Decision Could Spur a Rollback–Bar Leaders Eye Fla. Rule as a Model on Solicitation*, National Law Journal, p. 1, July 3, 1995.

19. Prior to her appointment as an associate Justice of the United States Supreme Court, Sandra Day O'Connor was a leading member of the State Bar of Arizona. Before her appointment as a Judge of the Arizona Court of Appeals in 1979 and her election in 1975 as a Judge of the Maricopa County Superior Court (Phoenix) she served as chairperson of the Maricopa County Bar Association Lawyer Referral Service and member of the state bar's Committees on Legal Aid, Public Relations, Lower Court Reorganization and Continuing Legal Education. *See* Biographical Data on Sandra Day O'Connor, provided by the United States Supreme Court, October 1995. As a member of the Arizona legal establishment one might infer that Judge, later Justice O'Connor, would not have been pleased by the legal clinic of Bates and O'Steen flouting the rules of the Arizona Supreme Court regulating lawyer advertising.

20. *See* In re R.M.J., 455 U.S. 191, 102 S.Ct. 929, 71 L.Ed.2d 64 (1982); Zauderer v. Office of Disciplinary Counsel, 471 U.S. 626, 105 S.Ct. 2265, 85 L.Ed.2d 652 (1985); Shapero v. Kentucky Bar Association, 486 U.S. 466, 108 S.Ct. 1916, 100 L.Ed.2d 475

mun was succeeded by Stephen G. Breyer, a person having little background in First Amendment jurisprudence relating to commercial speech. Breyer's vote provided O'Connor with the fifth vote she needed to unsettle nearly twenty years of lawyer advertising doctrine.

In *Florida Bar v. Went For It, Inc.*, two of the Florida Bar's rule on lawyer advertising were challenged by an individual lawyer and a lawyer referral service under the First and Fourteenth Amendments. Rule 4–7.4(b)(1) provides:

> "[a] lawyer shall not send, or knowingly permit to be sent, . . . a written communication to a prospective client for the purpose of obtaining professional employment if: (A) the written communication concerns an action for personal injury or wrongful death or otherwise relates to an accident or disaster involving the person to whom the communication is addressed or a relative of that person, unless the accident or disaster occurred more than 30 days prior to the mailing of the communication."

And Rule 4–7.8(a) states:

> "[a] lawyer shall not accept referrals from a lawyer referral service unless the service: (1) engages in no communication with the public and in no direct contact with prospective clients in a manner that would violate the Rules of Professional Conduct if the communication or contact were made by the lawyer."

Together, these rules create a 30–day blackout period after an accident during which lawyers may not, directly or indirectly, single out specific accident victims or their relatives in order to solicit their business.

The United States District Court for the Middle District of Florida entered summary judgment for the plaintiffs declaring the Florida Bar rules unconstitutional and enjoining their enforcement. The United States Court of Appeals for the Eleventh Circuit affirmed and the Supreme Court on certiorari reversed.

Writing for the Court Justice O'Connor concluded that the Florida bar rules met the tripartite test of *Central Hudson Gas & Electric Corp. v. Public Service Comm'n*[21] First, she had little trouble finding the bar's interest in suppressing lawyer advertising here to be substantial. The bases for this conclusion were the state's need to control the licensed professions for the health and safety of the public and the protection of potential law client's privacy from intrusion by lawyers.

That the bar rules advance these interests, as required by the second prong of *Central Hudson*, is established to Justice O'Connor's satisfaction by a 106–page summary of a two-year study of lawyer advertising and solicitation containing statistics and anecdotes but not the methodology employed in obtaining the statistics nor the supporting data. The study indicated that a majority of Floridians said that "con-

---

(1988); Peel v. Attorney Registration and Disciplinary Commission, 496 U.S. 91, 110 S.Ct. 2281, 110 L.Ed.2d 83 (1990).

21. 447 U.S. 557, 100 S.Ct. 2343, 65 L.Ed.2d 341 (1980).

tacting persons concerning accidents or similar events is a violation of privacy" and "27% of direct-mail recipients reported that their regard for the legal profession and for the judicial process as a whole was 'lower' as a result of receiving the direct mail."[22] Saying that the anecdotal record mustered by the bar was noteworthy for its breadth and detail, Justice O'Connor concluded that the Bar had satisfied the second prong of *Central Hudson*.

In justifying this conclusion Justice O'Connor was forced to distinguish the earlier direct mail solicitation case of *Shapero v. Kentucky Bar Association*.[23] She did this by attempting to demonstrate first that *Shapero* was not concerned with invasion of privacy of prospective clients but rather focused on the special dangers of overreaching inhering in targeted solicitation; second that *Shapero* involved a broad ban on all direct-mail solicitations, whatever the time frame and whoever the recipient, rather than a short-term ban of solicitation letters to accident victims; and third that in *Shapero* the state did not assemble evidence attempting to demonstrate actual harm caused by targeted direct mail.[24]

Regarding the third and final prong of *Central Hudson*, Justice O'Connor held that the Florida Bar's rules were narrowly drawn and were a reasonable "fit" with the interests the state was trying to protect primarily because of the limited period of the ban and the availability of many alternative means by which injured Floridians would be able to learn about the availability of legal representation during the thirty-day solicitation blackout.

The authors believe Justice O'Connor's opinion to be deeply flawed and the Court's ruling out of line with accepted First Amendment doctrine. Justice Kennedy, in a biting dissenting opinion concurred in by Justices Stevens, Souter and Ginsburg,[25] wasted no time in exposing those flaws. Kennedy began by stating that the majority's ruling undercuts the fundamental principle that attorneys who communicate their willingness to assist potential clients are engaged in speech protected by the Constitution.[26] While agreeing with Justice O'Connor that *Central Hudson* provides the analytical framework for determining the constitutionality of the Florida Bar rules, he strongly disagreed with the manner in which she applied that analysis.

According to Kennedy, the tripartite test of *Central Hudson* was properly applied in *Shapero v. Kentucky Bar Assn.*[27] and that lawyer mail solicitation case was controlling. The distinctions that Justice O'Connor makes are simply not persuasive to Kennedy. Her focus first on offensive intrusion on the privacy of prospective clients by targeted mail solicitations and the state's right to protect that privacy is misdirected and

22. Florida Bar, 515 U.S. at 625, 115 S. Ct. at 2377, 132 L. Ed. 2d at 551.

23. 486 U.S. 466, 108 S.Ct. 1916, 100 L.Ed.2d 475 (1988).

24. Florida Bar, 515 U.S. at 628, 115 S. Ct. at 2378, 132 L. Ed. 2d at 552–553.

25. *Id.* at 634, 115 S. Ct. at 2381, 132 L. Ed. 2d at 556.

26. *Id.*

27. 486 U.S. 466, 108 S.Ct. 1916, 100 L.Ed.2d 475 (1988).

doctrinally unsound. "[W]e do not allow restrictions on speech to be justified on the ground that the expression might offend the listeners."[28] Excepting the case of captive audiences, Justice Kennedy stated that the Court had never before held that " 'the Government itself can shut off the flow of mailings to protect those recipients who might potentially be offended.' "[29]

Turning to O'Connor's second claimed substantial interest that of protecting the reputation and dignity of the legal profession, Kennedy asserted that such claim assumes that direct mail solicitations are unethical, thereby creating public disrespect. "The fact is," according to Kennedy, "that direct solicitation may serve vital purposes and promote the administration of justice, and to the extent the bar seeks to protect lawyers' reputations by preventing them from engaging in speech deemed offensive, the State is doing nothing more . . . than manipulating the public's opinion by suppressing speech that informs us how the legal system works. . . . This, of course, is censorship pure and simple; and censorship is antiethical to the first principles of free expression."[30]

As to the second prong of *Central Hudson* that the state's regulation must advance its interest or interests in a direct and material way, Kennedy dismisses the Florida's Bar's compilation of material allegedly supporting the need for its letter solicitation rules because of its unscientific nature. "There is no description of the statistical universe or scientific framework that permits any productive use of the information the so-called Summary of Record contains. The majority describes this anecdotal matter as 'noteworthy for its breadth and detail' . . . but when examined, it is noteworthy for its incompetence."[31]

Getting to the Florida Bar's motive in promulgating the rules, Justice Kennedy stated that "[i]t is telling that the essential thrust of all the material adduced to justify the State's interest is devoted to the reputational concerns of the Bar."[32]

Addressing the third prong of *Central Hudson*, Justice Kennedy asserted that the means chosen to further the bar's interests were not a reasonable fit. "The Bar's rule creates a flat ban that prohibits far more speech than necessary to serve the purported state interest. . . . [T]here is a wild disproportion between the harm supposed and the speech ban enforced."[33] And he noted that while Justice O'Connor did not bother to discuss this disproportion, the Court's speech jurisprudence required her to do so.[34] Justice Kennedy ended his dissent with these telling remarks:

> "Today's opinion is a serious departure, not only from our prior decisions involving attorney advertising, but also from the principles

---

28. Florida Bar, 515 U.S. at 638, 115 S.Ct. at 2383, 132 L.Ed.2d at 558.

29. *Id.* at 638, 115 S. Ct. at 2383, 132 L. Ed. 2d at 559.

30. *Id.*

31. *Id.* at 640, 115 S. Ct. at 2384, 132 L. Ed. 2d at 560.

32. *Id.* at 640, 115 S. Ct. at 2384, 132 L. Ed. 2d at 560.

33. *Id.*

34. *Id.*

that govern the transmission of commercial speech. The Court's opinion reflects a new found and illegitimate confidence that it, along with the Supreme Court of Florida, knows what is best for the Bar and its clients. Self-assurance has always been the hallmark of a censor.... The general rule is that the speaker and the audience, not the government assess the value of the information presented....[35] By validating Florida's rule, today's majority, is complicit in the Bar's censorship.''[36]

6. Regulation of Other Professional Speech

The Court in *Ohralik, Zauderer, Shapero* and *Florida Bar* was, concerned, of course, with *lawyer* solicitation, and in *Ohralik* emphasized the particular danger posed by lawyer in-person solicitation from the profession's training in the art of persuasion.[37] A question not addressed in these cases is whether professionals not schooled in this art may be barred from engaging in in-person solicitation.

Certainly, in-person solicitation by physicians and surgeons, who are healers and not advocates, does not appear to pose nearly the degree of danger of overreaching and imposition presented by lawyer solicitation,

---

35. Quoting, Edenfield v. Fane, 507 U.S. 761, 770–773, 113 S.Ct. 1792, 1800–1801, 123 L.Ed.2d 543, 555–557 (1993).

36. Florida Bar, 515 U.S. at 645, 115 S. Ct. at 2386, 132 L. Ed. 2d at 562–563. One lower federal court wasted no time in upholding the censorship of lawyer mail solicitation in personal injury cases in Moore v. Morales, 63 F.3d 358 (5th Cir.1995), cert. denied, 516 U.S. 1115, 116 S.Ct. 917, 133 L.Ed.2d 847 (1996) (Texas statute prohibiting letter solicitations by professionals within 30 days of accidents), but another federal court has attempted to limit the reach of *Went for It* by refusing to apply it to mail solicitations in criminal traffic violation cases on the basis that by the end of the thirty days moratorium, such cases could well be disposed of and on the further basis that sparing one charged with a criminal act the distress and embarrassment of knowing that his arrest is a matter of public record and known to others, including criminal defense lawyers, is not a sufficient interest justifying restriction of commercial speech. Ficker v. Curran, 950 F.Supp. 123 (D.Md.1996). The judgment of the district court was affirmed by the Fourth Circuit 119 F.3d 1150 (4th Cir.1997). The appellate court distinguished *Florida Bar v. Went For It, Inc.* as one limited to solicitation letters aimed at accident victims and potential personal injury cases. *Id.* at 1155-1156. The court pointed out four major differences between personal injury and wrongful death situations and criminal cases. First,

in personal injury and wrongful death cases, the victims need a period to cope with their grief before being asked to redress an emotional loss. Second, while accident victims normally have years in which to file their claims, criminal defendants can lose rights if unrepresented for thirty days after arrest. Third, criminal defendants privacy concerns differ markedly from those of potential civil plaintiffs. And finally, unlike civil litigants, criminal or incarcerable traffic defendants enjoy the Sixth Amendment right to counsel. *Id.* But the Fourth Circuit panel's point that targeted letters do not carry the same potential for undue influence by prospective counsel as do in person solicitation is indistinguishable in the two cases. "[S]uch letters are no more likely to overwhelm the judgment of a potential client than an untargeted letter or newspaper advertisement." *Id.* at 1153. *See* Susan A. Moore, Note, Florida Bar v. Went For It, Inc.: *Refining The Constitutional Standard For Evaluating State Restrictions On Legal Advertising*, 45 Cath. U. L. Rev. 1351 (1996) for commentary critical of Justice O'Connor's opinion. "In upholding the Florida Bar's rule. ...the Court based its decision squarely on public opinion, and consequently ignored consumers' First Amendment interest in access to the free flow of commercial information." *Id.* at 1403; *see also* Symposium: *Lawyer Advertising*, 49 Ark. L. Rev. 671–794 (1997).

37. Ohralik, 436 U.S. at 464, 98 S. Ct. at 1923, 56 L. Ed. 2d at 458–459.

though invasion of privacy might still be a threat. In an accident situation, for instance, a lawyer's importuning a victim to employ him may be positively detrimental to the victim's welfare. But the offer of assistance by a physician or surgeon for a fee in an emergency may be of real benefit[38] and the governmental interest in banning direct in-person solicitation by doctors would be much less substantial.

The Supreme Court came to grips with the differing natures of the learned professions in *Edenfield v. Fane.*[39] There, after determining that the Florida Board of Accountancy's rules prohibiting all direct, in-person uninvited solicitation of business by certified public accountants failed the four-part commercial speech test laid down in *Central Hudson Gas & Elec. Corp.*,[40] the Court rejected the Board's alternative argument justifying its rule under *Ohralik* as a necessary prophylactic because more precise regulation of solicitation would be too difficult to administer. Justice Kennedy, speaking for the Court, explained that *Ohralik* did not stand for the proposition that blanket bans on personal solicitation by all types of professionals are always constitutional. Rather, because of differences in the professions, the constitutionality of such bans depends upon the identity of the parties and the precise circumstances of the solicitation.[41] Only where in-person solicitations are inherently conducive to overreaching and other forms of misconduct may they be prohibited.

The situation in *Ohralik* justified the ban because it involved an attorney trained in the art of persuasion importuning unsophisticated lay persons recently injured and distressed. But direct, in-person solicitation by CPAs pose none of the dangers identified in *Ohralik*. CPAs are not trained in the art of persuasion and advocacy. Prospective clients are far less susceptible to manipulation than young accident victims because they are normally sophisticated and experienced business executives who understand the services CPAs provide. Thus, the manner in which a CPA solicits business is conducive to rational and considered decision-making. A general prohibition of accountant in-person solicitation of business furthers no substantial state interest and violates the CPA's commercial speech rights.[42]

Edenfield suggests that even attorneys might engage in in-person solicitation in situations in which the prospective client is sophisticated as to the ways of the legal profession, the services attorneys provide and their customary charges. For instance, overt direct solicitation of busi-

---

38. *See* William C. Canby, Jr. & Ernest Gellhorn, *Physician Advertising: The First Amendment and the Sherman Act,* 1978 Duke L.J. 543, 563; *cf.* American Medical Ass'n. v. Federal Trade Comm'n, 638 F.2d 443 (2d Cir.1980), *aff'd per curiam by an equally divided court* 455 U.S. 676, 102 S.Ct. 1744, 71 L.Ed.2d 546 (1982) (AMA anti-solicitation ethical rule held to violate Federal Trade Commission Act).

39. 507 U.S. 761, 113 S.Ct. 1792, 123 L.Ed.2d 543 (1993).

40. *Id.* at 767–773, 113 S. Ct. at 1798–1802, 123 L. Ed. 2d at 553. The Court held that though the Board of Accountancy had a substantial governmental interest in protecting the integrity of the profession, it made no showing that that interest was advanced by its rule banning direct, in-person solicitation.

41. *Id.* at 774, 113 S. Ct. at 1802, 123 L. Ed. 2d at 559.

42. *Id.* at 773–777, 113 S. Ct. at 1802–1804, 123 L. Ed. 2d at 558.

ness executives by corporate lawyers may present a situation in which a general ban on such solicitation could violate the lawyer's First Amendment rights.

There is one other commercial speech issue arising from professionals soliciting business, specifically when they choose to wear more than one "hat" and suggest that they can provide clients with an array of services. In *Ibanez v. Florida Department of Business and Professional Regulation*,[43] the Florida professional board reprimanded a member of the Florida Bar who was also a certified public accountant (CPA) and Certified Financial Planner (CFP) for referring to all of these credentials in her advertising and other communications with the public in relation to her legal practice. Despite the accuracy of the listing of her credentials, the lawyer was sanctioned for using the CPA and CFP designations because the Board believed that such designations would mislead the public in that it communicates her subjection to the Florida Accountancy Act "when she believes and acts as though she is not." Yet the Board had never accused her of any specific violations of the act or produced any specific incidents of members of the public being mislead or being harmed.

Given these facts only Chief Justice Rehnquist and Associate Justice O'Connor dissented from the Court's determination, based heavily on *Peel v. Attorney Registration and Disciplining Commission*,[44] that the Board's decision reprimanding the professional was violative of the First Amendment's protection of commercial speech. "Ibanez has neither been charged with, nor found guilty of, any professional activity or practice out of compliance with the governing statutory or regulatory standards. And as long as Ibanez holds an active CPA license from the board we cannot imagine how consumers can be mislead by her truthful representation to that effect.... The Board's justifications for disciplining Ibanez for using the CFP designation are scarcely more persuasive.... Given 'the complete absence of any evidence of deception,' ... the Board's 'concern about the possibility of deception in hypothetical cases is not sufficient to rebut the constitutional presumption favoring disclosure over concealment.' "[45]

In summary, the following propositions can be distilled from the Supreme Court's solicitation decisions. First, in-person solicitation of business by professionals may be barred only in situations in which there is inherent or actual danger of overreaching, undue influence or substantial invasion of privacy. Second, solicitation through mass advertising media targeted at classes of persons with specific types of problems and professional service needs are fully protected by the First Amendment.

43. 512 U.S. 136, 114 S.Ct. 2084, 129 L.Ed.2d 118 (1994). For a detailed discussion of the case *see* Edward L. Birk, Note *Protecting Truthful Advertising by Attorney–CPA's*—Ibanez v. Florida Department of Business & Professional Regulation, Board of Accountancy, 23 Fla. St. U.L. Rev. 77 (1995).

44. 496 U.S. 91, 110 S.Ct. 2281, 110 L.Ed.2d 83 (1990), discussed in pp. 373-375 of the Practitioners Edition.

45. Ibanez v. Florida Dep't of Business and Prof. Reg., 512 U.S. 136, 144, 114 S.Ct. 2084, 2089, 129 L.Ed.2d 118, 127 (1994).

And third, truthful personal solicitation letters directed to individuals known to have specific legal problems requiring the services of lawyers may not be prohibited but may be regulated at least as to the timeframe within which they are sent.

7. The Supposed Special Problem of Mass Electronic Media Advertising

a. The source of the problem

In *Bates*, Justice Blackmun left an opening for elements of the organized bar and professional societies to mount serious resistance to truthful effective lawyer and other professional advertising when he wrote rather cryptically, "And the special problem of advertising on the electronic broadcast media will warrant special consideration. Cf. *Capital Broadcasting Co. v. Mitchell*, 333 F.Supp. 582 (D.D.C.1971), summarily aff'd *sub nom. Capital Broadcasting Co. v. Kleindienst*, 405 U.S. 1000, 92 S.Ct. 1289, 31 L.Ed.2d 472 (1972)."[46]

b. The print medium analogy

Since that statement was made the Court has not come to grips with the issue of regulation of professional advertising on television, radio and cable. The closest the Court has come to substantive consideration of electronic advertising is its analogous discussion in *Zauderer* regarding illustrations or photographs incorporated in print advertisements. There, an attorney employed a line drawing of a Dalkon Shield Intrauterine Device in his newspaper ad seeking clients who had been injured by the device. He was disciplined by the Ohio bar in part because its restrictive rule on advertising, patterned after the ABA's "Plan A," prohibited visual aids in order to protect the dignity of the bar. Besides questioning how the ban on visual representations would further the state interest in dignity, the Court expressed its doubt that dignity in communications with the public was an interest substantial enough to justify the abridgement of attorneys First Amendment rights.[47]

Nor did the Court accept the perennial argument that this advertising created risks of public manipulation and confusion that are too difficult to deal with on a particularized basis thereby justifying a general prophylactic rule. "[N]owhere does the State cite any evidence or authority of any kind for its contention that the potential abuses associated with the use of illustrations in attorneys advertising cannot be combated by any means short of a blanket ban."[48] Justice White,

---

46. Bates v. State Bar, 433 U.S. 350, 384, 51 Ohio Misc. 1, 97 S.Ct. 2691, 2709, 53 L.Ed.2d 810, 836 (1977). *Capital Broadcasting Co.* upheld the constitutionality of legislation banning cigarette advertising from the broadcast media, but its force is virtually nil because it was decided before the Court's about-face regarding constitutional protection for commercial speech and because of the summary nature of the affirmance of the district court's ruling.

47. Zauderer v. Office of Disciplinary Counsel, 471 U.S. 626, 648, 105 S.Ct. 2265, 2280, 85 L.Ed.2d 652, 670 (1985).

48. *Id.; compare* Grievance Committee v. Trantolo, 192 Conn. 15, 470 A.2d 228 (Conn. 1984) in which the Connecticut Supreme Court set aside discipline against an

speaking for the Court, then added, "Moreover, none of the State's arguments establish that there are particular evils associated with the use of illustrations in attorneys' advertisements. Indeed, because it is probably rare that decisions regarding consumption of legal services are based on a consumer's assumptions about qualities of the product that can be represented visually, illustrations in lawyer's advertisements will probably be less likely to lend themselves to material misrepresentations than illustrations in other forms of advertising."[49]

c. The resistance of certain courts and bars to electronic media advertising

Given the analogy provided by *Zauderer* and the words approving visual advertising by the Court, one might think that state bars would thereafter regulate visual and aural lawyer advertising only to prevent actual confusion or deception of the public. But that has not always been the case and attorneys have been disciplined or restrained for running truthful, nondeceptive commercials that run afoul of bar strictures regarding content and manner of presentation having nothing to do with the prevention of confusion, fraud and deception—strictures encouraged by the cryptic language in *Bates*.[50]

The most celebrated example of restricting the use of the electronic media as a conduit for attorney advertising is *Committee on Professional Ethics v. Humphrey*.[51] There, an Iowa law firm, rejecting the restrictive rules of the Iowa bar governing television advertising, ran a series of three commercials on a Des Moines television station featuring dramatizations by paid actors and actresses in which fictional characters have been injured allegedly by the negligence of others and the suggestion is made that the injured persons should have been talking to a lawyer. After each dramatization, the scene shifted to a receptionist in a law office. The name, address, phone number and areas of practice of the law firm was superimposed on the picture and a voice over stated: "If you're injured through the negligence of others, call the law firm of Humphrey, Haas & Gritzner. Cases involving auto accidents, work comp, serious personal injury and wrongful death handled on a percentage basis. No charge for initial consultation. Call now...."

attorney because he chose to use the television medium to convey his truthful, non-deceptive commercial message. "Freedom of speech simply does not tolerate the sort of blanket approach for which the plaintiff [grievance committee] argues. A total ban on advertising through the electronic media would not only exceed the state's legitimate interest in protecting potential consumers, but its over inclusiveness would also keep a great deal of information from consumers, thereby hindering their ability to make an informed choice." *Id.* at 233. *Compare also* In re Petition For Rule of Court, 564 S.W.2d 638, 643 (Tenn.1978) ("Advertising is advertising irrespective of the device or instrumentality employed.").

49. *Id.* at 648–649, 105 S. Ct. at 2280, 85 L. Ed. 2d at 671.

50. *See* Committee on Professional Ethics v. Humphrey, 355 N.W.2d 565, 573 (Iowa 1984) (dissenting opinion of Larson, J.).

51. 355 N.W.2d 565 (Iowa 1984), *vacated and remanded* 472 U.S. 1004, 105 S.Ct. 2696, 86 L.Ed.2d 712 (1985), *on remand* 377 N.W.2d 643 (Iowa 1985), *appeal dismissed for want of a substantial federal question* 475 U.S. 1114, 106 S.Ct. 1626, 90 L.Ed.2d 174 (1986), *rehearing denied*, 476 U.S. 1165, 106 S.Ct. 2293, 90 L.Ed.2d 734 (1986).

While the Iowa Bar's Committee on Professional Ethics did not find the television commercials to be deceptive, it did find them to be in violation of the bar's professional canons DR2–101 and DR2–105 setting out the rules for such advertising and recommended to the Iowa Supreme Court that the firm's attorneys be enjoined from further broadcasting the commercials. Iowa's DR2–101(B) provided as to the television medium that only the information included in the "Plan A" laundry list scheme could be conveyed and then only by "a single non-dramatic voice, not that of the lawyer, and with no other background sound.... [N]o visual display shall be allowed except that allowed in print as articulated by the announcer.... Any such information shall be presented in dignified manner...."[52]

The Iowa Supreme Court concurred in the recommendation issuing a permanent injunction relying on the abstruse language in *Bates*.[53] The Iowa court expressed concern that, in effect, the medium is the message and that the message can be misleading. That concern is clearly reflected in the following passage from its opinion. "We reject defendants' contention that the prohibition against background sound, visual displays, multiple dramatic statements, and self-laudatory statements is more extensive than necessary to serve the state interests. All that is prohibited are the tools which would manipulate the viewer's mind and will."[54]

On appeal, the United States Supreme Court vacated the judgment and remanded the case for further consideration in light of the decision in *Zauderer* which had been handed down after the Iowa Supreme Court's decision.[55] On the remand the Iowa court again issued a permanent writ, distinguishing *Zauderer* on the basis that Iowa's regulation of television advertising did not amount to a total ban on the use of visual advertising condemned in *Zauderer* and again embracing the electronic media language in *Bates*. The court in support of its conclusion that *Zauderer* was not even directed to television noted that the Supreme Court had said that *print* advertising poses much less risk of overreaching or under influence. What the Iowa court did not note was that Supreme Court observation was comparing print advertising to in-person solicitation and not to other communications media. Finally, the Iowa court expressed its continuing distrust of the visual medium when it said, "Electronically conveyed image-building was not part of the infor-

---

52. The question immediately comes to mind "who would want to use the television medium under these conditions?" The obvious answer and one the Iowa bar would likely approve is: "No lawyer in his right mind." See dissenting opinion of Larson, J., 355 N.W.2d at 572 where he writes, "As to the restrictions on *technique*, these are in fact a prescription for dullness, prohibiting all background music, dramatization, and other methods of stimulating viewer interest. It is undisputed that the effect of these limitations on technique is to substantially diminish the effectiveness of any television

advertising." Iowa has the "most extreme rules" limiting lawyer television advertising in the country. John J. Watkins, *Lawyer Advertising, The Electronic Media, and the First Amendment*, 49 Ark. L. Rev. 739, 741–742 (1997) (published as part of symposium on lawyer advertising).

53. *Id.* at 569–570.

54. *Id.* at 571.

55. 472 U.S. 1004, 105 S.Ct. 2696, 86 L.Ed.2d 712 (1985).

mation package which has been described as needed by the public. The special potential for abuse presented by electronic lawyers advertising is especially apparent at the important line we have tried our best to draw between the dissemination of protected information and crass personal promotion."[56]

This same distrust of the electronic media, has been exhibited by other bars and courts as well. In *Matter of Zang*, the Arizona Supreme Court said, "The dramatic sales pitch is especially troublesome when it is broadcast on radio or television which leaves little time for reflection and rational deliberation."[57] And in *Petition of Felmeister & Isaacs*, the New Jersey Supreme Court said, "We remain concerned ... with the potential adverse impact of such [visual] techniques and especially in television advertising.... "[58] Of more concern to would-be television advertisers of legal services, the New Jersey court interpreted the Supreme Court's dismissal of the appeal in *Humphrey* as a signal that broad bar restrictions on television commercials are constitutional.[59]

Given the ill-advised language regarding electronic mass media in *Bates*, the Supreme Court's dismissal of the second appeal in *Humphrey* for want of a substantial federal question and the intense hostility of certain state bars and courts to advertising by lawyers over radio, television and cable, prudence dictates that lawyers practicing in states with advertising rules restricting either content or mode of presentation or both should adhere to them. These jurisdictions are waging a serious rearguard action against effective lawyer commercial speech whether to protect the perceived dignitary interest of the bar or, more paternalistically, the public's interest in freedom from supposed lawyer manipulation. And until the Supreme Court clarifies its position on advertising through the electronic media, lawyers who break the rules can expect to be disciplined or enjoined and can further expect to expend countless hours, dollars and energy defending themselves against charges of ethical violations. While it is true the state bars cannot ban electronic advertising in its entirety, at the present time they can, if so inclined, make it too deadly boring to be useful and too expensive to be profitable.

8. *Other Pitfalls for Professionals Who Advertise*

Aside from the sanctions that may be imposed on them for violating the rules of their professional associations and societies, lawyers and

56. Committee on Professional Ethics, 377 N.W.2d at 647 (Iowa 1985). This time on appeal, the Supreme Court dismissed for want of a substantial federal question. 475 U.S. 1114, 106 S. Ct. 1626, 90 L. Ed. 2d 174 (1986).

57. 154 Ariz. 134, 741 P.2d 267, 279 (Ariz.1987).

58. 104 N.J. 515, 517, 518, 518 A.2d 188, 189, 201 (1986).

59. *Id; see also* Laura R. Champion & William M. Champion, *Television Advertising: Professionalism's Dilemma*, 23 St. Mary's Law Journal 331 (1991) (expressing serious reservations about television advertising by lawyers and exhibiting intense concern for the dignitary interests of the organized bar). *But see* John J. Watkins, *Lawyer Advertising, The Electronic Media, and the First Amendment*, 49 Ark. L. Rev. 739, 775–782 (1997) (expressing some doubt as to the constitutionality of state limitations on television as a medium of lawyer advertising but expressing strongly the belief that, constitutional or not, such limitations are unsound as a matter of policy).

other professionals face the normal sanctions that follow from false, deceptive or negligent advertising. Professionals, like other advertisers, may expect to be subjects of federal or state administrative proceedings and sanctions if their false or deceptive advertising comes to the attention of the Federal Trade Commission or parallel state agencies. There is no reason why professional advertising should be immune from the strictures of Section 5 of the Federal Trade Commission Act[60] or similar state statutes.[61] Criminal prosecution might also be pursued in extreme cases.

If professional advertising is negligently prepared, thereby causing injury to members of the audience, there seems on principle, to be no reason why the negligent advertiser cannot be sued in tort for damages.[62] For this reason, professionals who advertise should avoid giving even general advice in their ads which could conceivably be followed by members of the advertising audience to their detriment.

F. Access of the Public to the Private Advertising Media

Thus far in this section the thrust of the discussion has been the tort liability of or constitutional protection afforded to individuals and corporations involved in communicating commercial speech. As for the relationship of the First and Fourteenth Amendments to federal and state restrictions on freedom of such speech it is important to remember that these amendments are directed only to governmental action.[63] They do not require private advertising organizations and media owners to accept paid or unpaid editorial messages let alone commercial advertising, and, indeed, they protect private individuals and corporations against compelled carriage of editorial[64] and, by parity of reasoning, purely commercial[65] messages.

60. 15 U.S.C.A. § 45, as amended (West 1988). *Cf.* Federal Trade Comm'n v. Superior Court Trial Lawyers Ass'n, 493 U.S. 411, 110 S.Ct. 768, 107 L.Ed.2d 851 (1990) (trial lawyers held not immune from the Sherman Antitrust Act suits when they combine to boycott court-appointed cases in an effort to increase the fee schedule for representation of indigent criminal defendants).

61. *See e.g.*, Ark. Code Ann §§ 4–88–101 through 112 (1993); La. Rev. Stat. Ann. §§ 51: 411 through 414 (West 1987 and Supp. 1991); N.J. Stat. Ann. § 56:8–1 through 48 (West 1989 and Supp. 1990–1991); Wash. Rev. Code Ann. §§ 9.04.010 through .060 (West 1991).

62. Cf. Braun v. Soldier of Fortune Magazine, 968 F.2d 1110 (11th Cir.1992), cert. denied 506 U.S. 1071, 113 S.Ct. 1028, 122 L.Ed.2d 173 (1993) (wrongful death caused by an improperly screened ad announcing the availability for hire of a paid assassin); Weirum v. RKO General, Inc., 15 Cal.3d 40, 123 Cal.Rptr. 468, 539 P.2d 36 (1975) (automobile accident wrongful death occasioned by a radio station's promotional contest encouraging listeners to drive unsafely).

63. *See, e.g.*, Consolidated Edison Co. v. Public Service Comm'n 447 U.S. 530, 100 S.Ct. 2326, 65 L.Ed.2d 319 (1980).

64. *See* Pacific Gas & Elec. Co. v. Public Utilities Comm'n, 475 U.S. 1, 106 S.Ct. 903, 89 L.Ed.2d 1 (1986); Miami Herald Pub. Co. v. Tornillo, 418 U.S. 241, 94 S.Ct. 2831, 41 L.Ed.2d 730 (1974); Columbia Broadcasting System, Inc. v. Democratic National Committee, 412 U.S. 94, 93 S.Ct. 2080, 36 L.Ed.2d 772 (1973).

65. The Supreme Court made clear in *Central Hudson Gas & Elec. Corp. v. Public*

Service Comm'n, 447 U.S. 557, 563, 100 S.Ct. 2343, 2350, 65 L.Ed.2d 341, 348–349 (1980) that "[t]he Constitution ... accords a lesser protection to commercial speech than to other constitutionally guaranteed expression." Therefore, if the First Amendment protects against governmentally compelled editorial or political messages, it necessarily protects against the forced carriage of commercial messages.

Chapter Four

PRIVACY AND THE MEDIA

Analysis

4.1 Introduction

A. *The Importance of Privacy*

An inherent need of human beings to retain their individuality is personal space. That space encompasses both the psychic and the physical. While constantly interacting with others in a civilized society, the individual, for his physical and mental well-being, must be able to shut off the sensory stimuli generated by others and, perhaps more importantly, physically withdraw into secluded space away from the "madding crowd."

This is particularly true when an individual becomes the object of attention and curiosity of the governing body of his society and the organizations chiefly devoted to gathering and disseminating information about individuals, known collectively as the mass media.

In the twentieth century we have unfortunately come to learn that the surest way to glorify the interests of the state at the expense of the individual is to deprive the individual of that psychic and seclusive space we call privacy. When a totalitarian government takes over a society, the first liberty to be trampled is individual privacy. Neighborhood organizations are set up to monitor the activities of each member of the neighborhood and listening devices and powerful lenses become endemic. In short, the loss of individual privacy permits heightened state control which leads in turn to the loss of other individual freedoms and the rise of conformity and despair.[1]

B. *The Mass Media's Interference With Individual Privacy*

Not nearly as destructive of individual privacy as the modern totalitarian state are the modern media of mass communication. But under the banner of "the people's right to know," they are quite capable of interfering substantially with individual psychic and physical privacy.

In Western democracies, the belief is strongly held that there is a natural right of the people to receive information about individuals in their society, at least to the extent that such information is relevant to the healthy functioning of society. Thus, there are two significant interests that must be taken into account in determining the appropriate bounds for the media's gathering and disseminating information concerning specific persons. First is the individual's claim to psychic and seclusive space and his feelings and emotions when such space is invaded. Second is society's claim that it is entitled to news and information regarding its constituent members, especially so when such news and information may impact on the proper operation of the society. This second claim usually presented by the media, is made in the name of the social compact in which individuals give up some of the freedom that exists in the state of nature in return for the safety and cooperation found in a civilized society.[2]

In the United States, the recognition or rejection of these conflicting interests is determined largely by the common law of tort and to a lesser extent by federal and state legislation, with the constitutional limitations of the First Amendment ever present.

4.2 Nature of the Tort of Invasion of Privacy and Interests Protected

A. *Nature*

The tort of invasion of privacy is personal to the victim and, except for the appropriation branch of the tort, the cause of action is neither assignable nor descendible in the absence of statutory authority.[1] Survivors may not sue to vindicate the privacy interests of deceased individuals.[2] Again, because the tort action is a personal one, corporations, partnerships and other business and social entities may not sue in tort

---

1. *See* GEORGE ORWELL, 1984 (1949); Edward J. Bloustein, *Privacy as an Aspect of Human Dignity An Answer to Dean Prosser*, 39 N.Y.U. L. Rev. 962, 974 (1964).

2. *See* JEAN JACQUES ROUSSEAU, THE CONFESSIONS OF J.J. ROUSSEAU, open paragraph (C. Blanchard translation 1856–1857); *cf.* Pavesich v. New England Life Ins. Co., 122 Ga. 190, 294–205, 50 S.E. 68, 69–71 (1905).

1. Wood v. Hustler Magazine, Inc., 736 F.2d 1084, 1093 (5th Cir.1984); cert. denied

469 U.S. 1107, 105 S.Ct. 783, 83 L.Ed.2d 777 (1985); Bitsie v. Walston, 85 N.M. 655, 515 P.2d 659 (N.M.App.), cert. denied 85 N.M. 639, 515 P.2d 643 (1973); RESTATEMENT (SECOND) OF TORTS § 652I comment a (1977); WILLIAM L. PROSSER, HANDBOOK OF THE LAW OF TORTS 814 (4th ed. 1971).

2. Fitch v. Voit, 624 So.2d 542, 544 (Ala. 1993); RESTATEMENT SECOND OF TORTS § 652I, comment b (1977).

for invasion of claimed privacy interests, but will have to look elsewhere in the law for their vindication.[3]

B. Interests Protected

Because the tort of invasion of privacy is relatively new, was developed from a law review article motivated in large part by considerations personal to the authors,[4] has disparate branches, and overlaps or parallels a number of other torts including trespass, assault, defamation and intentional infliction of emotional distress, the interests protected by this tort are not yet well defined.[5] But if the tort action is ever to be properly rationalized and the results of litigation are to have coherence and a fair degree of predictability, the courts and commentators must achieve consensus as to the interests protected.

1. The Starting Point for Analyzing Interests

The starting point in dealing with the interests involved according to most commentators[6] is Judge Thomas M. Cooley's statement, made in the context of his general discussions of personal immunities, that each individual possesses a right (or interest) "to be let alone."[7] Cooley's statement was made before there was any recognition of a separate tort of invasion of privacy and there is no elaboration as to the parameters of this right. Taken to its logical extreme, such right would destroy the social compact supporting civilized society because it would bar any compulsion by society against the individual including levying of taxes, raising of armies and inoculating against communicable disease. Therefore, the challenge is to devise an interest theory that gives the catch phrase "the right to be let alone" a realistic meaning as to the individual and his relation to society.

2. The Human Dignity Approach

One approach that has been suggested is to equate Cooley's catch phrase with the need to protect the dignity of the individual that comes from having physical and emotional space to which he may withdraw.[8] Thus the tort of invasion of privacy despite its several manifestations or branches would have the unitary purpose of protecting the feelings of individuality and autonomy that come from not having to share *every-*

---

3. Joint Anti–Fascist Comm. v. McGrath, 341 U.S. 123, 71 S.Ct. 624, 95 L.Ed. 817 (1951); Southern Air Transport, Inc. v. American Broadcasting Co., Inc., 678 F.Supp. 8 (D.D.C.1988); *aff'd* 877 F.2d 1010 (D.C.Cir.1989); RESTATEMENT SECOND OF TORTS § 652I comment *c* (1977).

4. Samuel D. Warren and Louis D. Brandeis, *The Right to Privacy*, 4 Harv. L. Rev. 193 (1890).

5. *See* Diane L. Zimmerman, *Requiem for a Heavyweight: A Farewell to Warren and Brandeis's Privacy Tort*, 68 Corn. L. Rev. 291, 294–295 (1983); Raymond Wacks,

The Poverty of Privacy, 96 Law Q. Rev. 73, 75 (1980).

6. *See, e.g.*, W. PAGE KEETON, ET. AL., PROSSER AND KEETON, TORTS 849 (5th ed. 1984); William L. Prosser, *Privacy*, 48 Cal. L. Rev. 383, 389 (1960); Samuel D. Warren and Louis D. Brandeis, *The Right to Privacy*, 4 Harv. L. Rev. 193, 195 (1890).

7. THOMAS COOLEY, TORTS 29 (2d ed. 1888).

8. Edward J. Bloustein, *Privacy as an Aspect of Human Dignity: An Answer to Dean Prosser*, 39 N.Y.U. L. Rev. 962 (1964).

thing with one's neighbors. The limits of this protected space is, of necessity, not large but it is important.

Treating invasion of privacy as solely a human dignity tort would give it a unity that it does not presently appear to possess. For instance, the generally accepted view is that the appropriation branch of the tort exists at least in part to protect from usurpation whatever property interest resides in one's name, image and personality.[9] Therefore, the legal analysis will have little commonality with the analysis for publicity of private embarrassing facts, another branch of the tort. But if the exploitation of one's identity by another for the exploiter's benefit is viewed as an enslavement of the personality with the consequent damage to human autonomy, then the legal analysis and litigation results should be more consistent with that of the other branches of the tort which are viewed as more clearly dignitary.

3. Prosser's Experiential or Empirical Approach

The other major approach to defining the interest or interests protected by the tort of invasion of privacy is to look at the reported cases and attempt to glean from them what it is that the courts are protecting. This was Dean Prosser's methodology. He read all the reported cases to 1960 purporting to deal with invasions of privacy and then reported that "what has emerged from the decisions is no simple matter. It is not one tort, but a complex of four. The law of privacy comprises four distinct kinds of invasion of four different interests of the plaintiff, which are tied together by the common name, but otherwise have almost nothing in common except that each represents an interference with the right of the plaintiff, in the phrase coined by Judge Cooley 'to be let alone.' "[10]

The four branches of the tort found by Prosser are intrusion upon seclusion or private affairs; unreasonable publicity as to embarrassing private facts; publicity placing one in a false light; and appropriation for the appropriator's advantage of another's name likeness or other aspect of identity.[11]

The interest protected by "intrusion" is a mental one involving distress over the invasion but Prosser does not elaborate as to the exact nature of the mental distress.[12] The interest involved with publicity of embarrassing private facts is the reputation of the plaintiff and the mental distress that accompanies its destruction.[13] Despite numerous distinctions between the unwanted publicity of private facts branch and false light, Prosser asserts that the interest protected by a false light

---

9. C.E.G. Rogers v. Grimaldi, 875 F.2d 994, 1003 (2d Cir.1989); Snakenberg v. Hartford Cas. Ins. Co., Inc., 299 S.C. 164, 170, 383 S.E.2d 2, 5–6 (S.C.App.1989); State *ex. rel.* Elvis Presley Int'l. Memorial Found. v. Crowell, 733 S.W.2d 89, 97 (Tenn.App. 1987); Dan B. Dobbs, Remedies § 7.3 (5) (2d ed. 1993).

10. William L. Prosser, *Privacy*, 48 Cal. L. Rev. 383, 389 (1960).

11. *Id.*

12. *Id.* at 392.

13. *Id.* at 398.

action is the same—reputation and accompanying mental state.[14] Finally, he sees the appropriation tort as protecting a proprietary interest in the control of one's own name and likeness.[15]

If Prosser is correct, the supposed tort of invasion of privacy has no central meaning other than Cooley's imprecise concept of "the right to be let alone,"[16] and we must therefore deal with four disparate manifestations of that fuzzy idea.

Indeed, Prosser's view of the tort has become controlling, in large part because of its adoption by the American Law Institute in the second Restatement.[17] Though we might wish for some more coherent approach to privacy interests than Prosser and the Restatement provide, we must accept the world of privacy law as the courts now approach it and will discuss the tort or torts as a loosely related complex, with all the contradictions and inconsistencies that arise from the absence of a core definition.

4.3   History of the Tort and Its Proliferation

A.   *The Warren and Brandeis Article*

Context for the detailed analysis of privacy law that follows is provided by an exploration of the origin of the tort, its historical development and its proliferation. The tort, which is a major scourge of the news media, was in a broad sense stimulated by that self-same media. In genteel Boston in the closing years of the nineteenth century where "the Cabots spoke only to the Lodges and the Lodges spoke only to God" and nobody of breeding spoke to the press, "yellow journalism" was on the rise with its sensationalism and titillating gossip. Though perhaps not as extreme as the penny press of New York City, some of the Boston papers, particularly the *Saturday Evening Gazette*, annoyed proper Bostonians of that era by intrusive coverage of their social affairs and personal lives.[1] One who became especially annoyed over press coverage

---

14.   *Id.* at 400.

15.   *Id.* at 406.

16.   A number of respected commentators have differed with Prosser's conclusions regarding the interests protected by the tort of invasion of privacy. *See, e.g.,* Rodney A. Smolla, Defamation § 10.0 (2)(c) (1986), Diane L. Zimmerman, *Requiem for a Heavyweight: A Farewell to Warren and Brandeis's Privacy Tort*, 68 Corn. L. Rev. 291, 296–297 (1983) ("The gravamen of the 'false-light' offense is that publication of misinformation injures the plaintiff's dignity."). *See also* Southern Air Transport, Inc. v. American Broadcasting Co., 678 F.Supp. 8 (D.D.C.1988), *aff'd* 877 F.2d 1010 (D.C.Cir.1989).

17.   RESTATEMENT SECOND OF TORTS §§ 652–I (1977). Prosser was the reporter for the second Restatement until his death in 1972 when the work of restat-

ing the law of torts fell to John W. Wade of Vanderbilt, a co-author with Prosser of a casebook on torts. Craig Joyce, *Keepers of the Flame: Prosser and Keeton on the Law of Torts (Fifth Edition) and the Prosser Legacy*, 39 Vand. L. Rev. 851, 852 (1986) (Book Review Essay).

1.   *See* William L. Prosser, *Privacy*, 48 Cal. L. Rev. 383 (1960); Samuel D. Warren and Louis D. Brandeis, *The Right to Privacy*, 4 Harv. L. Rev. 193, 196 (1890) ("The press is overstepping in every direction the obvious bounds of propriety and of decency. Gossip is no longer the resource of the idle and the vicious, but has become a trade, which is pursued with industry as well as effrontery. To satisfy a prurient taste the details of sexual relations are spread broadcast in the columns of the daily papers. To occupy the indolent, column upon column is filled with idle gossip, which can only be

of social events at his home was Samuel D. Warren, a wealthy paper manufacturer and former practicing lawyer. Tired of having his social events reported in intimate detail in the newspapers and his lawn and gardens trampled by enterprising reporters, he turned to his law partner, Louis D. Brandeis to collaborate with him on a law review article arguing for the recognition of a common law tort of invasion of privacy making actionable the unauthorized publicity of private facts.[2] The two former law school classmates were concerned that modern inventions such as the movable camera and the willingness of the news media to use them for sensation and profit would inflict mental and emotional distress for which there would be no remedy.[3]

Resorting to the common law protection of intellectual and artistic property, they claimed to have found long-standing protection of personal privacy. They argued that the common law right of individuals to decide for themselves which if any of their thoughts, sentiments and emotions expressed in the form of words, signs, paintings, sculpture, musical compositions, or even gem collections should be made available to the public no matter how mundane and lacking in artistic virtue or intellectual context was a clear manifestation of the common law's protection of individual privacy.[4]

Their central authority for this argument was *Prince Albert v. Strange.*[5] There, Queen Victoria's consort brought action to enjoin not only the reproduction of etchings made by the royal couple for their own pleasure but also the publishing of even a summary description of the works. Going beyond common law protection of intellectual property as the court had to do because a mere summary description or simple listing of the etchings would hardly have qualified as an invasion of any property interest, Vice–Chancellor Knight Bruce said that the courts in proper cases would prevent injurious disclosures as to private matters.

It does not appear to have occurred to Warren and Brandeis that *Prince Albert v. Strange* might have been a sui generis hometown decision favoring the nominal ruler of the court handing down that decision. The authors also referred to a hypothetical case propounded by Lord Eldon that if one of the dying George III's court physicians had kept a diary of what he heard and saw during the king's illness, the court would not, in the king's lifetime, have permitted the physician to print and publish such diary.[6] Thus two of the major authorities cited dealt with the supposed privacy rights of ruling monarchs. But regarding

procured by intrusion upon the domestic circle."). But for a contrasting view of the behavior of the press of that period see DON R. PEMBER, PRIVACY AND THE PRESS 14–17 (1972).

2. Samuel D. Warren and Louis D. Brandeis, *The Right to Privacy*, 4 Harv. L. Rev. 193 (1890).

3. *Id.* at 196–197.

4. *Id.* at 198–203.

5. 2 DeGex & Sm. 652, 64 Eng. Rep. 293 (V.C. 1848).

6. Samuel D. Warren and Louis D. Brandeis, *The Right to Privacy*, 4 Harv. L. Rev. 193, 205 (1890), citing the opinion of Lord Chancellor Cottenham on the appeal of Prince Albert v. Strange, 1 McN. & G. 25, 64 Eng. Rep. 293 (1849).

all of the mere subjects of the realm, the English courts to this day have not recognized an independent right of privacy.[7]

Nevertheless, Warren and Brandeis proclaimed that the lesson to be learned from these authorities and a number of others permitting injunctions or awarding damages for breach of trust or contract in the publication of another's lectures,[8] drawings[9] photograph or visual image[10] was that the common law protected the personal privacy of the individual, or, in their words, tort law provided for "inviolate personality."[11] Thus, from a very few "strange" opinions and others that appeared inapposite because they dealt with property or contract rights, Warren and Brandeis discovered the existence of an individual right to privacy protected by the law of tort.

B.   Recognition of the Tort in the Courts and Legislatures— The Formative Period

While Warren and Brandeis were motivated by a desire to protect private facts from being widely publicized, their article did indicate that the perceived underlying interest of the tort in protecting against mental and emotional distress should also cover the case of private persons who wish to prevent the publication of their portraits.[12] The first judicial tests of Warren and Brandeis' theory of the existence of a tort of invasion of privacy arose in cases of unauthorized use of photographic images of individuals by business organizations for their commercial gain. The original attempt to turn law review theory into recognized law was *Roberson* v. *Rochester Folding Box Co.*[13] in which the defendants obtained a photograph of one Abigail M. Roberson and reproduced it on widely distributed flyers advertising Franklin Mills Flour. Above plaintiff's portrait was printed the dreadful pun "Flour of the Family." All of this was done without authorization and she sued both Rochester Folding Box Company, which did the lithography, and Franklin Mills Company which commissioned the advertising.

Plaintiff's theory followed that of Warren and Brandeis. While the appellate division of the New York Supreme Court could find little or no precedent for an invasion of privacy claim, it determined that a common law right of privacy did exist as an aspect of "the right to be let alone."[14]

---

7. SAMUEL HOFSTADTER AND GEORGE HOROWITZ, THE RIGHT OF PRIVACY, 13 (1964); Diane L. Zimmerman, *Requiem for a Heavyweight: A Farewell to Warren and Brandeis's Privacy Tort*, 68 Corn. L. Rev. 291, 342 n. 268 (1983).

8. Abernathy v. Huchinson, 1 H. & Tw. 33, 3 L.J. 209, 47 Eng. Rep. 1313 (1825).

9. Tuck v. Priester, 19 Q.B.D. 629 (1887).

10. Pollard v. Photographic Co., 40 Ch. Div. 345 (1888).

11. Samuel D. Warren and Louis D. Brandeis, *The Right to Privacy*, 4 Harv. L. Rev. 193 at 205, 207, 211, 213.

12. "The right of one who has remained a private individual, to prevent his public portraiture, presents the simplest case for such extension. . . . If you may not reproduce a woman's face photographically without her consent, how much less should be tolerated the reproduction of her face, her form, and her actions, by graphic descriptions colored to suit a gross and depraved imagination." *Id.* at 213–214.

13. 171 N.Y. 538, 64 N.E. 442 (1902).

14. *Id.* at 544, 64 N.E. at 443.

But the New York Court of Appeals reversed in a 4 to 3 decision, pointing out that the great commentators of the common law, Blackstone and Kent, had never mentioned such a right and, Brandeis and Warren to the contrary, no precedent (as opposed to dictum) could be found supporting its existence. Cognizant that the absence of precedent is hardly sufficient in and of itself to reject a proposed departure in the common law, the court justified its rejection of a right of privacy on the administrative ground that it would open the courts to massive new litigation of issues that could not be easily confined.[15]

While the New York Court of Appeals was certainly prescient regarding the flood of litigation of both serious and frivolous cases that would wash over the courts in the twentieth century once a tort action for invasion of privacy was recognized, people in New York and elsewhere were outraged that Miss Roberson was denied a remedy for suffering the humiliation associated with becoming a public commercial object without her consent.[16]

A result of the Court of Appeals unpopular decision was the enactment by the New York legislature of statutes making the conduct in Roberson a criminal offense and providing the victim with a civil action for injunction and damages.[17] This was the first important legal recognition of some form of a right to privacy, but there was yet no judicial acceptance of the right.

That acceptance was to come in a case strikingly like Roberson,[18] decided less than three years later—*Pavesich v. New England Life Ins. Co.*[19] There, Paolo Pavesich, a local artist, came face to face with a photographic image of himself in an advertisement in the *Atlanta Constitution*. In the ad Pavesich's likeness was placed next to that of a poorly dressed and sickly looking individual. Above the Pavesich image were the words "Do it now. The man who did." Above the less desirable image were the words "Do it while you can. The man who didn't." What it was that the reader should do without hesitation was purchase life insurance from New England Mutual Life Insurance Company. To underscore this

---

15. "If such a principle be incorporated into the body of the law through the instrumentality of a court of equity, the attempts to logically apply the principle will necessarily result not only in a vast amount of litigation, but in litigation bordering upon the absurd, for the right of privacy, once established as a legal doctrine, cannot be confined to the restraint of the publication of a likeness, but must necessarily embrace as well the publication of a word picture, a comment upon one's looks, conduct, domestic relations or habits. And, were the right of privacy once legally asserted, it would necessarily be held to include the same things if spoken instead of printed, for one, as well as the other, invades the right to be absolutely let alone." *Id.* at 544–545, 64 N.E. at 443.

16. *See* SAMUEL HOFSTADTER AND GEORGE HOROWITZ, THE RIGHT OF PRIVACY 28 (1964).

17. N.Y. Civ. Rights Law §§ 50, 51 (1909).

18. One possible explanation for such unauthorized appropriation of photographic images at this time is that photography was still in its technological infancy, photographs available for illustration were not commonplace and photographers' models almost unheard of. Thus photographers could be expected to turn to their photographic files of commissioned portraits to meet the need for illustrations.

19. 122 Ga. 190, 50 S.E. 68 (1905).

point Pavesich is quoted in the ad as saying, "In my healthy and productive period of life I bought insurance in the New England Mutual Life Insurance Co. of Boston, Mass., and to-day my family is protected and I am drawing an annual dividend on my paid-up policies."

As an artist unconcerned with commerce and finance, Pavesich claimed the ad to be offensive to him and sued for invasion of his privacy. The photograph was not reproduced by the defendant photographer with his consent. He had never uttered the words attributed to him and, indeed, he had never taken out a life insurance policy with the defendant company.

The Georgia Supreme Court, while agreeing with the New York Court of Appeals that an action enforcing a common law right of privacy was unprecedented,[20] reached the opposite conclusion. The absence for centuries of any precedent supporting a right of privacy suggested caution to the Georgia court, but it noted that "the common law will judge according to the law of nature and the public good."[21] Turning to natural law, the court found that the individual retained a liberty of privacy of some dimension in relationship to society as a whole within the social compact.[22]

Responding to the concerns expressed by the New York Court of Appeals about the volume and difficulty of the litigation that would follow from recognition of tort protection for a right of privacy, the Georgia Supreme Court wrote, "It may be said that to establish a liberty of privacy would involve in numerous cases the perplexing question to determine where this liberty ended, and the rights of others and of the public began. This affords no reason for not recognizing the liberty of privacy.... Each person has a liberty of privacy, and every other person has, as against him, liberty in reference to other matters, and the line where these liberties impinge upon each other may in a given case be hard to define; but that such a case may arise can afford no more reason for denying to one his liberty of privacy than it would deny to another his liberty, whatever it may be."[23] Recognizing a right of privacy protected by tort law and citing Warren and Brandeis approvingly, the Georgia Supreme Court reversed the order of the trial court sustaining the demurrer to Pavesich's complaint, thereby permitting him to have a trial on the merits of his claim that his "liberty of privacy" had been invaded by the unauthorized publication of his photograph and the false representations made concerning him in the commercial advertisement in the *Atlanta Constitution*.

With the decision in *Pavesich*, the enactment of legislation in New York protecting against unauthorized appropriation of one's name, likeness and personality and the earlier publication of the Warren and Brandeis article, the tort of invasion of privacy was on its way. But widespread recognition of what Warren and Brandeis had wrought was

20. *Id*. at 193, 50 S.E. at 69.   **22.** *Id*. at 194, 50 S.E. at 69–71.

21. *Id*. at 193, 50 S.E. at 69.   **23.** *Id*. at 200, 50 S.E. at 72.

not quick in coming. During the first fifty years after publication of their famous law review article, only fifteen states including Georgia had embraced some aspect of the tort by judicial decision and the courts of five others, Michigan, New York, Rhode Island, Washington and Wisconsin had rejected it.[24] The legislatures of four states—California, New York, Utah and Virginia—enacted legislation dealing primarily with the appropriation aspect of the tort.[25]

C. Recognition of the Tort in the Courts and Legislatures— The Modern Era

Typically in the development of this tort, two events in relatively modern times outside the courtroom gave impetus to the widespread judicial and even legislative acceptance today of the right of privacy. One was the promulgation by the American Law Institute of Section 867 of the first Restatement of Torts in 1939. The other was the publication of the second edition of Prosser's Handbook of the Law of Torts in 1955.

In the Restatement the American Law Institute unequivocally recognized the existence of an independent tort of "interference with privacy"[26] while indicating that the interest involved was similar in some respects to more fully legally protected interests in reputation and freedom from unwanted intentional contacts by others.[27] The Institute noted that forerunners of the tort included cases rationalized on property or contract basis involving the unauthorized publication of private letters or lectures or photographic likenesses but that "modern decisions allow recovery in situations in which it is not possible rationally to use the older bases of recovery, and the interest is now recognized as having an independent existence."[28] Given the unusual origins of the tort and the debate among courts and commentators whether it even existed, the Institute can hardly be faulted for originally treating invasion of privacy as a minor tort, placing it next to that of "interference with dead bodies."[29]

Nevertheless, the determination of the American Law Institute that an independent tort existed proved decisive in the courts. Two decades after the promulgation of Section 867, Prosser counted twenty-six states and the District of Columbia as recognizing the tort with several more jurisdictions likely to follow,[30] and another commentator announced that

---

24. *See* DON R. PEMBER, PRIVACY AND THE PRESS 58, 78, 82, 95 (1972). Professor Pember, a journalism instructor and former newsperson, provides an excellent decade by decade treatment of the historical development of the tort with particular reference to its impact on the press.

25. *Id.* at 58, 267–269.

26. "A person who unreasonably and seriously interferes with another's interest in not having his affairs known to others or his likeness exhibited to the public is liable

to the other." RESTATEMENT OF TORTS § 867 (1939). *See id.*, comments *b* and *d*.

27. *Id.*, comment *a*.

28. *Id.*, comment *b*.

29. *Id.*, at § 868.

30. *See* William L. Prosser, *Privacy*, 48 Cal. L. Rev. 383, 386–387 (1960). *See also* DON R. PEMBER, PRIVACY AND THE PRESS 122 (1972) (twenty states and the District of Columbia by 1950); *id.* at 146 (twenty-six states and the District of Columbia by 1960).

"the right of privacy had come of age."[31] Of the jurisdictions embracing the tort between 1939 and 1960, a majority had cited the Restatement.[32] All that was left was the mopping up of sporadic pockets of resistance and, ironically, by the Orwellian year 1984 every American jurisdiction except Minnesota[33] had recognized at least some aspect of the common law tort of invasion of privacy.[34]

The second major event in the modern development and acceptance of this tort was the publication of the second edition of Prosser's text. While perhaps not as influential in the proliferation of the tort as the Restatement, it gave a shape and compelling importance to the right of privacy not provided by the Restatement. In marked contrast to his first edition in which he placed the tort in a catchall chapter entitled, "Miscellaneous" and viewed it "as primarily concerned with the protection of a mental interest,"[35] in the second edition he gave the tort a chapter of its own[36] and declared it "to be a complex of four distinct wrongs, which have little in common except that each is an interference with the plaintiff's right 'to be let alone' ".[37] He then went on to list and describe its four branches, as intrusion, publicity of embarrassing private facts, false light and appropriation. By his formulation, Prosser provided the courts and legal profession with a conceptual framework for dealing with this newly accepted tort. Moreover, he persuaded the American Law Institute to adopt this framework as its own.[38]

31. Don R. Pember, Privacy and the Press 146 (1972).

32. *See* Smith v. Doss, 251 Ala. 250, 37 So.2d 118 (1948); Reed v. Real Detective Pub. Co., 63 Ariz. 294, 162 P.2d 133 (1945); Korn v. Rennison, 21 Conn.Sup. 400, 156 A.2d 476 (1959); Peay v. Curtis Pub. Co., 78 F.Supp. 305 (D.D.C.1948); Cason v. Baskin, 155 Fla. 198, 20 So.2d 243 (1944); Eick v. Perk Dog Food Co., 347 Ill.App. 293, 106 N.E.2d 742 (1952); Pallas v. Crowley, Milner & Co., 322 Mich. 411, 33 N.W.2d 911 (1948) (overruling Atkinson v. John E. Doherty & Co., 121 Mich. 372, 80 N.W. 285, 46 L.R.A. 219 (1899)); Martin v. Dorton, 210 Miss. 668, 50 So.2d 391 (1951) (accepting the tort by implication); Hinish v. Meier & Frank Co., 166 Or. 482, 113 P.2d 438 (1941); Roach v. Harper, 143 W.Va. 869, 105 S.E.2d 564 (W.Va.1958).

33. "Minnesota has never recognized, either by legislative or court action, a cause of action for invasion of privacy, even though many other states have done so." Hendry v. Conner, 303 Minn. 317 319, 226 N.W.2d 921, 923 (1975). *Hendry* was followed in Copeland v. Hubbard Broadcasting, Inc., 526 N.W.2d 402, 406 (Minn.App. 1995); Bohdan v. Alltool Mfg. Co., 411 N.W.2d 902, 906 (Minn.App.1987) (summary judgment granted); Sullivan v. Eginton, 406 N.W.2d 599 (Minn.App.1987); House v. Sports Films & Talents, Inc., 351

N.W.2d 684 (Minn.App.1984); Movie Systems, Inc. v. Heller, 710 F.2d 492, 496 (8th Cir.1983) (counterclaim dismissed). For a very long time Rhode Island was a hold-out against any recognition of the tort. *See* Henry v. Cherry & Webb, 30 R.I. 13, 43, 73 A. 97, 24 L.R.A. (N.S.) 991 (1909) (yet another appropriation of an individual's photographic likeness for commercial advertising purposes without consent); Gravina v. Brunswick Corp., 338 F.Supp. 1 (D.R.I. 1972). But in 1972 the legislature enacted legislation similar to that of New York providing a civil cause of action for the appropriation of another's name or likeness for purposes of commerce without permission. G.L. § 9–1–28 (1969 Reenactment). *See* Kalian v. People Acting Through Community Effort Inc., 122 R.I. 429, 408 A.2d 608 (1979) (reaffirming the common law view taken in the *Henry* case).

34. William L. Prosser and W. Page Keeton, Torts 851 (5th ed. 1984).

35. William L. Prosser, Torts, 1053 (1941).

36. William L. Prosser, Torts 635–644 (2d ed. 1955) (Chapter 20 "Privacy").

37. *Id.* 637. *See also* William L. Prosser, *Privacy*, 48 Cal. L. Rev. 383, 389 (1960).

38. William L. Prosser, *Privacy*, 48 Cal. L. Rev. 383 (1960); Stephen M. Fogel, Gerri

The discussion that follows accepts generally Prosser's division of common law invasion of privacy into four distinct torts for purposes of analysis. But it must be kept in mind that two or more of the torts may be implicated by a single set of facts.

4.4   The Intrusion Branch of the Tort

A.   Interest Involved

While intrusion into another's seclusion may often involve a physical invasion of a possessory interest in real property and thus a trespass, the interest injured by intrusion is entirely different—the mental or emotional state arising out of the belief that one is entitled to separate himself or his personal affairs from others.[1] The attempt to seclude oneself or one's affairs from society may be thwarted in many ways. Physical intrusion may be the most common but intrusion may also be effected by technological devices such as powerful telephoto lenses, shotgun microphones, audio and video recording devices and telephone taps employed beyond the victim's property lines.[2] And with the advent of the computer, data banks storing a person's private informational existence may be surreptitiously invaded, scanned and recorded by remote terminals resulting in actionable conduct by the terminal operator.[3]

Whatever the means or medium of intrusion the injury is the same—mental and emotional distress occasioned by the knowledge that one's physical or informational seclusion has been violated.

B.   Elements of Intrusion

An action under this branch of the tort requires that the plaintiff establish that the intrusion into his seclusion, however effected, was intentional and would be highly offensive to a reasonable person.[4] Thus, an inadvertent intrusion on an individual's privacy by someone entering through the wrong gate and finding a couple "skinny-dipping" in their backyard pool would not amount to an actionable intrusion,[5] provided the accidental intruder beats a hasty retreat. Staying on and viewing the proceedings for any length of time would convert the situation into an intentional intrusion. By the same token, negligently transposing a

---

L. Kornblut, and Newton P. Porter, *Survey of the Law on Employee Drug Testing,* 42 Miami L. Rev. 553 (1988).

1. *See* Phillips v. Smalley Maintenance Servs. Inc., 435 So.2d 705, 711 (Ala.1983); Magenis v. Fisher Broadcasting Inc., 103 Or.App. 555, 558, 798 P.2d 1106, 1108 (1990) William L. Prosser, *Privacy,* 48 Cal. L. Rev. 383, 392 (1960).

2. *See* Dietemann v. Time, Inc., 449 F.2d 245 (9th Cir.1971) (miniature microphone, radio transmitter and voice activated tape recorder).

3. *See* John A. McLaughlin, Comment, *Intrusion Upon Informational Seclusion in the Computer Age,* 17 J. Marshall L. Rev. 831, 843 (1984).

4. RESTATEMENT   SECOND   OF TORTS § 652B (1977).

5. McCormick v. Haley, 37 Ohio App.2d 73, 307 N.E.2d 34, 38 (1973); *cf.* Harris By Harris v. Easton Pub. Co., 335 Pa.Super. 141, 483 A.2d 1377 (1984) (publication of unsolicited government agency press release by defendant newspaper publisher exposing the status of a welfare recipient involved no intentional intrusion).

computer password and entering the wrong data bank is not actionable as an intrusion if the modem connection is immediately broken off.

While the issue of offensiveness is for the jury to decide under the objective standard of whether a person of reasonable sensitivity would find the conduct involved objectionable,[6] reported cases provide some idea of the quality of the conduct required. A reporter or investigator calling once or twice on the telephone or knocking on someone's front door or asking questions of neighbors to gather information for a story or report,[7] or a television camera operator, from the outside, filming the interior of a place of business through a front window for a short period of time in connection with a breaking news story[8] or a private detective attempting to gather evidence paying someone in a hospital, hotel or other place of public accommodation to retrieve discarded bandages or papers from a trash basket physically distant from the plaintiff's room[9] have been held not to be sufficient offensive.

But the unauthorized attendance of defendant newspaper's reporter, who took notes, and a photographer who took photographs at a private party held on an open hill some distance from passers-by to celebrate the recent divorces (not from each other) of the hosts,[10] the encouragement to readers by a newspaper columnist that they call a certain telephone number and "ask for Louise" if they wanted to hear "a sexy telephone voice," resulting in a deluge of phone calls to the plaintiff at her business office,[11] the unauthorized entry into a residence or private office[12] even when no one is present,[13] the entry under false pretenses into someone's

6. Rafferty v. Hartford Courant Co., 36 Conn.Sup. 239, 416 A.2d 1215, 1216 (1980); Harms v. Miami Daily News, Inc. 127 So.2d 715, 718 (Fla.App.1961); Steffen v. General Tel. Co., 60 Ohio App.2d 144, 395 N.E.2d 1346, 14 Ohio Op. 3d 111 (1978); *cf.* Varnish v. Best Medium Pub. Co., 405 F.2d 608 (2d Cir.1968), cert. denied 394 U.S. 987, 89 S.Ct. 1465, 22 L.Ed.2d 762 (1969); *see also* Harris By Harris v. Easton Pub., Co., 335 Pa.Super. 141, 483 A.2d 1377, 1384 (1984)

7. *See* Nicholson v. McClatchy Newspapers, 177 Cal.App.3d 509, 223 Cal.Rptr. 58 (1986) (emphasizing First Amendment protection for non-tortious and non-criminal reasonable newsgathering activities; Sofka v. Thal, 662 S.W.2d 502, 510–511 (Mo. 1983)); Dunlap v. McCarty, 284 Ark. 5, 678 S.W.2d 361 (1984) (dictum); Schupmann by Schupmann v. Empire Fire and Marine Ins., 689 S.W.2d 101 (Mo.App.1985); *see also* RESTATEMENT SECOND OF TORTS § 652, comment *b* (1977).

8. Mark v. King Broadcasting Co., 27 Wash. App. 344, 353, 618 P.2d 512, 519 (1980), *aff'd. sub. nom.* Mark v. Seattle Times, 96 Wash. 2d 473, 498, 635 P.2d 1081, 1094–1095 (1981), cert. denied 457 U.S. 1124, 102 S.Ct. 2942, 73 L.Ed.2d 1339 (1982).

9. *See* Froelich v. Werbin, 219 Kan. 461, 548 P.2d 482 (1976).

10. Rafferty v. Hartford Courant Co., 36 Conn.Sup. 239, 416 A.2d 1215 (1980).

11. Harms v. Miami Daily News, Inc., 127 So.2d 715 (Fla.App.1961); *cf.* CBM of Central Arkansas v. Bemel, 274 Ark. 223, 623 S.W.2d 518, 519–520 (1981) (approximately 70 phone calls over several months by a collection agency).

12. Miller v. National Broadcasting Co. 187 Cal.App.3d 1463, 1491–1491, 232 Cal. Rptr. 668, 678–679 (1986); Ritzmann v. Weekly World News, Inc., 614 F.Supp. 1336 (N.D.Tex.1985); Rawlins v. Hutchinson Pub. Co., 218 Kan. 295, 543 P.2d 988 (1975); Anderson v. WROC–TV, 109 Misc.2d 904, 441 N.Y.S.2d 220 (N.Y. 1981); Mark v. King Broadcasting Co., 27 Wash. App. 344, 618 P.2d 512 (1980).

13. Gonzales v. Southwestern Bell Tel. Co., 555 S.W.2d 219 (Tex.Civ.App.1977) (for purpose of removing phones for which sufficient deposits had not been made); *see* Pearson v. Dodd, 410 F.2d 701 (D.C.Cir.1969), cert. denied 395 U.S. 947, 89 S.Ct. 2021, 23 L.Ed.2d 465 (1969) (for purpose of removing and photo-copying business documents).

home or office with secreted photographic and recording devices[14] or entry into a hospital room to view an ill or dying patient[15] have been held to involve conduct offensive to a reasonable person.

While these cases can provide only a rough guide as to how the trier of fact will view the question of offensiveness in different factual contexts, they do suggest that physical intrusion into the interior of one's home or office will, in almost all cases, be viewed as offensive. In addition, the generation of a large number of telephone calls in a short span of time or even over an extended period is likely to be viewed as unreasonably intrusive.

The central element in an intrusion case is, of course, the seclusion of persons or information. That a plaintiff or private information concerning him was in a place which gives rise to a reasonable expectation of privacy must be established if the claimed intrusion is to be actionable.[16] One's home, office, automobile, hospital or hotel room, all of which can be secured to keep society out, are, of course, such places. Locked files and data banks requiring secret passwords are others. One need not have a possessory interest in the space if a reasonable expectation of privacy is fostered by its nature.[17]

Since the reasonable expectation of seclusion or separation is at the core of the tort, it follows that the absence of this element defeats the action. Thus, with but slight qualification, one is subject to observation, photographing, recording and even questioning when one is in a public or semi-public place where one could expect to be observed by others.[18]

---

14. Dietemann v. Time, Inc. 449 F.2d 245 (9th Cir.1971).

15. Barber v. Time, Inc. 348 Mo. 1199, 159 S.W.2d 291 (1942) (entry to photograph a woman with an exotic disease); Estate of Berthiaume v. Pratt, 365 A.2d 792 (Me. 1976) (physician entering hospital room to take photograph of dying man).

16. Nelson v. Maine Times, 373 A.2d 1221 (Me.1977); Tobin v. Michigan Civil Service Comm'n., 416 Mich. 661, 662, 331 N.W.2d 184, 189 (1982); Corcoran v. Southwestern Bell Tel. Co., 572 S.W.2d 212, 215 (Mo.App.1978); People for the Ethical Treatment of Animals v. Bobby Berosini, Ltd., 111 Nev. 615, 630–633, 895 P.2d 1269, 1279–1281 (Nev. 1995).

17. *E.g.*, Shulman v. Group W Prods., Inc., 18 Cal.4th 200, 74 Cal.Rptr.2d 843, 955 P.2d 469 (1998) (rescue helicopter may be viewed as an ambulance in which accident victims are ministered to); Harkey v. Abate, 131 Mich.App. 177, 180, 346 N.W.2d 74, 76 (1983) (ladies restroom in place of public accommodation equipped by defendant owner of premises with see-through panel in the ceiling permitting surreptitious observation).

18. *See* Ross v. Burns, 612 F.2d 271 (6th Cir.1980) (narcotics agent photographed in public near a courthouse by reporters for a small newspaper); Holman v. Central Arkansas Broadcasting Co., Inc. 610 F.2d 542 (8th Cir.1979) (audio tape recording made by broadcaster of person causing clamor in a police station); Schifano v. Greene County Greyhound Park, Inc., 624 So.2d 178, 180 (Ala.1993) (photographing of patrons seated in public area of dog track); Cefalu v. Globe Newspaper Co., 8 Mass.App.Ct. 71, 391 N.E.2d 935, 939 (Mass.App.1979), cert. denied 444 U.S. 1060, 100 S.Ct. 994, 62 L.Ed.2d 738 (1980) (photographing individual in unemployment compensation line in a government building open to public); People for the Ethical Treatment of Animals v. Bobby Berosini, Ltd., 111 Nev. 615, 630–633, 895 P.2d 1269, 1279–1281 (Nev. 1995) (videotaping of animal trainer "backstage before a performance"). Forster v. Manchester, 410 Pa. 192, 189 A.2d 147 (1963) (motion picture recording made of automobile accident claimant by insurance company while claimant was in public areas); Cox v. Hatch, 761 P.2d 556, 563 (Utah 1988) (postal employees photographed with candidate for

The same holds true for information and materials concerning one's personal affairs when they are in a public place and unsecured or are of public record.[19]

One qualification is that a person in a public area may not be hounded or harassed by constant and close-quarter attention from those who would record their activities.[20] *Galella v. Onassis* provides guidance as to the line between reasonable recording and photographing of persons in public and harassment. Ronald Galella, the self-styled "paparazzo" (Italian for an annoying insect), took it upon himself to photograph at length Jacqueline Kennedy Onassis and her children with the intention of selling the photographs for profit. Examples of his conduct included jumping into the path of John Kennedy while the boy was riding his bicycle in Central Park, causing concern for his safety, interrupting Caroline Kennedy while she was playing tennis, and constantly taking pictures of Mrs. Onassis and those in her party at very close range. Following his arrest, detention and acquittal for harassment, Galella sued Mrs. Onassis and her secret service agents for false arrest, malicious prosecution and tortious interference with his business. Mrs. Onassis counterclaimed for damages and injunctive relief based on, among other things, claimed violations of her common law, constitutional and statutory rights of privacy. The trial court dismissed Galella's complaint and on the counterclaim granted injunctive relief preventing Galella from, among other things, keeping Mrs. Onassis and her children under surveillance or following them; approaching within 100 yards of their home or schools or within 75 yards of either child or 50 yards of Mrs. Onassis. On appeal Galella attacked the injunction as a violation of his First Amendment right to gather news. Rejecting this claim[21] the United States Court of Appeals declared injunctive relief appropriate but eliminated the distance prohibition regarding home and school and reduced the prohibited zone around the person of Mrs. Onassis to 25 feet and around the children to 30 feet. The court expressed concern that the order "not unnecessarily infringe on reasonable efforts to 'cover' defendant."[22]

It seems clear from this case that so long as news gatherers, photographers, investigators and others remain a reasonable distance from their subjects and do not endanger them physically, such information gatherers may observe and record what can be sensed by the naked eye or ear or ask questions without tort liability.

public office at a postal facility); *see also* Stessman v. American Black Hawk Broadcasting Co., 416 N.W.2d 685, (Iowa 1987); RESTATEMENT SECOND OF TORTS § 652D, comment *b* (1977).

19. *See* Jaubert v. Crowley Post–Signal, Inc., 375 So.2d 1386, (La.1979) (plaintiff's "weatherworn and unkempt" home photographed from public street); Edwards v. State Farm Insurance, 833 F.2d 535 (5th Cir.1987).

20. Galella v. Onassis, 487 F.2d 986 (2d Cir.1973); *see also* Evans v. Detlefsen, 857 F.2d 330, 338 (6th Cir.1988); Nader v. General Motors Corp., 25 N.Y.2d 560, 307 N.Y.S.2d 647, 255 N.E.2d 765 (1970).

21. Galella's claim was rejected by the Second Circuit on the basis that the First Amendment does not provide immunity for criminal or tortious conduct engaged in while gathering news. 487 F.2d at 995–996.

22. *Id.* at 998.

One other qualification is that attempting to observe or record private aspects of an individual's person even while the person is in a public place would likely be considered an intrusion as, for instance, attempting to view or photograph someone's undergarments.[23]

C. Elements Not Required for Intrusion

The intrusive tort is completed when a physical, sensory, mechanical or electronic invasion of one's seclusion occurs. The tort does not require that information be obtained or material be taken and if it should be obtained or taken there is no requirement that it be done so surreptitiously or that the fruits of the intrusion be published or otherwise publicized.[24] Thus, if a reporter were allowed to enter the house of a reputed crime boss under the pretext of interviewing him for a story about his legitimate businesses and after being told to wait in the foyer until the host could meet with her, the reporter enters rooms into which she was not invited, opens desk and file drawers looking for evidence of criminal conduct on the part of the host, there is an intrusion. This is so even though there is no subsequent publicity or publication given to the host's alleged criminal activities by the reporter or her newspaper.

Because of the absence of any requirement of publicity or publication, intrusion is notably different than the other three branches of invasion of privacy and this difference can pose serious concerns for newsgatherers, particularly investigative reporters.

D. Dangers for the Newsgathering Media Posed by the Intrusive Tort

With other branches of the tort of invasion of privacy, the public interest in or newsworthiness or correctness of information, materials or images taken and publicized may prevent liability. That is not so regarding intrusion. All that matters is that someone's seclusion has been intentionally invaded and in such manner that the invasion would be considered offensive to a person of reasonable sensibilities. A reporter's motive in pursuing a legitimate story is irrelevant as is the quality of the information obtained by intrusion. Even if a newsgatherer obtains and publishes information of vital public interest through an intrusion, as for example evidence of corruption involving the mayor, an action will lie against the reporter and his media company. The press clause of the First Amendment provides no protection for the media and its representatives here. As the Supreme Court said in *Cox Broadcasting Corp. v.*

---

23. Daily Times Democrat v. Graham, 276 Ala. 380, 162 So.2d 474 (1964) (newspaper photographed woman with skirt blown up above her waist by a jet of air at a funhouse); *see* Phillips v. Smalley Maintenance Services, 435 So.2d 705, 711 (Ala.1983).

24. Dietemann v. Time, Inc., 449 F.2d 245, 247 (9th Cir.1971); Phillips v. Smalley Maintenance Services, 435 So.2d 705 (Ala.

1983) (constant questioning by male employer of an adult female employee concerning her sexual preferences and practices and just as constant refusal to answer by the employee held to be an intrusion); Lamberto v. Bown, 326 N.W.2d 305 (Iowa 1982); Hester v. Barnett, 723 S.W.2d 544 (Mo.App. 1987).

Cohn,[25] "[H]owever it may be ultimately defined, there *is* a zone of privacy surrounding every individual, a zone within which the State may protect him from intrusion by the press." A fine point is put on this statement by the United States Court of Appeals for the Ninth Circuit in *Dietemann v. Time, Inc.* [26] There, a male and female employee of Life Magazine went to the home of Dietemann, a plumber who practiced healing with clay, minerals and herbs. Through misrepresentations that they had been sent by a friend, that the pair were husband and wife and that they were seeking his medical assistance for the woman, they gained access to Dietemann's home. Once in Dietemann's den, the "wife" complained of a lump in one of her breasts. While examining the breast with an assortment of gadgets, Dietemann was secretly photographed by Life's male employee using a hidden camera. In addition, the conversation between the woman and Dietemann was transmitted by a radio hidden in the woman's purse to a tape recorder in a parked car occupied by another Life employee and officials from the Los Angeles district attorney's office and the California Department of Public Health.

The entire operation was a "sting"-type operation planned by employees of Life Magazine and public officials to get evidence against practitioners of quack medicine in southern California and thereafter to allow the magazine to write about the crackdown. Life published the story and pictures following Dietemann's arrest and plea of nolo contendere to criminal misdemeanor charges. Dietemann thereafter sued Time, Inc. in the United States District Court for invasion of privacy and won a judgment of $1,000.

In affirming this judgment, the Ninth Circuit was faced with the questions first whether under California Law the above facts established a cause of action for invasion of privacy and second, if they did, whether the First Amendment insulates the defendant from liability because defendant's employees performed those acts for the purpose of gathering material for a magazine story which was subsequently published utilizing some of the material.

Addressing the first question, the Court of Appeals had no trouble concluding that "clandestine photography of the plaintiff in his den and the recordation and transmission of his conversation without his consent resulting in his emotional distress warrants recovery for invasion of privacy in California."[27] According to the court, plaintiff's den was a

---

25. 420 U.S. 469, 487, 95 S.Ct. 1029, 43 L.Ed.2d 328 (1975) (emphasis by the Court).

26. 449 F.2d 245 (9th Cir.1971). *See also* Galella v. Onassis, 487 F.2d 986 (2d Cir.1973); Nicholson v. McClatchy Newspapers, 177 Cal.App.3d 509, 223 Cal.Rptr. 58 (1986).

27. 449 F.2d at 249. The court went on to say "One who invites another to his home or office takes a risk that the visitor may not be what he seems, and that the visitor may repeat all he hears and observes when he leaves. But he does not and should not be required to take the risk that what is heard and seen will be transmitted by photograph or recording, or in our modern world, in full living color and hi-fi to the public at large or to any segment of it that the visitor may select. A different rule could have a most pernicious effect upon the dignity of man and it would surely lead to guarded conversations and conduct where candor is most valued, *e.g.*, in the case of doctors and lawyers." *Id.* at 249.

sphere from which he could reasonably expect to exclude eavesdropping newspersons.

As to the defendant magazine publisher's claim that the newsgathering was protected by the First Amendment, the court, though agreeing with the publisher that newsgathering is integral to news dissemination, could find no First Amendment protection against liability of those who commit crimes or torts in the course of even legitimate newsgathering. "The First Amendment is not a license to trespass, to steal, or to intrude by electronic means into the precincts of another's home or office."[28]

The *Dietemann* case raises serious questions as to the acceptable boundaries of a newsgatherer's conduct in attempting to obtain sensitive personal information potentially for use in legitimate newsstories and articles. Does the resort to subterfuge alone to gain entry to premises or access to data constitute an intrusion? If so, what constitutes subterfuge? Or if subterfuge to gain access is in itself insufficient to constitute intrusion, what additional conduct must be present to establish the cause of action?

The Ninth Circuit's opinion deals with these important questions only indirectly. The court's language that "one who invites another to his home or office takes a risk that the visitor may not be what he seems" suggests that a reporter might engage in some degree of misrepresentation as to his status in order to gain entry or access. What really seems to have set the court on edge here was the use of concealed visual and aural recording devices. The court mentions this conduct disapprovingly three times in the course of its opinion. But hypothetically, if the Life Magazine employees had the gift of total recall unaided by recording devices and could dictate a verbatim record of the dialogue with Dietemann and describe scenes for a Life artist to sketch, Dietemann would, by the Ninth Circuit's own view, have had to accept this risk.[29] The potential audience could be just as great for a print transcript and sketches on paper as for an aural tape recording and photographs. And would Dietemann's emotional distress likely be any less?

Dietemann is thus something of an enigma.[30] But strongly analogous authorities subsequent to that case do affirm the proposition that the

28. *Id.* at 249; *cf.* Galella v. Onassis, 487 F.2d 986, 995–996 (2d Cir.1973) (harassment by photographer in public places); Belluomo v. KAKE TV & Radio, Inc., 3 Kan.App.2d 461, 596 P.2d 832, 840–842 (1979) (trespass by reporter and camera crew in place of public accommodation to cover health inspection); Le Mistral Inc. v. Columbia Broadcasting System, 61 A.D.2d 491, 493–94, 402 N.Y.S.2d 815, 817 (1978) (trespass by reporter and camera crew in place of public accommodation to cover story on health violations); Stahl v. State, 665 P.2d 839, 841 (Okla.Crim.App.1983), cert. denied 464 U.S. 1069, 104 S.Ct. 973, 79 L.Ed.2d 212 (1984) (criminal trespass by reporters on land of a public utility to cover

protest against construction of nuclear power generating facilities); Prahl v. Brosamle, 98 Wis.2d 130, 151, 295 N.W.2d 768, 781 (1980) (incompletely citing Dietemann v. Time, Inc., 449 F.2d 245, 249 (9th Cir. 1971)) (trespass by a television reporter accompanying police into a private home to cover a shooting incident).

29. *See* n. 27, *supra.*

30. An effort is made to pierce this enigma in an article appearing in the Hastings Journal of Communications and Entertainment Law. It is the authors' thesis that the Dietemann case should be understood as one involving simply the scope of consent. Entry into Dietemann's home, observation

use of cameras and other recording equipment by news gatherers on private property without the consent of the owners or occupants even to cover a legitimate news story constitutes tortious conduct for which damages will be assessed.[31] And this is true whether or not the entry is surreptitious.

If the newsmedia are to be protected from liability for tortious conduct in the course of newsgathering, either the state legislatures or the Congress (under the Commerce Clause) would have to enact legislation limiting the applicability of common law tort to legitimate newsgatherers, or the United States Supreme Court or the state supreme courts would have to be persuaded that the First and Fourteenth Amendments or various state constitutional provisions provide a privilege immunizing newsgatherers from traditional tort liability in the furtherance of the public's interest in the free flow of news and information.

There are, of course, serious obstacles to either approach. Regarding the statutory solution, persuading legislatures to reform the common law for the benefit of the news media would be extremely difficult given their low standing with the public. Furthermore, shaping the parameters of the statutory immunity would also be difficult because of the need to walk a tight-rope between the media's interests and the interests of individuals and corporations allegedly harmed by newsgathering opera-

of what was transpiring in the "office" area and subsequent reportage of words and events were impliedly consented to but sound recording and photographing of the plaintiff were not, and it was such activity that constituted the intrusion. Duncan A. Davidson and Jean A. Kunkel, *The Developing Methodology for Analyzing Privacy Torts*, 6 Comm/Ent L.J. 43, 46–47 (1983). But this explanation does not address the fact that entry into Dietemann's house was effected through misrepresentations.

31. *See* Miller v. National Broadcasting Co., 187 Cal.App.3d 1463, 232 Cal.Rptr. 668 (1986); Belluomo v. KAKE TV & Radio, Inc., 3 Kan.App.2d 461, 596 P.2d 832 (1979); Le Mistral Inc. v. Columbia Broadcasting System, 61 A.D.2d 491, 402 N.Y.S.2d 815 (1978); Prahl v. Brosamle, 98 Wis.2d 130, 295 N.W.2d 768 (1980); *contra:* McCall v. Courier–Journal, 4 Media L. Rptr. 2337 (Ky. Ct. App. 1980), *rev'd on other grounds* 623 S.W.2d 882 (Ky.1981), cert. denied 456 U.S. 975, 102 S.Ct. 2239, 72 L.Ed.2d 849 (1982) (agent of newspaper remained in lawyer's office under misrepresentation and recorded conversation with concealed audio tape recorder in purse); *and compare* Desnick v. American Broadcasting Cos., Inc., 44 F.3d 1345, 1352–53 (7th Cir.1995); Baugh v. CBS, Inc., 828 F.Supp. 745 (N.D.Cal.1993). These latter three cases seem wrong in principle because they immunize newsgatherers from liability

after they had exceeded the terms of consent under which they entered the private premises of the plaintiffs, be it a home or office.

An illuminating discussion of investigative journalism activities and consequent tort liability of the news media is presented in the Symposium, *Undercover Newsgathering Techniques: Issues and Techniques*, 4 Wm & Mary Bill Rights J. 1005–1163 (1996) featuring the articles: Robert M. O'Neil, *Tainted Sources: First Amendment Rights And Journalistic Wrongs* (1005–1025); Sandra S. Baron, et al., *Tortious Interference: The Limits of Common Law Liability for Newsgathering* (1027–1068); Jane E. Kirtley, *Vanity and Vexation: Shifting the Focus to Media Conduct* (1069–1109); John J. Walsh, et al., *Media Misbehavior And The Wages of Sin: The Constitutionality of Consequential Damages For Publication of Ill–Gotten Information* (1111–1144); Paul A. Lebel, *The Constitutional Interest In Getting the News: Toward A First Amendment Protection From Tort Liability For Surreptitious Newsgathering* (1145–1163). *See also* Ethan E. Litwin, Note, *The Investigative Reporter's Freedom and Responsibility: Reconciling Freedom of the Press With Privacy Rights*, 86 Geo. L.J.1093 (1998).

tions. Then there is the checkerboard problem. Unless the Congress imposed such immunity, each state's legislative solution would likely be different, creating problems for the national media, including forum shopping by plaintiffs aggrieved by claim tortious media activity.[32]

As for the constitutional solution, persuading at least five justices of the United States Supreme Court to change more than two hundred years of American tort law by finding a newsgatherers' privilege in the First Amendment would be very hard to accomplish.[33] The Court has never recognized a privilege protecting newsgathering apart from public access situations.[34] And since *New York Times Co.* v. *Sullivan* and its direct progeny, the Court has shown resistance to finding[35] or expanding[36] First Amendment privileges for the news media. But even assuming the Court could be persuaded to find such a privilege, the privilege would have to be very narrow so as not to trench too deeply regarding the rights of injured persons. At the very least the Court would likely place the burden on media defendants to establish clearly and convincingly that their newsgathering activities were designed to bring to light activities directly harmful to the public weal.

Given the highly problematic nature of protecting newsgatherers from potential tort liability, it appears probable that they will have to abide such liability as a risk of doing business for some time to come.

E.   Defenses to Actions for Intrusion

While there are a number of defenses that may be raised by way of rebuttal to the prima facie case of intrusion, there appear to be no privileged affirmative defenses actually excusing intrusive conduct. While on the surface this may seem strange given the fact that the various privileged defenses in tort law apply broadly, on reflection the absence of such defenses is quite consistent with the nature of the tort. First, affirmative defenses like truth or newsworthiness associated with

---

32. Tort actions may be brought in any jurisdiction in which a defendant is subject to process. *See* FLEMING JAMES, JR. CIVIL PROCEDURE 639–641 (1965). Forum shopping will often raise choice of law issues, and if the chosen forum wishes to apply its more plaintiff-oriented law it can often find an interest justifying the choice of the forum's own tort law, such as the interest in applying the forum's "better law." *See, e.g.,* ROBERT A. LEFLAR, AMERICANS CONFLICTS LAW 218–219, 224 (1959); BRAINERD CURRIE SELECTED ESSAYS ON THE CONFLICT OF LAW 177, 183 (1963).

33. But a strong case for the recognition of such a privilege is made by Paul A. Lebel, *The Constitutional Interest in Getting The News: Toward a First Amendment Protection From Tort Liability for Surreptitious Newsgathering*, 4 Wm & Mary Bill Rts. J. 1145 (1996).

34. *Compare* Richmond Newspapers, Inc. v. Virginia, 448 U.S. 555, 100 S.Ct. 2814, 65 L.Ed.2d 973 (1980) *with e.g.,* Houchins v. KQED, Inc., 438 U.S. 1, 98 S.Ct. 2588, 57 L.Ed.2d 553 (1978); Branzburg v. Hayes, 408 U.S. 665, 684, 92 S.Ct. 2646, 2658, 33 L.Ed.2d 626, 641 (1972) (dictum stating "It has generally been held that the First Amendment does not guarantee the press a constitutional right of special access to information not available to the public generally.)"

35. *See* Milkovich v. Lorain Journal Co., 497 U.S. 1, 110 S.Ct. 2695, 111 L.Ed.2d 1 (1990); Herbert v. Lando, 441 U.S. 153, 99 S.Ct. 1635, 60 L.Ed.2d 115 (1979).

36. *See, e.g.,* Gertz v. Robert Welch, Inc., 418 U.S. 323, 94 S.Ct. 2997, 41 L.Ed.2d 789 (1974); Saxbe v. Washington Post Co., 417 U.S. 843, 94 S.Ct. 2811, 41 L.Ed.2d 514 (1974).

torts involving publication or publicity are simply inapplicable to a tort which does not include the element of publication or publicity. Second, other more general privileged defenses developed by the courts such as "necessity" reflect a social policy that a defendant's conduct in particular circumstances may have value exceeding that of protecting a particular interest of the plaintiff in those same circumstances. But the value in a free society of protecting the interest in individuality and autonomy fostered by a zone of privacy or seclusion would rarely be exceeded by any other private interest because protection of individuality and autonomy of its members lies at the core of such a society.[37] However an action for intrusion is, of course, subject to accepted technical affirmative defenses such as the lapse of the statutory limitation period, estoppel and waiver.[38]

The important recurring defenses act to rebut the plaintiff's prima facie case that an intrusion has occurred. The plaintiff is alleging that the defendant, often a newsgatherer, has invaded a protected zone of privacy offensively and without plaintiff's consent. Thus, it must be established that it was the named defendant who intruded. But in the celebrated case of *Pearson v. Dodd*[39] it was the employees of the late Senator Dodd who rifled his files, made copies of sensitive documents and then turned them over to defendant Jack Anderson, who in turn made the documents available to his colleague, Drew Pearson. While the defendants, in publishing information from the documents, were aware of how the material was obtained, the United States Court of Appeals for the District of Columbia ruled that the two columnists could not be viewed as intruders simply because they knowingly accepted the fruits of others' misconduct.[40]

Information gatherers of all stripes can take comfort in the knowledge that they themselves commit no tort of intrusion in merely receiving information and material from intruders, even knowing the circumstances. But three cautionary notes must be sounded. First, if the

37. This is not to say that officials of the state may not be privileged to intrude when urgent state interests are implicated so long as such intrusion is in furtherance of the state's police power and is consistent with constitutional strictures. The one instance in which a private person might be privileged to intrude on one's seclusion would be to prevent a suicide or to save the life of or prevent serious injury to a third party menaced within or without the zone of privacy. Obviously the protection of life takes precedence over any other interest no matter how vital. The analogy here is with the privilege to defend third parties. *See* RESTATEMENT SECOND OF TORTS § 76 (1965); WILLIAM L. PROSSER & W. PAGE KEETON, TORTS 129–131 (5th ed. 1984).

38. Pinkerton National Detective Agency, Inc. v. Stevens, 108 Ga.App. 159, 132 S.E.2d 119 (1963) (waiver defense recognized but not established); *cf.* Bell v. Bir-mingham Broadcasting Co.; 266 Ala., 266 Ala. 266, 96 So.2d 263 (1957); Anderson v. Low Rent Housing Comm'n., 304 N.W.2d 239 (Iowa), cert. denied 454 U.S. 1086, 102 S.Ct. 645, 70 L.Ed.2d 621 (1981); Larsen v. Philadelphia Newspapers, Inc., 375 Pa.Super. 66, 543 A.2d 1181 (1988), cert. denied 489 U.S. 1096, 109 S.Ct. 1568, 103 L.Ed.2d 935 (1989).

39. 410 F.2d 701, 133 U.S. App. D.C. 279 (D.C.Cir.) cert. denied, 395 U.S. 947, 89 S.Ct. 2021, 23 L.Ed.2d 465 (1969).

40. *See also* McNally v. Pulitzer Pub. Co., 532 F.2d 69, 79 (8th Cir.1976), cert. denied 429 U.S. 855, 97 S.Ct. 150, 50 L.Ed.2d 131 (1976); Belluomo v. KAKE TV & Radio, Inc., 3 Kan.App.2d 461, 596 P.2d 832 (1979) (dictum); *compare* Liberty Lobby, Inc. v. Pearson, 390 F.2d 489, 129 U.S. App.D.C. 74 (1967).

information gatherer encourages intrusion by others, he may cross the line and become an aider and abetter and liable in tort as if he were the intruder.[41] Second, if the product of the intrusion is publicized, the one who gives currency to the information may be held to have invaded privacy by unreasonably publicizing private embarrassing facts.[42] Third, if a plaintiff's original documents or materials have commercial value and are turned over by the intruder to the information gatherer, he may be liable in tort for conversion[43] and criminally liable for receiving stolen goods.[44]

In addition to denying that he was the intruder, the defendant might also argue that no invasion of the plaintiff's protected zone of seclusion took place. This defense questions the scope of protection against intrusion afforded to the plaintiff or the extent of his *reasonable* expectation of privacy, looking at that expectation objectively. This defense appears in several variations, most of which involve the word "public" somewhere in defendant's argument. The most obvious is the defense that the plaintiff was physically in a public (as opposed to a private) place affording no reasonable expectation of privacy against approach or recordation.[45] Another variation is that of public records. Almost by definition if information about the plaintiff is embodied in a public record, he can have no reasonable expectation of privacy regarding that information no matter how deeply buried in the archives it may be and thus, for example, a reporter who mucks about in public records pertaining to the plaintiff cannot be held to have intruded on his seclusion.[46]

As for present and former public officials as plaintiffs, it has been suggested that they waive their right to privacy,[47] including the right to seclusion of their person and their private affairs. The idea of waiver of

41. *See* Pearson v. Dodd, 410 F.2d 701, 705, 133 U.S.App.D.C. 279 (D.C.Cir.) cert. denied, 395 U.S. 947, 89 S.Ct. 2021, 23 L.Ed.2d 465 (1969) (by implication); *see also* Fassett v. Delta Kappa Epsilon (N.Y.), 807 F.2d 1150, 1163 (3d Cir.1986), cert. denied 481 U.S. 1070, 107 S.Ct. 2463, 95 L.Ed.2d 872 (1987) (aiding and abetting negligent wrongful death).

42. *Id.* at 705–706.

43. *See* Iglesias v. United States, 848 F.2d 362, 364 (2d Cir.1988); A & E Supply Co. Inc. v. Nationwide Mutual Fire Ins. Co., 798 F.2d 669, 672–673 (4th Cir.1986); Pearson v. Dodd, 410 F.2d 701, 706–708, 133 U.S. App. D.C. 279 (D.C.Cir.1969); Mayer v. Morgan Stanley & Co., Inc., 703 F.Supp. 249, 254–255 (S.D.N.Y.1988).

44. *Cf.* New York Times Co. v. United States, 403 U.S. 713, 737, 91 S.Ct. 2140, 2153, 29 L.Ed.2d 822, 838 (1971) (White, J. concurring).

45. *See, e.g.,* Ross v. Burns, 612 F.2d 271 (6th Cir.1980); Gill v. Hearst Pub. Co., 40 Cal.2d 224, 253 P.2d 441 (1953); Cefalu v. Globe Newspaper Co., 8 Mass.App.Ct. 71, 391 N.E.2d 935, 939 (1979) cert. denied 444 U.S. 1060, 100 S.Ct. 994, 62 L.Ed.2d 738 (1980).

46. *See, e.g.,* Winegard v. Larsen, 260 N.W.2d 816 (Iowa 1977) (rephrasing of information in a judicial opinion by a lawyer for a reporter's benefit cannot amount to intrusion); Gill v. Snow, 644 S.W.2d 222 (Tex.App.1982); *cf.* Howard v. Des Moines Register & Tribune, 283 N.W.2d 289 (Iowa 1979) cert. denied 445 U.S. 904, 100 S.Ct. 1081, 63 L.Ed.2d 320 (1980). (plurality opinion upholding summary judgment in favor of defendant newspaper publisher whose employees used Iowa Freedom of Information Act to discover embarrassing facts about plaintiff contained in public records.)

47. Rawlins v. Hutchinson Pub. Co., 218 Kan. 295, 300, 543 P.2d 988, 993 (1975).

rights is incorrect here. The proper view of the issue of public officials requires recognition that such persons never have a claim to privacy regarding their public acts and other matters relevant to their public office.[48] Again, what is at issue here is the *scope* of the public official's right to seclusion. Even undercover law enforcement officials have no recognized expectation of seclusion when acting secretly on the public's business. In *Cassidy* v. *American Broadcasting Co.*,[49] the plaintiff, a Chicago police officer assigned to the vice control division, was engaged in an undercover investigation of a massage parlor. After paying a thirty dollar admission fee to see "de-luxe" lingerie modeling presented by one of the parlor's models, in a private room, the officer was filmed from an adjacent room through a two-way mirror by a "Channel 7 News" camera crew as he watched the model change her lingerie several times, made several physical advances toward her and finally made the arrest. When the camera crew was discovered someone cried out "Channel 7 News" and the crew exited filming as they went. The police officer sued the station owner and the camera crew for intrusion. The Illinois trial court granted the defendant's motion for summary judgment. In affirming the judgment, the appellate court said, "[I]t appears at once that plaintiff was not a private citizen engaged in conduct which pertained only to himself. He was a public official performing a laudable public service and discharging a public duty. In our opinion, under these circumstances no right of privacy against intrusion can be said to exist with reference to the gathering and dissemination of news concerning discharge of public duties."[50]

The analysis for candidates for public or quasi-public office and public figures is not quite so simple. Since these individuals are not directly conducting the public's business, the above rationale does not apply. Rather, the idea of waiver of an existing right of privacy may apply. The candidate is *seeking* the public's trust and can be said to waive an existing right against having his private affairs intruded upon but only to the extent necessary to assure the electorate that he is a worthy repository of their trust.[51] In the case of public figures there seems less justification for recognizing waiver. These transient or permanent public figures are not conducting the public's business or seeking positions of public trust. The only rationale for waiver here is public curiosity about their lives or the events that made them celebrated. This

---

48. Bell v. Courier–Journal and Times Co., 402 S.W.2d 84 (Ky.1966).

49. 60 Ill.App.3d 831, 17 Ill.Dec. 936, 377 N.E.2d 126, (1978).

50. *Id.* at 838, 17 Ill.Dec. at 942, 377 N.E.2d at 131–132; *see also* Bell v. Courier–Journal & Louisville Times Co., 402 S.W.2d 84 (Ky.1966); Fraternal Order of Police v. News and Sun–Sentinel, 12 Media L. Rep. 1619 (Fla.Cir.Ct.1985); *cf.* Rawlins v. Hutchinson Pub. Co., 218 Kan. 295, 300, 543 P.2d 988, 993 (1975).

51. *See* Beruan v. French, 56 Cal.App.3d 825, 128 Cal.Rptr. 869 (1976) (candidate for union office "voluntarily acceded to a searching inquiry into his fitness" and waived the right of privacy as to the flow of truthful information which may be relevant to the qualifications for office, here a long past criminal record); *cf.* Diaz v. Oakland Tribune, Inc., 139 Cal.App.3d 118, 188 Cal. Rptr. 762 (1983) (degree to which a newly elected student body president at a public community college exposed by defendant media organization as a transsexual opened her private life is a question of fact).

is a relatively weak reason for stripping one of a right against intrusion and justifies at best only a relatively narrow invasion limited to the event or events directly giving rise to the individual's celebrity.[52]

Since actionable intrusion requires that the finder of fact determine that the invasion is offensive to a reasonable person,[53] a defendant might deny that his intrusion was objectionable. Obviously the quality of offensiveness will, like the ideas of truth and beauty, vary among triers of fact. But while different juries might, for instance, differ as to the question of the offensiveness of reporters crashing a large and unusual wedding or "unwedding" party,[54] there seems little doubt that the peep holes or other secret viewing devices by news gatherers or others to maintain surveillance of private persons in private areas would be condemned.[55]

Finally, the tort of intrusion requires, as do other intentional torts,[56] lack of consent on the part of the plaintiff.[57] The rebuttal defense of consent appears in different guises. Not surprisingly, cases of express consent to intrusion are rare for one does not normally give such consent and then bring suit after the intrusion has occurred.[58] Whether the claim of express consent can be successfully pressed by a defendant may well depend on the scope of the consent given by the plaintiff[59] and whether the consent was in effect at the time the claimed intrusion took place.[60]

52. *See* Metter v. Los Angeles Examiner, 35 Cal.App.2d 304, 95 P.2d 491 (1939) (newspaper employee's entry into recent suicide's house and taking her portrait therefrom without permission held not intrusive); *cf.* Diaz v. Oakland Tribune, Inc., 139 Cal.App.3d 118, 188 Cal.Rptr. 762 (1983); Beresky v. Teschner, 64 Ill.App.3d 848, 21 Ill.Dec. 532, 381 N.E.2d 979, (1978); Williams v. KCMO Broadcasting Division Meredith Corp., 472 S.W.2d 1 (Mo.App. 1971).

53. Rafferty v. Hartford Courant Co., 36 Conn.Sup. 239, 243, 416 A.2d 1215, 1216 (1980); Froelich v. Werbin, 219 Kan. 461, 464, 548 P.2d 482, 484–85 (1976) Harkey v. Abate, 131 Mich.App. 177, 182, 346 N.W.2d 74, 76 (1983); *see* RESTATEMENT SECOND TORTS §§ 652B and comment *d* (1977) (by necessary implication).

54. *See* Rafferty v. Hartford Courant Co., 36 Conn.Sup. 239, 416 A.2d 1215 (1980).

55. *See* Harkey v. Abate, 131 Mich.App. 177, 346 N.W.2d 74 (1983); New Summit Associates Ltd. Partnership v. Nistle, 73 Md.App. 351, 533 A.2d 1350 (1987).

56. *See generally* William L. Prosser and W. Page Keeton, Torts 112–124 (5th Ed. 1984).

57. Parish Nat. Bank v. Lane, 397 So.2d 1282, 1286 (La.1981); Turner v. State, 494 So.2d 1292, 1297 (La.App.1986).

58. One of those rare instances is Turner v. State, 494 So.2d 1292 (La.App.1986) in which three adult female plaintiffs permitted a male Louisiana National Guard sergeant to enter their parents' home on a mission to recruit the three young women and one other for the Guard. He gave each of the potential recruits a physical examination. When it was subsequently discovered that the sergeant was not authorized to make such examinations, the home owner parents sued the sergeant and the state of Louisiana for intrusion. The Louisiana appeals court ruled that the parents could not recover because they were bound by the express consent to entry of the premises given with authority by their daughters. *See also* Wood v. Fort Dodge Messenger, 13 Media L. Rep. 1610, 1614 (Iowa Dist. Ct. 1986).

59. *Cf.* Hawkins By and Through Hawkins v. Multimedia, Inc., 288 S.C. 569, 344 S.E.2d 145 (S.C. 1986), cert. denied 479 U.S. 1012, 107 S.Ct. 658, 93 L.Ed.2d 712 (1986), in which there was apparent consent to being included in anonymous newspaper survey concerning teenage pregnancies but not to being identified in the news story.

60. *Cf.* Virgil v. Time, Inc., 527 F.2d 1122 (9th Cir.1975), cert. denied 425 U.S. 998, 96 S.Ct. 2215, 48 L.Ed.2d 823 (1976) in which following an extensive interview with

More common is consent implied either in fact or in law. Certain gestures, actions or conduct on the part of a plaintiff may give rise to the impression that consent has been given to another to intrude upon the plaintiff's seclusion. If that impression could be drawn by a reasonable person, the plaintiff may be found to have given consent even though his subjective intention might well be the opposite.[61] A shrug of the shoulders to a reporter seeking entry into a residence or private office might, in some contexts, be reasonably viewed as consent to enter when that is not the case at all.

From an information gatherer's perspective the most significant type of consent may be that implied by law. By custom and usage a reporter or other information gatherer may enter onto another's land for the limited purpose of asking permission to gather information or cover a story on that land unless "no trespassing" signs are visible.[62] But, of course, this limited license provided by law ends when the owner or possessor of the premises denies permission, at which point the information gatherer must withdraw or risk becoming a trespasser.

Members of the news media have, however, asserted a broader license to enter private property when they are invited to do so by public officials present on the property to deal with newsworthy occurrences requiring governmental action. In the leading case of *Florida Publishing Co.* v. *Fletcher*,[63] a fire broke out in the plaintiff's house while she was out of town, claiming the life of her seventeen-year-old daughter. When the fire marshal and the investigating police officer entered the house to make their official investigation, they invited representatives of the press to accompany them, a standard practice according to their depositions and the affidavits filed on behalf of some twenty-one media organizations. The media representatives entered solely for the purpose of newsgathering and did not damage or disturb anything. When the entourage entered the room from which the daughter's body had already been taken they discovered on the floor a silhouette of the deceased. Determining this to be important to the investigation, the fire marshal took a polaroid picture of the silhouette which did not come out clearly. Finding himself out of film the Marshall requested the defendant's news photographer to take a picture of the silhouette. The resulting photo-

a reporter from Sports Illustrated regarding an article supposedly about body surfing, plaintiff, one of the great practitioners of this sport, withdrew his permission even to being mentioned and sued when the magazine thereafter published the article which featured many peculiar activities of the plaintiff unrelated to body surfing. The trial court's denial of summary judgment for Time, Inc. was affirmed by the Ninth Court.

61. *Cf.* Wood v. Fort Dodge Messenger, 13 Media L. Rep. 1610, 1614 (Iowa Dist. Ct. 1986) (sheriff's employees giving out directions to a farm belonging to plaintiff which was a crime scene under sheriff's control held to amount to either express or implied consent for defendant newspaper's employees to enter, thereby negating trespass).

62. Prahl v. Brosamle, 98 Wis.2d 130, 295 N.W.2d 768, 780 (Wis.App.1980); *see* Florida Pub. Co. v. Fletcher, 340 So.2d 914 (Fla.1976), cert. denied 431 U.S. 930, 97 S.Ct. 2634, 53 L.Ed.2d 245 (1977) (by necessary implication); *cf.* Brabazon v. Joannes Bros. Co., 231 Wis. 426, 433, 286 N.W. 21, 25 (1939) (business visitors and solicitors).

63. 340 So.2d 914 (Fla.1976), cert. denied, 431 U.S. 930, 97 Sup. Ct. 2634, 53 L.Ed.2d 245 (1977).

graph became part of the official investigation file of the fire and police departments and, as might be expected, the photographer turned prints of it and other photographs over to the defendant newspaper which published the silhouette of the deceased.

The mother first learned of the fact surrounding her daughter's death from reading the newspaper account and viewing published photographs. She thereafter brought an action against the newspaper publisher for, among other things, trespass and intrusion. The defendant publisher, moved for summary judgment on the trespass-intrusion count, arguing that the entry was consented to under common custom and usage. The trial court accepted this argument and granted summary judgment. This decision was reversed by the District Court of Appeal because in its view the evidence before the trial court was not sufficient to demonstrate that there was an absence of genuine issues of material fact as to the implied consent issue.

Thereafter, the Florida Supreme Court reversed, reinstating the grant of summary judgment on this count, agreeing that there was no genuine issue of material fact and that, as a matter of law, common custom, usage and practice provides implied consent to the news media to enter private premises under the circumstances presented here. The court put great stock in the fact that the photographer and other media representatives entered the burned home at the invitation of the investigating officers. It was also impressed by the numerous media affidavits that stated this type of entry by news gatherers in the company of public officials occurred frequently in the newsgathering process.

However, the Wisconsin Court of Appeals has taken a decidedly different view of the media's claim of implied consent in these situations. In *Prahl* v. *Brosamle*,[64] the Madison police received a complaint that shots had been fired at four boys who had been bicycling near the plaintiff's residence and biochemical laboratory. Thereafter a SWAT team and other police and sheriff's officers took up positions on and around the plaintiff's property and demanded that the biochemist step out of his home. The scientist complied and after frisking him police searched the residence and laboratory, finding two guns and ammunition.

The defendant, a newscaster for a local television station, hearing the police calls on the station's radio scanner, grabbed a silent motion picture camera and went to the scene. He asked a sheriff's lieutenant, who was directing the operation, if he might enter the premises with the police and was told that he could come forward when the situation was under control. Shortly thereafter the newscaster rode to the residence with the lieutenant and entered the residence, positioning himself in the entranceway where he filmed the officers confiscating the guns and interviewing the plaintiff. The newsman had not requested or received permission from the plaintiff to enter the building or film events inside. Plaintiff did not object, believing the defendant to be a police officer or

64. 98 Wis.2d 130, 295 N.W.2d 768   (App.1980).

sheriff's deputy. The defendant returned to his station, drafted a news-script, edited the film and aired it the next day.

Plaintiff later brought suit against the newsman and his employer for trespass to land.[65] The defendants claimed that the plaintiff was bound by an implied consent arising from the custom and usage of newspersons accompanying police onto a crime scene with police acquiescence. They cited *Florida Publishing Co.* v. *Fletcher* as authority for this contention. The trial court dismissed the complaint.

The Wisconsin Court of Appeals reversed and ordered a trial on the trespass claim. While distinguishing *Fletcher* on grounds that no official here had requested the newscaster's assistance and that the defendants did not rely on record evidence of custom and usage, the Court made clear its doubt as to the correctness of the Florida precedent. The Wisconsin court pointed out that the authorities relied upon in *Fletcher* deal with the implied invitation by businessmen, tradesmen and professionals to the public to come to their places of business and the implied invitation by a householder to others to come to the home for business or information. But the defendant newscaster did not enter the plaintiff's land to do business with him or to obtain permission to gather news on the land or in the residence. Implied in law consent is narrow in scope and the defendants' case, according to the Wisconsin court, did not fall within it.[66]

In principle, the Wisconsin court is right and the Florida court is wrong. That representatives of the media frequently and customarily enter private premises with government officers in order to cover newsworthy events occurring thereon does not create implied in law consent to the intrusion. As discussed earlier, the protected interest in seclusion from society and the individualization that such seclusion or separation fosters is so central to a free society that few competing interests provide legal justification for intrusion. With the exception of *Fletcher*, only one appellate court outside Florida has ever held that the interest of the media in recording and reporting stories on private property overrides the interest protected by the tort of intrusion.[67] *Fletcher's* reliance on cases dealing with implied business invitation and implied invitation of householders for others to come to the door to solicit business and money or to seek permission to enter a building or information such as

---

65. While the interests protected by the torts of trespass to land and intrusive invasion of privacy are quite different, some elements of the two torts are congruent. *See e.g.,* Desnick v. American Broadcasting Cos., 44 F.3d 1345, 1352–1353 (7th Cir. 1995); Magenis v. Fisher, 103 Or.App. 555, 558, 798 P.2d 1106, 1108 (1990).

66. *See* Anderson v. WROC–TV, 109 Misc.2d 904, 441 N.Y.S.2d 220 (1981) which rejects *Fletcher* as unsound and compares the media's consent by custom and usage claim to the English general warrant or writ of assistance which was so odious to the American colonists. *See also* Ayeni v.

CBS, Inc., 848 F.Supp. 362 (E.D.N.Y.1994), aff'd 35 F.3d 680, cert. denied *sub nom.* Mottola v. Ayeni, 514 U.S. 1062, 115 S.Ct. 1689, 131 L.Ed.2d 554 (1995), which rejected the television network's claim to immunity from liability for intrusion because its television crew was invited to accompany a federal agent executing a search warrant in a private home when the occupants objected to the crew's presence.

67. *See* Desnick v. American Broadcasting Cos., Inc., 44 F.3d 1345, 1352–1353 (7th Cir.1995).

directions are inapposite because the intrusion, if any, in these cases is slight, momentary and unobjectionable to reasonable persons. The same cannot be said for reporters and camera operators entering land or buildings to record unusual or unseemly events and then reporting them.[68]

Moreover, the fact that government officers authorized to enter private premises under the state's police power customarily allow news gatherers to accompany them is not significant. The police power gives government officers such as police or fire officials the authority to enter private property only to protect the health, welfare and safety of the citizenry, and this authority may not be delegated to newsgatherers to witness, record and report events transpiring on such property.

F. Remedies for Intrusion

Because intrusion affects the mental and emotional state of the victim, the remedies for this tort are similar in nature to those available for other dignitary torts such as assault, battery and intentional infliction of mental or emotional distress. General, special and punitive damages may be awarded depending on the circumstances and, in rare instances, injunctions against threatened intrusions may be obtained.

General damages are based on the personal distress and injury to dignity caused by the intrusion. Because such injuries are difficult to measure, substantial sums rather than nominal amounts may be awarded, particularly by juries, even when no tangible harm can be established.

Apart from the question of punitive damages, the triers of fact may take into consideration the egregiousness of the circumstances of the intrusion in determining the amount of general damages to be awarded.[69] The fact of publicity relating to the intrusion is an important consideration. While significant damages may be awarded even when the intrusion is not accompanied by the obtaining or disclosing of information or subsequent publicity,[70] disclosures, publicity or publications made possible by intrusion add to the emotional injury and sense of loss of personal dignity and can be compensated for.[71] As stated in *Dietemann* v. *Time, Inc.*, the leading media intrusion case, "No interest protected by the First Amendment is adversely affected by permitting damages for intrusion to be enhanced by the fact of later publication of the information

---

68. *Cf.* Dietemann v. Time, Inc. 449 F.2d 245 (9th Cir.1971).

69. Dan B. Dobbs, Remedies 530–531 (1973); *cf.* Le Mistral, Inc. v. Columbia Broadcasting System, 61 A.D.2d 491, 402 N.Y.S.2d 815 (1978).

70. *See* Harkey v. Abate, 131 Mich.App. 177, 346 N.W.2d 74 (1983) (no evidence see-through ceiling panel in women's restroom ever utilized); Hamberger v. Eastman, 106 N.H. 107, 206 A.2d 239, 11 A.L.R. 3d 1288 (1964) (no allegation that listening device

planted in tenants' bedroom by landlord ever utilized).

71. Dietemann v. Time, Inc., 449 F.2d 245, 250 (9th Cir.1971); *cf.* Belluomo v. KAKE TV & Radio, Inc., 3 Kan.App.2d 461, 471, 596 P.2d 832, 842 (Kan.App.1979) (trespass to land with additional compensatory damages for publication of information acquired through the trespass); Prahl v. Brosamle, 98 Wis.2d 130, 295 N.W.2d 768, 781–782 (App.1980) (same).

that the publisher improperly acquired. Assessing damages [against the intruder] for the additional emotional distress suffered by a plaintiff when the wrongfully acquired data are purveyed to the multitude chills intrusive acts.''[72]

If an intrusion is accompanied by specific loss such as damage to premises, mental health expenses or even loss of income, special damages may be awarded to cover the proven monetary loss.[73] And punitive damages may be imposed for malicious intrusions, with the trier of fact entitled to consider the motive for and nature and scope of the intrusion in assessing the claim for such damages, just as in any other intentional tort action.[74]

In narrow circumstances, continuing or threatened intrusions may also be enjoined. Equitable relief will, of course, only be granted if the potential harm to the victim is irreparable and the remedy at law is inadequate. Intrusive invasions of privacy involve intangible personal injury to individual dignity which may never heal and which is difficult to measure in money terms. Add to this the hardship in returning to court to vindicate these intangible legal rights each time the intruder invades the plaintiff's seclusion and one may have a case for injunctive relief against threatened intrusion. Because intrusion, unlike other branches of invasion of privacy does not require any publication for its commission, First Amendment concerns regarding the enjoining of publication are not usually implicated here.[75]

Even without the obstacle of the First Amendment, injunctions against intrusions by news gatherers appear to be rare. Certainly there are few reported cases involving such remedies against the media. Perhaps this is because such invasions of privacy would normally be made in conjunction with specific newsstories and would end with those stories. To paraphrase an old saying, there is nothing so stale as yesterday's news and yesterday's newsmakers. But exceptions do occur, particularly in conjunction with persons of great celebrity. The leading example of this is *Galella* v. *Onassis*[76] in which the independent photographer Ronald Galella, the self-styled insect pest or "paparazzo," continually hounded Jacqueline Kennedy Onassis and her children in order to obtain photographs to sell to publications and individual collectors.

---

72. 449 F.2d 245, 250 (9th Cir.1971); *see* Pack v. Wise, 155 So.2d 909 (La.App.1963) (creditor's intrusion into debtor's employment relationship resulting in debtor's dismissal and ultimate award of both general damages for the intrusion and special damages for consequent loss of income).

73. Dan B. Dobbs, Remedies 530 (1973); *see* Le Mistral, Inc. v. Columbia Broadcasting System, 61 A.D.2d 491, 495, 402 N.Y.S.2d 815, 817–818 (1978) (defendant entitled in action for trespass to have jury consider its motive in sending a camera crew into a restaurant unannounced and uninvited with cameras rolling and bright lights on given defendant's claim for puni-

tive damages); *see* also Belluomo v. KAKE TV & Radio, Inc., 3 Kan.App.2d 461, 596 P.2d 832, 842 (1979).

74. *See generally* Dan B. Dobbs, Remedies 532–539 (1973).

75. For discussion of those concerns *see* New York Times Co. v. United States, 403 U.S. 713, 91 S.Ct. 2140, 29 L.Ed.2d 822 (1971); Near v. Minnesota, 283 U.S. 697, 51 S.Ct. 625, 75 L.Ed. 1357 (1931); T. Barton Carter, Juliet L. Dee, Martin J. Gaynes and Harvey L. Zuckman, Mass Communications Law 25–28 (4th ed. 1994).

76. 487 F.2d 986 (2d Cir.1973).

When these intrusions became unbearable and even dangerous to the safety of the children Mrs. Onassis obtained an injunction against Galella which, as modified by the Second Circuit, prohibited the photographer from entering her children's schools and play areas and coming within 30 feet of the children and 25 feet from her.[77]

Thus there is little doubt that in extreme cases, the courts will issue injunctions against newsgatherers for their continuing intrusions.

4.5   The Appropriation Branch of the Tort

A.   History

From a historical perspective, appropriation is the most interesting of the four branches of invasion of privacy. While Warren and Brandeis theorized in their landmark article about the existence of a common law right not to have one's private facts unreasonably publicized,[1] the existence of a right of privacy was first fought out in the courts at the turn of the twentieth century in the context of the appropriation of a person's name or image for another's advantage, normally commercial.

In *Roberson* v. *Rochester Folding Box Co.*[2] an attractive woman, upon discovering her photographic image printed on a widely distributed flyer advertising a particular brand of flour, sued for invasion of privacy. Her claim was rejected by the New York Court of Appeals, which held that no common law right of privacy existed. But in *Pavesich v. New England Life Ins. Co.*,[3] the Georgia Supreme Court held just the opposite when an Atlanta resident came face to face with his photograph and purported endorsement of New England Life Insurance Company policies in an ad in a local newspaper. The march of the cases in the twentieth century has been in step with Georgia and not New York in the recognition of the appropriation tort. And in a number of jurisdictions including New York the legislatures have made actionable by statute the taking without consent of another's identity for trade or advertising purposes.[4] Today, appropriation is the most widely accepted of the four branches of invasion of privacy.

By the middle of the twentieth century it was recognized that appropriation actually encompassed two distinct interests, one dignitary and the other proprietary. There were in reality two torts present under the rubric "appropriation," one of which was actually antithetical to the

---

77. *Id.* at 1001.

1. Samuel D. Warren and Louis D. Brandeis, *The Right to Privacy*, 4 Harv. L. Rev. 193 (1890).

2. 171 N.Y. 538, 64 N.E. 442 (1902).

3. 122 Ga. 190, 50 S.E. 68 (1905).

4. *See* Cal. Civ. Code §§ 990 (deceased personalities), 3344 (living persons) (West Supp. 1996); Fla. Stat. Ann. § 540.08 (West 1988); Ky. Rev. Stat. Ann. § 391.170 (Repl. Vol. 1984); Mass. Gen. Laws Ann. ch. 214 §§ 1B, 3A (West 1989); Neb. Rev. Stat. §§ 20–201, 20–202 (1991); N.Y. Civ. Rights Law §§ 50, 51 (McKinney 1992 and Supp. 1996); Okla. Stat. Ann. tit. 21, §§ 839.1, 839.2 (West 1983); R.I. Gen. Laws §§ 9–1–28 and 9–1–28.1(2) (1985) (general invasion of privacy statutes expressly encompassing the appropriation tort); Tenn. Code Ann. §§ 47–25–1101 through 47–25–1108 (1995); Utah Code Ann. §§ 45–3–1 through 45–3–6 (1993); Va. Code Ann. § 8.01–40 (Repl. Vol. 1992), § 18.2–216.1 (Repl. Vol. 1988); Wis. Stat. Ann. § 895.50 (West 1983).

idea of privacy. In *Haelan Laboratories, Inc.* v. *Topps Chewing Gum, Inc.*[5] the dichotomous nature of appropriation was judicially recognized for the first time when the Second Circuit held that in addition to one's right not to have his human dignity injured by the unauthorized commercial use of his photograph, one also "has a right in the publicity value of his photograph" which right has pecuniary worth.[6] This "right of publicity" as Judge Frank labeled it has now been recognized by the United States Supreme Court and the American Law Institute[7] and is so accepted that an entire treatise has been devoted to it.[8]

Thus, today when discussion is directed to the appropriation branch confusion can be avoided by remembering that that branch itself has two branches which grow out of the two very different interests involved.

B. Interests Involved

The Restatement Second of Torts in the comment to Section 652C states the interest protected by the tort of appropriation to be the individual's "exclusive use of his identity." But that statement hardly explains why the law should protect individual identity. The reason is, of course, that individuality is at the core of human autonomy and dignity. If another can take one's name or image or identity without permission for whatever purpose, the individual from whom these things are taken has been degraded to the status of involuntary servitude. It is this loss of autonomy and choice that led to Ms. Roberson's cry that 25,000 likenesses of her had been "conspicuously posted and displayed in stores, warehouses, saloons, and other public places; that they have been recognized by friends and other people, with the result that plaintiff has been greatly humiliated by the scoffs and jeers of persons who have recognized her face and picture on this advertisement. . . . "[9] Ms. Roberson had been impressed by a milling company to serve as its "Flour of the Family" to sell flour. It is to prevent such impressment and to preserve individual dignity that caused courts and legislatures overwhelmingly to recognize this interest in the twentieth century despite the New York Court of Appeals' refusal to do so in *Roberson*.[10]

---

5. 202 F.2d 866 (2d Cir.), cert. denied 346 U.S. 816, 74 S.Ct. 26, 98 L.Ed. 343 (1953).

6. *Id*. at 868; *see generally* H. Lee Hetherington, *Direct Commercial Exploitation of Identity: A New Age for the Right of Publicity*, 17 Colum.-VLA J.L. & Arts 1 (1993).

7. Zacchini v. Scripps–Howard Broadcasting Co., 433 U.S. 562, 97 S.Ct. 2849, 53 L.Ed.2d 965 (1977); RESTATEMENT THIRD OF THE LAW OF UNFAIR COMPETITION § 46 (1995).

8. J. Thomas McCarthy, The Rights of Publicity and Privacy (1987). Besides the *Haelan Laboratories* case, the major impetus for the recognition and development of this new tort in the second half of the twentieth century came from still another

law review article: Melville B. Nimmer, *The Right of Publicity*, 19 Law & Contemp. Probs. 203 (1954). For an excellent modern judicial discussion contrasting the torts of appropriation and invasion of the right of publicity *see* People for the Ethical Treatment of Animals v. Bobby Berosini, Ltd., 111 Nev. 615, 895 P.2d 1269 (1995), and for a thoughtful modern law review treatment of the right of publicity *see* Sheldon W. Halpern, *The Right of Publicity: Maturation of an Independent Right Protecting the Associative Value of Personality*, 46 Hastings L.J. 853 (1995).

9. Roberson v. Rochester Folding Box Co., 171 N.Y. 538, 64 N.E. 442 (1902).

10. *Id.*

While Ms. Roberson was not a celebrity but just another pretty face, celebrities too are entitled to autonomy and choice and may not be forced to promote commercial products such as cigarettes, flour, clothing, perfume or even bubblegum against their will.[11] For instance, in *Onassis v. Christian Dior–New York, Inc.,*[12] Dior–New York decided on a serial advertising campaign for the numerous Dior licensed products sold in the United States featuring a *menage a trois* of two male models and one female model known as the Diors and who were suggested to lead a sophisticated and unconventional lifestyle, or, as Newsweek Magazine put it in an article about the ad campaign, they were "idle rich, suggestively decadent and aggressively chic."[13] One of the sixteen ads featured a wedding between one of the male Diors and the female. For this "shoot" Dior's advertising agency obtained the appearance as wedding guests of Gene Shalit, the television personality, famous model Shari Belafonte, veteran actress Ruth Gordon and an unknown secretary named Barbara Reynolds, who was recruited for the ad by a celebrity look-alike outfit because of her extremely close resemblance to Jacqueline Kennedy Onassis. Mrs. Onassis, needless to say, was not invited to appear in the wedding scene and would have refused if she had been invited. It was, of course, the apparent image of Mrs. Onassis at the wedding of two of the Diors (the third would continue to hang around until the ad series terminated) that gave the ad the necessary cachet to make it succeed and help send sales of Dior licensed products "through the roof," as Dior–New York characterized the results.

Mrs. Onassis sued and moved for a preliminary injunction pursuant to New York's appropriation legislation[14] to prevent repetition of the offending ad. In granting the motion, the trial judge had no doubt that the use of a look-alike model amounted to a taking of Mrs. Onassis' image and an invasion of her privacy in violation of the New York statutory scheme. She had a protected privacy right to withhold her image and celebrity from commercial exploitation.[15]

11. *See, e.g.,* Motschenbacher v. R.J. Reynolds Tobacco Co., 498 F.2d 821 (9th Cir.1974) (famous racing car driver); Grant v. Esquire, Inc., 367 F.Supp. 876 (S.D.N.Y. 1973) (screen actor Cary Grant).

12. 122 Misc.2d 603, 472 N.Y.S.2d 254 (Sup. Ct. 1984).

13. *Id.* at 257.

14. N.Y. Civ. Rights Law §§ 50, 51 (McKinney 1992 and Supp. 1996). Section 50 provides:

"A person, firm or corporation that uses for advertising purposes, or for the purposes of trade, the name, portrait or picture of any living person without having first obtained the written consent of such person ... is guilty of a misdemeanor."

Section 51, which was amended in 1995 to include voice impersonations, provides:

"Any person whose name, portrait or picture is used within this state for advertising purposes or for the purposes of trade without the written consent first obtained as above provided may maintain an equitable action in the supreme court of this state against the person, firm or corporation to using his name, portrait, picture or voice, to prevent and restrain the use thereof; and may also sue and recover damages for any injuries sustained by reason of such use and if the defendant shall have knowingly used such person's name, portrait, picture or voice in such manner as is forbidden or declared to be unlawful by section fifty of this article, the jury, in its discretion, may award exemplary damages.... "

15. To similar effect *see* Ali v. Playgirl, Inc. 447 F.Supp. 723, 726 (S.D.N.Y.1978) involving a clearly recognizable drawing of Muhammad Ali portrayed as a boxer seated in a corner of the ring in the nude; *see also*

Mrs. Onassis also claimed in this case a violation of the common law right of publicity. While the trial court chose not to confront this claim,[16] the case suggests the point at which the appropriateable interests in privacy and publicity intersect.

Because the law secured her celebrity from unwanted exploitation so as to protect her privacy (a dignitary interest), that very celebrity takes on proprietary or publicity value which Mrs. Onassis could exploit in the marketplace if she chose. Precisely because Dior–New York invaded a *celebrity's* privacy by appropriating her likeness, it appropriated, at the same time, the commercial value of Mrs. Onassis' likeness. With privacy protection of one's identity comes property value, giving one imbued with celebrity the power of its exploitation—the "right of publicity."

This legal phenomenon of a proprietary publicity interest arising out of a dignitary privacy interest was first recognized in *Haelan Laboratories* v. *Topps Chewing Gum, Inc.*[17] There, one chewing gum manufacturer was alleged to have infringed on another chewing gum manufacturer's contractual right to exclusivity in distributing photographs of certain leading major league ballplayers as an inducement to the public to purchase its gum. In reversing and remanding the trial court's order dismissing the complaint, the Second Circuit recognized that the ballplayers, under New York statute, had a protected interest in their identity and, because of their celebrity, possessed a proprietary interest as well. But normally this interest would yield no monetary benefit unless it could be made the subject of an exclusive contractual grant of the right of exploitation. The claim of interference with the recognized right to cede to others this proprietary interest was held to state a cause of action in tort, and the "right of publicity" was on its way.

C. Elements of the Tort

While it is noted immediately above that the tort of appropriation protects two quite different interests, one of which is antithetical to personal privacy and the desire to be "let alone," the conduct of the appropriator necessary to the creation of the tort is the same whichever interest is present. But, in contrast, the status of the plaintiff, as will be discussed below, may make considerable difference in the result of litigation, depending upon which interest is asserted to have been violated.

Allen v. National Video, Inc., 610 F.Supp. 612 (S.D.N.Y.1985) (Woody Allen look-alike in an ad promoting a video tape rental club but with summary judgment granted to the actor-director on grounds of violation of Section 401 of the Lanham Act, 15 U.S.C.A. § 1125(a) (West 1994)); Prudhomme v. Procter & Gamble Co., 800 F.Supp. 390, 395–396 (E.D.La.1992) (Chef Paul Prudhomme look-alike promoting Folgers Coffee).

16. It was very doubtful at the time this case was decided that New York would recognize a common law right of privacy. Subsequently, the New York Court of Appeals ruled in Stephano v. News Group Pubs., Inc., 64 N.Y.2d 174, 485 N.Y.S.2d 220, 474 N.E.2d 580 (1984) that no common law cause of action to protect the right of publicity would be recognized in New York.

17. 202 F.2d 866 (2d Cir.), cert. denied 346 U.S. 816, 74 S.Ct. 26, 98 L.Ed. 343 (1953).

1. Taking

For the tort of appropriation to be committed, there must first be a taking of another's name,[18] image or likeness,[19] voice[20] or other characteristics.[21] But one's "likeness" or persona does not include events from a person's life, especially when fictionalized.[21a] Apparently the taking of the victim's persona or identity need not be intentional but, as with copyright infringement, may be negligent or even innocent.[22] What is critical here, is the result. Did third parties recognize the appropriated identity and act in a manner that tangibly benefited the taker or his successor.

18. See, e.g., Acme Circus Operating Co. v. Kuperstock, 711 F.2d 1538 (11th Cir. 1983) (appropriation of name of Clyde Beatty the famous animal trainer); Canessa v. J.I. Kislak, Inc., 97 N.J.Super. 327, 235 A.2d 62 (1967) (appropriation of name of non-celebrity to promote a real estate company that assisted the non-celebrity in finding a house for his family); cf. Carson v. Here's Johnny Portable Toilets, Inc., 698 F.2d 831 (6th Cir.1983) (use of the phrase "Here's Johnny" by a portable toilet company held to be an appropriation of the persona of the television entertainer Johnny Carson); Weingand v. Lorre, 231 Cal. App.2d 289, 41 Cal.Rptr. 778 (1964) (petition of actor to change his name to "Peter Lorie" rejected upon objection of the late actor Peter Lorre).

19. See, e.g., Pavesich v. New England Life Ins. Co., 122 Ga. 190, 50 S.E. 68 (1905) (photograph); Martin Luther King, Jr. Center For Social Change, Inc. v. American Heritage Prods., 250 Ga. 135, 296 S.E.2d 697 (1982) (plastic casting); Canessa v. J.I. Kislak, Inc., 97 N.J.Super. 327, 235 A.2d 62 (1967) (group photograph); Welch v. Mr. Christmas, Inc., 57 N.Y.2d 143, 454 N.Y.S.2d 971, 440 N.E.2d 1317 (1982) (video tape commercial); Kimbrough v. Coca-Cola/USA, 521 S.W.2d 719 (Tex.Civ.App. 1975) (reproduction of original painting of former college football star).

20. See N.Y. Civ. Rights Law § 51 (McKinney Supp. 1996); Midler v. Ford Motor Co., 849 F.2d 460 (9th Cir.1988) (use of voice imitator in a television commercial to suggest performance by the singer Bette Midler); see also Waits v. Frito–Lay, Inc. 978 F.2d 1093 (9th Cir.1992); compare Lahr v. Adell Chemical Co. 300 F.2d 256 (1st Cir.1962) (use of voice imitator in a television commercial to sound like the late comedian and actor Bert Lahr).

21. See, e.g., White v. Samsung Electronics America, Inc., 971 F.2d 1395, 1400 (9th Cir.1992) (appropriation of hair color and style, and dress of popular television game show hostess Vanna White along with a replica of her game show set); Groucho Marx Productions, Inc. v. Day and Night Co., 523 F.Supp. 485, 491 (S.D.N.Y.1981), rev'd on other grounds, 689 F.2d 317 (2d Cir.1982) (appropriation of stage and screen persona of the Marx Brothers); Chaplin v. Amador, 93 Cal.App. 358, 269 P. 544 (1928) (appropriation of Charlie Chaplin's "little tramp" character by another movie actor). The Vanna White case really pushes the envelope because what was appropriated there for a parody commercial, was Ms. White's style, a rather amorphous characteristic. For critical commentary on the case see David S. Welkowitz, Catching Smoke, Nailing Jello to the Wall: The Vanna White Case and the Limits of Celebrity Rights, 3 J. Intell. Prop. L. 67 (1995) (concluding that the case was incorrectly decided and collecting the critical commentary of others).

21a. See Matthews v. Wozencraft, 15 F.3d 432, 438 (5th Cir.1994); Toscani v. Hersey, 271 App.Div. 445, 65 N.Y.S.2d 814 (1946); WILLIAM L. PROSSER AND W. PAGE KEETON, TORTS 853 (5th ed. 1984).

22. See Douglass v. Hustler Magazine, Inc. 769 F.2d 1128, 1140 (7th Cir.1985) cert. denied 475 U.S. 1094, 106 S.Ct. 1489, 89 L.Ed.2d 892 (1986) (dictum); Fairfield v. American Photocopy Equipment Co., 138 Cal.App.2d 82, 87, 291 P.2d 194, 197 (1955); Welch v. Mr. Christmas, Inc., 57 N.Y.2d 143, 440 N.E.2d 1317 (1982) (interpreting the New York appropriation statutes); J. THOMAS MCCARTHY, THE RIGHTS OF PUBLICITY AND PRIVACY § 3.6 [F] (1987); cf. Kerby v. Hal Roach Studios, 53 Cal.App.2d 207, 127 P.2d 577 (1942) (a "false light" invasion of privacy case in which a motion picture company took the name of a real woman to promote its movie when the existence of this woman was unknown and use only of a fictitious character had been intended).

2. *Identification*

Such result requires both identification and benefit. If the complainant cannot be identified by third persons, actions for either invasion of privacy, infringement of the right of publicity or both will fail. It is thus not enough that a taking of another's identity be affected. Others besides the victim must be able to identify the object of the taking for it to be actionable.[23] Identifiability is, of course, a jury question.[24] A fanciful illustration of a non-actionable taking would be that of a very bad impersonator whose masquerade as the plaintiff in order to facilitate a commercial transaction goes unrecognized by the other parties to the transaction.

3. *Benefit to the Appropriator*

While identification of the plaintiff by third parties is necessary, it does not follow that benefits giving rise to a legal claim will always accrue. One may adopt another's well recognized name or character, without more, simply because he likes the sound or look of it or admires the other person.[25] So long as there is no attempt to capitalize on the other's identity, the mere psychic reward to the taker arising from the name or character change is not such benefit as will give rise to actionable appropriation.[26] However, in a common law action, the benefit involved need not be strictly commercial or pecuniary. For instance, the use of another's identity to influence the course of public affairs has been held to be actionable.[27]

Whether the benefit is commercial or non-commercial, it must further some specific interest of the appropriator or his successor. It is

23. Rawls v. Conde Nast Pub., Inc., 446 F.2d 313 (5th Cir.1971), cert. denied 404 U.S. 1038, 92 S.Ct. 712, 30 L.Ed.2d 730 (1972); Bayer v. Ralston Purina Co., 484 S.W.2d 473 (Mo.1972); Cohen v. Herbal Concepts., Inc., 63 N.Y.2d 379, 482 N.Y.S.2d 457, 472 N.E.2d 307 (1984) (interpreting the New York appropriation statute). *See* SAMUEL HOFSTADTER AND GEORGE HOROWITZ, THE RIGHT OF PRIVACY § 5.7, (1964); GEORGE B. TRUBOW (editor), PRIVACY LAW AND PRACTICE § 1.02(2) (1987).

24. Cohen v. Herbal Concepts, Inc., 63 N.Y.2d 379, 385, 482 N.Y.S.2d 457, 459, 472 N.E.2d 307, 309 (1984); GEORGE B. TRUBOW (editor), PRIVACY LAW AND PRACTICE § 1.02[2] (1987).

25. RESTATEMENT SECOND TORTS § 652C, comment *c* (1977); *See* Wrist–Rocket Mfg. Co. Inc. v. Saunders, 379 F.Supp. 902 (D.C.Neb.1974), *modified*, 516 F.2d 846 (8th Cir.1975), cert. denied 423 U.S. 870, 96 S.Ct. 134, 46 L.Ed.2d 100 (1975); Standard Oil Co. (Indiana) v. Standard Oil Co. (Ohio), 141 F.Supp. 876 (D.Wyo.1956).

26. RESTATEMENT SECOND TORTS § 652C, comment *c* (1977). One court has

gone so far as to rule that an appropriation which merely increases a commercial organization's general goodwill within a segment of the potential market is not actionable. *See* Benavidez v. Anheuser Busch, Inc., 873 F.2d 102 (5th Cir.1989); *see also* Moore v. Big Picture Co., 828 F.2d 270, 275 (5th Cir.1987); National Bank of Commerce v. Shaklee Corp., 503 F.Supp. 533 (W.D.Tex.1980); Gautier v. Pro–Football Inc., 304 N.Y. 354, 107 N.E.2d 485 (1952); Kimbrough v. Coca–Cola/U.S.A., 521 S.W.2d 719 (Tex.Civ.App.1975).

27. *See, e.g.*, Hinish v. Meier and Frank Co., 166 Or. 482, 113 P.2d 438 (1941) (telegram to governor urging veto of a bill over plaintiff's name inserted without permission by defendant held actionable); *cf.* Schwartz v. Edrington, 133 La. 235, 62 So. 660 (1913) (contempt citations upheld against newspaper publishers for publishing in violation of injunction a village incorporation petition knowing that some petitioners wished to dissociate themselves from the petition).

not enough that the use of another's name or likeness be simply of incidental benefit. As the Restatement Second of Torts states it, "The value of the plaintiff's name is not appropriated by mere mention of it, or by reference to it in connection with legitimate mention of his public activities; nor is the value of his likeness appropriated when it is published for purposes other than taking advantage of his reputation, prestige, or other value associated with him. . . . "[28] Thus, the publication in a magazine of a photograph of a group of persons including the plaintiff, who is clearly recognizable, to provide graphic interest to an article about modern sexual and social mores was held not to involve an actionable appropriation.[29] And the publication of the name and photograph of an airline pilot killed in a crash in a non-fiction book concerning his claimed reappearance as a ghost on subsequent flights, thus making him a central figure, was also held to be of incidental benefit to the author and publisher.[30] The argument is consistently made by plaintiffs in these cases that the benefit from using the names and images of others in a commercial enterprise such as publishing is ultimately financial profit for the enterprise. The equally consistent response of the courts is that the use of another's identify in these situations is not for the purpose of appropriating the commercial or other value associated with that identity as required for this action but simply a referencing to that identity.[31] A different response by the courts would have serious First Amendment implications because the news and information industry in this country is predominantly profit-seeking and would be hamstrung in facilitating the flow of news and information to the public if its members could be held liable in tort for using names and images of individuals associated with the events of our times.

4. Lack of Consent

Finally, it goes almost without saying, that the appropriation of another's identity must be without consent.[32] Since suits are rarely brought where consent is clearly given, this issue is normally raised in relationship to the interpretation, scope and expiration of written releases permitting the use of individual names and images for trade and commercial purposes.[33]

28. Section 652C, comment *d* (1977).

29. Tropeano v. Atlantic Monthly Co., 379 Mass. 745, 400 N.E.2d 847 (1980).

30. Loft v. Fuller, 408 So.2d 619. (Fla. App.1981).

31. *E.g.*, Loft v. Fuller, 408 So.2d 619, 623 (Fla.App.1981); Tropeano v. Atlantic Monthly Co. 379 Mass., 745, 748–749, 400 N.E.2d 847, 850 (1980); Arrington v. New York Times Co., 55 N.Y.2d 433, 440, 434 N.E.2d 1319, 1322, 449 N.Y.S.2d 941, 944 (1982), cert. denied 459 U.S. 1146, 103 S.Ct. 787, 74 L.Ed.2d 994 (1983); Nelson v. Maine Times, 373 A.2d 1221, 1224 (Me. 1977).

32. *See* Newton v. Thomason, 22 F.3d 1455 (9th Cir.1994); Neff v. Time, Inc., 406

F.Supp. 858 (W.D.Pa.1976); Faloona by Fredrickson v. Hustler Magazine, Inc., 607 F.Supp. 1341, 1353–1355 (N.D.Tex.1985), *aff'd*, 799 F.2d 1000 (5th Cir.1986), cert. denied, 479 U.S. 1088, 107 S.Ct. 1295, 94 L.Ed.2d 151 (1987); Andretti v. Rolex Watch, U.S.A., Inc., 56 N.Y.2d 284, 452 N.Y.S.2d 5, 437 N.E.2d 264 (1982) (interpreting the New York appropriation statute); Brinkley v. Casablancas, 80 A.D.2d 428, 438 N.Y.S.2d 1004 (1981) (same).

33. *See, e.g.*, Faloona by Fredrickson v. Hustler Magazine, Inc., 607 F.Supp. 1341, 1353–1355 (N.D.Tex.1985), *aff'd* 799 F.2d 1000 (5th Cir.1986), cert. denied 479 U.S. 1088, 107 S.Ct. 1295, 94 L.Ed.2d 151 (1987), Welch v. Mr. Christmas, Inc., 57

D. *Assignability and Descendibility of the Right of Publicity*

The actions for invasion of privacy are personal to the individual whose interest (or interests) is invaded and, as such, may not be asserted by others, assigned to others by contractual arrangement during the life of the injured party, or transferred by will or otherwise upon his death.[34] But a question arises as to the assignability or descendibility of the related right of publicity because of the proprietary interest represented by this right. If the right of publicity is assignable and descendible then who the specific plaintiff is will be of little concern in an action to vindicate the right. If, on the other hand, the right is viewed as not transferable the identify of the plaintiff may, as with the other branches of invasion of privacy, be determinative.

That the right of publicity has some aspects of private property cannot be denied, but the problem is to determine when transferability should be recognized as an aspect of that right by balancing the needs of society against the claims of individuals seeking to profit from another's identity or persons.

One facet of transferability is the contractual assignment of the right by the person whose identity is to be used or exploited. Because the right of publicity is indigenous to the person who possesses it, a direct assignment of the right to another would be like attempting transfer of one's personality to another—a practical impossibility. Rather, it is the right to exploit another's identity which is transferred, and the transfer is usually effected by the execution, for financial consideration, of an exclusive license or a release from liability.[35] Few legal issues arise from the inter vivos transfer of the power of exploitation other than those associated with the construction and scope of the license or release.

The major issue involving transferability arise at the death of persons whose identities retain publicity value. Does the deceased's right of publicity descend to others or does that right end with death, thereby permitting anyone who wishes to exploit the deceased's identity to do so without license? When this question was first presented the courts were seriously divided. The United States Court of Appeals for the Sixth Circuit became the chief advocate for the rule that the right of publicity

N.Y.2d 143, 440 N.E.2d 1317, 454 N.Y.S.2d 971 (1982); Brinkley v. Casablancas, 80 A.D.2d 428, 438 N.Y.S.2d 1004 (1981); *cf.* Leavy v. Cooney, 214 Cal.App.2d 496, 29 Cal.Rptr. 580 (1963) (written release with parol limitation as to use of plaintiff's image in motion picture theaters).

34. Memphis Dev. Found. v. Factors, Etc., 441 F.Supp. 1323 (W.D.Tenn.1977); Mac Donald v. Time Inc., 554 F.Supp. 1053 (D.N.J.1983); National Bank of Commerce v. Shaklee Corp., 503 F.Supp. 533 (N.D.Tex. 1980); Reeves v. United Artists Corp., 765 F.2d 79 (6th Cir.1985); Bell v. City of Milwaukee, 746 F.2d 1205 (7th Cir.1984); Young v. That Was The Week That Was, 25 Ohio Misc. 185, 423 F.2d 265 (6th Cir.

1970); Thompson v. Curtis Pub. Co., 193 F.2d 953 (3d Cir.1952).

35. For cases involving such releases, *see, e.g.*, Haelan Laboratories, Inc. v. Topps Chewing Gum, Inc., 202 F.2d 866 (2d Cir. 1953), cert. denied 346 U.S. 816, 74 S.Ct. 26, 98 L.Ed. 343 (1953); Ettore v. Philco Television Broadcasting Corp., 229 F.2d 481 (3d Cir.1956); Cepeda v. Swift and Co., 415 F.2d 1205 (8th Cir.1969); Martin Luther King, Jr. Center For Social Change, Inc. v. American Heritage Prods. Inc., 250 Ga., 135, 296 S.E.2d 697 (1982), Welch v. Mr. Christmas, Inc., 57 N.Y.2d 143, 440 N.E.2d 1317, 454 N.Y.S.2d 971 (1982).

was not descendible. In *Memphis Development Foundation* v. *Factors, Etc., Inc.*[36] the appeals court in a diversity case ruled that Elvis Presley's assignment of his right of publicity to Boxcare Enterprises, a corporation closely held by Presley, his manager, Colonel Tom Parker and a third person, did not survive Presley's death under Tennessee law, and thus the corporation's grant of exclusive license to yet another corporation to exploit Presley's persona following his death was not enforceable. As a result, the Memphis Development Foundation, a non-profit corporation was free to distribute to donors small pewter replicas of the bronze statute of Presley it planned to erect in downtown Memphis. The Court was concerned that recognition of descendibility of the right of publicity would create serious problems of judicial line-drawing such as the duration of the property interest, its taxability, the persons who might properly claim such interest, the extent of the interest once the claimant is determined to possess a right of publicity and the limitations which would be placed on the right by the First Amendment.[37] These problems would, according to the court, far outweigh any increase in creative endeavor that recognition of the right might encourage, and the court even doubted that any such increase would be stimulated by the knowledge that one's celebrity would be legally available for exploitation by one's heirs.[38]

The Sixth Circuit's decision in *Memphis Development Foundation* is wrong in principle and policy for a number of reasons. First, it questions the acquisitive nature of human beings and their normal desire to transmit their valuable tangible and intangible acquisitions to those related to them. Second, the decision discourages entrepreneurship by refusing to give continuing protection to publicity value created by hard work and enterprise. The decision seems badly at odds with the free enterprise system encouraged by the common law. Similarly, the decision encourages unjust enrichment of those who exploit a deceased's celebrity without having contributed to the market value that such persons and celebrity possesses. In addition, the decision is inconsistent with property and estates law that permits and sometimes requires those who acquire things of value to transmit them across generations. Finally, it

36. 616 F.2d 956 (6th Cir.), cert. denied 449 U.S. 953, 101 S.Ct. 358, 66 L.Ed.2d 217 (1980).

37. *Id.* at 959.

38. *Id.* at 959–960. This decision was accepted as binding authority by the Second Circuit in Factors Etc., Inc. v. Pro Arts, Inc., 652 F.2d 278 (2d Cir.1981), cert. denied 456 U.S. 927, 102 S.Ct. 1973, 72 L.Ed.2d 442 (1982). *See also* the Sixth Circuit's decisions interpreting Ohio law to similar effect in Reeves v. United Artists Corp., 765 F.2d 79 (6th Cir.1985) and Young v. That Was The Week That Was, 25 Ohio Misc. 185, 423 F.2d 265 (6th Cir. 1970). *Cf.* Cordell v. Detective Publications, Inc. 419 F.2d 989 (6th Cir.1969) (applying Tennessee law again to similar effect in an appropriation and unreasonable publicity case). The California Supreme Court in a confusing 4 to 3 decision also held the right of publicity not to be descendible in Lugosi v. Universal Pictures, 25 Cal.3d 813, 160 Cal.Rptr. 323, 603 P.2d 425, 10 A.L.R.4th 1150 (1979). *See also* Guglielmi v. Spelling–Goldberg Prods., 25 Cal.3d 860, 160 Cal. Rptr. 352, 603 P.2d 454 (1979). The California law was then applied by the Second Circuit in Groucho Marx Prods. v. Day and Night Co., Inc., 689 F.2d 317 (2d Cir.1982) to deny recovery to the assignees of the Marx Brothers rights of publicity against the producers of a musical play which used the appearance and comedy style of Groucho, Chico and Harpo.

ignores the fact that courts are created and judges are paid to decide the very kinds of difficult line-drawing issues that are avoided by the Sixth Circuit's refusal to permit the descendibility of the market valuable right of publicity. Concern for the courts should not be placed above consideration of individual rights and duties.

The erroneous nature of this decision has been recognized by other courts[39] and by commentators.[40] Moreover, as a result of legislative action and court decisions, the states that are home to most Americans who can claim a right of publicity—California, New York and Tennessee—now recognize the descendibility of that right.[41]

The only other issue concerning descendibility is whether celebrity must be commercially exploited during one's lifetime. While there is some dictum and superseded decisions suggesting the possible need for such exploitation,[42] the few operative holdings are to the

39. Martin Luther King, Jr. Center For Social Change Inc. v. American Heritage Prods. Inc., 694 F.2d 674, 682 (11th Cir. 1983); Estate of Presley v. Russen, 513 F.Supp. 1339, 1355 (D.N.J.1981); Martin Luther King, Jr., Center for Social Change, Inc. v. American Heritage Prods. Inc., 250 Ga. 135, 296 S.E.2d 697, 705 (1982); State ex rel. Elvis Presley Int'l. Memorial Found. v. Crowell, 733 S.W.2d 89, 97–99 (Tenn. App.1987) (Tennessee appellate court finally gets the opportunity to state the law of Tennessee). *See also* the strong attack on the Sixth Circuit's reasoning by Judge Mansfield dissenting in Factors Etc., Inc. v. Pro Arts, Inc., 652 F.2d 278, 284–290 (2d Cir.1981), cert. denied 456 U.S. 927, 102 S.Ct. 1973, 72 L.Ed.2d 442 (1982); McFarland v. Miller, 14 F.3d 912 (3d Cir.1994).

40. J. Thomas McCarthy, The Rights of Publicity and Privacy § 9.2 [B] [2] [b] (1987); Peter L. Felcher and Edward L. Rubin, *The Descendibility of the Right of Publicity: Is There Commercial Life After Death?*, 89 Yale L.J. 1125, 1132 (1980); Richard B. Hoffman, *The Right of Publicity—Heirs' Right, Advertisers' Windfall, or Courts' Nightmare?*, 31 DePaul L. Rev. 1, 37–38 (1981); Roberta R. Kwall, *Is Independence Day Dawning for the Right of Publicity?* 17 U.C. Davis L. Rev. 191, 212—214 (1983); Michael J. McLane, The Right of Publicity: *Dispelling Survivability Preemption and First Amendment Myths Threatening to Eviscerate a Recognized State Right*, 20 Cal. W.L. Rev. 415 420–422 (1984); *see also* J. Graham Matherne, *Descendibility of Publicity Rights in Tennessee*, 53 Tenn. L. Rev. 753 (1986).

41. *See* Cal. Civ. Code § 990 (West Supp. 1996) (effectively overruling Lugosi v. Universal Pictures, 25 Cal.3d 813, 160 Cal. Rptr. 323, 603 P.2d 425, 10 A.L.R. 4th 1150

(1979) and providing for a post mortem right of publicity of 50 years duration); Tenn. Code Ann. § 47–25–1103 (b) (Replacement Vol. 8B Michie 1995); Factors Etc., Inc. v. Pro Arts, Inc., 579 F.2d 215, 221–222 (2d Cir.1978), cert. denied 440 U.S. 908, 99 S.Ct. 1215, 59 L.Ed.2d 455 (1979) (diversity case applying perceived New York law); Hicks v. Casablanca Records, 464 F.Supp. 426, 429 (S.D.N.Y.1978) (dictum discussing New York law); Price v. Hal Roach Studios, Inc., 400 F.Supp. 836, 844–845 (S.D.N.Y.1975) (diversity case applying perceived New York law); State ex rel. Elvis Presley Int'l. Memorial Found. v. Crowell, 733 S.W.2d 89 (Tenn.App.1987). For a general treatment of the right of publicity in California and New York *see* Paul Cirino, Note, *Advertisers, Celebrities and Publicity Rights in New York and California*, 39 N.Y.L.S. L. Rev. 763 (1994). That these statutes and cases supporting the descendibility of the right of publicity have had a substantial commercial impact is demonstrated by the rise of post mortem sports and entertain agents. The client list of CMG Worldwide includes about 200 dead celebrities including Jackie Robinson, Babe Ruth, Amelia Earhart, Humphrey Bogart and even the great race horse Secretariat, whose individual likenesses are licensed to promote commercial products, some of which did not even exist during the lifetime of the particular deceased celebrity. *See* Marc Fisher, *Giving New Life to Dearly Departed Celebrities*, Wash. Post, Apr. 6, 1997, p. A17, col. 1.

42. Factors Etc., Inc. v. Pro Arts, Inc. 579 F.2d 215, 222 n. 11 (2d Cir.1978), cert. denied 440 U.S. 908, 99 S.Ct. 1215, 59 L.Ed.2d 455 (1979); Groucho Marx Prods. Inc. v. Day and Night Co., 523 F.Supp. 485,

contrary.[43]

Thus as a practical matter, the issue of descendibility has been resolved in favor of the assignees or heirs of those who, through their labor, have created a valuable market place interest in their persona or celebrity whether it is commercially exploited during their lifetime or not.

E.   Defenses of Special Application to the Media

In appropriation and right of publicity actions, news and entertainment media defendants will often raise First Amendment protection, newsworthiness and incidental use defenses. These defenses are related and are often put forth together.

Whenever an individual's name or likeness is utilized by the mass media in reporting or portraying some noteworthy event, the potential exists for conflict between the media's right guaranteed by the First Amendment to disseminate news and information and the individual's rights of privacy and publicity. From the very first, the appropriation tort has been tempered by the recognition that publicity about persons involved in noteworthy matters is essential to the public welfare.[44] Thus, there is no serious argument today against the proposition that the First Amendment protects the press and even the entertainment media against liability when they use persons' names or images legitimately in relationship to contemporary newsworthy events, truthfully presented.[45] The Supreme Court has clearly rejected the contention that First Amendment protections should not be made available because the media may profit financially from using names and personal images in disseminating news and information.[46] The fact that a media defendant seeks to profit from the publication, production, exhibition or circulation of news or information involving the names and likenesses of individuals is

490 (S.D.N.Y.1981), *rev'd*, 689 F.2d 317 (2d Cir.1982) (appeals court required application of California rather than New York law regarding descendibility); Hicks v. Casablanca Records, 464 F.Supp. 426, 429 (S.D.N.Y.1978); Guglielmi v. Spelling Goldberg Prods., 73 Cal.App.3d 436, 140 Cal.Rptr. 775, 779 (1977), *vacated* 25 Cal.3d 860, 160 Cal.Rptr. 352, 603 P.2d 454 (1979); State ex rel. Elvis Presley Int'l. Memorial Found. v. Crowell, 733 S.W.2d 89, 99 (Tenn. App.1987). *See* J. Thomas McCarthy, The Rights of Publicity and Privacy §§ 9.3 [B] [1]—[2] (1987).

43.   Martin Luther King, Jr. Center For Social Change Inc., v. American Heritage Prods. Inc., 694 F.2d 674, 682–683 (11th Cir.1983) (applying Georgia law); Price v. Hal Roach Studios, Inc. 400 F.Supp. 836, 846 (S.D.N.Y.1975) (applying New York law).

44.   *See* Pavesich v. New England Life Ins. Co., 122 Ga. 190, 204–205, 50 S.E. 68, 72–73 (1905).

45.   *See, e.g.*, Cox Broadcasting Corp. v. Cohn, 420 U.S. 469, 95 S.Ct. 1029, 43 L.Ed.2d 328 (1975); Lawrence v. A.S. Abell Co., 299 Md. 697, 705, 475 A.2d 448, 453 (1984); Donahue v. Warner Bros. Pictures Distrib. Corp., 2 Utah 2d 256, 266, 272 P.2d 177, 184 (1954).

46.   Time, Inc. v. Hill, 385 U.S. 374, 379, 87 S.Ct. 534, 537, 17 L.Ed.2d 456, 462 (1967). *See also* New York Times Co. v. Sullivan 376 U.S. 254, 266, 84 S.Ct. 710, 718, 11 L.Ed.2d 686, 698 (1964) (paid editorial advertising in a newspaper); Joseph Burstyn, Inc. v. Wilson, 343 U.S. 495, 501–502, 72 S.Ct. 777, 780, 96 L.Ed. 1098, 1106 (1952) (motion picture distributed for profit); Valentine v. C.B.S., Inc., 698 F.2d 430, 433 (11th Cir.1983) (use of plaintiff's name in a popular song about a newsworthy event); Guglielmi v. Spelling–Goldberg Prods., 25 Cal.3d 860, 868–869, 160 Cal. Rptr. 352, 357–358, 603 P.2d 454, 459–460 (1979) (concurring opinion of a majority of the justices).

simply not constitutionally significant.[47] What is significant is the public interest in or newsworthiness of that which is disseminated.

The limit of First Amendment protection is reached when the media engage in fraudulent commercial exploitation of an individual's name, likeness or persons to sell their product. The clearest example of this is the unauthorized use of either a celebrity or a non-celebrity's name or likeness to state or imply an endorsement of the defendant's media product, be it a newspaper, magazine, book, record, tape or film.[48] In *Cher v. Forum, Int'l., Ltd.,*[49] Forum magazine falsely stated in its advertising copy that the noted singer and actress Cher "tells Forum" things that she "would never tell US." The implication is of course, that Cher trusted and endorsed Forum magazine. The truth of the matter was that the Cher interview referred to was actually planned to run in US Magazine but was spiked. The interview was then offered to Forum by the interviewer without Cher's knowledge or approval. On these facts the Ninth Circuit ruled that there was sufficient evidence to support the trial court's finding of an implied endorsement and upheld the imposition of liability.

But the situation in *Cher* must be contrasted with cases in which the media simply promote, without fabrication, their product by making reference to future editorial content, including names and likenesses of individuals, or reprinting past such material. Such promotion referencing individuals without claim of endorsement by them is protected by the First Amendment because it encourages, without falsity, the dissemination of news, information and works of fiction to the public. Thus, the use of the name and image of Rudolph Valentino to promote a motion picture fictionalization about Valentino was held permissible[50] as was a subscription advertisement for Sports Illustrated magazine headed "How to Get Close to Joe Namath," accompanied by an action photograph of the football star published in a previous issue of the magazine and promising future coverage of his exploits.[51] Also approved were ads in the New Yorker and Advertising Age for Holiday magazine reprinting from Holiday a striking photograph of the late actress Shirley Booth in a large

47. Guglielmi v. Spelling-Goldberg Prods., 25 Cal.3d 860, 868–869, 160 Cal.Rptr. 352, 358, 603 P.2d 454, 460 (1979) (concurring opinion of Bird C.J. agreed with by a majority of the justices).

48. Cher v. Forum Int'l., Ltd., 692 F.2d 634, 639 (9th Cir.1982), cert. denied 462 U.S. 1120, 103 S. Ct. 3089, 77 L. Ed. 2d 1350 (1983) (falsely implied endorsement of magazine by actress-singer); Velez v. VV Pub. Corp., 135 A.D.2d 47, 54, 524 N.Y.S.2d 186, 189 appeal denied 72 N.Y.2d 808, 533 N.Y.S.2d 57, 529 N.E.2d 425 (1988) (unsuccessful claim of false endorsement of weekly newspaper); Anderson v. Fisher Broadcasting Co., 300 Or. 452, 465, 712 P.2d 803, 811

(1986) (dictum); *cf.* Fairfield v. American Photocopy Equip. Co., 138 Cal.App.2d 82, 291 P.2d 194 (1955) (false endorsement of photocopy machine).

49. 692 F.2d 634 (9th Cir.1982), cert. denied 462 U.S. 1120, 103 S. Ct. 3089, 77 L. Ed. 2d 1350 (1983).

50. *See* Guglielmi v. Spelling–Goldberg Prods., 25 Cal.3d 860, 160 Cal.Rptr. 352, 603 P.2d 454 (1979).

51. Namath v. Sports Illustrated, 48 A.D.2d 487, 371 N.Y.S.2d 10 (1975), *aff'd*, 39 N.Y.2d 897, 386 N.Y.S.2d 397 352 N.E.2d 584 (1976).

straw hat up to her neck in water at a Jamaican resort, with the caption "Shirley Booth and Chapeau, from a Recent Issue of Holiday."[52]

The *Valentino, Namath* and *Booth* cases illustrate the broad First Amendment protection enjoyed by the media. These cases do not directly involve the dissemination of news information or even fiction relating to individuals. Rather, they involve media self promotion—a commercial activity designed to sell movie tickets and magazines. But this self promotion encourages the dissemination of news, information and fiction to the public, a function consistent with First Amendment interests and is hence protected from liability.

The newsworthiness defense is simply a facet of the First Amendment privilege. The news media must be able to furnish the names and often the images of individuals legitimately related to news events of public interest. So long as what is disseminated has legitimate news value and the publicized individual has some rational link to the story, First Amendment protection is available to the disseminator.[53] This protection is very broad because most courts will usually defer to the judgment of the news media in determining newsworthiness and the relationship of individuals to reported events.[54]

The incidental use or benefit defense is still another aspect of First Amendment protection. This defense simply views the use of names and likenesses in relation to legitimate matters of public interest communicated to the public by profit-seeking media as not amounting to actionable appropriation of an individual's identity or persona.[55] To hold otherwise would deny to the profit-seeking media the First Amendment protection afforded to non-profit media, a distinction that is simply untenable in a free enterprise economy.

Closely related to the incidental use or benefit defense is that of the absence of advertising or trade purposes in utilizing names and likenesses. Again, the referencing of individuals by profit-seeking media in fair relation to matters of public interest is not actionable. Since the terminology "advertising or trade purposes" derives from state statutes concerning appropriation of names and likenesses, further discussion of

---

52. Booth v. Curtis Pub. Co., 15 A.D.2d 343, 223 N.Y.S.2d 737, *aff'd* 11 N.Y.2d 907, 228 N.Y.S.2d 468, 182 N.E.2d 812 (1962).

53. *Cf.* Murray v. New York Magazine Co., 27 N.Y.2d 406, 409, 267 N.E.2d 256, 258, 318 N.Y.S.2d 474, 477 (1971); Delan by Delan v. CBS, Inc., 91 A.D.2d 255, 258–259, 458 N.Y.S.2d 608, 613 (1983).

54. *See, e.g.*, Jenkins v. Dell Pub. Co., 251 F.2d 447, 451–452 (3d Cir.), cert. denied, 357 U.S. 921, 78 S.Ct. 1362, 2 L.Ed.2d 1365 (1958); Barbieri v. News-Journal Co., 189 A.2d 773, 776–777 (Del.1963); Cape Pubs., Inc. v. Bridges, 423 So.2d 426, 427–428 (Fla.App.1982), cert. denied 464 U.S. 893, 104 S.Ct. 239, 78 L.Ed.2d 229 (1983); Howard v. Des Moines Register and Trib-

une Co., 283 N.W.2d 289, 302–304 (Iowa 1979), cert. denied 445 U.S. 904, 100 S.Ct. 1081, 63 L.Ed.2d 320 (1980); *see also* Gertz v. Robert Welch, Inc., 418 U.S. 323, 346, 94 S.Ct. 2997, 3010, 41 L.Ed.2d 789, 809 (1974) (dictum); Diane L. Zimmerman, *Requiem for a Heavyweight: A Farewell to Warren and Brandeis' Privacy Tort*, 68 Corn. L. Rev. 291, 353–354 (1983).

55. *See, e.g.*, Loft v. Fuller, 408 So.2d 619, 623 (Fla.App.1981); Tropeano v. Atlantic Monthly Co., 379 Mass. 745, 748, 400 N.E.2d 847, 850 (1980); Nelson v. Maine Times, 373 A.2d 1221, 1224 (Me.1977); RESTATEMENT SECOND TORTS § 652C, comment *d* (1977).

this defense will be deferred to the section of this chapter dealing with these statutes.

F. A Major Limitation on the First Amendment Defense

As pointed out above, there are limits to the protection afforded the news and entertainment media by the First Amendment. Perhaps the most celebrated limit is a medium's appropriation of another's entire act, exhibition or commercial presentation. In *Zacchini* v. *Scripps—Howard Broadcasting Co.*,[56] a local television station's reporter, over Zacchini's objection, filmed his "human cannonball" act presented at a nearby county fair and the entire 15 second performance was then shown on a news program later the same day. Zacchini then brought an action in tort for unlawful appropriation of his professional property. The trial court's summary judgment for the defendant broadcasting company was reversed by the Ohio intermediate appellate court, which was in turn reversed by the Ohio Supreme Court. The latter court, while recognizing Zacchini's right of publicity in his act, reversed the lower appeal court on the basis that the television station's privilege under the First and Fourteenth Amendments to report in its newscasts matters of legitimate public interest overrode that personal right even when the entire performance was aired. The state court said that the news media had to be accorded broad latitude in their choice of how much of each story to present and the emphasis to be given.[57]

The United States Supreme Court reversed the Ohio Supreme Court, holding that the First and Fourteenth Amendments do not permit a news organization to exhibit an entire act or performance, thereby likely taking some or all of its economic value from the performer or owner in the guise of reporting the news. The Court made clear that Zacchini's right of publicity would not serve to prevent the television station from reporting newsworthy information about petitioner's act, but where the line was to be drawn was not suggested. One can speculate that the news report would likely have been accorded constitutional protection had it been limited to a verbal description of the act and perhaps a brief video byte of Zacchini in costume preparing to enter the cannon.

The Court was not concerned that television or other media audiences would not get to experience such acts because these performances are available to the public in person though for a price. Accordingly, First Amendment interests are not invaded by protecting the property value of entire performances.

Justice Powell, in dissent, argued strongly that the First Amendment should protect the station from a right of publicity suit when the film is legitimately used as news for a routine portion of a regular newscast.[58] This, of course, would avoid the problem of line drawing as to

---

56. 433 U.S. 562, 97 S.Ct. 2849, 53 L.Ed.2d 965 (1977).

57. 47 Ohio St.2d 224, 235, 351 N.E.2d 454, 461 (1976).

58. 433 U.S. 562, 581, 97 S.Ct. 2849,

the amount of an act or performance that could be aired and would place the burden on the plaintiff to establish that the broadcast was a subterfuge for the defendant's private or commercial benefit beyond its normal media operations.

Whatever the theoretical merits of this First Amendment debate, the practical truth is that a solid majority of the Supreme Court felt strongly that the First Amendment should not be used as a shield by those who would disseminate without permission the intellectual property of others and thereby diminish its value in the hands of the owners of such property.[59] This is a practical limitation today on First Amendment protection which the media ignores at its peril.

G. Statutory Protection Against Appropriation of Names and Likenesses

The New York Court of Appeals decision in *Roberson* v. *Rochester Folding Box Co.*[60] rejecting the idea of a common law right of privacy and permitting Miss Roberson's portrait to be emblazoned on advertising for a particular brand of flour without her permission, engendered substantial legal and public dissatisfaction. This dissatisfaction with the *Roberson* decision led, within the year, to enactment of sections 50 and 51 of the New York Civil Rights Law providing protection against name and likeness appropriation.[61] Similar legislation has now been adopted in

2860, 53 L.Ed.2d 965, 979 (1977).

59. *Compare* the parallel copyright case of Harper and Row Publishers, Inc. v. Nation Enterprises, 471 U.S. 539, 105 S.Ct. 2218, 85 L.Ed.2d 588 (1985) in which Harper and Row had exclusive rights to former President Gerald Ford's memoirs, "A Time To Heal", and granted rights to Time Magazine to excerpt, one week prior to publication of the book, 7500 words from Ford's account of his decision to pardon Nixon. The Nation magazine obtained an unauthorized copy of Ford's manuscript and published a 2,250 word article drawn exclusively from the manuscript before the scheduled appearance of the Time article. As a result Time did not publish its planned article and refused to pay Harper and Row the remaining $12,500 for the rights.

Harper and Row then sued the Nation for damages. In the course of its 6 to 3 judgment in favor of Harper and Row, the Court said, "[C]opyright assures those who write and publish factual narratives such as "A Time to Heal" that they may at least enjoy the right to market the original expression contained therein as just compensation for their investment. *Cf.* Zacchini v. Scripps—Howard Broadcasting Co., 433 U.S. 562, 575, 97 S.Ct. 2849, 2857, 53 L.Ed.2d 965 (1977)." While Harper and Row's victory was grounded in statutory copyright law and the inapplicability of the "fair use" defense in this case, the First Amendment implications are unmistakable. *See* Justice Brennan's dissent, 471 U.S. at 579, 105 S. Ct. at 2240, 85 L. Ed. 2d at 619; *see also* Roy Export Co. Estab. of Vaduz, Liechtenstein, Black Inc. v. Columbia Broadcasting System, Inc., 503 F.Supp. 1137, 1147–1148 (S.D.N.Y.1980), *aff'd* 672 F.2d 1095 (2d Cir.), cert. denied 459 U.S. 826, 103 S.Ct. 60, 74 L.Ed.2d 63 (1982). For a thoughtful and thought-provoking proposal to reconcile the protection of the right of publicity with the requirements of the First Amendment *see* Roberta R. Kwall, *The Right of Publicity vs. The First Amendment: A Property and Liability Rule Analysis,* 70 Ind. L.J. 47 (1994).

60. 171 N.Y. 538, 64 N.E. 442 (1902).

61. Section 50 Provides: [text in Practitioner's Edition only].

Section 51 as amended in 1995 provides: [text in Practitioner's Edition only].

The history of this legislation is summarized in Lawrence E. Savell, *Right of Privacy—Appropriation of a Person's Name, Portrait, or Picture for Advertising or Trade Purposes Without Prior Written Consent: History and Scope in New York,* 48 Albany L. Rev. 1, 3–14 (1983).

several other states primarily to fill the real or perceived gap in common law protection.[62]

The thrust of these statutes is that an individual's name, likeness or personality may not be used for advertising or trade purposes without permission. All of them authorize civil actions for injunctions and damages, and a few make the appropriation a criminal act.[63] Approximately half of them expressly provide for the descendibility of the right of publicity[64] and three expressly provide for transferability of the right.[65] A large proportion of the statutes exempt certain uses from liability either for policy or constitutional reasons.[66] Only one requires that the prohibited use or infringement be "knowingly" intended by the appropriator.[67] The others provide for civil actions simply when a prohibited use is made without first obtaining consent to the use.

The two basic issues regarding these statutes is their coverage and the defenses available against claims of violation. Because the body of judicial interpretation and analysis has developed, as might be expected in the great commercial state of New York under the oldest such statute,

62. See Cal. Civ. Code §§ 990 (deceased personalities); 3344 (living persons) (West Supp. 1996); Fla. Stat. Ann. § 540.08 (West 1988); Ky. Rev. Stat. Ann. § 391.170 (Repl. Vol. 1984); Mass. Gen. Laws Ann. ch. 214 § 3A (West 1989); Mass. Gen. Laws Ann. ch. 214 § 1B (West 1989) (general invasion of privacy statute which might encompass appropriation and right of publicty); Neb. Rev. Stat. §§ 20–201, 20–202 (1991); Okla. Stat. Ann. tit. 21, §§ 839.1, 839.2 (West 1983); R.I. Gen. Laws §§ 9–1–28 and 9–1–28.1(2) (1985) (general invasion of privacy statute expressly encompassing the appropriation tort); Tenn. Code Ann. §§ 47–25–1101 through 47–25–1108 (1995); Utah Code Ann. §§ 45–3–1 through 45–3–6 (1993); Va. Code Ann. § 8.01–40 (Repl. Vol. 1992), § 18.2–216.1 (Repl. Vol. 1988); Wis. Stat. Ann. § 895.50 (West 1983).

63. See, e.g., N.Y. Civ. Rights Law § 50 (McKinney 1992); Okla Stat. Ann. Tit 21, § 839.1 (West 1983).

64. See, e.g., Cal. Civ. Code § 990 (West Supp. 1996) (limited to deceased personalities); Fla. Stat. Ann. § 540.08(1)(c)(2) (West 1988); Ky. Rev. Stat. Ann. § 391.170 (1984); Neb. Rev. Stat. § 20–208 (1991); Tenn. Code Ann. § 47–25–1103 (1995); Va. Code Ann. § 8.01–40 (Repl. Vol. 1992).

65. Cal. Civ. Code § 990 (West Supp. 1996) (limited to deceased personalities); Fla. Stat. Ann. § 540.08 (1)(b), (2) (West 1988); Tenn. Code Ann. § 47–25–1103 (1995).

66. Cal. Civ. Code § 990 (West Supp. 1996) (regarding deceased personalities)

Fla. Stat. Ann. § 540.08(3) (West Supp. 1988) Mass. Gen. Laws Ann. ch. 214 § 3A (West 1989); Neb. Rev. Stat. § 20–202 (1995); N.Y. Civ. Rights Law § 51 (McKinney Supp. 1992); Okla. Stat. Ann. tit. 21, § 839.3 (West 1983); R.I. Gen. Laws § 9–1–28 (1985); Tenn. Code Ann. § 47–25–1107 (1995). Many of these statutes have adopted exemptions similar to those found in New York's legislation: (1) professional photographers may exhibit in their own shops specimens of their work until those portrayed object in writing; (2) anyone may use the name or likeness of an author, composer or artist in connection with such person's literary musical or artistic productions which he has sold or disposed of with such name or likeness used in connection with the creative product; (3) anyone may use the name or likeness of any manufacturer or dealer in connection with the goods, and merchandise manufactured, produced or distributed by him which he sold or otherwise disposed of with his name or likeness used in connection with the goods and merchandise; (4) anyone may sell or transfer any material containing names or likenesses in whatever medium to any users of such names or likenesses to third parties for sale or transfer directly or indirectly to such users for use in a manner lawful under the statutes. The last exempted use apparently refers to uses of names and likenesses protected under the First and Fourteenth Amendments.

67. Tenn. Code Ann. § 47–25–1105 (1995).

most of the references in this section will, of necessity be directed to the law of that state. Since however, a number of jurisdictions have patterned their legislation in whole or past on that of the Empire State, this body of law should be widely influential.

The focus on unauthorized use of names and likenesses for advertising and trade purposes makes the precise uses to which such names and likenesses are put a central concern in determining the applicability of this type of legislation. The phrase "for advertising purposes" has been broadly interpreted to cover not only advertising copy but any solicitation for patronage.[68] However, delineating prohibited advertising uses is not always as simple as it might seem. Advertising may be disguised as news[69] or it may include substantial information of public interest, as for example the modern "advertorial."[70] In borderline situations the courts may simply make an educated guess as to the primary purpose of the expression at issue in determining whether the statute has been violated.[71]

There appears to be little concern by the courts that statutory prohibition of unconsented use of names and likenesses in advertising, which is, after all, a form of expression, runs afoul of the First Amendment. A clear distinction is drawn between real world news and creative fiction utilizing names and likenesses of actual persons on the one hand and advertising on the other,[72] with news and fiction receiving greater protection than expression designed simply to further commerce.[73] Add

68. Flores v. Mosler Safe Co., 7 N.Y.2d 276, 284, 284, 164 N.E.2d 853, 857, 196 N.Y.S.2d 975, 981 (1959); Delan v. CBS Inc., 91 A.D.2d 255, 258, 458 N.Y.S.2d 608, 613 (1983); Sarat Lahiri v. Daily Mirror, Inc., 162 Misc. 776, 780, 295 N.Y.S. 382, 386 (N.Y.Sup.1937).

69. *See* Stephano v. News Group Pubs., Inc., 64 N.Y.2d 174, 485 N.Y.S.2d 220, 474 N.E.2d 580 (1984); Pagan v. New York Herald Tribune, Inc., 32 A.D.2d 341, 301 N.Y.S.2d 120 (1969), *aff'd without opinion* 26 N.Y.2d 941, 310 N.Y.S.2d 327, 258 N.E.2d 727 (1970); Selsman v. Universal Photo Books, Inc. 18 A.D.2d 151, 238 N.Y.S.2d 686 (1963); *see also* Zacchini v. Scripps—Howard Broadcasting Co., 433 U.S. 562, 581, 97 S.Ct. 2849, 2860, 53 L.Ed.2d 965, 979 (1977) (dissenting opinion of Justice Powell: "When a film is used, as here, for a routine portion of a regular news program, I would hold that the First Amendment protects the station from a 'right of publicity' or 'appropriation' suit, absent a strong showing by the plaintiff that the news broadcast was a subterfuge or cover for private or commercial exploitation.").

70. *Cf.* Central Hudson Gas and Elec. Corp. v. Public Service Comm'n., 447 U.S.

557, 563, 100 S.Ct. 2343, 2349, 65 L.Ed.2d 341, 348–349, (1980); Bolger v. Youngs Drug Prods. Corp., 463 U.S. 60, 64–68, 103 S.Ct. 2875, 2878–2881, 77 L.Ed.2d 469, 475–478 (1983).

71. *See, e.g.*, Selsman v. Universal Photo Books, Inc., 18 A.D.2d 151, 238 N.Y.S.2d 686 (1963); *cf.* Penthouse Int'l. Ltd. v. Koch, 599 F.Supp. 1338, 1344–1345 (S.D.N.Y.1984).

72. *See* Bolger v. Youngs Drug Prods. Corp., 463 U.S. 60, 64–65, 103 S.Ct. 2875, 2878–2879, 77 L.Ed.2d 469, 476, (1983); Ohralik v. Ohio State Bar Ass'n., 436 U.S. 447, 455–456, 98 S.Ct. 1912, 1918–1919, 56 L.Ed.2d 444, 452–454 (1978); J. Thomas McCarthy, The Rights of Publicity and Privacy §§ 8.2–8.4 (1987); Peter L. Felcher and Edward L. Rubin, *Privacy, Publicity, and the Portrayal of Real People by the Media*, 88 Yale L.J. 1577, 1597–1601 (1979).

73. *See* Posadas de Puerto Rico Assocs. v. Tourism Co., 478 U.S. 328, 106 S.Ct. 2968, 92 L.Ed.2d 266 (1986); Bolger v. Youngs Drug Prods. Corp., 463 U.S. 60, 64–65, 103 S.Ct. 2875, 2878–2879, 77 L.Ed.2d 469 (1983); Central Hudson Gas and Elec. Corp. v. Public Service Commission, 447 U.S. 557, 100 S.Ct. 2343, 65 L.Ed.2d 341 (1980).

to this the Supreme Court's penchant not to permit the media's exploitation of the property rights of others[74] and the conclusion can be drawn that statutes prohibiting the unconsented use of names and likenesses for advertising purposes are constitutional.

However, the phrase "purposes of trade" found in many of the same statutes poses a more difficult constitutional problem. That phrase, encompassing uses for the purposes of making a profit,[75] is both vague and broad[76] and could touch constitutionally protected expression where the profit motive is present.[77]

Sensitive to the constitutional issues raised by its appropriation statutes, the New York courts have leaned over backwards to avoid constitutional conflict. They have clearly held that the use of names and likenesses in legitimate conjunction with the reporting of matters of public information or public interest is privileged and not within the reach of the term "purposes of trade."[78] This newsworthiness privilege encompasses not only hard current news but that which though not strictly news is designed to be informative.[79] The privilege is recognized even when the media defendant is clearly profit-seeking and gives emphasis to the plaintiff's name or likeness to stimulate sales of its media product.[80]

74. *See* Zacchini v. Scripps—Howard Broadcasting Co., 433 U.S. 562, 97 S.Ct. 2849, 53 L.Ed.2d 965 (1977); Harper and Row Publishers, Inc. v. Nation Enterprises, 471 U.S. 539, 105 S.Ct. 2218, 85 L.Ed.2d 588 (1985).

75. Delan by Delan v. CBS, Inc., 91 A.D.2d 255, 259, 458 N.Y.S.2d 608, 613 (1983). Like advertising purpose, trade purpose, at its core, covers purely commercial dealings, and applications of the statutes to such dealings would likely be held constitutional.

76. *See* Davis v. High Society Magazine, Inc., 90 A.D.2d 374, 381–382, 457 N.Y.S.2d 308, 313 (1982); Sarat Lahiri v. Daily Mirror, Inc., 162 Misc. 776, 782–783, 295 N.Y.S. 382, 388 (N.Y.Sup.1937).

77. *See, e.g.,* Arrington v. New York Times Co., 55 N.Y.2d 433, 440, 449 N.Y.S.2d 941, 944, 434 N.E.2d 1319, 1322 (1982); cert. denied 459 U.S. 1146, 103 S.Ct. 787, 74 L.Ed.2d 994 (1983); Davis v. High Society Magazine, Inc., 90 A.D.2d 374, 382, 457 N.Y.S.2d 308, 313 (1982).

78. Arrington v. New York Times Co., 55 N.Y.2d 433, 440, 449 N.Y.S.2d 941, 944, 434 N.E.2d 1319, 1323 (1982); Murray v. New York Magazine Co., 27 N.Y.2d 406, 409, 318 N.Y.S.2d 474, 477, 267 N.E.2d 256, 258 (1971); Delan by Delan v. CBS, 91 A.D.2d 255, 259, 458 N.Y.S.2d 608, 613 (1983); Humiston v. Universal Film Mfg.

Co., 189 A.D. 467, 477, 178 N.Y.S. 752, 756–759 (1919); *see also* Tropeano v. Atlantic Monthly Co., 379 Mass. 745, 748, 400 N.E.2d 847, 850–851 (1980), (Massachusetts appropriation statute); *cf.* Johnson v. Harcourt, Brace, Jovanovich, Inc., 43 Cal.App.3d 880, 894–895, 118 Cal.Rptr. 370, 381 (Cal. App.1974).

79. Delan by Delan v. CBS, Inc., 91 A.D.2d 255, 259–260, 458 N.Y.S.2d 608, 613 (1983). *See* Murray v. New York Magazine Co., 27 N.Y.2d 406, 318 N.Y.S.2d 474, 267 N.E.2d 256 (1971) (feature story concerning Irish immigrants utilizing two year old photograph of plaintiff wearing typically Irish garb); Gautier v. Pro–Football, Inc., 304 N.Y. 354, 107 N.E.2d 485 (1952) (animal act televised during half-time of a professional football game); *see also* Tropeano v. Atlantic Monthly Co., 379 Mass. 745, 750–751, 400 N.E.2d 847, 851 (1980).

80. Arrington v. New York Times Co., 55 N.Y.2d 433, 440, 449 N.Y.S.2d 941, 944, 434 N.E.2d 1319, 1322 (1982); Murray v. New York Magazine Co., 27 N.Y.2d 406, 409, 318 N.Y.S.2d 474, 476, 267 N.E.2d 256, 258 (1971); Velez v. VV Pub. Corp., 135 A.D.2d 47, 52, 524 N.Y.S.2d 186, 188–189 (1988); Delan by Delan v. CBS, Inc., 91 A.D.2d 255, 259, 458 N.Y.S.2d 608, 613 (1983); *see also* Tropeano v. Atlantic Monthly Co., 379 Mass. 745, 748, 400 N.E.2d 847, 851 (1980).

This desire to avoid constitutional conflict on the part of the courts also extends to the "advertising purpose" branch of the New York statutes when it is the media doing the advertising. Apparently the theory, though not well articulated by the courts, is that such advertising using names and likenesses of individuals (preferably celebrities) aids in the future dissemination by the media of news and information and is thus protected by the First Amendment. This judicially created exemption from liability for the media is labeled "incidental use."[81]

Illustrative of the breadth of this media privilege is *Velez* v. *VV Publishing Corp.*[82] There, the Village Voice published a lengthy investigative report highly critical of the plaintiff, a well known Hispanic activist. The title of the report containing the plaintiff's name together with his photograph appeared on the cover of the publication. This cover was later reproduced as part of the Voice's advertising campaign for new subscriptions. But unlike earlier judicially approved incidental uses,[83] the reproduction of the cover featuring Mr. Velez was embellished with a cartoon balloon directed toward his photographic image containing the words "What's your address?" followed by an asterisk directing the reader to the Voice's subscription form below. Despite the enhancement of the plaintiff's image to encourage casual readers to subscribe, the Appellate Division ruled that Mr. Velez's photograph and name in the subscription was just another incidental use. One is left to wonder if, for instance, the Voice had turned its Velez cover upside down with a tag line in a cartoon balloon reading "people don't have to stand on their head for a subscription to the Village Voice" whether this too would be considered an incidental use.[84]

As long as the media stick to the dissemination of news and information or reasonable advertising to sell their product be it newspapers, magazines, film, tape or electronic data, they have little to fear from New York's or any other state's appropriation statutes. Names and likenesses are part of the news and information business and their legitimate use will not be interfered with.

---

81. *See* Velez v. VV Pub. Corp., 135 A.D.2d 47, 49, 524 N.Y.S.2d 186, 187 (1988); Namath v. Sports Illustrated, 48 A.D.2d 487, 488, 371 N.Y.S.2d 10, 11 (1975), *aff'd* 39 N.Y.2d 897, 386 N.Y.S.2d 397, 352 N.E.2d 584 (1976); Booth v. Curtis Pub. Co., 15 A.D.2d 343, 350–351, 223 N.Y.S.2d 737, 741, *aff'd* 11 N.Y.2d 907, 228 N.Y.S.2d 468, 182 N.E.2d 812 (1962); Humiston v. Universal Film Mfg. Co., 189 A.D. 467, 477, 178 N.Y.S. 752, 759 (1919) (root case for incidental use exemption).

82. 135 A.D.2d 47, 524 N.Y.S.2d 186 (1988).

83. Namath v. Sports Illustrated, 48 A.D.2d 487, 371 N.Y.S.2d 10 (1975), *aff'd* 39 N.Y.2d 897, 386 N.Y.S.2d 397, 352 N.E.2d 584 (1976) (action photograph of football star Joe Namath); Booth v. Curtis Pub. Co.,

15 A.D.2d 343, 223 N.Y.S.2d 737, *aff'd* 11 N.Y.2d 907, 228 N.Y.S.2d 468, 182 N.E.2d 812 (1962) (unaltered photograph portrait of the actress Shirley Booth).

84. Underscoring the First Amendment imperative for the "incidental use" exemption is the development by the New York courts of the contrasting idea of "collateral use." This concept views the use of past newsstories containing names or likenesses of individuals by commercial enterprises *other than the news media* to sell their goods and services as violative of New York's appropriation statutes. *See* Booth v. Curtis Pub. Co., 15 A.D.2d 343, 350, 223 N.Y.S.2d 737, 742, *aff'd* 11 N.Y.2d 907, 228 N.Y.S.2d 468, 182 N.E.2d 812 (1962).

H. Remedies for Tortious Appropriations

Given the interests protected by the appropriation tort, money damages are available here for both injuries to personal dignity and property value arising from the appropriation of one's name, likeness or persona which involves, of course, hurt feelings and impairment of the mental peace and comfort of the individual.[85] The injury, in short, is the impact on the psyche from being "used" against one's will. Thus, compensatory damages may be awarded for such misuse of another's identity, and it does not matter that such damages cannot be ascertained with any substantial degree of certainty. The measure of these damages for hurt feelings is for the trier of fact, and the trier is to be accorded wide latitude in making the award.[86] Of course, if the trier of fact is convinced that there was no real impact on the plaintiff's psyche, nominal damages may be awarded for the technical tortious invasion.[87] Special damages are available in these cases to compensate for the resulting out of pocket losses to the victim from such things as lost earnings from inability to work and fees for psychiatric counseling.[88] Punitive damages are also available where sufficient proof is adduced of maliciousness or recklessness in the appropriation.[89]

When the injury complained of relates to loss of commercial value arising from the unconsented taking of the individual's right of publicity, the measure of damage can be determined with a greater degree of precision, and the latitude of the trier of fact is correspondingly smaller. It is possible in most cases to calculate roughly the fair market value of the commercial loss sustained by the plaintiff from the unconsented use

85. *See* Waits v. Frito–Lay, Inc., 978 F.2d 1093, 1103 (9th Cir.1992); Fairfield v. American Photocopy Equipment Co., 138 Cal.App.2d 82, 86, 291 P.2d 194, 197 (1955); Eick v. Perk Dog Food Co., 347 Ill.App. 293, 301, 106 N.E.2d 742, 745–746 (1952); Candebat v. Flanagan, 487 So.2d 207, 212 (Miss.1986); Faber v. Condecor, Inc., 195 N.J.Super. 81, 90, 477 A.2d 1289, 1294 (1984); RESTATEMENT OF TORTS SECOND § 652H (1977); *but see* Cabaniss v. Hipsley, 114 Ga.App. 367, 378–379, 151 S.E.2d 496, 504–505 (1966).

86. Fairfield v. American Photocopy Equipment Co., 138 Cal.App.2d 82, 88, 291 P.2d 194, Faber v. Condecor, Inc., 195 N.J.Super. 81, 90, 477 A.2d 1289, 1294–1295 (1984); Hinish v. Meier & Frank Co., 166 Or. 482, 506, 113 P.2d 438, 448 (1941); Lerman v. Flynt Distrib. Co., Inc., 745 F.2d 123, 141 (2d Cir.1984) (award of seven million dollars reversed), cert. denied 479 U.S. 932, 107 S. Ct. 404, 93 L. Ed. 2d 357 (1986); Douglass v. Hustler Magazine, Inc., 769 F.2d 1128, 1144 (7th Cir.1985), cert. denied 475 U.S. 1094, 106 S.Ct. 1489, 89 L.Ed.2d 892 (1986) (case awarding $300,000 remanded for new trial). Rarely will extreme-

ly large general damage awards stand up on appeal.

87. *See* Lerman v. Flynt Distributing Co., Inc., 745 F.2d 123, 141 (2d Cir.1984) (plaintiff sought no professional help and completed a novel during relevant period after being erroneously identified in a pornographic magazine).

88. *See, e.g.,* Douglass v. Hustler Magazine, Inc., 769 F.2d 1128, 1143–1144 (7th Cir.1985), cert. denied 475 U.S. 1094, 106 S.Ct. 1489, 89 L.Ed.2d 892 (1986) (loss of income); Fairfield v. American Photocopy Equipment Co., 138 Cal.App.2d 82, 88, 291 P.2d 194, 198 (1955).

89. *See, e.g.,* Douglass v. Hustler Magazine, Inc., 769 F.2d 1128, 1145–1146 (7th Cir.1985), cert. denied 475 U.S. 1094, 106 S.Ct. 1489, 89 L.Ed.2d 892 (1986); Waits v. Frito–Lay, Inc. 978 F.2d 1093, 1104 (9th Cir.1992), cert. denied 506 U.S. 1080, 113 S.Ct. 1047, 122 L.Ed.2d 355 (1993); Leavy v. Cooney, 214 Cal.App.2d 496, 502, 29 Cal. Rptr. 580, 585 (1963) (exemplary damage award pursuant to statutory authority); Candebat v. Flanagan, 487 So.2d 207, 212 (Miss.1986).

to which his identity is put.[90] This fair market value can be determined by establishing what the plaintiff has received in the past for similar consented to uses of his celebrity and, through the testimony of expert witnesses, what others of comparable celebrity receive for their acquiescence in the commercial exploitation of their identity.[91] Of course, factors such as inflation, the present demand in the advertising market for the exploitation of celebrity and the depreciation of the residual value of celebrity caused by the particular use must be accounted for in the determination of damages.[92]

The award of fair market value alone to the plaintiff whose celebrity has been exploited without consent is, if one reflects upon it, quite unfair.[93] Fair market value denotes the monetary value that a willing buyer and a willing seller would agree to in the commercial market place. But when there is an invasion of an individual's right of publicity there is no meeting of minds on either exploitation of celebrity or the value thereof; there is only an unconsented taking. If justice is to be done in these cases, some premium or punitive award beyond fair market value should be made as a matter of course to compensate the plaintiff for having been improperly "used" and to let the defendant and others know that business must not be conducted in this fashion. But there is little authority for this proposition. Punitive damages are, of course, available in right of publicity cases along with nominal or

90. *See* Cabaniss v. Hipsley, 114 Ga. App. 367, 386, 151 S.E.2d 496, 509 (exotic dancer entitled to recover the advertising value for the time and manner her photograph was used by a rival night club without her consent); Hirsch v. S.C. Johnson & Son, Inc., 90 Wis.2d 379, 386, 280 N.W.2d 129, 132 (1979); J. Thomas McCarthy, The Rights of Publicity and Privacy § 11.8(B) (1987); Richard B. Hoffman, *The Right of Publicity—Heir's Right, Advertisers' Windfall, or Courts' Nightmare*, 31 DePaul L. Rev. 1, 13 (1981).

91. *See* Cher v. Forum Int'l., Ltd., 213 U.S.P.Q. 96, 103 (C.D.Cal.), *aff'd as to damages against Forum*, 692 F.2d 634, 640 (9th Cir.1982) (fair market value determined by earlier negotiations with the actress); Hirsch v. S.C. Johnson & Son, Inc., 90 Wis.2d 379, 386, 280 N.W.2d 129, 132 (1979) (Minimum compensation for the use of an athlete's name on an unrelated product was five percent according to expert testimony); Richard B. Hoffman, *The Right of Publicity—Heir's Right, Advertiser's Windfall or Court's Nightmare*, 31 DePaul L. Rev. 1, 13 (1981).

92. *Cf.* Douglass v. Hustler Magazine, Inc., 769 F.2d 1128, 1143 (7th Cir.1985), cert. denied 475 U.S. 1094, 106 S.Ct. 1489, 89 L.Ed.2d 892 (1986); ("Risk aversion" should be taken into account in computing

present value), Richard B. Hoffman, *The Right of Publicity—Heir's Right, Advertiser's Windfall, or Court's Nightmare*, 31 DePaul L. Rev. 1, 13 (1981).

93. This point is forcefully made by Professor J. Thomas McCarthy in his treatise The Rights of Publicity and Privacy: "An award of only a reasonable royalty in effect compels plaintiff to license defendant at a rate that, in some cases, defendant proposed and plaintiff originally refused. But in many cases, defendant did not even approach plaintiff for negotiation and permission. In those cases where defendant did ask and plaintiff refused, plaintiff is compelled by a court to merely 'license' defendant's past illegal use of plaintiff's identity at the 'going market rate.' Defendant suffers little: it is only required to pay for what is stolen. Plaintiff has lost something more: the right to make voluntary decisions about who is to make use of his or her identity, and when and where." *Id.* at § 11.8(B). *See* Douglass v. Hustler Magazine, Inc., 769 F.2d 1128, 1138 (7th Cir.1985), cert. denied 475 U.S. 1094, 106 S.Ct. 1489, 89 L.Ed.2d 892 (1986); Cher v. Forum Int'l., Ltd., 213 U.S.P.Q. 96, 101 (C.D.Cal.), *aff'd* 692 F.2d 634 (9th Cir.1982), cert. denied 462 U.S. 1120, 103 S. Ct. 3089, 77 L. Ed. 2d 1350 (1983).

compensatory damages when the traditional basis of malice or recklessness is present in the taking.[94]

While the foregoing discussion divides injury for which damages could be awarded between personal indignity and the loss of commercial value of celebrity, there is no reason why both kinds of injury may not be inflicted as the result of a single unauthorized appropriation of identity. For example, nude "stills" of a well-known respected actress taken from a serious motion picture and used without her permission to advertise a book about nudity in the movies would give rise to both special damages for the invasion of her right of publicity and general damages for the personal indignity of being displayed nude for crass commercial purposes. And if the unauthorized taking of the actress' name and nude image was done with ill will, spite or malice or was done recklessly, punitive damages would also be justified.

This discussion of common law damages is echoed in the state appropriation statutes though most of them do not provide expressly for exemplary or punitive damages.[95]

In addition to the remedy of damages, injunctive relief may be available to prevent continuing or threatened appropriations of identity. But because of the concern that protected communication to the public not be hindered, the courts must scrutinize such claims for injunction with great care in order to avoid prior restraint of protected expression.

Since most unauthorized appropriations of identity are made for trade or advertising purposes, injunctions in these cases may very occasionally be approved by the courts because of the lesser protection afforded commercial expression by the First Amendment.[96] This is particularly so given that the gravamen is expression which takes the names and likenesses of others without permission and is thus akin to theft.[97] Therefore, if success is to be achieved in obtaining an injunction in an appropriation case, the plaintiff should stress the commercial use to

---

94. *See* Douglass v. Hustler Magazine, Inc., 769 F.2d 1128, 1145 (7th Cir.1985), cert. denied 475 U.S. 1094, 106 S.Ct. 1489, 89 L.Ed.2d 892 (1986); Cher v. Forum Int'l., Ltd., 692 F.2d 634, 640 (9th Cir.1982) cert. denied 462 U.S. 1120, 103 S. Ct. 3089, 77 L. Ed. 2d 1350 (1983); Waits v. Frito–Lay, Inc., 978 F.2d 1093, 1104 (9th Cir.1992), cert. denied 506 U.S. 1080, 113 S.Ct. 1047, 122 L.Ed.2d 355 (1993) (right of publicity case); Cabaniss v. Hipsley 114 Ga.App. 367, 386, 151 S.E.2d 496, 509 (1966); Patrick Buckley, Comment, *The Implications of Waits v. Frito–Lay for Advertisers Who Use Celebrity Sound–Alikes*, 68 St. John's L. Rev. 241, 254–55 (1994).

95. *See* text at notes 62–63, *supra*.

96. *See* Posadas de Puerto Rico Assocs. v. Tourism Co., 478 U.S. 328, 106 S.Ct.

2968, 92 L.Ed.2d 266 (1986); Bolger v. Youngs Drug Prods. Corp., 463 U.S. 60, 103 S.Ct. 2875, 77 L.Ed.2d 469 (1983); Central Hudson Gas and Elec. Corp. v. Public Service Comm'n., 447 U.S. 557, 100 S.Ct. 2343, 65 L.Ed.2d 341 (1980).

97. *Cf.* Zacchini v. Scripps–Howard Broadcasting Co., 433 U.S. 562, 97 S.Ct. 2849, 53 L.Ed.2d 965 (1977) (damages approved for the taking of another's act in face of media defendant's First Amendment claim); Harper and Row Publishers, Inc. v. Nation Enterprises, 471 U.S. 539, 105 S.Ct. 2218, 85 L.Ed.2d 588 (1985) (damages approved for the taking of another's intellectual property in face of media defendant's First Amendment claim).

which his identity is put as well as the irreparable nature of the prospective injury and the inadequacy of money damages. Courts have granted injunctions in purely commercial appropriation cases as for example employment of celebrity look-alikes to huckster high fashion clothes and accessories[98] and video club rentals;[99] creation of false endorsements of products by real persons;[100] the use of a person's likeness on T-shirts;[1] and the use of names of and facts about professional athletes and other public figures in board games produced for sale.[2]

Those board game cases may well be on the edge of constitutionally permissible injunctive relief because they involve the communication to the public of a few highly selective biographical facts about the plaintiffs in the non-serious context of game playing. The line is clearly drawn against judicial prior restraint at real world biography, whether mere news reference, sketch or complete narrative and whether oral, visual or written. Howard Hughes discovered this when his own supposed exploitation company, Rosemont Enterprises, Inc., sought to enjoin Random House and its author from publishing a full-length biography of Hughes[3] and to enjoin McGraw–Hill Book Co. from publishing a fraudulent Hughes autobiography actually written by the author Clifford Irving.[4] The New York Supreme Court Special Term for New York County refused to enjoin publication in either case and lectured Hughes and his company on the central idea of the First Amendment: there must be no prior restraint of noncommercial expression except in the most extreme of cases, usually those involving national security.[5]

98. Onassis v. Christian Dior–New York, Inc., 122 Misc.2d 603, 472 N.Y.S.2d 254 (N.Y.Sup.1984). (Jacqueline Kennedy Onassis look-alike).

99. Allen v. National Video, Inc., 610 F.Supp. 612, 620–625 (S.D.N.Y.1985) (injunction actually granted under Lanham act to the real Woody Allen).

100. *E.g.,* Fairfield v. American Photocopy Equipment Co., 158 Cal.App.2d 53, 322 P.2d 93 (1958) (permanent injunction issued to prevent defendant's use of plaintiff lawyer's name in advertisements suggesting satisfaction with photocopy machine).

1. *See* Rosemont Enterprises, Inc. v. Choppy Prods., Inc., 74 Misc.2d 1003, 347 N.Y.S.2d 83 (N.Y.Sup.1972) (preliminary injunction issued to stop use of Howard Hughes' image on T-shirts sweatshirts and buttons).

2. Uhlaender v. Henricksen, 316 F.Supp. 1277 (D.Minn.1970) ("Big League Manager Baseball" using names and statistics of major league ballplayers); Palmer v. Schonhorn Enterprises, Inc., 96 N.J.Super. 72, 232 A.2d 458 (1967) ("Pro–Am Golf Game" using names and facts about 23 professional golfers); Rosemont Enterprises,

Inc. v. Urban Systems, Inc., 42 A.D.2d 544, 345 N.Y.S.2d 17 (1973) ("The Howard Hughes Game").

3. Rosemont Enterprises, Inc. v. Random House, Inc., 58 Misc.2d 1, 294 N.Y.S.2d 122 (1968), *aff'd without opinion* 32 A.D.2d 892, 301 N.Y.S.2d 948 (1969); *see also* Rosemont Enterprises, Inc. v. Random House, Inc., 366 F.2d 303 (2d Cir.1966), cert. denied 385 U.S. 1009, 87 S.Ct. 714, 17 L.Ed.2d 546 (1967); Corabi v. Curtis Pub. Co., 441 Pa. 432, 273 A.2d 899 (1971).

4. Rosemont Enterprises, Inc. v. McGraw–Hill Book Co., 85 Misc.2d 583, 380 N.Y.S.2d 839 (1975).

5. *See* Near v. Minnesota ex. rel. Olson, 283 U.S. 697, 51 S.Ct. 625, 75 L.Ed. 1357 (1931); New York Times Co. v. United States, 403 U.S. 713, 91 S.Ct. 2140, 29 L.Ed.2d 822 (1971). The Rosemont Enterprises cases involving publishers provide an instructive contrast with Rosemont Enterprises, Inc. v. Choppy Productions, Inc., (74 Misc.2d 1003, 347 N.Y.S.2d 83 (N.Y.Sup. 1972)), wherein Rosemont succeeded in obtaining a preliminary injunction against the use of Howard Hughes' image on T-shirts, sweatshirts and buttons.

Documentaries involving depiction of numerous individuals are viewed in the same way by the courts as biographies and, with but one erroneous exception, injunctions to prevent their exhibition have been denied.[6] The one exception is *Commonwealth v. Wiseman*[7] in which the Massachusetts Supreme Court approved an injunction against the noted documentary film maker Frederick Wiseman to prevent the commercial exhibition of his documentary "Titicut Follies." The film, about the Massachusetts correctional system and individuals involved with it, included scenes of nudity among mentally defective delinquents at the Bridgewater, Massachusetts correctional facility. State officials complained of the invasion of the inmate's privacy and ultimately obtained an injunction barring the exhibition of the film on a commercial basis, but the Massachusetts Supreme Court refused to go so far as to enjoin showings to professionals and organizations dealing with the social problems of custodial care and mental infirmity.

Despite attempts to justify the injunction here on the basis that Wiseman violated certain conditions imposed by the state when it granted him access to the facility and that the mentally defective inmates could not protect themselves as normal persons might,[8] the undisputed fact is that the film represents the expression of information and ideas about the Massachusetts correctional system—expression, in short, that is the reason for being of the First Amendment.[9] The Massachusetts court emphasized its error by distinguishing between educational and commercial exhibitions of the documentary. But the content of the work remains the same whatever the nature of the audience, and First Amendment protection is not withdrawn from the film because it is produced with an eye toward making money. If the opposite were true the First Amendment would provide little protection against prior restraint to the news and entertainment media, which are almost entirely profit based. What is critical to the availability of injunctive remedy in appropriation cases is whether the identity taken without permission is used to promote commercial services and commodities distinct from media products containing news, information and creative fiction. The Massachusetts courts apparently recognized the error of their ways 24 years later when the injunction was dissolved.[10]

6. *See* Cullen v. Grove Press, Inc., 276 F.Supp. 727 (S.D.N.Y.1967); Quinn v. Johnson, 51 A.D.2d 391, 381 N.Y.S.2d 875 (1976); *see also* In re Steinberg, 148 Cal. App.3d 14, 195 Cal.Rptr. 613 (1983).

7. 356 Mass. 251, 249 N.E.2d 610 (1969).

8. *See* DAN B. DOBBS, REMEDIES § 7.3(5) (2d ed. 1993) in which the author notes this attempted justification but chooses to reject it because of the film's exposure of conditions at a public institution.

9. *Compare* Cullen v. Grove Press, Inc., 276 F.Supp. 727 (S.D.N.Y.1967) (the very same "Titicut Follies film"); Delan by Delan v. CBS, Inc., 91 A.D.2d 255, 261, 458 N.Y.S.2d 608, 612–614 (1983) (depiction of mental hospital inmate in documentary); Quinn v. Johnson, 51 A.D.2d 391, 381 N.Y.S.2d 875 (1976) (depiction and interviews of children in state licensed institution for dependent and neglected children).

10. *See* Paul Langner, *Last Curb on Titicut Follies Is Lifted 24 Years After Ban*, Boston Globe, Aug. 2, 1991, p. 17.

4.6 False Light Publicity

A. *Historical Development*

According to Dean Prosser,[1] false light publicity seems to have made its debut in an 1816 literary case in which Lord Byron sought an injunction against a publisher to prevent publication of a collection of poems advertised as the work of the celebrated poet. Lord Byron denied authorship, and when the publisher declined to swear as to his belief that the poems were those of the great poet an injunction was issued. Of course, nothing was said in the very short report of this case about any invasion of Lord Byron's privacy.[2]

Little was heard from the courts in the United States in this area until the late 1940s and 1950s when a number of cases, often involving photographs of identifiable persons published out of context, held such conduct to be actionable.[3] While these cases did speak in terms of invasion of privacy or the right to be left alone, they often cited the Warren and Brandeis article, the *Pavesich* case and the New York Civil Rights legislation regarding appropriation of identity discussed earlier[4] without differentiating the false light problem they were actually dealing with. Perhaps the false communications bringing, as they did, unwanted publicity to the plaintiffs caused the courts to conclude instinctively that invasions of privacy had occurred.

Thus, for many years the tort was "rather nebulous" and without "independent recognition."[5] This all changed with the publication in 1960 of Dean Prosser's law review article on invasion of privacy in which he listed false light as one of the complex of four torts he determined from a review of the cases to make up the generic idea of invasion of privacy.[6] From this time on, rightly or wrongly, false light has been viewed by most courts and many prominent commentators as a discrete form of invasion of privacy.

B. *Nature of the Tort and Interests Involved*

The tort action of false light invasion of privacy is personal to the individual placed in a false light before the public or a substantial

---

1. William L. Prosser and W. Page Keeton, Torts 863 (5th ed. 1984).

2. Lord Byron v. Johnston, 2 Mer. 29, 35 Eng. Rep. 851 (1816).

3. *E.g.*, Leverton v. Curtis Pub. Co., 192 F.2d 974 (3d Cir.1951) (newspaper photograph of child injured on the street after being struck by careless motorist later employed in a magazine to illustrate article entitled "They Ask to be Killed" dealing with careless pedestrians); Peay v. Curtis Pub. Co., 78 F.Supp. 305 (D.D.C.1948) (photograph of a taxi driver employed to illustrate article about dishonest cabbies); Gill v. Curtis Pub. Co., 38 Cal.2d 273, 239 P.2d 630 (1952) (photograph of a married couple in an affectionate embrace in public employed to illustrate an article on illicit love); Martin v. Johnson Pub. Co., 157 N.Y.S.2d 409 (N.Y.Sup.1956) (plaintiff model's fashion photographs taken for use in one magazine employed in another magazine to illustrate lurid story about "man hungry" females); Metzger v. Dell Pub. Co., 207 Misc. 182, 136 N.Y.S.2d 888 (N.Y.Sup. 1955) (photograph of boy in a slum area who had no gang connection employed to illustrate article entitled "Gang–Boy").

4. *See*, pp. 423–426, 438 Practitioners Edition Vol. 1.

5. William L. Prosser and W. Page Keeton, Torts 863 (5th ed. 1984).

6. William L. Prosser, *Privacy*, 48 Cal. L. Rev. 383, 389 (1960).

segment thereof by a false communication concerning him.[7] Because the action is personal, it is neither transferrable nor descendible to others no matter how closely related[8] and dies with the victim unless previously filed, in which case the continuation of the litigation depends on the particular jurisdiction's survival statute. It is not available to corporate entities or associations.[9] The tort protection extends to all aspects of one's existence as an autonomous human being, including one's character,[10] work,[11] sex life,[12] social and sports activities[13] and thoughts, words and artistic or literary creations.[14]

7. *See* Clinton Community Hosp. Corp. v. Southern Maryland Medical Ctr., 374 F.Supp. 450, 456 (D.Md.1974), *aff'd* 510 F.2d 1037 (4th Cir.1975), cert. denied 422 U.S. 1048, 95 S.Ct. 2666, 45 L.Ed.2d 700 (1975).

8. *See* Gruschus v. Curtis Pub. Co., 342 F.2d 775, 776 (10th Cir.1965); Kelly v. Johnson Pub. Co., 160 Cal.App.2d 718, 325 P.2d 659, 660–662 (1958); Moore v. Charles B. Pierce Film Enters., Inc. 589 S.W.2d 489, 491 (Tex.Civ.App.1979) (numerous analogous authorities discussed); RESTATEMENT SECOND OF TORTS § 652I, comment *a* (1977); William L. Prosser, *Privacy*, 48 Cal. L. Rev. 383, 408 (1960).

9. *See* Clinton Community Hosp. Corp. v. Southern Maryland Medical Ctr., 374 F.Supp. 450, 456 (D.Md.1974), *aff'd* 510 F.2d 1037 (4th Cir.1975), cert. denied 422 U.S. 1048, 95 S.Ct. 2666, 45 L.Ed.2d 700 (1975); Diaz v. Stathis, 440 F.Supp. 634 (D.Mass.1977) *aff'd* 576 F.2d 9, (1st Cir. 1978); Mobile Oil Corp. v. FTC, 562 F.2d 170 (2d Cir.1977), L. Cohen & Co. v. Dun & Bradstreet, Inc., 629 F.Supp. 1419 (D.Conn. 1986); RESTATEMENT SECOND OF TORTS § 652I, comment *c* (1977).

10. *E.g.,* Douglass v. Hustler Magazine, Inc., 769 F.2d 1128 (7th Cir.1985), cert. denied 475 U.S. 1094, 106 S.Ct. 1489, 89 L.Ed.2d 892 (1986) (nude photograph of actress published in sleazy sex magazine when consent was for publication in a different and more respectable periodical); Colbert v. World Pub. Co., 747 P.2d 286 (Okla.1987) (erroneous identification of man as a convicted murderer).

11. *E.g.,* Peay v. Curtis Pub. Co., 78 F.Supp. 305 (D.D.C.1948) (photograph of a cab driver published in conjunction with article about uninformed and dishonest cabbies); Berkos v. National Broadcasting Co., 161 Ill.App.3d 476, 495–496, 113 Ill.Dec. 683, 694–695, 515 N.E.2d 668, 679–680 (1987) (photograph and discussion of sitting judge in a television news report about corruption in the local judiciary); Crump v. Beckley Newspapers, Inc., 173 W.Va. 699, 320 S.E.2d 70 (W.Va.1983) (photograph of

female West Virginia coal miner used to illustrate article about harassment of women miners in other states).

12. *E.g.,* Braun v. Flynt, 726 F.2d 245, rehearing denied 731 F.2d 1205 (5th Cir.), cert denied 469 U.S. 883, 105 S.Ct. 252, 83 L.Ed.2d 189 (1984) (unauthorized publication of plaintiff's photograph in an indecent magazine devoted to the sexual exploitation of women); Duncan v. WJLA–TV, Inc. 106 F.R.D. 4 (D.D.C.1984) (photograph of woman broadcast in course of a television report dealing with the widespread affliction of herpes); Gill v. Curtis Pub. Co., 38 Cal.2d 273, 239 P.2d 630 (1952) (photograph in a magazine of a married couple in an affectionate embrace printed in conjunction with an article on illicit love); Martin v. Johnson Pub. Co., 157 N.Y.S.2d 409 (N.Y.Sup.1956) (fashion model's photograph used to illustrate lurid story about "man hungry" females).

13. *E.g.,* Uhl v. Columbia Broadcasting Systems, Inc., 476 F.Supp. 1134 (W.D.Pa. 1979) (television film edited in such a way to give appearance that hunter had shot a goose not in flight); Fellows v. National Enquirer, 42 Cal.3d 234, 228 Cal.Rptr. 215, 721 P.2d 97 (1986) (photograph suggesting and caption stating that happily married film producer was dating a motion picture actress because they left a restaurant together); Rafferty v. Hartford Courant Co., 36 Conn.Sup. 239, 416 A.2d 1215 (1980) (newspaper coverage of an "unwedding ceremony" during a party to celebrate the hosts' respective divorces).

14. *See e.g.,* Tobin v. Michigan Civil Service Com'n, 416 Mich. 661, 331 N.W.2d 184 (1982); Beaumont v. Brown, 65 Mich. App. 455, 464, 237 N.W.2d 501, 506 (1975), *rev'd on other grounds* 401 Mich. 80, 257 N.W.2d 522 (1977) ("[T]his tort is found where defendants publicly falsely attribute some opinion or statement to plaintiff. . . . "); Spahn v. Julian Messner, Inc., 21 N.Y.2d 124, 286 N.Y.S.2d 832, 233 N.E.2d 840, 30 A.L.R.3d 196 (1967), appeal dismissed 393 U.S. 1046, 89 S.Ct. 676, 21

While the outline of the tort is clear, the exact interest protected is not. In his seminal article,[15] Dean Prosser, after reviewing the reported cases to that time, came to the conclusions that false light was a type of invasion of privacy[16] and that the interest protected was that of reputation, with the same overtones of mental distress as in defamation.[17] But if that is so what is the point of having an essentially duplicative tort? Indeed, Prosser expressed concern that the somewhat broader false light might swallow defamation, with its more numerous restrictions and limitations on the pursuit of money judgments, particularly against the press.[18]

With due deference to Dean Prosser, a privacy tort protecting the interest in reputation is anomalous. Concern for reputation presupposes interaction between the person attacked and those who perceive the victim's standing in the community. Such interaction is antithetical to the idea of being let alone by society, which is central to the concept of privacy.

A number of commentators have rejected Prosser's idea that the false light tort protects the reputational interest.[19] The interest that is really protected by false light is not very clear. It may be that all that can be said is that false light protects against the mental upset, embarrassment or humiliation from attention and publicity that is generated by false communications to the public,[20] or, if one is already in the public eye and not adverse to attention and publicity, the mental distress,

L.Ed.2d 600 (1969) (manufactured thoughts of and dialogue involving Boston and later Milwaukee Braves pitcher Warren Spahn in a supposed biography); Hemingway's Estate v. Random House Inc., 23 N.Y.2d 341, 244 N.E.2d 250, 296 N.Y.S.2d 771, 32 A.L.R.3d 605 (1968); Rinaldi v. Holt, Rinehart & Winston, Inc., 42 N.Y.2d 369, 366 N.E.2d 1299, 397 N.Y.S.2d 943 (1977), cert. denied 434 U.S. 969, 98 S.Ct. 514, 54 L.Ed.2d 456 (1977); Lord Byron v. Johnston, 2 Mer. 29, 35 Eng. Rep. 851 (1816) (anonymously written inferior poetry ascribed to Lord Byron).

15. William L. Prosser, *Privacy*, 48 Cal. L. Rev. 383 (1960).

16. *Id.* at 389.

17. *Id.* at 400.

18. *Id.* at 401. *See also* John W. Wade, *Defamation and the Right of Privacy*, 15 Vand. L. Rev. 1093, 1094–1095 (1962). But it is necessary to keep in mind that while actionable defamation necessarily involves placing the victim in a false light, not all false light actions involve defamation. *See, e.g.*, Magenis v. Fisher Broadcasting, Inc., 103 Or.App. 555, 558–559, 798 P.2d 1106, 1108–1109 (1990).

19. *See, e.g.*, Francis X. Beytagh, Jr. *Privacy and a Free Press: A Contemporary Conflict in Values,* 20 N.Y.L.F. 453, 502–

503 (1975); Harry Kalven, Jr., *Privacy in Tort Law—Were Warren and Brandeis Wrong*? 31 Law & Contemp. Probs. 326, 340–341 (1966); Melville B. Nimmer, *The Right to Speak from Times to Time: First Amendment Theory Applied to Libel and Misapplied to Privacy*, 56 Cal. L. Rev. 935, 963–64 (1968). The fifth edition of Dean Prosser's Hornbook prepared after his death backs off from his earlier position, stating "The action for defamation and the action for invasion of privacy should be carefully distinguished. The former is to protect a person's interest in a good reputation.... The latter is to protect a person's interest in being left alone.... " William L. Prosser and W. Page Keeton, Torts 864 (5th ed. 1984). The dispute over the interest protected by false light and the uncertainty, confusion and problems created in its wake are detailed in Ruth F. Walden and Emile Netzhammer, *False Light Invasion of Privacy: Untangling the Web of Uncertainty*, 9 Comm/Ent 347 (1987).

20. *See, e.g.*, Gill v. Curtis Pub. Co. 38 Cal.2d 273, 239 P.2d 630 (1952) (married couple humiliated by being held up to the public through photograph and accompanying story as being attracted to each other only for the sex).

embarrassment or humiliation resulting from the assault on dignity from false portrayal.[21] The tort simply has not been well rationalized, leading to its outright rejection in at least three jurisdictions[22] and its uncertain application elsewhere.[23]

C. Elements of the Tort

The Restatement of Torts Second Section 652 E sets out the elements of false light as (1) the giving of publicity (2) concerning another (3) which places the other before the public in a false light (4) that would be highly offensive to a reasonable person and (5) with knowledge or reckless disregard by the defendant of the falsity of the publicized matter and the resulting false light in which the other is placed. Except as to the fifth element which provides constitutionally based protection for the news media, there is little debate about the prima facie case of false light.

1. Publicity

If there is one requirement that reflects the essence of the tort it is the need on the part of the plaintiff to establish widespread publicity. In other words, the false communication must become *public* knowledge through the defendant's efforts.[24] Thus, plaintiffs have failed to establish their false light claims where an erroneous oral accusation of involvement in the failure to pay for a store layaway was communicated to a few persons in the store,[25] or where an erroneous oral statement about

21. *See, e.g.*, Spahn v. Julian Messner, Inc., 21 N.Y.2d 124, 286 N.Y.S.2d 832, 233 N.E.2d 840, 30 A.L.R.3d 196 (1967), appeal dismissed 393 U.S. 1046, 89 S.Ct. 676, 21 L.Ed.2d 600 (1969) (manufactured incidents, thoughts and dialogue involving a celebrated National League pitcher).

22. ELM Medical Lab, Inc. v. RKO General, Inc., 403 Mass. 779, 532 N.E.2d 675, 681 (Mass. 1989); Renwick v. News & Observer, Pub. Co., 310 N.C. 312, 322–323, 312 S.E.2d 405, 412–413, cert. denied 469 U.S. 858, 105 S.Ct. 187, 83 L.Ed.2d 121, (1984); Cain v. Hearst Corp., 878 S.W.2d 577 (Tex.1994) (5 to 4 vote). Ohio also appears to have rejected the false light tort but with some ambiguity. *See* Yeager v. Local Union 20, 6 Ohio St.3d 369, 372 and n. 1, 453 N.E.2d 666, 669–670 and n. 1 (1983); Rinehart v. Toledo Blade Co., 21 Ohio App.3d 274, 279, 487 N.E.2d 920, 923 (1985). *But see* Godbehere v. Phoenix Newspapers Inc., 162 Ariz. 335, 783 P.2d 781 (1989) (enthusiastic embrace of the tort).

23. *See* Mitchell v. Random House, Inc., 865 F.2d 664, 672 (5th Cir.1989); Sullivan v. Pulitzer Broadcasting Co., 709 S.W.2d 475 (Mo.1986) (en banc) (refusal to recognize false light in cases actionable under defamation); Hoppe v. Hearst Corp., 53 Wash.App. 668, 770 P.2d 203, 208 n. 5

(Wash.Ct.App.1989) ("We note that the trial court could have properly dismissed Hoppe's false light claim on the basis that thus far, Washington has not recognized the tort."); Zinda v. Louisiana Pac. Corp., 149 Wis.2d 913, 440 N.W.2d 548, 555 (Wis. 1989) (Wisconsin's statute "does not provide a cause of action for placing a person in a false light in the public eye"); *see also* Ruth F. Walden and Emile Netzhammer, *False Light Invasion of Privacy: Untangling the Web of Uncertainty*, 9 Comm/Ent 347, 373 (1987) (extensive case analysis).

24. Moore v. Big Picture Co., 828 F.2d 270, 273–274 (5th Cir.1987); Polin v. Dun & Bradstreet, Inc., 768 F.2d 1204, 1206 (10th Cir.1985); Kinsey v. Macur, 107 Cal.App.3d 265, 271–272, 165 Cal.Rptr. 608, 611–612 (1980) (letters to "perhaps twenty [people] at most" constituted sufficient publicity because they were a diverse and unconnected group living in several states); Early Detection Ctr. v. New York Life Ins. Co., 157 Mich.App. 618, 631, 403 N.W.2d 830, 836 (1986); *cf.* RESTATEMENT SECOND OF TORTS § 652D, comment *a* (1977).

25. Reed v. Ponton, 15 Mich.App. 423, 166 N.W.2d 629 (1968); *compare* Vogel v. W.T. Grant Co., 458 Pa. 124, 327 A.2d 133 (1974).

the source of inside information concerning operation of an air force base was communicated during a business meeting to no more than two of the eight persons in attendance[26] or where allegedly erroneous written credit reports were sent to a total of seventeen subscribers who were required by the subscription contract with the reporting service to keep them confidential.[27] Nor does plaintiff's own subsequent trumpeting to the public of a defendant's original limited false communication meet the publicity requirement.[28]

Because of the requirement of publicity the tort of false light is even more closely linked with the mass media than defamation, and newspersons must be particularly concerned that they not falsely portray the subjects of their stories to the public even when the false portrayal is not defamatory.

2. *Identification of the Plaintiff*

If one is to be successful in maintaining an action for false light, it goes almost without saying that the erroneous communication must be such that it identifies the plaintiff expressly or by clear implication.[29] And because the publicity required must be widespread,[30] it is necessary that the plaintiff be identifiable by a substantial number of the public.[31]

3. *False Publicity*

The publicity complained of must, of course, be false.[32] If it is correct, it is not actionable even when the plaintiff insists that it places him in a false light before the public.[33] But if the publicity, by the particular manner of presentation or the language chosen in conveying true facts suggests that the communicator intends to create a false impression from the facts publicized false light liability might still be found.[34] The choice of snide or accusatory words in a headline accompanying a newsstory or the juxtaposition of facts with other facts in a story which may lead the audience into drawing false impressions of the plaintiff may be actionable. For instance, the "ambush" interview practiced by the television networks and local stations may, on occasion,

26. Moore v. Big Picture Co., 828 F.2d 270, 273–275 (5th Cir.1987).

27. Polin v. Dun & Bradstreet, Inc. 768 F.2d 1204 (10th Cir.1985).

28. Moore v. Big Picture Co., 828 F.2d 270, 274 (5th Cir.1987).

29. *See* Brauer v. Globe Newspaper Co., 351 Mass. 53, 58, 217 N.E.2d 736, 740 (1966); *see also* Meeropol v. Nizer, 381 F.Supp. 29, 37 (S.D.N.Y.1974), *aff'd in part, rev'd in part*, 560 F.2d 1061 (2d Cir.1977), cert. denied 434 U.S. 1013, 98 S.Ct. 727, 54 L.Ed.2d 756 (1978).

30. *See* p. 451 in Practitioners Edition.

31. Brauer v. Globe Newspaper Co., 351 Mass. 53, 58, 217 N.E.2d 736, 740 (1966).

32. *See, e.g.*, White v. Fraternal Order of Police, 909 F.2d 512, 523, 285 U.S. App. D.C. 273, 284 (D.C.Cir.1990); Machleder v. Diaz, 801 F.2d 46, 53 (2d Cir.1986), cert. denied *sub nom.* Machleder v. CBS, Inc., 479 U.S. 1088, 107 S.Ct. 1294, 94 L.Ed.2d 150 (1987); Rinsley v. Brandt, 700 F.2d 1304, 1307 (10th Cir.1983); Brown v. Capricorn Records, Inc., 136 Ga.App. 818, 819, 222 S.E.2d 618, 619–620 (1975).

33. *See e.g.*, Machleder v. Diaz , 801 F.2d 46, 53 (2d Cir.1986), cert. denied 479 U.S. 1088, 107 S.Ct. 1294, 94 L.Ed.2d 150 (1987); Brown v. Capricorn Records, Inc., 136 Ga.App. 818, 222 S.E.2d 618 (1975).

34. *See* White v. Fraternal Order of Police, 909 F.2d 512, 523, 285 U.S. App. D.C. 273, 284 (D.C.Cir.1990).

create the unusual situation in which the on-screen conduct and words of the subject of the ambush are accurately recorded and broadcast but the portrait painted is distorted.[35] In *Machleder* v. *Diaz*,[36] for instance, a news crew from WCBS–TV, a New York television station owned and operated by CBS, Inc., confronted the plaintiff, an official of a company that manufactures paints, adhesives and coatings, at his plant which was located about 25 feet from an open area strewn with hundreds of rusting drums labeled "hazardous" and "flammable" and leaking noxious smelling substances. After filming the toxic dumps, the television reporter approached the official with audio recorders and video cameras rolling and asked him if he knew anything about the chemical barrels dumped next to his building. The plaintiff replied that he did not want to be on television and did not need the publicity but as he began retreating from the crew, he added, "We don't ... we didn't dump 'em.' " The reporter asked "Who did?" and the plaintiff replied, "You call the Housing Department. They have all the information." After the film report was aired the company official sued for, among other things, false light invasion of privacy and obtained a judgment totalling more than a million dollars in compensatory and punitive damages.

On appeal the United States Court of Appeals for the Second Circuit reversed the judgment and dismissed the complaint. The court held that the broadcast could not cast the plaintiff in a false light unless it were substantially false. His portrayal as intemperate and evasive could not be false since it was based on his own conduct accurately captured on film which had been broadcast virtually unedited.[37]

But even where, as in most false light cases, the publicity is demonstrably false, that alone is not enough to establish the tort. Such publicity must also *result* in a materially false portrayal of the plaintiff to the public.[38] Minor errors such as those relating to one's age and date of marriage (within reasonable limits), the condition of one's television set or the evidence in a marital dissolution proceeding are not actionable.[39] And the brief mention or portrayal of actual persons in obvious works of fiction to give a sense of authenticity to the invented character and plot

35. "Ambush journalism" has been defined as an investigative reporting technique in which a television reporter and crew "intercept an unsuspecting newsworthy subject on the street and bombard him with incriminating accusations ostensibly framed as questions." Kevin F. O'Neill, Note, *The Ambush Interview: A False Light Invasion of Privacy?* 34 Case W. Res. L. Rev. 72, 73 (1983). *See also* Machleder v. Diaz , 801 F.2d 46, 49 (2d Cir.1986). Almost inevitably the ambush victim looks guilty in dealing with the reporter.

36. 801 F.2d 46 (2d Cir.1986), cert. denied 479 U.S. 1088, 107 S.Ct. 1294, 94 L.Ed.2d 150 (1987).

37. *Id.* at 57–58.

38. Cordell v. Detective Publications, Inc., 307 F.Supp. 1212, 1220 (E.D.Tenn.

1968), *aff'd* 419 F.2d 989 (6th Cir.1969); Brown v. Capricorn Records, Inc., 136 Ga. App. 818, 819, 222 S.E.2d 618, 619 (1975); *see* Themo v. New England Newspaper Pub. Co., 306 Mass. 54, 27 N.E.2d 753 (1940).

39. *See* Cordell 307 F. Supp. at 1219 (E.D. Tenn. 1968); Carlisle v. Fawcett Publications, Inc. 201 Cal.App.2d 733, 747, 20 Cal.Rptr. 405, 415 (1962); Winegard v. Larsen, 260 N.W.2d 816, 823 (Iowa 1977); *see also* Varnish v. Best Medium Pub. Co., 405 F.2d 608, 612 (2d Cir.1968), cert. denied 394 U.S. 987, 89 S.Ct. 1465, 22 L.Ed.2d 762 (1969); Rinsley v. Brandt, 700 F.2d 1304, 1308 (10th Cir.1983); RESTATEMENT SECOND OF TORTS § 652E, comment *c* (1977).

would not amount to false light because the audience would understand that what they were perceiving was not real.[40]

A false portrayal to the public may arise however in cases where fact and fiction concerning the plaintiff are mixed, and the public cannot separate the two. Such was the situation in *Spahn v. Julian Messner, Inc.*[41] There, the defendants published a book purporting to be a biography of the great baseball pitcher Warren Spahn. In reality, the book contained much misinformation about its subject including the mistaken assertion that Spahn had been decorated during World War II with the Bronze Star for extraordinary valor. Other distortions of his military service suggesting heroism and of his relations with his wife and father abounded. Also included in the book were invented words, thoughts and feelings ascribed to the pitcher. Embarrassed by the book, Spahn sued for invasion of privacy and won an injunction prohibiting further publication and distribution of the book and money damages. The New York Court of Appeals ultimately affirmed the trial court's judgment.[42] The Spahn case also illustrates the point that the false light in which one is placed by false publicity need not be derogatory but may even be laudatory. The falsity of the portrayal is what is important and not the nature of that portrayal.

In summary, the publicity element requires false communication concerning the plaintiff which places him in a materially false light in the eyes of the public.

4. Offensiveness

For the false portrayal to amount to actionable false light it must be offensive. The generally accepted standard here is whether the false portrayal or mischaracterization of the plaintiff would be highly offen-

---

40. *See* University of Notre Dame v. Twentieth Century–Fox Film Corp., 22 A.D.2d 452, 457, 256 N.Y.S.2d 301, 304–305, *aff'd on opinion of the Appellate Division*, 15 N.Y.2d 940, 259 N.Y.S.2d 832, 207 N.E.2d 508 (1965); *but compare* Marcinkus v. NAL Pub. Inc., 138 Misc.2d 256, 522 N.Y.S.2d 1009 (N.Y.Sup.1987) (plaintiff a central figure in a novel). Whether a massive fictionalization concerning a living person clearly labeled as such would amount to placing the subject in a false light is an open question. *Compare* Hicks v. Casablanca Records, 464 F.Supp. 426 (S.D.N.Y. 1978) involving a book and motion picture presenting a purely fanciful explanation and narrative of the actual disappearance of the late mystery writer Agatha Christie for eleven days in 1926.

41. 43 Misc.2d 219, 250 N.Y.S.2d 529 (1964).

42. Spahn v. Julian Messner, Inc., 21 N.Y.2d 124, 286 N.Y.S.2d 832, 233 N.E.2d

840, 30 A.L.R.3d 196 (1967), appeal dismissed 393 U.S. 1046, 89 S.Ct. 676, 21 L.Ed.2d 600 (1969). *But compare* Carlisle v. Fawcett Pubs., Inc. 201 Cal.App.2d 733, 20 Cal.Rptr. 405 (1962) holding that numerous less dramatic inventions of dialogue and thoughts and feelings by the author of a motion picture magazine article purporting to be a biography of a screen star was not actionable and Leopold v. Levin, 45 Ill.2d 434, 259 N.E.2d 250 (1970) holding that substantial literary inventions in the contemporary historical or documentary novel "Compulsion" inspired by and closely paralleling the sensational Leopold Loeb murder case were not actionable. In *Leopold* the Illinois Supreme Court said, "[W]e consider that the fictionalized aspects of the book and motion picture were reasonably comparable to, or conceivable from facts of record from which they were drawn...." *Id.* at 443, 259 N.E.2d at 255–256.

sive to a reasonable person in the plaintiff's position.[43] Such determinations are made, of course, by the trier of fact in each case;[44] thus few generalizations concerning the application of the offensiveness standard can be presented. It is clear that minor errors concerning the plaintiff such as reporting the wrong date of birth or street address will not be considered offensive.[45] On the other hand, placing someone in a false moral or sexual light is generally viewed as offensive.[46]

There are only a few reported factual determinations of offensiveness falling between these polls. They include the portrayal of a family as living in poverty and in a dirty and dilapidated house,[47] and the innocent victim of an automobile accident as the careless party.[48]

5. Knowing Falsity or Reckless Disregard (The Constitutional Requirement)

The final requirement for a successful false light tort action that the disseminator know the publicity to be false or that he be reckless regarding its falsity is imposed to insure that this action not infringe upon the freedom of expression guaranteed to the communications media by the First Amendment.

This so-called "actual malice" requirement originated in the landmark defamation case of *New York Times Co. v. Sullivan,*[49] a case with strong civil rights overtones in which the New York Times published a paid advertisement setting out certain facts concerning private and governmental actions in Alabama violative of the civil rights of black citizens. The ad contained a number of erroneous and derogatory assertions of fact about unnamed local Montgomery, Alabama officials which errors could have been discovered prior to publication had someone checked the newspaper's own "morgue." A substantial judgment against the Times and in favor of one of the city officials was affirmed by the Alabama Supreme Court under the traditional common law of defamation. Several similar suits were pending with the potential of financial ruin for the newspaper when the United States Supreme Court granted certiorari. The judgment of the Alabama court was reversed, perhaps saving the New York Times Company from destruction. A major reason

---

43. Machleder v. Diaz , 801 F.2d 46, 58 (2d Cir.1986), cert. denied 479 U.S. 1088, 107 S.Ct. 1294, 94 L.Ed.2d 150 (1987); Braun v. Flynt, 726 F.2d 245, 252 (5th Cir.), cert. denied 469 U.S. 883, 105 S.Ct. 252, 83 L.Ed.2d 189 (1984); Winegard v. Larsen, 260 N.W.2d 816, 823 (Iowa 1977); RESTATEMENT SECOND OF TORTS § 652E, comment *c* (1977).

44. *See, e.g.,* Braun v. Flynt, 726 F.2d 245, 252 (5th Cir.), cert. denied 469 U.S. 883, 105 S.Ct. 252, 83 L.Ed.2d 189 (1984).

45. *Compare* note 39, *supra.*

46. *See, e.g.,* Braun v. Flynt, 726 F.2d 245, 252 (5th Cir.), cert. denied 469 U.S. 883, 105 S.Ct. 252, 83 L.Ed.2d 189 (1984).

(photograph of plaintiff in a swimsuit published in a hardcore men's magazine without permission); Douglass v. Hustler Magazine, Inc., 769 F.2d 1128 (7th Cir.1985), cert. denied 475 U.S. 1094, 106 S.Ct. 1489, 89 L.Ed.2d 892 (1986) (publication of nude photos of actress and model without her permission in a sexually degrading magazine suggesting lesbian behavior).

47. Cantrell v. Forest City Pub. Co., 419 U.S. 245, 95 S.Ct. 465, 42 L.Ed.2d 419 (1974).

48. Leverton v. Curtis Pub. Co., 192 F.2d 974 (3d Cir.1951) (by implication).

49. 376 U.S. 254, 84 S.Ct. 710, 11 L.Ed.2d 686 (1964).

for the reversal was the High Court's belief that money judgments against media organizations for honest mistake or negligence (as seemed to be the case here) in publishing defamatory materials concerning public officials interfered with the robust debate of public issues necessary for the continued vitality of our republican form of government. To insure that continued vitality the Court provided the media with a margin of error by requiring public officials (and later, public figures)[50] to prove with convincing clarity that false statements about them were published with knowledge that they were false or with "reckless disregard" for whether or not they were false.[51] Such proof was mandated by the First and Fourteenth Amendments.

This actual malice requirement was imposed in false light tort actions by the ruling of the Supreme Court in *Time, Inc.* v. *Hill*.[52] There, the seven plaintiffs, all members of the Hill family, had become the subjects of front page news stories after being held hostage in their suburban Philadelphia home for 19 hours in the late summer of 1952 by three escaped convicts. The family was released unharmed and Mr. Hill stressed to newspersons at that time that the convicts had treated the family courteously and had neither molested anyone nor had acted violently. Shortly after the incident the family moved to Connecticut and Mr. Hill discouraged all media efforts to keep the family in the public spotlight. Less than a year later Joseph Hayes' novel, "The Desperate Hours," was published depicting the experience of a family of four held hostage in their own home by three escaped prisoners. But, unlike the Hill family, Hayes' fictional family suffered violence at the hands of the convicts with the father and son beaten and the daughter subjected to verbal sexual assault.

A lawsuit by the Hills against Hayes and his publisher would have been doubtful at this point because of the difficulty of identifying the fictional family with the Hills; the author employed different names, numbers of family members and locales. No such suit was filed. But an action was subsequently brought against Hayes and the magazine publisher Time, Inc. for an article published in Life magazine which indicated that a Broadway play based upon Hayes' novel was an accurate portrayal of the Hill family's experience. Adding to the Hills' pain, Life staged in the Hills' former house numerous photographic scenes of incidents that never took place. The Hills won a substantial judgment in the New York Supreme Court which was ultimately affirmed by the New York Court of Appeals.[53]

50. *See* Curtis Pub. Co. v. Butts, 388 U.S. 130, 87 S.Ct. 1975, 18 L.Ed.2d 1094 (1967) reh. denied 389 U.S. 889, 88 S.Ct. 13, 19 L.Ed.2d 198 (1967), (famous college football coach); Associated Press v. Walker, 388 U.S. 130, 87 S.Ct. 1975, 18 L.Ed.2d 1094 (1967) (well-known controversial retired army general and political activist).

51. 376 U.S. at 279–283, 285–286, 84 S. Ct. at 726–727, 729, 11 L. Ed. 2d at 706–708, 710.

52. 385 U.S. 374, 87 S.Ct. 534, 17 L.Ed.2d 456 (1967).

53. Hill v. Hayes, 15 N.Y.2d 986, 260 N.Y.S.2d 7, 207 N.E.2d 604 (1965).

After argument and reargument of the case in the Supreme Court, with Richard M. Nixon appearing on behalf of Mr. Hill, the Court reversed the judgment, holding that the trial court committed error in failing properly to instruct the jury that liability could only be based on a finding of knowing falsity of the article by Time, Inc.'s employees or on their reckless disregard for the truth.[54]

The reason for the imposition of the actual malice standard in false light cases is the same one given originally for its imposition in defamation cases. "A broadly defined freedom of the press assures the maintenance of our political system and an open society. Fear of large verdicts in damage suits for innocent or merely negligent misstatements, even fear of the expense involved in their defense, must inevitably cause publishers to 'steer ... wider of the unlawful zone' ... and thus 'create the danger that the legitimate utterance will be penalized.' "[55] The Court was thus imposing a public interest standard.

On the other side of the balance, the actual malice standard makes it considerably more difficult for genuinely aggrieved plaintiffs placed in a false light to recover for their injury. But this is the price individuals may be called upon to pay to insure the survival of a society whose blessings they enjoy. And it should be kept in mind that recovery here, while rare, is not impossible. For instance, in *Cantrell* v. *Forest City Publishing Co.,*[56] the Supreme Court upheld a jury verdict and judgment against the publisher of the Cleveland Plain Dealer and one of its reporters and photographers for an article about the Cantrell family which had suffered the loss of its breadwinner Melvin Cantrell when a bridge collapsed over the Ohio River some months earlier. The reporter and photographer visited the Cantrell home while the widow was away and talked to the children and took some 50 photographs during the 60 to 90 minutes they were at the residence. Reporter Joseph Eszterhas's story and the accompanying selected photographs stressed the family's abject poverty; the children's old and ill-fitting clothes, the deteriorating condition of their home and the mother's mask of non-expression and refusal to talk about what happened and how the family was getting along.

The defendants conceded that the story contained a number of inaccuracies and false statements, notably that Mrs. Cantrell was home at the time, her appearance and her refusal to talk about the tragedy and its aftermath. Other misrepresentations related to descriptions of the Cantrells' poverty and the dirty and dilapidated condition of their home. The Cantrells, residents of West Virginia, brought a diversity action against the Ohio defendants for false light invasion of privacy and secured a jury verdict and judgment for compensatory damages in favor of two members of the family. The Court of Appeals for the Sixth Circuit reversed the judgment citing *Time, Inc.* v. *Hill.*

---

54. 385 U.S. at 394–396, 87 S. Ct. at 545–546, 17 L. Ed. 2d at 470–472.

55. *Id.* at 389, 87 S. Ct. at 543, 17 L. Ed. 2d at 468.

56. 419 U.S. 245, 95 S.Ct. 465, 42 L.Ed.2d 419 (1974); *see also* Peoples Bank and Trust Co. v. Globe Int'l. Pub. Inc., 978 F.2d 1065 (8th Cir.1992).

The Supreme Court in turn reversed the Sixth Circuit and ordered the appeals court to affirm the trial court's judgment holding that while in the *Hill* case the state trial judge's instructions had not confined the jury to a finding of actual malice, the United States District Judge in Cantrell had properly instructed the jury concerning knowing falsity or reckless disregard for the truth. Consequently, the only issue was whether there was sufficient evidence of actual malice to support the jury's finding on this point. The Court ruled that there was.[57]

While the reason for the importation of the actual malice rule of *New York Times* v. *Sullivan* into the tort of false light is clear, the precise theory followed by the Court for this importation in Hill is cryptic. "We find applicable here the standard of knowing or reckless falsehood, not through blind application of *New York Times Co.* v. *Sullivan*, relating solely to libel actions by public officials, but only upon consideration of the factors which arise in the particular context of the application of the New York statute in cases involving private individuals. This is neither a libel action by a private individual, nor a statutory action by a public official. Therefore, although the First Amendment principles pronounced in *New York Times* guide our conclusion, we reach that conclusion only by applying these principles in this discrete context."[58] Obviously, the meaning of this passage is subject to debate.

The debate over theory here is not an academic one for its resolution may have impact on the issue of the breadth of applicability of the actual malice requirement. In *Hill*, the Court made no distinction between public official-public figure plaintiffs on the one hand and private person plaintiffs on the other. But eight years after *Hill*, the Court in *Gertz* v. *Robert Welch, Inc.*[59] limited the reach of the *New York Times Co.* v. *Sullivan* actual malice requirement in defamation actions to cases involving public officials or public figures. Whether the distinction drawn in *Gertz* between public plaintiffs and private ones has relevance to false light cases might well be decided by divining the court's theory for imposing actual malice in false light cases in the first place.

If the theory is that false light is a close parallel to defamation, then arguably the applicability of the actual malice requirement for each tort should be parallel. If, on the other hand, the theory supporting the requirement has more to do with the promulgation of publicity about newsworthy events and persons such as hostage takings, then arguably the false light actual malice requirement should apply to *all* plaintiffs

---

57. Other rare examples of plaintiffs successfully establishing actual malice are: Varnish v. Best Medium Pub. Co., 405 F.2d 608 (2d Cir.1968), cert. denied 394 U.S. 987, 89 S.Ct. 1465, 22 L.Ed.2d 762 (1969) (article in National Enquirer presenting a substantially false and distorted picture of the relationship between surviving husband and his wife who killed their three children and committed suicide); Uhl v. Columbia Broadcasting Systems, Inc., 476 F.Supp. 1134, 1139–1141 (W.D.Pa.1979) (on motion for j.n.o.v., held actual malice established by the editing of film for a television documentary suggesting that a hunter had engaged in "fowl" play by shooting a wild goose on the ground).

58. 385 U.S. at 390–391, 87 S. Ct. at 543, 17 L. Ed. 2d at 468.

59. 418 U.S. 323, 94 S.Ct. 2997, 41 L.Ed.2d 789 (1974).

regardless of their status if they are of public interest. For the moment, the question of the scope of actual malice in false light tort actions is an open one,[60] with the commentators[61] and the courts[62] divided over this difficult question.

The prediction here is that ultimately the Supreme Court will overrule *Time, Inc.* v. *Hill* to the extent that it requires private persons to establish knowing falsity or reckless disregard for the truth on the part of false light defendants. We say this because there are marked similarities to defamation and the appeal of the apparent parallelism is a

60. The Court was able to avoid the question in the *Cantrell* case. "The District Judge in the case before us ... did instruct the jury that liability could be imposed only if it concluded that the false statements ... had been made with knowledge of their falsity or in reckless disregard of the truth. No objection was made ... to this knowing-or-reckless-falsehood instruction. Consequently, this case presents no occasion to consider whether a state may constitutionally apply a more relaxed standard of liability for a publisher or broadcaster of false statements injurious to a private individual under a false-light theory of invasion of privacy or whether the constitutional standard announced in *Time, Inc. v. Hill* applies to all false-light cases. *Cf.* Gertz v. Robert Welch, Inc., 418 U.S. 323, 94 S.Ct. 2997, 41 L.Ed.2d 789." 419 U.S. at 250–251, 95 S. Ct. at 469. And in a footnote to his concurring opinion in *Cox Broadcasting Co.* v. *Cohn*, 420 U.S. 469, 498 n. 2, 95 S.Ct. 1029 1035 n. 2, 43 L.Ed.2d 328, 351 n. 2 (1975), Justice Powell stated, "The Court's abandonment of the matter of general or public interest" standard as the determinative factor for deciding whether to apply the *New York Times* malice standard to defamation litigation brought by private individuals ... calls into question the conceptual basis of *Time, Inc. v. Hill*. In neither *Gertz* nor our more recent decision in *Cantrell v. Forrest City Publishing Co.*, ... however, have we been called upon to determine whether a state may constitutionally apply a more relaxed standard of liability under a false-light theory of invasion of privacy.

61. Making the case for retention of the actual malice requirement in false light cases based upon public interest in the publicity and not on the status of the plaintiffs are Ruth F. Walden and Emile Netzhammer, *False Light Invasion of Privacy: Untangling the Webb of Uncertainty*, 9 Comm/ Ent 347 (1987). *See also* Melville B. Nimmer, *The Right to Speak from Times to Time: First Amendment Theory Applied to Libel and Misapplied to Privacy*, 56 Cal. L. Rev. 935, 964 (1968) in which the author goes even further, arguing for a constitu-

tional privilege to protect false publicity that if true would be newsworthy and not actionable as an invasion of privacy. Making the case for the importation from *Gertz* of the limitation of the actual malice requirement to public official-public figure plaintiffs in false light cases are Donald M. Gillmor and Jerome A. Barron, Mass Communication Law 322 (4th ed. 1984); John E. Nowak, and Ronald D. Rotunda, Constitutional Law 1057 (4th ed. 1991); Francis X. Beytagh, Jr., *Privacy and a Free Press: A Contemporary Conflict in Values*, 20 N.Y.L.F. 453, 478–482 (1975); Alfred Hill, *Defamation and Privacy Under the First Amendment*, 76 Colum. L. Rev. 1205, 1274 (1976).

62. Decisions supporting continued application of the knowing falsity or reckless disregard actual malice standard on a public interest basis include Dodrill v. Arkansas Democrat Co., 265 Ark. 628, 639, 590 S.W.2d 840, 845 (1979), cert. denied 444 U.S. 1076, 100 S.Ct. 1024, 62 L.Ed.2d 759 (1980) ("Later decisions of the Supreme Court which have retreated from the malice standard in private individual defamation actions have not eroded the rule of *Time, Inc. v. Hill* ... as to 'false light' privacy actions."); McCall v. Courier–Journal and Louisville Times Co., 623 S.W.2d 882, 888 (Ky.1981), cert. denied 456 U.S. 975, 102 S.Ct. 2239, 72 L.Ed.2d 849 (1982) ("Until the Supreme Court has spoken, we must comply with the ruling in *Hill*, and recovery is predicated on the standards set out therein."); Colbert v. World Pub. Co., 747 P.2d 286, 291–292 (Okla.1987) ("The relaxation of the *Hill* rule may be premature because (1) the *Hill* decision was expressly limited to a private figure involved in a matter of public interest, (2) the *Hill* opinion was handed down prior to the extension of the constitutional standard to libel suits brought by public figures, (3) the common law restrictions on libel suits are more severe than the restrictions in false light privacy suits, and (4) false light cases often arise where no substantial danger to the sensitivities of the plaintiff appears from the face of the publication.").

strong one.[63] Moreover, the federalist philosophy which spawned the *Gertz* decision leaving to the states the standard of fault in defamation cases brought by private persons is, if anything, even stronger today following Reagan era appointments to the Court.

Under the *Gertz* approach, the state courts would be free to choose for themselves the standard of fault required in false light cases. They could opt to maintain the *Time, Inc.* v. *Hill* actual malice requirement if they wished.[64] More likely, most courts would choose to apply the common law negligence standard.[65] Less likely, the courts might choose a gross negligence standard.[66] Entirely prohibited to the courts, as a constitutional matter, would be the imposition of strict liability for the dissemination of false publicity.[67]

Whatever the fault standard adopted, the plaintiff would have the burden of proving the falsity of the publicity and that it placed him in a false light in the eye of the public.[68] If a negligence standard is chosen, the plaintiff will have the burden of establishing by a preponderance of the evidence both the falsity of the publicity and the defendant's negligence in its dissemination since truthfulness of the publicity would be inconsistent with negligence on the defendant's part. Obversely, the defendant would not be required to raise truth as an affirmative defense. Rather, defendant's claim of correctness of the publicity requires only simple rebuttal of the plaintiff's claims of falsity and negligence.

D. Comparison to Defamation

Many authorities have noted a strong similarity between false light and defamation.[69] And the highest court of two states have gone so far as

63. *See*, pp. 460–461 in Practitioners Edition, Vol. 1.

64. *Cf.* Walker v. Colorado Springs Sun, Inc., 188 Colo. 86, 538 P.2d 450 (Colo. 1975); cert. denied *sub nom.* Woestendiek v. Walker, 423 U.S. 1025, 96 S.Ct. 469, 46 L.Ed.2d 399 (1975); AAFCO Heating and Air Conditioning Co. v. Northwest Publications, Inc., 162 Ind.App. 671, 321 N.E.2d 580 (Ind.App.1974); cert. denied 424 U.S. 913, 96 S.Ct. 1112, 47 L.Ed.2d 318 (1976); Sisler v. Gannett Co., Inc., 104 N.J. 256, 516 A.2d 1083 (1986).

65. *See* Wood v. Hustler Magazine, Inc. 736 F.2d 1084, 1091–1092 (5th Cir.1984) cert. denied, 469 U.S. 1107, 105 S.Ct. 783, 83 L.Ed.2d 777 (1985) (making an educated guess that Texas courts would apply a negligence standard); Crump v. Beckley Newspapers, Inc., 173 W.Va. 699, 320 S.E.2d 70, 89 (W.Va. 1983) (applying negligence standard); *cf.* Rouch v. Enquirer & News of Battle Creek, 427 Mich. 157, 174, 398 N.W.2d 245, 252–265 (1986) (state authorities adopting negligence standard in defamation cases collected).

66. *Cf.* Chapadeau v. Utica Observer–Dispatch, Inc., 38 N.Y.2d 196, 199, 379 N.Y.S.2d 61, 64, 341 N.E.2d 569, 571 (1975) (plaintiff in a defamation action must show that the publisher "acted in a grossly irresponsible manner without due consideration for the standards of information gathering and dissemination ordinarily followed by responsible parties.")

67. *Cf.* Gertz v. Robert Welch, Inc. 418 U.S. 323, 347, 94 S.Ct. 2997, 3010, 41 L.Ed.2d 789, 809 (1974).

68. Rouch v. Enquirer & News of Battle Creek, 427 Mich. 157, 187, 398 N.W.2d 245, 266–267 (1986); *cf.* Philadelphia Newspapers, Inc. v. Hepps, 475 U.S. 767, 106 S.Ct. 1558, 89 L.Ed.2d 783 (1986).

69. *See e.g.*, Wood v. Hustler Magazine, Inc. 736 F.2d 1084, 1088 (5th Cir.), cert. denied 469 U.S. 1107, 105 S.Ct. 783, 83 L.Ed.2d 777 (1985); Rinsley v. Brandt, 446 F.Supp. 850, 856 (D.Kan.1977); Crump v. Beckley Newspapers, Inc., 173 W.Va. 699, 320 S.E.2d 70, 89 (W.Va. 1983); William L. Prosser, *Privacy*, 48 Cal. L. Rev. 383, 406 (1960); John W. Wade, *Defamation and the Right of Privacy*, 15 Vand. L. Rev. 1093, (1962).

to reject false light actions in part because such actions are duplicative of defamation.[70] The most obvious similarity is the requirement of a false statement and some dissemination of it. In addition, the statement must be of and concerning the plaintiff—the identification requirement. Both torts also require some degree of fault.[71] Moreover, many of the affirmative and rebuttal defenses are the same or parallel.

But there are differences between the torts that might justify their separate recognition and alleviate the fear that false light, with its lesser demands on plaintiffs, will swallow libel and slander. First, as previously noted,[72] the interests protected by the respective torts are different. Defamation protects the individual's interest in his reputation while false light apparently protects one's feelings or the mental and emotional tranquility that comes from being left alone by the rest of society. The invasion of these different interests result in different injuries. Related to this idea is the difference in the communication itself. In defamation, the expression must defame or adversely affect one's reputation. A false light communication need only give the public a false but not *necessarily* derogatory impression of the plaintiff.[73]

Then, too, unless *Time, Inc. v. Hill*[74] is overruled, most courts are likely to require private persons who are plaintiffs in false light cases to prove by clear and convincing evidence that the defendant knowingly or with reckless disregard for the truth disseminated false publicity. But, in contrast, most state courts in defamation cases, following *Gertz v. Robert Welch, Inc.*,[75] require only that private persons prove negligent publication of the communications complained of.[76] In addition, for a successful defamation action, the defamatory statement need only be communicated to one person other than the plaintiff.[77] Publication in the sense of mass distribution is not required for a defamation action. However, widespread publicity of a false statement is the essence of the tort of false light invasion of privacy.[78] This difference is, of course, more

---

70. Renwick v. News & Observer Pub. Co., 310 N.C. 312, 326, 312 S.E.2d 405, 413 (1984), cert. denied 469 U.S. 858, 105 S.Ct. 187, 83 L.Ed.2d 121 (1984); Cain v. Hearst Corp., 878 S.W.2d 577, 579 (Tex.1994); *see also* Sullivan v. Pulitzer Broadcasting Co., 709 S.W.2d 475 (Mo.1986) (en banc); *but see* Godbehere v. Phoenix Newspapers, Inc., 162 Ariz. 335, 783 P.2d 781 (1989).

71. *See* Gertz v. Robert Welch, Inc. 418 U.S. 323, 347, 94 S.Ct. 2997, 3010, 41 L.Ed.2d 789, 809 (1974); Time, Inc. v. Hill, 385 U.S. 374, 87 S.Ct. 534, 17 L.Ed.2d 456 (1967).

72. *See*, pp. 449–450 in Practitioners Edition, Vol. 1.

73. Prescott v. Bay St. Louis Newspapers, Inc., 497 So.2d 77, 80 (Miss.1986); WILLIAM L. PROSSER AND W. PAGE KEETON, TORTS 866 (5th ed. 1984).

74. 385 U.S. 374, 87 S.Ct. 534, 17 L.Ed.2d 456 (1967).

75. 418 U.S. 323, 94 S.Ct. 2997, 41 L.Ed.2d 789 (1974).

76. *See* Rouch v. Enquirer & News of Battle Creek, 427 Mich. 157, 188, 398 N.W.2d 245, 259 (1986), *on remand* 184 Mich.App. 19, 457 N.W.2d 74 (1990), *opinion vacated* 440 Mich. 1209, 488 N.W.2d 736 (1992), cert. denied 507 U.S. 967, 113 S.Ct. 1401, 122 L.Ed.2d 774 (1993), wherein the decisions of 24 jurisdictions expressly opting for the negligence standard are collected along with the decisions of eight states which have assumed the adoption of the negligence standard.

77. RESTATEMENT SECOND OF TORTS § 577(1) and comment *b* (1977).

78. *See, e.g.,* Moore v. Big Picture Co., 828 F.2d 270, 273–274 (5th Cir.1987); Polin v. Dun & Bradstreet, Inc. 768 F.2d 1204, 1206 (10th Cir.1985); Early Detection Ctr. v. New York Life Ins. Co., 157 Mich.App.

illusory than real when the defendant is a member of the communications industry since communication of false statements to the public obviously meets the requirements for both defamation and false light.

Also, the Restatement Second of Torts does not require that special damages be shown as part of the prima facie case of false light. In contrast, slander and, in most jurisdictions, libel per quod (statements libelous only in conjunction with certain extrinsic facts) require such showings unless the defamation involves allegations of (1) criminal conduct involving moral turpitude; (2) infection with a loathsome disease; (3) misconduct in or mismanagement of one's business, trade, profession or calling; or (4) unchastity or promiscuity.[79] The fear that this evidentiary safeguard for media defendants will be circumvented by labelling essentially defamation actions as invasions of privacy has caused some courts to impose the requirement of special damages in false light actions.[80]

Finally, and perhaps more as an effect of the differences already listed, some courts apply different statutes of limitation to actions for defamation and false light invasion of privacy. If, however, a complainant falls safely within the applicable statute or statutes of limitation, a single broadly disseminated false publication could, in many cases, give rise to causes of action both for defamation and false light.

E. The Statute of Limitations Employed

Because false light possesses both similarities to and differences with defamation and intentional or negligent infliction of mental or emotional distress as well, the question arises as to the proper statute of limitations to be applied. This question was addressed by the United States Court of Appeals for the Fifth Circuit in *Wood* v. *Hustler Magazine, Inc.*[81] There, the Fifth Circuit held that the Texas courts would apply the state's two-year general tort statute of limitations governing actions "for injury done to the person of another" to false light claims rather than the one-year statute "for injuries done to the character or reputation of another by libel or slander." The appeals court was persuaded by the difference in the interests protected by the respective torts.[82] On the other hand, the Washington Supreme Court in *Eastwood* v. *Cascade Broadcasting Co.*[83] held that the state's statute of limitations

618, 403 N.W.2d 830 (1986); *cf.* RESTATEMENT SECOND OF TORTS § 652D, comment *a* (1977).

79. *See* WILLIAM L. PROSSER AND W. PAGE KEETON, TORTS 788, 796 (5th ed. 1984).

80. *See* Fellows v. National Enquirer, Inc., 42 Cal.3d 234, 228 Cal.Rptr. 215, 721 P.2d 97 (1986); Fogel v. Forbes, Inc., 500 F.Supp. 1081, 1088 (E.D.Pa.1980); *but compare* William L. Prosser, *Privacy*, 48 Cal. L. Rev. 383, 409 (1960). Of course, there exists considerable congruity between the respective torts since actionable false defamatory communications always place the victims in a false light.

81. 736 F.2d 1084, 1087–1089 (5th Cir.), cert. denied 469 U.S. 1107, 105 S.Ct. 783, 83 L.Ed.2d 777 (1985).

82. *Accord*: Covington v. Houston Post, 743 S.W.2d 345, 347–348, (Tex.App.1987); *see* Jensen v. Times Mirror Co., 634 F.Supp. 304, 314–315 (D.Conn.1986); Colbert v. World Pub. Co., 747 P.2d 286, 288–289 (Okla.1987).

83. 106 Wash. 2d 466, 722 P.2d 1295 (1986).

for defamation actions applies to false light because of the duplication inherent in the two types of claims.[84]

It is a very close question whether a jurisdiction's general tort statute of limitations covering actions for mental and emotional distress should apply or whether the usually shorter specific defamation limitation governs. The closeness of the question is reflected by the split of authority in the reported cases[85] and counsel may not take the limitations issue for granted but should assume, for safety's sake, that the statute with the shorter limitation applies.

F. High Risk Activities of the Media

1. Erroneous Pictorial Captions

Now that parameters of the tort of false light invasion of privacy have been discussed, it seems appropriate to catalogue a number of pitfalls for the mass media presented by this tort. First and foremost, the news media often have problems with the photographs they print or the images they transmit. While the camera itself may not lie, the caption or accompanying story may portray the easily identifiable subject of the photograph falsely.[86] The Washington, D.C. based Reporters Committee for Freedom of the Press listed twenty-two reported cases of actionable or potentially actionable false light involving some form of visual imagery in its "1988 Photographer's Guide to Privacy" published for members of the news media. Illustrative of instances in which accompanying stories and captions place the subject of the photography in a false light is *Fellows v. National Enquirer, Inc.*[87] There, the National Enquirer published a photograph of television producer Arthur Fellows, a married man, with actress Angie Dickinson over the caption "ANGIE DICKINSON Dating a producer." The story accompanying the photograph said in part "Angie's steady-dating Fellows all over TinselTown, and happily posed for photographers with him as they exited the swanky Spago restaurant in Beverly Hills." In reality the photograph was not posed but was taken as the Fellows party, which included his wife and Ms. Dickinson, emerged from the restaurant. The California Court of Appeal held that the plaintiff might recover for false light on remand of the case for trial to the lower court, which had earlier dismissed the action because of plaintiff's failure to allege special damages. Even though the option was superseded and the holding reversed, the lesson of Fellows is for the graphics editor to determine accurately the circumstances in

---

84. 106 Wash. 2d at 474, 722 P.2d at 1299. *Accord*: Smith v. Esquire, Inc., 494 F.Supp. 967, 970–971 (D.Md.1980); *see* Gashgai v. Leibowitz, 703 F.2d 10, 13 (1st Cir.1983) (applying presumed Maine law); *cf.* Renwick v. News & Observer Pub. Co., 310 N.C. 312, 323, 312 S.E.2d 405, 412, cert. denied, 469 U.S. 858, 105 S.Ct. 187, 83 L.Ed.2d 121 (1984).

85. *See* nn. 81–84, *supra.*

86. *See e.g.*, Wood v. Hustler Magazine, Inc. 736 F.2d 1084 (5th Cir.), cert. denied 469 U.S. 1107, 105 S.Ct. 783, 83 L.Ed.2d 777 (1985); Crump v. Beckley Newspapers, Inc., 173 W.Va. 699, 320 S.E.2d 70 (W.Va. 1983).

87. 165 Cal.App.3d 512, 211 Cal.Rptr. 809 (1985), *review granted and opinion superseded*, 215 Cal.Rptr. 853, 701 P.2d 1171 (1985), *rev'd*, 42 Cal.3d 234, 228 Cal.Rptr. 215, 721 P.2d 97 (1986).

which the photograph, film or tape was exposed and to caption the visual images accordingly. Moreover, the question should always be asked *before* publication whether the image fully relates to what is being said in the accompanying caption or story.

2. Out of Context Photographs

Another dangerous activity occasionally engaged by the media is using photographic images in different context from those in which they were produced. An early but still leading case for the proposition that image juggling may result in tort liability is *Leverton* v. *Curtis Publishing Co.*[88] There, the plaintiff, when she was ten years of age, was struck on a city street through no fault of her own by a motor vehicle. A newspaper photographer who happened to be at the scene took a photograph of the child being assisted by a bystander. The photograph was published in a local newspaper the following day. At this point there could have been no cause of action because the context for the publication was appropriate and the picture newsworthy. But twenty months later, the photograph was used by the Saturday Evening Post to illustrate an article on traffic accidents emphasizing pedestrian carelessness and entitled "They Ask to Be Killed." Plaintiff, in this diversity action, received a substantial judgment affirmed by the United States Court of Appeals for the Third Circuit for falsely being made to appear careless of her own safety and thereby causing the accident.[89]

And in *Peoples Bank and Trust Co.* v. *Globe Int. Pub. Co.*,[90] a photograph taken of the plaintiff, a very old woman who had been distributing newspapers in her community for almost fifty years, and published originally by the defendant in conjunction with a fairly accurate feature story about her career was republished ten years later accompanying a fanciful story about a 101 year-old Australian woman who had to quit her paper route because an extramarital affair with a millionaire customer had left her pregnant. The plaintiff's judgment for compensatory and punitive damages was affirmed by the United States Court of Appeals for the Eighth Circuit, though a substantial remittitur of compensatory damages was ordered.

The moral provided by *Leverton* and *Peoples Bank and Trust Co.* is *never* use photographic images of recognizable human beings out of the context in which they were originally taken unless consent is first obtained from the subject or subjects. The subsequent context will almost never match the original and false light will very likely result.

3. Personal Updates After Newsworthiness Disappears

Somewhat akin to the "out of context" issue is that of time passage and its effect on the status of plaintiffs as public or private persons. The

88.   192 F.2d 974 (3d Cir.1951).

89.   *Compare* Crump v. Beckley Newspapers, Inc., 173 W.Va. 699, 320 S.E.2d 70 (W.Va.1983) (photograph of woman miner taken with knowledge and consent for a favorable story on women in local coal mines but later republished to illustrate article about harassment of women coal miners by their male peers around the country).

90.   978 F.2d 1065 (8th Cir.1992).

problem is often presented when the media revisit significant news events or newsworthy individuals long after the cause for publicity has ended. Since a society's attitudes and perceptions change with time, an individual highlighted in a "where are they now" type of story, for instance, may be perceived differently from the earlier time in which he was the subject of notoriety.

This is suggested by the "Stepin Fetchit" case.[91] Lincoln Theodore Perry was a celebrated black entertainer and motion picture actor whose stage name was "Stepin Fetchit." He appeared in numerous movies in the nineteen twenties and thirties often in the comic black role of an indolent, ignorant, fearful gambler and petty thief. Millions of moviegoers laughed at his antics and he was well rewarded by the studios that employed him.

But in the nineteen seventies and beyond, such racial stereotyping is no laughing matter, and when CBS developed and televised a series of programs entitled "Of Black America," Perry's stereotype of the black American male was roundly condemned in a narrative commentary by Bill Cosby, one of America's great entertainers and humorists.[92]

Perry sued CBS, the sponsor Xerox Corporation, the film's producer Twentieth Century–Fox Film Corporation and the owner of a CBS affiliate which aired the program for defamation and invasion of privacy. Perry complained in part that in using excerpts from his films made in the 1930s, he was being depicted in the 1970s as a tool of the white man who betrayed the members of his race and earned two million dollars portraying Negroes as inferior human beings. In affirming summary judgment for defendants, the Seventh Circuit determined, given Perry's continued active professional career up to the broadcast complained of, that he was a public figure for purposes of commentary concerning his career and that no showing of knowing untruthfulness or reckless disregard for the truth had been shown. But the court did not rule out the idea that the lapse of time might under different facts result in one being returned to the status of a private person and being placed in a false light.[93] The exposure and commentary on a person's past conduct, acceptable in the context of a different time, may cast that person in a false light in a contemporary setting where different standards and attitudes are in vogue.

---

91. Perry v. Columbia Broadcasting System Inc., 499 F.2d 797 (7th Cir.1974), cert. denied 419 U.S. 883, 95 S.Ct. 150, 42 L.Ed.2d 123 (1974).

92. "The tradition of the lazy, stupid, crapshooting, chicken-stealing idiot was popularized by an actor named Lincoln Theodore Monroe Andrew Perry. The cat made two million dollars in five years in the middle thirties. And everyone who ever saw a movie laughed at—Stepin Fetchit."

"It's too bad he was as good at it as he was. The character he played was planted in a lot of people's heads and they remember it the rest of their lives as clear as an auto accident." Perry, 499 F.2d at 799.

93. Id. at 801; cf. Wolston v. Reader's Digest Ass'n., Inc., 443 U.S. 157, 169–172, 99 S.Ct. 2701, 2708–2709, 61 L.Ed.2d 450, 461–463 (1979) (Blackmun, J. concurring).

4. *"Ambush" Interviews*

Regarding the "ambush" interview, it does not in and of itself create a false portrayal of the subject of such journalistic practice because the film or videotape captures the subject as he appears during the ambush.[94] While he may be entirely different when not ambushed, there is still no false light. But ambush journalism involves more than the interview. The editing of the film or tape for broadcast often requires the removal from the film or tape exposed some of the frames or electro-magnetic signals—the "out takes." This subtraction may distort the reality originally captured and give the subject a different appearance and cause the remaining utterances to have a different and distorted meaning. In the *Machleder* case,[95] the leading ambush litigation, the Second Circuit noted that the interview had been broadcast virtually unedited. But that is not always the case. Editing is a powerful tool that can be used to clarify or distort raw information gathered by reporters. It is incumbent upon the editors and producers of news and information programs and those lawyers who advise them to look carefully at the entire footage and to compare it with the edited version to insure as much as it is possible to do so that the editing does not distort the reality of the actual interview, especially the subject's responses.

5. *Mixing of Fact and Fiction*

Finally, the *mixture* of fact and fiction about individuals which leaves the audience at a loss to distinguish between the two may bring forth false light litigation. Fictionalized biographies and docudramas are particularly troublesome genre. The premier example of partially false biography leading to a monetary judgment against the publisher is, of course, *Spahn* v. *Julian Messner, Inc.*,[96] in which the biographer invented significant events, words and feelings in the life of the Hall of Fame pitcher Warren Spahn, resulting in an overall strongly favorable image of the athlete. Obviously, if Spahn could receive a substantial remedy for laudatory false light, the subjects of substantially invented and derogatory biographies should have little trouble establishing their causes of action.[97]

94. *See* Machleder v. Diaz, 801 F.2d 46, 57–58 (2d Cir.1986), cert. denied 479 U.S. 1088, 107 S.Ct. 1294, 94 L.Ed.2d 150 (1987).

95. *Id.*; *cf.* Herbert v. Lando, 73 F.R.D. 387, 391–396 (S.D.N.Y.), *rev'd* 568 F.2d 974 (2d Cir.1977), *rev'd* 441 U.S. 153, 99 S.Ct. 1635, 60 L.Ed.2d 115 (1979) (trial court order as to discovery relating, *inter alia*, to the editing process on CBS's "Sixty Minutes" reinstated).

96. 43 Misc.2d 219, 250 N.Y.S.2d 529 (1964), *aff'd* 21 N.Y.2d 124, 286 N.Y.S.2d 832, 233 N.E.2d 840 (1967), *appeal dismissed* 393 U.S. 1046, 89 S.Ct. 676, 21 L.Ed.2d 600 (1969).

97. Actionability for biographical invention is a matter of degree since minor inventions of dialogue, feelings and events would likely not be found by the trier of facts to be highly offensive to a reasonable person in the plaintiff's position as required by this tort. *Compare* Varnish v. Best Medium Pub. Co., 405 F.2d 608, 611–612 (2d Cir.1968), cert. denied 394 U.S. 987, 89 S.Ct. 1465, 22 L.Ed.2d 762 (1969); Carlisle v. Fawcett Publications, Inc., 201 Cal. App.2d 733, 742–743, 20 Cal.Rptr. 405, 415–416 (1962).

It must be kept in mind, however, that mere negligent errors concerning the lives of biographical subjects would not likely be actionable because such subjects are almost invariably public figures who are required to establish knowing untruthfulness or reckless disregard for the truth on the part of the defendants.[98]

Motion picture and television docudramas pose essentially the same risks for the visual media as invented biographies pose for the print media. But because audio-visual sensations are generally thought to have greater impact on the mind than the printed word and consequently have greater impact on the public, docudramas stimulate more costly litigation. While no docudramas so far presented to the public has yet resulted in the award of damages, it is not for want of trying by their subjects and others. Unsuccessful actions have been litigated regarding the motion picture "Compulsion," the fictionalized version of the Leopold–Loeb murder case;[99] the ABC television docudrama "Legend of Valentino: A Romantic Fiction" based in part on the life of the famous silent film star;[100] the NBC television drama "Judge Horton and the Scottsboro Boys," an account of the famous cross-racial gang rape trial of the 1930s containing dialogue beyond that of the trial transcript;[1] and "Tail Gunner Joe," another NBC television docudrama, this time about the life and times of Senator Joseph McCarthy and McCarthy aide Roy Cohn.[2]

Even *mention* of a proposed docudrama has drawn legal action. Following a Hollywood producer's announcement that his production company was planning a film entitled "The Elizabeth Taylor Story" for showing on ABC–TV, the famed actress filed suit in United States District Court to enjoin production and distribution of the film.[3] The complaint stated that since the proposed motion picture would be neither purely biographical nor documentary it would of necessity have to be a docudrama with manufactured dialogue and invented incidents, or as Ms. Taylor so colorfully put it in an interview with a Chicago newspaper, the film would have to be fiction unless somebody had been under her carpet or bed for the past fifty years.[4] The case was eventually dropped when the producer disclaimed his intention to make such a film.

98. *See* Time, Inc. v. Hill, 385 U.S. 374, 87 S.Ct. 534, 17 L.Ed.2d 456 (1967).

99. Leopold v. Levin, 45 Ill.2d 434, 259 N.E.2d 250 (1970).

100. Guglielmi v. Spelling—Goldberg Productions, 25 Cal.3d 860, 160 Cal.Rptr. 352, 603 P.2d 454 (1979).

1. Street v. National Broadcasting Co. 645 F.2d 1227 (6th Cir.), cert. denied 454 U.S. 815, 102 S.Ct. 91, 70 L.Ed.2d 83 (1981), cert. dismissed 454 U.S. 1095, 102 S.Ct. 667, 70 L.Ed.2d 636 (1981).

2. Cohn v. National Broadcasting Co., 67 A.D.2d 140, 414 N.Y.S.2d 906 (1979), *aff'd* 50 N.Y.2d 885, 430 N.Y.S.2d 265, 408 N.E.2d 672, cert. denied 449 U.S. 1022, 101 S.Ct. 590, 66 L.Ed.2d 484 (1980).

3. Taylor v. American Broadcasting Cos., Inc. (82 Civ. 6977, S.D.N.Y. 1982). False light invasion of privacy was not alleged in Ms. Taylor's complaint apparently because the film did not then exist and the requirement of widespread publicity could not therefore be met.

4. *See* Victor A. Kovner, *The Great Docudrama Controversy—Elizabeth Taylor and ABC*, 1 ABA Communications Lawyer 10 (No. 2, Spring 1982).

The point here is not the success or failure of these cases but the high risk that fictionalized biographies and docudramas will draw litigation with all the expenditures of time, money and energy that court battles entail. If, however, such projects are important enough to the writers and producers involved that they are prepared to proceed in the face of the known legal risks, there are defenses available to them that have a substantial probability of success if they act in good faith, deal with matters of public interest, extrapolate reasonably from the known to the unknown and keep invention to the minimum necessary for creative success.

G. Defenses to False Light Actions

Most of the defenses raised by media defendants in false light cases attempt to rebut elements of the plaintiffs' prima facie case but very occasionally affirmative defenses of privileged conduct will also be presented.

1. Truth

Because falsity of publicity is central to the plaintiff's case, truth of what was communicated is very often raised by the defendant in rebuttal.[5] Truth is a complete defense to the tort.[6] Immaterial errors of fact do not transform essentially truthful communications into false publicity.[7] Moreover, immaterial errors or untruths would not be considered offensive to reasonable persons of ordinary sensibility. Whether a material communication is true or false is a question for the trier of fact if it is in dispute.[8]

2. Waiver and Consent

Again, as with the other privacy torts waiver and consent, whether express or implied from the circumstances, are complete defenses to false light claims with the burden of proof on the defendant.[9] An obvious

---

5. At one time truth was a privileged defense to a common law defamation action because the falsity of defamatory statements was not an element of the plaintiff's action. That is not the case today. *See* Philadelphia Newspapers, Inc. v. Hepps, 475 U.S. 767, 106 S.Ct. 1558, 89 L.Ed.2d 783 (1986) (by necessary implication). And it has never been the case with false light because this tort has always required a showing by plaintiffs of the falsity of the publicity. *See* Machleder v. Diaz, 801 F.2d 46, 53 (2d Cir.1986), cert. denied 479 U.S. 1088, 107 S.Ct. 1294, 94 L.Ed.2d 150 (1987); Lord Byron v. Johnston, 2 Mer. 29, 35 Eng. Rep. 851 (1816); RESTATEMENT SECOND OF TORTS § 652E (1977).

6. *See* Machleder v. Diaz, 801 F.2d 46, 53 (2d Cir.1986), cert. denied 479 U.S. 1088, 107 S.Ct. 1294, 94 L.Ed.2d 150(1987); Rinsley v. Brandt, 700 F.2d 1304, 1307

(10th Cir.1983); Prescott v. Bay St. Louis Newspapers, Inc., 497 So.2d 77, 80 (Miss. 1986); *see also* Brown v. Capricorn Records, Inc., 136 Ga.App. 818, 222 S.E.2d 618 (1975).

7. *See* Rinsley v. Brandt, 700 F.2d 1304, 1308 (10th Cir.1983); *see also* Brueggemeyer v. Associated Press, 609 F.2d 825 (5th Cir.1980); Carlisle v. Fawcett Publications, Inc. 201 Cal.App.2d 733, 748, 20 Cal.Rptr. 405, 415 (1962); Winegard v. Larsen, 260 N.W.2d 816, 823 (Iowa 1977); Molony v. Boy Comics Pubs., Inc., 277 App.Div. 166, 171–172, 98 N.Y.S.2d 119, 124–125 (1950).

8. Rinsley v. Brandt, 700 F.2d 1304, 1307 (10th Cir.1983).

9. *See* Anderson v. Low Rent Housing Comm'n., 304 N.W.2d 239, 250–251 (Iowa 1981), cert. denied 454 U.S. 1086, 102 S.Ct. 645, 70 L.Ed.2d 621 (1981); *see also* RE-

example of consent is the television ambush interview. If the subject permits himself to be interviewed by a news crew the resulting broadcast of the film or tape not only reflects a truthful representation of those moments but such broadcast has been consented to as well, provided no substantial editing of the footage has taken place.[10]

But where one voluntarily approaches the news media prior to publication of an untruthful story about him, mentions the subject of the future story and then following publication provides rebuttal information to the media, there is neither consent to the false light publicity nor voluntary waiver of the right to sue for the invasion of privacy.[11] And where one merely mentions in the course of an interview with a media representative that members of his family suffer from a disfiguring disease, this does not give rise to either the defense of waiver or of consent when the interviewer thereafter broadcasts disparaging remarks about members of the family and their affliction such as to place them in a false right.[12]

Cases of waiver and consent are rare with regard to this form of invasion of privacy because it is not often that persons will knowingly and voluntarily assent to the spread of false publicity concerning themselves, and should they do so they will rarely wish to make such assent public by bringing suit.

3. Absence of Malice

Undoubtedly the most frequently employed defense utilized by the media in false light cases is the First Amendment defense of absence of actual malice in making the communications complained of. Since the Supreme Court's decision in *Time, Inc.* v. *Hill*,[13] every false light plaintiff has had to establish by clear and convincing evidence that the false publicity was spread by the defendant knowing it to be untrue or with reckless disregard for its truthfulness. This means that the plaintiff must establish either that the defendant actually knew at the time of the communication that it was untrue and would falsely portray the plaintiff to the public[14] or that the defendant was aware of a high probability that

---

STATEMENT SECOND OF TORTS § 652F, comment *b* (1977).

10. *Cf.* Machleder v. Diaz, 801 F.2d 46, 59 (2d Cir.1986) (consent to presence on premises where ambush interview took place).

11. Anderson v. Low Rent Housing Comm'n., 304 N.W.2d 239, 250–251 (Iowa 1981).

12. Kolegas v. Heftel Broadcasting Corp., 154 Ill.2d 1, 19, 180 Ill.Dec. 307, 607 N.E.2d 201, 210 (1992).

13. Because the decision in Gertz v. Robert Welch, Inc. 418 U.S. 323, 94 S.Ct. 2997, 41 L.Ed.2d 789 (1974) casts doubt as to the applicability of this constitutional requirement to cases involving plaintiffs who are neither public officials nor public figures, some courts have substituted a negligence standard for determining fault in false light cases brought by non-public plaintiffs thereby relieving them of the burden of proving actual malice. *See* Wood v. Hustler Magazine, Inc. 736 F.2d 1084, 1092 (5th Cir.), cert. denied, 469 U.S. 1107, 105 S.Ct. 783, 83 L.Ed.2d 777 (1985); Rinsley v. Brandt, 446 F.Supp. 850, 856 (D.Kan.1977); Crump v. Beckley Newspapers, Inc., 173 W.Va. 699, 320 S.E.2d 70, 89 (W.Va. 1983).

14. *See* Penwell v. Taft Broadcasting Co., 13 Ohio App.3d 382, 384, 469 N.E.2d 1025, 1028–1029 (1984); Dean v. Guard Pub. Co., Inc., 88 Or.App. 192, 194, 744 P.2d 1296, 1297 (1987).

the statement might be false and communicated it anyway.[15]

Establishing either of these alternatives of actual malice presents a substantial obstacle to plaintiffs succeeding in false light actions. It will take either direct testimony from someone close to the media defendant or compelling circumstances from which the inference of actual malice may be drawn. Neither the fact of publication without thoroughgoing investigation alone,[16] nor evidence of simple negligence in newsgathering, editing or disseminating by the media defendant nor lack of objectivity[17] is enough to permit such inference to be drawn clearly and convincingly. And even a showing of ill will on the part of the communicator toward the plaintiff might likewise be insufficient.[18] Because it is difficult to make a "clear and convincing" showing of actual malice,[19] this is an issue ripe for successful defense motions for summary judgment.[20]

4. Privileged Defenses

The rules governing the defenses of absolute and conditional privilege in defamation cases apply to the communication of false light publicity as well.[21] Perhaps because of the obviousness of this proposition, there are few reported cases on the point. But those few clearly demonstrate the availability of the defamation privileges here.

Persons who by statute are accorded an absolute privilege protecting them from liability for defamation because of the nature of their communications are also protected from liability for false light. Thus, where an

15. *See* Varnish v. Best Medium Pub. Co., 405 F.2d 608, 612 (2d Cir.1968), cert. denied 394 U.S. 987, 89 S.Ct. 1465, 22 L.Ed.2d 762 (1969); *cf.* St. Amant v. Thompson, 390 U.S. 727, 731, 88 S.Ct. 1323, 1325, 20 L.Ed.2d 262, 267 (1968); Garrison v. Louisiana, 379 U.S. 64, 74, 85 S.Ct. 209, 215, 13 L.Ed.2d 125, 133 (1964).

16. *See* Reader's Digest Ass'n. v. Superior Court, 37 Cal.3d 244, 259, 208 Cal.Rptr. 137, 146, 690 P.2d 610, 619 (1984), cert. denied 478 U.S. 1009, 106 S.Ct. 3307, 92 L.Ed.2d 720 (1986); *cf.* St. Amant v. Thompson, 390 U.S. 727, 733, 88 S.Ct. 1323, 1326, 20 L.Ed.2d 262, 268 (1968); Beckley Newspapers v. Hanks, 389 U.S. 81, 84–85, 88 S.Ct. 197, 199–200, 19 L.Ed.2d 248, 251–252 (1967) (per curiam).

17. *See* Reader's Digest Ass'n v. Superior Court, 37 Cal.3d 244, 258, 208 Cal.Rptr. 137, 146, 690 P.2d 610, 619 (1984), cert. denied 478 U.S. 1009, 106 S.Ct. 3307, 92 L.Ed.2d 720 (1986).

18. *Id.*

19. This is the standard of proof for actual malice rather than the preponderance of evidence test in false light cases. *See* Dodrill v. Arkansas Democrat Co., 265 Ark. 628, 638, 590 S.W.2d 840, 845 (1979), cert. denied 444 U.S. 1076, 100 S.Ct. 1024, 62 L.Ed.2d 759 (1980).

20. *See e.g.,* Bichler v. Union Bank & Trust Co., 745 F.2d 1006 (6th Cir.1984); Coughlin v. Westinghouse Broadcasting and Cable, Inc., 603 F.Supp. 377, 389 (E.D.Pa.), *aff'd* 780 F.2d 340 (3d Cir.1985), cert. denied 476 U.S. 1187, 106 S.Ct. 2927, 91 L.Ed.2d 554 (1986); Logan v. District of Columbia, 447 F.Supp. 1328, 1333–1334 (D.D.C.1978); Dodrill v. Arkansas Democrat Co., 265 Ark. 628, 637–639, 590 S.W.2d 840, 844–846 (1979), cert. denied 444 U.S. 1076, 100 S.Ct. 1024, 62 L.Ed.2d 759 (1980); Reader's Digest Ass'n v. Superior Court, 37 Cal.3d 244, 266, 208 Cal.Rptr. 137, 151, 690 P.2d 610, 624 (1984); McCammon & Assoc. v. McGraw–Hill Broadcasting Co., 716 P.2d 490, 492 (Colo.App.1986); McNabb v. Oregonian Pub. Co., 69 Or.App. 136, 142, 685 P.2d 458, 462 (1984), cert. denied 469 U.S. 1216, 105 S.Ct. 1193, 84 L.Ed.2d 339 (1985).

21. Bichler v. Union Bank & Trust Co., 745 F.2d 1006, 1011 (6th Cir.1984), (en banc); Lee v. Nash, 65 Or.App. 538, 542, 671 P.2d 703, 706 (1983) (absolute privilege); Crump v. Beckley Newspapers, Inc., 173 W.Va. 699, 320 S.E.2d 70, 83 n. 5 (W.Va. 1983); RESTATEMENT SECOND OF TORTS §§ 652F, 652G (1977).

attorney filed a motion in bankruptcy court affecting the wife of his client and the wife claimed that it placed her in a false light before her creditors, governmental agencies and the public, the Oregon Court of Appeals held that the statutory defamation privilege accorded to attorneys regarding relevant communications made in the course of judicial proceedings protected counsel against false light liability.[22] And similarly the New Jersey Superior Court found that a defendant private detective's report to a client repeated in an affidavit filed in a divorce proceeding asserting that the client's wife had been seen with the plaintiff in several compromising situations was absolutely privileged.[23] The court also determined that plaintiff's claim was subject to a qualified privilege base on the private detective-client relationship.[24]

The common law privilege of "fair comment" by the media on matters of legitimate public interest was recognized as applicable to false light claims in *Bichler* v. *Union Bank & Trust Co.*[25] There, a television station aired a report on the closing of the only dinner theater in West Michigan, the locking out of the production company employees, the plight of advance ticket holders and the financial problems of the theater's owner. Following a second broadcast on the closing, creditors repossessed most of the personal property within the theater and it never reopened. Claiming many false statements concerning the theater and himself, the owner brought suit for false light invasion of privacy. The trial court granted the station's motion for summary judgment. The reversal of this judgment by a panel of the United States Court of Appeals for the Sixth Circuit[26] was vacated following a rehearing en banc and the trial court judgment was affirmed. The appeals court held that the qualified fair comment privilege was applicable generally to false light claims. It also held that the closing for financial reasons of the only dinner theater in the station's service area was a matter of legitimate public interest thereby justifying application of this privilege. The further requirement of fair comment that the communication be made in good faith was also determined to have been met.[27]

Finally, while there appears to be no direct judicial authority on this point, it seems clear that the qualified privilege of fair and accurate

22. Lee v. Nash, 65 Or.App. 538, 540–542, 671 P.2d 703, 705–706 (1983).

23. Devlin v. Greiner, 147 N.J.Super. 446, 465, 371 A.2d 380, 390 (1977).

24. *Id.*

25. 745 F.2d 1006, 1011–1012 (6th Cir. 1984) (en banc).

26. 715 F.2d 1059 (6th Cir.1983), *rehearing granted and opinion vac'd* 718 F.2d 802.

27. The fair comment privilege, once the most popular of the common law privileged defenses, had been largely superseded by the broader constitutional privilege created by New York Times Co. v. Sullivan, 376 U.S. 254, 84 S.Ct. 710, 11 L.Ed.2d 686 (1964). However, where the plaintiff in a defamation or false light case is neither a public official nor a public figure, fair comment about him in relationship to a matter legitimate public interest may, under state law, shield the media defendant from liability. Further, it may be that the ruling in Milkovich v. Lorain Journal, 497 U.S. 1, 110 S.Ct. 2695, 111 L.Ed.2d 1 (1990), making opinion based on underlying false facts actionable as defamation, might again make this common law privileged defense fashionable though it too requires that underlying facts, if any, be accurate.

reporting by the media of governmental proceedings, meetings and actions extends to false light claims.[28]

H. Remedies for False Light Invasions

1. Damages

General compensatory damages are awarded in false light cases primarily for the mental distress caused by the false exposure to public view.[29] But such awards may also involve compensation for injury to reputation when the false light is also defamatory.[30] When these general damages are accompanied by actual monetary loss, as from lost wages, loss of profits, lost financial opportunities and mental health costs, special damages will be awarded to the extent such out of pocket losses can be proven.[31] But the presence of special damages is not a requirement for a successful false light action.[32]

The award of punitive damages for false light invasion of privacy is made upon essentially the same basis as in defamation actions—presentation of clear and convincing proof by the plaintiff that the erroneous publicity placing him in a false light was effected with knowledge that the material publicized was untrue or with reckless disregard for whether or not it was true.[33] Negligence in making a false light communication to the public would not, therefore, justify the award of punitive damages.[34]

2. Injunctive Relief

The issuance of an injunction to prevent continuing or threatened false light publicity is extraordinarily rare. As Professor Dan B. Dobbs, a leading authority on the law of remedies, has written, "Courts have always been reluctant to enjoin publication, as is shown by the fact that injunctions are almost never issued to forbid libel or slander. The reasons for this, of course, are that free speech policy, constitutional or otherwise, is opposed to any censorship of ideas or communication, and that even where damages would be awarded for libel, it is better to leave

---

28. *See* RESTATEMENT SECOND OF TORTS § 652G, (1977); *cf.* Kilgore v. Younger, 30 Cal.3d 770, 776–778, 180 Cal.Rptr. 657, 660–661, 640 P.2d 793, 797 (1982) (action based on general invasion of privacy "right to be left alone").

29. *See* Time, Inc. v. Hill, 385 U.S. 374, 385 n. 9, 87 S.Ct. 534, 541 n. 9, 17 L.Ed.2d 456, 465 n. 9 (1967); Brink v. Griffith, 65 Wash.2d 253, 259, 396 P.2d 793, 797 (1964).

30. *Id.*

31. *See* DAN B. DOBBS, REMEDIES 531–532 (1973).

32. *See* Kinsey v. Macur, 107 Cal.App.3d 265, 165 Cal.Rptr. 608, 614 (1980); William L. Prosser, *Privacy* 48 Cal. L. Rev. 383, 409 (1960); *cf.* Reed v. Real Detective Pub. Co., 63 Ariz. 294, 305, 162 P.2d 133, 139 (1945);

contra: Fogel v. Forbes, Inc., 500 F.Supp. 1081, 1088 (E.D.Pa.1980) (misinterpreting RESTATEMENT SECOND OF TORTS § 652E, comment *e* (1977)).

33. *Cf.* Gertz v. Robert Welch, Inc., 418 U.S. 323, 349, 94 S.Ct. 2997, 3011, 41 L.Ed.2d 789, 810 (1974).

34. Indeed, as matters apparently now stand, no case for liability could even be made out against a media defendant for false light invasion of privacy by any plaintiff without a showing of a defendant's knowing untruthfulness or reckless disregard for the truth. *See* Time, Inc. v. Hill, 385 U.S. 374, 87 S.Ct. 534, 17 L.Ed.2d 456 (1967).

the plaintiff to such a remedy than to shut off communication of ideas."[35] So that Professor Dobbs is not himself placed in a false light, it must be noted that he expressed a reservation as to the future attitude of the courts to the grant of injunctions in privacy cases based on publication.[36] But he was writing in 1973, less than a decade after the New York Court of Appeals had upheld an injunction to bar further publication and distribution of an unauthorized biography found to place the great pitcher Warren Spahn in a false light.[37] A careful review of the cases since *Spahn* fails to indicate any movement toward making injunctive relief more readily available in false light cases than it is in defamation actions. Writing in 1993, Professor Dobbs appears to agree with this assessment. "In others cases in which privacy is invaded by publication rather than by intrusion, free speech concerns are pressing. There may be no cause of action at all if the material published is true and if it is not illicitly obtained. But even when a cause of action exists, courts' have recognized that there are especially strong free speech reasons to deny the injunction...."[38] It is submitted that *Spahn* is aberrational because it enjoins publication and distribution of the truthful contents of the book as well as the false.

That decision is perhaps explicable in that it was brought under the only theory of invasion of privacy recognized in New York—appropriation of another's image or persona for purposes of advertising or trade in violation of sections 50 and 51 of the New York Civil Rights Act. This legislation provides injunctive relief to prevent such appropriations, and the New York courts have been relatively liberal over the years in issuing such injunctions.[39] But Spahn, however characterized by the plaintiff, is a false light case and not an appropriation case.[40] It involves, rather, the publication of an unauthorized and partially false biography with all the First Amendment implications that entails. It would be difficult, indeed, to argue that had the biography been correct in all material respects, the plaintiff could still have enjoined publication and distribution under the New York legislation. The First Amendment would prevent that. And it should prevent the enjoining of partially false biographies and other communications to the public as well.

35. DAN B. DOBBS, REMEDIES 537 (1973).

36. *Id.*

37. Spahn v. Julian Messner, Inc., 18 N.Y.2d 324, 274 N.Y.S.2d 877, 221 N.E.2d 543 (1966), *vacated and remanded*, 387 U.S. 239, 87 S.Ct. 1706, 18 L.Ed.2d 744 (1967), *earlier decision reaffirmed*, 21 N.Y.2d 124, 286 N.Y.S.2d 832, 233 N.E.2d 840, 30 A.L.R.3d 196, *appeal dismissed*, 393 U.S. 1046, 89 S.Ct. 676, 21 L.Ed.2d 600 (1969).

38. DAN B. DOBBS, REMEDIES § 7.3 (5) (2d ed. 1993).

39. *See e.g.*, Reilly v. Rapperswill Corp., 50 A.D.2d 342, 377 N.Y.S.2d 488 (1975) (preliminary injunction ordered); Doe v. Roe, 42 A.D.2d 559, 345 N.Y.S.2d 560 (1973) (preliminary injunction affirmed); Onassis v. Christian Dior—New York, Inc. 122 Misc.2d 603, 472 N.Y.S.2d 254 (N.Y.Sup.1984) (preliminary injunction issued); Durgom v. Columbia Broadcasting System, Inc., 29 Misc.2d 394, 214 N.Y.S.2d 752 (N.Y.Sup.1961) (temporary injunction issued).

40. This is as much as admitted by the New York Court of Appeals in placing emphasis on the falsity of much of the book's contents. *See* 21 N.Y.2d 124, 127, 286 N.Y.S.2d 832, 835, 233 N.E.2d 840, 842, 30 A.L.R.3d 196, 198 (1967); 18 N.Y.2d 324 328, 274 N.Y.S.2d 877, 879–880, 221 N.E.2d 543, 545 (1966).

4.7 Publication of Private Facts

A. *Historical Development and Modern Perspective*

The tort of publication of private embarrassing facts was first suggested by Samuel D. Warren and Louis D. Brandeis in their famous article "The Right to Privacy" in 1890.[1] It was this tort that the two proper Bostonians specifically had in mind when they wrote the article. They were motivated by the "yellow journalism" of the time that delighted in prying into the private affairs of people of influence and wealth.[2]

Their idea, distilled from fragments of language in bits and pieces of English precedents and one *sui generis* case, that there existed a common law tort of invasion of privacy involving the publication of private embarrassing facts, lay untouched by the courts for almost four decades. But in 1927, the Court of Appeals of Kentucky held that a complaint alleging that the defendant service garage owner placed a sign five feet by eight feet in size in his window stating that the plaintiff "owes an account here of $49.67. And if promises would pay an account this account would have been settled long ago." stated a cause of action in tort for unwarranted invasion of privacy even though the plaintiff did not contest the truthfulness of the communication.[3]

While this Kentucky case has had little celebrity, perhaps because of the prosaic nature of the facts and the lack of a media defendant, the "Red Kimono" case, decided a few years later, brought the tort to light with a vengeance because of its lurid nature and the involvement of a Hollywood film studio.[4] There, the defendant studio produced the true story of the plaintiff, a woman who had been a prostitute famous for her red kimono and who had been tried for and acquitted of murdering one of her clients. The silent film employed the plaintiff's true maiden name. After the film's release, Mrs. Melvin brought suit in California claiming, among other things, invasion of privacy. She alleged that after the murder trial she had reformed herself, married well and had led a virtuous and honorable life and that after release of the film identifying her as the notorious "red kimono" prostitute, friends turned against her, causing her severe mental and physical suffering. A demurrer to the complaint was sustained by the Los Angeles County Superior Court.

The California District Court of Appeal reversed and remanded the case for trial, holding that complaint stated a good cause of action. The appeals court, while mindful that the motion picture was based on facts contained in the public record, stated that the use of the plaintiff's true maiden name, thus identifying her with the life she had put behind, went too far and was an unwarranted invasion of her privacy.

---

1. 4 Harv. L. Rev. 193 (1890).

2. *See* William L. Prosser, *Privacy*, 48 Cal. L. Rev. 383, 383–384 (1960).

3. Brents v. Morgan, 221 Ky. 765, 299 S.W. 967 (1927) (citing the Warren and Brandeis article with approval).

4. Melvin v. Reid, 112 Cal.App. 285, 297 P. 91 (1931).

With the impetus of the *Melvin* case, the private facts tort became established in the nineteen thirties and forties. The signal event in setting the modern parameters of the tort was the decision in *Sidis v. F–R Publishing Corp.*[5] William James Sidis was a child prodigy in the field of mathematics. At the age of eleven, he lectured to distinguished mathematicians on the subject of four dimensional objects and at sixteen he was graduated from Harvard with considerable fanfare. A shy and retiring person, Sidis attempted to escape his fame and notoriety by concealing his identity, becoming a menial clerk and living in one small room in a shabby area of Boston.

Sidis succeeded in his quest for anonymity until he was tracked down by a writer for the New Yorker magazine who cornered him for an interview in his seedy lodgings. From this interview and the writer's observations came a "Where Are They Now?" feature detailing Sidis' present life with many of its oddities including Sidis' penchant for collecting streetcar transfers, his proficiency with an adding machine and his interest in the Okamakammesett Indians.

Sidis sued the New Yorker's parent company but the complaint was dismissed for failure to state a claim upon which relief could be granted.[6] The trial court's ruling was affirmed by the United States Court of Appeals for the Second Circuit even though the court described the feature story as "a ruthless exposure of a once public figure character, who has since sought and has now been deprived of the seclusion of private life."[7] The Second Circuit focused not on the injury to the plaintiff but on the justification, if any, of the defendant publisher in printing the biographical sketch.

The appeals court noted that the New Yorker article sketched the life of an unusual personality, and it possessed considerable popular news interest, thereby justifying the publication.[8] This was the first important judicial recognition of the idea that in later years was to dominate the tort—newsworthiness.

The development of the prima facie case and the defenses to the tort action have proceeded a pace since the *Sidis* case. Most American jurisdictions now clearly recognize it[9] and numerous commentators have attempted to deal with it.[10]

---

5. 113 F.2d 806 (2d Cir.), cert. denied 311 U.S. 711, 61 S.Ct. 393, 85 L.Ed. 462 (1940).

6. Sidis v. F–R Publishing Corp. 34 F.Supp. 19 (S.D.N.Y.1938), *aff'd* 113 F.2d 806, cert. denied 311 U.S. 711, 61 S.Ct. 393, 85 L.Ed. 462 (1940).

7. 113 F.2d at 807–808.

8. *Id.* at 809.

9. *See* note 30, section 4.3, *supra.*

10. *See* Gerald G. Ashdown, *Media Reporting and Privacy Claims—Decline in Constitutional Protection for the Press*, 66 Ky. L.J. 759 (1978); Randall P. Bezanson, *Public Disclosures as News: Injunctive Relief and Newsworthiness in Privacy Actions Involving the Press*, 64 Iowa L. Rev. 1061 (1979); Dorsey D. Ellis, Jr., *Damages and the Privacy Tort: Sketching a "Legal Profile,"* 64 Iowa L. Rev. 1111 (1979); Marc A. Franklin, *A Constitutional Problem in Privacy Protection: Legal Inhibitions on Reporting of Fact*, 16 Stan L. Rev. 107 (1963); Hugh Moore Jr., *A Newspaper's Risks in Reporting "Facts" From Presumably Reliable Sources: A study in the Practical Application of the Right of Privacy*, 22 S.C.L. Rev. 1 (1970); William L. Prosser, *Privacy*, 48 Cal. L. Rev. 383 (1960); Irwin L. Spiegel,

But recognition of the tort action is one thing and efficacy is another. The publication of private embarrassing facts is primarily a media tort; it was conceived as such by Warren and Brandeis. Yet in the more than 100 years since the publication of their now historic article, there have been less than a dozen appellate reports of successful actions against media defendants in this realm. Moreover, successful actions against media defendants seem even less likely in the future with the narrowing of the judicial view of what facts are private and embarrassing because of the expanding judicial view of what communications are newsworthy and because of doubts as to the constitutionality of the action. Thus, there is much sound and fury here but little real impact on the communications industry except for the substantial expenditures to defend against these actions. Nevertheless, the tort exists and because a few injured plaintiffs have recovered against media defendants, this tort will be examined in some detail.

B. *Nature of the Tort and Interests Involved*

Of the complex of four torts identified by Dean Prosser as making up the generic action of invasion of privacy, the publication of embarrassing private facts is the one at the core of invasion of personal privacy. The essence of the tort is publicizing of information that the subject of the public disclosure wishes, for good reason, to keep out of the hands of the public. It is information that while perhaps interesting is not of legitimate concern of the public.[11] Thus publicizing the style and color of a woman's undergarments,[12] a person's past sexual and criminal activities,[13] a hospital patient's rare and bizarre eating disorder,[14] and the fatherhood status of an unmarried teenager[15] may be actionable.

The gravamen of the tort is the personal humiliation and mental and emotional distress and suffering inflicted by the unwanted publicity and attendant public scorn, ridicule and ostracism.[16] Because the interest

Public Celebrity v. Scandal Magazines—The Celebrity's Right to Privacy, 30 S. Cal. L. Rev. 280 (1957); Peter N. Swan, *Publicity Invasion of Privacy: Constitutional and Doctrinal Difficulties With a Developing Tort*, 58 Or. L. Rev. 483 (1980); Linda N. Woito and Patrick McNulty, *The Privacy Disclosure Tort and the First Amendment: Should the Community Decide Newsworthiness?*, 64 Iowa L. Rev. 185 (1979); Jeffrey C. Martin, Comment, *First Amendment Limitations on Public Disclosure Actions*, 45 U. Chi. L. Rev. 180 (1977); Comment, *The Right of Privacy Normative–Descriptive Confusion in the Defense of Newsworthiness*, 30 U. Chi. L. Rev. 722 (1963); Comment, *An Accommodation of Privacy Interests and First Amendment Rights in Public Disclosure Cases*, 124 U. Pa. L. Rev. 1385 (1976).

11. *See* Virgil v. Time, Inc., 527 F.2d 1122, 1128–1129 (9th Cir.1975), cert. de-

nied 425 U.S. 998, 96 S.Ct. 2215, 48 L.Ed.2d 823 (1976); RESTATEMENT SECOND OF TORTS § 652D, comment *h* (1977).

12. *See* Daily Times Democrat v. Graham, 276 Ala. 380, 162 So.2d 474 (1964).

13. *See* Melvin v. Reid, 112 Cal.App. 285, 297 P. 91 (1931); Briscoe v. Reader's Digest Ass'n., 4 Cal.3d 529, 93 Cal.Rptr. 866, 483 P.2d 34 (1971).

14. *See* Barber v. Time, Inc., 348 Mo. 1199, 159 S.W.2d 291 (1942).

15. Hawkins by and Through Hawkins v. Multimedia, Inc., 288 S.C. 569, 344 S.E.2d 145, cert. denied 479 U.S. 1012, 107 S.Ct. 658, 93 L.Ed.2d 712 (1986).

16. *See, e.g.,* Briscoe v. Reader's Digest Ass'n., 4 Cal.3d 529, 93 Cal.Rptr. 866, 483 P.2d 34 (1971); Fry v. Ionia Sentinel–Standard, 101 Mich.App. 725, 731, 300 N.W.2d 687, 690 (1980).

here involves personal dignity, the tort action is available only to the individual injured, is not transferable to others and dies with the person.[17] Corporations and associations, therefore, may not bring invasion of privacy actions for media disclosures of their private facts.

C. Relationship of Public Records, Public Interest and Public Figures to the Action

The cases to date have not clearly rationalized the relationships of the three "publics"—records, interest and figures to the private facts tort. It would be wise to attempt this rationalization before beginning an analysis of the elements of the tort and the defenses thereto so as to avoid possible confusion. Information in records accessible by the public is by definition public information. Therefore, no matter how obscure the record or how embarrassing the facts contained therein may be, the facts *cannot* be *private facts* and their publicizing cannot be actionable.[18]

"Public interest" relates to the legitimate interest in the general public in being informed about private facts concerning the plaintiff. If there is a substantial public interest in the plaintiff or in events involving him, the party publicizing relevant private facts is privileged to do so, and if that party is a member of the media the privileged defense is loosely referred to as one of "newsworthiness."[19] Facts about public officials fall under this privilege. But the privilege obtains whether or not the plaintiff chooses to make himself a subject of public interest. A patron taken as a hostage in a failed bank robbery or an innocent person mistakenly arrested during a large drug bust may become the subject of legitimate public interest through no fault, desire or action of his own.[20]

Finally, "public figure" relates to the status of the plaintiff. If the plaintiff, through his conduct, has become a figure known to the public or a substantial segment thereof, such as an elected public official, certain private facts concerning him may be of legitimate public interest simply because of his status. Media parties publicizing such facts are privileged to do so under the rubric of newsworthiness.[21] The concept of public figure is necessarily an elastic one. The nature and extent of one's public status will determine the nature and extent of the private facts about him that may be publicized under privilege.[22] A public figure rarely

---

17. Melvin v. Reid, 112 Cal.App. 285, 291–292, 297 P. 91 (1931);

18. *See, e.g.*, Cox Broadcasting Corp. v. Cohn, 420 U.S. 469, 95 S.Ct. 1029, 43 L.Ed.2d 328 (1975);

19. *See* Sidis v. F–R Pub. Corp., 113 F.2d 806 (2d Cir.1940), cert. denied 311 U.S. 711, 61 S.Ct. 393, 85 L.Ed. 462 (1940); *see also* White v. Fraternal Order of Police, 909 F.2d 512, 528, 285 U.S. App. D.C. 273, 289 (D.C.Cir.1990).

20. *E.g.*, Angelotta v. American Broadcasting Corp., 820 F.2d 806 (6th Cir.1987); Penwell v. Taft Broadcasting Co. 13 Ohio

App.3d 382, 469 N.E.2d 1025 (1984); Covington v. The Houston Post, 743 S.W.2d 345 (Tex.App.1987).

21. Marzen v. Department of Health and Human Services, 825 F.2d 1148 (7th Cir.1987); McSurely v. McClellan, 753 F.2d 88, 243 U.S. App. D.C. 270 (D.C.Cir.), cert. denied 474 U.S. 1005, 106 S. Ct. 525, 88 L.Ed.2d 457 (1985); Tomson v. Stephan, 696 F.Supp. 1407 (D.Kan.1988); Huskey v. National Broadcasting Co., 632 F.Supp. 1282 (N.D.Ill.1986).

22. Sunward Corp. v. Dun & Bradstreet, 811 F.2d 511 (10th Cir.1987); Ollman v. Evans, 750 F.2d 970, 242 U.S. App.

if ever loses his right entirely to keep embarrassing facts private. But an individual who has chosen to become an actor and takes screen roles as a romantic leading man is unlikely to be successful in a private facts action against a movie fan magazine publisher who publicizes the actor's many love affairs.

This concept of public figure should not be confused with the public figure idea related to defamation actions. While the defamation public figure status also relates to the question of privilege to disclose, it is the contrasting privilege to publish *untrue* information unintentionally and non-recklessly about the individual.[23]

D. *Elements of the Tort*

The formal elements of the tort as set out in Section 652D of the Restatement Second of Torts as (1) publicity (2) of matters concerning the private life of another (3) of a kind that would be highly offensive to a reasonable person and (4) is not of legitimate concern to the public.

In apparent contradiction of the Restatement approach to the tort, Professor Alfred Hill has suggested that the real basis for explaining the few successful private facts actions against the media may simply be the one expounded in *Sidis* v. *F–R Publishing Corp.*, i.e., liability might be imposed when there are "relevations . . . so intimate . . . and unwarranted . . . as to outrage the community's notions of decency."[24] Professor Hill provides a strong analysis to support this point of view, but it is submitted that there is no substantial difference between his view and the more formal approach of the drafters of the second Restatement. Professor Hill emphasizes the "mores" standard of *Sidis* but Section 652D expresses a similar mores approach by requiring publicity "highly offensive to a reasonable person," and we can assume that the trier of fact would relate such standard to reasonable persons in the community in which disclosure is made. The Restatement Second formulation reflects the case law to date, has been adopted by numerous courts[25] and provides a sound framework for the analysis of the tort which follows.

1. *Publicity*

If disclosure of embarrassing private facts is to be actionable, the disclosure must result in substantial publicity as to those facts. As the Restatement Second drafters state it, "Publicity . . . means that the

D.C. 301 (D.C.Cir.1984), cert. denied 471 U.S. 1127, 105 S.Ct. 2662, 86 L.Ed.2d 278 (1985); Bichler v. Union Bank and Trust Co., 745 F.2d 1006 (6th Cir.1984); Littlefield v. Fort Dodge Messenger, 481 F.Supp. 919 (N.D.Iowa 1978), cert. denied 445 U.S. 945, 100 S.Ct. 1342, 63 L.Ed.2d 779 (1980).

23. *See* New York Times Co. v. Sullivan, 376 U.S. 254, 84 S.Ct. 710, 11 L.Ed.2d 686 (1964); Gertz v. Robert Welch, Inc. 418 U.S. 323, 94 S.Ct. 2997, 41 L.Ed.2d 789 (1974).

24. Alfred Hill, *Defamation and Privacy Under the First Amendment*, 76 Colum. L. Rev. 1205, 1258–1259 (1976) (quoting Judge Clark in Sidis v. F–R Publishing Corp., 113 F.2d at 809).

25. *See, e.g.*, Dotson v. McLaughlin, 216 Kan. 201, 208, 531 P.2d 1, 6 (1975); McCormack v. Oklahoma Pub. Co., 613 P.2d 737, 740 (Okl.1980); Hearst Corp. v. Hoppe, 90 Wash. 2d 123, 135, 580 P.2d 246, 253 (1978) (§ 652D adopted as standard for statutory right to privacy of state taxpayers); *see also* Cox Broadcasting Corp. v. Cohn, 420 U.S. 469, 493–495, 95 S.Ct. 1029, 1045–1046, 43 L.Ed.2d 328, 348–349 (1975).

matter is made public, by communicating it to the public at large, or to so many persons that the matter must be regarded as substantially certain to become one of public knowledge."[26] Stated more succinctly, the private facts must become public knowledge as a result of the defendant's conduct. Communication of private facts to a small number of persons does not meet the publicity requirement. However, disclosure by media defendants of private facts almost always results in the necessary publicity.[27] The one exception would be if the subject of the private facts disclosure is not identifiable by the public.[28] Where the defendant is not part of the media, closer scrutiny will be necessary to determine whether the disclosure results in the required publicity.[29]

Little judicial attention has been focused on the quality of the disclosure leading to the unwanted publicity. It seems clear, by analogy with United States Supreme Court decisions, that accidental, non-fault disclosures of private embarrassing facts, would not be actionable. Because of the "chill" on freedom of expression, strict liability has been rejected by the Court in libel cases involving public officials,[30] public figures[31] and private persons[32] and in all false light cases.[33] The "chill" would be even greater in cases where the publicity involved true facts and thus, a fortiori, strict liability is not an available theory."[34]

The difficult question is whether negligent disclosure would be actionable. There is little judicial authority pointing to an answer save for a statement in a Louisiana Supreme Court decision that "more than insensitivity or simple carelessness is required for the imposition of liability for damages when the publication is truthful, accurate and non-malicious."[35] A few cases state that liability may be predicated on facts indicating that the defendant should have known the publicity engen-

---

26. RESTATEMENT SECOND OF TORTS § 652D, comment *a* (1977); *see* Virgil v. Time, Inc., 527 F.2d 1122, 1126 (9th Cir.1975), cert. denied 425 U.S. 998, 96 S.Ct. 2215, 48 L.Ed.2d 823 (1976); Brown v. Mullarkey, 632 S.W.2d 507, 509–510 (Mo. App.1982).

27. *See* Tureen v. Equifax, Inc., 571 F.2d 411, 418 (8th Cir.1978).

28. *See* text, p. 482 and nn. 48, 49 in Practitioners Edition, Vol. 1.

29. *See e.g.*, Tureen v. Equifax, Inc., 571 F.2d 411 (8th Cir.1978) (no publicity by defendant retail credit company releasing report on plaintiff to defendant's clients); Beaumont v. Brown, 401 Mich. 80, 257 N.W.2d 522 (1977) (publicity by defendant employer sending letter detailing employment derelictions of plaintiff employee, a reserve Lt. Colonel, to a unit of the United States Army Reserve); Eddy v. Brown, 715 P.2d 74, 78 (Okla.1986) (no publicity where medical information in an employee's medical file released by employer only to a few co-workers).

30. New York Times Co. v. Sullivan, 376 U.S. 254, 84 S.Ct. 710, 11 L.Ed.2d 686 (1964).

31. Curtis Publishing Co. v. Butts, 388 U.S. 130, 87 S.Ct. 1975, 18 L.Ed.2d 1094 (1967).

32. Gertz v. Robert Welch, Inc. 418 U.S. 323, 94 S.Ct. 2997, 41 L.Ed.2d 789 (1974).

33. Time, Inc. v. Hill, 385 U.S. 374, 87 S.Ct. 534, 17 L.Ed.2d 456 (1967).

34. *See* Florida Star v. B.J.F., 491 U.S. 524, 109 S.Ct. 2603, 105 L.Ed.2d 443 (1989); *but see* Cape Publications, Inc. v. Hitchner, 514 So.2d 1136, 1138 (Fla.App. 1987) *decision quashed in part*, 549 So.2d 1374 (Fla.1989) where the court said "Invasion of privacy does not require that there be a knowing and willing public disclosure, only that private facts were publicly disclosed." If the Florida court is suggesting strict liability for publicity of private facts, then it's standard of liability seems constitutionally infirm.

35. Roshto v. Hebert, 439 So.2d 428, 432 (La.1983).

dered would be offensive to persons of ordinary sensibilities.[36] It is not clear whether such statements refer to ordinary negligence on the part of the publicizer or to recklessness, a higher standard of fault in tort.

The negligence standard is permitted in libel cases when the plaintiff is determined to be a private person.[37] This is, in part, because the victim of the libelous communication has not thrust himself into the limelight and made himself fair game for public commentary.[38] It may be argued, by parity of reasoning, that the negligence standard is permissible in private facts cases because the subject of the publicity tried to keep his private facts out of the limelight.

On the other hand, the difference between the torts of publicity of private facts and libel should not be lost sight of—truth and falsity. It is one thing to permit tort liability for negligent false statements but it is another matter to impose liability for negligent disclosure and publicity of private true facts. The latter situation may have a greater negative impact on freedom of expression and is more likely to conflict with First Amendment guarantees because of the public's larger interest in the availability of truthful facts and information.

For the present, all that can be said with certainty is that the question of whether negligence is a constitutionally acceptable standard for liability in private facts cases is an open one. But if a negligence standard proves not to be acceptable, then the lowest fault standard would be recklessness in disclosure.[39] This standard is analogous to the reckless disregard for the truth standard approved by the Supreme Court in *Time, Inc.* v. *Hill*,[40] a false light invasion of privacy case. Again, the difference is between truth and falsity but if the private facts tort is consistent with the First Amendment,[41] a reckless disclosure standard, which is quite imposing for plaintiffs, would seem to infringe minimally on First Amendment interests.

Of course, most private facts disclosures by the media are intended. Private facts are the grist, for instance, of investigative journalism, and news personnel want to make private facts public when they believe

---

36. Aquino v. Bulletin Co., 190 Pa.Super. 528, 533, 154 A.2d 422, 426 (1959); Truxes v. Kenco Enterprises, Inc., 80 S.D. 104, 119 N.W.2d 914, 917 (1963). RESTATEMENT OF TORTS § 867, comment d (1939).

37. *See e.g.*, Gertz v. Robert Welch, Inc. 418 U.S. 323, 94 S.Ct. 2997, 41 L.Ed.2d 789 (1974); Phillips v. Evening Star Newspaper Co., 424 A.2d 78 (D.C.1980), cert. denied 451 U.S. 989, 101 S.Ct. 2327, 68 L.Ed.2d 848 (1981); Triangle Publications, Inc. v. Chumley, 253 Ga. 179, 317 S.E.2d 534 (1984).

38. *See* Gertz v. Robert Welch, Inc. 418 U.S. 323, 345, 94 S.Ct. 2997, 3010, 41 L.Ed.2d 789, 808 (1974).

39. This may be what the Louisiana Supreme Court was suggesting by its state-

ment that "more than insensitivity or simple carelessness is required for the imposition of liability.... " Roshto v. Hebert, 439 So.2d 428, 432 (1983).

40. 385 U.S. 374, 87 S.Ct. 534, 17 L.Ed.2d 456 (1967). *See also* Cantrell v. Forest City Pub. Co. 419 U.S. 245, 95 S.Ct. 465, 42 L.Ed.2d 419 (1974).

41. That question was left open in Cox Broadcasting Corp. v. Cohn, 420 U.S. 469, 490–491, 95 S.Ct. 1029, 1044, 43 L.Ed.2d 328, 347, (1975). *But see* Florida Star v. B.J.F., 491 U.S. 524, 550, 109 S.Ct. 2603, 2618, 105 L.Ed.2d 443, 466 (1989) (dissenting opinion of Justice White suggesting that the tort is no longer consistent with the First Amendment).

them to have news value. Intentional disclosure is at the heart of the plaintiff's case against a media defendant, and, again by analogy with *Time, Inc.* v. *Hill*, the knowing disclosure of private embarrassing facts would be the clearest fault standard.

The only real question regarding knowing or even reckless disclosures is whether they must be accompanied by common law variety malice. In other words, must the publisher have an evil motive to embarrass, humiliate or otherwise injure the subject of the disclosure. If such were the case, plaintiffs would succeed in these actions even less than they already do because of the difficulty of proving that an embarrassing news story, for instance, was published with ill will toward the subject.

Normally common law malice is associated with the award of punitive damages in tort and not with the prima facie case,[42] but the question is raised here because of a troubling decision of the Idaho Supreme Court. In *Taylor* v. *K.T.V.B., Inc.*,[43] a television station filmed the arrest of a man who while in his own home had threatened a woman and then a police officer with a shotgun. Throughout the entire episode, the man was stark naked. When the cameraman realized that the suspect was nude he stopped filming the arrest. However, the station broadcast a clip the next day which included less than one second of film showing the man with his buttocks and genitalia exposed. The arrestee subsequently sued the station owner. At trial the court instructed the jury that the motives of the defendant in broadcasting the film were unimportant and not a matter of defense. The jury returned a verdict for the plaintiff and judgment was entered thereon.

On appeal the Idaho Supreme Court reversed the judgment because, among other things, the trial court erred in not requiring the jury to find that "the disclosure was made with 'malice,' i.e., for the purpose of embarrassing or humiliating the arrestee, or with reckless disregard as to whether that disclosure will result in such embarrassment or humiliation."[44] The Appellate court, after reviewing the record, concluded that there was sufficient testimony from which a jury might find that the airing of the film was malicious, and therefore remanded the case for a new trial.

Despite the fact that the Idaho court's ruling removed a money judgment from the shoulders of the media defendant in this case, the decision could prove troublesome for the media. It opens the defendant's editorial decision-making process and judgments to judicial scrutiny with all the intrusiveness into the media defendant's business that that implies.[45]

---

42. *See* Hawkins By and Through Hawkins v. Multimedia, Inc. 288 S.C. 569, 572, 344 S.E.2d 145, 146 (1986), cert. denied 479 U.S. 1012, 107 S.Ct. 658, 93 L.Ed.2d 712 (1986).

43. 96 Idaho 202, 525 P.2d 984 (1974).

44. *Id.* at 207, 525 P.2d at 988.

45. *Compare* Herbert v. Lando, 441 U.S. 153, 99 S.Ct. 1635, 60 L.Ed.2d 115 (1979) (public figure plaintiff in a libel case entitled to inquire into the media defendant's

K.T.V.B. appears to be the only decision making common law malice part of the plaintiff's prima facie case. On the other hand the South Carolina Supreme Court in the more recent case of *Hawkins By and Through Hawkins v. Multimedia, Inc.*,[46] held flatly in a case in which a newspaper specifically identified one unwed teenage father in a sidebar to a larger article generally surveying teenage pregnancy that malice need not be shown to recover for publicity of private embarrassing facts.[47] The South Carolina Court's view appears to be the better one because it is consistent with long proven principles of tort law and prevents the media's editorial processes from being opened to scrutiny by laymen with the chilling effect this can have on newsgathering and news dissemination.

2. *Identification of the Plaintiff*

Absent the public's ability to identify the plaintiff as the party to whom the disclosed private facts relate, there can be no publicity concerning the plaintiff.[48] In most private facts litigation, the plaintiff is all too clearly identified by name or photograph and identification is not a problem. Where the plaintiff is neither named nor pictured, the court will initially have the responsibility of deciding whether the embarrassing private facts are capable of being reasonably understood as relating to the plaintiff.[49] If they cannot be so understood, the case must be dismissed.

3. *Private Facts*

As a matter of definition, the facts disclosed must not be ones already in the possession of the public. The issue, then is to determine whether the alleged private facts were unknown and unknowable to the public prior to the complained of publicity.

a. *Public Records and Proceedings*

There are several facets to this issue, the most important being the existence of embarrassing facts concerning the plaintiff in public records

editorial process in order to establish knowing untruthfulness or reckless disregard).

46. 288 S.C. 569, 344 S.E.2d 145 (1986), cert. denied 479 U.S. 1012, 107 S.Ct. 658, 93 L.Ed.2d 712 (1986).

47. *See also* Sidis v. F–R Pub. Corp., 113 F.2d 806, 809 (2d Cir.), cert. denied 311 U.S. 711, 61 S.Ct. 393, 85 L.Ed. 462, (1940) *and* Meetze v. Associated Press, 230 S.C. 330, 339, 95 S.E.2d 606, 610 (1956) (stating the proposition that if the plaintiff cannot establish the private facts tort, proof of common law malice in publicizing the facts involved is immaterial).

48. Harris by Harris v. Easton Pub. Co., 335 Pa.Super. 141, 483 A.2d 1377, 1385 (Pa.Super.1984).

49. *Id.* In *Harris* the court held that sufficient evidence was present of identification of the plaintiffs, one of whom was described in defendant's newspaper as a public welfare applicant for medical assistance and food stamps for herself, a naturalized citizen who had married a GI in Germany, her 16–year-old pregnant daughter and her grandson who was living with her. The newspaper column also referred to a 19–year-old son living in the applicant's home, as well. The evidence established that seventeen members of the public identified the plaintiff-mother and other members of her family from the description in the column. *See also* Anonsen v. Donahue, 857 S.W.2d 700 (Tex.App.1993), cert. denied 511 U.S. 1128, 114 S.Ct. 2135, 128 L.Ed.2d 865 (1994).

and public proceedings. By definition facts contained in accessible public records or disclosed in public proceedings are not private facts.[50] Furthermore, publication of factual information found in the public record implicates First Amendment interests.[51] Therefore, the publicizing of such facts is generally held not to be actionable.[52] Illustrations of this include identification in a news broadcast of a rape victim's name which appeared first in a series of criminal indictments,[53] disclosure of information from government tax records that a police judge was delinquent in the payment of his personal and property taxes,[54] disclosure of an adult's earlier conviction for a hit-and-run violation while a juvenile,[55] a newspaper's report of a governor's commission meeting revealing that a family court judge in a juvenile proceeding had asked "would lashes help?"[56] and a newsstory quoting portions of a federal medical center report concerning plaintiff's mental competency to stand trial.[57]

Once embarrassing private facts enter accessible public records, the passage of time alone should not convert them to private facts no matter how musty the record might be. The lapse of nine years since a plaintiff had received twenty lashes pursuant to court imposed criminal punishment[58] or twenty years after conviction for the hit-and-run killing of a police officer[59] did not make newspaper publicity of these matters actionable.

A very few courts, failing to understand the nature of the private facts tort, have suggested that publicity of embarrassing facts encased in the public record may become actionable with the passage of time where

---

50. *See* Pemberton v. Bethlehem Steel Corp., 66 Md.App. 133, 502 A.2d 1101, 1118–1119 (Md.App.), cert. denied, 306 Md. 289, 508 A.2d 488, cert. denied 479 U.S. 984, 107 S. Ct. 571, 93 L. Ed. 2d 575 (1986) (circulation of criminal record and "mug shot" among members in a union dispute); Montesano v. Donrey Media Group, 99 Nev. 644, 649, 668 P.2d 1081, 1085–1088 (1983), cert. denied 466 U.S. 959, 104 S.Ct. 2172, 80 L.Ed.2d 555 (1984) (newspaper report of twenty-year old convictions for hit-and-run driving); Ayers v. Lee Enterprises, Inc., 277 Or. 527, 535–536, 561 P.2d 998, 1002–1003, 86 A.L.R.3d 72, 78 (1977) (identification of rape victim); William L. Prosser, Torts 810–811 (4th ed. 1971); *cf.* Winegard v. Larsen, 260 N.W.2d 816, 823 (Iowa 1977). *But compare* WILLIAM L. PROSSER AND W. PAGE KEETON, TORTS 858–859 (5th ed. 1984).

51. *See* Cox Broadcasting Corp. v. Cohn, 420 U.S. 469, 95 S.Ct. 1029, 43 L.Ed.2d 328 (1975).

52. *See, e.g.,* Cox Broadcasting Corp. v. Cohn, 420 U.S. 469, 95 S.Ct. 1029, 43 L.Ed.2d 328 (1975); Pemberton v. Bethlehem Steel Corp., 66 Md.App. 133, 502 A.2d 1101, 1118–1119, cert. denied 306 Md. 289, 508 A.2d 488 (1986), cert. denied 479 U.S.

984, 107 S. Ct. 571, 93 L. Ed. 2d 575 (1986); Ayers v. Lee Enterprises, Inc., 277 Or. 527, 535–536, 561 P.2d 998, 1002, 86 A.L.R.3d 72, 78 (1977).

53. Cox Broadcasting Corp. v. Cohn, 420 U.S. 469, 95 S.Ct. 1029, 43 L.Ed.2d 328 (1975). *See also* Ayers v. Lee Enterprises, Inc., 277 Or. 527, 535–536, 561 P.2d 998, 1002, 86 A.L.R.3d 72, 78 (1977).

54. Bell v. Courier–Journal and Louisville Times Co., 402 S.W.2d 84 (Ky.1966).

55. Montesano v. Donrey Media Group, 99 Nev. 644, 655, 668 P.2d 1081, 1088 (1983), cert. denied 466 U.S. 959, 104 S.Ct. 2172, 80 L.Ed.2d 555 (1984).

56. Reardon v. News–Journal Co., 164 A.2d 263 (Del.1960).

57. McNally v. Pulitzer Pub. Co., 532 F.2d 69 (8th Cir.1976), cert. denied 429 U.S. 855, 97 S.Ct. 150, 50 L.Ed.2d 131 (1976).

58. Barbieri v. News–Journal Co., 189 A.2d 773 (Del.1963).

59. Montesano v. Donrey Media Group, 99 Nev. 644, 668 P.2d 1081 (1983), cert. denied 466 U.S. 959, 104 S.Ct. 2172, 80 L.Ed.2d 555 (1984).

the publisher exposes such facts maliciously or for the purpose of exploiting the plaintiff.[60]

The important dissenters from the view that publicity of embarrassing facts taken from public records or proceedings is not actionable are the California courts. In *Melvin* v. *Reid*,[61] one of the first cases to recognize the private facts tort, the California District Court of Appeal held that a motion picture studio's identification of Mrs. Melvin from a criminal trial transcript as the notorious prostitute in "the red kimono" was actionable. More recently, the California Supreme Court affirmed this view in *Briscoe* v. *Reader's Digest Association*,[62] a case involving the exposure of a rehabilitated man's crime of truck hijacking eleven years after its commission. The California courts consider the passage of time in determining the actionability of publicity of embarrassing facts taken from the public record because of their expressed concern for the opportunity for rehabilitation over time.[63]

b. *Information in the Public Domain or Open to Public View*

It should follow from the strong majority view regarding public record facts that publicity of facts in the public domain[64] or open to public view[65] is also not actionable because the facts are not private. Thus, the dramatization on the "Dragnet" radio show of the celebrated events precipitated by the plaintiff's filing of a false report to police of the escape of a black panther in the Los Angeles area was not actionable,[66] nor was the publication of a photograph taken from the middle of a public street of the plaintiff's "weatherworn and unkempt" house.[67] And the mere passage of time does not transform public domain facts into private facts, the publication of which might be actionable.[68] If the facts involved are notorious enough, they remain in the public domain indefinitely as, for instance, the names and events surrounding the 1924 murder of Bobby Franks by Richard Loeb and Nathan F. Leopold, Jr.[69] But if public interest in an individual formerly in the limelight particu-

60. *See* Hall v. Post, 85 N.C.App. 610, 355 S.E.2d 819 (1987), *rev'd* 323 N.C. 259, 372 S.E.2d 711 (1988); *cf.* Taylor v. K.T.V.B., Inc., 96 Idaho 202, 525 P.2d 984 (1974).

61. 112 Cal.App. 285, 297 P. 91 (1931).

62. 4 Cal.3d 529, 93 Cal.Rptr. 866, 483 P.2d 34 (1971).

63. *See also* Diaz v. Oakland Tribune, Inc., 139 Cal.App.3d 118, 188 Cal.Rptr. 762, 771, (1983) (dictum).

64. *See* Diaz v. Oakland Tribune, Inc., 139 Cal.App.3d 118, 131, 188 Cal.Rptr. 762, 771, (1983); Boeke v. Williams, 721 S.W.2d 794 (Mo.App.1986).

65. *See* Hartman v. Meredith Corp., 638 F.Supp. 1015, 1018 (D.Kan.1986).

66. Smith v. National Broadcasting Co., 138 Cal.App.2d 807, 292 P.2d 600 (1956).

67. Jaubert v. Crowley Post–Signal, Inc., 375 So.2d 1386 (La.1979); *accord*: Wehling v. Columbia Broadcasting System, 721 F.2d 506, 509 (5th Cir.1983) (televised image of house viewed from street).

68. Smith v. National Broadcasting Co., 138 Cal.App.2d 807, 292 P.2d 600, 604 (1956).

69. *See* Leopold v. Levin, 45 Ill.2d 434, 259 N.E.2d 250 (1970) (the release of the novel and motion picture "Compulsion", based closely on the facts of the case, nearly a half century after the Franks murder, held not to invade Nathan Leopold's privacy). *See also* Forsher v. Bugliosi, 26 Cal.3d 792, 811, 163 Cal.Rptr. 628, 638–639, 608 P.2d 716, 726, (1980) (the Tate–LaBianco murders committed by the Charles Manson "family").

larly for criminal conduct fades with time, he sinks into relative anonymity and the facts regarding his notoriety are no longer readily accessible to the general public, later republication of the notorious facts might be actionable.[70]

Matters enter the public domain by their being given wide currency and, therefore, knowledge of private embarrassing facts concerning the plaintiff held by one other or by a small number of others are not in the public domain and their publication would not appear to preclude legal action.[71]

c. Information Concerning Public Officials, Candidates for Public Office and Public Figures

Very often courts will utilize the terminology of waiver or consent in denying recovery to public officials, political candidates and public figures who sue because media defendants made embarrassing disclosures concerning them.[72] The argument goes that when one chooses a public life or seeks the patronage of the public he or she becomes public property. But everyone is entitled to a private life and "the fact that they engage in an activity in which the public can be said to have a general interest does not render every aspect of their lives subject to public disclosure."[73]

Waiver requires the intentional or voluntary relinquishment of a known right[74] and consent means the voluntary agreement to make an intelligent choice to do something proposed by another[75] such as acquiescing in the violation of one's privacy. Neither concept is applicable to public officials or candidates for public office because no right of privacy exists in such context. Public officials and candidates have no right of privacy regarding the conduct of their offices or their qualifications to conduct the public's business.[76] Such concerns do not, as a matter of definition, involve *protected private* facts. Rather, they involve facts of legitimate public interest. Indeed, that public interest may even

70. *See* Briscoe v. Reader's Digest Ass'n., 4 Cal.3d 529, 539–540, 93 Cal.Rptr. 866, 873, 483 P.2d 34, 40 (1971) (plaintiff, convicted of highjacking a truck eleven years before the publication of an article discussing his crime, held to have a cause of action for invasion of privacy). But Briscoe is apparently a rare case even by California standards. *See* Forsher v. Bugliosi, 26 Cal.3d 792, 810–811, 163 Cal.Rptr. 628, 638–639, 608 P.2d 716, 726, (1980).

71. *Cf.* Virgil v. Time, Inc., 527 F.2d 1122, 1127 (9th Cir.1975), cert. denied 425 U.S. 998, 96 S.Ct. 2215, 48 L.Ed.2d 823 (1976).

72. *See, e.g.,* Briscoe v. Reader's Digest Ass'n., 4 Cal.3d 529, 535 n. 5, 93 Cal.Rptr. 866, 869–870 n. 5, 483 P.2d 34 37 n. 5 (1971); Cason v. Baskin, 159 Fla. 31, 36, 30 So.2d 635, 638 (1947); Pavesich v. New England Mut. Life Ins. Co., 122 Ga. 190, 199, 50 S.E. 68, 72 (1905); *cf.* Cassidy v. American Broadcasting Co., Inc., 60 Ill. App.3d 831, 838, 17 Ill.Dec. 936, 941–942, 377 N.E.2d 126, 131–132 (1978).

73. Virgil v. Time, Inc., 527 F.2d 1122, 1131 (9th Cir.1975), cert. denied 425 U.S. 998, 96 S.Ct. 2215, 48 L.Ed.2d 823 (1976).

74. BLACK'S LAW DICTIONARY 1417 (5th ed. 1979).

75. *Id.* at 276.

76. *See* Beruan v. French, 56 Cal.App.3d 825, 828, 128 Cal.Rptr. 869, 870–871 (1976); Rawlins v. Hutchinson Pub. Co., 218 Kan. 295, 300, 543 P.2d 988, 993 (1975); Bell v. Courier–Journal and Louisville Times Co., 402 S.W.2d 84, 88 (Ky. 1966).

carry over to certain facts relating to those in some relationship to officeholders or candidates.[77]

As for public figures who are not public officials or political candidates, the publication of information about them fairly related to their wanted or unwanted celebrity is not actionable because such information is also considered to be of legitimate public interest.[78] However, because they are not handling or asking to handle the public's business, the scope of privacy protection for public personages will likely be greater than for officeholders or candidates. Those related to public figures may also lose some of their privacy protection because of derivative public interest in them.[79] This idea of public interest negating actions for publicity of private embarrassing facts will be explored further in a later section dealing with "newsworthiness."

4. Offensiveness of the Publicity

The publicity tort is limited in scope to publicity of facts that would be highly offensive to the ordinary reasonable person in the plaintiff's position.[80] Thus, publishing photographs in a newspaper without consent of a woman taking a bath,[81] emerging from a fun house with her skirt blown up above her waist by a jet of air[82] or nursing her baby[83] would be actionable. But media descriptions of weddings meant to be private,[84] the eccentricities of a reclusive mathematical genius,[85] a burglary by very young children of the plaintiff lawyer's home involving the taking of three pieces of Swiss cheese, a piece of cake, some jello and a small amount of money[86] or a person's ordinary comings and goings[87] would

77. See Meyer v. Ledford, 170 Ga.App. 245, 316 S.E.2d 804 (1984). A number of private persons in recent years, particularly young women, have learned to their sorrow that their private lives have become "fair game" for the media because of their relationships with public office holders and even candidates for public office. Some of these women are so well known by virtue of their associations that it is unnecessary to name them. Needless to say they have no recourse to the protection of tort law when facts about their relationships with politicians are accurately recounted.

78. Cason v. Baskin, 159 Fla. 31, 30 So.2d 635, 638 (1947); Bilney v. Evening Star Newspaper Co., 43 Md.App. 560, 573, 406 A.2d 652, 660 (1979); RESTATEMENT SECOND OF TORTS § 652D, comments e, f and h (1977).

79. See Campbell v. Seabury Press, 614 F.2d 395 (5th Cir.1980) (sister-in-law of public figure); Johnson v. Harcourt Brace, Jovanovich, Inc., 43 Cal.App.3d 880, 892, 118 Cal.Rptr. 370, 379, (1974) (immediate family); Strutner v. Dispatch Printing Co., 2 Ohio App.3d 377, 380–381, 442 N.E.2d 129, 133 (1982) (father).

80. See Fry v. Ionia Sentinel–Standard, 101 Mich.App. 725, 728, 300 N.W.2d 687,

689 (1980); Langworthy v. Pulitzer Pub. Co., 368 S.W.2d 385, 390 (Mo.1963); Aquino v. Bulletin Co., 190 Pa.Super. 528, 533, 154 A.2d 422, 426 (1959); RESTATEMENT SECOND OF TORTS § 652D, (1977).

81. McCabe v. Village Voice, Inc., 550 F.Supp. 525 (E.D.Pa.1982).

82. Daily Times Democrat v. Graham, 276 Ala. 380, 162 So.2d 474 (1964).

83. RESTATEMENT SECOND OF TORTS § 652D, comment c, illustration 10 (1977).

84. Aquino v. Bulletin Co., 190 Pa.Super. 528, 533, 154 A.2d 422, 426 (1959) (dictum). Ironically, it was just such publicity that triggered Warren and Brandeis' celebrated law review article inventing the common law right of privacy. See William L. Prosser, Privacy, 48 Cal. L. Rev. 383 (1960).

85. Sidis v. F–R Pub. Corp., 113 F.2d 806, 809 (2d Cir.1940), cert. denied 311 U.S. 711, 61 S.Ct. 393, 85 L.Ed. 462 (1940).

86. Langworthy v. Pulitzer Pub. Co., 368 S.W.2d 385 (Mo.1963).

87. RESTATEMENT SECOND OF TORTS § 652D, comment c (1977).

not be actionable.

The dividing line seems to be dictated by community standards of decency.[88] It is not surprising, therefore, that most of the successful actions for publicity of embarrassing private facts involve the unconsented exposure of private bodily parts or functions.[89] Because the dividing line is fairly bright here, the media should normally not be in doubt when they are about to cross it and, unless the information is clearly newsworthy,[90] they may wish to seek consent to publish such facts or modify the story or illustration to avoid litigation.

5. Legitimate Public Interest or Concern (Loosely Known as the "Newsworthiness" Privilege)

Even after a plaintiff has established the requisite publicity of private facts that would be highly offensive to a reasonable person, the Restatement Second formulation of the publicity tort requires a showing that the facts disclosed are not of "legitimate concern to the public."[91] The reason for this additional requirement is clear—this tort with its imposition of civil liability for publicizing truthful facts implicates serious First Amendment interests.[92] The requirement that the publicity be of no legitimate public interest lessens the potential for conflicts with the First Amendment.

88. *See* Sidis v. F–R Pub. Corp., 113 F.2d 806, 809 (2d Cir.), cert. denied 311 U.S. 711, 61 S.Ct. 393, 85 L.Ed. 462 (1940); Aquino v. Bulletin Co., 190 Pa.Super. 528, 533, 154 A.2d 422, 426 (1959); *cf.* Linda N. Woito and Patrick McNulty, *The Privacy Disclosure Tort and the First Amendment: Should the Community Decide Newsworthiness?* 64 Iowa L. Rev. 185, 187 (1979).

89. *See e.g.,* McCabe v. Village Voice, Inc., 550 F.Supp. 525 (E.D.Pa.1982) (woman taking a bath); Daily Times Democrat v. Graham, 276 Ala. 380, 162 So.2d 474 (1964) (woman shown with her undergarments exposed); Hawkins By and Through Hawkins v. Multimedia, Inc. 288 S.C. 569, 344 S.E.2d 145 (1986), cert. denied 479 U.S. 1012, 107 S.Ct. 658, 93 L.Ed.2d 712 (1986) (teenage male identified as fathering a child out of wedlock); *see also* Diaz v. Oakland Tribune, Inc., 139 Cal.App.3d 118, 188 Cal.Rptr. 762 (1983) (woman exposed as a transsexual); Barber v. Time, Inc., 348 Mo. 1199, 159 S.W.2d 291 (1942) (hospital patient with eating disorder photographed against her will); *but see* McNamara v. Freedom Newspapers, Inc., 802 S.W.2d 901 (Tex.App.1991) (publication of action photograph of soccer player with his genitals exposed protected by First Amendment even though other photos of the game were available to the newspaper defendant).

90. *See* pp. 489–492 in Practitioners Edition, Vol. 1.

91. RESTATEMENT SECOND OF TORTS § 652D (1977). The broad scope of the concept of "legitimate concern to the public" is illustrated by the case of *Anonsen v. Donahue,* 857 S.W.2d 700 (Tex.App. 1993), cert. denied 511 U.S. 1128 , 114 S.Ct. 2135, 128 L.Ed.2d 865 (1994). There it was held that a woman's disclosure on the "Phil Donahue Show" that her adopted son was actually her own daughter's son conceived as a result of the rape of the daughter by the woman's then husband was a matter of legitimate public concern protected by the First Amendment. The Texas Court of Appeals in so holding said, "[W]e have no doubt that, as a matter of law, the crimes of incest and rape, the victimization of innocent people whose lives are touched by these crimes, and the importance of fostering understanding and healing of those victims are matters of public concern." *Id.* at 704. One can only wonder about the amount of healing that went on in the Anonsen family after such public disclosure.

92. *See* Cox Broadcasting Corp. v. Cohn, 420 U.S. 469, 95 S.Ct. 1029, 43 L.Ed.2d 328 (1975); Diaz v. Oakland Tribune, Inc., 139 Cal.App.3d 118, 130, 188 Cal.Rptr. 762, 770, (1983); RESTATEMENT SECOND OF TORTS § 652D, comment *d* (1977).

a. Burden of Proof

There is some division of judicial opinion regarding the allocation of the burden of proof on the public interest issue.[93] But the Restatement Second drafters have made the lack of newsworthiness an element of the plaintiff's prima facie case, and properly so, because it is consistent with the drafters' desire to avoid constitutional conflict. Placing the onus on media defendants to establish the existence of legitimate public interest in defending their disclosures would impose burdens on the media inconsistent with this goal and perhaps with the Constitution itself. Of course, media defendants would be given the opportunity to rebut the plaintiff's case on this element if they so desire.

Establishing the lack of legitimate public interest or concern in disclosures of private embarrassing facts is not easy for plaintiffs because the idea of "public interest" is both vague and complex[94] and because of the long standing judicial notion that if the media publishes something it must be "newsworthy" and if newsworthy it must be of legitimate public interest.[95]

b. Standard Employed

But the standard for determining legitimate public concern is not necessarily newsworthiness alone. California courts have often second-guessed editorial decisions to publish embarrassing facts by requiring the trier of fact to consider other factors as well.[96] These factors include the social value of the facts published (which is related to the determination of newsworthiness), the depth of the article's intrusion into private affairs and the extent to which the plaintiff voluntarily acceded to a position of public notoriety (factors unrelated to the issue of newsworthiness).[97] Societal interests militating against the disclosure of embarrassing or even life-threatening facts include the rehabilitation of criminals,[98]

---

93. *Compare* Diaz v. Oakland Tribune, Inc., 139 Cal.App.3d 118, 130, 188 Cal.Rptr. 762, 770, (1983) (burden placed on plaintiff) *with* Crump v. Beckley Newspapers, Inc., 173 W.Va. 699, 320 S.E.2d 70, 83–84 (W.Va. 1983) (burden placed on defendant).

94. For some of the complexities associated with the concept of "public interest" in the context of media disclosures of private embarrassing facts, *see* Randall P. Bezanson, *Public Disclosures as News: Injunctive Relief and Newsworthiness in Privacy Actions Involving the Press*, 64 Iowa 1061, 1065–1082 (1979).

95. *See, e.g.* Jenkins v. Dell Pub. Co., 251 F.2d 447, 451–452 (3d Cir.), cert. denied 357 U.S. 921, 78 S.Ct. 1362, 2 L.Ed.2d 1365 (1958); Howard v. Des Moines Register & Tribune Co., 283 N.W.2d 289, 302 (Iowa 1979), cert. denied 445 U.S. 904, 100 S.Ct. 1081, 63 L.Ed.2d 320 (1980); Don R. Pember and Dwight L. Teeter, Jr., *Privacy and the Press Since Time, Inc. v. Hill*, 50 Wash. L. Rev. 57, 69–73 (1974).

96. *See* Kapellas v. Kofman, 1 Cal.3d 20, 26, 81 Cal.Rptr. 360, 370, 459 P.2d 912, 914 (1969); Briscoe v. Reader's Digest Ass'n., 4 Cal.3d 529, 541, 93 Cal.Rptr. 866, 875, 483 P.2d 34, 43 (1971); Diaz v. Oakland Tribune, Inc., 139 Cal.App.3d 118, 133, 188 Cal.Rptr. 762, 772, (1983); Melvin v. Reid, 112 Cal.App. 285, 290–291, 297 P. 91, 93 (1931); *see also* Capra v. Thoroughbred Racing Ass'n. of North America, Inc., 787 F.2d 463, 464–465 (9th Cir.), cert. denied 479 U.S. 1017, 107 S.Ct. 669, 93 L.Ed.2d 721 (1986); *but see* Forsher v. Bugliosi, 26 Cal.3d 792, 810, 163 Cal.Rptr. 628, 638, 608 P.2d 716, 726 (1980) (apparently limiting the use of such factors to cases involving past criminal conduct of rehabilitated persons).

97. *Id.*

98. *See* Briscoe v. Reader's Digest Ass'n., 4 Cal.3d 529, 542, 93 Cal.Rptr. 866, 875, 483 P.2d 34, 43 (1971); Melvin v. Reid, 112 Cal.App. 285, 292, 297 P. 91, 93 (1931).

the encouragement of public testimony[99] and the protection of witnesses from physical harm.[100]

What little trend there is discernible here is toward adoption of a legitimate public interest standard utilizing criteria something like those set out by the California courts and away from the extreme deference to editorial judgment shown by the courts in the past.[1] As a matter of trial tactics, then, plaintiffs counsel, whatever the forum, should attempt to introduce in evidence the societal interest or interests being disserved by the publication of the embarrassing private facts about his client.

c. Newsworthiness of the Publicity

Whichever approach is taken to the public interest requirement, the newsworthiness of the facts publicized is of major importance in determining whether the disclosures are privileged. The blockbuster disclosure or "holy s---" story that seriously wounds someone is less likely to result in a judgment against the media defendant than one of minimal interest to the audience. Two comparative case studies vividly illustrate this.

In *Daily Times Democrat* v. *Graham*,[2] a photograph of the female plaintiff was published in the defendant's newspaper showing her body from the waist down except for that portion covered by her "panties." She was emerging from a fun house at a county fair with her two young sons when a jet of air blew her skirt above her waist. The newspaper's photographer captured the moment and, without the woman's consent, the paper ran the picture on its front page a few days later. The woman sued for invasion of her privacy and the newspaper company defended on the ground that publication of the photograph was a matter of legitimate public interest because of its relation to a story about the county fair. In affirming a judgment for the woman, the Alabama Supreme Court said, "We can see nothing of legitimate news value in the photograph. Certainly it discloses nothing as to which the public is entitled to be informed."[3]

But in the neighboring state of Florida, a female plaintiff's invasion of privacy action against a daily newspaper for publishing a more revealing photograph was not successful. In *Cape Publications, Inc.* v. *Bridges*,[4] the woman was abducted by her estranged husband at gunpoint, taken to their former apartment and forced to disrobe. Upon hearing a gunshot inside the apartment, the police stormed the place and rushed the plaintiff to safety. As she emerged from the apartment she

99. *See* Capra v. Thoroughbred Racing Ass'n. of North America, Inc., 787 F.2d 463, 465 (9th Cir.), cert. denied 479 U.S. 1017, 107 S.Ct. 669, 93 L.Ed.2d 721 (1986).

100. *Id.*; Times Mirror Co. v. Superior Court, 198 Cal.App.3d 1420, 1432, 244 Cal. Rptr. 556, 563–564 (1988).

1. *See* Hawkins By and Through Hawkins v. Multimedia, Inc. 288 S.C. 569, 571, 344 S.E.2d 145, 146 (1986), cert. denied 479

U.S. 1012, 107 S.Ct. 658, 93 L.Ed.2d 712 (1986).

2. 276 Ala. 380, 162 So.2d 474 (1964).

3. *Id.* at 383, 162 So. 2d at 477.

4. 423 So.2d 426 (Fla.App.1982), review denied 431 So.2d 988 (Fla.1983), cert. denied 464 U.S. 893, 104 S.Ct. 239, 78 L.Ed.2d 229 (1983).

was clutching a dish towel to her body in order to conceal her nudity. The defendant newspaper's photographer took several shots of the scene and one of them was run in connection with the story. The photograph revealed little more than could be seen had the woman been wearing a bikini bathing suit. In reversing a judgment on a jury verdict for the plaintiff the Florida District court of Appeal said, "just because the story and the photograph may be embarrassing or distressful to the plaintiff does not mean the newspaper cannot publish what is otherwise newsworthy."[5]

Even in California where other factors must be considered by the trier of fact in determining the presence or absence of legitimate public interest in the disclosure of private facts, the newsworthiness of the disclosure may be determinative. In *Sipple* v. *Chronicle Pub. Co.*,[6] the plaintiff, an ex-marine, after becoming a national hero for thwarting an assassination attempt against President Gerald R. Ford by grabbing or striking the arm of the would-be-assassin, Sara Jane Moore, as she was about to fire her weapon, was exposed as a homosexual by San Francisco newspaper columnist Herb Caen following a conversation with gay rights activists. Sipple's invasion of privacy action against Caen and his publisher was dismissed by the trial court. On Sipple's appeal the California District Court of Appeal affirmed the dismissal holding, *inter alia*, that the disclosure was newsworthy and therefore privileged. Here, according to the court, the newsworthiness stemmed from "legitimate political considerations, e.g., to dispel the false public opinion that gays were timid, weak and unheroic figures and to raise the equally important political question whether the President of the United States entertained a discriminatory attitude or bias against a minority group such as homosexuals."[7]

In contrast, the disclosure of the plaintiff's sexual orientation or gender was believed to be actionable in *Diaz* v. *Oakland Tribune, Inc.*[8] There, yet another columnist, Sidney Jones, wrote that the plaintiff, Toni Ann Diaz, the first woman student body president of the College of Alameda and student body representative to the college's board of trustees, was born a male. This column item was published at a time Ms. Diaz was claiming that student funds were being misused by the college's administrators and stated in its entirety: "More Education Stuff.

5. *Id*. at 428. *Compare* Macon Telegraph Pub. Co. v. Tatum, 263 Ga. 678, 436 S.E.2d 655 (1993), involving a story naming woman who shot and killed a knife-wielding intruder who had exposed his penis. In reversing the lower appeals court, the Georgia Supreme Court held the identification to be of public interest and nonactionable. "When she shot Hill, Tatum became the object of a legitimate public interest and the newspaper had the right under the Federal and State Constitutions to accurately report the facts regarding the incident, including her name." Id. at 679, 436 S.Ed.2d at 658. *Compare also* Cinel v. Connick, 15 F.3d

1338, 1345–1346 (5th Cir.1994), holding that the broadcast of a priest's own private videotape showing him engaging in homosexual activity with young males involved matters of public concern, particularly in light of the district attorney's decision not to prosecute.

6. 154 Cal.App.3d 1040, 201 Cal.Rptr. 665, (1984).

7. *Id*. at 1049, 201 Cal. Rptr. at 670.

8. 139 Cal.App.3d, 118, 188 Cal.Rptr. 762 (1983).

The Students at the College of Alameda will be surprised to learn their student body president, Toni Diaz, is not lady, but is in fact a man whose real name is Antonio. Now I realize, that in these times, such a matter is no big deal, but I suspect his female classmates in P.E. 97 may wish to make other showering arrangements."[9] In fact, the plaintiff had had sex change surgery and therapy. On appeal from a judgment entered on a large jury verdict for the plaintiff, the California District Court of Appeal, while reversing the judgment because of instructional errors, held that the disclosure was not newsworthy as a matter of law. The court suggested that a jury could, pursuant to proper instructions, find the item to be without newsworthiness because of the remoteness of connection to the plaintiff's student body offices. The columnist's attempt at humor did not amuse the court but rather persuaded it that the item was not meant to educate the reading public as to some matter of societal importance such as the role of women in public office or student body governance.

Without attempting to rationalize too deeply, it is important to note certain characteristics that make facts newsworthy. First, unlike history, the facts must have an element of timeliness. They must be important, in and of themselves, at the current moment. News, by and large, has a very short storage life.[10] Second, newsworthy facts must be ones that are out of the ordinary whether welcome or unwelcome.[11] Third, they must have some significance to the nature or functioning of society or a segment thereof.

Almost the antithesis of newsworthiness is idle curiosity, prying and the resulting gossip about others. Such gossip has little if any currency (it may be passed on for years) and cannot be related in any meaningful way to the nature or functioning of society. Such idle curiosity, prying and gossip is outside the newsworthiness protective shield.[12]

In the *Graham* and *Diaz* cases, the Alabama and California courts judged the respective disclosures to be more in the nature of prying and gossip than news. *Sipple*, on the other hand, seems clearly to meet the definition of news while *Bridges* is a close case in which the disclosure taken in context may say something about the human condition but which, at the same time, may be deeply offensive to community standards.

Finally, recent California cases raise the question as to whether there are categories of facts to which the newsworthiness protection may not relate, such as the names and addresses of persons involved in highly embarrassing or life-threatening situations.[13] In one case, a young moth-

---

9. *Id.* at 124, 188 Cal Rptr. at 766.

10. *See* Randall P. Bezanson, *Public Disclosures as News: Injunctive Relief and Newsworthiness in Privacy Actions Involving the Press*, 64 Iowa L. Rev. 1061, 1066 (1979).

11. *Id.* at 1068.

12. *See* Virgil v. Time, Inc., 527 F.2d 1122, 1129 (9th Cir.1975), cert. denied 425 U.S. 998, 96 S.Ct. 2215, 48 L.Ed.2d 823 (1976); RESTATEMENT SECOND TORTS § 652D, comment *h* (1977).

13. Pasadena Star—News v. Superior Court, 203 Cal.App.3d 131, 134–135, 249 Cal.Rptr. 729, 731 (1988); Times Mirror Co.

er who secretly gave birth and, with the help of her brother, abandoned the baby at a hospital, essentially conceded the newsworthiness of the event but argued that her name was not essential to an understanding of the story and was not newsworthy. The court disagreed, holding that no tort principle denies protection as a matter of law to the media for the disclosure of names in relation to otherwise newsworthy stories.[14]

At the same time, the court, in distinguishing a similar case,[15] recognized that in California the issue of newsworthiness is for the finder of fact and that a jury might attach no newsworthiness to reporting the name, incorporated in a dramatic news story, of an eye witness who could identify a murderer still at large and presumed dangerous.[16]

E. High Risk Activities of the Media

As with false light, there are a number of high risk activities engaged in by the media in the private facts area which may trigger litigation. The preeminent one is the naming of names. Except for gossip columns with their "blind" items, the media almost invariably report the names of the persons related to embarrassing private facts. The nature of news and information is such that the credibility of the news or information organization depends on linking factual matters to real persons.[17] When the media move away from specific identification or attribution, the result may be a "Jimmy's World" fiasco[18] or a gossip

v. Superior Court, 198 Cal.App.3d 1420, 244 Cal.Rptr. 556 (1988).

14. Pasadena Star—News, 203 Cal. App. 3d at 134–135, 249 Cal. Rptr. at 731 (1988); see McNutt v. New Mexico State Tribune Co., 88 N.M. 162, 166–167, 538 P.2d 804, 809, 84 A.L.R.3d 1148, 1155 (N.M. App),. cert. denied 88 N.M. 318, 540 P.2d 248 (1975).

15. Times Mirror Co. v. Superior Court, 198 Cal.App.3d 1420, 244 Cal.Rptr. 556, (1988), cert. dismissed 489 U.S. 1094, 109 S.Ct. 1565, 103 L.Ed.2d 931 (1989).

16. Pasadena Star—News, 203 Cal. App. 3d at 134, 249 Cal. Rptr. at 731–732 (1988); see Randall P. Bezanson, *Public Disclosures as News: Injunctive Relief and Newsworthiness in Privacy Actions Involving the Press*, 64 Iowa L. Rev. 1061, 1075–1076 (1979).

17. *See* Gilbert v. Medical Economics Co., 665 F.2d 305, 308 (10th Cir.1981); Ross v. Midwest Communications, Inc., 870 F.2d 271 (5th Cir.1989), cert. denied, 493 U.S. 935, 110 S.Ct. 326, 107 L.Ed.2d 316 (1989) Howard v. Des Moines Register & Tribune Pub. Co., 283 N.W.2d 289, 303 (Iowa 1979), cert. denied, 445 U.S. 904, 100 S.Ct. 1081, 63 L.Ed.2d 320 (1980); Montesano v. Donrey Media Group, 99 Nev. 644, 655, 668

P.2d 1081, 1088 (1983), cert. denied, 466 U.S. 959, 104 S.Ct. 2172, 80 L.Ed.2d 555 (1984); Diane L. Zimmerman, *Requiem for a Heavyweight: A Farewell to Warren and Brandeis's Privacy Tort*, 68 Corn. L. Rev. 291 356–357 (1983); *but see* Dorsey D. Ellis, Jr., *Damages and the Privacy Tort: Sketching a "legal Profile,"* 64 Iowa L. Rev. 1111, 1144 n. 229 (1979).

18. *See* Ross v. Midwest Communications, Inc., 870 F.2d 271, 274 (5th Cir.), cert. denied 493 U.S. 935, 110 S.Ct. 326, 107 L.Ed.2d 316 (1989). In the "Jimmy's World" fiasco, a Washington Post reporter did a series about a eight-year-old boy in Washington's urban ghetto identified only as "Jimmy." Others around him were also only vaguely identified. One revelation about Jimmy was that he was being supplied with narcotics by his mother and her boyfriend. Uneasy about the series, the Post began an internal investigation of the reporter's work after she was awarded a Pulitzer Prize. At this point it was revealed that Jimmy was a "composite" of the lives of numerous children in the ghetto and that the reporter had fabricated much of the series. The Pulitzer was returned and the reporter was dismissed.

Much of the blame for the fiasco has fallen upon the Washington Post and its

column. There may be times, however, when identification of the persons involved is of life and death consequence.[19] Only in such rare cases, would it be wise to counsel against publication of names to protect lives and avoid litigation.

A related activity is the publication of the identified person's address. Unless the individual's specific dwelling or neighborhood is of relevance to the story, publication of the address poses an unnecessary risk of litigation.[20] This truly "hits people where they live" and too often encourages intrusive behavior by members of the public.

Experience with the publicity tort suggests that while "sex sells," it also litigates. The publicity relating to sexual activity, orientation or bodily parts is more likely to draw litigation and liability for the media than any other subject.[21] This stands to reason since sex is perhaps the quintessential private activity. Responsible media when they treat sexual matters should do so with discretion and tact. A flip or leering approach should be avoided.[22]

As with the false light tort, the "where are they now?" story involves substantial risk of litigation because of the recurrence of painful emotions after the passage of time. "Where are they now" publicity prevents time from healing emotional scars caused by the initial embarrassing publicity and encourages the twice burned victim to sue his perceived tormentors. Revisitation journalism should be avoided unless there is a current news peg justifying a review of the plaintiff's embarrassing past. Examples of this type of case include the short biographical profile published without a current news peg which details an individu-

editors. The intense pressure to "make page one", propel the Post into even greater prominence, and conform to the Post system are all seen as factors which contributed to this situation. The Post was looking for a "flashy" slant to the drug and inner-city problems. Janet Cooke provided that angle with her "Jimmy" story. She also succumbed to the front page syndrome. *See generally* Janet Cooke, *Jimmy's World*, The Washington Post, April 19, 1981, p. 12, col. 1; Timothy Noah, *Jimmy's Big Brothers*, The New Republic, May 16, 1981, p. 14, col. 2.

19. *See e.g.*, Times Mirror Co. v. Superior Court, 198 Cal.App.3d 1420, 244 Cal. Rptr. 556, (1988), cert. dismissed 489 U.S. 1094, 109 S.Ct. 1565, 103 L.Ed.2d 931 (1989) (eye-witness who could identify at-large murderer identified in newspaper story about the murder).

20. *See, e.g.*, McNutt v. New Mexico State Tribune Co., 88 N.M. 162, 538 P.2d 804, 84 A.L.R.3d 1148, (N.M. App.), cert. denied 88 N.M. 318, 540 P.2d 248 (1975) (even though the media defendant prevailed here).

21. *See, e.g.*, Melvin v. Reid, 112 Cal. App. 285, 297 P. 91 (1931); Sipple v. Chronicle Pub. Co., 154 Cal.App.3d 1040, 201 Cal.Rptr. 665 (1984); Cape Publications, Inc. v. Bridges, 423 So.2d 426 (Fla.App. 1982), review denied 431 So.2d 988 (Fla. 1983), cert. denied 464 U.S. 893, 104 S.Ct. 239, 78 L.Ed.2d 229 (1983); Hawkins By and Through Hawkins v. Multimedia, Inc. 288 S.C. 569, 344 S.E.2d 145 (1986), cert. denied 479 U.S. 1012, 107 S.Ct. 658, 93 L.Ed.2d 712 (1986).

22. In Diaz v. Oakland Tribune, Inc., 139 Cal.App.3d 118, 188 Cal.Rptr. 762 (1983) involving an item in a newspaper column identifying a woman student body leader at a local college as a transsexual, the California Court of Appeals was not amused by a statement that read, "Now I realize, that in these times, such a matter is no big deal, but I suspect his female classmates in P.E.97 may wish to make other showering arrangements." The court doubted the newsworthiness of the item, saying, " ... Jones' attempt at humor at Diaz's expense removes all pretense that the article was meant to educate the reading public." *Id*. at 135, 188 Cal. Rptr. at 773.

al's past notoriety and updates the audience as to what has happened to him in the intervening years,[23] and the republication of old newsstories and photos merely to mark some anniversary or other.[24]

The major issue in these cases is whether facts on the public record or in the public domain can become private facts with the passage of time and the fading from public interest and attention of the individual.[25] Where there is current news justification for or educational value in republicizing embarrassing facts following a substantial lapse of time, the answer appears to be in the negative.[26] But the troublesome cases are the ones just described, in which there is no current news justification for republication. Here, the authorities provide no clear demarcation as to whether and when matters in the public domain may again become private.[27] The only agreement in the decided cases is that the passage of time alone is insufficient to transmute public facts into private ones.[28] Given the present uncertainty, media counsel may wish to question the wisdom of republishing private embarrassing facts about individuals formerly in the public limelight when no legitimate current news peg is apparent. While the existence of a news peg provides no shield against litigation, it makes it much more likely that a court will conclude as a matter of law or a jury will find as fact that the facts republicized are still of legitimate interest and concern to the public and thus their publication is protected.

F.   Defenses to the Private Facts Action

At the outset it is necessary to emphasize that, unlike the false light tort, truth is not a defense to an action for publicity of private embarrassing facts.[29] There is compelling logic supporting this proposition. If truth were a defense, it would wholly swallow the tort because the

---

23. *See* Sidis v. F–R Pub. Corp., 113 F.2d 806, 809 (2d Cir.1940).

24. *See* Roshto v. Hebert, 413 So.2d 927, (La.App.1982), *rev'd* 439 So.2d 428 (La.1983); *cf.* Estill v. Hearst Pub. Co., 186 F.2d 1017 (7th Cir.1951); Melvin v. Reid, 112 Cal.App. 285, 297 P. 91 (1931).

25. *See e.g.*, Briscoe v. Reader's Digest Ass'n., 4 Cal.3d 529, 538, 93 Cal.Rptr. 866, 872, 483 P.2d 34, 40 (1971); Roshto v. Hebert, 439 So.2d 428, 432 (La.1983); *cf.* Montesano v. Donrey Media Group, 99 Nev. 644, 652–654, 668 P.2d 1081, 1086–1088, 1089 (1983), cert. denied 466 U.S. 959, 104 S.Ct. 2172, 80 L.Ed.2d 555 (1984).

26. *See* Estill v. Hearst Pub. Co., 186 F.2d 1017 (7th Cir.1951); Barbieri v. News–Journal Co., 189 A.2d 773 (Del.1963); Montesano v. Donrey Media Group, 99 Nev. 644, 668 P.2d 1081, (1983), cert. denied 466 U.S. 959, 104 S.Ct. 2172, 80 L.Ed.2d 555 (1984); RESTATEMENT SECOND OF TORTS § 652D, comment *k* (1977).

27. *Compare* Briscoe v. Reader's Digest Ass'n., 4 Cal.3d 529, 93 Cal.Rptr. 866, 483

P.2d 34 (1971) *with* Roshto v. Hebert, 439 So.2d 428, (La.1983) *and compare* the majority opinion in Montesano v. Donrey Media Group, 99 Nev. at 654, 668 P.2d at 1088 *with* the dissent of Zenoff, Senior Justice, *id.* at 656, 688 P.2d at 1089.

28. *See* Briscoe v. Reader's Digest Ass'n., 4 Cal.3d 529, 539, 93 Cal.Rptr. 866, 872–873, 483 P.2d 34, 41 (1971); Barbieri v. News–Journal Co., 189 A.2d 773, 775 (Del. 1963); Roshto v. Hebert, 439 So.2d 428, 431 (La.1983); *see also* RESTATEMENT SECOND OF TORTS § 652D, comment *k* (1977).

29. *See* Cox Broadcasting Corp. v. Cohn, 420 U.S. 469, 489–491, 95 S.Ct. 1029, 1043–1044, 43 L.Ed.2d 328 346–347 (1975); Virgil v. Time, Inc., 527 F.2d 1122, 1127–1128 (9th Cir.1975), cert. denied 425 U.S. 998, 96 S.Ct. 2215, 48 L.Ed.2d 823 (1976); McCormack v. Oklahoma Pub. Co., 613 P.2d 737, 740 ((Okla. 1980).

gravamen is the giving of publicity to private embarrassing *facts* or truthful information. It is this liability for publicizing the truth that was a major factor in causing one court recently to reject this tort in its entirety.[30]

With the exception of truth, essentially the same defenses may be raised against publicity tort actions as may be raised against defamation and false light actions, including absolute and conditional privileges and waiver and consent.[31] Because the privilege to publicize private facts of legitimate public interest or concern has already been discussed in relation to plaintiff's prima facie case,[32] this defense will not be considered here.

Other absolute and conditional non-consensual defamation-type privileges are available, a fortiori, to prevent liability for publicity of private true facts.[33] Thus, for instance, publicity given to private embarrassing facts about government officers in the course of performing their official duties, attorneys, parties and witnesses relative to judicial proceedings, spouses in the conduct of their marital relationship with one another, and others in the protection of their lawful personal, family, third-party or public interests is not actionable.[34]

One privileged defense which cannot logically be analogized from defamation law is that of fair and accurate repetition of matter contained in reports of official proceedings or actions. The reason, of course, is that once private facts are included in a public report, those facts are no longer private[35] and, hence, no tort action for publicizing them can be maintained.[36]

The last defenses to be discussed are those of consent and waiver. Whether express or implied from the facts,[37] they are complete defenses often utilized by the media in attempting to defeat publicity tort claims.[38] The main issue with these defenses is often not the existence of a consensual relationship but rather the scope of the consent or waiver which was given. This is particularly true with regard to the consents or releases given by photographic models.[39]

30. *See* Hall v. Post, 323 N.C. 259, 372 S.E.2d 711 (1988).

31. *See* Crump v. Beckley Newspapers, Inc., 173 W.Va. 699, 320 S.E.2d 70, 83–85 (W.Va. 1983); RESTATEMENT SECOND OF TORTS §§ 652F–652G (1977).

32. *See*, pp. 487–492 in Practitioners Edition, Vol. 1.

33. *See* Crump v. Beckley Newspapers, Inc., 173 W.Va. 699, 320 S.E.2d 70, 83 (W.Va. 1983); RESTATEMENT SECOND OF TORTS §§ 652F–G (1977); *cf.* Kilgore v. Younger, 30 Cal.3d 770, 777, 180 Cal.Rptr. 657, 661, 640 P.2d 793, 797, (1982) (action for intentional infliction of emotional distress).

34. *Cf.* RESTATEMENT SECOND OF TORTS §§ 585–592, 594–598 (1977).

35. *See*, pp. 482–484 in Practitioners Edition, Vol. 1.

36. *See* Kilgore v. Younger, 30 Cal.3d 770, 777–778, 180 Cal.Rptr. 657, 661, 640 P.2d 793, 797, (1982).

37. *See* Crump v. Beckley Newspapers, Inc., 173 W.Va. 699, 320 S.E.2d 70, 84 (W.Va. 1983).

38. *See, e.g.*, Morgan v. Hustler Magazine, Inc., 653 F.Supp. 711 (N.D.Ohio 1987); *disapproved in* Angelotta v. American Broadcasting Corp., 820 F.2d 806 (6th Cir.1987); McCabe v. Village Voice, Inc., 550 F.Supp. 525 (E.D.Pa.1982); Hawkins By and Through Hawkins v. Multimedia, Inc. 288 S.C. 569, 344 S.E.2d 145 (1986), cert. denied 479 U.S. 1012, 107 S.Ct. 658, 93 L.Ed.2d 712 (1986).

There is nothing in the Restatement's formulation of the publicity tort to suggest that lack of consent is part of the prima facie case, and what authority there is places the burden of proof on the defendant to establish consent.[40] It would be logical to conclude that waiver, too, is an affirmative rather than denial defense.[41]

G. Remedies for Publicizing Embarrassing Private Facts

Any discussion of remedies for invasion of privacy in the nature at publicity of private embarrassing facts must of necessity be rather theoretical because in the entire history of this tort since its invention in 1890, only a small handful of plaintiffs have ever obtained relief of any kind from the courts. The common law and constitutional obstacles have simply proved too great for the overwhelming number of plaintiffs determined enough to seek judicial remedies. Thus discussion of such remedies cannot be moored too securely by judicial precedent.

1. General, Special and Punitive Damages

It is reasonable to think that the same damages available to plaintiffs for other types of invasion of privacy, *i.e.*, general, nominal, special and punitive, ought to be available in publicity of private facts actions whenever appropriate.[42] But it is also reasonable to assume that the First Amendment requires that recovery for this privacy action be confined to compensation for actual injury and not be extended to presumed or punitive damages, at least when liability for the complained of truthful disclosure is not based on the defendant's recklessness or wantonness in making such disclosure.[43] In other words, some functional equivalent of the requirement of actual malice in defamation or false light actions should be required here too to justify noncompensatory damages. Otherwise, greater liability could conceivably be imposed upon defendants who

39. *See* Morgan v. Hustler Magazine, Inc., 653 F.Supp. 711 (N.D.Ohio 1987), *disapproved in* Angelotta v. American Broadcasting Corp., 820 F.2d 806 (6th Cir.1987) (release held to extend to model's photographic image appearing on cover of sleazy men's magazine); McCabe v. Village Voice, Inc., 550 F.Supp. 525 (E.D.Pa.1982) (consent to plaintiff's nude photo appearing in a book did not extend to its reproduction in a newspaper); Pallas v. Crowley–Milner & Co., 334 Mich. 282, 54 N.W.2d 595 (1952) (waiver of privacy right by "showgirl" to control use of her publicity "stills" ordered taken by her employer); Crump v. Beckley Newspapers, Inc., 173 W.Va. 699, 320 S.E.2d 70, 84 (W.Va. 1983) (dictum).

40. *See* McCabe v. Village Voice, Inc., 550 F.Supp. 525, 530, (E.D.Pa.1982); Hawkins By and Through Hawkins v. Multimedia, Inc. 288 S.C. 569, 571, 344 S.E.2d 145,

146 (1986), cert. denied 479 U.S. 1012, 107 S.Ct. 658, 93 L.Ed.2d 712 (1986).

41. *Cf.* Anderson v. Low Rent Housing Comm'n., 304 N.W.2d 239, 249–250 (Iowa 1981), cert. denied 454 U.S. 1086, 102 S.Ct. 645, 70 L.Ed.2d 621 (1981) (false light invasion of privacy).

42. *See generally* RESTATEMENT SECOND OF TORTS § 652H, comment *a* (1977); DAN B. DOBBS, REMEDIES 528–532 (1973).

43. *See* RESTATEMENT SECOND OF TORTS § 652H, comment *c* (1977); *cf.* Gertz v. Robert Welch, Inc., 418 U.S. 323, 349, 94 S.Ct. 2997, 3011, 41 L.Ed.2d 789, 810 (1974); *but compare* Hawkins By and Through Hawkins v. Multimedia, Inc. 288 S.C. 569, 344 S.E.2d 145 (1986), cert. denied 479 U.S. 1012, 107 S.Ct. 658, 93 L.Ed.2d 712 (1986).

publicize true facts than could be imposed upon those who communicate false information.[44]

The sparse case law supports the availability of general and perhaps punitive damages. Thus, in *Brents* v. *Morgan*[45] the very first reported case involving this tort, the Kentucky Court of Appeals, while reversing a money judgment for the plaintiff because of instructional error, held that the plaintiff on retrial would be entitled to recover substantial damages for mental suffering even though such damages are not subject to a measurable pecuniary standard.[46] And in *Barber* v. *Time, Inc.*,[47] the first reported private facts tort action in which a judgment was actually upheld against a media defendant, the Missouri Supreme Court approved an award of $1,500 general damages on condition that the plaintiff enter a remittitur of the jury award of $1,500 in punitive damages.[48] Punitive damages were disapproved in *Barber* only because the plaintiff had failed to establish *common law* malice,[49] i.e., ill will, spite or other improper motive.

The most recent reported case affirming a judgment against a member of the media is *Hawkins by Hawkins* v. *Multimedia, Inc.*, involving the disclosure of an unwed teenager's fatherhood.[50] There, the South Carolina Supreme Court affirmed what must be the largest jury verdict and judgment that a plaintiff has ever actually collected in one of these cases—$1,500 general and $25,000 punitive damages.

Without addressing the issue of general damages, the court held, by necessary implication, that punitive damages were permissible upon a showing of common law malice.[51] While *Hawkins* was decided well after *Gertz* v. *Robert Welch, Inc.*,[52] a case proscribing punitive damages in defamation cases when the false publication is not made knowingly or recklessly, the South Carolina court did not address the question how, if at all, punitive damages might be imposed in publicity of private fact cases consistent with the First Amendment.

Regarding special damages, there is only scant authority, but can there be any doubt that if an actionable disclosure of private embarrassing facts led, for example, to a plaintiff's discharge from employment or

---

44. *Cf.* Florida Star v. B.J.F., 491 U.S. 524, 109 S.Ct. 2603, 105 L.Ed.2d 443 (1989); Gertz v. Robert Welch, Inc. 418 U.S. 323, 349, 94 S.Ct. 2997, 3011, 41 L.Ed.2d 789, 811 (1974); Time, Inc. v. Hill, 385 U.S. 374, 87 S.Ct. 534, 17 L.Ed.2d 456 (1967).

45. 221 Ky. 765, 767–768, 299 S.W. 967, 971 (1927).

46. *Id.* at 768, 299 S.W. at 971.

47. 348 Mo. 1199, 159 S.W.2d 291 (1942).

48. *Id.* at 1205, 159 S.W.2d at 296 (1942).

49. *Barber* v. *Time, Inc.* was, of course, decided long before *Gertz* v. *Robert Welch,*

Inc., 418 U.S. 323, 94 S.Ct. 2997, 41 L.Ed.2d 789 (1974) which raised constitutional questions concerning the availability of punitive damage awards in certain invasion of privacy cases.

50. 288 S.C. 569, 344 S.E.2d 145 (1986), cert. denied 479 U.S. 1012, 107 S.Ct. 658, 93 L.Ed.2d 712 (1986). *See also* Daily Times Democrat v. Graham, 276 Ala. 380, 162 So.2d 474 (1964) (approving a verdict and judgment of $4,166.00 in a case that might also be characterized as having sexual overtones).

51. *Id.* at 571, 344 S.E. 2d at 146.

52. 418 U.S. 323, 94 S.Ct. 2997, 41 L.Ed.2d 789 (1974).

his need for medical treatment, lost wages and doctor's fees would be recoverable?[53]

The dearth of authority on the question of damages in these cases underlines the general lack of success of plaintiffs with this tort action and tends to validate Professor Harry Kalven's prediction that the tort would be swallowed by the newsworthiness privilege,[54] a privilege which has its roots in the First Amendment.

2. *Injunctive Relief*

The publicity of private facts branch of invasion of privacy would seem to be one ripe for injunctive relief. Once embarrassing private facts are out of the bag, irreparable harm may be done to the individual exposed and the award of money damages would often be inadequate and immeasurable. It would be nearly impossible to compensate Mrs. Melvin with money, for instance, for the shambles made of her then respectable life by the silent film exposing her as the notorious prostitute in the red kimono who was charged but later acquitted of killing one of her clients.[55] Preventing the production or release of the motion picture would certainly be more effective in protecting Mrs. Melvin than any award of damages.

But while the publicity tort may fit the required profile for injunctive relief, there are even fewer cases in which injunctions have been granted than those in which damages have been awarded. There are two reasons for this paucity of authority. First, in the usual case the disclosure of private facts occurs in one episode without any opportunity for the plaintiff to seek an injunction to prevent the information from reaching the public. Therefore, except when the publicity is continuing and reaches new segments of the public serially, as may be the case of motion picture exhibition[56] or book sales,[57] the issuance of an injunction would normally be useless.

Second, and more importantly, injunctions to prevent communications to the public or a segment thereof constitute prior restraint of expression.[58] And if there is one thing that the First Amendment was created to do, it was to prevent such prior restraint in all but the most

---

53. *See* Doe v. Roe, 93 Misc.2d 201, 400 N.Y.S.2d 668, 679 (N.Y.Sup.1977) (semble).

54. Harry Kalven, Jr., *Privacy in Tort Law—Were Warren and Brandeis Wrong?*, 31 Law and Contemp. Probs. 326, 333 (1966); *see* Dorsey D. Ellis, Jr., *Damages and the Privacy Tort: Sketching a "Legal Profile,"* 64 Iowa L. Rev. 1111, 1133–1134 (1979); Diane L. Zimmerman, *Requiem for a Heavyweight: A Farewell to Warren and Brandeis's Privacy Tort*, 68 Corn. L. Rev. 291, 351 (1983).

55. *See* Melvin v. Reid, 112 Cal.App. 285, 297 P. 91 (1931).

56. *See* Commonwealth v. Wiseman, 356 Mass. 251, 249 N.E.2d 610 (1969), cert.

denied 398 U.S. 960, 90 S.Ct. 2165, 26 L.Ed.2d 546 (1970).

57. *See* Doe v. Roe, 42 A.D.2d 559, 345 N.Y.S.2d 560, *aff'd mem.*, 33 N.Y.2d 902, 307 N.E.2d 823, 352 N.Y.S.2d 626 (1973), cert. dismissed 420 U.S. 307, 95 S.Ct. 1154, 43 L.Ed.2d 213 (1975).

58. *See* Nebraska Press Ass'n. v. Stuart, 427 U.S. 539, 96 S.Ct. 2791, 49 L.Ed.2d 683 (1976); New York Times Co. v. United States, 403 U.S. 713, 91 S.Ct. 2140, 29 L.Ed.2d 822 (1971); Near v. Minnesota ex rel. Olson, 283 U.S. 697, 51 S.Ct. 625, 75 L.Ed. 1357 (1931).

extreme cases threatening national security or the public welfare, safety or morals.[59]

Extensive research reveals but one reported appellate case, *Commonwealth* v. *Wiseman*,[60] upholding the issuance of an injunction against a media defendant to prevent the communication of private embarrassing facts to the public, and that case is complicated by the defendant's breach of an agreement providing access to such facts in return for accepting certain conditions limiting publicity of the facts obtained.

In *Wiseman*, a documentary film maker obtained permission to make what he termed an educational film concerning the Massachusetts Correctional Institution at Bridgewater, to which mentally disturbed persons charged with crimes and defective delinquents may be committed. In return for permission to film at Bridgewater, Wiseman and his company Bridgewater Film Company, Inc. agreed to certain conditions imposed by the state including that the company would (1) use only photographs of inmates and patients legally competent to sign releases; (2) obtain releases from all patients appearing in the film; and (3) not release the film without the approval by the Commissioner of Correction and the superintendent of Bridgewater.

In three months of filming, 80,000 feet of film were exposed, some of the footage was of mentally incompetent patients in the nude and in the most personal and private circumstances. When they saw Wiseman's proposed final cut, the superintendent, the commissioner and the state attorney general all had serious objections to the film. The commissioner notified Wiseman that the film "could not be shown 'in its present form.' " Additionally, the attorney general stated that mentally incompetent patients were shown and that the releases, if any, obtained by the film maker were invalid.

At approximately the same time Wiseman entered into an agreement with a film distributing company for the general release of the completed film "Titicut Follies" to commercial motion picture theaters and ultimately television stations throughout the United States and Canada.

The film was shown both privately and to the public for profit in New York City with generally favorable reaction but without the necessary approvals from the Massachusetts officials. Thereafter, these officials and one inmate of Bridgewater sought an injunction to prevent further release of the film. The Massachusetts Superior Court trial judge issued a decree preventing further exhibition to any audience and ordering Wiseman and his company to deliver the negative and all prints to the attorney general for destruction.

---

59. *See, e.g.*, Near v. Minnesota ex. rel. Olson, 283 U.S. 697, 51 S.Ct. 625, 75 L.Ed. 1357 (1931); Laurence H. Tribe, American Constitutional Law 724 (1978); Thomas I. Emerson, *The Doctrine of Prior Restraint*, 20 Law and Contemp. Probs. 648, 650–652 (1955).

60. 356 Mass. 251, 249 N.E.2d 610, cert. denied 398 U.S. 960, 90 S.Ct. 2165, 26 L.Ed.2d 546 (1970), reh. denied 400 U.S. 954, 91 S.Ct. 231, 27 L.Ed.2d 260 (1970).

On appeal, the Supreme Judicial Court ordered modification of the decree to permit the continued limited exhibition of the film (because of its instructive nature) to legislators, judges, lawyers, sociologists, social workers, doctors, psychiatrists, students in such fields and organizations dealing with the social problems of custodial care and mental infirmity.

By this modification of the lower court's decree the appellate court acknowledged the social value of the information imparted by the film yet upheld the restraint of exhibition of the film to the general public, saying "The case is distinguishable from decisions which have permitted publication of newsworthy events where the public interest in reasonable dissemination of news has been treated as more significant than the private interests in privacy."[61] The court, however, did not favor the parties or the readers of its opinion with any real distinction.

The decision in *Wiseman* seems contradictory and doubtful because in one breath the Massachusetts court acknowledged the social value of the film but in another attempted to distinguish numerous cases in which the public interest in dissemination of news or information was held to be more significant than individual interests in privacy. The court never explains why it subordinated the privacy interests of the inmates and patients to the informational needs of legislators but refused to do so when it comes to the general public which elects these same legislators.

It is easy to understand how the court could have gone astray. First, there appears to have been a serious breach of contract and perhaps of faith on the part of the film maker,[62] second, an injunction would be very effective in preventing the serial spread of private facts about the inmates and patients by barring further exhibition of the film to the general public, and third, no other remedy for the patients and inmates would have been adequate. Regarding the inadequacy of remedy, many of those depicted could not even understand that they had a personal right of privacy, and thus the award of compensatory damages would be problematic. Nor has there been any intrusion on the patients' and inmates' privacy for which damages might be awarded to them because it was the *state's* zone of privacy which was violated and the patients and inmates could not themselves have had a reasonable expectation of privacy given their circumstances. Nor does there appear to be any actionable appropriation of the patients' and inmates' images or personas for which damages could be awarded because the appropriation was not directly for purposes of trade or commerce but rather for the

---

61. *Id.* at 261, 249 N.E.2d at 617.

62. Of the very few private facts cases in which injunctions have been granted, some have involved breaches of contract, confidentiality or faith which breaches made possible access to the private facts in the first place. *See* Doe v. Roe, 42 A.D.2d 559, 345 N.Y.S.2d 560, *aff'd mem.* 33 N.Y.2d 902, 307 N.E.2d 823, 352 N.Y.S.2d 626, cert. dismissed 420 U.S. 307, 95 S.Ct. 1154, 43 L.Ed.2d 213 (1975); *see also* Bazemore v. Savannah Hospital, 171 Ga. 257, 155 S.E. 194 (1930) (complaint for injunction to prevent distribution of photographs of a deceased nude infant with its heart on outside of its body held to state cause of action).

dissemination of news or information, albeit for profit.[63] Nevertheless, the issuance of any injunction in this case seems plainly wrong because of its effect of preventing communication to the public of matters of legitimate concern, i.e., about the state's penal system and mental institutions—a prior restraint almost certainly prohibited by the First Amendment.[64] The injunction was finally dissolved in 1991, 24 years after its issuance.[65]

Wiseman aside, it is unlikely that injunctive relief is, as a practical and constitutional matter, available to those whose newsworthy private facts are about to be divulged by the media.

4.8 Assessment of and Prognosis for the Common Law Complex of Torts of Invasion of Privacy

Because the operation of the complex of torts known collectively as invasion of privacy is so problematic and the interests protected by the individual torts subject to so much debate,[1] assessment of the present value of these torts in a rational and constitutional legal system and prognoses for their continued viability is in order.

The least troublesome of the privacy torts, at least from a communications media perspective, are intrusion and appropriation. This may be explained by the fact that, narrowly viewed, these torts protect property or financial interests and are not aimed directly at the media. Indeed, one, intrusion, does not even require publication for its commission. It is enough that the defendant invade without permission the plaintiff's legal protected zone of privacy. The other, appropriation, while often implicating advertising media, does not require mass communication for its perpetration. For example, the use of photographs of non-consenting subjects in a photographer's window would suffice.

This is not to say that media personnel will not, on occasion, commit these torts in the course of communicating to the public. It is not unheard of for investigative reporters, to invade a newsworthy subject's protected zone of privacy to obtain a story[2] or for the entertainment[3] or

63. *See, e.g.,* Loft v. Fuller, 408 So.2d 619, 623 (Fla.App.1981), review denied 419 So.2d 1198 (Fla.1982); Tropeano v. Atlantic Monthly Co., 379 Mass. 745, 748, 400 N.E.2d 847, 850 (1980); Nelson v. Maine Times, 373 A.2d 1221, 1224 (Me.1977); RESTATEMENT SECOND OF TORTS § 652C, comment d (1977).

64. *See* Cullen v. Grove Press, Inc. 276 F.Supp. 727 (S.D.N.Y.1967); *see also* Nebraska Press Ass'n. v. Stuart, 427 U.S. 539, 96 S.Ct. 2791, 49 L.Ed.2d 683 (1976); Near v. Minnesota ex. rel. Olson, 283 U.S. 697, 51 S.Ct. 625, 75 L.Ed. 1357 (1931).

65. *See* Paul Langner, *Last Curb on Titicut Follies is Lifted 24 Years After Ban,* Boston Globe, Aug. 2, 1991, p. 17.

1. *Compare, e.g.,* Edward J. Bloustein, *Privacy as an Aspect of Human Dignity: An Answer to Dean Prosser,* 39 N.Y.U.L. Rev 962 (1964) *with* William L. Prosser, *Privacy,* 48 Cal. L. Rev. 383 (1960); *and compare* Richard A. Posner, *The Right of Privacy,* 12 Ga.L.Rev. 393 (1978) *with* Edward J. Bloustein, *Privacy is Dear at Any Price: A Response to Professor Posner's Economic Theory,* 12 Ga.L.Rev. 429 (1978) *and* Richard A. Epstein, *Privacy, Property Rights and Misrepresentation,* 12 Ga.L.Rev. 455 (1978).

2. *See, e.g.,* Dietemann v. Time, Inc., 449 F.2d 245 (9th Cir.1971).

3. *See, e.g.,* Groucho Marx Prods., Inc. v. Day and Night Co., Inc., 689 F.2d 317 (2d Cir.1982) (appropriation not actionable be-

advertising[4] media to borrow, without permission or compensation, someone's image or identity for commercial gain. But these torts are designed to protect the individual's privacy, property and celebrity market value from invasion or misappropriation by anyone. Because the communication media and their publication processes are not specifically targeted by these particular torts, the potential for conflict with protected First Amendment interests is minimal and a major problem concerning the continued existence and operation of the torts is avoided.

That is all to the good because the interests involved with the intrusion and appropriation torts are fairly well defined, substantial and deserve protection in contemporary society. Intrusion represents little more than the extension of the ancient torts of trespass to real property and to chattels covering invasions of private spaces such as homes, offices and automobiles by the use of photographic and electronic devices not requiring apparent physical incursions. If the intrusive tort did not already exist it would have to be invented for an age obsessed with snooping and the facilitating devices capable of capturing and recording even the slightest movements and faintest whispers at considerable distances and behind even solid barriers.

As we noted at the beginning of this chapter, one of the inherent needs of human beings which must be met if they are to retain their individuality and dignity are zones of physical space to which they can truly retreat from the world. This need becomes more acute every day the population continues to increase. Legal protection for those physical zones of privacy is thus of paramount importance in a rational democratic society, and the tort of intrusion should only strengthen in the twenty-first century because of its noble purpose.

The appropriation tort is one realistically protecting whatever property value there may be in one's very being. Thus far this tort appears to be working reasonably well to prevent others from taking this value in a person's celebrity against his will.[5] The main problem here, given the tort's incorporation in statutes in a number of jurisdictions, most notably California,[6] New York,[7] and Tennessee,[8] is the scope of protection provided by such statutes. But this is merely a problem of statutory construction and does not go to the operation of the tort when it is applicable.

Fundamental justice would seem to dictate that the civil law permit one whose identity has commercial value to control the commerce in his identity. The law should protect such individuals so they may decide for themselves whether to defend their privacy by withholding their celebri-

---

cause right of publicity not descendible under facts of case).

4. *See, e.g.,* Midler v. Ford Motor Co., 849 F.2d 460 (9th Cir.1988), cert. denied 503 U.S. 951, 112 S.Ct. 1514, 117 L.Ed.2d 650 (1992).

5. *Id.*

6. *See* Cal. Civ. Code §§ 990 (deceased persons), 3344 (living persons) (West Supp. 1996).

7. *See* N.Y. Civ. Rights Law §§ 50, 51 (McKinney 1992 and Supp. 1996).

8. *See* Tenn. Code Ann. §§ 47–25–1101 through 1108 (1984).

ty from commerce or to waive privacy by making such celebrity available for a price. So long as protection is limited to purely commercial trading in human identity, there can be little objection to a tort that secures control of that commerce to the person whose identity is involved. While the privacy interest involved here is mainly financial and perhaps not as compelling as that protected by the intrusion tort, it too furthers individual autonomy and personhood and we may expect the appropriation tort to continue to be recognized in the twenty-first century.

On the other hand, the false light and publicity of private facts torts, because poorly rationalized, problematic in operation and aimed at publicity of news and information both false and true, seem poor candidates for long-term survival.

According to Prosser[9] the false light tort got its start in 1816 when Lord Byron succeeded in enjoining the advertising for sale of inferior poems falsely attributed to the great poet.[10] This was not a tort case but what might be characterized today as an action for unfair competition. The modern reported cases recognizing false light do not attempt to rationalize the value of the tort. Rather, they often rely on the Restatement Second codification of Dean Prosser's classification system to justify its existence.[11]

Prosser himself failed to rationalize the need for the tort apart from defamation when he stated "The interest protected is clearly that of reputation, with the same overtones of mental distress as in defamation."[12] He might have been influenced by Dean Wigmore's early twentieth century article, which he cited,[13] calling for the recognition of an actionable right of privacy to protect against certain classes of false statements whether or not falling within the accepted definition of defamation.[14] In support, Wigmore, the great master of the law of evidence, could cite only a handful of cases not involving defamation actions.[15] Of these cases not one sounded in tort, all were actions in equity for injunctive relief and, with the exception of Lord Byron's case where injunctions were issued without explanation, injunctive relief was granted because of the financial liability which might attach from being falsely linked to a business enterprise or to the birth of a child.[16] This is a far cry from supporting a tort right of privacy protecting some *personal* interest in freedom from being placed in a false light.

---

9. William L. Prosser, *Privacy*, 48 Cal. L. Rev. 383, 398 (1960).

10. Lord Byron v. Johnston, 2 Mer. 29, 35 Eng. Rep. 851 (1816).

11. *Compare* William L. Prosser, *Privacy*, 48 Cal. L. Rev. 383 (1960) *with* RESTATEMENT SECOND of TORTS §§ 652 A–E (1977).

12. *Id.* at 400.

13. *Id.* at 398 n.129.

14. J.H. Wigmore, *The Right Against False Attribution of Belief or Utterance*, 4 Ky. L.J. No. 8, p.3 (1916).

15. Vassar College v. Loose—Wiles Biscuit Co., 197 Fed. 982 (D.Mo.1912); Edison v. Edison Polyform Mfg. Co., 73 N.J.Eq. 136, 67 A. 392 (1907); Vanderbilt v. Mitchell, 72 N.J.Eq. 910, 67 A. 97 (1907); Walter v. Ashton, [1902] 2 Ch. 282; Dixon v. Holden, L.R. 7 Eq. 458 (1869); Routh v. Webster, 10 Beav. 561, 50 Eng. Rep. 698 (1847).

16. *See* Vanderbilt v. Mitchell, 72 N.J.Eq. 910, 67 A. 97 (1907) (false statement as to paternity on a birth certificate).

Interestingly, Wigmore, in formulating this new tort, reveals the same bias against the press of his day as that exhibited by Warren and Brandeis in theirs[17] when he stated in his article, "Finally there is the common situation in which the defendant falsely attributes to the plaintiff the *possession of some opinion* . . . . [I]t is a not uncommon form of injury in current journalistic practice. The irresponsible vendors of sensations, moved by the meanest motives of mankind, will recklessly attribute to this or that personage some view on current affairs which is alien to his actual thoughts and is calculated to make hard feelings that never can be assuaged by protestation"[18] (author's own emphasis). And like Warren and Brandeis he did not consider the impact of his proposed tort on the press clause of the First Amendment. Presumably he would have championed injunctions to prevent the dissemination of false statements by the press, given his citation almost exclusively to cases in equity granting this writ.

The appellate cases cited by Prosser[19] do justify the recognition of a false light category,[20] but they merely recognize such tort action as arising out of some general right of privacy or the even more general right to be let alone. They do not explain why the tort is needed, the interest or interests protected, how it can be harmonized with defamation and how it might be harmonized with the protections accorded freedom of expression.[21] Thus, the underpinnings of this twentieth century tort are shakey, but with the publication of Prosser's article the tort came to be accepted almost unquestioningly by the courts as an aspect of the common law right of privacy.[22]

Despite the lack of clear definition of the interest supposedly served, the prima facie case of false light is straight forward[23] enough. False statements of fact can be exposed as such by establishing the true facts. The effect of publicity of false statements in placing the plaintiff in a false light in the eyes of the public can be established by testimony of members of the public regarding the view they had of the plaintiff following their exposure to the false statement or statements. The finder of fact is then in a position to determine whether the false light would be highly offensive to a reasonable person in the plaintiff's position. Finally,

---

17. *See* p. 508, in Practitioners Edition, Vol. 1.

18. J. H. Wigmore, *The Right Against False Attribution of Belief or Utterance*, 4 Ky. L.J. No. 8, p.7 (1916). Apparently Wigmore, too, was "burned" by a journalist of the time who allegedly misquoted the great scholar to his considerable embarrassment. *Id.* at p.8.

19. William L. Prosser, *Privacy*, 48 Cal. L. Rev. 383, 398–400 nn. 131–143, 146 (1960).

20. *See* Alfred Hill, *Defamation and Privacy Under the First Amendment*, 76 Colum. L. Rev. 1205, 1270 (1976).

21. Many of the questions associated with recognition of false light are explored in Sullivan v. Pulitzer Broadcasting Co., 709 S.W.2d 475 (Mo.1986) (en banc) in which the Missouri Supreme Court refused to decide whether to recognize the tort because the action before it also sounded in traditional defamation. *See also* Prescott v. Bay St. Louis Newspapers, Inc., 497 So.2d 77, 80 (Miss.1986).

22. *See, e.g.*, Cantrell v. Forest City Pub. Co., 419 U.S. 245, 95 S.Ct. 465, 42 L.Ed.2d 419 (1974); Time, Inc. v. Hill, 385 U.S. 374, 87 S.Ct. 534, 17 L.Ed.2d 456 (1967).

23. *See* RESTATEMENT SECOND OF TORTS § 652 E (1977).

while the burden is great, the issue of whether the defendant publicized the false statement with knowledge of its falsity or with reckless disregard as to its falsity is merely one of proving the difficult element of actual malice.

The serious operational problem arises not from the elements of the prima facie case but from the very nature of the tort as going beyond defamation. This problem threatens the tort's very existence. While all actionable defamatory statements place the victim in a false light in the eyes of those who receive and accept such communications, the tort also encompasses false non-defamatory statements, thereby increasing the chill on free expression.

This chill can be substantial given the hierarchical nature of the news and information media. News and information is normally gathered by reporters and researchers and then presented to editors for processing and the decision whether to publish. Because defamatory material is that which injures reputation, such material usually provides a red warning flag to the editors of legal danger which can be countered by careful verification of the questionable material or even modification or excision. But false statements neutral or even laudatory regarding a subject's reputation provide no such warning to editors and publishers. They are thus unable to protect themselves from liability except at the expense of laboriously checking the accuracy of *all* statements of fact about individuals presented to them by the reporters and researchers. There are thus two alternatives presented to editors by the false light tort: either risk liability by not double checking *every* asserted fact about individuals or avoid such liability at great cost in time and money.

The media must accept the burden on free expression of potential civil liability for defamation because it was a part of the common law of England accepted by the American Colonies at the time of the Declaration of Independence and before adoption of the Constitution and Bill of Rights. This, of course, is not true of invasion of privacy generally or false light specifically. Thus the imposition of civil liability for publicizing false non-defamatory statements gives rise to potential conflicts with the First Amendment not posed by libel and slander. The requirement imposed on plaintiffs to establish actual malice on the part of those creating false light[24] does not fully eliminate the risk of this conflict.

The tension between false light and First Amendment protection for the media was first noted in the groundbreaking case of *Renwick* v. *News and Observer Pub. Co.*[25] There, the plaintiff, an associate dean at the University of North Carolina brought suit for libel and false light against two North Carolina newspapers which had published editorial comments about apparent bullying of the University by the Federal Government in regard to minority admissions. These newspaper pieces

---

24. *See* Time, Inc. v. Hill, 385 U.S. 374, 87 S.Ct. 534, 17 L.Ed.2d 456 (1967).

25. 310 N.C. 312, 312 S.E.2d 405 (1984), reh. denied 310 N.C. 749, 315 S.Ed.2d 704,

cert. denied 469 U.S. 858, 105 S.Ct. 187, 83 L.Ed.2d 121 (1984).

indicated that Washington's ire was raised by allegations made by Dean Renwick, who was formerly in charge of minority admissions at the school, that "between 1975 and 1978 about 800 black students had been denied admission." Renwick's actions were based on claimed falsity of the reported *number* of black students who had been denied admission. Amplifying on his contention Renwick stated in his complaints that the error in the opinion pieces gave "the impression that plaintiff is an extremist, a liar and is irresponsible in his profession".[26] The two claims were dismissed by the trial court but reinstated by the North Carolina Court of Appeals.

The North Carolina Supreme Court in turn reversed the decision of the intermediate appellate court. Regarding the action for libel *per se*, the high court found that the most obvious and natural meaning to be accorded the erroneous statement of fact incorporated by the defendant newspapers in their editorial commentaries was that it did not tend to defame the plaintiff.

Turning from defamation to the false light claim, the court indicated two basic concerns with the tort. First, the right to recover often overlaps actions for libel and slander[27] and second, judicial efficiency would not be served by recognizing an essentially duplicative tort action.

Of greater concern was the First Amendment issue. The court though that its recognition of false light would increase the tension already existing between the First Amendment and tort law because it would allow recovery for non-defamatory false statements. The court believed that it would be creating "a grave risk of serious impairment of the indispensable service of a free press in a free society if we saddle the press with the impossible burden of verifying to a certainty the facts associated in news articles with a person's name picture or portrait, *particularly as related to nondefamatory matter*"[28] (emphasis the court's).

Renwick is significant because it is the first appellate decision wholly and *specifically* rejecting the false light tort and doing so in part because of its redundant nature in substantially overlapping libel and slander and in part because the non-overlapping portion of the tort raises the specter of conflict with the First Amendment. While such conflict may be somewhat remote, the North Carolina court may be recognizing that the unrefined interest in protecting individuals from embarrassment and emotional upset arising out of publicity of false nondefamatory statements about them is not substantial enough to justify running the risk of First Amendment violations.

Recently the North Carolina court received support for its position rejecting false light from the Texas Supreme Court. In *Cain* v. *Hearst Corp.*[29] the Texas high court, in answer to a question certified to it by the

---

26. *Id.* at 319, 312 S.E.2d at 409.

27. *Compare* Mitchell v. Random House Inc., 865 F.2d 664, 672 (5th Cir.1989) (expressing concern that Mississippi defamation law would be diluted by recognition of the false light tort).

28. Renwick, 310 N.C. at 325, 312 S.E.2d at 413.

29. 878 S.W.2d 577 (Tex.1994). For comment on the case *see* Greg C. Wilkins, *The Night the Light Went Out in Texas*, 26 Tex. Tech. L. Rev. 249–264 (1995).

United States Court of Appeals for the Fifth Circuit, held, by a vote of five to four, that Texas did not recognize the tort. It gave as its reasons essentially the same ones given in *Renwick*, *i.e.*, overlap with other torts, particularly defamation, and the derogation of First Amendment rights.[30]

Now that two respected high state courts have, with persuasive reasoning, rejected false light by name, it seems likely to the authors that jurisdictions which have previously accepted the tort uncritically will eventually reappraise it, balancing the individual interest in freedom from embarrassment and mental upset against the societal interest in freedom of expression. If such a balance is struck, the false light tort may well disappear in the twenty-first century. But apparently the tort will not disappear without a fight. A recent Arizona Supreme Court decision embraces the tort in the face of the defendant newspaper company's First Amendment and overlap arguments. The Arizona court was not concerned that both the false light and intentional infliction of mental and emotional distress torts provide compensation for violation of virtually the same interest in emotional tranquility. As for the overlap with defamation, the court stated that the interests protected by the respective torts were different, with defamation actions compensating damage to reputation and false light actions protecting mental and emotional interests even when the private facts published are true.[31]

If the conception and operation of false light is doubtful, the tort of unreasonable publicity of private embarrassing facts seems downright ill-conceived. Warren and Brandeis chose *sui generis* or inapposite English precedents to support their notion that such a tort did exist in the English common law.[32] By their law review article they instigated Ameri-

---

30. The facts of this case are brutal, horrifying and bizarre. The plaintiff Cain (aptly named), was serving a life sentence for murder in a Texas prison when the Houston Chronicle published a story referring to him as a burglar, thief, pimp and killer. In recounting Cain's life of crime, the article stated:

> Cain is believed to have killed as many as eight people; Cain killed one of his lawyers in 1973 and married the lawyer's widow a few months later; Cain killed a 67 year old man in 1977; in 1983 he "bought" a prostitute from a friend to help finance his activities; Cain persuaded the prostitute to marry a trailer park owner named Anderson, so that Cain could kill Anderson and share the prostitute's inheritance from Anderson; when the prostitute balked, Cain threatened to kill her 5 year old daughter and "deliver her daughter's head in a wastepaper basket"; the prostitute married Anderson 3 days later, and on January 5, 1985 Cain killed Anderson.

878 S.W.2d at 577.

Cain's sole complaint was that the story contained erroneous information that he was a member of the so-called "Dixie Mafia" and that he had killed as many as eight people in his lifetime, thereby placing him in a false light with the public.

That Cain had murdered at least one person could not be denied. Nor did he deny the Chronicle's allegations that he was a burglar, thief and pimp. It would be almost legally impossible then for the alleged errors in the story regarding the number of people Cain had murdered and his membership in a criminal organization to place this man in a false light even if the tort were recognized in Texas.

31. *See* Godbehere v. Phoenix Newspapers, Inc., 162 Ariz. 335, 783 P.2d 781 (1989).

32. Their central authority for the existence of the tort, *Prince Albert* v. *Strange*, 2 De Gex & Am. 652, 64 Eng. Rep. 293 (V.C. 1848), concerned the threatened reproduction and summary description of certain etchings made by Queen Victoria and Prince Albert for their own amusement.

can common law development of the tort but without giving serious consideration to the substantiality of the interest to be protected or the dangers posed to freedom of expression by imposing civil liability for dissemination of truthful information.[33]

That they failed to come to grips with the interest their proposed tort would protect is not surprising given the motivation for their article. Their obvious concern was for putting down the popular press of the time when they say in sweeping terms, "The press is overstepping in every direction the obvious bounds of propriety and decency."[34] They did refer to the harm of "mental pain and distress, far greater than could be inflicted by mere bodily injury"[35] stemming from truthful but embarrassing publicity. But the authors did not consider that such real pain and distress endured by complaining parties is the result of having their true and more complete personas exposed to public view. While no doubt persons embarrassed by publicity would prefer "to be let alone," their interest in presenting a false or incomplete image to others is not one that seems very compelling.

But the argument is further made that the tort protects societal interests in maintaining social standards and a proper moral climate.[36] The authors might also have mentioned the societal interest in rehabilitation of criminals,[37] the encouragement of public testimony[38] and the protection of witnesses from physical harm.[39] But common law tort is designed to protect the interests of individuals and, more recently,

Going beyond common law protection of intellectual property as the court had to do because a mere summary description of the etchings would not have qualified as an invasion of any property interest, Vice Chancellor Knight Bruce said that the courts in proper cases would prevent injurious disclosures as to private matters. It apparently did not occur to Warren and Brandeis that this was a one of a kind case favoring the nominal ruler of the court handing down the decision. The other cases cited by them (4 Harv. L. Rev. at 207–210) deal with breaches of trust or contract. *See* Abernathy v. Huchinson, 1 H. & Tw. 33, 3 L.J. 209, 47 Eng. Rep. 1313 (1825); Tuck v. Priester, 19 Q.B.D. 629 (1887); Pollard v. Photographic Co., 40 Ch. Div. 345 (1888). To this day no common law tort of invasion of privacy is recognized in England. *See* Anderson v. Fisher Broadcasting Co., 300 Or. 452, 457, 712 P.2d 803, 808–809 (1986); REPORT OF THE COMMITTEE ON PRIVACY, CMD. 5, No. 5012 (1972); Diane L. Zimmerman, *Requiem for a Heavyweight: A Farewell to Warren and Brandeis's Privacy Tort*, 68 Corn. L. Rev. 291, 342 n. 268 (1983).

33. In fairness to the authors, it must be noted that at the time they wrote their article the United Supreme Court had not clearly adopted the theory of incorporation applying portions of the Bill of Rights to the States through the Fourteenth Amendment. See JOHN NOWAK & RONALD ROTUNDA, CONSTITUTIONAL LAW 382–388 (4th ed. 1991). It was not until 1925 that the Court applied the speech clause of the First Amendment to the states in Gitlow v. New York, 268 U.S. 652, 666, 45 S.Ct. 625, 630, 69 L.Ed. 1138, 1146 (1925) and not until 1931 that it so applied the press clause in Near v. Minnesota ex. rel. Olson, 283 U.S. 697, 701, 51 S.Ct. 625, 626, 75 L.Ed. 1357, 1363 (1931).

34. Samuel D. Warren and Louis D. Brandeis, *The Right to Privacy*, 4 Harv. L. Rev. 193, 196 (1890).

35. *Id.*

36. *Id.*

37. *See* Briscoe v. Reader's Digest Ass'n, 4 Cal.3d 529, 542, 93 Cal.Rptr. 866, 483 P.2d 34, 43 (1971); Melvin v. Reid, 112 Cal.App. 285, 291–292, 297 P. 91, 93 (1931).

38. *See* Capra v. Thoroughbred Racing Ass'n. of North America, Inc., 787 F.2d 463, 465 (9th Cir.), cert. denied 479 U.S. 1017, 107 S.Ct. 669, 93 L.Ed.2d 721 (1986).

39. *Id.*; Times Mirror Co. v. Superior Court, 198 Cal.App.3d 1420, 1426, 244 Cal. Rptr. 556, 563–564 (1988).

classes of individuals. It is not designed to protect society generally. That is best left to legislative action.

In short, the interest protected by Warren and Brandeis's tort is insubstantial,[40] which may explain why there have been so few successful actions and why contemporary courts are narrowing their view of what facts are private and embarrassing and, at the same time, expanding the newsworthiness privilege.[41]

Aside from raising serious doubt as to the need for this tort, the insubstantiality of the interest protected has serious constitutional ramifications. When truthful publicity is made the basis for civil liability there can be little doubt as to the chilling effect on free expression. Even in the absence of a broad absolutist view of the protection afforded expression by the First Amendment, the narrower ad hoc balancing approach requires some substantial state interest outweighing free expression before First Amendment protection is subordinated.[42] Thus, the vagueness and inconsequentiality of the countervailing interest vindicated by state recognition and enforcement of the tort makes it vulnerable to attack on constitutional grounds whatever First Amendment theory is employed.[43]

This tort is also problematic on a less philosophical level. One might think that after more than one hundred years acquaintance with the tort, American courts would be in agreement at least as to the elements of the prima facie case. Yet there is still uncertainty whether some kind of showing of fault analogous to actual malice in defamation law[44] must be made by plaintiffs in order to insure protection for truthful communications.[45]

---

40. *See* Richard A. Epstein, *Privacy, Property Rights, and Misrepresentations*, 12 Ga. L. Rev. 455, 463 (1978) ("Privacy, however lofty its pedigree is the least important tort for a civilized society."); Harry Kalven, Jr., *Privacy in Tort Law–Were Warren and Brandeis Wrong?*, 31 Law and Contemp. Probs. 327 328 (1966) (the author calls Warren and Brandeis's tort petty); Diane L. Zimmerman, *Requiem for a Heavyweight: A Farewell to Warren and Brandeis's Privacy Tort*, 68 Corn. L. Rev. 291, 323–324 (1983).

41. *See, e.g.*, Virgil v. Sports Illustrated, 424 F.Supp. 1286 (S.D.Cal.1976); *see also* Harry Kalven Jr., *Privacy in Tort Law— Were Warren and Brandeis Wrong?*, 31 Law and Contemp. Probs. 327, 336 (1966).

42. For discussion of the absolutist and ad hoc balancing approaches to the Bill of Rights, particularly with regard to the First Amendment, *see* John Nowak & Ronald Rotunda Constitutional Law 941–944 (4th ed. 1991); Laurence H. Tribe, American Constitutional Law 791–794 (2d ed. 1988); T. Barton Carter, Juliet L. Dee, Martin J. Gaynes & Harvey L. Zuckman, Mass Communications Law 7–10, 14–17 (4th ed. 1994).

43. This vulnerability has been noted by Professor Zimmerman. "[A] state can justify a content-based regulation of speech, such as the private-facts tort, only if it can demonstrate a clearly defined harm and a compelling interest in its prevention. But the nature of the harm done by publication of private facts has continued for almost a century to elude more than vague, subjective definition." Diane L. Zimmerman, *Requiem for a Heavyweight: A Farewell to Warren and Brandeis's Privacy Tort* 68 Corn. L. Rev. 291, 341 (1983).

44. *See* New York Times Co. v. Sullivan, 376 U.S. 254, 84 S.Ct. 710, 11 L.Ed.2d 686 (1964).

45. *Compare* Hawkins By and Through Hawkins v. Multimedia, Inc., 288 S.C. 569, 344 S.E.2d 145 (1986), cert. denied 479 U.S. 1012, 107 S.Ct. 658, 93 L.Ed.2d 712 (1986), with Anderson v. Fisher Broadcasting Co., 300 Or. 452, 712 P.2d 803 (1986); *but see* Florida Star v. B.J.F., 491 U.S. 524, 109 S.Ct. 2603, 105 L.Ed.2d 443 (1989) in which the Supreme Court seems to assume the need for some kind of scienter to accompa-

The conceptual and practical difficulties with the Warren and Brandeis tort have recently moved two jurisdictions too limit substantially its reach or to reject it entirely. In *Anderson* v. *Fisher Broadcasting Co.*,[46] the Oregon Supreme Court confronted the question whether truthfully publicizing a fact about a private individual which the individual would have preferred to keep private is, without more, a tort. The Oregon court, speaking through Justice Hans Linde, answered the question in the negative, holding that the complained of conduct must be designed to cause severe mental or emotional distress, whether for its own sake or as a means to some other end, and it must qualify as such extraordinary conduct that the finder of fact could determine that it went beyond the farthest reaches of socially tolerable behavior.[47] In other words, the invasion of privacy to be actionable would have to amount to the modern tort of intentional infliction of severe emotional distress, or "outrage."[48] Anything less in Oregon will not suffice.

Going beyond the Oregon Supreme Court, the North Carolina Supreme Court in *Hall* v. *Post*[49] pointedly refused to recognize the publicity of private facts tort because of the substantial overlap with "outrage."[50] A second and perhaps more important reason for the rejection of the Warren and Brandeis tort was its constitutionally suspect nature, the court saying, "[I]t would be entirely unrealistic to suggest that adoption of the private facts tort would do other than 'add to the tension already existing between the First Amendment and the law of torts.' "[51]

The *Anderson* and *Hall* cases are thus far unique[52] but they pinpoint questionable aspects of the tort created by Warren and Brandeis and may pressage a broader challenge, leading to this media tort's demise in the second century of its existence.[53]

---

ny the publicity of private facts. Other concerns about the tort on an operational level are expressed by Justice Linde in *Anderson*. 300 Or. at 457, 712 P.2d at 809. *See also* Harry Kalven, Jr., *Privacy in Tort Law—Were Warren and Brandeis Wrong?*, 31 Law and Contemp. Probs. 326, 331, 333–336 (1966).

46. 300 Or. 452, 712 P.2d 803 (1986).

47. *Id.* at 459, 712 P.2d at 807.

48. For a discussion of this tort *see generally* RESTATEMENT SECOND OF TORTS § 46 (1977); WILLIAM L. PROSSER AND W. PAGE KEETON, TORTS 55–66 (5th ed. 1984).

49. 323 N.C. 259, 372 S.E.2d 711 (1988).

50. *Id.* at 267–269, 372 S.E.2d at 716–717.

51. *Id.* at 269, 372 S.E.2d at 717.

52. The only other case which could be found even approaching them is *Brunson* v. *Ranks Army Store*, 161 Neb. 519, 73 N.W.2d 803 (1955) in which the Nebraska Supreme Court rejected the entire idea of common Law invasion of privacy in the setting of publicity of private embarrassing facts spread by a non-media defendant.

53. At least one Justice of the United States Supreme Court seems to think that this may already have happened. In *Florida Star* v. *B.J.F.*, 491 U.S. 524, 109 S.Ct. 2603, 105 L.Ed.2d 443 (1989), in which the Court reversed a judgment for negligent injury obtained by a rape victim identified by the defendant newspaper in violation of a Florida criminal statute, then Justice White said, "By holding that only 'a state interest of the highest order' permits the State to penalize the publication of truthful information, and by holding that protecting a rape victim's right to privacy is not among those state interests of the highest order, the Court accepts the appellant's invitation ... to obliterate one of the most noteworthy legal inventions of the 20th century: the tort of the publication of private facts ... Even if the Court's opinion does not say as much today, such obliteration will follow inevitably from the Court's conclusion here. If the First Amendment prohibits wholly

4.9 Select Federal and State Privacy Statutes Affecting Access to and Storage and Dissemination of News and Information

In the preceding sections of the chapter the discussion has focused on civil liability of media organizations and their representatives for the tortious invasion of the individual's common law right of privacy in its various guises. Statutes were referred to only as they modified or supplemented state common law. In this section we discuss selected federal and state privacy statutes which, by legislative mandate, prevent media access to news and information about individuals or have substantial impact on the media's ability to gather, store and disseminate news and information. Some of these statutes provide *criminal* penalties for their violation as well as civil remedies for those injured by media publicity.

A. *Federal Statutes*

1. *Freedom of Information Act Privacy Exemptions*

While the purpose of the Freedom of Information Act[1] (FOIA) is to make more readily available to the public information in the hands of the federal government concerning its operations,[2] the Act contains provisions exempting, on personal privacy grounds, the release of certain information concerning specific persons if the governmental agency involved properly invokes the applicable exemption or exemptions.[3] The act exempts from its general mandate to make disclosure "personnel and medical files and similar files the disclosure of which would constitute a clearly unwarranted invasion of personal privacy"[4] and "investigatory records compiled for law enforcement purposes, but only to the extent that the production of such records could . . . constitute an unwarranted invasion of personal privacy,[5] [or] . . . could reasonably be expected to

---

private persons (such as B.J.F.) from recovering for the publication of the fact that she was raped, I doubt that there remain any 'private facts' which persons may assume will not be published in the newspapers, or broadcast on television." *Id.* at 551 109 S. Ct. at 2618, 105 L. Ed. 2d at 459–460. *Compare* Macon Telegraph Publishing Co. v. Tatum, 263 Ga. 678, 436 S.E.2d 655 (1993) (newspaper story identifying woman who shot and killed a knife-wielding intruder who had exposed himself to her held to be nonactionable because of the legitimate public interest in the story, and thus publisher is protected by the First Amendment). However, some commentators are trying to keep the tort alive at least in cases not directly involving the media. *See, e.g.,* Jonathan B. Mintz, *The Remains of Privacy's Disclosure Tort: An Exploration of the Private Domain*, 55 Md. L. Rev. 425 (1996).

The Florida statute alleged to have been breached in *Florida Star* was declared to violate on its face both the United States and the Florida Constitutions in *State v. Globe Communications Corp.*, 648 So.2d 110 (Fla.1994).

1. 5 U.S.C.A. § 552, as amended (West 1977 and Supp. Pam. 1996).

2. *See* United States Dep't. of Justice v. Reporters Committee for Freedom of the Press, 489 U.S. 749, 773, 109 S.Ct. 1468, 1482, 103 L.Ed.2d 774, 796–797 (1989); Department of the Air Force v. Rose, 425 U.S. 352, 372, 96 S.Ct. 1592, 1604, 48 L.Ed.2d 11, 31 (1976); S. Rep. No. 813, 89th Cong. 1st. Sess. 3, 8 (1965).

3. *See* 5 U.S.C.A. § 552(b)(6), (7)(C), as amended (West 1977 and Supp. Pam. 1996). Consumer Product Safety Comm'n. v. GTE Sylvania Inc., 447 U.S. 102, 121, 100 S.Ct. 2051, 2062, 64 L.Ed.2d 766, 780 (1980).

4. 5 U.S.C.A. § 552 (b)(6) (West 1977).

5. *Id.* § (7)(C).

disclose the identity of a confidential source. . . . "[6]

The exemptions in the FOIA are to be narrowly construed consistent with the purpose of the Act[7] but, nevertheless, Exemptions six and seven have been successfully invoked at times to prevent access by the public and the media to personnel, medical and similar files and criminal investigative records and files. For instance, information concerning the identity of recipients of Veterans Administration housing loans, the addresses of the properties so financed in a particular suburb of Cleveland, Ohio and the loan amounts was withheld by the agency in the face of a request for such information motivated by a civil rights group's concern that the agency's loan program was being used to resegregate the suburb through "racial steering."[8] Likewise, a criminal identification record or "rap sheet" in the Federal Bureau of Investigation's files containing information concerning a businessman allegedly associated with organized crime figures and allegedly involved in corrupt dealing with a United States Congressman was held to have been properly withheld from a CBS news correspondent pursuing a story about the businessman.[9] Other information which may be withheld from public disclosure by the federal government under these personal privacy exemptions includes family relationships, medical conditions, job evaluations, welfare payments and involvement in criminal investigations.[10]

But generalization is often difficult here because in deciding whether to invoke the personal privacy exemptions, the agencies must determine whether the likely invasion of privacy is "unwarranted." They do this by balancing the public interest in disclosure of the particular information against the impact of disclosure on the persons referred to in the government's files and records.[11] However, the United States Supreme Court has now approved what it calls "categorical balancing" in which an agency is permitted to withhold whole categories of records and files such as "rap sheets" where the personal privacy interest of persons referred to will always be high and the disclosure interest in the *operations* of the involved government agency (the "what's the govern-

---

6. *Id.* § (7)(D) (West Supp. Pam. 1996).

7. *See, e.g.*, Department of the Air Force v. Rose, 425 U.S. 352, 361, 96 S.Ct. 1592, 1599, 48 L.Ed.2d 11, 21 (1976); Sharyland Water Supply Corp. v. Block, 755 F.2d 397, 398 (5th Cir.), cert. denied 471 U.S. 1137, 105 S.Ct. 2678, 86 L.Ed.2d 697 (1985); New England Apple Council v. Donovan, 725 F.2d 139, 141 (1st Cir.1984).

8. Heights Community Congress v. Veterans Admin., 732 F.2d 526 (6th Cir.), cert. denied 469 U.S. 1034, 105 S.Ct. 506, 83 L.Ed.2d 398 (1984).

9. United States Department of Justice v. Reporters Comm. for Freedom of the Press, 489 U.S. 749, 109 S.Ct. 1468, 103 L.Ed.2d 774 (1989); *see also* Brown v. Federal Bureau of Investigation, 658 F.2d 71 (2d Cir.1981).

10. *See* How to Use the Federal FOI Act 15–16 (Reporters Committee 5th ed. 1985); *see also* McCorstin v. United States Dep't. of Labor, 630 F.2d 242, 245 (5th Cir.1980), cert. denied 450 U.S. 999, 101 S.Ct. 1705, 68 L.Ed.2d 201 (1981).

11. *See* S. Rep. No. 813, 89th Cong., 1st Sess. p. 9 (1965); How to Use the Federal FOI Act 15–16 (Reporters Committee 5th ed. 1985); Susan Marble, Comment, *Is the Privacy Act An Exemption 3 Statute and Whose Statute Is It Anyway?*, 52 Fordham L. Rev. 1334, 1345–1346 (1984); *cf.* Department of the Air Force v. Rose, 425 U.S. 352, 380, 96 S.Ct. 1592, 1607–1608, 48 L.Ed.2d 11, 32 (1976).

ment up to" interest) will always be low.[12]

Because it is personal privacy that the Congress is attempting to protect here through exemptions 6 and 7, requests for information by members of the public and the media may be more readily granted if the requester is willing to have the names of individuals in the records and files redacted and settle for unascribed information.[13]

2. *Privacy Act of 1974, as amended.*

The Privacy Act of 1974, as amended,[14] affords broad protection for personal information contained in federal records. It provides that no federal agency may disclose any record contained in an agency's system of records to any person or even another agency except pursuant to written request by or prior written consent of the person to whom the record pertains unless such disclosure falls within one or more of twelve enumerated exceptions which include disclosures under the Freedom of Information Act.[15]

While the Privacy Act represents a commendable effort on the part of Congress to protect individual personal privacy, it must of necessity restrict access of the media to news and information which may be of value to the public. Unless the personal information covered by the Privacy Act can be disclosed under the Freedom of Information Act, media access to the government records containing the personal information is barred in the absence of written consent granted by the individuals to whom the records relate. But one of the major issues has been the relationship between the Privacy Act and FOIA.[16] If the Privacy Act anti-disclosure provisions were held to be incorporated into FOIA pursuant to its exemption 3 allowing non-disclosure of records specifically exempted from disclosure by other federal statutes,[17] then disclosure of information concerning identified individuals previously available to the media would be barred. Because the political complexion of the Congress changed only minimally between the time of enactment of FOIA and the passage of the Privacy Act it seemed unlikely that the public and media access to personal information granted by the legislators in FOIA would be taken back by them less than a decade later in the absence of major abuse and

---

12. *See* United States Dep't. of Justice v. Reporters Comm. for Freedom of the Press, 489 U.S. 749, 778–780, 109 S.Ct. 1468, 1484–85, 103 L.Ed.2d 774, 799–800, (1989); *cf.* NLRB v. Robbins Tire & Rubber Co., 437 U.S. 214, 223–224, 98 S.Ct. 2311, 2318, 57 L.Ed.2d 159, 166–168 (1978).

13. *See, e.g.,* Department of the Air Force v. Rose, 425 U.S. 352, 381, 96 S.Ct. 1592, 1608, 48 L.Ed.2d 11, 32 (1976); Frank A. Rosenfeld, Comment, *The Freedom of Information Act's Privacy Exemption and the Privacy Act of 1974,* 11 Harv. C.R.-C.L. L. Rev. 596, 623 (1976).

14. 5 U.S.C.A. § 552a, as amended (West 1977 and Supp. Pam. 1996).

15. 5 U.S.C.A. § 552a (b) (West 1977), as amended (West Supp. Pam. 1996).

16. For extended discussion of this problem of statutory construction *see* Susan Marble, Comment, *Is the Privacy Act an Exemption 3 Statute and Whose Statute is it Anyway?,* 52 Ford. L. Rev. 1334 (1984); Frank A. Rosenfeld, Comment, *The Freedom of Information Act's Privacy Exemption and the Privacy Act of 1974,* 11 Harv. CR–CL L. Rev. 596 (1976).

17. *See* 5 U.S.C.A. 552 (b)(3) (West 1977).

express legislative provision.[18] This view is confirmed by Congress' enactment of an amendment to the Privacy Act which provides that no agency may rely on any exemption in the act to withhold from individuals any records which are otherwise accessible to such individuals under the provisions of the Freedom of Information Act.[19] This amendment indicates the strong intent of Congress to reject the position that the Privacy Act is a disclosure withholding statute within the meaning of FOIA's exemption 3 and to require that the courts view the two acts as operating separately and independently of each other.[20] Given the amendment, the Freedom of Information and the Privacy Acts must be construed to allow maximum access of the public, the media and subject individuals to personal information in federal agency records consistent, of course, with the provisions of each act.

3. Driver's Privacy Protection Act of 1994

A little known piece of federal privacy legislation enacted as part of the Violent Crime Control and Law Enforcement Act of 1994[21] is the Driver's Privacy Protection Act of 1994[22] sponsored by Senator Barbara Boxer of California, apparently to curb stalkers like those who killed television actress Rebecca Shaefer and invaded the estate of singer and screen actress Madonna as well as to protect members of pro-choice organizations and abortion clinic personnel from physical retaliation by those who disagree with their activities.[23] The act provides that the states' motor vehicle departments and their personnel "shall not knowingly disclose or otherwise make available to any person or entity personal information about any individual obtained ... in connection with a motor vehicle record."[24]

Fourteen exceptions to this ban on disclosure are enumerated by the act, including use of such information by government agencies in carrying out their functions.[25] No exception is provided for news media inquiries, and this omission is very likely to interfere with legitimate news-gathering efforts because the media frequently rely on motor

18. See Porter v. United States Department of Justice, 717 F.2d 787 (3d Cir.1983); Provenzano v. United States Dept. of Justice, 717 F.2d 799 (3d Cir.1983), vacated as moot 469 U.S. 14, 105 S.Ct., 413, 83 L.Ed.2d 242 (1984); Greentree v. United States Customs Service, 674 F.2d 74 (D.C.Cir.1982) (detailing the legislative history of the Privacy Act); Susan Marble, Comment, Is the Privacy Act an Exemption 3 Statute and Whose Statute Is It Anyway?, 52 Fordham L. Rev. 1334, 1350–1356 (1984).

19. See Pub. L. 98–477 § 2(c), 98 Stat. 2211 (1984), codified at 5 U.S.C.A. § 552a (q)(2) (West Supp. 1996); see also Shapiro v. Drug Enforcement Admin., 762 F.2d 611 (7th Cir.1985) (construing 5 U.S.C.A. § 552a (q)(2)).

20. See H.R. Rep. No. 98–726, 98th Cong., 2d Sess., pt. 2, at 14–17 (1984); see also Shapiro v. Drug Enforcement Admin., 762 F.2d 611, 612 (7th Cir.1985).

21. Pub. L. 103–322, 108 Stat. 1796 (1994).

22. Pub. L. 103–322, § 300002, 108 Stat. 2099–2102 (1994), codified at 18 U.S.C.A. §§ 2721–2725 (West Supp. 1997).

23. See 139 Cong. Rec. S15745–01 (*S15762) (Nov. 16, 1993) (remarks of Senator Boxer).

24. 18 U.S.C.A. § 2721 (a) (West Supp. 1996).

25. The permissible uses or exceptional disclosures are: [text in Practitioner's Edition only.]

Id. § 2721(b).

vehicle departments to match descriptions, names, addresses and phone numbers with drivers' license applications, vehicle registrations and license plates and vice versa.

Besides the enumerated exceptions, the act permits the state motor vehicle departments to establish and utilize procedures under which they can, upon receiving a non-excepted request for information, mail a copy of the request to the individual about whom the information is sought to determine if that person wishes to waive his or her statutory right of privacy.[26]

Because the act has only recently become effective,[27] there are no appellate decisions determining its constitutionality and parameters.

4. The Privacy Protection Act of 1980

Perhaps the most unique privacy legislation ever enacted protects the privacy of newspersons and their sources from invasion through broad federal and state searches and seizures of work product and gathered documentary materials. The Privacy Protection Act of 1980[28] was passed in the wake of the United States Supreme Court's decision in *Zurcher* v. *Stanford Daily*[29] which, in a nutshell, held that searches and seizures in newsrooms pursuant to warrant did not violate First Amendment guarantees because the drafters of the Constitution had not, under the Fourth Amendment, forbidden search warrants directed to the press, did not require special showings that subpoenas would be impractical before warrants could be issued to search the premises of the press, and did not insist that if a press organization was named in a search warrant, the police would first have to show the organization's complicity in the alleged offense being investigated.[30]

Concerned that the use of the warrant process would allow the government to invade the personal privacy of nonsuspects in criminal investigations with consequent drying up of confidential news sources and other damage to the vigorous exercise of First Amendment rights,[31] Congress passed legislation limiting but not wholly eliminating warranted newsroom searches and seizures. The act makes it unlawful, with certain exceptions, for any government officer or employee in the course of a criminal investigation or prosecution to search for or seize any work product or documentary materials possessed by any person reasonably believed to have a purpose to disseminate to the public newspapers, books, broadcasts or other forms of public communication, in or affecting interstate or foreign commerce.[32]

26. *Id.* § 2721(d).

27. *See* note following § 2721(d) in 18 U.S.C.A. (West Supp. 1996).

28. 42 U.S.C.A. §§ 2000aa through 2000aa–12 (West 1994).

29. 436 U.S. 547, 98 S.Ct. 1970, 56 L.Ed.2d 525 (1978).

30. T. Barton Carter, Juliet L. Dee, Martin J. Gaynes and Harvey L. Zuckman, Mass Communications Law 290 (4th ed. 1994).

31. S. Rep. No. 96–874, 96th Cong. 2d Sess., at 4–5 (1980); *see* Doe v. Stephens, 851 F.2d 1457, 1464 (D.C.Cir.1988).

32. 42 U.S.C.A. § 2000aa(a), (b) (West 1994).

The exceptions[33] permit such searches and seizures where

(1) there is probable cause to believe that the person possessing such material has committed or is in the process of committing the criminal offense to which the materials relate;[34] (2) there is reason to believe that the immediate seizure of such materials is necessary to prevent the death of, or serious bodily injury to, a human being; (3) there is reason to believe that the giving of notice pursuant to a subpena duces tecum for the production of documentary material would result in the destruction, alteration, or concealment of such material; or (4) such documentary material has not been produced in response to a court order directing compliance with a subpena duces tecum and all appellate remedies have been exhausted or there is reason to believe that the delay in an investigation or trial occasioned by further proceedings relating to the subpena would threaten the interests of justice.

In conducting searches and seizures under the enumerated exceptions, federal officers and employees are to be governed by the Attorney General's guidelines promulgated pursuant to the mandate of the act.[35] This mandate requires the Attorney General to incorporate in his guidelines such matters as the recognition of the personal privacy interests of the newsperson possessing documentary materials and the requirements that the least intrusive methods be used in conducting newsroom searches and seizures and that applications for warrants to conduct searches governed by the act be approved by an attorney for the government, except that in an emergency the application may be approved by other appropriate supervisory officials if the appropriate United States Attorney is notified within 24 hours.[36]

The remedy for violation of the act is a civil cause of action for damages (1) against the United States, against a state which has waived its sovereign immunity or against any other governmental unit whose officers or employees who acted within the scope or under color of office or employment; and (2) against any officer or employee of a state while acting within the scope or under color of office or employment, if that state has not waived its sovereign immunity.[37] In addition, federal officers and employees violating the Attorney General's guidelines for

33. *Id.* at §§ 2000aa(a)(1)-(2), (b)(1)-(4).

34. This exception includes a proviso that "a government officer or employee may not search for or seize such materials under the provisions of this paragraph if the offense to which the materials relate consists of the receipt, possession, communication, or withholding of such materials or the information contained therein (but such a search or seizure may be conducted under the provisions of this paragraph if the offense consists of the receipt, possession, or communication of information relating to the national defense, classified information, or restricted data under the provisions of section 793, 794, 797, or 798 of Title 18, or section 2274, 2275 or 2277 of this title, or section 783 of Title 50). . . . " *Id.* at (b)(1).

35. 42 U.S.C.A. § 2000aa–11 (West 1994).

36. The Attorney General's guidelines are codified at 28 C.F.R. §§ 59.1–59.6 (1996).

37. 42 U.S.C.A. § 2000aa–6 (West 1994). Damages recoverable are limited to actual damages but not less than $1000 liquidated damages together with reasonable attorneys' fees and litigation costs. *Id.* at (f).

conducting searches and seizures pertaining to the news and information media are subject to disciplinary action by the agency or department by which he is employed.[38]

The lack of development of any significant body of reported case law construing the Privacy Protection Act of 1980 in more than fifteen years of its existence suggests that this legislation is probably working reasonably well to protect newspersons, their work product and their confidential sources from unnecessary privacy invasion by governmental officers and employees.

5.*   *Miscellaneous Federal Statutes Barring Access to Information*

B.*   **State Statutes**

State statutes attempting to protect personal privacy from invasion by the media and others are of two general kinds: those that bar access to personal information and those that impose sanctions for the dissemination of certain types of personal information. The presence in the state codes and compilations of statutes punishing the publicity of truthful personal information suggests inattention to the fundamental distinction drawn by the United States Supreme Court regarding the scope of protection afforded by the First Amendment. The Court has very consistently held that the Press Clause protects the dissemination of news and information and, almost as consistently, has held that it does not provide protection for the media in the news and information gathering process beyond that enjoyed by the general public.[39] This dichotomous approach to the reach of the First Amendment may explain the absence of *federal* legislation attempting to punish the publicity of sensitive personal information actually obtained by the media.

---

38. *See id.* at § 2000aa–12; 28 C.F.R. § 59.6 (1996).

* Published in Practitioners Edition

* Full text published in Practitioners Edition, Vol 1, only.Vol. 1.

39. *Compare, e.g.*, Smith v. Daily Mail Pub. Co., 443 U.S. 97, 99 S.Ct. 2667, 61 L.Ed.2d 399 (1979) and Landmark Communications, Inc. v. Virginia, 435 U.S. 829, 98 S.Ct. 1535, 56 L.Ed.2d 1 (1978) *with* Houchins v. KQED, Inc., 438 U.S. 1, 98 S.Ct. 2588, 57 L.Ed.2d 553 (1978). In *Houchins* the Supreme Court clearly expressed the dichotomy. "In discussing the importance of an 'untrameled press,' the Court in *Grosjean* readily acknowledged the need for 'informed public opinion' as a re-

straint upon misgovernment. 297 U.S., at 250. It also criticized the tax at issue because it limited 'the circulation of information to which the public [was] entitled.' *Ibid.* But nothing in the Court's holding implied a special privilege of *access* to information as distinguished from a right to publish information which has been obtained; *Grosjean* dealt only with government attempts to burden and restrain a newspaper's communication with the public. The reference to a public entitlement to information meant no more than that the government cannot restrain communication of whatever information the media acquire—and which they elect to reveal. *Cf. Landmark Communications, Inc.* v. *Virginia*, 435 U.S. 829, 838, 98 S.Ct. 1535, 56 L.Ed.2d 1 (1978)."

Chapter Five

THE NEW MEDIA LAW
OF DEFAMATION

Analysis

5.1 Introduction and Scope

In the view of the authors in this modern era with its all-pervasive media, defamation law plays a lesser role in society than privacy law because while the protection afforded by privacy law impacts our free society's ability to maintain itself against authoritarian tendencies of individuals and governments, the focus of defamation law is simply the protection of reputation of individual citizens. And thus contrary to accepted norms of treatise writing[1] the authors have chosen to place this chapter after the one on privacy and to devote less pages to it.

Within this chapter a conscious decision has also been made to limit the discussion of the common law of defamation[2] in favor of emphasizing the modern constitutional law. It is the media's constitutional claims to

---

1. *See, e.g.*, Rex S. Heinke, Media Law 69–140; 141–239 (1994); Prosser and Keeton, Torts 771–848; 849–69 (5th ed. 1984); Robert D. Sack & Sandra S. Baron, Libel, Slander, and Related Problems 63–550; 551–635 (2d ed. 1994); Bruce W. Sanford, Libel And Privacy 1–522; 523–86 (2d ed. 1991); Rodney A. Smolla, Law of Defamation §§ 1.01–9.14; 10.01–11.03 (1995).

2. For a comprehensive discussion of common law defamation, *see e.g.*, Laurence H. Eldredge, The Law Of Defamation (1978); William L. Prosser, & W. Page Keeton, Torts 771–814; 824–38, 840–48 (5th ed. 1984); Rodney A. Smolla, Law Of Defamation §§ 1.01–1.04, 4.01–4.13, 7.05–7.07, 8.01–9.12 (1995).

protection from liability that give rise to the important legal battles and judicial decisions of this era.[3]

Do not misunderstand. We do not wish to denigrate the venerable law of defamation. Rather, it is our purpose to emphasize the law that is most important to the modern media of communications. But a summary view of common law defamation follows because that law still forms a part of the predicate for plaintiffs' claims against the media.

5.2   The Common Law Action for Defamation

A.   *Definition of Defamation and the Elements of the Action*

1.   *Definition*

Defamation has been defined as the injury to reputation by "words [that] tend to expose one to public hatred, shame, ... contempt ... or disgrace, or to induce an evil opinion of one in the minds of right thinking persons and to deprive one of their confidence."[1] While this definition provides a good starting point for understanding the nature of defamation, it fails to place any emphasis on loss of reputation in one's business or profession. Moreover, the loss of reputation need only be with regard to a small but significant segment of the community, whose thinking is within normal bounds. Finally, as the late master of torts Dean William L. Prosser pointed out, one may be defamed by imputations of insanity or poverty, which would instead arouse pity or sympathy—feelings that diminish esteem and respect for the subject of the complained of communications.[2] Dean Prosser preferred the statement of the Restatement Second of Torts that a communication to be defamatory must tend to prejudice the subject in the eyes of a substantial and respectable minority of the community.[3]

2.   *Elements of the Tort*

Whatever the nuanced differences in definition put forth by courts and commentators, there is a consensus as to the essential common law elements of the tort action. They are (1) the making by the defendant of a false defamatory statement; (2) the publication to at least one other than the plaintiff of that statement; and (3) the identification in some way of the plaintiff as the person communicated about.[4] At common law

---

3.   *See e.g.,* New York Times v. Sullivan, 376 U.S. 254 84 S.Ct. 710, 11 L.Ed.2d 686 (1964); Philadelphia Newspapers, Inc. v. Hepps, 475 U.S. 767, 106 S.Ct. 1558, 89 L.Ed.2d 783 (1986); Milkovich v. Lorain Journal Co., 497 U.S. 1, 110 S.Ct. 2695, 111 L.Ed.2d 1 (1990).

1.   Kimmerle v. New York Evening Journal, 262 N.Y. 99, 102, 186 N.E. 217–18 (1933); *see* WILLIAM A. PROSSER & W. PAGE KEETON, TORTS 773 at n.17 (5th ed. 1984). *See also* RESTATEMENT SECOND OF TORTS § 559, Cmt. *b* (1977).

2.   WILLIAM A. PROSSER & W. PAGE KEETON, TORTS at 773.

3.   RESTATEMENT SECOND OF TORTS § 559, Cmt. *e* (1977).

4.   *Id.* § 558; ROBERT D. SACK & SANDRA S. BARON, LIBEL, SLANDER AND RELATED PROBLEMS 63–64 (2d ed. 1994); WILLIAM A. PROSSER & W. PAGE KEETON, TORTS 773–74, 797–98 (5th ed. 1984); LAURENCE H. ELDREDGE, THE LAW OF DEFAMATION 32 (1978); RODNEY A. SMOLLA, LAW OF DEFAMATION §§ 1.03, 1.08 (1995).

defamatory statements gave rise to the presumption that they were false which presumption could be rebutted by the defendant.[5]

a. The defamatory statement

The communication complained of must be such as to injure the reputation of a living person or existing organization because only the injured party may sue for defamation.[6] Some words such as "thief," "cheat," "murder" or "whore" are almost universally understood to hurt someone's reputation. Other words may have that effect in relation to the times and the victim's position. Falsely labeling one a Communist during the World War II period of United States–Soviet Union cooperation was not actionable.[7] But the same false identification was considered defamatory after the commencement of the "cold War."[8] And society's greater tolerance of homosexuality may eventually make its false imputation no longer actionable.[9]

The plaintiff's situation in life may also give a damaging effect to otherwise innocent words. The selling of pork is normally a respectable occupation, but suggesting that a kosher butcher sells bacon has been considered defamatory for clearly it would cause observant Jewish customers to think less of the butcher and to take their business elsewhere.[10]

Defamatory words can be presented in numerous ways. One need not attack with a verbal axe. The stiletto of ridicule may suffice. Provided that even one person other than the target of the communication understands it to be defamatory and such understanding is reasonable, given its content and context, a court may accept the plaintiff's argument that it is defamatory. Of course, the defendant may attempt to show that the communication had at least one nondefamatory meaning and others understand it in that sense, or that the communication was made in jest and could not reasonably be taken seriously.

---

5. *See, e.g.*, Philadelphia Newspapers, Inc. v. Hepps, 475 U.S. 767, 777, 106 S.Ct. 1558, 1564, 89 L.Ed.2d 783, 793 (1986); Milkovich v. Lorain Journal Co., 497 U.S. 1, 16, 110 S.Ct. 2695, 2704, 111 L.Ed.2d 1, 16 (1990).

6. *See, e.g.*, RESTATEMENT (SECOND) OF TORTS §§ 559–562, (1977); WILLIAM A. PROSSER & W. PAGE KEETON, TORTS at 778–80; ROBERT D. SACK & SANDRA S. BARON, LIBEL, SLANDER AND RELATED PROBLEMS at 165–68.

7. *See, e.g.*, Garriga v. Richfield, 20 N.Y.S.2d 544, 549, 174 Misc. 315, 320–21 (N.Y. 1940). *See also* WILLIAM A. PROSSER & W. PAGE KEETON, TORTS at 778 and nn. 95–97.

8. *See, e.g.*, Ward v. League for Justice, 93 N.E.2d 723, 726 (Ohio App.1950), appeal dismissed, 154 Ohio St. 367, 95 N.E.2d 769 (Ohio 1950); Herrmann v. Newark Morning Ledger Co., 138 A.2d 61, 71–72, 48 N.J.Super. 420, 438–40 (1958); Joopanenko v. Gavagan, 67 So.2d 434, 438 (Fla.1953); WILLIAM A. PROSSER & W. PAGE KEETON, TORTS at 778.

9. *See* MICHAEL A. MAYER, THE LIBEL REVOLUTION: A NEW LOOK AT DEFAMATION AND PRIVACY 35 (1987); Randy M. Fogle, Comment, *Is Calling Someone "Gay" Defamatory?: The Meaning of Reputation, Community Hores, Gay Rights, and Free Speech*, 3 Law & Sex 165, 166 (1993).

10. *See* Braun v. Armour & Co., 254 N.Y. 514, 173 N.E. 845 (1930).

b. *Publication*

Publication is a legal term of art meaning that the defamatory communication, whatever its form, has been perceived by at least one other than the person defamed.[11] Publication in the sense of printing and distribution of printed matter is not required. For example, publication occurs if a patient makes a serious statement in a loud voice in a crowded waiting room directly to a licensed physician that he or she is a "quack" and that statement is overheard by one or more of the other patients. In this situation, it is clear that the communicator either intends that others overhear his or her accusation or is so uncaring as to whether it is overheard as to be deemed reckless in his conduct.

On the other hand, where one does not intend the communication to be conveyed to anyone other than the target of his or her attack, and the means chosen to convey the communication will, in the normal course, prevent reception by third persons, there is no publication. For instance, Able writes his former business partner Baker a letter in which he accuses Baker of causing the failure of their business by "stealing the company blind." Able places the letter in a sealed envelope marks it "personal and confidential," addresses it to Baker and mails it to his house. Baker's son, curious about the letter from his father's former associate, opens and reads the letter. There is no publication and hence, no actionable defamation at this point.

Moreover, since it is the *defamer* who must intentionally or negligently promote publication, the requirement is normally not met by the victim himself publicizing the communication to others.[12] If in the above hypothetical, Baker opened the letter and then showed it to his son, the result would be the same—no publication. Where there is publication, however, foreseeable repetition of the original defamation by persons other than the victim constitutes republication for which the original defamer will be held responsible.[13] Of course, the person who republishes the original communication may also be held liable.[14]

A question of special significance to the print media is whether the distribution of each copy of a press run constitutes a separate publication permitting multiple defamation actions. American courts, for the most part, have adopted the "single publication rule."[15] The rule provides that

---

11. *See* RESTATEMENT SECOND OF TORTS § 577; WILLIAM A. PROSSER & W. PAGE KEETON, TORTS at 797; ROBERT D. SACK & SANDRA S. BARON, LIBEL, SLANDER, AND RELATED PROBLEMS at 121–25; LAURENCE H. ELDREDGE, THE LAW OF DEFAMATION at 206–07.

12. *See, e.g.*, RESTATEMENT SECOND OF TORTS § 577 (1); WILLIAM A. PROSSER & W. PAGE KEETON, TORTS at 802.

13. *See, e.g.*, WILLIAM A. PROSSER & W. PAGE KEETON, TORTS at 799–800; ROBERT D. SACK & SANDRA S. BARON, LIBEL, SLANDER AND RELATED PROBLEMS at 122–23.

14. *See, e.g.*, RESTATEMENT SECOND OF TORTS § 578; WILLIAM A. PROSSER & W. PAGE KEETON, TORTS at 799.

15. *See, e.g.*, Keeton v. Hustler Magazine, Inc., 465 U.S. 770, 777 n. 8, 104 S.Ct. 1473, 1480 n. 8, 79 L.Ed.2d 790, 799 n. 8 (1984); Gregoire v. G.P. Putnam's Sons, 298 N.Y. 119, 81 N.E.2d 45 (1948); McCutcheon v. State, 746 P.2d 461, 464–65 (Alaska 1987); Fellows v. National Enquirer, Inc., 42 Cal.3d 234, 245, 228 Cal.Rptr. 215, 223, 721 P.2d 97, 104 (1986); Firstamerica Dev. Corp. v. Daytona Beach News–Journal Corp., 196 So.2d 97, 101–02 (Fla.1966).

only one cause of action for defamation arises when the product of a press run or printing is released by the publisher for distribution, no matter how many separate transactions may result.[16] A corollary to this (though not a necessary one) is that the statute of limitations for defamation commences to run from the moment printed matter of a particular printing or press run is first released.[17]

Reinforcing this common law trend is the Uniform Single Publication Act promulgated by the National Conference on Uniform State Laws.[18] It extends the single publication idea to radio, television and motion pictures. The act has been adopted by statute in seven states, including California, Illinois and Pennsylvania and accepted by judicial decision in a number of others.[19]

c. Identification

Published defamation is not actionable unless the complaining party can establish that it was he who was defamed. Very often the target of a defamatory communication is not clearly named therein and thus linking the complaining party with the offending communication becomes a problem of analyzing extrinsic circumstances. The modern rule is that the courts will not entertain an action when the complainant is a member of a large group which is defamed. In contrast, the courts will permit actions by individual members of small groups. But how many people constitute a small group? There is no precise number, but groups under 100 may be small enough for a court to find that one or more of the members have been identified.[20] Often courts will pass this difficult question to the jury and ask it to determine the degree to which other people would find that the defamatory statement attached to the complaining group member. Finders of fact are more likely to find that a small group member was defamed the more inclusive the language of the attack.

---

16. *See, e.g.,* Keeton v. Hustler Magazine, Inc., 131 N.H. 6, 549 A.2d 1187, 1189–90 (N.H. 1988); Gregoire v. G.P. Putnam's Sons, 298 N.Y. 119, 124, 81 N.E.2d 45, 47–48 (1948).

17. *See, e.g.,* Gregoire v. G.P. Putnam's Sons, 298 N.Y. 119, 81 N.E.2d 45 (1948); BRUCE W. SANFORD, LIBEL AND PRIVACY § 13.2.4 (2d ed. 1991). *But see* Dominiak v. National Enquirer, Inc., 439 Pa. 222, 226–227, 266 A.2d 626, 629 (1970) ("We find that neither the wording of the statute [the Uniform Single Publication Act] nor the policy behind it requires a holding that the period of limitations begins to run from the time of the first publication.").

18. Uniform Single Publication Act, 14 U.L.A. 351 (1980). The act is restated in essence in RESTATEMENT SECOND OF TORTS § 577A (1977); *see* WILLIAM L. PROS-

SER & W. PAGE KEETON, TORTS 800 (5th ed. 1984).

19. *See* Keeton v. Hustler Magazine, Inc., 131 N.H. 6, 549 A.2d 1187, 1189 (N.H. 1988).

20. *See, e.g.,* Fawcett Publications v. Morris, 377 P.2d 42 (Okla.1962), cert. denied 376 U.S. 513, 84 S.Ct. 964, 11 L.Ed.2d 968 (1964), in which a member of the 1956 University of Oklahoma football team sued True Magazine after it had published an article implying that the "Sooners" had used stimulative drugs. Although no players were named in the article and there were more than 60 members of the team, the Oklahoma Supreme Court held that the suit could be maintained concluding that the defamatory language referred to everyone including the plaintiff.

Some courts will also allow individual actions when the defamatory communication is directed to a small segment of a group. Of course, in this situation the plaintiff must convince the finder of fact that he is or was a member of the segment at the time it was attacked.[21]

d. Economic loss

In addition to establishing the defamatory nature of the communication, its publication and the necessary identification, the plaintiff in certain cases must also plead and prove that he suffered actual pecuniary or economic loss, *i.e.*, special damages. In determining when this additional requirement must be met, we are confronted with the herculean task of sorting out libel from slander, libel *per se* from libel *per quod* and slander *per se* from all other slanders.

3. The Contrast Between Libel and Slander

Broadly differentiated, the tort of libel includes defamatory communications of a more or less permanent type such as printed material, photographs, paintings, motion pictures, signboards, effigies and even statutory (representations in stone of prominent persons as gargoyles). Slander, on the other hand, includes more ephemeral communications such as the spoken word, sign language and smoke signals. In wresting jurisdiction from the less severe ecclesiastical courts of England, which heard cases of slander, and in succeeding to the libel jurisdiction of the notoriously harsh Star Chamber, the common law courts kept the two types of defamation separate.[22]

While jurisdiction over both defamation torts are now lodged in our general courts of law, the need to distinguish between the torts remains a serious issue in some cases since whether special damages need be proven depends on the classification of the communication.[23] Generally, if the defamatory communication is held to constitute libel, the complaining party is not required to plead and prove as part of his case actual pecuniary loss resulting from the libel. On the other hand, if the communication is categorized as a slander, the complaining party generally has to establish such loss. As a practical matter many slander suits are quashed in the law office when the angry prospective plaintiff is informed by his counsel to forget filing suit because he cannot prove any out-of-pocket loss. However, there is a qualification to this financial loss requirement in some slander actions.

a. Special cases of slander

The early common law courts established three special categories of slander which were to be actionable without regard to the existence of

---

21. *See* Neiman–Marcus Co. v. Lait, 107 F.Supp. 96, (S.D.N.Y.1952); Hudson v. Guy Gannett Broadcasting Co., 521 A.2d 714 (Me.1987).

22. *See* R.C. Donnelly, History of Defamation, 1949 Wis. L. Rev. 99.

23. WILLIAM A. PROSSER & W. PAGE KEETON, TORTS 785–97 (5th ed. 1984); ROBERT D. SACK & SANDRA A. BARON, LIBEL, SLANDER, AND RELATED PROBLEMS 67–69 (2d ed. 1994); LAURENCE H. ELDREDGE, THE LAW OF DEFAMATION 77–81 (1978); RODNEY A. SMOLLA, LAW OF DEFAMATION §§ 7.01, 7.04 (1995).

special damages (slander per se): (1) imputation of crimes recognized by the common law courts; (2) imputation of certain loathsome diseases (limited to sexually transmitted diseases, leprosy and black plague); and (3) imputations affecting the victim in his or her business trade, profession or office.[24] Later, by common law decision or statute a fourth category, the imputation of unchastity to a woman, was added.[25] These four categories of slander continue to be recognized by most courts as permitting a slander victim to sue is or her slanderer without establishing special damages.[26]

While from a plaintiff's perspective the existence of these special categories provides a liberalizing element to the law of slander, a somewhat parallel development in the law of libel has had the opposite effect.

b. Libel per se and per quod

As the tort of libel developed, the rule became fixed that in contrast to slander actions, special damages need not be pleaded and proven in order for the plaintiff to recover. An explanation often given for this distinction is that written communications had greater potential for mischief because of their more permanent form. Therefore, some injury could be conclusively presumed.[27]

Initially, no distinction was drawn by the courts between those communications plainly libelous on their face (libel *per se*) such as "John Doe is a thief" and those which require reference to extrinsic circumstances in order to be found libelous (libel *per quod*). The classic example of libel *per quod* is the erroneous newspaper story stating that Mary Doe of 1234 Shady Lane rather than Cary Roe of 4321 Maiden Lane had just given birth to triplets at the local hospital. The story proves to be libelous to Mary Doe because of the extrinsic fact that Mrs. Doe had

---

24. RESTATEMENT SECOND OF TORTS §§ 570–573; WILLIAM A. PROSSER & W. PAGE KEETON, TORTS at 788–92; LAURENCE H. ELDREDGE, THE LAW OF DEFAMATION at 94–150; RODNEY A. SMOLLA, LAW OF DEFAMATION at § 7.05.

25. RESTATEMENT SECOND OF TORTS §§ 570(d), 574; WILLIAM A. PROSSER & W. PAGE KEETON, TORTS at 792–93; LAURENCE H. ELDREDGE, THE LAW OF DEFAMATION at 99, 117–23; ROBERT D. SACK & SANDRA S. BARON, LIBEL, SLANDER, AND RELATED PROBLEMS at 130; RODNEY A. SMOLLA, LAW OF DEFAMATION at § 7.05[5].

26. Modla v. Parker, 17 Ariz.App. 54, 56 n. 1, 495 P.2d 494, 496 n. 1 (Ariz.Ct.App.), cert. denied, 409 U.S. 1038, 93 S.Ct. 516, 34 L.Ed.2d 487 (1972); Fort v. Holt, 508 P.2d 792, 793 (Colo.Ct.App.1973), Spence v. Funk, 396 A.2d 967, 970 (Del.1978); Mittelman v. Witous, 135 Ill.2d 220, 238–39, , 142 Ill.Dec. 232, 240–41, 552 N.E.2d 973, 981–82 (1989); Ward v. Zelikovsky, 136 N.J. 516,

540–41, 643 A.2d 972, 984–85 (1994); Liberman v. Gelstein, 80 N.Y.2d 429, 435, 605 N.E.2d 344, 347–348, 590 N.Y.S.2d 857, 860–861 (1992).

The scope of the categories has not changed greatly over the years, despite the fact that the fourth category reflects our society's double standard: calling a woman unchaste or a whore is slander *per se*, but accusing a man of promiscuity is slander but not slander *per se*. But *compare* Rejent v. Liberation Publications, Inc., 197 A.D.2d 240, 245, 611 N.Y.S.2d 866, 868–869 (N.Y.App.Div.1994) (libel case in which court stated that gender distinction would violate constitutional protections).

27. *See, e.g.,* Mid–America Food Service Inc. v. ARA Services, Inc., 578 F.2d 691, 697 (8th Cir.1978); Braman v. Walthall, 215 Ark. 582, 593, 225 S.W.2d 342, 348 (1949); Lorillard v. Field Enterprises, 65 Ill.App.2d 65, 78, 213 N.E.2d 1, 7 (Ill.App.1965).

been married only one month before and a number of persons reading the story are aware of this fact.[28]

Originally, then, if the defamatory communication was broadly classified as libel, the showing of special damages was not essential to a successful action. This is still stated to be the majority rule by the American law Institute.[29] But Dean Prosser noted that at least 35 American jurisdictions draw a distinction between libel *per se* and *per quod* and hold that libel *per quod* is to be treated like slander, meaning that it is actionable only with the pleading and proving of special damages unless the libel falls within one or more of those four special categories associated with slander *per se*.[30]

    c. *Summary of the distinctions between the torts*

(1) Slander is actionable with a showing of special damages . . .

(2) . . . unless the slander imputes to the victim (a) criminal conduct recognized as involving moral turpitude; (b) infection with a sexually transmitted disease, leprosy or the plague; (c) misconduct or mismanagement in business trade, profession or office; or (d) unchastity (if the victim is a female).

(3) Libels *per se* in all jurisdictions and libels *per quod* in a minority of jurisdictions are actionable without the need for special damages.

(4) Libels *per quod* in a majority of jurisdictions are now actionable only with a showing of special damages unless they fall into one or more of the four special categories established originally for slander.

B. *Damages: The Central Remedy for Defamation*

Once the plaintiff has established his cause of action, and assuming the defendant has not interposed any valid defenses (discussed below), the focus of the defamation suit shifts from the question of liability to the question of remedies available to the defamed person. The central remedy at common law for injury to reputation is, of course, the award of monetary damages.[31]

---

28. *See* Morrison v. Ritchie & Co. [1902] 4 Fraser, Sess. Cas. 645, 39 Scot. L. Rep. 432.

29. RESTATEMENT SECOND OF TORTS § 569; Cmt. *b* (1977).

30. WILLIAM L. PROSSER, TORTS 763 (4th ed. 1971). A review of the cases cited by Dean Prosser supports his position. Moreover, the presumption of damage required for libel *per se* is now constitutionally suspect as to libelous media communications regarding private persons not made with "actual malice" as defined in New York Times v. Sullivan, 376 U.S. 254, 84 S.Ct.

710, 11 L.Ed.2d 686 (1964). "[T]he private defamation plaintiff who establishes liability under a less demanding standard than that stated by *New York Times* ['actual malice'] may recover only such damages as are sufficient to compensate him for actual injury." Gertz v. Robert Welch, Inc., 418 U.S. 323, 350, 94 S.Ct. 2997, 3012, 41 L.Ed.2d 789, 811 (1974).

31. *See* 2 DAN B. DOBBS, LAW OF REMEDIES: DAMAGES—EQUITY—RESTITUTION 265–70 (2d ed. 1993).

1. Special Damages

We have already seen that in cases of libel *per quod* in a majority of jurisdictions and in cases of slander, excluding the four special categories, proof of special damages is necessary for liability. Of course, such damages may be established in *any* defamation action. These damages require rather specific pleading and proof by the plaintiff of pecuniary or economic loss actually resulting from the defamatory communication and reasonable foreseeability of the plaintiff's loss by the defendant.[32] Obvious cases are the loss of one's employment, the loss of opportunity for business profits, impaired credit rating and the cost of therapy to deal with the mental and emotional injury from the defamation.

2. General Damages

The existence of special damages may influence the jury's award of general damages. These are damages awarded for actual losses to the plaintiff for such injuries as hurt feelings, embarrassment, mental and emotional distress and physical consequences. Special damages are not a prerequisite for the recovery of general damages unless the action is for a type of defamatory tort requiring the showing of special damages as part of the plaintiff's prima facie case.

Many factors may be considered by the finder of fact in attempting to determine reasonable and appropriate general damages. These are catalogued by Professor Dan B. Dobbs, a leading authority on remedies as including (1) the nature of the defamation (*e.g.*, irrational name calling or insinuation of serious wrongdoing); (2) the form and permanency of the communication; (3) the breadth of dissemination; (4) the degree to which the defamatory communication is believed; (5) the nature of the plaintiff's reputation; (6) in certain cases, the good faith of the defendant in publishing the defamatory matter; and (7) the defendant's subsequent conduct in retracting the complained of communication or in making apology.[33]

3. Punitive Damages

If spite, ill will or evil motive is present, the jury will be instructed that it may, but need not, award the plaintiff punitive damages. As the term implies, such damages are designed to punish the defamer and are not compensatory in nature. If such damages are to make the defendant "smart" for his tortious conduct and deter such conduct in the future, the jury is entitled to know the defendant's net work and to reduce it to where it hurts. Until very recently there were no Fifth Amendment guidelines controlling the award of punitive damages in tort actions. But finally in 1996, an egregious award in a case of fraud in the sale of an ostensibly new automobile led the Supreme Court to lay down three guideposts for triers of fact in imposing punitive damages.[34] They must

32. *See id*. 268–270, 292–295, 294–295.

33. *See* Dan B. Dobbs, Law of Remedies: Damages—Equity—Restitution   514–519 (1973).

34. BMW of North America, Inc. v. Gore, 517 U.S. 559, 116 S.Ct. 1589, 134 L.Ed.2d 809 (1996).

now give consideration to (1) the degree of reprehensibility of the defendant's conduct; (2) the ratio between the compensatory damages awarded and the punitive damages contemplated; and (3) the difference between the contemplated punitive damages and the civil or criminal sanctions which could be imposed for comparable misconduct.[35]

While the Supreme Court's ruling on punitive damages came in a case involving statutory fraud or deceit, the guideposts set out appear to have broad applicability and there is little doubt they will be applied in future defamation cases.

C. The Common Law Defenses

Once the plaintiff has provided sufficient evidence of the elements necessary to establish the prima facie case of defamation, the defendant is, of course, put to his defense. he may, of course, deny one or more aspects of the plaintiff's case such as the defamatory nature of the communication or that it was directed at the particular plaintiff. In addition or alternatively, he may attempt to establish one or more of the complete common law defenses of truth or privilege. In resorting to these defenses, the defendant accepts the burden of pleading them in his answer and proving them at trial by a preponderance of the evidence.[36]

1. Truth

Although British common law in the American colonies held that "the greater the truth the greater the libel," in criminal libel cases involving criticism of a public official,[37] even British common law respected truth as a defense in civil actions for defamation.[38]

But the defense of truth is not an easy one. Knowing something to be true and proving it in a court of law are two different things. In many situations only the plaintiff will have access to the necessary proof and, understandably, will not make it easy for the defendant to establish the defense.

Moreover, the defense must necessarily be as broad in its reach as the communication complained of. The defense will fail if only a portion of the allegation is verified. For example, a newspaper's charge that X is an habitual vice law offender is not justified by the paper establishing one conviction of X for a gambling violation. And a statement that a reliable source has informed the communicator that X is guilty of tax evasion is not justified by establishing that someone informed the defendant about X's conduct and that someone is a reliable source. The truth of the substantive charge itself must be established even though the defendant was not its originator.

35. *Id.* at 573–583, 116 S. Ct. at 1598–1603, 134 L. Ed. 2d at 826–832.

36. *See* McCORMICK, EVIDENCE 272 (4th Ed. 1992).

37. *See, e.g.,* Savannah News–Press, Inc. v. Hartridge, 138 S.E.2d 173, 176, 110 Ga.App. 203, 207 (Ga.Ct.App.1964).

38. *See* 2 BLACKSTONE, COMMENTARIES ON THE COMMON LAW OF ENGLAND 124–25 (2d ed. rev. 1876).

But this does not mean that defendants have to verify every detail of their communications. The defense of truth will be successful if the substance of the communications is established. An individual who publicly accuses his neighbor of embezzling $1,500 from the neighborhood homeowners association will escape liability by proving embezzlement of $150, for example.

2. Privilege

As with most intentional torts, the common law recognizes the defense of privilege in certain cases of defamation. Despite the fact that plaintiff suffers harm to his reputation, the defamer may be shielded from liability because the law accords supremacy to the conflicting interest of defendants in communicating the defamatory material, or of third persons in receiving the communication or of the public generally in encouraging free expression of matters of general concern. The defense, which is relatively narrow in scope, is divided into two categories depending on the parties involved and the circumstances: the absolute privilege to defame and the qualified one.

a. The absolute privilege

One who possesses an absolute privilege to defame or, perhaps more precisely, an absolute immunity from suit is not required to establish his or her good faith in making the defamatory communication.[39] Motivation is immaterial. The public proceedings in which the absolute privilege is available are divided into the legislative, judicial, executive and administrative. All who speak in a legislative forum—United States Congressmen and Senators, state house lawmakers, city and county council members—enjoy an absolute privilege to speak without fear of being sued for libel. But the comments must be made in the legislative forum.

The Supreme Court has ruled that although a senator's speech on the floor of the Senate is completely immune from a suit for libel, newsletters and press releases about such speech issued from a Senator's office are not immune because they are not essential to the deliberations of the legislature. In *Hutchinson v. Proxmire*,[40] then Senator William Proxmire of Wisconsin was famous for publicizing wasteful federal government spending by awarding the "Golden Fleece of the Month Award." In this particular case he made the award to federal agencies that had funded the plaintiff's study of emotional behavior by focusing on the aggressive behavior patterns of certain animals, particularly primates.

The award was announced in a speech given on the floor of the Senate and incorporated in a widely disseminated press release. Later, the award was also referred to in newsletters mailed by the senator, in a

---

39. *See, e.g.,* Briscoe v. LaHue, 460 U.S. 325, 331–32, 103 S.Ct. 1108, 1113–14, 75 L.Ed.2d 96, 105 (1983); ROBERT D. SACK AND SANDRA S. BARON, LIBEL, SLANDER, AND RELATED PROBLEMS 412 (2d ed. 1994); RODNEY A. SMOLLA, LAW OF DEFAMATION § 8.01[2] (1993).

40. 443 U.S. 111, 99 S.Ct. 2675, 61 L.Ed.2d 411 (1979).

television interview and in telephone calls made by the Senator's legislative assistant. In the speech, Proxmire, in referring to the research of the plaintiff, Dr. Ronald R. Hutchinson, then director of research at the Kalamazoo State Mental Hospital, said, "The funding of this nonsense makes me almost angry enough to scream and kick or even clench my jaw. It seems to me it is outrageous.... [i]t is time for the Federal Government to get out of this 'monkey business.' In view of the transparent worthlessness of Hutchinson's study of jaw-grinding and biting by angry or hard-drinking monkeys, it is time we put a stop to the bite Hutchinson and the bureaucrats who fund him have been taking [out] of the taxpayer."[41]

A better example of business or professional libel would be hard to find, and Dr. Hutchinson filed suit against Proxmire and his legislative assistant in the United States District Court for Wisconsin. The defendants responded with motions for change of venue and summary judgment, with the summary judgment motion based on the claim, *inter alia*, that all their acts and utterances were protected by the Speech and Debate Clause of the Constitution. Without ruling on venue, the district court concluded that the investigations and the speech were covered by the Speech or Debate Clause affording absolute immunity from civil liability. As for the press releases and other media disseminations, the district court concluded that the defendants were protected by the First Amendment. The United States Court of Appeals for the Seventh Circuit affirmed.

On certiorari the Supreme Court reversed and remanded, holding that the Speech or Debate Clause did not confer immunity for the Senator's defamatory activities related to the "Golden Fleece" speech engaged in outside the legislative chamber. "A speech by Proxmire in the Senate would be wholly immune and would be available to other Members of Congress and the public in the Congressional Record. But neither the newsletters nor the press release was 'essential to the deliberations of the Senate' and neither was part of the deliberative process."[42]

Thus, had the Senator limited himself to speaking about Dr. Hutchinson's research on the floor of the Senate and then merely calling attention to where in the Congressional Record the media might find his latest "Golden Fleece Award" presentation no civil liability would likely have attached.

The absolute privilege is also conferred on all communications in judicial forums such as courtrooms and grand jury rooms.[43] Judges,

---

41. *Id.* at 116, 99 S. Ct. at 2678–79, 61 L. Ed. 2d at 419; 121 Cong. Rec. 10803 (1975).

42. *Id.* at 130, 99 S. Ct. at 2686, 61 L. Ed. 2d at 428. The Court also ruled that the post-speech publicity generated by Proxmire and his legislative assistant was not protected by any First Amendment privilege.

43. Buckley v. Fitzsimmons, 509 U.S. 259, 271–72, 113 S.Ct. 2606, 2615, 125 L.Ed.2d 209, 225 (1993); Briscoe v. LaHue, 460 U.S. 325, 335–36, 103 S.Ct. 1108, 1115–16, 75 L.Ed.2d 96, 107–08 (1983); Imbler v. Pachtman, 424 U.S. 409, 426 n. 23, 96 S.Ct. 984, 993 n. 23, 47 L.Ed.2d 128, 141 n. 23 (1976); Ball Corp. v. Xidex Corp. 967 F.2d 1440, 1444 (10th Cir.1992); General Elec.

lawyers, witnesses, defendants and plaintiffs are immune from defamation actions provided their remarks occur during the official portions of a judicial proceeding such as pretrial discovery or trial and are relevant.[44]

Finally, people who work in the executive and administrative branches of government—presidents, governors, mayors, heads of government agencies—may also enjoy absolute immunity from civil suit for their official communications or statements. For example, in *Barr v. Matteo*,[45] a department head distributed a press release explaining why two federal employees had been fired. The fired individuals sued. In its decision rejecting liability of the government officer, the Supreme Court accorded government officials an absolute privilege to make defamatory statements within the bounds of their offices.

The reason for the absolute privilege of government officers are clear: if such persons are forced to analyze their remarks for defamatory content and strict legal relevance and to worry about the consequences if they act erroneously, their fearlessness and independence may be impaired and their actions on the public's behalf inhibited.

The one other universally recognized absolute privilege involves communications between husbands and wives. This one is accorded by society for the obvious reasons of insuring free communication between spouses, a necessary element in a healthy marital relationship and protecting their marital privacy.[46]

b.   The qualified privilege

In contrast to absolute privilege discussed above, the qualified privilege to communicate defamatory matter can be defeated by the plaintiff establishing malice on the part of the defendant communicator.[47] This entails the plaintiff proving that the complained of communication was motivated chiefly by some consideration other than furthering the interest for which the law accords the privilege in the first

Co. v. Sargent & Lundy, 916 F.2d 1119, 1125–26 (6th Cir.1990); Green Acres Trust v. London, 141 Ariz. 609, 612–14, 688 P.2d 617 620–22, (1984); Moore v. Conliffe, 7 Cal.4th 634, 649–50, 29 Cal.Rptr.2d 152, 161, 871 P.2d 204, 213–14 (1994) (construction of California Civil Code); Overman v. Klein, 103 Idaho 795, 796–800, 654 P.2d 888, 892–93, (1982).

44. Briscoe v. LaHue, 460 U.S. 325, 332, 103 S.Ct. 1108, 1114, 75 L.Ed.2d 96, 105 (1983); Buckley v. Fitzsimmons, 509 U.S. at 277 n. 8, 113 S.Ct. at 2618 n. 8, 125 L.Ed.2d at 229, n. 8; Imbler v. Pachtman, 424 U.S. at 426 n. 23, 96 S. Ct. at 993 n. 23, 47 L. Ed. 2d at 141 n.23; Ball Corp. v. Xidex Corp. 967 F.2d at 1444; General Elec. Co. v. Sargent & Lundy, 916 F.2d at 1125–27; Green Acres Trust v. London, 141 Ariz. at 613, 688 P.2d at 621; Overman v. Klein, 103 Idaho at 799, 654 P.2d at 892; Massen-

gale v. Lester, 403 S.W.2d 697 (Ky.1966), cert. denied, 385 U.S. 1019, 87 S.Ct. 747, 17 L.Ed.2d 556 (1967); Bailey v. Superior Court, 130 Ariz. 366, 636 P.2d 144, 146, (Ariz.Ct.App.1981); Moore v. Conliffe, 7 Cal. 4th at 649–50, 29 Cal.Rptr.2d at 161, 871 P.2d at 213.

45. 360 U.S. 564, 79 S.Ct. 1335, 3 L.Ed.2d 1434 (1959).

46. *See* McCormick, Evidence, 309–12 (West 4th Ed. 1992); 8 Wigmore, Evidence §§ 2228 (McNaughton Rev. 1961).

47. *See, e.g.,* McDonald v. Smith, 472 U.S. 479, 485, 105 S.Ct. 2787, 2791, 86 L.Ed.2d 384, 390 (1985); Catrone v. Thoroughbred Racing Ass'ns of North America, Inc., 929 F.2d 881, 889 (1st Cir.1991); Galvin v. New York, New Haven & Hartford Railroad Co., 341 Mass. 293, 296–297, 168 N.E.2d 262, 265–266 (1960).

place.[48] The law's recognition of this lesser privilege reflects the idea that some interests competing with that of reputation, while not as compelling as those which justify an absolute privilege or immunity for the communicator, are still sufficiently important to justify a lesser degree of protection. For example, there is a qualified privilege for an employer to comment on an employee's performance to someone requesting a reference for an employee, for communications to employers regarding employees' conduct toward customers and for company officials to tell employees that former employees were terminated because of theft of company property.[49] And there is a qualified privilege for bank officers to complain of forgery by customers to police officers.[50]

In the case of the media, the interests supporting the existence of the qualified privilege in reporting the proceedings of government and some private institutions and organizations are those of public oversight of governmental activity and legitimate public desire for information about matters affecting the public generally or a substantial segment thereof. And even when the oversight function is not involved, the public may have some legitimate interest in being informed of public proceedings of both governmental and private organizations in order to prepare for or guard against the consequences of those proceedings.

(1) Limitations on the scope of the privilege

The courts have placed certain limitations on the scope or availability of the privilege to the media in reporting on public proceedings. A majority of courts, for instance, led by Massachusetts[51] take the position that the privilege does not extend to reporting allegations or statements contained in complaints, affidavits or other pretrial papers unless and until such papers are brought before a judge or magistrate, the rationale being the prevention of scurrilous and defamatory matter being placed before the public with impunity and before it can be struck, if necessary, by a judicial officer. Thus, reporters must be alert to the law of their jurisdictions and must, in a majority of those jurisdictions, be wary of the content of court papers simply filled with the clerk of court and served but not yet acted upon by a judge or other judicial officer vested with discretionary authority.

The minority view, exemplified by New York,[52] is that the report of the contents of papers filed and served on the requisite parties are

---

48. See, e.g., Catrone v. Thoroughbred Racing Ass'ns of North America, 929 F.2d at 890; Roland v. d'Arazien, 685 F.2d 653, 655, 222 U.S. App. D.C. 203, 205 (D.C.Cir. 1982); Sheehan v. Tobin, 326 Mass. 185, 190–91, 93 N.E.2d 524, 527–28 (1950).

49. See, e.g., Garziano v. E.I. DuPont De Nemours & Co., 818 F.2d 380, 386–87 (5th Cir.1987); Tacket v. Delco Remy Div., 678 F.Supp. 1387, 1396 (S.D.Ind.1987), aff'd in part, rev'd in part, 836 F.2d 1042 (7th Cir.1987); Gonzalez v. Avon Products, Inc., 609 F.Supp. 1555 (D.Del.1985); Battista v. Chrysler Corp., 454 A.2d 286, 291–92

(Del.Super.Ct.1982); Torosyan v. Boehringer Ingelheim Pharmaceuticals, Inc., 234 Conn. 1, 28, 662 A.2d 89, 103 (1995). Compare Barr v. Matteo, 360 U.S. 564, 79 S.Ct. 1335, 3 L.Ed.2d 1434 (1959).

50. See Newark Trust Co. v. Bruwer, 51 Del. 188, 141 A.2d 615 (1958).

51. See Sanford v. Boston Herald–Traveler Corp., 318 Mass. 156, 61 N.E.2d 5 (1945).

52. See Campbell v. New York Evening Post, Inc., 245 N.Y. 320, 157 N.E. 153 (1927).

generally privileged, the rationale being that the filing and serving of pleadings and other papers authorized by the rules of the court are public and officials acts to which the public is entitled to be privy.

Reports of the activities of executive officers or administrative agencies are generally not privileged until the officer or agency has taken some definite action, such as a district attorney filing a criminal information or obtaining an indictment.[53] Th internal report of a district attorney would not be privileged in most jurisdictions. Police proceedings are especially dangerous for the newsperson to report because of the significant variations from state to state regarding the point at which the qualified privilege attaches. The status of the police blotter, record of arrests and charges and oral reports of police officers concerning their preliminary investigations has varied widely from jurisdiction to jurisdiction, but the recent trend is to declare them privileged.[54]

With regard to the legislative process, so long as the particular proceeding reported upon is authorized by the legislature, the report itself will be privileged, assuming conformity with the following criteria.

(2) General requirements of the privilege

First, proceedings must normally be public in nature unless a statute provides otherwise.[55] Thus, an investigative hearing such as "Iran—Contra" is privileged and defamatory material uttered by witnesses might be repeated by the newsmedia to inform the public without liability while the transcript of a legislative committee meeting held in executive session might not.

Second, the report of a public proceeding must be fair and accurate and motivated by the reporter's duty simply to make disclosure to those receiving his report.[56] The privilege is forfeited if it is held to be either an unfair or an inaccurate account of the portion of the proceeding covered.[57] The report need not be verbatim, but condensation, abridgment or paraphrasing must fairly and accurately reflect what transpired. An

---

53. *See, e.g.*, Phillips v. The Evening Star Newspaper Co., 424 A.2d 78, 88 (D.C. 1980) (by implication), cert. denied, 451 U.S. 989, 101 S.Ct. 2327, 68 L.Ed.2d 848 (1981); Village of Grafton v. American Broadcasting Co., 70 Ohio App.2d 205, 213, 435 N.E.2d 1131, 1136–37 (Ohio App.1980).

54. *See* DAVID A. ELDER, THE FAIR REPORT PRIVILEGE § 1.08 (1988).

55. Exceptions to the "public proceeding" requirement are occasionally recognized as in Coleman v. Newark Morning Ledger Co., 29 N.J. 357, 149 A.2d 193 (1959). There, the defendant newspaper published a fair and accurate report of Senator Joseph McCarthy's press conference summarizing the secret proceedings of his subcommittee's investigation into alleged communist activity at Fort Monmouth, New Jersey. The story was held to be privileged despite the fact pointed out in the dissenting opinion that there was no verification that the senator's press conference report of the secret legislative proceeding was itself fair and accurate. Such exceptions are rare. The public proceeding requirement and others are discussed in DAVID A. ELDER, THE FAIR REPORT PRIVILEGE §§ 1.01–1.26 (1988).

56. *See, e.g.*, Coleman v. Newark Morning Ledger Co., 29 N.J. 357, 377–83, 149 A.2d 193, 204–06 (1959).

57. *See, e.g.*, Schiavone Constr. Co. v. Time, Inc., 847 F.2d 1069, 1088 (3d Cir. 1988); Costello v. Ocean County Observer, 136 N.J. 594, 610–11, 643 A.2d 1012, 1020 (1994); McBurney v. Times Publishing Co., 93 R.I. 331, 341–42, 175 A.2d 170, 176, (1961); Express Publishing Co. v. Gonzalez, 326 S.W.2d 544, 547 (Tex.Civ.App.1959).

erroneous detail will not destroy the privilege so long as it does not affect the essential accuracy and fairness of the report. In contrast, a report may be literally accurate so far as it goes and yet unfairly and inaccurately portray the plaintiff's involvement in them because the report ends at a critical point or it omits important facts favorable to the plaintiff.

Third, if the defamatory report of a proceeding is made chiefly for a motive other than to inform those who have a need to know about that proceeding, the publication will be considered malicious and the privilege will be destroyed.[58] A fair and accurate account of a public proceeding containing defamatory matter communicated by one friend to another at a cocktail party during idle conversation would likely be considered malicious because the proper motivation for making such an account is missing. More clearly, the privilege will not obtain if the communication is motivated mainly by some selfish objective of the reporter or publisher such as enhancing the chance for a Pulitzer Price or furthering financial interests at the expense of a competitor who is unfavorably referred to in the public proceeding. But proving this will be extremely difficult.

3. Fair Comment

As traditionally viewed, common law fair comment involved the honest expression of the communicator's opinion on a matter of public interest based upon facts correctly stated in the communication or underlying it.[59] Such expression had to be free of speculation as to the motivation of the person whose public conduct is the subject of the criticism.[60] Chief among the unique characteristics of this defense are (1) its emphasis on opinion based on facts rather than the reporting of the facts themselves and (2) its broad scope, *i.e.*, permitting comment on all matters of public interest rather than simply proceedings of a public nature.[61] It is these characteristics of the privilege which made possible,

---

58. *See, e.g.,* Lavin v. New York News, Inc., 757 F.2d 1416–21 (3d Cir.1985); Mastandrea v. Lorain Journal Co., 65 Ohio App.3d 221, 233, 583 N.E.2d 984, 992 (Ohio App.1989), cert. denied, 498 U.S. 822, 111 S.Ct. 73, 112 L.Ed.2d 46 (1990); Molnar v. Star–Ledger, 193 N.J.Super. 12, 21, 471 A.2d 1209, 1214 (N.J.Super.1984). The privilege to publish an accurate and fair report of defamation is lost when the publication is made "solely for the purpose of causing harm to the person defamed." RESTATEMENT OF TORTS § 611 (1938). The modern view, however, has shifted away from the search for malice primarily as a result of the publication of the Restatement Second of Torts. The Second Restatement eliminates the element of malice and only requires that the report be fair and accurate. Some jurisdictions have adopted this new approach. *See* Rosenberg v. Helinski, 328 Md. 664, 677–78, 616 A.2d 866, 872–73, (1992), cert. denied 509 U.S. 924, 113 S.Ct.

3041, 125 L.Ed.2d 727 (1993); Read v. News–Journal, Co., 474 A.2d 119, 120–21 (Del.1984); Shafer v. Lamar Publishing Co., Inc., 621 S.W.2d 709, 713 (Mo.Ct.App.1981). *See also* ROBERT D. SACK & SANDRA BARON, LIBEL, SLANDER AND RELATED PROBLEMS 370–72 (2d ed. 1994).

59. *See, e.g.,* Milkovich v. Lorain Journal Co., 497 U.S. 1, 13–14, 110 S.Ct. 2695, 2703, 111 L.Ed.2d 1, 14 (1990); ROBERT D. SACK AND SANDRA S. BARON, LIBEL, SLANDER AND RELATED PROBLEMS 235–237 (2d ed. 1994); BRUCE W. SANFORD, LIBEL, AND PRIVACY § 5.2 (2d ed. 1993); RODNEY A. SMOLLA, LAW OF DEFAMATION §§ 6.02 [1]-[3] (1986).

60. *See, e.g.,* Foley v. Press Pub. Co., 226 App.Div. 535, 235 N.Y.S. 340 (App. Div. 1929).

61. *See* RESTATEMENT (SECOND) OF TORTS § 566, Comment *a* (1977); ROBERT D. SACK & SANDRA S. BARON, LIBEL, SLANDER

for instance, political, artistic and culinary criticism of those submitting themselves or their work for public approval before the advent of *New York Times v. Sullivan*.[62]

The courts traditionally gave broad meaning to the fair comment defense. Commentaries containing exaggeration, illogic, sarcasm, ridicule and even viciousness were protected if at all justified by the underlying facts. The classic example is the criticism leveled at the Cherry Sisters' vaudeville act by a now forgotten newspaper drama critic. "Effie is an old jade of 50 summers, Jessie a frisky filly of 40, and Addie, the flower of the family, a capering monstrosity of 35. Their long skinny arms, equipped with talons at the extremities, swung mechanically, and waved frantically at the suffering audience. The mouths of their rancid features opened like caverns, and sounds like the wailings of damned souls issued therefrom.... " The sisters, as might be expected, were not amused and sued for libel. In affirming a directed verdict for the newspaper, the Iowa Supreme Court held that the editor of a newspaper had the right, if not the duty, to publish, without malice, fair and reasonable comments, however, severe, about anything which is presented for the public's consideration by the complaining parties.[63] The great breadth of the privilege is clear from the Iowa court's opinion.

As the court noted, malice, if shown by the complaining party, would negate the defense but it cannot be inferred from the words chosen by the commentator. Malice can be found only from an examination of the commentator's motives in publishing.[64] The defense is also negated in a majority of jurisdictions if the comment or opinion is based on a major error of underlying fact as was noted in *Milkovich v. Lorain Journal Company*.[65] This privilege was largely eclipsed by the constitutional

---

AND RELATED PROBLEMS 234–42 (2d ed. 1994); WILLIAM A. PROSSER & W. PAGE KEETON, TORTS 831–32 (5th ed. 1984).

62. 376 U.S. 254, 84 S.Ct. 710, 11 L.Ed.2d 686 (1964).

63. Cherry v. Des Moines Leader, 114 Iowa 298, 86 N.W. 323 (1901).

64. *See, e.g.,* Potts v. Dies, 132 F.2d 734, 735, 77 U.S. App. D.C. 92, 93 (D.C.Cir. 1942), cert. denied, 319 U.S. 762, 63 S.Ct. 1316, 87 L.Ed. 1713 (1943); Beauharnais v. Pittsburgh Courier Pub. Co., 243 F.2d 705, 708 (7th Cir.1957).

65. Milkovich v. Lorain Journal Co., 497 U.S. 1, 18–19, 110 S.Ct. 2695, 2705–06, 111 L.Ed.2d 1, 17–18 (1990). *See* Phillips v. Evening Star Newspaper Co., 424 A.2d 78, 88 (D.C.1980), cert. denied 451 U.S. 989, 101 S.Ct. 2327, 68 L.Ed.2d 848.

The fair comment privilege experienced a turbulent period as a result of a passage in Gertz v. Robert Welch, Inc., 418 U.S. 323, 94 S.Ct. 2997, 41 L.Ed.2d 789 (1974), which said, "[U]nder the First Amendment there is no such thing as a false idea." Id. at 339–

40, 94 S. Ct. at 3007, 41 L. Ed. 2d at 805. As interpreted by the lower courts, this statement seemed to extend an absolute privilege to opinion. The Supreme Court ended this trend in Milkovich v. Lorain Journal Co., 497 U.S. 1, 110 S.Ct. 2695, 111 L.Ed.2d 1 (1990) when it stated that the *Gertz* passage "was [not] intended to create a wholesale defamation exemption for anything that might be labeled 'opinion'." *Id.* at 18, 110 S. Ct. at 2705, 111 L. Ed. 2d at 17. Presently, a defendant has two options in a defamation action based on unwelcome opinion. If the plaintiff is a public official or figure, then the *New York Times* "actual malice" constitutional standard may be relied on. If the plaintiff is a private individual and the actual malice standard is not available, then the common law fair comment privilege may be relied on by the defendant. The common law privilege can be defeated either by a showing that the facts expressed in the opinion are incorrect or that the opinion is based on erroneous underlying facts. If the opinion can be described as "pure" (meaning unrelated to

privilege recognized in *New York Times v. Sullivan* but perhaps resurrected to some as yet unknown degree in *Milkovich*, discussed below.

4. Incomplete Defenses

Certain defenses to defamation actions are labeled "incomplete" because they do not bar liability even if successful but only reduce the amount of damages recoverable by the plaintiff. Chief among them is retraction. If the defamer publishes a retraction punctually and with essentially the same prominence as was given the original defamatory communication, the potential for punitive damages is negated[66] and compensatory damages may be reduced.[67]

It should be emphasized that the retraction must be complete and unequivocal. Less than full retraction or a veiled continuance of the defamation will not mitigate damages but, in fact, may even increase them because of the repetition. It is not effective to state that "John Doe hasn't the morals of a tom cat" and then agree to "retract" by stating that "John Doe does have the morals of a tom cat." It should also be noted that the availability of the partial defense, the effects of retraction and the consequences of a refusal to retract are governed in a number of states such as California by statute.[68] The California statute figured prominently in a celebrated libel suit brought by comedienne and actress Carol Burnett against the National Enquirer.[69] The statute by its term applies to and provides partial protection for newspapers. In *Burnett* the trial court ruled that the National Enquirer was a magazine and thus, although it had published a retraction of the libelous material, it was not protected against the imposition of punitive damages.[70]

Somewhat akin to retraction is the idea of allowing defamed parties the right to reply to personal attacks. The voluntary agreement by media defamers to allow use of their facilities by victims to make reply does not necessarily establish the defamer's good faith and punitive damages remains a possibility.[71] But the actual injury to the defamed party may

---

any facts) then there is no recourse for the individual plaintiff no matter how malicious the opinion.

66. *See, e.g.*, Simonson v. United Press Int'l., Inc., 500 F.Supp. 1261, 1265 (E.D.Wis.1980), *aff'd* 654 F.2d 478 (7th Cir. 1981); Hinerman v. Daily Gazette Co., Inc., 188 W.Va. 157, 177, 423 S.E.2d 560, 580 (1992), cert. denied, 507 U.S. 960, 113 S.Ct. 1384, 122 L.Ed.2d 759 (1993) (common law retraction rule); Bock v. Plainfield Courier–News, 45 N.J.Super. 302, 310–11, 132 A.2d 523, 527–28 (N.J.Super.1957); 2 Dan B. Dobbs, Law of Remedies: Damages—Equity—Restitution, 290 (2d ed. 1993).

67. *See, e.g.*, Simonson v. United Press Intern., Inc., 500 F. Supp. at 1265, *aff'd* 654 F.2d 478 (7th Cir.1981); Webb v. Call Pub.

Co., 173 Wis. 45, 50–52, 180 N.W. 263, 264–65 (1920); 2 Dan B. Dobbs, Law of Remedies: Damages—Equity—Restitution at 290.

68. Cal. Civ. Code § 482 (West 1982). *See also, e.g.*, Ga. Code Ann. §§ 51–5–11 through 51–5–12 (1982 & Supp. 1995); Mass. Gen. Laws Ann. Ch. 231, § 93 (West 1985); N.J. Stat. Ann. 2A:43–2 (West 1987).

69. Burnett v. National Enquirer, Inc., 144 Cal.App.3d 991, 1000–05, 193 Cal.Rptr. 206, 210–14 (Cal.App.1983), appeal dismissed 465 U.S. 1014, 104 S.Ct. 1260, 79 L.Ed.2d 668 (1984).

70. 144 Cal. App. at 1004–05, 193 Cal. Rptr. at 213–14.

71. *See, e.g.*, Laurence H. Eldredge, The Law of Defamation 297–99 (1978).

be reduced because of the opportunity afforded to reach and favorably influence those whose good opinion of the victim has been affected.[72] Thus, voluntary action by defamers to allow their victims to respond may be rewarded by lesser damage awards, but any effort by government to mandate the right of reply, at least insofar as the print media are concerned, would be violative of the First Amendment.[73]

5.   Epilogue to the common law of defamation

The summary discussion of common law defamation is now concluded. This law is, in many respects, quite favorable to the defamed party's interest in reputation. Witness, for instance, its theory of strict liability. Conversely, this law imposes many restrictions upon and risks for those who seek to exercise their right of free expression under the First Amendment. Damage awards by juries in libel cases of millions of dollars against media defendants have become common and the costs to media defendants in defending against such suits may also run in the millions. Brown & Williamson Tobacco Company was awarded three million dollars in damages against CBS in 1987 and that award was upheld on appeal.[74] And entertainer Wayne Newton won a $19.3 million damage award against NBC in 1986 after the network broadcast a story linking him with organized crime. Fortunately for NBC, the United States Court of Appeals for the Ninth Circuit overturned the verdict and dismissed the case.[75] But even when the media win these cases, the expense of defending against them is very great. ABC allegedly spent seven million dollars defending itself against a series of actions brought by Synanon, and it cost CBS millions to defend itself against General William Westmoreland's libel action.[76]

The common law principles that have been considered in this section are still applicable to communications that do not involve public officials and public figures or matters of public concern, and in part to communications which do. They are thus worthy of continued discussion but the very serious question is raised whether the application of all aspects of the common law of defamation to the news and information media is consistent with the guarantees of the First Amendment. That question is addressed in the following sections of this chapter.

72. *Id.*

73. *See* Miami Herald Pub. Co. v. Tornillo, 418 U.S. 241, 94 S.Ct. 2831, 41 L.Ed.2d 730 (1974); RODNEY A. SMOLLA, LAW OF DEFAMATION § 9.13[2][a] (1986). At this time, it is not clear whether the distinction the Supreme Court once made between the print media and the broadcast media regarding governmentally mandated right of reply in Red Lion Broadcasting Co. v. F.C.C., 395 U.S. 367, 89 S.Ct. 1794, 23 L.Ed.2d 371 (1969) still exists. See the discussion of the "Fairness Doctrine" *infra*, chapter 14, section 14.5.B.4.

74. Brown & Williamson Tobacco Corp. v. Jacobson, 827 F.2d 1119 (7th Cir.1987).

75. Newton v. National Broadcasting Co., Inc., 930 F.2d 662 (9th Cir.1990), cert. denied, 502 U.S. 866, 112 S.Ct. 192, 116 L.Ed.2d 152 (1991).

76. Westmoreland v. Columbia Broadcasting Sys., Inc., 752 F.2d 16 (2d Cir.1984), cert. denied, 472 U.S. 1017, 105 S.Ct. 3478, 87 L.Ed.2d 614 (1985).

5.3 The Constitutionalization of Defamation Law

A. *The Landmark Decision of New York Times v. Sullivan*

1. *Moral and Political Imperatives for Constitutionalization*

New York Times v. Sullivan,[1] the case that constitutionalized defamation law at least so far as the news and information media are concerned, arose out of the turbulence of the civil rights struggle in the South in the 1950s and 1960s.[2] The suit against the New York Times can be viewed as a shot across the bow of the national news media that were covering the civil rights movement and bringing into America's living rooms daily the brutality of water cannons, tear gas, attack dogs and other devices employed by the southern white establishment against the mostly black demonstrators.

The ultimate success of the civil rights movement was due in no small part to the courage of southern white federal judges in making unpopular rulings supporting civil rights and the national media whose continuing coverage created a demand by a revulsed public that the federal government act forcefully to guaranty civil rights for everyone in the states of the former Confederacy.

But this victory for civil rights might never have been achieved if Montgomery, Alabama Public Affairs (Police) Commissioner L. B. Sullivan's libel suit against the New York Times Company had succeeded. The Times of the 1960s was not the financially strong media giant it is today. While the company might have been able to withstand the $500,000 judgement brought in by an all white Alabama jury, there is some doubt it could have survived another $2,500,000 in libel damages claimed by other individuals in pending related suits.[3] As it was, the litigation forced the Times to suspend distribution of the paper in Alabama for a time. Moreover, had Sullivan prevailed, his court victory would have sent a strong message to other media that they had better be very careful and cautious in reporting on the civil rights struggle. The common law of libel favored Sullivan and new law would have to be fashioned to prevent his victory—with all of the dangerous implications for a free press that would have arisen from it.

2. *Facts of the Case*

A civil rights group, Committee To Defend Martin Luther King and the Struggle for Freedom In The South, bought a full page fund-raising

---

1. 376 U.S. 254, 84 S.Ct. 710, 11 L.Ed.2d 686 (1964).

2. See BRUCE W. SANFORD, LIBEL AND PRIVACY § 7.2 (2d ed. 1991); *The Civil Rights Struggle: A Historic Movement That Spawned New York Times Co. v. Sullivan*, 2 ABA Communications Lawyer 21 (No. 3, Summer 1984) (compilation of photographs of scenes from the battle); Kermit Hall, Keynote Address at First Annual Symposium of the Constitutional Law Resource Center at Drake University Law School, New York Times v. Sullivan: *The Case and Its Times*, published in VALUES IN CONFLICT— TWENTY-FIVE YEARS AFTER NEW YORK TIMES V. SULLIVAN 22–36 (1990) (a detailed account of the civil rights context of the case).

3. New York Times, 376 U.S. at 278 n. 18, 84 S. Ct. at 725 n. 18, 11 L. Ed. 2d at 705 n.18.

advertisement in the New York Times entitled "Heed Their Rising Voices." The ad stated that non-violent demonstrations, seeking to live in human dignity as guaranteed by the Constitution and the Bill of rights, were being met by "an unprecedented wave of terror by those who would deny and negate that document. . . . "[4] Succeeding paragraphs represented the "wave of terror" by describing certain alleged events. The allegations that raised Commissioner Sullivan's ire and caused him to sue the Times for libel were the following:

> "In Montgomery, Alabama, after students sang 'My Country, Tis of Thee' on the State Capitol steps, their leaders were expelled from school, and truck loads of police armed with shotguns and tear-gas ringed the Alabama State College Campus. When the entire student body protested to state authorities by refusing to re-register, their dining hall was padlocked in an attempt to starve them into submission."

And

> "Again and again the Southern violators have answered Dr. King's peaceful protests with intimidation and violence. They have bombed his home almost killing his wife and child. They have assaulted his person. They have arrested him seven times—for 'speeding,' 'loitering' and similar 'offenses.' And now they have charged him with 'perjury'—a *felony* under which they could imprison him for *ten years* . . . . "[5]

There were a number of material errors of fact in the above statements. For instance, the college dining hall had never been padlocked and the only students who may have been barred were the few who had not applied to eat there. Nor did the police at any time "ring" the campus and they were not called to the campus in connection with the state capitol demonstration. Lesser factual errors were made with regard to the allegations concerning the bombings of Dr. King's house and his arrests. Had the Times checked its own files, particularly the reports of its Atlanta bureau chief Claude Sitton, it would have discovered the errors but it did not do so.

Under the common law of Alabama, Sullivan had merely to establish, as the trial judge instructed, that the statements complained of in the ad published by the Times were of and concerning him, *i.e.*, that he was identified as one of the "Southern violators;"[6] that they were defamatory and that they were published, *i.e.*, communicated to third persons.

4. *Id.* at 256, 84 S. Ct. at 713, 11 L. Ed. 2d at 692–93. The advertisement is set out in full in an appendix to the United States Supreme Court's opinion. *Id.*

5. *Id.* at 257–258, 84 S. Ct. at 714, 740–741, 11 L. Ed. 2d at 693.

6. Approximately 394 copies of the Times containing the ad were distributed in Alabama, of which approximately 35 copies were distributed in Montgomery County. The total circulation of the Times for the date the ad was published, March 29, 1960, was approximately 650,000 copies. *Id.* at 260 n. 3, 84 S. Ct. at 715 n.3, 11 L. Ed. 2d at 694 n. 3.

On appeal following the jury verdict for Sullivan and judgment thereon, the Alabama Supreme Court held that the allegations complained of injured Sullivan's professional reputation and were thus defamatory on their face; that Sullivan was identified as one of the "Southern violators" because it was common knowledge that the activities of the police in Montgomery, Alabama were under the control and direction of the police commissioner, *i.e.*, L.B. Sullivan; and that testimony of witnesses that they associated the allegations in the ad with Sullivan and would have thought less of him if they believed the statements in the ad to be true was admissible.[7]

Without the availability of truth or the fair comment privilege defenses, the newspaper company was left only with the claim that it was protected from civil liability for publishing an erroneous defamatory advertisement by the First and Fourteenth Amendments. This novel contention was summarily rejected by the Alabama court[8] which then affirmed Sullivan's judgment for $500,000.

Considering the Alabama Supreme Court's decision from a narrow common law perspective and within the confines of First Amendment jurisprudence of the time, it does not appear subject to criticism. But the dangers posed by it for the press in covering the activities of people like Sullivan and other public officials were serious ones and had to be addressed.

3.   *New York Times v. Sullivan in the Supreme Court*[9]

On certiorari, the New York Times Company reiterated its claim that the First and Fourteenth Amendments protected it from civil liability for inadvertent defamation of public officials in the course of criticizing their official acts. The United States Supreme Court, recognizing that the case went to the core of the First Amendment[10]—protection of political speech—held that Alabama's common law of defamation was "constitutionally deficient for failure to provide the safeguards for freedom of speech and of the press that are required by the First and Fourteenth Amendments in a libel action brought by public official

---

7. New York Times Co. v. Sullivan, 273 Ala. 656, 144 So.2d 25 (1962).

8. "The First Amendment of the U.S. Constitution does not protect libelous publications." 273 Ala. at 676, 144 So.2d at 40.

9. New York Times Co. v. Sullivan, 376 U.S. 254, 84 S.Ct. 710, 11 L.Ed.2d 686 (1964).

10. *Id.* at 273–276, 84 S. Ct. at 722–724, 11 L. Ed. 2d at 703–04. Referring to the Sedition Act of 1798, 1 Stat. 596, which made criminal "any false, scandalous and malicious writing or writings against the government of the United States, or either house of the Congress . . . or the President . . ., with intent to defame . . .," the Court said that while the Sedition Act was never tested before it, the attack upon its validity by Jefferson, Madison and the General Assembly of Virginia had carried the day in the court of history. *Id.* at 274–76, 84 S. Ct. at 722–23, 11 L. Ed. 2d at 702–03. "These views reflect a broad consensus that the Act, because of the restraint it imposed upon criticism of government and public officials, was inconsistent with the First Amendment." *Id.* at 276, 84 S. Ct. at 724, 11 L. Ed. 2d at 704. Though the Sedition Act was criminal in nature its obvious unconstitutionality provided an apt analogy for the Court because "[t]he fear of damage awards under a rule such as that invoked by the Alabama courts here may be markedly more inhibiting than the fear of prosecution under a criminal statute." *Id.* at 277, 84 S. Ct. at 724, 11 L. Ed. 2d at 705.

against critics of his official conduct."[11] The Court therefore reversed and remanded.

It did not matter that some of the statements in the editorial type ad ("advertorial") found to be defamatory by the Alabama courts were clearly untrue, because the First Amendment protected some untruth. Erroneous statements are inevitable in free debate, according to the Court, and they too must be protected if the freedoms of expression are to have the "breathing space that they need to survive."[12] Only with such broad protection could the country's "profound national commitment to the principle that debate on public issues should be uninhibited, robust, and wide-open"[13] be honored.

This does not mean that *all* untruthful defamations of public officials were to be protected. Rather, only inadvertent and negligent untruths are covered. To this end the Court fashioned its now famous "actual malice" rule. That rule, unlike common law malice which requires ill will, spite or bad motives for the imposition of punitive damages, prohibits a public official from recovering *any* damages for a defamatory falsehood relating to his official conduct unless he proves that the complained of communication was made "with knowledge that it was false or with reckless disregard of whether it was false or not."[14] Justice Brennan, speaking for the Court, thus rewrote the common law of malice in defamation cases involving public officials to make it conform to the central meaning of the First Amendment, *i.e.*, protection of political speech.

Justice Brennan then reviewed the record below and found that there was neither a proper instruction below on the Court's conception of actual malice nor proof of "convincing clarity" of such malice.[15] As to the petitioner New York Times Company (there were numerous individual petitioners before the Court) the Court found that the evidence that the Times failed to check the facts alleged in the ad for accuracy hardly amounted to actual malice when officials of the Company relied on people they knew to be of good reputation who apparently were associated with the ad. Nor did the Times' failure to retract when the accuracy of the ad was questioned amount to actual malice given the Times' reasonable doubt that the ad referred to Sullivan and that its request of Sullivan for an explanation as to his claim that he was a target of the ad was ignored.[16] "We think the evidence against the Times support at most a finding of negligence in failing to discover the misstatements, and is

11. *Id.* at 264, 283, 84 S. Ct. at 717, 727, 11 L. Ed. 2d at 697, 708.

12. *Id.* at 271–272, 84 S. Ct. at 721, 11 L. Ed. 2d at 701 (quoting N.A.A.C.P. v. Button, 371 U.S. 415, 433, 83 S.Ct. 328, 338, 9 L.Ed.2d 405 (1963)).

13. *Id.* at 270, 84 S. Ct. at 721, 11 L. Ed. 2d at 701.

14. *Id.* at 279–280, 84 S. Ct. at 726, 11 L. Ed. 2d at 706.

15. The Court mandated that the standard of proof of actual malice must be the intermediate one of "clear and convincing" proof if First Amendment requirements are to be met. *Id.* at 285–86, 84 S. Ct. at 729, 11 L. Ed. 2d at 710.

16. *Id.* at 286–88, 84 S. Ct. at 729–30, 11 L. Ed. 2d at 710–11.

constitutionally insufficient to show the recklessness that is requested for a finding of actual malice."[17]

But the Court did not stop with "actual malice" in constitutionalizing defamation law. Justice Brennan rejected the only evidence that the ad was "of and concerning" Sullivan as not meeting First Amendment standards. Brennan held that testimony of witnesses that they knew that Sullivan was in charge of the police of Montgomery was insufficient to establish that Sullivan was a target of the ad. The underlying proposition that attacks on governmental conduct necessarily involve the person who ostensibly control that conduct had disquieting implications for criticism of governmental conduct, according to the Court. It would sidestep the obstacle in our system that criticism of government may not be punished by transmuting such criticism into personal criticism and libel of the officials who make up government. "We hold that such a proposition may not constitutionally be utilized to establish that an otherwise impersonal attack on governmental operations was a libel of an official responsible for those operations."[18]

With its decision in *New York Times v. Sullivan*, the Court may have saved the New York Times from financial ruin and most certainly changed the law of defamation as applied to the news and information media. But, as with all great departures in the law, the decision left unanswered many questions, not the least of which is the reach of the First Amendment privilege created here.

B. *The Extension of New York Times v. Sullivan to Public Figures*

While the privilege covers cases involving "public officials,"[19] does constitutionalization of defamation law also involve "public figures" caught up in matters of public interest? This question was squarely presented in *Curtis Publishing Co. v. Butts* and *Associated Press v. Walker*.[20] In *Curtis*, its magazine The Saturday Evening Post published an article accusing Butts, a prominent former football head coach and then athletic director at the University of Georgia, of conspiring with the head coach of the University of Alabama to "fix" a football game between the two schools. While the University of Georgia is a state university, Butts was employed by the Georgia Athletic Association, a private corporation, rather than by the State of Georgia itself. The article was based on information supplied by one George Burnett, an Atlanta insurance salesman. Burnett claimed to have accidentally overheard, because of electronic error or crossed wires, a telephone conversation between Butts and Alabama head coach Paul "Bear" Bryant in

---

17. *Id.* at 287–88, 84 S. Ct. at 730, 11 L. Ed. 2d at 711.

18. *Id.* at 292, 84 S. Ct. at 732, 11 L. Ed. 2d at 713.

19. But who are encompassed within that description? This issue was first addressed in Rosenblatt v. Baer, 383 U.S. 75,

86 S.Ct. 669, 15 L.Ed.2d 597 (1966) and is discussed in Section 5.5 of this chapter.

20. 388 U.S. 130, 87 S.Ct. 1975, 18 L.Ed.2d 1094 (1967) (cases consolidated for argument and decision in the Supreme Court).

which Butts purportedly told Bryant about Georgia's offensive plays and defensive formations. The article went on to detail the alleged consequences of the phone conversation including Butts' resignation as athletic director when the present Georgia coach was informed of the situation. The Saturday Evening Post story concluded by saying that "[t]he chances are that Wally Butts will never help any football team again."[21] No attempt was made by the weekly magazine to check the veracity of Burnett's account though there was considerable lead time before the story was published. Butts brought suit for libel in the United States District Court for the Northern District of Georgia under diversity jurisdiction and won a jury verdict which was reduced by the trial judge. Both parties appealed. The United States Court of Appeals for the Fifth Circuit affirmed and the Supreme granted certiorari.

In *Associated Press*, the wire service moved a story on its wire to member newspapers giving an eyewitness account of a massive riot which broke out on the University of Mississippi campus protesting federal efforts to enforce a court decree ordering the enrollment of a black, James Meredith, as a student. The AP dispatch stated that Walker, a former Army general but private citizen at the time of the riot, had taken command of the violent crowd and had personally led a charge against federal marshals sent to the campus to effectuate the court's decree and to assist in preserving order. It also described Walker as encouraging rioters to resort to violence and giving them technical advice on combating the effects of tear gas. Walker, who after resigning his commission played a prominent public role in resisting the use of federal force in school desegregation, admitted to being on the campus at the time of the riot but denied fermenting it or leading the charge against the marshals and instead claimed to have counseled restraint and peaceful protest. The AP reporter who wrote the story was also present during the fastbreaking events just described and had reported them almost immediately to AP's office in Atlanta both orally and then by written dispatch. Only one minor discrepancy between the oral account and the subsequent written account was shown at trial.

The case was tried in Walker's home state of Texas. The state trial judge instructed the jury that an award of compensatory damages could be made if the dispatch was not substantially true[22] and that punitive damages could be added if the article was actuated by "ill will, bad or evil motive, or . . . entire want of care . . ."[23] The Texas jury returned a verdict of $500,000 compensatory damages and $300,000 punitive damages. The trial judge threw out the punitive damages because there was "no evidence to support the jury's answers that there was actual malice."[24] He also noted that this lack of "malice" would require a

---

21. *Id.* at 137, 87 S. Ct. at 1982, 18 L. Ed. 2d at 1100.

22. Two statements of fact were at issue in *Walker*, *i.e.*, that Walker assumed command of the crowd, and that he led a charge

against the marshals. *Id.* at 141 n. 4, 87 S. Ct. at 1984 n.4, 18 L. Ed. 2d at 1103 n.4.

23. *Id.* at 141, 87 S. Ct. at 1984, 18 L. Ed. 2d at 1103.

24. *Id.* at 141–42, 87 S. Ct. at 1984, 18 L. Ed. 2d at 1103.

verdict for the Associated Press if the "actual malice" rule were applicable. But he rejected its extension to private persons because there were "no compelling reasons of public policy requiring additional defenses to suits for libel. Truth alone should be an adequate defense."[25] Both sides appealed and the Texas Court of Civil Appeals affirmed the trial court's judgment and agreed without explanation that *New York Times* was inapplicable. The issue of whether *New York Times* reached private persons who were public figures was thus clearly joined by the Texas trial and appellate court in *Walker*. The Supreme Court of Texas refused review and the United States Supreme Court granted certiorari.

In choosing to take up the cases of *Curtis Publishing Co.* and *Associated Press*, Justice Harlan noted that the sweep of the *New York Times* rule in libel cases was a question not yet fully settled. Speaking for himself and three other justices, Harlan tried to limit *New York Times* in cases of concededly public figures by formulating narrower protection for the news media. "We consider and would hold that a 'public figure' who is not a public official may also recover damages for a defamatory falsehood whose substance makes substantial danger to reputation apparent, on a showing of highly unreasonable conduct constituting an extreme departure from the standards of investigation and reporting ordinarily adhered to by responsible publishers."[26]

Harlan could not actually hold this because five concurring and dissenting justices thought otherwise. Chief Justice Warren and Associate Justices Brennan, White, Black and Douglas[27] adhered to the actual malice rule of *New York Times*. Given the Court's "Rule of Five," *i.e.*, five votes rule, the "actual malice" rule was extended in *Curtis Publishing Co.* and *Associated Press,* to "public figure" cases. Even given this extension, five justices, including the Chief Justice, voted to uphold the judgement against Curtis Publishing Company at least in part because of the conscious policy of the publisher to provoke people with the magazine's stories and because of the slipshod, sketchy and minimalist efforts to check the veracity of the Butts–Bryant story even after the editors were notified by Butts and his daughter that Burnett's account was totally untrue.

In contrast, no justice voted to uphold the judgment against the Associated Press because the wire service's conduct could be characterized at worst as simple negligence given the fastbreaking and confusing nature of the events on the University of Mississippi campus, the

---

25. *Id.* at 142, 87 S. Ct. at 1984, 18 L. Ed. 2d at 1103.

26. *Id.* at 155, 87 S. Ct. at 1991–92, 18 L. Ed. 2d at 1111.

27. Justices Black and Douglas voted reluctantly because they held the view that the First Amendment was intended to leave the press free from *all* libel judgments and not just those where actual malice could not

be shown. *Id.* at 170–71, 87 S. Ct. at 1999–2000, 18 L. Ed. 2d at 1120 (Black, J., concurring). Since the actual malice rule is lesser included within their position they concurred in the extension of *New York Times* to public figure cases. But they, of course, dissented from the decision concurred in by five justices to affirm the judgment against Curtis Publishing Company.

apparent trustworthiness of its correspondent at the scene and the need for speed in moving this important story on the wire.

Now that the Court had voted to constitutionalize media defamation law in cases involving public officials and public figures, attention shifted to the question whether non-public figures involved in matters or events of public importance were also governed by *New York Times v. Sullivan* when they sued news organizations for libel.

C. To Be or Not to Be: The Extension of the New York Times Standard to Matters of Public Importance

1. Rosenbloom v. Metromedia, Inc.

The extension of the actual malice rule of *New York Times* to cases of non-public figures involved in stories of public interest or concern was considered inconclusively by the Court in *Rosenbloom v. Metromedia, Inc.*[28] because no position on the issue received more than three votes. There, a distributor of, among other things, nudist and "girlie" magazines was arrested by the police in a series of enforcement action's under Philadelphia's obscenity laws. Reports of the distributor's arrest on obscenity charges were broadcast on Metromedia's radio station WIP and the station continued to broadcast stories about the distributor, as a purveyor of obscenity, even after the station was informed that the courts and prosecutors had determined the magazines were not obscene and no laws had been violated. The distributor filed a libel action in the United States District Court against Metromedia and following trial the plaintiff magazine distributor won a jury verdict of $25,000 in general damages and $725,000 in punitive damages which was reduced by the trial judge to $250,000 on remitter and who then entered judgment.

In reversing the judgment of the trial court, the United States Court of Appeals for the Third Circuit emphasized that the broadcasts concerned matters of public interest, that they involved breaking news reported under deadline pressure and that the fact the plaintiff was not a public figure could not be accorded decisive importance if First Amendment interests in the reporting of matters of public concern were to be adequately protected. Therefore, the *New York Times* standard necessarily applied.

On certiorari, a plurality of three justices led by Brennan believe that the actual malice rule needed to be extended to this type of case to protect the First Amendment interests of the media. "If a matter is a subject of public or general interest, it cannot suddenly become less so merely because a private individual is involved, or because in some sense the individual did not 'voluntarily' choose to become involved. The public's primary interest is in the event; the public focus is on the conduct of the participant and the content, effect, and significance of the conduct, not the participant's prior anonymity or notoriety."[29] Justice

28. 403 U.S. 29, 91 S.Ct. 1811, 29 L.Ed.2d 296 (1971).

29. *Id.* at 43, 91 S. Ct. at 1819, 29 L. Ed. 2d at 311.

Black, held to his position that "the First Amendment does not permit the recovery of libel judgments against the news media,"[30] and had Justice Douglas, who agreed with Black, participated in *Rosenbloom*, there would have been the necessary five votes to extend the actual malice rule because it is lesser included within this absolutist position.

Justice Harlan, engaging in ad hoc balancing of the plaintiff's, defendant's and society's interests would not extend *New York Times* but would require that libel plaintiffs in suits against the news and information media establish a want of due care on the part of the defendant. Strict liability of the media would be abolished.

Justices Marshall and Stewart also refused to extend the actual malice rule thereby further dispossessing state common law because of their belief that the press could be adequately protected in these cases by restricting the award of damages to proved, actual injuries.[31] They also agreed with Justice Harlan that the First Amendment did not permit the imposition of strict liability.[32]

Justice White was the odd man out refusing to take a position on the standard of liability to be applied because he did not think the case forced such a judgment. He did, however, supply the fifth vote, along with votes by Chief Justice Warren, and Associate Justices Brennan, Black and Blackmun, to affirm the judgment of the Third Circuit.

Thus, while the media defendant prevailed here, the Court was unable to establish the standard for liability of the media in cases of non-public figures caught up in events of public interest. But the ideas espoused by a number of the justices would figure in the Court's next confrontation with this issue.

2. *Gertz v. Robert Welch, Inc.*

That confrontation occurred in the case of *Gertz v. Robert Welch, Inc.*[33] There, a Chicago Policeman named Nuccio shot and killed a juvenile name Nelson. Nuccio was subsequently prosecuted for murder in the second degree and convicted. Thereafter, the Nelson family retained petitioner Elmer Gertz, a reputable and prominent member of the bar, to represent them in civil litigation against Nuccio. Respondent, Robert Welch, Inc., publisher of the John Birch Society's monthly periodical American Opinion, apparently agitated by the belief that judicial and other challenges to police authority nationwide were a prelude to a Communist takeover of the United States, commissioned an article on the murder trial of Officer Nuccio. The published article entitled "FRAME–UP: Richard Nuccio And The War On Police," accused Gertz, among other things of being an architect of the criminal prosecution "frame-up;" having a police file that had to be lifted by "a big, Irish cop;" being an official of the "Marxist League for Industrial

30. *Id.* at 57, 91 S. Ct. at 1826, 29 L. Ed. 2d at 320 (Black, J., concurring).

31. *Id.* at 86, 91 S. Ct. at 1840, 29 L. Ed. 2d at 336 (Marshall, J., dissenting).

32. *Id.* at 86–87, 91 S. Ct. at 1841, 29 L. Ed. 2d at 336–37 (Marshall, J., dissenting).

33. 418 U.S. 323, 94 S.Ct. 2997, 41 L.Ed.2d 789 (1974).

Democracy" which advocated violent overthrow of government; being a "Communist-frontier;" and having been an officer of the National Lawyers Guild, an organization described as a "Communist organization." These statements were patently false. The magazine's managing editor had made no effort to verify or substantiate the charges made against Gertz, relying on the author's reputation for accuracy. The editor added insult to injury by including a photograph of the lawyer with the article bearing the caption he himself wrote "Elmer Gertz of Red Guild harasses Nuccio."

Following wide distribution of the article, Gertz brought a diversity action for libel in the United States District Court for the Northern District of Illinois. After filing its answer, the defendant publisher moved for summary judgment claiming a constitutional privilege to defame Gertz based on his status as a public official or public figure and its own lack of actual malice as defined by *New York Times v. Sullivan*. At trial and before the case was submitted to the jury, the court ruled in effect that petitioner was neither a public official nor a public figure and the defendant was not entitled to the privilege, overlooking the question whether the actual malice rule might be extended to non-officials and non-public figures involved in matters or events of public interest. Following submission to the jury, it returned with an award of $50,000. Then following the jury's verdict and on further reflection, the court concluded that the *New York Times* standard did extend to the case and entered judgment for the magazine publisher notwithstanding the jury verdict.

On appeal to the Seventh Circuit, while doubting the correctness of the trial court's finding that Gertz was not a public figure, the appeals court let that determination stand. It agreed, however, with the trial court that the actual malice rule applied to the case, citing, the plurality opinion in *Rosenbloom v. Metromedia, Inc.* which had been decided in the interim. The appeals court also agreed with the district court's conclusion that the plaintiff Gertz had failed to show by clear and convincing evidence that the defendant publisher had acted with actual malice.

The Supreme Court granted certiorari to reconsider the issue it had been unable to resolve in *Rosenbloom*. Writing for the Court and a bare five-member majority made possible by the willingness of Justice Blackmun finally to settle the issue,[34] Justice Powell rejected the extension of the actual malice rule to cases involving private non-public figures caught up in matters of public interest and reversed the judgment and remanded the case. While recognizing the news media's interest in avoiding self-censorship, Justice Powell recognized also the state's competing interest in providing compensation to victims of defamatory attacks through the judicial process. Engaging in ad hoc balancing of interest, he concluded that when purely private persons are libeled by the media, the state's interest is greater than the media's and a *per se*

---

34. *Id.* at 353–54, 94 S. Ct. at 3013–14, 41 L. Ed. 2d at 813.

constitutional requirement that plaintiffs establish actual malice on the part of the media defendant by clear and convincing proof too greatly disadvantages private libel plaintiffs.

According to Justice Powell private persons are not in the same class as public officials and public figures. Public officials and public figures usually enjoy significantly greater access to the channels of effective communication and thus have a more realistic opportunity to counteract false statements than do private individuals.[35] "Private individuals are therefore more vulnerable to injury, and the state interest in protecting them is correspondingly greater."[36] Moreover, those who seek public office or the public's attention must accept certain necessary consequences of that involvement in public affairs, including closer public scrutiny.[37] Powell doubted that there were very many truly *involuntary* public figures in need of protection. Rather, the overwhelming number have voluntarily assumed roles of prominence in society generally and are considered all-pervasive public figures or, more commonly, they have thrust themselves into the middle of public controversies. In either event, these public figures invite attention and comment whereas purely private persons do not.[38] "Thus, private individuals are not only more vulnerable to injury than public officials and public figures; they are also more deserving of recovery."[39] The Court, speaking through Justice Powell, therefore held that, so long as they do not impose liability without fault, the states may define for themselves the appropriate standard of liability for defamatory falsehoods published by the media directed against purely private persons.[40]

By this holding, Justice Powell gave a nod in the direction of federalism by allowing the states to choose the appropriate standard of liability, ranging from actual malice to negligence or something in between. On the other hand Powell read the First Amendment as preventing the states from imposing a strict liability standard in media libel cases because of the danger it posed for press freedom. In addition, Powell felt it necessary in accommodating the conflicting state and media interests here to limit a private person's recovery for defamation to compensation for *actual* injury suffered when the standard of liability employed is other than that requiring knowledge of falsity by the defendant or the defendant's reckless disregard for the truth, *i.e.*, the actual malice standard of *New York Times v. Sullivan*. Thus, if a negligence standard of fault is applied, a libel plaintiff cannot receive presumed or punitive damages.[41]

While the Court refused to mandate the application of the *New York Times* standard of liability, further constitutionalization of the state

---

35. *Id.* at 344, 94 S. Ct. at 3009, 41 L. Ed. 2d at 808.

36. *Id.*

37. *Id.*

38. *Id.* at 345, 94 S. Ct. at 3009–10, 41 L. Ed. 2d at 808.

39. *Id.* at 345, 94 S. Ct. at 3010, 41 L. Ed. 2d at 808.

40. *Id.* at 347, 94 S. Ct. at 3010, 41 L. Ed. 2d at 809.

41. *Id.* at 349–350, 94 S. Ct. at 3011–12, 41 L. Ed. 2d at 810–11.

common law of defamation continued in *Gertz* and, indeed, as Justice White pointed out in his dissent,[42] it was intensified by the Court's decision requiring the showing of actual damages in jurisdictions not imposing the *New York Times* standard[43] where once the common law permitted the presumption of damages and further requiring the elimination of punitive damages in those jurisdictions[44] where once the common law permitted such damages simply on a showing of ill will, spite or bad motive. Moreover, strict liability could no longer be imposed on the media by the states even when the plaintiffs are private persons.[45]

With the decision of *Gertz v. Robert Welch, Inc.*, the constitutionalization of the common law prima facie case for media defamation was essentially completed. The constitutionalization of the defenses of truth and fair comment are discussed below. At this point it would be useful to summarize the impact on the law of *New York Times Co. v. Sullivan* and its early progeny.

D. Impact of New York Times v. Sullivan and Its Early Progeny

The impact of *New York Times Co.* has been profound. Briefly summarized, the major effects on media defamation law include:

- Strict or absolute liability as a basis for liability of the media has been eliminated regardless of the status of the plaintiff.

- A new standard of "actual malice" is substitute for strict liability or negligence in media defamation law when the plaintiff is either a "public official" or a "public figure."

42. *Id.* at 370, 94 S. Ct. at 3022, 41 L. Ed. 2d at 822–23.

43. *See* Turf Lawnmower Repair, Inc. v. Bergen Record Corp., 139 N.J. 392, 404–405 n. 1., 655 A.2d 417, 423–424 n. 1 (1995), cert. denied 516 U.S. 1066, 116 S.Ct. 752, 133 L.Ed.2d 700 (1996) for a compendium of forty-two United States jurisdictions adopting the lesser negligence standard. The following jurisdictions have adopted the actual malice standard of New York Times v. Sullivan: Walker v. Colorado Springs Sun, Inc., 188 Colo. 86, 98–99, 538 P.2d 450, 457 (1975), cert. denied 423 U.S. 1025, 96 S.Ct. 469, 46 L.Ed.2d 399 (1975), *overruled on other grounds in* Diversified Management, Inc. v. Denver Post, Inc., 653 P.2d 1103 (Colo.1982); AAFCO Heating and Air Conditioning Co. v. Northwest Publications., Inc., 162 Ind.App. 671, 679, 321 N.E.2d 580, 586 (Ind.Ct.App.1974), cert. denied 424 U.S. 913, 96 S.Ct. 1112, 47 L.Ed.2d 318 (1976); Turf Lawnmower Repair, Inc. v. Bergen Record Corp., 139 N.J. 392, 655 A.2d 417, 425–428 (N.J. 1995) (limited to reporting on matters of important public interest; otherwise the lesser

negligence standard obtains); Sisler v. Gannett Co., Inc., 104 N.J. 256, 279, 516 A.2d 1083, 1095 (1986). New York has adopted its own "grossly irresponsible" standard. Chapadeau v. Utica Observer–Dispatch, Inc., 38 N.Y.2d 196, 199, 379 N.Y.S.2d 61, 64, 341 N.E.2d 569, 572 (1975); Gaeta v. New York News, Inc., 62 N.Y.2d 340, 348–51, 477 N.Y.S.2d 82, 85–86, 465 N.E.2d 802, 805–06 (1984). A few jurisdictions have not passed on the question.

44. *See, e.g.,* Cahill v. Hawaiian Paradise Park Corp., 56 Haw. 522, 535, 543 P.2d 1356, 1365–66 (1975). Some states have banned the use of punitive damages altogether. *See* Stone v. Essex County Newspapers, Inc., 367 Mass. 849, 851, 860, 330 N.E.2d 161, 164, 169 (1975). Wheeler v. Green, 286 Or. 99, 119, 593 P.2d 777, 789 (1979). *See also* DAVID A. ELDER, DEFAMATION: A LAWYER'S GUIDE, § 9:1(E)(2) (1993); ROBERT D. SACK & SANDRA S. BARON, LIBEL, SLANDER AND RELATED PROBLEMS 505 (2d ed. 1994); RODNEY A. SMOLLA, LAW OF DEFAMATION § 9.09[4] (1995).

45. Gertz, 418 U.S. at 347, 94 S. Ct. at 3010, 41 L. Ed. 2d at 809.

- "Public figures" are categorized in *Gertz v. Robert Welch, Inc.* as either all-pervasive or limited, *i.e.*, those who thrust themselves into specific public controversies in order to influence the outcome. Thus, if a limited public figure is defamed out of the context of the public controversy giving rise to his status, the actual malice standard is not *mandated* by the First Amendment.

- The common law definition of actual malice to mean evil motive, spite or ill will is rejected and the new constitutionalized definition of knowing untruthfulness or reckless disregard for the truth is *mandated* when the libel plaintiff is a public official or public figure and is *allowed* when the plaintiff is neither a public official nor a public figure.

- A higher standard of proof than mere preponderance of the evidence is now required to establish that a defamatory communication is "of or concerning" the plaintiff public official and that the defamatory communication is made with actual malice. This higher standard is the "convincing clarity" test.

- Effects associated with the "actual malice" standard and the higher "convincing clarity" standard of proof are the making of awards of summary judgment to media defendants or the entering of dismissals in their favor more prevalent and the reducing of the cost of trial litigation.

- Awards of presumed and punitive damages against the media are eliminated in cases involving private persons involved in matters of public interest where liability is based on other than the *New York Times* actual malice standard.

- As a necessary implication of the actual malice standard the defense of truth is impacted by shifting the burden of proof on the issue of truth or falsity to plaintiffs.[46]

The above list represents the major changes in defamation law wrought by its constitutionalization. These changes raise many important issues not fully addressed in *New York Times*, *Curtis Publishing*, *Associated Press* and *Gertz* such as the parameters of "actual malice" in specific contexts, the identification of public officials and public figures and the determination of the viability of the fair comment privilege. These and other issues are addressed below.

5.4   The Requirement of "Actual Malice"

As previously noted, the Constitution requires proof of some measure of fault on the part of a defendant accused of defamation.[1] Where

---

46. *See* Philadelphia Newspapers, Inc. v. Hepps, 475 U.S. 767, 106 S.Ct. 1558, 89 L.Ed.2d 783 (1986). The issue of truth or falsity of a defamatory communication is discussed in detail *infra*, section 5.6.

1. RESTATEMENT (SECOND) OF TORTS § 580B, comment *b* (1977); Gertz v. Robert Welch, Inc., 418 U.S. 323, 340, 94 S.Ct. 2997, 41 L.Ed.2d 789 (1974)("*Gertz*"). The *Gertz* decision confirmed that state courts may set the level of fault for recovery

plaintiffs in defamation cases are private persons, the requisite level of fault may be determined by the state courts. However, where plaintiffs are classified as public officials or "public figures" the Constitution requires them to prove that the defendant acted with "actual malice." A subsequent section discusses how plaintiffs come to be classified as public officials or public figures; the present section discusses the actual malice standard.

A. *New York Times v. Sullivan and "Actual Malice"*

The requirement of "actual" malice has its origins in *New York Times Co. v. Sullivan ("Sullivan")*.[2] In that case, a commissioner of the City of Montgomery, Alabama objected to a newspaper advertisement that accused local authorities of waging a "wave of terror" against civil rights demonstrators. The advertisement accused the police, in particular, of ringing the campus of Alabama State College in an effort to intimidate students who had demonstrated on the steps of the State Capitol. The advertisement also claimed that demonstrators had been padlocked out of a campus dining hall in order to "starve them into submission," and that Dr. Martin Luther King, Jr., had been subjected to a campaign of harassment that included bombing his home, arresting him seven times and charging him with perjury. The plaintiff alleged that because his duties as commissioner included police protection for the City of Montgomery, the advertisement could reasonably be read as accusing him of involvement in the actions described.

At trial to an Alabama state court, the plaintiff was able to show that a number of the statements in the advertisement were inaccurate and that he was not involved in many of the events described. The trial judge instructed the jury that the statements complained of were libelous *per se*, and that if the jury found that the defendants had published the statements and those statements were of or concerning the plaintiff, then the jury could make an award of compensatory damages without proof of fault on the part of the defendants.[3] The Supreme Court of Alabama affirmed a judgment for plaintiff and upheld the trial court's instructions to the jury.

The United States Supreme Court found that the instructions violated the right of free speech under the First and Fourteenth Amendments to the Constitution. Writing for a unanimous Court, Justice Brennan pointed out that in not requiring proof of fault in defamation

---

of actual damages in defamation suits brought by private plaintiffs, so long as proof of negligence at least is required. *Id.* at 347–48, 94 S. Ct. at 3010–11, 41 L. Ed. 2d at 809–10. For recovery of punitive damages, however, *Gertz* requires proof of actual malice even where the plaintiff is a not a public figure. *Id.* at 348–350, 94 S. Ct. at 3011–12, 41 L. Ed. 2d at 809–11.

2. 376 U.S. 254, 84 S.Ct. 710, 11 L.Ed.2d 686 (1964).

3. The trial court instructed the jury that in a case of libel *per se*, "falsity and malice are presumed" for the purpose of awarding compensatory damages. The judge told the jury, however, that in order to award punitive damages it must find proof of actual malice, which the court defined as something more than "mere negligence or carelessness."

cases, the Alabama courts effectively made speakers guarantors of the truthfulness of their utterances.[4] Where the statements complained of concern the official conduct of public officials, this standard "dampens the vigor and limits the variety of public debate."[5] The Court found that availability of the defense of truth does not cure this defect, since under a rule of strict liability for defamatory statements, "would-be critics of official conduct may be deterred from voicing their criticism, even though it is believed to be true and even though it is in fact true, because of doubt whether it can be proved in court or fear of the expense of having to do so."[6] Accordingly, the Supreme Court announced "a federal rule that prohibits a public official from recovering damages for a defamatory falsehood ... unless he proves that the statement was made with 'actual malice'—that is, with knowledge that it was false or with reckless disregard of whether it was false or not."[7] The Court also held that the proof of actual malice must be made, not according to the preponderance of the evidence standard usually applied in civil cases, but with "convincing clarity."[8]

After announcing the constitutionally-required standard, the *Sullivan* Court reviewed the evidence presented to the Alabama jury and found it wanting. This part of the Court's opinion gives some additional content to the actual malice standard. First, the Court found that at the time the advertisement was accepted for publication, the responsible persons at the *Times* believed the advertisement to be "substantially correct," and relied for this belief on the "good reputation of many of those whose names were listed as sponsors of the advertisement," as well as a letter from the labor leader A. Philip Randolph asserting that the use of those persons' names was authorized.[9] No one at the *Times* took the additional step of checking the events described in the advertisement against the *Times'* own news files. The Court found that while this evidence might be interpreted as showing negligence on the part of the *Times*, there was no evidence that anyone at the *Times* knew any part of the ad to be false or was recklessly indifferent to its truth or falsity.[10] The decision to accept the ad for publication, therefore, was not made with actual malice.

The *Times'* subsequent failure to publish a retraction upon demand from Commissioner Sullivan also failed to demonstrate actual malice. The Court declined to decide whether a refusal to retract ever might constitute actual malice but found that in the case before it the *Times* was uncertain that the advertisement could be taken to refer to Sullivan at all, and that in any case the refusal to publish a retraction was not final—the *Times* had asked Sullivan to explain why he believed that the

---

4. 376 U.S. at 279, 84 S.Ct. at 725, 11 L.Ed.2d at 706.

5. *Id.*

6. *Id.*

7. 376 U.S. at 279–80, 84 S.Ct. at 726, 11 L.Ed.2d at 706.

8. 376 U.S. at 285–86, 84 S.Ct. at 729, 11 L.Ed.2d at 710.

9. 376 U.S. at 286–88; 84 S.Ct. at 729–30, 11 L.Ed.2d at 710–11.

10. 376 U.S. at 287–88, 84 S.Ct. at 730, 11 L.Ed.2d at 710–11.

advertisement referred to him, and Sullivan had not answered that request. Accordingly, the circumstances of the failure to retract, like the decision to publish the advertisement in the first place, failed to show actual malice.[11]

The *Sullivan* case marks a milestone in First Amendment jurisprudence. Most fundamentally, *Sullivan* is the Supreme Court's first recognition that even erroneous defamatory speech—at least where it involves the central value of public criticism of the official conduct of government officials—is deserving of constitutional protection. The actual malice standard, however, has required case-by-case explication.

B. Refinements On the Actual Malice Standard

The Court has refined the actual malice standard in several post-*Sullivan* decisions. Notably, these decisions have affirmed that actual malice requires something more than negligence in confirming facts,[12] and has nothing to do with a defendant's ill-will toward the plaintiff or the fact that the defendant acted from self-interest.[13] Those cases also refined the definition of actual malice and have identified some of the circumstances in which a defendant may be found to have known that a statement was false or may be found to have acted with reckless disregard as to a statement's truth or falsity.

Among the cases refining the definition of actual malice is *St. Amant v. Thompson*,[14] in which the Court stated that a defendant in a public figure defamation case must at least have had "serious doubts" as to the truth of that statement. Similarly, in *Garrison v. Louisiana*,[15] the Court stated that a defendant in such a case must have published a false statement with a "high degree of awareness" of its "probable falsity."[16]

---

11. *Id.* The Times did, however, publish a retraction upon demand from the Governor of Alabama, and explained this decision by reference to the Governor's status as the "embodiment" of the State and the advertisement's specific references to actions of the Board of Education, of which the Governor was the ex officio chairman. The Court found this distinction to be reasonable and refused to find that the Times' subsequent retraction upon demand from the Governor proved actual malice as to Sullivan.

12. Garrison v. Louisiana, 379 U.S. 64, 85 S.Ct. 209, 13 L.Ed.2d 125 (1964).

13. The irrelevance of malice in the ordinary sense is demonstrated by *Hustler Magazine, Inc. v. Falwell*, 485 U.S. 46, 108 S.Ct. 876, 99 L.Ed.2d 41 (1988), in which the Court held that in the absence of proof of a defendant's knowledge of a statement's falsity or reckless disregard of the truth, a public figure plaintiff could not recover from a publisher for intentional infliction of emotional distress. The Court confirmed the irrelevance of a defendant's self-interest

in *Harte-Hanks Communications, Inc. v. Connaughton*, 491 U.S. 657, 109 S.Ct. 2678, 105 L.Ed.2d 562 (1989), in which the Court stated that "[i]f a profit motive could somehow strip communications of the otherwise available constitutional protection, our cases from New York Times to Hustler Magazine would be little more than empty vessels." 491 U.S. at 667, 109 S.Ct. at 2686, 105 L.Ed.2d at 576.

14. 390 U.S. 727, 88 S.Ct. 1323, 20 L.Ed.2d 262 (1968).

15. 379 U.S. 64, 85 S.Ct. 209, 13 L.Ed.2d 125 (1964).

16. *Id.* at 74, 85 S.Ct. at 216, 13 L.Ed.2d at 133. The Court also declined to follow a suggestion, made by Justice Harlan in his plurality opinion in *Curtis Publishing Co. v. Butts*, that would have created a kind of professional malpractice standard for defamation cases involving journalistic reporting on public figures. The Court's rejection of this proposed standard was unanimous "by the time of the Court's decision in *Gertz v. Robert Welch, Inc.*, 418 U.S. 323, 94

Among the Supreme Court decisions containing detailed discussions of the evidence on which an actual malice claim may be based is *Harte-Hanks Communications, Inc. v. Connaughton* ("*Harte-Hanks*").[17] In that case, an unsuccessful political candidate sued a newspaper for publishing charges that the candidate had promised favors to a grand jury witness and her sister in exchange for the witness's help in obtaining information concerning corruption in the incumbent's office. Reviewing the jury's findings along with the undisputed evidence in the case, the Court found clear and convincing evidence that the newspaper had acted with reckless disregard as to the truth or falsity of the charges. Specifically, the record showed that the newspaper published the story in spite of denials by the candidate and five other witnesses and in spite of internal inconsistencies in the charges as presented by the newspaper's source.[18] The record also showed that when the candidate offered the newspaper tapes of his telephone conversations with his accuser, the newspaper declined to listen to them. The record also showed that the newspaper did not attempt to interview one of the two women who allegedly had been offered favors by the candidate.[19]

The Supreme Court made it clear that if this evidence had amounted to no more than "failure to investigate," the evidence would not constitute proof of actual malice. The Court found, however, that the newspaper's failure to interview a key witness and listen to the proffered tapes showed "a deliberate decision not to acquire knowledge of facts that might confirm the probable falsity" of the accuser's charges. This was more than a careless failure to investigate: this was "purposeful avoidance of the truth ..." and constituted actual malice under the *Sullivan* standard.[20]

The Supreme Court confronted a somewhat different claim of actual malice in *Masson v. New Yorker Magazine*.[21] In *Masson*, a psychotherapist, agreed by the parties to be a public figure, complained that defendants had attributed statements to him that in fact were fabricated quotations. For purposes of the defendants' motion for summary judgment and appellate review of a decision granting summary judgment, the record showed that one of the defendants had tape recorded interviews with the plaintiff and had written articles containing a number of lengthy quotations that plaintiff regarded as both inaccurate and defam-

---

S.Ct. 2997, 41 L.Ed.2d 789 (1974) ..." Harte-Hanks Communications, Inc., 491 U.S. at 665–66, 109 S.Ct. at 2685, 105 L.Ed.2d at 576.

17. 491 U.S. 657, 109 S.Ct. 2678, 105 L.Ed.2d 562 (1989).

18. 491 U.S. at 682–85, 109 S.Ct. at 2693–94, 105 L.Ed.2d at 585–87.

19. *Id.*

20. 491 U.S. at 692, 109 S.Ct. at 2698, 105 L.Ed.2d at 591. The Court in *Harte-Hanks* also noted the similarity between that case and *Curtis Publishing*, in which a

plurality found proof of actual malice under the *Sullivan* standard. In *Curtis Publishing*, the Saturday Evening Post had published an informant's claim that a college athletic director had "fixed" a football game. Justices Brennan and White, along with Chief Justice Warren, found that the editors' failure to view films of relevant games or interview another witness to the alleged events, in spite of reasons to doubt the informant's reliability, satisfied the requirement of actual malice.

21. 501 U.S. 496, 111 S.Ct. 2419, 115 L.Ed.2d 447 (1991).

atory. The plaintiff complained about the quotations before they were published in an article in the New Yorker and subsequently in a book based on the New Yorker article.

The trial court had found that the evidence did not establish actual malice in the publication of the quotations and the United States Court of Appeals for the Ninth Circuit affirmed that finding. The Supreme Court assumed, for the sake of its analysis, that not all alterations of verbatim quotes are automatically false or amount—even where they are deliberate—to actual malice. Instead, the Court announced the principle that "deliberate alteration of the words uttered by a plaintiff does not equate with knowledge of falsity" for purposes of the actual malice standard of *Sullivan*.[22] The Court refused, however, to accept the version of the law adopted by the Court of Appeals, which had determined that "an altered quotation is protected so long it is a 'rational interpretation' of an actual statement . . . ."[23] In the Supreme Court's view, the use of quotation marks suggests to the reader that the person quoted is speaking for himself—not that the author is offering a rational interpretation of the words actually used by the person quoted.[24] Instead, the Court examined each of the quoted passages to determine whether the author's alterations were deliberate or reckless, and then asked, as to each quote that had been altered deliberately or recklessly, whether "the published passages differ materially in meaning from the tape-recorded statements so as to create an issue of fact for a jury as to falsity."[25]

The factors examined by the Court in order to ascertain whether the author's alterations were deliberate or reckless are particularly useful, and might be applied to any claim of actual malice in a journalistic context. Notably, the Court found from the record (taking all of the evidence in the light most favorable to the party resisting summary judgment below) that the author had the tapes of her conversations with the plaintiff in her possession while writing the article and "was not working under a tight deadline."[26] The Court also found it significant that the author had represented to her editor that all of the disputed quotations were taken from her tape recordings of conversations with the plaintiff.[27] Based on this and other evidence, the Supreme Court found that the record presented a jury question concerning whether the author "published the statements with knowledge or reckless disregard of the alterations."[28]

The Court next examined each of the author's alterations to the plaintiff's actual words to determine whether they resulted in material differences in meaning. Where such material differences did appear, the Court found that a jury question was presented as to the falsity of the

22. *Id.* at 517, 111 S.Ct. at 2433, 115 L.Ed.2d at 473.

23. *Id.* at 518, 111 S.Ct. at 2433, 115 L.Ed.2d at 473.

24. *Id.* at 519, 111 S.Ct. at 2434, 115 L.Ed.2d at 474.

25. *Id.* at 521, 111 S.Ct. at 2435, 115 L.Ed.2d at 475.

26. *Id.*

27. *Id.*

28. *Id.*

defendants' published versions of the plaintiff's statement. So, for example, in one tape-recorded conversation with the defendant author, the plaintiff stated that he was considered "much too junior within the hierarchy of [psycho]analysis for [more senior analysts] to be caught dead with him."[29] In the author's article and book, this statement was rendered, in quotation marks, as a supposed remark by the plaintiff that Anna Freud and another respected analyst considered him an "intellectual gigolo."[30] The Court found that a reasonable jury could find a material difference between these two statements and should be permitted to determine whether the quoted statement was defamatory.

In summary, the Supreme Court's decisions show that speakers who make statements about public figures are not liable for defamation, so long as they do not know the statements to be false or purposely avoid avenues of investigation that might demonstrate the falsity of the statements. Publishing statements known to be false includes the attribution to public figures of words that are prejudicially different from the words actually uttered. Deliberate avoidance of knowledge includes failure to view evidence proffered by the subject of an investigation or to interview persons who might be expected to dispute the prejudicial information. It is not necessary, however, that journalistic speakers comply with some standard of professional care, and liability cannot attach because speakers feel ill-will toward a public figure or act out of self-interest. Mere sloppiness, not amounting to deliberate avoidance of information that might refute the prejudicial statements, cannot give rise to liability.

5.5 Who Is a Public Official or Public Figure for Purposes of Applying the Actual Malice Standards?

Since *Sullivan*, the Supreme Court and lower federal courts have refined and expanded the class of plaintiffs required to prove actual malice when bringing claims of defamation. Specifically, the post-*Sullivan* case law imposes the burden of proving actual malice on three types of plaintiffs: public officials, "pervasive" or "all-purpose" public figures and "limited purpose" public figures.

A. Public Officials

The notion that public officials must prove actual malice begins with the *Sullivan* decision, which held that the higher scienter standard applies to "actions brought by public officials against critics of their official conduct." The *Sullivan* Court did not define the class of public officials, however, and said only that it would not at that time "determine how far down into the lower ranks of government employees the 'public official' designation would extend for purposes of this rule ..."[1]

---

29. *Id.* at 522, 111 S.Ct. at 2435, 115 L.Ed.2d at 475.

30. *Id.*

1. 376 U.S. at 283 n. 23, 84 S.Ct. at 728 n. 23, 11 L.Ed.2d at 709 n. 23.

Since *Sullivan*, the Court has offered guidance on the definition of "public official" only once. In *Rosenblatt v. Baer*[2], the Court established a two-part test under which a plaintiff would be classified as a public official if:

(1) the plaintiff has, or appears to the public to have, "substantial responsibility for or control over the conduct of public affairs" (the "apparent governmental authority" test);[3] and

(2) the plaintiff's position is of such "apparent importance that the public has an independent interest in the qualifications and performance of the person who holds it, beyond the general public interest in the qualifications ... of all government employees" (the "independent public interest" test).[4]

In practice, the public official category has not been confined to persons in the upper echelons of government but has been extended to all public employees in whose performance and qualifications the public may be said to have an interest. For example, the public official category has been found to include a naval officer,[5] a mid-level municipal employee,[6] an assistant public defender[7] and a college financial aid director.[8] Police officers and other law enforcement personnel consistently are found to be public officials.[9] In fact, where plaintiffs involved with government have been found not to be public officials, those plaintiffs typically have performed governmental duties only peripherally or episodically.[10]

B. *Public Figures*

Although the "public official" category has not proved all that difficult for the courts to apply, the broader category of "public figure" has been far more vexing. The Supreme Court first recognized this broader category in *Curtis Publishing Co. v. Butts*,[11] and the consolidated

2.   383 U.S. 75, 86 S.Ct. 669, 15 L.Ed.2d 597 (1966).

3.   *Id.* at 85, 86 S.Ct. at 676, 15 L.Ed.2d at 605.

4.   383 U.S. at 86, 86 S.Ct. at 676, 15 L.Ed.2d at 606. For useful discussions of the "public official" standard, *see* Peter S. Cane, *Defamation of Teachers: Behind the Times?*, 56 Fordham L. Rev. 1191 (1988); Rodney A. Smolla, *Dun & Bradstreet, Hepps, and Liberty Lobby: A New Analytic Primer on the Future Course of Defamation*, 75 Geo. L.J. 1519 (1987).

5.   Arnheiter v. Random House, Inc., 578 F.2d 804, 805 (9th Cir.1978).

6.   Grzelak v. Calumet Pub. Co., 543 F.2d 579, 582 (7th Cir.1975).

7.   Tague v. Citizens for Law & Order, Inc., 75 Cal. App. 3d Supp. 16, 21–23, 142 Cal.Rptr. 689, 691–93 (Cal.Super.1977).

8.   Van Dyke v. KUTV, 663 P.2d 52, 54–56 (Utah 1983).

9.   *See, e.g.*, Gray v. Udevitz, 656 F.2d 588, 591 (10th Cir.1981); Thuma v. Hearst Corp., 340 F.Supp. 867, 869 (D.Md.1972); Willis v. Perry, 677 P.2d 961, 963 (Colo.Ct. App.1983).

10.   So, for example, an attorney in private practice did not become a public official simply because he was appointed by the court to defend a criminal case, for which the attorney was paid from public funds. Steere v. Cupp, 226 Kan. 566, 572, 602 P.2d 1267, 1272 (1979). Similarly, a private citizen who acted as a police informant was found not to be a public official. Jenoff v. Hearst Corp., 644 F.2d 1004, 1005 (4th Cir.1981).

11.   388 U.S. 130, 87 S.Ct. 1975, 18 L.Ed.2d 1094 (1967).

case of *Associated Press v. Walker*.[12] Butts was the athletic director at the University of Georgia—a state institution—but performed these duties as the employee of a private corporation. Walker was a private citizen, heavily involved in politics, who held no governmental office. The articles that gave rise to the defamation claims accused Butts of "fixing" a football game and accused Walker of inciting a riot at the University of Mississippi.

Neither of the plaintiffs in *Butts* met the Supreme Court's definition of a public official and both plaintiffs accordingly argued that they were not required to prove that the defendants acted with actual malice. The Supreme Court agreed that the cases before them did not present the special circumstances of *Sullivan*. In the *Sullivan* case, the Court was confronted with a defamation claim by a government official—a claim that strongly resembled a charge of seditious libel.[13] Also, because Sullivan was a public official, he probably enjoyed a privilege against liability for his own defamation.[14] Under these circumstances, the Court in *Sullivan* had found that application of the ordinary rules of libel would chill debate on questions of public concern. As the Court acknowledged, Butts and Walker were not public officials enjoying immunity for their own defamatory statements, and their claims against the defendants contained no element of seditious libel. The Court nonetheless found that applying the ordinary rules of defamation to Butts's and Walker's claims threatened, as in *Sullivan*, to reduce the vigor of debate on matters of public concern. In determining how best to accommodate this constitutional concern, the Court applied a tort analysis that balanced the importance of the defendants' activities against the "prior activities and means of self-defense ..." of the plaintiffs. The Court found that in the cases before it, no less than in *Sullivan*, the public had an interest in "the circulation of the materials ...involved ..."[15] Also, as in *Sullivan*, the two plaintiffs "commanded a substantial amount of independent public interest"—Butts because of position alone, and Walker because of his "purposeful activity amounting to a thrusting of his personality into the 'vortex' of an important public controversy ..."[16] Because of the independent public interest they had generated, both plaintiffs "had sufficient [public] access to the means of counterargument to be able 'to expose through discussion the falsehood and fallacies' of the defamatory statements."[17] Accordingly, the Court concluded that it was appropriate to apply to Butts's and Walker's claims the same actual malice standard that the Court had adopted in *Sullivan*.

The boundaries of the public figure category have proved difficult to locate. The need for vigorous discussion of public issues notwithstanding, the law is rightly reluctant to require private persons to carry a higher

12. *Id.*

13. *Id.* at 153, 87 S.Ct. at 1990, 18 L.Ed.2d at 1110.

14. *Id.* at 153–54, 87 S.Ct. at 1991, 18 L.Ed.2d at 1110.

15. *Id.* at 154, 87 S.Ct. at 1991, 18 L.Ed.2d at 1111.

16. *Id.* at 154–55, 87 S.Ct. at 1991, 18 L.Ed.2d at 1111.

17. *Id.* at 155, 87 S.Ct. at 1991, 18 L.Ed.2d at 1111.

burden in defamation cases simply because of their inadvertent involvement with issues or events about which the public is curious. Such purely private persons lack the media access enjoyed by celebrities or persons who have thrust themselves into public controversies, and cannot readily defend their reputations through the give-and-take of public debate. For this reason, classification as a public figure requires a demonstration that the plaintiff has lost his or her claim to private status, either through a generalized celebrity or through some volitional involvement in a public issue. These propositions were clearly established in *Gertz v. Robert Welch, Inc.*[18]

1. *Gertz and the Public Person—Private Person Dichotomy*

In *Gertz*, a majority of the Court held that the privilege recognized in *Sullivan* was applicable only to cases involving defamation of public officials and public figures and rejected the idea that the actual malice rule extended to private persons caught up in matters of interest to the public.[19] Elmer Gertz was a reputable lawyer not generally know to the public and not then associated with any particular causes. He was retained by the family of a youth killed by a police officer to bring a civil suit against the officer. Gertz was viciously attacked in the John Birch Society's magazine American Opinion, which accused him of being a "Leninist," a "Communist-fronter," and of arranging a frame-up of the police officer.

Gertz sued for libel, and the Supreme Court ruled that despite his prominence in the civil rights area, Gertz was not a public figure for the purposes of this lawsuit. The Court explained that private persons are more in need of judicial redress and the state has a greater interest in providing it because they have not voluntarily invited public comment, thus choosing to put their reputations at risk. Moreover, the private person will normally have less access to the channels of effective communication (the media) to correct the record than will the public person.

The Supreme Court stressed the fact that Gertz had not achieved any general fame in the community—the jurors had never heard of him. Moreover, the Court did not think that simply because he was counsel in the civil litigation in question that he had "thrust himself into the vortex" of public controversy. In righting the perceived imbalance in constitutional protection between expression and reputation it was important for the Gertz majority to reduce the range of applicability of *Sullivan*. This could be accomplished by defining narrowly who was a public figure.

Gertz thus created the dichotomy between public figures and private persons and established the framework for distinguishing between two types of public figures: (1) the all-purpose public figure, such as Larry King, having such great general fame or notoriety that his or her name

18. 418 U.S. 323, 94 S.Ct. 2997, 41 L.Ed.2d 789 (1974).

19. That idea had been embraced by a plurality of the Court in *Rosenbloom v.*

Metromedia, Inc., 403 U.S. 29, 91 S.Ct. 1811, 29 L.Ed.2d 296 (1971).

is a household word, or (2) limited purpose public figures, who are further distinguished as being (a) voluntary or "vortex" public figures, referring to plaintiffs' thrusting themselves voluntarily into the vortex of a specific public controversy, or (b) involuntary public figures, referring to those who are placed in the media limelight by chance or against their will.[20]

2. The Progeny of Gertz

Within five years of the *Gertz* ruling, the Supreme Court agreed to hear three cases which would clarify the issue of who were public figures (who had to prove actual malice) and who were private persons (who merely had to prove negligence). These three cases established the truly restricted nature of the public figure category. The first case, *Time, Inc. v. Firestone*,[21] involved a highly publicized divorce between Mary Alice Firestone and her husband, an heir to the Firestone tire empire. After a lengthy and spicey public trial the judge granted the husband's request for a complete divorce. Time Magazine reported in its "Milestones" section that Russell Firestone was granted a divorce "on grounds of extreme cruelty and adultery." After her request for a printed retraction was rejected, Mrs. Firestone sued for libel. Time's report was false and defamatory because under Florida law at that time an adulterous wife could not receive alimony, but the Florida court had granted her $3000 per month in alimony.

Time argued that Mrs. Firestone was a public figure, which would require her to show that Time knew the story was false or had recklessly disregarded the truth. (Time was innocent of common law malice; its reporter had genuinely misunderstood the grounds for divorce).

But in rejecting Time's contention, the Supreme Court said that local social prominence is not enough to categorize a plaintiff as a public figure. Divorce is not the sort of "public controversy" referred to in *Gertz*; rather, it is a private matter.

The Court did not even mention Mrs. Firestone's open air press conferences or her hiring of a press agent designed to tell the public her side of the divorce story. Firestone considerably narrowed the public figure category, given Mrs. Firestone's notoriety. The category was further narrowed by two cases decided by the Supreme Court on the same day in its 1978–1979 term.

In *Wolston v. Reader's Digest Ass'n, Inc.*[22] defendant published a book about Soviet intelligence agents in the United States and listed Wolston as one of them. Sixteen years earlier Wolston had been subpoenaed to testify before a federal grand jury investigating the activity of

20. *See, e.g.*, Dameron v. Washington Magazine, Inc., 779 F.2d 736, 250 U.S. App. D.C. 346 (D.C.Cir.1985), cert. denied 476 U.S. 1141, 106 S.Ct. 2247, 90 L.Ed.2d 693 (1986).

21. 424 U.S. 448, 96 S.Ct. 958, 47 L.Ed.2d 154 (1976).

22. 443 U.S. 157, 99 S.Ct. 2701, 61 L.Ed.2d 450 (1979).

Soviet agents in this country. Because of claimed poor health he did not comply with the subpoena and he was cited for contempt.

Wolston denied any connection to the Soviet intelligence apparatus and sued the Reader's Digest Association for libel. Although the trial court granted the Association summary judgment and the United States Court of Appeals affirmed partly on the basis that Wolston was a public figure, the Supreme Court reversed, ruling that he was not a public figure because he had done nothing to thrust himself into a public controversy.

This holding restricts limited issue public figures to those who draw attention to themselves in order to advocate a particular view on a public matter and to affect public opinion. Thus, as in *Firestone*, mere involvement in a matter of public interest is not enough.

This same restrictive view of limited-issue public figures led the Court to reject the Association's other contention that any person who engages in criminal conduct automatically becomes a public figure regarding his trial conviction. As in *Firestone*, one involved in a public trial (here a criminal one) does not necessarily become a public figure.

In the companion case of *Hutchinson v. Proxmire*,[23] (1979), Senator William Proxmire awarded his decidedly uncoveted "Golden Fleece of the Month" awards to NASA and the Office of Naval Research for spending almost a half-million dollars to fund Dr. Hutchinson's research on the aggressiveness of animals, particularly monkeys, for the purpose of finding ways to reduce aggressiveness in humans thrown together in close quarters for extended periods of time. In his speech making the award, as well as in a related news release, Proxmire described Hutchinson's research as transparently worthless and called for an end to his making "a monkey out of the American taxpayer" and putting the "bite" on the taxpayer's resources. Dr. Hutchinson sued Senator Proxmire for libel. As in *Wolston*, the trial court granted summary judgment for Proxmire because the plaintiff was a public figure, and the United States Court of Appeals affirmed.

But, also as in *Wolston*, the Supreme Court reversed on the "public figure" issue, rejecting the view that local newspaper reports regarding Hutchinson's grants and research made him a limited-issue public figure. In so ruling the Court made the point that those charged with defamation cannot create their own defense by themselves making the victim a public figure. Furthermore, the access to the media required by *Gertz* is a regular and continuing one and not merely that made available to rebut a specific defamatory attack.

3. *Summarizing Gertz*

Regarding the public person-private person distinction, the importance of *Gertz* may be summarized as follows:

23. 443 U.S. 111, 99 S.Ct. 2675, 61 L.Ed.2d 411 (1979).

- Simply appearing in the newspapers in connection with some newsworthy story or stories does not make one a public figure;

- Social, professional or business prominence does not by itself make one a public figure, except in the case of those who are so famous that their names are household words such as Demi Moore or John Lennon, for example.

- Forced involvement in a public trial, either civil or criminal, does not by itself make one a public figure;

- Those charged with defamation cannot by their own conduct in making their victims notorious thereby create their own defense;

- Merely applying for, receiving or benefiting from public research grants does not make one a public figure;

- In order to meet the *Gertz* test of thrusting oneself into the forefront of a public issue or controversy, the issue or controversy must be a real dispute, the outcome of which affects the general public or some segment of it in an appreciable way. One's conduct must be calculated or clearly be expected to invite public comment respecting that issue or controversy, as for example, the value and conduct of a federal investigation into KGB activity in the United States during the McCarthy era.

- In order to meet the *Gertz* test of access to the media the access must be regular and continuing.

- Further, as an obvious extension of *Gertz*, businesses may also be pervasive or limited-purpose public figures. So, for example, in *Bose Corp. v. Consumers Union of the United States, Inc.*,[24] the Supreme Court found that a manufacturer of high-fidelity speakers that had heavily advertised the quality of its product was a public figure for the purpose of a suit arising out of an unfavorable published evaluation of one of its speakers.

All in all, following the *Firestone, Wolston, Proxmire* and *Bose Corp.* decisions, the category of public figures for purposes of *New York Times v. Sullivan* protection is much smaller than could have been imagined when *Gertz* was decided.

5.6 The Element of Truth in Media Defamation Cases

A. *The Issue at Common Law*

At common law, truth of that which was published, without more, was a complete defense to a civil action for defamation.[1] The English rule was modified primarily by statute in a few American jurisdictions making the affirmative defense available only if the truth were published

---

24. 466 U.S. 485, 104 S.Ct. 1949, 80 L.Ed.2d 502 (1984).

1. *See* RESTATEMENT OF TORTS § 582 (1938); RESTATEMENT (SECOND) OF TORTS § 581A (1976); 2 WILLIAM BLACK- STONE, COMMENTARIES ON THE LAWS OF ENGLAND 94 (19th ed. 1852); WILLIAM L. PROSSER AND W. PAGE KEETON, TORTS 840 (5th ed. 1984).

with good motives or for justifiable ends or both.[2] In a very few jurisdictions the truthful publication had to be for the purpose of informing the public or had to be made in relation to a matter of public concern.[3]

But whatever the requirements for the availability of the defense, it was the defendant upon whom was placed the burden of establishing the defense by a preponderance of the evidence.[4]

B.   The Burden of Proof After the Constitutionalization of Defamation Law

New York Times Co. v. Sullivan[5] imposed the constitutional requirement on public officials that in libel cases against the media they must establish defendant's fault in the form of actual malice. This fault requirement was extended to public figures in *Curtis Publishing Co. v. Butts* and *Associated Press v. Walker.*[6] And in *Gertz v. Robert Welch, Inc.,*[7] the Court permitted the states to choose for themselves the fault standard to be met by private persons in libel actions against the media, whether actual malice, negligence or something in between.

Whatever the standard, under these rulings it fell to the plaintiff as part of his prima facie case to establish by clear and convincing evidence that the media defendant was at fault. Closely related to fault is the falsity of the publication. It should follow that showing fault will virtually always involve the showing of false publication. That being so, it should also follow that to make their prima facie case, defamation plaintiffs have the burden of establishing that the complained of media publication is false.[8]

The Court soon recognized this inherent logic in the case of public officials. In *Garrison v. Louisiana,*[9] a case of criminal libel in which the district attorney of Orleans Parish, Louisiana was prosecuted for issuing a statement disparaging the judicial conduct of the judges of the local criminal court, the Supreme Court, in reversing the district attorney's conviction, read *Sullivan* as requiring that a public official is "allowed the civil remedy only if he establishes that the utterance was false."[10]

2. *See* RESTATEMENT OF TORTS § 582, *Special Note*; RESTATEMENT (SECOND) OF TORTS § 581A, *Comment a.*

3. *Id.*

4. *See* Philadelphia Newspapers, Inc. v. Hepps, 475 U.S. 767, 777, 106 S.Ct. 1558, 1563, 89 L.Ed.2d 783, 792 (1986); RESTATEMENT (SECOND) OF TORTS § 581A, *Comment c*; RESTATEMENT OF TORTS § 613, *Comment h*; WILLIAM L. PROSSER AND W. PAGE KEETON, TORTS 841 (5th ed. 1984).

5. 376 U.S. 254, 84 S.Ct. 710, 11 L.Ed.2d 686 (1964).

6. 388 U.S. 130, 87 S.Ct. 1975, 18 L.Ed.2d 1094 (1967) (the two cases consolidated for argument and decision in the Supreme Court).

7. 418 U.S. 323, 94 S.Ct. 2997, 41 L.Ed.2d 789 (1974).

8. *But see* WILLIAM L. PROSSER AND W. PAGE KEETON, TORTS 839–40 (5th ed. 1984) (disputing this logic).

9. 379 U.S. 64, 85 S.Ct. 209, 13 L.Ed.2d 125 (1964).

10. *Id.* at 74, 85 S. Ct. at 215, 13 L. Ed. 2d at 132. This reading is dictum, of course, since the case at hand involved a criminal prosecution and not a civil action.

And in *Herbert v. Lando*,[11] the Court said by way of dictum regarding a public figure that "the plaintiff must focus on the editorial process and prove a false publication attended by some degree of culpability."[12]

But for more than twenty years after *Sullivan* and more than a decade after *Gertz*, the Court was silent as to the placement of the burden of proof in cases of private persons bringing defamation actions against the media, and doubt remained in such cases whether the plaintiff's burden included establishing falsity.

The doubt was finally dispelled in *Philadelphia Newspapers, Inc. v. Hepps*.[13] There, the Philadelphia Inquirer ran a series of articles whose theme was that the plaintiffs, owners and franchisees of a chain of convenience stores, had links to organized crime and used those links to influence the state of Pennsylvania's governmental processes in order to gain competitive advantages particularly with regard to their sale of beer.[14]

They brought action in state court where, following the presentation of the parties' respective cases, the trial judge instructed the jury that the plaintiffs bore the burden of proving falsity of the assertions in the published articles. The jury found for the newspaper company and its reporters on the series but on appeal the Pennsylvania Supreme Court reversed the judgment and remanded the case for a new trial on the ground that a showing of fault did not require a showing of falsity by private person plaintiffs.

On certiorari the Supreme Court disagreed and reversed. It held that where the plaintiff is a private figure and the complained of publication is a matter of public concern the common law rule regarding burden of proof on the falsity issue "must ... fall ... to a constitutional requirement that the plaintiff bear the burden of showing falsity, as well as fault, before recovering damages."[15] In so ruling the Court recognized the very close connection between falsity and fault.[16]

11. 441 U.S. 153, 99 S.Ct. 1635, 60 L.Ed.2d 115 (1979).

12. *Id.* at 176, 99 S. Ct. at 1648, 60 L. Ed. 2d at 133.

13. 475 U.S. 767, 106 S.Ct. 1558, 89 L.Ed.2d 783 (1986).

14. *Id.* at 769, 106 S. Ct. at 1559–60, 89 L. Ed. 2d at 787–88.

15. *Id.* at 776, 106 S. Ct. at 1563, 89 L. Ed. 2d at 792. Where the plaintiff is a private person and the defamatory matter published is of exclusively private concern, the common law rule on burden of proof might not be constitutionally superseded: *See* Ramirez v. Rogers, 540 A.2d 475, 477–78 (Me.1988); *cf.* Dun & Bradstreet, Inc. v. Greenmoss Builders, Inc., 472 U.S. 749, 105 S.Ct. 2939, 86 L.Ed.2d 593 (1985) (plurality opinion stating that actual malice standard is unnecessary in such a case).

16. "We note that our decision adds only marginally to the burdens that the plaintiff must already bear as a result of our earlier decisions in the law of defamation. The plaintiff must show fault. A jury is obviously more likely to accept a plaintiff's contention that the defendant was at fault in publishing the statements at issue if convinced that the relevant statements were false. As a practical matter, then, evidence offered by plaintiffs on the publisher's fault in adequately investigating the truth of the published statements will generally encompass evidence of the falsity of the matters asserted." 475 U.S. at 778, 106 S.Ct. at 1565, 89 L.Ed.2d at 794.

C. The Standard of Proof and the Test for Proving Falsity

1. The Standard of Proof

In *Philadelphia Newspapers* the Court did not say what the First Amendment mandated in the way of the plaintiff's standard of proof in establishing falsity.[17] Two standards are possible: preponderance of the evidence or clear and convincing evidence. The "clear and convincing"[18] or "convincing clarity"[19] standard was adopted by the Court for the fault issue, and, because of the previously noted close link between fault and falsity, the higher standard of proof is the appropriate one here. The few lower courts that have passed on this question agree.[20]

2. The Hurdle of the "Substantial Truth" Test in Proving Falsity

Whether the standard of proof is clear and convincing evidence or the lesser and less likely preponderance test, the plaintiff must establish that the complained of publication by the media defendant is substantially false or, obversely, is not substantially true.[21] By this is meant that minor inaccuracies in detail, terminology or quotation are not actionable if the thrust or gist of the assertion is accurate.[22] For example, in *Strada v. Connecticut Newspapers, Inc.*[23] a former state senator believed that an allegedly defamatory newsstory cost him reelection. The story included a description of the plaintiff's relationship with reputed criminals, their associates and their enterprises and stated that the plaintiff had taken trips with or arranged by a reputed criminal, including one to Las Vegas and then to New Orleans for the Superbowl. The undisputed evidence showed, and the defendants conceded, that such a trip never took place. However, the plaintiff had taken a trip to Reno arranged by the same individual. In affirming summary judgment for the defendants, the Connecticut Supreme Court ruled that such an error of detail did not

17. Nor did the Court say what standard of proof would need to be utilized if a defamation plaintiff sued a nonmedia defendant. *See id.* at 779 n.4, 106 S. Ct. at 1565, n.4, 89 S. Ct. at 795 n.4. *See also* Linda Kalm Note, *The Burden of Proving Truth or Falsity in Defamation: Setting a Standard for Cases Involving Nonmedia Defendants*, 62 NYU L. Rev. 812 (1987) (supporting extension of the *Hepps* rule to every case involving public matters regardless of the status of the defendant).

18. Gertz v. Robert Welch, Inc., 418 U.S. 323, 342, 94 S.Ct. 2997, 3008, 41 L.Ed.2d 789, 807 (1974).

19. New York Times Co. v. Sullivan, 376 U.S. 254, 285–86, 84 S.Ct. 710, 729, 11 L.Ed.2d 686, 710 (1964).

20. *See* Auvil v. CBS 60 Minutes, 800 F.Supp. 928, 936 (E.D.Wash.1992); Riley v. Moyed, 529 A.2d 248, 250–51 (Del. Supr. 1987) (semble).

21. *See, e.g.,* Masson v. New Yorker Magazine Inc., 501 U.S. 496, 516–17, 111 S.Ct. 2419, 2433, 115 L.Ed.2d 447, 472–73

(1991); Chapin v. Knight–Ridder, Inc., 993 F.2d 1087, 1092 (4th Cir.1993); Desnick v. American Broadcasting Cos., Inc., 44 F.3d 1345, 1349–50 (7th Cir.1995); Strada v. Connecticut Newspapers, Inc., 193 Conn. 313, 317–19, 477 A.2d 1005, 1007–08 (1984); Bell v. Courier–Journal & Louisville Times Co., 402 S.W.2d 84, 87 (Ky.1966); RESTATEMENT (SECOND) OF TORTS § 581A, *Comment c* (1976); WILLIAM L. PROSSER & W. PAGE KEETON, TORTS 842 (5th ed. 1984).

22. *See, e.g.,* Masson v. New Yorker Magazine Inc., 501 U.S. at 516–17, 111 S. Ct. at 2432–33, 115 L. Ed. 2d at 472–73 (1991); Chapin v. Knight–Ridder, Inc., 993 F.2d 1087, 1092 (4th Cir.1993); Goodrich v. Waterbury Republican–American, Inc., 188 Conn. 107, 112–13, 448 A.2d 1317, 1322 (1982); WILLIAM L. PROSSER & W. PAGE KEETON, TORTS 842 (5th ed. 1984).

23. 193 Conn. 313, 477 A.2d 1005.

matter. "The sting of this excerpt ... does not arise from the trip location or purpose, but rather from the fact that the plaintiff had taken a trip in some way connected with De Poli ...: Where the 'main charge, or gist, of the libel' is true, minor errors that do not change a reader's perception of the statement do not make the statement actionable."[24] And in *Tschirgi v. Lander Wyoming State Journal*,[25] a newspaper article concerning a county and prosecuting attorney stated that in the course of his being arrested for a traffic violation he was wrestled to the ground by a highway patrolman. This account of the arrest was held to be substantially true and a summary judgment for the newspaper was affirmed because the plaintiff had been forced against his vehicle by the arresting officer.

Regarding inaccurate quotation, the United States Supreme Court in *Masson v. New Yorker Magazine Inc.*[26] said that "[i]f an author alters a speaker's words but effects no material change in meaning, including any meaning conveyed by the manner or fact of expression, the speaker suffers no injury to reputation that is compensable as a defamation."[27] And by fair extension, a third person who claims injury from such erroneous quotation has no course of action if the correct quotation would not have been actionable.

In all such cases the test is whether the alleged defamatory communication is more damaging to the plaintiff's reputation in the mind of the receiver of the communication than an accurate communication would be.[28] This test also necessarily implies that for material to be substantially true though containing erroneous details, the material must be reasonably related to the true facts. If it is not so related, the publication may be actionable. For instance, reporting that a woman is a known prostitute when her only recorded offense was the violation of an ordinance prohibiting nude dancing in an establishment selling alcoholic beverages would clearly be actionable because the violation does not support the assertion that the woman provided sexual services for money.[29]

Another necessary implication of this test for substantial truth is that even in cases in which the details of the publication are literally correct an action for defamation may lie. This happens where the details taken together convey an erroneous defamatory impression because other clarifying details are omitted or the context in which the details

---

24. *Id.* at 321–22, 477 A.2d at 1009–10. *See also* Ed Schory & Sons, Inc. v. Francis, 75 Ohio St.3d 433, 445, 662 N.E.2d 1074, 1083–84 (1996) (publicizing that a partner misappropriated $370,000 when the improper taking from the partnership was less than that is still a true representation).

25. 706 P.2d 1116 (Wyo.1985).

26. 501 U.S. 496, 111 S.Ct. 2419, 115 L.Ed.2d 447 (1991).

27. *Id.* at 516, 111 S. Ct. at 2432, 115 L. Ed. 2d at 472.

28. *See* Desnick v. American Broadcasting Cos., Inc., 44 F.3d 1345, 1350 (7th Cir. 1995); Goodrich v. Waterbury Republican–American, Inc., 188 Conn. 107, 113, 448 A.2d 1317, 1322 (1982); Gannett Co., Inc. v. Re, 496 A.2d 553, 557 (Del.1985); McIlvain v. Jacobs, 794 S.W.2d 14, 16 (Tex.1990).

29. *Compare* RESTATEMENT (SECOND) OF TORTS § 581A, *Comment c* (1977).

are presented is misleading.[30] For instance, in *Gannett Co., Inc. v. Re,*[31] the plaintiff, an inventor, claimed the Wilmington News–Journal libeled him in reporting that his compressed air-powered automobile had failed to start in a demonstration staged for the media. In fact, after several unsuccessful attempts to start it, the vehicle did subsequently start. A jury returned a verdict for the plaintiff and while the trial judge set aside the jury's award as excessive and ordered a new trial on the issue of damages, he let stand the verdict on liability. The judge's ruling was upheld on appeal to the Delaware Supreme Court.

The *Gannett* case and the few others like it are the other side of the coin from the substantial truth cases because while the material involved encompasses correct facts, the material, as a whole, is substantially untrue. And that case and the hypothetical above involving the allegation of prostitution suggest that even with the burden of proof placed on plaintiffs and the leeway given media defendants under the substantial truth doctrine, defendants are still vulnerable, particularly regarding plaintiffs characterized as private persons. In the end, the best defense against liability for defamation is accuracy in communicating *all* relevant facts and placing them in proper context.

5.7 The Opinion—Fact—Non-Fact Trichotomy Relating to Privileged Defenses

A. *Introduction to The Fair Comment Privilege*

Long before there was a *New York Times v. Sullivan,* American courts recognized the need in a democratic society for protection from defamation liability of robust, hard hitting commentary on matters of public interest and the people involved in them. Thus was born the privilege of "fair comment." The problem for the courts in fashioning the privilege was to protect vital public discourse while avoiding the extension of a license to the media to engage in professional and reputational assassinations. This privilege, whose parameters varied somewhat from jurisdiction to jurisdiction because of the difficulty in walking this fine line, protected from civil liability the newsmedia when they expressed their honest opinions concerning those who presented themselves, their ideas or their creations to the public for its approval, so long as such opinions are based on true or privileged statements of fact whether expressed or implied.[1] Those subject to the privilege include

---

30. *See* WILLIAM L. PROSSER & W. PAGE KEETON, TORTS 117 (West 1988 Pocket Part to 5th ed.).

31. 496 A.2d 553 (Del.1985). *See also* Church of Scientology v. Flynn, 744 F.2d 694, 698 (9th Cir.1984) (correct fact giving rise to unsupported *post hoc* inference of criminal activity *held* actionable); Batson v. Shiflett, 325 Md. 684, 726–28, 602 A.2d 1191, 1212–13 (1992) (correct assertion that the NLRB found that local union president had negotiated an illegal contract held not

to immunize further assertions of criminal activity by the union head); Marston v. Newavom, 629 A.2d 587, 591–92 (Me.1993) (correct assertion that employee charged personal expenses on employer's credit card held slanderous when other explanatory details of credit card usage omitted).

1. *See* RESTATEMENT OF TORTS § 606 (1938); WILLIAM F. SWINDLER, PROBLEMS OF LAW IN JOURNALISM 209 (1955); John E. Hallen, Comment, *Fair Comment,* 8 Tex. L. Rev. 41, 41 (1929).

public officers and candidates for public office,[2] scientists, artists, writers, actors and entertainers,[3] athletes,[4] and restauranteurs and chefs.[5]

B. Limitations and Difficulties With the Fair Comment Privilege

1. Distinguishing Opinion from Fact

Since the privilege only protects opinion or commentary, one question raised when the privilege is invoked, is whether a particular defamatory expression constitutes opinion or fact. This issue haunts the area of privilege in defamation law to this day[6] and no very satisfactory approach to making such distinction was ever worked out by the courts in relation to the fair comment privilege. Why this was so is answered at least in part by the great master of the law of Evidence, Dean John Henry Wigmore when he wrote, "In the first place no such distinction is scientifically possible.... [A]s soon as we come to analyze and define these terms for the purpose of that accuracy which is necessary in legal rulings, we find that the distinction vanishes.... If then our notion of the supposed firm distinction between 'opinion' and 'fact' is that the one is certain and sure, the other not, surely a just view of their psychological relations serves to demonstrate that in strict truth nothing is certain."[7]

2. Measuring Fairness of the Opinion

Even after the expression in question is deemed by the particular court to be opinion, the protection of the privilege obtains only if the trier of fact determines it to be fair commentary on the accurate factual predicate. Fairness, like "truth and beauty" is in the eye of the beholder and thus such a determination is subjective in the extreme and, because it is so subjective, trial judges could give very little guidance to juries and potentially undermined the protection of the privilege.[8]

But many juries and courts gave an elastic meaning to the idea of "fairness" and protected media defendants from liability for what may seem grossly unfair opinion or criticism. The classic case in which the outer limits of "fairness" may have been reached is *Cherry v. Des Moines Leader*.[9] There, a newspaper critic reviewing the famous Cherry Sisters vaudeville act wrote the following:

2. *See* RESTATEMENT OF TORTS § 607 (1938).

3. *Id.* § 609; Cherry v. Des Moines Leader, 114 Iowa 298, 86 N.W. 323 (1901).

4. *See, e.g.,* Cepeda v. Cowles Magazines & Broadcasting Inc., 328 F.2d 869 (9th Cir.), cert. denied 379 U.S. 844, 85 S.Ct. 51, 13 L.Ed.2d 50 (1964).

5. *See, e.g.,* Twenty–Five East 40th St. Restaurant Corp. v. Forbes, Inc., 37 A.D.2d 546, 322 N.Y.S.2d 408 (App. Div. 1971), *aff'd,* 30 N.Y.2d 595, 331 N.Y.S.2d 29, 282 N.E.2d 118 (1972).

6. *See*, pp. 588–593 in Practitioner Edition, Vol. 1.

7. 7 JOHN HENRY WIGMORE, EVIDENCE § 1919, at 14–16 (Chadbourn rev. ed. 1978).

8. *See, e.g.,* RODNEY A. SMOLLA, LAW OF DEFAMATION § 6.02[3] (1991).

9. 114 Iowa 298, 86 N.W. 323 (1901). The legal issue framed in the case was whether the reviewer was motivated by actual malice, *i.e.,* personal spite or ill will which could only be gleaned from the review itself. Thus, the necessary actual malice of the writer necessary to defeat the

Effie is an old jade of 50 summers, Jessie a frisky filly of 40, and Addie, the flower of the family, a capering monstrosity of 35. Their long skinny arms, equipped with talons at the extremities, swung mechanically, and anon waived frantically at the suffering audience. The mouths of their rancid features opened like caverns, and sounds like the wailings of damned souls issued therefrom. They pranced around the stage with a motion that suggested a cross between the danse du ventre and fox trot,_strange creatures with painted faces and hideous mien. Effie is spavined, Addie is stringhalt, and Jessie, the only one who showed her stockings, has legs with calves as classic in their outlines as the curves of a broom handle.[10]

One can only wonder today if such a nasty, mean-spirited review would first be tolerated by the newspaper's readership[11] and second be viewed as fair by *any* trier of fact.

3. The Requirement That the Express or Implied Facts Upon Which the Opinion Is Based Be True

For the most part the requirement of the privilege that the factual basis for the opinion had to be true or correct seems a reasonable safeguard against license to destroy reputations. But there are situations particularly in the heat of political campaigns, breaking stories, or social upheaval where some latitude for error by the newsmedia is necessary if they are to cover the news and report to the public in an aggressive and comprehensive manner. This was recognized by the Kansas Supreme Court in *Coleman v. MacLennan*[12] more than a half century before the constitutional revolution in libel law wrought by *New York Times v. Sullivan*.[13] In *Coleman*, a decidedly minority view, the Kansas court accorded the common law privilege to the Topeka State Journal which had published an article presenting erroneous facts in commenting about the fitness of a candidate for reelection to a commission charged with handling state school funds. The court took the view that in the interest of good government, the newsmedia must be given some latitude to make honest mistakes. " 'We unhesitatingly recognize the fact that in many cases, however damaging it may be to individuals, there should and must be legal immunity for free speaking, and that justice and the cause of good government would suffer if it were otherwise. With duty often comes a responsibility to speak openly and act fearlessly, ... and

privilege could only be determined by the unfairness of the review. The trial judge apparently did not think the review unfair for he granted directed verdict for defendants which was affirmed on appeal. *Id.* at 303–05, 86 N.W. at 324–25.

10. *Id.* at 299–300, 86 N.W. at 323.

11. Several years ago the drama critic of the Washington Post wrote a review of a dramatic reading by the late actress Viveca Lindfors in which he commented unflatteringly about the shape of her legs. A firestorm erupted over his comments about Ms.

Lindfors' lower extremities, with a vast number of letters to the paper heaping vitriol on the reviewer. Ms. Lindfors graciously did not sue the paper or the reviewer for libel.

12. 78 Kan. 711, 98 P. 281, 20 L.R.A. (n.s.) 361, 130 Am. St. Rep. 390 (1908); *see also e.g.*, Mulderig v. Wilkes–Barre Times, 215 Pa. 470, 64 A. 636 (1906); Bays v. Hunt, 60 Iowa 251, 14 N.W. 785 (1882).

13. 376 U.S. 254, 84 S.Ct. 710, 11 L.Ed.2d 686 (1964).

the party upon whom the duty was imposed must be left accountable to conscience alone, or perhaps to a supervising public sentiment, but not to the courts.' "[14] Nevertheless, the majority view is that errors of fact negate the privilege.[15] The majority rule can raise serious dangers to a free press and a free society.

C. The Eclipse of the Fair Comment Privilege by the United States Constitution

These dangers became evident during the civil rights struggle in the South during the 1960s. To the dismay of white supremacist southerners the national media covered the struggle extensively and in detail, and no news organization was more aggressive in its coverage than the New York Times. At one point the Times published a paid full page "advertorial" entitled "Heed Their Rising Voices" underwritten by civil rights supporters which, among other things, attacked unnamed "Southern violators" for violating the rights of blacks in Montgomery, Alabama by engaging in a number of unlawful acts. Some of the factual allegations were untrue, and Louis B. Sullivan, the Montgomery commissioner of public safety, brought a defamation action against the New York Times company and individuals signing the advertorial in an apparent attempt to send a message to the media.[16]

The defendants did not deny that some of the statements contained in the ad were erroneous[17] which may explain why they did not press the fair comment defense.[18] Rather, the New York Times Company, faced with potentially ruinous verdicts and judgments, had to rely primarily on the then untested theory that the First Amendment protected the press from liability for the publication of erroneous defamatory material about public officials so long as the error was honest in nature. While this theory was rejected out of hand by the Alabama Supreme Court, it was accepted by the United States Supreme Court which held that for defamation against public officials to be actionable, erroneous material

---

14. Coleman, 98 P. at 285 (quoting Thomas M. Cooley, Torts 246–47 (2d ed. 1888)).

15. *See, e.g.* Parsons v. Age–Herald Pub. Co., 181 Ala. 439, 61 So. 345, 350 (1913); Post Pub. Co. v. Hallam, 59 F. 530 (6th Cir.1893); Washington Times Co. v. Bonner, 86 F.2d 836, 66 App.D.C. 280, 110 A.L.R. 393 (D.C. Cir. 1936); Burt v. Advertiser Newspaper Co., 154 Mass. 238, 28 N.E. 1, 13 L.R.A. 97 (1891) (opinion by then judge Oliver Wendell Holmes, Jr.); Root v. King, 4 Wend. 113, 21 Am. Dec. 102, 8 Cow. 125 (N.Y.Sup.1828).

16. The racial context of the litigation is made clear by the New York Times' assignments of error on appeal to the Alabama Supreme Court that "(1) the courtroom was segregated during the trial below, and (2) the trial judge was not duly and legally

elected because of alleged deprivation of voting rights to negroes." New York Times Co. v. Sullivan, 273 Ala. 656, 681, 144 So.2d 25, 45 (1962), *rev'd* 376 U.S. 254, 84 S.Ct. 710, 11 L.Ed.2d 686 (1964). *See The Civil Rights Struggle. A Historic Movement That Spawned* New York Times Co. v. Sullivan, 2 A.B.A. Communications Lawyer 20 (No. 3, Summer 1984). These assignments of error were rejected by the Alabama Supreme Court at least ostensibly because the issues were not raised at trial.

17. New York Times Co. v. Sullivan, 376 U.S. 254, 258, 84 S.Ct. 710, 714, 11 L.Ed.2d 686, 694 (1964).

18. Alabama follows the majority rule that the fair comment privilege is lost if the commentary is predicated on erroneous facts. *See* Parsons v. Age–Herald Pub. Co., 181 Ala. 439, 61 So. 345, 350 (1913).

had to be published with actual malice, *i.e.*, with knowledge of its untruthfulness or reckless disregard for its truthfulness.[19] Later decisions extended the actual malice fault standard to cover defamation of candidates for public office[20] and public figures.[21]

Such constitutional protection for the news and information media is not dependent on whether the alleged defamatory communication involves fact or opinion but whether, if erroneous, it was published with that high degree of fault known as actual malice. Proving actual malice is a very large obstacle for plaintiffs to overcome.

Thus, the Supreme Court in *Sullivan* had provided the breathing room for a free press to make honest mistakes, something that a large majority of state jurisdictions refused to do in conjunction with the common law privileged defense of fair comment. Given that a great portion of the universe of defamation plaintiffs fall into the categories of public officials, candidates for public office and public figures, it is not surprising that the less protective fair comment defense covering such persons would be eclipsed (though not destroyed) by the greater constitutional protection offered the media by *New York Times Co. v. Sullivan*. For a time, then, the opinion-fact problem was essentially submerged under the weight of the actual malice rule. But it would soon reappear in a context somewhat different than the fair comment privilege.

D.   The Supposed Stand–Alone Constitutional Opinion Privilege

1.   The Dictum in Gertz v. Robert Welch, Inc.

In *Gertz v. Robert Welch, Inc.*,[22] in which the Court distinguished between public figures and private persons for the purpose of determining whether the actual malice standard had to be applied, Justice Powell in his opinion for the Court stated, by way of dictum, "Under the First Amendment there is no such thing as a false idea. However pernicious an opinion may seem, we depend for its correction not on the conscience of judges and juries but on the competition of other ideas."[23] While Justice Powell did not say that he meant to recognize a new stand-alone broad First Amendment opinion privilege, many lower federal and state courts read his dictum as meaning just that.

2.   Lower Court Reaction to the Dictum in Gertz v. Robert Welch, Inc.

Reacting to Justice Powell's dictum, a number of lower courts fashioned a broad constitutional privilege for expression labeled "opin-

19. New York Times Co. v. Sullivan, 376 U.S. at 279–80, 84 S. Ct. at 726, 11 L. Ed. 2d at 706 (1964).

20. *See* Ocala Star–Banner Co. v. Damron, 401 U.S. 295, 300, 91 S.Ct. 628, 631, 28 L.Ed.2d 57, 62 (1971); Monitor Patriot Co. v. Roy, 401 U.S. 265, 91 S.Ct. 621, 28 L.Ed.2d 35 (1971).

21. *See* Curtis Publ'g. Co. v. Butts, 388 U.S. 130, 87 S.Ct. 1975, 18 L.Ed.2d 1094 (1967).

22. 418 U.S. 323, 94 S.Ct. 2997, 41 L.Ed.2d 789 (1974).

23. *Id.* at 339–40, 94 S. Ct. at 3007, 41 L. Ed. 2d at 805.

ion."[24] But, of course, the labeling was problematic because it raised the old bugaboo of the common law fair comment privilege—distinguishing between fact and opinion. Various courts tried various approaches to the problem.[25]

Perhaps the most influential of the court opinions to grapple with the distinction after *Gertz* was that of then Circuit Judge Kenneth Starr writing for the majority of the United States Court of Appeals for the District of Columbia Circuit sitting *en banc*. In *Ollman v. Evans*,[26] a professor of political science at New York University was accused by syndicated columnists Robert Novak and Rowland Evans of being a Marxist who was using his position to convert his students to political Marxist philosophy and to prepare them for revolutionary action. Ollman sued the columnists for libel. The United States District Court granted summary judgment for the defendants, concluding that the column simply reflected the columnists opinion and therefore held that opinion was absolutely protected as a matter of law by the First Amendment. In affirming the summary judgment Judge Starr adopted a multi-factor approach to determining whether a communication involves fact which is actionable or opinion which is not. The factors identified by Judge Starr as significant in drawing the distinction were: (1) the common usage or meaning of the specific language of the complained of statements themselves; (2) the verifiability of the statements, *i.e.*, the ability of courts objectively to characterize the statements as true or false; (3) the narrow context in which the statements are made—here the syndicated column; and (4) the broader context or setting in which the statements are communicated—here the appearance generally of the column on editorial

24. *See, e.g.,* Ollman v. Evans, 750 F.2d 970, 242 U.S. App. D.C. 301 (D.C.Cir.1984), cert. denied 471 U.S. 1127, 105 S.Ct. 2662, 86 L.Ed.2d 278 (1985) (clearly the leading case); Hotchner v. Castillo–Puche, 551 F.2d 910, 913–14 (2d Cir.), cert. denied *sub nom.* Hotchner v. Doubleday & Co., Inc. 434 U.S. 834, 98 S.Ct. 120, 54 L.Ed.2d 95 (1977); Brown & Williamson Tobacco Corp. v. Jacobson, 827 F.2d 1119, 1129–31 (7th Cir. 1987), cert. denied *sub nom.* CBS, Inc. v. Brown & Williamson Tobacco Corp., 485 U.S. 993, 108 S.Ct. 1302, 99 L.Ed.2d 512 (1988); Janklow v. Newsweek, Inc., 788 F.2d 1300, 1302–1305 (8th Cir.1986) (en banc), cert. denied 479 U.S. 883, 107 S.Ct. 272, 93 L.Ed.2d 249 (1986); Steinhilber v. Alphonse, 68 N.Y.2d 283, 508 N.Y.S.2d 901, 501 N.E.2d 550 (1986).

25. *See* Ollman v. Evans 750 F.2d 970, 242 U.S. App. D.C. 301 (D.C.Cir.1984), cert. denied, 471 U.S. 1127, 105 S.Ct. 2662, 86 L.Ed.2d 278 (1985) for discussion of these approaches:

Some courts have in effect, eschewed any effort to construct a theory and simply treated the distinction between fact and opinion as a judgment call. *See, e.g.,*

Shiver v. Apalachee Publishing Co., 425 So.2d 1173 (Fla.Dist.Ct.App.1983). Other courts have concentrated on a single factor, such as the verifiability vel non of the allegedly defamatory statement. *See, e.g.,* Hotchner v. Castillo–Puche, 551 F.2d 910, 913 (2d Cir.) cert. denied sub nom. Hotchner v. Doubleday & Co., 434 U.S. 834, 98 S.Ct. 120, 54 L.Ed.2d 95 (1977). Still others have adopted a multi-factor test, attempting to assess the allegedly defamatory proposition in the totality of the circumstances in which it appeared. *See, e.g.,* Information Control Corp. v. Genesis One Computer Corp., 611 F.2d 781 (9th Cir.1980).

Id. at 977, 242 U.S. App. D.C. at 308. Writing for the District of Columbia Court of Appeals sitting en banc, then Circuit Judge Kenneth Starr opted for the multi-factor approach.

26. 750 F.2d 970, 242 U.S. App. D.C. 301 (D.C.Cir.1984), cert. denied 471 U.S. 1127, 105 S.Ct. 2662, 86 L.Ed.2d 278 (1985).

or "op ed" pages.[27]

As noted above, Judge Starr's multi-factor analysis was perhaps the most influential of the various schemes utilized to make the distinction between fact and opinion.[28] But in the end it did not matter which approaches were taken by the lower federal and state courts because the Supreme Court would have the final say.

E. End of the Supposed Stand–Alone Opinion Privilege

Sixteen years after Justice Powell had promulgated his dictum in *Gertz v. Robert Welch, Inc.* concerning false ideas and pernicious opinions, the Supreme Court finally addressed the supposed constitutional opinion privilege in *Milkovich v. Lorain Journal Co.*[29] There, a sports columnist for an Ohio newspaper in commenting upon the testimony of a former high school wrestling coach at a court proceeding related to an inter-school altercation involving the coach's team wrote:

> " 'Anyone who attended the meet, whether he be from Maple Heights, Mentor, or impartial observer, knows in his heart that Milkovich and Scott lied at the hearing after each having given his solemn oath to tell the truth.

> " 'But they got away with it.

> " 'Is that the kind of lesson we want our young people learning from their high school administrators and coaches?

> " 'I think not.' "[30]

The former coach brought an action for defamation alleging that a headline over the column and several passages in the column accused him of committing the crime of perjury and constituted libel per se. Following considerable litigation, the Ohio trial court, relying in part on the dictum in *Gertz* granted summary judgment to the defendants on the grounds that the article was an opinion protected from a libel action by constitutional law. Alternatively, the trial court ruled that as a public figure the plaintiff had failed to make out a prima facie case of actual malice. Ultimately, the Ohio Court of Appeals affirmed the trial court's grant of summary judgment for the defendants, concluding that "it has been decided, as a matter of law, that the article in question was constitutionally protected opinion."[31] The Ohio Supreme Court refused review and the Supreme Court granted certiorari.

27. *Id.* at 979–84, 242 U.S. App. D.C. at 310–15.

28. *See* Janklow v. Newsweek, Inc., 788 F.2d 1300, 1302–03 (8th Cir.1986) (en banc), cert. denied, 479 U.S. 883, 107 S.Ct. 272, 93 L.Ed.2d 249 (1986) (essentially adopting the Starr multi-factor approach); Steinhilber v. Alphonse, 68 N.Y.2d 283, 292, 508 N.Y.S.2d 901, 905, 501 N.E.2d 550, 554 (1986) (viewing the Starr approach favorably).

29. 497 U.S. 1, 110 S.Ct. 2695, 111 L.Ed.2d 1 (1990).

30. *Id.* at 5, 110 S. Ct. at 2698, 111 L. Ed. 2d at 9 (quoting from the Ohio Court of Appeals opinion below at 46 Ohio App.3d 20, 21, 545 N.E.2d 1320, 1322 (1989)).

31. *Id.* at 10, 110 S. Ct. at 2701, 111 L. Ed. 2d at 12 (quoting from the Ohio Court of Appeals opinion at 46 Ohio App. 3d at 23, 545 N.E.2d at 1324).

The Court reversed, rejecting the idea that the First Amendment required a separate privilege for expression labeled opinion. The Court reviewed the constitutional protection it had afforded the media against liability for allegedly defamatory communications and concluded that such protection was sufficient to insure the free flow of news and information to the public without adding yet another privilege.[32] The Court explained that the language in *Gertz*, read in context, equated the word "opinion" in the second sentence with the word "idea" in the first sentence.[33] Under this view, according to the Court, Justice Harlan's dictum was merely a reiteration of Justice Holmes' famous concept that the First Amendment protected the "marketplace of ideas" and not the enunciation of a new privilege protecting anything that might be labeled opinion.[34]

The Court criticized the idea of an opinion privilege because it ignores the reality that expressions of opinion may often imply an assertion of objective fact.

> If a speaker says, "In my opinion John Jones is a liar," he implies a knowledge of facts which lead to the conclusion that Jones told an untruth. Even if the speaker states the facts upon which he bases his opinion, if those facts are either incorrect or incomplete, or if his assessment of them is erroneous, the statement may still imply a false assertion of fact. Simply couching such statements in terms of opinion does not dispel these implications; and the statement, "In my opinion Jones is a liar," can cause as much damage to reputation as the statement, "Jones is a liar." As Judge Friendly aptly stated: "[It] would be destructive of the law of libel if a writer could escape liability for accusations of [defamatory conduct] simply by using, explicitly or implicitly the words 'I think.'" *See* Cianci, *supra*, at 64. It is worthy of note that at common law, even the privilege of fair comment did not extend to "a false statement of fact, whether it was expressly stated or implied from an expression of opinion. Restatement (Second) of Torts, § 566, Comment a (1977)."[35]

Having rejected a constitutional opinion privilege, the Court determined that assertions in the column and the attached headline were actionable because they inferred objectively verifiable facts supporting the assertion that Milkovich had perjured himself in a judicial proceeding.[36] "A determination whether petitioner lied in this instance can be made on a core of objective evidence by comparing *inter alia*, petitioner's

---

32. *Id.* at 14–21, 110 S. Ct. at 2703–07, 111 L. Ed. 2d at 14–19.

33. The entire passage reads:

Under the First Amendment there is no such thing as a false idea. However pernicious an opinion may seem, we depend for its correction not on the conscience of judges and juries but on the competition of other ideas. But there is no constitutional value in false statements of fact.

Gertz v. Robert Welch, Inc., 418 U.S. 323, 339–40, 94 S.Ct. 2997, 3007, 41 L.Ed.2d 789, 805 (1974).

34. Milkovich, 497 U.S. at 18, 110 S. Ct. at 2705, 111 L. Ed. 2d at 17.

35. *Id.* at 18–19, 110 S. Ct. at 2705–06, 111 L. Ed. 2d at 17–18.

36. *Id.* at 21–22, 110 S. Ct. at 2707, 111 L. Ed. 2d at 19.

testimony before the OHSAA [Ohio High School Athletic Association] board with his subsequent testimony before the trial court."[37] Thus, the Court developed a new dichotomy, not between opinion and fact but between objectively verifiable assertions and non-verifiable assertions.

Continuing, the Court scrutinized the offending column and added, "This is not the sort of loose, figurative, or hyperbolic language which would negate the impression that the writer was seriously maintaining that petitioner committed the crime of perjury. Nor does the general tenor of the article negate this impression."[38] Does this language mean that even if statements infer objectively verifiable facts, they are not actionable under the First Amendment if made in a loose, figurative or hyperbolic fashion? Adding to the uncertainty is the Court's language that the general tenor of the column did not negate the impression that the writer was implying underlying facts supporting the assertion that the wrestling coach lied in a judicial proceeding. The Court's insistence that courts focus on whether the assertions complained of have a factual predicate that is objectively verifiable seems at war with the idea it expresses later in its opinion that the communicator's language might be judged within the general tenor or context of the material surrounding it.

All in all, the Court's rejection of an opinion privilege has increased the risk of liability for media commentary, has done little to clarify First Amendment doctrine, and its attempt to protect the societal interest in individual reputation has caused much confusion in post-*Milkovich* defamation actions.[39]

F.   The Known, The Unknown and the Difficult After Milkovich v. Lorain Journal Co.

1.   The Known

Though adding to the complexity of distinguishing statements and assertions that are actionable and those that are not because of their connotational nature, *Milkovich v. Lorain Journal Co.* does confirm that certain expression is not actionable. Expression of ideas even though they implicate living individuals is not actionable.[40] Nor is hyperbole, gross exaggeration, invective, epithetical expression,[41] or speculation on

---

37. *Id.* at 21, 110 S. Ct. at 2707, 111 L. Ed. 2d at 19.

38. *Id.*

39. *See, e.g.,* Immuno AG. v. Moor–Jankowski, 77 N.Y.2d 235, 250, 566 N.Y.S.2d 906, 914, 567 N.E.2d 1270, 1278, cert. denied 500 U.S. 954, 111 S.Ct. 2261, 114 L.Ed.2d 713 (1991). *See also* Martin F. Hansen, *Fact, Opinion, and Consensus: The Verifiability of Allegedly Defamatory Speech,* 62 Geo. Wash. L. Rev. 43, 45 (1993); Kathryn D. Sowle, *A Matter of Opinion:* Milkovich *Four Years Later,* 3 Wm & Mary Bill Rts. J. 467, 471–75 (1994);

David A. Logan, *Of "Sloppy Journalism," "Corporate Tyranny," And Mea Culpas: The Curious Case of* Moldea v. New York Times, 37 Wm & Mary L. Rev. 161, 167 (1995); David C. Vogel, Note, *You Have the Right to Criticize This Casenote: Protecting Negative Reviews Within the Law of Defamation and the First Amendment,* 60 Mo. L. Rev. 445, 445 (1995).

40. Milkovich, 497 U.S. at 18, 110 S. Ct. at 2705, 111 L. Ed. 2d at 17.

41. *See* Collins v. Cox Enterprises, Inc., 215 Ga.App. 679, 680, 452 S.E.2d 226, 227 (Ga.Ct.App.1994) (suggestion that one

another's motives.[42] And, of course opinion is not actionable when couched in a way that is objectively unverifiable.[43]

2. *The Unknown*

As noted above the Court's statement regarding loose, figurative and hyperbolic language raises but does not answer the question whether the choice of words used to convey an opinion may have an effect on actionability even when the opinion is predicated on objectively verifiable facts. In addition, the Court doesn't provide a definition of "loose" language needed to permit lower courts to distinguish between "loose" and, if you will, "unloose" language as it might affect actionability under the First Amendment. More importantly, it is yet unknown if the context in which objectively verifiable assertions are made might properly be resorted to defeat or even support actionability. Some lower courts continue to rely, at least in part, on the context in which allegedly defamatory assertions are made in determining whether actions against the media will be allowed.[44]

Another unknown is whether and to what extent *Milkovich* affects what was once referred to as the common law qualified privilege of "fair comment." It can be expected that this privilege will be resorted to more

changed his name for base political motives held not actionable); Maynard v. Daily Gazette Co., 191 W.Va. 601, 606, 447 S.E.2d 293, 298 (1994) (statement that "[i]n hindsight, it appears that Maynard was interested chiefly in maintaining the athletic eligibility of his charges" *held* not actionable).

42. Milkovich, 497 U.S. at 16–17, 110 S. Ct. at 2704, 111 L. Ed. 2d at 16. *See, e.g.,* Phantom Touring, Inc. v. Affiliated Publications, 953 F.2d 724, 728 (1st Cir.), cert. denied 504 U.S. 974, 112 S.Ct. 2942, 119 L.Ed.2d 567 (1992) ("rip-off," "fraud," "scandal," "fake," "phony," "snake-oil job" held figurative and hyperbolic and not actionable); Greenhalgh v. Casey, 67 F.3d 299 (6th Cir.1995) (unpublished dissertation; calling one a "lying asshole" not actionable because objectively such rhetoric cannot be based on objective fact); Sagan v. Apple Computer, Inc., 874 F.Supp. 1072, 1075–76 (C.D.Cal.1994) (change of code name of new computer from "Carl Sagan" to "Butt–Head Astronomer" not actionable). *But see* Spence v. Flynt, 816 P.2d 771 (Wyo.1991) (Hustler Magazine's naming attorney Gerry Spence its "Asshole of the Month" might be actionable libel); cert. denied, 503 U.S. 984, 112 S.Ct. 1668, 118 L.Ed.2d 388 (1992). *See also* Kathryn D. Sowle, *A Matter of Opinion:* Milkovich *Four Years Later*, 3 Wm & Mary Bill Rts. J. 467, 540–48 (1994).

43. *See, e.g.,* Washington v. Smith, 80 F.3d 555, 556–57, 317 U.S. App. D.C. 79, 80–81 (D.C.Cir.1996) (statements in basket-

ball magazine that "[t]he [Kansas] Jayhawks are loaded with talent.... But coach Marian Washington usually finds a way to screw things up. This season will be no different." *held* not actionable because not objectively verifiable).

44. *See, e.g.,* Levin v. McPhee, 119 F.3d 189, 196–197 (2d Cir.1997) (applying New York law); Moldea v. New York Times Co. (II), 22 F.3d 310, 306 U.S. App. D.C. 1 (D.C. Cir.1994), cert. denied, 513 U.S. 875, 115 S.Ct. 202, 130 L.Ed.2d 133 (1994); Keohane v. Wilkerson, 859 P.2d 291, 296 (Colo.Ct. App.1993) ("[T]he phrasing of the statement, the context in which it appears, and the surrounding circumstances of its publication, are relevant.... "), *aff'd* 882 P.2d 1293 (Colo.1994); Kumaran v. Brotman, 247 Ill.App.3d 216, 228, 186 Ill.Dec. 952, 617 N.E.2d 191, 200 (Ill.App.1993) (context utilized in support of actionability of a statement accusing another of engaging in a "scam"); Gross v. New York Times Co., 82 N.Y.2d 146, 153, 603 N.Y.S.2d 813, 817, 623 N.E.2d 1163, 1167 (1993) ("In our State the inquiry, which must be made by the court ... entails an examination of the challenged statements with a view toward ... whether either the full context of the communication in which the statement appears or the broader social context and surrounding circumstances are such as to 'signal ... readers or listeners that what is being read or heard is likely to be opinion, not fact' ") (citations omitted).

frequently by media defendants when their allegedly defamatory assertions verge on opinion, thus increasing its importance.[45] But will the approach taken toward opinion in *Milkovich* encourage state courts to tighten their requirements for the availability of their fair comment or state constitutional defenses or reduce their scope of protection?

Some post-*Milkovich* cases provide clues to answering this last question. In *Immuno AG v. Moor–Jankowski*[46] after the New York Court of Appeals had initially decided a libel action in favor of the editor of a scientific journal who published a letter critical of the plaintiff company on the bases that the letter expressed opinion absolutely protected by the New York and United States Constitutions, and after the Supreme Court had vacated the New York Court's judgment and remanded for consideration in light of its decision in the interim in *Milkovich*, the state appellate court chose to adhere to its original decision. While reading *Milkovich* as not considering the contextual factors set out in *Ollman v. Evans*,[47] the New York court still found that the letter to the editor was not actionable under the First Amendment and that summary judgment for the defendant was properly entered.

The New York court analyzed the remanded case under the state constitution and reached the same conclusion. The court said that the language of the New York constitution was very expansive and often provided broader protection for expression than did the Federal Constitution.[48] Reflective of this, the court read the guarantee of free expression in the New York Constitution as requiring consideration of the context in which the complained of expression is made.[49]

Vail v. The Plain Dealer Publ'g Co.[50] involved a column in the Cleveland Plain Dealer complaining that a candidate for public office was a "gay-basher," "neo-numbskull," "bigot" and was engaging in "hate-mongering." The column ended with the writer saying, "Having learned long ago never to underestimate the neonumbskull vote, I won't hazard a guess on whether her hate-mongering will work. But although I personally don't have much use for bigots of any sort, I have a particular problem with those who can't even be up front about it. Honesty, it would appear, is one value on which Vail is not so 'pro.' "[51]

Ms. Vail brought a libel action which was dismissed by the trial court for failure to state a legal claim. This action was reversed by the

45. *See* RODNEY A. SMOLLA, LAW OF DEFAMATION § 6.02[4][b] (1991).

46. 77 N.Y.2d 235, 566 N.Y.S.2d 906, 567 N.E.2d 1270, cert. denied 500 U.S. 954, 111 S.Ct. 2261, 114 L.Ed.2d 713 (1991).

47. 750 F.2d 970, 982–85, 242 U.S. App. D.C. 301, 313–16 (D.C.Cir.1984), cert. denied 471 U.S. 1127, 105 S.Ct. 2662, 86 L.Ed.2d 278 (1985).

48. Immuno AG, 77 N.Y.2d at 249, 566 N.Y.S.2d at 913–15, 567 N.E.2d at 1277–78.

49. *Id.* at 252–255, 566 N.Y.S.2d at 916–18, 567 N.E.2d at 1280–82. *See* 600 W.

115th St. Corp. v. Von Gutfeld, 80 N.Y.2d 130, 143–45, 589 N.Y.S.2d 825, 832–33, 603 N.E.2d 930, 937–38 (1992), cert. denied 508 U.S. 910, 113 S.Ct. 2341, 124 L.Ed.2d 252 (1993); Gross v. New York Times Co., 82 N.Y.2d 146, 155–156, 603 N.Y.S.2d 813, 817–20, 623 N.E.2d 1163, 1167–69 (1993).

50. 72 Ohio St.3d 279, 649 N.E.2d 182 (1995), cert. denied 516 U.S. 1043, 116 S.Ct. 700, 133 L.Ed.2d 657 (1996).

51. *Id.* at 279–80, 649 N.E.2d at 184.

court of appeals. The intermediate appellate court believed that the columnist's description of the candidate as being anti-gay and fostering homophobia in an effort to get elected were statements capable of being proven false and were therefore actionable.

The Ohio Supreme Court disagreed. That court held that regardless of the decision in *Milkovich*, the Ohio Constitution provided protection for opinion and opinion would be distinguished from fact on an analysis based on the factors set out in *Ollman*, *i.e.*, the specific language used, whether the assertion is verifiable, the meaning of the statement in context and the broader social context in which the statement was made.[52] With this analysis, the Ohio court shifted the focus away from verifiability in *Milkovich* and back to the fact-opinion dichotomy. Applying the *Ollman* factors the court found that the assertions in the column were simply value laden opinions.

The above cases suggest that at least in heavily populated jurisdictions with major concentrations of media companies and a tradition of protecting expression, there will be no cutting back on the common law fair comment defense and perhaps even recognition or expansion of an opinion privilege under state constitutions. Whether the protection of opinion and commentary is based on common law or state constitution, defendant news and information media would do well to emphasize state law in their motions for dismissal or summary judgment where there is any credible argument that the expression complained of is opinion.

3. *The Difficult: Applying the Milkovich Verifiability Test*

In addition to the confusion wrought by *Milkovich*, its test of objective verifiability of complained of expression is difficult to apply. Objectivity and subjectivity are not always easy to distinguish and, as a result, the lower court decisions attempting to follow *Milkovich* have gone every which way.

a. *Miscellaneous examples of courts making misapplications*

Examples of inconsistency abound.[53] These include *Maynard v. Daily Gazette Co.*,[54] in which, among other things, a newspaper editorial accused a professor of education and, at the time, director of his university's student athletes program, of engineering a basketball scholarship for his son at his university because of his position. Resorting to a contextual analysis, the West Virginia Supreme Court of Appeals found these statements factually non-verifiable under *Milkovich*. But if it had focused on the language of these charges as *Milkovich* requires, would

---

52. *Id.* at 281–82, 649 N.E.2d at 185.

53. *See* Robert C. Vanderet, et al., *Media Law and Defamation Torts: Recent Developments*, 27 Tort & Ins. L. J. 333,340–342 (1992); Martin F. Hansen, *Fact, Opinion, and Consensus: The Verifiability of Allegedly Defamatory Speech*, 62 Geo. Wash. L. Rev. 43, 45 (1993); Kathryn D. Sowle, *A*

Matter of Opinion: Milkovich *Four Years Later*, 3 Wm & Mary Bill Rts. J. 467, 498–552(1994) (an exhaustive treatment of the history of, decision and issues in and operation of *Milkovich*).

54. 191 W.Va. 601, 447 S.E.2d 293 (1994).

not the court have had to reach the conclusion that objectively verifiable facts underlay the claim that the plaintiff used his position and influence to obtain a perhaps undeserved scholarship for his son?

And in *George v. International Society for Krishna Consciousness of California*[55] a Krishna newsletter commenting on the plaintiff's post Krishna activities stated in part, "For all we know now, her accounts of brutality and beatings [by her parents] were exaggerated or totally fabricated."[56] The California District Court of Appeal held this language non-actionable because it was "not a provably false statement of fact" about the plaintiff.[57] "The use of the prefatory language 'For all we know now' alerted readers" according to the appeals court, "that defendants were merely expressing their opinion.... "[58]

The *George* decision flies in the face of *Milkovich* and is clearly incorrect. The import of the quoted passage from the newsletter is that plaintiff lied to the Krishnas about being physically abused by her parents when she joined them—an objectively verifiable fact of the same order as the claim in *Milkovich* that the plaintiff had lied in a judicial proceeding.

That the statement in *George* was prefaced by the words "for all we know now" does not prevent the succeeding language from being held actionable.[59]

b. *Moldea v. New York Times Co.—the quintessential case of difficult application*

For the media one of the most dangerous vehicles giving rise to the difficult debate over what is opinion, what is fact and what is verifiable is literary, artistic or culinary criticism. The reviewer and the reviewee found this out the very hard way in *Moldea v. New York Times Co.*[60] There, the New York Times Book Review published a review by veteran Times sportswriter Gerald Eskenazi of the book "Interference: How Organized Crime Influences Professional Football" by Dan E. Moldea, an

---

55. 4 Cal.Rptr.2d 473 (Cal.App.1992) (ordered not published; no official report).

56. *Id.* at 489.

57. *Id.* at 503.

58. *Id.; compare* Levin v. McPhee, 119 F.3d 189 (2d Cir.1997) (words suggesting that published versions concerning how a Russian artist died in a studio fire were imagined made the versions opinion).

59. *See* Milkovich v. Lorain Journal Co., 497 U.S. 1, 18–19, 110 S.Ct. 2695, 2706, 111 L.Ed.2d 1, 18 (1990); *see also* Kathryn D. Sowle, *A Matter of Opinion:* Milkovich *Four Years Later,* 3 Wm & Mary Bill Rts. J. 467, 513–15 (1994). One case that got the application of the *Milkovich* verifiability standard right but with a nearly ludicrous result is Unelko Corp. v. Rooney, 912 F.2d 1049 (9th Cir.1990), cert. denied 499 U.S.

961, 111 S.Ct. 1586, 113 L.Ed.2d 650 (1991) in which in the course of a humorous disquisition on things viewers sent him, Andy Rooney of CBS's "60 Minutes" said that a windshield product designed to repel rain, sleet and snow and make the removal of bugs and dirt easier "didn't work." The United States Court of Appeals for the Ninth Circuit held that Rooney's statement was objectively verifiable and therefore actionable. However, the appeals court upheld summary judgment for Rooney and CBS, Inc. because the plaintiff had failed to create a triable issue of fact as to the falsity of the statement.

60. 15 F.3d 1137, 304 U.S. App. D.C. 406, *opinion modified and summary judgment affirmed* 22 F.3d 310, 306 U.S. App. D.C. 1 (D.C.Cir.), cert. denied 513 U.S. 875, 115 S.Ct. 202, 130 L.Ed.2d 133 (1994).

investigative journalist. The review was highly critical of the book and accused the author of "sloppy journalism."[61] In supporting this particular criticism Eskenazi made five assertions to which Moldea also took offense.[62] After the review of "Interference" was published sales of the book nosedived and Moldea's collateral sources of income dried up. After repeated efforts to obtain satisfaction from the Times were unsuccessful Moldea filed suit.

The United States District Court for the District of Columbia granted summary judgment in favor of the Times based on its determination that the portions of the Times review to which Moldea took exception consisted only of statements of nonverifiable opinion about the book or were so obviously true that reasonable jurors could not find them false.[63]

A panel of the United States Court of Appeals for the District of Columbia Circuit consisting of the Chief Judge Abner Mikva and Circuit Judges Patricia Wald and Harry Edwards split two to one in reversing the entry of summary judgment and remanding the case for trial. Writing for himself and Judge Wald, Judge Edwards first found that the complained of passages were capable of defamatory meaning by the reader and then reached the issue of verifiability. Relying quite literally on *Milkovich* Judge Edwards concluded that, "[i]n levying the charge of 'sloppy journalism,' it is inescapable that Eskenazi implies certain facts—that Moldea plays fast and loose with his sources, that his allegations are not to be believed.... Although 'sloppy' in a vacuum may be difficult to quantify, the term has obvious, measurable aspects when applied to the field of investigative journalism."[64] He also found that two of Eskenazi's assertions supporting the "sloppy journalism" criticism were also capable of objective verification and required jury determination of their truth or falsity, *i.e.*, the assertions that Moldea portrayed a meeting of two opposing NFL players as "sinister" and that Moldea revived the discredited notion that an NFL team owner had been murdered rather than having been an accidental drowning victim.[65]

In making these determinations Judge Edward expressly rejected consideration that the complained of material appeared in the context of a book review. "To permit a defendant to escape liability for libel merely because defamatory remarks are published in a book review would be as simplistic as permitting an author to insulate himself or herself by merely prefacing assertions with the words 'I think ...' and calling

61. The entire passage that gave Moldea offense read, "But there is too much sloppy journalism to trust the bulk of this book's 512 pages—including its whopping 64 pages of notes." Moldea, 15 F.3d at 1141, 304 U.S. App. D.C. at 410.

62. The five supporting passages as set out by the District of Columbia Circuit were: [text in Practitioner Edition only].

Id. at 1141–42, 304 U.S. App. D.C. at 410–11.

63. *Id.* at 1140–41, 304 U.S. App. D.C. at 409–10.

64. *Id.* at 1145, 304 U.S. App. D.C. at 414.

65. *Id.* at 1146–48, 304 U.S. App. D.C. at 415–17.

everything that followed nonactionable opinion."[66]

Chief Judge Mikva strongly dissented. He began with the proposition that the assertion of "sloppiness" in the context of a book review "is not verifiable, no matter what examples are used to sustain or reject the charge."[67] Continuing, he wrote that "the inherent imprecision of the phrase 'too sloppy' when coupled with its use to describe a book firmly pushes the statement at issue under the protective umbrella of nonverifiable opinion."[68]

Clearly Judge Mikva believed that the immediate context and tenor in which words are used must be looked to in determining their meaning and verifiability.

> [T]he overall tenor of the review suggests that the reviewer was not as much concerned with specific misstatements of objective and verifiable facts as he was with what he saw as Mr. Moldea's fundamental failure to prove the thesis of the book—his failure to produce a "smoking gun" linking the NFL to organized crime. At bottom, the review expresses a uniquely subjective evaluation of the quality of *Interference*.

> While another reader might disagree that Mr. Moldea fumbled the ball, it is difficult to see how one could prove the reviewer's assessment wrong as it is based largely on his particular tastes and standards. Furthermore, because the burden of proving that an allegedly defamatory statement is false lies with the plaintiff, defendants should prevail in cases like this where the verifiability of the statements at issue is doubtful.... Accordingly, the phrase "too much sloppy journalism" used in a book review to describe one's writing style or research methods is simply too subjective to be verified and therefore should be protected under *Milkovich*.[69]

He expressly decried the majority's refusal to consider the effect of the defendant's communicative vehicle upon the audience.[70]

A shocked and very concerned New York Times Company filed a motion with the appeals court for rehearing obviously hoping to persuade the entire membership that the panel had committed error.[71] But a funny thing happened on the way to an en banc proceeding. The panel confessed error and reversed itself thereby affirming the district court's entry of summary judgment for the New York Times Company.[72]

---

66. *Id.* at 1146, 304 U.S. App. D.C. at 415.

67. *Id.* at 1153, 304 U.S. App. D.C. at 422.

68. *Id.* at 1155, 304 U.S. App. D.C. at 424.

69. *Id.*

70. *Id.* at 1156, 304 U.S. App. D.C. at 425.

71. *See* David A. Logan, *Of "Sloppy Journalism," "Corporate Tyranny," and*

Mea Culpas: The Curious Case of Moldea v. New York Times, 37 Wm & Mary L. Rev. 161, 177–84 (1995) for a detailed description of the reaction of Times people and others to the decision in *Moldea (I)*.

72. This action by the *Moldea* panel is a real rarity in the law and is akin to a baseball umpire, after hearing dissent to his call from the players on the short end of the decision, walks away and then after one more outburst from the disappointed players says "what was I thinking. You guys are

In *Moldea (II)* Judge Edwards apologized for the panel's initial decision, saying that the majority was led into error by its too literal interpretation of *Milkovich* which did not consider context in finding a sports columnist's charge that Milkovich lied under oath was an objectively verifiable fact. Two factors persuaded Judge Edwards that *Milkovich* had not ruled out resort to context in the present situation involving literary criticism. First, the accusation of criminal conduct is a classic libel, and thus in *Milkovich* there was no need for the Supreme Court to consider the context in which the accusation was made.[73] Second, in *Masson v. New Yorker Magazine, Inc.*,[74] decided shortly after *Milkovich*, the Court resorted to context in another defamation case to determine whether words placed in quotation marks will be interpreted by readers as the actual statements of the speaker.[75]

In finally recognizing that context matters as to the meaning of words and the verifiability of assertions formed by the combination of words, Judge Edwards chose to accept the standard proposed by the New York Times Company for evaluating critical reviews made in its petition for rehearing. "The proper analysis would make commentary actionable only when the interpretations are unsupportable by reference to the written work."[76] In concluding that under this standard the Times book review was not actionable, Judge Edwards wrote

> Our initial decision in this case erred by basing its holding on a standard that failed to take into account the fact that the challenged statements appeared in the context of a book review, and were solely evaluations of a literary work.... Applying the "supportable interpretation" standard, the correct measure of the challenged statements' verifiability as a matter of law is whether no reasonable person could find that the review's characterizations were supportable interpretations of *Interference*. Applying this standard, we hold that the Times review is not actionable in defamation.[77]

With the decision of District of Columbia Circuit in *Moldea (II)* and the Supreme Court's denial of certiorari,[78] the legal contretemps over criticism of the book "Interference: How Organized Crime Influences Professional Football" came to an end. But problems relating to the verifiability standard of *Milkovich* will continue to arise, if not in the

---

right and I'm changing my call." How many times has anyone seen that happen at a professional baseball game? The need for two full-scale opinions in *Moldea* underlines the difficulty of applying the objective verifiability standard of *Milkovich*.

73. "We now recognize however, as has the First Circuit, that *Milkovich* did not disavow the importance of context, but simply 'discounted it in the circumstances of that case.' "*Moldea (II)*, 22 F.3d 310, 314, 306 U.S. App. D.C. 1, 5 (D.C.Cir.1994), cert. denied 513 U.S. 875, 115 S.Ct. 202, 130 L.Ed.2d 133 (1994) (quoting Phantom Touring, Inc. v. Affiliated Publications, 953

F.2d 724, 729 n. 9 (1st Cir.), cert. denied 504 U.S. 974, 112 S.Ct. 2942, 119 L.Ed.2d 567 (1992)).

74. 501 U.S. 496, 111 S.Ct. 2419, 115 L.Ed.2d 447 (1991).

75. *Id.* at 511–13, 111 S. Ct. at 2430–31, 115 L. Ed. 2d at 469–70.

76. Moldea (II), 22 F.3d at 315, 306 U.S. App. D.C. at 6.

77. *Id.* at 317, 306 U.S. App. D.C. at 8.

78. 513 U.S. 875, 115 S. Ct. 202, 130 L. Ed. 2d 133 (1994).

field of media criticism then in other areas. If nothing else, *Moldea* teaches us the difficulty of determining what is and what is not verifiable, particularly when context is ignored.[79]

G. *Assessment and Prognosis*

The area of defamation law involving the distinction between actionable fact and non-actionable opinion has always been a difficult one. For a time, however, guidance was provided by former Circuit Judge Starr's isolation of four factors that should be referred to in making the distinction.[80] They are common usage or meaning, verifiability, immediate context, and social context. But when the Supreme Court in *Milkovich* singled out one factor—verifiability—for determining whether assertions complained of are actionable, what was difficult became even more so for two reasons. First, lower courts could not be sure whether the contextual factors had been swept away, and second, if they were, common sense results might be sacrificed on the alter of objective verifiability.[81] Unless and until the Supreme Court clarifies its view regarding the availability of contextual analysis confusion in this area will continue.

If the Court ultimately permits the lower courts to consider the actionability of complained of assertions in context, the law will return part way to the *status quo ante*, though without a discrete First Amendment opinion privilege. Even if the law of defamation is clarified to allow consideration of immediate and societal contexts, media defendants should always consider whether they might be better off embracing state common law and constitutional privileges which, in some jurisdictions, may provide more protection for expression of opinion than the Supreme Court is willing to recognize under the First Amendment.

In the specific area of literary criticism, should the Supreme Court ultimately adopt the standard for actionability proposed by the New York Times Company and adopted by the District of Columbia Circuit in *Moldea (II)*, the media would have little to fear from the expression of honest and *relevant* opinion concerning at least written works offered for public approbation. The Times "supportable interpretation" standard makes the grant of summary judgment to media defendants in cases

---

79. A number of courts have developed contextual tests for separating fact from opinion following *Moldea II*. In *Hunter v. Hartman*, 545 N.W.2d 699 (Minn.Ct.App. 1996), for instance, a Minnesota appeals court fashioned this two-part test:

(1) When an allegedly defamatory statement, in its particular context, (*e.g.*, editorial, op-ed piece, sports column, review or television commentary), would be expected to be opinion, (2) it is protected so long as (a) it is tied to the work or event being reviewed or commented upon and (b) it is a supportable interpretation of the work or event.

Id. at 706–09. *See also* Partington v. Bugliosi, 56 F.3d 1147 (9th Cir.1995).

80. Ollman v. Evans, 750 F.2d 970, 979–984, 242 U.S. App. D.C. 301, 310–15 (D.C.Cir.1984), cert. denied 471 U.S. 1127, 105 S.Ct. 2662, 86 L.Ed.2d 278 (1985).

81. *See, e.g.*, Unelko Corp. v. Rooney, 912 F.2d 1049 (9th Cir.1990), cert. denied 499 U.S. 961, 111 S.Ct. 1586, 113 L.Ed.2d 650 (1991); Moldea v. New York Times Co. (I), 15 F.3d 1137, 304 U.S. App. D.C. 406 (D.C.Cir.), *opinion modified*, 22 F.3d 310 (1994), cert. denied 513 U.S. 875, 115 S.Ct. 202, 130 L.Ed.2d 133 (1994).

involving reviews quite likely because of its requirement that plaintiff establish to the trial judge's satisfaction that no reasonable person could find that the reviewer's assertions were supportable interpretations of the work reviewed. The standard, if adopted, would pose a high hurdle to plaintiffs in getting to a jury.

5.8 Other Constitutional Privileges

A. Nondisclosure of the Editorial Decision–Making Process

In *Herbert v. Lando*,[1] the Supreme Court held that in a defamation action brought by a "public figure" plaintiff, the defendant can be compelled in discovery to report on the editorial process and state of mind of those responsible for publication. Since the plaintiff must prove actual malice[2] regarding press circulation of damaging falsehoods injurious to plaintiff's reputation, he can use the discovery process to:

> obtain the necessary evidence to prove the critical elements of his cause of action.... New York Times and its progeny made it essential to proving liability that the plaintiff focus on the conduct and state of mind of the defendant. To be liable, the alleged defamer of public officials or of public figures must know or have reason to suspect that his publication is false. In other cases proof of some kind of fault, negligence perhaps, is essential to recovery. Inevitably, unless liability is to be completely foreclosed, the thoughts and editorial processes of the alleged defamer would be open to examination.[3]

Anthony Herbert, a retired Vietnam veteran, who had accused his superior officers of covering up reports of atrocities and other war crimes, was the subject of a program on the CBS network show "Sixty Minutes" and an article published in the *Atlantic Monthly*. Barry Lando, produced and edited the television program and wrote the magazine article, both of which challenged the existence of the war crimes. Mr. Herbert sued Mr. Lando, Mike Wallace, the "Sixty Minutes" on-air reporter, CBS and the *Atlantic Monthly* for defamation, alleging that the program and article falsely and maliciously portrayed him as a liar and person who had fabricated war crimes charges to explain his relief from command. Mr. Herbert sought substantial damages for injury to his reputation and to the value of a recently published autobiography.

The *Herbert* case offers guidance both in terms of what level of proof a plaintiff must show to prove defamation of a public figure and what opportunities the plaintiff should have to probe the state of mind of the defendant. Absent clear and convincing proof of actual knowledge of falsity or reckless disregard of probable falsity, media defendants are immune from liability for libel of public officials and figures. On the

1. 441 U.S. 153, 99 S.Ct. 1635, 60 L.Ed.2d 115 (1979).

2. *See* New York Times Co. v. Sullivan, 376 U.S. 254, 84 S.Ct. 710, 11 L.Ed.2d 686 (1964).

3. Herbert, 441 U.S. at 159–60, 99 S. Ct. at 1640, 60 L. Ed. 2d at 124.

other hand, plaintiffs are entitled to use the discovery process to seek evidence for determining whether a defendant acted with an "improper motive ... [and] the intent or purpose with which the publication was made, the belief of the defendant in the truth of his statement, or upon the ill will which the defendant might have borne toward the plaintiff."[4]

The Court rejected defendants' reference to *Miami Herald Pub. Co. v. Tornillo*,[5] and *Columbia Broadcasting Sys., Inc. v. Democratic Nat'l Comm.*,[6] as supporting unequivocal protection for the editorial process. "But holdings that neither a State nor the Federal Government may dictate what must or must not be printed neither expressly nor impliedly suggests that the editorial process is immune from any inquiry whatsoever."[7]

The court declined the invitation presented by the defense to expand and reinterpret *New York Times Co. v. Sullivan* in view of changed circumstances and developments in First Amendment jurisprudence:

> We are thus being asked to modify firmly established constitutional doctrine by placing beyond the plaintiff's reach a range of direct evidence relevant to proving knowing or reckless falsehood by the publisher of an alleged libel, elements that are critical to plaintiffs such as Herbert. The case for making this modification is by no means clear and convincing, and we decline to accept it.[8]

The Court reasoned that in view of the opportunity for media defendants to assert their good-faith belief in the truth of what they published, plaintiffs should face no impenetrable barrier to accessing evidence that may corroborate their side of the case. It rejected the need for an editorial privilege asserted by the media defendants on grounds that requiring disclosure of editorial conversations and reporters' conclusions about the veracity of collected material, would have an intolerable chilling effect on the editorial process and editorial decision making. The Court reasoned that case precedent[9] supports eliminating the risk of undue self-censorship and the suppression of truthful material, but not the fear of damages and liability for publishing knowing or reckless falsehoods.

4. *Id.* at 164, 99 S. Ct. at 1642–1643, 60 L. Ed. 2d at 126. "Courts have traditionally admitted any direct or indirect evidence relevant to the state of mind of the defendant and necessary to defeat a conditional privilege or enhance damages. The rules are applicable to the press and to other defendants alike, and it is evident that the courts across the country have long been accepting evidence going to the editorial processes of the media without encountering constitutional objections." *Id.* at 165, 99 S. Ct. at 1643, 60 L. Ed. 2d at 126–27.

5. 418 U.S. 241, 94 S.Ct. 2831, 41 L.Ed.2d 730 (1974).

6. 412 U.S. 94, 93 S.Ct. 2080, 36 L.Ed.2d 772 (1973).

7. Herbert, 441 U.S. at 168, 99 S. Ct. at 1644, 60 L. Ed. 2d at 128.

8. *Id.* at 169–170, 99 S. Ct. at 1645, 60 L. Ed. 2d at 129–130.

9. *Id.* at 171–172, 99 S. Ct. at 1646, 60 L. Ed. 2d at 130–131 (citing Gertz v. Robert Welch, Inc., 418 U.S. 323, 340, 94 S.Ct. 2997, 3006–3007, 41 L.Ed.2d 789, 805–806 (1974); Curtis Publishing Co. v. Butts, 388 U.S. 130, 87 S.Ct. 1975, 18 L.Ed.2d 1094 (1967); New York Times Co. v. Sullivan, 376 U.S. 254, 84 S.Ct. 710, 11 L.Ed.2d 686 (1964)).

In public figure cases, the plaintiff's inquiry into the editorial may therefore include:

1. [the reporter's or editor's] conclusions during his research and investigations regarding people or leads to be pursued, or not to be pursued . . .;

2. [the reporter's or editor's] conclusions about facts [imparted] by interviewees and his [or her] state of mind with respect to the veracity of persons interviewed;

3. [t]he basis for conclusions where [the reporter or editor] testified that he did reach a conclusion concerning the veracity of persons, information or events;

4. conversations [with journalistic colleagues and others] about matter to be included or excluded from the broadcast or publication; and

5. [the reporter's or editor's] intentions as manifested by his [or her] decision to include or exclude certain material.[10]

B. Neutral Reportage

1. Edwards v. National Audubon Society

In *Edwards v. Nat'l Audubon Soc'y Inc.*,[11] and *Edwards v. New York Times Co.*,[12] several prominent scientists and university professors brought a defamation action against employees of the National Audubon Society and the New York Times based on publication of an article accusing plaintiffs of being "paid liars" as regards their support for continued use of the insecticide DDT. The District Court rendered judgment for plaintiffs, with a jury concluding that the Audubon Society staff biologist and vice president had libeled the scientists by impugning their professional integrity. The jury also found the New York Times guilty of actual malice on the grounds that the reporter had serious doubts about the truth of the statement that the appellees were paid liars even if he did not have any doubt that he was faithfully reporting allegations of the Audubon representative.

The Second Circuit Court of Appeals held that a libel judgment against the newspaper was constitutionally impermissible, because the paper neutrally and accurately reported the facts of a newsworthy event and that the evidence did not support a finding of actual malice on the part of the newspaper. The Court created a new constitutional privilege of neutral reporting that would grant the press absolute immunity from libel judgments for accurately reporting "newsworthy" statements, regardless of the press's belief about the truth of the statements:

10. *Id.* at 181–182, 99 S. Ct. at 1651, 60 L. Ed. 2d at 137.

11. 556 F.2d 113 (2d Cir.) cert. denied, 434 U.S. 1002, 98 S.Ct. 647, 54 L.Ed.2d 498 (1977).

12. *Id.*

We believe that a libel judgment against the Times, in the face of this finding of fact, is constitutionally impermissible. At stake in this case is a fundamental principle. Succinctly stated, when a responsible, prominent organization like the National Audubon Society makes serious charges against a public figure, the First Amendment protects the accurate and disinterested reporting of those charges, regardless of the reporter's private views regarding their validity. . . . We do not believe that the press may be required under the First Amendment to suppress newsworthy statements merely because it has serious doubts regarding their truth. Nor must the press take up cudgels against dubious charges in order to publish them without fear or liability for defamation.[13]

The Court concluded that the benefits of having a robust and unintimidated press justify providing immunity from defamation suits where the journalist believes, reasonably and in good faith, that his report accurately conveys the charges made. However, this privilege does not extend to instances where a publisher espouses or concurs in the charges made by others, or deliberately distorts these statements to launch a person attack of his own on a public figure.[14] While not condoning mischievous and unwarranted assaults on the good name of individuals like the scientists favoring the use of DDT, the Court believed that the interest of a public figure in the purity of his reputation cannot obstruct "that vital pulse of ideas and intelligence on which an informed and self-governing people depend."[15]

2. *Cianci v. New Times Publishing Co.*

In *Cianci v. New Times Publishing Co.*,[16] the Mayor of Providence, Rhode Island, brought a libel action against a magazine that printed an article stating he had once been accused of rape but got the charges withdrawn after paying the accuser $3,000.00. While the United States District Court for the Southern District of New York dismissed the action, the Second Circuit held that the article was capable of defamatory meaning, was not protected as a statement of opinion and was not protected by the constitutional privilege of neutral reportage or the common-law privilege of fair report.

The Court applied the *New York Times v. Sullivan* standard which requires a public official and candidate for public office[17] to prove with "convincing clarity" that a defamatory statement was made with "actual malice" . . . [*i.e.*], with knowledge that it was false or with reckless disregard of whether it was false or not.[18] The Court decided that a jury could properly determine that a defamatory connotation was conveyed

---

13. Edwards v. Nat'l Audubon Soc'y, Inc., 556 F.2d at 120.

14. *See* RESTATEMENT SECOND OF TORTS, Section 580A (1976).

15. Edwards, 556 F.2d at 122.

16. 639 F.2d 54 (2d Cir.1980).

17. *See* Monitor Patriot Co. v. Roy, 401 U.S. 265, 91 S.Ct. 621, 28 L.Ed.2d 35 (1971).

18. *See* New York Times Co. v. Sullivan, 376 U.S. 254, 279–280, 84 S.Ct. 710, 726, 11 L.Ed.2d 686, 706 (1964).

by the article as a whole because readers might conclude that Mayor Cianci was in fact a rapist and an obstructor of justice, not simply a person who had been accused of being such. Likewise, the magazine could be considered a republisher of a libel and subject to liability just as if it had published it originally, even though it attributed the libelous statement to the original publisher, and even though it expressly disavowed the truth of the statement.

The republication of a rape and bribery allegation does not constitute reporting on someone's opinion, or referring to an expression so outlandish to be considered rhetorical hyperbole or an epithet:

> The principle of the Greenbelt–Letter Carriers–Gertz trilogy, of our own Buckley decision, and of the New York Court of Appeals decision in Rinaldi is (1) that a pejorative statement of opinion concerning a public figure generally is constitutionally protected, quite apart from Sullivan, no matter how vigorously expressed; (2) that this principle applies even when the statement includes a term which could refer to criminal conduct if the term could not reasonably be so understood in context; but (3) that the principle does not cover a charge which could reasonably be understood as imputing specific criminal or other wrongful acts.[19]

The Court concluded that "even if the article were to be read as only expressing the 'opinion' that Cianci committed the crimes of rape and obstruction of justice, it is not absolutely protected as distinguished from the protection afforded by *Sullivan*. The charges of rape and obstruction of justice were not employed in a 'loose, figurative sense' or as 'rhetorical hyperbole' [and therefore] [a] jury could find that the effect of the article was to convey the idea ... [that the Mayor had engaged in criminal conduct]."[20]

3. *Dickey v. CBS*

In *Dickey v. CBS Inc.*,[21] a Congressional candidate brought a defamation suit against the television station that aired a taped television debate during which the incumbent accused him of having accepted a bribe. On appeal from a judgment in favor of the television station, the United States Court of Appeals for the Third Circuit, held contrary to the Second Circuit in *Edwards*, that there was no privilege of neutral reportage. But the appeals court also held that the evidence in the case supported the finding that the television station had not acted with actual malice in broadcasting the debate including the allegedly defamatory statement. The Court affirmed the lower court's reading of *St.*

---

19. Cianci v. New Times Pub. Co., 639 F.2d at 64 (referring to Gertz v. Robert Welch, Inc., 418 U.S. 323, 94 S.Ct. 2997, 41 L.Ed.2d 789, (1974). Greenbelt Cooperative Publishing Assn., Inc. v. Bresler, 398 U.S. 6, 90 S.Ct. 1537, 26 L.Ed.2d 6 (1970), Letter Carriers v. Austin, 418 U.S. 264, 94 S.Ct. 2770, 41 L.Ed.2d 745 (1974) and Buckley v. Littell, 539 F.2d 882 (2d Cir.1976), cert. denied, 429 U.S. 1062, 97 S.Ct. 785, 50 L.Ed.2d 777 (1977)).

20. *Id.*

21. 583 F.2d 1221 (3d Cir.1978).

Amant v. Thompson,[22] implying that no such privilege could exist because it might permit a reporter to publish defamatory material even if he entertained serious doubts about the truth of the defamatory statement reported.[23] Proving reckless disregard requires the plaintiff to produce evidence that the media defendant proceeded with publication even though it could not reasonably infer the truth from such events as "an unverified anonymous telephone call ..., when the publisher's allegations are so inherently improbable that only a reckless man would have put them in circulation ... (or) where there are obvious reasons to doubt the veracity of the informant or the accuracy of his reports."[24]

4.   The Present Uncertain Status of the Privilege

Courts have struggled with the issue of neutral reportage and whether or not to adopt it as a Constitutional privilege. The Supreme Court in *Harte-Hanks Communications, Inc. v. Connaughton,*[25] did not validate neutral reportage as an absolute defense, but it did specify that a failure to investigate a potentially defamatory statement did not by itself establish reckless disregard for the truth.[26] In *Weaver v. Oregonian Publishing Co., Inc.,*[27] the United States Court of Appeals for the Ninth Circuit acknowledged that neutral reporting privilege was "an open and difficult question" such that the lower court erred in granting summary judgment for the defendant in a libel action based on a report of allegations made by an attorney. On the other hand, the Eighth Circuit appears to have adopted the privilege in *Price v. Viking Penguin, Inc.,*[28] where the Court considered a defamation suit by an FBI agent regarding allegations contained in a book covering the violence occurring during the Indian occupation of Wounded Knee, South Dakota and the Pine Ridge Reservation. If an author appears not to have espoused either side's point of view and refrained from distorting coverage, then it is reasonable to report accusations and counter-accusations.[29]

But all in all, the privilege is a shaky one that has never been approved by the Supreme Court and has gotten even shakier recently

22. 390 U.S. 727, 88 S.Ct. 1323, 20 L.Ed.2d 262 (1968).

23. Recklessness "is not measured by whether a reasonably prudent man would have published, or would have investigated before publishing." There must be sufficient evidence to permit the conclusion that the defendant in fact entertained serious doubts as to the truth of his publication. St. Amant v. Thompson, 390 U.S. at 731, 88 S. Ct. at 1325, 20 L.Ed.2d at 267.

24. *Id.* at 732, 88 S. Ct. at 1326, 20 L. Ed. 2d at 268.

25. 491 U.S. 657, 109 S.Ct. 2678, 105 L.Ed.2d 562 (1989).

26. *See id.* at 688, 109 S.Ct. at 2696, 105 L.Ed.2d at 588–589.

27. 878 F.2d 388 (9th Cir.1989). *See also* Khawar v. Globe Int'l, Inc., 54 Cal. Rptr.2d 92, 102–103, *review granted and opinion superseded,* 57 Cal.Rptr.2d 277, 923 P.2d 766 (Cal.1996), *aff'd* 19 Cal.4th 254, 79 Cal.Rptr.2d 178, 965 P.2d 696 (1998), cert. denied ___ U.S. ___, 119 S.Ct. 1760, ___ L.Ed.2d ___ (1999). (limiting the privilege, if any, to claims by public as opposed to private figures).

28. 881 F.2d 1426 (8th Cir.1989), cert. denied 493 U.S. 1036, 110 S.Ct. 757, 107 L.Ed.2d 774 (1990).

29. "Thus we focus on whether the reports were accurate reflections of what was said or done. Evidence of the author's general disposition toward his topic does not establish whether he espoused each particular allegation." *Id.* at 1434.

with the decision in *Khawar v. Globe Int'l Inc.*,[30] in which a California appeals court refused to extend the privilege when *private* figures are suing the newsmedia. The court reasoned that the newsmedia must not be accorded a privilege that may unreasonably undermine individual rights. "[A] reasonable degree of protection for a private individual's reputation is essential to a system of ordered liberty," according to the court.[31]

In addition, "the purposeful avoidance of the truth is in a different category."[32] A publisher who does not already have obvious reasons to doubt the accuracy of a story need not initiate an investigation that might create such doubt. However, once such doubt exists, the publisher must act reasonably to dispel it,[33] regardless of whether the events involved are current or historical.[34]

C. Non–Media Defendants and Matters of Public Concern

Dun & Bradstreet, Inc. v. Greenmoss Builders, Inc.[35] posed the question whether the *Gertz* standard for defamation, which restricts the damages that a private individual can obtain from a publisher for a libel involving a matter of public concern, applies as well to instances where false and defamatory statements involve matters only of private concern. The Supreme Court concluded that the First Amendment prohibition on presumed and punitive damages for false and defamatory statements absent proof of "actual malice" does not apply.

The case involved a construction contractor who brought a defamation action against a credit reporting agency that issued false credit reports to the contractor's creditors. The Supreme Court held that the false statements in the credit report did not involve matters of public concern[36] and accordingly the plaintiff could recover damages even if it could not produce evidence of actual malice.

In balancing the State's interest in compensating private individuals for injury to their reputation against the First Amendment interest in protecting this type of expression, the Court concluded that speech on

30. 51 Cal.App.4th 14, 54 Cal.Rptr.2d 92 (1996), *review granted* 57 Cal.Rptr.2d 277, 923 P.2d 766 (1996), *opinion superceded and judgment aff'd* 19 Cal4th 254, 79 Cal.Rptr.2d 178, 965 P.2c 696 (1998), cert. denied ___ U.S. ___, 119 S.Ct. 1760, ___ L.Ed.2d ___ (1999).

31. *Id.* at 30, 54 Cal. Rptr. 2d at 104. The shakiness of the privileged is underlined by the court's footnote 6 collecting the neutral reportage cases and referring to the privilege's "checkered history." *Id.* at 28, n.6, 54 Cal. Rptr. 2d at 103.

32. Peoples Bank & Trust Co. of Mountain Home v. Globe Int'l Pub., Inc., 978 F.2d 1065, 1070 (8th Cir.1992), cert. denied *sub. nom.*, Globe Int'l Pub., Inc. v. Peoples Bank and Trust Co. of Mountain Home, 510 U.S. 931, 114 S.Ct. 343, 126 L.Ed.2d 308 (1993) (finding that a jury had sufficient evidence to conclude that a tabloid newspa-

per purposefully avoided the truth in failing to investigate and confirm that an elderly women was or was not in fact dead before using a photograph of her and reporting that she had become pregnant).

33. *See* Masson v. New Yorker Magazine, Inc., 960 F.2d 896 (9th Cir.1992).

34. *See* Barger v. Playboy Enterprises, Inc., 564 F.Supp. 1151, 1156 (N.D.Cal. 1983), *aff'd* 732 F.2d 163 (9th Cir.), cert. denied 469 U.S. 853, 105 S.Ct. 175, 83 L.Ed.2d 110 (1984) (drawing no distinction between "hot" and "cold" news).

35. Dun & Bradstreet, Inc. v. Greenmoss Builders, 472 U.S. 749, 105 S.Ct. 2939, 86 L.Ed.2d 593 (1985).

36. "It was speech solely in the individual interest of the speaker and its specific business audience." *Id.* at 762, 105 S. Ct. at 2946–47, 86 L. Ed. 2d at 604.

matters of purely private concern is of less First Amendment concern, because there is no threat to the free and robust debate of public issues, or the possibility that the press will engage in self-censorship.[37] Accordingly, when allegedly defamatory statements are made in a private or commercial context, courts will not apply the actual malice standard.[38]

5.9 Attempts to Circumvent the *New York Times v. Sullivan* Privilege

Because the constitutional privilege recognized in *New York Times Co. v. Sullivan*[1] and its progeny poses such a formidable barrier to success in defamation actions against the newsmedia, some aggrieved persons have attempted to circumvent that barrier by alleging torts and statutory wrongs other than defamation. These include false light invasion of privacy, malicious interference with contractual rights and state "insulting words" statutes. The success of such claims is often defendant on how courts view the essence of plaintiffs' cases, particularly whether freedom to distribute news and information is involved, with its consequent need for "breathing space" for the newsmedia.[2]

A. Relying on Intentional Infliction of Emotional Distress: *Hustler Magazine v. Falwell*

Perhaps the premier example of attempts to circumvent the protection of *New York Times Co. v. Sullivan* is the embrace by defamation plaintiffs of the tort of intentional infliction of emotional distress. Such tort requires that a defendant's conduct be "so outrageous in character and so extreme in degree, as to go beyond all possible bounds of decency, and to be regarded as [so] atrocious and utterly intolerable in civilized [society]."[3] Under this judicially well recognized test of the Restatement Second of Torts, it would seem unlikely that persons aggrieved by the news media in their normal course of publication could ever meet the Restatement test for intentional infliction of emotional distress.

But the publication in *Hustler Magazine v. Falwell*[4] was anything

---

37. *Id.* at 759–60, 105 S. Ct. at 2945, 86 L. Ed. 2d at 602–603 (citing Connick v. Myers, 461 U.S. 138, 146–147 103 S.Ct. 1684, 1689–1690, 75 L.Ed.2d 708, 719–720 (1983)).

38. *See, e.g.*, U.S. Healthcare, Inc. v. Blue Cross of Greater Philadelphia, 898 F.2d 914 (3d Cir.1990) (comparative advertising campaigns of health insurer and health maintenance organization categorized as commercial speech to which the heightened protection of First Amendment's actual malice standard did not apply in court evaluation of defamation claim); Mutafis v. Erie Insurance Co., 775 F.2d 593 (4th Cir.1985) (where defamatory publication was merely an interoffice memorandum for use by only certain of insurance company's employees in dealing with its insured's loss of personal property there was no constitutional requirement of proof of actual malice); Sunward Corp. v. Dun & Bradstreet, Inc. 811 F.2d 511 (10th Cir. 1987) (because credit reports are not matter of public concern, agency's reports were not entitled to constitutional protection).

1. 376 U.S. 254, 84 S.Ct. 710, 11 L.Ed.2d 686 (1964).

2. Philadelphia Newspapers, Inc. v. Hepps, 475 U.S. 767, 772, 106 S.Ct. 1558, 1561, 89 L.Ed.2d 783, 790 (1986); New York Times Co. v. Sullivan, 376 U.S. at 272, 84 S. Ct. at 721, 11 L. Ed. 2d at 701.

3. RESTATEMENT (SECOND) OF TORTS § 46, Comment, *d* (1977).

4. 485 U.S. 46, 108 S.Ct. 876, 99 L.Ed.2d 41 (1988).

but normal and provided the Reverend Jerry Falwell with what his attorneys thought would be a strong vehicle for avoiding *New York Times v. Sullivan*. While Falwell did sue for defamation as well as intentional infliction, it became clear during litigation of the case that the defamation count would not succeed. Emphasis was placed on the emotional impact the Hustler Magazine parody advertisement had on the minister.

The ad parodied a series of Compari liquer ads in which celebrities talk about their "first time," referring, of course, to the first time they imbibed Compari. In Hustler's ad parody, the Reverend Falwell, in a fictitious interview, allegedly detailed an incestuous "first time" with his mother in an outhouse. Mother and son were portrayed in the vilest of terms. At the bottom of the "ad" was a disclaimer stating, "ad parody—not to be taken seriously."

After trial, the jury ruled for Larry Flynt, publisher of Hustler, regarding Falwell's libel claim because it found that no reasonable person would believe that the parody was describing actual facts about the minister. On the intentional emotional distress claim, however, the jury returned a $200,000 verdict and the United States Court of Appeals for the Fourth Circuit affirmed.[5]

On certiorari, the Supreme Court, in a rare unanimous decision reversed. Writing for the Court, Chief Justice Rehnquist explained that "robust political debate" will often produce sharp and caustic comments and vehement attacks.[6] But whether they are "outrageous" involves such a subjective judgment that imposition of liability would vary from jury to jury. The Court was clearly concerned that with a standard as subjective as "outrageousness," plaintiffs like Falwell could use the tort of intentional infliction of emotional distress to circumvent the actual malice standard of *New York Times Co. v. Sullivan*.

The Court was also concerned about the First Amendment implications of using the intentional infliction tort to impose liability for satire and parody generally, and for editorial cartoons specifically. The Court noted that the art of the cartoonist is often slashing and one-sided. "Despite their sometimes caustic nature, from the early cartoon portraying George Washington as an ass down to the present day, ... satirical cartoons have played a prominent role in public and political debate.... "[7] Allowing Falwell to by-pass the First Amendment protection afforded by *Sullivan* would, in the Court's view, have an immeasurable chilling effect on the cartoonists' and others speech.

Given the unanimity of the Court and the strength of its opinion in *Hustler* it is unlikely that the push to substitute other torts based on common law injurious falsehood for that of libel will be successful.[8]

---

5. 797 F.2d 1270 (4th Cir.1986).

6. Hustler Magazine, 485 U.S. at 51, 108 S. Ct. at 874, 99 L. Ed. 2d at 49.

7. *Id*. at 54, 108 S. Ct. at 881, 99 L. Ed. 2d at 51.

8. *See, e.g.*, Patrick v. The Superior Court of Los Angeles County, 27 Cal. Rptr.2d 883 (Cal.Ct.App.1994) (ordered depublished) (legal newspaper's description of a judge as a "despotic twit" and its repro-

B. Suing for Tortious Acts Committed In the Course of Newsgathering

Another approach to avoiding the rigors of *New York Times v. Sullivan* is that taken by Food Lion Inc. in its suit brought against Capital Cities/ABC in the wake of the network's broadcast expose' of unsanitary conditions at a Food Lion store.[9] Rather than sue for business defamation to recover damages for the subsequent loss of business, the company alleged successfully in the United States District Court trespass, fraud and unfair trade practices by the news organization and its reporters in the course of gathering the evidence and shooting tape for the broadcast.[10]

The plaintiff's theory accepted by the trial court was that the First Amendment does not protect newsgatherers when they violate generally applicable criminal or civil laws in the course of their newsgathering. While there is abundant authority for this general proposition,[11] it has not yet been tested as to tort law before the Supreme Court.[12]

Should the judgment with its imposition of substantial punitive damages be upheld on appeal, surreptitious investigative reporting such as engage in by the ABC Television Network in Food Lion will almost surely become a thing of the past because of its inherent need for some deception and trespassing in the course of exposing hidden wrongdoing.

duction of a fictitious memo purportedly written by judge declaring a court emergency and suspending election of his successor held to constitute nonactionable parody); *but see* Murray v. Schlosser, 41 Conn. Supp. 362, 574 A.2d 1339 (Conn.Super.Ct.1990) (trial court's refusal to dismiss action based on grossly insulting "Berate the Brides" radio program during which one disc joke described a recent bride as the "dog of the week" and awarded her a case of dog food and a dog collar).

9. Food Lion, Inc. v. Capital Cities/ABC, Inc., 887 F.Supp. 811 (M.D.N.C.1995).

10. *Id.* at 823.

11. *See, e.g.,*Cohen v. Cowles Media Co., 501 U.S. 663, 111 S.Ct. 2513, 115 L.Ed.2d 586 (1991) (broken promise of confidentiality leading to imposition of liability under common law promissory estoppel); Le Mistral, Inc. v. Columbia Broadcasting Sys., 61 A.D.2d 491, 402 N.Y.S.2d 815 (App. Div. 1978), *appeal dismissed* 46 N.Y.2d 940 (1979) (intrusion); Stahl v. State, 665 P.2d 839 (Okla.Crim.App.1983), cert. denied 464 U.S. 1069, 104 S.Ct. 973, 79 L.Ed.2d 212 (1984) (criminal trespass); Prahl v. Bro-

samle, 98 Wis.2d 130, 295 N.W.2d 768 (Wis. Ct.App.1980) (intrusion).

12. In *Cohen v. Cowles Media Co.*, 501 U.S. 663, 111 S.Ct. 2513, 115 L.Ed.2d 586 (1991), the Court held by a vote of 5 to 4 that newsgatherers were bound like all others by the general law of *contract*, specifically here promissory estoppel. The tribunal did not take kindly to a news organization going back on its promise of confidentiality to a news source. Twitting the news media, the majority observed that since journalist have long insisted that they should have the same privilege not to reveal a source as that enjoyed by physicians and priests, the refusal of editors and reporters to keep promises of confidentiality damages the credibility of the journalism profession's claim to a constitutional privilege. The *Cohen* decision does not endanger investigative reporting as a journalistic tool because it is within the power of newsgathers to honor their pledges of confidentiality under common law contract principles. Violations of general contract are not inherent in investigative reporting. The same cannot be said for violations of tort law in certain cases of newsgathering.

C. Statutory Circumvention: The Strange Cases of Veggie Libel

When a public interest group or the newsmedia communicated to the public that a normally edible product posed a serious hazard to the public health without substantial scientific evidentiary support, the effected producer or grower until recently had recourse only to the common law tort of injurious falsehood also known in this context as "slander of goods," "trade libel" or commercial disparagement.[13] But the requirements of the prima facie case of injurious falsehood pose numerous obstacles for the injured plaintiff in recovering damages for his pecuniary loss. As set down in the Restatement Second of Torts, the statement or statements disparaging the quality of the produce must be shown to be false; the publisher must be shown to have published the statement or statements with the intention to harm the plaintiff's pecuniary interests or have published recognizing or being in a position to recognize that pecuniary harm is likely to follow; and the publisher must be shown to have known that the statements were false or that he acted in reckless disregard of the statements' truth or falsity.[14]

The last element obviously reflects the actual malice requirement imposed by the Supreme Court in *New York Times Co. v. Sullivan*[15] for the parallel tort of defamation. The American Law Institute's application of the actual malice rule to commercial disparagement cases thereby effectively constitutionalizing the tort was confirmed by the Supreme Court in *Bose Corp. v. Consumers Union of United States, Inc.*,[16] a case involving a report in a consumer publication stating, *inter alia*, that a new and unique audio speaker system manufactured by the Bose Corporation caused the sound of individual musical instruments "to grow to gigantic proportions and tended to wander about the room."[17]

In ruling for the defendant Consumers Union, the Court required Bose Corporation to establish at trial that Consumers Union writers knew that their statements were false or were made with reckless disregard of the truth and to do so by clear and convincing evidence. The Court held that a review of the record indicated that Bose Corporation had not done so.[18]

Thus, between the requirements of proof imposed by the common law and the First Amendment, producers or growers filing injurious falsehood or commercial disparagement actions have a very difficult time prevailing against the newsmedia and public interest organizations communicating health warnings about food products to the public.

13. *See, e.g.*, WILLIAM L. PROSSER AND W. PAGE KEETON, TORTS 962–963 (5th ed. 1984).

14. RESTATEMENT (SECOND) OF TORTS § 623A (1977). The elements of the tort and burden of proof are set out in detail at *id*. §§ 623A, 629–630, 632–634, 651 and comments thereto.

15. 376 U.S. 254, 84 S.Ct. 710, 11 L.Ed.2d 686 (1964).

16. 466 U.S. 485, 104 S.Ct. 1949, 80 L.Ed.2d 502 (1984).

17. *Id*. at 488, 104 S. Ct. at 1953, 80 L. Ed. 2d at 509.

18. *Id*. at 511–514, 104 S. Ct. at 1965–1967, 80 L. Ed. 2d at 524–26.

1. *Auvil v. CBS 60 Minutes*

This difficulty for plaintiffs is born out by the decision in *Auvil v. CBS 60 Minutes*.[19] In this case the investigative news program publicized a report of the Natural Resources Defense Council ("NRDC") entitled "Intolerable Risk: Pesticides in Our Children's Food" outlining the health risks associated, *inter alia*, with daminozide, a pesticide and apparent carcinogen, commonly known as "Alar." The "Sixty Minutes" segment entitled " 'A' is for Apple" made statements concerning the danger of daminozide and its use on apples to keep them on the trees longer and make them look better. Following the broadcast consumer demand for apples and apple products plummeted, causing the loss of millions of dollars to growers and others. A number of Washington State apple growers brought suit, *inter alia*, against CBS, local CBS affiliates and the NRDC for, among other things, product disparagement. On cross-motions for summary judgment on the issue of falsity, the United States District Court granted CBS' motion because the growers did not produce evidence during discovery to create a triable issue of fact as to the falsity of statements made regarding daminozide and its use on apples.

The trial court did not reach the constitutional issue of actual malice.[20] The summary judgment for CBS was affirmed by the United States Court of Appeals for the Ninth Circuit which rejected the plaintiffs' argument that the broadcast's overall *message* was false even if none of the specific statements were erroneous.[21]

2. *State Perishable food disparagement statutes*

Apparently concerned after *Auvil* that growers and producers had insufficient legal recourse when the quality of their produce was questioned, a large number of states with substantial agricultural interests enacted legislation disparagingly referred to as "veggie libel" or "banana protection" acts.[22]

Common elements of these produce disparagement statutes distilled by one student commentator[23] are: (1) dissemination to the public in any manner (2) of false information the disseminator knows to be false[24] (3) stating or employing that a perishable food product is not safe for

---

19. 800 F.Supp. 928 (E.D.Wash.1992), *aff'd* 67 F.3d 816 (9th Cir.1995), cert. denied 517 U.S. 1167, 116 S.Ct. 1567, 134 L.Ed.2d 666 (1996). *See* David J. Bederman, et al., *of Banana Bills and Veggie Hate Crimes; The Constitutionality of Agricultural Disparagement Statutes*, 34 Harv. J. Legis 135, 141 (1997).

20. Auvil, 800 F. Supp. at 936–937 (dictum).

21. 67 F.3d 816, 822 (9th Cir.1995), cert. denied 517 U.S. 1167, 116 S.Ct. 1567, 134 L.Ed.2d 666 (1996).

22. *See, e.g.*, Ariz. Rev. Stat. Ann. § 3–113 (West Supp. 1997); Fla. Stat. Ann.

§ 865.065 (West Supp. 1997); Ga. Code §§ 2–16–1 through 2–16–4 (1996); Idaho Code §§ 6–2001 through 2003 (1996); La. Rev. Stat. Ann. §§ 3–4501 through 4504 (West Supp. 1997); Tex. Civ. Prac. & Rem. Code Ann. §§ 96.001 through 96.004 (West Supp. 1997).

23. Megan W. Semple, Note, *Veggie Libel Meets Free Speech: A Constitutional Analysis of Agricultural Disparagement Laws*, 15 Va. Envtl. L.J. 403 (1995–96).

24. Some of these statutes include the language "knows or should have known to be false." *See, e.g.*, Fla. Stats. Ann. § 865.065(2)(a) (West Supp. 1997); La. Stats. Ann. § 4502(1) (West Supp. 1997).

consumption by the consuming public (4) which information is presumed false when not based on reasonable and reliable scientific inquiry, facts or data. This disparagement provides a cause of action for damages which must be filed within one or two years of the disparagement.[25] The same commentator goes on to say that the very existence of the statutes with their relaxation of common law and constitutional burdens for growers and producers "may be enough to silence consumer activists and environmentalists fearing ruinous liability."[26]

3. Constitutionality of the State Statutes

Many of these state statutes would seem to conflict with First Amendment standards as determined by the Supreme Court in *New York Times Co. v. Sullivan* and its progeny by reducing the fault standard and shifting the burden of proof.

Growers and producers can be considered limited purpose "public figures" subject to the actual malice standard of *Sullivan* because their goods are sold to the public and their techniques in producing those vital goods are of the greatest public import.[27] This being so, the requirement of some of the statutes that the disseminator of information "knows or should have known" the information to be false[28] permits liability of the newsmedia and public interest groups on a mere negligence basis and not on the constitutionally mandated standard of reckless disregard of the truth.

Furthermore, statements are presumed to be false when "not based upon reasonable and reliable scientific inquiry, facts. or data."[29] This, of course, narrows the issue of falsity in plaintiffs favor and shifts the burden of proof to defendants to establish the truth of their statements in rebuttal to the statutes' presumption. This shift of the burden of proof on the issue of falsity to defendants is in direct conflict with the ruling in *Philadelphia Newspapers, Inc. v. Hepps*,[30] another of *Sullivan's* progeny, which places the burden of proof on the falsity issue with plaintiffs.

The conclusion seems clear that most or all of the so-called "Veggie Libel Acts" have the effect, if not the design, of circumventing the constitutional protections for the news and information media put in place by *Sullivan* and its progeny for the very purpose of insuring an informed public.

D. Suing for Libel in More Plaintiff–Friendly Foreign Jurisdictions

Another method of circumventing the *New York Times Co.* privilege is to bring libel actions against American citizens or residents in foreign

25. Semple, *supra* n. 23 at 413.

26. *Id.* at 415.

27. *Cf.* Bose Corp. v. Consumers Union of United States, Inc., 466 U.S. 485, 104 S.Ct. 1949, 80 L.Ed.2d 502 (1984) (by implication).

28. *See, e.g.,* Fla. Stat. Ann. § 865.065(2)(a) (West Supp. 1997); La. Stat. Ann. § 4502(1) (West Supp. 1997).

29. *See, e.g.,* Ga. Code § 2–16–2(1) (1996); Tex. Civ. Prac. & Rem. Code Ann. § 96.003 (West Supp. 1997).

30. 475 U.S. 767, 106 S.Ct. 1558, 89 L.Ed.2d 783 (1986).

forums when some nexus can be claimed between allegedly defamatory publications and plaintiff-friendly jurisdictions. Particularly, in the age of the Internet when specific communications may be received and published everywhere, suing in other jurisdictions to avoid the First Amendment privilege enjoyed by members of the media and others could become a serious problem for libel defendants if American courts were to enforce foreign judgments under long-standing principles of international comity.

Apparently, the forum of choice for plaintiffs attempting to avoid the rigors of *New York Times Co.* is the High Court of Justice of the Queen's Bench Division sitting in London. There are a number of reasons for this, including the fact that the court's judges and other personnel are, of course, English-speaking and London is a pleasant place in which to spend time while one's litigation is proceeding. More importantly, English law historically has strongly favored libel claimants.

Under English law, it is unnecessary for the plaintiff to establish fault—strict liability for defamation is alive and well in the United Kingdom.[31] In addition, defamation statements are presumed to be false unless the *defendant* proves them to be true.[32] Furthermore, a qualified privilege can be defeated by the plaintiff establishing common law malice, *i.e.*, spite, ill-will or improper motive, accompanying the defamatory communication. Plaintiff need not show knowing falsity or reckless disregard for the truth to defeat a claimed privilege or to obtain punitive damages.[33] In addition, context appears to be irrelevant in determining whether a statement is to be labeled fact or opinion.[34] In sum, English law totally rejects the principles set forth in *New York Times Co.* and its progeny.[35]

Because the libel law of England is so divergent from that of the United States, it is not surprising that the American courts that have considered whether English libel judgments should be enforced here have ruled in the negative.[36] In *Telnikoff v. Matusevitch*,[37] the only appellate decision thus far, the plaintiff Telnikoff, a British subject, was offended by a letter written during the period of the Cold War by the defendant, Matusevitch, a Maryland resident, to the Daily Telegraph, a London newspaper. The letter was in response to a freelance article

---

31. *See* Telnikoff v. Matusevitch, 347 Md. 561, 594, 702 A.2d 230, 247 (Md.1997) (opinion subject to revision or withdrawal); *Bachchan v. India Abroad Publications*, 154 Misc.2d 228, 231, 585 N.Y.S.2d 661, 663 (N.Y.Sup.1992).

32. *Id.* at 595, 702 A.2d at 247.

33. *Id.* at 596, 702 A.2d at 248.

34. *Id.* at 597, 702 A.2d at 248.

35. *Id.* at 597, 702 A.2d at 248 (citing RODNEY A. SMOLLA, LAW OF DEFAMATION § 1.03[3] (1996); Bachchan, 154 Misc. at 231–234, 585 N.Y.S.2d at 663–665.

36. Telnikoff v. Matusevitch, 347 Md. 561, 702 A.2d 230 (Md.1997) (opinion subject to revision or withdrawal); Bachchan v. India Abroad Publications, Inc., 154 Misc.2d 228, 585 N.Y.S.2d 661 (N.Y.Sup. 1992). *Cf.* DeRoburt v. Gannett Co., Inc. 83 F.R.D. 574 (D.Haw.1979) (the English common law of Nauru rejected in a choice of law ruling because its libel law failed to provide the free speech protections of the First Amendment).

37. 347 Md. 561, 702 A.2d 230 (Md.1997)(opinion subject to revisions or withdrawal).

written by Telnikoff for the same paper. In his letter to the editor, Matusevich wrote "Mr. Telnikoff demands that in the interest of more effective broadcasts the management of the BBC's Russian Service should switch from professional testing to a blood test [to insure that more real Russians rather than Russian-speaking minorities from the Soviet Union staff the BBC service]. Mr. Telnikoff is stressing his racialist recipe by claiming that no matter how high the standards and integrity _of ethnically alien_ people [on the] Russian staff might be, they should be dismissed. I am certain the Daily Telegraph would reject any article with similar suggestions of lack racial purity of the writer in any normal section of the British Media."[38]

After Matusevitch refused to apologize for his letter which Telnikoff took to mean, *inter alia*, that he was being called a racist and an anti-Semite, Telnikoff sued in the High Court of Justice and eventually won a judgment in the amount of £240,000. He then sought to have it enforced in the United States. He filed his petition for enforcement in the United States District Court for the District of Columbia which court held that enforcement of the English libel judgment would be "repugnant to the public policy of the State" of Maryland[39] within the meaning of its Uniform Foreign–Money Judgments Recognition Act.[40] Alternatively, the district court held that enforcement would violate the First and Fourteenth Amendments.[41] On appeal the District of Columbia Circuit certified to the Court of Appeals of Maryland the following question: "Would recognition of Telnikoff's foreign judgment be repugnant to the public policy of Maryland?"

In an opinion distinguished by an exhaustive scholarly analysis of the respective laws of libel and press freedom of England and Maryland (under both the federal and state constitutions), Judge Eldridge, writing for six of the seven members of the court held that English libel law underlying Telnikoff's judgment was so contrary to Maryland's public policy that recognition and enforcement of the judgment should be denied.

As reasons for the court's decision Judge Eldridge cited the striking divergence of the principles of libel law and press freedom[42] and the danger that enforcement "could well lead to wholesale circumvention of fundamental public policy in Maryland and the rest of the country."[43] As to the latter reason, the opinion quoted Professor Rodney A. Smolla, a noted expert on libel. "Plaintiffs with the wherewithal to do so now often choose to file suit in Britain in order to exploit Britain's strict libel laws, even when the plaintiffs and the publication have little connection to that country."[44]

---

38. 347 Md. at 565, 702 A.2d at 232.

39. Matusevitch v. Telnikoff, 877 F.Supp. 1, 3–4 (D.D.C.1995).

40. Md. Code Ann. § 10–704(b)(2) (1995 Repl. Vol).

41. Matusevich, 877 F. Supp. at 4–6.

42. Telnikoff, *supra* note 36 at 595–598, 702 A.2d at 247–248.

43. *Id.* at 601, 702 A.2d at 250.

44. *Id.* at 602, 702 A.2d at 250 (quoting RODNEY A. SMOLLA, LAW OF DEFAMATION § 1.03[3] (1996)). *See also* GEOFFREY ROBIN-

Summing up, Judge Eldridge wrote, "At the heart of the First Amendment, as well as Article 40 of the Maryland Declaration of Rights and Maryland public policy, is the recognition of the fundamental importance of the free flow of ideas and opinions on matters of public interest and concern.... The importance of that free flow of ideas and opinions on matters of public concern precludes Maryland recognition of Telnikoff's English libel judgment."[45]

This strong first appellate opinion may well discourage further attempts to circumvent *New York Times Co. v. Sullivan* by libel plaintiffs bringing their actions in the greener legal pastures of England, but, of course, there are other countries yet to be tried.

5.10 Defamation in Cyberspace

A. Introduction

In discussing defamation through the advanced technological medium of computer communications, we start with the obvious proposition that defamation is defamation so long as it meets the common law requirements for the tort. This is true whether we are communicating through smoke signals or computer modems. The new issues that are raised as a result of the employment of computer communications do not deal with the substance of the communications but rather with the nature of the medium and the allocation of liability between those who are involved with its operations and use.[1]

B. Nature of the Computer Communications Medium

One way to describe the computer communications medium is that it possesses a multiple personality. It has the capacity for both one-on-one personal communications through the computer's interconnection with an e-mail system, though, of course, the same e-mail message might be addressed to more than one person. At the same time, the same computer might be connected by modem and appropriate software to an on-line service where the computer's operator can post messages on one or more of an on-line service's bulletin board systems (BBS) for all

---

SON AND ANDREW NICOL, MEDIA LAW 65 (3d ed. 1992); BRUCE W. SANFORD, LIBEL AND PRIVACY § 2.2 (2d ed. 1996 Supp.).

45. *Id.* at 602, 702 A.2d at 251 (quoting in part Hustler Magazine v. Falwell, 485 U.S. 46, 50, 108 S.Ct. 876, 879, 99 L.Ed.2d 41, 48 (1988)). To like effect is *Bachchan v. India Abroad Publications, Inc.,* 154 Misc.2d 228, 585 N.Y.S.2d 661 (N.Y.Sup. 1992). There, a judgment was awarded in a libel action (also brought in the High Court of Justice in London) by an Indian national against a New York operator of a wire service that transmitted news and information to India. One of its stories stated that a Swedish newspaper had reported that Swiss authorities had frozen an account belonging

to the plaintiff into which money was transferred from a coded account of a Swedish arms manufacturer. The arms manufacturer contemporaneously was accused of making kickbacks to obtain a large munitions contract with the Indian government. Plaintiff denied possessing such an account, sued and obtained a substantial judgment against the New York company. On grounds very similar to those cited by the Maryland Court of Appeals, a New York trial court refused to extend comity to the London court's judgment.

1. *See* I. Trotter Hardy, *The Proper Legal Regime for "Cyberspace,"* 55 U. Pitt. L. Rev. 993, 999–1006 (1994).

bulletin board system subscribers to read on the Internet worldwide. While all of these computer signals are initially electronic, the messages they convey may be "downloaded" by anyone picking up the signals and "printed out."

1. Specific Issues Related to the Nature of Computer Communications

Because defamation comes in two varieties, slander and libel, with slander supposedly having a more fleeting and ephemeral character, thereby doing less damage to the victim's reputation, the nature of the computer medium might be thought to be relevant. But that issue was debated and resolved with the advent of radio. While defamatory words spoken over the air are fleeting and ephemeral, it was ultimately determined that the broad dissemination of those words made them sufficiently damaging to label them libelous.[2] The ubiquitous nature of computer generated words should establish beyond doubt that when defamatory computer communications are involved it is libel that the courts are dealing with.[3]

Further, because of the split personality of computer communications, the computer operator's choice of the scheme of distribution of his message may impact on the publication element of the tort. That element requires intentional or negligent communication of the libelous expression to a party other than the subject.[4] An e-mail message properly addressed to the subject so that supposedly only he could access it with his password would negate publication. And it would seem that if the defamed party disclosed his password to a third party so that the third party could "pick up the mail" for him there would not be publication if the sender of the e-mail had no reason to know of this arrangement.[5] Of course, if the sender chose instead to post the same message on his

---

2. *See* Wanamaker v. Lewis, 173 F.Supp. 126, 127 (D.D.C.1959); Coffey v. Midland Broadcasting Co., 8 F.Supp. 889, 890 (W.D.Mo.1934); First Indep. Baptist Church of Arab v. Southerland, 373 So.2d 647 (Ala.1979); Sorensen v. Wood, 123 Neb. 348, 243 N.W. 82 (1932); Shor v. Billingsley, 4 Misc.2d 857, 158 N.Y.S.2d 476, (1956) *order aff'd* 4 A.D.2d 1017, 169 N.Y.S.2d 416 (App. Div. 1957); RESTATEMENT SECOND OF TORTS § 568A (1977).

Before the determination that radio defamation was libel, one case went so far as to label words "ad libbed" over the air constituted slander while the same words read from a printed script were to be categorized as libel. *See* Summit Hotel Co. v. NBC, 336 Pa. 182, 8 A.2d 302 (1939). *But compare* Shor v. Billingsley, 4 Misc.2d 857, 158 N.Y.S.2d 476 480–481 (N.Y.Sup.Ct.1956); RESTATEMENT SECOND OF TORTS § 568A (1977).

3. In one of the very few reported cases thus far involving a claim of computer defamation, the trial court did not question the plaintiff's characterization of the alleged defamatory communication as libel. *See* Cubby, Inc. v. CompuServe Inc., 776 F.Supp. 135 (S.D.N.Y.1991).

4. *See* RESTATEMENT SECOND OF TORTS § 577 (1) (1977); WILLIAM L. PROSSER AND W. PAGE KEETON, TORTS § 113 (5th ed. 1984).

5. *Cf.* Barnes v. Clayton House Motel, 435 S.W.2d 616, 617 (Tex.Civ.App.1968) (court found no publication where defendant did not know that wife of plaintiff had authority to open sealed letter containing defamatory material); Weidman v. Ketcham, 278 N.Y. 129, 132–33, 15 N.E.2d 426, 428–29 (1938) (same).

favorite on-line bulletin board there would be no question as to its publication.

Another aspect of the nature of computer communications important to defamation law is its potential for anonymity.[6] Computer generated defamatory messages relayed through intermediary computers to the Internet are essentially impossible to trace, leaving the victim virtually no legal recourse since the author cannot be identified, and there is no real owner or controller of the Internet. It is essentially a cooperative association of all who make use of it.

2. Judicial Authority Directed to the Nature of Computer Communications

To date only one reported appellate decision could be found directly addressing the nature of computer communications and its scope is decidedly narrow. In *It's in the Cards, Inc. v. Fuschetto,*[7] the defendant posted a message on a bulletin board service of SportsNet, an on-line computer network, concerning a financial dispute between the defendant and the plaintiffs which was allegedly defamatory in nature. The defendant filed a motion for summary judgment asserting, *inter alia*, that the plaintiffs had failed to comply with a Wisconsin statute requiring the party alleged to have been defamed in a newspaper, magazine or periodical to give the alleged defamer an opportunity to retract the alleged libel prior to commencing suit.[8] This motion was granted. The sole issue before the Wisconsin appeals court was whether the computerized bulletin board was a "periodical" under the statute.

The court accepted Webster's Third New International Dictionary definition of a periodical publication which is "a magazine or other publication of which the issues appear at stated or regular intervals."[9] The appeals court then concluded that the posting of a message to a computer network bulletin board is a random communication analogous to the posting of a written notice on a public bulletin board and not a publication that appears at regular intervals. Thus, such message boards are not periodicals.

In addition, the statute requires retractions for defamatory writings in magazines, newspapers and other periodicals, and the court held that writings such as personal letters, billboards, computer bulletin boards and signs are not covered by the statute. Finally, the court held that the statute required that libelous publications be found exclusively in print media and a bulletin board on a computer network could not be classified as a print medium.

Reflecting on the Wisconsin libel legislation, the court said, "Applying the present libel laws to cyberspace or computer networks entails

---

6. *See* I. Trotter Hardy, *The Proper Legal Regime for "Cyberspace,"* 55 U. Pitt. L. Rev. 993, 1048 (1994).

7. 193 Wis.2d 429, 535 N.W.2d 11 (Wis. Ct.App.1995).

8. Wis. Stat. Ann. § 895.05(2) (West 1983 & Supp. 1995).

9. It's in the Cards, Inc., 193 Wis. 2d at 436, 535 N.W. 2d at 14 (Wis. Ct. App. 1995).

rewriting statutes that were written to manage physical, printed objects, not computer networks or services. Consequently, it is for the legislature to address the increasingly common phenomenon of libel and defamation on the information superhighway.''[10]

C. *Allocation of Liability for Defamation in Cyberspace*

During the developmental stage of law to cover a new field of human endeavor and in the absence of statutory regulation, the courts normally rely on analogic reasoning to resolve conflicts. This seems to be the case with claims of defamation by computer.

1. *The Analogic Approach*

Two analogies appear to be relevant. One of them is with established media and how they operate. Another is with the distinction in the publishing field between publishers and disseminators of the published product. Whether these analogies are applied separately or in combination, the application must be just and reasonable in light of this new medium and the particular circumstances of the allegedly defamatory communication.[11]

The Restatement Second of Torts distinguishes for purposes of liability between those who publish defamatory matter[12] and those who simply deliver or transmit such matter, *i.e.*, distributors.[13] Non-interactive media such as print publishing network broadcasting and cablecasting involve both categories. Publishers are those who write, edit or elect to distribute the particular expression. They have two things in common: knowledge of the contents of the expression and, to some extent, control over publication of the particular expression to third parties. Mere distributors or disseminators such as newsstand vendors and booksellers, on the other hand, normally have no knowledge of the contents of the material they distribute and certainly no control over the contents. Unless a distributor or disseminator knows or has reason to know of the defamatory nature of the material, he will not be held liable.[14]

---

10. *Id.* at 437, 535 N.W. 2d at 14.

11. *See* David R. Johnson and Kevin A. Marks, *Mapping Electronic Data Communications Onto Existing Legal Metaphors: Should We Let Our Conscience (And Our Contracts) Be Our Guide?*, 38 Vill. L. Rev. 487, 489 (1993) (a particularly thoughtful discussion of frontier issues of civil and criminal liability for cyberspace activities).

12. RESTATEMENT SECOND OF TORTS § 577 (1977).

13. *Id.* § 581(1).

14. *Id. See* Henry H. Perritt, Jr., *Tort Liability, The First Amendment, and Equal Access to Electronic Networks*, 5 Harv. J.L. & Tech. 65, 102–103 (1992); *cf.* Smith v. California, 361 U.S. 147, 152–155, 80 S.Ct. 215, 218–220, 4 L.Ed.2d 205, 210–12 (1959)

(obscenity prosecution of a book seller requires mens rea because of the demands of the First Amendment). Curiously, the Restatement would treat network affiliates who merely carry network originated programming as publishers, likening them more to newspaper or book publishers than to news vendors or booksellers. RESTATEMENT SECOND OF TORTS § 581(2) and *comment q* (1977). The one exception to broadcaster liability for the communication of defamatory matter is the case in which the broadcaster must, under the mandate of federal law, broadcast political messages without having any control over them. *Id.* § 592A. *See* Farmers Educ. and Co-op. Union of America v. WDAY, Inc., 360 U.S. 525, 79 S.Ct. 1302, 3 L.Ed.2d 1407 (1959).

The publisher—distributor dichotomy is an analogy that may be useful with regard to the interactive media. If the operator of a BBS simply opens his bulletin board to all subscribers without screening messages or choosing to edit them before they are posted, the system operator ("sysop") might claim merely to be a distributor and, therefore, not liable for defamatory material placed on the board by others.[15] Of course, under this analogy the sysop must act with reasonable dispatch to remove offending messages once he learns of it since he then has both knowledge of the contents of the communication and control over it.[16]

2. The Scant Judicial Authority

While some commentators have criticized the analogic approach to the development of rules allocating liability for defamation in cyberspace,[17] what little direct judicial authority presently existing takes this approach. In *Cubby, Inc. v. CompuServe Inc.*,[18] CompuServe Information Service (CIS) provided an on-line general information service or electronic library that subscribers might access from personal computers or terminals and operated numerous special interest "forums" comprising electronic bulletin boards, interaction online real-time conferences and topical databases. One of these forums, managed by an independent contractor focused on the journalism industry. One of the databases was "Rumorville USA" ("Rumorville"), a daily newsletter reporting on broadcast journalism and journalists published by defendant Don Fitzpatrick Associates (DFA). CompuServe had no employment, contractual or other direct relationship with DFA or defendant Don Fitzpatrick. DFA provided "Rumorville" to the journalism forum under contract with the independent contractor manager (CCI). The contract provided that DFA "accepts total responsibility for the contents" of Rumorville. The contract also required CCI to limit access to Rumorville to those CIS subscribers who had previously made membership arrangements directly with DFA.

For a time Rumorville had no competition but in 1990 plaintiffs Cubby, Inc. and Robert Blanchard developed a similar computer database, called "skuttlebut" designed to publish and distribute electronically news and gossip about the radio and television news business. Subscribers accessed Skuttlebut through their personal computers after completing access agreements with the plaintiffs.

---

15. *See* Cubby, Inc. v. CompuServe Inc., 776 F.Supp. 135 (S.D.N.Y.1991); Stratton Oakmont, Inc. v. Prodigy Servs. Co., 1995 WL 323710 (N.Y.Sup.1995) (not officially reported).

16. *See* RESTATEMENT SECOND OF TORTS § 581 (1977); David R. Johnson and Kevin A. Marks, *Mapping Electronic Data Communications Onto Existing Legal Metaphors: Should We Let Our Conscience (And Our Contracts) Be Our Guide?*, 38 Vill. L. Rev. 487, 497 (1993).

17. *See* Frank P. Dorr, *A Proposed Defamation Standard for Commercial Computer Information Systems*, 18 Comm/Ent L.J. 267, 277–279 (1996); David R. Johnson and Kevin A. Marks, *Mapping Electronic Data Communications Onto Existing Legal Metaphors: Should We Let Our Conscience (And Our Contracts) Be Our Guide?*, 38 Vill. L. Rev. 487, 491–497 (1993).

18. 776 F.Supp. 135 (S.D.N.Y.1991).

The plaintiffs brought suit, for among other things, libel because they claimed that Rumorville published false and defamatory statements relating to its new competitor and Robert Blanchard and that this libelous material was carried on CompuServe's journalism forum. The allegedly libelous statements included a suggestion that Skuttlebut gained access to information first published by Rumorville "through some back door", a statement that Blanchard was "bounced" from his previous employer, WABC in New York and an assertion that Skuttlebut was a "new start-up scam."

CompuServe had no opportunity to review Rumorville's content before DFA uploaded it into CompuServe's computer banks from which it was instantly available to approved CIS subscribers and claimed not to have had notice of complaints concerning the content of Rumorville. In addition, CompuServe received no part of fees DFA charged for access to Rumorville and provided no compensation to DFA for publishing the newsletter.

On these facts the United States District Court for the Southern District of New York granted CompuServe's motion for summary judgment. Accepting the distinction between publishers and distributors or disseminators found in the New York common law governing print media liability, the trial court held that before distributors such as news vendors, book sellers and libraries could be held liable for disseminating defamatory material published by others they must know or have reason to know of the nature of the material they are distributing.[19] Given the facts that CompuServe had no knowledge of the offending material before it was uploaded and made immediately available to third parties and that because of the nature of the electronic service and the contractual arrangements involved, it had "no more editorial control over such a publication than does a public library, bookstore, or newsstand," CompuServe could not be held liable here.

> Technology is rapidly transforming the information industry. A computerized database is the functional equivalent of a more traditional news vendor, and the inconsistent application of a lower standard of liability to an electronic news distributor such as CompuServe than that which is applied to a public library, book store, or newsstand would impose an undue burden on the free flow of information. Given the relevant First Amendment considerations, the appropriate standard of liability to be applied to CompuServe is whether it knew or had reason to know of the allegedly defamatory Rumorville statements.[20]

Reinforcing the analogy with print publishing and its constitutionally required distinction between publishers and distributors is *Stratton Oakmont, Inc. v. Prodigy Services Co.*,[21] another case involving computer

---

19. *Id.* at 139 (relying on the First Amendment and citing the bookseller prosecution case of Smith v. California, 361 U.S. 147, 152–153, 80 S.Ct. 215, 218–219, 4 L.Ed.2d 205, 210–11 (1959)).

20. *Id.* at 140–141.

21. 1995 WL 323710, 23 Med. L. Rptr. 1794 (N.Y.Sup.Ct.1995) (not officially reported).

bulletin boards. A Prodigy bulletin board carried statements about the plaintiffs, an incorporated securities investment banking firm and its president, asserting that they had committed criminal and fraudulent acts in connection with the initial public offering of another company. Specifically the posting asserted that Stratton was a "cult of brokers who either lie for a living or get fired."

A libel suit ensued against Prodigy, its joint venture partner IBM and its parent company Sears–Roebuck.

When Prodigy commenced operations in 1990 it attempted to gain marketshare by distinguishing itself as a family oriented computer network that exercised editorial control over the contents of messages posted on its bulletin boards and expressly likening itself to a newspaper. In furtherance of its family friendly policy, Prodigy (1) promulgated guidelines for its subscribers when posting messages; (2) used a software screening program which automatically prescreened all bulletin board postings for offensive language; and (3) employed Board Leaders to enforce the guidelines and operate an "emergency delete function" to remove inappropriate messages from the board.

The trial judge in *Stratton Oakmont* granted the plaintiffs' motion for partial summary judgment against the defendant on-line computer service because, based on the foregoing facts, it concluded that Prodigy had sufficient control over the content of what was posted on its bulletin board to be deemed a publisher thereof. The trial judge distinguished the present case from *Cubby*, whose principles he accepted, on two grounds. First, Prodigy held itself out as controlling the content of its bulletin boards. Second, Prodigy implemented this control through its automatic software screening program and the imposition of guidelines enforced by Board Leaders. By taking these steps "[p]rodigy has uniquely arrogated to itself the role of determining what is proper for its members to post and read on its bulletin boards."[22]

3. Legislative intervention

In *Stratton Oakmont*, the trial judge noted that the issue of allocation of liability for defamation by computer might be preempted by the Communications Decency Act as part of the then pending legislation to overhaul the 1934 Federal Communications Act.[23] And, indeed, that did

---

22. *Id.* at * 4, 23 Med. L. Rptr. at 1797. Because there is so little case law regarding cyberspace defamation, the commentators have had free rein to theorize about the development of the law in this area. Recent commentary includes Cynthia L. Counts and C. Amanda Martin, *Libel in Cyberspace: A Framework for Addressing Liability and Jurisdictional Issues in This New Frontier*, 59 Alb. L. Rev. 1083 (1996); Robert B. Charles and Jacob H. Zamansky, *Liability for online libel after* Stratton Oakmont Inc. v. Prodigy Services Co., 28 Conn. L. Rev. 1173 (1996); Jeremy S. Weber, Note; *Defin-*

ing Cyberlibel: A First Amendment limit for libel Against Individuals Arising from Computer Bulletin Boards Speech, 46 Case W. Res. L. Rev. 235 (1995); Noah Levine, Note, *Establishing Legal Accountability for Anonymous Communications in Cyberspace*, 96 Colum. L. Rev. 1526, 1550–1555, 1568–1569 (1996); Michael Johns, Comment, *The First Amendment and Cyberspace: Trying to Teach Old Doctrines New Tricks*, 64 U. Cin. L. Rev. 1383, 1424–1428 (1996).

23. 1995 WL 323710 at * 5, 23 Med. L. Rptr. at 1798.

happen. Section 230 of the Telecommunications Act of 1996[24] provides generally that "[n]o provider or user of an interactive computer service shall be treated as the publisher or speaker of any information provided by another information content provider."[25] And it further provides specifically, under the heading "Civil liability" that "no provider or user of an interactive computer service shall be held liable on account of—(A) any action voluntarily taken in good faith to restrict access to or availability of material that the provider or user considers to be obscene, lewd, lascivious, filthy, excessively violent, harassing, or otherwise objectionable, whether or not such material is constitutionally protected.... "[26] The legislative history makes it crystal clear that these provisions were designed to change the result in future cases like *Stratton Oakmont*. The Senate and House conference reports on the Telecommunications Act of 1996 referring to section 230 state, "one of the specific purposes of this section is to overrule *Stratton Oakmont v. Prodigy* and any other similar decisions which have treated such providers and users as publishers or speakers of content that is not their own because they have restricted access to objectionable material. The conferees believed that such decisions create serious obstacles to the important federal policy of empowering parents to determine the content of communications their children receive through interactive computer services."[27]

Some doubt has been cast as to the viability of section 230 because it is part of the Communications Decency Act, central portions of which were struck down by the Supreme Court in *Reno v. American Civil Liberties Union*[28] Should section 230 survive, it remains to be seen whether the courts will interpret its provisions as conferring such broad immunity from civil liability on operators of interactive computer services.

One court so far has spoken to this issue, though not directly in the context of a defamation action. In *Zeran v. America Online, Inc.* ("AOL")[29] the online service provider was sued for negligence in allowing defamatory messages to be communicated after receiving notice as to the nature of the messages. The messages applauded the bombing of the federal building in Oklahoma City in the grossest and most tasteless manner imaginable[30] and falsely listed the plaintiff Zeran as the author,

---

24. P.L. 104–104, 110 Stat. 137 (1996).

25. 47 U.S.C.A. § 230(c)(1) (West Supp. 1997).

26. *Id.* § 230(c)(2).

27. H.R. Rep. No. 458, 104th Cong., 2d Sess. 194 (1996),*reprinted in* 1996 U.S. Code Cong. and Admin. News 207–208; Sen. Rep. No. 230, 104th Cong., 2d Sess. 194 (1996).

28. 521 U.S. 844, 117 S.Ct. 2329, 138 L.Ed.2d 874 (1997). For detailed discussion of this landmark case *see* chapter two, section 2.4.C *supra* and chapter six, section

6.11, at pp. 755–761, of Practitioners Edition, Vol. 1.

29. 958 F.Supp. 1124 (E.D.Va.1997), *aff'd* 129 F.3d 327 (4th Cir.1997), cert. denied, __ U.S. __, 118 S.Ct. 2341, 141 L.Ed.2d 712 (1998).

30. The first messages included such slogans as a "Visit Oklahoma ... It's a Blast!!!" and "McVeigh for President 1996." Later slogans included "Forget the rescue, let the maggots take over—Oklahoma 1995" and perhaps the most disgusting one of all: "Finally a day care center

together with his telephone number. When Zeran began receiving vitriolic and threatening phone calls reacting to the first bulletin board message, he contacted AOL and asked that the message be stopped immediately. An AOL representative assured him that the offending message would be removed but, as a matter of company policy, declined to post a retraction on the system. However, while the first message was deleted, a new notice, at least as vulgar and tasteless, appeared on the AOL network followed by many more abusive calls to Zeran. Despite AOL's assurance that this second notice would be promptly deleted, various similar offensive communications continued to appear for approximately another week. So threatening and abusive were some of the calls to Zeran in response to the continuing messages that local police kept Zeran's house under protective surveillance.

In response to Zeran's suit, AOL filed, *inter alia*, a motion for judgment on the pleadings based on the theory that Zeran's action seeking damages for negligence on the part of one distributing material that he knows or should know is of a defamatory character was preempted by section 230 of the Communications Decency Act ("CDA"). In granting AOL's motion the United States District Court held that while Congress did not intend to occupy the entire field of liability for providers of online interactive computer services, it did intend to preempt state regulation of the private development of blocking and filtering technologies capable of restricting inappropriate online content.[31] Here, state common law tort rules would impose liability on distributors of online defamatory content of which they are or should be aware in direct conflict with the language of section 230(c)(1) of the CDA[32] specifically[33] and the purposes and objectives of Congress in enacting that provision generally.[34]

5.11 *The Last Word In Media Defamation Law: "Reform"

that keeps the kids quiet—Oklahoma 1995." *Id.* at 1127 nn. 3,5.

31. *Id.* at 1131.

32. Communications Decency Act § 230(c)(1), 47 U.S.C.A. § 230(c)(1) (West 1997) provides that "No provider or user of an interactive computer service shall be treated as the publisher or speaker of any information provided by another information content provider."

33. Zeran v. America Online, Inc., 958 F.Supp. 1124, 1131 (E.D.Va.), *aff'd* 129 F.3d 327 (4th Cir.1997), cert. denied, ___ U.S. ___, 118 S.Ct. 2341, 141 L.Ed.2d 712 (1998).

34. *Id.* at 1134–1135.

* Published in Modern Communication Law, Practitioners Edition, Vol. 1 only.

Chapter Six*

THE SUPPRESSION OR CONTROL OF OBSCENE, INDECENT AND VIOLENT EXPRESSION

* Published in Practitioners Edition only.

Chapter Seven

NEWSPERSONS' PRIVILEGES, RIGHTS AND RESPONSIBILITIES

Analysis

I. NEWSPERSONS' PRIVILEGES

7.1 Introduction to the Problem

Until the 1950s, there had been only a handful of cases involving attempts by government forcibly to obtain evidence from unwilling members of press and until the 1970s, the subpoenaing of newspersons by various branches and agencies of federal, state and local governments to testify about their sources and other information did not pose a major problem for the news media. As late as the advent of the Nixon Administration the problem was not one of major proportions.

But then a number of social and political forces combined to embolden prosecutors, judges, legislators and other government officials to seek unpublished material and "outtakes" as well as the identity of sources from newspersons. Mutual distrust and even enmity between public officials and reporters began to grow, particularly in the large urban areas, fueled at least in part by the Vietnam war, a troubled economy, widespread graft and corruption at all levels of government, doubtful media coverage of government and its personnel and what some might characterize as anti-establishmentarianism by elements of the media. In addition, stories about drug and sex subcultures and violence-prone drug dealers became of greater interest to the press. As a result, aggressive investigative reporting was encouraged and journalists became privy to information concerning apparent violations of law that prosecutors and legislators wanted and thought they could not obtain through traditional means. A prime example of newsgatherers having information coveted by government officials involved the Watergate scandal surrounding the Nixon Administration.

Thus, in the 1970s there was engendered a widespread attitude among government personnel that if reporters and editors had unpublished information concerning crimes and anti-establishment conduct, they had the same legal duty as anyone else to disclose it.

Though the social and political turmoil of those days has subsided and a kinder and gentler American society supposedly now exists, the attitude that journalists may be required against their will to give evidence acquired in the course of legitimate newsgathering persists. This poses difficult problems for the journalists. First, the ethics of their profession requires that they not divulge information obtained in confidence.[1] Second, any disclosure or the appearance of disclosure of sources or other information obtained in confidence will mark reporters as "unreliable" in the view of those from whom they are obtaining information and will inhibit the gathering of news.[2] Third, reporters think of themselves as "professionals" like doctors and lawyers. This gives them a rationale for claiming protection from disclosure of their non-published work product and confidential information. Requiring them to give evidence under subpoena strikes at the heart of their claim to professional status.[3]

---

1. *See* American Society of Newspaper Editors, A Statement of Principles, Article VI (1975); Society of Professional Journalists Code of Ethics, Part III Rule 5 (1987 revision).

2. *See, e.g.,* Caldwell v. United States, 434 F.2d 1081, 1084–1085 (9th Cir.1970),

rev'd sub nom. Branzburg v. Hayes, 408 U.S. 665, 92 S.Ct. 2646, 33 L.Ed.2d 626 (1972).

3. The status of journalists is legally in doubt. The National Labor Relations Board has ruled that journalists are not professionals within the statutory definition of

Whether or not the courts and other agencies of government consider them professionals, newspersons are refusing to obey subpoenas and choosing to face jail for contempt when claimed privileges are denied. There is thus a serious continuing confrontation with those who would use newsgatherers to provide information for governmental purposes. What makes the problem especially difficult is that both sides to this continuing dispute may say, with some justification, that by their actions they are serving the public interest.

7.2   The Lack of a Common Law Privilege of Confidentiality Covering the Newsgatherer–Source Relationship

While the same confidentiality rationale exists for journalists to encourage sources to disclose sensitive information that justifies the well-recognized privilege of government officials to protect the identities of their sources, the common law does not recognize testimonial privileges covering the newspersons-source relationship.[1] The reason for this is that the recognition of testimonial privileges makes the search for truth in the courtroom, grand jury room and legislative halls all the more difficult.[2] While the courts are forced to accept such long-recognized testimonial privileges as those involving government officials, husband and wife, attorney and client and physician and patient, they have generally not been inclined to permit additional ones no matter how compelling may be the rationale for their recognition.[3]

Therefore, if newspersons are to have a privilege against testimonial compulsion they must find it in state constitutions, statutes, rules of court or the United States Constitution.

---

that term because they are not " ... in a field that requires all of its members to have knowledge of an advanced type customarily acquired by a prolonged course of specialized intellectual instruction." The Express–News Corporation and San Antonio Typographical Union #172 A/W International Typographical Union, AFL–CIO, 223 NLRB 627, 628 (1976); *see* Reich v. Newspapers of New England, Inc., 44 F.3d 1060, 1070–1071 (1st Cir.1995); Reich v. Gateway Press, Inc., 13 F.3d 685, 697–698 (3d Cir.1994); Dalheim v. KDFW–TV, 918 F.2d 1220, 1228–1232 (5th Cir.1990). On the other hand the United States Court of Appeals for the Second Circuit has ruled that television news writers, editors and producers are "artistic professionals" under the Fair Labor Standards Act and thus exempt from its overtime wages provisions. Freeman v. NBC, Inc., 80 F.3d 78 (2d Cir. 1996). And the United States District Court for the District of Columbia has ruled that interpretative and analytical reporters and non-executive editors working for newspapers are professionals for purposes of monetary compensation and may not claim over-

time pay when they work more than 40 hours a week. *See* Sherwood v. Washington Post, 871 F.Supp. 1471 (D.D.C.1994); *see also* John Mintz, *The Battle Over a Reporter's Role; Former Post Staffer's Suit May Define Pay Rules and Journalists' Status*, Wash. Post., Jan. 2, 1993, p. C12; *Tom Sherwood Replies*, Wash. Post. Jan. 10, 1993, p. C6 (letter to the editor). Moreover, like other professions, journalists have their own ethical code which they are expected to observe in practicing their profession. *See* Society of Professional Journalists' Code of Ethics (1996). The Code has been in existence since 1926. *Id.*

1. *See* EDWARD W. CLEARY, McCORMICK ON EVIDENCE § 75 (3d ed. 1984); *see also* 8 J. H. WIGMORE, EVIDENCE § 2286 (McNaughton Rev. 1961).

2. *See* 8 J. H. WIGMORE, EVIDENCE § 2286 (McNaughton Rev. 1961).

3. *See, e.g.*, People *ex rel.* Mooney v. Sheriff of New York County, 269 N.Y. 291, 294, 199 N.E. 415, 416 (1936); 8 J. H. WIGMORE, EVIDENCE § 2286 (McNaughton Rev. 1961).

7.3 The Existence of Testimonial Immunity Under The First Amendment

A. Origin of the Claimed Privilege

The claim that the First Amendment provides newspersons with immunity from testimonial compulsion because such compulsion interferes with their access to sensitive and confidential news sources thereby restricting the flow of news and information to the public was first advanced at the appellate level in *Garland v. Torre*.[1] There, the great popular singer and actress Judy Garland had brought an action against Columbia Broadcasting System, Inc. (CBS) in which she alleged, among other things, that CBS executives had made false and defamatory statements about her and had orchestrated their campaign against her in newspapers and other media. An alleged example of such orchestration involved some paragraphs in Marie Torre's television and radio column printed in the New York Herald Tribune. In her column, Ms. Torre attributed to an unidentified CBS network executive certain statements about the plaintiff which Ms. Garland alleged were defamatory and highly damaging to her professional reputation. CBS denied these allegations. When Ms. Torre was deposed by Ms. Garland's attorney she verified the statements printed about Garland were exact quotes given to her over the telephone but refused under repeated questioning to reveal the network source. Contempt proceedings were then initiated against Torre and upon her continued refusal to disclose her source, Torre was held in criminal contempt and sentenced to serve 10 days in jail.

On appeal her counsel argued that she was protected from testimonial compulsion by the First Amendment.[2] In affirming her conviction, Judge, later Justice, Potter Stewart implied that the First Amendment might in certain circumstances provide newspersons with immunity from testifying when called upon to divulge their sources. But he rejected an absolute privilege, adopting instead a balancing approach to the problem. Where, as in *Garland*, the disclosure sought is very pointed and the need for the newsperson's testimony goes to the heart of the plaintiff's claim, the First Amendment confers no right on the newsperson to refuse to answer judicial inquiries.

On the other hand some state courts rejected the implication in *Garland* that a qualified newspersons's privilege existed[3] and thus the existence of a constitutional privilege remained in doubt until the United States Supreme Court passed on the question.

1. 259 F.2d 545 (2d Cir.), cert. denied, 358 U.S. 910, 79 S.Ct. 237, 3 L.Ed.2d 231 (1958) (opinion by circuit judge, later Justice, Potter Stewart).

2. Arguments were also advanced that the societal interest in the free flow of news compelled a holding that the identity of confidential news sources is protected by at least a qualified privilege and that in the particular circumstances of the case, the United States District Court should have ordered, pursuant to F.R. Crim. P. Rule 30, that no inquiry into the identity of the source be made. *Id.* at 548.

3. *See In re* Goodfader, 45 Haw. 317, 367 P.2d 472 (1961); State v. Buchanan, 250 Or. 244, 436 P.2d 729, cert. denied, 392 U.S. 905, 88 S.Ct. 2055, 20 L.Ed.2d 1363 (1968); *In re* Taylor, 412 Pa. 32, 193 A.2d 181 (1963).

B. The Supreme Court's Decision in the Branzburg-Pappas-Caldwell Trilogy

The issue was confronted by the Supreme Court in several cases which were consolidated for decision in *Branzburg v. Hayes*.[4] One of the cases (involving two judgments of the Kentucky Court of Appeals) pertained to Paul Branzburg, a staff reporter for the Louisville Courier–Journal,[5] another involved Earl Caldwell, a reporter for the New York Times[6] and the third involved Paul Pappas, a reporter-cameraman for a New Bedford, Massachusetts television station.[7]

In the two *Branzburg* cases, the journalist reported details of illegal drug activity in two counties in Kentucky. When subpoenaed to appear before a grand jury in one of the counties, Branzburg appeared but refused to identify the individuals he saw possessing marijuana or preparing hashish from the marijuana. A state trial judge ordered him to testify, rejecting his contention that the Kentucky reporters shield law or the First Amendment granted him testimonial immunity. The Kentucky Court of Appeals denied Branzburg's petition for writs of prohibition and mandamus, holding that he had abandoned his First Amendment claim and that the shield law did not cover reporters who personally observed criminal conduct taking place. In the other case another county's grand jury subpoenaed Branzburg to appear and testify about his article about the drug scene and drug users in the state's capital city of Frankfort. Utilizing numerous legal maneuvers raising the issue of reporters privilege, Branzburg managed to avoid appearing before this second grand jury to the time the Supreme Court granted certiorari in his cases.

In Caldwell's case subpoenas from a federal grand jury were served on the reporter to appear and testify concerning his knowledge of the Black Panther Party whose activities he was covering in the San Francisco area for the New York Times. Caldwell and his employer moved to quash, *inter alia*, on the ground that Caldwell would have to appear in secret before the grand jury and such appearance would destroy his working relationship with the Black Panthers thereby suppressing vital First Amendment freedoms "by driving a wedge of distrust and silence between the news media and the militants."[8] The district court denied the motion to quash on the ground that every person within the jurisdiction of the government is bound to appear upon being properly summoned. However, the court recognized Caldwell's First Amendment claims to the extent that he would not be required to reveal confidential associations, sources or information obtained by him in the course of legitimate newsgathering. Thereafter, Caldwell refused to appear and

4. 408 U.S. 665, 92 S.Ct. 2646, 33 L.Ed.2d 626 (1972).

5. *See* Branzburg v. Pound, 461 S.W.2d 345 (Ky.1970). A second decision in *Branzburg v. Meigs* is unreported.

6. For the United States Court of Appeals decision in this case, reversed by the Supreme Court in *Branzburg, see* Caldwell v. United States, 434 F.2d 1081 (9th Cir. 1970).

7. For the Massachusetts Supreme Judicial Court decision in this case, *see In re* Pappas, 358 Mass. 604, 266 N.E.2d 297 (1971).

8. 408 U.S. at 676, 92 S. Ct. at 2654, 33 L. Ed. 2d at 636.

was held in contempt. On appeal of the contempt order, the Ninth Circuit reversed, holding that the First Amendment provided a qualified testimonial privilege for newspersons to the extent of immunizing them from even appearing before grand juries when such appearances would deter informants from providing information in the future. The government then petitioned successfully for certiorari to review the Court of Appeals decision.

In Pappas' case, the television reporter was granted admission to the New Bedford headquarters of the Black Panthers to record a prepared statement by one of the organization's leaders and later the same day to film and report an anticipated police raid on the premises. As a condition of entry Papas agreed not to disclose anything else he saw or heard inside the headquarters. No raid took place and he filed no story and did not otherwise reveal what had transpired in the store while he was present. Two months later Pappas was summoned and appeared before the local grand jury but refused to answer questions about what had taken place inside the store-front headquarters, claiming that the First Amendment afforded him a privilege to protect confidential sources and their information. A second summons to appear was then served on him and his motion to quash on First Amendment and other grounds was denied by the trial judge and that denial was affirmed by the Supreme Judicial Court of Massachusetts, which rejected Pappas' First Amendment claims of privileges.

The common question in all of these cases whether the First Amendment provides newspersons with immunity against compelled appearance and testimony before grand juries was answered in the negative by an ostensible five-member majority in *Branzburg*. Speaking for the Court Justice White exalted the grand jury institution and its place in the Anglo–American system of justice and wrote that without access to reliable evidence the work of grand juries would be hampered. "Fair and effective law enforcement armed at providing security for the person and property of the individual is a fundamental function of government, and the grand jury plays an important, constitutionally mandated role in this process."[9] Justice White concluded that "[o]n the records before us, we perceive no basis for holding that the public interest in law enforcement and in ensuring effective grand jury proceedings is insufficient to override the consequential, but uncertain, burden on news gathering that is said to result from insisting that reporters, like other citizens, respond to relevant questions put to them in the course of a valid grand jury investigation or criminal trial."[10]

The Court's decision that no First Amendment privilege exists was seriously undermined by the concurring opinion of Justice Powell, one of the five justices comprising the apparent majority in *Branzburg*. Justice Powell seemed to recognize a limited newsperson's privilege when he wrote that "if the newsman is called upon to give information bearing

---

9. *Id*. at 690, 92 S. Ct. at 2661, 33 L. Ed. 2d at 644–645.

10. *Id*. at 690–691, 92 S. Ct. at 2661, 33 L. Ed. 2d at 645.

only a remote and tenuous relationship to the subject of the investigation, or if he has some other reason to believe that his testimony implicates confidential source relationships without a legitimate need of law enforcement, he will have access to the court on a motion to quash and an appropriate protective order may be entered. The asserted claim to privilege should be judged on its facts by the striking of a proper balance between freedom of the press and the obligation of all citizens to give relevant testimony with respect to criminal conduct."[11] But in a footnote,[12] Justice Powell made clear that newspersons had to appear in response to subpoenas and could not litigate at the outset the government's very authority to subpoena them. Rather, when a claim of privilege is presented to the court controlling the grand jury, it would be free to balance the competing interests of the newsperson and the government on the merits in the particular case.

What Justice Powell appears to be saying is that once a newsperson appears before a grand jury pursuant to subpoena he may be able to successfully claim a *qualified* constitutional privilege if the evidence sought does not relate to some substantial element of the government's investigation or if confidential source relationships may be jeopardized when the government has available to it alternative means of gaining the information or otherwise building its case.

Compare Powell's approach with that of Justices Stewart, Brennan and Marshall.[13] Writing for the three dissenters, Justice Stewart argued that the court's decision reflected a crabbed view of the First Amendment because the denial of a privilege for the newsperson-source confidential relationship would impede a full and free flow of information to the public. To protect that flow of information the dissenters would permit newspersons to challenge grand jury subpoenas by motions to quash *before* they are required to appear and would place the burden on the government to "(1) show that there is probable cause to believe that the newsman has information that is clearly relevant to a specific probable violation of law; (2) demonstrate that the information sought cannot be obtained by alternative means less destructive of First Amendment rights; and (3) demonstrate a compelling and overriding interest in the information."[14]

Reading the majority opinion, Powell's concurrence and Stewart's dissenting opinion together, substantial ambiguity in the Court's position is apparent. Clarity ends after stating the propositions that *Branzburg* holds that the First Amendment accords no absolute privilege to newspersons to refuse to appear and to testify when summoned before state and federal grand juries and accords no qualified privilege to refuse to *appear* before such bodies.

11. *Id.* at 710, 92 S. Ct. at 2671, 33 L. Ed. 2d at 656.

12. *Id.*

13. Justice Douglas filed a separate dissent espousing his absolutist view of the First Amendment. 408 U.S. at 711–725, 92 S. Ct. at 2686–2694, 33 L. Ed. 2d at 657–665.

14. 408 U.S. at 743, 92 S. Ct. at 2681, 33 L. Ed. 2d at 676.

Ambiguity arises from the fact that while White's majority opinion rejects *any* constitutional newsperson's privilege, *five* justices including Powell would find at least a qualified privilege of some dimension for newspersons to refuse to testify. Powell would require the newsperson to appear before the grand jury before invoking the qualified privilege. Stewart, Brennan and Marshall would permit a challenge to the compelled appearance itself. Justice Douglas would recognize an absolute immunity of newspersons against compulsory appearance and the giving of evidence.[15]

The parameters of a qualified privilege arising out of the First Amendment recognized by the four justices who passed directly on the questions is also not clear. The opinions of Powell and Stewart seem to agree that subpoenas of newspersons must seek evidence relevant to some important aspect of a government criminal investigation and may not be merely peripheral or tenuous.[16] The opinions also seem congruent in that confidential source relationships should not be jeopardized by subpoenaing newsperson when alternative means are available to the government to obtain needed information.[17]

Stewart, Brennan and Marshall differ from Powell in imposing a third requirement that the government "demonstrate a compelling and overriding interest in the information,"[18] citing by analogy Stewart's own Second Circuit opinion in *Garland v. Torre*.[19] Moreover, it is clear from the respective opinions that these three dissenters would place the burden on the government to defeat a claim of privilege while Powell would place the burden of establishing such claim on the newsperson. Where Powell and the three dissenters differ, the parameters of the privilege remain uncertain.

The one caveat in a trial proceeding regarding the balancing approach is that if it is immediately clear to the trial judge that if the entire case itself or the request to obtain evidence from a newsgatherer

---

15. 408 U.S. at 712–713, 92 S. Ct. at 2687, 33 L. Ed. 2d at 658. Of course, lesser included within an absolute newspersons privilege would be a qualified one.

16. Powell wrote "[I]f the newsman is called upon to give information bearing only a remote and tenuous relationship to the subject of the investigation ... he will have access to the court on a motion to quash and an appropriate protective order may be entered." 408 U.S. at 710, 92 S. Ct. at 2671, 33 L. Ed. 2d at 656. Stewart wrote, "[T]he government must (1) show that there is probable cause to believe that the newsman has information that is clearly relevant to a specific probable violation of law.... " *Id.* at 743, 92 S. Ct. at 2681, 33 L. Ed. 2d at 676.

17. Powell wrote, "[I]f he [the newsperson] has some other reason to believe that

his testimony implicates confidential source relationships without a legitimate need of law enforcement he will have access to the court on a motion to quash and an appropriate protective order may be entered." *Id.* at 710, 92 S. Ct. at 2671, 33 L. Ed. 2d at 656. Stewart wrote "[T]he government must ... (2) demonstrate that the information sought cannot be obtained by alternative means less destructive of First Amendment rights ..." *Id.* at 743, 92 S. Ct. at 2681, 33 L. Ed. 2d at 676.

18. *Id.* at 743, 92 S. Ct. at 2681, 33 L. Ed. 2d at 676.

19. 259 F.2d 545 (2d Cir.), cert. denied 358 U.S. 910, 79 S.Ct. 237, 3 L.Ed.2d 231 (1958), cited at 408 U.S. at 743 n. 33, 92 S. Ct. at 2681, n. 33, 33 L. Ed. 2d at 676–677 n. 33.

is insubstantial or frivolous, such evidence will not be compelled.[20] For instance, in *Cervantes v. Time, Inc.*[21] Former St. Louis Mayor Alfonso Cervantes sued Life magazine for suggesting that he had underworld connections. Cervantes said he could not prove malice without knowing the names of the FBI sources of the Life reporter. But Cervantes objected to only four paragraphs of an 87–paragraph, extremely well-documented story, and the court noted that the truth as to the vast amount of the other material in the article was either admitted or not explicitly denied. Because Cervantes did not ever make out a prima facie case showing that the Life article was false, the court refused to require the reporter to disclose his sources during pretrial discovery.

C. Lower Court Recognition of a Qualified Privilege After Branzburg

Perhaps emboldened by the Supreme Court's ambiguous position on qualified privilege in *Branzburg*, a number of state and lower federal courts have held that a qualified newsperson's privilege of some dimension does exist under the First Amendment.[22] Once that acknowledgment is made these courts are then compelled to deal with a number of difficult issues surrounding the qualified constitutional privilege against testimonial compulsion.

7.4 General Requirements and Scope of the Qualified Privilege

A. Meeting the Balancing Test

Most courts that have accepted the idea of a qualified privilege apply a balancing test similar to that put forward by Justice Stewart in his dissenting opinion in *Branzburg* and his earlier opinion for the Second Circuit in *Garland*,[1] though some also add a requirement that the party

---

20. *See, e.g.*, Cervantes v. Time, Inc., 464 F.2d 986, 994–995 (8th Cir.1972), cert. denied 409 U.S. 1125, 93 S.Ct. 939, 35 L.Ed.2d 257 (1973); Carey v. Hume, 492 F.2d 631, 637, 160 U.S.App.D.C. 365 (D.C.Cir.), cert. dismissed 417 U.S. 938, 94 S.Ct. 2654, 41 L.Ed.2d 661 (1974); *see also* Winegard v. Oxberger, 258 N.W.2d 847, 852 (Iowa 1977).

21. *Id.*

22. *See, e.g.*, Baker v. F & F Investment, 470 F.2d 778 (2d Cir.1972), cert. denied 411 U.S. 966, 93 S.Ct. 2147, 36 L.Ed.2d 686 (1973); Shoen v. Shoen, 48 F.3d 412 (9th Cir.1995); Silkwood v. Kerr–McGee Corp., 563 F.2d 433 (10th Cir.1977); Zerilli v. Smith, 656 F.2d 705, 710–714 (D.C.Cir.1981); Tribune Co. v. Huffstetler, 489 So.2d 722 (Fla.1986); Matter of Contempt of Wright, 108 Idaho 418, 700 P.2d 40 (1985); Winegard v. Oxberger, 258 N.W.2d 847 (Iowa 1977), cert. denied 436 U.S. 905, 98 S.Ct. 2234, 56 L.Ed.2d 402 (1978); State v. St. Peter, 132 Vt. 266, 315

A.2d 254 (1974); Brown v. Commonwealth, 214 Va. 755, 204 S.E.2d 429, cert. denied 419 U.S. 966, 95 S.Ct. 229, 42 L.Ed.2d 182 (1974); State *ex rel.* Hudok v. Henry, 182 W.Va. 500, 389 S.E.2d 188 (W.Va.1989); *see also* Romualdo P. Eclavea, Annot., *Privilege of Newsgatherer Against Disclosure of Confidential Sources or Information*, 99 A.L.R. 3d 37 (1980); *But see, e.g., In re* Grand Jury, 810 F.2d 580 (6th Cir.1987); Pankratz v. District Court, 199 Colo. 411, 609 P.2d 1101 (1980); Matter of Farber, 78 N.J. 259, 394 A.2d 330, cert. denied 439 U.S. 997, 99 S.Ct. 598, 58 L.Ed.2d 670 (1978); Texas ex rel. Healey v. McMeans, 884 S.W.2d 772, 775 (Tex.Crim.App.1994) (stating in no uncertain terms that newspersons have no constitutional privilege, qualified or otherwise, to withhold relevant evidence in criminal proceedings and citing *Branzburg*).

1. *See, e.g.*, United States v. Burke, 700 F.2d 70, 77 (2d Cir.), cert. denied, 464 U.S. 816, 104 S.Ct. 72, 78 L.Ed.2d 85 (1983); Miller v. Transamerican Press, Inc., 621

responsible for the issuance of the subpoena demonstrate that his case is not frivolous.[2]

Justice Stewart's balancing test requires the government or anyone seeking information by compulsion from newspersons to establish that (1) there is probable cause to believe that the newsperson has information that is clearly relevant to a specific probable violation of law; (2) the information cannot be obtained by alternative means less destructive of First Amendment rights; and (3) there exists a compelling and overriding interest in the information sought.[3]

Procedural requirements in striking the balance vary.[4] But under Justice Stewart's test the party seeking to compel testimony or production of material would have the burden of establishing the unavailability of the privilege in a separate hearing held by the judge supervising the grand jury proceeding or in the presiding judge's chambers during recess of a trial or pre-trial proceeding.[5]

In the *in camera* hearing, a determination first must be made whether the newsperson resisting the subpoena falls within the class of persons qualifying for the privilege. If that threshold question is determined in the affirmative, the material without inspection will be treated as presumptively privileged and the burden is on the requestor of the information to rebut that presumption by a preponderance of the evidence.[6] If the court is satisfied that the presumption has been rebutted, *in camera* inspection of the withheld information will be ordered. Following consideration of this information and any relevant collateral evidence, the court will rule finally, utilizing the balancing test, whether the evidence in the hands of the newsperson is protected from compelled disclosure by the qualified privilege.[7] Of course, the entire proceeding

F.2d 721, 726 (5th Cir.1980), cert. denied, 450 U.S. 1041, 101 S.Ct. 1759, 68 L.Ed.2d 238 (1981); Zerilli v. Smith, 656 F.2d 705, 712–714, 211 U.S. App. D.C. 116, 121–126 (D.C.Cir.1981); Matter of Contempt of Wright, 108 Idaho 418, 421, 700 P.2d 40, 43 (1985); WBAL–TV Div., Hearst Corp. v. State, 300 Md. 233, 243, 477 A.2d 776, 781 (1984).

2. *See* Bruno & Stillman, Inc. v. Globe Newspaper Co., 633 F.2d 583, 597 (1st Cir. 1980); Winegard v. Oxberger, 258 N.W.2d 847, 852 (Iowa 1977); WBAL–TV Div., Hearst Corp. v. State, 300 Md. 233, 243, 477 A.2d 776, 781 (1984).

3. Branzburg v. Hayes, 408 U.S. 665, 742, 92 S.Ct. 2646, 2681, 33 L.Ed.2d 626, 676 (1972) (dissenting opinion); *see* Garland v. Torre, 259 F.2d 545, 549–550 (2d Cir.), cert. denied, 358 U.S. 910, 79 S.Ct. 237, 3 L.Ed.2d 231 (1958); *see also* Shoen v. Shoen, 48 F.3d 412 (9th Cir.1995) (recent statement and application of this balancing test).

4. *See* Matter of Contempt of Wright, 108 Idaho 418, 421, 700 P.2d 40, 43 (1985).

5. *See* Lamberto v. Bown, 326 N.W.2d 305, 308–309 (Iowa 1982); *but see* Miami Herald Pub. Co. v. Morejon, 529 So.2d 1204, 1207 (Fla.App.1988), *approved* 561 So.2d 577 (Fla.1990).

6. *See* Shoen v. Shoen, 5 F.3d 1289, 1298 (9th Cir.1993); Lamberto, 326 N.W.2d at 308–309; *cf. In re* Farber, 78 N.J. 259, 276, 394 A.2d 330, 338, cert. denied, 439 U.S. 997, 99 S.Ct. 598, 58 L.Ed.2d 670 (1978) (procedure under New Jersey shield law); United States v. Nixon, 418 U.S. 683, 713, 94 S.Ct. 3090, 3110, 41 L.Ed.2d 1039, 1067 (1974) (procedure for considering claim of executive privilege).

7. This convoluted procedure is compelled by the need to avoid the unnecessary forcing of disclosure of the evidence even *in camera*. *See* Lamberto, 326 N.W.2d at 308–309; *In re* Farber 78 N.J. at 276, 394 A.2d at 338.

should be transcribed and specific findings should be placed on the record to facilitate appellate review.[8]

B. Information and Material Protected

1. Identification of Sources

If a jurisdiction recognizes a qualified privilege of any dimension, it will nearly always protect newspersons from being compelled to disclose the identity of their confidential sources.[9] In other words, the bedrock protection provided is as to matters concerning the sources of news and information. The protection covers not only direct identification but any information that would tend to expose the source.[10] But even here, the availability of the protection is subject to the balancing process previously described.[11]

2. Substantive Confidential Information

Going beyond protection for sources, the availability of the privilege becomes more problematic. Substantive information obtained by the newsgatherer under a promise of confidentiality is generally covered by the privilege[12] but because such information may be more compelling in judicial proceedings on the legal issues involved and its disclosure somewhat less likely to discourage sources from making themselves available to the news media, the balancing of interests may not turn out as favorably for the newsgatherers as it does regarding source identification.[13] Included within the protection of confidential information are such things as resource materials,[14] outtakes[15] and documents.[16]

---

8. *See* Matter of Contempt of Wright, 108 Idaho 418, 421, 700 P.2d 40, 43 (1985); *see also* Schreiber v. Multimedia of Ohio, Inc., 41 Ohio App.3d 257, 259, 535 N.E.2d 357, 360 (1987) (affect of unavailability of *in camera* transcript on appellate review of denial of privilege).

9. *See, e.g.,* Tribune Co. v. Huffstetler, 489 So.2d 722 (Fla.1986); Matter of Contempt of Wright, 108 Idaho 418, 700 P.2d 40 (Idaho 1985); Winegard v. Oxberger, 258 N.W.2d 847 (Iowa 1977), cert. denied, 436 U.S. 905, 98 S.Ct. 2234, 56 L.Ed.2d 402 (1978).

10. *Cf.* Mich. Comp. Laws Ann. § 767.5a(1) (Supp. 1990); Minn. Stat. Ann. § 595.03 (West 1988).

11. *See, e.g.,* Garland v. Torre, 259 F.2d 545, 549–550 (2d Cir.1958), cert. denied 358 U.S. 910, 79 S.Ct. 237, 3 L.Ed.2d 231 (1958); Shoen v. Shoen, 48 F.3d 412, 415–16 (9th Cir.1995); Tribune Co. v. Huffstetler, 489 So.2d 722 (Fla.1986), Senear v. Daily Journal–American , 97 Wash. 2d 148, 641 P.2d 1180, 1183–1184 (1982) (uniquely finding both the qualified privilege and the need to balance in the Washington common law).

12. *See, e.g.,* Winegard v. Oxberger, 258 N.W.2d 847 (Iowa 1977), cert. denied, 436 U.S. 905, 98 S.Ct. 2234, 56 L.Ed.2d 402 (1978); State v. Sandstrom, 224 Kan. 573, 574, 581 P.2d 812, 814 (1978) (dictum), cert. denied, 440 U.S. 929, 99 S.Ct. 1265, 59, L.Ed.2d 485, (1979); State *ex rel.* Hudok v. Henry, 182 W.Va. 500, 505, 389 S.E.2d 188, 193 (W.Va.1989); *see also* United States v. Cuthbertson, 630 F.2d 139, 147 (3d Cir.1980), cert. denied, *sub nom.* Cuthbertson v. CBS, Inc., 449 U.S. 1126, 101 S.Ct. 945, 67 L.Ed.2d 113 (1981) (unpublished material the confidentiality of which is waived by the source).

13. *See* Winegard v. Oxberger 258 N.W.2d 847, 852–853 (Iowa 1977); Knight–Ridder Broadcasting, Inc. v. Greenberg, 70 N.Y.2d 151, 160, 518 N.Y.S.2d 595, 600, 511 N.E.2d 1116, 1121 (1987).

14. *See* United States v. Cuthbertson, 630 F.2d 139 (3d Cir.1980), cert. denied *sub nom.* Cuthbertson v. CBS, Inc., 449 U.S. 1126, 101 S.Ct. 945, 67 L.Ed.2d 113 (1981) (statements given to reporter by non-witnesses); von Bulow By Auersperg v. von Bulow, 811 F.2d 136, 143–144 (2d Cir.),

---

15. See Note on page 508.

3. Non-confidential Information and Material

The availability of the privilege to protect from compelled disclosure non-confidential but unpublished information obtained in the course of newsgathering is even more problematic. The cases are in conflict[17] and seem to reflect two competing arguments. In opposition to the conferring of privilege here is the idea that the free flow of information to the public is not affected when information and material sought under compulsion is not gathered in confidence. There is no chilling of sources or of the information they impart. No expectation of confidentiality is raised and confidentiality is not an incentive for divulging information in this situation.[18]

The countervailing argument favoring availability of the privilege is that if newsmedia personnel are constantly bombarded with subpoenas and subpoenas *duces tecum* to provide to litigants non-confidential information in their possession this will have a seriously disruptive effect on the ability of the news media to do their job of informing the public.[19] This argument has been presented most forcefully by the New York Court of Appeals. "[B]ecause journalists typically gather information about accidents, crimes, and other matters of special interest that often give rise to litigation, attempts to obtain evidence by subjecting the press to discovery as a nonparty would be widespread if not restricted. The practical burdens on time and resources, as well as the consequent diversion of journalistic effort and disruption of newsgathering activity, would be particularly inimical to the vigor of a free press."[20]

While the New York Court's rationale would also be applicable to published non-confidential materials in the possession of newsgatherers

cert. denied 481 U.S. 1015, 107 S.Ct. 1891, 95 L.Ed.2d 498 (1987).

15. *See* State *ex rel.* Hudok v. Henry, 182 W.Va. 500, 389 S.E.2d 188 (W.Va.1989) (audio tape interview never aired).

16. *See* United States v. Burke, 700 F.2d 70, 76–77 (2d Cir.), cert. denied 464 U.S. 816, 104 S.Ct. 72, 78 L.Ed.2d 85 (1983).

17. *Compare, e.g.,* Gonzales v. National Broadcasting Co., 155 F.3d 618 (2d Cir. 1998) (privilege unavailable for television news outtakes); Miami Herald Pub. Co. v. Morejon, 561 So.2d 577 (Fla.1990) (privilege unavailable for eyewitness testimony); Carroll Contracting, Inc. v. Edwards, 528 So.2d 951 (Fla.App.1988) (privilege unavailable for unpublished news photos) *with* O'Neill v. Oakgrove Construction, Inc., 71 N.Y.2d 521, 526–530, 528 N.Y.S.2d 1, 3–5 523 N.E.2d 277 279–281 (1988) (privilege available for unpublished news photos); United States v. Cuthbertson, 630 F.2d 139, 147 (3d Cir.1980), cert. denied *sub nom.* Cuthbertson v. CBS, Inc., 449 U.S. 1126, 101 S.Ct. 945, 67 L.Ed.2d 113 (1981) (privilege

available for videotape portions of material which might be nonconfidential); Shoen v. Shoen, 5 F.3d 1289, 1293–1296 (9th Cir. 1993) (privilege available for notes and tapes utilized by author in publishing his book).

18. *See* Miami Herald Pub. Co. v. Morejon, 561 So.2d 577, 581 (Fla.1990).

19. *See* O'Neill v. Oakgrove Construction, Inc. 71 N.Y.2d 521, 526–530, 528 N.Y.S.2d 1, 3–5, 523 N.E.2d 277, 279–281 (1988) (breaking news photos).

20. O'Neill, 71 N.Y. 2d at 526–527, 528 N.Y.S. 2d at 3, 523 N.E. 2d at 279 (1988). *But see* Miami Herald Pub. Co. v. Morejon, 561 So.2d 577, 581 (Fla.1990) in which the Florida Supreme Court said, "The fact that journalists may be somewhat inconvenienced by having to appear in court or other related proceedings does not lessen their duty to testify. Ordinary citizens would not be excused from testifying as to what they observed, and the First Amendment should not be interpreted to make journalists' testimony privileged simply because they made their observations while on duty as a reporter."

as well, the few appellate cases to date hold that the qualified privilege is not available in this situation.[21]

4. Eye-witness Testimony

One type of evidence which is almost never protected from disclosure by the privilege is information concerning criminal matters obtained directly through the newsgatherer's own senses.[22] It does not matter whether the sensory information is obtained in the course of one's employment as a newsperson or outside of such employment.[23] Nor does it appear that eye witness evidence relevant to civil judicial proceedings is protected either.[24]

The reason for this judicial reluctance to strike the balance in favor of granting protection of the qualified privilege to eye witness testimony of newspersons is that they themselves are the source and such testimony is unique to the witness and may be particularly cogent. The idea that the judicial system is entitled to every person's testimony seems especially compelling to courts in this situation.[25]

5. Information Concerning Editorial Processes

Another type of evidence not protected by the newsperson's privilege is information concerning the editorial process, including the state of mind of the editors in dealing with a story. In *Herbert v. Lando*,[26] a libel plaintiff, an admitted public figure, deposed a news producer involved in the production and broadcast of a segment of CBS's program "Sixty Minutes," which the plaintiff, Army Col. Anthony Herbert, claimed defamed him. By the deposition Col. Herbert hoped to establish the actual malice of CBS[27] and the other defendants. To that end Col. Herbert's counsel attempted to elicit information about the thinking and editorial decisions leading to the presentation of the segment in the manner it was broadcast. The producer, Barry Lando, also a defendant in the libel action, refused to answer the questions on the ground that the First Amendment protected against inquiry into the state of mind of

---

21. *See* United States v. Criden, 633 F.2d 346 (3d Cir.1980), cert. denied *sub nom.* Schaffer v. United States, 449 U.S. 1113, 101 S.Ct. 924, 66 L.Ed.2d 842 (1981); State v. Hohler, 543 A.2d 364 (Me.1988).

22. *See* Branzburg v. Hayes, 408 U.S. 665, 92 S.Ct. 2646, 33 L.Ed.2d 626 (1972) (apparent majority opinion); Pankratz v. Colorado District Court, 199 Colo. 411, 609 P.2d 1101, 1103 (1980); Miami Herald Pub. Co. v. Morejon, 561 So.2d 577, 580 (Fla. 1990); ("We have found no case to support the proposition that a news reporter who actually witnesses the criminal act has a qualified constitutional privilege to refuse to respond to a subpoena"); *see also* Bell v. City of Des Moines, 412 N.W.2d 585, 588 (Iowa 1987) (dictum).

23. *See* Miami Herald Pub. Co. v. Morejon, 561 So.2d 577, 580 (Fla.1990).

24. *See* Bell v. City of Des Moines, 412 N.W.2d 585, 588 (Iowa 1987) (dictum).

25. *See* Branzburg v. Hayes, 408 U.S. 665, 686, 92 S.Ct. 2646, 2659, 33 L.Ed.2d 626, 642 (1972); Bell v. City of Des Moines, 412 N.W.2d 585, 588 (1987); *see also* 8 J. H. WIGMORE, EVIDENCE § 2192 (McNaughton Rev. 1961).

26. 441 U.S. 153, 99 S.Ct. 1635, 60 L.Ed.2d 115 (1979).

27. "Actual malice" in defamation actions involving public figures as plaintiffs means knowing untruthfulness or reckless disregard for whether the material published is false. *See* New York Times v. Sullivan, 376 U.S. 254, 279–280, 84 S.Ct. 710, 726, 11 L.Ed.2d 686, 706 (1964).

those who edit, produce, or publish news and information as well as into the editorial process.

Col. Herbert then sought and obtained an order from the United States District Court directing Lando to answer the questions. A divided panel of the Second Circuit reversed, holding under the First Amendment that Lando had an absolute privilege to refuse to answer questions about his thoughts, opinions and conclusions with respect to the information gathered by him and about his conversations with his editorial colleagues. On certiorari, the Supreme Court reversed, holding that the First Amendment does not accord such a privilege to evidence concerning the editorial process in libel cases when such evidence is material to a critical element of action, and a decision to the contrary would inappropriately enhance the burden on public figures of proving actual malice.

In public figure cases, the plaintiff's inquiry into the editorial process may therefore include: (1) the reporter's or editor's conclusions reached during research and investigation regarding people or leads to be pursued or not pursued; (2) the reporter's or editor's conclusions about facts imparted by interviewees and his subjective reaction as to the credibility of the persons interviewed; (3) the basis for the reporter's or editor's assessment of the credibility of the persons interviewed and the information imparted; (4) the gist of conversations with editorial colleagues and others regarding the manner in which particular stories should be approached, processed and published with special attention to discussions regarding the inclusion and exclusion of available material; and (5) the reporter's and editor's intentions relative to particular stories as reflected by their decisions to include or exclude particular material.[28]

In contrast to the development of the law following the Court's ambiguous decision in *Branzburg v. Hayes*,[29] the state and lower federal courts are following the Court's denial of a privilege covering evidence relating to the editorial process of the news media so long as what is requested is material.[30]

C. Persons Who May Be Covered By The Privilege

The qualified constitutional privilege is extended to members of the news media not because they are all-round good fellows (though they well may be) but because they are the instruments by which the citizenry receives its news and information, thus strengthening our

---

28. *See* Herbert v. Lando, 441 U.S. 153, 165–167 n. 15, 99 S.Ct. 1635, 1643–1644, n. 15, 60 L.Ed.2d 115, 127–128 n. 15 (1979).

29. 408 U.S. 665, 92 S.Ct. 2646, 33 L.Ed.2d 626 (1972) (see all opinions).

30. *See* Liberty Lobby, Inc. v. Rees, 111 F.R.D. 19, 22 (D.D.C.1986); Cape Publications, Inc. v. Bridges, 387 So.2d 436 (Fla.

App.1980), cert denied, 464 U.S. 893, 104 S.Ct. 239, 78 L.Ed.2d 229 (1983); Warford v. Lexington Herald–Leader Co., 789 S.W.2d 758, 772 (Ky.1990); *cf.* Hatchard v. Westinghouse Broadcasting Co., 516 Pa. 184, 532 A.2d 346, 349 (Pa. 1987) (determination under state shield law).

representative democracy.[31] It is this vital role of the news media in our society that defines the scope of the privilege at least insofar as those *who* may claim its protection. Therefore, even those who would ordinarily not be thought of as journalists may be covered if their activities are likely to result in the flow of news and information to the public.[32]

In *von Bulow by Auersperg v. von Bulow*,[33] Andrea Reynolds, an intimate friend of Claus von Bulow, the defendant in a civil action, was held in contempt when, under subpoena from the plaintiffs, she refused to produce certain private investigative reports commissioned by her on the lifestyle of the defendant's comatose wife's children, notes taken directly by her while observing the previous criminal trial of von Bulow for attempted murder of his wife and a manuscript of an unpublished book being written by her about the events surrounding the von Bulow prosecution. Although she submitted the investigative reports and the notes to the court *in camera*, for inspection, she refused to turn over the manuscript. And when the trial judge held all documents discoverable, she refused to produce them claiming, *inter alia*, that they were protected by the journalist's First Amendment privilege. The court ordered Ms. Reynolds to pay a fine of $500 per day until she purged herself of contempt but stayed the order pending determination of her appeal.

The United States Court of Appeals for the Second Circuit affirmed the contempt order, holding, among other things, that Ms. Reynolds was not a newsgatherer entitled to claim protection of the privilege. The Second Circuit's reasoning is very instructive on the question of who may be covered by the privilege. Particularly relevant here are the first three principles enunciated by the appeals court regarding an individual's eligibility to claim the First Amendment privilege. First the qualified First Amendment right resulting in the newsgatherer's privilege emanates, the Court said, "from the strong public policy supporting the unfettered communication of information by the journalist to the public. Second, whether a person is a journalist, and thus protected by the privilege, must be determined by the person's intent at the inception of the information-gathering process. Third, an individual successfully may

31. *See, e.g.*, dissenting opinion of Douglas, J. in *Environmental Protection Agency v. Mink*, 410 U.S. 73, 110–111, 93 S.Ct. 827, 847, 35 L.Ed.2d 119, 145 (1973), quoting James Madison in his letter to W. T. Barry, Aug. 4, 1822, "A popular Government, without popular information, or the means of acquiring it, is but a Prologue to a Farce or a Tragedy; or, perhaps both. Knowledge will forever govern ignorance: And a people who mean to be their own governors, must arm themselves with the power which knowledge gives." *See also* von Bulow By Auersperg v. von Bulow, 811 F.2d 136, 142–144 (2d Cir.), cert. denied *sub nom.* Reynolds v. von Bulow By Auersperg, 481 U.S. 1015, 107 S.Ct. 1891, 95 L.Ed.2d 498 (1987).

32. *See, e.g.*, von Bulow By Auersperg v. von Bulow, 811 F.2d at 144–145, (by implication a non-journalist taking notes at trial for use in a book to be sold to the public); Silkwood v. Kerr–McGee Corp., 563 F.2d 433 (10th Cir.1977) (free-lance documentary filmmaker); Apicella v. McNeil Laboratories, Inc., 66 F.R.D. 78 (E.D.N.Y.1975) (medical doctor as executive officer of a medical newsletter); see also Kraig L. Baker, Comment, *Are Oliver Stone and Tom Clancy Journalists? Determining Who Has Standing to Claim the Journalist's Privilege*, 69 Wash. L. Rev. 739, 748–754 (1994).

33. 811 F.2d 136 (2d Cir.), cert. denied *sub nom.* Reynolds v. von Bulow by Auersperg, 481 U.S. 1015, 107 S.Ct. 1891, 95 L.Ed.2d 498 (1987).

assert the journalist's privilege if he is involved in activities traditionally associated with the gathering and dissemination of news, even though he may not ordinarily be a member of the institutionalized press."[34]

Applying these principles to Ms. Reynolds, the Court found that she had ordered the investigative reports because the children's credibility in accusing their stepfather of wrongdoing was something she had to undermine not only for purposes of helping von Bulow with his defense at the criminal trial but also for her own peace of mind. Thus, at the time she directed the information be gathered, she was not intending to use the reports to disseminate information to the public and therefore the appeals court held the reports to be discoverable.[35]

As for the notes taken by Ms. Reynolds while watching the von Bulow criminal trial on television, her assertion that the notes were made because of an agreement with the New York Post for her to write about the criminal trial was rejected and the notes declared discoverable by the Second Circuit because she continued to take them even after contractual negotiations with the Post proved fruitless. The court noted that the trial judge had been unable to find that Ms. Reynolds was engaged in any meaningful way in the gathering and dissemination of news to the public while viewing the criminal trial.[36]

Finally, with regard to the manuscript itself, the privilege was found inapplicable because Ms. Reynolds had not demonstrated by competent evidence any intent at the time she commenced gathering information for the manuscript to disseminate it to the public. While she claimed to have acquired information from confidential sources her testimony was equally consistent with her gathering the evidence to assist von Bulow at trial. "Reynolds simply has not made the requisite showing that assurances of confidentiality were given by her out of journalistic necessity."[37]

While Andrea Reynolds was denied protection from compelled disclosure the clear implication from the Second Circuit's opinion is that even though she was not a member of the newsgathering profession, if she had in fact met the burden of proving that she had gathered information about von Bulow's criminal prosecution with the intent at the outset to disseminate it to the public, she would have been allowed to claim the privilege subject to the balancing standard laid down by the Second Circuit in *Garland* and echoed in Justice Stewart's dissent in *Branzburg*.[38]

34. *Id*. at 142.

35. *Id*. at 145.

36. *Id*.

37. *Id*. at 146.

38. *See* Shoen v. Shoen, 5 F.3d 1289, 1294–1295 (9th Cir.1993) adopting the test for the applicability of the privilege laid down in *von Bulow* and extending the qualified privilege to the author of a nonfiction book about a wealthy family's bitter internal feud. *See also* Summit Technology, Inc.

v. Healthcare Capital Group, Inc., 141 F.R.D. 381, 384 (D.Mass.1992) (investment analyst writing about publicly traded corporation). Once one establishes by a preponderance of the evidence that he or she is within the class of persons covered by the newsgatherer's qualified privilege, as in *Shoen*, the burden of proving whether, in the particular case, the privilege actually protects the newsgatherer under the accepted balancing standard is placed on the shoulders of the person seeking compelled

In accord with the principles set down in *von Bulow* is the earlier decision of the Tenth Circuit in *Silkwood v.Kerr-McGee Corp.*[39] involving an independent documentary filmmaker working on a factual film about the events surrounding the death of Karen Silkwood. Ms. Silkwood was employed by the defendant Kerr–McGee Corporation which was alleged in this civil action to have violated her civil rights through its agents by, among other things, willfully and wantonly contaminating her with toxic plutonium radiation.[40] During discovery proceedings, the filmmaker, Arthur (Buzz) Hirsch was called for deposition and simultaneously served with a subpoena *duces tecum* to produce all documents and writings in connection with his investigation. He moved to quash the subpoena and when that was denied, at the deposition, he refused to answer certain questions he believed would elicit confidential information from him claiming in justification the newsgatherer's privilege.

On appeal of the district court's order denying the protective order, the Tenth Circuit reversed the order, holding that Hirsch's mission was to carry out investigative reporting for use in the preparation of a documentary film and that there was an underlying public interest in the communication of his information and opinions throughout the film medium to citizenry.[41]

The emphasis in the *von Bulow* and *Silkwood* cases on who is a newsgatherer underscores the point that the privilege belongs to journalists and their publishing organizations[42] and not their sources.[43] If it

---

disclosure. *See* Shoen, 5 F.3d at 1296; May v. Collins, 122 F.R.D. 535, 540 (S.D.Ind. 1988); *see also* Pinkard v. Johnson, 118 F.R.D. 517 (M.D.Ala.1987).

39. 563 F.2d 433 (10th Cir.1977).

40. *Id.* at 434–435. Silkwood actually died in a mysterious automobile accident while on her way to a meeting with a reporter. *See* N.Y. Times, Nov. 19, 1974, p. 28, col. 1.

41. 563 F. 2d at 437. In support of its ruling the court cited Lovell v. Griffin, 303 U.S. 444, 58 S.Ct. 666, 82 L.Ed. 949 (1938) involving a city ordinance forbidding as a nuisance the distribution of any type of literature within the city limits of Griffin, Georgia without first obtaining written permission from the city manager. In the course of its opinion striking down the ordinance under the First and Fourteenth Amendments, the Supreme Court noted that the freedom of the press was not confined to newspapers and periodicals. *Id.* at 452, 58 S. Ct. at 669, 82 L. Ed. at 954. Interestingly, the film medium has had a prominent relationship with both the *Silkwood* and *von Bulow* cases. In addition to Buzz Hirsch's documentary on Karen Silkwood, a major commercial film *Silkwood* starring Meryl Streep in the title role (Mike

Nichols, director; ABC Films, Mike Nichols, Michael Hausman, producers 1983) was released. Another major studio film *Reversal of Fortune* (Barbet Schroeder, director; Warner Brothers, Edward R. Pressman, Oliver Stone producers 1990) detailed the successful efforts of Harvard law professor Alan M. Dershowitz to win Claus von Bulow a new trial following his original conviction for the attempted murder of his wife.

42. *See, e.g.*, Senear v. Daily Journal–American, 97 Wash. 2d 148, 157, 641 P.2d 1180, 1184 (1982).

43. *See* United States v. Cuthbertson, 630 F.2d 139, 147 (3d Cir.1980), cert. denied, 449 U.S. 1126, 101 S.Ct. 945, 67 L.Ed.2d 113 (1981); Palandjian v. Pahlavi, 103 F.R.D. 410 (D.D.C.1984) (by necessary implication); *see also* United States v. Criden, 633 F.2d 346, 359–360 (3d Cir.1980), cert. denied *sub nom.* Schaffer v. United States, 449 U.S. 1113, 101 S.Ct. 924, 66 L.Ed.2d 842 (1981); Shoen v. Shoen, 5 F.3d 1289, 1293 (9th Cir.1993); *cf.* New Jersey v. Boiardo, 83 N.J. 350, 360, 416 A.2d 793, 798 (1980) (construing New Jersey's shield statute); *but cf.* People v. Zagarino, 97 Misc.2d 181, 411 N.Y.S.2d 494 (N.Y.Sup.Ct. 1978) (construing New York's shield statute).

were otherwise sources could successfully waive the privilege forcing disclosure, but this is not the case.[44]

D. Proceedings to Which the Privilege Applies and Differences of Application

The qualified newsperson's privilege being of federal constitutional origin and operation is applicable in both federal and state governmental proceedings. Such proceedings include grand jury sessions,[45] criminal trials,[46] pretrial discovery[47] administrative proceedings[48] and legislative hearings.[49] The balancing of interests required by this privilege is less likely to be struck in favor of the newsperson when the individual case involves criminal investigation and prosecution[50] than when the claim of privilege is made in the context of non-libel civil litigation.[51] And it is not yet clear whether the newsperson will be protected as regularly and to the same degree at the *trial* of a civil case when a litigant seeks confidential information from a journalist which would likely have a decisive effect on the litigation as he would be protected during the *pretrial* stage when the relevance and materiality of the journalist's evidence may not be as clear or alternative sources of the evidence have not been as thoroughly explored.

1. Difference in the Availability of the Privilege in Civil Cases When the Newsperson is a Party to the Litigation

An obvious difference in the availability of the newsperson's privilege has developed in civil cases depending on whether those claiming the privilege are parties to the litigation. If the newsgatherer is not a

44. *See* United States v. Cuthbertson, 630 F.2d at 147.

45. *See, e.g.,* Lewis v. United States, 501 F.2d 418 (9th Cir.1974), cert. denied 420 U.S. 913, 95 S.Ct. 1106, 43 L.Ed.2d 386 (1975);

46. *See, e.g.,* United States v. Burke, 700 F.2d 70 (2d Cir.1983), cert. denied 464 U.S. 816, 104 S.Ct. 72, 78 L.Ed.2d 85 (1983); Brown v. Commonwealth, 214 Va., 755 204 S.E.2d 429, cert. denied 419 U.S. 966, 95 S.Ct. 229, 42 L.Ed.2d 182 (1974).

47. *See, e.g.,* United States v. Cuthbertson 630 F.2d 139 (3d Cir.1980), cert. denied 449 U.S. 1126, 101 S.Ct. 945, 67 L.Ed.2d 113 (1981) (criminal discovery); Silkwood v. Kerr–McGee Corp., 563 F.2d 433 (10th Cir. 1977) (civil discovery); Miami Herald Pub. Co. v. Morejon, 561 So.2d 577 (Fla.1990) (criminal discovery); O'Neill v. Oakgrove Construction, 71 N.Y.2d 521, 528 N.Y.S.2d 1, 523 N.E.2d 277 (1988) (civil discovery).

48. *See* State *ex rel.* Hudok v. Henry, 182 W.Va. 500, 389 S.E.2d 188 (W.Va.1989).

49. *Cf.* the multitude of cases in which either executive privilege or the privilege against self-incrimination has been invoked in federal and state legislative hearings.

50. *See* Continental Cablevision v. Storer Broadcasting Co., 583 F.Supp. 427, 433 (E.D.Mo.1984); Bell v. City of Des Moines, 412 N.W.2d 585, 587 (Iowa 1987); State v. Siel, 122 N.H. 254, 259, 444 A.2d 499, 503 (1982); *see also, e.g.,* Branzburg v. Hayes, 408 U.S. 665, 685, 92 S.Ct. 2646, 2658, 33 L.Ed.2d 626, 642 (1972) (grand jury proceeding); Lewis v. United States, 501 F.2d 418 (9th Cir.1974), cert. denied 420 U.S. 913, 95 S.Ct. 1106, 43 L.Ed.2d 386 (1975) (grand jury proceeding); Miami Herald Pub. Co. v. Morejon, 561 So.2d 577 (Fla.1990) (pretrial discovery in criminal prosecution); State v. Sandstrom, 224 Kan. 573, 581 P.2d 812 (1978) (trial of criminal case).

51. *See* Bell v. City of Des Moines, 412 N.W.2d 585, 587 (Iowa 1987); *see also, e.g.,* Zerilli v. Smith, 656 F.2d 705, 712, 211 U.S. App. D.C. 116, 121–122 (D.C.Cir.1981); Continental Cablevision v. Storer Broadcasting Co., 583 F.Supp. 427, 433 (E.D.Mo. 1984); O'Neill v. Oakgrove Construction, 71 N.Y.2d 521, 528 N.Y.S.2d 1, 523 N.E.2d 277 (1988).

party, he stands a fair chance of having the balance struck against testimonial compulsion.[52] But if the newsgatherer is a party (and this will normally occur only in defamation or invasion of privacy actions), the courts tend to look with disfavor upon the granting of the privilege.[53]

The reasons for this are clear. Very often the news media defendant will possess evidence that will permit a determination as to the truth or falsity of that which was published[54] or, in the case of public officials or public figures, whether a false statement was published with actual malice[55] and, of course, these issues go to the heart of a libel plaintiff's case.[56] In addition, the media defendant will normally be the *only* source of evidence on the editorial process as it relates to the question of actual malice in the publication of the challenged material, and, at times, may be the only one possessing admissible evidence on the issue of truth.[57]

Finally, when the newsperson is in the unusual position of being the plaintiff, he may not invoke the constitutional privilege to prevent the defendant from obtaining evidence material to his defense.[58] His bringing the action is deemed to waive the privilege.[59] The newsperson, by asserting the privilege against disclosure, "is attempting to use the

52. *See, e.g.*, Zerilli v. Smith, 656 F.2d 705, 211 U.S. App. D.C. 116 (D.C.Cir.1981); Lamberto v. Bown, 326 N.W.2d 305 (Iowa 1982); O'Neill v. Oakgrove Construction, 71 N.Y.2d 521, 528 N.Y.S.2d 1, 523 N.E.2d 277 (1988).

53. *See, e.g.*, Herbert v. Lando, 441 U.S. 153, 99 S.Ct. 1635, 60 L.Ed.2d 115 (1979); Miller v. Transamerican Press, Inc., 621 F.2d 721 (5th Cir.1980), cert. denied, 450 U.S. 1041, 101 S.Ct. 1759, 68 L.Ed.2d 238 (1981); Carey v. Hume, 492 F.2d 631 (D.C.Cir.), cert. dismissed 417 U.S. 938, 94 S.Ct. 2654, 41 L.Ed.2d 661 (1974); Cape Publications, Inc. v. Bridges, 387 So.2d 436 (Fla.App.1980), cert. denied 464 U.S. 893, 104 S.Ct. 239, 78 L.Ed.2d 229 (1983); Downing v. Monitor Pub. Co., 120 N.H. 383, 415 A.2d 683 (1980); *see also* Zerilli v. Smith, 656 F.2d 705, 714, 211 U.S. App. D.C. 116, 125–126 (D.C.Cir.1981); *but see, e.g.*, Mitchell v. Marin County Superior Court, 148 Cal.App.3d 360, 196 Cal.Rptr. 27 (1983), *aff'd*, 37 Cal.3d 268, 208 Cal.Rptr. 152, 690 P.2d 625 (1984); Gadsden County Times, Inc. v. Horne, 426 So.2d 1234 (Fla. App.), review denied 441 So.2d 631 (Fla. 1983).

54. Carey v. Hume, 492 F.2d 631, 636–637, 160 U.S. App. D.C. 365, 370–371 (D.C.Cir.1974), cert. dismissed 417 U.S. 938, 94 S.Ct. 2654, 41 L.Ed.2d 661 (1974).

55. *See* Herbert v. Lando, 441 U.S. 153, 169–170, 99 S.Ct. 1635, 1645, 60 L.Ed.2d 115, 129–130 (1979); Miller v. Transamerican Press, 621 F.2d 721, 726–727 (5th Cir.

1980), cert. denied 450 U.S. 1041, 101 S.Ct. 1759, 68 L.Ed.2d 238 (1981); Cape Publications, Inc. v. Bridges, 387 So.2d 436 (Fla. App.1980), cert. denied 464 U.S. 893, 104 S.Ct. 239, 78 L.Ed.2d 229 (1983); Downing v. Monitor Pub. Co., Inc., 120 N.H. 383, 386, 415 A.2d 683, 685–686 (1980).

56. *See* Herbert, 441 U.S. at 169–170, 99 S. Ct. at 1645, 60 L. Ed. 2d at 129–130 (1979); Branzburg v. Hayes, 408 U.S. 665, 742, 92 S.Ct. 2646, 2681, 33 L.Ed.2d 626, 676 (1972) (dissenting opinion of Justice Stewart); Garland v. Torre, 259 F.2d 545, 550 (2d Cir.), cert. denied 358 U.S. 910, 79 S.Ct. 237, 3 L.Ed.2d 231 (1958); Carey v. Hume, 492 F.2d 631, 636, 160 U.S. App. D.C. 365, 370 (D.C.Cir.1974), cert. dismissed 417 U.S. 938, 94 S.Ct. 2654, 41 L.Ed.2d 661 (1974); Downing v. Monitor Pub. Co., Inc., 120 N.H. 383, 386, 415 A.2d 683, 685–686 (1980).

57. *See* Carey, 492 F.2d at 636–637, 160 U.S. App. D.C. at 370–371.

58. *See* Driscoll v. Morris, 111 F.R.D. 459, 461–464 (D.Conn.1986); Anderson v. Nixon, 444 F.Supp. 1195, 1199–1200 (D.D.C.1978); Campus Communications, Inc. v. Freedman, 374 So.2d 1169 (Fla.App. 1979).

59. *See* Driscoll v. Morris, 111 F.R.D. 459, 461–464 (D.Conn.1986); Anderson v. Nixon, 444 F.Supp. 1195, 1199–1200 (D.D.C.1978); Campus Communications, Inc. v. Freedman, 374 So.2d 1169 (Fla.App. 1979).

shield of privilege as a sword to undermine the defendant's preparation of her defense"[60] and this he may not do.

2. Difference in Availability of the Privilege in Criminal Prosecutions Depending on the Purpose for Which the Newsperson's Evidence Is Sought

Prosecutors have been quite successful in overcoming claims to the newsperson's privilege in grand jury proceedings when the evidence sought is material to whether the target of the probe has committed a crime.[61] This is particularly true of a newsperson's eyewitness testimony.[62] Given the *absolute* stricture of the Sixth Amendment to the United States Constitution that "[i]n all criminal prosecutions, the accused shall enjoy the right . . . to have compulsory process for obtaining witnesses in his favor . . .", one might expect that criminal defendants would have at least as much success as prosecutors in overcoming the newsperson's *qualified* First Amendment privilege when invoked to deny them evidence to use in their defense. But this is not necessarily the case.

In order to prevail against the claim of privilege, the accused must demonstrate, in the words of the Second Circuit, that "the information is: highly material and relevant, necessary or critical to the maintenance of the claim, and not obtainable from other available sources."[63] Similar formulations have been set down in state prosecutions.[64] Properly analyzed the requirements that the criminal defendant must meet are materiality to his defense and unavailability of the evidence from other sources not implicating First Amendment interests. Whether the evidence sought from the newsperson is material depends on whether it goes toward disproving an element of the offense, or proving a defense

---

60. Driscoll, 111 F.R.D. at 463.

61. *See, e.g.,* Branzburg v. Hayes, 408 U.S. 665, 92 S.Ct. 2646, 33 L.Ed.2d 626 (1972); Lewis v. United States 501 F.2d 418 (9th Cir.1974), cert. denied, 420 U.S. 913, 95 S.Ct. 1106, 43 L.Ed.2d 386 (1975), *contempt order upheld,* 517 F.2d 236 (9th Cir. 1975); Pankratz v. District Court, 199 Colo. 411, 609 P.2d 1101 (Colo. 1980); Knight–Ridder Broadcasting, Inc. v. Greenberg, 70 N.Y.2d 151, 160, 518 N.Y.S.2d 595, 600, 511 N.E.2d 1116, 1121 (1987).

62. *See, e.g.,* Branzburg v. Hayes, 408 U.S. 665, 92 S.Ct. 2646, 33 L.Ed.2d 626 (1972); Pankratz v. District Court, 199 Colo. 411, 609 P.2d 1101 (Colo. 1980).

63. United States v. Burke, 700 F.2d 70, 77 (2d Cir.), cert. denied, 464 U.S. 816, 104 S.Ct. 72, 78 L.Ed.2d 85 (1983) (quoting Baker v. F & F Investment, 470 F.2d 778, 783–85 (2d Cir.1972), cert. denied, 411 U.S. 966, 93 S.Ct. 2147, 36 L.Ed.2d 686 (1973)).

64. *See, e.g.,* State v. Siel, 122 N.H. 254, 259, 444 A.2d 499, 503 (1982) ("[A] defen-

dant may overcome a press privilege to withhold a confidential source of news only when he shows: (1) that he has attempted unsuccessfully to obtain the information by all reasonable alternatives; (2) that the information would not be irrelevant to his defense; and (3) that, by a balance of probabilities, there is a reasonable possibility that the information sought as evidence would affect the verdict in his case."); State v. Rinaldo, 102 Wash. 2d 749, 755, 689 P.2d 392, 395–396 (1984) (to defeat the common law qualified privilege in a criminal proceeding, "the party seeking discovery must show (1) the claim is meritorious; (2) the information sought is necessary or critical to . . . the defense pleaded; and (3) a reasonable effort has been made to acquire the desired information by other means". The Washington court added a fourth requirement that the interest of the newsperson in nondisclosure be supported by a need to preserve confidentiality.)

asserted by the defendant, or reducing the classification or gradation of the offense charged or mitigating or lessening the sentence imposed.[65]

More specifically if the evidence sought is shown to be directly exculpatory the accused may succeed in forcing the reluctant newsgatherer to testify. For instance in *State v. Sandstrom*,[66] a first degree murder case, in which the accused was charged with murdering her husband, a reporter testified at the trial that a confidential source had told him that one of the state's witnesses had threatened to kill the husband shortly before the murder. The reporter refused to identify the informant, claiming privilege. The Kansas Supreme Court upheld the trial court's order holding the reporter in contempt for failing to disclose his source. But far more often than not the criminal defendant's request for a newsperson's evidence is simply a grasping at straws and the evidence is not really exculpatory or even material.[67]

Criminal accused also seek evidence from newspersons for purposes of impeachment. If, after *in camera* inspection, the trial judge is of the opinion that the impeaching evidence sought from the newsperson would likely affect the credibility of key prosecution witnesses or other critical evidence he may compel the newsperson to testify and, turn over documentary evidence in his possession[68] if the evidence is found to be material to guilt or innocence or the potential sentence to be imposed,[69] cannot be obtained from another source[70] and is not cumulative.[71]

Evidence least likely to be compelled from a newsperson is evidence of governmental misconduct. This is so because, except for the government concealing exculpatory evidence, such misconduct is normally not material to questions of guilt and innocence or punishment and the

65. *See* State v. Sandstrom, 224 Kan. 573, 576, 581 P.2d 812, 815 (1978); Brown v. Commonwealth, 214 Va. 755, 757, 204 S.E.2d 429, 431, cert. denied, 419 U.S. 966, 95 S.Ct. 229, 42 L.Ed.2d 182 (1974); State v. Rinaldo, 102 Wash. 2d 749, 754, 689 P.2d 392, 397 (1984) (concurring and dissenting opinion of Rossellini, J.); *see also*, Matter of McAuley, 63 Ohio App.2d 5, 22–23, 17 Ohio Op. 3d 222, 233, 408 N.E.2d 697, 709 (1979).

66. 224 Kan. 573, 581 P.2d 812 (1978); *see also* Matter of Farber, 78 N.J. 259, 266–267, 394 A.2d 330, 333–334, cert. denied 439 U.S. 997, 99 S.Ct. 598, 58 L.Ed.2d 670 (1978).

67. *See, e.g.*, Brown v. Commonwealth, 214 Va. 755, 204 S.E.2d 429, cert. denied 419 U.S. 966, 95 S.Ct. 229, 42 L.Ed.2d 182 (1974).

68. *See, e.g.*, United States v. Cuthbertson, 630 F.2d 139, 148 (3d Cir.1980), cert. denied 449 U.S. 1126, 101 S.Ct. 945, 67, L.Ed.2d 113 (1981); CBS, Inc. v. Cobb, 536 So.2d 1067, 1070–1071 (Fla.App.1988); *cf.* Hammarley v. Superior Court, 89 Cal.

App.3d 388, 400–402, 153 Cal.Rptr. 608, 614–616 (1979).

69. *See* United States v. Cuthbertson, 630 F.2d 139, 148 (3d Cir.1980), cert. denied 449 U.S. 1126, 101 S.Ct. 945, 67 L.Ed.2d 113 (1981); *see also* Brown v. Commonwealth, 214 Va. 755, 204 S.E.2d 429, cert. denied 419 U.S. 966, 95 S.Ct. 229, 42 L.Ed.2d 182 (1974).

70. *See* United States v. Cuthbertson, 630 F.2d 139, 148 (3d Cir.1980), cert. denied 449 U.S. 1126, 101 S.Ct. 945, 67 L.Ed.2d 113 (1981); *see also* Brown v. Commonwealth, 214 Va. 755, 204 S.E.2d 429, cert. denied 419 U.S. 966, 95 S.Ct. 229, 42 L.Ed.2d 182 (1974).

71. *See* United States v. Burke, 700 F.2d 70, 78 (2d Cir.), cert. denied 464 U.S. 816, 104 S.Ct. 72, 78 L.Ed.2d 85 (1983) (attempted further impeachment of witness Henry Hill of "Good Fellas" motion picture fame who had already been exposed at the trial as having been involved in extortion, drug trafficking, armed robbery, arson and hijacking).

government officials involved would normally be available to testify to what they themselves did or did not do.[72]

3. Unavailability of the Privilege when the Subpoena is for In-camera Review of Evidence

A number of cases have now held that the qualified privilege is inapplicable to judicial demands for *in-camera* review of evidence held by newspersons.[73] One rationale for this is that the trial judge must be able to determine whether the evidence is relevant or probative before passing on any claim of the privilege.[74]

E. Waiver of the Qualified Privilege

The qualified privilege may be waived but because the privilege belongs to newspersons and not their sources only newspersons are in a position to waive the protection against compelled testimony afforded by the First Amendment.[75] Waiver may be effected by such actions as newspersons voluntarily disclosing some or all of the sought after information in other public or private forums,[76] by their relying on the existence and veracity of a confidential source in defending against a civil action[77] or by their choosing to initiate civil actions themselves in which confidential information in their hands is relevant to the defense of the cause.[78]

7.5 State Shield Legislation

A. Introduction

Long before the idea was conceived that the First Amendment might protect newspersons against compelled testimonial disclosures, a few

72. *See* United States v. Calvert, 523 F.2d 895, 902 n. 4 (8th Cir.1975), cert. denied 424 U.S. 911, 96 S.Ct. 1106, 47 L.Ed.2d 314 (1976) (dictum on the question of materiality of the newsperson's evidence); United States v. Hubbard, 493 F.Supp. 202, 205 (D.D.C.1979) (FBI agent as an alternative source and requested evidence cumulative); *see also* United States v. Vastola, 685 F.Supp. 917 (D.N.J.1988); *but see* United States v. Criden, 633 F.2d 346 (3d Cir.1980), cert. denied *sub nom.* Schaffer v. United States, 449 U.S. 1113, 101 S.Ct. 924, 66 L.Ed.2d 842 (1981).

73. *See, e.g.*, Bruno & Stillman, Inc. v. Globe Newspaper Co., 633 F.2d 583, 598 (1st Cir.1980); United States v. Burke, 700 F.2d 70, 78 n. 9 (2d Cir.), cert. denied 464 U.S. 816, 104 S.Ct. 72, 78 L.Ed.2d 85 (1983); Minnesota v. Knutson, 539 N.W.2d 254 (Minn.App.1995).

74. *Id.*

75. *See* United States v. Cuthbertson, 630 F.2d 139, 147 (3d Cir.1980), cert. denied 449 U.S. 1126, 101 S.Ct., 945, 67 L.Ed.2d 113 (1981); Palandjian v. Pahlavi, 103 F.R.D. 410 (D.D.C.1984) (by necessary implication); Senear v. Daily Journal–American, 97 Wash. 2d 148, 156, 641 P.2d 1180, 1184 (1982) (state common law); *see also* United States v. Criden, 633 F.2d 346, 359–360 (3d Cir.1980), cert. denied *sub nom.* Schaffer v. United States, 449 U.S. 1113, 101 S.Ct. 924, 66 L.Ed.2d 842 (1981).

76. *See, e.g.*, Wheeler v. Goulart, 593 A.2d 173, 175–183 (D.C.App.1991) (disclosure to two private persons).

77. *Cf.* Dowd v. Calabrese, 577 F.Supp. 238, 243–244 (D.D.C.1983) (reliance upon existence and veracity of unidentified source for establishing truth or lack of actual malice in publication prohibited); Capuano v. Outlet Co., 579 A.2d 469, 475 (R.I. 1990) (waiver of Rhode Island shield law).

78. *See* Driscoll v. Morris, 111 F.R.D. 459, 461–464 (D.Conn.1986); Anderson v. Nixon, 444 F.Supp. 1195, 1199–1200 (D.D.C.1978); Campus Communications, Inc. v. Freedman, 374 So.2d 1169 (Fla.App. 1979).

states, concerned about the identification of sources and the consequent reduction of the flow of news to the public enacted what have become known as shield laws.[1] Even after state and lower federal courts began to recognize a qualified First Amendment privilege,[2] a number of states have continued to enact such legislation,[3] concerned perhaps by uncertainties surrounding the availability and parameters of the apparent common law constitutional privilege. Today thirty jurisdictions have some form of shield law on their books.[4]

There has been some debate as to the nature of shield legislation. Does it accord a statutory privilege to newspersons similar to that provided doctors, lawyers and priests[5] not to testify or merely an immunity from punishment for contempt for refusing to testify when properly required to do so?[6] As a practical matter, unless the newsperson or news

1. The first states to enact reporters shield legislation were Maryland in 1896 and New Jersey in 1933. *See* Law of April 2, 1896, Ch. 249, 1896 Md. Laws 437, *codified as amended at* Md. Cts. & Jud. Proc. Code Ann. § 9–112 (1989); 1933 N. J. Laws, Ch. 167 §§ 1–2, *codified as amended at* N. J. Stat. Ann § 2:97–11, *repealed 1960 and re-enacted and recodified as* N. J. Stat. Ann §§ 2A:84A–21 to 21.9, 2A:84A–29 (West 1976 and Supp. 1987); *see also* Bruce L. Bortz and Laurie R. Bortz, *"Pressing" Out the Wrinkles in Maryland's Shield Law for Journalists,* 8 U. Balt. 461, 462 (1979). This article provides an interesting historical discussion of how Maryland's shield statute came to be enacted. *Id.* at 461–462.

2. *See, e.g.,* Baker v. F & F Investment, 470 F.2d 778 (2d Cir.1972), cert. denied, 411 U.S. 966, 93 S.Ct. 2147, 36 L.Ed.2d 686 (1973); Silkwood v. Kerr–McGee Corp. 563 F.2d 433 (10th Cir.1977); Zerilli v. Smith, 656 F.2d 705, 710–714, 211 U.S. App. D.C. 116, 121–125 (D.C.Cir.1981); Tribune Co. v. Huffstetler, 489 So.2d 722 (Fla.1986); Winegard v. Oxberger, 258 N.W.2d 847 (Iowa 1977), cert. denied 436 U.S. 905, 98 S.Ct. 2234, 56 L.Ed.2d 402 (1978); State ex rel. Hudok v. Henry, 182 W.Va. 500, 389 S.E.2d 188 (W.Va.1989); *see also* Romualdo P. Eclavea, Annot., *Privilege of Newsgatherers Against Disclosure of Confidential Source or Information,* 99 A.L.R.3d 37 (1980).

3. *See, e.g.,* Colo. Rev. Stat. §§ 13–90–119, 24–72.5–101 to 106 (Supp. 1993); Ga. Code Ann. § 24–9–30 (Michie Supp. 1994); Mich. Comp. Laws Ann. § 767.5a (West 1982), as amended by P.A. 1986, No. 293, § 1 (West Supp. 1994).

4. *See* Confidential Sources & Information 3 (Reporters Committee 1993). These include: Ala. Code § 12–21–142 (1986); Alaska Stat. § 09.25.150–.220 (1983); Ariz. Rev. Stat. Ann. § 12–2237 (1982) and 12–2214 (Supp. 1993); Ark. Code Ann. § 16–

85–510 (Michie 1987); Cal. Const. art. 1 § 2(b) (West 1983) and Cal. Evid. Code § 1070 (West 1966 and Supp. 1994); Colo. Rev. Stat. §§ 13–90–119, 24–72.5–101 to 106 (1993); Del. Code Ann. tit. 10, §§ 4320–4326 (1975); D.C. Code Ann. § 16–4701 through 4704 (Supp. 1993); Ga. Code Ann. § 24–9–30 (Michie 1994); Ill. Ann. Stat. ch. 110, ¶¶ 8–901–8–909 (Smith–Hurd 1984 and Supp. 1992); Ind. Code Ann. § 34–3–5–1 (Burns 1986); Ky. Rev. Stat. Ann. § 421.100 (Michie/Bobbs–Merrill 1992); La. Rev. Stat. Ann. §§ 45:1451 to 1458 (West 1982 and Supp. 1990); Md. Cts. & Jud. Proc. Code Ann. § 9–112 (1989); Mich. Comp. Laws Ann. § 767.5a (West Supp. 1994); Minn. Stat. Ann. §§ 595.021–.025 (West 1988); Mont. Code Ann. §§ 26–1–901 through 903 (1993); Neb. Rev. Stat. §§ 20–144 through 147 (1991); Nev. Rev. Stat. § 49.275 (Michie 1986), N.J. Stat. Ann. §§ 2A:84A–21 through 21.9, 2A:84A–29 (Rules 27, 29) (West 1976 and Supp. 1993); N.M. Sup. Ct. R. 11–514 (Michie 1994); N.Y. Civil Rights Law § 79–h (McKinney 1992); N.D. Cent. Code § 31–01–06.2 (1976); Ohio Rev. Code Ann. §§ 2739.04, 2739.12 (Anderson 1992); Okla. Stat. Ann. tit. 12 § 2506 (West 1993); Or. Rev. Stat. §§ 44.510 to 44.540 (1989); 42 Pa. Cons. Stat. Ann. § 5942 (1982); R.I. Gen. Laws §§ 9–19.1–1 to 9–19.1–3 (1985); S.C. Code Ann. § 19–11–100 (Law Co-op Supp. 1993); Tenn. Code Ann. § 24–1–208 (1980 and Supp. 1994).

5. *See generally* 8 J. H. WIGMORE, EVIDENCE §§ 2197, 2285, 2286 (McNaughton Rev. 1961); EDWARD W. CLEARY, MCCORMICK ON EVIDENCE §§ 77–105 (2d ed. 1972).

6. *See e.g.,* Delaney v. Superior Court, 50 Cal.3d 785, 268 Cal.Rptr. 753, 789 P.2d 934 (1990); Mitchell v. Superior Court, 37 Cal.3d 268, 208 Cal.Rptr. 152, 690 P.2d 625 (1984); KSDO v. Superior Court, 136 Cal.

organization is a party to litigation and thus subject to judicial sanctions other than punishment for contempt, the privilege versus immunity debate is without practical significance.[7] Whether a shield statute creates a privilege not to testify or merely an immunity from punishment for contempt, the protection is personal to the newsperson and may only be waived by him.[8]

What is of significance regarding shield laws is their actual language and provisions and the attitude of the state judiciary to yet another exception to the idea that the courts are entitled to every person's evidence.

B. Public Policy Preambles

Apparently, as a signal to their judiciaries of the importance of shield laws to society, and the need for their liberal interpretation, three state legislatures, those of Colorado, Minnesota and Nebraska have enacted sections or preambles enunciating the public policy behind such legislation.[9] The Minnesota statute says simply that "[i]n order to protect the public interest and the free flow of information, the news media should have the benefit of a substantial privilege not to reveal sources of information or to disclose unpublished information." The statute goes on to say, "To this end, the freedom of press requires the protection of the confidential relationship between the newsgatherer and the source of information. The purpose of §§ 595.021 to 595.025 is to insure and perpetuate, consistent with the public interest, the confidential relationship between the news media and its sources."[10] The Nebraska legislature stated the policy behind its statutory scheme in the form of legislative findings as to the importance of protecting the free flow of news and other information to the public.[11]

App.3d 375, 186 Cal.Rptr. 211 (1982); Nora L. Rousso, Comment, *California's Newsgather's Shield: Inconsistent Interpretation Means Inadequate Protection,* 19 Golden Gate U.L. Rev. 347, 358–362 (1989).

7. *See* Mitchell v. Superior Court, 37 Cal.3d 268, 274, 208 Cal.Rptr. 152, 155, 690 P.2d 625, 628 (1984).

8. *See, e.g.,* Lightman v. State, 15 Md. App. 713, 725, 294 A.2d 149, 156, *aff'd* 266 Md. 550, 295 A.2d 212 (1972), cert. denied 411 U.S. 951, 93 S.Ct. 1922, 36 L.Ed.2d 414 (1973); State v. Boiardo, 83 N.J. 350, 360, 416 A.2d 793, 798 (1980).

9. *See* Colo. Rev. Stat. § 24–72.5–101 (Supp. 1993); Minn. Stat. Ann. § 595.022 (West 1988); Neb. Rev. Stat. § 20–144 (1991); *see also* Dumez v. Houma Mun. Fire and Police Civil Service Bd., 341 So.2d 1206 (La.App.1976), cert. denied, 344 So.2d 667 (La.1977); In re Farber, 78 N.J. 259, 394 A.2d 330, 99 A. L. R. 3d 1, cert. denied *sub nom.* New York Times Co. v. New Jersey, 439 U.S. 997, 99 S.Ct. 598, 58 L.Ed.2d 670 (1978).

10. Minn. Stat. Ann. § 595.022 (West 1988); *see* Colo. Rev. Stat. § 24–72.5–101 (Supp. 1993).

11. "The Legislature finds:

(1) That the policy of the State of Nebraska to insure the free flow of news and other information to the public, and that those who gather, write, or edit information for the public or disseminate information to the public may perform these vital functions only in a free and unfettered atmosphere.

(2) That such persons shall not be inhibited, directly or indirectly, by governmental restraint or sanction imposed by governmental process, but rather that they shall be encouraged to gather, write, edit, or disseminate news or other information vigorously so that the public may be fully informed;

(3) That compelling such persons to disclose a source of information or disclose unpublished information is contrary to the public interest and inhibits the free flow of information to the public;

Such statements of policy in the body of shield legislation may have the effect of heading off cramped interpretation by judiciaries notoriously hostile to any legislation limiting the availability of relevant evidence in judicial and other proceedings.[12]

C. Persons and Organizations Covered by Shield Legislation

Consistent with the idea that the privilege not to be compelled to testify or the narrower immunity from sanctions for contempt are designed to protect the flow of news and information to the public, shield legislation is limited to the protection of news organizations, newsgatherers, editors, publishers, owners and other news and information disseminators.[13] Certain statutes state explicitly that the protection is limited to those who are acting for the purpose of communicating news or information to the public.[14] Some acts place artificial limitations on those who may be covered by requiring them to be paid regular employees of recognized news organizations[15] or requiring association with news publications that publish or broadcast on a regular basis[16] or requiring the employing broadcast station to keep recordings or transcripts of the broadcast involved.[17] And only one statute expressly confers protection on those independently engaged in gathering information for publication or broadcast.[18]

The state judiciaries have only rarely been called upon to determine who is protected by shield legislation. In those rare cases, newspaper publishers have been held to be included within the legislative definitions of "reporter"[19] and "editorial employees."[20] And a weekly advertis-

(4) That there is an urgent need to provide effective measures to halt and prevent this inhibition;

(5) That the obstruction of the free flow of information through any medium of communication to the public affects interstate commerce; and

(6) That sections 20–144 to 20–147 are necessary to insure the free flow of information and to implement the first and fourteenth amendments and Article I, § 5, of the United States Constitution, and the Nebraska Constitution." Neb. Rev. Stat. § 20–144 (1991).

12. *See* section 7.8.B., *infra.*

13. *See, e.g.,* Cal. Const. Art. 1, § 2(b) (West 1983); Ga. Code Ann. § 24–9–30 (Michie 1994); Mich. Comp. Laws Ann. § 767.5a (1) (West Supp. 1994). A few statutes define "reporter" or "newsgatherer" to include authors, scholars and educators. *See, e.g.,* Del. Code Ann. tit. 10 § 4320 (3) (1975).

14. *See* Ga. Code. Ann. § 24–9–30 (Michie 1994); Minn. Stat. Ann. § 595.023 (West 1988); Neb. Rev. Stat. § 20–146 (1991); N.J. Stat. Ann. § 2A:84A–21 (West

Supp. 1990); N.M. Sup. Ct. R. 11–514 (Michie 1994); Or. Rev. Stat. § 44.520 (1989); *cf.* von Bulow By Auersperg v. von Bulow, 811 F.2d 136, 142 (2d Cir.), cert. denied, 481 U.S. 1015, 107 S.Ct. 1891, 95 L.Ed.2d 498 (1987).

15. *See, e.g.,* Ind. Code Ann. § 34–3–5–1 (Burns 1986); N.Y. Civil Rights Law § 79–h (a) (6)-(7) (McKinney 1992).

16. *See, e.g.,* Ill. Ann. Stat. ch. 110, ¶ 8–902(b) (Smith–Hurd Supp. 1992); Ind. Code Ann. § 34–3–5–1 (Burns 1986); La. Rev. Stat. Ann. § 45:1451 (West 1982); N.M. Sup. Ct. R. 11–514 (Michie 1994); N.Y. Civil Rights Law § 79–h (a) (1) (McKinney 1992).

17. *See* N.M. Sup. Ct. R. 11–514 (Michie 1994); 42 Pa. Cons. Stat. Ann. § 5942 (1982); *see also* Ohio Rev. Code Ann. § 2739.04 (Anderson 1992).

18. *See* Tenn. Code Ann. § 24–1–208(a) (Supp. 1994).

19. *See* Becnel v. Lucia, 420 So.2d 1173, 1175 (La.App.1982) (construing La. Rev. Stat. Ann. § 45:1451 (West 1982)).

20. *See* Las Vegas Sun, Inc. v. Eighth Judicial Dist. Court, 104 Nev. 508, 761 P.2d

er supported tabloid printed in Spanish and distributed without charge at newsstands and other commercial establishments is considered a "newspaper" within the listing of "news media" covered by the New Jersey shield law so as to permit the owner and publisher to claim the statutory protection.[21] But the courts have not been so generous regarding irregular journalists and members of the electronic news media. The Indiana Court of Appeals ruled that an environmentalist who did free lance work on an irregular basis for a small newspaper had no statutory privilege to refuse to testify at a civil pretrial deposition as to the identity of the source of a copy of a written report on a local environmental cleanup plan which she turned over to a local television station but not to her own newspaper.[22] And the Michigan Court of Appeals held that television news reporters were not within the protection of Michigan's former shield legislation protecting reporters of "newspapers or other publications" and their sources.[23] This crabbed view of who are to be protected was effectively overruled by amendment of the Michigan legislation almost immediately after the appeals court's decision.[24]

D. Information and Materials Covered and Under What Circumstances

1. Identity of Sources and the Information Obtained

The earliest shield laws focused on the confidential relationship between the newsperson and his sources and protected newspersons only from having to testify orally as to the identity of sources.[25] With experience it became clear that source identities might be disclosed through materials in the newspersons' possession and these materials

849, 854 n. 7 (Nev. 1988) (construing Nev. Rev. Stat. § 49.275 (Michie 1986)).

21. See In re Avila, 206 N.J.Super. 61, 501 A.2d 1018 (N.J.Super.A.D.1985) (construing N.J. Stat. Ann. § 2A:84A–21(a), (c) (West 1976)).

22. See Northside Sanitary Landfill, Inc. v. Bradley, 462 N.E.2d 1321, 1324–1325 (Ind.App.1984) (construing Ind. Code Ann. § 34–3–5–1 (Burns 1973)).

23. See In re Contempt of Stone, 154 Mich.App. 121, 125, 397 N.W.2d 244, 246 (1986), leave to appeal denied 426 Mich. 854 (1986) (construing Mich. Comp. Laws Ann. § 767.5a (West 1968)).

24. See Mich. Comp. Laws Ann. § 767.5a(1) (West 1982), as amended by P.A. 1986, No. 293 § 1, Dec. 22, 1986 (West Supp. 1994), which now provides:

Sec. 5a. (1) A reporter or other person who is involved in the gathering or preparation of news for broadcast or publication shall not be required to disclose the identity of an informant, any unpublished information obtained from an informant, or any unpublished matter or documentation, in whatever manner recorded, relating to a communication with an informant, in any inquiry authorized by this act, except an inquiry for a crime punishable by imprisonment for life when it has been established that the information which is sought is essential to the purpose of the proceeding and that other available sources of the information have been exhausted.

25. See Ala. Code § 12–21–142 (1986); Alaska Stat. § 09.25.150 (1983); Ariz. Rev. Stat. Ann. § 12–2237 (1982); Ark. Code Ann. § 16–85–510 (Michie 1987); Ill. Ann. Stat. ch. 110, ¶ 8–901 (Smith–Hurd Supp. 1992); Ind. Code Ann. § 34–3–5–1 (Burns 1986); Ky. Rev. Stat. Ann. § 421.100 (Michie/Bobbs–Merrill 1972); La. Rev. Stat. Ann. § 45:1452 (West 1982); Ohio Rev. Code Ann. §§ 2739.04, 2739.12 (Anderson 1992) 42 Pa. Cons. Stat. Ann. § 5942(a) (1982); see also Bruce L. Bortz and Laurie R. Bortz, "Pressing" Out the Wrinkles in

were protected in a few statutes to the extent that they might lead to exposure of confidential sources.[26]

The more modern shield statutes, recognizing that newspersons ought not be regarded as conscripts to the cause of litigants if they are to engage effectively in the business of facilitating the flow of news and information to the public,[27] protect not only the identity of confidential sources but *all* information gathered by the newsperson in the course of his professional responsibilities. The Georgia statute enacted in 1990 is among the most sweeping in terms of the information it potentially protects. It provides that news and information gatherers and disseminators "have a qualified privilege against disclosure of any information, document, or item obtained or prepared in the gathering or dissemination of news in any proceeding where the one asserting the privilege is not a party ... "[28] Other recent legislation is as broad or nearly as broad in its protection of information beyond mere source identification.[29]

2. *Fora in which the Information and Materials Are Protected*

Most shield laws specify rather broadly the fora or places in which the protection of newspersons and covered information applies. Alabama's statute first enacted in 1935 states that its protection against the compelled disclosure of news sources extends to "any legal proceeding or trial, before any court or before a grand jury of any court, before the presiding officer of any tribunal or his agent or agents or before any committee of the legislature or elsewhere ... "[30] Maryland's recently revised groundbreaking shield statute applies to "any judicial, legislative, or administrative body, or any body that has the power to issue subpoe-

---

Maryland's Shield Law for Journalists, 8 U. Balt. L. Rev. 461, 463 (1979).

26. *See* Mich. Comp. Laws Ann. § 767.5a(1) (West Supp. 1991); Minn. Stat. Ann. § 595.023 (West 1988).

27. *See, e.g.*, Bartlett v. Superior Court, 150 Ariz. 178, 183, 722 P.2d 346, 351 (Ariz. App.1986).

28. Ga. Code Ann. § 24–9–30 (Michie 1994).

29. *See* Cal. Const. Art. I, § 2(b) (West 1983) ("unpublished information"); Colo. Rev. Stat. §§ 13–90–119(2), 24–72.5–103 (1) (Supp. 1993) ("any news information"); Del. Code Ann. tit. 10, §§ 4321–4322 (1975) ("source or content of information"); Md. Cts. & Jud. Proc. Code Ann. § 9–112(2) (1989) ("any news or information ... including (i) Notes; (ii) Outtakes; (iii) Photographs or photographic negatives; (iv) Video and sound tapes; (v) Film; and (vi) Other data, irrespective of its nature not itself disseminated in any manner to the public.) (thorough revision in 1988 of earlier groundbreaking shield statute); Mont. Code Ann. § 26–1–902(1)-(2) (1993) ("any information ... or the source of that informa-

tion ... "); Neb. Rev. Stat. § 20–146 (1991) ("any unpublished or nonbroadcast information ... "); Nev. Rev. Stat. § 49.275 (Michie 1986) ("any published or unpublished information ... or the source of any information"); N.J. Stat. Ann. § 2A:84A–21 Rule 27 (West 1976 and Supp. 1990) ("The source, author, means, agency or person ... and ... [a]ny news or information ...); N.M. Sup. Ct. R. 11–514 (Michie 1994) ("the confidential source ... and any confidential information ... "); N.Y. Civil Rights Law § 79–h (b) (McKinney 1992) ("any news obtained or received in confidence or the identity of any source of any such news ... ") N.D. Cent. Code § 31–01–06.2 (1976) ("any information or the source of any information ... "); Okla. Stat. Ann. tit. 12, § 2506 (West 1993) ("[t]he source ... or [a]ny unpublished information ... "); R.I. Gen Laws § 9–19.1–2 (1985) ("any confidential information ... or the source of any confidential information ... "); Tenn. Code Ann. § 24–1–208(a) (Supp. 1994) ("any information or the source of any information ... ").

30. Ala. Code § 12–21–142 (1986).

nas ...."[31] Some legislation limits protection to judicial and adversarial proceedings.[32]

3. Sanctions Protected Against

While one shield statute specifically protects the newsperson from all types of sanctions for refusing to disclose sources or other information,[33] and a few statutes specifically limit the protection afforded to immunity from contempt proceedings,[34] most of the statutes simply do not state what the newsperson is protected from.[35] As to these latter statutes it should be assumed that no sanctions for the refusal to give evidence may be imposed because otherwise the legislation would have little practical meaning.

E. Limitations and Qualifications on the Availability of Shield Law Protection

What privileges the legislature may confer with one hand it may take back with the other. So long as shield legislation meets constitutional standards, the legislatures are free to qualify protection of newspersons in any way or ways they see fit. They have often seen fit.

1. Incorporation of Qualified First Amendment Balancing Tests

A number of more recently enacted or revised shield statutes incorporate some or all aspects of the balancing test determining the availability under the First Amendment of a newsperson's privilege[36] as propounded by the late Justice Potter Stewart first in his opinion for the Second Circuit in *Garland v. Torre*,[37] and later in his dissenting opinion in *Branzburg v. Hayes*.[38] The Colorado statute enacted in 1990 states that "notwithstanding the privilege of nondisclosure granted in subsection (2) ... any party to a proceeding who is otherwise authorized by law to issue or obtain subpoenas may subpoena a newsperson in order to obtain news information by establishing by a preponderance of the evidence, in opposition to a newsperson's motion to quash such subpoena: (a) that the news information is directly relevant to a substantial issue involved in the proceeding; (b) that the news information cannot be obtained by any other reasonable means; and (c) that a strong interest of the party seeking to subpoena the newsperson outweighs the interests

31. Md. Cts. & Jud. Proc. Code Ann. § 9–112(c) (1989); *see also, e.g.,* Colo. Rev. Stat. § 24–72.5–103(1) (Supp. 1993) (any "governmental entity").

32. *See* Ga. Code Ann. § 24–9–30 (Michie 1994); Ill. Ann. Stat. ch. 110, ¶ 8–901 (Smith–Hurd Supp. 1990); N. M. Sup. Ct. R. 11–514 (1986 and Supp. 1992).

33. *See* Colo. Rev. Stat. § 13–90–119(2) (Supp. 1993).

34. *See* Cal. Const. Art. 1, § 2(b) (West 1983); Cal. Evid. Code § 1070 (West 1966 and Supp. 1994); Mont. Code Ann. §§ 26–1–

902(2) (1993); N.Y. Civil Rights Law § 79–h(b) (McKinney 1992).

35. *See, e.g.,* Ark. Code Ann. § 16–85–510 (Michie 1987); Mich. Comp. Laws Ann. § 767.5a(1) (West Supp. 1994); Or. Rev. Stat. § 44.520 (1989); R.I. Gen. Laws § 9–19.1–2 (1985).

36. *See supra*, p. 10.

37. 259 F.2d 545, 549–550 (2d Cir.), cert. denied 358 U.S. 910, 79 S.Ct. 237, 3 L.Ed.2d 231 (1958).

38. 408 U.S. 665, 742, 92 S.Ct. 2646, 2681, 33 L.Ed.2d 626, 676 (1972).

under the first amendment to the United States constitution of such newsperson in not responding to a subpoena and of the general public in receiving news information."[39] A more amorphous balancing test is applied by the Delaware statute which states that a newsperson will be required to testify concerning the content of information obtained within the scope of his professional activities "if the judge determines that the public interest in having the reporter's testimony outweighs the public interest in keeping the information confidential."[40] The amorphousness of this public interest balancing is mitigated by a number of factors the judge must take into consideration in making his determination. But whether balancing tests are amorphous or not their employment in shield statutes means that until the balance is struck in some proceeding or other newspersons cannot be sure whether they and their sources will be protected.

2. The Confidential Relationship Requirement

Very few shield laws themselves specify that a confidential relationship must exist between newsperson and source or that the information involved be held in confidence. New Mexico in its supreme court rules accords a privilege only to newspersons to refuse to disclose confidential sources and confidential information obtained in the course of their professional activities.[41] And Rhode Island's statute covers only confidential associations, sources of confidential information and confidential information itself.[42] On the other hand, Maryland's recently revised statute protects against compelled disclosure of "[t]he source of any news or information procured by the person while employed by the news media whether or not the source has been promised confidentiality . . ."[43] Whatever problem there is concerning the need for confidentiality is created by a hostile judiciary reading such requirement into the legislation.[44]

3. The Disappearing Requirement that there Be Publication of the Information about which Source Identification Is Sought

A rather peculiar requirement for the availability of statutory protection for news sources which still persists in two older and not recently

---

39. Colo. Rev. Stat. § 13–90–119(3) (1990); *see also* Ga. Code Ann. § 24–9–30 (Supp. 1993); La. Rev. Stat. Ann. § 45:1459 (West 1982); Md. Cts. & Jud. Proc. Code Ann. § 9–112(d) (1989) (excepting source information); Mich. Comp. Laws Ann. § 767.5a(1) (West Supp. 1994); Minn. Stat. Ann. § 595.024 (West 1988); N.J. Stat. Ann. § 2A:84A–21.3(b) (West 1976 and Supp. 1993); N.M. Sup. Ct. R. 11–514 (Michie 1994); Okla. Stat. Ann. tit. 12, § 2506 (West 1993); Tenn. Code Ann. § 24–1–208(2) (Supp. 1994).

40. Del. Code Ann. tit. 10 § 4323 (1975); *see also* La. Rev. Stat. Ann. § 45:1453 (West 1982).

41. N.M. Sup. Ct. R. 11–514 (Michie 1994).

42. R.I. Gen. Laws § 9–19.1–2 (1985).

43. Md. Cts. & Jud. Proc. Code Ann. § 9–112(c)(1) (1989); *see also* N.Y. Civil Rights Law § 79–h(c) (McKinney Supp. 1992).

44. *See, e.g.,* Knight–Ridder Broadcasting, Inc. v. Greenberg, 70 N.Y.2d 151, 518 N.Y.S.2d 595, 511 N.E.2d 1116 (1987); Austin v. Memphis Pub. Co., 655 S.W.2d 146 (Tenn.1983) (reversing an intermediate appellate court order denying statutory protection without a showing that information was obtained in circumstances of confidentiality).

revised shield laws[45] is that there must first be publication of the information about which source identification is sought. This requirement can be traced back to the original shield statute enacted by Maryland in 1896.[46] The legislation protected newspersons from having to disclose "the source of any news or information procured or obtained by him for *and published in the newspaper* on and in which he is engaged, connected with or employed"[47] (emphasis supplied). The requirement was peculiar even in 1896 because journalism is a hierarchical profession. Newsgatherers cannot guarantee their sources that the information supplied will actually be published and that therefore their identities will not be disclosed in the face of legal compulsion. The decision to publish is, rather, in the hands of others, namely, the editors and publishers. Maryland has since eliminated the publication requirement[48] and Indiana and Nebraska specifically provide that the identity of sources are protected whether the information they provide is published or not.[49]

4. Limitations Imposed when the Newsperson Is a Party to the Proceedings or the Proceedings Involve Actions for Defamation

Apparently fearing that newspersons may use the shield privilege or immunity to thwart civil actions filed against them or their employers, a number of legislatures have included provisions in their statutes limiting the protection afforded. These provisions are of three general types. One type simply withholds protection from the newsperson where he is a party to the proceeding in which the statutory privilege would normally be invoked.[50]

A second type provides that if, in an action for damages for defamation, a legal defense of good faith is asserted by a reporter or news organization which defense is based on information supplied by a confidential source, the burden of proof in sustaining the defense is to be on the reporter or news organization.[51] This legislative device is obviously designed to prevent news media defendants from asserting defenses based on non-existent sources whose non-existence cannot be exposed by

45. *See* Ala. Code § 12–21–142 (1986); Ky. Rev. Stat. Ann. § 421–100 (1992).

46. *See* Law of April 2, 1896, Ch. 249, 1896 Md. Laws 437.

47. *Id.*; *see also* 63 Op. Md. Atty. Gen. 325 (1978).

48. *See* Md. Cts. & Jud. Proc. Code Ann. § 9–112(c) (1989).

49. *See* Ind. Code Ann. § 34–3–5–1 (Burns 1986); Neb. Rev. Stat. § 20–146 (1) (1991).

50. *See* Ga. Code Ann. § 24–9–30 (Michie 1994); "Any person, company, or other entity engaged in the gathering and dissemination of news for the public through a newspaper, book, magazine, or radio or tele-

vision broadcast, shall have a qualified privilege against disclosure of any information, document, or item obtained or prepared in the gathering or dissemination of news in any proceeding *where the one asserting the privilege is not a party* ..." (emphasis supplied).

51. *See* La. Rev. Stat. Ann. § 45:1454 (West 1982): "If the privilege granted herein is claimed and if, in a suit for damages for defamation, a legal defense of good faith has been asserted by a reporter or by a news media [sic] with respect to an issue upon which the reporter alleges to have obtained information from a confidential source, the burden of proof shall be on the reporter or news media [sic] to sustain this defense."

the plaintiff. Media defendants will have to persuade the trier of fact of the existence and reliability of their sources by either a preponderance of the evidence or clear and convincing evidence, depending on the standard of proof in defamation cases employed by the particular jurisdiction. This may mean that they will have to disclose their sources or fail in their defense.

The third class of provisions simply eliminate shield protection in defamation cases either when the plaintiff can demonstrate that identification of the source will lead to relevant evidence regarding actual malice[52] or when the defendant asserts a defense based on the content or source of allegedly defamatory information.[53]

Some seven state legislatures to date have demonstrated their skepticism as to the fairness of shield protection when those who would be protected or their employers are parties to the litigation.[54] On the other hand, one legislature, that of Colorado, appears to encourage the invocation of shield law protection by newspersons when they are parties to litigation. The Colorado shield statute provides that "[i]n any trial to a jury in an action in which a newsperson is a party as a result of such person's activities as a newsperson and in which the newsperson has invoked the privilege ... the jury shall be neither informed nor allowed to learn that such newsperson invoked such privilege or has thereby declined to disclose any news information."[55] This provision is unique and is one portion of recently enacted Colorado shield legislation. Whether the Colorado legislature sets a trend toward greater trust of media defendants remains to be seen.

As a practice matter plaintiffs attorneys should always join the primary newsgatherers in defamation actions even though they be without "deep pockets" in order to force waiver of the statutory privilege.

5. Miscellaneous Legislative Qualifications on the Availability of Shield Protection

Apart from the concern of legislatures regarding media defendants and shield law protection, a number of law-making bodies have expressed reservations in their statutes about the ready availability of the

---

52. *See* Minn. Stat. Ann. § 595.025 (1)-(2) (West 1988):

"Subdivision 1. The prohibition of disclosure provided in § 595.023   shall not apply in any defamation action where the person seeking disclosure can demonstrate that the identity of the source will lead to relevant evidence on the issue of actual malice.

Subd. 2. Notwithstanding the provisions of subdivision 1, the identity of the source of information shall not be ordered disclosed unless the following conditions are met:

(a) that there is probable cause to believe that the source has information

clearly relevant to the issue of defamation;

(b) that the information cannot be obtained by any alternative means or remedy less destructive of first amendment rights."

53. *See* Okla. Stat. Ann. tit. 12, § 2506(B)(2) (West 1993); Or. Rev.Stat. § 44.530(3) (1989); R.I. Gen. Laws § 9–19.1–3(b)(1) (1985) (sources only); Tenn. Code Ann. § 24–1–208(b) (Supp. 1994) (sources only).

54. *See* nn. 50–53, *supra.*

55. Colo. Rev. Stat. § 13–90–119(5) (Supp. 1993).

privilege in certain other situations. Rhode Island denies the privilege regarding the source of any information concerning details of grand jury or other proceedings required to be kept secret under state law. Thus leakers of Rhode Island state secrets cannot be sure that news media confidants will be able to keep them anonymous in the face of judicial compulsion. Only the ethics of the journalism profession protects sources in Rhode Island in such circumstances.

Louisiana has a provision in it's legislation withholding protection for newsperson where it's courts after hearing determine that compelled disclosure is essential to the "public interest."[56] North Dakota has a similar provision designed to prevent "miscarriage[s] of justice."[57] Michigan denies the statutory privilege in inquiries "for a crime punishable by imprisonment for life when it has been established that the information which is sought is essential for the purpose of the proceeding and that other available sources of the information have been exhausted."[58] Rhode Island, along the same lines as Michigan, divests shield protection if it's courts find after hearing that there is substantial evidence that disclosure is necessary to permit "criminal prosecution for the commission of a specific felony, or to prevent a threat to human life, and that such information or the source of such information is not available from other prospective witnesses ..."[59] The Colorado legislature has made clear that it's recently enacted statutory privilege does not apply to certain information already in the public domain.[60] And Arkansas rather amorphously permits defeat of the privilege when it is shown by those seeking disclosure that the article involved "was written, published, or broadcast in bad faith, with malice, and not in the interest of the public welfare."[61] While "bad faith" and "malice" may have reasonably settled meanings in the law, the meaning of the term "the public welfare" has to be subject to great debate, thus clouding the value of this old shield statute.[62]

6. Judicial Limitations on Protection for Newspersons' Eyewitness Testimony

With but two exceptions[63] limitation of shield statute protection for eyewitness testimony by newspersons derives from judicial interpreta-

56. La. Rev. Stat. Ann. § 45:1453 (West 1982).

57. N.D. Cent. Code § 31–01–06.2 (1976); *see* Grand Forks Herald v. District Court, 322 N.W.2d 850, 855 (N.D.1982).

58. Mich. Comp. Laws Ann. § 767.5a(1) (West Supp. 1994).

59. R.I. Gen. Laws § 9–19.1–3 (1985).

60. Colo. Rev. Stat. §§ 13–90–119(2)(a)-(b) and 24–72.5–103(1)(a)-(b) (Supp. 1993) provide in part: "[T]he privilege of nondisclosure shall not apply to the following: (a) News information received at a press conference; (b) News information which has actually been published or broadcast

through a medium of mass communication ..."

61. Ark. Code Ann. § 16–85–510 (Michie 1987).

62. The Arkansas statute was originally enacted in 1937. *See* 1937 Ark. Acts p. 1384.

63. *See* Colo. Rev. Stat. § 13–90–119 (2)(c)-(d) and 24–72.5–103(1)(c)-(d) (Supp. 1993) ("[T]he privilege of nondisclosure shall not apply to the following: ... (c) News information based on a newsperson's personal observation of the commission of a crime if substantially similar news information cannot reasonably be obtained by any other means; (d) News information based

tion and not from express provisions. Since the earliest forms of shield legislation were expressly drafted to protect against compelled disclosure of the identity of sources of information only,[64] the implication was drawn that personal observation by newsgatherers was not within the privilege.[65] In *Branzburg v. Pound*,[66] the Kentucky shield statute involved[67] provided that newspersons could not "be compelled to disclose ... the source of any information procured or obtained by him, and published in a newspaper or by a radio or television broadcasting station by which he is engaged or employed, or with which he is connected." The Kentucky Court of Appeals said in construing the statute that it merely granted immunity to a newsperson from disclosing the source of any information obtained but did not grant immunity against disclosing the information obtained itself. It then held that a reporter who witnessed the conversion of marijuana into the more potent drug hashish was not immune from testifying to his observations since he himself was the source of the information and the identities of those who engaged in the illegal activity was unprotected information. And in *Lightman v. State*[68] construing the groundbreaking 1896 Maryland shield statute,[69] which was identical to the later Kentucky statute in all material respects, the Maryland Court of Special Appeals came to the same conclusion as the Kentucky court that such statute protected only against the compelled disclosure of sources and upheld a civil contempt citation against a reporter who also refused to identify a person he personally observed engaging in illegal drug activity.

But once shield legislation is enacted to protect against forced disclosure of *both* sources and information, the personal observations of newspersons should be protected. In 1974, the California legislature

on a newsperson's personal observation of the commission of a class 1, 2, or 3 felony."); N.J. Stat. Ann. § 2A:84A–21 (Rule 27) (West 1976 and Supp. 1990) (incorporating limitation on eyewitness protection of N.J.S.A. § 2A:84A–29); *In re* Vrazo, 176 N.J.Super. 455, 423 A.2d 695, (N.J.Super.L.1980).

64. *See* Ala. Code § 12–21–142 (1986); Ariz. Rev. Stat. Ann. § 12–2237 (1982); Ark. Code Ann. § 16–85–510 (Michie 1987); Ill. Ann. Stat. ch. 110, ¶ 8–901 (Smith–Hurd Supp. 1992); Ind. Code Ann. § 34–3–5–1 (Burns 1986); Ky. Rev. Stat. Ann. § 421.100 (Michie/Bobbs–Merrill 1992); La. Rev. Stats. Ann. § 45:1452 (West 1982 and Supp. 1990); Ohio Rev. Code Ann. §§ 2739.04, 2739.12 (Anderson 1992); 42 Pa. Cons. Stat. Ann. § 5942 (a) (1982); Bruce L. Bortz and Laurie R. Bortz, *"Pressing" Out the Wrinkles in Maryland's Shield Law for Journalists*, 8 U. Balt. L. Rev. 461, 462 (1979) (setting out the text and describing the purpose of the very first shield statute).

65. *See* Branzburg v. Pound, 461 S.W.2d 345, 347–348 (Ky.1970), *aff'd sub nom.* Branzburg v. Hayes, 408 U.S. 665, 92 S.Ct.

2646, 33 L.Ed.2d 626 (1972); Lightman v. State, 15 Md.App. 713, 725, 294 A.2d 149, 156–157, *aff'd*, 266 Md. 550, 295 A.2d 212 (1972), cert. denied 411 U.S. 951, 93 S.Ct. 1922, 36 L.Ed.2d 414 (1973); *see also* Rosato v. Superior Court, 51 Cal.App.3d 190, 218–219, 124 Cal.Rptr. 427, 446 (1975); Delaney v. Superior Court (Kopetman), 249 Cal.Rptr. 60 (Cal.App.1988), *modified* 50 Cal.3d 785, 268 Cal.Rptr. 753, 789 P.2d 934 (1990).

66. 461 S.W.2d 345 (1970), *as modified on denial of rehearing*, (1971), *aff'd sub nom.* Branzburg v. Hayes, 408 U.S. 665, 92 S.Ct. 2646, 33 L.Ed.2d 626 (1972).

67. Ky. Rev. Stat. Ann. § 421.100 (Michie/Bobbs–Merrill 1992).

68. 15 Md.App. 713, 294 A.2d 149, *aff'd* 266 Md. 550, 295 A.2d 212 (1972), cert. denied, 411 U.S. 951, 93 S.Ct. 1922, 36 L.Ed.2d 414 (1973).

69. Law of April 2, 1896, Ch. 249, 1896 Md. Laws 437, as amended Md. Code Ann. Art. 35 § 2 (1957).

broadened its original 1935 shield statute protecting only newspersons' sources to include protection of "unpublished information."[70] The same protection is included in the California constitution[71] In *Delaney v. Superior Court (Kopetman),*[72] a reporter and a photographer for the Los Angeles Times were cited for contempt for refusing to answer questions at a suppression of evidence hearing relating to their personal observation while in a shopping mall of a search and arrest of an individual for illegal possession of brass knuckles. The accused denied that he had consented to the patdown search of his jacket yielding the contraband. He subpoenaed the newspersons to testify as to what had transpired. When their motions to quash were denied, they refused to testify as to the specifics of the search conducted in their presence.

The municipal court's citations for contempt were in effect reversed by the Los Angeles Superior Court, but that court's determination was in turn reversed by the California District Court of Appeal. The appellate court held that California's amended shield statute and its new constitutional provision did not grant newspersons the privilege of refusing to testify as to their observations of public events and ordered the superior court to vacate its orders granting the Times employees' petitions for habeas corpus even though the legislation now protected "unpublished information."

The California Supreme Court affirmed the judgment of the district court of appeal after holding that to do otherwise would violate the defendant's right afforded by the sixth amendment to have compulsory process to obtain witnesses in his favor. But the court also ruled that the protection of "unpublished information" in the shield statute and California constitution covered nonconfidential personal observations of events taking place in public places when such observations are part of the process of gathering news for dissemination to the public.[73] This statement of the California Supreme Court would seem to be determinative of the issue.[74]

70. 1974 Cal. Stats., ch. 1323, § 1, p. 2877 and ch. 1456, § 2, p. 3184; *see also* Assembly Const. Amend. No. 4, 1978 Cal. Stats. Res. ch. 77, pp. 4819–4820.

71. Cal. Const. Art. 1, § 2(b) (West 1983).

72. 50 Cal.3d 785, 268 Cal.Rptr. 753, 789 P.2d 934 (1990). *See* Ian W. Craig, Case Note, Delaney v. Superior Court: *Balancing Interests of Criminal Defendants and Newspersons Under California's Shield Law,* 22 Pac. L.J. 1371 (1991) (exhaustive discussion of *Delaney* and its ramifications and California's shield law.)

73. *Id.* at 796–805, 268 Cal. Rptr. at 758–764, 789 P. 2d at 938–945.

74. *See* Matter of Woodhaven Lumber and Mill Work, 123 N.J. 481, 589 A.2d 135 (1991) in which the New Jersey Supreme Court construed New Jersey's shield statute provision exempting from protection a reporter's eyewitness testimony as to "any act involving physical violence or property damage." N.J. Stat. Ann. 2A:84A–21(h)(West 1976; Supp. 1987). Taking an approach protective of the efficacy of the shield law similar to that taken by the California Supreme Court, the New Jersey court held that, in the context of fires of suspicious origin, photographers arriving at the scene of fires after they had been ignited could not be said to have been witnesses "any act involving ... property damage." All they witnessed was the product of such acts and not the acts of starting the fires. Therefore they could not be subpoenaed to produce unpublished photographs of the fires.

And in a ruling further protective of New Jersey's statutory newspersons privilege, the appellate division of the New Jersey

7.6   *Procedure Relative to Shield Legislation

7.7   *Waiver of the Statutory Privilege

7.8   *The Attitude of Courts to the Statutory Newspersons' Privilege—A Tale of Two Cities (Traveling from the Ridiculous (Albany) to the Sublime (Trenton))

7.9   Federal Regulatory Protection Against Compelled Disclosure by Newspersons

For reasons too numerous to mention, no federal shield legislation has ever been enacted.[1] However, the United States Department of Justice has adopted a set of guidelines that carefully define when and how a United States Attorney may obtain a subpoena directed to a member of the news media.[2]

The policy underlying the Department of Justice Guidelines clearly recognizes the needs of a free press in American society. "Because freedom of the press can be no broader than the freedom of reporters to investigate and report the news, the prosecutorial power of the government should not be used in such a way that it impairs a reporter's responsibility to cover as broadly as possible controversial public issues. This policy statement is thus intended to provide protection for the news media from forms of compulsory process, whether civil or criminal, which might impair the news gathering function."[3]

In striking the balance between the imperatives of the news media freely to gather and report the news and the Department's obligation to

Superior Court distinguished between subpoenas of reporters to give eyewitness testimony and subpoenas of reporters to give evidence establishing that they were eyewitnesses. As to the latter, they will be quashed as undermining the entire scheme of the New Jersey shield law. *See* New Jersey v. Santiago, 250 N.J.Super., 30, 38, 593, A.2d 357, 361, (N.J.Super.1991). "The very thought that a newsperson's testimony could be compelled in order to ascertain whether the newsperson actually witnessed the acts . . . and whether the events actually witnessed are relevant, material and necessary to the [criminal] defense 'would make the notion of a newsperson's privilege nothing more than an empty promise—the reasoning behind such rule would require the production of everything.'" (citation omitted). Id. at 38, 593 A.2d at 361. *But see* Minnesota v. Knutson, 523 N.W.2d 909, 912 (Minn.App.1994) (narrowly construing Minnesota's shield legislation so as not to cover a reporter's eyewitness information which does not identify a source).

* The text of this section is in Modern Communication Law, Practitioners Edition, Vol. 2.

1. *But see, e.g.*, Sam J. Ervin Jr., *In Pursuit of a Press Privilege*, 11 Harv. J. Legis. 233, 261–263 (1974) (divergence of views among newspersons themselves as to the need or desirability of federal shield legislation); David J. Smith Note, *News-Source Privilege in Libel Cases: A Critical Analysis*, 57 Wash. L. Rev. 349 (1982) (empirical data presented showing little or no need for federal legislation); Cynthia H. Plevin & Stevin M. Plevin, Note, *Journalists in the Court: Toward Effective Shield Legislation*, 8 U.S.F.L. Rev. 664, 675 (1974) (public interest in federal law enforcement thought to be paramount).

2. 28 C.F.R. § 50.10 (1993). The promulgation of subpoena and search warrant guidelines was mandated by the Privacy Protection Act of 1980 § 2000aa-ii, Pub.L. 103–141, 94 Stat. 1882 (1980), codified at 42 U.S.C.A. § 2000aa-ii (West 1994).

3. *Id.*

effective law enforcement and the fair administration of justice, members of the Department of Justice and other federal government personnel[4] must meet several requirements before requesting issuance of a subpoena directed to a member of the news media or to the local telephone company for his toll call records. As a threshold matter, all reasonable attempts should first be made to obtain the sought after evidence from alternative sources.[5] If thereafter, a subpoena is still contemplated, negotiations with the news media personnel involved *must* be pursued,[6] and where the nature of the investigation permits, the government representatives should make clear what the Department's needs are in the particular case and its willingness to respond to particular problems of the news media member in making the sought after evidence available.[7] But further negotiations are not required once it is clear that such efforts would be fruitless.[8]

If, after negotiations, an attorney for the United States decides to seek a subpoena, the Attorney General of the United States must expressly authorize its issuance.[9] The one exception to this requirement is the case in which the newsperson with whom negotiations were conducted expressly agrees to provide the material sought and such material was previously published or broadcast. In this event, a United States Attorney or the responsible assistant Attorney General may authorize issuance of the subpoena but must thereafter submit a report to the Department's Office of Public Affairs detailing the circumstances surrounding the issuance.[10] The government has no burden to show that the requirements of the guidelines have been met.[11]

Several principles control Department of Justice personnel in requesting the Attorney General's authorization. These include that (1) in criminal cases there should be reasonable belief based on non-media information that a crime has actually occurred; (2) in civil cases there should be reasonable belief based on non-media sources that the information sought is essential to the successful completion of the litigation in a case of substantial importance; (3) the government should have unsuccessfully attempted to obtain the information from alternative non-media sources; (4) except under exigent circumstances subpoenas should be limited to verification of published information; (5) even subpoena authorization requests for publicly disclosed information should be treated with care to avoid claims of harassment; and (6) subpoenas should, wherever possible, be directed at material information

---

4. See Maurice v. NLRB, 7 Media L. Rptr. 2221 (S.D.W.Va. 1981), *vacated and remanded*, 691 F.2d 182 (4th Cir.1982) (NLRB attorneys).

5. 28 C.F.R. § 50.10 (b); see Lewis v. United States, 517 F.2d 236, 239 (9th Cir. 1975).

6. *See* United States v. Blanton, 534 F.Supp. 295, 297 (S.D.Fla.1982); *cf.* Morton v. Ruiz, 415 U.S. 199, 235, 94 S.Ct. 1055, 1074, 39 L.Ed.2d 270, 294 (1974).

7. 28 C.F.R. § 50.10 (c) (1993); *see also id.* at § 50.10 (d) (telephone toll records under the control of the local telephone company).

8. *See* Lewis v. United States, 517 F.2d 236, 238 (9th Cir.1975).

9. 28 C.F.R. § 50.10(e) (1993).

10. *Id.*

11. *See In re* Lewis, 384 F.Supp. 133, 137 (C.D.Cal.1974), *aff'd sub nom.* Lewis v. United States, 517 F.2d 236 (9th Cir.1975).

regarding limited subject matter, should cover a reasonably limited period of time and should avoid requiring production of a large volume of the newsperson's unpublished material.[12]

Similar safeguards are included in the Department of Justice policy guidelines with regard to the subpoena of newspersons' telephone toll records[13] and authorizations to question, arrest or seek an arrest warrant for members of the news media, or to seek indictments or file information against such persons for offenses which they are suspected of having committed in the course of their professional responsibilities.[14] Failure to obtain the approval of the Attorney General for actions covered by the policy guidelines may result in administrative disciplinary action against the offender but does not give to newspersons adversely affected by violations any legally enforceable right against the government or its personnel.[15]

While the policy guidelines reflect the sensitivity of Department of Justice to the problem of compelling the disclosure of evidence by newspersons, they provide minimal and rather uncertain protection because they relate only to federal civil litigation and criminal prosecutions and are construed and applied by Department of Justice officials whose first concern must, of necessity, be for effective law enforcement.[16]

II. NEWSPERSONS RESPONSIBILITIES AND RIGHTS

7.10 Newspersons' Responsibilities to Safeguard Confidences

To this point in the chapter we have been concerned with the constitutional or statutory right, privilege or immunity of newspersons to resist under testimonial compulsion disclosure of news sources and other information gathered in the course of their professional activities. Now in this section we confront the question whether newspersons who obtain information under promises of confidentiality have a correlative legal duty to refrain voluntarily from disclosing the identity of sources and other unpublished information. Of course, newspersons have long had an ethical responsibility not to expose their sources and confidential information.[1] But until relatively recently the question of parallel legal responsibility had not been considered by the courts.[2]

---

12. 28 C.F.R. § 50.10(f) (1993).

13. *Id.* at § 50.10(g).

14. *Id.* at § 50.10(h)-(k).

15. *Id.* at § 50.10(n).

16. The weakness of this protection for newspersons is illustrated by the case of *In re Shain*, 978 F.2d 850 (4th Cir.1992) in which the court of appeals stated in dictum, that the violation of the Department of Justice regulations was an internal matter and would not provide a basis to quash subpoenas issued to compel testimony of media representatives. *Id.* at 853–854. The appeals court then went on to uphold the

contempt citations issued by the district court. *Id.* at 854.

1. *See* American Society of Newspaper Editors' Statement of Principles, Art. VI (1975); Society of Professional Journalists Code of Ethics, Part III, Rule 5 (1987 revision). But there is no central authority in journalism with mandatory enforcement power such as exists for the licensed professions.

2. Apparently the first case at all to consider this question was *Fries v. National Broadcasting Co.*, Civ. No. 456687 (Cal. Super. Ct. 1982), a contract action against a

The earliest reported appellate decision on this question is *Doe v. American Broadcasting Cos., Inc.*[3] There the plaintiffs, two rape victims and the boyfriend of one of them, were approached to appear on a special television reports about rape. They expressed great concern for their anonymity and only agreed to participate after repeated assurances that neither their faces nor their voices would be recognizable in the broadcasts. But the plaintiffs were not sufficiently disguised and were recognizable to viewers who knew them. They were thereafter approached by numerous persons who discussed their appearances on the broadcasts, and it was through the broadcasts that the family of one of the rape victims learned about the attack for the first time.

Plaintiffs brought actions for breach of contract and for the torts of negligent and intentional infliction of emotional harm. A majority of the New York Supreme Court's Appellate Division panel modified the trial court's across the board denial of the defendants' motions for summary judgment by ordering it granted as to the claims of intentional infliction of emotional distress. The majority held that defendants' actions as detailed by the plaintiffs did not constitute the intentional, deliberate and outrageous conduct required for this tort.[4] The dissenting judge pointed out that an excerpt from the videotape used by the station to promote the series of broadcasts permitted identification of one of the plaintiffs by her employer and another of the plaintiffs was clearly identifiable on the first of the series of actual broadcasts. Yet the defendant station failed to take effective additional steps to mask the identity of the plaintiffs on subsequent broadcasts. This failure raised in the dissenter's view questions of fact as to whether defendants' conduct

reporter for improperly releasing the name of a source. *See* 97 L. A. Daily J., Mar. 15, 1984, p. 1, col. 1; Michael Dicke, Note, *Promises and the Press: First Amendment Limitations on New Source Recovery for Breach of a Confidentiality Agreement,* 73 Minn. L. Rev. 1553, 1555 n. 14 (1989). The first trial ended in a hung jury and a settlement was reached before a second trial. *See* Marc A. Franking, Mass Media Law, Cases & Materials 588–589 (3d ed. 1987). The few other cases after *Fries* include *Ruzicka v. Conde Nast Publications, Inc.,* 733 F.Supp. 1289 (D.Minn.1990) *aff'd in part, remanded in part* 939 F.2d 578 (8th Cir.1991) *on remand* 794 F.Supp. 303 (D.Minn.1992) (summary judgment entered for defendant magazine publisher rejecting applicability of common law promissory estoppel), *judgment vacated* 999 F.2d 1319 (8th Cir.1993),; *Cohen v. Cowles Media Co.,* 14 Med. L. Rptr. 1460 (Minn.Dist.Ct.1987), 15 Med. L. Rptr. 2288 (Minn.Dist.Ct.1988), *aff'd in part, rev'd in part* 457 N.W.2d 199 (Minn. 1990), *rev'd* 501 U.S. 663, 111 S.Ct. 2513, 115 L.Ed.2d 586 (1991), *on remand* 479

N.W.2d 387 (Minn.1992); *Doe v. American Broadcasting Cos.* 152 A.D.2d 482, 543 N.Y.S.2d 455, *appeal dismissed,* 74 N.Y.2d 945, 550 N.Y.S.2d 278, 549 N.E.2d 480 (1989). Closely analogous cases include *Bindrim v. Mitchell,* 92 Cal.App.3d 61, 155 Cal.Rptr. 29, cert. dismissed 444 U.S. 984, 100 S. Ct. 490, 62 L. Ed. 2d 412 (1979) (writer who attended nude encounter group therapy under a written agreement not to write articles or otherwise disclose what she observed sued for breach of the agreement when she published a novel portraying just such a therapy group); *Virelli v. Goodson-Todman Enterprises, Ltd.,* 142 A.D.2d 479, 536 N.Y.S.2d 571 (1989) (reporter sued for tortious breach of confidence for breaking an alleged promise to permit plaintiffs to review article concerning them and their daughter before article entitled "Tormented by a Drug–Crazed Daughter," was published).

3. 152 A.D.2d 482, 543 N.Y.S.2d 455 (1989).

4. *Id.* at 482–483, 543 N.Y.S.2d at 455–456.

was so extreme and outrageous as to be regarded as intolerable by a civilized society.[5]

The case that has thus far caused the greatest stir in legal and journalistic circles in this emerging area is *Cohen v. Cowles Media Co.*[6] There, in the closing days of the 1982 Minnesota gubernatorial election campaign, Dan Cohen, an activist Republican and associate of the Independent Republican candidate for governor, approached reporters for the Minneapolis Star Tribune and the St. Paul Pioneer Press and indicated that he had important documents relating to a candidate in the coming election and that he would turn over to them copies of the documents provided they would promise him anonymity and would further promise not to inquire of him as to his own source of the documents. Both reporters promised to keep Cohen's identity secret. They did not indicate to Cohen that their promises might be overruled by their respective editors though they personally intended to keep their promises of confidentiality. Cohen then turned over to each reporter copies of two public court records concerning minor criminal matters involving the Democratic Farmer–Labor candidate for lieutenant governor. After the documents were presented to the editors of the respective papers and after investigation, the Star Tribune and the Pioneer Press editors, acting independently, decided that a major part of the story was Dan Cohen and his association with the Independent–Republican election campaign and that Cohen should be identified as the catalyst for the unfavorable last minute story about the DFL candidate. Cohen was so identified in both newspapers over the strong objections of the two reporters involved. Cohen was fired by the advertising agency that employed him on the day the story broke.

Cohen could not sue for defamation because the information published was true. He instead brought civil actions against the newspapers for fraudulent misrepresentations by their reporters and breach of contract. The Minnesota District Court refused to grant summary judgment for the defendants but did strike Cohen's claim for punitive

---

5. *Id.* at 483–484, 543 N.Y.S.2d at 456.

6. 14 Media L. Rep. 1460 (Minn.Dist.Ct. 1987) (on defendants' motions for summary judgment and to strike plaintiff's claim for punitive damages), 15 Med. L. Rptr. 2288 (Minn.Dist.Ct.1988) (on final judgment), *aff'd in part, rev'd in part,* 445 N.W.2d 248 (Minn.App.1989), *aff'd in part, rev'd in part,* 457 N.W.2d 199 (Minn.1990), *rev'd* 501 U.S. 663, 111 S.Ct. 2513, 115 L.Ed.2d 586 (1991), *on remand* 479 N.W.2d 387 (Minn.1992). *See also* Ruzicka v. Conde Nast Publications, Inc. 733 F.Supp. 1289 (D.Minn.1990) (defendant's motion for summary judgment granted in case involving same plaintiff's attorney and similar theories of liability as in *Cohen*). The *Cohen* case has been the subject of much legal commentary. *See* Kurt Hirsch, Note, *En-forcing Reporters' Promises and the Fallacy of Neutrality,* 18 N.Y.U. Rev.Law & Social Change 161 (1991); Kathryn M. Kase, *When a Promise Is Not a Promise: The Legal Consequences for Journalists Who Break Promises of Confidentiality to Sources,* 12 Comm/Ent L. J. 565 (1990) Daniel A. Levin & Ellen B. Rubert, *Promises of Confidentiality After* Cohen v. Cowles Media Company: *A Survey of Newspaper Editors,* 24 Golden Gate L. Rev. 423 (1994); David J. Smith, Note, *Promises and the Press: First Amendment Limitations on News Source Recovery for Breach of a Confidentiality Agreement,* 73 Minn. L. Rev. 1553 (1989); *see also* Lyle Denniston, *A Right to Expose Sources?,* Wash. Journ. Rev. 18 (Nov. 1988).

damages relating to the breach of contract claims.[7] The jury returned verdicts for Cohen, finding both willful misrepresentations and breach of contracts and awarded him $200,000 compensatory damages jointly and severally against the defendants and further awarded punitive damages on the tort claims of $250,000 against each defendant.

The trial court entered judgment on the verdicts, rejecting the contention that the First Amendment shielded the defendants from liability for common law torts[8] and breaches of contract committed in the legitimate course of gathering and disseminating news.

The Minnesota Court of Appeals affirmed the judgment in part and reversed it in part.[9] The appeals court held that Cohen's claims did not involve state action and therefore did not implicate the First Amendment; that further, even if First Amendment rights were implicated, those rights were outweighed by compelling state interests; and even further, that such constitutional rights were, in any event, waived by the newspapers under the circumstances. But the intermediate appellate court also ruled that there was insufficient evidence to support the misrepresentation tort and set aside the awards of punitive damages. What was left of the judgment was the joint and several award of $200,000 compensatory damages based on the jury's finding of breach of contract.

On further appeal,[10] the Minnesota Supreme Court sitting *en banc* affirmed the lower appeals court holdings regarding the claim of tortious misrepresentation and the setting aside of punitive damage. But the high court reversed the judgment affirming the award of compensatory damages for breach of contract. While conceding the apparent presence of a contract with an offer, acceptance and mutual consideration and an apparent breach thereof, the Minnesota court said the matter was not that simple. Looking at the traditional relationship of newsperson and source within the special milieu of newsgathering, the court was not persuaded that the parties actually intended to create a legally binding contract. Instead, the court said, "What we have here … is an 'I'll-scratch-your-back-if-you'll-scratch-mine' accommodation … In other words, contract law seems here an ill fit for a promise of news source confidentiality. To impose a contract theory on this arrangement puts an unwarranted legal rigidity on a special ethical relationship, precluding necessary consideration of factors underlying that ethical relationship."[11]

---

7. 14 Med. L. Rptr. 1460 (Minn.Dist.Ct. 1987).

8. The claim of newspersons and news organizations that the First Amendment immunizes them from liability for torts committed in the course of legitimate newsgathering has been uniformly rejected by the courts. *See, e.g.,* Galella v. Onassis, 487 F.2d 986 (2d Cir.1973) (public harassment); Dietemann v. Time, Inc., 449 F.2d 245 (9th Cir.1971) (trespass and invasion of privacy); Prahl v. Brosamle, 98 Wis.2d 130, 295 N.W.2d 768 (1980) (trespass); *cf.* Stahl v. State, 665 P.2d 839, 841–842 (Okl.Cr.App. 1983) (criminal trespass) (collecting cases generally on this point).

9. 445 N.W.2d 248 (Minn.App.1989).

10. 457 N.W.2d 199 (Minn.1990), *rev'd,* 501 U.S. 663, 111 S.Ct. 2513, 115 L.Ed.2d 586 (1991).

11. *Id.* at 203.

Turning to the possibility of promissory estoppel as an alternative theory of liability,[12] the court focused on the requirement that unsupported promises may be enforced if that is the only way to avoid injustice to the promisee—here, of course, Dan Cohen. Though noting that Cohen had lost his employment because of his exposure by the defendant papers, the court was unwilling to hold that an injustice would go unremedied if the reporters' promises were not enforced here. The court reasoned that the presence in the case of First Amendment interest required their balancing against the common law interest in protecting a promise of anonymity. In striking that balance "in the classic First Amendment context of the quintessential public debate in our society, namely a political source involved in a political campaign," the Minnesota Supreme Court held that the state's interest in enforcing the promise was outweighed by First Amendment imperatives.[13]

The two dissenting judges insisted that a valid enforceable contract existed or, at the very least, application of promissory estoppel was called for to insure evenhanded application of the law to powerful media organizations as well as to ordinary citizens.[14] Both dissenters also argued that the majority decision would discourage the free flow of information to the public because potential news sources will now be reluctant to risk exposure.[15] And one of the dissenters went so far as to deny that the First Amendment was implicated in the case.[16]

Given the unprecedented nature of the Minnesota Supreme Court's First Amendment ruling, it was not surprising that the United States Supreme Court granted certiorari. A bare majority of the High Court voted to reverse. The Court, in an opinion by Justice White, held that the First and Fourteenth Amendments did not bar application of laws of general applicability to the news media simply because the application has incidental effects on its ability to gather and report the news.[17] "There can be little doubt that the Minnesota doctrine of promissory estoppel is a law of general applicability. It does not target or single out the press. Rather, insofar as we are advised, the doctrine is generally applicable to the daily transaction of all citizens of Minnesota. The First Amendment does not forbid its application to the press."[18]

---

12. *See* RESTATEMENT SECOND OF CONTRACTS § 90 (1) (1981). This theory binds a promisor to his promise if it induces reasonably expected action by the promisee and injustice can only be avoided by enforcing the unsupported promise.

13. 457 N.W.2d at 204–205.

14. *Id*. at 205–207 (dissents of Yetka and Kelley, J.J.).

15. *Id*. at 206, 207.

16. *Id*. at 207 (dissent of Kelley, J.). Of course, if this is true, then the United States Supreme Court did not have jurisdiction to grant the writ of certiorari.

17. Cohen v. Cowles Media Co., 501 U.S. 663, 669, 111 S.Ct. 2513, 2518–2519, 115 L.Ed.2d 586, 597 (1991).

18. *Id*. Ironically, this unfavorable ruling for the press did not necessarily mean that Dan Cohen would be compensated for losses occasioned by the newspapers' failure to honor the agreement not to disclose his identity. The Court rejected Cohen's request that the jury verdict awarding him $200,000 in compensatory damages be reinstated. *Id* at 672, 111 S. Ct. at 2519–20, 115 L. Ed. 2d at 597. Rather, the Court remanded the case for further proceedings in which the question of whether a promissory estoppel claim had otherwise been established under Minnesota law. *Id*. In addition, the

Thus, the Court made clear that the First Amendment does not prevent the imposition of a legal duty under general state or federal law on news organizations and newspersons to honor their promises made in furtherance of newsgathering and in accordance with their accepted ethical obligation to do so.

There were two dissenting opinions, one by Justice Blackmun asserting that the First Amendment protected the press from incidental as well as direct regulation when the end product of its activity is a truthful communication to the public (here of the source's true identity)[19] and another by Justice Souter.[20] Souter's more sophisticated analysis rejected the majority's mechanical acceptance of the constitutionality of neutral incidental restrictions on the news media from laws of general applicability. Rather, he would "articulate, measure, and compare the competing interests involved in any given case to determine the legitimacy of burdening constitutional interests.... "[21] In determining that application of Minnesota common law promissory estoppel would violate the First Amendment in *this* case, Justice Souter emphasized the interest of the public in learning the identity of the source before they voted because the propriety of his conduct could be taken to reflect on his character and those he was associated with politically.[22] He did not rule out the possibility that imposition of civil liability under general contract law or its substitute might be constitutional in differing circumstances as when the identity of the source is of lesser importance to the public.[23]

As Justice Souter stated, the majority's approach is very mechanical and could be stretched to permit imposition of egregious restrictions and obligations on the news media resulting in constriction of the flow of news and information to the public. More should be required before civil liability is imposed on the newsgathering process than finding that the civil liability stems from neutral application of general statutory or common law. On the other hand, Justice Blackmun's test of whether the information communicated was truthful and lawfully obtained might countenance and protect some criminal and tortious conduct if engaged in by members of the newsmedia during the newsgathering process.[24]

Court indicated that the defendant newspapers could attempt to argue that the Minnesota constitution protects news media in the state from promissory estoppel actions such as the present one. *Id*. at 670–72, 111 S. Ct. at 2519–20, 115 L. Ed. 2d at 598. On remand the Minnesota Supreme Court upheld the jury verdict of $200,000 against the two newspapers on the promissory estoppel theory. 479 N.W.2d 387, 392 (Minn.1992).

19. *Id*. at 672, 111 S. Ct. at 2520–22, 115 L. Ed. 2d at 599–601.

20. *Id*. at 676, 111 S. Ct. at 2522, 115 L. Ed. 2d at 602–603.

21. *Id*.

22. *Id*. at 678, 111 S. Ct. at 2523, 115 L. Ed. 2d at 603.

23. *Id*.

24. *But compare, e.g.,* Dietemann v. Time, Inc., 449 F.2d 245, 249 (9th Cir.1971) (tort of intrusion during newsgathering case in which the appeals court observed "The First Amendment is not a license to trespass, to steal, or to intrude by electronic means into the precincts of another's home or office."); Le Mistral, Inc. v. Columbia Broadcasting System, 61 A.D.2d 491, 493–94, 402 N.Y.S.2d 815, 817 (1978) (tort of trespass); Stahl v. State, 665 P.2d 839, 841 (Okla.Cr.App.1983), cert. denied, 464 U.S. 1069, 104 S.Ct. 973, 79 L.Ed.2d 212 (1984) (crime of trespass); Prahl v. Brosamle, 98 Wis.2d 130, 151, 295 N.W.2d 768, 780–781 (1980) (tort of trespass).

Justice Souter's ad hoc balancing approach seems preferable here. Because one cannot tell beforehand how courts will strike the balance, it provides a legal amber light for the press as it approaches obvious ethical limits of the profession.[25] The problem with Justice Souter's analysis is that he fails to weigh in the balance the long-term interest of the public in encouraging the activity of confidential sources in divulging secret and sensitive information to the press in order to expose wrongdoing in high places and low. If sources come to realize that they can obtain no recompense for the willful failure of newspersons to keep their identities confidential, they may be less willing to engage in the often dangerous activity of providing information to the news media and, ultimately, the public.

7.11 Punishment for Civil and Criminal Contempt by Newspersons Who Refuse Lawful Orders to Make Disclosure

A. Introduction

The discussion concerning the constitutional and statutory newspersons privilege has thus far been conducted at a rather high level of abstraction. But the reasons for the strong resistance of journalists and their news organizations to testimonial compulsion are very practical. Testimonial compulsion of newspersons disrupts the newsgathering and disseminating process by forcing those involved in that process to expend time and resources better spent on getting the news out to the public. In addition, newspersons do not want to go to jail for what they are ethically bound to do—protect their sources and confidential information.

Of these two very practical reasons for insisting on a newspersons privilege, being jailed for contempt of court is, of course, the most dramatic. It is a real and omnipresent threat. Many journalists have spent time incarcerated, including Marie Torre, of the *New York Herald Tribune*,[1] Peter Bridge of the *Newark Evening News*,[2] William Farr of the *Los Angeles Herald Examiner*,[3] Myron Farber of the *New York Times*[4] and more recently Tim Roche, of the *Stuart* (Florida) *News*[5] to

---

25. For an excellent discussion of the impact of the *Cohen* case on the First Amendment and newsgathering, *see* Jerome A. Barron, Cohen v. Cowles Media *and its significance for First Amendment Law and Journalism,* 3 Wm. & Mary Bill of Rights Journal 419 (1994).

1. *See* Garland v. Torre, 259 F.2d 545 (2d Cir.) cert. denied, 358 U.S. 910, 79 S.Ct. 237, 3 L.Ed.2d 231 (1958).

2. *See In re* Bridge, 120 N.J.Super. 460, 295 A.2d 3 (App.Div.), cert. denied 62 N.J. 80, 299 A.2d 78 (1972), cert. denied, 410 U.S. 991, 93 S.Ct. 1500, 36 L.Ed.2d 189 (1973).

3. *See* Farr v. Superior Court, 22 Cal. App.3d 60, 99 Cal.Rptr. 342 (1971); Farr v. Pitchess, 522 F.2d 464 (9th Cir.1975), cert. denied 427 U.S. 912, 96 S.Ct. 3200, 49 L.Ed.2d 1203 (1976) (federal habeas corpus relief sought).

4. *See In re* Farber, 78 N.J. 259, 394 A.2d 330, cert. denied *sub. nom.* New York Times Co. v. New Jersey, 439 U.S. 997, 99 S.Ct. 598, 58 L.Ed.2d 670 (1978).

5. *See* Roche v. Florida, 589 So.2d 978 (Fla.App.1991).

name a few.[6] It is important, therefore, to examine the law of contempt as it relates to newspersons.[7]

B. Newspersons and the Contempt Power

Without a privilege to refuse to comply with a judicial or legislative subpoena, newspersons will almost surely be held in contempt if information withheld is deemed relevant and material to the work of the government or if a criminal or civil litigant is seeking the evidence. Sanctions for contumacious conduct depend upon how the conduct is classified. If the contempt is deemed to be civil, meaning in disregard of the rights of litigants seeking the information, indeterminate incarceration and payments to the parties injured by contemptuous conduct may be ordered to coerce compliance. The incarceration is indeterminate because the newsperson may choose at some point to purge himself of contempt by providing the sought after evidence. Release from legal custody would then follow.

However, if the contumacious behavior is deemed to challenge the lawful authority of the court, grand jury or other branch of government, the court attempting to enforce the subpoena may classify the contempt as criminal in nature and impose punishment including a specified jail term or a criminal fine or both. At this point it is too late for the newsperson to purge himself of contempt and, theoretically, release from his pledge by the one he promised confidentiality will have no bearing on the sentence to be served. The thrust here is punishment, not coercion to force cooperation.

But what is mainly at stake in the civil-criminal contempt dichotomy is the *procedures* to be followed in determining whether the newsperson is in contempt. If the citation is for criminal contempt not occurring in the presence of the court, there would be a jury trial which, of necessity, would be governed by criminal procedure requiring, for instance, proof of the contempt by the prosecution beyond reasonable doubt and other safeguards provided criminal accused.

If the contemptuous criminal conduct is exhibited in the immediate presence of the court and threatens the order of the proceedings as, for instance, the newsperson refusing, without privilege, to testify at trial after being called as a witness, the refusal could be dealt with summarily and the newsperson punished without further proceedings. But such

---

6. We should not forget John T. Morris of the *Baltimore Sun* whose incarceration in 1896 first triggered legal thinking about protection for newspersons who disobeyed subpoenas in order to protect their sources. Morris was sent to jail at the request of a grand jury for five days until the grand jury's term ended. The reporter literally spent five days in jail, and was let out at nightfall so that he might be with his family. See Bruce L. Bortz and Laurie R. Bortz, *"Pressing" Out the Wrinkles in Maryland's* *Shield Law for Journalists*, 8 U. Balt. L. Rev. 461, 462 (1979).

7. For general discussions of the law of contempt, *see e.g.*, JOHN C. FOX, THE HISTORY OF CONTEMPT OF COURT (1972); RONALD L. GOLDFARB, THE CONTEMPT POWER (1963); Dan B. Dobbs, *Contempt of Court: A Survey*, 56 Cornell L. Rev. 183 (1971); Robert J. Martineau, *Contempt of Court; Eliminating the Confusion Between Civil and Criminal Contempt*, 50 U. Cinn. L. Rev. 677 (1981).

punishment will have to fall within constitutional limits. Summary criminal contempt punishment may not exceed six months incarceration.[8] If the judge views the contempt, whether in or outside his presence, as a *serious* criminal matter involving potential punishment of more than six months imprisonment, the newsperson would be entitled to a jury trial as guaranteed by the Sixth and Fourteenth Amendments to the Constitution.[9] Whether the imposition alone of a fine of more than $500 against news organizations and individual newspersons would raise the contempt to the level of a serious crime depends on the circumstances surrounding the contumacious behavior.[10]

The serious and, by and large, unresolved question here is what the standards are for distinguishing between civil contempt and criminal contempt so that a choice can be made of the appropriate procedure to be followed *before* the contempt proceeding commences.[11] If the nature of the contempt is not determined at the outset, the choice of the procedure may not accord with the sanctions imposed as, for example, ordinary civil procedure employed in a contempt proceeding resulting in criminal punishment. Such discord between procedure and end result will often yield reversal.[12] This may even be true where criminal procedures are followed for civil contempts.[13]

Adding to the confusion are cases which inexplicably label civil contempts as criminal[14] or find both civil and criminal contempts arising out of the newsperson's act of disobedience of a lawful subpoena.[15] Where the court believes both civil and criminal contempt may be present, it will have to employ criminal procedures if it wishes to avoid Sixth Amendment issues.[16] But even then inappropriate criminal procedures may result in reversible error.

Subpoenas directed to newspersons and news organizations are

8. *See* Muniz v. Hoffman, 422 U.S. 454, 475–476, 95 S.Ct. 2178, 2190, 45 L.Ed.2d 319, 334–335 (1975); Cheff v. Schnackenberg, 384 U.S. 373, 378–379, 86 S.Ct. 1523, 1525–1526, 16 L.Ed.2d 629, 632–633 (1966).

9. *See* Bloom v. Illinois, 391 U.S. 194, 197–208, 88 S.Ct. 1477, 1480–1485, 20 L.Ed.2d 522, 526–533 (1968); Muniz v. Hoffman, 422 U.S. 454, 475–476, 95 S.Ct. 2178, 2190, 45 L.Ed.2d 319, 334 (1975).

10. *See* Muniz v. Hoffman, 422 U.S. 454, 476–477, 95 S.Ct. 2178, 2190–2191, 45 L.Ed.2d 319, 335, (1975).

11. *See* Robert J. Martineau, *Contempt of Court: Eliminating the Confusion Between Civil and Criminal Contempt*, 50 U. Cinn. L. Rev. 677, 681 (1981).

12. *See, e.g., In re* Kave, 760 F.2d 343, 351–353 (1st Cir.1985); Washington Metropolitan Area Transit Auth. v. Amalgamated Transit Union, 531 F.2d 617, 622, 174 U.S. App. D.C. 285, 290 (D.C.Cir.1976); Robert J. Martineau, *Contempt of Court: Eliminating the Confusion Between Civil and Crimi-* *nal Contempt*, 50 U. Cinn. L. Rev. 677, 683–684 (1981); Dan B. Dobbs *Contempt of Court: A Survey*, 56 Corn. L. Rev. 183, 238 (1971); *see also In re* Magwood, 785 F.2d 1077, 1081, 251 U.S. App. D.C. 389, 393 (D.C.Cir.1986).

13. *See, e.g., In re* Kave, 760 F.2d 343, 351 (1st Cir.1985).

14. *See, e.g.,* Garland v. Torre, 259 F.2d 545 (2d Cir.), cert. denied, 358 U.S. 910, 79 S.Ct. 237, 3 L.Ed.2d 231 (1958).

15. *See, e.g., In re* Farber, 78 N.J. 259, 394 A.2d 330 (1978), cert. denied *sub nom.* New York Times Co. v. New Jersey, 439 U.S. 997, 99 S.Ct. 598, 58 L.Ed.2d 670 (1978).

16. *See* United States v. United Mine Workers, 330 U.S. 258, 298–301, 67 S.Ct. 677, 698–700, 91 L.Ed. 884, 915–917 (1947); Dan B. Dobbs, *Contempt of Court: A Survey*, 56 Corn. L. Rev. 183, 236–237 (1971).

numerous and troublesome.[17] While the news media apparently comply with more than half of the thousands of subpoenas directed to them each year by both civil and criminal litigants,[18] the number of newspersons who refuse to obey subpoenas can be expected to rise. The best advice that a media lawyer can give to a newsperson confronted with a subpoena which he refuses to obey and against its enforcement no privilege exists is to be respectful of the court or grand jury when refusing to comply. In addition, counsel should make every effort to place on the record the journalistic imperatives that require his client's disobedience. This may avoid the enforcing court from classifying the contempt as criminal and imposing punishment that cannot be avoided. If the enforcing court does classify the contumacious behavior as criminal the only comforting note from the newsperson's viewpoint is the unlikelihood of incarceration for more than six months because of the burden on the judicial system of granting the newsperson a full-scale jury trial.

If the disobedience does not challenge the court's authority (and its manhood or womanhood), chances are enhanced that the court will view a continuing refusal to comply as civil contempt for which sanctions are imposed only to coerce compliance and to protect the private interests of those who initiated the subpoena. Beside avoiding criminal conviction and punishment, civil contempt has the advantages of allowing the newsperson to purge himself of contempt and requiring the subpoenaing party rather than the court to initiate the contempt proceeding[19] and to establish by clear and convincing evidence the contempt and the consequential monetary damage for which recompense is sought.[20]

C. Sanctions Alternative to Incarceration for Contempt

For numerous reasons including statutory prohibition in at least one jurisdiction against jailing newspersons for contempt,[21] the intransigence of many newspersons who are actually jailed for contempt[22] and the substantial number of cases in which the subpoenaed newsperson or media organization is a party to the litigation,[23] courts are shifting their tactics and choosing sanctions alternative to contempt in an effort to enforce subpoenas.[24]

---

17. See AGENTS OF DISCOVERY 6–11 (Reporters Committee for Freedom of the Press 1991).

18. Id. at 10.

19. See In re Magwood, 785 F.2d 1077, 1081 n. 9, 251 U.S. App. D.C. 389, 393 n. 9 (D.C.Cir.1986); CHARLES A. WRIGHT & ARTHUR R. MILLER, FEDERAL PRACTICE AND PROCEDURE § 2960 at 587 (1973).

20. See, e.g., In re Weiss, 703 F.2d 653, 662 (2d Cir.1983); Palmigiano v. Garrahy, 448 F.Supp. 659, 670–671 (D.R.I.1978) (thorough review of rules of procedure to be employed in civil contempt proceedings); Yalkowsky v. Yalkowsky, 93 A.D.2d 834, 834–835, 461 N.Y.S.2d 54, 55 (1983); see

also In re Kave, 760 F.2d 343, 351 (1st Cir.1985).

21. See N.Y. Civil Rights Law § 79–h(b) (McKinney Supp. 1992).

22. See e.g., Farr v. Superior Court, 22 Cal.App.3d 60, 99 Cal.Rptr. 342 (1971); Farr v. Pitchess, 522 F.2d 464 (9th Cir. 1975), cert. denied, 427 U.S. 912, 96 S.Ct. 3200, 49 L.Ed.2d 1203 (1976).

23. See AGENTS OF DISCOVERY 7 (Reporters Committee for Freedom of the Press 1991).

24. For a discussion of a number of alternative sanctions, see Dan B. Dobbs, Contempt of Court: A Survey, 56 Corn. L. Rev. 183, 278–282 (1971).

One tactic utilized in libel and invasion of privacy actions against newspapers and their employees when they refuse to disclose sources for their offending stories is for the courts to presume that such sources do not in fact exist. Such presumption would, for instance, aid public figure plaintiffs in establishing actual malice as required by *New York Times Co. v. Sullivan*[25] and *Time, Inc. v. Hill*[26] and private figure plaintiffs in making the showing of negligence on the part of media defendants as required in most jurisdictions following the ruling in *Gertz v. Robert Welch*.[27]

Another tactic employed by the courts to force compliance by defendant newspersons with subpoenas is to strike their pleadings and to enter default judgments for plaintiffs. Because this device raises serious questions of deprivation of due process, courts must be very careful in employing it.[28] The risk of reversal of court orders striking defenses and entering default judgments against media defendants is illustrated by the New York Court of Appeals decision in *Oak Beach Inn Corp. v. Babylon Beacon, Inc.*[29] There a small weekly newspaper published, without public attribution, an allegedly libelous letter to the editor and was sued by the subject of that letter. Plaintiffs served a show cause order demanding that defendants be compelled to disclose "the name and last known address of the writer or writers" of the letter. After unsuccessfully opposing the show cause order, defendants refused to comply with the order and plaintiffs moved to have them held in contempt and in the alternative to strike their answer and have default judgment entered against them. Plaintiffs argued that the information sought went to the heart of their case, relating to the necessary element of malice. In response defendants urged that there was no need for such drastic remedy because they did not intend to make "affirmative use" of the anonymous letter writer in defending the action.

The trial court held first that the remedy of contempt was barred by New York's shield statute[30] but, relying on New York's civil procedure law, the court ordered that defendants' answer be stricken and that plaintiffs be permitted to move for summary judgment or other appropriate relief if defendants did not make the actual letter available for inspection within fifteen days. The Appellate Division reversed and on appeal the Court of Appeals affirmed.

25. 376 U.S. 254, 84 S.Ct. 710, 11 L.Ed.2d 686 (1964).

26. 385 U.S. 374, 87 S.Ct. 534, 17 L.Ed.2d 456 (1967).

27. 418 U.S. 323, 94 S.Ct. 2997, 41 L.Ed.2d 789 (1974); *see, e.g.,* DeRoburt v. Gannett Co., 507 F.Supp. 880 (D.Haw. 1981); Caldero v. Tribune Pub. Co., 98 Idaho 288, 562 P.2d 791 (1977); Downing v. Monitor Pub. Co., 120 N.H. 383, 415 A.2d 683 (1980); Greenberg v. CBS, Inc. 69 A.D.2d 693, 419 N.Y.S.2d 988 (1979).

28. *See* Sierra Life Ins. Co. v. Magic Valley Newspapers, Inc. 101 Idaho 795, 623 P.2d 103 (1980); Dan B. Dobbs, *Contempt of Court: A Survey*, 56 Corn. L. Rev. 183, 279 (1971); *see also* Oak Beach Inn. Corp. v. Babylon Beacon, Inc. 62 N.Y.2d 158, 476 N.Y.S.2d 269, 464 N.E.2d 967 (1984).

29. 62 N.Y.2d 158, 476 N.Y.S.2d 269, 464 N.E.2d 967 (1984).

30. N.Y. Civil Rights Law § 79–h(b) (McKinney Supp. 1992).

New York's highest court first held that the sanction of contempt was barred by the plain language of the New York Civil Rights Law. Nor did the court permit imposition of the alternate sanction of striking defendants' answer because such action was draconian and lesser actions could have been taken by the trial court to achieve defendants' compliance or otherwise to aid the plaintiff. The court stated that orders could be entered prohibiting the noncomplying party from supporting or opposing specific claims, or introducing evidence on a particular issue. Putting a finer point on it, the court noted that the defendant publication had agreed to accept just such a limitation on its defense when it stated its willingness to defend the allegation of malice by relying on its own independent investigation and by not relying on the author of the letter.[31] In such a situation, "[a] newspaper should not be required to accept substantial financial loss as the price for continuing to honor a commitment to maintain the confidentiality of one of its sources."[32]

Obviously the willingness of the defendants to limit their defense here played a major role in the court's rejection of the order striking their answer entirely. Counsel for news media should consider this tactic showing good faith in litigation when confronted with similar situations. It should also be noted that the court's decision in *Oak Beach Inn Corp.* is particularly favorable to media defendants because, unlike in other jurisdictions, the alternative route of seeking a contempt citation was not available to plaintiffs. Even with this consideration present the New York Court of Appeals still refused to permit the striking of the answer.

It should be noted that in a jurisdiction that bars contempt citations against newspersons or news organizations when they refuse to disclose confidential news sources or information, newspersons and news organizations are effectively beyond the reach of any sanction if they are not parties to the civil litigation involved.[33] Therefore, counsel for plaintiffs should always consider the possibility of joining in their actions newspersons or organizations likely possessing relevant evidence.

7.12 Newsroom Searches and Seizures

A. Introduction

Searches for and seizures of material by law enforcement officers in the newsrooms of the nation have been rare in our history. One reason for this is that until 1967 it was thought that searches for and seizures of "mere evidence" of criminal activity, as opposed to the instrumentalities, fruits or contraband of crime, were not permitted by the fourth amendment to the Constitution.[1] In that year the Supreme Court held in *Warden v. Hayden,*[2] that whatever validity the distinction might once have had, it was no longer acceptable in contemporary society. Before

---

31. Oak Beach Inn Corp., 62 N.Y.2d at 167, 476 N.Y.S.2d at 273, 464 N.E.2d at 971.

32. *Id.*

33. *Id.* (by necessary implication).

1. *See* Warden v. Hayden, 387 U.S. 294, 300–301, 87 S.Ct. 1642, 1646–1647, 18 L.Ed.2d 782, 788 (1967).

2. 387 U.S. 294, 87 S.Ct. 1642, 18 L.Ed.2d 782 (1967).

Warden, prosecutors seeking evidence of crimes which they believed could be found in the desks, file drawers and computers of newsrooms simply subpoenaed some person in authority to bring the evidence to the grand jury or criminal trial. After 1967 it became clearly constitutional to obtain search warrants to look for and seize evidence of criminal activity in the hands of third parties such as news organizations not themselves involved in the activity.

A decade after *Warden*, the Santa Clara County California District Attorney took advantage of the decision to obtain a warrant to search for and seize evidence in the offices of the *Stanford Daily* so that it might be used against persons who had injured police officers and sheriffs deputies trying to restore order on the Stanford University campus after a riot had broken out. By his action the district attorney precipitated a major confrontation between the police power of the state and First Amendment protection of a free press.

B. The Zurcher Case

In *Zurcher v. Stanford Daily*,[3] the district attorney for the county encompassing Stanford University obtained a search warrant issued on a judge's finding of probable cause to believe that the *Stanford Daily*, the student newspaper, possessed photographs and negatives revealing the identity of demonstrators who had assaulted and injured several peace officers who were attempting to quell a riot at University Hospital. Two days after the riot, the campus newspaper had come out with a special edition devoted to the hospital protest and the violent clash between demonstrators and police that ensued. The published photographs carried the cut line of a Daily staff member and indicated that he had been located at a point where he could have photographed the actual assault and the assailants. The affidavit filed in support of the application for the warrant contained no allegation or indication that members of the *Daily* staff were in any way involved in unlawful acts at the hospital.

The search pursuant to the warrant covered the *Daily's* photographic laboratories, filing cabinets, desks and waste baskets but locked drawers and rooms were not opened. The search turned up only the photographs that had already been published in the special edition and no materials were removed from the paper's offices. Thereafter, the paper and certain staff members sought a judicial declaration that the search had deprived them of their constitutional rights under the First and Fourteenth Amendments and an injunction against further searches. The United States District Court for the Northern District of California denied the request for an injunction but, on the newspaper's motion for summary judgment, granted declaratory relief. The United States Court of Appeals for the Ninth Circuit affirmed the judgment of the District Court.

On certiorari, the respondent newspaper argued that such searches of newspaper offices for evidence of crimes committed by others seriously

3. 436 U.S. 547, 98 S.Ct. 1970, 56 L.Ed.2d 525 (1978).

threatened the ability of the press to gather, analyze and disseminate news thereby infringing the protections guaranteed by the First Amendment. More specifically, the newspaper argued first that searches would be physically disruptive to such an extent that timely publication of news would be impeded. Second, the paper contended that confidential sources of information would dry up and the press would lose opportunities to cover events because of participants' fear that press files would be reachable by law enforcement authorities. Third, the argument was made that reporters will be deterred from recording and preserving for future use their recollections of events if such information is subject to seizure. Fourth, the paper contended that searches would disclose internal editorial deliberations. Finally, the argument was advanced that the press would resort to self-censorship to conceal possession of sensitive information of potential interest to the police.[4]

By a vote of 6 to 3, the Court, in an opinion by Justice White, rejected all of these arguments, holding that properly issued and executed search warrants directed against news organizations, did not contravene the First Amendment's guarantees. Justice White reasoned that the drafters of the Bill of Rights had not forbidden under the Fourth Amendment search warrants directed to the press nor required special showings that subpoenas would be impractical before such warrants could be issued to search the premises of news organizations or newspersons. Nor did the drafters insist that if a press organization was named in a search warrant, the police would first have to demonstrate the organization's complicity in the alleged offense being investigated.[5] White then went on to state the majority's faith that issuing magistrates could guard against searches of the type, scope and intrusiveness that would actually interfere with the timely publication of a newspaper or intrude into or deter normal editorial and publication decisions.[6]

Warming to the subject of abuse of the search warrant process as directed toward the news media, Justice White said, "The fact is that respondents and *amici* have pointed to only a very few instances in the entire United States since 1971 involving the issuance of warrants for searches of newspaper premises. This reality hardly suggests abuse; and if abuse occurs, there will be time enough to deal with it."[7]

C. *Practical Effect of Zurcher*

While Justice White's preference in principle for fourth amendment procedure and the police power of the state over First Amendment protection for the news media here is subject to debate, his skepticism as to the practical effect of search warrants on the operation of the news media is supported by experience. A diligent search since *Zurcher* was decided reveals only three reported cases in which search warrants have

---

4. *Id.* at 563–564, 98 S. Ct. at 1980–1981, 56 L. Ed. 2d at 540.

5. *Id.* at 565, 98 S. Ct. at 1981, 56 L. Ed. 2d at 541.

6. *Id.* at 566, 98 S. Ct. at 1982, 56 L. Ed. 2d at 542.

7. *Id.*

been sought directed to news or information media[8] or in which police officers have actually seized material in the hands of the press.[9] Some other instances of searches and seizures involving the news media have been noted since *Zurcher*[10] but the number does not appear to be large.[11]

The obligations and rights of newspersons when confronted in those rare cases with a subpoena are clear. News personnel, like other citizens, may not hinder or obstruct the search.[12] On the other hand, they are not legally required to assist with it either.[13] Newspersons are entitled to reinforce the general reluctance of law enforcement officials to seek search warrants directed to the news media by quietly recording the entire newsroom search and seizure photographically and publishing the photographs in the next edition or on the next newscast. It is safe to say that law enforcement officers do not like to be photographed in this manner and most elected prosecutors would prefer to avoid this sort of publicity. Newspersons and news organizations may also sue the law enforcement officials involved in such actions for damages for violations of federal or state law and for the return of seized material.[14]

D. Newsroom Privacy Protection Acts

One reason for the dearth of search warrants directed to news media is the enactment of privacy protection legislation. Since *Zurcher* held only that the issuance of search warrants directed to the news media were constitutionally permissible, legislation controlling the issuance of such search warrants and searches and seizures made thereunder would be appropriate.[15] Following strong condemnation of the Supreme Court's ruling by nearly all segments of the press[16] as well as numerous legal commentators.[17] the Congress enacted the Privacy Protection Act of 1980,[18] substantially restricting the circumstances in which a newsroom

---

8. *See In re* Application of KMOT–TV, 7 Med. L. Rptr. 1443 (N.D.Dist.1981) (search warrant for video tape held by television station quashed).

9. Steve Jackson Games, Inc. v. United States Secret Service, 816 F.Supp. 432 (W.D.Tex.1993) *aff'd* 36 F.3d 457 (5th Cir. 1994) (warranted seizure of hardware and software from an information disseminating computer bulletin board); Minneapolis Star and Tribune Co. v. United States, 713 F.Supp. 1308 (D.Minn.1989) (warrantless seizure of reporters' photographic equipment, film and tape by the FBI at the scene of a drug "bust").

10. *See* NEWS MEDIA & THE LAW 4–5 (Reporters Committee for Freedom of the Press, Fall 1988).

11. *Id*. at 6.

12. *See* NEWS MEDIA & THE LAW 6 (Reporters Committee for Freedom of the Press, Fall 1988); *see also* WAYNE R. LAFAVE, SEARCH AND SEIZURE § 4.8(c) (1987).

13. *See* NEWS MEDIA & THE LAW 6 (Reporters Committee for Freedom of the Press, Fall 1988).

14. *See e.g.*, Minneapolis Star and Tribune Co. v. United States, 713 F.Supp. 1308 (D.Minn.1989); 42 U.S.C.A. § 2000 aa–6(f) (West 1981); *see also* N. J. Stat. Ann. § 2 A:84A–21.9 (West Supp. 1993); Or. Rev. Stat. § 44.520 (2)(1989).

15. *See* Zurcher v. Stanford Daily, 436 U.S. 547, 567, 98 S.Ct. 1970, 1983, 56 L.Ed.2d 525, 542 (1978).

16. *See, e.g.*, Susan K. Erburu, Note, *Zurcher v. Stanford Daily: The Legislative Debate*, 17 Harv. J. Legis. 152, 162 (1980).

17. *See, e.g.*, Jose M. Sariego, Note, *The Privacy Protection Act of 1980: Curbing Unrestricted Third–Party Searches in the Wake of* Zurcher v. Stanford Daily, 14 U. Mich. J. L. Ref. 519, 524 (1981).

18. Pub. L. No. 96–440, 94 Stat. 1879 (1980) *codified at* 42 U.S.C.A. § 2000aa

search and seizure may legally occur.

Part A of the statute divides evidence subject to search warrant into two categories: (1) work product materials possessed by those reasonably believed to have a purpose to communicate to the public generally;[19] and (2) all other documentary materials possessed by this same class of persons.[20] The act makes it unlawful for federal *and* state government officers or employees to search for or seize work product materials in the first category. But there are two exceptions to this. The first is where the person holding such materials has committed the criminal offense to which the sought after materials relate *unless* the offense consists simply of the receipt, possession, communication or withholding of the materials themselves or the information contained therein.[21] The second exception permitting the search for and seizure of work product involves cases in which there is reason to believe that the immediate seizure of such work product is necessary to prevent the death of or serious bodily injury to a human being.[22]

The federal act also makes it unlawful for federal *and* state government officers or employees to search for or seize material in the second category except in four distinct situations.[23] The first two exceptions are exactly the same as the exceptions for the first category of material.[24] The two additional exceptional situations permitting lawful searches and seizures of second category material in the hands of newspersons and certain others are (1) that reason exists to believe that the giving of notice pursuant to a subpoena duces tecum would result in the destruc-

(West 1981). This legislation has been much commented upon. *See* Birch Bayh, *Congressional Response to* Zurcher v. Stanford Daily, 13 Ind. L. Rev. 835 (1980) (providing substantial legal background for and legislative history of the Privacy Protection Act of 1980); Susan K. Erburuu, Note, Zurcher v. Stanford Daily: *The Legislative Debate*, 17 Harv. J. Legis. 152 (1980); Jose M. Sariego, Note, *The Privacy Protection Act of 1980: Curbing Unrestricted Third–Party Searches in the Wake of* Zurcher v. Stanford Daily, 14 U. Mich. J. L. Ref. 519 (1981); Stephanie Ann Christie, Note, *Media Searches after* Zurcher v. Stanford Daily: *A Statutory Approach*, 20 Santa Clara L. Rev. 491, 504–509 (1980); *see also* Alan A. Sant'Angelo, Note, *Protecting The Press from* Stanford Daily: *A Federal Newsman's Work Product Privilege from Search and Seizure*, 36 Wash. & Lee L. Rev. 1177, 1187–1194 (1979).

19. 42 U.S.C.A. § 2000aa (a) (West 1981).

20. *Id.* at § 2000aa (b).

21. *Id.* at § 2000aa (a)(1). There is a qualification to the exception. Work product may be searched for and seized though the possessor's crime consists of the receipt, possession, communication or withholding of work product information if that information relates to the national defense, classified information, certain restricted data "or if the offense involves the production, possession, receipt, mailing, sale, distribution, shipment, or transportation of child pornography, the sexual exploitation of children, or the sale or purchase of children under section 2251, 2251A, 2252 or 2252A of title 18, United States Code ..." This latter qualification was added as an amendment to the Privacy Protection Act by the Child Pornography Prevention Act of 1996, P.L. 104–208 § 121(6)(1), 110 Stat. 3009, 3030–3031 (1996) *codified at* 42 U.S.C.A. 2000aa, as amended (West 1996).

22. *Id.*

23. *Id.* at § 2000aa (b).

24. *Id.* at § 2000aa (b)(1), (2), as amended by the Child Pornography Prevention Act of 1996, Pub.L. 104–208, § 121(6)(2), 110 Stat. 3009, 3031 (1996) *codified at* 42 U.S.C.A. § 2000aa, as amended (West 1996). The language of the child pornography amendment here is the same as in § 121(6)(1), supra note 21.

tion, alteration or concealment of such materials[25] or (2) that such materials have not been produced in response to a court order directing compliance with a subpoena duces tecum and (a) all appellate remedies have been exhausted or (b) "there is reason to believe that the delay in an investigation or trial occasioned by further subpoena proceedings would threaten the interests of justice."[26] As to the quoted portion of the last exception, the person possessing the sought after material is afforded an opportunity under the Act to submit an affidavit setting forth the basis for his contention that the materials sought are not subject to seizure.[27]

Part B provides, among other things, for civil actions for damages for persons aggrieved by searches for and seizures of materials in violation of the act[28] and grants original jurisdiction of all such actions to the United States District Courts.[29] Remedies for aggrieved persons include recovery of actual damages but not less than liquidated damages of $1,000 and such reasonable attorneys' fees and other litigation costs reasonably incurred as the trial court may choose to award.[30] Violations of the act or the Attorney General's Guidelines under it[31] will also result in the imposition of administrative sanctions against the violating federal officer or employee.[32] But violation of the Guidelines may not be litigated and the courts may not entertain compliance or noncompliance as the basis for suppression or exclusion of the evidence obtained.[33] Some states have chosen not to emulate the federal government by enacting their own acts to complement the federal legislation.[34]

25. *Id.* at § 2000aa (b)(3).

26. *Id.* at § 2000aa (b)(4).

27. *Id.* at § 2000aa (c).

"(c) In the event a search warrant is sought pursuant to paragraph (4) (B) of subsection (b) of this section, the person possessing the materials shall be afforded adequate opportunity to submit an affidavit setting forth the basis for any contention that the materials sought are not subject to seizure."

28. *Id.* at § 2000aa–6(a).

"(a) A person aggrieved by a search for or seizure of materials in violation of this chapter shall have a civil cause of action for damages for such search or seizure–

(1) against the United States, against a State which has waived it sovereign immunity under the Constitution to a claim for damages resulting from a violation of this chapter, or against any other governmental unit, all of which shall be liable for violations of this chapter by their officers or employees while acting within the scope or under color of their office or employment; and

(2) against an officer or employee of a State who has violated this chapter

while acting within the scope or under color of his office or employment, if such State has not waived its sovereign immunity as provided in paragraph (1)."

29. *Id.* at § 2000aa–6(h).

30. *Id.* at §§ 2000aa–11 through 2000aa–12.

31. *Id.* at § 2000aa–6(f); *see* Minneapolis Star and Tribune Co. v. United States, 713 F.Supp. 1308 (D.Minn.1989).

32. *Id.* at § 2000aa–6(g); 28 C.F.R. § 59.6 (1993).

33. *Id.* at § 2000aa–12.

34. *See* Colo. Rev. Stat. §§ 13–90–119 and 24–72.5–106 (Supp. 1993) ("Nothing in this article shall preclude the issuance of a search warrant pursuant to the federal "Privacy Protection Act of 1980" . . .); Ill. Rev. Stat. ch. 38, par. 108–3 (Smith–Hurd Supp. 1988) [text of Illinois statute in Practitioner's Edition only]. N.J. Stat. Ann. § 2A:84A–21.9 (West Supp. 1990) [text of New Jersey statutes in Practioner's Edition only]. N. J. Stat. Ann. § 2A:84A–21.12(b) (West Supp. 1993); Or. Rev. Stat. § 44.520 (1989) ("(2) No papers, effects or work premises of a person connected with, em-

Thus far, there have been only two reported cases of federal or state officials actually having been adjudicated as violating the Privacy protection act. In *Steve Jackson Games, Inc v. United States Secret Service*,[35] an operator of a computer bulletin board and some of its consumers brought action against the Secret Service after its agents, pursuant to search warrant, and unaware of the Privacy Protection Act, raided the corporation, an entity having as its purpose the dissemination to the public of a book, *Gurps Cyberpunk*, or similar forms of public communication, and, seized computer equipment, software and documents. A proper investigation of the company by the Secret Service agent in charge before the issuance of the warrant would have disclosed that it was such a disseminator and protected by the act. And even after the Secret Service was specifically advised by company personnel of facts that put its agents on notice of their probable violations of the statute, the agents continued to search for and seize the corporation's work product pursuant to the warrant. Under these facts, the United States District Court had no trouble holding that the federal agents involved had violated the act and that the corporation was entitled to monetary damages against the government under the act's Part B.[36]

The only other case is *Minneapolis Star and Tribune Co.v. United States*,[37] in which an FBI agent seized without warrant photographic equipment at the scene of a drug bust from a newspaper reporter and a television station reporter who were photographing and videotaping the event. The agent feared the publication of the photos and videotape would reveal the identities of the government's undercover agents. The Office of the United States Attorney returned the equipment within three hours of the seizure.[38] Because of the lack of actual damages, the trial court ordered the award of liquidated damages to each of the reporters.[39]

---

ployed by or engaged in any medium of communication to the public shall be subject to a search by a legislative, executive or judicial officer or body, or any other authority having power to compel the production of evidence, by search warrant or otherwise. The provisions of this subsection, however, shall not apply where probable cause exists to believe that the person has committed, is committing or is about to commit a crime.").

The above state statutory provisions relating to searches and seizures of material in the hands of newspersons are all of recent vintage and additional states might be expected to enact such legislation in the future.

35. 816 F.Supp. 432 (W.D.Tex.1993), *aff'd* 36 F.3d 457 (5th Cir.1994).

36. 42 U.S.C.A. § 2000aa–6(f) (West 1981).

37. 713 F.Supp. 1308 (D.Minn.1989)

38. *Id.* at 1310. A third decision, in which a county prosecutor was found to have violated the act was reversed and remanded to determine whether she, in fact, "directed supervised, or otherwise engaged in the execution of the warrant to such an extent that a finding can be made that she 'searched for or seized'" a videotape in the possession of a television station operator. Citicasters v. McCaskill, 883 F.Supp. 1282 (W.D.Mo.1995), *rev'd* 89 F.3d 1350 (8th Cir. 1996).

39. 713 F. Supp. at 1310.

7.13　Rights and Responsibilities Under Business Laws Applicable to the Operation of News Organizations

A. *Introduction*

It is beyond argument today that organizations and individuals engaged in the business of gathering and disseminating news are not immunized by the First Amendment against non-discriminatory application of laws applicable to other businesses generally. The Supreme Court stated this idea succinctly in *Associated Press v. NLRB*.[1] "The business of the Associated Press is not immune from regulation because it is an agency of the press. The publisher of a newspaper has no special immunity from the application of general laws. He has no special privilege to invade the rights and liberties of others."[2] Thus, labor laws, antitrust laws, tax laws and even zoning laws may be applied to news organizations if done so in an equitable and even-handed manner unrelated to the content of what is published.

B. *Labor Laws*

1. News Organizations' Claims of Immunity Against Government Enforcement

In *Associated Press v. NLRB*, the Associated Press argued that in firing a news editor for engaging in union activity, it was exempt under the First Amendment from application of the National Labor Relations Act generally and Section 7[3] specifically which prohibited such employer conduct. The act seeks to confer certain rights on, among others, reporters and other non-management newspersons in their relations with the owners and managers of the news organizations which employ them. Correlatively, owners, publishers and management level editors have the legal responsibility to respect those statutory rights.

AP's position was that as a cooperative newgatherer and distributor it had to be wholly free from partisan activity and bias if it was to fulfill its responsibilities to its member newspapers to provide unslanted news. To insure an impartial news operation, the First Amendment protected management's right to hire and fire anyone who might inject a point of view into the news process as, for instance, a pro union slant. Therefore, any regulation protective of union activities or the right of employees to bargain collectively violated the free press guarantee of the First Amendment. The Supreme Court in a 5 to 4 decision rejected the idea that the statute in question had any relation whatsoever to the impartial distribution of news and held that the National Labor Relations Act was one of general application to labor relations in the country and that the First Amendment did not immunize the press from such non-discriminatory

1.　301 U.S. 103, 57 S.Ct. 650, 81 L.Ed. 953 (1937).

2.　*Id*. at 132–133, 57 S. Ct. at 656, 81 L. Ed. at 961; *see* Branzburg v. Hayes, 408 U.S. 665, 682–683, 92 S.Ct. 2646, 2657, 33 L.Ed.2d 626, 640 (1972).

3.　29 U.S.C.A. § 157 (West 1993).

governmental regulation of labor-management relations in the news business.[4]

The Court has never receded from this view of general nondiscriminatory regulation of the press.[5] In *Mabee v. White Plains Publishing Co.*,[6] and *Oklahoma Press Publishing Co. v. Walling*,[7] decided the same day, the Court upheld the constitutionality of applying to news organizations specific portions of the Fair Labor Standards Act[8] which, *inter alia*, sets standards as to wages and hours of workers.

In *Mabee*, the Court took up the question of what constituted discriminatory application of federal labor law regulation. There, the respondent publisher of a daily newspaper whose employees might be covered by all provisions of the Fair Labor Standards Act claimed the Act unconstitutionally discriminated against daily newspapers because it then exempted from certain coverage employees of weekly or semiweekly newspapers with a circulation of less than 3,000 copies where the major portion of the circulation is within the county in which the newspaper is printed and published.[9] The respondent publisher argued that volume of circulation, frequency of issue and area of distribution were improper bases of classification and therefore the act laid a discriminatory burden on the press in violation of the First Amendment. In rejecting this argument the Court held that the exemption was not a deliberate and calculated device to penalize a certain group of newspapers but was rather an attempt to put the small weeklies and semiweeklies more on a par with other small town enterprises.[10] Thus, discrimination against the news media in the application of the labor laws (and all other regulation) was to be determined, at least in part, by the motive behind the regulation.[11]

Having lost the war against nondiscriminatory labor law regulation, news organizations have taken to finding exemptions in the law applicable to their operations. A recent example of this is the effort to characterize employees involved in the editorial process as management executives or professionals not entitled to coverage under the National Labor Relations Act on the Fair Labor Standards Act.[12]

4. 301 U.S. at 132–133, 57 S. Ct. at 656, 81 L. Ed. at 961.

5. *See e.g.*, Cohen v. Cowles Media Co., 501 U.S. 663, 668–70, 111 S.Ct. 2513, 2518–2519, 115 L.Ed.2d 586, 597 (1991); Minneapolis Star & Tribune Co. v. Minnesota Com'r of Revenue, 460 U.S. 575, 581, 103 S.Ct. 1365, 1369–1370, 75 L.Ed.2d 295, 302 (1983).

6. 327 U.S. 178, 66 S.Ct. 511, 90 L.Ed. 607 (1946).

7. 327 U.S. 186, 66 S.Ct. 494, 90 L.Ed. 614 (1946).

8. 29 U.S.C.A. § 201, *et seq.* (West 1978).

9. Pub. L. 75–718, 52 Stat. 1067 (1938). This exemption has since been amended to

exempt from certain of its provisions employees of weekly, semiweekly and daily newspapers with a circulation of less than 4,000 if the major part of which is within the county of publication or counties contiguous thereto. 29 U.S.C.A. § 213 (a)(8) (West Supp. 1991).

10. 327 U.S. 178, 184, 66 S.Ct. 511, 514, 90 L.Ed. 607 613 (1946).

11. *See* Grosjean v. American Press Co., 297 U.S. 233, 250, 56 S.Ct. 444, 449, 80 L.Ed. 660, 668–669 (1936).

12. *See* Reich v. Gateway Press, 13 F.3d 685, 697–698 (3d Cir.1994) (reporters on a local weekly newspaper); Dalheim v. KDFW–TV, 918 F.2d 1220, 1228–1232 (5th Cir.1990) (general assignment reporters

2.*　*Employee Claims of Immunity Vis a Vis Union Organizations*

3.*　*Union Claims of Immunity Vis a Vis its Members*

C.　Antitrust Laws

1.　*Application of Sherman Antitrust Act and Clayton Act to News Media Organizations*

In order to preserve a free enterprise economy[13] the Congress has enacted antitrust legislation regulating the competitive operation of business entities.[14] This legislation is said to further First Amendment interests when applied to news organizations by encouraging a multiplicity of competing channels of news and information.[15]

In *Associated Press v. United States*,[16] the news cooperative restricted its membership by permitting existing members to insist on more difficult requirements of admission for newspapers that were competitors, requirements that made entry and access to AP gathered news extremely difficult if not impossible. In answer to the government's action to enjoin such allegedly anticompetitive practice, AP claimed, *inter alia*, that application of the Sherman Act to it violated guarantees afforded by the First Amendment to itself and its members.

In affirming the District Court order enjoining AP, the Supreme Court held news organizations subject to the antitrust laws and said, "it would be strange indeed ... if the grave concern for freedom of the press which prompted adoption of the First Amendment should be read as a command that the government was without power to protect that freedom.... Surely a command that the government itself shall not impede the free flow of ideas does not afford non-governmental combinations a refuge if they impose restraints upon that constitutionally guaranteed freedom."[17]

and producers); Wichita Eagle & Beacon Pub. Co. Inc. v. NLRB, 480 F.2d 52 (10th Cir.1973), cert. denied, 416 U.S. 982, 94 S. Ct. 2383, 40 L.Ed.2d 758 (1974) (editorial writer); Sherwood v. Washington Post, 677 F.Supp. 9 (D.D.C.1988), *rev'd* 871 F.2d 1144, 276 U.S. App. D.C. 404 (D.C.Cir. 1989); (reporters and non-executive editors); The Express–News Corporation and San Antonio Typographical Union #172 a/w International Typographical Union AFL–CIO, 223 NLRB 627 at 628 (1976) (typographical workers). To date this effort has been largely unsuccessful except where the employee formulates editorial policy. *See* Wichita Eagle & Beacon Pub. Co., *supra*.

** Text of this subsection published in Modern Communication Law, Practitioner's Edition, Vol. 2 only.

13. *See e.g.*, Associated Press v. United States, 326 U.S. 1, 14 n. 12, 65 S.Ct. 1416, 1421, n. 12, 89 L.Ed. 2013, 2027 n. 12 (1945); Paramount Famous Lasky Corp. v.

United States, 282 U.S. 30, 42, 51 S.Ct. 42, 44, 75 L.Ed. 145, 150 (1930); United States v. Colgate & Co., 250 U.S. 300, 307, 39 S.Ct. 465, 468, 63 L.Ed. 992, 997 (1919).

14. Sherman Antitrust Act §§ 1, 2, as amended, 15 U.S.C.A. §§ 1, 2 (West Supp. 1991); Clayton Act § 7, as amended, 15 U.S.C.A. § 18 (West Supp. 1991).

15. *See* Citizen Pub. Co. v. United States, 394 U.S. 131, 139–140, 89 S.Ct. 927, 931, 22 L.Ed.2d 148, 157 (1969), (quoting Associated Press v. United States 326 U.S. 1, 20, 65 S.Ct. 1416, 1424, 89 L.Ed. 2013, 2030 (1945)); United States v. Associated Press, 52 F.Supp. 362, 372 (S.D.N.Y.1943) (same case below; opinion by Judge Learned Hand).

16. 326 U.S. 1, 65 S.Ct. 1416, 89 L.Ed. 2013 (1945).

17. *Id.* at 20, 65 S. Ct. at 1424, 89 L. Ed. at 2030. Following the *AP* case the antitrust laws have been applied to the

Following the decision in *Associated Press*, antitrust actions (often unsuccessful) were brought against news organizations in a number of contexts for claimed violations of antitrust statutes including advertising tying arrangements,[18] use of undue economic power to expand circulation and advertising markets,[19] monopolization of newspaper distribution,[20] monopolization of the newspaper business itself through merger or acquisition,[21] refusal to accept advertising for anticompetitive reasons[22] and the entering into joint operating agreements providing for price fixing, profit pooling and division of the market.[23]

2. Statutory Exemption of Newspaper Organizations from Obligations Under the General Antitrust Laws

Stung by the decision in *Citizen Publishing Co.,* the newspaper industry went to the Nixon Administration and the Congress to restore the JOA *status quo ante Citizen*. In fact, the industry's lobbying was so successful that the resulting Newspaper Preservation Act of 1970 (NPA)[24] permits the arrangements disapproved in *Citizen* under an even weaker "failing newspaper" standard. This statutory standard requires a showing only that a daily or weekly newspaper "regardless of its ownership or affiliations, is in *probable* danger of financial failure."[25] (Italics supplied.)

The Congress promulgated this weaker standard because of the belief expressed in its declaration of policy that this standard would

---

other news and entertainment media. *See, e.g.,* National Collegiate Athletic Association v. Board of Regents, 468 U.S. 85, 104 S.Ct. 2948, 82 L.Ed.2d 70 (1984) (broadcasting); Broadcast Music, Inc. v. Columbia Broadcasting System, 441 U.S. 1, 99 S.Ct. 1551, 60 L.Ed.2d 1 (1979) (recording industry); United States v. Paramount Pictures, Inc. 334 U.S. 131, 68 S.Ct. 915, 92 L.Ed. 1260 (1948) (motion pictures); Crimpers Promotions, Inc. v. Home Box Office, Inc., 554 F.Supp. 838 (S.D.N.Y.1982) *aff'd* 724 F.2d 290 (2d Cir.1983), cert. denied, 467 U.S. 1252, 104 S.Ct. 3536, 82 L.Ed.2d 841 (1984) (cable television); Harriet L. Moses, *Antitrust and the Media*, 1984 Ann. Surv. Am. L. 723 (various media); Monroe E. Price & Mark S. Nadel, *Antitrust Issues in the News Video Media*, 3 Cardozo Arts & Ent. L.J. 27 (1984) (cable and satellite transmission). The antitrust laws obviously apply to the communications common carrier industry as well. *See, e.g.,* United States v. American Tel. & Tel. Co., 552 F.Supp. 131 (D.D.C.1982) (home of the modified final judgment (MFJ) breaking up the AT & T monopoly); Symposium: *The Divestiture of American Telephone & Telegraph Company,* 9 Comm/Ent 1 (1986).

18. *See* Times–Picayune v. United States, 345 U.S. 594, 73 S.Ct. 872, 97 L.Ed. 1277 (1953).

19. *See, e.g.,* Sun Newspapers, Inc. v. Omaha World–Herald Co., 713 F.2d 428 (8th Cir.1983) (metropolitan daily's expansion into suburban market).

20. *See, e.g.,* Auburn News Co. v. Providence Journal Co., 659 F.2d 273 (1st Cir. 1981), cert. denied, 455 U.S. 921, 102 S.Ct. 1277, 71 L.Ed.2d 461 (1982) (termination by newspaper of contracts with independent contractor distributors).

21. *See* United States v. Times Mirror Co. 274 F.Supp. 606 (C.D.Cal.1967), *aff'd without opinion* 390 U.S. 712, 88 S.Ct. 1411, 20 L.Ed.2d 252 (1968) (Times Mirror Co. ordered to divest itself of competing newspaper acquired by purchase).

22. *See* Lorain Journal Co. v. United States, 342 U.S. 143, 72 S.Ct. 181, 96 L.Ed. 162 (1951) (newspaper publishing company enjoined from refusing advertising from businesses also advertising on a local radio station).

23. *See* Citizen Pub. Co. v. United States, 394 U.S. 131, 89 S.Ct. 927, 22 L.Ed.2d 148 (1969).

24. Pub. L. 91–353, 84 Stat. 466 (1970), *codified at* 15 U.S.C.A. §§ 1801, *et seq.* (1982).

25. *Id.* § 1802(5).

serve the public interest in maintaining a newspaper press editorially and reportorially independent and competitive in all parts of the country.[26] Besides defining its operative terms,[27] the NPA ratified JOAs entered into before its effective date so long as not more than one of the newspapers involved was likely to remain or become a financially sound publication and so long as the terms of any renewal or amendment thereto are filed with the Department of Justice and amendments do not add any publications to the existing arrangement.[28]

As for JOAs entered into after the effective date of the act, exemption from the operation of the applicably antitrust statutes will not be granted unless prior written consent is received from the Attorney General of the United States.[29] Prior to granting such approval, the Attorney General must determine that not more than one of the newspapers involved is a nonfailing newspaper and that approval of the proposed arrangement would effectuate the policy and purpose of this chapter.[30] JOAs declared unlawful prior to the effective date of the NPA such as the one struck down in *Citizen Publishing Co.*[31] are permitted to be resurrected to the extent consistent with the act.[32] While exempting JOAs generally from the reach of the antitrust statutes if they are in conformity with its terms, the NPA makes clear that predatory pricing and practices designed to destroy competition are not so exempted.[33]

The constitutionality of this legislation has been upheld in the face of claims that the First Amendment rights of smaller newspapers competing with newspapers involved in an approved JOA are violated by the NPA's operation,[34] that its delegation of authority to the Attorney General is vague and overbroad in violation of the First Amendment,[35] and that it violated the right of competing newspapers generally to equal protection of the law[36] and, more specifically, because it discriminated invidiously in favor of papers publishing weekly or more often.[37]

D. Taxation

The First Amendment stands as a bulwark not only against the licensing and censorship of the news and information media but against

26. *Id.* § 1801.

27. *Id.* § 1802.

28. *Id.* § 1803(a); *see* Bay Guardian Co. v. Chronicle Pub. Co., 344 F.Supp. 1155, 1159 (N.D.Cal.1972).

29. *Id.* § 1803(b).

30. *Id.*

31. *See* Citizen Pub. Co. v. United States, 394 U.S. 131, 89 S.Ct. 927, 22 L.Ed.2d 148 (1969).

32. 15 U.S.C.A. § 1804(a) (West 1982); *see* Mark Fink, Note *The Newspaper Preservation Act of 1970: Help for the Needy or the Greedy?*, 1990 Det. C.L. Rev. 93, 100.

33. *Id.* § 1803(c).

34. *See* Committee for an Independent P–I v. Hearst Corp., 704 F.2d 467, 482–483,

(9th Cir.), cert. denied, 464 U.S. 892, 104 S.Ct. 236, 78 L.Ed.2d 228 (1983); Bay Guardian Co. v. Chronicle Pub. Co., 344 F.Supp. 1155, 1157–1158 (N.D.Cal.1972); *see also* Robbie Steel, *Joint Operating Agreements in the Newspaper Industry: A Threat to First Amendment Freedoms*, 138 U. Pa. L. Rev. 275 (1989).

35. *See* Committee for an Independent P–I, 704 F.2d 467 at 483 (9th Cir.), cert. denied 464 U.S. 892, 104 S.Ct. 236, 78 L.Ed.2d 228 (1983); Bay Guardian Co., 344 F.Supp. at 1159.

36. *See* Bay Guardian Co., 344 F.Supp. 1155.

37. *Id.*

any other activity of government that would unduly burden or destroy the media. The power to tax potentially involves the power to destroy[38] the media but there is little argument today that they are free from the obligation to support the operation of government through the payment of taxes.[39] The question is not whether taxes may be imposed but rather the manner of their imposition.

Unless government is prepared to disrupt society's entire economy through onerous general taxation (a self-defeating proposition at best), the media can only be targeted for retaliatory economic injury by singular and discriminatory tax laws. This is where First Amendment protection clearly comes into play. The task for the courts and particularly the Supreme Court is to determine when a tax law places or potentially places an unfair and unequal economic burden on news and information organizations.

The Supreme Court first confronted this problem in *Grosjean v. American Press Co.*[40] There the Huey Long administration through its subservient Louisiana legislature imposed a license tax on individuals or organizations engaged in the business of selling or charging for advertising in any newspaper, magazine or other publication in Louisiana having a circulation of more than 20,000 copies per week. This special tax of two percent of a publication's gross receipt was in addition to all other general taxes.

The Court, well aware of the Long administration's motive to silence and gain retribution against the larger and better financed daily papers in the state[41] which were opposing its populist policies, had no trouble striking down this legislation as violative of the First and Fourteenth Amendments. It saw the tax as a special burden on the press in two ways. First, its effect was to curtail the amount of revenue realized from advertising and second it had a direct tendency to restrict circulation.

Harkening back to the history surrounding the First Amendment, the Court found that one of the purposes of the drafters was to prevent

38. M'Culloch v. Maryland, 17 U.S. (4 Wheat.) 316, 427, 4 L.Ed. 579, 607 (1819) (per Marshall, C. J.).

39. *But see* Giragi v. Moore, 49 Ariz. 74, 64 P.2d 819, 822 (1937) (newspaper challenge to a general gross business income tax levy on First and Fourteenth Amendment grounds rejected); City of Corona v. Corona Daily Independent, 115 Cal.App.2d 382, 385, 252 P.2d 56, 59–60, cert. denied 346 U.S. 833, 74 S.Ct. 2, 98 L.Ed. 356 (1953) (newspaper challenge to a general business license tax rejected); Steinbeck v. Gerosa, 4 N.Y.2d 302, 311–316, 151 N.E.2d 170, 175–178, 175 N.Y.S.2d 1, 8–12, *appeal dismissed* 358 U.S. 39 79 S.Ct. 64, 3 L.Ed.2d 45 (1958) (novelist John Steinbeck's claim that as an author he was exempted by the First Amendment from paying New York's general business tax levied on revenues from the sale or licensing of rights to his literary works rejected).

40. 297 U.S. 233, 56 S.Ct. 444, 80 L.Ed. 660 (1936); *see, e.g.,* Randall P. Bezanson, *Political Agnosticism, Editorial Freedom and Government Neutrality Toward the Press: Observations on Minneapolis Star & Tribune Co. v. Minnesota Commissioner of Revenue,* 72 Iowa L. Rev. 1359 (1987); Todd F. Simon, *All the News That's Fit to Tax: First Amendment Limitations on State and Local Taxation of the Press,* 21 Wake Forest L. Rev. 59 (1985); David L. Medford, Note, Arkansas Writers' Project, Inc. v. Ragland: *Taxation of the Press,* 13 Okla. City U.L. Rev. 401 (1988).

41. *Id.* at 250, 56 S. Ct. at 449, 80 L.Ed. at 669.

suppression of a free press by burdensome special taxation.[42] The Louisiana tax was of the kind barred by the First Amendment because it was not measured in relationship to the volume of advertising revenue of the publication but rather by the amount of the publication's circulation "with the plain purpose of penalizing the publishers and curtailing the circulation of a selected group of newspapers."[43]

Because the Court's emphasis in *Grosjean* was on special taxation directed at the press, a clear implication of the decision is that non-discriminatory general business taxation applicable to the news media is permissible.[44] What was not clear from *Grosjean* was whether special taxation of the news media not motivated by malice but only a legislative desire to raise revenue might pass constitutional scrutiny.[45]

That question was answered nearly a half century later in *Minneapolis Star & Tribune Co. v. Minnesota Comm'r of Revenue*.[46] There, the state of Minnesota had exempted periodical publications such as newspapers from its general sales and use tax scheme until 1971. In that year, while leaving the exemption from the sales tax in place, the legislature amended the scheme to impose a use tax on the cost of paper and ink products used in the production of publications within the state. Three years later apparently at the behest of smaller circulation periodicals, the legislature again amended its use tax legislation to exempt the first $100,000 worth of ink and paper consumed by a publication in any calendar year, thereby in effect giving each publication an annual tax credit of $4,000.

In the first year after enactment of the use tax exemption, only eleven publishers, producing 14 of the 388 paid circulation newspapers in the state incurred a tax liability. The Star Tribune was one of the eleven, paying roughly two-thirds of the total revenue raised by the newsprint and ink use tax. The following year, 1975, the statistics were much the same and the Star & Tribune Company brought action against the commissioner of revenue for refund of all use taxes paid by it. The company claimed the use tax legislation violated the First and Fourteenth Amendments, citing *Grosjean v. American Press*. The Minnesota Supreme Court upheld the constitutionality of the legislation and the newspaper appealed.

While finding *Grosjean* not controlling because there was no legislative history indicating improper motive in enacting the use tax on periodical publications,[47] the Supreme Court nevertheless struck down

---

42. *Id.* at 245–248, 56 S. Ct. at 447–448, 80 L. Ed. at 666–667.

43. *Id.* at 251, 56 S. Ct. at 449, 80 L. Ed. at 669.

44. *See* Mabee v. White Plains Pub. Co., 327 U.S. 178, 184, 66 S.Ct. 511, 514, 90 L.Ed. 607, 613 (1946).

45. *See* Medlock v. Leathers, 499 U.S. 439, 111 S.Ct. 1438, 113 L.Ed.2d 494 (1991); Minneapolis Star & Tribune Co. v. Minnesota Comm'r of Revenue, 460 U.S. 575, 580, 103 S.Ct. 1365, 1369, 75 L.Ed.2d 295, 300 (1983).

46. 460 U.S. 575, 103 S.Ct. 1365, 75 L.Ed.2d 295 (1983).

47. 460 U.S. at 579–580, 592, 103 S. Ct. at 1369, 1375, 75 L. Ed. 2d at 301, 309.

the use tax scheme as violative of the First Amendment.[48] The Court characterized the tax treatment of publications as singular for at least two reasons. First, the legislation imposed a use tax that did not serve the function of protecting the sales tax from avoidance by purchasing goods subject to the sales tax out of state in jurisdictions with lower sales taxes. The normal use tax requires the resident who purchases goods out of state to pay a tax on in state use of the goods equivalent to the sales tax saving. While Minnesota designed its overall use tax scheme to serve this function, the use tax on newsprint and ink did not because it applied to goods *exempt* from the sales tax and was imposed on all uses of the goods whether or not they were purchased out of state. Second, the general rule in Minnesota was to tax only the ultimate retail sale to the ultimate user, but this use tax was applied to an intermediate transaction in the process of turning out the finished publication for sale.[49]

Having singled out the press for differential tax treatment, which the Court concluded placed a heavier burden on the press than generalized taxation does,[50] the state was required to establish an overriding governmental interest in the differential tax scheme if the legislation were to overcome First Amendment protections for the news media. The Court held that Minnesota's need to raise revenue did not establish overriding need here because it could have raised the additional revenue realized from the use tax on publications by increasing taxation on businesses generally thus "avoiding the censorial threat implicit in a tax that singles out the press."[51]

Beyond singling out print publications, the tax legislation was of concern to the Court because it targeted a small group of newspapers for actual payment of the tax. While not questioning the motives of the Minnesota legislature in creating this effect, the Court held that the exemption disfavoring the larger publications also violated the First Amendment because it resembled a penalty imposed on them without compelling reason.[52]

This last issue of targeting one group of publishers for payment of business taxes when others are exempted was revisited in *Arkansas Writers' Project, Inc. v. Ragland*.[53] There, Arkansas' general sales tax exempted gross receipts from sale of newspapers and religious, professional, trade and sports journals and publications printed and published within Arkansas when sold through regular subscription. This exemption from the sales tax did not cover the Arkansas Times, a general interest monthly magazine presenting articles on a variety of subjects including religion and sports, and the publisher was forced to pay taxes on its gross receipts from the sale of the magazine. Following the decision of the Supreme Court in *Minneapolis Star & Tribune Co.*, the

48. 460 U.S. at 593, 103 S. Ct. at 1376, 75 L. Ed. 2d at 310.

49. 460 U.S. at 581–582, 103 S. Ct. at 1370, 75 L. Ed. 2d at 302.

50. 460 U.S. at 583, 103 S. Ct. at 1371, 75 L. Ed. 2d at 303.

51. 460 U.S. at 586, 103 S. Ct. at 1372, 75 L. Ed. 2d at 305.

52. 460 U.S. at 591–592, 103 S. Ct. at 1375, 75 L. Ed. 2d at 309.

53. 481 U.S. 221, 107 S.Ct. 1722, 95 L.Ed.2d 209 (1987).

publisher sought a refund of all sales taxes paid claiming that the exemption for other journals and magazines had to be construed to include the more general Arkansas Times if it were to be constitutionally valid. The state refused to make refund and, not unexpectedly, the Arkansas courts refused to order the refund with the Arkansas Supreme Court holding, in effect, that the publisher of the non-exempt publication had no standing to claim discriminatory treatment because whatever the constitutionality of the exemption as to other favored publications, the publisher of the Arkansas Times would still have to pay the tax. It then went on to hold the state's sales tax scheme constitutional. Appeal was then taken to the Supreme Court which reversed, striking down the state's sales tax exemption scheme as then drafted.

The Court rejected the state's argument against the appellant publisher's standing to sue because if accepted it would insulate all invidiously underinclusive statutes from constitutional challenge. On the merits, the Court reaffirmed the principle that a discriminatory tax on the press burdens First Amendment rights and such burden may be justified only if the state can show an overriding compelling interest in imposing such a tax. Though the sales tax was broad in nature its newspaper and specialized magazine exemptions singled out for payment of the tax publishers of general interest and nonenumerated special interest magazines. Making matters worse, the singling out was done on the basis of editorial content rather than on the basis of the costs of the respective publishing operations, as was the case in *Minneapolis Star*. To determine whether a magazine is subject to the sales tax, Arkansas' enforcement authority would necessarily have to examine the content of the publication and "[s]uch official scrutiny of the content ... is entirely incompatible with the First Amendment's guarantee of freedom of the press."[54]

Thus, *Arkansas Writers' Project, Inc.* was an even clearer case than *Minneapolis Star* and the Court concluded that the state could not meet its very heavy burden of justifying content based discriminatory application of taxation to magazines. While the Court ruled the statutory discrimination between magazines violated the First Amendment, thus eliminating the differential treatment of newspapers and magazines, the Court left open the question whether discrimination between different *types* of communications media presented yet another reason for invalidating tax legislation.

From *Grosjean, Minneapolis Star* and *Arkansas Writers' Project,* the Court has drawn out the following propositions. First, differential taxation of First Amendment speakers is constitutionally suspect when it threatens to suppress the expression of particular ideas or viewpoints, and, absent a compelling justification, government may not exercise its taxing power to single out the press because of such threats. Second, a tax is also suspect if it targets a small group of speakers, particularly if the targeting is done on the basis of the content of taxpayer expression.

54.　481 U.S. at 230, 107 S. Ct. at 1728, 95 L. Ed. 2d at 220.

Third, however, when a discriminatory tax on media does not pose a threat of suppression of expression or target a small group of organizations within a medium, the legislation may be upheld.[55]

This last proposition was in issue in *Leathers v. Medlock*.[56] Here again the general Arkansas sales tax from the sale of tangible personal property and services was challenged, this time by a cable television subscriber, a cable television operator and the state cable television trade association. They claimed that the imposition of the tax was discriminatory as to the cable television medium and thus a violation of the First Amendment because newspapers sold over the counter and by subscription, magazines sold by subscription and satellite broadcast services delivered to home dish antennae owners were exempted from operation of the tax. The cable television interests were thus raising the issue left open in *Arkansas Writers' Project*, *i.e.*, whether taxation which discriminates *between* different media rather than within the same medium as in *Grosjean*, *Minneapolis Star* and *Arkansas Writers' Project* is constitutionally permissible.

Surprisingly, the answer from the United States Supreme Court was in the affirmative and Arkansas' inter-media discriminatory sales tax was upheld.[57] The Court held that the tax was general in nature, did not single out the press, was not content-based, was not motivated by a desire to interfere with First Amendment activities and did not, therefore, threaten to suppress free expression. Nor did the legislation select a narrow group to bear the burden of the levy within a particular medium. Every one of the approximately 100 cable systems then operating in the state was subject to the tax.

What the Court does not explain in upholding the Arkansas sales tax as it applies to cable is why this tax unlike those in *Grosjean*, *Minneapolis Star* and *Arkansas Writers' Project* does not possess the *potential* to cripple or destroy the one television medium singled out for its application.[58] It does not take a great imagination to spin a scenario in which a state legislature desperate for revenue raises its sales tax to twenty percent of gross receipts from all services, thereby driving many cable subscribers away from that First Amendment-protected medium[59] and crippling cable operations in the state. Under the ruling in *Leathers* the legislature's action would be destructive but not unconstitutional because it would be legislating a general tax and was not deliberately setting out to injure a medium of expression.

---

55. *See* Leathers v. Medlock, 499 U.S. 439, 111 S.Ct. 1438, 113 L.Ed.2d 494 (1991).

56. *Id.* at 449, 111 S. Ct. at 1445, 113 L. Ed. 2d at 505.

57. *Cf.* Regan v. Taxation with Representation of Washington, 461 U.S. 540, 103 S.Ct. 1997, 76 L.Ed.2d 129 (1983); Cammarano v. United States, 358 U.S. 498, 79 S.Ct. 524, 3 L.Ed.2d 462 (1959).

58. Leathers, 499 U.S. at 460–461, 111 S. Ct. at 1451, 113 L. Ed. 2d at 512–513 (Marshall And Blackmun, JJ. dissenting).

59. *See* Los Angeles v. Preferred Communications, Inc., 476 U.S. 488, 494, 106 S.Ct. 2034, 2037, 90 L.Ed.2d 480, 487 (1986).

The *Leathers* decision together with the noticeable shift of responsibility from the federal government to the states to raise money for social programs in the last fifteen years will only increase the kinds and amounts of taxes imposed on the media in the coming years. General business license taxes, general income taxes, general property taxes and general taxes on media sales and services are clearly permissible and taxation of advertising services is on the horizon.[60]

E. Miscellaneous Regulation Applicable to News Organizations and Newspersons.

In addition to the three major areas of general business regulation constitutionally applicable to news and information media organizations—labor law, antitrust law and taxation—there are other less prominent general statutes and regulations applicable to the news media and newspersons. A non-exhaustive list of such regulatory control passing First Amendment muster in the courts includes prohibition of door to door solicitation at private residences of magazine and other periodical subscriptions,[61] certain advertising restraints on media,[62] copyright protection for intellectual property of others,[63] and prohibition of gender discrimination under the 1964 Civil Rights Act.[64]

A somewhat different regulation of the media which the Supreme Court has recently upheld is the application of common law contractual liability to the obtaining of news and information from sources. This is a departure from past regulation in that it is applied directly to the First Amendment process of gathering truthful news for dissemination to the citizenry and involves common law principles and rules rather than statutory obligations and limitations.[65]

Finally, and again something of a departure from subjecting news organizations and persons to business laws of general application, the Supreme Court has time and again held or stated by way of dictum that newspersons are not absolutely exempted by the First Amendment from

---

60. *See* Barbara Steuart, *The 1991 Tax Threat*, Wash. Journ. Rev. 30, 31 (May 1991).

61. *See* Breard v. Alexandria, 341 U.S. 622, 71 S.Ct. 920, 95 L.Ed. 1233 (1951).

62. *See, e.g.,* Posadas de Puerto Rico v. Tourism Company of Puerto Rico, 478 U.S. 328, 106 S.Ct. 2968, 92 L.Ed.2d 266 (1986) (prohibition on local advertising of casino gambling directed to residents of Puerto Rico); Pittsburgh Press v. Pittsburgh Commission on Human Relations 413 U.S. 376, 93 S.Ct. 2553, 37 L.Ed.2d 669 (1973) (prohibition in city ordinance against publishing help wanted ads under headings designating job preference by sex); *see also* DONALD M. GILLMOR & JEROME A. BARRON, MASS COMMUNICATION LAW 605–637 (4th ed. 1984) (general survey of advertising restrictions on the media).

63. *See* Cohen v. Cowles Media Co., 501 U.S. 663, 669–670, 111 S.Ct. 2513, 2518–2519, 115 L.Ed.2d 586, 596–597 (1991); Harper & Row Publishers, Inc. v. Nation Enterprises, 471 U.S. 539, 105 S.Ct. 2218, 85 L.Ed.2d 588 (1985) (unfair use by magazine of another's autobiographical material of great public interest not protected by First Amendment); *cf.* Zacchini v. Scripps–Howard Broadcasting Co. 433 U.S. 562, 576–579, 97 S.Ct. 2849, 2858, 53 L.Ed.2d 965, 976–978 (1977) (appropriation of another's right to publicity value of his carnival act).

64. *See* Hausch v. Donrey of Nevada Inc., 833 F.Supp. 822 (D.Nev.1993).

65. *See* Cohen v. Cowles Media Co., 501 U.S. 663, 111 S.Ct. 2513, 115 L.Ed.2d 586 (1991).

obligation of citizens generally to obey subpoenas and give evidence in duly constituted grand jury proceedings.[66]

7.14 The Claimed Right of Access to News—An Introduction

James Madison expressed it best when he wrote "A popular Government, without popular information, or the means of acquiring it, is but a Prologue to a Farce or a Tragedy; or perhaps both. Knowledge will forever govern ignorance: And a people who mean to be their own Governors must arm themselves with the power which knowledge gives."[1] But whether the First and Fourteenth Amendment to the Constitution provide newsgatherer with special access to news and information beyond that available to the citizenry generally is a surprisingly complex matter.

The complexity begins with the ambiguous majority opinion in *Branzburg v. Hayes*.[2] There the Supreme Court seemed to recognize some constitutional protection for the newsgathering function when it said by way of dictum that "without some protection for seeking out the news, freedom of the press could be eviscerated."[3] But what the Court apparently giveth by dictum it tooketh away by dictum later in the same opinion when it stated that "[i]t has generally been held that the First Amendment does not guarantee the press a constitutional right of special access to information not available to the public generally."[4]

A possible explanation for the Court's view that the media with rare exceptions, are protected in publishing whatever they can gather,[5] but are accorded no special access in gathering news and information in the first place is that the Court views the Press Clause of the First Amendment as merely an aspect of the Speech Clause which, of course, is

---

66. *See id.* (dictum); Minneapolis Star & Tribune Co. v. Minnesota Comm'r of Revenue, 460 U.S. 575, 581, 103 S.Ct. 1365, 1370, 75 L.Ed.2d 295, 302 (1983); (dictum); Branzburg v. Hayes, 408 U.S. 665, 92 S.Ct. 2646, 33 L.Ed.2d 626 (1972) (holding).

1. Letter to W. T. Barry, Aug. 4, 1822, quoted in Environmental Protection Agency v. Mink, 410 U.S. 73, 110–111, 93 S.Ct. 827, 847, 35 L.Ed.2d 119, 145 (1973) (dissenting opinion of Douglas, J.); *see also* dissent of Stewart J. in *Branzburg v. Hayes*, 408 U.S. 665, 725–727, 92 S.Ct. 2646, 2672–2673, 33 L.Ed.2d 626, 667 (1972) ("a corollary of the right to publish must be the right to gather news ... News must not be unnecessarily cut off at its source for without freedom to acquire information, the right to publish would be impermissibly compromised.")

2. 408 U.S. 665, 92 S.Ct. 2646, 33 L.Ed.2d 626 (1972).

3. *Id.* at 681, 92 S. Ct. at 2656, 33 L. Ed. 2d at 639 (1972). *See* Davis v. East Baton

Rouge Parish School Bd., 78 F.3d 920, 926–927, 929–930 (5th Cir.1996) ("gag order" on school board release of information to media and public regarding deliberations and negotiations relating to proposed school desegregation plan held violative of First Amendment limited right of media to gather news).

4. *Id.* at 684, 92 S. Ct. at 2658, 33 L. Ed. 2d at 641, *citing inter alia*, Zemel v. Rusk, 381 U.S. 1, 16–17, 85 S.Ct. 1271, 1281, 14 L.Ed.2d 179, 189–191 (1965) ("The right to speak and publish does not carry with it the unrestrained right to gather information."); New York Times Co. v. United States, 403 U.S. 713, 728–730, 91 S.Ct. 2140, 2148–2149, 29 L.Ed.2d 822, 832–834 (1971) (Stewart, J. concurring).

5. *See, e.g.*, Near v. Minnesota, 283 U.S. 697, 51 S.Ct. 625, 75 L.Ed. 1357 (1931); New York Times Co. v. United States, 403 U.S. 713, 91 S.Ct. 2140, 29 L.Ed.2d 822 (1971) (all ten opinions).

designed to protect the right of the general citizenry to speak out and does not implicate newsgathering.[6] But this explanation is open to question raising the possibility that a limited special right of access may be accorded the media by the Press Clause. If such a qualified right of access does exist, the problem would be to determine under what legal tests and circumstances this right might be invoked. One approach, that taken by the late Justice Brennan, requires consideration of the information sought by the news media and the opposing interests involved.[7] While recognizing that the judicial task in such weighing is as much a matter of sensitivity to practical necessities as it is of abstract reasoning, Justice Brennan suggested two principles to guide judges in determining the access issue. First is whether there is a history and tradition of public access in the particular situation, and second, if there is such history and tradition, whether the access to particular government processes or information outweighs the government's interest in non-access to the processes or information involved.[8]

Another approach would be to require the government to establish a compelling interest in excluding the news media from places, processes and information under its control before access could be denied. This high standard, utilized in cases of direct limitation of free expression,[9]

---

6. Except by unclear implication from decided cases such as *Zemel v. Rusk*, 381 U.S. 1, 85 S.Ct. 1271, 14 L.Ed.2d 179 (1965); *Pell v. Procunier*, 417 U.S. 817, 94 S.Ct. 2800, 41 L.Ed.2d 495 (1974); *Saxbe v. Washington Post Co.*, 417 U.S. 843, 94 S.Ct. 2811, 41 L.Ed.2d 514 (1974); *Houchins v. KQED, Inc.* 438 U.S. 1, 98 S.Ct. 2588, 57 L.Ed.2d 553 (1978) and explicit enunciation by one former member of the Court, the late Chief Justice Burger, in a concurring opinion in *First National Bank v. Bellotti*, 435 U.S. 765, 796–802, 98 S.Ct. 1407, 1426–1429, 55 L.Ed.2d 707, 730–734 (1978), the Court has not explicated its position on the relationship of the Press and Speech Clauses. But as pointed out by Professor David A. Anderson, "If the Court has never given the press clause independent significance, neither has it foreclosed the possibility." David A. Anderson, *The Origins of the Press Clause*, 30 U.C.L.A. L. Rev. 455, 459 (1983). Because the dependence or independence of the Press Clause is central to, among others, the question of whether newsgatherers are specially privileged to access news and information, there is much debate on this subject by the commentators. For commentary favoring an independent construction of the Press Clause, *see e.g.*, Melville B. Nimmer, *Introduction—Is Freedom of the Press a Redundance? What Does It Add to Freedom of Speech?*, 26 Hastings L.J. 639 (1975) (general analysis); David A. Anderson, *The Origins of the* *Press Clause*, 30 U.C.L.A.L. Rev. 455 (1983) (historical analysis); Tom A. Collins, *The Press Clause Construed in Context: The Journalists' Right of Access to Places*, 52 Mo. L. Rev. 751 (1987) (historical and interest analysis); Randall P. Bezanson, *The New Free Press Guarantee*, 63 Va. L. Rev. 731 (1977)(case analysis). For commentary favoring a unitary construction of the Speech and Press Clauses *see* LEONARD W. LEVY, EMERGENCE OF A FREE PRESS (1985); David Lange, *The Speech and Press Clauses*, 23 U.C.L.A. L. Rev. 77 (1975); *cf.* William W. Van Alstyne, *The Hazards to the Press of Claiming a "Preferred Position,"* 28 Hastings L.J. 761 (1977) (arguing against special access for the news media under the Press Clause because of the danger it will backfire); Anthony Lewis, *A Preferred Position for Journalism?* 7 Hofstra L. Rev. 595 (1979), (arguing against special access for the news media because it might be balanced by the grant of greater latitude for government closure of its proceedings.)

7. *See* Richmond Newspapers, Inc. v. Virginia 448 U.S. 555, 587–589, 100 S.Ct. 2814, 2833–2834, 65 L.Ed.2d 973, 996–997 (1980) (concurring opinion).

8. *Id.* at 588–589, 100 S.Ct. at 2827–28, 2834, 65 L.Ed.2d at 989–90, 997–98.

9. *See, e.g.*, New York Times Co. v. United States 403 U.S. 713, 91 S.Ct. 2140, 29 L.Ed.2d 822 (1971) (per curiam opinion).

seems doubtful given the judiciary's previously demonstrated willingness (even eagerness) to deny access to the media.[10]

All that can be concluded from case authority and the analyses of knowledgeable commentators is that the existence of even a limited special right of access to news and the tests that might be applied in measuring access claims are in serious doubt. What is not in doubt is that in the overwhelming majority of cases in which assertions of special access under the First Amendment have been made they have been rejected.

7.15 Access to Private Property

A. Introduction

The most obvious failure of the claim that the First Amendment affords special access of the media relates to news occurring on private property. Much news, of course, does occur on or in property owned by private interests but, with a few minor exceptions,[1] the courts have rejected claims of protected access by newsgatherers and have held them tortiously or criminally liable for going upon private property without consent.[2]

The reasons for this seem to be either that private property is truly private property,[3] or that privacy interests of those lawfully occupying property must be protected.[4] Despite the desire of commentators to the contrary,[5] the appellate courts have not engaged in balancing First Amendment access interests against those interests emanating from the

10. *See, e.g.,* Houchins v. KQED, 438 U.S. 1, 98 S.Ct. 2588, 57 L.Ed.2d 553 (1978); Garrett v. Estelle, 556 F.2d 1274 (5th Cir.1977), cert. denied, 438 U.S. 914, 98 S.Ct. 3142, 57 L.Ed.2d 1159 (1978).

1. *See* Allen v. Combined Communications, 7 Media L. Rptr. 2417 (Colo. Dist. Ct. 1981); People v. Rewald, 65 Misc.2d 453, 457, 318 N.Y.S.2d 40, 45 (N.Y.Co.Ct.1971).

2. Galella v. Onassis, 487 F.2d 986, 995–996 (2d Cir.1973); Dietemann v. Time, Inc., 449 F.2d 245, 249–250 (9th Cir.1971); Belluomo v. KAKE TV & Radio, Inc., 3 Kan. App.2d 461, 465–469, 596 P.2d 832, 838–840 (1979); Le Mistral, Inc. v. Columbia Broadcasting System, 61 A.D.2d 491, 494, 402 N.Y.S.2d 815, 817 (1978), appeal dismissed 46 N.Y.2d 940 (1979); Anderson v. WROC–TV, 109 Misc.2d 904, 441 N.Y.S.2d 220 (N.Y.Sup.1981); Stahl v. State, 665 P.2d 839, 841–842 (Okl.Cr.1983), cert. denied 464 U.S. 1069, 104 S.Ct. 973, 79 L.Ed.2d 212 (1984); Prahl v. Brosamle, 98 Wis.2d 130, 149–150, 295 N.W.2d 768, 780–781 (Wis.App.1980); *see also* Thomas I. Emerson, *The Right of Privacy and Freedom of the Press*, 14 Harv. C.R.-C.L.L. Rev. 329,

332 (1979) ("Limitations upon newsgathering imposed by the law of trespass have never been thought to infringe upon any right of the press.")

3. *See* Belluomo v. KAKE TV & Radio, Inc. 3 Kan.App.2d 461, 468, 596 P.2d 832, 840–841 (1979); Le Mistral, Inc. v. Columbia Broadcasting System, 61 A.D.2d 491, 494, 402 N.Y.S.2d 815, 817 (1978) *appeal dismissed*, 46 N.Y.2d 940 (1979); Prahl v. Brosamle, 98 Wis.2d 130, 149–150, 295 N.W.2d 768, 780–781 (Wis.App.1980).

4. *See* Galella v. Onassis, 487 F.2d 986, 994–996 (2d Cir.1973); Dietemann v. Time, Inc., 449 F.2d 245 (9th Cir.1971) (tort of intrusion); Tom A. Collins, *The Press Clause Construed in Context: The Journalists' Right of Access to Places*, 52 Mo. L. Rev. 751, 791–793, 800–801 (1987).

5. *See* Alfred Hill, *Defamation and Privacy Under the First Amendment*, 76 Colum. L. Rev. 1205, 1278–1285 (1976); Tom A. Collins, *The Press Clause Construed in Context: The Journalists' Right of Access to Places*, 52 Mo. L. Rev. 751, 787–801 (1987); David F. Freedman, Note, *Press Passes and Trespasses*, 84 Colum. L. Rev. 1298 (1984).

ownership, control or occupation of private property.[6] Nor have these courts distinguished between private property privately utilized, private property open for public accommodation or private property permanently or temporarily controlled by government agents.[7] Arguments have been made that because places of public accommodations are open to the public[8] or may have aspects of public fora[9] or because the public has a strong interest in knowing what the government is doing on private property placed under its control,[10] the First Amendment should afford the news media access to such private property.

The first part of the argument is doubtful because it equates access of the public to the places of public accommodation for the narrow purposes prescribed by the owners with the access demanded by news gatherers for their own purposes in covering news occurring on those premises.[11] Moreover, recognizing that some private places of accommodation may have aspects of public fora requiring the protection of expression on the premises is not the same as recognizing the right of access of the media to the premises in order to gather news. It is almost a truism to say that newsgathering is a step or more removed from the expression being covered. The second argument has more substance if one accepts the so-called "checking function" of the newsmedia, *i.e.*, exposing wrongdoing by government.[12] But thus far the courts have not focused on this argument.

The doctrinaire position presently controlling is that the First Amendment provides newsgatherers no special access to private property originated in *Dietemann v. Time, Inc.*[13] There, a male and female employee of Life Magazine went to the home of Dietemann, a plumber

---

6. *See, e.g.*, Galella v. Onassis, 487 F.2d 986, 995–996 (2d Cir.1973); Dietemann v. Time, Inc., 449 F.2d 245 (9th Cir.1971); Le Mistral, Inc. v. Columbia Broadcasting System, 61 A.D.2d 491, 494, 402 N.Y.S.2d 815, 817 (1978), *appeal dismissed* 46 N.Y.2d 940 (1979).

7. *See, e.g.*, Dietemann v. Time, Inc. 449 F.2d 245 (9th Cir.1971) (office in private home sealed off by a locked gate); Le Mistral, Inc. v. Columbia Broadcasting System, 61 A.D.2d 491, 402 N.Y.S.2d 815 (restaurant open to the public); Stahl v. State 665 P.2d 839 (Okl.Cr.1983), cert. denied, 464 U.S. 1069, 104 S.Ct. 973, 79 L.Ed.2d 212 (1984) (property of power company and electric cooperatives heavily regulated by Nuclear Regulatory Commission); Prahl v. Brosamle, 98 Wis.2d 130, 295 N.W.2d 768 (Wis.App.1980) (crime scene on private property temporarily under control of law enforcement agencies); *but see* People v. Rewald, 65 Misc.2d 453, 318 N.Y.S.2d 40 (N.Y.Co.Ct.1971) (migrant work camp owned by produce cooperative).

8. *See* Le Mistral, Inc. v. Columbia Broadcasting System, 61 A.D.2d at 493 n.1,

402 N.Y.S.2d at 816 n.1; News Media & The Law 7 (Summer 1989) (Reporters Committee for Freedom of the Press).

9. *Id*. This argument apparently relies on the company town case of *Marsh v. Alabama*, 326 U.S. 501, 66 S.Ct. 276, 90 L.Ed. 265 (1946).

10. *See* Tom A. Collins, *The Press Clause Construed in Context: The Journalists' Right of Access to Places*, 52 Mo. L. Rev. 751, 793, 801 (1987). Professor Collins' argument relies on the so-called "checking" function of the press as a counterweight to government power and abuse of that power. *See id*. at 757–758; Vincent Blasi, *The Checking Value in First Amendment Theory*, 1977 Am. B. Found Res. J. 521.

11. *See* Le Mistral, Inc. v. Columbia Broadcasting System, 61 A.D.2d at 493 n.1, 402 N.Y.S.2d at 816–817 n.1.

12. *See* Tom A. Collins, *The Press Clause Construed in Context: The Journalists' Right of Access to Places*, 52 Mo. L. Rev. at 793, 801.

13.   449 F.2d 245 (9th Cir.1971).

who practiced healing with clay, minerals and herbs on the side. Through the misrepresentation that they had been referred to Dietemann by a friend they gained admittance to his house. Once inside, the woman falsely complained of a lump in one of her breasts. While examining the breast with an assortment of gadgets, Dietemann was secretly photographed by Life's male employee using a hidden camera. Further, the conversation between the woman and Dietemann was transmitted by a radio transmitter hidden in the woman's purse to a receiver and tape recorder in a parked car occupied by another employee of the magazine and officials from the local district attorney's office and the California Department of Public Health. The entire affair was a cooperative venture between Life and the public officials to aid in the crackdown on medical quackery in Southern California and to allow the magazine to cover this campaign. Life published its story and pictures following Dietemann's *nolo* plea to criminal misdemeanor charges.

Dietemann thereafter sued Time, Inc. in the United States District Court for invasion of privacy (the tort of intrusion) and won a judgment of $1,000 in general damages. In seeking reversal on appeal to the Ninth Circuit, Time, Inc. contended that the First Amendment immunized it from liability for its intrusion because its employees were gathering news and the photographic and recording equipment were indispensable tools of investigative reporting. Rejecting Time's claim to protection under the authority of the libel case of *New York Times Co. v. Sullivan*,[14] Judge Hufstedler distinguished the publication of the story and pictures from the earlier intrusion which made publication possible. Isolating the intrusion, Judge Hufstedler held without analysis that [t]he First Amendment has never been construed to accord newsmen immunity from torts or crimes committed during the course of newsgathering.[15] She then went on to say, without legal precedent, "The First Amendment is not a license to trespass, to steal, or to intrude by electronic means into the precincts of another's home or office."[16]

While *Dietemann* is troubling for both its lack of analysis of a serious First Amendment issue and the absence of any guidance for legitimate newsgatherers as to what constitutes intrusion on private property, and under what circumstances,[17] its doctrinaire approach has been followed in all appellate decisions involving intrusion and trespass by newspersons.[18] Therefore, unless the Supreme Court rules otherwise,

---

14. 376 U.S. 254, 84 S.Ct. 710, 11 L.Ed.2d 686 (1964).

15. Dietemann, 449 F.2d at 249.

16. *Id.*

17. "It is one thing to say that as a general matter one's home is sacrosanct from invasion by outsiders and that journalists are as responsible as the rest of us for illegal or improper eavesdropping ... It is quite another to conclude that when a person passes himself off as a doctor and uses his home as his office, journalists may not

act as prospective patients and record the illegal activities that occur there." Floyd Abrams, *The Press, Privacy and the Constitution*, New York Times Magazine, Aug. 21, 1977, p. 68.

18. *See* Le Mistral, Inc. v. Columbia Broadcasting System, 61 A.D.2d 491, 402 N.Y.S.2d 815 (1978), appeal dismissed 46 N.Y.S.2d 940 (1979); Stahl v. State, 665 P.2d 839 (Okl.Cr.1983), cert. denied 464 U.S. 1069, 104 S.Ct. 973, 79 L.Ed.2d 212 (1984); Belluomo v. KAKE TV & Radio, Inc., 3 Kan.App.2d 461, 596 P.2d 832 (1979); Prahl

the conclusion is that the First Amendment provides no special access to private property and the Court is not likely to.[18A]

B. State Constitutional, Statutory or Common Law Access

1. Constitutional and Statutory Access

While judicial construction of the First Amendment thus far provides no basis for special access of the media to private property, the Supreme Court in *PruneYard Shopping Center v. Robins*[19] stated that the individual states under their police power or limited sovereignty have the right to guarantee in their own constitutions individual liberties such as freedom of speech and of the press "more expansive than those conferred by the Federal Constitution" so long as such guarantees do not contravene the federal Constitution.[20] And one state trial court jurist wondered in one case why parties routinely and without reflection attach themselves to federal constitutional provisions, disregarding identical or frequently more liberal principles of state constitutions.[21] In that case the wondering New Jersey Superior Court jurist ruled that a limited right of access to a privately owned migrant farmworkers camp was accorded by the New Jersey constitution's guarantee of a free press[22] to members of the media including college newspaper reporters and photographers so they might report on living conditions of the residents. The public interest in such camps as reflected in several New Jersey statutes regulating the relationship of the landlord to the farmworker tenants justified this construction of the New Jersey constitution. This is a rare if not unique decision on news media access. But this case should be kept in mind by counsel for newspersons and news organizations as suggesting an optional course when confronted with criminal action for trespass or civil actions for intrusion and trespass against their clients, particularly in light of the uniform judicial rejection of access under the First Amendment.[23]

v. Brosamle, 98 Wis.2d 130, 295 N.W.2d 768 (Wis.App.1980); *see also* Galella v. Onassis, 487 F.2d 986, 994–996 (2d Cir.1973); Wolfson v. Lewis, 924 F.Supp. 1413 (E.D.Pa. 1996) (intrusion by use of electronic surveillance equipment from public areas); Food Lion, Inc. v. Capital Cities/ABC, Inc. 887 F.Supp. 811 (M.D.N.C.1995) (surreptitious investigation on plaintiff's premises).

The basic thrust of *Dietemann* was reaffirmed by the Ninth Circuit more than a quarter century later in *Berger v. Hanlon*, 129 F.3d 505, 513, (9th Cir.1997), *aff'd in part* 1999 WL 320818 (Sup.Ct.1999) (per curiam).

18A. *See* Berger v. Hanlon, 1999 WL 320818 (Sup.Ct.1999) (per curiam).

19. 447 U.S. 74, 100 S.Ct. 2035, 64 L.Ed.2d 741 (1980).

20. *Id.* at 81, 100 S. Ct. at 2040–2041, 64 L. Ed. 2d at 751.

21. Freedman v. New Jersey State Police, 135 N.J.Super. 297, 300, 343 A.2d 148, 150 (N.J.Super.L.1975); *see also* Lloyd Corp. v. Whiffen, 307 Ore. 674, 692, 773 P.2d 1294, 1304 (1989) (dissenting opinion).

22. N.J. Stat. Ann. Const. art. I, par. 6 (West 1971)("No law shall be passed to restrain or abridge the liberty of speech or of the press.")

23. It should also be kept in mind that two important media jurisdictions, California and Ohio have statutes that may be construed to permit special access of members of the news media to private property in an emergency situation. *See* Cal. Penal Code § 409.5(d) (West 1988 and Supp. 1991); Ohio Rev. Code Ann. § 2917.13(B) (Anderson 1992).

2. Common Law Access

a. Consent to entry

Tort actions for intrusion and trespass are, of course, avoided if the newsgatherer properly obtains express or implied consent from one authorized to give it to enter private property in search of news.[24] Therefore, newspersons should be advised to obtain permission to enter private premises whenever possible. Obviously, such course of action is not normally feasible for investigative reporting on sensitive or criminal matters. It is legally doubtful that investigative reporters who obtain assent to entry through misrepresentations as to their identity or mission are protected from civil or even criminal liability. For instance, in *Dietemann v. Time, Inc.*[25] concealment of the reporters' identity and the true reason for entering the plaintiff's home led to liability for intrusive invasion of privacy.

b. Custom

Closely related to consent as a basis for access to private property is local custom. If the custom of the community is to permit uninvited persons to pass through the front gate and to knock on a resident's door to sell things, solicit subscriptions, get petitions signed and the like, then newsgatherers should be able to ask a few brief questions.[26] Custom normally permits only minor and transient incursions on private property. But this concept was substantially expanded for Florida newsgatherers by the Florida Supreme Court in *Florida Publishing Co. v. Fletcher*.[27] There, the homeowner had gone out of town leaving her three young daughters in the house. While the oldest daughter was home alone a large fire of unknown origin broke out causing the girl's death. When the fire marshal and a police officer entered the house to make their official investigation, they invited members of the news media to accompany them—their standard practice. There was no one to object to the entry of the media representatives who entered solely for the purpose of providing news coverage. The fire had left a silhouette on the floor where the dead girl had fallen and the first marshal wanted a clear picture of the grisly reminder in order to establish that the body was already on the

24. *See* Prahl v. Brosamle, 98 Wis.2d 130, 147, 295 N.W.2d 768, 778–779 (Wis. App.1980); Anderson v. WROC–TV 109 Misc.2d 904, 907, 441 N.Y.S.2d 220, 223 (N.Y.Sup.1981); WILLIAM L. PROSSER & W. PAGE KEETON, TORTS 112 (5th ed. 1984); Tom A. Collins, *The Press Clause Construed in Context: The Journalists' Right of Access to Places*, 52 Mo. L. Rev. 751, 789–790 (1987).

25. 449 F.2d 245 (9th Cir.1971). *See* Belluomo v. KAKE TV & Radio, Inc., 3 Kan.App.2d 461, 596 P.2d 832, 844 (1979)("If the purported consent [for a camera crew to enter a non-public area of a restaurant] was fraudulently induced, there was no consent."); WILLIAM L. PROSSER AND W. PAGE KEETON, TORTS 119–120 (5th ed.

1984). *But see* McCall v. Courier–Journal, 6 Media L. Rptr. 1112 (Ky. Ct. App. 1980), *rev'd on other grounds* 623 S.W.2d 882 (Ky. 1981) (no intrusion or trespass when client was induced by reporters to bring concealed tape recorder into her lawyer's office and denied its existence when lawyer grew suspicious of her questions).

26. *See* Tom A. Collins, *The Press Clause Construed in Context: The Journalists' Right of Access to Places*, 52 Mo. L. Rev. 751, 791 (1987).

27. 340 So.2d 914 (Fla.1976), cert. denied, 431 U.S. 930, 97 S.Ct. 2634, 53 L.Ed.2d 245 (1977).

floor before the heat of the fire damaged the room. The marshal's own instant photographs were unsatisfactory and he requested a news photographer to take a photograph of the silhouette which was then made a part of the official investigation file. Copies of this photo and others taken at the scene were turned over to the photographer's newspaper. The silhouette shot and others were published in conjunction with the story of the fire. The mother first learned of the details of her daughter's death by reading the story and seeing the published photographs. She thereafter sued the newspaper publisher and certain of its employees for, among other things, trespass and intrusion.

The trial court granted summary judgment for the media defendants but was reversed by the Florida District Court of Appeal. On certiorari the Florida Supreme Court vacated the appeals court ruling on the trespass count. The Supreme Court held that summary judgment was appropriate because there was no genuine issue of material fact and the entry into the plaintiff's home by the defendant publisher's employees was lawful pursuant to the doctrine of common custom, usage and practice. The trial court had found, based on numerous affidavits of news editors and law enforcement officials, that it was common usage, custom and practice for newspersons to enter private premises under the circumstances presented here and thus consent to enter was implied in law. In upholding the trial court judgment, the Florida high court said, "Implied consent would, of course, vanish if one were informed not to enter at that time by the owner or possessor or by their direction. But here there was not only no objection to the entry, but *there was an invitation to enter by the officers investigating the fire*" (italics the court's).[28]

The court's ruling seems doubtful because first there was no one at the premises left alive who could have objected to the entry of the newspersons, second, no explanation is given as to how the state's police power to enter private disaster areas can be delegated by low level police and fire officials to non-officials even if there have been ostensible delegations in the past[29] and third, the extension of customary access goes well beyond anything that the common law has previously allowed. The decision has not been followed and, indeed, *Fletcher* has been questioned as even persuasive authority. In *Prahl v. Brosamle*[30] a television reporter at the scene of a shooting incident rode with a police lieutenant up a private driveway to a building from which the shots were apparently fired and housing the biochemist plaintiff's residence, his scientific research foundation offices and his laboratory. The defendant

---

28. *Id.* at 918.

29. *But see* Tom A. Collins, *The Press Clause Construed in Context: The Journalists' Right of Access to Places*, 52 Mo. L. Rev. 751, 791 (1987) wherein Professor Collins, using a privacy analysis argues that "A court cannot be seriously faulted for finding that it is customary for journalists to accompany government agents [to cover police and fire activity]. Indeed, if any customary right to enter is to be recognized, it should be recognized under these circumstances because the privacy interests have been diminished by the action of government agents."

30. 98 Wis.2d 130, 295 N.W.2d 768 (Wis.App.1980).

reporter went into the building with the police, positioned himself in the vestibule and filmed officers confiscating guns on the premises and interviewing the plaintiff. At no time did the newsperson request or receive permission from the plaintiff to enter the building or to take pictures therein. The plaintiff saw the reporter using his camera but thought that he was a police officer or deputy sheriff and did not tell the defendant to stop filming or to leave. Later when he found out who the man with the camera really was, the plaintiff brought an action against him, his employer, and certain peace officers for, among other things, trespass to real property.

The trial court held that the television reporter was not a trespasser and dismissed the entire complaint following presentation of the plaintiff's case. The Wisconsin Court of Appeals reversed the judgment of the trial court insofar as it dismissed the claim for damages for trespass and ordered a new trial on that cause of action. On the appeal the reporter and the television station owner, relying on *Fletcher*, had argued that by virtue of custom and usage, plaintiff had impliedly consented to the presence of newsmen on his premises. While distinguishing *Fletcher* on the facts that no official requested the television newsperson's assistance in the investigation and that the news media defendants did not rely on evidence of a custom such as affidavits entered in the Florida case, the Wisconsin appeals court went on to question the rationale of *Fletcher*. "We will not imply a consent as a matter of law. It is of course well known that news representatives want to enter a private building after or even during a newsworthy event within the building. That knowledge is no basis for an implied consent by the possessor of the building to the entry. . . . We conclude that custom and usage have not been shown in fact or law to confer an implied consent upon news representatives to enter a building under the circumstances of this case."[31]

Given that no court outside of Florida has ever followed *Fletcher* and courts have questioned or rejected outright its rationale,[32] caution should be exercised in counseling reliance upon it. Where access to private

---

31. *Id.* at 149, 295 N.W.2d at 780; *see* Anderson v. WROC–TV, 109 Misc.2d 904, 907, 441 N.Y.S.2d 220, 223 (1981) ("The gathering of news and the means by which it is obtained does not authorize, whether under the First Amendment or otherwise, the right to enter into a private home by an implied invitation arising out of a self-created custom and practice."); *compare Berger v. Hanlon*, 129 F.3d 505 (9th Cir.1997) (federal agent wired for sound pursuant to contract with a private newsgathering organization violated plaintiffs' constitutional rights during execution of search warrant of their premises).

32. *Id. See also* Ayeni v. CBS, Inc. 848 F.Supp. 362 (E.D.N.Y.1994) *aff'd* 35 F.3d 680 (2d Cir.1994), *cert. denied* 514 U.S. 1062, 115 S.Ct. 1689, 131 L.Ed.2d 554 (1995) (news organization held to have no immunity from liability for videotaping in a private home at the invitation of a federal agent executing a search warrant); *Berger v. Hanlon*, 129 F.3d 505, 511, (9th Cir. 1997), *aff'd in part* per curiam, 1999 WL 320818 (Sup.Ct.1999), the appeals court saying, "We find even further support of this view [that federal agents inviting representatives of the media to witness or record the execution of search warrants on private property violate the possessor's fourth amendment rights] when we observe that no circuit decision has ever upheld the constitutionality of a warranted search where the broadcast media were present to document the incident for non-law enforcement purposes, and where the videotaping

property is concerned, seeking express permission to enter is clearly the best policy.[33]

7.16 Access to Government Controlled News and Information

A. Introduction

Without question, the most significant sources of news and information of importance to the citizenry are governmental entities at all levels—federal, state and local. For the information held and the news made by governments ultimately determines the nature of society. Access to governmentally controlled news and information then is critical to the continuance of our existing representative democracy.[1] At the same time there is an almost undoubted right of governments to attempt to keep secret certain information and bar access of the citizenry and its news media agents to this information.[2] Examples of information or news that could cost the country its independence or might seriously undermine or destroy the system of government established by the Constitution easily come to mind. No one would seriously suggest that the news media should have had access to Enrico Fermi's physics laboratory at the University of Chicago where secret experiments leading to the development of the atomic bomb were taking place during the life and death struggle of World War II. Nor would they likely suggest that the press was entitled to access to the Navy Department files indicating that American cryptographers had cracked Japan's "Purple Code."[3]

But there is much news and information that governments may wish to suppress such as the results of serious errors of judgment or the corrupt practices of elected and appointed officials.[4] Without access to

and sound recording were outside the scope of the warrant."

33. Obtaining the permission of the tenant on the premises rather than the landlord who may not want newspersons snooping around his property may be sufficient. See Lal v. CBS, Inc., 726 F.2d 97, 100 (3d Cir.1984) (Under Pennsylvania common law the out of possession lessor of improved land cannot maintain an action for trespass absent injury to the reversionary interest, and consent of the lessee to entry is a complete defense to a trespass action).

1. See, e.g., Richmond Newspapers, Inc. v. Virginia, 448 U.S. 555, 575, 100 S.Ct. 2814, 2826, 65 L.Ed.2d 973, 988 (1980); Time, Inc. v. Hill, 385 U.S. 374, 389, 87 S.Ct. 534, 543, 17 L.Ed.2d 456, 461 (1967); New York Times Co. v. Sullivan, 376 U.S. 254, 270, 84 S.Ct. 710, 720–721, 11 L.Ed.2d 686, 700 (1964); Letter of James Madison to W. T. Barry, August 4, 1822, quoted in Environmental Protection Agency v. Mink, 410 U.S. 73, 110–111, 93 S.Ct. 827, 847, 35 L.Ed.2d 119, 145 (1973) (dissenting opinion of Douglas, J.); Kathleen A. Dockry, Note, The First Amendment Right of Access to Government–Held Information: A Re–Evaluation After Richmond Newspapers, Inc. v. Virginia, 34 Rutgers L. Rev. 292, 303–304 (1982).

2. See United States v. Nixon, 418 U.S. 683, 703–713, 94 S.Ct. 3090, 3105–3110, 41 L.Ed.2d 1039, 1061–1067 (1974); United States v. Reynolds, 345 U.S. 1, 73 S.Ct. 528, 97 L.Ed. 727 (1953).

3. But in fact the Chicago Tribune somehow did get access to this information and published a short article about it, causing President Roosevelt to exclaim that if the publisher, Col. Robert B. McCormick were in the same room he (Roosevelt) would kill him with his bare hands.

4. See, e.g., United States v. Nixon, 418 U.S. 683, 94 S.Ct. 3090, 41 L.Ed.2d 1039 (1974) (the Nixon White House Tapes) New York Times Co. v. United States, 403 U.S. 713, 91 S.Ct. 2140, 29 L.Ed.2d 822 (1971) (the "Pentagon Papers"); Near v. Minnesota, 283 U.S. 697, 51 S.Ct. 625, 75 L.Ed. 1357 (1931) (stories about corrupt city officials appearing in a sleazy Minneapolis weekly scandal sheet).

this news and information the citizenry will be powerless to effect peaceful change and preserve the essence of our democratic system.[5] The question, then, is to what extent the nation's legal structure insures access of the news media as representatives of the public to news and information controlled by government.

B. Access Provided by the Common Law

There is a very limited common law right of access to public records and documents permitting their inspection and copying.[6] One commentator has synthesized the common law right to mean that "[a] person may inspect public records in which he has an interest or make copies or memoranda thereof when necessity for inspection is shown and the purpose does not seem improper, and where the disclosure would not be detrimental to the public interest."[7] This right applies only to "a written memorial, made by a public officer authorized by law to make it. It is required by law to be kept, in the discharge of a duty imposed by law or directed by law to serve as a written memorial and evidence of something written, said or done."[8] Given the narrow definition of a public record or document, many, if not most, of the records and papers held by governmental entities would not be available under the common law right. The common law exempts from disclosure those records which are private, secret or privileged and even those clearly public in a legal sense but sufficiently sensitive that their disclosure would likely do more harm than good to the public interest.[9] Such judgment is left to the sound discretion of the trial court.[10] Examples of the exercise of discretion to bar access to public records and documents include sordid details of marital life embodied in divorce papers, libelous statements in public filings and the disclosure of trade secrets.[11]

Because of the narrowness of the common law access privilege and its very uncertain application given the wide discretion of trial courts to withhold it, the news media more often than not make their claims to access to governmentally held news and information on other bases.

---

5. See n.4, *supra.*

6. See Nixon v. Warner Communications, Inc. 435 U.S. 589, 597, 98 S.Ct. 1306, 1312, 55 L.Ed.2d 570, 579 (1978); Application of National Broadcasting Co., Inc., 635 F.2d 945, 949 (2d Cir.1980); HAROLD L. CROSS, THE PEOPLE'S RIGHT TO KNOW: LEGAL ACCESS TO PUBLIC RECORDS AND PROCEEDINGS (1953); Kathleen A. Dockry, Note, *The First Amendment Right of Access to Government–Held Information: A Re–Evaluation After Richmond Newspapers, Inc. v. Virginia*, 34 Rutgers L. Rev. 292, 295 (1982).

7. HAROLD L. CROSS, THE PEOPLE'S RIGHT TO KNOW: LEGAL ACCESS TO PUBLIC RECORDS AND PROCEEDINGS 29 (1953).

8. Amos v. Gunn, 84 Fla. 285, 343, 94 So. 615, 634 (1922).

9. See HAROLD L. CROSS, THE PEOPLE'S RIGHT TO KNOW: LEGAL ACCESS TO PUBLIC RECORDS AND PROCEEDINGS 75 (1953); Project, *Government Information and the Rights of Citizens*, 73 Mich. L. Rev. 971, 1170–1171 (1975).

10. See Nixon v. Warner Communications, Inc., 435 U.S. 589, 599, 98 S.Ct. 1306, 1313, 55 L.Ed.2d 570, 577 (1978).

11. *Id.* at 598, 98 S. Ct. at 1312, 55 L. Ed. 2d at 598; David S. Cohen, Note, *The Public's Right to Access Under the First Amendment*, 51 Chi–Kent L. Rev. 164, 169–170 (1974).

C. Special Access Under the First Amendment

1. The Supreme Court's Doctrine

Given the critical importance of access to news and information controlled by the government and the very weak privilege provided by the common law, it is not surprising that members of the news media have laid claim to access under the Press Clause of the First Amendment. But the United States Supreme Court, while recognizing the need for some protection for newsgathering,[12] has consistently rejected any special right of access to governmentally controlled news and information beyond that accorded to the general public.[13]

The claim to special access was first presented to the high court in a somewhat oblique manner in *Zemel* v. *Rusk*.[14] There, shortly after the Cuban missile crisis in 1962, a private citizen applied to the Department of State to have his valid United States passport validated for travel to Cuba as a tourist, stating that the purpose of the proposed trip was "to satisfy my curiosity about the state of affairs in Cuba and to make me a better informed citizen."[15] When his request was denied, he filed suit against the Secretary of State and the Attorney General seeking a judgment declaring, *inter alia*, that he was entitled under the Constitution to travel to Cuba and to have his passport validated for that purpose. He also claimed that the Secretary of State's refusal to validate his passport violated rights guaranteed to him by the Constitution. His constitutional claims were grounded in part in the First Amendment. A divided three-judge district court granted the Secretary's motion for summary judgment and dismissed the action against the Attorney General.

On the appeal the Supreme Court affirmed the judgments of the trial court. Regarding the appellant's contention that the First Amendment protected unrestrained travel abroad for fact-finding purposes, the Court held that the First Amendment did not have such broad reach. "There are few restrictions on action which could not be clothed by ingenious argument in the garb of decreased data flow.... The right to speak and publish does not carry with it the unrestrained right to gather information."[16] No authority or overarching constitutional theory was offered by the Court in fashioning its limiting position on access to news and information under the First Amendment.

---

12. *See* Branzburg v. Hayes, 408 U.S. 665, 681, 92 S.Ct. 2646, 2656, 33 L.Ed.2d 626, 639 (1972).

13. Access of the news media to news and information concerning judicial process is based on the general public's historic right to such news and information and is dealt with in the following section of this chapter.

14. 381 U.S. 1, 85 S.Ct. 1271, 14 L.Ed.2d 179 (1965).

15. *Id.* at 4, 85 S. Ct. at 1274, 14 L. Ed. 2d at 183.

16. *Id.* at 16–17, 85 S. Ct. at 1281, 14 L. Ed. 2d at 190. The Court, in attempting to reduce the appellant's contention to absurdity gave the following example: "[T]he prohibition of unauthorized entry into the White House diminishes the citizen's opportunities to gather information he might find relevant to his opinion of the way the country is being run, but that does not make entry into the White House a First Amendment right." *Id.* at 17, 85 S. Ct. at 1281 14 L. Ed. 2d at 190.

Later in *Branzburg* v. *Hayes*,[17] not an access case but one involving claims of reporters to a First Amendment privilege not to disclose information to grand juries obtained in the course of newsgathering, the Supreme Court said more pointedly by way of dictum, and still without offering any theory, "It has generally been held that the First Amendment does not guarantee the press a constitutional right of special access to information not available to the public generally."[18]

In its first access cases involving actual newsgatherers, *Pell* v. *Procunier*[19] and *Saxbe* v. *Washington Post*,[20] decided on the same day, a closely divided Court turned the pointed dictum of *Branzburg* into holding. In *Pell*, the reporters' requests for face to face interviews with individual inmates held by the California Department of Corrections was denied pursuant to a Department regulation barring interviews by members of the news media with specific inmates. In *Saxbe*, a reporter's similar request of the Federal Bureau of Prisons to conduct interviews with a specific list of inmates in the federal prisons at Lewisburg, Pennsylvania and Danbury, Connecticut was denied pursuant to the Bureau's standing policy statement. Deeming the cases constitutionally indistinguishable, Justice Stewart, writing for the Court, rejected the claims of the newsgatherers involved that the First Amendment accorded them access broader than that accorded members of the public generally, including face to face interviews with specifically designated inmates.[21] In his opinion in *Pell*, Justice Stewart touched on a theory, developed elsewhere[22] which might, for want of a better term, be labeled the "cat and mouse" theory[23] with the cat being government and the mouse being the news media. Under this theory the government is free to attempt to keep news and information secret and the news media is free to attempt furtively (though not unlawfully) to snatch news and information from the very jaws of its adversary. Or, in Justice Stewart's own words, "It is one thing to say that a journalist is free to seek out sources of information not available to members of the general public, that he is entitled to some constitutional protection of the confidentiality of such sources, *cf. Branzburg v. Hayes, supra*, and that government cannot restrain the publication of news emanating from such sources.... It is quite another thing to suggest that the Constitution imposes upon government the affirmative duty to make available to journalists sources of information not available to members of the public

---

17. 408 U.S. 665, 92 S.Ct. 2646, 33 L.Ed.2d 626 (1972).

18. *Id.* at 684, 92 S. Ct. at 2658, 33 L. Ed. 2d at 641 (citing Zemel).

19. 417 U.S. 817, 94 S.Ct. 2800, 41 L.Ed.2d 495 (1974).

20. 417 U.S. 843, 94 S.Ct. 2811, 41 L.Ed.2d 514 (1974).

21. Pell, 417 U.S. at 834, 94 S. Ct. at 2810, 41 L. Ed. 2d at 508; Saxbe, 417 U.S.

at 850, 94 S. Ct. at 2815, 41 L. Ed. 2d at 519–520.

22. *See* Potter Stewart, *"Or of the Press,"* 26 Hastings L.J. 631 (1975); Randall P. Bezanson, *The New Free Press Guarantee*, 63 Va. L. Rev. 731 (1977).

23. Actually, Professor Randall P. Bezanson has coined a better though less colorful name for this theory—"libertarian." *See* Randall P. Bezanson, *The New Free Press Guarantee*, 63 Va. L. Rev. 731, 734–735, 752 (1977).

generally. That proposition finds no support in the words of the Constitution or in any decision of this Court."[24]

Justice Stewart suggested that while the Press Clause does confer protection on the media to publish the news it obtains from whatever source, the Founding Fathers did not accord a special privilege to the fourth estate to gather news, since to have done so would have compromised it's independence from government in exercising the desired checking function against government. There are serious shortcomings in Justice Stewart's reading of the First Amendment including the lack of a guarantee of *any* receipt by the public of vital news and information controlled by government should the "mouse" prove to be ineffectual in snatching it and the failure to explain why the independence of the press will inevitably be compromised if special access is bestowed by the very amendment that guarantees the press' independence in the first place. Nevertheless, the Court continued to embrace Stewart's theory in *Houchins* v. *KQED, Inc.,*[25] another prison access case reaching essentially the same result, *i.e.,* barring press access to portions of a jail and to the prisoners therein. The jail regulation went beyond that in *Pell* and *Saxbe* in banning the use of cameras and tape recorders on the narrowly restricted public tours that were permitted. This difference led Justice Stewart to file a concurring opinion based on the premise that news media access equal to that of the touring members of the public encompassed cameras and recording equipment so that effective presentation of what could actually be seen and heard on the tours could be made to those not present for the tours.[26]

It is clear, then, that existing Supreme Court doctrine is to the effect that there is no right of access of the news media to governmentally controlled information under the First Amendment beyond that made available by government to the public generally. And this is true whether the Court views the Press Clause as redundant of the Speech Clause or accepts the late Justice Stewart's view that although the Press Clause has independent meaning, it may not be read as conferring a guarantee of special access on the news media. The Court's doctrine, is of course, binding on the lower federal and state courts when they confront claims of special access in a multitude of newsgathering situations.

24. 417 U.S. at 834–835, 94 S. Ct. at 2810, 41 L. Ed. 2d at 508–509.

25. 438 U.S. 1, 14–15, 98 S.Ct. 2588, 2597, 57 L.Ed.2d 553, 564–565 (1978). Between the cases of *Pell, Saxbe* and *Houchins,* the Court decided the analogous case of *Greer* v. *Spock,* 424 U.S. 828, 96 S.Ct. 1211, 47 L.Ed.2d 505 (1976) in which the famous pediatrician Benjamin Spock and others sought access to Fort Dix for the purpose of exercising their claimed First Amendment right to distribute election campaign literature and to hold a meeting to discuss election issues with service personnel and their dependents. When their request for access was rejected by the commanding general, they obtained a permanent injunction barring military authorities from interfering with the political activity in areas of the fort open to the general public. The judgment was ultimately reversed by the Court under an historical analysis establishing the unquestioned power of commanding officers summarily to exclude civilians from the area of their commands. *Id.* at 838, 96 S. Ct. at 1217, 47 L. Ed. 2d at 514.

26. *Id.* at 18, 98 S. Ct. at 2598, 57 L. Ed. 2d at 567.

2. Lower Federal and State Court Decisions

The lower courts have encountered claims of special access under the First Amendment in a number of news source contexts. The more recurring ones are discussed below.

a. Government Owned or Regulated Land and Buildings.

The fact that buildings or land are publicly owned and used for governmental purposes provides no basis for access thereto unless the public generally is encouraged to enter and gather information by the authorities in control. This is true of penitentiaries,[27] state mental hospitals,[28] voting areas within buildings[29] and federally regulated nuclear power plants.[30] Even where the public is encouraged to enter publicly owned facilities used for proprietary rather than governmental purposes such as a civic center auditorium leased to promoters for a rock concert[31] or an ice skating competition,[32] the news media may be barred from bringing in photographic equipment to record the activities.

b. Disaster and Crime Scenes.

Whether there exists some limited special access of the news media to the scene of disasters and crimes is a rather complex issue. On the one hand the Wisconsin Supreme Court has ruled that no such special access to disaster scenes exists, relying on *Zemel, Branzburg, Pell, Saxbe* and *Houchins*.[33] And the New Jersey Supreme Court, while purporting to find a limited right of special access for newspersons at accident scenes under the First Amendment, upheld the conviction of a newspaper photographer as a "disorderly person" simply because of his heated refusal to obey the order of the lone police officer present to leave the

---

27. *See, e.g.,* Garrett v. Estelle, 556 F.2d 1274 (5th Cir.1977) (television reporter denied access to "death row" and execution area to film interviews with condemned prisoners and photographically record an execution); Jersawitz v. Hanberry, 783 F.2d 1532, 1534 (11th Cir.1986), cert. denied 479 U.S. 883, 107 S.Ct. 272, 93 L.Ed.2d 249 (1986); *see also* Houchins v. KQED, Inc. 438 U.S. 1, 98 S.Ct. 2588, 57 L.Ed.2d 553 (1978); Saxbe v. Washington Post Co., 417 U.S. 843, 94 S.Ct. 2811, 41 L.Ed.2d 514 (1974); Pell v. Procunier, 417 U.S. 817, 94 S.Ct. 2800, 41 L.Ed.2d 495 (1974).

28. *See* Mann v. State's Attorney for Montgomery County, 298 Md. 160, 171–172, 468 A.2d 124, 129–130 (1983) (television reporter denied access to state mental hospital to interview criminally insane patient); *but see* North Broward Hospital Dist. v. ABC, 13 Media L. Rptr. 1509 (Fla.Cir.Ct. 1986) (First Amendment held to protect access of television crew to film comatose patient with the consent of her attorneys and guardians).

29. *See* Firestone v. News–Press Pub. Co., Inc., 538 So.2d 457, 460 (Fla.1989).

30. *See* Stahl v. State, 665 P.2d 839, 841–842 (Okl.Cr.1983), cert. denied 464 U.S. 1069, 104 S.Ct. 973, 79 L.Ed.2d 212 (1984).

31. *See* D'Amario v. Providence Civic Center, 639 F.Supp. 1538 (D.R.I.1986), *aff'd mem.* 815 F.2d 692 (1st Cir.), cert. denied 484 U.S. 859, 108 S.Ct. 172, 98 L.Ed.2d 125 (1987).

32. *See* Post Newsweek Stations–Connecticut, Inc. v. Travelers Ins. Co., 510 F.Supp. 81 (D.Conn.1981).

33. *See* City of Oak Creek v. King, 148 Wis.2d 532, 541, 436 N.W.2d 285, 291–293 (1989) (television reporter's conviction for disorderly conduct in failing to leave air crash scene after being ordered to do so by police officer upheld); *see also* Prahl v. Brosamle, 98 Wis.2d 130, 149–150, 295 N.W.2d 768, 780–781 (Wis.App.1980) (civil liability of television reporter for entering crime scene on private property without consent of owner upheld).

immediate vicinity of a gory fatal automobile accident.[34] Though ostensibly accepting the idea that a balancing approach to special newsgatherer access to accident scenes was required under the First Amendment, the New Jersey Court seemed to pay mere lip service to the reporter's claim of a constitutional right.[35]

On the other hand, one federal trial court has unequivocally recognized such a claim. In *Westinghouse Broadcasting Co., Inc.* v. *National Transportation Safety Board*,[36] the United States District Court for Massachusetts adopted, in an oral opinion from the bench, a balancing test for according special access to the scene of a plane crash scene in the Boston area.[37] The court weighed the Board's need to prevent tampering with the area and remnants of the airliner against the facts that the runway involved was not in use, the fuselage was out in the open where cameramen and news reporters could fulfill their responsibilities without touching the wreckage in any way and the Board's inspection of the actual wreckage had been temporarily suspended.[38] Given these facts, the court ruled that the Board's "one hour per day" order violated the news media's evolving First Amendment right of special access to news scenes. But the decision, is flawed by the court's misreading of the approach to special access taken by the Supreme Court in *Houchins* and *Zemel*[39] and the almost total lack of authority for its reading of the First Amendment.[40] As much as some commentators would prefer to have it otherwise,[41] there does not yet appear to be any substantial recognition of a constitutional right of special access to disaster and crime scenes.

This is not to say that state and federal legislators are barred from providing special access by statute[42] or that local authorities, by extra-

---

34. *See* State v. Lashinsky, 81 N.J. 1, 13–14, 19, 404 A.2d 1121, 1127–1128, 1130–1131 (1979); *see also* Kent R. Middleton, *Journalists Interference with Police: The First Amendment, Access to News and Official Discretion,* 5 Comm/Ent L.J. 443 (1983) (highly critical analysis of *Lashinsky* ruling).

35. *See* dissenting opinion of Pashman, J., 81 N.J. at 21, 404 A.2d at 1131; Middleton, 5 Comm/Ent L.J. at 449.

36. 8 Med. L. Rptr. 1177 (D.Mass.1982).

37. *Id.* at 1184. In so doing the trial court misread the plurality opinion in *Houchins* v. *KQED, Inc.,* 438 U.S. 1, 98 S.Ct. 2588, 57 L.Ed.2d 553 (1978) and the majority opinion in *Zemel* v. *Rusk,* 381 U.S. 1, 85 S.Ct. 1271, 14 L.Ed.2d 179 (1965) as applying some kind of balancing test for special access under the First Amendment. *Id.* at 1182.

38. *Id.* at 1184.

39. *See* note 37, *supra.*

40. The authority the district judge in *Westinghouse* most heavily relied upon is *Cable News Network, Inc.* v. *American Broadcasting Companies, Inc.,* 518 F.Supp. 1238 (N.D.Ga.1981) in which the district court adopted a balancing approach in the context of access of television networks to pool coverage of White House events. Unless one takes an extremely cynical view, this case does not deal with disaster scenes.

41. *See* Kent R. Middleton, *Journalists' Interference with Police: The First Amendment, Access to News and Official Discretion,* 5 Comm/Ent L.J. 443, 452 (1983); Karen S. Precella, Comment, *Freedom of the Press: Does the Media Have a Special Right of Access to Air Crash Sites?,* 56 J. Air L. & Com. 641, 679–687 (1990).

42. *See* Cal. Penal Code § 409.5 (West Supp. 1991): [text in Practitioners Edition, Vol. 2 only].

The California statute was construed broadly in favor of news person access in *Leiserson* v. *City of San Diego,* 184 Cal. App.3d 41, 229 Cal.Rptr. 22 (1986). *But see* Los Angeles Free Press, Inc. v. City of Los Angeles, 9 Cal.App.3d 448, 457, 88 Cal.Rptr. 605 (1970), cert. denied 401 U.S. 982, 91 S.Ct. 1193, 28 L.Ed.2d 334 (1971) (discre-

legal arrangements,[43] cannot provide for such access to crime and disaster scenes for members of the news media.

c. *Access to War Zones and Military Installations.*

(1) constitutional access.

There has been a long and checkered history regarding special access of news media representatives to war zones and military installations under the control of the United States military.[44] What access there has been is of a *de facto* nature through administrative grace. And, of course, it has been accompanied by military censorship.[45] Until relatively recently in our history there has been no case law considering whether the news media have a constitutionally protected *right* to access to such areas and installations. Then in *Cafeteria Workers* v. *McElroy*,[46] and *Greer* v. *Spock*,[47] the Supreme Court stated that "[a] necessary concomitant of the basic function of a military installation has been 'the historically unquestioned power of [its] commanding officer summarily to exclude civilians from the area of his command.' "[48] While neither of these cases involved the news media, they did implicate constitutional claims of civilians relating directly (*Spock*) or indirectly (*Cafeteria Workers*) to access to military installations, which claims were summarily rejected by the Court.

tion placed in law enforcement officers to decide whether to permit certain members of news media to cross police lines); 66 Ops. Atty. Gen. 497 (1983) (state law enforcement officers may assist federal authorities to exclude members of the news media from plane crash site under control of the federal officers).

43. *See* ACCESS TO PLACES 8–9 (Reporters Committee for Freedom of the Press 1989); Kent R. Middleton, *Journalists' Interference with Police: The First Amendment, Access to News and Official Discretion*, 5 Comm/Ent 443, 448 (1983). Police department guidelines for police—media relations and press pass systems as unofficial attempts to resolve access issues are beyond the scope of this section.

44. *See* Paul G. Cassell, *Restrictions on Press Coverage of Military Operations: The Right of Access, Grenada, and "Off-the-Record Wars,"* 73 Geo. L.J. 931, 932–948 (1985); Roger W. Pincus, *Press Access to Military Operations: Grenada and the Need for a New Analytical Framework*, 135 U. Pa. L. Rev. 813, 836–838 (1987); Michelle D. Boydston, Note, *Press Censorship and Access Restrictions During the Persian Gulf War: A First Amendment Analysis*, 25 Loyola L.A. L. Rev. 1073, 1074–1088 (1992).

45. There seems little doubt on the part of the federal judiciary that such censorship is constitutional if limited to immediate intelligence of a nature posing a serious risk of danger to the country's military operations or national security. *See* New York Times Co. v. United States, 403 U.S. 713, 91 S.Ct. 2140, 29 L.Ed.2d 822 (1971) (concurring opinions of Brennan, Stewart, White and Marshall, J.J. and dissenting opinions of Burger, C. J. and Harlan and Blackmun, J.J.); Haig v. Agee, 453 U.S. 280, 308–309, 101 S.Ct. 2766, 2782–2783, 69 L.Ed.2d 640, 663 (1981); Near v. Minnesota, 283 U.S. 697, 716, 51 S.Ct. 625, 631, 75 L.Ed. 1357, 1367 (1931) (dictum); *see also* Roger W. Pincus, *Press Access to Military Operations; The Right of Access, Grenada and the Need for a New Analytical Framework*, 135 U. Pa. L. Rev. 813, 836 (1987); Michelle D. Boydston, Note, *Press Censorship and Access Restrictions During the Persian Gulf War: A First Amendment Analysis*, 25 Loyola L.A. L. Rev. 1073, 1098–1099 (1992).

46. 367 U.S. 886, 81 S.Ct. 1743, 6 L.Ed.2d 1230 (1961).

47. 424 U.S. 828, 96 S.Ct. 1211, 47 L.Ed.2d 505 (1976).

48. 367 U.S. at 893, 81 S. Ct. at 1743, 6 L. Ed. 2d at 1230; 424 U.S. at 838, 96 S. Ct. at 1217, 47 L. Ed. 2d at 514.

Apparently the first reported case to consider a claim to news media access to a war zone was *Flynt* v. *Weinberger*.[49] There, Larry Flynt, publisher of *Hustler* magazine, and others challenged the Department of Defense order banning press coverage of the initial stages of the Grenada invasion. While conceding that in the early going a total news blackout was imposed and the only information made available to the public about the military intervention was that issued by official government sources, the district court dismissed the action with prejudice on grounds of mootness since the swift military action was over and the anti-press access order had been lifted by the time Flynt's action was considered. By way of dictum the trial judge stated that even if there were a live controversy and the temporary press ban violated the plaintiffs' First Amendment rights (which he doubted), he would not issue an injunction restraining the government from restricting press access to future military operations. "An injunction such as the one plaintiffs seek would limit the range of options available to the commanders in the field in the future, possibly jeopardizing the success of military operations and the lives of military personnel and thereby gravely damaging the national interest."[50]

The District of Columbia Circuit affirmed the dismissal order solely on grounds of mootness but found the district judge's remarks on the underlying merits and his dismissal of the complaint with prejudice to be inappropriate. The appeals court therefore vacated the district court's opinion.[51] Thus even after Grenada there was no firm holding by any court on the constitutional access claim of the news media. But by then the pro-military attitude of the federal judiciary had become increasingly apparent.[52]

(2) administrative access.

The Grenada news blackout and the high handed treatment of news media personally by the military[53] engendered such controversy and

49. 588 F.Supp. 57 (D.D.C.1984), *affirmed but opinion vacated* 762 F.2d 134, 246 U.S. App. D.C. 40 (D.C.Cir.1985).

50. *Id.* at 60.

51. 762 F.2d at 135–136, 246 U.S. App. D.C. at 41–42.

52. In other contexts, conflicts between claimed military necessity and First Amendment rights of individuals have been resolved by the federal courts in favor of the military. *See, e.g.,* Goldman v. Weinberger, 475 U.S. 503, 106 S.Ct. 1310, 89 L.Ed.2d 478 (1986) (claim of right to free exercise of religion by Air Force officer and ordained rabbi who wished to wear prayer cap on duty rejected); Ben–Shalom v. Marsh, 881 F.2d 454 (7th Cir.1989), cert. denied 494 U.S. 1004, 110 S.Ct. 1296, 108 L.Ed.2d 473 (1990) (claim of Army Reserve sergeant that her right to freedom of speech was violated by her being barred from reen-listment after making public statements concerning her lesbian sexual orientation rejected; her claim of violation of constitutionally protected privacy also rejected); Dash v. Commanding General, Fort Jackson, South Carolina, 307 F.Supp. 849 (D.S.C.1969), *aff'd* 429 F.2d 427 (4th Cir. 1970)(claims that servicemembers' rights of freedom of speech and peaceable assembly were violated by post commander's refusal to permit them to hold an open public meeting to discuss legal and moral questions relating to Vietnam War rejected). After reviewing the cases one might be tempted to conclude that in such Constitutional conflicts the American military always wins.

53. The Commander of Task Force in Grenada, Vice Admiral Joseph Metcalf, III, was quoted as saying, "Well, I know how to stop those press boats. We've been shooting

enmity between the press and the government[54] that the Department of Defense was forced to confront the access issue in a systematic manner.[55] The Chairman of the Joint Chiefs of Staff, General John W. Vesey, Jr. appointed a panel of military and media people under the chairmanship of retired General Winant Sidle, a military spokesperson during the Vietnam War. The panel's final report released less than a year after the Grenada invasion[56] recommended that news pools should be instituted to insure early access to military operations. Further, it recommended that operational planning should provide for the largest press pool practical and minimize the length of time pooling is necessary before "full coverage" of military operations is feasible.[57] The panel also recommended that "a basic tenet governing media access to military operations should be voluntary compliance by the media with security guidelines or ground rules established and issued by the military" with violations thereof resulting in "exclusion of the correspondent(s) concerned from further coverage of the operation."[58] In addition, recommendations were made to provide pool members with military communications facilities, transportation support and military escorts.[59] Other suggestions peripheral to the issue of access were also made.

The Sidle panel's recommendations were generally accepted by the Secretary of Defense[60] and, despite warnings that the news media would be tying their own hands or would be coopted in reporting war news by embracing the panel's report,[61] the major news organizations went

at them. We haven't sunk any yet, but how are we to know who's on them?" *Admiral Says It Was His Decision to Tether the Press*, N.Y. Times, Oct. 31, 1983, p. A12, col. 3 (AP wire report). Four experienced journalists were actually stopped from filing news reports by being held virtually incommunicado for 18 hours aboard Admiral Metcalf's flagship the *U.S.S. Guam* after being led to believe by "a good-hearted marine colonel" that they might be able to use that ship's communications facilities. Edward Cody, *The Invasion of Grenada; U.S. Forces Thwart Journalists' Reports*, Wash. Post, Oct. 27, 1983, p. A16; William E. Farrell, *U.S. Allows 15 Reporters to Go to Grenada for Day*, N.Y. Times, Oct. 28, 1983, p. A13, col. 5.

54. *See, e.g.*, THE MEDIA AT WAR: THE PRESS AND THE PERSIAN GULF CONFLICT 15 (The Gannett Foundation 1991) Paul G. Cassell, 73 Geo. L.J. 931, 932 (1985); William E. Farrell, *U.S. Allows 15 Reporters to Go to Grenada for Day*, N.Y. Times, Oct. 28, 1983, p. A13, col. 5. The Farrell article quoted a spokesperson for the American Society of Newspaper Editors as saying that the restrictions on coverage of the Grenada invasion "go beyond the normal limits of military censorship." *Id*. The same article quoted Jerry Freidheim, executive vice president of the American Newspaper

Publishers Association as saying the restrictions were "unprecedented and intolerable." He called upon Congress to investigate what he called a "policy of secret wars hidden from the American people." *Id*.

55. *See, e.g.*, THE MEDIA AT WAR: THE PRESS AND THE PERSIAN GULF CONFLICT 15–16 (The Gannett Foundation 1991).

56. Chairman of the Joint Chiefs of Staff Media–Military Relations Panel, Sidle Report [hereafter referred to as the Sidle Report], *reprinted in* Office of Assistant Secretary of Defense (Public Affairs) News Release No. 450–84 (Aug. 23, 1984); *see* N.Y. Times, Aug. 24, 1984, p. 6, col. 1 (key sections of Sidle Report set out in full text).

57. Sidle Report at 4.

58. *Id*. at 5.

59. *Id*.

60. *See* Office of Assistant Secretary of Defense (Public Affairs) News Release No. 450–84 (Aug. 23, 1984); Richard Halloran, *Pentagon Issues News Guidelines for Combat Zones*, N.Y. Times, Aug. 24, 1984, p. A1, col. 1.

61. *See, e.g.*, Harvey L. Zuckman, *Don't Be Co-opted by the Folks Who Brought Us Vietnam, Grenada and the Iranian Rescue Fiasco*, 3 ABA Communications Lawyer 15

along.[62] The first attempt to implement the Sidle Panel's recommendations came with the invasion of Panama. The implementation was not a success for either the media or the military.[63]

In his special report to the Assistant Secretary of Defense for Public Affairs,[64] a Pentagon official listed numerous shortcomings of the Panama pool arrangement including the military's failure to provide regular operational briefings for the pool representatives; the breakdown of communications causing serious delays in getting out print media reports and still photos; the lateness of the arrival of the pool representatives in Panama from Washington; and the ineffectiveness of the military's public affairs officers or "escorts" in getting pool reporters to the scenes of action.[65] The official then made several recommendations for improving the operation of the Department of Defense National Media Pool in future combat situations.[66]

In the Persian Gulf engagement, the National Media Pool faced its first truly major challenge, given the size of the theater of operations. Logistical problems developed in providing news media access to the combat zones, particularly in the early stages of the fighting[67] which

(No. 1, Winter 1985) (editorial); *Covering the Next War*, Wash. Post, Aug. 31, 1984, p.A20, col. 1 (editorial); Richard Halloran, *The Pentagon, Weinberger and the Press: An Ebb in the Flow*, N.Y. Times, Aug. 25, 1984, § 1, A6, col. 3.

62. *See* Caroline Rand Herron, Michael Wright and Katherine Roberts, *Taking the Press Along*, N.Y. Times, Aug. 26, 1984, § 4, p. 2, col. 2.

63. *See, e.g.*, Report of Fred Hoffman to Pete Williams, Assistant Secretary of Defense for Public Affairs, reprinted as an attachment to DoD Memorandum for Correspondents, Mar. 20, 1990; Patrick J. Sloyan, *Candor Panama's 1st Casualty; U.S. Press Restrictions Guarded Military's Image, Curbed News*, Newsday, Jan. 14, 1990, Sec. "News," p. 5; Arthur A. Lord, *The Flow of Combat News Was a Strangled Media Trickle: The Sequestering of Reporters After the Panama Invasion Proves the Pentagon's Openness to Coverage a Sham*, L.A. Times, Jan. 23, 1990, Sec. Metro, Part B, p. 7 col. 1 (op-ed piece); Kevin Merida, *The Panama Press Pool Fiasco; the Military Let Journalists Do Everything Except Cover the News*, Wash. Post, Jan. 7, 1990, p. B2 (opinion piece); Patrick E. Tyler, *Officially, Pentagon Takes Blame, Media Pool Had Problems in Panama After Bush Worried About Secrecy*, Wash. Post, Mar. 21, 1990, p. A19; Michael R. Gordon, *Cheney Blamed for Press Problems in Panama*, N.Y. Times, Mar. 20, 1990, p. A8, col. 4.

64. Report of Fred Hoffman to Pete Williams, Assistant Secretary of Defense for

Public Affairs, reprinted as an attachment to DoD Memorandum for Correspondents, Mar. 20, 1990.

65. *Id.* at 2.

66. *Id.* at 17–19. The 17 recommendations included requiring all operational plans drafted by the Joint Staff to have an annex spelling out measures to assure that the pool would move with the lead elements of United States forces and cover the earliest stages of operations; encouraging the Chairman of the Joint Chiefs of Staff to send a message ordering all commanders to give full cooperation to the pool and escorts, such message making clear that necessary transportation and communications resources must be earmarked specifically for pool use; that the pool *"must"* have ready access to the earliest action (report author's emphasis) and safety of pool members must not be used as a reason to keep the pool reporters from combat action; that during deployments, there should be held regular briefings for the pool by senior operations officers; and that the pool escort system be overhauled. *Id.* at 17–18.

67. *See* REPORT: THE MEDIA AT WAR: THE PRESS AND THE PERSIAN GULF CONFLICT 16–20 (Gannett Foundation 1991); Howard Kurtz, *News Media Ask Freer Hand in Future Conflicts*, Wash. Post, July 1, 1991, p. A4, col. 1; Howard Kurtz *Journalists Say 'Pools' Don't Work; Lack of Access Hampers Coverage*, Wash. Post, Feb. 11, 1991, p.A1, col. 5; Guy Gugliotta, *Signs of Breakdown in Pool System; Dispatches Arrive Late, Lack of Firsthand Accounts of*

problems were compounded by ground rules and supplementary guidelines seemingly designed to thwart the successful operation of the Department of Defense's pool system.[68] Members of the news media protested the use and operation of the pools in a letter to the Secretary of Defense following the Persian Gulf War, which stated that independent reporting should be the principal means of coverage for all future United States military operations.[69] The letter further asserted that pools should be employed only for the first 24 to 36 hours of any military deployment.[70]

Some news and civil rights organizations did more than send a letter complaining about the lack of access. They sued the Department of Defense. Only one such case reached the merits. In *JB Pictures, Inc.* v. *Department of Defense*,[71] various news media personnel and veterans groups sought on First Amendment grounds an emergency preliminary injunction to prevent the Defense Department from closing Dover Air Force Base to the public and the news media so as to prevent the viewing there of the arrival of the bodies of service personnel killed in the Gulf War.[72] Dover AFB in Delaware is the East Coast receiving point for military members killed in action abroad. In its motion to dismiss, the government asserted that the First Amendment did not guarantee to the public and media access to all events or information within its control.[73] The trial judge denied the request for preliminary injunction.[74] More than two years later the same judge dismissed the action as failing to state a claim upon which relief could be granted because there was no First Amendment right of access to the military installation involved.[75]

A gulf war access decision that did not reach the merits but is informative on peripheral matters is *Nation Magazine* v. *United States Department of Defense*[76] in which numerous members of the news media

---

Ground Battle, Wash. Post, Feb. 27, 1991, p. A27, col. 1.

68. These ground rules and guidelines are reprinted as appendices to *Nation Magazine v. United States Department of Defense*, 762 F.Supp. 1558, 1575–1582 (S.D.N.Y.1991) and REPORT: THE MEDIA AT WAR: THE PRESS AND THE PERSIAN GULF CONFLICT 98–101 (Gannett Foundation 1991).

69. Howard Kurtz, *News Media Ask Freer Hand in Future Conflicts; Executives Tell Cheney Independent Reporting Should Be "Principal Means of Coverage"*, Wash. Post., July 1, 1991, p. A4, col. 1; Jason DeParle, *17 News Executives Criticize U.S. for "Censorship" of Gulf Coverage*, N.Y. Times, July 3, 1991, p. A4, col. 5.

70. *Id.* In an initial response to the letter from news media members, the Assistant Secretary of Defense for Public Affairs said, "Everyone hates pools. We hate pools because they are tough to administer. News organizations hate pools because they go against the grain [of competition]." But he

further stated that they could not be ruled out in some circumstances. *Id.*

71. 1993 WL 166918, 21 Med. L. Rptr. 1564 (D.D.C.1993), *aff'd* 86 F.3d 236 (D.C.Cir.1996) *and unofficially reported in* REPORT: THE MEDIA AT WAR: THE PRESS AND THE PERSIAN GULF CONFLICT 22 (Gannett Foundation 1991); Legal Times, Mar. 18, 1991, p. 15; N.Y. Times, Mar. 9, 1991, § 1, p. 4, col. 5 (Reuters wire report).

72. *See* Legal Times, Mar. 18, 1991, p. 15.

73. *Id.*

74. *Id.*; *see also* REPORT: THE MEDIA AT WAR: THE PRESS AND THE PERSIAN GULF CONFLICT 22 (Gannett Foundation 1991) (synopsis of trial judge's oral opinion from the bench); N.Y. Times, Mar. 9, 1991, § . 1, p. 4, col. 5 (Reuters wire report); Wash. Post, Feb. 26, 1991, p. A12 (denial of temporary restraining order in same case).

75. 21 Med. L. Rptr. 1564 (D.D.C.1993).

76. 762 F.Supp. 1558 (S.D.N.Y.1991).

brought an action challenging the Gulf War Ground Rules and Supplementary Guidelines governing access to military operations. Consolidated with this action was *Agence France—Presse* v. *United States Department of Defense*[77] in which the French wirephoto service sought access to the Department of Defense's photographic pool. The thrust of the plaintiffs claim was that the news media have a First Amendment right to unlimited access to foreign combat zones in which United States forces are engaged. More specifically they claimed that Department of Defense pool regulations restricting access to such zones to a limited numbers of press representatives and subjecting them to certain restrictions in gathering the news violated the First Amendment. Less emphasis was placed in the complaint on restrictions as to what could be published.[78] In response the Department of Defense argued as it had in *JB Pictures* that the First Amendment did not prevent the government from restricting access to areas of combat activity and that the regulations were narrowly tailored to deal with compelling national security interests.[79]

While stating that the issues raised by the complaint were profound and novel as to the existence and scope of a First Amendment right of special access in this context, the United States District Court for the Southern District of New York dismissed the complaint. The court held that the plaintiffs did have standing to raise their constitutional claims[80] and that the political question doctrine[81] did not stand in the way of litigation.[82] Regarding the mootness issue, the District Court held that since the ground rules and supplementary guidelines, though having been lifted with the cessation of hostilities, could be reimposed in future armed conflicts the controversy was one capable of repetition yet evading review.[83] In such situation the action itself was held to survive a challenge of mootness.[84] But because the court was being asked to enjoin enforcement of the Department of Defense rules as they might apply to the next combat situation, it found the issue of whether application of the rules in the future would be a reasonable time, place and manner restriction under the First and Fifth Amendments "too abstract and conjectural for judicial resolution.... "[85] The district court also refused declaratory relief on the right of access claim because of the long settled policy of the federal courts to refrain from deciding constitutional issues presented in a highly abstract form.[86] Accordingly the court dismissed the count of the complaint based on this claim.[87]

77. *Id.*

78. *Id.* at 1561.

79. *Id.*

80. *Id.* at 1561, 1565–1566.

81. *See* Goldwater v. Carter, 444 U.S. 996, 998, 100 S.Ct. 533, 534, 62 L.Ed.2d 428, 429 (1979) (Powell, J. concurring) (statement of the doctrine).

82. 762 F. Supp. at 1561, 1566–1568.

83. *Id.* at 1562; *see* Southern Pacific Terminal v. Interstate Commerce Commission, 219 U.S. 498, 515, 31 S.Ct. 279, 283, 55 L.Ed. 310, 316 (1911).

84. 762 F. Supp. at 1562, 1568–1569.

85. *Id.* at 1562, 1570.

86. *Id.* at 1572.

87. The claim of Agence France–Presse of discriminatory treatment is not discussed.

Thus, even after the Gulf War there is still no substantial authority on the issue of First Amendment special access for the news media to combat zones though most indications are to the effect that no such constitutional access will be found to exist.[88] Moreover, after two applications of the new ground rules and guidelines, access by administrative grace of the Department of Defense has proven to be uneven and at times ineffectual, particularly in the early going of combat in both the Panamanian and the Persian Gulf conflicts.

d.   Access for Media Equipment.

In situations in which media personnel may have personal access to news sources, the question may arise whether they may employ their photographic and recording equipment in aid of newsgathering. In *Houchins* v. *KQED, Inc.*[89] Alameda County Jail regulations permitted scheduled public tours of portions of the facility which news media personnel could sign up for but prohibited tour members from using cameras and tape recorders to record what they were viewing and hearing. The United States District Court's order preliminarily enjoining the sheriff from denying news media personnel reasonable access to the entire facility and from preventing their use of photographic and sound recording equipment was affirmed by the Ninth Circuit but reversed by a badly divided Supreme Court with but seven members participating. Three of the justices held that neither the First nor the Fourteenth Amendments provided any right of access for the news media and their equipment to information or sources of information within the government's control beyond that afforded the general public. Since the public could not bring along cameras and recording equipment neither could representatives of the news media.

The fourth and deciding vote to reverse was cast by Justice Stewart because he believed the trial court's preliminary injunction was overbroad in requiring the sheriff to allow reporters into a portion of the facility off limits to the general public and further requiring him to let news media representatives randomly interview encountered inmates when ordinary tour members could not. But in his opinion concurring in the judgment to reverse[90] Stewart argued that if a television reporter on the public jail tour is to convey to those members of the public not

---

88.   *See, e.g.,* JB Pictures v. Department of Defense, 1993 WL 166918, 21 Med.L.Rptr 1564 (D.D.C.1993) *aff'd* 86 F.3d 236 (D.C.Cir.1996); REPORT: THE MEDIA AT WAR: THE PRESS AND THE PERSIAN GULF CONFLICT 22–24 (1991). *But see* Nation Magazine v. United States Department of Defense, 762 F.Supp. 1558, 1572 (S.D.N.Y.1991) (dictum stating "If the reasoning of these recent access cases were followed in a military context, there is support for the proposition that the press has at least some minimal right of access to view and report about major events that affect the functioning of government, including, for example, an overt combat operation. As such, the government could not wholly exclude the press from a land area where a war is occurring that involves this country. But this conclusion is far from certain since military operations are not closely akin to a building such as a prison, nor to a park or a courtroom." [and citing, *inter alia*, Richmond Newspapers, Inc. v. Virginia, 448 U.S. 555, 100 S.Ct. 2814, 65 L.Ed.2d 973 (1980)]).

89.   438 U.S. 1, 98 S.Ct. 2588, 57 L.Ed.2d 553 (1978).

90.   *Id.* at 16–19, 98 S. Ct. at 2597–2599, 57 L. Ed. 2d at 565–567.

taking the tour the sights and sounds of the jail made available by government to those on the tour he must use cameras and sound equipment. In this situation, according to Stewart the First Amendment protects access with audio and visual equipment because the equipment equalizes the access of members of the public not able personally to take the *public* tours. "[T]erms of access that are reasonably imposed on individual members of the public [including the prohibition against cameras and tape recorders] may, if they impede effective reporting without sufficient justification, be unreasonable as applied to journalists who are there to convey to the general public what the visitors see."[91]

The dissent,[92] accepting the "checking" function of the press,[93] found a constitutional right of access of members of the news media to areas of the jail the sheriff was concealing in order that the citizenry might be informed of the conditions in which their fellow citizens were being confined. The citizenry, in a democracy is entitled to this information and therefore the news media has a First Amendment right to access it on their behalf.[94] Obviously included within this reasoning of the dissent is equipment which makes the press' access on behalf of the public effective. One might argue, then, that a majority in *Houchins* rejected prohibitions on news media equipment when news personnel have access to a source of news. But since there was no opinion for the court and all the majority could officially agree on was a judgment of reversal, this argument is doubtful.

The lower state and federal court decisions are few in number and show little consistency on the issue. The leading case not involving judicial proceedings[95] is *Sigma Delta Chi* v. *Speaker, Maryland House of Delegates*.[96] There the rules of the legislature prohibited cameras either explicitly or implicitly and recording devices in the two chambers without permission of the presiding officers. Though a certain number of reporters were allowed by the rules to be on the Senate and (apparently) House floors,[97] they were not permitted to bring cameras and tape recorders with them. Certain members of the public might also be admitted to the floors of the legislative bodies to view the proceedings personally. A number of reporters attacked the rules as violative *inter alia*, of the Press Clause of the First Amendment and the Due Process and Equal Protection Clauses of the Fourteenth Amendment because the prohibition of tape recorders hindered their ability to report news from

91. *Id.* at 17, 98 S. Ct. at 2598, 57 L. Ed. 2d at 566.

92. *Id.* at 19–40, 98 S. Ct. at 2599–2610, 57 L. Ed. 2d at 567–581 (dissenting opinion of Stevens, J., joined by Brennan and Powell, JJ.).

93. *Id.* at 31–34, 98 S. Ct. at 2605–2606, 57 L. Ed. 2d at 575–577.

94. *Id.* at 36–38, 98 S. Ct. at 2608–2609, 57 L. Ed. 2d at 578–579.

95. The issue of news media cameras, recording equipment and sketch artists in the courtroom is discussed *infra*, section 7.17F, pp. 144–153.

96. 270 Md. 1, 310 A.2d 156 (1973).

97. The rules of the House of Delegates were not clear on newsperson and equipment access to that chamber's proceedings. *See id.* at 2–3 nn. 1–2, 310 A.2d at 157 nn. 1–2.

the legislature to the public with speed and accuracy and interfered with the pursuit of their livelihood as newsgatherers.

In an opinion distinguished by an almost total absence of persuasive reasoning, the Maryland Court of Appeals denied constitutional protection for access to the legislative floor of even unobtrusive media sound recording equipment. The court found no curtailment of the reporters' access to the legislature because all the tape recorders would do is promote greater accuracy and speed in their reporting. The court was unwilling to include those enhancements on newsgathering within the protection of the First Amendment.[98] By the same token the court found no due process or equal protection violations because it doubted that the restriction on recording devices interfered with the reporters' right to pursue the newsgathering profession.

No consideration was given to the idea that those members of the public unable to attend sessions of the legislature might be disadvantaged by not being able to hear what those in attendance at the legislative sessions could hear.[99] The Maryland court's rejection of the reporters' leading authority *Nevens* v. *City of Chino*,[100] is also doubtful.[1] The court seized upon one questionable supporting analogy in *Nevens*, a California case, to discredit its basic premise that news media personnel and others in attendance at public meetings of bodies such as city councils should have a right to use nondisrupting and unobtrusive recording devices to insure the accuracy of what they report as having transpired. In reversing an order by the trial court sustaining a demurrer to a newspaper reporter's complaint that the First Amendment was being violated by a rule of the Chino, California City Council forbidding the use of sound recording devices in the council's chamber, the California District Court of Appeal said, "Accuracy in reporting the transactions of a public governing body should never be penalized, particularly in a democracy where truth is often said to be supreme".[2] But neither *Nevens* nor the similar cases citing or quoting it with approval[3] have ruled unambiguously that there is a First Amendment protected right of access for cameras and recording equipment to open public meetings,

---

98. *See also* Dean v. Guste, 414 So.2d 862, 864–865 (La.App.) cert. denied 459 U.S. 1070, 103 S.Ct. 489, 74 L.Ed.2d 632 (1982) (taking an extremely crabbed view of public access to government controlled information under the First Amendment, saying "[T]he States are altogether without *constitutional* impediment should they decide to close the doors of their legislative chambers and other governmental bodies. It follows then that if the states are free to prohibit public attendance at meetings of governmental bodies, they are free to prohibit the tape recording of those proceedings by those who are enabled to attend not by virtue of the Constitution, but by statute." *Id*. at 865); CBS, Inc. v. Lieberman, 439 F.Supp. 862, 867 (N.D.Ill.1976) (saying that existing precedent was against consti-

tutional access of television cameras and sound recording equipment to public meetings of a state's public utilities commission but refusing to take a position on the issue without a full hearing).

99. *Compare* Belcher v. Mansi, 569 F.Supp. 379, 382 (D.R.I.1983).

100. 233 Cal.App.2d 775, 44 Cal.Rptr. 50 (1965).

1. Sigma Delta Chi, 270 Md. at 8, 310 A.2d at 160.

2. Nevens v. City of Chino, 233 Cal. App. 2d at 778, 44 Cal. Rptr. at 52.

3. *See* Belcher v. Mansi, 569 F.Supp. 379 (D.R.I.1983); Sudol v. Borough of North Arlington, 137 N.J.Super. 149, 348 A.2d 216 (Ch.Div.1975).

tours or other executive and legislative proceedings. The decisions in those cases rely at least in part on state open meetings legislation.

Thus, the right of access for news media equipment under the Constitution remains ambiguous but clearly the better reasoning here is that of Justice Stewart in *Houchins*. If newsgatherers have entry to government controlled information by virtue of the access afforded the public, media access should include such equipment as is necessary to make the reporting to members of the public not in attendance the functional equivalent of their having been there.

e.   *Access to Polling Places and Voters.*

A somewhat different approach is taken by the courts to news media claims of access to polling areas and voters. In this context the access claim is viewed as one falling primarily under the Freedom of Speech Clause of the First Amendment because of the political dialogue between media representatives and voters necessary to the gathering of information on the behavior and attitudes of the electorate.[4]

Governmental attempts to regulate access to voters on election day arise primarily out of a concern that early broadcast projections of the results of national elections discourage late voters beyond the Eastern Time Zone, particularly in the West, from going to the polls.[5] A number of state legislatures,[6] though not the Congress,[7] responded to the perceived threat to the franchise by enacting legislation attempting to curtail the exit polling on which such network projections are based.

4. *See* National Broadcasting Co., Inc. v. Cleland, 697 F.Supp. 1204, 1213–1214 (N.D.Ga.1988). But the position has been advanced that members of the news media are entitled to access to voting areas because the general public is entitled to such access. *See* Note, *Exit Polls and the First Amendment*, 98 Harv.L.Rev. 1927, 1930–1931 (1985). This position misperceives the kind of access involved. The general citizenry may enter voting areas to vote and even engage in informal conversation with other voters. Reporters may do the same and of course observe what is going on. But the general citizenry is not entitled to conduct systematic exit polling and thus representatives of the news media would need constitutionally protected special access to engage in such polling if their freedom of speech were not also implicated.

5. *See* Note, *Exit Polls and the First Amendment*, 98 Harv.L. Rev. 1927 (1985); Anthony M. Barlow, Comment, *Restricting Election Day Exit Polling: Freedom of Expression vs. the Right to Vote,* 58 U. Cinn. L. Rev. 1003, 1004 (1990); Mary A. Doty, Note, *Clearing* CBS, Inc. v. Smith *from the Path to the Polls: A Proposal to Legitimize*

States' Interests in Restricting Exit Polls, 74 Iowa L. Rev. 737 (1989); Wallace Turner, *How the West Was Made to Feel that Its Votes Would Not Count,* N.Y. Times, Nov. 6, 1980, p.A32, col. 1.

6. *See* Cal. Elec. Code § 29470(b) (West 1989); Fla. Stat. Ann. § 102.031(3)(a)-(b) (West. 1985); Ga. Code Ann. § 21–2–414(a) (1993); Haw. Rev. Stat. Ann. § 11–132 (1985); Ky. Rev. Stat. Ann. § 117.235(3) (Supp. 1993); Minn. Rev. Stat. Ann. § 204 C.06(1) (West 1992); Mo. Ann.Stat. § 115.637(18) (West Supp. 1994); Mont. Code Ann. § 13–35–211(3)(1993); Neb. Rev. Stat. § 32–1221 (1988); R.I. Gen. L. § 17–23–15 (Michie 1988); S.D. Codified L. § 12–18–3 (Michie Supp. 1994); Wash. Rev. Code Ann. § 29.51.020(1)(e) (West 1993); Wyo. Stat. § 22–26–114 (1977).

7. *See* Anthony M. Barlow, Comment, *Restricting Election Day Exit Polling: Freedom of Expression vs. the Right to Vote,* 58 U. Cinn. L. Rev. 1003, 1005 n. 17, 1011–1013 (1990) (providing a thorough review of the legislative history of Congress' failure to enact a solution to the problem caused by exit polling).

Typically, this legislation prohibits polling of voters within a specified distance from the actual voting area.[8]

The constitutionality of this type of legislation has been addressed only indirectly by the Supreme Court. In *Burson v. Freeman*,[9] the campaign treasurer for a candidate for municipal office in metropolitan Nashville challenged Tennessee's statute limiting campaign activity within 100 feet of the entrance to a polling place on the basis that it limited her ability to communicate with voters in violation, *inter alia*, of the First Amendment. The trial court dismissed the action for declaratory judgment and injunction but was reversed by the Tennessee Supreme Court which held the statute to be content based restriction on speech and did not meet the requirements of constitutional strict scrutiny.

On certiorari the Supreme Court reversed and upheld the constitutionality of the statute. In a plurality opinion, Justice Blackmun, speaking for himself and three other justices, held that while the statute was facially content based it did meet the exacting standards of strict scrutiny. There was a compelling state interest expressed by the statute to protect voters from intimidation and the electorial system from fraud.[10] And, though conceding that it is a rare case in which government action regulating the content of speech can be constitutionally justified as necessary to further a compelling state interest, Justice Blackmun found this to be such a case because the statute did protect an essential institution of a democratic society.[11] Regarding the issue of the narrowness of the regulation which translated here into the question of how large a restricted zone is permissible, the justice simply did not view the question whether the 100–foot boundary, could be somewhat reduced as a question of constitutional dimension. He rejected as a difference only in degree the Tennessee Supreme Court's suggestion that reducing the boundary to 25–feet would make the restriction on speech here narrowly tailored.[12]

Justice Scalia concurred in the judgment of the Court thereby providing the fifth vote to sustain the statute. He believed that the area around polling places is traditionally not considered a public forum and thus restrictions on speech there are not subject to strict scrutiny. Rather he holds that under a more relaxed standard of review such statutes as Tennessee's, though content based, are constitutional because they provide reasonable, viewpoint neutral regulation.[13]

---

8. *See, e.g.*, Cal. Elec. Code § 29470(b) (West 1989) (no polling within 100 feet of voting area); Haw. Rev. Stat. § 11–132 (1985) (no polling within 1000 feet of voting area); Neb. Rev. Stat. § 32–1221 (1988) (no polling within 20 feet from door of polling place or if within the polling place building, 100 feet from the voting booths). Oklahoma enacted an atypical statute permitting exit polling within 300 feet of the ballot boxes upon notification of the secretary of the county election board approximately one week preceding the election. Okla.Stat.Ann. tit. 26, § 7–108.1 (West 1991).

9. 504 U.S. 191, 112 S.Ct. 1846, 119 L.Ed.2d 5 (1992).

10. *Id.* at 206–211, 112 S. Ct. at 1855–1858, 119 L. Ed. 2d at 20–21.

11. *Id.* at 210–211, 112 S. Ct. at 1857–1858, 119 L. Ed. 2d at 21.

12. *Id.* at 210, 112 S. Ct. at 1857, 119 L. Ed. 2d at 21.

13. *Id.* at 214–215, 112 S. Ct. at 1859, 119 L. Ed. 2d at 22.

It is not yet clear whether the ruling in *Burson* upholding the 100–foot boundary around polling places is transferable to statutes extending the distance from the polls to thwart access by the media to voters particularly *after* they vote. In this situation the rationale behind the plurality opinion in *Burson* is not applicable, *i.e.*, prevention of voter intimidation and electoral fraud. Only Justice Scalia's rationale would seem broad enough to justify such regulation.

In the only federal appellate decision directly confronting this type of media regulation and one decided before *Burson*, the United States Court of Appeals for the Ninth Circuit ruled a Washington statute to be in violation of the First Amendment. In *Daily Herald Co.* v. *Munro*,[14] the Washington legislature in 1983 amended its statute regulating conduct in and around polling places so as to extend the controlled area from 100 feet to 300 feet from the polls and prohibited within that area the conduct of any exit or public opinion poll of voters.[15] Several print and electronic news media challenged the constitutionality of the amended statute and sought to have its enforcement enjoined, claiming the statute infringed their First Amendment rights to gather and disseminate election news. The United States District Court for the Western District of Washington ultimately found that the media plaintiffs conducted their exit polling in a systematic and statistically reliable manner; that information obtained from exit polling could not be obtained by other means; that the 300 foot restriction precluded exit polling, and that exit polling was not inherently disruptive of the voting place. The court then held the statute unconstitutional as applied to the plaintiffs.

On appeal, the Ninth Circuit applied the standard of whether the *speech* to be regulated in the course of exit polling occurred in a traditional public forum. Ruling that public areas within 300 feet of the entrance to polling places are public forums, the appeals court applied a strict scrutiny standard and held that the Washington statute unconstitutionally regulated speech content in public forums because it was not narrowly tailored to achieve the state's compelling interest in maintaining peace, order and decorum at the polls and preserving the integrity of the electoral process. Nor did the statute employ the least restrictive means available to achieve that interest, according to the appeals court.

The statute was not sufficiently narrowly tailored because it prohibited *all* exit polling. Prohibiting non-disruptive exit polling did not advance the state's interest and, moreover, rendered the statute constitutionally overbroad.[16] Regarding the requirement that regulation of speech in a public forum had to be the least restrictive possible in achieving the state's compelling interest, the court pointed out that Washington already had a statute specifically prohibiting disruptive

---

14. 838 F.2d 380 (9th Cir.1988).

15. Wash.Rev.Code   Ann. § 29.51.020(1)(e) (West. 1988) (held unconstitutional).

16. Daily Herald Co. v. Munro, 838 F.2d at 385; *cf.* Clean–Up '84 v. Heinrich, 759 F.2d 1511, 1513–1514 (11th Cir.1985) (polling area restriction on gathering signatures for petitions struck down as overbroad).

behavior at the polls[17] and that other less restrictive devices to prevent disruption were available, including requiring the media to explain that their polls are voluntary and requiring polling places to have separate entrances and exits.[18]

The court then assumed, *arguendo*, that the statute was content neutral and involved time, place and manner regulation only. In that case, such regulation would be unreasonable because it was not, as the court held earlier in its opinion, narrowly tailored to achieve the government's interest.[19] Moreover, it left open no viable alternative channels for the news media to obtain the information uniquely generated by exit polling.[20]

Finally, the appeals court turned to the news media's contention and the trial court's finding that a real purpose of the statute was to prevent broadcasting of early returns.[21] The court held that, assuming at least one purpose was to prevent the broadcast of early returns, the statute was unconstitutional because this purpose to prevent dissemination of information to the electorate is impermissible and because, again, the statute was not sufficiently narrowly tailored and did not provide the least restrictive alternative in preventing the media's dissemination.[22]

From this strict scrutiny and meticulous analysis the Ninth Circuit concluded that the statute was facially invalid and not merely unconstitutional as applied.[23] A number of lower federal courts have reached similar results generally following *Daily Herald*.[24] No court has finally upheld a statute restricting exit polling more than 25 feet beyond the exit to buildings where voting is taking place. *Burson* of course, upheld a

---

17. Wash. Rev. Code Ann. § 29.51.020(1)(d) (West 1993).

18. Daily Herald Co., 838 F.2d at 385; see Note, *Exit Polls and the First Amendment*, 98 Harv. L. Rev. 1927, 1935 (1985).

19. Daily Herald Co., 838 F.2d at 386.

20. *Id.*

21. *See* Note, *Exit Polls and the First Amendment*, 98 Harv. L. Rev. 1927, 1932–1933 (1985); Anthony M. Barlow, Comment, *Restricting Election Day Exit Polling: Freedom of Expression vs. the Right to Vote*, 58 U. Cinn. L. Rev. 1003, 1016 (1990).

22. Daily Herald Co., 838 F.2d at 387–388.

23. *Id.* at 386; *cf.* Clean-Up '84 v. Heinrich, 759 F.2d 1511 (11th Cir.1985).

24. *See* CBS, Inc. v. Smith, 681 F.Supp. 794 (S.D.Fla.1988) (essentially following the freedom of speech analysis of *Daily Herald Co.* in enjoining enforcement of Fla. Stat. Ann. § 102.031(3)(a)-(b) (West Supp. 1988) but also accepting a special right of access of the media to news under the Press Clause. *Id.* at 802–803); National Broadcasting Co., Inc. v. Cleland, 697 F.Supp.

1204, 1210–1215 (N.D.Ga.1988) (limiting enforcement of Ga. Code Ann. § 21-2-414(a) (1987) beyond 25 feet of the exit of any building in which a polling place is located in order to preserve the sanctity and decorum of the polls *and* the constitutional rights of members of the news media to gather polling information); Journal Broadcasting, Inc. v. Logsdon, No. 99–Civ.–0147 (W.D. Ky. Mar. 8, 1988) (cited in *Cleveland* as temporarily enjoining Ky. Rev. Stat.Ann. § 117.235(3) (Michie/Bobbs–Merrill Supp. 1988) which prohibited exit polling within 500 feet of polling areas); CBS, Inc. v. Growe, 15 Media L. Rep. 2275 (D.Minn. 1988) (invalidating Minn. Stat. Ann. § 204 C.06(1) (West Supp. 1988) as overbroad in its prohibition of exit polling within 100 feet of the voting area); National Broadcasting Co. v. Colburg, 699 F.Supp. 241 (D.Mont.1988) (invalidating Mont. Code Ann. § 13–35–211(3) (1988) as not sufficiently narrowly tailored and not providing the least restrictive means to achieve a compelling state interest); National Broadcasting Co. v. Karpan, No. C88–0320–B (D. Wyo. Oct. 21, 1988) (invalidating clause in Wyo. Stat. Ann. § 26–113 (1977) prohibiting exit polling by news media).

100–foot boundary but to curb rather different problems than those associated with exit polling and its application here is doubtful. For those concerned about the possible skewing of electoral results because of early media projections, one likely constitutional route would be a uniform national poll closing time law.[25]

D. Fair and Equal Access If Not Special Access

Running through the cases denying constitutionally protected special access for the news media is the admonition to government that when it voluntarily sets up a system to provide access to news sources and information within its control, it must do so fairly and nondiscriminatorily.[26] The first proposition here is that once the government has opened its doors to the public the press is guaranteed equal access to news and information along with the public.[27] The theory is that the area of access becomes dedicated to public communications use.[28] And when government specifically grants to the news media access to persons or places, it may not arbitrarily discriminate between individual media representatives.[29] Thus the Secret Service, which had the responsibility of issuing press passes for access to the White House, was required to publish the standard employed in determining whether an otherwise eligible journalist will obtain the credential necessary to cover the activities of the President.[30] Should a journalist be denied the credential, he is entitled to due process, including notice of the factual bases for the denial, opportunity to respond to the denial and, after his response, a written statement of the reasons for the denial should the press pass still not be issued.[31] Nor may governments or even recognized political parties arbitrarily distinguish between specific news organizations[32] and kinds of media[33] for purposes of access.

25. *See, e.g.*, Anthony M. Barlow, Comment, *Restricting Election Day Exit Polling: Freedom of Expression vs. the Right to Vote*, 58 U. Cinn. L. Rev. 1003, at 1011–1012 (1990).

26. *See, e.g.*, Legi–Tech, Inc. v. Keiper, 766 F.2d 728 (2d Cir.1985); Sherrill v. Knight, 569 F.2d 124 (D.C.Cir.1977); Nation Magazine v. United States Department of Defense, 762 F.Supp. 1558, 1573–1574 (S.D.N.Y.1991).

27. *See* Houchins v. KQED, Inc., 438 U.S. 1, 16, 98 S.Ct. 2588 2597, 57 L.Ed.2d 553, 565–567 (1978) (Stewart, J. concurring); Pell v. Procunier, 417 U.S. 817, 94 S.Ct. 2800, 41 L.Ed.2d 495 (1974) (by implication); Saxbe v. Washington Post. Co., 417 U.S. 843, 94 S.Ct. 2811, 41 L.Ed.2d 514 (1974) (by implication); Legi–Tech, Inc. v. Keiper, 766 F.2d 728 (2d Cir.1985).

28. *See* American Broadcasting Cos., Inc. v. Cuomo, 570 F.2d 1080, 1083 (2d Cir.1977); Nation Magazine v. United States Department of Defense, 762 F.Supp. 1558, 1573 (S.D.N.Y.1991).

29. *See* Sherrill v. Knight, 569 F.2d 124 (D.C.Cir.1977); American Broadcasting Cos., Inc., 570 F.2d at 1083; Borreca v. Fasi, 369 F.Supp. 906, 909–910 (D.Haw.1974).

30. Sherrill, 569 F.2d at 130.

31. "This first amendment interest undoubtedly qualifies as liberty which may not be denied without due process of law under the fifth amendment." *Id.*

32. *See* American Broadcasting Cos., 570 F.2d at 1083 (exclusion of ABC Television Network from various Democratic Party campaign facilities); Nation Magazine v. United States Department of Defense, 762 F.Supp. 1558, 1573–1574 (S.D.N.Y.1991) (dictum) (exclusion of Agence France–Presse from Gulf War official news pool).

33. *See* Legi–Tech, Inc. v. Keiper, 766 F.2d 728 (2d Cir.1985) (exclusion of a private computer service as opposed to other non-computer media from subscription to New York legislature's Legislative Retrieval Service not permitted); Cable News Network v. American Broadcasting Cos., Inc.,

When individual news persons, particular news organizations or forms of news media are denied the access accorded to others, government has the difficult burden of establishing that it has a compelling interest in making such exclusion and is not engaging in invidious discrimination.[34] In the few instances in which exclusion of particular newsgatherers has been upheld, the courts have found the exclusion to be neither arbitrary nor invidious because the newsgatherers were not of the class normally covering the events or places to which access had been otherwise granted.[35]

7.17 Access to the Judicial System

A. Introduction

Readers who are at all acquainted with the law of media access may wonder why scant attention is paid in the preceding section to the landmark case of *Richmond Newspapers, Inc.* v. *Virginia.*[1] That precedent (created without a majority opinion) is now more than a decade old and in that time little authority has developed holding or even suggesting that it should be construed as going beyond its judicial setting to establish a right under the First Amendment of special access *generally* to news and information held or controlled by government. What authority there is for such a broad proposition comes from a handful of federal trial courts.[2] It is therefore the position of the authors that unless and until substantial appellate authority develops holding that *Richmond Newspapers* requires a reading of the First Amendment so as to provide limited special access across the board to news sources under govern-

518 F.Supp. 1238, 1242–1245 (N.D.Ga. 1981) (by necessary implication television coverage of White House events cannot be barred when print media are permitted access).

34. *See* Houchins v. KQED, Inc., 438 U.S. 1, 17–18, 98 S.Ct. 2588, 2598, 57 L.Ed.2d 553, 566–567 (1978) (Stewart, J. concurring) (by necessary implication); Sherrill v. Knight, 569 F.2d 124, 129–130 (D.C.Cir.1977); Nation Magazine v. U.S. Dept. of Defense, 762 F.Supp. 1558, 1573 (S.D.N.Y.1991) (dictum); Borreca v. Fasi, 369 F.Supp. 906, 909–910 (D.Haw.1974).

35. *See* Jersawitz v. Hanberry, 783 F.2d 1532 (11th Cir.1986), cert. denied, 479 U.S. 883, 107 S.Ct. 272, 93 L.Ed.2d 249 (1986); Los Angeles Free Press, Inc. v. City of Los Angeles, 9 Cal.App.3d 448, 88 Cal.Rptr. 605 (1970), cert. denied, 401 U.S. 982, 91 S.Ct. 1193, 28 L.Ed.2d 334 (1971); *see also* WPIX v. League of Women Voters, 595 F.Supp. 1484 (S.D.N.Y.1984) (denial of preliminary injunction sought by television station to force sponsor of presidential debate to permit its own cameras to cover event outside of television pool previously arranged).

1. 448 U.S. 555, 100 S.Ct. 2814, 65 L.Ed.2d 973 (1980).

2. *See* Westinghouse Broadcasting Co., Inc. v. National Transportation Safety Board, 8 Med. L. Rptr. 1177, 1181–1184 (D.Mass.1982)(airplane crash scene) WPIX v. League of Women Voters, 595 F.Supp. 1484, 1489 (S.D.N.Y.1984) (presidential debate); Nation Magazine v. Department of Defense, 762 F.Supp. 1558, 1572 (S.D.N.Y. 1991) (dictum) (combat zones); Cable News Network, Inc. v. American Broadcasting Cos., Inc., 518 F.Supp. 1238, 1242–1245 (N.D.Ga.1981) (White House events); Society of Professional Journalists v. Secretary of Labor, 616 F.Supp. 569, 574–577 (D.Utah 1985), *appeal dismissed and judgment vacated and remanded as moot*, 832 F.2d 1180 (10th Cir.1987) (administrative fact-finding hearings); *see also* Lewis v. Baxley, 368 F.Supp. 768, 775–777 (M.D.Ala.1973) (access to state buildings and officials); Allen v. Combined Communications, 7 Media L. Rptr. 2417, 2419–2420 (Colo.Dist.Ct.1981) (private Property).

ment control, that decision should be read as relating only to the judicial system in most of its facets.

The decision in *Richmond Newspapers* to find a right of access of newsgathers to criminal trials under the First Amendment was an obvious reaction to the decision the year before in *Gannett Co., Inc.* v. *DePasquale*[3] featuring an almost unfathomable majority opinion by Justice Stewart holding that the sixth amendment guarantee of a public trial was for the benefit of the defendant alone and provided no access of the public to criminal pretrial proceedings. And since the public did not have guaranteed access neither did the press. The broad implication from the opinion was that the public and press could also be excluded from criminal trials as well though such trial closings would fly in the face of nearly 200 years of American judicial history.[4]

The major confusion in Stewart's opinion was in its treatment of Gannett's First Amendment claim.[5] Stewart denied that Gannett's *assumed* right of access had to be balanced against the defendant's right to a fair trial but then in assuming *arguendo* a need to balance he failed to lay out the factors that a trial judge would have to consider in striking the balance. Adding to the confusion Stewart wrote that any denial of First Amendment access was temporary, for as soon as the danger of prejudicial publicity had dissipated, a transcript of the suppression hearing involved was made available to the public and press. In a breathtaking *non sequitur*, Stewart concluded for the five person majority that therefore no *assumed* First Amendment right of Gannett to *attend* the criminal proceeding was violated.[6] But the opinion never came to grips with whether there was indeed a First Amendment right of access in the first place. If the opinion for the Court itself was not enough to boggle the mind three of the five justices in the majority filed concurring opinions trying to explain in disparate ways what they had just done.[7]

---

3. 443 U.S. 368, 99 S.Ct. 2898, 61 L.Ed.2d 608 (1979).

4. *See In re* Oliver, 333 U.S. 257, 266, 68 S.Ct. 499, 504, 92 L.Ed. 682, 690 (1948).

5. At the time *Gannett Co., Inc.* v. *DePasquale* was decided there was widespread recognition by jurists, journalists and Commentators that the decision was confusing if not plain wrong. *See, e.g.,* Richmond Newspapers, Inc. v. Virginia, 448 U.S. 555, 602 nn.1–2, 100 S.Ct. 2814, 2816 nn.1–2, 65 L.Ed.2d 973, 978–979 nn.1–2 (1980) (confusion of commentators and journalists collected); Sacramento Bee v. United States Dist. Ct. 656 F.2d 477, 481 (9th Cir.1981), cert. denied 456 U.S. 983, 102 S.Ct. 2257, 72 L.Ed.2d 861 (1982) (*"Richmond Newspapers* followed a confusing decision in *Gannett Co.* v. *DePasquale....*"); James C. Goodale, *Gannett Means What It Says; But Who Knows What It Says?*, National L.J., Oct. 15, 1979, p. 20; Arthur J. Keefe, *The*

Boner Called Gannett, 66 A.B.A.J. 227 (1980); Richard M. Schmidt, Jr. & Gregory M. Schmidt, *Some Observations on the Swinging Courthouse Doors of Gannett and Richmond Newspapers*, 59 Den. L.J. 721, 721–722 (1982); *The Supreme Court, 1978 Term,* 93 Harv. L. Rev. 1, 65–66 (1979); Baltimore Sun, Sept. 22, 1979, p. A14 (decision said to be "incoherent"); Newsweek, Aug. 27, 1979, p. 69 (decision a "muddle").

6. 443 U.S. at 391–393, 99 S. Ct. at 2912, 61 L. Ed. 2d at 628.

7. *Id.* at 394–406, 99 S. Ct. at 2913–2919 61 L. Ed. 2d at 631–638 (concurring opinions of Burger, C. J. and Powell and Rehnquist, JJ.). Justice Blackmun wrote a lengthy dissent stating that the Court had not found any First Amendment right of access to judicial or other governmental proceedings and emphasizing instead access through the sixth amendment and the dangers of secret judicial proceedings. *Id.* at

Fortuitously, another case raising essentially the same issues as in *Gannett* v. *DePasquale* but directed to criminal trials rather than pretrial proceedings was working its way through the judicial system of Virginia and would quickly give the Court an opportunity to dissipate the confusion generated by *Gannett*.

B. *Richmond Newspapers, Inc. v. Virginia*

1. *The Facts of the Case*

In *Richmond Newspapers, Inc.* v. *Virginia*,[8] decided precisely one year after *Gannett*, a murder conviction had first been reversed because of the improper admission into evidence of a bloodstained shirt purportedly belonging to the accused and two subsequent prosecutions ended in mistrials with the third trial apparently aborted because a prospective juror had read a newspaper account of the accused's two previous trials and had told other prospective jurors on the panel about the case. Refusing to give up in its quest for justice, the state of Virginia prosecuted a fourth time. Before this trial began counsel for the defendant moved that it be closed to the public and the press because the defense did not want information being shuffled back and forth during recesses as to what particular witnesses had testified to. Neither the prosecutor nor the reporters covering the trial for Richmond Newspapers, objected to the motion at the time it was made and the trial judge quickly granted it and ordered that the courtroom be kept clear of all parties except the witnesses as they testified. Later the same day counsel for Richmond Newspapers sought and obtained a hearing on their motion to vacate the closure order on constitutional grounds. A hearing with the reporters excluded was held at the close of the day's trial proceedings at which time the judge reaffirmed his closure order. The next day the judge struck the state's evidence, excused the jury and found the defendant not guilty, all in the absence of the public and press. Subsequently he did permit Richmond Newspapers to intervene *nunc pro tunc* in the case to allow a challenge of his closure order on appeal. However, the Virginia Supreme Court dismissed the newspaper company's petitions for writs of mandamus and prohibition directed to the trial judge and denied its petition for leave to appeal. Thereafter, the Supreme Court granted a petition for certiorari and, after rejecting a suggestion that the case was moot, reversed the closure order. There were no more than three votes for any one opinion and of the eight justices who participated in the case seven felt compelled to file opinions. Six of these opinions supported a judgment of the Court reversing the order closing the criminal trial as constitutionally erroneous. Seven

406–448, 99 S. Ct. at 2919–2940, 61 L. Ed. 2d at 639–665; *see* Richard M. Schmidt, Jr. & Gregory M. Schmidt, *Some Observations on the Swinging Courthouse Doors of Gannett and* Richmond Newspapers, 59 Den.

L.J. 721, 727–728 (1982) (listing the benefits of open judicial proceedings).

8. 448 U.S. 555, 100 S.Ct. 2814, 65 L.Ed.2d 973 (1980).

justices found some right of the public and news media to access to criminal trials arising out of the First Amendment.[9]

2. Analysis of the Opinions

It would serve little purpose to attempt to parse all of the opinions in the case but because Chief Justice Burger's opinion announcing the judgment of the Court commanded three votes and because Justice Brennan's opinion joined in by Justice Marshall provides compelling reasoning for finding public access to court proceedings, those two opinions are analyzed below.

The Chief Justice began by attempting to distinguish *Gannett* by saying that there the Court was not called on to decide whether a right of access to trials as opposed to pretrial hearings was constitutionally guaranteed. He repeated what he had said in his concurring opinion in *Gannett* that a hearing on a motion prior to trial to suppress evidence is not a trial. Having made this point he felt free to consider the question as a matter of first impression whether the First and Fourteenth Amendments guaranteed a right of the public to attend criminal trials.

His answer, of course, was that it did, and he gave as reasons for this conclusion the long history of public attendance at criminal trials in this country, and the related need of the citizenry in a democracy to receive information through such attendance concerning the important governmental function of conducting criminal trials. "Freedom of speech carries with it some freedom to listen. In a variety of contexts this Court has referred to a First Amendment right to 'receive information and ideas' ... What this means in the context of trials is that the First Amendment guarantees of speech and press, standing alone, prohibit government from summarily closing courtroom doors which had long been open to the public at the time that Amendment was adopted."[10] The Chief Justice concluded that absent an overriding governmental interest articulated in findings by the trial judge, the trial of criminal cases must be open to the public.

Justice Brennan began his opinion by making clear his agreement with the other justices who held that, *without more*, agreement of the trial judge and the parties cannot under the First Amendment close a trial to the public.[11] Brennan too appealed to history in saying that "the case for a right of access has special force when drawn from an enduring and vital tradition of public entree to particular proceedings or information.... Such a tradition commands respect in part because the Constitution carries the gloss of history."[12]

---

9. *See* Globe Newspaper Co. v. Superior Court, 457 U.S. 596, 603, 102 S.Ct. 2613, 2618, 73 L.Ed.2d 248, 254 (1982). Only Rehnquist, J. dissented from the judgment of the Court. 448 U.S. at 604, 100 S. Ct. at 2842, 65 L. Ed. 2d at 1007. Powell, J. did not participate. *Id*. at 581, 100 S. Ct. at 2830, 65 L. Ed. 2d at 992.

10. *Id*. at 576, 100 S. Ct. at 2817, 65 L. Ed. 2d at 989.

11. *Id*. at 584–585, 100 S. Ct. at 2831, 65 L. Ed. 2d at 994.

12. *Id*. at 589, 100 S. Ct. at 2834, 65 L. Ed. 2d at 997.

But more than history was involved in justifying a reading of the First Amendment to include public access to criminal trials, according to Brennan. Public access is necessary as a safeguard against attempts to employ the courts as instruments of persecution or for the suppression of political and religious heresies. Open trials are indispensable to First Amendment political and religious freedoms.[13] In short, open and public trials are a structural part of the judicial process and, more broadly, of the entire constitutional system of free and democratic government.

The opinions of Chief Justice Burger and Justice Brennan have much in common. Both rely on the long Anglo–American tradition of open and public trials antedating the adoption of the Bill of Rights. And while the Chief Justice emphasizes the right of the citizenry to receive information in a democracy, this emphasis is consistent with the thrust of Justice Brennan's opinion that access to trials is critical to the checking function preventing government abuse and, more broadly, the preservation of our constitutional system of government. The right to receive information in Burger's opinion is the means to various desirable ends including those central to Brennan's position. Thus, in *Richmond Newspapers*, there were at least five votes for a historical analysis justifying public and press access to criminal trials under the First Amendment and at least those same five votes accepting the additional analysis that such access was a structural part of our system of self-government encompassed by the Constitution.

The decision in *Richmond Newspapers* relegates *Gannett Co., Inc.* v. *DePasquale* to the scrap heap of legal history at least insofar as it suggests or holds that there is no first Amendment access to criminal trials and very likely also discarded *Gannett's* holding as to hearings on pretrial motions. As to the latter point, the reasoning in *Richmond Newspapers* regarding the structural importance of public and press access to *trials*, of necessity, carries over to pretrial and post trial criminal proceedings given their importance in our constitutional judicial framework as well.

C.   *Richmond's Progeny*

1.   *Globe Newspaper Co.*

The above analysis is confirmed by the line of cases spawned by *Richmond Newspapers*. In *Globe Newspaper Co.* v. *Superior Court*,[14] the Boston Globe was excluded from a criminal trial in which the defendant was charged with forcible rape of three minor girls pursuant to a Massachusetts statute requiring trial judges at trials for specified sexual offenses involving victims under the age of eighteen to exclude the press and public from the courtroom during the victims' testimony. The closure order was entered during a pretrial hearing. The Globe Newspaper Company then moved that the court revoke the order, hold hearings on any such future orders and permit the Globe to assert its right to

---

13. *Id.* at 592, 100 S. Ct. at 2835–2836, 65 L. Ed. 2d at 999.

14. 457 U.S. 596, 102 S.Ct. 2613, 73 L.Ed.2d 248 (1982).

access to pretrial proceedings and the trial. The trial court denied the motions and reaffirmed its trial closure order. The accused objected to the exclusion and the prosecution made clear that it had not requested such action. Before the Globe's appeal could be decided, the trial proceeded and the defendant was acquitted. Nine months after the trial, the Massachusetts Supreme Judicial Court dismissed the Globe's appeal. That court held that the case was then moot but nevertheless rendered an opinion on the merits that the statute did not require the exclusion of the press from the *entire* criminal trial but only during the testimony of minor victims. Exclusion during other portions of such trials was a matter within the judge's sound discretion. The Globe then appealed to the Supreme Court which vacated the state high court's judgment and remanded for further consideration in light of the recently decided *Richmond Newspapers* case. On remand, the Supreme Judicial Court held that while generally criminal trials were traditionally open, there was an exception regarding trials of sexual assaults allowing portions of such trials to be closed to some segments of the public even when the victim was an adult in order to further important state interests. The state court, therefore, did not believe *Richmond Newspapers* required the invalidation of the provision closing sexual assault trials when victims were testifying and again dismissed the Globe's appeal.

On the second appeal the Supreme Court this time reversed and held that even the narrow mandatory closure rule of the state statute violated the First Amendment. Writing for the majority Justice Brennan quickly dismissed the mootness issue and, reaching the merits, he reiterated much of what was said in his and the Chief Justice's opinions in *Richmond Newspapers*.[15] Then recognizing that the First Amendment right of access to criminal trials is not absolute, he turned to the state's contention that closing portions of sexual assault trials served compelling governmental interest and were narrowly tailored to serve those interests. He viewed those interests as two in number: the protection of minor victims of sex crimes from further trauma and embarrassment and the encouragement of such victims to come forward and testify in a truthful and credible manner.[16]

While agreeing with the state that the first interest, that of protecting the physical and psychological well-being of minor victims, is compelling, Justice Brennan held that it did not justify mandatory closure in each case because the circumstances of the particular case may affect the significance of the interest and the determination whether to close the trial at the point the victim testifies. Among the factors which must be weighed in each case are the minor's age, psychological maturity and understanding, the nature of the crime, the desires of the victim and the interests of parents and relatives. In short, the Massachusetts statute could not be viewed as a narrowly tailored means to achieve the state's

15. *Id*. at 603–606, 102 S. Ct. at 2618–2620, 73 L. Ed. 2d at 255–257.

16. *Id*. at 607, 102 S. Ct. at 2620, 73 L. Ed. 2d at 257.

interest and therefore violated the constitutional right of the press and public to access to criminal trials.[17]

As to the second interest, that of encouraging minor victims of sex crimes to come forward with accurate testimony, Justice Brennan noted that there was no empirical support for this claim in the record and the claim was open to serious question as a matter of logic and common sense because the news media could still publicize victims' testimony since access to the transcript and other sources providing accounts of the testimony was not barred by the statute.[18] This interest could not therefore be established to justify the statute's mandatory partial trial closure.[19] Thus, even as to very sensitive criminal trials the public and press may be accorded a right of access under the First Amendment.

2. *Press-Enterprise Co. (I)*

One aspect of a criminal proceeding that is fundamentally part of yet preliminary to the actual trial on the merits is the *voir dire* of prospective jurors. In *Press-Enterprise Co.* v. *Superior Court (I)*,[20] the Press–Enterprise Company moved that the *voir dire* in a sensational rape and murder trial involving a teenage girl be open to the public and press. The State of California opposed the newspaper company's motion arguing that if the press were present, individual juror responses to the questioning would lack the candor necessary to assure a fair trial. While permitting members of the news media to be present for the general *voir dire* of the jury panel, the trial judge ruled that individual *voir dire* would be conducted in a closed proceeding to insure fairness. The *voie dire* was of six weeks duration with all but approximately three days of it closed to the public. The trial judge also refused to release the transcript of the closed *voir dire* because of concern for the jurors' privacy. After the accused had been convicted and sentenced to death, the newspaper company again unsuccessfully sought release of the transcript. The company then petitioned the California District Court of Appeal for a writ of mandate (mandamus) directing the trial court to release the transcript and to vacate the original order closing the *voir dire* proceedings. The petition was denied and the California Supreme Court refused to review the matter. The Supreme Court then granted certiorari and reversed the order of the intermediate appellate court.

17. *Id.* at 607–609, 102 S. Ct. at 2620–2621, 73 L. Ed. 2d at 257–259.

18. *Id.* at 609–610, 102 S. Ct. at 2621–2622, 73 L. Ed. 2d at 258–260.

19. In a footnote at the end of his opinion for the majority, Justice Brennan emphasized the narrowness of the Court's holding. "We emphasize that our holding is a narrow one: that a rule of mandatory closure respecting the testimony of minor sex victims is constitutionally infirm. In individual cases, and under appropriate circumstances, the First Amendment does not necessarily stand as a bar to the exclusion from the courtroom of the press and general public during the testimony of minor sex-offense victims. But a mandatory rule, requiring no particularized determinations in individual cases, is unconstitutional." *Id.* at 611 n.27, 102 S. Ct. at 2622 n.27, 73 L. Ed. 2d at 260 n.27. Regardless of the narrowness of the holding itself, *Globe Newspaper Co.* is significant in incorporating much of Chief Justice Burger's plurality opinion and Justice Brennan's concurring opinion in *Richmond Newspapers* in the opinion of the Court.

20. 464 U.S. 501, 104 S.Ct. 819, 78 L.Ed.2d 629 (1984).

Harkening back to history, Chief Justice Burger writing for the majority demonstrated that at least since the sixteenth century, the selection of jurors had been essentially a public process in England. This tradition had carried over to colonial America and was in existence when the Constitution was adopted.[21] Extolling the virtues of open and public trials and recalling the support for openness in *Richmond Newspapers* and *Globe Newspaper*, the Chief Justice ruled that the presumption of open and public *voir dire* of prospective jurors could be overcome only by an overriding interest based on findings that closure is essential to the preserving of higher values and is narrowly tailored to serve such interest.[22]

The two interests identified by the trial judge—protection of a fair trial for the accused and protection of privacy for the prospective jurors—were found constitutionally not to justify closing the individual *voir dire* proceedings because they were not supported by findings that an open proceeding in fact threatened these interests and because the trial court failed to consider whether alternatives to closure and suppression of the transcript were available to protect the privacy interest of the prospective jurors.[23]

3. *Press-Enterprise Co. (II)*

By its decision in *Press-Enterprise Co. (I)* the Court had begun the expansion of the First Amendment right of access beyond the core criminal trial proceeding. This expansion continued in *Press-Enterprise Co. v. Superior Court (II)*.[24] There the same newspaper and the public were excluded on the defendant's motion from attending the preliminary hearing on a complaint filed by the state against a nurse charging him with the murders of 12 patients and seeking the death penalty. In granting the unopposed motion the magistrate found closure to be necessary because the case had attracted national publicity and "only one side may get reported in the media."[25] The closed preliminary hearing went on for 41 days at the end of which the accused was held to answer on all charges. After the conclusion of the hearing the Press–Enterprise Company asked that the transcript be released. The magistrate refused the request and sealed the record. Then, with the company joining, the state moved in Superior Court for release of the transcript. The court overruled the motion because there was a reasonable likelihood that the release might prejudice the defendant's right to a fair and impartial trial. While the California District Court of Appeal was considering the application of the newspaper company for a writ of mandate, the accused waived his right to a jury trial and the Superior Court released the transcript. Thereafter the appeals court held the controver-

21. *Id.* at 506–508, 104 S. Ct. at 822–823 78 L. Ed. 2d at 635–637.

22. *Id.* at 510, 104 S. Ct. at 824, 78 L. Ed. 2d at 638.

23. *Id.* at 510–511, 104 S. Ct. at 824–825, 78 L. Ed. 2d at 638–639; *see* Providence Journal Co. v. Superior Court, 593 A.2d 446, 448 (R.I.1991).

24. 478 U.S. 1, 106 S.Ct. 2735, 92 L.Ed.2d 1 (1986).

25. *Id.* at 4, 106 S. Ct. at 2738, 92 L. Ed. 2d at 7.

sy not to be moot, but denied the writ. The California Supreme Court also denied the writ, holding that there was no general First Amendment right of access to preliminary hearings. Under California's access statute, according to that court, if the defendant established a "reasonable likelihood of substantial prejudice"[26] the burden shifted to the prosecution or the media to show by a preponderance of the evidence that there is no reasonable probability of prejudice. The Supreme Court granted certiorari and reversed.

Again the Chief Justice delivered the opinion of the Court and summarily rejected any claims of mootness. Turning to the merits he first observed that the First Amendment question could not be resolved solely on the basis of the given event to which access is sought, particularly where the preliminary hearing functions somewhat like a trial. Rather, constitutional access had to be determined on considerations of historical openness and whether such access plays a significant role in the functioning of the particular process in question.[27] The Chief Justice then found a historical tradition of open preliminary hearings from the time of the case of *United States v. Burr*[28] to the present day[29]. He also found that public access to preliminary hearings in California played a significant positive role in the functioning of preliminary proceedings leading to trial because in many cases it will be the sole occasion for public scrutiny of the criminal justice system as a check on corrupt or overzealous prosecutors and biased or eccentric judges. Moreover, openness of such proceedings has a community therapeutic value.

Thus, being subject to the First Amendment, preliminary proceedings cannot be closed unless specific findings are made on the record that closure is necessary to preserve higher values and is narrowly tailored to serve those values. If the values asserted involve the right of the accused to a fair trial, closure may only be ordered if specific findings are made demonstrating first that there is a substantial probability that the defendant's right to a fair trial will be prejudiced by publicity that closure would prevent, and, second, that reasonable alternatives to closure cannot adequately protect the accused's fair trial rights.[30]

Reversal here was necessary because the California Supreme Court employed too low a standard for closure and failed to consider whether alternatives short of complete closure would have protected the interests of the accused.[31] Thus the Supreme Court, with its decision in *Press-Enterprise (II)* clearly moved beyond construing the First Amendment as providing access merely to criminal trials. The tests embraced by the Court to determine public and news media access to any type of criminal proceeding is whether there is substantial historical tradition of public

---

26. Cal. Penal Code § 868 (West 1985).

27. 478 U.S. at 8–9, 106 S. Ct. at 2741, 92 L. Ed. 2d at 10.

28. 25 Fed.Cas. 1 (No. 14,692) (C.C.D. Va. 1807).

29. 478 U.S. at 10–11, 106 S. Ct. at 2741–2742, 92 L. Ed. 2d at 11–12.

30. *Id.* at 13–14, 106 S. Ct. at 2742, 92 L. Ed. 2d at 13.

31. *Id.* at 14–15, 106 S. Ct. at 2743, 92 L. Ed. 2d at 14.

access and whether openness of the proceedings serves a substantial purpose in furthering the particular process.

4. *El Vocero De Puerto Rico*

More recently the Court emphasized that the tradition of openness of particular preliminary proceedings is to be measured by the experience of jurisdictions throughout the United States. In *El Vocero de Puerto Rico* v. *Puerto Rico*,[32] a reporter for the largest circulation newspaper in Puerto Rico requested to attend, criminal preliminary hearings of the Commonwealth's superior court. His request was denied under its Rule of Procedure 23(c) which provided that probable cause hearings were to be held privately unless the defendant requested otherwise. The newspaper then brought an action in the superior court challenging the constitutionality of the rule on the basis of the ruling in *Press-Enterprise (II)*. The trial court's dismissal of the newspaper company's suit was affirmed by the Puerto Rico Supreme Court on the basis that Puerto Rico's preliminary hearing was substantially different than California's and that Puerto Rican tradition favored closed preliminary hearings.

On the grant of certiorari the Supreme Court, in a per curiam decision, reversed. It first rejected as insubstantial the differences between the preliminary hearings.[33] Second, and more significantly, the Court refused to accept the tradition or experience of any one American jurisdiction as a constitutionally adequate basis for closing criminal proceedings. "As the First Circuit Court of Appeals has correctly stated, the 'experience' test ... does not look to the particular practice of any one jurisdiction, but instead 'to the experience in that *type* or *kind* of hearing throughout the United States ...' "[34]

History does matter when a trial court has to decide whether to close any type of hearing as one state high court recently noted.[35] But the procedure employed in ordering closure or the sealing of records, files, transcripts, exhibits and documents may matter even more. Very often where the news media have been successful in having a closure or sealing order reversed or vacated on appeal, it has been because the trial court failed to follow the procedural requirements laid down in *Richmond Newspapers*, *Press-Enterprise (I)* and *Press-Enterprise (II)*.[36]

---

32. 508 U.S. 147, 113 S.Ct., 2004, 124 L.Ed.2d 60 (1993).

33. *Id.* at 148–149, 113 S. Ct. at 2005–2006, 124 L. Ed. 2d at 64.

34. *Id.* at 150, 113 S. Ct. at 2006, 124 L. Ed. 2d at 65.

35. Johnson Newspaper Corp. v. Melino, 77 N.Y.2d 1, 5–8, 563 N.Y.S.2d 380, 381–383, 564 N.E.2d 1046, 1047–1049 (1990); *see* Westmoreland v. Columbia Broadcasting System, 752 F.2d 16, 23 (2d Cir.), cert. denied *sub nom.* Cable News Network v. United States Dist. Ct., 472 U.S. 1017, 105 S.Ct. 3478, 87 L.Ed.2d 614 (1985) (citing

lack of historical precedent in closing trial to television cameras); Publicker Industries v. Cohen, 733 F.2d 1059, 1066–1070 (3d Cir.1984).

36. *See, e.g.,* United States v. Cojab, 996 F.2d 1404, 1407 (2d Cir.1993) (failure to give timely public notice of closing of pretrial hearing); Application of the Herald Co., 734 F.2d 93 (2d Cir.1984) (failure to state on the record adequate reasons for closing courtroom during pretrial hearing and failure to give public notice before closure ordered); *In re* State–Record Co., Inc., 917 F.2d 124 (4th Cir.1990) (use of wrong

Following the Supreme Court's two-prong constitutional standard and required procedures thereunder, lower courts have at times recognized the right of the news media to access to such diverse proceedings and materials as pretrial hearings,[37] trial motion hearings,[38] post trial hearings[39] and court records, documents and files.[40] On the other hand, access is often denied under the Court's standards.[41] A reading of the access cases decided since the *Richmond News* and its progeny gives the firm impression that the lower courts are more likely to recognize the First Amendment right when access is sought to documents, files and records which can be easily redacted and controlled as to time of release than when access is sought to live hearings.[42] In addition, there is considerable reluctance, based perhaps on the Supreme Court's earlier decision in the *Nixon Tapes Case*,[43] to permit access under the First

standard of proof of damage); Oregonian Pub. Co. v. United States. Dist. Ct., 920 F.2d 1462 (9th Cir.1990) (placement of burden of proof on party *opposing* sealing of plea agreement); Des Moines Register & Tribune v. Iowa Dist. Ct., 426 N.W.2d 142 (Iowa 1988) (failure to state specific findings on record in closing preliminary hearing); *Ex parte* South Carolina Press Assoc., 281 S.C. 52, 314 S.E.2d 321 (1984), cert. denied *sub. nom.* Patterson v. South Carolina, 471 U.S. 1036, 105 S.Ct. 2056, 85 L.Ed.2d 329 (1985) (failure to state specific findings on record in closing preliminary hearing).

37. *See, e.g., In re* Washington Post Co., 807 F.2d 383 (4th Cir.1986) (plea hearing); *Ex parte* Consolidated Pub. Co., Inc., 601 So.2d 423, 426–430 (Ala.) cert. denied, 506 U.S. 1024, 113 S.Ct. 665, 121 L.Ed.2d 590 (1992) (thorough analysis of relevant authorities); Buzbee v. Journal Newspapers, Inc., 297 Md. 68, 465 A.2d 426 (1983) (suppression hearing) (collects access cases decided under state constitutions and statutes); State *ex rel.* The Repository v. Unger, 28 Ohio St.3d 418, 504 N.E.2d 37 (1986) (all pretrial hearings and deposition); Vermont v. Schaefer, 157 Vt. 339, 346, 599 A.2d 337, 342 (1991), *cert. denied,* 502 U.S. 1077, 112 S.Ct. 981, 117 L.Ed.2d 144 (1992) (suppression hearing).

38. *See* Houston Chronicle Pub. Co. v. Shaver, 630 S.W.2d 927 (Tex.Crim.App. 1982) (evidentiary hearing); *see also* Shiras v. Britt, 267 Ark. 97, 589 S.W.2d 18 (1979) (evidentiary hearing).

39. *See* United States v. Simone, 14 F.3d 833 (3d Cir.1994) (post verdict hearing on alleged jury misconduct); *In re* Washington Post Co., 807 F.2d 383 (4th Cir.1986) (sentencing hearing).

40. *See, e.g.,* Globe Newspaper Co. v. Pokaski, 868 F.2d 497 (1st Cir.1989); *In re*

Washington Post Co., 807 F.2d 383 (4th Cir.1986); Application of National Broadcasting Co., Inc., 828 F.2d 340 (6th Cir. 1987); Washington Post v. Robinson, 935 F.2d 282, 290 U.S. App. D.C. 116 (D.C.Cir. 1991); State v. Densmore, 160 Vt. 131, 624 A.2d 1138 (1993).

41. *See e.g., In re* Globe Newspaper Co. 729 F.2d 47 (1st Cir.1984) (bail hearing); In re Grand Jury Subpoena, 103 F.3d 234, 242–243 (2d Cir.1996) (grand jury proceeding); *In re* Greensboro News Co., 727 F.2d 1320, 1322–1324, 1326 (4th Cir.1984), cert. denied, 469 U.S. 829, 105 S.Ct. 114, 83 L.Ed.2d 57 (1984) (voir dire) (Press–Enterprise (I) distinguished in supplemental opinion); United States v. Chagra, 701 F.2d 354 (5th Cir.1983) (bail reduction hearing); United States v. Hegge, 636 F.Supp. 119 (E.D.Wash.1986) (pretrial hearings); Lexington Herald–Leader Co., Inc. v. Meigs, 660 S.W.2d 658 (Ky.1983) (voir dire); Poughkeepsie Newspapers, Inc. v. Rosenblatt, 92 A.D.2d 232, 459 N.Y.S.2d 857 (1983), *aff'd* 61 N.Y.2d 1005, 475 N.Y.S.2d 370, 463 N.E.2d 1222 (1984) (mid-trial evidentiary hearing). For an exhaustive collection of cases involving access to criminal proceeding see Dan Paul, Richard J. Ovelmen and Laura Besvinick, *Access,* Communications Law 1989 611, 642–690 (Practising Law Institute 1989).

42. *See, e.g., In re* Greensboro News Co., 727 F.2d 1320, 1321 (4th Cir.), cert. denied, 469 U.S. 829, 105 S.Ct. 114, 83 L.Ed.2d 57 (1984); Phoenix Newspapers, Inc. v. Superior Court, 140 Ariz. 30, 34–35, 680 P.2d 166, 170–171 (Ariz.App.1983); Poughkeepsie Newspapers, Inc. v. Rosenblatt, 92 A.D.2d 232, 236, 459 N.Y.S.2d 857, 860 (1983), *aff'd* 61 N.Y.2d 1005, 475 N.Y.S.2d 370, 463 N.E.2d 1222 (1984).

43. Nixon v. Warner Communications, Inc., 435 U.S. 589, 98 S.Ct. 1306, 55

Amendment to inspect and copy audio and video tape trial exhibits and pretrial depositions.[44] Rather, if access is allowed it is pursuant to the common law right recognized in *Nixon*.[45]

D. Access to Civil Judicial Proceedings

1. Constitutional Access

In *Richmond Newspapers*, the Supreme Court in a footnote observed that historically both civil and criminal trials have been presumptively open[46] but thus far it has not held squarely that there is a First Amendment right of access to civil judicial proceedings. However, a number of federal appeals courts have concluded that such right exists.

In *Publicker Industries, Inc.* v. *Cohen*,[47] the Third Circuit held in a case involving a proxy fight to determine control of a publicly traded corporation that employees of Philadelphia Newspapers, Inc. publisher of the Philadelphia Inquirer and Dow Jones & Company, Inc. publisher of the Wall Street Journal, had, along with the public, a First Amendment right to attend a hearing on motions for preliminary injunctions and to have access to the transcript of the hearing. The trial court had closed the hearing, sealed the transcript and ordered the publishing company's own attorneys not to disclose to their clients certain supposedly confidential information disclosed at the hearing. The trial judge refused to make detailed findings of the need to close the hearing and, after the hearing, to unseal the transcript. He also refused to consider seriously the suggestion of counsel for the papers to close only those parts of the hearing that involved the confidential information. By the admission of the corporate party which had sought the closure and sealing orders, more than two-thirds of the transcript contained no confidential information, and, before the publishers appeal was decided, the corporation made public the supposedly confidential information.

The corporation's argument that the appeal was therefore moot was rejected by the Third Circuit because closure orders were capable of repetition yet likely to evade review because trials and hearings are of

L.Ed.2d 570 (1978) (no access under First Amendment to copy White House audio tapes admitted in criminal trial of members of Nixon's staff).

44. *See In re* Application of National Broadcasting Co., 635 F.2d 945 (2d Cir. 1980); United States v. Criden, 648 F.2d 814 (3d Cir.1981); United States v. Webbe, 791 F.2d 103, 105 (8th Cir.1986); United States v. McDougal, 103 F.3d 651 (8th Cir. 1996) (review of cases denying access to audio and video tapes); Group W Television, Inc. v. State, 96 Md.App. 712, 719, 626 A.2d 1032, 1035, (Md.Sp.App.1993) (stating flatly that there is no First Amendment right of the public or the media to copy tape evidence); *but see* United States v. Carpentier,

526 F.Supp. 292, 294–295 (E.D.N.Y.1981), *aff'd*, 689 F.2d 21 (2d Cir.1982), cert. denied 459 U.S. 1108, 103 S.Ct. 735, 74 L.Ed.2d 957 (1983).

45. *See* In re Application of CBS, Inc. 828 F.2d 958 959–960 (2d Cir.1987); *In re* Application of National Broadcasting Co., 635 F.2d at 949–953; United States v. Criden, 648 F.2d at 823–826; United States v. Carpentier, 526 F. Supp. at 295–296.

46. Richmond Newspapers, Inc. v. Virginia, 448 U.S. 555, 580 n. 17, 100 S.Ct. 2814, 2829 n. 17, 65 L.Ed.2d 973, 992 n. 17 (1980); *see* Gannett Co. v. DePasquale, 443 U.S. 368, 386 n. 15, 99 S.Ct. 2898, 2908 n. 15, 61 L.Ed.2d 608, 625–626 n. 15 (1979).

47. 733 F.2d 1059 (3d Cir.1984).

such short duration.[48] On the merits, the appeals court first held that the news media and the public possess a common law right of access to civil trials. Then, engaging in reasoning parallel to that in *Richmond Newspapers*, and *Globe Newspaper Co.*, the Third Circuit concluded "that the public and the press possess a First Amendment and a common law right of access to civil proceedings; indeed, there is a presumption that these proceedings will be open."[49] The court then added, "The trial court may limit this right, however, when an important countervailing interest is shown."[50] In determining when the right of access may be limited, the court imposed the procedural requirements laid down in *Press-Enterprise Co.* (I).[51] It then reversed the lower court's orders because the trial judge had not explained on the record what standards it was following and why it was closing the hearing and sealing the transcript. No countervailing interests were articulated, no specific findings were made and no alternatives to closure and sealing were considered.

The First Amendment was also read as providing access to the civil judicial process in *Brown & Williamson Tobacco Corp.* v. *Federal Trade Commission*.[52] There a United States District Court placed under seal all documents filed by the FTC in the tobacco corporation's suit against the agency preventing a public interest health group from examining documents submitted to the agency by several tobacco companies. Saying that the Supreme Court's analysis in *Richmond Newspapers* and *Globe Newspaper Co.* of historical and structural justifications and policy considerations for constitutional access to the criminal courtroom "apply as well to the civil trial,"[53] the Sixth Circuit vacated the trial court's order sealing the documents because the confidentiality agreement between the parties to the litigation did not bind the court and the court's order did not meet the requirements for closing the civil judicial process to the public and the press. All that was shown was that the information in the documents would harm the company's reputation and such showing is not sufficient to overcome the presumption in favor of public access.[54]

Shortly after these Third and Sixth Circuit holdings, the Second Circuit weighed in with its decision to the same effect in *Westmoreland* v. *Columbia Broadcasting System, Inc.*[55] There, while recognizing the First Amendment right of the public and press to *attend* civil trials, it upheld on historical grounds the order of the United States District Court denying one television network's application to televise another television network's "libel trial of the decade."[56]

---

48. *Id.* at 1065–1066 (citing *Richmond Newspapers*).

49. *Id.* at 1071.

50. *Id.*

51. *Id.* at 1072–1073.

52. 710 F.2d 1165 (6th Cir.1983), cert. denied, 465 U.S. 1100, 104 S.Ct. 1595, 80 L.Ed.2d 127 (1984).

53. *Id.* at 1178, 1179.

54. *Id.* at 1179.

55. 752 F.2d 16, 23–24 (2d Cir.1984), cert. denied *sub nom.* Cable News Network v. United States Dist. Ct., 472 U.S. 1017, 105 S.Ct. 3478, 87 L.Ed.2d 614 (1985).

56. *Id.* at 23. *See also* NBC Subsidiary (KNBC–TV) Inc. v. Superior Court, 49 Cal. App.4th 487, 56 Cal.Rptr.2d 645, appeal granted 60 Cal.Rptr.2d 1, 928 P.2d 485 (1996) (recent thorough statement of the

2. *Protective Orders in Discovery Proceedings Preventing Access*

Westmoreland, Brown & Williamson and *Publicker* form the predicate for the conclusion that the federal courts recognize constitutional access to civil trials, hearings and records, files and documents similar to that involving the criminal process.[57] Some state jurisdictions are in accord at least in principle.[58] There is however, one line of federal and state cases involving protective orders in discovery proceedings[59] that appears to be in conflict with normal constitutional access to the civil process and its fruits. The generally accepted First Amendment standard for limiting public and media access is whether denial serves an important governmental interest and no narrower feasible way of protecting the government's interest is available.[60] But in *Seattle Times Co.* v. *Rhinehart*[61] the Supreme Court ruled that protective orders entered pursuant to Washington Rule of Civil Procedure 26(c) (and by necessary implication, Federal Rule of Civil Procedure 26(c)) to prevent the dissem-

rationale for fully opening civil trials to the public and press; issue on appeal limited to question whether there is a First Amendment right of public access to civil trials).

57. *See also* Rushford v. New Yorker Magazine, Inc., 846 F.2d 249, 253 (4th Cir. 1988); *In re* Continental Illinois Securities Litigation, 732 F.2d 1302, 1308–1309 (7th Cir.1984) (semble as to constitutional basis for access); Wilson v. American Motors Corp., 759 F.2d 1568, 1569–1570 (11th Cir. 1985) (semble as to constitutional basis for access); United States *ex rel.* McCoy v. California Medical Review, 133 F.R.D. 143, 147–148, (N.D.Cal.1990); *but see* Cincinnati Gas & Elec. Co. v. General Elec. Co., 854 F.2d 900 (6th Cir.1988) (no constitutional access on historical grounds to summary jury trial proceeding); *In re* Reporters Committee for Freedom of the Press, 773 F.2d 1325, 1330–1341, 249 U.S. App. D.C. 119, 124–135 (D.C.Cir.1985) (no immediate constitutional access to discovery documents) (lengthy historical and structural analysis by Judge, now Justice, Scalia).

58. *See* Courier–Journal v. Peers, 747 S.W.2d 125, 127–130 (Ky.1988); State v. Cottman Transmission Systems, Inc., 75 Md.App. 647, 654–658, 542 A.2d 859, 862–864 (Md.Sp.App.1988) (cases collected); New Jersey Div. of Youth and Family Services v. J.B., 120 N.J. 112, 117–123, 576 A.2d 261, 264–267 (1990); Hutchison v. Luddy, 398 Pa.Super. 505, 581 A.2d 578, 582–583 (1990), *rev'd on other grounds* 527 Pa. 525, 594 A.2d 307 (1991); *but see* Bowlen v. District Court, 733 P.2d 1179 (Colo. 1987) (protective order entered to prevent disclosure of discovery material to third parties); Minneapolis Star & Tribune Co. v. Schumacher, 392 N.W.2d 197, 203–205 (Minn.1986) (rejecting constitutional access

to settlement agreements and related transcripts in a civil case under a historical analysis); Johnson Newspaper Corp. v. Melino, 77 N.Y.2d 1, 563 N.Y.S.2d 380, 564 N.E.2d 1046 (1990) (rejecting constitutional access to an administrative professional disciplinary proceeding on historical grounds): Rhinehart v. Seattle Times Co., 98 Wash.2d 226, 236, 654 P.2d 673, 679 (1982), *aff'd* 467 U.S. 20, 104 S.Ct. 2199, 81 L.Ed.2d 17 (1984) (protective order entered to prevent disclosure of discovery material to third parties). It should be remembered, of course, that access to various criminal and civil proceedings, transcripts, records and files may also be provided by state constitutional and statutory provisions and court rules. *See, e.g.*, Atlanta Journal v. Long, 258 Ga. 410, 369 S.E.2d 755 (1988); KUTV v. Conder, 635 P.2d 412 (Utah 1981); Matter of Estates of Zimmer, 151 Wis.2d 122, 442 N.W.2d 578 (Wis.App.1989). For an exhaustive collection of cases involving access to civil proceedings in both state and federal courts see Dan Paul, Richard J. Ovelmen and Laura Besvinick, *Access*, Communications Law 1989 611, 690–710 (Practicing Law Institute).

59. *See* F.R. Civ. P. 26(c) and counterpart rules in state civil procedure codes such as Colo. R. Civ. P. 26(c) and Wash. R. Civ. P. 26(c).

60. *See, e.g.*, Brown & Williamson Tobacco Corp. v. Federal Trade Commission, 710 F.2d 1165, 1179 (6th Cir.1983), cert. denied, 465 U.S. 1100, 104 S.Ct. 1595, 80 L.Ed.2d 127 (1984); Publicker Industries, Inc. v. Cohen, 733 F.2d 1059, 1070 (3d Cir.1984); Rushford v. New Yorker Magazine, 846 F.2d 249, 253 (4th Cir.1988).

61. 467 U.S. 20, 104 S.Ct. 2199, 81 L.Ed.2d 17 (1984), *affirming* 98 Wash.2d 226, 654 P.2d 673 (1982).

ination to the public and press of material and information obtained solely through the discovery process were not subject to the normal heightened level of First Amendment scrutiny. Rather, if the standard embodied in Rule 26(c) of "good cause" is factually demonstrated by the moving party to the satisfaction of the trial court, the court is justified in issuing a protective order preventing dissemination of discovered information.[62] Such order would only be overturned for abuse of discretion. "The trial court is in the best position to weigh fairly the competing needs and interests of parties affected by discovery. The unique character of the discovery process requires that the trial court have substantial latitude to fashion protective orders."[63] Following *Rhinehart* the only debate over limiting access to discovery information under the Federal Rules scheme appears to be whether any constitutional scrutiny of protective orders remains.[64]

3. Sealing of Settlement Agreements by Action of the Parties

Another major obstacle to full access of the public and news media to the civil process is the recent and growing practice fully documented by the Washington Post[65] of parties to litigation agreeing to seal their

62. *See* Anderson v. Cryovac, Inc., 805 F.2d 1, 5–8 (1st Cir.1986); Bowlen v. District Court, 733 P.2d 1179, 1181–1183 (Colo.1987); *see also* Gregory G. Sarno, Annot., *Restriction on Dissemination of Information Obtained Through Pretrial Discovery Proceedings as Violating Federal Constitution's First Amendment—Federal Cases*, 81 A.L.R. Fed. 471 (1987); Gary L. Wilson, Note, *Seattle Times: What Effect on Discovery Sharing?* 1985 Wis. L. Rev. 1055; *cf. In re* Reporters Comm. for Freedom of the Press, 773 F.2d 1325, 1330–1341 (D.C.Cir.1985) (intervention by press organization third party in order to obtain access to discovery material sealed pursuant to discovery order). Criteria that may be considered in determining good cause includes the factual assessment of the magnitude and imminence of the harm threatened by disclosure, the effectiveness of the protective order in preventing the harm, the availability of less restrictive means of doing so and the breadth of the requested protective order. *See In re* San Juan Star Co., 662 F.2d 108, 116 (1st Cir. 1981); Anderson, 805 F.2d at 7–8.

63. Rhinehart, 467 U.S. at 36, 104 S. Ct. at 2209 81 L. Ed. 2d at 29. The supposedly "unique" aspects of the discovery process justifying lessened if not wholly eliminated constitutional scrutiny include the extreme breadth of what can be discovered including irrelevant prejudicial and privacy-invading information regarding parties and nonparties alike as well as its private nature as opposed to the public nature of actual trials. *See id.* at 33–35, 1045 S. Ct. at 2207–2209,

81 L. Ed. 2d at 27–28; *In re* San Juan Star Co., 662 F.2d 108, 115 (1st Cir.1981); Bowlen v. District Court, 733 P.2d 1179, 1182 (Colo.1987).

64. *Compare* Anderson v. Cryovac, Inc., 805 F.2d 1, 6–7 (1st Cir.1986) (lower level of scrutiny still required) *with* Cipollone v. Liggett Group, Inc., 785 F.2d 1108, 1118–1120 (3d Cir.1986) (no First Amendment scrutiny permitted). There is a split of authority on the alternative question whether there is a *common law* right of access to discovery motions and supporting material. *See* Anderson, 805 F.2d at 13 *and* Leucadia, Inc. v. Applied Extrusion Technologies, Inc., 998 F.2d 157, 167 (3d Cir.1993) (no common law access); Mokhiber v. Davis, 537 A.2d 1100 (D.C.1988) (common law access found).

65. The influential *Washington Post* series on judicial sealings of court records insisted upon by the parties in their settlement agreements was published under the general title "Public Courts, Private Justice" and included six major articles. *See* Elsa Walsh & Benjamin Weiser, *Court Secrecy Masks Safety Issues*, Wash. Post, Oct. 23, 1988, p. A1; Elsa Walsh & Benjamin Weiser, *Hundred of Cases Shrouded in Secret*, Wash. Post, Oct. 24, 1988, p. A1; Benjamin Weiser & Elsa Walsh, *Drug Firms Strategy: Avoid Trial, Ask Secrecy*, Wash. Post, Oct. 24, 1988, p. A1; Benjamin Weiser & Elsa Walsh, *Settlements Kept Former Drug Salesman's Story Under Wraps*, Wash. Post, Oct. 24, 1988, p. A13; Benjamin

settlement agreements and all related court papers.[66] When this practice is challenged by the news media and public interest organizations seeking to examine the filings particularly in product liability cases, the courts have split on whether to make the papers available.[67] Two important public policies come into conflict when access is sought. On the one hand there is, of course, the policy that the public is entitled to know what is happening in *its* courtrooms, particularly when the litigation may impact on the public's health and safety. On the other hand, there is a strong policy to encourage parties to settle there disputes by themselves thereby reducing the burden on the public's judicial system. Sealing agreements and court files may, in some cases, be the only way to achieve this end.

But trial courts should not lose sight of the constitutional standard that must be met before civil court records and documents may be kept from the public's gaze. The parties seeking the sealing pursuant to a settlement agreement must establish good cause meaning that there is a compelling governmental interest justifying such action,[68] that the sealing order furthers that interest and that the requested order is narrowly tailored. A balancing of the public's interest in disclosure and the parties' interests in secrecy is involved, with the burden of proof placed on the party or parties seeking the sealing order.[69]

Weiser & Elsa Walsh, *Secret Filing Settlement Hides Surgeon's Record*, Wash. Post, Oct. 26, 1988, p. A1; Benjamin Weiser, *Forging a "Convenant of Silence,"* Wash. Post, Mar. 13, 1989, p. A1; *see also* concurring opinion of Judge Pratt in City of Hartford v. Chase, 942 F.2d 130, 137–138 (2d Cir.1991); Benjamin Weiser, *Lawsuits Spur A Debate Over Secrets vs. Safety*, Wash. Post, July 26, 1994, p. A1, A7 (updating the issue of judicial secrecy and public safety and reporting that on June 28, 1994 the United States Senate rejected, on a procedural vote of 51–49, a bill that would require federal judges to weigh the public interest involved before deciding to seal records in civil suits).

66. *See, e.g.*, City of Hartford v. Chase, 942 F.2d 130 (2d Cir.1991); United States v. Kentucky Utilities Co., 927 F.2d 252 (6th Cir.1991); Society of Professional Journalists v. Briggs, 687 F.Supp. 1521 (D.Utah 1988); Holland v. Eads, 614 So.2d 1012 (Ala.1993); Anchorage Daily News v. Anchorage School Dist., 803 P.2d 402 (Alaska 1990); *In re* Estates of Zimmer (WISC–TV v. Mewis), 151 Wis.2d 122, 442 N.W.2d 578 (App.1989).

67. *Compare, e.g.*, City of Hartford v. Chase, 942 F.2d 130, (2d Cir.1991) *and* Holland v. Eads, 614 So.2d 1012 (Ala.1993) (denying access to records sealed pursuant to settlement agreements) *with, e.g., In re* Johnson, 232 Ill.App.3d 1068, 174 Ill.Dec.

209, 598 N.E.2d 406 (1992) *and In re* Estates of Zimmer (WISC–TV v. Mewis), 151 Wis.2d 122, 442 N.W.2d 578 (App.1989) (granting access to news media representatives).

68. The *parties'* desire for privacy or to avoid embarrassment is not a sufficient interest. *See In re Johnson*, 232 Ill.App.3d 1068, 1071–1075, 174 Ill.Dec. 209, 598 N.E.2d 406, 409–411 (1992). Nor is the avoidance of public expenditure for the conduct of trials. *See In re* Estates of Zimmer (WISC–TV v. Mewis), 151 Wis.2d 122, 133, 442 N.W.2d 578, 583 (App.1989).

69. *See* Pansy v. Borough of Stroudsburg, 23 F.3d 772 (3d Cir.1994) (thorough discussion of all issues associated with requests to seal settlement agreements); Brown v. Advantage Engineering, Inc., 960 F.2d 1013 (11th Cir.1992); *In re* Johnson, 232 Ill.App.3d 1068, 1071–1075, 174 Ill.Dec. 209, 598 N.E.2d 406, 409–411 (1992); *cf. e.g.*, Publicker Industries, Inc. v. Cohen, 733 F.2d 1059, 1067–71 (3d Cir.1984); Rushford v. New Yorker Magazine, Inc., 846 F.2d 249, 253 (4th Cir.1988); Brown & Williamson Tobacco Corp. v. Federal Trade Comm'n, 710 F.2d 1165, 1177–79 (6th Cir. 1983); Wilson v. American Motors Corp., 759 F.2d 1568, 1570–71 (11th Cir.1985). An effort of manufacturing groups to weaken the standard by simply allowing federal judges to seal settlement agreements at the

Should sealing orders be entered without meeting this high standard, they should be vacated on the petition of members of the news media or the general public.[70] The one plausible justification for a court to refuse to unseal in such situation would be a showing of irreparable harm from disclosure to one or more of the parties brought about by justifiable reliance on the trial court's order.[71]

E. Summary Analysis of Richmond Newspapers and Its Progeny

Certain propositions have become clear more than two decades after the decision in *Richmond Newspapers*. On the procedural front there is no doubt that the news media have standing to assert their First Amendment right of access to the judicial process and that as a function of standing they may intervene in the litigation in question and appeal adverse access rulings and orders.[72] And because trials and hearings may terminate before appellate review can be obtained, the appellate courts will reject objections to such review based upon grounds of mootness.

On the merits, a limited constitutional right of access to criminal proceedings including trials, hearings, court records, files and documents is recognized if there is historical precedent for such access and access will aid the criminal justice system and governmental process. The access is limited because it may be defeated by parties seeking closure or sealing orders if they can shoulder the burden of establishing that there is a compelling state interest to be served and the proposed closure or sealing order is narrowly tailored to serve that interest.

The judge in issuing closure or sealing orders must make specific findings on the record as to what the compelling state interest is (often the interest in a fair trial and how closure or sealing orders will serve that interest). Findings must also be made demonstrating that reasonable less drastic alternatives to closure or sealing will not serve the state interest adequately. Unless adequate findings are made, anti-access orders will be reversed or vacated on appeal.

request of the parties was rejected in 1995 by the Judicial Conference of the United States. *See* Saundra Torry, *Judges Reject Record-Secrecy Rule*; *Federal Meeting Opens Door to New Courtroom Camera Experiments*, Wash. Post, Mar. 15 1995, p.A8, cols. 4–6; *see also* In re Purcell, 879 P.2d 468 (Colo.App.1994) (similar claim of party control of sealing process rejected pursuant to state statute); *but see* In re Cincinnati Enquirer, 94 F.3d 198 (6th Cir.1996) (apparently adopting a *per se* rule that summary jury trials designed to reach settlement of a civil action are not open to the public or the media).

70. *See* Brown v. Advantage Engineering, Inc., 960 F.2d 1013, 1016 (11th Cir. 1992).

71. *See* Sogeclif U.S.A., Ltd. v. Xavier Decludt, 16 Med. L. Rptr. 1765 (D.D.C. 1989) (dictum).

72. Intervention is required in at least one jurisdiction (*see* Courier–Journal v. Peers, 747 S.W.2d.125, 130 (Ky.1988)) and would be the preferred way for news media challenges to protective orders to proceed (*see, e.g.*, In re Reporters Comm. for Freedom of the Press, 773 F.2d 1325, 1327, 249 U.S. App. D.C. 119, 121 (D.C.Cir.1985)), though some courts may not require it (*see* United States v. Beckham, 789 F.2d 401 (6th Cir.1986) (Post–Newsweek Stations, Michigan, Inc. listed as a "Non–Party Appellant" in caption of appeal challenging the denial of the opportunity to copy tape recording exhibits in a criminal trial)).

While the Court has not squarely ruled on the question of constitutional access to civil judicial proceedings, a number of federal appeals courts have recognized such access on reasoning parallel to that of *Richmond Newspapers* and the Supreme Court decisions following it. Some state courts have also recognized this federal constitutional right of access. But this right of access is qualified by *Seattle Times Co.* v. *Rhinehart* regarding protective orders entered in discovery proceedings to prevent dissemination to third parties including representatives of the new media of material obtained solely through those proceedings.

F. Access of Cameras and Recording Equipment to the Courtroom

1. History

Before the late 1930s, still and motion picture cameras, microphones and recording equipment were regularly permitted in state courtrooms.[73] They were present at the Scopes evolution theory trial in Tennessee and the celebrated Leopold–Loeb murder trial in Illinois. Their presence was no more questioned than the pencils and note-books of print journalists attending newsworthy trials or more recently the pens, pastels and sketch pads of sketch artists in the United States Supreme Court. But the 1935 circus-like New Jersey trial of Bruno Hauptmann for the kidnap-murder of the Lindbergh baby caused the legal establishment to reexamine, fairly or unfairly, the practice of permitting cameras and broadcasting and recording equipment in courtrooms.[74] In 1937 the American Bar Association adopted Canon 35 of its Canons of Judicial Ethics banning photographic and broadcasting equipment from courtrooms.[75] Most states adopted the Canon and its modifications through the years.[76] The ABA's ban was adopted for the federal courts in Federal

---

73. *See* Diane Kiesel, *Will There Ever Be Cameras in the Federal Courtrooms?* 1 ABA Communications Lawyer 1, 12 (No. 4, Fall 1983).

74. *Id.; see also* Estes v. Texas, 381 U.S. 532, 597, 85 S.Ct. 1628, 1667, 14 L.Ed.2d 543, 589 (1965); S. L. Alexander, *Cameras in the courtroom: a case study,* 74 Judicature 307, 313 (1991); Carolyn S. Dyer & Nancy R. Houserman , *Electronic Coverage of the Court: Exception to Exposure,* 75 Geo. L.J. 1633, 1641 (1987).

75. This canon provided: "Proceedings in court should be conducted with fitting dignity and decorum. The taking of photographs in the courtroom, during sessions of the court or recesses between sessions, and the broadcasting of court proceedings are calculated to detract from the essential dignity of the proceedings, degrade the court and create misconceptions with respect thereto in the mind of the public and should not be permitted."

76. *See* Carolyn S. Dyer & Nancy R. Hauserman, *Electronic Coverage of the Courts: Exceptions to Exposure,* 75 Geo. L.J. 1633, 1641 (1987); Diane Kiesel, *Will there Ever Be Cameras in the Federal Courtrooms?* 1 ABA Communications Lawyer 1, 12 (No. 4, Fall 1983). Canon 35 was amended and renumbered 3A(7) of the ABA Code of Judicial Conduct in 1972. Canon 3A provided, "A judge should prohibit broadcasting, television recording or taking photographs in the courtroom and areas immediately adjacent thereto during sessions of court or recesses between sessions, except that a judge may authorize: a. The use of electronic or photographic means for the presentation of evidence, or for the perpetuation of a record; and b. The broadcasting, televising, recording. or photographing of investigative, ceremonial, or naturalization proceedings."

Rule of Criminal Procedure 53.[77]

The ban on photographic and electronic coverage was approved by a plurality of the Supreme Court in *Estes* v. *Texas*.[78] There, Texas, one of the few states that had not adopted Canon 35, was prosecuting a nationally notorious fraud case involving politically well-connected Billy Sol Estes and at the commencement of the trial television and still and motion picture cameras and microphones for radio broadcasting were present in the courtroom. At that time counsel for Estes, decrying the publicity being given to the case, moved to ban all cameras and microphones from the trial. The hearing on this motion was televised, broadcast and photographed with so much personnel and equipment as to cause considerable disruption. While the motion to ban the telecasts, broadcasts and photography was denied, another motion asking for continuance was granted and in the interim a booth was constructed at the back of the courtroom to which all television and newsreel cameras were relegated. Live television, coverage was severely though not totally limited but videotaping of the entire proceeding without audio accompaniment was permitted except for defense summations to the jury. No camera or broadcast coverage of any kind was permitted as to those summations. Following his conviction for swindling, Estes claimed that the television and broadcasting of his trial deprived him of due process of law guaranteed him by the Fourteenth Amendment. This claim was rejected by the trial court and the Court of Criminal Appeals.

The United States Supreme Court reversed the conviction. Justice Clark's opinion held that the showing of actual prejudice to Estes' right to a fair trial was not essential to reversal but could be presumed. The justices agreeing with Clark's opinion presumed prejudice because of their concern about (1) the potential psychological impact on the jurors; (2) the effect of the presence of the cameras on the testimony of witnesses; (3) the increased burdens imposed on the trial judge by television; and (4) the mental harassment of the defendant by the presence of the cameras.[79] But, of course, none of this could be documented and the fifth justice voting to reverse, Harlan, stated in his concurring opinion that the day might come when television was so common-place as to dissipate any likelihood that it could adversely affect the judicial process and those involved with it.[80] Because of other reservations in Justice Harlan's concurring opinion, *Estes* was read in

---

77. F.R Crim. P. 53 provides: "The taking of photographs in the court room during the progress of judicial proceedings or radio broadcasting of judicial proceedings from the court room shall not be permitted by the court." Though the Rule has not been formally amended to include television (*see* F.R. Crim. P. 53 (18 U.S.C.A. Federal Rule of Criminal Procedure 53) (West Supp. 1991)), there is no doubt that it encompasses civil trials and television broadcasting as well. *See* Westmoreland v. Columbia Broadcasting System, Inc., 752 F.2d 16 (2d Cir. 1984), cert. denied *sub nom.* Cable News Network v. United States Dist. Ct., 472 U.S. 1017, 105 S.Ct. 3478, 87 L.Ed.2d 614 (1985); REVISED REPORT OF THE JUDICIAL CONFERENCE COMMITTEE OF THE OPERATION OF THE JURY SYSTEM ON THE "FREE PRESS—FAIR TRIAL" ISSUE, 87 F.R.D. 519, 535–536 (1980).

78. 381 U.S. 532, 85 S.Ct. 1628, 14 L.Ed.2d 543 (1965).

79. *Id.* at 545–550, 85 S. Ct. at 1634–1636, 14 L. Ed. 2d at 551–554.

80. *Id.* at 595, 85 S. Ct. at 1666, 14 L. Ed. 2d at 588.

Chandler v. *Florida* as *not* announcing a constitutional rule barring still photographic, radio and television coverage in all cases and under all circumstances.[81]

2. Cameras and Electronic Recording Equipment in State Courtrooms

In *Chandler*, pursuant to a resolution overwhelmingly approved by the Conference of State Chief Justices allowing the highest court of each state to promulgate standards and guidelines regulating radio, television and photographic coverage of court proceedings, the Florida Supreme Court ended the complete ban on such coverage. That court, after an experimental one-year program, promulgated a revised Canon 3A(7) of its Code of Judicial Conduct permitting, subject to the authority of the presiding judge, electronic media and still photography coverage of public judicial proceedings in the appellate and trial courts of Florida without requiring the consent of any of the parties or participants. Implementing guidelines specified the kind of equipment that might be used and the manner in which it might be used.

The defendants in *Chandler*, then Miami Beach police officers, were charged with several criminal offenses relating to the breaking and entering into a Miami Beach restaurant. The case attracted substantial media attention. Counsel for the defendants moved during pretrial proceedings to have then experimental Canon 3A(7) declared unconstitutional. The trial court denied the motion and the Florida Supreme Court declined to rule on the question on the ground it was not directly relevant to the pending criminal charges. After several other attempts by defense counsel to prevent electronic coverage of the trial, the jury was selected. During *voir dire*, defense counsel asked each prospective juror whether he or she could be fair and impartial despite the presence of a television camera in the courtroom during some, or all, of the trial. Each juror selected to hear the case answered that television coverage would not affect his or her deliberation in any way. The *voir dire* was recorded by television. A defense motion was also made and denied to sequester the jury but the court instructed the jurors not to watch or read anything about the case in the media and suggested that they avoid local news and watch only national news on television.

During the trial itself a television camera was present for one entire afternoon session, during which the State presented the testimony of its chief witness. No camera was present for any part of the case for the defense. Thereafter, television coverage resumed only to cover closing arguments. Less than three minutes of the trial were actually broadcast and no part of the defendants' case was included.

Following their conviction on all counts, the defendants moved for a new trial, claiming that the television coverage had denied them a fair

81. 449 U.S. 560, 571–573, 101 S.Ct.   (1981).
802, 808–809, 66 L.Ed.2d 740, 749–751

and impartial trial but no evidence of specific prejudice was presented in support of the motion. The motion was denied and the convictions were affirmed by the District Court of Appeal, which declined to discuss the facial validity of experimental Canon 3A(7). The appeals court reasoned that since the Florida Supreme Court had permitted television coverage of criminal trials, it had implicitly determined that such coverage was constitutional. The court also found that the canon was not unconstitutional as applied since there was no evidence to indicate that the defendants were actually prejudiced by the television coverage. On certification of the constitutional question, the Florida Supreme Court denied review holding the matter to be moot.

On appeal to the United States Supreme Court, the high court discounted *Estes* because the constitutional ruling was supported only by a plurality of the justices. Not feeling constrained by the so-called "opinion of the court" in *Estes,* Chief Justice Burger, speaking for a true majority in *Chandler,* rejected the defendant-appellants proposed *per se* rule that television coverage of criminal trials over objection violated due process. "The risk of juror prejudice in some cases does not justify an absolute ban on news coverage of trials by the printed media; so also the risk of such prejudice does not warrant an absolute constitutional ban on all broadcast coverage.... [T]he appropriate safeguard against such prejudice is the defendant's right to demonstrate that the media's coverage of his case—be it printed or broadcast—compromised the ability of the particular jury that heard the case to adjudicate fairly."[82] Such right was granted the defendants by the state according to the Court but the record did not indicate that they requested an evidentiary hearing to demonstrate adverse impact on their case from the television coverage.[83] All that was presented were generalized allegations of prejudice and the Court refused to presume prejudice.[84] In affirming the convictions the Court held that the Constitution did not prohibit states from experimenting with media coverage of trials.[85]

This ruling should not be read as necessarily implying a constitutional right of the media to bring their photographic and electronic equipment into the courtroom to televise, broadcast, record or photograph judicial proceedings.[86] At one point in *Chandler* the Court quoted from its opinion in *Nixon* v. *Warner Communications,* Inc.[87] to the effect that the sixth amendment guarantee of a public trial did not require that trials be broadcast live or on tape. The court did not address any First Amendment claim of electronic access in *Warner* but the United States Court of Appeals for the Second Circuit rejected just such a claim in *Westmoreland* v. *Columbia Broadcasting System, Inc.*[88] Unless and until

82. *Id.* at 575, 101 S. Ct. at 810, 66 L. Ed. 2d at 752.

83. *Id.* at 577, 101 S. Ct. at 811, 66 L. Ed. 2d at 753.

84. *Id.* at 577, 581–582, 101 S. Ct. at 811, 813, 66 L. Ed. 2d at 753, 755–756.

85. *Id.* at 583 101 S. Ct. at 814, 66 L. Ed. 2d at 757.

86. *See id.* at 569, 101 S. Ct. at 807, 66 L. Ed. 2d at 748.

87. 435 U.S. 589, 610, 98 S.Ct. 1306, 1318, 55 L.Ed.2d 570, 587 (1978).

88. 752 F.2d 16, 21–24 (2d Cir.1984),

the Supreme Court determines there is First Amendment protection for electronic and photographic access to the courtroom, such access will be accorded only by the supervisory authority overseeing the operation of each individual court system.[89]

Prior to *Chandler* only eight states besides Florida had adopted rules permitting electronic coverage of trials.[90] But with the decision in *Chandler* the floodgates opened and a decade later more than one half of the state jurisdictions had adopted permanent rules permitting at least limited access to judicial proceedings of cameras, microphones and recording equipment.[91] At the same time eight states permitted limited access of the equipment on an experimental basis.[92] Only three states and the District of Columbia now totally bar radio, television, film and recording coverage in accordance with original Canon 3A(7).[93] Most jurisdictions permit film and electronic coverage of trials and appeals in both criminal and civil proceedings.[94]

cert. denied *sub nom.* Cable News Network v. United States District Court, 472 U.S. 1017, 105 S.Ct. 3478, 87 L.Ed.2d 614 (1985).

89. *See* Chandler, 449 U.S. at 569–570, 101 S. Ct. at 807, 66 L. Ed. 2d at 748–749; Westmoreland, 752 F.2d at 23–24.

90. *See* Chandler, 449 U.S. at 565 n.5, 101 S. Ct. at 805 n.5, 66 L. Ed. 2d at 745 n.5; News Media and the Law 31 (Fall 1991) (chart).

91. *See* Ala. R. Crim. P. 9.4 and Canons of Jud. Ethics 3(A)(7) (7A), (7B); Alaska R. Civ. P. 46 and Admin. R. 50; 17A Ariz. Rev. Stat. Ann. Sup. Ct. R. 81, Canon 3A(7) (West. Supp. 1991); Cal. R. Ct. Misc. R. 980; Colo. Code Jud. Conduct Canon 3A(7); Conn. Code Jud. Conduct Canon 3A(7), (7A), (7B); Fla. Code Jud. Conduct Canon 3A(7); Ga. R. Unif. Super Ct. R. 22 and Ga. R. Unif. Prob. Ct. R.18; Haw. R. Sup. Ct. R.5; Ill. Sup. Ct. R. 61, Canon 1; Iowa Ct. R. 119 Canon 3A(7)3(b); Kan. Sup. Ct. R. 601 Canon 3A(7); Ky. Sup. Ct. R. 4.300, Canon 3A(7) and R.4 App; La. Code of Jud. Conduct, Canon 3A(7) (appellate proceedings only); Md. R. Ct. Admin. R. 1209; Mass. R. Sup. Jud. Ct. R. 3:09, Canon 3A(7); Mich. Sup. Ct. Admin. Order 1989–1 (Jan. 13, 1989); Minn. Code. Jud. Conduct, Canon 3A(7); Neb. Sup. Ct. R. Prac. R.17 (Supreme Court proceedings only); Nev. Sup. Ct. R. 229–247; N.H. Sup. Ct. R. 19, Super. Ct. R. 78, Dist. and Mun. Cts. R. 1.4 and Prob. Ct. R. 15; N.J. Code of Jud. Conduct, Canon 3A(8)(b); N.Y.R. Chief J. § 29.1; N.C. Super. and Dist. Cts. R.15 and Code of Jud. Conduct, Canon 3A (7); N.D. R. Local Ct. Admin. R. 21; Ohio Sup. Ct. R. 15, Common Pleas Cts. R. 11, Mun. and County Cts. R.9 and Claims Ct. Local R.18; Okl. Code of Jud. Conduct, Canon 3A(7); Or.

Unif. Trial Ct. R. 3.180 and Code of Jud. Conduct, Canon 3A(7); R.I. Sup. Ct. Art. VII, R. 1–13; S. C. App. Ct. R. 605; Tenn. Sup. Ct. R.10, Canon 3A(7); Vt. R. Civ. Proc. 79.2, R. Crim. Proc. 53, R. Prob. Proc. 79.2, R. App. Proc. 35 and Dist. Ct. Civ. R. 79.2; Wash. Code of Jud. Conduct, Canon 3A(7); W. Va. Jud. Code of Ethics 3A(7); Wis. Sup. Ct. R. 61.02–12; Wyo. R. Crim. Proc. R. 53. But in the wake of the O.J. Simpson murder trial there is a debate whether the California rule (Cal. R. Ct. Misc. R. 980) should be withdrawn. *See Point–Counter Point: Should cameras be banned from California courts?*, Cal. Bar J. 12–13 (Feb. 1996). Doubts concerning the wisdom of allowing cameras in courtrooms are expressed by numerous criminal defense attorneys. See, *e.g.*, Anton R. Valukas, et. al, *Cameras in the Courtroom: An Overview*, 13 ABA Comm. Lawyer 1, 21 (No. 3, Fall 1995).

92. *See* News Media & the Law 31 (Spring 1991) (chart listing Arkansas, Delaware, Maine, Pennsylvania, Texas, Utah and Virginia). Missouri has now joined these ranks. *See* Joseph E. Martineau & Mary B. Schultz, *Cameras in Missouri's Courtrooms: Supreme Court Administrative Rule 16*, 49 Mo. Bar J. 379 (1993).

93. *See* Carolyn S. Dyer & Nancy R. Hauserman, *Coverage of the Courts: Exceptions to Exposure*, 75 Geo. L.J. 1633, 1635, 1639 n.13 (1987); S. L. Alexander, *Cameras in the courtroom: a case study*, 74 Judicature 307, 310 (No. 6, April—May, 1991) (chart); News Media & the Law 31 (Fall 1991) (chart); Tony Mauro, *Simpson Trial Aftermath: Courts Closing Doors*, First Amendment News 1 (Mar. 1996, No. 3) The remaining holdout states are Indiana, Mississippi and South Dakota.

The major issue with the revised access rules is whether they require the consent of any or all of the parties to the proceeding.[95] Alabama's rule for instance, requires consent of all parties and leading attorneys in civil litigation and all accused persons in criminal prosecution,[96] thereby, in practice, insuring little or no electronic or film coverage. On the other hand New Jersey's rules state specifically that consent need not be obtained from any party, attorney or participant in the proceedings.[97] Of course, even where consent of participants is not required they may always object and for good cause shown the presiding judge may exercise his inherent authority to order that objecting persons not be photographed or otherwise recorded.[98]

Beyond consent, coverage may be limited somewhat by the need to obtain judicial permission to cover proceedings with photographic and electronic equipment[99] and by rules specifying detailed procedures to be followed by media personnel[100] and the equipment that may be employed.[1]

94. *See, e.g.*, Fla. Code Jud. Conduct, Canon 3A(7) ("Subject at all times to the authority of the presiding judge to (i) control the conduct of proceedings before the court, (ii) ensure decorum and prevent distractions, and (iii) ensure the fair administration of justice in the pending cause, electronic media and still photography coverage of public judicial proceedings in the appellate and trial courts of this state shall be allowed in accordance with standards of conduct and technology promulgated by the Supreme Court of Florida."); Iowa Ct. R. 119, Canon 3A(7) ("Subject at all times to the authority of the presiding judge to control the conduct of proceedings before the court to ensure decorum and prevent distractions and to ensure the fair administration of justice in the pending cause, electronic media and still photography coverage of public judicial proceedings in the trial and appellate courts of this state shall be allowed in accordance with rules of procedure promulgated by the Supreme Court of Iowa."); Kan. Sup, Ct. R. 1001 ("The news media and educational television stations may photograph and record public proceedings before the Appellate District and Municipal Courts of this state in accordance with the following applicable conditions and procedures.... "); *see also* News Media & the Law 31 (Spring 1991) (chart).

95. *See* Ala. R. Crim. P. 9.4 and Canons of Jud. Ethics 3A(7)(b)-(c) (consent of all accused in criminal cases and all litigants and leading attorneys); Alaska Admin. R. 50 (c) (consent of all parties in family law proceedings); Iowa Code Jud. Conduct, Canon 3B(2)(d) (consent of all parties to juvenile, marital dissolution, adoption, child

custody and trade secret proceedings); Md. R. Ct. Admin. R. 1209(d)(1) (consent of all parties to trial court proceedings except governmental entities and persons sued or suing in their official governmental capacity); Minn. Code Jud. Conduct Canon 3A(7) (consent of all parties to trial proceedings); Okla. Code of Jud. Conduct Canon 3A(7)(c) (witnesses, jurors and parties who do not consent to coverage may not be photographed nor their particular participation in trial proceedings be otherwise broadcast or televised); Or. Unif. Trial Ct. R. 3.180(1)(e) (witnesses, except party witnesses in civil cases, who do not consent may not be subject to television coverage); Tenn. Sup. Ct. R.10, Canon 3A(7)(a)(ii) (written consent of accused in criminal proceedings); Texas R. Civ. P. 18c and R. App. P. 21 (consent of all parties and witnesses); Wash. Code of Jud. Conduct Canon 3A(7)(c) (witnesses, jurors or parties who object may not be photographed nor may their particular participation in the trial proceedings be broadcast or televised).

96. Ala. R. Crim. P. 9.4 and Canon of Jud. Ethics 3a(7)(b)-(c).

97. N.J. R. Sup. Ct. Media Coverage Guideline 11.

98. *See, e.g.*, Conn. Code Jud. Conduct Canon 3(7A)(8); Kan. Sup. Ct. R. 100 (6); Wis. Sup. Ct.R. 61.11(1).

99. *See, e.g.*, Ariz. Sup. Ct. R. 81, Canon 3A(7)(f); Cal. R. Ct. Misc. R. 980(b)(1); Colo. Code Jud. Conduct, Canon 3A(8)(f).

100. *See, e.g.*, Colo. Code Jud. Conduct, Canon 3A(8)(e); Neb. Sup. Ct.R. 17E; N.J. R. Sup. Ct. Media Coverage Guideline 3.

3.   Cameras, Microphones and Electronic Recording Equipment in Federal Courtrooms

Newsmedia cameras, microphones and electronic recording equipment had been barred from federal courtrooms beginning in 1946.[2] For nearly 45 years thereafter every effort by the news media to breach the federal courts' stone wall with their photographic and electronic equipment was rebuffed.[3] Then in 1990 the Judicial Conference of the United States, on the recommendation of its Ad Hoc Committee on cameras in the Courtroom, voted to permit an experimental program of photographic and electronic coverage of certain civil proceedings in a maximum of two circuit courts of appeal and six district courts beginning July 1, 1991.[4]

1. *See e.g.,* Fla Code of Jud. Conduct; Canon 3A(7), Schedule A; Ill. Supp. Ct. R. 61; Canon 1, Schedule A; N.Y. R. Chief Admin. § 131.13. Some of these rules on equipment access to the courtroom are quite specific. For instance § 131.13 of the Rules of the Chief Administrator of the New York Courts provides:

"The following equipment shall be deemed acceptable for use in audio-visual coverage of trial court proceedings pursuant to **Part 131** of the Rules of the Chief Administrator of the Courts:

(a) Video Cameras.

Sony: BVP–3, BVP–3A, BVP–3U, BVP–5, BVP–30, BVP–33AM, BVP–50J, BVP–110, BVP–150, BVP–250, BVP–300, BVU–300, BVV–1, BVV–5, DXC–3000, M–3

IKegami: HL–79, HL–79D, HL–79E, HL–83, HL–95, ITC–170, SP–3A, 75–D, 79–E, 95, 730, 730a, 730ap

JVC: KY–1900, KY–2000, KY–2700, BY–110

RCA:TK–76

Thompson: 501, 601

NEC: SP–3A

Sharp: XC–800

Panasonic: X–100 (the recam system in a camera/recorder combination)

Ampex: Betacam

(b) Still Cameras.

Leica: M

Nikon: FE, F–3, Fm–2, 2000

Canon: F–1, T–90

(c) Any other audio or video equipment may be used with the permission of the presiding trial judge."

2. *See* F.R. Crim. P. 53; F.R. App. P. 54; Diane Kiesel, *Will There Ever Be Cameras in the Federal Courtrooms?*, 1 ABA Communications Lawyer 1 (No. 4, Fall 1983).

3. *See, e.g.,* Carolyn S. Dyer & Nancy R. Hauserman *Electronic Coverage of the Courts: Exceptions to Exposure*, 75 Geo. L.J. 1633, 1640n.15 (1987): *see also* Diane Kiesel, 1 ABA Communications Lawyer 1 (No. 4 Fall 1983). Warren Burger when he was Chief Justice of the United States is reported to have said that there would be cameras in the Supreme Court when they carried him out of the building on a catafalque. He could make his personal objections to cameras in *all* federal courtrooms into policy as the *ex officio* chairman of the Judicial Conference of the United States. Present Chief Justice William Rehnquist is proving to be less doctrinaire on this issue. *See* S. L. Alexander, *Cameras in the courtroom: a case study*, 74 Judicature 307 (Apr.-May 1, 1991), Linda Greenhouse, *Federal Courts Moving to Permit Trial Coverage by Radio and TV*, N.Y. Times, Sept. 13, 1990, p. A18, Col. 5.

4. *See* REPORT OF THE JUDICIAL CONFERENCE AD HOC COMMITTEE ON CAMERAS IN THE COURTROOM, Agenda E–22 p. 8 (Sept. 1990); 22 The Third Branch 1 (Nov. 10, Oct. 1990) (official newsletter of the Federal Courts published by the Administrative Office of United States Courts); *see also* S. L. Alexander, *Cameras in the courtroom: a case study*, 74 Judicature at 313; Linda Greenhouse, *Federal Courts Moving to Permit Trial Coverage by Radio and TV*, N.Y. Times, Sept. 13, 1990, p. A8, Col. 5. The breaching of the federal judicial stone wall actually began in 1990 when the United States Court of Military Appeals, which is not administered by the Judicial Conference, allowed live television camera coverage of selected oral arguments. *See* Alexander at 307. The United States Court of Appeals apparently jumped

Participation of the federal courts in the approved pilot program was voluntary[5] and the volunteer courts selected by the Ad Hoc Committee were the Second and Ninth Circuits and the District Courts for the Southern District of Indiana, District of Massachusetts, Eastern District of Michigan, Southern District of New York, Eastern District of Pennsylvania and Western District of Washington.[6] These courts were governed in the experimental coverage by detailed guidelines fashioned by the Ad Hoc Committee which were obviously influenced by the experience of the state courts with photographic and electronic coverage.[7] During the

the gun on the federal court experiment starting date when it permitted live coverage by C–SPAN of one of its appellate arguments held in Boise, Idaho on June 28, 1991. *See* 77 ABA J. 26, 27 (Sept. 1991) ("News" column); Wash. Post, June 29, 1991, p. A4 ("Around the Nation" column).

5. *See* REPORT OF THE JUDICIAL CONFERENCE AD HOC COMMITTEE ON CAMERAS IN THE COURTROOM, Agenda E–22, p. 6 (Sept. 1990); 22 The Third Branch, 1, 2 (No. 10, Oct. 1990).

6. FINAL REPORT OF THE JUDICIAL CONFERENCE AD HOC COMMITTEE ON CAMERAS IN THE COURTROOM, Agenda p.2 (Mar. 1991); *see* Alexander at 313; 77 ABA J. at 27.

7. GUIDELINES FOR THE PILOT PROGRAM ON PHOTOGRAPHING, RECORDING, AND BROADCASTING IN THE COURTROOM, REPORT OF THE JUDICIAL CONFERENCE AD HOC COMMITTEE ON CAMERAS IN THE COURTROOM, Agenda E–22 Appendix C (Sept. 1990). These guidelines provide:

"1. General Provisions.

(a) Media coverage of federal court proceedings under the pilot program on cameras in the courtroom is permissible only in accordance with these guidelines.

(b) Reasonable advance notice is required from the media of a request to be present to broadcast, televise, record electronically, or take photographs at a particular session. In the absence of such notice, the presiding judicial officer may refuse to permit media coverage.

(c) A presiding judicial officer may refuse, limit, or terminate media coverage of an entire case, portions thereof, or testimony of particular witnesses, in the interests of justice to protect the rights of the parties, witnesses, and the dignity of the court; to assure the orderly conduct of the proceedings; or for any other reason considered necessary or appropriate by the presiding judicial officer.

(d) No direct public expense is to be incurred for equipment, wiring, or personnel needed to provide media coverage.

(e) Nothing in these guidelines shall prevent a court from placing additional restrictions, or prohibiting altogether,

photographing, recording, or broadcasting in designated areas of the courthouse.

(f) These guidelines take effect July 1, 1991, and expire June 30, 1994.

2. Limitations

(a) Coverage of criminal proceedings, both at the trial and appellate levels, is prohibited.

(b) There shall be no audio pickup or broadcast of conferences which occur in a court facility between attorneys and their clients, between co-counsel of a client, or between counsel and the presiding judicial officer, whether held in the courtroom or in chambers.

(c) No coverage of the jury, or of any juror or alternate juror, while in the jury box, in the courtroom, in the jury deliberation room, or during recess, or while going to or from the deliberation room at any time, shall be permitted. Coverage of the prospective jury during voir dire is also prohibited.

3. Equipment and Personnel.

(a) Not more than one television camera, operated by not more than one camera person, shall be permitted in any trial court proceeding. Not more than two television cameras, operated by not more than one camera person each, shall be permitted in any appellate court proceeding.

(b) Not more than one still photographer, utilizing not more than one camera and related equipment, shall be permitted in any proceeding in a trial or appellate court.

(c) If two or more media representative apply to cover a proceeding, no such coverage may begin until all such representatives have agreed upon a pooling arrangement for their respective news media. Such pooling arrangements shall include the designation of pool operators, procedures for cost sharing, access to and dissemination of material, and selec-

experimental period three methods of data collection were utilized in determining permanent rules regarding the accessibility to the federal courts of photographic and electronic broadcasting and recording equipment: (1) case studies of the courts involved; (2) information collected by survey; and (3) information as to what coverage actually reaches the public.[8] Recommendations based on the experience gained from this pilot program were prepared by the Federal Judicial Center in November 1993 but not then publicly disclosed.[9]

These recommendations, which would have extended to all federal courts the pilot program, were rejected by the Judicial Conference of the

tion of a pool representative if appropriate. The presiding judicial officer may not be called upon to mediate or resolve any dispute as to such arrangements.

(d) Equipment or clothing shall not bear the insignia or marking of a media agency. Camera operators shall wear appropriate business attire.

4. Sound and Light Criteria

(a) Equipment shall not produce distracting sound or light. Signal lights or devices to show when equipment is operating shall not be visible. Motorized drives, moving lights, flash attachments, or sudden light changes shall not be used.

(b) Except as otherwise approved by the presiding judicial officer, existing courtroom sound and light systems shall be used without modification. Audio pickup for all media purposes shall be accomplished from existing audio systems present in the court facility, or from a television camera's built-in microphone. If no technically suitable audio system exist in the court facility, microphones and related wiring essential for media purposes shall be unobtrusive and shall be located in places designated in advance of any proceeding by the presiding judicial officer.

5. Location of Equipment and Personnel.

(a) The presiding judicial officer shall designate the location in the courtroom for the camera equipment and operators.

(b) During the proceedings, operating personnel shall not move about nor shall there be placement, movement, or removal of equipment, or the changing of film, film magazines, or lenses. All such activities shall take place each day before the proceeding begins, after it ends, or during a recess.

6. Compliance.

Any media representative who fails to comply with these guidelines shall be subject to appropriate sanction, as determined by the presiding judicial officer.

7. Review.

It is not intended that a grant or denial of media coverage be subject to appellate review insofar as it pertains to and arises under these guidelines, except as otherwise provided by law."

8. FINAL REPORT OF THE JUDICIAL CONFERENCE AD HOC COMMITTEE ON CAMERAS IN THE COURTROOM, p.3 (Mar. 1991). To facilitate cooperation between the Federal Judicial Center, which monitored and evaluated the pilot program, and the selected pilot courts, these courts were required, with some modifications to:

"1. Provide detailed records of all requests for media coverage as provided in Guideline 1(b). To assure receipt of uniform information, the FJC will prepare a package of evaluation materials for each court that will include, among other things, forms the media should use in requesting permission to broadcast, record, or photograph.

2. Provide information relevant to refusing, limiting, or terminating media coverage, as provided by Guideline 1(c).

3. Provide specific information identifying participants in a pool, along with names, addresses, and phone numbers of contacts for each organization.

4. Require media organizations, as a condition of the court's decision to grant a broadcasting, recording, or photographing request, to provide the actual footage, photographs, etc., of court proceedings that are aired or published.

5. Assign an individual from the court to serve as liaison to the FJC in connection with the study." *Id.*

9. REPORT OF THE FEDERAL JUDICIAL CENTER TO THE COMMITTEE ON COURT ADMINISTRATION AND CASE MANAGEMENT OF THE JUDICIAL CONFERENCE OF THE UNITED STATES: ELECTRONIC MEDIA COVERAGE OF FEDERAL CIVIL PROCEEDINGS (Nov. 1993).

United States in a secret vote on September 20, 1994.[10] No explanation was given but a Conference spokesperson said that "the tenor of concern was potential impact on jurors and witnesses. . . ."[11] According to the spokesperson the vote ratio was about "2 to 1" against.[12]

7.18 *Access to Government News and Information Through Open Meetings Legislation

7.19 *Statutory Access to Federal Governmental Information, Records and Documents—The Freedom of Information Act

7.20 *Electronic Freedom of Information Act Amendments of 1996

7.21 The Constitutional Right to Disseminate News and Information Once Media Access Has Been Obtained

A. *Historical Background*

1. *Reaction to England's Odious Tradition of Censorship*

Once access to news and information has been obtained by the media, the only legal recourse available to those who would conceal news and information from the public is to persuade a court of competent jurisdiction to issue an injunction preventing publication. But if the First Amendment Press Clause means anything, it means that government, including the courts, may not, except in the most extreme circumstances, restrain expression and that newspersons have a very broad right to disseminate whatever news and information they gather.[1] The founding fathers were acutely aware of England's odious licensing and censorship laws imposed both in the mother country and the colonies and were

---

10. REPORT OF THE PROCEEDINGS OF THE JUDICIAL CONFERENCE OF THE UNITED STATES 46–47, 67 (Sept. 20, 1994).

11. Joan Biskupic, *Vote on Cameras Reveals Judges' Deep Concern; Mistrust of Media Is Called a Factor in Decision Against Televising Federal Court Hearings,* Wash. Post, Sept. 23, 1994, p. A3, cols. 3–6.

12. Id. But apparently the Judicial Conference can't quite make up its mind because on March 14, 1995, it voted 17 to 9 to allow a committee of judges this time to formulate a pilot program to allow cameras to cover civil cases in the federal courts. *See* Saundra Torrey, *Judges Reject Record–Secrecy Rule; Federal Meeting Opens Door to New Courtroom Camera Experiment,* Wash. Post, Mar. 15, 1995; p. A8, cols. 4–6. And on March 12, 1996 it voted to approve a resolution stating that "Each court of ap-

peals may decide for itself whether to permit the taking of photographs and radio and television coverage of appellate arguments" in some cases. *See* News Release of the Administrative Office of the U.S. Courts (Mar. 12, 1996); Joan Biskupic, *A New Eye on Federal Courts,* Wash. Post, March 13, 1996, p. A12. In addition, the Judicial Conference urged each circuit court of appeals judicial council to adopt an order reflecting the Conference's September 1994 decision not to permit the taking of photographs or the broadcasting of United States District Court proceedings. *Id.*

* Published in Modern Communication Law, Practitioners Edition, Vol. 2, only.

1. *See* Near v. Minnesota ex rel. Olson, 283 U.S. 697, 51 S.Ct. 625, 75 L.Ed. 1357 (1931).

determined not to permit such suppression of expression in the new independent state they were creating.[2]

2. *Near v. Minnesota and Judicial Censorship*

When judicially imposed restraint on the dissemination of news and information is attempted, such effort very nearly always fails. The first noteworthy attempt at prior restrain of the press to reach the courts was in *Near* v. *Minnesota ex rel. Olson*.[3] There, a Minnesota statute provided for the abatement as a public nuisance of "malicious, scandalous, and defamatory publications." The statute further provided that all persons guilty of such a nuisance could be permanently enjoined from further publication of malicious, scandalous and defamatory matter. The Hennepin County (Minneapolis) attorney, who was himself a target of some of the defendant's articles, brought an action under the statute to enjoin the defendant from publishing his newspaper, The Saturday Press. The state alleged that the paper had run articles charging in substance that a Jewish Gangster was in control of gambling, bootlegging and racketeering in Minneapolis and that law enforcement officers including the mayor, the chief of police and the county attorney were not performing their duties to end this lawlessness.

Angered by the charges made against him and other officials and by expressions of concern from the Jewish community that the paper was fanning the flames of antisemitism, the county attorney sought and obtained a temporary injunction preventing further circulation of issues of the paper already published and barring any future publication of the paper "containing malicious, scandalous and defamatory matter of the kind alleged in plaintiff's complaint herein or otherwise."[4]

Jay Near, the publisher, through his attorneys, demurred to the complaint, *inter alia*, on the then novel ground that such an injunction violated the fourteenth amendment which incorporated the protections of the First Amendment. The district court overruled the demurrer but certified the question of the statute's constitutionality to the Minnesota Supreme Court which upheld the validity of the statute. On remand of the case, the trial court made the temporary injunction permanent. Thereafter, Jay Near could not produce, edit, publish, circulate, possess, sell or give away The Saturday Press or any other publication containing similar material. Near appealed to the Minnesota Supreme Court which pointed to its earlier decision in the case and upheld the injunction.

On appeal, the United Supreme Court, by a vote of 5 to 4, reversed. Speaking for the majority, Chief Justice Hughes held that the object and effect of the statute was to suppress further publication of the newspaper. This he equated to prior restraint of the press which is, except for

---

2. *See* Leonard W. Levy, *On the Origins of the Free Press Clause*, 32 UCLA L. Rev. 177, 202–206, 212–214 (1977); David A. Anderson, *The Origins of the Press Clause*, 30 UCLA L. Rev. 455, 462–486 (1983). *See also Patterson v. Colorado*, 205 U.S. 454, 462, 27 S.Ct. 556, 558, 51 L.Ed. 879, 881 (1907).

3. 283 U.S. 697, 51 S.Ct. 625, 75 L.Ed. 1357 (1931).

4. *Id.* at 704–705, 51 S. Ct. at 627, 75 L. Ed. at 1361.

exceptional cases, not permitted by the First Amendment.[5] Moreover, if the person enjoined wished to publish anything in the future he would have to submit the material to the appropriate judicial officer for clearance if he wished to avoid being held in contempt of court for violating the injunction. To the court this constituted censorship generally prohibited by the First Amendment.[6]

If we cut through mere details of procedure, the operation and effect of the statute in substance is that public authorities may bring the owner or publisher of a newspaper or periodical before a judge upon a charge of conducting a business of publishing scandalous and defamatory matter—in particular that the matter consists of charges against public officers of official dereliction—and unless the owner or publisher is able and disposed to bring competent evidence to satisfy the judge that the charges are true and are published with good motives and for justifiable ends, his newspaper or periodical is suppressed and further publication is made punishable as a contempt. This is of the essence of censorship.

The question is whether a statute authorizing such proceedings in restraint of publication is consistent with the conception of the liberty of the press as historically conceived and guaranteed. In determining the extent of the constitutional protection, it has been generally, if not universally, considered that it is the chief purpose of the guaranty to prevent previous restraints upon publication. The struggle in England, directed against the legislative power of the licenser, resulted in renunciation of the censorship of the press. The liberty deemed to be established was thus described by Blackstone: "The liberty of the press is indeed essential to the nature of a free state; but this consists in laying no *previous* restraints upon publications, and not in freedom from censure for criminal matter when published"[7] (footnote omitted).

But the Chief Justice, speaking for the majority, did not say that the constitutional prohibition against prior restraint was absolute. By way of dictum he stated that the limitation of the prohibition has been recognized "only in exceptional cases."[8]

"When a nation is at war many things that might be said in time of peace are such a hindrance to its effort that their utterance will not be endured so long as men fight and that no Court could regard them as protected by any constitutional right." *Schenck v. United States*, 249 U.S. 47, 52, 39 S.Ct. 247, 249, 63 L.Ed. 470. No one would question but that a government might prevent actual obstruction to its recruiting service or the publication of the sailing dates of transports or the number and location of troops. On similar grounds, the primary requirements of decency may be enforced

---

5. *Id.* at 711–712, 51 S. Ct. at 629, 75 L. Ed. at 1365.

6. *Id.* at 712–713, 51 S. Ct. at 629–630, 75 L. Ed. at 1365–1366.

7. *Id.* at 713, 51 S. Ct. at 630, 75 L. Ed. at 1366.

8. *Id.* at 716, 51 S. Ct. at 631, 75 L. Ed. at 1367.

against obscene publications. The security of the community life may be protected against incitements to acts of violence and the overthrow by force of orderly government. The constitutional guaranty of free speech does not "protect a man from an injunction against uttering words that may have all the effect of force. *Gompers v. Bucks Stove & Range Co.,* 221 U.S. 418, 439, 31 S.Ct. 492, 55 L.Ed. 797, 34 L.R.A. (N.S.) 874." *Schenck v. United States,* supra. These limitations are not applicable here. Nor are we now concerned with questions as to the extent of authority to prevent publications in order to protect private rights according to the principles governing the exercise of the jurisdiction of the courts of equity.

The exceptional nature of its limitations places in a strong light the general conception that liberty of the press, historically considered and taken up by the Federal Constitution, has meant, principally although not exclusively, immunity from previous restraints or censorship"[9] (footnotes omitted).

The decision in *Near* is a landmark one for many reasons. It was the Supreme Court's first definitive statement concerning the constitutionality of prior restraint on expression and more particularly on expression by the press. More than this, it made clear that what was important was not the form governmental action took, but its *effect* on speech and press. And because it indicated that the constitutional ban on prior restraints was not absolute and did permit narrow exceptions, it opened up the question of the precise limits of First Amendment protection.

Finally, borrowing from Blackstone, it made the point very clearly that while expression was generally protected from prior restraint, it might subsequently be punished if it were determined that the expression was unlawful. This dichotomy between prior restraint and subsequent punishment continues to the present day, particularly in the context of national security, and was relied upon or alluded to by five justices in the next important press restraint case to come before the Supreme Court.

B. *Modern Rejection of Judicial Restraint of Expression*

1. *New York Times Co. v. United States*

In *New York Times Co. v. United States*[10] (the "Pentagon Papers Case") the federal government sought to enjoin the New York Times and the Washington Post from publishing the contents of a classified study of American involvement in southeast Asia entitled "History of U.S. Decision–Making Process on Viet Nam Policy." The study had been surreptitiously copied by a former government official and then distributed to the newspapers sought to be enjoined and other publications as well. When the two papers began publishing excerpts, the Department of Justice demanded return of the copies of the classified study and when

9. *Id.,* 51 S. Ct. at 631, 75 L. Ed. at 1367–1368.

10. 403 U.S. 713, 91 S.Ct. 2140, 29 L.Ed.2d 822 (1971).

this demand was rejected, the Department sought injunctions against the defendants. Ultimately, the United States Court of Appeals for the Second Circuit reversed the district court's order refusing to enter an injunction against the Times and issued its own stay while the United States Court of Appeals for the District of Columbia upheld the district court's similar refusal to enter an injunction against the Post, which then continued to publish excerpts from the papers while the Times was being restrained.

The Supreme Court granted certiorari in the two cases and, within one week of the appeals courts' decisions, the justices heard argument, decided the cases, and issued ten opinions. The heart of the short per curiam opinion (concurred in by six justices) is that:

> "Any system of prior restraints of expression comes to this Court bearing a heavy presumption against its constitutional validity." *Bantam Books, Inc. v. Sullivan*, 372 U.S. 58, 70 83 S.Ct. 631, 639, 9 L.Ed.2d 584 (1963); see also *Near v. Minnesota ex rel. Olson*, 283 U.S. 697, 51 S.Ct. 625, 75 L.Ed. 1357 (1931). The Government "thus carries a heavy burden of showing justification for the imposition of such a restraint." *Organization for a Better Austin v. Keefe*, 402 U.S. 415, 419, 91 S.Ct. 1575, 1578, 29 L.Ed.2d 1 (1971). The District Court for the Southern District of New York in the *New York Times* case, [328 F.Supp. 324], and the District Court for the District of Columbia and the Court of Appeals for the District of Columbia Circuit, 446 F.2d 1327, in the *Washington Post* case held that the Government had not met that burden. "We agree."[11]

The per curiam opinion is hardly a ringing endorsement of a free press or a stirring denunciation of prior restraints and censorship. Such endorsements were left to less than a majority of the individual justices, particularly the First Amendment absolutists Black and Douglas who continued to argue that the language of the First Amendment that "Congress shall make no law ... abridging the freedom of speech, or of the press" means what it says leaving "no room for governmental restraint of the press."[12]

Justice Brennan took a less doctrinaire approach allowing for prior restraint to protect national security but only when the government can establish that publication "must inevitably, directly, and immediately cause the occurrence of an event kindred to imperiling the safety of a transport already at sea.... "[13] Justice Brennan did not find such evidence in the case.

Similarly, Justice Stewart would allow for prior restraint in cases where the President, in whom the Constitution reposes primary responsibility for international relations and national defense, establishes that prior restraint is necessary to prevent disclosure that will "surely result

---

11. *Id.* at 714, 91 S. Ct. at 2144, 29 L. Ed. 2d at 824.

12. *Id.* at 720, 91 S. Ct. at 2144, 29 L. Ed. 2d at 828.

13. *Id.* at 726–727, 91 S. Ct. at 2148, 29 L. Ed. 2d at 832.

in direct, immediate, and irreparable damage to our Nation or its people."[14] For Justice Stewart publication of the "Pentagon Papers" did not pose such danger.

Justice White, with whom Justice Stewart concurred, apparently believed that Congress could constitutionally have authorized prior restraint in the case but did not, and thus the government could not obtain an injunction because it did not meet the very heavy burden set out in the Court's per curiam opinion.[15] Justice White added, however, that legislation did exist authorizing prosecution of the defendant newspaper corporations here.[16]

Justice Marshall noted the rejection by Congress of many proposed statutes authorizing prior restraint in the name of national security and suggested that the government was asking the Court to enact such legislation which, of course, the Court has no power to do.[17] He, too, alluded to the existence of legislation seemingly authorizing criminal prosecutions for engaging in activity similar to that involved in the case.[18]

The consistent themes of the dissenters Chief Justice Burger and Associate Justices Harlan and Blackmun were that the case was being decided in unseemly haste[19] and that criminal prosecution was possible.[20]

The good news for the press in the *Pentagon Papers Case* is that a clear majority of the justices indicated serious concern about prior restraint of the news media even in the context of a claimed continuing breach of national security;[21] the chilling news is that five of the justices

14. *Id.* at 730, 91 S. Ct. at 2149, 29 L. Ed. 2d at 834.

15. *Id.* at 730–733, 91 S. Ct. at 2150–2151, 29 L. Ed. 2d at 833–836.

16. *Id.* at 733–740, 91 S. Ct. at 2151–2155, 29 L. Ed. 2d at 835–840.

17. *Id.* at 740–743, 91 S. Ct. at 2155–2156, 92 L. Ed. 2d. at 839–842.

18. *Id.* at 745, 91 S. Ct. at 2157, 92 L. Ed. 2d at 842.

19. *Id.* at 748–752, 752–755, 759–763, 91 S. Ct. at 2158–2161, 2161–2164, 2164–2165, 92 L. Ed. 2d at 844–846, 846–848, 850–852.

20. *Id.* at 752, 755, 759, 91 S. Ct. at 2160, 2162, 2164, 92 L. Ed. 2d at 846, 848, 850.

21. The courts, following the *Pentagon Papers* case, have occasionally been swayed by the federal government's claim that censorship and prior restraint had to be imposed on writers and publishers in order to safeguard national security. See *Snepp v. United States*, 444 U.S. 507, 100 S.Ct. 763, 62 L.Ed.2d 704 (1980); McGehee v. Casey, 718 F.2d 1137, 231 U.S. App. D.C. 99 (1983); Alfred A. Knopf, Inc. v. Colby, 509

F.2d 1362, 29 A.L.R. Fed. 593 (4th Cir. 1975), cert. denied 421 U.S. 908, 95 S.Ct. 1555, 43 L.Ed.2d 772, (1975), United States v. Marchetti, 466 F.2d 1309 (4th Cir.), cert. denied 409 U.S. 1063, 93 S.Ct. 553, 34 L.Ed.2d 516 (1972); United States v. Progressive, Inc., 467 F.Supp. 990 (W.D.Wis. 1979).

Snepp and *Marchetti* involved injunctions obtained by the government preventing former employees of the Central Intelligence Agency (CIA) from disclosing information about their service without first submitting their material to the CIA for prepublication review. Such prepublication review was required by secrecy agreements entered into by them when they joined the CIA. *Alfred A. Knopf, Inc.* involved the same former CIA agent and book as in *Marchetti*. Here the former agent, with his co-author and publisher, sued the CIA to prevent the deletions it had demanded following prepublication review from taking effect. The United States District Court permitted publication of all but 26 of the 168 passages the CIA demanded be deleted. The Fourth Circuit ruled that deletions were to be upheld on remand if the government could prove that they disclosed classified information

also referred to the existence of legislation that might be utilized by the government to mount criminal prosecutions against the news media in such situations.

Shortly after the *Pentagon Papers* case the Court again spoke out against prior restraints, this time in the context of a trial court attempting to insure a fair criminal proceeding. In *Nebraska Press Association* v. *Stuart*[22] the Court unanimously reversed restrictive orders of Nebraska courts barring newspersons from (1) reporting testimony and evidence presented in an open preliminary hearing concerning the ghastly multiple murders of a family of six in a small Nebraska town; (2) reporting the existence and nature of any confessions or admissions made by the accused to law enforcement officers or others; and (3) reporting any other facts "strongly implicative" of the accused.

In striking down this general judicial order restricting publication, the Court took the opportunity to make clear that its distaste for prior restraints on the press first expressed in *Near* v. *Minnesota ex rel. Olson* had not abated. After reviewing *Near* and the *Pentagon Papers* case, among others, Chief Justice Warren E. Burger wrote that "[t]he thread running through all these cases is that prior restraints on speech and publication are the most serious and the least tolerable infringement on First Amendment rights.... A prior restraint ... has an immediate and irreversible sanction. If it can be said that a threat of criminal or civil sanctions after publication 'chills' speech, prior restraint 'freezes' it at least for the time. The damage can be particularly great when the prior restraint falls upon the communication of news and commentary on current events."[23]

and such information had been obtained during CIA service. Ultimately the CIA agreed to permit all but one of the deleted passages to be published.

The contract rationale supporting prior restraint and censorship in these cases can be gleaned from the words of the Fourth Circuit in the *Knopf* case:

[2] We decline to modify our previous holding that the First Amendment is nor bar against an injunction forbidding the disclosure of classifiable information within the guidelines of the Executive Orders when (1) the classified information was acquired, during the course of his employment, by an employee of a United States agency or department in which such information is handled and (2) its disclosure would violate a solemn agreement made by the employee at the commencement of his employment. With respect to such information, by his execution of the secrecy agreement and his entry into the confidential employment relationship, he effectively relinquished his First Amendment rights. 509 F.2d at 1370.

See also Snepp, 444 U.S. at 509 n.3, 100 S. Ct. at 765 n.3, 62 L.Ed. 2d at 708 n.3.

The only case in which an injunction was issued to prevent a publication assertedly harmful to national security that did not have a contract rationale is the *Progressive* case. There the Progressive magazine was about to publish an article by free-lance writer Howard Morland entitled "The H-Bomb Secret: How We Got It, Why We're Telling It." The United States District Court issued a preliminary injunction against publication after concluding that some of the information would probably violate the Atomic Energy Act of 1954. The *Progressive's* appeal of the injunctive order was aborted following oral argument and before decision when a small Wisconsin alternative newspaper published a letter written by a California computer programmer containing essentially the same information as The Progressive's article. The court of appeals dissolved the injunction and dismissed the case.

22. 427 U.S. 539, 96 S.Ct. 2791, 49 L.Ed.2d 683(1976).

23. *Id.* at 559, 96 S. Ct. at 2803, 49 L. Ed. 2d at 697–698.

2. Other Significant Rejections of Judicial Censorship

Given the Supreme Court's distaste for prior restraints, it is very rare for courts to issue injunctions preventing publication. This does not seem to stop those who would prevent disclosure of news and information to the public from seeking them. But such attempts very nearly always fail. Recent appeals cases are typical in rejecting requests to restrain the news media.

In *CBS, Inc.* v. *Davis*,[24] as part of a continuing investigation into unsanitary practices in the meat packing industry CBS obtained videotape footage of conditions in a Federal Beef Processors, Inc. (Federal), factory in South Dakota from a federal employee stationed on the premises. Before the network could air the tape on its investigative news program "48 Hours," Federal went into the South Dakota Circuit Court and, in what can only be described as "home town decisions" obtained first a temporary restraining order and then a preliminary injunction preventing CBS from "disseminating, disclosing, broadcasting, or otherwise revealing" any images of Federal's plant interior. The South Dakota trial court, displaying considerable ignorance regarding the large body of law on the subject of prior restraint of the news media, concluded that because the videotape was obtained by CBS surreptitiously on Federal's premises, conventional First Amendment doctrine was inapplicable and any injury to CBS resulting from injunctive delay was outweighed by the potential economic harm to Federal.

On February 8, 1994, the South Dakota Supreme Court denied CBS' application for a stay of the injunction and ordered the circuit judge to either rescind the injunction or show cause on March 21 why a preemptory writ of mandamus directing dissolution of the injunction should not be issued. But the "48 Hours" program on which the videotape was to be exhibited was scheduled for the evening of February 9, 1994 and thus the South Dakota Supreme Court's order, in effect, perpetuated the prior restraint imposed by the trial court.

As soon as the state high court's order was handed down, CBS filed an emergency petition with Associate Justice Harry A. Blackmun, the circuit justice for the Eighth Federal Circuit which encompasses South Dakota. Recognizing that a single Supreme Court Justice may only stay a lower court's order under extraordinary circumstances, Justice Blackmun found such circumstances to exist in the case. Further recognizing that the prohibition against prior restraints is not absolute, he emphasized that "the gagging of publication has been considered acceptable only in 'exceptional cases.'"[25] Exceptional cases are presented "only where the evil that would result from the reportage is both great and certain and cannot be mitigated by less intrusive measures."[26]

---

24. 510 U.S. 1315, 114 S.Ct. 912, 127 L.Ed.2d 358 (1994).

25. *Id.* at 1317, 114 S. Ct. at 914, 127 L. Ed. 2d at 361 (citing Near v. Minnesota ex rel. Olson, 283 U.S. 697, 716, 51 S.Ct. 625, 631, 75 L.Ed. 1357, 1367 (1931)).

26. *Id.* (citing Nebraska Press Association v. Stuart, 427 U.S. 539, 562 96 S.Ct. 2791, 2804, 49 L.Ed.2d 683, 699 (1976)).

Justice Blackmun concluded that Federal had not met this high standard, that indefinite delay of the broadcast would cause irreparable harm to CBS which is "intolerable under the First Amendment," that if the network has breached South Dakota law the First Amendment requires Federal to seek remedy for its alleged harms through a damages proceeding "rather than through suppression of protected speech" and that a stay of the state trial court's injunction was appropriate under the federal All Writs Act.[27] The stay was issued on February 9, 1994 and CBS broadcast the videotape that same evening.

Perhaps the most significant recent lower federal appeals court rejection of judicial restraint of expression can be found in *Procter & Gamble Co.* v. *Bankers Trust Co.*[28] a decision of the United States Court of Appeals for the Sixth Circuit. There, Procter & Gamble sued Bankers Trust in United States District Court to recover over $100 million allegedly lost in derivatives purchases resulting from alleged fraud by the seller Bankers Trust. The parties stipulated to a broad protective order allowing them to conduct discovery in secret and sealing documents and exhibits filed during the discovery process. The United States district judge agreed to this unusual procedure but died during discovery and was succeeded by a senior federal judge who acquiesced to the secret proceedings.

Apparently the P & G lawyers didn't communicate their desire for secrecy to others in the company because a P & G employee in the company's public relations department made an off-the-record phone call to an editor at Business Week magazine suggesting that some documents about to be filed in the case would be of interest to Business Week's readers. One of the editor's associates had an acquaintance who was a partner at the New York law firm representing Bankers Trust in the litigation. The partner, upon request, obligingly provided Business Week with copies of the documents. Apparently, none of the people involved were aware that the documents had been filed under seal. Thus, while the lawyers were trying to keep a lid of secrecy on the proceedings, their co-workers and partners were acting to make the documents public through publication in a widely circulated and respected business magazine.

When counsel discovered the leaks from their own organizations, they notified the trial judge, who, without notice to Business Week or its parent corporation McGraw–Hill Companies and without providing the concerned parties an opportunity to be heard, transmitted by facsimile on September 13, 1995, an order to McGraw–Hill enjoining the company

---

27. *Id.* at 1318, 114 S. Ct. at 914–915, 127 L. Ed. 2d at 361–362. Following remand to the South Dakota Circuit Court, the case was removed to the United States District Court for the District of South Dakota where the state court's preliminary injunction was dissolved. Federal Beef Processors, Inc. v. CBS Inc., 864 F.Supp. 127 (D.S.D.1994). For an extremely insightful discussion of lessons to be learned from direct prior restraint cases such as *Davis*, see Bruce E.H. Johnson, *CBS, Inc.* v. *Davis: Oddball Lessons From a Typical Prior Restraint Case*, 13 ABA Communications Lawyer 1 (No. 2, Summer 1995) (ruminations by one of CBS, Inc.'s lawyers in the case).

28. 78 F.3d 219 (6th Cir.1996).

from publishing the documents without consent of the court. The order had no termination date and set no date for hearing. Confronted with this very questionable order entered without notice and hearing, Business Week pulled its story just hours before deadline.[29]

The following day McGraw–Hill filed with the Sixth Circuit a request for stay of the district court's order and an expedited appeal with the Sixth Circuit. The appeals court dismissed the appeal on September 19th on the ground that the order was a temporary restraining order and thus not final and appealable. The panel never considered exercising its discretion by mandamus to set aside the prior restraint under the All Writs Act of the United States Judicial Code.[30] Later that same day McGraw–Hill sought an emergency stay from Justice Stevens, who, on September 21st denied the staying, doubting his jurisdiction and believing the wiser course was to return the case to the district court for a fact-finding hearing.[31] That same day the district court began a hearing that extended until October 3rd when McGraw–Hill was permanently enjoined from publishing its story based on the documents filed under seal, because, according to the trial judge, it knowingly violated the court's protective order. At the same time, the trial judge entered a second order withdrawing his sealing order on the documents and releasing them into the public domain.[32]

In attempting to punish McGraw–Hill by entering a permanent injunction against publication while at the same time publicly releasing the very documents forming the predicate for the injunction, the district court, perhaps unwittingly, opened the door for an appeal to the Sixth Circuit, which this time clearly had jurisdiction.

In reversing and vacating the permanent injunction, Chief Judge Gilbert Merritt, speaking for the Sixth Circuit, quickly dismissed the claim of mootness based on the documents now being in the public domain and provided a strong defense of press freedom while condemning the restraint of free expression engaged in by the district judge. In addition, he pointed out that the trial judge's violation of the First Amendment would never have occurred had he not improperly deferred to counsel in sealing the documents in the first place.

Judge Merritt recognized what the trial judge apparently did not—that the permanent injunction against publication created a classic case of prior restraint in the mode of *Near* v. *Minnesota ex rel. Olson.*[33]

> "[A]t no time—even to the point of entering a permanent injunction . . . did the District Court appear to realize that it was engaging in a practice that, under all but the most exceptional circumstances, violates the Constitution: preventing a news organization from

29. *Id.* at 222.

30. *Id.* The All Writs Act is 28 U.S.C.A. § 1651 (West 1994).

31. McGraw–Hill Cos. v. Procter & Gamble Co., 515 U.S. 1309, 116 S.Ct. 6, 132 L.Ed.2d 892 (1995); see also Procter &

Gamble Co. v. Bankers Trust Co., 78 F.3d 219, 222 (6th Cir.1996).

32. *Id.* at 222–223.

33. 283 U.S. 697, 51 S.Ct. 625, 75 L.Ed. 1357 (1931).

publishing information in its possession on a matter of public concern." [34]

And Judge Merritt had no difficulty in determining that the circumstances here did not amount to such "exceptional circumstances."

Despite the Sixth Circuit's eventual condemnation of the temporary stays and permanent injunction, the fact remains that Business Week, as a result of these judicially imposed prior restraints, was prevented from publishing its story for 175 days—nearly six months, the longest officially reported gagging of a news organization since the *Near* case. And the damage is not mitigated by the fact that several federal judges simply appeared unaware of their constitutional responsibilities. Rather, this case gives cause for alarm even though ultimately reaching a correct resolution because it suggests that some of those who swear to uphold the Constitution may not understand what the Press Clause of the First Amendment commands.

34. Procter & Gamble Co., 78 F.3d at 225.

Chapter Eight

FREE PRESS AND FAIR TRIAL

Analysis

8.1 Introduction to the Problem of Free Press and Fair Trial

The supposed conflict between the protection of the right of the citizenry to a free press and the protection of the right to fair trials particularly for those accused of criminal violations may well be the subject of more discussion among members of the bench, bar and news media than any other legal issue.[1] And a lengthy discussion it has been beginning as far back as the treason trial of Aaron Burr when the defendant and his lawyers lamented that it would be difficult if not impossible for him to find any unprejudiced jurors in the land because of the widespread publicity about the case.[2] But as shrill, voluminous and

1. Robert E. Drechsel, *An Alternative View of Media–Judiciary Relations: What the Non–Legal Evidence Suggests About the Fair Trial—Free Press Issue*, 18 Hofstra L. Rev. 1, 2 (1989). Professor Drechsel's point is supported in part by the large number of books and articles devoted to the issue written by lawyers, judges and newspersons. *See, e.g.*, ROBERT E. DRECHSEL, NEWS MAKING IN THE TRIAL COURTS (1983); ALFRED FRIENDLY & RONALD GOLDFARB, CRIME AND PUBLICITY (1967); DONALD M. GILLMORE, FREE PRESS AND FAIR TRIAL (1966); H. SULLIVAN, TRIAL BY NEWSPAPER (1961); Arthur L. Alarcón et al., *Fair Trial v. Free Press: Who's On First?*,

14 U. West L.A. L. Rev. 1 (1982)(sitting judge's analysis); Scott M. Matheson Jr., *The Prosecutor, the Press, and Free Speech*, 58 Fordham L. Rev. 865 (1990); Newton N. Minow & Fred H. Cate, *Who Is An Impartial Juror in an Age of Mass Media?*, 40 Am. U. L. Rev. 631 (1991); Jack B. Swerling, *The Right to Free Speech Versus The Right to Fair Trial—Balancing Competing Constitutional Interests*, 42 S. C. L. Rev. 901 (1991); Joel H. Swift, *Restraints on Defense Publicity in Criminal Jury Cases*, 1984 Utah L. Rev. 45 (1984).

2. *See* United States v. Burr, 25 Fed. Cas. 49, 51 (C.C.D.Va.1807) (No, 14,692); J.

629

lengthy the debate on the free press-fair trial issue has been, the reality of its importance probably does not warrant all the attention it receives. A number of well conceived studies on the controversy suggest that pretrial and trial publicity and news media misconduct rarely have had any measurable effect on the outcome of trials.[3]

Whatever the true dimensions of the problem, there have been enough notorious cases through the years raising questions about excessive trial and pretrial publicity and undue media influence on trials. Thus, attention is necessarily drawn to the question of the proper relationship between the First,[4] Fifth[5] and Sixth[6] Amendments to the Constitution.

8.2   The Constitutional Dimension of the Problem

The Sixth Amendment guarantees that in criminal prosecutions the accused shall be entitled to a speedy and public trial "by an impartial jury." A necessary implication of this constitutional mandate is that jurors must not be influenced in their determination of the guilt or innocence of the accused by forces outside the courtroom or by information or material not admitted into evidence at the trial. But news stories concerning a criminal case published before or during trial, particularly those containing information adverse to the accused not presented to the

GERALD, NEWS OF CRIME: COURTS AND PRESS IN CONFLICT 70–72 (1983); Minow & Cate, *supra* note 1, at 639–640.

3. *See* Robert E. Drechsel, *supra* note 1, at 11–16. From his review of the studies, Drechsel, a professor of journalism, concluded "Taken together, the research suggests that in an absolute quantitative sense, prejudicial publicity is a small problem. At worst, the data indicate only a potential for prejudicial impact." Drechsel, *supra* note 1, at 16; *see* LAURENCE H. TRIBE, AMERICAN CONSTITUTIONAL LAW 860 (2d ed. 1988) ("[The actual risk that a trial's result will be tainted by such news media] publicity is slight. Only a small percentage of criminal cases ever reach a jury, most jury trials generate no publicity and much crime news goes unnoticed."). *but see* Minow & Cate, *supra* note 1, at 649. Minow, a practicing attorney and Cate, a professor of law report that recent studies (Jonathan D. Casper et al. *Juror Decision Making, Attitudes, and the Hindsight Bias*, 13 L. & Hum. Behav. 291, 308 (1989); Geoffrey P. Kramer et al. *Pretrial Publicity, Judicial Remedies, and Jury Bias*, 14 L. & Hum. Behav. 409, 431 (1990)) suggest that pretrial bias created by publicity may affect the ways in which jurors recall, recount and weigh evidence resulting in biased deliberations. Minow & Cate, *supra* note 1, at 649.

4. U.S. CONST. Amend. I: "Congress shall make no law respecting an establish-ment of religion, or prohibiting the free exercise thereof; or abridging the freedom of speech, or of the press; or the right of the people peaceably to assemble, and to petition the Government for a redress of grievances."

5. U.S. CONST. Amend. V: "No person shall be held to answer for a capital or otherwise infamous crime, unless on a presentment or indictment of a Grand Jury, except in cases arising in the land or naval forces, or in the Militia, when in actual service in time of War or public danger; nor shall any person be subject for the same offence to be twice put in jeopardy of life or limb; nor shall be compelled in any criminal case to be a witness against himself, nor be deprived of life, liberty, or property, without due process of law; nor shall private property be taken for public use, without just compensation."

6. U.S. CONST. Amend. VI: "In all criminal prosecutions, the accused shall enjoy the right to a speedy and public trial, by an impartial jury of the State and district wherein the crime shall have been committed; which district shall have been previously ascertained by law, and to be informed of the nature and cause of the accusation; to be confronted with the witnesses against him; to have compulsory process for obtaining witnesses in his favor, and to have the assistance of counsel for his defence."

jury at trial such as a past criminal record or some incriminating statement or confession, may influence individual jurors and destroy their impartiality. And because the Constitution promises accused persons only "impartial" juries and not favorably biased ones, this constitutional guarantee, binding on the states through the Fourteenth Amendment,[1] might also be violated by publicity adverse to the prosecution.

As for the relevance here of the Fifth Amendment, it guarantees to every person, including criminal accused, that he or she will not be deprived "of life, liberty, or property without due process of law." Due judicial process may be affected by the news media and their representatives by the generation of publicity that prevents a fair trial by an impartial jury, by the generation of undue pressures on the trial judge through the substance of editorial comment and by disruption of the decorum of the courtroom through unseemly conduct making fair trial procedure and calm deliberation difficult if not impossible.

The problem in attempting to safeguard an accused's Fifth and Sixth Amendment rights arises from the potentially conflicting protection of press freedom by the First Amendment. Its language that "Congress shall make no law ... abridging the freedom of ... the press" has by long usage come to include court orders. Therefore, orders designed to assure fair and impartial trials may directly or indirectly restrict the newsgathering and news disseminating functions of the press. In addition, some orders, particularly those that bar newspersons from the courtroom may also violate a defendant's right to a "public trial" granted by the Sixth Amendment itself.

8.3 Confrontation of the Problem by the Supreme Court

A. The Initial Cases

Given the relationship of the three amendments and their apparent conflict when they address news media coverage of crimes and trials, it was inevitable that the United States Supreme Court would eventually address the issue. It did so for the first time in *Marshall v. United States*,[1] but there only in the exercise of its supervisory authority over the lower federal courts. In *Marshall*, the Court was confronted with jurors who had read in newspapers during trial that the defendant, who was accused of unlawfully dispensing drugs without valid prescriptions, had previously practiced medicine without a license including the prescription of dangerous drugs. This information had been offered in evidence and had been ruled inadmissible as extremely prejudicial. When the trial judge learned that several jurors had read about the defendant's previous misconduct in the newspapers he summoned them into his chamber separately and was told by each juror that he would not be influenced and would decide the case only on the evidence presented.

---

1. *Cf.*, *e.g.*, Washington v. Texas, 388 U.S. 14, 87 S.Ct. 1920, 18 L.Ed.2d 1019 (1967); Pointer v. Texas, 380 U.S. 400, 85 S.Ct. 1065, 13 L.Ed.2d 923 (1965); Gideon v. Wainwright, 372 U.S. 335, 83 S.Ct. 792, 9 L.Ed.2d 799 (1963).

1. 360 U.S. 310, 79 S.Ct. 1171, 3 L.Ed.2d 1250 (1959) (per curiam).

The trial judge, stating that he felt there was no prejudice, denied the defendant's motion for a new trial and conviction was obtained.

The Supreme Court, exercising its supervisory power to formulate and apply proper standards for enforcement of the criminal code in the federal courts and without touching on the underlying constitutional issue, reversed the conviction in a *per curiam* opinion.[2] While the decision was extremely narrow, it may have triggered the Court's interest in constitutional questions arising from trial and pretrial publicity, for two years later it granted certiorari to consider some of those questions.

In *Irvin v. Dowd*[3] the habeas corpus petitioner had been arrested in the wake of six murders committed in a short period of time in the Evansville, Indiana area. As might be expected the crimes generated extensive news coverage in the area, including Vanderburgh County, where Evansville is located, and adjoining Gibson County. Shortly after the petitioner's arrest the Vanderburgh County prosecutor and Evansville police officials issued press releases, which were widely publicized, stating that the petitioner had confessed to the six murders. Following indictment the lawyer appointed to defend the petitioner moved for a change of venue from Vanderburgh County. The motion was granted but only to adjoining Gibson County. A second motion for a second change of venue was filed, this time to a county sufficiently removed from the Evansville locality that a fair trial would not be prejudiced. This motion was denied apparently because an Indiana statute allows for only one change of venue in a criminal proceeding. Further motions were filed during voir dire for changes of venue and continuances which were also denied.

At trial 268 members of the 430–person jury panel were excused for cause as having fixed opinions as to the guilt of the petitioner. Of the twelve jurors ultimately selected, eight thought the petitioner was guilty but said they would be able to decide the case on the evidence presented in court. Following trial the petitioner was found guilty of the one murder for which he had been charged and was sentenced to death. His petition to the United States District Court for a writ of habeas corpus was dismissed. The dismissal was affirmed by the United States Court of Appeals for the Seventh Circuit.

On certiorari the Supreme Court recognized that in an era of pervasive mass communications important cases can be expected to arouse the interest of the public. Most of those best qualified to serve as jurors will have formed some impression or opinion as to the merits of notorious cases and to hold the mere existence of any preconceived view of guilt or innocence of an accused, without more, is sufficient to rebut the presumption of jury impartiality would be to establish an impossible standard for the prosecution.[4] But the Court vacated the dismissal order

---

2. *Id.* at 313, 79 S. Ct. at 1173, 3 L. Ed. 2d at 1252.

3. 366 U.S. 717, 81 S.Ct. 1639, 6 L.Ed.2d 751 (1961).

4. *Id.* at 722–23, 81 S. Ct. at 1642–43, 6

and remanded the case for further proceedings because the force with which the jurors' preconceived notions of guilt were held would have had to be very strong given the amount, breadth and nature of the pretrial publicity in the area in which the crime charged was perpetrated. The Court set out examples of that publicity in great detail, including the petitioner's extensive criminal record, his alleged confession to all six murders as well as 24 burglaries and his offer to plead guilty to avoid the death penalty which was rejected by the prosecutor. Some of the news stories themselves reflected the bitter and angry feelings of the local populace toward the accused and the difficulty of finding impartial jurors in the area to try him.[5]

The Court then pointed to the number of jurors empaneled who admitted to holding the belief that the petitioner was guilty and the number of ways in which they expressed such belief in order to support the conclusion that due process in the form of trial by an impartial jury had been denied the petitioner given the specific facts of this case. The Court said, "With his life at stake, it is not requiring too much that petitioner be tried in an atmosphere undisturbed by so huge a wave of public passion and by a jury other than one in which two-thirds of the members admit, before hearing any testimony, to possessing a belief in his guilt."[6]

The emphasis of the Court in *Irvin v. Dowd* was on the deep-seated prejudice held by members of the jury however formed. Obviously, extensive publicity, particularly that relating to confessions and prior criminal activities released or leaked by the prosecutor and the police, played a part in the creation of that prejudice against the accused and partiality for the prosecution.

Two years later, the Court revisited this area of constitutional law in *Rideau v. Louisiana*.[7] In that case a man had robbed a bank, kidnapped three of the bank's employees and murdered one of them. A few hours after these events the accused was taken into custody by the police and lodged in the Calcasieu Parish (county) jail in Lake Charles, Louisiana. The next morning a motion picture film with sound track was made of an interrogation of the accused by the sheriff lasting approximately 20 minutes. In the film the accused admitted that he had perpetrated the bank robbery, kidnapping and murder. Later the same day the film was broadcast over a television station in Lake Charles to some 24,000 people in the community. The film was rebroadcast the next day and the day after that to 53,000 and 29,000 viewers respectively. At the time Calcasieu Parish had a population of approximately 150,000 people. Shortly thereafter, the accused was arraigned on charges of armed robbery, kidnapping and murder. His two appointed lawyers filed a motion for change of venue on the ground that to try their client in Calcasieu

L. Ed. 2d at 756.

5. *Id.* at 725–27, 81 S. Ct. at 1644–45, 6 L. Ed. 2d at 757–59.

6. *Id.* at 728, 81 S.Ct. at 1645, 6 L.Ed.2d at 759.

7. 373 U.S. 723, 83 S.Ct. 1417, 10 L.Ed.2d 663 (1963).

Parish after the three television broadcasts would deprive him of his constitutional right to a fair and impartial trial. The motion was denied. During voir dire three members of the jury stated that they had seen and heard the televised interrogation and admissions at least once. Two other members of the jury were Calcasieu Parish deputy sheriffs. By the time these jurors were examined for fitness to serve, defense counsel had exhausted all of their peremptory challenges and their challenges for cause were denied by the trial judge. The accused was thereafter tried, convicted and sentenced to death. The conviction was affirmed by the Louisiana Supreme Court and certiorari was granted.

The Supreme Court reversed the conviction, holding that it was a denial of due process to refuse the request for a change of venue after the people in the parish had been exposed repeatedly and in depth to the accused personally confessing in detail to the crimes with which he was later to be charged. Presuming prejudice from the broadcast, the Court said, "Any subsequent court proceedings in a community so pervasively exposed to such a spectacle could be but a hollow formality."[8] Due process required a trial before a jury which had not seen or heard the accused's interrogation.

The Court emphasized in its decision to reverse the active cooperation and participation of local law enforcement officers in making and then releasing the film of the interrogation[9] and the "kangaroo court" proceedings that resulted in a death sentence for the accused.[10]

Shifting its focus on cameras from those outside the courtroom to those inside, the Court reversed another conviction in *Estes v. Texas*.[11] There, in a case involving charges of massive fraud by an entrepreneur with ties to the Texas Democratic Party and President Lyndon Johnson, a pretrial hearing on whether to permit television cameras, microphones and still cameras to be present at trial was itself broadcast by television and radio and photographed with considerable disruption of the proceedings. The television broadcasting was initially live and then repeated on tape, reaching approximately 100,000 viewers. During the hearing the courtroom was a mass of wires, television cameras, microphones, camera persons and still photographers. The witnesses and the lawyers were all exposed to this situation and four of the jurors selected to hear the case saw or heard all or part of the broadcasts. The judge himself was distracted following his decision to allow television coverage of the trial itself by having to make numerous decisions regulating the television coverage. Relying, *inter alia,* upon *Rideau*, the Court presumed from the presence of the television cameras and attendant equipment and the resulting broadcasts a denial of the accused's right to a fair trial guaranteed by the Due Process Clause of the Fourteenth Amendment.[12]

8. *Id.* at 726, 83 S. Ct. at 1419, 10 L. Ed. 2d at 665.

9. *Id.* at 725, 83 S. Ct. at 1418–19, 10 L. Ed. 2d at 665.

10. *Id.* at 726, 83 S. Ct. at 1419, 10 L. Ed. 2d at 665.

11. 381 U.S. 532, 85 S.Ct. 1628, 14 L.Ed.2d 543 (1965).

12. The Court's concern about the presence of television cameras in the courtroom would eventually change. *See* Chandler v.

B. *The Court's Most Extensive Consideration of the Issue: Sheppard v. Maxwell*

The Court's consideration of the free press and fair trial issue in *Marshall, Irvin, Rideau* and *Estes* was merely the prologue to its more extensive statement of the problem and possible solutions in *Sheppard v. Maxwell*.[13] This is the classic case of excessive and abusive pretrial and trial publicity, improper courtroom behavior by the news media and abdication by a public official—the presiding judge—of his responsibility to insure a fair trial for the accused.

Dr. Samuel Sheppard's pregnant wife, Marilyn, was brutally bludgeoned to death in an upstairs bedroom of her home in a suburb of Cleveland. Dr. Sheppard's story was to the effect that at the time of the murder he was asleep on a couch in the living room. He heard his wife cry out and he rushed upstairs where, in the dim light from the hall, he saw a "form" standing near his wife's bed. As he struggled with the "form" he was struck on the back of the neck and fell to the floor unconscious. When he regained consciousness he found his wife dead.

From the beginning, the coroner and the police believed Sheppard guilty of murder and interrogated him at great length and without benefit of counsel. He was also pressed by the police to take an "infallible" lie detector test or an injection of "truth serum" or to confess. Sheppard resisted. The local newspapers, which took great interest in the case, played up Sheppard's refusal to subject himself to a lie detector test and the injections, as well as a so-called "protective ring" thrown up around him by his family.

Thereafter, an editorial writer opened fire with a front page charge that somebody was "getting away with murder." The editorial attributed the ineptness of the investigation to "friendship, relationships, hired lawyers, a husband who ought to have been subjected instantly to the same third-degree to which any other person under similar circumstances is subjected." The following day another front page editorial was headed: "Why No Inquest? Do It Now, Dr. Gerber." The coroner called the inquest the same day. It was staged in a school gymnasium, televised live to the people of the Cleveland area, covered by a swarm of reporters and photographers and ended after three days in a public brawl.

Throughout the period prior to Sheppard's arrest the newspapers emphasized facts that tended to incriminate Sheppard and highlighted discrepancies in his statements. Much of this "evidence" was never introduced at trial and the editorials became more insistent as to Sheppard's guilt. An editorial entitled "Why Don't Police Quiz Top Suspect" demanded that Sheppard be taken to police headquarters and another asked: "Why Isn't Sam Sheppard in Jail?" Immediately thereafter Sheppard was arrested and charged with murder. Then the publicity intensified. Cartoons, editorials, news stories and features, mostly unfavorable to Sheppard, poured forth from the local presses and radio and

Florida, 449 U.S. 560, 101 S.Ct. 802, 66 L.Ed.2d 740 (1981).   **13.** 384 U.S. 333, 86 S.Ct. 1507, 16 L.Ed.2d 600 (1966).

television stations. Headlines announced, among other things, "Sheppard 'Gay Set' is revealed by Houk [Sheppard's neighbor and mayor of the town in which the murder took place]," "Blood Is Found In Garage," "New Murder Evidence Is Found, Police Claim," "Dr. Sam Faces Quiz At Jail On Marilyn's Fear Of Him." The publicity continued unabated until Sheppard's conviction in December 1954 and the press clippings alone from the three Cleveland newspapers filled five volumes of the record.

The conduct of the trial was equally depressing. Before the case was set the names of the prospective jurors were published along with their addresses. Consequently, anonymous letters and telephone calls concerning the prosecution were received by all of the prospective jurors. Most of the space in the small courtroom was set aside for the use of the media, including a large area inside the bar where traditionally only those directly involved in the conduct of trials are permitted. Representatives of the news media used all the rooms on the courtroom floor, and private telephone lines and telegraphic equipment were installed in these rooms for their convenience. Live newscasts were made from a temporary broadcasting facility set up on another floor of the courthouse. Everywhere around the courthouse and nearly everywhere within, there were newsreel and still photographers with all of their paraphernalia, intent on capturing all the participants on film as often as possible.

All of these arrangements with the representatives of the media were permitted to continue throughout the nine weeks of trial, and the courtroom remained crowded to capacity with news personnel. The confusion caused by their movement in and out of the courtroom made it difficult for witnesses and counsel to be heard. Because of the close quarters and crowding it was almost impossible for Sheppard and his counsel to hold confidential discussions in the courtroom. Participants in the trial had to run a human gauntlet of media representatives just to get into and out of the courtroom. It was all reminiscent of the circus atmosphere that pervaded the Bruno Hauptmann trial for kidnapping and murder of the Lindbergh child some thirty years earlier. The trial judge, who was running for reelection, did nothing to stop it. He failed to sequester the jury during the presentation of evidence. Consequently, the jurors were exposed to the publicity generated during the trial. The Supreme Court in its opinion in the Sheppard case listed several instances of highly prejudicial publicity during that period. Repetition of only a few of them will suffice to suggest the environment in which the jurors decided Sheppard's fate.

On the second day of voir dire examination of the prospective jurors a debate was presented over WHK radio. The participants, newspaper reporters, accused Sheppard's counsel of throwing roadblocks in the way of the prosecution and claimed that Sheppard had admitted his guilt by hiring a prominent criminal lawyer to defend him. When defense counsel complained about the broadcast to the judge, he refused to take any protective action. During the trial, a Cleveland police officer gave testimony that tended to contradict portions of Sheppard's written statement made to the police. Two days later, in a broadcast again over WHK, Robert Considine, Hearst feature writer and radio personality, likened Sheppard to a perjurer and compared the episode to Alger Hiss' confrontation with Whittaker Chambers. Defense counsel asked the judge to question the jury to determine how many had heard the broadcast and, again, the judge refused and overruled a motion for a continuance based on the same incident. Later, a story dealing with the defendant's temper appeared under an eight column headline reading "Sam Called A 'Jekyll–Hyde' by Marilyn, Cousin To Testify." No such testimony was ever produced at trial. Similarly, two weeks later a police captain not at the trial and never called as a witness denied certain trial testimony given by Sheppard under the headline " 'Bare–Faced Liar,' Kerr says of Sam."

Only after the case was submitted to the jurors were they sequestered. However, after the guilty verdict was returned, defense counsel discovered that jurors had been allowed to make telephone calls every day and no record was kept of the calls. The trial judge had failed to instruct the bailiffs to prevent such calls. Defense counsel moved for a new trial. The motion was overruled. Sheppard's initial state appeals were unsuccessful and review of his conviction by the United States Supreme Court was denied.[14] He served ten years in the Ohio penitentiary before obtaining a review of the conviction in the federal courts on a habeas corpus application.

In that ten-year period the Court had decided *Marshall*, *Irvin*, *Rideau* and *Estes* and, apparently as a result, realized that it had not fairly scrutinized Sheppard's claims of denial of fair trial occasioned by the undue publicity and courtroom disruption generated by the media and left unchecked by the trial judge.

In ordering Sheppard's release from custody, the Supreme Court signalled its determination to end free-wheeling media coverage of important criminals cases. While noting that a responsible press is regarded as an indispensable handmaiden of fair and effective judicial administration, Justice Clark speaking for the Court in *Sheppard* recognized that in cases involving probable jury exposure to massive publicity relating to information not introduced in evidence at trial, jurors might be improperly influenced in their deliberations and decisions.[15] The Court then ruled, relying on almost a decade of its precedents, that in

14. Sheppard v. Ohio, 352 U.S. 910, 77 S.Ct. 118, 1 L.Ed.2d 119 (1956). *See* Memorandum of Frankfurter, J., reflecting the Sheppard's claim of denial of due process because of the Roman Circus that passed for a trial. Id. at 910–911, 77 S. Ct. at 118, 1 L. Ed. 2d at 119. This whole sorry episode in the history of American Justice is recapitulated in great detail in an article in the Washington Post. *See* Peter Finn, The Wrong Man, Wash. Post, Jan. 28, 1996, pp. F1, F4–5.

15. 384 U.S. at 357, 362, 86 S. Ct. at 1519, 1522, 16 L. Ed. 2d at 617, 620. As-

suming arguendo that Dr. Sheppard was innocent, the Supreme Court's belated recognition of prejudice in the trial proceedings is emblematic of the adage "Justice delayed is justice denied." Sheppard's life was ruined. His attempt to return to the practice of medicine was a failure and his final days were spent earning a living as a professional wrestler attracting the morbidly curious to his matches. Richard G. Zimmerman, *Letter to the Editor*, Washington Post, Oct. 16, 1993, p. A20, Col. 3.

cases involving a high probability of prejudice to one or the other of the parties stemming from pretrial and trial publicity, such prejudice could be presumed to exist and actual evidence of the exposure to and the effect on individual jurors of such publicity need not be presented.[16] Sheppard's case was held to be one of those in which that presumption would apply.

The Court further stated that the trial judge compounded the problem of undue publicity in the case by acting pursuant to the erroneous belief that he lacked power to control it in any way.[17] The Supreme Court catalogued a number of approaches and tactics that the judge might have utilized to guarantee Sheppard the fair trial guaranteed by the Fourteenth Amendment without imposing restrictions or sanctions *directly* against press coverage, including imposing strict rules of courtroom and courthouse decorum, isolating witnesses from obtaining trial information, controlling the release of information and misinformation generally by those participating in the trial, continuing cases until the threat of undue publicity abates, ordering changes of venue to places not so saturated with publicity and ordering the sequestration of juries at the outset of high profile trials.[18] These judicial devices intended to insure fair trials for accused in cases of great public interest and widespread publicity will be discussed below.[19]

8.4 Publicity Alone Is Not the Touchstone of Unfair Trials

A. Sheppard v. Maxwell—The Dictum

Despite the pervasive publicity in *Sheppard v. Maxwell*, it seems unlikely that publicity without more would have persuaded the Court that Dr. Sheppard had been denied a fair trial and that, after ten years of incarceration, he should be released from prison. The Court suggested as much when it said, "While we cannot say that Sheppard was denied due process by the judge's refusal to take precautions against the influence of pretrial publicity alone, the court's later rulings must be considered against the setting in which the trial was held."[1] The Court then went on to lambast the trial judge, who was, at the time, standing for reelection, for failing to insure even the fundamentals of a fair trial. "[W]e believe that the arrangements made by the judge with the news media caused Sheppard to be deprived of that 'judicial serenity and calm to which [he] was entitled. *Estes v. Texas, supra* at 536.' "[2] The Court underlined its disgust with the trial proceedings by adding, "The fact is that bedlam reigned at the courthouse during the trial and newsmen

---

16. 384 U.S. at 352–55, 86 S. Ct. at 1516–18, 16 L. Ed. 2d at 614–16.

17. 384 U.S. at 357–58, 86 S. Ct. at 1519–20, 16 L. Ed. 2d at 617–18.

18. 384 U.S. at 358–63, 86 S. Ct. at 1519–23, 16 L. Ed. 2d at 617–21.

19. *See* section 8.5, *infra.*

1. Sheppard v. Maxwell, 384 U.S. 333, 354–55, 86 S.Ct. 1507, 1517–18, 16 L.Ed.2d 600, 615–16 (1966).

2. *Id.* at 355, 86 S. Ct. at 1518, 16 L. Ed. 2d at 616.

took over practically the entire courtroom, hounding most of the participants in the trial, especially Sheppard."[3]

The conclusion that extensive pretrial and trial publicity does not by
itself render trials unfair which may be drawn from *Sheppard* is strongly
supported by practical necessity and subsequent decisions of the Court.
The idea that massive publicity concerning criminal trials automatically
results in the denial of a fair trial to one or the other parties defies
common sense. If that proposition were correct the more notorious the
alleged criminal conduct the less the likelihood of obtaining a valid
conviction in this age of mass communications. It has often been suggested that if Lee Harvey Oswald had lived to stand trial of President
Kennedy no conviction would have survived because a fair trial would
have been impossible anywhere. Such reasoning presupposes the requirement that jurors be ignorant of the case before trial and not merely that
they be impartial. But the judicial system will not allow itself to be
paralyzed by such a requirement. If the presumed prejudice of prospective jurors who have knowledge provided by news media is clearly
rebutted on voir dire examination, no denial of a fair trial should be
found merely on the basis of publicity. On the other hand, where
publicity is so intense and virulent that all surrounding indicia suggest
that the presumption of prejudice cannot be overcome, then a fair trial
will not be possible at the time and place designated.[4] But this will
seldom be the case. These propositions are suggested by the Supreme
Court's decisions in *Murphy v. Florida*,[5] *Patton v. Yount*[6] and Justice
Kennedy's dissent in *Mu'Min v. Virginia*.[7]

B. Cases Holding That Publicity Alone Will Not Justify Re-versal of Criminal Convictions

In *Murphy v. Florida*, a notorious thief was charged with breaking
and entering a home while armed with intent to commit robbery therein
and for assault with intent to commit robbery. Before trial on these
charges in Dade County, Florida, the accused was convicted in a Florida
state court of murder in connection with another robbery and pleaded
guilty in federal court to a charge involving stolen securities. The
murder and securities cases drew extensive press coverage in south
Florida and elsewhere. Jury selection in *Murphy* began after the notoriety of the earlier criminal cases and many of the prospective jurors were
aware of the accused's previous convictions. In the process of jury

---

3. *Id.*

4. *See, e.g.,* Rideau v. Louisiana, 373
U.S. 723, 83 S.Ct. 1417, 10 L.Ed.2d 663
(1963).

5. 421 U.S. 794, 95 S.Ct. 2031, 44
L.Ed.2d 589 (1975).

6. 467 U.S. 1025, 104 S.Ct. 2885, 81
L.Ed.2d 847 (1984).

7. 500 U.S. 415, 448, 111 S.Ct. 1899,
1917, 114 L.Ed.2d 493, 520 (1991). Even
when the Dallas Morning News broke the

sensational and disputed story on its web
page that accused Oklahoma courthouse
bombing suspect Timothy J. McVeigh had
confessed to his counsel, outraged defense
attorney Stephen Jones at first said that he
was "confidant that Federal District Court
Judge Richard P. Matsch would see that we
get a fair jury." Tom Kenworthy, *The
McVeigh Story and Its Impact*, Wash. Post,
Mar. 2, 1997, p. A7, col. 1.

selection 78 persons were questioned. Of these, 30 were excused for miscellaneous personal reasons, 20 were excused by the court as having prejudged the case and of the remaining eight six served as jurors and two served as alternates.

Petitioner moved to dismiss the selected jurors on the ground that through publicity surrounding his earlier convictions they were aware that he had been involved in the infamous "Star of India" jewel theft and murder. This motion was denied as was his motion for change of venue necessitated by allegedly prejudicial pretrial publicity. At trial the accused did not testify, or put in any evidence or cross-examine the state's witnesses. He was convicted on both counts of the indictment and, after an unsuccessful appeal, he sought a writ of habeas corpus from the federal courts. The district court refused to issue the writ and the then Fifth Circuit affirmed.

In the Supreme Court, the petitioner relied upon *Irvin, Rideau, Estes* and *Sheppard* in arguing that the attendant publicity had denied him a fair trial guaranteed by the Fourteenth Amendment. But the Court distinguished those cases on the basis that the influence of the news media, either in the community at large or in the courtroom so pervaded the proceedings that juror prejudice was presumed and the presumption could not be adequately rebutted. "The proceedings in these cases were entirely lacking in the solemnity and sobriety to which a defendant is entitled in a system that subscribes to any notion of fairness and rejects the verdict of the mob. They cannot be made to stand for the proposition that juror exposure to information about a state defendant's prior convictions or to news accounts of the crime with which he is charged alone presumptively deprives the defendant of due process."[8]

The Court was therefore compelled to determine whether any of the indicia of fundamental unfairness present in those cited cases were present in Murphy's case. In making this determination the Court started with the proposition that the constitutional standard of fairness requires that an accused be judged by a panel of impartial and indifferent jurors, not jurors totally ignorant of the facts and issues involved.[9] But the Court would not accept jurors' assurances alone that they could lay aside their opinions on the case and would render a verdict based solely on the evidence presented in court. Rather, the Court scrutinized the transcript of the voir dire examination of the jurors and found no indicia of prejudice toward the accused of any great significance. Rather, the indicia suggested the opposite.[10]

Indicia of impartiality exhibited during voir dire might, however, be disregarded, according to the Court, in cases where the general atmo-

---

8. Murphy v. Florida, 421 U.S. 794, 799, 95 S.Ct. 2031, 2035, 44 L.Ed.2d 589, 594 (1975).

9. *Id.* at 799–800, 95 S. Ct. at 2035–36, 44 L. Ed. 2d at 594–95; *see* Irvin v. Dowd,

366 U.S. 717, 722, 81 S.Ct. 1639, 1642, 6 L.Ed.2d 751, 755–56 (1961).

10. Murphy, 421 U.S. at 800–02, 95 S. Ct. at 2036–37, 44 L. Ed. 2d at 594–96.

sphere in the community or the courtroom is sufficiently inflammatory. But that was not the situation in Murphy's case. Mostly the publicity had appeared seven to eight months prior to trial and was largely factual in nature, unlike the accusatory publicity in *Sheppard*.[11] Also bolstering the conclusion that the trial had not been poisoned was the fact that only 20 venireman out of 78 had to be excused because they held an opinion as to the accused's guilt. In contrast in *Irvin* 90 percent of those questioned on the point leaned toward the defendant's guilt.[12]

What *Murphy* clearly establishes is that the presence of publicity surrounding a trial and juror knowledge of that publicity will not, by itself, result in a denial of due trial process. Rather, voir dire of prospective jurors as to their opinions and the subsequent conduct of the trial itself will more likely determine whether media coverage can be said to have had an adverse affect on the trial.

These themes were repeated in *Patton v. Yount*,[13] where the petitioner sought habeas corpus from a United States District Court following his incarceration for murder in part because he claimed that excessive publicity surrounding the case had deprived him of his right to a fair trial by an impartial jury guaranteed by the Sixth and Fourteenth Amendments. The petitioner, a high school mathematics teacher had been charged with the particularly brutal murder of one of his female students after confessing to the police. Once the confession was read at the petitioner's arraignment a torrent of publicity followed. His 1966 conviction of first degree murder and rape was reversed on appeal because of inadequate *Miranda* warnings.

Prior to the second trial in 1970, the trial court ordered suppression of the petitioner's written confessions and the portion of the oral confession that was obtained after he was legally in custody. As a result the prosecution dismissed the rape charge.

There was extensive voir dire at the second trial directed in part to the petitioner's claim that widespread dissemination of prejudicial publicity could not be eradicated from the minds of potential jurors. Jury selection took ten days, seven jury panels, 292 veniremen and 1186 pages of testimony before twelve jurors and two alternates were seated. Petitioner moved before and several times during the voir dire for a change of venue. The motions were denied, the trial court noting that the news stories merely reported events without editorial comment, that few if any of the jurors actually seated had prior or present fixed opinions about the petitioner's guilt or innocence and that there had been "little, if any, talk in public" between the first and second trials. Petitioner was convicted a second time of first degree murder and he was resentenced to life imprisonment. The trial court denied a motion for a new trial finding that practically no publicity had been given to the case between the two

11. *Id*. at 802, 95 S. Ct. at 2037, 44 L. Ed. 2d at 596:

12. *Id*. at 803, 95 S. Ct. at 2037, 44 L. Ed. 2d at 596–97.

13. 467 U.S. 1025, 104 S.Ct. 2885, 81 L.Ed.2d 847 (1984).

trials, that little public interest was exhibited regarding the second trial and that the jury was without bias. The Pennsylvania Supreme Court affirmed the conviction and the trial court's findings.

In 1981 the petitioner filed his petition for a writ of habeas corpus which was denied by the district court. The United States Court of Appeals for the Third Circuit reversed relying primarily on the analysis presented in *Irvin v. Dowd*[14] In analyzing the publicity surrounding the second trial, the voir dire testimony as a whole and the voir dire testimony of the jurors actually seated, the appeals court concluded that the pretrial publicity had made a fair trial impossible in the county in which the murder had occurred. This publicity revealed the petitioner's prior conviction for the murder, his confession and his prior plea of temporary insanity none of which was admitted into evidence at the second trial. Of the 163 veniremen actually questioned about the case, all but two had heard about it and 126 or 77 percent admitted that they would carry an opinion into the jury box.[15] Finally, the Court of Appeals found that eight of the fourteen jurors and alternates actually seated admitted that at some time between Yount's original arraignment in 1966 and the voir dire in the second trial they had formed an opinion as to his guilt, that some of these jurors gave equivocal response to the question whether they could set their opinions aside and that one juror and both alternates would have required evidence from Yount to overcome their beliefs as to his guilt. The appellate court concluded that despite assurances of impartiality, the jurors could not set aside their opinions and render a verdict based solely on the evidence presented— the test for an impartial jury and a fair trial.

Nevertheless, the Supreme Court reversed, reinstating the trial court's denial of the writ. The Court criticized the Third Circuit for ignoring the rule set down in *Irvin* that a trial court's findings of jury impartiality might be overturned only for "manifest error."[16] The Court also pointed out that while in *Irvin* there had been for six or seven months prior to trial a barrage of newspaper headlines, articles, cartoons and pictures ... unleashed against the defendant, in *Patton* the prejudicial publicity had greatly diminished by the time of the second trial. According to the Court the record showed that in the year and a half from the reversal of the first conviction to the start of the second voir dire each of the two local newspapers published less than one article per month and though coverage increased to almost a daily basis during voir dire it was purely factual reporting of the lengthy jury selection process and not the crime itself.[17]

Turning to the jurors who were actually seated, the Court argued that time had weakened or eliminated any opinion as to the petitioner's

14. 366 U.S. 717, 81 S.Ct. 1639, 6 L.Ed.2d 751 (1961).

15. This was a higher percentage than in *Irvin*, where 62 percent of the 430 veniremen were dismissed for having fixed opinions concerning the accused's guilt.

16. Patton, 467 U.S. at 1031–35, 104 S. Ct. at 2888–91, 81 L. Ed. 2d at 854–56 (1984).

17. *Id.* at 1032; 104 S. Ct. at 2889, 81 L. Ed. 2d at 854–55.

guilt they might once have had arising from the earlier publicity and the later factual publicity had not inflamed or prejudiced them against the petitioner.[18] "[I]t is clear that the passage of time between a first and a second trial can be a highly relevant fact. In the circumstances of this case, we hold that it clearly rebuts any presumption of partiality or prejudice that existed at the time of the initial trial. There was fair, even abundant, support for the trial court's findings that between the two trials of this case there had been 'practically no publicity given to this matter through the news media,' and that there had not been 'any great effect created by any publicity.' "[19]

Underlining just how much the Court's thinking had changed about pretrial and trial publicity since *Irvin*, Justice Stevens in a dissent joined by Justice Brennan noted that the majority's own statement of the facts ought to give "the reader a strong feeling about how this case should be decided."[20] Justice Stevens went on to analyze the record in the case and, contrary to the Court's reading concluded that the voir dire established that the case was still a "cause cèlebrè" in the county in which it was tried and that the jurors were not neutral.[21]

The main difference on the law between Justice Stevens and the majority was as to the nature of the issue of whether a juror holds a disqualifying opinion. The majority held that the issue was one purely of fact and the trial court's finding on juror prejudice was entitled to the statutory presumption of correctness. Justice Stevens would hold that it was a mixed question of law and fact not subject to the presumption of correctness but requiring independent review on appeal. He noted that his position was the one the Court had previously taken in *Irvin* and had now abandoned to the detriment of accused seeking to raise on appeal the issue of the denial of their right to a fair trial because of undue publicity tainting the jury process.[22]

The decision in *Patton* leads to the tentative conclusion that, with an entirely new Court in place since *Irvin* having an entirely different mindset about the constitutional rights of accused, *Irvin* no longer provides any basis for appellate reversal of a trial court ruling that a fair trial had not been denied the accused because of media publicity.

This tentative conclusion became fixed with the Court's recent ruling in *Mu'Min v. Virginia*.[23] There, a prison inmate serving time for first degree murder and assigned to a work detail in Northern Virginia outside the penitentiary, escaped and made his way to a nearby shopping center where he stabbed to death a retail establishment owner in the course of robbing her store. His criminal conduct was discovered and he was thereafter tried. About three months before trial, the accused moved

---

18. *Id.* at 1033–34, 104 S. Ct. at 2889–90, 81 L. Ed. 2d at 855–56.

19. *Id.* at 1035, 104 S. Ct. at 2890–91, 81 L. Ed. 2d at 856.

20. *Id.* at 1040, 104 S. Ct. at 2893, 81 L. Ed. 2d at 859–60.

21. *Id.* at 1041–53, 104 S. Ct. at 2894–2900, 81 L. Ed. 2d at 860–67.

22. *Id.* at 1050–53, 104 S. Ct. at 2898–2900, 81 L. Ed. 2d at 865–67.

23. 500 U.S. 415, 111 S.Ct. 1899, 114 L.Ed.2d 493 (1991).

for a change of venue and in support thereof submitted 47 newspaper articles relating to the murder that had been published either in a large circulation newspaper, the Washington Post, or in a small circulation Northern Virginia paper, the Potomac News. One or more of these articles discussed the details of the murder and investigation, and included information about the accused's prior criminal record, his rejection for parole six times, accounts of his prison infractions, details about the prior murder, including the fact that the death penalty had not been available when he was convicted, and indications that he had confessed to killing the shop owner. The trial judge deferred ruling on the request for change of venue until after attempting to seat a jury. Once a jury was seated the motion was denied.

Shortly before the beginning of the trial, the accused submitted to the trial judge a number of proposed voir dire questions including some directed to eliciting the content of articles read or seen by the prospective jurors and he asked for individual voir dire. The motion for individual voir dire was denied but the judge decided to question the veniremen in panels of four. He refused questions about the content of the news items the jurors might have seen or heard. Twenty-six prospective jurors were summoned into the courtroom and first questioned as a group with a verbal response only required if a juror wished to admit to knowledge of the case or prejudice against the accused. Questions included whether anyone had acquired information about the case from the news media or any other source, to which question 16 potential jurors responded affirmatively, and whether such information would affect their impartiality to which question one juror responded affirmatively and was excused.[24] Petitioner then moved for removal for cause all of the potential jurors who indicated exposure to pretrial publicity and for a change of venue. Both motions were denied.

The trial court then conducted additional voir dire in panels of four, again with the questions posed in such manner as to require a response only if a juror wished to admit prior knowledge of the case, possession of an opinion about guilt or innocence or an inability to fairly judge the evidence at trial. Of the twelve jurors selected eight admitted to having read or heard something about the case but none stated that he or she had formed an opinion or gave any indication of prejudice. All swore that they could enter the jury box with an open mind and hear the evidence before reaching a conclusion as to guilt or innocence.[25] This jury subsequently found petitioner guilty of capital murder and recommended the death penalty which recommendation was accepted by the trial judge. A divided Virginia Supreme Court affirmed the conviction and sentence, holding that a defendant does not have a constitutional right to explore on voir dire the content of a juror's previously acquired information but is only entitled to know whether jurors can be impartial in light of that information.

24. *Id.* at 419, 111 S. Ct. at 1902, 114 L. Ed. 2d at 501–02.

25. *Id.* at 421, 111 S. Ct. at 1903, 114 L. Ed. 2d at 503–04.

The United States Supreme Court affirmed in a particularly revealing majority opinion ignoring the damaging nature of the publicity as detailed in the opinion itself. It again distinguished *Irvin v. Dowd* on the basis of numbers of veniremen who held opinions on guilt or innocence, the difference in the respective county populations involved and the nature of the news accounts surrounding the two cases. As to the latter point the Court made much of the fact that in *Irvin* the publicity included details of 24 burglaries and six murders, Irvin's offer to plea bargain in order to avoid the death sentence and numerous editorial opinions as to his guilt and the appropriate punishment. Guilty itself of considerable understatement the Court compared the case at hand saying that the news reports about Mu'Min were not favorable, but, looking on the bright side, found that they did not contain the same sort of damaging information.[26] The Court's comparison glossed over the facts that the 47 Washington Post and Potomac News articles did contain information about the defendant's prior criminal record, his poor prison behavior and indications that he had confessed to the murder of the shop owner.

The dissent by Justice Marshall, joined by Justices Blackmun and Stevens, did not gloss over these facts. "Much of the pretrial publicity was of the type long thought to be uniquely destructive of a juror's ability to maintain an open mind about a case—in particular, reports of Mu'Min's confession . . . ; statements by prominent public officials attesting to Mu'Min's guilt . . . ; and reports of Mu'Min's unsavory past. . . . "[27] Justice Marshall went on to observe that such publicity, which eight of the twelve jurors admitted to being exposed to, may well have rendered them incapable of reaching any other verdict but guilty.[28] "The majority holds that the trial court was entitled to seat those jurors . . . based solely on their assertions of impartiality. Far from 'tak[ing] strong measures to ensure that the balance [was not] weighed against the accused,' the procedures undertaken in this case amounted to no more than the trial court going through the motions."[29]

Justice Kennedy's separate dissent first attempted to make sense of the Court's precedents from *Irvin* through *Murphy* to *Mu' Min*. He found that the cases fell into two main categories: those involving allegations that individual jurors might have been prejudiced by exposure to pretrial publicity (*Patton, Murphy* and *Mu'Min*) and those involving the separate problem of cases tried in such a corruptive atmosphere that the Court was required to presume the absence of a fair trial (*Sheppard, Rideau* and probably *Irvin*). The latter category involved cases in which the trial court or the prosecutor may have been remiss in failing to protect the defendant from a carnival atmosphere created by press coverage.[30]

26. *Id.* at 429, 111 S. Ct. at 1907, 114 L. Ed. 2d at 508.

27. *Id.* at 444, 111 S. Ct. at 1915, 114 L. Ed. 2d at 517–18.

28. *Id.* at 444–45, 111 S. Ct. at 1917, 114 L. Ed. 2d at 520.

29. *Id.*

30. *Id.*

While it would have been easier for Justice Kennedy to dissent if Mu'Min's case had been in the second category because the Court in the past had been particularly concerned about corruption of trial decorum, he did not place it there. Justice Kennedy then tackled the first category, indicating that the inquiry should be directed to the question of the actual impartiality of the seated jurors and the related question whether the trial judge conducted an adequate voir dire of the eight jurors who acknowledged some exposure to press accounts of the trial. He then found the voir dire to be inadequate to assess the individual juror's ability to be impartial. "The questions were asked of groups, and the individual jurors attested to their own impartiality by saying nothing."[31] Justice Kennedy would have held, contrary to the majority, that when a juror admits exposure to pretrial publicity, the trial court must conduct a sufficient colloquy with the individual juror to make an assessment of the juror's ability to be impartial.[32] Since, as far as Justice Kennedy was concerned, "impartiality must be based on something more than the mere silence of the individual in response to questions asked *en masse*,"[33] he dissented.

When five justices accept the impartiality of jurors subjected to considerable publicity based solely upon their "say so,"—actually their failure to say otherwise—in a death penalty case no less, it seems clear beyond peradventure that claims of unfair trial falling within Justice Kennedy's first category simply will not result in reversal on appeal, at least in the federal courts. Thus, unless the conduct of the press results in courtroom disorder or prejudice admitted on the record, there seems little point today in appealing federal convictions on the ground of undue publicity or seeking writs of habeas corpus from the federal courts directed to state penitentiary custodians on that ground.[34]

As a corollary to the decisions in *Patton* and *Mu'Min*, the judicial devices developed to mitigate the dangers to fair trials by pretrial and trial publicity are reduced in their significance. Nevertheless, those trial judges who are serious about protecting defendants' rights to fair trials

31. *Id.* at 452, 111 S. Ct. at 1919, 114 L. Ed. 2d at 522–23.

32. *Id.*

33. *Id.* The shortcomings generally of voir dire to ferret out juror bias or prejudice are catalogued in a recent article. *See* Joseph F. Flynn, Note, *Prejudicial Publicity in Criminal Trials: Bringing* Sheppard v. Maxwell *Into the Nineties*, 27 New England L. Rev. 857, 871–874 (1993).

34. Two commentators make the *Mu'Min* voir dire holding, combined with the dictum on the permissiblity of judicial "gag orders" in Sheppard, the centerpiece of their thesis that, even in light of the highly publicized prosecutions of O.J. Simpson, the Menendez brothers, the police officers involved in the Rodney King beating and the two men accused of the Okla-

homa City bombing, the preservation of both fair trials and freedom of the press is still possible. "The best solution is the *Sheppard-Mu'Min* remedy which strikes the proper balance between the defendant's interest in a fair trial and the media's interest in informing the public. Under the *Sheppard-Mu'Min* remedy, trial courts impose a gag order on the trial participants from the beginning of the proceedings and, when selecting a jury, fashion the *voir dire*, after the standard set in *Mu'Min v. Virginia*." Charles H. Whitebread and Darrell W. Contreras, *Free Press v. Fair Trial: Protecting the Criminal Defendant's Rights In A Highly Publicized Trial By Applying The Sheppard—Mu'Min Remedy*, 69 S. Cal. L. Rev. 1587, 1619–1620 (1996).

in notorious cases may wish to choose to rely on them and therefore examination of these devices is still called for.

8.5 Judicial and Extra–Judicial Actions to Counter Undue Pretrial and Trial Publicity

A. Cooperation Between Bench, Bar and News Media Through Employment of Voluntary Guidelines

An extra-judicial device to avoid undue publicity sometimes employed by those intimately involved in the conduct and coverage of judicial proceedings is voluntary guidelines for controlling publicity subscribed to by judges, lawyers and members of the news media. Voluntary guidelines are in effect in more than half of the states and are strongly backed by such organizations as the American Bar Association, the American Society of Newspaper Editors and the American Newspaper Publishers Association.

An example of these guidelines is the "Free Press—Fair Trial Guidelines for the State of North Carolina" published by the North Carolina Bar Association and by the School of Journalism of the University of North Carolina.[1] The guidelines are ten in number and provide detailed guidance for newsgatherers, lawyers and judges involved with criminal proceedings. They range from categorizing the kinds of information which may be made public in criminal cases to admonishing trial

---

1. THE NEWS MEDIA AND THE COURTS (3d ed. undated). The guidelines are published in cooperation with the Institute of Government of the University of North Carolina and the News Media Administration of Justice Council of North Carolina. The Council is a quasi-public organization composed of selected representatives of the North Carolina Judicial Conference, the North Carolina Bar Association, the North Carolina Press Association and the North Carolina Association of Broadcasters. *Id.* at 2. For other examples *see* F. SIEBERT, et al., FREE PRESS AND FAIR TRIAL SOME DIMENSIONS OF THE PROBLEM 118–33 (1970) (guidelines for the states of Minnesota, Oregon and Washington and the city of Burlington, Vermont); FREE PRESS AND FAIR TRIAL 95–119 (1967) (a report of the American Newspaper Publishers Association reprinting guidelines for the states of Kentucky, Louisiana, Massachusetts, North Carolina (original version), Oregon, Washington, and Wyoming and the city of Philadelphia). The National Judicial College has also weighed in with its "top ten" suggestions, from the judiciary's perspective, for smoothing relations between the bench and the media: (1) encourage and establish continuing interdisciplinary educational opportunities and dialogue among judges, journalists and lawyers; (2) assume there is access to all court proceedings and records and place the burden of proof for closure on the entity seeking it; (3) refrain from imposing gag orders on the news media or attorneys except in extraordinary cases; (4) establish and support bench-bar-media committees which will meet regularly in every community to address issues of mutual concern; (5) establish, after consultation with media representatives, guidelines for trial-press management in high profile cases; (6) consider non-binding professional standards for journalists; (7) assume that cameras should be allowed in the courtroom, including the federal court system, and that access should be limited or excluded only for strong reasons; (8) encourage judges to explain on the record, the reasons for their rulings; (9) determine when and if it is appropriate to compel reporters to testify or produce notes, tapes and other evidence, understanding that the news media is not an arm of law enforcement; and (10) encourage media organizations to develop an ombudsman system to hear recommendations from the courts and the public. *Top 10 Significant Issues for Judges, Journalists and Lawyers on Court–Media Issues and Relationships*, 11 NJC Alumni 27 (No. 3, Summer 1996).

judges to release promptly information as to the disposition of their cases.[2] Separate guidelines are provided for juvenile proceedings.[3]

While such guidelines have been helpful in reducing the level of conflict between the press and the bench and bar over access to information and publicity regarding judicial proceedings,[4] they have at least two major shortcomings, one obvious and one not so obvious. The obvious one is that because they are voluntary, newsgatherers, lawyers and even judges (especially those who are elected) may choose to ignore the guidelines when it suits their purpose. The temptation to do so may be great when an especially notorious case is presented that could enhance one's journalistic, legal or judicial career.

The not so obvious shortcoming is that the judiciary may choose to use the voluntary guidelines as implements of involuntary coercion. While the coercion may often be subtle and unchallenged, there have been at least two reported instances where coercion to comply with existing guidelines were, to say the least, very direct. In the celebrated case of *Nebraska Press Association v. Stuart*[5] involving several ghastly murders that wiped out an entire family in a small Nebraska town, the local County and District Courts entered orders requiring members of the press covering the case to observe the supposedly voluntary Nebraska Bar–Press Guidelines, and not disclose certain information which they might possess.[6] And in *Federated Publications, Inc. v. Swedberg*,[7] a trial judge conditioned attendance by members of the press at an evidence suppression hearing in connection with the notorious "Hillside Strangler" serial murder case on the journalists signing an agreement to abide by the Washington State Bench–Bar–Press Guidelines. When the press challenged the condition the Washington Supreme Court held that in furtherance of an accused's sixth amendment rights, which include the right to an unbiased and unprejudiced jury, a trial judge may condition news media access to pretrial hearings when unconditional access might result in the prejudice of jurors who would be selected following publicity concerning such hearings.[8]

Obviously the trial judges in *Nebraska Press Association* and *Federated Publications, Inc.* were doubtful that the existence of extra-judicial voluntary guidelines were enough to prevent prejudicial publicity depriving accused of fair trials. This same doubt may motivate trial judges to exercise their discretion to employ other more direct judicial devices to guarantee fairness.

---

2. The guidelines in their entirety are: [text in Practitioners Edition, Vol. 2].

3. *Id.* at 38–39.

4. Telephone interview with Hugh H. Stevens, Jr., Esquire, general counsel of the North Carolina Press Association (June 1, 1992) (regarding the North Carolina guidelines).

5. 427 U.S. 539, 96 S.Ct. 2791, 49 L.Ed.2d 683 (1976).

6. *Id.* at 542, 544, 96 S. Ct. at 2794–95, 2795–96, 49 L. Ed. 2d at 687–88, 688–89. A description of the Nebraska guidelines is provided in the opinion of the case. *Id.* at 542 n.1, 96 S. Ct. at 2795 n.1, 49 L. Ed. 2d at 688 n.1.

7. 96 Wash. 2d 13, 633 P.2d 74 (1981), cert. denied, 456 U.S. 984, 102 S.Ct. 2257, 72 L.Ed.2d 862 (1982) (Brennan & Marshall, JJ., dissenting).

8. *Id.* at 20–22, 633 P.2d at 77–78.

B. Continuing Judicial Proceedings Until the Threat to Fair Trial Abates

The first direct judicial device that the Supreme Court in *Sheppard* recommended that trial courts employ in avoiding prejudice from publicity is continuance of trials until the threat of unfairness reflected in the voir dire or other aspects of the record abates.[9] On the face of it, such tactic seems unlikely to succeed in sensational and well publicized criminal cases because they tend to remain in the public consciousness for a long period of time or there may be a reprise of the publicity when these cases are finally tried.[10] Nevertheless, the Supreme Court and lower courts have indicated their faith in the efficacy of continuances as a counter to prejudicial publicity. For instance, in *Patton v. Yount*[11] the Supreme Court pointed to the fact that jury selection for the accused's second trial for murder occurred four years after the first one at a time when prejudicial publicity had greatly diminished and community sentiment had softened in rejecting the claim that the accused had been denied a fair trial the second time around.[12] Admittedly, continuances, if granted, are not likely to extend beyond six months to one year.[13] Nevertheless, the Court in *Patton* exhibited a ready acceptance of the ameliorative effect of the passage of time.

More directly, while the overwhelming number of reported cases have rejected claims of error by trial judges denying motions for continuance based on claims of prejudicial publicity, courts, on rare occasions, have granted such motions in the belief that delay of proceedings will help insure fair trials.[14] But delay is the antithesis of speedy trial

9. Sheppard v. Maxwell, 384 U.S. 333, 363, 86 S.Ct. 1507, 1522, 16 L.Ed.2d 600, 620–21 (1966).

10. *See, e.g.,* United States v. Haldeman, 559 F.2d 31, 63–64 n. 42, 181 U.S. App. D.C. 254, 287 n. 42 (1976), cert. denied *sub nom.* Ehrlichman v. United States and Mitchell v. United States, 431 U.S. 933, 97 S. Ct. 2641, 53 L. Ed. 2d 250 (1977) (prevoir dire motions for continuance or change of venue based on pretrial publicity of the Watergate conspiracy denied in part because there was little reason to believe the news media would not continue their coverage at least until trial whenever that might take place); *see also* United States v. Moreno Morales, 815 F.2d 725, 737 (1st Cir. 1987); United States v. Hoffa 156 F.Supp. 495, 500 (S.D.N.Y.1957); People v. Manson, 61 Cal.App.3d 102, 176–177, 132 Cal.Rptr. 265, 309–310 (1976), cert. denied 430 U.S. 986, 97 S.Ct. 1686, 52 L.Ed.2d 382 (1977); People v. Moore, 42 N.Y.2d 421, 434, 397 N.Y.S.2d 975, 984, 366 N.E.2d 1330, 1338 (1977), cert. denied, 434 U.S. 987, 98 S.Ct. 617, 54 L.Ed.2d 482 (1977); Andrew M. Schwartz, Note, *Gagging the Press in Criminal Trials*, 10 Harv. C.R.—C.L. L. Rev. 608, 617–18 (1975).

11. 467 U.S. 1025, 104 S.Ct. 2885, 81 L.Ed.2d 847 (1984).

12. *Id*. at 1032–33, 104 S. Ct. at 2889–90, 81 L. Ed. 2d at 854–55; *see also, e.g.,* Thomas v. State, 539 So.2d 375, 392–93 (Ala.Crim.App.1988); State v. Smith, 340 So.2d 222, 224 (La.1976); Commonwealth v. Martin, 465 Pa. 134, 147–49, 348 A.2d 391, 398 (1975).

13. The postponement in the second trial of Officer Powell in the notorious Rodney King beating case extended slightly less than six months from the date of the verdicts in the first trial (April 29, 1992 to October 19, 1992, *see* L.A. Times, May 23, 1992, p. A1, col. 5), keeping in mind that few criminal prosecutions in the country's history have generated more pervasive news media coverage and commentary.

14. *See* United States v. Daniels, 282 F.Supp. 360, 361–62 (N.D.Ill.1968); Maine v. Superior Court, 68 Cal.2d 375, 383–84, 66 Cal.Rptr. 724, 729–30, 438 P.2d 372, 377–78 (1968) (adopting standards for fair trial proposed in the American Bar Association Project on Minimum Standards for Criminal Justice Standards Relating to Fair Trial

guaranteed by the Sixth Amendment and undue media attention requiring accused persons to seek continuances may result in the forced waiver of their constitutional right.[15]

C. Change of Venue

A parallel judicial device to mitigate the danger posed by prejudicial publicity is the change of situs of the trial. Where it becomes apparent before trial that prejudice may infect the criminal proceedings the trial judge may order a change of venue.[16] Perhaps the most celebrated recent example of resorting to this device was the movement of the state trial from Los Angeles County to Ventura County of the four Los Angeles Police Department officers accused of unlawfully beating of motorist Rodney King following his capture after a high speed chase, which beating was recorded on video tape and later broadcast extensively.[17]

If a criminal case is too heinous or shocking and the publicity too intense, pervasive and widespread, changes of venue may be of doubtful value and trial courts in the exercise of their discretion may refuse to grant them on that basis.[18] Other significant factors influencing trial courts in denying or granting motions for change of venue include the gravity and nature of the crime charged, the extent and nature of the publicity surrounding it, the size and nature of the community in which the crime was committed, status of the victim and of the accused, indications from voir dire that publicity had prejudicial effect,[19] the extent to which publicity focuses on the crime rather than on the accused, the extent to which government is responsible for generating

and Free Press (Tentative Draft 1966)); State v. Montgomery, 248 La. 713, 715–30, 181 So.2d 756, 758–62 (1966); Commonwealth v. Brado, 470 Pa. 306, 368 A.2d 643 (1977).

15. *Cf.* United States v. Abbott Laboratories, 505 F.2d 565, 573 (4th Cir.1974), cert. denied, 420 U.S. 990, 95 S.Ct. 1424, 43 L.Ed.2d 671 (1975).

16. *See, e.g.,* United States v. Mabry, 809 F.2d 671, 683 (10th Cir.1987); United States v. Addonizio, 313 F.Supp. 486, 494 (D.N.J.1970), *aff'd* 451 F.2d 49 (3d Cir. 1971), cert. denied 405 U.S. 936, 92 S.Ct. 949, 30 L.Ed.2d 812 (1972); Fain v. Superior Court, 2 Cal.3d 46, 84 Cal.Rptr. 135, 465 P.2d 23 (1970); Commonwealth v. Cohen, 489 Pa. 167, 177–87, 413 A.2d 1066, 1072–77 (1980); State v. Dandy, 151 W.Va. 547, 153 S.E.2d 507 (1967).

17. *See* Powell v. Superior Court (People) 232 Cal.App.3d 785, 283 Cal.Rptr. 777 (1991).

18. *See* United States v. Haldeman 559 F.2d 31, 64 n. 43, 181 U.S. App. D.C. 254, 287 n. 43, (D.C.Cir.1976), cert. denied *sub nom.* Ehrlichman v. United States and Mitchell v. United States, 431 U.S. 933, 97

S. Ct. 2641, 53 L. Ed. 2d 250 (1977) ("Moreover, on the basis of the record we note that a change of venue would have been of doubtful value. Many of the articles appellants submitted in support of their motions were taken from nationally circulated news magazines. The network news programs and legislative hearings of which appellants also complain were similarly national in their reach."); People v. Manson, 61 Cal. App.3d 102, 175–77, 132 Cal.Rptr. 265, 308–10 (1976), cert. denied, 430 U.S. 986, 97 S.Ct. 1686, 52 L.Ed.2d 382 (1977). *See also* Note, *Prejudicial Publicity in Trials of Public Officials,* 85 Yale L.J. 123 n.2 (1975). But the easy assumption that pervasive publicity negatives change of trial location as a useful device to insure fair trials may have been exploded by the jury verdicts of acquittal in the first Rodney King beating prosecution though the argument continues whether the changed venue from Los Angeles to the Simi Valley resulted in a fair trial for the prosecution.

19. *See, e.g.,* People v. Price, 1 Cal.4th 324, 389–90, 3 Cal.Rptr.2d 106, 139, 821 P.2d 610, 643 (1991). State v. Mayberry, 248 Kan. 369, 379–80, 807 P.2d 86, 96 (1991).

that publicity,[20] the exercise or failure to exercise the allotted peremptory challenges following voir dire[21] and whether a "cooling off period" has occurred in which the complained of publicity has abated.[22]

Just as with the continuance procedure, the Sixth Amendment impacts on the change of venue device. The Sixth Amendment guarantees all accused the right to be tried in the state and federal district in which the crime charged was committed and state constitutions generally require trial in the county or judicial district in which the indictment or information is issued.[23] Therefore, it is the accused who must move for a change of venue or acquiesce in a motion made by the prosecution, thereby waiving his constitutional right. If an accused opposes change of venue the trial must be held in the state, county or district in which the crime occurred[24] and other judicial devices will have to be resorted to in order to counter prejudicial publicity.

D. Sequestration of Jurors

To prevent subversion of the right of all parties to a fair trial after proceedings are commenced, the trial judge, *sua sponte* or on motion of either the defendant or the prosecution, may order the jury to be sequestered or separated from society for the period of the trial. Numerous courts have expressed their belief in the efficacy of this option in countering the danger of jury prejudice from undue publicity *during* trial.[25] Factors to be considered in deciding whether to sequester include the likelihood of undue publicity following selection of a jury, the nature of the publicity as inflammatory or noninflammatory, the quantity and breadth of the publicity, the sensational or nonsensational nature of the case,[26] the expected length of the trial,[27] the passage of time between the

20. *See, e.g.,* United States v. Maldona-do–Rivera, 922 F.2d 934, 967 (2d Cir.1990); State v. Jones, 593 So.2d 1301, 1315 (La. App.1991); State v. Jeffries, 105 Wash. 2d 398, 409, 717 P.2d 722, 729, cert. denied, 479 U.S. 922, 107 S.Ct. 328, 93 L.Ed.2d 301 (1986).

21. *See, e.g.,* United States v. Ebens, 800 F.2d 1422, 1427 (6th Cir.1986); State v. Bradley, 236 Neb. 371, 386, 461 N.W.2d 524, 536 (1990); State v. Jeffries, 105 Wash. 2d 398, 409, 717 P.2d 722, 729, cert. denied 479 U.S. 922, 107 S.Ct. 328, 93 L.Ed.2d 301 (1986).

22. *See, e.g.,* State v. Bradley, 236 Neb. 371, 385, 461 N.W.2d 524, 536 (1990); Commonwealth v. Cohen, 489 Pa. 167, 177, 413 A.2d 1066, 1072 (1980); Childress v. State, 807 S.W.2d 424, 428 (Tex.App.1991).

23. *See, e.g.,* Gilliland v. State 291 Ala. 89, 277 So.2d 901 (1973); Mississippi Publishers Corp. v. Coleman, 515 So.2d 1163, 1165 (Miss.1987).

24. *See* Mississippi Publishers Corp. v. Coleman, 515 So.2d 1163, 1165 (Miss.1987).

25. *See, e.g.,* United States v. Shiomos, 864 F.2d 16 (3d Cir.1988) (sequestration on

court's own motion); United States v. Peters, 791 F.2d 1270, 1298–1299 (7th Cir. 1986), cert. denied *sub nom.* Odoner v. United States, 479 U.S. 847, 107 S.Ct. 168, 93 L.Ed.2d 106 (1986); People v. Vialpando, 809 P.2d 1082, 1083–84 (Colo.App.1990); Hughes v. State, 437 A.2d 559, 576–78 (Del. 1981); Welch v. United States, 466 A.2d 829, 837–38 (D.C.1983); State v. Guloy, 104 Wash. 2d 412, 427–30, 705 P.2d 1182, 1192–93, cert. denied 475 U.S. 1020, 106 S.Ct. 1208, 89 L.Ed.2d 321 (dictum); *see also* Abby Propis Simms, Note, *Sequestration: A Possible Solution to the Free Press—Fair Trial Dilemma,* 23 Am. U. L. Rev. 923, 933–36 (1974). *But see* Joseph F. Flynn, Note, *Prejudicial Publicity in Criminal Trials: Bringing* Sheppard v. Maxwell *Into the Nineties,* 27 New England L. Rev. 857, 878–79 (1993).

26. *See* State v. Heath, 35 Wash. App. 269, 270–72, 666 P.2d 922, 923–24 (1983).

27. *See* People v. Hernandez, 47 Cal.3d 315, 338, 253 Cal.Rptr. 199, 211, 763 P.2d 1289, 1301 (1988).

crime and publicity and the trial[28] and the actual location of the trial in relation to the place of the crime.[29]

No federal constitutional right to jury sequestration exists directly[30] and thus unless guaranteed by state constitutional provision, the ordering or denying of sequestration will be found violative of a criminal defendant's constitutional rights only if the trial judge's determination is found to result in jury prejudice or his action otherwise compromises a fair trial.[31] The determination to sequester is wholly within the discretion of the judge[32] and he may order sequestration because of the threat of prejudicial publicity on his own motion.[33] If the court in exercising its discretion does not order jury sequestration, it may still issue strong cautionary instructions to the jury to avoid all news accounts of the case during the course of the trial. However, the ameliorative effect of such instructions is doubtful and they may even be counterproductive by drawing juror attention to prejudicial publicity.[34]

8.6 Judicial Actions to Prevent Prejudicial Pretrial and Trial Publicity by Restricting Sources of News and Information

A. Limiting Access of the News Media—Pretrial, Trial and Post Trial Rules and Orders Preventing Trial Participants From Commenting Publicly

1. Introduction

One means suggested by the Supreme Court in *Sheppard v. Maxwell* to reduce pretrial, trial and even post trial publicity is for trial courts to promulgate standing rules or issue orders directed to those involved in trials, including law enforcement personnel, court personnel, the lawyers, witnesses, parties, and even judges, preventing them from communicating to the public about pending cases.[1] The thrust of such no-

---

28. *See* Ruiz v. State, 299 Ark. 144, 155–56 772 S.W.2d 297, 303 (1989); State v. Washington, 430 So.2d 641, 645 (La.1983).

29. *See* Ruiz, 299 Ark. at 155–56, 772 S.W.2d at 303.

30. *See* Young v. Alabama, 443 F.2d 854, 856 (5th Cir.1971), cert. denied 405 U.S. 976, 92 S.Ct. 1202, 31 L.Ed.2d 251 (1972); Powell v. Spalding, 679 F.2d 163, 166 n. 3 (9th Cir.1982); State v. Clay, 812 S.W.2d 872, 875 (Mo.App.1991); People v. D'Alvia, 171 A.D.2d 96, 104–05, 575 N.Y.S.2d 495, 501 (1991).

31. *See* Powell, 679 F.2d at 166; People v. D'Alvia, 171 A.D.2d at 104–07, 575 N.Y.S.2d at 501–02 (semble).

32. *Id.*

33. *See, e.g.,* United States v. Shiomos, 864 F.2d 16, 18 (3d Cir.1988); United States v. Peters, 791 F.2d 1270, 1299 (7th Cir.

1986); People v. Avery, 736 P.2d 1233, 1236 (Colo.App.1986).

34. *See* United States v. Simon, 664 F.Supp. 780, 794 (S.D.N.Y.1987), *aff'd sub nom.* In re Dow Jones & Co., 842 F.2d 603 (2d Cir.), cert denied 488 U.S. 946, 109 S.Ct. 377, 102 L.Ed.2d 365 (1988); Newton N. Minow & Fred H. Cate, *Who Is an Impartial Juror in an Age of Mass Media?*, 40 Am. U. L. Rev., 631, 648 (1991) (collecting psychological studies of mock jurors and juries); Mark R. Stabile, Note, *Free Press-Fair Trial: Could They Be Reconciled in a Highly Publicized Criminal Case?*, 79 Geo. L. J. 337, 345 (1990).

1. 384 U.S. 333, 363, 86 S.Ct. 1507, 1522, 16 L.Ed.2d 600, 620 (1966); *see* Nebraska Press Association v. Stuart, 427 U.S. 539, 564, 96 S.Ct. 2791, 2805, 49 L.Ed.2d 683, 700 (1976); In re Inquiry of Broadbelt, 146 N.J. 501, 511, 683 A.2d 543, 548 (1996),

comment rules or orders, referred to pejoratively as "gag orders," is to prevent trial participants from talking to the news media. The Court apparently finds no Press Clause problem with such orders because of its long held belief that this clause of the First Amendment protects dissemination of news and information once obtained by the news media but not the process of gathering news and information in the first instance.[2] The *Sheppard* Court also paid no attention to another constitutional issue whether this indirect method of reducing trial publicity infringed on the free speech rights of both willing and unwilling trial participants.[3] And finally the Court failed to consider that "no comment" rules and orders may have more than the indirect restraining effect on newsgatherers of drying up their sources. If sources violate a no comment order or rule by providing information in confidence, reporters may be held in contempt if they refuse to disclose the identity of the sources.[4] Over the years a number of reporters have found themselves in this position and some have landed in jail.[5]

2. Standards for Silencing Trial Participants

Despite the difficult constitutional issues presented by standing rules of court or specific judicial orders muzzling trial participants,[6] a

cert. denied 520 U.S. 1118, 117 S.Ct. 1251, 137 L.Ed.2d 332 (1997) (disapproval of sitting judge commenting on pending cases in other jurisdictions while appearing on television).

2. *Compare, e.g.,* Vance v. Universal Amusement Co., Inc., 445 U.S. 308, 100 S.Ct. 1156, 63 L.Ed.2d 413 (1980); New York Times Co. v. United States, 403 U.S. 713, 91 S.Ct. 2140, 29 L.Ed.2d 822 (1971)(the "Pentagon Papers" case); Near v. Minnesota ex rel. Olson, 283 U.S. 697, 51 S.Ct. 625, 75 L.Ed. 1357 (1931) *with* Houchins v. KQED, Inc., 438 U.S. 1, 98 S.Ct. 2588, 57 L.Ed.2d 553 (1978); Saxbe v. Washington Post Co., 417 U.S. 843, 94 S.Ct. 2811, 41 L.Ed.2d 514 (1974); Zemel v. Rusk, 381 U.S. 1, 85 S.Ct. 1271, 14 L.Ed.2d 179 (1965); *and see* News–Journal Corp. v. Foxman, 939 F.2d 1499, 1512–1516 (11th Cir. 1991).

3. But in Gentile v. State Bar of Nevada, 501 U.S. 1030, 111 S.Ct. 2720, 115 L.Ed.2d 888 (1991) the Court was willing to assume *arguendo* that lawyers participating in judicial proceedings might be subjected, consistent with the First Amendment, to speech restrictions that could not be imposed on the press or general public. *Id.* at 1037, 111 S. Ct. at 2726, 115 L. Ed. 2d at 900. Such assumption would clearly be more difficult to make with regard to witnesses who may not have the same voluntary choice to participate in criminal proceedings as do legal counsel. *See* Marcy Strauss, *From Witness to Riches: The Con-*

stitutionality of Restricting Witness Speech, 38 Ariz. L. Rev. 291 (1996) (concluding that California statutes passed in the wake of the O.J. Simpson prosecution to curb "checkbook journalism" enticing witnesses to sell their stories are violative of the First Amendment); Erwin Chemerinsky, *Should Witnesses be Allowed to Sell Their Stories Before the Trial,* L.A. Times Aug. 22, 1994, p. B7 (same).

4. *See* United States v. Bingham, 769 F.Supp. 1039, 1045 (N.D.Ill.1991), Sheryl A. Bjork, Comment, *Indirect Gag Orders and the Doctrine of Prior Restraint,* 44 U. Miami L. Rev. 165, 177, 179 n.115 (1989).

5. *See, e.g.,* Farr v. Pitchess, 522 F.2d 464 (9th Cir.1975), *cert. denied* 427 U.S. 912, 96 S.Ct. 3200, 49 L.Ed.2d 1203 (1976), *connected case* Farr v. Superior Court, 22 Cal.App.3d 60, 99 Cal.Rptr. 342 (1971); Rosato v. Superior Court, 51 Cal.App.3d 190, 124 Cal.Rptr. 427 (1975), cert. denied, 427 U.S. 912, 96 S.Ct. 3200, 49 L.Ed.2d 1204 (1976); see also United States v. Bingham, 769 F.Supp. 1039, 1045 (N.D.Ill.1991); In re Decker, 322 S.C. 212, 471 S.E.2d 459 (S.C. 1995) (incarceration of reporter ordered in connection with the notorious case of the mother who drowned her two young sons by rolling the family automobile into a lake; state shield law narrowly read and First Amendment qualified privilege rejected).

6. *See id.* (all opinions); *see also* Chicago Council of Lawyers v. Bauer, 522 F.2d 242, 247–49 (7th Cir.1975), cert. denied *sub*

number of legal organizations have issued reports, rules and standards encouraging the use of such orders or rules of court since the Court's suggestion in *Sheppard*. The first and perhaps most influential of these is the American Bar Association's Standards Relating to Fair Trial and Free Press.[7] Under the leadership of Paul C. Reardon, a then justice of the Supreme Judicial Court of Massachusetts, the ABA published standards which it recommended be incorporated in bar codes of professional responsibility enjoining lawyers from releasing or authorizing the release of information or opinion for public dissemination in connection with pending or imminent criminal litigation with which they are associated.[8] The no comment standards further specified the kinds of information and opinions not to be publicly communicated, including prior criminal records, the existence or contents of any confessions, admissions or statements given by accused and any opinions as to guilt or innocence.[9] Other ABA no comment standards related to the conduct of law enforcement agencies,[10] court personnel such as court stenographers and clerks,[11] and judges.[12]

nom. Cunningham v. Chicago Council of Lawyers, 427 U.S. 912, 96 S.Ct. 3201, 49 L.Ed.2d 1204 (1976); Scott M. Matheson Jr., *The Prosecutor, the Press, and Free Speech*, 58 Fordham. L. Rev. 865, 897–904 (1990); Jack B. Swerling, *The Right to Free Speech Versus the Right to a Fair Trial Balancing Competing Constitutional Interests*, 42 S. C. L. Rev. 901, 906–19 (1991); Michael E. Swartz, Note, *Trial Participant Speech Restrictions: Gagging First Amendment Rights*, 90 Colum. L. Rev., 1411, 1421–33 (1990).

7.   Other organizations weighing in with similar reports, rules and standards include the Judicial Conference of the United States with its REPORT OF THE COMMITTEE ON THE OPERATION OF THE JURY SYSTEM ON THE "FREE PRESS–FAIR TRIAL" ISSUE, 45 F.R.D. 391 (1969), 51 F.R.D. 135 (1970)(supplemental report); 87 F.R.D. 519 (1980)(revised report); the United States Department of Justice with its statement of policy regarding release of information by personnel relating to criminal and civil proceedings, 28 C.F.R. § 50.2 (1994), supplemented in 2 DOJ Manual § 1–7.001 (1987); and the Association of the Bar of the City of New York with its FINAL REPORT OF THE SPECIAL COMMITTEE ON RADIO, TELEVISION, AND THE ADMINISTRATION OF JUSTICE, FREEDOM OF THE PRESS AND FAIR TRIAL (1967) (the so-called Medina Report) and its REPORT OF THE AD HOC COMMITTEE ON PRETRIAL PUBLICITY (1987).

The Reardon and Medina Committee reports justifying organized bar codes designed to suppress trial publicity generated

by counsel are severely criticized for their methodology and conclusions in Lloyd B. Snyder, *Rhetoric, Evidence, and Bar Agency Restrictions on Speech by Attorneys*, 28 Creighton L. Rev. 357, 391–395 (1995).

8.   *See* AMERICAN BAR ASSOCIATION PROJECT ON STANDARDS FOR CRIMINAL JUSTICE: STANDARDS RELATING TO FAIR TRIAL AND FREE PRESS § 1.1 (1968).

9.   *Id.* The current revised ABA standards relating to controlling attorney communications are: [text in Practitioners Edition only].

10.   The standards for law enforcement agencies are: [text in Practitioners Edition, Vol. 2, only].

11.   The standards for court personnel are:

"Court personnel shall not disclose to any unauthorized person information relating to a pending criminal case that is not part of the public records of the court and that may be prejudicial to that right of the people or the defendant to a fair trial. Particular reference should be made in this rule to standards 8–3.2 and 8–3.6(d). Appropriate disciplinary action should be provided for infraction of this rule." *Id.* § 8–2.2.

12.   The standard for judges is to "refrain from any conduct of the making of any statements that may be prejudicial to the right of the people or of the defendant to a fair trail." *Id.* § 8–2.3.

With the incorporation of the ABA standards in state bar codes of professional responsibility or rules of professional conduct[13] governing attorney behavior the constitutional issues come to the fore. Because freedom of speech under the First Amendment is not absolute, the expression of lawyers and other involved in trial proceedings like everyone else is subject to some restriction if the government's interest is great enough. Here, of course, the interest is insuring fair trials for all accused. To be consistent with the First Amendment no comment orders must be no broader than necessary to prevent prejudice at trial and may be entered only after trial courts find that no alternative to such orders will be effective.[14] The major constitutional issue presented by no comment rules and orders is the proper standard to be applied in determining when such content regulation of expression is permissible.

a. "Clear and present danger" test

A split of authority as to the appropriate standard developed almost immediately upon the proliferation of the ABA's no comment rules. Some courts believed that only communications to the public that posed something like a "clear and present danger" to fair trial justified restriction of the speech of attorneys involved in trials,[15] particularly since such speech is often political in nature[16] and regulation has features akin to prior restraint.[17] This high standard is also said to be

---

13. As of 1991 eleven states had adopted code provisions patterned after some version of ABA Model Code of Professional Responsibility Disciplinary Rule 7–107 (1981), which utilized the standards recommended in the Reardon Committee report. *See* Gentile v. State Bar of Nevada, 501 U.S. 1030, 1068 n. 2, 111 S.Ct. 2720, 2741 n. 2., 115 L.Ed.2d 888, 919 n. 2 (1991). DR 7–107 on trial publicity provides: [text in Practitioners Edition, Vol. 2].

14. *See* United States v. Salameh, 992 F.2d 445–447 (2d Cir.1993); Breiner v. Takao, 73 Haw. 499, 505, 835 P.2d 637, 641 (1992).

15. *See* Bailey v. Systems Innovation, Inc., 852 F.2d 93, 99 (3d Cir.1988); United States v. Ford, 830 F.2d 596, 600 (6th Cir.1987)("serious and imminent threat"); CBS v. Young, 522 F.2d 234, 238 (6th Cir. 1975)("clear and present danger" language); Levine v. United States Dist. Ct., 764 F.2d 590, 598 (9th Cir.1985), cert. denied, 476 U.S. 1158, 106 S.Ct. 2276, 90 L.Ed.2d 719 (1986)("serious and imminent threat"); Breiner v. Takao, 73 Haw. 499, 505, 835 P.2d 637, 641 (1992) ("serious and imminent threat"); Markfield v. Association of the Bar of the City of New York, 49 A.D.2d 516, 517, 370 N.Y.S.2d 82, 85 (1975), *appeal dismissed*, 37 N.Y.2d 794, 375 N.Y.S.2d 106, 337 N.E.2d 612 (1975)("clear and present danger"); In re

Lasswell, 296 Or. 121, 126 n. 3, 673 P.2d 855, 858 n. 3 (1983)("highly probable serious prejudice to an imminent procedure").

16. *See e.g.*, State v. Hohman, 138 Vt. 502, 420 A.2d 852 (1980) (prosecutor's re-election campaign ad advocating a change in the bail laws and promising to obtain a murder conviction in a pending case); Michael E. Swartz, Note, *Trial Participant Speech Restrictions: Gagging First Amendment Rights*, 90 Colum. L. Rev. 1411, 1428 (1990); *see also* Gentile v. State Bar of Nevada, 501 U.S. 1030, 111 S.Ct. 2720, 115 L.Ed.2d 888 (1991); *cf.* Landmark Communications, Inc. v. Virginia, 435 U.S. 829, 839, 98 S.Ct. 1535, 1541–42, 56 L.Ed.2d 1, 10 (1978) ("The article published by Landmark provided accurate factual information about a legislatively authorized inquiry pending before the Judicial Inquiry and Review Commission, and in so doing clearly served those interests in public scrutiny and discussion of governmental affairs which the First Amendment was adopted to protect.").

17. *See* CBS, Inc. v. Young, 522 F.2d 234, 239 (6th Cir.1975)(per curiam)(lack of rationale for prior restraint conclusion); Chicago Council of Lawyers v. Bauer, 522 F.2d 242, 249 (7th Cir.1975)(no comment rules "have some of the inherent features of 'prior restraints' which have caused the judiciary to review them with particular

necessary to avoid the overbreadth and vagueness of such rules.[18]

b. "Reasonable likelihood" and "substantial likelihood" tests

On the other hand a number of courts[19] have opted for the apparently less demanding reasonable likelihood of interference with a fair trial standard first suggested in dictum in *Sheppard v. Maxwell*[20] and echoed in the original ABA standards relating to fair trial and free press.[21] It appears that when this lesser standard is utilized specific applications of no comment rules and orders are more likely to be upheld.[22] While the

care."); Journal Pub. Co. v. Mechem, 801 F.2d 1233, 1236 (10th Cir.1986); Connecticut Magazine v. Moraghan, 676 F.Supp. 38, 42 (D.Conn.1987); *see also* Sheryl A. Bjork, Comment, *Indirect Gag Orders and the Doctrine of Prior Restraint*, 44 U. Miami L. Rev. 165, 181–85 (1989); Michael E. Swartz, Note, *Trial Participant Speech Restrictions: Gagging First Amendment Rights*, 90 Colum. L. Rev. 1411, 1429–30 (1990); *but see* In re Dow Jones & Co., 842 F.2d 603, 609 (2d Cir.), cert. denied, 488 U.S. 946, 109 S.Ct. 377, 102 L.Ed.2d 365 (1988) (no prior restraint from no comment rule); Radio & Television News Association v. United States District Court, 781 F.2d 1443, 1447 (9th Cir.1986)(same); KPNX Broadcasting Co. v. Superior Court, 139 Ariz. 246, 254, 678 P.2d 431, 439 (1984) (same); Florida Freedom Newspapers v. McCrary, 520 So.2d 32, 35–36 (Fla.1988)(same). The latter cases involved news media challenges to no comment orders formally directed not to the media but to trial participants.

18. *See* Chicago Council of Lawyers v. Bauer, 522 F.2d 242, 249–50 (7th Cir.1975) cert. denied, *sub nom.* Cunningham v. Chicago Council of Lawyers, 427 U.S. 912, 96 S.Ct. 3201, 49 L.Ed.2d 1204 (1976); Levine v. United States Dist. Ct., 764 F.2d 590, 599 (9th Cir.1985), cert. denied, 476 U.S. 1158, 106 S.Ct. 2276, 90 L.Ed.2d 719 (1986); Laurence H. Tribe, American Constitutional Law 860 (2d Ed. 1988).

19. *See, e.g.,* United States v. Cutler, 58 F.3d 825, 834 (2d Cir.1995); In re Dow Jones & Co., 842 F.2d 603, 610 (2d Cir.), cert. denied 488 U.S. 946, 109 S.Ct. 377, 102 L.Ed.2d 365 (1988); Hirschkop v. Snead, 594 F.2d 356, 369 (4th Cir.1979); *see also* United States v. Tijerina, 412 F.2d 661, 667 (10th Cir.), cert. denied 396 U.S. 990, 90 S.Ct. 478, 24 L.Ed.2d 452 (1969) (maintenance "of atmosphere essential to the preservation of a fair trial" standard).

20. 384 U.S. 333, 363, 86 S.Ct. 1507, 1522, 16 L.Ed.2d 600, 620 (1966) ("'[w]here there is a reasonable likelihood that prejudicial news prior to trial will prevent a fair trial ... [t]he courts must take such steps by rule and regulation that will protect their processes from prejudicial outside interferences.")

21. AMERICAN BAR ASSOCIATION PROJECT ON STANDARDS FOR CRIMINAL JUSTICE STANDARDS RELATING TO FAIR TRIAL AND FREE PRESS § 1.1 (Approved Draft 1968). The ABA Model Code of Professional Responsibility (1981) utilizes this standard. See DR 7–107(D), (E). The ABA Model Rules of Professional Conduct (1987) use a slightly different formulation which may or may not be substantively different, *i.e.,* "substantial likelihood of materially prejudicing an adjudicative proceeding." Rule 3.6(a). *See* Matter of Sullivan, 185 A.D.2d 440, 444–445, 586 N.Y.S.2d 322, 326 (1992) which employs essentially the language of Rule 3.6(a) while adjudicating the case under DR 7–107.

22. *Compare, e.g.,* CBS v. Young, 522 F.2d 234 (6th Cir.1975)(clear and present danger standard applied; no comment order vacated); Chicago Council of Lawyers v. Bauer, 522 F.2d 242 (7th Cir.1975), *cert. denied sub nom.* Cunningham v. Chicago Council of Lawyers, 427 U.S. 912, 96 S.Ct. 3201, 49 L.Ed.2d 1204 (1976) (serious and imminent threat applied; declaratory and injunctive relief ordered to prevent enforcement of local no comment rule and ABA disciplinary rule); Markfield v. Association of the Bar of the City of New York, 49 A.D.2d 516, 370 N.Y.S.2d 82 (1975), *appeal dismissed*, 37 N.Y.2d 794, 375 N.Y.S.2d 106, 337 N.E.2d 612 (1975) ("clear and present danger" standard applied; order of bar association sanctioning attorney vacated); *In re* Lasswell, 296 Or. 121, 673 P.2d 855 (1983)("highly probable serious prejudice" standard applied; attorney found not guilty of violation of state bar disciplinary rule DR 7–107(B)) *with* United States v. Cutler, 58 F.3d 825 (2d Cir.1995) (reasonable likelihood of interference with a fair trial or administration of Justice); *In re* Dow Jones & Co., 842 F.2d 603 (2d Cir.), cert. denied, 488 U.S. 946, 109 S.Ct. 377,

lower standard may be criticized as infringing on the First Amendment rights of trial participants and, derivatively, newsgatherers attempting to inform the public about pending trials, a semantic variation of it has recently been upheld by the Supreme Court. In *Gentile v. State Bar of Nevada*[23] the petitioner, a member of the Nevada Bar, held a press conference just hours after his client was indicted for theft of illegal drugs and travelers' checks worth hundreds of thousands of dollars from a safety deposit box at a private vault company. The box was being used by the Las Vegas Metropolitan Police Department in an undercover operation. The petitioner's client was the owner of the safety deposit company, and while he may have had access to the police safety deposit box so too did two police officers. The police "cleared" the two officers and thereafter the vault owner was indicted.

In the press conference, which took place six months prior to trial, the accused's defense counsel in opening remarks asserted the innocence of his client, the guilt of one of the two police officers, the complicity of the police department in a coverup of the truth about the theft and the lack of credibility of a number of potential witnesses against his client. During questioning from the audience on the credibility of potential witnesses defense counsel was asked to elaborate on their backgrounds and interests in the case. He declined to do so saying, "I can't because ethics prohibit me from doing so."[24]

But counsel's understanding of the reach Nevada Supreme Court Rule 177, patterned closely after ABA Model Rule 3.6,[25] was different than that of the state bar and the Nevada Supreme Court. Those two bodies found that counsel knew or should have known that there was "a substantial likelihood that his statements would materially prejudice the trial of his client" and approved a private reprimand for his press conference remarks.[26] The standard for sanctioning counsel was taken from Rule 177.

102 L.Ed.2d 365 (1988) ("reasonable likelihood" of prejudice standard applied; pretrial judicial no comment order upheld); United States v. Tijerina, 412 F.2d 661 (10th Cir.), cert. denied, 396 U.S. 990, 90 S.Ct. 478, 24 L.Ed.2d 452 (1969) (maintenance of "atmosphere essential to the preservation of a fair trial" standard applied; criminal contempt conviction for violation of no comment order upheld). *See also* Gentile v. State Bar of Nevada, 501 U.S. 1030, 111 S.Ct. 2720, 115 L.Ed.2d 888 (1991); Michael E. Swartz, Note, *Trial Participant Speech Restrictions: Gagging First Amendment Rights*, 90 Colum. L. Rev. 1411, 1414–15 (1990).

23. 501 U.S. 1030, 111 S.Ct. 2720, 115 L.Ed.2d 888 (1991).

24. *Id.* at 1049, 111 S. Ct. at 2731, 115 L. Ed. 2d at 907. His full response to the question was: "I can't because ethics prohibit me from doing so."

"Last night before I decided I was going to make a statement, I took a close look at the rules of professional responsibility. There are things that I can say and there are things that I can't. Okay?"

"I can't name which of the people have the drug backgrounds. I'm sure you guys can find that by doing just a little bit of investigative work." *Id.*

25. *See* n.13, *supra.* The Nevada rule is set out in full text as Appendix B to the opinion of Kennedy, J., 501 U.S. at 1060, 111 S. Ct. at 2737–38, 115 L. Ed. 2d at 914–15.

26. *Id.* at 1062, 111 S. Ct. at 2738, 115 L. Ed. 2d at 914–15; *see also* 106 Nev. 60, 62–63, 787 P.2d 386, 387 (1990).

In seeking relief from the discipline imposed at the state level, counsel contended in the Supreme Court that the First Amendment required application of a higher standard before speech by an attorney may be punished. He argued that these must be a finding of "actual prejudice or a substantial and imminent threat to fair trial,"[27] in other words a standard more closely akin to "clear and present danger."

A majority of the Court rejected this argument and held, despite the political nature of the defense counsel's remarks at the press conference, that the "substantial likelihood of material prejudice" standard applied by Nevada and most other states passed constitutional muster and provided sufficient protection to the speech interests of lawyers involved in judicial proceedings.[28] The Court added that "the speech of lawyers representing clients in pending cases may be regulated under a less demanding standard than that established for regulation of the press...."[29]

However, a different majority reversed the judgment of the Nevada Supreme Court thereby setting aside the disciplinary action. This majority found the Nevada Supreme Court rule void for vagueness. In their view section 3 of the rule which permits counsel to communicate publicly certain facts about pending cases without elaboration was too vague to provide adequate guidance and misled counsel who had, in good faith attempted to stay within its bounds.[30]

What *Gentile* means is that some regulation of attorney speech is constitutional. The states in regulating such expression may, if they wish, use a relatively low standard of speech protection, thereby decreasing substantially the amount of information concerning trial proceedings that can safely be made available to the press and public.

3. Legal Standing of the Media to Challenge "No Comment" Orders and Rules

Whatever the standard or standards chosen to suppress public communication by lawyers and other trial participants, the legal issue of greatest concern to the news media here is whether they have standing to challenge inappropriate and overbroad application of these no comment orders and rules, particularly when those directly bound may not be in a position to question them. While there is an early and ill-considered United States District Court decision denying standing to plaintiff newspersons and journalism organizations to question no comment orders because the court could find no harm to the plaintiffs from such orders,[31] the overwhelming position of both federal and state

---

27. 501 U.S. at 1063, 111 S. Ct. at 2738, 115 L. Ed. 2d at 914–15.

28. *Id.*

29. *Id.* at 1074, 111 S. Ct. at 2744, 115 L. Ed. 2d at 922–23; *see* Nebraska Press Association v. Stuart, 427 U.S. 539, 96 S.Ct. 2791, 49 L.Ed.2d 683 (1976).

30. 501 U.S. at 1048–52, 111 S. Ct. at 2731–32, 115 L. Ed. 2d at 906–08.

31. *See* Central South Carolina Chapter, Society of Professional Journalists, Sigma Delta Chi v. Martin, 431 F.Supp. 1182 (D.S.C.), *aff'd in part, criticized in part*, 556 F.2d 706 (4th Cir.1977), cert. denied, 434 U.S. 1022, 98 S.Ct. 749, 54 L.Ed.2d 771

appellate courts is that news persons and organizations do have legal standing in such matters.[32]

The most compelling analysis supporting standing is provided by the United States Court of Appeals for the Second Circuit in *In re Dow Jones & Co., Inc.*[33] Though rejecting on the merits the contention of several news organizations that a district court's no comment order directed to prosecutors, defendants and defense counsel in the Wedtech public fraud prosecutions was a prior restraint on the press, the Second Circuit held that the news media had a First Amendment right to receive speech communications from willing speakers. Their standing to sue could be upheld based on the claim that no comment orders infringe on that right by preventing the news media from receiving speech communications from otherwise willing counsel and other trial participants.[34] After citing a number of Supreme Court precedents in support,[35] the appeals court said, "Throughout all these cases the First Amendment unwaveringly protects the right to receive information and ideas. A challenge by news agencies must certainly be permitted when the restrained speech, as here, concerns allegations of corruption by public officials in obtaining federal contracts."[36] Because it held that the news organizations had standing as recipients of speech to appeal the district court's no comment order, the Second Circuit found it unnecessary to address the

---

(1978) (trial judge's opinion considering news media challenge to his own no comment order).

32. *See In re* Dow Jones & Co., Inc., 842 F.2d 603, 606–08 (2d Cir.1988), cert. denied 488 U.S. 946, 109 S.Ct. 377, 102 L.Ed.2d 365 (1988); CBS, Inc. v. Young, 522 F.2d 234, 237–38 (6th Cir.1975); Radio & Television News Association v. United States Dist. Ct., 781 F.2d 1443, 1445–46 (9th Cir. 1986); Journal Pub. Co. v. Mechem, 801 F.2d 1233, 1235 (10th Cir.1986); *In re* Subpoena to Testify Before Grand Jury, 864 F.2d 1559, 1561 (11th Cir.1989) (challenge by several newspaper companies and journalism organizations of a grand jury no comment order); KPNX Broadcasting Co. v. Superior Court, 139 Ariz. 246, 254–57, 678 P.2d 431, 439–42 (1984) (by necessary implication from court's decision on merits of broadcaster's petition); Florida Freedom Newspapers, Inc. v. McCrary, 520 So.2d 32, 35–36 (Fla.1988) (by necessary implication from court's decision on merits of newspaper company's petition); National Broadcasting Co., Inc. v. Cooperman, 116 A.D.2d 287, 289, 501 N.Y.S.2d 405, 406 (1986).

33. 842 F.2d 603, 606–08 (2d Cir.1988), cert. denied 488 U.S. 946, 109 S.Ct. 377, 102 L.Ed.2d 365 (1988).

34. *Id.* at 607–08.

35. The Second Circuit cited the following Supreme Court decisions to support the proposition that the First Amendment protects the right of an audience to receive the willing speech of others and that members of the audience may assert that right in court: Virginia State Bd. of Pharmacy v. Virginia Citizens Consumer Council, Inc., 425 U.S. 748, 96 S.Ct. 1817, 48 L.Ed.2d 346 (1976)(holding that consumers of prescription drugs have standing to challenge state restrictions on drug price advertising); Procunier v. Martinez, 416 U.S. 396, 94 S.Ct. 1800, 40 L.Ed.2d 224 (1974) (holding that censorship of prisoners' mail violates rights of non-inmate addresses); Kleindienst v. Mandel, 408 U.S. 753, 92 S.Ct. 2576, 33 L.Ed.2d 683 (1972) (stating that American scholars have the theoretical right to hear and debate alien Marxist theoretician having no personal right to enter the country) (dictum); Red Lion Broadcasting Co. v. FCC, 395 U.S. 367, 89 S.Ct. 1794, 23 L.Ed.2d 371 (1969) (holding that public has a First Amendment right to receive speech communication through broadcasting media); Stanley v. Georgia, 394 U.S. 557, 89 S.Ct. 1243, 22 L.Ed.2d 542 (1969) (holding that the right to receive information extends to possession of obscene materials in one's own home); Lamont v. Postmaster General, 381 U.S. 301, 85 S.Ct. 1493, 14 L.Ed.2d 398 (1965)(holding that public has First Amendment right to receive communist political publications from abroad).

36. *In re* Dow Jones & Co., Inc., 842 F.2d at 607.

alternative question whether the applicants' status as newsgatherers also afforded them standing.[37] Standing of the news media would have been even clearer here if the court had held that no comment rules worked a prior restraint on the press, but, as noted earlier, it rejected such claim.[38]

B.   *Limiting Access of the News Media to Trial Proceedings*

Following the Supreme Court's decision in *Nebraska Press Association v. Stuart*,[39] which made it extraordinarily difficult for trial judges to enjoin the news media from publishing information concerning pending criminal trials, a number of courts attempted to avoid that ruling by simply closing their doors to the press.[40] This effort flew in the face of more than two hundred years of American judicial history and tradition of open trials.[41] But within a relatively short time of the commencement of this court-closing movement, Chief Justice Burger, recognizing its dangerous nature, stated in a plurality opinion in *Richmond Newspapers, Inc. v. Virginia*,[42] that the First Amendment prohibited the closing of courtrooms in criminal cases absent an overriding governmental interest articulated in specific findings of the trial judge.[43] "We hold that the right to attend criminal trials is implicit in the guarantees of the First Amendment; without the freedom to attend such trials, which people have exercised for centuries, important aspects of freedom of speech and 'of the press could be eviscerated.' "[44] The Chief Justice left largely unarticulated the circumstances in which all or parts of a

37. *Id.* at 608.

38. *Id.* at 608–609. *See* Sheryl A. Bjork, Comment, *Indirect Gag Orders and the Doctrine of Prior Restraint*, 44 U. Miami L. Rev. 165 (1989) for a persuasive argument in favor of treating no comment orders and rules as prior restraints of the news media and therefore subject to a much higher level of constitutional scrutiny in the course of legal challenges brought by newsgatherers.

39. 427 U.S. 539, 96 S.Ct. 2791, 49 L.Ed.2d 683 (1976). *See* section 8.7B, *infra*, pp. 301–304.

40. *See, e.g.*, Martineau v. Perrin, 601 F.2d 1196 (1st Cir.1979); Detroit Free Press, Inc. v. Recorder's Court Judge, 409 Mich. 364, 294 N.W.2d 827 (1980)(order closing trial reversed on appeal; newspaper held to have standing to appeal closure order); State v. Lane, 60 Ohio St.2d 112, 397 N.E.2d 1338, 14 O.O.3d 342 (1979); Cumbee v. Commonwealth, 219 Va. 1132, 254 S.E.2d 112 (1979)(conviction obtained in closed trial reversed on appeal).

41. *See In re* Oliver, 333 U.S. 257, 266, 68 S.Ct. 499, 504, 92 L.Ed. 682, 690 (1948); Richmond Newspapers, Inc. v. Virginia 448 U.S. 555, 564–69, 100 S.Ct. 2814, 2820–23, 65 L.Ed.2d 973, 981–85 (1980).

42. 448 U.S. 555, 100 S.Ct. 2814, 65 L.Ed.2d 973 (1980). While Chief Justice Burger's opinion speaks only for himself and Justices White and Stevens, the opinion of Justice Brennan joined in by Justice Marshall has much in common with it and therefore the Chief Justice's opinion has been generally accepted as authoritative.

43. *Id.* at 579–81, 100 S. Ct. at 2828–30, 65 L. Ed. 2d at 991–92. One year earlier a Court majority in Gannett Co., Inc. v. DePasquale, 443 U.S. 368, 99 S.Ct. 2898, 61 L.Ed.2d 608 (1979) had held that the Sixth Amendment guarantee of a public trial was for the benefit of the accused alone and provided no access of the public and press to criminal pretrial proceedings. Such might also have been said for trial proceedings that follow. The opinion in the case by Justice Stewart, being almost unfathomable and having been bypassed for all intents and purposes by *Richmond Newspapers*, will be referred to in this work as little as possible in order to avoid unnecessary confusion.

44. Richmond Newspapers, Inc., 448 U.S. at 580, 100 S. Ct. at 2829, 65 L. Ed. 2d at 991–92 (quoting in part Branzburg v. Hayes, 408 U.S. 665, 681, 92 S.Ct. 2646, 2656–57, 33 L.Ed.2d 626, 639 (1972)).

criminal trial might be closed to the public,[45] but did require a finding of unavailability of reasonable alternative means to avoid prejudicial publicity.[46]

This barrier to trial closure extends even to the most sensitive sex crime prosecutions. In *Globe Newspaper Co. v. Superior Court*,[47] the state of Massachusetts closed a rape trial involving minor victims because of a statute requiring that trials be closed without exception when juvenile victims of specified sexual assaults are on the stand. The Supreme Court struck down the statute as violative of the First Amendment right of the press and public to have access to criminal trials. While the constitutional prohibition on closed trials is not absolute, the Court held that closures must be justified by a showing that they are necessitated by a compelling government interest and narrowly tailored to serve such interest.[48] Massachusetts mandatory trial closing statute did not permit consideration of whether closure served a significant government interest in particular cases.[49] In other words, the government must make a strong factual showing of its compelling interest in each case and demonstrate that exclusion of the press and public in the particular case is as narrow as possible in achieving its ends. These showings must, of course, be reflected in the trial court's findings. And news media have standing to dispute such showings and any closure orders based upon them.[50] With such standing newsgatherers must be accorded due process to assert their interests particularly regarding notice of closure and the opportunity to be heard in opposition to exclusion from the courtroom.[51]

Left unmentioned by the Supreme Court in its trial access decisions is the question whether there is any right of press and public access to civil proceedings or whether they may be closed without constitutional concern. In *State v. Cottman Transmission Systems, Inc.*,[52] the Maryland Court of Special Appeals held in a civil case in which the Baltimore Sun Newspapers had intervened that the trial court had no authority to exclude the press and public from a hearing at which testimony would be taken on the merits of the state's motion for an interlocutory injunction

---

45. *Id.* at 581 n.18, 100 S. Ct. at 2830 n.18, 65 L. Ed. 2d at 992–93 n.18.

46. *Id.* at 580–81, 100 S. Ct. at 2829–30, 65 L. Ed. 2d at 991–92.

47. 457 U.S. 596, 102 S.Ct. 2613, 73 L.Ed.2d 248 (1982).

48. *Id.* at 607, 102 S. Ct. at 2620, 73 L. Ed. 2d at 257.

49. *Id.* at 607–09, 102 S. Ct. at 2620–22, 73 L. Ed. 2d at 257–59. *See also* Renkel v. State, 807 P.2d 1087 (Alaska App.1991); Pritchett v. State, 566 So.2d 6 (Fla.Dist.Ct. App.1990).

50. This is evident from the Court's decisions on the merits of the closings in *Richmond Newspapers, Inc.* and *Globe Newspaper Co.*

51. *See, e.g.,* Globe Newspaper Co., 457 U.S. at 609 n.25, 102 S. Ct. at 2621 n.25, 73

L. Ed. 2d at 259 n.25; United States v. Raffoul, 826 F.2d 218, 221–25 (3d Cir.1987); Gannett River States Pub. Co. v. Hand, 571 So.2d 941, 944–45 (Miss.1990). The United States Court of Appeals for the Third Circuit has given considerable thought to the procedures that should be employed in giving notice to newsgatherers inside and outside the courtroom when closure is contemplated in both trial and pretrial proceedings and the procedures that should be followed in according newsgatherers the opportunity to respond. *See* United States v. Raffoul, 826 F.2d at 221–25 (trial closure) and United States v. Criden, 675 F.2d 550, 557–60 (3d Cir.1982) (pretrial hearing closure).

52. 75 Md.App. 647, 542 A.2d 859 (1988).

barring the defendant automobile repair company from engaging in allegedly unfair and deceptive trade practices. The Maryland court based its holding primarily on dictum in *Richmond Newspapers, Inc. v. Virginia*[53] and holdings in seven United States Court of Appeals decisions that both the common law and the First Amendment granted access of the press and public to civil proceedings, making no distinction between evidentiary materials, transcripts pretrial hearings and the trials themselves.[54]

The *Cottman* case is significant because it involved closure of an evidentiary proceeding akin to a trial. It is also significant for its ringing declaration of access of the press and public to nearly all aspects of the judicial system. "To close a court to public scrutiny of the proceedings is to shut off the light of the law. How else will the citizenry learn of the happenings in the courts—their government's third branch—except through access to the courts by the people themselves or through reports supplied by the media?"[55] Finally, the decision is significant because it presents a persuasive case for the proposition that the constitutional standards involved in closure in civil trials are the same as for criminal trials—the presence of a compelling governmental interest in closure in each case which is furthered by a narrowly tailored order.[56] It rejected protection of civil litigants from harm to professional or corporate reputation as such an interest.[57] When a trial judge believes a compelling government interest is present to justify closure, he must, as in criminal cases, insure that fair notice of any contemplated closure is given to the press and public and afford an opportunity to those opposing closure to be heard.[58]

Given both the substantive constitutional obstacles and the procedural requirements for closing both criminal and civil trials, such closure is an unlikely device for avoiding the risks to fair trial posed by news coverage.

53. 448 U.S. 555, 580 n. 17, 100 S.Ct. 2814, 2829 n. 17, 65 L.Ed.2d 973, 992 n. 17 (1980).

54. Federal Trade Commission v. Standard Financial Management Corp., 830 F.2d 404 (1st Cir.1987) (access to sworn personal financial statements); Joy v. North, 692 F.2d 880 (2d Cir.1982)(access to report of special litigation committee); Publicker Industries v. Cohen, 733 F.2d 1059 (3d Cir.1984)(access to hearing on motion for preliminary injunction and transcripts of proceedings); Rushford v. The New Yorker Magazine, 846 F.2d 249 (4th Cir.1988) (access to pleadings and documents accompanying motion for summary judgement); Brown & Williamson Tobacco Corp. v. Federal Trade Commission, 710 F.2d 1165 (6th Cir.1983) (access to documents); In re Continental Illinois Securities Litigation, 732 F.2d 1302 (7th Cir.1984) (access to report of special litigation committee); Newman v. Graddick, 696 F.2d 796 (11th Cir.1983) (ac-

cess to judicial records and pretrial hearing); *but see* Minneapolis Star & Tribune Co. v. Schumacher, 392 N.W.2d 197 (Minn. 1986)(no access to sealed documents and pretrial transcripts under common law standard of abuse of trial court discretion and no access to such materials under First Amendment).

55. State v. Cottman Transmission Systems, Inc., 75 Md. App. at 657–59, 542 A.2d at 864.

56. *Id.* at 656, 542 A.2d at 863.

57. *See* Brown & Williamson Tobacco Corp. v. Federal Trade Commission, 710 F.2d 1165, 1179 (6th Cir.1983); State v. Cottman Transmission Systems, Inc., 75 Md. App. at 657–59, 542 A.2d at 864.

58. *See* Rushford v. New Yorker Magazine, Inc., 846 F.2d 249, 253–54 (4th Cir. 1988); Newman v. Graddick, 696 F.2d 796, 803–04 (11th Cir.1983).

C. Limiting Access of the News Media to Voir Dire, Pretrial Proceedings, Trial Transcripts, Court Records, Tapes, Documents and Other Evidence

While extensive trial closure is very difficult to justify historically and constitutionally, trial courts are more likely to close pretrial proceedings and seal documents, transcripts and specific evidentiary materials. Even resorting to these more limited devices, trial courts may still face substantial common law and constitutional difficulties.

1. Pretrial Proceedings

In *Waller v. Georgia*[59] the Supreme Court, in a state racketeering prosecution, held that accuseds' Sixth Amendment right to a public trial extended to pretrial evidence suppression hearings. The Court ruled that such hearings could not be closed at the request of the prosecution over the objection of defendants unless it could be shown that the government has an overriding interest in closure; that the closure is no broader than necessary to protect that interest and that reasonable alternatives to closure have been considered and found unavailing.[60] The trial court must make and place on the record specific findings as to these requirements.[61] While the Court did not address the question whether the press and public had a First Amendment right of access to criminal pretrial proceedings, its reliance on *Richmond Newspapers, Inc.* and *Globe Newspaper Co.* in reaching its decision strongly suggested the existence of such right.

Shortly after *Waller*, in *Press-Enterprise Co. v. Superior Court II*,[62] the Court confirmed that a First Amendment right of access to criminal pretrial proceedings did exist. In that case a California court had, at the request of the accused, closed a preliminary hearing on the state's complaint that the accused, a nurse, had murdered 12 patients by administering lethal doses of drugs to them. Thereafter, a newspaper company sought a writ of mandate directing the trial court to release the transcript of the hearing. The California Supreme Court denied the writ, holding that there was no general First Amendment right of access to preliminary hearings. The California court was concerned about the generation of pretrial publicity that would attend an open hearing and which might prejudice potential jurors.[63]

The United States Supreme Court ruled otherwise on First Amendment access to California preliminary hearings based upon a history of public access to such proceedings and their institutional importance in the criminal justice process.[64] The Court then held that to overcome the press and public's qualified constitutional right of access, it must be

---

59. 467 U.S. 39, 104 S.Ct. 2210, 81 L.Ed.2d 31 (1984).

60. 467 U.S. at 45, 104 S. Ct. at 2214–15, 81 L. Ed. 2d at 37–38.

61. *Id.*

62. 478 U.S. 1, 106 S.Ct. 2735, 92 L.Ed.2d 1 (1986).

63. *Id.* at 5, 106 S. Ct. at 2738, 92 L. Ed. 2d at 8.

64. The Court pointed out that the preliminary hearing is often the final step in a given criminal proceeding. *Id.* at 12, 106 S. Ct. at 2742, 92 L. Ed.2d at 12.

found specifically on the record that closure is essential to preserve "higher values" and that the closure order is narrowly tailored to achieve this.[65] When the interest asserted is the right of the accused to a fair trial, the preliminary hearing can be closed only if specific findings are made demonstrating that, first, there is a substantial probability that the defendant's right to a fair trial will be prejudiced by publicity that court closure would prevent and, second, reasonable alternatives to closure cannot adequately protect the accused's right to a fair trial.[66] Of course, members of the news media, by clear implication, have standing to challenge closing of pretrial proceedings.

By parity of reasoning, the First Amendment right of access extends to all other criminal pretrial proceedings that have been historically open to the public and play an important part in the criminal justice system. A number of lower courts have so held.[67] Constitutional protection for access is also recognized with regard to civil pretrial proceedings.[68]

2. Voir Dire

Prior to its ruling in *Press-Enterprise Co. II*, regarding access to a pretrial proceeding, the Supreme Court in *Press Enterprise Co. I*,[69] a case excluding the press from a nearly six-week-long voir dire proceeding to select jurors to decide a notorious rape-murder prosecution involving a 13–year-old victim, held that the First Amendment extended to the questioning of prospective jurors as well as to the trial itself. In a unanimous opinion, the court found that jury selection was historically held in public and that open selection was important to the criminal justice system because it assures society that criminal trials will be conducted fairly.[70] The standard to be met for closing voir dire to the press and public are essentially the same as for the closing of pretrial proceedings and the trials themselves. Voir dire is to be open unless it can be specifically found by the trial court that there is a compelling governmental interest presented under the facts of the case such as protection of fair trial or juror privacy; that the closure is no broader or longer than absolutely necessary to protect that interest; and that

---

65. *Id.* at 13–14, 106 S. Ct. at 2742–43, 92 L. Ed. 2d at 13–14.

66. *Id.* at 14, 106 S. Ct. at 2743, 92 L. Ed. 2d at 13–14. *See, e.g.,* Rockdale Citizen Pub. Co. v. Georgia, 266 Ga. 92, 93–94, 463 S.E.2d 864, 866, (1995).

67. *See, e.g., In re* Washington Post Co., 807 F.2d 383, 388–89 (4th Cir.1986)(plea hearing); Baltimore Sun v. Colbert, 323 Md. 290, 217–300, 593 A.2d 224, 227–28 (1991) (hearing on pretrial motion to enforce plea bargain agreement); State ex rel. The Repository v. Unger, 28 Ohio St.3d 418, 420–21, 504 N.E.2d 37, 40 (1986) (pretrial hearing and videotape deposition); Associated Press v. Bell, 70 N.Y.2d 32, 37–38, 517 N.Y.S.2d 444, 447, 510 N.E.2d 313, 316

(1987) (suppression hearing); State v. Schaefer, 157 Vt. 339, 344–46, 599 A.2d 337, 341–42 (1991) (suppression hearing).

68. *See, e.g.,* Publicker Industries v. Cohen, 733 F.2d 1059 (3d Cir.1984); Grove Fresh Distrib., Inc. v. Everfresh Juice Co., 24 F.3d 893 (7th Cir.1994); Newman v. Graddick, 696 F.2d 796 (11th Cir.1983); State v. Cottman Transmission Systems, Inc., 75 Md.App. 647, 542 A.2d 859 (1988).

69. Press–Enterprise Co. v. Superior Court, 464 U.S. 501, 104 S.Ct. 819, 78 L.Ed.2d 629 (1984).

70. *Id.* at 506–10, 104 S. Ct. at 822–24, 78 L. Ed. 2d at 635–39.

reasonable alternatives have been considered and found unavailing.[71] In assessing whether the interest in a fair trial is compelling enough in a given case, the test to be applied is whether there is a substantial probability of prejudice if the particular proceeding is not closed.[72]

3.   Court Records, Documents, Tapes, Hearing Transcripts and Exhibits

Press-Enterprise Co. II also involved the sealing of the transcript of the preliminary hearing. As to the transcript as well as the closure, the Court held that a First Amendment right of access attached and required specific findings that a substantial probability of prejudice to a fair trial existed and reasonable alternatives to protect against prejudice were unavailable before the hearing transcript could be sealed.[73] On the fair extension of *Press-Enterprise Co. II*, alone, sealed court transcripts records, documents, tapes and exhibits would seem to be subject to public access.[74]

In addition, analogizing to *Richmond Newspapers, Inc. v. Virginia*,[75] it would seem that, if historically the public and press were allowed access to particular judicial material and the material is important to the operation of the criminal justice system and the public's confidence in that system, access should follow unless the same high constitutional standards associated with judicial closures are met.

Historically, the common law allowed the public to inspect and copy judicial records and materials in the discretion of the trial judge.[76] This should provide the historical foundation justifying access to most materi-

71. *Id.* at 509–13, 104 S. Ct. at 823–26 78 L. Ed. 2d at 637–40; *see In re* South Carolina Press Association, 946 F.2d 1037, 1040–44 (4th Cir.1991) (press access to voir dire denied because of compelling governmental interest and absence of reasonable alternatives to closure); Providence Journal Co. v. Superior Court 593 A.2d 446, 448 (R.I.1991); *see also* In re Gannett River States Pub. Corp., 630 So.2d 351, 352 (Miss. 1994) (access of media to voir dire based on state common law standards); State *ex rel.* Storer Broadcasting Co. v. Gorenstein, 131 Wis.2d 342, 388 N.W.2d 633 (Wis.App.1986) (access of media to voir dire based on state statutory standards).

72. *See In re* South Carolina Press Association, 946 F.2d 1037, 1041 (4th Cir.1991); Associated Press v. Bell, 70 N.Y.2d 32, 38, 517 N.Y.S.2d 444, 447–48, 510 N.E.2d 313, 316–17 (1987); State v. Schaefer, 157 Vt. 339, 347–49, 599 A.2d 337, 343 (1991); *cf.* Press–Enterprise Co. v. Superior Court, 478 U.S. 1, 14, 106 S.Ct. 2735, 2743, 92 L.Ed.2d 1, 13–14 (1986) (standard for voir dire).

73. Press–Enterprise Co. v. Superior Court II, 478 U.S. 1, 13–14, 106 S.Ct. 2735, 2742–43, 92 L.Ed.2d 1, 13–14 (1986).

74. *See, e.g.*, United States v. Haller, 837 F.2d 84, 87 (2d Cir.1988) (plea agreement access); *In re* State–Record Co., 917 F.2d 124, 127–28 (4th Cir.1990) (access to court documents); Oregonian Pub. Co. v. United States Dist. Ct., 920 F.2d 1462, 1465–66 (9th Cir.1990) (access to plea agreement and related documents); United States v. Poindexter, 732 F.Supp. 165, 167–70 (D.D.C.1990) (denial of access to deposition taking of former President Reagan); Russell v. Miami Herald Pub. Co., 570 So.2d 979, 982–83 (Fla.Dist.Ct.App.1990) (access to criminal records); State v. Schaefer, 157 Vt. 339, 347–49, 599 A.2d 337, 343 (1991) (access to affidavits of probable cause).

75. 448 U.S. 555, 100 S.Ct. 2814, 65 L.Ed.2d 973 (1980).

76. *See* Nixon v. Warner Communications, Inc., 435 U.S. 589, 597–99, 98 S.Ct. 1306, 1311–13, 55 L.Ed.2d 570, 579–80 (1978); Globe Newspaper Co. v. Pokaski, 868 F.2d 497, 503–05 (1st Cir.1989); Baltimore Sun Co. v. Colbert, 323 Md. 290, 305, 593 A.2d 224, 231 (1991).

al, and if it can be shown that the particular material sought for inspection is significant in the fair operation of the judicial system then access here should also follow.

A major caveat to First Amendment access to judicial materials arises out of the judiciary's discomfort with the copying by the news media and public of audio and video tapes under the control of the courts. This undoubtedly stems from the Supreme Court's decision in the *Nixon Tapes Case*.[77] There, the Court denied a media request to copy, broadcast and sell portions of audio tapes made by President Nixon which were played in open court during the Watergate prosecutions. The Court first held that the common law right of access was subject to the discretion of the trial judge, who initially refused access, *inter alia,* out of concern for the Watergate defendants' rights on appeal. The judge's discretion was held to have been properly exercised.[78]

The Court then ruled that there was no First Amendment right of access to the tapes accruing to the news media because the public never had *physical* access to them, and newsgatherers' had no greater right than that possessed by the public.[79] However, the public has a historic common law right to physical access to copy court-held documents and other materials whatever the form they are in, and a majority of justices in the later case of *Richmond Newspapers, Inc.* recognized that the historic right to access to criminal justice proceedings provides one of the two major pillars of a First Amendment right of access of both public and press. *Nixon* seems clearly inconsistent with the First Amendment thrust of *Richmond Newspapers, Inc.* though concededly that case involved access not to trial evidence but to the trial itself.

Nevertheless, there is now real doubt whether the courts, perhaps because of fear of pretrial publicity, or of the impact on personal privacy of mass dissemination of the voices and images of the parties involved in sensational trials or the unseemliness of the commercialization of evidence, will ever extend copy access to tapes presented at trial, particular-

77. Nixon v. Warner Communications, Inc., 435 U.S. 589, 98 S.Ct. 1306, 55 L.Ed.2d 570 (1978).

78. *Id.* at 602–08, 98 S. Ct. at 1314–17, 55 L. Ed. 2d at 582–86.

79. *Id.* at 609–10, 98 S. Ct. at 1317–19, 55 L. Ed. 2d at 586–88. Justice Powell's rather simplistic reasoning on behalf of the Court is, in its entirety, the following:

"Thus the issue presented in this case is not whether the press must be permitted access to public information to which the public generally is guaranteed access, but whether these copies of the White House tapes—to which the public has never had *physical* access—must be made available for copying. Our decision in *Cox Broadcasting* simply is not applicable.

The First Amendment generally grants the press no right to information about a trial superior to that of the general public. 'Once beyond the confines of the courthouse, a news-gathering agency may publicize, within wide limits, what its representatives have heard and seen in the courtroom. But the line is drawn at the courthouse door; and within, a reporter's constitutional rights are no greater than those of any other member of the public.' *Estes v.Texas*, 381 U.S. 532, 589 (1965) (Harland, J. concurring). *Cf.* Saxbe v. Washington Post Co., 417 U.S. 843 (1974); Pell v. Procunier, 417 U.S. 817 (1974). *See also* Zemel v. Rusk, 381 U.S. 1, 16–17 (1965)." *Id.*

ly when, as in *Nixon*, transcripts of the tapes are made available to the public and press.[80]

D. Limiting Access to Post Verdict Proceedings and Materials and Jurors Following Their Discharge

1. Post Verdict Proceedings and Materials

The same constitutional reasoning that prevents closure of criminal and civil trials, pretrial hearings and voir dire examinations and the sealing of court records, transcripts, documents, tapes and exhibits except for the most compelling reasons would seem to apply to post-trial hearings and materials if they were historically accessible to the public and press and are significant in the fair administration of the criminal or civil justice systems. What little direct authority there is on this issue supports such conclusion.

In *CBS, Inc. v. United States District Court*,[81] the broadcast network sought access to sealed documents filed relative to a sentence reduction proceeding in a federal narcotics and tax evasion prosecution. The trial court denied the network's motion to unseal the documents and mandamus was sought. In granting the writ the United States Court of Appeals for the Ninth Circuit speaking through Judge (now Justice) Kennedy held that there was no principled basis to distinguish between post-trial documents and proceedings and pretrial matters in regard to closures and sealings. "The primary justification for access to criminal proceedings, first that criminal trials historically have been open to the press and to the public, and, second, that access to criminal trials plays a significant role in the functioning of the judicial process and the governmental system ... apply with as much force to post-conviction proceedings as to the trial itself."[82]

The Ninth Circuit's reasoning was followed by the Massachusetts Supreme Judicial Court in *Globe Newspaper Co. v. Commonwealth*[83] in which a trial judge closed a post conviction hearing held to investigate allegations of extraneous prejudicial influence on the jury. The Globe's motion to open the hearing was denied and on appeal the Massachusetts court, quoting now Justice Kennedy, held that formal post trial hearings may not be closed unless accepted constitutional standards are met justifying closure.[84]

Finally, in *United States v. Simone*,[85] another case involving a post-trial proceeding ordered to consider allegations of juror misconduct, the criminal defendant's motion to have the jurors examined *in camera* was denied as was a media motion to intervene and be given access to the

---

80. *See* United States v. Poindexter, 732 F.Supp. 173 (D.D.C.1990)(videotape deposition of former President Reagan prepared for use in trial of Iran–Contra figure not available for viewing and copying prior to trial though printed transcript made available).

81. 765 F.2d 823 (9th Cir.1985).

82. *Id.* at 825.

83. 407 Mass. 879, 556 N.E.2d 356 (1990).

84. *Id.* at 884 n.7, 556 N.E.2d at 360 n.7.

85. 14 F.3d 833 (3d Cir.1994).

hearing. The proceedings were then stayed by the United States Court of Appeals for the Third Circuit. After the stay was issued, the trial judge concluded that no further juror examination was needed and entered an order denying the defendant's motions for acquittal, new trial and arrest of judgement. At the same time the judge released a transcript of the proceedings with the jurors' names redacted.

In disapproving of the trial court's refusal to permit direct media access, a majority of the Third Circuit relied on the Supreme Court's policy prong in *Richmond Newspapers*. The appeals court concluded that "[p]ublic access to such proceedings helps provide the public with the assurance that the system is fair to all concerned."[86]

The appeals court majority rejected the argument of the United States that the district court's release of the redacted transcript met all access concerns under the First Amendment. "We do not doubt that the ten-day interval between the hearing and the release of the transcript had very little effect on the value of this information as news. But ... this argument unduly minimizes, if it does not entirely overlook, the value of 'openness' itself, a value that is threatened whenever immediate access to ongoing proceedings is denied."[87] Beyond the value itself of direct access, the court noted its practical importance. "[A] transcript is not the equivalent of presence at a proceeding; it does not reflect the numerous verbal and non-verbal cues that aid in the interpretation of meaning."[88]

2. Shielding Jurors From the News Media Following Discharge

The news media have rarely, if ever, claimed any common law or First Amendment right of access to jurors themselves during trial proceedings because such access would almost surely be viewed as jury tampering and lead to mistrials.[89] But because of the natural curiosity of the public regarding jury deliberations in major criminal cases, news-

---

86. *Id.* at 839.

87. *Id.* at 842.

88. *Id.*

89. One cable television network discovered this truth the hard way. During a criminal trial in Austin, Texas, Court TV caused a mistrial when one of its producers approached sitting jurors and told them that she wished to talk to them after the trial. When her superiors at the network heard of the incident they quickly notified the presiding judge who then declared a mistrial. In his letter to the head of the network, the judge said, "a juror looking forward to either being interviewed on TV or being lambasted by another juror on TV might be less than candid during deliberations." The network voluntarily agreed to pay about $500 to cover the costs of the mistrial. *See* Howard Kurtz, *Media Notes: Lights, Camera, Mistrial*, Wash. Post, June 20, 1992, p. B1. *See also* Journal Pub. Co. v. Mechem, 801 F.2d 1233, 1236 (10th Cir.

1986) ("[T]he threat to justice caused by news media contact with jurors is much lower after trial than it is during trial.... "). But obtaining access to information about currently sitting jurors without actually making contact with them might be allowed in certain cases. *See* Times Pub. Co. v. Florida, 632 So.2d 1072 (Fla.Dist.Ct. App.1994). *And see* Abraham Abramovsky & Jonathan I. Edelstein, *Cameras In The Jury Room: An Unnecessary and Dangerous Precedent*, 28 Ariz. St. L. J. 865 (1996), discussing instances in which television cameras were allowed to film actual jury deliberations and arguing against such practice. "If jury deliberations are routinely recorded, any gain in accountability [to the public] is offset by the damage to free debate in the jury room, jury privacy, and the centuries-old tradition of jury deliberation secrecy." *Id.* at 892.

gatherers have often sought to question jurors following completion of trials and their discharge from jury service.

The efforts of trial judges to prevent post trial access to jurors must necessarily have a different rationale than closure and sealing orders entered before or during trial because such access poses no threat to an accused's fair trial rights under the Fifth and Sixth Amendments. The trial is over and though an appeal may be pending appellate judges are not likely to be influenced by extra-record statements of individual jurors. And while, on occasion, appellate courts order new trials, reporting about discussions and votes of former jurors are unlikely to have much if any impact on new jurors selected for the retrial. If there is any such impact, it can be neutralized by the same judicial devices employed to neutralize any other pretrial publicity.[90]

Rather, the rationale for orders directing jurors to refrain from talking to the news media and members of the news media to refrain from approaching jurors following trial must involve protection of the jury system generally from degradation of the freewheeling process of deliberation and decision-making in the jury room,[91] protection of jurors' privacy[92] and protection of jurors from harassment.[93] But while these are clearly legitimate interests, such "nonfraternization" orders are subject to scrutiny under First Amendment standards similar to those imposed in *Richmond Newspapers, Inc. v. Virginia*[94] and *Globe Newspaper Co. v. Superior Court*[95] for criminal trial closures[96] or constitutional standards akin to those applied in cases involving prior restraint of news and information dissemination if the orders are viewed as a direct restraint on newsgathering.[97]

90. *See* section 8.5, *supra*; *see also* United States v. Sherman, 581 F.2d 1358, 1361 (9th Cir.1978).

91. *See* Miller v. United States, 403 F.2d 77, 81–82 (2d Cir.1968); United States v. Doherty, 675 F.Supp. 719, 722 (D.Mass.1987)(semble); United States v. Antar, 839 F.Supp. 293, 295 (D.N.J.1993), *aff'd in part, rev'd in part* 38 F.3d 1348 (3d Cir.1994); United States v. Franklin, 546 F.Supp. 1133, 1139 (N.D.Ind.1982); State *ex rel.* Cincinnati Post v. Court of Common Pleas, 59 Ohio St.3d 103, 106–07, 570 N.E.2d 1101, 1104 (1991); Abraham S. Goldstein, *Jury Secrecy and the Media: The Problem of Post Verdict Interviews*, 1993 U. Ill. L. Rev. 295, 308–11 (article triggered by the flood of post verdict juror interviews in the Rodney King beating trial); Note, *Public Disclosures of Jury Deliberations*, 96 Harv. L. Rev. 886, 889–91 (1983).

92. *See* United States v. Harrelson, 713 F.2d 1114, 1118 (5th Cir.1983), cert. denied *sub nom.* El Paso Times, Inc. v. United States District Ct., 465 U.S. 1041, 104 S.Ct. 1318, 79 L.Ed.2d 714 (1984); United States v. Franklin, 546 F.Supp. 1133, 1142

(N.D.Ind.1982); *cf.* United States v. Gurney, 558 F.2d 1202, 1210 n. 12 (5th Cir.1977), cert. denied *sub nom.* Miami Herald Pub. Co. v. Krentzman, 435 U.S. 968, 98 S.Ct. 1606, 56 L.Ed.2d 59 (1978); Abraham S. Goldstein, *Jury Secrecy and the Media: The Problem of Post Verdict Interviews*, 1993 U. Ill. L. Rev. 295, 308–11.

93. *See, e.g., In re* Express—News Corp., 695 F.2d 807, 810 (5th Cir.1982); United States v. Sherman, 581 F.2d 1358, 1361 (9th Cir.1978); Journal Pub. Co. v. Mechem, 801 F.2d 1233, 1236 (10th Cir. 1986); State *ex rel.* Cincinnati Post v. Court of Common Pleas, 59 Ohio St.3d 103, 105, 570 N.E.2d 1101, 1103 (1991).

94. 448 U.S. 555, 100 S.Ct. 2814, 65 L.Ed.2d 973 (1980).

95. 457 U.S. 596, 102 S.Ct. 2613, 73 L.Ed.2d 248 (1982).

96. *See In re* Express—News Corp., 695 F.2d 807, 810 (5th Cir.1982); State *ex rel.* Cincinnati Post v. Court of Common Pleas, 59 Ohio St.3d 103, 105, 570 N.E.2d 1101, 1103 (1991); United States v. Doherty, 675 F.Supp. 719, 721–24 (D.Mass.1987).

An example of employment of the latter prior restraint standard is *United States v. Sherman*[98] in which the trial judge, following receipt of the verdict in a sensational prosecution for armed robbery committed by members of a revolutionary terrorist organization bent on the overthrow of the government, forbade the jurors from discussing the case with anyone and ordered everyone, including the news media, to stay away from the jurors.[99] The petition for a writ of mandamus filed by the Seattle Times Company under the federal All Writs Act[100] was granted by the United States Court of Appeals for the Ninth Circuit primarily on the basis that the order restrained the press prior to any attempt to contact the jurors involved and thereby gather information about their deliberations.

Viewing the order very much like a classic prior restraint of news and information *dissemination*, the court stated there was "a heavy presumption against its constitutional validity."[1] Amplifying on this, the appeals court held that the government had to establish that the newsgathering activity restrained posed a "clear and present danger or a serious and imminent threat to a protected competing interest" and that the restraint was both narrowly drawn and had the least impact on First Amendment freedoms of any reasonable alternative available.[2] Believing that the government had failed to meet its heavy burden, the court issued the writ requiring vacation of the order.

The reasoning and standards of *Sherman* were applied in *Journal Publishing Co. v. Mechem*[3] despite the fact that the trial judge's verbal order following the civil trial of a police brutality claim was directed to the jurors alone and not the news media.[4] The United States Court of Appeals viewed the instruction as if it were a prior restraint of the press and granted the newspaper's petition for writ of mandamus.

The heavy burden on the government to sustain the orders imposed in *Sherman* and *Journal Publishing Co.* seems questionable in light of precedent. These cases involve *access* to an aspect of criminal or civil trial proceedings and even when representatives of the news media are themselves included in post verdict orders, classic prior restraint of the press, *i.e.*, direct governmental interference with dissemination of news and information already obtained, is not involved.[5]

---

97. *See* United States v. Sherman, 581 F.2d 1358, 1361 (9th Cir.1978); Journal Pub. Co. v. Mechem, 801 F.2d 1233, 1236 (10th Cir.1986).

98. 581 F.2d 1358 (9th Cir.1978).

99. *Id.* at 1360.

100. 28 U.S.C.A. § 1651 (West 1966).

1. United States v. Sherman, 581 F.2d at 1361 (citing Bantam Books v. Sullivan, 372 U.S. 58, 70, 83 S.Ct. 631, 639, 9 L.Ed.2d 584, 593 (1963)).

2. *Id.*

3. 801 F.2d 1233 (10th Cir.1986).

4. The order stated, "You should not discuss your verdict after you leave here with anyone. If anyone tries to talk to you about it, or wants to talk to you about it let me know. If they wish [to] take the matter up with me, why, they may do so, but otherwise don't discuss it with anyone." *Id.* at 1235.

5. *Compare, e.g.*, Nebraska Press Association v. Stuart, 427 U.S. 539, 96 S.Ct. 2791, 49 L.Ed.2d 683 (1976); New York Times Co. v. United States, 403 U.S. 713, 91 S.Ct.

Mechem is especially doubtful because the "no discussion" order there was limited to the jurors involved. The effect on newsgathering was thus indirect and of the same nature as standing no comment court rules directed to counsel. In *Gentile v. State Bar*[6], which involved such rules, the Supreme Court approved the lesser standard for justifying indirect interference with newsgathering of "substantial likelihood of material prejudice."[7] The Court specifically rejected the idea that the "clear and present danger" test was required to be met under the First Amendment before no comment rules could be imposed on counsel prior to and during trials.[8] Since these standing court rules are designed in part to prevent prejudice to fair trials—an overarching concern of government—and since jury no comment orders do not have the same compelling goal, the *Gentile* approach would seem to apply with even more force to these post verdict orders.

Because it is access to aspects of trial proceedings, *i.e.*, jury deliberations and voting, that is really involved, the constitutional standards imposed in *Richmond Newspapers, Inc.* and *Globe Newspaper Co.* seem more appropriate. Such standards are reflected in *In re Express–News Corp.*[9] There the Fifth Circuit considered the district court's application of a local rule preventing anyone from interviewing jurors or their relatives, friends or associates except by leave of court upon the showing of good cause.[10] The Fifth Circuit followed *Globe Newspaper Co.* in holding the local rule was unconstitutional as applied because the government made no showing that a compelling governmental interest was being furthered by application of the rule and the application was not narrowly tailored but instead open-ended as to time and scope. "A court may not impose a restraint that sweeps so broadly and then require those who would speak freely to justify special treatment by carrying the burden of showing good cause. The first amendment right to gather news is 'good cause' enough. If that right is to be restricted, the government must carry the burden of demonstrating the need for curtailment."[11] The Fifth Circuit did not suggest that this demonstration entailed a clear and present danger to the administration of justice. The court expressed no view concerning the validity of a rule narrowly tailored to prevent the disclosure of the ballots of individual jurors, saying only, "That unrestrained post-verdict inquiry into every juror's

2140, 29 L.Ed.2d 822 (1971) ("Pentagon Papers" case); Bantam Books v. Sullivan, 372 U.S. 58, 83 S.Ct. 631, 9 L.Ed.2d 584 (1963); Near v. Minnesota *ex rel.* Olson, 283 U.S. 697, 51 S.Ct. 625, 75 L.Ed. 1357 (1931).

6. 501 U.S. 1030, 1060–1062, 111 S.Ct. 2720, 2738, 115 L.Ed.2d 888, 914–15 (1991).

7. *Id*. at 1069–1076, 111 S. Ct. at 2742–45, 115 L. Ed. 2d at 919–24.

8. *Id*. at 1074, 111 S. Ct. at 2744, 115 L. Ed. 2d at 923.

9. 695 F.2d 807 (5th Cir.1982).

10. Local Rule 500–2 of the Western District of Texas provided that no person

shall "interview ... any juror, relative, friend or associate thereof ... with respect to the deliberations or verdict of the jury in any action, except on leave of court granted upon good cause shown." *Id*. at 808.

11. *Id*. at 810; *see also* State *ex rel.* Cincinnati Post v. Court of Common Pleas, 59 Ohio St.3d 103, 105, 570 N.E.2d 1101, 1103 (1991). The Fifth Circuit now appears to have backpedaled from this tough stand against trial judges restraining post-trial interviews of jurors. *See* United States v. Cleveland, 128 F.3d 267 (5th Cir.1997).

vote and every jury's deliberations in every trial might be harmful cannot validate a categorical denial of all access."[12]

The same local district court rule was involved in a subsequent ruling of the Fifth Circuit in *United States v. Harrelson*.[13] In denying a writ of mandamus in this case the appeals court stated the First Amendment standard to be whether restrictions on approaches to jurors following discharge were imposed "to prevent a substantial threat to the administration of justice."[14] Here, the Fifth Circuit held that the trial judge's specific order issued pursuant to the authority of the local rule met this standard and was narrowly tailored. The order, issued in light of the ruling in *In re Express–News Corp.*, stated, *inter alia*, that (1) no juror had any obligation to speak to any person about this case; (2) no person may make repeated requests for interviews after a juror has expressed his or her desire not to be interviewed; (3) no interviewer may inquire into the specific vote of any juror other than the juror being interviewed; and (4) no interview could take place with a willing juror until each juror had received a copy of the court's final order.[15]

In seeking a writ of mandamus the El Paso Times complained *inter alia*, about the bans on repeated requests for interviews and inquiries into the specific votes of other jurors. In rejecting these complaints the Fifth Circuit held that invasion of juror privacy, harassment of jurors and potential damage to freedom of jury deliberations in the future amounted to a substantial threat to the administration of justice and the trial judge's order was narrowly tailored to forestall such threat.[16]

Clearly, the "substantial threat" standard implied in *Express-News Corp.* and set down and applied specifically in *Harrelson* is a different and lesser standard than the "clear and present danger" standard of *Sherman* and *Mechem* and one which seems more appropriately applied to complaints about denial of access to trial proceedings raised by newsgathers under the First Amendment.

It goes almost without saying that regardless of the nature of the no juror comment rule or order involved or the constitutional standard applied, the news media do have standing to complain and to seek writs of mandamus[17] in the federal courts or writs of prohibition or mandamus in the state courts.[18]

---

12. *In re Express–News Corp.*, 695 F.2d at 811. But access is dependent on being able to identify the jurors. The issue of access to particular jury lists is a somewhat different issue involving affirmative action on the part of the trial court to release the names of jurors, something trial courts may sometimes be reluctant to do. *Compare In re Globe Newspaper Co.*, 920 F.2d 88 (1st Cir.1990) *with* United States v. Edwards 823 F.2d 111 (5th Cir.1987).

13. 713 F.2d 1114 (5th Cir.1983), cert. denied *sub nom.* El Paso Times, Inc. v. United States Dist. Ct., 465 U.S. 1041, 104 S.Ct. 1318, 79 L.Ed.2d 714 (1984).

14. *Id.* at 1116.

15. *Id.*

16. *Id.* at 1118.

17. *See In re* Express–News Corp., 695 F.2d 807, 808 n. 1(5th Cir.1982); United States v. Sherman, 581 F.2d 1358, 1360–61 (9th Cir.1978); Journal Pub. Co. v. Mechem, 801 F.2d 1233, 1235–36 (10th Cir. 1986).

18. *See* State *ex rel.* Cincinnati Post v. Court of Common Pleas, 59 Ohio St.3d 103, 107, 570 N.E.2d 1101, 1105 (1991).

None of the cases discussed above should be read in any way as *requiring* jurors to make themselves available to the news media for interviews following trial[19] or providing authority for parties or counsel to interview jurors following trial.[20] The First Amendment protects the right of jurors not to speak about their experiences if that is their preference.[21] And First Amendment protection accorded representatives of the news media in gathering information about trial proceedings for the benefit of the public certainly does not extend to lawyers and parties seeking information from jurors for their own narrow purposes such as impeachment of the verdict.[22]

It is clear from the cases involving juror access following trial that the trial courts do have some latitude under the First Amendment to restrict interviews with former jurors. That latitude is reflected in the following proposed instruction. "Ladies and gentlemen of the jury, thank you for your dedicated service in the trial just concluded. Before I discharge you from jury duty, I have one final set of instructions for you. First, you are advised that you have no legal obligation to speak to members of the news media or anyone else about your jury service. You have a First Amendment right, if you wish to exercise it, to refuse any and all requests to discuss your experience as a juror. Second, if you are contacted by members of the news media or anyone else and, after clearly indicating to them that you do not wish to answer their questions, you are further importuned or badgered to cooperate, you are to contact me so that I may put an end to any harassment or invasion of your privacy. Third, in the interest of preserving for future jurors the same feeling of freedom to speak one's mind and to vote the way one's conscience dictates that you enjoyed in your deliberations in this case, you are instructed not to divulge to anyone the positions taken by your fellow jurors and their votes. You may, if you wish, indicate to others your own views of the case and how you yourself voted."[23]

19. *See* In re Express–News Corp., 695 F.2d at 811; Sherman, 581 F.2d at 1361–62; Journal Pub. Co., 801 F.2d at 1236–37; Cincinnati Post, 59 Ohio St. 3d at 105, 570 N.E.2d at 1103.

20. *See* Haeberle v. Texas International Airlines, 739 F.2d 1019 (5th Cir.1984); Big John, B.V. v. Indian Head Grain Co., 718 F.2d 143 (5th Cir.1983); United States v. Antar, 839 F.Supp. 293, 295 (D.N.J.1993), *aff'd in part, rev'd in part* 38 F.3d 1348 (3d Cir.1994).

21. *See In re* Express–News Corp., 695 F.2d at 811.

22. *See* Big John, B.V., 718 F.2d at 149; *see also* Haeberle, 739 F.2d at 1021–22 (juror interviews sought by counsel to satisfy their curiosity and improve their advocacy techniques).

23. Compare the instructions or orders given or suggested in United States v. Harrelson, 713 F.2d 1114, 1116–18 (5th Cir. 1983), cert. denied *sub nom.* El Paso Times, Inc. v. United States Dist. Ct., 465 U.S. 1041, 104 S.Ct. 1318, 79 L.Ed.2d 714 (1984); *In re* Express–News Corp., 695 F.2d 807, 811 (5th Cir. 1982); Journal Pub. Co. v. Mechem, 801 F.2d 1233, 1236–37 (10th Cir.1986); Sullivan v. National Football League, 839 F.Supp. 6, 7 (D.Mass.1993); United States v. Franklin, 546 F.Supp. 1133, 1145 (N.D.Ind.1982); State *ex rel.* Cincinnati Post, 59 Ohio St. 3d at 105–07, 570 N.E.2d at 1103–1104, (1991); *see also* United States v. Antar, 839 F.Supp. 293, 295 (D.N.J.1993), *aff'd in part, rev'd in part* 38 F.3d 1348 (3d Cir.1994).

E. Limiting Access to the Courtroom of Cameras and Recording Equipment

1. State Courtrooms

Between the mid 1930s and the 1970s, cameras and recording devices were easy targets of restrictive court rules and orders designed to improve the decorum of the courtroom and reduce or eliminate the visual and aural impact of publicity on criminal trials. As a result of the 1935 circus-like trial of Bruno Hauptmann for the kidnapping and murder of Charles Lindbergh and Anne Morrow Lindbergh's son at which still and newsreel cameras and microphones were in abundance, the American Bar Association adopted Canon 35 of its Canons of Judicial Ethics effectively banning photographic and broadcasting equipment from most American courtrooms.[24] The ABA ban was extended to the federal courts in Federal Rule of Criminal Procedure 53.[25]

The innate judicial suspicion of coverage of court proceedings beyond that embodied in the printed word came dramatically to the fore in *Estes v. Texas*.[26] There, Texas, one of the few states that had not adopted Canon 35, was prosecuting a nationally notorious fraud case involving politically well-connected Billy Sol Estes. At the commencement of the trial television and still and motion picture cameras and microphones for radio broadcasting were present in the courtroom. At that time counsel for Estes, decrying the publicity being given to the case, moved to ban all cameras and microphones from the trial. The hearing on this motion was televised, broadcast and photographed with so much personnel and equipment as to cause considerable disruption. While the motion to ban the telecasts, broadcasts and photography was denied, another motion

---

24. This canon provided: "Proceedings in court should be conducted with fitting dignity and decorum. The taking of photographs in the courtroom, during sessions of the court or recesses between sessions, and the broadcasting of court proceedings are calculated to detract from the essential dignity of the proceedings, degrade the court and create misconceptions with respect thereto in the mind of the public and should not be permitted." *See* Carolyn Dyer & Nancy R. Hauserman, *Electronic Coverage of the Courts: Exceptions to Exposure*, 75 Geo. L.J. 1633, 1641, (1987); Diane Kiesel, *Will There Ever Be Cameras in the Federal Courtrooms?* 1 A.B.A. Comm. Law. 1, 12 (No. 4, 1983). Canon 35 was amended and renumbered 3A(7) of the ABA Code of Judicial Conduct in 1972. Canon 3A provides, "A judge should prohibit broadcasting, television recording or taking photographs in the courtroom and areas immediately adjacent thereto during sessions of court or recesses between sessions, except that a judge may authorize: a. The use of electronic or photographic means for the presentation of evidence, or

for the perpetuation of a record; and b. The broadcasting, televising, recording, or photographing of investigative, ceremonial, or naturalization proceedings."

25. Fed. R. Crim. P. 53 provides: "The taking of photographs in the courtroom during the progress of judicial proceedings or radio broadcasting of judicial proceedings from the courtroom shall not be permitted by the court." Though the Rule has not been formally amended to include television (*see* 18 U.S.C.A. Fed. R. Crim. P. 53 (West Supp. 1991)), there is no doubt that it extends to civil trials and television coverage as well. *See* Westmoreland v. Columbia Broadcasting System, Inc., 752 F.2d 16 (2d Cir.1984), cert. denied *sub nom.* Cable News Network v. United States Dist. Ct., 472 U.S. 1017, 105 S.Ct. 3478, 87 L.Ed.2d 614 (1985); REVISED REPORT OF THE JUDICIAL CONFERENCE COMMITTEE ON THE OPERATION OF THE JURY SYSTEM ON THE "FREE PRESS—FAIR TRIAL" ISSUE, 87 F.R.D. 519, 535–36 (1980).

26. 381 U.S. 532, 85 S.Ct. 1628, 14 L.Ed.2d 543 (1965).

asking for continuance was granted and in the interim a booth was constructed at the back of the courtroom to which all television and newsreel cameras were relegated. Live television coverage was severely though not totally limited, but videotaping of the entire proceeding without audio accompaniment was permitted except for defense summations to the jury. No camera or broadcast coverage of any kind was permitted as to those summations. Following his conviction for swindling, Estes claimed that the television and broadcasting of his trial deprived him of due process of law guaranteed him by the Fourteenth Amendment. This claim was rejected by the trial court and the Texas Court of Criminal Appeals.

The United States Supreme Court reversed the conviction. Justice Clark's plurality opinion held that the showing of actual prejudice to Estes' right to a fair trial was not essential but could be presumed. The justices agreeing with Clark's opinion presumed prejudice because of their concern about the potential psychological impact on the jurors; the effect of the presence of the cameras on the testimony of witnesses; the increased burdens imposed on the trial judge by television; and the mental harassment of the defendant by the presence of the cameras.[27] But, of course, none of this could be documented and the fifth justice voting to reverse, Harlan, stated in his concurring opinion that the day might come when television was so commonplace as to dissipate any likelihood that it could adversely affect the judicial process and those involved with it.[28]

Because of other reservations in Justice Harlan's concurring opinion, *Estes* was read in the Court's revisitation of the issue in *Chandler v. Florida* as *not* announcing a constitutional rule barring still photographic, radio and television coverage in all cases and under all circumstances.[29] Not feeling constrained by the so-called "opinion of the court" in *Estes*, Chief Justice Burger, speaking for a true majority in *Chandler*, rejected the defendant-appellants proposed *per se* rule that the allowance of television coverage of criminal trials over objection violated due process. "The risk of juror prejudice in some cases does not justify an absolute ban on news coverage of trials by the printed media; so also the risk of such prejudice does not warrant an absolute constitutional ban on all broadcast coverage.... [T]he appropriate safeguard against such prejudice is the defendant's right to demonstrate that the media's coverage of his case—be it printed or broadcast—compromised the ability of the particular jury that heard the case to adjudicate fairly."[30]

Such right was accorded to the defendants by the state but the record did not indicate that they requested an evidentiary hearing to demonstrate the adverse impact on their case from the television coverage.[31] All that was presented were generalized allegations of prejudice.

27. *Id.* at 545–50, 85 S. Ct. at 1634–37, 14 L. Ed. 2d at 551–55.

28. *Id.* at 595, 85 S. Ct. at 1666, 14 L. Ed. 2d at 587–88.

29. 449 U.S. 560, 571–73, 101 S.Ct. 802, 808–09, 66 L.Ed.2d 740, 749–51 (1981).

30. *Id.* at 575, 101 S. Ct. at 810, 66 L. Ed. 2d at 752.

31. *Id.* at 577, 101 S. Ct. at 811, 66 L.

The Supreme Court refused to presume prejudice here.[32] In affirming the convictions the Court necessarily held that the Constitution did not prohibit *states* from permitting media coverage of trials.[33] But this ruling should not be read as necessarily implying a constitutional right of the *media* to bring their photographic and electronic equipment into the courtroom to televise, broadcast, record or photograph judicial proceedings.[34] Indeed, at one point in *Chandler* the Court quoted from its opinion in *Nixon v. Warner Communications, Inc.*[35] to the effect that the sixth amendment guarantee of a public trial did not require that trials be broadcast live or on tape. The court did not address the First Amendment claim of media to camera access in *Warner* but the United States Court of Appeals for the Second Circuit rejected just such a claim in *Westmoreland v. Columbia Broadcasting System, Inc.*[36] Unless and until the Supreme Court recognizes First Amendment protection for electronic and photographic access to the courtroom, such access is afforded only by the administrative grace of the supervisory authority overseeing the operation of each individual court system.[37]

Prior to *Chandler* only eight states besides Florida had adopted rules permitting access to the courtroom of electronic coverage of trials.[38] But with the decision in *Chandler* the logjam was broken and a decade later 36 state jurisdictions had adopted permanent rules permitting at least limited access to judicial proceedings of cameras, microphones and recording equipment.[39] At the same time seven states permitted limited

Ed. 2d at 753.

32. *Id.* at 577, 581–82, 101 S. Ct. at 811, 813–14, 66 L. Ed. 2d at 753, 755–57.

33. *Id.* at 583, 101 S. Ct. at 814, 66 L. Ed. 2d at 757.

34. *See id.* at 569, 101 S. Ct. at 807, 66 L. Ed. 2d at 748.

35. 435 U.S. 589, 610, 98 S.Ct. 1306, 1318, 55 L.Ed.2d 570, 587 (1978).

36. 752 F.2d 16, 21–24 (2d Cir.1984), cert. denied *sub nom.* Cable News Network v. United States Dist. Ct., 472 U.S. 1017, 105 S.Ct. 3478, 87 L.Ed.2d 614 (1985); *see* Associated Press v. Bost, 656 So.2d 113, 117–18 (Miss.1995) (utilizing the rational basis test for determining constitutionality of Canon 3A(7) of state's code of judicial conduct and collecting cases on this issue).

37. *See* Chandler, 449 U.S. at 569–70, 101 S. Ct. at 807–08, 66 L. Ed. 2d at 748–49; Westmoreland, 752 F.2d at 23–24.

38. *See* Chandler, 449 U.S. at 565 n.5, 101 S. Ct. at 805 n.5, 66 L. Ed. 2d at 745 n.5; News Media and the Law 31 (Fall 1991) (Reporters Committee for Freedom of the Press) (chart).

39. *See* Ala. R. Crim. P. 9.4 and Canons of Jud. Ethics 3(A)(7)(7A), 7(B); Alaska R. Civ. P. 46 and Admin. R. 50; 17A Ariz. Rev. Stat. Ann. Sup. Ct. R. 81, Canon

3A(7)(West. Supp. 1991); Cal. R. Ct. Misc. R. 980 (amended effective Jan. 1, 1997 in wake of O.J. Simpson criminal prosecution to emphasize trial judges' discretion to prohibit cameras and recording equipment in their courtrooms); Colo. Code Jud. Conduct Canon 3A(7); Conn. Code Jud. Conduct Canon 3A(7), 7(A), 7(B); Fla. Code Jud. Conduct Canon 3A(7); Ga. R. Unif. Super. Ct. R. 22 and Ga. R. Unif. Prob. Ct. R. 18; Haw. R. Sup. Ct. R. 5; Ill. Sup. Ct. R. 61, Canon 1; Iowa Ct. R. 119 Canon 3A(7); 3(b); Kan. Sup. Ct. R. 601 Canon 3A(7); Ky. Sup. Ct. R. 4300, Canon 3A(7) and R.4 App.; La. Code of Jud. Conduct, Canon 3A(7) (appellate proceedings only); Md. R. Ct. Admin. R. 1209; Mass. R. Sup. Jud. Ct. R. 3: 09, Canon 3A(7); Mich. Sup. Ct. Admin. Order 1989–1 (Jan. 13, 1989); Minn. Code. Jud. Conduct, Canon 3A(7); Neb. Sup. Ct. R. Prac. R17 (Supreme Court proceedings only); Nev. Sup. Ct. R. 229–247; N.H. Sup. Ct. R. 19, N.H. Super. Ct. R. 78, Dist. and Min. Cts. R. 1.4 and Prob. Ct. R. 15; N.J. Code of Jud. Conduct, Canon 3A(8)(b); N.M. R. Civ. P. 3–102 and R. Crim. P. 6–102, 7–1025 8–102; N.Y. R. Chief J. § 29.1; N.C. Sup. and Dist. Cts. R. 15 and Code of Jud. Conduct, Canon 3A(7); N.D. R. Local Ct. Admin. R. 21; Ohio Sup. Ct. R. 15, Common Pleas Cts. R. 11, Mun. and County Cts. R. 9 and Claims Ct. Local R. 18;

access of the equipment on an experimental basis.[40] Only five states and the District of Columbia continue to bar radio, television, film and recording coverage in accordance with the original ABA Canon.[41] Most state jurisdictions now permit film and electronic coverage of trial and appellate courts in both criminal and civil proceedings,[42] and in those states blanket trial court orders excluding such coverage without compelling reason are not likely to be upheld.[43]

The major issue with the revised access rules is whether they require the consent of any or all of the parties to the proceeding. Alabama's rule for instance, require consent of all parties and lead attorneys in civil litigation and all accused persons in criminal prosecution,[44] thereby, in practice, insuring little or no electronic or film coverage. On the other hand New Jersey's rules state specifically that consent need not be obtained from any party, attorney or participant in the proceedings.[45] Of course, even where consent of participants is not required they may always object and, for good cause shown, the presiding judge may exercise his inherent authority to order that objecting persons not be photographed or otherwise recorded.[46] Beyond consent, coverage may be limited by the need to obtain judicial permission to cover proceedings with photographic and electronic equipment[47] and further by rules specifying detailed procedures to be followed by media personnel[48] and the equipment they may use.[49]

2. Federal Courtrooms

News media cameras, microphones and electronic recording equip-

Okla. Code of Jud. Conduct, Canon 3A(7); Or. Unif. Trial Ct. R.3.180 and Code of Jud. Conduct, Canon 3A(7); R. I. Sup. and Dist. Cts. Crim. R. 53; Tenn. Sup. Ct. R. 10, Canon 3A(7); Vt. R. Civ. P. 79.2, R. Crim. P. 53, R. P. P. 79.2, R. App. P. 35 and Dist. Ct. Civ. R. 79.2; Wash. Code of Jud. Conduct, Canon 3A(7); W. Va. Jud. Code of Ethics 3A(7); Wis. Sup. Ct. R. 61.02–12.

40. *See* News Media & the Law 31 (Spring 1991) (Reporters Committee for Freedom of the Press) (chart listing Arkansas, Delaware, Maine, Pennsylvania, Texas, Utah and Virginia).

41. *See* Carolyn S. Dyer & Nancy R. Hauserman, *Electronic Coverage of the Courts: Exceptions to Exposure*, 75 Geo. L.J. 1633, 1635, 1639 n.13 (1987); S.L. Alexander, *Cameras in the courtroom: a Case study*, 74 Judicature 307, 310 (No. 6, April—May 1991) (chart); News Media & the Law 31 (Spring 1991) (chart). The five holdout states were then Indiana, Missouri, Mississippi, South Carolina and South Dakota. Missouri has since begun an experimental program permitting camera access.

42. *See, e.g.,* Fla. Code Jud. Conduct, Canon 3A(7); Iowa Ct. R. 119, Canon 3A(7); Kan. Sup. Ct. R. 1001; *see also* News Media

& the Law 31 (Spring 1991) (chart). A reaction to cameras in the state courts may be setting in in light of the O.J. Simpson murder case. See, *e.g.,* Steven Brill & Rory K. Little, *Point Counterpoint*, Cal. Bar J. 12 (Dec. 1994) (debate).

43. See, *e.g.,* Hearst Corp. v. Justices of the Superior Court, 24 Med. L. Rptr. 1478 (Mass.1996).

44. Ala. R. Crim. P. 9.4 and Canon of Jud. Ethics 3a(7)(b)-(c).

45. N.J. R. Sup. Ct. Media Coverage Guideline 11.

46. *See, e.g.,* Conn. Code Jud. Conduct Canon 3(7A)(8); Kan. Sup. Ct. R. 100 (6); Wis. Sup. Ct. R. 61.11(1).

47. *See, e.g.,* Ariz. Sup. Ct. R. 81, Canon 3A(7)(f); Cal. R. Ct. Misc. R. 980(b)(1); Colo. Code Jud. Conduct, Canon 3A(8)(f).

48. *See, e.g.,* Colo. Code Jud. Conduct, Canon 3A(8)(e); Neb. Sup. Ct.R. 17E; N.J. R. Sup. Ct. Media Coverage Guideline 3.

49. *See, e.g.,* Fla. Code of Jud. Conduct; Canon 3A(7), Schedule A; Ill. Sup. Ct. R. 61, Canon 1, Schedule A; N.Y. R. Chief Admin. § 131.13.

ment had been barred from federal courtrooms since 1946.[50] For nearly 45 years thereafter every effort by the news media to breach the federal courts' stone wall with their photographic and electronic equipment was rebuffed.[51] Then in 1990 the Judicial Conference of the United States, on the recommendation of its Ad Hoc Committee on Cameras in the Courtroom, voted to permit an experimental program of photographic and electronic coverage of certain civil proceedings in a maximum of two circuit courts of appeal and six district courts beginning July 1, 1991.[52]

Participation in the federal courts in the approved pilot program was voluntary.[53] The volunteer courts selected by the Ad Hoc Committee were the Second and Ninth Circuits and the District Courts for the Southern District of Indiana, District of Massachusetts, Eastern District of Michigan, Southern District of New York, Eastern District of Pennsylvania and Western District of Washington.[54] These courts were governed in the experimental coverage by detailed guidelines fashioned by the Ad Hoc Committee which guidelines were obviously influenced by the experience of the state courts.[55]

In an evaluation of the pilot program issued on November 4, 1993,[56] the Federal Judicial Center found that (1) during the two-year period

---

50. *See* F.R. Crim. P. 53; F.R. App. P. 54; Diane Kiesel, *Will There Ever Be Cameras in the Federal Courtrooms?* 1 A.B.A. Comm. Law. 1 (No. 4, 1983).

51. *See, e.g.,* Carolyn S. Dyer & Nancy R. Hauserman, *Electronic Coverage of the Courts: Exceptions to Exposure,* 75 Geo. L.J. 1633, 1640 n.15 (1987); *see also* Diane Kiesel, *supra* note 44, at 1. It may be apocryphal but Warren Burger, when he was Chief Justice of the United States allegedly said that there would be cameras in the Supreme Court when they carried him out of the building on a catafalque. Apocryphal or not, Burger's enmity toward cameras was well known and he could make his personal objections to them into policy as ex officio chairman of the Judicial Conference of the United States. Present Chief Justice William Rehnquist is proving to be less doctrinaire on this issue. *See* S. L. Alexander, *Cameras in the courtroom: a case study,* 74 Judicature 307 (Apr.–May 1, 1991); Linda Greenhouse, *Federal Courts Moving to Permit Trial Coverage by Radio and TV,* N.Y. Times, Sept. 13, 1990, at A18, Col. 5.

52. *See* Report of the Judicial Conference Ad Hoc Committee on Cameras in the Courtroom, Agenda E–22, at 8 (Sept. 1990); 22 The Third Branch 1 (Nov. 10, Oct. 1990) (official newsletter of the Federal Courts published by the Administrative Office of the United States Courts), *see also* Alexander, *supra* note 45, at 313; Linda Greenhouse, *Federal Courts Moving to Permit Trial Coverage by Radio and TV,* N.Y. Times, Sept. 13, 1990, at A8, Col. 5. The

breaching of the federal judicial stone wall actually began in 1990 when the United States Court of Military Appeals, which is not governed by the Judicial Conference, allowed live television camera coverage of selected oral arguments. *See* Alexander at 307. The United States Court of Appeals for the Ninth Circuit apparently jumped the gun on the federal court experiment starting date when it permitted live coverage by C–SPAN of one of its appellate arguments held in Boise, Idaho on June 28, 1991. *See* 77 A.B.A. J. 26, 27 (Sept. 1991) ("News" column); Wash. Post, June 29, 1991, at A4 ("Around the Nation" column).

53. *See* Report of the Judicial Conference Ad Hoc Committee on Cameras in the Courtroom, Agenda E.22, AT 6 (SEP. 1990); The Third Branch 1, 2 (No. 20, Oct. 1990).

54. Final Report of the Judicial Conference Ad Hoc Committee on Cameras in the Courtroom, Agenda, at 2 (Mar. 1991); *See* Alexander, *supra* Note 45, at 313; 77 A.B.A. J. 26, 27.

55. *See* Guidelines for the Pilot Program on Photographing, Recording, and Broadcasting in the Courtroom, Report of the Judicial Conference Ad Hoc Committee on Cameras in the Courtroom, Agenda E–22 Appendix C (Sept. 1990).

56. Report of the Federal Judicial Center to the Committee on Court Administration and Case Management of the Judicial Conference of the United States: Electronic Media Coverage of Federal Civil Proceedings (Nov. 1993).

July 1, 1991 through June 30, 1993, the media filed applications for coverage in 257 cases of which 82 percent were approved; (2) the most common type of coverage was the televising of trials; (3) overall, attitudes of judges toward coverage of civil proceedings were initially neutral but became more favorable after experience with electronic media coverage; (4) judges and attorneys who had experience with electronic media coverage under the program generally reported observing little or no effect of camera presence on participants in the proceedings, courtroom decorum or the administration of justice; (5) judges, media personnel and court staff found the guidelines governing the program to be generally workable; (6) overall, judges and court staff reported that members of the media were very cooperative and complied with the guidelines and any other restrictions imposed; and (7) most television broadcast footage submitted for content analysis (a) employed courtroom footage to illustrate a reporter's narration rather than to tell the story through the words and actions of participants; (b) provided basic verbal information to the viewer about the nature and facts of the case covered; and (c) provided little verbal information to viewers about the legal process.[57]

The Federal Judicial Center's recommendations were not made public at the time of the report but were, instead, forwarded separately to the Committee on Court Administration and Case Management, the committee responsible for the final recommendations to the Judicial Conference of the United States regarding cameras in federal courtrooms.[58] It seems safe to say that, given the mostly favorable findings in the report, it is likely the Federal Judicial Center recommended opening to some extent Federal courtrooms to television cameras, microphones and recording devices or at least extending and enlarging the experimental program to allow for further evaluation. The Center's recommendations were rejected by the Judicial Conference of the United States in a secret vote on September 20, 1994, but then on March 12, 1996 the Judicial Conference voted by a narrow margin to permit cameras in the courts of appeal in civil cases if the circuit judges acquiesce.[59]

It must be kept in mind that even if the federal courts do eventually permit photographic coverage, such access and that to the state courts is by administrative grace and trial court discretion. Individual judges will still be able to ban cameras and recording equipment from their courtrooms wholly or in part subject only to reversal for abuse of discretion, a standard rarely met on appeal. To this point in our history the First Amendment is not being read as protecting the access of cameramen to the courthouse.

3.   The Gatekeeping Role of Individual Judges and the Responsibility of the Media to Respect the Judicial Process

With the increasing access to the courtroom of media cameras, microphones and recording devices, the gatekeeping function of the trial

---

57. *Id.* at 2.

58. *Id.* at 14.

59. *See* Joan Biskupic, *A New Eye on Federal Courts; Committee Votes to Permit*

Cameras in Appeals Hearings, Wash. Post, Mar. 13, 1996, p. A12, C.4.

judge takes on greater importance. Abdication of responsibility properly to control media representatives and their equipment can result in injustice in civil and criminal trials such as occurred in *Sheppard*. Correspondingly, the media must be sensitive to the needs of the judiciary in its effort to insure fair trial proceedings.

In *Iowa v. Douglas*[60] the trial judge failed to exercise sound judgment when he allowed live microphones to be placed by local television stations at the counsel tables over the objection of the defendant's lawyers. Though the judges and defense counsel were twice assured that the media representatives would act responsibly and would not air in any manner confidential communications, one of the defense lawyers watched a television news program following the second day of trial which allegedly broadcast a confidential communication of her co-counsel. When she complained the next day and sought verification, the television station, in what can only be described as unacceptable hubris, refused to cooperate immediately and to deliver a copy of the tape of the broadcast to the judge voluntarily. By the time a subpoena was served on the station and it understood which tape it was being requested to supply, station personnel had already erased it and counsel's complaint could not be verified.

While on appeal of the defendant's criminal conviction the Iowa Supreme Court found no prejudice arising out of the episode, it had much to say about the judgment of the trial judge and the behavior of the media.

> "[W]e view with alarm the distainful attitude displayed by the media in this case. The impression given is that once expanded media coverage was granted, media conduct was above reproach and beyond review. Despite assurances of responsibility, the media representative's promise to not broadcast confidential communications was apparently violated. Efforts to verify this were met with the media's reaction of outright rejection, delay, delivery of substituted tape and destruction of evidence.... *The professional standards of the media were badly undermined by this episode.*
>
> It is clear that the presence of live microphones at the counsel table creates a real potential for prejudicing a defendant's constitutional rights ... Viewed in retrospect, the trial court would have been well advised in denying the media's request for the type of live microphones at the counsel table used in this case.
>
> Our rules allowing expanded media coverage have been drafted to give the public increased access to judicial proceedings. This access is, nevertheless, subject to the duty and authority of the presiding judge to control the conduct proceedings to prevent distractions, and to ensure the fair administration of justice."[61] (Emphasis supplied).

60. 485 N.W.2d 619 (Iowa 1992).

61. *Id.* at 625–26; *see also* Marin Independent Journal v. Marin County Municipal Court, 12 Cal.App.4th 1712, 16 Cal.Rptr.2d 550 (1993) (willful failure of newspaper photographer to follow rules regarding

As suggested by the Iowa Supreme Court's opinion, if either the judge fails to exercise his gatekeeping function properly or the media fails to act responsibly, injustice may result. Repeated episodes similar to that in *Douglas* and the O.J. Simpson murder prosecution could lead to a change of attitude by those who control the courtrooms of the country and to a return to the exclusionary policies imposed following the *Hauptmann* and *Sheppard* cases.[62] It bears repeating that at this time the First Amendment has not been construed to insure the access of cameras and other media paraphernalia to the courtroom. If the public's electronic access to our courts is to be safeguarded, it must be through the work of responsible judges and responsible media personnel.

8.7 Direct Judicial Restrictions on Publication—"Gag Orders"

A. Introduction

In the preceding section the focus of the discussion was on judicial devices and techniques to reduce or prevent prejudicial trial publicity having a more or less indirect effect on newsgathering by the media relative to current or future trial proceedings. In this section, we consider direct efforts by the courts to prevent the news media from disseminating news and information in their possession. These direct efforts are usually in the form of injunctive orders directing the news media not to publish certain information and are known pejoratively as "gag orders."

For most of our history as a nation, for whatever reason, direct injunctions preventing publication of trial news were rare. But increasingly during the late 1960s and early to mid–1970s trial courts chose to issue such injunctions.[1] While very nearly all such restrictive orders that were challenged on appeal were ultimately reversed,[2] their issuance was exceedingly disruptive to targeted news organizations in terms of conducting business and spending time, energy and money litigating in court. Finally, because of the serious constitutional issues raised by these orders the Supreme Court took action for the first time in this area.[3]

courtroom photography in a pretrial criminal proceeding).

62. See Daniel M. Kolkey and Brian Goebel *Point-Counterpoint: Should Cameras be Banned from California's Courts?*, Cal. Bar J. 12 (Feb. 1996).

1. *See, e.g.,* United States v. CBS, Inc., 497 F.2d 102 (5th Cir.1974); Schuster v. Bowen, 347 F.Supp. 319 (D.Nev.1972), *remanded* 496 F.2d 881 (9th Cir.1974); Phoenix Newspapers, Inc. v. Superior Ct., 101 Ariz. 257, 418 P.2d 594 (1966); Cooper v. Rockford Newspapers, Inc., 34 Ill.App.3d 645, 339 N.E.2d 477 (1975); New York Times Co. v. Starkey, 51 A.D.2d 60, 380 N.Y.S.2d 239 (1976); State *ex rel.* Beacon Journal Pub. Co. v. Kainrad, 46 Ohio St.2d 349, 75 Ohio Op. 2d 435, 348 N.E.2d 695 (1976).

2. *Id.*

3. *But cf.* Near v. Minnesota, *ex rel.* Olson, 283 U.S. 697, 51 S.Ct. 625, 75 L.Ed. 1357 (1931); New York Times Co. v. United States, 403 U.S. 713, 91 S.Ct. 2140, 29 L.Ed.2d 822 (1971).

B. *Nebraska Press Association v. Stuart*[4]

On the evening of October 18, 1975, local police found an entire family of six murdered and sexually assaulted in their home in Sutherland, Nebraska, a town of approximately 850.[5] Shortly after the crimes were discovered, the townspeople were alerted by a special announcement broadcast over the local television station and were requested to stay off the streets and exercise caution as to whom they admitted into their homes.[6] When an investigation implicated Erwin Charles Simants as a suspect, his name and description were provided to the press and then disseminated to the public.[7] He was subsequently apprehended and charged with the crimes.

Representatives of local, regional and national newspapers and radio and television stations descended upon the town, and the county prosecutor and the accused's attorney joined in asking the courts to enter a restrictive order relating to matters that might or might not be publicly reported or disclosed to the public because of massive media coverage and the consequent reasonable likelihood of prejudicial news tending to prevent a fair trial.[8] Ultimately the state district court, after permitting several press and broadcast associations, publishers and individual reporters to intervene, entered a restrictive order "because of the nature of the crimes charged in the complaint that there is a clear and present danger that pre-trial publicity could impinge upon the defendant's right to a fair trial."[9]

The order applied until the jury was impaneled and prohibited the intervening newsgatherers from reporting on five subjects: the existence or contents of a confession Simants had made to law enforcement officers, which had been introduced in open court at arraignment; the fact or nature of statements Simants had made to other persons; the contents of a note he had written the night of the crime; certain aspects of the medical testimony at the preliminary hearing; and, finally, the identity of the victims of the alleged sexual assault and the nature of the assault. It also prohibited reporting the exact nature of the restrictive order itself. This order incorporated the Nebraska Bar–Press Guidelines as mandatory requirements.[10] The intervenors immediately applied to the Nebraska Supreme Court for a writ of mandamus, a stay and an expedited appeal from the order. Following oral argument the Nebraska Supreme Court modified the trial court's order to better accommodate the accused's right to a fair trial and the news media's interest in reporting pretrial events. The order as modified prohibited reporting of only three subjects: the existence and nature of any confessions or admissions made by the defendant to law enforcement officers; any

---

4. 427 U.S. 539, 96 S.Ct. 2791, 49 L.Ed.2d 683 (1976).

5. *Id.* at 542, 573, 96 S. Ct. at 2795–2809, 49 L. Ed. 2d at 687, 705–06.

6. *Id.* at 573, 96 S. Ct. at 2809, 49 L. Ed. 2d at 705–06.

7. *Id.*

8. *Id.* at 542, 96 S. Ct. at 2795, 49 L. Ed. 2d at 687.

9. *Id.* at 543, 96 S. Ct. at 2795, 49 L. Ed. 2d at 688.

10. *Id.* at 543–44, 96 S. Ct. at 2795–96, 49 L. Ed. 2d at 688–89.

confessions or admissions made to any third parties, except members of the news media; and other facts "strongly implicative" of the accused. The Nebraska Supreme Court's modification did not rely on the Nebraska Bar–Press Guidelines.[11]

The modified order expired by its own terms when the jury was impaneled and before the United States Supreme Court could consider it on certiorari. Nevertheless, the high court rejected the state's claim of mootness because the controversy was one capable of repetition yet otherwise evading review.[12]

On the merits the Court recognized the temporary order for what it was—a prior restraint of the press[13] that could be justified only by the proponent of the prior restraint overcoming the heavy presumption against its constitutionality.[14] The reason for imposing this high First Amendment standard was stated succinctly, "A prior restraint ... by definition, has an immediate and irreversible sanction. If it can be said that a threat of criminal or civil sanctions after publication 'chills' speech, prior restraint 'freezes' it at least for the time."[15] The presumption of unconstitutionality had special force as applied to reporting of criminal proceedings to the public, according to the Court.[16]

To meet the heavy presumption, the proponent of the judicial restrictive order must establish that the gravity of the evil here—prejudice to a fair trial from trial or pretrial publicity—justified the invasion of press freedom to avoid the danger.[17] More specifically, there is a four-fold burden. First, a substantial showing must be made that the pretrial or trial news coverage would be intense and pervasive. Second, it would have to be shown that alternative judicial measures such as those discussed in *Sheppard v. Maxwell*,[18] would be unlikely to mitigate the effects of pretrial publicity. Third, it would be necessary to establish the effectiveness of the restraining order in preventing trial prejudice. And finally, the order must be shown not to be vague and overbroad in its reach.[19]

While the trial judge met his burden regarding the first element of the constitutional test given that the pretrial record was replete with evidence of news media interest,[20] he fell short of meeting the burden

11. *Id.* at 545, 96 S. Ct. at 2796, 49 L. Ed. 2d at 689.

12. *Id.* at 546–47, 96 S. Ct. at 2796–97, 49 L. Ed. 2d at 690–91.

13. *Id.* at 556, 560, 96 S. Ct. at 2801, 2803, 49 L. Ed. 2d at 695–96, 698.

14. *Id.* at 558–59, 570, 96 S. Ct. at 2802–03, 2808, 49 L. Ed. 2d at 697–98, 704.

15. *Id.* at 559, 96 S. Ct. at 2802–03, 49 L. Ed. 2d at 697–98.

16. *Id.*

17. *Id.* at 562, 96 S. Ct. at 2804, 49 L. Ed. 2d at 699. This test first enunciated by Hand, J., in United States v. Dennis, 183 F.2d 201, 212 (2d Cir.1950), *aff'd*, 341 U.S. 494, 71 S.Ct. 857, 95 L.Ed. 1137 (1951)

undermined the "clear and present danger" test enunciated by Holmes, J., in Schenck v. United States, 249 U.S. 47, 39 S.Ct. 247, 63 L.Ed. 470 (1919). *See* Christopher P. Wells, Comment, *Confidentiality Statutes and the First Amendment: A Landmark Opinion*, 31 Fed. Comm. L. J. 85, 106 n.89 (1978).

18. 384 U.S. 333, 358–62, 86 S.Ct. 1507, 1520–22, 16 L.Ed.2d 600, 617–20.

19. Nebraska Press Association, 427 U.S. at 562, 568, 96 S. Ct. at 2804, 2807, 49 L. Ed. 2d at 699, 702–03.

20. *Id.* at 562–63, 96 S. Ct. at 2804–05, 49 L. Ed. 2d at 699–700.

regarding the other elements and the Nebraska Supreme Court judgment was reversed.

The Supreme Court found that the record contained no finding and no evidence that alternative measures or devices would not have protected the accused's right; that the restraining order would likely be ineffective because the constitutional requirements for *in personam* jurisdiction to bind all news media could not be met and the unrestrained media could circulate their coverage of the trial in the community of the trial; that the restraining order would likely be ineffective also because the community was small and rumors about the trial could travel swiftly by word of mouth; and that the order on the face of it was not narrowly tailored and clear. The Court reached this last conclusion because the order covered reporting of evidence adduced at an *open* preliminary hearing and its prohibition regarding reporting of facts "strongly implicative" of guilt of the accused was too broad and too vague to pass constitutional muster.[21]

Despite striking the Nebraska order, the majority was quick to point out that no matter how difficult it would be to justify a prior restraint on trial reporting, it was not ruling out the possibility that such justification could be made. "This Court has frequently denied that First Amendment rights are absolute and has consistently rejected the proposition that a prior restraint could never be employed."[22] But at the time of the decision it seemed that for all practical purposes, prior restraints on reporting on judicial proceedings were a thing of the past. This apparent reality was underscored in Justice White's concurring opinion. While joining the opinion of the Court, he added "that for the reasons which the Court itself canvasses, there is grave doubt in my mind whether orders with respect to the press such as were entered in this case would ever be justifiable."[23] One of White's concerns was undoubtedly the difficulty of trial courts fashioning restraining orders that are effective in safeguarding the accused's right to a fair trial and, at the same time, are so narrow and precise as to satisfy settled constitutional doctrine. Walking this constitutional tightrope can never be easy, and at the time of the decision in *Nebraska Press Association* it was difficult to envision a scenario in which a prior restraint would be upheld.

C. *Walking the Nebraska Press Association Prior Restraint Tightrope and Falling Off*

For approximately fifteen years the decision in *Nebraska Press Association* brought stability to this area of constitutional law and few

---

21. *Id.* at 563–69, 96 S. Ct. at 2804–08, 49 L. Ed. 2d at 700–04.

22. *Id.* at 570, 96 S. Ct. at 2808, 49 L. Ed. 2d at 704. *See also* Kansas v. Alston, 256 Kan. 571, 887 P.2d 681, 686 (1994); Ohio ex rel. New World Communications v. Character, 100 Ohio App.3d 773, 775–76, 654 N.E.2d 1301, 1302–03 (1995) ("The concerns recited at the hearing which prompted the restraining order . . . were (1) the parties' right to a fair trial, one untainted by pretrial publicity which could adversely affect potential jurors, and (2) the parties ability to negotiate effectively. Neither of these concerns is sufficient to overcome the presumption of unconstitutionality in this case.")

23. *Id.* at 570–71, 96 S. Ct. at 2808–09, 49 L. Ed. 2d at 704–05.

orders directly restraining the news media from reporting judicial proceedings regarding any significant cases were upheld as meeting the Supreme 'Court's demanding requirements for such orders.[24] And then came the infamous *Noriega Tapes Case.*

Following the American invasion of Panama, the Panamanian dictator Manuel Antonio Noriega was captured and forcibly brought to Miami to stand trial for violation of American drug laws. During his pretrial incarceration in the Metropolitan Correctional Center (MCC) he made several telephone calls to his attorneys and other members of his defense team which were apparently recorded by officials in violation of MCC's policy against monitoring attorney client conversations. Seven of the tapes were obtained by the Cable News Network (CNN) from an unidentified source. On November 6, 1990, CNN representatives appeared at the law office of Noriega's counsel and informed him of CNN's possession of the tapes. They played a portion of one of the tapes for counsel, who identified the voices as those of Noriega, the counsel's secretary and a legal assistant. According to counsel, the portion of the recording played contained discussions of trial strategy and investigation of the pending criminal charges against Noriega. The CNN representatives informed counsel that the cable network intended to air a story about the government's wiretapping and recording on its 6 PM broadcast on November 8, 1990. On November 7th counsel filed an emergency motion for an injunction prohibiting CNN from broadcasting any tape recording of any privileged communication between himself and any of his lawyers or members of the defense staff.[25]

Because the United States District Court believed that broadcast of the tapes would interfere with Noriega's right to a fair trial by having his trial strategy and tactics disclosed to the prosecution if the tapes in CNN's hands contained such material, it issued a temporary restraining order before 6 PM on November 8th barring their broadcast and requiring CNN to produce them for inspection.[26] The restraining order was extended the following day in a supplemental order to provide time for the court to review the tapes.[27] In neither the original restraining orders

24. *See, e.g., In re* the Charlotte Observer, 921 F.2d 47 (4th Cir.1990); CBS, Inc. v. United States Dist. Ct., 729 F.2d 1174 (9th Cir.1984); KPNX Broadcasting Co. v. Maricopa County Superior Ct., 139 Ariz. 246, 250–54, 678 P.2d 431, 435–39 (1984); Miami Herald Pub. Co. v. Morphonios, 467 So.2d 1026 (Fla.Dist.Ct.App.1985); Minneapolis Star & Tribune Co. v. Lee, 353 N.W.2d 213 (Minn.App.1984); State *ex rel.* Chillicothe Gazette, Inc. v. Ross County Court of Common Pleas, 2 Ohio St.3d 24, 442 N.E.2d 747 (1982); *but see* KUTV, Inc. v. Wilkinson, 686 P.2d 456 (Utah 1984) (restraining order prohibiting publication of allegedly prejudicial information not related to the trial itself upheld), criticized in Scott A. Hagen, Note, KUTV v. Wilkinson; *Another Episode* in the Fair Trial/Free Press Saga, 1985 Utah L. Rev. 739, 747–57.

25. United States v. Noriega, 752 F.Supp. 1045, 1047 (S.D.Fla.1990).

26. United States v. Noriega, 752 F. Supp. at 1035–36.

27. *Id.* at 1034–35 *quoted in* United States v. Noriega, 917 F.2d 1543, 1547 (11th Cir.), cert. denied 498 U.S. 976, 111 S.Ct. 451, 112 L.Ed.2d 432 (1990). To CNN's argument that an alternative means short of ordering the network to produce the tapes existed, namely compelling the government to turn over its copies, the district court responded, "It is entirely possible that CNN is in possession of communications between Noriega and his lawyers

nor the supplemental order was there any indication that Noriega had carried the burden of justification for the imposition of this prior restraint on the news organization nor was any finding made that restraint of the coming broadcast was necessary to protect Noriega's right to a fair trial. It was simply assumed by the court that the restraining order was constitutionally permissible because of the potential threat to a fair trial posed by broadcast of the tapes and because the court could not decide whether an injunction should issue without first examining the tapes. "It seems fundamentally unfair to allow CNN to benefit from its refusal to disclose the contents of the tapes to the court—that is, to allow CNN to argue that no prior restraint should issue because no clear and immediate harm yet appears is because CNN has so far prevented this court from reviewing the content of the tapes in its possession."[28]

CNN filed an emergency motion with the United States Court of Appeals for the Eleventh Circuit seeking vacation of the orders and also filed a petition for a writ of mandamus or prohibition to prevent the trial court from hearing Noriega's motion for imposition of sanctions against the news network for alleged violation of the orders. The United States Court of Appeals for the Eleventh Circuit, acting with appropriate haste, announced its decision on November 10th. For jurisdictional reasons the appeals court treated CNN's emergency motion as a petition for a writ of mandamus and then denied both petitions. Relying almost entirely upon cases involving *access* to judicial proceedings[29] rather than prior restraint decisions with their higher standard of constitutional justification,[30] the Eleventh Circuit ignored the issue of where the burden of proof lies to justify the prior restraint no matter how short its duration. It simply agreed with the district court that "[t]he District Court must possess the subject tapes in order to make its *in camera* determination of whether the attorney-client communications are privileged or, while not privi-

---

and staff which the Government did not record, since it appears that the Government did not tape all of Noriega's attorney-client conversations." *Id.*

28. United States v. Noriega, 917 F.2d at 1545–46.

29. *See* Press–Enterprise Co. v. Superior Ct. (II), 478 U.S. 1, 106 S.Ct. 2735, 92 L.Ed.2d 1 (1986); Press–Enterprise Co. v. Superior Ct. (I), 464 U.S. 501, 104 S.Ct. 819, 78 L.Ed.2d 629 (1984); Waller v. Georgia, 467 U.S. 39, 104 S.Ct. 2210, 81 L.Ed.2d 31 (1984); Gannett Co. v. DePasquale, 443 U.S. 368, 99 S.Ct. 2898, 61 L.Ed.2d 608 (1979); Nixon v. Warner Communications, Inc., 435 U.S. 589, 98 S.Ct. 1306, 55 L.Ed.2d 570 (1978); *In re* Application of Dow Jones & Co., 842 F.2d 603 (2d Cir.), cert. denied, 488 U.S. 946, 109 S.Ct. 377, 102 L.Ed.2d 365 (1988); Belo Broadcasting Corp. v. Clark, 654 F.2d 423 (5th Cir.1981);

United States v. Gurney, 558 F.2d 1202 (5th Cir.1977), cert. denied *sub nom.* Miami Herald Pub. Co. v. Krentzman, 435 U.S. 968, 98 S.Ct. 1606, 56 L.Ed.2d 59 (1978); Columbia Broadcasting System v. Young, 522 F.2d 234 (6th Cir.1975); Levine v. United States Dist. Ct., 764 F.2d 590 (9th Cir. 1985), cert. denied, 476 U.S. 1158, 106 S.Ct. 2276, 90 L.Ed.2d 719 (1986). *But see* United States v. Columbia Broadcasting System, Inc., 497 F.2d 107 (5th Cir.1974)(contempt proceeding for violation of a district court order restraining CBS from televising sketches of courtroom scenes in a highly publicized criminal trial; case remanded for trial of the contempt action).

30. *See* Gentile v. State Bar, 501 U.S. 1030, 1073–75, 111 S.Ct. 2720, 2744, 115 L.Ed.2d 888, 922–23 (1991) (opinion of the Court per Rehnquist, C.J.)

leged, are of such a nature that disclosure would impair Noriega's Sixth Amendment rights."[31] And while not addressing in detail CNN's other petition for a writ directing the district court to refrain from hearing Noriega's motion seeking contempt sanctions, the appeals court did say, "While appealing to our nation's judicial system for relief, CNN is at the same time defiant of that system's reasonable directions.... No litigant should continue to violate a district court's order and attempt to have that district court's order reviewed at the same time."[32] The perceived violation of the trial court's orders by CNN may very well have contributed to the doubtful determination here.

Doubtful though the decision may be in upholding the placement of the burden of proof on the newsgatherer to prevent imposition of the order and utilizing a number of inapposite access cases, *Noriega* remains the law in the Eleventh Circuit[33] with the refusal of the Supreme Court, over the dissent of two Justices, to review the decision.[34]

31. United States v. Noriega, 917 F.2d 1543, 1550 (11th Cir.), cert. denied, 498 U.S. 976, 111 S.Ct. 451, 112 L.Ed.2d 432 (1990). In the only comparable case the could be found, the United States Court of Appeals for the Ninth Circuit vacated a restraining order requiring the news media target to establish that tape in its possession would not prejudice a fair trial. Goldblum v. NBC, 584 F.2d 904 (9th Cir.1978).

32. Noriega, 917 F.2d at 1551, 1552.

33. To date no other jurisdiction has chosen to follow the Eleventh Circuit decision.

34. Cable News Network, Inc. v. Noriega, 498 U.S. 976, 111 S.Ct. 451, 112 L.Ed.2d 432 (1990). In his dissent Marshall, J., joined by O'Connor, J., reviewed the Court's precedents recognizing the heavy presumption against the constitutional validity of prior restraints of the press and stated, "I do not see how the prior restraint imposed in this case can be reconciled with these teachings." More ominously, Marshall observed, "[I]f the lower courts in this case are correct in their remarkable conclusion that publication can be *automatically* restrained pending application of the demanding test established by *Nebraska Press*, then I think it is imperative that we re-examine the premises and operation of *Nebraska Press* itself." *Id.* at 977, 111 S. Ct. at 451, 112 L. Ed. 2d at 433.

Whatever the current state of *Nebraska Press Association v. Stuart*, Judge Hoeveler did proceed to impose sanctions on CNN for criminal contempt in United States v. Cable News Network, Inc., 865 F.Supp. 1549,

(S.D.Fla.1994). He ordered CNN to pay a fine of $85,000 to the Administrative Office of the United States to reimburse the judiciary for fees paid to the special prosecutor in the case, to pay a special assessment of $100 and to broadcast an agreed statement several times over its facilities. The statement reads:

> On November 1, 1994, the United States District Court for the Southern District of Florida found CNN guilty of criminal contempt after a trial. The court held CNN in contempt because CNN broadcast tape recordings of General Manuel Noriega's telephone conversations with his attorney in November 1990. CNN's broadcast of these recordings violated an explicit order of the United States District Court not to broadcast.
>
> On further consideration, CNN realizes that it was in error in defying the order of the court and publishing the Noriega tape while appealing the court's order. We do now and always have recognized that our justice system cannot long survive if litigants take it upon themselves to determine which judgments or orders of court they will or will not follow. Ours is a nation of laws under which the very freedoms we espouse can be preserved only if those laws are observed. In the event unfavorable judgments are rendered, the right of appeal is provided. This is the course on which we should have relied. We regret that we did not.

United States v. Cable News Network, Inc., 865 F.Supp. 1549 (1994).

D. Judicial Evasion of the Requirements of Nebraska Press Association and the Dilemma for Newsgatherers Posed Thereby

The questionable *Noriega* decision aside, *Nebraska Press Association* seemingly stands as a bulwark of constitutional doctrine against the facile resort by trial court to prior restraints to prevent feared prejudice to fair trial rights. But as a practical matter if appellate courts are unwilling or unable to act with uncharacteristic dispatch to vacate restraints on the press before they have any real effect,[35] a trial court, for what it sees as a compelling interest of justice, may choose to impose short term restraints on publication in clear violation of constitutional requirements knowing the order will be effective long enough to serve the perceived interest.

Such actions by trial courts place newsgatherers in a difficult position. On the one hand the newsgatherer with trial information to communicate to the public may know that in his jurisdiction an "expedited appeal" will be futile because the restraint on publication will almost surely expire before the appeals court hears and decides the case, with the information literally becoming yesterday's news. On the other hand if the newsgatherer chooses to publish in violation of the order, he will likely be held in contempt. And there is no certainty he will escape punishment even though the order violated is an unconstitutional one.

More than one reporter can attest to this state of the law. In *United States v. Dickinson*[36] a pretrial hearing was held to consider whether Louisiana's motive in prosecuting a black civil rights activist on a charge of conspiring to murder the mayor of Baton Rouge was legitimate or contrived. At the hearing, the trial judge announced an order from the bench barring publication by any news media of the testimony to be given in open court and threatening sanctions for its violation. Notwithstanding the order and understanding that their professional actions violated its terms, reporters for the Baton Rouge Morning Advocate and the Baton Rouge State Times wrote articles for their respective papers reporting in detail the day's testimony. Thereafter, a show cause order was issued and the reporters were found guilty of criminal contempt and fined $300 each.

On appeal, and even before the Supreme Court in *Nebraska Press Association* set the standard for prior restraint of the press in trial settings, the Fifth Circuit held the verbal restraining order unconstitutional as not overcoming the heavy presumption of unconstitutionality attaching to prior restraints because it did not meet the "clear and present danger test."[37]

But the Fifth Circuit quickly pointed out that holding the restraining order unconstitutional did not end the matter. The appeals court

---

35. In Nebraska Press Association, for instance, the Nebraska Supreme Court did not decide the newsgatherers' expedited appeal from the district court's restrictive order for 31 days. 427 U.S. at 544, 96 S. Ct. at 2795–96, 49 L. Ed. 2d at 688–89.

36. 465 F.2d 496 (5th Cir.1972), cert. denied 414 U.S. 979, 94 S.Ct. 270, 38 L.Ed.2d 223 (1973).

37. *Id.* at 501, 507–508.

reiterated the then well-established principle in proceedings for criminal contempt that an injunction duly issued by a court with subject matter and personal jurisdiction had to be obeyed, *irrespective of its ultimate validity.* "Invalidity," said the court, "is no defense to criminal contempt."[38] The court rejected the argument that these rules were inapplicable to the press but vacated the judgments of contempt because of a narrow technical error and remanded the case to see if the district judge still thought the judgment of contempt and the punishment therefor were appropriate in light of the unconstitutionality of his order.[39]

The Fifth Circuit in *Dickinson* sent two very strong signals. First, by reaching out to vacate the judgment for a very technical reason, the court was suggesting that the matter be dropped on remand. Second, by saying, "Having disobeyed the Court's decree, they [the reporters] must, as civil disobeyers, suffer the consequences,"[40] the appeals court was indicating that it did not wish to see judicial authority undermined by willful disobedience of court orders by members of the press.

But who really brings the judicial system into disrepute in these situations? Is it the reporter who comes by information in open court or otherwise legally and simply wishes to do his job by communicating it to the public or is it the trial judge who through ignorance of the law or cynical calculation enters a clearly unconstitutional restraining order against the press?[41]

Confronting this question may lead to a reevaluation of the rule that denies to press violators the defense of unconstitutionality. In *Matter of Providence Journal Co.*[42] the newspaper and a Providence television station pursuant to a Freedom of Information Act (FOIA) request obtained certain logs and memoranda from the FBI pertaining to illegal Bureau electronic surveillance of a reputed member of the Mafia. By this time the surveillance target was deceased and his son filed suit against the Bureau, the newspaper and the television station complaining that

---

38. *Id.* at 509 (citing among other authorities, Walker v. City of Birmingham, 388 U.S. 307, 87 S.Ct. 1824, 18 L.Ed.2d 1210 (1967) and United States v. United Mine Workers, 330 U.S. 258, 67 S.Ct. 677, 91 L.Ed. 884 (1947)); *see* P.H. Vartanian, Annot., *Right to Punish for Contempt for Failure to Obey Court Order or Decree Either Beyond Power or Jurisdiction of Court or Merely Erroneous,* 12 A.L.R. 2d 1059, 1107–16 (1950).

39. Dickinson, 465 F.2d at 514.

40. *Id.* at 513.

41. *See* Note, *Defiance of Unlawful Authority,* 83 Harv. L. Rev. 626, 635 (1970) in which the student author observed, "Behind the concern for 'integrity' [of judicial authority] appear to lie fears that such vindication of defiance would reduce respect for law and would encourage disobedience

of judicial commands which would later be found lawful. On the contrary refusing to hear collateral attacks may, by seeming to sanction judicial lawlessness, work against the societal interest in fostering respect for judicial processes." *See also* Goldblum v. NBC, 584 F.2d 904 (9th Cir.1978) (semble); Phoenix Newspapers, Inc. v. Superior Ct. 101 Ariz. 257, 418 P.2d 594 (1966) (decided under state constitution); Dailey v. Superior Ct., 112 Cal. 94, 44 P. 458 (1896) (decided under state constitution); Cooper v. Rockford Newspapers, Inc., 50 Ill.App.3d 250, 8 Ill.Dec. 508, 365 N.E.2d 746 (1977); State v. Coe. 101 Wash. 2d 364 369–78, 679 P.2d 353, 357–61 (1984) (decided under state constitution).

42. 820 F.2d 1342 (1st Cir.1986), *modified,* 820 F.2d 1354 (1st Cir.1987)(en banc per curiam order), cert. denied, 485 U.S. 693, 108 S.Ct. 1502, 99 L.Ed.2d 785 (1988).

the logs and memoranda were wrongfully released and sought injunctive relief to prevent the defendants from publishing the material. In this connection a temporary restraining order was sought to suppress the material until an injunction might issue. At the conference concerning the TRO on November 13, 1985, the argument of counsel for the Providence Journal that any restraining order would constitute a prior restraint forbidden by the First Amendment, was rejected by the district court and the TRO was entered. The court set a hearing for November 15th at which time it would decide whether to vacate the order. The order was later vacated and a preliminary injunction denied, but on November 14th while the TRO was in effect the Journal published an article on the deceased that included information taken from the logs and memoranda. Following hearing the district court found the Journal guilty of criminal contempt and imposed an 18–month jail term on its executive editor which was suspended in lieu of his performing 200 hours of public service. The newspaper was fined $100,000.[43]

On appeal, the United States Court of Appeals for the First Circuit held that the appellants should have been allowed to challenge collaterally the constitutionality of the restraining order at the contempt proceedings, and because the order was found by the appeals court to be "transparently invalid" it reversed the criminal contempt order entered by the trial court.[44]

Citing dictum in *Walker v. City of Birmingham*[45] the First Circuit held that the Supreme Court had established the rule there that a transparently invalid order cannot form the basis for a contempt citation and may be collaterally attacked.[46] The appeals court then engaged in an extensive analysis of the order and proceedings below to demonstrate the transparent invalidity of the order. The court first found that the three grounds assertedly supporting the request for injunctive relief, the Fourth Amendment, FOIA and Title III of the Omnibus Crime Control and Safe Streets Act of 1968 did not do so.[47] Second, the court found that the district court had failed to make findings to support its order required by *Nebraska Press Association* that publication will result in "damage to a near sacred right;" that the prior restraint order will be effective; and that no less extreme alternatives to prior restraint are available to safeguard the judicial interest involved.[48] Regarding the efficacy of the order, the appeals court believed, given the record in the case, that no finding of effectiveness could be made. Other media not restrained had the same information that the government had disclosed to the Providence Journal and had already published portions of it.[49] Third, as a procedural matter, the prior restraint was issued prior to a

---

43. *Id.* at 1344–45.

44. *Id.* at 1353.

45. 388 U.S. 307, 315, 87 S.Ct. 1824, 1829, 18 L.Ed.2d 1210, 1216–17 (1967).

46. Matter of Providence Journal Co., 820 F.2d at 1346–47.

47. *Id.* at 1349–50.

48. *Id.* at 1351.

49. *Id.*

full and fair hearing thus making the unconstitutionality of the order even more patent.[50]

Providence Journal is a very helpful precedent for the news media because it qualifies the absolutist rule reiterated in *Dickinson* that unconstitutional prior restraints may not be challenged in collateral contempt proceedings. They now may be, narrowly at least, in the First Circuit,[51] but it must be kept in mind that if a prior restraint is held by the reviewing court to be unconstitutional though not transparently so, even the First Circuit would bar collateral challenge of the order in a criminal contempt proceeding involving news media violators.[52] Courts will only go so far in allowing the sanctity of court orders to be challenged by violators[53] and members of the news media must be made aware that they are gambling with their freedom and their pocketbooks when they choose to violate restraining orders and injunctions rather than appealing them directly. Appeals, of course, may not be expeditious and the value of the news restrained from publication may be lost but the risk of criminal sanctions for violation of court orders must be taken into account in deciding whether to defy judicial authority in order to get the story out.

Counsel may be of help in reducing the risk in these difficult situations. If some time exists between the imposition of a prior restraint and the date when a story will lose its news value, an emergency or expedited appeal and petition for mandamus or prohibition should be filed with the appropriate appellate court clearly setting out the time constraints in the case. To be certain that the court understands the urgency of the situation counsel may wish to discuss the need for expedition with the chief clerk as well. If the court acts with dispatch the very great likelihood is that the order will be vacated or rendered unenforceable[54] and journalistically nothing will have been lost.

If, on the other hand it becomes clear that the appellate process will not move the case to resolution within the requisite time needed to

---

50. *Id.*

51. Collateral challenge would also seem to be permitted in the Ninth Circuit. *See* Goldblum v. NBC, 584 F.2d 904 (9th Cir. 1978) in which counsel for a television network was imprisoned for contempt when his media client refused to produce certain film for the United States District Court's inspection. In a mandamus action brought by the network, the Ninth Circuit vacated the inspection order and the order jailing counsel saying, "a broadcaster or publisher should not, in circumstances such as those in this case, be required to make a sudden appearance in Court and then to take urgent measures to secure appellate relief, all the while weighing the delicate question of whether or not refusal to comply with an apparently invalid order constitutes a contempt." *Id.* at 907. Some state jurisdictions also permit collateral challenges in narrow situations. *See* Phoenix Newspapers, Inc. v. Superior Ct., 101 Ariz. 257, 418 P.2d 594 (1966); Dailey v. Superior Ct., 112 Cal. 94, 44 P. 458 (1896) (decided under state constitution); Cooper v. Rockford Newspapers, Inc., 50 Ill.App.3d 250, 8 Ill.Dec. 508, 365 N.E.2d 746 (1977); State v. Coe, 101 Wash. 2d 364, 369–78, 679 P.2d 353, 357–61 (1984) (decided under state constitution).

52. Matter of Providence Journal Co., 820 F.2d at 1347; *see In re* "S" Children, 140 Misc.2d 980, 982–87, 532 N.Y.S.2d 192, 194–96 (Fam. Ct., Orange Co. 1988).

53. Matter of Providence Journal Co., 820 F.2d at 1347–48.

54. This is because very few prior restraints of the press have ever been upheld on appeal.

prevent loss of the story, the newspersons involved can, at this point, decide whether they will violate the trial court's order. Again, nothing is lost journalistically in choosing after the appeal is filed to violate the order and something may even be gained legally. If the order is now violated and the violators are held in contempt, on appeal from the contempt order media counsel can argue that his client acted in good faith throughout but was forced to vindicate his First Amendment rights in the way he did because the appeals court could not or would not act in the time required.[55] At the very least this argument should give the appeals court pause in ruling that collateral attack on the validity of the order is not permitted or even that the order is not transparently unconstitutional. The proposed procedure appears to be mandatory in the First Circuit.[56]

E. Assessment of the Law of Prior Restraint Regarding Coverage of Judicial Proceedings and Prognosis for the Future

1. Assessment

On their face the standards laid down in *Nebraska Press Association v. Stuart*[57] are more than sufficient to prevent prior restraints on the dissemination on news and information relating to judicial proceedings. As Justice White noted in his concurring opinion, the standards imposed raised considerable doubt whether such restraints could ever by justified.[58] But then apparently no one thought at that time that a newsgatherer might actually interfere with the attorney-client relationship by broadcasting allegedly privileged communications. The Cable News Network may have obtained the one type of information that judges will not permit to be made public, *i.e.*, privileged attorney-client communications. From practically their first day of law school, lawyers are taught that such communications are sacrosanct and may not be divulged. This may explain the trial court in *United States v. Noriega* imposing a temporary gag order without requiring the proponent of the order to meet the standards imposed in *Nebraska Press Association* and then the Eleventh Circuit upholding such order.[59] Rather than representing serious erosion

---

55. *See* Matter of Providence Journal Co., 820 F.2d at 1354–55 (*en banc* per curiam op. on rehearing); James C. Goodale, *The Press Ungagged: The Practical Effect on Gag Order Litigation of* Nebraska Press Association v. Stuart, 29 Stan. L. Rev. 497, 507–510 (1977); *see also* New York Times Co. v. Starkey, 51 A.D.2d 60, 380 N.Y.S.2d 239 (1976).

56. Matter of Providence Journal Co., 820 F.2d at 1355.

57. 427 U.S. 539, 96 S.Ct. 2791, 49 L.Ed.2d 683 (1976).

58. *Id.* at 570, 96 S. Ct. at 2808, 49 L. Ed. 2d at 704.

59. United States v. Noriega, 917 F.2d 1543 (11th Cir.1990); *See* Randall Rothen-

berg, *Noriega Tape Case Reviving Clash Over First Amendment*, N.Y. Times, Nov. 14, 1990, p. A1, col. 2 (article focusing on effect of broadcasting the tapes on the attorney-client relationship). Of course, it didn't hurt Noriega's position at the appellate level that the Eleventh Circuit perceived that CNN was violating the trial court's order while at the same time it was challenging it. *Noriega*, 917 F.2d at 1551, 1552. The mini constitutional crisis created by CNN here should never have occurred. CNN used questionable news judgement in airing one of the tapes. The story was the taping by the government of some or all of Noriega's phone conversations with his defense team and not the content of the tapes. Problems may also have been compounded

of *Nebraska Press Association* doctrine, *Noriega* may simply be *sui generis* because it involves a perceived interference with the attorney-client relationship which could have influenced the judges involved to ignore the Supreme Court's dictates out of ingrained special reverence for the lawyer-client relationship.[60]

The more important problem regarding prior restraints is the evasion of *Nebraska Press Association* by trial courts engaging in expedient conduct to achieve short term objectives free from appellate court interference. This conduct will continue to undermine the First Amendment guarantee of a free press so long as appellate courts are slow to act to set aside unconstitutional prior restraint orders directly and refuse to permit collateral challenges by newspersons on their appeal of criminal sanctions imposed for violation of these restraining orders.

2. *Prognosis*

While the Supreme Court has clearly signalled its intention in *Gentile v. State Bar*[61] not to waver in permitting and even encouraging *indirect* obstacles to the gathering and ultimate publication of news and information pertaining to judicial proceedings, it seems unlikely that the Court will retreat in the foreseeable future from the strong position it took in *Nebraska Press Association* against the application of *direct* prior restraints or "gag orders" against the press.

By a number of recent decisions a clear majority of the current justices—some veterans of the court and some relatively recent appointees—have shown a continuing sensitivity to the importance of free expression to our society.[62] This sensitivity should translate into determi-

---

by some of the legal advice given the network. *See* Stuart Taylor Jr., *CNN's First Amendment Hubris*, Legal Times, Nov. 19, 1990, p. 23; Marcia Chambers, *CNN Takes Wrong Tack in Tape Row, The Tale of the Tapes: Bad Law, Bad Case*, Nat'l. L. J., Dec. 10, 1990, p. 13; Anthony Lewis, *Abroad at Home: Despite CNN's Folly*, N.Y. Times, Nov. 16, 1990, p. A39, col. 1; *Odd Behavior in the Noriega Case*, N.Y. Times, Dec. 1, 1990 Sec. 1, p. 24, col. 1 (editorial); Jim McGee, *Tale of the Noriega Tapes; How CNN's Constitutional Battle Was Joined*, Wash. Post, Nov. 25, 1990, p. A1, col. 5 (good exposition of the facts leading up to the constitutional confrontation over the Noriega tapes). The opinion of these journalists was vindicated ultimately by CNN's acceptance of sanctions for criminal contempt in United States v. Cable News Network, Inc., 865 F.Supp. 1549 (S.D.Fla.1994). *See* note 34, p. 307, *supra*.

60. That the Supreme Court denied certiorari does not necessarily mean that the Court approves of the Eleventh Circuit's decision. A denial of certiorari does not signify approval of the decision below. *See*,

e.g., Hughes Tool Co. v. Trans World Airlines, Inc., 409 U.S. 363, 364 n. 1, 93 S.Ct. 647, 650 n. 1, 34 L.Ed.2d 577, 581 n. 1 (1973); Parker v. Ellis, 362 U.S. 574, 576, 80 S.Ct. 909, 911, 4 L.Ed.2d 963, 966 (1960); Griffin v. United States, 336 U.S. 704, 716, 69 S.Ct. 814, 820, 93 L.Ed. 993, 1000 (1949). Floyd Abrams, an eminent First Amendment practitioner, speculates that granting certiorari and the necessarily concomitant stay of the district court's order would have been perceived as an endorsement of CNN's actions in refusing to turn over the tapes in its possession to the court and in broadcasting one of them in apparent violation of the temporary restraining order. Floyd Abrams, *Prior Restraints*, 1 Comm. L. 1991 318 (Practising Law Institute).

61. 501 U.S. 1030, 111 S.Ct. 2720, 115 L.Ed.2d 888 (1991).

62. *See* R.A.V. v. City of St. Paul, Minnesota, 505 U.S. 377, 112 S.Ct. 2538, 120 L.Ed.2d 305 (1992); Simon & Schuster, Inc. v. Members of the New York State Crime Victims Board, 502 U.S. 105, 112

nation that prior restraint of the press, the most dangerous kind of assault on First Amendment freedom, will not be tolerated. In this connection, the *Noriega Tapes Case* will likely be seen by appellate judges, at least, as an aberration to be treated like a derelict on the legal waters.[63]

As for short term efforts by some trial courts to evade the constitutional standards laid down in *Nebraska Press Association*, they are likely to become fewer in number as appellate courts are sensitized to the extraordinary nature of prior restraint orders against the press no matter how temporary, to the need for immediate direct review of these orders and to the need to permit collateral attack on them in criminal contempt proceedings where their unconstitutionality is arguably patent. Here, *Matter of Providence Journal Co.* represents the more modern thinking. *United States v. Dickinson*, decided before *Nebraska Press Association* and out of step with its spirit, displays antiquated absolutist thinking regarding the sanctity of restraining orders against the press and may eventually be discarded.

Finally, the Supreme Court's current position that large-scale publicity surrounding criminal trials is not, by itself, any reason to reverse criminal convictions should have the effect of lessening the propensity of trial judges to turn to the prior restraint device in sensational criminal trials to control unwanted publicity.[64]

8.8 Subsequent Punishment of Members of the News Media for Contempt of Court for Violating Statutes Controlling Information Regarding Judicial Proceedings

A. Introduction

It has long been believed that as between prior restraint of the press by government licensors and censors, and subsequent punishment of the

S.Ct. 501, 116 L.Ed.2d 476 (1991); United States v. Eichman, 496 U.S. 310, 110 S.Ct. 2404, 110 L.Ed.2d 287 (1990); Texas v. Johnson, 491 U.S. 397, 109 S.Ct. 2533, 105 L.Ed.2d 342 (1989). And yet one Justice (Stevens) refused to intervene on jurisdictional grounds to stay a United States District Court restraining order preventing a Magazine, Business Week, from publishing information from documents filed under seal without the prior consent of the District Court. "Even if I have jurisdiction to pass on the merits of the District Court's order of September 13 [1995]—a matter which is doubtful at best—I am satisfied that the wiser course is to give the District Court an opportunity to find the relevant facts, and to allow both that Court and the Court of Appeals to consider the merits of the First Amendment issue before it is addressed in this court." McGraw–Hill Cos. v. Procter & Gamble Co., 515 U.S. 1309, 1311,

116 S.Ct. 6, 7, 132 L.Ed.2d 892, 894 (1995). By Justice Stevens' decision, the District Court's "gag order" effectively remained in force until October 3, 1995 when the District Court made the sealed documents part of the public record. Technically, though, its 'restraining order remained in effect until it was finally vacated by the Sixth Circuit on March 5, 1996. *See* Procter & Gamble Co. v. Bankers Trust Co., 78 F.3d 219 (6th Cir.1996). Thus, Business Week was legally restrained from publishing for 175 days.

63. *Compare* Goldblum v. NBC, 584 F.2d 904 (9th Cir.1978).

64. *See* Mu'Min v. Virginia, 500 U.S. 415, 111 S.Ct. 1899, 114 L.Ed.2d 493 (1991); Patton v. Yount, 467 U.S. 1025, 104 S.Ct. 2885, 81 L.Ed.2d 847 (1984); Murphy v. Florida, 421 U.S. 794, 95 S.Ct. 2031, 44 L.Ed.2d 589 (1975).

press for publication of news and information displeasing to the ruling authorities, the former was by far the worse evil because the public was denied access to the news and information suppressed.[1] Or, as the Supreme Court stated it, "If it can be said that a threat of criminal or civil sanctions after publication "chills" speech, prior restraint "freezes" it at least for the time."[2]

But it goes almost without saying that the threat of incarceration or the imposition of heavy fines may dissuade even the most courageous members of the press from publishing that which they know will bring down upon them the wrath of government. And thus subsequent punishment for publication poses an extremely serious threat to press freedom and ultimately the freedom of society. Because for more than half a century, the Supreme Court has recognized the gravity of the threat, constitutional standards nearly as high as for prior restraints have been imposed upon those who would justify punishing members of the media for what they publish about the judiciary and the judicial system.

The major difference in the standards, if any really exists, is that the oft stated idea that prior restraints come before the judiciary bearing a heavy presumption against their constitutional validity[3] is not mentioned in the subsequent punishment cases. This omission may represent merely a semantic difference because the Supreme Court continues to view subsequent punishment of members of the press with great wariness.[4]

1. Professor Thomas I. Emerson compared the evils of prior restraint with the evils of subsequent punishment in his classic article *The Doctrine of Prior Restraint*, 20 Law & Contemp. Probs. 648 (1955). According to Emerson, a system of prior restraint is broader in its coverage, more uniform in its effect and more easily and effectively enforced than a system of subsequent punishment. Everything which is publicly uttered is subject to the scrutiny of licensors or censors while some publications which are displeasing to the government will not be noticed and punished. In addition, expression which is banned never sees the light of day and that which is not banned may be so delayed in the administrative bureaucracy that it loses its value when it is finally "cleared." Then, too, the procedural safeguards of the criminal justice system, including open courtrooms and public scrutiny, are not present to the same degree in the administrative censorial process. Finally, the entire prior restraint system is premised on suppression and the censor is impelled to find things to suppress. *Id.* at 656–59. *See* Near v. Minnesota *ex rel.* Olson, 283 U.S. 697, 713, 51 S.Ct. 625, 630, 75 L.Ed. 1357, 1366 (1931); *see also* the dissenting opinion of Warren, C.J.,

in Times Film Corp. v. Chicago, 365 U.S. 43, 50, 81 S.Ct. 391, 395, 5 L.Ed.2d 403, 408 (1961) (detailing the dangers of prior restraint throughout history).

2. Nebraska Press Association v. Stuart, 427 U.S. 539, 559, 96 S.Ct. 2791, 2803, 49 L.Ed.2d 683, 697 (1976) (paraphrasing Alexander Bickel, The Morality Of Consent 61 (1975)).

3. *See* New York Times Co. v. United States, 403 U.S. 713, 714, 91 S.Ct. 2140, 2141, 29 L.Ed.2d 822, 824 (1971); Organization for a Better Austin v. Keefe, 402 U.S. 415, 419, 91 S.Ct. 1575, 1577–78, 29 L.Ed.2d 1, 5 (1971); Bantam Books, Inc. v. Sullivan, 372 U.S. 58, 70, 83 S.Ct. 631, 639, 9 L.Ed.2d 584, 593 (1963).

4. *But cf.* the concurring opinion of White, J., in New York Times Co. v. United States, 403 U.S. 713, 730, 91 S.Ct. 2140, 2149, 29 L.Ed.2d 822, 833–34 (1971) (the "Pentagon Papers" case) in which he argued that while the prior restraint of publication for asserted national security reasons involved there did not meet the high constitutional standards required for its validity, criminal prosecution for violation of a number of relevant federal statutes would have been permissible.

B.   **Punishment for Criminal Contempt*

C.   **Punishment for Violation of Statutes Protecting Confidentiality in the Judicial System*

D.   **Assessment and Prognosis Regarding the Law of Subsequent Punishment*

* This section published in Modern Communication Law, Practitioners Edition, Vol. 2, only.

Chapter Nine

THE TELECOMMUNICATIONS ACT OF 1996

Analysis

9.1 An Introduction to the 1996 Telecommunications Act

On February 8, 1996, President Clinton signed into law the most comprehensive telecommunications legislation since the passage of the Communications Act of 1934.[1] The new statute, styled the Telecommunications Act of 1996,[2] confirmed the transformation of telecommunications in the United States from a closed system of regulated monopolies to an industry driven by competition and technological advance.

The new legislation was badly needed and long overdue. In the decades that had followed passage of the first Communications Act, evolving technology and the FCC's deregulatory initiatives had strained the rules and policies of the 1934 Act to the breaking point. At the same time, oversight of the industry had grown increasingly balkanized, with state regulations and the AT & T divestiture consent decree restricting competition in ways that often were in conflict with the policy preferences of the FCC. Long before the 1996 Act was passed, therefore, it was clear that statutory reform was needed in a number of areas.

One pressing need was to streamline—and in the view of many, to eliminate—the federal system of common carrier regulation to which many telecommunications service providers still were subject. As codified

---

1. Communications Act of 1934, 48 Stat. 1064 (1934), *codified as amended at* 47 U.S.C.A. §§ 151 *et seq.* (West 1991 and Supp. 1997).

2. Telecommunications Act of 1996, Pub. L. 104–104, 110 Stat. 56 (1996)(hereinafter "1996 Act").

in Title II of the 1934 Act,[3] common carrier regulation required all carriers to adhere to published schedules of rates and to seek the permission of the FCC before building or extending facilities or discontinuing service. These requirements, which had been designed to promote universal service and limit abuses of market power by telephone and telegraph monopolies, seemed increasingly inappropriate in an age of competition.

A second problem was the persistence of legal barriers to the participation of certain carriers in certain markets. Most notably, the AT & T antitrust consent decree prohibited the Bell operating companies from offering interexchange telephone service or manufacturing telecommunications equipment;[4] and the Cable Act of 1984[5] prevented telephone companies (both Bell and nonBell) from providing cable television service in the areas in which they also provided telephone service. These restrictions became increasingly anachronistic in the 1990s, and the Bell companies already were eroding them piecemeal through litigation.

Finally, the industry needed an orderly transition to competition in local telephone service. This was considered vital in itself, and also as a logical precondition to Bell company provision of interexchange service.

The Act signed into law in February, 1996 addressed all of these concerns, along with other subjects ranging from indecent communications on the Internet to restrictions on ownership of broadcast stations. The provisions of the new Act, which add new sections to the 1934 Act and amend a number of existing sections, are allocated among six titles.

Title I of the Act ("Telecommunications") is devoted to the reform of the telephone industry. This title establishes the framework for the emergence of competition in local telephone markets, sets conditions for entry of the Bell operating companies into long-distance service and telecommunications equipment manufacturing and mandates the continued subsidization of telephone service for rural and high-cost customers. Title I also establishes rigorous deadlines for FCC enactment of regulations implementing its provisions and gives the states a substantial role in enforcing those regulations and establishing concurrent rules of their own.

Title II of the Act ("Broadcast Services") reduces the regulatory burdens on broadcast licensees. Among other provisions, Title II eases restrictions on ownership of multiple broadcast licenses by a single entity, extends the terms of broadcast licenses and creates a stronger presumption in favor of renewal of licenses already granted.

3. 47 U.S.C.A. §§ 201–226 (West 1991 and Supp. 1997).

4. United States v. Western Elec. Co., 569 F.Supp. 1057 (D.D.C.1983), *aff'd mem. sub nom.* California v. United States, 464 U.S. 1013, 104 S.Ct. 542, 78 L.Ed.2d 719 (1983).

5. Cable Communications Policy Act of 1984, Pub. L. 98–549, 98 Stat. 2780 (1984), *codified as amended at* 47 U.S.C.A. §§ 601–639 (West 1991 and Supp. 1997).

Title III ("Cable Services") ends the statutory ban on telephone company ownership of cable television operations in the telephone companies' service areas, and creates a quasi-common carrier type of cable television service called an open video system ("OVS"). Title III also sets a timetable for reduction of cable television rate regulation and preempts any effort by local franchising authorities to prevent or regulate the offering of telephone services by cable television systems.

Title IV ("Regulatory Reform") eliminates certain regulations—including some foreign ownership restrictions and the requirement that common carriers obtain approval before extending their lines—and gives the FCC sweeping authority to scrutinize other regulations and eliminate those that no longer serve the public interest. To ensure that regulatory reform will become an ongoing process, the Act requires the Commission to review and eliminate needless regulations again in 1998 and to repeat the process every two years thereafter.

Title V of the Act ("Obscenity and Violence") imposed restrictions on obscene, indecent and violent communications. Notably, this title criminalized the transmission of indecent materials through interactive computer services where those communications might reach minors and also criminalized the knowing provision of facilities through which those transmissions are provided. These provisions were declared unconstitutional on their face in *Reno v. ACLU*.[6] The Act also required cable operators to take certain measures to limit the availability of indecent or sexually explicit programming, gave television program distributors one year in which to develop program ratings and required the FCC to develop rules requiring television set manufacturers to include a blocking device (the so-called "V-chip") through which viewers can block programming carrying particular ratings.

Title VI ("Effect on Other Laws") declares that the AT & T, GTE and McCaw consent decrees[7] are superseded by the 1996 Act and also preempts local taxation of direct broadcast satellite ("DBS") services.

Title VII ("Miscellaneous Provisions") addresses a number of concerns that do not fit logically within any of the preceding titles. Notably, Title VII requires the Bell operating companies to protect proprietary information obtained from their customers, requires utilities to make their poles and conduits available to cable television and telecommunications companies and creates a private, nonprofit corporation to receive federal funding and spur private investment for the development and improvement of education technology infrastructure.

While some provisions of the Act are relatively complete in themselves, the meaning of many of the most significant provisions had to await the outcome of a long list of accelerated regulatory proceedings mandated by the Congress. The following sections, after examining in more detail the legal and factual background of the Act, consider the

---

6.   521 U.S. 844, 117 S.Ct. 2329, 138 L.Ed.2d 874 (1997).

7.   *See* section 9.7, *infra*.

substantive provisions of all seven titles together with the scope and outcome of the associated regulatory proceedings.

9.2 Title I Of The 1996 Act—Telephone Competition and Regulation

Title I of the 1996 Act amends the 1934 Act by adding 16 new sections[1] and amending two existing sections.[2] The purpose of Title I is to reform the regulation of telecommunications services. As noted earlier, its most important provisions concern the opening of the local telephone market to competition, the elimination of barriers to Bell operating company entry into the interLATA long-distance market, and the creation of a framework for continuing support of universal service. The Act's treatment of each of these goals merits detailed review.

A. *Opening The Local Exchange Market*

As recently as 1984, when AT & T was divested of its local telephone operations under the terms of an antitrust consent decree, local telephone service was widely believed to be a natural monopoly—*i.e.*, a service that could be provided most efficiently by a single carrier. Accordingly, the Justice Department's lawsuit against AT & T did not seek to open the local market to competition; instead, the Department concentrated on separating AT & T's control of the local market from its long-distance and manufacturing operations. The Department believed that manufacturing and long-distance could be subject to efficient, effective competition, but only after AT & T no longer controlled its competitors' access to the local exchange "bottleneck."

The AT & T divestiture, therefore, left in place the exclusive franchise of the existing telephone companies—both Bell and nonBell—to provide telephone service within local calling areas. And the state public service commissions, which historically had favored intrastate monopolies as a means of preserving subsidies for basic, residential service, gave every indication that they would protect the exclusive local franchises of their incumbent telephone companies into the indefinite future.

Through the latter 1980s and early 1990s, however, a number of developments challenged the belief that local service is a natural monopoly. Some of these developments involved new businesses and technologies that made local exchange competition appear more plausible. Others showed a gradual shift in the climate of opinion, especially among policy makers, in favor of reliance on competitive markets over regulated monopoly.

---

1. The new sections are sections 251–261 and sections 271–276, all codified at 47 U.S.C.A. §§ 251–261 and 271–276 (West Supp. 1997).

2. The 1996 Act amends sections 214 and 251 of the 1934 Act. The 1996 Act also includes amendments to The Public Utility Holding Company Act of 1935, 15 U.S.C.A. §§ 79 *et seq.* (West 1997), for the purpose of permitting gas, electric and other utilities to offer telecommunications services. 1996 Act § 103.

Among the business and technical developments making local competition appear more plausible was the emergence of the competitive access provider (CAP) industry. A number of entrepreneurs learned that by running optical fiber through the business centers of cities, they could create networks capable of connecting business customers with their long-distance service providers. These new networks, by eliminating the local telephone company as a source of interexchange access, avoided the steep charges normally paid by the long-distance carriers for access to the local networks.

The CAP industry received a substantial boost when the FCC enacted rules requiring the local exchange carriers ("LECs")to sell the CAPs the facilities they needed in order to provide access over a combination of LEC and CAP facilities.[3] These rules, which allowed CAPs to enter the market more quickly and economically, demonstrated that with some regulatory encouragement, wireline competition inside the local exchange was possible. The next obvious step was to create similar rules for switched local telephone service.

Other business and technical factors favoring local competition included the rise of cellular telephony and the rapid expansion of cable television systems. The cellular telephone, while still not a perfect substitute for wireline service (chiefly because of cost), taught an important lesson—*i.e.*, that new technologies could enable new entrants to compete with wireline telephony without duplicating the embedded networks of the established carriers. And cable television, by carrying a new wireline transmission channel to most of the neighborhoods in the country, suggested that the backbone for a second, wireline telephone network might actually be at hand.

The movement toward local competition also was aided by a change in the attitude of many state regulators. A number of states, under pressure from long-distance carriers and others who expected to benefit from increased competition, began to permit interexchange carriers to offer intraLATA[4] long-distance service in competition with the LECs. With that precedent established, would-be local competitors (including CAPs and cable companies) argued persuasively that the public interest would be served by opening the local exchange market, as well, to competition.

By the time the 1996 Act was passed, the local competition initiatives at the state level had gone far enough to permit some conclusions. First, it was clear that the states still varied widely in the speed with

3. *See, e.g.*, Expanded Interconnection with Local Telephone Company Facilities, 7 FCC Rcd 7369 (1992).

4. LATAs, or local administrative and transport areas, were established in the AT & T divestiture proceeding to define the areas within which the Bell operating companies would be permitted to offer telecommunications services. Some LATAs covered only a single metropolitan area, while oth-

ers covered an entire state. The Bells were not permitted to provide long-distance service between LATAs, but were permitted to provide telecommunications service (both local and long-distance) between points within any LATA. *See, e.g.*, MICHAEL K. KELLOGG, JOHN THORNE and PETER W. HUBER, FEDERAL TELECOMMUNICATIONS LAW 227–34 (1992).

which they were permitting new entry into the local loop and in the restrictions they were prepared to impose on competition. Second, it was clear that the all-important terms on which new entrants would be allowed to interconnect their facilities with those of the established carriers would vary widely from state to state, depending on the attitude of the local carriers and the willingness of the state commissions to set rules or resolve complaints. Under these circumstances, it appeared that local competition would arrive piecemeal and would encounter less favorable conditions in some markets than in others.

The local competition provisions of the 1996 Act, while preserving a large role for the states, were designed to bring order and direction to this process by setting a uniform, nationwide policy in favor of local competition, and by establishing (with the aid of the FCC) a set of rules to guide the implementation of local competition. The most stringent of these provisions fall upon the incumbent local exchange carriers ("ILECs"), which must interconnect with the new competitors upon reasonable terms and conditions. And in order to increase the motivation of the Bell companies, in particular, to comply with these requirements, the Act makes compliance with the interconnection standards a precondition to Bell operating company entry into interLATA long-distance service and manufacturing.

1. Removing Legal Barriers to Local Competition

Logically and practically, the Congress's first task in promoting local competition was to remove existing legal prohibitions—and foreclose future legal prohibitions—on new entry into the local telephone service market. The existing prohibitions included state statutes forbidding, or establishing substantial barriers to, the provision of service by firms other than the established telephone companies and statutory limitations on provision of telephone service by electrical power companies and other nontelephone utilities. Potential prohibitions included the likelihood that municipalities might use their local franchise authority over cable television systems to prevent or limit participation by cable operators in the local telephone service market.

Of the existing legal impediments to local competition, the most fundamental was the states' traditional control over licensing telephone companies. Accordingly, Section 253 of the 1996 Act provides that "[n]o State or local statute or regulation . . . may prohibit or have the effect of prohibiting the ability of any entity to provide any interstate or intrastate telecommunications service."[5] While Section 253 preserves to the states the right to impose "competitively neutral" rules for the promotion of universal service, public safety and other public-interest concerns and permits states and municipalities to control access to public rights-of-way, the section also gives the FCC express authority to preempt state and local enactments that it finds to be anticompetitive.

---

5. 1996 Act § 253(a), *codified at* 47 U.S.C.A. § 253(a) (West Supp. 1997).

To remove the second impediment, the Act amends the Public Utilities Holding Company Act ("PUHCA") which limited the ability of gas and electric utilities to offer telecommunications and other nontraditional services. Specifically, Section 103 of the Act amends PUHCA to permit gas and electrical power companies, upon application to the FCC, to offer telecommunications services.[6]

The third concern is addressed by Section 303 of the Act, which preempts any attempt by state and local authorities to franchise the providing of telecommunications service by cable companies, or to use the franchising authority to limit or prohibit the providing of telecommunications service by a cable company.[7]

With these three sections of the new Act, the Congress removed the principal *de jure* obstacles to local telephone competition.[8] If the Congress had stopped there, however, the Act's promise of local competition would have rung hollow. Notably, unless the incumbent telephone companies completed calls placed to their customers by subscribers of the new networks and delivered calls from the telephone companies' customers to subscribers served by the new networks, the new carriers would only be able to offer closed systems carrying conversations between their own customers. Some level of mandated cooperation between the telephone companies and their competitors, therefore, was required. And in fact, the 1996 Act mandates a degree of cooperation among competitors unprecedented in the history of American law.[9] In order to appreciate the scope and depth of these obligations, they will be reviewed in some detail.

2.   *Mandating Cooperation With Local Competitors*

Section 251 of the 1996 Act imposes some level of interconnection obligation on all telecommunications service providers. The stringency of the Act's interconnection requirements varies dramatically, however, depending on whether a service provider is a one of the monopoly, incumbent local exchange carriers ("ILECs"), a new, competing LEC ("CLEC"), or a nonLEC. This section describes each of these sets of obligations, beginning with the modest duties imposed on all telecommunications carriers and concluding with the dramatic obligations of the incumbent telephone companies.

6. *Id.* § 103, *codified at* 47 U.S.C.A. § 34 (West 1997).

7. *Id.* § 3(d), *codified at* 47 U.S.C.A. § 541(b)(3)(A) (West Supp. 1997).

8. The Act also restrains other, less fundamental, state and local limitations on local competition. Specifically, the Act preempts local taxation of direct-to-home satellite services (also known as direct broadcast satellite, or DBS) and declares that state and local governments may not prohibit the placement, construction or modification of facilities used for wireless personal communications services. The Act also provides that in their exercise of regulatory authority over wireless facilities, states and localities may not discriminate among functionally equivalent services. *Id.* §§ 602, 704, *codified at* 47 U.S.C.A. notes § 152, § 332(a) (West Supp. 1997).

9. For a critique of the efficacy of these rules, see section 9.9, *infra.*

a. Obligations of Telecommunications Carriers

The Act's least specific interconnection obligations are set out in Section 251(a), which applies to all "telecommunications carriers"—a category that includes "any provider of telecommunications services," including local exchange carriers, commercial mobile radio service providers and long-distance carriers.[10] Since all nonLEC carriers lack market power and therefore have little incentive *not* to link their networks and services with those of others, the Act merely gives such carriers a nonspecific obligation to interconnect—either directly or indirectly—with the facilities and equipment of other such carriers and forbids them to install equipment or features that discourage interconnectivity with other networks and equipment or that fail to comply with the Act's requirements concerning access by persons with disabilities.[11] Section 251(a) does not specify the type or quality of interconnection arrangements that telecommunications carriers must provide and sets no standards for the pricing of such interconnections. The Commission's implementing order, similarly, confirms that the general interconnection obligation of Section 251(a) does not require telecommunications carriers to offer direct interconnection with other carriers, and that "indirect connection [*e.g.*, two non-incumbent LECs interconnecting with an incumbent LEC's network] satisfies a telecommunications carrier's duty to interconnect pursuant to section 251(a)."[12]

b. Obligations of Local Exchange Carriers ("LECs")

Somewhat more stringent obligations are imposed on local exchange carriers (LECs)—a category that includes both the incumbent telephone companies and the new, competing local exchange carriers (CLECs).[13] Specifically, all LECs must permit resale of their services; they must, where feasible, allow their customers to use the same telephone numbers when they switch their service to a competitor (a capability known as number portability); they must offer dialing parity to subscribers of competing networks; they must provide their competitors with reason-

---

10. 47 U.S.C.A. § 153(44) (West Supp. 1997). The Commission's implementing order confirms that the Act's definition of "telecommunications carrier" extends to cellular and other commercial mobile radio service ("CMRS") providers. Implementation of the Local Competition Provisions in the Telecommunications Act of 1996, CC Docket No. 96–98, and Interconnection between Local Exchange Carriers and Commercial Mobile Radio Service Providers, CC Docket No. 95–185, First Report and Order (rel. Aug. 8, 1996) ("Interconnection Order") at para. 993.

11. 1996 Act § 251(a), *codified at* 47 U.S.C.A. § 251(a) (West Supp. 1997).

12. Interconnection Order at para. 997.

13. The 1996 Act defines a local exchange carrier as "any person that is engaged in the provision of telephone exchange service or exchange access," and expressly excludes from the definition "a person insofar as such person is engaged in the provision of a commercial mobile radio service ... , except to the extent that the Commission finds that such service should be included in the definition of such term." 1996 Act § 153(26), *codified at* 47 U.S.C.A. § 153(26) (West Supp. 1997). Because this definition includes both incumbent and competing LECs (ILECs and CLECs, respectively), the obligations of section 251(b) apply equally to both classes of carrier. Only ILECs, however, must also comply with the more stringent obligations of section 251(c). Competing LECs need only comply with the obligations of section 251(b).

able access to their poles, conduits and rights-of-way; and they must establish reciprocal compensation arrangements with other service providers for the transport and termination of communications.[14] Each of these obligations, and the FCC's corresponding rulemaking proceedings, merit discussion.

(1) LEC Resale Obligations

The resale obligation imposed on nonincumbent LECs by the 1996 Act is notable for what it does not include. Specifically, the competing LECs, unlike the incumbent LECs subject to the obligations of section 251(c) of the Act, are not expressly obligated to make their retail services available to resellers at a discount from the LECs' retail rates. Accordingly, the CLECs will satisfy the requirements of section 251(a) if they simply do not discriminate between end users and resellers in the rates, terms and conditions by which they offer their retail services.

(2) The LEC Number Portability Obligation

The 1996 Act defines number portability as "the ability of users of telecommunications services to retain, at the same location, existing telecommunications numbers without impairment of quality, reliability, or convenience when switching from one telecommunications carrier to another."[15] Section 251(b)(2) requires all LECs to offer this capability "to the extent feasible" and leaves to the Commission the task of enacting rules to determine when and how number portability must be made available.

The Commission addressed the number portability obligation in an order released on July 2, 1996[16] directing all LECs to begin the phased deployment of number portability in the 100 largest metropolitan statistical areas (MSAs) by October 1, 1997, and to complete that deployment by December 31, 1998.[17] The Commission's *Number Portability Order* did not endorse a particular number portability technology, but established performance criteria that any number portability method should meet.[18]

(3) Dialing Parity and Related LEC Obligations

Dialing parity is the ability of a service provider's customer to access the service provider's facilities without dialing "extra digits."[19] Dialing

---

14. *Id.* § 251(b), *codified at* 47 U.S.C.A. § 251(b) (West Supp. 1997).

15. *Id.* § 3(a)(2)(46), *codified at* 47 U.S.C.A. § 153(30) (West Supp. 1997).

16. Telephone Number Portability, 11 FCC Rcd 8352 (1996)("*Number Portability Order*").

17. *Id.* at 8393. After December 31, 1998, LECs are required to provide number portability in areas outside the 100 largest MSAs within six months of receiving a specific request. *Id.* at 8394.

18. The *Number Portability Order* also requires certain commercial mobile radio service providers (CMRSs) to provide number portability by June 30, 1999. *Id.* at 8433.

19. The definitional section of the Act says that dialing parity "means that a person who is not an affiliate of a local exchange carrier is able to provide telecommunications services in such a manner that customers have the ability to route automatically, without the use of any access code, their telecommunications to the telecommunications services provider of the

parity first became an issue when the FCC mandated competition in the interexchange telephone market and competitors of AT & T wanted to offer their customers the ability to dial long-distance calls without first dialing a separate number to reach the competing carrier's switch.

In the interexchange context, dialing parity was implemented by a process called presubscription. Customers would select a long-distance carrier and that choice would be entered in the programmed memory of the local telephone company switch. When the customer dialed an interexchange call the switch automatically routed the call to the customer's presubscribed interexchange carrier.

The 1996 Act does not specify a method or implementation schedule for the dialing parity obligation it imposes. It simply requires all LECs to provide dialing parity to competing providers of telephone exchange service and toll service and also requires LECs to give competitors nondiscriminatory access to telephone numbers, operator services, directory assistance and directory listings.[20]

The Commission addressed these obligations in a companion order to its *Interconnection Order* that we may call, for convenience, the *Second Interconnection Order*.[21] Specifically, the Commission determined that the Act required all LECs to offer dialing parity for intrastate, interstate and international calls.[22] For toll calling, LECs must at least permit customers to select two presubscribed carriers—one for intra-LATA toll calling and another for interLATA toll calling—and must have that presubscription capability in place not later than February 8, 1999. The Commission also anticipated that dialing parity for local calling would be achieved once the number portability and interconnection requirements of Section 251 were implemented.[23]

The *Second Interconnection Order* also addressed the LECs' obligation to afford competing carriers nondiscriminatory access to telephone numbers, operator services, directory assistance and directory listings. Specifically, the Commission found that LECs must give competitors the same access to telephone numbers and directory assistance that the LECs offer to themselves. Customers of competitors providing operator services should be able to access a specified list of LEC operator services capabilities by dialing "0" or "0–plus" the desired telephone number, and LECs must share directory listings with their competitors in tape or electronic formats upon request.

---

customer's designation from among 2 or more telecommunications services providers (including such local exchange carrier)." 1996 Act § 3(a)(2)(39), *codified at* 47 U.S.C.A. § 153(15) (West Supp. 1997).

20. *Id.* § 251(b)(3), *codified at* 47 U.S.C.A. § 251(b)(3) (West Supp. 1997).

21. Implementation of the Local Competition Provisions in the Telecommunications Act of 1996, Second Report and Order and Mem. Op. and Order (Aug. 8, 1996)("Second Interconnection Order").

22. The Commission declined to impose dialing parity obligations on commercial mobile radio service (CMRS) providers. Second Interconnection Order, *supra*, note 21 at para. 29.

23. *Id.* at para. 71.

(4) Access to LEC Poles, Conduits and Rights-of-way

Two sections of the 1996 Act create an obligation of LECs—and other utility companies, as well—to make capacity on their poles, in their ducts and along their rights-of-way available to competitors. Specifically, Section 251(b)(4) of the Act requires LECs to grant other providers of telecommunications services access to these facilities upon "rates, terms, and conditions that are consistent with section 224 [of the Act]." Section 224 of the 1934 Act, in turn, is amended to impose a similar obligation on all "utilities" (including LECs) to make their poles, conduits and rights-of-way available to any "cable television system . . . or telecommunications carrier."[24]

(5) LEC Reciprocal Compensation Obligations

The Act requires all LECs to "establish reciprocal compensation arrangements for the transport and termination of telecommunications."[25] The Act supplements this requirement with a pricing provision directing state commissions not to approve reciprocal compensation arrangements as just and reasonable unless those arrangements provide for the "mutual and reciprocal recovery by each carrier of costs associated with the transport and termination on each carrier's network facilities of calls that originate on the network facilities of the other carrier," and "determine such costs on the basis of a reasonable approximation of the additional costs of terminating such calls."[26] The Act left the states with the task, in the course of arbitration or review of interconnection agreements, of determining how charges for these mutual compensation arrangements should be set.

In creating rules to implement the mutual compensation requirements, the Commission concentrated on establishing a standard to guide the states in reviewing the charges imposed for transport and termination of calls. The Commission gave the states three alternatives: set rates based on total element long-run incremental cost ("TELRIC"), a standard described at subsection 9.2.A.2C, *infra*; adopt one of a range of default prices established in the Commission's Order; or adopt a "bill-and-keep" methodology, under which each party to a mutual compensation agreement bears its own costs and no money changes hands between them.[27] Each of these approaches is controversial. As discussed further below, the ILECs attacked the TELRIC approach as confiscatory, and the default ranges also have been characterized as arbitrary and

---

24. The Act permits electrical utilities—but not LECs or other nonelectrical utilities—to deny access "where there is insufficient capacity and for reasons of safety, reliability and generally applicable engineering purposes." 1996 Act § 703, *codified at* 47 U.S.C.A. § 224 (West Supp. 1997). The Commission's implementing Order, however, notes that LECs and other nonelectrical utilities may raise similar concerns in resisting access, although those claims will be scrutinized closely. Second Interconnection Order, *supra*, note 21 at para. 1177.

25. 1996 Act § 251(b)(5), *codified at* 47 U.S.C.A. § 251(b)(5) (West Supp. 1997).

26. *Id.* § 252(d)(2), *codified at* 47 U.S.C.A. § 252(d)(2) (West Supp. 1997).

27. If a state commission adopts a default price, that price eventually must be replaced with a price based on a TELRIC study or with a price based on the FCC's subsequent generic cost model. Interconnection Order, *supra*, note 10 at para. 1055.

insufficient to recover the ILECs' costs. Similarly, the bill and keep approach, which effectively assumes that ILECs and CLECs incur similar costs to terminate traffic, was criticized by the ILECs as failing to recognize the greater investment in ILEC networks, which are engineered for universal service and high reliability under peak service loads.[27A]

c. Obligations of Incumbent LECs

The most stringent interconnection obligations fall on incumbent LECs, or ILECs—*i.e.*, carriers that were offering local exchange service as of the date of enactment of the Act. All ILECs are entrenched carriers formerly protected as lawful monopolies, with nearly a 100 percent share of the local exchange market in most areas. Only these carriers (unlike new, competing LECs) have the power to prevent effective competition by closing off access to their networks, and therefore have strong incentives to refuse reasonable interconnection arrangements. Accordingly, the 1996 Act imposes on ILECs all of the obligations applicable to LECs generally, and adds to those obligations a set of more stringent detailed requirements. These requirements fall into four broad categories: first, interconnection with the facilities of competing providers of exchange and access service; second, sale to competitors of various facilities and functions of the ILECs' networks for the competitors' use in providing competing services; third, sale of ILEC services, at a discount, to firms who will resell those services to retail telephone customers; and fourth, negotiation in good faith of interconnection agreements with other carriers. Each of these sets of obligations is to be implemented in negotiated agreements between ILECs and new entrants into the local service market,[28] and the negotiation process, in turn, is subject to mediation and arbitration by the state commissions having jurisdiction.[29] Each of these sets of obligations, as supplemented by implementing rules of the FCC, is complex and requires explanation.

27A. The United States Court of Appeals for the Eighth Circuit, on a petition for review of the Commission's Order, vacated the reciprocal compensation pricing rules on the ground that the 1996 Act gives the States—not the FCC—the power to set rates for local access, inter-connection, transport and termination. Iowa Utilities Board v. FCC, 120 F.3d 753 (8th Cir.1997). These rules were reinstated by the United States Supreme Court. ___ U.S. ___, 119 S.Ct. 721, 142 L.Ed.2d 835 (1999).

28. The requirement to negotiate interconnection agreements in good faith is set out at section 251(c)(1) of the Act. 1996 Act § 251(c)(1), *codified at* 47 U.S.C.A. § 251(c)(1) (West Supp. 1997). Where the parties enter into negotiated agreements, those agreements are not required to comply with the standards of section 251. *See id.* § 252(a)(1), *codified at* 47 U.S.C.A. § 252(a)(1) (West Supp. 1997). Those

agreements must be submitted to the state commission having jurisdiction for review, however, and the state may reject the agreement if it finds that the agreement discriminates against third parties or is contrary to the public interest. *See id.* § 252(e), *codified at* 47 U.S.C.A. § 252(e) (West Supp. 1997).

29. Any party to a negotiation for interconnection may ask the state commission to mediate at any time. *Id.* § 252(a)(2), *codified at* 47 U.S.C.A. § 252(a)(2) (West Supp. 1997). Any party may ask the state commission to arbitrate any open issues, so long as the request is made from the 135th day to the 160th day (inclusive) after the ILEC has received the interconnection request. *Id.* § 252(b)(1), *codified at* 47 U.S.C.A. § 252(b)(1) (West Supp. 1997). The state commission then must resolve the issues presented to it within nine months after the

(1) Interconnection

As we noted earlier, all telecommunications carriers have a general obligation to interconnect, either directly or indirectly, with the facilities and equipment of other telecommunications carriers. In the case of ILECs, however, the general obligation to interconnect is bolstered by more detailed requirements. ILECs must interconnect with the facilities of requesting carriers "for the transmission and routing of telephone exchange service and exchange access," and must do so "at any technically feasible point within the [ILEC's] network." ILEC interconnection arrangements provided to competitors also must be "at least equal in quality" to those offered to the ILECs' own affiliates, and must be provided at rates and other terms that are "just, reasonable, and nondiscriminatory."[30]

To the statute's statement of the ILECs' interconnection obligation, the FCC added detailed requirements of its own. Specifically, the Commission directed ILECs to offer interconnection to competing carriers providing either exchange service (*i.e.*, service between customers) or exchange access service (*i.e.*, service connecting customers with their long-distance carriers),[31] and to do so at any of a minimum list of physical network locations.[32] The Commission also imposed on the ILECs the burden of demonstrating the infeasibility of interconnection at any network location, in addition to those on the Commission's list, for which a request is received. Specifically, any ILEC wishing to show that interconnection at a requested physical point in its network is not feasible must make that demonstration to its state commission and may not rely on the fact that interconnection will be costly or will require changes to the ILEC's network. An ILEC may, however, rely on "legitimate threats to network reliability and security" in resisting a request for interconnection at a particular point. On the other hand, the fact that the ILEC, or another carrier with comparable facilities, already has granted interconnection at a particular point will be taken as evidence that similar interconnections are feasible for an ILEC attempting to prove infeasibility.

The Commission also set guidelines for the terms and conditions of ILEC interconnection arrangements.[33] Specifically, the Commission de-

---

date on which the interconnection request was received. *Id.* § 252(b)(4)(C), *codified at* 47 U.S.C.A. § 252(b)(4)(C) (West Supp. 1997). The FCC may resolve the open issues if the state commission fails to act, and the FCC's decision, in turn, will be subject to the usual judicial review remedy provided for FCC final actions. *Id.* § 252(e)(6), *codified at* 47 U.S.C.A. § 252(e)(6) (West Supp. 1997). (Any party aggrieved by a state commission action under Section 252 must seek judicial review in "an appropriate Federal district court.")

30. *Id.* § 251(c)(2), *codified at* 47 U.S.C.A. § 251(c)(2) (West Supp. 1997).

31. The Commission distinguished the physical interconnection of ILEC and competitors' facilities, mandated at section 251(c)(2) of the Act, from the obligation to establish reciprocal compensation arrangements for the transport and termination of calls imposed by section 251(b)(5). Interconnection Order, *supra* note 10 at para. 176.

32. *Id.* at para. 210. At minimum, ILECs must interconnect with requesting carriers at "the line-side of a local switch, ... the trunk-side of a local switch; the trunk interconnection points for a tandem switch; and central office cross-connect points in general." *Id.*

termined that for any telecommunications carrier requesting interconnection, an ILEC must provide a level of quality that is "at least indistinguishable from that which the incumbent provides itself, a subsidiary, an affiliate, or any other party."[34] At the same time, if a requesting carrier asks for an interconnection arrangement that is superior or inferior to the arrangements offered by the ILEC to itself or others, interconnection of the kind requested must be provided if technically feasible.[35]

The Act also requires ILECs to permit other carriers to collocate their equipment, as needed for interconnection or access to the ILECs' unbundled network elements,[36] at the ILECs' premises. Collocation must be provided on "just, reasonable, and nondiscriminatory" terms and conditions, except where the ILEC convinces its state commission that it lacks space for physical collocation at its premises, or demonstrates that physical collocation is technically impractical. In these cases, the ILEC may substitute "virtual" collocation for physical collocation.[37]

The physical collocation provisions of the Act resulted in some of the Commission's most detailed rules. Concerned that the incumbents may have circumvented its past collocation orders, the Commission defined ILEC "premises" expansively to include central offices, serving wire centers and tandem offices, as well as "all buildings or similar structures owned or leased by the incumbent LEC that house LEC network facilities."[38] The Commission also extended to the local market essentially all of the collocation rules from its earlier *Expanded Interconnection* orders, suggesting at the same time that those detailed rules eventually might be supplanted by the statutory provisions and the regulations adopted in the *Interconnection Order*.[39]

(2) Unbundled Network Elements

Of all the requirements imposed on ILECs by Section 251 of the Act, the most radical and controversial is the requirement that ILECs offer their competitors access to so-called "unbundled network elements."[40]

---

33. *Id.* at para. 213–225. The pricing guidelines for interconnection are the same as those the Commission established for pricing of unbundled elements, discussed immediately above in text. These pricing guidelines were vacated by the Eighth Circuit in the *Iowa Utilities Board* decision, *supra* n. 27A but reinstated by the Supreme Court. ___ U.S. ___, 119 S.Ct. 721, 142 L.Ed.2d 835 (1999).

34. Interconnection Order, *supra* note 10 at para. 224–25.

35. *Id.* The FCC's requirement that an ILEC provide forms of interconnection to other carriers that are superior to arrangements already in place was vacated in *Iowa Utilities Bd.* decision, *supra* n. 27A.

36. For an explanation of the obligation to provide unbundled network elements, see the following subsection 9.2A.2.c.(2).

37. 1996 Act § 251(c)(6), *codified at* 47 U.S.C.A. § 251(c)(6) (West Supp. 1997). The statutory physical collocation requirement was necessitated by a court's earlier finding that the Commission lacked statutory authority to impose such a requirement by regulation. Bell Atlantic Tel. Cos. v. FCC, 24 F.3d 1441, 306 U.S. App. D.C. 333 (D.C.Cir.1994).

38. Interconnection Order, *supra* note 10 at para. 573.

39. *Id.* at para. 612.

40. 1996 Act § 251(c)(3), *codified at* 47 U.S.C.A. § 251(c)(3) (West Supp. 1997).

Quite simply, these provisions mean that ILECs must sell (or, more accurately, rent) to their competitors the use of the lines, switches, databases, and related services through which the ILECs serve their own customers so that the competitors may use them to provide their own telecommunications services. This requirement is comparable to a government agency ordering a private railroad to allow other railroads to use its tracks or requiring Ford to let General Motors make cars in Ford's factories and sell them at Ford's dealerships.[41]

Obviously, a statute that requires businesses to act with such direct prejudice to their self-interest will not be self-enforcing: it can only be implemented by clear rules, and those rules must be sufficiently detailed to anticipate every likely tactic of evasion. While the Act expressly gives the states the primary role in implementing its interconnection provisions, the Commission chose to impose its own, detailed regulations implementing the technical and pricing requirements of the unbundled network elements provisions.

The heart of the Commission's rules is the adoption of a pricing standard for network elements that does not rely on the ILECs' pricing preferences, or even on the costs actually incurred by ILECs in providing network elements. Instead, the Commission adopted a pricing standard called total element long-run incremental cost, or "TELRIC".[41A] The Commission decided that although the states could approve interim rates based on a range of "default" charges set out in the *Interconnection Order*, charges for unbundled elements eventually must be set based on TELRIC studies. The significance of the TELRIC standard, and the reason it has been controversial, is that it is *forward-looking* and based only on the *incremental cost* of providing the facilities or services provided. Each of these features of the standard requires a word of explanation.

First, to say that TELRIC is forward-looking is to say that it permits the ILECs' prices to recover, not the costs actually incurred to provide network elements, but the cost that would be incurred to provide those elements today over an optimally-efficient network. This means, for example, that if an ILEC provides network elements in a particular exchange over an old but serviceable switch that costs more to operate than a new, digital switch, the ILEC may not charge prices based on the greater cost of the old switch; its rates must reflect the lower cost of a newer, more efficient switch. By imposing this forward-looking standard, the FCC hopes to force ILECs to become more efficient, by ensuring that they will charge only the prices they would charge if they *were*, in fact, more efficient.[42]

---

41. The rationale for this requirement, and a critique of that rationale, are set out at section 9.9, *infra*, pp. 361–368.

41A. The FCC's imposition of the TELRIC standard was vacated by the Eighth Circuit in *Iowa Utilities Bd, supra* n. 27A

and reinstated by the Supreme Court. ___ U.S. ___, 119 S.Ct. 721, 142 L.Ed.2d 835 (1999). The TELRIC Standard is the choice of many states in setting or approving rates for access and interconnection between ILEC's and their local competitors.

Second, to say that the TELRIC standard is based on incremental cost means that the prices charged for access to a network element will recover only the costs incurred to provide that network element and will not recover any investment made in connection with other products and services. More specifically, to use the language of the *Interconnection Order*, TELRIC includes only "the forward-looking costs directly attributable to the specified element, as well as a reasonable allocation of forward-looking common costs."[43] In order to understand the importance of this definition, it is necessary to know what it includes and what it leaves out.

First, the "forward-looking costs directly attributable" to a network element include all costs incurred as a direct result of providing the network element or that can be avoided if the ILEC ceases to provide the network element.[44] So, for example, the forward-looking direct cost of the access lines[45] provided to new entrants is a projection of the costs that will be incurred to purchase the copper wire, install telephone poles and string the lines as well as the expenses that will be incurred to maintain and repair the lines. The direct costs of the access lines also will include the salaries of technicians that work on the lines as well as the costs of supervising those technicians and other "back office" costs that are incurred directly to provide those lines.[46] These direct costs, divided by the number of access lines that the ILEC expects the new entrants to purchase, yield a portion of the price that the TELRIC approach permits the ILEC to charge for each line.

As we saw, however, TELRIC also includes a "reasonable allocation of forward-looking common costs." Common costs, simply put, are costs incurred in the provision of more than one product or service. Some of these costs, such as the salaries of the president and other top-level officers of the corporation, are "incurred by the firm's operations as a whole" and therefore are common to all products and services, including network elements furnished to competitors. Other costs (such as the cost of maintaining a switch) are common only to the switched subset of the ILEC's products and services. TELRIC recognizes that some portion of these common costs should be attributed to each service for which those

---

42. Specifically, the Commission found that ILECs would be allowed to recover "forward-looking economic cost ... based on the most efficient technology deployed in the incumbent LEC's current wire center locations." Interconnection Order, *supra* note 10 at para. 685. In their petitions for review of the FCC's Interconnection Order, the ILECs argued that by imposing a pricing standard that does not permit recovery of costs actually incurred, the Commission committed an impermissible, uncompensated taking of the ILECs' property.

43. *Id.* at para. 682.

44. *Id.* at para. 691.

45. Access lines are the copper wires, strung along poles or buried in underground conduit, that connect telephone company customers with the nearest telephone company switch.

46. Interconnection Order, *supra*, note 10 at para. 691.

costs are incurred and permits them to be allocated to individual network elements on any reasonable basis.[47]

While TELRIC includes many of the costs that ILECs will want to recover in their network element prices, it also leaves out some of those costs. Specifically, TELRIC excludes from network element prices the ILECs' embedded costs and opportunity costs. Each of these terms, also, requires some explanation.

Embedded, or accounting, costs recognize that network elements may be provided over facilities that were constructed before the accounting period in which those network elements will be sold and that expenses incurred in connection with those elements also may have been incurred during earlier accounting periods. To the extent these past costs were capital costs, they appear on the books today as depreciation. To the extent they were incurred as expenses, they appear on the books as past operating expenses.[48] If those costs must be recovered through present or future prices, and if the cost of those inputs has declined or technology has become more efficient since those historic costs were incurred, then the embedded cost of providing a network element may exceed the forward-looking incremental cost of providing that element. Accordingly, network element prices based only on forward-looking incremental cost will be insufficient to recover the costs actually incurred.

Opportunity cost, simply put, recognizes that an ILEC might earn a better return on investment by using its network elements as part of its own service rather than selling those elements to competitors. Some economists argue that in a competitive market, a firm would have the freedom to choose the most profitable use for its property; and that since the purpose of the Act is to replicate as closely as possible the incentives of competition, the Commission should permit these opportunity costs to be recovered in the course of the coerced transactions mandated by the Act.[49] So, for example, if an ILEC would have earned five percent more profit by selling the use of an access line to its own customer, rather than to a CLEC, that lost profit should be included in the price the ILEC is allowed to charge the CLEC for use of the line.

However esoteric it may appear, the debate over embedded and opportunity costs is a fundamental clash of business and regulatory goals. By adopting a pricing standard that ignores these costs, the FCC and many state commissions have chosen to err on the side of new entry by ensuring that CLECs will pay low prices for the items they need in order to enter the local exchange market quickly. At the same time, the adoption of TELRIC is another step in the FCC's gradual abandonment of the traditional regulatory goal of ensuring that regulated entities

---

47. *Id.* at para. 696. The Commission concludes, for example, that it would be reasonable to allocate common costs by a uniform mark-up to each of the direct costs or by overallocating those costs to products and services that are less critical to competitors. The Commission will not, however, sanction an allocation formula that overallocates costs to those network elements most needed by competitors. *Id.*

48. *Id.* at para. 675.

49. W. J. BAUMOL AND J. G. SIDAK, TOWARD COMPETITION IN LOCAL TELEPHONY 95–116 (1994).

recover all costs prudently incurred. Local telephone companies, like unregulated businesses of all kinds, assume the risk of loss if their investment decisions, however prudent, prove less astute than those of their competitors.

(3) Sale of Incumbent Local Exchange Carriers ("ILECS") Services to Resellers

Finally, in addition to interconnecting with their competitors, arranging for the mutual termination of calls and offering access to unbundled network elements, ILECs also must sell their competitors the same services they sell to their own subscribers and must do so at a discount from their retail rates.[50] This requirement gives the ILECs' competitors the option of foregoing the construction of networks or the assembly of the ILECs' network elements into facilities-based services. With mandated sale of ILEC services to new entrants, new entrants simply can buy ILEC services at wholesale and sell them at retail—the fastest, if not necessarily the most profitable, method of entering the local telephone market.

The Act does little to define the extent of the resale obligation, except to state that the ILECs must offer to resellers any service that the ILECs sell at retail and must do so at "wholesale" rates that reflect a discount from the ILECs' retail charges. That discount, in turn, must reflect those costs—such as customer billing and retail marketing—that are incurred at the retail level but avoided when an ILEC sells at wholesale.

In crafting rules to implement the resale provisions, the Commission paid particular attention to the calculation of wholesale rates. Notably, by requiring those rates to be based on a discount from the ILECs' retail charges, the Congress had foreclosed the use of the TELRIC method that the Commission had adopted for pricing of interconnection and unbundled network elements.[51] While TELRIC builds a price "from the bottom up," based on the costs incurred to provide a network element, wholesale prices must be set from the top down, by subtracting avoided costs from the carrier's retail price.

In order to guide the states in establishing wholesale rates, the Commission listed a number of particular cost account items that would be presumed to be avoided when ILECs offer services in the wholesale market and left to the parties and the states the task of applying those presumptions in particular cases. The Commission also adopted a range of "default" discounts, ranging from 17 to 25 percent, that states could adopt in the interim before avoided cost studies could be completed.[51A] With these rules in place, resellers were free to begin immediate negotia-

---

50. 1996 Act § 251(c)(4), *codified at* 47 U.S.C.A. § 251(c)(4) (West Supp. 1996).

51. See section 9.2c.(2), *supra*.

51A. These discounts were vacated by the Eighth Circuit in Iowa Utilities Bd,

supra, n. 27A. The discounts were reinstated by the Supreme Court. ___ U.S. ___, 119 S.Ct. 721, 142 L.Ed.2d 835 (1999).

tion for the purchase of ILEC services and the sale of those services, in turn, to customers.

(4) Duty of ILECS to Negotiate in Good Faith

Section 251(c)(1) of the 1996 Act requires both ILECs and carriers requesting interconnection to negotiate interconnection agreements in good faith. The Commission's *Interconnection Order* finds that it "would be futile to try to determine in advance every possible action that might be inconsistent with the duty to negotiate in good faith"[52] but does identify some types of nonconforming behavior. Specifically, the Commission finds that parties may not mislead or coerce others into concluding agreements they would not otherwise have made,[53] may not refuse a clause in an agreement that permits it to be changed in the event of a change in state or FCC rules,[54] may not engage in tactics intended to delay negotiations,[55] may not unreasonably refuse to provide information needed to conclude an agreement[56] and may not impose "bona fide request" requirements as a condition of negotiation.[57]

3. Bell Operating Company Entry Into Manufacturing and Long-distance

As noted earlier, one of the principal objectives of the 1996 Act is to make an orderly transition toward Bell operating company participation in interexchange and other telecommunications markets from which they were barred by the AT & T divestiture consent decree.[58] This goal, which had been the subject of a number of legislative false starts during the 1980s and 1990s, was complicated by the continuing domination by the Bells of their local telephone service markets. Policy makers believed that only after the Bells had lost control of the local "bottleneck" would their entry into markets that relied on access to the local exchange serve the public interest.

Section 271 of the Act,[59] accordingly, requires the Bell Operating Companies ("BOCs") to obtain FCC authorization before they may offer interexchange service originating within their local service areas.[60] In

---

52. Interconnection Order, *supra*, note 10 at para. 142.

53. *Id.* at para. 148.

54. *Id.* at para. 152.

55. *Id.* at para. 154.

56. *Id.* at para. 155. The Commission recognizes, however, that carriers may have a legitimate interest in protecting proprietary information. *Id.*

57. *Id.* at para. 156.

58. United States v. Western Elec. Co., 552 F.Supp. 131 (D.D.C.1982).

59. 1996 Act § 271, *codified at* 47 U.S.C.A. § 271 (West Supp. 1997). One district court has found that the requirements of section 271 are an unconstitutional "bill of attainder." SBC Communica-

tions v. FCC, 981 F.Supp. 996 (N.D.Tex. 1997). This ruling was reversed by the Fifth Circuit. 154 F.3d 226 (5th Cir.1998). *See* BellSouth Corp. v. FCC, 144 F.3d 58, 330 U.S.App.D.C. 109 (D.C.Cir.1998).

60. The Bell operating companies are permitted to offer out-of-region and "incidental" interexchange services, however, immediately after enactment of the 1996 Act. *Id.* § 271(b)(2)-(3), *codified at* 47 U.S.C.A. § 271(b)(2)-(3) (West Supp. 1997). Incidental services include BOC provision of interexchange audio, video or other programming services to subscribers or distributors, alarm monitoring services, interactive video or Internet services to or for elementary or secondary schools, commercial mobile radio services, information stor-

reviewing those requests, the FCC is required to consult with the Attorney General and the state public utilities commissions and assure itself, as to each state in which interexchange authorization is requested:

(1) that the Bell operating company has complied with the interconnection requirements of sections 251 and 252 of the Act; and

(2) that at least one facilities-based carrier competes with the Bell operating company in the service area for which interexchange authorization is sought, and does so primarily over its own facilities.

In determining compliance with these conditions, the FCC is to consult a "competitive checklist" that specifies the scope of interconnection the Bell must have provided to at least one competitor before it may provide in-region interexchange services.[61] Alternatively, a Bell company is deemed to comply with the checklist if, after 10 months from the date of enactment of the Act, no competitor has requested interconnection before the date which is three months prior to the Bell's application to the FCC.

The Act also imposes conditions on Bell entry into the manufacturing of telecommunications equipment. Specifically, a BOC may not engage in manufacturing until after it has received approval to provide in-region interLATA services and a BOC and its affiliates may not engage in manufacturing in conjunction with another BOC and its affiliates.[62]

In addition to these constraints on BOC entry into certain markets, Section 272 of the Act requires the Bells to offer certain services through separate affiliates. Specifically, BOCs providing manufacturing, in-region interLATA service or interLATA information service (other than electronic publishing or alarm monitoring) must do so through structurally separate affiliates.[63] Each affiliate must operate independently, have separate books and records, have separate officers, directors and employees and must conduct transactions with its affiliated BOC on an arm's-

---

age and retrieval services and certain types of network signaling information. *Id.* § 271(g), *codified at* 47 U.S.C.A. § 271(g) (West Supp. 1997).

61. The checklist includes nondiscriminatory interconnection; nondiscriminatory access to network elements; nondiscriminatory access to poles, ducts, conduits and rights-of-way; nondiscriminatory access to 911, directory assistance and operator call completion services; white pages directory listings; nondiscriminatory access to signaling necessary for call routing and completion; nondiscriminatory access to information needed to implement local dialing parity; reciprocal compensation arrangements; nondiscriminatory number assignment and number portability; and availability of services for resale. *Id.*

§ 271(c)(2)(B), *codified at* 47 U.S.C.A. § 271(c)(2)(B) (West Supp. 1997).

62. A BOC may, however, engage in research relating to manufacturing or enter into royalty agreements with manufacturers. *Id.* § 273(b), *codified at* 47 U.S.C.A. § 273(b) (West Supp. 1997).

63. *Id.* § 272(a), *codified at* 47 U.S.C.A. § 272(a) (West Supp. 1997). BOCs have provided information services for a number of years, but have not been required to offer those services through separate affiliates. Accordingly, the Act gives the BOCs one year from the date of enactment to bring any nonconforming services into compliance with the separate affiliate requirements. *Id.* § 272(h), *codified at* 47 U.S.C.A. § 272(h) (West Supp. 1997).

length basis. BOCs and their affiliates are subject to strict nondiscrimination requirements, including a requirement that BOCs impute to themselves charges for access used in the provision of their own services.

The separate affiliate requirements for in-region interLATA service and manufacturing are subject to a sunset provision of three years after the BOC is authorized to provide in-region interLATA services. The separate affiliate requirement for interLATA information services is subject to a sunset provision of four years after enactment.

9.3 Title II of the 1996 Act—Broadcasting Regulation

Title II of the new Act—and especially the provisions of Sections 202, 203 and 204—mandates changes in the regulation of radio and television broadcasting. While these changes are less dramatic than the Act's provisions opening the local telephone market to competition, they have a similar purpose—to bring regulation in line with evolving technological and economic realities. Specifically, the Title II provisions recognize that in the multichannel world of cable television, direct broadcast satellite and the Internet, the broadcast industry, which transmits signals over scarce radiofrequency spectrum assigned by the FCC, no longer controls the only source of electronic mass communication. Accordingly, statutes and rules based on the premises of spectrum scarcity and broadcaster power are becoming just as obsolete as common carrier regulation based on the notion of the natural monopoly telephone company.

The most important of the Title II provisions concern restrictions on broadcast license ownership and rules governing the duration of broadcast licenses and the process and standards for renewal of those licenses. This section considers each of these subjects in turn.[1]

A. Section 202: Broadcast Ownership

The FCC's ownership rules, like most of the Commission's radio and television regulations, have been based on the scarcity of radiofrequency spectrum suitable for broadcasting.[2] Spectrum scarcity meant that only a

1. Title II also includes a number of provisions that are not treated in detail here. Notably, Section 336 of the 1996 Act (new section 336 of the Communications Act) requires the FCC to limit any advanced television (ATV) licenses it awards to current broadcast licensees, and to adopt regulations permitting ATV licensees to offer ancillary or supplementary services over ATV frequencies. 1996 Act § 336, *codified at* 47 U.S.C.A. § 336 (West Supp. 1997). Section 205 of the new Act (section 303(v) of the Communications Act) gives the FCC exclusive jurisdiction to regulate direct broadcast satellite service. *Id.* § 205, 47 U.S.C.A. § 303(v) (West Supp. 1997). Section 207 authorizes the Commission to prohibit zoning and other local restrictions on the use of antennas for direct broadcast satellite and other broadcast and direct-to-home services. *Id.* § 207, 47 U.S.C.A. nt. § 303 (West Supp. 1997). Finally, section 206 of the new Act, if approved by the U.S. Coast Guard, exempts ships from carrying a radio telegraph station operated by one or more radio operators where those ships comply fully with the Global Maritime Distress and Safety System. *Id.* § 365, 47 U.S.C.A. § 363 (West 1996).

2. *See, e.g.,* National Broadcasting Co. v. United States, 319 U.S. 190, 226, 63 S.Ct. 997, 1014, 87 L.Ed. 1344, 1368 (1943); Red Lion Broadcasting Co. v. Federal Communications Commission, 395 U.S. 367, 386–88, 89 S.Ct. 1794, 1804–06, 23 L.Ed.2d 371, 387–89 (1969).

limited number of radio and television stations could be licensed in each market. If a single person or entity controlled most or all of the broadcast licenses in a market, that entity might engage in monopolistic behavior and might control the range of information available to the public—a situation with obvious antidemocratic potential.

Historically, the Commission has responded to this concern with elaborate rules limiting the number of broadcast licenses that a single entity could own or control—both nationally, and within particular markets. Nationally, at the time the new Act was passed the Commission allowed a single entity to own no more than twelve television stations and to reach no more than 25 percent of the nationwide television audience; the Commission also permitted radio licensees to have a "cognizable interest" in no more twenty AM stations and twenty FM stations nationwide, but with no limitation on the percentage of the national audience those radio stations could reach. Within local markets, the Commission's so-called "duopoly" rules permitted an entity to control no more than one television station in a single market.[3] A single licensee also could control no more than two FM stations and two AM stations in any market with fifteen or more stations,[4] or more than three radio stations in a market with fewer than fifteen stations.[5]

The Commission's ownership restrictions may have played a useful role when broadcast stations were the only source of electronic mass communication.[6] As cable television, direct broadcast satellite and other alternatives to conventional, over-the-air broadcasting became nearly ubiquitous, however, it seemed unlikely that anyone could build an electronic information monopoly—either locally or nationally—simply by acquiring broadcast licenses.[7] At the same time, a number of radio and television stations, struggling to compete with the new outlets for advertising dollars, were seeking to consolidate under common ownership.[8]

3. The Commission also did not permit a single licensee to own a VHF television station and a radio station in the same market. 47 C.F.R. § 73.3555(c)(1997).

4. No single licensee in a market of more than fifteen stations, however, could have more than a 25 percent share of that market. *Id.* § 73.3555(a)(1)(ii).

5. No entity in a smaller market could control more 50 percent of the stations in that market, and only two of the stations owned by the entity could be in the same service (*i.e.*, AM or FM). *Id.* § 73.3555(a)(1)(i).

6. In fact, some commentators question whether the ownership rules were needed to achieve programming diversity. *See, e.g.,* THOMAS H. KRATTENMACHER AND LUCAS H. POWE, JR., REGULATING BROADCAST PROGRAMMING 95 (1994).

7. This is not to suggest that the growth of new programming outlets has made the concern over concentration of media ownership obsolete. In fact, while the number of "pipelines" into the home has grown, horizontal concentration of programming providers and vertical integration of those providers with cable systems and other distribution channels continues to worry many commentators and has attracted the attention of the Justice Department.

8. In the early 1990s, broadcast radio was an industry at risk of widespread financial collapse. The crisis was the result of a number of causes, including over-valuation of radio and television stations, the FCC's program of expanding the number of available frequencies and the growth of new media alternatives to broadcasting. For all of these reasons, "[b]y 1991, more than half of all commercial radio stations were operating in the red, and for small market stations the percentage was even higher."

Long before the passage of the 1996 Act, the Commission had begun to address this problem by liberalizing its broadcast station ownership regulations. Notably, in the early 1990s the Commission began to approve local marketing agreements (LMAs), under which one station sold advertising for another station serving the same market—usually with one of the stations acquiring rights toward a future purchase of the other, FCC rules permitting. In response to the economic plight of radio licensees, the FCC upheld these arrangements against charges that they violated the duopoly rules.[9] Later, the Commission relaxed its local and national ownership rules outright.[10]

The 1996 Act directs the FCC to take this liberalization process still farther. Specifically, Section 202 directs the Commission to:

(1) permit a single entity to own or control an unlimited number of television, or AM or FM radio, stations nationwide;[11]

(2) permit a party to own, operate or control up to eight commercial radio stations in any market with 45 or more such stations,[12] or up to seven commercial radio stations in a market with between 30 and 44 such stations (inclusive),[13] or up to six commercial radio stations in a market with between 15 and 29 such stations (inclusive),[14] or up to 5 commercial radio stations in a market with 14 or fewer such stations;[15]

(3) permit a single licensee to own, operate or control stations that reach, in the aggregate, up to 35 percent of the nationwide

David M. Hunsaker, *Duopoly Wars: Analysis and Case Studies of the FCC's Radio Contour Overlap Rules*, 2 COMMLAW CONSPECTUS 21, 22 (1994).

9. *See* Letter from Roy J. Stewart, Chief, Mass Media Bureau, to Roy R. Russo, Counsel, Spanish Radio Network, 5 FCC Rcd 7586, 68 Rad. Reg. 2d 1028 (P & F 1990); Letter from Edythe Wise, Chief, Complaints and Investigations Branch, Enforcement Division, Mass Media Bureau, to Joseph A. Belisle, Esq., 5 FCC Rcd 7585, 68 Rad. Reg. 2d 1031 (P & F 1990).

10. Before the Commission revised its rules, a licensee could control no more than twelve AM and twelve FM stations nationwide, and could not own two AM or two FM stations in the same market. In an Order released in 1992, the Commission announced that a single licensee would be allowed to own as many as thirty AM and thirty FM stations nationwide and as many as three AM and three FM stations in markets with forty or more radio stations so long as the licensee's total local audience share did not exceed 25 percent. Lower local ownership thresholds were established for three additional classes of smaller markets. Revision of Radio Rules and Policies, *Report and Order*, 7 FCC Rcd 2755, 70 Rad. Reg. 2d 903 (P & F 1992), *recons. granted*

in part, 7 FCC Rcd 6387, 71 Rad. Reg. 2d 227 (P & F 1992). Because of adverse congressional and industry reaction to these changes, the FCC changed the national limit to an eventual twenty stations of each class and changed its four-tier classification of local markets to a two-tier classification. Revision of Radio Rules and Policies, Mem. Op. and Order and Further Notice of Proposed Rule Making, 7 FCC Rcd 6387, *supra*.

11. 1996 Act § 202(a), 202(c)(1)(A). These provisions of the Act require the FCC to revise section 73.3555 of its rules. 47 C.F.R. § 73.3555 (1997).

12. 1996 Act § 202(b)(1)(A). Not more than five of the eight stations, however, may be in the same service (*i.e.*, AM or FM). *Id.*

13. *Id.* § 202(b)(1)(B). Not more than five of the seven stations, however, may be in the same service (*i.e.*, AM or FM).

14. *Id.* § 202(b)(1)(C). Not more than four of the six stations may be in the same service.

15. *Id.* § 202(b)(1)(D). Not more than three of the stations may be in the same service, and a party may not own, operate or control more than 50 percent of the stations in the market. *Id.*

television audience;[16] and

(4) consider the modification, or outright elimination, of the regulations limiting the number of television stations that a single entity may control in a local market.[17]

In addition to these requirements, section 202 directs the Commission to extend its policy of granting waivers of its one-to-a-market rule to the top 50 markets.[18] The section also permits a single entity, under certain conditions, to own more than one broadcast network[19] and directs the FCC to change its rules to permit a single entity to own both a broadcast network and a cable system.[20]

The Congress also makes clear, in section 202, that it intends the liberalization of broadcast ownership regulation to extend beyond the express provisions of the new Act. Notably, section 202 requires the Commission to review all of its broadcast rules every two years and to repeal any such regulations that no longer serve the public interest.[21]

B. Sections 203 and 204: Terms of Licenses And License Renewals

The FCC's authority to award and renew radio and television broadcast licenses has been one of its principal instruments for control of broadcast content. The renewal process, in particular, permits rival license applicants and members of the public to argue that incumbent licensees are not meeting their obligations under the vague public interest standard of the Act. Depending upon political fashion and the agendas of different FCC commissioners, the renewal authority has been wielded with varying severity in the service of shifting visions of the programming mix the public should enjoy.

By the time the 1996 Act was passed, however, the licensing and renewal process as an instrument of content control was approaching entropy. The FCC had made and abandoned various efforts to quantify and micromanage the public interest standard as applied to broadcasters,[22] and licensing and renewal had deteriorated into an expensive

---

16. *Id.* § 202(c)(1)(B).

17. *Id.* § 202(c)(2).

18. *Id.* § 202(d). The one-to-a-market rule prohibits common ownership of a radio and television station in the same market. Before enactment of the 1996 Act, the Commission's policy of waiving this rule extended only to the top 25 markets.

19. *Id.* § 202(e). This change does not extend to common ownership of two of the major networks (ABC, CBS, NBC or Fox), and does not extend to acquisition, by one of the four major networks, of one of the smaller English-language networks. *Id.*

20. *Id.* § 202(f). The Act also repeals the statutory ban on common ownership of a local broadcast station and a cable system operating in the same market, and repeals

the cable/MMDS cross-ownership ban in areas that have effective competition as defined in sec. 623(*l*) of the Act.

21. *Id.* § 202(h). "The Commission shall revise its rules adopted pursuant to this section and all of its ownership rules biennially as part of its regulatory reform review under section 11 of the Communications Act of 1934 and shall determine whether any of such rules are necessary in the public interest as the result of competition. The Commission shall repeal or modify any regulation it determines to be no longer in the public interest." *Id.*

22. Examples include the FCC's abandonment of the notion that programming quality requires some amount of unsponsored programming; the abandonment of

process of "litigation over trivia."[23]

The 1996 Act reduces the burdensomeness of the renewal process, both by extending the term of broadcast licenses (thereby making renewals less frequent) and by placing limits on the Commission's discretion to deny renewals. Specifically, Section 203 of the Act extends the maximum license term for both radio and television stations to eight years—an increase from the former limits of seven and five years, respectively.[24] And Section 204 of the Act establishes a two-step renewal process, under which a renewal application must be granted if the station has served the public interest and has committed no serious violations of the Communications Act or the Commission's regulations. Only if the licensee has failed this first stage of the inquiry may the Commission take other action, including denial of the renewal application; and only after the renewal has been denied may the Commission accept applications for construction permits from other parties.[25]

9.4   Title III of the 1996 Act—Cable Television and Video Services Regulation

By 1996 the cable television industry, while considerably newer than the telephone and broadcasting industries, was also subject to regulations that the Congress had come to regard as outmoded. Notably, the 1992 Cable Television Consumer Protection and Competition Act,[1] which had imposed price regulation on basic cable services, already had proved to be a cumbersome disappointment.[2] Similarly, the rules under which the Commission had permitted telephone companies to provide cable television services on a common-carrier basis (the so-called "video dial-tone" rules) had been overtaken by events. Accordingly, the Congress addressed these and other concerns in Title III of the new Act.

A. Deregulating Cable Television Rates

Regulation of cable television rates has had a complex history. In the early years of the cable industry, some cable systems were subject to rate regulation by state and local authorities. In 1969, the FCC preempted those rules in favor of a flexible set of pricing guidelines.[3] Later, the

the Commission's 1973 *Processing Guidelines*, which conditioned *pro forma* license renewals on the broadcast of 10 percent nonentertainment programming; and the abandonment of the *Ascertainment Primer*, which required stations to conduct "random surveys of the community, plus interviews with community leaders, taken from nineteen specified categories, to determine the problems—not the programming desires—of the community." THOMAS J. KRATTENMACHER AND LUCAS H. POWE, JR., REGULATING BROADCAST PROGRAMMING, *supra* note 6 at 80.

23. Revision of Application for Construction Permit for Commercial Broadcast Station, Mem. Op. and Order, 50 Rad. Reg. 2d 381, 382–83 (P & F 1981).

24. 1996 Act § 203, *codified at* 47 U.S.C.A. § 307(c) (West Supp. 1997).

25. *Id.* § 204(a)(1), *codified at* 47 U.S.C.A. § 309(k) (West Supp. 1997).

1. Cable Television Consumer Protection and Competition Act of 1992, Pub. L. 102–385, 106 Stat. 1460 (1992).

2. *See, e.g.,* JOHN THORNE, PETER W. HUBER AND MICHAEL K. KELLOGG, FEDERAL BROADBAND LAW 400–403 (1995).

3. Community Cable T.V., Inc., 95 F.C.C. 2d 1204 (1983).

Commission restored some of the authority it had preempted and even ordered local authorities to set initial rates for basic cable services and review subsequent rate increases.[4] Still later, in 1976, the Commission decided to make local regulation of basic cable rates permissive rather than mandatory[5] and most jurisdictions chose not to engage in ongoing cable rate supervision.

The 1984 Cable Act completed the FCC's program of cable rate deregulation. Specifically, the 1984 Act confirmed that rates for nonbasic cable services may not be regulated and permitted regulation of basic cable service rates only of cable operators that did not face "effective competition."[6] In its rules implementing these provisions, the FCC adopted a definition of "effective competition" for which all but a small percentage of cable service markets qualified.[7] By the end of 1986, when the 1984 Act and the Commission's rules were fully implemented, cable television service was effectively an industry no longer subject to state, local or federal rate regulation.

Although the deregulatory provisions of the 1984 Cable Act were intended to lower cable rates by stimulating competition,[8] the real-world results were disappointing. Expected competition from direct broadcast satellite and wireless cable technologies was slow to develop and most consumers continued to depend on broadcast stations and monopoly cable franchises for all of their television programming. Responding to consumer complaints about the cost of service, the Congress ordered a General Accounting Office study of cable rates. That study, completed in 1992, showed that cable rates had risen at three times the rate of increase of the Consumer Price Index since the passage of the 1984 Cable Act.[9] Accordingly, the Congress decided to reregulate rates for basic cable television service.

In the 1992 Cable Act, Congress determined that all cable systems not meeting a new, more exacting definition of "effective competition" would be subject to state, local and federal regulation of the rates they charged for certain services. For this purpose, cable services were divided into four categories:

---

4. *See* Cable Television Report and Order, 36 F.C.C. 2d 143 (1972). Basic services included broadcast channels carried by the cable system and excluded "specialized programming for which a per-program or per-channel charge is made." Amendment of Part 74, Subpart G of the Commission's Rules and Regulation Relative to Program Origination by Cable Television Systems, 46 F.C.C. 2d 175, 199 (1974).

5. Amendment of Subpart C, Part 76 of the Commission's Rules and Regulations Regarding the Regulation of Cable Television System Regular Subscriber Rates, 60 F.C.C. 2d 672, 685 (1976). The FCC had preempted local regulation of rates for nonbasic cable programming in 1974. Amendment of Part 74, Subpart G of the Commis-

sion's Rules and Regulations Relative to Program Origination by Cable Television Systems, 46 F.C.C. 2d 175, 199 (1974); *see also* Community Cable T.V., Inc., 95 F.C.C. 2d 1204, 1216 (1983).

6. Cable Communications Policy Act, 47 U.S.C.A. § 543(b)(1) (West 1992).

7. 47 C.F.R. § 76.33(1)(2) (1997).

8. *See, e.g.,* Rafael G. Prohias, *Longer than the Old Testament, More Confusing than the Tax Code: An Analysis of the 1992 Cable Act,* 2 COMMLAW CONSPECTUS 81, 83 (1994).

9. H.R. Rep. No. 862, 102d Cong., 2d Sess. 55 (1992).

(1) the basic-service tier, which included local broadcast signals, and any public, educational and governmental ("PEG") channels that the cable operator was required to carry as a condition of its local franchise;

(2) "cable programming service," which included all programming not in the basic-service tier, but for which the system did not assess a per-channel or per-program charge;

(3) programming (often called "premium" programs) for which customers pay on a per-channel or per-program basis; and

(4) "commercial leased access" programming.[10]

The 1992 Act subjected the first, or basic-service, category to state and local rate regulation, or to FCC regulation in the event state and local governments did not act. It subjected the second category to regulation only in the event of particular complaints, deregulated the third category, and subjected the fourth category to regulation by the FCC.

This Act required regulators to ensure that rates for regulated cable service were "reasonable"—*i.e.*, that they equalled the rates that would be set by a system subject to effective competition.[11] The Commission, in turn, responded to this mandate by issuing a series of complex pricing regulations. Among other decisions, the Commission set new benchmark rates based on those charged by systems found to be subject to effective competition and ordered a rollback of rates that exceeded the benchmark. The Commission also "capped" the rolled-back rates, and permitted increases above that level only to account for inflation. The 1992 Act also permitted cable systems to avoid rate regulation but only where their markets met a new, more stringent definition of "effective competition" that counted only competition from another cable system or other multichannel distributor—not competition from broadcast stations.

Unfortunately, the 1992 Act's reregulation of rates proved no more successful than the 1984 Act's deregulation of rates. As critics soon pointed out, the consumer benefits of the 1992 Act proved questionable while the burden the pricing rules imposed—both on the industry and on the FCC's Cable Services Bureau—were undeniable. Accordingly, the Telecommunications Act of 1996 set out a timetable under which cable rates, once again, would be deregulated. Specifically, the 1996 Act deregulates most rates of smaller cable systems immediately and ends regulation of all but the basic-service tier of larger systems on March 31, 1999. The 1996 Act also relaxes the effective competition test of the 1992

---

10. Leased access is the providing of channels on a cable system, for a fee, to independent programmers. The 1984 Act had extended a presumption of reasonableness to cable systems' leased access rates, and parties seeking the use of such channels complained that cable operators took advantage of the presumption by charging prohibitive rates.

11. The Act did not regulate nonbasic service rates, but authorized the Commission to review those rates in response to individual complaints.

Act and no longer permits cable service subscribers to file rate complaints with the FCC.

The deregulatory provisions of the 1996 Act may represent, at last, a permanent policy of permitting the market to decide the prices at which subscribers will obtain multichannel video services. With direct broadcast satellite already a reality, and with the telephone companies authorized to offer video service in competition with the established cable operators, the monopoly cable franchise is eroding. If these trends continue, there should be no economic or public-interest rationale for reregulating cable rates in the future.

B. Telephone Company Provision of Video Services

Section 302 of the 1996 Act also opens the cable television market to greater competition by defining methods by which telephone companies may enter the video services market—whether as providers of video programming, or as carriers of programming provided by others. Among other provisions, section 302 removes existing restrictions on telephone company video services, creates a new kind of video delivery system called "open video service," or OVS, and limits the ability of telephone companies to enter the video market by purchasing existing cable systems.

The most fundamental of the section 302 provisions is the removal of the so-called cable-telco cross-ownership restriction. This restriction, first adopted as a Commission rule in 1970 and later incorporated in the 1984 Cable Act, generally prohibited telephone companies from offering video programming in any area in which they also provided telephone service. Originally intended to protect the cable industry from unfair competition by LEC monopolists, the ban seemed increasingly anachronistic when cable operators, themselves, came under fire for abuse of their monopoly franchise. When several LECs obtained judicial relief from the restriction on the ground that it violated their First Amendment rights,[12] the question became not whether, but when and on what terms, LECs would enter the video market.

The FCC, in the meantime, had abandoned its support for the restriction and tried to relieve its impact through a series of regulatory initiatives. Chief of these was the adoption of the "video dialtone" rules. Under the video dialtone rules, LECs still were not permitted to provide video programming but were allowed to provide a common carrier service through which other entities could offer video programming. Specifically, the FCC authorized two "levels" of video dialtone service: a so-called basic platform, offering video programmers access to switching, transmission, and other basic functions needed to reach their customers;

---

12. *See* Chesapeake & Potomac Tel. Co. v. United States, 830 F.Supp. 909 (E.D.Va. 1993), *aff'd* 42 F.3d 181 (4th Cir.1994), vacated as moot 516 U.S. 415, 116 S.Ct. 1036, 134 L.Ed.2d 46 (1996); US West, Inc. v. United States, 855 F.Supp. 1184 (W.D.Wash.1994), *aff'd* 48 F.3d 1092 (9th Cir.1994); BellSouth Corp. v. United States, 868 F.Supp. 1335 (N.D.Ala.1994); Ameritech Corp. v. United States, 867 F.Supp. 721 (N.D.Ill.1994).

and a noncommon-carrier, unregulated set of enhanced services also offered to video programmers.[13] The FCC also required LECs to request authority under section 214 of the 1934 Communications Act before constructing video dialtone facilities. Proceedings pursuant to those applications proved to be long and contentious. In fact, few video dialtone systems were built, as the LECs awaited congressional or judicial developments that might permit them to provide content as well as transport.

The 1996 Act changed this picture radically. It eliminated the cable-telco cross-ownership restriction,[14] repealed the video dialtone rules and defined five methods by which LECs might choose to offer video programming. Specifically, under Title III of the 1996 Act, LECs may:

(1) offer video programming through radio-based technologies, such as direct broadcast satellite (DBS) and multichannel multipoint distribution service (MMDS);

(2) provide common-carrier delivery systems for video service providers;

(3) provide video programming as cable system operators;

(4) distribute video programming to subscribers over switched networks on an on-demand, point-to-point basis (*i.e.*, offer interactive on-demand services); or

(5) offer programming over an open video system—a new delivery system, similar to video dialtone, over which the LEC may carry its own programming and that of third-party programmers on nondiscriminatory terms and conditions.

A telephone company's choice among these options will determine the kind of regulation to which its video services will be subject. If a LEC chooses to offer a DBS or other radio-based video service, it must comply with Title III of the Communications Act and the FCC's broadcast regulations but is not subject to Title II (common carrier) regulation or Title VI (cable) regulation.[15] If the LEC chooses to deliver the program-

13. The Commission did not define in advance the enhanced services that LECs might offer at this second level but gave the example of a "video gateway," through which a customer might access and select from a menu of video services. Telephone Company–Cable Television Cross–Ownership Rules, Sections 63.54–63.58, 7 FCC Rcd 5781, 5784 n. 5 (1992).

14. Some LECs already had challenged the cross-ownership restriction as an unlawful limitation on their First Amendment rights and had prevailed in every court before which the claim was brought. *See, supra* note 12. By the time the 1996 Act was passed, therefore, the ban was moribund at best and the question before the Congress was not whether, but when and on what

terms, LECs would become video programming providers.

15. As discussed elsewhere in this treatise, broadcasters are subject to content-based requirements affecting political speech, children's programming and other subjects; common carriers are not subject to content-based regulation but are subject to economic regulation; while cable operators are subject to a hybrid regulatory scheme set out in Title VI of the 1934 Act, including some economic regulation and rules (such as program access, must carry/retransmission consent and access for public, educational and governmental programming) that are content-based and specific to cable operators.

ming of others as a common carrier, or offers interactive on-demand service, it will be subject only to the common-carrier provisions of Title II of the Communications Act. If the LEC becomes a cable system operator, it is required only to meet all of the obligations imposed on cable operators by Title VI of the Act. Finally, if the LEC operates an OVS system certified by the Commission, it will be subject to certain Title VI requirements but will not need a local franchise in order to operate; if the OVS system is not certified by the FCC, it will be subject to local franchising requirements.[16]

As the section 302 provisions show, the Congress by 1996 had decided that the benefits of LEC entry into the video market outweighed any risks that such entry posed to competition. The Congress was concerned, however, that telephone companies might choose to buy existing cable systems rather than build systems of their own—an option that would not increase competition and might even lead to a more concentrated cable marketplace. The Act therefore provided that, with some exceptions, no LEC or its affiliate may acquire more than a 10 percent financial interest in a cable operator that provides video programming in the LEC's telephone service area; and no cable operator may acquire more than a 10 percent interest in a LEC that provides telephone service in the cable operator's franchise area. The principal exceptions to these "buy-out" restrictions apply in rural areas or to LEC interests in cable systems that face significant competition.

9.5 Title IV of the 1996 Act—Common Carriers

As noted earlier, the FCC had tried for a number of years to reduce the burden of common carrier regulation on providers of interstate telecommunications services. The process began with the FCC's decision to permit competition in interstate, private line service.[1] In the Commission's view, requiring new competitors in this market to file tariffs and obtain permission before constructing facilities imposed needless compliance costs and deprived these carriers of the flexibility they needed in order to compete effectively with AT & T. In order to relax those requirements, however, the Commission needed a rationale that could be squared with the plain requirements of Title II of the Communications Act.

The Commission accordingly adopted an antitrust-based theory of common carrier regulation. Specifically, the Commission decided that common carrier regulation, as defined in the 1934 Communications Act, was intended to protect consumers from carriers with the ability to control price and output in a relevant market (*i.e.*, carriers with market

---

16. Anyone seeking to provide service over an open video service must certify to the FCC that it complies with all applicable Commission regulations. The FCC must act on certification requests within ten days.

1. *See, e.g.,* Establishment of Policies and Procedures for Consideration of Applications to Provide Specialized Common Carrier Services in the Domestic Public Point-to-Point Microwave Radio Service, 29 F.C.C. 2d 870 (1971), *aff'd*, 31 F.C.C. 2d 1106 (1971), *aff'd sub nom.*, Washington Util. and Transp. Comm. v. FCC, 513 F.2d 1142 (9th Cir.), cert. denied, 423 U.S. 836, 96 S.Ct. 62, 46 L.Ed.2d 54 (1975).

power). Where carriers enjoy such power, they can exploit it to charge monopoly rates, engage in predatory pricing and cross-subsidization and otherwise exploit consumers and inhibit competitors. Tariff filings, accompanied by disclosure of the cost of providing the service described in the tariff, were effective counterweights to market power because they permitted the Commission and the public to determine whether rates charged were reasonable and nondiscriminatory. And the requirement that common carriers charge no rates not disclosed in the tariffs insured that once rates had been found to be reasonable, the public interest would not be subverted by transactions that deviated from those rates.[2]

The competing carriers who were entering various markets in competition with AT & T lacked market power and were incapable, in the Commission's view, of engaging in any of the abusive conduct that the common carrier provisions were intended to prevent. Accordingly, in a series of decisions entered between 1979 and 1985, the Commission relaxed the common carrier requirements for a number of carriers and service providers serving a variety of interstate markets in which competition had been permitted.[3]

Unfortunately for the Commission's deregulatory enterprise, an appeals court ruled in 1992 that the Commission lacked the discretion, under the 1934 Act, to eliminate any of the tariffing and other requirements of Title II.[4] This decision was upheld by the United States Supreme Court, with Justice Scalia's opinion effectively conceding the correctness of the FCC's approach as a matter of policy, but emphasizing the inability of any agency lawfully to exceed the authority conferred by its enabling statute.[5]

It was against this background that the Congress drafted the regulatory forbearance provisions of the Act.[6] Under these provisions the FCC not only is permitted to, but must, forbear from applying any provision of the Act or any FCC regulation to carriers that the Commission finds do not require such oversight in order to insure just and reasonable rates, consumer protection and service in the public interest.[7]

2. For a complete statement of the Commission's "market power" theory of common carrier regulation, *see* Policy and Rules Concerning Rates for Competitive Common Carrier Services and Facilities Authorizations Therefor, 85 F.C.C. 2d 1 (1980).

3. *Id.*; Second Report and Order, 91 F.C.C. 2d 59 (1982); Third Report and Order, 48 Fed. Reg. 46,791 (1983); Fourth Report and Order, 95 F.C.C. 2d 554 (1983); Fifth Report and Order, 98 F.C.C. 2d 1191 (1984); Sixth Report and Order, 99 F.C.C. 2d 1020 (1985), *vacated*, MCI Telecomm. Corp. v. FCC, 765 F.2d 1186, 247 U.S. App. D.C. 32 (D.C.Cir.1985).

4. American Tel. & Tel. Co. v. Federal Communications Commission, 978 F.2d 727, 298 U.S. App. D.C. 230 (D.C.Cir.1992) *aff'd sub nom.*, MCI Telecomm. Corp. v.

American Tel. & Tel. Co., 512 U.S. 218, 114 S.Ct. 2223, 129 L.Ed.2d 182 (1994).

5. *Id.* at 234, 114 S. Ct. at 2233, 129 L. Ed. 2d at 234.

6. These provisions also had a prelude. In 1993, the Congress enacted an amendment to the 1934 Communications Act that gave the FCC authority to forbear from common carrier regulation for commercial mobile radio service ("CMRS") providers. 47 U.S.C.A. § 332(c)(1) (West Supp. 1997); *see* Implementation of Sections 3(n) and 332 of the Communications Act, 9 FCC Rcd 7988 (1994). The forbearance provisions of the 1996 Act borrow heavily from this amendment.

7. 1996 Act § 401, *codified at* 47 U.S.C.A. § 160 (West Supp. 1997). The Act also prohibits the states from enforcing any

In order to effect an ongoing process of deregulation by the FCC, the 1996 Act also requires the Commission to conduct a biennial review of all of its regulations, beginning in 1998.[8] The Act also eliminates certain regulations outright and gives the FCC the ability to adopt a number of streamlining measures, including the elimination of depreciation schedules,[9] annual ship radio inspections[10] and construction permits for minor changes to broadcast stations.[11]

The forbearance authority conferred by the 1996 Act is strikingly comprehensive. Not only does the Act require the Commission to decline to enforce its own regulations where such action will serve the public interest, but it requires the Commission, in effect, to repeal particular provisions of its enabling statute where the public interest requires. While this authority is somewhat confined by the requirement that the Commission make public interest findings before it exercises forbearance, the authority is sufficiently unconstrained to raise serious questions of delegation of legislative authority.[12]

9.6   Title V of the 1996 Act—Obscenity, Indecency and Violence

Some of the most controversial provisions of the 1996 Act were those of Title V, which the Congress styled the "Communications Decency Act of 1996" and which is often called, for convenience, the "CDA." The CDA provisions were intended to control the content of information moving over the proliferating electronic communications media, including cable television and the Internet. Some of these provisions were declared facially unconstitutional upon judicial review and others present constitutional and practical issues that have not yet been resolved. This subsection reviews the provisions of the CDA and briefly discusses their treatment in the courts.

A.   Section 502: Obscene or Harassing Use of Telecommunications Facilities

Section 223 of the Communications Act had, for many years, prohibited the making of obscene or harassing interstate or foreign telephone calls. Section 502 of the 1996 Act expanded the reach of section 223 to reach, not just telephone calls, but communications carried through all kinds of telecommunications devices and "interactive computer services," including the Internet and other systems that facilitate on-line, computer-to-computer communications. The most controversial of these

---

statute or regulation that the Commission has declined, under the authority granted in this section, to enforce. *Id.*

8. *Id.* § 402, *codified at* 47 U.S.C.A. § 161 (West Supp. 1997).

9. *Id.* § 403(d), *codified at* 47 U.S.C.A. § 220(b) (West Supp. 1997).

10. *Id.* § 403(n), *codified at* 47 U.S.C.A. § 360(b) (West Supp. 1997).

11. *Id.* § 403(m), *codified at* 47 U.S.C.A. § 319(d) (West Supp. 1997).

12. *See, e.g.,* Mistretta v. United States, 488 U.S. 361, 109 S.Ct. 647, 102 L.Ed.2d 714 (1989); Skinner v. Mid–America Pipeline Co., 490 U.S. 212, 109 S.Ct. 1726, 104 L.Ed.2d 250 (1989); Yakus v. United States, 321 U.S. 414, 64 S.Ct. 660, 88 L.Ed. 834 (1944).

provisions, codified at subsections (a)(1)(B) and (d) of section 223 of the Communications Act, were considered especially threatening to the interests of on-line service providers and their users.

Subsections (a)(1)(B) and (d) of section 223 define three principal offenses. One is the use of a telecommunications device to make, create, solicit or transmit "any [prohibited communication] knowing that the recipient of the communication is under 18 years of age, regardless whether the maker of such communication placed the call or initiated the communication." A second offense, set out at section 223(d)(1)(A), is the use of an interactive computer service to "send [a prohibited communication] to a specific person or persons under 18 years of age." The third offense, set out at section 223(d)(1)(B), is the use of an interactive computer service to "display [a prohibited communication] in a manner available to a person under 18 years of age . . ." For the offense defined at subsection (a)(1)(B), the prohibited communications include "any comment, request, suggestion, proposal, image, or other communication which is obscene or indecent;" for the offenses defined at subsection (d), prohibited communications include "any comment, request, suggestion, proposal, image, or other communication that, in context, depicts or describes, in terms patently offensive as measured by contemporary community standards, sexual or excretory activities or organs, regardless of whether the user of such service placed the call or initiated the communication . . ."[1]

For users and providers of on-line services, these proscriptions threatened a drastic curtailment of free expression on the Internet. They effectively criminalized not only the creation and communication of words and images that others might find offensive but the mere offering of a service or facility over which those communications are made. The potential, chilling effect of the CDA extended from individual users of the Internet, to small providers of on-line bulletin boards and news groups, all the way to the largest and best-known on-line service providers. In apparent recognition of these risks, the CDA included some defenses to a claim of violation of subsections (a)(1)(B) and (d). Specifically, one who does no more than provide "access or connection to or from a facility, system or network not under that person's control," and "who does not creat[e] . . . the content of the [prohibited] communication," has not violated the CDA.[2] Also, anyone who has taken "good

---

1. The CDA also would have been violated when someone "knowingly permits any telecommunications facility under such person's control to be used for an activity prohibited by [section 223(d)(1)(A)-(B)]." 47 U.S.C.A. § 223(d)(2) (West Supp. 1997). And the 1996 Act also amended the criminal obscenity provisions of Title 18 of the United States Code to make clear that those prohibitions include the transmission of obscene materials—and certain abortion-related material—by computer. 1996 Act § 507, *codified at* 18 U.S.C.A. § 1462 (West Supp. 1997).

2. 47 U.S.C.A. § 223(e)(1) (West Supp. 1997). This defense is not available, however, to anyone who conspires with an entity that violates the CDA, or who "provides access or connection to a facility, system, or network engaged in the violation of this section that is owned or controlled by such person." *Id.* at § 223(e)(2)-(3). This defense also is unavailable, of course, where a third party has transmitted an offending commu-

faith, reasonable, effective, and appropriate actions" to prevent access to prohibited communications by minors, or who "has restricted access to such communication by requiring use of a verified credit card, debit account, adult access code, or adult personal identification number," might assert a successful defense to a claim under the CDA.[3]

Taken together, these provisions of section 502 created strong incentives for anyone who sends information over an on-line service, or who controls facilities over which such communications are made, to take measures to restrict access to those communications by minors. As the plaintiffs who raised First Amendment challenges to the CDA pointed out, however, the duties imposed on the on-line community by the CDA and the measures identified in the statute as establishing potential defenses were impractical and risked limiting the lawful speech available to adults.

The CDA's difficulties begin with the fact that section 502 imposed content-based restrictions on constitutionally-protected speech. All of the offenses defined in subsections (a)(1)(B) and (d) may be committed by the transmission of words and images that are not obscene, but merely indecent.[4] The courts have recognized that indecency, which is largely a concept invented by the FCC in the course of broadcast regulation, defines kinds of expression that may be restricted only to serve a compelling state interest and through regulation that is narrowly tailored to achieve that interest.[5] And restrictions on indecent speech that are overbroad—*i.e.*, that "penaliz[e] a substantial amount of speech that is constitutionally protected"—may not be upheld.[6]

nication over a facility the defendant does control.

3. *Id.* § 223(e)(5), *codified at* 47 U.S.C.A. § 223(e)(5) (West Supp. 1997). The CDA also exempted providers or users of interactive computer services from liability for any actions taken to restrict access to obscene, indecent, excessively violent or otherwise objectionable material and declared that users or providers of interactive computer services shall not be treated as publishers or speakers of information provided by other content providers. *Id.* § 509, *codified at* 47 U.S.C.A. § 230(c) (West Supp. 1997).

4. Obscene speech, which may be criminalized, "portray[s] sexual conduct in a patently offensive way" and, taken as a whole, lacks "serious literary, artistic, political or scientific value." *See, e.g.,* Miller v. California, 413 U.S. 15, 93 S.Ct. 2607, 37 L.Ed.2d 419 (1973). Indecent speech is constitutionally protected, but may be regulated for certain purposes, such as protection of minors. *See* Federal Communications Commission v. Pacifica Found., 438 U.S. 726, 98 S.Ct. 3026, 57 L.Ed.2d 1073 (1978). Section 223(a)(1)(B) of the Act uses the word "inde-

cent" to describe one of its classes of prohibited speech while section 223(d) incorporates a definition of indecent speech—as "the description or depiction of sexual or excretory activities or organs in a patently offensive manner as measured by contemporary community standards …"—first used by the Federal Communications Commission in regulating broadcast speech and so-called "dial-a-porn" service. *See* Regulations Concerning Indecent Communications by Telephone, 5 FCC Rcd 4926, 4927 (1990).

5. *See, e.g.,* Sable Communications of California, Inc. v. Federal Communications Commission, 492 U.S. 115, 126, 109 S.Ct. 2829, 2836–37, 106 L.Ed.2d 93, 105 (1989).

6. Forsyth County v. Nationalist Movement, 505 U.S. 123, 130, 112 S.Ct. 2395, 2401, 120 L.Ed.2d 101, 111 (1992); *see also* Broadrick v. Oklahoma, 413 U.S. 601, 612–13, 93 S.Ct. 2908, 2915–16, 37 L.Ed.2d 830, 840 (1973); Gooding v. Wilson, 405 U.S. 518, 520–21, 92 S.Ct. 1103, 1105–06, 31 L.Ed.2d 408, 413–14 (1972).

Section 502 was challenged before two three-judge district court panels,[7] and both panels entered preliminary injunctions against enforcement of the indecency restrictions of section 502, finding a likelihood that the plaintiffs would succeed on their claim that those restrictions were unconstitutionally overbroad.[8] Notably, both panels found that the defenses offered by the statute could not be implemented, or could be implemented at a cost sustainable only by commercial providers of Internet content and services.[9] Smaller and noncommercial service providers, faced with their technical or financial inability to adopt solutions such as credit card verification or password technology, simply would cease to create or transmit speech on subjects that might be regarded as unsuitable for minors. As a result, under the guise of protecting minors, the CDA would deprive adults of many kinds of constitutionally-protected communication.[10]

On direct appeal from the three-judge District Court for the District of Columbia, the United States Supreme Court ruled by a seven-member majority that the CDA violated the First Amendment because it was overbroad.[11] For a thorough discussion of this historic ruling and its implications, see the text at chapter two, section 2.4.C. and chapter six, section 6.11.B.2, *supra*. The other provisions of Title V of the 1996 Act, however, remain in effect and are described briefly in the following section.

B. Other Provisions of Title V

Besides its controversial provisions criminalizing obscene and indecent communication on the Internet, the 1996 Act includes a number of other limitations on offensive or violent programming and communications. Notably, section 504 of the Act requires cable operators, upon subscriber request and at no cost, to scramble or block any programming to which the customer has not subscribed; and section 505 requires cable and other multichannel video programmers to fully scramble or block all sexually explicit or indecent programming so that customers who do not subscribe to that programming receive neither the video nor audio portion of such programs.[12] In addition, Section 508 makes it a felony to

7. The 1996 Act established this procedure for judicial challenges to the constitutionality of the Communications Decency Act. 1996 Act § 561.

8. American Civil Liberties Union v. Reno, 929 F.Supp. 824 (E.D.Pa.1996) ("ACLU v. Reno"); Shea v. Reno, *et al.*, 930 F.Supp. 916 (S.D.N.Y.1996) ("Shea v. Reno"). Two of the judges on the panel in *ACLU* also found the language of section 223(d), incorporating the FCC's definition of "indecent," to be unconstitutionally vague. The panel in *Shea* did not agree with this conclusion. In neither case did the plaintiffs challenge the CDA's prohibitions against obscene speech.

9. ACLU v. Reno, *supra*, 929 F. Supp. at 846–49, 856; Shea v. Reno, *supra*, 930 F. supp. at 942–48.

10. ACLU v. Reno, *supra*, 929 F. Supp. at 855, 858, 879; Shea v. Reno, *supra*, 930 F. Supp. at 950.

11. Reno v. American Civil Liberties Union, 521 U.S. 844, 117 S.Ct. 2329, 138 L.Ed.2d 874 (1997).

12. The 1996 Act also permits cable systems to refuse to carry any program, or portion of a program, on a public access or leased access channel that contains obscenity, nudity or indecency. 1996 Act § 506, *codified at* 47 U.S.C.A. § 531(e) (West 1996).

use a telecommunications device knowingly to lure, entice or coerce a minor into prostitution or a sexual crime or to attempt to do so.[13]

After the Internet obscenity and indecency provisions, perhaps the best-publicized requirements of Title V have to do with the so-called "V-chip"—an electronic device built into a television set that can be activated to block programming identified by the broadcaster as violent or otherwise objectionable. Section 551 of the 1996 Act gives video program distributors one year voluntarily to develop ratings for programming that contains violent, sexual or other indecent material and to agree to transmit signals that contain those ratings.[14] If no industry consensus is reached within one year of enactment of the 1996 Act, then the FCC must, in consultation with an advocacy committee, adopt such a ratings system and corresponding rules requiring its implementation by broadcasters. In either event, the FCC must prescribe rules requiring television set manufacturers to include a V-chip device in their television receivers sold to the public. The V-chip provisions are discussed in detail in chapter 14, section 14.5.C.3.

Finally, Title V includes a nonmandatory provision, urging broadcast, cable, satellite, syndication and other video programming distributors to encourage the television equipment industry to develop a technology that will allow parents to block television programming that they deem inappropriate for their children.[15]

9.7 Title VI—Effect on Other Laws

In addition to the legal changes the 1996 Act effects through direct amendment of the Communications Act and other federal statutes, Title VI clarifies the Act's effect on certain other provisions of existing state and federal law.

The most dramatic of these provisions is the express displacement of the antitrust consent decrees that had guided much of the telecommunications industry for several years. Most famous of these decrees is the so-called Modified Final Judgment, or MFJ, under which the Bell operating companies had been prevented from entering the interexchange telecommunications market or manufacturing telecommunications equipment.[1] That decree is expressly replaced by the plan of deregulation set out at sections 271 and 272 of the 1996 Act.[2] Similarly, the GTE consent decree, imposing certain restrictions on the conduct of the GTE operating companies,[3] and the more recent McCaw consent decree, imposed in the wake of the merger of the McCaw cellular telephone network with AT & T,[4] are effectively terminated.[5]

13. *Id.* § 508, *codified at* 18 U.S.C.A. § 2422 (10(b)) (West Supp. 1997).

14. *Id.* § 551(b), *codified at* 47 U.S.C.A. § 303(w) (West Supp. 1996).

15. *Id.* § 552, *codified at* 47 U.S.C.A. § nt. 303 (West Supp. 1997).

1. United States v. American Tel. and Tel. Co., 552 F.Supp. 131 (D.D.C.1982).

2. 1996 Act § 601(a)(1), *codified at* 47 U.S.C.A. § nt. 152 (West 1996).

3. United States v. GTE Corp., 1985–1 Trade Cas. (CCH) 66,355 (1984).

4. United States v. AT & T Corp. and McCaw Cellular Communications, Inc., Civil Action No. 94–01555 (1994).

The other, principal provision of Title VI is contained in section 602 of the Act, which preempts the authority of any local taxing authority to collect any tax or fee on direct-to-home satellite service (also known as direct broadcast satellite, or "DBS.")[6] This provision does not, however, preempt taxation of a DBS service provider by a state.[7]

9.8 Title VII—Miscellaneous Provisions

Title VII of the 1996 Act addresses a number of subjects that do not fit logically within any of the preceding titles. Some of the Title VII provisions involve important public-interest questions and merit a brief discussion.

Section 702 of the 1996 Act addresses the vexing question of protection of private or proprietary information obtained by telecommunications carriers in the course of providing their services. The section requires all carriers to protect the confidentiality of proprietary information of other telecommunications carriers, equipment manufacturers and customers, and forbids carriers from using the proprietary information of other carriers, in particular, for marketing or other purposes that exceed the purpose for which the information is provided.[1] Similarly, proprietary information provided by customers (customer proprietary network information, or "CPNI") may only be disclosed in the course of providing the service in connection with which the information was disclosed by the customer or for billing, protection of property and protection of the carrier from fraud. Section 702 does not, however, restrain carriers from selling or otherwise disclosing subscriber listing information.

Another significant section of Title VII addresses the ability of state and local governments to control the placement of towers used for cellular telephone and other personal wireless services—an issue with considerable political resonance in many communities. Under section 704 of the 1996 Act, the authority of state and local governments over the placement, construction and modification of radio towers and other facilities used for personal wireless services is preserved but subjected to certain limitations. Notably, state and local governments may not impose regulations that have the effect of prohibiting the provision of personal wireless services and they must act upon requests for permission to place towers or other facilities within a reasonable time. Denials of requests must be in writing and supported by substantial evidence in a written record, and state and local authorities may not regulate based on the environmental effects of radio emissions, so long as facilities comply with the FCC radio frequency emissions requirements.[2]

5. 1996 Act § 601(a)(2)-(3), *codified at* 47 U.S.C.A. § note 152 (West 1996).

6. *Id.* § 602(a), *codified at* 47 U.S.C.A. § nt. 152 (West 1996).

7. *Id.* § 602(b), *codified at* 47 U.S.C.A. § nt. 152 (West 1996).

1. 1996 Act § 702, *codified at* 47 U.S.C.A. § 222 (West Supp. 1997).

2. *Id.* § 704, *codified at* 47 U.S.C.A. § 332(c)(7) (West Supp. 1997).

Other sections of Title VII include section 701, which creates certain protections against abusive billing practices associated with pay-per-call services offered in conjunction with toll-free numbers;[3] section 703, concerning access to the poles, ducts, conduits and rights-of-way of utilities;[4] and sections 706, 707 and 708, which respectively require the Commission to study the public availability of advanced telecommunications services,[5] create a loan fund for small businesses involved in telecommunications services[6] and authorize a non-profit corporation to assist in the development of educational technology infrastructure.[7]

9.9 Questions About The 1996 Act and the Public Interest

In crafting the 1996 Act, the Congress had at least three goals in mind. One goal was to promote consumer welfare by breaking up local telephone company monopolies and subjecting local telephone service to the rigors of competition.[1] Another was to reduce or eliminate regulation of telecommunications services—especially telephone service, but to some extent broadcast and cable television service, as well.[2] A third was to ensure that ratepayers in rural and high-cost areas would continue to enjoy access to affordable, basic telephone service.[3] While many provisions of the Act are well-calculated to serve one or more of these goals, others are likely to disserve one or more of the statutory objectives—either because they undermine the goal they expressly are intended to serve, or because they serve one of the congressional objectives at the expense of one or more of the other goals the Congress intended the Act to achieve.

The following sections of this chapter examine some aspects in which the Congress and the Commission, in drafting and implementing the Telecommunications Act of 1996, may have served or failed to serve the public interest most effectively. They also consider a related question, posed primarily by the extensive regulations adopted by the FCC to implement the Act, *i.e.*, whether the Commission has usurped the scheme of federalism contained in the 1934 Communications Act and largely preserved, with modification, in the Telecommunications Act of 1996.

3. *Id.* § 701, *codified at* 47 U.S.C.A. § 228(c) (West Supp. 1997).

4. *Id.* § 703, *codified at* 47 U.S.C.A. § 224 (West Supp. 1997).

5. *Id.* § 706(b), *codified at* 47 U.S.C.A. § nt. 157 (West Supp. 1997).

6. *Id.* § 707, *codified at* 47 U.S.C.A. § 714 (West Supp. 1997).

7. *Id.* § 708.

1. This is the purpose and intended effect of the interconnection provisions of section 251, the negotiation, mediation and arbitration provisions of section 252 and the various provisions of the 1996 Act eliminating state, local and federal statutory re-strictions on the provision of telecommunications service by cable companies, utilities and competing local exchange carriers.

2. This is the purpose and effect of the 1996 Act's provisions imposing on the FCC a duty to forbear from enforcing common carrier regulations that no longer serve the public interest. *See* 1996 Act §§ 401, 402 *codified at* 47 U.S.C.A. §§ 160, 161 (West Supp. 1997).

3. This is the purpose and intended effect of the provisions of section 254 of the 1996 Act.

A. *Do The Interconnection Provisions Encourage Competition?*

The Act expressly states that it is intended to bring the benefits of competition to local telephone service ratepayers.[4] In order to ascertain whether the Act is well-calculated to achieve this result, it is useful to remind ourselves what the benefits of competition are, and how those benefits are achieved. Briefly put, competition is valued because it allocates scarce resources in a way best calculated to achieve consumer welfare—a condition in which consumers realize more of their needs, given their incomes and the technological limitations of the society, than they would realize through any alternative allocation of resources. Competition achieves consumer welfare, in turn, by encouraging two kinds of efficiency: allocative efficiency and productive efficiency. The former is achieved when prices are set at the cost of production; the latter is achieved when the costs of production match the marginal cost of a firm of optimally efficient size for the industry.[5]

The consumer welfare benefits of competition can be frustrated in two ways. One method is through governmental enactments that prevent firms from achieving productive and allocative efficiency. The other is through the limitation of total output in the market by one or more dominant or colluding firms. In trying to open the local market to competition, the Congress faced problems of both kinds.

During the long reign of monopoly telecommunications a broad range of governmental requirements, ranging from exclusive franchises to universal service policies to common carrier regulations, have limited both the number of competitors and their flexibility in moving rates closer to costs. Unquestionably, these constraints called for deregulatory legislation. By removing the ability of states to grant monopoly franchises, permitting entry into telephone service by nontelephone utilities and limiting the ability of states and monopolies to restrict participation in telephone markets by cable companies and utilities, the Act creates an environment in which all would-be competitors, regardless of the technology on which they are based, can compete for local telephone customers.

Second, the established telephone companies plainly have some degree of market power. While the extent of this power can be debated, there is little doubt, for example, that the incumbents could strangle competition in its cradle simply by refusing to interconnect with their rivals. In imposing affirmative obligations on incumbents to cooperate with competitors, however, it is critical to remember that all such requirements risk inhibiting, rather than promoting, robust competition.

---

4. The stated purpose of the 1996 Act is "to provide for a pro-competitive, deregulatory national policy framework designed to accelerate rapidly private sector deployment of advanced telecommunications and information technologies and services to all Americans by opening all telecommunications markets to competition ..." Conference Report to accompany S. 652, Jan. 31, 1996 at 1.

5. *See, e.g.,* Charles H. Kennedy, An Introduction to U.S. Telecommunications Law 121 (1994).

Accordingly, unless those obligations are necessary to prevent abuses of market power they will become, themselves, the source of inefficiency and will reduce consumer welfare. This is why imposing disabilities on some competitors simply to improve the prospects of other competitors—rather than to correct for market power—is unsound regulatory policy. Unfortunately, the interconnection requirements of the 1996 Act cross this line at several points.

There is no question that in order to achieve meaningful competition in the local telephone service market, the Congress had to mandate *some* level of cooperation among incumbents and their rivals. To understand why this is so, we need only remind ourselves that telephone service is provided over networks—*i.e.*, systems that connect each user of the service to all other users of the service. As with other networked services, the value of telephony to its users increases in proportion to the number of points it allows its customers to reach.[6] In a world of competing networks, therefore, each service provider has incentives both to expand its own network as far as possible, and to interconnect its network with those of its competitors.

The incentives are very different, however, where one network is ubiquitous and controls essentially the entire market. Under these conditions, the utility to the monopolist of connecting with small, competing networks is far outweighed by the temptation to prevent competition altogether—something the monopolist can achieve simply by refusing to interconnect its network with those of its competitors.

Unfortunately, the local competition provisions of the 1996 Act go well beyond the modest goal of mandated interconnection. They also require ILECs to resell service and furnish competitors with unbundled network elements. These requirements not only may have anticompetitive effects; they also severely undermine the Congress's objective of deregulating the telecommunications industry.

To understand why this is so, we must recall that the Congress did not mandate new entry into the local telephone market as an end in itself: the purpose of new entry is to improve the cost and quality of local telephone service available to consumers.[7] This goal is best achieved through a market populated by a large number of competing, *facilities-based* service providers. Service providers that build their own networks contribute the most to consumer welfare because they can lower the costs for *all* inputs that make up their service and because they put pressure on the incumbent to do the same. By contrast, competitors that resell the service of the incumbent telephone company, or that offer service through switching capacity and other facilities purchased from the incumbent, do not put competitive pressure on the incumbent to reduce the cost or improve the quality of the incumbent's infrastructure.

6. *See, e.g.*, Michael L. Katz and Carl Shapiro, *Systems Competition and Network Effects*, 8 J. Econ. Perspectives 93 (1994); Jeffrey Church and Neil Gandal, *Network Effects, Software Provision and Standardization*, 40 J. Indus. Econ. 85 (1992).

7. *See* Conference Committee statement, at n. 4, *supra*.

At most, they can exert pressure on the incumbent's retail pricing at the margin by cutting the cost of those few functions—such as retail marketing and billing—that the resale-based competitor provides independently of the incumbent.

If the Congress had wished only to encourage facilities-based competition, it would simply have removed legal barriers to new entry and mandated interconnection between incumbent networks and new, competing networks. Then, if investors and business persons found that the technology and economics of local telephony supported the building of new networks, the way would have been clear for them to do so.

In going beyond these few, obvious measures and requiring resale and access to unbundled network elements, the Congress took two substantial risks. First, it risked discouraging, rather than encouraging, the more beneficial facilities-based entry in favor of resale-based competitive strategies with lower potential for enhancing consumer welfare; and second, because ILECs could not be counted on to obey these mandates without detailed regulation and ongoing supervision, it risked reregulating, rather then deregulating, the telecommunications industry.

If the Congress was justified in taking these risks, it can only be on the assumption that facilities-based competition would not develop at the level required to yield a true competitive market. If this was the Congress's assumption, however, that belief seems entirely misplaced. In fact, the Act itself, by clearing the way for market entry by cable television operators and gas and electric power companies, expands a universe of potential service providers that already was growing rapidly to accommodate new generations of wireless services. With all of these options available or soon to be available, there is no basis for believing that facilities-based competition will be scarce.

In short, the local competition provisions of the new Act combine healthy—even necessary—regulatory initiatives with requirements that are unnecessary, anticompetitive and tend to perpetuate, rather than dismantle, regulation.

B. Does The Act Deregulate The Industry?

The 1996 Act declares the intention of Congress to create a "deregulatory national policy framework" for telecommunications. In fact, as a deregulatory instrument the Act combines dramatic progress with backsliding and missed opportunities.

In order to assess the Act's deregulatory impact, we should keep in mind that regulation of telecommunications (defined broadly to include broadcast and cable television as well as wireless and wireline telephone service) is of at least three kinds. The first category might be called entry regulation—i.e., rules that determine who may participate in certain markets, or to what extent particular players may participate in certain markets. Examples of this kind of regulation are the line-of-business restrictions of the AT & T consent decree, the cable-telco cross-ownership restriction and the broadcast license cross-ownership rules. A second category is rate regulation, such as state and federal regulation of telephone rates and the cable television rate provisions of the 1992 Cable Act. The third category is content regulation, typified by the Commission's efforts to regulate broadcast speech and the many rules—such as program access and must-carry—that dictate certain carriage decisions of cable operators. It is fair to say that the 1996 Act does at best a partial job of eliminating regulations of all three kinds.

Removal of entry regulation is perhaps the Act's most consistent deregulatory achievement. By ending the AT & T and GTE consent decrees, prohibiting states from preventing new entry into the local telephone service market and removing restrictions on local telephone service by utilities, the Congress has thrown open the monopoly local exchange to new entry of all kinds. The Commission's treatment of broadcast market entry restrictions, however, seems needlessly timid. The present multichannel environment justifies, not merely the relaxation of cross-ownership restrictions achieved in the 1996 Act, but outright elimination of those restrictions. A thorough reform of this kind would leave responsibility for preventing undue concentration in this industry where it lies with every other industry—*i.e.*, with the Antitrust Division of the Department of Justice.

The Act's record with respect to rate regulation is, if anything, more inconsistent than its treatment of entry regulation. The Act gives the FCC a bold grant of authority to end common carrier regulation but sets only a gradual timetable for elimination of the failed price controls of the 1992 Cable Act. And sections 251 and 252 of the Act, with their new regime of control over the pricing of local network access and interconnection, will bring a dramatic increase in the overall burden of rate regulation on incumbent local exchange carriers.

Finally, content regulation is not reduced by the 1996 Act, but in fact is increased. All of the Commission's rules dictating the programming decisions of broadcasters and cable television operators remain in place, and the new provisions concerning obscenity, indecency and violence subject on-line services, broadcasters and cable companies to new— and, in some cases, constitutionally questionable—burdens on content.

While the 1996 Act leaves much regulation intact, it also leaves the FCC with enormous discretion to eliminate its own rules, and even to forbear from enforcing provisions of the Communications Act. Completion of the Congress's deregulatory program, therefore, is now largely a matter for the FCC.

C. Does The Act Promote Universal Service?

Of all the objectives Congress expressed in the 1996 Act, perhaps the most unequivocal is its commitment to universal service. Specifically, Section 254 of the Act[8] mandates affordable access to basic and advanced telecommunications service for all Americans, whether rural or urban, and whether they are cheap or costly to serve; and the section describes

---

8. 1996 Act § 254, *codified at* 47 U.S.C.A. § 254 (West Supp. 1997).

this condition, not as a goal, but as a mandate.[9] In keeping with that mandate, the Congress directs the FCC to enact rules that will ensure universal service, and will require all telecommunications carriers to contribute to the maintenance of universal service.

Section 254 gives the FCC a mandate to reform, without dismantling, a universal service system that was increasingly at odds with the competitive telecommunications environment. In essence, universal system was a complex process by which long-distance carriers, through the access charges they paid to local telephone companies for completing long-distance calls, subsidized the local service rates of rural and high-cost customers. Using a separations formula set by the FCC, local telephone companies reported the interstate portion of the costs they incurred to build and maintain access lines and other facilities used to reach their subscribers. Where those costs exceeded 115 percent of the national average, an amount equal to a percentage of the above-average costs would be returned to the company from a so-called "high-cost fund" of access charge revenues. With these support funds in hand, rural and high-cost companies could cover their costs of service without charging local service rates dramatically higher than those charged by nonrural carriers.

Even before passage of the 1996 Act, the FCC had announced its intention to revamp the universal service system. Specifically, the Commission believed that the system unfairly singled out long-distance carriers as the sole segment of the industry supporting universal service. The Commission also viewed the existing method of calculating support payments, which relied entirely on the reported costs of the rural companies, as a vestige of "cost-plus" rate regulation that discouraged efficiency and perpetuated an excessive level of supports.

Beginning in 1994, the Commission had conducted a rulemaking in which it clearly proposed to reduce the availability of supports for local service in rural and high-cost areas of the country, either by basing those supports on "proxy" costs that may not equal the actual costs incurred by rural carriers to serve their customers or by auctioning the right to receive universal service supports to the lowest bidder.[10] The FCC apparently intended to force rural companies to become more efficient by tying support payments, not to actual costs, but to the costs of a

---

9. Section 254 states that the FCC and its advisory Federal–State Joint Board "*shall* base policies for the preservation and advancement of universal service" on certain principles, including the principle that "[c]onsumers in all regions of the Nation, including low-income consumers and those rural, insular, and high-cost areas, should have access to telecommunications and information services, including interexchange services and advanced telecommunications services, that are reasonably comparable to those services provided in urban areas and that are available at rates that are reasonably comparable to rates charged for similar services in urban areas." 1996 Act § 254(b)(3), *codified at* 47 U.S.C.A. § 254(b)(3) (West Supp. 1997) (*emphasis added*).

10. *See* Amendment of Part 36 of the Commission's Rules and Establishment of a Joint Board, 9 FCC Rcd 7404 (1994); Amendment of Part 36 of the Commission's Rules and Establishment of a Joint Board, 10 FCC Rcd 12309 (1995).

theoretical, optimally efficient company. The FCC was still considering, but had not yet adopted, this approach when the 1996 Act was passed.

While section 254 reflects some of the Commission's concerns, it rejects the Commission's apparent solution. In fact, the Conference Committee Report to the 1996 Act refers pointedly to this proceeding, and states that it is not "an appropriate foundation on which to base" the Commission's implementation of section 254.[11] Instead, the Act requires the Commission, with the advice of a Federal–State Joint Board, to devise a universal service system to which all telecommunications carriers contribute and that is sufficient and effective to insure reasonable parity between the quality and cost of service available to rural and urban ratepayers.

Responding to the Congress's directive, the Commission in 1996 initiated an entirely new rulemaking to address the issue of universal service, including mechanisms to make advanced telecommunications services available to schools, libraries and health care facilities.

D.   Federalism And The Act

One of the most troubling questions posed by the new Act and the FCC's implementing rules is the impact of those enactments on the states' historic authority to regulate intrastate telecommunications. Section 2(b) of the 1934 Act[12] preserved this role for the states in unequivocal language, and the 1996 Act appeared to confirm the states' authority by giving the state regulatory commissions the power to approve and arbitrate interconnection agreements between incumbent LECs and their competitors and by giving states the authority to set prices for interconnection, resale and access to unbundled network elements.

When the FCC came to write rules implementing the Act, however, it chose to emphasize, not these expansive grants of state authority but rather the brief directions to the FCC to make rules implementing various provisions of the Act. Relying on these statements, the Commission found that unless it offered detailed guidance to the states in the discharge of their responsibilities, a crazy-quilt of regulations and arbitration results would delay and confuse the advent of competition in local service markets.[13]

To many observers, the Commission's action seemed contrary to the rule announced by the U.S. Supreme Court in *Louisiana Public Service Commission v. Federal Communications Commission*[14], which holds that the FCC may preempt state jurisdiction only where necessary to avoid frustrating a goal that is within the FCC's jurisdiction under the Communications Act, and then may only preempt as to those aspects of

---

11. Conference Report to Accompany S. 652, *supra* note 4 at 131.

12. 47 U.S.C.A. § 152(b) (West 1991).

13. Implementation of the Local Competition Provisions in the Telecommunications Act of 1996, CC Docket No. 96–98, and Interconnection between Local Ex-

change Carriers and Commercial Mobile Radio Service Providers, CC Docket No. 95–185, First Report and Order (rel Aug. 8, 1996) para. 114.

14. 476 U.S. 355, 106 S.Ct. 1890, 90 L.Ed.2d 369 (1986).

regulation that cannot be separated into interstate and intrastate components. Accordingly, a number of petitions for review were brought asserting that the Commission had exceeded its jurisdiction. Those petitions were consolidated before the United States Court of Appeals for the Eighth Circuit. The Court of Appeals then stayed the effect of the FCC's pricing regulations pending its decision on the merits and noted particularly that the petitioners were likely to prevail on their claim that the pricing regulations exceeded the Commission's jurisdiction. Subsequently, the Court of Appeals determined that the FCC's pricing rules infringed on prerogatives expressly committed to the states in the 1996 Act.[15] But most of the appeals court's rulings were reversed by the Supreme Court.[16]

15. Iowa Utilities Board v. Federal Communications Commission, 120 F.3d 753 *modified* 1997 WL 65871 (8th Cir. 1997), *aff'd in part, rev'd in part,* __ U.S. __, 119 S.Ct. 721, 142 L.Ed.2d 835 (1999).

16. __ U.S. __, 119 S.Ct. 721, 142 L.Ed.2d 835 (1999).

Chapter Ten

THE FEDERAL COMMUNICATIONS COMMISSION: JURISDICTION, STRUCTURE AND PROCEDURES

Analysis

10.1 Introduction

Electronic communications services in the United States are regulated primarily by the Federal Communications Commission—an agency created by the Congress in the Communications Act of 1934.[1] (For convenience, in this chapter we shall often refer to the Communications Act of 1934 as the "Act," and the Federal Communications Commission as the "FCC" or the "Commission.") The Act, as amended from time to time, defines the organization and procedures of the FCC, grants the Commission the power to regulate "all interstate and foreign communications by wire or radio," and defines, in broad terms, the Commission's authority to regulate particular services and service providers. The Act also prescribes generally the procedures under which the FCC makes rules, enforces the Act and its regulations and adjudicates disputes that come within its jurisdiction.

The FCC is a so-called independent agency, *i.e.*, an administrative body created by Congress and not placed under the direct control of either the legislative or executive branch. Like other independent agencies, however, the FCC is controlled in various ways by all three constitutional branches of the federal government. So, for example, the Congress writes the legislation under which the Commission operates,

1. 47 U.S.C.A. § 151 *et seq.* (West 1991 and Supp. 1997).

742

controls its budget and exercises legislative oversight of its operations;[2] the President, with the advice and consent of the Senate, appoints the commissioners and chooses one of them to serve as Chairman;[3] and the federal judiciary reviews the Commission's actions when those actions are challenged as violative of the Constitution or the statutes to which the Commission is subject.[4]

The FCC has one of the broadest and most complex mandates of all federal agencies. The industries the Commission regulates are based on a variety of electronic technologies, in a state of rapid evolution, that strain the statutory categories within which the Commission must work. The skills the Commission must bring to its tasks range from technical fields such as engineering and microeconomics, at one extreme, to policy judgments in such socially and politically sensitive areas as obscenity, indecency and the content of children's television programs, at the other. The substantive rules by which the Commission regulates particular services and service providers are discussed elsewhere in this book. The task of this chapter is to describe the Commission's organization, jurisdiction and procedures, as well as the constitutional and statutory constraints on the Commission's powers and processes. Each of these subjects merits a word of introduction.

The first section of this chapter describes briefly some of the constitutional limits within which the Commission must confine its actions: specifically, the extent to which the FCC, as an independent federal agency, may perform legislative, executive and judicial functions without violating the constitutional prerogatives of the Congress, the President and the federal judiciary, and without violating the principle that each of those powers should be exercised by a separate branch of government. These subjects, which often are referred to as delegation questions, involve fundamental issues of administrative law.

The second section describes the Commission's organization, which is prescribed generally in the Act and more particularly in the Commission's regulations. This section briefly describes the responsibilities of the commissioners, staff offices and bureaus, and leaves to other chapters the task of describing in detail how the principal line organizations—such as the Common Carrier Bureau and the Mass Media Bureau—carry out their specialized tasks.

The next section discusses the Commission's jurisdiction, which is perhaps the most vexing of all the subjects covered in this chapter. One source of jurisdictional confusion is the advent of new technologies, not foreseen in 1934, that test the limits of the Commission's subject-matter authority. The other is the ongoing puzzle of drawing the line between state and federal authority over telecommunications services and facilities and deciding when the Commission has the power to cross that line by preempting state authority.

2. *See, e.g., id.* § 154(k) (West 1991).
3. *Id.* § 154(a).

4. *Id.* § 402; 28 U.S.C.A. § 2342 (West 1996).

Finally, the section on Commission procedures describes the particular methods by which the Commission makes and enforces regulations, adjudicates disputes and carries out licensing and other specialized functions. A complete understanding of these subjects requires some knowledge, not only of the Act and the rules, but of the broader constraints on agency action imposed by the Constitution, the Administrative Procedure Act and the process of judicial review. Those wishing a deeper understanding of these questions should consult an administrative law treatise.

10.2   The Federal Communications Commission's Place in the Constitutional Scheme

As a federal administrative agency, the FCC is part of what some have called the "fourth branch" of the United States government.[1] The proper role of the federal regulatory agencies has never been free from controversy, and the ambiguity of their status makes them vulnerable to challenge when their powers appear to usurp the prerogatives of one of the constitutional branches of government. Because these issues can have practical consequences for the FCC and those it regulates, they merit a brief discussion here.

A.   *Delegation and Separation of Powers Generally*

The Constitution vests legislative, executive and judicial power in the Congress, the President and the courts respectively, and does not expressly authorize the delegation of those powers to other organs of government, or the mingling of the functions of one of the constitutional branches with those of another. Often, however, the political branches have made limited delegations of their constitutional powers to specialized agencies with authority to regulate particular industries or address particular problems. These agencies often are granted the power to make rules (a legislative function), to enforce those rules and investigate alleged violations (executive functions) and to adjudicate claims that their rules or the standards set out in their governing statutes have been violated (a judicial function).

These grants of authority to specialized agencies raise a number of closely-related constitutional questions. One such issue is the extent to which the Congress may delegate its legislative responsibility to the Executive branch or to independent agencies that are not directly accountable to the electorate. Another question is the legality of congressional delegations of judicial authority to agencies, rather than courts and judges created under Article III of the Constitution. And still another question is the legality, under the separation-of-powers scheme of the Constitution, of statutes that limit the ability of the President to appoint and remove high-level officers of federal agencies. While the courts generally have upheld delegations against challenges raising these

---

1. *See, e.g.*, Peter Strauss, *The Place of Agencies in Government: Separation of Pow-*   *ers and the Fourth Branch*, 84 Colum. L. Rev. 573 (1984).

issues, they also have made it clear that the discretion to delegate is not unlimited.

The courts have been most indulgent in reviewing delegations of rulemaking, or legislative, authority, often taking the view that to require the Congress to impose detailed standards on agencies would limit the flexibility that the regulatory process is meant to achieve. The courts have upheld legislative delegations both by applying a lenient standard of review,[2] and by construing statutes so as to ensure that the standard is almost always met.[3] This approach does not mean, however, that constitutional challenges to legislative delegations will never succeed: extreme cases of standardless delegation still are vulnerable to attack,[4] and there is substantial academic support for strengthening the delegation doctrine as a means of curbing the ability of Congress to pass responsibility for unpopular decisions to bureaucrats who lack political accountability.[5]

Delegations of judicial authority also invite constitutional scrutiny, chiefly because agency adjudications are not made by judges with the salary protection and lifetime tenure guaranteed to federal judges by Article III. Judicial delegations nonetheless were generally upheld until 1982,[6] when they appeared to be called into question by the Supreme Court's *Northern Pipeline* decision.[7] In *Northern Pipeline*, the Court struck down the system of bankruptcy courts established under the 1978 Bankruptcy Act, noting that the Congress could not constitutionally delegate the wide range of private rights adjudications contemplated by that Act to a court that did not meet the requirements of Article III of

2. Legislative delegations generally are upheld unless the statutory language is so broad that "it would be impossible in a proper proceeding to ascertain whether the will of Congress has been obeyed." Yakus v. United States, 321 U.S. 414, 426, 64 S.Ct. 660, 668, 88 L.Ed. 834, 849 (1944); *see also* Skinner v. Mid–America Pipeline Co., 490 U.S. 212, 109 S.Ct. 1726, 104 L.Ed.2d 250 (1989); Mistretta v. United States, 488 U.S. 361, 109 S.Ct. 647, 102 L.Ed.2d 714 (1989).

3. Courts may "save" a broad delegation of legislative power by supplementing the statutory language with standards derived from the legislative history of related statutes (*see, e.g.,* Amalgamated Meat Cutters v. Connally, 337 F.Supp. 737 (D.D.C. 1971)), or simply by adopting a narrow reading of the statutory text (*see, e.g.,* National Cable Television Ass'n v. United States, 415 U.S. 336, 94 S.Ct. 1146, 39 L.Ed.2d 370 (1974); Kent v. Dulles, 357 U.S. 116, 78 S.Ct. 1113, 2 L.Ed.2d 1204 (1958)). Similarly, a court may find that supplementation of the statutory delegation with administrative standards, and the susceptibility of those standards to judicial review, is sufficient to cure the arbitrariness and lack of notice to regulated persons that

an overbroad delegation otherwise might entail. *See, e.g.,* Amalgamated Meat Cutters v. Connally, *supra.*

4. Justice (now Chief Justice) Rehnquist, in a concurring opinion written in 1980, stated that he would have struck down the Secretary of Labor's regulation concerning worker exposure to benzene, not on the ground on which the majority relied (failure of the Secretary to make adequate findings), but on the ground that the statute itself was an impermissible delegation. Industrial Union Dep't, AFL–CIO v. American Petroleum Inst., 448 U.S. 607, 100 S.Ct. 2844, 65 L.Ed.2d 1010 (1980); *see also* American Textile Mfrs. Inst. v. Donovan, 452 U.S. 490, 101 S.Ct. 2478, 69 L.Ed.2d 185 (1981) (concurring opinion of Justices Burger and Rehnquist).

5. *See, e.g.,* JOHN HART ELY, DEMOCRACY AND DISTRUST 131–32 (1980); J. Skelly Wright, *Beyond Discretionary Justice*, 81 Yale L.J. 575, 582–87 (1972).

6. Crowell v. Benson, 285 U.S. 22, 52 S.Ct. 285, 76 L.Ed. 598 (1932).

7. Northern Pipeline Construction Co. v. Marathon Pipe Line Co., 458 U.S. 50, 102 S.Ct. 2858, 73 L.Ed.2d 598 (1982).

the Constitution. The rationale of *Northern Pipeline* appeared to apply to administrative adjudications, as well; but subsequent decisions involving agency action have upheld delegations of judicial power on the ground that the rights adjudicated were primarily "public rights," and that the challenged statute empowered the agency to judge private rights only to the extent necessary to secure those "public rights."[8] Future challenges to judicial delegations, therefore, are likely to succeed only where those delegations empower an agency to settle private disputes that could, without detriment to the agency's legitimate mission, be resolved by the courts.

Independent agencies—*i.e.*, the SEC, FERC, FCC and other agencies created by the Congress and not placed within the Executive branch—have been especially problematic because while those agencies perform executive functions, the Congress has limited the President's power to appoint and remove their highest-ranking officials. These statutes, too, are upheld where they are found not to "impede the President's ability to perform his constitutional duty,"[9] and particularly where the function of the officer involved is found to be more judicial or legislative than executive.[10]

B. *Delegation and Separation of Powers Issues at the FCC*

Courts confronted with a challenge to agency action are far more likely to find that the agency has exceeded its statutory mandate, than they are to find that in enacting the statute the Congress has made an unconstitutional delegation of legislative authority. As might be expected, therefore, delegation-doctrine challenges to the Communications Act have been rare and uniformly unsuccessful.

An early—and quite fundamental—challenge attacked the Act's "public interest" standard as an impermissible delegation. Specifically, in *National Radio Broadcasting Co., Inc. v. United States*, a radio broadcasting network petitioned for review of the so-called "chain broadcasting" rules, through which the Commission sought to curb the power of networks over their affiliates.[11] The petitioners argued that the regulations, which the Commission had based on its broad authority to regulate wire and radio communication in the public interest, convenience and necessity, exceeded the scope of that authority. The petitioners further argued that even if the public interest standard was broad enough to embrace the challenged regulations, it should be rejected as excessively vague, amounting to an impermissible delegation of legislative authority.

8. CFTC v. Schor, 478 U.S. 833, 106 S.Ct. 3245, 92 L.Ed.2d 675 (1986); Thomas v. Union Carbide Agricultural Products Co., 473 U.S. 568, 105 S.Ct. 3325, 87 L.Ed.2d 409 (1985).

9. Morrison v. Olson, 487 U.S. 654, 108 S.Ct. 2597, 101 L.Ed.2d 569 (1988).

10. *See* Wiener v. United States, 357 U.S. 349, 78 S.Ct. 1275, 2 L.Ed.2d 1377 (1958); Myers v. United States, 272 U.S. 52, 47 S.Ct. 21, 71 L.Ed. 160 (1926).

11. 319 U.S. 190, 63 S.Ct. 997, 87 L.Ed. 1344 (1943).

The Supreme Court rejected all of the petitioners' claims. On the delegation question, in particular, the Court found that the public interest standard was not an unbounded grant of discretion, but was limited by "[t]he purpose of the Act, the requirements it imposes, and the context of the provision in question ..." Since the overall scheme and specific provisions of the Act permitted the will of Congress to be ascertained,[12] the challenged regulations were upheld.

Somewhat later, in a case brought in the 1960s, a broadcasting company challenged a 1959 amendment to section 315 of the Communications Act as an impermissible delegation of legislative authority.[13] The amendment codified the FCC's Fairness Doctrine, which required broadcasters to seek a reasonably balanced presentation of all viewpoints on controversial issues of public importance. The petitioners argued that the amendment's use of expressions such as "reasonable opportunity for the discussion of conflicting view" and "issues of public importance" failed to set "adequate standards or ascertainable criteria" for the exercise of the Commission's discretion.[14] And since the Fairness Doctrine implicated First Amendment rights, the petitioners argued that section 315 was required—and failed—to meet the especially stringent standard of precision imposed on legislation affecting basic freedoms.[15]

The court of appeals found that the challenged provisions of the Act offered sufficient guidance for a court to determine whether regulations enacted under those provisions violated the intent of Congress. The court noted that the broad, public interest standard on which the Fairness Doctrine was based had been upheld against a delegation challenge in *National Broadcasting Co.,* and found that the particular provisions of the amendment to section 315, in particular, when read in the context of the entire scheme of broadcast regulation contained in the Act, constituted a sufficient set of statutory standards and policies to guide the Commission's exercise of judgment in implementing the amendment.[16] In a later delegation case presenting a more specific question, the National Cable Television Association challenged regulations by which the Commission assessed certain charges against cable television systems.[17] According to the plaintiff the charges were not regulatory "fees," intended to offset the costs of regulatory benefits conferred upon the cable companies, but were "taxes" intended merely to raise revenue for the federal treasury. If the charges were authorized by the Act, then the Act made an impermissible delegation of the

12. *Id.* at 226, (quoting New York Central Securities Corp. v. United States, 287 U.S. 12, 24–25, 53 S.Ct. 45, 77 L.Ed. 138 (1932)).

13. Red Lion Broadcasting Co., Inc. v. Federal Communications Commission, 381 F.2d 908, 127 U.S.App.D.C. 129 (D.C.Cir. 1967), *aff'd* 395 U.S. 367, 89 S.Ct. 1794, 23 L.Ed.2d 371 (1969).

14. *Id.* at 920, 121 U.S. App. D.C. at 141.

15. *Id. See* N.A.A.C.P. v. Button, 371 U.S. 415, 438, 83 S.Ct. 328, 9 L.Ed.2d 405 (1963); *see also* Aptheker v. Secretary of State, 378 U.S. 500, 514, 84 S.Ct. 1659, 1668, 12 L.Ed.2d 992 (1964).

16. Red Lion Broadcasting Co., 381 F.2d at 922, 121 U.S. App. D.C. at 143.

17. National Cable Television Association v. United States, 415 U.S. 336, 94 S.Ct. 1146, 39 L.Ed.2d 370 (1974).

congressional power to tax. In this case the Supreme Court avoided reaching the question whether the FCC could tax cable companies by finding that the charges were permissible fees that did not raise a delegation question.[18]

As this brief review of the principal cases shows, the delegation doctrine has not played an important role in judicial review of FCC actions. It should not be assumed, however, that petitioners will not find the doctrine useful in the future. Notably, the new Telecommunications Act of 1996 grants sweeping discretion to the FCC to transform the regulation of telecommunications and broadcasting, and persons aggrieved by the FCC's exercise of that discretion may discover plausible claims that the authority granted in the new Act goes beyond even the lenient limits of the existing delegation doctrine.

10.3 Structure of the FCC

The FCC is made up of five commissioners appointed by the President with the advice and consent of the Senate.[1] One Commissioner is named by the President to serve as Chairman;[2] only the smallest number of commissioners needed to form a majority may be members of the same political party.[3] FCC commissioners are appointed for a term of five years, plus any additional time needed for their successors to be confirmed and take the oath of office.[4]

The Act authorizes the Commission to hire staff personnel and to organize its staff into "integrated bureaus" and "such other divisional organizations as the Commission may deem necessary."[5] The integrated bureaus are to function according to the Commission's "principal workload operations," and may be assigned such legal, engineering and other specialized personnel as the Commission thinks necessary.[6]

The Chairman, as chief executive officer of the Commission, delegates substantial management responsibility to the Managing Director, who makes administrative policy and oversees the operations of the various bureaus and staff offices.[7] These bureaus and staff offices, in turn, perform most of the Commission's day-to-day work, and a number of these are worth describing in some detail.[8]

---

18. In a later case involving another agency, however, the Supreme Court faced the question and found that there is no *per se* rule against congressional delegation of its taxing power. Like other delegations, statutes permitting agencies to tax must be judged according to whether the agencies' discretion is sufficiently circumscribed so that a reviewing court can decide, in a particular case, whether the will of Congress has been violated. Skinner v. Mid–America Pipeline Co., *supra*, note 2.

1. 47 U.S.C.A. § 154(a) (West 1991).

2. *Id.*

3. *Id.* § 154(b)(5).

4. *Id.* § 154(c). In any event, no commissioner may serve "beyond the expiration of the next session of Congress subsequent to the expiration of said fixed term of office . . ." *Id.* A commissioner appointed to fill a vacancy may not serve beyond the unexpired term of the commissioner he succeeds. *Id.*

5. *Id.* § 155(b).

6. *Id.*

7. The functions of the Office of Managing Director are described at 47 C.F.R. § 0.11 (1997).

8. Occasionally, bureaus and offices are added, eliminated or reorganized. These

A. *Commission Offices*

The staff offices support the work of the Commission in a broad range of policy, technical, legal, legislative and other areas. Unlike the operating bureaus (described below), the offices generally do not deal directly with the persons and entities the Commission regulates.

The Office of Plans and Policy (OPP) is the Chairman's chief resource for studies of long-term policy and agenda items requiring particular economic and technical expertise. Among other functions, the OPP is charged with weighing the effect of alternative policy choices on domestic and international communication industries and services. The OPP also recommends funding levels and priorities for research related to the Commission's business, and supervises research projects conducted by outside contractors.[9]

The Office of Inspector General (OIG) is the Commission's internal auditor and investigator, with ongoing responsibility to find and correct deficiencies in the Commission's operations and to conduct special investigations at the direction of the Chairman.[10] In addition to its responsibilities to the Chairman, however, the OIG also has a statutory obligation to make periodic reports directly to the Congress, and to advise the Congress independently of any instances of fraud or inefficiency it discovers.[11] The Chairman is prevented by statute from interfering with the OIG's compliance with these investigatory and reporting requirements.[12]

The Office of Legislative and Intergovernmental Affairs (OLA) is the Commission's liaison with the Congress and with the Executive Branch to the extent the Executive proposes, or requests information concerning, legislation.[13] The OLA keeps the Congress informed of Commission actions, responds to congressional inquiries and presents the Commission's views concerning pending legislation that affects the FCC's operations or the effectiveness of its policies and rules.

The Office of Engineering and Technology is the Commission's technology advisor and also has direct responsibility for administering the Commission's regulations concerning frequency allocations, radio equipment certification and other specified rules that primarily involve technical issues.[14] The Office of Engineering and Technology also represents the Commission at international technical and standards-making conferences that involve electronic communications.

changes are summarized most conveniently in the FCC's Annual Reports, available from the Government Printing Office.

9. 47 C.F.R. § 0.21 (1997).

10. *Id.* § 0.13.

11. *Id.* The duties of federal inspectors general to the Congress are set out in the Inspector General Act of 1978 *codified as*

amended (5 U.S.C.A.) (West 1996 & West Supp.1998) and the Inspector General Act Amendments of 1988 (Pub. L. 100–504).

12. *Id.*

13. 47 C.F.R. § 0.17 (1997).

14. *Id.* § 0.31.

The Office of General Counsel (OGC) is the Commission's legal advisor and advocate.[15] Among other functions, the OGC represents the Commission when the Commission is a party to litigation, interprets statutes, international agreements and treaties that affect the Commission and makes recommendations to the Commission concerning proposed legislation. The OGC also provides legal memoranda on such questions as the Commission may direct and acts as the Commission's lawyer with respect to internal legal issues.

Finally, the Office of Public Affairs (OPA) informs the public and the press of the FCC's regulatory requirements and policies, and is charged with involving the public in the FCC's decision-making process.[16] The OPA's News Media Division, in particular, issues daily news releases and public notices and prepares the Commission's Annual Report and other publications.

B. The Commission's Operating Bureaus

While the Commission's staff office personnel are generalists, the operating bureau personnel are specialists. Each bureau deals with specific industries and services subject to the Commission's jurisdiction and administers regulations unique to the activities it is charged to regulate. These organizations—the Mass Media Bureau, the Common Carrier Bureau, the Wireless Telecommunications Bureau, the Cable Services Bureau, the International Bureau and the Compliance and Information Bureau—are the FCC's front-line units. Each merits a brief description.

The Mass Media Bureau is in charge of licensing of radio and television broadcast stations, and also makes rules and policies pursuant to its statutory mandate to regulate broadcasting in "the public interest, convenience and necessity."[17] The Bureau's Enforcement Division oversees compliance with the broadcasting rules, responds to private and congressional complaints brought against broadcast licensees and imposes sanctions ranging from monetary forfeitures to revocation—or refusal to renew—station licenses.

The Common Carrier Bureau (CCB) makes rules and policies and adjudicates complaints concerning the interstate communications services of wireline telephone and telegraph companies.[18] Because the regulation of these "common carrier" services is uniquely pervasive, including detailed oversight of the terms and conditions on which services are offered and interconnections among carriers (and with customer-provided equipment) are made, the activities of the Common Carrier Bureau are extensive and involve the work of a number of specialized divisions. Notably, the Competitive Pricing Division reviews the publicly-filed rates under which common carrier communications services are offered; the Network Services Division oversees reliability, numbering and other issues concerning the operation of the nationwide

15. *Id.* § 0.41.

16. *Id.* § 0.15.

17. *Id.* § 0.61.

18. *Id.* § 0.91.

telecommunications network; the Enforcement Division adjudicates complaints brought against common carriers, monitors consumer protection questions and reviews common carrier mergers and acquisitions; the Industry Analysis Division collects, analyzes and publishes common carrier industry statistics; the Accounting and Audits Division manages the complex pooling process by which universal service is supported and oversees the FCC's cost accounting rules for common carriers; and the Policy and Program Planning Division is charged with developing procompetitive policies for common carrier regulation.

The Wireless Telecommunications Bureau (WTB) regulates all domestic, terrestrial, wireless telecommunications services, including paging, cellular telephone, personal communications service (PCS) and public safety radiocommunication. The WTB carries out its mandate through several divisions: the Commercial Wireless Division regulates cellular, PCS and other commercial applications of wireless telecommunications; the Enforcement and Consumer Information Division monitors compliance with the rules and orders applicable to wireless telecommunications and responds to complaints; the Policy Division formulates proposed rules and policies concerning services within the Bureau's jurisdiction; the Auctions and Industry Analysis Division sets the procedures for competitive bidding on electromagnetic spectrum and conducts the auctions; and the Public Safety and Private Wireless Division regulates public safety, marine, fixed microwave, aviation and other wireless services that fall outside the purview of the Commercial Wireless Division.

The Cable Services Bureau ("CSB") was formed in response to the Cable Television Consumer Protection and Competition Act of 1992, which reregulated the rates charged by cable operators for their basic tier of services. In addition to implementing the 1992 Act, the CSB is responsible for policy development and rulemaking for the cable television industry.

The International Bureau coordinates the development of Commission policy concerning international communications and oversees the Commission's regulation of international telecommunication services that come within its jurisdiction. Notably, the International Bureau is responsible for authorizing and regulating international services and the associated facilities, and regulating domestic and international satellite systems. The Bureau is also heavily involved in the development of the United States position concerning international radiofrequency allocations and the assignments of orbital locations for communication satellites and this country's compliance with international and bilateral agreements concerning the use of those resources.

Finally, the Compliance and Information Bureau operates the field offices through which the Commission inspects radio stations, assists public service agencies, monitors uses of the radio spectrum to guard against unauthorized use and interference and answers public inquiries. The Bureau also initiates and carries out enforcement activities against persons deemed to be in violation of the Communications Act and the rules and orders of the Commission.

In recent years, as technology and the Commission's regulatory policies have evolved, changes to the FCC's organization have become more frequent. Those wanting to confirm the present status of the offices and bureaus described here should contact the Commission's Office of Public Affairs.

10.4 Jurisdiction of the FCC

In order to determine whether (and how) the Act permits the Commission to deal with any particular rate, facility or service, we first must know whether the regulation falls within the Act's definition of communication by wire or radio and which of the Act's various regulatory schemes applies to the regulated activity. We also must know whether the activity is interstate or foreign, as those terms are defined by the Congress and the courts. In the discussion that follows, we address each of these jurisdictional questions in some detail; after which, we discuss the procedures and organization through which the FCC carries out its jurisdictional mandate.

A. Jurisdiction Over Communications by Wire or Radio

As we have noted, the Act grants the FCC the power to regulate "all interstate or foreign communication by wire or radio."[1] The Act does not define the terms "wire or radio," but does define "communications" as "the transmission of writing, signs, signals, pictures and sounds of all kinds . . ., including all instrumentalities, facilities, apparatus, and services incidental to such transmission."[2]

While this definition is expansive, the Act's specific regulatory provisions have not kept pace with advancing technology. When the Act was passed, the world of electronic communications could be neatly divided among common carrier services (telephones and telegraphs), radio broadcasting, and nonbroadcast radio applications such as maritime and public safety communication. The structure of the Act reflected this tidy classification: Title II regulation applied to common carriers and governed entry, exit and terms of service; Title III regulation applied to noncommon carrier radio services and governed licensing and (in the case of broadcasting) various provisions intended to ensure that the scarce set of available frequencies was used by licensees in the public interest.

B. Ancillary Jurisdiction

Where electronic communication technologies—such as cable television—have appeared that do not fit within the traditional categories of broadcasting or common carriage, the Commission has been forced either to wait for a suitable amendment of the Act before asserting its

---

1. 47 U.S.C.A. § 152(a) (West 1991).   **2.** *Id.* § 153(b).

jurisdiction or to find some basis for regulation within the language enacted in 1934. The courts have recognized this problem, and have held that technologies and services not contemplated in the 1934 Act may nonetheless come within the FCC's so-called "ancillary" jurisdiction. In support of this catchall jurisdictional category, the courts have pointed to section 152(a) of the Act, giving the Commission the power to regulate "all interstate and foreign communication by wire or radio. .;" and to section 154(i), which empowers the Commission to "make such rules and regulations, . . . not inconsistent with this chapter, as may be necessary in the exercise of its functions." As the courts also have made clear, however, the FCC's ancillary jurisdiction is something less than a blank check: regulation of new services still must comport with the Act and with past Commission treatment of similar services. More adventuresome regulation of new technologies will require new legislation.

The principal case on the Commission's ancillary jurisdiction is *United States v. Southwestern Cable Company.*[3] In *Southwestern Cable,* a cable television operator argued that the Commission lacked jurisdiction, under the Act, to interfere with its carriage of distant broadcast signals in competition with local television stations. In support of its claim, the cable operator pointed out that cable television systems are not common carriers, which are regulated under Title II of the Act; and are not broadcasters, which are regulated under Title III of the Act. In response to the Commission's argument that regulation of cable television could be based on section 152(a) of the Act, which gives the FCC jurisdiction over "all interstate and foreign communication by wire or radio . . ." the cable operator contended that section 152(a) only prescribes the kinds of communication to which Title II and Title III regulation may be applied, and does not independently confer jurisdiction over any service not within those categories.

The Supreme Court rejected these arguments on two grounds. First, the Court found no language in Section 152(a), or elsewhere in the language or history of the Act, to suggest that the reach of section 152(a) is limited to the categories of common carrier and radio regulation addressed in Titles II and III. Second, the Court found that regulation of cable television so as to limit its impact on local stations was well within the Commission's statutory mandate to preserve the viability of local broadcasting. Accordingly, the Court determined that section 152(a) permitted the FCC to issue rules for cable television to the extent those rules were "reasonably ancillary to the effective performance of the Commission's various responsibilities for the regulation of television broadcasting."[4]

While the ancillary jurisdiction recognized in *Southwestern Cable* gives the Commission some ability to regulate new services, the Supreme Court confirmed in a later case that discretion is limited. In *Midwest Video,* the Court held that section 152(a) did not empower the Commis-

3. 392 U.S. 157, 88 S.Ct. 1994, 20 L.Ed.2d 1001 (1968).

4. *Id.* at 178, 88 S. Ct. at 2005, 20 L.Ed.2d at 1016.

sion to require cable operators to make their facilities available to third-party providers of certain types of programming.[5] The Court found that while the FCC order reviewed in *Southwestern Cable* promoted the statutory goals of the Act's broadcast provisions, and therefore was reasonably ancillary to the jurisdiction granted by those provisions, nothing in the broadcast provisions supported the imposition of common carrier obligations, which the Act expressly states may *not* be imposed on broadcasters. Regulations imposing common carrier obligations, therefore, cannot be ancillary to the Commission's jurisdiction over broadcasting.

C. Limitations on Jurisdiction

As the *Midwest Video* decision suggests, nothing in the Communications Act, including the broad grant of subject-matter jurisdiction in section 152(a), gives the Commission unfettered discretion to regulate new technologies as it thinks best. In fact, the courts have found that while the Commission may experiment with different methods of regulation where a service or technology presents novel questions, any regulations the FCC adopts must be within its statutory authority and must be rationally reconcilable with the Commission's regulation of other, similar services.

This point is well stated in the opinion of the United States Court of Appeals for the District of Columbia Circuit in *National Association of Broadcasters v. Federal Communications Commission*.[6] In that case the FCC had adopted interim regulations for direct broadcast satellite ("DBS") service, which retransmits television programming from satellites to small receiving dishes located at the viewers' premises. Although DBS fit the statutory definition of a broadcast service, the Commission wished to relieve some DBS providers of certain restrictions imposed on broadcasters by Title III of the Act. Specifically, the Commission allowed some DBS satellite owners to operate as common carriers, leasing satellite space to programmers but exercising no control over the content of the programming provided by those lessees. The lessees, in turn, would be exempt from the usual requirements that broadcasters make their facilities reasonably available to political candidates and that where one candidate is granted access, other qualified candidates be given an equal opportunity to respond.[7]

The Commission offered three reasons for its novel treatment of lessee-providers of DBS. First, the Commission noted that the provision of broadcast services through the facilities of a common carrier was not contemplated in the 1934 Act and concluded on this ground that the restrictions placed by the Act on traditional broadcasters did not apply to this new, hybrid entity. Second, the Commission concluded that since

---

5. Federal Communications Commission v. Midwest Video Corp., 440 U.S. 689, 99 S.Ct. 1435, 59 L.Ed.2d 692 (1979).

6. 740 F.2d 1190, 239 U.S. App. D.C. 87 (D.C.Cir.1984).

7. 47 U.S.C.A. §§ 312(a)(7), 315 (West 1991).

traditional carriers continued to bear the political programming obligations, the public interest was not disserved by relieving the lessee-providers of those requirements. And third, the Commission pointed out that its treatment of these providers was consistent with its regulation of customers of Multipoint Distribution Service ("MDS") services, which also were exempt from the political programming requirements.[8]

In spite of the FCC's rationale, the court found that the Commission's exemption of lessee-providers from the political broadcasting provisions of the Act could not be reconciled with the Act or with the FCC's past decisions. The court pointed out that lessee-providers, no less than terrestrial broadcasters and DBS providers who own satellite facilities, are broadcasters within the meaning of the Act. Nothing in the statute offered any basis for treating one broadcaster differently from another. Further, the court found that the Commission's treatment of lessee-providers could not be reconciled with its earlier decision, in a rulemaking involving subscription television, that the touchstone dividing broadcast from nonbroadcast services is the intention of the service provider to "provide radio or television service to as may members of the general public as can be interested in the particular program as distinguished from a point-to-point message service to specified individuals ... , even though a segment of the public is unable to view programs without special equipment ..."[9]

Since lessee-providers of DBS service plainly are "broadcasters" within the Commission's earlier definition, the court noted that they could not—in the absence of a rational explanation—be treated as nonbroadcasters under the DBS rules.

10.5   The Limits of the FCC's "Interstate or Foreign" Jurisdiction

The most perplexing feature of the FCC's jurisdiction is the Communications Act's denial of Commission authority to regulate intrastate communication.[1] This reservation of power to the states forces the Commission to make artificial distinctions between the intrastate and interstate components of geographically indivisible services, and to confine its regulations to those services and service elements it reasonably identifies as interstate.[2] The Act's confinement of FCC regulation to the interstate jurisdiction also limits the Commission's power to preempt state enactments that are inconsistent with the Commission's regulations.[3]

---

8. *National Association of Broadcasters v. FCC, supra,* 740 F.2d at 1200, 239 U.S. App. D.C. at 97.

9. *Id.* at 1200, 239 U.S. App. D.C. at 97.

1. 47 U.S.C.A. § 152(b) (West 1991).

2. The Act preempts state authority over certain activities, notably including the licensing of radio stations. *Id.* § 301. For activities as to which no such statutory preemption is available, however, the Commission must respect the Act's reservation of regulatory power to the states.

3. *See, e.g.,* Louisiana Public Service Commission v. FCC, 476 U.S. 355, 106 S.Ct. 1890, 90 L.Ed.2d 369 (1986).

While the limits of federal and state jurisdiction, on the one hand, and the circumstances under which the FCC may preempt intrastate jurisdiction, on the other, are often discussed together and are easily confused, it is useful to keep these issues separate. Accordingly, this section considers, first, the efforts of the Commission and the courts to find the line separating federal from state jurisdiction over electronic communications services and facilities; and second, the extent of the Commission's authority, once the jurisdictional line is drawn, to step over that line where needed to fulfill the FCC's regulatory mandate.

A. *Federal and State Jurisdiction Defined*

Under the Supremacy Clause of Article VI of the Constitution, the states may not impose their own requirements in areas that the Congress has chosen to regulate exclusively.[4] Congress may show its intention to displace, or preempt, state law by expressing that intention in, or concurrently with the enactment of, a statute;[5] or by legislating so comprehensively that no scope for state regulation remains.[6] Preemption also will be given effect when simultaneous compliance with federal and state law is physically impossible,[7] or where the laws of the two jurisdictions are in outright conflict,[8] or where preemption can fairly be implied from the federal law[9] or where enforcement of the state law would frustrate the objectives of Congress.[10]

Until passage of the 1934 Act, the extent to which Congress meant to displace state regulation of telecommunications was unclear. The 1910 Mann–Elkins Act merely added telephone and telegraph services to the mandate of the Interstate Commerce Commission (ICC), suggesting to many that federal jurisdiction over those services had been made coextensive with the ICC's jurisdiction over rail service.[11] When the Supreme Court later ruled that the ICC was empowered to regulate railroad rates for goods transported entirely within a state,[12] therefore, the ICC well might have relied on that authority to assert jurisdiction over wholly

4. "This Constitution, and the Laws of the United States which shall be made in Pursuance thereof; and all Treaties made, or which shall be made, under the Authority of the United States, shall be supreme Law of the Land; and the Judges in every State shall be bound thereby, any Thing in the Constitution of Laws of any State to the Contrary notwithstanding." U.S. Const. Art. VI.

5. Jones v. Rath Packing Co., 430 U.S. 519, 97 S.Ct. 1305, 51 L.Ed.2d 604 (1977).

6. Rice v. Santa Fe Elevator Corp., 331 U.S. 218, 67 S.Ct. 1146, 91 L.Ed. 1447 (1947).

7. Florida Lime & Avocado Growers, Inc. v. Paul, 373 U.S. 132, 83 S.Ct. 1210, 10 L.Ed.2d 248 (1963).

8. Free v. Bland, 369 U.S. 663, 82 S.Ct. 1089, 8 L.Ed.2d 180 (1962).

9. Shaw v. Delta Air Lines, Inc., 463 U.S. 85, 103 S.Ct. 2890, 77 L.Ed.2d 490 (1983).

10. Hines v. Davidowitz, 312 U.S. 52, 61 S.Ct. 399, 85 L.Ed. 581 (1941). As we discuss below, a federal agency may preempt state law where that action is within the authority delegated to the agency by Congress. Capital Cities Cable, Inc. v. Crisp, 467 U.S. 691, 104 S.Ct. 2694, 81 L.Ed.2d 580 (1984); Fidelity Federal Savings & Loan Ass'n v. de la Cuesta, 458 U.S. 141, 102 S.Ct. 3014, 73 L.Ed.2d 664 (1982).

11. 36 Stat. 539 (1910).

12. Houston, E. & W. Tex. Ry v. United States, 234 U.S. 342, 34 S.Ct. 833, 58 L.Ed. 1341 (1914). This decision usually is referred to as the *Shreveport Rate Case.*

intrastate telephone and telegraph transmissions, as well—displacing state regulation altogether. The ICC did not take this approach, however, and by the time the Communications Act was passed there were 45 state commissions regulating the activities of telephone companies within their borders. The state regulators were fully aware, however, that they were exercising a jurisdiction for which they possessed no statutory guarantee.

The 1934 Act clarified the situation by expressly displacing state regulation of *interstate* communications and making an equally clear reservation of state power to regulate *intrastate* communications. Specifically, the Act gives the FCC the power to regulate all "interstate and foreign commerce in communication by wire and radio,"[13] and gives the states the power to regulate "intrastate communication service by wire or radio."[14] The Act also makes it clear, as to both jurisdictional grants, that the power to regulate is expansive: wire communication and radio communication are defined to include "all instrumentalities, facilities, apparatus, and services" incidental to those communications,[15] and the intrastate jurisdiction, in particular, extends to all "charges, classifications, practices, services, facilities, or regulations for or in connection with" intrastate communication services.[16]

While the Act's language is simple enough, in practice it has not always been easy to determine whether a regulated service or facility is jurisdictionally interstate or intrastate. A particular service may include both interstate and intrastate communications or may include communications that are not clearly interstate or intrastate. Similarly, a telecommunications facility may be located entirely within a state but may be used for both interstate and intrastate communications—requiring the federal and state authorities to determine how jurisdiction of the facility should be shared between them.

Fortunately, the efforts of the Commission and the courts to make sense of these problems have yielded some fairly definite rules. In summary, the cases show that a service that includes an interstate communication at any point is subject to regulation as an interstate service; and that a facility used in connection with any interstate communication is jurisdictionally interstate, and therefore subject to exclusive federal regulation, to the extent of its interstate use. A complete understanding of these rules requires a brief review of the principal cases.

1. *Interstate and Intrastate Services and Communications*

In ascertaining whether particular services involve interstate communications and therefore are within the jurisdiction of the FCC, the courts have resisted efforts to divide interstate transmissions into smaller, intrastate components as a means of defeating federal jurisdic-

---

13. 47 U.S.C.A. § 151 (West Supp. 1997).

14. *Id.* § 152(b).

15. *Id.* §§ 153(a)-(b) (West 1991).

16. *Id.* § 152(b) (West Supp. 1997).

tion but rather treated any interstate communication made in connection with a service as sufficient to bring the service within the authority of the FCC.

Two of the leading cases involve retransmission of broadcast signals by telephone and cable companies. In *Southwestern Cable*,[17] a cable company carried the signals of Los Angeles broadcast television stations into the San Diego area for distribution to the cable company's customers. In response to a complaint from a San Diego broadcast station, alleging that competition from the cable company was not in the public interest, the Commission ordered the cable company not to expand its operations pending a resolution of the complaint on the merits. The Supreme Court found that the FCC had acted within its statutory authority and rejected an argument that the cable company's only interstate involvement was through "connection . . . with the facilities of another carrier."[18] The Court found that the cable systems were "engaged in interstate communication, even where, as here, the intercepted signals emanate from stations located within the same State in which the CATV system operates."[19] The Court took notice that many broadcast television programs originate in different states for distribution to national audiences, and that the cable companies therefore were engaged in the "simultaneous retransmission of communications that very often have originated in other States."[20] Because the stream of communication passing through the cable systems was "uninterrupted and properly indivisible," failure to characterize the transmissions as interstate would be artificial.

A similar rationale was used in the District of Columbia Circuit Court of Appeals' decision in *General Telephone v. FCC*.[21] In that case, a telephone company that delivered broadcast signals between points within a state argued that because the service was delivered only to customers within a single state, the FCC lacked jurisdiction to regulate the service. The court disagreed, finding that the service was jurisdictionally interstate because the broadcast signals the company delivered to its customers originated outside California.[22]

17. United States v. Southwestern Cable Co., 392 U.S. 157, 88 S.Ct. 1994, 20 L.Ed.2d 1001 (1968).

18. *Id.*, at 169 n. 29 88 S.Ct. at 1994 n. 29, 20 L.Ed.2d at 1001 n. 29; *see* 47 U.S.C.A. § 152(b) (West Supp. 1997).

19. *Id.* at 168–69, 88 S. Ct. at 2000, 20 L.Ed.2d at 1011.

20. *Id.* at 169, 88 S. Ct. at 2001, 20 L.Ed.2d at 1011.

21. 413 F.2d 390, 134 U.S. App. D.C. 116 (D.C.Cir.), cert. denied, 444 U.S. 839, 100 S.Ct 77, 62 L.Ed.2d 50 (1979).

22. The FCC has plenary jurisdiction over the regulation of radio communications in the United States even where radio signals originate and terminate within a single state. *See* 47 U.S.C.A. § 301 (West 1991); *see also* Federal Communications Commission v. Pottsville Broadcasting Co., 309 U.S. 134, 137, 60 S.Ct. 437, 84 L.Ed. 656 (1940). The FCC's jurisdiction over radio communications does not, however, prevent states from enforcing their common carrier regulations where carriers happen to provide intrastate services using wireless, rather than wireline, technologies. California v. Federal Communications Commission, 798 F.2d 1515, 255 U.S. App. D.C. 84 (D.C.Cir.1986).

The FCC and the courts have faced more difficult jurisdictional questions in connection with so-called enhanced services, which connect customers to remote databases and information processing equipment. But those disputes, too, have yielded to the principle that any interstate transmission made in connection with a service is sufficient to confer federal jurisdiction.

In the *Georgia MemoryCall* case, for example, an FCC decision affirmed by the Eleventh Circuit Court of Appeals, the Georgia Public Service Commission ("PSC") had ordered BellSouth's voice mail service "frozen" until the state could develop a scheme of regulation for that service. BellSouth brought a petition to the FCC seeking a declaration that its voice mail service was not exclusively intrastate because the service could be accessed through calls placed from outside Georgia.

In response to BellSouth's petition, the Georgia commission conceded that the voice mail service could be accessed through an interstate call, but argued that the interstate call to the system was not part of the voice mail service: only the intrastate transmission from the telephone company switch, forwarding the call to the voice mail platform, was jurisdictionally part of the service.[23]

The FCC was unpersuaded by Georgia's analysis. The Commission's Memorandum Opinion and Order pointed out that when a caller in another state calls a Georgia voice mail customer, or when a voice mail customer calls the service from out of state to check for messages, "there is a continuous path of communications across state lines between the caller and the voice mail service, just as there is when a traditional out-of-state long distance voice telephone call is forwarded by the local switch to another location in the state and answered by a person, a message service bureau or customer premises answering device."[24] Relying on the principle that jurisdiction over a communication must be determined on an end-to-end basis, therefore, the Commission found that interstate calls to BellSouth's voice mail service were jurisdictionally interstate.

Where a service is used exclusively for intrastate communications, however, the FCC may lack jurisdiction even if the service is capable of interstate use. For example, in *McDonnell Douglas Corp. v. General Telephone Co. ("McDonnell Douglas")*,[25] the United States Court of Appeals for the Ninth Circuit found that a Centrex service used by a customer exclusively for intrastate calls was not subject to the nondiscrimination requirements of § 202 of the Communications Act.[26] Notably, the court refused to find that the service's technical potential to be used

---

23. Investigation into Southern Bell Telephone and Telegraph Company's Provisions of MemoryCall Service, Docket No. 4000–U, 123 P.U.R.4th 83 (Ga.P.S.C.1991).

24. Petition for Emergency Relief and Declaratory Ruling Filed by the BellSouth Corp., 7 FCC Rcd 1619, 1620 (1992). The FCC was upheld by the Court of Appeals for the Eleventh Circuit. Georgia Public Service Commission, 5 F.3d 1499 (1993).

25. 594 F.2d 720 (9th Cir.), cert. denied, 444 U.S. 839, 100 S.Ct. 77, 62 L.Ed.2d 50 (1979).

26. *Id.*, 594 F.2d at 724–25.

for interstate calling conferred federal jurisdiction so long as the service was not in fact used for that purpose.[27]

The Ninth Circuit refined its approach to the regulation of dual-use services, however, in *State of California v. Federal Communications Commission* ("California"). In that case the FCC, as part of its rulemaking concerning the provision of enhanced services by the Bell operating companies ("BOCs") had ordered the BOCs to file tariffs covering certain features (known as basic service elements or "BSEs") that might be used with interstate services offered to enhanced service providers. At the same time, the Commission permitted state tariffing of those services for use with intrastate communications. California objected, arguing on the authority of *McDonnell Douglas* that the FCC could regulate "only those BSEs which are *actually used* for interstate services."[28]

The court found, however, that potential use of BSEs in connection with interstate communications did, in fact, justify the Commission's requirement that those services be federally tariffed. The court distinguished *McDonnell Douglas* as a case involving regulation of services already provided by the carrier which were known to have been used exclusively for intrastate communications. By contrast, the BSEs covered by the FCC's tariffing requirements had the potential to be used for interstate communications, and the FCC proposed to regulate the rates charged for those BSEs only to the extent they were so used. Accordingly, the Ninth Circuit found no conflict between the interstate tariffing requirement for BSEs and the result in *McDonnell Douglas*.[29]

2. Facilities Used for Both Interstate and Intrastate Communications

Most switches, wires, interoffice trunks and other physical telecommunications facilities are located entirely in one state, but are used for both interstate and intrastate calls. Not surprisingly, the states would prefer that jurisdiction over these mixed-use facilities, and services provided through the use of those facilities, be determined by the facility's location, while the FCC prefers that jurisdiction be based on use. The courts have adopted the FCC's position, and have made it clear that any facility used for interstate communication is subject to federal regulation to the extent of its interstate use.

The most complete discussion of this principle by an appellate court is found in *California v. FCC*.[30] The underlying dispute in that case began when the Commission ordered the Bell Operating Companies

---

27. *Id.* at 724 n. 3.

28. 798 F.2d 1515, 1518–20 (D.C.Cir. 1986).

29. *Id.* The *California* case also shows that where a service is used in connection with both interstate and intrastate communications, federal and state authorities both may regulate the service where that approach is feasible. The Ninth Circuit pointed out in *California* that the FCC's orders

"establish a dual federal and state tariffing structure, and the states will retain authority to set rates for those BSEs which are used for intrastate service." *Id.* at 1519.

30. California v. Federal Communications Commission, 567 F.2d 84, 185 U.S. App. D.C. 217 (D.C.Cir.1977)(per curiam), cert. denied, 434 U.S. 1010, 98 S.Ct 721, 54 L.Ed.2d 753 (1978).

(then owned by AT & T) to interconnect their local exchange facilities with the interexchange facilities of Southern Pacific Communications Company (SPCC)—a competing long-distance carrier—so that SPCC could provide certain interstate services to its customers.[31] The State of California, concerned that interexchange competition would divert revenues the Bell System needed in order to support basic telephone service, challenged the order as a usurpation of state jurisdiction over intrastate communications. In support of its position, the State argued that the FCC lacked jurisdiction over Bell's local exchange facilities because those facilities were located entirely within California.

The Ninth Circuit disagreed with California, and found (adopting the language of the Commission) that for purposes of determining jurisdiction over telephone facilities "[t]he key issue ... is the nature of the communications which pass through [the] facilities, not the physical location of the lines." Because the record afforded no reason to doubt the FCC's finding that the interconnected facilities were "an integral part of a dedicated interstate communications network," the Court found that the FCC could order interconnection in support of its obligation to regulate interstate communications.[32]

B. The Power of the FCC to Preempt State Regulation

Even where communications services or facilities are jurisdictionally intrastate, the FCC still has the authority, in some circumstances, to preempt state regulation of those service and facilities. The development of the law governing preemption is, if anything, more complex than the law's efforts to determine the respective spheres of federal and state jurisdiction and can only be understood fully in the context of the cases in which the doctrine has developed.

The modern law of preemption is a result of the FCC's efforts, beginning in the 1960s, to introduce competition into particular telecommunications markets. Many of the states disagreed with those policies, perceiving competition as a threat to the subsidized rate structures that kept rates for local calling relatively lower, in relation to the cost of service, than rates for long-distance, business and premium services. When the Commission preempted state regulation in order to advance competition, the states sought review of those preemption orders in the appellate courts.

The first cases arose from a conflict between the FCC and some of the states over attachment of customer-provided equipment ("CPE") to the public telephone network. In 1974, the North Carolina Public Utilities Commission ordered that telephone subscribers could not connect their own equipment to the network unless that equipment was used strictly for interstate calling. The FCC, which already had enacted rules

31. In re AT & T, 56 F.C.C.2d 14 (1974).

32. The Court also noted the Commission's conclusion that it was impractical to separate interstate Foreign Exchange ("FX") service from intrastate FX service and assert jurisdiction over only the former. California v. FCC, *supra*, note 30.

permitting connection of customer-provided equipment, then issued an order preempting contrary state regulation.[33] North Carolina appealed the preemption order, arguing that the Act gave it plenary authority over telephone equipment located within the state. In response to the FCC's argument that a state prohibition against customer-provided equipment prevented the exercise of the interconnection rights granted to customers by the Commission, the state pointed out that customers theoretically could purchase their own equipment for interstate calling and use telephone company-provided equipment for intrastate calling. The Court of Appeals for the Fourth Circuit rejected the state's arguments, finding that North Carolina's proposed regulation effectively precluded customers from exercising their federal right to attach their own equipment for use in interstate calling, thereby frustrating the FCC's legitimate exercise of its authority to regulate interstate and foreign communications.[34]

The FCC then went further in its efforts to end the telephone company monopoly over CPE by ruling, not simply that attachment of customer-provided equipment must be allowed, but that the telephone companies *may not provide* such equipment as part of their tariffed, end-to-end interstate telephone service. The basis for this decision was a determination that CPE is not a Title II (*i.e.*, common carrier) service, and therefore may be offered by telephone companies only on a contract basis not subject to common-carrier regulation. In order to facilitate its deregulation of CPE, the Commission also preempted all state regulations that purported to treat the provision of CPE as a common carrier service.[35]

The FCC's decision to deregulate CPE, like its earlier decision to permit attachment of CPE to the telephone network, was challenged as a usurpation of a prerogative reserved to the states by the Communications Act. The Court of Appeals for the District of Columbia Circuit upheld the FCC, noting that the same CPE is used for both interstate and intrastate calling, and finding that tariffing CPE with the states would frustrate the FCC's determination that CPE should be provided on a deregulated basis. These early FCC victories, however, were followed by a series of reversals. The first of these defeats—and the most important, because it resulted in a Supreme Court opinion that defined the limits of the Commission's preemption authority—resulted from the FCC's efforts to liberalize depreciation of telephone plant.

33. Telerent Leasing Corp., 45 F.C.C.2d 204 (1974), *aff'd sub nom.* North Carolina Utilities Comm'n v. FCC, 537 F.2d 787, 791 (4th Cir.), cert. denied, 429 U.S. 1027, 97 S.Ct. 651, 50 L.Ed.2d 631 (1976)("NCUC I").

34. *Id.* at 791–93.

35. Amendment of Sec. 64.702 of the Commission's Rules, 77 F.C.C.2d 384 *modi-*fied by Mem. and Order, 84 F.C.C.2d 50 (1980), *aff'd on further recons.*, 88 F.C.C.2d 512 (1981), *aff'd sub nom.* CCIA v. FCC, 693 F.2d 198, 224 U.S. App. D.C. 83 (D.C.Cir.1982), cert. denied, 461 U.S. 938, 103 S.Ct 2109, 77 L.Ed.2d 313 (1983), *aff'd on second further recons.*, 56 Rad. Reg. 301 (P & F 1984).

When telephone markets were opened to competition, local telephone companies responded by seeking permission to accelerate the depreciation of their tangible capital assets. Because both the states and the FCC prescribed accounting rules for assets used in telecommunications, the telephone companies pressed their case before both jurisdictions.

In 1980 and 1981, the FCC made three changes in its depreciation rules for the capital assets of telephone companies subject to its jurisdiction. Specifically, the Commission allowed the companies to group their assets according to estimated service life, rather than the year of installation;[36] allowed them to adjust their estimates of the remaining life of assets if those estimates proved inaccurate;[37] and permitted wiring on customers' premises to be "expensed" rather than capitalized.[38] All of these changes, in the view of the FCC and the companies, resulted in more adequate depreciation of the companies' assets.

While there was no controversy concerning the FCC's authority to impose these accounting changes on the ratemaking process for interstate services, the FCC went further: it found that it had the power to preempt inconsistent accounting rules imposed by the states in their regulation of intrastate rates. The United States Court of Appeals for the Fourth Circuit upheld the FCC's preemption order.

The Supreme Court disagreed.[39] The Court found that while the Supremacy Clause of the United States Constitution permits Congress to preempt state law, a regulatory agency acting by delegated authority may exercise that power only where the Congress has occupied the field by regulation or otherwise shown a clear intent to preempt, or where it is physically impossible to comply with both state and federal law or where the state law clearly "stands as an obstacle to the accomplishment and execution of the full objectives of Congress."[40] Depreciation accounting, in the Court's view, met none of these tests.

Looking for evidence of congressional policy concerning preemption by the FCC, the Court reviewed the language of the Communications Act. The Court noted that while section 151 of the Act grants the FCC a sweeping mandate to promote "efficient, Nation-wide, and world-wide wire and radio communication service,"[41] section 152(b) of the Act contains an equally broad disclaimer of intent to "give the Commission jurisdiction with respect to (1) charges, classifications, practices, services, facilities, or regulations for or in connection with intrastate communication service ..."[42] In the Court's view these two provisions, read together, support the view that the Act contemplates a system of dual regula-

36. Property Depreciation Order, 83 F.C.C. 2d 267 (1980), *recons. denied*, 87 F.C.C. 2d 916 (1981).

37. *Id.*

38. Uniform System of Accounts, 85 F.C.C. 2d 818 (1981).

39. Louisiana Public Service Comm'n v. FCC, 476 U.S. 355, 106 S.Ct. 1890, 90 L.Ed.2d 369 (1986) ("Louisiana PSC").

40. *Id.* at 369, 106 S.Ct. 1899, 90 L.Ed.2d 378.

41. 47 U.S.C.A. § 151 (West 1991).

42. *Id.* § 152(b).

tion under which the FCC must tolerate state policies that differ from its own. The Commission, therefore, lacks the power to preempt simply to promote policies that it thinks best.

Given this evidence of congressional intent, the Court found that the Commission may preempt state regulation only where *necessary* to achieve some valid goal that is within the Commission's jurisdiction under the Act; and that even where this requirement is met, the Commission may preempt only those aspects of regulation that cannot be separated into interstate and intrastate components.

The next reversal involved a challenge to the FCC's decision to preempt state regulation of so-called inside wiring—*i.e.*, the wiring on the customer's premises that connects the customer's CPE to the telephone company's access line. The Commission had decided that inside wiring, like CPE, could be provided on a competitive basis and had preempted all state rules that permitted inside wiring to be tariffed as a common carrier service.

Responding to a petition for review brought by the National Association of Regulatory Utilities Commissioners ("NARUC"), the FCC offered two arguments in favor of its preemption order. First, the Commission argued that because inside wiring is not a common carrier service, the Act's reservation of intrastate regulatory authority to the states—which by its terms only involves regulations applicable to *carriers*—did not apply to inside wiring. Second (and somewhat more persuasively), the Commission made the same argument it had made in support of preemption of state regulation of CPE—*i.e.*, that separate "intrastate" and "interstate" inside wiring was not a practical possibility, and therefor a separate system of state tariffing requirements for inside wiring would defeat the FCC's determination that the provision of those facilities should not be tariffed.

In a decision that has come to be known as *NARUC III*, the Court of Appeals found that the Commission had not shown a sufficient basis for preemption of all state tariffing requirements for inside wiring. The court quite sensibly rejected the Commission's first argument—that section 2(b)(1) guarantees state jurisdiction only over intrastate common carrier services—as circular, pointing out that the Commission's reading of section 2(b)(1) permitted it to oust state jurisdiction over any service merely by declaring it to be "private carriage" rather than a common carrier service.[43] The court also rejected the second argument, however, without adequately explaining how its decision could be harmonized with its earlier decision that CPE, which also is used for both interstate and intrastate service, could not be subject to tariffing at the state level. The court merely found that the Commission could accommodate dual regu-

---

43. National Association of Regulatory Utility Commissioners v. Federal Communications Commission, 880 F.2d 422, 429, 279 U.S. App. D.C. 99, 106 (D.C.Cir. 1989)("NARUC III").

lation of inside wiring through the separations process—an alternative the same court had rejected in the case of CPE.[44]

While finding that state tariffing requirements for inside wiring could not be preempted altogether, the court did note that state approval of particular tariffs might frustrate federal goals and subject those tariffs to preemption. The court noted, for example, that state approval of below-cost intrastate rates for inside wiring would permit predatory pricing, and that this practice might deprive customers of the competitive inside wiring market the FCC had mandated. Tariff regulation of this kind could be preempted by the Commission.[45]

The FCC's next defeat was especially disheartening, because it threatened to undo one of the most arduous rulemakings in the Commission's history. In the series of proceedings known collectively as *Computer III*,[46] the Commission had defined the conditions under which the Bell Operating Companies could provide enhanced services using the same facilities through which they offered basic telephone service. These rules, which replaced an earlier regime (known as "structural separation") that required BOCs to provide these services only through separate subsidiaries, would permit the BOCs to exploit the efficiencies of integrated operations without imposing unfair disabilities on competing enhanced service providers.

The FCC had concluded that inconsistent state regulation of enhanced services would defeat its *Computer III* policies and had preempted state regulation accordingly. Specifically, the Commission decided that the states could not impose structural separation requirements on BOC provision of intrastate enhanced services, could not require intrastate enhanced services to be tariffed and could not impose competitive safeguards on enhanced services that were inconsistent with, or more burdensome than, the FCC's requirements.

The petition to review *Computer III* was brought before the Court of Appeals for the Ninth Circuit. That court found that while preemption of some kinds of state regulation of enhanced services might be justified under the *Louisiana* standard,[47] the Commission had not shown that preemption of *all* state regulation in the three enumerated areas was necessary in order to achieve its policy objectives.[48] Accordingly, the

44. *Id.* at 428, 279 U.S. App. D.C. at 105.

45. *Id.* at 430, 279 U.S. App. D.C. at 107.

46. State of California v. FCC, 905 F.2d 1217 (9th Cir.1990).

47. In *Louisiana PSC, supra,* n. 39, the Supreme Court found that the FCC may preempt state regulation only to the extent necessary to achieve a valid goal that is within the FCC's jurisdiction. Applying this principle to enhanced services, the Ninth Ciruit noted that a state regulation requiring all BOC intrastate enhanced services to be provided through separate subsidiaries would guarantee, as a practical matter, that BOC interstate services would be provided through those same subsidiaries. Such a regulation clearly would frustrate the FCC's policy that basic and enhanced interstate services should be provided on an integrated basis. *Id.* at 1244.

48. In addition to its rejection of the Commission's preemption order, the court of appeals also found the record inadequate to justify the FCC's principal, substantive decision in the *Computer III* proceeding—

court remanded *Computer III* to the FCC for further proceedings.[49] The court directed that on remand, the Commission must justify any preemption order, not merely "by showing that *some* of the preempted state regulation would, if not preempted, frustrate FCC regulatory goals," but rather by demonstrating that "the order is narrowly tailored to preempt *only* such state regulations as would negate valid FCC regulatory goals."[50]

The remand proceeding in *Computer III* was a milestone in the FCC's approach to preemption. Determined to salvage an historic regulatory effort, the Commission crafted preemption decisions that observed the Ninth Circuit's mandate to preempt only those regulations that "negate[] the exercise by the FCC of its own lawful authority over interstate communication."[51] Accordingly, the FCC decided that states could not require separation of facilities and personnel used to provide "jurisdictionally mixed" enhanced services, but could require structural separation for the provision of intrastate enhanced services and could require a separate corporate entity, with separate books of account, for the intrastate portion of jurisdictionally mixed enhanced services. The Commission also preempted certain kinds of state regulation concerning customer proprietary network information (CPNI) and disclosure of technical information concerning changes to telephone company networks.[52]

Although the states challenged the FCC's remand decision, the Ninth Circuit Court of Appeals upheld the limited scheme of preemption the Commission had adopted. The appellate court's ruling addresses two important issues.

First, the states had argued that the FCC's preemption decisions on remand were improperly based, not on the specific regulatory power over common carrier regulation granted to the Commission under Title II of the Communications Act, but only on the general grant of jurisdiction set out in Title I of the Act. In the states' view, "the FCC may preempt state action only when it is acting pursuant to specified regulatory duties under Title II of the Act, such as setting tariffs."[53] The court rejected this argument, pointing out that nothing in the Supreme Court's *Louisi-*

---

i.e., that nonstructural safeguards, rather than structural separation, would prevent anticompetitive conduct by the BOCs in the enhanced services market. *Id.* at 1230–39.

49. In *Computer III*, as in *NARUC III*, the Commission argued that it could preempt state regulation of enhanced services under section 2(b)(1) of the Act because that section applies only to carrier services. Like the District of Columbia Circuit in the earlier case, the Ninth Circuit rejected this argument as giving the Commission the power to preempt intrastate regulation of any service it chose to deregulate at the interstate level. *Id.* at 1240.

50. *Id.* at 1243 (emphasis in original).

51. State of California v. Federal Communications Commission, 905 F.2d 1217, 1243 (9th Cir.1990), quoting *NARUC III*, *supra*, 880 F.2d at 429, 279 U.S. App. D.C. at 106.

52. Computer III Remand Proceedings: Bell Operating Company Safeguards and Tier 1 Local Exchange Company Safeguards, 6 FCC Rcd 7571, 7625 (1991), *vacated in part and remanded sub nom.* California v. Federal Communications Commission, 39 F.3d 919 (9th Cir.1994), cert. denied, 514 U.S. 1050, 115 S.Ct. 1427, 131 L.Ed.2d 309 (1995).

53. State of California, 39 F.3d at 932.

ana decision supports such a limitation on the permissible bases of preemption.[54]

The states also argued that the FCC had not met its burden, under the *Louisiana* standard, of proving the impossibility of compliance with both the federal rules and state rules of the kind that the FCC had chosen to preempt. The court, however, was satisfied that the FCC had met the *Louisiana* test. Specifically, the Commission had shown that if states required structural separation of BOC facilities "for the intrastate portion of enhanced services that are offered both interstate and intrastate," BOCs would be forced, as a matter of economic feasibility, to "comply with state requirements and provide such services entirely on a structurally separated basis."[55] As a result, the FCC's goal of allowing BOCs to provide interstate enhanced services on an integrated basis would be negated. This prospect, while it would result from economic and operational infeasibility rather than literal impossibility, was sufficient to satisfy the "impossibility" exception recognized in *Louisiana*.[56]

The Telecommunications Act of 1996 ("1996 Act"),[57] and the FCC's efforts to implement that statute, have opened a new chapter in the preemption debate. The 1996 Act imposed extensive requirements on the incumbent local exchange telephone companies to interconnect their facilities with those of new, competing local carriers, and to do so at cost-based rates that would be subject to review by state regulatory commissions.[58] The 1996 Act also empowered the FCC to promulgate regulations implementing the interconnection provisions of the 1996 Act, but gave the states the more specific obligation to "establish any rates for interconnection, services, or network elements ..." provided to competing carriers by the incumbent telephone companies.[59]

In its order implementing the interconnection provisions of the 1996 Act, the FCC imposed on the states a detailed pricing methodology to govern the setting, review and approval of interconnection arrange-

---

54. *Id., citing* Louisiana Public Service Comm'n v. FCC, 476 U.S. 355, 106 S.Ct. 1890, 90 L.Ed.2d 369 (1986).

55. *Id.*

56. *Id.* at 933. As the court pointed out, the earlier cases concerning preemption of state regulation of customer premises equipment (CPE) also presented a case in which compliance with federal rules and contrary state rules would not have been literally impossible, but entirely infeasible. In those cases, as discussed earlier, the FCC had deregulated CPE, which meant that telephone company customers could purchase and use CPE from sources other than the telephone company. If the states continued to prohibit use of customer-provided CPE for intrastate calling, the only way for a customer to comply simultaneously with both rules would have been through the purchase of separate equipment for inter-

state and intrastate calling. This result was infeasible and the Fourth Circuit Court of Appeals held that this infeasibility was sufficient to justify preemption of contrary state regulations. North Carolina Utilities Commission v. Federal Communications Commission, 537 F.2d 787 (4th Cir.), cert. denied, 429 U.S. 1027, 97 S.Ct. 651, 50 L.Ed.2d 631 (1976); North Carolina Utilities Commission v. Federal Communications Commission, 552 F.2d 1036 (4th Cir.), cert. denied, 434 U.S. 874, 98 S.Ct. 222, 54 L.Ed.2d 154 (1977). In the *Louisiana PSC* case the Supreme Court endorsed the Fourth Circuit's reasoning in the CPE cases. *See supra*, note 3.

57. Telecommunications Act of 1996, Pub. L. No. 104–104, 110 Stat. 56.

58. *Id.* § 252(e)(1), *codified at* 47 U.S.C.A. § 252(e)(1) (West Supp. 1997).

59. *Id.* § 252(c).

ments.[60] A number of petitioners sought review of the order, and the state public utilities commissions, in particular, contended that the Commission had overstepped its authority under the 1996 Act by effectively preempting ratemaking authority that the Congress plainly had granted to the states.

The Eighth Circuit Court of Appeals vacated the pricing provisions of the FCC's order, and found that the 1996 Act did not permit the FCC to set interconnection rates.[61] The court pointed out that the state commissions had historically determined the rates for "intrastate communications services," and found in the 1996 Act a clear statement of the Congress's intention to preserve that realm of state authority.

As the Eighth Circuit correctly pointed out, the 1996 Act, which represented an obvious opportunity for the Congress to limit or remove the inconvenience of federalism in communications law, contained instead a clear confirmation of the continuing state role. Accordingly, the FCC and the states will continue to wrestle with the complex, and ultimately artificial, task of defining their respective spheres of authority over technologies that are intended to make geographic boundaries meaningless.

10.6   The Procedures of the FCC

The FCC, like many other regulatory agencies, makes rules, executes those rules and adjudicates the rights of persons engaged in activities that are within its jurisdiction. The procedures under which the FCC conducts these activities are set out in Part 1 of Title 47 of the United States Code of Federal Regulations. What follows is a (by no means exhaustive) overview of some of the principal provisions under which the FCC's activities are conducted.

A.   Rulemaking Proceedings

Agency rulemaking, unlike adjudication, is binding not only on the parties to the particular proceeding, but is "addressed to and sets a standard of conduct for all to whom its terms apply."[1] The FCC is empowered to exercise this authority as to all matters committed to its jurisdiction. While some FCC rulemakings are formal *i.e.,* conducted through evidentiary hearings most are informal, "paper" proceedings. Those proceedings follow the procedures prescribed at subpart C of Part 1 of Title 47 of the Code of Federal Regulations.[2]

---

60. First Report and Order, Implementation of the Local Competition Provisions in the Telecommunications Act of 1996, CC Docket No. 96–98 (Aug. 8, 1996).

61. Iowa Utilities Board v. Federal Communications Commission, 120 F.3d 753 (8th Cir.1997), *aff'd in part, rev'd in part,* ___ U.S. ___, 119 S.Ct. 721, 142 L.Ed.2d 835 (1999).

1. Columbia Broadcasting System v. United States, 316 U.S. 407, 418, 62 S.Ct. 1194, 1201, 86 L.Ed. 1563, 1571 (1942).

2. Formal rulemakings are those which "are required by law to be made on the record after opportunity for a Commission hearing," and are governed by the regulations for hearing proceedings. 47 C.F.R.§§ 1.201 *et seq.* (1997). In practice, the FCC only holds formal rulemakings in connection with common carrier ratemak-

Rulemakings may be initiated by the FCC or by any interested person pursuant to a Petition for Rulemaking.[3] If a Petition for Rulemaking is granted or the Commission elects to initiate a rulemaking upon its own motion, the process will begin with the issuance of a Notice of Proposed Rulemaking ("NPRM"). The NPRM must contain "either the terms or substance of the proposed rule or a description of the subjects or issues involved."[4] A summary of the NPRM will be published in the Federal Register, and the Commission will set a date for filing of written comments on the proposed rules, along with a subsequent date for filing of reply comments. Any interested person may file comments and reply comments directed to an NPRM.[5]

Once notice has been afforded and comments have been received, the FCC may take any of a number of actions. It may adopt the proposed rules, in whole or in part, or may decline to adopt new rules. If the Commission decides that some or all of the issues raised in the NPRM and comments require a more complete record before a decision is made, the Commission may issue a further NPRM devoted to those questions. At the same time, the Commission may choose to issue an order covering those questions as to which the record is adequate to support a decision.

Interested persons who disagree with a rulemaking order may ask the Commission to reconsider that order,[6] or may petition for review in a United States Court of Appeals.[7]

In some cases the Commission will wish to receive comment on an issue that is within its jurisdiction but as to which it is not prepared to propose specific rules. In such cases the Commission may initiate a "notice of inquiry," which must observe the same notice-and-comment procedures as an informal rulemaking, but as to which a notice is not required to be published in the Federal Register.[8]

B. Adjudicatory Hearings

The Commission conducts adjudicatory and quasi-adjudicatory proceedings in a number of contexts. Historically, the most important occasion for FCC adjudication has been the granting, renewal, and revocation of construction permits and radio licenses—particularly broadcast licenses, which are scarce and valuable resources awarded and renewed by the Commission according to which applicant will best serve the public interest. Adjudications also are conducted, however, in other contexts, including enforcement proceedings brought by the Commission

ing proceedings, a business in which the FCC is effectively no longer engaged.

3. 47 C.F.R. § 1.401 (1997). Rulemakings also may be prompted by legislation or a judicial decision.

4. 5 U.S.C.A. § 553(b)(3) (West 1996).

5. 47 C.F.R. § 1.415 (1997).

6. 47 U.S.C.A. § 405 (West 1991); 47 C.F.R. § 1.429 (1997). A petition for reconsideration must be filed within 30 days from the date of public notice of the action

to which it relates. Oppositions to the petition must be filed within 15 days of public notice of the filing of the petition, and replies must be filed within 10 days after the time for filing of oppositions has expired. *Id.*

7. *Id.* § 1.429; 47 U.S.C.A. § 402 (West 1991 and Supp. 1997); 28 U.S.C.A. 2342 (West 1994).

8. 47 C.F.R. § 1.430 (1997).

against persons believed to have violated the Act and complaints brought by private parties against common carriers alleging that those parties have been injured by unreasonable rates or other violations of Title II of the Communications Act.

Most of the Commission's adjudicatory and quasi-adjudicatory proceedings are conducted informally—*i.e.*, without trial-type hearings. In those cases in which the Commission chooses, or is required, to hold a formal adjudicatory hearing or formal rulemaking, the Commission follows the procedures set out in subpart B of Part 1 of Title 47 of the Code of Federal Regulations.[9] Under those rules, hearings are initiated by Commission order naming the parties to the hearing and listing the issues upon which evidence will be taken. The Chief Administrative Law Judge then will name a presiding officer, set a time and place for an initial prehearing conference and set another date when the hearing itself will begin. Persons named as parties and desiring to participate must file notices of appearance within 20 days of the Commission's order.[10]

Where a hearing involves an adjudication rather than a formal rulemaking, parties have a right to discovery in the form of "taking the deposition of any person (including a party), . . . interrogatories to parties, and . . . orders to parties relating to the production of documents or things and . . . entry upon real property."[11] Parties also may request the issuance of subpoenas by the presiding officer, either to secure the attendance of witnesses or to compel the production of documents.[12]

An initial prehearing conference must be held thirty days after the effective date of an order designating a matter for hearing, "unless good cause is shown for scheduling such conference at a later date."[13] At this and such other prehearing conferences as the Commission may schedule, the parties will attempt to limit or clarify the issues as to which evidence will be taken, agree as to uncontested facts and the admissibility or genuineness of documents, and agree as to the number of witnesses to be called and the procedures to be followed at the hearing.[14]

At the hearing itself, the order of presentation of evidence will depend upon the nature of the issues. So, for example, where a hearing is brought upon a "formal complaint or petition or in a proceeding for any instrument which the Commission is empowered to issue," the complainant, petitioner or applicant will present its evidence first unless the

9. Respondents in enforcement proceedings have a right to a hearing if the Commission has issued an order to show cause why a station license or construction permit should not be revoked or has issued a cease and desist order. *Id.* § 1.91. Hearings also may be held upon applications for licenses, where the staff or Commission finds that the public interest will be served by that approach.

10. *Id.* § 1.221. Anyone not named as a party may petition to intervene. *Id.* § 1.223.

11. *Id.* § 1.311. Where a hearing is not adjudicatory, parties may still take discovery for the purpose of preserving evidence. *Id.*

12. *Id.* §§ 1.331–1.340.

13. *Id.* § 1.248(a).

14. *Id.* § 1.248(c).

Commission otherwise directs.[15] Where a hearing concerns an order to show cause, to cease and desist or to revoke or modify a radio station license, the Commission will open and close the taking of evidence.[16] In proceedings for which the rules do not designate a particular order of presentation, "the Commission or presiding officer shall designate the order of presentation."[17]

Aside from these particularized procedures, formal adjudications at the FCC resemble civil trials. Testimony is taken under oath, the rules of evidence are applied and a transcript of the proceeding is prepared. At the close of the record of the hearing, the presiding officer will prepare an initial or recommended decision containing "findings of fact and conclusions, as well as the reasons or basis therefor, upon all the material issues of fact, law, or discretion presented on the record ...," and also containing the presiding officer's recommended rule or order.[18]

The presiding officer's initial or recommended decision will not become effective until 50 days after public release of its full text.[19] Within 30 days after the text is released, any party may appeal to the full Commission by filing exceptions to the decision. Within 20 days after the time for filing exceptions expires, the Commission on its own motion may elect to review the decision.[20] If exceptions are filed, the full Commission may permit oral argument, and subsequently will issue a final decision that will include "findings of fact and conclusions, as well as the reasons or basis therefor, upon all the material issues of fact, law or discretion presented ... ;" and will also rule on each "relevant and material exception filed," and issue an appropriate rule or order.[21]

1. *Award of Radio Licenses Through Comparative Hearings*

As noted earlier, the chief source of formal adjudicatory proceedings throughout most of the FCC's history has been the award of broadcast radio licenses in cases where two or more mutually exclusive applications for those licenses have been received. Through most of the FCC's history, the rights of competing applicants for broadcast licenses have been decided through comparative hearings.[22] While comparative hearings ensure a full airing of relevant public interest concerns and protect the rights of competing applicants to due process, they also tend to be

---

15. *Id.* § 1.255(a).

16. *Id.* For the order of presentation in other types of adjudications, *see id.* § 1.255(a)-(c).

17. *Id.* § 1.255(c).

18. *Id.* § 1.267(b). The parties may file proposed findings of fact and conclusions, briefs or memoranda of law "within 20 days after the record is closed, unless additional time is allowed." *Id.* § 1.263(a). The presiding officer may require the filing of proposed findings of fact and conclusions of law, and a party's failure to do so "may be

deemed a waiver of the right to participate further in the proceeding." *Id.* § 1.263(c).

19. *Id.* § 1.276(d).

20. *Id.* § 1.276(a)-(d).

21. *Id.* § 1.282. Where exceptions are deemed to be irrelevant or "not of decisional significance," the Commission may deny them without giving a statement of reasons. *Id.* § 1.282(b)(2).

22. 47 U.S.C.A. § 309(e) (West 1991); *see also* Comparative Broadcast Hearings, 1 F.C.C.2d 393, 394–400 (1965).

lengthy and burdensome, to encourage frivolous challenges to applications and renewals, and to cause delay in the construction and operation of radio stations.[23]

2. *Award of Licenses Through Employment of Lotteries*

In order to avoid some of the shortcomings of the comparative hearings process, the FCC has assigned certain kinds of radio licenses by lottery.[24] Lotteries, however, have led to problems and abuses of their own, including the sale of licenses by lottery winners who had no intention of using their licenses to serve the public, and litigation by losing applicants seeking to deny the award of licenses to the winners.[25]

As new spectrum-based technologies created new services and new licensing opportunities, many commentators and public officials saw a way to avoid the defects of comparative hearings and lotteries and generate revenue for the public treasury at the same time. Support grew for the use of competitive bidding, implemented through government-sponsored auctions, as a means of awarding broadcast spectrum for a wide range of uses.[26]

3. *Award of Licenses Through Employment of Auctions*

Auctions became official policy with the Omnibus Budget Reconciliation Act of 1993 ("Budget Act"),[27] which permitted competitive bidding to be used to award wireless licenses.[28] Under section 309(j)(3) of the Act, the Commission was to give special attention to the development of new technologies, service to rural areas, and promotion of minorities, women and entrepreneurs.[29]

The Commission first used its new authority in establishing a competitive bidding program for the award of personal communication service ("PCS") licenses. The Commission allocated six broadband frequency blocks for auctioning and adopted a number of rules intended to fulfill a congressional mandate to ensure that "designated entities"—*i.e.,* small business, rural telephone companies and businesses owned by

---

23. The FCC has described the comparative hearings process as "elaborate and costly," and has questioned whether the process "results in a material benefit to the public." Amendment of the Commission's Rules to Allow the Selection from among Competing Applicants for new AM, FM, and Television Stations by Random Selection (Lottery), 4 FCC Rcd 2256 para. 2 (1989).

24. Mobile telephone and low power television licenses have been awarded through lotteries.

25. *See* Implementation of Section 309(j) of the Communications Act: Competitive Bidding, 74 Rad. Reg. 2d 700 para. 4 (P & F 1994).

26. Economists have advocated auctions of radiofrequency spectrum for many years. *See, e.g.,* Ronald H. Coase, *The Federal Communications Commission,* 2 J.L. & Econ. 1 (1959). FCC Chairman Fowler suggested the use of auctions as early as 1985.

27. Pub. L. No. 103–66, 107 Stat. 312 (1993).

28. The Budget Act authorized auctions only for spectrum to be used in a service that would be provided to subscribers for compensation. 47 U.S.C.A. § 309(j)(1) (West Supp. 1997).

29. These concerns are expressed at *id.* §§ 309(j)(3)(A)-(B).

minorities or women—had an opportunity to participate in the provision of spectrum-based services. In particular, the rules included more favorable terms—including installment payment options and bidding credits—for minority and female owned businesses than for other bidders.[30]

More recently, as a result of the Supreme Court's decision in *Adarand Constructors, Inc. v. Pena*,[31] the Commission has revised its auction rules to eliminate preferences available only to businesses owned by minorities and women, and has retained preferences that apply to small businesses regardless of their ownership.

The use of auctions to award licenses for frequency-based services is likely to become commonplace, even in broadcast applications. In July of 1996, for an example, the FCC opened a rulemaking to consider the use of auctions to allocate frequencies that will be recovered from certain existing broadcast channels in exchange for allocation of channels for high definition television ("HDTV"). Others have urged that when new HDTV channels are allocated, they should be auctioned rather than simply assigned to present broadcast licensees. There is considerable support in Congress for these proposals, and in light of the billions of dollars already earned from FCC auctions of spectrum for mobile telephone applications, it seems likely that the competitive bidding approach will expand as new spectrum-based services appear.

C. *Obtaining Judicial Review of FCC Actions*

Final actions of the FCC, like those of other federal agencies, are subject to judicial review upon petition of anyone aggrieved by those actions.[32] Petitions to review FCC actions may be brought in any of the United States circuit courts of appeals;[33] venue is proper wherever the petitioner resides or has its principal office, or in the Court of Appeals for the District of Columbia Circuit.[34]

The courts favor the right of aggrieved persons to obtain judicial review of agency action, and they construe procedural bars to those actions narrowly. Persons seeking review of FCC actions must be aware of certain such limitations, however. Specifically, a petitioner must

---

30. For a summary of these provisions, *see* Implementation of Section 309(j) of the Communications Act: Competitive Bidding, 10 FCC Rcd 11872 para. 6 (1995).

31. 515 U.S. 200, 115 S.Ct. 2097, 132 L.E.2d 158, (1995). The Supreme Court in *Adarand* held that federal programs that make distinctions based on race must demonstrate that those distinctions serve a compelling governmental interest and are narrowly tailored to serve that interest. *Adarand* effectively overruled *Metro Broadcasting, Inc. v. Federal Communications Commission*, 497 U.S. 547, 564–65, 110 S.Ct. 2997, 3009, 111 L.Ed.2d 445, 463

(1990), to the extent that the latter decision subjected minority preferences for radio licenses to only an intermediate standard of scrutiny.

32. 5 U.S.C.A. § 702 West (1991).

33. 47 U.S.C.A. § 402(a) (West 1991); 28 U.S.C.A. § 2342 (West 1994).

34. 28 U.S.C.A. § 2343 (West 1994). Petitions to review certain FCC actions, including denials of broadcast station licenses and revocations of radio operator licenses, must be brought in the District of Columbia Circuit Court of Appeals. 47 U.S.C.A. § 402(b) (West 1991 and Supp. 1997).

ascertain whether the FCC action complained of is an "action" for purposes of judicial review, and may not seek review before the action is final. Petitioners also may be barred if the action complained of is based on grounds found to be nonreviewable; or if the petitioner lacks standing to bring the petition; or if the petition is not "ripe" for review or is otherwise untimely.

Chapter Eleven

COMPUTER COMMUNICATIONS LAW

Analysis

11.1   Introduction

No serious discussion of modern communications law can ignore the computer. Along with the printing press, the telephone, the telegraph, radio and television, the computer is one of the transforming technologies in the history of human communication. Like other technological changes before it, the computer has strained the familiar rules and categories in many areas of substantive law. Some of the questions posed by the computer involve the law of intellectual property: notably, protection of the creative work of designers of computers and computer programs and protection of information transmitted from one computer to another. Useful computer programs, in particular, are highly valuable and almost inconceivably difficult to write. The law of intellectual property has had to move with unaccustomed speed to give these new creations fair and rational protection.

Computers also invite various kinds of criminal and tortious misconduct—including unauthorized access to sensitive or commercially valuable databases, interception of electronic mail and other private communications, electronic transmission of defamatory, obscene or indecent materials and "hacking" activities that breach the security of computer systems simply to cause havoc or demonstrate the intruder's cleverness. State and federal statutes have been enacted to deal with some of these problems, and the courts have used common-law principles to address others; but many of these approaches are both incomplete and controversial.

The use of telephone lines to carry data among computers has presented novel problems of telecommunications regulation. Notably, the Federal Communications Commission—and some state regulators, as well—have enacted elaborate rules to ensure that providers of computer communications obtain access to the telephone network on reasonable terms and conditions. More recently, the explosive growth of the Internet and its use to carry voice telephone calls and audio programming have created uncertainty as to the appropriate model for regulation of this new medium.

Beyond these specific concerns, the ability of computers to store information efficiently and in enormous quantity, and the ability of interconnected computers to pass information instantaneously among them, have challenged familiar beliefs about the protection of informational privacy. In particular, many have questioned whether the present patchwork of laws affecting access to databases, interception of electronic communications and the right of individuals to control the collection, accuracy and use of private information about themselves are adequate in the face of the explosion of data-gathering technology. The law's fitful response to this problem is very much a work in progress.

While the subject matter of this chapter is legal rather than technical, a complete understanding of the law of computer communications—especially the intellectual property problems posed by software design—requires, inevitably, some familiarity with the technology. For those readers who will find it helpful, therefore, the next section explains in nontechnical terms how computers, computer software and computer networks do their work. The succeeding sections then explore the impact of these systems and devices on the law of privacy, intellectual property, telecommunications regulation and antitrust.

11.2 The Technological Background of Computer Law

Computers vary widely in size and appearance—from huge mainframes that occupy entire rooms to notebook computers that can be carried in a purse or pocket. Whatever their architecture, computers are collections of hardware (devices we can touch and feel) and software (information and instructions encoded in a machine-readable language). Each of these systems requires some explanation.

A. *Computer Hardware*

A computer may house all of its hardware in a single enclosure or may divide it among several interconnected devices. Its components may be linked with those of other computers by wire, cable, optical fiber or radio, or they may be linked only with each other.

Whatever its size or architecture, a computer is likely to have at least four distinguishable kinds of hardware: an input device (or devices) through which information can be fed to the computer; a central processing unit that manipulates data fed to the computer; a medium for storage of information; and an output device (or devices) through which the computer can convey information to its users or to other computers with which it shares a network.

The nerve center of any computer is its central processing unit, or CPU. The CPU directs the computer's functions and executes our commands to solve equations, draw pictures or form sentences on a page. In most modern computers, the CPU accomplishes these tasks through a network of millions of silicon switches (transistors) connected by minute strands of aluminum and housed on a tiny chip. This complex of switched circuits is etched into the chip by its manufacturer and cannot be altered by the user.

Information storage devices may include the CPU's chips or specialized storage media such as hard disks, floppy disks and magnetic tape. Disks of various kinds are the primary vehicle for long-term information storage.

The most common pieces of input hardware today are the typewriter-style keyboard and the "mouse." These are not the only input devices in use, however: notebook computers may use a stylus because they are too small to accommodate a keyboard, and older mainframes may use input devices based on magnetic tape or punchcards. In the future, the spread of speech recognition technology will make the human voice an increasingly common input device.

Common output devices include cathode-ray monitors, liquid crystal display screens, printers and magnetic tape. Modems and other communications hardware, including radio devices used to connect with wireless computer networks, also may be classified as output devices.

While CPUs, storage media, input devices and output devices are the principal types of computer hardware, many other devices—such as scanners and cables—work with computers to improve their versatility and performance.

B. *Machine Language and Software*

The fundamental fact about a modern, electronic computer is that it is a dense array of millions of interconnected switches. Like other switches with which we are familiar, these minute devices—called transistors—have two fundamental states: when they are open, or "on," they permit electrical current to flow through them; when they are closed, or "off," they prevent electrical current from flowing through them. The genius of the computer is that it represents and manipulates information, ranging from ordinary numbers to human language to elaborate graphical displays, simply by turning these switches on and off.[1]

It is no small trick, of course, to build complex structures of information with a toolbox containing only "on" and "off." The key is to translate the information we want to process, and the commands that tell the computer how to manipulate that information, into a language that itself is made up of only two symbols. Once we have such a language, an "on" switch can represent one of the two symbols and an "off" switch can represent the other.

In the world of computers, the language of choice is the language of binary numbers. Just as switches have only two positions, binary numbers are combinations of only two symbols—1 and 0. Each place in a binary number represents a multiple of 2 (rather than the multiples of 10 that make up our familiar, decimal system) with zeroes acting as placeholders and the value of the places ascending in magnitude from right to left. So, for example, a binary equivalent of the number 1 is 0001; a binary equivalent of the number 2 is 0010; and a binary equivalent of the number 6 is 0110.

To make switches represent binary numbers, we need only make an "on" switch stand for 1 and an "off" switch stand for 0. To represent a particular binary number, we simply turn a series of switches on and off in sequence. So, for example, to represent 0110, which we know to be the binary equivalent of the decimal number 6, we turn one switch off, two adjacent switches on, and the fourth switch off.[2]

Computers use binary numbers, encoded in open and closed switches, to represent both information and the commands that tell the computer how to use that information.[3] The encoding of this information and the execution of these commands are among the most complex products of human intelligence, but a simple example will give some idea of how the process works.

Suppose that Ada Augusta, a computer programmer, has trouble calculating the amount of money she sends to her mother each month.[4]

---

1. Obviously, a complete explanation of the ways in which transistorized circuits represent information and logical operations is somewhat more complex, and beyond the scope of this chapter. A number of excellent introductions to the subject, written for nonengineers, are available. *See, e.g.* RON WHITE, HOW COMPUTERS WORK (Ziff–Davis Press 1993); RON WHITE, HOW SOFTWARE WORKS (Ziff–Davis Press 1993); PETER NORTON, INSIDE THE PC (Sams Publishing 1995); LARRY GONICK, THE CARTOON GUIDE TO THE COMPUTER (HarperCollins Publishers 1991).

2. Personal computers typically use microprocessors (the devices on which the computers' logic chips are located) that can work with binary numbers of 16 or 32 places, or *bits*. The largest 32–bit binary number, which is written as a row of 32 ones, is equivalent to the decimal number 4,294,967,296.

3. Programmers often use less cumbersome digital languages, such as the hexadecimal (base 16) language, that are built on translations of two-place binary numbers into larger sets of symbols.

4. The original Ada Augusta, Lady Lovelace, was the daughter of the poet Lord Byron and is regarded by history as the first writer of coded instructions for use in

Her mother sends Ada a monthly statement of her expenses, and Ada's friend Babbage sends Ada his month's winnings—if any—from the racetrack. Ada then sends her mother Babbage's winnings, along with an amount equal to the difference between the winnings and the total shown in her mother's statement of expenses. (If Babbage's winnings exceed Ada's mother's expenses, Ada will return the surplus to Babbage.) Ada decides to write a program (a set of instructions) that will tell her computer how to make the monthly calculation.

Ada's computer accepts original programs written in a language called BASIC. Using that language, Ada writes the following program:

```
10     PRINT "MOTHER'S EXPENSES"
20     INPUT M
30     PRINT "BABBAGE WON"
40     INPUT B
50     IF B > M THEN 80
60     PRINT "ADA WILL SEND MOTHER"; (M–B)
70     GO TO 90
80     PRINT "ADA WILL SEND BABBAGE"; (B–M)
90     END
```

Ada types this program on her computer's keyboard, along with the name of her new program and instructions to add the name of the program to her computer's menu screen. Her computer translates the instructions into binary language and records them magnetically on a disk, called the hard drive, that is permanently installed in the computer.[5] The program, as written by Ada in BASIC, can be read by humans and is called source code; the program, as stored by the computer in binary form, can be read only by machines and is called object code.

Ada decides to try her new program the following day. She turns on the computer and selects the name of her program from the menu. The computer locates the program on the hard drive and transfers it to a group of memory chips designed to hold random access memory, or RAM. The RAM version of the program, created by opening and closing a series of switches on the memory chips, will exist only so long as Ada is using the program.

Ada's program now asks her to type in the amount of her mother's expenses (Line 10 of the program). Ada types "$500." The program next executes Line 30, asking Ada to type in the amount of Babbage's winnings, and she duly types "$220," thereby executing Line 40 of the

a programmable computer. She worked closely with Charles Babbage (1792–1871), whose proposed "analytical engine" introduced many principles later adopted for electronic computers in the Twentieth Century.

5. For purposes of this example, we assume that the instructions are compiled and stored as machine-readable language before the program is run. In fact, BASIC, unlike most programming languages, is not compiled but is translated into machine language each time the program is run.

program. Now her computer's central processing unit, following the instructions in the RAM version of the program, compares B with M and finds that B is not greater than M. Accordingly, the program does not advance directly to Line 80, but moves on to Line 60 and tells Ada to send her mother $380.

The reader may have noticed that Ada's computer is doing a great many things that go well beyond calculating the difference between B and M. The computer also is taking commands from the keyboard, locating the program on the hard drive, moving the program to RAM, coordinating the RAM chips with the CPU and sending information to the monitor. Ada's program does not tell the computer how to do any of this. What is the source of these commands?

Our question introduces the vital distinction between operating software and application software. Ada's program is a piece of application software—*i.e.*, a program that tells the computer how to perform a specialized task. In order to carry out the instructions contained in that program, however, the computer must execute other instructions that tell it how to read files, retrieve data from memory and perform many other routine, but indispensable, tasks. The programs containing these instructions are called operating software.

It is entirely possible, of course, to write each application program so that it also includes a complete operating program. If Ada had written her program this way it would have included instructions, not only for calculating the amount she needs to send to her mother (or Babbage), but also for reading disks, moving information within the computer, sending data to the monitor and so forth; but that would be inefficient. Since these routine tasks are common to all application programs, it makes more sense to write the operating software once and store it in the computer for different application programs to use. And this is how modern, multipurpose computers—including personal computers—are designed to work.

C. Computer Networks

In the early days of data automation, computers were standalone devices attended by humans who fed them information encoded on punchcards or tape. Eventually, engineers made data processing more convenient by adapting computers for use with teletype devices—*i.e.*, machines that translated strokes on a typewriter-style keyboard into encoded bits of data and passed those data to the computer. The engineers then made computing even more convenient by linking different devices together in networks so that the more expensive devices (such as large database storage units) could be centralized for access by user devices.

The first computer networks (like many of the networks in use today) were private systems located on the premises of a single business or government agency. Devices in these so-called local area networks were connected by wires or cables installed entirely on the using organization's property.

Some large governmental, academic and business users, however, needed to move data among computers and peripheral devices located at great distances from each other. The obvious way to accomplish this was to encode the data in a form that could move over voice telephone lines, and use the telephone network to move information among these computers and devices.

Unfortunately, voice telephone signals usually are carried from the home or office in analog form, while the signals generated by computers are digital (on-off) signals.[6] In order to move data signals over the telephone network, therefore, it was necessary to convert the computer's digital signals into an analog equivalent. This was accomplished by the modulator-demodulator, or modem, which converted the computer's on-off signals into a series of analog tones.

Aided by the modem and the invention of the personal computer, telephonic computer communication quickly became a pervasive feature of our society. What began as an esoteric method of transferring data among research laboratories and defense installations now has reached homes and small offices in the form of credit card verification systems, electronic mail, on-line information and entertainment services, bulletin boards and chat lines of all kinds.

The most dramatic development in computer networking has been the explosive growth of the Internet—a network of computer networks using a common communications protocol that began as a means of exchanging information among computers operated by the United States Department of Defense and some of its research contractors. In only a few short years this little-known military and scientific system has become the host for millions of civilian users. Access to the Internet now is considered so vital to full participation in our society that the Telecommunications Act of 1996 mandates a program of discounted access to the Internet for schools and libraries.[7] As we discuss at greater length later in this chapter, the growth of the Internet has given increased urgency to the legal issues posed by on-line dissemination of information.

11.3 Computers and the Law of Intellectual Property

Some of the most troubling legal problems posed by the computer involve the adaptation of the law of intellectual property—*i.e.*, the rules by which the creators of inventions, literary works and other products of mental effort control the reproduction and use of their creations—to computer programs and data compilations. These creations strain the

6. This is not always the case. Businesses with substantial data communication needs can obtain data lines that carry transmissions from the customer's premises in digital form, eliminating the need for a modem.

7. Telecommunications Act of 1996, Pub. L. 104–104 § 254(h), *codified at* 47 U.S.C.A. § 254(h)(West 1996).

familiar rules of intellectual property, broadly, for two reasons: first, because the programs that make computers work are themselves difficult to fit within the traditional categories of intellectual property; and second, because the novel ways in which computers manipulate, store and distribute information make it more difficult to protect proprietary interests in that information. In responding to these problems the Congress, the courts and the affected parties have had to accommodate an explosively developing technology with a set of intellectual property concepts derived from the age of the printing press. Fortunately, these concepts have proved remarkably adaptable.

We begin the discussion of intellectual property issues with the application of copyright and patent law to the protection of computer programs and data compilations. We then discuss intellectual property protection of information stored within, and transferred among, computers and computer databases.

A. Copyright Protection Of Computer Programs and Data Compilations

Copyright is the exclusive right of an author or other copyright owner to copy, distribute, perform or display a work.[1] Copyright protection does not require formal registration or the placing of any form of notice on the work: protection inheres in a work of authorship as soon as it is fixed in a tangible medium of expression.[2] In the United States the right is primarily statutory and federal and is good for the life of the author plus fifty years—or, in the case of works for hire, for seventy-five years.[3] Where one of the exclusive rights has been infringed, the copyright owner may sue the infringer for damages and injunctive relief.[4] Violations of copyright also are punishable under the criminal provisions of the United States Code.[5]

Copyright is the most popular means of protecting computer programs from unauthorized duplication. Unlike the formal and rigorous patent law regime, copyright protection may be achieved with little formality and expense.[6] Unlike trade secret protection, copyright is not lost when protected information becomes public. These features of copyright are a good fit with much of the software industry's open, informal and entrepreneurial character.

At the same time, however, the law of copyright has not adapted smoothly to the protection of computer software. In fact, many courts

---

1. 17 U.S.C.A. § 106 (West 1996).

2. 2 MELVILLE B. NIMMER and DAVID NIMMER, COPYRIGHT §§ 7.02[B], 7.16[A] (1996) (hereinafter "Nimmer"). Registration of a copyright with the Copyright Office does, however, confer definite benefits, including the right to recover attorney's fees in a successful copyright infringement suit. Nimmer § 14.01[A].

3. NIMMER § 9.01[A].

4. NIMMER §§ 14.01 et seq.

5. As discussed further below, copyright also is the subject of international agreements that are acquiring greater importance as technology markets become increasingly global.

6. The chief limitation of copyright protection, as compared to the patent regime, is that a copyright holder is not protected against independent creation of an identical or substantially similar work.

have had difficulty deciding whether various kinds of expression contained within computer programs may be copyrighted at all. In other cases, courts have had to determine whether various activities, including replication of programs through reverse engineering, copying of programs into a computer's memory chips and transmission of information from one computer to another constitute infringement of a program's copyright. And still other courts are working out the extent to which operators of on-line services may be liable for copyright infringement committed by users of their facilities.

The discussion of these questions begins with the most fundamental issue, *i.e.*: whether particular, expressive elements of computer programs may be copyrighted at all. We first consider the copyrightability of the literal, coded instructions in which programs are written by their creators, and then discuss the extent to which copyright law extends beyond those literal instructions to protect the structure and organization of programs and the way in which programs interact with their human users. Finally, we describe a statutory form of intellectual property protection for semiconductor chips and the problem of copyright protection for information electronically stored in computer databases.

1. Copyrightability of Literal Elements of Computer Programs

The Copyright Act extends its protections to "original works of authorship fixed in any tangible medium of expression...."[7] The Act expressly recognizes a nonexclusive list of eight categories of these protectible "works of authorship," including literary works, musical works, dramatic works, motion pictures and sound recordings.[8]

The Copyright Act also excludes some elements of works of authorship from the scope of copyright. Specifically, § 102(b) of the Act states that:

> In no case does copyright protection for an original work of authorship extend to any idea, procedure, process, system, method of operation, concept, principle, or discovery, regardless of the form in which it is described, explained, illustrated, or embodied in such work.[9]

The exceptions of § 102(b) serve two important purposes in defining the scope of copyright protection. First, the exception for "any idea" ensures that authors will enjoy a monopoly over their original expressions of ideas but not over the ideas they express. Second, the references to any "process, system [or] method of operation" distinguish the subject-matter of copyright from the subject-matter of patents. Accordingly, authors may copyright their particular descriptions of processes, systems or methods of operations, but may not copyright those processes, systems or methods of operation themselves.

---

7. 17 U.S.C.A. § 102(a) (West 1996).　　**9.** *Id.* § 102(b).

8. *Id.*

While the Copyright Act does not list computer programs among the eight categories of "works of authorship" expressly protected by the Act, there no longer is any serious question that software enjoys copyright protection.

The Congress first confronted the question of copyrightability of computer programs in 1974, when it created the Commission on New Technological Uses of Copyrighted Works ("CONTU").[10] In its final report (issued in 1979, after passage of the 1976 Copyright Act), CONTU recommended amendments to the Act "to make it explicit that computer programs, to the extent that they embody an author's original creation, are proper subject matter of copyright."[11] CONTU also recommended specific amendments, including a new section 117 to permit rightful possessors of computer programs to make backup copies[12] and a definition of "computer program" for inclusion among the definitions set out in section 101 of the Act.[13]

In 1980, Congress amended the Act to adopt the CONTU recommendations. Specifically, Congress added a new section 117 that allowed the owner of a copy of a computer program to copy or adapt the program when necessary to "the utilization of the computer program" or "for archival purposes ..."[14] It also added to section 101 the following definition of "computer program":

> A "computer program" is a set of statements or instructions to be used directly or indirectly in a computer in order to bring about a certain result.[15]

While these amendments still do not *declare* the copyrightability of software or list software among the enumerated categories of "works of authorship," they leave no serious doubt as to the intention of Congress to adopt CONTU's conclusion that "computer programs ... are proper subject matter of copyright."[16] And when read in conjunction with the

---

10. The Copyright Office began accepting applications to copyright computer software in 1964.

11. NATIONAL COMMISSION ON NEW TECHNOLOGICAL USES OF COPYRIGHTED WORKS, FINAL REPORT 1 (1979) (hereinafter "CONTU Report"). Although the 1976 Act was passed without the benefit of the CONTU Report, the legislative history suggests that Congress intended computer programs to be classified as "literary works" within the meaning of the Act. H.R. Rep. No. 1476, 94th Cong., 2d Sess. 54 (1976), *reprinted in* 1976 U.S. Code Cong. and Admin. News 5659, 5667.

12. CONTU Report, *supra* at 1. As enacted in the 1976 Act, section 117 was a *status quo* provision that protected computerized versions of copyrighted material. The 1976 version of section 117 did not protect computer programs. H.R. Rep. No.

1476 at 166, *reprinted in* 1976 U.S. Code Cong. & Admin. News at 5731. As discussed further below, § 117 as enacted permitted only owners of copies of programs, rather than the licensees contemplated in the CONTU Report, to make archival copies and copies needed to run their programs.

13. CONTU Report, *supra* at 12.

14. 17 U.S.C.A. § 117 (West 1996). This statutory provision, which creates an exception to the rule that the owner of a copy of a copyrighted work is presumptively not entitled to make additional copies of that work, is one of two legislative enactments that make substantive changes in copyright law for the purpose of accommodating computer technology. The other such provision is the so-called "Mask Act," which is discussed at Section 11.6, *infra*.

15. 17 U.S.C.A. § 101 (West 1996).

16. CONTU Report, *supra* at 1.

Act's definition of "literary works," they anticipate and resolve at least two issues concerning the scope of copyright protection of software.

First, the definition of "computer program," by including instructions to be used *directly or indirectly* in a computer, settles the question whether both source code (readable directly by humans but not by machines) and object code (readable directly by machines but not by humans) are protected.[17]

Second, the definition of "literary works," by including works expressed in "numbers, or other ... numerical symbols or indicia," disposes of the question whether object code must be excluded from copyright because it is not expressed in words.[18]

2. Cases Discussing the Copyrightability of Literal Elements

While the intent of Congress to protect computer software seemed clear enough, some district courts in the late 1970s and early 1980s nonetheless took a contrary view. Notably, in 1979 a trial court in the Northern District of Illinois, interpreting the 1909 Copyright Act, held that the copying of a ROM chip did not infringe the copyright of the program encoded on the chip. The court found that when the object code version of the program was "burned" on the chip, the result was not a copy of the program but a mere "mechanical tool or a machine part engaged in the computer to become an essential part of the mechanical process ..."[19] Since machines may be patented but may not be copyrighted, no infringement had occurred when the chip was copied. Fortunately, the Seventh Circuit Court of Appeals, in affirming the district court's decision, did not adopt the trial court's refusal to extend copyright to programs encoded in ROM. Instead, the Court affirmed on the narrow ground that the plaintiff's ROM did not include a copyright notice.[20]

Similarly, in 1982 a trial court refused to grant a preliminary injunction against Franklin Computer Corporation ("Franklin"), which had made verbatim copies of fourteen separate operating system programs developed by Apple Computer, Inc. ("Apple"). In finding that Apple was unlikely to prevail on the merits of its infringement claim, the court expressed doubt that object code, ROMs and operating systems

17. CONTU debated this question, and the majority expressly concluded that source code and object code are equally deserving of copyright protection. The minority argued that copyright should apply only to works directed at a human audience, and therefore should not extend to object code. CONTU Report, *supra*, at 21 and 28–30.

18. 17 U.S.C.A. § 101 (West 1996). Article 4 of the World Intellectual Property Organization Copyright Treaty, adopted on December 20, 1996 and not yet ratified by the United States, also grants express copyright protection to computer programs

"whatever may be the mode or form of their expression." World Intellectual Property Organization Copyright Treaty, adopted by the Diplomatic Conference on December 20, 1996, Art. 4.

19. Data Cash Systems, Inc. v. JS&A Group, Inc., 480 F.Supp. 1063 (N.D.Ill. 1979).

20. Data Cash Systems, Inc. v. JS&A Group, Inc., 628 F.2d 1038 (7th Cir.1980). The lawsuit had been brought under the 1909 Copyright Act, which denied copyright protection to works published without notice of copyright.

could be copyrighted.[21] Apple appealed the denial of its petition for preliminary injunction.

On appeal, Franklin raised three principal arguments in support of the district court's decision: first, that programs in object code (as opposed to source code) could not be copyrighted because those programs are not communicated to human beings; second, that software embedded in the computer's memory, rather than embodied in a traditional writing, is not "fixed in a tangible medium of expression" as required by the Act; and third, that even if application programs may be copyrighted, operating programs may not.[22]

Franklin's first argument was based on the decision of the Supreme Court in *White-Smith Publishing Co. v. Apollo Co.*,[23] in which the Court had declined to extend copyright protection to a player-piano roll because the information on the roll could not be read and understood by human beings. Franklin argued that object code, which also is encoded in a form (binary numbers recorded on a chip) intelligible to machines but not human beings, was no more copyrightable than the piano roll in *White-Smith Music*.

The Court of Appeals found the answer to this argument in the plain language of the 1976 Act. Specifically, the opinion notes that the Act protects works in any form of expression *"from which they can be perceived*, reproduced, or otherwise communicated, either directly or *with the aid of a machine or device."*[24] Similarly, the definition of "computer program" in the 1980 amendments to the Act includes "sets of statements or instructions to be used *directly or indirectly* in a computer in order to bring about a certain result."[25] This language, which is reinforced by the legislative history, shows that the 1976 Act limits the scope of the *White-Smith Music* rule.[26]

Franklin's second argument—that the program's embodiment on a read-only memory chip does not satisfy the "fixation" requirement of

---

21. Apple Computer, Inc. v. Franklin Computer Corp., 545 F.Supp. 812 (E.D.Pa. 1982).

22. Apple Computer, Inc. v. Franklin Computer Corp., 714 F.2d 1240, 1249–50 (3d Cir.1983), cert. dismissed, 464 U.S. 1033, 104 S.Ct. 690, 79 L.Ed.2d 158 (1984) (hereinafter "Franklin").

23. 209 U.S. 1, 28 S.Ct. 319, 52 L.Ed. 655 (1908) (hereinafter "White-Smith Music").

24. Franklin, *supra*, n. 22 at 1248.

25. *Id.*, *citing* 17 U.S.C.A. § 101 (West 1996) (*emphasis by Court*). The opinion also notes that copyrightable "literary works" are defined in the statute to include works using "numbers, or other ... numerical symbols or indicia." *Id.* at 1249, *citing* 17 U.S.C.A. § 101 (West 1996). (This seems unresponsive to Franklin's argument, which is based not on object code's numerical form, but on the fact that such code is

intelligible to machines rather than humans.)

26. In a 1989 decision, the United States District Court for the Northern District of California considered a challenge to the copyrightability of microcode—a set of instructions even lower than object code in the software hierarchy. NEC Corp. and NEC Electronics, Inc. v. Intel Corp., 1989 Copr.L.Dec. 26,379 (N.D.Cal.1989). Among other claims, the defendant argued that plaintiff's microcode, which was designed to "tell[] a microprocessor which of its thousands of transistors to actuate in order to perform [particular] tasks ...," was not a program but a noncopyrightable part of the computer. The court rejected this argument, which it characterized as "semantic," and found that microcode is as much a computer program as object code is.

the Act—also was rejected. In the Court's view, fixation in a ROM chip is as valid as fixation in more traditional literary forms.[27]

Franklin's third argument—that operating software is less deserving of copyright protection than application software—was based on two propositions: first, that operating systems are not copyrightable works but "processes, systems or methods of operation;" and second, that operating systems may not be copyrighted because they are ideas that have merged with their expression.

The claim that operating systems are processes, systems or methods of operation derives from the Supreme Court's decision in *Baker v. Selden*,[28] in which the Court declined to extend copyright protection to a bookkeeping method described in a book, as opposed to the book's particular expression of that method. Franklin contended that an operating system, as opposed to an application system, is a utilitarian device that directs the operations of a machine and is no more copyrightable than the bookkeeping method in *Baker*.

The Court disagreed. Notably, the Court found that Apple had not tried to "copyright the method which instructs the computer to perform its operating functions but only the instructions themselves."[29] The Court also found no difference between the function performed by an operating system and an application system, either in practice or in the language of the statute.

Finally, Franklin argued that the operating system's expression was inseparable from the ideas contained in the system, so that the program consisted only of a noncopyrightable idea.[30] The Court declined to find on the record before it whether other programs could be written that performed the same function as Apple's operating system, but it noted that if other such programs could be written, then the operating system could be copyrighted.

Franklin is a significant case, if only because no subsequent appellate decision has seriously entertained the idea that the literal elements of a computer program, in whatever form they are expressed, are *per se* outside the realm of copyright protection. The *Franklin* Court's treatment of these issues, with its solid grounding in the intent and language of the Act, must be regarded as definitive.

11.4 Copyrightability of a Program's Nonliteral Elements

As the previous section shows, some fundamental issues concerning copyright protection of software may be taken as resolved. Notably, there is no serious question that an original program is copyrightable whether

---

27. Franklin, *supra* n. 22 at 1249. The Court relied for this result on its previous decision in *Williams Electronics, Inc. v. Artic International, Inc.*, 685 F.2d 870 (3d Cir.1982), in which it also was argued that "a computer program is not infringed when the program is loaded into electronic memory devices (ROMs) and used to control the activity of machines." *Id.* at 876.

28. 101 U.S. 99, 25 L.Ed. 841 (1879) (hereinafter "Baker").

29. Franklin, *supra*, n. 22 at 1251.

30. *Id.* at 1252.

it is encoded as source code, object code, microcode or read only memory (ROM).[1] Similarly, there no longer is any doubt that operating systems enjoy the same protection as application programs.[2]

These principles are sufficient to resolve most challenges to the copyrightability of the literal, coded instructions in which programs are written by programmers and "read" by computers. But the most troubling cases are not those in which an alleged infringer has made a verbatim copy of substantially all of the code of a plaintiff's program: the hard cases are those in which the allegedly infringing program contains only a small part of the coded instructions of the original, or mimics some element of the original's structure or organization without copying any of the original's coded instructions literally.

In dealing with cases of this kind, the courts have not seriously doubted that a program may be infringed, at least in theory, by something short of literal copying of the program's code. The courts have long recognized, for example, that imitation of the plot, characters and other features of a novel or play, short of verbatim copying of the work's language, may infringe copyright if done at a sufficient level of detail.[3] There is no *a priori* reason not to entertain similar, nonliteral infringement claims involving copyrighted computer programs.

The challenge of these cases is not the courts' reluctance to recognize the copyrightability of nonliteral elements of software, but the difficulty of ascertaining the extent of that protection and the elements of computer programs to which it should apply. The problems, in fact, are of two kinds: one is the need, present in all cases of nonliteral copying, to draw the line between exploitation of the nonprotectible idea of a work and copying of an author's particular, copyrighted expression of that idea; the other is the concern that in a utilitarian work such as a computer program, some elements of the work may be neither ideas nor expressions but processes or methods of operation that may be protected, if at all, only by patent.[4]

In a case alleging nonliteral copying, therefore, the court's hardest task is to determine whether a defendant has copied protected expression contained in the plaintiff's work. As a procedural matter, the court may address this problem in either of two ways: by isolating the protectible elements of the original and then comparing those elements with their counterparts in the allegedly infringing work; or by first comparing the two works in their entirety to ascertain whether they are substantially similar, and then determining whether the substantial similarity between the works extends to protectible elements of the

1. *See* Apple Computer, Inc. v. Franklin Computer Corp., 714 F.2d 1240 (3d Cir. 1983); Williams Electronics, Inc. v. Artic International, Inc., 685 F.2d 870 (3d Cir. 1982); NEC Corp. and NEC Electronics, Inc. v. Intel Corp., 1989 Copr.L.Dec. 26,379 (N.D.Cal.1989).

2. Franklin, *supra.*

3. *See* Nichols v. Universal Pictures Corp., 45 F.2d 119 (2d Cir.1930), cert. denied, 282 U.S. 902, 51 S.Ct. 216, 75 L.Ed. 795 (1931).

4. 17 U.S.C.A. § 102(b) (West 1996).

original.[5] Whichever method is chosen, proof of infringement may only be based on copying of elements of the original program that are protected by copyright.

In order to understand the law's response to claims of nonliteral infringement, it is necessary to identify the kinds of nonliteral elements that plaintiffs in software copyright cases seek to protect. Once this is understood, the courts' efforts to fit those elements within traditional categories of protectible and nonprotectible expression can profitably be explored.

A. *The Nonliteral Elements of Computer Programs*

The design of a program typically begins with a more or less concise statement of the purpose the program will serve.[6] The overall purpose might be as simple as "word processing" or "computer-aided design of roof trusses" or might include more precise specifications such as the particular inputs the program must accept, the outputs it must produce, and the type of hardware and operating system with which the program must be compatible.

Once the programmer knows the overall purpose the program must serve, he or she may create a flowchart depicting, among other things, the order in which a program serving that purpose might receive data inputs, manipulate the data and create outputs. The programmer also might work out some of the data structures and algorithms to be used by the program. At this point—before he or she has written any source code—the programmer also will break the program into a manageable set of subprograms, known as modules or subroutines, and may subdivide these further into additional modules or subroutines. Finally, the programmer will write source code through which each module will

---

5. While the former approach has the virtue of screening out irrelevant (*i.e.*, nonprotectible) elements of the original before the two programs are compared, some courts have noted that comparison of the two programs in their entirety—including both protectible and nonprotectible elements—is useful to the trier of fact on the issue of copying. *See, e.g.*, Gates Rubber Co. v. Bando Chemical Industries, Inc., 9 F.3d 823, 832 n. 7 (10th Cir.1993); *see also* Atari, Inc. v. North American Philips Consumer Electronics Corp., 672 F.2d 607, 618 (7th Cir.), cert. denied, 459 U.S. 880, 103 S.Ct. 176, 74 L.Ed.2d 145 (1982). Professor Nimmer, for example, argues that merger of idea and expression should bar a finding of substantial similarity, but should not be tested at an earlier stage of the inquiry to determine copyrightability. NIMMER § 13.03[A] at 13–33 to 13–34, *commenting on* Morrissey v. Procter & Gamble Co., 379 F.2d 675 (1st Cir.1967).

6. The account of program creation given here is based on various descriptions given by courts and academic com-

mentators. The steps involved in creating a program vary widely in practice: in infringement cases, courts will rely on expert testimony to reconstruct the development and structure of the specific programs at issue. *See, e.g.*, Gates, *supra* note 5, at 834–836; Lotus Development Corp. v. Paperback Software Int'l, 740 F.Supp. 37, 44–45 (D.Mass.1990); 5 MCGRAW-HILL ENCYCLOPEDIA OF SCIENCE AND TECHNOLOGY 531 (7th ed. 1992); Steven R. Englund, Note, *Idea, Process, or Protected Expression?: Determining the Scope of Copyright Protection of the Structure of Computer Programs.* 88 Mich. L. Rev. 866, 871, 899 (1990); Andrew H. Rosen, *Virtual Reality: Copyrightable Subject Matter and the Scope of Judicial Protection*, 33 Jurimetrics J. 35 (1992); John W.L. Ogilvie, *Defining Computer Program Parts Under Learned Hand's Abstractions Test in Software Copyright Infringement Cases*, 91 Mich. L. Rev. 526 (1992).

perform its function, and also will write source code to govern the data flows and interactions between one module and another.

When the program is complete, its structure will reflect the process of its creation. A lay observer might suppose that the finished program consists only of its overall purpose and the expression of that purpose in a single, linear series of coded instructions. To a knowledgeable observer, however, the program's purpose and its coded instructions will represent only the two extremes of abstraction and detail between which lie a complex, hierarchical set of intermediary elements that may constitute the program's most creative and valuable features. In most programs, these intermediate elements will include the following.

1. The Program's Overall Structure or Architecture

This is the program as it may have been depicted in the programmer's first flowchart. It consists of a functional description of each of the modules into which the program is divided and the way those modules interact with each other. The process of interaction among modules, in turn, may be described in terms of control flow (*i.e.*, the sequence in which the various modules perform their tasks), data flow (*i.e.*, the movement of data among modules and the way in which the data are operated upon by the modules) and nesting (*i.e.*, the relationships between modules and their subordinate submodules). So, for example, the overall structure or architecture of a payroll program might consist of a description of the interactions, including control flows and data flows, among modules that calculate gross pay, quantify various deductions and yield a net pay figure based on those calculations.

2. The Program's Modules

The next level of abstraction, below the program's structure or architecture, consists of the functions and internal workings of the modules themselves. Each module may be understood as the performance of a certain operation or operations on a defined data type. So, for example, a single module within a payroll program may subtract an employee's tax withholding amount from the employee's pre-tax salary. This module will consist of two data types—the pre-tax salary and the withholding amount—and the operation for subtracting the latter from the former.

3. Algorithms and Data Structures

Algorithms and data structures are the constituent elements of the operations and data types contained within the individual modules. An algorithm is the series of steps through which an operation (such as calculating a net pay figure in a payroll program) is accomplished, while a data structure is the precise way in which a data type is represented. Of these various elements of computer programs, all but the source code and object code are abstract, nonliteral features. Structure, architecture, modules, control flows, data flows and the other elements that reside somewhere between the program's overall purpose and its literal code resemble the themes, characters, plots and interactions depicted in a novel or play. Like these features of literary works, the nonliteral elements of a program can be imitated without verbatim duplication of a single line of the language of the original work.

B. *Distinguishing Protectible From Nonprotectible Elements*

As the analogy with literary works suggests, the tools for distinguishing protectible from nonprotectible expression in cases of nonliteral copying of software were first developed in connection with more traditional works of authorship. Many authors of novels and plays have brought infringement suits to protect the plots, scenes and characters of their works from imitation by other authors. The task of the courts in these cases has been to ascertain whether the defendant's work resembles the original at a level of detail sufficient to infringe, not just the idea of the original, but the idea's particular expression in the original work. While the line is difficult to draw, the distinction is central to copyright's policy of protecting an author's original expression while leaving others free to create works expressing the same ideas in different and novel ways. As Judge Learned Hand put it, the law will not permit a plagiarist to escape liability by "immaterial variations" from another author's work.[7] At the same time, the law will not "grant property status to a mere idea," because such a policy would "permit withdrawing the idea from the stock of materials that would otherwise be open to other authors."[8] The courts have given the idea/expression dichotomy more content through a number of closely-related doctrines, including merger, *scenes a faire*, and the doctrine that expression may not be protected where it is essential to the use of a process or cannot be separated from a utilitarian work's functional features.

1. *Merger Doctrine*

The merger doctrine dates at least from the Supreme Court's decision in *Baker*,[9] which found that if the idea of a work cannot be used unless some expressive elements of the work are copied by the user, then those expressive elements may not enjoy copyright protection. In *Baker*, the author of a book describing a method of bookkeeping, and incorporating a set of forms by which the method could be implemented, contended that no one should be able to use those forms without paying the author a royalty. The Court found that the idea expressed in the author's book (*i.e.*, the method of bookkeeping) could not be used without copying the forms, and that protection of the forms therefore would amount to copyright protection of the author's idea. Since ideas are not protectible in copyright, the Court rejected the author's claim. Defendants have relied upon the rule of *Baker* to argue that their

7. Nichols, *supra* note 3, at 121.

8. *Id.*

9. Baker v. Selden, 101 U.S. 99, 25 L.Ed. 841 (1879). The rule of *Baker* is codi-

fied at § 102(b) of the 1976 Copyright Act. 17 U.S.C.A. § 102(b)(West 1996).

copying of certain elements of software programs was essential to the use of nonprotectible ideas contained in those programs.[10]

2. Scene a Faire Doctrine

A *scene a faire* is, literally, a scene that "must be done." The *scenes a faire* cases deal primarily with plays, novels and other literary works, and define a class of incidents, characters and settings without which it is impossible to treat a given topic. (So, for example, no play about Henry VIII can be written without the character of Henry VIII, his wives and ministers.) To hold otherwise would be to permit the author of the first work on a topic to foreclose future works, however original, on that same topic.[11]

The courts also have found that the copyright in the description of a process may not be used to obtain a monopoly of the process itself,[12] and that copyright does not extend to those elements of the design of functional items that cannot be separated from their utilitarian features.[13] Only expression that is subject to copyright apart from the processes it describes, or the functional features with which it is associated, may be protected by copyright law.

All of these doctrines, which often are hard to distinguish from one another in practice, serve a similar function in copyright litigation: they enable courts to deny protection to expression, otherwise copyrightable, that is essential to the further dissemination of ideas, processes or other elements that are not proper subjects of copyright.

3. Application of Doctrines

The first effort by an appellate court to apply the idea/expression dichotomy to a computer program was a 1986 decision of the United States Court of Appeals for the Third Circuit. In *Whelan Associates, Inc.*

---

10. *See, e.g.,* Whelan Associates, Inc. v. Jaslow Dental Laboratory, 797 F.2d 1222 (3d Cir.1986), cert. denied, 479 U.S. 1031, 107 S.Ct. 877, 93 L.Ed.2d 831 (1987) ("*Whelan*").

11. As one court has expressed it, "a second author does not infringe even if he produces verbatim the first author's expression, if that expression constitutes stock scenes or scenes that flow necessarily from common unprotectable ideas, because to hold otherwise would give the first author a monopoly on the commonplace ideas behind the *scenes a faire*." Landsberg v. Scrabble Crossword Game Players, Inc., 736 F.2d 485, 489 (9th Cir.), cert. denied 469 U.S. 1037, 105 S.Ct. 513, 83 L.Ed.2d 403 (1984). *See also* Hoehling v. Universal City Studios, Inc., 618 F.2d 972, 979 (2d Cir.1980).

12. This doctrine is a variant of the merger doctrine of *Baker, supra,* note 9; *see also* Brief English Systems, Inc. v. Owen, 48 F.2d 555 (2d Cir.), cert. denied, 283 U.S. 858, 51 S.Ct. 650, 75 L.Ed. 1464 (1931).

13. This exception to copyright protection sometimes is called the "useful article" doctrine. So, for example, the standard "QWERTY" keyboard arrangement and the "H" pattern of automobile gearshifts have utilitarian functions and do not merely convey information or contribute to the appearance of the items in which they appear. To the extent these expressive elements cannot be separated from their function, they may not be copyrighted. *See* Mazer v. Stein, 347 U.S. 201, 74 S.Ct. 460, 98 L.Ed. 630 (1954); *see also* Plains Cotton Co-op. Ass'n v. Goodpasture Computer Serv., Inc., 807 F.2d 1256, 1262 (5th Cir.), cert. denied, 484 U.S. 821, 108 S.Ct. 80, 98 L.Ed.2d 42 (1987); Kitchens of Sara Lee, Inc. v. Nifty Foods Corp., 266 F.2d 541 (2d Cir.1959); Rosenthal v. Stein, 205 F.2d 633, 636 (9th Cir.1953).

v. Jaslow Dental Laboratory, Inc. (*"Whelan"*), the Court confronted a case of nonliteral copying of a program for the operation of a dental laboratory.[14] Whelan had written a program, called Dentalab, in the EDL language used by IBM minicomputers. Dentalab was written for Jaslow and was patterned closely on the operation of Jaslow's dental laboratory. Later, Jaslow wrote his own dental laboratory program in BASIC, a language used by personal computers. Jaslow's program, called Dentcom, was not a literal translation of Dentalab into BASIC but resembled Dentalab in its logical structure.

Whelan sued Jaslow for infringement, and the district court entered judgment for Whelan finding that the Dentalab copyright was valid and was infringed by Dentcom.[15] On appeal, the only substantive question was whether Jaslow infringed Dentalab's copyright in creating the Dentcom program.

Jaslow's principal argument before the Court of Appeals was that there was insufficient evidence at trial of substantial similarity between the two programs. This claim was based on two grounds: first, that the district court found no similarity between the source code and object code of the programs, but only between their "overall structures," which Jaslow claimed could not be copyrighted; and second, that even if the non-literal elements of a program may be copyrighted, the evidence was insufficient to establish substantial similarity between the non-literal elements of Dentalab and Dentcom.[16]

Jaslow's claim that a program's structure may not be copyrighted was based on the merger doctrine of *Baker v. Selden*. According to Jaslow's argument, the structure of a program "is, by definition, the idea and not the expression of the idea," and therefore cannot be covered by the program's copyright.[17]

The Court of Appeals disagreed, and announced its own version of the rule of *Baker v. Selden*. According to the Court, "the purpose or function of a utilitarian work would be the work's idea, and everything that is not necessary to that purpose or function would be part of the expression of the idea."[18] Accordingly, "[w]here there are various means of achieving the desired purpose, then the particular means chosen is not necessary to the purpose; hence, there is expression, not idea."[19] The Court reinforced its treatment of the idea/expression dichotomy with two lines of copyright cases: those related to *scenes a faire*, and those related to "fact-intensive works."[20]

In the Court's view, both the *scene a faire* and fact-intensive work cases suggest a method of distinguishing idea from expression in the structure of a computer program. Where some feature of a program's logical structure is indispensable to the program's purpose, then that

---

14. Whelan, *supra*, note 10.

15. Whelan Associates v. Jaslow Dental Laboratory, 609 F.Supp. 1307 (E.D.Pa. 1985).

16. Whelan, *supra*, note 10 at 1233.

17. *Id.* at 1235.

18. *Id.* at 1236.

19. *Id.* at 1236–37.

20. *Id.* at 1236.

feature, like a *scene a faire* or a device integral to a fact-intensive work, is part of the program's idea. If, on the other hand, the feature is one of a number of ways in which the program's purpose or function may be achieved, then that feature is protectible as part of the program's expression.[21]

The Court acknowledged that its version of the idea/expression dichotomy might be a poor fit with many nonutilitarian literary works but found it to be a good tool for analyzing the Dentalab and Dentcom programs.[22] Specifically, the Court noted that the purpose of the Dentalab program was to "aid in the business operation of a dental laboratory."[23] The Court then affirmed the district court's finding that the commercial availability of software that achieved this same purpose through different logical structures demonstrated that the particular structure of the Dentalab program was not essential to its purpose. On the strength of this analysis, the Court of Appeals upheld the entry of judgment for Whelan on its claim of copyright infringement.

While some courts have applied the analysis set out in *Whelan*,[24] many courts—and most academic commentators—have found the analysis inadequate.[25] Specifically, courts and commentators have noted that

---

21. The Court's opinion also rejects some arguments, made chiefly in the academic literature, against copyright protection of the nonliteral elements of computer software. Notably, one commentator had argued that copyright law should not discourage the immense creative effort required to copy the structure, but not the literal elements, of a program. Another had argued that "the concept of structure in computer programs is too vague to be useful in copyright cases;" and still another had argued that progress in computer software development is uniquely incremental and cannot be achieved without plagiarism. *Id.* at 1237–38 and authorities cited therein. As to the first argument, the Court noted that copyright protection has nothing to do with the ease or difficulty of infringement. As to the second and third arguments, the Court expressed its confidence that the rule it had announced cured any vagueness in the concept of program structure and declined to find any unique need for plagiarism in the software industry. The Court also buttressed its conclusion with the language of the 1976 Copyright Act, which extended copyright protection to compilations—*i.e.*, to the assembly of preexisting works according to a different method of organization. *Id.* at 1239.

22. The Court also rejected an argument that the CONTU Report "recommend[ed] that copyright protection be limited to protection of the literal elements of computer programs ..." *Id.* at 1241. The

Court found that the CONTU Report contains no such limitation and would not be authoritative on this point if it had, since § 102(b) is not among the sections of the Copyright Act amended in response to the CONTU Report. *Id.* at 1240–42.

23. *Id.* at 1238.

24. *See, e.g.*, Bull HN Information Systems, Inc., v. American Express Bank, Ltd., 1990 Copyright Law Dec. (CCH) 26,555 at 23,278 (S.D.N.Y. 1990); Dynamic Solutions, Inc. v. Planning & Control, Inc., 1987 Copyright Law Dec. (CCH) 26,062 at 20,912 (S.D.N.Y. 1987); Broderbund Software, Inc. v. Unison World, Inc., 648 F.Supp. 1127, 1133 (N.D.Cal.1986).

25. *See, e.g.*, Computer Associates International, Inc. v. Altai, Inc., 982 F.2d 693, 705 (2d Cir.1992); Plains Cotton, *supra*, note 13 at 1262; Apple Computer, Inc. v. Microsoft Corp., 799 F.Supp. 1006, 1024 (N.D.Cal.1992); 3 NIMMER § 13.03(F); Steven R. Englund, Note, *Idea, Process, or Protected Expression?: Determining the Scope of Copyright Protection of the Structure of Computer Programs*, 88 Mich. L. Rev. 866, 881 (1990); Peter S. Menell, *An Analysis of the Scope of Copyright Protection for Computer Programs*, 41 Stan. L. Rev. 1045, 1074, 1082 (1989); Mark T. Kretschmer, Note, *Copyright Protection for Computer Architecture: Just Say No!*, 1988 Colum. Bus. L. Rev. 823, 837–39 (1988); Peter G. Spivack, Comment, *Does Form Follow Function? The Idea/Expression Di-*

computer programs do not have a single purpose, any more than a complex work of literature has a single "idea."[26] Programmers break the task of a program into a group of interacting subroutines, each of which has its own purpose. As *Whelan's* critics effectively pointed out, the assumption that each program will display a single idea reflects an inadequate grasp of software technology.

More fundamentally, the *Whelan* analysis has been criticized—and with considerable justice—as anticompetitive. If each computer program expresses only one idea, then all expressive elements of a program that are not essential to the expression of that program's single idea must be classified as protectible expression. In practice, this could mean that the first programmer to write software for a particular purpose—*e.g.*, word processing, spreadsheet creation, bridge design, or operation of a dental laboratory—will enjoy a monopoly over all elements of the program that are not inherent in the very notion of word processing, spreadsheet creation, bridge design or operation of a dental laboratory. A broad monopoly of this kind may extend to ideas and other noncopyrightable elements of modules or subroutines within the program that are entirely independent of the program's overall purpose. A monopoly over these elements will stifle competition, not only in the market for programs serving the overall purpose of the original, but in the markets for other types of programs, as well.[27]

Other critics have argued that *Whelan* erred in declaring the protectibility of a program's structure, sequence and organization. In the view of these commentators, structure, sequence and organization lie inherently on the idea side of the idea/expression dichotomy and are so broad that recognition of their protectibility will stifle progress in the software industry.[28]

A second, and somewhat more discriminating, approach to nonliteral copying of programs was that of the District Court of Massachusetts in *Lotus Development Corp. v. Paperback Software International* ("*Paper-*

---

chotomy in Copyright Protection of Computer Software, 35 UCLA L. Rev. 723, 747–55 (1988).

26. *See, e.g.*, Computer Associates v. Altai, Inc., 982 F.2d 693, 705 (2d Cir.1992); Julian Velasco, *The Copyrightability of Nonliteral Elements of Computer Programs*, 94 Colum. L. Rev. 242 (1994); Mark T. Kretschmer, Note, *Copyright Protection for Software Architecture: Just Say No!*, 1988 Colum. Bus. L. Rev. 823, 837–39.

27. *See, e.g.*, JONATHAN BAND AND MASANOBU KATOH, INTERFACES ON TRIAL: INTELLECTUAL PROPERTY AND INTEROPERABILITY IN THE GLOBAL SOFTWARE INDUSTRY 95–96 (Westview Press 1995); Marc T. Kretschmer, Note, *Copyright Protection for Software Architecture: Just Say No!*, 1988 Colum. Bus. L. Rev. 823–837–39. For an extreme example, imagine a word processing program that also

includes a complete operating program. Under a strict application of the *Whelan* analysis all of the device drivers and other software routines contained in the operating system, because they are not essential to the word processing function, must be considered part of the protectible expression of the idea of word processing. Common sense tells us, however, that the dichotomy is false: operating system functions are adaptable to all kinds of applications programs and are neither essential to, nor expressive of, the overall purpose of any particular application program.

28. *See, e.g.*, Michael A. Jacobs, *Copyright and Compatibility*, 30 Jurimetrics J. 91, 103 (1989); Peter G. Spivak, Comment, *Does Form Follow Function? The Idea/Expression Dichotomy in Copyright Protection of Computer Software*, 35 UCLA L. Rev. 723, 747 (1988).

back"). In that case Lotus, maker of the industry standard "1–2–3" spreadsheet program, sued the developer of an electronic spreadsheet program that closely emulated the "user interface" of the Lotus program. Specifically, the defendant had not copied the literal code of Lotus's program, but used the same L shaped layout, many of the same keystroke commands, a similar two-line moving cursor menu and a similar menu hierarchy. Lotus alleged that each of these elements, wholly apart from the instructions in which they were expressed, was protected by copyright.

The district court, like the Third Circuit in *Whelan*, accepted the premise that a program's copyright could be infringed by nonliteral copying and that separation of protectible from nonprotectible expression in a program required application of the idea/expression dichotomy. Unlike the *Whelan* court, however, the *Paperback* court did not suggest that each program has a single function that is the equivalent of the "idea" of a literary work, and that all elements of the program not essential to that idea must be classed as expression. Instead, the district court concluded that the line between a program's idea and its expression may be found at a level of abstraction somewhere between the overall function of the program and its coded instructions.[29]

In formulating this approach, the district court was aided by Judge Learned Hand's famous "abstractions" test. In *Nichols v. Universal Pictures Corp.* ("*Nichols*"), the Court was asked to find that a copyright in a play could be infringed by a subsequent play that used the same comic premise and similar characters and situations. Judge Hand noted that the case required a trier of fact to find the point at which imitation of a work was sufficiently detailed to cross the line from idea to expression:

> Upon any work and especially upon a play a great number of patterns of increasing generality will fit equally well, as more and more of the incident is left out. The last may perhaps be no more than the most general statement of what the play is about and at times consist only of its title, but there is a point in the series of abstractions where they are no longer protected since otherwise the playwright could prevent the use of his ideas to which apart from their expression his property is never extended.[30]

The district court in *Paperback* determined that applying Learned Hand's approach to nonliteral copying of computer programs called for a three-step analysis. First, the court must examine the element or elements of the program that are alleged to be infringed and determine the idea which those elements may be said to express. The district court acknowledges that a program may include more than one such idea, each at a different level of abstraction within the program. Second, the court must determine whether the allegedly infringed element of the program

---

29. The Paperback court also rejected the "total concept and feel" standard as a means of identifying copyrightable elements of a user interface. Paperback, 740 F. Supp. at 62–63.

30. Nichols, 45 F.2d at 121.

is essential to the expression of that idea, or includes expression not essential to every expression of that idea. Finally, when the court has found protectible expression, it must determine whether that expression is a substantial part of the plaintiff's program.

Applying this analysis to the case before it, the district court found that the spreadsheet programs at issue included not only the general idea of a spreadsheet, but also such ideas as having a readily available method of invoking the command system and the idea of a menu command structure. Some of the elements of the Lotus program, the court found, merged with these ideas. For example, the court found that the idea of a spreadsheet merges with the L shape layout used by Lotus, the keys used to invoke the menu command system, and the use of the arithmetic operation keys. Similarly, the idea of having a readily available method of invoking the menu command system merges with the slash key. The court found that the idea of a menu command structure, however, can be expressed in many ways, and the court therefore found that Lotus's overall menu command structure was protected by copyright. Since the evidence of defendant's copying of the Lotus menu command structure was "so 'overwhelming and pervasive' as to preclude any assertion of independent creation," the court found that Lotus's copyright in its user interface had been infringed.

The *Paperback* analysis, with its acknowledgment that a computer program may embody and express any number of ideas, is a considerable advance on the "one idea" approach of *Whelan*. In fact, to the extent the *Paperback* analysis has been criticized by judicial and academic commentators, those criticisms have focussed chiefly on the protectibility of user interfaces rather than on the appropriateness of the *Paperback* approach for nonliteral infringement claims generally.[31]

Still another approach to claims of nonliteral infringement of software copyrights was adopted in the case of *Brown Bag Software v. Symantec Corp.*, 960 F.2d 1465 (9th Cir.1992)("*Brown Bag*"). In *Brown Bag*, the Ninth Circuit Court of Appeals followed its own precedents in finding that nonliteral elements of a program could be copyrighted. The legal test of substantial similarity it applied, however, was the Ninth Circuit test, known as the extrinsic/intrinsic test, for ascertaining substantial similarity in any copyright case.[32]

---

31. *See* Gerard J. Lewis, Jr., Comment, *Lotus Development Corp. v. Paperback Software International: Broad Copyright Protection for User Interfaces Ignores the Software Industry's Trend Toward Standardization*, 52 U. Pitt. L. Rev. 689, 692–93 (1991); Joseph T. Verdesca, Jr., Comment, *Copyrighting the User Interface: Too Much Protection?*, 45 Sw. L. J. 1047, 1075–80 (1991). As discussed further below, some courts have taken the view that user interface cases should not be resolved through the abstraction-filtration-comparison approach, but generally should be decided against plaintiffs on the ground that user interfaces are noncopyrightable "methods of operation." *See, e.g.*, Lotus Development Corporation v. Borland International, Inc., 49 F.3d 807 (1st Cir.1995), *aff'd by an equally divided Court*, 515 U.S. 1191, 116 S.Ct. 39, 132 L.Ed.2d 921 (1995); *see also* Synercom Technology, Inc. v. University Computing Co., 462 F.Supp. 1003 (N.D.Tex.1978).

32. *See* Sid & Marty Krofft Television Productions, Inc. v. McDonald's Corp., 562 F.2d 1157, 1164–65 (9th Cir.1977); *see also*

The first part of the test—the extrinsic phase—may be conducted with the aid of expert testimony. At this stage, the plaintiff's work is dissected, and protectible and nonprotectible elements of the work are identified. This stage determines the scope of the plaintiff's copyright in the work. The second part—the intrinsic phase—is reached only after the court has identified protected expression in the original work. This test is a subjective, nonexpert comparison of the similarity between the allegedly infringing work and copyrighted elements of the original work.

In the *Brown Bag* case, the district court had granted summary judgment for defendant on the strength of the extrinsic phase of the inquiry, which showed that the allegedly infringed features of plaintiff's program either had merged with their expression, were *scenes a faire* or were purely functional. Accordingly, the intrinsic phase of the examination never was reached. The Court of Appeals upheld this result.

Brown Bag's application of the extrinsic/intrinsic test to computer programs has been criticized on a number of grounds. Notably, commentators have pointed out that the extrinsic test involves a dissection of the program into its copyrightable and noncopyrightable elements, and a plaintiff's failure to survive the extrinsic phase precludes the intrinsic inquiry. Thus, the trier of fact may have no chance to assess the copyrightability of the plaintiff's program as a whole.[33] More fundamentally, critics have pointed out that the intrinsic phase of the test, which calls for a trier of fact to make a purely impressionistic judgment, may be appropriate in cases involving plays and popular songs but cannot be squared with the complexity—and impenetrability to the lay mind—of computer software.[34]

Fortunately for the future of competition and innovation in the software industry, the *Whelan*, *Paperback* and *Brown Bag* approaches were eclipsed by a more refined and procompetitive judicial analysis. For what is unquestionably the most influential approach to cases of nonliteral copying of software, we turn to the so-called "abstraction-filtration-comparison" test proposed by David Nimmer and applied in a groundbreaking decision of the United States Court of Appeals for the Second Circuit.

4. *Abstraction-filtration-comparison Approach*

In *Computer Associates, Inc. v. Altai, Inc.* ("*Computer Associates*"),[35] the plaintiff (Computer Associates or "CA") had created a program called CA–SCHEDULER, which established and controlled the sequence in which IBM mainframe computers performed multiple tasks. Among CA–SCHEDULER's sub-programs was a program called CA–ADAPTER,

Shaw v. Lindheim, 919 F.2d 1353 (9th Cir. 1990).

33. *See* Mitchell Zimmerman, *Substantial Similarity of Computer Programs After*

Brown Bag, 9 Computer Law 6 (No. 7 1992).

34. *See, e.g.,* Nimmer § 13.03[E][4].

35. 982 F.2d 693 (2d Cir.1992).

which permitted applications software to run on any of the three operating systems used by the IBM System 370 family of computers.[36]

The defendant, Altai, developed its own task scheduling program for IBM 370 computers. The first iteration of this program, which Altai called ZEEK, could run on only one of the three System 370 operating systems. Altai decided to upgrade ZEEK so that it could interface with a second System 370 operating system, as well.[37]

The ZEEK upgrade project was aided considerably when Altai hired one of CA's employees—a software designer who had worked on ADAPT-ER and brought copies of the ADAPTER source code with him to his new job at Altai. The ex-CA employee created a new version of ZEEK, called OSCAR, that made ZEEK compatible with both the VSE and MVS IBM operating systems.[38] However, as the trial court found, the employee "had copied approximately 30% of OSCAR's code from CA's ADAPTER program."[39]

When CA sued Altai for copyright and trade secret violations, Altai rewrote the OSCAR program to eliminate the literal copying, replaced all copies of OSCAR already in customers' hands with the newer version, and shipped only the new version in response to subsequent orders.

At trial, CA sought to prove that both the first version of OSCAR (the version that was copied 30% from CA–ADAPTER) and the second version were substantially similar to CA–ADAPTER and infringed CA's copyright. The district court agreed with CA as to the first version of OSCAR, but found no substantial similarity between CA–ADAPTER and the sanitized OSCAR. CA appealed the latter finding.

In reviewing the district court's decision, the Court of Appeals considered—and rejected—the *Whelan* approach to proof of substantial similarity.[40] Instead, the Court adopted a three-step analysis, along the lines suggested in Nimmer's treatise on the law of copyright,[41] by which similarities involving nonprotectible elements of the two programs could be identified and the substantiality of the remaining similarities—*i.e.*, those involving protected expression—could be assessed.

The first stage in this process is called the "abstraction" phase and borrows from the similarity analysis announced many years earlier by Judge Learned Hand. The court at this stage must retrace the software designer's creative process, which typically begins with the identification of the program's overall purpose, then divides that task into manageable subroutines, and then defines and encodes the interactions among those subroutines.[42] Through this process, the court can identify the various

36. *Id.* at 698–99.

37. *Id.* at 699.

38. *Id.* at 700.

39. *Id.*

40. The district court also had considered and declined to follow *Whelan*.

41. Nimmer § 13.03[F].

42. Computer Associates, Inc., 982 F.2d at 697–98. This analytical process is followed by the reduction of the program to source code and its translation (or "compilation") into object code.

"abstraction levels" contained in the allegedly infringed program.[43]

The second step is the "filtration" process, by which the nonprotectible elements of the allegedly infringed program are identified. This inquiry, which is conducted for each level of abstraction identified in the "abstractions" phase, involves the court in a search for three categories of nonprotectible expression.

The first of the three unprotected categories includes all "elements dictated by efficiency."[44] As the decision points out, programmers strive to create software that achieves its purposes through the most direct and economical series of commands. To the extent the programmer achieves this goal the resulting software's structure will "approximate the idea or process embodied in [each] aspect of the program's structure" and may be said to have merged with that idea or process.[45] Under the traditional copyright doctrine of merger, therefore, program structure dictated by efficiency falls on the "idea" side of the idea/expression dichotomy and may not be protected.

The second category of unprotected expression consists of "elements dictated by external factors."[46] These are programming design choices imposed by the hardware on which the program will run, by the specifications of other software with which the program will interact, by computer manufacturers' design standards, by the requirements of the business or industry that will use the program or by "widely accepted programming practices with the computer industry."[47] Where such factors have determined the choice of an element of the software's design, the traditional *scene a faire* doctrine requires that the design element not receive copyright protection.

The third category consists of "elements taken from the public domain."[48] As the Court of Appeals notes, much software has been offered over public software exchanges or otherwise has entered the public domain.[49] These elements would not be protected if contained in any other work of authorship and the court declined to create an exception for software.

Once the court has finished its search for the three categories of nonprotected elements, whatever remains is the allegedly infringed program's "core of protectable expression."[50] Now the *Computer Associates* court's analysis moves on to the final, "comparison" stage, at which point "the court's substantial similarity inquiry focuses on whether the defendant copied any aspect of this protected expression and assesses the copied portion's relative importance with respect to the plaintiff's overall program."[51]

43. *Id.* at 706–07.

44. *Id.* at 707.

45. *Id.* at 708.

46. *Id.* at 709.

47. *Id.* at 710.

48. *Id.* at 710.

49. *Id.*

50. *Id.*

51. *Id.*

Having set out and explained its analysis, the Court of Appeals found that the district court had taken the three-step approach and that its application of that method was not clearly erroneous. Specifically, the trial court first had identified levels of abstraction within the OSCAR program and then had applied the filtration approach to each level so identified.[52] Where the district court found substantial similarity (as it did, for example, with respect to some of the "lists and macros" in the two programs and the programs' organizational charts), most of those expressions were in the public domain, "dictated by the functional demands of the program,"[53] required by other software with which the program was to interact or were so obvious as to be covered by the doctrine of *scene a faire*.[54] Since these conclusions were consistent with the Court of Appeals' analytical standard and not clearly erroneous in light of the record they were affirmed.

Computer Associates is the most influential judicial decision in the short history of computer software copyright litigation. The analysis announced in this case has two great virtues that other courts quickly recognized: first, it adapts copyright concepts to the realities of computer program design, thereby permitting courts to fashion rules that the software industry can understand and follow; and second, the decision establishes for software a procompetitive, "thin" version of copyright protection appropriate to these purely utilitarian creations.[55] Not surprisingly, a number of appellate courts have expressly endorsed the *Computer Associates* analysis.

The first application of *Computer Associates* in an appellate decision was the Federal Circuit's disposition of a claim involving computer game

---

52. *Id.* at 714. The appellate Court criticized the trial court, however, for applying the filtration analysis to the allegedly infringing program, rather than the allegedly infringed program. The Court cautioned that district courts in the future should analyze the plaintiff's program, rather than the defendant's program, to avoid wasteful identification of protectible expression in the defendant's program that is not found in the plaintiff's program. *Id.*

53. *Id.*

54. *Id.*

55. The decision also has been well-received in the academic press. *See, e.g.,* Dennis M. McCarthy, *Recent Decision, Copyright Infringement—Redefining the Scope of Protection Copyright Affords the Non–Literal Elements of a Computer Program—Computer Associates, Inc. v. Altai, Inc.,* 99 Temple L. Rev. 273 (1993); Timothy S. Teter, Note, *Merger and the Machines: An Analysis of the Pro–Compatibility Trend in Computer Software Copyright Cases,* 45 Stan. L. Rev. 1061, 1084–86 (1993). As might be expected, however, that support is not unanimous and unqualified. Notably, the analysis has been criticized as leaving insufficient incentive for the arduous labor reflected in many of the design elements it labels as nonprotectible—a criticism the Court itself considered in response to extensive briefing by the parties and various *amici.* The Court defended its analysis as a sound application of copyright principles, particularly in light of the Supreme Court's rejection of the "sweat of the brow" doctrine in *Feist Publications, Inc. v. Rural Telephone Service Co.,* 499 U.S. 340, 111 S.Ct. 1282, 113 L.Ed.2d 358 (1991) and noted that any defects in the result should prompt further consideration of the appropriateness of patent, as opposed to copyright, protection of computer programs. *Id.* at 711. Other critics have suggested that in denying protection for program features dictated by efficiency, *Computer Associates* gives infringers the power, by defending their preference for a given programming approach, to place that approach outside the scope of copyright. *See, e.g.,* RAYMOND T. NIMMER, THE LAW OF COMPUTER TECHNOLOGY: RIGHTS, LICENSES, AND LIABILITIES, Special Update 45 (2d ed. 1992).

programs. In *Atari Games Corporation v. Nintendo of America, Inc.* ("*Atari*"), the Federal Circuit upheld an order granting a preliminary injunction on behalf of Nintendo, which alleged that Atari had copied the software that allowed games to be played on Nintendo's game consoles.[56] Nintendo's program, called 10NES, consisted of a "lock" programmed into the console and a "key" programmed into each game cartridge. Atari, allegedly, had made a nonliteral, but quite similar and highly functional, copy of the 10NES "key."

In reviewing the district court's granting of a preliminary injunction for Nintendo, the Court first applied the abstraction phase of the *Computer Associates* test to "separat[e] the program into manageable components." The Court then moved to the filtration phase by analyzing those components to determine whether they were mere ideas, expressions necessarily incident to ideas, expressions dictated by external factors, or otherwise within one of the unprotected categories identified by *Computer Associates*.[57] The district court already had found that the "idea" of Nintendo's program was "the generation of a data stream to unlock a console," and that Nintendo's program went well beyond this idea and did not merge with it because it was one of "a multitude of different ways to generate a data stream which unlocks the NES console."[58] The Court of Appeals found that the Nintendo program was also not dictated by external factors and was not taken from the public domain.[59] Accordingly, the Court found that the district court had acted correctly when it found that Nintendo's program contained protectible expression.[60]

The Ninth Circuit Court of Appeals, like the Federal Circuit, elected to follow *Computer Associates* in a case involving a program designed to prevent use of unauthorized cartridges on computer game consoles. In *Sega Enterprises, Ltd. v. Accolade, Inc.* ("*Sega*"),[61] the defendant—Accolade—had "reverse engineered" the plaintiff's lock and key program, resulting in a nonverbatim, but functionally equivalent, version of the original. The defendant claimed that its reverse engineering of the original constituted fair use, and in the course of upholding this claim the Court of Appeals endorsed the *Computer Associates* approach to determining copyrightability.[62] More importantly, when asked to reconsider its finding of fair use in light of *Atari, supra*, the *Sega* court applied the *Computer Associates* analysis to distinguish *Atari*. Specifically, the Ninth Circuit found that while the Nintendo console in *Atari* could have

56. 975 F.2d 832 (Fed.Cir.1992). The jurisdiction of the U.S. Court of Appeals for the Federal Circuit is limited to appeals involving patents, international trade and claims against the Federal Government. In the *Atari* case, the Federal Circuit had jurisdiction over Nintendo's copyright claim because Nintendo also had brought a claim of patent infringement.

57. Atari, *supra*, 975 F.2d at 839–40.

58. *Id.* at 840.

59. *Id.*

60. *Id.*

61. 977 F.2d 1510 (9th Cir.1992).

62. Specifically, the Court used the *Computer Associates* analysis to determine the "nature of the copyrighted work"—the second of the four-part test of fair use. The concept of reverse engineering, and the *Sega* court's treatment of this claim, are discussed at section 11.8.B.2, *infra*.

been unlocked by any of a multitude of programs, Sega's lock could be opened only by a key consisting of "29 bytes of initialization code plus the letters S–E–G–A."[63] Accordingly, the expression of the Sega key effectively had merged with its idea and could not be protected by copyright.

The Fifth Circuit Court of Appeals has also endorsed the *Computer Associates* analysis. In *Engineering Dynamics, Inc. v. Structural Software, Inc.*,[64] the Court addressed the copyrightability of the input formats and sequences of a program used to design offshore oil platforms and other structures. The district court had dismissed the plaintiff's complaint in part, finding that "computer/user interface in the forms of input and output formats are uncopyrightable."[65] The Court of Appeals reversed this finding, and directed the district court to apply the *Computer Associates* analysis to determine whether the plaintiff's formats were dictated by industry standards and whether they had been infringed by the defendant.

The Tenth Circuit Court of Appeals also has endorsed the *Computer Associates* analysis. In *Gates Rubber Co. v. Bando Chemical Industries, Inc.*,[66] the Court reversed a district court decision finding that copyright protection extended to a program for the design of rubber belts. The district court, relying primarily on *Whelan*, had found that program elements such as numerical constants, control flow and data flow and engineering algorithms of the plaintiff's program were expressive of the program's "idea" and therefore protectible in copyright.[67]

The Tenth Circuit responded with what is perhaps the most careful and thorough appellate discussion so far of the *Computer Associates* analysis. The Court noted that "a computer program can often be parsed into at least six levels of generally declining abstraction: (i) the main purpose, (ii) the program structure or architecture, (iii) modules, (iv) algorithms and data structures, (v) source code, and (vi) object code."[68] The Court stated that of these various levels of abstraction, both the main purpose of the program and the individual purpose of each module always are unprotectible ideas, while source code and object code always are protectible unless otherwise required by the doctrines of merger and *scene a faire*.[69] According to the Court, all levels of abstraction between these abstractions must be examined for protectible elements under the Second Circuit's filtration process. Because the district court had "failed

---

63. Sega, note 61, *supra*, at 1524 n. 7.

64. 26 F.3d 1335 (5th Cir.1994), *opinion supplemented* 46 F.3d 408 (5th Cir.1995).

65. 785 F.Supp. 576, 582 (E.D.La.1991). The district court had relied on the Fifth Circuit's decision in *Plains Cotton, supra*, note 13, as holding that input formats cannot be separated from the uncopyrightable processes or ideas they implement. The holding of *Plains Cotton* was clarified, however, by the Fifth Circuit's subsequent decision in *Kepner-Tregoe, Inc. v. Leadership Software, Inc.*, 12 F.3d 527 (5th Cir.1994),

stating that "nonliteral aspects of copyrighted works—like structure, sequence and organization—*may* be protected under copyright law ..." 12 F.3d at 536, n. 20 (*emphasis in original*).

66. 9 F.3d 823 (10th Cir.1993).

67. Gates Rubber Co. v. Bando American, Inc., 798 F.Supp. 1499 (D.Co.1992).

68. Gates Rubber, 9 F.3d at 835.

69. *Id.* at 836.

to undertake a proper filtration analysis with respect to several elements and ... erroneously found other elements to be protectable," the case was remanded for application of a proper filtration analysis.[70]

While enormously and deservedly influential, the abstraction-filtration-comparison test remains a largely *ad hoc* approach that places severe demands on the technical expertise of courts. The importance of the test will decline if courts follow the lead of the recent decision in *Lotus Development Corp. v. Borland International, Inc.,*[71] and reject the application of abstraction-filtration-comparison to cases alleging infringement of user interfaces.

11.5 Protecting the User Interface

The user interface of a computer program is the set of input commands, screen outputs, menus and other features through which the program and its human user interact. Depending on the program, the user interface may include a set of keystroke commands, macro commands, a hierarchy of menus and submenus from which users can select functions and explanatory text to assist the user.

So long as computers were used only by professional programmers and hobbyists, software designers paid little attention to the ease with which users could interact with these exotic devices. For the most part, early computers demanded mastery of an extensive vocabulary of commands that were far from intuitive and required some understanding of the logical structure of the programs on which they were based.

All of this changed dramatically when the microchip turned data processing into a consumer industry. Software designers found that the most marketable feature of a program might have nothing to do with its efficiency at performing its particular task but everything to do with the ease with which a nontechnical customer could master its operation. Quite naturally, as the user interfaces of programs became a greater element of their commercial value, software companies looked for ways to protect their user interfaces against infringement. At the same time, designers of applications programs found that the marketability of their product depended on the degree of resemblance between their user interfaces and those with which users already were familiar.

In cases involving the alleged infringement of features of user interfaces, litigants have urged three different lines of analysis. One approach is the so-called "look and feel" theory, which urges courts to view the allegedly infringed program's user interface as a whole and ascertain whether the allegedly infringing program has copied its overall concept and feel. This theory has resisted clear articulation and has attracted few judicial or academic adherents.[1] Two other approaches, however, have proved more successful.

70. *Id.* at 842.

71. 49 F.3d 807 (1st Cir.1995), *aff'd by an equally divided Court,* 516 U.S. 233, 116 S.Ct. 804, 133 L.Ed.2d 610 (1996).

1. The "total concept and feel" approach first was applied in Roth Greeting Cards v. United Card Co., 429 F.2d 1106 (9th Cir.1970), in which the court held that

A number of courts have chosen to apply to user interfaces the same analysis used in cases involving other nonliteral features of computer programs. Notably, in *Lotus Development Corp. v. Paperback Software International* (*"Paperback"*),[2] the district court rejected the "look and feel" approach in favor of an analysis based on the abstraction analysis described by Learned Hand in *Nichols*. Similarly, in *Engineering Dynamics, Inc. v. Structural Software, Inc.*,[3] the Court of Appeals held that input and output formats are copyrightable and remanded the case to the district court to decide whether industry standards precluded copyrightability and to determine whether the plaintiff's user interface was infringed.[4]

Still another approach, far less congenial to plaintiffs, views user interfaces as mere methods by which users "operate" the computer, and therefore no more deserving of copyright protection than the H pattern of an automobile gearshift. This is the approach taken by the First Circuit Court of Appeals in *Lotus Development Corp. v. Borland International, Inc.* (*"Borland"*).[5] In *Borland*, the Court held that the menu command hierarchy of the Lotus 1–2–3 spreadsheet program is a mere method of operation, no more susceptible of copyright protection than "the buttons for operating a VCR . . . ."[6]

The scope of the *Borland* analysis is unclear and should not, pending judicial explication in future cases, cause undue alarm to the authors of user interfaces. Notably, the Court was careful to point out that in the case at hand it was called upon only to consider the copyrightability of the Lotus "menu command hierarchy standing on its own (*i.e.*, without other elements of the user interface, such as screen displays, in issue)." The Court also noted that other elements of the Lotus interface, including the long prompts and screen displays, are not necessary to the operation of the program and presumably are not methods of operation. Nonetheless, the *Borland* approach, which trumps the abstraction-filtration-comparison analysis wherever a user interface feature can be characterized as a method of operation, has led to interest in the use of trademark concepts (especially the notion of "trade dress") as an alternative to copyright protection of user interfaces.[7]

although the text of the allegedly infringed greeting cards was in the public domain, all elements of the cards taken together, including text, artwork, and the relationship between artwork and text, constituted copyrightable expression. The courts have not found this concept helpful in infringement cases involving computer programs, and Professor Nimmer, among other commentators, suggests that it be abandoned. *See* NIMMER § 13.03[A][1][c].

2.   740 F.Supp. 37 (D.Mass.1990).

3.   26 F.3d 1335 (5th Cir.1994), *opinion supplemented*, 46 F.3d 408 (5th Cir.1995).

4.   *See also* Autoskill, Inc. v. National Educational Support Systems, Inc., 994

F.2d 1476 (10th Cir.1993), cert. denied, 510 U.S. 916, 114 S.Ct. 307, 126 L.Ed.2d 254 (1993).

5.   49 F.3d 807 (1st Cir.1995), *aff'd by an equally divided Court*, 516 U.S. 233, 116 S.Ct. 804, 133 L.Ed.2d 610 (1996).

6.   A similar analysis was applied by the district court for the Northern District of Texas. Synercom Technology, Inc. v. University Computing Co., 462 F.Supp. 1003, 1013 (N.D.Tex.1978).

7.   *See, e.g.*, Two Pesos, Inc. v. Taco Cabana, Inc., 505 U.S. 763, 112 S.Ct. 2753, 120 L.Ed.2d 615 (1992).

11.6   Semiconductor Chips and the Mask Act

While most computer-related products have found intellectual property protection within the framework of laws that precede the invention of the computer, one category of product now is protected by a special-purpose statute that creates a hybrid form of intellectual property. This product is the semiconductor chip, which is protected under the so-called Mask Act.

As its popular name suggests, the Semiconductor Chip Protection Act ("SCPA")[1] protects semiconductor chips only indirectly, by protecting the circuit layout and stencils ("masks") by which electronic circuits are etched on a chip. The Congress concluded that a special statute was needed in order to prevent piracy of chips because of the inadequacy of existing intellectual property law. Specifically, mask works may not be protectible in patent because they do not meet the rigorous requirements of novelty and nonobviousness, and they do not qualify for copyright protection because they are utilitarian objects.

While the Mask Act is therefore *sui generis*, it draws heavily on established copyright principles. Notably, SCPA protection requires a modicum of creativity[2] and directly incorporates the copyright exceptions of idea/expression dichotomy and merger. Similarly, SCPA protection does not extend to any procedure, process, system, method of operation, concept, principle or discovery, or to similarities dictated by function.

The Mask Act does, however, appear to permit copying by reverse engineering, which the SCPA defines as reproducing the mask for the purpose of "analyzing or evaluating the concepts or techniques embodied in the mask work or the circuitry, logic flow, or organization of the components used in the mask work."[3] This exception, with its potential to swallow the Mask Act scheme of protection whole if liberally interpreted, has proved the most troubling of the SCPA's provisions.[4]

11.7   Copyright Protection of Computer Databases

One of the computer's greatest advantages is its ability to store and retrieve enormous quantities of data at a cost unattainable through nonelectronic means. Both private and governmental users of electronic data processing have exploited this capability to develop databases for applications ranging from census taking to payroll administration to marketing.

While electronic databases may have substantial value and represent significant investment, their eligibility for copyright protection is limited. In fact, where a database merely compiles information in the public

---

1.   17 U.S.C.A. §§ 901–914 (West 1996).

2.   H.R. Rep. No. 781, 98th Cong., 2d Sess. 19 (1984).

3.   17 U.S.C.A. § 906 (West 1996).

4.   *See* Brooktree Corp. v. Advanced Micro Devices, Inc., 705 F.Supp. 491 (S.D.Cal. 1988).

domain without adding any original matter, copyright protection may be entirely unavailable.

The law on this point is set out most authoritatively in the decision of the Supreme Court in *Feist Publications, Inc. v. Rural Telephone Service Co., Inc.* (*"Feist"*).[1] The plaintiff in *Feist* had claimed copyright protection for names and telephone numbers compiled in its telephone directory. The Court, rejecting lower court decisions finding that copyright protection could be based merely on the effort required to compile directories and other factual collections,[2] held that compilations of fact may be protected only insofar as they are "selected, coordinated, or arranged ... in an original way."[3] Facts themselves may not be copyrighted, and compilations of facts arranged in ways that are merely mechanical or routine may not be copyrighted.[4] To hold otherwise, in the Court's view, would overturn the constitutional requirement that copyright protection extend only to original works. The *Feist* decision is a matter of substantial concern to the owners of databases. While *Feist* allows database owners to protect the creative selection and organization of factual material, it offers no protection against wholesale copying of the facts themselves, regardless of the effort and expense their collection represents. This prospect has resulted in considerable lobbying for revision of the Copyright Act, and more recently for adoption of an international Database Treaty that, if adopted and ratified by the United States Senate, will overturn *Feist* in part by creating a *sui generis* property right in electronically compiled factual material.[5]

The Database Treaty is still under discussion within the World Intellectual Property Organization.[6] Even if the Treaty is adopted and ratified by the U.S. Senate, however, an amendment of the Copyright Act will be required before the Treaty's database protection provisions will be enforceable in the United States. Until then, copyright protection for database compilations remains "thin," as *Feist* requires.[7]

1. 499 U.S. 340, 111 S.Ct. 1282, 113 L.Ed.2d 358 (1991).

2. *See, e.g.,* Leon v. Pacific Telephone and Telegraph Co., 91 F.2d 484 (9th Cir. 1937); Jeweler's Circular Publishing Co. v. Keystone Publishing Co., 281 F. 83 (2d Cir. 1922).

3. *Feist, supra* note 12. As the opinion in *Feist* points out, the requirement of originality is not stringent and does not demand novelty but only some modicum of creativity. *Id.* at 345, 111 S.Ct. at 1287–88, 113 L.Ed.2d at 369. *See, e.g.,* West Publishing Company v. Mead Data Central, Inc., 799 F.2d 1219 (8th Cir.1986).

4. *Id.*

5. *See* John B. Kennedy and Shoshana R. Dweck, *WTO Pacts Go Digital*, The National Law Journal, Jan. 27, 1997 p. C–1. The proposed treaty is based in part on a Database Directive adopted by the European Union in 1996. *Id.*, p. C–29.

6. In the meantime, the World Intellectual Property Organization has adopted Article 5 of its Copyright Treaty, which provides that "[c]ompilations of data ... in any form, which by reason of the selection or arrangement of their contents constitute intellectual creations, are protected as such," but which also provides that copyright "protection does not extend to the data or the material itself and is without prejudice to any copyright subsisting in the data or material contained in the compilation." World Intellectual Property Organization Copyright Treaty, adopted by the Diplomatic Conference on December 20, 1996, Art. 5. This Article appears to be entirely consistent with *Feist*.

7. Even an appropriate amendment to the Copyright Act, creating copyright protection for facts contained in databases, will likely be challenged as a violation of the constitutional requirement of originality.

11.8 Proving Infringement of Computer Program Copyrights

A copyright gives its owner certain exclusive statutory rights. Specifically, these are: (1) the right to reproduce (*i.e.*, copy) the work; (2) the right to prepare derivative works based upon the copyrighted work; (3) the right to distribute copies of the work to the public; (4) the right to perform the work in public; and (5) the right to display the work in public.[1] In order to establish a claim for copyright infringement, the copyright owner must prove that the defendant violated one or more of these rights.

A. Tests for Infringement

1. Access Plus Substantial Similarity

Most infringement suits involving software allege violation of the reproduction right—*i.e.*, unlawful copying. Such claims may be proved in either of two ways: a plaintiff may offer direct evidence of copying, such as the testimony of a witness who saw the defendant copy the work; or the plaintiff may prove that the defendant had access to the work and that the plaintiff's and defendant's works are substantially similar.[2] Because direct evidence of copying rarely is available, all but a small number of infringement cases rely on proof of access and substantial similarity. In most infringement cases involving computer programs, the defendant's access to the allegedly infringed program is readily established. Proof of substantial similarity of the two programs, however, may present procedural and substantive difficulties to which traditional methods of proof are inadequate.

2. Audience Test

In cases involving traditional works of authorship, the courts have given considerable weight to a jury's spontaneous reaction to the works at issue. This so-called "ordinary observer" or "audience" test calls upon the trier of fact to decide whether an ordinary member of the intended audience, when exposed to both works, would immediately find them substantially similar "without any aid or suggestion or critical analysis by others."[3] The audience test has the advantage of simplicity, but also has at least two important limitations: it leaves the court little discretion to dismiss an infringement claim on a motion for summary judgment where substantial similarity is the dispositive issue;[4] and it makes little

---

1. 17 U.S.C.A. § 106 (West 1996).

2. 3 NIMMER § 13.01[B] at 13–11, 13–12.

3. Harold Lloyd Corp. v. Witwer, 65 F.2d 1, 18 (9th Cir.1933); *see also* Dawson v. Hinshaw Music Inc., 905 F.2d 731, 736 (4th Cir.), cert. denied 498 U.S. 981, 111 S.Ct. 511, 112 L.Ed.2d 523 (1990).

4. In spite of the inconsistency of the audience test with the disposition of substantial similarity claims by summary judg-

ment, a number of decisions granting summary judgment in such cases have been upheld. *See, e.g.,* Narell v. Freeman, 872 F.2d 907, 910 (9th Cir.1989); Olson v. National Broadcasting Co., 855 F.2d 1446 (9th Cir.1988). To the extent the audience test places the question of substantial similarity beyond the reach of summary judgment, it also is in tension with the Supreme Court's admonition that summary judgment be

sense when applied to complex creations and factual questions (such as a claim of similarity between a computer program and an alleged nonliteral copy of that program) as to which nonexperts cannot form a meaningful, spontaneous impression.

Fortunately, even before the advent of copyright litigation involving computer programs, some courts had adopted variants of the audience test that limit the role of the "ordinary observer." Notably, a number of decisions have divided the similarity analysis into two steps. The first step may be supported by expert testimony and be determined as a matter of law, and the second may be decided impressionistically (without analysis) under the audience test. The Second Circuit's version of a two-step test was articulated in *Arnstein v. Porter* ("*Arnstein*")[5] and calls for the trier of fact first to determine whether copying occurred and then to decide whether the copying was so extensive as to be unlawful. The Ninth Circuit's version of such a test was first stated in *Sid & Marty Krofft Television Productions, Inc. v. McDonald's Corp.* ("*Krofft*")[6] and calls for the trier of fact first to decide whether the general ideas of the two works are substantially similar (the "extrinsic test") and then to decide whether the expressions of those ideas in the two works are substantially similar (the "intrinsic test").

The audience test has shown particular strain when applied to software copyright cases. As a number of courts and commentators have recognized, it is pointless to pretend that lay triers of fact will have meaningful, impressionistic reactions to competing versions of source code, object code and nonliteral elements of computer programs.[7] Accordingly, some courts have abandoned the audience test altogether in infringement cases involving software or have adopted versions of the test that give a substantial role to objective analysis aided by expert testimony.

3. Modern Substitutes for the Audience Test

Among the courts that effectively have abandoned the audience test for complex works such as software are the Courts of Appeals for the Second and Third Circuits. The Second Circuit, while disclaiming any intention to displace the audience test for more traditional works of authorship, has given the district courts considerable latitude to decide the extent to which they will rely on expert opinion to resolve claims of

---

treated, not as a "disfavored procedural shortcut," but as "an integral part of the Federal Rules as a whole, which are designed 'to secure the just, speedy and inexpensive determination of every action.'" Celotex Corp. v. Catrett, 477 U.S. 317, 327, 106 S.Ct. 2548, 2555, 91 L.Ed.2d 265, 276 (1986).

5. 154 F.2d 464 (2d Cir.1946).

6. 562 F.2d 1157 (9th Cir.1977); *see also* Shaw v. Lindheim, 919 F.2d 1353 (9th Cir. 1990).

7. *See, e.g.*, Nimmer § 13.03[E][4] at 13–111, 13–112 ("...[I]t is meaningless to attempt to isolate the 'spontaneous and immediate' reaction of the lay observer to two sets of object code"); *see also* Whelan Associates, Inc. v. Jaslow Dental Lab., Inc., 797 F.2d 1222, 1232 (3d Cir.1986), cert. denied 479 U.S. 1031, 107 S.Ct. 877, 93 L.Ed.2d 831 (1987); Michael F. Sitzers, Note, *Copyright Infringement Actions: The Proper Role for Audience Reactions in Determining Substantial Similarity*, 54 S. Cal. L. Rev. 385 (1981).

substantial similarity involving computer programs. This appeals court has prescribed for software cases an "abstraction-filtration-comparison" analysis that cannot meaningfully be applied without extensive reliance on expert testimony.[8] Similarly, the Third Circuit Court of Appeals expressly has rejected the "ordinary observer test in copyright cases involving exceptionally difficult materials, like computer programs, [and] instead [has adopted] a single substantial similarity inquiry to which both lay and expert testimony would be admissible."[9]

Among the courts that have modified, rather than abandoned, the audience test in software cases are the Courts of Appeals for the Fourth and Ninth Circuits. In *Dawson v. Hinshaw Music Inc.* (*"Dawson"*)[10], the Fourth Circuit suggested modifying the audience test by replacing the "ordinary observer" with the "intended observer" as the person whose reaction will guide the determination of substantial similarity. This approach applies the two-step analysis of *Arnstein* but permits the second step to depart from reliance on lay reaction where the intended audience of the work possesses specialized expertise.[11] Similarly, while the Ninth Circuit has declined to reject its intrinsic/extrinsic variant of the audience test outright, it has permitted both lay and expert testimony as part of the intrinsic phase of the test.[12]

As these cases suggest, the continued vitality of the audience test is in doubt, particularly as applied to computer software and other works that cannot be understood without expert knowledge. The task of those who advocate outright abandonment of the test is made considerably easier by the Supreme Court's decision in *Feist*,[13] which sets out the elements of an infringement claim without mentioning the audience test. As Professor Nimmer suggests, the time may be right for "a paradigm shift of Copernican proportions ... in the law of copyright," involving the explicit abandonment of the audience test.[14] In the meantime, even

---

8. Computer Associates International, Inc. v. Altai, Inc., 982 F.2d 693, 705 (2d Cir.1992). The Second Circuit's abstraction-filtration-comparison test has proved to be enormously influential, and effectively displaces the audience test wherever it is applied.

9. Whelan Associates, Inc. v. Jaslow Dental Laboratory, Inc., 797 F.2d 1222, 1233 (3d Cir.1986), cert. denied 479 U.S. 1031, 107 S.Ct. 877, 93 L.Ed.2d 831 (1987); see also Gates Rubber Co. v. Bando Chemical Industries, Ltd., 9 F.3d 823, 835 (10th Cir.1993); Plains Cotton Coop. Assoc. v. Goodpasture Computer Service, Inc., 807 F.2d 1256, 1259 (5th Cir.1987), reh'g denied, 813 F.2d 407 (5th Cir.1987)(en banc), cert. denied 484 U.S. 821, 108 S.Ct. 80, 98 L.Ed.2d 42 (1987); E.F. Johnson Co. v. Uniden Corp. of America, 623 F.Supp. 1485, 1493 (D.Minn.1985).

10. 905 F.2d 731, 736 (4th Cir.), cert. denied 498 U.S. 981, 111 S.Ct. 511, 112 L.Ed.2d 523. (1990).

11. Although the particular work at issue in *Dawson* was not a computer program, the Court's opinion expressly includes computer programs among the categories of works to which application of the "intended audience" test would be justified.

12. *See, e.g.*, Brown Bag Software v. Symantec Corp., 960 F.2d 1465 (9th Cir.), cert. denied 506 U.S. 869, 113 S.Ct. 198, 121 L.Ed.2d 141 (1992). In Professor Nimmer's view, the *Brown Bag* case "signals potential abandonment of the audience test" by the Ninth Circuit. NIMMER § 13.03[E][4] at 13–112 n. 270.

13. Feist Publications, Inc. v. Rural Telephone Service Co., 499 U.S. 340, 111 S.Ct. 1282, 113 L.Ed.2d 358 (1991).

14. NIMMER § 13.09[E][1][b] at 13–90, 13–91.

courts that officially employ the audience test will continue to rely heavily on expert testimony to resolve claims of substantial similarity of computer programs.

B. Clean Rooms and Reverse Engineering

As the preceding section shows, where a program developer with access to another developer's copyrighted program writes a new program that is substantially similar to the original, the developer of the new program is likely to be found liable for infringement. In some cases, however, software developers have used techniques that permit them to copy or use information contained in existing programs to develop competing programs without incurring liability for infringement. These methods of software development are known as *clean room* and *reverse engineering* techniques.

1. Clean Room Technique

The clean room approach to software development divides the task of writing software between two programmers or teams of programmers. One team has access to an existing program and derives from that program a set of specifications for use by the second team. The second team does not have access to the existing program but develops a new program to meet the specifications provided by the first team.

If careful records of the clean room process are kept, those records may be used in an infringement suit to show that the defendant did not have access to the allegedly infringed program when it wrote the allegedly infringing program—thereby defeating the first prong of the "access-plus-substantial-similarity" test for proof of infringement. If established to the satisfaction of the court, strict observance of the clean room routine theoretically is equivalent to independent creation, which provides a complete defense to a claim of infringement.

It should be clear, however, that if the rights of copyright owners are to be protected, courts must impose a high evidentiary burden on defendants who offer to prove that a program was written through a clean room procedure. Since a defendant making this claim admits that someone under its control had access to the plaintiff's program before the new program was written, courts are properly concerned about the possibility that the conversation between the defendant's two programming teams went beyond the mere exchange of specifications. Also, the process by which the team with access to the plaintiff's program developed its list of specifications may have involved reverse engineering. Therefore, this process might support a wholly independent claim of unlawful copying.

The *Computer Associates* case offers an example of judicial skepticism toward the clean room approach.[15] In that case Computer Associates

---

15. Computer Associates International,   1992).
Inc. v. Altai, Inc., 982 F.2d 693 (2d Cir.

("CA") had developed CA–SCHEDULER, a job scheduling program that directed the tasks performed by IBM mainframe computers. In conjunction with and as part of CA–SCHEDULER, CA also had developed a program called ADAPTER that made CA–SCHEDULER compatible with different IBM operating systems. The defendant, Altai, wrote its own job scheduling program for IBM computers, and one of Altai's employees wrote an equivalent of ADAPTER, called OSCAR, to permit the Altai job scheduling program to run with different types of operating software.[16]

Unfortunately, Altai discovered, after receiving a demand from Computer Associates, that the employee who had written OSCAR had acquired a copy of ADAPTER while employed by CA and had copied substantial parts of the CA program. Accordingly, Altai ceased distribution of OSCAR and developed a new version through use of a clean room procedure. The former CA employee was barred from the rewrite process, which was conducted by one James P. Williams and a team of eight programmers. Williams provided the team with a description of the job scheduling program with which the new program would have to be compatible, and the eight programmers wrote the new program without access to ADAPTER or any portions of OSCAR that had been copied from ADAPTER.[17]

The district court, while conceding that "an argument could be made that Altai did not have access [to ADAPTER] because of the precautions attempted by Altai [during the rewrite process]. .,"[18] nonetheless noted unspecified conflicts in the evidence as to Williams' access to ADAPTER when that process was underway. Accordingly, the district court found that Altai had access to ADAPTER when it wrote its new program and moved on to determine whether ADAPTER and the clean room version of OSCAR were substantially similar.[19]

2.   Reverse Engineering

Reverse engineering presents somewhat different issues from the clean room procedure. Reverse engineering, broadly defined, is the examination of a finished product to determine how the product is made.[20] In the software context, reverse engineering is most commonly used to discover those unprotected elements of a program that must be emulated in order to write a second program that is compatible with the original.[21] Software engineers may accomplish reverse engineering in a number of ways, including the study of manuals and documentation. The

16. *Id.* at 698–99.

17. *Id.* at 700.

18. Computer Associates International, Inc. v. Altai, Inc., 775 F.Supp. 544, 558 (E.D.N.Y.1991).

19. *Id.*

20. *See* Kewanee Oil Co. v. Bicron Corp., 416 U.S. 470, 476, 94 S.Ct. 1879, 1883, 40 L.Ed.2d 315, 322 (1974) (defining reverse engineering as "starting with the known product and working backward to divine the process which aided in its development or manufacture").

21. So, for example, a designer writing a new word processing program might examine a popular operating system to discover the interface specifications with which the new word processing program must conform in order to run on that operating system.

most powerful method of software reverse engineering, however, is disassembly—*i.e.*, converting the electronic version of the program back into the series of ones and zeros that constitute the program's object code, storing the object code in a computer's memory, then translating the object code into readable source code.[22] Because this process involves the making of a copy of the original program, copyright owners have argued that reverse engineering through disassembly is an act of infringement, even where the ultimate product of the process—*i.e.*, the alleged infringer's new program—does not contain copyrightable elements of the original. Defenders of the practice, on the other hand, argue that designers are entitled to copy programs in order to learn how they are made, so long as any new program resulting from that effort does not contain protected elements of the original.

Two federal appellate courts have examined the legality of reverse engineering of software and both have concluded that although the practice does involve the making of an infringing copy, such copying may constitute "fair use" of the original that does not give rise to liability for infringement. Both cases involved the making of video game software that could be played on the "game consoles" of other, market-leading makers of video games.

In *Sega Enterprises Ltd. v. Accolade, Inc.*[23], defendant Accolade, Inc. ("Accolade") made game cartridges that could be played on the consoles of various game systems, including those manufactured by plaintiff Sega Enterprises Ltd. ("Sega"). Because each manufacturer's console contained software with unique interface specifications, and because game software that did not meet those specifications could not be played on those consoles, knowledge of the leading game systems' interfaces was essential to Accolade's business. Accolade failed to obtain a license for Sega's Genesis interface specifications and used a decompiler program to produce a source code version of the Genesis software from which the interface specifications could be derived. The result was a series of Accolade games that were compatible with, but did not contain protectible elements of, the Sega console software.

Sega sought and obtained a preliminary injunction preventing, *inter alia*, Accolade's disassembly of Sega's programs and the development and sale of Genesis-compatible games created through reverse engineering. In support of the entry of the preliminary injunction, the district court found that Sega probably would succeed in its claim that Accolade's disassembly of Sega's program was an act of copying not covered by the doctrine of fair use. Accolade appealed the grant of the preliminary injunction to the Ninth Circuit Court of Appeals where it argued that reverse engineering for the purpose of making a noninfringing program is *per se* lawful. Accolade also argued, in the alternative, that even if its conduct established a *prima facie* case of infringement the

---

22. Special programs called "decompilers" or "disassemblers" perform the task of reading a program in its electronic form (*e.g.*, imprinted on a microchip) and translating the program into object code and source code.

23. 977 F.2d 1510 (9th Cir.1992).

facts supported a defense of fair use. The appellate court's response to each of these arguments is worth recounting.

Accolade's claim that its conduct was *per se* lawful rested on three arguments. First, Accolade urged that no right of the copyright owner is infringed by "intermediate" copying that is done as part of the creation of a final product that is not substantially similar to the original. Second, Accolade contended that disassembly of a program does not infringe copyright because it is necessary in order to discover "ideas and functional concepts" of the original program that are not protected by copyright. Finally, Accolade claimed that its conduct was lawful under § 117 of the Copyright Act, which authorizes the owner of a copy of a program to make further copies for archival purposes or as an essential step in the use of the program.[24]

The Court rejected each of these arguments. Most fundamentally, the Court found that where an act presents all of the elements of copying under the Copyright Act, the fact that the copy is only an intermediate step in the creation of a noninfringing program does not make the copying *per se* lawful. The Court rejected the second argument, based on the idea/expression dichotomy, as assuming the discredited notion that object code is not fully protected by copyright. Finally, the Court found that the limited protection of § 117 of the Act, whatever its precise extent, cannot be stretched to cover "a user who disassembles object code, converts it from assembly into source code, and makes printouts and photocopies of the refined source code version."[25]

The Court did, however, uphold Accolade's reliance on the equitable defense of fair use. That doctrine, as set out in § 107 of the Copyright Act, requires the Court to assess the alleged infringer's conduct under four, nonexclusive criteria. These are:

(1) the purpose and character of the use, including whether such use is of a commercial nature or is for nonprofit or educational purposes;

(2) the nature of the copyrighted work;

(3) the amount and substantiality of the portion used in relation to the copyrighted work as a whole; and

(4) the effect of the use on the potential market for or value of the copyrighted work.[26]

Of these four factors, the Court found that only the third supported Sega's case. As to the first factor, the Court found that while Accolade's use of the Genesis program was commercial, the primary purpose of the copying—studying the functional requirements for compatibility with Genesis—was legitimate and not intended to misappropriate copyrighted elements of Sega's program or "avoid performing [Accolade's] own

---

24. *Id.* at 1517–18.

25. *Id.* at 1520.

26. 17 U.S.C.A. § 107 (West 1996).

creative work ...''[27] As to the second factor, the Court concluded that because the Genesis program was available only in object code and disassembly of that code was necessary in order to examine unprotected features of Sega's program, the "nature of the work" test weighed in favor of the defense.[28] Finally, as to the fourth (and most important) element of the defense, the Court found that Accolade's creation of competing programs did not substantially harm the marketability of Sega's games, and that in any event the exploitation of unprotectible interface specifications to maintain a monopoly "runs counter to the statutory purpose of promoting creative expression and cannot constitute a strong equitable basis for resisting the invocation of the fair use doctrine."[29] Taken together, factors one, two and four outweighed the fact the third factor—the "amount and substantiality" of Accolade's copying of the Genesis program—clearly favored Sega.

In addition to its discussion of the four nonexclusive, statutory elements of fair use, the *Sega* Court offered a useful discussion of the policy implications of reverse software engineering. The Court acknowledged the apparent incongruity of its finding that fair use permitted Accolade, "a commercial competitor of Sega, [to engage] in wholesale copying of Sega's copyrighted code as a preliminary step in the development of a competing product." But the Court defended this result as necessary to avoid conferring a monopoly over nonprotectible ideas and functional concepts. Specifically, the Court pointed out that where computer programs are distributed to the public in the form of object code, reverse engineering may be the only means of access to those ideas and functional concepts, including interface specifications, that will facilitate further creative work in the field. Permitting such copying as fair use is consistent with the purpose of the Copyright Act, which is to "stimulate artistic creativity for the public good," and with the Supreme Court's teaching that largely functional works are entitled only to weak copyright protection.[30]

In *Atari Games Corp. v. Nintendo of America, Inc.* ("*Atari*"),[31] the United States Court of Appeals for the Federal Circuit confronted a far less straightforward fact situation than the one presented in *Sega*. Like Accolade in the *Sega* case, Atari wanted to make and sell computer games that were compatible with a rival manufacturer's consoles—in this case the consoles made by Nintendo for Nintendo's computer games. Unlike Accolade, however, Atari did not simply disassemble publicly-available object code of the console program, but bolstered its reverse engineering effort with a copy of Nintendo's source code obtained by

27. Sega, 977 F.2d at 1522.

28. *Id.* at 1524.

29. *Id.* at 1523–24.

30. *Id.* at 1527, *citing* Feist Publications, Inc. v. Rural Telephone Serv. Co., Inc., [499 U.S. 340, 350] 111 S.Ct. 1282, 1290, [113 L.Ed.2d 358, 372 (1991)]. Sega also argued that to allow reverse engineering of its programs would permit others to become "free riders" on the effort and expense that Sega had incurred in developing those programs. The Court rejected this argument as an attempt to revive the "sweat of the brow doctrine," which had been put to rest by the Supreme Court in Feist, *supra* n. 13.

31. 975 F.2d 832 (Fed.Cir.1992).

making a false representation to the Copyright Office. Also, the program that Atari eventually developed included more of the Nintendo program than absolutely necessary to make Atari's game compatible with the Nintendo console. On these facts, a district court granted a preliminary injunction against Atari.

On appeal, the Federal Circuit found that Atari had infringed Nintendo's copyright when it copied the source code Nintendo had filed with the Copyright Office[32] and had also copied protected expression when it incorporated, in its own game program, elements of the Nintendo console program that were not necessary to ensure that Atari's game could be played on Nintendo's console. The Court considered, however, whether Atari's disassembly of the Nintendo program, apart from its wrongful acquisition of Nintendo's deposited source code and use of protected elements in its own game programs, constituted fair use. Relying on the purpose of the fair use doctrine, rather than the four-part test set out in the statute and applied in *Sega*, the Court determined that object code may be disassembled and an intermediate copy made for the purpose of understanding the unprotected "ideas and processes in a copyrighted work ..."[33] The Court cautioned, however, that "fair use reproductions of a computer program must not exceed what is necessary to understand the unprotected elements of the work," and may not be used "to misappropriate protectable expression."[34] Because the fair use doctrine is equitable and must be applied with careful attention to the facts of each case, *Sega* and *Atari* must not be read as supporting all disassembly and copying of computer programs to create programs that are compatible with the originals. Those cases do, however, support a general rule that disassembly of object code to make an intermediate copy is fair use when it is the only means of gaining access to the unprotectible elements of a program and the person disassembling the program does so for a legitimate purpose.

While the fair use doctrine plainly offers substantial protection for reverse engineering of software, owners of program copyrights often try to preempt the fair use defense by including terms in their software licenses that forbid reverse engineering. A number of defenses may plausibly be raised, however, to efforts by copyright owners to enforce these provisions under state contract law. Notably, where the prohibition against reverse engineering is contained in a "shrink-wrap" license, the prohibition may be attacked as a contract of adhesion.[35] Similarly, where

---

32. *Id.* at 841–42. Although the Copyright Act permits the copying of deposited material so long as Copyright Office regulations are observed, the means by which Atari's counsel had obtained Nintendo's deposited source code violated those regulations. Accordingly, Atari could not avail itself of the statutory exemption.

33. *Id.* at 843. The Court did rely on the second part of the test—the nature of the work—to point out that because the nature of object code requires disassembly and intermediate copying in order to understand the ideas and processes expressed in object code, the second part of the fair use test supports such disassembly and intermediate copying.

34. *Id.*

35. Software sold to the mass market typically is packaged with a "shrink-wrap" license. While such licenses obviously are not negotiated with the purchasers of the

enforcement of the license prohibition in state court would create rights that are equivalent to those protected by the Copyright Act, a defendant might argue that the enforcement action is preempted by the Act.[36] Finally, an action to enforce such a license provision might constitute misuse of copyright.[37]

11.9 Other Intellectual Property Protections of Computer Programs

While copyright is the most common choice for intellectual property protection of software, the scope of copyright protection for these works suffers from important limitations. Notably, as discussed earlier in this chapter, some of the most valuable features of computer programs are nonliteral elements that may be classified as noncopyrightable ideas, processes or methods of operation.[1] And as a previous section of this chapter also points out, even where a program or program element proves eligible for copyright protection, the copyright owner is not protected against independent creation of a similar or identical program.[2]

For program designers seeking to avoid these limitations of copyright, the principal alternative is patent law. Patents may protect the systems, processes and methods of operation that expressly are excluded from the copyright regime. Patents also create comprehensive rights against infringing inventions, even where those inventions are the products of independent creation rather than copying.

But patent law, no less than copyright law, poses some obstacles to program designers seeking to protect their creations. One obstacle is the high threshold of novelty and nonobviousness that a patentable invention must meet and the correspondingly rigorous disclosure and review process that would-be patentees must undergo. Another, more fundamental obstacle is the limited extent to which the Patent Office and the courts treat computer programs as patentable subject matter. This chapter considers each of these problems in turn.

A. Statutory Requirements for Patent Protection

A patent is a twenty-year monopoly on the manufacture, use and sale of a useful process, machine, manufacture or composition of matter.[3]

programs, the packaging and installation programs of mass-marketed software typically declare that the purchaser accepts the terms of the license by opening the package or proceeding with the installation program. The software industry is seeking recognition of shrink-wrap licenses in a pending, revised version of Article 2 of the Uniform Commercial Code. For an appellate decision upholding the enforceability of shrink-wrap licenses generally, *see* ProCD, Inc. v. Zeidenberg, 86 F.3d 1447 (7th Cir.1996).

36. 17 U.S.C.A. § 301(a) (West 1996).

37. *See* Lasercomb America v. Reynolds, 911 F.2d 970 (4th Cir.1990).

1. *See* section 11.4, *supra.*

2. *See* section 11.3A at n. 6, *supra.*

3. Until the Congress amended the Patent Act in 1994, patents were good for seventeen years from the date the patent was granted. Under the current statute, patent protection begins on the date the patent is granted and ends twenty years from the date of filing of the application. Uruguay Round Agreements Act, Pub. L. 103–465, *reprinted in* 1994 U.S. Code Cong. & Admin. News 4809, 4984 (1994).

In order to qualify for patent protection, an invention must come within one of these categories and must meet additional statutory requirements of utility, novelty, nonobviousness and enabling disclosure. The Patent and Trademark Office ("PTO") will issue a patent only after an examiner determines that each of these requirements has been met.

The utility and novelty requirements are less exacting than the requirements of nonobviousness and disclosure. To show utility, the applicant merely describes the use or uses to which the invention will be put.[4] To establish novelty, the applicant asserts—and the patent examiner must confirm—that the invention has not previously been completely disclosed.[5]

The third requirement—nonobviousness—is the most difficult of the statutory standards to satisfy. Specifically, the applicant must establish that the invention is not only novel but improves upon the existing technology ("prior art") in a way that would not be obvious to "a person having ordinary skill" in that technology.[6] Determining whether a claimed invention satisfies this requirement demands an exercise of expert judgment by the patent examiner, based on an exhaustive search of the relevant prior art.[7]

Finally, a patent will issue only for a fully-disclosed invention. Section 112 of the Patent Act requires the inventor to provide "a written description of the invention and of the manner and process of making and using it, in such full, clear, concise, and exact terms as to enable any person skilled in the art to which it pertains ... to make and use the same, and shall set forth the best mode contemplated by the inventor of carrying out his invention."[8] The disclosure requirement is much more than a procedural hurdle: disclosure of the invention, so that it becomes part of the publicly available pool of useful knowledge, is the primary consideration for grant of the patent monopoly.[9]

---

4. 35 U.S.C.A. § 101 (West 1996).

5. 35 U.S.C.A. §§ 101, 102 (West 1996).

6. 35 U.S.C.A. § 103 (West 1996).

7. The patent law requirements of novelty and nonobviousness bear little resemblance to the copyright law concept of originality. Although the Copyright Act limits its protection to original works of authorship, originality in copyright means only that the person seeking protection for a work, and not someone else, is the works's author, and that the work displays some minimal element of creativity. So long as the work is original to the author, of more than trivial scale and not a mere collection of facts organized in an obvious way, it will be protected even if it is tired, cliched, and represents no creative advance over other works of its kind.

8. 35 U.S.C.A. § 112 (West 1996). *See also* 35 U.S.C.A. § 119 (West 1996), which requires "such full and complete disclosure of the preferred embodiment of the invention as enables one skilled in the art to make it without undue experimentation." Until the patent is issued, however, and thereafter if a patent is not granted, the disclosures in the application are treated as confidential. 35 U.S.C.A. § 122 (West 1996).

9. Here, too, the patent law regime is substantially more rigorous than copyright. In the software context, for example, a program submitted to the Patent Office must be sufficiently detailed to permit replication of the program by anyone reading the application. A program submitted for copyright registration, on the other hand, is permitted to contain no more than 50 pages of the program's code, and is not required to facilitate duplication of the program. The different approaches reflect the fact that a patent application must disclose technology, while deposit of a work for copyright purposes only identifies the work for which protection is claimed.

The designer of a program must carefully consider its ability to meet the statutory requirements of utility, novelty, nonobviousness and disclosure before deciding whether to seek patent protection. Even where these requirements are satisfied, however, a designer's ability to secure patent protection will be determined by whether that program, or any computer program, is regarded by the Patent Office and the courts as patentable subject matter.

B. *Computer Programs as Patentable Subject Matter*

Patent, like copyright, is intended to protect certain intellectual creations and exclude others. No matter how useful, novel and nonobvious an invention is, it may be patented only if it falls within one of the four statutory categories of "process, machine, manufacture, or composition of matter," or represents a "new and useful improvement " upon an invention that falls within one of those four categories.[10]

While the four categories of patentable subject matter are not defined in the statute, they have been given some content by the courts. A process is "[t]he transformation and reduction of an article to a different state or thing . . . "[11] and may be patented even where the result of the process is not, itself, a patentable invention. A machine is a physical device that accomplishes some useful work, and also may be referred to as an "apparatus."[12] "Manufacture" has been judicially defined as "the production of articles for use from raw or prepared materials by giving to these materials new forms, qualities, properties, or combinations, whether by hand labor or by machinery."[13] Finally, "composition of matter" has been defined to include "all compositions of two or more substances and . . . all composite articles, whether they be the results of chemical union, or of mechanical mixture, or whether they be gases, fluids, powders or solids."[14] Because the first category refers to acts rather than objects, while the second, third and fourth categories refer to things, the patent universe often is divided between process patents, on the one hand, and product (*i.e.*, machine, manufacture and composition of matter) patents, on the other.[15]

---

10. 35 U.S.C.A. § 101 (West 1996); *see* Kewanee Oil Co. v. Bicron Corp., 416 U.S. 470, 94 S.Ct. 1879, 40 L.Ed.2d 315 (1974). In addition to these statutory categories of patentable subject matter, the Patent Act also recognizes plant patents and design patents. Plant patents cover new plant varieties that reproduce asexually, and design patents cover the appearance of articles of manufacture. 35 U.S.C.A. §§ 161–164, 171–173 (West 1996).

11. Diamond v. Diehr, 450 U.S. 175, 184, 101 S.Ct. 1048, 1055, 67 L.Ed.2d 155, 164 (1981), *quoting* Gottschalk v. Benson, 409 U.S. 63, 68–70, 93 S.Ct. 253, 256–57, 34 L.Ed.2d 273, 278 (1972).

12. In re Prater, 415 F.2d 1393, 1395 n. 11 (C.C.P.A. 1969).

13. Diamond v. Chakrabarty, 447 U.S. 303, 100 S.Ct. 2204, 65 L.Ed.2d 144 (1980), *quoting* American Fruit Growers, Inc. v. Brogdex Co., 283 U.S. 1, 11, 51 S.Ct. 328, 330, 75 L.Ed. 801, 807 (1931).

14. *Id.*, *quoting* Shell Development Co. v. Watson, 149 F.Supp. 279, 280 (D.D.C. 1957).

15. The categories may overlap in particular inventions: for example, an applicant may claim patent protection for an invention that includes both a product and the process by which the product is made.

In the course of applying the statutory categories of patentable subject matter to particular patent claims, the courts have identified certain intellectual creations that fall outside the statutory categories. Notably, the courts have found that patents may not issue for phenomena of nature, even where those phenomena were unknown before the applicant discovered them.[16] Similarly, scientific principles, or the mathematical expressions of such principles, may not be patented;[17] nor may patent protection be claimed for a process that consists entirely of the steps one would follow to apply a mathematical principle to solve a mathematical problem.[18] The application of a law of nature or scientific principle to a "new and useful end," however, may be patented.[19]

Unfortunately for patent protection of computer programs, both the Patent Office and some courts have tended to view programs as mere writings, which are *per se* outside the categories of patentable subject matter, or as unpatentable mathematical formulae or "algorithms."[20] In fact, for several years the Patent Office simply refused to grant patents on computer programs or programmed computers—a situation that began to change only in 1969, when the Court of Customs and Patent Appeals ("CCPA")reversed some of those decisions. As a result of the CCPA's action, a number of computer program patents were issued between 1969 and 1972.

In 1972, however, the United States Supreme Court issued its decision in *Gottschalk v. Benson* ("*Benson*"). In *Benson*, the Court considered the patentability of a program that converted binary-coded decimal (BCD) numbers to pure binary numbers.[21] According to the applicant, the conversion of numbers from one form to another, as accomplished by the program, was a "process" within the meaning of Section 101 of the Patent Act. Justice Douglas, writing for the Court, found that the process claim was for a "generalized formulation for programs to solve mathematical problems of converting one form of numerical representation to another"—a claim so "abstract and sweeping" as to amount to an attempt to patent an idea, rather than a process. Specifically, the Court concluded that because the BCD-to-binary conver-

---

16. *See, e.g.,* Gottschalk v. Benson, *supra* n. 11; Funk Bros. Seed Co. v. Kalo Inoculant Co., 333 U.S. 127, 130, 68 S.Ct. 440, 441, 92 L.Ed. 588, 592 (1948).

17. Mackay Radio & Telegraph Co. v. Radio Corp., 306 U.S. 86, 94, 59 S.Ct. 427, 431, 83 L.Ed. 506, 510 (1939).

18. *See, e.g.,* Diamond v. Diehr, *supra* note 11 at 185, 101 S.Ct. at 1056. 67 L.Ed.2d at 165–66 (1981).

19. Kalo, *supra,* note 16.

20. Broadly defined, an algorithm is any "step-by-step procedure for solving a problem or accomplishing some end." In re Freeman, 573 F.2d 1237, 1245 (C.C.P.A. 1978), *quoting Webster's New Collegiate Dictionary* (1976). Defined in this way, many patentable processes are algorithms.

Accordingly, the Patent Office does not deny protection to all algorithms, but only to so-called mathematical algorithms, which are defined as "procedure[s] for solving . . . given type[s] of mathematical problem[s]." Gottschalk, *supra,* n. 16, at 65, 93 S.Ct. at 254, 34 L.Ed.2d at 276.

21. A BCD is a way of representing decimal, rather than binary, numbers. The BCD number represents each digit of a decimal number with a 4–bit binary code. Because computers can use only true binary numbers, each incoming BCD digit must be converted to a 16–bit or 32–bit binary number before the computer can execute the program.

sion program had "no substantial practical application except in connection with a computer," a patent on the program effectively would grant a monopoly on use of the mathematical algorithm itself, no matter what the particular application. While the Court in *Benson* was careful to deny that its decision "preclud[ed] a patent for any program servicing a computer," the *Benson* decision discouraged patent attorneys and their clients from seeking patent protection for computer programs and programmed computers, and encouraged the Patent Office to grant very few such patents.

The chilling effect of the *Benson* decision was reinforced in 1978, when the Court issued its decision in *Parker v. Flook* ("*Flook*" [22]). In *Flook*, the claim was for a patent on a program for updating alarm limits in catalytic converters. Catalytic converters convert hydrocarbons and are useful in a number of industrial processes. In the course of the conversion process, catalytic converters measure such variables as temperature, pressure, and flow rates and signal an alarm when any of the variables exceeds a defined limit. The subject invention included an "algorithm" by which the alarm limits could be changed to take into account conditions, such as start-up, in which the standard alarm limits might not be sufficient.

The Court of Customs and Patent Appeals had held that while the alarm limit algorithm itself might not be patentable, the entire process of which the algorithm was a part was a patentable process. The CCPA distinguished the invention before it from the program in *Benson*, pointing out that since solution of the algorithm alone was insufficient to infringe the claimed patent before it, granting the patent would not amount to conferring a monopoly on a principle alone.[23]

Urging the Supreme Court to uphold the CCPA's decision on appeal, the applicant in *Flook* argued that even if the algorithm itself was an unpatentable principle, the invention also involved "post-solution activity"—*i.e.*, a patentable process that occurred after the solution of the algorithm to update the alarm limits. Specifically, the applicant argued that the "the adjustment of the alarm limit to the figure computed according to the formula" made the invention more than a mere principle.[24]

The Supreme Court, however, found that the process for which the patent was claimed was not novel, and that the algorithm—which was novel—could not be patented. On the issue of patentability, Justice Stevens' opinion for the Court confused the issue drastically by finding, not that the invention fell outside the categories of patentable subject matter, but that the claimed invention failed to meet the criteria of novelty and inventiveness. Specifically, Justice Stevens found that be-

22. 437 U.S. 584, 98 S.Ct. 2522, 57 L.Ed.2d 451 (1978).

23. In re Flook, 559 F.2d 21, 23 (C.C.P.A. 1977) *rev'd*, 437 U.S. 584, 98 S.Ct. 2522, 57 L.Ed.2d 451 (1978).

24. *Id.* at 590, 98 S.Ct. at 2525, 57 L.Ed.2d at 454.

cause a mathematical formula is one of the "basic tools of scientific and technological work," it cannot be new and inventive and must be treated as within the prior art; and "once [the] algorithm is assumed to be within the prior art, the application, considered as a whole, contains no patentable invention."[25]

Fortunately, the Supreme Court's most recent teaching on the patentability of computer programs confirms that while programs alone may not qualify for patent protection, otherwise patentable inventions incorporating programs may be patented. In *Diamond v. Diehr* ("*Diehr*"),[26] the Court reviewed a process for molding raw synthetic rubber into cured products. The applicants had claimed that their process improved upon prior art by constantly measuring the temperature inside the rubber mold. Those measurements then were fed to a computer that recalculated the cure time as the temperature in the mold fluctuated, using an equation already well-known in the industry. When the cure time had elapsed, the computer automatically sent a command to open the press.

The patent examiner had rejected these claims, finding that the functions carried out by a programmed computer were not patentable subject matter and that the remaining steps were "conventional and necessary to the process and [could] not be the basis of patentability."[27] The Patent and Trademark Office Board of Appeals upheld the rejection of the patent, but the Court of Customs and Patent Appeals reversed that decision.

The Supreme Court concluded that the patent claim in *Diehr* described a patentable process—specifically, the "transformation of an article, in this case raw, uncured synthetic rubber, into a different state or thing . . ."[28] Having found that the claims described a patentable process, the Court then refused to find that the process became nonstatutory simply because "in several steps of the process a mathematical equation and a programmed digital computer are used."[29] The Court in

---

25. 437 U.S. at 591, 594, 98 S.Ct. at 2526, 2527–2528, 57 L.Ed.2d at 458, 459. Justice Stevens' opinion was severely criticized, both in the dissent in *Parker* and in a subsequent decision of the Court of Customs and Patent Appeals. Application of Bergy, 596 F.2d 952 (C.C.P.A. 1979), *vac'd in part,* 444 U.S. 1028, 100 S.Ct. 696, 62 L.Ed.2d 664 (1980). The principal criticism was that Justice Stevens had confused the categories of patentable subject matter in § 101 of the Act with the requirements for patentable inventions set out in § 102. "It is one thing to say that a natural cause, or formula, *per se,* is not within the categories of § 101, but quite another to say it is 'prior art' in determining the nonobviousness of an invention predicated on it even though the inventor discovered it." *Bergy, supra,* 596 F.2d at 966. In the view of the CCPA, Justice Stevens' reading jeopardized

"the long-standing proposition of law that patentability may be predicated on discovering the cause of a problem even though, once that *cause* is known, the solution is brought about by obvious means." *Id.* Justice Stevens' duel with the Court of Customs and Patent Appeals continued with his dissent in Diamond v. Diehr, in which he criticized "the lower court's expansive approach to § 101 during the past 12 years . . ." 450 U.S. at 205, 101 S.Ct. at 1066, 67 L.Ed.2d at 177.

26. Diamond v. Diehr, *supra,* note 11.

27. *Id.* at 181, 101 S.Ct. at 1054, 67 L.Ed.2d at 161.

28. *Id.* at 184, 101 S.Ct. at 1055, 67 L.Ed.2d at 162.

29. *Id.* at 185, 101 S.Ct. at 1056, 67 L.Ed.2d at 163.

Diehr was careful to distinguish the process patent before it from the claims it rejected in *Benson* and *Flook*. In *Benson*, the Court explained, the respondent had sought to patent an algorithm "the sole practical application [of which] was in connection with the programming of a . . . digital computer." [30] In that case, therefore, to patent the claimed process was equivalent to patenting the algorithm. Similarly, in *Flook* the respondent sought patent protection for an "alarm limit," and contained no disclosure concerning such patentable subject matter as "the chemical processes at work, the monitoring of process variables, or the means of setting off an alarm or adjusting an alarm system." [31] The claim in *Flook* was confined entirely to an algorithm. The rubber curing process in *Diehr*, by contrast, did not seek to preempt the use of the mathematical equation employed in the process—only to preclude the use of the equation by others "in conjunction with all of the other steps in their claimed process." [32]

In a series of decisions entered both before and after *Diehr*, the Court of Customs and Patent Appeals and its successor, the Court of Appeals for the Federal Circuit, developed a two-part test for evaluation of process claims involving computers. First, the Patent Office is to determine whether the claim recites a mathematical algorithm. In applying this step of the analysis, the Patent Office is to distinguish mathematical algorithms, which are procedures for solving mathematical problems and are not patentable subject matter, from other algorithms that may be patentable processes. [33] If the claim does not involve a mathematical algorithm, then the Patent Office will not reach the second step. If the claim does include a mathematical algorithm, then the Patent Office must determine whether remaining elements of the claim are "otherwise statutory." [34] While the courts and the Patent Office have not offered an exhaustive list of criteria to guide this second step, the Patent Office has suggested that it will be helpful to determine whether the mathematical algorithm is "applied to any patentable process steps." If the invention proves to be patentable under the second step of the analysis, then the use of a mathematical algorithm as part of the invention will not, in itself, defeat the applicant's claim.

The teaching of *Diehr* and subsequent cases is reasonably clear. A computer program, standing alone, almost certainly will be classified as a mathematical algorithm rather than a statutory process and will not qualify for patent protection. Where a computer program is part of a patentable process, however, or is an element of an invention belonging to one of the other statutory categories, the use of a computer program

30. *Id.* at 185–86, 101 S.Ct. at 1056, 67 L.Ed.2d at 163.

31. *Id.* at 187, 101 S.Ct. at 1057, 67 L.Ed.2d at 164.

32. *Id.*

33. *See, e.g.,* Paine, Webber, Jackson & Curtis, Inc. v. Merrill Lynch, Pierce, Fenner & Smith, 564 F.Supp. 1358, 1367 (D.Del. 1983)("The CCPA [has] . . . held that a computer algorithm, as opposed to a mathematical algorithm, is patentable subject matter"). As noted earlier, "every step-by-step process" is an algorithm, but not all are mathematical algorithms. *See, e.g.,* In re Grams, 888 F.2d 835 (Fed.Cir.1989).

34. In re Abele, 684 F.2d 902 (C.C.P.A. 1982).

in the invention will not deprive that invention of patent protection. Given this legal context, software designers are well advised to regard copyright, rather than patent, as their primary source of intellectual property protection.

C. Trade Secret Protection of Computer Programs

In the early years of commercial computer technology, when most transactions were negotiated sales of mainframe computers and software to large customers, trade secret was a more important method of protecting computer technology than it is today. By requiring their employees and customers alike to sign trade secret agreements, hardware and software manufacturers could prevent disclosure of valuable technology at a time when the availability of copyright and patent protection for computer programs and programmed computers was less certain than it is today.

While the development of a mass computer and software market has made trade secret protection less practical for many companies, and judicial recognition of the copyrightability and patentability of programs has made the trade secret alternative less critical, mainframe computer manufacturers and designers of custom software may still sometimes rely on trade secret law. Also, even in the mass software market, designers use trade secret to protect the source code on which the object code programs distributed to the public are based.

In order to prevent, or obtain compensation for, disclosure of information that they regard as trade secrets, hardware and software makers must comply with the trade secret laws of the states in which they will seek to enforce those rights. While the elements of a cause of action for a trade secret violation vary somewhat from state to state, the following elements generally apply:[35]

>   (1) the plaintiff must possess commercially valuable information, the value of which is attributable in part to its secrecy;

>   (2) the plaintiff must have taken reasonable steps to preserve the secrecy of the information;

>   (3) the defendant must have agreed to keep the information confidential or must have acquired the information through wrongful means; and

>   (4) the defendant must have disclosed or used the information, or there must be a likelihood that the defendant will disclose or use the information, in a way that is inequitable to the plaintiff.

Both conceptually and practically, it is important to keep in mind that unlike patent and copyright, trade secret law does not protect information *per se* but rather protects information that is kept in certain

---

35. The states have three recognized sources of trade secret law from which to fashion their own rules. These are RESTATEMENT OF TORTS § 757 (1938); the UNIFORM TRADE SECRETS ACT (1985 Approved Draft), 14 UNIFORM LAWS ANNOTATED 537 (1979) (adopted in more than forty states); and the RESTATEMENT (THIRD) OF UNFAIR COMPETITION (1995).

ways against persons who engage in certain kinds of wrongful conduct with respect to that information. The chief limitation of trade secret protection is that it can be so readily lost either by inadvertent public disclosure, failure to secure sufficient confidentiality commitments from employees or customers, or because the realities of the marketplace make it impossible to maintain a policy of secrecy. The chief advantage of trade secret protection is that by taking sufficient measures to secure the confidentiality of commercially valuable information, hardware and software makers may acquire enforceable rights against disclosure of information that is not protected by patent or copyright.

D. Trademarks and the Computer

Trademarks are names, symbols and other devices used by makers and vendors of goods to distinguish their products from those made and sold by others.[36] Where a person has adopted and used a trademark in commerce, he or she may prevent others from using that trademark in ways that cause confusion as to the origin of goods or that harm the property rights associated with the trademark.

Unlike copyrights and patents, trademarks are not mentioned in the United States Constitution. Accordingly, trademark law first developed in the state courts as a branch of the common law of unfair competition. Today, however, the most important source of trademark law is the national registration scheme set out in the Lanham Act.[37] While this complex body of law cannot be discussed here in detail, a brief review of the subject will assist in understanding the application of trademark law to computer technology.

Trademark rights are based largely on priority of use, and the most important tool in determining priority is the system of federal registration. In order to quality for registration, a trademark must meet two criteria: it must be distinctive and it must not present a likelihood of confusion with another trademark.

The distinctiveness requirement means that in order to function as a trademark, a name, symbol or device must distinguish the goods made or sold by one person from the goods made or sold by others or, in other words, the mark must be distinctive. Certain marks, known to the law as generic and descriptive marks, are incapable of performing this function unless they have acquired a secondary meaning that associates them with a particular producers' goods.[38] Other marks, categorized as suggestive, arbitrary or fanciful marks, are purely or primarily distinctive.

---

36. *See* 15 U.S.C.A. § 1127 (West 1996). The law also protects service marks, which include "any word, name, symbol, or device, or any combination thereof [used] to identify and distinguish the services of one person ... from the services of others and to indicate the source of the services." *Id.* Because the procedural and substantive law governing trademarks and service marks is essentially the same, we use the term "trademark" here to refer to devices of both kinds.

37. 15 U.S.C.A. §§ 1127 *et seq.* (West 1996).

38. Descriptive marks indicate some feature (*e.g.*, "light" or "nonshrink") of a product, while generic marks identify the category of product or service (*e.g.*, "car" or "videocassette recorder") of which a partic-

The requirement that a mark not present a likelihood of confusion means simply that in order to be registered, a mark must not so resemble a mark registered in the Patent and Trademark Office, or a mark or trade name previously used in the United States and not abandoned, as to be likely, when used, to "cause confusion, or to cause mistake, or to deceive . . ."[39] Whether a mark is likely to cause confusion will depend on a number of factors, including the similarity of the mark to one previously used and the similarity of the products to which the two marks are applied, as well as the nature of the markets and the sophistication of consumers in those markets.

When a trademark meets these criteria and is registered with the Patent and Trademark Office, the registration is effective for ten years and may be renewed at ten-year intervals.[40] So long as the trademark is not abandoned, the trademark owner may bring legal action against anyone who infringes the trademark—*i.e.*, against anyone who uses, in commerce, a copy or imitation of the trademark that is likely to cause confusion, mistake or deception.[41]

Where an infringement action is brought, and assuming the plaintiff's trademark is found to be valid and enforceable,[42] the focus of the trier of fact will turn to the "likelihood of confusion" caused by the defendant's allegedly infringing use. Determining whether a subsequent use is likely to cause confusion is a complex inquiry that includes examination of the following factors:

(1) the similarity of the plaintiff's and the defendant's marks;

(2) the similarity of the goods or services in connection with which the marks are used;

(3) the nature of the markets in which the plaintiff's and defendant's goods or services are sold;

(4) the strength of the plaintiff's mark; and

---

ular producer's product or service is a member. Unlike descriptive marks, generic marks are not eligible for trademark protection even where they have acquired secondary meaning.

39. 15 U.S.C.A. § 1051(a)(1)(A) (West 1996).

40. 15 U.S.C.A. § 1058 (West 1996).

41. 15 U.S.C.A. § 1114(1) (West 1996). Trademarks that have not been registered with the Patent and Trademark Office also may be enforced against subsequent, infringing uses, but such actions will lack certain procedural and substantive benefits conferred by federal registration. Notably, federal registration gives the registrant nationwide rights in the trademark, confers federal court jurisdiction over any enforcement action, and makes the trademark incontestable after five years continuous use. 15 U.S.C.A. § 1065 (West 1996).

42. The notion of incontestability becomes important at this stage of the inquiry. Before a trademark becomes incontestable through five years of federally-registered use, enforcement may be denied on the ground that the trademark is merely descriptive—*i.e.*, that it indicates a characteristic of the product rather than its origin. After the trademark becomes incontestable, enforcement may be denied only if the trademark is generic—*i.e.*, if it defines the product to which it refers. So, for example, if the Ace Typewriter Company made a small, lightweight typewriter that it marketed as its "portable" model, and brought an action to enforce the trademarks "portable" and "typewriter," it might succeed in enforcing the first mark—but not the second—after those marks achieved incontestability.

(5) the defendant's intent.[43]

Of these criteria, the most important are the similarity of the marks, the similarity of the goods or services and the nature of the markets. The fourth element—strength of the mark—may be persuasive but rarely is dispositive.[44] The last element—the defendant's intent—does not itself affect the likelihood of confusion, but evidence of intent may have some value in the liability element of a close case[45] and becomes directly relevant where a plaintiff seeks equitable relief.[46]

In addition to the protections it affords to trademarks, the Lanham Act regulates certain unfair trade practices that are independent of trademark infringement and affect interstate commerce. Specifically, section 43(a) of the Lanham Act[47] creates a federal right of action for false statements of fact about a defendant's products or services that are likely to deceive consumers and cause injury to plaintiff. The section 43(a) cause of action reaches the common law tort of "palming off," or representing one's own goods as those of another, and also reaches other false statements, such as claiming properties for a product that the product does not have, where those statements are likely to cause confusion and harm competitors.[48] Where the elements of a section 43(a) cause of action are established, the plaintiff may obtain injunctive relief without proving actual damages.[49]

Trademark law is, or may become, especially important to the computer hardware and software industries in at least three ways. First, where software and hardware makers design their products for compatibility with those of other suppliers, they will wish to advertise this fact

43. *See, e.g.,* White v. Samsung Electronics of America, Inc., 971 F.2d 1395 (9th Cir.1992); Electronic Design and Sales, Inc. v. Electronic Data Systems Corp., 954 F.2d 713 (Fed.Cir.1992).

44. Purely fanciful marks—*i.e.,* marks that convey no information about the nature of the product except through their association with that product in the public mind—are stronger than marks that also have descriptive meanings. A fanciful mark may present a good case for a finding of infringement, both because subsequent uses of such a mark are unlikely to be innocent and because limiting the commercial use of such marks will not reduce the available stock of useful, descriptive phrases.

45. For example, if the independent evidence of likelihood of confusion is inconclusive, the fact that the defendant intended to use the trademark to mislead the public as to the origin of goods or to trade on the goodwill of plaintiff becomes an effective admission that confusion is likely.

46. The equitable nature of trademark law also makes it appropriate for the courts to recognize certain kinds of noninfringing "fair use" of trademarks. Notably, a trademark may be used, even in a commercial context, for the purpose of fair comment—*i.e.,* comparing one supplier's product or service to that of another supplier. The law also permits collateral use of trademarks, as where a manufacturer uses a trademarked product as part of another product. Both the fair comment and collateral use defenses, however, will be defeated by uses of the trademark that are deceptive or likely to cause confusion.

47. 15 U.S.C.A. § 1125 (West 1996).

48. For example, a defendant's claim to manufacture "potato chips" that were in fact processed potato products was found to violate section 43(a) of the Lanham Act on the ground that the false statement was likely to confuse consumers and harm defendant's competitors. Potato Chip Institute v. General Mills, Inc., 333 F.Supp. 173 (D.Neb.1971), *aff'd,* 461 F.2d 1088 (8th Cir. 1972).

49. Monetary damages will be awarded under section 43(a), however, only where the plaintiff proves actual financial loss. *See* Johnson & Johnson v. Carter–Wallace, Inc., 631 F.2d 186 (2d Cir.1980).

and to use the trademarks of compatible suppliers in the course of that advertising. Because interoperability and compatibility with market-leading operating systems, in particular, are so vitally important to success in the software industry, the ability to use trademarks in this way may become a matter of survival for makers of applications programs. Second, the continuing uncertainty concerning the scope of copyright protection for the user interfaces of computer programs makes trademark, and especially the trademark concept of "trade dress," or the distinctive manner of presentation of one's product or service including its overall composition and design, including size, shape, color, texture and graphical presentation,[49A] attractive as an alternative source of protection. Third, the growing importance of the World Wide Web as a commercial outlet for products and services of all kinds has made trademark protection for domain names, which identify sites on the Web, an area of growing controversy.

Use of trademark to advertise similarity between computer products has been considered in two reported cases. In *Sierra On-Line, Inc. v. Phoenix Software, Inc. ("Sierra")*,[50] the Ninth Circuit Court of Appeals affirmed the entry of a preliminary injunction against the defendant's use of the expression "Hi–Res Adventure" in advertisements for its computer games. Plaintiff used this same expression, for which trademark registration was pending, to indicate that its games offered a realistic and detailed high-resolution graphic display. The Court of Appeals affirmed the trial court's determination that the plaintiff had a reasonable chance of proving that the subject expression, although descriptive, had acquired a secondary meaning and that defendant's use of the phrase in its advertising was not a non-trademark fair use of the expression. In the other reported decision, *Apple Computer, Inc. v. Formula International, Inc. ("Formula International")*[51], a computer manufacturer was enjoined from using the word "Pineapple" as a trademark for a kit from which a functionally identical computer to those of Apple Computer, Inc. could be made. The trial court found that the defendant's use of the name "Pineapple" on its kits was confusingly similar to plaintiff's use of the name "Apple" as a trademark for similar goods.[52]

There are no reported decisions determining whether trademark may be used to protect the user interfaces of computer programs. Some commenters have found encouragement for this idea, however, in the Supreme Court's decision in *Two Pesos, Inc. v. Taco Cabana, Inc. ("Two*

49A. *See* Coach Leatherware Co. v. AnnTaylor, Inc., 933 F.2d 162, 168 (2d Cir. 1991).

50. 739 F.2d 1415 (9th Cir.1984).

51. 562 F.Supp. 775 (C.D.Cal.1983).

52. The trademark concept of trade-dress is also available as a means of protecting the nonfunctional graphical elements of a user interface. *See* Two Pesos, Inc. v.

Taco Cabana, Inc., 505 U.S. 763, 112 S.Ct. 2753, 120 L.Ed.2d 615 (1992); Engineering Dynamics, Inc. v. Structural Software, Inc., 26 F.3d 1335, 1350 (5th Cir.1994), supplemented on denial of rehearing 46 F.3d 408 (5th Cir.1995); Interactive Network, Inc. v. NTN Communications, Inc. 875 F.Supp. 1398, 1408 (N.D.Cal.1995).

Pesos").[53] In that case, the Court held that a Mexican restaurant chain's distinctive method of decoration could be protected from infringement under section 43(a), and that so long as the trade dress was nonfunctional and distinctive, there was no requirement that the trade dress also have acquired a secondary meaning. Accordingly, under *Two Pesos*, the nonfunctional, graphical elements of a user interface are potentially protectible under trademark law.

11.10 Intellectual Property and Networked Communications

The growth of on-line communications among computers, including the Internet and thousands of network services ranging from large, international information gateways to bulletin board services run by hobbyists, has raised new questions of copyright and trademark protection. Some commentators have suggested that the on-line environment stretches the traditional doctrines of copyright law, in particular, so severely that some copyright doctrines cannot be applied meaningfully to on-line services.[1] Protection of trademarks in cyberspace also has been complicated, not only by the new avenues of infringement that on-line services provide, but by the creation of a new device—the World Wide Web domain name—in which trademark rights are claimed and through which those rights may be violated.

A. Copyright in Cyberspace

According to the Copyright Act, copyright protects "works of authorship fixed in any tangible medium of expression . . . from which they can be perceived, reproduced, or otherwise communicated, either directly or with the aid of a machine or device."[2] Neither this language, nor the Copyright Act's definitions of particular categories of works of authorship, limits the physical media or technical methods by which works may be "fixed in [a] tangible medium of expression."[3] Accordingly, works of authorship are protected in their digital as well as their analog incarnations.

---

53. 505 U.S. 763, 112 S.Ct. 2753, 120 L.Ed.2d 615 (1992).

1. *See, e.g.*, David Nimmer, *Brains and Other Paraphernalia of the Digital Age*, 10 Harv. J. Law & Tech. 1 (1996); *see also* Egbert J. Dommering, *Copyright Being Washed Away through the Electronic Sieve*, in THE FUTURE OF COPYRIGHT IN A DIGITAL ENVIRONMENT, (P. Bernt Hugenholtz ed. 1996); Wendy M. Malone, *Contributory Liability for Access Providers: Solving the Conundrum Digitalization Has Placed on Copyright Laws*, 49 Fed. Comm. L.J. 491 (1997); John Perry Barlow, *The Economy of Ideas: A Framework for Rethinking Patents and Copyrights in the Digital Age (Everything You Know about Intellectual Property is Wrong)*, Wired, Mar. 1994 p. 84.

2. 17 U.S.C.A. § 102(a) (West 1996).

3. So, for example, the Copyright Act defines literary works as "works, other than audiovisual works, expressed in words, numbers, or other verbal or numerical symbols or indicia . . ." *Id.* § 101. Audiovisual works, in turn, are defined as "works that consist of a series of related images which are intrinsically intended to be shown by the use of machines or devices such as projectors, viewers, or electronic equipment . . ." *Id.* Nothing in these definitions excludes literary or audiovisual works fixed as binary code on a compact disk, computer hard drive, microchip or other tangible medium from which those works can be perceived reproduced or otherwise communicated.

The scope of copyright protection for digital works is complicated, however, by the movement of digitized works from one computer to another, which presents questions of direct and indirect infringement that have no precise counterparts in the nondigital world.

The issues might usefully be approached through a hypothetical. Suppose that Ada Augusta, a computer programmer and poetry lover, wants to form an on-line poetry club. She decides to start by downloading poetry from the Internet and sharing it with her friends. Ada's old computer is not Internet-ready, so she buys and installs a fast modem and a communications software package. She also must subscribe to an Internet access provider, or ISP, that will connect her telephone line to the Internet backbone network.[4] She calls her friend Zeke, who operates an ISP service called ZekeCom, and arranges a subscription to his service.

Ada is now ready to log onto the Internet. She instructs her modem to dial ZekeCom, and a welcoming page from her friend Zeke appears on the monitor of her computer. She undertakes an on-line search and finds a bulletin board service, or BBS, called "Beats On-line," run by someone named Carlo Marx. Beats On-line, which reaches the Internet through a large ISP called Scorched Earth Communications, claims to have an exhaustive collection of works by Kerouac, Ginsberg, Snyder, Ferlinghetti and the other major Beat poets, as well as works by relative unknowns. Some of Beats On-line's poems were scanned into the BBS server and posted to the BBS by Carlo Marx, while others were "uploaded" by third parties who subscribe to Beats On-line. Ada browses through the Beats On-line poetry collection, scanning several pages of poetry by Snyder and Ginsberg. She decides her friends might want to read Ginsberg's "Howl", so she stores that poem in her computer's hard drive and prints a copy of the poem on her laser printer. She then exits the BBS.

Each stage of the process we have described presents incidents of arguable copyright infringement. Some of those incidents—for example the posting of poems to Beats On-line and Ada's making of a permanent copy of "Howl"—involved deliberate actions that fit more or less comfortably within our intuitive understanding of copyright infringement. Other incidents, however—such as Ada's mere act of browsing through poems that she did not copy in her hard drive or send to her printer—may not strike us intuitively as violations of copyright owners' rights. And still other incidents—such as the postings of poems to the BBS by subscribers and the automatic replication of the poems in the ISPs' servers as those poems are transmitted from the BBS to Ada's computer—raise troubling questions concerning the liability of human agents

---

4. Internet service providers ("ISPs") purchase high-capacity, dedicated lines that connect their servers—directly or indirectly—to a point of access to the Internet backbone. Subscribers to these services gain access to the Internet by connecting their computers to the ISP's server. Business subscribers typically use a dedicated, private line for this purpose, while residential subscribers' modems dial their ISPs' servers over the subscribers' home telephone lines.

who merely provide the facilities through which postings and replications of digital works are made.[5]

As our hypothetical suggests, cyberspace can be a hazardous environment for BBS operators, ISPs, and ordinary Internet users who post, transmit, and gain access to copyrighted works. ISPs, in particular, are threatened by the difficulty of controlling the uses others make of their facilities: a threat made especially harsh when the ISP's involvement is scrutinized under the strict liability standard of direct copyright infringement, which takes no account of the ISP's inability to supervise the content of the data it carries.

The following sections discuss the application of current law to all of the players and incidents in our hypothetical, beginning with the law of direct liability for infringement and continuing with the indirect theories of contributory infringement and vicarious liability.

1. Direct Infringement in Cyberspace

As noted earlier, direct infringement of copyright is a strict liability offense. The offense is established whenever a defendant has violated one of more of the following, exclusive rights of the copyright owner:

(1) the right to reproduce the work;

(2) the right to prepare derivative works based upon the work;

(3) the right to distribute copies of the work to the public;

(4) the right to display the work in public; and

(5) the right to perform the work in public.[6]

To understand the application of these rights to our hypothetical, we might begin with Carlo Marx's scanning of poems into his server for posting to the Beats On-line BBS. Because these are Marx's own deliberate acts, the liability questions are relatively straightforward. By scanning copyrighted poems into his server without permission, Marx created digitized copies that violated the copyright owners' reproduction rights. By placing those copies in a publicly available place for viewing and downloading by others, Marx probably violated the copyright owners' display and distribution rights, as well.[7]

The postings to the Beats On-line BBS by subscribers present more difficult issues. The liability of subscribers for their own postings, like Marx's liability for scanning poems into his server, is straightforward: by

---

5. The poems also may have been replicated and stored in other facilities along the transmission path.

6. 17 U.S.C.A. § 106 (West 1996).

7. Copyright owners have the exclusive rights to distribute and display protected works to the public, but they may not, for example, prevent the distribution and display of lawfully-acquired copies to a group of friends and acquaintances of the person owning the copy. See 2 MELVILLE B. NIMMER,

COPYRIGHT § 8.14[c] at 8–169 (1993). This requirement could present a fact issue where postings are made to a BBS or other on-line service with a particularly small, closed group of users. The fact that access to the BBS was limited to paid subscribers, however, would not preclude a finding of public distribution and display. See Playboy Enterprises, Inc. v. Frena, 839 F.Supp. 1552, 1557 (M.D.Fla.1993).

sending copyrighted poems to Marx's server for storage, display and downloading, the subscribers violated the copyright owners' reproduction rights and arguably violated the rights of distribution and display, as well. More controversially, however, at least one judicial decision concludes that BBS operators like Marx may be directly liable for their subscribers' infringing postings, simply because the ISPs provided a facility or service through which those works were publicly distributed.[8]

Marx and his subscribers are not the only parties to the infringing postings. Those postings also were stored and transmitted through the facilities of Marx's ISP, Scorched Earth Communications. Is Scorched Earth also a direct infringer in this case? In part, this question presents the same issue as imposition of liability on Marx for third party posting: *i.e.*, can someone be found liable merely for providing a facility or service that others use to commit infringing acts? However, purely passive ISPs like Scorched Earth also are sometimes said to present another question—specifically, whether they should enjoy the same immunity from liability for the content of communications made over their systems that common carrier telephone and telegraph companies traditionally have enjoyed.

This question has been posed in two reported decisions, and both courts have concluded that ISPs are not common carriers. In *Netcom*, a case in which the ISP defendant *wished* to be treated as a common carrier, the court pointed out that the common carrier immunity was created in order to facilitate the responsibility of monopoly telephone and telegraph companies to serve all customers indifferently—an obligation not imposed on ISPs, which may refuse to deal.[9] The court in *CompuServe Inc. v. Cyber Promotions, Inc.*,[10] a case in which the ISP defendant *resisted* treatment as a common carrier, reached the same conclusion. These decisions undoubtedly are correct: the common carrier regime, which is declining as a legal model even in the industries to which it traditionally applied,[11] should not be extended to industries that

---

8. *Id.*; *see also* Sega Enterprises, Inc. v. MAPHIA, 857 F.Supp. 679, 683 (N.D.Cal. 1994). In the *Playboy* case, a BBS operator made his facilities available for uploading and downloading of digital copies of photographs in which plaintiff owned copyrights. The court found that merely by making the photographs available on his system the defendant violated both the distribution and display rights of the copyright owner. The better approach is to treat Marx's liability under the standards for contributory infringement and vicarious liability, which will take into account Marx's knowledge of, contribution to, ability to control and financial interest in the infringing activity. Otherwise, as one court has pointed out, those who commit conscious acts of infringement will be no more liable than those whose contribution to the infringement is entirely passive and unconscious. Religious Technol-

ogy Center v. Netcom On-line Communication Services, Inc. ("Netcom"), 907 F.Supp. 1361, 1372–73 (N.D.Cal.1995).

9. *Id.* at 1369 n. 12.

10. 962 F.Supp. 1015 (S.D.Ohio 1997). In *Netcom, supra*, the ISP sought to avoid responsibility for a subscriber's infringement by invoking the common carrier exemption. In *Cyber Promotions, Inc. v. American Online, Inc.*, 948 F.Supp. 436 (E.D.Pa. 1996), the plaintiff, a sender of bulk, unsolicited electronic mail (known in the on-line world as "spam") characterized the ISP defendant as a common carrier in order to impose on the ISP an obligation to transmit the plaintiff's messages.

11. *See* Telecommunications Act of 1996, Pub. L. No. 104–104, 110 Stat. 56, § 401, *codified at* 47 U.S.C.A. § 159 (West 1996). This section of the 1996 Telecommu-

do not enjoy regulatory monopolies and therefore have none of the corresponding common carrier obligations.

Ada's downloading of copyrighted poems from the Beats On-line BBS presents its own set of infringement questions. Ada's acts of downloading were of two kinds. First, Ada scanned through a number of poems on her computer's monitor without loading them into her hard drive or creating any hard copies on her printer. Second, Ada placed a copy of Ginsberg's "Howl" in permanent memory in her computer's hard drive and printed a hard copy of that poem as well. These two incidents of downloading present somewhat different infringement issues.

When Ada downloaded poems in order to browse through them, her computer arguably made two copies of those poems: a digital copy stored temporarily in random access memory ("RAM") and another copy in the form of a display on her computer's monitor. Each of these "copies" had disappeared by the time Ada stopped browsing and logged off her computer. Is Ada's browsing through these poems an act of copying within the meaning of the Copyright Act?[12] And if browsing is an act of copying, and thereby *prima facie* an infringement of an exclusive right of the copyright owner, should it be immunized from liability as fair use?

The notion that mere browsing might lead to liability for copyright infringement has been the source of considerable contention. One argument against such liability is that the temporary copies made in RAM, or displayed on the computer's monitor, are too ephemeral to satisfy the "fixation" requirement of the Copyright Act. Proponents of this argument correctly point out that the Copyright Act protects only works of authorship that are "fixed in [a] tangible medium of expression"—a requirement that is satisfied when a work's "embodiment in a copy or phonorecord ... is sufficiently permanent or stable to permit it to be perceived, reproduced, or otherwise communicated for a period of more than transitory duration."[13] No court, however, has so far found that RAM copies and screen displays fail to satisfy the fixation requirement, and some decisions lend support to a contrary result.[14]

The question of fixation by RAM copying was squarely presented in *MAI Systems Corp. v. Peak Computer, Inc.*[15] MAI Systems, Inc. ("MAI") accused Peak Computer, Inc. ("Peak"), a computer maintenance company, of infringing MAI's computer program copyright when it performed

nications Act gives the Federal Communications Commission broad discretion to dismantle the traditional structure of common carrier regulation in the U.S. telecommunications industry.

12. Because Ada does not make the RAM or audiovisual versions of the works available to others, the rights of public distribution and display are not implicated in her browsing.

13. 17 U.S.C.A. § 101 (West 1996).

14. *See* MAI Systems Corp. v. Peak Computer, Inc., 991 F.2d 511 (9th Cir. 1993); Stern Electronics, Inc. v. Kaufman, 669 F.2d 852 (2d Cir.1982); Williams Electronics, Inc. v. Artic International, Inc., 685 F.2d 870 (3d Cir.1982); *but see* NLFC, Inc. v. Devcom Mid–America, Inc., 45 F.3d 231 (7th Cir.1995); Lewis Galoob Toys, Inc. v. Nintendo of America, Inc., 964 F.2d 965 (9th Cir.1992).

15. 991 F.2d 511 (9th Cir.1993).

testing and maintenance on a computer manufactured by MAI and owned by a customer of Peak. The alleged copying occurred when Peak's technician switched on the customer's computer and ran an operating system of which MAI owned the copyright. While conceding that the customer that owned the copies of the programs contained in the hard drive was entitled to download and run those programs, MAI argued that third parties could not do so without infringing MAI's copyright. In its defense, Peak argued that the RAM version of MAI's program was too ephemeral to qualify as a copy of a protected work. The Court of Appeals, however, upheld the district court's finding that "by showing that Peak loads the software into the RAM and is then able to view the system error log and diagnose the problem with the computer, MAI has adequately shown that the representation created in the RAM is 'sufficiently permanent or stable to permit it to be perceived, reproduced, or otherwise communicated for a period of more than transitory duration.' "[16]

Screen displays also have been found to satisfy the fixation requirement. In *Williams Electronics, Inc. v. Artic International, Inc.* ("*Artic*"),[17] the defendant was accused of infringing the plaintiff's copyrights in the visual displays of a video arcade game. The defendant argued that the two audiovisual displays, known as the "attract mode" and "play mode" of the arcade game, were insufficiently fixed to qualify as protected works.[18] Specifically, the defendant pointed out that the game's attract mode was constantly changing (albeit in a repetitive sequence of images), and that the play mode changed each time the player interacted with the program. The Court of Appeals, however, found that the shifting visual displays generated by plaintiff's game programs were "sufficiently permanent or stable to permit [them] to be perceived, reproduced or otherwise communicated for a period of more than transitory duration."[19]

MAI and *Artic* notwithstanding, it is likely that some RAM copies and audiovisual displays will be found to be too evanescent to satisfy the fixation requirement. Those cases, however, are unlikely to involve browsing: if a copyrighted document remains in memory or on a screen long enough to be browsed, then courts are likely to find that it has been

---

16. The Court of Appeals also found support for its conclusion in the district court decision in Apple Computer, Inc. v. Formula International, Inc., 594 F.Supp. 617 (C.D.Cal.1984), which concluded that loading software into RAM creates a copy; and in those authorities holding generally that "loading of software into a computer constitutes the creation of a copy under the Copyright Act." MAI, 991 F.2d at 519, *citing* Vault Corp. v. Quaid Software Ltd., 847 F.2d 255, 260 (5th Cir.1988); 2 Melville B. Nimmer, Copyright, § 8.08 at 8–105 (1983); FINAL REPORT OF THE NATIONAL COMMISSION ON THE NEW TECHNO-LOGICAL USES OF COPYRIGHTED WORKS at 13 (1978).

17. 685 F.2d 870 (3d Cir.1982).

18. The "attract mode" is the shifting visual display shown on the arcade game's screen when no one is playing the game. The "play mode" is the video display presented when the game is played, which changes in response to inputs from the player's "joystick" or other device.

19. Williams Electronics, Inc. v. Artic International, Inc., 685 F.2d 870, 874 (3d Cir.1982). *See* 17 U.S.C.A. § 101 (West 1996).

"perceived, reproduced or otherwise communicated for a period of more than transitory duration."[20]

2. *The Right to Read and "Fair Use"*

Yet another argument against liability for browsing suggests that temporary browsing is indistinguishable from reading a book, which no one treats as an act of copying.[21] According to this view, the digital copying that occurs in the course of downloading should not be counted as an infringing act so long as the only result is the reading of the document on the screen of a computer's monitor.

However appealing this so-called "right to read" argument may be, it is a matter for congressional rather than judicial action: the courts cannot apply such a doctrine in derogation of exclusive rights plainly reserved to copyright owners under the present Copyright Act. If Ada's browsing results in the making of a copy within the meaning of the Copyright Act, then Ada's right to read the document must be protected, if at all, by the defense of fair use, and by the various protections the Copyright Act affords for so-called "innocent infringers."[22] The former will preclude a finding of liability at all, while the latter will reduce the penalties the infringer otherwise might suffer.

In most cases of downloading on-line material for browsing and other private, noncommercial purposes, the fair use defense will have a strong probability of success. The Copyright Act provides that "the fair use of a copyrighted work ... for purposes such as criticism, comment, news reporting, teaching, ... scholarship or research, is not an infringement of copyright."[23] The statute also lists four factors that courts are to consider in deciding the fair use defense in particular cases:

(1) the purpose and character of the use, including whether such use is of commercial nature or is for nonprofit educational purposes;

(2) the nature of the copyrighted work;

(3) the amount and substantiality of the portion used in relation to the copyrighted work as a whole; and

(4) the effect of the use upon the potential market for or value of the copyrighted work.[24]

20. 17 U.S.C.A. § 101 (West 1996).

21. *See* Jessica Litman, *The Exclusive Right to Read*, 13 Cardozo Arts & Ent. L.J. 29 (1994). In traditional media, "[t]o read a copyright text is no violation, only to copy it in writing." *See also* Ithiel De Sola Pool, Technologies of Freedom 214 (1983).

22. For example, criminal liability for copyright infringement is incurred only by those who act wilfully and for commercial advantage or private financial gain; and even civil liability, while it requires no intent on the part of the infringer, may be moderated by the discretion given the courts to impose only token penalties on innocent infringers. 17 U.S.C.A. §§ 504(c)(2), 506(a) (West 1996).

23. *Id.* § 107.

24. *Id.* Of these four factors, the last—the effect of the alleged infringement on the potential market for the work—is the most important. Harper & Row Publishers, Inc. v. Nation Enterprises, 471 U.S. 539, 566, 105 S.Ct. 2218, 2233, 85 L.Ed.2d 588, 611 (1985).

In fact, the courts have shown themselves willing to uphold defenses of fair use in cases of noncommercial downloading of copyrighted material. In *Religious Technology Center v. F.A.C.T.NET, Inc.*,[25] the defendant, F.A.C.T.NET, was a nonprofit organization involved in the ongoing controversy concerning the practices, teachings and tax-exempt status of the Church of Scientology. In connection with this activity, the defendant had obtained certain unpublished works in which the Church of Scientology claimed copyright and had scanned those works into the F.A.C.T.NET computer. It appeared that the defendant also had given copies of the materials to a F.A.C.T.NET director, one Arnold P. Lerma, who posted some of those materials on the Internet. Except for the Lerma posting, the allegedly copyrighted works had been held in a "private portion of the FACNET library" that was not available to the public, through the Internet or otherwise.[26]

On the plaintiff's motion for preliminary injunction, the district court found that the plaintiff had not shown a substantial likelihood of success on the merits. Specifically, the court found that all of the alleged activity, including the scanning of the Church of Scientology materials into F.A.C.T.NET's computer and Lerma's posting of some of those materials on the Internet, appeared to fall within the defense of fair use. The court relied for this conclusion on the noncommercial nature of the defendant's enterprise and on the absence of any evidence to show that the posting of the Church of Scientology documents to the Internet would have any effect on the potential market for those works.[27] In a district court case involving some of the same parties as *F.A.C.T.NET*, *supra*, the Religious Technology Center sued Arnaldo Lerma, The Washington Post, an Internet access provider and two reporters for copyright infringement. Mr. Lerma had posted certain documents on the Internet through the facilities of the Internet access provider, Digital Gateway Systems ("DGS").[28] The documents in question were 69 pages of so-called "Advanced Technology" works in which the Church of Scientology claimed a copyright. The works originally had been appended to an affidavit filed in open court by Steven Fishman, a former member of the Church of Scientology. The Washington Post and its reporters, who received a copy of the materials from Lerma, then independently acquired a copy of the materials from the court in which Fishman's affidavit had been filed.

Upon defendants' motion for summary judgment, the court had little difficulty finding that all of the conduct complained of satisfied the requirements of fair use. The court found that the defendants used the documents for news gathering, news reporting and responding to litigation; that the materials were more informative than creative, justifying a "broader fair use approach"; that the portions of the total works appropriated by defendants were no more than fragmentary; and that

---

25. 901 F.Supp. 1519 (D.Colo.1995).

26. *Id*. at 1521.

27. *Id*. At 1526.

28. Religious Technology Center v. Lerma, 908 F.Supp. 1362 (E.D.Va.1995).

the alleged infringement would have no significant effect on the potential market for the complete works.[29] Accordingly, the court entered summary judgment for defendants.

As these cases suggest, the defense of fair use is fact-specific and favors noncommercial uses that have no significant economic impact on the copyright owner. Returning to our hypothetical, these factors would provide a defense for Ada, whose downloading of a few poems for a noncommercial purpose may not have had much impact on the market for those works. They provide less comfort for the website operator, however, whose ongoing enterprise (even if noncommercial) might have a more substantial impact on the market for the copyrighted works of the Beat poets. Fair use is also an uncertain defense for passive infringers, such as the operators of intermediate servers, who cannot know the character or market impact of the bytes moving over their facilities.

From the standpoint of the on-line community, in fact, fair use, the "innocent infringer" provisions of the Copyright Act and other protections that are available only after a *per se* case of infringement is established must seem a poor corrective to the perceived unfairness of applying traditional notions of direct infringement to the digital world. From this perspective, a more satisfactory solution would be a broad exemption from direct liability for violations of the exclusive rights that do not involve conscious action or result in the making of permanent copies. The courts cannot recognize such *per se* exemptions, however, without a change in the Copyright Act.[30]

As might be expected, a number of legislative and international treaty initiatives have been proposed that seek to clarify liability for direct copyright infringement in cyberspace. The most notable such initiative had its origins in the so-called National Information Infrastructure White Paper ("White Paper"), written by a task force that had been formed by President Clinton in 1993.[31] The White Paper recommended an amendment to § 106(3) of the Copyright Act that would supplement the copyright owner's right of distribution with a right of transmission. (The present Copyright Act recognizes transmission only in connection with performances or displays of a work.) The White Paper recommended a definition of transmission of a reproduction as distribution "by any device or process whereby a copy or phonorecord of the work is fixed beyond the place from which it was sent."[32]

The intent of the White Paper proposal, which has not yet led to new legislation, is to ensure that the copyright owner's exclusive right to distribute copies of a work applies in the digital environment. The transmission right addresses a subtle conceptual difficulty posed by digitized copying: *i.e.*, the fact that when a digitized copy of a document

29. *Id.* at 1366–67.

30. Nor, as discussed further below, is this necessarily the best solution.

31. INTELLECTUAL PROPERTY AND THE NATIONAL INFORMATION INFRASTRUCTURE: THE REPORT OF THE

WORKING GROUP ON INTELLECTUAL PROPERTY RIGHTS (*"White Paper"*) (1995).

32. White Paper, n.2 at app. 1 § 1(b)(2).

is distributed over the Internet, the original copy is replicated rather than transferred.[33] The new language expands the notion of distribution to take this feature of digital transmission into account.

More importantly, the right of transmission contemplated by the White Paper confers an important benefit on copyright owners. The transmission right, by augmenting the right of distribution rather than the right of reproduction, avoids the difficulty of determining at what point a replication of a digitized work in a server or random access memory is too fleeting to qualify as a copy.

But there is also a pro-user dimension to the proposed transmission right. The White Paper does not propose removal of the requirement that an infringing distribution must be to the "public." While the scope of public distribution in the on-line world is unclear, the White Paper concedes, for example, that transmitting a "copyrighted work from one person to another in a private e-mail message would not constitute a distribution to the public."[34] The White Paper also cautions, however, against assuming that the notion of "public" in the distribution right for copies is coextensive with the counterpart notion in the context of public performance or display.[35] The point at which on-line distribution of copyrighted documents will violate the White Paper's proposed transmission right, therefore, is unclear.

Although the White Paper's transmission right has not been enacted into law, a movement in the World Intellectual Property Organization ("WIPO") may ultimately have a similar effect. In December of 1996, WIPO adopted a Copyright Treaty intended to digitize the international copyright regime. Among the document's less controversial provisions was the inclusion of computer programs in the definition of literary works and recognition of copyright protection for compilations of data. More controversially, however, Article 8 of the Copyright Treaty gives authors the exclusive right to distribute their works so as to make them available to the public from a place and at a time individually chosen by them. With this provision, WIPO effectively gave copyright owners the ability to control distribution of their works from BBSs and web sites.

WIPO, however, rejected proposed Article 7, which would have expanded the reproduction right to include "direct and indirect reproduction of . . . works, whether permanent or temporary, in any manner or form."[36] This Article would have settled the question whether copies of digital documents downloaded temporarily into random access memory violate the copyright owner's reproduction right. Passage of Article 7 would have reinforced the trend of American case law, which supports the inclusion of RAM copying within the reproduction right, and might

---

33. *Id.* at 218.

34. *Id.* n. 10 at 215.

35. *Id.* at 28–32.

36. World Intellectual Property Organization, Basic Proposal for the Substantive

Provisions of the Treaty on Certain Questions Concerning the Protection of Literary and Artistic Works to be considered by the Diplomatic conference, Draft Treaty, Aug. 30, 1996 at art. 7.

have foreclosed efforts to amend the Copyright Act to secure a different result.

B. Contributory and Vicarious Infringement in Cyberspace

Copyright law imposes liability for infringement, not only on those who directly copy, distribute, publicly display or publicly perform protected works, but also on those who facilitate infringement by providing a physical or commercial channel for the dissemination of protected material to others. These types of indirect legal responsibility, referred to as contributory and vicarious liability, have been applied for many years to night clubs, photo processing labs, bookstores and other businesses through which copyrighted works are duplicated, performed or sold.[37]

Contributory liability for infringement is imposed upon those who induce, cause or materially contribute to the infringing activity of others and who do so with knowledge of the infringing activity.[38] Specifically, findings of contributory infringement have been made against those who provided services to the direct infringer—such as selecting infringing material for the direct infringer to reproduce[39]—and on those who provided goods or equipment used by the direct infringer to violate a copyright owner's exclusive rights.[40]

Vicarious liability may be imposed upon persons who lack actual knowledge of the infringing activity of another but who have the "right and ability" to supervise the activity of the direct infringer and who also have a direct financial interest in that activity.[41] This is the basis upon which bookstores, dance hall owners and others have been found responsible for copyright infringement by dance bands, publishers and other direct infringers with whom they have business relationships.[42]

As the discussion in the preceding section demonstrated, imposition of direct liability on the operators of Internet access facilities and services often seems inappropriate because those parties have committed no conscious act that is proximately linked to the alleged infringement. Indirect liability theories, which permit an inquiry into the defendant's

---

37. Both doctrines are essentially judge-made and are not mentioned in the Copyright Act. The Copyright Act does, however, grant to copyright owners the right to "authorize" the exercise of their exclusive rights. This provision clarifies the liability of contributory infringers for any purported "authorization" by which they direct or permit others to infringe. *See* H.R. Rep. No. 1476, 94th Cong. 2d Sess. 47 (1976), *reprinted in* 1976 U.S. Code Cong. & Admin. News 5674.

38. *See* Gershwin Publishing Corp. v. Columbia Artists Management, Inc., 443 F.2d 1159, 1162 (2d Cir.1971).

39. *See* Universal Pictures Co. v. Harold Lloyd Corp., 162 F.2d 354, 366 (9th Cir. 1947).

40. *See, e.g.,* Sega Enterprises Ltd. v. MAPHIA, 857 F.Supp. 679 (N.D.Cal.1994); Cable/Home Communication Corp. v. Network Productions, Inc., 902 F.2d 829, 845–47 (11th Cir.1990).

41. Shapiro, Bernstein & Co. v. H. L. Green Co., 316 F.2d 304, 307 (2d Cir.1963).

42. *See, e.g.,* Dreamland Ball Room, Inc. v. Shapiro, Bernstein & Co., 36 F.2d 354 (7th Cir.1929); Famous Music Corp. v. Bay State Harness Horse Racing & Breeding Ass'n, Inc., 554 F.2d 1213 (1st Cir.1977); Boz Scaggs Music v. KND Corp., 491 F.Supp. 908, 913 (D.Conn.1980).

knowledge of, contribution to and financial interest in the infringing activity, provide a more discriminating way of dealing with these defendants.

Contributory liability, in particular, with its requirement of actual knowledge of infringing activity, provides a standard of liability with which few Internet service providers ("ISPs") can reasonably quarrel. For example, in *Sega Enterprises, Inc. v. MAPHIA*,[43] the defendant ran an on-line bulletin board service ("BBS") devoted entirely to the uploading and downloading of copyrighted video game software made by plaintiff Sega Enterprises Inc. ("Sega"). The plaintiff presented evidence to show that defendant "specifically solicited this copying and expressed the desire that these video game programs be placed on the MAPHIA bulletin board for downloading purposes."[44] The defendant's purpose, the evidence showed, was entirely commercial: not only did the defendant charge a direct fee for downloading privileges (or, in some cases, barter by exchanging downloading privileges in exchange for a user's uploading of new, pirated Sega software), but the defendant also used the bulletin board to advertise a piece of hardware that could be used to play pirated video game software on a Sega game cartridge.

On the facts, the court had little difficulty entering a preliminary injunction against the defendant. In particular, the court found a substantial likelihood that Sega would prove a case of contributory infringement. Defendant's open encouragement of posting of pirated software to his bulletin board clearly showed knowledge of the infringing activity, and his operation of his BBS for this express purpose amounted to inducing, causing or materially contributing to that activity.[45]

While few will express sympathy for the system operator in *Sega v. MAPHIA*, not all claims of contributory infringement in cyberspace are similarly straightforward. In *Religious Technology Center v. Netcom On-Line Communication Services, Inc., (Netcom)*,[46] *supra*, the ISP had no notice of infringing activity until he received a telephone call from the Church of Scientology. The caller advised the system operator, Netcom On-line Communication Services ("Netcom") that one Dennis Ehrlich had posted copyrighted material to a Usenet Newsgroup, using Netcom's facilities as his means of accessing the Internet.[47] After receiving this call, Netcom took no action against Ehrlich. The court found that while Netcom was not contributorily liable for Ehrlich's postings made before

---

43. 857 F.Supp. 679 (N.D.Cal.1994).

44. *Id.* at 683.

45. The court also found a substantial probability that Sega would prove direct infringement, but in support of this conclusion found merely that "games were uploaded to the MAPHIA bulletin board ... with the knowledge of Defendant Scherman." 857 F.Supp at 686. The court's reliance on knowledge, of course, is relevant to a finding of contributory—but not direct—infringement.

46. 907 F.Supp. 1361 (N.D.Cal.1995).

47. Usenet newsgroups provide a forum for postings on particular subjects. The Usenet, itself, is a "community of electronic BBSs associated with the Internet and the Internet Community ... Each Usenet site distributes its users' postings to other Usenet sites based on various implicit and explicit configuration settings, and in turn receives postings from other sites." Netcom, 907 F.Supp. at 1365 n. 4.

the call from the Church of Scientology was received, a question of fact was presented as to whether Netcom had knowledge of, and contributed to, the alleged infringement when it continued to provide Ehrlich with access to the Internet after the call from the Church of Scientology was received.

The *Netcom* decision raises the possibility that an Internet access provider will be required to deny access to anyone about whom it receives a mere complaint of infringement. The consequences of such a rule can be especially severe when (as Netcom claimed) the only way to deny access to an individual is to deny access to all users of a Newsgroup or other service to which the controverted postings occurred.

Vicarious liability poses even more difficult questions for ISPs. Vicarious liability does not require knowledge of infringing activity, but may be imposed on any system operator that has the right and ability to supervise the conduct of its users and stands to benefit financially from an alleged infringement. In cyberspace, each of these two elements of vicarious liability presents vexing factual questions, some of which were raised in the *Netcom* case.

In *Netcom*, the system operator's right and ability to supervise his users was found to present a factual question. On the question of Netcom's *right* to supervise, the court found a factual question in the written agreement between Netcom and its users, which specified that Netcom reserved the right to "control its users' postings before they occur[red]," prohibited copyright infringement and required users to indemnify Netcom for infringing activity. On the question of Netcom's *ability* to supervise, the court noted a dispute in the evidence as to the practicality of denying access to infringing users. Netcom argued that it could not, as a technical matter, deny access to Ehrlich without denying access to all users of Klemesrud's service. A plaintiff's expert, however, testified that Netcom could have used software screening to block certain postings without denying access to innocent parties.

On the second element of the vicarious liability standard—defendant's receipt of direct financial benefit from the infringing activity—the court entered summary judgment for Netcom on the ground that because Netcom charged its users a fixed fee for Internet access, "[t]here [was] no evidence that infringement by Ehrlich, or any other user of Netcom's services, in any way enhances the value of Netcom's services to subscribers or attracts new subscribers."[48]

C. *Browsing and ISP Liability: Are New Rules Needed?*

Of the various kinds of liability for on-line copyright infringement we have described, two stand out as presenting an apparent potential for unfairness: first, the imposition of direct liability for browsing in an on-line document; and second, the imposition of liability on ISPs, website operators and bulletin board operators for infringing material transmit-

---

48. *Id.* at 1377.

ted through their facilities. Commentators have argued for legislative relief for both groups of defendants.[49] The judicial process, however, is well-suited to the development of fair and efficient rules to govern these cases.

Consider first, the matter of browsing in on-line documents. Those who advocate a browsing exemption argue that browsing in an on-line document never causes the harm that the Copyright Act is intended to prevent and, in fact, is no different from browsing through a book found on a friend's shelf. In fact, however, it is by no means clear that browsing never harms copyright owners. Imagine, for example, that someone puts a copyrighted encyclopedia on a website, and makes it available for anyone to download. A person who acquired the habit of accessing the on-line encyclopedia will have found an entirely suitable substitute for purchasing the original, since browsing—*i.e.*, dipping episodically into individual articles—is precisely the purpose for which encyclopedias are bought. Browsing of this kind poses a severe threat to the market for the encyclopedia and might not qualify as fair use. A *per se* rule protecting browsing would be bad policy as applied to this and other cases that would not qualify as fair use under present law.

The desire to immunize ISPs from all liability for infringement of which they lack actual knowledge also is easy to understand. While contributory liability, which involves actual knowledge of and participation in the infringing activity, seems as applicable to ISPs as to anyone else, commentators have more difficulty with the imposition of vicarious liability on ISPs. Specifically, some commentators have emphasized the difficulties ISPs face in monitoring the billions of bytes of encoded information that may flow through their services daily, many of them from individuals or groups that the ISP does not know or control. Under these circumstances, it may seem futile to expect ISPs to exercise a purely theoretical "right and ability" to control users of their systems and unfair to subject ISPs to liability for failure to do so. Accordingly, some have contended that ISPs should be held liable only where they have actual knowledge of the infringing activity and the actual (not merely theoretical) ability and authority to prevent the infringement. Should these views prevail, ISPs whose subscribers infringe copyrights would escape the risk of vicarious liability borne by bookstore owners, sellers of recorded music and others.

In assessing this argument, we first should understand the rationale for imposing vicarious liability on more familiar kinds of enterprises and then determine whether that rationale applies with equal force to ISPs. It is fair to say that one rationale for imposing vicarious liability is that it forces distributors to exercise some degree of supervision over the

---

49. Niva Elkin–Koren, *Copyright Law and Social Dialogue on the Information Superhighway: The Case Against Copyright Liability of Bulletin Board Operators*, 13 Cardozo Arts & Ent. L.J. 346, 390 (1993); Jessica Litman, *The Exclusive Right to Read*, 13 Cardozo Arts & Ent. L.J. 29 (1994); Kevin M. Caws, Comment, *Online Service Providers and Copyright Law: The Need for Change*, 1 Syr. J. Legis. & Pol'y 197, 202 (1995).

works they distribute. The expectation is that if enterprises may be found liable regardless of *scienter*, so that they will gain nothing by deliberate ignorance, those enterprises will become part of the apparatus of copyright enforcement. So long as the supervisory burden is not excessive—that is, so long as the cost of compliance does not discourage more socially useful activity than it promotes—and so long as the sanctions for good-faith violation do not offend our sense of justice, imposition of vicarious liability is reasonable.

In the familiar kinds of cases, the supervisory burden is not excessive, risk shifting is feasible and the law is sufficiently flexible to avoid unjust results. In the dance hall cases, for example, proprietors need not monitor each song their performers play in order to ensure compliance with copyright: they need only pay license fees to ASCAP and BMI, thereby eliminating the risk of liability. In the bookstore cases, proprietors can lower their risk of copyright liability by dealing only with reputable publishers with whom they are familiar. And in both kinds of cases, distributors can seek contractual indemnification from publishers and performers for any copyright infringement actions that may arise.

Where the distributor does not successfully carry its supervisory burden but has not acted willfully, the law permits courts to impose lesser damages or confine the remedy to injunctive relief. So, for example, in *D.C. Comics Inc. v. Mini Gift Shop*,[50] the court awarded a plaintiff only the statutory minimum of $200 in damages because "the lack of business sophistication and the absence of a copyright notice on the infringing goods formed a proper basis for a determination of innocent infringement and explained the failure of defendants to inquire as to the source of the goods."[51]

An ISP's ease of supervision will vary with the type and volume of communications that move over the on-line service. In *Playboy Enterprises, Inc. v. Frena*,[52] the defendant operated a bulletin board service (BBS) that could be accessed by anyone who paid a fee or purchased products from the defendant. The undisputed facts showed that a large number of copyrighted photographs, first published in Playboy magazine, had been uploaded to Frena's BBS and subsequently downloaded by subscribers. Frena admitted that the photographs were posted to his BBS and further admitted that some of his subscribers had downloaded those photographs to their own computers; but he denied knowledge of the infringement and particularly denied uploading the photographs, which he insisted had been uploaded by subscribers to his service. The court found that while "Defendant Frena may have been unaware of the copyright infringement," no finding of intent was necessary to establish liability.[53] Accordingly, the court entered summary judgment on behalf of

---

50. 912 F.2d 29 (2d Cir.1990).

51. *Id.* at 36.

52. 839 F.Supp. 1552 (M.D.Fla.1993).

53. "Intent or knowledge is not an element of infringement, and thus even an innocent infringer is liable for infringement; rather, innocence is significant to a trial court when it fixes statutory damages, which is a remedy equitable in nature." *Id.* at 1559.

Playboy for infringement of the copyrights in the photographs posted to Frena's BBS.

The finding of vicarious liability in *Playboy* does not appear to suggest an impossible supervisory burden for ISPs. While the court's opinion does not address the point in detail, it appears that the defendant's bulletin board was a relatively small operation in which the posting and downloading of Playboy photographs was a prominent, ongoing activity. This is far from the case of a large on-line service found liable for an errant, infringing communication lost among billions of bits of unrelated message traffic.

The *Sega* case is even less appealing as a demonstration of the need to relieve ISPs of traditional liability. The undisputed evidence in that case showed that the system operator was aware of the infringing activity, and in fact "solicited this copying and expressed the desire that these video game programs be placed on the MAPHIA bulletin board for downloading purposes."[54] The record also included evidence (although defendant denied this) that the BBS benefitted economically from the infringing activity by charging fees or engaging in barter transactions for the privilege of downloading copyrighted game software,[55] and further that defendants, in addition to facilitating the downloading of Sega games, sold devices that had no apparent use except to make unauthorized copies of Sega game programs.[56] On all of these facts, the court found that the defendants were contributory—not merely vicarious—infringers of Sega's programs and entered a preliminary injunction against those infringing activities.

As these cases suggest, a statutory exemption from vicarious liability, created exclusively for ISPs, would deprive the courts of the ability to distinguish innocent from culpable conduct and eliminate any incentive for ISPs to supervise the conduct of their subscribers, even when they clearly are in a position to do so. The judicial process is much better adapted than legislative action to engage in the gradual refinement of existing law that this emerging technology requires.

D.   *Trademarks in Cyberspace*

There is no serious question that trademarks, no less than copyrights, may be infringed by misuse in on-line communications. In *Playboy*, for example, the court found that the BBS operator and his subscribers had violated trademark rights of Playboy Enterprises, Inc. in two ways. First, Frena stripped the Playboy text from some of the uploaded materials and added his own name and telephone number, thereby creating confusion as to the origin of the photographs.[57] Second, the BBS retained Playboy Enterprises' registered trademarks to identify many of the files containing the photographs, wrongly suggesting that

---

54. Sega, 857 F. Supp. at 683.

55. *Id*. The court also found that the defendants enjoyed a number of indirect economic benefits from making copyrighted games available for downloading. *Id*. at 684.

56. *Id*. at 684–85.

57. Playboy Enterprises, *supra*, n. 52 at 1559.

Playboy had authorized their distribution through Frena's BBS.[58] The court had no difficulty granting summary judgment for plaintiff on its claims of trademark infringement and unfair competition under the Lanham Act.[59]

For the most part, trademark infringement in cyberspace does not present new or difficult conceptual issues of the kind we encountered in our discussion of on-line copyright. Cyberspace has created a new device, however, that presents novel questions of trademark enforcement.

In recent years, the most popular region of cyberspace has been the World Wide Web—a graphics-rich environment of services using the HTML protocol, which permits users to "click" on key words in one page of text and go directly to material of related interest. As the popularity of the Web has grown, commercial enterprises have established websites and learned to use the Web as an important marketing tool.

Each "site" on the World Wide Web has a unique address, identified by a so-called domain name, that identifies a computer at which the website may be accessed. Each domain name consists of a prefix (often an identifiable word), followed by a suffix that identifies the system as, for example, governmental, educational, or commercial.

Difficulties arise because most domain names are registered with an organization called Network Solutions, Inc., which began operation under the auspices of the National Science Foundation.[60] (The organization's popular name is InterNIC.)[61] On several occasions, persons have registered domain names with InterNIC that incorporated trademarks registered to other persons or companies under the national registration scheme of the Lanham Act. Sometimes these websites were used to post information critical of the trademark owner; in other cases, the person registering the domain name simply wished to secure a fee from the trademark owners as the price of abandoning the domain name registration.

There is no serious question that a World Wide Web domain name can infringe a trademark and that actions to enjoin such infringement and secure damages may be brought. The presence of a domain name registration system parallel to the registration scheme of the Lanham Act creates difficulties, however—especially for InterNIC. In order to reduce its own exposure in these cases, InterNIC has adopted procedures under which a party claiming that a domain name infringes a trademark may trigger a suspension of the domain name registrant's use of the domain name. This procedure, in turn, has led to protests from domain

---

58. *Id.*

59. 15 U.S.C.A. §§ 1114, 1125(a) (West 1996).

60. The National Science Foundation discontinued its involvement in domain name registration in March, 1998.

61. The federal government was scheduled to end its involvement with Network

Solutions, Inc. on October 7, 1998. However, under an agreement that provides for eventual privatization of the domain name registration system, the government extended its agreement with the corporation until Sept. 30, 2000. *See Commerce, NSI to Open Management of Domain System,* 67 U.S.L.Wk. 2205 (Oct. 13, 1998).

name registrants. Efforts to develop fair domain name registration procedures are continuing.

11.11 Informational Privacy and Data Protection

A. Introduction

Electronic technologies have made it feasible to transmit, collect, store, manipulate and retrieve information more rapidly and in greater quantities than was conceivable before the late Twentieth Century. As discussed elsewhere in this treatise, these technologies have strained familiar legal rules in many substantive areas, including freedom of expression, regulation, defamation and protection of intellectual property. This section considers another set of issues posed by electronic information technologies: *i.e.*, the protection of electronically transmitted and stored information from wrongful access, tampering, alteration, destruction, disclosure and use—a range of problems that we may call, for convenience, the problems of informational privacy and data protection. This complex set of legal issues involves both the protection of individuals from the wrongful acquisition and use of their transmitted and stored personal information and the protection of the owners of computer systems and stored information from unlawful alteration and destruction of their property. In dealing with these issues, the law defines rights and obligations affecting those who create and disclose information, those who store, process and transmit information and those who seek to acquire information.

The law's efforts to address the protection of personal information are especially complex. Personal information pertains to individuals and includes their personal histories, their criminal, medical, financial, employment and educational records, their spending habits and their private communications with others in the form of conversations, telephone calls, facsimile transmissions and electronic mail. Where electronically stored and transmitted information of this kind is concerned, the law defines rights and obligations affecting a number of different players.

First, the law gives individuals limited rights to prevent (or seek redress for) unauthorized interceptions of private communications and unauthorized disclosure of personal information stored in databases. The law also gives individuals more specific rights concerning information in the hands of particular kinds of entities such as credit reporting bureaus, government agencies and financial institutions.

These rights of individuals in their own personal information are enforced by the imposition of corresponding obligations upon services that transmit and store personal information, and upon third parties (including governmental agencies) that might wish to acquire, disclose and use such transmitted and stored personal information for purposes ranging from criminal prosecution to compilation of marketing databases. The law also gives service providers and third parties certain rights, including the right of communications service providers to intercept and access personal communications when necessary for the protection of their customers and property and the right of government to intercept or seize information pursuant to warrants, interception orders and other legal process.

The law also recognizes the property rights of owners of computer systems, programs and stored information. Notably, both the Congress and most of the states have passed legislation that criminalizes "hacking"—*i.e.*, the destruction or alteration of computer programs and stored information, or the denial of authorized access to those programs and stored information.

The following sections discuss these rights and obligations in more detail: first, as they involve the protection of personal information; and second, as they involve the protection of computer systems and databases from harmful intrusion.

B. Protection of Electronically Transmitted and Stored Personal Information

Informational privacy has been defined as "the claim of individuals, groups or institutions to determine for themselves when, how and to what extent information about them is communicated to others."[1] Before the invention of electronic communications, this right was secured primarily by the primitiveness of the available methods of gathering and distributing information. The advent of electronic technologies made it far more difficult for individuals to control the acquisition, disclosure and use of information about themselves. For example, the telephone and telegraph carried personal messages by wire over great distances, exposing the users of these technologies to electronic eavesdropping at any point along the circuit. The digital computer and the compilation of huge governmental and private databases raised the threat of unauthorized access to, and disclosure and use of, personal information stored in—and capable of instantaneous transfer among—networked computers.

These threats to informational privacy have multiplied with the growing popularity of the personal computer and the ubiquitous interconnection of those personal computers over telephone lines. With the growth of electronic mail, bulletin boards, electronic funds transfer and remote computing services of all kinds, we are conducting more and more of our private conversations and business transactions over insecure telephone lines, and feeding more and more information (knowingly or unknowingly) to public and private networks and databases.

Against this volatile social and technological background, efforts to define and protect informational privacy must accommodate competing values and interests. If our society simply placed privacy interests ahead of all other claims, the law's task would be much simpler. Individuals would have a plenary right to prevent others—including agencies of government—from intercepting their communications or gaining access to private information stored in commercial or governmental databases.

---

1. ALAN F. WESTIN, PRIVACY AND FREEDOM 7 (1967).

Individuals also would have a comprehensive right to know the contents of any stored information concerning them and could demand correction of that information where it was inaccurate. Similarly, where individuals provided information to private and governmental agencies—in the course of obtaining drivers' licenses, credit, medical care or other private and governmental goods and services—they would have a right to prevent the sale or use of that information for any other purpose. But no societal consensus supports such absolute rights largely because the widespread accumulation and exchange of personal information facilitates many activities, from law enforcement to easy access to credit, that powerful interests—and many individuals, as well—may value more highly than personal privacy. These competing interests and values, combined with rapid technological change, have produced the complex, evolving patchwork of privacy protections described in the following sections.

C. Rights against interception of personal communications

Of all of the means of invading privacy, perhaps the most troubling is electronic eavesdropping. Having our conversations overheard is, if anything, more invasive than having our private documents seized. Written records and correspondence, even at their most casual, are prepared with some level of deliberation and self-censorship: the very act of making a written record increases the likelihood that a communication may one day be exposed and lowers, however subtly, our expectation of privacy. But a spontaneous, unguarded conversation with a friend is a far different matter: we all make incautious or potentially embarrassing statements in private conversation, and we rely heavily on our belief that our spoken statements are private and ephemeral—that they will not be overheard, recorded or repeated by persons who are not parties to our conversation.

The law reinforces this expectation by making the use of wiretaps, electronic bugging devices and other means of intercepting private communications unlawful in most circumstances. Some of these prohibitions are constitutional and are, of course, good only against governmental action; others are statutory and establish rights against both private and public acts of interception. All are subject to important exceptions.

D. Constitutional challenges to governmental electronic surveillance

The Supreme Court has found that electronic surveillance by government, in circumstances in which the target of the surveillance had a reasonable expectation of privacy, is a "search" within the meaning of the Fourth Amendment to the United States Constitution.[2] Where an act

---

2. *See* Smith v. Maryland, 442 U.S. 735, 99 S.Ct. 2577, 61 L.Ed.2d 220 (1979). The Fourth Amendment provides that "[t]he right of the people to be secure in their persons, houses, papers, and effects, against unreasonable searches and seizures, shall not be violated, and no warrants shall issue, but upon probable cause, supported by oath or affirmation, and particularly describing the place to be searched, and the persons or

of surveillance is undertaken without a proper order, therefore, or is otherwise constitutionally unreasonable, evidence obtained through that act of surveillance may be suppressed. The Supreme Court reached its determination that the Fourth Amendment applies to electronic eaves-dropping, however, by a circuitous route.

The issue was first presented to the Court in *Olmstead v. United States*,[3] in which a divided Court found that the interception of calls through a wire attached to a telephone line, where the attachment was made at a point outside the suspect's property, did not violate the Amendment because the police had neither entered physically upon the plaintiff's property nor searched and seized any tangible item. In the majority's view, the language of the Fourth Amendment itself "shows that the [prohibited] search is to be of material things—the person, the house, his papers or his effects."[4] Accordingly, any legal protection against eavesdropping not accomplished by physical trespass must come from the Congress—not through judicial extension of the Fourth Amendment "beyond the possible practical meaning of houses, persons, papers, and effects, or so to apply the words 'search and seizure' as to forbid [the acquisition of information through] hearing and sight."[5]

Justice Brandeis responded to the *Olmstead* majority with a famous and prescient dissent. As Justice Brandeis saw it, the Fourth Amendment's references to houses and to searches and seizures of persons and material objects reflected only the technology of the Eighteenth Century—not the intention of the Framers. To freeze the Fourth Amendment in time would prevent its extension, not only to wiretapping, but to surveillance technologies as yet unknown; and would leave the Amendment powerless against all but the most primitive methods of government surveillance.[6]

Justice Brandeis's objections notwithstanding, the Court applied its "physical trespass" analysis in a series of post-*Olmstead* electronic surveillance cases. Notably, in *Goldman v. United States*,[7] the Court found no physical trespass, and therefore no violation of the Fourth Amendment, when police placed a listening device against the wall of an office adjoining a suspect's office. Similarly, in *On Lee v. United States*,[8]

---

things to be seized." U.S. Const., Amend. IV.

3. 277 U.S. 438, 48 S.Ct. 564, 72 L.Ed. 944 (1928).

4. *Id.* at 464, 48 S.Ct. at 568, 72 L.Ed. at 950.

5. *Id.* at 465, 48 S.Ct. at 568, 72 L.Ed. at 951.

6. *Id.* at 474, 48 S.Ct. at 5701, 72 L.Ed. at 954.

7. 316 U.S. 129, 62 S.Ct. 993, 86 L.Ed. 1322 (1942), *overruled in part by* Katz v. United States, 389 U.S. 347, 88 S.Ct. 507, 19 L.Ed.2d 576 (1967).

8. 343 U.S. 747, 72 S.Ct. 967, 96 L.Ed. 1270 (1952). *Goldman* and *On Lee* were

decided after passage of the Communications Act of 1934, which prohibited the interception and divulgence of wire and radio communications. 47 U.S.C.A. § 605 (West 1990). The Communications Act did not, however, address the use of electronic listening devices that intercept oral, rather than wire or radio, communications. *See Silverman v. United States*, 365 U.S. 505, 508, 81 S.Ct. 679, 681, 5 L.Ed.2d 734, 737 (1961); *see also* Irvine v. California, 347 U.S. 128, 131, 74 S.Ct. 381, 382, 98 L.Ed. 561, 568 (1954); Goldman, 316 U.S. at 134, 62 S.Ct. at 996, 86 L.Ed. at 1327.

the Court found that a federal agent who lawfully entered a suspect's place of business wearing a listening device and transmitter did not commit an unlawful search or seizure.

The trespass doctrine was showing some strain, however, by the time of the Court's 1961 decision in *Silverman v. United States*.[9] In that case the police, suspecting gambling activity in a Washington, D.C. row house, had obtained permission to use the adjoining row house as a listening post. The police pushed a so-called "spike microphone" through the wall between the two houses until they encountered a heating duct that conducted the sound of conversations taking place in the suspect's house.

The government urged the Court to find, as it had in *Olmstead* and *Goldman*, that no violation of the Fourth Amendment had occurred because the police had not physically trespassed on the suspect's property. This time, however, the Court signalled its discomfort with these precedents by straining to find a trespass. Specifically, the majority found that "the officers overheard the petitioners' conversations only by usurping part of the petitioners' house or office—a heating system which was an integral part of the premises occupied by the petitioner ..."[10] This, the Court found, was eavesdropping accomplished by trespass; and in an ironic reference to the minute distinctions the trespass doctrine now seemed to require, the Court declared that while it would not "re-examine Goldman here," it would "decline to go beyond it, by even a fraction of an inch."[11]

Eventually, of course, the Court did abandon *Goldman*. In 1967, in *Katz v. United States*,[12] the Court was asked to scrutinize the actions of police who, without first obtaining a warrant, attached a listening device to the outside of a telephone booth. The government, relying on *Olmstead* and *Goldman*, argued that the Fourth Amendment was not implicated because the listening device had not physically entered a house or other "constitutionally protected area."[13] The Court, however, found that the authority of *Olmstead* had been "so eroded" by the Court's subsequent decisions that the " 'trespass' doctrine there enunciated can no longer be regarded as controlling."[14] The Court found that the petitioner's Fourth Amendment rights had been violated, not because of a physical invasion or usurpation of a protected space, but because the government's use of a recording device had "violated the privacy upon which [the plaintiff] justifiably relied while using the telephone booth ..."[15]

9. Silverman, 365 U.S. 505, 81 S.Ct. 679, 5 L.Ed.2d 734 (1961).

10. *Id.* at 511, 81 S.Ct. at 682, 5 L.Ed.2d at 739.

11. *Id.* at 512, 81 S.Ct. at 683, 5 L.Ed.2d at 739.

12. 389 U.S. 347, 88 S.Ct. 507, 19 L.Ed.2d 576 (1967), *superseded by statute as*

stated in United States v. Koyomejian, 946 F.2d 1450 (9th Cir.1991).

13. *Id.* at 351, 88 S.Ct. at 511, 19 L.Ed.2d at 582.

14. *Id.* at 353, 88 S.Ct. at 512, 19 L.Ed.2d at 583.

15. *Id.* The phrase "reasonable expectation of privacy," which often is attributed

After *Katz*, any warrantless use by Government of a wiretap, concealed microphone or other eavesdropping device violates the Fourth Amendment if the suspect reasonably expects that he or she will not be overheard. As elaborated in cases subsequent to *Katz*, the standard is that the suspect must have a subjective expectation of privacy and this expectation must be objectively reasonable.[16]

Not all petitioners have met this two-part test. In *Smith v. Maryland*,[17] for example, a criminal suspect complained that a pen register—a device that records the numbers dialed from a telephone—could not lawfully be placed on his telephone line without a warrant. The Court found that while the petitioner may have had a subjective expectation that the numbers dialed from his telephone would remain private, society need not treat that expectation as reasonable. According to *Smith*, users of telephones reasonably may expect the contents of their conversations to be private but should understand that telephone numbers, which are captured and used by the telephone company for billing purposes, may be disclosed.[18]

While the liberalized rule of *Katz* brought all forms of electronic surveillance within the ambit of the Fourth Amendment, the protections afforded by the Constitution remained limited and uncertain. Most obviously, only surveillance activities initiated or carried out by government could be challenged under the Fourth Amendment. Also, the exclusionary rule for illegally obtained evidence did not automatically require suppression of evidence obtained through unlawful electronic surveillance, but applied only to criminal cases in which the Government sought to use illegally seized evidence to incriminate the victim of the unlawful search.[19] Similarly, the Fourth Amendment did not create a private right of action for damages, did not subject the perpetrators of unlawful surveillance to criminal penalties, did not regulate the purposes

to the majority opinion, appears in Justice Harlan's concurring opinion. *Id.* at 360, 88 S.Ct. at 516, 19 L.Ed.2d at 587. *See also* Berger v. New York, 388 U.S. 41, 87 S.Ct. 1873, 18 L.Ed.2d 1040 (1967).

16. *See, e.g.,* Terry v. Ohio, 392 U.S. 1, 88 S.Ct. 1868, 20 L.Ed.2d 889 (1968).

17. 442 U.S. 735, 99 S.Ct. 2577, 61 L.Ed.2d 220 (1979).

18. *Id.* at 742, 99 S.Ct. at 2581, 61 L.Ed.2d at 228.

19. *See* Mapp v. Ohio, 367 U.S. 643, 81 S.Ct. 1684, 6 L.Ed.2d 1081 (1961); *see also* United States v. Calandra, 414 U.S. 338, 94 S.Ct. 613, 38 L.Ed.2d 561 (1974); Brown v. United States, 411 U.S. 223, 93 S.Ct. 1565, 36 L.Ed.2d 208 (1973); Alderman v. United States, 394 U.S. 165, 89 S.Ct. 961, 22 L.Ed.2d 176 (1969). The exclusionary rule, in fact, is not mandated by the Constitution but is a "judicially created means of effectuating the rights of the Fourth Amend-

ment." Stone v. Powell, 428 U.S. 465, 482, 96 S.Ct. 3037, 3046, 49 L.Ed.2d 1067, 1081 (1976); *see also* Brewer v. Williams, 430 U.S. 387, 421, 97 S.Ct. 1232, 1250–51, 51 L.Ed.2d 424, 450 (1977). As such, the rule has never been treated as an absolute but is subject to balancing against other interests, including effective law enforcement. *See, e.g.,* United States v. Calandra, *supra*, finding that application of the exclusionary rule to grand jury proceedings would "unduly interfere with the effective and expeditious discharge of the grand jury's duties." 414 U.S. at 350, 94 S.Ct. at 621, 38 L.Ed.2d at 573. *See also* United States v. Place, 462 U.S. 696, 103 S.Ct. 2637, 77 L.Ed.2d 110 (1983), in which the Court noted that Fourth Amendment jurisprudence generally requires a balancing "of the nature and quality of the intrusion on the individual's Fourth Amendment interests against the importance of the governmental interests alleged to justify the intrusion." *Id.* at 703, 103 S.Ct. at 2642, 77 L.Ed.2d at 118.

for which surveillance could be conducted and did not require the obtrusiveness of surveillance to be minimized. For all of these kinds of protection, statutory relief was required.[20]

11.12 Federal Legislation Involving Electronic Surveillance

A. Background

Until the enactment of the Communications Act of 1934, no federal statute comprehensively regulated wiretapping or other forms of electronic surveillance.[1] Section 605 of the 1934 Act remedied this deficiency in part, by prohibiting the unauthorized interception and divulgence of telephone calls and radio communications.[2] Section 605 did not, however, prohibit interceptions not accompanied by divulgence, and did not prevent the placing of listening devices in the walls of homes or offices.[3]

The Congress's first attempt to regulate all forms of electronic surveillance was Title III of the Omnibus Crime Control and Safe Streets Act of 1968, which prohibited the willful interception of "any wire or oral communication" and the disclosure or use of the contents of any unlawfully intercepted communication.[4] The statute created exceptions for use of electronic surveillance by law enforcement, but only for enumerated crimes, pursuant to court order and executed under continuing judicial supervision. For the first time, a federal statute appeared to embrace all forms of electronic surveillance. But the ink was barely dry on the 1968 Act before new communications technologies began to make its protections obsolete.

20. For a discussion of these limitations of *Katz*, *see* United States v. Torres, 751 F.2d 875, 889, 891 (7th Cir.1984) (concurring opinion of Cudahy, J.); *see also* United States v. Koyomejian, 946 F.2d 1450, 1454–55 (9th Cir.1991).

1. A number of states, however, enacted statutes prohibiting or limiting the use of wiretaps. Most states today have statutes criminalizing the use of unauthorized wiretaps and the laws of many states permit civil actions against electronic eavesdroppers for invasion of privacy. *See* Todd R. Smyth, Annot., *Eavesdropping on Extension Telephone as Invasion of Privacy*, 49 A.L.R. 4th 430 (1977).

2. 47 U.S.C.A. § 605 (West 1991); *see* Nardone v. United States, 302 U.S. 379, 58 S.Ct. 275, 82 L.Ed. 314 (1937); Nardone v. United States, 308 U.S. 338, 60 S.Ct. 266, 84 L.Ed. 307 (1939). The 1968 Wiretap Act, discussed *infra*, displaced § 605 as the principal federal anti-wiretapping statute. Section 605 now prohibits the interception of certain radio communications but addresses only unauthorized disclosure—rather than interception—of wire communications. *See*

Laurie Thomas Lee, *U.S. Telecommunications Privacy and Caller ID*, 30 Cal. Wes. L. Rev. 1, text accompanying n. 32 (1993).

3. Silverman v. United States, 365 U.S. 505, 507–08, 81 S.Ct. 679, 681, 5 L.Ed.2d 734, 737 (1961); Irvine v. California, 347 U.S. 128, 131, 74 S.Ct. 381, 382, 98 L.Ed. 561, 568 (1954).

4. Pub. L. No. 90–351, 82 Stat. 197 (1968), 18 U.S.C.A. §§ 2510–2520 (West 1996). The 1968 legislation was a response to the Supreme Court's decisions in *Katz* v. *United States*, 389 U.S. 347, 88 S.Ct. 507, 19 L.Ed.2d 576 (1967) and *Berger* v. *New York*, 388 U.S. 41, 87 S.Ct. 1873, 18 L.Ed.2d 1040 (1967), which made it clear that the Fourth Amendment applies to governmental wiretaps and electronic eavesdropping. Congressional proponents of the new statute had expressed their dissatisfaction with the vague and uncertain protections against electronic surveillance enunciated in *Katz* and *Berger*. *See* S. Rep. No. 1097, 90th Cong., 2d Sess., *reprinted in* 1968 U.S. Code Cong. & Admin. News 2112, 2153–63. *See* United States v. Koyomejian, 946 F.2d 1450, 1455 (9th Cir.1991).

One such advance was the exchange of information between computers over telephone lines. Many such communications (electronic mail, in particular) presented significant privacy concerns; but because the 1968 Act protected only wire and oral communications, and because the 1968 Act's definitions of those terms covered only communications that could be overheard and understood by the human ear, it was entirely lawful under the Wiretap Act to intercept transmissions of electronic mail and other digitally-encoded information.[5]

Another, equally significant technological advance was the advent of cellular telephone service.[6] People using cellular telephones might well have the same privacy expectations as people using landline telephones. But because the radio portion of a cellular call was neither a wire nor an oral communication as those terms were defined in the 1968 Act, interception of cellular calls was lawful. (And in fact, radio "scanning" devices designed for this purpose became quite popular in the mid–1980s.)[7]

A third development that troubled privacy advocates was the proliferation of noncommon-carrier providers of various communications services—including specialized data communication providers and private, corporate telephone and computer networks. The 1968 Act prohibited only the interception of communications transmitted by common carriers and appeared to offer no protection for information transmitted over other networks.[8]

B.   *Electronic Communications Privacy Act—Title I*

1.   *Purpose of the Act*

Title I of the Electronic Communications Privacy Act ("ECPA") was Congress's attempt to update the 1968 Wiretap Act.[9] In addition to the

5. *See* United States v. Seidlitz, 589 F.2d 152, 157 (4th Cir.1978), cert. denied 441 U.S. 922, 99 S.Ct. 2030, 60 L.Ed.2d 396 (1979); *see also* United States v. New York Telephone Company, 434 U.S. 159, 167, 98 S.Ct. 364, 370, 54 L.Ed.2d 376, 386 (1977).

6. The first licensed cellular telephone service began operation in 1983. *See* George Calhoun, *Digital Cellular Radio* 63 (1988). By mid–1987 884,000 cellular mobile telephones were in use, and the market was growing at an estimated 34,000 users each month. *See The Celling of America*, U.S. News & World Report, Aug. 31, 1987, p. 45.

7. Until passage of the Electronic Communications Privacy Act in 1986, the Congress had prohibited only the unauthorized interception and disclosure—not mere interception—of radio communications. *See* subsection B.3, *infra*. Accordingly, amateur radio operators and others routinely scanned the airwaves for interesting transmissions on short wave, police, fire, ship-to-shore, cellular telephone and other frequen-

cies. Because radio communications were not covered by the 1968 Wiretap Act, courts hearing challenges to the interception of radio communications applied the *Katz* expectation of privacy test. *See* United States v. Hoffa, 436 F.2d 1243, 1247 (7th Cir. 1970), cert. denied 400 U.S. 1000, 91 S.Ct. 464, 27 L.Ed.2d 452 (1971); Edwards v. Bardwell, 632 F.Supp. 584, 589 (M.D.La.), *aff'd* 808 F.2d 54 (5th Cir.1986); Willamette Subscription Television v. Cawood, 580 F.Supp. 1164, 1168–69 (D.Or.1984).

8. *See* Seidlitz, 589 F.2d at 157 (finding that acquisition of a transmission made over a computer network is not an interception forbidden by the 1968 Act).

9. Pub. L. 99–508, 100 Stat. 1848 (1986), *codified at* 18 U.S.C.A. §§ 2510–2522, 2701–2710, 2711 (West 1996). According to the Senate Report on the new legislation, its purpose was "to update and clarify Federal privacy protections and standards in light of dramatic changes in new comput-

1968 Act's prohibitions against interception of wire and oral communications, the ECPA prohibited the intentional interception of "electronic communications," which it defined comprehensively as "any transfer of signs, signals, writing, images, sounds, data or intelligence of any nature transmitted in whole or in part by a wire, radio, electromagnetic, photoelectronic or photooptical system."[10] These provisions brought interception of electronic mail and other computer-to-computer communications under federal statutory protection for the first time. The ECPA also extended statutory protection to wire and electronic communications not transmitted by common carriers and adopted a definition of "wire" communication that was carefully crafted to include the radio portion of a cellular telephone call.[11] And the ECPA made it an offense intentionally to disclose or use the contents of any communication, with the knowledge that the communication was intercepted in violation of the Act.

2. *Shortcomings of the Act*

But the new Act also was riddled with exceptions and limitations— some expressly identified as such, and others scattered more obscurely through the definitions and enforcement provisions. So, for example, the ECPA forbids only the acquisition of the "contents" of a communication and permits the acquisition of information (such as telephone numbers) that relate to the identity of the parties to a communication. Similarly, interceptions of oral communications are unlawful only where the circumstances of those communications disclose a "reasonable expectation of privacy." Also, court orders for interceptions of electronic communications are more easily obtained than orders to intercept wire and oral communications; evidence obtained through wrongful interception of electronic communications may not be suppressed under the ECPA's exclusionary rule; many unencrypted radio communications may be intercepted without penalty; and acquisition of the contents of a stored electronic communication is not an interception under the ECPA, although acquisitions of stored wire and oral communications are interceptions.

As these examples suggest, in order to determine whether a particular communication is protected by Title I of the ECPA it is necessary to work through all of the relevant provisions, with particular attention to the definitions, exceptions and enforcement language. The following sections are intended as a guide to that process.

er and telecommunications technologies." S. Rep. No. 541, 99th Cong., 2d Sess. 1 (1986), *reprinted in* 1986 U.S. Code Cong. & Admin. News 3555 (hereinafter referred to as "Senate Report").

10. *Id.* § 2510(1).

11. In this discussion the phrase "cellular telephone" will be used generically to refer to all forms of mobile radiotelephony, including cellular communications, personal communications service ("PCS") and enhanced specialized mobile radio ("ESMR") service. The ECPA definition of "wire communication" covers all of these technologies and services.

3. Analysis of the Act

a. Were the Contents of a Communication Intentionally Intercepted?

Section 2511 of the ECPA states that any person who "intentionally intercepts, endeavors to intercept, or procures any other person to intercept or endeavor to intercept, any wire, oral, or electronic communication;" or "intentionally uses, endeavors to use, or procures any other person to use or endeavor to use any electronic, mechanical device to intercept any oral communication;" or "intentionally discloses, or endeavors to disclose, to any other person the contents of any wire, oral, or electronic communication, knowing or having reason to know that the information was obtained through the interception of a wire, oral, or electronic communication ... ;" or "intentionally uses, or endeavors to use, the contents of any wire, oral, or electronic communication, knowing or having reason to know that the information was obtained through the interception of a wire, oral, or electronic communication ..." is subject to the criminal penalties and civil remedies prescribed in the statute.[12] The key word here is "intercept," which the ECPA defines as "the aural or other *acquisition* of the *contents* of any wire, electronic, or oral communication through the use of any electronic, mechanical or other device ..."[13]

The term "acquisition", while not itself defined, is limited by the definition of "intercept" to acquisitions made through the use of an "electronic, mechanical or other device."[14] Acquisitions covered by the statute would appear, therefore, to exclude interceptions accomplished with the unaided human ear, but to cover the overhearing, monitoring or recording of communications with the aid of microphones, radio transmitters, tape recorders, clip-on telephone sets, computer terminals and receiving and recording devices of all kinds.[15]

The requirement that a prohibited interception must acquire the *contents* of a communication is especially important. The 1968 Wiretap Act defined "contents" to include information concerning the identity of the parties; the ECPA deletes that language and defines "contents" to include only "information concerning the substance, purport, or meaning of [any wire, oral, or electronic] communication."[16] This means that a person or entity may acquire the identities of the calling and called parties, their telephone numbers, and information establishing the time

---

12. *Id.*

13. *Id.* § 2510(4) *(emphasis added)*. It also is an offense under chapter 119 to "endeavor [to intercept, or procure] any other person to intercept or endeavor to intercept, any wire, oral, or electronic communication." *Id.*

14. *Id.* § 2510(4).

15. The Act defines "electronic, mechanical, or other device" to include any "device or apparatus which can be used to

intercept a ... communication other than" a telephone or similar device used by a subscriber or provider of telephone service, or a device being used by an investigative or law enforcement officer, or a hearing aid. *Id.* § 2510(5). Listening in on an extension telephone is not an interception under Title I, although placing a tap on an extension line is an interception. *See* Williams v. Poulos, 11 F.3d 271, 279–80 (1st Cir.1993).

16. 18 U.S.C.A. § 2510(8)(West 1996).

and other circumstances surrounding the making of a communication, without violating the Act.[17]

In order to determine whether a communication has been intercepted, it is necessary to keep in mind not only the definition of "interception," but also the definitions of the kinds of communications—wire, oral and electronic—that the ECPA covers. We turn now to those definitions.

b. Does the Communication Meet the Definition of a Wire, Oral or Electronic Communication?

The ECPA's definitions of wire, oral and electronic communications are sufficiently comprehensive to include telephone conversations, private oral communications, electronic mail, certain radio transmissions and information transmitted to computing services for processing or storage. The definitions themselves are quite technical, however, and must be reviewed carefully before a determination is made that a particular communication is covered by the ECPA.

(1) Definition of Wire Communication

If a communication is an aural transfer (a transfer containing the human voice at any point),[18] made "in whole or in part through the use of facilities for the transmission of communications by the aid of wire, cable or other like connection between the point of origin and the point of reception ... furnished or operated by any person engaged in providing or operating such facilities for the transmission of interstate or foreign communications or communications affecting interstate or foreign commerce ... ," then the communication is a wire communication.[19] Such communications may be transmitted by common carriers or by noncommon carrier service providers. The definition includes wire communications in the process of transmission and wire communications in electronic storage.[20] Telephone calls, including the radio portions of cellular and cordless telephone calls, are classified as wire communications.[21]

---

17. The Federal Communications Commission has relied on this provision to establish the legality, under the ECPA, of so-called "Caller ID" services, which transmit the telephone number of a calling party for display on a piece of equipment at the called party's premises. Rules and Policies Regarding Calling Number Identification Service—Caller ID, 9 FCC Rcd 1764 (1994).

18. 18 U.S.C.A. § 2510(18)(West 1996). Transmissions containing the digitized human voice, as well as those containing the human voice in an analog form of electronic representation, qualify as "aural transfers" under the Act. Senate Report, *supra*, note 9 at 12 (1986), *reprinted in* 1986 U.S. Code Cong. & Admin. News at 3566.

19. 18 U.S.C.A. § 2510(1) (West 1996).

20. *Id.* Electronic storage is defined as "any temporary, intermediate storage of a wire or electronic communication incidental to the electronic transmission thereof; and ... any storage of such communication by an electronic communication service for purpose of backup protection of such communication." *Id.* § 2510(17). Under this definition, a seizure of a storage device containing voice mail messages is an interception of wire communications. As discussed more fully below, the seizure of a storage device containing recorded oral or electronic communications is not an interception under the ECPA. *See* text at section 11.12.-B.3.e., *infra*, discussing *Steve Jackson Games, Inc.* v. *United States Secret Service*, 36 F.3d 457 (5th Cir.1994).

21. This definition carefully brings the radio portion of a cellular telephone conversation within its reach by providing that if such a conversation passes through a wire

(2) Definition of Oral Communication

The ECPA defines an oral communication simply as "any oral communication uttered by a person exhibiting an expectation that such communication is not subject to interception under circumstances justifying such expectation," and expressly excludes "any electronic communication."[22] The most striking feature of this definition is its use of the *Katz* standard to limit the rights of targets of electronic bugging devices.[23] Oral communications are intercepted within the meaning of the Act only if the circumstances of their making reflect the speaker's objectively reasonable expectation of privacy.[24] The ECPA does not place this same limitation on wire and electronic communications. So, for example, a person whose oral statements made in a crowded public place are secretly recorded is not the victim of an interception under the ECPA; but if a person makes the same statement, at the same public place, into a telephone mouthpiece, then a wiretap on the telephone line does accomplish an interception because the definition of wire communication does not require the person making the communication to exhibit a reasonable expectation of privacy.[25] The definition of oral communication, unlike the definition of wire communication, does not include a communication in electronic storage. Accordingly, if a person seizes a tape recording of an oral communication, even where that communication was made under circumstances exhibiting a reasonable expectation of privacy, no interception has occurred under the ECPA.[26]

(3) Definition of Electronic Communication

Any "transfer of signs, signals, writing, images, sounds, data, or intelligence of any nature transmitted in whole or in part by wire, radio [or other electronic means] that affects interstate or foreign commerce" is an electronic communication unless certain other exceptions apply.[27] The exceptions are:

— any wire or oral communication;

or switch an any point along the transmission path all links in the transmission path become wire communications. In fact, most cellular telephone conversations link a mobile and a landline telephone and pass through a telephone company switch at the originating or terminating end of the call. And even so-called "mobile to mobile" cellular calls at least pass through a switch at the cellular telephone company's office. This contact with the switch is sufficient to transform the radio portions of those calls into wire communications under the ECPA definition. The wire communication definition, therefore, creates an exception to the ECPA's classification of radio transmissions as electronic communications. *See* Senate Report, *supra* note 9.

22. 18 U.S.C.A. § 2510(2) (West 1996). The legislative history shows that an oral communication is one carried by sound waves, rather than a method of electronic transmission. Senate Report, *supra* note 9 at 12.

23. *See* Katz v. United States, 389 U.S. 347, 88 S.Ct. 507, 19 L.Ed.2d 576 (1967).

24. 18 U.S.C.A. § 2510(2) (West 1996). Oral communications must be "uttered by a person" and expressly do not include "any electronic communication."

25. According to the House Judiciary Committee's Report on the proposed ECPA, a party's utterances into the telephone mouthpiece are an oral communication.

26. *See* Steve Jackson Games, Inc. v. United States Secret Service, 816 F.Supp. 432 (W.D.Tex.1993), *aff'd*, 36 F.3d 457 (5th Cir.1994).

27. 18 U.S.C.A. § 2510(12) (West 1996).

— any communication made through a tone-only paging device;[28] or

— any communication from a tracking device.[29]

By excluding wire and oral communications, the definition of electronic communication excludes wireline voice communications and the radio portion of any cellular or cordless telephone conversation. The definition of electronic communication includes, however, voice and other communications carried entirely by radio (except for tone-only paging devices and tracking devices) and wireline communications (such as electronic mail) that do not involve the human voice.[30]

As we discuss further at section 11.12.B.3.e, *infra*, one federal appellate court has found that because the definition of electronic communication (in contrast to the definition of wire communication) does not include such a communication in electronic storage, the seizure of undelivered electronic mail stored in a service provider's computer is not an "interception" within the meaning of the ECPA.[31]

c. Does the Interception Come Within an Exception?

Title I of the ECPA includes a long list of situations in which intentional interceptions of protected communications do not violate the Act. Some of these exceptions are available only to law enforcement agencies, others are intended to protect the rights of system operators, and still others permit the interception of certain communications by anyone. Several of these exceptions are worth reviewing in detail.

(1) Interception of Protected Communications by Law Enforcement Agencies

Perhaps the most important—and certainly the most complex—exception provisions of Title I of the ECPA define the circumstances under which state and federal law enforcement agencies may intercept wire, oral and electronic communications in the course of criminal investigations. These provisions are divided among four sections of the Act: Section 2516, which lists the officers who may request court orders authorizing interceptions and the offenses in connection with which such orders may be sought; Section 2517, which governs the disclosure and

---

28. Paging transmissions that contain alphanumeric characters or other intelligence do not fall within this exception; they are electronic communications. Also, voice pager messages are treated as continuations of the wire communication made by the caller to the paging service. Report of the Committee of the Judiciary on the Electronic Communications Privacy Act, H.R. Rep. No. 647, 99th Cong., 2d Sess., 24–25 (1986).

29. 18 U.S.C.A. § 2510(12)(West 1996).

30. The Senate Report includes the following discussion of the scope of "electronic communication":

As a general rule, a communication is an electronic communication protected by the federal wiretap law if it is not carried by sound waves and cannot fairly be characterized as containing the human voice. Communications consisting solely of data, for example, and all communications transmitted only by radio are electronic communications. This term also includes electronic mail, digitized transmissions, and video teleconferences.

S. Rep. No. 541, 99th Cong., 2d Sess. (1986), *reprinted in* 1986 U.S. Cong. Code & Admin. News 3555 ("Senate Report").

31. Steve Jackson Games, Inc. v. United States Secret Service, 36 F.3d 457 (5th Cir. 1994).

use of information obtained through authorized law enforcement interceptions; Section 2518, which sets out an elaborate procedure for judicial issuance and supervision of law enforcement interception orders; and Section 2519, which requires periodic reports concerning interception activities to be made to the Administrative Office of the United States Courts and the Congress.[32]

Section 2516 distinguishes federal law enforcement interceptions of wire and oral communications, on the one hand, from federal law enforcement interceptions of electronic communications, on the other. Any federal government attorney may request a judicial order authorizing the interception of electronic communications and particularly "when such interception may provide or has provided evidence of *any Federal felony.*"[33] But judicial authorizations for interceptions of wire or oral communications may be requested only by certain, specified officers, and only in connection with a limited (although lengthy) list of federal offenses.[34]

Section 2518 specifies the contents of an application for an interception order, the mandatory elements of such an order, the scope of such an order, some procedural safeguards and a supervision process that the court ordering the interception must implement. As discussed further below, section 2518 also provides for emergency interception orders to be entered in defined situations.

Where a law enforcement official (state or federal) requests a judicial order authorizing the interception of wire, oral or electronic communications, the application must be made in writing and upon oath or affirmation.[35] The application must identify the officers making and authorizing the application, must state the applicant's authority to request an interception order and must include a "full and complete statement of the facts and circumstances relied upon by the applicant, to justify his belief that an order should be issued." The statement of facts and circumstances, in turn, must include, among other matters, "details as to the particular offense that has been, is being, or is about to be committed" and descriptions of the communications to be intercepted and the identity of the person whose communications are to be intercepted.[36] The applicant also must certify to the court that other investigative procedures have been unsuccessful or will be futile or dangerous; and

---

32. Another exception to the prohibitions of Chapter 119 has to do with so-called pen registers and trap-and-trace devices. *See* 18 U.S.C.A. § 2511(2)(h)(i)(West 1996). The conditions under which these devices may be used are set out at section 206 of title 18 of the United States Code.

33. 18 U.S.C.A. § 2516(3) (West 1996) (emphasis added).

34. *Id.* at § 2516(1). Section 2516(2) contains counterpart provisions for state law enforcement: the principal prosecuting attorney of any state, or of any political subdivision of a state, if authorized, may apply to a state court judge for an interception of wire, oral or electronic communications when "such interception may provide or has provided evidence of" the commission of certain enumerated offenses, or of any other offense "dangerous to life, limb, or property, and punishable by imprisonment for more than one year . . ."

35. *Id.* at § 2518(1). This is in contrast to applications for search warrants, which may be made by telephone.

36. *Id.* at § 2518(1)(b).

must state the period of time for which the interception will be required.[37]

A court may enter an interception order when it finds, from the facts submitted to it, that there is probable cause that someone is committing, has committed or is about to commit one of the offenses specified in the Act and that the requested interception will yield "communications concerning that offense."[38] The court also must find that the applicant has made the required showing that normal investigative procedures have been tried and failed, or are likely to fail or are too dangerous.[39]

Every interception order entered by a court must specify, among other things, the identity of the person (if known) whose communications will be intercepted, the type of communication to be intercepted, the offense to which the communication relates and the period of time during which the interception is authorized. The order may also include directions to landlords, service providers and others to assist the law enforcement agency in conducting the interception.[40] The order, in addition, may require the applicant to report to the court on the progress of, and continued need for, the interception.[41]

Section 2518 also imposes time limits on interception orders. Each authorization may be for no longer than necessary to achieve the purpose of the interception, and in any case no longer than thirty days. Extensions may be granted, but only upon application, subject to the same standards as an initial application and requiring the applicant to present a statement of the results obtained thus far, or "a reasonable explanation of the failure to obtain such results."[42] Extensions, like initial authorizations, must be for no longer than necessary and in any event for no longer than thirty days.[43]

Section 2518 also requires that the contents of any authorized interception shall, whenever possible, be recorded and the recordings tendered to the court. The court will order the recordings sealed and kept in a place of the court's choosing for at least ten years. Unless the court's seal is present on the recordings or a satisfactory explanation for

---

37. *Id.* at §§ 2518(c)-(d). The applicant also must describe "the nature and location of the facilities from which or the place where the communication is to be intercepted" (*id.* at § 2518(b)(ii)) unless the applicant can show that such specification of the facilities is impractical (for example, because the object of the interception is attempting to prevent interception by changing facilities (*id.* at § 2518(11))).

38. *Id.* at § 2518(3)(a)-(b).

39. *Id.* at § 2518(3)(c). The court also must find, from the description given in the application, that there is probable cause to believe that the "facilities from which, or the place where, the wire, oral, or electronic communications are to be intercepted are

being used, or are about to be used, in connection with the commission of such offense, or are leased to, listed in the name of, or commonly used by such person." *Id.* at § 2518(3)(d). This finding is not necessary, however, if the applicant has shown that a description of the facilities or place would be impractical. *Id.* at § 2518(11).

40. *Id.* at § 2518(4). Such persons are entitled to compensation for their reasonable expenses incurred in assisting in the interception. *Id.*

41. *Id.* at § 2518(6).

42. *Id.* at §§ 2518(5) and 2518(1)(f).

43. *Id.*

the seal's absence is provided, the contents may not be used or disclosed in connection with any court or other proceeding.[44]

The Act also provides for interceptions to be made before a court order is obtained if one of a specified group of law enforcement officers reasonably determines that grounds for a court order exist but that the interception must begin immediately because of an emergency involving death, serious physical injury, a breach of national security or "conspiratorial activities characteristic of organized crime."[45] Law enforcement officers relying on this provision must apply for a court order within forty-eight hours after interception begins. If no order is requested or if a request for an order is denied the contents of the communication "shall be treated as having been obtained in violation of [chapter 119] . . . ."[46]

Within ninety days after the expiration of an interception order, or after the denial of an application for authorization of an emergency interception already completed, the court must serve on the persons named in the interception a so-called "inventory", including the fact of the entry of the order or application, the date of entry and the period of authorized approved or disapproved interception, or the denial of the application and the fact that communications were or were not intercepted.[47] The court also may, in its discretion, give the targets of the interceptions access to as much of the communications, applications and orders "as the judge determines to be in the interest of justice."[48]

The ECPA also contains an exclusionary rule but makes it applicable only to evidence from wrongfully intercepted wire and oral (not electronic) communications.[49] The Act provides that an aggrieved person may move to suppress the contents of any intercepted wire or oral communication, or any evidence derived from that communication, on the grounds that the interception was unlawful, or that the application or order under by which the interception was authorized was legally insufficient, or that the interception "was not made in conformity with the order of authorization or approval."[50]

Section 2519 of the ECPA requires all courts that grant or deny interception orders (and extensions of such orders) to report the circumstances of the grant or denial to the Administrative Office of the United States Courts. Designated state and federal law enforcement officials must make similar reports to the Administrative Office in January of each year concerning all applications and interceptions undertaken during the preceding year. The Director of the Administrative Office of the

---

44. *Id.* at §§ 2518(8)(a) and 2517(3).

45. *Id.* at § 2518(7).

46. *Id.*

47. *Id.* at § 2518(8)(d).

48. *Id.* The contents of any intercepted wire, oral or electronic communication must be excluded from evidence, whether in state or federal court, unless "each party, not less than ten days before the trial, hearing, or proceeding, has been furnished with a copy of the court order, and accompanying application, under which the interception was authorized or approved." *Id.* at § 2518(9).

49. *Id.* § 2515.

50. *Id.* at § 2518(10)(a).

United States Courts, in turn, must give Congress each April "a full and complete report concerning the number of applications for orders authorizing or approving the interception of wire, oral, or electronic communications pursuant to this chapter ... during the preceding calendar year."[51]

(2) Cooperation With Interception Orders

In order to ensure that service providers will cooperate with law enforcement actions taken under sections 2516 through 2519, the ECPA provides that such entities and persons may, without violating the Act, "provide information, facilities, or technical assistance to persons authorized by law to intercept wire, oral, or electronic communications ..."[52] This exception applies only where the service provider has been furnished with a court order directing such assistance, or a certification that no warrant or court order is required and specifying the assistance required and the time during which it will be required.[53] The same section of Title I prohibits the system operator from telling anyone about the authorized surveillance with which it is assisting, and immunizes the system operator from liability for its cooperation with an authorized interception or surveillance by law enforcement authorities.[54]

(3) Interceptions of Communications Accessible to the Public

Another exception states that it shall not be unlawful for anyone to intercept or access an electronic communication made through an electronic communication system that is configured so that such electronic communication is readily accessible to the general public.[55] This exception applies primarily to on-line services and broadcast radio transmissions.

Where on-line services are concerned, this exception means that it is not unlawful to access communications to and from bulletin boards, chat lines and other services that are meant to be available to the public.

Where radio is concerned, the phrase "readily accessible to the general public" is defined at section 2510(16) and means that it is not unlawful to intercept a radio transmission that is not scrambled, encrypted, transmitted over a common carrier system or within certain other categories. This exception is likely to become more troubling as people use new, noncommon-carrier radio services to carry transmissions that they wish to keep confidential. Under the ECPA, users of such services will be forced to encrypt their communications if they wish to bring them within the protection of the Act.[56]

---

51. *Id.* at § 2519(3).

52. *Id.* at § 2511(2)(a)(ii).

53. *Id.* The certification must come from the court ordering the surveillance or one of the officials listed in § 2511(a)(ii)(B) or § 2518(7).

54. *Id.*

55. *Id.* at § 2511(2)(g)(i). The ECPA expressly makes this exception available under both Title I and Title II of the Act. Title II of the ECPA, which deals with access to stored communications, is discussed at section 11.13, *infra.*

56. For a discussion of encryption technologies and the governmental response to

(4) Protection of System Operators and Their Customers

Another, potentially quite broad, exception is for switchboard operators, wire and electronic system operators and other providers of communication facilities, who may intercept, disclose or use a wire communication carried over their facilities in the normal course of employment while "engaged in any activity which is a necessary incident to the rendition of his service or to the protection of the rights or property of the provider of that service."[57] (This exception does not permit the provider of a *wire* communication service to monitor communications at random "except for mechanical or service quality control checks.")[58]

A related exception provides that electronic communication system operators may "record the fact that a wire or electronic communication was initiated or completed in order to protect such provider, another provider furnishing service toward the completion of a wire or electronic communication, or a user of that service from fraudulent, unlawful or abusive use of such service."[59]

These "operator protection" provisions may prove useful to employers who provide communication systems for their employees' use. Employers who monitor employees' conversations, for example, may argue that in so doing they are protecting their rights or property as system providers.[60] It is questionable, of course, whether such claims will succeed where the interest protected is not the security or integrity of the employer-provided communication system itself but rather competitive or other interests of the employer.[61]

(5) The "One Party Consent" Exception

The ECPA permits a person "acting under color of law" to intercept a wire, electronic or oral communication where that person is a party to

those technologies, see section 11.12.F, *infra*.

57. 18 U.S.C.A. §§ 2511(2)(a)(i) and 2511(3)(b)(West 1996).

58. *Id.; see also* United States v. Christman, 375 F.Supp. 1354 (N.D.Cal.1974) (finding that private telephone installations, but not "communications common carriers," are permitted to engage in random monitoring). The application of this provision only to wire communications is deliberate. As the Senate Report on the proposed ECPA points out, "[t]he provider of electronic communications services may have to monitor a stream of transmissions in order to properly route, terminate, and otherwise manage the individual messages they contain." Senate Report at 20, *reprinted in* 1986 U.S. Code Cong. & Admin. News at 3574. Since these functions do not require system operators to listen in on voice conversations and may be necessary to provisioning of the service, they are permitted

for electronic (but not wire) service operators.

59. 18 U.S.C.A. § 2511(2)(h)(ii) (West 1996).

60. Although no reported cases have directly construed this exemption, a number of decisions have upheld the right of employers to monitor employees' telephone calls in order to protect legitimate interests of the employer. *See* Epps v. St. Mary's Hospital, Inc., 802 F.2d 412, 417 (11th Cir. 1986); Briggs v. American Air Filter Co., 630 F.2d 414, 420 (5th Cir.1980); James v. Newspaper Agency Corp., 591 F.2d 579, 581 (10th Cir.1979).

61. Of course, the Act already permits interception of information—such as telephone numbers—that may disclose the identities of the parties to a conversation. For employers who are concerned that their employees are talking to the press or to competitors, for example, this much information may suffice.

the communication or one of the parties to the communication has given his or her consent to the interception;[62] and it extends the same immunity to persons not acting under color of law who intercept those same communications under the same conditions, so long as those persons are not intercepting the communication "for the purpose of committing any criminal or tortious act in violation of the Constitution or laws of the United States or of any State."[63]

This "one party consent" exception is less stringent than the laws of many states that forbid interception of telephone conversations (and in some states, other types of communications as well) unless both parties to the conversation consent to the interception.[64] Persons planning to intercept a communication with the consent of only one party to the communication, therefore, should consult the laws of the state in which the interception will occur.

(6)   The Foreign Intelligence Exception

The ECPA immunizes the conduct of any officer, employee or agent of the United States who conducts electronic surveillance as defined in the Foreign Intelligence Surveillance Act of 1978.[65] The Act also expressly does not affect the ability of government agents involved in foreign surveillance through foreign communications and foreign electronic communication systems to perform electronic surveillance; but it also makes clear that the procedures in chapter 119 and in the Foreign Intelligence Surveillance Act of 1978 are the only means by which electronic surveillance and interception of domestic wire and oral communications may be conducted.[66]

(7) Exceptions for Disclosure or Divulgence by Electronic Communications Service Providers

The Act states that anyone providing an electronic communication service to the public shall not intentionally disclose or divulge the contents of any communication (unless sent to the system operator) while in transmission on that service to any person or entity other than an addressee or intended recipient.[67] The Act also includes certain exceptions to this rule, i.e.: an electronic system operator may divulge

62.   18   U.S.C.A.   § 2511(2)(c)   (West 1996).

63.   Id. § 2511(2)(d); see Manufacturas International, LTDA v. Manufacturers Hanover Trust Co., 792 F.Supp. 180, 192 (E.D.N.Y.1992); but see Deal v. Spears, 980 F.2d 1153, 1156–57 (8th Cir.1992). The ECPA eliminated the phrase "other injurious act," included in the one-party consent language of the 1968 legislation, in a conscious decision to overrule Boddie v. American Broadcasting Companies, 731 F.2d 333 (6th Cir.1984). In that case, a reporter's alleged desire to embarrass the subject of an intercepted conversation was found to satisfy the 1968 Act's exception to the one-party consent rule for interceptions made in connection with any "other injurious act."

64.   See, e.g., Cal. Penal Code §§ 631–32 (West 1996).

65.   18   U.S.C.A.   § 2511(2)(e)   (West 1996). For the provisions of the Foreign Intelligence Surveillance Act, see 50 U.S.C.A. §§ 1401–1408 (West 1996).

66.   18   U.S.C.A.   § 2511(2)(f)   (West 1996).

67.   Id. §§ 2511(1)(c) and 2511(3)(a).

the contents of communications when needed to render service,[68] protect the service provider's rights or property,[69] to comply with a court order or certification,[70] to comply with the request of the originator or any addressee or intended recipient,[71] to assist someone authorized to forward the communication to its destination,[72] or to cooperate with a law enforcement agency where the communication was inadvertently obtained and appears to relate to the commission of a crime.[73]

(8)   Other Exceptions

Title I contains an exception for interception of certain types of radio communications, including ship and aircraft distress signals, police and fire transmissions and amateur and citizens' band broadcasts.[74] The Act also permits interception of any wire or electronic communication that is causing harmful interference to other stations or equipment to the extent necessary to identify the source of the interference,[75] and it permits FCC employees to exercise their monitoring responsibilities under chapter 5 of the Communications Act, which may require the interception, disclosure or use of wire or electronic communications, or of "oral communication[s] transmitted by radio."[76]

d.   The Penalty Provisions of Chapter 119 of the ECPA

The penalty provisions of Chapter 119, like the rest of the statute, are complex. They set out two tiers of criminal penalties, a special injunction procedure, a civil right of action and a provision that decriminalizes certain (otherwise violative) conduct altogether.

Except as otherwise provided, violations of Chapter 119 are so-called "five-year felonies," calling for a maximum prison term of five years and a maximum fine set out in section 3623 of Title 18 of the United States Code.[77] These penalties apply to all intentional interceptions of wire communications including interceptions of the radio portion of a cellular telephone call.[78]

Lesser penalties are provided, however, for certain interceptions of radio communications. Specifically, if a defendant is a first offender and has intercepted the unscrambled, unencrypted radio portion of a cellular telephone communication, public land mobile service communication or paging service communication[79] and the interception was not made for a tortious or criminal purpose or for commercial gain, then the offender shall be fined not more than $500. If the defendant is a first offender and has intercepted an unscrambled, unencrypted radio communication

---

68. *Id.* § 2511(2)(a)(i).

69. *Id.*

70. *Id.*   §§ 2511(3)(b)(i),   2511(1), (2)(a)(ii) and 2517.

71. *Id.* § 2511(3)(b)(ii).

72. *Id.* § 2511(3)(b)(iii).

73. *Id.* § 2511(3)(b)(iv).

74. *Id.* § 2511(2)(g)(ii).

75. *Id.* § 2511(2)(g)(iv).

76. *Id.* at § 2511(2)(b).

77. *Id.* § 2511(4)(a). The specific schedule of fines is set out at § 3623 of title 18.

78. *See* 1986 U.S. Code Cong. & Admin. News 3575.

79. 18 U.S.C.A. § 2511(4)(b) (West 1996). This section also acknowledges that the radio portion of a cellular telephone call is a wire communication under the Act.

that is not the radio portion of a cellular telephone, public land mobile service or paging communication and the interception was not made for a tortious or criminal purpose or for commercial gain, then the defendant is subject to fine or imprisonment for not more than one year, or both.[80]

The penalty provisions of the ECPA also decriminalize certain conduct altogether. Specifically, section 2511(4)(c) permits the interception (except where done for financial gain) of satellite transmissions that are not encrypted or scrambled and that are transmitted to a broadcast station for retransmission to the public (*i.e.*, so-called "network feeds" from networks to local broadcasting stations) or to an "audio subcarrier intended for redistribution to facilities open to the public" (*i.e.*, music programming transmitted to broadcast stations, cable television operators, or the public areas of hospitals or office buildings.)[81] This provision does not decriminalize the interception of data transmissions or telephone calls that are otherwise protected by the Act.

The ECPA also creates a special enforcement procedure for wrongful interceptions of certain other radio transmissions. Specifically, section 2511(5) provides that if someone not acting for a tortious or criminal purpose or for financial gain intercepts either: (1) an unscrambled, unencrypted private satellite video communication for private viewing or (2) an unscrambled, unencrypted communication under subpart D of Part 74 of the FCC's rules, that person may be sued by the Government for injunctive relief (if the violation is a first offense) or will be subject (for a second or subsequent offense) to a mandatory $500 civil fine.[82] The first set of transmissions covered by section 2511(5) are private satellite communications, including those used for private videoteleconferencing.[83] The second set of transmissions covered by the section (so-called subpart D transmissions) generally are remote video feeds from mobile facilities to a broadcaster's studio.[84]

Finally, the ECPA authorizes a private right of action for persons aggrieved by violations of Title I. Successful plaintiffs may obtain injunctive relief and may recover actual or statutory damages, punitive damages and reasonable attorneys' fees and costs. Damage awards will equal the greater of (1) the sum of the plaintiff's actual damages and any profits the violator made by reason of the violation or (2) statutory damages of $100 a day or $10,000, whichever is greater.[85] The ECPA also provides for reduced civil remedies where the offense is the private viewing of a private satellite video communication that is scrambled or encrypted or where the communication is a radio communication under

80. *Id.*

81. *Id.* § 2511(4)(c); *see* Senate Report No. 99–541, 104th Cong., 2d Sess. 22, *reprinted in* 1986 U.S. Code Cong. & Admin. News 3576.

82. *Id.* § 2511(5).

83. *Id.*

84. *Id.* Subpart D of Part 74 can be found at 47 C.F.R. § 74.401 *et seq.* (1997).

85. 18 U.S.C.A. § 2520 (West 1996).

subpart D of Part 74 of the FCC's rules, so long as those interceptions are not made for a tortious or illegal purpose or for commercial gain.[86]

Subsection 2520(d) permits defendants in civil or criminal actions under the Act to establish a good faith defense where they have intercepted communications pursuant to court orders, warrants or similar authorizations, or in a good faith belief that their conduct was permitted by § 2511(e).[87] These good faith provisions establish an absolute defense to a civil or criminal action brought under the ECPA or any other law.[88]

e. Interception of Communications in Electronic Storage: the Steve Jackson Games Decision

One federal appellate court has found that the prohibitions of Chapter 119 do not apply to a seizure, by law enforcement officials, of undelivered electronic mail stored in a service provider's computer.

The *Steve Jackson Games* case[89] began with a raid on a publisher of books and games that also operated an electronic bulletin board and an electronic mail (E-mail) service. The Secret Service, which had obtained a search warrant but had not obtained an interception order, was seeking evidence concerning the alleged theft of a computer file concerning BellSouth's 911 emergency system as well as evidence of suspected "hacking" activity by a co-operator of the bulletin board system. Among the items seized and removed by the Secret Service was a computer containing "162 items of unread, private E-mail . . ."[90]

Steve Jackson Games, Inc., which operated the system on which the seized E-mail was stored, brought suit under Titles I and II of the ECPA and under the provisions of the Privacy Protection Act of 1980.[91] The district court found that while the seizure of the computer violated the Privacy Protection Act of 1980 (governing seizure of materials made or kept by publishers)[92] and Title II of the ECPA (governing unauthorized access to, and disclosure of, stored communications), it did not violate Title I of the Act because no interception had occurred.[93]

The Fifth Circuit Court of Appeals agreed with the district court. The Court of Appeals considered the appellant's commonsense argument that seizure of E-mail that has been sent, but not retrieved by the addressee, is an interception of a communication.[94] But the court nonetheless found that Congress, in defining "electronic communication" so as to exclude electronic communications in electronic storage, meant to distinguish electronic transmissions from wire communications which are defined to include communications in electronic storage. The court

86. *Id.* § 2520(c)(1).

87. *Id.* § 2511(d).

88. *Id.*

89. Steve Jackson Games, Inc. v. United States Secret Service, 36 F.3d 457 (5th Cir. 1994).

90. *Id.* at 459.

91. The Privacy Protection of Act of 1980 is discussed at section 11.13.B.4, *infra.*

92. 42 U.S.C.A. § 2000aa (West 1996).

93. Steve Jackson Games, Inc. v. United States Secret Service, 816 F.Supp. 432, 442 (W.D.Tex.1993).

94. Steve Jackson Games, 36 F.3d at 461.

found that while wire communications in electronic storage may be intercepted within the meaning of Title I of the ECPA, electronic communications in electronic storage may not be intercepted. Under the rule of *Steve Jackson Games*, therefore, persons seeking the protection of the ECPA against a seizure of stored E-mail must bring their actions under Title II of the Act.

C. Section 705 of the Communications Act

Section 705 of the Communications Act of 1934 complements, and to some extent overlaps with, the provisions of Title I of the Electronic Communications Privacy Act.[95] Specifically, section 705 prohibits (with some exceptions) the disclosure of wire or radio communications by persons involved in their receipt or transmission, and forbids the use or divulgence of certain unlawfully intercepted radio transmissions, including scrambled cable television programming transmitted by satellite.[96] Section 705 does not apply, however, to interceptions of wire or radio communications that do not result in disclosure or use of those communications: such interceptions are the province of Title I of the Electronic Communications Privacy Act.[97]

While section 705's restrictions on divulgence or use of wire communications apply only to persons involved in their receipt or transmission, the restrictions on interception, divulgence and use of radio communications apply to all persons.[98] Specifically, the section makes it unlawful for anyone not authorized by the sender to intercept a radio communication and divulge its existence or contents to anyone.[99] The section also prohibits anyone not entitled to do so to receive or assist in receiving a radio communication (or its contents) for "his own benefit or for the benefit of another not entitled thereto."[100] Also, anyone who obtains the contents of an intercepted radio communication knowing that it was intercepted will violate the section if he or she divulges the communication or uses it "for his own benefit or for the benefit of another not entitled thereto."[1]

---

95. Communications Act of 1934 § 705, 47 U.S.C.A. § 605 (West 1996).

96. The prohibition on divulgence of radio communications was first adopted by statute in 1912. Radio Act of 1912, Pub. L. No. 62–264, 37 Stat. 302 (1912).

97. *See, e.g.,* United States v. Seidlitz, 589 F.2d 152 (4th Cir.1978), *cert. denied,* 441 U.S. 922, 99 S.Ct. 2030, 60 L.Ed.2d 396 (1979). As discussed *supra,* the ECPA prohibits the interception of wire, oral and electronic communications, including the radio portion of a radio or cordless telephone call, and generally prohibits the interception of radio communications made over systems that are not configured so as to be accessible to the general public. *See* § 11.12.B, *supra* pp. 480–490.

98. Since passage of the 1968 Wiretap Act, section 705 does not cover unlawful interception and use of protected communications by law enforcement personnel. *See* United States v. Hall, 488 F.2d 193, 195 (9th Cir.1973).

99. 47 U.S.C.A. § 605(a) (West 1996). Section 705, unlike the ECPA, does not limit its prohibitions to divulgence of the contents of a communication. Instead, the section comprehensively addresses divulgence of the "existence, contents, substance, purport, effect, or meaning of such intercepted communication ..." *Id.*

100. *Id.*

1. *Id.*

As with the ECPA, a number of exceptions limit the application of section 705. Notably, persons receiving or involved in the transmission of wire or radio communications may disclose the "existence, contents, substance, purport, effect or meaning" of those communications to "the addressee, his agent, or attorney;" to anyone "employed or authorized to forward such communication to its destination;" or to "accounting or distributing officers of the various communicating centers over which the communication may be passed."[2] Exceptions also are provided for disclosure to the master of a ship on which the operator is serving, or in response to subpoenas, or "on demand of other lawful authority."[3]

The section also permits the receipt and divulgence of broadcast radio communications, distress calls and transmissions by amateur or citizens band radio operators and permits the interception or receipt of unscrambled, satellite cable programming for private viewing if no system for marketing those transmissions for private viewing exists, or where a marketing system does exist and the person viewing the programming has obtained authorization for private viewing under that system.[4]

The criminal penalties for violations of section 705 vary according to the purpose and intent of the wrongful conduct. If the defendant violated the section "willfully and for purposes of direct or indirect commercial advantage or private financial gain," then the offender faces a fine of not more than $50,000 or imprisonment for not more than 2 years, or both, for the first offense; and a fine of not more than $100,000 and imprisonment of not more than 5 years, or both, for any subsequent conviction.[5] Where the offense was willful but not committed for commercial advantage or financial gain, the offender faces a fine of not more than $2,000 or imprisonment for not more than 6 months, or both.[6]

The available civil remedies for violations of section 705 include both injunctive relief and damages along with awards of attorneys' fees and costs. The prevailing party may elect a damage award based either on: (1) the sum of his or her actual damages plus profits earned by the offender by reason of the offense; or (2) statutory damages under a formula set out in the Act.[7] The court also is granted discretion to increase the award of damages, whether actual or statutory, by not more than $100,000 for each violation or to reduce the award to a sum of not less than $250 where the violator "was not aware and had no reason to believe that his acts constituted a violation" of section 705.[8]

Since enactment of the 1968 Wiretap Act and the Electronic Communications Privacy Act, section 705 of the Communications Act no longer is the primary statutory constraint on misuse of wiretaps and intercepted radio transmissions. As amended from time to time, howev-

---

2. *Id.*

3. *Id.*

4. *Id.* § 605(b).

5. *Id.* § 605(e)(2).

6. *Id.* § 605(e)(1).

7. *Id.* § 605(e)(3)(C)(I).

8. *Id.* §§ 605(e)(3)(C)(ii)-(iii).

er, section 705 has a considerable role in the control of video piracy,[9] and is a useful supplement to the ECPA's constraints on interception of wire and radio communications.[10]

D. Trap And Trace Devices And Pen Registers

The Congress also has adopted statutory protections against particular surveillance techniques known as "pen registers" and "trap and trace" devices. A pen register records all telephone numbers dialed from a particular telephone, while a trap and trace device records the telephone numbers from which calls are placed to a particular telephone. After the Supreme Court, in *Smith v. Maryland*,[11] found that use of a pen register does not violate a reasonable expectation of privacy and therefore is not a "search" under the Fourth Amendment, the Congress enacted the provisions of chapter 206 of title 18 of the United States Code, regulating the use of both pen registers and trap and trace devices.[12]

Section 3121(a) of Chapter 206 provides, generally, that "no person may install or use a pen register or a trap and trace device without first obtaining a court order."[13] Such a device may be employed, however:

(1) in the operation, maintenance, and testing of a wire or electronic communication service or in protecting the rights or property of such provider or in protecting against abuse of service or unlawful use of service;

(2) to record the fact that a wire or electronic communication was initiated or completed in order to protect such provider from fraudulent, unlawful or abusive use of service; or

(3) where the consent of the user of that service has been obtained.[14]

---

9. Quincy Cablesystems, Inc. v. Sully's Bar, Inc., 640 F.Supp. 1159 (D.Mass.1986); Hoosier Home Theater, Inc. v. Adkins, 595 F.Supp. 389, 396 (S.D.Ind.1984). Theft of cable television service is covered at § 633 of the Communications Act of 1934, 47 U.S.C.A. § 553 (West 1996). Title I of the ECPA seeks to clarify the relationship between the ECPA and the video piracy and theft of cable service provisions of the Communications Act by providing that conduct prohibited by § 633 or permitted by § 705(b) of the Communications Act does not violate Title I of the ECPA. 18 U.S.C.A. § 2511(2)(g)(iii) (West 1996).

10. Because Title I of the ECPA prohibits interceptions of certain communications, while § 705 prohibits only interceptions accompanied by disclosure or misuse of the intercepted communications, violations of § 705 will generally violate the ECPA as well. The Congress was aware of this overlap, including the possibility of prosecutions under both statutes for the same conduct, when it enacted the ECPA. *See* 132 Cong.

Rec. S14, 452–53 (daily ed. Oct. 1, 1986) (Statement of Sen. Byrd); *see also* United States v. Crawford, 52 F.3d 1303, 1306 (5th Cir.1995)(finding that prosecution under both § 705 and Title I of the ECPA does not violate the Double Jeopardy Clause of the U.S. Constitution).

11. 442 U.S. 735, 99 S.Ct. 2577, 61 L.Ed.2d 220 (1979); *see also* United States v. New York Telephone Co., 434 U.S. 159, 98 S.Ct. 364, 54 L.Ed.2d 376 (1977), finding that a pen register does not violate Title I of the ECPA because the device does not acquire the "contents" of a protected communication.

12. 18 U.S.C.A. §§ 3121 *et seq.* (West 1985).

13. *Id.* § 3121(a).

14. *Id.* § 3121(b). The protection afforded by chapter 206 also is limited by the fact that no statutory exclusionary rule applies to information obtained through an unlawful trap and trace device or pen register. *See* United States v. Thompson, 936 F.2d

Knowing violations of these statutory limitations on the use of pen registers and trap and trace devices are punishable by fine, imprisonment for not more than one year, or both.[15]

E.   *The Foreign Intelligence Surveillance Act*

Until 1978, the authority of the executive branch of the federal government to engage in warrantless electronic surveillance for national security, rather than criminal investigative purposes was unclear.[16] The lack of comprehensive rules in this area invited government to abuse civil liberties by citing national security concerns in order to avoid the usual requirements for warrants and interception orders. The Foreign Intelligence Surveillance Act ("FISA") attempted to fill this vacuum with specialized tribunals and warrant procedures for use in connection with legitimate national security investigations.[17]

FISA's procedures apply to all "electronic surveillance" in connection with foreign intelligence rather than criminal conduct. FISA's definition of electronic surveillance includes electronic acquisitions of the contents of wire communications within the United States, or any wire or radio communication sent by or intended to be received by any "United States person"[18] in the United States where that United States person is the target of the surveillance and has a reasonable expectation of privacy and where a warrant would be required if the surveillance was in connection with a criminal investigation.[19] Electronic surveillance includes radio communications when both the sender and all intended recipients are in the United States.[20] In addition to these specific types of communications, electronic surveillance is defined to include the acquisition of information "other than from a wire or radio communication" where the target of the surveillance has a reasonable expectation of privacy and a warrant would be required if the surveillance was in connection with a criminal investigation.[21]

Applications for FISA warrants are heard by a special panel of seven district court judges, and the decisions of that panel may be appealed to another, special panel also established by the statute.[22] Applications are

---

1249 (11th Cir.1991), cert. denied 502 U.S. 1075, 112 S.Ct. 975, 117 L.Ed.2d 139 (1992).

15. 18 U.S.C.A. § 3121(d) (West 1985).

16. *See* United States v. United States District Court, 407 U.S. 297, 92 S.Ct. 2125, 32 L.Ed.2d 752 (1972); *see also* United States v. Brown, 484 F.2d 418 (5th Cir. 1973); United States v. Butenko, 494 F.2d 593 (3d Cir.1974) (en banc); Zweibon v. Mitchell, 516 F.2d 594 (D.C.Cir.1975).

17. 50 U.S.C.A. §§ 1801–1808 (West 1996).

18. A "United States person" is a U.S. citizen, a resident alien, an unincorporated association with substantial U.S. membership or a corporation organized under the laws of the United States. A corporation controlled by a foreign government is not a United States person. 50 U.S.C.A. § 1801(i) (West 1996).

19. *Id.* § 1801(f)(1).

20. *Id.* § 1801(f)(4).

21. *Id.* § 1801(f)(4). This language is sufficiently broad to bring electronic mail and other computer-to-computer communications within the reach of FISA.

22. 50 U.S.C.A. § 1803(a) (West 1996). Warrantless surveillance is permitted of communications between foreign powers where that surveillance is unlikely to acquire the contents of a communication in which a "United States person" is involved, and in certain other circumstances. *Id.* § 1802.

filed under seal, and must include the Attorney General's certification that the application complies with FISA as well as other certifications from the President's assistant for national security or another official designated by the President.[23] No surveillance authorized under FISA may exceed one year.[24]

Although FISA may seem far removed from the concerns of computer users and network operators, the fact is that the line between national security concerns and investigations of domestic criminal activity, such as terrorist acts, is a difficult one to draw.[25] Inevitably, therefore, some computer system operators and users who are not involved—knowingly or otherwise—with foreign intelligence activities will find themselves the targets of surveillance activities covered by FISA.

F.   The Encryption Debate

Many observers have concluded that the best protection against electronic surveillance is the conversion of communications into a form that is unintelligible to eavesdroppers. In contemporary communications technologies, this goal is advanced in two ways. First, persons who send and receive wire and electronic communications may deliberately encrypt those communications for transmission. Second, the digitization of transmissions over wireline telephone, cellular telephone and other communications systems and the disassembly of transmissions by packet switching and similar systems has the incidental effect of making those transmissions inaccessible and incomprehensible to persons seeking to intercept those communications through ordinary means.

While digitization and encryption are lawful, government views these technologies as a threat to its ability to engage in electronic surveillance—an activity that it finds enormously helpful in the investigation of crime. Accordingly, the federal government has urged the implementation of systems that facilitate eavesdropping on encrypted communications and has secured the passage of legislation that requires common carriers to make their networks "wiretap friendly."

1.   The Clipper Chip

Modern encryption technologies tend to be of two kinds—public key and private key. With public key methods, the user instructs a cryptography program to generate two keys.[26] One key is the user's private key that he or she keeps secret. The other is a public key that the user gives to the persons with whom he or she will exchange communications. Persons sending messages to the holder of the private key will use the

---

23. *Id.* §§ 1804(a)(4)-(6), 1804(a)(5), 1804(a)(7)(c).

24. *Id.* § 1802(a)(1).

25. *See* United States v. Sarkissian, 841 F.2d 959, 964 (9th Cir.1988), upholding electronic surveillance under FISA rather than the ECPA, in an investigation of terrorist activities that violated criminal law.

26. A "key" is merely a long sequence of characters. The best-known public key system is the Pretty Good Privacy ("PGP") program, developed by Phil Zimmerman and available free of charge on the Internet.

public key to encrypt the message before transmission. The recipient then uses the private key to decrypt the message.[27]

Private key systems are simpler than public key systems but also are less secure. With a private key method, the key used by the sender to encrypt the message is sent to the recipient, who uses the same key to decrypt the message. Obviously, the need to send the private key to all recipients of a message increases the risk that the key will become available to others.[28]

The Clinton Administration has proposed a public key encryption system that would facilitate government eavesdropping on encrypted communications. The so-called Clipper Chip initiative, announced by the White House in April of 1993, proposed that a standard microprocessor be installed in telephones, personal computers and other communications devices. The actual encryption algorithm contained in the Clipper Chip, called Skipjack, would be classified. Two agents of the United States government would hold so-called "escrowed keys," which would be released to law enforcement personnel upon presentation of a warrant or other sufficient authorization to conduct electronic surveillance.

An example will help to show how the Clipper Chip is supposed to work. Each device equipped with a Clipper Chip will contain a serial number, a unit key and a family key. While the serial number and unit key will be unique to the particular chip, the family key will be uniform among Clipper Chips and known only to the government. The Clipper Chip's serial number will be reported to the government when the telephone or other device is sold. Then, each time the device makes a call to another device equipped with the Clipper Chip, the two devices will create a session key according to which the conversation will be encrypted and decrypted. The Clipper Chip will combine the session key with the unit key, serial number and family key to produce the Law Enforcement Access Field ("LEAF"), which will be transmitted ahead of the actual conversation or other substantive transmission between the parties to the call.

If a law enforcement agency wants to eavesdrop on your call it simply records the conversation, uses the family key to decrypt the LEAF and derives the serial number and session key. Next, the law enforcement agency requests the two escrow keys from the escrow agents, and uses the escrow keys to decrypt the transmissions.

Not surprisingly, the Clipper Chip proposal has generated considerable controversy. Some of the objections are practical, rather than legal or philosophical. Opponents of the intitiative point out that because the Skipjack algorithm is classified, the algorithm cannot be independently

27. Public key programs generate private keys that cannot be "reverse engineered" from the public key.

28. The U.S. Commerce Department has adopted a private key system, known as the Data Encryption Standard, for protection of unclassified data in U.S. government computers.

tested to determine its reliability and susceptibility to compromise. Other critics point out that a government-imposed encryption technology will not deter the most sophisticated criminal and terrorist elements who will simply deploy alternative encryption systems of their own and evade any surveillance dependent on the Clipper Chip.

More fundamental objections assume that government eventually will mandate the use of Clipper Chip or other "key escrow" encryption and forbid the use of alternative technologies.[29] If this occurs, lawful encryption no longer will be available as a means of avoiding government surveillance. The arguments against this result tend to be of three kinds.

The first category of argument is more philosophical than legal and decries the possible loss of a tool that promises to make governmental surveillance—whether lawful or unlawful—more difficult. On this view, the democratization of encryption technology tips the scale of privacy strongly in the direction of individual freedom and against the interests of the state.[30] For those who feel that privacy outweighs the crime-control utility of electronic surveillance this argument has considerable appeal.

The second category of argument emphasizes the likelihood that law enforcement will misuse its monopoly of the escrowed keys to engage in unauthorized surveillance and that foreign governments or private parties may gain access to the escrowed keys or the government's surveillance database.[31] The weakness of these arguments is that the danger of unlawful surveillance, once the system has been compromised in one of these ways, is still no greater than it is in the present, generally unencrypted, communications environment.

The third category suggests that the government, by forcing private citizens to install and use a device designed to facilitate government surveillance, would violate protections ensured by the First, Fourth and Fifth Amendments to the United States Constitution.[32] These arguments, too, are somewhat doubtful so long as orders authorizing interception through escrowed keys continue to be issued by neutral magistrates who enforce the established constitutional safeguards.

At this writing, neither the Clipper Chip nor any other key escrow proposal has been enacted into law. Until encrypted communications become more common the government probably will not bring this politically charged idea forward again. That legislation mandating technological cooperation with governmental surveillance can succeed, how-

---

29. In its Clipper Chip announcement, the Clinton Administration emphasized that use of the technology would be entirely voluntary.

30. *See e,g,,* John Perry Barlow, "Jackboots on the Infobahn," *Wired*, April 1994.

31. *See* ANDRE BACARD, THE COMPUTER PRIVACY HANDBOOK 101–102 (1995).

32. A. Michael Froomkin, *The Constitutionality of Mandatory Key Escrow—A First Look*, in BUILDING IN BIG BROTHER 413 (1994) (Lance J. Hoffman, ed.); *see also Cryptographic Issue Statements: Letter to the Computer System Security and Privacy Advisory Board*, in *id.* at 408.

ever, is demonstrated by the passage of the Communications Assistance for Law Enforcement Act.

2. The Communications Assistance for Law Enforcement Act

Even where communications are not deliberately encrypted, the increasing digitization of wireline and wireless networks, along with intelligent network features such as call forwarding, may pose obstacles to conventional methods of electronic surveillance. Notably, a law enforcement officer who merely taps into a line or radio signal carrying digitized information will hear nothing but meaningless electronic chatter. In order to make sense of the transmission—whether containing data or the digitized human voice—the officer must have the means to decode the bit stream. Similarly, an officer who obtains an order authorizing a tap on a particular line will not intercept calls that have been automatically forwarded, through a telephone company's call forwarding service, to a different telephone number.

All of these obstacles created by technology can, of course, be overcome by technology, and there is no evidence that law enforcement has been unable to carry out interception orders because of technical obstacles.[33] Nonetheless, federal law enforcement officials proposed, and the Congress enacted, a statute that requires all telecommunications carriers to make electronic surveillance a design criterion for telecommunications networks. Under what is popularly known as the Communications Assistance for Law Enforcement Act ("CALEA"),[34] carriers must ensure the ability of government to isolate and intercept both call-identifying information and the substance of wire and electronic communications transmitted over the carriers' facilities.[35] The responsibility for developing the capabilities required to comply with CALEA is left to the carriers in the first instance, but the Federal Communications Commission is empowered to impose specific requirements by regulation if necessary.[36] The government is required to pay carriers their costs of compliance with the Act.[37]

CALEA, like the Clipper Chip proposal, represents government's desire to preserve the ease with which electronic eavesdropping was accomplished in the analog, pre-encryption age of telecommunications. Rather than meet the challenge of new technologies through its own ingenuity, the government prefers to conscript private citizens, equipment manufacturers and carriers as part of the apparatus of law enforcement. While this approach may be lawful, it represents a new chapter in the aggrandizement of state power.

---

33. In 1992 William Sessions, the head of the Federal Bureau of Investigation, admitted to Congress that no interception orders had issued that could not be executed. *See* New York Times, Mar. 27, 1992, p. A19.

34. Communications Assistance for Law Enforcement Act, Pub. L. 103–414, 108 Stat. 4279 (1994), *codified at* 47 U.S.C.A. §§ 1001 *et seq.* (West Supp. 1997).

35. *Id.* § 103(a), *codified at* 47 U.S.C.A. § 1002(a) (West Supp. 1997).

36. *Id.* § 107, *codified at* 47 U.S.C.A. § 1006 (West Supp. 1997).

37. *Id.* § 109, *codified at* 47 U.S.C.A. § 1008 (West Supp. 1997).

11.13   Privacy Issues Involving Stored Personal Information: Control of Access, Accuracy, Disclosure and Use

While interception of communications is an especially dramatic form of intrusion, misuse of personal information already stored in written or electronic form also is a substantial challenge to personal privacy. Under present law, the rights of individuals to control access to and disclosure of stored personal information, and to ensure that such information is accurate, vary widely depending upon the type of information that is collected, the purpose for which it is collected and the nature of the public or private institution or enterprise that is doing the collecting. This section reviews the principal sources of statutory, constitutional and common law protection for the privacy interest in stored personal information.

A.   Constitutional Challenges to Governmental Access to Stored Information

Persons aggrieved by governmental collection and use of personal information have sought redress in the constitutional right of privacy and in the protections of the Fourth Amendment to the United States Constitution. While these efforts have met with little practical success, they have resulted in judicial recognition that, in a proper case, the Constitution will restrain the government's collection and use of personal information.

The first Supreme Court case articulating a right of privacy is *Griswold v. Connecticut* ("*Griswold*")[1], a decision involving a challenge to a state anti-contraception statute. The Court found in *Griswold* that a right to privacy is fairly implied from the specific guarantees of the Bill of Rights. (As the Court's opinion famously puts it, the right is among the "penumbras" of the Bill of Rights "formed by emanations from those guarantees that help give them life and substance.")[2]

Cases subsequent to *Griswold* have defined the right of privacy primarily as a guarantee of noninterference by government in such private matters as marriage and abortion.[3] The Court has declined to place the interest in nondisclosure of personal information in the same

---

1. 1 381 U.S. 479, 85 S.Ct. 1678, 14 L.Ed.2d 510 (1965).

2. *Id.* at 484, 85 S.Ct. at 1681, 14 L.Ed.2d at 514. The majority opinion located these penumbras around the First Amendment's guarantee of peaceful assembly, the Third Amendment's prohibition of quartering of troops, the Fourth Amendment's prohibition of unreasonable searches and seizures, and the Fifth Amendment freedom from compelled self-incrimination. Justice Goldberg, concurring, found the rationale in the Ninth Amendment's reservation of nonenumerated rights to the people; while Justice Harlan opined that the right

to privacy is to be found in the liberty guaranteed by the Due Process Clause of the Fourteenth Amendment. In a later decision, the Court settled on the Fourteenth Amendment's concept of personal liberty as the source of the right. Roe v. Wade, 410 U.S. 113, 152, 93 S.Ct. 705, 726, 35 L.Ed.2d 147, 176 (1973).

3. Loving v. Virginia, 388 U.S. 1, 87 S.Ct. 1817, 18 L.Ed.2d 1010 (1967); Roe v. Wade, 410 U.S. 113, 93 S.Ct. 705, 35 L.Ed.2d 147 (1973); Moore v. East Cleveland, 431 U.S. 494, 97 S.Ct. 1932, 52 L.Ed.2d 531 (1977).

class as these matters,[4] but the Court has acknowledged that government inquiry into, and disclosure of, purely personal matters might violate the right of privacy where the inquiry and disclosure involve one of the fundamental rights.[5]

The principal Supreme Court decision concerning the privacy right in nondisclosure of personal information is *Whalen v. Roe* ("*Whalen*"). In that case, a group of physicians and patients challenged a New York State statute requiring the collection and maintenance of a database of all prescriptions written for drugs that had both lawful and unlawful uses.[6] In the plaintiffs' view, the statute invaded their privacy in two ways: first, it threatened them with harm to their reputations if the information in the database was disclosed; and second, it inhibited the physicians' willingness to write, and the patients' willingness to use, prescriptions for certain drugs. A three-judge district court reviewing the statute had found that "the doctor-patient relationship" is one of the zones of privacy accorded "constitutional protection" and that in requiring physicians to disclose the identities of patients for whom they had written prescriptions the statute had invaded the doctor-patient relationship with a "needlessly broad sweep."[7]

The Supreme Court found, however, that the New York statute did not "pose a sufficiently grievous threat" to either of the two kinds of privacy rights recognized by the Court—*i.e.*, the "interest in avoiding disclosure of personal matters," and the "interest in independence in making certain kinds of important decisions"—to violate the United States Constitution. [8]Notably, the Court found no evidence that the security provisions of the New York data-gathering process were inadequate to protect prescription records from unauthorized disclosure. The Court also found that the compilation of the database, while it might discourage some persons from seeking needed medication, had not "deprive[d] the public of access to drugs" or "deprived any individual of the right to decide independently, with the advice of his physician, to acquire and to use needed medication."[9] On this record, the Court concluded that the patient-identification requirements of the statute did not "constitute an invasion of any right or liberty protected by the Fourteenth Amendment."[10]

The *Whalen* decision did, however, give some comfort to privacy advocates by expressly recognizing, in *dicta*, that unwarranted disclosure by government of personal information could present a constitutional question:

4. *See* Paul v. Davis, 424 U.S. 693, 713, 96 S.Ct. 1155, 1166, 47 L.Ed.2d 405, 421 (1976).

5. *See* Whalen v. Roe, 429 U.S. 589, 97 S.Ct. 869, 51 L.Ed.2d 64 (1977); *see also* Paul v. Davis, *supra*, 424 U.S. at 713–14, 96 S.Ct. at 1166, 47 L.Ed.2d at 421.

6. Whalen, 429 U.S. at 591, 97 S.Ct. at 872, 51 L.Ed.2d at 68.

7. *Id.* at 596, 97 S.Ct. at 874–75, 51 L.Ed.2d at 71.

8. *Id.* at 599–600, 97 S.Ct. at 876–77, 51 L.Ed.2d at 73–74.

9. *Id.* at 603, 97 S.Ct. at 878, 51 L.Ed.2d at 75.

10. *Id.*

We are not unaware of the threat to privacy implicit in the accumulation of vast amounts of personal data in computerized data banks or other massive government files. The collection of taxes, the distribution of welfare and social security benefits, the supervision of public health, the direction of our Armed Forces, and the enforcement of the criminal law all require the orderly preservation of great quantities of information, much of which is personal in character and potentially embarrassing or harmful if disclosed.

The right to collect and use such data for public purposes is typically accompanied by a concomitant statutory or regulatory duty to avoid unwarranted disclosures. Recognizing that in some circumstances that duty arguably has its roots in the Constitution, nevertheless New York's statutory scheme, and its implementing administrative procedures, evidence a proper concern with, and protection of, the individual's interest in privacy. We therefore need not, and do not, decide any question which might be presented by the unwarranted disclosure of accumulated private data—whether intentional or unintentional—or by a system that did not contain comparable security provisions.[11]

Challenges to disclosure of stored personal information also have been brought under the Fourth Amendment. In the principal Supreme Court case—*United States v. Miller*—the Court found that a criminal suspect had no Fourth Amendment interest in checks and deposit slips obtained through subpoenas served upon the suspect's banks.[12] The Court found that records maintained by a depositor's bank are not the depositor's "private papers," but instead are business records of the bank.[13] Responding to the argument that a depositor makes his or her records available to a bank for a limited purpose and retains a "reasonable expectation of privacy" in those records, the Court stated that persons lose any reasonable expectation of privacy in information that they voluntarily convey to others.[14] Where bank records, in particular, are concerned, the Court concluded that "[t]he depositor takes the risk,

11. *Id.* Justice Brennan, concurring, also expressed concern about the potential for abuse of large governmental databases but agreed that the New York statute's "provisions for computer storage, on their face, [did not] amount to a deprivation of constitutionally protected privacy interests ..." *Id.* at 607. 97 S.Ct. at 880, 51 L.Ed.2d at 78. *See also* United States Department of Justice v. Reporters Committee for Freedom of the Press, 489 U.S. 749, 109 S.Ct. 1468, 103 L.Ed.2d 774 (1989) (recognizing "a strong privacy interest ... in the nondisclosure of compiled computerized information ...").

12. 425 U.S. 435, 96 S.Ct. 1619, 48 L.Ed.2d 71 (1976).

13. *Id.* at 440, 96 S.Ct. at 1623, 48 L.Ed.2d at 77–78. In Boyd v. United States, 116 U.S. 616, 622, 6 S.Ct. 524, 528, 29 L.Ed. 746, 748 (1886), the Supreme Court had held the Fourth Amendment applicable to "compulsory production of a man's private papers."

14. In rejecting the respondent's *Katz* argument, the *Miller* Court pointed to the language in that decision stating that "[w]hat a person knowingly exposes to the public ... is not a subject of Fourth Amendment protection." 425 U.S. at 442, 96 S.Ct. at 1623, 48 L.Ed.2d at 78, *quoting* Katz v. United States, 389 U.S. 347, 351, 88 S.Ct. 507, 511, 19 L.Ed.2d 576, 582 (1967).

in revealing his affairs to another, that the information will be conveyed by that person to the Government."[15]

Although the Supreme Court has not yet found a reasonable expectation of privacy in stored communications held by third parties, the Court of Appeals for the Armed Forces has held that users of electronic mail systems have a reasonable expectation of privacy in electronic mail stored in their service providers' computers. In *United States v. Maxwell* (*"Maxwell"*),[16] an Air Force colonel had engaged in a sexually explicit, electronic mail correspondence with a junior officer and had used his personal computer to download child pornography. The Court of Appeals for the Armed Forces found that the defendant's service provider, America On-line, had divulged the contents of some communications that were not covered by the warrant served upon America On-line. The court found that the production of those communications violated the Fourth Amendment,[17] and expressly stated that persons have a reasonable expectation of privacy in their electronic mail because their "individually assigned passwords" create an objectively low risk that electronic mail, either transmitted to other subscribers or stored in the service provider's computers, will be accessed by others.[18]

As *Whalen* and *Miller* demonstrate, protection of rights in stored personal information under the United States Constitution is highly uncertain.[19] For more specific and reliable—if less than comprehensive—protections, it is necessary to look to a patchwork of statutes enacted by the Congress and the state legislatures.

B. Statutory Protection Of Stored Personal Information

The United States lacks a broad, statutory scheme governing the collection and use of personal information by private and governmental agents. Instead, the federal and state governments have enacted laws that restrain some actors—such as government agencies and credit

---

15. Miller, 425 U.S. at 443, 96 S.Ct. at 1624, 48 L.Ed.2d at 79. The *Miller* case led directly to passage of the Right to Financial Privacy Act of 1978, which in most circumstances requires law enforcement agencies to obtain a warrant, subpoena or court order as a predicate to obtaining a depositor's records from a financial institution. 12 U.S.C.A. §§ 3401 *et seq.* (West 1996).

16. 42 M.J. 568 (A.F.Ct.Crim.App.1995), *rev'd in part on other grounds,* 45 M.J. 406 (1996). The Court of Military Appeals hears cases from the highest courts of each branch of the Armed Services. Its judges are civilians appointed for terms of fifteen years. The Supreme Court has jurisdiction to hear appeals from this court by writ of certiorari.

17. The court rejected the government's argument that American On-line's disclosure of items not called for in the warrant was purely private action.

18. Because the most serious charges against Colonel Maxwell were established by evidence obtained through a separate, properly-executed warrant, the convictions on those charges were allowed to stand. The case was remanded for possible reconsideration of the court martial's sentence.

19. *But see* Merriken v. Cressman, 364 F.Supp. 913 (E.D.Pa.1973), in which a district court found that questions put to students by school officials asking for intimate information concerning the students' family lives violated the constitutional right of privacy because they intruded excessively on the parent-child relationship. Among the record facts that influenced the court's decision was evidence that parental consent to the program was obtained upon less than full disclosure and that strict confidentiality of the information provided in response to the questions was not maintained.

reporting bureaus—fairly stringently while leaving a number of other actors and activities either unregulated or thinly regulated. Even where detailed statutory restrictions are in place, those statutes tend to rely upon affected individuals, rather than regulators, to enforce the protections they provide.

This section reviews the principal federal statutes offering protection against misuse of stored personal information.

1. The Electronic Communications Privacy Act—Title II

The federal government's most comprehensive response to the problem of informational privacy is the Electronic Communications Privacy Act of 1986, or ECPA. Title I of the ECPA, already discussed, protects electronic communications from unauthorized interception during transmission.[20] Title II of the ECPA protects electronic communications from unauthorized acquisition while those communications are in electronic storage.[21] We deal in this section with Title II of the Act, which is codified at Chapter 121 of Title 18 of the United States Code.[22]

Title II of the ECPA protects two kinds of electronic communications. First, the ECPA protects electronic mail, transmissions to electronic bulletin boards and other communications carried by providers of so-called "electronic communication services."[23] Second, the ECPA protects electronic communications between "remote computing services" and their customers—e.g., communications and funds transfers among bank computers, computerized transfers of medical records between physicians and hospitals and "transmission of proprietary data among the various offices of a company."[24]

Specifically, the ECPA makes it a criminal offense for anyone intentionally to access, without authorization, a facility through which an electronic communication service is provided (or intentionally to exceed an authorization to access that facility) and through such access to obtain, alter or prevent authorized access to a wire or electronic communication while it is in electronic storage.[25] The ECPA also makes

---

20. For a discussion of the provisions of Title I of the ECPA, *see* section 11.12.B, *supra*.

21. The Act also includes a Title III, which applies to so-called pen registers and trap and trace devices. *See* section 11.13.D, *infra*.

22. 18 U.S.C.A. §§ 2701 *et seq.* (West 1996).

23. The Act defines "electronic communication service" as "any service which provides to users thereof the ability to send or receive wire or electronic communications." *Id.* at § 2510(15). The definitions of wire and electronic communications are the same as those for Title I of the ECPA discussed *supra*.

24. Sen. Rep. No. 541, 99th Cong. 2d Sess. (1968), *reprinted in* 1968 U.S. Code Cong. & Admin. News 3562. The Act defines a "remote computing service" as "the provision to the public of computer storage or processing services by means of an electronic communications system." 18 U.S.C.A. § 2710(2) (West 1996). An electronic communications system, in turn, is defined as "any wire, radio, electromagnetic, photooptical or photoelectronic facilities for the transmission of electronic communications, and any computer facilities or related electronic equipment for the electronic storage of such communications." *Id.* at § 2510(14).

25. *Id.* § 2701(a).

it a crime for any provider of electronic communication service or remote computing service to the public to knowingly divulge the contents of a communication stored in, or carried or maintained on, that electronic communication service or remote computing service.[26] The penalties for violations of Title II vary, depending on whether the offense is committed "for purposes of commercial advantage, malicious destruction or damage, or private commercial gain." Where these motives are present, the offender may be fined not more $250,000 or imprisoned not more than one year, or both, for a first offense; and may be fined not more than $250,000 or imprisoned for not more than two years, or both, for any subsequent offense.[27] The ECPA also creates a private right of action for those harmed by unauthorized access to, and disclosure of, their stored communications.

Title II includes a number of exceptions to its prohibitions, some of which apply to private actors and some of which apply exclusively to "governmental entities." First, anyone may *access* stored information, and thereby obtain, alter, or prevent authorized access to a wire or electronic communication while it is in electronic storage in that system, if such conduct is authorized by the service provider or a user of the service with respect to a communication "of or intended for that user."[28] Second, anyone may *divulge* the contents of a communication to an addressee or intended recipient of the communication (or such addressee or intended recipient's agent), or with the lawful consent of the originator, addressee (or subscriber, in the case of remote computing service), or to anyone employed or authorized to forward the communication to its destination.[29] Finally, a system operator may divulge the contents of a communication where such disclosure is "necessarily incident to the rendition of the service or to the protection of the rights or property of the provider of that service" or to a law enforcement agency where the system operator inadvertently obtained the contents of the communication and those contents appear to pertain to the commission of a crime.[30]

---

26. *Id.* § 2702(a). Where a remote computing service is involved, the prohibition on disclosure of contents applies to "divulgence [of] ... the contents of any communication which is carried on that service (A) on behalf of, and received by means of electronic transmission from (or created by means of computer processing of communications received by means of electronic transmission from) a subscriber or customer of such service; and (B) solely for the purpose of providing storage or computer processing services to such subscriber or customer, if the provider is not authorized to access the contents of any such communications for purposes of providing any services other than storage or computer processing." *Id.* § 2702(a)(2). This narrow prohibition does not forbid the disclosure, for example, of customer data that merchants transmit to compilers of telemarketing databases or any other information transmitted for purposes other than "storage or computer processing."

27. *Id.* § 2701. Where the offense is not committed for commercial advantage, malicious destruction or damage, or private commercial gain, the penalties are a fine of not more $5,000 or imprisonment for not more than six months, or both. *Id.*

28. *Id.* § 2701(c). The Act defines a "user" as "any person or entity who (A) uses an electronic communication service; and (B) is duly authorized by the provider of such service to engage in such use ..." *Id.* § 2510(13).

29. *Id.* §§ 2702(b)(1), (3) and (4).

30. *Id.* § 2702(b)(6). The Act does not define "system operator."

a.   Section 2703 of the Act

Disclosure of stored communications to governmental entities under Title II are governed by section 2703 of the Act. Section 2703 defines certain circumstances under which the government must obtain a search warrant in order to compel disclosure of communications in electronic storage, and defines other circumstances in which the government must give the system operator, subscriber or user notice and an opportunity to resist disclosure. The rules vary according to whether the communication is stored in an electronic communication service or a remote computing service.

Where a communication is in electronic storage in an electronic communication service, the rules vary according to whether the communication has been in storage in that system for 180 days or less or has been in storage in that system for more than 180 days. If the communication has been stored in the system for 180 days or less the service provider may be compelled to disclose the content of the communication only "pursuant to a warrant issued under the Federal Rules of Criminal Procedure or equivalent State warrant."[31] If the communication has been stored in the system for more than 180 days, then disclosure may be compelled pursuant to warrant or, if a warrant is not obtained, pursuant to an administrative subpoena, Federal or state grand jury subpoena or trial subpoena, or pursuant to a special procedure established by the ECPA.[32]

The special ECPA procedure for governmental access to stored communications requires the requesting governmental entity to give notice to the subscriber or customer before the order is executed, and to demonstrate to the court from which the order is requested that "there is reason to believe that the contents of a wire or electronic communication ... are relevant to a legitimate law enforcement inquiry."[33] If the service provider brings a prompt motion to quash, the court may quash or modify an order under the ECPA procedure "if the information or records requested are unusually voluminous ... or compliance with such order otherwise would cause an undue burden on such provider."[34]

Title II also recognizes that in some circumstances, notice to the subscriber or customer may result in destruction of the communications as to which the governmental entity is seeking disclosure. Accordingly,

31. Id. § 2703(a). The 180–day requirement captures most electronic mail, which typically is stored in a communication service for a limited time. By requiring a warrant for compelled disclosure of such communications, the ECPA limits their disclosure to cases in which there is probable cause to believe that the communications contain evidence of a crime. See United States v. Rundle, 327 F.2d 153, 162–63 (3d Cir.1964). At the same time, the warrant procedure permits communications described in the warrant to be seized without notice to the system operator or subscriber. See, e.g., Zurcher v. Stanford Daily, 436 U.S. 547, 573, 98 S.Ct. 1970, 1985, 56 L.Ed.2d 525, 546 (1978) (Stewart, J., dissenting).

32. 18 U.S.C.A. § 2703(b) (West 1996). Unlike a warrant, a subpoena or order issued under the special ECPA procedure will not permit disclosure without prior notice to the customer or subscriber.

33. Id. § 2703(d).

34. Id.

Title II permits the governmental entity to include in its subpoena or court order, before notice is given to the customer or subscriber, a request to the service provider to create a backup copy of the communications as to which disclosure is sought.[35] The government may include such a request if in its sole discretion it determines that notice of a subpoena or court order may result in the destruction of, or tampering with, the evidence.[36] The system operator may not notify the customer or subscriber of the request and must create the backup copy within two business days and notify the government that the backup copy has been made. After confirmation from the system operator is received, the government must notify the subscriber or customer within three days unless certain exceptions set out in section 2705 apply. The service provider must preserve the backup copy until the information is delivered or any judicial proceedings concerning the subpoena or order have been resolved, whichever event occurs later.[37]

Within fourteen days after the notice to the subscriber or customer is made of the subpoena or court order, the subscriber or customer may move to quash the subpoena or vacate the court order. A motion to vacate must be made with the court that issued the order, and a motion to quash must be made "in the appropriate United States district court or State court."[38] A motion to quash or vacate must recite that the applicant is a customer or subscriber to the service from which the information is sought and must state "the applicant's reasons for believing that the records sought are not relevant to a legitimate law enforcement inquiry or that there has not been substantial compliance with the provisions of this chapter in some other respect."[39]

If the court finds that the applicant has made the required showing, it will order the government to file a sworn response (which may be filed *in camera*, if appropriate) and may conduct additional proceedings as required.[40] The statute provides that orders denying a motion to quash or application to vacate are not final orders, and therefore are not subject to interlocutory appeal.[41]

The rules for compelled disclosure of communications stored in a remote computing service are somewhat different from those for communications stored in an electronic communication service.[42] Specifically, *all* communications stored in a remote computing service (not just those

35. *Id.* § 2704(a).

36. *Id.* § 2704(a)(5).

37. *Id.* § 2704(a)(3).

38. *Id.* § 2704(b)(1).

39. *Id.*

40. *Id.* § 2704(b)(3).

41. *Id.* § 2704(b)(5).

42. A warrant, subpoena or order pursuant to section 2703(d) is required for compelled disclosure of any electronic communication held in or maintained on a remote computing service (A) on behalf of, and received by means of electronic transmission from (or created by means of computer processing of communications received by means of electronic transmission from), a subscriber or customer of such remote computing service; and (B) solely for the purpose of providing storage or computer processing services to such subscriber or customer, if the provider is not authorized to access the contents of any such communications for purposes of providing any services other than storage or computer processing. *Id.* § 2703(b)(2).

that have been in storage for more than 180 days) may be disclosed pursuant to warrant, subpoena or the special procedure set out in § 2703(d).[43] The procedure for backup storage of communications sought by the governmental entity apply to communications held in remote computing services as well as communications held in electronic communication services.

Title II also governs the disclosure to governmental agencies of records or other information pertaining to users or subscribers, as distinguished from the contents of the users' or subscribers' communications. A provider of electronic communication or remote computing service may disclose such information to a governmental entity only where that entity has the consent of the customer or subscriber or has a warrant, subpoena or court order under the special procedure set out in the Act.

b.   Miscellaneous Provisions of the Act

The statute provides for the government to reimburse service providers for costs incurred in complying with a subpoena or court order and creates a private right of action for service providers, subscribers or customers who are injured by any action in violation of the statute.[44] Civil actions may be brought where the defendant's conduct was "engaged in with a knowing or intentional state of mind ..."[45] The relief authorized in a civil action includes equitable and declaratory remedies, actual damages (in an amount not less than $1,000) and reasonable attorney's fees and other costs reasonably incurred.

The statute also provides for certain defenses to a civil action. Specifically, if the defendant relied in good faith on a court warrant, order, grand jury subpoena, legislative or statutory authorization, or on a request of an investigative or law enforcement officer for an emergency interception[46] or on a good faith determination that the conduct was permitted by certain exceptions enumerated at § 2511(3) of the Act then no damages or other relief may be awarded against that defendant.[47]

Finally, the Act provides that any civil action must be brought within two years after the claimant first discovered (or had a reasonable opportunity to discover) the claimed violation; and the remedies provided for are made exclusive for nonconstitutional violations of Title II.

2.   The Privacy Act of 1974

The Privacy Act of 1974 limits the use the federal government may make of the information it maintains concerning individual persons.[48] While the Act's provisions apply to paper as well electronic governmental

---

43.   *Id.* § 2703(b). As discussed *supra*, communications that have been in electronic storage in an electronic communication service for 180 days or less may only be disclosed to a governmental entity pursuant to a warrant.

44.   *Id.* §§ 2706 and 2707.

45.   *Id.* § 2707(a).

46.   These are provided for at § 2518(7) of the Act.

47.   *Id.* at § 2707(d).

48.   5 U.S.C.A. § 552a (West 1996).

records, the legislative history makes it clear that the Act was prompted by the growing computerization of the government's files.[49]

Under the Privacy Act, an agency of the federal government may not disclose any record concerning an individual to anyone—including another agency—except upon written request of, or with the written permission of, the person to whom the record pertains.[50] The Act also requires federal agencies to grant individuals access to agency records that pertain to those individuals, and to entertain requests for amendments of those records that individuals believe to be inaccurate, irrelevant or incomplete.[51] The Act restricts the government's maintenance of data records to those "relevant and necessary to accomplish a purpose of the agency required to be accomplished" by statute or executive order[52] and establishes criminal and civil penalties for violations of its provisions.[53] The requirements of the Privacy Act also apply, in some circumstances, to government contractors.[54] The Privacy Act's provisions contain significant limitations on the obligations they impose. Notably, the Act does not apply to all files maintained by an agency but only to "records" as defined in the Act. This term is defined to include files that contain not only information "about an individual" but also "his name, or the identifying number, symbol, or other identifying particular assigned to the individual, such as finger or voice print or a photograph."[55] Accordingly, records that pertain to individuals and include information from which those individuals can be identified but that do not contain their names or other "identifying particulars" are not covered by the Privacy Act.

The Act's limitations on data collection and disclosure by federal agencies are also not particularly strong. The Act limits agencies' records to those that are "relevant and necessary" to accomplish the agency's purpose—a criterion that few agency personnel will interpret narrowly. Similarly, the Act permits disclosure of records without the permission of the subject of those records, so long as the purpose of the disclosure is consistent with the purpose for which the data were collected. Again, this criterion is subject to liberal interpretation by those whose actions the Act is intended to control.

49. S. Rep. No. 1183, 93rd Cong., 2d Sess. 1 (1974).

50. 5 U.S.C.A. § 552a(b) (West 1996). There is an exception to this requirement for disclosures that are compatible with the purpose for which the data were collected. *Id.*

51. *Id.* § 552(d).

52. *Id.* § 552a(e)(1).

53. *Id.* §§ 552a(g). The Privacy Act also requires federal agencies to keep accurate records of all record disclosures and corrections, and to maintain records with "such

accuracy, relevance, timeliness, and completeness as is reasonably necessary to assure fairness" to persons about whom records are maintained. *Id.* §§ 552a(c) and 552a(e)(5). Federal agencies also must develop and implement security and confidentiality safeguards for all records subject to the Act. *Id.* § 552a(e)(10).

54. *Id.* § 552a(m)(1). The Privacy Act obligations apply to any contractor that operates "by or on behalf of the agency ... a system of records to accomplish an agency function ..." *Id.*

55. *Id.* § 552a(a)(4).

3. Computer Matching and Privacy Protection Act of 1988

In addition to the limitations on federal data collection and disclosure contained in the Privacy Act of 1974, federal law also imposes some limits on the federal government's use of cross-matching—*i.e.*, the comparison of data maintained on an individual by one agency with data maintained on that individual by another agency or organization. Cross matching is a powerful tool for locating income not declared to the Internal Revenue Service, confirming eligibility for government benefits and other purposes for which the responsible agency's files may be incomplete or inaccurate. Limitations on federal use of this practice are set out in the Computer Matching and Privacy Act of 1988 ("Matching Act").[56]

For activities covered by the Matching Act, the principal regulatory device is a written agreement that agencies must execute before implementing a program to compare their records.[57] The written agreement must specify, *inter alia*, the matching program's purpose, the legal authority for the program, the records that will be matched, verification procedures for matched records and procedures under which persons submitting information to an agency will be notified that the information they submit will be matched. Written agreements for matching programs are public documents and may be effective for no more than eighteen months.

The Matching Act also establishes procedural protections for persons affected by adverse agency decisions based on use of a matching program. Specifically, an agency may not take adverse action based on a matching program until it first undertakes an independent verification of the records on which the proposed, adverse action is based. In addition, the agency proposing to take adverse action must give the affected individual an opportunity to contest the agency's findings.

As with the Privacy Act of 1974, the requirements of the Matching Act are subject to important limitations. Notably, the Act only covers matching programs that are intended to verify eligibility for federal benefit programs, or to recoup payments due or debts owed under such programs, or to match payroll records of government personnel.[58] The Matching Act does not cover matching programs in connection with law enforcement or foreign intelligence investigations or matching activities that are within the statutory authority of the Internal Revenue Service. The Matching Act also contains broad loopholes for matches that gather "aggregate statistical data without any personal identifiers" and matches that will not be used as a basis for agency decisions concerning particular individuals.[59]

4. The Privacy Protection Act of 1980

The impetus for the Privacy Protection Act of 1980 is often traced to a 1971 police raid on the offices of the Stanford Daily, a student

---

56. *Id.* § 552a.

57. *Id.* § 552a(*o*)(1).

58. *Id.* § 552a(a)(8)(A).

59. *Id.* § 552a(a)(8)(B).

newspaper.[60] The newspaper had published photos of an assault on police who were attempting to remove demonstrators from the Stanford University Hospital. Hoping to find additional photos of the assailants, the police obtained a warrant and conducted an exhaustive, unannounced search of the newspaper's offices.

The paper brought an action against the police chief and other officials, alleging that the unannounced search was disruptive, intimidating and violative of the newspaper's First Amendment rights. The newspaper argued that when law enforcement wishes to obtain the files of a publication that is not, itself, suspected of involvement in a crime, the police should be required to use a subpoena procedure under which the target of the inquiry receives notice, has an opportunity to bring a motion to quash or modify the subpoena and, if necessary, conducts the search for relevant material itself. The United States Supreme Court, however, found nothing in the record to suggest that the warrant was not properly issued or executed and refused to find that the press enjoys special immunity from searches and seizures that comply with the Fourth Amendment.[61]

The Privacy Protection Act's principal effect is to give publishers notice and an opportunity to be heard before materials they are preparing for publication may be taken by law enforcement officers conducting criminal investigations. The Act also provides other (somewhat weaker) protections for research materials and other resource documents found on publishers' premises.

The higher level of protection is for "work product materials possessed by a person reasonably believed to have a purpose to disseminate to the public a newspaper, book, broadcast, or other similar form of public communication, in or affecting interstate or foreign commerce . . ."[62] Materials of this kind, which are defined as materials possessed in anticipation of communicating them to the public and including mental impressions, conclusions, opinions or theories of the person who prepared them,[63] may not be searched for or seized unless there is probable cause to believe the person possessing those materials has committed or is committing a criminal offense to which the work product materials

60. For a useful discussion of the background and provisions of the Privacy Protection Act, *see* Charles Currier, *We Have a Warrant to Search your Files*, 19 Tenn. B.J. 12 (1983).

61. Zurcher v. Stanford Daily, 436 U.S. 547, 98 S.Ct. 1970, 56 L.Ed.2d 525 (1978).

62. 42 U.S.C.A. § 2000aa(a) (West 1996). Under this standard, the state of knowledge of law enforcement personnel may determine when a warrant becomes an improper means of obtaining work-product material of a publisher. In *Steve Jackson Games* v. *United States Secret Service*, 36 F.3d 457 (5th Cir.1994), a case involving a raid on the offices of a publisher of games and a related magazine, the agents who executed the search warrant were told after their arrival at the publisher's premises that the organization was engaged in publication of a magazine. At that point, the court found, the officers should have ceased execution of the warrant and followed the procedures prescribed for disclosure of work-product materials under the Privacy Protection Act of 1980.

63. 42 U.S.C.A. § 2000aa-7 (West 1996).

relate or there is reason to believe that the immediate seizure of the materials is necessary to prevent death or serious bodily injury.[64]

A lower level of protection is provided for "documentary materials, other than work product materials, possessed by a person in connection with a purpose to disseminate to the public a newspaper, book, broadcast, or other similar form of public communication, in or affecting interstate or foreign commerce ..."[65] These materials may be seized by law enforcement for the two reasons applicable to work product materials, or on the ground that the giving of notice to the person in possession of the materials would result in their "destruction, alteration, or concealment" or where a subpoena duces tecum has been served and not obeyed, all appellate remedies for that refusal have been exhausted and "there is reason to believe that ... further proceedings relating to the subpena would threaten the interests of justice."[66]

In addition to these provisions, the Privacy Protection Act contains some limitations that favor the interests of law enforcement. Notably, the statute expressly disclaims an exclusionary rule[67] and makes the civil remedies it provides exclusive of other remedies.[68] The statute also contains a "good faith defense" providing that no damages may be recovered against a government officer or employee who "had a reasonable good faith belief in the lawfulness of his conduct."[69]

5.   The Right to Financial Privacy Act

The Right to Financial Privacy Act ("RFPA"),[70] passed in 1978, is Congress's response to the Supreme Court's decision in *United States v. Miller, supra*, and is the model for Title II of the Electronic Communications Privacy Act.

The RFPA applies to individual customer records maintained by financial institutions[71] and defines the circumstances under which such institutions may be compelled to disclose customer records to an authority of the United States government.[72] Like Title II of the ECPA, the RFPA permits records within its protection to be produced pursuant to a warrant (in which case the customer does not received prior notice of the disclosure)[73] or pursuant to administrative subpoena or summons.[74] If a warrant is not used, disclosure may be compelled only where there is reason to believe that the records sought are relevant to a legitimate law

---

64. *Id.* § 2000aa(a). Except for certain exceptions related to national security, the offense to which materials relate may not consist of the possession, communication or withholding of the seized materials or the information contained in those materials. So, for example, if the only criminal offense to which work product materials relate is violation of an obscenity statute, the materials may not be searched for and seized.

65. *Id.* § 2000aa(b).

66. *Id.* §§ 2000aa(b)(3)-(4).

67. "Evidence otherwise admissible in a proceeding shall not be excluded on the basis of a violation of this Act." *Id.* § 2000aa-6(e).

68. *Id.* §§ 2000aa–6(2)(d)-(e).

69. *Id.* § 2000aa–6(2)(b).

70. 12 U.S.C.A. §§ 3401 *et seq.* (West 1996).

71. *Id.* § 3401(1)-(2).

72. *Id.* § 3401(3).

73. *Id.* § 3406.

74. *Id.* § 3405.

enforcement inquiry and after a copy of the subpoena or summons has been served upon the customer.[75]

While the RFPA is a significant source of rights for customers of financial institutions, bank customers still are subject to constraints on their privacy. Notably, the RFPA does not prevent informal access to bank records by the Internal Revenue Service.[76] In addition, banks remain subject to the Bank Secrecy Act of 1970 which requires them to create and hold records of their depositors' dealings that are deemed by the government to be useful to regulation and law enforcement.[77]

6. The Educational Privacy Act

Federal law also offers some protection against promiscuous disclosure of student records by educational institutions that receive federal funding. Specifically, the Family Educational Rights and Privacy Act (popularly referred to as the "Buckley" Act)[78] prohibits the disclosure of student records except in response to a subpoena or unless the disclosure will be made to the student, his or her parents, school officials who have a legitimate need for information contained in the files, organizations engaged in research or public officials with responsibility for education.

The Family Educational Rights and Privacy Act creates no private right of action for persons aggrieved by violations of the Act.[79] The penalty for noncompliance is withdrawal of federal funding from the institution found to be in violation.

7. The Fair Credit Reporting Act

In the United States, the most stringent and comprehensive statutory constraints on the private use and collection of personal data are those imposed on consumer credit reporting agencies. Under the Fair Credit Reporting Act ("FCRA"),[80] organizations that regularly collect information on individuals and use that information to prepare and furnish credit reports to third parties must exercise care in the preparation of those reports and provide for notice to persons who are adversely affected by those reports. Consumer credit reporting agencies also must disclose the content of credit reports upon request from the individuals to whom they pertain and must correct errors contained in those reports.

---

75. *Id.* The statute also permits disclosure pursuant to judicial subpoena and formal written request from agencies that authorize such requests by regulation. *Id.* §§ 3407–08. Like Title II of the ECPA, the RFPA, in certain circumstances, permits governmental agencies to request the making of backup copies of requested records, before notice is given to the customer. *Id.* § 3409(a).

76. *Id.* § 3413(c); *see* Raikos v. Bloomfield State Bank, 703 F.Supp. 1365 (S.D.Ind.1989).

77. 12 U.S.C.A. § 1829(a) (West 1996).

78. 20 U.S.C.A. § 1232g (West 1990 and Supp. 1997).

79. At least one court, however, has been willing to imply a private right of action under the Act. Fay v. South Colonie Central School District, 802 F.2d 21 (2d Cir.1986).

80. 15 U.S.C.A. §§ 1681 *et seq.* (West 1996).

The duty of care in the preparation of credit reports is set out at section 1681e(b) of the FCRA, which provides that "[w]hen a consumer reporting agency prepares a consumer report, it shall follow reasonable procedures to assure maximum possible accuracy of information concerning the individual about whom the report relates."[81] Failure to comply with this standard gives affected consumers a private right of action.[82] The FCRA does not impose a strict liability standard on credit reporting agencies but establishes "only a duty of reasonable care in preparation of the report," including an ongoing duty to exercise care in the updating of the report.[83]

An example of a credit reporting agency's violation of the FCRA duty of care is the case of *Thompson v. San Antonio Retail Merchants Association* ("*Thompson*").[84] In that case, a credit reporting agency used a system under which subscribing merchants sent the agency on-line inquiries containing personal information on persons who had applied for credit. The agency then would "search its records and display on the subscriber's terminal the credit history file that most nearly match[ed] the consumer." If the merchant's terminal operator accepted the file as a good match with the credit applicant, the credit agency's computer automatically updated that file with all personal information furnished in the merchant's inquiry.

Following this procedure, the agency had erroneously matched personal information on one consumer, furnished by a subscriber, with one of the agency's files on a different person. By updating its file with the information furnished by the merchant, the agency had erroneously created a file for plaintiff that included a different person's bad debt history. At this point, the agency's file "became a potpourri of information on both the plaintiff" and the consumer with the delinquent debt history and even associated the plaintiff's name and other personal information with the delinquent consumer's social security account number. The agency not only created this "potpourri" automatically, without any effort at verification; it failed to detect and correct the error after another merchant—Gulf Oil Corporation—expressly asked the agency to recheck the information. As a result, Gulf Oil and another merchant denied credit to the plaintiff.

The district court found that the credit reporting agency had been negligent and awarded damages accordingly. On appeal, the Fifth Circuit Court of Appeals found no error in the district court's decision. Specifically, the appellate court found that the agency had "failed to exercise reasonable care in programming its computer to automatically capture information into a file without requiring any minimum 'points of correspondence' between the consumer and the file or having an adequate

---

81. *Id.* § 1681e(b).

82. *Id.* § 1681o states that a "consumer reporting agency" is liable to "any consumer" for negligent failure to comply with "any requirement imposed" by the FCRA.

83. Thompson v. San Antonio Retail Merchants Association, 682 F.2d 509, 513 (5th Cir.1982).

84. *Id.*

auditing procedure to foster accuracy,"[85] and it had "failed to employ reasonable procedures designed to learn the disparity in social security numbers [between the two consumers] when it revised [the file] at Gulf's request."[86]

The duty to disclose information to the subjects of credit reports is not automatic: the subject of a report must request disclosure. When such a request is received, the agency must disclose the substance of the information in its files, the sources of the information and all information provided to third parties within the preceding six months.[87] If the subject then questions the accuracy of any of the information in his or her file, the agency must reinvestigate the information and delete data that either are found to be inaccurate or cannot be confirmed. If the disputed information is not deleted then the requesting subject is entitled to insert a statement in the file explaining the subject's disagreement with the information.

The FCRA also imposes obligations on users of information supplied by credit reporting agencies. Specifically, when a merchant, employer or other user takes action adverse to any person based on a credit report, the user must disclose that fact to the person as to whom adverse action is taken.[88] Users of credit reports also are criminally liable for obtaining information from credit agencies under false pretenses.[89]

8. *The Freedom of Information Act*

The federal Freedom of Information Act ("FOIA")[90] is discussed at length in Chapter Seven of this treatise, but one aspect of that statute impinges directly on informational privacy and must be mentioned here. Specifically, although FOIA is a disclosure statute and creates a presumption in favor of the right of the public and the media to inspect governmental documents, FOIA also includes a number of exemptions.

---

85. *Id.* at 513. "Points of correspondence" are commonly used by credit agencies to decide whether a file in their computer matches the personal information furnished in a subscriber's inquiry. Under this procedure, different items of personal information are assigned point values depending on the likelihood that they will be unique to a single person. When a subscriber inquiry is received, the agency will compare the information in the request with the personal information files maintained in the computer. Only files that correspond with the inquiry in items of personal information totaling a minimum number of points will be furnished to the merchant. *See, e.g.,* Lowry v. Credit Bureau, Inc. of Georgia, 444 F.Supp. 541 (N.D.Ga.1978) (credit bureau required at least 50 points of correspondence between personal information furnished by a subscriber and a file in the bureau's database).

86. Thompson, 682 F.2d at 513.

87. 15 U.S.C.A. § 1681g (West 1996). If reports have been furnished for purposes of employment, then the agency must disclose the recipients of such reports during the two years prior to the request.

88. *Id.* § 1681m. Upon request, the user also must disclose any other basis for refusal to extend credit.

89. *Id.* § 1681g.

90. 5 U.S.C.A. § 552 (West 1996). The Freedom of Information Act amends the Administrative Procedure Act. The statute covers executive branch agencies except the president and the president's immediate staff, and provides that "upon any request for records which ... reasonably describes such records and is made in accordance with published rules," any agency covered by the statute shall make those records "promptly available to any person." *Id.* § 552(a)(3).

One of those exemptions is for medical and other records "the disclosure of which would constitute a clearly unwarranted invasion of personal privacy."[91]

The privacy exemption of FOIA does not permit federal agencies to withhold all information of a personal nature. Instead, it requires agencies to determine whether the invasion of privacy is warranted. Where governmental records relating to an individual or individuals also involve matters of legitimate public concern, this balancing test can be difficult to administer.

The leading case construing the FOIA privacy exemption is *United States Department of Justice* v. *Reporters Committee for Freedom of the Press* (*"Reporters Committee"*), decided by the Supreme Court in 1989.[92] In *Reporters Committee*, news organizations had asked the Federal Bureau of Investigation to release its "rap sheets" on four members of the Medico family, which owned a business that had been identified by the Pennsylvania Crime Commission as dominated by organized crime figures. The FBI released the requested information on four of the Medico family members after their deaths but continued to resist disclosure of much of the rap sheet information on the fourth member, Charles Medico.

The news organizations pointed out that a rap sheet is merely an FBI compilation and summary of an individual's criminal history, and contains arrests, charges, convictions and incarcerations that are a matter of public record in the court houses and police stations where those events first were recorded. The news organizations argued that the privacy interest in such public-record information approaches zero while the criminal histories of persons who may be involved in organized crime are matters of legitimate public interest.

The Supreme Court found, however, that Medico's interest in non-disclosure of his FBI rap sheet is "the sort of 'personal privacy' interest Congress intended [the privacy exemption] to protect."[93] The Court refused to find that because individual events in a person's criminal history may be matters of public record at various locations around the country, a computerized summary of those events also should be readily accessible to the public. The Court found a substantial difference, "in terms of personal privacy, between scattered disclosure of the bits of information contained in a rap sheet and revelation of the rap sheet as a whole."[94] In the Court's view, "there is a vast difference between the public records that might be found after a diligent search of courthouse files, county archives, and local police stations throughout the country and a computerized summary located in a single clearinghouse of information."[95] Accordingly, the Court found that individuals have a strong

91. *Id.* § 552(b).

92. 489 U.S. 749, 109 S.Ct. 1468, 103 L.Ed.2d 774 (1989).

93. *Id.* at 762, 109 S.Ct. at 1476, 103 L.Ed.2d at 782.

94. *Id.* at 764, 109 S.Ct. at 1477, 103 L.Ed.2d at 783.

95. *Id.*

privacy interest in the non-disclosure of compiled, computerized information, regardless of the sources from which those compilations are assembled.[96]

The Court also acknowledged, however, that FOIA's privacy exemption prevents only *unwarranted* disclosures of private information and therefore requires disclosure of information in which an individual may have a privacy interest where such disclosure is warranted by the purpose of the Act. In this connection, the Court determined that private information should be disclosed where such disclosure served to "open agency action to the light of public scrutiny."[97] The Court found no such purpose in the disclosure of Medico's rap sheet. Medico was accused of "improper dealings with a corrupt Congressman and [of serving as] an officer of a corporation with defense contracts."[98] In the Court's view, Medico's rap sheet would not serve the purpose of informing the public about the conduct of the Congressman. Similarly, the public interest in the conduct of the Department of Defense in awarding contracts to Medico's company could be more directly served by FOIA requests to the Department of Defense asking for records related to those contracts or to the Department's procedures for determining whether prospective contractors have criminal records. Accordingly, disclosure of the rap sheets, containing only particularized information about an individual's criminal history, would not be warranted under FOIA's privacy exemption.

Despite the result in *Reporters Committee*, FOIA requests are a tool with significant potential to compromise personal privacy. The categorical balancing test endorsed by the Supreme Court is at best an imprecise instrument and could easily have supported a contrary decision on the facts of *Reporters Committee* itself.[99] Where an agency or reviewing court finds that information on a private person held by an agency is sufficiently illuminating on the subject of an agency's behavior, that information is likely to be disclosed pursuant to a proper FOIA request.[100]

C. Informational Privacy and State Legislation

Although this discussion has concentrated on federal constitutional and statutory protections for informational privacy, practitioners in this

96. *Id.* at 765, 109 S.Ct. at 1477, 103 L.Ed.2d at 783. The Court found support for its conclusion in the Privacy Act of 1974, which demonstrated, in the Court's view, the Congress's concern about the threat to privacy posed by centralized databases.

97. *Id.* at 772, 109 S.Ct. at 1481, 103 L.Ed.2d at 795, citing Department of the Air Force v. Rose, 425 U.S. 352, 372, 96 S.Ct. 1592, 1604, 48 L.Ed.2d 11, 27 (1976).

98. *Id.* at 774, 109 S.Ct. at 1482, 103 L.Ed.2d at 796.

99. Medico's rap sheet certainly would have helped the public decide whether the Department of Defense, in particular, was remiss in entering into contracts with his family's company. The alternative suggest-

ed by the Supreme Court—*i.e.*, that the news organizations obtain the Department's records concerning those contracts and the Department's contracting procedures generally—may not have been of comparable value for this purpose. In fact, any disparity between the information in the rap sheet and the Department's own information may have been essential to demonstrate dereliction on the part of the Department in this case.

100. The record in *Reporters Committee* showed that at the time of the news organizations' FOIA request, the FBI maintained computerized rap sheets on 24,000,000 individuals.

area of the law also must be aware of the role of the states. Notably, state constitutions have provided an additional, and in some cases more favorable, avenue for constitutional challenges to interceptions of personal communications and unauthorized disclosure and use of stored personal data. Similarly, most states have enacted some combination of anti-wiretap, anti-hacking and other kinds of data protection statutes. While this discussion does not attempt to identify and consider all of these state laws, a brief review will give a fair idea of the scope of protection that they afford.

First, we should note that the constitutions of California and some other states expressly recognize a right of privacy—a right that is only implicit in the United States Constitution.[1] In these jurisdictions, a privacy claim brought under the state constitution might supply a cause of action not supported by the United States Constitution or federal statutes.[2] And even in some states that do not expressly recognize privacy rights in their constitutions, state courts have extended constitutional protection to forbid practices that might have been permitted under the federal Constitution's privacy and Fourth Amendment guarantees.[3]

Some states also have strong statutory protection against wiretapping and other forms of electronic surveillance. Notably, they do not permit interception of telephone calls when only one party to the call consents to the interception.[4] These statutes are more favorable to privacy rights than the federal ECPA, which permits interceptions with the consent of one party to a conversation.

Most states also have enacted statutes that protect the privacy interest in stored communications. The most common of these are statutes that impose obligations on state agencies similar to those established for federal agencies in FOIA (including its privacy exemption) and the Privacy Act of 1974. Many of these statutes are based at least partly on the Uniform Information Practices Code.[5] In addition, many states have enacted anti-hacking statutes similar to the federal Computer Fraud and Abuse Act and counterparts to the federal Elec-

---

1. *See, e.g.*, Griswold v. Connecticut, 381 U.S. 479, 85 S.Ct. 1678, 14 L.Ed.2d 510 (1965); Roe v. Wade, 410 U.S. 113, 93 S.Ct. 705, 35 L.Ed.2d 147 (1973).

2. For example, a California court has held that the California constitution forbids the seizure of an unlisted telephone number without a warrant. People v. Chapman, 36 Cal.3d 98, 201 Cal.Rptr. 628, 679 P.2d 62 (1984). Smith v. Maryland, 442 U.S. 735, 99 S.Ct. 2577, 61 L.Ed.2d 220 (1979), suggests that a different result would have been reached under the Fourth Amendment to the U.S. Constitution.

3. *See, e.g.*, State v. Hunt, 91 N.J. 338, 450 A.2d 952 (N.J. 1982), in which the New Jersey Supreme Court found a reasonable expectation of privacy in a customer's telephone billing records. *See also* Burrows v. Superior Court, 13 Cal.3d 238, 118 Cal. Rptr. 166, 529 P.2d 590 (1974) (disclosure of bank records protected by privacy rights guaranteed in state constitution).

4. *See* Barasch v. Pennsylvania Public Utility Commission, 133 Pa.Cmwlth. 285, 576 A.2d 79 (1990) (invalidating a telephone company's caller identification service as a violation of Pennsylvania wiretap statute).

5. Uniform Information Practices Code, 13 U.L.A. 277 (1986).

tronic Communications Privacy Act.[6] Finally, a number of states have enacted legislation to protect particular kinds of stored communications, including medical treatment records and insurance records, from unauthorized disclosure and use.[7]

In bringing claims under state privacy legislation, practitioners will find that many of the statutes are of recent vintage and have not been tested in the state courts. Practitioners also must be sensitive not only to the varying scope of subject-matter these statutes address but to subtle differences in *scienter* requirements and other elements that can drastically affect their usefulness to particular litigants.

D. Informational Privacy and the Common Law

From its earliest beginnings, the law has recognized a legitimate interest in the protection of persons and property from wrongful injury. Accordingly, a rich body of civil and criminal law has grown around such notions as assault, battery, wrongful homicide, trespass, conversion, theft and fraud. The law took more slowly, however, to the notion that mental tranquility, no less than property or the integrity of the body, might in some cases be a protectible interest. In fact, much of this law—the law of privacy—is a product of the last hundred years. Its development and parameters are discussed in detail in Chapter Four of this work.

E. An Alternative Approach to Informational Privacy: The Data Directive of the European Union

As this section demonstrates, the United States does not impose comprehensive restrictions on the collection and use of personal data. Instead, data protection in this country is a patchwork of laws that impinge primarily on government and certain specialized providers of database services—such as credit reporting agencies—but that leave many forms of data collection and use largely unregulated. And even where the law imposes specific obligations on public and private compilers of personal data, those laws rely on action taken after violations are discovered, rather than ongoing regulatory supervision, to enforce their requirements.

The countries of the European Union ("EU") generally have taken a different approach to informational privacy and data protection. While the most important example of the European approach is the EU Data Protection Directive, about which more will be said in a moment, a number of European countries regulated collection of personal data before that Directive was adopted in 1995. For example, the United Kingdom long has required registration of all databases containing personal information and has imposed penalties, including cancellation

---

6. *See, e.g.*, Cal. Ann. Penal Code § 502 (West 1988); Minn. Stat. Ann. §§ 270B.01 *et seq.* (West 1989); 21 Okl.Stat.Ann. § 1953 (West 1983); Wis. Stat. Ann. § 943.70 (West 1996).

7. *See. e.g.*, Conn. Gen. Stat. Ann. §§ 38a–97 *et seq.* (West 1992); Ariz. Rev. Stat. Ann. §§ 20–2101 *et seq.* (West 1990); Wis. Stat. Ann. § 51.61(n) (West 1997).

of registration, for database operators that misuse personal data. Similarly, Sweden licenses database operators and empowers a Data Inspection Board to impose and enforce the terms under which licenses are granted. Through this licensing approach, individual countries of the European Union have made the compilation of personal information in databases a governmental privilege subject to close oversight backed by the threat of revocation.[8]

In 1995, at Cambridge, England, the EU adopted the Data Protection Directive, which strengthens data protection throughout the EU by requiring each member nation to implement a minimum set of data protection practices.[9] The Directive governs the regulation of all governmental and private compilations of personal data intended for more than personal use.[10]

The Directive prevents the collection and processing of personal information, with certain exceptions, unless the subject has given his or her "unambiguous consent" to that activity.[11] Where data gathering falls within a recognized exception to the right of unambiguous consent, the subject of the data collection still has a "right to object" to that activity.[12] And where information is collected for direct marketing purposes, the subject has an absolute right to prevent that activity.[13]

The requirement of unambiguous consent, and the companion right to object, would be useless without a mechanism for notification to individuals of data collection activity. Accordingly, where a database operator or other collector of data collects information directly from the subject, the collector's identity must be disclosed to the subject along with the purpose of the data collection.[14] Where information about an individual is not obtained from the subject, the duty to disclose is not triggered until the collector or processor of the information first discloses it to a third party, and does not arise at all under certain circumstances.[15]

The Directive also imposes significant minimization, accuracy and use standards on collectors and processors of personal data. Notably, a data controller must collect data for a specified purpose and may not use it in a way not compatible with that purpose.[16] Individuals have a right

---

8. *See, e.g.,* CHARLES H. KENNEDY AND M. VERONICA PASTOR, AN INTRODUCTION TO INTERNATIONAL TELECOMMUNICATIONS LAW 140–141 (1996).

9. Directive of the European Parliament and of the Council on Protection of Individuals With Regard to the Processing of Personal Data and the Free Movement of Such Data, 12004/4/94 COR 3 (en), Brussels (July 20, 1995).

10. Data Protection Directive § 28.

11. Data Protection Directive art. 7(a). Most data protection obligations under the

Directive will be imposed on "data controllers," which are defined as "natural or legal person[s], public authorit[ies], agenc[ies] or any other bod[ies] which alone or jointly with others determine[] the purposes and means of the processing of personal data . . ." *Id.* art. 2(d).

12. *Id.* art. 14(a).

13. *Id.* art. 14(b).

14. *Id.* art. 10.

15. *Id.* art. 15.

16. *Id.* § 28.

to know what personal data are maintained in a data controller's database and to access that personal data and obtain correction of errors and elimination of information that exceeds the purpose of collection or otherwise violates the Directive.[17] The Directive also requires data controllers to implement adequate security and confidentiality procedures, and limits the use of stored personal data to make automated decisions concerning credit and other decisions with direct effects on individual welfare.[18]

In order to comply with the Data Directive, each EU country not only must enact the substantive and procedural provisions just described but must create an appropriate regulatory body and provide for civil remedies for persons aggrieved by violation of data protection laws, including a right of damages.[19]

Potentially, one of the most consequential features of the Data Directive and related enactments is the question of transborder data transfers. The Directive provides that computerized personal data may be transferred to a third country only if that country ensures an adequate level of protection for personal data.[20] While this provision does not seem to require third countries to offer protection at a level precisely equivalent to that of the Data Directive, there is considerable question as to whether particular non-EU countries, including the United States, qualify to receive transfers of personal data originating in the EU under this standard. In the absence of such qualification, third countries may have to satisfy certain exception standards provided in the Directive's clearance procedure[21] or satisfy the transferor country that protections established by contract or otherwise are sufficient to ensure protection of the particular data being transferred.[22]

The EU Data Directive is an ambitious framework for regulation of personal data collection and use. The Directive effectively imposes upon all collectors and aggregators of personal data a set of obligations roughly comparable to those imposed upon credit reporting agencies in the United States. At the same time, it mandates ongoing regulation by a specialized agency, rather than the private enforcement mechanism under which United States data protection laws tend to be implemented. The Directive's approach is sharply at odds with the deregulatory climate of official opinion in the United States, and therefore is unlikely to be adopted as a model for further American initiatives in this area. United States policy makers should consider, however, whether a partial implementation of the European approach, such as imposition of FCRA-type obligations on all aggregators of personal data, enforced primarily through private remedies, might beneficially strengthen privacy protections without creating new bureaucracies.

17. *Id.* art. 6.
18. *Id.* art. 15.
19. *Id.* arts. 22, 23, 28.
20. *Id.* art. 25(1).

21. *Id.* art. 31.
22. *Id.* art. 26(2).

11.14   Protection Against Theft, Alteration or Destruction of Programs and Data

A.   *The Computer Fraud and Abuse Act*[1]

The Computer Fraud and Abuse Act[2] ("CFAA"), enacted in 1984, attempts to protect information stored on computer systems from unauthorized access or destruction and to deter actions that disrupt the use of a computer. The CFAA as it stands today is the product of several amendments[3] that, like the original Act, were passed in response to the evolving threats facing the nation's increasingly interlinked computer systems.

1.   *History and Development of the Statute*

The development of the CFAA is best described as a process of action and reaction. Before 1984, there was "no specific Federal legislation in the area of computer crime."[4] In order to prosecute computer-related crime, federal prosecutors had to shoehorn the action into statutes designed for other offenses such as mail fraud or wire fraud statutes. In *United States v. Seidlitz,*[5] federal prosecutors used the wire fraud statutes[6] to convict a former government contractor who remotely accessed a Federal Energy Administration computer and copied some of the software maintained on the system. However, according to the Department of Justice, had the defendant not made any telephone calls across state lines, "there would have been no basis for Federal prosecution."[7] Congress also was aware of the gap in the law concerning "hackers"—that is, people who access ("trespass into") public and private computer systems without authorization.[8]

Congress attempted to fill these gaps in the criminal code by enacting the Computer Fraud and Abuse Act. The initial version of the Act only protected classified information maintained by the federal government, financial information and computer systems used by the federal government.[9] To deter those who sought to access such information, the Act imposed "criminal sanctions upon 'hackers' and other

1. This discussion of the Computer Fraud and Abuse Act was researched and drafted by Daniel J. Smith, J.D., University of Virginia, while a summer associate at Morrison & Foerster LLP.

2. Counterfeit Access Device and Computer Fraud and Abuse Act of 1984, Pub. L. 98–473, §§ 2101–03, 98 Stat. 2190 (1984), *codified at* 18 U.S.C.A. § 1030 (West Supp. 1997).

3. *See* Pub. L. 99–474, § 2, 100 Stat. 1213 (1986); Pub. L. 100–690, § 7065, 102 Stat. 4404 (1988); Pub. L. 101–73, § 962(a)(5), 103 Stat. 502 (1989); Pub. L. 101–647, §§ 1205(e), 2597(j), 3533, 104 Stat. 4831, 4910, 4925 (1990); Pub. L. 103–322, § 290001(b)-(f), 108 Stat. 2097–99

(1994); Pub. L. 104–294, § 201, 110 Stat. 3488 (1996).

4. H.R. Rep. 894, 98th Cong., 2d Sess. 6 (1984), *reprinted in* 1984 U.S. Code Cong. & Admin. News 3689, 3691.

5. 589 F.2d 152 (4th Cir.1978), cert. denied, 441 U.S. 922, 99 S.Ct. 2030, 60 L.Ed.2d 396 (1979).

6. 18 U.S.C.A. § 1343 (West 1996).

7. H.R. Rep. No. 894, *supra* note 4 at 6, *reprinted in* 1984 U.S. Code Cong. & Admin. News 3691.

8. *Id.* at 10, *reprinted in* 1984 U.S. Code Cong. & Admin. News at 3695.

9. *See* 18 U.S.C.A. § 1030(a)(1)-(3)(West Supp. 1997).

criminals who access computers without authorization."[10] The 1984 Act established "a specific Federal felony for unauthorized access to computers" when the defendant either financially gained from an unauthorized access or accessed classified information.[11] The Act also created "three misdemeanor crimes of unauthorized access or computer abuse."[12]

The first amendments to the Act were proposed in 1986.[13] Noting that the "technological explosion has made the computer a mainstay of our communications system,"[14] experience had shown to members of Congress that computer crimes posed threats not "solely financial in nature."[15] In this vein, Congress sought to respond to the "pirate bulletin boards" that had "sprung up around the country for the sole purpose of exchanging passwords to other people's computer systems."[16] Thus, in addition to modifying the CFAA's scienter requirement, the 1986 amendments included language that made the Act applicable to "acts of simple trespass,"[17] and added sections that covered fraud, malicious mischief and trafficking in computer passwords.[18]

Additional problems with the CFAA surfaced in *United States v. Morris*.[19] Morris, a graduate student at Cornell University, was prosecuted under the Act after a "worm"[20] he released into the Internet in the fall of 1988 caused computers on the system to crash, resulting in thousands of dollars of damage.[21] Morris raised two arguments on appeal of his conviction. First, he challenged his conviction on the ground that the scienter requirement of the CFAA required him not only intentionally to make an unauthorized access of a covered computer but also intentionally to cause damage.[22] Second, Morris argued that the subsection criminalizing trespass offenses only applied to people who lacked access to any covered computer.[23] Because he was authorized to use such computers, Morris argued that he only exceeded his access, thereby

10. H.R. Rep. No. 894 at 21, *reprinted in* 1984 U.S. Code Cong. & Admin. News 3707.

11. *Id.* at 12, *reprinted in* 1984 U.S. Code Cong. & Admin. News 3698.

12. *Id.*

13. Pub. L. 99–474, § 2, 100 Stat. 1213 (1986).

14. S. Rep. No. 432, 99th Cong., 2d Sess. 2 (1986), *reprinted in* 1986 U.S. Code Cong. & Admin. News 2479, 2480.

15. *Id.*, *reprinted in* 1986 U.S. Code Cong. & Admin. News 2480. The Report cited the example of the "414 Gang." This group of hackers broke into the computer system at a cancer center and accessed the radiation treatment records of over 6,000 patients. *Id.* "[T]he potentially life-threatening nature of such mischief is a source of serious concern." *Id.* at 3, *reprinted in* 1986 U.S. Code Cong. & Admin. News 2480.

16. *See* Pub. L. 99–474, § 2(d), *codified at* 18 U.S.C.A. § 1030(a)(4)-(5) (West Supp. 1997).

17. S. Rep. No. 432 at 7, *reprinted in* 1986 U.S. Code Cong. & Admin. News 2484.

18. Pub. L. 99–474, § 2(d), 100 Stat. 1213 (1986).

19. 928 F.2d 504 (2d Cir.), cert. denied, 502 U.S. 817, 112 S.Ct. 72, 116 L.Ed.2d 46 (1991).

20. A "worm" is a program that travels from one computer system to another. Unlike a "virus," a worm does not attach itself to the operating software of the infected system. United States v. Morris, 928 F.2d 504, 504–505 n. 1 (2d Cir.1991).

21. *Id.* at 505. In fact, Morris tried to warn users but his message could not get through because the worm had clogged the network. *Id.* at 506.

22. *Id.* at 507.

23. *Id.* at 511. The relevant statutory provision is 18 U.S.C.A. § 1030(a)(5)(West 1986).

making the subsection inapplicable.[24] Morris grounded his argument in one phrase of the Senate report that accompanied the 1986 amendments.[25] The court nonetheless found that the statute "does not require the Government to demonstrate that the defendant intentionally prevented authorized use and thereby caused loss" and that "Morris acted 'without authorization' within the meaning of [the] section."[26]

In 1994, Congress acted to close what it had identified, after *Morris*, as another "potential loophole in the computer crime statute."[27] To accomplish this, Congress totally revamped one subsection of the CFAA[28] to place "the focus on harmful intent and resultant harm, rather than on the technical concept of computer 'access.' "[29] This revision established a misdemeanor offense for the act of recklessly accessing a "Federal interest computer"[30] without authorization that either affects the information stored on the computer or prevents the use of the computer.[31] In an effort to "boost the deterrence of the statute," the 1994 amendments included a civil action remedy[32] "allowing aggrieved individuals to obtain relief."[33]

In October of 1996, the Congress again decided that events had overtaken the CFAA and required its amendment. Notably, as Senator Leahy pointed out, the 1994 version of the Act protected computerized information of financial institutions and consumer reporting agencies, but did not protect all computers used in interstate and foreign commerce and communications and did not protect Federal government computers from unauthorized access to information.[34] Also, the 1994 version of the Act did not reach the transmission of computer viruses or other harmful programs from outside the United States and did not reach activities that harmed government or financial institution computers that were not used in interstate commerce.[35] Finally, the Congress was concerned that the CFAA did not prohibit extortionate hacking

---

24. *Id.* at 510.

25. *Id.* The Report stated that the Act was aimed at "outsiders," *i.e.*, those lacking authorization to access any covered computer. 1986 U.S. Code Cong. & Admin. News at 2488. However, the court observed that the Report also stated that the Act covered acts that are "interdepartmental in nature." 928 F.2d at 510.

26. *Id.* at 505.

27. H.R. Rep. No. 681, 101st Cong., 2d Sess., pt. I, at 71 (1990), *reprinted in* 1990 U.S. Code Cong. & Admin. News 6472, 6475. *See also* S. Rep. No. 544, 101st Cong., 2d Sess. 5 (1990)(discussing the Morris incident).

28. *See* Pub. L. 103–322, § 290001(b), 108 Stat. 2097–98 (1994).

29. 140 Cong. Rec. S12313 (daily ed. Aug. 23, 1994) (insertion of legislative history).

30. "Federal interest computer" was defined to include any computer used by the United States Government, a financial institution or "one of two or more computers used in committing the offense, not all of which are located in the same State." 18 U.S.C.A. § 1020(e)(2)(A) and (B) (West 1996).

31. *See* Pub. L. 103–322, § 290001(b), 108 Stat. 2098 (1994).

32. *Id.* § 290001(d), 108 Stat. 2098 (1994), *codified at* 18 U.S.C.A. § 1030(g) (West 1996).

33. 139 Cong. Rec. S16421 (daily ed. Nov. 19, 1993) (statement of Sen. Leahy, author of bill).

34. 142 Cong. Rec. S10886 (daily ed. Sep. 18, 1996) (statement of Sen. Leahy).

35. *Id.*

activities[36] and that the definition of "damage" in the CFAA was not sufficiently comprehensive to reach all activities that might cause physical injury to persons or threaten the public health and safety. In order to correct these perceived weaknesses of the CFAA, the Congress amended the statute in 1996 with the passage of the National Information Infrastructure Protection Act of 1996.[37]

As computer technology advances and more and more computer users and business move "on line," it is certain that legislative changes in this area have yet to be exhausted. Senator Laxalt's statement in 1986 remains true today: we should "fully expect Congress to continue to review the problems caused by computer fraud and abuse and to respond to them with appropriate remedies."[38]

2. *The Statute's Provisions*

Subsection (a)(1) of Section 1030 creates a felony offense for "knowingly" accessing a computer without authorization or in excess of authorized access and by means of such access obtaining certain kinds of classified or restricted data "with reason to believe that such information so obtained could be used to the injury of the United States, or to the advantage of any foreign nation." Satisfaction of the knowing state of mind requirement[39] can be made "by proof that the actor was aware of a high probability of the existence of the circumstance."[40] This scienter requirement is intended to include "the situation that has been called 'willful blindness.' "[41]

Subsection (a)(2) punishes one who "intentionally" accesses without authorization or in excess of authorized access a computer and "obtains information" contained in the financial records of a "financial institution",[42] card issuer or consumer reporting agency. Pursuant to the 1996 amendments to the Act, subsection (a)(2) also makes it a crime to intentionally access without authorization, or in excess of authorization, a computer and thereby to obtain "information from any department or agency of the United States" or "information from any protected computer if the conduct involved an interstate or foreign communication."[43] The use of the "intentional" standard is meant to cover conduct that "evinces a clear intent to enter, without proper authorization, computer

---

36. Sen. Leahy particularly noted a case in which "a person threatened to crash a computer system unless he was given free access to the system and an account." *Id.*

37. Pub.L. 104–294, § 201, 110 Stat. 3488 (1996).

38. 132 Cong. Rec. S14453 (daily ed. Oct. 1, 1986) (statement of Sen. Laxalt).

39. *See id.* at 20, *reprinted in* 1984 U.S. Code Cong. & Admin. News at 3706.

40. *Id.* at 16, *reprinted in* 1984 U.S. Code Cong. & Admin. News at 3702.

41. *Id.* at 16–17, *reprinted in* 1984 U.S. Code Cong. & Admin. News 3702. Willful

blindness is defined as the condition in which an actor is "aware of the probable existence of a material fact but does not satisfy himself that it does not in fact exist." *Id.* at 17, *reprinted in* 1984 U.S. Code Cong. & Admin. News 3702. *See also United States v. Jewell*, 532 F.2d 697, 700 n. 7 (9th Cir.), *cert. denied* 426 U.S. 951, 96 S.Ct. 3173, 49 L.Ed.2d 1188 (1976).

42. This term is defined at § 1030(e)(4).

43. 18 U.S.C.A. § 1030(a)(2)(B)-(C) (West Supp. 1997).

files or data belonging to another.''[44] The section is not intended to cover "mistaken, inadvertent, or careless" acts resulting in unauthorized access.[45] The phrase "obtains information" in the context of this section includes "mere observation of the data."[46] Evidence of "[a]ctual asporation, in the sense of physically removing the data from its original location or transcribing the data," is not required to "establish a violation of this subsection."[47]

Subsection (a)(3) makes it an offense to "intentionally" access without authorization "any nonpublic computer of a department or agency of the United States" or "a computer of that department or agency that is exclusively for the use of the Government of the United States . . ."[48] This subsection also forbids unauthorized access to nonpublic computers of a United States department or agency where that computer is not exclusively used by the United States Government, where the computer is used by or for the Government and the offending conduct affects the use of the computer by the United States Government.[49]

The CFAA also includes a fraud provision that is found in subsection (a)(4). This section makes it an offense to "knowingly and with intent to defraud" access a "protected computer"[50] in a manner that "furthers the intended fraud" and thereby to "obtain anything of value."[51] The offense does not apply where "the object of the fraud and the value of such use is not more than $5,000 in any 1–year period." The purpose is to penalize "thefts of property via computer that occur as a part of a scheme to defraud."[52] The section is not intended to cover schemes in which use of a computer is "wholly extraneous" to the fraud, such as using a computer to keep records of a fraudulent scheme.[53] In addition, mere acts of "computer trespass" are not to be treated as "an attempt to defraud a service provider of computer time."[54] Rather, to fall under this provision, "the use of the computer must be more directly linked to the intended fraud."[55] For example, a violation occurs when the unautho-

---

44. S. Rep. No. 432 at 6, *reprinted in* 1986 U.S. Code Cong. & Admin. News 2484.

45. *Id.* at 5, *reprinted in* 1986 U.S. Code Cong. & Admin. News at 2483.

46. *Id.* at 6, *reprinted in* 1986 U.S. Code Cong. & Admin. News at 2484.

47. *Id.* at 6–7, *reprinted in* 1986 U.S. Code Cong. & Admin. News at 2484.

48. 18 U.S.C.A. § 1030(a)(3) (West Supp. 1997).

49. *Id.*

50. A "protected computer" is a computer "exclusively for the use of a financial institution or the United States Government, or, in the case of a computer not exclusively for such use, used by or for a financial institution or the United States Government and the conduct constituting the offense affects that use by or for the

financial institution or the Government . . ." The definition also includes any computer "used in interstate or foreign commerce or communication." "Protected computer" replaces the expression "Federal interest computer," used in the Act prior to the 1996 amendments. 18 U.S.C.A. §§ 1030(e)(2)(A) and (B) (West Supp. 1997).

51. 18 U.S.C.A. § 1030(a)(4).

52. S. Rep. No. 432 at 6–7, *reprinted at* 1986 U.S. Code Cong. & Admin. News at 2486–87.

53. *Id.*, *reprinted in* 1986 U.S. Code Cong. & Admin. News at 2487.

54. *Id.* at 9–10, *reprinted in* 1986 U.S. Code Cong. & Admin. News at 2487.

55. *Id.* at 9, *reprinted in* 1986 U.S. Code Cong. & Admin. News at 2487.

rized access of the computer is used "to obtain property of another" that furthers the intended fraud.[56] The scienter requirement utilizes the same standard used in the credit card fraud provisions of section 1029 of title 18 of the United States Code.[57]

Section 1030(b)(5) of the Act is aimed at a wide variety of harmful conduct. The section makes it a criminal offense knowingly to cause "the transmission of a program, information, code, or command, and as a result of such conduct, intentionally cause damage without authorization, to a protected computer . . ."[58] and prohibits the intentional accessing of a protected computer without authorization, where the result of that conduct is to cause damage[59] or recklessly cause damage.[60]

Section 1030(a)(6) of the Act makes it an offense to traffic in any password or similar information, where such action is taken knowingly and with intent to defraud, through which a computer may be accessed without authorization if trafficking affects interstate or foreign commerce or "such computer is used by or for the Government of the United States."[61]

In addition to the criminal penalties the CFAA imposes,[62] the Act also authorizes a civil cause of action to recover "compensatory damages" and "other equitable relief" under subsection (g) for "[a]ny person who suffers damage or loss by reason of a violation of this section." To bring a cause of action a plaintiff must satisfy a threshold of $5,000 in damages for any 1–year period unless the injury is to medical care, involves physical injury to any person or involves a threat to public health or safety.[63] The action also must be brought within 2 years of the date of the act or the discovery of the damage.

B. Mass Electronic Mail: The Problem of Spamming

Spamming is the transmission of mass, unsolicited electronic mail (e-mail) on subjects as diverse as "get-rich-quick ads, weight loss ads, health aid promises and even phone sex services."[64] Spammers tend to send their messages in large bursts to long lists of e-mail addresses: a large ISP may receive millions of such messages for delivery to its customers in a single day.[65]

Spamming is attractive to advertisers because it achieves wide coverage at very low cost. Mass e-mail is substantially cheaper than bulk rate mailing, telemarketing and other methods of direct-to-customer advertising and has the additional advantage that recipients of spam must usually read the spammers' messages in order to determine that

56. *Id.*

57. *Id.* at 10, *reprinted in* 1986 U.S. Code Cong. & Admin. News at 2488.

58. 18 U.S.C.A. § 1030(a)(5)(A) (West Supp. 1997).

59. *Id.* § 1030 (a)(5)(c).

60. *Id.* § 1030(a)(5)(B).

61. *Id.* § 1030(a)(6).

62. *Id.* § 1030(c).

63. *Id.* § 1030(e)(8).

64. Cyber Promotions, Inc. v. America Online, Inc., 948 F.Supp. 436, 438–39 (E.D.Pa.1996) ("AOL").

65. *Id.*

they are unwanted. These advantages have spawned new companies that offer advertisers the capability to send spam to millions of unsuspecting recipients.

Spamming causes a number or problems, both for the addressees and for the ISPs that receive and store junk e-mail addressed to their subscribers. Addressees may incur downloading charges each time they receive a spammed message. ISPs are harmed when their servers are "clogged" by junk e-mail, interrupting customer service and possibly damaging ISP software. ISPs that deliver spam also may lose customer goodwill.

As the following discussion shows, while spamming is not *per se* unlawful, spamming that harms the facilities, reputation or customer relationships of an ISP may give rise to civil or criminal liability. As the following material also points out, ISPs may lawfully take a number of measures to protect themselves and their customers from unsolicited email.

1. *The Legality of "Spamming"*

The Congress has not yet enacted an e-mail equivalent of the so-called "Junk Fax Act," which makes it unlawful for any person to "use any telephone facsimile machine, computer or other device to send an unsolicited advertisement to a telephone facsimile machine ..."[66] Until such a statute is enacted, the mere transmission of junk e-mail, without more, is not unlawful. Where spam causes harm to an ISP or its customers, however, the spammer may be liable under a number of theories, including the Computer Fraud and Abuse Act, the Lanham Act and tort theories such as trespass to chattels.[67] Each of these theories merits a brief discussion.

a. *The Computer Fraud and Abuse Act and State Anti-hacking Statutes*

The federal Computer Fraud and Abuse Act ("CFAA") and similar state laws establish civil and criminal liability for certain acts that result in damage to computer systems, destruction or alteration of programs or data stored in those systems or denial of authorized access to those systems.[68] Although no court has ruled on the application of these statutes to spamming, at least one reported case involves CFAA claims against both a spammer and an ISP whose customers were spammed.[69]

The CFAA provides a promising cause of action when spammers clog ISP servers, preventing subscribers from accessing the system or other-

---

66. 47 U.S.C.A. § 227(b)(1)(c) (West 1996).

67. This list is not exhaustive but includes the claims that fit the typical spamming scenario. In a proper case other theories, including fraud and interference with contractual relationships, may be appropriate. Also, the contents of spamming mes-

sages may give rise to additional claims ranging from defamation to copyright infringement.

68. 18 U.S.C.A. § 1030(a)(5) (West 1996).

69. AOL, *supra*, note 64.

wise harming the system, its facilities or programs. Under amendments to the statute adopted in 1994, it no longer is necessary to prove that a defendant gained access to the plaintiff's system without authorization.[70] Also, the defendant's actions must cause at least $5,000 in economic damages during any one-year period in order to support a private action—a threshold that should not be difficult to meet where a spammer has prevented an ISP from serving its subscribers for an appreciable period of time.[71] The relief available under the CFAA's private right of action includes injunctions and other equitable remedies, as well as damages.[72]

ISPs also should be aware of anti-hacking statutes in the criminal codes of the states in which their facilities are located. The provisions of the state laws are remarkably diverse, and some statutes may be more favorable to plaintiffs than the CFAA. Accordingly, complainants alleging CFAA violations by spammers typically would do well to include state claims, as well.

b.   Trespass to Chattels

In a case brought by CompuServe against Cyber Promotions, Inc., a United States district court in Ohio enjoined Cyber Promotions from sending any unsolicited advertisements to any e-mail address maintained by CompuServe.[73] In support of its action, the court found it likely that CompuServe could establish a claim against Cyber Promotions for the tort of trespass to chattels, which is defined in the Restatement Second of Torts as the intentional use of, or intermeddling with, a chattel in the possession of another.[74]

Cyber Promotions argued that trespass to chattels cannot be established unless a defendant "actually takes physical custody of the property or damages it . . ."[75] The court, however, applying Ohio law supplemented by relevant provisions of the Restatement, found that an actionable trespass occurs whenever a defendant's conduct diminishes the value of a plaintiff's property.[76] Applying this view of the law to the case before it, the court held that Cyber Promotions' electronic transmissions to CompuServe's facilities were sufficiently tangible to constitute a trespass. The court further found that "the enormous volume of mass mailings that CompuServe receives places a tremendous burden on its equipment," with the result that data processing and storage resources are diverted from the task of serving CompuServe's subscribers.[77] Similarly, the court found that receipt of unwant-

---

70. 18 U.S.C.A. § 1030(a)(5)(A)(West Supp. 1997). If access was not unauthorized, however, the damage caused by the intruder must be the result of intent to cause harm rather than mere recklessness. *Id.* § 1030(a)(5)(B).

71. *Id.* § 1030(e)(8)(A). The right to bring a private action under the CFAA is set out at § 1030(g).

72. *Id.*

73. CompuServe, Inc. v. Cyber Promotions, Inc., 962 F.Supp. 1015 (S.D.Ohio 1997) ("CompuServe").

74. RESTATEMENT (SECOND) OF TORTS § 217 (1965).

75. CompuServe, 962 F.Supp. at 1022.

76. *Id.*

77. *Id.*

ed e-mail caused harm to "plaintiff's business reputation and goodwill with its customers."[78] These forms of injury, while concededly involving no physical damage to CompuServe's equipment, diminished the value of that equipment to CompuServe and satisfied the injury element of the tort.

While the *CompuServe* decision is useful precedent, two cautionary notes concerning that case are in order. First, the court in *CompuServe* stated that in order to prove a trespass—*i.e.*, unauthorized entry—an ISP arguably is required to show that the spammer was given notice that its transmissions no longer were welcome on the ISP's system.[79] Second, the court's conclusion that mass e-mail that burdens, but does not damage or prevent the operation of, an ISP's facilities constitutes an actionable trespass is somewhat adventurous and may not be supported by the tort law of other states in which similar actions are brought.

c. Trademark Infringement and Unfair Competition

Spammers sometimes conceal the source of their messages by falsifying the point of origin information in the message header, removing sender information in the header and replacing it with another address or configuring their servers to simulate other computers. In many cases the false information generated by spammers suggests that their messages originate with other entities, including reputable, well-known ISPs that have no relationship with the spammers.

Conduct of this kind violates criminal statutes and gives rise to both state and federal causes of action. For example, when a spammer misuses a domain name or other identifying information that is protected as a trademark, the victim of the practice may bring a trademark infringement action under the Lanham Act[80] and state anti-dilution statutes. Even where the identifying information misappropriated by the spammer is not trademarked, the spammer's conduct may constitute unfair competition under section 43(a) of the Lanham Act[81] and may violate state consumer protection statutes, as well.

---

78. *Id.* at 1023. For a thorough exposition of "spamming" and the theory of spamming as a trespass to chattels *see* Anne E. Hawley, *Taking Spam Out of Your Cyber–Space Diet: Common Law Applied to Bulk Unsolicited Advertising Via Electronic Mail,* 66 UMKC L.Rev. 381 (1997).

79. *Id.* at 1024. A spammer might argue that if an ISP's system is programmed to accept any e-mail addressed to its subscribers, whether "solicited" or not, then no properly addressed e-mail transmission reaching that ISP's system can be characterized as a trespass. In order to rebut this presumption, an ISP should be prepared to prove that it revoked the spammer's "permission" to access the system. A simple statement of policy, not expressly communicated to the spammer, might not suffice for this purpose. *Id.*

80. 15 U.S.C.A. §§ 1051 *et seq.* (West 1997).

81. *Id.* § 1125. The elements of a cause of action under this section are: (1) false statements of fact concerning defendant's products or services; (2) deception of consumers or its likelihood; (3) materiality of the deception; (4) introduction of the product or service into interstate commerce; and (5) injury to plaintiff or its likelihood. *See* Skil Corp. v. Rockwell International Corp., 375 F.Supp. 777 (N.D.Ill.1974).

2. *Legality of ISP Actions to Counter "Spamming"*

ISPs have taken a number of measures to protect their subscribers from mass, unsolicited e-mail. One approach is simply to refuse to deliver e-mail that originates with known spammers. Another is to "bomb" the sender by returning undelivered or undeliverable e-mail in bulk to the originating server. Still another is to implement software that permits the ISP's subscribers to decide whether they wish to receive spam and that blocks spam addressed to any subscriber who has not elected to receive it.

All of these measure are lawful, although the "bombing" approach may present some legal risk where the practice causes harm to a spammer's server or system. As the following discussion shows, the courts so far have supported self-help measures adopted by ISPs to deal with spam and have endorsed the fundamental principle that ISPs have no obligation to deliver all e-mail that reaches their systems.

a. *Refusal to Deliver "Spam"*

Spammers are legally helpless against ISPs' refusals to deliver their messages unless they can find some "right" to have their messages delivered, or some "obligation" of ISPs to transmit or deliver all communications that reach their systems. Cyber Promotions has tried to establish that ISPs are obligated under the First Amendment or as common carriers to deliver bulk e-mail messages to their subscribers, but those efforts so far have failed.

In *Cyber Promotions, Inc.* v. *America Online, Inc.*,[82] Cyber Promotions argued that AOL's refusal to deliver bulk e-mail constituted a form of state action, subject to the free speech provisions of the First Amendment. Cyber Promotions' principal argument was that AOL was in the same position as the company town in *Marsh* v. *Alabama*[83] and the shopping center in *Amalgamated Food Employees Union v. Logan Valley Plaza*[84], which the Supreme Court found to be state actors when they suppressed certain expressive activity. The court rejected this argument, however, finding that AOL is not equivalent to a state actor because it does not serve any exclusively public function and because Cyber Promotions had numerous, alternative outlets for advertising messages.

When Cyber Promotions raised its First Amendment argument again in *CompuServe Inc. v. Cyber Promotions, Inc.*,[85] the court merely recounted with approval the reasoning of the *AOL* court. The *CompuServe* court also made short work of an alternative argument to the effect that large ISPs must serve everyone indifferently because they are a kind of common carrier. The court found that CompuServe's service was neither "essential to society" in the same sense as a traditional

---

82. 948 F.Supp. 436 (E.D.Pa.1996).

83. 326 U.S. 501, 66 S.Ct. 276, 90 L.Ed. 265 (1946).

84. 391 U.S. 308, 88 S.Ct. 1601, 20 L.Ed.2d 603 (1968).

85. 962 F.Supp. 1015 (S.D.Ohio 1997) *citing* Cyber Promotions, Inc. v. America Online, Inc., 948 F.Supp. 436 (E.D.Pa. 1996).

public utility service, nor a monopoly service of the kind traditionally regulated under common carrier principles.[86]

b. *"Bombing"*

If an ISP has no obligation to deliver spam, then logically it has the right to return spam to its point of origin. Cyber Promotions, however, claimed in the *AOL* case that AOL violated the CFAA and committed various torts when its "bombing" allegedly caused other ISPs to terminate their contracts with Cyber Promotions or refuse to enter into contracts with Cyber Promotions.[87] While the court in *AOL* did not rule on this claim and it seems unlikely that such complaints will garner much sympathy, the most conservative approach an ISP might take is to delete, rather than return, undelivered e-mail from spammers.[88]

c. *Blocking Software*

An ISP's safest response to spamming is to offer its subscribers the choice to elect whether or not they wish to receive spam. AOL, for example, has implemented a program through which AOL's servers can be programmed to deliver messages from known spammers only to those subscribers who have elected to receive bulk e-mail. This approach limits the ISP's exposure by making the subscriber, rather than the ISP, the decision maker. It also requires spammers, if they wish to reach all of the ISP's subscribers, to take deceptive measures to evade the blocking software—conduct that will make the spammers especially vulnerable to charges of computer fraud and abuse, trespass to chattels, unfair competition, trademark infringement and other claims.

11.15 Control of Content on the Internet

The Internet is, above all, a powerful medium of communication and, like other media, its content will, on occasion, give offense to individuals and groups. Major concerns regarding Internet content involve obscenity, indecency and defamation. Persons and groups aggrieved by allegedly defamatory, obscene and indecent transmissions will often seek to impose civil liability or criminal penalties on offenders. The issue of civil liability for defamatory communications over the Internet is considered in chapter five, section 5.10, *supra*. The issue of criminal liability for obscene or indecent communications over the Internet is discussed in chapter six, section 6.11 in volume two of the Practitioners Edition.

86. *Id.* at 182. *See also* Religious Technology Center v. Netcom On-Line Communication Services, Inc., 907 F.Supp. 1361 (N.D.Cal.1995) (refusing to find that an ISP is a common carrier).

87. AOL, *supra* note 85.

88. It seems especially improbable that a court would find for the spammer on such a claim without also finding for the ISP, since any harm the spamming messages do to the spammer's facilities on their return trip can hardly be any greater than the harm they did to the ISP's facilities when they arrived, in equal or greater volume, at the ISP's server.

11.16   *Computers and the Regulation of Telecommunications

11.17   *Antitrust and the Computer Industry

* Published in Modern Communication
Law, Practitioners Edition, vol. 2 only.

Chapter Twelve

REGULATION AND DEREGULA-
TION OF COMMUNICATIONS
COMMON CARRIERS

Analysis

12.1 General Historical Foundation for Defining and Regulating Common Carriers

The definition of common carriage in the Communications Act of 1934[1] and the FCC's Rules and Regulations provides no evidence of the time, effort and challenge in reaching a common view of what the term means,[2] or the importance of common carriage in telecommunications. Section 3(10) of the Communications Act defines common carrier as "any person engaged as a common carrier for hire."[3] The FCC's Rules and Regulations provides an equally unhelpful definition: "Any person

---

1. Communications Act of 1934, Pub. L. No. 73–416, 48 Stat. 1064, *codified as amended at* 47 U.S.C.A. § 151 et seq. (West 1991).

2. The Conference Report of the Bill creating the Communications Act of 1934 and specifically Section 3(h) defining common carriage noted that "the definition

does not include any person if not a common carrier in the ordinary sense of the term." H.R. Conf. Rep. No. 1918, 73d Cong., 2d Sess. 46 (1934), *reprinted in* [Current Service] Rad. Reg.2d (Pike and Fischer) ¶ 10.1011.

3. Communications Act, § 3(10), *codified at* 47 U.S.C.A. § 153(10) (West 1996).

engaged in rendering communication service for hire to the public."[4]

Common carrier regulation contained in Title II of the Communications Act does not contain a definition either. The Communications Act incorporates an extensive body of law developed for transporters such as railroads and other occupations displaying a public character[5] and applies it to telecommunication carriers. In the late seventeenth century Matthew Hale articulated the view that certain private businesses are "clothed and superinduced with a *jus privaturm*," *i.e.*, a common and public interest.[6] Lord Hale and others developed the view that common carriers operate as quasi-public undertakings with: (1) a higher duty of care owed to customers; (2) an obligation to serve all persons indiscriminately; and (3) a requirement that they balance commercial interests with the "public interest,"[7] thereby accepting an obligation to make service widely available, even though the particular service may be useful only to a small portion of the population.

These obligations first applied to recipients of royal charters for the privilege of soliciting the public's business. They extended to other businesses, such as innkeepers, barge operators and ferriers. While the definition easily applied to enterprises that physically carried something, *e.g.*, railroads and steamboats, it could be extrapolated to apply to carriers of messages via telecommunications.

A. Telegraph and Telephone Companies as Common Carriers

The United States Congress expressly decreed that telegraph and telephone providers operated as common carriers in the Mann–Elkins Act of 1910.[8] Without modifying existing definitions, this Act amended the Interstate Commerce Act of 1887[9] which had codified the duties and liabilities of railroad common carriers. "Indeed, comments of various legislators during floor debate uniformly suggest that Congress transferred the meaning of the term common carrier intact from its [traditional] use in the amended Interstate Commerce Act."[10] Thus, the content of modern day regulation of telecommunication common carriers

---

4. 47 C.F.R. § 21.2 (1994).

5. *See* Robert Frieden, *Continuation of the Common Carrier Conception in Telecommunications*, 19 Telecom. Policy 685–697 (No.9, Dec.1995).

6. MATTHEW HALE, A TREATISE IN THREE PARTS, in 1 Collection of Tracks Relative to The Law of England, 1, 84 (F. Hargrave ed. 1787); *see also* MATTHEW HALE, THE ANALYSIS OF LAW (1713).

7. *See* Walton H. Hamilton, *Affectation with Public Interest*, 39 Yale. L. J. 1089, 1093 (1930); *see also* Munn v. Illinois, 94 U.S. 113, 24 L.Ed. 77 (1876)(upholding a state statute setting maximum rates for grain storage and setting the basis for state economic regulation of an industry); Budd v. New York, 143 U.S. 517, 12 S.Ct. 468, 36 L.Ed. 247 (1892) (regulation of grain elevators upheld because the business is charged with a public interest and must serve the common good in a manner analogous to that of common carriers); Breck P. McAllister, *Lord Hale and Business Affected with a Public Interest*, 43 Harv. L. Rev. 759 (1930).

8. Mann–Elkins Act, Pub. L. No. 61–218, § 7, 36 Stat. 539, 544 (1910).

9. Interstate Commerce Act, ch. 104, 24 Stat. 379 (1887) (codified as amended throughout 49 U.S.C. A. (West 1994)).

10. Phil Nichols, *Redefining 'Common Carrier': The FCC's Attempt At Deregulation By Redefinition*, 1987 Duke. L. J. 501, 511.

is primarily a product of railroad regulation. The Supreme Court had established a working definition for common carrier in 1858 as:

> [O]ne who undertakes for hire to transport the goods of those who may choose to employ him from place to place. He is, in general, bound to take the goods of all who offer, unless his complement for the trip is full, or the goods be of such a kind as to be liable to extraordinary danger, or such as he is unaccustomed to convey.[11]

Over time telegraph and telephone companies began to be described as public service corporations and by analogy, came to be treated as the functional equivalent of public utility common carriers. Their growing importance as carriers of information and assumptions that a single enterprise could most efficiently operate in any particular locality supported the view that telecommunication services had become an essential social and commercial resource.

B. Contemporary Definitions of Telecommunications Carriage

While not changing the fundamental definition of common carrier, the Telecommunications Act of 1996, which amended the Communications Act of 1934, provides supplemental definitions, including one for telecommunications carrier[12] and telecommunications service: "the offering of telecommunications for a fee directly to the public, or to such classes of users as to be effectively available directly to the public, regardless of the facilities used."[13] This latter definition emphasizes that common carriers market services to the general public, rather than target and serve a small segment of the user population.

The two key modern cases addressing the definition of communications common carriage considered whether to apply a conventional, undifferentiated common carrier status to telecommunication enterprises. In assessing cable television[14] and specialized mobile radio[15] the reviewing courts in the 1970s refused to classify such endeavors as common carriage. In *FCC v. Midwest Video*,[16] the Supreme Court held that the FCC could not impose common carrier obligations on cable television systems, because, *inter alia*, such systems do not make a " 'public offering to provide [communications facilities] whereby all members of the public who choose to employ such facilities may communicate or transmit intelligence of their own design and choosing.... ' "[17]

---

11. Propeller Niagara Co. v. Cordes, 21 How. 7, 62 U.S. 7, 22, 16 L.Ed. 41, 46 (1858) *quoted in* David Cosson, *Development of Regulation of Common Carrier Communications*, 28 Fed. Comm. Bar J. 132, 133 (1975).

12. Communications Act of 1934, § 3(44), *as amended and codified at* 47 U.S.C.A. § 153(44) (West 1991).

13. *Id.* Sec. 3(46), 47 U.S.C.A. § 153(46).

14. FCC v. Midwest Video Corp. 440 U.S. 689, 701, 99 S.Ct. 1435, 1442, 59 L.Ed.2d 692 (1979).

15. National Ass'n. of Regl. Utility Commissioners v. FCC, 525 F.2d 630, 173 U.S. App. D.C. 413 (D.C.Cir.1976), cert. denied 425 U.S. 992, 96 S.Ct. 2203, 48 L.Ed.2d 816 (1976).

16. 440 U.S. 689, 99 S.Ct. 1435, 59 L.Ed.2d 692 (1979).

17. FCC v. Midwest Video Corp., 440 U.S. 689, 701, 99 S.Ct. 1435, 1442, 59

The Court rejected attempts by the FCC to impose public access responsibilities because cable television operators had no common carrier duty to abdicate their own programming freedom. And earlier in *National Association of Regulatory Utility Commissioners v. FCC,*[18] the Court of Appeals for the District of Columbia affirmed an FCC decision to refrain from applying common carrier status to a new type of terrestrial mobile radio service. The FCC chose to classify Specialized Mobile Radio Service ("SMRS") as a non-common carrier system because operators would enter the marketplace without a captive subscriber base, *i.e.*, users having no option but to use SMRS, and no market power, *i.e.*, the ability to affect the price or supply of land mobile radio services. Using a functional analysis of SMRS operations, [19]the court upheld the FCC's non-common carrier determination, because it could find no "substantial likelihood that SMRS [operators] will hold themselves out to serve indifferently those who seek to avail themselves of their particular services."[20] A telecommunications common carrier must "offer indiscriminate service to whatever public its service may legally and practically be of use."[21] The court noted that SMRS operators typically offer service on a medium-to-long term contractual basis and concluded that the FCC acted reasonably in classifying SMRS as a non-common carrier service.

The court's functional analysis considered the nature of the services proposed, *i.e.*, the extent to which they are essential and should be made available to all requesting services. The analysis also considered the operator and whether it had the ability to control the supply or price of the services it proposed to offer. A functional analysis considers the state of supply and demand rather than engage in results-oriented decision-making where political and economic philosophies drive the regulatory process.

C. *Requirements Imposed by Title II of the Communications Act*

Title II of the Communications Act sets out the rights and responsibilities of common carriers. Collectively, these regulations impose burdens that can affect carrier revenues and restrict the latitude and discretion customarily available in commercial transactions. Title II regulation "entails more than just a nondiscriminatory service duty. It also calls into being the full panoply of public utility regulation—supervision of rates, entry, construction, and a great deal else—under Title II . . . and associated state regulatory legislation."[22] While the FCC

L.Ed.2d 692, 702–03 (1979) (citing Report and Order, Industrial Radio location service, Docket No. 16106, 5 F.C.C. 2d 197, 202 (1966)).

18. 525 F.2d 630, 173 U.S. App. D.C. 413 (D.C.Cir.1976), cert. denied, 425 U.S. 992, 96 S.Ct. 2203, 48 L.Ed.2d 816 (1976).

19. *See id.*, at 644, 173 U.S. App. D.C. at 427.

20. *Id.* at 642, 173 U.S. App. D.C. at 425.

21. *Id.*

22. Roland Hornet Jr., *Getting the Message: Statutory Approaches to Electronic Information Delivery and the Duty of Carriage*, 37 Fed. Comm. L.J. 217, 252 (1985) (citing ALFRED KAHN, PRINCIPLES OF REGULATION, 52, 79–80 (1970)).

has attempted to streamline Title II regulations,[23] and even to forbear from regulating non-dominant carriers[24] (those carriers that lack the ability to affect the price or supply of a good or service), it cannot ignore or deny applicability of legislated requirements.[25]

1. Section 10: Forbearance

However, Section 10 of the Telecommunications Act of 1996 provides legislative authority for the Commission to "forbear from applying any regulation or any provision of this Act to a telecommunications carrier or telecommunications service"[26] if enforcement of such regulation or provision is no longer needed to guard against unjust and unreasonable discrimination, is unnecessary for consumer protection and such forbearance would serve the public interest.[27] The FCC wasted no time in using its newly granted discretion to propose that it adopt a mandatory detariffing policy for domestic services provided by non-dominant interexchange carriers and permit the bundling by such carriers of long distance services and customer premises equipment.[28]

With passage of the Telecommunications Act of 1996 and the ensuing implementation proceedings by the FCC, some of the fundamental requirements of telecommunications common carriers will no longer be enforced.

2. Section 201: Service and Charges

Section 201 of the Communications Act establishes the duty of common carriers to furnish service upon reasonable request and to establish reasonable charges, practices, classifications and regulations regarding service. This means that a carrier must "furnish reasonably adequate communication facilities to the public it serves ... [that] by

23. *See, e.g.*, Streamlining the International Section 214 Authorization Process and Tariff Requirements, IB Docket No. 95–118, Notice of Proposed Rulemaking, FCC 95–286, 10 FCC Rcd. 13477 (1995), Report and Order, 11 FCC Rcd. 12884 (1996).

24. Policy and Rules Concerning Rates for Competitive Common Carrier Services and Facilities Authorizations Therefor, CC Docket No. 79–252, First Report and Order 85 FCC2d 1 (1980), Second Report and Order 91 FCC2d 59 (1982), *recon.*, 93 FCC2d 54 (1983), Third Report and Order, 48 Fed. Reg. 46,791 (Oct. 6, 1983), Fourth Report and Order., 95 FCC2d 554 (1983), Fifth Report and Order, 98 FCC2d 1191 (1984), Sixth Report and Order, 99 FCC2d 1020 (1985), *rev'd sub nom.* MCI v. FCC, 765 F.2d 1186, 247 U.S. App. D.C. 32 (D.C.Cir. 1985).

25. For example, despite the clear language in Section 203 requiring carriers to file service charges in the form of a tariff, the FCC sought to eliminate the require-

ment for non-dominant carriers in the *Competitive Carrier* rulemaking. On appeal the Court of Appeals for the District of Columbia overturned the Commission and reinstated the tariff filing requirement for all carriers, regardless of market share. MCI Corp. v. FCC, 765 F.2d 1186, 247 U.S. App. D.C. 32 (D.C.Cir.1985).

26. Communications Act of 1934, *as amended*, § 10(a), *codified at* 47 U.S.C.A. § 160(a) (West 1991).

27. *Id.* at § 160(a)(1)-(3).

28. Policy and Rules Concerning the Interstate, Interexchange Marketplace, CC Docket No. 96–61, Notice of Proposed Rulemaking, FCC 96–123, 11 FCC Rcd. 7141 (1996), First Report and Order, 11 FCC Rcd. 9564 (1996), Second Report and Order, 11 FCC Rcd. 20730 (1996), First Mem. Op. and Order on Recons, 12 FCC Rcd. 11812 (1997), on Further Recons, 12 FCC Rcd. 15014 (1997), partial stay denied, 12 FCC Rcd. 15739 (1997), Third Report and Order, 12 FCC Rcd 15756 (1997).

necessity, [include] those services offered in the carrier's tariffs."[29] However, the duty to furnish a service and the tariffing of such service does not translate into the absolute right of a user to demand immediate service or to specify the type of facilities and services the carrier must provide. A carrier will not be liable for the inability to provide service immediately or to incur the obligation and expense to provide services in unanticipated volume, locations, or configurations.

In *Southwestern Bell Telephone v. FCC,*[30] the District of Columbia Circuit remanded an order of the Commission that required local exchange carriers ("LECs") to continue offering "dark fiber" (installed, but unused fiber optic cable) under a general tariff rather than on an individually, negotiated basis. The court rejected the Commission's view that a common carrier undertaking had occurred simply because the carriers had voluntarily negotiated access on an individualized basis and thereby met the "holding out" test established in *National Association of Regulatory Utility Commissioners v. FCC,*[31] (NARUC–I) and *National Association of Regulatory Utility Commissioners v. FCC,*[32] (NARUC–II).

Section 201 also addresses the extent to which a common carrier must provide interconnection with its facilities and services to other carriers and to end users. With the onset of competitive inter-exchange, "long distance" service[33] and more recently local-exchange service competition,[34] incumbent carriers have balked at having to interconnect lines with competitors. In most instances, telecommunication service competition requires incumbent LECs to hand off and receive traffic from recent market entrants. For example, long distance carriers may seek to interconnect their limited transmission facilities with the vastly more extensive network of an incumbent. New carriers typically need to have traffic routed through the "Public Switched Telephone Network" ("PSTN") operated by the incumbent LEC. While market entry and technological innovations may challenge the view that the LEC operates an essential facility[35] or bottleneck,[36] most switched traffic continues to originate and

---

29. Coastal Auto Parts, Inc. v. Coastal Utilities Inc., 20 FCC2d 316 (1969) (ordering a public hearing to determine whether defendant had violated Section 201(a) by refusing to provide a private line for interstate communications use upon request).

30. 19 F.3d 1475, 305 U.S. App. D.C. 272 (D.C.Cir.1994).

31. 525 F.2d 630, 173 U.S. App. D.C. 413 (D.C.Cir.1976), cert. denied 425 U.S. 992, 96 S.Ct. 2203, 48 L.Ed.2d 816 (1976).

32. 533 F.2d 601, 174 U.S. App. D.C. 374 (D.C.Cir.1976).

33. *See, e.g.,* MCI Telecommunications Corp. v. FCC, 561 F.2d 365, 182 U.S. App. D.C. 367 (D.C.Cir.1977), cert. denied 434 U.S. 1040, 98 S.Ct. 781, 54 L.Ed.2d 790 (1978)(authorizing switched long distances services).

34. *See, e.g.,* Petition of Rochester Telephone Corp. for Approval of Proposed Restructuring Plan, Opinion and Order Approving Joint Stipulation and Agreement, Case 93–C–0101, Opinion No. 94–25 (N.Y. Pub. Serv. Comm'n Nov. 19, 1994); Rochester Telephone Corp., Pet. for Waivers to Implement Its Open Market Plan, FCC 95–96, 10 FCC Rcd. 6776 (1995) (petition for waiver of access charge rules to permit Rochester Telephone Corp. to establish a competitive interexchange carrier while continuing local exchange carrier operations).

35. *See, e.g.,* Bell System Tariff Offerings, 46 FCC 2d 413 (1974), *aff'd. sub nom.* Bell Telephone Co. v. FCC, 503 F.2d 1250 (3d Cir.1974), cert. denied 422 U.S. 1026, 95 S.Ct. 2620, 45 L.Ed.2d 684, *rehearings denied* 423 U.S. 886, 96 S.Ct. 163, 46 L.Ed.2d 118 (1975); MCI Telecommunica-

terminate over LEC facilities, frequently referred to as the first and last mile of the network, or the "local loop".

Section 201 addresses the terms, conditions and nature under which an incumbent carrier must interconnect its facilities with newcomers that can migrate traffic and revenues. The lengthy and contentious interconnection disputes between market entrants like MCI and the former Bell System evidence the scope of Section 201's obligations and the stakes involved. Throughout the 1960s the FCC promoted market entry by facilities-based carriers who offered private lines via point-to-point microwave facilities, *i.e.*, dedicated links between two or more locations.[37] These "Specialized Common Carriers" initially did not provide the functional equivalent of switched long distance service, although typically they required access to LEC facilities to link subscribers with their facilities. While the FCC had duly certified and licensed such new carriers,[38] incumbent operators, like the Bell Operating Carriers, refused to make their local distribution facilities available.[39]

tions Corp. v. FCC, 580 F.2d 590, 188 U.S. App. D.C. 327 (D.C.Cir.1978), cert. denied 439 U.S. 980, 99 S.Ct. 566, 58 L.Ed.2d 651 (1978) (access to local exchange facilities mandated); Establishment of Domestic Communications Satellite Facilities by Non-governmental Entities, 22 FCC 2d 86, 97 (1970), *policy reaffirmed*, 34 FCC 2d 9, 64–5, *adopted*, 35 FCC 2d 844, 856 (1972), *on recons.*, 38 FCC 2d 665 (1972) (domestic satellite policy mandates non-discriminatory, diverse, and flexible access to domestic satellites and earth station facilities); *accord* Specialized Common Carrier Services, 29 FCC 2d 870, 940 (1971) (AT & T required to afford local exchange facility access to competing inter-city carriers), *on recons.*, 31 FCC 2d 1106 (1971), *aff'd. sub nom.*, Washington Utilities and Transportation Comm. v. FCC, 513 F.2d 1142 (9th Cir.), cert. denied 423 U.S. 836, 96 S.Ct. 62, 46 L.Ed.2d 54 (1975).

36. "A firm controlling bottleneck facilities has the ability to impede access of its competitors to those facilities. We must be in a position to contend with this type of potential abuse. We treat control of bottleneck facilities as prima facie evidence of market power requiring detailed regulatory scrutiny. Control of bottleneck facilities is present when a firm or group of firms has sufficient command over some essential commodity or facility in its industry or trade to be able to impede new entrants. Thus bottleneck control describes the structural characteristic of a market that new entrants must either be allowed to share the bottleneck facility or fail." Policy and Rules Concerning Rates for Competitive Common Carrier Services and Facilities Authorizations Therefor, CC Docket No. 79–252, First Report and Order, 85 FCC 2d 1, 21–22 (1981). *See also* United States v. Ter-

minal Railroad Ass'n, 224 U.S. 383, 32 S.Ct. 507, 56 L.Ed. 810 (1912) (antitrust court ordered railroads to provide competitors equivalent access to bottleneck railway terminal facilities), *appeal after remand*, 236 U.S. 194, 35 S.Ct. 408, 59 L.Ed. 535 (1915); Cellular Communications Systems, 86 FCC2d 469, 495–96 (1981) (Commission required telephone companies to furnish interconnection to cellular systems upon terms no less favorable than those used by or offered to wireline carriers), *modified*, 89 FCC2d 58 (1982), *further modified*, 90 FCC2d 571 (1982); Need to Promote Competition and Efficient Use of Spectrum for Radio Common Carrier Services, 59 Rad. Reg. 2d (Pike & Fischer) 1275 (1986), *clarified*, 2 FCC Rcd. 2910 (1987), *aff'd on recons.*, 4 FCC Rcd 2369 (1989) (Commission clarified policies regarding interconnection of cellular and other radio common carrier facilities to landline network); Lincoln Tel. & Tel. Co. v. FCC, 659 F.2d 1092, 1102, 1103–06, 212 U.S.App.D.C. 208, 218, 219-222 (D.C.Cir.1981)(court upheld Commission's order requiring Lincoln to provide interconnection facilities to MCI); MCI Telecommunications Corp. v. FCC, 580 F.2d 590, 188 U.S.App.D.C. 327(D.C.Cir.), *cert. denied* 439 U.S. 980, 99 S.Ct. 566, 58 L.Ed.2d 651 (1978); Bell Tel. Co. v. FCC, 503 F.2d 1250 (3d Cir.1974), *cert. denied* 422 U.S. 1026, 95 S.Ct. 2620, 45 L.Ed.2d 684 (1975), *rehearing denied* 423 U.S. 886, 96 S.Ct. 163, 46 L.Ed.2d 118 (1975).

37. *See* Allocation of Frequencies in the Bands Above 890 Mc., 27 F.C.C. 2d 359 (1959), *recons. denied* 29 F.C.C. 2d 825 (1960).

38. *See, e.g.*, Microwave Communications Inc., 18 F.C.C. 2d 953 (1969), *recon. den.*, 21 FCC2d 190 (1970) (approving

AT & T had also attempted to justify its restrictions of interconnection with competitors as consistent with Section 201. For example, in responding to a 1984 civil antitrust suit filed by the Southern Pacific Communications Company (now known as Sprint), AT & T claimed immunity from liability for refusing to interconnect its facilities with other carriers simply because the FCC pervasively regulated it pursuant to Title II of the Communications Act.[40] The United States Court of Appeals for the District of Columbia agreed with AT & T, holding that the carrier did not have to provide absolute equality of access even to essential facilities because a non-specific public interest based interconnection requirement should not automatically apply. However, the court did qualify AT & T's regulatory justification defense by requiring the carrier to justify its interconnection policies as reasonable and established in good faith rather than being made on the basis of competitive considerations.[41] The court defined reasonableness in terms of "concerns for the public interest that are concrete, articulatable, and recognized as legitimate by the appropriate regulatory agencies."[42]

The good faith component, adopted from a Seventh Circuit case[43] includes both subjective and objective elements:

> a carrier has an obligation under the Communications Act to interconnect, but may deny interconnections if it determines that the public interest is to the contrary; and that if the carrier at the time had a reasonable basis in regulatory policy to conclude, and in good faith concluded, that denial of interconnections is required by concrete, articulatable concerns for the public interest, then there is no liability under the antitrust laws.[44]

The FCC's consideration of the reasonableness of a carrier's interconnection decision-making also includes an assessment of the impact on customers, particularly because some users may lack service options and bargaining leverage.[45] While most users currently have multiple carriers and technologies from which to choose, in 1980 the FCC viewed the

MCI's application to provide facilities-based, private line service between Chicago and St. Louis). *See also* Establishment of Policies and Procedures for Consideration of Applications to Provide Specialized Common Carrier Services in the Domestic Public Point-to-Point Microwave Radio Service, 29 F.C.C. 2d 870 (1971).

39. *See, e.g.,* American Satellite Corp. v. Southwestern Bell Telephone Co., 64 F.C.C. 2d 503 (1977) (ordering local exchange carrier to make distribution services and facilities available on a non-discriminatory basis to all satellite carriers).

40. Southern Pacific Communications Co. v. FCC, 682 F.2d 232, 220 U.S.App.D.C. 397 (D.C.Cir.1982).

41. *Id.* at 1009, 238 U.S. App. D.C. at 338.

42. *Id.*

43. MCI Communications Corp. v. AT & T, 708 F.2d 1081 (7th Cir.1983), cert. denied 464 U.S. 891, 104 S. Ct. 234, 78 L. Ed. 2d 226 (1983).

44. 740 F.2d at 1010, 238 U.S. App. D.C. at 339 (*quoting* MCI Communications Corp. v. AT & T, 708 F.2d 1081, 1138).

45. RCA American Communications, Inc. 84 FCC2d 353 (1980)(a domestic satellite carrier's decision to modify tariff terms and conditions should be considered under the reasonableness standard in Section 201(b), both in terms of its impact on carriers and the public as consumers).

unfettered ability of carriers to change the terms and conditions of service as potentially unfair and unreasonable. The Commission formally declared "a carrier may not alter a long term service tariff, except as provided in the tariff itself, or if the carrier establishes ... that substantial cause exists for a departure from the original tariff terms."[46] On the other hand, the Filed Rate Doctrine[47] specifies that tariff terms and conditions prevail over any inconsistent term or condition previously negotiated and contained in a contract.[48]

3.   Other Implications of Section 201

The FCC has interpreted Section 201's requirement for just, reasonable and nondiscriminatory charges as requiring cost-based rates.[49] This obligates the Commission to assess the reasonableness of carrier rates in terms of the manner in which joint and common costs are allocated, *i.e.*, how the carrier assigns costs incurred to install plant that can provide a number of services. Changes and developments in regulatory economic theory have affected the Commission's view of what is reasonable on such marketplace competition issues as carrier tariffing and the ease in which tariffs can be changed to meet competition.

The FCC's evaluation of reasonableness also includes a determination whether the carrier can bundle telecommunication services and equipment. The Commission ordered carriers to separate telephone service from the sale or lease of telephone handsets[50] to access such services. Common carriers would continue to provide the former on tariffed terms and conditions while a competitive and unregulated market would operate regarding the manufacture, sale or lease of equipment. This unbundling eliminated "the seller's exploitation of its control over the tying product ... [thereby preventing it from coercing a] buyer into the purchase of a tied product that the buyer either did not want at all, or might have preferred to purchase elsewhere on different terms."[51]

In 1988, the FCC deemed an AT & T-designed financial compensation plan as violating Section 201(b). Under the nullified plan AT & T

---

46.   *Id*. at 363.

47.   *See* Maislin Inds., Inc. v. Primary Steel, Inc., 497 U.S. 116, 126, 110 S.Ct. 2759, 2766, 111 L.Ed.2d 94, 108 (1990).

48.   *See* American Broadcasting Cos., Inc. v. FCC, 643 F.2d 818, 207 U.S. App. D.C. 68 (D.C.Cir.1980); *see also* Showtime Networks, Inc. v. FCC, 932 F.2d 1, 289 U.S. App. D.C. 348 (D.C.Cir.1991) (carrier must demonstrate substantial cause to revise a tariff providing for long term service arrangement).

49.   *See. e.g.*, Separation of Costs of Regulated Telephone Service from Costs of Nonregulated Activities, CC Docket No. 86–111, Report and Order, 2 FCC Rcd. 1298 (1987), *on recon.*, 2 FCC Rcd. 6283 (1987), *on further recons.*, 3 FCC Rcd. 6701 (1988), *aff'd sub nom.*, Southwestern Bell Corp. v.

FCC, 896 F.2d 1378, 283 U.S. App. D.C. 80 (D.C.Cir.1990).

50.   *See* Telerent Leasing Corp., 45 FCC 2d 204 (1974), *aff'd sub nom.* North Carolina Utilities Commission v. FCC, 537 F.2d 787 (4th Cir.), cert. denied 429 U.S. 1027, 97 S.Ct. 651, 50 L.Ed.2d 631(1976); Terminal Equipment Registration, 56 FCC 2d 593 (1975), 58 FCC 2d 736 (1976), *aff'd sub nom.*, North Carolina Utilities Commission v. FCC, 552 F.2d 1036 (4th Cir.) cert. denied 434 U.S. 874, 98 S.Ct. 222, 54 L.Ed.2d 154 (1977).

51.   AT & T's Private Payphone Commission Plan, 3 FCC Rcd. 5834, 5837, ¶ 24, 65 Rad. Reg.2d 609 (P & F 1988) (quoting Jefferson Parish Hosp. Dist. No. 2 v. Hyde, 466 U.S. 2, 12 104 S.Ct. 1551, 1558, 80 L.Ed.2d 2, 13 (1984)).

provided a higher commission to the operators of private payphones if they agreed to deliver all long distance calls to AT & T:

> AT & T is using its power to induce PPCs [Private Payphone Companies to purchase "1+" [direct dialed long distance] service from it that the PPC may have wanted to purchase elsewhere. This tie-bundling effectively forecloses competition for the PPC's "1+" service because of the unrelated choice as to a "0+" operator-assisted long distance call] provider. AT & T has not provided any justification why this practice should be viewed as reasonable. Thus, we find that based on the record before us AT & T's tying ... is an unreasonable practice under Section 201(b).[52]

Thus, tying or exclusive agreements, which foreclose or thwart competition, may constitute a violation of Section 201(b).

12.2   Development of Tariffs Governing Common Carriers

A.   *Discrimination and Preferences*

1.   *Section 202*

Section 202 of the Communications Act prohibits unjust or unreasonable discrimination in the provisioning of and charging for service. While it applies more typically to practices of carriers, this section also prevents the FCC from adopting rules that allow such discrimination to occur.[1] The section does not prohibit carriers from offering different services at diverse unit costs to different categories of users. Carriers simply must offer "like" and "functionally equivalent" services[2] to "similarly situated" users[3] under the same terms and conditions. For example, in *Western Union International, Inc.* v. *FCC,*[4] the reviewing court determined that the services provided to international record

---

52. *Id.* at ¶ 28, 5837, 65 Rad. Reg.2d at 614.

1. In Nat'l. Assn. of Regl. Util. Comm'rs v. FCC, 737 F.2d 1095, 237 U.S. App. D.C. 390 (D.C.Cir.1984) the Court of Appeals held the FCC did not discriminate against carriers subject to the carrier common line charge in favor of interstate users of exchange facilities. However, the FCC did not adequately explain certain decisions relating to party line access charges and average schedule companies.

2. *See* AT & T Communications, Revisions to Tariff F.C.C. No. 12, Memorandum Opinion and Order on Remand, 6 FCC Rcd. 7039, 7041, ¶ 9 (1991); Ad Hoc Telecommunications Users Committee v. FCC, 680 F.2d 790, 796, 220 U.S. App. D.C. 241, 247 (D.C.Cir.1982). To determine whether a carrier has violated Section 202(a) of the Communications Act, the Commission undertakes a three-step analysis: "(1) whether the services [in question] are 'like'; (2) if they are 'like,' where there is a price differ-

ence; and (3) if there is a difference, whether it is reasonable." MCI Telecommunications Corp. v. FCC, 917 F.2d 30, 39, 286 U.S. App. D.C. 316, 325 (D.C.Cir.1990).

3. "The requirement that AT & T make its ... discount offering available to all 'similarly situated' customers is mandated, not only by ... [language in the] tariff ... but also by Sections 201(b), 202(a) and 203(c) of the Act." Letter From Thomas D. Wyatt, Chief, Formal Complaints and Investigations Branch, Common Carrier Bureau Re: Affinity Network, Inc. v. AT & T, DA 93–771, File No. E–93–007, 8 FCC Rcd. 4384 (1993). *See also* Competitive Telecommunications Association v. FCC, 998 F.2d 1058, 302 U.S. App. D.C. 423 (D.C.Cir. 1993); Nader v. FCC, 520 F.2d 182, 172 U.S. App. D.C. 1 (D.C.Cir.1975)(carriers may not unjustly or unreasonably discriminate against classes of service and the actual rate structure chosen must be free of unreasonable discrimination).

4. 568 F.2d 1012 (2d Cir.1977).

carriers, *i.e.*, providers of text services like telex and telegraph, were functionally similar[5] irrespective of whether they were offered under a contract or tariff.[6] Accordingly, a price differential would constitute discrimination.

The FCC must develop a neutral and rational basis for assessing functional similarity and determining whether discrimination in charges and practices has occurred. *In National Association of Regulatory Utility Commissioners* v. *FCC*,[7] the United States Court of Appeals for the District of Columbia found a rational basis for the FCC's decision regarding the interstate allocation of local telephone company plant costs. In finding no discrimination against long distance (interexchange) carriers subject to an access charge for use of local exchange facilities, the court endorsed a costing scheme that increased the level of compensation due from long distance service competitors of AT & T to reflect near parity of access opportunities and equivalent costs incurred by local exchange carriers to provide access.[8]

Additionally, the court made clear that Section 202 does not prohibit all discrimination. In response to a claim that the FCC had discriminated against facilities-based long distance carriers and basic service resellers in favor of enhanced service providers which offer value added services like credit card verification using leased basic transmission lines, the court held that the "Communications Act does not prevent all discrimination—disparities in prices for similar service—but only unreasonable discrimination."[9]

Reasonable discrimination may exist when a dominant carrier,[10] faces a "competitive necessity" to lower rates to a level set by a non-

5. *Id.* at 1018, n. 11; *see also* MCI Telecommunications Corp. v. FCC, 917 F.2d 30, 286 U.S. App. D.C. 316 (D.C.Cir.1990)(Sec. 202(a) analysis requires: (1) an assessment of whether "like" services or facilities are involved; (2) calculation of the disparity in price for the service; and (3) consideration of whether any discrimination that exists can be deemed just and reasonable); *see also* Ad Hoc Telecommunications Users Comm. v. FCC, 680 F.2d 790, 220 U.S. App. D.C. 241 (D.C.Cir.1982) (the functional equivalency test is an appropriate method for determining "likeness" within the meaning of the statute prohibiting unjust and unreasonable discrimination in charges for or in connection with like communication services).

6. The FCC required AT & T to eliminate a discrimination by which it charged international record carriers lower rates under contracts than it charged other common carriers for "like" services under tariff. The Court of Appeals held that evidence supported a finding of "likeness" regarding the facilities used by different international and domestic carriers. Having determined

the "likeness" of facilities used for access, the burden shifted to the international carriers to disprove the discrimination in their favor.

7. 737 F.2d 1095, 237 U.S. App. D.C. 390 (D.C.Cir.1984); *see also* Reservation Telephone Cooperative v. FCC, 826 F.2d 1129, 264 U.S. App. D.C. 113 (D.C.Cir.1987) (finding no discrimination if a neutral, rational basis exists supporting disparate charges).

8. The Court viewed the FCC's decision as "rationally necessary to minimize difficulties in administering the access charges and ... within ... the Commission's discretion." *Id.* 737 F.2d at 1133, 237 U.S. App. D.C. at 428.

9. *Id.* at 1136, 237 U.S. App. D.C. at 431 (*quoting* Associated Press v. FCC, 452 F.2d 1290, 1300–01, 146 U.S. App. D.C. 361, 371–372 (D.C.Cir.1971)).

10. The Competitive Carrier proceeding created a dichotomy between carriers with market power, *i.e.*, the ability to affect the price or supply of a service and those carri-

dominant carrier.[11] In its consideration of AT & T's Tariff F.C.C. No. 15, the FCC approved rates established on a customer-specific basis in response to evidence that a competitor had charged a rate below what AT & T had previously tariffed.[12] Despite the fact that penalties for early service termination made it difficult for existing customers from taking service at the now lower rates, the Commission and a reviewing court found no unreasonable discrimination.

On the other hand, a court found AT & T to have violated Section 202 when the company filed a tariff that was so narrowly drawn as to prevent even similarly situated users from qualifying to take service under the tariff.[13] A carrier may tailor a tariff to serve the specific requirements of a single customer, but it must provide service under the very same tariff to other customers who meet the usage criteria established by the "customized" tariff. For consumers, tariffed terms and conditions govern even if preceded by a negotiated contract containing different terms or conditions.[14]

A carrier may opt to negotiate and execute a contract with another carrier in lieu of a tariff.[15] For instances where carriers use contracts

ers lacking market power. The former are considered dominant and are subject to conventional common carrier regulations streamlined to reflect an increasingly competitive marketplace. The latter are considered non-dominant and are subject to "regulatory forbearance" meaning that the FCC will eliminate as far as possible all conventional common carrier regulations. *See* Policy and Rules Concerning Rates for Competitive Common Carrier Services and Facilities Authorizations Therefor, Notice of Inquiry and Proposed Rulemaking, 77 FCC2d 308 (1979); First Report and Order, 85 FCC2d 1 (1980); Second Report and Order, 91 FCC2d 59 (1982), *recons. denied*, 93 FCC2d 54 (1983); Third Report and Order, 48 Fed. Reg. 46,791 (1983); Fourth Report and Order, 95 FCC2d 554 (1983) *rev'd and remanded sub nom.*, AT & T v. FCC, 978 F.2d 727, 298 U.S. App. D.C. 230 (D.C.Cir.1992); Fifth Report and Order, 98 FCC2d 1191 (1984); Sixth Report and Order, 99 FCC2d 1020 (1985), *rev'd and remanded sub nom.* MCI Telecommunications Corp. v. FCC, 765 F.2d 1186, 247 U.S. App. D.C. 32 (D.C.Cir. 1985).

11. In the Competitive Carrier proceeding, the FCC found that carriers lacking market power are presumptively unable to engage in unreasonable discrimination. Policy and Rules Concerning Rates for Competitive Common Carrier Services and Facilities Authorizations Therefor, First Report and Order, 85 FCC 2d at 21 and 31.

12. *See* AT & T Communications Tariff F.C.C. No. 15, Competitive Pricing Plan No. 2 Resort Condominiums Int'l, CC Docket

No. 90–11, 6 FCC Rcd. 5648 (1991), *remand granted*, No. 91–1504 (D.C. Cir. Jan. 21, 1992), *on remand*, 7 FCC Rcd. 3456 (1992).

13. AT & T Communications, Revisions to Tariff F.C.C. No. 12, Mem. Op. & Order, 4 FCC Rcd. 4932, *recons. denied*, 4 FCC Rcd. 7928 (1989), reversed and remanded sub nom., MCI Telecommunications Corp. v. FCC, 917 F.2d 30, 286 U.S. App. D.C. 316 (D.C.Cir.1990).

14. "The 'filed rate doctrine' specifies that rates charged by common carriers must be clear from the face of the tariff in which those rates are filed. The Supreme Court has held, therefore, that 'the rights as defined by the tariff cannot be varied or enlarged by either contract or tort of the carrier.'" Section 208 Complaints Alleging Violations of the Commission's Rate of Return Prescription for the 1989–1990 Monitoring Period, Mem. Op. and Order, 10 FCC Rcd. 3657 n. 18 (1994) (quoting Keogh v. Chicago & Northwestern R.R. Co., 260 U.S. 156, 163, 43 S.Ct. 47, 49, 67 L.Ed. 183, 187 (1922)). In application this means that for non-carrier consumers tariffed terms and conditions will prevail in disputes, even if subsequently filed. *See* Maislin Industries v. Primary Steel, Inc., 497 U.S. 116, 110 S.Ct. 2759, 111 L.Ed.2d 94 (1990).

15. Section 211(a) of the Communications Act requires "[e]very carrier subject to this Act [to] file with the Commission copies of all contracts ... with other carriers...." 47 U.S.C.A. § 211(a) (West 1991). The FCC can examine any carrier-to-carrier contract to assess whether it complies with

typically the terms and conditions negotiated therein govern, even if subsequently the service provider seeks to change the deal by filing a tariff or the consuming customer seeks to abrogate the deal.

2. Discrimination Under Section 202

Courts have subjected a number of carrier practices and policies to scrutiny under Section 202. For example, a finding of discrimination can lie where a carrier attempts to disconnect service to a particular type of user who has lawfully secured service. "Section 202(a) prohibits a carrier from subjecting a person to unreasonable prejudice or disadvantage."[16] The FCC found a violation of Section 202 tariff restrictions on the resale or shared use of domestic telecommunication services.[17] The Commission sought to promote arbitrage as a way to force carriers to price all services on the basis of cost and to reduce the extent of a discount between high and low volume users.

B. Section 203—Schedule of Charges (Tariffing)

Section 203(a) of the Communications Act imposes a tariffing obligation on all carriers[18] and as well a duty on the FCC's part to respond to such applications in a timely manner.[19] Tariffs are public contracts that set forth the terms and conditions for service. They reduce carriers' transaction costs and limit liability for outages and damages[20] in provid-

all Communications Act requirements, such as the common carrier provisions in Title II. *See, e.g.*, ACC Long Distance Corp. v. Yankee Microwave, Inc., Memorandum Opinion and Order, 10 FCC Rcd. 654 (1995) (carrier that secured microwave services from another carrier by contract not entitled to demand rate reduction that would abrogate the contract); *see also* United Gas Pipe Line Co. v. Mobile Gas Service Corp., 350 U.S. 332, 76 S.Ct. 373, 100 L.Ed. 373 (1956); FPC v. Sierra Pacific Power Co., 350 U.S. 348, 76 S.Ct. 368, 100 L.Ed. 388 (1956)(regulatory agency must meet a strict public interest standard before it can modify the terms of a private contract freely negotiated between carriers), *principal applied in* Bell Telephone Company of Pennsylvania v. FCC, 503 F.2d 1250 (3d Cir. 1974), cert. denied, 422 U.S. 1026, 95 S.Ct. 2620, 45 L.Ed.2d 684 (1975) (AT & T could not abrogate a contract with Western Union Telegraph Co. simply by replacing a local distribution facilities contract with a tariff) and MCI Telecommunications Corp. v. FCC, 665 F.2d 1300, 214 U.S. App. D.C. 482 (D.C.Cir.1981) (carriers contracts and tariffs are not always mutually exclusive, but the contract governs the legality of any subsequent tariff filing); Western Union Telegraph Co. v. FCC, 815 F.2d 1495, 259 U.S. App. D.C. 294 (D.C.Cir.1987) (intercarrier agreement setting specific and con-

trolling procedures for changing negotiated rates).

16. Edwards Industries, Inc. v. Bell Telephone Co. of Nevada, 74 FCC 2d 322, 326, 46 Rad. Reg.2d 576, 580 (P & F 1979).

17. Regulatory Policy Concerning Resale and Shared Use of Common Carrier Domestic Public Switched Network Services, 83 FCC2d 167 (1980).

18. Section 203(a) of the Communications Act of 1934, as amended, states that "every common carrier ... shall ... file with the Commission and print and keep open for public inspection schedules showing all charges ... and showing the classifications, practices, and regulations affecting such charges."

19. *See* MCI Telecommunications Corp. v. FCC, 627 F.2d 322, 200 U.S.App.D.C. 269 (D.C.Cir.1980) ("rule of reason" used to assess timeliness of FCC action in suspending, investigating and deciding whether to approve a tariff filing).

20. *See* Christy C. Kunin, Note, *Unilateral Tariff Exculpation in the Era of Competitive Telecommunications*, 41 Cath. U. L. Rev. 907 (1992) (arguing that communications common carriers should not be able to avoid liability for outages, tortious conduct, etc. in the new competitive and regulatory environment where parties negotiate and execute service contracts).

ing service to a large number of users who generate insubstantial traffic volumes. While carriers can serve such users under the terms and conditions of a single tariff, typically large volume users and ones with complex service requirements motivate carriers to establish additional narrowly drawn tariffs to include different service and pricing packages.

In serving sophisticated users who typically have a number of carrier options available and who might construct their own facilities, carriers generally want to use contracts in lieu of the tariffs. Courts have interpreted Section 203 as prohibiting the elimination of the tariff filing requirement.[21] However, Section 10 of the Telecommunications Act of 1996 authorizes the FCC to eliminate any regulatory burden if such enforcement is unnecessary to guard against discrimination to ensure just and reasonable services, to safeguard consumers and to serve the public interest.[22] Section 203 does not prohibit carriers and customers from negotiating contracts which will be subsequently memorialized in tariff filings by carriers. Such "contract carriage" affords carriers flexibility in customizing price and service packages. However even such customer-specific arrangements must be made available to any other "similarly situated" user whose requirements and characteristics parallel the initial contracting user.[23]

1. The Tariff Filing Requirement

The FCC's Competitive Carrier proceeding[24] reduced regulation of a number of carrier-provided services and attempted to eliminate the mandatory tariff filing requirements for some carriers. In a series of proceedings commencing in 1979 the Commission sought to forbear from

21. *See* MCI Telecommunications Corp. v. AT & T, 512 U.S. 218, 114 S.Ct. 2223, 129 L.Ed.2d 182 (1994) (rejecting FCC's order that certain common carrier must detariff service).

22. *See* 47 U.S.C.A. § 160 (a)(1)-(3) (West Supp. 1997).

23. "Nor do we think that our contract carriage proposal will present an undue risk of discrimination. First, we would require the price cap LECs to make its [sic] contracts generally available to similarly situated customers so as to comply with the Section 202(a) nondiscrimination provisions of the Communications Act. [citation omitted] Second, contract carriage would only be allowed for services subject to substantial competition. Such competition would help to ensure that all customers purchasing services subject to streamlined review would receive just, reasonable and nondiscriminatory rates, regardless of whether the purchase is made pursuant to generic or contract-based tariffs." Price Cap Performance Review for Local Exchange Carriers, Second Further Notice of Proposed Rulemaking in CC Docket No. 94–1, Further Notice of Pro-

posed Rulemaking in CC Docket No. 93–124, and Second Further Notice of Proposed Rulemaking in CC Docket No. 93–197, FCC 95–393, 1995 WL 564434 (F.C.C. at 57 149, rel. Sep. 20, 1995). *See also* Price Cap Performance Review for Local Exchange Carriers, 4th Report and Order in CC Docket No. 94–1, Second Report and Order in CC Docket No. 96-262, 12 FCC Rcd. 16642 (1997).

24. Policy and Rules Concerning Rates for Competitive Common Carrier Services and Facilities Authorizations Therefor, Notice of Inquiry and Proposed Rulemaking, 77 FCC2d 308 (1979); First Report and Order, 85 FCC2d 1 (1980); Second Report and Order, 91 FCC2d 59 (1982), *recons. denied*, 93 FCC2d 54 (1983); Third Report and Order, 48 Fed. Reg. 46,791 (1983); Fourth Report and Order, 95 FCC2d 554 (1983), *rev'd and remanded sub nom.*, AT & T v. FCC, 978 F.2d 727, 298 U.S. App. D.C. 230 (D.C.Cir.1992); Fifth Report and Order, 98 FCC2d 1191 (1984); Sixth Report and Order, 99 FCC2d 1020 (1985), *rev'd and remanded sub nom.* MCI Telecommunications Corp. v. FCC, 765 F.2d 1186, 247 U.S. App. D.C. 32 (D.C.Cir.1985).

regulating an increasing large category of non-dominant carriers, *i.e.*, carriers "not possessing the market power necessary to sustain prices either unreasonably above or below costs."[25]

In its First Report and Order, the FCC decided to "streamline" the tariff filing process for all interexchange carriers other than AT & T. In application this meant that every long distance carrier except AT & T could file a new or modified tariff with an effective date of 14 days, absent suspension or investigation by the FCC. The FCC's new streamlined regulatory treatment of non-dominant carriers included a presumption that all such tariff filings were prima facie lawful, while retaining the general requirements in Title II of the Communications Act, such as prohibiting unreasonable rates and discrimination between similarly situated users.

The FCC's Second Report and Order contained an interpretation of Section 203 to support exempting carriers, on a permissive, non-mandatory basis, from filing tariffs if the costs incurred exceed the public interest benefits. The Commission's Third Report and Order applied permissive forbearance regarding tariffs to resellers of domestic interexchange services and the Fourth Report and Order extended the optional tariff exemption to facilities-based carriers, including satellite operators and non-dominant long distance telephone companies such as MCI and Sprint.

The Commission's rationale for such substantial deregulation was the view that strict interpretation of Section 203(a) would impose unnecessary expense and burden on non-dominant carriers that could retard service innovation, inhibit price competition and facilitate collusion among carriers.[26] The Commission tried to convert its permissive tariff filing policy into a mandatory prohibition in its Sixth Report and Order.

Two portions of the FCC's forbearance policy have generated major appellate court reversals. In *MCI v. FCC*,[27] the District of Columbia Court of Appeals found that the FCC acted arbitrarily and in violation of its statutory authority when in its Sixth Report and Order in the *Competitive Carrier* proceeding[28] the Commission mandated all carriers subject to regulatory forbearance to cancel their filed tariffs within six months. The court ruled that the Commission's change of policy from one of permissive forbearance of the tariff filing requirement for non-dominant carriers to one of prohibiting tariff filing violated the clear

25. Policy and Rules Concerning Rates For Competitive Common Carrier Services and Facilities Authorizations Therefor, First Report and Order, 85 FCC2d 1, 6 (1980). In 1995 the FCC reclassified AT & T as a non-dominant carrier thereby qualifying it for substantial deregulation. *See* Motion of AT & T To Be Reclassified as a Non–Dominant Carrier, Order, 11 FCC Rcd. 3271 (1995). The Commission extended the non-dominant classification to AT & T's international services in 1996. *See* Mo-

tion of AT & T to be Declared Non–Dominant for International Service, Order, 11 FCC Rcd. 17963 (rel. May 14, 1996).

26. Competitive Carrier, Fourth Report and Order, 95 FCC2d at 555, n.1.

27. 765 F.2d 1186, 247 U.S. App. D.C. 32 (D.C.Cir.1985).

28. Competitive Carrier, First Report and Order, 85 FCC 2d 1 (1985).

language of Section 203 containing a congressional mandate that every common carrier, except connecting carriers, *shall* file tariffs. The court ruled that the Commission could use its discretion only to modify tariff filing requirements and that a modification could not result in the "wholesale abandonment or elimination of a requirement."[29]

In 1992 the District of Columbia Court of Appeals considered the legality of the FCC's Fourth Report and Order in the Competitive Carrier proceeding in the context of whether the Commission could accord some carriers the option not to file tariffs. AT & T filed a formal complaint with the FCC, under Section 208 of the Communications Act, alleging MCI was violating Section 203(a) of the Communications Act by charging certain customers special unfiled, negotiated rates and by ignoring the terms and conditions of previously tariffed services in order to accommodate the requirements of particular customers. AT & T sought a cease and desist order from the FCC and damages from MCI for violation of Section 203.[30]

The FCC issued an order dismissing AT & T's complaint, stating that the issues raised, including the lawfulness of its permissive forbearance policy, should be considered in a new rulemaking, rather than in the context of its ongoing *Competitive Carrier Proceeding*.[31] The FCC refused to consider awarding AT & T any financial damages because the Commission believed that even if the permissive forbearance policy contained in the Fourth Report and Order in the *Competitive Carrier Proceeding* was deemed unlawful, new interpretations of the Communications Act should not be applied retroactively.[32]

The FCC failed to respond to AT & T's complaint on a timely basis, apparently because it lacked confidence that its Fourth Report and Order, upon which MCI had relied in its decision not to file tariffs, would pass judicial muster. The court rejected the Commission's administrative maneuvering, *i.e.*, the initiation of another rulemaking proceeding to consider further the deregulatory initiative sought by the Fourth Report and Order, as an improper vehicle to delay responding to AT & T's complaint.[33] Refusing to act because the Commission planned on taking another opportunity to justify optional tariffing "is similar," according to the appeals court, "to a judge who dismisses a complaint based on a federal statute because he has been informed that Congress is conducting hearings on whether to change the statute. Like the judge, the

---

29. MCI, 765 F.2d at 1192, 247 U.S. App. D.C. at 38.

30. AT & T Communications v. MCI Telecommunications Corp., File No. E–89–297, 7 FCC Rcd. 807 (1992).

31. Tariff Filing Requirements for Interstate Common Carriers, Notice of Proposed Rulemaking, 7 FCC Rcd. 804 (1992).

32. 7 FCC Rcd. at 809.

33. "It is rather apparent that, because the Commission fears the Fourth Report cannot withstand judicial scrutiny (at least in our court), it wants to avoid judicial review of the rule." AT & T Co. v. FCC, 978 F.2d 727, 731, 298 U.S. App. D.C. 230, 234 (D.C.Cir.1992). "When presented with AT & T's complaint, the Commission had an obligation to answer the questions it raised and to decide whether MCI had violated the statute." *Id*. at 732.

agency has an obligation to decide the complaint under the law currently applicable."[34]

The court reversed the Commission's decision to initiate a new rulemaking on the tariff filing question while dismissing AT & T's complaint against MCI. The court held that the Commission acted arbitrarily and capriciously, thereby violating the Administrative Procedure Act in refusing to consider the lawfulness of regulatory forbearance.[35] On the substantive issue of whether the Commission had properly interpreted Section 203 to grant such tariff filing flexibility, the court held that its "is simply not defensible in this court" to modify the clear requirements imposed by the Communications Act.[36] The court held the Commission lacked authority to eliminate the tariff filing requirement for a class of carriers on either a permissive or mandatory basis.

> Whether detariffing is made mandatory, as in the Sixth Report, or simply permissive, as in the Fourth Report, carriers are, in either event, relieved of the obligation to file tariffs under section 203(a). That step exceeds the limited authority granted the Commission in Section 203(b) to "modify" requirements of the Act.[37]

As to the refusal of the Commission to consider a damage award to AT & T, the court instructed the FCC to reconsider AT & T's claim and to explain why the reversal of its legal interpretation should not apply retroactively[38] in view of the court's order that the no filing of tariffs policy cease and the court's decision that any carrier's failure to file tariff leaves it open to damage claims in the federal district court.[39]

While "understand[ing] fully why the Commission wants the flexibility to apply the tariff provisions ... differently"[40] based on market power, the court had to apply the clear language of Congress in Section 203 of the Communications Act which makes no distinction between carrier types for purposes of the tariff filing requirement.[41] Less than two weeks after the court's decision, the FCC completed its rulemaking proceeding established to respond to AT & T's complaint about MCI's practice of only sometimes filing tariffs and of failing to apply terms and conditions of previously filed tariffs in other instances.[42] The Commission rearticulated a permissive detariffing policy as a reasonable exercise of

---

34. *Id.* at 732, 298 U.S. App. D.C. at 235.

35. *Id.* at 733, 298 U.S. App. D.C. at 238.

36. *Id.* at 735–36, 298 U.S. App. D.C. at 238–239.

37. *Id.* at 736, 298 U.S. App. D.C. at 239.

38. *Id.* at 737, 298 U.S. App. D.C. at 240.

39. *Id.*

40. *Id.* at 736, 298 U.S. App. D.C. at 239.

41. AT & T v. FCC, 978 F.2d 727, 298 U.S. App. D.C. 230 (D.C.Cir.1992). The court stated that "[w]hether detariffing is made mandatory, as in the Sixth Report [in the Competitive Carrier proceeding], or simply permissive, as in the Fourth Report, carriers are, in either event, relieved of the obligation to file tariffs under section 203(a). That step exceeds the limited authority granted the Commission in section 203(b) to 'modify' requirements of the Act." *Id.* at 736, 298 U.S. App. D.C. at 239 (footnote omitted).

42. Tariff Filing Requirements for Interstate Common Carriers, 7 FCC Rcd. 8072 (1992), *stayed* 7 FCC Rcd. 7989 (1992).

its authority under Section 203(b) of the Communications Act to modify tariffing requirements. The Court of Appeals granted AT & T's motion for summary reversal,[43] and the Supreme Court affirmed.[44]

Even if the FCC could make a strong case for the view that tariff filing by some common carriers is unnecessary and counterproductive, the Commission cannot unilaterally ignore Congressional directives embodied in statutes.

> [O]ur estimations, and the Commission's estimations, of desirable policy cannot alter the meaning of the Federal Communications Act of 1934. For better or worse, the Act establishes a rate-regulation, filed-tariff system for common-carrier communications, and the Commission's desire "to 'increase competition' cannot provide [it] authority to alter the well-established statutory filed rate requirements" [quoting Maislin Industries, U.S., Inc. v. Primary Steel, Inc., 497 U.S. 116, 135, 110 S.Ct. 2759, 111 L.Ed.2d 94 (1990)]. . . . [S]uch considerations address themselves to Congress, not to the courts. [quoting Armour Packing Co. v. United States, 209 U.S. 56, 82, 28 S.Ct. 428, 52 L.Ed. 681 (1908)][45]

Despite clear language in several court judgments, the FCC initiated yet another rulemaking proceeding with an eye toward finding some way to relax the rate filing requirements of nondominant carriers. The Commission tentatively concluded that "while tariff regulation is required by the [Communications] Act, traditional tariff regulation of nondominant carriers is not only unnecessary to ensure just and reasonable rates, but is actually counterproductive, since it can inhibit price competition, service innovation, entry into the market, and the ability of carriers to respond quickly to market trends."[46] The Commission established a "significantly streamlined" tariff filing requirement allowing nondominant carriers to implement new or revised tariffed terms and conditions on not less than one day's notice,[47] and setting a fixed rate or a "reasonable range of rates."[48]

Once again an appellate court rejected the FCC's attempt to relax the tariff filing requirement for nondominant carriers. In *Southwestern Bell Corp. v. FCC*, the District of Columbia Court of Appeals vacated the FCC's order proposing to allow nondominant carriers the option of filing

---

43. AT & T v. FCC, No. 92–1628, 1993 WL 260778 (D.C.Cir.1993) (per curiam), *affirmed sub. nom.* MCI v. FCC, 765 F.2d 1186, 247 U.S.App.D.C. 32 (1985).

44. MCI Telecommunications Corp. v. AT & T, 512 U.S. 218, 114 S.Ct. 2223, 129 L.Ed.2d 182 (1994). The Court held that: (1) FCC's ability to modify the requirements of the Communications Act does not permit the Commission to make basic and fundamental changes in the regulatory scheme; and (2) that its detariffing policy exempting nondominant long distance telephone carriers from tariff filing require-

ment exceeded it statutory authority. *Id.* at 231–232, 234, 114 S. Ct. at 2232, 2233, 129 L. Ed. 2d at 193–194.

45. *Id.* at 234, 114 S. Ct. at 2233, 129, L. Ed.2d at 195.

46. Tariff Filing Requirements for Nondominant Carriers, 8 FCC Rcd. 6752 *codified at* 47 C.F.R. §§ 6120 et seq. (1995).

47. *Id.* at 6756–57, *codified at* 47 C.F.R § 61.23(c) (1995).

48. *Id.* at 6758–59, *codified at* 47 C.F.R. § 61.22 (1995).

a range of rates instead of specific rates.[49] In undertaking a statutory analysis, the court deemed irrelevant the question whether the law supports rational economic policy. The court held that Section 203(a), which mandates every common carrier to file schedules showing all charges, does not permit the FCC to allow some common carriers to file a range of charges. The court referred to the clear language of the Act, cases interpreting parallel provisions in the Interstate Commerce Act, which served as the template for the Communications Act and the Supreme Court's decision in *MCI v. AT & T*.[50]

On remand,[51] the FCC eliminated the provision allowing a range of rates and reinstated liberal policies that permit the tariff filings of nondominant carriers to take effect on one day's notice,[52] without the inclusion of cost support data.[53] In 1996, as part of its implementation of the Telecommunications Act of 1996, the Commission proposed a mandatory detariffing policy for domestic services provided by non-dominant interexchange carriers, and to permit the bundling by such carriers of long distance services and customer premises equipment.[54] Again a reviewing court stayed implementation, but the Commission appears determined to support detariffing as procompetitive.

a. Deviation From Tariffed Terms and Conditions

Just as the FCC cannot alter statutory requirements,[55] neither carriers nor users can evade the requirement that they adhere to the terms and conditions of an applicable tariff. This is true regardless of whether they previously negotiated contracts and the existing or revised tariffs deviate from the terms and conditions contained in the contracts. In *American Broadcasting Co. v. FCC*,[56] the appellate court affirmed the Commission's refusal to give any weight to the provision of a service

---

49. 43 F.3d 1515, 310 U.S. App. D.C. 90, (D.C.Cir.1995).

50. 512 U.S. 218, 114 S.Ct. 2223, 129 L.Ed.2d 182 (1994).

51. Tariff Filing Requirements for Nondominant Common Carriers, CC Docket No.93–36, Order, 10 FCC Rcd. 13653 (1995).

52. Tariff Filing Requirements for Nondominant Common Carriers, CC Docket No. 93–36, Memorandum Opinion and Order, 8 FCC Rcd. 6752 (1993).

53. Policy and Rules Concerning Rates for Competitive Common Carrier Services and Facilities Authorizations Therefor, CC Docket No. 79–252, First Report and Order, 85 FCC 2d 1, 34 (1980).

54. Policy and Rules Concerning the Interstate, Interexchange Marketplace, CC Docket No. 96–61, Notice of Proposed Rulemaking, FCC 96–123 (rel. Mar. 25, 1996), 11 FCC Rcd. 7141 (1996); 11 FCC Rcd. 9564 (1996). Second Report and Order, 11 FCC

Rcd. 20730 (1996), *stayed in* MCI Telecommunications Corp. v. FCC, No. 96-1459 (D.C. Cir., Feb. 13, 1997), on recons., 12 FCC Rcd. 15014 (1992). The Commission has interpreted the new act to permit mandatory detariffing in title IV (Regulatory Reform) section 401(a)(1)-(3), *codified at* 47 U.S.C.A. § 160(a)(1)-(3) (West Supp. 1997).

55. In AT & T v. FCC, 487 F.2d 865 (2d Cir.1973), AT & T successfully challenged an FCC decision denying it "special permission" to file revisions to its occasional user private line video programming transmission service. The Second Circuit Court of Appeals held that the Communications Act does not authorize the FCC to require carriers to secure its permission to file new rates.

56. 643 F.2d 818, 207 U.S. App. D.C. 68 (D.C.Cir.1980); *see also* Eternal Word Television Network v. AT & T Co., 2 FCC Rcd. 1369, 62 Rad. Reg.2d 669 (P & F 1987) (a contract cannot supersede any provisions in a filed tariff, even if the carrier subsequently revises the tariff).

contract that prohibited the filing of a rate increase.[57] When the carrier subsequently raised rates in a revised tariff, the Commission refused to prohibit the increase. Tracing the origins of Section 203 to the Interstate Commerce Act of 1887, the court noted that tariffing works to eliminate an "elaborate system of secret special rates, rebates, drawbacks, and concessions, to foster monopoly, to enrich favored shippers, and to prevent free competition."[58] Because equality of rates works to destroy favoritism, the Commission could refuse to enforce the contracted rate hike prohibition as "just the kind of unpublished contractual alteration of a tariff which the Act condemns."[59]

b. Contract Tariffs

The FCC has recognized that increasing competition in the interexchange services marketplace can support reduced regulatory oversight of the tariffing process. The Commission permitted AT & T to convert individually negotiated contracts into a tariff, but initially only for services subject to streamlined regulation, *i.e.*, business services.[60] Residential and small business services were included in 1995.[61] These "contract tariffs" must be made generally available to similarly situated customers under substantially similar circumstances.[62] In 1995 the FCC deemed AT & T non-dominant and, with some conditions, granted AT & T the opportunities for tariffing flexibility other inter-exchange carriers already enjoyed. [63]

2. Tariff 12: Discriminatory Pricing of Like Services or Necessary Pricing Flexibility?

The Commission, courts and carriers have struggled to determine what constitutes appropriate tariffing flexibility[64] and what represents

---

57. *See also* Midwestern Relay Company, Mem. Op. and Order, 59 FCC2d 477 (1976) (rate provision in a carrier negotiated contract can be superseded by a subsequently filed tariff rate increase); cf. RCA American Communications, Inc., Mem. Op. and Order 84 FCC2d 353 (1980) (initiating rate investigation); 86 FCC2d 1197 (1981); *on recons.*, 2 FCC Rcd. 236 (1987) (carrier must show substantial cause to support tariff revisions that alter a long-term service arrangement).

58. American Broadcasting Co. Inc., 643 F. 2d at 821, 207 U.S. App. D.C. at 71.

59. *Id*. at 826, 207 U.S. App. D.C. at 76.

60. Competition in the Interstate Interexchange Marketplace, CC Docket No. 90–132, Report and Order, 6 FCC Rcd 5880 (1991); Order, 6 FCC Rcd 7255 (1991); Mem. Op. and Order, 6 FCC Rcd 7569 (1991) ("Sua Sponte Reconsideration Order"); Mem. Op. and Order on Recons., 7 FCC Rcd 2677 (1992) ("Reconsideration Order"); Mem. Op. and Order on Recons., 8 FCC Rcd 2659 (1993) ("March 1993 Or-

der"), *petitions for recons. pending*; Second Report and Order, 8 FCC Rcd 3668 (1993) ("Second Report").

61. Motion of AT & T Corp. To Be Classified as a Non–Dominant Carrier, Order, FCC 95–427, 11 FCC Rcd. 3271 (1995); *see also* Commission Declares AT & T Non-dominant, Report No. CC 95–60, 1995 WL 600854 (F.C.C. rel. Oct. 12, 1995).

62. Competition in the Interstate Interexchange Marketplace, CC Docket No. 90–132, Report and Order, 6 FCC Rcd 5880, 5896–97, *recons. in part*, Mem. Op. and Order, 6 FCC Rcd 7569 (1991), *further recons.*, Mem. Op. and Order *on Recons.*, 7 FCC Rcd 2677 (1992) (Interexchange Order).

63. *See* Motion of AT & T To Be Reclassified as a Non–Dominant Carrier, Order, 11 FCC Rcd. 3271 (1995).

64. While the FCC cannot eliminate a requirement imposed by the Communications Act, *e.g.*, the tariff filing obligation of common carriers, courts will affirm some

discrimination and potentially anticompetitive practices. In response to an increasingly competitive marketplace predominated by non-dominant carriers freed of most tariffing obligations, AT & T filed a new set of services and rates in Tariff F.C.C. No. 12 in the late 1980s.[65] In the service options provided under this tariff, AT & T proposed to package a number of services that previously were available on an individual basis, typically at higher rates. Competing carriers argued AT & T had repackaged already available "like" services and provided such similar services at a lower rate thereby discriminating against users taking such services at the previously available terms and conditions.

The appellate court identified the "core issue in this case [as being] whether a carrier must justify a lower rate it charges for integrated packages than for an aggregation of the individually-tariffed services comprising the packages."[66] To assess whether Tariff 12 violated Section 202 of the Communications Act which prohibits discrimination, the court applied a three-part test established in *MCI Telecommunications Corp. v. FCC*:[67]

> (1) whether the services are "like;" (2) if they are "like," whether there is a price difference; and (3) if there is a difference, whether it is reasonable.[68]

To consider whether a new tariff discriminates against users of previously offered services, the FCC conducts a "functional equivalency test" that "focuses on whether the services in question are 'different in any material functional respect.'"[69] This assessment ignores any cost

flexibility in interpretation and applications. For example, in American Telephone and Telegraph Company v. Federal Communications Commission, 503 F.2d 612 (2d Cir.1974), the Second Circuit affirmed an FCC ruling that revised procedures governing the filing of interstate tariffs by common carriers. The court held that provision of Communications Act of 1934 which gives the FCC power in its discretion and for good cause shown to "modify" its requirements permitted a rule revision which enlarged from 30 days to 60 days the required notice period for communications common carriers filing rate increases.

65. AT & T Communications, Revisions to Tariff F.C.C. No. 12, Mem. Op. & Order, 4 FCC Rcd. 4932 (1989) *recons. den.*, 4 FCC Rcd. 7928 (1989), *rev'd and remanded sub nom.*, MCI Telecommunications Corp. v. FCC, 917 F.2d 30, 286 U.S. App. D.C. 316 (D.C.Cir.1990).

66. MCI Telecom. Corp. v. FCC, 917 F.2d at 39, 286 U.S. App.D.C. at 325.

67. 842 F.2d 1296, 269 U.S. App. D.C. 1 (D.C.Cir.1988).

68. MCI Telecom. Corp. v. FCC, 842 F.2d 1296, 1303, 269 U.S. App. D.C. 1, 8 (D.C.Cir.1988) (remanding to FCC for ex-

amination whether AT & T's shared network facilities agreements with the BOCs are discriminatory relative to special access rates paid by other interexchange carriers); *see also* American Broadcasting Co. v. FCC, 663 F.2d 133, 139, 213 U.S. App. D.C. 369, 375 (D.C.Cir.1980) (carrier offering an integrated service package bears the burden of justifying any price disparity with an aggregation of the services as unpackaged).

69. Ad Hoc Telecom. Users Comm. v. FCC, 680 F.2d 790, 795, 220 U.S. App.D.C. 241, 246 (D.C.Cir.1982) (comparison of dial-up long distance telephone service with inbound and outbound 800 service and holding that a "likeness" assessment focuses on whether the services in question are different in any material functional aspect) (quoting American Trucking Ass'n v. FCC, 377 F.2d 121, 127, 126 U.S. App. D.C. 236, 241 (D.C.Cir.1966) cert. denied 386 U.S. 943, 87 S.Ct. 973. 17 L.Ed.2d 874 (1967)); *see also* Am. Tel. & Tel. Co., 61 FCC2d 587 (1976), *aff'd in part and vacated in part sub nom.*, Aeronautical Radio, Inc. v. FCC, 642 F.2d 1221, 206 U.S. App. D.C. 253 (D.C.Cir. 1980) (affirming use of fully distributed costing methodology for assessing adequacy of cost allocation), cert. denied 451 U.S. 920, 101 S.Ct. 1998, 68 L. Ed.2d 311 (1981).

differential[70] and looks solely at the nature of the service offered and whether users perceive the two services as performing the same functions. Because the FCC did in fact look at cost differentials to determine whether Tariff 12 was discriminatory, the court remanded the cases "with directions that the FCC resolve it without regard for differentials in cost to the carrier and price to the customer."[71]

On remand the FCC again determined that Tariff 12 was not "like" the individually tariffed services previously provided by AT & T on a desegregated basis. The Commission applied a functional equivalency test to assess likeness on the basis of customer perceptions and determined that customers considered Tariff 12 services functionally different than AT & T's individually tariffed services because of AT & T's flexibility in provisioning lines, its network monitoring functions and the "turnkey", "one stop shopping" nature of the service.[72]

Contrary to its previous decision that the different option plans under Tariff 12 were "like" each other and therefore had to be made generally available to any "similarly situated customers to avoid discriminating unreasonably among Tariff 12 customers,"[73] the FCC on remand determined that the various Tariff 12 option plans had different terms and conditions than previously available services.[74] The Commission determined that various Tariff 12 options resulted from extensive negotiation between AT & T and prospective customers. Each negotiated option contained various types of transmission capabilities and features that were not like an available service option. The Commission also concluded that the terms contained in AT & T's tariff provided adequate assurance that the carrier would make available any service option to a qualified user and that AT & T had complied with the Commission's guidelines on the structuring and discounting of private lines[75] and on their availability for resale and shared use.

---

70. "Pricing differences a fortiori cannot be a basis for finding the services unlike—otherwise, the very discrimination Section 202 attempts to prevent would be the grounds for finding that section inapplicable." MCI Telecom. Corp. v. FCC, 917 F.2d at 39, 286 U.S. App.D.C at 325. "[C]onsideration of cost differentials and competitive necessity are properly excluded [from the likeness determination] and introduced only when determining whether the discrimination is unreasonable or unjust." Id., quoting ABC, 663 F.2d at 139, 213 U.S. App. D.C. at 374 and citing Western Union Int'l v. FCC, 568 F.2d 1012, 1019, n. 15 (2d Cir.1977) (deeming "like" access facilities used by domestic and international carriers), cert. denied 436 U.S. 944, 98 S.Ct. 2845, 56 L.Ed.2d 785 (1978).

71. MCI Telecom. Corp. at 40, 286 U.S. App.D.C at 326.

72. AT & T Communications Revisions to Tariff F.C.C. No. 12, CC Docket No, 87–568, Mem. Op. & Order on Remand, 6 FCC Rcd. 7039, 7047 57 43 (1991)[hereinafter cited as Tariff 12 Order on Remand].

73. *Id.* at 7040, 57 3 (1991) *citing* Tariff 12 Order, 4 FCC Rcd. at 4937–38, *pet. for rehearing denied sub nom.*, Competitive Telecomms. Ass'n. v. FCC, 998 F.2d 1058, 302 U.S. App. D.C. 423 (D.C.Cir.1993).

74. "The proper frame of reference in evaluating the likeness of such packages vis-a-vis other packages is to look at the function of the package as a whole: Is the package, as a whole, functionally equivalent to other, individually negotiated packages? Viewed in this light, the four Tariff 12 options at issue in this remand proceedings are not 'like.' " Tariff 12 Order on Remand at 7048, ¶ 52.

75. *See* Private Line Rate Structure and Volume Discount Practices, 97 FCC2d 923 (1984), *codified at* 47 C.F.R. §§ 61.40 (1990).

The District of Columbia Court of Appeals affirmed the Commission solely on the ground that provisioning flexibility made the Tariff 12 packaged services unlike other previously available services. As to network monitoring and turnkey servicing, the court found that likeness could exist within the meaning of Section 202 of the Communications Act if a carrier simply provides additional service features at a lower price.[76] Had the Commission found unlikeness based on a pricing difference, then it would have violated the holding in the prior court decision that rejected the use of price as the basis for finding unlikeness.[77]

3. Tariff 15: Competitive Pricing Plans

On August 1, 1991, the FCC ruled AT & T's Tariff 15 Competitive Pricing Plan for Resort Condominiums International (RCI) was unreasonably discriminatory in violation of Section 202(a) of the Communications Act.[78] That plan contained special discounts to AT & T's general 800 Service and Software Defined Network rate schedules. AT & T had asserted that the RCI discount was justified by the doctrine of "competitive necessity" as a necessary pricing response to keep a customer who had received a lower priced service offer from MCI. The Commission concluded the discrimination was unlawful because it resulted from a tariffed price matching mechanism that could generate an anticompetitive impact on the interstate interexchange communications marketplace.[79] The Commission ordered AT & T to file tariff revisions removing the RCI plan,[80] after which AT & T successfully obtained a stay. The FCC subsequently requested a voluntary remand of the case for further consideration and later reinstated the RCI plan after AT & T revised the tariff to include language making the service available to other customers who could demonstrate the receipt of a substantially similar offer from a competing interexchange carrier.[81]

4. Contract Carriage

In seeking to foster greater service pricing flexibility and competition, the FCC has permitted non-dominant carriers[82] the option of using

---

76. "By providing only a benefit and nary a detriment to the user, the network monitoring function and the 'turnkey' feature of Tariff 12 each constitute an in-kind bonus, which is the functional equivalent of a price discount." Competitive Telecom. Ass'n. v. FCC, 998 F.2d 1058, 1062, 302 U.S. App. D.C. 423, 427 (D.C.Cir.1993).

77. MCI Telecom. Corp. v. FCC, 917 F.2d at 39, 286 U.S. App. D.C. at 325.

78. AT & T Communications, Tariff FCC No. 15, Competitive Pricing Plan No. 2, Resort Condominiums International (CC Docket 90–11), 6 FCC Rcd 5648 (1991) (RCI Order), *remanded*, AT & T v. FCC, Order, D.C. Circuit No. 91–1504 (filed January 21, 1992), *on remand*, 7 FCC Rcd. 3465 (1992).

79. *Id*. at 5649–50.

80. *Id*. at 5650.

81. *See* RCI Order, 6 FCC Rcd at 5648. In its description and justification for the tariff transmittal establishing this language, AT & T stated that its "Tariff 15 regulations ... make CPP2 rates available to any customer that can demonstrate that it has been made a substantially similar off-tariff offer by MCI." AT & T Transmittal 1854, Description and Justification at 11.

82. In the Competitive Carrier proceeding, the FCC found that carriers lacking market power, *i.e.*, non-dominant carriers, are presumptively unable to engage in unreasonable discrimination. Policy and Rules Concerning Rates for Competitive Common Carrier Services and Facilities Authorizations Therefor, First Report and Order, 85 FCC 2d at 21 and 31.

service contracts, provided such subsequently agreements are memorialized by a tariff. Tariff filings by nondominant common carriers are presumed lawful.[83] Because of AT & T's prior market dominance, the Commission delayed the reclassification of non-dominance for 800 services until end users could use any interexchange carrier for a particular telephone number, also known as "number portability,"[84] and for residential and small business services until the Commission could conclude that the market had become substantially competitive.[85]

The Commission imposed slightly more burdensome tariff filing requirements on AT & T in contrast to other carriers. Specifically, AT & T must file "a tariff summarizing [the] contract and containing the following information: (1) the term of the contract, including any renewal options; (2) a brief description of each of the services provided under the contract; (3) minimum volume commitments for each service; (4) the contract price for each service or services at the volume levels committed to by the customers; (5) a general description of any volume discounts built into the contract rate structure; and (6) a general description of other classifications, practices, and regulations affecting the contract rate."[86]

The FCC established the contract carriage option to promote planning by both users and interexchange carriers through greater availability of long-term commitments and price protection. The Commission noted this benefit would be reduced if carriers using contracts unilaterally altered the terms of their contracts.[87] The Commission recognizes that the Filed Rate Doctrine supports the supremacy of a tariff even if subsequently filed and containing changes unilaterally made by the carrier which are at odds with the previously negotiated contract.[88]

83. *See* 47 C.F.R. § 1.773 (1997).

84. Competition in the Interstate Interexchange Marketplace, CC Docket No. 90–132, Second Report and Order, 8 FCC Rcd. 3668 (1993) (streamlining regulation of AT & T 800 services except for Directory Assistance upon occurrence of number portability), *recons. denied*, 10 FCC Rcd. 4421 (1995).

85. Competition in the Interstate Interexchange Marketplace, CC Docket No. 90–132, 6 FCC Rcd. at 5880–82, 5893–94 (excluding AT & T's residential and small business services basket, including operators services and international message telephone service from further regulatory streamlining because of insufficient evidence that these services were subject to substantial competition). The Commission reconsidered the scope of competition in 1995 and decided that the marketplace had grown sufficiently competitive to warrant further streamlining of AT & T. *See* Motion of AT & T Corp. To Be Reclassified as a Non–Dominant Carrier, Order, FCC 95–47, 11 FCC Rcd. 3271 (1995).

86. Competition in the Interstate Interexchange Marketplace, CC Docket No. 90–132, Report and Order, 6 FCC Rcd. 5880, 5902 (1991), *recons.*, Mem. Op. and Order, 6 FCC Rcd. 7569 (1991), *further recons.*, Mem. Op. and Order on *recons.*, 7 FCC Rcd. 2677 (1992), *further recons.*, 8 FCC Rcd. 2659 (1993).

87. Competition in the Interstate Interexchange Marketplace, CC Docket No. 90–132, Mem. Op. and Order on Recons., FCC 95–2, 10 FCC Rcd. 4562, 57 25 (rel. Feb. 17, 1995).

88. "It is a well-established principle that, when a filed tariff rate differs from a rate set in a carrier-customer contract, the tariffed rate is the legal one. Likewise, if a carrier initiates a unilateral rate change altering a contract rate by filing a tariff revision, the new filed rate becomes the lawful one unless the revised rates are found to be unjust or unreasonable under Section 201(b) of the Communications Act, 47 U.S.C. § 201(b), or otherwise unlawful." AT & T Communications Contract Tariff

However, it will not allow carriers to use the tariffing option indiscriminately and unilaterally in ways that deprive users of the benefit of the bargains they negotiated. While refraining from absolutely embracing the law of contracts as the foundation for evaluating tariff revisions the Commission did state its willingness to consider contract law principles in assessing whether carriers had "substantial cause"[89] to file revised tariffs.

> Given the special nature of contract-based tariffs, we believe that commercial contract law principles are highly relevant to an assessment of whether a contract based tariff revision is just and reasonable under the substantial cause test. We are not prepared, however, to say at this time that these principles provide definitive parameters for a substantial cause showing. Instead, we will consider on a case-by-case basis in light of all relevant circumstances whether a substantial cause showing has been made.[90]

While the FCC's non-dominant classification currently does not apply to local exchange carriers, the Commission initiated a proposed rulemaking that asked whether LECs should be permitted to offer contract carriage for services governed by streamlined regulation, therefore subject to the same conditions as AT & T.[91] The Commission sought comment on whether it should adopt rules defining the conditions "price cap LECs" must meet to be considered nondominant, what those conditions should be and whether a LEC should be regulated as nondominant for certain services or within certain geographic markets, but not for others.

No. 374 Transmittal Nos. 2952 and 3441, DA 95–1061, 10 FCC Rcd. 7950 (1995) (suspending and ordering the investigation of unilateral changes to a contract for carriage established in a subsequently filed tariff revision and citing Competition in the Interstate Interexchange Marketplace), CC Docket No. 90–132, Mem. Op. and Order on Recons., FCC 95–2, para. 23 (rel. February 17, 1995) and American Broadcasting Companies, Inc. v. F.C.C., 643 F.2d 818, 207 U.S. App. D.C. 68 (D.C.Cir.1980).

89. In RCA American Communications, Inc., 84 FCC2d 353, 358 (1980) (ordering investigation of revised tariff filing), *rejecting tariff*, 86 FCC2d 1197, 1201 (1981), *on recons.*, 2 FCC Rcd. 236 (1987) the Commission established a standard for assessing whether changed circumstances warranted the filing of revised tariffs with more expensive rates than previously negotiated. The Commission held that a satellite carrier had "substantial cause" to raise rates when launch failures constrained transponder capacity and the carrier incurred higher than anticipated expenses, *e.g.*, a launch failure not fully compensated by insurance.

90. Competition in the Interstate Interexchange Marketplace, CC Docket No. 90–132, Report and Order, 6 FCC Rcd. 5880, 5898 n. 155 (1991)(citing RCA Americom Communications, Inc., 84 FCC2d at 358, 86 FCC2d at 1201 and 2 FCC Rcd. 236 (1987)).

91. Price Cap Performance Review for Local Exchange Carriers, CC Docket No. 94–1, in CC Docket No. 94–1, Further Notice of Proposed Rulemaking in CC Docket No. 93–124, and Second Further Notice of Proposed Rulemaking in CC Docket No. 93–197, Second Further Notice of Proposed Rulemaking, 1995 WL 564434 (FCC rel. Sep. 20, 1995) (proposing to streamline price cap regulation of local exchange carriers); Fourth Report and Order in CC Docket No. 94–1 and Second Report and Order in CC Docket No. 96–262, 12 FCC Rcd. 16642 (1997).

12.3 Administrative Regulation of Tariffs

A. *Section 204: Hearings as to Lawfulness of New Charges; Suspension*

Section 204 of the Communications Act provides for public-and Commission-initiated hearings on the legality and reasonableness of tariff filings.[1] Typically the carrier filing the tariff bears the burden of proving its reasonableness.[2] *MCI v. FCC*,[3] endorsed two options for the FCC to take upon receiving a carrier-filed tariff revision. Under Section 204(a) the Commission must first decide whether to hold hearings, or to allow revisions to become effective immediately after the customary public notice period. If the Commission decides to conduct a hearing, it must decide whether to suspend the proposed revision or to permit them to take effect on an interim basis subject to the possibility of subsequent rejection and refunds. Section 204(a) limits the suspension period to five months after which the tariff takes effect in the absence of Commission action on the merits of the filing. Section 204(b) establishes streamlined and expedited process for partial approvals of tariff changes on a temporary basis without a hearing or determination that the provisions are just and reasonable.[4]

The major appellate cases addressing Section 204 generally endorse the Commission's right to suspend and investigate a tariff, provided the Commission acts in a timely manner. In *Nader v. FCC*,[5] the United States Court of Appeals for the District of Columbia Circuit affirmed the FCC's decision not to accept a carrier's proposed rate of return and to

---

1. 47 U.S.C.A. § 204 (West Supp. 1997).

2. "Although carriers who file new or revised rates bear the burden of proof in Section 204 proceedings, it is well settled that complainants in Section 208 formal complaint proceedings bear the burden of proof. Beehive, as the complainant in this proceeding, has the burden of proving that the disputed rates are unjust and unreasonable." Beehive Telephone, Inc., and Beehive Telephone Nevada, Inc. v. The Bell Operating Companies, File No. E–94–57, Mem. Op. and Order, 10 FCC Rcd. 10562, 10566 (1995) (determination of who bears the burden of proving whether a new tariff complies with Title II of the Communications Act).

3. 627 F.2d 322, 200 U.S. App. D.C. 269 (D.C.Cir.1980).

4. Section 204(b) provides in part: "[T]he Commission may allow part of a charge, classification, regulation, or practice to go into effect, based upon a written showing by the carrier or carriers affected, and an opportunity for written comment thereon by affected persons, that such partial authorization is just, fair, and reasonable. Additionally, or in combination with a partial authorization, the Commission, upon a similar showing, may allow all or part of a charge, classification, regulation, or practice to go into effect on a temporary basis pending further order of the Commission." 47 U.S.C.A. § 204(b) (1995). "Section 204(b) of the Act empowers the Commission to allow part of a charge or other tariff provision to become effective or to allow all or part of a tariff provision to become effective on a temporary basis. Thus, Section 204 gives the Commission a choice of remedies in cases of proposed tariff revisions that appear to be unlawful." Annual 1987 Access Tariff Filings, Mem. Op. and Order, 2 FCC Rcd. 866, 880, 57 134 (1986). "Section 204(b) requires that a partial authorization be based on a written showing by the carrier affected, and opportunity for written comment thereon by affected persons, that a partial authorization would be just, fair and reasonable." *Id.* at 881, 57 136. *See also* MCI Telecommunications Corp. v. FCC, 627 F.2d 322, 200 U.S.App.D.C. 269 (D.C.Cir.1980) (concluding that § 204(a) and § 204(b) are complementary and designed to serve different purposes).

5. 520 F.2d 182, 172 U.S. App. D.C. 1 (D.C.Cir.1975).

prescribe its own rate after investigation. However, the court deemed untimely the Commission's failure to reach closure on some issues after ten years of consideration. In another case, a reviewing court rejected the FCC's decision to suspend and investigate MCI's Execunet service tariffs because the Commission had no general authority to insist that carriers receive its approval before filing tariffs proposing new services or rates.[6]

B.   Section 205: Prescribing Rates

Section 205 of the Communications Act authorizes the FCC to prescribe, *inter alia*, just and reasonable maximum charges after having provided the full opportunity for a hearing, to determine whether any carrier charge, classification, regulation or practice of any carrier violates any provision of the Act.[7] The rate prescription process once involved lengthy and administratively exhausting analysis of a carrier's cost of capital for both debt and equity, an assessment of risk and the determination of a "fair" rate of return. Following the lead of other nations and states, the FCC has replaced traditional rate of return regulation with incentive regulation that uses a more easily implemented "price cap" formula.[8]

Part 65 of the Commission's rules[9] establishes procedures and methodologies for prescribing and enforcing the rate of return certain

---

6. *See* MCI v. FCC, 561 F.2d 365, 182 U.S. App. D.C. 367 (D.C.Cir.1977) (only if the FCC has determined that the public convenience and necessity may require that new services receive advance approval can it then reject a tariff as unauthorized).

7. 47 U.S.C.A. § 205 (West 1991).

8. Policy and Rules Concerning Rates for Dominant Carriers, Second Report and Order, 5 FCC Rcd. 6786 (1990) and Erratum, 5 FCC Rcd. 7664 (1990) (LEC price cap order), *modified on recons.*, 6 FCC Rcd 2637 (1991), *petitions for further recons. dismissed*, Mem. Op. and Order 6 FCC Rcd. 7482 (1991), *further modified on recons.*, 6 FCC Rcd. 4524 (1991) (ONA/Part 69 order), *petition for recons. of ONA/Part 69 Order pending*, LEC Price Cap Order *aff'd. sub nom.* National Rural Telecom Ass'n v. FCC, 988 F.2d 174, 300 U.S. App. D.C. 226 (D.C.Cir.1993); Policy and Rules Concerning Rates for Dominant Carriers, Report and Order, and Second Further Notice of Proposed Rulemaking, 4 FCC Rcd 2873 (1989) (AT & T price cap order), *recons.*, 6 FCC Rcd 665 (1991) (AT & T price cap recons. order), *remanded on other grounds sub nom.* AT & T v. FCC, 974 F.2d 1351, 298 U.S. App. D.C. 1 (D.C.Cir.1992). The Commission has conducted a performance review of the AT & T price cap plan. Price Cap Performance Review for AT & T, CC Docket No. 92–134, Report, 8 FCC Rcd 6968 (1993). The Commission proposed relatively minor adjustments to the AT & T price cap plan based on the performance review. Revisions to Price Caps Rules for AT & T, CC Docket No. 93–197, Notice of Proposed Rulemaking, 8 FCC Rcd 5205 (1993); Revisions to Price Cap Rules for AT & T, CC Docket No. 93–197, Report and Order, FCC 95–18, 10 FCC Rcd. 3009 (rel. Jan. 12, 1995). The Commission also initiated a performance review of the LEC price cap plan. Price Cap Performance Review for Local Exchange Carriers, CC Docket No. 94–1, Notice of Proposed Rulemaking, 9 FCC Rcd 1687 (1994); First Report and Order, 10 FCC Rcd. 8961(1995) Second Further Notice of Proposed Rulemaking in CC Docket No. 94–1, Further Notice of Proposed Rulemaking in CC Docket No. 93–124, and Second Further Notice of Proposed Rulemaking in CC Docket No. 93–197, FCC 95–393, 1995 WL 564434 (F.C.C. rel. Sep. 14, 1995) (proposing modifications to the price cap regime for LECs to facilitate the transition to competition for local exchange services). *See also* Access Charge Reform, Price Cap Performance Review for Local Exchange Carriers, CC Docket No. 96-262, 94-1, Notice of Proposed Rulemaking, Third Report and Order and Notice of Inquiry, 11 FCC Rcd. 21354 (1996).

9. 47 C.F.R. Part 65 (1993).

local exchange carriers ("LECs") may earn on interstate access service. The Commission finetuned the Part 65 rules from 1987 to 1992,[10] a process upheld by the District of Columbia Circuit as part of the Commission's discretion to consider how best to process evidence and methodologies in the represcribing of rates of return.[11] The Commission finalized rule changes in 1995 to reflect the migration from rate of return to incentive regulation.[12] Rather than initiate a new represcription proceeding every two years regardless of conditions in capital markets, the Commission established a rule that considers the yields on ten-year United States Treasury securities to determine when represcription might be warranted. Under this system the Commission will issue a notice asking whether it should institute a represcription proceeding only if, for six consecutive months, the six-month average of those yields deviates by 150 basis points or more from the yield on these securities when considered by the Commission during its prior represcription. After evaluating the responses to such notice, the Commission will decide whether a represcription proceeding is necessary and will then issue an order that either sets forth a procedural schedule for the proceeding or announces that a represcription proceeding is not necessary.

The current rules also establish a "paper hearing" process for represcription proceedings that is modeled after the system used in evidentiary hearings. Because this process contains procedural steps beyond those necessary for a full and complete record, the Commission adopted streamlined procedures that reduce the inordinate delays and costs experienced in previous represcription proceedings, yet provide parties full opportunity to present and evaluate relevant evidence.

Part 65 previously required the Regional Bell Holding Companies ("RHCs") to undertake complex studies and to submit the resulting data for inclusion in the record in represcription proceedings. The Commission found the cost of equity studies unnecessary and the cost of debt and capital structure studies unduly complex. Accordingly, the Commission replaced them with specified methodologies to be used in future represcription proceedings unless the record in those proceedings showed

---

10. *See* Refinement of Procedures and Methodologies for Represcribing Interstate Rates of Return for AT & T Communications and Local Exchange Carriers, CC Docket No. 87–463, Notice of Proposed Rulemaking, 2 FCC Rcd. 6491 (1987), *terminated*, 7 FCC Rcd. 5949 (1992); Refinement of Procedures and Methodologies for Represcribing Interstate Rates of Return for AT & T Communications and Local Exchange Carriers, CC Docket No. 87–463, Order, 5 FCC Rcd. 197, 202–03 (1989), *recons. denied* Mem. Op. and Order, 7 FCC Rcd 5949 (1992); Represcribing the Authorized Rate of Return for Interstate Services of Local Exchange Carriers, Order, 5 FCC Rcd 7507 (1990), *recons. denied*, Mem. Op and Order, 6 FCC Rcd. 7193 (1991), *aff'd*

sub nom. Illinois Bell Telephone Co. v. FCC, 988 F.2d 1254, 300 U.S. App. D.C. 296 (D.C.Cir.1993).

11. *See* Illinois Bell Telephone Co. v. FCC, 988 F.2d 1254, 300 U.S. App. D.C. 296 (D.C.Cir.1993).

12. Amendment of Parts 65 and 69 of the Commission's Rules to Reform the Interstate Rate of Return Represcription and Enforcement Processes, CC Docket No. 92–133, Report and Order, FCC 95–134, 10 FCC Rcd. 6788 (1995); *see also* Regulatory Reform for Local Exchange Carriers Subject to Rate of Return Regulation, Report and Order, CC Docket No. 92–135, 8 FCC Rcd. 4545 (1993).

that the methodologies would produce unreasonable results. Part 65 had authorized an automatic refund, including accrued interest, of earnings exceeding what the rules referred to as "the maximum allowable rate of return."[13] In *AT & T v. FCC*,[14] the United States Court of Appeals for the District of Columbia Circuit remanded this rule to the Commission which subsequently decided to eliminate it. The Commission decided to rely on its tariff review and complaint processes to guard against rates of return in excess of the maximum permissible prescribed rate. Practically speaking, incentive regulation through a price cap scheme established the basis for allocating any return in excess of the prescribed rate between shareholders and ratepayers.

1. The "Old School" Rate of Return Prescription Model

The rate of return prescription process previously served as an essential component in the FCC's economic regulation of most telephone companies. Under this form of regulation, telephone companies computed their revenue requirements, *i.e.*, the total revenues their tariffs should generate in a year based on demand estimates using the following formula: Revenue requirements equal total plant investment less accumulated depreciation, meaning the rate base times the prescribed rate of return plus expenses (including current year depreciation, taxes and operating expenses).[15] The rate for any given service equaled its revenue requirement divided by the demand anticipated for that service.

The FCC first prescribed an interstate rate of return in 1967 as part of a comprehensive investigation into the reasonableness of AT & T's interstate rates.[16] Between 1967 and 1984, the Commission represcribed rates of return four times, with prescription proceedings involving lengthy evidentiary hearings held before an Administrative Law Judge.[17] The proceedings resulted in prescribed rates of return that AT & T used to calculate its long distance rates and to compensate the Bell Operating Companies ("BOCs") and independent telephone companies for use of their facilities to originate and terminate interstate calls.

With the divestiture of AT & T in 1984 the FCC decided to regulate directly the access charges LECs impose for originating and terminating interstate calls.[18] In Docket 84–800, the Commission sought to develop

---

13. 47 C.F.R. § 65.700 (1996).

14. 836 F.2d 1386, 267 U.S. App. D.C. 38 (D.C.Cir.1988) (per curiam).

15. For an extensive analysis of traditional public utility ratemaking *see* ALFRED E. KAHN, THE ECONOMICS OF REGULATION—PRINCIPLES AND INSTITUTIONS (1988).

16. American Tel. & Tel. Co., CC Docket No. 16258, Interim Decision and Order, 9 FCC2d 30 (1967).

17. American Telephone and Telegraph Co., Modification of Prescribed Rate of Return, 86 FCC2d 221 (1981), *aff'd sub nom.* United States v. FCC, 707 F.2d 610, 227

U.S. App. D.C. 413 (D.C.Cir.1983); AT & T Co. Charges For Interstate Telephone Service (Docket 20376), 57 FCC2d 960 (1976); AT & T and the Associated Bell Sys. Cos. (Docket 19129), 38 FCC2d 213 (1972), *aff'd sub nom.* Nader v. FCC, 520 F.2d 182, 172 U.S. App. D.C. 1 (D.C.Cir.1975); AT & T (Dockets 16258 and 15011), 9 FCC2d 30 (1967), *mod.* Mem. Op. and Order on Recons., 9 FCC 2d 960 (1967), *further mod.* 10 FCC2d 705 (1967).

18. *See* MTS and WATS Market Structure, CC Docket No. 78–72, Phase I, Third Report and Order, 93 FCC2d 241 (1983), *mod. on further recons.*, Mem. Op. and Or-

procedures and methodologies to address the increased complexity of rate of return regulation in the post-divestiture environment.[19] The resulting Part 65 rules were designed to enable the Commission to represcribe authorized rates of return for LEC interstate access service and AT & T's interstate communications services without engaging in traditional evidentiary hearings.[20]

The new rules for represcribing authorized interstate rates of return incorporate a streamlined administrative process. Only under limited circumstances do the rules permit cross examination, oral argument and use of separated trial staff. The rules require the Regional Bell Operating Companies to:

- file notices of appearance;
- undertake complex studies using particular methodologies, to include the data resulting from these studies in their initial submissions;
- respond to Bureau information requests; and
- comply with any discovery orders.[21]

2. Incentive Regulation

The FCC grew to realize traditional rate of return regulation created little incentive or reward for telephone companies to operate efficiently. The Commission replaced rate of return regulation of AT & T and the LECs with price cap plans that reward carrier innovation and increased productivity by regulating prices directly, rather than indirectly through the examination of projected costs and demand as under traditional rate of return regulation. These plans took effect July 1, 1989 and January 1, 1991 respectively.[22] Both plans require telephone companies to adjust their price cap indexes to reflect inflation,[23] certain productivity offsets,[24]

der, 97 FCC2d 682 (1983), *mod. on second further recons.*, 97 FCC2d 834 (1984), *aff'd in pertinent part sub nom.* National Ass'n of Regulatory Util. Comm'rs v. FCC, 737 F.2d 1095, 237 U.S. App. D.C. 390 (D.C.Cir. 1984), cert. denied 469 U.S. 1227, 105 S.Ct. 1224, 84 L.Ed.2d 364 (1985), *modified on further recons.*, Mem. Op. and Order, 99 FCC2d 708 (1984), *aff'd sub nom.* American Tel. and Tel. Co. v. FCC, 832 F.2d 1285, 266 U.S. App. D.C. 47 (D.C.Cir.1987), *modified on further recons.*, Mem. Op. and Order, 101 FCC2d 1222 (1985), *recons. denied*, Mem. Op. and Order, 102 FCC2d 849 (1985).

19. Authorized Rates of Return for the Interstate Services of AT & T Communications and Exchange Telephone Carriers, CC Docket No. 84–800, Notice of Proposed Rulemaking, FCC 84–395, 49 Fed. Reg. 32871 (August 17, 1984); Authorized Rates of Return for the Interstate Services of AT & T Communications and Exchange Telephone Carriers, CC Docket No. 84–800,

Supplemental Notice of Proposed Rulemaking, FCC 85–458, 50 Fed. Reg. 33786 (August 21, 1985).

20. Authorized Rates of Return for the Interstate Services of AT & T Communications and Exchange Telephone Carriers, Report and Order, CC Docket No. 84–800, Phase II, 51 Fed. Reg. 1795 at ¶ ¶ 3, 70–72 (Jan. 15, 1986) (Phase II Order), Mem. Op. and Order on Recons., 104 FCC2d 1404 (1986) (Phase II Reconsideration).

21. *See, e.g.,* 47 C.F.R. §§ 65.100(a)(1), 65.102(a), 65.103(a), 65.200 (1996).

22. Policy and Rules Concerning Rates for Dominant Carriers, Report and Order and Second Further Notice of Proposed Rulemaking, 4 FCC Rcd at 2968 (1989); Policy and Rules Concerning Rates for Dominant Carriers, Second Report and Order, 5 FCC Rcd. at 6837 (1990).

23. The inflation adjustments reflect changes in the Gross National Product Price Index (GNP–PI) as reported by the

and exogenous costs.[25] The LEC price cap plan also requires LECs whose earnings exceed certain levels to share those additional earnings with customers through prospective rate reductions.[26] The Commission adopted an optional incentive plan giving non-price cap regulated LECs, which are willing to assume more risk, the opportunity to realize increased profits while remaining under rate of return regulation.[27] This plan permits non-price cap LECs to retain earnings up to 1.5 percent above the rate of return prescribed for LEC interstate access service. In exchange, LECs electing this form of regulation must file tariffs that remain in effect for two-year periods. The LECs must target these rates to earn the prescribed interstate rate of return. During the two-year period, these LECs may increase their tariff rates only if necessary to produce earnings 0.75 percent below the prescribed interstate rate of return.[28]

C.　Section 208: The Complaint Process

Section 208 of the Communications Act provides the basis for interested parties to file complaints alleging carrier violation of one or more statutory provisions, Commission rules or regulations. The com-

United States Department of Commerce. 47 C.F.R. § 61.3(p) (1996). This is a broad-based index computed by the Federal government that reflects changes in the cost factors of production for a wide spectrum of economic sectors. It is also known as the fixed-weight GNP deflator.

24. The productivity offset for AT & T is 3.0 percent. Policy and Rules Concerning Rates for Dominant Carriers, CC Docket No. 87–313, Report and Order and Second Further Notice of Proposed Rulemaking, 4 FCC Rcd. 2873, 2989, 3001(1989), *erratum*, 4 FCC Rcd. 3379 (1989), *on recons.*, 6 FCC Rcd. 665 (1991). *See also* Revisions to Price Cap Rules for AT & T Corp., CC Docket No. 93–197, Report and Order, 10 FCC Rcd. 3009 (1995). LECs may elect productivity offsets of either 3.3 percent or 4.3 percent with the latter factor qualifying the carrier to capture a greater share of profits. Policy and Rules Concerning Rates for Dominant Carriers, CC Docket No. 87–313, Second Report and Order, 5 FCC Rcd. 6796, 6801(1990), *on recons.*, 6 FCC Rcd. 2637 (1991), *aff'd sub nom.* Nat'l Rural Telecom. Ass'n v. FCC, 988 F.2d 174, 300 U.S. App. D.C. 226 (D.C.Cir.1993).

25. Under price caps, most increases and decreases in a carrier's cost of providing regulated service are treated as "endogenous" changes, *i.e.*, expected in internal costs borne by the carrier. Such costs do not result in adjustments to the carrier's price cap indexes. The Commission, however, has identified certain types of "exogenous" cost changes, triggered by adminis-

trative, legislative, or judicial action that are beyond the carrier's control that should result in adjustments to those indexes. LEC Price Cap Order, 5 FCC Rcd. at 6807; AT & T Price Cap Order, 4 FCC Rcd. at 3187. The Commission concluded that failing to recognize these cost changes through price cap index adjustments would unjustly punish or reward the carrier. LEC Price Cap Order, 5 FCC Rcd at 6807. Accordingly, the Commission found that those types of cost changes should be considered as exceptional and unpredictable in order to ensure that price cap regulation did not lead to unreasonably high or unreasonably low rates.

26. Price cap regulated LECs may increase their interstate rates to the extent necessary to earn a 10.25 percent interstate rate of return. LECs electing the 3.3 percent productivity offset may retain all interstate earnings up to 12.25 percent, 50 percent of interstate earnings between 12.25 percent and 16.25 percent, and no interstate earnings above 16.25 percent. LECs electing the 4.3 percent productivity offset may retain all interstate earnings up to 13.25 percent, 50 percent of interstate earnings between 13.25 percent and 17.25 percent, and no interstate earnings above 17.25 percent. LEC Price Cap Order, 5 FCC Rcd. at 6801–02, ¶¶ 123–27.

27. Regulatory Reform for Local Exchange Carriers Subject to Rate of Return Regulation, Report and Order, CC Docket No. 92–135, 8 FCC Rcd. 4545, 4547(1993).

28. *Id.* at 4550.

plainants bear the burden of proof. Only after meeting the burden of making a *prima facie* case will the burden shift to the carriers to show the reasonableness of the practice about which the complaints are filed. For example, to establish such a case of discrimination under Section 202 of the Communications Act, "the complainant must show that: (1) a customer seeks substantially the same service arrangement under the same terms and conditions that were made available to another customer; and, (2) the carrier refused to make service available to that customer on those terms. Alternatively, the complainant may show that the contract is, by its terms, not generally available to other similarly situated customers."[29] A complainant could establish such a prima facie case by showing that the contract contained impermissible restrictions on geographic availability.

If a complainant establishes this *prima facie* case the burden then shifts to the carrier to show that the discrimination was reasonable. Courts have recognized the sufficiency in a given instance of any proffered justification is, by nature, a fact-intensive inquiry requiring a case-by-case adjudication in the complaint process.[30] Courts have upheld the FCC's decision to approve a tariff, despite evidence of discrimination, if factors such as cost differences or competitive necessity justify such discrimination.[31]

D.   *Section 214: Extension of Lines*

Prior to enactment of the Telecommunications Act of 1996, Section 214 of the Communications Act[32] required all common carriers to apply for certificates of public convenience and necessity from the Commission for the construction of new interstate or international lines. Before a carrier can begin to construct and operate a new line, it must submit an application that includes a "summary of the factors showing the public need for the proposed facilities"[33] and a description of current service with "reasons why existing facilities are inadequate."[34] This provision also applies to discontinuance, reduction or impairment of service and ensures that interested parties and the public have an opportunity to investigate and comment on a carrier's line expansion or reduction

---

29. Competition in the Interstate Interexchange Marketplace, CC Docket No. 90–132, Report and Order, 6 FCC Rcd. 5880, 5903, ¶ 131.

30. *See, e.g.*, L.T. Barringer & Co. v. United States, 319 U.S. 1, 13–14, 63 S.Ct. 967, 974–975, 87 L.Ed. 1171, 1181–82 (1943); Dresser Industries, Inc. v. ICC, 714 F.2d 588, 599–602 (5th Cir.1983).

31. American Broadcasting Co. v. FCC, 663 F.2d 133, 139, 213 U.S. App. D.C. 369, 375 (D.C.Cir.1980); AT & T v. FCC, 449 F.2d 439, 449–50 (2d Cir.1971) (deeming unreasonably discriminatory sharing restrictions contained in AT & T's Telpak private line service tariff).

32. In 1997 the Commission proposed to forbear from applying its Section 214 authority to carriers who may be subject to price-cap regulation, average schedule carriers, and domestic, non-dominant carriers offering local or long-distance services. *See* Elimination of Section 214 Applications for Extension of Lines, CC Docket No. 97–11, Notice of Proposed Rulemaking, 12 FCC Rcd. 1111 (1997). The Telecommunications Act of 1996 added § 214(e) Provision of Universal Service which provides a legislative mandate for universal service and the means by which carriers shall help achieve this mandate.

33. 47 C.F.R. § 63.01(1) (1997).

34. *Id*. at § 63.01(n).

plans. The process may seem perfunctory now because the FCC believes no carrier would commit the financial and other resources to construct unnecessary facilities. But before the FCC's reliance on marketplace forces, the Section 214 evaluation afforded the Commission and the public an opportunity to determine whether current or near term consumer demand justified construction of a particular facility.

Under conventional rate base regulation, carriers might have perceived a financial incentive to overinvest in facilities for which a prescribed rate of return would apply.[35] Similarly, a carrier might seek authorization to construct and operate facilities, which might not be justified on the basis of consumer demand, to "warehouse" capacity or to acquire a massive amount of capacity that could be dumped on the market at predatory rates to drive out incipient, or established competition. The FCC now discounts such potential anticompetitive practices even as it refrains from conducting a rigorous analysis of transmission capacity supply and demand. The Commission is predisposed to accept any carrier's assertion of public need, either on the basis of demand or on other grounds including routing diversity, redundancy and national security. Likewise, it now will grant blanket certification for a carrier's anticipated annual circuit growth rather than require individual applications for each type of facility.[36]

Courts previously supported the view that Section 214 mandated close scrutiny of carrier facility construction plans. In *Hawaiian Telephone Co. v. FCC*,[37] the Court of Appeals for the District of Columbia Circuit held that the FCC did not comply with statutory requirements when it considered competition in terms of its effect on carriers instead of the potential for public benefit.[38] The Commission "cannot merely assert the benefits of competition in an abstract, sterile way"[39] but must demonstrate how facilities-based competition will serve the public interest and not simply promote competition for the sake of competition.

---

35. "The Commission has identified two economic phenomena tending to create inefficient results. The Averch–Johnson effect occurs when carriers have an incentive to adopt inefficient, capital intensive approaches to business operations when the allowed rate of return exceeds the cost of capital, and to adopt inefficient, labor intensive approaches when the cost of capital exceeds the allowed rate of return. Harvey Averch & Leland L. Johnson, *Behavior of the Firm Under Regulatory Constraints*, 52 Am. Econ. Rev. 1052 (1962). The term "X-inefficiency" refers to a second phenomenon describing the lack of incentive for utilities to control expenses when expenses are included in a firm's annual revenue requirement. Harvey Leibenstein, *Allocative Efficiency vs. X–Efficiency*, 56 Am. Econ. Rev. 392, 392–415 (1966)." Policy and Rules Concerning Rates for Dominant Carriers,

CC Docket No. 87–313, Second Report and Order, 5 FCC Rcd. 6786, 6790, n. 30 (1990).

36. *See e.g.*, AT & T Co., DA 94–760, Order & Auth. 9 FCC Rcd. 3381(1994) (granting blanket authorization pursuant to Section 214 of the Communications Act of 1934, as amended, to lease and operate satellite voice-grade bearer circuits between the United States and points in Central America, South America, the Caribbean Area and Africa during the years 1993–1997).

37. 498 F.2d 771, 162 U.S. App. D.C. 229 (D.C.Cir.1974).

38. *Id.* at 774, 162 U.S. App. D.C. at 232.

39. *Id.* at 776, 162 U.S. App. D.C. at 234 (citing FCC v. RCA Communications, Inc., 346 U.S. 86, 94, 73 S.Ct. 998, 1003, 97 L.Ed. 1470, 1478 (1953)).

The court provided the following interpretation of Section 214:

When the FCC considers an application for certification of a new line, it must start from the situation as it then exists, and must apply the statutory standard to determine whether indeed the public convenience and necessity requires more or better service. If it determines that more or additional competitive service would be in the public interest, then it can consider how much added service is necessary, and finally to whom the opportunity for providing service should be awarded. In this latter determination the [FCC] can balance equities and opportunities among the various carriers. The initial question for the [FCC], however, must be whether the public interest requires more or different service.[40]

Just as the FCC cannot promote competition for competition's sake, it cannot use its authority under Section 214 to restrict the kinds of services available from an authorized line unless it explicitly identifies a public interest justification. In *MCI Telecommunications Corp. v. FCC*,[41] the court reversed FCC orders requiring MCI to stop offering its Execunet switched long distance services. The court stated the "primary purpose of Section 214(a) is prevention of unnecessary duplication of facilities, not regulation of services. Because of this, Section 214 would appear to have a limited office with respect to regulation of service offerings on existing lines."[42] While the FCC may have intended to limit new facilities-based competition to private line services, its failure to state affirmatively why switched services would not serve the public interest meant that it could not impose restrictions on the use of MCI's microwave facilities for switched services.

ITT World Communications, Inc. v. FCC,[43] which considered whether the FCC appropriately authorized additional facilities-based competition for international record services, provides a summary of the requirements imposed by Section 214(a):

Section 214(a) prohibits new common carrier communication "lines" in the absence of a certificate from the [FCC] that "the present or future public convenience [and necessity] require" it. Section 214(a) itself imposes no procedural requirements. However, the [FCC] has laid down quite elaborate specifications for the contents of an application under § 214, 47 C.F.R. § 63.01 et. seq.; and has provided that any interested party may file an application to deny it. 47 C.F.R. § 63.52(c). The applicant may then file an opposition and the opposer a reply. Allegations of fact not subject to official notice must be supported by affidavit.[44]

Section 214(a) does not mandate an evidentiary hearing, nor does the FCC have to grant one. Courts typically will affirm the Commission's

---

40. *Id.* at 776, 162 U.S. App. D.C. at 234.

41. 561 F.2d 365, 182 U.S. App. D.C. 367 (D.C.Cir.1977).

42. *Id.* at 375, 182 U.S. App. D.C. at 377 (citations omitted).

43. 595 F.2d 897 (2d Cir.1979).

44. *Id.* at 900.

refusal to grant a hearing unless a petitioner can demonstrate the Commission's refusal was "arbitrary, capricious, and abuse of discretion , or otherwise not in accordance with law."[45]

Section 214 does not provide the basis for challenging tariff revisions, even though one could argue that the removal of a rate discount constitutes a discontinuance, reduction or impairment of service. In *Aeronautical Radio, Inc. v. FCC*,[46] the court affirmed the FCC's decision to accept a proposal from AT & T to eliminate certain "Telpak" bulk service discounts. The court held AT & T did not have to file for Section 214 approval simply to change the terms of a service offering.

The Section 214 application process does provide an opportunity for interested persons to file comments stating how construction or extension of facilities would or would not serve the public interest. Even with efforts to expedite the pleading cycle, the need to consider the merits of such filings takes time. In *Southern Pacific Communications Co. v. American Telephone and Telegraph Co.*,[47] the court dismissed a private antitrust suit, and, *inter alia*, rejected plaintiff's contention that the ability of AT & T to file comments on Section 214 applications of new and prospective competitors enabled it to delay and discourage market entry.[48]

Carriers (both private and common) typically seek licenses to operate from the FCC pursuant to Section 214 and Sections 308, 309 and 319 for services that use radio spectrum, *e.g.*, microwave links, satellites and earth stations. Unless the proposed use of spectrum complies with the United States Table of Frequency Allocations (47 C.F.R. § 2.1), the applicant must petition for a reallocation of spectrum or waiver to permit non-conforming operations.[49] Applicants for a new service typically seek spectrum reallocations in the context of a Petition for Rulemaking. In conjunction with its consideration of a Rulemaking petition and

45. *Id.* at 901 (citing 5 U.S.C.A. § 706(2)(A) (West 1995)).

46. 642 F.2d 1221, 206 U.S. App. D.C. 253 (D.C.Cir.1980), cert. denied 451 U.S. 920, 101 S. Ct. 1998, 68 L. Ed. 2d 311 (1981).

47. 556 F.Supp. 825 (D.D.C.1982).

48. "[I]t is the FCC not AT & T that requires new entrants ... to obtain the necessary microwave permits. 47 U.S.C. § 214. Moreover, AT & T has a right to file comments to the new applications, just like any other interested party.... Any delays that result from AT & T's petitions in this regard are a result not of AT & T's attempt to obfuscate the issues, but rather of the various regulatory bodies' close scrutiny of the obviously meritorious petitions." 556 F. Supp. at 881.

49. For example Motorola Satellite Services, Inc. proposed to provide a mobile voice and data service via a constellation of 66 low earth orbiting "IRIDIUM" satellites using spectrum allocated for radio determination (position indication) satellite services ("RDSS"). Application of Motorola Satellite Communications, Inc. for Authority to Construct, Launch, and Operate a Low Earth Orbit Satellite System in the 1616–1626.5 MHz Band, File Nos. 9–DSS–P–91(87); CSS–91–010; 43–DSS–AMEND–92; 15–SAT–LA–95; 16–SAT–AMEND–95, 10 FCC Rcd 2268; (1995). Both the International Telecommunication Union and the FCC revised the RDSS spectrum allocation to include mobile satellite services thereby mooting the need for a waiver. *See* International Telecommunication Union, Final Acts of the World Administrative Radio Conference (WARC–92), Malaga–Torremolinos (1992), Report and Order, ET Docket No. 92–28; *see also* Preparation for International Telecommunication Union World Radiocommunication Conferences, IC Docket No. 94–31, Report, 10 FCC Rcd. 12783 (1995).

having decided not to pursue competitive bidding, the FCC also accepts applications to construct, launch (where applicable) and operate facilities to provide new services. In a manner parallel to broadcast licensing, the Commission places the initial application on public notice and creates a filing window during which time it will accept additional applications. Qualified applicants filing within the window are considered for license grants at the same time as the initial applicant. The licensing process also provides a pleading cycle for interested parties to file comments and petitions relating to any application. These comments, often filed by the other applicants, supply the Commission with additional information for its consideration whether a particular applicant is legally, financially and technically qualified to provide the proposed service and whether licensing the particular applicant would serve the public interest.

Before placing a carrier application on public notice, the FCC typically makes a threshold evaluation of the application and the applicant's legal, financial and technical qualifications. While the Commission has adhered to a "letter perfect" standard for applications involving some preexisting services, for example, Multi-channel Multipoint Distribution Service,[50] it may request additional information and accept an application with some filing flaws. For new services the Commission may permit applicants to revise and amend their applications as more precise technical details become available.

Before accepting an application for filing and placing it on public notice, the Commission usually considers whether the applicant possesses or has access to capital sufficient to support construction of all required facilities and operation for at least one year.[51] The Commission also may consider whether the applicant has the technical know-how to provide the service and whether the application contains sufficient detail to provide the Commission with a basis to assess the technical merits of the application. The Commission also may consider whether the applicant possesses all legal credentials to become a licensee, for instance,

---

50. "We propose that the standard to be met for LMDS applications be the 'letter perfect' standard, rather than the present Part 21 standard of substantial compliance and opportunity to amend. The latter standard has proved to be administratively burdensome and may have contributed to delays in licensing MMDS stations. Accordingly, LMDS applicants not meeting the proposed rule's requirements would be dismissed rather than, under the current Part 21 practice, being allowed to perfect their applications." Rulemaking to Amend Part 1 and Part 21 of the Commission's Rules to Redesignate the 27.5—29.5 GHz Frequency Band and to Establish Rules and Policies for Local Multipoint Distribution Service, 8 FCC Rcd 557 (1993).

51. Thus, the Commission has, since Domsat I, traditionally required all appli-

cants to demonstrate that they are financially qualified to construct, launch and operate their proposed systems promptly. This scrutiny ensures that an applicant is capable of implementing its proposed . . . system promptly. 101 FCC2d 223, 231 ¶ 18, *citing* Domestic Communications Satellite Facilities, Second Report and Order, 35 FCC2d 844 (1972) and Ultravision Broadcasting, Mem. Op. and Order, 1 FCC 2d 544 (1965). *See also* Amendment of the Commission's Rules to Establish Rules and Policies Pertaining to a Mobile Satellite Service in the 1610–1626.5/2483.5–2500 MHz Frequency Bands, CC Docket No. 92–166, Report and Order, 9 FCC Rcd. 5936 (1994) (establishing a strict financial requirement, *e.g.*, irrevocably committed external financing, given the expense of proposed systems and limited available spectrum).

that the foreign ownership composition does not exceed limits established in Section 310 of the Communications Act.[52]

In contrast to the lengthy and administratively complex comparative licensing process for broadcasting, the FCC prefers to find ways to expedite the grant of licenses for carriers. While the Commission initially held comparative hearings for cellular radio, it quickly moved to a lottery scheme. For satellite services, the Commission has adopted an "open skies" policy[53] that favors granting as many licenses as can be accommodated by the available spectrum and orbital arc. This has required complex coordination among licensees including the reduction of spacing between satellites and occasional orders by the Commission to relocate an in-orbit satellite.[54]

Only recently has the FCC had to consider licensing alternatives for situations in which more applicants existed than could be accommodated by the available spectrum, even after conducting a preliminary threshold assessment of financial, technical, and legal qualifications. For mobile satellite services provided via geostationary orbiting satellites the Commission concluded marketplace factors and the need to complete satellite coordination with operators in other countries justified forcing eight applicants to merge into a single consortium.[55] The Commission required each applicant to contribute five million dollars to capitalize the consortium. One applicant that failed to make the capital contribution and subsequently had its application dismissed by the FCC claimed that the

52. *See* Orion Satellite Corporation, Application for modification of authorization to construct, launch and operate an international communications satellite system consistent with current separate systems policies, 9 FCC Rcd 4077(1994)(scrutinizing extent of foreign control of U.S. private carrier proposing to provide international satellite services).

53. 35 FCC2d 844 (1972), *recons. in part* 38 FCC 2d 665 (1972).

54. "For example, GE Americom has moved its in-orbit Satcom 4 satellite one degree in order to conform to its new assignment. Indeed, to accommodate Hughes's Galaxy 5–W satellite (formerly Westar 5–R) when it is launched in November 1991. AT & T will be required to relocate its Telstar 303 satellite before its end-of-life." Assignment of Orbital Locations to Space Stations in the Domestic Fixed–Satellite Service, Mem. Op. and Order, 5 FCC Rcd. 179 n. 37 (1990); GTE Spacenet Corp., Application for Modification of License for the GSTAR III Domestic–Fixed Satellite and Application for Temporary Orbital Assignment for GSTAR III, 5 FCC Rcd 1182 (1990) (permitting relocation of satellite to an unoccupied but previously assigned location).

55. Amendment of Parts 2, 22 and 25 of the Commission's Rules to Allocate Spectrum for, and to Establish Other Rules and Policies Pertaining to the Use of Radio Frequencies in the Land Mobile Satellite Service for the Provision of Various Common Carrier Services, GEN Docket No. 84–1234, Report and Order, 2 FCC Rcd. 1825, *recons. den.*, 2 FCC Rcd. 6830 (1987), *further recons. den.* 4 FCC Rcd. 6016 (1989) (allocating spectrum for land mobile services provided via geostationary orbiting satellites); Second Report and Order, 2 FCC Rcd. 485 (1987), *recons. den.*, Mem. Op. and Order, 4 FCC Rcd. 6029 (1989) (establishing licensing procedures); Mem. Order and Authorization, 4 FCC Rcd. 6041 (1989) (authorizing a single consortium to construct, launch an operate a mobile satellite system), *remanded sub nom.* Aeronautical Radio, Inc. v. FCC, 928 F.2d 428, 289 U.S. App. D.C. 16 (D.C.Cir.1991) (requiring the FCC to consider further the rationale for a single consortium in lieu of comparative hearings and the manner in which the FCC required applicants to invest $5 million cash in the consortium), Tentative Decision on Remand, 6 FCC Rcd. 4900 (1991); Final Decision on Remand, 70 Rad. Reg. 2d 271 (P & F 1992); *aff'd sub nom.* Aeronautical Radio, Inc. v. FCC, 983 F.2d 275, 299 U.S. App. D.C. 250 (D.C.Cir.1993).

Commission failed to comply with its licensing rules and the *Ashbacker Doctrine*[56] that holds that qualified, mutually exclusive applicants are entitled to a comparative hearing. The Commission and the appellate court considered the *Ashbacker Doctrine* inapplicable because the FCC had legitimate public interest grounds to mandate a consortium that procedurally reduced the number of applicants before the Commission to one.

> ARINCs application was not denied as a consequence of the Commission's grant of AMSC's application without a hearing. To the contrary, the Commission rejected ARINC's application because it was inconsistent with the Commission's spectrum allocation orders, and this rejection came a full two years before the MSS license was awarded to AMSC.[57]

In the case of mobile services provided via low earth orbiting satellites, the Commission has dismissed or deferred consideration of applicants it deemed inadequate in demonstrating financial qualifications.[58] To accommodate all qualified applicants, the Commission granted licenses based on a frequency band segmentation plan.[59]

12.4 Historical Foundation for Defining and Regulating Common Carriers: Accounting, Records and Depreciation

A. *Section 220: Accounts, Records, and Memoranda; Depreciation Charges*

Section 220 of the Communications Act addresses record keeping and depreciation, two key elements for scrutinizing carrier performance and determining service rates. The rates charged by carriers in large part depend on how costs are allocated and how investments are depreciated. Accordingly, cost allocation and depreciation issues often divide the FCC which typically wants to promote speedy depreciation to spur innovation and most states which have greater concern for service affordability and universal service.

The FCC may seek to preempt state jurisdiction on matters involving cost allocation and depreciation pursuant to Section 220. The Commission has persuaded many courts that a prevailing federal interest supports preemption of state jurisdiction to prevent the proliferation of

---

56. Ashbacker Radio Corp. v. FCC, 326 U.S. 327, 66 S.Ct. 148, 90 L.Ed. 108 (1945).

57. Aeronautical Radio, Inc. v. FCC, 928 F.2d 428, 438, 289 U.S. App. D.C. 16, 26 (D.C.Cir.1991)

58. *See, e.g.*, Application of Constellation Communications, Inc. for Authority to Construct, Launch, and Operate a Low Earth Orbit Satellite System in the 1610–1626.5 MHz/2483.5–2500 Mhz Band Order, 10 FCC Rcd. 2258 (1995)(deferring consideration to accord applicant an opportunity

to provide more complete evidence of financial qualifications).

59. Application of Motorola Satellite Communications, Inc. for Authority to Construct, Launch and Operate a Low Earth Orbit Satellite System in the 1616–1626.5 MHz Band, Order and Authorization, 10 FCC Rcd. 2268 (1995); *see also* Amendment of the Commission's Rules to Establish Rules and Policies Pertaining to a Mobile Satellite Service in the 1610–1626.5/2483.5–2500 Mhz Frequency Bands, 9 FCC Rcd. 5936 (1994).

inconsistent state policies harmful to interstate commerce and a single, uniform policy.[1] However, language in the Communications Act safeguards state jurisdiction over intrastate service. The FCC has not been able to preempt the states on depreciation issues when it is possible to have parallel, and even inconsistent federal and state policies applicable to plant that can be allocated between interstate and intrastate service.[2]

Section 152(b) of the Communications Act expressly denies the FCC "jurisdiction with respect to (1) charges, classifications, practices, services, facilities, or regulations for or in connection with intrastate communication service. . . . "[3] In *Louisiana Public Service Commission v. FCC*,[4] the Supreme Court reversed an FCC ruling that Section 220 of the Communications Act authorized the Commission to preempt inconsistent state depreciation regulations for intrastate ratemaking purposes.[5] The Commission sought to stimulate innovation and modernization of the telecommunications infrastructure by prescribing faster depreciation schedules thereby allowing telephone companies to recoup plant investment over a shorter period of time. Faster depreciation schedules would result in unpopular and politically undesirable upward pressures on local rates. Fearing the potential for higher rates resulting from FCC regulatory initiatives, state public utility commissions challenged the assertion of jurisdiction as an illegal attempt to regulate intrastate "charges" under Section 152(b) of the Communications Act.

1. *See, e.g.,* National Association of Regulatory Utility Commissioners v. FCC, 880 F.2d 422, 279 U.S. App. D.C. 99 (D.C.Cir. 1989) (remanding case for a determination by the FCC whether state regulation of wiring inside premises would thwart achievement of a federal policy promoting free and competitive inside wiring market); Illinois Bell Telephone Co. v. FCC, 883 F.2d 104, 280 U.S. App. D.C. 32 (D.C.Cir.1989) (upholding FCC preemption of state regulation on the issue of unbundling customer premises equipment from network services and conditioning the marketing of such equipment by local exchange telephone companies on their agreement to provide independent vendors with the opportunity to market equipment and to resell network services on a bundled basis); Public Utility Commission of Texas v. FCC, 886 F.2d 1325, 281 U.S. App. D.C. 25 (D.C.Cir.1989) (preempting order of state utilities commission that prohibited a local exchange telephone company from interconnecting with an FCC-licensed microwave facility originating traffic in the franchise region of another local exchange telephone company); California v. FCC, 905 F.2d 1217 (9th Cir. 1990) (affirming FCC's Second Computer Inquiry Policies maintaining common carrier regulation of basic services but not regu-

lating enhanced services that add computer enhancements to basic transport capacity); MCI Telecommunications v. FCC, 750 F.2d 135, 242 U.S. App. D.C. 287 (D.C.Cir.1984) (affirming an FCC-prescribed formula that separated costs for telephone equipment used in both interstate and intrastate services, but invalidating a plan to phase out costs of embedded customer premises equipment).

2. The FCC might preempt state regulation of intrastate service when "it is not possible to separate the interstate and intrastate components of the asserted FCC regulation." Louisiana Public Service Commission v. FCC, 476 U.S. 355, 375 n. 4, 106 S.Ct. 1890, 1902, n. 4, 90 L.Ed.2d 369, 386 n. 4 (1986).

3. 47 U.S.C.A. § 152(b) (West Supp. 1997).

4. 476 U.S. 355, 106 S.Ct. 1890, 90 L.Ed.2d 369 (1986).

5. Amendment of Part 31, Uniform Sys. of Accounts for Class A and Class B Tel. Co., Mem. Op. and Order, 92 FCC 2d 864 (1983), *aff'd. sub nom.,* Virginia State Corp. Comm'n v. FCC, 737 F.2d 388 (4th Cir. 1984) *rev'd sub nom.* Louisiana Pub. Serv. Comm'n v. FCC, 476 U.S. 355, 106 S.Ct. 1890, 90 L.Ed.2d 369, (1986).

In reviewing the Commission's orders the Fifth Circuit applied the test established in *North Carolina Utilities Commission v. FCC*[6] and found that allowing states to set depreciation schedules different from the federal rate would "substantially affect" federal policy favoring a more competitive industry.[7] On certiorari, the Supreme Court reversed using a basic legislative analysis of the Communications Act to determine "whether Congress intended that federal regulation supersede state law."[8] The Court declined to "assess the wisdom of the asserted federal policy of encouraging competition within the telecommunications industry"[9] and whether inconsistent state policies would frustrate the Commission's initiative. Instead, it scrutinized Sections 151 and 152 of the Communications Act and determined that Section 152(b) explicitly "fences off from FCC reach or regulation intrastate matters ..., including matters 'in connection with' intrastate service."[10] While acknowledging "the realities of technology and economics belie ... a clean parceling of responsibility" between federal and state regulatory agencies,[11] the Court referenced Section 410(c) of the Communications Act that establishes a "jurisdictional separations" process by which the FCC and state regulators determine "what portion of an asset is employed to produce or deliver interstate as opposed to intrastate service."[12] With separate cost allocational mechanisms in place, the Court concluded that it was possible to distinguish between a matter involving jurisdiction over depreciation and instances "where it was not possible to separate the interstate and the intrastate components of the asserted FCC regulation."[13] The Court stated:

> [Section] 220 directs the FCC to prescribe the classes of property for which depreciation charges may be included under operating expenses, and prohibits carriers from departing from FCC-set regulations respecting depreciation. While it is, no doubt possible to find some support in the broad language of the section for ... [this] position, we do not find the meaning of the section so unambiguous or straightforward as to override the command of [Section] 152(b) that "nothing in this chapter shall be construed to apply or to give the [FCC] jurisdiction" over intrastate service.[14]

6. 537 F.2d 787 (4th Cir.1976), *cert. denied* 429 U.S. 1027, 97 S. Ct. 651, 50 L. Ed. 2d 631 (1976).

7. Virginia State Corp. Comm'n v. FCC, 737 F.2d 388, 392 (4th Cir.1984), *reversed sub nom.*, Louisiana Pub. Serv. Comm'n v. FCC, 476 U.S. 355, 106 S.Ct. 1890, 90 L.Ed.2d 369 (1986).

8. *Id.* at 369, 106 S. Ct. at 1899, 90 L. Ed.2d at 382.

9. *Id.* at 359, 106 S.Ct. at 1893, 90 L.Ed.2d at 376.

10. *Id.* at 370. 106 S.Ct. at 1899, 90 L.Ed.2d at 382–83. The Court read Section 152 of the Communications Act as establishing a substantive jurisdictional limita-

tion on the FCC's power and a rule of statutory construction. While Section 220 of the Communications Act authorizes the FCC to set depreciation rules, it does not allow the FCC to exceed the jurisdictional limits established in Section 152 of the Communications Act. *Id.* at 376–78, 106 S.Ct. at 1902–1904, 90 L.Ed.2d at 386–387.

11. *Id.* at 360, 106 S.Ct. at 1894, 90 L.Ed.2d at 376.

12. *Id.* at 375, 106 S.Ct. at 1902, 90 L.Ed.2d at 386.

13. *Id.* at 375, n.4, 106 S.Ct. at 1902, 90 L.Ed.2d at 386.

14. *Id.* at 377, 106 S.Ct. at 1903, 90 L. Ed. 2d at 387.

Put more bluntly, Section 152(b) "fences off from FCC reach or regulation intrastate matters—indeed, including matters 'in connection with' intrastate service."[15]

B. Section 221: Special Provisions Relating to Telephone Companies/Jurisdiction and Federal Preemption in Telecommunications

Cases supporting federal preemption by the FCC do so primarily on the practical grounds that the same telecommunications infrastructure supports both interstate and intrastate service. As interstate services typically "contaminate"[16] a line also providing intrastate service, federal policies may prevail if the FCC can supply convincing reasons for a single, uniform policy. For example, in *California v. FCC*,[17] the District of Columbia Circuit held the FCC could assert jurisdiction over interstate services provided by a long distance competitor of AT & T even though all facilities were physically situated in a single state and used to provide both interstate and intrastate service. Notwithstanding the facilities did provide some intrastate services, the fact that they also provided interstate services prevented the assertion of state jurisdiction where it was " 'technically and practically difficult' to separate the two types of communications."[18]

1. Specialized Mobile Radio

In *National Association of Regulatory Utility Commissioners v. FCC*,[19] the court upheld an FCC order on spectrum allocation for a new specialized mobile radio service to be provided by private operators free of common carrier regulations. The Court supported the Commission's option to designate the service as private carriage and agreed the Commission could preempt the states' regulation to ensure a uniform regulatory status. Allowing each individual state to make the decision between private and common carriage would have created an unworkable, "balkanization" of policy. Accordingly, the court rejected petitioners' assertion that Section 221(b) of the Communications Act, which denies FCC jurisdiction over telephone exchange service, bars federal

---

15. *Id.*

16. "The term 'contamination doctrine' has been used to describe the view that any private line that is used to transmit any interstate communications is jurisdictionally interstate." Petition of the New York Telephone Co. for a Declaratory Ruling with Respect to the Physically Intrastate Private Line and Special Access Channels Utilized for Sales Agents to Computer New York State Lottery Communications, Memorandum Opinion and Order, 5 FCC Rcd. 1080, 1083 (1990) (deeming access lines subject to intrastate jurisdiction even though a de minimis amount of traffic, *i.e.*, less than 10% was interstate in nature).

17. 905 F.2d 1217 (9th Cir.1990), cert. denied 434 U.S. 1010, 98 S.Ct. 721, 54 L.Ed.2d 753 (1978).

18. *Id.* (quoting AT & T and Associated Bell Syst, Cos. Interconnection with Specialized Carriers, Mem. Opinion & Order 56 FCC2d 14, 19 (1975)). Likewise in 1982, the D.C. Circuit affirmed the FCC's preemption of the states on the issue of customer premises equipment and regulatory blueprint for basic and enhanced services. Computer and Communications Indus. Ass'n v. FCC, 693 F.2d 198, 224 U.S. App. D.C. 83 (D.C.Cir. 1982), cert. denied 461 U.S. 938, 103 S.Ct. 2109, 77 L.Ed.2d 313 (1983).

19. 525 F.2d 630, 173 U.S. App. D.C. 413 (D.C.Cir.1976).

preemption of state regulation affecting specialized mobile radio carriers.[20]

2. Commercial mobile radio service

Section 6002(b) of the Omnibus Budget Reconciliation Act of 1993 ("Budget Act")[21] amended Section 332 of the Communications Act of 1934 ("Communications Act") by creating two categories of mobile services, each subject to a uniform regulatory framework. The legislation replaced common carrier and private land mobile service definitions for mobile radio operators, created in amendments to the Communications Act enacted in 1982,[22] with two new classifications: commercial mobile radio service ("CMRS") and private mobile radio service ("PMRS"). The 1993 legislation defined CMRS as "any mobile service (as defined in section 3(n)) that is provided for profit and makes interconnected service available (A) to the public or (B) to such classes of eligible users as to be effectively available to a substantial portion of the public."[23] PMRS is defined as "any mobile service (as defined in section 3(n)) that is not a commercial mobile service or the functional equivalent of a commercial mobile service."[24]

By creating a CMRS/PMRS dichotomy Congress made it easier for the FCC to establish a single regulatory framework for all profit-seeking mobile radio ventures like cellular radio telephone service and a different regulatory system for private ventures. The old common carrier/private carrier model proved unworkable, particularly since the FCC had permitted private land mobile service operators to "patch" into the public switched telephone network[25] and thereby provide the kind of services

---

20. *Id.* at 646, 173 U.S. App. D.C. at 429.

21. Omnibus Budget Reconciliation Act of 1993, Pub. L. No. 103–66, Title VI, § 6002(b)(2)(A), 6002(b)(2)(B), 107 Stat. 312, 392 (1993).

22. In 1982, Congress amended the Communications Act by adding Section 3(gg) and Section 332(c). The purposes of adding these provisions were: (1) to define private land mobile service; (2) to distinguish between private and common carrier land mobile services; and (3) to specify the appropriate authorities empowered to regulate these same services. *See* H.R. Rep. No. 97–765, 97th Cong., 2d Sess., at 54 (1982). Section 3(gg) defined private land mobile service as "a mobile service ... for private one-way or two-way land mobile radio communications by eligible users over designated areas of operation." Communications Act of 1934, as amended, § 3(gg), 47 U.S.C.A. § 153(gg) (West 1991), stricken and replaced with new definitions in Budget Act, § 6002(b)(2)(B)(ii)(II). Section 332(c)(3) preempted state authority to im-

pose rate or entry regulation upon any private land mobile service. *See also* Telocator Network of America v. FCC, 761 F.2d 763, 245 U.S. App. D.C. 360 (D.C.Cir.1985) (upholding FCC's interpretation of Sec. 332(c)(1), 47 U.S.C.A. § 332(c)(1) regarding preemption of state regulation).

23. *Id.* § 332(d)(1), 47 U.S.C.A. § 332(d)(1) (West 1991).

24. *Id.* § 332(d)(2), 47 U.S.C.A. § 332(d)(2) (West 1991).

25. "Under current law, private carriers are permitted to offer what are essentially common carrier services, interconnected with the public switched telephone network, while retaining private carrier status." United States Congress, Omnibus Budget Reconciliation Act of 1993, Report of the Committee on the Budget, H.R. Rep. No. 111, 259–260, 103d Cong. 1st Sess. (1993)[hereinafter cited as Committee Report]. *See also* United State Congress, Omnibus Budget Reconciliation Act of 1993, H.R. Conf. Rep. No. 213, 103d Cong., 1st Sess. (1993).

previously available only from common carriers.[26]

The 1993 legislation accorded the FCC flexibility to establish appropriate levels of regulation for mobile radio services providers. Section 332(c) required the FCC to treat CMRS operators as common carriers but granted the Commission authority to forbear from applying the common carrier regulatory provisions contained in Title II of the Communications Act, except for Sections 201(just and reasonable charges for service); 202 (no unjust or unreasonable discrimination); and 208 (resolution of complaints filed with the FCC).

The statute also authorized the FCC to preempt state regulation of entry and rates for both CMRS and PMRS providers but permitted the states to regulate "other terms and conditions" of CMRS.[27] The legislative history provides an "illustrative" list of what constitutes "other terms and conditions":

> By "terms and conditions", the Committee intends to include such matters as customer billing information and practices and billing disputes and other consumer protection matters; facilities siting issues (e.g., zoning); transfers of control; the bundling of services and equipment; and the requirement that carriers make capacity available on a wholesale basis or such other matters as fall within a state's lawful authority.[28]

In contrast to language favoring federal preemption, Congress permitted the grandfathering of any rate regulation concerning CMRS in effect as of June 1, 1993, provided the rate regulatory authority petitioned the FCC by August 9, 1994 and demonstrated that either: (1) "market conditions with respect to such services fail to protect subscribers adequately from unjust and unreasonable rates or rates that are unjustly or unreasonably discriminatory;" or (2) "such market conditions exist and such service is a replacement for land line telephone exchange service for a substantial portion of the telephone land line exchange service within such State." [29]

The FCC interpreted the language in amended Section 332 of the Communications Act to be a strong endorsement of its federal authority because "Congress has explicitly amended the Communications Act to preempt state and local rate and entry regulation of commercial mobile radio services without regard to Section 2(b)" which reserves to the states regulatory authority over intrastate telecommunications.[30] In view of the Congressional desire for a uniform regulatory framework and explicit preemptive authority, the FCC "vigorously implemented the

---

26. "Functionally, these 'private' carriers have become indistinguishable from common carriers but private land mobile carriers and common carriers are subject to inconsistent regulatory schemes." Committee Report at 260.

27. *See* 47 U.S.C.A. § 332(c)(3)(A) (West Supp. 1997).

28. Committee Report at 261.

29. *See* 47 U.S.C.A. § 332(c)(3)(A) (West Supp. 1997).

30. Implementation of Sections 3(n) and 332 of the Communications Act, Regulatory Treatment of Mobile Service, GEN. Docket No. 93–252, Second Report and Order, 9 FCC Rcd. 1411, 1463–1493 ¶ 5 (1994).

preemption provisions of the Budget Act to ensure that state rate regulation of CMRS providers will be established only in the case of demonstrated market conditions in which competitive forces are not adequately protecting the interests of CMRS subscribers."[31]

The FCC imposed a substantial evidentiary threshold when considering petitions by states to maintain rate regulation:

> [W]e conclude that a state must do more than merely show that market conditions for cellular service have been less than fully competitive in the past. In order to retain regulatory authority, a state must show that, given the rapidly evolving market structure in which mobile services are provided, the conduct and performance of CMRS providers ill-serve consumer interests by producing rates that are not just and reasonable, or are unreasonably discriminatory.[32] The Commission rejected petitions from several state petitions seeking to continue rate regulation of all or some types, *e.g.*, wholesale cellular service rates. [33]

3. *Customer Premises Equipment*

Many states did not support the FCC's decision in the late 1960s and early 1970s to separate telephone company delivery of telecommunication services from the leasing of telephones and other customer premises equipment (CPE).[34] The FCC sought to separate the provision of CPE, which it assumed could support a competitive marketplace, from the provision of telephone service, which it assumed would continue to be subject to joint federal and state regulation.[35] In *North Carolina Utilities Commission* v. *FCC* (NCUC–I),[36] the Fourth Circuit Court of Appeals affirmed an FCC order that preempted inconsistent state regulation of CPE used for both intrastate and interstate communications. In rejecting the petitioner's argument that Section 221 prohibited federal jurisdiction, the court stated that "this restriction is intended to do no more than to prevent the circumstance that a single telephone exchange serves an area that includes parts of more than one state [e.g., the metropolitan Washington D.C. region] from enlarging the jurisdiction of ... [the] FCC over the business and facilities of that exchange."[37] Accordingly, Section 221(b) simply assures a local carrier, which operates

---

31. *Id.* at ¶ 16.

32. Petition of the State of Ohio for Authority to Continue to Regulate Commercial Mobile Radio Services, PR Docket No. 94–104, Report and Order, 10 FCC Rcd. 7842, 7843 ¶ 6, (1995) (denying petition to continue rate regulation).

33. *See, e.g.*, Petition of the People of the State of California and the Public Utilities Commission of the State of California to Retain Regulatory Authority over Intrastate Cellular Service Rates, PR Docket No. 94–105, Report and Order, 10 FCC Rcd. 7486 (1995)(petition denied), *recons. den.*, 10 FCC Rcd. 12427 (1995); Petition of New York State Public Utility Commission to Extend Rate Regulation, Report and Order, PR Docket No. 94–108, 10 FCC Rcd. 8187 (1995)(petition denied).

34. *Cf.* Use of the Carterfone Device in Message Toll Tel. Serv., Decision, 13 FCC2d 420 (1968).

35. Telerent Leasing Corp., 45 FCC 2d 204 (1974), *aff'd sub nom.*, North Carolina Utilities Comm'n v. FCC, 537 F.2d 787 (4th Cir.), *cert. denied* 429 U.S. 1027, 97 S.Ct. 651, 50 L. Ed. 2d 631 (1976).

36. 537 F.2d 787 (4th Cir.1976).

37. *Id.* at 795.

in a multi-state region, the same insulation from federal regulation provided by Section 2(b) of the Communications Act, *i.e.*, reserving to the states jurisdiction over intrastate communications.

The *North Carolina Utilities Commission cases*[38] affirm the FCC's primary authority over CPE used for both intrastate and interstate communication. The court reiterated that the purpose of Section 221(b) is "to enable state commissions to regulate local exchange service in metropolitan areas … which extend across state boundaries" and does not apply to CPE.[39] The court concluded the FCC's assertion of jurisdiction over CPE matters did not jeopardize state regulatory powers to subsidize rates for particular offerings, such as local exchange services.[40]

Section 152(b) proscribes federal jurisdiction only as to local matters "that in their nature and effect are separable from and do not substantially affect the conduct or development of interstate communications."[41] This section limits FCC regulatory authority only regarding "local services, facilities and disputes that in their nature and effect are separable from and do not substantially affect the conduct or development of interstate communications."[42] In a related case, the court reached the same conclusion as to the scope of Section 221(b).[43]

The Court of Appeals for the District of Columbia Circuit has also affirmed a sweeping assertion of FCC jurisdiction over customer premises equipment and enhanced services that add information processing functions to basic telecommunications transport capacity.[44] The court in *Computer and Communications Industry Association v. FCC* affirmed the Commission's ancillary jurisdiction[45] over CPE on grounds that such equipment cannot be separated into intrastate and interstate facilities under Section 152(b).

---

38. *See* North Carolina Utilities Comm'n v. FCC, 537 F.2d 787 (4th Cir.), cert. denied 429 U.S. 1027, 97 S.Ct. 651, 50 L.Ed.2d 631(1976); North Carolina Utilities Comm'n v. FCC 552 F.2d 1036 (4th Cir. 1977) cert. denied 434 U.S. 874, 98 S.Ct. 222, 54 L.Ed.2d 154 (1977).

39. North Carolina Utilities Comm'n, 552 F.2d at 1045.

40. *Id.* at 1048.

41. *See* Telerent Leasing Corp., Mem. Op. and Order, 45 FCC2d 204 (1974) *aff'd sub nom.*, North Carolina Util. Comm'n v. FCC, 537 F.2d 787, 793 (4th Cir.), cert. denied 429 U.S. 1027, 97 S.Ct. 651, 50 L.Ed.2d 631(1976).

42. *Id.* at 793.

43. North Carolina Util. Comm'n v. FCC, 552 F.2d 1036 (4th Cir.), *cert. denied*, 434 U.S. 874, 98 S.Ct. 222, 54 L.Ed.2d 154 (1977).

44. Computer and Communications Indus. Ass'n. v. FCC, 693 F.2d 198, 224 U. S. App. D. C. 83 (D.C.Cir.1982), cert. denied 461 U.S. 938, 103 S. Ct. 2109, 77 L. Ed. 2d 313 (1983).

45. Ancillary jurisdiction allows the FCC to extend oversight from one medium or regulatory category, which the FCC has direct legislative authority, *e.g.*, broadcasting under Title II of the Communications Act and common carriage under Title II of the Communications Act, to another medium or area that the Commission has a less defined regulatory role or one not specified by law, *e.g.*, cable television. *See* United States v. Southwestern Cable Co., 392 U.S. 157, 88 S.Ct. 1994, 20 L.Ed.2d 1001 (1968) (affirming FCC jurisdiction over cable television as ancillary to its regulation of broadcasting).

Louisiana PSC provides a boundary line beyond which FCC asser-tions of jurisdiction cannot go.[46] Section 151 of the Communications Act grants expansive powers to the FCC.[47] But Section 152(b) specifies that the Commission cannot assert jurisdiction regarding "charges, classifica-tions, practices, services, facilities, or regulations for or in connection with intrastate communication.... "[48] The juxtaposition of Sections 151 and 152(b) presents the prospect of conflict between the states and the FCC over the permissible scope of federal preemption.[49]

4. Post-Louisiana PSC Cases Favoring State Jurisdiction

a. Use of FM Radio Sub-Carriers

A number of cases decided after *Louisiana PSC* bolster that deci-sion. In *California v. FCC* ("FM Subcarrier"),[50] the District of Columbia Circuit reversed the FCC's preemption of state regulation regarding rules on market entry by radio common carriers operating on FM radio subcarriers. The FCC preempted the states on grounds that Section 301 of the Communications Act, which establishes the FCC's broadcast regulatory authority, superseded the states' authority to regulate intra-state radio common carrier service. While courts once favored the view that interstate service and lawful FCC jurisdiction would contaminate and thereby preclude state jurisdiction, they now seem inclined to favor parallel and possible conflicting regulatory policies based on the sever-ability of the equipment or service or on the severability of the subject for state or federal regulation. The court in FM Subcarrier held that the FCC had no power to preempt state regulation of clearly in-state service because to do so "would reduce section 152(b) to a nullity, violating the congressional intent to establish a system of dual regulatory con-trol.... "[51] The court's holding rejected the view that FCC preemption should proceed simply because inconsistent state policies would frustrate a uniform, FCC-driven policy.[52]

46. For more extensive analysis of *Loui-siana PSC* and federal preemption in tele-communications *see* Richard R. McKenna, *Preemption Under the Communications Act*, 37 Fed. Com. L. J. 1 (1985); Richard R. McKenna, *Preemption Reversed: The Su-preme Court's Decision in Louisiana Public Service Commission v. FCC*, 39 Admin. L. Rev. 43 (1987); Rita M. Cain, *Constitutional Struggle Over Telecommunications Regula-tion*, 10 Comm/Ent L. J. 1 (1987); John Haring & Kathleen Levitz, *The Law and Economics of Federalism in Telecommuni-cations*, 41 Fed. Comm. L. J. 261 (1989). A comprehensive analysis of FCC preemption post-Louisiana PSC is provided by Michael J. Zpevak, *FCC Preemption After Louisiana PSC*, 45 Fed. Com. L. J. 185 (1993).

47. Congress created the FCC "[f]or the purpose of regulating interstate and foreign commerce in communication by wire and radio so as to make available, so far as possible, to all the people of the United States ... a rapid, efficient, nationwide and worldwide wire and radio communication service." 47 U.S.C.A. § 151 (West 1991 and Supp. 1997).

48. *Id.* § 152(b).

49. "For many years the regulatory phi-losophy of state regulators and the FCC was consistent, and the issue of jurisdiction rarely arose. However, as the FCC began to promote policies of competitiveness and de-regulation, this regulatory harmony unrav-eled and the states and the FCC have been involved in a turf battle ever since." Ann E. Rendahl, *California v. FCC: A Victory for the States*, 13 Comm/Ent. L. J. 233, 248 (1991).

50. 693 F.2d 198, 224 U.S. App. D.C. 83 (D.C.Cir.1982).

51. *Id.* at 1519, 255 U.S. App. D.C. at 88.

52. *Id.*

b. The Computer Inquiries

In *California v. FCC*,[53] the Ninth Circuit reversed three FCC orders that preempted state regulation of intrastate and local enhanced services, including carrier tariff filings and requirements that conflicted with the Commission's plan for nonstructural separation between carrier-provided basic and enhanced services. The court held the FCC acted arbitrarily and capriciously by adopting non-structural safeguards in the Third Computer Inquiry to replace the separate subsidiary requirements of the Second Computer Inquiry.[54] The court also held the clear language of the Communications Act forecloses federal preemption of state regulation affecting intrastate enhanced services.[55] The court applied the *NARUC-III* view that Section 152(b) could apply to intrastate non-common carrier service, including inside wiring and enhanced services provided "in connection with intrastate communication service by wire or radio of any carrier."[56] The court also considered rare instances where the FCC and states could not segregate interstate and intrastate services for purposes of dividing regulatory authority. The court considered an inseverability exception to Section 152(b) to be "limited."[57] On remand, the FCC preempted again, albeit on narrower grounds.[58]

c. Preemption of Local Regulation of Satellite Earth Stations

On the matter of FCC preemption of satellite earth station zoning by states and municipalities, the Telecommunications Act of 1996 removes some of the doubt as to whose policy predominates. Section 207 of the Act directs the Commission to promulgate regulations "to prohibit restrictions that impair a viewer's ability to receive video programming services through devices designed for over-the-air reception of television broadcast signals multichannel, multipoint distribution service, or direct broadcast satellite services."[59] Prior to the enactment of the Telecommunications Act of 1996, the FCC adopted a Notice of Proposed Rulemaking[60] that reiterated the claim of federal preemption but proposed to review local disputes over the installation of satellite dishes only after

---

53. 905 F.2d 1217 (9th Cir.1990), *vacated in part after remand to the FCC*, 39 F.3d 919 (9th Cir.1994), cert. denied 514 U.S. 1050, 115 S. Ct. 1427, 131 L.Ed.2d 309 (1995).

54. *Id.* at 1246.

55. *Id.* at 1240, 1242–45.

56. *Id.* at 1239.

57. *Id.* at 1243 (quoting Nat'l Assn. of Reg. Util. Comm'rs, 880 F.2d at 430, 279 U.S. App. D.C. at 1107: "a valid FCC preemption order must be limited to [state regulation] that would necessarily thwart or impede' the FCC's goals. . . . ").

58. Bell Operating Co. Safeguards and Tier I Local Exchange Co. Safeguards, Report and Order, 6 FCC Rcd. 7571, 7625 (1991); Computer III Remand Proceedings, Notice of Proposed Rulemaking, 5 FCC Rcd. 5242 (1990); Computer III Remand Proceedings, Report & Order, 5 FCC Rcd. 7719 (1990).

59. Telecommunications Act of 1996, Pub. L. 104–104, § 207, 110 Stat. 56, *codified at* 47 U.S.C.A. § 151 et seq. (West Supp.1997). Restrictions on Over-the-Air Reception Devices; *see also* Preemption of Local Zoning Regulation of Satellite Earth Stations, IB Docket No. 95–59, Report and Order and Further Notice of Proposed Rulemaking, FCC 96–78, 11 FCC Rcd. 5809 (1996); Report and Order, Mem. Op. and Order and Further Notice of Proposed Rulemaking, 11 FCC Rcd. 19276 (1996).

60. Preemption of Local Zoning Regulation of Satellite Earth Stations, 10 F.C.C. Rcd. 6982 (1995).

the parties have exhausted non-federal administrative remedies but not all non-federal legal remedies. The Commission proposed new standards to determine the reasonableness of non-federal regulations and proposed procedures by which state and local governments authorities can request a waiver of the rule in cases where unusual circumstances are demonstrated.

Prior to enactment of the Telecommunications Act of 1996, the FCC adopted a rule preempting local regulation that differentiated between satellite receive-only earth stations, the kind of relatively small and unobtrusive devices used for direct-to-home reception of video programming, and other types of antenna facilities, absent a reasonable and clearly defined health, safety or aesthetic objective that does not impose unreasonable user costs and limitations on antenna usage.[61] Without invalidating the FCC's assertion of jurisdiction an appellate court did reject the Commission's requirement that satellite-antenna users exhaust all other legal remedies before petitioning the FCC for a declaratory ruling on the validity of a local zoning ordinance.[62]

The FCC continues to face a quandary in establishing the proper balance between acting on its interest in promoting access to satellite services and respecting local zoning regulation:

> On the one hand, we are responsible for promoting the federal interest in nationwide communications systems, including access to satellite-delivered communications where appropriate. In pursuit of this federal interest, we have stated many times the strong federal interest in ensuring that users have reasonable access to satellite signals. Such is our mandate from Congress, and when nonfederal regulation "stands as an obstacle to the accomplishment of a congressional purpose," such regulation is subject to preemption. On the other hand, we must, to the maximum extent possible, respect principles of federalism. Those principles are particularly weighty in this case because the nonfederal regulations in question are not overt attempts to assert control over interstate communications; they are local land-use restrictions that lie at the core of state and local police powers.[63]

61. Preemption of Local Zoning Regulations of Receive–Only Satellite Earth Stations, Report and Order, 51 Fed. Reg. 5519 (Feb. 14, 1986), *codified at* 47 C.F.R. § 25.104 (1996). The Commission relied on the broad mandate of Section 1 of the Communications Act, 47 U.S.C.A. § 151 "to make communications services available to all people of the United States," the numerous powers granted by Title III of the Act regarding establishment of a unified communications system and the recently added 47 U.S.C.A. § 705 that creates certain rights to receive unscrambled and unmarketed satellite signals. The Commission articulated its federal interest in preventing dis-

criminatory local regulation that reduces the range of consumer choices. *Id.* at ¶ 26.

62. Town of Deerfield, New York v. FCC, 992 F.2d 420 (2d Cir.1993).

63. Preemption of Local Zoning Regulations (notice at 41, citing Capital Cities Cable, Inc. v. Crisp, 467 U.S. 691, 699, 104 S.Ct. 2694, 81 L.Ed.2d 580 (1984) (quoting Hines v. Davidowitz, 312 U.S. 52, 61 S.Ct. 399, 85 L.Ed. 581 (1941)); Michigan Canners and Freezers Ass'n, Inc. v. Agricultural Marketing and Bargaining Bd., 467 U.S. 461, 104 S.Ct. 2518, 81 L.Ed.2d 399 (1984)); Florida Lime & Avocado Growers, Inc. v. Paul, 373 U.S. 132, 83 S.Ct. 1210, 10 L.Ed.2d 248 (1963).

The FCC stated that it did "not intend to operate as a national zoning board ...[but will] expect that local authorities will conform their regulations to our standards and that they will make determinations which are in the best interests of their communities that reflect federal policy."[64]

5. Post–Louisiana PSC Cases Favoring Federal Preemption

In *Hawaiian Telephone Co.* v. *Hawaii Public Utilities Commission*[65] the FCC's jurisdictional separations system came up for a post *Louisiana PSC* review. The cost allocational process between interstate and intrastate jurisdictions has been scrutinized by courts previously[66] and is recognized as a joint federal-state undertaking by Section 410(c) of the Communications Act. This section authorizes the creation of a Joint Board, comprised of three FCC Commissioners and four commissioners of state regulatory commissions appointed by the National Association of Regulatory Utility Commissioners, for joint decision-making on matters of mutual interest and possibly shared jurisdiction such as allocation of costs incurred by telephone companies in providing service.

When the Hawaii Public Utilities Commission ("HPUC") implemented a new cost allocation system requiring increases in intrastate rates, the Hawaiian Telephone Company objected to the Joint Board's defined system and to the refusal of the HPUC to authorize the total amount of rate increases sought by the company. The Ninth Circuit held that HPUC was preempted from applying a separations procedure for determining intrastate rates because the state process was inconsistent with what the FCC had adopted for interstate services.[67] While the court could have reached its decision by referring to Section 410(c) of the Communications Act, the court concentrated on *Louisiana PSC* in determining the states could be preempted, even as to intrastate rate making matters, when a uniform federal-state formula has been created.[68]

In *National Association of Regulatory Utility Commissioners* v. *FCC* (*NARUC-III*),[69] the FCC received a somewhat revived judicial view that its broad mandate under Section 151 of the Communications Act could encompass federal preemption. The court granted a conditional endorsement of federal preemption over state regulation of depreciation schedules for inside wiring, namely, the wiring inside businesses and residences to connect one or more phones with outside wiring and plant owned and maintained by the telephone company. The court required the FCC to show with some specificity that such regulation would negate

---

64. *Id.* at 39.

65. 827 F.2d 1264 (9th Cir.1987), cert. denied 487 U.S. 1218, 108 S.Ct. 2870, 101 L.Ed.2d 906 (1988).

66. *See, e.g.*, MCI Telecommunications v. FCC, 750 F.2d 135, 242 U.S. App. D.C. 287 (D.C.Cir.1984) (affirming an FCC prescribed formula that separated costs for telephone equipment used in both interstate and intrastate services, but invalidat-

ing its plan to phase out costs embedded customer premises equipment).

67. Hawaiian Telephone Co. v. Hawaii Public Util. Comm'n., 827 F.2d 1264, 1276 (9th Cir.1987).

68. *Id.*

69. 880 F.2d 422, 279 U.S. App. D.C. 99 (D.C.Cir.1989).

the Commission's policy [70]of deregulating the installation and maintenance of inside wiring and separating competitively provided wiring installation services from the common carrier provision of telephone service.[71] The Commission reasoned that having "unbundled" inside wiring from common carrier telephone service, Section 152(b) should no longer apply.

The District of Columbia Circuit rejected this view and recognized the applicability of Section 152(b). Following the *Louisiana PSC* rationale, the court held that inside wiring constitutes a facility or service offered "for or in connection with" a common carrier communication service, meaning that it connects CPE with lines used for either intrastate or intrastate service.[72] The court also rejected the Commission's view that inside wiring could not be divided into an interstate and interstate components on grounds that, pursuant to FCC orders, it no longer fell within the cost allocation and revenue division process administered by a joint board comprised of FCC and state public utility commissioners under Section 410(c) of the Communications Act. The court also refused to allow the FCC to make unilateral decisions on the severability of services and equipment on jurisdictional grounds, because this would lead to "unchecked authority [by the FCC] to force state deregulation of any activity [the FCC] chose to deregulate at the interstate level."[73]

Nevertheless the court held that as to inside wiring policies, separation of dual jurisdiction property constituted a "practical and economic impossibility."[74] The court concluded that the Commission, pursuant to its broad mandate under Section 151, still had authority to assert ancillary jurisdiction over inside wiring policies, particularly ones inconsistent with its stated deregulatory mission.[75] Additionally, the court expressed concerns about policy balkanization. "[T]he FCC may preempt inconsistent state regulation so long as it can show that the state regulation negates a valid federal policy."[76]

Rather than decide broadly that the Commission had the right to preempt the states, the court ruled more narrowly that the FCC could not preempt all possible state regulation. It remanded to the Commission

---

70. *Id.* at 430, 279 U.S. App. D.C. at 107

71. Detariffing the Installation and Maintenance of Inside Wiring, CC Docket No. 79–105, Third Report & Order., 7 FCC Rcd. 1334 (1992) (preempting state regulation that requires or allows telephone companies to bundle charges for simple inside wiring services with charges for tariffed services, but monitoring and not preempting state regulation of telephone company pricing of inside wiring services). *See also* Detariffing the Installation and Maintenance of Inside Wiring, Second Further Notice of Proposed Rule Making, 5 FCC Rcd 3407 (1990), *partially reversed and remanded sub*

nom, National Association of Regulatory Utility Commissioners v. FCC, 880 F.2d 422, 279 U.S. App. D.C. 99 (D.C.Cir.1989).

72. *Id.* 880 F.2d at 428, 279 U.S. App. D.C. at 105.

73. *Id.* at 429, 279 U.S. App. D.C. at 106.

74. *Id.*

75. *Id.* at 429–430, 279 U.S. App. D.C. at 106–107.

76. *Id.* at 431, 279 U.S. App. D.C. at 108.

the task of more narrowly articulating the scope of its preemption to that which might be "thwarted" by inconsistent state regulation.[77]

In *Illinois Bell Telephone Co.* v. *FCC*,[78] the District of Columbia Court of Appeals affirmed FCC preemption of state regulation to prevent inconsistent policies that would frustrate the use of non-structural safeguards replacing requirements that the Bell Operating Companies and AT & T form separate subsidiaries to market Customer Premises Equipment and enhanced services. While allowing the carriers to integrate telephone service with marketing of CPE, the FCC required the BOCs to enter into sales agency agreements with unaffiliated CPE vendors and to afford them an equal opportunity to vie with BOC affiliates for CPE sale commissions. The FCC believed sales agency contracts would provide non-structural safeguards ensuring that the BOCs would not favor their CPE marketing affiliates or engage in cross-subsidization by shifting the cost of CPE commissions to regulated services. Thus the Commission preempted the states from adopting different arrangements such as reinstating a separate subsidiary requirement.

The court upheld FCC preemption on grounds that no regulatory agency could separate equipment functions or regulatory responsibilities between interstate and intrastate jurisdictions: "[F]ederal regulation of the entire subject matter (which may include preemption of state regulation) ... [will pass muster with a reviewing court] if necessary to fulfill a valid federal regulatory objective."[79] The court reasoned that "strict separation of state and federal regulatory spheres ... would require construction of wholly independent intrastate and interstate networks and facilities."[80]

In *Public Utility Commission of Texas* v. *FCC*,[81] the District of Columbia Circuit affirmed FCC preemption of state regulation that would have denied customers the right to choose which local exchange carrier would handle traffic originating or terminating on the customers' private microwave network. In this case Atlantic Richfield decided to disconnect its private microwave network from the local exchange facilities of GTE Southwest, the carrier certified by the Texas Public Utility Commission to provide service in the area, and to reconnect them with nearby Southwestern Bell. The court rejected the Texas PUC's argument that the exercise of federal preemption would result in federal jurisdiction over a local matter, namely the determination of local exchange service territories. Federal preemption was permissible in this case not because the lines in question provided access to both interstate and intrastate service, but because the FCC could not separate its regulation into interstate and intrastate components.[82]

77. *Id.* at 430, 279 U.S. App. D.C. at 107.

78. 883 F.2d 104, 280 U.S. App. D.C. 32 (D.C.Cir.1989).

79. *Id.* at 115, 280 U.S. App. D.C. at 43.

80. *Id.* at 116, 280 U.S. App. D.C. at 44.

81. 886 F.2d 1325, 281 U.S. App. D.C. 25 (D.C.Cir.1989).

82. *Id.* at 1334, 281 U.S. App. D.C. at 34; *accord* Maryland Pub. Serv. Comm'n v. FCC, 909 F.2d 1510, 285 U.S. App. D.C. 329 (D.C.Cir.1990) (federal preemption will not

Overall, telecommunications preemption involves a three step assessment: (1) a court first will determine whether the issue involves mixed federal and state jurisdiction. If a court determines that the matter is purely intrastate, federal preemption cannot occur; (2) if the matter is found to be jurisdictionally mixed, a court will assess whether both state and federal jurisdiction can coexist through some segregation that will not frustrate federal policies or result in state regulation of interstate communications; and (3) if a court determines inseverability of jurisdictions, it will uphold preemption of state regulation if such regulation otherwise would negate a valid federal regulatory goal.[83] This three-step process continues to generate uncertainty and fails to provide a simple template for resolving jurisdictional disputes between state regulatory agencies and the FCC.

12.5   The Telecommunications Act of 1996 and the Concept of Common Carriage

Enactment of the Telecommunications Act of 1996 has created substantial upheaval in the telecommunications landscape. It changes the rights and responsibilities of common carriers, creating broad deregulatory opportunities but providing greater specificity of the duties common carriers must assume. The Telecommunications Act creates a presumption that telecommunications carriers will operate as common carriers.[1] However, it authorizes the FCC to abandon regulatory requirements that heretofore have defined what it means to be a common carrier if doing so would serve the public interest.[2]

Soon after the Telecommunications Act became law the FCC proposed to eliminate the tariff filing requirement of non-dominant interexchange carriers,[3] something the Commission had unsuccessfully attempted prior to enactment of the statute.[4] The FCC also proposed to eliminate the requirement that carriers seek approval from the Commission before expanding phone services to consumers within any new geo-

---

be denied on unsupported grounds that there might be a way to sever interstate and intrastate traffic).

83. *See* Michael J. Zpevak, *FCC Preemption After Louisiana PSC*, 45 Fed. Comm. L. J. 185, 206 (1993).

1. "A telecommunications carrier shall be treated as a common carrier under this Act only to the extent that it is engaged in providing telecommunications services...." Telecommunications Act of 1996, P.L. 104–104, § 3(44), 110 Stat. 56, *codified at* 47 U.S.C.A. § 153(44)(West Supp. 1997).

2. The Act authorizes the FCC to forbear from enforcing any regulation or provision of the Act if the Commission determines that such enforcement is unnecessary to guard against discrimination, to ensure just and reasonable services, to

safeguard consumers and serve the public interest. *Id.* Title IV—Regulatory Reform, Sec. 401(a)(1)-(3), *codified at* 47 U.S.C.A. § 160 (a) (1)-(3) (West Supp. 1997).

3. *See* Policy and Rules Concerning the Interstate Interexchange Marketplace Implementation of Sec. 254(g) of the Communications Act of 1934, as amended, CC Docket No, 96–61, Report and Order, 11 FCC Rcd. 9564 (1996).

4. On two separate occasions an appellate court has ruled that the FCC could not accord non-dominant carriers the option of refraining from filing tariffs. *See* AT & T v. FCC, 978 F.2d 727 (D.C.Cir.1992)(voluntary detariffing); MCI Telecommunications Corp. v. FCC, 765 F.2d 1186, 247 U.S.App. D.C. 32 (D.C.Cir.1985), *aff'd sub nom.* MCI Telecom. Corp. v. Am. Tel. & Tel. Co., 512 U.S. 218, 114 S.Ct. 2223, 129 L.Ed.2d 182 (1994)(mandatory detariffing).

graphic area that they are otherwise eligible to serve.[5] On the other hand, the Telecommunications Act of 1996 specifies common carrier requirements. The legislation imposes greater and more specific duties, particularly on incumbent local exchange carriers ("LECs"), with an eye toward promoting full and fair competition.

The Telecommunications Act of 1996 overhauls the Communications Act of 1934 and provides a foundation for facilities-based competition in every sector of the industry. The Act contemplates a "network of networks" with each operator interconnected and competing with all others. The Telecommunications Act provides greater specificity of what obligations a telecommunications carrier has toward other carriers, particularly LECs, and the terms and conditions for interconnection and access to another carrier's facilities. To implement its new policies, the Congress directed the FCC to initiate dozens of rulemakings, many on an expedited basis even as stakeholders pursued litigation to stay or overturn completed aspects of the overall package of implementing dockets.[6] At the time of this writing the FCC had not yet completed all implementation proceedings, particularly in light of appeals and requests for stays that slowed the process. However, even now one can understand how telecommunications common carriage is affected by the legislation and the FCC's regulatory implementation.

The Telecommunications Act and FCC's implementation strive to stimulate more resale and facilities-based competition while at the same time fostering a level competitive field among incumbents and market entrants and promoting a more robust concept of what constitutes universal service in telecommunications. The Telecommunications Act can be characterized as removing previous legislative and judicially imposed barriers to market entry. For example, the Act eliminates cross-ownership restrictions on telephone company provision of cable television service and vice versa. Likewise, the Act eliminates the remaining lines of business restrictions imposed on the Regional Bell Operating Companies ("RBOCs") by the Modification of Final Judgment,[7] *i.e.*,

---

5. Elimination of Section 214 Applications for Extension of Lines, CC Docket No. 97–11, Notice of Proposed Rulemaking, 12 FCC Rcd. 1111 (1997). The Commission also proposed to forbear from applying any remaining Section 214 authority to carriers who may be subject to price-cap regulation, average schedule carriers, and domestic, non-dominant carriers offering local or long-distance services.

6. *See* Implementation of the Local Competition Provisions in the Telecommunications Act of 1996, CC Docket No. 96–98, First Report and Order, 11 FCC Rcd. 15499, 15612 (1996) (Local Competition Order), Order on Recons., CC Docket No. 96–98, 11 FCC Rcd. 13042 (1996), *petition for review pending and partial stay granted, sub nom.* Iowa Utilities Board v. FCC, No. 96–3321 and consolidated cases (8th Cir., Oct. 15,

1996), *partial stay lifted in part*, Iowa Utilities Board v. FCC, No. 96–3321 and consolidated cases, 109 F.3d 418 (8th Cir.1996). Implementation of the Local Competition Provisions in the 1996 Telecommunications Act, CC Docket No. 96–98, Second Report and Order, and Mem. Op. and Order, FCC 96–333, 11 FCC Rcd. 19392 (rel. Aug. 8, 1996) (Second Interconnection Order); *partially rev'd and remanded sub nom.* Iowa Utilities Bd. v. FCC, 120 F.3d 753 (8th Cir.1997), State of California v. FCC, No. 96–3519 (8th Cir. Sept.23, 1996), SBC Communications Inc. v. FCC, No. 96–1414 (D.C. Cir. Nov. 1, 1996).

7. United States v. AT&T, Western Elec. Co., 552 F.Supp. 131 (D.D.C.1982), *aff'd sub nom.* Maryland v. United States, 460 U.S. 1001, 103 S.Ct. 1240, 75 L.Ed.2d 472 (1983).

inter-Local Access and Transport Area ("LATA"),[8] long distance telephone service and telecommunications equipment manufacturing, after the companies meet a fourteen point competitive check list evidencing full and fair interconnection and facilities access by other carriers.[9]

Congress leaves to the FCC and state public utility commissions the task of ensuring full and fair interconnection as well as a host of other issues requiring complex economic analysis. For example, the FCC and state public utility commissions must determine appropriate discounts for resold LEC services and the actual cost of providing switching and routing of traffic generated by interconnecting with competing LECs, interexchange carriers ("IXCs") and end users. Billions of dollars in carrier revenues and cross-subsidies to promote universal service are at stake as the FCC attempts to define a national framework for rational cost-based pricing and to move from implicit to explicit universal service subsidies. For example, IXCs pay LECs an access charge of about three cents a minute for the use of LEC facilities to originate and terminate long distance toll calls. IXCs estimate that the actual cost of such access lies in a range from 0.4–1.2 cents, meaning that current access charges exceed cost by 250–700 percent and provide a large sources of funds for either profits or universal service subsidies.[10] The FCC has the unenviable task of sorting out complex pricing issues and determining competitively neutral facilities interconnection and access issues for local and long distance carriers, and as well as for end users.

This Section will address how the Telecommunications Act of 1996 and the FCC's implementation will affect the concept of common car-

8. Under the Telecommunications Act of 1996, a "local access and transport area" (LATA) is "a contiguous geographic area (A) established before the date of enactment of the [1996 Act] by a [BOC] such that no exchange area includes points within more than 1 metropolitan statistical area, consolidated metropolitan statistical area, or State, except as expressly permitted under the AT & T Consent Decree; or (B) established or modified by a [BOC] after such date of enactment and approved by the Commission." 47 U.S.C.A. § 153(25) (West Supp. 1997). LATAs were created as part of the Modification of Final Judgment's (MFJ) "plan of reorganization" under which the BOCs were divested from United States v. AT&T, Western Elec. Co., 552 F.Supp. 131 (D.D.C.1982), *aff'd sub nom.* Maryland v. United States, 460 U.S. 1001, 103 S.Ct. 1240, 75 L.Ed.2d 472 (1983); United States v. Western Elec. Co., 569 F.Supp. 1057 (D.D.C.1983) (Plan of Reorganization), *aff'd sub nom.* California v. United States, 464 U.S. 1013, 104 S.Ct. 542, 78 L.Ed.2d 719 (1983); *see also* United States v. Western Elec. Co., 1996 WL 255904 (D.D.C.1996), (vacating the MFJ). Pursuant to the MFJ, "all Bell territory in

the continental United States [was] divided into LATAs, generally centering upon a city or other identifiable community of interest." United States v. Western Elec. Co., 569 F.Supp. 990, 993 (D.D.C.1983).

9. *See* 47 U.S.C.A. §§ 271(c)(2)(B)(i)-(xiv) (West Supp. 1997). *See* Regulatory Treatment of LEC Provisions of Interexchange Services originating in the LEC's Local Exchange Area, Second Report and Order in CC Docket No. 96–149 and Third Report and Order in CC Docket No. 96–61, 12 FCC Rcd. 15756 (1997).

10. "AT & T asserts, for instance, that the current average per-minute access rates of the BOCs are nearly seven times the forward-looking economic cost of providing that service, and that total interstate access charges collected today from interexchange carriers exceed forward-looking economic cost by $11 billion, or 70 percent of the total." Access Charge Reform Price Cap Performance Review for Local Exchange Carriers, CC Docket No. 96–262, Notice of Proposed Rulemaking, Third Report and Order, and Notice of Inquiry, FCC 96–488, 1996 WL 733469 (F.C.C.) at 11 (rel. Dec. 24, 1996).

riage with particular emphasis on changes to local and long distance competition, carrier-to-carrier interconnection and universal service funding.

A. *Local Competition*

The Telecommunications Act of 1996 orders the removal of statutory, regulatory, and operational barriers to local telephone services competition. The local competition provisions of the 1996 Act added new sections 251, 252, and 253 to the Communications Act of 1934. Section 251 establishes general interconnection obligations for all telecommunications carriers[11] delineates further obligations for LECs[12] and prescribes additional requirements for incumbent LECs ("ILECs").[13] Section 251 requires an incumbent LEC to provide interconnection at any technically feasible point, with equivalent quality as that provided to itself and affiliates and at just, reasonable, and nondiscriminatory rates.[14] Section 252 establishes procedures that state commissions, ILECs and new entrants must follow to implement the requirements of section 251, including the examination and approval of carrier-to-carrier interconnection arrangements. Finally, Section 253 bars state and local regulations that prohibit or have the effect of prohibiting entities from offering telecommunications services.[15]

The legislation contemplates that incumbent LECs and market entrants will negotiate terms and conditions for interconnection and resold services.[16] If an incumbent LEC and requesting carrier are unable to reach a negotiated agreement, either party may ask a state to arbitrate the disputed issues. As required by the 1996 Act, incumbent LECs must provide interconnection and nondiscriminatory access to network elements on an unbundled basis.[17] In implementing the Act, the FCC identified the following minimum set of network elements that incumbent LECs must provide to requesting telecommunications carriers, many of which are analogous to interstate access rate elements: network interface devices; local loops; local and tandem switches (including all software features provided by such switches); interoffice transmission facilities; signaling and call-related database facilities; operations support systems and information; and operator and directory assistance facilities.[18] States may require unbundling of additional elements.

---

11. 47 U.S.C.A. § 251(a)(1)-(2) (West Supp. 1997).

12. *Id.* § 251(b)(1)-(5).

13. *Id.* § 251(c)(1)-(6).

14. *See especially Id.* §§ 251(c)(2) and (c)(3).

15. *Id.* § 253(a). Section 253 also authorizes the Commission to preempt any law or regulation that is violative of this section. *Id.* § 253(d).

16. *Id.* § 252(a)(1).

17. *Id.* § 251(c)(3).

18. Implementation of the Local Competition Provisions in the Telecommunications Act of 1996, CC Docket No. 96–98, Notice of Proposed Rulemaking, 11 FCC Rcd. 14121 (1996) at ¶ 366 [hereinafter cited as Local Competition NPRM]. *See also* Implementation of the Local Competition Provisions in the Telecommunications Act of 1996, First Report and Order, CC Docket No. 96–98, 11 FCC Rcd. 15499, 15510, para. 16 (1996) (Local Competition Order), *aff'd in part and vacated in part sub nom.* Competitive Telecommunications Assoc. v. FCC, 117 F.3d 1068 (8th Cir.1997), *aff'd in part and vacated in part sub nom.* Iowa Utils.

Section 251(a) of the Telecommunications Act imposes general common carrier interconnection obligations on all telecommunications carriers. Section 251(b) imposes on all LECs additional requirements, including the obligation to lease services to other telecommunication carriers for resale to end users, to provide access to rights-of-way, and to establish reciprocal compensation arrangements for transport and termination of traffic, including that generated by Commercial Mobile Radio Service providers, such as mobile cellular radio and personal communication service operators. In addition to the above requirements, Section 251(c) of the Act requires incumbent LECs to make available to new entrants interconnection and access to unbundled network elements and to offer LEC retail services for resale to telecommunications carriers at wholesale rates.[19] Access to unbundled elements and resale opportunities makes it possible for new ventures to enter local exchange markets without incurring the time and expense in duplicating the existing facilities operated by incumbent carriers.

In implementing the Telecommunications Act, the FCC seeks to promote full facilities-based entry, resale of incumbent LEC services or a hybrid of the two whereby market entrants purchase only those unbundled network elements they need to erect a complete service. To achieve such facilities-based or resale competition, Section 251(c)(2) of the 1996 Act requires incumbent LECs to provide interconnection to any requesting telecommunications carrier at any technically feasible point. The interconnection must be at least equal in quality to that provided by the incumbent LEC to itself or its affiliates, and must be provided on rates, terms, and conditions that are just, reasonable, and nondiscriminatory.

Additionally, Section 251(c)(6) requires incumbent LECs to provide physical collocation of equipment necessary for interconnection or access to unbundled network elements at the incumbent LEC's premises, except that the incumbent LEC may provide virtual collocation if it demonstrates to the appropriate state regulatory commission that physical collocation is not practical for technical reasons or because of space limitations. Incumbent LECs are required to provide any technically feasible method of interconnection or access requested by a telecommunications carrier, including physical collocation virtual collocation and interconnection at meet points, a location where one carrier's geographi-

Bd. v. FCC, 120 F.3d 753 (8th Cir.1997) (Iowa Utils. Bd.), Order on Recons., 11 FCC Rcd. 13042 (1996) (Local Competition First Recons. Order), Second Order on Recons., 11 FCC Rcd. 19738 (1996) (Local Competition Second Recons. Order), Third Order on Recons. and Further Notice of Proposed Rulemaking, FCC 97–295 (rel. Aug, 18, 1997) (Local Competition Third Recons. Order), further recons. pending.

19. Section 251(f)(1) of the 1996 Act provides for exemption of the requirements in section 251(c) for rural telephone companies (as defined by the 1996 Act) under certain circumstances. Section 251(f)(2) permits LECs with fewer than 2 percent of the nation's subscriber lines to petition for suspension or modification of the requirements in sections 251(b) or (c). States are primarily responsible for interpreting the provisions of section 251(f) through rulemaking and adjudicative proceedings, and are responsible for determining whether a LEC in a particular instance is entitled to exemption, suspension, or modification of section 251 requirements.

cal service coverage ends and another carrier's begins or starts to overlap.

The Act also requires the FCC to establish procedures for nondiscriminatory access by cable television systems and telecommunications carriers to poles, ducts, conduits and rights-of-way owned by utilities or LECs.[20] The Commission's implementing Order includes several specific rules as well as a number of more general guidelines designed to facilitate the negotiation and mutual performance of fair, pro-competitive access agreements without the need for regulatory intervention.[21] Additionally, an expedited dispute resolution process is provided when good faith negotiations fail concerning such matters as modifications to poles, ducts, conduits, and rights-of-way and the allocation of the costs of such modifications.

1. Number Portability, Dialing Parity and Other Numbering Issues

Section 251(b) of the Communications Act of 1934, as amended, requires all LECs to offer, "to the extent technically feasible, number portability in accordance with requirements prescribed by the Commission."[22] The Act defines number portability as "the ability of users of telecommunications services to retain, at the same location, existing telecommunications numbers without impairment of quality, reliability, or convenience when switching from one telecommunications carrier to another."[23] In implementing this requirement the FCC first required all LECs to implement a long-term number portability method in the 100 largest Metropolitan Statistical Areas ("MSAs") according to a phased deployment schedule concluding on December 31, 1998.[24] Thereafter, for areas outside the 100 largest MSAs, each LEC must make long-term number portability available within six months after a specific request by another telecommunications carrier. In addition, the First Report and Order required all cellular, broadband personal communications services and covered Specialized Mobile Radio providers to be able to deliver calls from their networks to dialed numbers by December 31, 1998 and also required these wireless carriers to offer number portability throughout their networks and to have the capability to support roaming nationwide by June 30, 1999.

Rather than choosing a particular technology for the provision of number portability, the FCC established performance criteria that any long-term number portability method selected by a LEC must meet. The Commission required the maintenance of regional numbering databases by one or more independent administrators selected by the North

---

20. 47 U.S.C.A. § 224 (West Supp. 1997).

21. Amendment of Rules and Policies Governing Pole Attachments, CS Docket No. 97–98, Notice of Proposed Rule Making, 12 FCC Rcd. 11725 (1997), Report and Order, 13 FCC Rcd. 6772 (1998).

22. 47 U.S.C.A. § 251(b)(2) (West Supp. 1997).

23. *Id.* § 153(30) (West Supp. 1997).

24. *See* Telephone Number Portability, CC Docket No. 95–116, First Report and Order and Further Notice of Proposed Rulemaking, 11 FCC Rcd. 8352 (1996); First Mem. Op. and Order on Recons. 12 FCC Rcd. 7236 (1997) Second Report and Order, 12 FCC Rcd. 12281 (1997).

American Numbering Council empaneled to address telephone numbering issues.[25]

Section 251(b)(3) of the Communications Act, as amended, requires all LECs to provide dialing parity to providers of telephone exchange and toll services. This means that customers can choose different carriers for different services without having to dial extra digits. To achieve this objective, the Commission established minimum federal standards for interstate, intrastate, local, and toll calls.[26] The Commission also concluded that customers should have the option of selecting different carriers for routing intraLATA and interLATA toll calls. It imposed a deadline of no later than February 8, 1999 for LECs to make it possible for customers the option of pre-selecting two different "Primary Interexchange Carriers" for direct dial (0+ and 1+) access.[27]

Section 251(e)(1) of the Communications Act, as amended, vests the FCC with exclusive jurisdiction over "those portions of the North American Numbering Plan[28] that pertain to the United States ... [with authority to delegate to] State commissions or other entities all or any portion of such jurisdiction."[29] On the matter of abbreviated dialing codes, *i.e.*, the use of fewer than seven digits to complete a call as is the case with 911 access to police and emergency services, the FCC authorized the continuing use of 311 for a non-emergency service, and 611 and 811 for access to LEC repair and business service offices.[30] The Commission prohibited LECs from offering enhanced services via any three digit code unless it offers access to the code on a reasonable, nondiscriminatory basis to competing enhanced service providers in the local service area

25. "[T]he North American Numbering Council will make recommendations to the Commission, develop policy, initially resolve disputes and guide the North American Numbering Plan Administrator. The North American Numbering Plan Administrator will process number assignment applications and maintain administrative number databases." Administration of the North American Numbering Plan, CC Docket No. 92–237, Report and Order, 11 FCC Rcd. 2588, 2590 (1995). *See also* Administration of the North American Numbering Plan, Report and Order, 11 FCC Rcd 2588, 2593–94 (1995).

26. Implementation of the Local Competition Provisions in the Telecommunications Act of 1996, CC Docket No. 96–98, Notice of Proposed Rulemaking, FCC 96–182, 11 FCC Rcd. 14171, ¶¶ 202–219 (rel. Apr. 19, 1996), 61 Fed. Reg. 18311 (Apr. 25, 1996); Second Report and Order and Mem. Op. and Order, FCC 96–333, 11 FCC Rcd. 19392 (rel. Aug. 8, 1996) (implementing the dialing parity, non-discriminatory access, network disclosure and numbering administration requirements of the 1996 Act).

27. The Commission applied dialing parity requirements to pay telephones. *See*

Implementation of the Pay Telephone Reclassification and Compensation Provisions of the Telecommunications Act of 1996, CC Docket No. 96–128, Report and Order, FCC 96–388, 1996 WL 547458 (rel. Sept. 20, 1996).

28. The North American Numbering Plan is the basic numbering scheme, *e.g.*, areas codes, for the telecommunications networks located in Anguilla, Antigua, Bahamas, Barbados, Bermuda, British Virgin Islands, Canada, Cayman Islands, Dominica, Dominican Republic, Grenada, Jamaica, Montserrat, St. Kitts & Nevis, St. Lucia, St.Vincent, Turks & Caicos Islands, Trinidad & Tobago, and the United States (including Puerto Rico, the U.S. Virgin Islands, Guam and the Commonwealth of the Northern Mariana Islands).

29. 47 U.S.C.A. § 251(e)(1) (West Supp. 1997).

30. Use of N11 Codes and Other Abbreviated Dialing Arrangements, CC Docket No. 92–105 First Report and Order and Further Notice of Proposed Rulemaking, 12 FCC Rcd. 5572 (1997).

for which it is using the code to facilitate distribution of their enhanced services.

2. New Structural and Accounting Safeguards and Methodologies

To ensure a level competitive playing field between incumbent and recent market entrants, the FCC had to erect significant structural[31] and accounting safeguards,[32] particularly in view of new market opportunities for the Bell Operating Companies ("BOCs"), *viz.*, interLATA long distance services and manufacturing, and the need for new LECs to access the facilities and services of incumbent LECs. Also the FCC and state public utility commissions needed a basis for assessing what constitutes fair compensation when a market competitor requires access to an incumbent LEC's installed network or simply desires discounted charges when reselling local retail services of the incumbent LEC.

Section 271 and 272 of the Communications Act, as amended, condition a BOC's entry into interLATA long distance telephone services and manufacturing. Congress required the BOCs to establish separate manufacturing and long distance service subsidiaries to ensure that in the absence of full competition in the local exchange marketplace, the BOC would not engage in anticompetitive, discriminatory or cost-shifting practices designed to favor its new ventures which would enter competitive markets. Under traditional rate of return regulation and even under incentive regulation involving price caps, a BOC might "allocate improperly to its regulated core business costs that would be properly attributable to its competitive ventures."[33]

The FCC has developed a cost allocation methodology for use by state regulators when establishing actual rates for interconnection and the purchase of unbundled elements. The Commission used a controversial cost-based pricing methodology based on "forward-looking" econom-

---

31. Implementation of the Non–Accounting Safeguards of Section 271 and 272 of the Communications Act of 1934, as Amended, CC Docket No. 96–149, First Report and Order and Further Notice of Proposed Rulemaking, 11 FCC Rcd. 21905 (1996), Second Report and Order, 12 FCC Rcd. 15756 (1997), *aff'd sub nom.* Bell Atlantic Telephone Cos. et al. v. FCC, 131 F.3d 1044, 327 U.S.App.D.C. 390 (D.C.Cir. 1997). *See also* Implementation of the Telecommunications Act, CC Docket No. 96–115, Second Report and Order and Fourth Notice of Proposed Rulemaking, 13 FCC Rcd. 8061 (1998) [hereinafter cited as Non–Accounting Safeguards].

32. Implementation of the Telecommunications Act of 1996:Accounting Safeguards under the Telecommunications Act of 1996, CC Docket No. 96–150, Report and Order, 12 FCC Rcd. 2993 (1996).

33. Non–Accounting Safeguards at ¶ 11. "For example, a BOC may have an incentive to degrade services and facilities furnished to its affiliate's rivals, in order to deprive those rivals of efficiencies that its affiliate enjoys. Moreover, to the extent carriers offer both local and interLATA services as a bundled offering, a BOC that discriminates against the rivals of its affiliates could entrench its position in local markets by making these rivals' offerings less attractive. With respect to BOC manufacturing activities, a BOC may have an incentive to purchase only equipment manufactured by its section 272 affiliate, even if such equipment is more expensive or of lower quality than that available from other manufacturers." *Id. See also* Implementation of the Telecommunications Act of 1996: Telecommunications Carriers' Use of Customer Proprietary Network Information and Other Customer Information, CC Docket No. 96–115, Second Report and Order and Further Notice of Proposed Rulemaking, 13 FCC Rcd. 8061 (1998).

ic costs, an estimate of the costs an efficient LEC would incur to provide such interconnection rather than an estimate of the carrier's actual or historical costs.[34] The Commission pricing methodology is based on a staff study of the "Total Service Long–Run Incremental Cost" ("TSLRIC") incurred by LECs to provide network elements needed for interconnection and access to unbundled elements. Because the TSLRIC studies pertain to network elements, the FCC renamed them "Total Element Long Run Incremental Cost" ("TELRIC") studies. The Commission ordered that prices be set at TELRIC plus a reasonable share of forward-looking joint and common costs. The Commission contemplated that most states regulatory bodies would use its proposed methodology when assessing the merits of a LEC access proposal or when resolving a request for arbitration between incumbent LECs and their competitors. For states not yet adopting this methodology, the Commission also established default proxies, *i.e.*, actual rate ranges of 0.2–0.4 cents per minute for switching, and a ceiling of 0.15 cents per minute for tandem switching, that a state commission may use to resolve arbitrations even before completion of a TELRIC study. Language in the Telecommunications Act also directs the FCC to determine rates on an "avoided cost standard," *i.e.*, reducing charges to carriers on the basis of costs the incumbent carrier would not have to incur in providing such access or services for resale, *e.g.*, sales and marketing expenses.

In April 1996 the FCC issued a Notice of Proposed Rulemaking to allow the public to comment on the establishment of regulations to implement interconnection requirements. Under the Act incumbent LECs must

- negotiate interconnection agreements in good faith;

- provide interconnection to their networks on just, reasonable, and nondiscriminatory terms and conditions;

- provide access to each separate network element such as subscriber numbers, databases, or signaling systems;

- offer resale of their telecommunications services at wholesale rates;

- provide reasonable public notice of changes to their networks; and

- provide physical collocation (facilities sharing), or virtual collocation if physical collocation is impractical.

B.   The Eight Circuit's Rejection of the FCC's Local Competition First Report and Order

Despite its best efforts the FCC could not quickly implement the 1996 Act. Implementation was delayed by extensive litigation, a predictable outcome given the stakes involved and the ability of litigation to tilt

---

34. ILECs can recover "forward-looking economic cost ... based on the most efficient technology deployed in the incumbent LEC's current wire center locations." Implementation of the local Competition Provisions in the Telecommunications Act of 1996, CC Docket No. 96–98, First Report and Order, 11 FCC Rcd 15499, ¶ 685 (1996).

the competitive playing field in favor of one category of operator over another. Soon after the FCC released it Local Competition First Report and Order in August, 1996, many ILECs and state public utility commissions filed motions for partial or complete stays on grounds that the Commission exceeded its jurisdiction in establishing pricing policies that address local intrastate telecommunication services. The petitioners convinced the United States Court of Appeals for the Eighth Circuit that it should temporarily stay pricing provisions and the "pick and choose"[35] rule[36] of the Report and Order.

In deciding the merits of numerous appeals, the court identified the following defects in the FCC's Local Competition First Report and Order:

- allowing requesting LECs the "pick and choose" option when negotiating an interconnection agreement;[37]

- specifying the terms and conditions exempting rural and small LECs from the ILEC requirements;[38]

- establishing the FCC, instead of federal district courts, as the forum for reviewing and hearing complaints about ILEC agreements approved by state commissions;[39]

- requiring state commission approval of interconnection agreements negotiated prior to enactment of the '96 Act.[40]

In each instance, the appeals court rejected the Commission's decisions as exceeding its jurisdiction and the scope of authority established by the 1996 Act.[41] Simply put the Eighth Circuit rejected the assertion of federal jurisdiction over intrastate service pricing in view of the clear

---

35. The FCC's "pick and choose" rule would allow requesting LECs the opportunity to incorporate any individual provision of any interconnection agreement that an ILEC previously had negotiated with one or more other carriers.

36. Iowa Utilities Bd. v. FCC, 109 F.3d 418 (8th Cir.) *motion to vacate stay denied,* 519 U.S. 978, 117 S. Ct. 429, 136 L. Ed. 2d 328 (1996), *decision on the merits,* 120 F.3d 753 (8th Cir.1997), cert. granted ___ U.S. ___, 118 S.Ct. 879, 139 L.Ed.2d 867 (1998), *aff'd in part, rev'd in part sub nom.* AT&T Corp. v. Iowa Utilities Board, ___ U.S. ___, 119 S.Ct. 721, 142 L.Ed.2d 835 (1999) (endorsing FCC jurisdiction to implement local competition provisions of the '96 Act and largely reversing the 8th Circuit court's rejection of the FCC's implementation).

37. Iowa Utilities Bd., 120 F.3d at 792. The Commission based its pick and choose rule (codified at 47 C.F.R. § 51.809 (1996)) on subsection 252(i) of the '96 that provides: "A local exchange carrier shall make available any interconnetion, service, or network element provided under an agree-

ment approved under this section to which it is a party to any other requesting telecommunications carrier upon the same terms and conditions as those provided in the agreement." 47 U.S.C.A. § 252(i) (West Supp. 1997).

38. Iowa Utilities Bd., 120 F.3d at 801–803.

39. "We believe that state commission retain the primary authority to enforce the substantive terms of the [interconnection] agreements made pursuant to sections 251 and 252." *Id.* at 804.

40. *Id.* at 804–806.

41. "Our review of the extensive arguments in this case has confirmed our initial belief that the FCC exceeded its jurisdiction in promulgating the pricing rules regarding local telephone service. We also remain convinced that the FCC's 'pick and choose' rule would frustrate the Act's design to make privately negotiated agreements the preferred route to local telephone competition." *Id.* at 792.

language of Section 152(b) of the Communications Act[42] and the failure of the 1996 Act explicitly to authorize federal rate regulation of such service as had acquired with earlier amendments of the 1934 Communications Act relating to cable television service.[43]

The court rejected the "impossibility" exception narrowly drawn by the Supreme Court in *Louisiana Public Service Commission* v. *FCC*,[44] whereby the FCC may preempt state regulation only if (1) it is impossible to separate the interstate and intrastate components of FCC Regulation and (2) the state regulation would negate the FCC's lawful authority over interstate communication.[45] In contrast to federal cable television "no provision of the [1996] Act unambiguously requires *rates* for the local competition provisions to comply with FCC-prescribed requirements, no provision unambiguously directs the FCC to issue such *pricing* regulations, and there is no straightforward and unambiguous modification of section 2(b) in the Act."[46]

However, the FCC's network unbundling rules largely passed muster with the appellate court. The court acknowledged that a requesting carrier need not have built or acquired any portion of a telecommunications network before qualifying to purchase unbundled elements despite ILEC assertions that this would lead to "cherry-picking" of choice customers[47] without any efficiency or technology gains and that market entrants would opt for unbundled network access instead of resale.[48]

42. "Any ambiguity regarding the FCC's vacuum of authority over local telecommunications] pricing under the [Communications] Act is resolved by the operation of section 2(b) of the Communications Act of 1934. 47 U.S.C.A. § 152(b). Section 2(b) provides that 'nothing in this chapter shall be construed to apply or to give the [FCC] jurisdiction with respect to ... charges, classifications, practices, services, facilities, or regulations for or in connection with intrastate communication service.' " *Id.* at 796.

43. "In sharp contrast to the Telecommunications Act, several provisions of the Cable Act explicitly grant the Commission the authority to regulate the rates of cable companies and explicitly require state authorities to follow the Commission's rate-making rules [*citing* 47 U.S.C.A. § 543(a)(2)(3)(b)(1994)] ... Consequently, we conclude that the Act plainly grants the state the local competition provisions of the Act." *Id.* at 795–796.

44. 476 U.S. 355, 106 S.Ct. 1890, 90 L.Ed.2d 369 (1986).

45. Iowa Utilities Bd., 120 F.3d at 796–800, *citing* Louisiana Pub. Serv. Comm'n v. FCC, 476 U.S. at 375–76 n.4, 106 S. Ct. at 1902 n.4, 90 L.Ed.2d at 386 n.4; California v. FCC, 39 F.3d 919, 931 (9th Cir.1994)

cert. denied, 514 U.S. 1050, 115 S. Ct. 1427, 131 L. Ed. 2d 309 (1995); National Assoc. of Regulatory Utility Comm'rs v. FCC, 880 F.2d 422, 429, 279 U.S. App. D.C. 99, 106 (D.C.Cir.1989).

46. Iowa Utilities Bd., 120 F.3d at 797.

47. Having vacated the FCC's pricing rules and discount proxy and without knowing what state-determined rates will be the petitioners' arguments that "competing carriers will incur only minimal costs in gaining access to incumbent LECs' networks ... [with] no incentive to build their own network is merely speculative at best." *Id.* at 816. The court noted that while Congress may have envisioned facilities-based competition for local services in the future, the rules favor expedited market entry presumably by resellers and operators with only partially constructed networks. *Id.* at 816.

48. A "reseller is able to purchase only as many services ... as it needs to satisfy its customer demand. A carrier providing services through unbundled access, however, must make an up-front investment that is large enough to pay for the cost of acquiring access to all of the unbundled elements of an incumbent LEC's network that are necessary to provide local telecommunications services without knowing whether

Likewise the court rejected as not ripe for review, in view of having vacated parts of the FCC's unbundling rules, claims that they interfere with intellectual property rights of third parties or constitute a taking of ILEC property.[49] The court agreed with the Commission that it could reasonably conclude that subsection 251(c)(3) of the new Act included as a network element ILEC operational support systems, operator services, directory assistance and vertical switching features including caller identification, call forwarding and call waiting.[50] The court also accepted the Commission's definition of what constitutes a "technically feasible point" for direct interconnection and access to unbundled network elements,[51] but specified that this term applies to points where such access may occur, not which elements must be unbundled.[52] The court also accepted the FCC's use of requesting carrier need for access to a proprietary network element if the ILEC's failure to offer such access would impair the requesting carrier's ability to provide service.[53] But it rejected the Commission's quality of service rules which it interpreted as requiring ILECs to provide service superior to that which they provide for themselves.[54]

C. Universal Service

Section 254 of the Telecommunications Act of 1996 memorializes for the first time an explicit mandate for the FCC to promote universal access to telecommunication services.[55] The Act directs the Commission to commence a proceeding to implement sections 254 and 214(e) of the Act, and to refer such proceeding to a Federal–State Joint Board. The Joint Board was given nine months to make recommendations to the Commission, including a definition of the services to be supported by federal universal service support mechanisms and a timetable for the implementation of such recommendations. The FCC initiated the Joint Board proceeding in March 1996,[56] and the Joint Board issued its *Recommended Decision* in November 1996.[57]

1. Requirements

The 1996 Act established several requirements for federal universal service support mechanisms. It directed the Joint Board and the FCC to base the preservation and advancement of universal service on six

---

consumer demand will be sufficient to cover such expenditures." *Id.* at 815. The court also rejected the FCC's requirement that ILECs recombine elements on request. *Id.* at 813.

49. *Id.* at 817–818. The court also approved the FCC's determination of ILEC resale obligations because the Commission did not specify a specific methodology or rate. *id.* at 818–819.

50. *Id.* at 808–810.

51. *Id.* at 810–812.

52. *Id.* at 810.

53. *Id.* at 811–812.

54. *Id.* at 812–813.

55. 47 U.S.C.A. § 254 (West Supp. 1997).

56. Federal–State Joint Board on Universal Service, Notice of Proposed Rulemaking and Order Establishing Joint Board, CC Docket No. 96–45, FCC 96–93, 11 FCC Rcd. 18092 (rel. Mar. 8, 1996)[hereinafter cited as Universal Service NPRM].

57. Federal–State Joint Board on Universal Service, CC Docket No. 96–45, Recommended Decision, FCC 96J–3, 1996 WL 656113 12 FCC Rcd. 87 (1996) [hereinafter

general principles, but stipulated that additional appropriate principles might be considered. These six principles are:

(1) quality services should be available at just, reasonable, and affordable rates;

(2) access to advanced services should be available in all regions of the nation;

(3) access to basic and advanced services should be available to customers in rural and high cost areas and to low-income consumers at rates comparable to those in urban areas;

(4) equitable and nondiscriminatory contributions should be made by all telecommunications providers to the preservation and advancement of universal service;

(5) specific and predictable support mechanisms should exist at both the federal and state level; and

(6) schools, health care facilities, and libraries should have access to advanced telecommunications services.

The Commission, after receiving the recommendations of the Joint Board, must identify specific services for federal universal service support[58] and target subsidies for the provision, maintenance and upgrading of the specifically identified facilities and services. [59]Such support is to be available to all telecommunications carriers eligible to receive universal service subsidies. [60]The legislation requires explicit universal service funding [61]and mandates equitable and non-discriminatory sharing of the financial burden among all telecommunications carriers providing interstate telecommunications services.[62]

In its *Recommended Decision*, the Federal–State Joint Board concluded that several universal service mechanisms currently implemented through the jurisdictional separations and access charge structures must be replaced or modified to meet the amended Communication Act's requirements that support mechanisms be explicit, specific, predictable and sufficient to preserve and advance universal service. Accordingly, the Joint Board recommended that changes be made to the high cost assistance fund[63] and that the Dial Equipment Minutes ("DEM") weighting program[64] and Long Term Support ("LTS")[65] be phased out and

cited as Joint Board Recommended Decision].

58. 47 U.S.C.A. § 254(c) (West Supp. 1997).

59. *Id.* § 254(e), (k).

60. *Id.* §§ 254(e), 214(e); *see also* Joint Board Recommended Decision at ¶ ¶ 155–62; Joint Statement of Managers, S. Conf. Rep. No. 230, 104th Cong. 2d Sess. at 131 (1996) ("The conferees intend that only eligible telecommunications carriers should receive support from specific Federal universal service support mechanisms.... ")[hereinafter cited as Joint Explanatory Statement].

61. 47 U.S.C.A. 254(e) (West Supp. 1997); *see also* Joint Explanatory Statement at 131 ("In keeping with the conferees' intent that universal service support should be clearly identified, [section 254(e)] states that such support should be made explicit ... ").

62. 47 U.S.C.A. § 254(d) (West Supp. 1997).

63. 47 C.F.R. §§ 36.601 *et seq.* (1997).

64. *Id.* § 36.125(b).

65. See note 65 on page 974.

replaced by a new explicit universal service mechanism.[66] The Joint Board's recommendations will obligate the FCC to revise its access charge rules to eliminate any implicit universal service subsidization, to prevent incumbent LECs from recovering the same costs twice and to provide the same subsidies to non-incumbent LECs as are provided to incumbent LECs for serving high-cost or low-income subscribers.

In its *Universal Service NPRM*, the FCC asked whether current charges imposed on IXCs contained an implicit universal service support mechanism.[67] While the Joint Board did not reach this question, it suggested that it would be desirable for per minute access charges to be restructured and collected on a flat-rate basis, because per-minute collection is economically inefficient.[68]

The Telecommunications Act of 1996 identified specific beneficiaries of the universal service mission: schools, health care provider facilities, and libraries. Additionally the Act directs the FCC and state commissions to promote in all regions of the nation services "that are reasonably comparable to those services provided in urban areas and that are available at rates that are reasonably comparable to rates charged for similar services in urban areas."[69] The law established the principle of guaranteeing that some set of telecommunications services are available to all at affordable rates. According to the Act, the FCC will articulate what this "universal service" package constitutes and how it will evolve over time and take into account advances in telecommunications and information technologies and services.

2. Infrastructure Sharing

Section 259 of the Telecommunications Act of 1996 broadens the public interest duty of ILECs to share "public switched network infrastructure, technology, information and telecommunications facilities and functions" with "qualifying carriers" entitled to receive federal universal service financial support and which lack economies of scale or scope that would make it possible for them to provide advanced telecommunications and information services in the most efficient manner possible. This section provides certain carriers with a means for tapping the economies of scale and scope possessed by incumbent LECs, but only for purposes of bolstering a universal service commitment and not to enhance one carrier's competitive prospects *vis a vis* another carrier. Unlike the general interconnection requirements of Sections 251 and 252, this section permits access under particular circumstances where the carrier accessing LEC facilities is not a direct competitor. Such a scenario typically would involve an independent, rural-based carrier that could use nearby facilities of a Bell Operating Company in its provision of

65. *Id.* §§ 69.105, 69.502, 69.603(e), 69.612.

66. Joint Board Recommended Decision at ¶¶ 268–82.

67. Universal Service NPRM at ¶¶ 113–14.

68. Joint Board Recommended Decision at ¶¶ 775–76.

69. *See* 47 U.S.C.A. § 254(b)(3) (West Supp. 1997).

advanced telecommunication services. Section 259 complements section 254 [universal service] by requiring incumbent LECs to make available, under certain conditions, public switched network infrastructure and other capabilities to qualifying carriers that are making available universal service outside the providing incumbent LEC's telephone exchange area.[70]

In implementing Section 259 of the Communications Act the FCC emphasized the use of negotiations between carriers rather than a Commission-managed process. Because the carriers will not directly compete with each other, the Commission concluded that the carrier providing infrastructure access would have no incentive to exploit any inequality for the sake of competitive advantage.[71] The FCC will expect incumbent carriers to provide access to any facility regardless of whether it provides interstate services, but the Commission does not expect incumbent LECs "to develop, purchase, or install network infrastructure, technology, and telecommunications facilities and functions solely on the basis of a request from a qualifying carrier to share such elements when such incumbent LEC has not otherwise built or acquired, and does not intend to build or acquire, such elements."[72] Likewise, the FCC will permit an infrastructure-providing incumbent LEC to withdraw from a sharing agreement upon demonstrating that the arrangement has become economically unreasonable or is otherwise not in the public interest.

D. The FCC's 1997 Universal Service Order and Reconsideration

On May 8, 1997 the FCC issued a Report and Order on universal service that largely adopted the Joint Board recommendations.[73] The FCC determined that the following services warranted subsidization to achieve ubiquity:

- voice grade access to the public switched network, with the ability to place and receive calls;

- "Dual Tone Multifrequency" ("touch tone") signaling or its functional equivalent;

- single-party service;

- access to emergency services, including 911 and Enhanced 911 (which identifies a caller's location);

- access to operator services;

70. Implementation of Infrastructure Sharing Provisions in the Telecommunications Act of 1996, CC Docket No. 96–237, Report and Order, FCC 97–36, at ¶ 3, 1997 WL 49598 (FCC rel. Feb. 7, 1997).

71. *Id.* at ¶ 8.

72. *Id.* at ¶ 12.

73. Federal–State Joint Board on Universal Service, Report and Order, CC Docket No. 96–45, 12 FCC Rcd. 8776 (1997) [hereinafter cited as Universal Service Report and Order], *on recons.* 12 FCC Rcd. 18514 (1997) [hereinafter cited as Universal Service Reconsideration Order], Fourth Order on Recons. in CC Docket No. 96–45, Report and Order in CC Docket Nos. 96–45, 95–72, 96–262, 94–1, 91–213, 13 FCC Rcd. 2372 (1997).

- access to interexchange services;
- access to directory assistance; and
- "Lifeline and Link Up" services for qualifying low-income consumers.

As recommended by the Joint Board, the FCC required eligible carriers[74] seeking universal service subsidization to offer each of the designated services. The Commission will allow a transition period for carriers currently unable to provide single-party service, enhanced 911 service and toll limitation services. Additionally as recommended by the Joint Board, the Commission will convene another Federal–State Joint Board to review the definition of universal service on or before January 1, 2001.

On the matter of telephone service affordability, the FCC accepted the Joint–Board's recommendation that states should monitor rates and non-rate factors, such as subscribership levels, to ensure local telephone service remains affordable. The Report and Order noted that a correlation exist between subscribership and affordability.[75] To achieve universal service the Commission concluded that eligible telecommunications carriers should be free to use any available technology to achieve universal service, including wireless options. As to service to rural, insular, and high cost areas, the Commission found that carriers should use forward-looking economic costs but conceded that the cost estimation methodologies presented thus far had not proved sufficiently reliable. Pending completion of an additional processing on costing methodologies, the FCC offered states the option of using the Commission's existing TELRIC mechanisms or their own forward-looking cost studies for determining universal service support. Until the FCC releases a new forward-looking costing mechanism, non-rural carriers will continue to receive high cost loop support and long term support based on existing universal service mechanisms.

Consistent with the Joint Board's recommendation, rural carriers will continue to receive the full level of support they receive under the current mechanism, with some minor modifications. The Commission contemplates working with the Joint Board on developing an appropriate forward-looking mechanism for rural carriers and has recommended that the Joint Board establish a rural task force to work on it. Because a forward-looking methodology will generate less total funds for supporting high costs areas, the FCC established a mechanism taking effect in 1999 for sharing by interstate and intrastate carriers of the difference in

74. Section 214(e) of the Communications Act of 1934, as amended, defines eligible telecommunications carriers as common carriers eligible to receive universal service support in accordance with Section 254 based on their designation of eligibility by state commissions for intrastate service and by the FCC for unserved interstate services.

75. "We agree with the Joint Board that there is a correlation between subscribership and affordability and we further agree that joint examination by the Commission and the states of the factors that may contribute to low penetration is warranted in areas, such as insular areas, where subscribership levels are particularly low." Universal Service Report and Order at ¶ 23.

support funds with a national benchmark level being funded by the Federal Universal Service Fund. In the interest of fairness among rural and more urbanized states, the FCC determined that states should be free to develop their own universal service programs. Additionally, the Commission will refer this issue to the Joint Board for further review. As recommended by the Joint Board, the Commission will also continue to explore the use of competitive bidding as a mechanism to provide universal service.

The FCC's Report and Order also modifies the Lifeline program that reduces qualifying low-income consumers' monthly phone charges. The related Link Up program provides federal support that reduces qualifying low-income consumers' initial incumbent wireline LEC connection charges by up to one half and is currently funded by contributions from IXCs. The Commission's Report and Order expands the Lifeline program to make it available in every state, territory and commonwealth. It increases the federal Lifeline support amount to $5.25 in federal funding with an additional $1.00 federal contribution for every $2.00 of state support up to a maximum of $1.75 making the maximum federal support $7.00. The Report and Order also makes the contribution and distribution of low-income support competitively and technologically neutral by requiring all providers of interstate telecommunications services to contribute, including non-common carriers and payphone aggregators, and by allowing all eligible telecommunications carriers, including, for example, wireless carriers, to receive support for offering Lifeline and Link Up service.

The FCC also adopted the Joint Board's recommendations for providing eligible schools and libraries discounts on the purchase of all commercially available telecommunications services, Internet access, and internal connections. Eligible schools will qualify for discounts ranging from 20% to 90%, with the higher discounts available to the most disadvantaged schools and libraries and to those in high cost areas. The Commission capped total expenditures for universal service support for schools and libraries at $2.25 billion per year, with a roll-over into following years of funding authority for funds not disbursed in any given year. Additionally, all public and not-for-profit health care providers located in rural areas will receive universal service support not to exceed an annual cap of $400 million. A health care provider may obtain telecommunications service at a transmission capacity up to and including 1.544 megabits per second, the bandwidth equivalent of a T1–line, at rates comparable to those paid for similar services in the nearest urban area with more than 50,000 residents within the state in which the rural health care provider is located. Rural health care providers also will receive support for both distance-based charges and a toll-free connection to an Internet service provider. Each health care provider that lacks toll-free access to an Internet service provider also may receive the lesser of 30 hours of Internet access at local calling rates per month of $180 per month in toll charge credits for toll charges imposed for connecting to the Internet.

As the Joint Board recommended, and in light of concerns about affordability, the FCC decided not to raise the monthly subscriber line charge for primary residential and single-line business lines to pay for the increased universal service financial burden.[76] Additionally the Commission endorsed the Joint Board's conclusion that a mechanism used to balance carrier common line charges among ILECs carrier constituted an implicit support mechanism and therefore must be removed from CCL charges.

E. Access Charge Reform

The third major prong of the FCC's implementation of the Telecommunication Act involves reforming the charges imposed on interexchange carriers ("IXCs") accessing local exchange carrier ("LEC") facilities to originate and terminate long distance telecommunications. In view of the cost reductions imposed by the Telecommunications Act on interconnection charges between LECs and the impending entry by the Bell Operating Companies ("BOCs") into interexchange services, the FCC also had to consider the even greater disparity in rates imposed by LECs on IXCs.[77] The technological nature of interconnection is quite similar for access among LECs and between an IXC and a LEC. Accordingly, absent compelling public interest justifications, such as an explicit requirement that IXCs primarily underwrite universal service funding, the charges incurred for local and interexchange carriers should be similar.

76. Part of the Universal Service Funding problem results from the exemption of enhanced services providers, including Internet Service Providers that now have the ability to provide services functionally equivalent to telecommunications provided by regulated common carriers subject to Universal Service Funding obligations. *See* Federal–State Joint Board on Universal Service (Report to Congress), Docket No. 96–45, 11 Comm.Reg. 1312 (P&F 1998), 1988 WL 166178 (F.C.C.) (rel. April 15, 1998).

77. "Current access charges distort competition in the markets for local exchange access. Our access charge rules create incentives for IXCs to bypass the LEC switched access network for reasons that have nothing to do with the economics of operating an access network. This uneconomic bypass may occur for a variety of reasons; rates may be too high, or our access charge rules may require rates for a LEC access service to be too high in relation to the rates for an alternative LEC service or for a comparable service offered by an alternative supplier. Inefficient entry may occur if the price for a package of jointly-provided services is above economic cost, even if the LEC would actually be the most efficient provider of the service. Conversely, if a package of jointly-provided services, including access, is priced too low because of regulatory requirements, efficient entry by an otherwise efficient provider may be precluded. In either case, the total cost of telecommunications service will not be as low as it could be if all services were priced at economic levels, thereby providing accurate price signals to all market participants. High access charges may also keep long-distance rates higher than they would otherwise be, which restricts demand for service and harms long-distance consumers. We describe more fully some of the causes of uneconomic bypass below." Access Charge Reform, Price Cap Performance Review For Local Exchange Carriers, Transport Rate Structure and Pricing, Usage of the Public Switched Network by Information Service and Internet Access Providers, CC Docket Nos. 96–262, 94–1, 91–213, 96–263, Notice of Proposed Rulemaking, Third Report and Order, and Notice of Inquiry, 11 FCC Rcd. 21354 (1996), First Report and Order, 12 FCC Rcd. 15982 (1997), Second Order on Recons. and Mem. Op. and Order, 12 FCC Rcd. 16606 (1997), *see also* Fourth Report and Order in CC Docket No. 94–1, and Second Report and Order in CC Docket No. 96–262, 12 FCC Rcd. 16642 (1997).

In late 1996 the FCC contemporaneously initiated two proceedings to consider reforms to the access charge regime: (1) a Notice of Proposed Rulemaking seeking to reform the access charge system in view of the Telecommunications Act of 1996 and with an eye toward fostering efficiency; and (2) a Notice of Inquiry on Internet and interstate information services seeking to identify what policies would best facilitate the development of the high-bandwidth data networks of the future, while preserving efficient incentives for investment and innovation in the underlying voice network.[78]

1. *Access Charge NPRM*

The FCC commenced a review of its Part 69 interstate access charge rules, together with its Part 61 price cap rules

> to determine the extent to which we must revise these rules to take account of the local competition and Bell entry provisions of the 1996 Act and state actions to open local networks to competition; to reflect the effects of potential and actual competition on incumbent LECs' ("ILEC's") pricing for interstate access; to implement the Act's direction to end implicit universal service subsidies in favor of a system of explicit subsidies; and to establish fair rules of competition for both the local exchange and interexchange markets, especially as carriers begin to offer service packages that bundle local and interexchange offerings.[79]

The Commission noted that the current access charge system imposes traffic-sensitive, per minute carrier common line ("CCL") fees, which compensate LECs for the shortfall resulting from less than fully compensatory flat-rated Subscriber Line Charges,[80] *viz.*, monthly access payments by end users, even though local loop costs do not vary with the amount of traffic carried by the loop.[81] Likewise the Commission's access

---

78. Access Charge Reform, Price Cap Performance Review For Local Exchange Carriers, Transport Rate Structure and Pricing, Usage of the Public Switched Network by Information Service and Internet Access Providers, CC Docket Nos. 96–262, 94–1, 91–213, 96–263, Notice of Proposed Rulemaking, Third Report and Order, and Notice of Inquiry, 11 FCC Rcd. 21354 (1996) [hereinafter cited as Access Charge Reform NPRM].

79. Access Charge Reform NPRM at 5.

80. "[I]n the original *Access Charge Order*, [93 FCC 2d at 279]the Commission found that recovering NTS [non-traffic sensitive] costs through flat monthly charges imposed on end users by incumbent LECs would promote optimal utilization of telecommunications facilities. The Commission decided at that time, however, to place a limit on the SLC [Subscriber Line Charge], and, consequently, required incumbent LECs to recover the remainder of their

common line costs through per-minute CCL rates. The current CCL charge has been uniformly criticized by both incumbent LECs and IXCs because it discourages efficient use of the network and encourages uneconomic bypass." Access Charge Reform NPRM at 58.

81. "We tentatively conclude that several provisions in Part 69 of our rules compel incumbent LECs to impose charges for access services in a manner that does not accurately reflect the way those LECs incur the costs of providing those services. For example, generally the costs associated with the local loop are non-traffic-sensitive (NTS), but our rules require incumbent LECs to recover a portion of those costs through per-minute CCL charges. Similarly, at least some portion of the costs of local switching is NTS, but our rules require incumbent LECs to recover all local switching costs through per-minute charges." Access Charge Reform NPRM at ¶ 55.

charge rules required IXCs to pay per-minute charges for local switching, even though a portion of such costs correlated to the number of lines connected to the switch, rather than the number of minutes of traffic routed by the switch. The Commission's access charge rules also imposed a non-facilities-based, per-minute transport interconnection charge ("TIC") on all switched access customers regardless of whether they used the incumbent LEC's transport facilities.

The Commission concluded that "[r]ather than fostering efficient pricing and competition, these mandatory rate structures inflate usage charges and reduce charges for connection to the network, in essence overcharging high-volume end users in order to reduce rates for low-volume end users."[82] The current access charge rules place

> the incumbent LEC at a regulatorily-imposed disadvantage in competing for high-volume end users, and jeopardizes the source of revenue that permits the incumbent LEC to cover its costs of providing service to low-volume end users. At the same time, these inefficient rate structures and implicit support flows also create artificial impediments to any new entrants that might seek to serve the subsidized end users, because they must attempt to do so without the benefit of a subsidy. As a result, these access rate structures may inhibit the development of competition for service to low-volume end users.[83]

In the sections that comprise the Third Report and Order in the Price Cap Performance Review for Local Exchange Carriers, the FCC eliminated the lower service band indices, which it considered unnecessarily restricting the ability of LECs subject to price cap regulation to lower their access prices.[84] In the Notice of Proposed Rulemaking portion, the Commission outlined two possible approaches "for addressing claims that existing access charge levels are excessive, for establishing a transition to access charges that more closely reflect economic costs, and for deregulating incumbent LEC exchange access services as competition develops in the local exchange and exchange access market."[85]

Under a market-based, incremental approach the FCC would "rely on potential and actual competition from new facilities-based providers and entrants purchasing unbundled elements to drive prices for interstate access services toward economic cost."[86] The Commission gradually would relax and ultimately remove existing Part 69 rate structure requirements and Part 61 restrictions on rate level changes as marketplace forces support self-regulation. The FCC's incremental approach

82. *Id*. at ¶ 7.

83. *Id*. at ¶ 8.

84. "Under our existing rules a price cap LEC must specifically justify a proposal to lower its access charges below the pricing floors established by the indices. Thus, our rules currently discourage price cap LECs from lowering prices even when it would be economically efficient to do so. These rules also hamper a price cap LEC in responding to lower-priced access service offerings by competing access service providers. To encourage the development and prompt deployment of new switched access services, we also streamline the process for price cap LECs to offer such services." *Id*. at ¶ 12.

85. *Id*. at ¶ 14.

86. *Id*.

would require an ILEC to demonstrate that certain circumstances exist before the Commission would permit greater access pricing flexibility. The incremental approach has two phases. In the first phase, where partial deregulation can occur, an ILEC would have to show that its local market has been opened to competition and that potential rivals are able to enter through any of the three avenues mandated by the Telecommunications Act, *viz.*, interconnection, unbundled network elements, or resale. In the second phase full deregulation of price cap and local access tariff filings can occur if the LEC proves that it is subject to substantial competition.

The FCC identified an alternative to market-based, incrementalism: a prescriptive approach to access reform, whereby the FCC "would specify the nature and timing of the changes to the existing rate levels."[87] Under a prescriptive approach, the FCC would compensate for the inability of marketplace forces alone to drive access rates to forward-looking economic costs. Under this approach, the Commission asked for comment whether it should require ILECs to move prices for interstate access in their service areas to more economically-efficient levels based on rules adopted in this proceeding rather than simply on the basis of marketplace conditions. As with a market-based approach, the FCC proposed to remove ILEC access services subject to substantial competition from price cap and tariff regulation.

The FCC sought comment on whether and when one approach or the other is preferable, or if a combination of these approaches should be used. To the extent that implementation of access charge reform is expected to cause a significant reduction in ILEC access revenues from current levels, the Commission also sought comment on whether such LECs are entitled or should be permitted to recover some or all of that difference through a temporary special recovery mechanism.

The FCC and the Federal State Joint Board examining universal service funding both recognized the economic inefficiency of a mechanism that only partially recovers non-traffic sensitive costs through a fixed charge. The Joint Board suggested that the Commission change the existing rate structure so that ILECs are no longer required to recover any of the NTS cost of the local loop from IXCs on a per-minute basis as had been done through Carrier Common Line charges.[88] The Commission considered the Joint Board's recommendation that LECs recoup the unrecovered costs from end user monthly payments (subscriber line charges). The FCC also proposed to increase or eliminate the cap on subscriber line charges for the second and additional lines for residential customers and for all lines for multi-line business customers so that such services bear the full per-line loop costs assigned to the interstate jurisdiction.[89]

---

87. *Id.*

88. *See* Joint Board Recommended Decision at 776.

89. Access Charge Reform NPRM at 65.

As to local switching costs the FCC noted that while Section 69.106 of its rules requires incumbent LECs to charge per-minute rates for local switching,[90] a significant portion of local switching costs, like line cards or line-side ports, appear to vary with the number of loops connected to the switch and not traffic volume. The Commission tentatively concluded that LECs should recover dedicated line card costs through flat charges[91] but refrained from concluding that other switching functions, like call setup (the process of establishing a transmission path over which a phone call will be routed) should be charged on a flat-rated basis even if LECs provide this service on a shared basis to multiple IXCs.

The FCC's Access Charge Reform NPRM also considered transport services, *i.e.* the use of LEC facilities to deliver traffic from LEC switching facilities to IXCs' switching and routing facilities commonly referred to as Points of Presence ("POP"). The Modification of Final Judgment required the spun-off Bell Operating Companies ("BOCs") to provide transport services on an "equal charge per unit of traffic" basis, ostensibly to prevent discrimination between AT & T and other IXCs that had never had a corporation affiliation with the BOCs.[92] The FCC required incumbent LECs to establish flat rates for: (1) "entrance facilities," transport service from the IXC POP to the LECs' switching facility commonly referred to as the Serving Wire Center ("SWC"), and (2) "direct-trunked transport," *i.e.* dedicated line transport service from a SWC to an end office (the LEC's switching facility closest to the call originator or recipient) without routing via other LEC switching facilities, typically ones located higher up in the hierarchy of call switching and routing facilities, and commonly referred to as tandem switches.[93] In addition, incumbent LECs were directed to establish usage-based charges for "tandem-switched transport," a transport service from the SWC to the end office that provides switching via a tandem switch. The tandem-switched transport service charge includes an inter-office transmission charge and a charge for using the tandem switch.[94] Because of the rate averaging requirement in the MFJ, the FCC authorized LECs to establish a non-cost-based transport interconnection charge ("TIC") to recover the revenue difference between what the LECs would have realized under the equal charge rate structure and what they would realize based on routing and the types of switching facilities used.[95]

90. *See* 47 C.F.R. § 69.106 (1997).

91. Access Charge Reform NPRM at 72.

92. *See* United States v. American Tel. & Tel. Co., 552 F.Supp. 131, 233–34 (D.D.C. 1982), *aff'd sub nom.*, Maryland v. United States, 460 U.S. 1001, 103 S.Ct. 1240, 75 L.Ed.2d 472 (1983).

93. *See* 7 FCC Rcd. at 7009–10.

94. *Id.* at 7010.

95. *See* First Transport Order, 7 FCC Rcd. at 7038. The TIC is a non-facilities-based, usage-sensitive charge that currently accounts for some 70 percent of incumbent LEC transport revenues. In Competitive Telecommunications Association v. FCC, 87 F.3d 522, 318 U.S.App.D.C. 288 (D.C.Cir. 1996), the D.C. Circuit Court of Appeals directed the FCC to eliminate the TIC, or to provide a reasoned explanation for retention of this non-cost-based rate element. *Id.* at 532, 318 U.S. App. D.C. at 298. The TIC is sometimes referred to as the Residual Interconnection Charge (RIC) or Residual Charge, because it was initially priced on a residual basis.

The FCC subsequently required incumbent LECs to offer two pricing options for tandem-switched transport service: (1) usage-sensitive rates with any mileage component computed on the basis of the distance between the SWC and the end office, regardless of the actual physical routing; or (2) flat-rated direct-trunked transport between the SWC and the tandem office and usage-sensitive tandem-switched transport between the tandem office and the end office, with any tandem-switched transport mileage component computed on the basis of the distance between the tandem office and the end office.[96]

The Access Charge Reform NPRM proposed to divide transport into three components: (1) charges for entrance facilities; (2) charges for direct-trunked transport service, *i.e.,* transport without intermediate tandem switching; and (3) charges for tandem-switched transport service.

The Commission proposed flat-rated charges for entrance facilities and direct-trunked transport service because it tentatively concluded that "these transport facilities appear to be dedicated to individual customers, and we believe that flat rates reflect the way incumbent LECs incur costs for dedicated facilities."[97] For tandem switched transport, the Commission proposed several options: (1) retention of the two existing options discussed above; (2) reversion back to the Commission's initial view that LECs should assess flat-rated charges for the circuit between the SWC and the tandem, which typically is a dedicated circuit, and to apply usage-based rates for the tandem-to-end office link; or (3) development of a peak load pricing system.

2. *Notice of Inquiry on Internet Access and Service Providers*

On the subject of Internet service providers and other "enhanced service providers" the Commission noted that previously it exempted such ventures from paying access charges in addition to their ordinary line rental fees. In 1983, the FCC classified enhanced service providers as "end users" rather than "carriers" for purposes of the access charge rules.[98] The Commission tentatively concluded that ISPs should not be

---

96. First Transport Reconsideration Order, 8 FCC Rcd. at 5372. *See also* Third Transport Reconsideration Order, 10 FCC Rcd at 3036 and 3037, Figure 2; 47 C.F.R. §§ 69.111, 69.112 (1997); Transport Order, 7 FCC Rcd at 7009 n.7, and 7077, Diagram 3.

97. Access Charge Reform NPRM at 86.

98. "In 1983 we adopted a comprehensive 'access charge' plan for the recovery by local exchange carriers (LECs) of the costs associated with the origination and termination of interstate calls. [citing MTS and WATS Market Structure, Memorandum Opinion and Order, 97 FCC 2d 682 (1983)]. At that time, we concluded that the immediate application of this plan to certain providers of interstate services might unduly

burden their operations and cause disruptions in provision of service to the public. Therefore, we granted temporary exemptions from payment of access charges to certain classes of exchange access users, including enhanced service providers." Matter of Amendments of Part 69 of the Commission's Rules Relating to Enhanced Service Providers, CC Docket No. 87–215, Notice of Proposed Rulemaking, 2 FCC Rcd. 4305 (1987)(proposing to imposed access charges on enhanced service lines), *terminated,* Order 3 FCC Rcd. 2631(1988)(proposal abandoned on ground that despite the apparent discrimination in charges "a period of change and uncertainty" besetting the enhanced services industry justified ongoing exemption from access charge pay-

subject to access charges as currently constituted.[99] Instead, enhanced and Internet service providers should only have to pay "business line rates and the appropriate subscriber line charge, rather than interstate access rates."[100] However, the Commission did note that "usage continues to grow, [and that] such services may have an increasingly significant effect on the public switched network."[1]

For the time being, the Commission chose to consider the issue broadly in terms of how to "provide incentives for investment and innovation in the underlying networks that support the Internet and other information services"[2] rather than narrowly as a matter of whether enhanced and Internet service providers should pay access charges.[3] With that perspective in mind, the Commission noted:

> the development of the Internet and other information services raise many critical questions that go beyond the interstate access charge system that is the subject of this proceeding. Ultimately, these questions concern no less than the future of the public switched telephone network in a world of digitalization and growing importance of data technologies. Our existing rules have been designed for traditional circuit-switched voice networks, and thus may hinder the development of emerging packet-switched data networks. To avoid this result, we must identify what FCC policies would best facilitate the development of the high-bandwidth data networks of the future, while preserving efficient incentives for investment and innovation in the underlying voice network. In particular, better empirical data are needed before we can make informed judgments in this area. [4]

The FCC initiated a Notice of Inquiry seeking comment generally on the implications of information services such as Internet access for the telephone network and what the Commission should do to encourage development of packet switching hardware able to route data traffic around incumbent LEC switches, or by installing new high-bandwidth access technologies such as asymmetric digital subscriber line ("ADSL") or wireless solutions.

---

ments). Currently the FCC requires users of ISDN services to pay only one Subscriber Line Charge, an access payment, despite the fact that ISDN circuits can derive more than one voice-grade equivalent channel.

99. Access Charge Reform Price Cap Performance Review for Local Exchange Carriers, CC Docket No. 94–1; Transport Rate Structure and Pricing, CC Docket No. 91–213, Usage of the Public Switched Network by Information Service and Internet Access Providers, CC Docket No. 96–263, Notice of Proposed Rulemaking, Third Report and Order and Notice of Inquiry, FCC 96–488, 1996 WL 733469 (rel. Dec. 24, 1996); *see* also First Report and Order, FCC 97–158, 62 Fed. Reg. 3140, 1997 WL 268841

(rel. May 16, 1997). *See also* Robert Frieden, *Dialing for Dollars: Will the FCC Regulate Internet Telephony?*, 23 Rutgers Computer and Tech. L.J. 47–79 (1997).

100. *Id.* at ¶ 285.

1. *Id.* at ¶ 282.

2. *Id.* at ¶ 283.

3. "The mere fact that providers of information services use incumbent LEC networks to receive calls from their customers does not mean that such providers should be subject to an interstate regulatory system designed for circuit-switched interexchange voice telephony." *Id.* at ¶ 288.

4. *Id.* at ¶ 311.

F. The FCC's 1997 Access Charge Report and Order

In May, 1997 the FCC's Access Charge Reform Report and Order[5] largely implemented what the Commission had previously proposed. The Report and Order adopts numerous reforms to the existing rate structure for interstate access that collectively reduce the cost differential IXCs pay for local exchange access and what similarly situated LECs pay. To move closer to parity of charges, the Commission had to revamp the IXC access charge rate structure to eliminate implicit subsidies for universal service and other public policy initiatives and to identify explicit subsidy elements that IXCs should incur. Toward that end the FCC adopted changes to the Common Line and Local Switching rate elements proposed in the Notice of Proposed Rulemaking ("NPRM"). The Commission generally removed from minute-of-use access charges costs that are not incurred on a usage-sensitive, per-minute-of-use basis. The Commission concluded that LECs should recover such non-traffic sensitive costs though flat-rated charges.

The Commission also adopted changes included in the NPRM regarding the rate structure for interstate transport. The reforms are designed to move the charges for those services to more cost-based levels and to promote competition for interstate transport services. Additional-

---

5. Access Charge Reform, Price Cap Performance Review for Local Exchange Carriers, Transport Rate Structure and Pricing and End User Common Line Charge, First Report and Order, CC Docket Nos. 94–1, 96–262; 94–1; 91–213; 95–72 12 FCC Rcd. 15982 (1997) [hereinafter cited as Access Charge Reform First Report and Order] *petitions for review den. sub nom.,* Southwestern Bell Telephone Co. v. Federal Communications Commission, 153 F.3d 523 (8th Cir.1998). Deeming the FCC's decisions acceptable because they were not arbitrary or capricious, the appellate court rejected long distance carriers' assertions that the FCC's Access Charge Report and Order overemphasized concern for retaining universal service subsidies and did not order on a timely basis the transition to competitive access rates. The court also rejected the argument from incumbent LECs that the FCC's emphasis on universal service made it possible for market entry and unfair competition from inefficient local exchange carriers. Specifically, the court deemed as a reasonable interpretation of the 1996 Act the FCC's decision to eliminate implicit subsidies embedded in interstate access charges prior to the full implementation of a new, explicit mechanism for universal service support, and the Commission's decision on how LECs shall recover their investment in plant used to provide long distance carrier access, *e.g.,* the Commission's decision to retain a $3.50 cap on the monthly fee for first lines to residences while raising

charges for second residential and business lines. The court also accepted the FCC's rationale for exempting Internet Service Providers from access charges.

In parallel to the above proceeding, the Fifth Circuit Court of Appeals overturned a lower court's decision that provisions in the Act specifically applicable to the Bell Operating Companies, *e.g.,* a prohibition on inter–LATA long distance service, constituted an unconstitutional "bill of attainder" by singling out the BOCs for punishment without the benefit of a trial. *See* SBC Communications, Inc. v. Federal Communications Commission, 154 F.3d 226 (5th Cir.1998), *reversing* SBC Communications, Inc. v. Federal Communications Commission, 981 F.Supp. 996 (N.D.Tex.1997). The court rejected SBC's position that particularized legislation, *i.e.,* the specialized provisions in the Act that restrict the BOCs from inter–LATA long distance markets until compliance with a 14 point competitive checklist, imposed punishment. Citing, *inter alia, Nixon v. Administrator of General Services,* 433 U.S. 425, 97 S.Ct. 2777, 53 L.Ed.2d 867 (1977) (ordering a class comprised of one individual to turn over his presidential papers), the court held that legislation with a legitimately nonpunitive function, purpose, and structure does not constitute punishment for purposes of the Bill of Attainder Clause even if it bars designated individuals from engaging in certain professions.

ly, the Order affirms the tentative conclusion reached in the NPRM that ILECs may not assess interstate access charges on information service providers ("ISPs"). The Commission found that its existing policy promotes the development of the information services industry, advances the goals of the 1996 Act and creates significant benefits for the economy and the American people.[6] The Commission said it will address fundamental questions about ISP usage of the public switched network as part of a broader set of issues under review in a related Notice of Inquiry.

With respect to the actual rates at which LECs should set access charges, the FCC rejected proposals for the immediate application of TSLRIC to each rate element. Instead, the Commission chose to rely on the marketplace option, discussed in the NPRM, to drive interstate access prices toward competitive levels.[7] The Commission believes that this process will give carriers progressively greater flexibility in setting rates as competition develops, gradually replacing regulation with competition as the primary means of setting prices and facilitating investment decisions. However, in the absence of competitive self-regulation, the Commission adopted a prescriptive safeguard that would bring access rates to competitive levels even in the absence of competition. For all services then still subject to price caps and not deregulated in response to competition, the Commission will require ILECs subject to price caps to file TSLRIC studies no later than February 8, 2001.[8] Because competition, forward looking costs and other access charge reforms may "strand" preexisting ILEC investments, the Commission stated that it would address in a subsequent order "historical cost" recovery issues including whether and to what extent ILECs carrier should receive compensation for the recovery of such previously incurred and now unrecoverable costs.[9]

1. Immediate and Future Financial Consequences

The FCC touted its Access Charge Order as generating almost immediate consumer savings by way of lower long distance bills. However, the Order does impose new or higher fees for residential and business users having more than one phone line. The Commission now considers such additional lines a luxury for which users must bear the full cost of LEC facilities access. Beginning in 1998, the Subscriber Line Charge, which currently is $3.50 per line and will remain so for single line residences and businesses, will increase for second and additional residential lines to the lesser of $5.00 or one-twelfth of annual common line revenues permitted under the Commission's price cap rules divided by total access lines. In 1999, the SLC ceiling for these additional residential lines will increase to the lesser of $6.00 per line or one-twelfth of annual common line revenues permitted under the price cap rules divided by total access lines. In subsequent years an inflation adjusted increase can occur up to a cap of $9.00 per month. The SLC ceiling for

6. *Id.* at ¶ 50.   **8.** *Id.* at ¶ 48, 267.

7. *Id.* at ¶ 44.   **9.** *Id.* at ¶ 14, 49.

some multi-line business customers will increase in July 1997 from $6.00 to the lesser of $9.00 or one-twelfth of annual common line costs allocated to the interstate jurisdiction divided by total access lines. However, the Commission estimates that after phased-in increases the SLC payments to most incumbent LECs will stabilize at about $7.60.

2. The Presubscribed Interexchange Carrier Charge

The FCC also replaced the per-minute Carrier Common Line ("CCL") charge imposed on IXCs[10] with a flat-rated, per-line Presubscribed Interexchange Carrier Charge ("PICC") as discussed in the NPRM. The PICC will recover LEC common line revenues not otherwise recovered through SLCs, and in the future also may recover a portion of costs currently collected through the per-minute Transport Interconnection Charge ("TIC"). In 1998, the ceiling on the monthly PICC associated with primary residential and single line business lines will be the lesser of 53 cents or one-twelfth the annual common line revenues permitted under the FCC's price cap rules divided by total access lines minus $3.50 and any applicable universal support payments received by the incumbent LEC. IXCs currently pay a per-line charge of $.53 to contribute to existing universal high cost and low-income support programs and this amount will thus remain unchanged. In 1999 and subsequent years, the Commission will adjust the monthly PICC ceiling for inflation and increased the charge $.50. The monthly PICC ceiling may never exceed the sum of one-twelfth of the annual permitted common lines revenues and residual TIC revenues divided by total access lines, minus $3.50 and all universal service support received by the incumbent LEC for such lines.

Effective January 1, 1998, the PICC for second and additional residential lines will be the lesser of $1.50 or one twelfth of the annual common line revenues permitted to be recovered under the Commission's price cap rules minus the annual common line revenues permitted to be recovered through all SLCs and the PICC assessed on primary residential and single-line business lines, divided by the number of second and additional residential lines and multi-line business lines. In 1999, the monthly ceiling on the PICC for such multiple line users will

10. The CCL elimination will occur only after a transition to full PICC recovery. Initially the per-minute CCL charge shall be assessed on originating minutes and shall not exceed annual common line revenues permitted under the Commission's price cap rules less the common line revenues that incumbent LECs are permitted to recover from SLCs and PICCs, divided by forecasted originating interstate access minutes. To the extent that the sum of a LEC's per-minute local switching charge and any residual per-minute CCL, TIC, and marketing expense charges exceeds the sum of its local switching, CCL, and TIC charges on originating access on December 31, 1997, the excess shall be collected through a per-minute charge on terminating access. This circumstance is expected to affect only a few price cap LECs and none beyond 1998. As a result of these policies, the average price cap LEC will have to charge lower rates for terminating than originating access. Originating access charges are more likely to be subject to competition than terminating access. *See also* Tariffs Implementing Access Charge Reform, Mem. Op. and Order, FCC 98–106, 1998 WL 278896 (FCC) (rel. June 1998); Access Charge Reform for Incumbent Local Exchange Carriers Subject to Rule of Regulation, CC Docket No. 98–101, Notice of Proposed Rulemaking, FCC 98–101, 1998 WL 289161 (FCC) (rel. June 4, 1998).

be adjusted for inflation and increased by an additional $1.00. In each subsequent year, the monthly ceiling shall be adjusted for inflation and again increased by $1.00. However, the Commission noted that the actual PICC for second and additional residential lines paid by IXCs will decrease over time, as the ceilings on the PICC for primary residential and single-line business lines gradually increase. It estimated that the average second residential line PICC will never exceed $2.00, and that this average will decline from 1999 onwards. Decreases are expected to begin for some incumbent price cap LECs in 1999 and for all LECs no later than 2001. Eventually, the PICC for second and additional residential lines will be one-twelfth of the annual common line and residual TIC revenues permitted under the Commission's price cap rules, divided by total access lines, minus the ceiling on the SLC for those lines, plus certain expenses that LECs incur in marketing their retail services. In 1998, the PICC for multi-line business lines will be the lesser of $2.75 or one twelfth of the annual common line revenues permitted under the Commission's price cap rules, minus the annual common line revenues permitted to be recovered through all SLCs and the PICC assessed on all residential and single-line business lines, divided by the number of multi-line business lines. In 1999 and 2000, the PICC ceiling will be adjusted annually for inflation and, if necessary for certain carriers, increased by an additional $1.50 on average. However even for multi-line business users the FCC estimates that the PICCs will begin to decline and reach a level below $1.00 in 2001.

3. Switching

Effective January 1, 1998, the Commission ordered price cap regulated LECs to recover the non-traffic-sensitive ("NTS") costs associated with local switching associated with line ports to the common line charges discussed above. Price cap LECs also may assess a monthly flat-rated charge directly on end users that are subscribing to ISDN, digital subscriber line or other services that have higher line port costs than basic, analog service. This charge will recover the amount by which the cost of the line port exceeds the cost of a line port for basic, analog service. Also effective January 1, 1998, the FCC directed price cap regulated LECs to move the NTS costs of local switching attributable to dedicated trunk ports to the trunking basket and to recover them through flat-rated monthly charges collected from the user of the trunk port. The NTS costs attributable to shared trunk ports continue to be recovered through per-minute local switching charges. In addition, price cap LECs may, but are not required to, recover some of their local switching revenue through a call set-up charge that is assessed on a per call basis.

4. Transport

Effective 1998, the FCC eliminated the unitary rate structure option for tandem-switched transport and created a three-part rate structure for recovering the costs of tandem-switched transmission. The NTS costs of tandem switching attributable to dedicated ports will be recovered through a new flat-rated monthly charge, with multiplexing of high capacity lines linking tandem switches and end offices recovered through a new per-minute rate element. The FCC also ordered the calculation of tandem-switched transport volume rather than a the previously used assumption of 9000 minutes.

12.6   Bellwether Cases in Common Carrier Deregulation

From its debut until the 1970s telecommunications was considered a "natural monopoly"[1] whose technological and economic characteristics necessitated government regulation. Government designated telecommunication service providers as common carriers to guard against potential abuse of monopoly power and as well to achieve social goals presumed otherwise to be unattainable.[2] As businesses "clothed" or "affected with" the public interest,[3] telecommunications common carriers were subjected to public utility regulation whereby government intervened on matters such as prices, profits and availability of service.

Common carrier regulation serves as a surrogate for marketplace functions and presumably operates unless and until the marketplace can operate in an unfettered manner. Critics of government involvement with telecommunications believe that technological innovations will promote efficient market resource allocation because then less heavily capitalized enterprises can operate efficiently and compete with incumbents. Government can support market entry by enforcing the antitrust laws to guard against anticompetitive practices of incumbents and by dismantling pro-incumbent regulatory structures when they are deemed no longer necessary.

The federal government started such a deregulatory course on two tracks by (1) engaging in close antitrust scrutiny of AT & T leading to several civil actions and negotiated consent decrees, culminating in divestiture of the Bell System; and (2) permitting progressively more liberal market entry authorizations based on the view that certain telecommunication markets will become or already have become competitive.[4]

---

1. "A natural monopoly is generally said to exist if there are declining costs to scale or a massive capital outlay is required to provide service, or both, and thus customer demand for a particular service can be satisfied at the lowest cost by a single firm." NTIA REGULATORY ALTERNATIVES REPORT 8 (1987).

2. Economists use the term "market failure" to represent the view of government officials that marketplace resource allocation, unfettered by government involvement, would underserve particular segments of society. Markets clear available supply relative to demand, but under the rubric of marketplace failure, policy-

makers deem inadequate the resulting output and accordingly institute policies and requirements to increase output, even if it requires subsidies and distorts the marketplace. Government justifies its financial support for public education, libraries, fire and police departments, public utilities and other public safety and welfare enhancements on grounds that market will underallocate resources relative to public need and benefit.

3. *See* Munn v. Illinois, 94 U.S. (4 Otto) 113, 24 L.Ed. 77 (1876).

4. The FCC must support any procompetitive initiative with substantive evidence outlining how the public interest will be

A. Unbundling Telephone Service From Telephone Attachments and Devices

One of the FCC's first major deregulatory initiatives established the right of users to attach non-electrical devices to their telephones. While such an opportunity to secure and attach equipment not manufactured by the telephone company's affiliate seems quite uncontroversial today, the 1955 *Hush-A-Phone* decision[5] was a major departure providing a qualified endorsement of the telephone user's right to attach a plastic device to enhance the privacy of telephone calls. That the Commission even there was swayed by the telephone companies' arguments about the potential financial and technical harm from such an acoustic device underscores the concern that federal regulators exhibited that they do nothing to undermine the ability of regulated carriers to meet pricing and universal service objectives. On appeal of the *Hush-A-Phone* case, the court was less solicitous and established a broader standard that would allow users to attach any device that was privately beneficial without being publicly detrimental to the telephone system.[6]

The FCC later changed its attitude and began to favor policies that would stimulate innovation and competition over concerns for "systemic integrity." In its *Carterfone* decision, the Commission authorized customer attachment of electrical devices[7] and adopted the appeals court's language requiring only a network harm evaluation. The Commission subsequently approved expanded use of "foreign attachments" and ordered carriers to amend their tariffs to allow attachment of non-Bell System equipment.

B. Transmission Facility Competition

In 1959 the FCC overturned its previous policy of restricting access to microwave radio frequencies to common carriers and government agencies. The Commission's *Above 890* decision authorized private microwave systems to link multiple facilities.[8] The end user's right to erect microwave networks and to attach network customizing equipment established new intracorporate options. It established the idea that users should not have to rely on outside companies to meet all service and equipment requirements. The Commission grew to adopt this view first with terminal equipment and subsequently with transmission facilities. The next deregulatory step would involve the licensing of common

---

served. FCC v. RCA, 346 U.S. 86, 73 S.Ct. 998, 97 L.Ed. 1470 (1953) (rejecting a pro-competitive initiative that appeared to promote competition for competition's sake rather than evidence public benefits).

5. Hush–A–Phone Corp., 20 FCC 391 (1955), *reversed sub nom.* Hush–A–Phone v. United States, 238 F.2d 266, 99 U.S. App. D.C. 190 (D.C.Cir.1956).

6. 238 F.2d at 269, 99 U.S. App. D.C. at 193.

7. Use of the Caterfone Device in Message Toll Telephone Service, Initial Decision of Hearing, Examiner Chester F. Naumewicz, Jr., 13 FCC2d 430 (1967), *recons. denied*, Mem. Op. and Order, 14 FCC2d 571 (1968).

8. Allocation of Microwave Frequencies in the Bands Above 890 Mc, 27 F.C.C. 2d 359 (1959), *recons. denied*, 29 F.C.C. 2d 825 (1960).

carrier competitors who would challenge the legal and economic justification for an incumbent carrier monopoly.

C.   *Facilities–Based Common Carrier Competition*

1.   *Terrestrial Microwave Facilities*

More robust competition in telecommunication occurred with market entry by facilities-based carriers providing service to the general public. The most prominent and iconoclastic market entrant was Microwave Communications, Inc. ("MCI"), which in 1969 received authority from the FCC initially to provide "private line" services between Chicago and St. Louis.[9] The FCC limited MCI and other "Specialized Common Carriers" to the provision of dedicated lines for single users, inaccessible to the dial-up, public switched telephone network.[10] In limiting MCI and other market entrants to this private line market, the FCC responded to protests from AT & T that new competitors would "cream-skim" profits by only serving lucrative, high density routes leaving AT & T as the carrier of last resort on less dense and presumably less profitable routes. In limiting facilities-based competition to private-line services the Commission believed that it had insulated AT & T from significant traffic and revenue diversion:

> [W]e do not see how there could be any diversion of revenues of a magnitude to have the impact claimed by AT & T, in view of the very small percentage of AT & T's existing total market that is vulnerable to competition of the kind proposed here, the growth rate of Bell's basic services, and the likelihood that AT & T would obtain a very substantial share of the potential market for specialized service.[11]

The FCC did not foresee the extent to which Specialized Common Carriers would thrive and the scope of services for which they would seek to provide. The designation given them by the FCC contemplated specialized applications and augmenting services of incumbent carriers. In limiting such carriers to private lines, the FCC sought to stimulate competition in niche markets while safeguarding incumbent carriers from the larger, switched service markets.

Such a regulatory line of demarcation did not last long. Having secured the right to demand interconnection with local exchange carriers for access needed to originate and terminate their private line services, MCI sought to extend its scope of services to include the functional

---

9. Microwave Communications, Inc., 18 FCC2d 953 (1969), *recons. denied*, 21 F.C.C. 2d 190 (1970).

10. Establishment of Policies and Procedure for consideration of Applications to Provide Specialized Common Carrier services in the Domestic Public Point-to-Point Microwave Radio Service and Proposed Amendments to Parts 21, 43, and 61 of the Commission's Rules, First Report and Order, 29 FCC2d 870 (1971), *aff'd*, Mem. Op. and Order, 31 F.C.C. 2d 1106 (1971) *aff'd sub nom.*, Washington Util. & Transp. Comm'n v. FCC, 513 F.2d 1142 (9th Cir. 1975), cert. denied *sub nom.*, Nat'l Ass'n of Regl. Util. Com'rs v. FCC, 423 U.S. 836, 96 S.Ct. 62, 46 L.Ed.2d 54 (1975).

11. 29 F.C.C. 2d at 910.

equivalent of dial-up long distance calling.[12] The FCC rejected MCI's attempt to expand into switched public services, but the Court of Appeals for the District of Columbia Circuit in turn rejected the Commission's view that it could restrict the scope of services that a common carrier might offer over existing transmission facilities.[13] The court in *Execunet-1* held that the Commission's failure to restrict MCI to private line services explicitly and its failure to hold that AT & T was entitled to a long distance service monopoly precluded the Commission from denying MCI the opportunity to provide conventional long distance telephone services:

> In granting the facilities authorizations on the basis of that public interest finding, the Commission did not perhaps intend to open the field of common carrier communications generally, but its constant stress on the fact that specialized carriers would provide new, innovative, and hitherto unheard-of communications services clearly indicates that it had no very clear idea of precisely how far or to what services the field should be opened. As indicated in the staff report, a decision was apparently made to consider the consequences of future developments in appropriate future proceedings. There being no affirmative determination of public interest need for restrictions, MCI's facility authorizations are not restricted and therefore its tariff applications could not properly be rejected.[14]

Immediately after the court's *Execunet-I* decision, AT & T petitioned the FCC for a declaratory ruling that the Bell System did not have to provide other common carriers with access to local exchange facilities.[15] While the FCC again sided with AT & T, the appellate court once more responded favorably to an MCI complaint.[16] The court directed the FCC to dismiss its order rejecting any right of access by MCI to Bell System switched, local exchange facilities and any other order absolving AT & T of the duty to provide such access on reasonable tarriffed terms and conditions.[17]

AT & T responded to long distance service competition with discount pricing targeted to high volume users.[18] Its Telpak service tariff

---

12. MCI Telecommunications Corp., 60 FCC2d 25 (1976) (rejecting proposed tariffs for consumer services involving dial up access to long distance calling).

13. MCI Telecommunications Corp. v. FCC, 561 F.2d 365, 182 U.S. App. D.C. 367 (D.C.Cir.1977), cert. denied 434 U.S. 1040, 98 S.Ct. 780, 54 L.Ed.2d 790 (1978) (Execunet–I).

14. *Id.* at 379, 182 U.S. App. D.C. at 381.

15. Petition of AT & T for a Declaratory Ruling and Expedited Relief, 67 F.C.C. 2d 1455 (1978).

16. MCI Telecommunications Corp. v. FCC, 580 F.2d 590, 188 U.S. App. D.C. 327

(D.C.Cir.1978), cert. denied 439 U.S. 980, 99 S. Ct. 566, 58 L.Ed.2d 651 (1978) (Execunet–II).

17. In Lincoln Telephone and Telegraph Co. v. FCC, 659 F.2d 1092, 212 U.S. App. D.C. 208 (D.C.Cir.1981) (Execunet–III), the D.C. Circuit Court of Appeals extended the right of access to include independent telephone company local exchange facilities.

18. Telpak, 37 F.C.C. 2d 1111 (1964), *tent. decision in* 38 F.C.C. 2d 370 (1964), *rehearing granted in part, denied in part,* 38 F.C.C. 2d 761 (1964), *aff'd sub nom.,* American Trucking Ass'n, Inc. v. FCC, 377 F.2d 121 126 U.S. App. D.C. 236 (D.C.Cir. 1966), cert. denied 386 U.S. 943, 87 S.Ct. 973, 17 L.Ed.2d 874 (1967); AT & T Long

provided four separate discount classes based on volume usage commitments. While the discounting plan simply repackaged services already available, albeit at higher rates, the FCC initially viewed the service as completely new and hence non-discriminatory relative to "like" services.[19] However, the Commission did have concerns about whether the services were cost-compensatory and whether the rationale for segregating the discount plan into four different classes was sound. Given the level of competition in the late 1960s and early 1970s, the FCC was unwilling to support Telpak on the basis of competitive necessity, *i.e.*, the need to match competitors' prices to retain market share. The Commission stated that "the specialized carriers [in operation] do not present a sufficient competitive threat along their few routes to justify nationwide discriminatory pricing on the basis of competitive necessity."[20]

2. *Domestic Satellites*

In addition to terrestrial microwave facilities competition, the FCC sought to stimulate facilities competition via satellites.[21] In 1972 the Commission adopted a qualified "open skies" policy for satellites, *viz.*, a commitment to find a suitable orbital slot for operations and to grant a license to all technically, financially and legally qualified applicants:[22]

Lines Dept., 61 FCC 2d 587 (1976), *rehearing granted in part, and modified sub nom.*, Aeronautical Radio, Inc. v. FCC, 642 F.2d 1221, 206 U.S. App. D.C. 253 (D.C.Cir. 1980), cert. denied 451 U.S. 920, 101 S. Ct. 1988, 68 L.Ed.2d 311 (1981).

19. Telpak, 37 FCC at 378–79.

20. AT & T Long Lines Dept., 61 FCC2d at 658.

21. Domestic Communications–Satellite Facilities, First Report and Order, 22 FCC2d 86 (1970), Second Report and Order, 35 F.C.C. 2d 844 (1972), *aff'd sub nom.* Network Project v. FCC, 511 F.2d 786, 167 U.S. App. D.C. 220 (D.C.Cir.1975) (affirming "open skies" policy for satellite communications, in which multiple entries would be accepted).

22. The FCC had to order a reduction in spacing between satellites to accommodate all qualified applicants. *See* Assignment of Orbital Locations to Space Stations in the Domestic Fixed–Satellite Service, Mem. Op. and Order, 84 F.C.C. 2d 584 (1981) (1980 Assignment Order); Assignment of Orbital Locations to Space Stations in the Domestic Fixed–Satellite Service, Mem. Op. and Order, 94 F.C.C. 2d 129 (1983) (1983 Assignment Order), *recons.* FCC 84–32 (February 2, 1984), *further recons.*, FCC 84–181 (1984); Assignment of Orbital Locations to Space Stations in the Domestic Fixed-Satellite Service Mem. Op.

and Order, 50 Fed. Reg. 35228 (August 30, 1985) (1985 Assignment Order). Licensing of Space Stations in the Domestic Fixed–Satellite Service, 54 Rad. Reg. 2d 577, 589 (P & F 1983) (Reduced Orbital Spacing). *See also* Establishment of an Advisory Committee on Implementation of Reduced Orbital Spacing Between Domestic Fixed–Satellites, 102 F.C.C. 2d 390 (1985); Amendment of Part 25 of the Commission's Rules and Regulations To Reduce Alien Carrier Interference Between Fixed–Satellites at Reduced Orbital Spacings and to Revise Application Processing Procedures for Satellite Communications Services, CC Docket No. 86–496, First Report and Order, 6 FCC Rcd. 2806 (1991).

To avoid having to conduct a comparative hearing to assess the merits of applicants in excess of what the marketplace and the satellite orbital arc could accommodate, the FCC mandated creation of a consortium. *See* Amendment of Parts 2, 22 and 25 of the Commission's Rules to Allocate Spectrum for and to Establish Other Rules and Policies Pertaining to the Use of Radio Frequencies in a Land Mobile Satellite Service for the Provision of Various Common Carrier Services, GEN. Docket 84–1234, 4 FCC Rcd 6041 (1989) (hereinafter MSS Licensing Order); *remanded* Aeronautical Radio, Inc. v. FCC, 928 F.2d 428, 289 U.S. App. D.C. 16 (D.C.Cir.1991), *on remand* Tentative Decision, 6 FCC Rcd 4900 (1991), Final

We are further of the view that multiple entry is most likely to produce a fruitful demonstration of the extent to which the satellite technology may be used to provide existing and new specialized services more economically and efficiently than can be done by terrestrial facilities.... Our decision in favor of multiple entry does not mean that we have opted for a policy of 'unlimited or unrestricted open entry.' Our aim ... is to afford qualified applicants a reasonable opportunity to demonstrate the public advantages in use of the satellite technology as a means of communications. But such entry cannot be 'open' in the sense that it is without any restrictions or limitations. Pursuant to statute we must require showings of financial, technical and other qualification and make the requisite finding that a grant of the particular proposal will serve the public interest, convenience and necessity.[23]

The Commission reasoned that multiple satellite service providers would stimulate the development of satellite technology, promote innovation in services and generate downward pressure on rates.[24] To ensure that AT & T did not extend its terrestrial facilities market domination to satellites, the FCC imposed a 7 year moratorium on AT & T's construction and operation of satellites to provide private line services to nongovernment users.[25] The Commission expressed concern that it could not detect cross subsidies from monopoly to competitive services and that AT & T could fully load satellites from traffic generated by its existing customer base, while other market entrants initially would likely not be able efficiently to load its new satellites.

D. Non–Facilities–Based Competition Through Resale and Shared Use

In addition to facilities based competition, the FCC predicted that the public would benefit if the Commission authorized enterprises to resell bulk private line services.[26] The Commission subsequently expanded its pro-resale policy to include large volume calling services like WATS lines, which initially had been made available only to individual companies generating high volumes of long distance calls.[27]

Private line resale involves the aggregation of small volume users whose collective demand qualifies for a bulk, volume discount otherwise unavailable to any single small volume user. The FCC viewed this option as putting pressure on "underlying [facilities-based] carrier[s] ... to

Decision on Remand, 7 FCC Rcd. 266 (1992).

23. Domestic Communications–Satellite Facilities, 35 F.C.C. 2d 844 at ¶¶8 and 18.

24. 35 F.C.C. 2d at 847.

25. 38 F.C.C. 2d at 665, 676–77 (1972).

26. *See* Regulatory Policies Concerning Resale and Shared Use of Common Carrier Services and Facilities, Report and Order, 60 F.C.C. 2d 261 (1976), [hereinafter cited as Domestic Resale Policy] *modified*, Mem. Op. and Order, 61 F.C.C. 2d 70 (1976), *further modifications*, Mem. Op. and Order, 62 F.C.C. 2d 588 (1977), *aff'd sub nom.*, AT & T v. FCC, 572 F.2d 17 (2d Cir.1978), cert. denied, 439 U.S. 875, 99 S. Ct. 213, 58 L.Ed.2d 190 (1978).

27. Regulatory Policies Concerning Resale and Shared Use of Common Carrier Domestic Public Switched Network Ser-

realign the relationship between unit and bulk prices to make that relationship wholly cost-[based].... ''[28]

E. Reforming the Cost Allocation Process and Pricing Access to Local Exchange Facilities

Facing a strong judicial admonition to get on with the task of ensuring full and fair interconnection of long distance and local exchange facilities, the FCC in 1978 initiated a broad inquiry into the market structure for basic inter-exchange long distance services.[29] With an eye toward determining "what delineation of single source and competitive markets is in the public interest for long distance MTS and WATS,"[30] the Commission began to address matters involving cost allocation for local and long distance services and what constituted the appropriate charge interexchange carriers should pay for access to the local loop.

These issues presented a daunting task because much of the telecommunication infrastructure involves sunk, embedded investments, whose costs do not vary with usage.[31] Additionally, carriers typically make facilities investments for a variety of interstate and intrastate services. Over time the cost allocation process had become a politicized matter with the terms and conditions for access to local exchange facilities set to recover a disproportionate share of total plant costs. The "jurisdictional separations" used by local exchange carriers ostensibly to allocate plant investment costs between local, primarily intrastate and interexchange, primarily interstate pools had purposefully loaded costs onto the interstate, long distance service sector. This attribution of costs to interstate long distance calling built in a subsidy mechanism to reduce the end user cost of politically sensitive local exchange rates.[32] Ironically, new long distance carriers largely avoided the cross-subsidy obligation because of the inferior nature of the facilities interconnection the Bell System decided to provide. Because the new carriers could not secure 1 + dialing for their customers, called trunk-side interconnection, they initially secured access to their long distance networks via ordinary local

---

vices, Report and Order, 83 F.C.C. 2d 167 (1980), *on recons.*, 86 FCC 2d 820 (1981).

28. Domestic Resale Policy, 60 F.C.C. 2d at 298–99.

29. MTS and WATS Market Structure, CC Docket 78–72, Notice of Inquiry and First Notice of Proposed Rulemaking, 67 FCC 2d 757 (1978) (Phase I), Third Report and Order, 93 F.C.C. 2d 241 (1983), *modified on recons.*, Mem. Op. and Order, 97 F.C.C. 2d 682 (1983), *further modification on recons.*, Mem. Op. and Order, 97 F.C.C. 2d 834 (1984), *partially aff'd and partially remanded sub nom.*, Nat'l Ass'n Regl. Util. Comm'rs v. FCC, 737 F.2d 1095, 237 U.S. App. D.C. 390 (D.C.Cir.1984), cert. denied 469 U.S. 1227, 105 S. Ct. 1224, 84 L.Ed.2d 364 (1985), *further modification*, Mem. Op. and Order, 99 F.C.C. 2d 708 (1984), Mem. Op. and Order, 101 F.C.C. 2d 1222 (1985),

further recons. denied, Mem. Op. and Order, 102 F.C.C. 2d 849 (1985).

30. 67 F.C.C. 2d at 758.

31. Non-traffic sensitive facility investment "consist primarily of the costs of installing and maintaining the local loop between each subscriber's premises and the local telephone company." Hence, such costs are a function of such factors as the number of subscribers connected to the network and the distance between the subscriber premises and local telephone company central offices. Mark Fowler et al, *"Back to the Future": A Model for Telecommunications*, 38 Fed. Com. L. J. 145, 174 n. 82 (1986).

32. For a history of how the FCC and state regulatory commissions agreed to allocate plant costs, *see id.* at 175–184.

exchange lines typically charged on a monthly flat rate.[33] Competitors of AT & T paid access charges at a discount to what AT & T paid,[34] and later continued to pay the same rate when they secured the same terms and conditions for access to local exchange carrier facilities.[35]

The FCC proposed to consider whether and how it could move the cost allocation process from one that underwrote below cost provision of local exchange services to a more equitable "reimbursement [mechanism based] ... on a cost causational basis."[36] With further refinements throughout the 1980s,[37] the FCC devised a cost allocation and local exchange facilities access charge system that attempted to avoid market disruptions by requiring users to pay the full amount of the costs they required carriers to incur in providing service.

12.7 Local Exchange Carrier Issues

At the macro-level, telecommunications can be divided into three major components: (1) local exchange services; (2) interexchange, "long distance" services and (3) customer premises equipment, including the telephone handset used to originate and terminate calls. This section will examine trendsetting developments in local services prior to enactment of the Telecommunications Act of 1996.

A. *Duty to Interconnect*

Local exchange telecommunications once was considered a natural monopoly service meaning that it could most efficiently be provided in terms of per unit costs and scale by a single service provider. Even as the interexchange marketplace began to evolve into a competitive market starting in the 1970s, a single Local Exchange Carrier ("LEC") operated within a particular geographical region. Because the LEC was perceived

---

33. "[O]n the one hand, the OCCs [Other Common Carriers like MCI] were able to avoid making the contribution for local plant costs required of AT & T Long Lines despite the fact that ... [they] used local facilities in originating and terminating their customers' interstate calls. On the other hand, the access provided ... [them] was inferior in many respects to that provided AT & T...." *Id.* at 177–78.

34. *See* Exchange Network Facilities for Interstate Access, 71 FCC 2d 440 (1979); *see also* MCI Telecom. Corp. v. FCC. 712 F.2d 517, 523, 229 U.S. App. D.C. 203, 209 (D.C.Cir.1983).

35. *See* discussion of access charges regarding Local Exchange Carriers, section 12.7, pp. 634–642, *infra.*

36. 67 FCC 2d at 759.

37. *See* Amendment of Part 67 of the Commission's Rules and Establishment of a Joint Board, Recommended Decision and Order, 46 Fed. Reg. 63,344 (1981), *partially modified*, 89 FCC2d 1 (1982), *aff'd on re-*

cons., Mem. Op. and Order, 91 FCC2d 558 (1982), *aff'd sub nom.*, MCI Telecommunications Corp. v. FCC, 750 F.2d 135, 242 U.S. App. D.C. 287 (D.C.Cir.1984). Because local exchange carriers, particularly ones operating in high cost areas, had become reliant on a subsidy from interstate services, the FCC adopted the Joint Board's recommendation that it establish a universal service fund and make temporary exceptions to the 25 percent cap on the allocation of interstate plant cost to the interstate jurisdiction. *See* MTS/WATS Market Structure and Amendment of Part 67, Decision and Order, 50 Fed. Reg. 939 (1985), *aff'd on recons.*, Mem. Op. and Order, FCC 86–56, 1986 WL 292605 (FCC rel. Jan. 30, 1986), *aff'd sub nom.*, Rural Tel. Coalition v. FCC, 838 F.2d 1307, 267 U.S. App. D.C. 357 (D.C.Cir.1988)(deeming carefully considered the FCC decision to allocate 25 percent of non-traffic sensitive plant to the interstate service).

as having bottleneck control[1] over local facilities used to originate and terminate both local and long distance calls, pervasive common carrier regulation applied. Regulators imposed substantial requirements and limitations on LECs because of the view that, absent regulation, controllers of the local loop could extract monopoly rents from users, engage in unreasonable or anticompetitive conduct (particularly in response to incipient market entry) and favor corporate affiliates.

As controllers of the local loop bottleneck, LECs have a duty as common carriers to provide access to their facilities by other carriers and end users.[2] Technological innovations have challenged the view that the local loop supports a natural monopoly held by LECs. The advent of digital transmissions over fiber optic cables made it possible for private, non-common carriers to install facilities in the central business district of large and medium sized cities. These Competitive Access Providers ("CAPS"); now more commonly referred to as Competitive Local Exchange Carriers ("CLECs"), provide high speed voice and data service primarily to high volume business users on flexible terms and conditions.[3] Cable television operators and other wireless service providers also may provide local services.

The development of competition for local exchange services raises questions regarding the permissible scope of competition relative to the universal service mission of incumbent LECs. On the other hand, to the extent that the FCC and state public utility commissions have authorized facilities-based competition, these agencies must devise regulations and monitor compliance of orders designed to foster full and fair competition, particularly since LEC competitors will continue to need access to some of the incumbent carrier's facilities.

1. Access Charges

The FCC, state public utility commissions and telecommunication carriers have engaged in a decades long battle over what constitutes the best way for carriers to allocate costs between interstate and intrastate jurisdictions and to recoup expenses and investments. The cost allocation

---

1. "A monopoly provider of an essential service to a rival can subject its rival to a 'price squeeze.' Since the interconnector is both customer and competitor of the LEC, an interconnector's price for the service it provides to its retail customers depends on the price at which the LEC sells bottleneck facilities that are the critical productive inputs for the interconnector. Because the interconnector would flow through any increased overhead loading levels to its retail customers, the interconnector's retail prices would rise." Local Exchange Carriers' Rates, Terms, and Conditions for Expanded Interconnection Through Virtual Collocation for Special Access and Switched Transport, CC Docket No. 94–97, Phase I, 10 FCC Rcd. 637, ¶ 71 (1995).

2. *See* Bell System Tariff Offerings, 46 FCC2d 413 (1974), *aff'd sub nom.* Bell Telephone Co. of Pennsylvania v. FCC, 503 F.2d 1250 (3d Cir.1974), cert. denied, 422 U.S. 1026, 95 S.Ct. 2620, 45 L.Ed.2d 684 (1975). The Telecommunications Act of 1996 codified and specified the general terms and conditions for such interconnection. *See* Communications Act of 1934, *as amended*, 47 U.S.C.A. § 251 (West Supp. 1997).

3. *See* discussion of CAPs in Bell Atlantic Tel. Cos. v. FCC, 24 F.3d 1441, 306 U.S.App.D.C. 333 (D.C.Cir.1994)(reversing FCC orders requiring LECs to permit CAPs to connect their facilities to LEC network through physical collocation).

process for local exchange services has greater significance in a competitive environment, because carriers that compete with incumbent LECs typically also need some incumbent LEC facilities and services to originate or terminate calls.[4] When incumbent LECs did not face competition for local services and when they participated in a Bell System managed long distance network, the allocation of costs between jurisdictions affected how much a particular constituency paid and whether they had to underwrite other services. But in a competitive environment, both at the local exchange and interexchange levels, the cost allocation process and cost recoupment through access charges can affect market share and profitability.

a. The FCC's Access Charge System

The FCC had to devise an access charge system[5] that eliminated cross-subsidies between jurisdictions and service categories unless justified on public policy grounds, *e.g.*, underwriting "lifeline" services to the poor and helping defray extraordinarily high costs of providing service in

4. The group of carriers competing with the LECs and subject to an access charge payment requirement includes mobile commercial radio services like cellular radio. *See* Equal Access and Interconnection Obligations Pertaining to Commercial Mobile Radio Services, Notice of Proposed Rulemaking and Notice of Inquiry, CC Docket No. 94–54, 9 FCC Rcd. 4957 (1994). On the other hand, the FCC, responding to pressure from users of computer bulletin boards and data base services like CompuServe and America On-line, preliminarily determined that access to enhanced services via lines that provide multiple voice-grade equivalent channels will not trigger multiple Subscriber Line Charges. *See* Public Notice, Common Carrier Bureau Will Not Enforce Current Rules on Application of Subscriber Line Charges to ISDN Service, DA 95–1168, 10 FCC Rcd. 13473 (FCC rel. May 30, 1995) (despite finding that Section 69.104 of the Commission's rules, 47 C.F.R. § 69.104, require payment of a Subscriber Line Charge (SLC) for each derived channel of Integrated Services Digital Network (ISDN) service, the FCC refrain from enforcement provided that LECs calculate their Carrier Common Line charges as if they were imposing a SLC for each voice-grade-equivalent derived channel of the ISDN service, except for D channels used for signaling); *see also* End User Common Line Charges, CC Docket No. 95–72, Notice of Proposed Rulemaking, 10 FCC Rcd. 8565 (1995)(proposing a number of options for Subscriber Line Charge cost recovery in ISDN services).

5. MTS/WATS Market Structure (Phase I), Third Report and Order, 93 F.C.C. 2d

241 (1983), *modified on recons.*, Mem. Op. and Order, 97 F.C.C. 2d 682 (1983), *further modification on recons.*, Mem. Op. and Order, 97 F.C.C. 2d 834 (1984), *partially aff'd and partially remanded sub nom.* National Ass'n Regl. Util. Comm'rs v. FCC, 737 F.2d 1095, 237 U.S. App. D.C. 390 (D.C.Cir. 1984), cert. denied 469 U.S. 1227, 105 S.Ct. 1224, 84 L.Ed.2d 364 (1985); *further modification*, 99 FCC2d 708 (1984), *aff'd sub. nom.* American Tel. & Tel. Co. v. FCC, 832 F.2d 1285, 266 U.S. App. D.C. 47 (D.C.Cir. 1987), *modified on further recons.*, Mem. Op. and Order, 101 F.C.C. 2d 1222 (1985), *further recons. denied* Mem. Op. and Order, 102 F.C.C. 2d 849 (1985). Additionally, Modification of Final Judgment ("MFJ") requires the spun-off Bell Operating Companies to provide local exchange facilities access on an "equal charge per unit of traffic basis." United States v. American Tel. & Tel., 552 F.Supp. 131, 227 (D.D.C. 1982), *aff'd sub nom.* Maryland v. United States, 460 U.S. 1001, 103 S.Ct. 1240, 75 L.Ed.2d 472 (1983) (Modification of Final Judgment or "MFJ"). "Equal access allows end users to access facilities of a designated [IXC] by dialing '1' only." Investigation of Access and Divestiture Related Tariffs, CC Docket No. 83–1145, Phase I, Mem. Op. & Order, 101 FCC2d 911 (1985) (end user also has the capability to use other IXCs by dialing access codes). *See also* Access Charge Reform, CC Docket No. 96–262, First Report and Order, 12 FCC Rcd. 15982 (1997), Second Order on Recons. and Mem. Op. and Order, 12 FCC Rcd. 16606 (1997).

some rural locales.[6] Cost-based pricing also ensures that all carriers pay the same rates for equivalent service even though one carrier may be affiliated with the carrier providing the service.

Much of the complexity of the Commission's mission arises from the fact that most local exchange carrier investments constitute "sunk," "fixed costs." These investments are needed to make both interstate and intrastate services available. Such investments have to be made regardless of how much traffic the plant is used to transport. Such traffic insensitivity means that a plant investment is sunk regardless of how many minutes of revenue generating traffic occurs. Recouping such investments on a per minute basis, which has been a common practice,[7] burdens heavy volume users with excess payments while relieving low volume users of a proportionate burden even though there may be little difference in the extent to which either type of user causes the carrier to make a plant investment. Likewise, an arbitrary decision to load interstate services with a disproportionate share of plant investment builds in a mechanism for cross-subsidization of intrastate services.

Before adopting a new access charge system, the FCC noted that the current cost allocation system had skewed cost recovery to the interstate jurisdiction and primarily to interstate, long distance services. In 1980, AT & T reported that actual plant usage for interstate services constituted 7.8 percent, but that 25.8 percent of local exchange costs were assigned to AT & T's interstate rate base.[8] While the 7.8 percent usage-based figure may not have represented actual costs attributable to interstate services, using a multiple of minutes of use to determine the interstate share of investment overstated the amount, resulting in a substantial cross-subsidy from interstate to local services.

6. *See* Amendment of Part 67 of the Commission's Rules and Establishment of a Joint Board, 96 FCC2d 781 (1984) (ordering creation of a Universal Service Fund as part of a new access charge system).

7. Until the holding in *Smith v. Illinois Bell Telephone Co.*, 282 U.S. 133, 51 S.Ct. 65, 75 L.Ed. 255 (1930), inter-exchange services made no contribution to the recoupment of plant investment incurred by local exchange carriers to provide either switched, local or long distance services. This "board-to-board" approach deemed local and interexchange services mutually exclusive. After the *Smith* case, the Bell System in coordination with the National Association of Regulatory Utility Commissioners developed a "Separations Manual" to allocate costs between interstate and intrastate jurisdictions and between local and interexchange services. The Manual adopted a cost allocation scheme that considered costs from the originating telephone handset (station) to the terminating one. The Manual established minutes of use ("Subscriber Line Usage") as the basis for cost recovery and over time expanded the degree to which an interexchange minute of use was treated as more expensive, *i.e.*, a Subscriber Plant Factor weighed every interstate, interexchange minute of use by a multiple of 3.3. *See* Prescription of Procedures for Separating and Allocating Plant Investment, Operating Expenses, Taxes and Reserves Between the Intrastate and Interstate Operations of Telephone Companies, Report and Order, 26 F.C.C. 2d 247 (1970). Jurisdictional Separation Reform and Referral to the Federal–State Joint Board, CC Docket No. 80–286, Notice of Proposed Rulemaking, 12 FCC Rcd. 22120 (1997). *See also* Amendments to Uniform System of Accounts for Interconnection, CC Docket No. 97–212, NPRM, 12 FCC Rcd. 16577 (1997) (Telecommunications Act of 1996 mandated revisions).

8. Mark S. Fowler, et al, *"Back to the Future": A Model for Telecommunications*, 38 Fed. Com. L. J. 145, 176, n.88 (1983).

In 1980, pursuant to Section 410(c) of the Communications Act,[9] the FCC convened a Federal–State Joint Board to examine the growing gap between actual interstate minutes of usage and attributed percentage of investment to be borne by interstate ratepayers. The FCC adopted the Joint Board's recommendation to phase-in an interstate plant allocation factor fixed at 25 percent.[10]

The FCC has committed to developing rules and regulations that will ensure that both interexchange carriers (the long-distance telephone companies) and end users pay fair, cost-based rates for use of LEC facilities to originate and terminate interstate telephone traffic.[11] In addition to the FCC's campaign to eliminate cross-subsidies and allocate costs on a more equatable basis, the Modification of Final Judgment ("MFJ") breaking up AT & T required the spun-off Bell Operating

---

9. Section 410(c) of the Communications Act requires the FCC to establish a board comprised of FCC and state public utility Commissioners to address matters pertaining to separation of property and expenses between intrastate and interstate jurisdictions. 47 U.S.C.A. § 410 (c), *as amended* (West Supp. 1997). *See, e.g.,* Crockett Telephone Co. v. FCC, 963 F.2d 1564, 295 U.S.App.D.C. 397 (1992) (affirming Joint Board "average schedule" cost allocation scheme used by some carriers); Public Service Commission of the District of Columbia v. FCC, 906 F.2d 713, 285 U.S. App. D.C. 19 (D.C.Cir.1990)(affirming use of same cost allocation schedule by both small and large carriers).

10. *See* Amendment of Part 67 of the Commission's Rules and Establishment of a Joint Board, Recommended Decision and Order, 46 Fed. Reg. 63,344 (1981), *partially modified*, 89 FCC2d 1 (1982), *aff'd on recons.*, Mem. Op. and Order, 91 F.C.C. 2d 558 (1982), *aff'd sub nom.*, MCI Telecommunications Corp. v. FCC. 750 F.2d 135, 242 U.S. App. D.C. 287 (D.C.Cir.1984). Because LECs, particularly ones operating in high cost areas, had become reliant on a subsidy from interstate services, the FCC adopted the Joint Board's recommendation that it establish a universal service fund and make temporary exceptions to the 25 percent cap on the allocation of interstate plant cost to the interstate jurisdiction. *See* MTS/WATS Market Structure and Amendment of Part 67, Decision and Order, 50 Fed. Reg. 939 (1985), *aff'd on recons. by inviting further comments*, Mem. Op. and Order on Recons. and Order Inviting Comments, 1 FCC Rcd. 1287 (1986), Recommended Decision and Order, 4 FCC Rcd. 1352 (1989).

11. MTS/WATS Market Structure (Phase I), Third Report and Order, 93 F.C.C. 2d 241 (1983), *modified on recons.*, 97 F.C.C. 2d 682 (1983), *further modification on recons.*, 97 F.C.C. 2d 834 (1984), *partially aff'd and partially remanded sub nom.*, Nat'l Ass'n Regl. Util. Comm'rs v. FCC, 737 F.2d 1095, 237 U.S. App. D.C. 390 (D.C.Cir.1984), *cert. denied,* 469 U.S. 1227, 105 S.Ct. 1224, 84 L.Ed.2d 364 (1985), *further modification,* Mem. Op. and Order, 99 F.C.C. 2d 708 (1984), *aff'd. sub nom.*, Amer. Tel. & Tel. Co. v. FCC, 832 F.2d 1285, 266 U.S. App. D.C. 47 (D.C.Cir.1987), *mod. on further recons.*, 101 F.C.C. 2d 1222 (1985), *further recons.*, Mem. Op. and Order, 102 F.C.C. 2d 849 (1985). *See also* MCI Telecommunications Corp. v. FCC, 712 F.2d 517, 229 U.S. App. D.C. 203 (D.C.Cir.1983) (affirming interim access charge scheme). *See also* Investigation of Access and Divestiture Related Tariffs, Mem. Op. and Order, 101 F.C.C. 2d 911 (1985) (Allocation Order), *recons. denied*, Mem. Op. and Order, 102 F.C.C. 2d 503 (1985) (Reconsideration Order); Investigation of Access and Divestiture Related Tariffs, Mem. Op. and Order, 101 F.C.C. 2d 935 (1985) (Waiver Order); *see also* Expanded Interconnection with Local Telephone Company Facilities, CC Docket No. 91–141, Notice of Proposed Rulemaking and Notice of Inquiry, 6 FCC Rcd. 3259 (1991), Rep. & Order & Notice of Prop. Rulemaking, 7 FCC Rcd. 7369 (1992); Transport Rate Structure and Pricing, Report and Order and Further Notice of Proposed Rulemaking, CC Docket No. 91–213, 7 FCC Rcd 7006 (1992), *on recons.*, First Mem. Op. and Order on Recons., 8 FCC Rcd 5370 (1993) *on further recons.*, Second Mem. Op. and Order on Recons., 8 FCC Rcd 6233 (1993) *on further recons.*, Third Mem. Op. and Order on Recons. and Supplemental Notice of Proposed Rulemaking, 10 FCC Rcd. 3030 (1994)[hereinafter cited as Third Reconsideration Order], *on further recons.*, Fourth Mem. Op. and Order on Recons., FCC 95–404, 10 FCC Rcd. 12979 (rel. Sep. 22, 1995).

Companies to provide local exchange facilities access on an equal charge per unit of traffic basis.[12]

Over a number of years, the FCC has devised a regulatory regime for categorizing and pricing access to the local loop and for subsidizing service in high cost areas.[13] The Commission's Access Charge Plan shifted most non-traffic sensitive ("NTS") costs from a per-minute rate paid by interexchange carriers to a flat-rated Subscriber Line Charge paid by end users on a monthly basis.[14] The FCC sought to require the "cost causative" user to pay the full cost incurred by the carrier to provide access. However, the Commission found it politically infeasible to adopt a "pure" system that eliminated entirely all per minute charges added to long distance rates. Instead, the Commission adopted a transition system starting with a $1.00 monthly residential and single-line businesses subscriber line charge in 1985 and a $6.00 fee charged larger businesses.[15] Because the compromise access charges imposed on end users did not fully fund all NTS costs, the FCC opted to continue a type of usage sensitive charge on interexchange carriers when assessing the facilities of local exchange carriers.[16] This Carrier Common Line Charge

---

12. United States v. American Tel. & Tel., 552 F.Supp. 131, 227 (D.D.C.1982), *aff'd sub nom.* Maryland v. United States, 460 U.S. 1001, 103 S.Ct. 1240, 75 L.Ed.2d 472 (1983) (Modification of Final Judgment or "MFJ"). "Equal access allows end users to access facilities of a designated [IXC] by dialing '1' only." Allocation Order, 101 F.C.C. 2d at 911 (end user also has the capability to use other IXCs by dialing access codes).

13. The access charges imposed on interexchange carriers include a per minute fee that underwrites a Universal Service Fund designed to subsidize local exchange services in high cost, primarily rural areas. Amendment of Part 67 of the Commission's Rules and Establishment of a Joint Board, Decision and Order, 96 F.C.C. 2d 781 (1984). In 1993, the FCC proposed an interim rule limiting growth of this fund while it and a Federal State Joint Board completed an examination of the funding system. Amendment of Part 36 of the Commission's Rules and Establishment of a Joint Board, CC Docket No. 80-286, 8 FCC Rcd. 7114 (1993). The Joint Board recommended an interim rule that would establish an index cap on increases in funding, based on the increased number of local access lines for the previous year. Recommended Decision, 9 FCC Rcd. 334 (1993). The FCC adopted the Joint Board's recommendation 9 FCC Rcd. 303 (1993) and in 1995 initiated two proceedings to extend interim rules so that the Commission could launch a rulemaking to improve the Part 36 jurisdictional separations rules, which allocate costs among service categories, and establish the frame-

work for subsidizing service to high cost areas. The Commission seeks to target subsidies to high cost areas and to individual subscribers more precisely. *See* Amendment of Part 36 of the Commission's Rules and Establishment of a Joint Board, CC Docket No. 80-286, Notice of Proposed Rulemaking and Notice of Inquiry, FCC 95-282, 10 FCC Rcd. 12309 (1995)(seeking comment on proposals and policy changes to calibrate subsidy mechanism from interstate to local exchange service).

14. MTS/WATS Third Report and Order, 93 FCC2d at 281-82.

15. The FCC implemented the $1.00 fee starting on June 1, 1985, raised it to $2.00 the following year. MTS/WATS Second Reconsideration, 97 FCC2d at 837. The subscriber line charge was $3.60 for residential and single-line businesses in 1995.

16. There are two basic types of access to local exchange carrier facilities:

1) *Special Access*—"a form of interstate access that uses dedicated transmission lines between two points, without switching the traffic on those lines;" Expanded Interconnection with Local Telephone Company Facilities, CC Docket No. 91-141, Order on remand, Mem. Op. and Order, 9 FCC Rcd. 5154, n. 2 (1994); and

2) *Switched Access*—"another form of interstate access comprising the transmission of traffic between interexchange carriers '(or other customers)' points of presence [i.e., operating facil-

("CCLC"),[17] initially administered exclusively by the National Exchange Carrier Association, makes up for the NTS shortfall and also underwrites a subsidy for service in high cost areas ("High Cost" and "Universal Service Fund")[18] and for "life line" assistance for individuals with low incomes.[19]

In *National Association of Regulatory Utility Commissioners v. FCC,*[20] the Court of Appeals for the District of Columbia Circuit upheld the FCC's flat rate access charge regime deeming it within the Commission's broad "statutory discretion to balance the multiple goals embodied in the Communications Act."[21] The court held that the plan fell within the Commission's "broad zone of expertise and discretion which must be granted . . . in a proceeding which touches the very core of the rapidly developing telecommunications industry."[22] The court affirmed the FCC's decision to impose the flat rated access scheme, which many consumer groups had opposed as burdensome and detrimental to the goal of achieving universal service, precisely because the Commission had asserted that its plan and the rates charged were "structured to avoid disruptive service impacts."[23]

b.   Limits on Access Charge Ratemaking

In 1988 the FCC determined that Illinois Bell and other LECs had set access charge rates at overly compensatory levels.[24] Without having first suspended the tariffs, or issuing an accounting order requiring the

---

ities that aggregate and switch traffic] and local telephone companies' end offices, where the traffic is switched and routed to end users." *Id.*

The Commission previously considered Wide Area Telephone Service ("WATS") access. The Commission directly assigned WATS access lines between interstate and intrastate jurisdictions. MTS/WATS Market Structure and Amendment of Part 67, Recommended Decision and Order, 50 Fed. Reg. 47,774, 47,778 (1985), Decision and Order, 51 Fed. Reg. 7,942, 7,943 (1986). It also replaced a usage-sensitive CCLC with a flat monthly access charge. *See* WATS–Related and Other Amendments of Part 69, 59 Rad. Reg. 2d (Pike & Fischer) 1418 (1986).

17. MTS/WATS Third Report and Order, 93 FCC2d at 328.

18. MTS/WATS Market Structure and Amendment of Part 67, Decision and Order, 50 Fed. Reg. 940 (1985).

19. *Id.* at 941–43.

20. In 1997, the FCC shifted more costs onto end users through the Presubscribed Interexchange Carrier Charge. *See* subsection 12.5.F.2, *supra,* 737 F.2d 1095, 237 U.S. App. D.C. 390 (D.C.Cir.1984), cert. denied, 469 U.S. 1227, 105 S.Ct. 1224, 84 L.Ed.2d 364 (1985).

21. *Id.* at 1134, 237 U.S. App. D.C. at 429.

22. *Id.* at 1138, 237 U.S. App. D.C. at 433. While the Commission failed to specify "a plan of pristine quality," (*Id.* at 1147, 237 U.S. App. D.C. at 441), the court would not require perfection in the necessary balancing of interests and reconciling of diverse policy goals and constituencies. *See id.* at 1138, 237 U.S.App.D.C. at 433 (finding that the Commission's decision was reasonable given its expertise and the degree of discretion afforded the expert regulatory agency).

23. *Id.* at 1135, 237 U.S.App.D.C. at 430. "The Communications Act authorizes the Commission to impose reasonable charges to promote a rapid, efficient, and modern telecommunications network in which technological innovations are encouraged in order to permit the development of facilities adequate to provide this service." *Id. Cf.* Chevron U.S.A. v. Natural Resources Defense Council, 467 U.S. 837, 104 S.Ct. 2778, 81 L.Ed.2d 694 (1984) (affirming discretion afforded the Environmental Protection Agency to interpret and implement the Clean Air Act).

24. *See* 1988 Access Tariff Filings, 4 FCC Rcd. 3965 (1988).

LECs to track access charge costs and revenues during the duration of a hearing, the FCC ordered an investigation. The Commission subsequently ordered lower rates and determined that the rates should apply both prospectively and retroactively through a one-time refund. On appeal, the Court of Appeals agreed with Illinois Bell that the FCC failed to comply with Section 204(a)(1) of the Communications Act that specifies the Commission's powers regarding refund orders. That section permits the FCC to suspend or investigate a tariff filing. During the Commission's investigation, it may require an accounting of revenues collected. After completing its investigation the Commission may establish a proper and lower rate and may order a refund. But by failing to order a suspension of the access charge filing, the FCC could not subsequently order a refund.[25] The Commission could still remedy the problem pursuant to Section 205, but that section authorizes only prospective relief.[26] By ordering a refund without having suspending the rates pending an investigation, the FCC engaged in impermissible retroactive ratemaking.[27]

c. Different Access Charges Based on Traffic Density and Competitive Necessity

The FCC's access charge rules previously required LECs to charge uniform carrier common line, local switching, and transport interconnection charges throughout each LEC's study area, typically representing all locations within a single state. The Commission subsequently accorded LECs greater pricing flexibility and opportunities to deviate from absolute rate uniformity in view of expanded requirements to interconnect facilities with competing local service providers[28] and the competitive necessity to bring access rates more in line with costs.

25. "We conclude that when the FCC investigates and remedies an unreasonable rate which it has theretofore permitted to become fully effective without a suspension order, it acts under § 205, not § 204. We further conclude that the Commission has no authority under § 205 to order the refunds contemplated only under § 204." Illinois Bell v. FCC. 966 F.2d 1478, 1483, 296 U.S. App. D.C. 197, 202 (D.C.Cir.1992).

26. "In § 205 Congress provided the mechanism for prospective relief from unreasonable rates. In § 204 it provided the mechanism for preventing an unreasonable rate from being filed, or at least from taking effect only subject to an accounting order and such further order as would be required. The one supposes prospective relief, the other the possibility of refund." *Id.* at 1482, 296 U.S. App. D.C. at 201.

27. The "rule against retroactivity is 'a cardinal principle of ratemaking: a utility may not set rates to recoup past losses, nor may the Commission prescribe rates on that principle.' " City of Piqua v. FERC, 610 F.2d 950, 954, 198 U.S. App. D.C. 8, 12

(D.C.Cir.1979) (quoting Nader v. FCC, 520 F.2d 182, 202, 172 U.S. App. D.C. 1, 21 (D.C.Cir.1975)); *see also* MCI Telecommunications Corp. v. FCC, 59 F.3d 1407, 313 U.S. App. D.C. 419 (D.C.Cir.1995)(FCC cannot allow local exchange carriers to use overcharges paid by an interexchange carrier as an offset against underpayment for another type of service even if incurred during the same time period).

28. *See* Expanded Interconnection with Local Telephone Company Facilities, Report and Order and Notice of Proposed Rulemaking, 7 FCC Rcd 7369 (1992) (Special Access Physical Collocation Order), *on recons.*, Mem. Op. and Order, 8 FCC Rcd 127 (1992), *vacated in part and remanded sub nom.* Bell Atlantic Telephone Co. v. FCC, 24 F.3d 1441, 306 U.S. App. D.C. 333 (D.C.Cir. 1994); Second Mem. Op. and Order on Recons., 8 FCC Rcd 7341 (1993); Second Report and Order and Third Notice of Proposed Rulemaking, 8 FCC Rcd 7374 (1993); Mem. Op. & Order, 9 FCC Rcd. 5154 (1994).

The Commission authorized LECs to establish a system of traffic density-related rate zones within a study area, with different special access rates in each zone.[29] To implement this additional pricing flexibility, the Commission permitted each affected LEC to establish, subject to Commission approval, zones within each study area and required each central office in that study area to be assigned to one of the zones. Once plans were approved, LECs could file tariffs establishing differing rates in each zone. The Commission required the LECs to show they assigned each central office to a zone using criteria reflecting cost-related characteristics, such as the amount of traffic that passes through a central office. Geographic contiguity could, under certain conditions, be a secondary consideration.

d. Switched Access Transport Pricing Flexibility

The FCC also has afforded LECs greater flexibility in pricing switched access transport services.[30] Transport constitutes the transmission of switched traffic between the access customer's point of presence and the LEC's end office.[31] In the provision of transport service, the LECs use both dedicated circuits, available to a single access customer, and shared circuits that carry the access traffic of several customers in addition to other types of traffic within the LEC network.[32] The Modified Final Judgment ("MFJ") "equal charge" rule requires uniformity regardless of whether the facilities provide non-traffic sensitive dedicated circuits or the usage-sensitive shared circuits. The rule was scheduled to terminate,[33] but the FCC extended it pending a complete reevaluation of

29. See Expanded Interconnection with Local Telephone Company Facilities, Report and Order and Notice of Proposed Rulemaking, 7 FCC Rcd 7369, 7373, 7454 (1992) (Special Access Expanded Interconnection Order). See also Bell South Telecommunications, Inc., GTE Service Corporation, Lincoln Telephone and Telegraph Co., NYNEX Telephone Companies, Pacific Bell, Rochester Telephone Corporation Zone Density Pricing Plans, Order, 8 FCC Rcd 4443 (1993) (First Zone Density Order); see also Bell Atlantic Telephone Companies, Centel Telephone Company, Southwestern Bell Telephone Company, United Telephone Companies, Zone Density Pricing Plans, Order, 8 FCC Rcd 5529 (1993); US West Communications and Ameritech Operating Companies Zone Density Pricing Plans, Order, 8 FCC Rcd 7267 (1993).

30. See Transport Rate Structure and Pricing, Report and Order and Further Notice of Proposed Rulemaking, CC Docket No. 91–213, 7 FCC Rcd 7006 (1992)[hereinafter cited as First Transport Order], on recons., First Mem. Op. and Order on Recons., 8 FCC Rcd 5370 (1993) on further recons., Second Mem. Op. and Order on Recons., 8 FCC Rcd 6233 (1993) on further recons., Third Mem. Op. and Order on Re-

cons. and Supplemental Notice of Proposed Rulemaking, 10 FCC Rcd 3030 (1994)[hereinafter cited as Third Reconsideration Order], on further Recons., Fourth Memorandum Op. and Order on Recons., 10 FCC Rcd. 12979 (1995).

31. "To place transport services in perspective with the other LEC interstate access services, transport revenues, based on projected Bell Operating Company (BOC) revenues under the interim rate structure, comprise roughly 19% of all BOC interstate access revenues. Under our expanded interconnection policies, competitive access providers (CAPs) and the IXCs themselves may compete with the LECs to provide all or portions of transport service." Transport Rate Structure and Pricing, CC Docket No. 91–213, Third Mem. Op. and Order On Recons. and Supplemental Notice of Proposed Rulemaking, 10 FCC Rcd 3030, 3033 (1994).

32. For a more detailed description of transport service, see Third Recons. Order, 10 FCC Rcd at 3033–35, paras. 5–7. Figure 1.

33. See Third Recons. Order, 10 FCC Rcd at 3035, ¶ 7 (citing United States v.

the transport rate structure and pricing rules.[34]

The FCC has sought to reform the transport rate structure to: (1) encourage efficient use of transport facilities; (2) facilitate full and fair interexchange competition; and (3) avoid interference with the development of interstate access competition. In October 1992, the Commission released the First Transport Order that adopted an interim transport rate structure that attempted to align pricing more closely with costs as the best way to advance these objectives in the near term. The interim structure, which was set to remain in place until October 31, 1995, includes flat-rated elements for entrance facilities and direct-trunked transport, and usage-based charges for tandem-switched transport and the interconnection charge.[35] In addition, the First Transport Order based initial transport rates on the rate structure and associated pricing of special access facilities and made future transport rate changes subject to existing price cap rules.[36] The Reconsideration Orders that followed in 1993 and 1994 affirmed the interim transport rate structure and clarified various implementation issues.

e. Waivers for Special Conditions

In view of changing and increasingly competitive conditions, the FCC has become receptive to some LEC petitions for more expansive waivers, or even changes in the rules themselves. The Commission granted the former regional Bell Operating Company NYNEX, now Bell Atlantic, a waiver to use a different cost-recovery methodology and to deaverage its rates for the transport interconnection charges.[37] The waiver allowed NYNEX to reduce its per-minute access charges for the carrier common line, local switching, and transport interconnection charges throughout its entire region (*i.e.*, New York and the New England states), and to recover most of the revenues corresponding to those rate reductions from long-distance carriers in a manner other than that prescribed by the existing rules.

The FCC granted the waiver in response to NYNEX's assertion that it needed greater pricing flexibility to reduce per-minute access charges in order to meet switched access competition and to limit the bypass of its system that could result from uneconomic access pricing required by

American Tel. & Tel. Co., 552 F.Supp. 131, 233, Appendix B, ¶ B(3) (D.D.C. 1982), *aff'd sub nom.* Maryland v. United States, 460 U.S. 1001, 103 S.Ct. 1240, 75 L.Ed.2d 472 (1983)).

34. Transport Rate Structure and Pricing, Order and Further Notice of Proposed Rulemaking, 6 FCC Rcd 5341 (1991) (requiring LECs to maintain the equal charge rate structure pending further Commission action, while at the same time proposing a new transport rate structure and new pricing rules). *See also* First Transport Order, 7 FCC Rcd at 7007, 7016, paras. 1, 20; Third Recons. Order, 10 FCC Rcd at 3035–36, ¶ 8.

35. *See* First Transport Order, 7 FCC Rcd at 7016–22, 7038, paras. 21–29, 61. *See also* Third Recons. Order, 10 FCC Rcd at 3036, paras. 9–10.

36. *See* First Transport Order, 7 FCC Rcd at 7028, 7043–44, paras. 42, 74–76. *See also* Third Recons. Order, 10 FCC Rcd at 3038–39, 3040, paras. 12, 16.

37. Transport Rate Structure and Pricing, CC Docket No. 91–213, First Mem. Op. and Order on Recons., 8 FCC Rcd. 5370 (1993); Third Mem. Op. and Order on Recons. and Supplemental Notice of Proposed Rulemaking, 10 FCC Rcd. 3030 (1994).

the Commission's rules. NYNEX also noted that overpricing switched access reduces economic efficiency by discouraging usage. The FCC allowed NYNEX to assess two charges on interexchange carriers "(IXCs") in lieu of the single carrier common line charge. First, NYNEX could recover the portion of the carrier common line charge that recovers its long-term support costs through an assessment based on interstate toll minutes of use. Absent the waiver, NYNEX would have had to pay the National Exchange Carrier Association on a nationwide average for its administration of a carrier common line pool. Second, NYNEX could recover the carrier common line revenues associated with the originating and terminating interstate access usage attributable to multi-line business customers in the New York City metropolitan area through a charge assessed on IXCs based on the number of subscriber lines in the region presubscribed to that carrier.

The Commission also granted NYNEX additional flexibility to reduce transport interconnection charges in the New York City area. The waiver allowed the company to respond to developing competition by lowering its interconnection charge on less than a region-wide basis. The Commission conditioned this waiver on NYNEX meeting several requirements. NYNEX was not allowed to raise any interconnection charge above the tariffed rate in effect the day before the new waiver-permitted rate and it could not raise the rate for any interconnection charge to offset a reduction elsewhere. The FCC established a floor for these charges based on tandem switching costs that are included in the interconnection charge category.

The FCC also reacted favorably to a petition from Rochester Telephone Company to implement an "open market" plan for full and fair local exchange competition.[38] Rochester Telephone spun off a competitive local and long distance service provider (Frontier) and agreed to provide full and fair access to its local exchange facilities to all carriers on the same terms and conditions.

f. Restructuring the Elements of Facilities Access

The FCC continues to finetune its cost allocation mechanism for local exchange access, particularly in view of the elimination of the MFJ provision requiring the divested Bell Operating Companies to provide access on an equal charge per unit of traffic basis[39] regardless of traffic volume generated.[40] Because the FCC expects expanded local exchange

---

38. Rochester Telephone Corporation Petition for Waivers to Implement Its Open Market Plan, Order, 10 FCC Rcd. 6776 (1995).

39. Section II(A) of the Modification of Final Judgment requires the divested Bell Operating Companies to provide exchange access "on an unbundled, tariffed basis that is equal in type, quality and price to that provided to AT & T." United States v. AT&T, 552 F.Supp. 131, 234 (D.D.C.1982),

aff'd sub nom., Maryland v. United States, 460 U.S. 1001, 103 S.Ct. 1240, 75 L.Ed.2d 472 (1983).

40. *See* Transport Rate Structure and Pricing, CC Docket No. 91–213, Report and Order and Further Notice of Proposed Rulemaking, 7 FCC Rcd 7006 (1992) (First Transport Order), *recon.*, Third Mem. Op. and Order on Recons. and Supplemental Notice of Proposed Rulemaking, 8 FCC RCD 5370 (1993), *further recons.*, 8 FCC

service competition, it has begun the process of unbundling and revamping the access elements within the local loop that both end users and competitors typically require.

In 1992 the FCC reexamined the switched transport services of LECs with an eye toward desegregating them into discrete, cost-based elements: entrance facilities, dedicated transport typically used by a single IXC with substantial traffic volume, common transport typically shared by two or more IXCs with lower traffic volumes into and out of a particular local loop service territory and a contribution charge imposed on all IXCs to make up for any financial shortfall created by the rate restructuring.[41] Entrance facilities and dedicated transport would be flat-rated while common transport would be usage sensitive. To safeguard users of less competitive local exchange services which might otherwise face substantial rate increases to offset reductions in competitive services, the FCC revised its price cap ratemaking system.[42] The FCC also created a new "trunking basket" by pulling from the existing transport sensitive services basket all transmission related elements, including tandem switching, and interconnection. Much of the Commission's work on access charge reform flowed into its reexamination of the issue in the context of changes in local exchange carrier interconnection rules and universal service funding required by the Telecommunications Act of 1996.

g. Promoting "Seamless" Interconnection Between Incumbent Wireline LEC and New Wireless Networks

The FCC has recognized the consumer benefits in having wireline and wireless local carriers interconnect facilities[43] so that the telecommunication infrastructure can become an integrated array of connected networks.[44] The Commission first ordered such carriers to negotiate access terms and conditions in good faith.[45] It later expressed concern

---

Rcd. 6233 (1993), *pets. for recons. pending, appeal dismissed sub nom.*, New England Tel. and Tel. Co. v. FCC, No. 93–1494 (D.C.Cir. Sept. 7, 1993); *see also* 47 C.F.R. § 69.127 (1997).

41. First Transport Order, 7 FCC Rcd. at 7042–7044.

42. Transport Rate Structure and Pricing, CC Docket No. 91–213, Second Report and Order, 9 FCC Rcd. 615 (1994).

43. "The ability to interconnect has become more important because today telecommunications is increasingly provided by a system of independent, interconnected networks, often referred to as a 'network of networks.' " Interconnection Between Local Exchange Carriers and Commercial Mobile Radio Service Providers, Notice of Proposed Rulemaking, CC Docket No. 95–185, 11 FCC Rcd. 5020, para. 11 (1996) [hereinafter cited as LEC–CMRS Interconnection NPRM].

44. *See, e.g.*, Amendment of the Commission's Rules to Permit Flexible Service Offerings in the Commercial Mobile Radio Services, WT Docket No. 96–6, Notice of Proposed Rule Making, 11 FCC Rcd. 2445 (1996) (proposing to allow wireless Commercial Mobile Service Operators to provide both mobile and fixed services on a primary basis), First Report and Order and Further Notice of Proposed Rulemaking, 11 FCC Rcd. 8965 (1996).

45. The Commission ordered wireline LECs to provide cellular radio carriers with: (1) the type of interconnection the mobile carrier requested; (2) interconnection to the nonwireline carrier that is not less favorable than that furnished to its affiliated wireline cellular carrier; and (3) reasonable interconnection arrangements with the nonwireline carrier that may not be the same as those used by the wireline cellular carrier. *See* The Need to Promote Competi-

"that existing general interconnection policies may not do enough to encourage development of CMRS [Commercial Mobile Radio Services], especially in competition with LEC-provided wireline services."[46] In 1996 the Commission proposed that at least for an interim period LECs and CMRS operators should interconnect facilities used to provide services for more than one carrier on a reciprocal basis, *i.e.*, both carriers agree to route the other carrier's traffic at the same charge.[47]

The Commission's proposal contrasts with the way in which wireline and wireless carriers historically have interconnected facilities. Wireless carriers have compensated wireline carriers for terminating calls originated on wireless networks but destined for wireless subscribers, *e.g.*, a cellular radio subscriber's call from the car phone to someone at his home. However, wireline carriers have not compensated wireless carriers when calls originated on the wireline network destined for wireless network subscribers, *e.g.*, when someone at home calls a cellular subscriber's car phone.

The FCC's plan for reciprocal termination of traffic between LECs and CMRS operators supported a diverse, robust and multiple local telecommunication infrastructure and the Telecommunications Act of 1996 ordered similar reciprocal compensation for both wire and wireless carriers. The Commission will encourage the development of "seamless connectivity" between networks by promoting fair and administratively convenient interconnection agreements.

h. Other Access Charge Issues

(1) Presubscription and Number Portability

The access charge system also established a mechanism by which users can select the interexchange carrier that customarily will carry their long distance traffic. This "presubscription" process enables each customer to select one primary IXC from among several available carriers, for the customer's phone line(s).[48] Just as users now can select from among several long distance carriers, the possibility of local exchange carrier competition requires similar user flexibility. The FCC has proposed that end users retain their existing telephone numbers even if they opt for a different carrier or move within the local calling area.[49]

---

tion and Efficient Use of Spectrum for Radio Common Carrier Services, Mem. Op. and Order, 59 Rad. Reg. 2d 1275, 1283–84 (P & F 1986) *citing* An Inquiry Into the Use of the Bands 825–845 MHz and 870–890 MHz for Cellular Communications Systems, CC Docket No. 79–318, Report and Order, 86 FCC2d 469, 495–96 (1981), *on recons.*, Mem. Op. and Order on Recons., 89 FCC 2d 58, 81–82 (1982).

46. LEC–CMRS Interconnection NPRM at 2.

47. *Id.* at para. 3.

48. Allocation Order, 101 FCC2d at 928. A customer accesses the primary IXC's services by dialing "1" only. *Id.* at 911. *See also* Administration of the North American Numbering Plan Carrier Identification Codes (CICS), CC Docket No. 92–237, Declaratory Ruling, 12 FCC Rcd. 8687, Order on Recons. and Order on Application for Review, 12 FCC Rcd. 17876 (1997).

49. *See* Telephone Number Portability, CC Docket No. 95–116, Notice of Proposed Rulemaking, 10 FCC Rcd. 12350 (1995); *see also* Provision of Access for 800 Service, Notice of Proposed Rulemaking, CC Docket

The lack of such number portability "appears to deter customers who wish to select new and different services or who wish to choose among competing service providers."[50]

(2) Billed Party Preference, Alternative Operator Services and Payphones

The access charge system substantially affects the multi-billion dollar pay telephone business by requiring changes in the manner in which owners and users of such phones acquire and pay for long distance service. The high stakes involved necessitated that the FCC promulgate rules on how owners of pay phones presubscribe to a long distance carrier and how users can override the presubscription. The FCC has articulated a Billed Party Preference ("BPP") system for routing collect or credit card long distance telephone calls that typically begin with callers dialing a zero.[51] Under the BPP, the person financially responsible for the charge has the right to determine which interexchange carrier should carry the call instead of the owner of the pay phone used to make the call. The BPP requires expensive network intelligence to identify and route calls to a customer specified interexchange carrier. Because this plan would promote access to non-presubscribed interexchange carriers, the Commission ordered these carriers to pay monthly compensation to the payphone operators initially at a collective rate of $6.00 but later on a per-call basis.[52]

No. 86–10, 102 F.C.C. 2d 1387 (1986); Mem. Op. and Order on Recons. and Second Supplemental Notice of Proposed Rulemaking, 6 FCC Rcd. 5421 (1991), Order, 7 FCC Rcd. 8616 (1992). The FCC needed to examine the telephone number dialing system because demand has necessitated the proliferation of new area codes and a second toll-free prefix (888) and because of its view that Bell Communications Research, Inc. ("Bellcore") a Bell Operating Company research and development venture, should relinquish administrative responsibilities. *See* Administration of the North American Numbering Plan., CC Docket No. 92–237, Notice of Inquiry, 7 FCC Rcd. 6837 (1992), Notice of Proposed Rulemaking, 9 FCC Rcd. 2068 (1994); Report and Order, FCC 95–283 (1995), 11 FCC Rcd. 2588 (rel. July 13, 1995); Toll Free Service Access Codes, CC Docket No. 95–155, Notice of Proposed Rulemaking, 10 FCC Rcd. 13692 (1995), Report and Order, 11 FCC Rcd. 2496 (1996).

50. 10 FCC Rcd. at 12351, para. 2. *See also* Telephone Number Portability, CC Docket No. 95–116, Third Report and Order, FCC 98–82, 1998 WL 238481 (F.C.C.) (rel. May 17, 1998).

51. Billed Party Preference for Inter-LATA 0+ Calls, CC Docket No. 92–77, Second Report and Order and Order on Recons., 13 FCC Rcd. 6122 (1998).

52. Each IXC will pay a percentage of the $6.00 based on its toll revenues. *See* Policies and Rules Concerning Operator Service Access and Pay Telephone Compensation, CC Docket No. 91–35, Second Report and Order, 7 FCC Rcd 3251, 3259 (1992) (implementing the Telephone Operator Consumer Services Improvement Act, Pub.L. No. 101–435, 104 Stat. 986 (1990), *codified at* 47 U.S.C.A. § 226 (West 1991 and Supp. 1997)), Mem. Op. and Order on Recon., 8 FCC Rcd 7151 (1993), Mem. Op. and Order on Further Recons. and Second Further Notice of Proposed Rulemaking, 10 FCC Rcd. 11457 (1995)(proposing a per call compensation plan). *See also* Implementation of the Pay Telephone Reclassification and Compensation Provisions of the Telecommunications Act of 1996, CC Docket No. 96–128, Report and Order, 11 FCC Rcd. 20,541, on recons., 11 FCC Rcd. 21,233 (1996) *aff'd in part, vacated in part, sub nom.* Illinois Public Telecomm. Assoc. v. FCC, 117 F.3d 555, 326 U.S.App.D.C. 1 (D.C.Cir.1997), Second Report and Order, 13 FCC Rcd. 1778 (1997) (pet. for recons. and appeals pending).

The Commission also undertook an investigation of "Alternative Operator Services"[53] ("AOS") and the terms and conditions by which they compensate payphone owners for agreeing to route all long distance calls to a particular AOS.[54] The divestiture of AT & T led to the entry of competitors into the interstate operator service provider ("OSP") industry that had previously been dominated by the Bell System. The newer AOS companies generally lease lines from telephone carriers and combine these transport elements with their own operator services. Then, like the more traditional OSPs, they enter into contracts to provide operator services to call aggregators. Call aggregators market long distance services of other facilities-based carriers and operating sales agents rather than carriers. A caller using an aggregator's telephone system will automatically be connected to this "presubscribed" OSP unless an access code is dialed.

The proliferation of operator services has generated confusion and "widespread consumer dissatisfaction over the rates and practices of many ... providers."[55] In response to this situation, the FCC in 1989, responded to a complaint filed by two consumer advocacy groups and ordered the defendant companies *inter alia* to (1) provide written information about their services to be posted on or near presubscribed telephones; (2) identify themselves audibly at the beginning of calls, a process known as "call branding"; (3) discontinue the blocking of access to other OSPs; and (4) cease "call splashing" to the extent technically possible.[56] In 1990, the FCC adopted the initial Notice of Proposed

---

53. The term "operator services" refers to "any interstate telecommunications service initiated from an aggregator location that includes, as a component, any automatic or live assistance to a consumer to arrange for billing or completion, or both, of an interstate telephone call through a method other than—(A) automatic completion with billing to the telephone from which the call originated; or (B) completion through an access code used by the consumer, with billing to an account previously established with the carrier by the consumer." 47 U.S.C.A. § 226(a)(7) (West 1991). A call "aggregator" is "any person that, in the ordinary course of its operations, makes telephones available to the public or to transient users of its premises, for interstate telephone calls using a provider of operator services." 47 U.S.C.A. § 226(a)(2) (West 1991).

54. A full discussion of the development of the operator services industry and the proceedings related to operator service issues is contained in Policies and Rules Concerning Operator Service Providers' Notice of Proposed Rulemaking, CC Docket No. 90–313, 5 FCC Rcd 4630, 4630–31 (1990) (hereinafter NPRM). *See also* Further Notice of Proposed Rule Making, CC Docket

No. 90–313, 6 FCC Rcd. 120 (1990); Policies and Rules Concerning Operator Service Access and Pay Telephone Compensation, CC Docket No. 91–35, Second Report and Order, 7 FCC Rcd 3251, 3259 (1992) (implementing the Telephone Operator Consumer Services Improvement Act, Pub.L. No. 101–435, 104 Stat. 987 (1990), *codified as amended at* 47 U.S.C.A. § 226 (West 1991 & Supp. 1997)), Mem. Op. and Order on Recons., 8 FCC Rcd 7151 (1993), Mem. Op. and Order on Further Recons. and Second Further Notice of Proposed Rulemaking, 10 FCC Rcd. 11457 (1995) (proposing a per call compensation plan). *See also* Performance Measurements and Reporting Requirements for Operations Support Systems, Interconnections, Operator Services and Directory Assistance, CC Docket No. 98–56, Notice of Proposed Rulemaking, FCC 98–72, 11 Comm. Reg. 51–5025 (P & F 1998), 1998 WL 180809 (F.C.C.) (rel. April 12, 1998).

55. NPRM, 5 FCC Rcd. at 4630.

56. "Call splashing occurs when the OSP [Operators Services Provider] transfers a call to another carrier at a location different from the originating consumer and the second carrier cannot tell the originating location, resulting in an incorrect charge to the consumer which is not based

Rulemaking in CC Docket No. 90–313 and proposed specific rules addressing consumer information, call blocking, call splashing, interexchange carrier access and equipment capabilities. During the comment period for CC Docket No. 90–313, the Telephone Operator Consumer Services Improvement Act of 1990[57] was signed into law. The Act, among other things, required the Commission to conduct rule making proceedings to adopt "general" regulations, and specific rules on payphone access and compensation issues. The Commission responded generally with rules ordering the AOS companies to provide the means for users to access any interexchange carrier and with rules as to what compensation interexchange carriers owe AOS when callers use an alternative to the presubscribed long distance carrier.[58]

(3) "Slamming"

The FCC's system of long distance carrier selection created financial incentives for employees and agents of carriers to encourage telephone subscribers to change carriers, even without their informed consent. The FCC defines the practice, commonly referred to as "slamming," as the "unauthorized conversion of a customer's interexchange carrier by another interexchange carrier, interexchange resale carrier or a subcontracted telemarketer."[59] The Commission established rules requiring a long distance telephone company to establish some evidence that a customer really intends to change carriers.[60]

on originating location." Further Forbearance from Title II Regulation for Certain Types Of Commercial Mobile Radio Service Providers, GN Docket No. 94–33, Notice of Proposed Rulemaking, 9 FCC Rcd. 2164, 2169 (1994). The FCC also defined it as the practice of some AOS [Alternative Operators Services] to distort the call mileage calculations by determining the distance of the call from a point other than the location of the pay phone. Telecommunications Research and Action Center and Consumer Action v. Central Corp. Int'l Telecharge, Inc., 4 FCC Rcd. 2157 (1989). Call blocking refers to the practice of some OSPs to prevent callers from accessing a particular interexchange carrier by "dialing around" the presubscribed carrier through a dialing sequence that the FCC has ordered local exchange carriers to make available.

57. Pub. L. 101–435, 104 Stat. 987 (1990) ("Operator Services Act") *codified as amended at* 47 U.S.C.A. § 226 (West 1991 and Supp. 1997). The President signed the Act on October 17, 1990.

58. Policies and Rules Concerning Operator Service Access and Pay Telephone Compensation, CC Docket No. 91–35, Second Report and Order, 7 FCC Rcd 3251, 3259 (1992) (implementing the Telephone Operator Consumer Services Improvement

Act Pub.L. No. 101–435, 104 Stat. 987 (1990), *codified at* 47 U.S.C.A. § 226 (West 1991)), Mem. Op. and Order on Recons., 8 FCC Rcd 7151 (1993), Mem. Op. and Order on Further Recons. and Second Further Notice of Proposed Rulemaking, 10 FCC Rcd. 11457 (1995) (proposing a per call compensation plan). *See also* Implementation of the Pay Telephone Reclassification and Compensation Provisions of the Telecommunications Act of 1996, CC Docket No. 96–128, Report and Order, 11 FCC Rcd. 20541 (1996), on recons. 11 FCC Rcd. 21233 (1996), *aff'd in part and reversed in part,* Illinois Public Telecomm. Assoc. v. FCC, 117 F.3d 555, 326 U.S.App.D.C. 1 (D.C.Cir. 1997).

59. Cherry Communications, Inc., Order, 9 FCC Rcd. 2086, 2087 (1994).

60. Policies and Rules Concerning Unauthorized Changes of Consumers' Long Distance Carriers, CC Docket No. 94–129, Report and Order, 10 FCC Rcd. 9560 (1995)(prescribing the general form and content of the letter of agency (LOA) used to authorize a change in a consumer's primary long distance telephone company). *See also* Amendment of Policies and Rules Concerning Operator Service Providers and Call Aggregators, CC Docket No. 94–158, Notice of Proposed Rulemaking and Notice

(4) Toll Free Number Access

The FCC's access charge policy and the MFJ's equal access requirements also apply to 800 Wide Area Telephone Service ("WATS"). The LECs have upgraded their switching capability to provide a uniform and more versatile type of WATS access to all IXCs. Previously, 800 and 888 access prefixes (the first three digits) were assigned exclusively to particular IXCs, meaning that only one carrier could provide service to a automobile rental company that wanted a WATS line number equating to CAR–RENT.[61] In CC Docket No. 86–10, the FCC conducted a rule making regarding WATS data base services in which it prescribed a rate structure and filing dates for data base WATS access service tariffs with an eye toward fostering "number portability,"[62] *i.e.*, the opportunity for WATS access users to retain the same telephone number regardless of changes in the physical location and the interexchange carrier chosen to provide WATS services. The Commission required the tariffing of the Service Management System (SMS/800) to provide number portability.[63] The SMS/800 is a centralized data base through which customer records and routing instructions for each WATS telephone number are entered and updated and WATS numbers are reserved.

of Inquiry, 10 FCC Rcd. 1533 (1995), Report and Order and Further Notice of Proposed Rulemaking, CC Docket No. 94–158, 11 FCC Rcd. 4532 (1996). *See also* Implementation of the Subscriber Carrier Selection Changes Provisions of the Telecommunications Act of 1996 and Policies and Rules Concerning Unauthorized Changes of Long Distance Carriers, CC Docket No. 94–129, Further Notice of Proposed Rulemaking and Mem. Op. and Order on Recons., 12 FCC Rcd. 10674 (1997).

61. The matter of telephone numbers and dialing regimes has generated increasing interest. Telephone number demand has required modification of the North American Numbering Plan ("NANP") to include area codes with a second digit other than 0 or 1. For example, portions of Northern Virginia now have the 540 area code. Prior to divestiture, the NANP was administered by the Bell System. After divestiture, the Bell Operating Companies' research and development arm, Bell Communications Research ("Bellcore") took over the administrative responsibility. In 1994, the FCC issued a Notice of Proposed Rulemaking to determine whether a different entity, unaffiliated with the BOCs should take over responsibility for administering the NANP. *See* In the Matter of Administration of the North American Numbering Plan, Notice of Proposed Rulemaking, Phases One and Two, CC Docket No. 92–237, 9 FCC Rcd. 2068 (1994), Report and Order, FCC 95–283, 11 FCC Rcd. 2588 (rel. July 13, 1995).

62. "Number portability" here refers to the ability of a customer to change 800 service providers without being forced to change phone numbers. Under the data base system, all 800 numbers are stored in a computer data base that includes for each number a field identifying the carrier selected by the customer. LECs generally use their common channel Signaling System 7 (SS7) networks to query this data base and determine the proper routing for all 800 calls. Pacific Bell Petition for Waiver of 800 Data Base Access Time Requirements BellSouth Petition for Waiver of 800 Data Base Access Time Requirements, CC Docket No. 86–10, DA 95–375, 11 FCC Rcd 4436 (rel. Feb. 28, 1995). *See also* Telephone Number Portability, CC Docket No. 95–116, Notice of Proposed Rulemaking, 10 FCC Rcd. 12350 (1995).

63. Provision of Access for 800 Service, CC Docket No. 86–10, Notice of Proposed Rule Making, 102 FCC2d 1387 (1986); Supplemental Notice of Proposed Rule Making, 3 FCC Rcd 721 (1988); Report and Order, 4 FCC Rcd 2824 (1989); Mem. Op. and Order on Recons. and Second Supplemental Notice of Proposed Rule Making, 6 FCC Rcd 5421 (1991); Order, 7 FCC Rcd 8616 (1992); Second Report and Order, 8 FCC Rcd 907 (1993) (Rate Structure Order); Mem. Op. and Order on Further Recons., 8 FCC Rcd 1038 (1993); Order, 8 FCC Rcd 1423 (1993); Order, DA 93–294 (March 11, 1993). In 1995, the FCC initiated a rulemaking addressing the need for number portability in other types of telephone services.

2. *Expanded Interconnection*

In 1992 the Commission authorized "expanded interconnection"[64] opportunities for new carriers, particularly providers of alternative access to interexchange carrier services and local telephone services.[65] These carriers, commonly referred to as Competitive Access Providers ("CAPS") and Competitive Exchange Carriers ("CLECs"), along with new services of cable television and wireless operators, have generated the potential for competition with incumbent local exchange carriers. However, CAPS do not construct an infrastructure parallel to that of the incumbent carrier. Instead, they typically concentrate on serving densely populated areas and central business districts often providing direct access to fiber optic facilities. To serve other customers and to secure call completion to telephone subscribers not directly accessed by their facilities, CAPS need to interconnect with facilities of the incumbent local exchange carrier.[66] CAPS need to receive from and hand off to a competitor possibly disinclined to help foster competition and motivated to provide inferior or costly access. Accordingly, regulators must determine what constitutes fair competition, including the terms and conditions for access to incumbent carrier facilities.

Regulators have confronted vastly divergent characterizations of CAPs. Incumbent carriers typically consider them "cherry pickers" who can serve the most profitable customers with cutting edge technology, thereby "bypassing" the incumbent carriers' facilities and in turn reducing revenues needed to support price averaging of dense and sparse routes. On the other hand, CAPS consider themselves underdogs in the quest to foster, for the first time, true competition in the local exchange service marketplace, previously considered a natural monopoly. Regulators have encouraged competition from CAPS by classifying them as private carriers who can negotiate contracts with customer-specific terms, conditions, and prices. While incumbent LECs have achieved some pricing flexibility, they still remain subject to more extensive regulatory oversight that limits their flexibility and speed in responding

---

64. Expanded interconnection is a LEC offering that enables parties to compete on a facilities basis with certain LEC services by interconnecting their circuits with those of the LEC at the LEC central office. Expanded interconnection through virtual collocation enables an interconnector to terminate its circuits in central office transmission equipment owned by the LEC and under the physical control of the LEC. The interconnector has the right to designate its choice of central office equipment, which is dedicated to the exclusive use of the interconnector, and installed, maintained and repaired by the LEC. Expanded Interconnection With Local Telephone Company Facilities, CC Docket No. 91–141, 9 FCC Rcd 5154, 5158 (1994).

65. *See* Expanded Interconnection with Local Telephone Company Facilities, CC Docket No. 91–141, Report and Order and Notice of Proposed Rulemaking, 7 FCC Rcd. 7369 (1992), *on recons.*, Mem. Op. and Order, 8 FCC Rcd. 127 (1992), *on further recons.*, Second Mem. Op. and Order on Recons., 8 FCC Rcd, 7341 (1993), *vacated in part and remanded sub nom.* Bell Atlantic Telephone Cos. v. FCC, 24 F.3d 1441, 306 U.S. App. D.C. 333 (D.C.Cir.1994).

66. "Since the CAP networks are still limited in coverage, they need to interconnect with the LECs to reach customers not part of the CAP network and at times to interconnect with interexchange carriers to complete long distance phone calls." Leonard M. Baynes, *The on-Ramp to the Information Superhighway: a Case Study of the New York Collocation and Telecommunications Policy*, 7 DePaul Bus. L.J. 1, 9 (1994).

to customer requirements. Additionally, the incumbent LECs must provide service throughout a certificated region, often at subsidized rates to rural and low volume subscribers.

B. Fostering Local Exchange Competition

The FCC authorized the CAPS initially to provide special access services, such as direct links between an enduser and an interexchange carrier providing interstate services. The Commission later viewed the CAPs as a key competitive force and considered ways to improve the type and quality of LEC facilities interconnection.[67] The FCC recognized that fostering such competition will generate ample public dividends,[68] but also will require incumbent LECs to revamp the physical manner in which they interconnect lines and facilities with users and competitors and the terms and conditions for such interconnections.[69] As to physical interconnection of incumbent[70] and new carrier/end user facilities, the Commission considered two types of arrangements: (1) *co-location*—permitting third parties to install their own facilities at an incumbent LEC's central switching office, in much the same way as one would acquire access to property through a commercial real estate lease; and

67. Expanded Interconnection with Local Telephone Company Facilities, CC Docket No. 91–41, Report and Order and Notice of Proposed Rulemaking, 7 FCC Rcd. 7369 (1992)[hereinafter cited as Expanded Interconnection Order], *recons.* 8 FCC Rcd. 127 (1992)(modifying the scope of geographical availability of expanded interconnection to be tariffed initially) *on further recons.*, 8 FCC Rcd. 7341 (1993) (modifying rate structure and requirements permitting access customers to have a "fresh look" at LEC service alternatives), *vacated in part and remanded sub nom.* Bell Atlantic, Inc. v. FCC, 24 F.3d 1441, 306 U.S. App. D.C. 333 (D.C.Cir.1994), *on remand*, Mem. Op. and Order, 9 FCC Rcd. 5154 (1994) [hereinafter cited as Expanded Interconnection Remand Decision]. *See also* Local Exchange Carriers' Rates, Terms and Conditions for Expanded Interconnection Through Virtual Collocation For Special Access and Switched Transport, CC Docket No. 94–97, Phase I, Report and Order, 10 FCC Rcd. 6375 (1995), Phase II, Order Designating Issues for Investigation, 10 FCC Rcd. 11116 (1995). In an increasing number of states, Public Utility Commissions have also permitted CAPs to provide switched services, *e.g.*, conventional business and residential services often referred to as "Plain Old Telephone Service" (POTS).

68. "Our decisions mandating expanded interconnection and collocation are fundamental to opening the interstate special access and switched transport markets to greater competition. Our simultaneous grant of greater pricing flexibility to the local telephone companies enables those companies to compete more vigorously as well, while assuring that we retain necessary controls on dominant access providers. We believe that expanded interconnection, by fostering increased competition in interstate access markets, should increase economic growth. Competition should lead to lower special access and switched transport charges which in turn will make it possible for long-distance companies to offer service at lower rates, thus stimulating demand for communications services. Lower prices for communications services not only benefit consumers directly, they also make resources available for productive investment elsewhere in the economy." Expanded Interconnection Remand Decision, 9 FCC Rcd 5154, ¶ 1 (1994).

69. *See* Transport Rate Structure and Pricing, CC Docket No. 91–213, Report and Order and Further Notice of Proposed Rulemaking, 7 FCC Rcd. 7006 (1992), *recons.*, First Mem. Op. and Order on Recons., 8 FCC Rcd. 5370 (1993), *on further recons.*, Mem. Op. and Order, 8 FCC Rcd. 6233 (1993), Third Mem. Op. & Order on Recons. and Supplemental Notice of Proposed Rulemaking, 10 FCC Rcd. 3030 (1994).

70. The FCC imposed expanded interconnection requirements on "Tier 1" local exchange carriers, (these carriers whose annual revenues exceed $100 million). Expanded Interconnection Order, 7 FCC Rcd. at 7489–7492.

(2) *virtual co-location*—in lieu of direct physical interconnection of equipment at LEC premises, the LEC provides third parties with the facilities and lines necessary for interconnection at a point near, but not inside the switching office, for instance, a manhole or remote office.

Co-location constitutes an essential element for competitive services from CAPS. Without a direct interconnection of facilities CAPS would have to secure usage based services of the incumbent LEC to handle traffic on a metered basis. Such access charges as applied to interexchange carriers like AT & T, MCI and Sprint constitute over 40 percent of their revenues. If applied to CAPS these rates would render these carriers nothing more than low profit resellers of LEC services. Congress recognized the benefit of facilities-based local exchange service competition by requiring " 'physical collocation of equipment necessary for interconnection or access to unbundled network elements at the premises of the local exchange carrier, . . . [with] virtual collocation if the local exchange carrier demonstrates to the State commission that physical collocation is non practical. . . . ' " [71]

The FCC expressed a preference for physical collocation, but offered to accept waiver petitions upon a showing of insufficient floor space or where formal state action mandated virtual co-location. In exchange for opening up its facilities for interconnection with competitors, incumbent LECs were to receive expanded pricing flexibility for high capacity services, such as digital lines with throughput capacity of 1.544 and 45 Megabits per second. [72] In the context of price cap regulation of LEC rates, the expanded flexibility would have allowed a tariffed rate decrease with additional cost justification and regulatory review. The FCC also would have allowed partial deaveraging of rates to reflect differences in traffic density and presumably as well, differences in the costs of providing service. The Commission had proposed to allow LECs to reduce rates in selected areas as much as 10 percent to reflect higher traffic density, and upward by as much as 5 percent to reflect higher per unit costs for rural routes. Such rate averaging presumably would not constitute discrimination among similarly situated users for like services because traffic density could evidence differences in the cost of providing even the same type of service.

The Court of Appeals for the District of Columbia Circuit vacated in part the FCC's expanded interconnection orders on grounds that the Commission did not have authority under the Communications Act of 1934 to mandate physical collocation. The court held that Section 201(a) of the Communications Act, which authorizes the FCC to order carriers "to establish physical connections with other carriers," [73] did not authorize the Commission "to grant third parties a license to exclusive

71. Communications Act of 1934, as amended, Sec. 251(6), Collocation, *codified at* 47 U.S.C.A. § 251(6)(West Supp. 1997); *see also* Implementation of the Local Competition Provisions of the Telecommunications Act of 1996, CC Docket No. 96–98,

Notice of Proposed Rulemaking, FCC 96–182, 61 Fed. Reg. 18,311 (April 25, 1996).

72. 7 FCC Rcd. at 7453–7456.

73. 47 U.S.C.A. § 201(a) (West 1991).

physical occupation of a section of the LECs' central offices."[74] In the court's view mandatory physical co-location, even if provided for compensation, constituted a "taking" of property under the Fifth Amendment standard established by the Supreme Court in *Loretto v. Teleprompter Manhattan CATV Corp.*[75] Accordingly, the court remanded to the Commission the matter of whether and how to impose a virtual collocation requirement.

The FCC acted quickly to resurrect the mandatory virtual collocation requirement for both special access and switched transport services, with exemptions granted to LECs that choose instead to maintain or offer physical collocation options.[76] While the Commission reiterated its preference for physical collocation as the less costly and technologically superior option,[77] it reendorsed expanded interconnections through virtual collocation as a way

> to facilitate competition for special access and switched transport services, essentially by making it possible … [for end users and LEC competitors] to buy only those LEC transmission and distribution links that a customer wants, and to combine those links with the services of a competitor. This policy enables the LECs' competitors to offer transmission segments that can substitute for the previously bundled segments offered by the LECs, and to connect their own transmission segments with transmission and distribution links that the LECs continue to provide.[78]

The FCC's decision on remand emphasized the inapplicability of *Loretto* and the absence of a taking of property from virtual collocation, because "unlike physical collocation, interconnectors have no right to enter LEC-owned premises or to install their own equipment at such locations."[79] The LEC may dedicate certain equipment for the exclusive use of a

74. Bell Atlantic Telephone Cos. v. FCC, 24 F.3d 1441, 1446, 306 U.S. App. D.C. 333, 338 (D.C.Cir.1994).

75. 458 U.S. 419, 426, 102 S.Ct. 3164, 3170, 73 L.Ed.2d 868 (1982) (deeming as an unconstitutional taking a New York statute requiring landlords to permit cable television installation).

76. Expanded Interconnection Remand Proceeding, 9 FCC Rcd. 5154, 5156, ¶ 3.

77. *Id.* at 5159, ¶ 10. The Commission noted that virtual collocation requires an interconnector to procure from the LEC transport services to link lines and equipment that would not have been required in a physical co-location environment. Additionally, the length of such "cross-connect" lines typically cannot exceed 450 feet. *Id.* at paras. 10–11. Virtual co-location requirements include the duty of a LEC to provide signaling information necessary for competitors to provide tandem switching, switching at a high level of traffic aggregation, in competition with the LECs. *See* Expanded Interconnection with Local Telephone Company Facilities, CC Docket No. 91–141, Transport Phase II, Third Report and Order, 9 FCC Rcd. 2718 (1994).

78. 9 FCC Rcd. at 5159, ¶ 9. The Commission has closely examined cost allocation and rate setting for co-location tariffs. *See* Local Exchange Carriers' Rates, Terms, and Conditions for Expanded Interconnection Through Virtual Collocation for Special Access and Switched Transport, CC Docket No. 94–97, Report and Order, 10 FCC Rcd. 6375 (1995)(holding that the LECs have failed to meet their burden under Sec. 204(a) of the Communications Act to demonstrate the justness and reasonableness of overhead loading levels); *see also* Order Designating Issues for Investigation, CC Docket No. 94–97, Phase II, DA 95–2001, 10 FCC Rcd. 11116 (rel. Sep. 19, 1995).

79. Expanded Interconnection Remand Proceeding, 9 FCC Rcd. 5154, 5163, ¶ 25.

particular customer—a customary practice in telecommunications—but no physical occupation or invasion by an outsider takes place.[80]

C. Local Exchange Service Pricing Flexibility—Price Caps

A monumental change in the manner in which the FCC regulated the rates and profitability of carriers occurred when the Commission adopted price caps in lieu of conventional rate of return regulation. Prior to adopting a more flexible approach that attempts to create incentives for carriers to operate efficiently, the FCC applied traditional public utility ratemaking "based directly on cost. .[with] rates [set] no higher than necessary to obtain 'sufficient revenue to cover ... [a carrier's] costs and achieve a fair return on equity.' "[81]

The Commission grew to recognize that regulation based on carrier-reported costs plus a prescribed rate of return created perverse incentives[82] including:

- rate base padding, *i.e.*, overinvestment in plant and other facilities that qualify for inclusion in the amount of investment to which the prescribed rate of return applies;

- the ability to pass any cost to ratepayers, often without regard for ways to economize;

- the incentive to shift costs from unregulated and competitive activities to regulated and often monopolized services regardless of which service necessitated carrier investment and expenses; and

- the involvement of accountants, lawyers, expert witnesses and others in a lengthy and costly processes ostensibly to determine a fair rate of return on proper investments and reimbursement of reasonably incurred expenses.

1. Price Cap Mechanics

In 1990, the FCC adopted price cap regulation[83] for LECs and for

80. *See, e.g.,* FCC v. Florida Power Corp., 480 U.S. 245, 251–53, 107 S.Ct. 1107, 1111–1113, 94 L.Ed.2d 282, 289–91 (1987) The element of "required acquiescence is at the heart of the concept of occupation" under *Loretto*.

81. Nat'l Rural Telecom Ass'n v. FCC, 988 F.2d 174, 177–78, 300 U.S. App. D.C. 226, 229–230 (D.C.Cir.1993) (quoting Policy and Rules Concerning Rates for Dominant Carriers, Further Notice of Proposed Rulemaking, 3 FCC Rcd. 3195, 3211 (1988)).

82. "By the late 1980s, however, the FCC began to take serious note of some of the inefficiencies inherent in rate-of-return regulation. First, the resulting cost incentives are perverse. Because a firm can pass any cost along to ratepayers (unless it is identified as imprudent), its incentive to

innovate is less sharp than if it were unregulated. There is even a temptation toward 'gold-plat[ing]'—using equipment or services that are not justifi[ed] in purely economic terms, especially when their use improves the lot of management (elegant offices, company jets, etc.)." 988 F.2d at 178, 300 U. S. App. D.C. at 230 (citing LEC Price Cap Order, 5 FCC Rcd. at 6853, n. 450).

83. The price cap rules are codified at Sections 61.41–61.49 of the Commission's Rules, 47 C.F.R. §§ 61.41–61.49 (1997). *See also* Policy and Rules Concerning Rates for Dominant Carriers, CC Docket No. 87–313, Second Report and Order, 5 FCC Rcd. 6786 (1990), *recons.*, Order on Recons., 6 FCC Rcd. 2637 (1991), *further recons.*, Report and Order & Order on Further Recons. &

some AT & T services.[84] The Commission began to realize that the old cost plus a set rate of return model created disincentives for efficiency and productivity. An efficient carrier would have to pass along cost savings and earnings in excess of the revenue requirement to rate payers through rate reductions,[85] while an inefficient carrier could pad its rate base and expenses with the expectation that tariffs would increase to meet the revenue requirement.

A price cap regulatory regime attempts to rely on marketplace mechanisms and the existence of competition in lieu of a lengthy and speculative regulatory mechanism.[86] In price cap regulation carriers have incentives to operate more efficiently and productively because they can capture monetary savings rather than have to pass them on to users through refunds or lower rates. Instead of prescribing a rate of return, which purports to reflect a carrier's market risks and cost of attracting holders of its stock and bonds, the Commission accepts its current price levels as a starting point.[87]

Supplemental Notice of Proposed Rulemaking, 6 FCC Rcd. 4524 (1991), *second further recons.*, 7 FCC Rcd. 5235 (1992), *aff'd sub nom.*, National Rural Telecom Ass'n v. FCC, 988 F.2d 174, 300 U.S. App. D.C. 226 (D.C.Cir.1993). The Commission had previously imposed price cap regulation on AT & T, *see* Report and Order and Second Further Notice of Proposed Rulemaking, 4 FCC Rcd. 2873 (1989). The Commission has investigated whether the price cap regime might have an adverse impact on service quality. *See* Policy and Rules Concerning Rates for Dominant Carriers, CC Docket No. 87–313, Mem. Op. and Order, 6 FCC Rcd 2974 (1991) (Service Quality Order), *mod.*, Mem. Op. and Order, 6 FCC Rcd 4819 (1991), *further mod.*, Public Notice, Adjustments to Price Cap Carriers' Service Quality and Infrastructure Reports in ARMIS, Public Notice, 7 FCC Rcd 3590 (rel. Mar. 31, 1992), *further mod.*, Public Notice, Modifications to Service Quality Infrastructure Reporting, 7 FCC Rcd 4632 (released July 7, 1992), *mod.*, ARMIS Filing Requirements, Public Notice, 7 FCC Rcd 8795 (1992) and Erratum, DA 92–1696 (rel. Dec. 18, 1992), *further mod.*, 8 FCC Rcd 7259 (1993) (modified service quality order).

84. Traditional public utility rate regulation involved calculation of a carriers revenue requirement, namely the total sum of annual revenues the carrier should generate from tariffed service. The revenue requirement was calculated by adding operating expenses, taxes, current year depreciation to the rate base, the value of working physical assets minus accumulated depreciation multiplied by a regulatory agency determined rate of return.

85. The carrier may refund the over earnings. *See, e.g.*, AT & T v. FCC, 836 F.2d 1386, 267 U.S. App. D.C. 38 (D.C.Cir.1988) (reversing the FCC rule requiring carriers to refund excess earnings and interpreting the Communications Act as limiting the Commission's remedial power to prospective relief). However, Sec. 204(a) of the Communications Act does allow the FCC to order refunds where it has allowed rates to take effect subject to an accounting order that subsequently evidences unreasonable and excessive rates.

86. For an extensive review of the price cap mechanism *see* Sutapa Ghosh, *The Future of FCC Dominant Carrier Rate Regulation: The Price Caps Scheme*, 41 Fed. Com. L. J. 401 (1989).

87. *See* Policy and Rules Concerning Rates for Dominant Carriers, CC Docket No. 87–313, Notice of Proposed Rulemaking, 2 FCC Rcd. 5208 (1987) (proposing price cap regulation of AT & T), Further Notice of Proposed Rulemaking, 3 FCC Rcd. 3195 (1988), Report and Order and Second Further Notice of Proposed Rulemaking 4 FCC Rcd. 2873 (1989), *erratum*, 4 FCC Rcd. 3379 (1989), *on further recons.* 6 FCC Rcd. 665 (1991), *mod.*, Order and Recons., 6 FCC Rcd. 2637 (1991); *see also* Motion of AT & T to be Reclassified as a Non–Dominant Carrier, Order, FCC 95–427, 11 FCC Rcd. 3271, (rel. Oct. 23, 1995).

The FCC subsequently applied price caps to major local exchange carriers. Policy and Rules Concerning Rates for Dominant Carriers, Second Report and Order, 5 FCC Rcd. 6786 (1990), *erratum*, 5 FCC Rcd. 7664 (1990), *modified on recons.*, 6 FCC Rcd. 2637 (1991), *petitions for further recons.*

The price cap system starts by simply accepting as lawful a baseline for all current rates.[88] then classifies services into "baskets"[89] and "bands" based on common characteristics.[90] Service baskets are broad categories of services, for instance shared common line services and individually used traffic sensitive services. Bands are further refinements of service baskets and are further subdivided into "service categories." Within AT & T's Residential and Small Business Basket, for instance, there are subelements by time of day along with categories for special calling plans and for directory assistance and credit card calling.

Rates charged by price-cap-regulated carriers can rise in parallel with an overall measurement of consumer prices, namely the Gross National Product fixed weight price index as offset by a productivity factor to reflect declining costs and expected efficiency gains in telecommunications. However, the FCC also established rules limiting the maximum aggregate prices for each basket and permitted streamlined processing of price increases or decreases for each service category within a basket that fall within a band.[91] To prevent cross-subsidization between service baskets, the FCC will not allow a LEC to justify an increase in rates in one basket because rates have dropped in another one. But to allow flexibility to respond to varying degrees of service demand and the extent to which a user group can secure alternative services, also known

dismissed, 6 FCC Rcd. 7482 (1991) *aff'd sub nom.* Nat'l Rural Telecom Ass'n v. FCC, 988 F.2d 174, 300 U.S. App. D.C. 226 (D.C.Cir.1993) (affirming FCC requirements that a local exchange carrier electing price caps must do so permanently and for all affiliates); *see also* Regulatory Reform For Local Exchange Carriers Subject to Rate of Return Regulation, CC Docket No. 93–179, 8 FCC Rcd. 4415 (1993) (allowing adjustment in following year's price cap calculations to reflect previous year's rate of return that was 1 percent or more below the prescribed level).

The FCC still later applied a price cap regime to medium and small local exchange carriers, including ones not affiliated with the Regional Bell Operating Companies. Regulatory Reform For Local Exchange Carriers Subject to Rate of Return Regulation, CC Docket No. 92–135, Notice of Proposed Rulemaking, 7 FCC Rcd. 5023 (1992), *erratum,* 7 FCC Rcd. 5501 (1992) Report and Order, 8 FCC Rcd. 4545 (1993).

88. "Under a price cap scheme, the regulator sets a maximum price, and the firm selects rates at or below the cap. Because cost savings do not trigger reductions in the cap, the firm has a powerful profit incentive to reduce costs. Nor is there any reward for shifting costs from unregulated activities into regulated ones, for the higher costs will not produce higher legal ceiling prices. Finally, the regulator has less need to collect detailed cost data from the regulated firms

or to devise formulae for allocating the costs among the firm's services." National Rural Telecom. Ass'n., 988 F.2d at 178, 300 U.S. App. D.C. at 230.

89. Prior to creating the trunking basket, the Commission divided LEC charges into four baskets: common line, traffic sensitive, special access and interexchange.

90. Currently, there are three service baskets for AT & T: (1) residential and small business; (2) 800 services; and (3) other business services. Local exchange carriers have five different service baskets: (1) "common line services"; (2) "traffic sensitive services" [containing subelements for local switching, local transport, information, tandem switched transport, interconnection and data base access]; (3) "special access services"; (4) "interexchange services" and (5) a later created "trunking basket" formed by pulling from the existing transport sensitive services basket all transmission related elements, including tandem switching, and interconnection. *See* LEC Price Cap Order, 5 FCC Rcd. at 6811; Transport Rate Structure and Pricing, CC Docket No. 91–213, Second Report and Order, 9 FCC Rcd. 615 (1994).

91. The FCC requires cost support information to justify rates changes, upward or downward, that do not fit within the established ceiling and floor set for price baskets and service categories.

as demand and supply elasticities, the FCC allows streamlined review of rates increases and decreases that are within plus or minus 5 percent.[92] In other words, price cap regulation presumes as lawful any individual service rate set by a carrier, provided the overall basket of services meets the required annual reduction and no individual rate exceeds or falls below a 5 percent zone of reasonableness without carrier justification.[93] The Commission also recognized that it should allow carriers to pass through one time, "exogenous" changes in costs that would result, for example, if cost allocation and accounting rules change.[94]

In the early 1990s, the price cap regime required carriers to reduce total rates by a 3.3 percent "X-factor." The FCC established the lower figure to reflect its estimate of obtainable efficiency gains of 2.8 percent, based on historical data, plus a 0.5 percent "consumer productivity" dividend to reflect the consumer benefits from marketplace competition and incentive regulation. As a "backstop" to prevent LECs from greatly exceeding this productivity goal without having to share any portion with ratepayers, the FCC established a three-tier sharing rule when the carrier exceeds the Commission prescribed rate of return.

- For the first 1 percent the carrier can keep the entire amount;[95]

- For returns between 1 and 5 percent in excess of the prescribed rate, the carrier can retain half and rebate to users the other half; and

- For returns in excess of 5 percent, the carrier must rebate the entire amount.[96]

The FCC recently proposed changes to the LEC price cap plan with an eye toward enabling the LECs to lower prices more quickly in response to competition and eventually to eliminate price cap regulation for services subject to substantial competition. In the First Report and Order in CC Docket No. 94–1, the Commission acknowledged the emer-

---

92. LEC Price Cap Order, 5 FCC Rcd. at 6811–12.

93. Carriers do not receive streamlined regulatory consideration and bear a substantial burden to justify rates that exceed or fall below the zone of reasonableness. *See* Policy and Rules Concerning Rates for Dominant Carriers, Report and Order and Second Further Notice of Proposed Rulemaking, 4 FCC Rcd. 2873, 3100–03 (1989); AT & T Price Cap Recons. Order, 6 FCC Rcd. 666 (1991).

94. Exogenous costs are "in general those costs that are triggered by administrative, legislative or judicial action beyond the control of the carriers." 5 FCC Rcd. at 6807. Because of the carriers' lack of control, adjustments for such changes presumably do not undermine the price caps' incentive structure. The Commission considered in advance several likely instances for exogenous cost treatment, including

changes in amounts paid or received under certain pooling arrangements and accounting changes, *e.g.*, changes made by the Commission itself in its Uniform System of Accounts. *Id.* at 6807; *see also* 47 CFR § 61.45(d)(1) (1996); Southwestern Bell Tel. Co. v. FCC, 28 F.3d 165, 307 U.S.App.D.C. 298 (D.C.Cir.1994) (holding that exogenous cost treatment had improperly been denied to changes in accounting treatment of certain post-retirement worker benefits); Bell Atlantic Tel. Cos. v. FCC, 79 F.3d 1195, 316 U.S. App. D.C. 395 (D.C.Cir.1996)(affirming FCC's revised price cap methodology including the "X-factor" productivity offset).

95. The FCC provided LECs with a higher 4.3 percent productivity offset which if elected would enable a LEC to begin sharing at 2 percent over the benchmark rate of return.

96. 5 FCC Rcd. at 6801.

gence of competition for certain LEC interstate services and granted the LECs greater pricing flexibility, expanding the lower pricing limits from 5 to 10 percent for most of the service categories within the traffic sensitive and trunking baskets, and from 10 to 15 percent for those that apply to density pricing zones.[97] In a Further Notice, the Commission asked for comment on whether its new service rules for LEC price cap services should be relaxed further by reducing the notice and cost support requirements to facilitate the introduction of some new services.[98] It also asked whether it should replace the requirement that a LEC obtain a waiver of Part 69 of the rules before introducing new switched access services with a more streamlined procedure for introducing new switched access rate elements. The Commission also asked whether the lower service band index limit should be eliminated and whether it should permit any other additional downward pricing flexibility. In addition, the Commission asked for comments on whether any revisions of the price cap baskets should be made and whether any service categories should be consolidated.

The Commission further asked for comment on whether any or all of its proposals for relaxed regulatory treatment and additional pricing flexibility should be conditioned on a demonstration that barriers to entry to the local exchange market have been removed, and, if so, what showing should be required. In addition, it invited parties to comment on the appropriate product and geographic markets that should be used for any such assessment of competitive conditions. It also asked what impact these changes might have on interstate toll rates.

The Commission next sought comment on the requirements for removing LEC interstate access services from price caps and placing them under streamlined regulation. It asked whether LEC services should be removed from price cap regulation and made subject to streamlined regulation upon the same standard as AT & T services, and whether the Commission should consider the same factors—demand responsiveness, supply responsiveness, pricing history and market share—in evaluating whether that standard has been met. In addition, the Commission asked whether LECs should be permitted to offer contract carriage for services that are subject to streamlined regulation, subject to the same conditions as AT & T. The Commission also sought comment on whether it should adopt rules now that would define the conditions "price cap LECs" must meet to be considered nondominant, what those conditions should be and whether a LEC should be regulated

97. Price Cap Performance Review for Local Exchange Carriers, CC Docket No. 94–1, First Report & Order, 10 FCC Rcd. 8961 (1995).

98. Price Cap Performance Review for Local Exchange Carriers, Second Further Notice of Proposed Rulemaking in CC Docket No. 94–1, Further Notice of Proposed Rulemaking in CC Docket No. 93–124, and Second Further Notice of Proposed Rulemaking in CC Docket No. 93–

197, 11 FCC Rcd. 858 (1995) (seeking comment on achieving greater pricing flexibility to reflect marketplace competition, but still in a price cap environment); Price Cap Performance Review for Local Exchange Carriers, Fourth Further Notice of Proposed Rulemaking, CC Docket No. 94–1, 10 FCC Rcd. 13659 (1995) (seeking comment on calculating the productivity factor in the future).

as nondominant for certain services or within certain geographic markets but not for others. Finally, the Commission asked for comments on whether changes in access prices charged by CAPs should receive exogenous cost treatment under the AT & T price cap plan, as such changes by price-cap LECs do now.

2. Revised Price Caps Under the 1996 Telecommunications Act

In 1997 as part of its implementation of the Telecommunications Act of 1996 and reform of local exchange carrier interconnection rules, access charges and universal service funding, the FCC revised the price cap plan for incumbent local exchange carriers.[99] The Commission's new price cap plan requires LECs subject to price caps to reduce their price cap indices by a single 6.5 percent X factor annually, less an adjustment for inflation—an increase from the previous highest rate of 5.3%. On the other hand, the new rules eliminate the requirement that LECs earning more than certain specified rates of return on interstate investment "share" all or a portion of such excess price cap earnings with their access customers during the next year in the form of lower rates. The Commission concluded that sharing substantially undercuts the efficiency incentives of price cap regulation.

The FCC imposed a more aggressive price cap formula with the idea that it would expedite the elimination of all forms of rate regulation. The Commission reiterated that price cap rules attempt to create incentives for efficiency, innovation, and responsiveness to consumer demand like that established by a competitive market for interstate access services. The revised rules seek to encourage LECs to become more productive by permitting then to capture the upside financial gains, while at the same time limiting the prices they may charge for interstate access services. If a LEC's earnings fall below a 10.25 percent floor in any calendar year, the carrier may increase its interstate access rates in their next annual filing to levels targeted to such a rate of return.

The FCC's order required price cap incumbent LECs to file revisions to their interstate access tariffs in compliance with the new rules, to be effective July 1, 1997. It also directed the LECs to set their 1997 price cap indices for the coming year at the levels they would be if the new 6.5 percent X–Factor had been in effect at the time of the 1996 tariff filing.

D. Duty to Provide "Dark" Fiber

The scope of a local exchange carrier's common carrier service obligation was examined by the District of Columbia Circuit in *Southwestern Bell Telephone Co. v. FCC*.[100] The FCC considered as common carriage the provision of "dark" fiber optic cable, *i.e.*, broadband transmission capacity that has been installed but not equipped with the laser

---

99. Price Cap Performance Review for Local Exchange Carriers, CC Docket No. 94–1, Fourth Report and Order, 12 FCC Rcd. 16642 (1997).

100. 19 F.3d 1475, 305 U.S. App. D.C. 272 (1994).

and other electronic components needed for operation.[1] After having received LEC contracts for leasing dark fiber on an individual case basis (an ad hoc negotiated basis specifically tailored to meet the needs of a single customer), the FCC subsequently received revisions for broadband capacity using "lit" fiber optic cables equipped with the necessary power and laser equipment. The Commission investigated whether the rate differential between dark and lit fiber service constituted "unjust or unreasonable discrimination" in violation of Section 202(a) of the Communications Act.[2]

The Commission considered individual case basis ("ICB") pricing as an acceptable practice until a carrier had acquired enough experience and service demand to file average cost rates.[3] Accordingly, the Commission asserted Title II jurisdiction over both types of fiber optic cable services and expected carriers to file generally available, tariffed and average cost rates for both.[4] The LECs did not want to make dark fiber generally available at averaged cost and sought to withdraw the service by filing an application pursuant to Section 214 of the Communications Act. The Commission denied the application on grounds that the carriers had failed to meet their burden of showing that such a withdrawal would not adversely affect the public convenience or necessity.[5]

The Court was not persuaded that just because the LECs had made dark fiber facilities available only on an individual case basis, they had acceded to the full array of common carrier regulation under Title II of the Communications Act:

> Whether an entity in a given case is to be considered a common carrier or a private carrier turns on the particular practice under surveillance. If the carrier chooses its clients on an individual basis and determines in each particular case "whether and on what terms to serve" and there is no specific regulatory compulsion to serve all indifferently, the entity is a private carrier for that particular service and the Commission is not at liberty to subject the entity to regulation as a common carrier.[6]

The Court of Appeals reiterated its holding in *NARUC-I* and *II* that a common carrier can qualify for non-common carrier status regarding certain services.[7] While a common carrier cannot "vitiate its common

---

1. Bell Atlantic Telephone Companies, Revisions to Tariff F.C.C. No. 1, 6 FCC Rcd. 1436 (1991) *on review*, 6 FCC Rcd. 4891 (1991). Southwestern Bell Telephone Co., 8 FCC Rcd. 2589 (1993) (refusing permission to withdraw offering of dark fiber).

2. Local Exchange Carriers' Individual Case Basis DS3 Service Offerings, Mem. Op. and Order, 4 FCC Rcd. 8634 (1989).

3. *Id.* at 8642.

4. The Commission assumed that the filing of ICBs by the carriers constituted an acceptance of common carrier status and FCC jurisdiction.

5. Southwestern Bell Telephone Co., 8 FCC Rcd. at 2589.

6. Southwestern Bell Telephone Co. v. FCC, 19 F.3d at 1481, 305 U.S. App. D.C. at 278 (citing NARUC–II, 533 F.2d at 608–09, 174 U.S. App. D.C. at 381–382; NARUC–I, 525 F.2d at 643, 173 U.S. App. D.C. at 426).

7. "It is at least logical to conclude that one can be a common carrier with regard to some activities but not others." NARUC–II, 533 F. 2d at 608, 174 U.S. App. D.C. at 381.

carrier status merely by entering into private contractual relationships with its customers ... it does not make sense that the filing of the terms of any contract—no matter how customer tailored—with the FCC, without more, reflects a conscious decision to offer the service to all takers on a common carrier basis."[8]

The Court endorsed the FCC's requirement that carriers file ICB contracts to ensure that carriers do not use contracts to circumvent Title II regulation.[9] But on the other hand, the filing of a contract, when it is permissible to do so, does not "supply the bootstrap for Title II common carriage rate regulation of virtually any service provided by an entity"[10] that provides other types of service on a common carrier basis.[11]

E. Calling Number Identification

Significant commercial opportunities and privacy questions result when telephone companies commercialize signaling technologies that make it possible to identify the telephone number of calling parties. Calling Number Identification, commonly known as "Caller–ID," makes it possible for retailers to verify credit and billing information almost instantaneously thereby reducing transaction and processing time. On the other hand, without opportunities to block the Caller–ID function, a caller seeking anonymity for lawful purposes might lose that opportunity.[12] The FCC concluded that interstate callers should have a simple, uniform way of assuring privacy on an interstate call. The Commission amended its rules to require common carriers using the SS7 signaling system, which makes Caller–ID possible with little additional expense, to provide the service without charge, including the mechanism for blocking the service.[13] Many, but not all states parallel the FCC requirement by requiring carriers to provide local and intrastate callers with Caller–ID service and the ability for calling parties to block the transmission of

---

8. Southwestern Bell Telephone Co, 19 F.3d at 1481, 305 U.S. App. D.C. at 278.

9. *Id.* at 1483, 305 U.S. App. D.C. at 280 (citing 47 U.S.C.A. § Sec. 211(a) (West 1991)).

10. *Id.*

11. "While the Commission has ancillary jurisdiction over private offerings of common carriers under section 152 [of the Communications Act] any may require common carriers to supply information regarding their private carriage offerings pursuant to section 211, only common carrier activity falls within the Commission's regulatory powers under Title II." *Id., citing* MCI Telecommunications Corp. v. FCC, 765 F.2d 1186, 1188, 247 U.S. App. D.C. 32, 33 (D.C.Cir.1985); Computer and Communications Inds. Ass'n v. FCC, 693 F.2d 198, 211, 224 U.S.App.D.C. 83, 96 (D.C.Cir.1982).

12. "The Commission recognized that passage of CPN [the calling party's number] could invade the privacy of calling parties wishing to remain anonymous. While the Commission recognized the privacy right of the called party to know who is calling, it found that the federal model governing passage of CPN should also offer the calling party a means of remaining anonymous." Rules and Policies Regarding Calling Number Identification Service—Caller ID, CC Docket No. 91–281, FCC 95–187, Mem. Op. and Order on Recons., Second Report and Order and Third Notice of Proposed Rulemaking, 10 FCC Rcd. 11700, 11706, ¶ 13 (1995), Order, 10 FCC Rcd. 13819 (1995); *see also*, Rules and Policies Regarding Calling Number Identification—Caller ID, Order and Fourth Notice of Proposed Rulemaking, 10 FCC Rcd. 13796 (1995).

13. Rules and Policies Regarding Calling Number Identification Service—Caller ID, CC Docket No. 91–281, Report and Order and Further Notice of Proposed Rulemaking, 9 FCC Rcd. 1764 at paras. 3, 17.

the number of the telephone originating the call by dialing *67 on a per-call basis.[14]

12.8 Divestiture of the Bell System (The Modification of Final Judgement or "MFJ")

Telecommunications marketplace domination by the American Telephone and Telegraph Company triggered frequent antitrust concerns resulting in three major consent decrees in 1914,[1] 1956[2] and 1982.[3] The antitrust law suits initiated by the Department of Justice required a court to consider whether and how vertical and horizontal market integration and corporate strategies designed to maintain market domination trigger antitrust liability, despite extensive regulatory oversight. While none of the cases reached a verdict,[4] the ruling by Judge Harold H. Greene denying AT & T's motion to dismiss the government's 1974 suit, after conclusion of the government's case in chief, did identify problem

---

14. *Id.* at ¶ 15.

1. In 1913, the federal government filed a civil antitrust suit to block AT & T's acquisition of a small long distance telephone company. The government had expressed concern that the Bell System was attempting to monopolize the local and long distance telephone market. In a consent decree, commonly referred to as the Kingsbury Commitment, AT & T agreed to refrain from acquiring competing independent telephone companies and to provide facilities access to other telephone companies. For a complete analysis of Bell System antitrust issues *see* MICHAEL W. KELLOGG, JOHN THORNE AND PETER W. HUBER, FEDERAL TELECOMMUNICATIONS LAW, 199–248 (1992).

2. In 1949 the federal government filed another antitrust suit alleging attempted monopolization of telecommunications equipment and services through the manner in which the Bell System acquired and licensed patents. The parties settled in 1956 with a Consent Decree that obligated AT & T to grant nonexclusive licenses for all existing and future Bell System patents, furnish licensees with technical information sufficient for them to manufacture equipment in competition with Western Electric, which would be limited to the manufacture of telephone equipment, and to provide only common carrier communication services. *See* United States v. Western Elec. Co., 1956 Trade Cases (CCH) ¶ 68,246 (D.N.J. 1956). The latter restriction would grow increasingly limiting in view of technological innovations that integrated data processing with conventional common carrier functions.

3. United States v. AT & T, 552 F.Supp. 131, 226–234 (D.D.C.1982), cert. denied, 460 U.S. 1001, 103 S.Ct. 1240, 75 L.Ed.2d 472 (1983). This consent decree, stylized as a modification of the 1956 "Final Judgment," settled an antitrust suit brought by the federal government in 1974 in the United States District Court for the District of Columbia alleging an unlawful combination within the Bell System resulting in the monopolization of both long distance telephone service and the manufacture of telecommunications equipment. The MFJ text is set out at 552 F. Supp. at 226–234.

4. By agreeing to the terms and conditions set out in a Consent Decree, AT & T avoided having a large factual record with *res judicata* value for private antitrust litigants. However, AT & T did not avoid liability in such cases. In 1980, MCI won a $1.8 billion antitrust suit, later reduced by the presiding judge. *See* MCI Communications Corp. v. AT & T, 462 F.Supp. 1072 (N.D.Ill.1978), *aff'd*, 594 F.2d 594 (7th Cir. 1978), *cert. denied*, 440 U.S. 971, 99 S.Ct. 1533, 59 L.Ed.2d 787 (1979); Litton Systems, Inc. v. AT & T, 700 F.2d 785 (2d Cir.1983), cert. denied, 464 U.S. 1073, 104 S.Ct. 984, 79 L.Ed.2d 220 (1984); Mid–Texas Communications Sys., Inc. v. AT & T, 615 F.2d 1372 (5th Cir.1980); Woodlands Telecommunications Corp. v. Southwestern Bell Tel. Co., 449 U.S. 912, 101 S.Ct. 286, 66 L.Ed.2d 140 (1980); Northeastern Tel. Co. v. AT & T, 651 F.2d 76 (2d Cir.1981), cert. denied 455 U.S. 943, 102 S.Ct. 1438, 71 L.Ed.2d 654 (1982). However, U.S. Sprint failed to recover damages in its antitrust litigation. Southern Pacific Comms. Co. v. AT & T, 556 F.Supp. 825 (D.D.C. 1982).

areas:[5] exclusion of competition by restricting interconnection to local facilities, cross-subsidization of long distance services from monopoly local exchange services and restricting the option of users to attach equipment to the telephone network.[6]

After a number of false starts and negotiation quagmires, AT & T and the federal government reached the basis for a settlement: divestiture of the local Bell Operating Companies from AT & T[7] in exchange for lifting the 1956 consent decree prohibition on AT & T's provision of information processing and other non-communications common carrier services. The maneuvering necessary to achieve this outcome required coordination between the New Jersey District Court, which retained jurisdiction over the 1956 Consent Decree, and the District Court for the District of Columbia that presided over the government's 1974 suit. With jurisdiction to modify the 1956 "Final Judgment," *i.e.*, a 1982 Modification of Final Judgment ("MFJ"), Judge Greene was in a position to assess the public interest merits of the proposed settlement and to modify its terms.[8] To assist in this assessment the Judge allowed intervenors to file comments on the proposed settlement. Additionally, he identified areas where the agreement would have to be modified and established pleading cycles for considering how to carry out the division of personnel and resources. In July, 1993 the Judge issued an extensive opinion, conditionally approving the Plan of Reorganization implementing the Bell Operating Companies ("BOCs") divestiture provided certain additional modifications were made, for instance, AT & T guaranteeing the BOCs' recovery of equal access and network reconfiguration costs, agreeing to assign to the BOCs the Bell name and logo, granting royalty-free licenses to all existing patents then owned or controlled by AT & T and all patents issued within five years after divestiture.[9]

---

5. United States v. AT & T, 524 F.Supp. 1336 (D.D.C.1981).

6. AT & T's defense was based primarily on the premise that pervasive state and federal regulation made it impossible for the Bell System to control prices, exclude competitors and earn excessive rates of return. The interplay of regulatory regimes with the antitrust laws has been a problem for the courts. In the telecommunications area the claim of implied immunity has been raised frequently with little success. *See, e.g.*, MCI Communications Corp. v. AT & T, 708 F.2d 1081 (7th Cir.1983); Phonetele, Inc. v. AT & T, 664 F.2d 716 (9th Cir.1981), cert. denied 459 U.S. 1145, 103 S.Ct. 785, 74 L.Ed.2d 992 (1983); Northeastern Telephone Co. v. AT & T, 651 F.2d 76 (2d Cir.1981), cert. denied 455 U.S. 943, 102 S.Ct. 1438, 71 L.Ed.2d 654 (1982); Sound, Inc. v. AT & T, 631 F.2d 1324 (8th Cir.1980); Mid–Texas Communications Systems, Inc. v. AT & T, 615 F.2d 1372 (5th Cir.), cert. denied 449 U.S. 912, 101 S.Ct. 286, 66 L.Ed.2d 140 (1980); Essential Com-

munications Systems, Inc. v. AT & T, 610 F.2d 1114 (3d Cir.1979).

7. The Justice Department sought divestiture of the BOCs from AT & T, dissolution of Western Electric, the manufacturing arm of the Bell System and a surrender by Western Electric of its 50 percent ownership of Bell Labs, the Bell System's research and development group. *See* Paul Dempsey, *Adam Smith Assaults Ma Bell with His Invisible Hands: Divestiture, Deregulation, and the Need for New Telecommunications Policy*, 11 Comm/Ent L. J. 527, 551 (1989).

8. For example, Judge Greene required revisions to the proposed Modification of Final Judgment to allow the spun-off Bell Operating Companies to market customer premises equipment and to stay in the yellow pages business.

9. United States v. Western Elec. Co., 569 F.Supp. 1057 (D.D.C.1983), *aff'd sub nom.* California v. United States, 464 U.S. 1013, 104 S.Ct. 542, 78 L.Ed.2d 719 (1983).

A. Terms of the MFJ

The 1982 Modification of Final Judgment, contained four basic provisions:

(1) divestiture of the BOCs[10] from AT & T;

(2) specification of the core lines of businesses of the divested BOCs as exchange telecommunications systems and exchange access, *i.e.*, local and long distance services within a geographical service region known as a Local Access and Transport Area[11] ("LATA") and providing access services, on a non-discriminatory basis,[12] to long distance carriers providing inter-LATA services and to other information service providers;

(3) prohibiting the BOCs generally from providing any product or service besides local telephone service "that is not a natural monopoly service actually regulated by tariff"[13] and specifically from certain markets, *i.e.*, inter-LATA telecommunications,[14] in-

10. The MFJ applied as well to any enterprise in which a BOC "controls or possesses a direct or indirect ownership interest greater than 50 percent." MFJ § IV(A). Provisions of the MFJ other than the equal access requirement applied to "affiliated enterprises" which execute contractual arrangements that give BOCs a direct and continuing interest in another enterprise's revenues. *See* United States v. Western Electric Co., 12 F.3d 225, 304 U.S. App. D.C. 199 (D.C.Cir.1993).

11. Section IV(G) of the MFJ defined a LATA as "one or more contiguous local exchange areas serving common social, economic, and other purposes, even where such configuration transcends municipal or other local governmental boundaries." The 163 LATAs created by the MFJ can be as large as a state, *e.g.*, New Mexico, but typically represent only a portion of one state.

12. Section II(A) of the MFJ required the BOCs to provide exchange access "on an unbundled, tariffed basis, that is equal in type, quality, and price to that provided to AT & T." Equal access obligations applied to both private and public telephones, including payphones. *See* United States v. Western Electric Co., 698 F.Supp. 348, 353 (D.D.C.1988) (authorizing owners of the premises where a payphone is located to select the interexchange carrier for direct access). The FCC has examined the matter of interexchange carrier access from payphones and has established as a goal access that meets the billed party's preference, *i.e.*, allowing the person responsible for paying for the call to determine which interexchange carrier shall carry the call. *See* Billed Party Preference for 0 + Inter–LATA

Calls, CC Docket No. 92–77, Notice of Proposed Rulemaking, 7 FCC Rcd. 3027 (1992), Further Notice of Proposed Rulemaking, 9 FCC Rcd. 3320 (1994) (proposing automatic carriage of pay telephone long distance calls by a preselected operator services provider selected by the party being billed for the call instead of the pay phone owner).

The equal access requirement of the MFJ and the FCC's access charge policies also apply to 800 service, commonly referred to as Wide Area Telephone Service ("WATS"). *See* Provision of Access for 800 Service, CC Docket No. 86–10, Notice of Proposed Rule Making, 102 FCC 2d 1387 (1986); Supplemental Notice of Proposed Rule Making, 3 FCC Rcd 721 (1988); Report and Order, 4 FCC Rcd 2824 (1989); Mem. Op. and Order on Recons. and Second Supplemental Notice of Proposed Rule Making, 6 FCC Rcd 5421 (1991); Order, 7 FCC Rcd 8616 (1992); Second Report and Order, 8 FCC Rcd 907 (1993) (Rate Structure Order); Mem. Op. and Order on Further Recons., 8 FCC Rcd 1038 (1993); Order, 8 FCC Rcd 1423 (1993); Order, 8 FCC Rcd. 1844 (1993).

13. MFJ § II(D)3, 552 F.Supp. at 228.

14. The MFJ defined interexchange telecommunications as "telecommunications between a point or points located in one exchange telecommunications area [a LATA] and a point or points located in one or more other [LATAs] ... or a point outside [a LATA]." MFJ § IV(K). The MFJ authorized some inter-LATA traffic such as internal administrative lines. *See* United States v. Western Elec. Co., 569 F.Supp. 1057, 1100 (D.D.C.1983), *aff'd sub nom.* California v. United States, 464 U.S. 1013, 104 S.Ct. 542, 78 L.Ed.2d 719 (1983) ("offi-

formation processing and telecommunications equipment manufacture unless and until a BOC could demonstrate "no substantial possibility that it could use its monopoly power to impede competition in the market it seeks to enter;"[15] and

(4) freeing AT & T from the lines of business limitations contained in the 1956 Consent Decree except that the MFJ contained a seven year moratorium on AT & T providing electronic publishing over its own transmission facilities.[16]

1. Line of Business Restrictions

a. Interexchange Services

Section II(D)(1) of the MFJ prohibited the BOCs from providing "interexchange telecommunication services," *i.e.*, inter-LATA services. This restriction addressed concerns that the BOCs would subvert the MFJ's equal access provisions by engaging in the same sorts of preferential treatment of its inter-exchange affiliates as the Justice Department alleged to have occurred within the Bell System.[17] Accordingly, the BOCs could not deliver inter-LATA traffic, without a MFJ waiver, even where efficiency, financial and traffic management factors support consolidation of data bases and resources, as for instance, a central gateway for handling information services generated by numerous enterprises located in several LATAs.[18]

---

cial services" defined as "communications between personnel or equipment of an Operating Company and their customers."). The District Court has interpreted the MFJ to permit the RBOCs to engage in some interexchange *service. See, e.g.*, United States v. Western Elec. Co., 690 F.Supp. 22 (D.D.C.1988) (deeming no violation of the MFJ the use of switching, signaling and call processing technology that involves carriage across a LATA boundary provided the originating call terminates within the same LATA or transfers to an inter-exchange carrier).

In other instances, the Court refused to accept an assertion that an inter-LATA line crossing was necessary on financial and efficiency grounds. *See, e.g.*, United States v. Western Elec. Co., 627 F.Supp. 1090 (D.D.C.), *rev'd in part on other grounds*, 797 F.2d 1082, 254 U.S. App. D.C. 415 (D.C.Cir.1986), cert. denied 480 U.S. 922. 107 S.Ct. 1384, 94 L.Ed.2d 698 (1987) (deeming resale of interexchange services as part of share tenant services, marketing of such services and selection of interexchange carriers for a third party violations of the MFJ prohibition on interexchange services); United States v. Western Elec. Co., 1989–1 Trade Cases (CCH) at para. 68,400, 1989 WL 21992 (D.D.C.1989), *aff'd sub nom.* United States v. Western Elec. Co., 907

F.2d 160, 285 U.S. App. D.C. 90 (D.C.Cir. 1990) (requiring a BOC to secure a Line of Business waiver to offer centralized processors for "gateway" access from across a LATA boundary to information services).

15. MFJ § VIII(C). This Section was added to the MFJ in United States v. Western Elec. Co., 592 F.Supp. 846, 852–853 (D.D.C.1984), *mod.* 1991–2 Trade Cases P 69532, 1991 WL 193534 (1991).

16. MFJ § VIII(D), 552 F.Supp. at 225.

17. The interexchange prohibition did not apply to BOC investment in foreign interexchange ventures or to an internal network.

18. *See* United States v. Western Elec. Co., 1989–1 Trade Cases (CCH) ¶ 68,400 1989 WL 21992 (D.D.C.1989) (deeming inter-LATA, interexchange service the provision of gateway access to information service providers across a LATA boundary), *aff'd sub nom.* United States v. Western Elec. Co., 907 F.2d 160, 285 U.S.App.D.C. 90 (D.C.Cir.1990). *See also* Application of Ameritech Michigan Pursuant to Sec. 271 of the Communications of 1934, as amended to provide In-Region InterLATA Services in Michigan, CC Docket No. 97–137, Mem. Op. and Order, 12 FCC Rcd. 20543 (1997) (denying inter-LATA long distance authority

b. *Information Services*

The MFJ also prohibited the BOCs from providing information services defined as "the offering of a capability for generating, acquiring, storing, transforming, processing, retrieving, utilizing, or making available information which may be conveyed via telecommunications."[19] Until its repeal in 1990, this restriction prevented the BOCs from providing services to the public that integrated aspects of data processing, electronic publishing, voice mail, videotext, electronic yellow pages and cable television. Even when in force, the restriction was not intended to limit "any use of such capability for the management, control, or operation of a telecommunications system or the management of a telecommunications service."[20]

Such a restriction grew increasingly difficult to support on public interest and technological grounds because it prevented the BOCs from marketing desirable services that integrated information processing with conventional local exchange services, such as Caller–ID services that use automatic number identification to display the telephone number of a calling party. Nevertheless, Judge Greene considered past anticompetitive practices as "the most probable consequence of such entry by the Regional Companies [RBOCs] ... [leading to] the elimination of competition from that market and the concentration of the sources of information of the American people in just a few dominant, collaborative, conglomerates, with the captive local telephone monopolies as their base."[21] Judge Greene previously had refused to grant a modification of the MFJ, despite consensus support for the change from the Department of Justice and the parties bound by the MFJ.[22]

As to information services, the United States Court of Appeals for the District of Columbia found that the record supported the parties' conclusions that there was no substantial risk that removing this line of business restriction would lessen competition either through BOC control over essential, bottleneck local exchange facilities or through cross-subsidization. The court emphasized the existence of regulatory oversight as substantially minimizing the potential for anticompetitive prac-

because of failure to meet competitive checklist requirements in the 1996 Act).

19. MFJ § IV(J), 552 F. Supp. at 229.

20. *Id.*

21. United States v. Western Elec. Co., Inc., 767 F.Supp. 308, 326 (D.D.C.1991).

22. In United States v. Western Elec. Co., 673 F.Supp. 525 (D.D.C.1987) Judge Greene held that the RBOCs had failed to make an affirmative showing that they would lack ability to use their monopoly power anticompetitively because they retained bottleneck power over the local loop. He declined to amend that decision (690 F.Supp. 22 (D.D.C.1988)) but subsequently allowed the RBOCs to engage in transmission of information, including voice storage and retrieval, but not in the generation of content. 714 F.Supp. 1 (D.D.C.1988). On appeal, the Court of Appeals affirmed in part but reversed the lower court's decision to use the more burdensome Line of Business waiver standard established in § VII(c) of the MFJ instead of the more liberal standard established in § VII applicable when no party to the MFJ opposes a waiver grant. 900 F.2d 283, 283 U.S. App. D.C. 299 (D.C.Cir.1990), cert. denied 498 U.S. 911, 111 S.Ct. 283, 112 L.Ed.2d 238 (1990). On remand, Judge Greene held that while the RBOCs still possessed market power information services within the meaning of the antitrust laws, he had to apply the more liberal waiver standard as mandated by the Court of Appeals.

tices from such beneficial line of business.[23] Moreover, the court noted that uncontested proposed modifications to the MFJ warranted a more lenient public interest evaluation under Section VII as compared to the requirements imposed by Section VIII(C) for removal of a line of business restriction opposed by AT & T or the Justice Department. On remand, Judge Greene removed the restriction because he could not conclude with certainty that removal would lessen competition in information services. The District of Columbia Circuit affirmed this decision.[24] The Telecommunications Act of 1996 requires the BOCs to provide electronic publishing services via a separate subsidiary[25] and prohibits many forms of joint marketing with other BOC affiliates. [26]

c. Manufacturing Telecommunications Equipment

Section II(D)(2) of the MFJ prohibited the BOC from manufacturing telecommunications products or customer premises equipment while Section VIII(A) permitted sales and lease of such equipment. The manufacturing restriction had been interpreted as covering the design and development of both equipment and software "integral to" the hardware.[27] While this did not prevent the BOCs from performing basic research related to network enhancement, the question of how integral the work must be "may be more meaningful to lawyers than to software designers."[28]

2. Line-of-business Restriction Waivers

Almost as soon as the MFJ became effective, the BOCs sought waivers of various restrictions.[29] Frequently they received waivers. The MFJ established two criteria for evaluating a line of business waiver request: (1) Section VII establishes a general public interest basis for proposals uncontested by AT & T or the Justice Department;[30] and (2)

---

23. United States v. Western Elec. Co., Inc., 900 F.2d 283, 283 U.S. App. D.C. 299 (D.C.Cir.1990), cert. denied 498 U.S. 911, 111 S.Ct. 283, 112 L.Ed.2d 238 (1990).

24. United States v. Western Elec. Co., Inc., 993 F.2d 1572, 301 U.S.App.D.C. 268 (D.C.Cir.1993), cert. denied *sub nom.* Consumer Federation of America v. United States, 510 U.S. 984, 114 S.Ct. 487, 126 L.Ed.2d 438 (1993).

25. 47 U.S.C.A. § 274 (West 1996).

26. *Id.* at § 274(c).

27. United States v. Western Elec. Co., 894 F.2d 1387, 1390–1393, 282 U.S. App. D.C. 347, 350–353 (D.C.Cir.1990)(manufacturing includes design and development of equipment and software programming that is "integral" to the operation of hardware).

28. MICHAEL W. KELLOGG, JOHN THORNE & PETER W. HUBER, FEDERAL TELECOMMUNICATIONS LAW 335 (1992).

29. In addition to the waiver route, the MFJ contained a provision for judicial re-

view of the decree every three years to consider lifting restrictions on the BOCs. United States v. AT & T, 552 F. Supp. at 195. In the first such triennial review, which occurred in 1987, the Justice Department recommended that the court modify the inter-LATA services restriction and remove other line-of-business restrictions. *See* Report and Recommendation of the United States Concerning the Line of Business Restrictions Imposed on the Bell Operating Companies by the Modification of Final Judgment, discussed in United States v. Western Elec. Co., 673 F.Supp. 525 (D.D.C. 1987), *aff'd in part and rev'd and remanded in part* 900 F.2d 283, 283 U.S. App. D.C. 299 (D.C.Cir.) (per curiam), cert. denied *sub nom.* MCI Communications Corp. v. United States, 498 U.S. 911, 111 S.Ct. 283, 112 L.Ed.2d 238 (1990).

30. A BOC might apply to the court retaining jurisdiction over the MFJ "at any time for such further orders or directions as may be necessary or appropriate for the

Section VIII(C) establishes a more burdensome standard involving an antitrust assessment whether the BOC has market power and the ability to impede competition in the event of AT & T or Justice Department opposition.[31]

In response to the deluge of waiver requests, the court established a process whereby a regional Bell Operating Company ("RBOC") would first apply to the Justice Department for preliminary evaluation. Absent opposition from AT & T or the Justice Department, the court would apply the more liberal Section VII standard created by the MFJ.[32] However, the court responded to the growing number of waiver request by emphasizing the need to ensure that the RBOCs did not impede competition.[33] Judge Greene interpreted the MFJ as supporting RBOC diversification only to the extent that they could still demonstrate the centrality of their corporate responsibilities to provide permissible services identified in the MFJ and not to engage in anticompetitive conduct in new lines of business.

3. Example of Denied Waivers

a. International Interexchange Services

In *United States v. Western Elec. Co., Inc.*,[34] Judge Greene issued an order denying NYNEX a waiver to enter the international telecommunications market through acquisition of Private Transatlantic Telecommunications System, Inc. ("PSI"). PSI and its British partner Cable & Wireless were constructing a fiber optic submarine cable between the United States, Bermuda, Ireland and the United Kingdom. The court determined that an ownership share in PSI's cable would violate the interexchange services restriction even though the cable would make its United States landfall in New Jersey outside the territory where NYNEX provides local exchange services. In contrast, in the same year Pacific Telesis secured a Line of Business waiver to participate in an international submarine cable venture.[35] The court granted a waiver to Pacific Telesis on the grounds that it would not own the portion of the cable making United States landfalls and on the basis of the carrier's small equity position in the venture.

construction or carrying out of this Modification of Final Judgment, for the modification of any provisions hereof.... " MFJ § VII, United States v. AT & T, 552 F. Supp. at 186.

31. The MFJ line of business restrictions "shall be removed upon a showing by the petitioning BOC that there is no substantial possibility that it could use its monopoly power to impede competition in the market it seeks to enter." MFJ § VII, United States v. AT & T, 552 F. Supp. at 231.

32. United States v. Western Elec. Co., Inc., 592 F.Supp. 846 (D.D.C.1984).

33. Judge Greene may have been reluctant to grant Line of Business waivers in

view of his concern that the RBOCs had a predilection to engage in anticompetitive conduct. He found NYNEX in criminal contempt and fined it $1 million for permitting a subsidiary to provide information services to MCI. *See* United States v. NYNEX Corp., 814 F.Supp. 133 (D.D.C.1993), *rev'd and vac'd* 8 F.3d 52, 303 U.S.App.D.C. 399 (D.C.Cir.1993).

34. 1989–1 Trade Cases ¶ 68,434 (D.D.C.1989).

35. United States v. Western Elec. Co., Inc., 1989–1 Trade Cases ¶ 68,444 (D.D.C. 1989).

b. Interexchange Services to Provide Common Channel Signaling Across LATA Boundaries

In 1992 the District of Columbia Circuit Court of Appeals upheld the District Court's refusal to modify or waive the MFJ restriction on BOC inter-LATA, interexchange service permitting the BOCs to provide common-channel signaling across LATA boundaries.[36] This type of signaling uses a channel, separate from the one carrying telecommunication traffic, to provide network management functions.[37] Several BOCs sought to install centralized switches rather than deploy such devices in each LATA. The court held that the MFJ required the BOCs to provide a signaling interconnection point for interexchange carriers in each LATA because the functions performed constitute interexchange telecommunication service prohibited by Section II(D)(1) of the MFJ:

> It is therefore plain to us that the CCS waiver would not merely change the details of existing exchange access service, but would allow the BOCs to expand their monopolies over exchange access into a slice of the competitive interexchange services market-maybe a narrow slice, involving (for now) only the transmission of traditional network control signaling between the LATAs in each Company's region, but a slice nevertheless.[38]

Because AT & T opposed the waiver grant, the court used the stricter criterion established in Section VIII(c) of the MFJ.[39]

c. Shared Manufacturing Royalties

In 1993 the Court of Appeals affirmed the lower court's decision[40] refusing to grant the Justice Department's Petition for Declaratory Ruling that a proposed funding/royalty arrangement between an RBOC and another company constituted manufacturing directly or through an "affiliated enterprise" within the meaning of the MFJ. The court held that the manufacturing Line of Business restriction on collaboration with an "affiliated enterprise" covers all arrangements, contractual or otherwise, in which AT & T's former subsidiaries have direct and

---

36. United States v. Western Elec. Co., Inc., 969 F.2d 1231, 297 U.S. App. D.C. 231 (D.C.Cir.1992).

37. "In 'out-of-band' or Common Channel Signaling (CCS), the signals are transmitted over a system of switches and circuits separate from that of the communications they control. The CCS and communications networks are not parallel but rather linked only at special CCS switches known as Signal Transfer Points (STPs).... [CCS] reduces call set-up time—the time between dialing on one end and ringing on the other—a particular benefit ... to long distance service. It also frees circuits for communications by not clogging them while callers listen to busy signals or service announcements. And it provides the technological foundation for a

variety of new telecommunications services, including some for which the signaling functions as part or all of the communicated information." *Id.* at 1234, 297 U.S. App. D.C. at 234.

38. *Id.* at 1237, 297 U.S. App. D.C. at 237.

39. "We are thus persuaded by AT & T's argument that the CCS waiver must be judged according to section VIII(C)'s standard, for whenever a modification implicates the line-of-business restrictions and is contested by any of the parties to the decree, the section VIII(c) test governs." *Id.* at 1241, 297 U.S. App. D.C. at 241.

40. United States v. Western Elec. Co., Inc. 12 F.3d 225, 304 U.S.App.D.C. 199 (D.C.Cir.1993).

continuing share in revenues of entities engaged in prohibited businesses. The appeals court affirmed the lower court and remanded the case to it for a determination whether the RBOCs qualified for a waiver.

4. *Waiver Grants—Inter-LATA Services Via Cellular Radio*

The increasingly important role of wireless mobile communications has created a number of occasions for MFJ interpretations. The RBOCs were qualified as "wireline carriers" to apply for one of the two licenses granted by the FCC for cellular radio service in any geographical region.[41] They compete with "non-wireline" operators who have no local loop ownership and face none of the restrictions imposed by the MFJ. Non-wireline carriers have provided services that cross LATA boundaries, either as part of the local call or as long distance calling. The RBOCs have sought a more competitive position by seeking Line of Business waivers to achieve the same kind of call routing, forwarding and scope of service provided by non-wireline carriers.

To a large extent, Judge Greene has granted the necessary waivers to permit inter-LATA cellular radio service. For example the court granted waivers so that the RBOCs could provide inter-LATA cellular service to regions sharing common social and economic ties.[42] Other waiver requests involved intersystem handoff; automatic call delivery and systems integration, all of which involved the carriage of traffic across a LATA boundary. Intersystem handoff permits the mobile telephone switching office (MTSO) of a particular RBOC to interconnect with the MTSO of an adjacent cellular system so that cellular telephone calls already in progress can be handed off between systems. Automatic call delivery permits a cellular phone user to receive calls while visiting ("roaming") a territory served by a cellular system other than the home cellular system to which he or she subscribes. The automatic call delivery waivers permit the RBOCs to provide the inter-LATA intelligence necessary to locate the user roaming in the visited system, to route

---

41. *See* Cellular Communications Systems, 86 FCC2d 469 (1981), *modified*, 89 FCC2d 58 (1982), *further modified*, 90 FCC2d 571 (1982), *appeal dismissed sub nom.* United States v. FCC, No. 82–01526 (D.C. Cir. March 3, 1983).

42. The MFJ granted the RBOCs the right to carry inter-LATA traffic on a limited basis (for example, extended area service (EAS) and limited interstate traffic). Judge Greene also granted Line of Business Waivers for inter-LATA "corridor" service. *See* United States v. Western Elec. Co., Inc. 578 F.Supp. 668 (D.D.C.1983) (granting waivers for cellular service in nine corridors like the greater New York City area which includes portions of New Jersey and Connecticut). Judge Greene had ruled that the RBOC could not purchase interests in cellular radio systems that provide extraregional exchange services. United States v. Western

Elec. Co., 627 F.Supp. 1090, 1106 (D.D.C. 1986). However, on appeal the Court of Appeals reversed. 797 F.2d 1082, 1089–92, 254 U.S. App. D.C. 415, 422–425 (D.C.Cir. 1986). As a result, the RBOCs began aggressively purchasing interests in non-wireline companies outside their own exchange regions. *See also* United States v. Western Elec. Co., Inc., 1989 WL 11455 (D.D.C.1989) (granting a waiver for Bell Atlantic to provide cellular mobile telephone service in the New Jersey counties of Mercer, Warren, and Hunterdon through its existing Philadelphia–Wilmington cellular system). *See also* United States v. Western Elec. Co., 890 F.Supp. 1 (D.D.C.1995), *vacated,* 84 F.3d 1452, 318 U.S.App.D.C. 78 (D.C.Cir.1996) (allowing conditional resale of inter-LATA long distance telephone service via cellular radio and other wireless ventures).

the call to the user and to provide the inter-LATA transmission of messages.

In 1994, the District Court for the District of Columbia granted a waiver to permit AT & T's acquisition of McCaw Cellular which, *inter alia*, held minority interests in cellular radio ventures with RBOCs.[43] In 1995, the court granted a waiver so that the RBOCs, acting as cellular radio operators, could resell long distance services provided they formed a separate subsidiary to provide the long distance resale, submitted an equal access plan to enable users to secure the long distance services of other operators without handicaps, separately tariffed local and long distance services and did not dedicate more than 45 percent of their long distance capacity to any one interexchange carrier.

B. Supersession of the MFJ By the Telecommunications Act of 1996

The Telecommunications Act of 1996 supersedes the MFJ by providing the BOCs with conditional opportunities to engage in inter-LATA long distance telephone service and telecommunication equipment manufacturing lines of business. Section 271 of the Telecommunications Act of 1996 permits the BOCs to provide inter-LATA services subject to several conditions. Upon enactment of the Telecommunications Act BOCs could provide such services outside of the region where it provides local exchange service. For "in-region" inter-LATA services a BOC must face local exchange service facilities-based competition as evidenced by the completion of one or more binding interconnection agreements that comply with a 14-point competitive checklist established in Section 251 of the Telecommunications Act and the regulatory approval process established in Section 252. Alternatively Section 271(B) permitted BOC entry if it had not received any access and interconnection request 10 months after enactment of the Telecommunications Act. Section 272 requires BOCs to form separate inter-LATA, long distance service subsidiaries.

Section 273 of the Telecommunications Act conditionally authorizes a BOC to manufacture telecommunications equipment including devices used on customer premises, for instance, telephones and private branch exchanges ("PBXs"). A BOC can secure manufacturing authority if it satisfies the criteria established in Section 271(d) to provide inter-LATA long distance telephone services. Section 272 expressly permits a BOC to collaborate with another telecommunications equipment manufacturer in research and such joint activities can include a royalty payment

43. While it refused to issue a ruling that the MFJ did not apply to the transaction, United States v. Western Elec. Co., 154 F.R.D. 1 (D.D.C.1994), the court granted a waiver, subject to equitable conditions, but independent of an attempt by several RBOCs to secure a generic waiver of the MFJ to provide wireless services. United States v. Western Elec. Co., 158 F.R.D. 211 (D.D.C.1994), *aff'd sub nom.* United States v. Western Elec. Co., 46 F.3d 1198, 310 U.S. App. D.C. 281 (D.C.Cir.1995). *See also* Amendment of the Commission's Rules to Establish Competitive Service Safeguards for Local Exchange Carriers Provision of Commercial Mobile Radio Services, WT Docket No. 96–162, Report and Order, 12 FCC Rcd. 15668 (1997).

agreement. This section includes a variety of competitive safeguards including mandatory disclosure of protocols and technical requirements relating to interconnection with telephone exchange facilities and the establishment of a separate manufacturing affiliate.

12.9   Interexchange Telecommunications

Interexchange telecommunications involves the carriage of traffic between local exchanges by long distance telephone companies like AT & T, MCI and Sprint. Until the 1970s, AT & T dominated the interexchange marketplaces and made it a component within the array of services provided by the Bell System. A revenue sharing arrangement, known as "separations and settlements,"[1] established a mechanism for cross-subsidization of local exchange services by long distance calling. Technological innovations, *e.g.*, low cost microwave transmitters, conversion from analog to digital transmission, the onset of satellites and fiber optic transmission media and FCC deregulatory initiatives have now made it more likely that large volume users can secure alternative traffic routing arrangements that avoid the cross subsidy obligation.

A.   *Initial FCC Deregulatory Market Entry Initiatives*

Most of the FCC's procompetitive initiatives have addressed ways to stimulate private transmission facilities and market entry in the provision of private line services, such as dedicated voice and data links between two locations primarily for large volume corporate users. In 1960, the Commission allocated frequencies for microwave transmissions for use by private businesses.[2] The *Above 890* decision evidenced the Commission's willingness to support private use of a developing technology to meet specialized needs not fully met by the general, tariffed offerings of communications common carriers and to stimulate innovation in equipment manufacturing.

The FCC also supported facilities-based, microwave competition between incumbent carriers and market entrants called Specialized Common Carriers ("SCCs"). In 1969, the FCC granted MCI's application to provide private line, common carrier services between Chicago, St. Louis and nine intermediate points.[3] The Commission supported niche market competition "designed to meet the interoffice and interplant communications needs of small businesses,"[4] acknowledging that MCI's facilities would duplicate routes already served by such incumbent carriers as AT & T and Western Union.[5]

---

1. *See* Smith v. Illinois Bell. Tel. Co., 282 U.S. 133, 51 S.Ct. 65, 75 L.Ed. 255 (1930).

2. Allocation of Frequencies in the Bands Above 890 Mc., 27 F.C.C. 359 (1959), *mod.*, 29 F.C.C. 825 (1960).

3. Microwave Communications, Inc., 18 F.C.C. 2d 953 (1969), *mods. granted*, 27 F.C.C. 2d 380 (1970).

4. *Id.* at 953.

5. *Id.* at 958–59. One of the rationales for maintaining a regulated monopoly is the concern that competition would result in wasteful duplication of resources. In authorizing MCI to compete the Commission believed that MCI would stimulate market demand rather than simply migrate traffic from incumbent carriers.

The MCI decision stimulated market entry by other carriers, eventually leading the FCC to commence a rulemaking to address the scope of SCC service and the procedures for licensing such carriers.[6] The Commission confirmed that the public interest favored permitting the entry of new carriers in the specialized communications field because entrants would customize services to meet an end user's particular requirements.[7] The Commission rejected the interpretation of Section 214 suggested by incumbent carriers that the Commission could authorize additional facilities-based carriers if and only if "there is a need for the proposed services which existing carriers are not now adequately meeting and could not in the future adequately meet."[8]

The FCC could not promote competition for competition's sake[9] but would have to articulate with specificity why market entry would generate competition that serves the public interest. The Commission met this standard by articulating that the public interest would not be served by maintaining the status quo simply on the statements of incumbent carriers that they would lose revenues, traffic and perhaps the ability to operate at the lowest per unit costs:

> [I]f an applicant is found qualified, obtains the necessary financial backing, and makes a business judgment to risk that investment ..., we are not inclined to place further obstacles in its path.[10]

Instead, the Commission was willing to sponsor a marketplace test to determine who operated efficiently, who could achieve economies of scale and whether consumer requirements could grow and support increased specialization.[11] While it may have underestimated the extent to which it would have to police access terms and conditions, the FCC sought to ensure that new SCCs would have reasonable access to local exchange facilities despite the fact that the Bell Operating Companies had a financial incentive to favor its corporate affiliate AT & T Long Lines.[12]

---

6. Specialized Common Carrier Service, Notice of Inquiry to Formulate Policy, Notice of Proposed Rulemaking and Order, 24 F.C.C. 2d 318 (1970), First Report and Order, 29 F.C.C. 2d 870 (1971), *aff'd sub nom.* Washington Util. & Transp. Comm'n v. FCC, 513 F.2d 1142 (9th Cir.), cert. denied *sub nom.* National Ass'n of Regl. Util. Comm'rs v. FCC, 423 U.S. 836, 96 S.Ct. 62, 46 L.Ed.2d 54 (1975).

7. 29 F.C.C. 2d at 906–08.

8. *Id.* at 900.

9. *See* FCC v. RCA Communications, Inc., 346 U.S. 86, 73 S.Ct. 998, 97 L.Ed. 1470 (1953).

10. Specialized Common Carrier Service, First Report and Order, 29 FCC2d at 927.

11. It is important to emphasize that as much as it appeared revolutionary for the FCC to embrace marketplace resource allocation, the private line service market only constituted four percent of AT & T's total revenues (*id.* at 911) and at the time, no carrier could compete for conventional switched, long distance services.

12. The FCC ordered "established carriers with exchange facilities ... upon request, [to] permit interconnection of leased channel arrangements on reasonable terms and conditions to be negotiated with the new carriers." Specialized Common Carrier Service, First Report and Order, 29 F.C.C. 2d at 940; *accord:* Bell Sys. Tariff Offerings, Decision, 46 F.C.C. 2d 413, 426–427 (requiring Bell System to provide same types of facilities that it provided AT & T Long Lines), *aff'd sub nom.* Bell Tel. Co. v. FCC, 503 F.2d 1250 (3d Cir.1974), cert. denied 422 U.S. 1026, 95 S.Ct. 2620. 45 L.Ed.2d 684 (1975). *See also* MCI Telecommunications Corp. v. FCC, 627 F.2d 322, 200 U.S. App. D.C. 269 (D.C.Cir.1980); MCI Telecommunications Corp. v. FCC, 712 F.2d

B. *Satellite Competition*

In addition to supporting microwave facilities-based competition, the FCC endorsed an "open skies" policy for domestic satellite carriers, meaning that it would license any legally, technically and financially qualified applicant.[13] To support the prospect of multiple satellite carriers, the FCC decided to impose a seven year moratorium on AT & T's ownership of satellites providing private line services to non-governmental users.[14] The Commission had concerns that the marketplace might not support multiple carriers if, at the outset, AT & T could construct, launch and operate satellites that it could load with competitive private lines and still monopolize switched long distance traffic. Likewise, the Commission lacked confidence that it could detect any cross-subsidization achieved by overpricing service to captive customers while underpricing competitive, private line services.[15]

C. *Resale and Shared Use*

Resale is an exercise in arbitrage: securing bulk capacity intended for use by a single large volume user and subdividing it for use by a number of customers with lower individual capacity requirements. There are two kinds of resale: (1) pure or simple resale where the arbitrageur simply subdivides bulk transmission capacity; and (2) enhanced resale where the service provider adds value to, and enhances leased lines typically with information processing functions like data storage and manipulation functions, *e.g.,* credit card verification. The FCC grew to believe that resale reduces the potential for facilities-based carriers to discriminate against small volume users and engenders the benefits of competition without the delay and expense of parallel facilities construction.

517, 229 U.S. App. D.C. 203 (D.C.Cir.1983)(review of the initial terms and conditions of access provided MCI under the negotiated Exchange Network Facilities for Interstate Access agreement).

13. Establishment of Domestic Communication–Satellite Facilities by Non–Governmental Entities, Docket No. 16495, First Report & Order, 22 F.C.C. 2d 86 (1970) Second Report & Order, 35 F.C.C. 2d 844 (1972), *on recons.* Mem. Op. and Order, 38 F.C.C. 2d 665 (1972). "Our decision in favor of multiple entry does not mean that we have opted for a policy of 'unlimited or unrestricted open entry.' Our aim, as outlined above, is to afford qualified applicants a reasonable opportunity to demonstrate the public advantages in use of the satellite technology as a means of communications. But such entry cannot be 'open' in the sense that it is without any restrictions or limitations. Pursuant to statute we must require showings of financial, technical and other qualification and make the requisite finding that a grant of the particular proposal will serve the public interest, convenience and necessity. Although, as discussed in paragraph 15 above, it is our intention to make such determinations with due regard for the unique circumstances involved here, each applicant must make a sufficient showing of potential public benefit to justify the assignment of orbital locations and frequencies. Moreover, we believe it necessary to impose certain conditions to protect the public from possible detriment and to further the implementation of our policy objectives. In addition to the conditions discussed below, we will require a reasonable showing by any common carrier applicant now engaged in providing essential communications services that revenue requirements related to the proposed domestic satellite venture will not be burden or detriment to customers for such essential services." 35 F.C.C. 2d at 844, para. 18.

14. Domestic Communications–Satellite Facilities, 38 F.C.C. 2d at 676–77.

15. Domestic Communications–Satellite Facilities, 34 F.C.C. 2d at 52.

The FCC first addressed niche market enhanced resale services proposed by "value-added carriers" in the early 1970s.[16] The Commission expanded the scope of permissible resale activities and the potential for competition and downward pressure when it began a series of proceedings affecting the private line and switched, long distance markets. The Commission predicted that private line service resale[17] would accrue ample public benefits by pressuring "underlying [facilities-based] carrier[s] . . . to realign the relationship between unit and bulk rates to make that relationship wholly cost related. . . . "[18] The Commission subsequently expanded its pro-resale policy to include large volume calling services like WATS lines which were initially provided by AT & T only to individual high volume long distance users.[19]

D. *Facilities–Based Switched Services Competition*

Switched long distance service competition initially was the product of judicial activism instead of a deliberate FCC policy to extend private line competition to dial-up services. In *MCI Telecommunications Corp.*, v. *FCC*[20] the District of Columbia Court of Appeals reversed the FCC's holding that its *Specialized Common Carrier* proceeding had authorized MCI only to offer private line services. The Commission had refused to open the switched toll service market to competition.[21] The Court of Appeals reversed on the ground that having failed to state clearly why such market entry would not serve the public interest, the Commission could not deny new, specialized common carriers the opportunity to enter that market:

> [T]he Commission did not perhaps intend to open the field of common carrier communications generally, but its constant stress

---

16. *See, e.g.,* Telenet Communications Corp., Mem. Op. Order and Certificate, 46 F.C.C. 2d 680 (1974); Graphnet Sys., Inc., Mem. Op. Order and Certificate, 44 F.C.C. 2d 800 (1974); Packet Communications, Inc., Mem. Op. Order and Certificate, 43 F.C.C. 2d 922 (1973).

17. *See* Regulatory Policies Concerning Resale and Shared Use of Common Carrier Services and Facilities, Report and Order, 60 F.C.C. 2d 261, [hereinafter cited as Domestic Resale Policy] *mod.,* Mem. Op. and Order, 61 F.C.C. 2d 70 (1976) *further mods.,* Mem. Op. and Order, 62 F.C.C. 2d 588 (1977), *aff'd sub nom.,* AT & T v. FCC, 572 F.2d 17 (2d Cir.1978), cert. denied 439 U.S. 875, 99 S.Ct. 213, 58 L.Ed.2d 190 (1978). AT & T initially sought to limit its bulk private line (TELPAK) capacity to large volume users by inserting tariff terms prohibiting shared use. On appeal, the Second Circuit Court of Appeals affirmed the Commission's action striking down the tariffed ban on shared use, but reversed the Commission as to its order that AT & T extend sharing privileges to all private line

customers on grounds that the Commission had not explained how such extension would be just, reasonable and in the public interest. *See* TELPAK Tariff Sharing Provisions of American Tel. & Tel. Co. and the Western Union Tel. Co., Recommended Decision of the Chief of the Common Carrier Bureau, 23 F.C.C. 2d 639 (1969), Decision, 23 F.C.C. 2d 606 (1970) *aff'd in part and rev'd in part sub nom.* AT & T v. FCC, 449 F.2d 439 (2d Cir.1971).

18. Domestic Resale Policy, 60 FCC 2d at 298–99.

19. Regulatory Policies Concerning Resale and Shared Use of Common Carrier Domestic Public Switched Network Services, Report and Order, 83 F.C.C. 2d 167 (1980), *on recons.,* 86 F.C.C. 2d 820 (1981).

20. 561 F.2d 365, 182 U.S. App. D.C. 367 (D.C.Cir.1977), cert. denied 434 U.S. 1040, 98 S.Ct. 781, 54 L.Ed.2d 790 (1978).

21. *See* MCI Telecom. Corp., Mem. Op. and Order, 57 FCC2d 271 (1975), Decision, 60 FCC 2d 25 (1976).

on the fact that specialized carriers would provide new, innovative, and hitherto unheard-of-communications services clearly indicates that it had no very clear idea of precisely how far or to what services the field should be opened.[22]

AT & T subsequently discontinued its FCC-mandated interconnection with MCI on grounds that the access was limited to private line service. While the FCC again agreed with the restricted market opening viewpoint,[23] the District of Columbia Circuit in an even more strident tone admonished both the Commission and incumbent carriers to accept the fact of facilities-based competition and the duty of local exchange carriers to provide access to the local loop:

> MCI has met with almost continuous resistance from AT & T in its efforts to provide communications services. We had thought that this process finally culminated in our Execunet decision upholding MCI's authority to offer Execunet pending further rulemaking by the Commission. Now, however, we are faced with a new effort by AT & T, with the approval of the Commission, to arrest the development of Execunet service, and the question for immediate disposition is whether protection of the integrity of our Execunet mandate requires that this new effort be terminated through an order directing compliance with our mandate. We believe it does.[24]

E.   Post–Divestiture AT & T

Soon after divestiture of AT & T's Bell Operating Companies, the FCC completed its *Competitive Carrier* rulemaking that assessed the competitiveness of the long distance services marketplace.[25] The Commission decided to "forbear" from exercising full Title II regulation of AT & T's competitors, but retained all such requirements for AT & T based on the determination that "AT & T possessed substantial market power in the provision of transmission services that its competitors did not."[26]

22. MCI Telecom. Corp. v. FCC, 561 F.2d at 379, 182 U.S. App. D.C. at 381.

23. AT & T, Mem. Op. and Order, 67 F.C.C. 2d 1455 (1978), *rev'd sub nom.*, MCI Telecom. Corp. v. FCC, 580 F.2d 590, 188 U.S. App. D.C. 327 (D.C.Cir.) cert. denied *sub nom.* United States Independent Telephone Association v. MCI Telecommunications Corporation, 439 U.S. 980, 99 S.Ct. 566, 58 L.Ed.2d 651 (1978).

24. MCI, 580 F.2d at 591, 188 U.S. App. D.C. at 328.

25. Policy and Rules Concerning Rates for Competitive Common Carrier Services and Facilities Authorizations Therefor, Notice of Inquiry and Proposed Rulemaking, 77 F.C.C. 2d 308 (1979); First Report and Order 85 F.C.C. 2d 1 (1980); Further Notice of Proposed Rulemaking, 84 F.C.C. 2d 445 (1981); Second Report and Order, 91 F.C.C.

2d 59 (1982), *recons. denied*, Order on Recons., 93 F.C.C. 2d 54 (1983); Second Further Notice of Proposed Rulemaking, 47 Fed. Reg. 17308 (1982); Third Further Notice of Proposed Rulemaking, 48 Fed. Reg. 46791 (1983); Third Report and Order, 48 Fed. Reg. 46791 (1983); Fourth Report and Order, 95 F.C.C. 2d 554 (1983); Fourth Further Notice of Proposed Rulemaking, 49 Fed. Reg. 11856 (1984); Fifth Report and Order, 98 FCC 2d 1191 (1984); Sixth Report and Order 99 F.C.C. 2d 1020 (1985), *rev'd and remanded sub nom.*, MCI Telecommunications Corp. v. FCC, 765 F.2d 1186, 247 U.S. App. D.C. 32 (D.C.Cir.1985).

26. Competition in the Interstate Interexchange Marketplace, CC Docket No. 90–132, Report and Order, 6 FCC Rcd 5880, 5881, ¶ 2 (1991)[hereinafter cited as Interstate Interexchange Marketplace], *on re-*

Increasing competition, particularly for large business customers, motivated the FCC to extend the deregulation established in *Competitive Carrier* to AT & T's business services not subject to price cap regulation,[27] including Wide Area Telephone Services and analog private line services.

> With minor exceptions, we now conclude that the business services market is substantially competitive. We base this conclusion in part on our finding that the business services marketplace is characterized by substantial demand and supply elasticities that limit AT & T's ability to exercise market power in this market segment. We also rely on AT & T's pricing of business services under price cap regulation and unrefuted evidence that AT & T's market share is substantially lower in business services than it is in other markets.[28]

The FCC allowed AT & T to file business service tariffs with the expectation that they would take effect fourteen days after public notice, provided the Commission, in its preliminary review, found no conflict with a statute, regulation or order that would warrant suspension or rejection of the tariff. In light of the competitiveness of business services, the Commission stated its intention to presume the lawfulness of AT & T's tariff filings, to relieve AT & T of the need to file cost support data and to fit such services within price cap ceilings, bands, and rate floors.

The Commission did continue to afford interested parties the opportunity to file petitions against these tariffs within seven days after the tariff filing. It also retained authority to institute at any time on its own motion investigations of AT & T tariffs after they become effective and to declare tariffs unlawful, if necessary. The Commission also would adjudicate in the complaint process claims of unlawful actions by AT & T, but it stated its desire to reduce "opportunities for gamesmanship by parties participating in the regulatory process and minimizing unnecessarily intrusive regulation, while at the same time preserving for the present both advance and subsequent scrutiny of AT & T's business services tariffs."[29]

The Commission decided that the existing rules imposed unnecessary costs on consumers by:

cons., Mem. Op and Order on Recons., 7 FCC Rcd. 2677 (1992), *on further recons.*, Mem. Op. and Order on Recons., 8 FCC Rcd. 2659 (1993), Second Report and Order, 8 FCC Rcd. 3668 (1993), *on further recons.* Mem. Op. and Order on Further Recons., 10 FCC Rcd. 4562 (1995)(reducing scope of AT & T's dominant carrier status and allowing provision of service based on customized tariffs preceded by a contract for carriage), *further recons. denied* Mem. Op. and Order on Recons., 10 FCC Rcd. 4421 (1995).

27. The streamlining applied to all services in AT & T's price cap Basket 3, except for analog private lines services, which the Commission feared would increase in price in the absence of price cap rules and without adequate digital substitutes (Interstate Interexchange Marketplace at 6 FCC Rcd. 5880 at ¶ 81) and all services not under price cap regulation, including Tariff 12 services, but excepting special construction services relating to non-streamlined services and promotional offerings for non-streamlined services. *Id.* at ¶ 72.

28.   6 FCC Rcd. 5880 at ¶ 36.

29.   *Id.* at 5894 at para. 74.

- denying AT & T the full pricing flexibility needed to react to market conditions and customer demands thereby diminishing its ability to compete as a full-fledged competitor;

- creating regulatory delays and uncertainty reducing the value of AT & T's service offerings;

- affording AT & T's competitors as much as ninety days advance notice (more if the tariff is suspended) of AT & T price and service changes, fostering a reactive market, rather than a proactive one, and reducing incentives for AT & T's competitors to "stay on their competitive toes;" and

- negating, in whole or in part, AT & T's ability to take advantage, as its competitors can, of being a "first-mover" in the market, lessening AT & T's incentive to initiate pro-consumer price and service changes.[30]

The FCC defended the lawfulness of its deregulatory campaign by referring to Section 203(b)(2) of the Communications Act that grants the Commission authority "for good cause shown" to "modify" the notice period for tariff filings. The Commission also cited to *Southern Motor Carriers Rate Conference v. United States*,[31] as support for the option to recognize special circumstances or conditions. The Commission distinguished *Maislin Industries v. Primary Steel, Inc.*,[32] which held that the rate filing requirement for a regulated carrier was essential to administration of the Interstate Commerce Act by the Interstate Commerce Commission. *Maislin Industries* addressed the duty of a carrier to file a tariff and not the notice requirements or the necessary scope of preliminary tariff reviews. In the deregulation proposed by the Commission, AT & T would still have to file tariffs and the Commission "will still have an opportunity to review these tariffs before they go into effect and to investigate and, if necessary, find them unlawful after they go into effect."[33]

1.   *800, 888 and 788 Wide Area Telephone Service Competition*

In 1991, the FCC refrained from streamlining regulation of AT & T's Basket 2 Services (WATS numbers) because the market had not yet become competitive. This was primarily because the local exchange carrier infrastructure was not yet able to switch any WATS number dialing sequence to interexchange carriers. The Commission deemed the lack of such "number portability"[34] "an impediment to full competition

---

30.   *Id.* at ¶ 80.

31.   773 F.2d 1561 (11th Cir.1985).

32.   497 U.S. 116 110 S.Ct. 2759, 111 L.Ed.2d 94 (1990).

33.   Interstate Interexchange Marketplace, 6 FCC Rcd. 5880 at ¶ 89.

34.   Number portability means that any interexchange carrier can provide transport services via any 800 number dialing se-

quence. Previously, a single interexchange carrier had exclusive access to a batch of dialing prefixes, thereby limiting the scope of competition. For example, if an automobile rental firm wanted to use 1–800–CAR–RENT, it would have to do business with the one and only IXC that had control over the CAR dialing prefix (227).

in 800 services."[35]

The FCC expressed concern that AT & T might be able to use market power in outbound or inbound WATS services as leverage to gain a comparative advantage in competitive service negotiations with prospective customers. Accordingly, the Commission precluded AT & T from including in contracts and new Tariff 12 options any WATS services until WATS numbers became portable.[36] While refraining from invalidating all Tariff 12 options already on file that contained WATS services, the Commission required AT & T to allow customers of such Tariff 12 packages a "fresh look" option to terminate such packages within 90 days of the time 800 numbers become portable without incurring any liability for premature termination of service.[37]

Two years later, the FCC extended the streamlined, tariff filing system for AT & T to include 800 services.[38] The Commission concluded that it could include such services because local exchange carriers had reprogrammed their switches to provide number portability. The Commission assumed that the implementation of number portability rendered the WATS services marketplace substantially competitive and that the elimination of price cap regulation of AT & T's WATS services would serve the public interest.[39] Under its "fresh look" policy, the FCC allowed preexisting AT & T customers with service packages that included WATS services, to terminate such arrangements. Customers had ninety days after implementation of number portability to exercise this option.

In 1995 the FCC extended the scope of remaining price cap regulation over commercial services provided to small business users who do not qualify for volume discounts.[40] The Commission authorized AT & T to file new or revised tariffs on fourteen days notice and eliminated the requirement that AT & T submit cost support data.

2. AT & T Considered a Thoroughly Non-dominant Carrier

In late 1995 the FCC found that AT & T lacked market power in the interstate, domestic, interexchange telecommunications services markets.[41] The Commission decided that it could refrain from continuing to

35. Interstate Interexchange Marketplace, 6 FCC Rcd. 5880 at ¶ 146.

36. *Id.* at ¶ 149.

37. *Id.* at ¶ 151.

38. Competition in the Interstate Interexchange Marketplace, CC Docket No. 90–132, Second Report and Order, 8 FCC Rcd. 3668 (1993).

39. The Commission excluded AT & T's Residential and Small Business Services Basket (Basket One), including operator and international services, from further streamlining, because of insufficient evidence that the marketplace for these services was substantially competitive. *See* Competition in the Interstate Interexchange Marketplace, CC Docket No. 90–132, 6 FCC Rcd. 5880, 5906–08 (1991), *on recons.*, Mem. Op. and Order, 6 FCC Rcd. 7569 (1991), *on further recons.*, Mem. Op. and Order on Recons., 7 FCC Rcd. 2677 (1992), *further recons.*, Mem. Op. and Order on Recons., 8 FCC Rcd. 2659 (1993).

40. Revisions to Price Cap Rules for AT & T Corp., CC Docket No. 93–197, Report and Order FCC 95–132, 10 FCC Rcd. 8961 (1995), Further Notice of Proposed Rulemaking, FCC 95–198, 10 FCC Rcd. 7854 (rel. May 18, 1995).

41. Motion of AT & T Corp. To Be Reclassified as a Non–Dominant Carrier, Order, 11 FCC Rcd. 3271 (1995). *See also*

regulate AT & T as a dominant carrier, a decision that culminated the incremental steps taken over a decade to deregulate AT & T and accord it the same pricing flexibility available to other interexchange carriers. To encourage the FCC to grant its motion for non-dominant status, AT & T made voluntary service commitments that would benefit low volume long distance users.

In 1981 the FCC classified AT & T as dominant when the company managed the vertically integrated Bell System serving over 80 percent of the nation's phones and provided virtually all the nation's interexchange services. Now AT & T faces competition in the interexchange market from hundreds of facilities-based and resale carriers. It no longer controls local access facilities and has voluntarily divested itself of independent telecommunication services, equipment and data processing companies.[42] As a non-dominant carrier, AT & T will no longer be subject to price cap regulation and will be able to file tariffs that are presumed lawful on one day's notice absent suspension and investigation by the Commission. AT & T will no longer have to file cost support data and other additional information now required for certain price cap filings, and it will be relieved of certain annual reporting requirements. It can apply for blanket Section 214 authorization for a wide range of facilities construction projects and for expedited authority to discontinue a service.

F. Contract Carriage

As part of its AT & T deregulatory initiatives, the FCC allowed AT & T to join the other interexchange carriers in offering services based on individually negotiated contracts that subsequently become the terms and conditions in a tariff. Increasingly, interexchange carriers provide service to large volume customers through negotiations or under competitive bidding arrangements.[43] Contract carriage,[44] provides needed flexi-

Motion of AT & T Corp. to be Declared Non–Dominant for International Service, Order, 11 FCC Rcd. 17963 (1996).

42. "In the first breakup, AT & T opted to keep its telecommunications equipment manufacturing operation and to spin off its local telephone service. Now, it is divesting itself of its manufacturing operations and preparing to re-enter the local phone business. One antitrust problem that prompted the original divestiture was that the local Bell telephone companies were preferentially buying equipment from AT & T because of the family ties. One problem that is now spurring AT & T to spin off its manufacturing operations is that some of the local phone companies are increasingly wary of buying AT & T equipment because they view the company as a competitor in telephone service." Andrew Pollack, *AT & T Move Is a Reversal Of Course Set in 1980's*, N.Y. Times, Sep. 22, 1995, § D, p. 4 (reporting AT & T's plans

to divide itself into three separate companies to pursue telecommunication services, equipment, manufacturing and computer markets on a separate basis). *See also AT & T Unveils Spinoff: Lucent Technologies; Offerings: SEC Filing Gives No Details on Number of Shares for $20–Billion Phone Equipment Business*, L.A. Times, Feb. 6, 1996, part D, p. 3 (announcing identity of AT & T's telecommunication equipment spin-off company).

43. "Contract carriage would further benefit consumers by unleashing competitive forces for business services to the maximum extent possible. By permitting customers to seek competitive bids from all carriers in the long-distance market—and allowing AT & T to offer customers the same types of contract deals that its competitors are already offering—contract carriage will expand customers' choices." In-

44. See note on page 1043.

bility to tailor service to meet the particular needs of individual customers.[45]

The FCC supported the lawfulness of contract carriage by referring primarily to the general flexibility afforded by Section 203 and secondarily to Section 211(b) of the Communications Act which authorizes the Commission to require the filing of any other contracts of any carrier and Section 219(a) which authorizes the Commission to require carriers to file annual reports containing information in relation to charges or regulations concerning charges, or agreements, arrangements, or contracts affecting the same. Additionally, the Commission referred by analogy to *Sea–Land Service, Inc. v. ICC*,[46] which upheld the ICC's contract rate policy and *Associated Gas Distributors v. FERC*,[47] upholding the Federal Energy Regulatory Commission's selective discounting policy.

Section 203(a) requires carriers to file "schedules" showing their charges, classifications, practices and regulations affecting such charges. The FCC reasoned that the information filed by AT & T relating to the terms and conditions of a negotiated contract satisfied this requirement.[48] The Commission also concluded that contract carriage would not constitute discrimination under Section 202(a) of the Communications because it would require AT & T to make the service available on the same terms and conditions to other similarly situated customers.

However, users need to recognize that under the "Filed Rate Doctrine" the terms and conditions contained in the tariff supersede what the parties establish in a contract even if the tariff conflicts with the contract and establishes less attractive, more burdensome or inconsistent terms and conditions.[49] The ability to revise tariffs can create

terstate Interexchange Marketplace, 6 FCC Rcd. 5880 at para. 105.

44. The FCC required "AT & T to file, fourteen days prior to the effective date of each of its customer contracts, a tariff summarizing that contract and containing the following information: (1) the term of the contract, including any renewal options; (2) a brief description of each of the services provided under the contract; (3) minimum volume commitments for each service; (4) the contract price for each service or services at the volume levels committed to by the customers; (5) a general description of any volume discounts built into the contract rate structure; and (6) a general description of other classifications, practices, and regulations affecting the contract rate." *Id.* at 5902, para. 121.

45. "Limiting AT & T to 'plain vanilla' generic tariffs, on the other hand, would substantially restrict the availability of these types of service arrangements because no single tariff can adequately incorporate all of the individually designed variables that customers desire." *Id.* at 5899, ¶ 104.

46. 738 F.2d 1311, 238 U.S. App. D.C. 165 (D.C.Cir.1984).

47. 824 F.2d 981, 263 U.S. App. D.C. 1 (D.C.Cir.1987).

48. "Requiring AT & T to provide section 203 information in the form of a contract-based tariff is clearly within our permissible discretion under this provision." Interstate Interexchange Marketplace at 6 FCC Rcd. 5880 at para. 127 *citing* MCI Telecom. Corp. v. FCC, 917 F.2d 30, 37–38, 286 U.S. App. D.C. 316, 323–324 (D.C.Cir. 1990) (generally endorsing AT & T's customized service arrangements under Tariff 12, but remanding the case to the FCC for a determination, without regard to price differentials, whether such tariffs constitute discrimination).

49. Maislin Indus., Inc. v. Primary Steel, Inc., 497 U.S. 116, 110 S.Ct. 2759, 111 L.Ed.2d 94 (1990); *accord:* Keogh v. Chicago & Northwestern Ry. Co., 260 U.S. 156, 43 S.Ct. 47, 67 L.Ed. 183 (1922)(contracts cannot vary or enlarge the rights defined by tariff); American Broadcasting

problems particularly for users who have executed multi-year service contracts and who think they enjoy insulation from unilateral modification of the contract's terms and conditions. Before it allows a tariff modification of a preexisting multi-year service arrangement to become effective, the FCC can assess whether the carrier has "substantial cause" to make the changes.[50] The Commission "believe[s] that commercial contract law principles are highly relevant to the assessment of whether a contract-based tariff revision is just and reasonable under the substantial cause test."[51] Still, it opted not to enforce conventional contract law.[52]

12.10 *Video Program Delivery by Local Exchange Carriers

    A. *The FCC's Reconsideration of the Ban on Video Delivery by Local Exchange Carriers (Video Dialtone)

    B. *Constitutional Challenges by Local Exchange Carriers to the 1984 Cable Act Ban on LEC Provision of Video Programming

    C. Open Video System ("OVS") Replacement of Video Dialtone

With enactment of the Telecommunications Act of 1996, the video dialtone option was eliminated, and the FCC no longer needed to craft a mechanism that would enable LECs to participate in the video marketplace in a manner consistent with the statutory telephone-cable cross-ownership restriction.[1] The Telecommunications Act repealed the telephone-cable cross-ownership restriction imposed by the Cable Communications Policy Act of 1984 ("1984 Cable Act"),[2] which generally prohibited common carriers from providing video programming directly to

---

Cos., Inc. v. FCC, 643 F.2d 818, 207 U.S. App. D.C. 68 (D.C.Cir.1980).

50. RCA American Communications, Inc., Mem. Op. and Order, 84 F.C.C. 2d 353 (1980) (designating tariff revision issues for investigation), Mem. Op. and Order, 86 F.C.C. 2d 1197 (1981) (rejecting tariff revisions), on recons., 2 FCC Rcd. 2363 (1987), aff'd, D.C. Cir. 81–1558 (Mar. 8, 1984); see also Showtime Networks, Inc. v. FCC, 932 F.2d 1, 289 U.S.App.D.C. 348 (D.C.Cir. 1991) (substantial cause test applies to ordinary tariff review prior to authorization and does not impose a separate and more extensive burden).

51. Competition in the Interstate Interexchange Marketplace, CC Docket No. 90–132, Mem. Op. & Order on Recons., 10 FCC Rcd. 4562, 4574, ¶ 25 (1995).

52. "Given the special nature of contract-based tariffs, we believe that commercial contract law principles are highly relevant to an assessment of whether a contract-based tariff revision is just and reasonable under the substantial cause test. We are not prepared, however, to say at this time that these principles provide definitive parameters for a substantial cause showing. Instead, we will consider on a case-by-case basis in light of all relevant circumstances whether a substantial cause showing has been made. In the unlikely event that a material change to a contract-based tariff meets the substantial cause test, we will also consider on a case-by-case basis whether to permit customers taking service under that contract-based tariff to terminate their contract." Id.

* Published in Modern Communication Law, Practitioners Edition, vol. 2.

1. See Telecommunications Act of 1996, § 332(b)(3), codified at 47 U.S.C.A. § 332(b)(3)(West Supp. 1997).

2. Id. § 302(b)(1).

subscribers in their telephone service areas.[3] In repealing the Commission's video dialtone rules and policies, the 1996 Act provided that

> The Commission's regulations and policies with respect to video dialtone requirements issued in CC Docket No. 87–266 shall cease to be effective on the date of enactment of this Act. This paragraph shall not be construed to require the termination of any video-dialtone system that the Commission has approved before the date of enactment of this Act.[4]

As required by the Telecommunications Act of 1996 the FCC (1) eliminated its rules implementing the telephone-cable cross-ownership restriction; (2) eliminated the video dialtone rules and policies; (3) terminated a preexisting proceeding that established its video dialtone rules and policies (CC Docket No. 87–266); and (4) did not require currently approved video dialtone systems to cease operations.[5]

Section 651 of the Communications Act, as amended by the Telecommunications Act of 1996 now provides four options for common carriers entering the video programming marketplace:

> (1) provision of video programming to subscribers through "wireless cable television" radio communication under Title III of the Communications Act;[6]

> (2) provision of transmission of video programming on a common carrier basis under Title II of the Communications Act;[7]

> (3) provision of video programming as a cable system under Title VI of the Communications Act;[8] or

> (4) provision of video programming by means of an "open video system" under new Section 653 of the Communications Act.[9]

The open video system framework provides common carriers with the opportunity to enter video programming delivery markets without having to become a "cable system" subject to all of the provisions

---

3. Cable Communications Policy Act of 1984, Pub. L. No. 98–549, § 613(b) (codified at 47 U.S.C.A. § 533(b) (West 1991)).

4. 47 U.S.C.A. § 332(b)(1) (West 1996). Similarly, the Conference Report to the Telecommunications Act of 1996 Act states: "Repeal of the Commission's video dialtone regulations is not intended to alter the status of any video dialtone service offered before the regulations required by this section become effective." Telecommunications Act of 1996, Conf. Report, S. Rep. 230, 104th Cong., 2d Sess. 179 (1996).

5. *See* Implementation of Section 302 of the Telecommunications Act of 1996, Report and Order and Notice of Proposed Rulemaking, CS Docket No. 96–46, FCC 96–99, 11 FCC Rcd. 14639 (rel. Mar. 11, 1996), 61 Fed. Reg. 10496 at ¶¶ 75–76 (Mar. 14, 1996). *See also* Second Report and Order in CS Docket No. 96–46, 61 Fed. Reg. 28698 (June 5, 1996), FCC 96–249, 11 FCC Rcd. 18223 (rel. June 3, 1996); Third Report and Order and Second Order on Recons., FCC 96–334, 11 FCC Rcd. 20227 (1996). *See also* Annual Assessment of the Status of Competition in Markets for the Delivery of Video Programming, CS Docket No. 97–141, Fourth Annual Report, 13 FCC Rcd 1034 (1998).

6. Pub. L. 104–104, § 651(a)(1), *codified at* 47 U.S.C.A. § 571(a)(1) (West Supp. 1997).

7. *Id.* § 651(a)(2), *codified at* 47 U.S.C.A. § 571(a)(2).

8. *Id.* § 651(a)(3), *codified at* 47 U.S.C.A. § 571(a)(3).

9. *Id.* § 651(a)(3)-(4), *codified at* 47 U.S.C.A. § 571(a)(3)-(4).

contained in Title VI of the Communications Act and without having to acquire municipal franchises and other authorizations prior to entry.[10] If a telephone company agrees to permit carriage of unaffiliated video programming providers under just, reasonable and non-discriminatory rates and terms, including access to as much as one-third of the available transmission capacity,[11] it can qualify to operate an open video system and be subject to streamlined regulation under Title VI.[12]

The OVS option makes it possible for telephone companies to enter video programming under streamlined regulation. It reduces Title VI regulatory requirements and exempts telephone companies from many of the traditional common carrier regulatory burdens imposed by Title II of the Communications Act.[13] An open video system operator's certification request must state that it complies with the Commission's regulations implementing the requirements in Section 653(b), which (1) prohibit the operator from discriminating among video programmers regarding carriage on its system; (2) require the operator to establish rates, terms and conditions of carriage that are just, reasonable and not unjustly or unreasonably discriminatory; (3) prohibit the operator or its affiliate, if carriage demand exceeds capacity, from selecting the video programming on more than one-third of its activated channels; (4) permit the operator to use channel sharing arrangements that provide subscribers with ready and immediate access to programming; (5) extend the Commission's sports exclusivity, network non-duplication and syndicated exclusivity regulations to open video systems; and (6) prohibit the operator from unreasonably discriminating in favor of its affiliates with regard to information provided to subscribers for the purpose of selecting programming. The Commission must approve or disapprove any open video system certification request within ten days of receipt.[14] Subsection 653(c)(2)(A) directs the Commission to take all actions necessary (including any reconsideration) to prescribe regulations applying, to the extent possible, Title VI "must-carry" and public, educational and governmental ("PEG") access obligations and Title III retransmission consent obligations, to open video systems operators.

D. Dial-a-Porn and the Concept of Common Carriage

The traditional model of telecommunication common carriage involved a transparent conduit function used to transport content. The

---

10. *See* Communications Act of 1934, as amended, § 653(a)(3), *codified at* 47 U.S.C.A. § 573(c) (West Supp. 1997).

11. Section 653(b)(1)(B)of the Telecommunications Act of 1996 provides "if demand exceeds the channel capacity of the open video system, [the FCC shall] prohibit an operator of an open video system and its affiliates from selecting the video programming services for carriage on more than one-third of the activated channel capacity on such system, but nothing in this subparagraph shall be construed to limit the num-

ber of channels that the carrier and its affiliates may offer to provide directly to subscribers." 47 U.S.C.A. § 573(b)(1) (West Supp. 1997).

12. Telecommunications   Act § 653(a)(1), *codified at* 47 U.S.C.A. § 573(a)(1) (West Supp. 1997).

13. *Id.* § 653(c)(3) *codified at* 47 U.S.C.A. § 573(c)(3).

14. *Id.* § 673(a)(1) *codified at* 47 U.S.C.A. § 573(a)(1).

common carrier did not generate the content and had no business making qualitative decisions on what content warranted carriage and what did not. In *Sable Communications, Inc. v. FCC*,[15] the Supreme Court upheld a federal statute prohibiting obscene telephone messages but overturned the statute's absolute denial of adult access to indecent messages holding that such messages are entitled to First Amendment protection.[16] Indecent messages, which are commercially packaged and commonly referred to as "dial-a-porn,"[17] can be regulated to some extent.

> The Government may … regulate the content of constitutionally protected speech in order to promote a compelling interest if it chooses the least restrictive means to further the articulated interest. We have recognized that there is a compelling interest in protecting the physical and psychological well-being of minors.[18]

Time, place and manner restrictions applied to dial-a-porn have involved the required use of credit cards, access codes and signal scrambling to ensure that such programming remains outside the reach of children.[19] However, the Supreme Court in *Sable* emphasized the difference between common carrier delivery and broadcast[20] of such material:

> [T]he dial-it medium requires the listener to take affirmative steps to receive the communication. There is no "captive audience" problem here; callers will generally not be unwilling listeners.… Placing a telephone call is not the same as turning on a radio and being taken by surprise by an indecent message.[21]

---

15. 492 U.S. 115, 109 S.Ct. 2829, 106 L.Ed.2d 93 (1989) (invalidating a total ban on indecency contained in the Telephone Indecency Act of 1988, Pub. L. 100–297, § 6101, 102 Stat. 424 (1988)).

16. For an analysis of telephone company First Amendment rights, *see* Angela J. Campbell, *Publish or Carriage: Approaches to Analyzing the First Amendment Rights of Telephone Companies*, 70 N.C. L. Rev. 1071 (1992).

17. Dial-a-porn is the colloquial term for sexually explicit services delivered to telephone subscribers typically on a pay-per-call basis. *See* Carlin Communications, Inc. v. FCC, 749 F.2d 113, 114 (2d Cir.1984). For an in depth analysis of dial-a-porn in the context of the First Amendment and the definition of common carriage, *see* Jerome A. Barron, *The Telcos, the Common Carrier Model and the First Amendment— The 'Dial–A–Porn' Precedent*, 19 Rutgers Computer & Tech. L. J. 371 (1993); Angelyn M. Wright, *Indecent Exposure on the Information Superhighway: Regulating Pornography on Integrated Broadband Telecommunications Networks*, 11 Ga. St. U. L. Rev. 465 (1995).

18. Sable Communications, Inc. v. FCC, 492 U.S. 115, 126, 109 S.Ct. 2829, 2836, 106 L.Ed.2d 93, 105 (1989).

19. *See* Carlin Communications, Inc. v. FCC, 837 F.2d 546 (2d Cir.), cert. denied, 488 U.S. 924, 109 S.Ct. 305, 102 L.Ed.2d 324 (1988).

20. The Supreme Court has shown far greater willingness to narrow the scope of First Amendment protections accorded broadcasters, initially on scarcity grounds and the use of publicly owned radio spectrum. *See* Red Lion Broadcasting Co. v. FCC, 395 U.S. 367, 89 S.Ct. 1794, 23 L.Ed.2d 371 (1969). In FCC v. Pacifica Foundation, 438 U.S. 726, 98 S.Ct. 3026, 57 L.Ed.2d 1073 (1978), the Court upheld an FCC fine for the radio broadcast of indecent speech during afternoon hours when it could be expected that children would make up a part of the listening audience. The Court emphasized the accessibility of the medium to children and its pervasive presence in society.

21. Sable Communications, Inc., 492 U.S. at 127–28, 109 S.Ct. at 2837, 106 L.Ed.2d at 106.

As telephone companies enter video distribution markets the question arises whether the common carrier model will persist and whether common carriers must carry objectionable messages that may adversely affect the carrier's business. As noted above, the FCC contemplated video dialtone to contain common carrier transport functions coupled with non-common carrier enhanced services. The Commission's model was based on the view that telephone companies will not operate as electronic speakers, editors or publishers, because the requirements of common carriage prohibit discrimination. However, courts have affirmed decisions by telephone companies to refrain from carrying certain categories of messages, such as dial-a-porn, despite their common carrier status. In *Carlin Communications, Inc. v. Mountain States Telephone and Telegraph*,[22] the Ninth Circuit Court of Appeals upheld the right of a telephone company to terminate a dial-a-porn service because adverse publicity might affect public relations and profits.[23] The court also held that providing the type of service used by Carlin Communications, known as audiotext[24] which uses a 7 digit local telephone with a 976 prefix, or an 11 digit number with a 1 + 800 or 1 + 900 prefix did not constitute common carriage:[25]

> Moreover, we question whether state public utility law in its traditional form makes sense as applied to Mountain Bell's 976 network. The technology of that network differs fundamentally from that of basic phone service.... Under these circumstances the telephone is serving as a medium by which Carlin broadcasts its messages. The phone company resembles less a common carrier than it does a small radio station.[26]

Traditional expectations of telephone companies and conventional interpretation of what constitutes common carriage[27] will require revi-

---

22. 827 F.2d 1291 (9th Cir.1987), cert. denied 485 U.S. 1029, 108 S.Ct. 1586, 99 L.Ed.2d 901(1988).

23. *Id.* at 1293.

24. For an extensive analysis of the legislative, regulatory and legal development in the pay-per-call business, *see* William W. Burrington and Thaddeus J. Burns, *Hung Up on the Pay-Per-Call Industry?: Current Federal Legislative and Regulatory Developments*, 17 Seton Hall Legis. J. 359 (1993); *see also* Ellen L. Nagel, Note, *First Amendment Constraints on the Regulation of Telephone Pornography*, 55 U.Cin. L. Rev. 237 (1986); Cindy L. Petersen, Note, *The Congressional Response to the Supreme Court's Treatment of Dial-a-Porn*, 78 Geo. L. J. 2025 (1990).

25. Carlin Communications, Inc. v. Mountain States Tel. & Tel. Co., 827 F.2d 1291, 1294–95 (9th Cir.1987). *Accord* Carlin Communication, Inc. v. Southern Bell Tel. & Tel. Co., 802 F.2d 1352 (11th Cir.1986) (tariff containing content restrictions on

material qualifying for First Amendment protection nevertheless deemed permissible as legitimate business judgment); Network Communications v. Michigan Bell Tel. Co., 703 F.Supp. 1267 (E.D.Mich.1989) (affirming telephone company decision to cut off billing and collection services for a dial-a-porn operator).

26. Carlin Communications, Inc., 827 F.2d at 1294.

27. Traditionally common carriers have not been able "to make individualized decisions, in particular cases, whether and on what terms to deal." National Ass'n of Regl. Util. Comm'rs v. FCC, 525 F.2d 630, 641, 173 U.S. App. D.C. 413, 424 (D.C.Cir. 1976); *see* discussion of common versus private carriage in FCC v. Midwest Video Corp., 440 U.S. 689, 99 S.Ct. 1435, 59 L.Ed.2d 692 (1979) (rejecting a common carrier classification for cable television); *see also* 47 U.S.C.A. § 202(a) (West 1991) that prohibits common carriers from making "any unjust or unreasonable discrimi-

sion if carriers can resort to business judgment to decide whether or not to carry a particular category of messages and if courts exempt new technologies or services from falling within the definition of common carriage.[28] Professor Jerome A. Barron considers "[b]usiness judgment in these cases [as sounding] suspiciously like editorial judgment"[29] which broadcasters and newspaper publishers frequently exercise, but which does not correspond to the traditional non-discrimination expectation of common carriers.[30] He sees "a disturbing willingness to grant exemptions from the common carrier principle when that principle proves troublesome to the carriers, particularly in light of their direct involvement in information and video services."[31] Perhaps sympathy with the telcos' reticence to upset its standing in the community by carrying salacious material bolsters the government's willingness to tinker with First Amendment protections.[32] Congress and the FCC have attempted to

nation in charges, practices, classifications, regulations, facilities or services. . . . "

28. If a court determines that dial-a-porn constitutes a public, rather than private communication medium, then it may abandon application of the traditional common carrier definition: "Once the telephone company becomes a medium for public rather than private communication, the fit of traditional common carrier law becomes less snug." Carlin Communications, Inc., 827 F.2d at 1294. A telephone company "may refuse to provide access to information providers whose messages it does not wish to be associated with, in a relationship outside the scope of the utility's role as a common carrier. . . . " Network Communications v. Michigan Bell Tel. Co., 703 F.Supp. 1267, 1276 (E.D.Mich.1989).

29. Jerome A. Barron, *The Telcos, the Common Carrier Model and the First Amendment—The "Dial–A–Porn" Precedent*, 19 Rutgers Computer & Tech. L. J. 371, 386 (1993).

30. The Judge in *Carlin Communications*, v. *Mountain States Telephone and Telegraph* "is really saying here that the telco can censor an information service even though a state statute could not. The reason the state could not effect such censorship is that it would amount to state action violating the First Amendment. But if one views the telco as a private actor, then a telco's decision to prohibit the transmission of a certain category of messages—in this case, Carlin's 'adult entertainment service'—is simply an editorial decision such as broadcasters and newspapers make all the time." *Id.* at 388, n. 44. Professor Barron rejects this analysis on the view that it might be possible for the telephone company "to become the dominant informa-

tion provider—overtaking broadcasting, cable broadcasting and newspapers" with "more power than government" to affect speech, yet freely able to do so. *Id.* Most courts have rejected the view that telephone company decisionmaking on carriage represents state action. *See, e.g.,* Dial Information Services Corp. v. Thornburgh, 938 F.2d 1535 (2d Cir.1991), cert. denied *sub nom.* Dial Information Services Corp. v. Barr, 502 U.S. 1072, 112 S.Ct. 966, 117 L.Ed.2d 132 (1992) (finding no government compulsion whether to bill or not bill for dial-a-porn services). Such a finding would make the refusal to carry or bill for such material more difficult as the First Amendment analysis would have to be undertaken with closer scrutiny. *See* Jackson v. Metropolitan Edison Co., 419 U.S. 345, 95 S.Ct. 449, 42 L.Ed.2d 477 (1974) (action of a private company will be attributed to the state when the company exercises powers traditionally and exclusively reserved to the state such as eminent domain). Censorship, as opposed to editing and business decisionmaking, would constitute state action. *See* Carlin Communications, Inc. v. South Central Bell Telephone Co., 461 So.2d 1208 (La.App. 1984) (dial-a-porn messages deemed obscene and not indecent may be censored by the telco to serve the traditional state concern about minors' exposure to obscenity).

31. "If the telcos as information providers are too quickly suited with First Amendment armor and labeled speakers or editors, they can too easily shed the non-discriminatory access obligations of the common carrier. The end result could be that the regional telco will not only control who enters the conduit but also what can be said on it." *Id.*

32. *See, e.g.,* FCC Authorization Act of 1983, Pub. L. 98–214, 97 Stat. 1467–68,

channel to late night hours or condition dial-a-porn access by requiring credit card payment and pre-authorizations.[33] While likely sympathetic to the goals of such restrictions, some courts have subjected them to close scrutiny when the content involved is indecent (and not obscene) and therefore entitled to First Amendment protection.

The United Stated Court of Appeals for the Second Circuit in *Carlin Communications, Inc. v. FCC*,[34] held that the FCC failed to demonstrate that its regulatory scheme was narrowly tailored to achieve its purpose and that no less restrictive means were available. While protecting minors from "salacious matter" served a compelling governmental interest,[35] the manner in which such protection occurs will be subjected to "exacting scrutiny."[36] The court found that the FCC regulations were both over and under inclusive because they denied access to adults at times but not access of minors who at times could meet the credit card requirement without providing evidence of age.

The Second Circuit subsequently rejected regulations that required adults first to obtain access or identification codes from audiotext providers or required payment by credit card before access could be achieved.[37] The court held that the regulations were not the least restrictive because the Commission could have considered the feasibility of blocking per line access at customer election by devices on customer premises or through telephone company facilities.[38] In 1988, the court finally upheld a regulatory scheme that required access codes, message scrambling and credit card payment.[39]

In 1989 the Supreme Court rejected a Congressional attempt to revise Section 223 of the Communications Act to prohibit all obscene or indecent communications for commercial purposes in *Sable Communications*.[40] With the Supreme Court's reversal of an absolute ban on indecent commercial communications, Congress again amended Section 223 of the Communications Act[41] and the FCC faced yet another labor of codifying regulations that serve a compelling government interest in

codified as amended at 47 U.S.C.A. § 223 (West 1991 and Supp. 1997) (amending the Communications Act to prohibit the use of a telephone to transmit obscene or indecent communications to persons under the age of 18).

33. The FCC created two defenses to a violation of Sec. 223: (1) limiting operations to the hours between 9 p.m. and 8 am; and (2) requiring payment by credit card before transmission of the message. Enforcement of Prohibition Against the Use of Common Carriers for the Transmission of Obscene Material, 49 Fed. Reg. 24,996, 25,003 (1984).

34. 749 F.2d 113 (2d Cir.1984).

35. Carlin Communications, Inc. v. FCC, 749 F.2d 113, 120–121 (2d Cir.1984).

36. *Id.*

37. Carlin Communications, Inc. v. FCC, 787 F.2d 846 (2d Cir.1986).

38. *Id.* at 855–56.

39. Carlin Communications, Inc. v. FCC, 837 F.2d 546 (2d Cir.1988).

40. *See* Augustus F. Hawkins–Robert T. Stafford Elementary and Secondary School Improvement Amendments of 1988, Pub. L. 100–297, § 6101, 102 Stat. 424, *codified as amended at* 47 U.S.C.A. § 223(b) (West 1992), *held unconstitutional in part* in Sable Communications, Inc. v. FCC, 492 U.S. 115, 109 S.Ct. 2829, 106 L.Ed.2d 93 (1989).

41. The amendments to Section 223 of the Communications Act were contained in Section 521 of the Department of Labor, Health and Human Services, and Education, and Related Agencies Appropriations Act of 1990, Pub. L. 101–166, § 512,

protecting minors from indecent but not obscene[42] dial-a-porn, while not placing an unnecessarily restrictive burden on adult access.[43] The Commission adopted a "reverse blocking" scheme that required dial-a-porn service providers and adults wishing to access such programming to take several affirmative steps to provide and secure such material.[44] Service providers must inform the telephone company that indecent communications will be transmitted.[45] Prospective customers must pay by credit card or use an authorized access code before transmission. Alternatively, the service provider may scramble the message rendering it unintelligible to any calling party lacking an on-premises descrambler. The Second Circuit upheld the statute imposing such conditions as being narrowly drawn to serve a compelling governmental interest and this time the Supreme Court denied review.[46]

12.11   *The Viability of the Common Carrier Regulatory Model

103 Stat. 1159, 1192–93, *codified at* 47 U.S.C.A. § 223 (West 1991).

42. The Court in *Sable* reiterated that "protection of the First Amendment does not extent to obscene speech." Sable Communications, Inc., 492 U.S. at 124, 109 S. Ct. at 2835, 106 L. Ed. 2d at 103–04, citing Paris Adult Theatre I v. Slaton, 413 U.S. 49, 69, 93 S.Ct. 2628, 2641, 37 L.Ed.2d 446, 464 (1973).

43. Regulations Concerning Indecent Communications By Telephone, Report and Order, 5 FCC Rcd. 4926 (1990) *codified at* 47 C.F.R. § 64.201 (1996). *See also,* Policies and Rules Concerning Interstate 900 Telecommunications Services, Report and Order, 6 FCC Rcd. 6166 (1991), *codified at* 47 C.F.R. §§ 64.318(c)(2) and 64.709–64.716 (1996).

44. *See* Information Providers' Coalition for Defense of the First Amendment v. FCC, 928 F.2d 866 (9th Cir.1991) (supporting reverse blocking as a more effective vehicle than blocking at telephone company switching facilities, to prevent minors from accessing dial-a-porn).

45. 47 C.F.R. § 64.201(b) (1996).

46. Dial Information Services v. Thornburgh, 938 F.2d 1535 (2d Cir.1991), cert. denied 502 U.S. 1072, 112 S.Ct. 966, 117 L.Ed.2d 132 (1992).

* Published in Modern Communication Law, Practitioners Edition, Vol. 2.

Chapter Thirteen

REGULATION OF CABLE TELEVISION

Analysis

13.1   Background

Few communications industries have been subjected to the extreme pendulum swings of regulation versus deregulation as has been the cable television industry. Federal regulation began in the 1960s as a response to increasing competition with traditional broadcasters, and was designed to limit growth of the industry. Local regulation, in the form of franchising, was, at least initially, directed more toward the control of local land use and business practices. The pendulum moved away from these regulatory approaches with passage of the 1984 Cable Act, but swung back again with passage of the highly regulatory Cable Competition and Consumer Protection Act of 1992. Within four years, Congress acted again to lighten certain cable regulations with passage of the Telecommunications Act of 1996.

In many ways, the nature and scope of cable television regulation evolved along with the industry. Community antenna television ("CATV"), as cable television was known originally, developed first in "fringe areas"—markets that were too small to support a local television station and where over-the-air reception was not satisfactory.[1] The first noncommercial operation was in Astoria, Oregon in 1949 and the first commercial system was started in Lansford, Pennsylvania in 1950. By 1959 there were a few hundred CATV systems operating throughout the

---

1. First Report and Order, 18 R.R. 1573, 1578 (P & F 1959).

country.[2] Growth of the industry was slow at first, and by the early 1970s one study of the industry noted that "only recently has it begun to warrant notice on the front pages of the daily press."[3] Nevertheless, the report indicated that cable television was "[s]preading quietly into every corner of the United States—slowly and unevenly and yet with its own air of inevitability."[4]

The prophesy came true. By 1996, the Supreme Court found that cable television was as accessible to viewers as over-the-air broadcasting. A plurality of the Court concluded that cable television had established a pervasive presence in American television households.[5] This finding is supported by annual FCC surveys of the video marketplace. By 1997 cable television was available to more than 97 percent of all television households, or over 94 million homes.[6] Of this potential audience, 66 percent subscribed to the service.[7] In addition, the cable industry expanded from a service that only retransmitted television signals to one that provided well over a hundred specialized programming networks, including such services as Home Box Office, C–Span, Cable News Network, Court TV, A&E Television Networks, the History Channel, Black Entertainment Television, the Discovery Channel and Lifetime Television. By 1995 there were 129 different cable programming services.[8] Accordingly, Congress concluded that "[c]able television has become our Nation's dominant video distribution medium."[9]

Such industry growth made regulation inevitable. Although most cable regulation had been accomplished through local franchises, federal

2. *Id.* at 1579–80. Even at that early stage of development, television broadcasters claimed that the CATV industry had resulted in a "substantial adverse economic impact" upon the television broadcasting community.

3. ON THE CABLE 1 (Report of the Sloan Commission on Cable Communications 1971).

4. *Id.* In 1959 there were approximately 550 CATV systems providing approximately three signals to their subscribers. In contrast, in 1965 there were approximately 1,300 CATV systems providing approximately 5 or more signals. By 1966 there were 1,565 CATV systems with the capacity to provide approximately 12 channels. Second Report and Order, 6 Rad.Reg. 2d 1717, 1773 (P&F 1996). In a 1966 Report and Order the FCC noted the rapid growth of CATV systems in cities and metropolitan areas. The Commission pointed to "the asserted intent of CATV interests to wire up almost all American cities—large and small." *Id.* at 1741 (quoting address by Milton J. Schapp, "CATV—Past, Present, Future," December 8, 1964, reprinted in Television Digest Special Supplement, Vol. 4, No. 50, December 14, 1964, page 1.).

5. Denver Area Educational Telecommunications Consortium, Inc. v. FCC, 518 U.S. 727, 116 S.Ct. 2374, 2386, 135 L.Ed.2d 888, 903 (1996) (citation omitted).

6. Annual Assessment of the Status of Competition in the Market for the Delivery of Video Programming, 13 FCC Rcd.1034, para. 14 (1998)("Fourth Video Competition Report"). *See also* Annual Assessment of the Status of Competition in the Market for the Delivery of Video Programming, 12 FCC Rcd. 4358; FCC rel. 96–496 ¶ 13 (Jan. 2, 1997) ("Third Video Competition Report"). *See also* Annual Assessment of the Status of Competition in the Market for the Delivery of Video Programming, Second Annual Report, 11 FCC Rcd. 2060 (1996) ("Second Video Competition Report"); Annual Assessment of the Status of Competition in the Market for the Delivery of Video Programming, First Report, 9 FCC Rcd 2896 (1994) ("First Video Competition Report").

7. Fourth Video Competition Report at ¶ 14.

8. Second Video Competition Report, 11 FCC Rcd. at 2066.

9. S. Rep. No. 92, 102d Cong, 1st Sess. 3 (1992), *reprinted in* 1978 U.S. Code Cong. & Admin. News, 1135.

rules became increasingly important over time. For example, in 1961 the FCC denied an application to construct a microwave radio communications system to transmit signals received from television stations of distant cities to CATV systems in several towns in Wyoming.[10] The Commission reasoned that allowing Carter Mountain Transmission Company to bring outside stations into local communities "would result in the 'demise' of the local station ... and the loss of service to a substantial rural population not served by the [CATV] systems, and to many other persons who did not choose (or were unable) to pay the cost of subscribing to the [CATV] systems."[11] The United States Court of Appeals for the District of Columbia Circuit affirmed the FCC's decision.[12]

As cable television began to evolve into "a national communications system," the Commission "began to express more regulatory interest."[13] During 1965 and 1966, the FCC promulgated extensive regulations over the cable systems, in response to what the agency described as the explosive growth of CATV systems.[14] Consistent with the FCC's earlier rulings, the rules were intended to restrict the importation of distant broadcast signals and thereby to protect local broadcasters from competition. The FCC's 1966 Report and Order noted that the goal of the regulations was to "integrate the CATV service into the national television structure in such a way as to promote maximum television service to all people of the United States, both those who are cable viewers and those dependent on off-the-air service."[15] In 1968, the Supreme Court held that the FCC had the authority to regulate the CATV industry but clarified that the decision did not address the validity of the specific rules promulgated by the Commission for the regulation of CATV.[16] The Court noted that the FCC's jurisdiction was limited to actions "reasonably ancillary to the ... Commission's various responsibilities for the regulation of television broadcasting."[17]

In 1972, the FCC adopted more comprehensive cable television rules that helped define the federal-state relationship, cross-ownership issues, technical standards and programming issues, including local origination, syndicated exclusivity and must carry.[18] Although the Supreme Court

10. Carter Mountain Transmission Corp. v. FCC, 321 F.2d 359, 361, 116 U.S. App. D.C. 93, 95 (1963), cert. denied 375 U.S. 951, 84 S.Ct. 442, 11 L.Ed.2d 312 (1963).

11. *Id*. at 361.

12. *Id*. at 366.

13. *See* Cable Television Ass'n of New York, Inc. v. Finneran, 954 F.2d 91, 95 (2d Cir.1992) (citation omitted).

14. First Report and Order, 38 FCC 683, 711 (1965).

15. Second Report and Order, 6 R.R. at 1746. *See* United States v. Midwest Video Corp., 406 U.S. 649, 92 S.Ct. 1860, 32 L.Ed.2d 390 (1972).

16. United States v. Southwestern Cable Co., 392 U.S. 157, 88 S.Ct. 1994, 20 L.Ed.2d 1001 (1968).

17. *Id*. at 178, 88 S.Ct. at 2005, 20 L.Ed.2d at 1001.

18. Cable Television Report and Order, 36 FCC 2d. 143 (1972). In *FCC v. Midwest Video Corp.*, 440 U.S. 689, 99 S.Ct. 1435, 59 L.Ed.2d 692 (1979), the Supreme Court struck down requirements of the 1972 rules that required cable operators to set aside channel capacity for public, educational and governmental channels and for leased access. The Court held that such requirements exceeded the FCC's statutory authority.

initially upheld certain FCC rules requiring cable program origination as being subject to the FCC's ancillary jurisdiction,[19] it subsequently restricted FCC authority. In *FCC v. Midwest Video Corp.*, the Court held that rules requiring cable systems to allocate channels to public, educational, local governmental and leased access users exceeded the FCC's ancillary jurisdiction.[20]

Beginning with the 1972 rules, the FCC attempted to establish a "deliberately structured dualism" whereby local governments would be responsible for selecting franchises pursuant to minimum standards established by the FCC, while the Commission retained exclusive authority over all operational aspects of cable communication, including technical standards and signal carriage.[21] The Commission subsequently ceded virtually all franchising authority to the states,[22] although many local regulations were preempted by federal authority.[23]

To respond to the "fluid and ever-changing balance between state and federal authority," Congress passed the Cable Communications Policy Act of 1984 ("1984 Cable Act").[24] The Act to a large degree deregulated cable television and established rules governing local franchise agreements. Six years later, the pendulum swung in the other direction with passage of the Cable Television Consumer Protection and Competition Act of 1992.[25] That Act reimposed extensive rate regulations, established program access requirements, reimposed must carry and retransmission consent obligations, established new ownership limits and various other requirements. Just four years later, Congress passed the Telecommunications Act of 1996, Title III of which relaxed many of the rules adopted pursuant to the 1992 Act.[26] Most notably, the Act established an expiration date of March 21, 1999 for federal rate regulation of cable programming services.[27]

13.2   Regulation and Cable Franchising

A.   *Dual Nature of Franchising*

Cable companies operate "under a complex, dual system of regulation, subject both to franchise agreements made with states and munici-

---

19. United States v. Midwest Video Corp., 406 U.S. 649, 92 S.Ct. 1860, 32 L.Ed.2d 390 (1972) ("Midwest Video I").

20. 440 U.S. 689, 99 S.Ct. 1435, 59 L.Ed.2d 692 (1979) ("Midwest Video II").

21. *See* Cable Television Ass'n of New York, Inc. v. Finneran, 954 F.2d 91, 96, (*quoting* New York State Commission on Cable TV. v. FCC, 749 F.2d 804, 242 U.S. App. D.C. 126 (1984)).

22. Finneran, 954 F.2d at 96.

23. *See* Capital Cities Cable, Inc. v. Crisp, 467 U.S. 691, 104 S.Ct. 2694, 81 L.Ed.2d 580 (1984) (FCC regulations preempt state law prohibiting cable companies from retransmitting out-of-state alcoholic beverage commercials); ACLU v. FCC, 823 F.2d 1554, 1558–1559, 262 U.S. App.

D.C. 244, 248-249 (1987), cert. denied, 485 U.S. 959, 108 S.Ct. 1220, 99 L.Ed.2d 421 (1988) (FCC preemption of local rate regulation of premium cable services and limitations on franchise fees upheld).

24. Pub. L. 98–549, 98 Stat. 2779 (1984), *codified at* 47 U.S.C.A. §§ 521 et. seq.

25. Pub. L. 102–385, 106 Stat. 1460 (1992), *codified at* 47 U.S.C.A. §§ 521 et. seq.

26. Telecommunications Act of 1996, Pub. L. No. 104–104, 110 Stat. 56 (1996).

27. 47 U.S.C.A. § 301(b)(4) (West Supp. 1997).

palities … and FCC regulation designed to protect [federal interests]."[1] The precise boundaries between federal power and state authority were never clear until passage of the Cable Act of 1984. The 1984 Act expressly recognized the authority of state and local governments to award cable television franchises.[2] Historically, this authority rested on local government police power over the public streets and highways. The consent of the state was necessary for cable operators to place their cables either above or below the public streets. Consequently, a franchise was granted when the appropriate governmental entity authorized the use of the streets for a private purpose, such as that of a cable operator.[3] The power of localities to grant franchises also encompassed the right of local governments to condition local consent upon the fulfillment of certain terms and conditions by the franchisee, so long as these requirements do not clash with the federal statutory scheme or any contrary state direction.[4] The nature of this process is contractual.[5]

The Cable Acts recognize the dual nature of franchises. For instance, contractual conditions contained in a franchise agreement that conflict with the Act were grandfathered by the 1984 Act if the provisions are part of an "existing franchise," as defined by the Act.[6] In addition, the statute authorizes the inclusion of certain provisions in a franchise agreement, such as Public, Educational or Governmental ("PEG") access requirements, which traditionally had been negotiated conditions in franchise agreements.[7] The law also ratifies the right of cable operators and franchise authorities to contract for the modification or renewal of franchises.[8]

While a franchise granted by a locality constitutes a contract, the arrangement typically is authorized and regulated by a local ordinance as well. The regulatory ordinance establishes the terms under which a cable operator must operate, and under which the franchise is issued.[9] Sometimes, the ordinance and the contract are combined to create a franchise ordinance. Because of the contractual nature of the franchise ordinance, it may not be unilaterally modified by the municipality.[10]

1. Cable Television Ass'n of New York, Inc. v. Finneran 954 F.2d 91, 96 (2d Cir. 1992).

2. 47 U.S.C.A. § 541 (West 1991).

3. James C. Goodale, All About Cable §§ 4–5 to 4–6 (Update by Mark D. Director, 1995).

4. *Id.* at § 4–6.

5. *See e.g.,* Nashoba Communications Ltd. Partnership No. 7 v. Town of Danvers, 893 F.2d 435, 440–41 (1st Cir.1990).

6. 47 U.S.C.A. § 557(a) (West 1991).

7. *Id.* § 531(c).

8. *Id.* §§ 545 and 546.

9. *See* Jones Intercable of San Diego, Inc. v. City of Chula Vista, 67 F.3d 846, 850 (9th Cir.1995) ("It is difficult to see what the City was doing, if not regulating, when it precluded Jones from installing more cable infrastructure and from servicing customers unless Jones first obtained a citywide franchise.").

10. Franchises are contracts within the meaning of the Contract Clause of the Constitution. U.S. Const. art I, § 10, cl. 1. Local governments may also exercise police powers to the extent they do not impair the contract. *See* Cox Cable San Diego Inc. v. City of San Diego, 188 Cal.App.3d 952, 233 Cal.Rptr. 735 (Cal.Ct.App.1987).

B. Cable Act Franchising Requirements

1. Statutory Framework

The 1984 Cable Act codified the established practice of franchising by local authorities but also established a legal framework within which the franchising process must operate.[11] The Cable Act specifies that a cable operator may not operate without a franchise,[12] but grandfathered systems that legally operated without a franchise prior to 1984.[13] Franchise authorities are authorized by the law to grant one or more franchises within their jurisdiction, and the 1992 Act explicitly prohibits the grant of exclusive franchises.[14] In addition, the franchise authority may not unreasonably deny the award of an additional competitive franchise.[15]

The extent to which local authorities control cable television is governed by state law. Some states, preempt local franchising and a state agency serves as franchising authority.[16] In other states, local franchising is authorized by statute.[17] Even in states where local governments act as franchising authorities, the state may nevertheless exert regulatory authority over various aspects of cable service. Some states have regulatory commissions to govern cable services,[18] while other states provide more limited jurisdiction to state agencies over cable television issues. Local authorities, including cities, counties or other political subdivisions, may exercise only those powers granted by the state.

The 1984 Cable Act also authorizes the use of public rights of way by a cable operator.[19] This includes the use of easements that "have been dedicated for compatible uses."[20] This allowance provides a cost-effective means to construct cable systems since existing utility easements may be utilized. This authorization by the statute does not compel owners of private property, including owners of private easements, to grant franchisees access to their land or easements. Rather, the Cable Act grants a franchise cable operator a right of access only to "dedicated easements"

---

11. The FCC had previously established minimum procedural requirements for franchising that were rescinded after passage of the 1984 Act. *See* 58 Rad. Reg. 2d 1 (P&F 1985).

12. 47 U.S.C.A. § 541(b)(1) (West 1991). This requirement has been challenged in the courts. In particular, it has been challenged as a violation of the First Amendment. *See* Preferred Communications, Inc. v. City of Los Angeles, 754 F.2d 1396 (9th Cir.1985), *aff'd on narrower grounds*, 476 U.S. 488, 106 S.Ct. 2034, 90 L.Ed.2d 480 (1986). Preferred Communications challenged cable franchising regulations after unsuccessfully seeking to bypass the City of Los Angeles' franchising regulations.

13. 47 U.S.C.A. § 541(b)(2) (West 1991).

14. *Id.* § 541 (West Supp. 1997).

15. *Id.* § 541(a)(1).

16. *See, e.g.,* Conn. Gen. Stat. § 16–1 (West 1993 & Supp. 1997); Nev. Rev. Stat. Ann. § 711 (Michie 1993 & Supp. 1995); R.I. Gen. Laws § 39–19 (1990 & Supp. 1996); Vt. Stat. Ann. tit. 30, §§ 501–08 (Supp. 1982).

17. Mass. Ann. Laws ch. 166A, §§ 1–22, (West 1976 & Supp. 1997) (Michie Law. Co-op. 1979 & Supp. 1984); N.J. Stat. Ann. § 48:5A (Supp. 1997); NY Public Service Law §§ 211–230 (McKinney Supp. 1997); Minn. Stat. Ann. §§ 238.01–238.43 (West 1980 & Supp. 1997); Del. Code Ann. tit. 26, §§ 601–16 (1989 & Supp. 1987).

18. Mass. Ann. Laws ch. 166A, § 3 (MichieLaw. Co-op. 1979); NY Public Service Law §§ 215–16 (McKinney 1997).

19. 47 U.S.C.A. § 541(a)(2) (West 1991).

20. *Id.*

that (1) have been publicly recorded, (2) that are specific in their description as to location and dimension and (3) over which the property owners have relinquished the right of exclusion.[21] Some states, on the other hand, have adopted more extensive access to property laws.[22]

The Cable Act also imposes certain limitations on franchise authorities. For example, while cable operators may be required "under the terms of any franchise to pay a franchise fee,"[23] the amount of fees are capped at five percent of gross annual revenues from cable service.[24] Moreover, franchise authorities are limited in their ability to contract for certain provisions that regulate services, facilities and equipment that are unrelated "to the establishment or operation of a cable system."[25] Congress adopted these provisions out of concern that some franchise authorities had abused the franchising system by requiring that cable operators agree to provide unrelated benefits to the city (*e.g.*, building a park) in order to receive a franchise.[26] Under the Cable Act, cities can only bargain for such regulatory provisions that relate to the cable system itself. The Act also is intended to protect cable operators from excessive franchise demands. Accordingly, the statute created a federally defined process by which operators of both existing and new franchises are protected from overreaching by local franchise authorities. Denial of a franchisee's modification request may be appealed to a federal court.[27]

The 1992 Act also limited local regulation of services, facilities, and equipment. Under the Act, franchise authorities are permitted in their request for proposals ("RFPs") to establish requirements for facilities and equipment but generally cannot establish specific requirements for video programming or other information services.[28] Some exceptions to this restriction include the ability of franchise authorities to require the provision of "broad categories of programming" and to require a cable

---

21. *See* Century Southwest Cable Television, Inc. v. CIIF Associates, 33 F.3d 1068 (9th Cir.1994); TCI of North Dakota, Inc. v. Schriock Holding Co., 11 F.3d 812 (8th Cir. 1993); Media General Cable of Fairfax, Inc. v. Sequoyah Condominium Council of Co–Owners, 737 F.Supp. 903 (E.D.Va.1990), *aff'd* 991 F.2d 1169 (4th Cir.1993); Cable Holdings of Georgia v. McNeil Real Estate, 953 F.2d 600 (11th Cir.1992) (holding that provision of 1984 Cable Act does not authorize access to private, nondedicated easements for particular utilities in multi-unit apartment buildings), cert. denied 506 U.S. 862, 113 S.Ct. 182, 121 L.Ed.2d 127 (1992); Cable Investments, Inc. v. Woolley, 867 F.2d 151 (3d Cir.1989). *See also* Loretto v. Teleprompter Manhattan CATV Corp., 458 U.S. 419, 102 S.Ct. 3164, 73 L.Ed.2d 868 (1982) (requiring use of private property for installation of cable wire is a taking for which the Fifth Amendment requires just compensation).

22. *See* ACS Enterprises, Inc. v. Comcast Cablevision of Philadelphia, 857 F.Supp. 1105 (E.D.Pa.1994), *aff'd* 60 F.3d 813 (3d Cir.1995); American Cablecom Limited Partnership v. Cablevision of Pennsylvania, Inc., 1994 WL 675193 (E.D.Pa.1994); AMSAT Cable Ltd. v. Cablevision of Connecticut Limited Partnership, 6 F.3d 867 (2d Cir.1993).

23. 47 U.S.C.A. § 542(a) (West 1991).

24. *Id.* § 542(b).

25. 25. *Id.* § 544.

26. H. R. Rep. No. 98–934 at 21, 24 (1984) *reprinted in* 1984 United States Code Cong. and Admin. News at 4655.

27. 47 U.S.C.A. § 545(b) (West 1991). *See* Cablevision Sys. Corp. v. Town of East Hampton, 862 F.Supp. 875 (E.D.N.Y.1994), *aff'd* 57 F.3d 1062 (2d Cir.1995); Tribune–United Cable v. Montgomery County, 784 F.2d 1227 (4th Cir.1986).

28. 47 U.S.C.A. § 544(b) (West Supp. 1997).

operator to (1) provide thirty days advance written notice of any change in channel assignment or video programming; and (2) inform subscribers in writing that comments on programming and channel position changes are being recorded by a designated franchise authority office.[29] Otherwise, the Cable Act generally preempts local authority over "the provision or content of cable services," unless authorized by the Act.

The 1992 Cable Act required the FCC to prescribe minimum technical standards relating to cable system's operation and signal quality and enabled franchising authorities to enforce such standards through their control over franchise modifications, renewals or transfers.[30] Local enforcement of the FCC technical standards was eliminated, however, by the Telecommunications Act of 1996. It deleted language permitting local authorities to require, as part of a franchise, provisions for the enforcement of federal technical standards. Additionally, the 1996 law barred states and franchising authorities from prohibiting, conditioning or restricting a cable system's use of any type of subscriber equipment or any transmission technology.[31]

2. *Definition of a Cable System*

One issue of critical importance involves the determination of which providers of video programming services are considered to be cable operators and require a local franchise. This question has gained added importance as various technologies have emerged to provide the same or similar types of programming services. Accordingly, the Cable Act specifically defines what constitutes a "cable system."

The 1984 and 1992 Cable Acts defined a cable system as:

a facility, consisting of a set of closed transmission paths and associated signal generation, reception, and control equipment that is designed to provide cable service which includes video programming and which is provided to multiple subscribers within a community, but such term does not include (A) a facility that serves only to retransmit television signals of one or more television broadcast stations; (B) a facility that serves only subscribers in one or more multiple dwelling units under common ownership control, or management, unless such facility or facilities uses any public right-of-way; (c) a facility of a common carrier which is subject, in whole or in part, to the provisions of title II of this Act, except that such facility shall be considered a cable system ... to the extent such facility is used for the transmission of video programming directly to subscribers; or (D) any facilities of any electric utility used solely for operating its electric utility system.[32]

29. *Id.* §§ 544(b)(2)(B), 544(h).

30. *Id.* § 544(e).

31. Telecommunications Act of 1996, Pub. L. 104–104, § 301(e), 110 Stat. 56,

(1996), *codified as amended at* 47 U.S.C.A. § 544 (West Supp. 1997).

32. 47 U.S.C.A. § 522(7) (West 1991 and Supp. 1997).

In 1993 the Supreme Court upheld the statutory definition of a cable system in *FCC v. Beach Communications, Inc.*[33] Under the definition that existed at that time, the FCC had concluded that certain satellite master antenna television ("SMATV") systems qualified as cable systems requiring franchises, while others did not. It had concluded that SMATV systems that did not use public rights-of-ways or that commonly owned managed or controlled buildings that were interconnected did not require a franchise. On the other hand, SMATV systems that connected separately owned buildings were considered cable systems even if no public rights-of-way were used.[34] The Supreme Court upheld the regulatory distinction against statutory, First Amendment and equal protection challenges, finding that the definition did not infringe fundamental rights nor create a suspect classification.[35] The Court held that it was not necessary for the government to articulate its reasons for creating the distinction and that there were conceivable reasons for Congress to have treated separately owned buildings differently from commonly owned buildings served by SMATV systems.[36] On remand, United States Court of Appeals for the District of Columbia Circuit held that this conclusion was unaltered by passage of the 1992 Cable Act.[37]

Congress eliminated the different treatment of "commonly owned" versus "separately owned" buildings served by SMATV systems in the 1996 Telecommunications Act. Section 301(a) of the 1996 Act amended the definition of "cable system" to exclude any facilities that served subscribers without using public rights-of-way. Consequently, systems serving separately owned, managed, or controlled multipledwelling units need not obtain a cable franchise so long as they do not use any public rights-of-way.[38] The 1996 Act also clarified that Congress did not intend to regulate entities that provide "interactive on-demand services" as cable systems.[39] This clarification is reflected in the statutory definitions of both "cable system" and "cable service." Congress altered the definitions to reflect "the evolution of cable to include interactive services such as game channels and information services ... and enhanced services" but did not intend "to affect Federal or State regulations ... to

---

33. 508 U.S. 307, 317, 113 S.Ct. 2096, 2103, 124 L.Ed.2d 211, 220–21 (1993).

34. *In re* Definition of a Cable System, 5 FCC Rcd. 7638, 7642 (1990).

35. FCC v. Beach Communications, Inc., 508 U.S. 307, 313–14, 113 S.Ct. 2096, 2100–01, 124 L.Ed.2d 211, 221 (1993).

36. *Id.* at 315–20, 113 S.Ct. at 2102–04, 124 L.Ed.2d at 224–25.

37. Beach Communications, Inc. v. FCC, 10 F.3d 811, 304 U.S. App. D.C. 36 (D.C.Cir.1993) (per curiam). *See also* Liberty Cable Co. v. City of New York, 60 F.3d 961, 963 (2d Cir.1995), *cert. denied*, 516

U.S. 1171, 116 S.Ct. 1262, 134 L.Ed.2d 210 (1996).

38. 47 U.S.C.A. § 522(7) (West 1996). In 1998, the FCC ruled that a SMATV operator that transmitted video signals through public rights-of-way solely by means of a common carrier video transmission facility was not a cable operator. Entertainment Connections, Inc., FCC 98–111 (rel. June 30, 1988).

39. Telecommunications Act of 1996 § 302(b)(2)(A), 110 Stat. 56 (1996), *codified as amended* at 47 U.S.C.A. § 522(7) (West Supp. 1997).

cause dial-up access information services over telephone lines to be classified as a cable service."[40]

3. Judicial Challenges to Franchising Requirements

Because the franchising provisions of the Cable Act established general procedures governing the franchising process, it did not resolve questions raised about specific franchise requirements or fundamental constitutional questions. Consequently, the Cable Act franchising provisions have sparked a substantial amount of litigation that seek to define the appropriate level of local control. Results have been mixed.

A significant case in this regard is *City of Los Angeles v. Preferred Communications, Inc.,*[41] in which the Supreme Court, without resolving the merits, held that the First Amendment governed cable television franchising requirements. The Court, however, declined to identify the applicable level of constitutional scrutiny.[42] On remand, the district court held that an exclusive franchise provision was unconstitutional, as were other franchising requirements including leased access rules, universal service requirements, financial and technical qualifications requirements and customer service requirements.[43] The United States Court of Appeals for the Ninth Circuit affirmed, but limited the scope of this decision. It upheld the lower court's decision that the exclusive franchise limitation was broader than necessary to achieve the government's asserted interests.[44] The Court deferred passing on other franchise requirements, however, because it was uncertain whether Preferred Communications would obtain a cable franchise. Without a franchise, the Court held that Preferred would lack standing and that any resolution of the remaining constitutional issues would be premature.[45] On the other hand, the Ninth Circuit in *Preferred* upheld the local government's ability to condition the ability to provide cable service on the grant of a franchise.[46]

Lower courts have reached inconsistent conclusions regarding the validity of various franchising requirements. While some courts have held that the Constitution significantly limits the ability of local governments to impose franchise restrictions,[47] other courts have held that local authorities have far greater discretion in limiting the number of fran-

40. S. Conf. Rep. No. 104–230 104th Cong., 2d Sess. 378 (1996). *See* Implementation of Cable Act Reform Provisions of the Telecommunications Act of 1996, 11 FCC Rcd. 5937, 5959 (1996).

41. 476 U.S. 488, 106 S.Ct. 2034, 90 L.Ed.2d 480 (1986).

42. *Id.* at 494–95, 106 S.Ct. at 2038, 90 L.Ed.2d at 487–88.

43. Preferred Communications v. City of Los Angeles, Civ. No. A. 83–5846 (C.D.Cal.1990).

44. Preferred Communications, Inc. v. City of Los Angeles, 13 F.3d 1327, 1332 (9th Cir.), cert. denied, 512 U.S. 1235, 114 S.Ct. 2738, 129 L.Ed.2d 859 (1994).

45. *Id.* at 1333–34. Those portions of the District Court decision deciding the constitutionality of various franchising requirements were vacated.

46. *Id.* at 1332. *See also* Telesat Cablevision, Inc. v. City of Riviera Beach, 773 F.Supp. 383, 394–399 (S.D.Fla.1991), *appealed dismissed*, No. 91–5908 (11th Cir., July 26, 1993).

47. *See, e.g.,* Pacific West Cable Co. v. City of Sacramento, 672 F.Supp. 1322, 1340 (E.D.Cal.1987); Group W Cable, Inc. v. City of Santa Cruz, 669 F.Supp. 954, 967 (N.D.Cal.1987); Century Federal, Inc. v. City of Palo Alto, 648 F.Supp. 1465, 1478 (N.D.Cal.1986).

chises or in imposing conditions.[48] For example, in *Communications Systems, Inc. v. City of Danville*,[49] the United States Court of Appeals for the Sixth Circuit held that a city may reject an application for a competing franchise on the ground that the market could not support two cable operators. Similarly, in *Nor-West Cable Communications Partnership v. City of St. Paul*,[50] the court held that a would-be cable operator lacked standing to attack the grant of a single franchise "unless he or she would have had a 'realistic chance' of some benefit in the absence of the [city's] constitutional violation."[51] Other courts have held that local governments are not obligated to grant more than one cable franchise for any area,[52] and that various specific franchise requirements are valid.[53]

The 1992 Cable Act modified the franchising requirements to eliminate disputes regarding exclusive franchises. Section 7 of the Act prohibited franchising authorities from granting exclusive franchises and for unreasonably refusing to award an additional competitive franchise.[54] This provision was upheld by the United States Court of Appeals for the Eleventh Circuit in *Cox Cable Communications, Inc. v. United States*.[55] The court also held that the provision applies retroactively, thus voiding franchise provisions granting exclusivity that were entered into prior to the effective date of the 1992 Act. Accordingly, cable operators do not have a constitutionally protected right to be free from competition.[56]

C. The Franchisee

1. Municipalities

Not all cable operators are private entities. The Cable Act of 1984 authorized local governments to own and operate their own cable television systems.[57] This authority was expanded in the 1992 Act, which

48. *See*, e.g., City Communications, Inc. v. City of Detroit, 650 F.Supp. 1570, 1581 (E.D.Mich.1987), *aff'd*, 888 F.2d 1081, 1091 (6th Cir.1989); Towner Cable TV, Inc. v. City of Towner, No. A4–89–060 (D. N.D. Feb. 4, 1991).

49. 880 F.2d 887, 892 (6th Cir.1989).

50. 924 F.2d 741, 749 (8th Cir.1991), cert. denied, 501 U.S. 1231, 111 S.Ct. 2853, 115 L.Ed.2d 1021 (1991).

51. *Id.* (citation omitted).

52. Madison Cablevision, Inc. v. City of Morgantown, 948 F.2d 1281 (4th Cir.1991) (per curiam), cert. denied, 503 U.S. 985, 112 S.Ct. 1670, 118 L.Ed.2d 390 (1992).

53. *See*, e.g., Chicago Cable Communications v. Chicago Cable Commission, 879 F.2d 1540 (7th Cir.1989), cert. denied, 493 U.S. 1044 110 S.Ct. 839, 107 L.Ed.2d 835 (1990); Telesat Cablevision, Inc. v. City of

Riviera Beach, 773 F.Supp. 383, 411–413 (S.D.Fla.1991).

54. 47 U.S.C.A. § 541(a)(1) (West Supp. 1997).

55. 992 F.2d 1178 (11th Cir.1993).

56. Cox Cable Communications, Inc. v. United States, 866 F.Supp. 553 (M.D.Ga. 1994). *See* Warner Cable Communications, Inc. v. City of Niceville, 911 F.2d 634, 637 (11th Cir.1990), cert. denied 501 U.S. 1222, 111 S.Ct. 2839, 115 L.Ed.2d 1007 (1991) ("[t]he right to be free from competition is not within [the cable operator's First Amendment rights], even when the cable operator's most formidable competitor is a municipality"). *But see* James Cable Partners, L.P. v. City of Jamestown, 43 F.3d 277 (6th Cir.1995) (section 7 of the 1992 Cable Act does not operate retroactively to terminate an exclusive franchise).

57. 47 U.S.C.A. § 533(e) (West 1991).

provided that a local government could operate a cable service without a franchise.[58]

In *Warner Cable Communications, Inc. v. City of Niceville*,[59] the United States Court of Appeals for the Eleventh Circuit upheld the creation of a local municipal franchise over various challenges, including a constitutional challenge. First, the court rejected the cable operator's First Amendment claim, noting that the city was not attempting to regulate private speech, but was only seeking to "increas[e] speech in the cable marketplace."[60] It found the First Amendment does not require that the federal courts "prevent the City from communicating its own message to an audience that would like to receive it."[61] The court also rejected the company's due process claim. It found that the city's dual role as regulator and competitor could be a reason for concern, but pointed out that "Warner has brought no matter before the City for decision, and the City is threatening no regulatory action that will result in redressible injury" and that consideration of such claims would be premature. The court also rejected claims that the state constitution barred local ownership of the cable system.

2. Electric Utilities

The Telecommunications Act of 1996 amended the Public Utility Holding Company Act to permit certain public utility holding companies to affiliate with telecommunications companies that provide a range of services that may include telecommunications, information services, other services subject to FCC jurisdiction or other products or services related to or incidental to the provision of telecommunications and information services.[62] Pursuant to this statutory authority, the FCC was empowered to implement rules governing entry into such services, including cable service.[63]

3. Telephone Companies

Congress removed long-standing restrictions on telephone companies operating as cable operators with passage of the Telecommunications Act of 1996. Section 302 of the Act repealed the previous cross-ownership restrictions and provided multiple ways in which common carriers might provide video service. Section 302 permits telephone companies and other common carriers to provide video service to consumers either as a spectrum-based provider (*e.g.*, MMDS), as a common carrier open video system ("OVS") or as a franchised cable system.[64]

---

58. 47 U.S.C.A. § 541(f)(2) (West Supp. 1997).

59. 911 F.2d 634 (11th Cir.1990).

60. *Id.* at 640.

61. *Id.*

62. Telecommunications Act of 1996, Pub. L. 104–104 § 103, 110 Stat. 56 (1996), (codified as amended at 47 U.S.C.A. § 103 (1996)).

63. *In re* Implementation of Section 34(a)(1) of the Public Utility Holding Company Act of 1935, as added by Section 103 of the Telecommunications Act of 1996, Report and Order, 11 FCC Rcd. 11377 (1996).

64. 47 U.S.C.A. § 571(a) (West Supp. 1997). The FCC found that telephone companies had acquired cable franchises in dozens of communities as of 1997, but did not represent a national presence in the cable

D. Franchise Modifications

When it established franchising requirements in the Cable Act, Congress understood that the franchising process sometimes led cities to demand, and prospective operators to promise, more features in a cable system than could be realistically or economically delivered. Accordingly, the Cable Act established a process to permit a cable operator to negotiate modifications in existing and new franchises.

Section 625 of the 1984 Cable Act allows the operator to modify requirements governing facilities and equipment, including Public, educational and government ("PEG") access, if it can demonstrate that: (1) it is "commercially impracticable" to comply with the requirements for facilities or equipment; and (2) its proposal for modification is appropriate in light of the commercial impracticability.[65] The Act also allows a cable operator to modify service requirements to the extent it can demonstrate that the "mix, quality and level of services" required by the franchise will be maintained after it implements the proposed modification.

In applying the modification provisions, the United States Court of Appeals for the Fourth Circuit barred a franchising authority from enforcing penalties against the operator until the parties resolved a pending request for modification.[66] The practical effect of the holding is to allow cable operators to file prospective modification requests to cure past breaches of a franchise agreement. Similarly, modification requests have been filed to avoid revocation of a franchise.[67]

E. Franchise Renewals

Section 626 of the Cable Act establishes a specific procedure governing franchise renewal. This section was intended to balance the interests of cable operators and franchising authorities in the renewal process. On one hand, Section 626 protects cable operators against arbitrary or capricious denials of renewal applications. Thus, it was designed to "establish an orderly process for franchise renewal which protects cable operators against unfair denials of renewal where the operator's past performance and proposal for future performance meet the standards established by this subchapter."[68] On the other hand, Section 626 also establishes a process by which franchising authorities may seek to

---

television market. Fourth Video Competition Report at ¶ ¶ 108, 112–115.

65. 47 U.S.C.A. § 545(a)(1)(A) (West 1991). Commercial impracticability is defined by the act as "that it is commercially impracticable for the operator to comply with such requirements as a result of a change in conditions which is beyond the control of the operator and the nonoccurrence of which was a basic assumption on which the requirement was based." *Id.* § 545(f) (West 1991).

66. Tribune–United Cable v. Montgomery County, 784 F.2d 1227 (4th Cir.1986).

67. Cablevision Systems Corp. v. Town of East Hampton, 862 F.Supp. 875 (E.D.N.Y.1994), *aff'd,* 57 F.3d 1062 (2d Cir. 1995).

68. 47 U.S.C.A. § 521(5) (West 1991). The provision was retained without material change in the 1992 Cable Act.

ensure that the cable operator complies with the franchise terms and otherwise serves community needs.

The Cable Act authorizes both formal or informal renewal agreements between franchising authorities and cable operators. Thus, Section 626 does not require that the formal procedures be used in every case. Congress anticipated that "the vast majority of franchises will be renewed without regard to this section."[69] A cable operator and a franchising authority may negotiate the renewal of a franchise without going through the procedures of Section 626. Moreover, independent of the Cable Act, the local government and cable operator may reach agreement on franchise renewal at any time during the process, even if formal procedures had already been initiated. The law provides formal procedures that either party can initiate if necessary.[70] Once formal procedures have been invoked, however, the parties must comply with Cable Act requirements unless the parties reach an informal agreement to the contrary.[71]

Section 626 establishes a time period during which a franchise authority should initiate renewal proceedings. The franchise authority must notify the public and invite their participation to identify future cable-related needs of the community and to review the performance of the incumbent cable operator during the six month period beginning with the thirty-sixth month before the expiration of the franchise.[72] Likewise, a cable operator may initiate this process by submitting during the six month a written renewal notice requesting the commencement of a formal renewal process.[73] In response to such a notice, the franchise authority must commence the proceeding within six months.[74]

The first phase of the formal renewal process, community ascertainment, involves public proceedings by which the franchising authority reviews the cable operator's past performance and seeks to identify future cable-related community needs and interests. There is no statutory time limit on the length of ascertainment proceedings. After this ascertainment process is completed, the cable operator seeking renewal may, on its own initiative or at the request of the franchise authority, submit a proposal for renewal. If the franchising authority sets a deadline by which the proposal must be submitted, as the Cable Act permits, the local authority must provide written notice of the deadline.[75]

69. H.R. Rep. No. 98–934, at 72 (1984).

70. *Id.*

71. TCI of South Carolina, Inc. v. City of Bennettsville, No. 4:89–334–12, slip op. at 8 (D.S.C. 1990) (not published in F.Supp.).

72. 47 U.S.C.A. § 546(a) (West 1991).

73. *Id.* the 1992 Cable Act clarified the requirement that the cable operator must provide specific written notice to invoke the formal renewal procedures. 47 U.S.C.A. § 546(a) (West Supp.1997).

74. In addition to clarifying that the cable operator's renewal request for formal renewal proceedings be in writing, the 1992 Cable Act specified that after a written renewal request, the franchising authority is required to commence formal proceedings within six months.

75. 47 U.S.C.A. § 546(b) (West 1991). *See* Eastern Telecom Corp. v. Borough of East Conemaugh, 872 F.2d 30 (3d Cir. 1989), cert. denied, 493 U.S. 811, 110 S.Ct. 55, 107 L.Ed.2d 24 (1989) (franchising authority is required to notify the franchise

In the second stage of the formal renewal process, the franchising authority must evaluate the sufficiency of the operator's proposal. Within four months after submission of the proposal, the franchise authority must either renew the franchise or issue a preliminary assessment that the franchise should not be renewed.[76] Upon the request of the operator or on its own initiative, the franchise authority must then commence a formal administrative proceeding.

The renewal hearing is the third stage of the formal process and, the Cable Act establishes certain due process requirements for the proceeding. The public must be given notice of the administrative proceeding and a transcript must be made of the hearing.[77] The cable operator may introduce evidence regarding both the franchising authority's needs, and its proposal.[78] At the completion of the proceeding the franchising authority must issue a written decision based upon the record.[79] The Cable Act requires the franchising authority to consider whether:

(1) the cable operator has substantially complied with the material terms of the existing franchise and with applicable law;

(2) the quality of the operator's service, including signal quality, response to consumer complaints and billing practices, but without regard to whether the mix or quality of cable services or other services provided over the system, has been reasonable in light of community needs;

(3) the operator has the financial, legal, and technical ability to provide the services, facilities, and equipment as set forth in its proposal; and

(4) the operator's proposal is reasonable to meet the future cable-related community needs and interests, taking into account the costs of meeting such needs and interests.[80]

A decision to deny a proposal must be founded upon one or more adverse findings made with respect to the four statutory factors.[81]

holder in writing of the deadline for submission of a renewal proposal).

76. The 1992 Act also clarified the four month period governing the franchising authority's review of a renewal proposal does not begin until after the cable operator has submitted its proposal. 47 U.S.C.A. § 546(c)(1) (West 1991 & Supp. 1997).

77. *Id.* § 546(c)(1)-(2) (West 1991).

78. The franchising authority must permit the cable operator to conduct adequate discovery during this phase of the renewal process. *See* Continental Cablevision, Inc. v. Irwin, No. 91–11256–N (D. Mass., July 15, 1991) (not published in F.Supp.).

79. 47 U.S.C.A. § 546(c)(3) (West 1991).

80. *Id.* § 546(c)(1) (West 1991 & Supp. 1997). The 1992 Act amended the law with

respect to the second factor, specifying that the franchising authority could not evaluate the "mix or quality" of cable or other services provided over the system, rather than the "mix, quality or level" of service. *Id.* at § 546(c)(1)(B) (West Supp. 1997). The amendment indicates that franchising authorities can take into account, at least in part, whether the operator had increased a number of cable services to the community, even if it could not regulate particular programming services.

81. 47 U.S.C.A. § 546(c) (West 1991). *See also* Rolla Cable System, Inc. v. City of Rolla, 761 F.Supp. 1398 (E.D.Mo.1991) (holding that preponderance of evidence supported franchising authority's determination that cable operator did not have technical competence to provide service set forth in renewal proposal).

However, denial based upon the operator's failure to comply with the franchise agreement or upon the quality of service is only allowed where the operator has been given notice and opportunity to cure the problem.[82] If, however, the franchise authority has received written notice from the cable operator of failure or inability to cure, and the franchise authority has failed to object to the noncompliance within a reasonable time from the date of notice, then it may not deny renewal.[83] Cable operators have the right to question any witnesses. The renewal decision must be in writing and based on the record of the hearing.[84] Cable operators have the right to judicial review in state or federal court within 120 days of a final administrative decision to deny their proposal by a franchise authority. A cable operator whose proposal for renewal has been denied may, following the administrative proceeding, appeal to a state or federal district court.[85] The court may grant relief if it finds that the franchising authority's findings upon which a franchise renewal was denied is not supported by a preponderance of the evidence submitted in the formal proceeding or if the franchising authority failed to comply with the Act's procedural requirements.[86] The 1992 Cable Act specified that a reviewing court shall not overturn a franchising authority's denial of renewal if the challenge is based on an infraction of procedural requirements that the court considers "harmless error."[87]

In *Union CATV, Inc. v. City of Sturgis*,[88] the United States Court of Appeals for the Sixth Circuit upheld the denial of a cable franchise based upon the city's finding, after a hearing, that the city had identified a need for a five-year franchise renewal term as opposed to the operator's proposal for a twenty-year term. The court concluded that judicial review of a municipality's identification of its cable-related needs and interests is very limited and that courts should defer to the franchising authority's identification of community needs and interests.[89] Under this standard, the court held that it could not review the city's stated "need" for a five-year renewal term without evidence that the cost in diminished profits or higher subscriber rates outweighs the need.[90]

As noted above, cable operators and franchise authorities have the option of following the formal procedures for renewal outlined above or

---

82. 47 U.S.C.A. § 546(d) (West 1991). *See also* Rolla Cable System, Inc. v. Rolla, 761 F.Supp. 1398 (E.D.Mo.1991) (holding that communications to the cable operator by city officials were inadequate to give operator proper notice of problems regarding poor signal quality and consumer service, and, therefore, franchising authority's findings regarding those problems could not serve as basis for nonrenewal of franchise).

83. 47 U.S.C.A. § 546(d) (West 1991). The 1992 Cable Act specified that the cable operator must provide written notice of its failure to comply and gave the franchising authority "reasonable time" within which

to object. This amendment replaced the previous statutory standard, that permitted franchise violations where the authority was deemed to have "effectively acquiesced" in the non-compliance period.

84. *Id.* § 546(c).

85. *Id.* § 546(e).

86. *Id.* § 546(e)(2).

87. *Id.* § 546(e)(2)(A).

88. 107 F.3d 434 (6th Cir.1997).

89. *Id.* at 441.

90. *Id.* at 442.

of using informal renewal procedures, and Congress expected the "vast majority" of franchises to be renewed by informal means.[91] However, when informal renewal procedures are utilized, the Cable Act requires that the public be given adequate notice and opportunity to comment.[92] Any decision to deny franchise renewal informally does not affect the cable operator's statutory rights under the formal renewal process.

F. Franchise Transfers

The ability of cable operators to buy and sell cable systems provides a case study of the pendulum swings of the cable regulation. Generally, such issues were governed by the terms of the franchising agreement and were not the subject of federal regulation. Transfers of cable franchises generally were recognized under the 1984 Act, but the 1992 Act significantly expanded regulatory authority over the process by which ownership and control of cable television systems are transferred.[93] The 1992 Act imposed strict limits on the transfer of cable systems, most notably through anti-trafficking limitations. Within four years, however, Congress altered course once again, repealing the anti-trafficking rules in the 1996 Telecommunications Act.[94]

Section 617(a) of the 1992 Cable Act had established a three-year holding requirement for cable systems.[95] That provision provided that "no cable operator may sell or otherwise transfer ownership in a cable system within a 36–month period following either the acquisition or initial construction of such system by such operator."[96] The FCC was empowered to waive the prohibition on transfers for public interest reasons, subject to the approval of the franchising authority. For any transfer or sale after the three-year period, the law required the franchising authority to act within 120 days of a request by the cable operator. Failure by a franchising authority to act within the 120–day period was treated as an approval of the transfer unless the parties agreed to an extension of time.[97]

In the Telecommunications Act of 1996, Congress repealed the transfer provision of the 1992 Act except for the 120–day time limit on action by local franchising authorities.[98] Consequently, what began as a restriction on the ability of cable operators to transfer their systems, ended as a procedural limitation on the ability of franchising authorities to block such transfers.

---

91.   H.R. Rep. No. 98–934, at 72 (1984).

92.   47 U.S.C.A. § 546(h) (West 1992).

93.   *Id.* § 533.

94.   Telecommunications Act of 1996, Pub. L. 104–104, § 301(i), 110 Stat. 56, 117 (1996); *codified as amended at* 47 U.S.C.A. 537 (West Supp. 1997).

95.   Cable Television Consumer Protection and Competition Act of 1992, Pub. L. No. 102–385, § 13, 106 Stat. 1460, 1489

(1992), *codified as amended at* 47 U.S.C.A. 537 (West Supp. 1997).

96.   *Id.* § 537(a).

97.   *Id.* § 537(e).

98.   Telecommunications Act of 1996, § 301(i), 110 Stat. 56, 117 (1996), *codified as amended at* 47 U.S.C.A. § 537 (West 1996).

G. *Franchise Fees*

Local franchise authorities traditionally require cable operators to pay a portion of their proceeds to the government as a condition of obtaining the franchise. Section 622 of the Cable Act limits the amount that a local government may charge to five percent of the operator's gross revenues from the provision of cable service.[99] The Act defines a franchise fee as "any tax, fee, or assessment of any kind imposed by a franchising authority or other governmental entity on a cable operator or cable subscriber, or both, solely because of their status as such."[100] The term franchise fee excludes: (1) any tax, fee or assessment of general applicability that is not unduly discriminatory against cable operators or subscribers; (2) PEG access payments required by pre-Cable Act franchises; (3) PEG capital costs; (4) charges incidental to the awarding or enforcing of the franchise; and (5) copyright fees.[1] The Telecommunications Act of 1996 amended the definition of franchise fee to exclude the imposition of such fees on revenue from the provision of non-cable services.[2]

Quite naturally, disputes have arisen between cable operators and franchising authorities regarding the definition and calculation of franchise fees. Franchising authorities have sought to minimize the nature and amount of fees subject to the five percent limit while maximizing the types of charges excluded from treatment as franchise fee exclusions. Cable operators, predictably, have advocated the opposite position. Generally, except for the five percent limit, the FCC is barred from regulating the amount of a franchise fee or how it is used by local authorities.[3] Accordingly, the FCC generally will not resolve conflicts over whether particular local taxes are considered "franchise fees" pursuant to the Cable Act, unless such disputes directly affect national cable policies or implicate the Commission's expertise.[4]

Certain local authorities have attempted to pay significant legal and consulting fees associated with franchise renewal on the theory that the Cable Act exempts from the five percent limit "charges incidental to the awarding or enforcing of the franchise."[5] However, reviewing courts have held that such charges cannot be considered "incidental" and must be considered part of the franchise fees subject to statutory limits.[6]

---

99. 47 U.S.C.A. § 542 (West 1992).

100. *Id.* § 542(g)(1).

1. *Id.* § 542(g)(2) (A)-(E).

2. Telecommunications Act of 1996, § 303 (b), 110 Stat. 56, 125 (1996), *codified as amended at* 47 U.S.C.A. § 542(g) (West 1996).

3. 47 U.S.C.A. § 542(i) (West 1991).

4. *See* ACLU v. FCC, 823 F.2d 1554, 1563, 262 U.S. App. D.C. 244, 253 (1987), cert. denied, 485 U.S. 959 108 S.Ct. 1220, 99 L.Ed.2d 421 (1988).

5. 47 U.S.C.A. § 542(g)(2)(D) (West 1991).

6. *See* Time Warner Entertainment Co. v. Briggs, No. CIV. A. 92–40117–GN, 1993 WL 23710 (D.Mass. July 22, 1992); Birmingham Communications, Inc. v. City of Birmingham, No. Civ. A. 87–L–0755–S, 1989 WL 253850 (N.D.Ala. May 5, 1989); Robin Cable Systems, L.P. v. City of Sierra Vista, 1993 WL 434094 (D.Ariz.1993), *op. amended*, 842 F.Supp. 380 (D.Ariz.1993).

Other disputes involve the definition of "gross revenues" by which the five percent fee is calculated. In one case, the FCC held that the franchise fees a cable operator collects from subscribers are not part of the operator's "gross revenues" for the purpose of determining the operator's franchise fee obligation.[7] The cable industry had argued that to allow local authorities to charge franchise fees on subscriber payments that ultimately were paid to the local government amounted to an unjustified surcharge. Local governments, on the other hand, argued that franchising authorities historically had collected franchise fees on total revenues, and that fees should be based on the total amount subscribers pay to cable operators and not the total revenues that the operators ultimately receive. The FCC had held that a "franchise fee on the franchise fee" violated the Cable Act.

The United States Court of Appeals for the Fifth Circuit rejected the FCC's reasoning and held that the amount to be paid in franchise fees is to be considered part of "gross revenues" under the Cable Act.[8] The Court disagreed with FCC's argument that the term "gross revenues" as used in the Act was ambiguous and held that Congress intended the term to have its normal, ordinary, and common meaning. Additionally, the Court rejected the FCC's characterization of franchise fees as taxes, holding that they are "essentially a form of rent; the price paid to rent use of public right-of-ways."[9] Accordingly, it found that franchise fees imposed upon the cable operator "are part of a cable operator's expense of doing business," and should be calculated based on the total amount of revenue collected from subscribers.[10]

The Cable Act permits cable operators to identify on subscriber bills the amounts of money paid to local governments for franchise fees. Specifically, bills may identify verifiable costs attributable to franchise fees, amounts necessary for support and use of PEG access channels and any other governmental assessments on transactions between a cable operator and a subscriber.[11] Where a cable operator itemizes costs, it must do so in a manner consistent with the FCC's regulation of cable rates. Section 623 of the Act provides that rules governing basic cable service rates must take into account "the reasonably and properly allocable portion" of amounts assessed as franchise fees, taxes and other governmental charges.[12]

Various cable operators have challenged the constitutionality of franchise fees with mixed results. Certain courts have held that franchise fees are constitutional to the extent they are related to the local government's costs of administering the franchise or the fair market value of the public right-of-way.[13] Other courts have held that, by

7. United Artists Cable of Baltimore, 11 FCC rcd. 18158 (1996).

8. City of Dallas, Texas v. FCC, 118 F.3d 393 (5th Cir.1997).

9. *Id.* at 397.

10. *Id.* at 398.

11. 47 U.S.C.A. § 542(c) (West Supp. 1997).

12. *Id.* § 543.

13. *See* Telesat Cablevision, Inc. v. City of Riviera Beach, 773 F.Supp. 383, 406–407 (S.D.Fla.1991); Group W Cable, Inc. v. City

singling out a speaker for burdensome financial obligations, the franchise fee violates the First Amendment.[14] In still other cases, courts have ruled that cable operators may waive their rights to challenge the constitutionality of franchise fees by signing a release as part of a settlement of other litigation.[15]

13.3 Cable Television Rate Regulation

A. *The Rise and Fall and Rise and Fall of Rate Regulation*

Rate regulation was a common feature of many early cable franchises and was institutionalized by federal law, beginning with the 1984 Cable Act.[1] However, very different philosophies toward rate regulation were embodied in the 1984 and 1992 Cable Acts, and in the Telecommunications Act of 1996. The 1984 Cable Act permitted local rate regulation while, at the same time, significantly limiting its scope.[2] The 1992 Act, by sharp contrast, adopted an intricate and confusing body of rate regulations, implemented both at the local and federal levels.[3] More recently, the 1996 Act established a "sunset" for most rate regulations, moving back to a system of limited local regulation of basic service.[4]

Under the 1984 Cable Act, franchising authorities could regulate rates only for basic cable service in communities in which the cable system was not subject to "effective competition."[5] The FCC defined the term "effective competition" as applying to communities that received three over-the-air broadcast signals, a standard that effectively deregulated almost all cable communities.[6] In 1991, the Commission revised the standard as applying to communities that received six unduplicated broadcast signals and/or communities in which there was an independent, competing multichannel video delivery system.[7] A principal question under the 1984 rate regulations involved the extent to which federal law preempted local regulations. Some courts imposed a restrictive reading of the Act and preempted almost all local attempts at regulation,[8] while other courts allowed greater local authority.[9] In one case, the

of Santa Cruz, 669 F.Supp. 954, 974–75 (N.D.Cal.1987).

14. *See, e.g.*, Century Federal, Inc. v. City of Palo Alto, 710 F.Supp. 1559 (N.D.Cal.1988).

15. *See, e.g.*, Erie Telecommunications, Inc. v. City of Erie, 853 F.2d 1084 (3d Cir.1988).

1. Cable Communications Policy Act of 1984, Pub. L. 98–549, 98 Stat. 2779 (1984).

2. *Id.*

3. Cable Television Consumer Protection and Competition Act of 1992, Pub. L. 102–385, 106 Stat. 1460 (1992).

4. Telecommunications Act of 1996, Pub. L. 104–104, § 301(c)(4) 110 Stat. 56, 115 (1996) (codified as amended at 47 U.S.C.A. 543(c)(3) (West Supp. 2997)).

5. Cable Communications Policy Act of 1984, Pub. L. 98–549, 98 Stat. 2779 (1984).

6. *See* Re-examination of the Effective Competition Standard for the Regulation of Cable Television Basic Service Rates, Carriage of Television Broadcast Signals By Cable Television Systems, Report and Order and Second Further Notice of Proposed Rulemaking, 6 FCC Rcd. 4545, 4546 (1991).

7. *Id.* at 4547.

8. *See, e.g.*, Westmarc Communications, Inc. v. Connecticut Department of Public Utility Control, 807 F.Supp. 876, 888–889 (D.Conn.1990); Town of Norwood v. Adams–Russell Co., 406 Mass. 604, 549 N.E.2d 1115, 1119–1120 (1990).

9. *See, e.g.*, Cable Television Ass'n. of N.Y., Inc. v. Finneran, 954 F.2d 91 (2d Cir.1992) (local regulation of "downgrade"

United States Court of Appeals for the First Circuit suggested that the 1984 Act did not preempt "contractual commitment(s)" entered as part of the franchise agreement, such as a rate freeze, so long as the franchising authority did not attempt to impose a rate regulation regime.[10]

The 1992 Act dramatically expanded rate regulation authority, effectively extending local authority over basic rates in most communities and creating federal authority to regulate rates for tiers of service above the basic tier.[11] In 1993, pursuant to a statutory deadline imposed by the 1992 Act, the FCC adopted rules governing rate regulation that became effective on September 1, 1993. In the 28 months between May 1993, when the initial rate regulations were adopted, and September 1995, the FCC issued complex regulations followed by 13 orders on reconsideration alternately strengthening, relaxing and otherwise "refining" the rate rules.[12] Ultimately, rules adopted pursuant to the 1992 Act resulted in overlapping regulations that established different rate "benchmarks" depending on the time period under review, different obligations for large and small cable systems, cost-based pricing as an alternative to the benchmarks for service rates (but as an absolute requirement for equip-

charges not preempted by 1984 Cable Act); Comcast Cablevision v. City of Sterling Heights, 178 Mich.App. 117, 443 N.W.2d 440 (Mich.Ct.App.1989) (same); Ventura v. Cox Cable Jefferson Parish, Inc., 583 So.2d 1237 (La.Ct.App.1991).

10. Nashoba Communications Ltd. Partnership No. 7 v. Town of Danvers, 893 F.2d 435, 440–441 (1st Cir.1990).

11. 47 U.S.C.A. § 543 (West Supp. 1997).

12. Implementation of Sections of the Cable Television Consumer Protection and Competition Act of 1992, 8 FCC Rcd. 5631 (1993) ("First Report and Order"); Implementation of Sections of the Cable Television Consumer Protection and Competition Act of 1992; Rate Regulation, First Order on Reconsideration, Second Report and Order and Third Further Notice of Proposed Rulemaking, 9 FCC Rcd. 1164 (1993); Implementation of Sections of the Cable Television Consumer Protection and Competition Act of 1992: Rate Regulation, Second Order on Reconsideration, Fourth Report and Order, and Fifth Notice of Proposed Rulemaking, 9 FCC Rcd 4119 (1994); Implementation of Sections of the Cable Television Consumer Protection and Competition Act of 1992: Rate Regulation and Buy–Through Prohibition, Third Order on Reconsideration, 9 FCC Rcd. 4316 (1994); Implementation of Sections of the Cable Television Consumer Protection and Competition Act of 1992: Rate Regulation, Fifth Order on Reconsideration and Further No-

tice of Proposed Rulemaking, 9 FCC Rcd. 5327 (1994); Implementation of Sections of the Cable Television Consumer Protection and Competition Act of 1992: Rate Regulation, Sixth Order on Reconsideration, Fifth Report and Order, and Seventh Notice of Proposed Rulemaking, 10 FCC Rcd. 1226 (1994); Implementation of Sections of the Cable Television Consumer Protection and Competition Act of 1992: Rate Regulation, Seventh Order on Reconsideration, 10 FCC Rcd. 3225 (1995); Implementation of Sections of the Cable Television Consumer Protection and Competition Act of 1992; Eighth Order on Reconsideration, 10 FCC Rcd. 5179 (1995); Implementation of Sections of the Cable Television Consumer Protection and Competition Act of 1992; Ninth Order on Reconsideration, 10 FCC Rcd. 5198 (1995); Implementation of Sections of the Cable Television Consumer Protection and Competition Act of 1992; Tenth Order on Reconsideration, 10 FCC Rcd. 6870 (1995); Implementation of Sections of the Cable Television Consumer Protection and Competition Act of 1992; Rate Regulation, Sixth Report and Order and Eleventh Order on Reconsideration, 10 FCC Rcd. 7393 (1995); Implementation of Sections of the Cable Television Consumer Protection and Competition Act of 1992: Rate Regulation, Twelfth Order on Reconsideration, 11 FCC Rcd. 785 (1995); Implementation of Sections of the Cable Television Consumer Protection and Competition Act of 1992; Rate Regulation, Thirteenth Order on Reconsideration, 11 FCC Rcd. 388 (1995).

ment prices), a special regime governing newly-offered services and a host of other legal prescriptions. This led one observer to describe the rules as "Longer Than the Old Testament [and] More Confusing Than the Tax Code."[13]

Notwithstanding this history and the complexity of the rules, the United States Court of Appeals for the District of Columbia Circuit upheld the rate regulation provisions of the 1992 Act as well as most of the regulations promulgated by the FCC. In *Time Warner Entertainment Co. v. FCC*,[14] the court upheld the Commission's rate regulation rules, issuing three separate opinions. The court rejected challenges brought both by cable operators and franchising authorities, upholding the Commission's rules under the deferential standard enunciated by the Supreme Court in *Chevron U.S.A., Inc. v. Natural Resources Defense Council*.[15] Although it upheld most of the rate regulations, the court rejected certain of the FCC's policy choices, such as its refusal to permit cable operators to recover "external costs" for the period after the Act passed and before FCC implementing rules were adopted.[16] It also rejected the FCC's restrictive definition of "effective competition" for determining which systems would remain unregulated[17] and voided the FCC's decision to apply uniform rate structure requirements to systems otherwise exempt from rate regulation.[18] The court also held that the Act's prohibition against negative option billing did not preempt state consumer laws unless they amount to "rate regulation."[19] The court held that the FCC's rate regulations rules did not violate the First Amendment, and that, pursuant to intermediate scrutiny, the rules were appropriately tailored to deal with the problem of monopoly pricing.[20] Other aspects of the FCC's rate regulation rules were upheld in *Adelphia Communications Corp. v. FCC*.[21] There, the court upheld restrictions on the ability of cable operators to offer unregulated a la carte channels as part of a bundled package. The District of Columbia Circuit rejected a facial constitutional challenge to the rate requirements in *Time Warner*

---

13. Rafael G. Prohias, *Longer Than the Old Testament, More Confusing Than the Tax Code: An Analysis of the 1992 Cable Act*, 2 COMMLAW CONSPECTUS 81 (1994).

14. 56 F.3d 151, 312 U.S. App. D.C. 187 (D.C.Cir.1995) (per curiam), cert. denied, 516 U.S. 1112, 116 S. Ct. 911, 133 L.Ed.2d 842 (1996) ("Time Warner I").

15. 56 F.3d at 163, 312 U.S. App. D.C. at 199 (opinion of Ginsburg, J.) (citing Chevron, U.S.A. Inc. v. Natural Resources Defense Council, Inc., 467 U.S. 837, 104 S.Ct. 2778, 81 L.Ed.2d 694 (1984)).

16. *Id.* at 173, 312 U.S. App. D.C. at 197.

17. *Id.* at 189–90, 312, U.S. App. D.C. at 213 (opinion Rogers, J.).

18. *Id.* at 191, 312 U.S. App. D.C. at 227.

19. *Id.* at 194–95, 312 U.S. App. D.C. at 230–31. *See* Time Warner Cable v. Doyle, 66 F.3d 867 (7th Cir.1995), cert. denied, 516 U.S. 1141, 116 S.Ct. 974, 133 L.Ed.2d 894 (1996) (Wisconsin negative option billing statute preempted by federal law); Kentucky *ex rel.* Gorman v. Comcast Cable, 881 F.Supp. 285 (W.D.Ky.1995) (Kentucky Consumer Protection Act prohibition on negative option billing not preempted). *Cf.* Total TV v. Palmer Communications, Inc., 69 F.3d 298 (9th Cir.1995), cert. dismissed, 517 U.S. 1152, 116 S.Ct. 1459, 134 L.Ed.2d 576 (1996) (California Unfair Practices Act prohibiting predatory pricing not preempted by federal law).

20. Time Warner I, 56 F.3d at 184–185, 312 U.S. App. D.C. at 210–11 (opinion of Randolph, J.).

21. 88 F.3d 1250, 319 U.S. App. D.C. 187 (D.C.Cir.1996).

II.[22] As in Time *Warner I*, the court sustained the rate requirements under intermediate First Amendment review.[23] The court found that the basic service tier requirements were not content-based even though the law provided that broadcast and public access channels must be contained on the basic tier.[24]

After all this effort, Congress significantly relaxed cable rate regulation in the Telecommunications Act of 1996.[25] Most importantly, the 1996 Act imposed a "sunset" on upper-tier regulation of programming services after March 31, 1999.[26] The law immediately eliminated upper-tier rate regulation for small cable operators in franchise areas with 50,000 or fewer subscribers, and modified a number of regulations that could fairly be characterized as micromanagement of the industry.

The decision to end the rate regulation experiment cannot be considered as a rousing endorsement of detailed federal price regulation. Nevertheless, in its first annual report on cable industry prices issued after passage of the 1996 Telecommunication Act, the FCC concluded that "the intent of the 1992 Cable Act's rate regulation, to stimulate the effects of a competitive market, was met."[27] The Commission compared cable rates before and after the introduction of rate regulation and concluded that the price differential between unregulated competitive cable systems and regulated systems narrowed during the period of regulation.[28] The data showed that the average monthly rate for cable service on noncompetitive regulated systems declined by 10 cents during the study period from $21.69 in August 1993 to $21.59 in January 1995. During this period the FCC also found that the per-channel rate declined.[29] Other independent economic analyses suggested that rate regulation lead cable operators to adjust the quality of their service offerings with the effect of making basic cable service less attractive to consumers. One study found statistically significant declines in basic subscribership during the period of regulation,[30] and concluded that "reregulation did not succeed in lowering quality-adjusted prices" or "increasing basic cable TV penetration."[31]

Continuing the uneven level of interest in cable television rate regulation, by 1998 federal regulators and legislators began to express a renewed faith in regulatory approaches. FCC Chairman William Kennard asked whether regulation might be imposed on the practice of

---

22. Time Warner Entertainment Co. v. FCC, 93 F.3d 957, 320 U.S. App. D.C. 294 (1996) (per curiam) ("Time Warner II").

23. Time Warner I, 56 F.3d at 1984, 312 U.S. App. D.C. at 210.

24. *Id.* at 966–67, 320 U.S. App. D.C. at 303–04.

25. Telecommunications Act of 1996, § 301, Pub. L. 104–104, 110 Stat. 56 (1996).

26. 47 U.S.C.A. § 543(c)(4) (West 1997).

27. Statistical Report on Average Rates for Basic Service, Cable Programming and Equipment, 12 FCC Rcd. 3239, 3252 (1997).

28. *Id.* at 3252.

29. *Id.* at 3252–53.

30. Thomas W. Hazlett, *Prices and Outputs Under Cable TV Reregulation*, 12 J. of Regulatory Econ. 173 (1997).

31. *Id. See also* ROBERT CRANDALL AND HAROLD FURCHGOTT-ROTH, CABLE TV: REGULATION OR COMPETITION? (Brookings Inst. 1996).

marketing cable programming in tiers, among other things.[32] Legislation was introduced in the 105th Congress that would revoke the March 1999 sunset of upper tier rate regulation, or would permit local franchising authorities to lift the sunset unless the cable operator offered "economically reasonable" tiers.[33] Although no such legislation passed, prospects for the future are hard to predict.

B. Threshold Issues of Rate Regulation

1. The "Effective Competition" Standard

Federal law presumes that market forces will hold prices for cable service in check. Consequently, since passage of the 1984 Act, rate regulation has been permitted only in systems that lack "effective competition."[34] Although the concept of "effective competition" has been a constant feature of federal law, its meaning has changed over time.[35] The FCC first defined the term to include communities that received three broadcast signals then subsequently modified the rule to mean six unduplicated broadcast signals.[36]

Under the 1992 Cable Act, "effective competition" was considered to exist in communities in which: (1) fewer than 30 percent of the households in the franchise area subscribe to one cable system;[37] (2) the franchise area is served by at least two unaffiliated multichannel video programming distributors ("MVPDs") that each offer comparable programming to at least 50 percent of the households in the franchise area, and the number of households subscribing to MVPDs other than the largest MVPD exceeds 15 percent of the households in the franchise area;[38] or, (3) a MVPD operated by the franchising authority offers video programming to at least 50 percent of the households in that franchise area.[39] Under this regime, the FCC presumed that effective competition

---

32. Annual Assessment of the Status of Competition in the Market for the Delivery of Video Programming, 13 FCC Rcd. 1034 (1998) (statement of Chairman Kennard).

33. See e.g., Video Competition and Consumer Choice Act of 1998, H.R. 4352, 105th Cong., 2d Sess. (introduced July 29, 1998); Cable Consumer Protection Act of 1998, H.R. 3258, 105th Cong., 2d Sess. (introduced Feb. 25, 1998).

34. 47 U.S.C.A. § 543(a)(1) (West 1991 & Supp. 1997).

35. Id.

36. See Re-examination of the Effective Competition Standard for the Regulation of Cable Television Basic Service Rates, 6 FCC Rcd 4545 (1991).

37. 47 U.S.C.A. § 543(l)(1)(A) (West Supp. 1997).

38. Compare Time Warner, 56 F.3d at 188–90 with Implementation of Section of the Cable Television Consumer Protection and Competition Act of 1992: Rate Regula-

tion, Report and Order Further Notice of Proposed Rulemaking, 8 FCC Rcd 5631, 5664–65 (1993). The Court of Appeals modified the Commission's interpretation of these definitions. The FCC had determined that only those multichannel video programming distributors which offered service to at least 50 percent of the households would be included in the determination of whether 15 percent of the households in the franchise area subscribe to the non-dominant system. The Court disagreed, stating that only the largest multichannel video programming distributor should be excluded from the 15 percent calculation, and not overbuild systems that fail to reach 50 percent of the franchise area. The court concluded that the Commission's definition of effective competition is narrower than was Congress intended. 56 F.3d at 189.

39. 47 U.S.C.A. § 543(l)(1)(c) (West Supp. 1993).

did not exist in a given community until proven otherwise.[40] Cable companies had the burden to demonstrate the existence of effective competition.

The 1996 Act expanded the effective competition test to include communities in which a local exchange carrier or its affiliate offers comparable video programming services to subscribers.[41] Unlike the previous definition of effective competition, the new test does not include minimum standards for either the availability of competing service in a franchise area or minimum penetration requirements.[42] Additionally, the test recognizes multichannel competition without regard to the technology used. Other than through Direct Broadcast Satellite ("DBS") service, a LEC providing video service in a cable community will be considered an effective competitor if it obtains a separate cable franchise, provides open video service ("OVS") or provides "wireless cable" service such as through multichannel multipoint distribution service ("MMDS").[43] Rather than providing a penetration test, the 1996 Act recognizes effective competition where a LEC is "physically able" to offer service to subscribers "in the franchise area" and where it provides "comparable programming."[44] "Comparable programming" is defined as "at least twelve channels of programming, at least some of which are television broadcasting signals."[45]

2.   *Local and Federal Jurisdiction*

The nature of rate regulation—and the identity of the regulator—depends on how cable service is offered to subscribers. Tier placement of a particular programming service determines whether federal or local authorities will regulate rates, whether rates must be approved in advance, and whether the service is subject to rate regulation at all. These programming platforms include the Basic Service Tier ("BST"), the Cable Programming Service Tier ("CPST") and premium per-channel or per-program offerings.[46]

Basic service is regulated by local authorities subject to FCC oversight. The Cable Act requires that BST rates must be "reasonable."[47] The BST must include, at a minimum, must carry channels, PEG channels, all broadcast television signals except superstations, and any

---

40. 47 C.F.R. § 79.906 (1993).

41. Telecommunications Act of 1996, § 301(b)(3), *codified at* 47 U.S.C.A. § 543(l)(1) (West Supp. 1997). The Act generally defines an "affiliate" as an entity in which a LEC holds a ten percent or greater equity stake. *Id.* at § 153(1) (West Supp. 1997).

42. *Id.*

43. *Id.* at § 543(l)(1)(D).

44. *See* Implementation of Cable Act Reform Provisions of the Telecommunications Act of 1996, 11 FCC Rcd. 5937, 5941–5942 (1996) [hereinafter Cable Act Reform

Provisions of the Telecommunications Act of 1996].

45. *Id.* at 5942. *See* Conf. Rep. No. 458, 104th Cong. 2d Sess. 170 (1996).

46. In addition to these statutory categories, the FCC further subdivided this regulatory framework by designated certain types of offerings as New Product Tiers ("NPTs") and Migrated Product Tiers ("MPTs").

47. 47 U.S.C.A. § 543(b)(1) (West Supp. 1997).

other programming the cable operator chooses to add to the tier.[48] This is the tier to which all cable subscribers have access, and it is the most heavily regulated. Rates for equipment and service installation are also regulated as basic cable services. Local franchising authorities, subject to FCC certification and review, oversee regulation of the basic tier.[49] The Commission, however, may regulate the BST if the franchising authority acts inconsistently with the Commission's administering regulations.[50] Before a local franchising authority may regulate the basic rates, it must file a written request for certification with the FCC.[51] Once a local authority is certified, the cable operator must seek approval for its existing rates for basic service and equipment. The operator must demonstrate that the rates charged are "reasonable."[52]

The cable programming services tier, or CPST, is regulated for large cable systems at the federal level, at least until March 31, 1999.[53] This tier consists of any programming on the cable service other than programming carried as basic, or programming offered to subscribers on a per-channel (*e.g.*, HBO, Showtime) or per-program (*e.g.*, pay-per-view) basis.[54] The FCC regulates CPST rates only upon receiving a complaint following a rate increase.[55] Whereas a single disgruntled subscriber could trigger the enforcement authority of the federal government under the 1992 Cable Act,[56] this was changed in 1996. Under the Telecommunications Act, CPST regulation occurs only after a franchising authority (which has received complaints from multiple customers) files a complaint with the FCC.[57] The local authority is permitted, but not required, to file with the FCC if multiple subscribers have complained within 90 days of a rate increase.[58] The Act does not impose a time limit on the complaint filed by the franchising authority, but the FCC implementing regulations established a 180–day limit.[59] Before filing an FCC complaint, the franchising authority must provide written notice to the cable operator of its intentions and allow at least 30 days for the operator to file FCC forms justifying the rate increase with the franchising authori-

---

48. *Id.* § 543(b)(7)(A). FCC rules require that public access channels be carried on the BST unless the franchising agreement provides otherwise. 47 C.F.R. § 76.901(a) (1997). The requirements regarding the composition of the basic tier were upheld in *Time Warner II*, 93 F.3d at 966–67, 320 U.S. App. D.C. at 303–04.

49. *Id.* § 543(a).

50. *Id.* § 543(a)(2)(A); § 543(a)(6).

51. *Id.* § 543(a)(3); § 543(a)(4).

52. *Id.* § 543(b)(1).

53. *Id.* § 543(a)(2)(B); *See also* 47 U.S.C.A. § 543(c) (establishing requirements and factors Commission must consider in regulating unreasonable rates on CPST). *See* Telecommunications Act of 1996, Pub. L. No. 104–104, § 301, 110 Stat. 114 (1996) (sunset of CPST regulation).

54. 47 U.S.C.A. § 543(l)(2) (West Supp. 1997).

55. *Id.* § 543(c)(1).

56. Cable Telecommunication Consumer Protection and Competition Act of 1992, Pub. L. 102–385, § 3(a), 106 Stat. 1468 (1992).

57. The Telecommunications Act of 1996 § 301(b)(1)(C). Under the 1992 Act, the FCC was obligated to initiate a proceeding if it received a subscriber complaint within 45 days of a CPST rate increase. Cable Television Consumer Protection and Competition Act of 1992, Pub. L. 102–385, § 6, 106 Stat. 1482 (1992).

58. The Telecommunications Act of 1996 § 301(b)(1)(c).

59. *See* Cable Act Reform Provisions of the Telecommunications Act of 1996, *supra* note 44 at para. 21.

ty.[60] If the local authority rejects the operator's justification and proceeds to the FCC, the cable operator must demonstrate that the CPST price is "not unreasonable."[61]

Cable services offered to subscribers on a per-program or per-channel basis are unregulated. Although the Commission initially decided that "a la carte" tiers (programming packages composed of channels also made available individually) should be unregulated, it subsequently determined that collective "a la carte" offerings introduced by cable to evade regulation are subject to CPST treatment.[62] The District of Columbia Circuit noted the irony of the Commission's initial policy regarding certain service offerings "oxymoronically called an 'a la carte package' in FCC jargon," and upheld the decision to tighten the regulations.[63]

C. Regulation of the Basic Service Tier

1. Certification

Before a local franchising authority may regulate basic tier rates, it must be certified by the FCC.[64] The local authority must file a written request with the FCC certifying that it will adopt and administer regulations that are consistent with those of the Commission, that it has the legal authority and personnel to adopt and administer such regulations and that it will provide reasonable opportunities to consider the views of interested parties.[65] The FCC rules also require that franchising authorities certify that the cable operator is not subject to effective competition, "[u]nless the franchising authority has actual knowledge to the contrary."[66] A certification becomes effective within 30 days unless the FCC finds that the franchising authority has not satisfied the statutory requirements.[67] Any franchising authority unable to meet the standards may petition the FCC to regulate rates if the local authority lacks the resources or legal authority to regulate.[68]

Certification may be blocked in two different ways. First, a cable operator or other interested party may challenge a certification application by filing a petition with the FCC.[69] If the petition alleges that effective competition exists, rate regulation by the local authority is stayed. However, it is the cable operator's burden to overcome the presumption that effective competition does not exist.[70]

---

60. *Id.*

61. 47 U.S.C.A. § 543(c).

62. Implementation of Sections of the Cable Television Consumer Protection and Competition Act of 1992; Rate Regulation, Sixth Order on Reconsideration, Fifth Report and Order, and Seventh Notice of Proposed Rulemaking, 10 FCC Rcd. 1226, paras. 45–53, *codified at* 47 C.F.R. § 76.986 (1997).

63. Adelphia Communications Corp., 88 F.3d at 1251, 319 U.S. App. D.C. at 187.

64. 47 U.S.C.A. § 543(a)(3) (West Supp. 1997).

65. *Id.*

66. 47 C.F.R. § 76.910(b)(4) (1997).

67. *Id.* § 76.910(e).

68. *Id.* § 76.913(b). The FCC also may assume interim jurisdiction over basic rate regulation until certification is approved. *Id.* §§ 76.911(e), 76.913(a).

69. *Id.* § 76.911(a)(1).

70. *Id.* § 76.911(b)(1). A cable operator who frivolously alleges that effective competition exists when it does not may be fined by the FCC. *Id.* § 76.911(d).

As an alternative, a cable operator or other interested party may petition the FCC to revoke a local franchising authority's certification.[71] The local regulations remain in effect while a revocation petition is pending unless the FCC orders a stay. If the Commission finds that local regulations are inconsistent with the Cable Act, it may allow the local authority to cure any defect or it may revoke the certification.[72] If the FCC denies certification, or subsequently revokes a local franchising authority's certification, it assumes jurisdiction over local rates in that community until the franchising authority can file a new certification that meets Cable Act requirements.[73]

2. Local Rate Regulation Procedures

Before it may regulate rates, a certified franchising authority must adopt procedural rules within 120 days of certification.[74] After rules have been adopted and the cable operator notified, any changes in basic rates must be approved by the franchising authority.[75]

The process of establishing initial rates is complex. First, the cable operator must submit a proposed schedule of basic rates to the franchise authority.[76] This schedule must cover the costs both for programming services and also for equipment and installation costs,[77] presented in an unbundled format.[78] The operator may elect to have this proposed rate schedule analyzed under the "benchmark" methodology or under a "cost-of-service" showing.[79] Whichever analysis the cable system elects, however, it must use the same method to determine the "reasonableness" of rates for both the BST and the CPST.[80] A cable operator seeking to increase basic rates must provide notice to the local franchising authority 30 days before the proposed increase is to become effective. [81] Additionally the operator must notify subscribers in writing at least 30 days before the increase.[82] The local authority must provide an opportunity for public comment on the proposed increase.[83]

Generally, a franchising authority should approve or disapprove the rate within 30 days of the request.[84] It has the option, however, of extending this time by issuing a tolling order.[85] Thus, where the cable operator is seeking to justify rates based upon the regulatory benchmark, the period may be extended an additional 90 days; where cable operators seek to justify rates based on cost of service, the franchising authority may extend the time for approval by 120 days.[86]

---

71. *Id.* 47 C.F.R. § 76.914.

72. 47 U.S.C.A. § 543(a)(5) (West Supp. 1997).

73. *Id.* § 543(a)(6).

74. 47 C.F.R. § 76.910(e)(1) (1997).

75. *Id.*

76. *Id.* § 76.930.

77. *Id.* § 76.923(a).

78. 47 U.S.C.A. § 543(b)(3) (West Supp. 1997); 47 C.F.R. § 76.923 (1997).

79. 47 C.F.R. § 76.922(b) (1997).

80. *Id.* § 76.934(a).

81. *Id.* § 76.932.

82. *Id.*

83. *Id.* § 76.935.

84. *Id.* § 76.933(a).

85. 47 C.F.R. § 76.933 (1997).

86. *Id.* § 76.933(b).

If the franchising authority cannot complete its evaluation within the designated time, it may issue an accounting order which puts the cable operator on notice that it may decide in the future to order refunds or rate reductions.[87] In order to complete its task, the franchising authority is empowered to seek discovery of information reasonably necessary to determine compliance with the rate regulations.[88] Information submitted to local authorities is subject to the open record laws of the jurisdiction at issue. Thus, in some states, all filings are open for press and public inspection regardless of any need for confidentiality. If the franchising authority does not issue a written decision or accounting order within the FCC deadlines, the rate filed is deemed accepted.[89] It is not necessary that the franchising authority issue a decision—it may simply permit the proposed rate to take effect, or remain in effect.[90] Where the authority wishes to formally accept or modify the rate, however, it must issue a written decision accepting the rate, rejecting it or prescribing an alternative rate.[91] There are two limitations on this authority. First, the local authority cannot simply announce a reduced rate without a reasoned basis as described in the order. Second, the local authority may not prescribe a rate below the amount permitted by FCC rules.[92]

FCC rules authorize local franchising authorities to order refunds within certain limits.[93] A local authority cannot order refunds unless it has provided an opportunity for comment by the cable operator, although this may be accomplished as part of the rate proceeding.[94] Additionally, a local authority may not order a refund unless it reached a final decision on the rate request within the prescribed time frames or unless it issued an accounting order. If it does order a refund, the period covered cannot extend back in time for more than one year.[95] The cable operator has discretion as to how refunds should be implemented.[96]

The cable operator may appeal any local order prescribing a rate within 30 days.[97] The FCC generally will defer to factual findings made by local franchising authorities. Disputes over procedural issues, such as due process, confidentiality or other matters, are subject to judicial review.[98]

D. *Regulation of Cable Programming Services*

The 1992 Cable Act gave the FCC jurisdiction to regulate rates for upper tier cable services ("CPST rates.")[99] In contrast with local regulation of basic rates, which requires that rates in affected systems generally be "reasonable," the 1992 Act directed the Commission to prescribe

87. *Id.* § 76.933(c).

88. *Id.* §§ 76.937, 76.938 and 76.939.

89. *Id.* § 76.933(g).

90. *Id.*

91. *Id.* § 76.936 (1997).

92. *Id.* § 76.936.

93. *Id.* § 76.942.

94. *Id.* § 76.942.

95. *Id.* § 76.942(b).

96. *Id.* § 76.942(d).

97. 47 C.F.R. § 76.944.

98. *Id.*

99. *Id.*

rules to identify "in individual cases" where rates for cable programming services are "unreasonable."[100] Pursuant to this provision, the FCC established a complaint process by which any subscriber, franchising authority or other "relevant" state entity could trigger federal regulatory authority over a cable system's CPST rates.[1] Under the FCC's initial rules, a complaint could be filed within 45 days after a subscriber received a bill that reflected a change in upper tier rates.[2] Cable operators were required to respond to complaints within 30 days.[3] Under the 1992 Act, challenges to upper tier rates were permitted from the effective date of rate regulation until February 28, 1994.[4] After that, the Commission would entertain complaints only after a change in CPS rates. Until 1995, however, the FCC would review both the rate increase and the underlying CPS rate upon receiving a complaint.[5] This policy ended in late 1995, and the FCC "grandfathered" existing upper tier rates in communities where a complaint had not yet been filed. Thereafter, only the rate increase would be reviewed for reasonableness.[6]

Under its rate regulations, the FCC could order rate reductions, prescribe a "reasonable" rate, or order refunds with interest accruing from the date the complaint was filed.[7] It could also impose fines for a noncompliance with a rate order. The rules did not require cable operators to obtain advance approval for a rate increase. However, if a complaint was pending at the FCC, the cable operator was required to advise the Commission 30 days in advance of any proposed change.[8] Also, if the FCC had ordered the operator to reduce its rates, the new price was required to remain in effect for one year unless the operator obtained FCC approval for an increase. At the height of the Commission's rate regulation activities, it reviewed over 11,000 rate complaints and issued more than 700 rate decisions.[9]

The Telecommunications Act of 1996 imposed a sunset date of March 31, 1999 for CPST regulation by the FCC but also imposed certain reforms during the interim.[10] Under the Act, FCC review cannot be triggered by a single subscriber complaint.[11] Instead, multiple subscribers must submit complaints to the local franchising authority, not to the FCC.[12] The franchising authority may, but is not required, to file an official complaint with the FCC. On the other hand, the Act expanded the time within which a complaint may be filed from 45 to 90 days after

---

100. 47 U.S.C.A. § 543(c) (West Supp. 1997).

1. *Id.*

2. Implementation of Sections of the Cable Television Consumer Protection and Competition Act of 1992: Rate Regulation, Thirteenth Order on Recons. 11 FCC Rcd. 388, 399 (1995).

3. *Id.*

4. *Id.* at 449.

5. *Id.* at 448.

6. *Id.* at 450.

7. *Id.* at 390.

8. *Id.* at 391.

9. Federal Communications Commission, 61st Ann. Rep., Fiscal Year 1995 at 70.

10. Telecommunications Act of 1996, Pub. L. 104–104, § 301(b)(4), 110 Stat. 115, 147 (1996).

11. *Id.* § 301(b)(1).

12. *Id.*

a rate increase.[13] The franchising authority must file its complaint with the FCC within 180 days of the rate increase.[14] Before filing a complaint, the franchising authority must first give the cable operator written notice of its intention to do so and must allow at least 30 days for the operator to file a justification for the increase.[15] Under this change, the amount of operator liability is limited to the amount of the rate increase, and not to its pre-existing rate structure. Once a complaint is submitted to the FCC, the 1996 Act requires Commission action within 90 days.[16]

E. Establishing "Reasonable" Rates

Congress gave the FCC wide discretion in determining how to regulate rates.[17] The 1992 Cable Act requires the Commission to adopt a regulatory structure that ensures reasonable rates for subscribers while at the same time preserves an incentive for cable system innovation.[18] Additionally, the regulations must reduce the administrative burdens on subscribers, cable operators, franchising authorities, and the Commission.[19]

The Act establishes criteria for determining in individual cases whether rates for cable programming services are "unreasonable."[20] The statutory factors include:

(1) the rates for similarly situated cable systems offering comparable cable programming services, taking into account similarities in facilities, regulatory and governmental costs, the number of subscribers, and other relevant factors;

(2) the rates for cable systems, if any, that are subject to effective competition;

(3) the history of the rates for cable programming services of the system, including the relationship of such rates to changes in general consumer prices;

(4) the rates, as a whole, for all the cable programming, cable equipment, and cable services provided by the system other than programming provided on a per-channel or per-program (basis);

(5) the operating costs of the cable system; and

(6) the revenues received by the cable operator from advertising carried on cable programming service tiers.

Based on the statutory criteria, the FCC established two different methods by which cable operators could demonstrate the reasonableness of the price for cable programming services. Operators could either compare their rates to "benchmarks" based on mathematical formulas

---

13. *Id.* § 301(b)(3).

14. *Id.*

15. *Id.*

16. 47 U.S.C.A. § 543(c)(3) (West Supp. 1997).

17. *See, e.g.,* S. Rep. No. 92, 102d Cong., 1st Sess. 73 (1991) ("This provision ...

gives the FCC broad discretion to ensure rates are reasonable.").

18. 47 U.S.C.A. § 543(b)(1) (West Supp. 1997).

19. *Id.* § 543(b)(2)(A).

20. *Id.* § 543(c)(1).

developed at the FCC or they could seek to demonstrate reasonableness by comparing rates to the actual cost of providing service.[21]

The "benchmark" rate is a national per-channel average rate for programming services. It is the result of a mathematical equation that compares the rate of a non-competitive cable system with certain service characteristics with the rate charged by a competitive cable system with similar service characteristics.[22] The difference between the average national "non-competitive" rates and the benchmark rate is referred to as the "competitive differential."[23] The cable system's rate schedule is then compared to the benchmark rate and rolled-back to the lesser of the benchmark or the competitive differential (currently 17 percent, adjusted forward for inflation).[24] The Commission treats the resulting rate as "reasonable."[25]

The cable operator may elect whether to justify rates based on the benchmark or on a cost-of-service showing.[26] Once the initial permitted rate is calculated it may be adjusted, again at the operator's election, by a rate determined pursuant to a "mini" cost-of-service showing, or a rate determined pursuant to a "price cap" which allows for adjustments based on changes in inflation and "external costs."[27] External costs include franchise fees, cost of complying with franchise requirements, state and local taxes based on the provision of cable service, retransmission consent fees, copyright fees, programming license fees and other costs that generally are "uncontrollable" for the cable operator.[28]

As an alternative to the benchmark analysis, a cost-of-service showing may justify initial rates higher than what may be permitted by the benchmark rate.[29] Under a cost-of-service showing, an operator may demonstrate that the national benchmark rate does not reflect the specific operator's investments, revenues and expenses. Cost-of-service showings are made by cable operators seeking to justify rate increases greater than the levels determined under the price-cap approach. This

---

21. 47 C.F.R. 76.922(a) (1997).

22. 47 C.F.R. § 76.922(b)(3) (1997). These characteristics included, at least initially, the number of channels offered by the system, the number of subscribers it serves, and the number of satellite-delivered signals.

23. *But see* Stanley M. Besen and John R. Woodbury, *Rate Regulation, Effective Competition, and the 1992 Cable Act*, 17 Hastings Comm/ Ent L.J. 203 (1994) (arguing that the FCC applied poor statistical methodology in performing the multiple regression analysis that produced the benchmark differential between competitive and non-competitive systems).

24. *Id.* at 205–06.

25. One factor that the Commission did not include in initial benchmark calculation was the increase in external costs during the "gap period" (extending from September 30, 1992 until the operator became sub-

ject to rate regulation at some point after September 1, 1993). The rules provided that, to determine a benchmark rate, operators must reduce their September 30, 1992 rates by 17 percent, then adjust forward for inflation. But the Commission did not allow operators an adjustment for increases in external costs. The District of Columbia Circuit struck down this methodology in *Time Warner Entertainment Co. v. FCC*, 56 F.3d 151, 312 U.S. App. D.C. 187 (1995), holding that the FCC must permit operators to recover for increases in external costs during the "gap period." *Id.* at 178, 312 U.S. App. D.C. at 214.

26. 47 C.F.R. § 76.922(b)(1) (1997).

27. *Id.* § 76.922(c)-(d).

28. *Id.* § 76.922(e)(2)(ii)(A).

29. *Id.* § 76.922(a).

method of rate modification allows the cable system to recover its operating expenses plus a fair return on investments.[30]

The FCC first adopted interim rules to govern cost-of-service proceedings in 1994.[31] The cost-of-service rules were intended to permit operators that faced unusually high costs to justify rates above the benchmark, as the Act required.[32] The rules were temporary, since the FCC had not yet been able to complete studies of cost within the cable industry. In 1996, the FCC reaffirmed and modified some of its cost-of-service rules.[33]

The FCC's cost-of-service formula calculated reasonable revenues by adding the cable operator's expenses plus the rate base times a reasonable rate of return. The rules established 11.25 percent as the reasonable rate of return.[34] However, there was a great deal of dispute regarding calculation of the rate base. For example, the interim rules presumed that start-up losses incurred by cable operators during the first two years of system operation would be included in the rate base, but excluded losses after the initial two year period. This presumption was eliminated in the final rules, and cable operators were permitted to include their actual "accumulative net losses plus interest expenses."[35] A significant issue in the cost-of-service regime involved the question of allocating costs between basic and upper tier services. In late 1995, the FCC adopted final rules to govern cost-of-service rate justifications by cable companies. Another issue involved the extent to which a cable system could include acquisition-related intangible assets in the rate base.[36]

1. *Adjustments to "Reasonable" Rates*

After establishing the initial regulated rate, that rate must be adjusted over time to reflect cost increases in the marketplace and provide an incentive to improve service. Over the years since rate regulation began, the Commission developed several methods for making such adjustments, including price caps, cost-of-service showings, the going forward rules, new product tiers and an upgrade incentive plan ("social contracts").[37]

---

30. *Id.* § 76.922(g).

31. Implementation of Sections of the Cable Television Consumer Protection and Competition Act of 1992: Rate Regulation and Adoption of an Uniform Accounting System for Provision of Regulated Cable Service, Report and Order and Further Notice of Proposed Rulemaking, 9 FCC Rcd. 4527 (1994).

32. *Id.* at 4532.

33. Implementation of Sections of the Cable Television Consumer Protection and Competition Act of 1992, Rate Regulation and Adoption of a Uniform Accounting System for Provision of Regulated Cable Service, Second Report and Order, First Order on Reconsideration, and Further Notice of Proposed Rulemaking, 11 FCC Rcd. 2220 (1996).

34. 47 C.F.R. § 76.922(g)(7).

35. This change was codified in the 1996 Telecommunications Act, which expressly permits operators to recover any system losses incurred prior to September 4, 1992. 47 U.S.C.A. § 543 (West Supp. 1997).

36. The cost-of-service rules are codified at 47 C.F.R. § 76.922(i) (1997).

37. *Id.* § 76.922(c).

Price cap adjustments allow cable operators to change their rates to reflect inflation and other increases in external costs, such as taxes, franchise fees, or retransmission consent fees.[38] Adjustments can also reflect the addition of new program services to a cable system. Initially, cable operators were allowed a return on such programming of costs plus a 7.5 percent markup, an amount ultimately considered insufficient to encourage the addition of new services.[39] Under this adjustment method, when external costs decrease from previous levels, cable operators must reduce their rates by the amount of those savings plus a 7.5 percent markdown.[40]

The FCC adopted what it called "going forward" rules as a variation of the price cap method to permit cable operators to increase rates when channels were added to a programming tier. Operators were given the option to use the price cap method of increasing rates for channel additions (*i.e.*, a pass-through of programming costs plus 7.5 percent) or the "going forward" method.[41] Under "going forward," the cable operator was allowed to impose a flat fee per-channel markup for each new channel added to a CPST. The operator was permitted to charge an additional $.20 per channel (per subscriber), limited by an operator's cap to a total of $1.20 for the two-year period ending December 31, 1996 and $1.40 for the three-year period that ended December 31, 1997.[42] Corresponding rate decreases were required by the rules if the operator moved, dropped, or replaced a channel.[43] This was designed to deter channel retiering intended to evade the regulations.

The Commission also established "New Product Tiers" ("NPT") as an incentive for cable systems to add new programming.[44] An NPT can consist of either new programming or programming duplicated from an existing tier, with restrictions on programming transferred from a regulated tier.[45] The NPT, like per channel and per program offerings, is not subject to rate regulation on the theory that the service is less subject to market power pricing, and that the service is not as essential to consumers as is the BST or CPST.

NPTs were intended to allow cable operators to introduce an entirely new program package largely free from rate regulation. While channels offered on existing tiers were not permitted to be offered exclusively on the NPT, such channels could be "cloned" on the NPT.[46] The Commission's rationale for allowing this unregulated tier is its belief

---

38. *Id.* § 76.922(d).

39. 47 C.F.R. § 76.922(d)(3)(xi) (1995).

40. *Id.*

41. *Id.* at § 76.922(e)(I).

42. *Id.* § 76.922(e)(3)(I).

43. *Id.* § 76.922(e)(4)-(e)(6).

44. 47 C.F.R. § 76.987 (1997). Under this concept, channels could be offered simultaneously on more than one tier.

45. Implementation of Sections of the Cable Television Consumer Protection and Competition Act of 1992: Rate Regulation, Sixth Order on Recons., 10 FCC Rcd. 1226 at paras. 22–37 (1995). The NPT follows the general policy goals of the 1992 Act to whenever possible give cable operators incentives to expand service and to rely on the marketplace to determine optimal levels of cost and service. *See id.* at ¶ 16 (listing policy goals of 1992 Cable Act).

46. *Id.* at 1331 (Statement of Commissioner Ness).

that consumers will not select the NPT over the CPST if the tier is unreasonably priced, since subscribers have sufficient choices among the regulated tiers.[47] The NPT must succeed on the strength of its mix of pricing and exclusive channels.

2. Other Restrictions (Buy Through; Negative Option; Uniform Rate Structure)

The 1992 Cable Act contained a number of provisions designed to prevent cable operators from evading rate regulations. The most important of these provisions include a no buy-through prohibition, the "negative option" billing prohibition, and the requirement of a uniform rate structure throughout the franchise area.[48]

a. Anti–Buy–Through Restrictions

Under the no buy-through prohibition, cable operators may not require a customer to subscribe to any tier of service other than the BST as a condition for access to channels offered on a per program or per channel basis (*e.g.*, HBO, Showtime, or pay-per-view service).[49] Further, the operator may not discriminate between subscribers to the BST and subscribers to other tiers regarding the rates charged for such services.[50] The provision was intended to prevent cable operators from tying premium services to the purchase of tiers and to provide subscribers with more flexibility.

The buy-through prohibition does not apply to cable systems that cannot offer premium or pay-per-view services to "basic only" households "by reason of the lack of addressable converter boxes or other technological limitations" at least until October 5, 2002.[51] The FCC has interpreted this exception liberally, so that the rule generally does not apply unless the cable operator can provide all of its premium services to "basic only" subscribers. Thus, if for technical reasons, a cable operator could provide one premium channel to basic subscribers but could not provide other premium services without providing access to CPST channels, the rule does not apply.[52] Additionally, the anti buy-through restriction does not apply to cable systems that are not subject to rate regulation because they face effective competition.

b. Prohibition on Negative Option Billing

The 1992 Cable Act prohibits cable operators from charging a subscriber for service or equipment that the subscriber has not affirmatively requested by name.[53] Congress enacted the provision out of concern that some cable operators had engaged in the practice of providing

---

47. *Id.*

48. Cable Television Consumer Protection and Competition Act of 1992, Pub. L. 102–385, § 3, 106 Stat. 1460, 1469 (1992), *codified as amended* at 47 U.S.C.A. § 543(f) (West Supp. 1997).

49. 47 U.S.C.A. § 543(b)(8).

50. 47 C.F.R. § 76.921(b) (1997).

51. 47 U.S.C.A. § 543(b)(8)(B) (West Supp. 1997).

52. 47 C.F.R. § 76.921(c) (1997).

53. 47 U.S.C.A. § 543(f) (West Supp. 1997).

new premium services to subscribers, and increased their monthly rates, without the subscribers' consent. The subscriber was then given the "negative option" of canceling the new service or retaining it at the higher rate.[54] Under this provision, Congress made clear that a subscriber's silence in the face of an offer of service was not to be construed as consent.

The negative option billing provision prohibits a cable operator from charging a customer for any programming service or equipment that the subscriber has not affirmatively requested.[55] A customer's failure to respond to a cable operator's offer is not an affirmative response.[56] However, this prohibition does not cover minor adjustments in rates or channel selection.[57] As implemented by the FCC, the law does not "preclude the addition or deletion of a specific program from a service offering, the addition or deletion of specific channels from an existing tier of service, or the restructuring or division of existing tiers of service that do not result in a fundamental change in the nature of an existing service or tier of service."[58]

Certain of the FCC's policies with respect to negative option billing have been challenged by states which sought to provide more restrictive requirements. In *Time Warner Cable v. Doyle*,[59] the Seventh Circuit held that state negative options requirements are preempted by federal law. Although states are allowed to adopt consumer protection laws that affect cable service, the Court found that such laws could not conflict with the FCC's rate regulations.[60] It noted that federal regulations permit a "limited range of negative option billing whose prohibition by the states would interfere with the execution of the Commission's rate rules."[61]

c. Uniform Rate Structure

A cable operator is required to have a geographically uniform rate structure.[62] The provision is designed to provide average rates for customers in the franchise area, regardless of the cost to provide the service, and to prevent cable operators from manipulating rates to undermine competition. While the uniformity requirement prohibits rate de-averaging, cable operators were permitted to establish separate rates for reasonable categories of both service and customers.[63] Thus, cable opera-

---

54. *Id.*

55. *Id.*

56. *Id.*

57. 47 C.F.R. § 76.981(b) (1997).

58. *Id.*

59. 66 F.3d 867 (7th Cir.1995), cert. denied, 516 U.S. 1141, 116 S.Ct. 974, 133 L.Ed.2d 894 (1996).

60. *Id.* at 882.

61. *Id. But see* Kentucky ex rel. Gorman v. Comcast Cable, 881 F.Supp. 285 (W.D.Ky.1995).

62. 47 U.S.C.A. § 543(d) (West Supp.) This provision has been found not to confer a right on private parties to bring an action Hahn v. Rifkin/Narragansett South Florida CATV Ltd. Partnership, 941 F.Supp. 1196, 1202 (S.D.Fla.1996).

63. 47 C.F.R. § 76.984(b).

tors can offer discounted rates to, as an example, multiple-dwelling units or clients with duration contracts.[64]

The FCC initially applied the uniform rate structure requirement to systems facing effective competition, and thus exempt from rate regulation, as well as systems without effective competition. This interpretation was rejected by the District of Columbia Circuit, which barred the Commission from applying the rule to competitive cable systems.[65] The court's holding was codified in the Telecommunications Act of 1996, which amended the statute to clarify that uniform rate requirements do not apply to any geographic area in which a cable system faces effective competition, or to any video programming offered on a per channel or per program basis.[66] The 1996 Act also made clear that cable operators are permitted to offer bulk discounts to multiple dwelling units so long as they do not engage in predatory pricing.

F. Rate Regulation and Small Cable Systems

The 1992 Cable Act required the FCC to design regulations to reduce the administrative burdens and costs of compliance for small cable systems and small cable companies.[67] The Commission made several attempts to implement this requirement under the 1992 Act, and these efforts were supplemented by the 1996 Telecommunications Act, which deregulated certain rates for "small systems" owned by "small cable operators."[68] Under the 1996 Act, rate regulation was eliminated for small cable systems, defined as franchise areas with 50,000 or fewer subscribers, that are owned or affiliated with small cable operators, which serve fewer than one percent of all subscribers in the United States[69] and which are not affiliated with any entity whose gross annual revenues exceed $250 million dollars.[70] The FCC adopted rules implementing the statutory amendments.[71] The Commission defined "affiliate" for purpose of the small system exemption to include entities that have a twenty percent or greater equity interest in the operator or entities that hold *de jure* or *de facto* control over the operator.[72]

The rate deregulation for small systems contained in the 1996 Act did not entirely supplant pre-existing FCC rules governing small systems. Under the law, only those cable systems that had a single tier of service (basic only) as of December 31, 1994 were exempted from rate

64. *Id.*

65. Time Warner Entertainment Co. v. FCC, 56 F.3d 151, 190, 312 U.S. App. D.C. 187, 226 (D.C.Cir.1995).

66. Telecommunication Act of 1996, Pub. L. 104–104, § 301(b)(2), 110 Stat. 56, 114–15 (1996).

67. Cable Television Consumer Protection and Competition Act of 1992, Pub. L. 102–385, § 3(a), 106 Stat. 1460, 1470 (1992) *codified as amended at* 47 U.S.C.A. § 543(i).

68. Telecommunications Act of 1996, Pub. L. 104–104, § 301(c), 110 Stat. 56, 116 (1996) (codified as amended at 47 U.S.C.A. § 543(m)) (West Supp. 1997).

69. *Id.*

70. *Id.*

71. Implementation of Cable Act Reform Provisions of the Telecommunications Act of 1996, 11 FCC Rcd. 5937, 5947 (1996).

72. *Id.* at 5948.

regulation on all tiers.[73] Any system that had more than one tier as of the qualifying date was deregulated only with respect to upper tier services.[74] Additionally, the exemption applies only after the date of enactment of the 1996 Act—February 8, 1996.[75] In all other instances, FCC rules governing small systems apply.

In its 1995 "small system order," the FCC significantly relaxed rate regulation for small cable systems.[76] It defined small systems as those with 15,000 or fewer subscribers and small cable companies as having 400,000 or fewer subscribers.[77] A "small system" owned by a "small cable company" is eligible for several forms of relief under the FCC rules, including streamlined cost-of service analysis, deferral of deadlines for filing rate justifications, and special going-forward rules.

The streamlined cost-of-service analysis permits eligible cable systems to supply just five pieces of data in order to determine if its rate is reasonable.[78] The five pieces of data include total operating expenses, net rate base, rate of return, number of channels and number of subscribers.[79] If this information demonstrates that the system's per channel rate is less than $1.24, then the rate is presumptively reasonable.[80] Small system operators may submit this information to regulators in a streamlined form. The approved rate can be used to justify an existing rate or to support a rate increase. When the rules were adopted, small system operators were given a 90 day "grace period" to file rate justifications, notify subscribers of rate changes and to implement restructured rates.[81]

The Commission also adopted special going forward rules to benefit small system operators. These rules permit small systems to pass through to subscribers the costs of headend equipment for new channels (with costs capped at $5,000 per channel).[82] The cost of the headend equipment must be amortized over the useful life of the equipment and operators are permitted to take an 11.25 percent rate of return on the undepreciated expense.[83]

G. Social Contracts and Settlements

As an alternative to the established rate adjustment mechanisms discussed above, the Commission adopted what it called an Upgrade Incentive Plan, or "social contract" which involves a cable operator's agreement to a BST rate-freeze in exchange for more relaxed regulation

---

73. *Id.*

74. *Id.*

75. *Id.*

76. Implementation of Sections of the Cable Television Consumer Protection and Competition Act of 1992. Rate Regulation, Sixth Report and Order and Eleventh Order on Recons., 10 FCC Rcd. 7393 (1995).

77. 47 C.F.R. § 76.901(c)(e) (1997). This definition is a departure from the 1992 Act, which defined small systems as those with 1,000 or fewer subscribers.

78. *Id.* § 76.924(d).

79. *Id.*

80. Implementation of Sections of the Cable Television Consumer Protection Act of 1992; Rate Regulation, Sixth Report and Order and Eleventh Order on Recons., 10 FCC Rcd. 7393, 7395 (1995).

81. 47 C.F.R. § 76.934(f).

82. *Id.* at 76.922(e)(7).

83. *Id.*

of new services.[84] This "social contract" between operators and customers was designed to provide greater assurance of stable rates to customers for existing services while also generating profit incentives for operators to upgrade their systems in cost-effective ways.[85] The "contract" is intended to remain in effect for a fixed period of years.[86]

After this alternative approach to rate regulation was announced, most major cable MSOs entered into some form of social contract or rate settlement with the FCC. After the first such agreement was reached with Continental Cablevision in 1995, other operators, including Telecommunications, Inc., Time Warner, Cox Cable, Comcast Cable, Cablevision Systems, Adelphia Cable and others entered similar arrangements, thus supplanting many of the formal rate rules.

In the arrangement entered by Continental Cablevision, for example, the operator agreed to reduce BST rates to at least 15 percent below permitted levels while gaining additional flexibility for pricing on the CPST. Additionally, the operator was permitted to set equipment and installation prices on an average regional basis, rather than a strictly cost-based method. All pending rate complaints were resolved with the payment of $9.5 million in-kind subscriber refunds. In addition, Continental agreed to invest $1.35 billion in system upgrades through the year 2000. The upgrades related to both system capacity and technical sophistication. The agreement was later amended to encompass new systems acquired by the cable operator after the initial social contract. It provided for additional subscriber refunds, a heightened upgrade commitment and an agreement to provide services to public schools within its franchise area, among other things. Local franchising authorities were given the opportunity to "opt out" of the settlement, but none did so.

The Continental social contract demonstrated the Commission's willingness to dispense with formal rate regulations in favor of more tailored arrangements, and others quickly followed. Some, like the arrangements with Time Warner and Comcast Cable, resembled the Continental social contract.[87] In other cases, the arrangements were straightforward settlements of outstanding complaints.[88] Through these

84. Implementation of Sections of the Cable Television Consumer Protection and Competition Act of 1992: Rate Regulation and Adoption of a Uniform Accounting System for Provision of Regulated Cable Service, Report and Order and Further Notice of Proposed Rulemaking, 9 FCC Rcd. 4527, 4689–91 (1994).

85. *Id.* at 4689.

86. *Id.*

87. Social Contract for Time Warner, 11 FCC Rcd. 2788 (1995); Social Contract for Comcast Cable Communications, Inc., Public Notice, 12 FCC Rcd. 5248 (1997).

88. Cablevision Systems Corp., Resolution of Cable Programming Service Rate Complaints, FCC 98-193 (rel. Aug. 11, 1998); Adelphi Communications Corporation, Final Resolution of Cable Programming Service Rate Complaints, Order, 12 FCC Rcd. 6344 (1997); TCI Communications, Inc., Final Resolution of Cable Programmers Service Rate Complaints, Order, 11 FCC Rcd. 14696 (1996); Viacom Cable, Inc., Final Resolution of Cable Programming Service Rate Complaints, Order 12 FCC Rcd. 5058 (1997); Cox Communications Inc. and Times Mirror Cable Television, Inc., Rate Complaints, Order, 11 FCC Rcd. 1972 (1995); Century Communications Corp., Resolution of Rate Complaints, Order, 11 FCC Rcd. 11188 (1996); Social Con-

procedures, most of the cable industry became subject to "regulation by contract" rather than by formal rules.

13.4 Regulation of Cable Programming

Cable programming regulation is emerging as an area of increasing importance. Unlike broadcast licensees, that were subjected to various programming requirements by virtue of their license to use the radio spectrum, cable operators historically faced less regulation of programming content. Federal programming requirements related generally to providing assistance to local broadcast stations rather than imposing direct content requirements. Local efforts to regulate content generally were unsuccessful. Beginning with the 1992 Cable Act, federal authorities began to show greater interest in regulating such things as "indecent" programming on cable television.[1] This trend continued with adoption of the Telecommunications Act of 1996.[2]

A. Access Requirements and Other Structural or Economic Regulations

1. Must Carry Rules and Retransmission Consent

a. Judicial Approval of Must Carry Rules

"Must carry" rules require cable operators to transmit the signals of local television stations. The requirement was adopted to preserve the viability of marginal television stations in the face of competition from cable television operators. After more than a decade of litigation involving various must carry rules, a divided Supreme Court upheld must carry rules in the face of a First Amendment challenge in *Turner Broadcasting System v. FCC* ("Turner II").[3] The Court's 5–4 decision surprised most observers of the litigation.[4] The Court had previously remanded the case to determine whether Congress' predicted judgment about the need for must carry rules was supported and whether the provisions burdened more speech than necessary to further those interests. Upon review, the Court concluded that the must carry rules served three interrelated interests: "preserving the benefits of free over-the-air local broadcast television, promoting the widespread dissemination of information from a multiplicity of sources, and promoting fair competition in the market for television programming."[5] The Court also found that the must carry rules did not impose significant adverse effects on cable operators and programmers.[6]

---

tract for Continental Cable Television Inc., Order, 10 FCC Rcd. 12651 (1995).

1. Cable Television Consumer Protection and Competition Act of 1992, Pub. L. 102–385, § 10, 106 Stat. 1460, 1486 (1992) *codified as amended* at 47 U.S.C.A. 532 (West Supp. 1997).

2. Telecommunications Act of 1996, Pub. L. 104–104, § 551, 110 Stat. 56, 139–42 (1996) *codified as amended at* 47 U.S.C.A. § 303 (West Supp. 1997).

3. 520 U.S. 180, 117 S.Ct. 1174, 137 L.Ed.2d 369 (1997).

4. *Id.*

5. *Id.* at 189, 117 S.Ct. at 1186, 137 L.Ed.2d at 388.

6. *Id.* at 214–215, 117 S. Ct. at 1198, 137 L. Ed. 2d at 403 (94.5 percent of cable systems have not had to drop any programming; the remaining 5.5 percent have had to drop on average 1.22 services; operators

Three years earlier, in *Turner I*, the Supreme Court had determined that the must carry requirements were content-neutral, and that an intermediate standard of constitutional review should be applied.[7] It concluded that such regulations may be appropriate to the extent cable operators act as a "bottleneck" restricting transmission of broadcast signals to their intended audience.[8] Despite these findings the *Turner I* majority declined to uphold the rules, and expressed skepticism about the congressional findings.[9] The Court noted that even where the "government's asserted interests are important in the abstract[, it] does not mean ... that the must-carry rules will in fact advance those interests."[10] It found that the government had not demonstrated that the "recited harms are real" or that the regulation "will in fact alleviate these harms in a direct and material way."[11] The Court found it significant that the government had not presented "any evidence that local broadcast stations have fallen into bankruptcy, turned in their broadcast licenses, curtailed their broadcast operations, or suffered a serious reduction in operating revenues as a result of their being dropped from, or otherwise disadvantaged by, cable systems."[12] It also noted the lack of findings regarding adverse effects of the rules "on the speech of cable operators and cable programmers."[13]

The majority in *Turner II* appeared to hold Congress to a somewhat different standard of proof.[14] The majority stated that Congress was not just concerned over the loss of "a few voices,"[15] but instead was concerned that the market shift from broadcast television to cable resulting from increased market penetration, combined with expanding horizontal concentration and vertical integration, gave cable system operators the incentive and ability to delete, reposition or decline carriage of local broadcasters.[16] The majority concluded that "the Congress was under no illusion that there would be a complete disappearance of broadcast television nationwide in the absence of must carry."[17] Rather, it was concerned that significant numbers of broadcast stations would be refused carriage and that those stations would either "deteriorate to a substantial degree or fail altogether."[18]

nationwide carry 99.8 percent of the programming they carried before the must carry rules were implemented).

7. Turner Broadcasting System, Inc. v. FCC, 512 U.S. 622, 661–62, 114 S.Ct. 2445, 2469, 129 L.Ed.2d 497, 530 (1994) ("Turner I").

8. *Id.* at 660–61, 114 S.Ct. at 2468, 129 L.Ed.2d at 529.

9. *Id.* at 665–66, 114 S. Ct. at 2470–71, 129 L. Ed. 2d at 530–31.

10. *Id.* at 664, 114 S. Ct. at 2470, 129 L. Ed. 2d at 531.

11. *Id.* at 664, 114 S. Ct. at 2470, 129 L. Ed. 2d at 531 (quoting Edenfield v. Fane, 507 U.S. 761, 770–771, 113 S.Ct. 1792, 1798–99 123 L.Ed.2d 543 (1993)).

12. *Id.* at 667, 114 S. Ct. at 2472, 129 L. Ed. 2d at 533.

13. *Id.*, at 667–68, 114 S.Ct. at 2472, 129 L.Ed.2d at 533.

14. Turner II, 520 U.S. 180, 117 S.Ct. 1174, 137 L.Ed.2d 369 (1997).

15. *Id.* at 191, 117 S.Ct. at 1187, 137 L.Ed.2d at 388.

16. *Id.* at 191, 117 S.Ct. at 1187, 137 L.Ed.2d at 389.

17. *Id.*

18. *Id.* at 191–192, 117 S.Ct. at 1183, 137 L.Ed.2d at 384. Justice Breyer, who was the fifth vote in the majority, did not agree with the antitrust rationale for must carry. *Id.* at 225, 117 S.Ct. at 1203, 137

Justice O'Connor's dissent questioned the new majority's statement of the government interest being to prevent a "significant reduction in the multiplicity of broadcast programming sources available to non-cable households."[19] Justice O'Connor contrasted this statement with the decision in *Turner I*,[20] in which she said a far greater threat to the structure to the local broadcast system than the loss of "a few" stations runs through virtually every passage in the principal *Turner* opinion.[21]

A major point of contention between the majority and dissent, as it had been in *Turner I*, was the question of whether must carry rules are content-based. The majority held that intermediate First Amendment scrutiny was appropriate because the rules served as a check on anticompetitive behavior by cable operators and preserved a multiplicity of broadcast voices to ensure access to television by non-cable households.[22] Justice Stevens, in a brief concurring opinion, repeated that must carry rules are "intended to forestall the abuse of monopoly power," but added that "[i]f this statute regulated the content of speech rather than the structure of the market, our task would be quite different."[23] Justice Breyer, on the other hand, concurring only in part, did not base his agreement on governmental efforts to promote fair competition but focused instead on the goal of promoting the widespread dissemination of information from a multiplicity of sources.[24] Justice Breyer acknowledged that compulsory carriage of broadcast stations carries "a serious First Amendment price" amounting to a "suppression of speech" but he balanced the interests of broadcast viewers against those of cable operators and programmers, finding that "Congress could reasonably conclude that must carry will help the over-the-air viewer more than it will hurt

L.Ed.2d at 410. (Breyer, J., concurring in part). Instead, he favored the statute's "non-economic purpose" to prevent a too precipitous decline in the quality and quantity of programming choice for an ever-shrinking segment of the public that does not subscribe to cable. *Id.* at 226, 117 S.Ct. at 1204, 137 L.Ed.2d at 411.

19. *Id.* at 232, 117 S.Ct. at 1206, 137 L.Ed.2d at 414.

20. Turner Broadcasting System, Inc. v. FCC, I, 512 U.S. 622, 673, 114 S.Ct. 2445, 2475–76, 129 L.Ed.2d 497, 538 (1994).

21. *See id.* at 647, 114 S.Ct. at 2461, 129 L.Ed.2d at 520 (recognizing substantiality of interest in protecting non-cable households from loss of regular television broadcasting service due to competition from cable) (citation omitted); 512 U.S. at 652, 114 S.Ct. at 2464, 129 L.Ed.2d at 522, ("Congress sought to preserve the existing structure of the Nation's broadcast television medium ... and, in particular, to ensure that broadcast television remains available as a source of video programming for those without cable"); 512 U.S. at 663,

114 S.Ct. at 2469, 129 L.Ed.2d at 531 (recognizing interest in "maintaining the local broadcasting structure"); 512 U.S. at 664–65, 114 S.Ct. at 2470–71, 129 L.Ed.2d at 532 (characterizing inquiry as whether government "has adequately shown that the economic health of local broadcasting is in genuine jeopardy"); 512 U.S. at 665, 114 S.Ct. at 2470, 129 L.Ed.2d at 532 (noting government's reliance on congressional findings that "absent mandatory carriage rules, the continuing validity of local broadcast television would be 'seriously jeopardized' ") (quoting Cable Act, § 2(a)(16)); 512 U.S. at 666, 114 S.Ct. at 2471, 129 L.Ed.2d at 533 (recognizing government's assertion that "the must-carry rules are necessary to protect the viability of broadcast television").

22. Turner II, 520 U.S. at 180, 117 S.Ct. at 1188, 137 L.Ed.2d at 390–91.

23. *Id.* at 225, 117 S.Ct. at 1203, 137 L.Ed.2d at 410 (Stevens, J., concurring) . .

24. *Id.* at 226, 117 S. Ct. at 1203–1204, 137 L.Ed.2d at 410 (Breyer, J., concurring in part).

the typical cable subscriber."[25] The four dissenting justices found that the justification of increasing the "multiplicity" of broadcast voices to be heavily content based.[26] Justice O'Connor wrote that "the must-carry provisions should be subject to strict scrutiny, which they surely fail."[27]

Lower courts had not been as sympathetic when reviewing earlier must carry requirements. In 1985, the United States Court of Appeals for the District of Columbia Circuit, in *Quincy Cable TV, Inc. v. FCC*,[28] held that FCC must carry rules were invalid. The court found the must carry rules failed under a First Amendment challenge for two reasons. First, the court held that the Commission failed to prove that a substantial governmental interest existed.[29] Second, the court found that even if the rules were found to serve a substantial interest, they would not survive because the rules were overbroad.[30] In reaching its decision, the court struggled with whether the cable regulations deserved the higher level of scrutiny afforded print and film media.[31] However, the court concluded that it did not need to reach the question of whether the rules warranted a more exacting level of scrutiny than the balancing test set out in *United States v. O'Brien*, because the rules failed even under the intermediate *O'Brien* test.[32]

Under pressure from Congress and the broadcasting industry, the FCC reluctantly revised the must-carry rules following *Quincy*.[33] The revised must carry rules were a two-part regulatory program.[34] The first part involved educating the consumer regarding the capability of receiv-

---

25. *Id.*

26. *Id.* at 232–234, 117 S.Ct. at 1207, 137 L.Ed.2d at 415 (O'Connor, J., dissenting).

27. *Id.* at 235, 117 S.Ct. at 1208, 137 L.Ed.2d at 416.

28. 768 F.2d 1434, 248 U.S.App.D.C. 1 (D.C.Cir.1985), cert. denied, 476 U.S. 1169, 106 S.Ct. 2889, 90 L.Ed.2d 977 (1986). The Quincy case was a consolidation of a case brought by a cable programmer (TBS) and a cable system operator (Quincy). Prior to their consolidation the claims were brought before the FCC. The programmer argued that the must carry rules caused a significant number of channels to be occupied by over-the-air broadcast stations. This diminished the number of channels available for cable programmers and created "artificially stiff competition" for programmers. *Id.* at 1445, 248 U.S. App. D.C. at 12. Quincy Cable Television, Inc. argued that the must carry rules interfered with editorial discretion and subscriber preference. *Id.* at 1446–47, 248 U.S. App. D.C. at 13–14.

29. *Id.* at 1444–45, 248 U.S. App. D.C. at 1–12.

30. *Id.*

31. *Id.* at 1450, 248 U.S. App. D.C. at 17.

32. *Id.* at 1448, 248 U.S. App. D.C. at 14. The court was not convinced that the government's interest was unrelated to speech, as was the court in *Home Box Office, Inc. v. FCC*, 567 F.2d 9, 185 U.S. App. D.C. 142 (D.C.Cir.) cert. denied, 434 U.S. 829, 98 S.Ct. 111, 54 L.Ed.2d 89 (1977). *Home Box Office* involved several FCC regulations limiting programming fare a cablecaster could offer its subscribers.

33. S. Rep. No. 102–92, at 39 (1992), *reprinted in* 1992 United States Code Cong. and Admin. News 1133, 1172.

34. *See* Amendment of Part 76 of the Commission's Rules Concerning Carriage of Television Broadcast Signals by Cable Television Systems, Report and Order, 1 FCC Rcd. 864 (1986). The FCC pointed to the fact that cable systems predominated in transmitting satellite-delivered programs to consumers. *Id.* In addition, the cable industry had begun to provide locally originated programming and some systems had started to sell time to advertisers in order to generate revenue. *Id.* "In offering alternative program services to their subscribers, cable operators now function as independent media voices exercising broad editorial control over content." *Id.* at 879.

ing broadcast television and the use of input selector devices called "A/B switches."[35] The second part was the provision of interim must carry rules to protect broadcast television during the transition.[36] The interim must carry rules were to remain in effect five years.[37] The Commission believed the five-year transition period would be a sufficient time to allow consumers to become aware of their choices.[38] The rules were in place approximately eleven months before they were struck down by an unanimous panel in *Century Communications Corp. v. FCC*.[39] The court concluded that the FCC did not meet the burden of proving the rules advanced a substantial governmental interest to justify the intrusion upon protected First Amendment rights.[40] Similar to the *Quincy* decision, the court did not find it necessary to determine whether strict scrutiny was the appropriate standard of review to apply to cable regulations because the FCC's revised regulations failed even under intermediate scrutiny.

b.   *Must Carry Rules Under the 1992 Cable Act*

In adopting the 1992 Cable Act, Congress found a "substantial governmental interest in promoting the continued availability of ... free television programming, especially for viewers who are unable to afford other means of receiving programming."[41] To protect broadcast viewers, Congress declared that the "[f]ederal Government has a substantial interest in having cable systems carry the signals of local commercial television stations[.]"[42] Congress concluded that the "economic viability of local broadcasting will be seriously jeopardized" because there is an economic incentive for cable systems to "delete, reposition, or not carry local broadcast signals."[43] According to Congress, the 1992 Cable Act serves the goals of the Communication Act of 1934, in that it "provid[es] fair, efficient, and equitable distribution of broadcast services."[44] Congress also found that the must carry rules provided an improved alternative to input selector switches and antennas, to ensure access to local broadcasting.[45] This governmental purpose was found to be sufficient to uphold the must carry rules in *Turner II*.

---

35. *Id.* at 886. This required cable operators to offer subscribers "input selector switches" that would be used along with antennas to access over-the-air broadcasts once the must carry rules were eliminated. It also included a consumer education program regarding the need for switches and antennas.

36. *Id.*

37. *Id.*

38. *Id.*

39. Century Communications Corp. v. FCC, 835 F.2d 292, 266 U.S. App. D.C. 228 (D.C.Cir.1987).

40. *Id.* at 293, 266 U.S. App. D.C. at 229.

41. 47 U.S.C.A. § 521(a)(12) (Historical and Statutory Note) (West Supp. 1997).

42. *Id.* § 521(a)(9); 47 C.F.R. § 76.64 (a)-(b) (1997). In 1998, the FCC initiated a proceeding to determine whether to extend must carry rules to digital broadcast channels. Carriage of the Transmissions of Digital Television Broadcast Stations, Notice of Proposed Rulemaking, FCC–98–153 (rel. July 10, 1998).

43. 47 U.S.C.A. § 521(a)(15)-(16) (West Supp.1997).

44. *Id.* § 521(a)(9).

45. *Id.* § 521(a)(18). Congress found the input selector switch and antenna requirements were not "an enduring or feasible" options. *Id.* The 1992 Cable Act abolished the 1986 requirement that cable operators provide or make available any input selector devices and provide information to sub-

(1) Requirements for Commercial Television Stations

Under the 1992 Act, the number of local stations a cable system is required to carry depends upon the number of "usable activated channels."[46] The 1992 Act requires that cable systems with 12 or fewer usable activated channels carry three commercial[47] and one noncommercial stations.[48] Cable systems with thirteen to thirty-six usable activated channels must carry "up to one-third of the aggregate number of usable activated channels"[49] and at least one but not more than three noncommercial stations.[50] Cable systems with greater than thirty-six usable activated channels must carry "up to one-third of the aggregate number of usable activated channels"[51] and all nonduplicative noncommercial stations that request carriage.[52] If there are not enough local commercial stations to fill the channels set aside under this regulation, a system with thirty-five or fewer stations, is required to carry one "qualified low power station."[53] A cable system with more than thirty-five usable activated channels is required to carry two qualified low power stations.[54]

The cable operator has the discretion to select among local commercial stations if the number of local stations available exceeds the maximum number of signals a cable system is required to carry.[55] There are two exceptions to this provision. First, "under no circumstances shall a cable operator carry a qualified low power station in lieu of a local commercial television station."[56] Second, "if the cable operator elects to carry an affiliate of a broadcast network ... such cable operator shall carry the affiliate of such broadcast network whose city of license

---

scribers about input selector switches or similar devices. 47 U.S.C.A. § 534(e)(1)-(2) (West Supp. 1997).

46. 47 U.S.C.A. § 534(b)(1) West Supp.(1997); 47 C.F.R. § 76.56(b)(1)-(2) (1997). Usable activated channels are defined as "[t]hose activated channels of a cable system, except those channels whose use for the distribution of broadcast signals would conflict with technical and safety regulations [under Subpart K of Part 76 of the FCC's ruling]." 47 C.F.R. § 76.56 (b) (1997).

47. Id. § 534(b)(1)(A) (West Supp. 1997); 47 C.F.R. § 76.56(b)(1) (1997). Cable systems with 300 or fewer subscribers, are not subject to must carry requirements, as long as such systems do not delete any signal of a broadcast television station already being carried. Id.

48. Id. § 535(b)(2)(A); 47 C.F.R. § 76.56(a)(1)(i) (1997). In cases where a cable system with 12 or fewer activated channels operates beyond the presence of any qualified local noncommercial educational ("NCE") stations, the cable operator will import one qualified NCE station. 47 U.S.C.A. § 535(b)(2)(B)(i); 47 C.F.R. § 76.56(a)(2)(i) (1997).

49. Id. § 534(b)(1)(A); 47 C.F.R. § 76.56(b)(2) (1997).

50. Id. § 535(b)(3); 47 C.F.R. § 76.56(a)(1)(ii) (1997). A cable operator or a cable system with between 13 and 36 activated channels, that operates beyond the presence of any qualified local NCE station, will import at least one qualified NCE station. 47 U.S.C.A. § 535(b)(3)(B); 47 C.F.R. § 76.56(a)(2)(ii) (1997).

51. Id. § 534(b)(1)(B) Id.; 47 C.F.R. § 76.56(b)(2) (1997).

52. Id. § 535(b)(3)(D) Id.; 47 C.F.R. § 76.56(a)(1)(iii) (1997).

53. Id. at § 534(c)(1)(A) Id. at 47 C.F.R. § 76.56(b)(3) (1997). A "qualified low power station" is defined as "any television broadcast station conforming to the low power television rules contained in part 74 of this chapter," and meets identified requirements designated in 47 C.F.R. § 76.55(d)(1)-(6). 47 C.F.R. § 76.55(d) (1997).

54. Id. § 534(c)(1)(B) Id.; 47 C.F.R. § 76.56(b)(3) (1997).

55. Id. § 534(b)(2) Id.

56. Id. at § 534(b)(2)(A).

reference point ... is closest to the principal headend of the cable system."[57]

The 1992 Act also establishes requirements regarding content, quality, duplication and channel positioning. The cable operator is required to carry the programming of local commercial stations programming in their entirety unless carriage of a specific program is prohibited.[58] The signals of the local stations must be carried "without material degradation."[59] A cable operator is not required to carry a local commercial television station's signal if it "substantially duplicates" the signal of another local commercial television station which is already carried on the cable system.[60] While the cable operator is not required to carry the signals of more than one local commercial station affiliated with the same network,[61] if it chooses to carry stations whose signals are substantially duplicative or who are affiliated with the same network, "all such signals shall be counted toward the number of signals the operator is required to carry under the [must carry rules]."[62] Unless mutually agreed otherwise, the cable operator is required to carry the local commercial station's broadcast on the same channel as it is broadcast over the air or on the channel it was carried on as of July 19, 1985 or January 1, 1992.[63]

The 1992 Cable Act requires that every cable subscriber shall receive the must carry signals which means that the signals must be provided on the basic service tier.[64] If additional equipment is required to receive local signals but the cable operator does not provide such equipment, the cable operator will notify the subscriber that the broadcast stations cannot be viewed without the necessary equipment and shall sell or lease the equipment to the subscriber at rates in accordance with rate regulations.[65] In addition, a cable operator must provide, upon request, the identification of signals carried on its system.[66]

The 1992 Act specifically prohibits cable operators from accepting or requesting "monetary payment or other valuable consideration in exchange either for carriage of local commercial television stations" in fulfillment of the requirements or for the channel positioning rights provided under the Act.[67] A cable operator must provide written notifica-

---

57. *Id.* at § 534(b)(2)(B).

58. *Id.* at § 534(b)(3)(A)-(B).

59. *Id.* at § 534(b)(4)(A).

60. 47 U.S.C.A. § 534(b)(5) (West Supp. 1997); 47 C.F.R. § 76.56(b)(5) (1997). A station will be deemed to 'substantially duplicate' the programming of another station if it "regularly simultaneously broadcasts the identical programming as another station for more than 50 percent of the broadcast week." 47 C.F.R. § 76.56(b)(5) (1997).

61. *Id.*

62. *Id.* § 534(b)(5) (West Supp. 1997).

63. *Id.* § 534(b)(6); 47 C.F.R. § 76.57(a), (c) (1997). For noncommercial

stations, the cable operator must carry the broadcast on the same station that the NCE broadcast is carried over the air, or on the channel it was carried on as of July 19, 1985. 47 C.F.R. § 76.57(b) (1997).

64. *Id.* § 534(b)(7) (West Supp. 1997); 47 C.F.R. § 76.56(d)(1) (1997).

65. *Id.* § 534(b)(7); 47 C.F.R. § 76.56(d)(3) (1997).

66. *Id.* § 534(b)(8); 47 C.F.R. § 76.56(e) (1997).

67. *Id.* § 534(b)(10); 47 C.F.R. § 76.60 (1997). There are several exceptions to this provision which include allowing payment for the costs associated with delivering a

tion to a local commercial station at least thirty days before deleting that station or channel repositioning.[68] In addition, any deletion or repositioning cannot occur during sweeps weeks—the "period in which major television ratings services measure the size of audiences of local television stations."[69]

If a local commercial station or qualified low power station believes the cable operator has not complied with the must carry requirements, the local station must notify the operator in writing, explaining how the cable operator has not complied.[70] The cable operator is required to respond within thirty days of receipt of such written notification.[71] A station that is denied carriage may file a complaint with the FCC for review.[72] If the Commission determines that the cable operator has not complied with the carriage regulations, then it will order compliance within 45 days of the decision.[73] If the Commission determines the cable operator has complied with the regulations the complaint will be dismissed.[74]

(2) Requirements for Noncommercial Television Stations

As with commercial television stations, the number of local noncommercial educational television stations (NCE) a cable system is required to carry varies depending upon the number of "usable activated channels."[75] The Act requires that cable systems with 12 or fewer usable activated channels carry one noncommercial station.[76] Cable systems with thirteen to thirty-six usable activated channels are required to carry at least one but not more than three noncommercial stations.[77] Cable systems with greater than thirty-six usable activated channels are required to carry all nonduplicative noncommercial stations that request carriage.[78] "[H]owever, a cable system with more than thirty-six channels shall not be required to carry an additional qualified local NCE station whose programming substantially duplicates the programming of another qualified local NCE station being carried."[79]

good quality signal, payments from stations with distant signals, and payments from stations pursuant to a retransmission consent agreement. 47 C.F.R. § 76.60(a)-(c) (1997).

68. 47 U.S.C.A. § 534(b)(9) (West Supp. 1997); 47 C.F.R. § 76.58 (1997).

69. *Id.* § 534(b)(9); 47 C.F.R. § 76.58(a) (1997) (note).

70. *Id.* § 534(d)(1); 47 C.F.R. § 76.61(a)(1) (1997).

71. *Id.* § 534(d)(1); 47 C.F.R. § 76.61(a)(2) (1997).

72. *Id.* § 534(d)(1); 47 C.F.R. § 76.61(a)(3) (1997).

73. 47 C.F.R. § 76.61(a)(4) (1997).

74. *Id.* § 534(d)(3) (West Supp. 1997); 47 C.F.R. § 76.61(a)(4) (1997).

75. *Id.* § 535; 47 C.F.R. § 76.56(a) (1997).

76. *Id.* § 535(b)(2)(A); 47 C.F.R. § 76.56(a)(1)(i) (1997).

77. 47 U.S.C.A. § 535(b)(3); 47 C.F.R. § 76.56(a)(1)(ii) (1997). The cable operator of a cable system with between 13 and 36 activated channels, that operates beyond the presence of any qualified local NCE station, will import at least one qualified NCE station. 47 U.S.C.A.A. § 535(b)(3)(B); 47 C.F.R. § 76.56(a)(2)(ii) (1997).

78. *Id.* § 535(b)(3)(D); 47 C.F.R. § 76.56(a)(1)(iii) (1997).

79. *Id.* § 535(e). *See also* 47 C.F.R. § 76.56(a)(1)(iii) (1997). A noncommercial station "substantially duplicates" the programming of another station if it broadcasts the same programming, simultaneous or

If a cable system with up to twelve activated channels operates beyond the market presence of any qualified local NCE station, it must import one qualified NCE station.[80] A cable system with thirteen to thirty-six activated channels, which operates beyond the presence of any qualified local NCE stations, must import at least one qualified NCE station.[81] In the case of those cable stations that imported a NCE station as of March 29, 1990, the systems "shall continue to import such signal until such time as a qualified local NCE station is available."[82] A cable system with fewer than twelve activated channels is not required to remove any programming service provided to subscribers in order to satisfy the 1992 Cable Act requirements.[83] A cable system with thirteen to thirty-six activated channels is not required to carry more than one qualified NCE station affiliated with a state public television network, if the programming would be "substantially duplicative."[84] Furthermore, all cable operators must continue to provide carriage to all qualified local NCE stations whose signal was carried as of March 29, 1990.[85]

Just as with the requirements applicable to commercial broadcast stations, a cable operator must retransmit the entirety of the NCE broadcast without material degradation.[86] The channel position for NCE stations must be the same channel number on which the station is broadcast over the air, unless mutually agreed otherwise.[87] If a signal is repositioned the cable operator must provide the station and all subscribers with written notice.[88] The 1992 Act does not require cable operators to carry signals of any qualified local NCE which does not deliver a good quality signal or presents an increased copyright liability to the cable system.[89]

Signals carried by a cable systems operator in fulfillment of the must carry rules must be made available to all subscribers as part of the "lowest priced service tier that includes the retransmission of local commercial television broadcast signals."[90] A cable operator must identify all the signals carried upon request of any person.[91] As in the commercial station provisions, "[a] cable operator shall not accept monetary payment or other valuable consideration in exchange for carriage of

non-simultaneous, for more than 50 percent outside of prime time over a three-month period. 47 C.F.R. § 76.56(a)(1)(iii) (1997)(note).

80. 47 U.S.C.A. § 535(b)(2)(A) (West Supp. 1997); 47 C.F.R. § 76.56(a)(2)(i) (1997).

81. *Id.* § 535(b)(3)(B); 47 C.F.R. § 76.56(a)(2)(ii) (1997).

82. *Id.* § 535(b)(3)(B); 47 C.F.R. § 76.56(a)(5) (1997).

83. *Id.* § 535(b)(2)(B)(iii); 47 C.F.R. § 76.56(a)(3) (1997).

84. *Id.* § 535(b)(3)(C); 47 C.F.R. § 76.56(a)(4) (1997).

85. *Id.* § 535(c); 47 C.F.R. § 76.56(a)(5) (1997).

86. *Id.* § 535(g)(1)-(2) (West Supp. 1997); 47 C.F.R. § 76.62 (a)-(b) (1997).

87. 47 U.S.C.A. § 535(g)(5); 47 C.F.R. § 76.57(b) (1997).

88. *Id.* § 535(g)(3); 47 C.F.R. § 76.58(a) (1997). Written notice must be at least 60 days prior to any change in designation of its principal headend. 47 C.F.R. § 76.58(c) (1997).

89. *Id.* § 535(g)(4) (West Supp. 1997); 47 C.F.R. § 76.58(d)(1)-(2) (1997).

90. *Id.* § 535(h); 47 C.F.R. § 76.56(d)(2) (1997).

91. *Id.* § 535(k); 47 C.F.R. § 76.56(e) (1997).

the signal of any qualified local noncommercial educational television station," carried to fulfill the requirements of this Act, except if the payment is associated with delivering a good quality signal.[92]

If a NCE station believes a cable operator has failed to comply with the signal carriage requirements, then the station can file a complaint directly with the Commission.[93] The complaint must explain how the cable operator has failed to comply and state the basis for such allegations.[94] The law requires Commission action within 120 days after the complaint is filed.[95]

(3) Determining Qualified Stations and Broadcast Markets

The Cable Act must carry rights for television stations in the same local television market as the cable operator, as initially defined by Arbitron's areas of dominant influence ("ADI") but eventually as measured by Nielsen's designated market areas (DMAs').[96] There are two exceptions to this carriage requirement: first, a local commercial broadcaster that is considered to be a "distant signal" under the Copyright Act does not qualify for carriage unless it agrees to indemnify the cable operator for any increased copyright liability.[97] Second, a local broadcast station is ineligible for must carry unless it delivers a good quality signal to the principal headend of the cable system.[98] However, the broadcaster may qualify for carriage if it bears the cost associated with delivering a good quality signal by such means as improved antennas, increased tower height or microwave relay equipment.[99]

The market designations in the FCC must carry rules are effective for periods of three years, coinciding with broadcasters' must-carry elections, beginning in 1993. A broadcaster is considered local in each county listed in its ADI.[100] If a cable system serves more than one county, then it must carry all local commercial broadcasters in its home counties, even if they are assigned to different ADIs.[1]

92. 47 U.S.C.A. § 535(i)(1); 47 C.F.R. § 76.60 (1997).

93. *Id.* § 535(j)(1); 47 C.F.R. § 76.61(b)(1) (1997).

94. *Id.*

95. *Id.* § 535(j)(3) (West Supp. 1997).

96. *Id.* § 534(h)(1)(c). The FCC's rules provided that ADIs, as defined in Arbitron's 1991–1992 Television Market Guide, should be used for initial implementation of must carry rules. The Commission later switched to Nielsen's DMAs for must carry–retransmission consent elections. See Definition of Markets for Purposes of the Cable Television Broadcast Signal Carriage Rules, 11 FCC Rcd. 6201 (1996). However, the FCC postponed the switch to DMAs until October 1, 1999 and continued to use the 1991–1992 ADIs for the 1996 must carry election.

97. 47 U.S.C.A. § 534(h)(1)(B)(ii) West Supp. 1997.

98. *Id.* § 534(h)(1)(B)(iii). The broadcast signal must register a signal level of–45dBm for UHF signals and 49dBm for VHF signals at the input terminal of the signal processing equipment.

99. 47 C.F.R. § 76.55(c)(3) (1997).

100. *Id.* § 76.55(e). Stations also are considered local in their home counties even if the county is in a different ADI. Alaska and Hawaii stations use Nielsen's Designated Market Areas ("DMAs"), instead of the ADI.

1. This obligation may be limited by the total must-carry requirement or the "substantial duplication" and "network affiliation" restrictions. *See* 47 U.S.C.A. § 534(b)(5) (West Supp. 1997) (cable operator need not carry a broadcast station that

The Cable Act permits cable operators or broadcasters to request modification of the local market designation from the FCC.[2] Any such request for special relief must provide relevant evidence that the local market differs from that designated by the rules. This may include the station's signal coverage area, historic carriage of the station and the station's connection to the community (local viewing patterns or coverage of community events).

c. Retransmission Consent

Under the 1992 Cable Act, no cable system operator can retransmit the signal of a broadcast station without the consent of the station or unless it is transmitted as a must carry signal.[3] The law includes four exceptions: (1) retransmission of noncommercial broadcasting station; (2) retransmission of a signal directly to a home satellite antenna of a broadcasting station that is not owned, operated, or affiliated with a broadcasting network; (3) retransmission of a signal of a broadcasting station that is owned, operated, or affiliated with a broadcasting network directly to a home satellite antenna of an unserved household; (4) a cable operator's retransmission of a superstation's signal that was obtained from a satellite carrier, if the originating signal was a superstation on May 1, 1991.[4]

The regulations require that the television stations make an election every three years between the right of retransmission consent and the right of signal carriage under the must carry rules.[5] Those stations that fail to make an election by the deadline are deemed to have elected must carry status for the subsequent three-year period.[6] New stations must make their election during a 90–day window, beginning sixty days before commencing broadcast and ending thirty days after commencing service.[7] The election takes effect ninety days after notifying the cable operator of the choice.[8] Television stations that subsequently become eligible for must carry status must make their election within thirty days of the effective date of their new eligibility.[9]

"substantially duplicates" the signal of another local station already carried); 47 C.F.R. § 76.55(f) (1997) (cable operator need not carry more than one network affiliate licensed to its home market).

2. 47 U.S.C.A. § 534(h)(1)(C); 47 C.F.R. § 76.59 (1997).

3. *Id.* § 325(b) (West Supp. 1997); 47 C.F.R. § 76.64 (1997).

4. *Id.* § 325(b)(2); 47 C.F.R. § 76.64(b) (1997).

5. *Id.* § 325(b)(3)(B); 47 C.F.R. § 76.64(f) (1997). Broadcasters made their first such election by June 17, 1993 and their second election by October 1, 1996. 47 C.F.R. § 76.64(f)(1)-(2). *See* Implementation of the Cable Television Consumer Protection and Competition Act of 1992: Broadcast Signal Carriage Issues Recommendation of the Effective Competition Standard for the Regulation of Cable Television Basic Service Rates, Report and Order, 8 FCC Rcd at 3002 (1993). The second election became effective January 1, 1997. Subsequent election dates are October 1999, taking effect on January 1, 2000 and continuing at three year intervals. 47 C.F.R. § 76.6(f)(2) (1997).

6. 47 C.F.R. § 76.64(f)(3) (1997).

7. *Id.* § 76.64(f)(4).

8. *Id.*

9. *Id.* § 76.64(f)(5). Carriage is required ninety days after must carry is elected.

Once a station has elected either retransmission or must carry status, the television station must place copies of the decision in its public file and send notification to the cable operator.[10] Retransmission consent agreements must be in writing and must specify whether the consent is for transmission of all or part of a signal.[11] Exclusive retransmission consent agreements are not permitted.[12]

2. PEG Access Channels

Section 611 of the 1984 Cable Act empowers local franchising authorities to establish rules and procedures designating channel capacity for public, educational, or governmental ("PEG") use.[13] This provision reflected the fact that almost all of the franchise agreements at the time the 1984 Cable Act was adopted provided for access by local governments, schools, and non-profit and community groups on "PEG" channels. Such requirements are implemented and enforced by local cable franchising agreements, not by federal rule.

Not all cable franchises require PEG channels. Also, because they are regulated locally, it is difficult to generalize when describing such channels. Nevertheless, it is typical that "public" channels are those available for use by members of the general public on a first-come, first-served nondiscriminatory basis; educational channels are those available for use by local educational authorities and institutions; and "government" channels are those available for use by municipal and state government institutions.[14]

Where PEG channel capacity provided in a franchise is underused, the 1984 Cable Act provides that the cable operator should be permitted to utilize those channels for commercial services.[15] Section 611(d) of the Act directs franchising authorities to prescribe rules and procedures for the use of unused PEG channel capacity by the cable operator.[16] The 1992 Cable Act adds specific circumstances whereby unused PEG capacity can be used, including the carriage of must-carry non-commercial stations and, in limited circumstances, carriage of qualifying low-power must-carry stations.[17]

In *Time Warner Entertainment Co. v. FCC,*[18] the court upheld the facial validity of statutory PEG access channel provisions under interme-

---

10. *Id.* § 76.64(h).

11. *Id.* § 76.64(k).

12. *Id.* § 76.64(m).

13. Cable Communications Policy Act of 1984, Pub. L. 98–549, § 611, 98 Stat. 2782, (1984) *codified at* 47 U.S.C.A. § 531 (West 1991 & Supp. 1997).

14. *See* Time Warner Cable v. City of New York, 943 F.Supp. 1357, 1372 n. 11 (S.D.N.Y.1996) *aff'd* Time Warner Cable v. Bloomberg, L. P., 118 F.3d 917, 929 (2d Cir.1997); Berkshire Cablevision of Rhode Island v. Burke, 571 F.Supp. 976, 980 (D.R.I.1983), *vacated as moot,* 773 F.2d 382, 385 (1st. Cir.1985).

15. Cable Communications Policy Act of 1984, Pub. L. 98–549, § 611(d), 98 Stat. 2779, 2782 (1984) *codified at* 47 U.S.C.A. § 531(d) (West 1991 & Supp. 1997).

16. *Id.*

17. Cable Television Consumer Protection and Competition Act of 1992, Pub. L. 102–385, § 614(c)(2), 106 Stat. 1460, 1447 (1992) *codified at* 47 U.S.C.A. § 534(c)(2) (1994) (West Supp. 1997). The franchising authority's approval is required for such uses.

18. 93 F.3d 957, 320 U.S. App. D.C. 294 (D.C.Cir.1996). *See also* Telesat Cablevision, Inc. v. City of Riviera Beach, 773 F.Supp. 383, 411–13 (S.D.Fla.1991).

diate constitutional review. The Court declined to hold that the law was facially invalid because Time Warner did not prove that local access requirements would be unconstitutional in every instance. Although the Court conceded that it could "imagine PEG franchise conditions that would raise serious constitutional issues," it also could imagine circumstances in which local requirements serve an important purpose unrelated to the suppression of free expression and are narrowly tailored.[19] The Court expressed no view on the constitutionality of particular local PEG requirements.

In another case involving Time Warner, the company challenged a decision by the City of New York to place a competing news service on public access channels.[20] Time Warner filed for declaratory and injunctive relief alleging violation of its First Amendment rights.[21] The dispute arose from contract negotiations between Time Warner and Fox for the carriage of the Fox News Service on the New York City cable system.[22] After negotiations with Fox broke down during consummation of the Time Warner–Turner Broadcasting System merger, the City of New York announced that it would provide carriage for the Fox News Service and another news service by Bloomberg, L.P. on governmental and municipal channels.[23] The district court held that the City's decision was a content-based effort designed to punish Time Warner for its exercise of editorial discretion.[24] The court applied strict scrutiny and found that the City's actions violated the First Amendment.[25] The decision was upheld on appeal by the United States Court of Appeals for the Second Circuit, although the court did not reach the constitutional issue.[26] Rather, it held that an injunction was justified because the City's actions were inconsistent with the Cable Act and breached the franchise agreements.[27]

3. *Leased Access Channels*

Congress established the structure for commercial leased access in Section 612 of the 1984 Cable Act by requiring cable operators to make available between ten and fifteen percent of their channels for lease to unaffiliated programmers.[28] The Act requires that channels be set aside for "commercial use by persons unaffiliated with the [cable] operator," generally prohibits editorial control by the cable operator, and establishes FCC jurisdiction over channel pricing.[29] The statutory purpose is "to assure that the widest possible diversity of information sources are

---

19. *Id.* at 973, 320 U.S. App. D.C. at 310.

20. Time Warner Cable, 943 F. Supp. at 1364.

21. *Id.* at 1399–40.

22. *Id.* at 1378–79.

23. *Id.* at 1364.

24. *Id.* at 1400.

25. Time Warner Cable v. City of New York, 943 F.Supp. 1357, 1400–1402 (S.D.N.Y.1996).

26. Time Warner Cable v. Bloomberg L.P., 118 F.3d 917 (2d Cir.1997).

27. *Id.* at 919–20.

28. Cable Communications Policy Act of 1984, Pub. L. 98–549, § 612, 98 Stat. 2779, 2782 (1984) *codified as amended at* 47 U.S.C.A. § 532(b) (West 1991 & Supp. 1997).

29. *Id.*

made available to the public from cable systems in a manner consistent with growth and development of cable systems."[30]

The amount of channel capacity that must be set aside depends on system capacity. An operator with 36 or more, but less than 55 activated channels, must designate ten percent of capacity for leased access.[31] An operator with 55 to 100 channels is required to set aside 15 percent of activated channels, while a cable operator with more than 100 channels must designate 15 percent of all channels.[32] The Act permits cable operators to continue using unused capacity otherwise designated for leased access until an unaffiliated entity enters a contract for its use.[33]

With certain exceptions, cable operators are prohibited from exercising editorial control over video programming on leased access channels.[34] As described in greater detail later in this chapter, a cable operator may adopt a policy against carriage of leased access programming considered to be indecent. Additionally, a cable operator may use up to one-third of the channel capacity otherwise designated for leased access for carriage of programming "from a qualified minority programming source or from any qualified educational programming source."[35] Otherwise, a cable operator cannot consider the content of the leased access provider except "to the minimum extent necessary to establish a reasonable price for the commercial use of designated channel capacity."[36]

The 1984 Act also directed cable operators to set "the price, terms, and conditions of such use which are at least sufficient to ensure that such use will not adversely affect the operation, financial condition, or market development of the cable system."[37] In particular, section 612 was intended to counter a cable operator's incentive to keep opposing social or political viewpoints off the system, or to block competing

30. *Id.* § 532(a).

31. *Id.* § 532(b)(1)(A) (West 1991). However, an operator with less than 36 channels is not required to set aside leased access capacity unless the franchise in effect on October 30, 1984 required leased channels. *Id.* § 532(b)(1)(D). "Activated channels" are defined as those channels engineered at the cable system's headend for the provision of services generally available to residential subscribers, regardless of whether the channels are actually provided. *Id.* § 532(b)(5)(A) (West 1991). *See* Sierra East Television, Inc. v. Weststar Cable Television, Inc., 776 F.Supp. 1405 (E.D.Cal. 1991) (equipment must actually be in place at cable headend for channel to be considered "activated," and channel service must be available throughout the cable system); Media Ranch, Inc. v. Manhattan Cable Television, Inc., 757 F.Supp. 310 (S.D.N.Y. 1991).

32. 47 U.S.C.A. § 532(b)(1)(B)-(C) (West 1991).

33. *Id.* § 532(b)(4).

34. *Id.* § 532(c)(2).

35. *Id.* § 532(i)(1) (West Supp. 1997). A "qualified minority programming source" must devote substantially all of its programming coverage to minority viewpoints or to members of minority groups, and must be more than 50 percent minority owned. *Id.* § 532(i)(2). A "qualified educational programming source" must devote substantially all of its programming to educational or instructional programming that promotes public understanding of mathematics, the sciences, the humanities and the arts and has a documented annual programming expenditure of $15 million. *Id.* § 532(i)(3). This reservation does not apply to minority or educational programming sources that were carried on the cable system as of July 1, 1990. *Id.* § 532(i)(1).

36. *Id.* § 532(c)(2).

37. Cable Communications Policy Act, Pub. L. 98–549, § 612(c)(1), 98 Stat. 2779, 2783 (1984) *codified as amended at* 47 U.S.C.A. § 532(2) (West 1991 & Supp. 1997).

program services. However, the low rate of leased access channel usage led Congress in 1992 to amend section 612.[38] The 1992 Cable Act empowered the FCC to set maximum reasonable rates for leased access programming. The FCC adopted new rate regulations for leased access channels in 1993, but the overall level of leased access usage did not markedly increase.[39]

As a result, the FCC in 1997 revised the rules and established a new formula for setting the maximum reasonable leased access rate.[40] To replace the previous formula, the FCC adopted a new rule based on what it called the "average implicit fee."[41] The "implicit fee" represents the average amount of subscriber revenue that programmers cede to the operator to permit the operator to cover costs and earn a profit.[42] For example, if a subscriber pays an average of fifty cents per channel for a particular tier, and the average programming or license fee for that tier is ten cents, then programmers on the tier are implicitly "paying" the operator forty cents for carriage. The new formula effectively lowered leased access rates because it was based on the "average" fee for channels with greater than 50 percent penetration, rather than a "highest implicit fee" as under the FCC's original rule. However, the FCC retained the highest implicit fee approach for channels sold on a per program or á la carte basis to the subscriber. But on such channels, any subscriber revenue from an á la carte leased access service must be passed through to the leased access programmer.[43]

The Commission also refined its rules governing the provision of leased access channels. For example, it affirmed its previous rule requiring cable operators to lease time in half-hour increments even though such part-time arrangements are not expressly required by the Cable Act. The FCC also reaffirmed its policy that a cable operator is not required to open additional leased access capacity if a programmer's request can be accommodated "in a comparable time slot" on an existing leased channel. What kind of time is "comparable" will be determined by "objective factors" such as day of the week, time of day and audience share. Even if a cable operator has unused capacity, it is not required to open a new leased access channel if comparable time can be made available on an existing channel.

Cable operators are not required to open an additional channel for part-time leased access until existing part-time channels are substantially filled. For purposes of the rule, the Commission considers a channel "substantially filled" with leased access programming if leased access

---

38. *Id.*

39. Implementation of Section of the Cable Television Consumer Protection and Competition Act of 1992 Rate Regulation, Report and Order and Further Notice of Proposed Rulemaking, 8 FCC Rcd. 5631 (1993).

40. Implementation of Sections of the Cable Television Consumer Protection and

Competition Act of 1992, Leased Commercial Access, Second Report and Order and Second Order on Recons.of the First Report and Order, 12 FCC Rcd. 5267 (1997).

41. *Id.* at para. 33.

42. *Id.*

43. *Id.*

programming occupies 75% or more of its programming day. This means that an operator need open a new channel only if its existing leased access channel is transmitting 18 hours of programming per day. Additionally, a cable operator is required to open a new part-time channel if a programmer (or collective) agrees to provide programming for a minimum eight continuous hours every day for at least one year.

The Commission set the response time for leased access requests at 15 calendar days from the time the programmer makes a written request. All requests must be made in writing and specify the date that they are sent to the operator. Small systems have 30 days to provide the required information. In response to such a request, an operator must provide a complete schedule of the operator's full-time and part-time leased access rates, how much of the cable operator's leased access set-aside capacity is available, rates associated with technical and studio costs and, if specifically requested, a sample leased access contract.

The United States Court of Appeals for the District of Columbia Circuit upheld the FCC's revised lease access rules in *ValueVision Int'l, Inc. v. FCC*.[44] Petitioners, which included low power broadcast stations, home shopping stations and various public interest advocacy groups, contended that the FCC had shown "too much concern for the financial health of cable operators and too little concern for the ability of programmers to afford leased access."[45] But the court found that the FCC adequately reconciled the statutory purpose of promoting leased access without economically burdening cable operators. Congress anticipated that leased access might not be economically viable, according to the court, and did not intend for cable operators to subsidize leased access programmers.[46]

In other cases, cable operators have mounted constitutional challenges to the statutory leased access requirements but without success. For example, the United States Court of Appeals for the District of Columbia Circuit rejected a facial First Amendment challenge to leased access requirements in *Time Warner Entertainment Co. v. FCC*.[47] With respect to leased access obligations, the Court noted that the generally low usage of such channels indicated a lack of any real First Amendment harm.[48] It stressed, however, that it was dealing only with the facial validity of leased access provisions and noted that a cable operator may challenge the rules "as applied" if the level of channel usage increases.[49]

4. Network Nonduplication and Syndicated Exclusivity Rules

FCC rules give local broadcasters the right to demand that cable operators delete certain duplicate programming where the broadcaster

---

44. 149 F.3d 1204, 331 U.S.App.D.C. 331 (D.C.Cir.1998).

45. *Id.* at 1208, 331 U.S.App.D.C. at 335.

46. *Id.* at 1209, 331 U.S.App.D.C. at 336.

47. 93 F.3d 957, 320 U.S. App. D.C. 294 (D.C.Cir.1996).

48. *Id.* at 971, 320 U.S. App. D.C. at 308.

49. *Id.* at 971 n.4, 320 U.S. App. D.C. at 308 n.4.

has retained contractual exclusivity in a specified geographic area.[50] Generally, the network non-duplication rules relate to programming that is delivered simultaneously to broadcast station groups, while syndicated exclusivity rules apply to non-network programming that is made available in more than one market.

Under the network non-duplication rules, network affiliates may request exclusivity protection within specified zones.[51] Protection for stations in larger markets is given priority over those in smaller broadcasting markets.[52] Somewhat anachronistically, the rules define "network" as "one of the three major national television networks [ABC, CBS, NBC] with which it has a primary affiliation."[53] Where the rules apply, the cable operator must block out duplicative network programming even if it is not aired simultaneously.[54] To claim such protection, broadcasters must provide notice of their request for non-duplication protection within 60 days of signing a new affiliation agreement.[55]

The FCC has created a number of exceptions to the network non-duplication rules. Such protection need not be provided in cable systems with fewer than 1000 subscribers, where the duplicated programming is in a different language, for network programming aired within one hour following a live sports event or for network programming aired on a station that has a lower priority of exclusivity protection.[56] Additionally, programming need not be deleted on local stations considered "significantly viewed."[57] FCC rules prescribe the reference points for identifying major and smaller television markets.[58]

Commercial television broadcasters and programming distributors may seek non-duplication protection under the syndicated exclusivity rules.[59] To claim protection, the broadcaster or programming distributor must have a valid contract that specifically grants syndicated exclusivity protection. For contracts signed after August 18, 1988, the rules specify the language necessary to invoke protection.[60]

---

50.   47 C.F.R. §§ 76.97, 76.163 (1997).

51. Major market network affiliates may claim protection within a 35–mile zone that includes the cable community. *Id.* § 76.92(b)-(c). Smaller market affiliates may claim protection within a 55–mile zone. Translator stations (which duplicate the programming of a primary station) may also claim protection under certain conditions. *Id.* § 76.92(d)-(e).

52.   *Id.* § 76.92(b).

53.   *Id.* § 76.5(j).

54.   *Id.* § 76.92(a).

55.   *Id.* § 76.94(b).

56.   *Id.* § 76.94(b) (1997). For example, where a major market broadcaster is also located within the zone of protection for a smaller market broadcaster, exclusivity need not be provided. *Id.* § 76.54. Nor must the cable operator delete programming

from a translator station that is licensed to the cable community. *Id.* § 76.92(d).

57.   *Id.* § 76.54. Stations considered significantly viewed are determined by FCC surveys conducted in the 1970s. As an alternative, a broadcast station may establish its status as being significantly viewed by an independent professional audience survey of non-cable television homes as prescribed by FCC rules. *Id.*

58.   *Id.* § 76.53. Major television markets are listed in the Commission's rules. *Id.* § 76.51.

59.   *Id.* § 76.153. Low power stations, non-commercial broadcasters and translator stations are not entitled to protection.

60.   *Id.* § 76.159. The contract must state either "the licensee shall, by the terms of this contract, be entitled to invoke the protection against duplication of pro-

Where syndicated exclusivity protection exists, the cable operator must delete protected programming within a specified geographic zone.[61] The size of the zone is generally prescribed by contract, although FCC rules prohibit its extension beyond 35 miles.[62] Program distributors, on the other hand may exert exclusivity nationwide except in areas where the program has already been licensed.[63] Exclusivity for distributors is limited to a one year period.[64] As with network non-duplication rules, those seeking protection must notify cable operators of their request within 60 days of signing a contract.[65] Exceptions for syndicated exclusivity are somewhat more limited than for network non-duplication. The rules do not apply to cable systems with less than 1000 subscribers or to a second local station that carries the syndicated programming.[66]

5. Sports "Blackout" Rules

FCC rules prohibit cable television carriage, via distant television broadcast signals, of live sports events which are played locally but which are not made available for local conventional television broadcast.[67] The rule is based on the concept that owners of television rights to sporting events often limit local telecast in the belief that such coverage depresses ticket sales. Broadcasts outside the local market were permitted because no such effect on ticket sales was perceived. This changed with the advent of cable television, where distant signals—along with the telecast of sporting events—could be imported into the market.[68]

The FCC's sports blackout rule permits owners of television rights to distribute sports programming in distant markets while precluding local broadcasts. Under the rules, no cable operator located within the specified zone of a television station licensed to a community in which the sporting event is taking place may carry the live television broadcast of the event upon the request of the rights holder.[69] The rule does not apply if the event is being carried on a television station license whose Grade B signal covers the local community.[70] Communities with less than

---

gramming imported under the Compulsory Copyright License, as provided in Section 76.151 of the FCC rules," or "the licensee shall, by the terms of this contract, be entitled to invoke the protection against duplication of programming imported under the Compulsory Copyright License, as provided in the FCC's syndicated exclusivity rules." *Id.*

61. 47 C.F.R. § 76.151 (1997).

62. *Id.* §§ 76.151, 73.658.

63. *Id.* § 73.658(e).

64. *Id.* § 76.153(b).

65. *Id.* § 76.155(b).

66. *Id.* § 76.156(a)-(b).

67. *Id.* § 76.67.

68. Cable Television Systems and the Carriage of Sports Programs on Cable Television Systems, Mem. Op. and Order, 56

F.C.C.2d 561 (1975); Amendment of Part 76 of the Commission's Rules and Regulations Relative to Cable Television Systems and the Carriage of Sports Programs on Cable Television Systems, Report and Order, 54 F.C.C. 2d 265 (1975).

69. 47 C.F.R. § 76.67(a) (1997).

70. If no television station is licensed to the community in which the sports event takes place, then the specified zone is that of the television station licensed to the community with which the sports event or team is identified. If the local team is not identified with a particular community, then the specified zone is based on the nearest community to which a television station is licensed. *Id.*

1,000 cable subscribers are exempt from the rule.[71]

To take advantage of the rule, the owner of television rights must provide advance notice to the cable operator of events to be deleted.[72] For non-regularly scheduled events, or if an earlier event is rescheduled, notice must be provided within 24 hours after the time of the event is known and in no case less than 24 hours prior to the event.[73] A special exemption to sports blackout requirements applies to National Football League games that have been sold out before the broadcast. The NFL agreed to allow carriage of home market games sold out 72 hours in advance of the starting time of the game.[74] In such circumstances, the cable operator is obligated to determine whether the game has been sold out, since such information is widely available.[75]

In the 1992 Cable Act, Congress directed the FCC to study the effect of the migration of sports programming from broadcast to cable television.[76] The Commission was directed to determine "the extent to which preclusive contracts between college athletic conferences and video programming vendors have artificially and unfairly restricted the supply of sporting events of local colleges for broadcast on local television stations," as well as the "economic causes and the economic and social consequences" of such migration.[77] In an interim report, the FCC found slight evidence of migration.[78] Accordingly, the Commission did not recommend any changes in policies regarding sports migration.[79]

B. Federal Regulation of Programming Content

1. Restrictions on Indecency

a. Direct Regulation of Programming

The FCC and local governments generally have far less authority to regulate indecency on cable television compared to over-the-air broadcasting. As a general proposition, the Supreme Court has rejected the application to cable of the lesser constitutional protections reserved for broadcasters. In *Turner Broadcasting System v. FCC*,[80] the Court stated categorically that "the rationale for applying a less rigorous standard of First Amendment scrutiny to broadcast regulation, whatever its validity in the cases elaborating it, does not apply in the context of cable regulation." Applying much the same reasoning, various courts have

---

71. *Id.* § 76.67(f).

72. For regularly scheduled events, notice must be given no later than the Monday preceding the calendar week of the event. *Id.* § 76.67(c).

73. *Id.*

74. Single Notice Provision of Sports Program Deletion Rule Affirmed, Public Notice, 61 F.C.C.2d 455 (1976).

75. *Id.* at 456.

76. Cable Television Consumer Protection and Competition Act of 1992, Pub. L. 102–385, § 26, 106 Stat 1460, 1502–03

(1992) *codified as amended at* 47 U.S.C.A. § 521 (West 1991 & Supp. 1997).

77. *See* Implementation of Section 26 of the Cable Television Consumer Protection and Competition Act of 1992, Final Report, 9 FCC Rcd. 3440 (1994) (citation omitted).

78. *Id.*

79. *Id.* at 3512.

80. 512 U.S. 622, 637, 114 S.Ct. 2445, 2456, 129 L.Ed.2d 497, 514 (1994).

invalidated efforts to directly regulate indecent speech on cable television, citing the fundamental differences between the two technologies.[81]

These earlier cases found that none of the special characteristics cited in *FCC v. Pacifica Foundation*,[82] pertained to cable television. First, they found that the physical scarcity of spectrum that justified more intrusive regulation of broadcasting—including content regulation—"is not present" in the cable medium.[83] Second, earlier cases indicated that cable television does not have a pervasive presence in the same way as broadcasting. Cable television is not an "uninvited intruder."[84] Rather, a subscriber "must make the affirmative decision to bring [cable] into his home."[85] Additionally, a subscriber must make the additional decision about whether to subscribe to premium services, such as Playboy Television or HBO.[86] Moreover, the subscriber may discontinue the service at any time. Courts have noted that "there is no possibility that a non-cable subscriber will be confronted with materials carried only on cable."[87] Third, courts have found that cable services are not uniquely available to children because of the availability of "lockboxes," as required by the 1984 Cable Act.[88] Additionally, program guides provide viewers with sufficient warnings to protect them from unexpected or unwanted exposure to offensive programming.[89]

These conclusions are not as firm in the wake of the Supreme Court's decision in *Denver Area Educational Telecommunications Consortium v. FCC*,[90] in which a plurality of the Court found that cable television is a "pervasive" medium that is as accessible to children as over-the-air broadcasting. In that case, however, the Court upheld regulations that permit cable operators to use their own editorial judgment to carry, or not carry, indecent programs on leased access channels. The Court struck down a similar provision relating to public access channels as well as a requirement that indecent programs on leased channels be

81. Community Television of Utah, Inc. v. Wilkinson, 611 F.Supp. 1099 (D.C.Utah 1985), *aff'd sub nom.* Jones v. Wilkinson, 800 F.2d 989 (10th Cir.1986), *aff'd mem.* 480 U.S. 926, 107 S.Ct. 1559, 94 L.Ed.2d 753 (1987); Cruz v. Ferre, 755 F.2d 1415 (11th Cir.1985); Community Television of Utah, Inc. v. Roy City, 555 F.Supp. 1164 (D.Utah 1982); Home Box Office, Inc. v. Wilkinson, 531 F.Supp. 987 (D.Utah 1982).

82. 438 U.S. 726, 98 S.Ct. 3026, 57 L.Ed.2d 1073 (1978).

83. *Wilkinson*, 611 F. Supp. at 1112.

84. *Id.* at 1113.

85. *Cruz*, 755 F.2d at 1419.

86. *Id.* at 1420.

87. *Id.* Alliance for Community Media, 56 F.3d 105, 139, 312 U.S. App. D.C. 141, 175 (D.C.Cir.1995), *aff'd in part, rev'd in part*, 518 U.S. 727, 116 S.Ct. 2374, 135

L.Ed.2d 888 (1996) (Wald, J., dissenting) ("Subscribers not only consent to, but must affirmatively request cable service."). *See also* Action for Children's Television v. FCC, 58 F.3d 654, 660, 313 U.S. App. D.C. 94, 99 (D.C.Cir.1995) ("Unlike cable subscribers, who are offered such options as 'pay-per-view' channels, broadcast audiences have no choice but to 'subscribe' to the entire output of traditional broadcasters.").

88. Section 544(d)(2) of the Act requires cable operators to provide lockboxes that enable subscribers to block out specified channels. 47 U.S.C.A. § 544(d)(2) (West 1991 & Supp. 1997). *See* Cruz, 755 F.2d at 1420–21; Community Television of Utah, Inc., 611 F.Supp. at 1113–14.

89. Cruz, 755 F.2d at 1420; Wilkinson, 611 F. Supp. at 1114.

90. 518 U.S. 727, 748, 116 S.Ct. 2374, 2388, 135 L.Ed.2d 888, 906 (1996).

blocked and segregated onto a separate channel.[91] Given this mixed holding, it is not yet clear how the Court will evaluate a more direct regulation of indecency on cable television. Nevertheless, the Court in *Denver* invalidated indecency regulations for cable television that would likely have been upheld in the broadcasting context.

b. *Indirect Regulation of Access Channels*

As the discussion above suggests, the 1992 Cable Act introduced new First Amendment questions with respect to regulation of indecency on cable television.[92] Section 10(a) of that Act permitted cable operators to refuse to carry indecent programming on leased access channels.[93] In other respects, cable operators were prohibited from exerting editorial control over the content of programming on leased access channels. Pursuant to Section 10(b), any operator that permitted indecent programming on leased channels was required to segregate the programming on a separate channel, access to which was blocked in advance.[94] Access to such channels would be provided to subscribers only upon written request.[95] Similarly, Section 10(c) required the FCC to adopt regulations enabling cable operators to prohibit the use of public access channels for "any programming which contains obscene material, sexually explicit conduct, or materials soliciting or promoting unlawful conduct."[96]

The District of Columbia Circuit, sitting *en banc* upheld the legislation in *Alliance for Community Media v. FCC*.[97] Although the Court compared leased access channels to broadcast services in terms of their wide availability, it did not conclude that the government may constitutionally regulate the content of cable services. Instead, the Court found that the law served only to restore a measure of editorial discretion to cable operators by allowing them to control, to a greater degree than previously, leased and public access channels, and that the rules lacked state action necessary to support a constitutional challenge.[98] Indeed, the court stressed that "[i]f decisions of cable operators not to carry indecent programs on leased or PEG access channels ... were treated as decisions of the government, the Commission and the United States would be hard put to defend the constitutionality of these provisions."[99] In another case, a United States District Court stayed the operation of the access rules on indecency in New York.[100] The court found that a requirement

---

91. 518 U.S. at 730, 116 S. Ct. at 2379, 135 L. Ed. 2d at 892.

92. Cable Television Consumer Protection and Competition Act of 1992, Pub. L. 102–385, § 10, 106 Stat. 1460, 1484 (1992) *codified as amended at* 47 U.S.C.A. § 532(h) (West 1991 & Supp. 1997).

93. 47 U.S.C.A. § 532(h) (West 1991 & Supp. 1997).

94. *Id.* § 532(i).

95. *Id.* § 532(j).

96. *Id.* § 531. "Historical and Statutory Notes."

97. 56 F.3d 105, 312 U.S. App. D.C. 141 (D.C.Cir.1995) (en banc), *aff'd in part, rev'd in part*, sub nom. Denver Area Educ. Telecom. Consortium v. FCC, 518 U.S. 727, 116 S.Ct. 2374, 135 L.Ed.2d 888 (1996).

98. *Id.* at 110–13, 312 U.S. App. D.C. at 146–49.

99. *Id.* at 113, 312 U.S. App. D.C. at 148.

100. Goldstein v. Manhattan Cable Television, Inc., 916 F.Supp. 262 (S.D.N.Y. 1995).

that indecent access programming be scrambled and blocked, constituted a potential burden on First Amendment rights.[1] The district court concluded that requiring a written request from subscribers would significantly deter access to protected speech.[2]

In *Denver Area Educational Telecommunications Consortium, Inc. v. FCC*, the Supreme Court reversed in part the District of Columbia Circuit's *Alliance* decision and invalidated significant portions of Section 10. The Court struck down Sections 10(b) and 10(c) of the 1992 Cable Act which required a written request from subscribers before they could have access to indecent communications on cable leased access channels and which permitted operators to ban indecency on public access channels. However, the court upheld Section 10(a) of the Act which restored cable operators' editorial discretion to ban indecent programming on leased access channels.[3]

The Court's long and complex decision is divided among six opinions. In general, the decision appeared to extend broadcast-type indecency regulation to cable television—something the Court previously had refused to do—by concluding that *Pacifica Foundation v. FCC* applies equally to the technology of cable television as it does to broadcast TV.[4] But that is too facile a conclusion. The Court only upheld a *permissive* regulation that allows, but does not require, cable operators to ban indecent speech on leased access channels.[5] It applied heightened constitutional scrutiny and invalidated the directly regulatory portions of the law.

All nine Justices agreed that heightened First Amendment scrutiny applies to regulation of cable television in this context notwithstanding dictum about *Pacifica*. Indeed, five of the Justices indicated that they would apply strict scrutiny.[6] Justices Kennedy and Ginsburg applied strict scrutiny and voted to invalidate Section 10 in its entirety.[7] Paradoxically, Justices Thomas, Scalia and Rehnquist[8] applied strict scrutiny but would have upheld the entire statutory provision.[9] However, their judgment appeared to be affected by the special nature of access channels. The remaining four Justices, while declining to endorse strict scrutiny by name, applied a standard that closely resembles strict scrutiny, and in this case was strict enough to invalidate the segregation and blocking requirement of Section 10(b).

The Court's plurality specifically found that the indecency standard is not vague because such determinations are made in a particular

---

1. *Id.*

2. *Id.* at 264.

3. 518 U.S. 727, 116 S.Ct. 2374, 135 L.Ed.2d 888.

4. *Id.* at 744-745, 116 S.Ct. at 2386–87, 135 L.Ed.2d at 903.

5. *Id.* at 743, 1165 S.Ct. at 2386, 135 L.Ed.2d at 902–903.

6. *Id.* at 743, 782, 818, 116 S.Ct. at 2385, 2405, 2422, 135 L.Ed.2d at 903, 927–928, 952.

7. 518 U.S. at 782, 116 S.Ct. at 2405, 135 L.Ed.2d at 931.

8. 518 U.S. at 812, 116 S.Ct. at 2419, 135 L.Ed.2d at 946.

9. *Id.*

context.[10] Although this finding was endorsed by only four votes, Justices Thomas, Scalia, and Rehnquist also seemed untroubled by the imprecision of the indecency standard (although they did not specifically discuss it). Conclusions about the relative vagueness of the indecency standard, however, may be limited to the context of the case. First, Justice Kennedy made clear that the Court's analysis did not include changes in the indecency definition that were added in the Telecommunications Act of 1996.[11] Second, the plurality stressed that a *private* decision to limit indecency would not be found unconstitutional so long as it was accomplished pursuant to a "written and published policy" specifically defining indecency.[12] This requirement might set the stage for more rigorous constitutional review of indecency decisions where policies are not as well defined.[13]

c. Regulation of Signal Bleed

Section 505 of the Telecommunications Act of 1996 imposed a unique scrambling requirement on "sexually explicit adult programming or other programming that is indecent" transmitted on a channel "primarily dedicated to sexually oriented programming."[14] The law required that any such channel must be fully scrambled even without a request by the customer for such blocking.[15] Until a cable operator complied with this requirement, it was required to cease transmitting such channels "during the hours of the day (as determined by the [Federal Communications] Commission) when a significant number of children are likely to view it."[16] All other programming channels, including those showing some of the same sexually oriented adult programming, are covered by the voluntary blocking provision of Section 504 of the Act, which requires blocking only after a subscriber's request and does not limit the hours sexually explicit adult programming can be shown on such channels.[17]

Section 505 was adopted as an amendment to the Senate telecommunications bill on the final day of consideration without any hearing or debate.[18] Congress issued no findings, either on the extent that cable subscribers may receive partially scrambled signals of premium services, or the extent that such exposure, however fleeting, could be considered harmful to minors. Section 505 was adopted despite substantial voluntary efforts by the major trade organizations of the cable television industry to ensure that consumers would be able to exercise control over any signals coming into their homes. For example, in February 1995, the National Cable Television Association adopted a policy that included

---

10. *Id.* at 753, 116 S.Ct. at 2390, 135 L.Ed.2d at 909.

11. *Id.* at 782, 116 S. Ct. at 2404, 135 L.Ed.2d at 927.

12. *Id.* at 753, 116 S.Ct. at 2390, 135 L.Ed.2d at 909.

13. *E.g.,* Reno v. ACLU, 521 U.S. 844, 117 S.Ct. 2329, 138 L.Ed.2d 874 (1997).

14. 47 U.S.C.A. § 561 (West Supp. 1997).

15. *Id.* at § 561(b).

16. *Id.*

17. *Id.* § 560.

18. *Id.* § 561.

voluntary blocking on request plus a number of other measures to facilitate parental control. Such a voluntary approach was embodied in Section 504 of the Act.[19]

Section 505 was challenged on constitutional grounds by Playboy Entertainment Group, Inc., whose video channels include Playboy Television and Adult Vision. A three-judge federal district court held that the law violated the First Amendment and permanently enjoined its enforcement in *Playboy Entertainment Group, Inc. v. United States.*[20] The court held that strict scrutiny is the applicable standard of review because the section is a content-based restriction on speech.[21] It found that Section 505 served a compelling governmental interest, but was troubled by the lack of evidence marshalled in support of that interest.[22] Despite this finding, the court concluded that Section 505 was unconstitutional because it was not the least restrictive means of serving the government's purpose. It compared the subscriber-initiated blocking approach of Section 504 with the blanket mandate of Section 505 that applies "irrespective of whether a household has children," and concluded that Section 504 was the less restrictive option. "In fact," the court found, "two-thirds of all households in the United States have no children."[23] In light of the less restrictive alternative of Section 504, the court found that Section 505 infringed the First Amendment because the time channeling requirement "diminishes Playboy's opportunities to convey, and the opportunity of Playboy's viewers to receive, protected speech."[24]

2. The V-Chip

Section 551 of the Telecommunications Act implemented the so-called V-chip provision of the law.[25] Although this section of the legislation purports to regulate televised violence, its provisions apply to a much broader array of programming content. Section 551(b) of the Act amended Section 303 of the Communications Act, empowering the FCC to prescribe "guidelines and recommended procedures for the identification and rating of video programming that contains sexual, violent, and other indecent material about which parents should be informed before it is displayed to children."[26] The subsection stressed that nothing in the

---

19. *Id.* § 560.

20. 30 F.Supp.2d 702 (D.Del.1998). Previously, the district court had granted a temporary restraining order that initially barred enforcement of Section 505, Playboy Entertainment Group, Inc. v. United States, 918 F.Supp. 813 (D.Del.1996), but subsequently denied plaintiff's request for a preliminary injunction. Playboy Entertainment Group, Inc. v. United States, 945 F.Supp. 772 (D.Del.1996), *aff'd mem.* 520 U.S. 1141, 117 S.Ct. 1309, 137 L.Ed.2d 473 (1997).

21. Playboy Entertainment Group, Inc. v. United States, 30 F.Supp.2d at 713–15.

22. *Id.* at 716. The court recognized that empirical proof is not required in such cases, but noted that "[t]he mere articulation of a theoretical harm is not enough," and that "some evidence of harm short of definitive scientific proof must be presented."

23. *Id.* at 718.

24. *Id.*

25. Telecommunications Act of 1996, Pub. L. 104–104, § 551, 110 Stat. 56, (1996), *codified as amended at* 47 U.S.C.A. § 303(x) (West Supp. 1997).

26. 47 U.S.C.A. § 303(w)(1) (West Supp. 1997).

legislation "shall be construed to authorize any rating of video programming on the basis of its political or religious content."[27]

After a one-year period, in which the television industry was permitted to devise its own program ratings system, the Act authorized the FCC to either approve the system or propose an alternative. Such ratings would be devised "on the basis of recommendations from an advisory committee established by the Commission"[28] composed of "parents, television programming producers, cable operators, appropriate public interest groups, and other interested individuals from the private sector."[29] The FCC would provide staff and resources for the advisory committee, which is required to issue a final report within one year after the appointment of its members.[30]

Pursuant to these requirements, the television industry submitted a ratings system for FCC approval in early 1997. Jointly developed by the National Association of Broadcasters, the National Cable Television Association and the Motion Picture Association of America, the proposed guidelines established six ratings categories: TV–Y (appropriate for all children), TV–Y7 (appropriate for children age 7 and above), TV–G (appropriate for a general audience), TV–PG (parental guidance suggested), TV–14 (some material may be unsuitable for children under age 14) and TV–MA (program designed for adult audiences and may be unsuitable for children under 17).[31] The proposed rating system ran into sharp criticism immediately after it was unveiled. Various members of Congress claimed that the system was too vague and was inconsistently applied to television programs. Several members of Congress introduced legislation designed to correct perceived deficiencies in the system.[32]

The controversy over the rating system, combined with pressure from Congress, lead to the creation of a compromise rating system to provide more detailed information. Under the revised system, additional letters were added to the ratings to provide more content information. Thus, in the TV–PG, TV–14 and TV–MA categories, the new ratings would include (where appropriate) V for violence, S for sexual situations, L for language, and D for dialogue. In the TV–Y7 category, FV for fantasy violence would be added where appropriate.[33] Based on the

---

27. *Id.*

28. *Id.*

29. *Id.* § 303. "Historical and Statutory Notes: Advisory Committee Requirements."

30. *Id.*

31. *See* Commission Seeks Comments on Industry Proposal for Rating Video Programming, Public Notice, CS Docket No. 97–55, FCC 97–34 (rel. Feb. 7, 1997); Modification of Industry Proposal for Rating Video Programming, CS Dkt. No. 97–55, DA 97–518 (rel. March 12, 1997).

32. United States Senator Ernest Hollings (D–SC) introduced S.363, the "Children's Protection from Violent Programming Act." It would direct the FCC to issue regulations prohibiting "violent video programming" during hours when children are "reasonably likely to comprise a substantial portion of the audience," unless the programming is rated to enable a V–Chip to block it on the basis of violent content. In addition, Senator Dan Coats (R–IN) introduced S.409, the "Family Television Viewing Information and Empowerment Act." It provided that the FCC could not grant or renew a television broadcast license unless the applicant submitted a plan for implementing a content-based rating system.

33. *See* Implementation of Section 551 of the Telecommunications Act of 1996, Video Programming Ratings, 13 FCC Rcd. 8232 (1998).

compromise, key members of the House and Senate said they would recommend FCC approval and that "there should be a substantial period of governmental forbearance during which further legislation or regulation concerning television ratings, content or scheduling should be set aside."[34] Under the agreement, Congress would forebear from threatening new legislation for a period of three years.[35] However, not all members of the industry went along with the modified ratings. Most notably, NBC announced that it would not be a part of the new agreement. The broadcast network stated its concern "that the ultimate aim of the current system's critics is to dictate programming content. NBC has consistently stated that, as a matter of principle, there is no place for government involvement in what people watch on television."[36] Additionally, Black Entertainment Television declined to use ratings at all.

In spite of the intense legislative pressures brought to bear, the resulting content-based ratings were described by legislators as a voluntary system. One key participant in Congress noted that "[t]his was voluntary in that we [in Congress] did not dictate the terms of the agreement, and yes, we expect everyone to comply with it." He added that there had been "the threat of legislation, but the end result ... is something that American families will be very happy with."[37]

Throughout the legislative history of the V–chip requirement, its proponents asserted that the ratings provisions were voluntary as to the industry. Although the 1996 Act empowered the FCC to "prescribe ... guidelines and recommended procedures for the identification and rating of video programming,"[38] the Conference Committee analysis of the provision stated that the law does not establish legal requirements:

> [T]he guidelines and recommended procedures for a rating system are not rules and do not include requirements. They are intended to provide industry with a carefully considered and practical system for rating programs if industry does not develop such a system itself. However, nothing in subsection (b)(1) authorizes, and the conferees do not intend that, the Commission require the adoption of the recommended rating system nor that any particular program be rated.[39]

Other requirements, on the other hand, are plainly mandatory. Distributors of video programming are required to transmit the rating of the programming being distributed as part of the television signal

---

34. Dear colleague letter from United States Senator John McCain (R.-AZ), United States Senate (July 8, 1997).

35. Letter from Edward J. Markey, U.S. Congressman, U.S. Congress, to the National Cable Television Association, (July 7, 1997).

36. *See* NBC Statement on TV Ratings Deal (July 10, 1997).

37. Paul Farhi, *TV Ratings Agreement Reached: NBC Refuses to Join Deal for Stronger Advisories*, Wash. Post, July 10, 1997, p. A1 (quoting statement of Senator John McCain).

38. 47 U.S.C.A. § 303(w) (West Supp. 1997).

39. H.R. Conf. Rep. No. 104–458, at 421–22 (1996).

(whether or not the ratings were devised by the FCC).[40] Also, televisions 13–inches or larger newly manufactured or imported for use in the United States must be equipped with circuitry to enable viewers to block the display of channels, programs, and time slots; and "shall enable viewers to block display of all programs with a common rating."[41]

Given these provisions, and in light of the extensive congressional involvement in fashioning a "compromise" in the ratings system presented to the FCC for approval, it may not be entirely accurate to characterize Section 551 as truly voluntary.[42] Even if private industry created the system, it quickly became clear that the "voluntary" ratings would be "acceptable to the Commission" only after key members of Congress added refinements based on perceptions of program content. Moreover, apart from the approved ratings system, the law is clear that the "rules prescribed for transmitting a rating are requirements."[43]

The cable television and broadcast industries decided to go along with the V-chip requirements rather than mount a constitutional challenge. The industry's acquiescence to the law does not mean that its constitutionality is free from doubt. To the contrary, the nature of the regulation and the tactics used to impose it raise a number of questions.

In certain circumstances, courts have been unwilling to endorse such "indirect" censorship or to treat such measures as voluntary. The Supreme Court has held that, in certain circumstances, mere speeches given by government officials can have "at least as much coercive effect as an ordinance."[44] In *Lombard v. State of Louisiana*,[45] for example, the mayor and police superintendent made widely publicized statements that no sit-in demonstrations would be permitted in the city. Subsequently, when civil rights demonstrators were arrested for trespassing in violation of the public pronouncements, the Court overturned the convictions. It brushed aside the assertions by local officials that sit-in demonstrations were not in the "public interest" of the community and held that informal statements "must be treated exactly as if [the city] had an ordinance prohibiting such conduct."[46] The Court ruled that the government could not be permitted to do indirectly what it was barred from doing directly.

That same year, the Court decided *Bantam Books, Inc. v. Sullivan*,[47] the classic example of informal censorship. There, the Rhode Island legislature established an advisory committee, the Rhode Island Commis-

40. 47 U.S.C.A. § 303(w) (West Supp. 1997).

41. *Id.* § 303(x).

42. *See generally* Robert Corn–Revere, *"Voluntary" Self–Regulation and the Triumph of Euphemism*, in RATIONALES AND RATIONALIZATIONS 183–14 (Media Institute 1997); Robert Corn–Revere, *Television Violence and the Limits of Voluntarism*, 12 Yale J. on Reg. 187 (Winter 1995).

43. H.R. Conf. Rep. No. 104–458, at 422 (1996).

44. Lombard v. State of Louisiana, 373 U.S. 267, 273, 83 S.Ct. 1122, 1125, 10 L.Ed.2d 338, 342 (1963).

45. *Id.* at 271 n.3, 83 S.Ct. at 1124 n.3, 10 L.Ed.2d at 340–41 n.2.

46. *Id.* at 272–73, 83 S.Ct. at 1125, 10 L.Ed.2d at 342.

47. 372 U.S. 58, 83 S.Ct. 631, 9 L.Ed.2d 584 (1963).

sion to Encourage Morality in Youth.[48] Members of the Commission would notify bookstores that certain books and magazines were considered "objectionable" for sale or display to youths under the age of 18.[49] The written notice included a reminder that the Commission also had a mandate to recommend prosecution for purveyors of obscenity. Soon after the Commission's notice was sent, a local policeman would visit bookstores to determine what action they took in response, if any. The Supreme Court described the Commission's practice as a "blacklist,"[50] and found that "informal censorship may sufficiently inhibit the circulation of publications to warrant injunctive relief."[51] The Court discounted the Commission's claim that it was only providing legal advice, concluding that "the Commission deliberately set about to achieve the suppression of publications deemed 'objectionable' and succeeded in its aim."[52]

Similarly, concern over informal pressure by the government twenty years ago led a court to strike down a drive to restrict violent TV shows. In the mid–1970s broadcasters adopted the "family viewing policy" as a result of a concerted effort by Congress and the FCC. Then Chairman Richard Wiley, pursuant to a congressional directive, initiated a series of meetings with network, independent TV and NAB officials "to serve as a catalyst for the achievement of meaningful self-regulatory reform."[53] The Chairman's message was amplified in speeches before broadcast groups and in suggestions to the press that public hearings would be convened if voluntary action was not forthcoming.[54] The FCC's "suggestions" were adopted by the networks and were to be enforced through an industry code. The self-regulation program was adopted just in time for the FCC to report to Congress on the status of televised sex and violence.

In a lawsuit brought by writers and producers of television programs, the United States District Court for the Central District of California invalidated the policy. The court held that "[t]he existence of the threats, and the attempted securing of commitments coupled with the promise to publicize non-compliance . . . constituted per se violations of the First Amendment."[55] The court characterized the FCC's tactics as "backroom bludgeoning," and found them to be in violation of the First Amendment, the Communications Act and the Administrative Procedure

---

48. *Id.* at 59, 83 S.Ct. at 633, 9 L.Ed.2d at 587.

49. *Id.* at 61–62, 83 S.Ct. at 634–35, 9 L.Ed.2d at 588.

50. *Id.* at 68–69, 83 S.Ct. at 638, 9 L.Ed.2d at 592.

51. *Id.* at 67. 83 S.Ct. at 637–38, 9 L.Ed.2d at 591.

52. *Id.* at 67, 83 S.Ct. at 637, 9 L.Ed.2d at 591. The Court found that the Commission's practices "plainly serve as instruments of regulation independent of the law against obscenity." *Id.* at 68–69, 83 S.Ct. at 638, 9 L.Ed.2d at 592. *See also* Playboy Enterprises, Inc. v. Meese, 639 F.Supp. 581 (D.D.C.1986). *But see* Penthouse Interna-

tional, Ltd. v. Meese, 939 F.2d 1011, 291 U.S.App.D.C. 183 (D.C.Cir.1991).

53. Report on the Broadcast of Violent, Indecent, and Obscene Material, 51 F.C.C.2d 418, 420 (1975).

54. Writers Guild of America, West Inc. v. FCC, 423 F.Supp. 1064, 1098, 1105, 1117 (C.D.Cal.1976), *vacated and remanded on jurisdictional grounds sub nom.* Writers Guild of America, West v. ABC, 609 F.2d 355 (9th Cir.1979), cert. denied, 449 U.S. 824, 101 S.Ct. 85, 66 L.Ed.2d 27 (1980).

55. *See* Writers Guild of America, West, Inc., 423 F. Supp. at 1151.

Act.[56] The District Court opinion was vacated on appeal for other reasons, but the Court of Appeals agreed that "the use of these techniques by the FCC presents serious issues involving the Constitution, the Communications Act and the APA."[57]

Ultimately, if a judicial challenge should take place the constitutionality of V–chip requirements might turn on whether courts accepted the government's claim that the ratings provisions are voluntary. If courts did not perceive some actual or threatened imposition of governmental power,[58] or if the system were perceived simply as a non-judgmental exercise in product labeling,[59] then the V–chip requirements would likely be considered constitutional.[60] But if, on the other hand, the requirements were viewed in the larger context of the government using its power over licensed media to alter programming content, then V–chip requirements might not survive a judicial challenge.

After resolving the question of whether the V-chip involves governmental action, it is necessary to determine whether the V–chip requirements impose a content-based restriction on speech. Courts have consistently invalidated government use of such ratings systems to serve as a proxy for parental choices. This is true even when the ratings initially were developed by the private sector.

With respect to the V-chip requirements, the law's sponsors suggested their intention to affect the type of television programs that are produced. It will likely have such effect. All households are likely to be restricted in their viewing preferences, not just those with children or who activate the chip. The legislative history includes sponsors' claims that they expect V-chips to result in a reduction of violent programming by making such shows less attractive to advertisers. Congressman Markey said, for example, that "[e]ven if a small percentage of parents used [V–Chip] technology, the networks will see declining ratings for violent programs.[61] The result will be less violence on [t]elevision."[62] Similarly, Congressman Spratt has claimed that V-chips "will send a message to the broadcasters and the producers. It will have an inhibiting effect ... on the kind of scripting that they do today ..."[63] In this way, one

---

56. *Id.* at 1142. The court also held that the networks and NAB were liable for damages for acting in concert with the government to suppress speech.

57. Writers Guild of America, West, Inc., 609 F.2d at 365. It should be noted, however, that the court was most concerned by the fact that the Commission had acted without express congressional authority. That is not the case here.

58. *See* Laird v. Tatum, 408 U.S. 1, 11, 92 S.Ct. 2318, 2324–25, 33 L.Ed.2d 154, 162 (1972); Lamont v. Postmaster General, 381 U.S. 301, 85 S.Ct. 1493, 14 L.Ed.2d 398 (1965); Penthouse International Ltd. v. Meese, 939 F.2d 1011, 1015, 291 U.S.App. D.C. 183, 187 (1991).

59. Meese v. Keene, 481 U.S. 465, 482, 107 S.Ct. 1862, 1871, 95 L.Ed.2d 415, 430 (1987).

60. *But see* International Dairy Foods Assn. v. Amestoy, 92 F.3d 67 (2d Cir.1996).

61. *See* Patricia M. Wald, *Doing Right by Our Kids: A Case Study in the Perils of Making Policy on Television Violence*, 23 U. Balt. L. Rev. 397, 416 (1994).

62. 141 Cong. Rec. E1436 (daily ed. July 13, 1995). *See* Wald, *supra,* note 61.

63. 141 Cong. Rec. H8487 (daily ed. August 4, 1995).

possible effect of the law would be to "reduce the adult population ... to [viewing] only what is fit for children."[64]

In the context of film ratings, courts have similarly struck down governmental attempts to "adopt" a ratings system created by private entities. For example, in *Engdahl v. City of Kenosha*,[65] the court found that the adoption of a city ordinance incorporating the MPAA film ratings code to limit children's access to theaters was an unconstitutional prior restraint. An identical finding doomed a state law in *Motion Picture Association of America v. Specter*.[66] These decisions resulted in the demise of various laws even though the government was not attempting to ban the rated programming. Rather, the courts found First Amendment violations where governments sought to provide special licenses for adult movies, restrict children's access or simply provide prior warnings for movies above a specified rating. Similarly, in *Swope v. Lubbers*,[67] the United States District Court for the Western District of Michigan invalidated the government's attempt to use the MPAA ratings system as a mechanism to deny student funding for X-rated films shown on a state university campus. The court held that "it is well-established that Motion Picture ratings may not be used as a standard for a determination of constitutional status."[68]

The constitutionality of V-chip requirements has also been defended based upon judicial approval of FCC rules regulating "indecent" speech.[69] It is argued that the courts generally have approved regulation to protect children, and have approved "time channeling" or "safe harbor" approaches to regulate content.[70] However, courts have historically treated indecency regulation as a special case that does not necessarily translate to other areas, such as violence. The District of Columbia Circuit expressly declined to define the scope of the indecency definition, noting that it was a matter for the Supreme Court.[71] For its part, the Supreme Court has emphasized the "narrowness" of the *Pacifica* holding on indecency.[72] To add "violence" and "other material about which parents should be informed" to the list of regulable content is a significant expansion of the government's ability to control programming content.

It also represents an expansion of authority that courts have been unwilling to approve. For example, in *Winters v. New York*,[73] the Su-

---

64. *See* Butler v. Michigan, 352 U.S. 380, 383, 77 S.Ct. 524, 526, 1 L.Ed.2d 412, 414 (1957).

65. 317 F.Supp. 1133, 1135 (E.D.Wis. 1970).

66. 315 F.Supp. 824 (E.D.Pa.1970).

67. 560 F.Supp. 1328, 1334 (W.D.Mich. 1983).

68. *Id.*

69. *See, e.g.,* Action for Children's Television v. FCC, 58 F.3d 654, 313 U.S. App. D.C. 94 (D.C.Cir.1995).

70. *Id.* at 664–68, 313 U.S. App. D.C. at 104–108.

71. *Id.* at 659, 313 U.S. App. D.C. at 99.

72. Bolger v. Youngs Drug Products Corp., 463 U.S. 60, 74, 103 S.Ct. 2875, 2884, 77 L.Ed.2d 469, 482 (1983); Federal Communications Comm. v. Pacifica Foundation, 438 U.S. 726, 750, 98 S.Ct. 3026, 3041, 57 L.Ed.2d 1073, 1094 (1978).

73. 333 U.S. 507, 68 S.Ct. 665, 92 L.Ed. 840 (1948).

preme Court invalidated a state law that curbed the publication of magazines "devoted principally to criminal news and stories of bloodshed, lust or crime."[74] In doing so, the Court pointedly stated: "What is one man's amusement, teaches another's doctrine. Though we can see nothing of any possible value to society in these magazines, they are as much entitled to the protection of free speech as the best of literature."[75] Similarly the Seventh Circuit has noted that "violence on television ... is protected speech, however insidious. Any other answer leaves the government in control of all the institutions of culture, the great censor and director of which thoughts are good for us."[76] In another appeals court case invalidating restrictions on videotape rentals to minors, the Eighth Circuit has held that violent video programming is entitled to "the highest degree of [First Amendment] protection."[77]

A law review article by Chief Judge Edwards of the United States Court of Appeals for the District of Columbia Circuit addressed the constitutionality of regulating televised violence.[78] Judge Edwards concluded that "there must be full First Amendment protection for all violent speech short of the violence equivalent of obscenity."[79] He noted that the constitutional weakness of any scheme to regulate violence turns on the definition that the law uses. Judge Edwards and his co-author concluded that "[w]hen it comes to televised violence, we cannot imagine how regulators can distinguish between harmless and harmful violent speech, and we can find no proposal that overcomes the lack of supporting data."[80] They added: "We cannot imagine how a regulator might fix rules designed to ferret out gratuitous violence without running the risk of wholesale censorship of television programming."[81]

Various courts have borne out the concern about the ability to fashion a constitutionally defensible definition of "violence." In striking down a Missouri law that prohibited rental of violent video tapes to minors, the Eighth Circuit found it "virtually impossible" to determine if the law could be narrowly applied so as to survive constitutional review.[82] Similarly, in other contexts, courts have invalidated restrictions on providing materials depicting "excess violence" to minors on the ground that the laws were unconstitutionally vague.[83] Indeed, the Supreme Court of Tennessee described such a statutory restriction as

---

74. *Id.* at 511, 68 S.Ct. at 668, 92 L.Ed. at 847.

75. *Id.* at 510–11, 68 S. Ct. at 667, 92 L. Ed. at 846.

76. American Booksellers Ass'n, Inc. v. Hudnut, 771 F.2d 323, 330 (7th Cir.1985), *aff'd mem.*, 475 U.S. 1001, 106 S.Ct. 1172, 89 L.Ed.2d 291 (1986).

77. Video Software Dealers Association v. Webster, 968 F.2d 684, 688 (8th Cir. 1992).

78. *See* Harry T. Edwards and Mitchell N. Berman, *Regulating Violence on Television*, 89 Nw. U. L. Rev. 1487 (1995). *See also* Patricia M. Wald, *Doing Right by Our*

Kids: A Case Study in the Perils of Making Policy on Television Violence, 23 U. Balt. L. Rev. 397 (1994).

79. *See* Edwards and Berman *supra*, note 78 at 1524.

80. *Id.* at 1565.

81. *Id.* at 1502 (emphasis in original).

82. Video Software Dealers' Assoc., 968 F.2d at 689.

83. Davis–Kidd Booksellers, Inc. v. McWherter, 866 S.W.2d 520, 522 (Tenn. 1993).

"entirely subjective."[84] That court also noted that "every court that has considered the issue has invalidated attempts to regulate materials solely based on violent content, regardless of whether that material is called violence, excess violence, or included within the definition of obscenity."[85]

Unless a proposed regulation applies to an established category in which speech is accorded less constitutional protection, the diminished level of First Amendment protection applied to broadcasting will be unlikely, by itself, to support the regulation of television violence. The Supreme Court has expressed a decreased tolerance for broadcast content controls, and it has expressly declined to extend the theory for such controls to cable television. As the Court noted in 1994, "the FCC's oversight responsibilities do not grant it the power to ordain any particular type of programming that must be offered by broadcast stations."[86] Nor may the government "impose upon [broadcasters] its private notions of what the public ought to hear."[87]

The fact that broadcast and cable television are regulated media may be a reason to more carefully scrutinize ratings requirements. The Supreme Court made clear in a case involving the Dallas film ratings board, that the problem of a vague rating scheme "is particularly pronounced where expression is sought to be subjected to licensing."[88] Such concerns apply with special force to industries such as cable television that are subject to federal regulation. Similar concerns led the United States Court of Appeals for the District of Columbia Circuit to strike down a requirement that noncommercial radio stations make audio tapes of programs in which "issues of public importance" were presented.[89] It found that both commercial and noncommercial broadcasters are subject to "a variety of sub silentio pressures and 'raised eyebrow' regulation of program content."[90] Accordingly, even a seemingly neutral regulation could be invalid to the extent it increases the likelihood that regulatees "will censor themselves to avoid official pressure and regulation."[91] Section 551 may create such a risk for cable television operators, as well as for traditional broadcasters.[92]

84. *See id* at 532. *See also* Allied Artists Pictures Corp. v. Alford, 410 F.Supp. 1348 (W.D.Tenn.1976).

85. Davis–Kidd Booksellers, 866 S.W.2d at 531.

86. Turner Broadcasting System, Inc. v. FCC, 512 U.S. 622, 650–51, 114 S.Ct. at 2445, 2463–64, 129 L.Ed.2d 497, 522 (1994).

87. *Id.* at 650, 114 S. Ct. at 2463, 129 L. Ed. 2d at 522 (quoting En Banc Programming Inquiry, 44 F.C.C.2d 2303, 2312 (1960)).

88. Interstate Circuit, Inc. v. City of Dallas, 390 U.S. 676, 683, 88 S.Ct. 1298, 1303, 20 L.Ed.2d 225, 232 (1968).

89. Community–Service Broadcasting of Mid–America, Inc. v. FCC, 593 F.2d 1102,

1105, 192 U.S.App.D.C. 448, 451 (D.C.Cir. 1978) (en banc).

90. *Id.* at 1116.

91. *Id.*

92. Telecommunications Act of 1996, Pub. L. 104–104, § 551, 110 Stat. 56, 139–40 (1996) *codified at* 47 U.S.C.A. § 303 (West Supp. 1997) ("Historical and Statutory Notes, Parental Choice in Television Programming"). For a contrary analysis of V-chip requirements, *see* Matthew L. Spitzer, *An Introduction to the Law and Economics of the V-Chip*, 15 Cardozo Arts & Ent.L.J. 429 (1997).

3. Closed Captioning Requirements

In 1990, Congress adopted the Television Decoder Circuitry Act of 1990 to require all television receivers with screen sizes 13 inches or larger to be capable of receiving and displaying closed captions for the hearing impaired.[93] By 1995, 25 million decoder-equipped television sets were sold in the United States, and the FCC estimated that between 50 and 60 million American homes were capable of receiving closed captioning.[94] Although program producers increased the amount of captioned programming to coincide with the increase in equipment, Congress became concerned that the growth of programming was insufficient to ensure accessibility of video programming to persons with disabilities.[95]

Accordingly, Congress adopted Section 305 of the Telecommunications Act of 1996 "to ensure that video services are accessible to hearing impaired and visually impaired individuals."[96] The Telecommunications Act requires the FCC to conduct an inquiry into issues relevant to video programming accessibility and to establish regulations and implementation schedules to ensure that video programming is fully accessible through closed captioning.[97] The inquiry addressed the extent to which existing or previously published programming was closed captioned, the relative size of video programming providers and programming owners that provide closed captioning, size of the markets served, relative market shares and other issues.[98] In keeping with the Congressional interest in assisting visually impaired individuals, the FCC study also examined "video descriptions" of programming, a method of providing voice-over narratives of video programming.[99]

The Act required the FCC, within 18 months of passage, to adopt regulations including "an appropriate schedule of deadlines for the provision of closed captioning of video programming."[100] Through such requirements, the Commission was directed to ensure that "video programming first published or exhibited after the effective date . . . is fully accessible through the provision of closed captions," and that "video programming providers or owners maximize the accessibility of video programming first published or exhibited prior to the effective date of such regulations through the provision of closed captions."[1] The Act empowered the FCC to establish exemptions for certain programs, classes of programs or services for which the requirement would be economically burdensome or if the requirement would violate existing

---

93. Pub. L. No. 101–431, 104 Stat. 960 (1990) *codified at* 47 U.S.C.A. §§ 303(u), 330(b) (West Supp. 1997).

94. Closed Captioning and Video Description of Video Programming, Notice of Proposed Rulemaking, 12 FCC Rcd 1044 (1997).

95. H.R. Rep. No. 204, 104th Cong., 1st Sess. 113–14 (1995).

96. H.R. Conf. Rep. No. 104–458, 104th Cong., 2nd Sess. 182 (1996).

97. Telecommunications Act of 1996, Pub. L. No. 104–104, § 305, 110 Stat. 56, 126–28 (1996) *codified at* 47 U.S.C.A. § 613 (West Supp. 1997).

98. Closed Captioning and Video Description of Video Programming, Report, 11 FCC Rcd. 19214 (1996).

99. *Id.* at 19253–69.

100. 47 U.S.C.A. § 613(c) (West Supp. 1997).

1. *Id.* § 613(b).

contracts. It also provided a process for seeking exemptions from the Commission.[2] Programmers seeking an exemption are required to demonstrate that compliance would cause an "undue burden."[3] The requirements apply to all types of video programming regardless of transmission medium.

Pursuant to this section, the FCC established a timetable requiring video programmers to provide captioning for programming initially produced or exhibited over an eight-year period, by January 1, 2006.[4] The programming requirement is to be phased-in over two-year increments, with the first "benchmark" occurring on January 1, 2000.[5] For programming produced before the effective date of the rules, the FCC requires that 75 percent of such programming must contain closed captions at the end of a 10–year transition period, by January 1, 2008.[6] The rules also establish a number of exemptions to prevent particular networks from bearing an undue economic burden.

4. Derivative Broadcasting Requirements

It is widely held that the rationale for more intrusive government regulation of broadcast television content is related to spectrum usage, and therefore inapplicable to cable television. In *Turner Broadcasting System v. FCC* ("Turner I"), the Supreme Court made clear that "the rationale for applying a less rigorous standard of First Amendment scrutiny to broadcast regulation, whatever its validity in the cases elaborating it, does not apply in the context of cable regulation."[7] Nevertheless, various Communications Act provisions and FCC regulations of broadcast content have been applied to cable television as if no such distinction existed.

a. Political Broadcasting Rules

Congress amended Section 315 of the Communications Act, the "equal opportunities" provisions, to apply to cable television systems.[8] Under the FCC's rule implementing this provision, cable operators who offer time on their facilities to legally qualified candidates for public office must provide equal opportunities for all other candidates for that office.[9] The channels to which the rule applies are not well defined in the rules. The heading to the equal opportunities rule indicates that it applies only to "origination cablecasts" by legally qualified candidates

---

2. *Id.* § 613(d).

3. *Id.* § 613(e). An "undue burden" means significant difficulty or expense, involving such factors as the nature and cost of closed captions, the impact on the operation of the provider or program owner, the financial resources of the provider and the type of operations involved.

4. Closed captioning and Video Description of Video Programming, 13 FCC Rcd. 3272 (1997). *See* chapter 14.5 [B][5].

5. 47 C.F.R. § 79.1 (1998).

6. *Id.*

7. 512 U.S. 622, 637, 114 S.Ct. 2445, 2456, 129 L.Ed.2d 497, 514 (1994).

8. 47 U.S.C.A. § 315(a) (West 1991). *See* Federal Election Campaign Act of 1971, Pub. L. 92–225, 86 Stat. 3 (1972).

9. 47 C.F.R. § 76.205 (1997).

for public office.[10] The rules generally define "origination cablecasting" as programming carried on a cable system "subject to the exclusive control of the cable operator."[11] The rules also require that cable operators offer candidates the "lowest unit charge" for political advertising.[12] Cable operators also are required to maintain public files, listing all requests for political advertising time made on behalf of candidates.[13] Finally, a cable operator "engaging in origination cablecasting" is required to adhere to remnants of the broadcast fairness doctrine, such as the personal attack rules.[14]

b. Children's Television Rules

Commercial limits imposed on children's programming established in the Children's Television Act of 1990 apply to cable operators.[15] Under the FCC's rules, no cable operator may air more than 10.5 minutes of commercial matter per hour during children's programming on weekends, or more than 12 minutes of commercial matter per hour on weekdays.[16] Additionally, cable operators are required to maintain records sufficient to verify compliance with the rule.[17]

In addition to the overarching constitutional question of whether broadcast-type content controls can be applied to cable television, the application of children's television requirements to cable operators is somewhat ironic. In adopting a three-hour programming requirement for broadcast stations under the Children's Television Act, the FCC expressly excluded consideration of cable television programming.[18] It reached this conclusion despite the fact that the Supreme Court has accepted the argument that "cable television broadcasting . . . is as 'accessible to children' as over-the-air broadcasting, if not more so" and that most people receive television via cable, which provides entire networks dedicated to education.[19]

c. Restrictions on Lotteries

FCC rules prohibit a cable system operator from transmitting "any advertisement of or information concerning any lottery, gift, enterprise, or similar scheme, offering prizes dependent in whole or in part upon lot

---

10. *Id.*

11. *Id.* § 76.5(p). The rule itself, however, applies to any "use" of a cable operator's "facilities."

12. *Id.* § 76.206.

13. *Id.* § 76.207.

14. *Id.* § 76.209. Unlike the equal opportunities requirements, the rule relating to personal attacks specifies that it applies only to "origination cablecasting," and not to other channels carried by the operator.

15. Children's Television Act of 1990, Pub. L. 101–437, 104 Stat. 996 (1990).

16. 47 C.F.R. § 76.225(a) (1997). Although the rules specify the limitations do not apply to broadcast stations carried

"passively" or to access channels over which the cable operator has no editorial control, it evidently applies to other satellite channels carried by the operator. *See id.* § 76.225(b). Thus, the rule is not limited to "origination cablecasting."

17. *Id.* 76.225(c).

18. Policies and Rules Concerning Children's Television Programming, Report and Order, 11 FCC Rcd. 10661, 10681 (1996).

19. Denver Area Educational Telecommunications Consortium, Inc. v. FCC, 518 U.S. 727, 116 S.Ct. 2374, 2386, 135 L.Ed.2d 888, 903 (1996).

or chance."[20] This restriction applies specifically only to "origination cablecasting channel or channels."[21] The prohibition does not apply to lotteries conducted by state governments in specified situations or to lotteries or other gaming enterprises conducted by Native Americans.[22]

The determination whether a particular program falls within the restriction depends on the facts of each case. Generally, however, a "lottery, gift, enterprise, or similar scheme" contains three elements: (1) distribution of prizes; (2) distribution based on chance, rather than skill; and (3) consideration.[23] Recently, the constitutionality of the lottery restrictions has been called into question.[24]

d. *Sponsorship Identification*

FCC broadcast rules requiring disclosure of sponsorship identification have also been applied by rule to "origination cablecasting."[25] Where any individual or group furnishes money, services or other valuable consideration, either directly or indirectly in exchange for transmitting any program, the rule requires the operator to identify all relevant sponsors.[26] The rule also requires the operator to exercise reasonable diligence in determining the sponsor of the programming in question.[27]

The rule does not apply to programming that advertises commercial products or services to the extent the program states the sponsor's corporate or trade name and it is clear that the sponsor has been identified.[28] Additionally requirements are waived for transmission of "want ad" or classified advertisements sponsored by an individual.[29]

C. *Local Regulation of Programming Content*

By virtue of the Cable Act and franchising requirements, local governmental officials may exert a certain level of control over cable television programming. The Act permits local authorities to establish franchising requirements governing "broad categories of video programming or other services,"[30] permits a franchising authority to require channels be set aside for public, educational, and governmental ("PEG") uses,[31] and permits enforcement of state and local laws regarding defamation, obscenity, incitement, invasions of privacy, false or misleading advertising or other similar laws.[32] Although these provisions recognize a

---

20. 47 C.F.R. § 76.213(a) (1997).

21. *Id.*

22. *Id.* § 76.213(c).

23. *Id.* § 76.213(a). *See* FCC v. American Broadcasting Co., 347 U.S. 284, 295, 74 S.Ct. 593, 600, 98 L.Ed. 699, 705 (1954).

24. *See* Valley Broadcasting Co. v. United States, 107 F.3d 1328 (9th Cir.1997). *But see* Greater New Orleans Broadcasting Assn. v. FCC, 149 F.3d 334 (5th Cir.1998) cert. granted, ___ U.S. ___, 119 S.Ct. 863, 142 L.Ed.2d 716 (1999).

25. 47 C.F.R. § 76.221(a) (1997).

26. *Id.*

27. *Id.* § 76.221(b).

28. *Id.* § 76.221(e).

29. *Id.* § 76.221(f).

30. 47 U.S.C.A. § 544(b)(2)(B) (West 1991).

31. *Id.* § 531. The section precludes cable operators from exercising editorial control over PEG channels.

32. 47 U.S.C.A. § 558 (West 1991 and Supp. 1997).

local ability to regulate programming content, they are subject to statutory and constitutional limitations.

Local government authority to enforce franchise provisions relating to "broad categories of video programming or other services"[33] does not authorize municipalities to require the provision of particular networks or programs. In *Jones Intercable, Inc. v. City of Stevens Point*,[34] a cable operator challenged the franchising authority's demand that the system retain the USA Network and WWOR on its channel lineup. The court agreed with the operator and held that the Cable Act did not permit the city to demand carriage of specific cable services.[35] On the other hand, the court affirmed the authority's ability to enforce requirements for "broad categories" of programming, and found that the city could require carriage of certain program types, such as "East Coast programming" or sports programming.[36] The court granted summary judgment in favor of the operator, holding that it did not violate the terms of its franchise by dropping the USA Network. [37] Similarly, in *Time Warner Entertainment Company, L.P. v. FCC*,[38] the District of Columbia Circuit held that franchising authorities could not prescribe which channels must be contained in the basic service tier. Nor may a franchising authority alter "the programming mix" chosen by a cable operator by forcing the operator to carry a particular commercial network that the operator had rejected.[39]

Courts have accorded a greater degree of discretion to local governments to require specified amounts of local programming. For example, in *Chicago Cable Communications v. Chicago Cable Commission*,[40] the Seventh Circuit held that the government could require the cable operator to produce four and-one-half hours of local origination programming as a condition of the franchise. Such authority is not unlimited, however. In *Time Warner* cable, for example, the court has held that a city may not use its PEG access channels to require a cable operator to carry a commercial cable news service.[41] The district court held that it was a violation both of the Cable Act and the operator's First Amendment rights because the action was a viewpoint-based restriction on the operator's editorial discretion.[42] Additionally, it is impermissible for a franchising authority to eliminate its public access channels and return

33. 47 U.S.C.A. § 544(b)(2)(B) (West 1991).

34. 729 F.Supp. 642, 643 (W.D.Wis. 1990).

35. *Id.* at 650.

36. *Id.* at 648–49.

37. *Id.* at 650.

38. 56 F.3d 151, 197, 312 U.S. App. D.C. 187, 233 (D.C.Cir.1995), cert. denied, 516 U.S. 1112, 116 S. Ct. 911, 133 L.Ed.2d 842 (1996).

39. Time Warner Cable of New York City v. Bloomberg L.P., 118 F.3d 917, 924 (2d. Cir.1997).

40. 879 F.2d 1540, 1551 (7th Cir.1989), cert. denied, 493 U.S. 1044, 110 S.Ct. 839, 107 L.Ed.2d 835 (1990). *See also* Telesat Cablevision, Inc. v. City of Riviera Beach, 773 F.Supp. 383, 411–413 (S.D.Fla.1991).

41. Time Warner Cable v. City of New York, 943 F.Supp. 1357 (S.D.N.Y.1996), *aff'd*, Time Warner Cable of New York City v. Bloomberg L.P., 118 F.3d 917 (2d Cir. 1997).

42. *Id.* at 1399–1400. The court of appeals affirmed without reaching the constitutional issues. Time Warner Cable of New York City, 118 F.3d at 919–920.

them to cable operator control for the specific purpose of precluding access by an unpopular speaker.[43]

Certain local efforts to control programming are preempted by federal authority. For example, the Cable Act generally preempts local efforts to control programming except as allowed by the statute.[44] The Supreme Court generally upheld federal preemptive authority over cable programming regulation in *Capital Cities Cable, Inc. v. Crisp.*[45] There, the State of Oklahoma had attempted to require cable operators to delete the retransmission of liquor commercials carried on out-of-state broadcast signals. The advertisements were considered to violate the state ban on alcoholic beverage advertising. The Supreme Court preempted the enforcement of Oklahoma law because of federal authority contained in the Communications Act. Similarly, in *Playboy Enterprises, Inc. v. Public Service Commission of Puerto Rico,*[46] the United States Court of Appeals for the First Circuit upheld federal preemptive authority over a local obscenity prosecution for programming transmitted over a leased access channel.

13.5 Program Access Requirements and Channel Occupancy Limits

Section 628 of the 1992 Cable Act prohibits cable operators, vertically integrated "satellite programming vendors" or satellite broadcasting programming vendors from engaging in "unfair methods of competition or unfair or deceptive acts or practices, the purpose or effect of which is to hinder significantly or to prevent any multichannel video programming distributor from providing satellite cable programming or satellite broadcast programming to subscribers or consumers."[1] Pursuant to this general mandate, the FCC established rules to prevent cable operators from unduly influencing their affiliated programming services to disadvantage competitors, to prohibit discrimination in the prices, terms, or conditions of sale or delivery of satellite cable programming to competing vendors and to prohibit practices, understandings, arrangements and activities, including exclusive contracts between operators and vertically integrated programming services, that prevent competitors from obtain-

43. Missouri Knights of the Ku Klux Klan v. Kansas City, 723 F.Supp. 1347, 1352 (W.D.Mo.1989) ("[A] state may only eliminate a designated public forum if it does so in a manner consistent with the First Amendment. The complaint alleges Channel 20 was eliminated to censor the viewpoint of the Missouri Knights. At this stage of the proceedings, that is sufficient.").

44. 47 U.S.C.A. § 544 (West 1991 & Supp. 1997). *Cf.* United Video, Inc. v. FCC, 890 F.2d 1173, 281 U.S. App. D.C. 368 (D.C.Cir.1989). *See* 47 U.S.C.A. § 544 (f)(1) (West 1991).

45. 467 U.S. 691, 104 S.Ct. 2694, 81 L.Ed.2d 580 (1984).

46. 906 F.2d 25 (1st Cir.1990), cert. denied, *sub nom.* Rivera Cruz v. Playboy Enterprises, Inc. 498 U.S. 959, 111 S.Ct. 388, 112 L.Ed.2d 399 (1990). The Cable Act provision that preempted local obscenity actions against cable operators for leased access programming was deleted in the 1992 Cable Act. *See* 47 U.S.C.A. § 558 (West Supp. 1997).

1. Cable Television Consumer Protection Act of 1992, Pub.L. 102–385, § 625(b), 106 Stat. 1460, 1484 (1992), *codified as amended at* 47 U.S.C.A. § 548(b) (West Supp. 1997).

ing such programming.[2] This provision was expanded by the 1996 Act to include any common carrier or its affiliate that provides video programming by any means to subscribers.[3] In addition, the FCC in 1998 strengthened its procedures by creating a damages remedy for rule violations, by permitting discovery of documents relied upon by defendants before the agency and by setting time limits for the resolution of program access complaints.[4]

A. Rules Prohibiting "Unreasonable Refusals to Sell" Cable Programming

Section 628(c)(2)(B) of the 1992 Act prohibits discrimination by vertically-integrated programming vendors against unaffiliated providers of multichannel video service. Pursuant to this statutory mandate, the FCC adopted a rule prohibiting discrimination "in the prices, terms, and conditions of sale or delivery of satellite cable programming ... among or between competing cable systems, competing cable operators, or any competing multichannel video programming distributors."[5] More generally, Commission rules prohibit "unfair methods of competition or unfair or deceptive acts and practices, the purpose or effect of which is to hinder significantly or prevent any multichannel video programming distributor from providing satellite cable programming ... to subscribers or consumers."[6] The Commission has interpreted its rules to prohibit various forms of non-price discrimination, including "unreasonable refusal to sell" or refusal to initiate discussions to sell programming to competitors.[7]

Although the FCC has not had many occasions to apply this restriction on refusals to sell, the Commission's Cable Services Bureau decided that SportsChannel Associates, an affiliate of Cablevision Systems Corporation, violated the rule by refusing to sell programming to CellularVision of New York, an operator of an LMDS system.[8] In that case, the Bureau found that SportsChannel had unreasonably dragged its feet in its negotiations with CellularVision.[9] In particular, SportsChannel continued to raise doubts and questions about signal security beyond what

2. Id.

3. Telecommunications Act of 1996, Pub. L. 104–104, § 301(j), 110 Stat. 56, 118 (1996) codified as amended at 47 U.S.C.A. § 548(j) (West Supp. 1997).

4. See Implementation of the Cable Television Consumer Protection and Competition Act of 1992: Petition for Rulemaking of Ameritech New Media, Inc. Regarding Development of Competition and Diversity in Video Programming Distribution and Carriage, FCC 98–189 (rel. Aug. 10, 1998). The Rules require resolution of complaints dealing with exclusive contracts and unreasonable refusals to sell programming within five months and all other program access complaints within nine months.

5. 47 C.F.R. § 76.1002(b) (1997).

6. Id. § 76.1001.

7. Implementation of Sections 12 and 19 of the Cable Television Consumer Protection and Competition Act of 1992—Development of Competition and Diversity in Video Programming Distribution and Carriage, Report and Order, 8 FCC Rcd. 3359, 3412 (1993) ("First Report and Order").

8. Cellular Vision of New York, L.P. v. SportsChannel Associates, Program Access Complaint Pursuant to 47 C.F.R. § 76.1003, Mem. Op. and Order, 10 FCC Rcd. 9273, 9274 (1995).

9. Id.

was reasonable.[10] The fact that discussions were ongoing did not insulate SportsChannel from liability. The Cable Bureau noted that "defendant unreasonably has refused to sell its programming to CellularVision, not that defendant has refused to deal with CellularVision."[11] It added that, although the record showed continuing communications between the parties, "the fact that defendant has engaged in communications does not preclude a finding that defendant unreasonably has refused to sell its programming."[12]

In bringing a complaint to the FCC, an injured party must demonstrate that the defendant: (1) "is a vertically-integrated satellite cable programming vendor"; (2) "has engaged in some form of non-price discrimination, such as an unreasonable refusal to sell its programming to a complainant"; (3) that there is some overlap in the actual or proposed service area of the video competitor and the cable operator to whom the vendor has licensed programming.[13]

Section 628(c) of the Cable Act does not establish a threshold burden of proof requiring injured parties to show that a cable programmer's discriminatory behavior caused either specific or generalized harm to competition.[14] Thus, where discriminatory behavior is established, competitive harm is presumed.[15] To avoid liability, a defendant must demonstrate that its refusal to sell programming is not unreasonable. Factors in a "reasonable" refusal to sell programming might include the existence of an impasse on specific contractual terms, the complainant's history of defaulting on other contracts or the programming provider's refusal to sell programming outside its established geographic area of distribution in the case of a regional network.[16]

B.   Cable Act Restrictions on Exclusive Contracts

Section 628 generally prohibits exclusive programming contracts for programming offered by vertically integrated vendors in areas where there is no cable service, and permits such contracts in areas where cable service exists only upon FCC approval. Any agreement between a vertically integrated programming vendor and a cable operator that grants the operator exclusive right to distribute programming within its franchise area must be approved by the Commission before it may be enforced.[17] A party seeking an FCC determination that such an agreement meets the statutory public interest standard bears the burden of demonstrating that the proposed exclusivity provides sufficient public interest benefits to outweigh the presumptively anti-competitive effect on competing distributors. The FCC examines such petitions for exclusivity case-by-case.[18] Although the Cable Act gives the FCC the discretion

---

10. *Id.*

11. *Id.* at 9277.

12. *Id.* at 9279.

13. *Id.* at 9276–77.

14. 47 U.S.C.A. § 548(c) (West Supp. 1997).

15. First Report and Order, 8 FCC Rcd. at 3377.

16. *Id.* at 3412.

17. *Id.* at 3386.

18. *Id.* at 3385.

to allow exclusive contracts in areas served by cable systems, such exclusivity is prohibited in unserved areas.[19]

The Commission has emphasized that the congressional policy is to "disfavor such exclusive contracts."[20] Accordingly, the Commission has stated that it will not approve exclusivity simply to improve the prospective profitability of a new service. Rather, it examines the effect of each case on the broader public interest, with a heavy emphasis on potential anti-competitive effects.[21] The programming vendor must demonstrate that exclusivity is necessary to preserve the viability of its service.[22]

In determining whether an exclusive contract serves the public interest, Section 628 directs the Commission to consider five specific factors:

(1) the effect of such exclusive contract on the development of competition in local and national multichannel video programming distribution markets;

(2) the effect of such exclusive contract on competition from multichannel video programming distribution technologies other than cable;

(3) the effect of such exclusive contract on the attraction of capital investment in the production and distribution of new satellite cable programming;

(4) the effect of such exclusive contract on diversity of programming in the multichannel video programming distribution market; and

(5) the duration of the exclusive contract.[23]

The FCC has exercised its waiver authority in only a handful of cases, and has applied it rather strictly. It has granted exclusivity waivers for two regional news networks (New England Cable News and NewsChannel), but has rejected waiver requests for such networks as Court TV, the Sci–Fi Channel, Outdoor Life Network and Speedvision Network, which are distributed nationally.[24] The Commission also grant-

---

19. 47 U.S.C.A. § 548(c)(2)(C) (West Supp. 1997).

20. *See* Time Warner Cable, Petition for Public Interest Determination under 47 C.F.R. § 76.1002(c)(4) Relating to Exclusive Distribution of Courtroom Television, Mem. Op. and Order, 9 FCC Rcd. 3221, 3229 (1994).

21. *Id.*

22. NewsChannel, a Division of Lenfest Programming Services, Inc., Petition for Public Interest Determination under 47 C.F.R. § 76.1002(c)(4) Relating to Exclusive Distribution of NewsChannel Mem. Op. and Order, 10 FCC Rcd. 691, 693–95 (1994) ("NewsChannel").

23. *See* 47 U.S.C.A. § 548(c)(4)(A)-(E) (West Supp. 1997).

24. *See generally,* New England Cable News, Petition for Public Interest Determination Under 47 C.F.R. § 76.1002(c)(4) Relating to Exclusive Distribution of New England Cable News, Mem. Op. and Order, 9 FCC Rcd. 3231 (1994) ("New England Cable News"); Newschannel, a division of Comcast Programming Services, Inc., Petition for Public Interest Determination under 47 C.F.R. § 76.1002(c)(4) Relating to Exclusive Distribution of Newschannel, Mem. Op. and Order, 10 FCC Rcd. 691 (1994); Cablevision Industries Corporation and Sci–Fi Channel, Petition for Public Interest Determination under 47 C.F.R. § 76.1002(c)(4) Relating to the Exclusive Distribution of the Sci–Fi Channel, Mem. Op. and Order, 10 FCC Rcd. 9786 (1995)

ed a limited waiver for the Disney Channel, but only to the extent it was carried in hotels at the Walt Disney World resort complex.[25]

The cases both granting and denying waiver requests provide an indication of the strictness of Commission scrutiny. The Commission has held that a vertically integrated programmer must demonstrate "unique obstacles or limitations in attracting investments and security carriage agreements ... such that its viability requires the ability to offer [it] the additional incentive of exclusivity."[26] The Commission also has closely scrutinized the geographic scope of proposed exclusivity and has granted waivers only where the programming service was available on a regional basis.[27] The Commission rejected an exclusivity waiver request filed for Court TV because it found that Time Warner had not demonstrated that exclusivity was necessary for the service to gain acceptance and because its belief that "even a modest detrimental effect on competing distributors is strongly disfavored by the statute."[28] Similarly, the FCC denied an exclusivity waiver request for the Sci–Fi Channel even though the exclusivity agreements were entered before Sci–Fi was vertically integrated and despite the fact that no parties opposed the exclusivity request.[29]

An indication of the strictness with which the Commission views waiver requests is also provided by its grant of an exclusivity waiver for distribution of the Disney Channel over hotel systems in Walt Disney World. Although the Cable Services Bureau noted that the Disney World system "cannot in any meaningful way be viewed as a 'traditional cable system,' " it required Disney to seek additional approval if it should "begin residential distribution or expand the number of non-Disney owned hotels to which it provides service beyond the current two."[30]

C. Discriminatory Prices, Terms or Conditions

Section 628(c)(2)(B) of the Cable Act generally prohibits vertically-integrated program services from discriminating in the prices, terms, and conditions for the sale or delivery of programming.[31] The Commission's rules implement this statutory limitation essentially as written.[32]

Neither the Act nor Commission rules prohibit all contractual differences in the terms of affiliation agreements. Rather, the rules permit

("Cablevision Industries Corporation"); Outdoor Life Network and Speedvision Network, Mem.Op. and Order DA 98–1241 (Cable Services Bureau, rel. June 26, 1998).

25. Petition of Walt Disney Company for Waiver of Program Access Rules, Mem. Op. and Order, 9 FCC Rcd. 4007 (1994) ("Walt Disney Company").

26. NewsChannel, 10 FCC Rcd. at 695.

27. *Id.*; New England Cable News, 9 FCC Rcd. 3231, 3236 (1994). *See also* Time Warner Cable, Petition for Public Interest Determination Under 47 C.F.R. § 76.1000(c)(4) Relating to Exclusive Distri-

bution of Courtroom Television, Mem. Op. and Order, 9 FCC Rcd. 3221, 3230 (1994).

28. Time Warner Cable, 9 FCC Rcd. at 3228.

29. Cablevision Industries Corporation, 10 FCC Rcd. at 9791.

30. Walt Disney Company, 9 FCC Rcd. at 4008.

31. *See* Cable Television Consumer Protection and Competition Act of 1992, Pub. L. 102–385, § 628(c)(2)(B), 106 Stat. 1460, 1494–95 (1992) *codified as amended at* 47 U.S.C.A. § 548(c)(2)(B) (West Supp. 1997).

32. 47 C.F.R. § 76.1002(b) (1997).

differences based on: (1) cost differences at the wholesale level among distributors; (2) volume differences; (3) differences based on the financial stability and creditworthiness of multichannel distributors; and (4) differences in the "offering of service."[33] Different arrangements based on "offering of service" include such factors as subscriber penetration levels, the retail price of programming for pay services, the level of promotion provided by a distributor, distribution of programming as a package as opposed to à la carte, channel positioning, contract duration, prepayment discounts or other legitimate factors.[34] Such terms must be applied in a technology-neutral fashion.[35]

To bring an actionable complaint against a programming vendor, a multichannel video provider must first establish that it is a "competing distributor." This means that there must be some overlap in the actual or proposed service area of the complainant and a cable operator that receives the programming service.[36] Additionally, the complainant must establish that it has been offered or is paying a higher price or has received less favorable terms.[37] In evaluating a complaint, the Commission must consider whether the parties are "similarly situated" and whether the differences in contracts are justified by the statutory factors governing permissible price differentials.

The Commission's rules establish a two-step analysis. First, it compares the differences in contract prices, terms or conditions. Minimal differences are not actionable.[38] Second, the Commission allows the defendant programmer to justify any differences in price or contract terms under the factors listed above, or by submitting an alternative contract from a more "similarly situated" distributor.[39] Generally, it is the defendant's burden to justify differences in the contract terms on a case-by-case basis, or to demonstrate that a different "similarly situated" contract should be the focus of comparison. The Commission has emphasized that "faithful implementation of the statute requires us to allow for differences based on the permissible factors enumerated" in Section 628.[40]

Although a number of complaints have been filed with the Commission alleging discrimination, the parties usually settle complaint proceedings before a decision is reached.[41] Complaints alleging discriminatory prices or terms are more difficult for the Commission to decide than

---

33. First Report and Order, 8 FCC Rcd. at 3405; 47 C.F.R. § 76.1002(b) (1997).

34. First Report and Order, 8 FCC Rcd. at 3409.

35. *Id.*at 3409–10.

36. *Id.* at 3400.

37. *Id.*

38. 47 C.F.R. § 76.1003(d)(6)(ii) (1997). The Commission will not act on price differentials of less than or equal to 5 cents per subscriber or 5 percent, whichever is greater. *Id.*

39. First Report & Order, 8 FCC Rcd. at 3401–02. 47 C.F.R. § 76.1003(d)(6)(iii) (1997).

40. First Report & Order, 8 FCC Rcd. at 3403.

41. *E.g.*, Complaint of Consumer Satellite Systems, Inc. d/b/a National Programming Service v. Lifetime Television, *Order*, 9 FCC Rcd. 3212 (1994); Private Network Cable Systems v. SportsChannel Associates, *Order*, 9 FCC Rcd. 5326 (1994).

cases involving exclusive contracts, because of the number of statutory factors the Commission must consider. This is particularly true where the defendant may submit an alternative contract involving a more "similarly situated" video program provider as the basis of comparison. Nevertheless, the Commission in 1998 upheld a discrimination complaint in part against CNN. Several vendors of C-Band satellite programming had complained that CNN charged competitors substantially lower rates for Cable News Network and Headline News networks. Although it found that the complaint process does not lend itself to definitive information, and that CNN had justified most of the price differential, the Commission directed the parties to renegotiate the rates charged to C-Band retailers.[42]

D. Antitrust Remedies for Refusals to Sell Cable Television Programming

In addition to administrative remedies under the Cable Act, it is possible to seek judicial remedies through relevant antitrust laws. Section 1 of the Sherman Act prohibits agreements, combinations, and conspiracies that restrain trade.[43] This section relates to concerted conduct by two independent entities and generally does not reach actions of a parent and a majority-controlled subsidiary. Section 2 of the Sherman Act prohibits monopolization, conspiracy or an attempt to monopolize.[44] Unlike a Section 1 action, a Section 2 violation does not depend on concerted action. In addition to the Sherman Act, the Federal Trade Commission Act prohibits unfair methods of competition and unfair or deceptive acts and practices.[45] Although a number of cable program-related cases have been litigated under these laws, they are rarely successful. Additionally, such litigation is far more cumbersome than the procedures established under Section 628 of the Cable Act.[46]

Several courts have dismissed Sherman Act claims for refusals to sell cable programming. In *Futurevision Cable Systems of Wiggins, Inc. v. Multivision Cable TV Corp.*,[47] the court dismissed Sherman Act Section 1 and Section 2 claims regarding exclusive contracts for the distribution of The Learning Channel, ESPN and TNT. Similarly, in *TV Communications Network, Inc. v. Turner Network Television, Inc.*, the court dismissed Sherman Act claims arising from a refusal to sell TNT and ESPN to a wireless cable operator. The court held that a party cannot be accused of attempting to monopolize its own product, that the program providers lacked monopoly power in the relevant markets and that there was no support for a conspiracy claim.[48] Finally, in *Nishimura v.*

42. Turner Vision, Inc., Satellite Receivers, Ltd., Consumer Satellite Systems, Inc., and Programmers Clearing House, Inc. v. Cable News Network, Inc., DA 98–1295 (Cable Services Bureau, rel. June 30, 1998).

43. Sherman Anti–Trust Act, § 1 (1890) (current version at 15 U.S.C.A. § 1 (West 1997)).

44. *Id.* § 2.

45. *Id.* § 45.

46. 47 U.S.C.A. § 548.

47. 789 F.Supp. 760 (S.D.Miss.1992), *aff'd* 986 F.2d 1418 (5th Cir.1993).

48. 964 F.2d 1022 (10th Cir.), *cert. denied*, 506 U.S. 999, 113 S.Ct. 601, 121 L.Ed.2d 537 (1992).

Dolan,[49] the court found that a competing overbuilder did not have standing to challenge exclusive contracts between Cablevision and its sports programming services and that there was no evidence to support a conspiracy allegation. The case was settled before appeal. Although not all courts have dismissed antitrust claims outright,[50] such cases are difficult to win.

E. Channel Occupancy Limits

The 1992 Cable Act required the FCC to promulgate rules to establish "reasonable limits on the number of channels on a cable system that can be occupied by a video programmer in which a cable operator has an attributable interest."[51] The Senate report on the Act stated that the provision "is designed to increase the diversity of voices available to the public." It noted that some multiple system operators own "many programming services" and concluded that it would be "unreasonable for them to occupy a large percentage of channels on a cable system."[52]

Pursuant to this authority, the FCC adopted rules to limit the number of affiliated programming services that could be carried on a cable system.[53] The rules provide that no cable operator may devote more than 40 percent of its activated channels to the carriage of national video programming services in which it has an attributable interest.[54] These limits apply only to channel capacity up to 75 channels on a cable system.[55] A cable operator may devote two additional channels (or up to 45 percent of its channel capacity, whichever is greater) to the carriage of minority-controlled programming services in which the operator has an attributable interest.[56] The rules do not apply to channels that were being carried on a cable system as of December 4, 1992.[57] Cable operators are required to maintain records in their public file for three years regarding the nature and extent of their attributable interest in video programming services, as well as information regarding which services they carry on their systems.[58]

49. 599 F.Supp. 484 (E.D.N.Y.1984).

50. *See e.g.,* Fort Wayne Telsat v. Entertainment & Sports Programming Network, 753 F.Supp. 109 (S.D.N.Y.1990).

51. 47 U.S.C.A. § 533(f)(1)(B) (West Supp.1997).

52. S.Conf.Rep. No. 102–92, 102d Cong., 1st Sess. 80 (1991).

53. Implementation of Sections 11 and 13 of the Cable Television Consumer Protection and Competition Act of 1992: Horizontal and Vertical Ownership Limits, Second Report and Order, 8 FCC Rcd. 8565 (1993); Implementation of Section 11(c) of the Cable Television Consumer Protection and Competition Act of 1992: Vertical Ownership Limits, Memorandum Opinion and Order, 10 FCC Rcd. 7361 (1995).

54. 47 C.F.R. § 76.504(a)(1997). Generally, any voting stock interest amounting to 5 percent or more of the outstanding voting stock is considered to be attributable, unless there is another party who owns more than 50 percent of the outstanding voting stock. *Id.* §§ 76.504(h); 76.501.

55. *Id.* § 76.504(b).

56. *Id.* § 76.504(c). Minority controlled programming services are those in which members of a minority group have a greater than 50 percent interest. *Id.* § 76.504(f).

57. *Id.* § 76.504(d).

58. *Id.* § 76.504(e).

As with many of the provisions of the 1992 Cable Act, the section relating to channel occpancy limits was challenged on constitutional grounds. In *Daniels Cablevision, Inc v. United States*, the United States District Court for the District of Columbia declined to rule on the facial validity of the channel occupancy limits.[59] However, the court noted that the channel occupancy limits "appear unrelated to content" and should be evaluated under intermediate constitutional scrutiny.[60] It added that whether or not the regulations ultimately promulgated by the FCC will pass constitutional muster is "at this point unclear."[61] On appeal, the United States Court of Appeals for the District of Columbia Circuit held its review of the channel occupancy rules in abeyance pending FCC reconsideration of the horizontal and vertical ownership limits.[62]

13.6   Cable Television Ownership Restrictions

A.   Cable–Telco Cross–Ownership

1.   The Telecommunications Act of 1996 and the Presumption of Competition

The Telecommunication Act of 1996 ended the historic prohibitions on cross ownership of cable systems by telephone companies that had been imposed by Congress, the FCC and federal courts. Section 302 of the Act repealed the former cross-ownership restriction of the Cable Act and terminated FCC rulemaking proceedings on telephone company provision of video services.[1] Section 302 of the Act expressly permits common carriers to provide video programming to subscribers in one of four ways: (1) a telephone company may provide video service as a "wireless cable" operator; (2) a telephone company may provide video transport service on a common carrier basis; (3) a telephone company may obtain a franchise and operate as a cable system; or (4) a local exchange carrier may provide video programming as an open video system. ("OVS").[2] The OVS option, which replaced the FCC's attempt to

---

59.   835 F.Supp. 1 (D.D.C.1993), *aff'd in relvant part*, Time Warner Entertainment Co. v. FCC, 93 F.3d 957, 320 U.S.App.D.C. 294 (D.C.Cir.1996).

60.   *Id.* at 7 n.11.

61.   *Id.*

62.   Time Warner Entertainment Co., 93 F.3d. at 980, 320 U.S.App.D.C. at 317. Following the release of its *Reconsideration Order* on horizontal ownership limits, the FCC asked the court to resume appellate proceedings in this matter. *See* Implementation of Section 11(c) of the Cable Television consumer Protection and Competition Act of 1992: Horizontal Ownership Limits, Memorandum Opinion and Order on Reconsideration and Further Notice of Proposed Rulemaking, FCC 98–138 (released June 26, 1998).

1.   Telecommunications Act of 1996, Pub. L. 104–104, § 302, 110 Stat. 56, 118

(1996) *codified as amended at* 47 U.S.C.A. § 571 (West Supp. 1997).

2.   *Id.* Although the 1996 Act generally repealed the cross-ownership ban, the law prohibits more than a 10 percent financial interest, or any management interest, by a telephone company in any cable operator that already provides cable service within the exchange carrier's service area.   47 U.S.C.A. § 572(a)(West Supp. 1997).   Cable operators similarly are barred from acquiring such interests in a telephone company within its franchise area.   *Id.* § 572(b). The law also prohibits joint ventures in the same markets.   *Id.* § 572(c). The 1996 Act exempts rural cable systems from the anti-buy out provision in communities of less than 35,000 population outside rural areas. *Id.* § 572(d).   It also permits telephone companies to acquire an interest in a small cable operator in competitive markets below

create a video dialtone service, enables common carriers to provide video service in a hybrid form in which carriers are subject to only some of the Cable Act requirements.[3]

Just as the Telecommunication Act permits telephone companies to provide cable service, it also opened the door to cable systems providing telecommunications service. Section 303 of the Act provides that franchising authorities "may not impose any requirement ... that has the purpose or effect of prohibiting, limiting, restricting, or conditioning the provision of a telecommunications service by a cable operator or an affiliate thereof."[4] The Act also emphasizes that telecommunications services provided over a cable system are not subject to Cable Act requirements, such as the need to obtain a franchise. Among other things, the law prohibits the collection of franchise fees on telecommunications or non-cable services. Local governments are permitted to regulate telecommunications service only to the extent necessary to manage their public rights-of-way and to ensure reasonable rates.[5] The Act also provides the FCC with preemptive authority over local regulation that would effectively prohibit the provision of telecommunication services.[6]

2. History of the Cross-Ownership Rules

The promotion of competition between different industries embodied in the 1996 Act represents a sharp break with the traditional balkanization of telecommunications and video services. Statutory and regulatory barriers existed virtually from the beginning of cable that had the effect of creating and perpetuating monopoly status of the cable industry as a wireline provider of video services. Although the rules that created and enforced the separation of industries were intended to be pro-competitive, the net effect of the regulatory structure was profoundly anti-competitive.

the top 25 markets. *Id.* § 572(d)(3). Small telephone companies also may acquire cross-ownership interests in certain suburban areas. *Id.* § 572(d)(5). Finally, telephone companies may acquire small cable systems not owned by large cable operators outside the top 100 markets.

3. 47 U.S.C.A. § 573 (West Supp. 1987). OVS resembles common carriage to the extent it is designed to be a nondiscriminatory platform for offering video services. The operator of an OVS system cannot select the programming services for carriage on more than one-third of its channel capacity where demand for carriage exceeds the supply of activated channels. 47 C.F.R. § 76.1503(c)(1997). The OVS provider cannot discriminate among the video programmers that use its channel capacity, and is required to maintain just and reasonable rates. *Id.* §§ 76.1503(a), 76.1504. OVS operators are not required to obtain a cable franchise, although certain Cable Act

obligations apply. *Id.* § 76.1510 (EEO rules, negative option billing, ownership restrictions regulation of carriage agreements). In addition, OVS operators must comply with PEG channel requirements, must carry rules, program access requirements, network nonduplication rules, syndicated exclusivity rules, and franchise fee requirements. *Id.* §§ 73.7505, 73.1506. 73.1507, 73.1508, 73.1509, 73.1511. The FCC must certify OVS operators. *Id.* § 76.1502. A cable operator may be certified only in markets with effective competition. *Id.* § 1501.

4. Telecommunication Act of 1996, Pub. L. 104–104, § 303, 110 Stat. 56, 124–25 (1996), *codified as amended at* 47 U.S.C.A. § 254 (West Supp. 1997).

5. 5. H.R. Conf. Rep. No. 458, 104th Cong., 2nd Sess. 403 (1996).

6. 47 U.S.C.A. § 253(d) (West Supp. 1997).

a. FCC Rules

Telephone companies were prohibited from providing cable television service since the early years of the cable television industry. The initial technology of cable television systems entailed building large antennas in rural areas and in locations unable to receive clear television signals over the air, and stringing cables, often on telephone poles, from the central antenna to the CATV customers.[7] Several concerns motivated the FCC to adopt cross-ownership regulations. First, the telephone company-cable television cross-ownership rules were meant to prevent local telephone companies from monopolizing the cable television business.[8] The FCC's telephone-cable rules were developed at a time when the cable television industry was in its infancy and the FCC was concerned that telephone companies would frustrate the development of this emerging industry. The FCC sought to preserve a competitive environment within the market for telecommunications services so that consumers received cable services at the lowest possible cost. The Commission feared that cross-ownership would extend the telephone company's monopoly position from telecommunications into the cable industry.[9]

Another FCC concern was the ability of the telephone company to partially avoid rate-of-return regulation on its telephone service by attributing a greater portion of its capital costs to the regulated telephone division and its revenues to an unregulated cable division. A telephone company would have an unfair competitive advantage over non-affiliated entities in establishing cable systems since it could cross-subsidize the cost of cable construction and services from its carrier revenues.[10]

The FCC cited as another justification the ability of telephone companies to deny access to independent cable systems through their control over pole attachment and conduit space.[11] Prior to action by the FCC in 1970, telephone companies could refuse to grant pole space to independent CATV operators for the placing of their cable facilities, thereby virtually barring them from entering into competition with telephone company affiliates. When access was allowed, rates charged by the telephone companies for pole attachment often were unrelated to the cost of providing such service.[12] Through its cross-ownership ban, the FCC sought to ensure that telephone companies would not use their control over telephone poles and underground conduits to prevent cable system operators from constructing cable systems.[13]

7. *See generally* Chesapeake and Potomac Telephone Co. of Virginia v. United States, 42 F.3d 181, 186 (4th Cir.1994), *vacated*, 516 U.S. 415, 116 S.Ct. 1036, 134 L.Ed.2d 46 (1996) (discussing early history of cable television).

8. *See* Applications of Telephone Companies for Section 214 Certificates for Channel Facilities Furnished to Affiliated Community Antenna Television Systems,

Final Report and Order, 21 F.C.C.2d 307, 324–25 (1970).

9. *Id.*

10. *Id.* at 308.

11. *Id.* at 327.

12. *Id.* at 311–12.

13. *Id.* at 324.

In 1968, the FCC ruled that telephone companies must obtain certification pursuant to section 214 of the Communications Act of 1934 prior to constructing, acquiring or operating any video transmission facilities.[14] The resulting section 214 applications revealed varying degrees of ownership affiliation between telephone companies and cable television operators, and the FCC initiated a rulemaking proceeding to ascertain whether telephone companies, either directly or through affiliates, should be permitted to provide cable television service to the public.[15]

In 1970, as a result of the proceeding, the FCC banned telephone companies from owning cable systems in their geographic area of operations.[16] The FCC ban precluded both direct telephone ownership and indirect ownership through an affiliate owned by, controlled by, or under the common control of the telephone company.[17] Specifically, the telephone-cable rule prohibited "any financial or business relationship whatsoever by contract or otherwise, directly or indirectly, between the carrier and the customer, except only the carrier-user relationship."[18] The Commission's rules also precluded telephone companies from providing channel or pole line conduit space, or other rental arrangements to any entity affiliated with the carrier, where such facilities or arrangements are to be used for the provision of cable service to the viewers within the telephone carrier's service area.[19]

However, the Commission's rules did not create a total barrier to telephone ownership of cable. A telephone company could own and operate cable systems outside of its telephone service area. Furthermore, a telephone company could own cable facilities where the facilities are leased back to an independent cable system. In each case, the telephone carrier was required to obtain prior FCC approval to construct the proposed cable television facilities under section 214 of the Communica-

---

14. General Telephone Co. of California, (formerly California Water and Telephone Company), The Associated Bell System Companies, The General Telephone System and United Utilities, Inc. Companies, Applicability of Section 214 of the Communications Act with Regard to Tariffs Source for Use by Community Antenna Television Systems, 13 F.C.C.2d 448 (1968), *aff'd sub nom.*, General Tel. Co. v. FCC, 413 F.2d 390, 134 U.S.App.D.C. 116 (D.C.Cir.1969). Section 214 provides in pertinent part:

No carrier shall undertake the construction of a new line or of an extension of any line, or shall acquire or operate any line, or extension thereof, or shall engage in transmission over or by means of such additional or extended line, unless and until there shall first have been obtained from the Commission a certificate that the present or future public convenience and necessity require or will require the construction, or operation, or construc-

tion and operation, of such additional or extended line. . . .

47 U.S.C.A. § 214 (West Supp. 1997).

15. Applications of Telephone Common Carriers for Section 214 Certificates for Channel Facilities Furnished to Affiliated Community Antenna Television Systems, Notice of Inquiry and Notice of Proposed Rulemaking, 34 Fed. Reg. 6290 (1969).

16. Applications of Telephone Companies for Section 214 Certificates for Channel Facilities Furnished to Affiliated Community Antenna Television Systems, Final Report and Order, 21 F.C.C.2d 307 (1970), *recon. granted in part*, 22 F.C.C.2d 746 (1970), *aff'd sub nom.*, General Telephone Co. of the Southwest v. United States, 449 F.2d 846 (5th Cir.1971).

17. 47 C.F.R. § 63.54(a) (1971).

18. *Id.* § 63.54(c).

19. *Id.* § 63.54(b).

tions Act.[20] Telephone companies wishing to enter into a lease-back arrangement within their service area were required to include a showing that they are not related or affiliated in any way with the proposed cable television operator.[21] FCC rules also provided that independent cable systems be allowed the option of constructing their own facilities. Telephone companies could not force the cable systems to accept a telephone company owned facility.[22]

The cross-ownership rules included provisions allowing the FCC to grant waivers. The rules permitted a telephone company to enter the cable television business under two circumstances: (1) in communities where cable service "demonstrably could not exist" unless provided by the local telephone company; or (2) in other circumstances where "other good cause" could be shown.[23]

The FCC later adopted an amendment attempting to better define those areas where cable service otherwise could not exist and to streamline the procedures for seeking waivers. In 1979, the FCC adopted a presumptive waiver policy giving a petitioning telephone company a rebuttable presumption that independent cable television service is not feasible in jurisdictions with population densities of less than thirty homes passed per cable mile.[24] The waiver mechanism and its amendment were designed to reduce the impediments to the development of rural cable television service caused by the general cross-ownership prohibition.

In 1978, the FCC stated that the waiver for "other good cause" included cases that are in the "public interest" and required telephone companies to demonstrate the general benefits which could flow from joint operation of cable television and telephone facilities.[25] In 1980, the FCC stated that a telephone company's burden of demonstrating good cause could be satisfied by a showing of clear and substantial economies in telephone company construction or operation.[26] However, the FCC also stated that the burden would not be met by a mere showing of possible marginal advantage in joint operation over independent operation.[27]

Despite the waiver mechanism, the FCC found in 1981 that many rural areas remained unserved by cable television.[28] Therefore, to ensure

20.   47 U.S.C.A. § 214 (West 1997).

21.   47 C.F.R. § 63.55 (1971).

22.   *Id.* § 63.57.

23.   *Id.* § 63.55.

24.   Revision of the Processing Policies for Waivers of the Telephone Company– Cable Television "Cross–Ownership Rules," Sections 63.54 and 64.601 of the Commission's Rules and Regulations, Report and Order, 82 F.C.C.2d 233 (1979); 47 C.F.R. § 63.56(b) (1980).

25.   Revision of the Processing Policies for Waivers of the Television Company–

Cable Television "Cross–Ownership Rules," Sections 63.54 and 64.601 of the Commission's Rules and Regulations, Clarification and Notice of Proposed Rulemaking, 69 F.C.C.2d 1097, 1110–11 (1978).

26.   Petition of Sugar Land Telephone Company for Waiver of Sections 63.54 and 64.601 of the Commission's Rules and Regulations, Mem. Op. and Order, 76 F.C.C.2d 230, 235–36 (1980).

27.   *Id.*

28.   Elimination of the Telephone Company—Cable Television Cross–Ownership Rules, Sections 63.54–63.56, for Rural Ar-

that rural areas enjoy the benefits of cable service and to reduce the expense and delay associated with the waiver process, the FCC supplemented its policy by granting an exemption from the cross-ownership rules for those carriers serving "rural areas."[29] This exemption, also required that no cable system be under construction or in existence within the proposed rural service area.

b.   Modification of Final Judgment or "MFJ"

In addition to the FCC rules, the nation's largest local telephone companies faced additional restrictions on cable-related activities. The provision of cable services was construed as an "information" service that could not be provided by former Bell Companies under the terms of the Modified Final Judgment in connection with the AT & T divestiture.

In 1982, AT&T settled the government's antitrust suit against it by entering into the Modification of Final Judgment ("MFJ").[30] Under the MFJ, AT&T divested its local telephone operations, known as Bell Operating Companies ("BOCs"), which were organized into regional holding companies.[31] AT&T retained its long-distance telephone and other businesses and was released from certain restrictions on its entry into certain unregulated lines of business, such as computers, imposed by an earlier 1956 consent decree.[32]

The MFJ imposed various restrictions on the BOCs' "lines of business." These restrictions were intended to prevent the BOCs from using their monopoly positions in the local telephone business to disadvantage competitors in other markets. Specifically, the MFJ prohibited the BOCs from becoming involved, directly or indirectly, in (1) providing interexchange telecommunications services; (2) manufacturing telecommunications equipment; or (3) providing information services. The limit on involvement in the information services business was broad, and it included cable television services.[33] Thus, the MFJ prohibited the BOCs from providing any type of cable television service.[34]

c.   1984 Cable Act

The Cable Communications Policy Act of 1984 generally codified the

---

eas, Report and Order, 88 F.C.C.2d 564, 565 (1981).

29. *Id., partial recons. denied.,* Mem. Op. and Order, 91 F.C.C.2d 622 (1982). The FCC adopted the definition of "rural area" prepared and used by the Bureau of the Census. Thus, a carrier would be exempt from the prohibition if that area did not contain:

1) any incorporated place of 2,500 inhabitants or more, or any part thereof;

2) any unincorporated place of 2,500 inhabitants or more, or any part thereof; or

3) any other territory, incorporated or unincorporated, included in an urbanized area.

47 C.F.R. § 63.58. (1982).

30. *See* United States v. AT&T, 552 F.Supp. 131 (D.D.C.1982) *aff'd sub nom.,* Maryland v. United States, 460 U.S. 1001, 103 S.Ct. 1240, 75 L.Ed.2d 472 (1983).

31. AT&T, 552 F. Supp. at 200.

32. *Id.* at 170.

33. *Id.* at 186–95.

34. *Id.* at 189–95.

FCC's cross-ownership rules.[35] The Act prohibited a telephone common carrier from providing (1) video programming to subscribers in its telephone service area; and (2) channel capacity, or pole line, or conduit space to any affiliate to be used in connection with the provision of video programming directly to subscribers in the telephone company's service area.[36]

Like the FCC's cross-ownership rule, the statutory test for waiver in the 1984 Act was whether a cable system "demonstrably could not exist" without telephone company involvement or whether "good cause" can be shown.[37] However, the 1984 Act altered the FCC waiver process by directing the Commission to narrowly construe its waiver authority in a manner that would not undermine the "basic policy" of the 1984 Act's cross-ownership rule. This basic policy was to prohibit telephone companies from providing video programming directly to subscribers in their telephone service areas.[38]

The most significant difference from the FCC cross-ownership rules was the 1984 Act's treatment of the rural exemption. Under the 1984 Act, telephone companies were granted a blanket exemption to provide cable service in rural areas.[39] The legislative history expressed congressional desire to eliminate as an absolute precondition the prior FCC requirement that there be no cable system under construction or in existence in the rural area. Congress found that this condition had prevented some rural telephone companies from offering cable television service in rural areas.[40] Thus, under section 613(b)(3), a telephone company was permitted to compete with traditional cable operators for a franchise in any area which met the FCC's definition of a rural area. The telephone company needed only to certify that it served a rural area to come within the exemption.

3. Erosion of the Prohibitions

a. Lifting the MFJ Restriction

As part of the 1982 MFJ, the district court retained jurisdiction over the decree and the Department of Justice pledged to report to the court every three years as to the continuing need for the line of business restrictions.[41] Since divestiture was not actually accomplished until 1984, the first such "triennial review" was held in 1987. The 1987 report recommended the complete removal of the manufacturing and information services restrictions as well as the modification of the interexchange restrictions. However, after considering the DOJ's report, as well as the comments of the other parties and dozens of other individuals and organizations, the district court largely left intact the interexchange,

---

35. 47 U.S.C.A. § 533(b) (West 1991).

36. *Id.* § 533(b)(1)-(2).

37. *Id.* § 533(b)(4).

38. 130 Cong. Rec. H12237 (daily ed. Oct. 11, 1984).

39. 47 U.S.C.A. § 533(b)(3) (West 1991).

40. House Comm. on Energy and Commerce, Report on Cable Franchise Policy and Communications Act of 1984, H.R. Rep. No. 98–934, at 57 (1984).

41. AT&T, 552 F. Supp. at 231.

manufacturing, and information services restrictions including the cable cross-ownership ban.[42]

In 1990, the United States Court of Appeals for the District of Columbia Circuit affirmed the district court's ruling with regard to the manufacturing and interexchange restrictions.[43] However, the appeals court instructed the district court to use a different standard than it had been using to determine whether the BOCs should be allowed to provide information services in their local telephone service areas.[44] The district court had required the BOCs to show that there was "no substantial possibility" that they could use their monopoly power to impede competition.[45] The District of Columbia Circuit held that the proper standard was whether or not allowing the BOCs to provide information services "comports with the 'public interest.' "[46]

On remand, the district court reluctantly eliminated the restriction on information services.[47] For over fifty pages, the court chronicled the anticompetitive practices of the BOCs and presented a forceful case against eliminating the information services restrictions. The court added that "were the Court free to exercise its own judgment, it would conclude without hesitation that removal of the information services restriction is incompatible with the decree and the public interest."[48] But the district court interpreted the appeals court's opinion as requiring it to defer to the judgment of the Department of Justice on the question of whether to allow telephone companies to provide information services.[49] In addition, the district court felt constrained to allow telephone companies to provide those services unless it was certain that the effect would be anticompetitive.[50] Accordingly, the court lifted the bar against the provision of information services contained in the MFJ.[51] The court of appeals affirmed the district court's removal of the information services line of business restriction from the MFJ in 1993.[52]

b. Judicial Challenges to Cable Act Cross-Ownership Limits

When Congress adopted the Telecommunications Act, the existing cross-ownership rules were under substantial pressure from constitutional litigation. Several United States district courts and the United States Courts of Appeals for the Fourth and Ninth Circuits had held that section 613(b) of the Cable Act violated the First Amendment rights of telephone companies. In the first case, *Chesapeake and Potomac Tele-*

---

42. *See* United States v. Western Elec. Co. Inc., 673 F.Supp. 525 (D.D.C.1987).

43. United States v. Western Elec. Co., 900 F.2d 283, 289, 283 U.S. App. D.C. 299, 305 (D.C.Cir.), cert. denied 498 U.S. 911, 111 S.Ct. 283, 112 L.Ed.2d 238 (1990).

44. Western Elec. Co., 900 F.2d at 309, 283 U.S. App. D.C. at 325.

45. *Id.* at 300, 283 U.S. App. D.C. at 316.

46. *Id.* at 305, 283 U.S. App. D. C. at 321.

47. United States v. Western Elec. Co. Inc., 767 F.Supp. 308 (D.D.C.1991).

48. *Id.* at 327.

49. *Id.* at 329.

50. *Id.* at 330–32.

51. *Id.* at 332.

52. United States v. Western Elec. Co., 993 F.2d 1572 (D.C.Cir.1993), cert. denied, 510 U.S. 984, 114 S.Ct. 487, 126 L.Ed.2d 438 (1993).

phone Co. of Virginia v. United States,[53] Bell Atlantic, through its subsidiary C&P Telephone, challenged the cross-ownership restriction as violative of the First Amendment, both on its face and as applied to Bell Atlantic's proposal to provide cable service in Alexandria, Virginia.[54] The court agreed with Bell Atlantic, and applied an intermediate level of First Amendment scrutiny to the law.[55] The court determined that although the government's interests in promoting competition and facilitating the availability of multiple information sources are significant, the ban on telephone company provision of video programming was not sufficiently narrowly tailored.[56] The Fourth Circuit also held that section 613(b) did not leave telephone companies with ample alternative channels for communication.[57]

In *US West v. United States,*[58] the Court of Appeals for the Ninth Circuit similarly applied an intermediate scrutiny test and agreed with the Fourth Circuit that Section 613(b) was not sufficiently narrowly tailored. The court found that the evidence submitted by US West demonstrated that the pro-competitive goals of the ban could be "achieved through a variety of less speech-restrictive means."[59] Unlike the Fourth Circuit, however, the Ninth Circuit, did not reach the issue of the availability of "ample alternative channels of communication."[60] Several district courts similarly held that Section 613(b) violates the First Amendment.[61] The Supreme Court granted certiorari in *Chesapeake & Potomac Telephone Company of Virginia*. The case was briefed and argued in the Supreme Court's 1995 Term.[62] In the interim, however, Congress adopted Section 302 of the Telecommunications Act which eliminated the statutory ban on cross-ownership. Accordingly, the Supreme Court terminated the proceeding and vacated the lower court rulings.[63]

c. Changing Federal Policies

Before Congress changed the law to allow telephone entry, the FCC had begun to relax its policies in various respects. Even as the government was defending the cross-ownership ban in court, the FCC had

53. 830 F.Supp. 909 (E.D.Va.1993), *aff'd* 42 F.3d 181 (4th Cir.1994), *vac'd,* 516 U.S. 415, 116 S.Ct. 1036, 134 L.Ed.2d 46 (1996).

54. *Id.*

55. *Id.* at 917.

56. Chesapeake and Potomac Telephone Company of Virginia, 42 F.3d 181 (4th Cir. 1994), *vac'd,* 516 U.S. 415, 116 S.Ct. 1036, 134 L.Ed.2d 46 (1996).

57. *Id.* at 202–03.

58. 48 F.3d 1092, 1106 (9th Cir.1994), *cert. granted, judgment vac'd,* 516 U.S. 1155, 116 S.Ct. 1037, 134 L.Ed.2d 186 (1996).

59. *Id.* at 1105.

60. *Id.* at 1106.

61. Ameritech Corp. v. United States, 867 F.Supp. 721, 736 (N.D.Ill.1994); Bell-South Corp. v. United States, 868 F.Supp. 1335 (N.D.Ala.1994); Nynex Corp. v. United States, 1994 WL 779761, at *1 (D.Me.1994). *See also* Southwestern Bell v. United States, 1995 WL 444414 (N.D.Tex.1995) (holding that Section 613(b) abridges plaintiff telephone company's First Amendment rights because it is not narrowly tailored).

62. 515 U.S. 1157, 115 S.Ct. 2608, 132 L.Ed.2d 852 (1995), *vacated,* 516 U.S. 415, 116 S.Ct. 1036, 134 L.Ed.2d 46 (1996).

63. United States v. Chesapeake and Potomac Telephone Co. of Virginia, 516 U.S. 415, 116 S.Ct. 1036, 134 L.Ed.2d 46 (1996).

recommended that Congress should repeal the cross-ownership prohibition. In 1987, the FCC instituted a Notice of Inquiry to reassess the telephone company-cable television cross-ownership rules.[64] The Notice generally supported repeal or relaxation of the cross-ownership rules. The FCC questioned whether there remained any need for those protective rules in light of the fact that the cable television business is "robustly competitive and comparatively mature" and not the fledgling industry it was in 1972.[65] In 1988, the FCC issued a Further Notice of Inquiry in which it tentatively recommended that Congress repeal the cross-ownership rules and allow cable ownership by telephone companies.[66]

Additionally, the FCC relaxed its cross-ownership rules to allow some telephone company involvement in the video programming industry. In 1992, the FCC issued a Second Report and Order that modified its cross-ownership rules to permit, but not require, telephone companies to provide video dialtone service in their telephone service areas.[67] The FCC modified the cross-ownership rules in order to advance its goals of "creating opportunities to develop an advanced telecommunications infrastructure, increasing competition in the video marketplace, and enhancing the diversity of video services to the American public."[68]

Under the FCC's video dialtone rules, telephone companies were permitted to make available to video programmers a basic platform to deliver video programming and other services to consumers within the telephone companies' local service areas.[69] The "basic platform" was defined as a common carriage transmission service coupled with a means by which consumers could gain access to any or all video program providers making use of the program.[70] The telephone company was required to offer transmission capacity on its basic platform on a nondiscriminatory common carrier basis and the platform was to contain sufficient capacity to serve multiple video programmers.[71]

The video dialtone rules also permitted telephone companies to provide, on a separate platform, enhanced and non-common carrier services to customers of the common carrier platform.[72] Such services could include the offering of video menus or "gateways," video processing services, billing and collection, video customer premises equipment and other services related to video programming.[73] The video dialtone rules prohibited a telephone company from selecting video programming

---

64. Telephone Company–Cable Television Cross–Ownership Rules, Sections 63.54–63.58, Notice of Inquiry, 2 FCC Rcd. 5092 (1987).

65. *Id.* at 5093.

66. Telephone Company–Cable Television Cross–Ownership Rules, Sections 63.54–63.58, Further Notice of Inquiry and Notice of Proposed Rulemaking, 3 FCC Rcd. 5849 (1988).

67. Telephone Company–Cable Television Cross–Ownership Rules, Sections 63.54–63.58, Second Report and Order, Recommendation to Congress, and Second Fur-

ther Notice of Proposed Rulemaking, 7 FCC Rcd. 5781 (1992).

68. *Id.* at 5783.

69. *Id.* at 5787.

70. *Id.* at 5783, n.3.

71. *Id.* at 5787.

72. *Id.* at 5788.

73. *Id.* Telephone Company—Cable Television Cross–Ownership Rules, 7 FCC Rcd. at 5788 (1992).

by determining how programming is presented for sale to customers.[74] The rules also prohibited a telephone company from having a cognizable financial interest in, or exercising editorial control over, video programming provided directly to subscribers within their telephone service areas.[75]

In a separate Memorandum Opinion and Order, the FCC reaffirmed its conclusion that neither telephone companies offering video dialtone services nor the customer-programmers of such services would be required to obtain a local cable television franchise in order to provide video programming to end users.[76] An appeal filed by the National Cable Television Association, the National Association of Telecommunications Officers and Advisors and other cable, local government, and interested parties challenged the FCC's decision on the franchise issue. However, the United States Court of Appeals for the District of Columbia Circuit rejected the petitioners' arguments and upheld the FCC's decision.[77]

Finally, in 1995, the Commission issued a Third Report and Order to respond to the court decisions declaring section 613(b) unconstitutional.[78] In its Third Report and Order, the FCC concluded that it had the legal authority to grant waivers to allow telephone companies to provide video programming directly to subscribers in their telephone service areas over video dialtone networks if they comply with certain conditions.[79] The FCC derived this authority from section 613(b)(4) which permits the FCC to waive the cross-ownership ban upon a showing of "good cause."[80] The FCC explained that "good cause" commonly is interpreted to include changed circumstances, and that the circumstances that led the FCC to institute the cross-ownership rule in 1970 had changed dramatically.[81] Accordingly, the FCC concluded that it has good cause to routinely grant waivers to the cross-ownership prohibition under certain conditions.[82]

The FCC stated that its reading of the waiver provision avoided the constitutional difficulties associated with section 613(b) that were identified by the courts.[83] By construing the waiver provision to authorize telephone companies to provide video programming, the FCC contended that telephone companies' free speech interests are not unduly bur-

---

74. *Id.* at 5789.

75. *Id.*

76. Telephone Company–Cable Television Cross–Ownership Rules, Sections 63.54–63.58, Mem. Op. and Order on Recons., 7 FCC Rcd. 5069 (1992).

77. National Cable Television Ass'n Inc. v. FCC, 33 F.3d 66, 75 (D.C.Cir.1994). In November 1994, the FCC released a Reconsideration Order that generally affirmed the video dialtone service rules adopted in the Second Report and Order, and made only minor clarifications to those rules. *See* Telephone Company–Cable Television Cross–Ownership Rules, Sections 63.54–63.58 and Amendments of Parts 32, 36, 61, 64 and 69

of the Commission's Rules to Establish and Implement Regulatory Procedures for Video Dialtone Service, Mem. Op. and Order on Recons. and Third Further Notice of Proposed Rulemaking, 10 FCC Rcd. 244 (1994).

78. Telephone Company–Cable Television Cross–Ownership Rules, Sections 63.54–63.58, Third Report and Order, 10 FCC Rcd. 7887 (1995).

79. *Id.*

80. *Id.*

81. *Id.* at 7889.

82. *Id.*

83. *Id.* at 7888.

dened.[84] Thus, the FCC concluded that its waiver policy made it unnecessary for the courts to decide whether a complete prohibition on video programming by telephone companies is constitutional.[85] Less than a year later, these issues were rendered moot by the passage of the Telecommunications Act of 1996.

B. Cross–Ownership Restrictions Governing Other Video Technologies

Cross-ownership rules also apply to various types of wireless delivery of video signals. The 1992 Cable Act amended section 613(a) of the Communications Act of 1934 by adding a prohibition against common ownership of a cable system and either a multichannel multipoint distribution ("MMDS") service or a satellite master antenna television ("SMATV") service in the franchise area served by the cable system.[86] The cross-ownership provision addressed congressional concern that common ownership of different means of video distribution might reduce competition and limit the diversity of voices available for the public.[87] The cross-ownership provisions also were intended to promote competition by preventing a cable operator from "warehousing its potential competition."[88]

1. MMDS

Section 613(a)(2) of the Cable Act prohibits a cable operator from holding a MMDS license in any portion of the franchise area served by the cable operator's cable system.[89] The Commission concluded that the MMDS-cable cross-ownership rules it adopted in a 1991 rulemaking, with certain modifications and additions, effectively implemented the MMDS-cable restriction in the 1992 Act. Those rules "prohibited" directly or indirectly, ownership interests in, control of, or leasing of ... MMDS ... by cable television companies in geographic areas which overlap the ... MMDS protected service areas ... for cable franchise areas lacking two or more competing cable television companies."[90] The Commission made several modifications to these rules to bring them into compliance with the 1992 Act. First, the FCC's rules previously had

---

84. Telephone Company–Cable Television Cross–Ownership Rule, Section 63.54–63.58, Third Report and Order, 10 FCC Rcd. 7887, 7890 (1995).

85. *Id.* at 7888.

86. 47 U.S.C.A. § 533 (West Supp. 1997). MMDS systems, often referred to as "wireless cable," transmit programming to subscribers through 2 GHz microwave frequencies, using channels allocated to MDS service and leased excess capacity on instructional microwave ("ITFS") channels. SMATV, or satellite master antenna television systems, transmit signals to high density locations, such as multiple dwelling units, without using public rights-of-way.

87. S. Rep. No. 102–92, at 46 (1991).

88. *Id.* at 47. *See* Implementation of Sections 11 and 13 of the Cable Television Consumer Protection and Competition Act of 1992: Horizontal and Vertical Ownership Limits, Cross–Ownership Limitations and Anti–Trafficking Provisions, Report and Order and Further Notice of Proposed Rulemaking, 8 FCC Rcd. 6828 (1993) ("Report and Order For Sections 11 and 13").

89. 47 U.S.C.A. § 533(a)(2) (West Supp. 1997).

90. Amendments of Parts 21, 43, 74, 78, and 94 of the Commission's Rules Governing Use of the Frequencies in the 2.1 and 2.5 GHz Bands, Order on Recons., 69 Rad. Reg. 2d 477, 1491 (P & F 1991).

prohibited a cable operator from obtaining an MMDS license if the protected MMDS service area overlapped in any part with the cable operator's franchise area, regardless of whether the cable system actually served those portions of its franchise area that overlapped the MMDS service area.[91] The FCC amended these rules to prohibit MMDS-cable cross-ownership only to the extent that the MMDS service area overlaps the actual cable service area of the cable system.[92] Pursuant to the Telecommunications Act of 1996, the FCC amended the rules to eliminate the cross-ownership restriction in communities with "effective competition."[93]

The FCC's rules establish attribution limits on cross-ownership of cable systems and MMDS services. Under the current rule, a cable operator is considered to have an attributable interest in an MMDS system only if the cable operator holds five percent or more of the stock of the licensee.[94] However, the FCC did not adopt a single majority shareholder exception and decided that all officer and director positions and general partnership interests are attributable.[95] A cable operator also is considered to have an attributable interest if it owns a limited partnership interest of five percent or greater, regardless of insulation.[96]

The Commission's rules previously had permitted a cable operator to own an interest in an MMDS system if another cable operator provided cable service in the franchise area. The Commission eliminated this exception as inconsistent with the cross-ownership bar under Section 613.[97] The FCC also eliminated the rural exemption to its cross-ownership prohibition as inconsistent with the 1992 Act.[98] However, cable operators can seek a waiver for ownership of an MMDS license in rural areas if, consistent with section 613(a), such waiver is necessary to ensure that all significant portions of a cable franchise area are able to obtain video programming.[99] A waiver will be granted only if no other MMDS operator desires to provide video programming service in the area.[100] Finally, the FCC's rules had contained an exception to the cross-ownership restriction which permitted cable operators to lease one MMDS channel in an MMDS service area to provide local programming not otherwise available within the franchise area. The FCC retained the exception.[1]

2.   SMATV

Section 613(a)(2) of the 1992 Cable Act prohibits a cable operator from offering SMATV service "separate and apart" from its franchised

91. *Id.*

92. Report and Order of Sections 11 and 13, 8 FCC Rcd. at 6843 (1993).

93. Implementation of Sections 202(f), 202(i) and 301(i) of the Telecommunications Act of 1996, 11 FCC Rcd. 15115 (1996); 47 C.F.R. § 21.912 (1997).

94. *Id.* at 6843.

95. *Id.*

96. *Id.*

97. *Id.* at 6842–43.

98. *Id.* at 6844.

99. *Id.* at 6843–44.

100. *Id.* at 6844.

1. *Id.* The FCC has opened an inquiry to review its attribution rules, Review of the Commission's Cable Attribution Rules, CC Docket No. 98–82 (rel. June 26, 1998).

cable service in any portion of the franchise area served by the cable operator's cable system.[2] The FCC modified SMATV-cable cross-ownership rules adopted in 1991 to conform to the statutory cross-ownership restriction.[3] The rules were modified again after passage of the Telecommunications Act of 1996 to exclude franchise areas where there is "effective competition."[4]

The FCC interpreted the 1992 Act's "separate and apart" language to permit cable operators to construct stand-alone or integrated SMATV systems within its actual service area, provided that such cable-owned SMATV systems comply with all provisions of the applicable cable franchise agreement.[5] However, the FCC initially interpreted the statutory language to prohibit cable operators from acquiring existing SMATV facilities within the cable operator's actual service area, even if the operator intended to integrate the SMATV facility into its existing system.[6] The FCC concluded that allowing cable operators to acquire existing SMATV facilities would undermine competition between cable operators and SMATV providers, reinforce existing cable monopolies, and reduce competitive opportunities for SMATV providers within the cable service area.[7]

Although a cable operator was initially prohibited from acquiring an existing SMATV system in its actual service area, the FCC permitted cable operators to acquire or build SMATV systems located in unserved portions of their franchise areas.[8] However, cable operator-owned SMATV systems that are acquired or built in unserved portions of franchise areas must still be operated in compliance with the franchise agreements.[9]

In 1995, the FCC removed the prohibition against cable operators' acquisitions of SMATV systems within their actual service areas and eliminated the regulatory distinction drawn in the Report and Order that accorded disparate regulatory treatment based upon distinctions between the construction and acquisition of SMATV systems. The modification permits a cable operator to acquire an SMATV system located within its franchise area, provided that the acquired SMATV facility is operated in accordance with the terms and conditions of the franchise agreement.[10]

---

2. 47 U.S.C.A. § 533(a) (West Supp. 1997); see generally, Report and Order for Sections 11 and 13, 8 FCC Rcd. at 6844.

3. Report and Order of Section 11 and 13, 8 FCC Rcd. at 6845.

4. Implementation of Sections 202(f), 202(i) and 301(i) of the Telecommunications Act of 1996, 11 FCC Rcd. 15115 (1996); 47 C.F.R. § 76.501(f) (1997).

5. Id.

6. Id. at 6846.

7. Id.

8. Id. at 6846.

9. Id.

10. See Implementation of Sections 11 and 13 of the Cable Television Consumer Protection and Competition Act of 1992: Horizontal and Vertical Ownership Limits, Cross–Ownership Limitations and Anti–Trafficking Provisions, Mem. Op. and Order on Recons. of First Report and Order, 10 FCC Rcd. 4654 (1995) ("Mem. Op. and Order on Recons.").

The Commission applied the same attribution criteria adopted in connection with the MMDS-cable cross-ownership restrictions to SMATV-cable restrictions.[11] Thus, a cable operator is considered to have an attributable interest in a SMATV system if the cable operator holds five percent or more of the stock of the SMATV system.[12] In addition, all officer and director positions and general partnership interests are attributable, as are limited partnership interests of five percent or greater.[13]

Section 613(a)(2)(A) provides that the FCC shall waive the ownership restrictions for all existing MMDS and SMATV services that were "owned by a cable operator [on the date of enactment of this paragraph.]"[14] The FCC clarified that cable ownership interests in MMDS and SMATV services as of October 5, 1992 are grandfathered.[15] It is unclear whether a grandfathered MMDS or SMATV system can expand the number of households currently served.

The 1992 Act does not address enforcement of the cross-ownership provisions, and the FCC declined to adopt additional enforcement mechanisms or reporting requirements.[16] The Commission enforces the cross-ownership restrictions on a case-by-case complaint basis.[17] Complaints regarding violations of these restrictions must be filed with the FCC pursuant to the special relief procedures set forth in section 76.7 of the FCC rules.[18]

3. Broadcasting

The FCC historically prevented cable systems from owning broadcast stations in their service areas or affiliating with broadcast networks. In 1992, the FCC significantly relaxed the network restrictions and allowed major broadcast networks to own cable systems in certain circumstances.[19] The rule allowed a network to own cable systems so long as the network-owned systems did not pass more than ten percent of homes passed nationwide and fifty percent of the homes passed within the Area of Dominant Influence in which the cable system was located.[20] The 1996 Act eliminated the network cross-ownership rule. Section 202(f) of the Act required the FCC to revise its rules to "permit a person or entity to own or control a network of broadcast stations and a cable system."[21] The Telecommunications Act also eliminated a statutory

---

11. Report and Order For Sections 11 and 13, 8 FCC Rcd. at 6846.

12. Id.

13. Id.

14. 47 U.S.C.A. § 533(a)(1) (West Supp. 1997).

15. Implementation of Sections 11 and 13 of the 1992 Cable Act: Horizontal and Vertical Ownership Rules, Cross-Ownership Rules and Anti–Trafficking Provisions, Erratum, 8 FCC Rcd. 6212 (1993).

16. Report and Order For Sections 11 and 13, 8 FCC Rcd. at 6847.

17. Id.

18. Id.

19. 47 C.F.R. § 76.501 (b)(i)-(ii) (1993).

20. Id. However, the fifty percent limit was inapplicable if the cable system was subject to effective competition.

21. Implementation of Sections 202(f), 202(i) and 301(i) of the Telecommunications Act of 1996; Cable Television Anti–Trafficking Network Television, and MMDS/SMATV Cross–Ownership Rules, Order, 11 FCC Rcd. 15115 (1996).

prohibition against common ownership of a local broadcast station and a cable system, but FCC rules continue to preclude cross-ownership of a cable system and a broadcast station within the same local market.[22]

C. Horizontal Ownership Restrictions

In 1990, the FCC found that ownership of cable systems became significantly more concentrated following the passage of the 1984 Act.[23] It concluded that horizontal concentration in the cable industry is a serious concern because concentration can facilitate anti-competitive conduct.[24] In 1992, Congress echoed the FCC's concerns about horizontal concentration and added section 613(f) to the Cable Act. That section required the FCC to prescribe "reasonable limits on the number of cable subscribers a person is authorized to reach through cable systems owned by such person, or in which such person has an attributable interest."[25] However, due to a judicial challenge to the horizontal ownership restrictions, the FCC stayed their effective date, and the rules have never gone into effect.[26]

The FCC rules prohibit "any one entity from having an attributable interest in cable systems that in the aggregate reach more than 30 percent of cable homes passed nationwide."[27] The FCC concluded that the 30 percent limit was reasonable to prevent the types of anticompetitive conduct that concerned Congress.[28] It further concluded that 30 percent was not so low as to diminish unreasonably the efficiencies and program financing benefits still to be gained from additional horizontal consolidation by the largest multiple systems operators.

The 30 percent limit is measured by reference to all cable systems in which an entity has an attributable interest. The FCC adopted the broadcast attribution criteria contained in section 73.3555 of the FCC's rules to determine compliance with the horizontal ownership limit.[29] In general, and subject to certain exceptions enumerated in the attribution rules, an entity will have an attributable interest in a cable system in

---

22. 47 C.F.R. § 76.501(a) (1997). In 1998, the FCC initiated an inquiry to determine whether to eliminate the cross-ownership ban on broadcast stations in the same market. Review of the Commission's Broadcast Ownership Rules and Other Rules Enacted Pursuant to Section 202 of the Telecommunications Act of 1996, FCC 98-37 (rel. Mar. 13 (1998).

23. Competition, Rate Deregulation and the Commission's Policies Relating to the Provision of Cable Television Service, Report, 5 FCC Rcd. 4962, 5004 (1990).

24. *Id.* at 5006.

25. 47 U.S.C.A. § 533(f)(1)(A) (West Supp. 1997).

26. Implementation of Section 11(c) of the Cable Television Consumer Protection Act of 1992: Horizontal Ownership Limits,

Mem.Op. and Order on Recons. and Further Notice of Proposed Rulemaking, FCC 98-138 (rel. June 26, 1998).

27. Implementation of Sections 11 and 13 of the Cable Television Consumer Protection Act of 1992: Horizontal and Vertical Ownership Limits, Second Report and Order, 8 FCC Rcd. 8565, 8576-77 (1993). ("Horizontal and Vertical Ownership Limits").

28. *Id.* at 8577. *See* 47 C.F.R. § 76.503 (1997).

29. Horizontal and Vertical Ownership Limits, 8 FCC Rcd. at 8580-81. The FCC has since reopened the question of how to define what constitutes a cognizable interest. *See* Review of the Commission's Cable Attribution Rules, Notice of Proposed Rule-Making, FCC 98-112 (rel. June 26, 1998).

which it owns or controls at least five percent of the voting stock, any general partnership interest, or any limited partnership interest.[30] However, minority stock interests will not be attributed where there is a single 51 percent shareholder.[31] Additionally, the interests of "insulated" limited partners are not attributable.[32]

The FCC did not adopt a proposal that would have excluded from a multichannel system operator's "homes passed" calculation those homes in areas of "effective competition."[33] Nor did the Commission prorate the calculation according to the size of the attributable interest in the particular system that passes those homes. The FCC stated that the presence of effective competition does not directly respond to congressional concerns about the exercise of undue control by a single entity at the national level.[34]

The rule requires periodic review of the ownership limits in view of the fact that the cable industry is so dynamic and fluid.[35] Accordingly, the subscriber limits are subject to review every five years to determine if they are still necessary under prevailing market conditions.[36]

The FCC rules provide one exception to the 30 percent limit on horizontal ownership. The rules allow the ownership of additional cable systems reaching up to 35 percent of cable homes passed if at least five percent of those homes are subscribers of minority-controlled cable systems.[37] The attribution rules define "minority-controlled" as a system "more than 50 percent owned by one or more members of a minority group."[38] The 35 percent exception was designed to encourage a diversity of viewpoints in cable programming.[39]

The FCC prescribed a certification system to enforce the horizontal ownership limits. Entities holding attributable interests in cable systems reaching 20 percent or more of homes passed nationwide will be required to certify to the FCC, prior to the acquisition of any additional cable systems, that such acquisition will not result in a violation of the horizontal ownership limits.[40] Where a transaction will result in a cable operator exceeding the limit, the rules permit the cable operator to seek either a temporary or permanent waiver from the FCC.[41] Generally, waivers apply requests only in limited circumstances where an acquisition temporarily places a cable operator over the permissible number of subscribers or where a cable operator seeks to expand service into an otherwise unserved rural area.[42]

30. Horizontal and Vertical Ownership Limits, 8 FCC Rcd. at 8580.

31. *Id.* at 8581.

32. 8 FCC Rcd. 8568, 8581 (1993); *see* 47 C.F.R. § 73.3555 (1997).

33. Horizontal and Vertical Ownership Limits, 8 FCC Rcd. at 8579.

34. *Id.*

35. *Id.* at 8583.

36. *Id.*

37. 47 C.F.R. § 76.503(b) (1997).

38. *Id.* 76.503(d).

39. Horizontal and Vertical Ownership Limits, 8 FCC Rcd. at 8578–79.

40. *Id.* at 8582–83.

41. *Id.*

42. *Id.* at 8583.

In 1998, the FCC decided to continue its stay preventing enforcement of the ownership limits, but lifted the stay as it related to certain reporting requirements.[43] Previously, the United States District Court for the District of Columbia had found that the horizontal ownership limitation was violative of the First Amendment, and the FCC stayed enforcement pending reconsideration.[44] On review, the United States Court of Appeals for the District of Columbia Circuit decided to hold court proceedings on the horizontal limits in abeyance pending FCC reconsideration.[45] In this proceeding the FCC decided to retain the 30 percent limit, but sought comment on how the limit should be applied.[46] In the interim, the Commission directed entities owning cable systems reaching 20 percent or more of homes nationwide to notify the FCC of any incremental ownership changes.[47]

13.7   Cable Consumer Protection Issues

A.   *Subscriber Privacy*

The 1984 Cable Act created statutory privacy rights for cable subscribers. The Act requires notice to subscribers that personally identifiable information is being collected, prohibits the unauthorized collection or disclosure of any such data and provides private causes of action for any violations of these rights.[1]

Subscribers must be notified of their privacy rights when they first subscribe to cable service. Notice must be provided annually thereafter. Subscriber notices must describe what personally identifiable information might be collected, how it may be disclosed and how long the operator retains the information.[2] The notice also must describe the limits of operator liability, and provide a method for gaining access to the subscriber data.[3] Generally, the notice requirements have been strictly construed.[4]

The Act prohibits collection of personally identifiable data without the subscriber's prior consent.[5] Such consent may be given electronically or in writing.[6] There are two exceptions to this requirement: (1) the operator may collect personally identifiable information in order to "render a cable service or other service provided by the cable operator to

---

43. Implementation of Section 11(c) of the Cable Television Consumer Protection and Competition Act of 1992: Horizontal Ownership Limits, Memorandum Opinion and Order on Reconsideration and Further Notice of Proposed Rulemaking, FCC 98–138 (rel. June 26, 1998).

44. Daniels Cablevision, Inc. v. United States, 835 F.Supp. 1, 10 (D.D.C.1993).

45. Time Warner Entertainment Co., L.P. v. FCC, 93 F.3d 957, 979–980, 320 U.S. App.D.C. 294, 316–317 (D.C.Cir.1996).

46. *See* note 43 *supra*, at 101.

47. *Id.* ¶ 76.

1. 47 U.S.C.A. § 551 (1985) as *amended by* 47 U.S.C.A. § 551 (West 1991 and Supp. 1997).

2. *Id.* § 551(a)(1)(A) (West 1991).

3. *Id.* § 551(a)(1).

4. *See* Scofield v. Telecable of Overland Park, Inc., 751 F.Supp., 1499 (D.Kan.1990), *rev'd*, 973 F.2d 874 (10th Cir.1992); Warner v. American Cablevision of Kansas City, Inc., 699 F.Supp. 851 (D.Kan.1988). The *Warner* case was settled and the District Court ruling was vacated.

5. 47 U.S.C.A. § 551(b)(1) (West 1991).

6. *Id.*

the subscriber," or (2) to "detect unauthorized reception of cable communications."[7] Additionally, the provision does not apply to aggregate data which do not contain "personally identifiable information," such as individual programming choices.[8]

The requirement of subscriber consent before disclosure also contains exceptions. First, it is not necessary to obtain consent in order "to render or conduct a legitimate business activity related to a cable service or other service provided by the cable operator to the subscriber."[9] Additionally, the cable operator may disclose the name and address of a subscriber so long as the disclosure does not include any information regarding the nature of service provided or viewing habits.[10] Additionally, information may be disclosed pursuant to a court order, subject to various conditions.[11] The 1992 Cable Act strengthened subscribers' rights by requiring cable operators to take precautions to prevent unauthorized access to information covered by the section.[12]

The Cable Act gives subscribers the right to access data collected by the cable operator as well as the right to correct any erroneous information.[13] Operators also have an affirmative duty to delete any subscriber data that is no longer necessary.[14] The Act provides a private right of action for subscribers whose rights have been violated. Successful litigants may obtain $100 per day for a violation, or a minimum of $1000 punitive damages, and attorneys' fees.[15] One court has held that claims under this section may not be brought as a class action.[16] The federal privacy protections do not preempt state or local laws protecting subscriber privacy, so long as they are consistent with the Cable Act.[17]

B. Customer Service Standards—Consumer Protection

Good customer service has traditionally been a concern of franchising authorities and cable subscribers.[18] The 1992 Cable Act greatly expanded government authority in this area by empowering the FCC to establish federal customer service standards that could be adopted and supplemented by local authorities.[19] The federal standards include, as a

7. *Id.* § 551(b)(2).

8. *See* Metrovision of Livonia, Inc. v. Wood, 864 F.Supp. 675 (E.D.Mich.1994).

9. 47 U.S.C.A. § 551(c)(1) (West 1991 & Supp. 1997).

10. *Id.* § 551(c)(2)(ii) (West 1991).

11. *Id.* § 551(h). When the government seeks to obtain protected data, it must offer "clear and convincing evidence" that the subscriber is reasonably suspected of a crime and that the information would be relevant to its prosecution. The subscriber must be provided the opportunity to contest any such demand. *Id.* § 551(h)(1). If a private party is seeking the information, the subscriber need only be notified of the demand. *Id.* § 551(c)(2)(B).

12. *Id.* § 551(c)(1) (West Supp. 1997).

13. *Id.* § 551(d) (West 1991).

14. *Id.* § 551(e).

15. *Id.* § 551(f).

16. Wilson v. American Cablevision of Kansas City, Inc., 133 F.R.D. 573 (W.D.Mo. 1990).

17. 47 U.S.C.A. § 551(h) (West 1991).

18. *See* Telesat Cablevision, Inc. v. City of Riviera Beach, 773 F.Supp. 383 (S.D.Fla. 1991) (upholding requirement for "efficient service"); Ventura v. Cox Cable Jefferson Parish, Inc., 583 So.2d 1237 (La.App.1991).

19. 47 U.S.C.A. § 552(b) (West Supp. 1997).

statutory minimum, requirements governing cable system office hours and telephone availability, installations, outages, service calls and communications between the cable operator and subscriber regarding such matter as bills and refunds.[20] The Act specifically preserved local authority, stating that non-federal consumer protection laws would be valid unless "specifically preempted by this subchapter."[21] In particular, the law allows state or local governments to impose customer service requirements that exceed the federal standards or that address issues not covered by the FCC's rules. Additionally, franchising authorities and cable operators are permitted to reach customer service agreements that are more stringent than the federal rules.[22]

The FCC adopted specific customer service standards in 1993.[23] The rules provide for local enforcement of the FCC customer service standards. The Commission specifically noted that the 1992 Act did not contemplate a federal enforcement role. Nevertheless, the FCC stated that it will "retain the authority to address, as necessary, systemic abuses that undermine the statutory objectives."[24] Before a local franchising authority may enforce customer service standards it must notify the cable operator of its intention to do so in writing. The rules cover cable operations in minute detail. For example, the FCC rules provide that telephone answer time (including time on hold) cannot exceed 30 seconds and, if the call must be transferred, transfer time must not exceed an additional 30 seconds.[25] The standards must be met at least 90 percent of the time, measured quarterly. Cable systems with 1,000 or fewer subscribers are eligible to seek waiver of the customer service rules.

C. Notice Requirements

The Cable Act imposes various requirements on cable operators to provide information to subscribers. These requirements relate to such issues as the collection of personally identifiable information, services offered and billing practices, changes in cable service and notice regarding the provision of free previews of premium movie channels.

Many of the notice requirements are derived from the rate regulation requirements of the Act. Cable operators are required to provide adequate notice to all subscribers of the availability of basic cable service.[26] In addition, any increase in basic rates must be preceded by at least 30 days' notice to the franchising authority.[27] The FCC's rules further provide that a franchising authority must be notified of any

---

20. *Id.* § 552(b) (1)-(3).

21. *Id.* § 552(d)(1).

22. *Id.* § 552(d)(2).

23. Implementation of Section 8 of the Cable Television Consumer Protection and Competition Act of 1992, Consumer Protection and Customer Service, Report and Order, 8 FCC Rcd. 2892 (1993).

24. *Id.* at 2897.

25. *Id.* at 2904; 47 C.F.R. § 76.309(c)(1).

26. 47 U.S.C.A. § 543(b)(7) (West Supp. 1997).

27. *Id.* § 543(b)(6).

increase or decrease in rates for service or equipment.[28] No prior notice to subscribers is required where rate changes are caused by fees imposed by federal agencies, or by state or local franchising authorities.[29] Like the provisions relating to subscriber privacy, the FCC's customer service standards require cable operators to provide written information at the time of installation, and at least annually thereafter or upon a subscriber's request.[30] The required information must describe the products and services being offered, prices and options for programming services and conditions of subscription, installation and service maintenance policies, instructions as to how to use the particular cable service, channel positions of services carried on the system and billing and complaint procedures, including the address and telephone number of the franchising authority.[31] The rules also require that subscriber bills be fully itemized and broken down into charges for basic and premium services and equipment.[32]

Another provision of the 1992 Act requires cable operators to provide advance notice for any free previews of "premium channels" that offer movies rated by the Motion Picture Association of America as X, NC–17, or R.[33] Although this provision was initially found to be unconstitutional by the United States District Court for the District of Columbia, it was subsequently upheld by the United States Court of Appeals for the District of Columbia Circuit.[34] The appeals court held that the law required only that the cable operator provide notice to subscribers, and for that reason it did not prevent "a cable operator from running any program a subscriber desires."[35] It found that such notice requirements were necessary to make such measures as "lockboxes" an effective mechanism for screening programs coming into subscribers' homes.[36] The court acknowledged that the MPAA ratings "do not measure which movies are constitutionally protected and which are not" but added, "[w]e are dealing with a disclosure statute, not a direct restriction on speech." [37]

D. *Compatibility with Electronics Equipment*

The 1992 Cable Act included detailed requirements intend to ensure compatibility between television, cable systems and other consumer electronic products, such as VCRs.[38] The Act required that the FCC implement rules affecting various issues of equipment compatibility, including clarifying what is meant by a "cable ready" TV, notifying

28. 47 C.F.R. § 76.964 (1997).

29. 47 U.S.C.A. § 552(c) (West Supp. 1997).

30. 47 C.F.R. § 76.309(c)(3)(i)(A) (1997).

31. *Id.* § 76.309(c)(3)(i)(A)(1)-(6).

32. *Id.* § 76.309(c)(3)(ii)(A).

33. 47 U.S.C.A. § 544(d)(3)(B) (West Supp. 1997). The Section also provides that subscribers may have such free previews blocked upon request.

34. Daniels Cablevision, Inc. v. United States, 835 F.Supp. 1 (D.D.C.1993), *rev'd in relevant part, sub nom.* Time Warner Entertainment Co. v. FCC, 93 F.3d 957, 320 U.S. App. D.C. 294 (D.C.Cir.1996).

35. Time Warner Entertainment Co., 93 F.3d at 981, 320 U.S. App. D.C. at 318.

36. *Id.* at 982, 320 U.S. App. D.C. at 319.

37. *Id.*

38. 47 U.S.C.A. § 544A(c)(2) (West Supp. 1997).

subscribers where converter boxes may limit a subscribers' ability to watch one program while simultaneously taping another, taping consecutive programs on different channels, preserving the option to forego the need for a converter box and preserving the subscriber's ability to obtain converter boxes and remote controls from competitive sources. These requirements were limited slightly by passage of the Telecommunications Act of 1996, which required that the compatibility regulations be limited to the equipment functions set out in the 1992 Act.[39]

Where a cable operator rents remote control devices, it must notify subscribers that they can purchase the devices from a competing source rather than renting them from the operator.[40] Cable operators are required to supply subscribers when they first subscribe, and annually thereafter, with information on electronic equipment compatibility.[41]

The 1996 Act requires the FCC to adopt rules to guarantee the competitive availability of "navigation devices."[42] A navigation device is any equipment used to access multichannel video programming, such as a converter box or other interactive communication equipment.[43] The provision was adopted to ensure that unaffiliated entities may provide navigation devices to subscribers.

The Act empowers the FCC to waive the requirements if necessary to aid in the development of new or improved programming services.[44] Additionally, the FCC cannot adopt rules that would jeopardize security of programming signals.[45] Under rules promulgated by the FCC, subscribers have the right to attach any compatible navigation devices (such as set top boxes, cable modems, and other devices) to a multichannel video programming system. Multichannel video programming distributors are required to separate security functions of such devices from non-security functions by July 1, 2000. Video service providers are permitted to continue offering navigation devices with integrated security functions during a transition period, but the sale of such devices will be prohibited after January 1, 2005. The rules on navigation devices will sunset when the FCC determines that the multichannel video market is fully competitive, that the market for navigation devices is fully competitive and that elimination of the rules will promote competition.[46]

13.8   *Technical Regulations

A.   *Generally*

The 1992 Cable Act required the FCC to establish minimum technical standards for cable television signal quality, and to periodically

---

39. *Id.* § 544(a)(4).

40. *Id.* § 544A(c)(2)(E)(I).

41. 47 C.F.R. § 76.630(d) (1997).

42. 47 U.S.C.A. § 549(a) (West Supp. 1997).

43. *Id.*

44. *Id.* § 549(c).

45. *Id.* § 549(b).

46. Implementation of Section 304 of the Telecommunications Act of 1996: Commercial Availability of Navigation Devices, FCC 98–116 (rel. June 24, 1998). *See* 47 C.F.R. §§ 76.1200–76.1210 (1998).

* Entire section published in Modern Communication Law, Practitioners Edition, Vol. 3.

update such standards.[1] Pursuant to an agreement between organizations representing cable operators and franchising authorities, the FCC in 1992 had adopted new technical standards for cable television systems. It was the first major revision of such standards in two decades.[2] The 1992 revisions, which were mandatory for all cable systems, replaced the Commission's voluntary guidelines for signal quality. These rules were incorporated as part of the 1992 Act's requirements.[3]

The 1992 law permitted local franchising authorities to enforce technical standards as part of local franchising requirements.[4] In addition, local authorities could petition the FCC for permission to impose more stringent standards.[5] The 1996 Telecommunications Act, however, repealed these provisions, making enforcement of technical signal quality a matter of exclusive federal jurisdiction.[6] The 1996 law bars states and franchising authorities from prohibiting, conditioning or restricting a cable system's use of any type of subscriber equipment or any transmission technology.[7]

Other federal regulations relate to various aspects of cable system operation. For example, consumer electronics components of a cable system such as converter boxes are governed by FCC equipment verification standards.[8] In addition, rules adopted pursuant to the 1992 Cable Act require that consumer electronics devices and cable systems be compatible.[9] Additionally, the FCC and the Federal Aviation Administration jointly administer regulations governing notification and other technical requirements effecting the construction of antenna towers.[10] FCC rules also require cable systems to maintain a technical inspection file which is generally available only to regulatory bodies.[11]

B.   Cable Television Relay Service ("CARS")*

C.   Frequency Coordination*

D.   Emergency Alert System*

E.   Home Wiring*

13.9   *Miscellaneous Issues

1. 47 U.S.C.A. § 544(e) (West Supp. 1997).

2. Cable Television Technical and Operational Requirements, Review of the Technical and Operational Requirements of Part 76, Cable Television, Report and Order, 7 FCC Rcd. 2021 (1992).

3. Cable Television Technical and Operational Requirements, Review of the Technical and Operational Requirements of Part 76, Cable Television, Petitions for Reconstruction, Mem. Op. and Order, 7 FCC Rcd. 8676 (1992).

4. 47 U.S.C.A. § 544 (West Supp. 1997).

5. *Id.*

6. Telecommunications Act 1996, Pub. L. 104–104, § 301(8), 110 Stat. 56, 116 (1996) *codified as amended* at 47 U.S.C.A. § 544(e) (West Supp.1997).

7. *See* Implementation of Cable Act Reform Provisions of the Telecommunications Act of 1996, Order and Notice of Proposed Rulemaking, 11 FCC Rcd. 5937 (1996).

8. 47 C.F.R. pt. 15 (1997).

9. 47 U.S.C.A. § 544A (West Supp. 1997).

10. 47 C.F.R. pt. 17 (1997).

11. *Id.* § 76.601 (c) (1997).

* Published in Modern Communication Law, Practitioners Edition, Vol. 3.

* Published in Modern Communication
Law, Practitioners Edition, Vol. 3.

Chapter Fourteen

REGULATION OF BROADCASTING

Analysis

14.1 Broadcast Regulation And The Public Interest

A. *The Elusive Public Interest Standard*

The public interest standard is the "touchstone of authority" for the Federal Communications Commission ("FCC").[1] The standard was first adopted as part of the Radio Act of 1927, which created the Federal Radio Commission ("FRC"). Recognizing the importance of the new medium of communications, the Washington Post described the Radio Act as the "most important legislation of the session."[2] The Act directed the FRC to perform various tasks, including classifying radio stations, describing the type of service to be provided, assigning frequencies, making rules to prevent interference, establishing the power and location of transmitters and establishing coverage areas in a way that maximized the public good. But this did not address the larger question of what constitutes "the public good." The FRC took the position that the Supreme Court eventually would define the public interest case by case. Nevertheless, it outlined the primary attributes of the public interest in its policy statements and licensing decisions. [3]

---

1. FCC v. Pottsville Broadcasting Co., 309 U.S. 134, 60 S.Ct. 437, 84 L.Ed. 656 (1940).

2. *See* PHILIP T ROSEN, THE MODERN STENTORS: RADIO BROADCASTING AND THE FEDERAL GOVERNMENT 106 (Greenwood Press 1980).

3. *E.g.*, Great Lakes Broadcasting Co., F.R.C. Ann. Rep. 32 (1929), *aff'd in part and rev'd in part* Great Lakes Broadcasting v. FRC, 37 F.2d 993, 59 App. D.C. 195 (D.C.Cir.), *cert. dismissed*, 281 U.S. 706, 50 S.Ct. 467, 74 L.Ed. 1129 (1930). The *Great Lakes* decision established programming service as one of the public interest criteria governing radio station renewal. *See generally* Robert Corn–Revere, *Economics and Media Regulation*, in MEDIA ECONOMICS THEORY AND PRACTICE 71–90 (Alexander, Owers & Carveth, eds, 1993).

Congress borrowed the expression "public interest, convenience or necessity" from the field of railroad regulation, and its use in the context of radio regulation was almost accidental. The terms had been used previously in the Transportation Act of 1920.[4] Senator Clarence C. Dill, who drafted the Communications Act, later recounted that "[a] young man on the committee staff had worked at the Interstate Commerce Committee for several years ... and he said, 'Well, how about "public interest, convenience and necessity"? That's what we used there.' That sounded pretty good, so we decided we would use it, too."[5]

By shifting the context of the regulatory mandate from railroads to radio, however, its meaning became less certain. Judge Henry Friendly wrote in his classic study *The Federal Administrative Agencies* that the use of the "public convenience and necessity" standard "conveyed a fair degree of meaning" in the Transportation Act "when the issue was whether new or duplicating railroad construction should be authorized or an existing line abandoned." However, the standard "was almost drained of meaning" in the context of radio regulation "where the issue was almost never the need for broadcasting service but rather who should render it."[6]

The Communications Act of 1934 uses various formulations of the "public interest" language,[7] and like the Radio Act before it, does not define the terms.[8] The absence of specific statutory direction has been a distinguishing characteristic of communications regulation. As one contemporary observer wrote regarding the standard as employed in the Radio Act, " '[p]ublic interest, convenience or necessity' means about as little as any phrase that the drafters of the Act could have used.... "[9] The Communications Act did not improve the situation. Former FCC Commissioner Glen O. Robinson has noted the frequent criticism that

---

4. 41 Stat 456 (1920), *codified at* 49 U.S.C.A. § 10901 (West 1997). For a general discussion *see* Glen O. Robinson, *The Federal Communications Act: An Essay on Origins and Regulatory Purpose* in A Legislative History of the Communications Act of 1934 (Max Paglin, ed. 1989) pp. 3–24.

5. Newton N Minow and Craig L. Lamay, Abandoned in the Wasteland 4 (Hill and Wang: New York 1995).

6. Henry Friendly, The Federal Administrative Agencies 54–55 (Harvard University Press 1962) *See also* Robinson, note 4 *supra* at pp. 14–16.

7. *See, e.g.,* 47 U.S.C.A. §§ 201(b), 215(a), 319(c) and 315(a) ("public interest"); §§ 214(a) and 214(c) ("public convenience and necessity"); § 214(d) ("interest of public convenience and necessity"); §§ 307(c), 309(a) and 319(d) ("public interest, convenience and necessity"); § 307(a) ("public convenience, interest or necessi-

ty"); §§ 311(b) and 311(c)(3) ("public interest, convenience or necessity").

8. Office of Communication of the United Church of Christ v. FCC, 707 F.2d 1413, 1429, 228 U.S. App. D.C. 8, 24 (D.C.Cir. 1983) ("the [Communications] Act provides virtually no specifics as to the nature of those public obligations inherent in the public interest standard"). Despite the lack of a categorical definition of the public interest, various provisions of the Act operationally define at least part of what Congress intended. For example, the Act directs the FCC to provide, to the extent possible, rapid and efficient communication service, adequate facilities at reasonable charges, provision for national defense and safety of lives and property, and a fair, efficient and equitable distribution of radio service to each of the states and communities.

9. Louis Caldwell, *The Standard of Public Interest, Convenience or Necessity as Used in the Radio Act of 1927,* 1 Air Law Rev 291, 295 (1930).

the public interest standard "is vague to the point of vacuousness, providing neither guidance nor constraint on the agency's action," adding that "[w]hat the act itself does not define, the legislative history does not illuminate."[10]

Accordingly, "[b]ecause the act did not define what the public interest meant," former FCC Chairman Newton Minow has written, "Congress, the courts, and the FCC have spent sixty frustrating years struggling to figure it out."[11] Two prominent communications lawyers have suggested that "[p]erhaps no single area of communications policy has generated as much scholarly discourse, judicial analysis, and political debate over the course of the last 70 years as has that simple directive to regulate in 'the public interest.' "[12] It has also generated conflict. Since broadcast regulation began, the meaning of the public interest has been the focal point for the clash of values at the FCC, and at the FRC before it.[13]

But there is another eye-of-the-beholder problem embedded in this regulatory puzzle. Not only does the public interest standard provide scant guidance for selecting among particular policy options in a given instance, there is robust debate as to whether it is a "good" standard. At one end of the spectrum, it has been described as the "intellectual knife of collectivism's sacrificial guillotine."[14] At the other, it has been said that all of the FCC's actions would be "without meaning" in the absence of the public interest standard.[15] As a consequence, the FCC has been "a storm center of criticism from the left and the right."[16] One thing that all can agree on, however, is that the meaning of the "public interest" has changed over time.

The nature of the public interest has fluctuated in part because of the political outlook of those who administer the law. "At various times in its history the Federal Communications Commission has taken a broad view of its power and responsibility to further what it deemed to be in the public interest" while at others it has promoted "rapid moves toward deregulation."[17] As former FCC Commissioner Ervin Duggan put it, "successive regimes at the FCC have oscillated wildly between enthusiasm for the public interest standard and distaste for it."[18] While this

---

10. Robinson, *supra* note 4 at 14.

11. MINOW and LAMAY, *supra* note 5 at 5.

12. Erwin G. Krasnow, and Jack Goodman, *The "Public Interest" Standard: The Elusive Search for the Holy Grail*, 50 Fed. Comm.L.J. 605, 606 (1998).

13. NEWTON N. MINOW, EQUAL TIME, THE PRIVATE BROADCASTER AND THE PUBLIC INTEREST 4 (NEW YORK: ATHENAEUM 1964).

14. AYN RAND, CAPITALISM: THE UNKNOWN IDEAL 121–122 (New American Library 1966) ("the 'public interest'. .amounted to a blank check on totalitarian power over the broadcasting industry, granted to whatever bureaucrats happened to be appointed to the Commission").

15. Newton N Minow, *Commemorative Messages*, in A LEGISLATIVE HISTORY OF THE COMMUNICATIONS ACT OF 1934 (Max Paglin, ed. 1989) at p. xvi.

16. J Roger Wollenberg, *The FCC as Arbiter of "The Public Interest, Convenience, and Necessity,"* in A LEGISLATIVE HISTORY OF THE COMMUNICATIONS ACT OF 1934 (Max Paglin, ed. 1989) p. 77.

17. *Id* at 77–78.

18. Ervin Duggan, *Congressman Tauzin's Interesting Idea*, Broadcasting & Cable, Oct 20, 1997 at S18.

has led some to criticize the FCC for being overly political, Judge E. Barrett Prettyman of the United States Court of Appeals for the District of Columbia Circuit has described it as being "political in the high sense of that abused term."[19] Still, the inherently political nature of the regulatory mandate creates special tensions since "the 'public interest' standard necessarily invites reference to First Amendment principles."[20]

The invitation to apply First Amendment principles, however, has done little to clarify the statutory mandate or reduce the Commission's political mood swings. From the beginning, the public interest standard permitted the government to regulate broadcast content while simultaneously prohibiting censorship. Section 29 of the Radio Act, and Section 326 of the Communications Act, specifically prohibited "giv[ing] the licensing authority the power of censorship over the radio communications...."[21] At the same time, the FRC promulgated as an early statement of policy that programming would be considered in license renewal decisions, that stations should meet the "tastes, needs and desires of substantial groups among the listening public" as opposed to "propaganda"[22] and that operators that failed to meet the Commission's expectations would lose their licenses.[23] The Commission and the courts resolved this evident paradox by concluding that the "application of the regulatory power of Congress in a field within the scope of its legislative authority" is not "a denial of freedom of speech."[24] Similarly, comparing the FCC to a "traffic cop," the Supreme Court decided that the Act "does not restrict the Commission merely to supervision of the traffic. It puts upon the Commission the burden of determining the composition of that traffic."[25] What none of the decisions established, however, was how far the cop could go in issuing citations.

The meaning of the public interest also varies because of the nature of technology. Congress purposefully left the regulatory standard open,

19. Pinellas Broadcasting Co. v. FCC, 230 F.2d 204, 206, 97 U.S. App. D.C. 236, 238 (D.C.Cir.1956), cert. denied, 350 U.S. 1007, 76 S.Ct. 650, 100 L.Ed. 869 (1956) ("Commissions themselves change, underlying philosophies differ, and experience often dictates change. Two diametrically opposite schools of thought in respect to the public welfare may both be rational.").

20. CBS, Inc. v. Democratic National Committee, 412 U.S. 94, 122, 93 S.Ct. 2080, 2096, 36 L.Ed.2d 772 (1973). *See* Wollenberg, *supra*, note 16 at 61 ("[I]t seems passing strange that a society traditionally fearful of government should have subjected one of its major communications media to sweeping, vaguely defined administrative powers").

21. 47 U.S.C.A. § 29 (West 1927); 47 U.S.C.A. § 326 (West 1991).

22. Great Lakes Broadcasting Co, 3 FRC Ann. Rep. 32.

23. *See* KFKB Broadcasting Ass'n v. FRC, 47 F.2d 670, 671, 60 App. D.C. 79, 80

(D.C.Cir.1931) (self-promoting program the "Medical Question Box" which aired on station licensed to a controversial doctor held to violate the public interest); Trinity Methodist Church, South v. FRC, 62 F.2d 850, 61 App. D.C. 311 (D.C.Cir.1932), cert. denied, 288 U.S. 599, 53 S.Ct. 317, 77 L.Ed. 975 (1933) (license renewal denied to radio minister who campaigned against corruption and attacked the Catholic Church, Jews, local law enforcement officers and public officials). *Compare* Near v. Minnesota, 283 U.S. 697, 51 S.Ct. 625, 75 L.Ed. 1357 (1931) (injunction against "nuisance publication" that attacked local public officials struck down as prior restraint).

24. Trinity Methodist Church, South, 62 F.2d at 852, 61 App. D.C. at 313.

25. National Broadcasting Co. v. United States, 319 U.S. 190, 215–216, 63 S.Ct. 997, 1009, 87 L.Ed. 1344 (1943).

with the details to be filled in by the FCC over time because radio was a new and complicated technology. The FCC's broad powers were based on the assumption that "Congress could neither foresee nor easily comprehend ... the highly complex and rapidly expanding nature of communications technology."[26] The Supreme Court described the public interest standard in *FCC v. Pottsville Broadcasting Co.* as "a supple instrument for the exercise of discretion" that is "as concrete as the complicated factors for judgment in such a field of delegated authority permit."[27]

At various times the underlying focus on technological issues has been made explicit. For example, in 1983 Congress added a new section to the Communications Act establishing "the policy of the United States to encourage the provision of new technologies and services to the public."[28] The Telecommunications Act of 1996 also placed great emphasis on promoting innovation and technology. Similarly, the Supreme Court has recognized that "because the broadcast industry is dynamic in terms of technological change[,] solutions adequate a decade ago are not necessarily so now, and those acceptable today may well be outmoded 10 years hence."[29]

For all of these reasons, in seeking to apply a vague statutory mandate, the Commission has revised its substantive public interest requirements over time. In 1941, the Commission decided that broadcast editorials violated the public interest, only to reconsider that policy eight years later.[30] Similarly, in 1945 the Commission withheld renewal of a radio station license until the station agreed to sell time for paid editorials to the United Auto Workers.[31] Since then, however, the Commission determined that licensees cannot be forced to sell time to a particular group. This more current view of the public interest was upheld by the Supreme Court.[32]

Even when the basic policies have not changed, the Commission has modified their application to the extent audience needs and expectations are different today than they were in the early days of radio. The FCC's "indecency" restrictions have existed since radio regulation began, but their scope has shifted along with social change. For example, in late 1937, hundreds of radio listeners complained about an episode of NBC's

---

26. National Ass'n of Regulatory Utility Commissioners v. FCC, 525 F.2d 630, 638 n. 37, 173 U.S. App. D.C. 413, 421 n. 37 (D.C.Cir.1976).

27. 309 U.S. at 138, 60 S.Ct. at 439, 84 L.Ed. at 659.

28. 47 US.C.A. § 157 (West 1991).

29. CBS v. Democratic National Committee, 412 U.S. 94, 102, 93 S.Ct. 2080, 2086, 36 L.Ed.2d 772, 783–784 (1973).

30. *Compare* Mayflower Broadcasting Corp 8 F.C.C. 333 (1941) *with* Opinion on Editorializing by Broadcasters, 13 F.C.C. 1246 (1949). *See also* Syracuse Peace Council, 2 FCC Rcd. 5043 (1987), *aff'd sub nom.*

Syracuse Peace Council v. FCC, 867 F.2d 654, 276 U.S. App. D.C. 38 (D.C.Cir.1989), cert. denied, 493 U.S. 1019, 110 S.Ct. 717, 107 L.Ed.2d 737 (1990) (fairness doctrine does not serve the public interest); FCC v. League of Women Voters of California, 468 U.S. 364, 104 S.Ct. 3106, 82 L.Ed.2d 278 (1984) (ban on editorials by public broadcast stations is unconstitutional).

31. *E.g.*, United Broadcasting Co., 10 F.C.C. 515 (1945).

32. CBS, Inc. v. Democratic National Committee, 412 U.S. 94, 93 S.Ct. 2080, 36 L.Ed.2d 772 (broadcasters may not be compelled to provide a generalized right of access to discuss controversial issues).

"Charlie McCarthy" program in which Charlie McCarthy and Mae West portrayed the title characters in a sketch entitled "Adam and Eve." The FCC investigated the matter and found nothing in the script objectionable. But some of Mae West's inflections were considered "suggestive." On this basis, the Commission sent NBC and its affiliates letters concluding that the program was "vulgar, immoral or of such other character as may be offensive to the great mass of right-thinking, clean-minded American citizens."[33] Although the indecency rules continue to be a major point of contention, there is little doubt that the standard upheld in *FCC v. Pacifica Foundation*,[34] with its focus on "filthy words," is not as restrictive as the rules once were.

The same is true for some of the Commission's other programming requirements. For example, eight Georgia radio stations were given only temporary renewals in 1958 because the stations were devoted to a "news and music" format. The Commission informed the stations by letter that full-term license renewals had been denied because their program schedules consisted "almost entirely of recorded music."[35] The Commission has since left questions of programming format up to the listeners, who may express their preferences as choices in the marketplace.[36]

Similar examples abound. The Commission has suggested in the past that the public interest was not served when stations scheduled commercials within news programs, or when they aired "too many" soap operas.[37] In 1937 the Commission questioned the license renewal of a station that produced a program called "The Friendly Thinker" that offered advice on business affairs, love and marriage. Although the show's host was not an astrologer and disclaimed any supernatural powers, the Commission concluded that such advice programs were objectionable because of their tendency to mislead the public. The Commission renewed the license only after the station discontinued the program.[38] The FCC has moved away from such a rigid approach, and it is not difficult to find such programs as "The Friendly Thinker" on the air today.

The FCC's approach to broadcast advertising similarly evolved. In 1936, it ordered a renewal hearing for a licensee that had aired commercials that made "exaggerated claims" for a weight loss product.[39] But as then-Chairman James H. Quello wrote in 1993, "[j]ust imagine the number of minor celebrities that would have to find honest work if the

33. *See "FCC Issues Rebuke for Mae West Skit,"* Broadcasting, January 15, 1938 at 13.

34. 438 U.S. 726, 98 S.Ct. 3026, 57 L.Ed.2d 1073 (1978).

35. *See Closed Circuit,* Broadcasting, March 31, 1958 at 5; *Closed Circuit,* Broadcasting, July 7, 1958 at 10

36. FCC v. WNCN Listeners Guild, 450 U.S. 582, 101 S.Ct. 1266, 67 L.Ed.2d 521 (1981).

37. *See generally* Public Service Responsibility of Broadcast Licensees (March 7, 1946) (the "Blue Book")

38. Radio Broadcasting Corp, 4 F.C.C. 125 (1937).

39. Don Lee Broadcasting System, 2 FC.C. 642 (1936).

Commission mounted a new crusade to ensure the effectiveness of diets."[40] The notion of what may be considered "excessive" advertising also changed over time. In 1930, William S. Hedges, then president of the National Association of Broadcasters, testified before Congress regarding the quantitative advertising limits that the NAB then enforced. He said that at his station, "no more than one minute out of the 30 minutes is devoted to advertising sponsorship. In other words, the radio listener gets 29 minutes of corking good entertainment, and all he has to do is to learn the name of the organization that has brought to him this fine program."[41]

Not only does today's audience expect to give up more than a minute in exchange for a corking good sitcom, the Commission concluded that the viewers are the best judge of how much advertising is too much. The FCC found in 1984 that the number of alternative choices available to viewers is the best protection against over-commercialization.[42] The Commission assumed that the remote control is a better regulator of broadcaster behavior than the government. This conclusion found further support in the fact that, in the interval of a few years, the broadcast networks experienced sharp declines in audience share, from over 90 percent in the mid–1980s to less than 60 percent in the early 1990s.[43]

Such a market-oriented approach had not been persuasive to the Federal Radio Commission. In 1928 it rejected the argument that listeners could shift away from "irksome" broadcasts and it placed four radio stations on probation for having too many commercials. The FRC noted that the listeners' "only alternative, which is not to tune in on the station, was not satisfactory, particularly when in a city such as Erie only the local stations could be received during a large part of the year. When a station is [devoted to excessive advertising] the entire listening public is deprived of the use of a station for a service in the public interest."[44]

The FRC's approach to the public interest was deemed to be necessary because of the economic and technological factors unique to broadcasting. The same considerations informed the FCC's interpretation of the public interest, as affirmed by the Supreme Court in *National Broadcasting Co. v. United States*[45] and *Red Lion Broadcasting Co. v.*

40. Implementation of Section 4(g) of the Cable Television Consumer Protection and Competition Act of 1992, Home Shopping Station Issues, 8 FCC Rcd 5321, 5335 (1993) (Statement of Chairman Quello).

41. Senate Committee on Interstate Commerce, Hearings on S. 6, 71st Cong., 2d Sess. (1930). William S. Paley of CBS similarly testified that seven-tenths of one percent of the network's air time was devoted to advertising. *Id.*

42. The Revision of Programming and Commercialization Policies, Ascertainment Requirements, and Program Log Require-

ments for Commercial Television Stations, 98 F.C.C. 2d 1076, 1101–05 (1984), *aff'd in relevant part sub nom.* Action for Children's Television v. FCC, 821 F.2d 741, 261 U.S. App. D.C. 253 (D.C.Cir.1987).

43. Evaluation of the Syndication and Financial Interest Rules, 58 Fed Reg. 28927 (May 18, 1993).

44. FRC Decision on Stations WRAK, WABF, WBRE and WMBS, discussed in the Blue Book at 41.

45. 319 U.S. 190, 63 S.Ct. 997, 87 L.Ed. 1344.

FCC.[46] The Telecommunications Act of 1996, however, was based on the premise that economic regulation had become less necessary, and that many rules could be lifted. Nevertheless, every provision of the Telecommunications Act relating to speech content added new regulations.[47] In this aspect, the Act signaled a shift back to defining the "public interest" through content controls. At the same time, the FCC reemphasized content regulation in pursuit of the public interest. For example, it adopted guidelines quantifying the amount of educational programming required of television licensees.[48] Former FCC Chairman Reed Hundt forcefully advocated numerous other measures, including mandating free time for political candidates and public service announcements, arguing that the public interest standard should be implemented through quantified programming requirements.[49]

In 1997, by Executive Order, President Bill Clinton initiated another effort to define the public interest by establishing an Advisory Committee on the public interest obligations of digital broadcasters.[50] The committee, dubbed the "Gore Commission" because of its mandate to report conclusions to the Vice President, was chartered to define "the public interest obligations digital television broadcasters should assume." The Committee recommended that the FCC adopt a set of "mandatory minimum public interest requirements for digital broadcasters" but could not reach consensus about what the standards should be.[51] The Gore Commission's effort continued a process begun exactly seventy years earlier with the Radio Act's search for the public interest.

B. *Public Interest Rationales*

Although broadcasting "is clearly a medium affected by a First Amendment interest,"[52] the public interest standard has been interpreted over the years to permit a greater degree of government regulation of speech than for the print media. The primary rationale advanced for this differential treatment has been the limited capacity of the broadcast

---

46. 395 U.S. 367, 89 S.Ct. 1794, 23 L.Ed.2d 371 (1969).

47. *See generally* The Telecommunications Act of 1996, Pub L. 104–104, 110 Stat. 56 (1996) Title V of the law, the Communications Decency Act, implemented the V-chip regime, added scrambling and time-shifting requirements on "adult" video services and included the Exon amendment to regulate "indecent" speech on the Internet. In addition, Section 713 of the Act required the FCC to establish regulations and implementation schedules requiring closed captioning for video programming.

48. Policy and Rules Concerning Children's Television Programming, 11 FCC Rcd. 10660 (1996).

49. *See, e.g.,* Reed E. Hundt and Karen Kornbluh, *Renewing the Deal Between Broadcasters and the Public: Requiring Clear Rules for Children's Educational*

Television, 9 Harv. J. Law & Tech. 11, 16–17 (1996); FCC News Release, Chairman Hundt Says More Campaign Free Political Time, And Direct Communications Between Candidates And Public Is Needed; Praises Belo Broadcasting Initiative (Sept. 24, 1996).

50. Executive Order 13038, Advisory Committee on the Public Interest Obligations of Digital Broadcasters (rel Mar. 11, 1997).

51. Report of the Advisory Committee on Public Interest Obligations of Digital Television Broadcasters (Dec. 18, 1998) at 47–48.

52. Red Lion Broadcasting Co, 395 U.S. at 386, 89 S. Ct. at 1805, 23 L. Ed.2d at 386–387.

spectrum. As the Supreme Court put it in *Red Lion Broadcasting Co. v. FCC*, "[b]ecause of the scarcity of radio frequencies, the Government is permitted to put restraints on licensees in favor of others whose views should be expressed on this unique medium."[53] An important question is whether broadcasting necessarily receives a lower level of First Amendment protection, or if it may grow out of its less favored position.

The Supreme Court appears to have taken the position that the heightened level of government intervention permitted under the public interest standard may not be permanent. In *FCC v. League of Women Voters of California*, for example, the Court invalidated a statutory prohibition on editorializing by public broadcasting stations that received funds from the Corporation for Public Broadcasting and questioned the continuing validity of the scarcity rationale.[54] Subsequently, after an extended inquiry, the FCC in 1987 found that the scarcity rationale was no longer valid.[55] Additionally, in drafting the legislation that became the Telecommunications Act of 1996, the House Commerce Committee concluded that the audio and video marketplace has undergone significant changes over the past 50 years "and the scarcity rationale for government regulation no longer applies."[56]

Despite these findings, the level of content regulation permitted pursuant to the public interest standard has persisted, and, in recent years, has tended to increase. Professor Robert O'Neil has called it "a singular tribute to the sanctity of precedent that *Red Lion Broadcasting Co. v. FCC* continues to validate a second-class constitutional status for licensed broadcasting in the name of 'scarcity,' long after the array of electronic media options has become one of genuine abundance."[57] Some more recent decisions suggest that "scarcity" is an inherent feature of a spectrum-based medium, regardless of the number of choices available to consumers. Thus, for example, the United States Court of Appeals for the District of Columbia Circuit upheld significant public interest requirements for DBS operators on the basis that the radio spectrum is inherently finite.[58]

---

53. *Id.* at 390, 89 S. Ct. at 1806, 23 L. Ed. 2d at 389.

54. 468 U.S. 364, 377 n. 11, 104 S.Ct. 3106, 3115 n. 11, 82 L.Ed.2d 278, 289 n. 11 (1984) (noting criticisms of scarcity rationale, the Court indicated that it would be willing "to reconsider our longstanding approach" if given "some signal from Congress or the FCC that technological developments have advanced so far that some revision of the system of broadcast regulation may be required").

55. Complaint of Syracuse Peace Council Against Television Station WTVH, 2 FCC Rcd 5043 (1987), *aff'd sub nom.* Syracuse Peace Council v. FCC, 867 F.2d 654, 276 U.S. App. D.C. 38 (D.C.Cir.1989), cert. denied, 493 U.S. 1019, 110 S.Ct. 717, 107 L.Ed.2d 737 (1990).

56. Communications Act of 1995, H Rep. 204, 104th Cong. 1st Sess. 54 (July 24, 1995).

57. Robert M O'Neil, *Dead or Alive: How Long Will the Red Lion Specter Haunt Free Speech and Broadcasting?*, in RATIONALES AND RATIONALIZATIONS 19 (Robert Corn-Revere, ed., Media Institute 1997).

58. Time Warner Entertainment Company v. FCC, 93 F.3d 957, 973–977, 320 U.S. App. D.C. 294, 309–313 (D.C.Cir.1996). In a denial of rehearing on this issue, five judges of the court issued a dissent, sharply criticizing the scarcity rationale. They concluded that "DBS is not subject to anything remotely approaching the 'scarcity' that the Court found in conventional broadcast in 1969 and used to justify a peculiarly relaxed First Amendment regime for such broad-

Economists, and some judges, have suggested that the notion of "scarcity" that has been used to support the public interest standard does not distinguish broadcast spectrum from any other economic good. Professor Ronald Coase in a seminal 1959 essay described it as a "commonplace of economics" that "almost all resources used in the economic system (and not simply radio and television frequencies) are limited in amount and scarce, in that people would like to use more than exists." He added that "[l]and, labor, and capital are all scarce, but this, of itself, does not call for government regulation."[59] Nor does scarcity distinguish broadcasting from other mass media. Judge Robert Bork wrote that "[a]ll economic goods are scarce, not least the newsprint, ink, delivery trucks, computers and other resources that go into the production and dissemination of print journalism."[60] Since "scarcity is a universal fact," he pointed out, "it can hardly explain regulation in one context and not the other."[61] Others have suggested that scarcity is more an artifact of regulation than it is an inherent characteristic of the medium. Indeed, former FCC Chief Economist Thomas Hazlett has written that the Federal Radio Commission actually increased scarcity by refusing to expand the band available for radio stations.[62]

But whether or not scarcity is real, or even relevant to broadcast regulation, it is clear that the debate over the public interest standard will continue. Former FCC Chairman Reed Hundt, a believer in the doctrinal importance of scarcity, has written that "[s]carcity is not the only justification on which we can appropriately base minimal, nonburdensome requirements for broadcast licensees to serve the public interest." He suggested that affirmative programming obligations may be based on the government's duty to promote "robust public debate on public issues." In addition, the broadcast spectrum may be viewed as public property, for which the government may demand programming commitments as the condition of license. Alternatively, the spectrum might be characterized as a "public forum," for which First Amendment doctrine creates a general right of access.[63]

It is unsettled whether such theories will propel the current understanding of the public interest standard into the next century. The

cast." Time Warner Entertainment Company v. FCC, 105 F.3d 723, 323 U.S. App. D.C. 109 (D.C.Cir.1997) (Williams, J., dissenting). The dissenters pointed out that "[w]hile *Red Lion* is not in such poor shape that an intermediate court of appeals could properly announce its death, we can think twice before extending it to another medium."

59. Ronald H Coase, *The Federal Communications Commission*, 2 J. Law & Econ. 1, 14 (1959).

60. Telecommunications Research and Action Center v. FCC, 801 F.2d 501, 508, 255 U.S. App. D.C. 287, 294 (D.C.Cir.1986).

61. *Id.*

62. *See* Thomas W Hazlett, *The Rationality of U.S. Regulation of the Broadcast Spectrum*, 33 J. Law & Econ. 133 (1990). *See also* Matthew L. Spitzer, Seven Dirty Words and Six Other Stories 9–27 (Yale Univ. Press 1986).

63. Statement of Chairman Reed E Hundt, In the Matter of the Repeal or Modification of the Personal Attack and Political Editorial Rules (rel. Aug. 11, 1997). *But see* Arkansas Educational Television Commission v. Forbes, 523 U.S. 666, 118 S.Ct. 1633, 140 L.Ed.2d 875 (1998) (public broadcasting stations generally are not public forums).

various rationales have received more attention as a growing number of proposals for content regulation paradoxically has coincided with increasing media abundance.[64] The five District of Columbia Circuit judges who dissented from the denial of rehearing in *Time Warner Entertainment Company v. FCC* considered the other possible theories of regulation and offered various insights.

They concluded that a required set-aside requirement for "educational" or "informational" programming is content-based, and "as a simple government regulation of content, the DBS requirement would have to fall."[65] They discussed the licensing scheme as a method of making conditioned grants of government property (the subsidy theory underlying the social compact) and found "good reason for the Court to have hesitated to give great weight to the government's property interest in the spectrum."[66] Among other things, the judges foresaw "rather serious First Amendment problems if the government used its power of eminent domain to become the only lawful supplier of newsprint and then sold the newsprint only to licensed persons, issuing the licenses only to persons that promised to use the newsprint for papers satisfying government-defined rules of content."[67] The dissenters also expressed doubt about applying the public forum doctrine to licensing the spectrum.[68]

None of these theories were fully adjudicated in *Time Warner,* or in any other case thus far. The dissenting statement is nothing more than a first peek at the thinking of five judges on the issues that will become the intellectual battleground over the public interest in the 21st Century. But the beginning of this discourse is revealing, and it suggests that the debate over the meaning of the public interest that began in 1927 will continue for the foreseeable future.

14.2   The Broadcast License

A. *Nature of the License*

The licensing process is the primary means by which the Federal Communications Commission regulates broadcasters.[1] Under the terms of the Communications Act of 1934, a broadcast license is a grant of a discrete portion of the publicly-controlled electromagnetic spectrum for a set period of time for the purpose of broadcasting radio or television transmissions to the public and in furtherance of the "public interest, convenience and necessity."[2] Under the Telecommunications Act of 1996, both radio and television station broadcast licenses are granted for

---

64. *See generally* RATIONALES AND RATIONALIZATIONS (Robert Corn–Revere, ed, Media Institute 1997).

65. Time Warner Entertainment Company v FCC, 105 F.3d at 726, 323 U.S. App. D.C. at 112 (Williams, J., dissenting).

66. *Id* at 727, 323 U.S. App. D.C. at 113.

67. *Id* at 728, 323 U.S. App. D.C. at 114.

68. *Id.* at 727, 323 U.S. App. D.C. at 113.

1. The Communications Act of 1934 states, "It is the purpose of this chapter, among other things to maintain the control of the United States over all the channels of radio transmission." 47 U.S.C.A. § 301 (West 1991).

2. *Id.* §§ 301, 303.

a period not to exceed eight years.[3] Previously, under amendments to the Communications Act adopted in the 1980s, license terms of seven years and five years were granted for radio and television stations respectively.[4] Before that, license terms for both radio and television stations lasted three years.[5]

In its traditional form, the broadcast license is granted without a fee and is not intended to create a cognizable property interest in favor of the licensee.[6] Congress specified in Section 301 of the Communications Act that a broadcast license "provide(s) for the use of such channels, but not the ownership thereof" and "no ... license shall be construed to create any right, beyond the terms, conditions and periods of the license."[7] However, once obtained, licenses are transferable with Commission approval, and the purchase and sale of broadcast licenses has developed into an active market. The market for the transfer of broadcast licenses is a powerful indicator that licenses could be allocated initially using market mechanisms, but early policymakers developing the concept of the broadcast license were skeptical that the limited nature of available spectrum would support a market-based allocation of broadcast stations.[8]

The idea of having the government auction spectrum to the highest bidder was first proposed in the 1950s,[9] but it was not until the early 1990s that Congress authorized auctions for certain non-broadcast services.[10] Currently, part of the spectrum allocated for Direct Broadcast Satellite services has been distributed by auction,[11] as have licenses for certain "wireless cable" services[12] and for Digital Audio Radio Service.[13] The Balanced Budget Act of 1997 expanded the FCC's competitive bidding authority to include mutually exclusive initial license applications for certain types of broadcast stations.[14] Based on this authority,

3. Telecommunications Act of 1996, Pub. L. No. 104–104, § 203, 110 Stat. 56 (1996), *amending* 47 U.S.C.A. § 307(c) (West Supp. 1997).

4. 47 U.S.C.A. § 307(c) (West Supp. 1997).

5. Act of June 19, 1934, c. 652, Title III, § 307, 48 Stat. 1083.

6. *See* Tak Communications, Inc., 985 F.2d 916 (7th Cir.1993) (holding a lender unable to claim a security interest in a broadcast license because such license is not a property right).

7. 47 U.S.C.A. § 301 (West 1991). *See* FCC v. Sanders Bros. Radio Station, 309 U.S. 470. 475, 60 S.Ct. 693, 697, 84 L.Ed. 869, 874 (1940) ("the (Communications) Act is clear that no person is to have anything in the nature of a proprietary right as a result of the granting of a license.").

8. ITHIEL DE SOLA POOL, TECHNOLOGIES OF FREEDOM 138 (1983).

9. Leo Herzel, *"Public Interest" and the Market in Color Television Regulation*, 18

U. Chi. L. Rev. 802 (1951); Ronald A. Coase, *The Federal Communications Commission*, 2 J. Law & Econ. 1 (1959).

10. 1993 Budget Act, § 6002(a), (b) (1), Pub. L. 103–66, 107 Stat. 387, 392 (Aug.10, 1993).

11. Revision of Rules and Policies for the Direct Broadcast Satellite Service, Report and Order, 11 FCC Rcd. 9712 (1995).

12. Amendment of Parts 21 and 74 of the Commission's Rules With Regard to Filing Procedures in the Multipoint Distribution Service and in the Instructional Television Fixed Service and Implementation of Section 309(j) of the Communications Act—Competitive Bidding, 10 F.C.C. Rcd. 9589 (1995).

13. Establishment of Rules and Policies for the Digital Audio Radio Satellite Service, 12 FCC Rcd. 5754 (1997).

14. Pub. L. No. 105–33, 111 Stat. 251 (1997). *See* 47 U.S.C.A. § 309(j) (West Supp. 1997).

the Commission adopted auction procedures to resolve mutually exclusive applications for all initial broadcast licenses except for non-commercial stations and initial licenses or construction permits for digital television service by existing terrestrial broadcast licenses.[15] It should be noted that a license obtained through an auction is still subject to term and renewal requirements that characterize a license awarded through more traditional means.

Potential capital financiers interested in investing in the broadcast industry face a dilemma due to the intangible nature of the license. The license is the mainspring of a station's value, yet a broadcast license in itself is not granted as a property interest. As a result, capital investment in broadcast stations can be problematic, as traditional security and reversionary interests attach only to a station's tangible assets and real estate. The FCC has examined ways to encourage investment in the broadcast industry.[16] Similarly, banking institutions, concerned about the effect of foreclosure on the physical property of a bankrupt station, the value of which is considerably diminished without an interest in the license, have encouraged the Commission to create some type of security interest.[17] A major challenge facing the FCC is finding a solution that makes investors secure without making broadcasters too susceptible to the influence of investors.[18]

B. Qualifications of the Licensee

The Communications Act requires that broadcast licensees must meet certain legal, technical and financial qualifications. Although the requirements for holding a broadcast license have been streamlined over the years, an applicant generally must be financially, legally and technically qualified and be of good character.[19]

15. FCC Adopts Auction Procedures For Commercial Broadcast Licenses, Report No. MM98–11 (rel. Aug. 7, 1998). *See* Implementation of Section 309(j) of the Communications Act—Competitive Bidding for Commercial Broadcast and Instructional Television Fixed Service Licenses, FCC 97–397, MM Docket No. 97–234 (rel. Nov. 26, 1997). *See* 47 U.S.C.A. § 309(j) (West Supp. 1997).

16. Review of the Commission's Regulations and Policies Affecting Investment in the Broadcast Industry, Report & Order, 10 FCC Rcd. 5670 (1995); Review of the Commission's Regulations and Policies Affecting Investment in the Broadcast Industry, Notice of Proposed Rulemaking, 10 FCC Rcd. 3606 (1995); Review of the Commission's Regulations and Policies Affecting Investment in the Broadcast Industry, Notice of Proposed Rulemaking and Notice of Inquiry, 7 FCC Rcd. 2654 (1992).

17. *See* Shorenstein and Stein, *FCC Proposals Relating to Financing the Purchase and Sale of Broadcast Properties,* NAB Broadcasters Law and Regulation Conference Papers, 22, 24 (1994).

18. Broadcast Regulation: A Mid Year Report, 26 (National Association of Broadcasters Legal Department 1994).

19. Beginning in 1981, the Commission streamlined its process for collecting data on individual application criteria. *See, e.g.,* Revision of Form 301, 87 F.C.C.2d 200 (1981) (allowing applicant to certify financial qualification, versus producing actual proof of financing); Character Qualifications in Broadcast Licensing, 102 F.C.C.2d 1179 (1989) (character qualifications will focus on broadcast related misconduct and on certain specified categories of nonbroadcast-related misconduct); Enactment of the Telecommunications Act of 1996, Pub. L. No. 104–104, has streamlined the process even further. *See, e.g.,* § 204(k) (1) (simplifying renewal process for qualified licensees).

Section 310 of the Communications Act of 1934 mandates a license "shall not be granted to, or held by any foreign government or representative thereof", nor shall any broadcast license be granted "to any alien or representative of any alien."[20] The restrictions on alien ownership apply to partnerships with alien members, foreign corporations or other corporations where one fifth of the capital stock is owned and voted by aliens, and to corporate parents of licenses where more than one-fourth of the capital stock is owned or voted by aliens.[21] Pursuant to this statutory mandate, the Commission examines the economic realities underlying corporate arrangements that include aliens.[22]

The Communications Act also requires that broadcast licensees be of good character. As might be expected, the nature of this qualification has evolved over time. Prior to 1986, a host of broadcast-related misconduct issues could be considered by the Commission, including matters related to the content of programming.[23] In 1986, the Commission refocused the character requirement to emphasize "FCC-related" misconduct, such as misrepresentation and lack of candor before the agency and abuse of process.[24] Abuse of the FCC process may encompass such matters as unacceptable behavior toward competing applicants during the application process. The Commission subsequently made clear that its character rules to include consideration of any felony convictions the applicant has received, as well as misrepresentations before other government entities, media-related antitrust violations and similar activities.[25]

As a character issue, lack of candor before the FCC is the most serious breach of a licensee's or applicant's duty, and it can have a devastating effect in a particular case. Lack of candor can involve either a false statement of fact or a failure to fully disclose pertinent information.[26] For example, FCC concern over lack of candor led the agency to find that RKO General lacked sufficient character to be a licensee after it failed to disclose that its corporate parent had engaged in bribery, fraud and other anti-competitive activities. After administrative and judicial proceedings that continued for fifteen years, the FCC ruled that RKO was unqualified to hold its radio and television licenses. The egregious corporate conduct by a licensee's parent, compounded by a

---

20. 47 U.S.C.A. § 310(a)(b) (West 1991).

21. *Id.* § 310(a)-(b)(3).

22. *See* In re Application of Fox Television Stations, Inc., 11 FCC Rcd. 7773 (1996); Prime Media Broadcasting, Inc., 3 FCC Rcd. 4294 (1988) (voting trust with United States trustees but with alien beneficiary violated prohibition on alien ownership).

23. *See, e.g.,* Palmetto Broadcasting Co., 33 F.C.C. 250 (1962) (lying to Commission); WSAL, 8 F.C.C. 34 (1940); Independent Broadcasting Co. v. FCC, 193 F.2d 900, 89 U.S. App. D.C. 396 (D.C.Cir.1951) (broadcaster engaged in personal attacks); Bran-

dywine–Main Line Radio, Inc. v. FCC, 473 F.2d 16, 25 Rad. Reg. 2d (P&F) 2010, *aff'd,* 473 F.2d 16, 153 U.S.App.D.C. 305 (D.C.Cir. 1972) (sudden change in programming to controversial content, found to be deceptive).

24. Character Qualifications in Broadcast Licensing, 102 F.C.C.2d 1179 (1986); 47 U.S.C.A. § 312 (West 1991).

25. Character Qualifications Policy, 5 FCC Rcd. 3252 (1990).

26. Cf. Application of Fox Television Stations, Inc., 10 FCC Rcd. 8452, 8478 (1995).

failure to disclose the misconduct, led to the non-renewal of the licenses.[27]

A broadcast license applicant also must be financially qualified and certify to the Commission that it has sufficient financial resources to acquire, construct and operate the station without revenue for a three-month period. Before the FCC revised the financial showing requirement in 1981, applicants were obligated to show they could operate a station without revenue for a full year. Applicants for construction permits are required to submit information regarding the source of their funding, including names, addresses, relationship to the applicant, and the amount financed.[28]

An applicant also must be legally and technically qualified in order to obtain a broadcast license. The technical requirements are designed to insure that the licensee will be able to broadcast a transmission of sufficient quality and without interference.[29] With respect to applicant's legal qualifications, the Commission will inquire into several areas as set out in the Communications Act. For example, the FCC may revoke the license of any licensee who is found to have willfully used the station to distribute or assist in the distribution of controlled substances.[30]

C. The Broadcast License Application Process

1. New Stations

Applications for broadcast licenses are filed with the Commission's Mass Media Bureau and processed on a first-come, first-served basis.[31] Once an application for a new station is determined by the Bureau to be substantially complete, a thirty day cut-off period is triggered during which mutually exclusive applications for the same spectrum may be filed.[32] After the cut-off date is established, any major amendment to the application (*e.g.*, a fifty percent or greater ownership change, change of location, or a change in the power of the proposed station) will shift the cut-off date to the date of the major amendment.[33]

If an application remains unopposed as of the cut-off date, the license will be summarily granted if the following criteria are satisfied: (1) the applicant is legally, technically, financially and otherwise qualified to hold a broadcast license; (2) the applicant is not in violation of the law, FCC rules, or established policies; and (3) a grant of the application would serve the public interest, convenience and necessity.[34] If a competing application is filed within the thirty-day filing window, the Commission must choose which of the applicants will obtain the license.

---

27. *See* RKO General, Inc. v. FCC, 670 F.2d 215, 216 U.S. App. D.C. 57 (D.C.Cir. 1981) cert. denied, 456 U.S. 927, 102 S.Ct. 1974, 72 L.Ed.2d 442 (1982).

28. Revision of Form 301, 84 F.C.C.2d 200 (1981).

29. 47 U.S.C.A. § 308(b). *See, e.g.*, 47 C.F.R §§ 73.300–73.333 (1997).

30. 47 U.S.C.A. § 312(a) (West 1991).

31. 47 C.F.R. § 73.3564 (1997).

32. *Id.*

33. 47 C.F.R. § 73.3571 (1997).

34. *Id.* § 73.3591.

In 1997 Congress broke with historic methods of selecting between competing applicants, and authorized the FCC to select from between mutually exclusive broadcast license applications by competitive bidding.[35] The change requires the FCC to use auctions to resolve most initial licensing proceedings involving mutually exclusive applications. However, the competitive bidding authority does not apply to licensees or construction permits for digital television service given to existing terrestrial broadcast licensees to replace their analog television service licenses. In addition, the FCC is not authorized to auction licenses for non-commercial educational broadcast stations and public broadcast stations.

Pursuant to this authority, the FCC in 1998 adopted a system of competitive bidding to award new broadcast licenses.[36] The rules established auction procedures for all primary broadcast services (except for DTV and non-commercial licenses) as well as for secondary commercial broadcast services, such as low power TV, FM translator and TV translator services.[37]

Before mutually exclusive applications were subject to the competitive bidding process, comparative hearings were the norm for selecting the prevailing applicant. The requirement was established in *Ashbacker Radio Corp. v. Federal Communications Commission*.[38] In *Ashbacker*, a construction permit was granted to a licensee whose choice of frequency foreclosed another applicant's request to expand its service. The Supreme Court invalidated the Commission's summary decision, holding that Section 309(e) of the Communications Act of 1934 requires that all similarly situated, mutually exclusive, applications be accorded a comparative hearing.[39]

Various parties have standing to challenge a license application, including competing applicants, existing licensees to whom grant of the new application would potentially cause interference, and members of the community. In years past, the Commission considered economic harm that might be caused to an incumbent broadcaster in competition with the proposed station. The "Carroll doctrine"[40] required a three tier

35. Balanced Budget Act of 1997, Pub. L. No. 105–33, 111 Stat. 251 (1997). *See* 47 U.S.C.A. § 309(j) (West Supp. 1997). *See* FCC Adopts Auction Procedures for Commercial Broadcast Licenses, Report No. MM98–11 (rel. Aug. 7, 1998).

36. Implementation of Section 309(j) of the Communications Act—Competitive Bidding for Commercial Broadcast and Instructional Television Fixed Service Licenses, First Report and Order, FCC 98–194 (rel. Aug. 18, 1998) ("Competitive Bidding Order"). *See* 47 C.F.R. §§ 73.5000–73.5009. 47 U.S.C.A. § 309(j)(West Supp. 1997).

37. Competitive Bidding Order at ¶ ¶ 7–19.

38. 326 U.S. 327, 333, 66 S.Ct. 148, 90 L.Ed. 108 (1945).

39. *Id*. Section 309(e) of the Communications Act provides: "If in the case of any application ... a substantial and material question of fact is presented, or the Commission for any reason is unable to make the finding so specified ... it shall formally designate the application for hearing." 47 U.S.C.A. § 309(e) (West 1991). Once the Commission begins the hearing process it is required to notify "all known parties in interest of such action, specifying with particularity the matters and things in issue." 47 C.F.R. § 73.3593 (1997).

40. Carroll Broadcasting Co. v. FCC, 258 F.2d 440, 103 U.S. App. D.C. 346 (D.C.Cir.1958).

showing that the presence of the new station would result in economic hardship which would negatively affect the existing broadcasters programming and this loss of programming would not be offset by any potential programming of the applicant. The Commission, which never actually upheld a "Carroll" claim, eliminated the use of the Carroll doctrine as anti-competitive in 1988.[41] Community groups may also participate in the licensing process. Once denied a voice by the Commission,[42] listeners and community groups also have standing to participate in licensing proceedings[43] so long as they raise issues of public, rather than private interest.[44]

The comparative hearing process was designed to determine which applicant was most likely to operate the station in the public interest. The FCC articulated two primary objectives for the hearing process: to obtain the best practicable service to the public and to ensure maximum diffusion of control of the media of mass communication.[45] Diversification of media control was given primary significance in the Commission's licensing scheme. Other factors were considered relevant for predicting which applicant would provide the best service. One crucial comparative factor was the integration of a station's ownership and management. The Commission believed that an owner-operator involved in running the station was more likely to provide better service to the public.[46]

A series of decisions by the United States Court of Appeals for the District of Columbia Circuit questioned the Commission's continued adherence to the integration policy and criticized its failure to articulate a justification for the assumption that an owner-operator is more able to serve the public interest than a station manager who is an employee. In *Bechtel v. FCC*, the United States Court of Appeals for the District of Columbia Circuit invalidated the use of comparative criteria such as "integration of ownership and management," "local ownership," and "civic participation" because the FCC could not demonstrate the nexus between the selection criteria and the public interest. According to the plaintiff in that case, the Commission was unable to "identify a single instance in which the applicant who won his station on the basis of his integration credit proposal continued to operate the station as promised for an appreciable period of time."[47] The court was concerned that many applicants would structure ownership integration solely for the purpose of obtaining a license grant and then sell the station after one year to a

41. Policies Regarding Detrimental Effects of Proposed New Broadcasting Station on Existing Broadcasting Stations, 3 FCC Rcd. 638 (1988).

42. Northern Pacific Radio Corp., 23 Rad. Reg. (P&F) 186 (1962); Gordon Broadcasting of San Francisco, Inc., 22 Rad. Reg. (P&F) 236 (1962).

43. Office of Communication of United Church of Christ v. FCC, 359 F.2d, 994, 123 U.S. App. D.C. 328 (D.C.Cir.1966).

44. *See, e.g.,* Tele–Vue Systems, Inc., 32 F.C.C.2d 876 (1971).

45. Policy Statement on Comparative Broadcast Hearings, 1 F.C.C.2d 393, 394, (1965).

46. *Id.* at 395.

47. *See* 957 F.2d 873, 294 U.S. App. D.C. 124 (D.C.Cir.1992) ("Bechtel I"); Bechtel v. FCC, 10 F.3d 875, 879, 304 U.S. App. D.C. 100, 104 (D.C.Cir.1993) ("Bechtel II").

non-integrated owner.[48] Because the Commission failed to support the proposition that an owner-operator would be more responsive to community needs, the Court of Appeals found the integration credit to be arbitrary and capricious.[49]

To further the Commission's long-standing public interest goal of promoting "diversity of voices" the FCC also had a long-established policy of giving credit for minority participation in licensing decisions.[50] In 1990, the Supreme Court by a 5–4 vote, upheld the use of such criteria in *Metro Broadcasting, Inc. v. FCC.*[51] That case involved an equal protection challenge to the Commission's minority preference policies in comparative hearings and station transfers. The Court, applying an intermediate level of constitutional scrutiny, upheld the provisions because they were considered to be substantially related to the promotion of broadcast diversity—an important governmental objective.[52] However, the current constitutional status of minority credits is uncertain. Five years after *Metro Broadcasting*, the Court revisited the issue in *Adarand Constructors v. Pena.*[53] There, the Court held that strict scrutiny is the appropriate standard of review for minority preferences and specifically overruled the portion of *Metro Broadcasting* that had adopted intermediate scrutiny as the applicable standard.[54] A growing number of cases have questioned the viability of minority preferences.

In an earlier case, the United States Court of Appeals for the District of Columbia Circuit struck down Commission policies favoring women in the context of granting a construction permit. In *Lamprecht v. FCC,*[55] the Commission was called upon to justify its policy of awarding credit to female station operators in the face of a equal protection challenge by a disappointed radio license applicant. The court was presented with a federal government study that demonstrated only a tenuous link between the gender of a station's owner and programming of any particular type.[56] Based on the lack of factual support, the

---

48. Bechtel I, 57 F.2d at 878, 294 U.S. App. D.C. at 129.

49. Bechtel II, 10 F.3d at 887, 304 U.S. App. D.C. at 112.

50. *See, e.g.,* Statement of Policy on Minority Ownership of Broadcasting Facilities, 68 F.C.C.2d 979 (1978); Commission Policy Regarding Advancement of Minority Ownership in Broadcasting, 92 F.C.C.2d 849 (1982). The Commission also prohibits discrimination in the employment practices of licensees. *See* Bilingual Bicultural Coalition on Mass Media v. FCC, 595 F.2d 621, 629, 193 U.S. App. D.C. 236 (D.C.Cir.1978); Black Broadcasting Coalition of Richmond v. FCC, 556 F.2d 59, 64, 181 U.S. App. D.C. 182, 187 (D.C.Cir.1977); Nondiscrimination in the Employment Policies and Practices of Broadcast Licensees, 54 F.C.C.2d 354 (1975); Petition for Rulemaking to Require Broadcast Licensees to Show Nondiscrimi-

nation in Their Employment Practices, 13 F.C.C.2d 766 (1965).

51. 497 U.S. 547, 110 S.Ct. 2997, 111 L.Ed.2d 445 (1990).

52. *Id.* at 556, 110 S.Ct. at 3004, 111 L.Ed.2d at 457.

53. 515 U.S. 200, 115 S.Ct. 2097, 132 L.Ed.2d 158 (1995).

54. *Id.* at 227, 115 S.Ct. at 2112, 132 L.Ed.2d at 181. *See also* Lutheran Church–Missouri Synod v. FCC, 141 F.3d 344, 329 U.S.App.D.C. 381 (D.C.Cir.1998).

55. 958 F.2d 382, 294 U.S. App. D.C. 164 (D.C.Cir.1992) (striking down gender-based licensing preferences).

56. *Id.* at 398, 294 U.S. App. D.C. at 180. The Congressional Research Service study, entitled *Minority Broadcast Station Ownership and Broadcasting Programming: Is There a Nexus?*, found that female-

Commission could not justify treating applicants of different genders differently based on gender, even under the intermediate level of scrutiny established in *Metro Broadcasting*. As a result, the gender preference was ended.[57]

Many comparative hearings were resolved by settlement among the parties. Similarly, many licensing proceedings in which petitions to deny were filed were settled informally. Any such settlement by competing applicants must be approved by the Commission to satisfy the statutory requirement that any grant of a broadcast license serves the public interest. To prevent creating incentives for fraudulent competing applications or objections to applications, the Commission must approve in detail any settlement by the parties who must certify that the consideration exchanged does not exceed the party's legitimate expenses to prosecute its application.[58] This policy was strengthened after the FCC found that its rules had previously encouraged various forms of "greenmail."

After the FCC's comparative criteria were invalidated by the Court of Appeals, a significant backlog of cases developed when the FCC had difficulty fashioning new selection criteria. The FCC stayed all on-going comparative cases pending resolution of the issues raised regarding the comparative hearing criteria.[59] As part of the Balanced Budget Act of 1997, Congress acted to resolve the backlog of licensing cases. For applications filed before July 1, 1997, the Act empowered the FCC to conduct a competitive bidding proceeding to award the licenses. In addition, the Act created a limited period during which the FCC was required to waive any provision of its regulations necessary to permit parties to enter settlement agreements.[60]

A winning applicant, regardless of the method of selection, is awarded a construction permit. Typically, a construction permit granted by the Commission requires the permittee to build and operate a new television station within 24 months of the issuance of the permit, and other stations within 18 months of the grant.[61] Failure to make the station operational in the time specified can result in forfeiture of the permit. However, extensions of time for construction may be granted.[62] After the

owned stations broadcast "female oriented" programming in 35 percent of the cases, contrasted with male owned stations, which broadcast "female oriented" programming in 25 percent of the cases. *Id.* at 397, 294 U.S. App. D.C. at 179.

57. *Id.* at 399, 294 U.S. App. D.C. at 181.

58. Amendment of Sections 1.420 and 73.3584 of the Commission's Rules Concerning Abuses of the Commission's Processes, 5 FCC Rcd. 3911 (1990); Formulation of Policies and Rules Relating to Broadcast Renewal Applicants, Competing Applicants, and Other Participants to the Comparative Renewal Process and to the

Prevention of Abuses of the Renewal Process, 4 FCC Rcd. 4780 (1989). *See* 47 C.F.R. § 73.3588(a)(1) (1997).

59. Public Notice: FCC Freezes Comparative Hearings, 9 FCC Rcd. 1055 (1994), *modified*, 9 FCC Rcd. 6689 (1994), *further modified*, 10 FCC Rcd. 12182 (1995).

60. Balanced Budget Act of 1997, Pub.L. No. 105–33, 111 Stat. 251 (1997). *See* FCC Adopts Auction Procedures for Commercial Broadcast Licenses, Report No. MM 98–11 (rel. Aug. 7, 1998).

61. 47 C.F.R. § 73.3598 (1997).

62. 47 C.F.R. § 73.3534 (1997).

initial construction period, the permitee can seek FCC permission to extend the deadline where the permittee can show that it has undertaken substantial steps to complete the station or where outside forces have prevented the completion of the station.[63] Once the station is built, the permittee must file for and obtain a license to commence operations.[64]

2. License Renewals

The Telecommunications Act of 1996 authorized the FCC to change the term of a broadcast license from a seven year term for radio stations and a five year term for television stations to a flat term not to exceed eight years for both services.[65] The 1996 Act also significantly altered the broadcast license renewal process by eliminating comparative hearings for all renewal applications after May 1, 1995.[66]

Before these changes, a licensee which had demonstrated "substantial service" and programming consistent with the public interest mandate was granted a "renewal expectancy." The renewal expectancy provided a powerful position for an incumbent licensee facing a challenger and would generally outweigh more favorable structural and personnel "public interest" credits of a competing applicant.[67] The Commission reasoned that an existing broadcaster performing "substantial service" would likely continue that service in comparison to the untested promises of a challenger and would be more likely to invest in equipment to improve service. The FCC predicted that denying license renewals to incumbent licensees and awarding licenses to challengers would cause market uncertainty and lead to a reduction in service to the public.[68]

The renewal expectancy was awarded based on overall performance of the applicant and focused generally on the following factors: (1) the amount of non-entertainment programming presented, the time of day of its presentation and its service of local needs and interests; (2) the amount of programming produced locally; and (3) the reputation of the station in the community.[69] In one extreme case, an expectancy was denied an incumbent station that devoted 48 percent of its air time to non-entertainment, informational programming.[70]

---

63. Id.

64. 47 C.F.R. §§ 73.3536, 73.3598 (1997).

65. Telecommunications Act of 1996, Pub. L. No. 104–104, § 203, 110 Stat. 56 (1996) amending 47 U.S.C.A. § 307(c) (West Supp. 1997). Implementation of Section 203 of the Telecommunications Act of 1996, Report and Order, 12 FCC Rcd. 1720 (1997).

66. Id. For the remaining comparative hearings left over after passage of the Balanced Budget Act of 1997, the FCC authorized hearings in which the applicants can present "whatever evidence they believe relevant," with renewal expectancy remaining the most important factor. Competitive Bidding Order, supra note 36 at ¶ 1.

67. Cowles Broadcasting, Inc., 86 F.C.C.2d 993, 1015 (1981) ("Cowles II"), aff'd sub nom. Central Florida Enterprises, Inc. v. FCC, 683 F.2d 503, 221 U.S. App. D.C. 162 (D.C.Cir.1982).

68. Id.

69. Formulation of Policies and Rules Relating to Broadcast Renewal Applicants, Third Further Notice of Inquiry and Notice of Proposed Rulemaking, 4 FCC Rcd. 6363 n.11 (1989).

70. Simon Geller, 90 F.C.C.2d 250, 264–267 (1982), recons. denied, 91 F.C.C.2d 1253, aff'd in relevant part sub nom. Committee for Community Access v. FCC, 737 F.2d 74, 77–78, 237 U.S. App. D.C. 292, 295–296 (D.C.Cir.1984).

Over time, the FCC renewal process became less burdensome to renewal applicants. Before that station renewal had been an elaborate process that involved an "ascertainment procedure" whereby a survey of the general public, station program logs and reports of "community needs" were presented to the Commission.[71] This process was substantially reformed in radio and television deregulation proceedings in the 1980s. The Commission determined that market forces were sufficient to enforce the needs of the community and that audiences and revenues would decline for stations that failed to satisfy community needs.[72]

Before the Telecommunications Act of 1996 was enacted, a competing applicant could file for an expiring broadcast license, claiming to be better equipped to serve the public interest.[73] Such challenges were eliminated by the 1996 Act. The Commission must issue a renewal if it finds that the licensee has served the public interest, convenience and necessity, has not been found to be in serious violation of the Commission's rules and has not engaged in a pattern of abusing the Commission's rules or the provisions of the Communications Act.[74] If the Commission finds an applicant to be in violation of these criteria, it may deny the renewal. A station denied a renewal after a hearing by the Commission may appeal the decision directly to the United States Court of Appeals for the District of Columbia.[75] However, members of the public may still file a petition to deny the renewal application of a broadcast station based on allegations that the licensee has failed to serve the public interest. In such a case the FCC may require a renewal hearing.

71. Report and Statement of Policy Re: Commission en banc Programming Inquiry, 44 F.C.C. 2303 (1960); Primer on Ascertainment of Community Problems by Broadcast Applicants, 27 F.C.C.2d 650 (1971).

72. Deregulation of Radio, 84 F.C.C.2d 968 (1981), *aff'd in part, remanded in part sub nom.* Office of Communication United Church of Christ v. FCC, 707 F.2d 1413, 228 U.S. App. D.C. 8 (D.C.Cir.1983). Revision of Programming and Commercialization Practices, Report and Order, 98 F.C.C.2d 1076 (1984), *recons. denied,* 104 F.C.C.2d 358 (1986), *rev'd in part,* Action for Children's Television v. FCC, 821 F.2d 741, 261 U.S. App. D.C. 253 (D.C.Cir.1987).

73. *See* Cellular Mobile Systems of Pennsylvania v. FCC, 782 F.2d 182, 251 U.S. App. D.C. 100 (D.C.Cir.1985), *quoting* Ashbacker Radio Corp. v. FCC, 326 U.S. 327, 333, 66 S.Ct. 148, 90 L.Ed. 108 (1945) Even under the FCC's previous procedures, a license challenger did not have a "right" to a comparative hearing. *See id.* (*Ashbacker* hearing rights apply only to "similarly situated" applicants). *See also* FCC v. National Citizens Committee for Broadcasting,

436 U.S. 775, 98 S.Ct. 2096, 56 L.Ed.2d 697 (1978); Black Citizens for a Fair Media v. FCC, 719 F.2d 407, 231 U.S. App. D.C. 163 (D.C.Cir.1983), *cert. denied,* 467 U.S. 1255, 104 S.Ct. 3545, 82 L.Ed.2d 848 (1984). In order to successfully initiate a comparative hearing at the license renewal stage, a challenger was required to demonstrate that "a grant of the application would be prima facie inconsistent with [the public interest, convenience and necessity]." 47 U.S.C.A. § 309(d) (1)(West 1991 and Supp. 1997). The challenger was also required to raise a "substantial and material question of fact" regarding the renewal, 47 U.S.C.A. § 309(e)(West 1991). The Commission had broad discretion to review and act on competing applications. Columbus Broadcasting Coalition v. FCC, 505 F.2d 320, 324, 164 U.S. App. D.C. 213, 217 (D.C.Cir.1974).

74. In the Matter of Implementation of Sections 204(a) and 204(c) of the Telecommunications Act of 1996 (Broadcast License Renewal Procedures), 11 FCC Rcd. 6363 (1996).

75. 47 U.S.C.A. § 402(b) (West Supp. 1997).

The license renewal process often included a review of licensee's compliance with the Commission's equal employment opportunities ("EEO") policy, and a station with inadequate employment practices could be forced to undergo a renewal hearing.[76] If the Commission determined that a station had submitted a pattern of inconsistent or inaccurate EEO records, that fact would be addressed at the hearing.[77] Renewal was evaluated under the Commission's benchmark integration percentages, known as the "Employee Profile Screening Guidelines." Under the guidelines, stations were expected to recruit women and minorities based upon their availability in the labor force.[78] However, in *Lutheran Church–Missouri Synod v. FCC,* the U.S. Court of Appeals for the District of Columbia Circuit held that the FCC's EEO program requirements were unconstitutional under the Equal Protection Clause.[79] In response, the FCC initiated a proceeding to determine if a valid EEO policy with respect to licensing decisions could be adopted.[80]

An incumbent licensee must file for renewal four months before expiration of the current license.[81] The broadcaster must maintain a public file containing a copy of its application for public inspection.[82] Finally, a detailed public notice requirement, alerting the public to the licensee's intention to renew its license, must be published and broadcast at various stages of the renewal process.[83]

D.   *License Assignments and Transfers*

The FCC must approve any transfer or assignment of a broadcast license based upon its determination that the transfer satisfies the "public interest convenience and necessity."[84] In making this finding, the Commission is required to focus solely on the applicants before it and cannot consider any other applicants for the license.[85] However, an entity may seek to acquire involuntary control over a corporate entity that has broadcast licenses. Also, interested parties may file petitions to deny an assignment or transfer. The prohibition on alien control of a broadcast

76. *See, e.g.,* Beaumont Branch of the NAACP v. FCC, 854 F.2d 501, 510, 272 U.S. App. D.C. 92, 101 (D.C.Cir.1988), Bilingual Bicultural Coalition on Mass Media v. FCC, 595 F.2d 621, 629, 193 U.S. App. D.C. 236, 244 (D.C.Cir.1978), Black Broadcasting Coalition of Richmond v. FCC, 556 F.2d 59, 64, 181 U.S. App. D.C. 182, 187 (D.C.Cir. 1977).

77. Beaumont Branch of the NAACP v. FCC, 854 F.2d 501, 272 U.S. App. D.C. 92 (D.C.Cir.1988).

78. *See e.g.,* Sun Mountain Broadcasting, 9 FCC Rcd. 2124 (1994) (applicant must adopt procedures "so as to attract an adequate pool of minority or female applicants or hires for at least 66% of all vacancies during the license term").

79. 141 F.3d 344, 329 U.S.App.D.C. 381 (D.C.Cir.1998), *rehearing denied,* Sept. 15, 1998.

80. Review of the Commission's Broadcast and Cable EEO Rules and Policies, FCC 98–305 (rel. Nov. 20, 1998.)

81. 47 C.F.R. § 73.3539(a) (1997).

82. *Id.* § 73.3539(b).

83. *Id.* § 73.3580.

84. 47 U.S.C.A. §§ 308, 310(d) (West 1991). A transfer of control generally occurs when a corporation or other entity holding a license remains the same, but the actual control of the corporation or entity changes. An assignment, or sale occurs when the license itself changes hands.

85. *Id.* § 310(d). This is known as the *Crosley* rule, *see* Powell Crosley, Jr., 11 F.C.C. 3 (1945).

station, direct or indirect, applies to any transfer or assignment of a broadcast station.[86]

In a corporation, transfer of affirmative control occurs when an entity acquires a controlling interest, or when shareholders owning fifty percent or more of the stock sell to a third party. The transfer also occurs when an entity gains negative control by acquiring fifty percent of the voting stock.[87] A transfer can also occur when a family group or an individual in a family group loses affirmative or negative control or when a group in privity gains or loses affirmative or negative control.[88] In each of these situations, Commission approval must be obtained.[89]

The FCC has adopted special procedures to govern transfers in various circumstances. For example, not all transfers are voluntary. In the situation of a tender offer, a trustee is appointed to control the station in question, while the FCC considers the offeror's application.[90] During this time the Commission will grant the trustee a special temporary authorization ("STA") to operate the station while it considers the transfer.[91] In the interim, the trustee must act as a fiduciary towards the station and insure that the station continues to operate in the public interest.[92] If the application is rejected, the trustee must find another purchaser.[93]

As part of the Commission's policy to promote diversity of ownership, it in the past authorized "distress sales" when a station facing nonrenewal, or a renewal hearing, agrees to sell the station to a minority-controlled enterprise.[94] Under the distress sale policy the minority purchaser could acquire the distressed station for up to 75 percent of the station's value.[95] Both buyer and seller were required to submit to the Commission independent assessments of the fair market value of the station which could not differ by more than five percent. If they exceeded this margin, a third evaluation had to be submitted from a party selected by both buyer and seller and the three assessments were averaged.[96] The seller in a distress sale situation was allowed to obtain a tax certificate

86. 47 U.S.C.A. § 310(a) and (b) (West 1991 and Supp. 1997).

87. Report and Order in MM Docket No. 83–46, 97 F.C.C.2d 997, 1018 n. 47 (1984).

88. *Id.*

89. FCC Form 314 is required for an assignment of a license; FCC Form 315 is used when a transfer of control occurs; and FCC Short Form 316 is used when the change of control is temporary, or involuntary (as in the case of a trustee), or when the change will not materially affect control of the station.

90. Tender Offers and Proxy Contents, 59 Rad. Reg. 2d 1536 (P&F 1987).

91. *Id.* at ¶ 45.

92. *Id.* at ¶ 66.

93. *Id.* at ¶ 71. *See also* J.B. Acquisition Corp., 60 Rad. Reg. 2d 1288 (P&F 1986);

McFadden Acquisition Corp., 60 Rad. Reg. 2d 1366 (P&F 1986).

94. Statement of Policy of Minority Ownership of Broadcast Facilities, 68 F.C.C.2d 978, 983 (1978). A distress sale was upheld against a constitutional challenge in Metro Broadcasting, Inc. v. FCC, 497 U.S. 547, 110 S.Ct. 2997, 111 L.Ed.2d 445 (1990) (distress sale held substantially related to goal of promotion of diversity). *But see* Adarand Constructors v. Pena, 515 U.S. 200, 115 S.Ct. 2097, 132 L.Ed.2d 158 (1995) (requiring strict scrutiny for minority preferences).

95. Legal Guide to Broadcast Law and Regulation 142 (National Association of Broadcasters 4th ed. 1994).

96. *Id.*

from the Internal Revenue Service that permitted it to defer taxation on capital gains.[97] However, in 1995 Congress repealed the portion of the Internal Revenue Code under which the FCC administered the tax certificate program.[98]

14.3 Traditional and Advanced Broadcast Services

A. *Traditional Broadcast Services*

1. *Audio Services*

The FCC licenses radio stations for operation under various classifications and conditions. The terms of a particular license specify what class of station may be operated based on its frequency, its power levels and, for some classes, its hours of operation. The purpose of the radio classification scheme is to provide a system of national, regional and local stations and to prevent frequency interference.

a. *AM Broadcast Service*

AM stations, also known as standard broadcast stations, operate on a frequency range from 535 to 1705 kilohertz ("KHz").[1] AM is an untabled service. This means that channels for AM stations are allocated by the application of engineering standards to ensure that a new station will not cause interference with other broadcasters based on criteria established by the FCC.[2] Stations licensed to other broadcast services receive license assignments from a "table of allotments." AM station operations are licensed according to various classifications established in the FCC's rules. AM stations are classified as "clear channel," "regional," or "local" stations, and the rules create specific station types within each category.

Class A stations serve wide areas and operate at power levels from 10 to 50 kilowatts ("kW").[3] Class A stations are the most powerful type of clear channel station and are intended to render both primary and secondary radio service over an extended range.[4] Although the range of a

---

97. Statement of Policy on Minority Ownership of Broadcasting Facilities, 68 F.C.C.2d 979 (1978).

98. *See* Implementation of Section 309(J) of the Communications Act—Competitive Bidding for Commercial Broadcast and Instructional Television Fixed Service Licenses, FCC 98–194 at n. 216 (rel. Aug. 18, 1998).

1. "AM" is an abbreviation for amplitude modulation, which describes the way in which sound waves are propagated. The various powers of the wave and their corresponding wave heights are interpreted by the receiving apparatus and reproduced as sounds. 47 C.F.R § 73.14 (1997). AM transmissions include both "ground waves," which create a long range primary service, and "sky waves," which can cause unpred-

ictably long range service, particularly at night. In the early 1990s, due to congestion in the AM service, the FCC expanded the AM band from 1605 KHz to 1705 KHz and allowed certain stations to "migrate" to the expanded band. *See* Review of the Technical Assignment Criteria for the AM Broadcast Service, 6 FCC Rcd. 6273 (1991); 47 C.F.R. § 73.30 (1997).

2. *See, e.g., id.* §§ 73.182—73.190.

3. *Id.* § 73.21(a)(1).

4. The primary service area is an area in which the groundwave is not subjected to objectionable interference or objectionable fading; the secondary service area is the service area of the station served by the skywave and not subject to objectionable interference and in which the signal is sub-

clear channel station is affected by many variables, such as atmospheric conditions and time of day, such stations can transmit signals for hundreds of miles. The FCC protects Class A stations from interference in their primary service areas on the same and adjacent channels and protects them on the same channel in their secondary service areas.[5]

Class B and D stations may be licensed as either clear channel or regional channel stations. Class B clear channel stations operate twenty-four hours a day at power levels of between .25 and 50 kW but are licensed to provide service only over a primary service area.[6] Class D clear channel stations are restricted to daytime operation and reduced-power nighttime operation. Class D stations operate at power levels of .25 to 50 kW during the day and less than .25 kW at night. Nighttime operation is not protected from interference.[7]

Regional channels are allocated to serve primarily a principal center of population and the contiguous rural area.[8] Class B and D stations may be licensed as regional channels, and FCC rules specify which channels are available for regional use.[9] Local channels are allocated to serve small areas or rural communities, and stations authorized for this purpose operate at very low power levels. The Commission licenses Class C stations as local channels, which operate at power levels between .25 and 1 kW. Class C stations are permitted to operate for an unlimited broadcast time, but the primary service area may be reduced by interference protections.[10]

b. FM Broadcast Service

FM radio is licensed for operation on frequencies between 88 and 108 megahertz ("MHz").[11] The band is divided into 100 channels of 200 KHz each. FM broadcasting was first authorized in the 1940s, and from the beginning could be received in stereo and was less subject to objectionable interference than AM broadcasting. Despite its technical advantages, FM service grew slowly, making few inroads into the previously established AM service. As late as the 1960s, radio executives would refer to FM as the "Forgotten Medium."[12] FM service began to take off in the 1970s because of its superior sound quality, and by the mid–1980s, had captured 70 percent of the radio audience.[13] The high

---

ject to intermittent variations in strength. *Id.* § 73.14 (1997).

5.   47 C.F.R. § 73.21 (a)(1). *See also id.* § 73.182.

6.   *Id.* § 73.21(a)(2).

7.   *Id.* § 73.21(a)(3).

8.   *Id.* § 73.21(b).

9.   *Id.* § 73.26(a).

10.   *Id.* § 73.21(c).

11.   "FM" is the abbreviation of frequency modulation. It produces a transmission of uniform wave height, but at varying frequencies. Unlike AM transmissions, FM radio waves do not follow the surface of the

earth. 47 C.F.R. § 73.681 (1997). *See* MARC A. FRANKLIN and DAVID A. ANDERSON, MASS MEDIA LAW 631 (Foundation Press 5th ed. 1995).

12.   Robert Corn–Revere, *Economics and Media Regulation*, in MEDIA ECONOMICS THEORY and PRACTICE 76 (Alexander, Owers and Carveth, eds. 1993).

13.   Amendment of Section 73.242 of the Commission's Rules and Regulations in Regard to AM–FM Program Duplication, 59 Rad. Reg. 2d 1611, 1613 (P&F 1986).

demand for FM services in the 1980s led the Commission to authorize a significant number of new FM stations in a practice known as creating "drop ins."[14]

Unlike the AM service, which is allotted on a patchwork arrangement based on zones of interference, the FCC devised a table of allotments in which FM stations were reserved for designated communities.[15] The allotment table is not set in stone, however, and it changes frequently based on requests by prospective licensees.[16] An applicant wishing to add a new station to the table must submit a petition for rulemaking to the Commission which includes a detailed engineering report, a demonstration that the proposed station will comply with existing allotment principles, and proof that it will not interfere with the spacing contours of existing stations.[17] The petitioner must indicate an intention to apply for and operate the station, if the allotment is made.[18] Upon a finding that the proposal is feasible, the Commission issues a notice of proposed rulemaking to modify the table of allotments. During the notice period other parties may file petitions proposing alternative allotments. Once a new allotment is approved by the Commission, competing applicants may file for the new license.

A licensee wishing to improve its existing facilities over the specifications permitted by the rules must also seek a change in the table of allotments from the Commission.[19] However, in that situation, the incumbent broadcaster's application is considered exclusively. If the Commission approves its application and grants the new allotment, only the abandoned frequency is open to competing applicants.[20]

FCC rules establish different classes of FM stations and prescribe permissible power levels and antenna heights for each class. There is an inverse proportion between permitted power levels and permissible antenna heights. The rules also establish minimum distance separation requirements between stations to prevent interference. FM stations are designated as Class C and C1 (effective radiated power level of up to 100 kW); Class C2 and C3 (power levels of 50 kW and 25 kW, respectively); Class B and B1 (effective radiated power levels of 50 kW and 25 kW, respectively) and Class A (effective radiated power level of 6 kW).[21]

2. Television Services

The FCC first began licensing television broadcast stations in 1941 but because of the disruption of World War II, it did not issue a

14. Modification of FM Broadcast Station Rules to Increase Availability of Commercial FM Broadcast Assignment, Report and Order, 94 F.C.C.2d 152 (1984).

15. 47 C.F.R. § 73.202 (1997).

16. *Id.* § 73.203(b).

17. *Id.* §§ 1.401(d), 1.420 *see* Amendment of Policies and Procedures for Amending the FM Table of Assignments, Section

73.202(b) of the Commission's Rules, 88 F.C.C.2d 631 (1981).

18. *Id.*

19. *Id.*

20. Legal Guide To Broadcast Law And Regulation 180 (National Association of Broadcasters, 4th ed. 1994).

21. *See generally*, 47 C.F.R. §§ 73.210–73.215 (1997).

comprehensive table of television assignments until the end of 1945.[22] In 1948 the Commission froze its assignments of channels because of a natural phenomenon involving tropospheric interference that created reception problems. The freeze ended in 1952 and the Commission began to assign television channels in the VHF and UHF frequencies.[23]

FCC rules make channel assignments by number (*e.g.,* channel 2 operates in the frequency band at 54–60 MHz, channel 3 from 60–66 MHz, etc.)[24] and designate the communities in which stations are licensed based on a table of allotments.[25] The table lists both the community of license, and the channel number of the broadcast station. As in the FM service, an applicant may seek authorization for a station not listed on the table only by filing a petition to amend the table of allotments.

Like the different classes of radio stations, FCC rules authorize several types of television stations. A television translator station retransmits the signals of a television station on a separate channel in areas where reception of the original signal is difficult because of terrain barriers or distances.[26] A translator may only transmit the signal of the primary station for which it is licensed to augment the signal.[27] A television booster station provides a function similar to the translator station in relaying the signal of a primary station. However, the booster station operates on the same channel as the primary station. Like a translator, a booster station is prohibited from broadcasting any signal other than that of the primary station.[28]

A low power television ("LPTV") station is a hybrid which can either broadcast original programming to the public, operate as a translator station or operate as a subscription service.[29] Low power television is a secondary service, and stands in a subordinate position to primary television stations. If a LPTV station causes interference to primary stations, the LPTV station must correct the interference or seek to change channels.[30] Interference to LPTV stations is not considered when the Commission approves a change in the table of allotments by adding a primary station. Additionally, low power stations typically do not have a right to demand "must carry" status on local cable systems.[31] A broadcaster can hold more than one LPTV license in the same community,

22. *See* Network Broadcasting, H.R. Rep. 1297, 85th Cong., 2d Sess. 18–20 (1955). Television channel allocation began with 400 VHF channels allotted to 140 regional markets.

23. Amendment to the Commission's Rules, Regulations and Engineering Standards Concerning the Television Broadcast Service, Sixth Report and Order, 41 F.C.C. 148 (1952). Television stations operate on either the Very High Frequency ("VHF") band (channels 2–13) at frequencies of 54 MHz to 88 MHz and 174 to 216 MHz, or on the Ultra High Frequency ("UHF") band

(channels 14–69) at frequencies between 470 MHz and 806 MHz.

24. 47 C.F.R. § 73.603 (1997).

25. *Id.* § 73.606.

26. *Id.* § 74.701.

27. *Id.* § 74.784(c).

28. *Id.* at § 74.784(d).

29. *Id.* at § 74.701(f).

30. *Id.* at § 74.703.

31. *Id.* §§ 76.55(d) and 76.56(b).

and the LPTV license is not counted for purposes of the Commission's multiple ownership rules.[32]

3. Multichannel Video Services

The FCC authorizes various over-the-air technologies that provide multichannel video service to the public. While some of the services are not "broadcasting" in a technical sense, they are licensed by the Commission to provide video programming using radio spectrum and are required to serve the public interest.

a. "Wireless Cable" Service

"Wireless cable" uses microwave channels for over-the-air distribution of video programming to individual reception antennas. While generally similar to wired cable television in its programming, the transmission range of wireless cable is determined by transmitter power, the capability of the receive antenna and the viability of a line-of-sight path between the transmitter or signal booster and the antenna.

Various microwave services licensed by the FCC can be used for wireless cable. They include multipoint distribution service ("MDS"), multichannel multipoint distribution service ("MMDS"), local multipoint distribution service ("LMDS"), instructional television fixed service ("ITFS") and operational fixed service ("OFS"). The FCC has allotted spectrum for MDS, which provides for one or two channels in a community; MMDS, which provides four channels in two different groups; and ITFS, which consists of 20 channels. Up to 33 microwave channels are available for each market, allowing for 150 to 200 channels through compressed digital video technology.

The ability to use these microwave services to provide wireless cable evolved over a period of years. In 1974, the Commission established the MDS rules, which provided for two MDS channels in the 50 largest metropolitan areas.[33] To encourage competition and allow for increased demand, the Commission later reallocated eight of 28 original ITFS channels to create MMDS and authorized ITFS licenses to lease excess capacity to MMDS operators.[34]

Beginning in 1995, the FCC changed its licensing scheme and began to distribute unused MDS and MMDS spectrum through competitive bidding.[35] The auction of this spectrum in 1996 distributed MMDS authorizations in 493 geographic Basic Trading Areas ("BTAs"). Auction

---

32. *Id.* § 74.732(b).

33. *See* Report and Order, Amendment of Parts 1, 2, 21 and 43 of the Commission's Rules to Provide for Licensing and Regulation of Common Carrier Radio Stations in the Multipoint Distribution Service, 45 F.C.C.2d 616 (1974), *recons. denied*, 57 F.C.C.2d 301 (1975).

34. Report and Order in Gen. Docket No. 80–112 and CC Docket No. 80–16, 94 F.C.C.2d 1203 (1983).

35. Report and Order In the Matter of Amendment of Parts 21 and 74 of the Commission's Rules With Regard to Filing Procedures in the Multipoint Distribution Service and in the Instructional Television Fixed Service and Implementation of Section 309(j) of the Communications Act—Competitive Bidding, 10 F.C.C. Rcd. 9589 (1995).

winners were authorized to build and license wireless cable facilities during a five-year build-out period within each BTA subject to interference limitations and other restrictions.[36] An authorization granted by auction lasts for ten years, and the licensee may receive a renewal expectancy by demonstrating substantial service and compliance with the Commission's orders.[37]

The MMDS channels may be augmented by the use of other microwave services.[38] Subject to certain restrictions, a programming provider may lease ITFS channels for the transmission of wireless cable. Under the FCC's rules, ITFS channel permits and licenses are restricted generally to accredited institutions, educational governmental units and nonprofit educational organizations.[39] Additionally, the ITFS licensee must transmit a specified number of hours of educational and instructional programming over its frequencies.[40] However, the rules also permit a wireless cable operator to lease excess capacity from ITFS licensees provided that the ITFS licensee meets certain requirements, such as maintaining specified minimum amounts of ITFS programming per channel.[41]

LMDS is another microwave service established by the FCC for use as wireless cable (among other applications). Because of its propagation characteristics, LMDS systems operate with multiple "cells" with radii of three to six miles in order to provide service in metropolitan areas. LMDS service is authorized to operate in the 28 and 31 GHz bands. The 28 GHz band is shared with fixed satellite service. The FCC authorized LMDS to provide broadband two-way video communications, including video distribution and data services in order to provide competition to cable companies and local exchange carriers.[42]

LMDS service emerged from an experimental authorization that was initially granted in 1986. The FCC had granted a waiver permitting CellularVision of New York to provide point-to-multipoint LMDS service in the 28 GHz band, which was at that time reserved for point-to-point service. Pursuant to the waiver, CellularVision constructed an LMDS system in the New York City Primary Metropolitan Statistical Area. By mid–1996, CellularVision was providing LMDS service in competition

---

36. *See, e.g.,* 47 C.F.R. §§ 21.930(a)(1), 21.938 (1996). Existing MDS and MMDS licensees were grandfathered as of June 15, 1995, and their service areas are protected from interference under the new scheme.

37. *See* Memorandum and Order on Reconsideration in MM Docket No. 94–131 (October 27, 1995) at ¶ 8.

38. Frequencies in the 18 GHz band allocated for Operational Fixed Microwave Service ("OFS") may be used for the transmission of video entertainment programming within certain limits. Specifically, OFS frequencies may not be used to provide the final RF link in the chain of transmission of program material to cable television

systems, multipoint distribution systems or master antenna TV systems, except in the frequency bands 6425–6525 and 18,142–18,-580 MHz and on frequencies above 21,200 MHz. 47 C.F.R. § 101.603 (1997).

39. *See id.* § 74.932.

40. *See id.* § 74.931. For the most part, ITFS programming must be "formal educational programming offered for credit to enrolled students of accredited schools."

41. *See id.* § 74.931(e). In addition, the ITFS permittee/licensee must remain in control of the construction and operation of the licensed facilities.

42. *See id* §§ 101.1001–101.1017.

with cable operators in the Brighton Beach area of New York. After an initial freeze of new point-to-point applications in the 28 GHz band,[43] the FCC authorized the grant of LMDS licenses by competitive bidding. The FCC defined the service area for LMDS based on BTAs and allocated 1,000 MHz of spectrum to LMDS. Two licenses for LMDS service are authorized in each of 493 BTAs.[44]

b. Direct Broadcast Satellite Service

Direct Broadcast Satellite service ("DBS"), is a satellite broadcasting service which delivers a focused, powerful transmission to a discrete area using frequencies in the Ku-band.[45] The DBS signal, in contrast to a traditional communication satellite signal, allows reception via small, relatively low-cost dishes of approximately 18 inches in diameter. A DBS licensee provides cable television-type service by contracting with other programming providers, and packaging a service offering for subscribers. The first high-powered DBS service was launched in mid–1994 and within one year had well over one million subscribers. By mid-1997, there were four major providers of DBS service with more than five million subscribers. In addition, two other operators provided "medium power" DBS service. The number of subscribers was projected to increase to up to fifteen million by the year 2000.[46] One reason for the rapid growth rate is the ability of DBS to penetrate markets that cable television could not effectively reach.[47]

Despite its rapid growth after introduction to the market, DBS represents an overnight success that was years in the making. In 1980 the FCC first announced it would begin to develop DBS regulations based on its policy of promoting new media technologies.[48] The first

43. *See* In the Matter of Petitions for Redesignation of the Common Carrier Point-to-Point Microwave Radio Service Frequency Band 27.5 GHz–29.5 GHz, 7 FCC Rcd. 7201 (Common Carrier Bureau 1992).

44. Auction of Local Multipoint Distribution Service, Auction Notice and Filing Requirements for 986 Basic Trading Area ("BTA") Licenses in the 28 Ghz and 31 Ghz Bands, 13 FCC Rcd. 7754 (1997).

45. The Ku-band refers to a band of frequencies at approximately 12 GHz. DBS broadcasting services licensed under 47 C.F.R. part 25, operate at 11.7 to 12.2 GHz downlink frequencies. *See* Implementation of Section 25 of the Cable Television Consumer Protection Act of 1992, 8 FCC Rcd. 1589 n.4, 1591 n.10 (1993). This is to be distinguished from C–band satellite service, that requires much larger dishes (10–feet) to receive satellite transmissions. Also, the FCC has licensed entities to provide satellite service in the high-powered Ka-band, which will provide additional broadband

services to the home. *See* Assignment of Orbital Locations to Space Stations in the Ka-band, DA 97–967 (rel May 9, 1997); Teledesic Corp., 12 FCC Rcd. 3154 (1997).

46. Annual Assessment of the Status of Competition in the Market for the Delivery of Video Programming, 13 FCC Rcd. 1034, para. 55 (1997). By early 1998, the FCC estimated that high-powered DBS and traditional satellite dishes served a combined subscriber base of 8.5 million households. Policies and Rules for the Direct Broadcast Satellite Service, Notice of Proposed Rulemaking, 13 FCC Rcd. 6907 (1998).

47. Dwight L. Teeter, Jr. and Don R. LeDuc, Mass Communications and Government 434 (8th ed. 1995).

48. Notice of Proposed Policy Statement and Rulemaking, Gen. Docket No. 80–603, 86 F.C.C.2d 719 (1981). *See also,* Inquiry into the Regulatory Policy in Regard to Direct Broadcasting Satellites for the Period Following the 1983 World Administrative Radio Conference, 90 F.C.C.2d 676 (1982).

application for a DBS license was submitted in 1979 by the Satellite Television Corporation, a subsidiary of COMSAT. The Commission accepted the application in 1981, along with several other prospective DBS service providers.[49] The Commission responded the following year with simplified regulations applicable to DBS, including exemptions from the Commission's ownership and political broadcasting requirements.[50]

However, clouds would soon appear in the "open skies" policy the Commission was attempting to foster. Traditional broadcasters challenged what they considered to be deregulatory favoritism toward DBS. Notwithstanding the Commission's public interest mandate to promote new technologies, the United States Court of Appeals for the District of Colombia Circuit held that DBS met the statutory definition of broadcasting and that the FCC could not justify its disparate treatment of DBS.[51]

In response, the FCC initiated a proceeding "to determine what criteria may be used by the Commission to determine whether a communications service should be treated as 'broadcasting' under the Communications Act."[52] The Commission determined that subscription video services should be classified as "non-broadcast" services and freed from broadcast regulation. The appropriate classification hinged on the operator's intent: the service is not considered to be broadcasting if the licensee does not intend to serve the public generally.[53] Based on the *Subscription Video* rules, a DBS operator could opt for regulatory treatment as a broadcaster, a non-broadcaster or a common carrier. The United States Court of Appeals for the D.C. Circuit upheld this approach to regulatory classification.[54]

Before commercial DBS service was successfully launched, however, Congress decided that certain broadcast-type public interest obligations should be imposed on the service. Section 25 of the 1992 Cable Act requires DBS operators to set aside four to seven percent of channel capacity for "public interest" programming.[55] The District of Columbia

49. Notice of Proposed Policy Statement and Rulemaking in General Docket 80–603, 88 F.C.C.2d 100 (1981). The other applicants included CBS, RCA, and Western Union.

50. Inquiry Into the Development of Regulatory Policy in Regard to Direct Broadcasting Satellites, 90 F.C.C.2d 676 (1982).

51. National Association of Broadcasters v. FCC, 740 F.2d 1190, 239 U.S. App. D.C. 87 (D.C.Cir.1984).

52. Subscription Video, Report and Order, 2 FCC Rcd 1001, 1003 (1987).

53. *Id.* at 1006. As indicia of intent, the Commission focused on whether the customer needs a special encoder to receive the transmission, the information is encrypted and the operator and subscriber are in a contractual relationship.

54. National Ass'n For Better Broadcasting v. FCC, 849 F.2d 665, 270 U.S. App. D.C. 334 (D.C.Cir.1988). *See generally* Symposium: Telecommunications Law: Unscrambling the Signals, Unbundling the Law: Howard A. Shelanski, *The Bending Line Between Conventional "Broadcast" and Wireless "Carriage"*, 97 Columb. L. Rev. 819, 1048 (1997). As of this writing, all DBS providers have chosen to be classified as subscription video services. Policies and Rules for the Direct Broadcast Satellite Service, 13 FCC Rcd 6907 (1998).

55. Section 25, Cable Television Consumer Protection and Competition Act of 1992, Pub. L. 102–385, 106 Stat. 1460, *codified at* 47 U.S.C.A. § 335(b)(1)(West Supp. 1997).

Circuit upheld the requirement using the traditional scarcity rationale for broadcast content controls.[56] Following the affirmance the Commission adopted rules requiring DBS licensees to comply with political broadcasting rules and to set aside four percent of channel capacity for educational and informational programming.[57]

Another legal challenge arose from a change in the Commission's method for assigning DBS channels. The original DBS assignments had been made through a fairly traditional application process. After the successful launch of DBS service, however, the FCC found numerous bidders willing to pay for a DBS authorization. When the Commission in 1995 withdrew its grant of fifty-one channels initially made to Advanced Communications Corporation,[58] it decided to distribute the reclaimed channels by auction rather than on a first-come, first-served basis to existing permit holders, as previously decided.[59] The FCC concluded that an auction would be preferable to other licensing alternative by promoting efficiency, minimizing delay and speeding the development of the new service.[60] In 1996 the Commission auctioned licenses for the reclaimed channels plus one previously unassigned orbital slot.[61]

Regulation of DBS service also includes an inherent international aspect because DBS transmissions cross national boundaries, and satellite frequencies are allocated by treaty. After the successful launch of the domestic DBS industry, the Commission began to reevaluate regulatory restrictions affecting the provision of DBS service by American and foreign corporations. In 1996, the FCC eliminated its "transborder" policy, thus allowing domestic satellite service operators, including DBS, more flexibility to provide international service. The Commission also modified the "separate systems" policy, which allowed the provision of international service, but restricted domestic service.[62] The Commission decided that United States licensees that provide DBS service internationally do not need additional FCC approval beyond existing domestic DBS authorization.[63]

---

56. Time Warner Entertainment Company v. FCC, 93 F.3d 957, 973–977, 320 U.S. App. D.C. 294, 309–313 (D.C.Cir.1996).

57. Implementation of Section 25 of the Cable Television Consumer Protection and Competition Act of 1992, Direct Broadcast Satellite Service Obligations, FCC 98–307 (rel. Nov. 25, 1998).

58. Advanced Communications Corp., 11 FCC Rcd. 3399 (1996). The FCC concluded that Advanced failed to make sufficient progress in constructing its satellites or initiating DBS service.

59. Continental Satellite Corp., 4 FCC Rcd. 6292, 6299 (1989), *partial recons. denied*, 5 FCC Rcd. 7412 (1990).

60. Revision of Rules and Policies for the Direct Broadcast Satellite Service, Report and Order, 11 FCC Rcd. 9712 (1996).

61. Annual Assessment of the Status of Competition in the Market for the Delivery of Video Programming, 12 FCC Rcd. 4358, 4383 (1997) MCI placed the winning bid of $682 million dollars.

62. Amendment to the Commission's Regulatory Policies Governing Domestic Fixed Satellites and Separate International Satellite Systems, ("DISCO I"), 11 FCC Rcd. 2429 (1996).

63. *Id. See also* In the Matter of the Application of TelQuest Ventures, L.L.C. for a License for a Fixed–Satellite Transmit/Receive Earth Station to Communicate with a Canadian DBS Satellite to be Located at 91 Degrees W.L., Report and Order, 11 FCC Rcd. 13943 (1996).

The FCC also indicated its intention to allow provision of DBS service within the United States by foreign licensees, provided the foreign government instituted reciprocal treatment of American DBS licensees. Such treatment is evaluated through an examination of competitive opportunities and barriers in the home market and "route markets" of the non-United States provider.[64] While foreign governments may impose conditions on an American DBS provider, the Commission will not enforce foreign rules under United States laws. Relying on the Universal Declaration of Human Rights, the Commission stated "international law does not give any nation an absolute right of 'prior consent' before information is sent across its borders."[65] Pending approval of the World Trade Organization's Basic Telecommunications Agreement, the United States proposes to regulate participation by foreign licensees in the United States satellite market by reviewing license applications for United States earth stations to ensure that American satellite systems have effective competitive opportunities in the respective countries involved. WTO members would receive streamlined treatment under this process.[66]

DBS service is also affected by very local concerns. Accordingly, the Telecommunications Act of 1996 lowered regulatory barriers for DBS by giving the FCC preemptive authority over local restrictions on the reception of satellite service.[67] Some local zoning laws and other restrictions had limited the ability of homeowners and others to place satellite dishes and antennas at their residences. The Commission adopted rules preempting local and state restrictions on DBS receiving equipment but created certain exceptions in special cases.[68] The FCC action extended beyond restrictions imposed by local zoning rules to include decisions of homeowners associations and other bodies.

B. Advanced Broadcasting Services

1. Digital Television

In furtherance of the Communications Act mandate to encourage the provision of new technologies and services to the public, the FCC has authorized a shift from analog to digital broadcasting service. Known by the various acronyms of Advanced Television ("ATV"), High Definition

---

64. This is known as the effective competitive opportunities for satellites ("ECO–Sat") test. The route markets are the other international markets which the satellites seek to serve. Amendment to the Commission's Regulatory Policies to Allow Non–U.S.-Licensed Space Stations to Provide Domestic and International Satellite Service, ("DISCO II") 11 FCC Rcd. 18178 (1996). The Commission proposed eliminating the ECO–Sat test for signatories to the World Trade Organization's Basic Telecommunications Agreement. IB Docket No. 96–111, Further Notice of Proposed Rulemaking (released July 18, 1997).

65. *See* DISCO I, 11 FCC Rcd. at 2439–40 n. 87.

66. Amendment of the Commission's Regulatory Policies to Allow Non–U.S.-Licensed Space Stations to Provide Domestic and International Satellite Service in the United States, 12 FCC Rcd. 14220 (1997); DISCO II, 11 FCC Rcd. at 18187–88.

67. Telecommunications Act of 1996, Pub. L. 104–104, § 207 110 Stat. 56 (1996).

68. 47 C.F.R. § 1.4000(a) (1996); Preemption of Local Zoning Regulations of Satellite Earth Stations, 11 FCC Rcd. 19276 (1996).

Television ("HDTV") and Digital Television ("DTV"), this service promises to deliver superior video and sound quality by means of digital transmission. The new service also makes possible a range of multichannel and interactive applications. A television broadcaster may transmit a high definition signal with superior picture quality or, through digital compression, multiple channels of standard definition television.

In 1992 the Commission announced plans to adopt a universal technical standard for ATV and began assigning UHF frequencies for ATV transmission to existing broadcasters. The broadcasters were to be given six years to either begin operation on the new frequencies or face comparative hearings when their existing licenses expire.[69] By 1994 the Commission had developed and adopted various technical aspects of the DTV standard in cooperation with a consortium of companies and institutions,[70] and in 1996, the Commission formally adopted the complete DTV standard.[71]

The Telecommunications Act of 1996 required the Commission to implement a series of procedural rules for establishing the new service.[72] In general terms, the Act restricted the eligibility for DTV licenses to existing VHF and UHF broadcasters.[73] The FCC adopted rules requiring broadcasters to provide a free digital programming service of at least identical quality as existing analog service by the year 2006.[74] The rules provide broadcasters with some flexibility regarding the nature of the digital service to be provided. Broadcasters are not required to provide high definition service, but have the option to provide multicasting, software distribution, interactive services, non-broadcast data transmission and other services to the public.[75]

Network affiliates in the top ten broadcast markets voluntarily agreed to initiate digital broadcasting by the end of 1998, while network affiliates in the forty largest markets are required to build DTV facilities by November 1, 1999. All other commercial stations must build DTV facilities by May 1, 2002. Non-commercial television licensees have a May 1, 2003 deadline for digital service.[76] The Commission also estab-

69. Memorandum Opinion and Order, Third Report and Order, Third Further Notice of Proposed Rule Making in MM Dkt. 87–268, 7 FCC Rcd. 6924 (1992).

70. Fourth Further Notice of Proposed Rulemaking, Third Notice of Inquiry in MM Docket 87–268, 10 FCC Rcd. 10541 (1995). The entities involved included AT&T, Zenith Electronics, General Instruments, MIT, Phillips Consumer Electronics, David Sarnoff Research, and Thompson Consumer Electronics.

71. Fourth Report and Order in MM Docket No. 87–267, 11 FCC Rcd. 17771 (1996).

72. Advanced Television Systems and Their Impact upon the Existing Television Broadcast Service, Fifth Report and Order, 12 FCC Rcd. 12809 (1997) ("Fifth Report

and Order"); see also Advanced Television Systems and Their Impact Upon the Existing Television Broadcast Service, Mem.Op. and Order on Recons. of the Fifth Report and Order, 13 FCC Rcd. 6860 (1998). See 47 C.F.R. § 73.624 (1997).

73. Telecommunications Act of 1996, Pub. L. 104–104 § 336(a)(1), 110 Stat. 56 (1996).

74. Fifth Report and Order, 12 FCC Rcd. at ¶ 28.

75. *Id.* at ¶ 29.

76. *Id.* at ¶ 76. Two six-month exceptions may be granted by the Mass Media Bureau for unforeseen problems beyond the control of the licensee.

lished a simulcasting phase-in schedule, during which time a station can broadcast the same programming in both analog and digital formats. DTV channels must simulcast fifty percent of the video programming of their analog channel by April 21, 2003; seventy five percent by April 21, 2004; and one hundred percent by April, 1 2005.[77]

Broadcasters providing digital service will be licensed under a streamlined process that allows a broadcaster to renew its license by filing a form affirming that certain technical and environmental requirements have been met.[78] By 2006, if DTV receivers achieve a specified level of market penetration, broadcasters will be required to return one of two assigned channels to the Commission which will then use the recovered portion of the spectrum, channels 60–69, for additional DTV broadcasting requirements.[79]

The FCC also adopted a table of allotments and procedures for assigning DTV frequencies.[80] In allotting DTV channels, the FCC sought to accommodate all eligible broadcasters with a second channel for DTV service. All television licensees (except licensees of low power TV and translator stations) and holders of construction permits for full-power stations are eligible for initial DTV authorizations. The Commission attempted to replicate existing analog service areas, with the DTV allotments. The Commission recognized that development of DTV will displace some existing LPTV and TV translator stations. In these situations, while LPTV and translator stations still retain their secondary status, the Commission decided to permit a displaced station to apply for non-interfering operation on an existing channel using a simplified application procedure. If the Commission determines that no previous request has been made for the vacant channel it will assign the channel to the applicant within thirty days, barring any objections.[81]

The Commission confined its rulemaking to procedural and technical issues and deferred resolving issues related to the public interest obligations and must-carry requirements for DTV broadcasters.[82] However, in December 1998, the Vice–President's Advisory Commission on the Public Interest Obligations of Digital Television Broadcasters recommended that the FCC adopt "mandatory minimum public interest requirements for digital broadcasters."[83]

2. Digital Audio Radio Service ("DARS")

Digital Audio Radio Service ("DARS") is a satellite-delivered nationwide radio service that will provide nationwide compact disc-quality

77. Id. at ¶ 54.

78. Id. at ¶ 72.

79. Id. at ¶ 100.

80. Advanced Television Systems and Their Impact Upon the Existing Television Broadcast Service, Sixth Report and Order, 12 FCC Rcd. 14588 (1997) ("Sixth Report and Order"). The FCC made some minor revisions to the table of allotments and technical rules on reconsideration. See Memorandum Opinion and Order on Recon-

sideration of the Sixth Report and Order, 13 FCC Rcd. 7418 (1998). See also 47 C.F.R. §§ 73.622–73.623 (1997).

81. Sixth Report and Order at ¶ 144.

82. Fifth Report and Order, 12 FCC Rcd. at ¶ 50.

83. Report of the Advisory Committee on Public Interest Obligations of Digital Broadcasters (Dec. 18, 1998) at 47.

sound for the broadcast of music on a subscription basis. In 1995 the Commission concluded that DARS would compliment rather than compete with existing broadcasting services and would fulfill the congressional desire for a nationwide radio service.[84] Applications of four prospective licensees were then on file with the FCC seeking authorization to provide DARS service. In order to resolve mutually exclusive assignments, the Commission conducted an auction among the four competing applicants.[85] In the interim, Congress directed the Commission to auction the spectrum initially assigned to DARS for the provision of a new wireless communications service.[86] The Commission responded by assigning bands in the 2310 MHz to 2320 MHz and 2345 to 2360 MHz range for satellite DARS.[87]

The FCC did not classify this service for regulatory purposes, and allowed licensees substantial flexibility in meeting subscriber needs and market requirements.[88] Accordingly, DARS applicants submitted proposals that would allow for a mix of both subscription and advertiser-supported services.[89] Although the Commission declined to classify DARS as a broadcast service, it nevertheless decided to impose the same eight-year license term that applies to broadcast licensees.[90] In addition, the Commission imposed political programming requirements on DARS licensees, including the "reasonable access" obligation of Section 312(a) and the "equal opportunities" requirement of Section 315 of the Communications Act. The FCC left open the question of whether to apply additional public interest broadcast requirements to DARS licensees.

14.4 Structural Regulations

A. *Ownership Limits*

Over the years the FCC has imposed various limits on the number and types of broadcasting outlets which can be controlled by a single entity, both nationwide and in local markets. Ownership rules arose from concerns over potential concentration of power in the broadcast industry and were intended to promote a "diversity of voices" in

---

84. Amendment to the Commission's Rules with Regard to the Establishment and Regulation of New Digital Audio Radio Service, Report and Order in Docket 90–357, 10 FCC Rcd. 2310 (1995).

85. Establishment of Rules and Policies for the Digital Audio Radio Satellite Service, 12 FCC Rcd. 5754 (1997). Winning bids in excess of $170 million were submitted by Satellite CD Radio, Inc. and American Mobile Radio Corp. Public Notice, FCC Announces Auction Winners for Digital Audio Radio Service, 12 FCC Rcd. 18727 (1997).

86. Omnibus Consolidated Appropriations Act, 1997 Pub L. 104–208, 110 Stat. 3009 (1996).

87. Establishment of Rules and Policies for the Digital Audio Radio Satellite Service, 12 FCC Rcd. 5754, (1997). *See* In the Matter of Amendment to the Commission's Rules to Establish Part 27, The Wireless Communication Services ("WCS"), Notice of Proposed Rulemaking, Docket No. 96–228 (released Nov. 12, 1996).

88. Establishment of Rules and Policies for the Digital Audio Radio Satellite Service, 12 FCC Rcd. 5754 (1997).

89. *Id.*

90. *Id.* at ¶ 111. The Commission had earlier proposed a ten year license term.

furtherance of the public interest.[1] At the same time, ownership restrictions reflected a tension between the desire to promote free expression by limiting private concentrations of power and the effort to preserve a system of free private broadcasting without excessive government control. Before enactment of the Radio Act of 1927, Herbert Hoover, then the Secretary of Commerce, testified that "we cannot allow any single person or group to place themselves in [the] position where they can censor the material which shall be broadcast to the public, nor do I believe that the government should ever be placed in the position of censoring this material."[2] Some members of Congress argued that broadcast stations should be classified as common carriers and required to transmit any and all messages,[3] but Congress rejected this approach in the Radio Act of 1927.[4] As established by the Act, the Federal Radio Commission determined that the public interest would best be served by "the free and fair competition of opposing views."[5]

Over time, the Commission has regulated ownership of broadcast outlets in a number of ways. In 1940 the Commission issued rules to restrict the number of FM broadcast outlets one could own in a single community.[6] Rules prohibiting network ownership followed a year later that applied both horizontally, to prohibit the ownership of more than one broadcast network and vertically to forbid the network ownership of more than one station in a community.[7] The Commission declined to prohibit newspaper ownership of local broadcast outlets in the 1940s and instead relied on a case-by-case approach.[8] It later reversed course and adopted a cross-ownership rule in the 1970s.[9] Nationwide limits on the number of stations that could be owned by a single entity have been in place since the 1950s. The FCC has modified the limits from time to time but the underlying premise in favor of ownership limits remained constant.

The Telecommunications Act of 1996 Act questioned this underlying premise by enacting sweeping changes in the broadcast ownership rules. The 1996 Act removed the limit on the number of broadcast stations that can be controlled nationally by a single entity and relaxed various

1. *See e.g.,* Multiple Ownership of Standard, FM and Television Broadcast Stations, 45 F.C.C. 1467, 1467–1477 (1964). *See also* National Broadcasting Co. v. United States, 319 U.S. 190, 63 S.Ct. 997, 87 L.Ed. 1344 (1943).

2. Hearings on H.R. 7357 before the House Committee on Merchant Marine and Fisheries, 68th Cong., 1st Sess., 8 (1924).

3. 67 Cong. Rec. 5483 (1926) (statement of Rep. Davis).

4. Radio Act of 1927, § 18, 44 Stat. 1170.

5. Great Lakes Broadcasting Co., 3 F.R.C. Ann. Rpt. 32, 33 (1929), *aff'd in part, rev'd in part on other grounds,* Great Lakes Broadcasting Co. v. FRC, 37 F.2d 993, 59 App. D.C. 195 (D.C.Cir.), *cert. dismissed,*

281 U.S. 706, 50 S.Ct. 467, 74 L.Ed. 1129 (1930).

6. Rules Governing Standard and High Frequency Broadcast Stations, § 3.228(a), 5 Fed. Reg. 2382, 2384 (1940).

7. Rules and Regulations Governing Commercial Television, § 4.226, 6 Fed. Reg. 2284, 2284, 2285 (1941).

8. Newspaper Ownership of Radio Stations, Notice of Dismissal of Proceeding, 9 Fed. Reg. 702 (1944).

9. Rules Relating to Multiple Ownership of Standard FM and Television Broadcasting Stations, Second Report and Order, 50 F.C.C.2d 1046 (1975).

other restrictions but retained limits on the total audience reach for commonly-owned television stations, as well as restrictions on the number of stations that can be acquired in a particular market. Pursuant to the 1996 Act, the FCC in 1998 initiated a review of the continuing validity of various ownership rules, including the newspaper-broadcasting cross-ownership rule, the cable television-broadcasting cross-ownership rule, the UHF discount for measuring audience reach, the national television audience cap, the local radio ownership restrictions and the dual network rule.[10]

1. Ownership Attribution

To enforce ownership rules it is necessary to establish a threshold for what constitutes ownership or control of a broadcast license. The FCC makes such determinations through its "attribution rules." Under these rules, various types of ownership are considered to be cognizable or attributable. Generally, any entity that owns five percent or more of the outstanding voting stock in a corporation that holds a broadcast license has an attributable interest. However, under the "single majority shareholder" rule, where 50 percent or more of voting stock is held by a single entity, only that entity is attributable for purposes of the broadcast ownership rules. Passive investors such as investment companies, insurance companies, or, trust departments of banks are considered to have attributable interests if their stock ownership amounts to 10 percent of voting shares, provided the passive investor has not attempted to exert influence over the corporation and has no representative among the officers or board of the corporation.[11] Attributable interests are also counted for stations acquired in bankruptcy proceedings.[12]

Any person who votes stock or has the sole or joint right to determine how stock will be determined is considered to be the owner under the attribution rules. All shares of stock for which a person has such rights are aggregated to determine ownership even if record title to the stock is held in one or different names. Trust beneficiaries may be considered attributable owners under certain circumstances, such as where the beneficiary has the sole power to sell the stock or to revoke the trust at will.[13]

Ownership interests that are held indirectly through one or more intervening corporations are calculated by successive multiplication of the ownership percentages for each link in the vertical ownership chain.[14] In general, all officers and directors of a corporation are deemed to have attributable interests. If a corporation engages in both media-related and non-media-related activities, a corporate officer who has no

10. 1998 Biennial Regulatory Review—Review of the Commission's Broadcast Ownership Rules Adopted Pursuant to Section 202 of the Telecommunications Act of 1996, FCC 98–37 (rel. Mar. 13, 1998).

11. 47 C.F.R. § 73.3555, notes 2(b), (c) (1997).

12. *See e.g.*, Paramount Communications, Inc., 7 FCC Rcd. 1390 (1992) (6.45% interest acquired in bankruptcy proceeding is attributable).

13. 47 C.F.R. § 73.3555 note (e) (1997).

14. *Id.* § 73.3555, note (d).

involvement in media-related activities may be able to obtain non-attributable status but only if the Commission grants a waiver request. The officers and directors of a parent company of a broadcast licensee, with an attributable interest in any such subsidiary company, shall be deemed to have an attributable interest in the subsidiary unless the duties and responsibilities of the officer or director are wholly unrelated to the activities of the licensee.[15]

Not all stock ownership in a corporation is attributable. For example, non-voting shares do not create a cognizable interest under the FCC's rules. This is true even if non-voting stock is convertible to voting stock. Attribution is required only when the conversion to voting stock occurs. Similarly, warrants to buy stock, stock options and convertible debt do not create attributable interests until converted to voting shares.

In the case of partnerships, general partnership interests are attributable, regardless of the size, while limited partnership interests typically are not. However, all general partners and limited partners who are materially involved in the broadcast business of the partnership are considered to have attributable interests.[16] The Commission will not recognize the presence of a limited partner or investor who is "not materially involved, directly or indirectly, in the management or operation of the media related activity of the partnership and the licensee or system so certifies."[17] However, failure to disclose the involvement, even temporarily, of a limited partner or investor will result in full attribution of the ownership interest of that individual or partner.

The FCC also employs a "cross interest policy" to scrutinize relationships that may not otherwise fall under the rules. Under the policy, the FCC considers the intertwining of interests of stations through common employees, common participation in other business ventures or ownership interests short of those found to be attributable under the ownership rules. Although the FCC has reduced its emphasis on cross interests and has considered eliminating the policy, such scrutiny may still take place.[18]

2. *Multiple Ownership Restrictions*

Under the Telecommunications Act of 1996, the Commission does not prescribe the number of radio or television stations a single entity may own. However, such restrictions have long been a feature of FCC regulation. Multiple ownership rules were first adopted in 1953.[19] The

15. *Id.* § 73.3555, note (h).

16. *Id.* § 73.3555, note (g)(1).

17. Reexamination of the Commission's Rules and Policies Regarding the Attribution of Ownership Interests in Broadcast, Cable Television and Newspaper Entities, 50 Fed. Reg. 27,438, 27,449 (1985), *codified at* 47 C.F.R. § 73.3555 note 2 (1996). Coast TV, 5 FCC Rcd. 2751, 2752 (1990).

18. *See* Reexamination of the Commission's Cross–Interest Policy, Notice of In-

quiry, 2 FCC Rcd. 3699 (1987); Reexamination of the Commission's Cross–Interest Policy, Further Notice of Inquiry and Notice of Proposed Rulemaking, 4 FCC Rcd. 2035 (1989); Further Notice of Proposed Rulemaking, 10 FCC Rcd. 3606 (1994). *See also* Telemundo Group, Inc., 10 FCC Rcd. 1104, 1107 (1994).

19. Amendment of Sections 3.35, 3.240 and 3.636 of Rules and Regulations of Multiple Ownership of AM, FM and Television

"rule of seven" prohibited a broadcaster from owning more than seven AM, FM and television stations. Three years after it was adopted, Storer Broadcasting Company challenged the rule because it allowed the Commission to deny a hearing without regard to whether the acquisition would serve the public interest. In *United States v. Storer Broadcasting Co.*, the Supreme Court upheld the rule.[20] The Court found that the rule of seven, while not specifically authorized by the Communications Act of 1934, was nevertheless justified under the Commission's public interest mandate. The court determined that the rule was not an absolute prohibition, and a potential owner alleging a sufficient public interest rationale might persuade the Commission to waive its rules in a particular case.

The Commission has repeatedly revisited and revised its multiple ownership rules. With respect to radio concentrations, the Commission in 1985 raised the ownership limit to twelve AM and FM stations.[21] Subsequently, in 1992 the Commission raised the total to eighteen AM and eighteen FM stations, with the limit expanding to twenty AM and FM broadcast stations after 1994.[22] Finally, all national numerical limits on radio station ownership were eliminated by the Telecommunications Act of 1996.

The Commission raised the ownership limits for television broadcast stations from seven to twelve in 1985.[23] The rule permitted an owner to exceed the 12 station cap and to hold 14 stations, if at least two of those stations were minority-controlled enterprises or small businesses.[24] After the FCC relaxed the television ownership limits in 1985, various influential members of Congress expressed disapproval with the extent of the liberalization. As a result, the Commission revised the television ownership rule to include a national cap on audience reach to supplement the numerical limits on station ownership.[25] Specifically, the limitation on audience reach prohibited an owner from holding multiple television stations reaching more than 25 percent of the national audience.[26] The

Broadcasting Stations, Report and Order, 18 F.C.C. 288, 291 (1953).

20. 351 U.S. 192, 76 S.Ct. 763, 100 L.Ed. 1081 (1956).

21. Amendment to Section 73.3555, Report and Order, 100 F.C.C.2d 17 (1984).

22. Revision of Radio Rules and Policies, 7 FCC Rcd. 6387 (1992).

23. Amendment to Section 73.3555, Report and Order, 100 F.C.C.2d 17 (1984). The FCC considered a further expansion of the number to between eighteen and twenty-four commonly held stations in 1995, but did not adopt the proposal. *See* Review of the Commission's Regulations Governing Television Broadcast Stations Television Satellite Stations Review of Policy and Rules, 60 Fed. Reg. 6490 (Jan. 17, 1995).

24. The FCC defines minority ownership in a corporation as a 50 percent or greater control of stock by a member of a minority group. Recognized minorities include, Blacks, Hispanics, American Indians, Alaska Natives, Asian or Pacific Islanders. *See* Policy Statement on Minority Ownership of Broadcasting Facilities, 68 F.C.C.2d 979, 980 n. 8 (1978). The Commission defines small businesses as individual or business entities and all affiliated enterprises, under common control, with assets less than $1 million and annual revenues less than $500,000. Revision of the Radio Rules and Policies, 7 FCC Rcd. 6387, (1992).

25. Multiple Ownership (12–12–12 Reconsideration) 100 F.C.C.2d 74 (1985).

26. *Id.* For purposes of this rule, UHF stations are attributed with only 50 percent of the households in their respective markets.

audience reach limit also contained an exception for minority controlled stations, allowing the owner to acquire stations that reach 30 percent of the national audience, provided that at least five percent of the audience is served by minority-controlled stations.[27]

As with the radio ownership rules, the Telecommunications Act eliminated the numerical limits on television station ownership. However, it retained the audience reach limitation first adopted in 1985, but expanded the limit to 35 percent of the overall national audience.[28]

3. Local Ownership Restrictions

a. Newspaper–Broadcast Cross Ownership Rules

The newspaper-broadcast cross-ownership rule forbids a direct or indirect ownership interest in a daily newspaper and an AM, FM or television station in the same community.[29] The rule applies to daily newspapers published in English four or more days per week and circulated in the community of publication.[30] The Commission calculates ownership interests according to its attribution rules which generally apply to general partnership interests or corporate ownership of more than five percent of voting stock.[31]

The cross-ownership rules were adopted in 1975 although the Commission first began considering such restrictions in the 1940s. After its initial inquiry, the Commission rejected a bright-line rule, preferring instead to examine cross-ownership issues case-by-case.[32] By the 1970s, the Commission revisited the issue and determined to impose a ban on newspaper-broadcast cross-ownership. In a 1970 investigation, the Commission had found that 94 television stations were owned in common with daily newspapers serving the same broadcast community.[33] It compared the situation to common ownership of the two or more broadcast stations in the same market which was then prohibited under the one-to-a-market rule.[34]

---

27. *Id.*

28. Telecommunications Act of 1996, Pub. L. 104–104, § 202(c), 110 Stat. 56 (1996). The revised audience reach cap retained the 50 percent "discount" for measuring the audience reach of UHF stations. 47 C.F.R. § 73.3555(e)(2)(i) (1997). Pursuant to the 1996 Act, the FCC initiated an inquiry into the methodology of measuring national audience reach. *See* In the Matter of Broadcast Television National Ownership Rules, Notice of Proposed Rule Making, 11 FCC Rcd. 19949 (1996).

29. 47 C.F.R. § 73.3555(e) (1997). The rule applies where: (1) the 2mV/m contour of an AM station encompasses the entire community in which the daily newspaper is published; (2) the 1 mV/m contour of the FM station encompass the entire communi-

ty in which the newspaper is published; or (3) the grade A contour of the television station encompasses the entire community in which the newspaper is published.

30. *Id.* § 73.3555, note 6. College newspapers are not considered newspapers for the purpose of this rule.

31. *Id.* § 73.3555, note 2(a)–(b).

32. Newspaper Ownership of Radio Stations, Notice of Dismissal of Proceeding, 9 Fed. Reg. 702 (1944).

33. Further Notice of Proposed Rulemaking, Docket No. 18110, 22 F.C.C.2d 339 (1970).

34. Multiple Ownership of Standard FM and Television Broadcast Stations, 45 F.C.C. 1476 (1964).

The newspaper-broadcast prohibition was for the most part prospective, but required divestitures in what the Commission called "egregious" cases.[35] The FCC required divestiture in situations where there was common ownership of the sole daily newspaper and either the sole television or radio station with a clear signal in a particular community.[36] Accordingly, it ordered divestiture for seven television-newspaper combinations and for nine radio-newspaper combinations.[37] Going forward, the owner of a broadcast station that acquires a newspaper in the same community generally must divest its broadcast station within one year of the acquisition, or by the date of its next license renewal, whichever was longer.[38]

The constitutionality of the cross-ownership rule was challenged in *FCC v. National Citizens Committee for Broadcasting*.[39] The United States Court of Appeals for the District of Columbia Circuit held that the rule lacked a rational basis and invalidated the divestiture order as arbitrary.[40] The Supreme Court reversed, holding that it was not arbitrary for the Commission to grandfather most of the existing combinations given the agency's concern over the disruption that would be caused by an inflexible divestiture rule.[41] The Court held that the Commission could draw certain lines in an effort to promote a diversity of voices, provided those lines were not drawn arbitrarily.[42]

One reason the Supreme Court upheld the cross-ownership rules was because they provided for a waiver when the public interest so requires.[43] Accordingly, the Commission has granted both temporary and permanent waivers of the rule. The FCC has identified various factors upon which a waiver could be justified, including a demonstration that the licensee would have to sell its station at a distressed price, a showing that separate ownership and operation of a newspaper and broadcast station could not be supported otherwise or that the purposes of the rule would not be served by divestiture.[44] Temporary waivers under this policy have been granted in various cases.[45]

35. Rules Relating to Multiple Ownership of Standard FM and Television Broadcasting Stations, Second Report and Order, 50 F.C.C.2d 1046 (1975).

36. 47 C.F.R. § 73.3555(e)(3)(i) (1970).

37. Second Report and Order, 50 F.C.C.2d at 1080–1081.

38. *Id.* at 1076 n. 25. This is an "automatic" temporary waiver of the cross-ownership rule.

39. 436 U.S. 775, 98 S.Ct. 2096, 56 L.Ed.2d 697 (1978).

40. National Citizens Committee for Broadcasting v. FCC, 555 F.2d 938, 181 U.S. App. D.C. 1 (D.C.Cir.1977), *aff'd in part, rev'd in part*, 436 U.S. 775, 98 S.Ct. 2096, 56 L.Ed.2d 697 (1978).

41. *Id.* at 804, 98 S.Ct. at 2117, 56 L.Ed.2d at 720.

42. *Id.* at 814, 98 S.Ct. at 2122, 56 L.Ed.2d at 726.

43. *Id.* at 802 n.20, 98 S.Ct. at 2116 n. 20, 56 L.Ed.2d at 719 n.20. However, the United States Court of Appeals for District of Columbia Circuit held that a licensee could not challenge the cross-ownership rule on its face in a waiver proceeding, but must first exhaust administrative remedies. Tribune Co. v. FCC, 133 F.3d 61, 328 U.S.App.D.C. 198 (D.C.Cir.1998).

44. Second Report and Order, 50 FCC 2d at 1085.

45. *See, e.g.,* Metromedia Radio & Television, Inc., 102 FCC 2d 1334 (1985), *aff'd,* Health & Medicine Policy Research v. FCC, 807 F.2d 1038, 257 U.S. App. D.C. 123 (D.C.Cir.1986); Crosby N. Boyd, 57 F.C.C. 2d 475 (1976).

Permanent waivers of the rule are available but the burden on an applicant for such a waiver is considerably heavier than for a temporary one.[46] In 1993, the FCC granted a permanent waiver of the rule to permit Fox Television Stations to reacquire the New York Post despite its ownership of a New York television station because of the newspaper's imminent demise.[47] The FCC granted the waiver over claims that it should, at a minimum, convene a hearing on the request. Chairman James H. Quello pointed out that the delay associated with such a hearing in a previous case had led to the closure of the *Washington Star* when a local broadcaster had requested a waiver in order to acquire it.[48]

Decisions to grant or deny a cross-ownership waiver cannot be based on the government's approval or disapproval of the licensee. In *News America Publishing, Inc. v. FCC*, the United States Court of Appeals for the District of Columbia Circuit invalidated a restriction in an appropriations bill that prevented the FCC from extending any then-outstanding temporary waivers of the cross-ownership rule. At that time, only one waiver existed, permitting Rupert Murdoch to own a television station and newspaper in Boston. The Court of Appeals found that the appropriations amendment "strikes at Murdoch with the precision of a laser beam," and invalidated the restriction on First Amendment grounds.[49]

The House report for the 1994 FCC appropriations bill encouraged the Commission to liberalize its restriction on the newspaper cross-ownership rule, suggesting a waiver policy that would allow combinations in the top twenty-five markets, where thirty independent stations would remain after the combination.[50] In addition, the House version of the Telecommunication Act of 1996 would have eliminated the rule, but the provision did not survive the conference committee.[51] In 1996 the FCC began an inquiry into its own waiver policies to consider whether to modify the cross-ownership rule, and in 1998 it initiated a proceeding to consider whether to eliminate the rule.[52]

b. Broadcast-Cable Cross Ownership Rules

In 1970 the FCC adopted rules prohibiting common ownership of a television station and a cable television system in the same community.[53]

---

46. News America Publishing, Inc. v. FCC, 844 F.2d 800, 803, 269 U.S. App. D.C. 182, 185 (D.C.Cir.1988).

47. Metropolitan Council of NAACP Branches v. FCC, 46 F.3d 1154, 310 U.S. App. D.C. 237 (D.C.Cir.1995). The FCC had previously granted a permanent waiver only in one other case. *See* Field Communications Corp., 65 F.C.C. 2d 959 (1977).

48. Fox Televisions Stations, Inc., 8 FCC Rcd. 5341 (1993) (separate statement of Chairman James H. Quello). *See* Washington Star Communications, Inc., 54 FCC 2d 669, 690–691 (1975) (Commissioner Robert E. Lee dissenting).

49. 844 F.2d 800, 814, 269 U.S. App. D.C. 182 196 (D.C.Cir.1988).

50. H.R. Rep. No. 103–293, 103rd Cong., 1st Sess. at 40.

51. See 141 Cong. Rec. E–1571 (Aug. 1, 1995)(statement of Rep. Markey).

52. In the Matter of Newspaper/Radio Cross Ownership Waiver Policy, 11 FCC Rcd. 13003 (1996); 1998 Biennial Review— Review of the Commission's Broadcast Ownership Rules and Other Rules adopted pursuant to Section 202 of the Telecommunications Act of 1996, FCC 98–37 (rel. Mar. 13, 1998).

53. CATV, Second Report and Order, 23 F.C.C.2d 816 (1970). The rules prohibited the ownership of a cable system and a television station where the television station's

Congress subsequently codified the rules as part of the Cable Communications Policy Act of 1984.[54] The United States Court of Appeals for the Fifth Circuit upheld the cross-ownership rule, finding that divestiture of a cable interest under the 1984 Act did not violate the First Amendment rights of a television broadcaster.[55]

The Telecommunications Act of 1996 eliminated the statutory broadcast-cable cross-ownership restriction.[56] However, the Act did not eliminate the FCC's cross-ownership rules, and the Conference Report made clear that Congress did not intend to "prejudge the outcome of any review by the Commission of its own rules."[57] Congress, however, was more definite with respect to network-cable cross-ownership rules. The 1996 Act eliminated cross-ownership restrictions that barred common ownership of cable systems and broadcast networks.[58]

c.   One-to-a-Market Rule

The FCC's one-to-a-market rule prohibited the ownership of more than one overlapping type of broadcast station (AM, FM or television) within a broadcast market.[59] The FCC adopted the rule in 1964 to promote the goal of ownership diversity.[60] The Telecommunications Act significantly relaxed the restrictions by increasing significantly the number of radio stations an entity can own within overlapping contours.[61]

Both before and after passage of the 1996 Act, the FCC moderated the effect of the one-to-a-market rule through exceptions for certain markets. For example, under the "top 25 markets–30 voices" exception, the Commission waived the rule in the top 25 markets in the United States if, after the combination, there continued to be at least 30 separately-owned television and radio broadcast stations.[62] The Telecom-

grade B contour overlaps the service area of a cable system.

54. 47 U.S.C.A. § 533(a) (West Supp. 1997).

55. Marsh Media, Ltd. v. FCC, 798 F.2d 772 (5th Cir.1986), cert. denied, 479 U.S. 1085, 107 S.Ct. 1287, 94 L.Ed.2d 145 (1987).

56. Telecommunications Act of 1996, Pub. L. No. 104–104 § 202(I), 110 Stat. 56 (1996).

57. Conf. Rep. No. 458, 104th Cong., 2d Sess. 164 (1996). The FCC has since initiated a proceeding to determine whether to retain the rule. 1998 Biennial Review—Review of the Commission's Broadcast Rules and Other Rules Adopted Pursuant to Section 202 of the Telecommunications Act of 1996, FCC 98–37 (Rel. Mar. 13, 1998).

58. *Id.* at 59. *See* Section 202(f). Such ownership restrictions had been previously relaxed somewhat by Commission rules. *See* Amendment of Section 73.555 of the Commission's Rules, the Broadcast Ownership

Rules Second Report and Order, 4 FCC Rcd. 1741 (1989).

59. 47 C.F.R. § 73.3555(c) (1996). However, the Commission permitted local AM–FM combinations and considered the ownership of UHF television-radio combinations case-by-case. Multiple Ownership of Standard, FM and TV Broadcast Stations, 28 F.C.C.2d 662 (1971).

60. Multiple Ownership of Standard, FM and Television Broadcast Stations, 45 F.C.C. 1467 (1964).

61. The Telecommunications Act of 1996, Pub.L. 104–104, § 202, 110 Stat. 56 (1996).

62. 47 C.F.R. § 73.3555, note 7(1) (1997). The "market" for purposes of the one-to-a-market rule is the Area of Dominant Influence ("ADI"), television market defined by the Arbitron Ratings Company, *Id.* § 73.3555, note 7(c)(1). Voices are calculated by counting all full power commercial television and AM and FM radio stations licensed in the ADI market. The overlap is

munications Act of 1996 further liberalized the waiver policy by extending it "to any of the top 50 markets, consistent with the public interest, convenience, and necessity."[63]

Even if the "top 50 markets–30 voices" test is not met, the Commission may consider waiver requests under the general public interest standard. In such a case, the Commission considers: (1) the potential public service benefits of joint operation of the facilities; (2) the types of facilities involved; (3) the number of media outlets owned by the applicant; (4) the financial difficulties of the station involved; and (5) the nature of the relevant market in light of the level of competition and diversity after the joint operation is implemented.[64] In addition, the Commission may grant a waiver of the one-to-a-market rule when a proposed combination includes a "failed" broadcast station.[65]

d. Duopoly Rule

(1) Radio

Beginning with individual licensing decisions and eventually applying the policy as a rule, the FCC historically prohibited licensees from owning more than one station of a particular service within the same market. In 1992, the Commission began to relax the rule in particular radio markets.[66] The FCC generally permitted local radio ownership to two AM and two FM stations in the largest markets as long as the combined radio audience share did not exceed 25 percent.

The Telecommunications Act of 1996 significantly changed the local radio ownership limits. It established four tiers of permissible ownership levels: In a market with fourteen or fewer radio stations, a single owner may acquire up to five stations, provided no more than three are of the same service, AM or FM. In addition, the permitted combinations cannot represent more than 50 percent of the radio stations in a given market. In a market with fifteen to twenty-nine stations, a single entity may acquire six stations, provided that no more than four stations are of the same service. In markets with between thirty and forty-three stations, a single entity may own seven stations, with no more than four in the

---

determined by the signal area if the 2mVm groundwave contour of an AM station, or the 1mVm contour of an FM station covers the entire community in which the television station is licensed, or in the case of television, if the grade A contour of the television station covers the entire community in which the radio station is licensed. *See* Amendment of Section 73.555 of the Commission's Rules, the Broadcast Ownership Rules Second Report and Order, 4 FCC Rcd. 1741 (1989). *See also* The Helen Broadcasting Co., L.P., 5 FCC Rcd. 2829, 2833 (1990); Group W Radio Acquisition Co., 4 FCC Rcd. 8343 (1989).

63. Telecommunications Act of 1996, Pub. L. 104–104, 110 Stat. 56, § 202(d).

64. *See* Revision of Radio Rules and Policies, 7 FCC Rcd. 6394 n. 40 (1992). *See also* Greater Los Angeles Radio, 12 FCC Rcd. 10501 (1997) (permitting waiver despite multiple ownership of television and two same service radio stations); Pennino Broadcasting Corp., 12 FCC Rcd. 10752 (1997) (permitting waiver in small market).

65. The failed station must be one which has not broadcast for a substantial amount of time or is involved in a bankruptcy proceeding. 47 C.F.R. § 73.3555, Note 7(c)(2) (1997).

66. Revision of Radio Rules and Policies, 7 FCC Rcd. 2755 (1992).

same service. Finally, in markets with over forty-four stations, an entity may own up to eight stations, with no more than five in the same service.[67]

The change in ownership restrictions opened questions of antitrust enforcement. Prior to the Act, the FCC's limits on local radio ownership were such that neither the Federal Trade Commission ("FTC") nor the Department of Justice ("DOJ") questioned individual radio mergers. Almost immediately following the passage of the Act, the DOJ, either through the Hart–Scott–Rodino ("HSR") reporting process, or by its independent review of trade press stories on proposed mergers, began investigating the competitive effects of proposed radio acquisitions. In late 1996, for example, the Justice Department ordered American Radio Systems Corp. to dissolve a joint sales agreement and divest three radio stations in Rochester, NY even though the statutory ownership limits would not have been breached.[68] In 1997, DOJ filed suit to block the acquisition of a Long Island radio station that would consolidate the ownership of three FM stations in Suffolk County, N.Y.[69]

(2) Television

The television duopoly rule generally prohibits the ownership of more than one television station in a market where either of the station's grade B contours overlap.[70] As with its other ownership rules, the Commission has the authority to waive the rule when appropriate.[71] For example, it has allowed television duopolies in situations in which the overlap is "minimal."[72] The Commission has also waived the duopoly rule in markets where there were a large number of independent voices, or where the public interests so required.[73] The Telecommunications Act directed the Commission to open an inquiry on the continuing status of the local television ownership restrictions.[74] In November 1996 the Commission initiated a proceeding to consider possible modifications of its television duopoly rules.[75] The FCC proposed revising the duopoly

---

67. Telecommunications Act of 1996, Pub.L. 104–104, § 202(b), 110 Stat. 56 (1996).

68. *See* Elizabeth A. Rathbun, *Justice Tells ARS to Sell Stations*, Broadcasting & Cable, Oct. 28, 1996 at 10.

69. *See* Chris McConnell, *Justice Puts Brakes on SFX, Chancellor*, Broadcasting & Cable, Nov. 10, 1997 at 16.

70. 47 C.F.R § 73.3555(b) (1997).

71. Multiple Ownership of Standard, FM and Television Stations, 45 F.C.C. 1476 (1964).

72. *See e.g.*, Taft Broadcasting Partners Ltd. Partnership, 7 FCC Rcd. 855 (1992); John Hay Wireless, 28 F.C.C. 736, 752 (1971).

73. *See e.g.*, Channel 33, Inc., 4 FCC Rcd. 855 (1992)(exception permitted in market with 22 stations available); Capital Cities Communications, Inc. 59 Rad. Reg.2d

451, 464–465 (P&F 1985)(exception permitted in light of programming and other public interest rationales).

74. Telecommunications Act of 1996, Pub.L. 104–104 § 202(c)(2)(1996). The Conference report made a number of recommendations to the Commission including suggesting that the FCC retain a prohibition on VHF–VHF combinations, except in "compelling" circumstances, Conf. Rpt. No. 458, 104th Cong., 2d Sess. 163 (1996). The House version of the Telecommunications Act would have permitted UHF–UHF and UHF–VHF combinations but this change was deleted in the Conference. In its place, the Committee suggested that the FCC study the local television ownership rules.

75. *See* Review of the Commission's Regulation's Governing Television Broadcasting; Television Satellite Stations Review of Policy and Rules, Second Further

rules to authorize common ownership of television stations that are in separate markets and whose Grade A contours do not overlap. It also proposed permitting common ownership within a market if there is not Grade B overlap.

e. Quasi-ownership: Local Marketing Agreements

Local Marketing Agreements ("LMAs"), or "time brokerage agreements" are arrangements by which a broadcaster sells time on its station to air programming produced by another. LMAs may take many forms, including arranging for the provision of original programming for the station, or the provision of programming which is aired on other stations within the community.[76] A station may enter an LMA with another licensee or some other party,[77] and the agreement may involve a small portion of the licensee's broadcast time or take up the entire broadcast day.[78] Time brokerage typically involves the broker buying the airtime, filling that time with programming and selling commercial time to advertisers. While distinct from LMA, some time brokerage agreements may be considered LMAs.

In 1992 the Commission recognized that LMAs could be critical for the survival of small stations.[79] At the same time, the Commission sought to ensure that brokered stations fulfilled their non-delegable responsibility to abide by the terms of their licenses and to comply with FCC rules and policies. The Commission required brokered stations to provide a certification verifying continued FCC compliance.[80] Brokerage agreements must be placed in the brokered station's public files, and a copy must be filed with the FCC thirty days after execution.[81]

The Commission was also concerned about the effect of LMAs on its ownership rules. Accordingly, it decided that where a radio station brokers over 15 percent of its airtime, the station that acquires the time should be counted as the station's owner for purposes of the Commission's ownership restrictions including both local limits and national numerical limits.[82] Additionally, the Commission's rules prohibit the simulcast of more than 25 percent of the broker's programming where both stations broadcast in the same community.[83]

Notice of Proposed Rule Making, 11 FCC Rcd. 21655 (1996). *See also* 1998 Biennial Review—Review of the Commission's Broadcast Ownership Rules and Other Rules Pursuant to Section 202 of the Telecommunications Act of 1996, FCC 98–37 (rel. Mar. 13, 1998).

76. Revision of Radio Rules and Policies, 7 FCC Rcd. at 2787. *See* LEGAL GUIDE TO BROADCAST LAW AND REGULATION 136 (National Association of Broadcasters, 4th ed. 1994).

77. *Id.*

78. *Id.*

79. Revision of Radio Rules and Policies, 7 FCC Rcd. at 2787.

80. *Id.* at 2728 n.124. While an LMA can provide a station with programming efficiencies, it could lead to a challenge at renewal time based on allegations of an unauthorized transfer of control. *See* LEGAL GUIDE TO BROADCAST LAW AND REGULATION, *supra* note 76 at 136.

81. Revision of Radio Rules and Policies, 7 FCC Rcd. at 2789.

82. *Id.* at 2788, 2789.

83. *Id.* at 2789; 47 C.F.R. § 73.3556 (1997).

The Conference Report to the 1996 Act acknowledged the "positive contribution" of television LMAs and encouraged the Commission to approve future LMAs, consistent with its rules.[84] The Commission began to address the ownership implications of television LMAs shortly after passage of the Telecommunications Act. In particular, the Commission proposed treating some LMAs as an attributable interest for purposes of its restrictions on broadcast-newspaper cross-ownership, radio-television cross-ownership and the one-to-a-market rule.[85] The FCC also conducted a separate inquiry on the treatment of LMAs in counting national audience reach for purposes of television station ownership limits.[86]

4. Foreign Ownership Restrictions

Section 310 of the Communications Act of 1934 prohibits foreign ownership or control of broadcast licensees.[87] The Act restricts alien ownership in various forms. First, no license may be granted to "any alien or the representative of any alien."[88] Similarly, no license may be granted to "any corporation organized under the laws of any foreign government." [89] Nor may a license be granted to any foreign government or the representative of such government.[90] Section 310 does permit foreign involvement in American corporations that hold broadcast licenses, but the extent of the involvement is limited by the statute. For example, a domestic corporation that holds a broadcast license cannot have one-fifth or more of the capital stock owned or voted by aliens, their representatives or by a corporation organized under the laws of a foreign country.[91] In addition, an American corporation is prohibited from holding a broadcast license if its corporate parent is directly or indirectly controlled by a corporation that has more than one-fourth of its capital stock owned or voted by aliens or their representatives.[92] Section 310 previously focused on board membership and corporate officers as well, but under the Telecommunications Act of 1996 the Commission no longer considers the citizenship of either directors or corporate officers in evaluating foreign control issues.[93] The Communications Act gives the FCC some discretion to determine whether such

---

84. Conf. Rep. No. 458, 104th Cong. 2d. Sess. at 59.

85. Review of the Commission's Regulations Governing Attribution of Broadcast and Cable/MDS Interests, 11 FCC Rcd. 19895 (1996).

86. Broadcast Television National Ownership Rules, 11 FCC Rcd. 19949 (1996).

87. 47 U.S.C.A. § 310 (West 1991). Congress considered eliminating the foreign ownership restrictions as part of the 1996 Telecommunications Act, but this provision was deleted from the final version of the Act. H.R. 1555, Title III, § 303(b), (1st Sess. 104th Cong. 1995).

88. 47 U.S.C.A. § 310(b)(1) (West 1991).

89. *Id*. § 310(b)(2).

90. *Id*. § 310(a).

91. *Id*. § 310(b)(3) (West 1991 and Supp. 1997). When applying for a license, a corporation must satisfy the Commission that its shares are not held by foreign persons or entities. The Commission requires an accounting of the citizenship of shareholders, either through a statistical sample, or by an inquiry of the shareholders. *See* TVEU Associates, Inc., 45 F.C.C. 1275 (1964) (accounting of 7,000 shareholder was determined to be "reasonable" by the Commission).

92. § 310(b)(4).

93. Telecommunications Act of 1996, Pub. L. 104–104, § 403(k)(1)(2), 110 Stat. 56 (1996).

ownership would be in the public interest.[94] It is empowered to waive the restrictions on foreign ownership in a vertical ownership chain case-by-case where the public interest so requires.[95]

The foreign ownership limits historically focused on corporate control rather than the level of foreign investment. The FCC modified this approach after investigating the level of investment by News Corporation, an Australian corporation, in the Fox Broadcasting Network. In that case, the foreign parent corporation owned twenty-four percent of the capital stock of the licensee corporation, giving it less than the twenty-five percent limit on voting control. However, the parent had contributed ninety-nine percent of the capital invested in the licensee. As a result, the Commission reevaluated its foreign ownership rules and decided it would begin to consider the amount of equity capital contributed by a corporate parent.[96] Based on its reappraisal of the way in which foreign control should be measured, the FCC found that the level of foreign ownership of Fox exceeded the limit established in Section 310(b)(4), even after corporate restructuring.[97] However, the Commission found that "under the unique facts before it," it would be "consistent with the public interest to allow [Fox] to retain its present level of alien equity."[98]

B. Network Rules

Almost from the beginning of commercial radio the broadcasting medium has been dominated by networks.[99] By 1938, more than half of the radio stations across the United States had entered into affiliation agreements with national networks which at the time included the National Broadcasting Company, ("NBC"), which operated two national networks ("Red" and "Blue"); the Columbia Broadcasting System ("CBS"); and the Mutual Broadcasting System.[100] In addition to their affiliates, the networks owned and operated 23 radio stations.[1] In the

---

94. *Id.*

95. 47 U.S.C.A. § 310(b)(4) (West 1991 and Supp. 1997) (by necessary implication). The Commission has declined to enforce the restrictions in certain instances, such as where an individual was in the process of becoming a United States citizen, Metromedia Radio and Television, Inc., 102 F.C.C.2d 1334 (1985), and where the foreign control of stock of a corporate parent was counterbalanced by the citizenship of the corporate board, or vice versa. GRC Cablevision, Inc., 47 F.C.C.2d 467 (1974); Request of Millicom, Inc. for Declaratory Ruling Concerning Section 310(4)(b) of the Communications Act of 1934, 4 FCC Rcd. 4846 (1988).

96. *See* Application of Fox Television Stations, Inc., 10 FCC Rcd. 8452 (1995).

97. Application of Fox Televisions Stations, Inc., 11 FCC Rcd 5714 (1995).

98. *Id.*

99. *See* 47 C.F.R. § 73.658(g)(1)(2) (1997). Networks are defined by the Commission as "any person, entity, or corporation which offers an interconnected program service on a regular basis for 15 or more hours per week to at least 25 affiliated television licensees in 10 or more states." *See also* 47 U.S.C.A. § 153(p) (West 1991) (defining "chain broadcasting;" chain broadcasting was the precursor to the networks of today).

100. Many of the network affiliates were AM clear channel stations, operating at the maximum permitted power of 50 kW. Of the 660 commercial radio stations within the United States, 341 were affiliated with national networks. *See* National Broadcasting Co. v. United States, 319 U.S. 190, 63 S.Ct. 997, 87 L.Ed. 1344 (1943).

1. *Id.*, 63 S. Ct. at 1001, 87 L. Ed. at 1352–1353.

years before Arbitron ratings, it was estimated that network affiliated stations utilized 97 percent of the total nighttime broadcasting power in the United States.[2]

Concern over network dominance led to the adoption by the FCC of the "chain broadcasting rules."[3] The Commission found that "chain broadcasting makes possible a wider reception for expensive entertainment and cultural programs of national and regional significance" and provides "a strong incentive for advertisers to finance the production of expensive programs."[4] But the FCC was also concerned about the exercise of network power over affiliates and therefore implemented regulations designed to limit the NBC, CBS and Mutual networks. The rules dealt with: (1) programming exclusivity, barring an affiliation agreement with a network which would preclude the broadcast of programming from any other network; (2) territorial exclusivity, prohibiting the exclusive sale of network programming to a single affiliate in a given area; (3) term restrictions, prohibiting an affiliate from being bound for a period of more than two years; (4) restrictions on the networks' authority to require "option time" from its affiliates, which allowed the networks to reserve broadcast time; (5) freedom of affiliates to reject network programming; (6) ownership limits, prohibiting network ownership of more than one station within a service area; and (7) prohibitions on agreements that would allow networks to control the price of advertising time charged by affiliates during non-network programming.[5]

The networks challenged the chain broadcasting rules, arguing that they exceeded the FCC's authority.[6] The networks maintained that the Commission's power was confined to the technical concerns of broadcasting. In *National Broadcasting Co. v. United States*, the Supreme Court rejected this contention and affirmed the regulations. In upholding the rules, the Court emphasized that "the Act does not restrict the Commission merely to the supervision of traffic. It puts upon the Commission the burden of determining the composition of that traffic."[7] The Court explained that this discretion was not unlimited and in regulating broadcasting, the Commission was bound by the public interest mandate.[8] The decision cited antitrust concerns as part of the Commission's public interest inquiry.[9]

---

2. *Id.*

3. Chain broadcasting, defined as the "simultaneous broadcasting of an identical program by two or more interconnected stations," 47 U.S.C.A. § 153(p) (West 1991), allowed potential nationwide broadcasts via radio. Originally *codified at* 47 C.F.R. § 3.101–108 (1941), the rules have been repealed with respect to radio and now apply to television. *See* 47 C.F.R. § 73.658 (1996).

4. National Broadcasting Co., 319 U.S. at 198, 63 S.Ct. at 1001, 87 L.Ed. at 1353.

5. *Id.* at 198–209, 63 S.Ct. at 1001–1007, 87 L.Ed at 1353–1359.

6. 47 U.S.C.A. § 303 (h), now *codified at* § 303(i) (West 1991) (granting FCC "authority to make special regulations applicable to radio stations involved in chain broadcasting").

7. National Broadcasting Co. v. United States, 319 U.S. 190, 215–216, 63 S.Ct. 997, 1009, 87 L.Ed. 1344, 1362–1363 (1943).

8. *Id.* at 219, 63 S.Ct. at 1010, 87 L.Ed. at 1364.

9. *Id.* at 222, 63 S.Ct. at 1012, 87 L.Ed at 1365–1366. The networks argued unsuccessfully that Section 311 of the Act, which prohibits the Commission from issuing a

The network rules now apply only to television, and the remaining rules are similar to the chain broadcasting limits upheld in *National Broadcasting Co.* Generally, the rules prohibit affiliated stations from broadcasting the programs of any other network.[10] Additionally, the rules prohibit network affiliation agreements from imposing territorial exclusivity, thus barring other stations from transmitting network programming rejected by the affiliate.[11] The rules prohibit "option time," defined as any contract, arrangement, or understanding between a station and the network which prevents the station from scheduling programs before the network agrees to utilize the time.[12] The rules also require that affiliates retain the ability to reject network programming and to substitute programs which "in the station's opinion, is of greater local or national importance."[13] Affiliation with more than one network generally is prohibited, at least with respect to established networks,[14] and networks cannot exert formal or informal control over advertising rates charged by their affiliates.[15] FCC rules also require that network affiliation agreements be filed with the Commission.[16]

In 1995, citing dramatic changes in the market since the network rules were adopted, the Commission initiated several proceedings to examine whether it should eliminate or modify its network rules. In one notice of proposed rulemaking, the FCC asked whether it should eliminate five principal network rules, including the rule granting affiliates the right to reject network programming, the rule regarding option time, the exclusive affiliation rule, the dual network rule and the rule governing network territorial exclusivity.[17] The Commission also opened a proceeding to consider elimination of rules governing network control of station advertising rates and network advertising representation of its affiliates.[18] It also considered deleting the rule that requires the filing of network affiliation agreements.[19] The Commission in 1995 eliminated two network rules, including the network station ownership rule[20] and

broadcast license to one convicted of violating the antitrust laws, was the extent of the Commission's authority in this area. *See also* United States v. Radio Corporation of America, 358 U.S. 334, 79 S.Ct. 457, 3 L.Ed.2d 354 (1959)(although FCC does not enforce antitrust laws, consideration of station acquisition may include antitrust inquiry).

10. 47 C.F.R. § 73.658(a) (1997).

11. *Id.* § 73.658(b). Non-network program suppliers are also covered by restrictions against territorial exclusivity. *Id.* § 73.658(m).

12. *Id.* § 73.658(d).

13. *Id.* § 73.658(e).

14. *Id.* § 73.658(g). The rules permit multiple network affiliations unless the entities in question were considered to be "networks" under the rules as of February 8, 1996.

15. *Id.* § 73.658(h). Broadcast networks also are prohibited from representing their affiliates in the sale of advertising time, except in the case of owned and operated stations.

16. 47 C.F.R. § 73.3613(a) (1997).

17. Review of the Commission's Regulation Governing Programming Practices of Broadcast Television Networks and Affiliates, 10 FCC Rcd. 11951 (1995).

18. Review of the Commission's Regulations Governing Broadcast Television Advertising, 10 FCC Rcd. 11853 (1995).

19. Amendment of Part 73 of the Commission's Rules Concerning the Filing of Network Affiliation Contracts, 10 FCC Rcd. 5677 (1995).

20. 47 C.F.R. § 73.658(f) (1997). The network station ownership rule prohibited network ownership of television broadcast stations in markets that had so few stations

the "secondary affiliation" rule.[21] The Commission concluded that these rules were obsolete.[22]

The elimination of network rules was part of a trend that began in the mid–1990s with the repeal of the Financial Interest and Syndication Rules ("Fin–Syn") and the Prime Time Access Rule ("PTAR"). These rules had regulated the networks' ability to enter the programming market, either by acquiring financial interests in network programming, or by owning and marketing syndicated programming.

The PTAR, adopted in 1970, prohibited network affiliates in the top fifty markets (with three or more operating television stations) from providing network programming for more than three hours per day during "prime time."[23] The rules were successively modified, first to limit the non-network programming requirement,[24] and then to create a number of content-based carve-outs for network programming.[25] The PTAR survived two judicial challenges, although at least one court was skeptical about whether the rule produced the beneficial results that prompted its creation.[26] Subsequently the FCC determined that the market for programming had sufficiently changed with respect to the market influence of the networks and the increased availability of non-network programming. The Commission eliminated PTAR in August, 1996.[27]

---

or stations of such unequal desirability that "competition would be substantially restrained" by permitting network ownership.

21. Id. § 73.658(l). The secondary affiliation rule limited secondary affiliations in markets where two stations were affiliated with two of the three established broadcast networks and there was at least one independent station with comparable facilities. The rule required a third network seeking an affiliate in the market to offer its programming first to the independent station.

22. Review of the Commission's Regulations Governing Television Broadcasting, 10 FCC Rcd. 4538 (1995).

23. Amendment of Part 73 of the Commissions Rules and Regulations with Respect to Competition and Responsibility in Network Television Broadcasting, 23 F.C.C.2d 382, 384 (1970). Exceptions were made for fast-breaking and on-the-spot coverage of news events and broadcasts by political candidates.

24. Consideration of Prime Time Access Rule, 44 F.C.C.2d 1081 (1974) ("PTAR II"). PTAR II was overruled in *National Association of Independent Television Producers & Distributors v. FCC*, 502 F.2d 249 (2d Cir. 1974) (effective date of PTAR II harmed independent producers relying to their detriment on PTAR I).

25. The Prime Time Access Rule, Section 73.658(k), Second Report and Order, 50 F.C.C.2d 829 (1975). Exceptions included children's programming, public affairs coverage, documentaries, news coverage, political broadcasts, network news connected to local news, sports runovers and simultaneous live broadcasts between differing time zones.

26. Mt. Mansfield Television, Inc. v. FCC, 442 F.2d 470, 477 (2d Cir.1971) ("far from violating the First Amendment, [the rule] appears to be a reasonable step towards its fundamental precepts, for it is the stated purpose of that rule to encourage the [d]iversity of programs and development of diverse and antagonistic sources of program service"). In a subsequent review of the rules as modified, the Second Circuit noted that the actual result of PTAR was not the "diverse and antagonistic" speech envisioned by the Commission. The court pointed to the fact that over 40 percent of access programming constituted game shows and another substantial portion of the time was devoted to animal shows. National Association of Independent Television Producers & Distributors v. FCC, 516 F.2d 526, 533–537 (2d Cir.1975).

27. Review of the Prime Time Access Rule, Section 73.658(k) of the Commission's Rules, Report and Order, 11 FCC Rcd. 546 (1995).

Elimination of PTAR coincided with the demise of the other network rules adopted in 1970, the Fin–Syn rules.[28] The Fin–Syn rules were intended to limit network power over the market for syndicated programming by prohibiting networks from either selling or licensing the broadcast rights of any non-network program to an independent station, whether foreign or domestic, or sharing in the syndication profits of non-network programming.[29] The rules also prohibited the acquisition of any other financial or proprietary right in the distribution or "other commercial uses" of non-network programming.[30]

Because of the significant financial stakes involved in the television programming market, the Fin–Syn rules became the focus of a pitched regulatory battle that lasted more than a decade. A Commission staff report in 1980 concluded that the rules were outdated, ineffective, and counterproductive, and the FCC opened a proceeding to consider their elimination.[31] This effort was cut short, however, by what was reported to be White House intervention in the Commission proceeding. The issue was reopened in 1990 because of pressure placed on the rules by the emergence of a new network, the Fox Broadcasting Network. Following a highly contentious proceeding the FCC, on a 3–2 vote, decided not to repeal the Fin–Syn rules, but instead to modify them.[32] The United States Court of Appeals for the Seventh Circuit remanded the decision to the Commission, finding no support in the record for the agency's conclusion that diversity and the public interest were advanced by the new rules.[33] On remand, the FCC adopted a timetable for phasing out the Fin–Syn rules,[34] and the Commission subsequently decided to eliminate rules earlier than scheduled.[35]

14.5 Regulation of Broadcast Content

A. *The Public Interest Standard and the First Amendment Tightrope*

Broadcasters are subject to various forms of content regulation under the public interest standard of the Communications Act. The Act imposes certain specific requirements—such as those for educational programming—as well as general public interest mandates that are

28. Review of the Syndication and Financial Interest Rules, Report and Order, 10 FCC Rcd. 12165 (1995).

29. 47 C.F.R. § 73.658(j)(1)(1990).

30. In 1981, the Commission modified its rules to allow network syndication of non-broadcasting sources, such as cable television, video cassettes, and video discs. Mem. Op. and Order, 87 F.C.C.2d 301 (1981), *aff'd,* Viacom International, Inc. v. FCC, 672 F.2d 1034 (2d. Cir.1982).

31. Tentative Decision and Request for Further Comments, 94 F.C.C.2d 1019 (1983).

32. Evaluation of Syndication and Financial Interest Rules, Report and Order, 6

FCC Rcd. 345 (1991). While similar in concept to the old rules, the new rules most notably prohibited networks from broadcasting more than forty hours per week of their own programming in prime-time.

33. Schurz Communications, Inc. v. FCC, 982 F.2d 1043, 1050 (7th Cir.1992).

34. Second Report and Order in MM Docket No. 90–162, 8 FCC Rcd. 3282 (1993), *aff'd,* Capital Cities v. FCC, 29 F.3d 309 (7th Cir.1994).

35. Review of the Syndication and Financial Interest Rules, Report and Order, 10 FCC Rcd. 12165 (1995).

unlike anything that may be applied to the print media. At the same time, Congress recognized that broadcasters "are engaged in a vital and independent form of communicative activity,"[1] and conferred upon licensees " 'the widest journalistic freedom consistent with their public [duties].' "[2] For example, Section 326 of the Communications Act prohibits censorship and expressly withholds from government the power to "interfere with the right of free speech by means of radio communication." This denies to the FCC "the power of censorship" as well as the ability to promulgate any "regulation or condition" that interferes with freedom of speech.[3] These policies "were drawn from the First Amendment itself [and] the 'public interest' standard necessarily invites reference to First Amendment principles."[4]

This obvious tension between public interest regulation and traditional First Amendment concepts has been blunted somewhat to the extent the FCC approached broadcast licensees with a certain degree of sensitivity to the competing values at stake. From the beginnings of broadcast regulation, Congress and the FCC (and its predecessor agency, the Federal Radio Commission), appeared to approach the business of regulation with the understanding that constitutional limitations might prevent too great a reliance on specific programming mandates. One of the bills submitted prior to passage of the Radio Act of 1927 included a provision that would have required stations to comply with programming priorities based on subject matter. However, the provision was eliminated because "it was considered to border on censorship."[5] Similarly, the Federal Radio Commission sought to "chart a course between the need of arriving at a workable concept of the public interest in station operation, on the one hand, and the prohibition laid on it by the First Amendment to the Constitution of the United States . . . on the other."[6]

In 1960 the FCC emphasized that "[i]n considering the extent of the Commission's authority in the area of programming it is essential [first] to examine the limitations imposed upon it by the First Amendment to the Constitution and Section 326 of the Communications Act."[7] After an extensive analysis of the meaning of the public interest, the FCC found that the required constitutional and statutory balance barred the government from implementing programming requirements that were too specific. It noted:

> [S]everal witnesses in this proceeding have advanced persuasive arguments urging us to require licensees to present specific types of

1. League of Women Voters v. FCC, 731 F.2d 995, 235 U.S.App.D.C. 293 (1984).

2. CBS, Inc. v. FCC, 453 U.S. 367, 395, 101 S.Ct. 2813, 2829, 69 L.Ed.2d 706, 728 (1981), (quoting CBS, Inc. v. Democratic National Committee, 412 U.S. 94, 110, 93 S.Ct. 2080, 2090, 36 L.Ed.2d 772 (1973)).

3. 47 U.S.C.A. § 326 (West 1991).

4. CBS, Inc., 412 U.S. at 121, 93 S. Ct. at 2095, 36 L.Ed.2d at 794.

5. *See* FCC v. WNCN Listeners Guild, 450 U.S. 582, 597, 101 S.Ct. 1266, 1276, 67 L.Ed.2d 521, 536 (1981).

6. Report and Statement of Policy re: Commission En Banc Programming Inquiry, 44 F.C.C. 2303, 2313 (1960).

7. *Id.* at 2306.

programs on the theory that such action would enhance freedom of expression rather than to abridge it. With respect to this proposition we are constrained to point out that the First Amendment forbids governmental interference asserted in aid of free speech, as well as governmental action repressive of it. The protection against abridgment of freedom of speech and press flatly forbids governmental interference, benign or otherwise. The First Amendment while regarding freedom in religion, in speech, in printing and in assembling and petitioning the government for redress of grievances as fundamental and precious to all, seeks only to forbid that Congress should meddle therein.[8]

Such considerations led the Commission to conclude that it could not "condition the grant, denial or revocation of a broadcast license upon its own subjective determination of what is or is not a good program."[9] To do so, the Commission concluded, would "lay a forbidden burden upon the exercise of liberty protected by the Constitution."[10] In order to maintain a balance between a free competitive broadcast system, on the one-hand, and the requirements of the public interest standard on the other, the Commission found that "as a practical matter, let alone a legal matter, [its role] cannot be one of program dictation or program supervision."[11]

The FCC has attempted to balance the constitutional imperative of the First Amendment with the public interest aspirations of the Communications Act. It has found that while it may "inquire of licensees what they have done to determine the needs of a community they propose to serve, the Commission may not impose upon them its private notions of what the public ought to hear."[12] In particular, public interest "standards or guidelines should in no sense constitute a rigid mold for station performance, nor should they be considered as a Commission formula for broadcasts in the public interest."[13] The Commission emphasized that it did "not intend to guide the licensee along the path of programming; on the contrary the licensee must find his own path with the guidance of those whom his signal is to serve."[14]

Recognizing this delicate balance, courts have noted that the Commission must "walk a 'tightrope'" to preserve the First Amendment values written into the Radio Act and its successor, the Communications Act.[15] The Supreme Court has described this balancing act as "a task of great delicacy and difficulty," and stressed that "we would [not] hesitate to invoke the Constitution should we determine that the [FCC] has not

8. *Id.* at 2308 (citation omitted).

9. *Id.*

10. *Id.* quoting Cantwell v. Connecticut, 310 U.S. 296, 307, 60 S.Ct. 900, 906 84 L.Ed. 1213 (1940).

11. *Id.* at 2309.

12. *Id.* at 2308.

13. *Id.* at 2313.

14. *Id.* at 2316.

15. CBS, Inc. v. DNC, 412 U.S. at 117, 93 S. Ct. at 2094, 36 L.Ed.2d at 792; Banzhaf v. FCC, 405 F.2d 1082, 1095, 132 U.S. App. D.C. 14, 27 (D.C.Cir.1968), cert. denied. *sub. nom.* Tobacco Institute, Inc. v. FCC, 396 U.S. 842, 90 S.Ct. 50, 24 L.Ed.2d 93 (1969).

fulfilled with appropriate sensitivity to the interest of free expression."[16] The Court found that the Communications Act was designed "to maintain—no matter how difficult the task—essentially private broadcast journalism."[17] For that reason, licensees are to be held "only broadly accountable to public interest standards."[18] In *Turner Broadcasting System, Inc. v. FCC*, the Supreme Court quoted the *1960 En Banc Policy Statement*, and reiterated that "although 'the Commission may inquire of licensees what they have done to determine the needs of the community they propose to serve, the Commission may not impose upon them its private notions of what the public ought to hear.' "[19]

Specific program requirements generally are considered the most constitutionally suspect among the requirements imposed by broadcasting regulations. The United States Court of Appeals for the District of Columbia Circuit has noted that the "power to specify material which the public interest requires or forbids to be broadcast ... carries the seeds of the general authority to censor denied by the Communications Act and the First Amendment alike."[20] Public interest requirements relating to specific program content create a "high-risk that such rulings will reflect the Commission's selection among tastes, opinions, and value judgments, rather than a recognizable public interest," and "must be closely scrutinized lest they carry the Commission too far in the direction of the forbidden censorship."[21]

In those instances in which Congress has adopted affirmative obligations—such as the requirement of Section 312(a)(7) of the Communications Act that broadcast licensees provide "reasonable" access to federal political candidates—it has stressed that the requirement must be implemented "on an individualized basis" and not on the basis of "across-the-board policies."[22] The Commission has never attempted to specify what amount of candidate access is "reasonable" and the Supreme Court's First Amendment analysis of the law assumed that the broadcaster's editorial discretion would be accorded appropriate deference.[23]

In *Turner Broadcasting System, Inc. v. FCC*, the Supreme Court emphasized "the minimal extent" that the government may influence the programming provided by broadcast stations. The Court noted that

16. CBS, Inc. v. DNC, 412 U.S. at 102, 93 S. Ct. at 2086, 36 L.Ed.2d at 783.

17. *Id*. at 120, 93 S. Ct. at 2095, 36 L. Ed.2d at 793–794.

18. *Id*.

19. 512 U.S. 622, 650, 114 S.Ct. 2445, 2463, 129 L.Ed.2d 497, 523 (1994) (citation omitted).

20. Banzhaf, 405 F.2d at 1095, 132 U.S. App. D.C. at 27.

21. *Id*. at 1096, 132 U.S. App. D.C. at 28. *See also* Public Interest Research Group v. FCC, 522 F.2d 1060, 1067 (1st Cir.1975), cert. denied, 424 U.S. 965, 96 S.Ct. 1458, 47

L.Ed.2d 731 (1976) ("[we] have doubts as to the wisdom of mandating ... government intervention in the programming and advertising decisions of private broadcasters"); Anti–Defamation League of B'Nai B'rith v. FCC, 403 F.2d 169, 172, 131 U.S. App. D.C. 146, 149 (D.C.Cir.1968) ("the First Amendment demands that [the FCC] proceed cautiously [in reviewing programming content] and Congress ... limited the Commission's powers in this area").

22. CBS, Inc. v. FCC, 453 U.S. at 387, 101 S. Ct. at 2825, 69 L.Ed.2d at 723.

23. *Id*. at 396–397, 101 S. Ct. at 2829–30, 69 L.Ed.2d at 728–729.

Sec. 14.5   **REGULATION OF BROADCAST CONTENT**   **1217**

"the FCC's oversight responsibilities do not grant it the power to ordain any particular type of programming that must be offered by broadcast stations."[24] Similarly, the United States Court of Appeals for the District of Columbia Circuit expressly avoided approving "a more active role by the FCC in oversight of programming" on educational stations because it would "threaten to upset the constitutional balance struck in *CBS v. DNC*."[25] The challenge facing broadcast content regulation is the need to reconcile public interest mandates with constitutional commands and statutory restrictions.

B. *Affirmative Programming Mandates*

1. *General Requirements*

As a general matter, broadcast licensees have a public interest obligation to provide programming that is responsive to the needs of the community of license.[26] To ensure compliance, the FCC requires radio and television broadcasters to file quarterly reports listing the programs that have provided the station's most significant treatment of community issues during the proceeding three month period. This list must include a brief narrative statement describing what issues were given significant treatment and which programs addressed the particular issues. The report must list the air date, day part, as well as program length and title of the programs.[27] The station's overall performance in serving the community is evaluated at license renewal time.

The FCC previously enforced such programming requirements in a far more detailed way. In its 1960 *En Banc Programming Inquiry*, for example, the Commission listed 14 categories of programs generally considered necessary to serve the public interest, including programs that provided an opportunity for local self-expression, programs that used local talent, children's programs, religious programs, educational programs, public affairs programs, editorials, political broadcasts, agricultural programs, news, weather and market reports, sports programs, service to minority groups and (finally) entertainment programming.[28] Although the Commission did not prescribe the transmission of particular programs, noting that the specified categories should not be considered "a rigid mold of fixed formula for station operation," it nevertheless concluded that the listed programming types, provided in some reasonable mix, provided evidence that a licensee was operating in the public interest.[29] This was enforced through the use of formal ascertainment procedures, which required applicants for broadcast licenses to interview

24. 512 U.S. 622, 650–652, 114 S.Ct. 2445, 2463–2464, 129 L.Ed.2d 497, 523–524 (1994).

25. Accuracy in Media v. FCC, 521 F.2d 288, 296–297, 172 U.S. App. D.C. 188, 195 (D.C.Cir.1975). *See also* Community–Service Broadcasting v. FCC, 593 F.2d 1102, 1115, 192 U.S.App.D.C. 448, 461 (D.C.Cir. 1978) (en banc) (FCC and courts have generally eschewed "program-by-program re-

view" schemes because of constitutional dangers).

26. 47 C.F.R. §§ 3526(a)(8)(i), 3527(a)(9) (1997).

27. *Id.*

28. En Banc Programming Inquiry, 44 F.C.C. at 2314.

29. *Id.*

community leaders in 19 specified categories ranging from agriculture to religion.[30]

The FCC eliminated these requirements during a deregulatory period in the 1980s. In 1981, it deleted rules and policies requiring radio stations to keep program logs and conduct ascertainment of community problems, imposing non-entertainment programming requirements and limiting the amount of commercial time.[31] The FCC similarly deregulated television, eliminating ascertainment and other requirements in 1984.[32] The Commission greatly simplified the renewal process, eliminating the detailed program-related questions that had accompanied the ascertainment process.[33] Generally, the FCC moved away from examining the programming formats chosen by broadcast stations, leaving such decisions to marketplace forces.[34]

2. Educational Programming

One exception to the general preference for private editorial choices involves educational programming for children. The Children's Television Act of 1990 ("CTA") requires the FCC, in its review of each television broadcast license renewal application, to "consider the extent to which the licensee ... has served the educational and informational needs of children through the licensee's overall programming, including programming specifically designed to serve such needs."[35] The CTA also imposes specific limits on the amount of the advertising that can be aired during children's programming.[36] Although the objective of the legislation was "to increase the amount of educational and informational broadcast television available to children,"[37] it is not clear that Congress intended the FCC to adopt specific programming requirements. Thus, in 1991, the FCC's implementing regulations contained "no requirement as to the number of hours of educational and informational programming that stations must broadcast or the time of day during which such programming may be aired."[38] The FCC's initial reading of the law

---

30. *See* Primer on Ascertainment of Community Problems by Broadcast Applicants, 27 F.C.C. 2d 650 (1971).

31. Deregulation of Radio, 84 F.C.C.2d 968 (1981), *aff'd. in part and remanded in part*, Office of Communication of the United Church of Christ v. FCC, 707 F.2d 1413, 228 U.S. App. D.C. 8 (D.C.Cir.1983).

32. Revision of Programming and Commercialization Policies, Ascertainment Requirements, and Program Requirements for Commercial Television Stations, 98 F.C.C.2d 1078 (1984); Revisions of Programming Policies and Reporting Requirements Related to Public Broadcasting Licensees, 96 F.C.C.2d 74 (1984). *See* Action for Children's Television v. FCC, 821 F.2d 741, 261 U.S. App. D.C. 253 (D.C.Cir.1987) (remanding FCC decision to eliminate commercial guidelines for children's programming).

33. *See* Black Citizens for a Fair Media v. FCC, 719 F.2d 407, 231 U.S. App. D.C. 163 (D.C.Cir.1983), cert. denied, 467 U.S. 1255, 104 S.Ct. 3545, 82 L.Ed.2d 848 (1984).

34. *See* FCC v. WNCN Listeners Guild, 450 U.S. at 604, 101 S. Ct. at 1279, 67 L.Ed.2d at 540.

35. Children's Television Act of 1990, Pub. L. 101–437, 104 Stat. 996–1000, *codified at* 47 U.S.C.A. §§ 303a, 303b, 394 (West 1991).

36. *Id.* § 303b.

37. S. Rep. No. 227, 101st Cong., 1st Sess. 1 (1989).

38. *See* Policy and Rules Concerning Children's Television Programming and Revision of Programming Policies for Television Broadcast Stations, Notice of Proposed

appeared to be consistent with legislative intent. Committee reports as well as statements of key legislators emphasized that Congress did not intend to impose—or have the FCC adopt—a specified number of hours of mandatory educational programming. Both the Senate and House Reports on the CTA stated that:

> The Committee does not intend that the FCC interpret this section as requiring a quantification standard governing the amount of children's educational and informational programming that a broadcast licensee must broadcast to [obtain license renewal] pursuant to this section or any section of this legislation.[39]

Similarly, Congressman Edward Markey, who sponsored the law, explained that "[t]he legislation does not require the FCC to set quantitative guidelines for educational programming, but instead requires the Commission to base its decision upon an evaluation of a station's overall service to children."[40] Senator Daniel Inouye stated that each broadcast licensee should be afforded the "greatest possible flexibility in how it discharges its public service obligation to children" and that the "Committee expects that the Commission will continue to defer to the reasonable programming judgments of licensees."[41]

Despite this legislative history, the FCC revised its children's television rules in 1996 to adopt a quantitative approach to compliance. The rules emerged from a spirited debate within the agency about how to implement the CTA. On one side of the debate, then-Chairman Reed Hundt strongly advocated quantitative programming requirements.[42] On the other side, senior Commissioner James H. Quello sought to avoid imposing what he saw as intrusive regulations that would violate the First Amendment.[43] When the quantitative guidelines for compliance eventually were adopted, the Commission acknowledged the contrary legislative history, but reconciled its approach by explaining that Congress did not "prohibit us from seeking to provide greater clarity and guidance through a processing guideline."[44]

Under the revised rules, television stations are required to transmit a certain amount of programming "specifically designed to serve the educational and informational needs of children" although the precise method of meeting that requirement may vary.[45] Stations that transmit

---

Rulemaking, 10 FCC Rcd. 6308, 6315 (1995).

39. S. Rep. No. 227, 101st Cong., 1st Sess. 23 (1989); H.R. Rep. No. 385, 101st Cong. 1st Sess. 17 (1989).

40. 136 Cong. Record H8537 (Oct. 1990).

41. 136 Cong. Record S10121–10122 (July 19, 1990).

42. *See, e.g.*, Speech of FCC Chairman Reed E. Hundt at the National Press Club, July 27, 1995.

43. *See, e.g.*, James H. Quello, *The FCC's Regulatory Overkill*, Wall Street Journ. July 24, 1996, p.A20.

44. Policy and Rules Concerning Children's Television Programming, 11 FCC Rcd. 10660, 10722 (1996) ("Children's Television Order"). *But see* Robert Corn–Revere, *"Voluntary" Self-Regulation and the Triumph of Euphemism*, in Rationales & Rationalizations 183, 198–201 (Robert Corn–Revere, ed. Media Institute, 1997).

45. Children's Television Programming Order, 11 FCC Rcd. 10,660 (1996). *See* 47 C.F.R. §§ 73.671–73.673 (1997).

three hours per week of "core programming" may have their licenses renewed by the FCC staff without the need for review by the full Commission. Core programming is defined as that which serves the educational and informational needs of children as a significant purpose, is aired between the hours of 7:00 a.m. and 10:00 p.m., is regularly scheduled at least weekly, is at least 30 minutes in length, and for which the educational or informational objective and the target child audience has been specified in writing by the broadcaster in advance.[46]

The rules define "educational and informational television programming" as any programming "which furthers the positive development of children 16 years of age and under in any respect, including the child's intellectual/cognitive or social/emotional needs."[47] The guidelines call for the Commission to "ordinarily rely on the good faith judgments of the licensee" in determining whether programming has a significant educational and informational purpose. However, the FCC will review programming content to ensure compliance "as a last resort."[48]

Noncommercial television stations are not required to meet a quantitative programming guideline. The rules state simply that "[e]ach noncommercial television broadcast station licensee has an obligation to serve, over the term of its license, the educational and informational needs of children through the licensee's overall programming, including programming specifically designed to serve such needs."[49]

A commercial licensee who fails to satisfy the quantitative "guideline" for core programming may still have its license renewed at the staff level if it airs "slightly less than" three hours of per week of core programming, but demonstrates a commitment "that is at least equivalent to airing three hours per week," making up the slight deficit with public service announcements, short-form programs and regularly scheduled non-weekly programs.[50] Licensees that fail to meet the FCC's "processing guidelines" will be referred to the Commission, "where they will have a full opportunity to demonstrate compliance with the CTA."[51] Such stations may point to their sponsorship of core educational programs on other stations in the market and/or special non-broadcast efforts that "enhance the value of children's educational and informational television programming."[52]

In addition to the programming and scheduling requirements, television licensees are required to maintain quarterly reports in their public files that describe programming efforts during the preceding quarter and outline planned efforts for the next quarter. The rules require stations to list the name of the individual at the station responsible for collecting

46. *Id.* § 73.671(b).

47. *Id.* § 73.671(b), Note.

48. *Id.* § 73.671, Note 1.

49. *Id.* § 73.672(a).

50. *Id.* § 73.671, Note 2.

51. Children's Television Order, 11 FCC Rcd. at 10,719.

52. *Id.*

comments on the station's compliance with the CTA and require licensees to file the quarterly reports with the FCC on an annual basis.[53]

Commercial television stations are also required to provide advance notice to the public of the educational programs they air. At the beginning of each educational show, the licensee must provide an on-screen identifier. The rules do not prescribe the form of the notice, but leave it to the licensee's discretion.[54] Broadcasters also are required to provide information on educational programming to publishers of television program guides. The published information must identify the age group for which the program is intended.[55]

3. Political Broadcasting

From the beginning of federal regulation, special rules have applied to the broadcasts of political candidates. The law has required broadcasters to provide "equal opportunities" for the use of their stations by candidates and has prohibited censorship of candidates' messages.[56] The Communications Act also creates special access rights for federal candidates.[57] These political broadcasting requirements have resulted in a detailed body of FCC rules and judicial decisions interpreting their scope.[58]

a. Equal Opportunities

Section 315(a) of the Communications Act obliges broadcasters to make their facilities available to all legally qualified candidates for a given office if they have allowed one candidate for that office to "use" the facilities. While reasonable access to airtime by federal candidates is required by Section 312(a)(7), no station is required to permit the "use" of its facilities by a qualified candidate under Section 315.[59] The equal opportunities obligation is triggered only after a station has permitted a political candidate, for federal, state or local office, to use its facilities for either a free or paid appearance.[60]

Equal opportunities are provided only to "legally qualified candidates" for public office. In general, a person is legally qualified if he has publicly announced his intention to run for nomination or office, is qualified under the applicable, local, state or federal law to hold the

53. 47 C.F.R. § 73.3526(a)(8)(iii)(1997). The annual filings are required as part of a three-year "experiment" regarding enforcement of the children's television rules.

54. *Id.* § 73.673(a).

55. *Id.* § 73.673(b).

56. 47 U.S.C.A. § 315(a)(re-enacting § 18 of the 1927 Radio Act, Pub. L. 632 69th Cong. (1927)). This is often referred to as the "equal time" rule.

57. 47 U.S.C.A. § 312(a)(7) (West 1991).

58. *See, e.g.,* The Law of Political Broadcasting and Cablecasting: A Political Primer, 100 F.C.C.2d 1476 (1984); Codification of the Commission's Political Pro-

gramming Rules, 6 FCC Rcd. 5707 (1991); Codification of the Commission's Political Programming Rules, Report and Order, 7 FCC Rcd. 678 (1991).

59. 47 C.F.R. § 73.1941(a) (1997). However, at license renewal time the Commission may take in to account a stations' refusal to transmit political broadcasts.

60. *See* Codification of the Commission's Political Programming Rules, 6 FCC Rcd. 5707, 5713 n.22 (1991); Interpretation of Second Sentence in Section 315(a), 40 F.C.C. 1088 (1963).

office in question and can make a substantial showing that he is a bona fide candidate.[61] A "substantial showing" of bona fide candidacy means evidence that the person seeking equal opportunities has engaged to a substantial degree in activities commonly associated with political campaigning. These activities normally include making campaign speeches, distributing campaign literature, issuing press releases, maintaining a campaign committee and establishing campaign headquarters (which may be located in some cases at the candidate's residence or at the home of his campaign manager). The list of campaign activities is non-exclusive and the bona fides of a particular candidacy is considered by the FCC case-by-case.[62] Ballot status alone does not determine whether a person is a bona fide candidate.[63] At the same time, a licensee cannot deny equal opportunities because of its subjective judgment that a candidate has no chance of winning a party nomination or an election.[64] Nevertheless, the candidate requesting equal opportunities pursuant to Section 315 has the burden of proving that he is a legally qualified candidate.[65]

The FCC has special rules regarding presidential and vice presidential candidates. To be considered a bona fide candidate for the presidential election in all states, a candidate must be considered "ballot qualified" in at least ten states.[66] If a presidential or vice presidential candidate does not meet the ten-state test he is considered a legally qualified candidate only in those states in which he has qualified for the ballot or made a substantial showing of being a bona fide candidate.[67] In addition, the 90-day limit on being considered a bona fide candidate before a primary does not apply to presidential and vice presidential candidates.

The next question raised by Section 315(a) is whether the first candidate's appearance was a "use" of broadcast facilities. "Use" is a term of art in the Communication Act, and is subject to a number of significant qualifications. To be considered a "use" under Section 315, a candidate's voice or image must be readily identifiable to the audience. The FCC considers all such appearances (except for fleeting appearances) to be "uses" regardless of the political or non-political nature of the program. Under that interpretation, the FCC has held that the appearance of a movie actor in a televised film constituted a "use" if broadcast when the actor later became a candidate.[68] Even the appearance of a

61. 47 C.F.R. § 73.1940(a), (e) (1997). This rule provides that no person (except presidential and vice presidential candidates) shall be considered a legally qualified candidate for nomination prior to 90 days before the beginning of the party convention, caucus or similar procedure by which the candidate seeks nomination.

62. *Id.* § 73.1940(f). *See* Legally Qualified Candidates for Public Office, 43 Rad. Reg.2d 905 (P&F 1978).

63. Anthony R. Martin–Trigona, 2 FCC Rcd. 109 (1987); Flory v. FCC, 528 F.2d 124 (7th Cir.1975).

64. Letter to CBS, Inc., 40 F.C.C. 244 (1952).

65. 47 C.F.R. § 73.1941(e) (1997).

66. *Id.* § 73.1940(c). The District of Columbia is counted as a state for purposes of this rule.

67. *Id.* § 73.1940(c), (e).

68. Adrian Weiss, 58 F.C.C.2d 342 (1976) (broadcast of Ronald Reagan movies

comedian who waged a "joke" presidential campaign was found to have "used" a broadcast facility during a subsequent appearance in a children's program.[69] The Commission also held that news reporters or other station employees who appeared on the air as part of their regular duties, but in a non-political capacity, had engaged in a "use" when those employees become candidates.[70] On the other hand, an employee-candidate whose voice is not well known to the public would not trigger a "use" by performing voice-overs for commercials, public service and station identification announcements.[71]

The FCC in the early 1990s narrowed its interpretation of the types of appearances that constitute a "use," excluding certain appearances where a candidate does not voluntarily appear as a performer, celebrity or station employee in a non-exempt program. Thus, for example, the transmission of movies featuring an actor-turned-candidate or a candidate appearance in unauthorized, independently sponsored advertisements were not considered to be "uses." [72] Subsequently, however, the Commission decided to return to its broader definition of "use" of a broadcast facility. Although it continued to believe that the reasons for adopting the narrower interpretation were valid, the FCC concluded that the issue warranted "more comprehensive examination." [73]

The Section 315(a) requirement is often inaccurately referred to as the "equal time" rule. In actuality, the time that a broadcaster makes available to a candidate need not be identical to that of the first "use" in order to be considered an "equal opportunity." However, it must be comparable in terms of exposure to the listening or viewing audience.[74] A station cannot satisfy the equal opportunity requirement by making a single "take-it-or-leave-it" offer of time to a candidate and must provide a candidate who declines such an ultimatum a comparable opportunity to appear.[75] However, once a candidate accepts a given format, he cannot reject it during the broadcast and subsequently demand equal access.[76] The time offered to a candidate under the equal opportunity requirement must be on the same basis as the time provided to the first candidate. Thus, if a station sold time to one candidate it must offer to

during the campaign periods constitutes a "use" for purposes of Section 315).

69. Paulsen v. FCC, 491 F.2d 887 (9th Cir.1974).

70. Branch v. FCC, 824 F.2d 37, 262 U.S. App. D.C. 310 (D.C.Cir.1987), cert. denied, 485 U.S. 959, 108 S.Ct. 1220, 99 L.Ed.2d 421 (1988); Letter to KUGN, 40 F.C.C. 293 (1958); Letter to KTTV, 40 F.C.C. 279 (1956).

71. Letter to WNEP, 40 F.C.C. 431 (1965). Whether the announcer's voice is well-known or identifiable to the public is a matter left to the broadcaster's good faith judgment. Letter to A. W. Davis, 17 F.C.C.2d 613 (1969).

72. One reason for the change was to prevent "double dipping" by a candidate

who broadcast a negative campaign ad that pictured an opponent, which led to a demand for response time to the candidate's own advertisement. *See* Codification of the Commission's Political Programming Policies, 7 FCC Rcd. at 685.

73. Codification of the Commission's Political Programming Policies, 9 FCC Rcd. 651 (1984).

74. Use of Broadcast and Cable Facilities by Candidates for Public Office, 34 F.C.C.2d 510 (1972).

75. Senate Committee on Commerce, 40 F.C.C. 357 (1962).

76. Complaint by Ishmail Flory, 49 F.C.C.2d 521 (1974).

sell time to the second. The station must offer free broadcast time if the first candidate appeared without charge.[77] The equal opportunities requirement is not breached simply because one candidate may be able to afford to purchase more advertising time than his opponent.[78]

Equal opportunities requirements do not apply to all candidate appearances on a broadcast facility. In 1959 Congress amended Section 315 to exempt certain appearances by candidates on news programs, thus reversing an FCC ruling that had applied the rule to a local newscast on which the incumbent mayor of Chicago had appeared.[79] Congressional alarm over the Commission's ruling was heightened by the fact that the FCC's decision gave a statutory right of access to a perennial fringe candidate—Lar Daly. "Campaigning in an Uncle Sam costume and using the nickname 'America First' in many of the ballots on which he appeared, Daly ran unsuccessfully for more than 40 elections until his death in 1978."[80] Concerned that the ruling would deter broadcasters from presenting political news coverage, Congress responded by amending the statute within three months of the FCC decision.[81]

The 1959 amendments to Section 315 created an exemption for four categories of news coverage from the equal opportunities requirement:

(1) bona fide newscasts;

(2) regularly scheduled news interviews;

(3) bona fide news documentaries; and

(4) on-the-spot-coverage of bona fide news events.[82]

One significant issue that was not directly addressed by the 1959 amendments was the extent to which the exemptions applied to candidate debates. An immediate confrontation over the issue of debate coverage was avoided because Congress suspended equal opportunities requirements for the 1960 presidential debates.[83] After that, the FCC interpreted the exemptions narrowly and excluded political debates from their reach. Beginning in 1975, however, the Commission changed its interpretation and ruled that broadcast coverage of candidate debates qualifies as "on-the-spot coverage of bona fide news events."[84] Initially, the exemption was extended to broadcast debates only to the extent a

---

77. William H. Branch, 101 F.C.C.2d 901 (1985); Letter to RKO General, Inc., 25 F.C.C.2d 117 (1970); Alan Y. Naftalin (WNEP–TV), 40 F.C.C. 431 (1965).

78. Letter to Mrs. M. R. Oliver, 40 F.C.C. 253 (1952).

79. Telegram to CBS, Inc. (Lar Daly), 18 Rad. Reg. 238 (P & F 1959).

80. Fulani v. FCC, 49 F.3d 904, 908 n. 5 (2d Cir.1995).

81. *See* Thomas G. Krattenmaker and Lucas A. Powe, Jr., Regulating Broadcast Programming 67 (MIT Press 1994).

82. 47 U.S.C.A. § 315(a)(1)-(4)(West 1991). *See* Fox Broadcasting Co., 11 FCC Rcd. 11101, 11107–11 (1996) (discussing history of exemptions).

83. Pub. L. 86–677, 74 Stat. 554 (1960).

84. *See* Aspen Inst. Program on Communications & Society, 55 F.C.C.2d 697 (1975), *aff'd sub nom.* Chisholm v. FCC, 538 F.2d 349, 176 U.S. App. D.C. 1 (D.C.Cir.), cert. denied, 429 U.S. 890, 97 S.Ct. 247, 50 L.Ed.2d 173 (1976). *Accord* Ross Perot, 11 FCC Rcd. 13109, 13116 (1996).

third party—such as the League of Women Voters—sponsored the debate and acted as moderator.

In 1983, the Commission extended the Section 315 exemption to include broadcaster-sponsored debates.[85] It reasoned that the identity of a debate's sponsor does not affect the program's news value. The FCC also found that exempting broadcaster-sponsored debates "should serve to increase the number of such events" because "a broadcaster may be the ideal, and perhaps the only, entity interested in promoting a debate between candidates for a particular office, especially at the state or local level."[86] The Commission has since further broadened its view of what constitutes an exempt news program, thus allowing candidate appearances on a wide variety of programs without triggering the equal opportunities rule.[87]

The Commission's decision to exempt broadcaster-sponsored debates was based on the conclusion that sponsoring a debate is an exercise of news judgment. Thus, the "common denominator" of a broadcaster's decision to sponsor a debate, to determine its format and to limit participation to selected candidates is "bona fide news value."[88] The Commission may consider the format, content and level of participation by qualified candidates,[89] but the FCC generally will not interfere with the broadcaster's " 'good-faith news judgment.' "[90] " '[A]bsent evidence of broadcaster intent to advance a particular candidacy, the judgment of the newsworthiness of an event is left to the reasonable news judgment of professionals.' "[91] Applying these principles, the Commission has sustained broadcasters' decisions to limit debate participation to the major candidates in a campaign and to exclude minor party candidates.[92]

85. Henry Geller, 95 F.C.C.2d 1236 (1983), *aff'd. sub. nom.* League of Women Voters Educ. Fund v. FCC, 731 F.2d 995, 235 U.S. App. D.C. 293 (D.C.Cir.1984).

86. Henry Geller, 95 F.C.C.2d at 1244–45.

87. Exempt programs have included such interview-type shows as the Donahue Show, which initially was denied a news exemption. Multimedia Entertainment, Inc., 56 Rad.Reg.2d 143 (P & F 1984). The Commission has determined that an exemption can be invoked for a show if it reports "some area of current events." Paramount Pictures Corp. 3 FCC Rcd. 245, 246 (1988). *See also* Multimedia Entertainment, Inc., 6 FCC Rcd. 1798 (1991) (exemption for "Sally Jessy Rafael"); CBS, Inc., 2 FCC Rcd. 4377 (1987) (exemption for "The Morning Show").

88. Henry Geller, 95 F.C.C.2d at 1244.

89. Request of KFI, Inc. for Declaratory Ruling, 8 FCC Rcd. 8561 (1993). *See also* Declaratory Ruling—Bona Fide News Interview Programs, 7 FCC Rcd. 4681 (1992).

90. King Broadcasting Co., 6 FCC Rcd. 4998, 4999 (1991) (quoting Kennedy for President Comm., 77 F.C.C.2d 964, 969, *aff'd*, Kennedy for President Comm. v. FCC, 636 F.2d 417, 204 U.S. App. D.C. 145 (D.C.Cir.1980)). The Commission, "places considerable reliance on the exercise of a broadcaster's journalistic discretion to determine [a program's] 'newsworthiness.' " *Id.*

91. Kennedy for President Comm., 636 F.2d at 427, 204 U.S. App. D.C. at 155 (quoting Chisholm, 538 F.2d at 359, 176 U.S. App. D.C. at 10).

92. *See also* Ross Perot, 11 FCC Rcd. at 13116 (Reform Party candidate's exclusion from debate sponsored by Commission on Presidential Debates to be broadcast by commercial television networks did not trigger equal opportunity requirement); Arthur R. Block, Esq., 7 FCC Rcd. 1784, 1785 (1992) (equal opportunity requirement not triggered by exclusion of legally qualified presidential candidate from debate produced by McNeil/Lehrer Productions to be aired on PBS stations because candidate failed to present "objective evidence," such as polling data, "sufficient to demonstrate that she [wa]s a major presidential candi-

However, if a broadcaster exhibits favoritism in the presentation of a debate, the FCC may require the station to provide an equal opportunity for the disfavored candidate to present his or her views.[93]

In one case involving a state-owned noncommercial network, the United States Court of Appeals for the Eighth Circuit held that a public broadcasting station created a limited public forum when it sponsored a candidate debate.[94] This ruling suggested that all legally qualified candidates have a First Amendment right to participate in a debate sponsored by a public station. Although the court agreed that the licensee's decision to invite only the major party candidates "was made in good faith" and involved "exactly the kind of journalistic judgment routinely made by newspeople," it pointed out that, unlike commercial broadcast stations, public stations are run by state employees. It characterized the exclusion of any candidate who attains ballot status as a bureaucratic "ipse dixit" and held that all legally qualified candidates have a First Amendment right to appear in the debate.[95]

date"); Mitchell Rogovin, Esq., 7 FCC Rcd. 1780, 1781 (1992) (presidential debate sponsored by Democratic National Committee and aired on commercial television station did not trigger equal opportunities for candidate who did "not present[] objective criteria sufficient to demonstrate that he [wa]s a major presidential candidate"); Carl E. Person, Esq., 6 FCC Rcd. 7477 (1991) (upholding exclusion of legally qualified presidential candidate from debates to be aired on commercial stations and PBS); Jim Trinity, 7 FCC Rcd. 3199 (1992) (upholding public television station decision to exclude candidate from Republican senatorial debate where candidate was behind in polls and failed to "demonstrate that the participating candidates were not chosen on the basis of their newsworthiness"). Lenora B. Fulani, 3 FCC Rcd. 6245, 6246 (1988) (commercial networks' coverage of presidential debate between major party presidential candidates did not trigger equal opportunities provision where excluded candidate failed to show that broadcasters' decision "was motivated by bad faith rather than the requisite good faith intent to air what was perceived as a bona fide news event"); John W. Spring, 1 FCC Rcd. 589, 590 (1986) (upholding commercial radio station decision to air debate on talk radio show among Republican senatorial candidates although six qualified candidates were excluded); Cyril E. Sagan, 1 FCC Rcd. 10 (1986) (upholding noncommercial television station decision to exclude candidate from Democratic senatorial debate based on candidate's low standing in public opinion poll).

93. *See* WPRY Radio Broadcasters, Inc., 40 F.C.C.2d 1183, 1193–1200 (1973) (license renewal denied and fine imposed where part owner of station who was also a candi-

date used station to advance his own candidacy and to discriminate against others in the race); WANV, Inc., 54 F.C.C.2d 432 (1975) (station fined for discriminating between candidates); Western Connecticut Broadcasting Co., 43 F.C.C.2d 730 (1973) (station fined for requiring all candidates in a race—except the Republican—to submit in advance scripts for political announcements); Linda Jenness, 26 F.C.C.2d 485 (1970) (equal opportunities ordered where news staff which disproportionately focused on the Republican and Democratic candidates to the exclusion of a third party candidate during a debate).

94. Forbes v. Arkansas Educational Television Comm'n, 93 F.3d 497 (8th Cir. 1996) (en banc), *rev'd*, 523 U.S. 666, 118 S.Ct. 1633, 140 L.Ed.2d 875 (1998). After *Forbes*, another panel of the Eighth Circuit found that a news interview program was a limited public forum, but that the licensee was justified in restricting the forum to "newsworthy" candidates. Marcus v. Iowa Public Television, 150 F.3d 924 (8th Cir. 1998). The *Forbes* decision created a split in the circuit courts of appeal. *See* Chandler v. Georgia Pub. Telecomm. Comm'n, 917 F.2d 486 (11th Cir.1990), cert. denied, 502 U.S. 816, 112 S.Ct. 71, 116 L.Ed.2d 45 (1991); Muir v. Alabama Educ. Television Comm'n, 688 F.2d 1033, 1042 (5th Cir.1982) (en banc), cert. denied, 460 U.S. 1023, 103 S. Ct. 1274, 75 L.Ed.2d 495 (1983).

95. The *Forbes* court initially defined the class of speakers qualifying for a right of access as including all "legally qualified candidates." It subsequently modified its holding to exclude certain debates and candidates. *See* Forbes v. Arkansas Educational

The Supreme Court reversed the Eight Circuit decision, holding that the debates in question were a non-public forum, not a designated public forum. The Court found that most public television programming could not be considered a public forum, but that candidate debates were "a forum of some type" because they focused on the unedited messages of the invited candidates. However, it determined that the debates at issue were non-public forums since they were designed to be news programs and were not intended to be an "open microphone" available to all candidates. Importantly, participation in the debates was not based on the candidates' viewpoints.[96]

During the 1996 election cycle the FCC permitted broadcasters to experiment with various formats for providing free time to political candidates. The appearances were treated as exempt under the news programming exceptions. Some of the major commercial networks made time available to presidential and vice presidential candidates in prime time or on regularly scheduled newscasts. The Commission also approved a PBS proposal to telecast unmoderated statements by certain presidential candidates selected by such criteria as national polling data. The Commission concluded that the presentations would not trigger the equal opportunities requirement because there was no "basis to question the good faith news judgment of PBS with respect to its decision to broadcast the event."[97] The Commission has also approved programming produced in cooperation with local broadcast stations that made free air time available to major candidates in senatorial, congressional, and gubernatorial races.[98]

When none of the exemptions apply to a candidate's "use" of broadcast facilities, his opponents must follow FCC rules in order to obtain access to air time. To take advantage of the requirements, a candidate must notify the licensee that he is seeking time within one week of the first candidate's use.[99] If a candidate is aware of a specific future use by his opponent of a broadcast station, the request may be made before the actual air date.[100] Multiple uses by an opponent within the week will afford an opponent an equal access opportunity for each initial use and subsequent uses as well.[1] While the licensee generally does not have an affirmative duty to notify the candidate regarding his chance to invoke equal opportunities,[2] a notice obligation may arise when

Television Comm'n, 93 F.3d 497 (8th Cir. 1996) (deleting access requirements for "write-in candidates" and for debates "organized by people or groups other than the defendants").

96. Arkansas Educational Television Commission v. Forbes, 523 U.S. 666, 118 S.Ct. 1633, 140 L.Ed.2d 875 (1998).

97. Fox Broadcasting Co., 11 F.C.C.R. at 11,113.

98. A. H. Belo Corp., 11 F.C.C.R. 12,-306, 12,309–10 (1996).

99. 47 C.F.R. § 73.1941(c) (1997).

100. KLAS-TV, 42 F.C.C.2d 894 (1973); Letter to Socialist Worker's Party, 15 F.C.C.2d 96 (1968).

1. Hughes Toll Co., 42 F.C.C.2d 894 (1973).

2. *See, e.g.,* Jose DeLeon, Jr., 9 FCC Rcd. 595 (1994); Notice of Apparent Liability Issued to Surrey Front Range Ltd. Partnership, 7 FCC Rcd. 6361 (1992).

a broadcaster offers free air time to one candidate immediately before an election without notifying his opponents.[3]

A candidate that alleges a denial of equal opportunities must make a prima facie case for the violation in a complaint to the FCC.[4] Acceptance by the candidate of air time offered by the station does not cut off his right to file an FCC complaint,[5] nor does the refusal of the offer of broadcast time, if the licensee's proposed access is inadequate.[6] To facilitate enforcement of equal opportunities and other political broadcasting regulations, Commission rules require broadcasters to maintain a political file.[7] The file must contain all requests for time and their disposition and the time, number and cost of political spots which aired on the station. The file must also disclose any free time provided to candidates.[8] The station must enter information into the political file immediately when it becomes available and is required to retain information in the political file for two years.[9]

b. Reasonable Access Requirements

Section 312(a)(7) of the Communications Act, requires that broadcast stations provide federal candidates with "reasonable access" to their facilities during political campaigns.[10] The Act provides that station licenses may be revoked for "willful or repeated failure to allow reasonable assess or to permit purchase of reasonable amount of time for the use of a broadcasting station by a legally qualified candidate for federal elective office on behalf of his candidacy."[11] As a practical matter, the FCC reviews compliance with the reasonable access requirements on a case-by-case basis.

Generally, reasonable access must be provided to federal candidates at least 45 days before a primary and 60 days before a general or special election. Ultimately, however, the FCC may determine when a campaign is underway. In doing so, it will consider factors such as announcements of candidacy, the establishment of campaign organizations, fundraising activities, endorsements, media coverage or delegate selection activities.[12]

---

3. Complaint by James Spurling, 30 F.C.C.2d 675, 676 (1971).

4. There is no private right of action to raise an equal opportunities claim outside the FCC's administrative process. *See* Belluso v. Turner Communications Corp., 633 F.2d 393, 397 (5th Cir.1980); Daly v. CBS, 309 F.2d 83, 85 (7th Cir.1962). *See also* Exclusive Jurisdiction with Respect to Potential Violations of the Lowest Unit Charge Requirements of Section 315(b), Declaratory Ruling, 6 FCC Rcd. 7511, (1991).

5. Radio Station KLIF, 40 F.C.C. 1096 (1964); Complaint Under Section 315 of the Communications Act (D.L. Grace), 40 F.C.C. 296 (1958).

6. Radio Station KTRM, 40 F.C.C. 335 (1962).

7. 47 C.F.R. § 73.1943 (1997).

8. *Id.* § 73.1943(a)-(b).

9. *Id.* § 73.1943(c).

10. 47 U.S.C.A. § 312(a)(7) (West 1991). These requirements apply to candidates for federal elective office including the President, Vice President and members of Congress. State or local candidates have no right of access under Section 312(a)(7). Political Programming Policies, 7 FCC Rcd. at 682.

11. 47 U.S.C.A. § 312(a)(7) (West 1991).

12. *See* Carter/Mondale Presidential Committee, Inc., 74 F.C.C.2d 631 (1979), *aff'd sub nom.*, CBS v. FCC, 629 F.2d 1, 202 U.S. App. D.C. 369 (D.C.Cir.1980), *aff'd*, 453 U.S. 367, 101 S.Ct. 2813, 69 L.Ed.2d 706 (1981).

The right of access created by Section 312(a)(7) applies only to a "use" of a broadcast station by a federal candidate. The definition of what constitutes a "use" is the same for "reasonable access" as it is for "equal opportunities" under Section 315. A station is not obligated to sell time to political action committees or other supporters of a candidate.[13]

The heart of a Section 312(a)(7) inquiry is determining whether access is "reasonable." It is not measured in specific numbers, but depends on the circumstance of a particular broadcast station and a particular campaign. For example, in a broadcast market that encompasses a small number of federal campaigns for office, stations are expected to provide each candidate with more air time than stations in markets with many candidates.[14]

Reasonable access imposes an affirmative obligation on licensees, who must either make free time available or provide the opportunity for candidates to purchase campaign commercials.[15] If a station makes reasonable amounts of commercial time available to federal candidates, it is under no obligation to provide free time.[16] By the same token, a commercial station that provides reasonable amounts of free time to candidates is not required to sell political advertisements as well. However, a station that chooses to donate rather than sell time to candidates must make available free spot time in the same lengths, classes and periods that are available to commercial advertisers.[17]

Non-commercial stations, which are precluded by federal law from selling advertising, nevertheless must comply with Section 312(a)(7). A non-commercial station must provide spot announcements to federal candidates if it utilizes spot time for underwriting announcements.[18] Public broadcast stations may not charge candidates for political spots, nor may they reject materials submitted by a candidate merely because the advertisement was prepared originally for broadcast on a commercial station.[19]

The FCC generally relies on the reasonable, good-faith judgment of licensees to determine what constitutes reasonable access by federal candidates. Broadcasters generally may not adopt across-the-board policies that fail to account for the circumstances of a particular candidate.[20]

13. National Conservative Political Action Committee v. Kennedy, 563 F.Supp. 622 (D.D.C.1983); National Conservation Political Action Committee, 89 F.C.C.2d 626 (1982); You Can't Afford Dodd Committee, 81 F.C.C.2d 579 (1980).

14. *See* Public Notice, 43 Rad. Reg.2d 1353, 1395 (P & F 1978). *See also* Primer on Political Broadcasting & Cablecasting, 100 F.C.C.2d 1476, 1524 (1984).

15. *See* D.J. Leary, 69 F.C.C.2d 1265 (1978).

16. Kennedy for President Committee v. FCC, 636 F.2d 432, 204 U.S. App. D.C. 160 (D.C.Cir.1980).

17. Public Notice, 43 Rad. Reg.2d 1353, 1396 (P & F 1978).

18. Political Programming Policies, 7 FCC Rcd. at 681.

19. *Id.*

20. Commission Policy in Enforcing Section 312(a)(7) of the Communications Act, 68 F.C.C.2d 1079 (1978). The Commission will examine such factors as the amount of time previously sold to a candi-

The Communications Act does not entitle federal candidates to particular placement of political announcements in a particular program on a station's broadcast schedule.[21] In addition, the FCC has upheld the right of broadcasters to deny political advertisements during newscasts.[22] Similarly, licensees are not required to sell advertising spots of lengths (*e.g.*, five minutes) that are not generally made available to commercial advertisers. Broadcasters are required only to provide federal candidates with commercial lengths generally offered to others in the year preceding an election.[23]

Section 312(a)(7) requires broadcast licensees to provide federal candidates with access to a wide array of day parts and programs for the placement of political announcements.[24] In particular, broadcasters generally must make available program time during "prime time" absent unusual circumstances.[25] Unusual circumstances may exist where, for example, a broadcast station serves an area that has dozens of federal candidates. In that circumstance, a station might not be required to provide access during prime time because of the disruptive effect on the broadcast schedule.[26]

The Supreme Court upheld Section 312(a)(7) of the Communications Act and FCC policies adopted thereunder in *CBS, Inc.* v. *FCC*.[27] The Court held that the Act imposed an obligation that went beyond the usual "public interest" requirements, and that requiring such access did not violate the First Amendment rights of broadcasters.[28] The Court also confirmed that no request for access must be honored under Section 312(a)(7) unless the candidate is willing to pay for the time sought.[29] The Court affirmed the FCC's "rule of reason," whereby licensees are not permitted to adopt blanket policies regarding the sale or denial of advertising time but must consider request for access individually.

c. *Prohibition Against Censorship*

Section 315 provides that no licensee shall have the "power of censorship over the material broadcast under the provisions of this

date, the disruptive impact on regular programming and the likelihood of request for equal time by rival candidates under the equal opportunities requirements.

21. *Id.* at 1091.

22. Political Programming Policies, 7 F.C.C. Rcd. at 682; Law of Political Broadcasting and Cablecasting: A Political Primer, 100 F.C.C.2d at 1525.

23. Request for Declaratory Ruling of National Association of Broadcasters Regarding Section 312(a)(7) of the Communications Act, 9 F.C.C. Rcd. 5778 (1994). Broadcast stations must make program-length time available to federal candidates of the same lengths they have transmitted as programs during the proceeding year, whether or not such spots have actually been sold to commercial advertisers.

24. Commission Policy in Enforcing Section 312(a)(7) of the Communications Act, 68 F.C.C.2d at 1091; Political Programming Policies, 7 F.C.C. Rcd. at 682.

25. Commission Policy in Enforcing Section 312(a)(7) of the Communications Act, 68 F.C.C.2d at 1094; The Law of Political Broadcasting and Cablecasting, 69 F.C.C.2d 2209, 2289 (1978).

26. Political Broadcasting and Cablecasting; A Political Primer, 100 F.C.C.2d at 1524.

27. 453 U.S. 367, 101 S.Ct. 2813, 69 L.Ed.2d 706 (1981).

28. *Id.* at 377–378, 394–396, 101 S.Ct. at 2821, 2829–30, 69 L.Ed.2d. at 717–18, 727–29.

29. *Id.* at 382 n.8, 101 S. Ct. at 2823 n.8, 69 L.Ed.2d. at 720 n.8.

section." Accordingly, the Commission has ruled that a broadcast licensee cannot control the content of a candidate's speech.[30] At the same time, the courts have been sensitive to the extent to which broadcasters are required to transmit—without editing—the speech of others. Therefore, when the Supreme Court found that Section 315 prohibited a station from removing potentially defamatory comments by a candidate, it also held that the Communications Act preempts state defamation laws.[31] The Court reasoned that broadcasters cannot be subject to potential liability for speech over which they have no editorial control.

The "no censorship" rule extends even to political broadcasts considered to be highly offensive or inflammatory, including racial slurs. The Commission found that "[a] contrary conclusion would permit anyone to prevent a candidate from exercising his rights under Section 315 [simply] by threatening a violent reaction."[32] In such a circumstance, however, a station may transmit a content-neutral disclaimer informing viewers that the political sentiments "are not necessarily the views of the station."[33] If the station transmits such disclaimers in connection with a particular candidate's advertisements, it must use an identical disclaimer with all subsequent spots on behalf of all candidates for the same office.

Despite the blanket "no censorship" prohibition, broadcasters may review in advance, and may reject, certain political messages. For example, a broadcaster may request an advanced tape or script of a political broadcast to determine whether it would be a "use," whether it includes the proper sponsorship identification and to ensure that it meets other technical and scheduling requirements.[34] Television stations generally have the right to pre-screen political advertisement to ensure compliance with the sponsorship identification rules.[35] Radio stations, on the other hand, cannot require advanced submissions and are responsible for adding the necessary sponsorship identification prior to airing the political advertisement.[36] Although a broadcaster cannot edit the content of a political advertisement, it may slightly alter the political message for the purpose of ensuring that it has proper sponsorship identification.[37]

Another exception to the "no censorship" rule involves the transmission of obscene or indecent material. Although Section 312(a)(7)

---

30. *See, e.g.*, WANV, Inc., 50 F.C.C.2d 177 (1974) (station policy restricting scope of candidate's response to station editorial found to be impermissible censorship), Gray Communications Systems, Inc., 14 F.C.C.2d 766 (1968); Letter to WMCA, Inc,, 40 F.C.C. 241 (1952); Letter to Congressman Allen Oakley Hunter, 40 F.C.C. 246 (1952).

31. Farmers Educational & Cooperative Union v. WDAY, Inc., 360 U.S. 525, 79 S.Ct. 1302, 3 L.Ed.2d 1407 (1959).

32. Letter to Mr. Lonnie King, 36 F.C.C.2d 635, 637 (1972).

33. Letter to Wayne Brewies, 5 FCC Rcd. 4643, 4644 (1990).

34. Political Broadcasting and Cablecasting, 100 F.C.C.2d at 1512. When requesting a tape or transcript in advance, the broadcaster must inform the candidate that licensee cannot censor the content of the spot.

35. Sponsorship Identification Reconsideration, 7 FCC Rcd. 1616 (1992).

36. Political Programming Policies, 7 FCC Rcd. at 687.

37. Sponsorship Identification Reconsideration, 7 FCC Rcd. at 1618 n.19. Joint Agency Guidelines for Broadcast Licensees, 69 F.C.C.2d 1129 n. 2 (1978).

requires broadcast licensees to provide reasonable access to federal candidates, Section 312(a)(6) of the Act authorizes the FCC to revoke any station license for the transmission of obscene or indecent material. A potential dilemma involving these two statutory provisions confronted the Commission in the 1980s when it was rumored that *Hustler Magazine* publisher Larry Flynt planned to run for federal office and to transmit obscene images in his political advertisements. In response, the Commission staff issued an opinion that a broadcaster "would be justified in refusing access to a candidate who intended to utter obscene or indecent language, because Section 312(a)(6) ... must be granted to carve an exception to Section 312(a)(7)."[38]

The FCC staff opinion averted a clash over the indecency issue. However, in the early 1990s, a number of anti-abortion candidates launched campaigns with the intent to use the "no censorship" and "reasonable access" provisions as a means to present graphic abortion-related images to the public. In response, one federal district court found that the graphic images were "indecent" and held that a broadcast station could channel the broadcast of a candidate's anti-abortion advertisements to "safe harbor" hours.[39] In a subsequent declaratory ruling, the Commission disagreed that the advertisements were indecent, but nevertheless decided that a licensee could reschedule political advertisements containing graphic abortion images to time periods where children are less likely to be in the audience.[40]

The United States Court of Appeals for the District of Columbia Circuit rejected the FCC's analysis of Section 312(a)(7).[41] The court reasoned that the FCC's interpretation would permit broadcasters to limit the scheduling of political advertisements containing any "graphic images" considered to be "harmful to children" and that it would be impossible to determine whether the licensee had rescheduled the advertisement because of disagreement with its message. It expressly rejected the FCC's conclusion that "channeling" graphic political advertisements to a time of day when fewer children in the audience did not constitute "censorship" under Section 315(a). "Not only does the power to channel confer on a licensee the power to discriminate between candidates," the Court noted, "it can force one of them to back away from what he considers to be the most effective way of presenting his position on a controversial issue less he be deprived of the audience he is most anxious to reach."[42] By allowing licensees to channel political advertisements, the FCC's policy interfered with political access by requiring a candidate "to choose between what he wished to say and the audience he wishes to

38. Letter from Chairman Mark Fowler to Congressman Thomas A. Luken, January 19, 1984 (enclosing staff memorandum). *See* Gillett Communications of Atlanta, Inc. v. Becker, 807 F.Supp. 757, 762 (N.D.Ga. 1992), *dismissed without opinion and remanded*, 5 F.3d 1500 (11th Cir.1993).

39. *Id.* The court also held the station's actions were not a prior restraint.

40. Petition for Declaratory Ruling Concerning Section 312(a)(7) of the Communications Act, 9 FCC Rcd. 7638 (1994).

41. Becker v. FCC, 95 F.3d 75, 320 U.S. App. D.C. 387 (D.C.Cir.1996).

42. *Id.* at 83, 320 U.S. App. D.C. at 395.

address."[43] Permitting channeling, according to the court enabled broadcast licensees to relegate a candidate's advertisements to "broadcasting Siberia."[44]

d. Lowest Unit Charge

Section 315(b) of the Communications Act requires broadcast stations to provide the "lowest unit charge" for advertising time purchased by legally qualified candidates during political campaigns.[45] Before Section 315(b) was enacted, a licensee was permitted to charge a candidate a premium for airing political advertisements, and channel those ads to specific time slots.[46] Congress, unhappy with this situation, amended the Act in 1952 and required that broadcasters charge candidates their standard rates available to other advertisers.[47] Congress again amended the Act in 1972, and required stations to charge the "lowest unit charge" during the forty-five days prior to a primary election and sixty days prior to a general election.[48]

Under Section 315(b) licensees are prohibited from charging candidates more than the licensee's most favored commercial advertiser for the same classes, amounts, and periods of time.[49] For each class of advertising time, licensees are required to charge uniform rates to all candidates seeking a particular elected office. Broadcasters also must disclose to candidates all information about rates, terms, conditions and any value-enhancing discount privileges offered to commercial advertisers.[50] Outside the campaign period, the charge for political advertisements "shall not exceed the charges made for comparable use of such station by other users thereof."[51]

For purposes of enforcing Section 315(b), the FCC recognizes four separate classes of advertising time: non-preemptible advertising, preemptible with notice, immediately preemptible (without notice) and run-of-schedule (no guarantee that advertisements will run at a fixed time or that they will run at all).[52] The FCC's rules also permit broadcasters to establish and define their own reasonable classes of immediately preemptible time so long as the differences between the classes are based on "demonstrable benefits." Such benefits may include varying levels of preemption protection, scheduling flexibility or associated privileges, such as guaranteed time-sensitive "make goods."[53] Stations may also establish reasonable classes of time that are preemptible with notice, and non-preemptible time, so long as the various classes are well-defined and fully disclosed to candidates. However, stations may not

43. *Id*. at 84, 320 U.S. App. D.C. at 396.

44. *Id*.

45. 47 U.S.C.A. § 315(b) (West 1991).

46. *See* Hernstadt v. FCC, 677 F.2d 893, 219 U.S. App. D.C. 305 (D.C.Cir.1980).

47. Communications Act Amendments of 1952, Pub. L. 82–544, 66 Stat. 711 (1952).

48. 47 U.S.C.A. § 315(b)(1)(West 1991); 47 C.F.R. § 73.1942 (1997).

49. *Id*. § 73.1942(a)(1)(i).

50. *Id*.

51. 47 U.S.C.A. § 315(b)(2) (West 1991).

52. 47 C.F.R. § 73.1942(a)(1)(i) (1997).

53. *Id*. § 73.1942(a)(1)(iii).

establish a separate, premium-period class of time that is sold only to candidates.[54]

Discount rates charged as part of a special package must be included in the calculation of the lowest unit charge. In this respect, candidates are not required to purchase advertising in every program or day part in a package in order to obtain the discount rate.[55] "Bonus spots" made available to commercial advertisers also must be factored into the lowest unit charge calculation.[56] A station must honor a candidate's "make good" spots (preempted advertising that is rescheduled) prior to election day if the station has provided a time-sensitive make good during the year preceding the election periods. Stations must disclose and make available to candidates any make good policies provided to commercial advertisers.[57]

Although the FCC has held that broadcast stations may not create special classes of advertising for candidates in general, such classes may be created if they provide a special discount to political candidates. These classes of time are permissible to the extent they confer a "greater benefit" upon candidates than that afforded the licensee's most favored commercial advertiser. A class of "candidate-only" non-preemptible time will be considered legitimate if a station can show that a commercial advertiser buying preemptible time at the same rate would run a genuine risk of preemption. In addition, it must be shown that commercial advertisers cannot buy any time that is the functional equivalent of the candidate class, and the station must disclose and offer all preemptible rates to candidates.[58]

4. The Fairness Doctrine

Although no longer enforced by the Commission, the fairness doctrine is considered by many to be the touchstone for the weakened constitutional status of broadcasting compared to other media. The doctrine gave the government the authority to oversee broadcasters' coverage of controversial issues of public importance. The fairness doctrine grew out of a 1946 FCC report entitled *Public Service Responsibility of Broadcast Licensees.*[59] Known as the "Blue Book" because of the color of its cover, the report is identified as the genesis of the fairness doctrine even though only 2 of its 59 pages were devoted to the "discussion of public issues" as a component of the public interest.[60] At the time, the fairness doctrine was thought to expand broadcasters' rights, because it replaced a previous policy that banned altogether editorializing by broadcasters.[61] The doctrine was officially formulated in

---

54. *Id.* § 73.1942(a)(1)(iv), (v), (vi).

55. *Id.* § 73.1942(a)(1)(x).

56. *Id.* § 73.1942(a)(1)(xi). Non-cash promotional merchandising incentives need not be included so long as the inducements are also made available to candidates.

57. *Id.* § 73.1942(a)(1)(xii), (xiii).

58. Political Programming Policies, 7 FCC Rcd. at 692.

59. FCC, Public Service Responsibility of Broadcast Licensees (March 7, 1946) ("The Blue Book").

60. *Id.* at 39–40.

61. Mayflower Broadcasting Corp., 8 FCC 333 (1940).

a 1949 Commission report entitled *Editorializing by Broadcast Licensees.*[62] It imposed dual responsibilities on broadcast licensees. First, the broadcaster was required to devote a reasonable percentage of time to the coverage of public issues. Second, such coverage was subject to the broadcaster's duty to provide an opportunity for the presentation of contrasting points of view.[63]

The fairness doctrine gave rise to several corollary doctrines, some of which are still enforced by the Commission. In 1963, for example, it adopted the Cullman doctrine, which provided that if only one side of a controversial issue was presented during a sponsored program, the other side must be presented even if no one was willing to pay for the presentation.[64] Under the Zapple doctrine, a station that sells time to political supporters of one candidate during an election campaign is required to provide comparable time to supporters of his opponents.[65] The fairness doctrine also had special application to news reports regarding ballot issues, such as bond authorization measures. Additionally, under the "political editorializing" rule, broadcasters that endorse or oppose political candidates are required to notify the subject of the editorial and offer time to respond.[66] Finally, under the personal attack rule, individuals whose honesty, character, integrity or like personal qualities are attacked during a broadcast regarding a controversial issue of public importance must be notified of the attack and offered a reasonable opportunity to respond.[67]

The Supreme Court upheld the fairness doctrine's constitutionality in *Red Lion Broadcasting Co. v. FCC.*[68] The licensee had challenged an FCC order under the personal attack rule on general First Amendment grounds. The Supreme Court, however, pointing to spectrum scarcity, found that "it is idle to posit an unabridgable First Amendment right to broadcast comparable to the right of every individual to speak, write, or publish."[69] Instead, it concluded that, under the public interest standard, "it is the right of the viewers and listeners, not the right of the broadcasters, which is paramount."[70] At the same time, the Court noted that if such regulations "have the net effect of reducing rather than enhancing the value of speech, there will be time enough to reconsider the constitutional implications."[71]

---

62. 13 F.C.C. 1246, 1258 (1949).

63. Handling of Public Issues Under the Fairness Doctrine and the Public Interest Standards of the Communications Act, 48 F.C.C.2d 1 (1974).

64. Cullman Broadcasting Co., 40 FCC 576 (1963).

65. Letter to Nicholas Zapple, 23 F.C.C.2d 707 (1970); First Report, Docket No. 19260, 36 F.C.C.2d 40 (1972). This is also known as the "quasi-equal opportunities" rule.

66. 47 C.F.R. § 73.1930 (1997).

67. *Id.* § 73.1920.

68. 395 U.S. 367, 374, 89 S.Ct. 1794, 1798, 23 L.Ed.2d 371, 380 (1969).

69. *Id.* at 388, 89 S. Ct. at 1806, 23 L.Ed.2d at 388.

70. *Id.* at 390, 89 S. Ct. at 1806, 23 L.Ed.2d at 389. Even at the height of its vitality, however, the fairness doctrine was never found to require broadcasters to carry editorial advertisements. CBS, Inc. v. Democratic National Committee, 412 U.S. 94, 93 S.Ct. 2080, 36 L.Ed.2d 772 (1973).

71. Red Lion, 395 U.S. at 393, 89 S. Ct. at 1808, 23 L.Ed.2d at 391. *See also* FCC v. League of Women Voters of California, 468

The Supreme Court has yet to engage in such a reconsideration.[72] However, during the mid–1980s the FCC embarked upon a rigorous re-examination of the fairness doctrine and its underpinnings. In 1985 the Commission concluded, among other things, that the fairness doctrine was no longer needed because "the public has access to a multitude of viewpoints without the need or danger of regulatory intervention."[73] It also found that the doctrine chills speech by discouraging licensees from airing controversial topics which invoke the doctrine's requirements, thus discouraging diversity.[74]

The Commission's ability to act on its conclusions depended upon the extent to which the fairness doctrine was codified by Section 315 of the Communications Act. If the doctrine was a statutory requirement, the FCC would have no choice but to enforce it. On the other hand, if the doctrine was nothing more than an agency policy, the Commission could eliminate it at will. In *Telecommunications Research and Action Center v. FCC*, the United States Court of Appeals for the District of Columbia Circuit answered that question, holding that the fairness doctrine was a creation of the FCC, not Congress.[75] The Court examined 1959 amendments to the Communications Act and found that the language did not make the fairness doctrine a binding obligation. Instead, "it ratified the Commission's longstanding position that the public interest standard authorizes the fairness doctrine."[76] A plurality of judges on the United States Court of Appeals for the Eighth Circuit subsequently agreed with this conclusion, although on different grounds.[77]

As the FCC reviewed its overall policies under the fairness doctrine, it was also considering a complaint against a Syracuse, New York television station. The Commission found that the station had failed to meet its fairness doctrine obligations with respect to a series of spot editorial advertisements for the Energy Association of New York in support of nuclear power.[78] Notwithstanding its recent fairness doctrine inquiry, the Commission declined to consider the broadcaster's First Amendment challenge, finding that "Congress and the court are more appropriate than us for reacting to the constitutional questions."[79] The

U.S. 364, 104 S.Ct. 3106, 82 L.Ed.2d 278 (1984).

72. *See* Robert M. O'Neill, *Dead or Alive: How Long Will the Red Lion Specter Haunt Free Speech and Broadcasting?* in Rationales and Rationalizations 19–42 (Robert Corn–Revere, ed. Media Institute 1997).

73. Inquiry Into Section 73.1910 of the Commission's Rules and Regulations Concerning Alternatives to the General Fairness Doctrine Obligations of Broadcast Licensees, 102 F.C.C.2d 143, 244 (1985). The Commission cited the vast increase in the number of broadcast outlets, the growing number of alternative technologies and development of spectrum efficiencies since its 1949 report. *Id.* at 196–199.

74. *Id.* at 169.

75. 801 F.2d 501, 255 U.S. App. D.C. 287 (D.C.Cir.1986), cert. denied, 482 U.S. 919, 107 S.Ct. 3196, 96 L.Ed.2d 684 (1987).

76. *Id.* at 517, 255 U.S. App. D.C. at 303.

77. *See* Arkansas AFL–CIO v. FCC, 11 F.3d 1430, 1436–42 (8th Cir.1993) (en banc). *See also* Coalition for a Healthy California v. FCC, 87 F.3d 383 (9th Cir.1996) (declining to reach the issue).

78. Complaint of Syracuse Peace Council, 99 F.C.C.2d 1389 (1984).

79. Complaint of Syracuse Peace Council, 59 Rad.Reg.2d 179, 182 n. 4 (P&F 1985).

United States Court of Appeals for the District of Columbia Circuit remanded the case, however, finding that the FCC could not evade ruling on the constitutional question. The Court found that the Commission ducked the issue because of "non-legislative expressions of congressional concern" but found "no precedent that permits a federal agency to ignore a constitutional challenge to the application of its own policy merely because the resolution would be politically awkward."[80]

On remand, after extensive public comment, the FCC concluded that the fairness doctrine was inconsistent with the First Amendment and contravened the public interest.[81] As a result, the Commission vacated its earlier decision that WTVH had violated the fairness doctrine. On a broader scale, the Commission found that "many broadcasters are in fact inhibited by fairness doctrine burdens from covering controversial issues of public importance." Accordingly, it found that "the overall net effect of the doctrine is to reduce the coverage of controversial issues of public importance, in contravention of the standard announced in *Red Lion*."[82]

Additionally, the Commission found that spectrum scarcity was no longer a significant problem, pointing to its 1985 Fairness Report.[83] The FCC also concluded that scarcity was not a relevant characteristic by which to distinguish the electronic and print media.[84] Based on its findings, the Commission called upon the Supreme Court to "reconsider its use of a constitutional standard based on scarcity."[85] At the same time, the FCC submitted to Congress a comprehensive report on alternatives to the fairness doctrine.[86] The report, delivered the same day as the Commission's *Syracuse Peace Council* decision, concluded that the "best alternative to the doctrine and the one that best achieves the First Amendment principles underlying the doctrine" would be "an unregulated marketplace of ideas."[87]

The United States Court of Appeals for the District of Columbia Circuit upheld the FCC's decision to cease enforcement of the fairness doctrine, but did not reach the First Amendment issue.[88] The Court found that it was unnecessary to address the constitutional question

---

80. Meredith Corp. v. FCC, 809 F.2d 863, 873–74, 258 U.S. App. D.C. 22, 32–34 (D.C.Cir.1987), cert. denied, 493 U.S. 1019, 110 S.Ct. 717, 107 L.Ed.2d 737 (1990). The FCC's general counsel in oral argument had sought to justify the Commission's position by saying "we are not talking law school enforcement, legal text book argument, we're talking political reality here." *Id.* at 873, 258 U.S. App. D.C. at 32.

81. Complaint of Syracuse Peace Council, 2 FCC Rcd. 5043 (1987).

82. *Id.* at 5050.

83. *Id.* at 5053–54.

84. *Id.* at 5055.

85. *Id.*

86. Inquiry into Section 73.1910 of the Commission's Rules and Regulations Concerning Alternatives to the General Fair-ness Doctrine Obligations of Broadcast Licensees, 2 FCC Rcd. 5272 (1987) ("Fairness Doctrine Alternatives"). The inquiry was compelled by a congressional directive as an appropriations rider. *See* Continuing Appropriations for Fiscal Year 1987, Pub. L. 99–500 (signed into law on October 18, 1986).

87. Fairness Doctrine Alternatives, 2 FCC Rcd. at 5295.

88. Syracuse Peace Council v. FCC, 867 F.2d 654, 276 U.S.App.D.C. 38 (D.C.Cir. 1989). A subsequent decision to drop the fairness doctrine in cases involving ballot issues was upheld by the United States Court of Appeals for the Eighth Circuit. Arkansas AFL–CIO v. FCC, 11 F.3d 1430, 1438, 1443 (8th Cir.1993) (en banc).

where the case could be resolved solely by reference to the FCC's conclusion that the fairness doctrine disserves the public interest.[89] In a concurring opinion, Judge Kenneth Starr wrote that the court should have reached the First Amendment issue, and described its decision to avoid the question "a bit cheeky, in light of *Meredith's* generous terms of remand."[90] The Supreme Court did not take the Commission up on its request that the Court review the scarcity rationale and denied certiorari.[91]

The FCC's *Fairness Doctrine Alternatives* report and the *Syracuse Peace Council* decision provoked an immediate adverse reaction in Congress. In particular, Congressman John D. Dingell, then Chairman of the House Committee on Energy and Commerce demanded that FCC Chairman Dennis Patrick explain the scope of its decision. In response to Congressman Dingell, Chairman Patrick wrote that the Syracuse Peace Council decision left intact certain fairness doctrine corollaries. He wrote that "[u]ntil such time as the Commission makes a formal determination as to the scope of *Meredith* beyond general fairness doctrine cases, the Commission will continue to accept, investigate and act upon complaints on matters that do not clearly fall within the scope of *Meredith* decision," including personal attack, political editorializing, Zapple and ballot issues cases.[92] Congress also passed legislation to codify the fairness doctrine, but it was vetoed by President Ronald Reagan.[93]

With the fairness doctrine out of the way, action shifted to the remaining corollaries. In 1992, in a split decision, the FCC eliminated the remaining fairness doctrine obligations that applied to news reports of ballot issues.[94] The Commission found that the earlier decision to repeal a doctrine because of its chilling effects "applies to the fairness doctrine's application to ballot issues as well."[95] This action was upheld by the United States Court of Appeals for the Eighth Circuit, which found that in the absence of a congressional mandate, the Commission was not required to enforce any element of the fairness doctrine.[96] In an interesting turn of events, however, the FCC reversed its earlier position and asked the Eighth Circuit to remand the decision. The FCC explained that remand was needed "to allow the Commission to give further consideration to whether Congress codified the fairness doctrine when it amended Section 315 of the Communications Act in 1959."[97] It is

89. Syracuse Peace Council, 867 F.2d at 657–660, 276 U.S. App. D.C. at 41–44.

90. *Id*. at 677, 276 U.S. App. D.C. at 61 (Starr, J., concurring).

91. Syracuse Peace Council v. FCC, 493 U.S. 1019, 110 S.Ct. 717, 107 L.Ed.2d 737 (1990).

92. Letter from FCC Chairman Dennis R. Patrick to Congressman John D. Dingell, September 22, 1987.

93. Pres. Doc. 715 (June 29, 1987). The Senate then returned the bill to committee

without attempting an override. 133 Cong. Rec. S8438 (1987).

94. Complaint of the Arkansas AFL–CIO and the Committee Against Amendment 2, 7 FCC Rcd. 541 (1992).

95. *Id*.

96. Arkansas AFL–CIO v. FCC, 11 F.3d 1430 (8th Cir.1993)(en banc).

97. Public Notice, Commission Instructs General Counsel to Support Remand in Arkansas AFL–CIO, Inc. v. FCC, 8 FCC Rcd. 2360 (1993).

probably not a coincidence that the FCC's change in position accompanied a change in administrations.

Perhaps for the same reason its overall attitude toward the fairness doctrine changed, the Commission deadlocked on whether to repeal or modify the remaining fairness doctrine corollaries in 1997 and 1998. The FCC's consideration of the corollaries was prompted by a petition filed 14 years earlier by the Radio–Television News Director's Association ("RTNDA"). When the FCC failed to act, RTNDA filed a petition for mandamus with the United States Court of Appeals for the District of Columbia Circuit. Although the court denied mandamus, it invited RTNDA to renew its request "should the Federal Communications Commission fail to make significant progress within the next six months, toward the possible repeal or modification of the personal attack and political editorial rules."[98] The FCC attempted to act on the RTNDA petition within the time frame implied by the court's order but was evenly split on how to respond. In opposing repeal or modification of the personal attack and political editorial rules, former FCC Chairman Reed Hundt advocated reexamining the Commission's earlier decision in *Syracuse Peace Council*.[99] A year later, after the composition of the FCC changed, the agency was still split on the question of the personal attack and political editorial rules.[100]

Until the FCC decides to repeal or modify these policies, or until a court intervenes, the remnants of the fairness doctrine embodied in the personal attack and political editorial rules remain on the books. The personal attack rule is implicated when a licensee airs an attack upon the character, honesty or integrity of a person or group during a broadcast of a controversial issue of public importance. When a personal attack takes place, the rule requires the licensee to notify the targeted individual within one week of the broadcast and to provide the individual with a reasonable opportunity to respond, free of charge, over the licensee's facilities.[1]

The rule only applies to attacks that occur within a program that addresses "controversial issues of public importance."[2] Also, the rule exempts attacks that occur during bona fide news coverage, attacks made by political candidates, or attacks on foreign groups or foreign

---

98. In re Radio–Television News Directors Association, 1997 WL 150084 (D.C.Cir.1997) (not reported in F.3d).

99. In the Matter of the Repeal or Modification of the Personal Attack and Political Editorial Rules, Statement of Chairman Reed E. Hundt (FCC rel. Aug. 11, 1997).

100. Radio-Television News Directors Assn. and National Assn. of Broadcasters, FCC 98–126 (rel. June 22, 1998).

1. 47 C.F.R. § 73.1920(a). Failure by the licensee to provide adequate notice or otherwise comply with the rule does not give rise to a private cause of action. *See* Lechtner v. Brownyard, 679 F.2d 322 (3d Cir.1982); Schnapper v. Foley, 667 F.2d 102, 116, 215 U.S.App.D.C. 59, 73, (D.C.Cir. 1981), cert. denied 455 U.S. 948, 102 S.Ct. 1448, 71 L.Ed.2d 661 (1982).

2. The public importance of an issue is determined case-by-case, taking into account the amount of coverage an issue receives in the press and the attention it receives from community and public leaders. Fairness Doctrine Report, 48 F.C.C.2d 1, 12 (1974). The controversial nature of the issue is based on an examination of whether the issue is one of substantial debate that divides significant elements of the community. *Id.*

leaders.[3] The personal attack rule does not apply to general allegations of bias,[4] or to personal insults.[5]

The final fairness doctrine corollary, the political editorial rule, applies to campaign endorsements by a licensee either opposing or supporting a particular political candidate. When such an editorial airs, the station is required to provide the opposing candidate with notice within twenty-four hours of the editorial and to offer free response time.[6] The licensee is not required to allow the candidate to respond in person since that may trigger equal opportunities requirements. Such responses typically are provided by a spokesperson for the candidate.[7] Political editorial requirements do not apply where a station merely has taken a position on a public issue upon which a candidate has expressed an opinion. Rather, the rule is triggered only by endorsement of, or opposition to, a particular candidate.[8]

5. Closed Captioning Requirements

Section 713 of the Telecommunications Act of 1996 was enacted "to ensure that video services are accessible to hearing impaired and visually impaired individuals."[9] It requires the Commission to ensure that "video programming first published or exhibited after the effective date [of the rules] is fully accessible through the provision of closed captions," and that "video programming providers or owners maximize the accessibility of video programming first published or exhibited prior to the effective date of such regulations through the provision of closed captions."[10] Pursuant to this section, the FCC in 1997 adopted regulations establishing "an appropriate schedule of deadlines for the provision of closed captioning of video programming."[11] The requirements apply to all types of video programming regardless of transmission medium. The statutory requirement divides programming into two groups: pre-rule programming (defined as programming "first published or exhibited on or

3. 47 C.F.R. § 73.1930(b) (1997).

4. Personal Attack Complaint of Bree Walker Lampley, 7 FCC Rcd. 1385, (1992).

5. Application of Eagle Radio, 9 FCC Rcd. 1294 (1994).

6. 47 C.F.R. § 73.1930 (1997).

7. See, e.g., letter to Charles F. Massart, 10 F.C.C.2d 968 (1967).

8. Taft Broadcasting Co. (WDAF), 53 F.C.C.2d 126 (1975).

9. Section 713, Telecommunications Act of 1996, Pub. L. 104–104, 110 Stat. 56 (1996) codified at 47 U.S.C.A. § 613 (West Supp. 1997). See Conf. Rep. 104–458, 104th Cong., 2d. Sess. 182 (1996). The provision was adopted to supplement existing, nonmandatory captioning policies. Congress adopted the Television Decoder Circuitry Act of 1990 to require all television receiv-

ers with screen sizes 13 inches or larger to be capable of receiving and displaying closed captions for the hearing impaired. Pub. L. 101–431, 104 Stat. 960 (1990), codified at 47 U.S.C.A. §§ 303(u), 330(b) (West 1991). Although program producers had voluntarily increased the amount of captioned programming to coincide with the increase in equipment, Congress became concerned that the growth of programming was insufficient to ensure accessibility of video programming to persons with disabilities. H.R. Rep. 104–204, 104th Cong., 1st Sess. 113–114 (1995).

10. 47 U.S.C.A. § 613(b) (West Supp. 1997).

11. Report and Order, Closed Captioning and Video Description of Video Programming, 13 FCC Rcd. 3272 (1997) ("Closed Captioning Order"). See 47 U.S.C.A. § 613(c) (West Supp. 1997).

before" January 1, 1998)[12] and new programming (programming first published or exhibited after that date). Beginning in the first calendar quarter of 2000, new programming is subject to a series of benchmarks requiring that a specified number of hours of such programming is captioned per calendar quarter, as follows: In years 2000–2001, at least 450 hours of programming per calendar quarter must be captioned; in years 2002–2003, at least 900 hours per quarter must be captioned; and in years 2004–2005 at least 1350 hours per quarter must be captioned.[13] After January 1, 2006, 95 percent of all new, non-exempt programming must be captioned. Pre-rule programming is subject to no specific requirements until the first calendar quarter of 2008. After that time, 75 percent of all pre-rule programming aired or shown by broadcasters must be captioned.[14]

The Act empowered the FCC to establish exemptions for certain programs, classes of programs or services for which closed captioning would be economically burdensome.[15] Pursuant to this authority, the Commission exempted various programming types from captioning requirements, including foreign language programming,[16] primarily textual programming,[17] advertisements (of less than five minutes in duration), interstitials, promotionals, and public service announcements (of less than 10 minutes in duration), primarily non-vocal music programming,[18] certain locally produced programming[19] and late-night programming.[20] In addition, the Commission has exempted from captioning requirements programming prepared specifically for digital television, which will be

12. Closed Captioning Order 13 FCC Rcd. at 3300.

13. Any broadcaster that airs less than the specified number of hours of new, non-exempt programming is required to caption 95 percent of all new programs each quarter. *Id.* at 3294–95 & n.121. In addition, broadcasters cannot fall below the average hourly amount of captioned programming that was transmitted during the first six months of 1997 even if the amount of captioned programming exceeds the amount required under the benchmarks. *Id.*

14. *Id.* at 3301. Although no captioning benchmark for pre-rule programming becomes effective until 2008, the Commission will review the requirement after four years.

15. Programmers seeking an exemption are required to demonstrate that compliance would cause an "undue burden." This means a significant difficulty or expense involving such factors as the nature and cost of closed captions, the impact on the operation of the provider or program owner, the financial resources of the provider and the type of operations involved. 47 U.S.C.A. § 613(e) (West Supp. 1997).

16. The rules exempt programming in all foreign languages but require any pro-

gramming that is "readily captioned through the ENR technique" to be captioned. Closed Captioning Order at 13 FCC Rcd. at 3344. On reconsideration the FCC excluded Spanish language programming from this exemption. Closed Captioning Reconsideration Order, FCC 98–236 (rel. Oct. 2, 1998).

17. The "primarily textual" exemption applies only to programming that has "little or no relevant audio track," such as community bulletin boards, but not "sports, shopping or weather programming." *Id.*

18. Non-vocal music programming is exempt if 80 percent of the programming has no verbal elements.

19. The Commission defined exempted locally produced programming as programming that is locally created, is not networked outside of the local service area or market, is not readily captioned through ENR means (such as local news), and does not have much, if any, repeat value.

20. This applies to programs that are distributed between 2 a.m. and 6 a.m. local time (within the contiguous 48 states) or within any four-hour time period between 12 a.m. and 7 a.m. if the programming is distributed to two or more time zones.

uniformly designated as "pre-rule programming" until "such time as the necessary decoder standard rules have been adopted by the Commission and are effective."[21] Finally, the rules include exemptions for several types of programming providers, including companies that have devoted two percent of annual gross revenues to closed captioning expenses.

The FCC established a petition process to permit requests for "undue burden" waivers. Any party with an interest in the programming (including producers, owners or distributors) may file a waiver request, which is subject to a public comment period. The petitioner may put forth any evidence relevant to the statutory factors for an undue burden waiver, including the costs of captioning and the possibility of alternate means of providing information. The petitioner may also propose alternate mechanisms by which the programming may be made more accessible without captioning.[22] Complaints regarding non-compliance with captioning requirements must first be sent to the video distributor, not the FCC. A complaint must "state with specificity the Commission rule violated and should provide some information which supports the alleged rule violation."[23] The licensee must respond in writing within 45 days after the end of the quarter in which the violation allegedly occurred or within 45 days after receipt of the written complaint, whichever is later. Only if the distributor does not respond and resolve the situation or if there is reason to believe that the distributor's response is inaccurate may the complaint be filed with the FCC. If a violation is found, the Commission may then impose penalties ranging from forfeitures to increased captioning requirements.[24]

6. Sponsorship Identification

The Communications Act and FCC rules require that a broadcast licensee identify the sponsor of any paid matter transmitted over the station.[25] This provision applies if "any money, service or other valuable consideration is directly or indirectly paid, or promised to or charged or accepted by" the broadcast station.[26] Such consideration does not include any service or property furnished "without charge or at a nominal charge."[27] However, even where property is furnished without charge, the rules require sponsorship identification if the mention of a brand name, trademark, service, product or person exceeds what is "reasonably related to the use of such service or property on the broadcast."[28] The Communications Act also requires licensees to "exercise reasonable

---

21. *Id.* at 3300–01.

22. *See id.* at 3364.

23. *Id.* at 3381.

24. *See id.* at 3382–83. The FCC declined to impose formal recordkeeping requirements to demonstrate compliance with the captioning regulations. Licensees must only maintain sufficient records to respond to any complaint. *Id.* at 3383.

25. 47 U.S.C.A. § 317 (West 1991); 47 C.F.R. § 73.1212 (1997).

26. 47 U.S.C.A. § 317(a)(1) (West 1991).

27. *Id.*

28. *Id.* The practice of visibly inserting a product in a broadcast with its trademark prominently displayed is called "plugola."

diligence" to learn the identity of the sponsor so that appropriate identification can be transmitted.[29]

The sponsorship identification requirements were originally adopted as part of the Radio Act of 1927. However, the requirements "occupied a humble position in the regulatory design and went virtually unnoticed."[30] The sponsorship provisions provoked little controversy until scandals rocked the broadcast industry in the late 1950s. Information surfaced in a series of congressional subcommittee hearings that a popular quiz show called "Twenty One" was rigged by producers who provided popular contestants with answers.[31] At nearly the same time, disc jockeys at several radio stations were exposed for accepting cash and other bonuses ("payola") from record companies in return for broadcasting the companies' records.[32] Congress reacted by amending Section 317 and strengthening the sponsorship identification requirements.[33] Another section was added to the Act to address the abuses related to quiz shows where assistance had been provided to seemingly independent contestants.[34] The provision also prohibits the use of persuasion, bribery or intimidation to influence a contestant to refrain from using his or her knowledge or skills.[35]

Commercial advertisements fall directly within the reach of the sponsorship identification requirements since such messages by definition represent programming material for which a station receives money or other consideration. However, there is usually little confusion about the fact that advertisements are paid announcements. Accordingly, the FCC's rules provide that mention of the sponsor's corporate name or trade name, or the name of the sponsor's product in the body of the advertisement shall be deemed sufficient "when it is clear that the mention of the name of the product constitutes a sponsorship identification."[36]

Special rules apply to programs involving political announcements or discussions of controversial issues of public importance. Where any film, record, transcription, talent, script, or other material is provided to a station for a political announcement, the licensee is required to provide sponsorship identification at the beginning and end of such program-

---

29. 47 U.S.C.A. § 317(c). The section requires broadcasters to obtain from "its employees, and from other persons with whom it deals directly" information regarding the identity of sponsors.

30. *See* Loveday v. FCC, 707 F.2d 1443, 228 U.S. App. D.C. 38 (D.C.Cir.1983).

31. Investigation of Television Quiz Shows: Hearings Before the Legislative Oversight Subcommittee of the House Comm. on Interstate and Foreign Commerce, 86th Cong. 1st Sess. (1959); Investigation of Regulatory Commissions and Agencies, Interim Report of the Subcommittee on Legislative Oversight, H.R. Rep. No. 1258, 86th Cong., 2d Sess. (1960).

32. Responsibilities of Broadcasting Licensees and Station Personnel: Hearings on Payola and Other Deceptive Practices in the Broadcasting Field Before the Legislative Oversight Subcommittee of the House Comm. on Interstate and Foreign Commerce, 86th Cong., 2d Sess. (1960).

33. *See* Loveday v. FCC, 707 F.2d at 1453–54, 228 U.S. App. D.C. at 48–49.

34. 47 U.S.C.A. § 509(a)(1) (West 1991).

35. *Id.* § 509(a)(2).

36. 47 C.F.R. § 73.1212(f) (1997).

ming.[37] Sponsorship identification requirements for political announcements are quite specific. The announcement must make clear that the spot is "paid for" or "sponsored by" the identified sponsor.[38] FCC rules also require licensees to keep on public file a list of the officers, board members or executive committee members of the corporation or other entity that sponsors any broadcast involving discussion of a controversial issue of public importance. Licensees are required to use "reasonable diligence" to determine the identity of the sponsors of such broadcasts, even where the sponsored programming has been arranged by an agent.[39]

The Commission has taken varying approaches to the level of investigation required by licensees. In the 1980s the FCC concluded that radio and television stations were not required to investigate allegations that the tobacco industry was sponsoring an advertising campaign related to a California ballot issue. Although the industry had provided virtually all of the funds for the campaign, the Commission concluded that the broadcast stations had not acted unreasonably in declining to conduct a sponsorship investigation. The United States Court of Appeals for the District of Columbia Circuit upheld this decision in *Loveday v. FCC*.[40] More recently, the FCC, reached a contrary conclusion on similar facts. The Commission required sponsorship identification for advertisements aired during an Oregon ballot proposition that allegedly were sponsored by the tobacco industry.[41] While acknowledging that broadcasters need not act as private investigators to ascertain whether the persons with whom they deal are the "true" sponsors of an advertisement, and noting that licensees normally may rely on the plausible assurances of the person paying for the broadcast time, the Commission nevertheless concluded that a challenger may make "so strong a circumstantial case" that further investigation would be required. The Commission cautioned that the ruling does not require sponsorship identification of entities who provide funding for advertisements unless there is credible evidence that the funding entities also exercise editorial control.

C. *Negative Programming Mandates*

1. *General*

The public interest, as interpreted by regulators, demands more than affirmative action by broadcasters. The Communications Act and the Commission's rules contain a number of prohibitions designed to protect listeners and viewers from exposure to certain types of broadcast content. Although much of the public interest doctrine is justified by its

---

37. 47 U.S.C.A. § 317(a)(2)(West 1991); 47 C.F.R. § 73.1212(d) (1997). For broadcast of five minute's duration or less, only one sponsorship announcement must be made, either at the beginning or end of the broadcast.

38. Letter to Dalton Moore, 7 FCC Rcd. 3587 (1992); Letter to KOOL Radio-Television, Inc., 26 F.C.C.2d 42 (1970).

39. 47 C.F.R. § 73.1212(e) (1997).

40. 707 F.2d at 1447, 1457; 228 U.S. App. D.C. at 42, 52.

41. Trumper Communications of Portland, Ltd., 11 FCC Rcd. 20415 (1996).

supporters as being speech enhancing,[42] an inherent aspect of the public interest includes speech restrictions.[43] With government-imposed limits on speech, it is the decisions of regulators, not the rights of viewers or listeners, which is paramount.

2. *Indecent Programming*

Section 1464 of the United States Criminal Code provides criminal and civil penalties for persons who utter "obscene, indecent, or profane language by means of radio communication."[44] In addition, Section 312(a)(6) of the Communications Act authorizes the FCC to revoke the license of any broadcaster who violates Section 1464.[45] The prohibition against profane or indecent broadcasts was adopted originally as Section 29 of the Radio Act of 1927, which, at the time, contained both the indecency ban and the denial to the government of the "power of censorship."[46] The indecency prohibition was transferred to the United States Criminal Code in 1948.[47] Although the indecency concept is discussed in greater detail in Chapter 6, this Section addresses some aspects of indecency enforcement that relate to the broadcast public interest mandate.

Ten years after the Supreme Court upheld enforcement of the indecency rules with respect to the "seven dirty words,"[48] the FCC broadened its enforcement efforts to encompass a "generic" definition of the proscribed speech.[49] The Commission defines "indecent" speech as "language or material that, in context, depicts or describes, in terms patently offensive as measured by contemporary community standards for the broadcast medium, sexual or excretory activities or organs."[50] In addition, the material must be transmitted at a time of day when

---

42. *See, e.g., Red Lion*, 395 U.S. at 390, 89 S.Ct. At 1806, 23 L.Ed.2d at 389 ("it is the right of the viewers and listeners, not the right of the broadcasters which is paramount").

43. *See e.g.*, FCC v. Pacifica Foundation, 438 U.S. 726, 748–751, 98 S.Ct. 3026 3039–3041, 57 L.Ed.2d 1073, 1092–1094 (1978).

44. 18 U.S.C.A. § 1464 (West 1991). The FCC usually enforces this provision through civil forfeitures and licensing proceedings. However, it has in the past threatened and, in some cases obtained, criminal sanctions. *See, e.g.*, Pacifica Found. Inc., 2 FCC Rcd. 2698 (1987). *See also* CB Abuser Convicted of Obscenity, FCC Public Notice 4833 (Sept. 14, 1987) (conviction under 18 U.S.C.A. § 1464 was based on "use of threats and profanity in [defendant's] CB transmissions"); United States v. Simpson, 561 F.2d 53 (7th Cir.1977) (conviction for uttering obscene, indecent, or profane radio broadcast on CB radio reversed); Tallman v. United States, 465 F.2d 282, 284 (7th Cir. 1972) (conviction under 18 U.S.C.A. § 1464

for "obscene, indecent or profane... radio communication" upheld); Duncan v. United States, 48 F.2d 128, 134 (9th Cir.), cert. denied, 283 U.S. 863, 51 S.Ct. 656, 75 L.Ed. 1469 (1931) (conviction for profane radio broadcast upheld where words "damned" and "By God" were used "irreverently").

45. 47 U.S.C.A. § 312(a)(6) (West 1991).

46. 44 Stat. 1172–1173. This dual mandate was continued in Section 326 of the Communications Act of 1934, as originally adopted by Congress. June 19, 1934, c. 652, Title III, § 326, 48 Stat. 1091 (1934).

47. Ch. 645, § 21, 62 Stat. 862 (June 24, 1948).

48. FCC v. Pacifica Foundation, 438 U.S. 726, 98 S.Ct. 3026, 57 L.Ed.2d 1073 (1978).

49. *See* New Indecency Enforcement Standards to be Applied to All Broadcast and Amateur Radio Licenses, 2 FCC Rcd. 2726 (1987).

50. Infinity Broadcasting Corp. of Pennsylvania, 2 FCC Rcd. 2705 (1987).

children are likely to be in the audience. In its most recent pronounce-ment on the subject, the FCC ruled that material may be broadcast during a "safe harbor" period, between the hours of 10 p.m. and 6 a.m., without violating the rules.[51]

Because "[s]exual expression which is indecent but not obscene is protected by the First Amendment,"[52] the FCC was able to finalize its "safe harbor" policy only after protracted litigation. In *Action for Children's Television v. FCC*, ("*ACT I*"), the United States Court of Appeals for the District of Columbia Circuit rejected vagueness and overbreadth challenges to the generic indecency standard, but remanded to the FCC a midnight to 6 a.m. "safe harbor" as being arbitrary.[53] As the Commis-sion began to fashion a new safe harbor period, Congress enacted legislation directing the agency to institute a twenty-four hour ban on indecency.[54] The Commission complied,[55] but the flat ban was invalidated in *ACT II*.[56] Once again, before the FCC could reach a decision, Congress defined the safe harbor legislatively.[57] The District of Columbia Circuit upheld the new safe harbor (for the most part) in *ACT III*.[58] The court, sitting en banc, upheld most of the rule, but found no justification for the difference in safe harbor hours between commercial and noncommer-cial licensees.[59] Finally, in *ACT IV*, the United States Court of Appeals for the District of Columbia Circuit upheld the procedures by which the FCC assesses forfeitures in indecency cases.[60]

Although the principal questions regarding the FCC's indecency enforcement policies have been resolved through two decades of litiga-tion, there is a continuing tension between the indecency prohibition of Section 1464 and the "no censorship" requirement in Section 326 of the Communications Act. Section 326 provides that "[n]othing in this chap-ter shall be understood or construed to give the Commission the power of censorship over ... radio communications ... and no regulation or condition shall be promulgated or fixed by the Commission which shall

---

51. Enforcement of Prohibitions Against Broadcast Indecency in 18 U.S.C.A. Section 1464, 10 FCC Rcd. 10558 (1995).

52. Sable Communications of Cal., Inc. v. FCC, 492 U.S. 115, 126, 109 S.Ct. 2829, 2836, 106 L.Ed.2d 93, 105 (1989).

53. 852 F.2d 1332, 271 U.S. App. D.C. 365 (D.C.Cir.1988).

54. Pub. L. 100–459 § 608, 102 Stat. 2186 (1988).

55. Enforcement of Prohibitions Against Broadcast Indecency in 18 U.S.C.A.A. Section 1464, 4 FCC Rcd. 457 (1988).

56. Action for Children's Television v. FCC, 932 F.2d 1504, 290 U.S. App. D.C. 4 (D.C.Cir.1991), cert. denied, 503 U.S. 913, 112 S.Ct. 1281, 117 L.Ed.2d 507 (1992). The court ordered the Commission to resume its safe harbor inquiry that began after *ACT I*.

57. Public Telecommunications Act of 1992, Pub. L. 102–356, § 16(a), 106 Stat.

949 (1992). The law created a safe harbor of 10 p.m. to 6 a.m. for certain public stations and from midnight to 6 a.m. for all other stations.

58. Action for Children's Television v. FCC, 58 F.3d 654, 313 U.S. App. D.C. 94 (D.C.Cir.1995) (en banc), cert. denied *sub nom.*, Pacifica Foundation v. FCC, 516 U.S. 1043, 116 S.Ct. 701, 133 L.Ed.2d 658 (1996).

59. The court required the Commission to impose a 10 p.m. to 6 a.m. safe harbor uniformly on commercial and noncommer-cial licensees alike. 58 F.3d at 669, 670, 313 U.S. App. D.C. at 108, 109.

60. Action for Children's Television v. FCC, 59 F.3d 1249, 313 U.S. App. D.C. 261 (D.C.Cir.1995)("*ACT IV*"), cert. denied, 516 U.S. 1072, 116 S.Ct. 773, 133 L.Ed.2d 726 (1996).

interfere with the right of free speech by means of radio communication."[61] The *Pacifica* Court harmonized the seemingly conflicting provisions through a historical analysis of the law. It defined "censorship" as the absence of prior restraint and noted that the Commission historically had been permitted to evaluate the public interest value of programming after it was broadcast.[62] Additionally, the Court pointed out that Sections 1464 and 326 evolved from the same statutory section in the Radio Act, thus supporting the conclusion that "Congress intended to give meaning to both provisions."[63]

Subsequent opinions have fleshed out judicial thinking on the relationship between "channeling" objectionable broadcast content to safe harbor hours and censorship. More recently, the United States Court of Appeals for the District of Columbia Circuit in *ACT III* described the process as "a balancing of irreconcilable interests."[64] In a contest between the government's compelling interest in protecting children, and what the court recognized as a "burden [on] the rights of many adults," Judge James Buckley, writing for the *en banc* court, concluded that it was "entirely appropriate that the marginal convenience of some adults be made to yield to the imperative needs of the young."[65] After all, Judge Buckley wrote, "adults have alternative means of satisfying their interest in indecent material at other hours that pose no risk to minors."[66] The District Court in *ACT IV* was even more direct regarding "channeling" and censorship: "This court will not construe the FCC [indecency enforcement] scheme as a system of censorship when that system only operates for two-thirds of the broadcast day." Any chilling effect on broadcasters, according to the court, "disappears with the daylight."[67]

Such decisions appear to settle the matter. Yet the unease embedded in the concept that a prohibition for two-thirds of the broadcast day is not censorship came to the fore in a 1996 decision of the United States Court of Appeals for the District of Columbia Circuit. That case involved an FCC declaratory ruling that permitted broadcasters to channel political advertisements that contained graphic imagery that, in the good faith judgment of the licensees, posed a risk to children.[68] The Commission had found that the presentation of graphic abortion imagery in political advertisements "can be psychologically damaging to children" and ruled that broadcasters had discretion to transmit such materials at times when children were less likely to be in the audience. The FCC concluded that such a decision would be reasonable, so long as it was not based on

61. 47 U.S.C.A. § 326 (West 1991).

62. Pacifica, 438 U.S. at 736–737, 98 S.Ct. at 3033–34, 57 L. Ed.2d at 1085–1086.

63. *Id*. at 738, 98 S.Ct. at 3034, 57 L. Ed.2d at 1086.

64. 58 F.3d at 667, 313 U.S. App. D.C. at 107.

65. *Id*.

66. *Id*. at 666, 313 U.S. App. D.C. at 106.

67. Action for Children's Television v. FCC, 827 F.Supp. 4, 19 (D.D.C.1993), *aff'd*, 59 F.3d 1249, 313 U.S. App. D.C. 261 (D.C.Cir.1995). In point of fact, the court had it backwards. The chilling effect rises with the sun, since the rules relegate indecent speech to late night hours.

68. Petition for Declaratory Ruling Concerning Section 312(a)(7) of the Communications Act, 9 FCC Rcd. 7638 (1994).

the candidate's political viewpoint and only to the extent the candidate was allowed access at times when "the audience potential is broad enough to meet ... reasonable access obligations."[69] One United States District Court similarly found that graphic anti-abortion images could have a negative psychological impact on children, and held that such political advertisements were indecent.[70]

Notwithstanding these findings, the District of Columbia Circuit held in *Becker v. FCC* that the imperative needs of the young did not outweigh the marginal needs of some candidates. Judge James Buckley, again writing for the court, concluded that channeling political advertisements violated the "no censorship" provision of Section 315 of the Communications Act. In sharp contrast to the conclusion in *ACT III*, the court in *Becker* found that "censorship, ... as commonly understood, connotes any examination of thought or expression in order to prevent discussion of 'objectionable' material."[71] The court concluded that it would not be possible to assure a candidate "broad audience potential" while at the same time avoiding large numbers of children in the audience, and that the safe harbor hours amounted to "broadcasting Siberia."[72] It also found that the ability to channel speech would give broadcasters too much power to discriminate between candidates which would exert a chilling effect on speech.[73]

The court's divergent responses to similar problems is perplexing. In evaluating the "competing interests [of] the licensee's desire to spare children the sight of images that are not indecent but may nevertheless prove harmful" and a political candidate's interest in "access to the time periods with the greatest audience potential," the court held that time channeling unquestionably violated the "no censorship" prohibition of Section 315 of the Communications Act.[74] Yet in evaluating the "irreconcilable interests" of adults' access to constitutionally protected speech on matters related to sex and protecting children from exposure to such

---

69. *Id.*

70. Gillett Communications of Atlanta, Inc. v. Becker, 807 F.Supp. 757, 763 (N.D.Ga.1992), *appeal dismissed*, 5 F.3d 1500 (11th Cir.1993).

71. Becker v. FCC, 95 F.3d 75, 82, 320 U.S. App. D.C. 387, 395 (D.C.Cir.1996), quoting Farmers Educ. & Coop. Union of Am. v. WDAY, Inc., 360 U.S. 525, 527, 79 S.Ct. 1302, 1304, 3 L.Ed.2d 1407, 1410 (1959).

72. Becker, 95 F.3d at 80, 84, 320 U.S. App. D.C. at 392, 396.

73. *Id.* at 83, 320 U.S. App. D.C. at 395 ("Not only does the power to channel confer on a licensee the power to discriminate between candidates, it can force one of them to back away from what he considers to be the most effective way of presenting his position on a controversial issue lest he be deprived of the audience he is most anxious to reach."). Although the Commis-

sion stressed that it intended to permit licensees no discretion to channel political advertisements on the basis of a candidate's political position, but only as a response to graphic imagery (Petition for Declaratory Ruling Concerning Section 312(a)(7) of the Communications Act, 9 FCC Rcd. at 7647–48) the court found that "[i]n many instances ... it will be impossible to separate the message from the image." Becker, 95 F.3d at 81, 320 U.S. App. D.C. at 393. This statement is difficult to reconcile with the Supreme Court's assurance with respect to "indecent" speech that "[t]here are few, if any, thoughts that cannot be expressed by the use of less offensive language." Pacifica, 438 U.S. at 743 n.18, 98 S. Ct. at 3037 n.18, 57 L.Ed.2d at 1089 n.18.

74. Becker, 95 F.3d at 80, 320 U.S. App. D.C. at 392.

material, the court found that channeling did not violate the "no censorship" provision of Section 326, and that such rules did not require much "precision" or "fine tuning" to minimize the burdens on speech.[75]

The unarticulated distinction appears to be the court's assumption that the graphic political advertisements have greater merit than any other arguably indecent speech. However, as Judge Patricia Wald of the United States Court of Appeals for the District of Columbia Circuit pointed out in another case, " '[i]ndecency' is not confined merely to material that borders on obscenity—'obscenity lite.' "[76] Indecency encompasses a broad category of speech that includes works of great merit, she wrote, and in many instances "the programming's very merit will be inseparable from its seminal 'offensiveness.' "[77] The Supreme Court lent support to this view when it struck down portions of the Communications Decency Act in *Reno v. ACLU*. The Court acknowledged the governmental interest in protecting children from harmful material but concluded that it "does not justify an unnecessarily broad suppression of speech addressed to adults."[78] Among the problems it found with the CDA's indecency standard was that it provided too little consideration of the potential "societal value" of indecent speech.[79] These developments suggest that constitutional questions arising from the FCC's indecency regulations may be far from settled.

3. *Violent Programming*

Concerns about violence in the mass media historically have preoccupied policymakers. After World War I (and through the 1960s), there was great concern with the impact of cinema, particularly its depictions of sex and violence.[80] In the 1940s attention was diverted to crime magazines, with their emphasis on bloodshed, lust or crime. Such publications were believed to encourage or incite the social violence.[81] This concern was focused on comic books in the 1950s when Senate Hearings investigated a purported link between violent comics and juvenile delinquency.[82] The on-going debate over televised violence repre-

75. *ACT III*, 58 F.3d at 666–667, 313 U.S. App. D.C. at 106–107.

76. Alliance for Community Media v. FCC, 56 F.3d 105, 130, 312 U.S. App. D.C. 141, 166 (D.C.Cir.) (en banc) (Wald, J., dissenting), *rev'd in part and aff'd in part sub nom.* Denver Area Educ. Telecomms. Consortium v. FCC, 518 U.S. 727, 116 S.Ct. 2374, 135 L.Ed.2d 888 (1996).

77. *Id.*

78. 521 U.S. 844, 875, 117 S.Ct. 2329, 2346, 138 L.Ed.2d 874, 899 (1997).

79. *Id.* at 873, 117 S. Ct. at 2345, 138 L. Ed. 2d at 899. The Court distinguished regulation of broadcasting from control over Internet communication. In doing so, however, it largely limited *Pacifica* to its facts. *Id.* at 866–867, 117 S. Ct. at 2341–42, 138 L. Ed. 2d at 893–894.

80. To head off film censorship, legislation by the states, Hollywood established the Motion Picture Producers and Distributors of America, headed by former Postmaster General Will H. Hays. The Hays office was set up to be the industry's own censorship bureau. A study of censors in 1928 found that 56.4 percent of deletions related to depictions of crime. *See* Thomas G. Krattenmaker & Lucas A. Powe, *Televised Violence: First Amendment Principles and Social Science Theory*, 64 Va. L. Rev. 1123, 1289 (1978).

81. *See* Winters v. New York, 333 U.S. 507, 510–11, 68 S.Ct. 665, 667–668, 92 L.Ed. 840, 847–848 (1948).

82. Hearings Before the Subcomm. to Investigate Juvenile Delinquency of the Senate Comm. on the Judiciary, 83d Cong.,

sents a continuation of this trend. Senate Judiciary Committee hearings on juvenile delinquency in the mid–1950s and early 60s examined the effects of television on young people, and, in the mid–1970s, both Congress and the FCC again expressed concerns about depictions of violence on TV.[83]

In the early 1990s Congress considered a wide variety of bills designed to address the issue of televised violence, some more regulatory than others.[84] In the Telecommunications Act of 1996, Congress adopted Section 551 which imposed a requirement that television manufacturers install V-chips, decoder circuitry designed to block programs based on ratings, and established a timetable by which industry could devise a "voluntary" ratings system.[85] Congressional proponents of the V-chip

2d Sess. (1954). This led to the voluntary creation of the Comic Book Code. *See* Krattenmaker and Powe, *supra* n.80, at 1291.

83. *See* Report on the Broadcast of Violent, Indecent, and Obscene Material, 51 F.C.C.2d 418 (1975). The Commission's 1975 report to Congress on such programming concluded that industry self-regulation should be emphasized over legislation because of First Amendment concerns and the subjective nature of what type of violence is inappropriate. *Id.* at 419–420. The FCC's behind-the-scenes activities in preparation of the report led to adoption by the networks of the "family viewing policy." However, the extent to which the policy was an exercise in "self-regulation" was questioned by the reviewing court and the policy was invalidated. Writers Guild of America, West v. FCC, 423 F.Supp. 1064 (C.D.Cal.1976), *vacated and remanded on jurisdictional grounds sub nom.* Writers Guild of America, West v. ABC, 609 F.2d 355 (9th Cir.1979), cert. denied, 449 U.S. 824, 101 S.Ct. 85, 66 L.Ed.2d 27 (1980).

84. *See, e.g.,* S. 2136, the Federal Advertisement Reform Act, 103d Cong., 2d Sess. (proposing to prohibit sponsorship of television programs by federal government agencies); S. 943, The Children's Television Violence Protection Act of 1993, 103d Cong., 1st Sess. (proposing to require warnings prior to programming depicting 'violence or unsafe gun practices'); S. 973 and H.R. 2159, the Television Violence Report Card Act of 1993, 103d Cong., 1st Sess. (proposing to require the FCC to evaluate and publicly report on violence contained in TV programs); S. 1383, the Children's Protection from Violent Programming Act of 1993, 103d Cong., 1st Sess. (proposing to prohibit the telecast of violent programming at times when children are likely to be in the broadcast audience); S. 1556, 103d Cong., 1st Sess. (proposing to require oversight of violent commercials and program

promotions); H.R. 2609, the Presidential Commission on TV Violence and Children Act, 103d Cong., 1st Sess. (proposing to create a presidential commission to investigate and propose solutions to reduce broadcasting of violence on television); H.R. 2756, the Parents Television Empowerment Act of 1993, 103d Cong., 1st Sess. (proposing to require the FCC to establish a toll free telephone number to collect complaints regarding televised violence); H.R. 2837, the Television and Radio Program Violence Reduction Act of 1993, 103d Cong., 1st Sess. (proposing to require the FCC to prescribe standards to reduce violent programming on broadcast stations and cable systems and require license revocation for repeated violations); S. 1811, 103d Cong., 2d Sess. and H.R. 2888, the Television Violence Reduction Through Parental Empowerment Act of 1993, 103d Cong., 1st Sess. (proposing to require new television sets to be equipped with circuitry to block the transmission of violent programs—the so-called "V-chip").

85. Section 551(b) of the 1996 Act amended Section 303 of the Communications Act and empowered the FCC to prescribe "guidelines and recommended procedures for the identification and rating of video programming that contains sexual, violent, and other indecent material about which parents should be informed before it is displayed to children." 47 U.S.C.A. § 303(w)(1) (West Supp. 1997). Under this section, program ratings would be devised "on the basis of recommendations from an advisory committee established by the Commission" composed of "parents, television programming producers, cable operators, appropriate public interest groups, and other interested individuals from the private sector," but only if the FCC determined that video programming distributors had not "established voluntary rules for rating video programming that ... are acceptable to the Commission" and "agreed voluntari-

provision characterized it as non-regulatory.[86] In addition, the Conference Committee analysis of Section 551 stated that "nothing in [the law] authorizes, and the conferees do not intend that, the Commission require the adoption of the recommended rating system nor that any particular program be rated."[87]

In early 1997 the television industry implemented—and proposed for FCC acceptance—a six-tier rating system conceptually similar to the MPAA rating system for feature films. The proposed system included the ratings of TV–Y (program is appropriate for all children), TV–Y7 (appropriate for children seven and above), TV–G (appropriate for all ages), TV–PG (parental guidance suggested), TV–14 (appropriate for children fourteen and above) and TV–MA (appropriate for mature audiences). News and sports programming were exempt. The system was criticized immediately for being insufficiently "content-based" and for being applied inconsistently.[88] In response to intense congressional pressure, the industry in mid–1997 revised its ratings plan to include content-designators to be added at the end of a rating. They included "S" (for sex), "V" (for violence), "L" (for language) "D" (for suggestive dialogue) and "FV" (for fantasy violence). In addition, the industry created a 19-person Oversight Monitoring Board to ensure "accuracy, uniformity and consistency" in the use of ratings.[89] The FCC accordingly cancelled a scheduled hearing on the industry system[90] and key members of Congress pledged "a substantial period of governmental forbearance during which further legislation or regulation concerning television ratings, content or scheduling should be set aside."[91] The FCC approved the

---

ly to broadcast signals that contain ratings of such programming." Section 551(b)(1) provides for rules prescribing the transmission of ratings information adopted in accordance with the industry-devised system. 47 U.S.C.A. § 303(w)(2)(West Supp. 1991).

86. Senator Kent Conrad stated that "Section 551 does not mandate a government ratings system, or that a program be rated if a broadcaster refuses to rate programming." 142 Cong. Rec. S702 (Feb. 1, 1996). He added that "[n]o penalties are established by this provision if a television broadcaster's cable operator refuses to develop ratings, or apply whatever ratings or identification system is established voluntarily, or by the advisory committee under the FCC. The development of any rating or other television program identification is entirely voluntary—the effectiveness of the V–Chip technology as an aid for parents rests with television broadcasters and cable operators, not the Federal Government." *Id.* Similarly, Congressman Edward Markey, sponsor of the V-chip legislation in the House, stated that "[a]ll of the ratings will be done voluntarily by the broadcasters. There is no mandate. There is no enforcement mechanism. There is absolutely no

connective tissue between this bill and any first amendment violation." 141 Cong. Rec. H8486 (Aug. 4, 1995).

87. Conf. Rpt. No. 458, 104th Cong., 2d Sess. 195 (Jan. 31, 1996).

88. Marcia S. Smith, V-Chip and TV Ratings: Helping Parents Supervise Their Children's Television Viewing 3 (Cong. Res. Serv., Aug. 1, 1997).

89. Agreement on Modifications to the TV Parental Guidelines, released with Joint Statement of the Motion Picture Association of America, National Association of Broadcasters and the National Cable Television Association (July 10, 1997). The NBC Television Network and Black Entertainment Television did not agree to the industry plan.

90. *See* Smith, *supra* note 88 at 3.

91. "Dear Colleague" Letter from Senator John McCain, *et. al.*, July 8, 1997; Letter to Jack Valenti, Decker Anstrom and Eddie Fritts from Congressman Edward Markey, *et. al.*, July 7, 1997 (proposing a three-year moratorium on "legislation or regulations designed to influence the airing of controversial content").

industry's rating system in 1998.[92]

Despite assurances in the legislative history regarding the non-regulatory nature of V-chip requirements, the significant extent of government participation in developing an "acceptable" ratings plan in advance of the official FCC decision on the issue casts doubt on whether the scheme is truly voluntary. A Congressional Research Service analysis acknowledged that President Clinton exerted political pressure on the industry to develop a ratings system, and noted that "Congress has been deeply involved in the TV ratings debate both formally and informally."[93] On its face, the opportunity for the television industry to adopt a voluntary ratings system was written into federal law, with the proviso that the FCC would make its own "recommendation" if business failed to develop an "acceptable" scheme. Moreover, Senator John McCain, Chairman of the Senate Commerce Committee warned one network that if it failed to adopt the modified ratings system he would "pursue a series of alternative ways of safeguarding, by law and regulation, the interests that [you] refuse to safeguard voluntarily."[94] Other members of Congress introduced legislation that would require broadcasters to time channel violent programming to safe harbor hours.[95] Apart from questions about whether the rating system is voluntary or mandatory, the V-chip provisions of the Telecommunications Act and continuing legislative proposals raise important questions regarding the government's constitutional authority to regulate violent programming. Although there is little direct precedent on the precise question, proponents of such measures have assumed that the government's constitutional ability to regulate violent speech flows naturally from its authority to regulate indecency. Attorney General Janet Reno informed Congress that the industry could be required to make specific proposals to curb violent programming and that if it failed to comply voluntarily the government could compel such results through legislation. The constitutional authority the Attorney General cited for these conclusions was *FCC v. Pacifica Foundation*.[96]

Despite such rhetoric, the FCC has rejected direct appeals to regulate televised violence. In 1998 a citizens group petitioned the Commission to deny the license renewals of television stations in Denver based

---

92. Implementation of Section 551 of the Telecommunications Act of 1996, Video Programming Ratings, 13 FCC Rcd. 8232 (1998). The FCC also approved technical standards for the V–chip. Technical Requirements to Enable Blocking of Video Programming Based on Program Ratings, FCC 98–36 (rel. Mar. 13, 1998).

93. Smith, *supra* note 88 at 2, 4. *See also* Pres. Documents, Mar. 4, 1996, Vol. 32, No 9, 386–389.

94. Letter from Senator John McCain to Robert Wright, President and CEO of the National Broadcasting Company (Sept. 29, 1997). Senator McCain wrote that he would

urge the FCC to subject the network's owned stations to license renewal hearings if it did not adopt the FCC-approved ratings system, and would support legislation that would require the network to channel violent programming to late night hours.

95. *See* S. 363, 105th Cong., 1st Sess.(1997); H.R. 910, 105th Cong. 1st Sess. (1997). *See also* Smith, *supra* note 88 at 4–5.

96. *See Reno Endorses Bills to Deal With TV Violence, Communications Daily*, October 21, 1993 at 2; TV Rocked by Reno Ultimatum, McAvoy and Coe, Broadcasting and Cable, October 25, 1993 at 6.

on content analysis of local evening newscasts. It alleged that 45 to 55 percent of the newscasts was devoted to stories about crime, disasters, war and terrorism. According to the petition, the newscasts suffered from "toxic TV news syndrome." The FCC rejected the petition, however, "for reasons rooted in the First Amendment and the no censorship provision of Section 326 of the Communications Act."[97] Similarly, courts have rejected regulations that attempted to target violent speech. The Supreme Court invalidated a state law that curbed the publication of magazines "devoted principally to criminal news and stories of bloodshed, lust or crime."[98] The United States Court of Appeals for the Eighth Circuit struck down restrictions on rentals of violent videotape to minors, finding that violent video programming is entitled to "the highest degree of First Amendment protection."[99] As the United States Court of Appeals for the Seventh Circuit noted, "violence on television . . . is protected speech, however insidious. Any other answer leaves the government in control of all the institutions of culture, the great censor and director of which thoughts are good for us."[100] Consistent with these decisions, the Tennessee Supreme Court has noted that "every court that has considered the issue has invalidated attempts to regulate materials solely based on violent content, regardless of whether that material is called violence, excess violence, or included within the definition of obscenity."[1]

4.   *Advertising*

The FCC historically has used its broadcast licensing power to exert some control over advertising. In its 1946 report, Public Service Responsibility of Broadcast Licensees (the "Blue Book"), the FCC examined the advertising practices of broadcast licensees as a component of the public interest. The report reviewed instances in which renewals had been denied because of over-commercialization. The Commission applied such policies case by case and had no formal rules prohibiting stations from carrying too many commercials. Such a rule was proposed in the 1960s,

---

97. Letter to Dr. Paul Klite, 1998 WL 208060 (1998).

98. Winters v. New York, 333 U.S. at 510–11, 68 S. Ct. at 667–668, 92 L.Ed. at 847–848. ("What is one man's amusement, teaches another's doctrine. Though we can see nothing of any possible value to society in these magazines, they are as much entitled to the protection of free speech as the best of literature.").

99. Video Software Dealers Association v. Webster, 968 F.2d 684 (8th Cir.1992).

100. American Booksellers Ass'n, Inc. v. Hudnut, 771 F.2d 323, 330 (7th Cir.1985), *aff'd mem.*, 475 U.S. 1001, 106 S.Ct. 1172, 89 L.Ed.2d 291 (1986). *See also* Harry T. Edwards and Mitchell N. Berman, *Regulating Violence on Television*, 89 Nw. U.L. Rev. 1487, 1565 (1995) ("When it comes to televised violence, we cannot imagine how regulators can distinguish between harmless and harmful violent speech, and . . . can find no proposal that overcomes the lack of supporting data."); Patricia M. Wald, *Doing Right by Our Kids: A Case Study in the Perils of Making Policy on Television Violence*, 23 U.Balt.L.Rev. 397 (1994).

1. Davis-Kidd Booksellers, Inc. v. McWherter, 866 S.W.2d 520, 531 (Tenn. 1993). *See also* Eclipse Enterprises, Inc. v. Gulotta, 134 F.3d 63 (2d Cir.1997); Olivia N. v. National Broadcasting Co., 126 Cal. App.3d 488, 178 Cal.Rptr. 888, 894 (Cal.Ct. App.1981) (rejecting relevance of *Pacifica* outside the context of "indecent" programming); Zamora v. Columbia Broadcasting System, 480 F.Supp. 199 (S.D.Fla.1979).

however, by former Chairman Newton Minow.[2] Although this policy was never adopted, license renewal applications required licensees to disclose the amount of time devoted to commercials. Based on that information, and relying on industry-developed codes of conduct, the FCC staff implemented an informal "processing guideline" that limited commercial content to 18 minutes per hour in most circumstances.[3] These standards were briefly incorporated into the FCC's rules, but were eliminated in the 1980s.[4] Apart from the Commission's historic use of the licensing process to limit broadcast advertising, its efforts to regulate advertising under its "inherent" authority are fairly rare. During one seven year period, between 1967 and 1974, the FCC experimented with directly regulating cigarette advertising under its public interest mandate.[5] At the end of that period and following an extensive proceeding reevaluating its policies, the FCC concluded that it had been a "great mistake" to attempt such regulation and that "it is questionable whether this Commission has a mandate so broad as to permit it to scan the airwaves for offensive material with no more discriminating a lens than the 'public interest' or even the 'public health.' "[6]

Accordingly, FCC authority over advertising typically flows from specific statutory grants of jurisdiction. With respect to cigarettes, for example, Congress banned the advertising of cigarettes and little cigars from "any medium of electronic communication subject to the jurisdiction of the Federal Communications Commission."[7] Federal law also prohibits any broadcast station from knowingly permitting "the broadcasting of any advertisement of or information concerning any lottery, gift, enterprise, or similar scheme."[8] In addition, the Children's Television Act of 1990 limits the amount of advertising in children's programming,[9] and political advertising is subject to special statutory requirements.[10] Finally, the Communications Act requires broadcasters to identify sponsored programming.[11]

2. *See* Erwin G. Krasnow, Lawrence D. Longley and Herbert A. Terry, The Politics of Broadcast Regulation 192–205 (St. Martin's Press, 3rd ed. 1982).

3. *See* Deregulation of Radio, 84 F.C.C.2d 968, 1092 (1981).

4. *Id.*

5. *See* WCBS–TV, 8 F.C.C.2d 381, (1967), *stay and recons. denied*, 9 F.C.C.2d 921 (1967); The Handling of Public Issues Under the Fairness Doctrine and the Public Interest Standards of the Communications Act, 48 F.C.C.2d 1 (1974) ("Fairness Doctrine Report"), *aff'd*, National Citizens Committee for Broadcasting v. FCC, 567 F.2d 1095, 186 U.S. App. D.C. 102 (D.C.Cir. 1977), cert. denied, 436 U.S. 926, 98 S.Ct. 2820, 56 L.Ed.2d 769 (1978).

6. Fairness Doctrine Report, 48 F.C.C.2d at 25, n. 22, quoting Banzhaf v. FCC, 405 F.2d 1082, 1099, 132 U.S. App. D.C. 14, 31 (D.C.Cir.1968), cert. denied, 396 U.S. 842, 90 S. Ct. 50, 24 L.Ed.2d 93 (1969).

Similarly, in a 1969 Notice of Proposed Rulemaking on tobacco advertising, the Commission stressed that the "question of an across-the-board [cigarette advertising] ban is of course one solely for the Congress." Amendment of Part 73 of the Federal Communications Commission Rules With Regard to the Advertisement of Cigarettes, 16 F.C.C.2d 284, 289 (1969).

7. 15 U.S.C.A. § 1335 (West 1991).

8. 18 U.S.C.A. § 1304 (West 1991). The law exempts advertising for certain lotteries or other gambling enterprises, such as state-conducted lotteries (18 U.S.C.A. § 1307 (West 1991)), and gambling enterprises on Native American reservations. *See* Indian Gaming Regulatory Act, 25 U.S.C.A. § 2701 (West 1991); 47 C.F.R. § 73.1211(c)(3) (1997).

9. Pub. L. 101–437, 104 Stat. 996–1000, *codified at* 47 U.S.C.A. § 303b (West 1991).

10. 47 U.S.C.A. §§ 312(a)(7), 315 (West 1991).

a. Cigarette Advertising

Since the early 1970s, the advertisement of tobacco products on any medium of electronic communications regulated by the FCC has been prohibited.[12] The ban has survived a constitutional challenge but the decision predated the Supreme Court's extension of First Amendment protection to commercial speech.[13] The district court decision upholding the tobacco ad ban reiterated the attenuated First Amendment protections afforded to the broadcast medium and relied upon the limited First Amendment protections applicable to advertising.[14] The court noted that the law did not impose a complete ban on speech since broadcasters could present non-commercial pro-smoking messages.[15] It also rejected an equal protection challenge based on the distinction made by Congress between broadcasting and the print media.[16]

Even before the law was enacted the FCC had experimented with requiring counter-advertising for cigarette product advertising under the fairness doctrine.[17] The Commission reasoned that advertisement that promoted smoking presented one side of a controversial issue of public importance and that counter-advertising was necessary to provide a balanced presentation of views. In upholding this policy, the United States Court of Appeals for the District of Columbia Circuit found that the obligation to run counter-advertising arose "not from any esoteric requirements of a particular doctrine but from the simple fact that the

---

11. *Id.* §§ 317, 508. *See* 47 C.F.R. § 73.1212 (1997).

12. 15 U.S.C.A. § 1335 (West 1991).

13. In 1976, the Supreme Court abandoned what it described as a "simplistic" and "highly paternalistic" approach that enabled the government to "suppress the dissemination of concededly truthful information about entirely lawful activity" on the theory that the government knew best how to protect the health of the public. Virginia State Board of Pharmacy v. Virginia Citizens Consumer Council, 425 U.S. 748, 759, 769, 772, 96 S.Ct. 1817, 1824, 1829, 1831, 48 L.Ed.2d 346, 356–357, 362–363, 365 (1976). Since then, the Supreme Court has invalidated restrictions on the advertising of contraceptives that government considered "offensive" or that it thought "would legitimize sexual activity of young people." Carey v. Population Services Int'l, 431 U.S. 678, 701, 97 S.Ct. 2010, 2024, 52 L.Ed.2d 675, 694–695 (1977); Bolger v. Youngs Drug Products Corp., 463 U.S. 60, 103 S.Ct. 2875, 77 L.Ed.2d 469 (1983). The Supreme Court's most recent pronouncements on the subject accorded stronger First Amendment protection to commercial speech relating to alcohol. 44 Liquormart, Inc. v. Rhode Island, 517 U.S. 484, 116 S.Ct. 1495, 134 L.Ed.2d 711 (1996); Rubin v. Coors Brewing Co., 514 U.S., 476, 115 S.Ct. 1585, 131 L.Ed.2d 532 (1995). *See also* Martin Redish, *Tobacco Advertising and the First Amendment*, 81 Iowa L. Rev. 589, 631–632 (1996) ("the decision originally upholding the [cigarette advertising] ban should be deemed to have no precedential force, because it was decided long before the Supreme Court extended substantial First Amendment protection to commercial speech"). *But see* Anheuser–Busch, Inc. v. Schmoke, 101 F.3d 325 (4th Cir.1996), cert. denied, 520 U.S. 1204, 117 S.Ct. 1569, 137 L.Ed.2d 714 (1997) (allowing the City of Baltimore to regulate the locations of billboards for alcohol products).

14. Capital Broadcasting Co. v. Mitchell, 333 F.Supp. 582, 584 (D.D.C.1971), *aff'd sub nom.* Capital Broadcasting Co. v. Kleindienst, 405 U.S. 1000, 92 S.Ct. 1289, 31 L.Ed.2d 472 (1972).

15. *Id.*

16. *Id.* at 857.

17. WCBS–TV, 8 F.C.C.2d 381, *stay and recons. denied*, 9 F.C.C.2d 921 (1967).

public interest means nothing if it does not include ... a responsibility" to inform listeners of the other side.[18]

Despite the FCC's stated intention to apply the policy only to cigarettes, it was quickly overrun with demands for counter-advertising in a wide variety of situations. Demands for time arose from retail store advertising during a labor dispute,[19] automobile advertisements,[20] gasoline advertising,[21] institutional advertising praising commercial television,[22] advertisements advocating oil exploration,[23] institutional advertisements for a power company,[24] army recruiting advertisements,[25] advertisements for snowmobiles[26] and even advertisements for dog food.[27] Although the FCC rejected some demands for counter-advertising (army recruiting, gasoline additives, snowmobiles, etc.), it accepted others (oil exploration, utility rates, retail advertising). Even in cases where the FCC did not mandate responsive ads, the court of appeals did. Thus, in *Friends of the Earth v. FCC*, the District of Columbia Circuit reversed the denial of a complaint regarding advertisements for high-powered cars. The court rejected the FCC's claim that cigarettes are a "unique" product and was "unable to see how the Commission can plausibly differentiate the case presently before us from *Banzhaf*."[28]

The Commission's problem in fashioning a coherent "public interest" response to issues arising from product advertising resulted in an extensive examination of the issues. It led to a five-year proceeding in which 120 written comments were filed. The Commission also convened a week-long series of panel discussions and oral arguments. At the conclusion of this extensive fact-finding, the FCC concluded that it had been a "great mistake" to impose counter-advertising requirements and it expressly declined to do so in the future.[29] In particular, the FCC found that the policy had become "particularly troublesome" because it could not be limited to cigarette advertising as planned.[30] The United States Court of Appeals for the District of Columbia Circuit agreed that the Commission had "great difficulties" in fashioning a rational policy regarding counter-advertisements and found that "if anything, [the

18. Banzhaf v. FCC, 405 F.2d 1082, 1093, 132 U.S. App. D.C. 14, 25 (D.C.Cir. 1968), cert. denied, 396 U.S. 842, 90 S. Ct. 50, 24 L.Ed.2d 93 (1969).

19. Retail Store Employees Union, Local 880 Retail Clerks International Ass'n, AFL–CIO v. FCC, 436 F.2d 248, 141 U.S. App. D.C. 94 (D.C.Cir.1970).

20. Friends of the Earth v. FCC, 449 F.2d 1164, 146 U.S. App. D.C. 88 (D.C.Cir. 1971).

21. Neckritz v. FCC, 502 F.2d 411, 163 U.S. App. D.C. 409 (D.C.Cir.1974).

22. Anthony R. Martin–Trigona, 19 F.C.C.2d 620, 622 (1969).

23. National Broadcasting, 30 F.C.C.2d 643 (1971).

24. Media Access Project, 44 F.C.C.2d 755 (1973).

25. Green v. FCC, 447 F.2d 323, 144 U.S. App. D.C. 353 (D.C.Cir.1971).

26. Public Interest Research Group v. FCC, 522 F.2d 1060 (1st Cir.1975), cert. denied, 424 U.S. 965, 96 S.Ct. 1458, 47 L.Ed.2d 731 (1976).

27. Complaint by Mrs. Fran Lee, Director, Children Before Dogs, Concerning Fairness Doctrine re Stations WNBC–TV–AM–FM, 37 F.C.C.2d 647 (1972).

28. Friends of the Earth, 449 F.2d at 1170, 146 U.S. App. D.C. at 94.

29. Fairness Doctrine Report, 48 F.C.C. 2d at 26.

30. *Id.* at 25.

FCC] understated the problem."[31] Both the Commission and the court subsequently retreated from the view that the FCC could implement such a policy under its general public interest mandate.[32]

One reason the FCC abandoned the counter-advertising policy was the perception that the FCC was "not really encouraging a balanced debate but, rather, [was] simply imposing [its] view that discouraging smoking was in the public interest."[33] Ultimately, the FCC defended its policy decisions regarding cigarette advertisements by pointing to the unique dangers inherent in the "normal use of the product" that "threatens a substantial body of the population, not merely a peculiarly susceptible fringe group."[34] The FCC concluded that there was no "debate" over the health effects of smoking, based on scientific reports, government studies and congressional action, and therefore no need to present "the other side."

b. Lottery Advertising

The United States Criminal Code and FCC rules prohibit the broadcast of "any advertisement of, or information concerning any lottery."[35] Although seemingly quite categorical, the lottery ad ban has been modified over the years through a series of exceptions. For example, the law permits the advertisement of lotteries run by state governments[36] for legal charity lotteries,[37] and for lotteries conducted on Native American Land.[38]

A prohibited lottery must include three elements: prize, chance, and consideration.[39] That is, there must be a valuable prize at stake which does not require skill to win and for which the contestant gives something in exchange. Although the test is easily stated, it is not always a simple matter to distinguish skill from chance. A guessing game obviously involves luck whereas picking the winner of a sporting even might be a game of skill. The question of consideration also requires some analysis. Generally, consideration entails paying money, buying the sponsor's product or expending substantial time or effort.[40] The Supreme Court

---

31. National Citizens Committee for Broadcasting, 567 F.2d at 1100, 186 U.S. App. D.C. at 107.

32. *Id.* at 1108, 186 U.S. App. D.C. at 115.

33. Fairness Doctrine Report, 48 F.C.C.2d at 25. *See id.* at 25 n.21 ("Following the Congressional ban on cigarette advertising, the Commission was criticized even more strongly for taking sides on this issue.").

34. Formulation of Appropriate Further Regulatory Policies Concerning Cigarette Advertising and Anti–Smoking Presentations, 27 F.C.C.2d 453, 457 (1970) (citation omitted), *aff'd* Larus & Brother Co. v. FCC, 447 F.2d 876 (4th Cir.1971).

35. 18 U.S.C.A. § 1304 (West 1991); 47 C.F.R. § 73.1211 (1997).

36. *Id.* § 1307.

37. *Id.* § 1307(2)(A).

38. 25 U.S.C.A. § 2701 (West 1991); 47 C.F.R. § 73.1211(c)(3) (1997).

39. FCC v. American Broadcasting Co., 347 U.S. 284, 74 S.Ct. 593, 98 L.Ed. 699 (1954).

40. 47 C.F.R. § 73.1211 (1997). Based apparently on a staff complaint, Commission personnel investigated "Allyns Pants Ranch," which advertised on six Washington, D.C. radio stations a promotion involving "the Pants Ranch Wheel of Fortune." Four attorneys from the Commission's staff concluded that to participate, one indeed had to purchase a pair of pants. Although the licensees had been assured by the advertiser that its promotion was not a lot-

has held that simply listening to the sponsor's broadcast does not represent sufficient consideration to trigger the lottery rules.[41]

The Commission has developed analyses for coping with advertising for casinos. The word "casino" may be used only if it is part of the official name of the business establishment. Additionally, the advertisement must focus on food, entertainment or some other attribute unrelated to gambling activities. Otherwise, the advertisement will be considered a prohibited spot.

The continuing validity of the lottery advertising ban is uncertain as courts subject the rule to First Amendment scrutiny. In *United States v. Edge Broadcasting Co.*, the Supreme Court upheld against a First Amendment challenge of the lottery restriction in states that do not sponsor a government lottery.[42] However, the Court's decision was highly fragmented, with seven justices writing opinions and none relying on *Red Lion Broadcasting* or other broadcast-related precedent. The decision ultimately relied on the commercial speech doctrine. However, subsequent decisions cast doubt on the continuing constitutionality of the lottery advertising ban. In *Valley Broadcasting Co. v. United States*, the United States Court of Appeals for the Ninth Circuit held that the ban on broadcast advertising for casino gambling violated the First Amendment.[43] For further discussion of the ban on lottery and casino advertising see Chapter 3, section 3.15.B.5, *supra*.

c. Children's Advertising

The Children's Television Act of 1990 and implementing regulations limit commercial matter to twelve minutes per hour during children's programming on week days, and ten and a half minutes per hour on weekends.[44] The restrictions apply only to programming directed toward children twelve years and younger regardless of when it is transmitted or the actual audience demographics.[45] Since the rules became effective in 1992, the FCC has vigorously enforced the commercial time limits. It has issued numerous fines for violations, some in excess of $100,000.[46] In

tery, the FCC fined the station for running the advertisements. Metromedia, Inc., 60 F.C.C.2d 1075 (1976).

41. American Broadcasting Co., 347 U.S. at 290–294, 74 S. Ct. at 597–599, 98 L.Ed. At 705–708.

42. 509 U.S. 418, 113 S.Ct. 2696, 125 L.Ed.2d 345 (1993).

43. 107 F.3d 1328 (9th Cir.1997), *cert. denied* ___ U.S. ___, 118 S.Ct. 1050, 140 L.Ed.2d 114 (1998). *See also* Players Int'l, Inc. v. United States, 988 F.Supp. 497 (D.N.J.1997). *But see* Greater New Orleans Broadcasting Association v. United States, 149 F.3d 334 (5th Cir.1998) (upholding lottery advertising ban), cert. granted ___ U.S. ___, 119 S.Ct. 863, 142 L.Ed.2d 716 (1999).

44. 47 U.S.C.A. § 303(b) (West 1991); 47 C.F.R. § 73.670 (1997).

45. Policies and Rules Concerning Children's Television Programming, Report and Order, 6 FCC Rcd. 7199 (1990). *See also* 47 C.F.R. §§ 73.670–73.672 (1997).

46. After completing an audit of station compliance with the advertising limits in 1998, the Mass Media Bureau found that 26 percent of commercial television stations could not certify full compliance. Mass Media Bureau Advises Commercial Television Licensees Regarding Children's Television Commercial Limits, DA 98–950 (rel. May 20, 1998). The Bureau noted that forfeitures had been assessed against at least 85 licensees for exceeding the commercial limits. *See, e.g.*, Notice of Apparent Liability to Jasas Corp., FCC 97–190 (rel. June 3, 1997) ($115,000); Clear Channel Television, Inc. (KTTU–TV), 10 FCC Rcd. 3773 (1995)

addition to forfeitures, license renewal is tied to compliance with the advertising limits.

The FCC's rules also prohibit "host-selling" during children's television programming as well as program-length commercials. Host-selling occurs where the host of a children's program, or a character from the program, delivers advertising or endorses a product, in character, in (or adjacent to) a program in which the host or character appears. The prohibition applies to all characters in a children's program, and not just the "host" or main character. A program-length commercial is a children's program that is associated with a product or service in which commercials for that product or service are aired. The rules require that commercial materials must be separated from a children's program to which it is related by "intervening and unrelated program material."[47] If a show is classified as a program-length commercial, the entire program is counted as commercial time.[48]

FCC rules include public file requirements to monitor compliance with the children's advertising rules. Records documenting commercial time during children's programming must be placed in the public file on a quarterly basis. The records must be maintained for the entire renewal term. The licensee must also list the name of the individual at the station who is responsible for compliance with the children's television rules.[49]

5. News Slanting and Hoaxes

FCC policies prohibit the deliberate staging or distortion of news events. In 1969, the Commission investigated the presentation of a documentary called "Hunger in America" in which the producers presented a "malnourished" infant, who was later discovered to be suffering from an unrelated medical condition.[50] As a result of that investigation, the Commission articulated policies requiring the presentation of authentic news events while otherwise deferring to the editorial judgment of licensees.[51] When investigating allegations of news slanting, the Commission first examines whether the story is deliberately misleading, and

($125,000); Stainless Broadcasting Co., (WICZ–TV), 10 FCC Rcd. 9961 (1995) ($110,000). *See also* Paramount Stations of Houston, Inc. 9 FCC Rcd. 149 (1993) ($80,000); Koplar Communications, 8 FCC Rcd. 7884 (1993) ($30,000); Independent Communications, Inc. 8 FCC Rcd. 7886 (1993) ($27,500); Paramount Stations Group of Kerrville, Inc. 8 FCC Rcd. 7064 (1993) (15,000); Big Horn Communications, Inc., 8 FCC Rcd. 5081 (1993) ($15,000); WKPD, Inc. 8 FCC Rcd. 5079 (1993) ($15,000); KEVN, Inc. 8 FCC Rcd. 5077 (1993) ($15,000); Bay Television, Inc., 8 FCC Rcd. 412 (1993) ($10,000); Tampa Bay Television, Inc. 8 FCC Rcd. 411, (1993) ($10,000); Le-Sea Broadcasting Corp., 8 FCC Rcd. 336 (1993) ($20,000).

47. *See* Children's Television Programming, 6 FCC Rcd. at 2118.

48. *Id.*

49. 47 C.F.R. § 73.3526(a)(8)(iii) (1997).

50. Hunger in America, 20 F.C.C.2d 143 (1969). *See* Serafyn v. FCC, 149 F.3d 1213, 331 U.S.App.D.C. 340 (D.C.Cir.1998) (holding that the FCC had established too high a threshold for evaluating extrinsic evidence of news slanting in complaint against CBS news program "60 Minutes").

51. Galloway v. FCC, 778 F.2d 16, 250 U.S. App. D.C. 143 (D.C.Cir.1985).

is supported by extrinsic evidence.[52] Under the FCC policy, any distortion must relate to a significant aspect of the story rather than something incidental to the news report. Thus, if an event is staged but it does not affect the overall accuracy of the report, the Commission is unlikely to intervene.[53] Staging may also be acceptable if fully disclosed.[54]

The news staging policy requires the Commission to carefully balance its public interest concerns with the First Amendment rights of journalists. On one hand, press conferences and photo opportunities are, essentially, staged events, yet both are widely reported.[55] In one early case, an inexperienced reporter producing a documentary about the use of marijuana invited college students to stage a "pot party" which was later made part of the documentary. The station employing the reporter was sanctioned by the Commission, despite its instructions to the reporter not to stage the event.[56] On the other hand, a reporter who told disgruntled customers of a business he would be filming the next day in Small Claims Court was deemed not to have staged a news event because the customers were, in fact, disgruntled.[57]

The FCC has also adopted policies regarding news hoaxes. The most famous broadcast hoax involved Orson Welles' presentation of the "War of the Worlds" on Halloween night in 1938. His dramatic presentation of a fictional Martian invasion, which caused widespread panic, is considered a milestone of American broadcasting. Nevertheless, a station airing a contemporary interpretation of the event, which included disclaimers airing prior to and forty-seven minutes into the broadcast, resulted in Commission sanctions against the station.[58] In instances of April Fool's pranks, licensees that took remedial steps, such as firing the responsible personnel, have simply been admonished.[59] More serious violations have resulted in the imposition of sizable forfeitures, as for example, the St. Louis radio station that broadcast an emergency broadcasting alert tone, and reported that the United States was under nuclear attack.[60]

Based on the St. Louis incident, the FCC clarified its policy against hoaxes. It now prohibits the broadcast of false information concerning a crime or catastrophe if the licensee knows the information is false, if it is foreseeable the broadcast will cause "substantial public harm" and if the

52. Hunger in America, 20 F.C.C.2d at 151.

53. WPIX, Inc. 68 F.C.C.2d 381. *See also* Oscar B. White, 87 F.C.C.2d 954, 959–960 (1981).

54. WBBM–TV, 18 F.C.C.2d 124, 132–133 (1969).

55. Another example of permissible staging involves an interview, where the reporter, after finishing with the subject, is then filmed asking the questions. This is known as a "reverse" and is inserted into the interview to create the appearance of a dialogue. *See* Galloway, 778 F.2d at 20, n.3, 250 U.S. App. D.C. at 147 n.3.

56. WBBM–TV, 18 F.C.C.2d 124 (1969).

57. Taft Broadcasting Co., 2 FCC Rcd. 6622, 6624–6625 (1987).

58. Capital Cities Communications, Inc. 54 F.C.C.2d 1035 (1975).

59. Station KSLX (FM), Scottsdale Arizona, Oct. 2, 1989, ref. No. 8310–TD, C6–220,(station taken over by Indians); WCCC–FM, Hartford, Connecticut, July 26, 1990, ref. No. 8310–TD, C5–820, Newsweek, April 14, 1980 at 35 (volcano eruption in Connecticut).

60. Emmis Broadcasting Corp. of St. Louis, 6 FCC Rcd. 2289 (1991).

broadcast actually causes "substantial public harm."[61] The rule does not apply to programming accompanied by a disclaimer that characterizes the program as fiction and that is "reasonable under the circumstances."[62] The FCC made clear that licensees will not be held accountable for unreasonable or unpredictable public reactions. However, the timing of a broadcast (*i.e.*, April Fool's Day), and the "inherent unbelievability" of a story are simply factors the Commission may consider in assessing a complaint. The Commission reaffirmed that licensees are accountable for the actions of their employees.[63]

14.6   Enforcement of Broadcast Rules

A.   *Private Enforcement: Petitions to Deny*

The process of enforcing FCC rules includes members of the public[1] and competing broadcasters[2] who are authorized to file petitions to deny the grant of a license or a transfer. The Commission must schedule a hearing on matters raised in the petition if the petitioner presents a "substantial or material question of fact" that grant of the license would not be in the public interest or that the licensee is unqualified.[3] Upon such a demonstration, the FCC formally designates the application for hearing, and notifies both the applicant and all other known parties in interest.[4]

For most services, a petition to deny may be filed any time prior to the grant of a license. In some cases, Commission rules establish a specific cut-off date for petitions.[5] Licensees generally have thirty days to respond to a petition to deny to which the petitioner has twenty days for a reply.[6] Even if a petition to deny is rejected for procedural defects the Commission generally will treat the petition as an informal objection and address the substance of the petition.[7] Competing broadcasters often file petitions to deny where the grant of a license or the modification of its terms will cause interference.[8]

Individual members of the listening or viewing public have standing to file petitions to deny to the extent that their concerns are representa-

---

61.   47 C.F.R. § 73.1217 (1997). "Public harm" must begin immediately and cause direct and actual damage to property or to the health or safety of the general public. Public harm may include the diversion of law enforcement or other public health or safety personnel form their duties.

62.   *Id.*

63.   Amendment of Part 73 Regarding Broadcast Hoaxes, 7 FCC Rcd 4106 (1992).

1.   Office of Communication of United Church of Christ v. FCC, 359 F.2d 994, 123 U.S. App. D.C. 328 (D.C.Cir.1966).

2.   Northern Pacific Radio Corp., 23 Rad. Reg. 186 (P&F 1962); Gordon Broadcasting of San Francisco, Inc., 22 Rad. Reg. 236 (P&F 1962). However, the Telecommu-

nications Act of 1996 effectively removed competing broadcasters from the license renewal process. Telecommunications Act of 1996, Pub. L. 104–104, § 204, 110 Stat. 56 (1996).

3.   47 U.S.C.A. § 309(d) (West Supp. 1997).

4.   *Id.* § 309(e) (West 1991).

5.   47 C.F.R. § 73.3584 (1997).

6.   *Id.* § 73.3584(b).

7.   *Id.* § 1.717.

8.   47 U.S.C.A. § 316(a)(2)(West 1991). *See e.g.*, Cornwell Broadcasting Corp. 89 F.C.C.2d 716 (1981); Amendment of Section 73.202(b), Table of Assignments, FM Broadcast Stations, 70 F.C.C.2d 2007 (1979).

tive of "broad public interest values."[9] Petitions filed by the public generally seek to achieve non-financial goals, such as obtaining certain programming by the licensee, forcing the broadcaster to address issues of community concern or encouraging the broadcaster to improve its record of hiring minorities.[10]

While standing may be readily conferred on a petitioning party, the Commission has been reluctant to act on the vast number of petitions filed. One study found that the Commission acted on only five percent of the petitions it had received,[11] and in only one instance did it deny the license.[12] However, formal FCC action is not the only measure of the impact of such petitions. A licensee may make concessions either to the FCC or to the petitioner in order to resolve the proceeding. In this regard, the Commission has found it necessary to police the settlement arrangements between petitioners and incumbent broadcasters. In 1981, the FCC began an inquiry out of concern that many petitions to deny had been initiated for the sole purpose of obtaining a cash settlement with the incumbent licensee.[13] The Commission subsequently adopted rules requiring FCC approval of all settlements, and limiting cash settlements to the parties' "prudent and legitimate" expenses.[14] This policy was extended in 1990 to cover non-financial agreements between citizen's groups and licensees.[15]

Under the Terms of the Telecommunication Act of 1996, comparative hearings have been eliminated for license renewals.[16] With this development, competing broadcasters are now generally foreclosed from filing petitions to deny, which was done almost exclusively at the renewal phase. However, the Commission will still consider petitions to deny filed by members of the public.

B. Public Enforcement

The FCC has a variety of administrative tools which it can bring to bear on a licensee to insure compliance with its rules. Public enforcement options range from sanctions such as admonishment or forfeiture to the ultimate penalty—license revocation.

9. Such standing cannot be based on economic interests of the petitioner. *See* Tele–Vue Systems, Inc., 32 F.C.C.2d 876 (1971) (minority stockholders petition to deny barred on basis of pecuniary motives).

10. Formulation of Policies and Rules Relating to Broadcast Renewal Applicants, First Report and Order, 4 FCC Rcd. 4780, 4785 (1989). *But see* Lutheran Church–Missouri Synod v. FCC, 141 F.3d 344, 329 U.S.App.D.C. 381 (D.C.Cir.1998) (invalidating FCC EEO rules).

11. Harold L. Nelson and Dwight L. Teeter, Jr., Law of Mass Communications 567 (3d ed. 1978).

12. Alabama Educational Television Commission, 50 F.C.C.2d 461 (1975).

13. Notice of Inquiry in BC Docket No. 81–742, 88 F.C.C.2d 120 (1981).

14. Formulation of Policies and Rules Relating to Broadcast Renewal Applicants, First Report and Order, 4 FCC Rcd. 4780, 4786 (1989).

15. Amendment of Sections 1.420 and 73.3584 of the Commission's Rules Regarding Abuses of the Commission's Processes, 5 FCC Rcd. 3911 (1990).

16. Telecommunications Act of 1996, Pub. L. 104–104 § 309, 110 Stat. 56 (1996).

1. FCC Orders and Forfeitures

The FCC may employ either formal or informal means to enforce its rules. Before it decides to impose more formal sanctions, the Commission, or a Bureau Chief on delegated authority, may send an admonishment to a licensee. Such action generally takes the form of a cautionary letter to the licensee regarding an infraction of the Commission's rules. An admonishment usually is sent in cases of inadvertent violations or on issues of first impression. Typically a letter of admonishment directs the licensee to cease violating FCC rules and requires the licensee to place the letter in its public inspection file.[17] Such letters can be considered at license renewal time, and will be taken into account in assessing any subsequent violation of the same rule.[18]

If a letter of admonishment fails to encourage a licensee to modify its behavior, the Commission may impose more formal sanctions. The Communications Act empowers the FCC to issue cease and desist orders to licensees for a variety of reasons,[19] such as failing to operate substantially under the terms of the license or violating any FCC rule or regulation. Such infractions may include being off the air for a prolonged time,[20] broadcasting obscenity or indecency, engaging in fraudulent practices or violating some other rule.[21] Before a cease and desist order may be issued, the licensee must be served with an order to show cause wherein the Commission specifies the inquiry and the matter in question.[22] A licensee that receives a cease and desist order has a right to a hearing on the matter.[23] A licensee may waive the hearing expressly or by failing to appear. In such cases, the matter is certified to the Commission for final action.[24]

A formal cease and desist order may be avoided where a licensee and the FCC agree to a consent order regarding violations of Commission rules or policies. However, a consent order cannot acknowledge a violation that undermines the licensee's basic statutory qualifications to hold a license.[25] Negotiations for a consent order may be initiated by either party and can be undertaken at any time before the hearing.[26] If an agreement is reached, the designated officer or Chief Administrative Law Judge will either sign the consent order, require the parties to renegotiate or reject the order, whereupon the hearing will proceed.[27] The Commission has final authority over any action on a consent order.[28]

---

17. *See e.g.*, Letter to Henry Broadcasting Co., 9 FCC Rcd. 597 (1994) (admonishment sent to licensee who put set limits on the number of spots a qualified candidate could purchase).

18. *Id.*

19. 47 U.S.C.A. § 312(b) (West 1991).

20. *See, e.g.*, Debrine Communications, Inc., 7 FCC Rcd. 2118 (1992).

21. 47 U.S.C.A. § 312(a) (West 1991).

22. *Id.* § 312(c).

23. *Id. See* 47 C.F.R. § 1.91 (1997). The rules provide that a licensee has at least thirty days to respond to a cease and desist order. The thirty-day limit may be modified in matters where "safety of life or property" is involved.

24. *Id.* § 1.92.

25. *Id.* § 1.93.

26. *Id.* Each party is asked whether it wishes to enter negotiations for a consent order at the pre-hearing conference.

27. *Id.* § 1.94.

28. *Id.* § 1.94(e).

The Commission is also empowered by the Communications Act to assess forfeitures for violations of the Act or FCC rules.[29] A broadcaster may be subject to a forfeiture if it "willfully and repeatedly" fails to comply substantially with the terms of the license, the rules of the Act, treaty obligations or the rules and regulations of the Commission.[30] The Act provides a statute of limitations on forfeiture actions, precluding such penalties for violations that are more than one year old or that took place prior to the date of the current license term, whichever is earlier.[31] Factors the Commission will consider in deciding whether or not to impose a forfeiture include "the nature, circumstances, extent and gravity of the violation; and with respect to the violator, the degree of culpability, any history of prior offenses, and ability to pay and such other matters as justice requires."[32] The Commission had initially assessed forfeitures on a case-by-case basis.[33] In 1989, Congress increased the forfeiture amounts for individual acts to $25,000 for a single violation and $250,000 for a continuing violation.[34] Following this adjustment, the Commission adopted guidelines establishing base forfeitures for specific offenses and adjustment criteria based on various factors, such as willfulness and past history.[35] The United States Court of Appeals for the District of Columbia Circuit vacated the forfeiture guidelines on procedural grounds.[36] However, this did not affect the Commission's substantive ability to assess forfeitures so long as it could justify the amount assessed in particular cases.[37]

The forfeiture procedure is a two-step process. The Commission first sends the licensee a Notice of Apparent Liability ("NAL") that describes the licensee's act, the violation and the proposed forfeiture liability.[38] The licensee is given thirty days to file a written response to the NAL. After considering the response, the Commission may cancel the NAL, modify it or assess the forfeiture.[39] A licensee can challenge a forfeiture

---

29. 47 U.S.C.A. § 503 (West 1991 and Supp. 1997). Forfeitures for violations of common carrier regulations, radio equipment and shipboard radio, and violations of the Great Lakes Agreement are dealt with elsewhere in the Act.

30. *Id.* § 503(b)(1). "Willfully" is defined as a conscious and deliberate commission or omission, irrespective of intent; "repeatedly" means the commission or omission of any act, if continuous, for more than one day. *Id.* § 312(f).

31. 47 C.F.R. § 1.80(b)(4)(C) (1997).

32. *Id.* § 1.80(b)(4). *See* 47 U.S.C.A. § 503(b)(2)(D).

33. In the Matter of Standards for Assessing Forfeitures, Policy Statement, 6 FCC Rcd. 4695 (1991), *modified*, 8 FCC Rcd. 6215 (1993).

34. 47 U.S.C.A. § 503(b)(2)(A)(West 1991).

35. Under the 1991 guidelines, for example, a licensee who intentionally violated

the children's programming advertising requirements, but who later informed the FCC of its conduct, would be assessed a base forfeiture of $10,000, increased as an intentional violation (70 percent + $7,000) and then mitigated by a "good faith disclosure" (–30 percent = $3,000). Following the various calculations, the station would be assessed $14,000 for the violation.

36. USTA v. FCC, 28 F.3d 1232, 307 U.S. App. D.C. 365 (D.C.Cir.1994).

37. *See, e.g.,* KVEO–TV, 12 FCC Rcd. 3324 (1997).

38. 47 C.F.R. § 1.80(f)(1) (1997). This procedure does not apply in a renewal proceeding. *See id.* § 1.80(e).

39. *Id.* § 1.80(f)(4). If a licensee declines to pay the forfeiture, the Department of Justice has the responsibility of enforcing the judgment by filing a collection action in district court. 47 U.S.C.A. § 504(a)(West 1991). Such collection actions are decided in a trial de novo before the district court.

order in United State District Court.[40] Also, if a licensee is involved in another proceeding before the Commission, such as license renewal, the forfeiture component will be addressed at that hearing.[41] In such a case, the Commission is not required to issue a NAL, but must provide the licensee with notice and an opportunity for a full evidentiary hearing prior to execution of the forfeiture.[42]

In 1994, a diverse group of plaintiffs initiated a facial challenge to the FCC's forfeiture procedures in the indecency context.[43] Plaintiffs noted that the procedure lacked safeguards and was based on informal determinations of indecency by Commission staff. Additionally, it was alleged that the Commission would "bootstrap" subsequent forfeitures that had not been subject to a court order and charge the licensee questioning the initial determination with "an apparent pattern of indecent broadcasting."[44] The United States Court of Appeals for the District of Columbia Circuit upheld the forfeiture procedures, declining to grant a facial challenge to the basic forfeiture section and holding that it lacked evidence of an actual chilling effect to support an "as applied" challenge.[45]

2. Licensing Proceedings

The United States maintains primary control over the broadcast channels of mass communication through the licensing process.[46] The Commission's ability to conduct hearings is one of its most powerful enforcement tools. The Commission may conduct hearings for various reasons, both initially in the context of the construction permit, and later, in the renewal context.[47] The Commission in a hearing may examine the character of the applicant,[48] the content of the licensee's broadcasts, violations of the Commission's EEO policy,[49] or any past infraction of the Communications Act or the Commission's rules and regulations. The Commission may schedule a hearing in response to a petition to deny or on its own order.[50]

40. *Id.* § 505.

41. 47 C.F.R. § 1.80(g) (1997).

42. *Id.* § 1.80(g)(1).

43. Action for Children's Television v. FCC, 59 F.3d 1249, 313 U.S. App. D.C. 261 (D.C.Cir.1995) (en banc) ("ACT IV"), *cert. denied*, 516 U.S. 1072, 116 S.Ct. 773, 133 L.Ed.2d 726 (1996).

44. *Id.* at 1255, 313 U.S. App. D.C. at 267.

45. *Id.* at 1261–1262, 313 U.S. App. D.C. at 272–273. However, the Court invited aggrieved broadcasters to initiate such a challenge in an appropriate case.

46. 47 U.S.C.A. § 301 (West 1991).

47. While renewal hearings have been eliminated in most cases by the Telecom-

munications Act of 1996, Pub. L. 104–104, § 204, 110 Stat. 56 (1996), a renewal hearing may still be initiated by the Commission based on a "pattern of abuse" of its rules.

48. *See* Character Qualifications in Broadcast Licensing, 102 F.C.C.2d 1179 (1986).

49. *See, e.g.*, Bilingual Bicultural Coalition on Mass Media v. FCC, 595 F.2d 621 193 U.S. App. D.C. 236 (D.C.Cir.1978); Black Broadcasting Coalition of Richmond v. FCC 556 F.2d 59, 181 U.S. App. D.C. 182 (D.C.Cir.1977). *But see* Lutheran Church—Missouri Synod v. FCC, 141 F.3d 344, 329 U.S.App.D.C. 381 (D.C.Cir.1998).

50. 47 U.S.C.A. § 403 (West 1991).

Section 307 of the Communications Act empowers the Commission to grant a station license for a term of not more than eight years[51] to an applicant that will serve the public interest convenience and necessity.[52] In a hearing on an existing license, the Commission must notify the licensee and interested parties that a hearing will take place.[53] The general public is notified by broadcast announcements and local publications.[54] A non-party who informs the Commission of an interest in the proceeding will be notified of the hearing, and will not be excluded from giving competent, relevant testimony.[55] Hearings generally are conducted by an administrative law judge but may also be convened by the Commission or one or more Commissioners.[56]

The Communications Act specifies that at a hearing on a construction application, the burden of proof rests with the applicant for a license.[57] However, in the case of a hearing to revoke a license the burden rests with the Commission. Hearings are governed by the Federal Rules of Evidence for civil trials.[58] In addition to license revocation, the agency has the option of granting a license for a shorter term, imposing a forfeiture or issuing a specific cease and desist order. Final Commission action in a licensing case is appealable to the United States Court of Appeals for the District of Columbia.[59]

14.7 *Noncommercial Broadcasting

51. Telecommunications Act of 1996, Pub. L. 104–104, § 203, 110 Stat. 56 (1996) (modifying 47 U.S.C.A. 307(c))(West 1991 and Supp.1997).

52. 47 U.S.C.A. § 307(a) (West 1991).

53. 47 C.F.R. § 1.221 (1997).

54. *Id.* § 73.3539.

55. *Id.* § 1.225.

56. *Id.* § 1.241.

57. 47 U.S.C.A. § 309(e) (West 1991).

58. 47 C.F.R. § 1.351 (1997).

59. 47 U.S.C.A. § 402(b) (West 1991 and Supp. 1997).

* Published in Modern Communication Law, Practitioners Edition, Vol. 3.

Chapter Fifteen*

MANAGEMENT OF THE RADIO SPECTRUM

* This chapter published in Modern Communication Law, Practitioners Edition, Vol. 3, only.

Chapter Sixteen*

ORGANIZATION AND REGULATION OF INTERNATIONAL TELECOMMUNICATIONS

* This Chapter published in Modern Communications Law, Practitioners Edition, Vol. 3, only.

APPENDIX A

TERMINOLOGY, DEFINITIONS, ABBREVIATIONS AND ACRONYMS

A/B Switch—an input selector switch to a television set that switches signals from one source of input, such as a cable television system to another, such as a broadcast antenna.

Accounting rate—a unit of currency negotiated by international carriers as the amount of compensation to cover the cost of completing an international call. This amount includes all satellite or submarine cable transmission costs and the use of domestic tail circuits used to link an international gateway with the call originator and recipient. Carriers typically divide the accounting rate in half when settling accounts.

Administrative Procedure Act—an Act of the United States Congress setting forth required procedures that administrative and regulatory agencies must use to provide for public participation and due process in the setting rules and policies.

ADR: Alternative Dispute Resolution—the use of conflict resolution alternatives to litigation and conventional administrative channels, including negotiations managed by a private facilitator or mediator.

Ad Valorem Tariff—A tariff calculated as a percentage of the value of foreign goods clearing customs.

Algorithm—a specification of a series of steps required to obtain a result. A mathematical algorithm is a procedure for solving a mathematical problem.

AM Broadcast Service—Standard radio broadcast service which operates on a frequency range from 535 to 1705 kiloHertz.

Analog Communication—in electronic communication, analog technologies represent information by creating a continuous electronic equivalent of a nonelectronic input. For example, an analog telephone converts the varying acoustic waveform of the human voice into an electronic waveform with equivalent variations in frequency and intensity.

ANI: Automatic Number Identification—a feature in advanced telecommunication routing that provides the calling party's telephone number as the call is set up. Telephone companies have packaged this feature as a way to screen calls in residences and as a marketing and billing tool in commercial applications.

ANSI: the American National Standards Institute—a non-profit organization addressing standard setting, primarily by certifying other expert bodies to formulate standards in a narrow area of expertise.

Anti-Buy–Through Rules—FCC rules that prohibit a cable operator from requiring a customer to subscribe to any service tier other than the basic tier as a condition for access to premium channels.

Application Program—a program that works with a computer's operating program to perform a specialized task, such as word processing or preparation of a spreadsheet.

Arbitrage—a brokering function by which a business acquires bulk capacity and resells it to individual users who singularly could not qualify for the discounts accruing to large volume customers.

AVT—Advanced Television which uses twice the lines of the current NTSB standard for greater image definition.

Basic services—the switching, routing and transmission of voice or data provided by facilities-based carriers traditionally subject to common carrier regulation. Enhanced service providers use basic services as "plain vanilla" building blocks over which additional services and features are added.

BBS—acronym for bulletin board service—a site on the Internet to which computer users can post information and from which they can retrieve information posted by the BBS operator or others.

Bell Operating Company (BOC)—the telephone service operating companies of the Regional Holding Companies divested from AT & T. For example, the Regional Holding Company Bell Atlantic—NYNEX operates five BOCs: New York Telephone, New England Telephone, Bell Atlantic, Diamond State Telephone and New Jersey Bell.

Binary Numbering—a base–2 numbering system in which all values are represented by combinations of 1 and 0. Binary numbers typically are written as combinations of four digits. For example, the number 2 is represented in binary as 0010; the number 7 is represented in binary as 0111. Binary numbers, which can be represented by combinations of any two voltage levels or other electronic states, are the basis of all digital computer programs.

Bit—"binary digit;" the smallest unit of measurement in the transmission of data having only two values called 0 or 1.

Bit error rate—the extent to which a digital transmission network generates an error. The rate can be reduced through error detection and correction.

Bit rate (also known as "throughout")—the speed at which bits are transmitted, usually expressed in terms of bits per second. For example, a reasonably fast modem can handle data at the rate of 33,600 bits per second.

Bombing—in Internet parlance, the practice of returning mass, unsolicited electronic mail in bulk to the originating Internet server.

BOO: Build, Own, Operate—a method of infrastructure development by which a foreign enterprise agrees to build and operate a facility. This arrangement creates a service franchise and the incentive for the operator to upgrade and maintain facilities without fear of nationalization.

Bottleneck—a facility or portion of a route where traffic aggregates often, according the operator or service provider the opportunity to charge monopoly rates and to engage in anticompetitive practices.

Broadcast network—an interconnected program service by which programs are transmitted via affiliated local stations.

BSA: Basic Serving Arrangement—a term used by the Federal Communications Commission in its *Third Computer Inquiry* to identify the components in generic connections between Enhanced Service Providers and facilities-based carriers providing basic services. BSAs consist of the access links between facilities as well as the transport and routing functions.

BSE: Basic Serving Elements—a term used by the Federal Communications Commission in its *Third Computer Inquiry* to identify optional network features, available on an unbundled, "ala carte" basis, such as ANI.

BST—Basic Service Tier; the lowest tier of cable television service, consisting of public access channels, local broadcast channels and other channels selected by the cable operator.

Bundled—the process by which two or more possibly segregated features are offered jointly.

Bypass—the use of facilities or services alternative to what incumbent carriers offer, *e.g.*, the use of cable television systems or Digital Termination Systems to access interexchange carrier facilities rather than the incumbent telephone company's wireline network.

Byte—an intermediate unit of data transmission capacity comprised of 8 bits.

Cablehead—the oceanfront location where a submarine cable makes landfall and where power, amplification and multiplexing functions take place.

CATV—Community Antenna Television, an early abbreviation for cable television.

CAP—acronym for competitive access provider. CAPs offer business customers a connection with long-distance companies that bypasses the access service of the local telephone company.

CEI—Comparatively Equivalent Interconnection, a precondition imposed by the FCC before the BOCs could provide basic and enhanced services without structural separation.

Cellular radio—a terrestrial radio service designed primarily for mobile applications using microwave transmitters whose low powered operations enable frequency reuse and integrated service throughout a region.

Central Office—a telephone company facility that provides centralized management of switching, routing and line transport functions that may traverse other facilities closer to the end user.

Central Processing Unit (CPU)—the part of an electronic computer that performs the mathematical and other logical operations required to carry out program instructions.

Clean Room Process—a method of writing a computer program in which one programmer or team of programmers, with access to an existing program, develops a set of specifications based on that existing program and provides those specifications to a separate programmer or team of programmers that does not have access to the original. The second, or "clean room" programmer then writes a computer program based on the specifications supplied by the first programmer. Clean room procedures also may be used for development of microchips and other components.

CLEC—acronym for competitive local exchange carrier. CLECs offer local telephone service in competition with Bell operating companies and other established carriers.

Closed Captioning—program captions that are visible to television viewers with special decoder circuitry.

Collection rate—the end user charge for service, typically set out in a tariff.

Collocation—the physical interconnection of lines and equipment owned and operated by different carriers typically on the premises of the major incumbent carrier.

C3I: Command, Control, Communications and Intelligence—tactical requirements of the military.

Common carrier—a legal and regulatory classification that requires a telecommunication facility or service provider to serve any user within a certificated geographical region, and to provide service in a non-discriminatory manner typically through public tariffs.

Communications Act of 1934—the primary United States law establishing the Federal Communications Commission and the general scope of broadcast and common carrier regulation. It was broadly amended by the Telecommunications Act of 1996.

Comparably Efficient Interconnection—the requirement of the Federal Communications Commission that the Bell Operating Companies provide a plan demonstrating that they will not discriminate against unaffiliated enhanced services providers when the BOC decides to provide similar services. While the Second Computer Inquiry required the BOCs to provide enhanced services through a separate subsidiary, the Third Computer Inquiry eliminated structural separate subsidiaries provided the BOCs filed a CEI plan for each enhanced service.

Comparative Hearing—an administrative hearing conducted by the FCC to select from among competing applicants for a license.

Compatibility—the ability of users and carriers to interconnect equipment, lines and facilities while maintaining services with a reasonable degree of reliability and quality.

Complementary products—products that add to the value and utility of other products, *e.g.*, sugar with coffee and modems with personal computers.

Compression—the application of techniques for reducing the amount of frequency spectrum or channel capacity needed to derive a circuit. For example, 4 to 1 compression provides the means for deriving 4 channels where previously only one channel was available.

Computer Inquiries—a set of proceedings of the Federal Communications Commission beginning in the 1970s designed to erect a regulatory system that permits facilities based carriers to enter enhanced services markets without cross-subsidization by users of the carrier's basic services.

Conscious parallelism—the deliberate matching of prices and services by carriers to avoid more aggressive competition and price wars.

Consent Decree—a remedy in an antitrust case by which the proceeding concludes without a verdict in exchange for an agreement by the defendant to refrain from continuing to engage in certain activities or practices. AT & T agreed to Consent Decrees in 1918, 1956 and 1982 to settle antitrust suits.

Convergence—the merger of technologies that previously served discrete markets leading to integrated, additional offerings, *e.g.*, computer terminals serving entertainment applications (in addition to information processing) and television sets serving information processing applications (in addition to entertainment).

CPB—Corporation for Public Broadcasting, which aids in funding of programming for public broadcasting organizations.

CPE: Customer Premises Equipment—telecommunication equipment, including telephones and Private Branch Exchanges, located on user premises.

CPNI: Customer Proprietary Network Information—information about a customer's basic services usage that can provide marketing leads to enhanced service providers. The *Computer Inquiries* established rules requiring the BOCs to withhold such information from enhanced service affiliates or competitors unless authorized to do so by the user.

CPST—Cable Programming Service Tier; the level of cable television service beyond basic service.

Cross-subsidization—using revenues accrued from one service to underwrite the provision of another service at less than fully compensatory rates.

Cyberspace—popular expression for the communications environment created by the Internet and other computer networks and their users.

DAB: Digital Audio Broadcasting—the transmission of audio signals in a higher quality digital format rather than the conventional analog method.

DAMA: Demand Assigned Multiple Access—a queuing method by which a larger number of users may share transmission capacity by allocating that capacity on an as needed basis.

DARS—Digital Audio Radio Service.

DBS: Direct Broadcast Satellite—the use of medium to high powered signals for direct broadcasting to satellite terminals located on the premises of the recipient.

Dedicated—reserved for the use of one or more specified users. For example, a private line or satellite transponder may be dedicated for the use by a particular lessee. Non-dedicated capacity is provided on a virtual or on-demand basis.

De facto standard setting—the creation of a dominant or single standard by the interplay of market forces rather than promulgation of a standard through the standard setting process.

De jure standard setting—the formation of a standard by legislation or through the rulemaking process of the appropriate regulatory agency.

Dialing Parity—the ability of a telephone customer to reach any telecommunications service provider by dialing the same number of digits.

Digital—the use of a binary form, comprised of on and off pulses to represent the continuously varying signals of images and sounds. Information, entertainment, voice traffic and other forms of communication can be encoded, stored, processed and transmitted in a numeric as opposed to analog form.

Digitization—the use of computer readable bit streams for transmitting, switching and routing information.

Direct access—the opportunity for end users and service providers to acquire satellite capacity directly from the operator, *e.g.*, Intelsat and Eutelsat instead of having to deal with an intermediary.

Direct Broadcast Satellite—the use of a satellite to transmit programming, including audio and video, directly to end users equipped with receiving dishes and the necessary electronic components; also known as Direct to Home Broadcasting.

Divestiture—severing part of a corporation and creating a separate business entity on a voluntary basis or as part of an antitrust settlement or verdict.

Dominant carrier—an FCC classification of common carriers who because of their market power require closer regulatory scrutiny. Such carriers have less flexibility to change tariff terms and conditions. The classification applied to AT & T, foreign-owned carriers on a route-specific basis, Comsat in its Intelsat and Inmarsat Signatory functions and carriers operating the only earth station in an off-shore point, for example, Guam.

DOV/DUV: Data-over-voice/Data-under-voice—a technique for transmitting voice and data over a single channel through multiplexing or other signal splitting technology.

Downlink—the transmission of traffic from a satellite to receiving locations.

DTS: Digital Termination Systems—digital microwave transmission systems that provide a "bypass" alternative to conventional local exchange carrier wireline facilities.

DTV—Digital Television, a video system using binary numerics of zeros and ones to create images for transmission.

Duopoly—a monopoly shared by two enterprises.

Earth Station—terrestrial equipment used to transmit and receive satellite telecommunications. Some earth stations provide receive-only functions.

Economies of scale—a measurement of economic efficiency that identifies who produces a good or service at the lowest per unit cost and the optimal amount of production.

Economies of scope—a measurement for assessing how efficiently an enterprise will operate when serving adjacent markets, for example, whether a telephone company can efficiently use its network to provide cable television and information services.

Electronic Data Interchange—the use of telecommunications and information processing to conduct business transactions, often in an integrated network combining different media, such as voice, text and data processing.

Electronic Funds Transfer—the use of telecommunications and information processing to achieve a transfer of money, typically from one bank to another.

E-mail—common expression for electronic mail, which permits messages to be sent between networked computers for storage and retrieval by intended recipients.

Encryption—in electronic communication, the alteration of a signal so that it cannot be intercepted during transmission in intelligible form.

End office—the telephone company switching facility closest to a particular user.

End-on-end routing—the segmentation of a route into two or more segments typically priced individually.

End-to-end routing—a complete traffic routing arrangement typically priced at one composite rate.

Enhanced services—enhancements to basic common carrier transmission services involving computer processing that acts on the code, content, protocol or format of the information in such a way as to change the output and possibly store it for subsequent retrieval and manipulation.

Enterprise Networks—diversified, customized and complex international telecommunications and information networks primarily used by multinational enterprises to serve particular requirements. These networks often require the assistance of system integrators and outsourcers who plan, procure and manage the network.

FCC: Federal Communications Commission—the expert regulatory agency created by federal law to allocate, allot and assign spectrum and to oversee broadcasting and common carrier telecommunications.

FDC: Fully Distributed Costs—costing that includes a contribution to fixed costs by all consumers.

Feeder Link—a radio link to and from satellites conveying information, including the tracking, telemetry and network control needed to maintain a satellite in proper orbit.

Fixed Satellite Service—the use of satellites to provide service between users at fixed locations.

FM Broadcast Service—radio service license for operation on frequencies between 88 and 108 megaHertz.

Footprint—the range of geographical coverage of a satellite transmission.

Forbearance—the FCC articulated concept of refraining from regulating certain common carriers lacking market power thereby affording greater flexibility in pricing and providing service.

Frame Relay—a new data transmission technology that quickly switches and routes digital packets with a low bit error rate.

Franchise Fee—a fee charged by a local government to a cable operator as a condition of the franchise that is limited by federal law to five percent of gross revenues of the cable system.

Geostationary—the location above the earth where launched objects appear stationary relative to earth. Satellites become geostationary at 22,300 miles in altitude. Placing satellites in geostationary orbit above the equator maximizes the scope of geographical coverage.

GigaHertz (GHz)—a measure of radio frequency equivalent to 1 billion Hertz (cycles per second).

GNP—Gross National Product, an aggregate measure of income generated from all goods and services.

Greenmail—an agreement to withdraw a petition to deny a broadcast license in exchange for a cash settlement.

HDTV: High Definition Television—the development of a video transmission and production standard calling for higher resolution and better sound quality, usually digital in nature.

Headend—the part of a cable television system at which satellite signals are received for distribution to cable subscribers.

ILEC—acronym for incumbent local exchange carrier. ILECs are the Bell operating companies and other established, local telephone companies that were providing service when the Telecommunications Act of 1996 became effective.

Incentive regulation—alternatives to the conventional rate base regulation designed to reward innovation and efficiency by allowing carriers to capture financial gains rather than automatically flowing them to ratepayers through refunds or lower rates.

Incumbent carriers—carriers that have installed an extensive network and heretofore have faced limited, if any, competition.

Infrastructure—a system essential to the public health and welfare, *e.g.*, water, sewerage, electricity, currency, telecommunications and roadways.

Intelligent Network—the architecture and plans for a future telecommunications infrastructure with advanced features made possible by expanded network switching, signal processing and intelligence.

Interactive—the ability of users to request, manipulate, process and change data through on-line commands. Interactivity converts one-way information sources into two-way media.

Interconnect—the physical connection of equipment and lines to secure a complete route and service arrangement. Users physically interconnect CPE to a telecommunication network through a plug physically attached to a jack.

Interexchange telecommunications—long haul services that link local exchanges. In the United States, the Modification of Final Judgment precludes Bell Operating Companies from providing those interexchange services that cross Local Access and Transport boundaries.

Interface—a shared boundary, for instance, between CPE and the telecommunication plant owned and operated by a telephone company.

Internet—a dispersed, noncentralized network of computers among which data are transferred in discrete, individually addressed and routed packets of digitized information. The Internet began as a network of defense and research computers in the United States and is now a worldwide conduit for commerce and communication available to the public at large.

ISDN: Integrated Services Digital Networks—a telecommunication standard envisioning interconnected digital networks capable of simultaneous delivery of voice and data services.

ITU: International Telecommunication Union—a specialized agency of the United Nations that formulates policy, regulations and recommendations for telecommunications, including spectrum allocation, satellite orbital arc registration, telecommunications development, standard setting and conflict avoidance/resolution.

ITFS—Instructional Television Fixed Service.

IXC: interexchange carrier—a provider of long haul telecommunications services;

KiloHertz—a measurement of radio waves equal to 1000 cycles per second.

LATA: Local Access and Transport Area—a geographical region sharing common cultural, social and economic interests within which the divested Bell Operating Companies may provide local and interexchange services.

Leased Access Channels—channels that federal law require federal operators to set aside for commercial use by unaffiliated entities.

LEC: local exchange carrier—the provider of local services, often considered a natural monopoly and bottleneck through which most interexchange traffic traverses.

LEOs: Low Earth Orbiting satellites—satellites operating in orbits below the geostationary orbiting arc where service can be provided to low powered handheld terminals. Big LEOs provide a variety of voice and data services while small LEOs provide data and emergency position location services.

Level Competitive Playing Field—the goal of market entrants who claim that regulators and other decision makers must take affirmative steps to reduce unfair market access opportunities accruing to incumbent carriers as a function of their earlier market entry, bottleneck control, customer base and regulatory status.

Liberalization—the relaxation of rules and service obligations, *e.g.*, subsidized and under-priced local services, imposed on incumbent carriers, often occurring contemporaneously with privatization, deregulation and market entry initiatives.

Line-side interconnection—interconnection that takes place at a low level in the switching hierarchy, typically for end users.

LMA—local marketing agreement; an arrangement by which a broadcaster brokers time on its station.

LMDS—Local Multi-point Distribution Service.

Local area network—a network of work stations and personal computers linked by wiring installed by the operator or the telephone company or by a wireless application.

Local loop—local exchange facilities comprising the first and last legs of a telecommunications route.

Low Earth Orbit—the use of non-geostationary orbits for satellites primarily providing mobile telecommunications to lightweight transceivers. LEO satellites operate only a few hundred miles above the earth surface thereby reducing launch costs and the power needed to transmit to and from the satellites. On the other hand, the closer proximity to earth requires a larger number of satellites to achieve desired regional or global coverage.

LPTV—Low Power Television.

LRIC: Long Run Incremental Cost—a measure of the additional cost incurred over the long term to provide a particular amount of a good or service. This measure accounts only for the additional costs incurred without regard to embedded, fixed costs that could be shared by additional users.

MFJ: Modification of Final Judgment—modifications to the 1956 Consent Decree agreed to by AT & T and the Justice Department thereby settling an antitrust suit. The MFJ required AT & T to divest its Bell Operating Companies in exchange for the opportunity to serve data processing markets. The spun-off Bell Operating Companies were initially limited to local exchange services.

Microcode—coded instructions that direct the activation of transistors on a computer's central processing unit as required to perform particular tasks.

MMDS—Multi-channel Multipoint Distribution Service; a form of "wireless cable" television.

Modem—common name for modulator-demodulator, a device that converts digital signals from a computer into analog signals for transmission over the telephone network and converts analog signals from the telephone network into digital signals usable by a computer.

MTS: Message Telephone Service—conventional dial-up voice telephone service also known by the acronym POTS ("Plain Old Telephone Service").

Multimedia—the integration of various media previously considered available only by separate pipelines or marketing channels, *e.g.*, using television for new interactive data processing, consumer order entry and utility monitoring.

Multiplexing—subdividing a circuits into more than one channel to derive more throughout and capacity.

Multipoint—using telecommunication services to serve more than one physical location, *e.g.*, originating a video program for delivery to numerous cable systems using the broad geographical coverage of a satellite.

Must Carry—A requirement that cable television systems transmit designated local broadcast signals.

NAL—Notice of Apparent Liability; a notice issued to an FCC licensee denoting a forfeiture.

Negative Option Billing—charging a cable subscriber for service or equipment that the subscriber has not affirmatively requested by name.

NII: National Information Initiative—a plan for using government to stimulate primarily private ventures that will upgrade and expand the telecommunications and information processing infrastructure in the

United States. The government initiative includes a vision of ubiquitous access to a feature-rich information highway.

Node—a point in a telecommunications or information processing network configuration where two or more lines, routes or pathways come together, *e.g.*, at a switch, earth station or PBX.

Non-common carrier—a classification that reduces or eliminates regulation in recognition of the carrier's lack of market dominance and the non-essentialness of the services offered.

NTB: non-tariff barrier—barriers to trade that are not documented in a customs duty or tariff.

NTIA: National Telecommunications and Information Administration—the United States Executive branch agency, located in the Department of Commerce, that serves as the President's researcher and advisor on telecommunications and information processing policy issues.

NTSC—National Television Standards Committee, the developer of a broadcast color television standard in the United States and implemented in North America and Japan.

Number Portability—the ability of a telephone service subscriber to change service providers without changing his or her telephone number. A secondary meaning of number portability is the ability of a customer to be reached through the same telephone number at different geographic locations.

Object Code—machine-readable computer program expressed in binary numbers.

One+ dialing—a calling arrangement for direct connections with a prearranged billing commitment.

One-stop shopping—the provision of a number of functions, like telecommunication network, design, procurement and management by a single enterprise as an alternative to the end user performing these functions or securing the services from a number of enterprises.

Open Network Architecture—an FCC articulation of a blueprint for providing enhanced services providers with access to local exchange facilities distilled into basic elements that such providers can secure on an as-needed basis.

Operating Program—a computer program that directs tasks common to all applications programs, such as reading disks, moving information within the computer and transferring data to and from input and output devices.

Origination Cablecasting—programming originated by, and under the exclusive control of, a cable operator.

OVS—Open Video System; a form of multi-channel video service authorized primarily for telephone companies.

Ownership Attribution Rules—FCC rules establishing the threshold for having a cognizable interest in a broadcast station or other licensed entity.

Packet switching—a transmission technology that reduces messages and data into individually routed packets and reassembles them before reaching the final destination.

PBS—Public Broadcasting Service, an interconnected television network providing primarily educational and public affairs programming funded in part by the Corporation for Public Broadcasting, a quasi-governmental entity.

PBX: private branch exchange—equipment on customer premises for managing a bank of telephones.

PCS: Personal communication services—a variety of new terrestrial and satellite-delivered services to handheld terminals operating at low power.

PEG Channels—cable television franchise requirements for public, educational or governmental access channels on local cable systems.

Pen Register—a device that records all telephone numbers dialed from a particular telephone.

Petition to Deny—a petition filed with the FCC to deny an application for a broadcast license or transfer.

Point-to-multipoint—traffic routing from a single location to many recipients, for instance, video programming distribution to numerous cable operators.

POTS: Plain Old Telephone Service—conventional telephone services provided to residential and small business users.

Power Flux Density—a measure of power radiated from a transmitter like a satellite.

Preemption—assertion of jurisdiction by one regulatory authority that would replace and dislodge the assertion of jurisdiction by another agency.

Premium Channels—cable television channels typically marketed on a pay per-channel or per-program basis.

Price Cap—a form of incentive regulation where carriers and regulators agree to replace conventional rate base regulation for a cap on rates and the requirement that the rates drop by a certain percentage each year, to reflect productivity improvements, as offset by a measure of overall increased costs to producers. Carriers are permitted to capture all or part of increased profits.

Primary Rate Interface—the large standard unit of capacity in an Integrated Services Digital Network comprised of twenty-three 64 kilobits per second (''kbps'') bearer channels and one 16 kbps data channel totaling 1.54 megabits per second.

Primary Status—the designation for a particular radio service that qualifies users for maximum permissible protection from interference by users of services holding a lower priority.

Private line—dedicated capacity designed to link a single user with requirements in two international locations. Carriers now provide "virtual" private lines by partitioning capacity from public networks through the application of software.

PSTN: Public Switched Telecommunications Network—the publicly available local and long haul facilities of the incumbent carrier.

PTAR—Prime Time Access Rule requiring the making of time available during the half hour before prime time (8PM—11PM EST) to independent programmers and syndicators for the telecasting of their programming.

RAM—acronym for random access memory, the volatile, nonpermanent memory to which computer programs and data are transferred from longer-term storage media, such as a hard drive, memory for use by the computer's central processing unit.

Ramsey Pricing—charging users on the basis of their demand elasticity, *i.e.*, users with numerous telecommunications options, including dedicated facilities and leased lines from a number of carriers, qualify for rates below those charged users with fewer options.

RBOC: Regional Bell Operating Company—upon divestiture from AT & T, the Bell Operating Companies were reformulated initially into 7 new corporations representing particular geographic regions of the United States.

Redundancy—the availability of backup capacity to restore service in the event of a facility outage or peak demand condition.

Resale—the acquisition of bulk transmission capacity and other services for subsequent resale to individual users who singularly do not generate the demand for large capacity offerings. Resellers perform an arbitrage function and profit by acquiring discounted bulk capacity from underlying, facilities based carriers and repackaging it at rates less than what an individual user could secure directly from the carrier.

Retransmission Consent—permission required by a cable operator to transmit the signal of a broadcast station that does not avail itself of "must carry" rights.

Reverse Engineering—examination of a finished product to ascertain the method of its design or manufacture.

RFP: Request For Proposals—a tender offer soliciting bids by parties interested in securing a contract to perform some form of work, often in the telecommunications industry.

Roamer—an individual desiring to use a mobile telecommunication device, such as, a cellular radiotelephone, while away from the location where service is usually provided.

Roll-off—the manner in which signal strength drops off at locations increasingly distant from the targeted service location.

Rulemaking—the process by which a United States administrative or regulatory agency establishes a binding rule, regulation or policy. Procedural due process requirements obligate the agency to notify the public of proposed actions and to provide opportunities for participation, through filed comments or testimony.

Sender Keep All—a toll revenue division arrangement whereby the originating carrier keeps all charges.

Sender Pay All—a charging mechanism whereby the calling party pays all charges.

Signal Bleed—the visible or audible portion of a premium cable television channel that is received by non-subscribers due to imperfect scrambling technology.

Smart card—a credit card sized instrument containing microchips and associated electronics for providing credit and other data for facilitating transactions.

SMATV—Satellite Master Antenna Television; a "private cable" system typically serving a multi-unit dwelling.

Software defined network—the use of software to partition transmission capacity from public networks for private use making it appear to be the functional equivalent of capacity dedicated for a single user.

Source Code—computer program expressed in language that can be read and written by human programmers.

Spam—in Internet parlance, any mass transmission of unsolicited electronic mail.

Spectrum—a term depicting the range of frequencies used in telecommunications.

STA—Special Temporary Authorization; a temporary grant of authority to operate a broadcast station without a license.

Switch—the portion of the telecommunications infrastructure where traffic is received by a device that identifies the intended destination and selects the routing for delivering traffic onward to that point.

T–1—a unit of transmission capacity equal to 1.544 megabits per second in throughput.

Tariff—a contract for service setting out the terms and conditions under which the general public will secure service.

Teledensity—the penetration of telecommunication access lines typically measured per 100 inhabitants.

Telepoint—a new generation of pay telephones and one-way wireless communications based on micro-cellular radio technology.

Teleport—a satellite earth station with extensive access to terrestrial facilities and a broad base of users, situated on real estate developments adjacent to the earth stations or at other locations.

Teletext—slow speed transmission of textual information through the vertical blanking intervals of broadcast television signals.

Television Booster Station—a station that boosts the signal of a primary television station, operating on the same channel to increase the range of the signal.

Television Translator Station—a station that retransmits the signal of a television station on a separate channel.

TELRIC—acronym for total element long run incremental cost. TELRIC is a method of establishing the price at which incumbent telephone companies will make their unbundled network elements available to competitors. The TELRIC price for a network element is the forward looking cost directly attributable to providing the network element. As defined by the Federal Communications Commission, TELRIC does not include embedded costs, opportunity costs or costs attributable only to other products or services. A TELRIC price may, however, include a reasonable allocation of forward-looking common costs.

Throughput—the amount of data carried over a particular amount of capacity in a specified timespan (see also bit rate).

Traffic—the messages, programming, files and other intelligence requiring transport from one location to another.

Transceiver—a devices that contains componetry that transmits and receives radio signals.

Transiting—the carriage of international traffic via the facilities of an intermediary, third country between the sender and recipient.

Transponder—the components in a satellite able to transmit and receive traffic. Satellite capacity is typically stated in the number of available 36 MHz equivalent transponders.

Trap and Trace—a device that records the telephone numbers from which calls are placed to a particular telephone.

TVRO: Television Receive–Only—satellite dishes equipped for one-way reception of television signals.

UHF—Ultra High Frequency television service providing electromagnetic signals in the 300 to 3000 MHz frequencies, corresponding to channels 14 through 83 on the television dial.

Unbundled—separation of services and equipment into discrete elements available on an individual, ala carte basis.

Unbundled Network Element—a subscriber access line, switch port or other component of an incumbent telephone company's network that must be made available to competitors under the Telecommunications Act of 1996.

Uplink—the process of transmitting traffic from earth to a satellite.

URL—acronym for Uniform Resource Locator, an addressing format for reaching other computers linked on the World Wide Web.

Usenet Newsgroup—an on-line community of BBSs that provides a forum for postings of information on particular subjects.

V–Chip—A computer chip integrated into electronic circuitry placed primarily in television sets addressable by signals encoded in nearly all television transmissions to permit the set owner to screen out undesired violent and indecent programs.

Vertical blanking interval—the black space between frames visible only when a television set's vertical hold control fails and the frames holding the images roll. This space has a total of 42 lines which may be used for signals such as those that address V-chips.

VHF—Very High Frequency television service providing electromagnetic signals in the 30 to 300 MHz frequencies, corresponding to channel 2 through 13 on the television dial.

Videotext—slow speed transmission of textual information over closed circuits.

WAN: Wide Area Network—a interconnected network of personal computers and work stations situated in different locations.

WATS—Wide Area Telephone Service, toll-free calling to the call originator provided by many retailing and service organizations.

Windowing—segmenting the distribution of a product, *e.g.*, a movie, into sequences based on consumer demand elasticities and time from initial availability. Movie producers attempt to extract the greatest amount of rent by calibrating availability and charges, *e.g.*, $6–8 at a theater, $2–3 on rented video tape and no charge to viewers on broadcast television.

Wireless Local Loop—the use of unwired transmission facilities to provide connections to the wireline public switched telecommunication network; many of these technologies also provide mobile services.

Wireless networks—the use of radio technology to serve increasingly diverse applications, including mobile services and some applications heretofore provided via wireline facilities.

Wireless Cable—various methods of microwave delivery of subscription video services including MMDS, LMDS, ITFS and OFS.

Wireline—the conventional wire-based telecommunication infrastructure installed and managed by incumbent carriers.

World Wide Web—a client/server application on the Internet that uses hypertext transfer protocol (HTTP) and hypertext markup language (HTML) to produce documents and establish links among them. The World Wide Web offers users a graphics-rich environment and the ability to move from one document or Internet site to another with the click of a mouse.

*

APPENDIX B

PROVISIONS OF THE UNITED STATES CONSTITUTION INVOLVED WITH COMMUNICATIONS

Provision of the Constitution:

Article I, Section 8:

The Congress shall have Power . . .

To regulate Commerce with foreign Nations, and among the several States, and with the Indian Tribes; . . .

Amendments to the Constitution:

Amendment I:

Congress shall make no law respecting an establishment of religion, or prohibiting the free exercise thereof; or abridging the freedom of speech, or of the press; or the right of the people peaceably to assemble, and to petition the Government for a redress of grievances.

Amendment IV:

The right of the people to be secure in their persons, houses, papers, and effects, against unreasonable searches and seizures, shall not be violated, and no Warrants shall issue, but upon probable cause, supported by Oath or affirmation, and particularly describing the place to be searched, and the persons or things to be seized.

Amendment V:

No person shall be held to answer for a capital, or otherwise infamous crime, unless on a presentment or indictment of a Grand Jury, except in cases arising in the land or naval forces, or in the Militia, when in actual service in time of War or public danger; nor shall any person be subject for the same offence to be twice put in jeopardy of life or limb; nor shall be compelled in any criminal case to be a witness against himself, nor be deprived of life, liberty, or property, without due process of law; nor shall private property be taken for public use, without just compensation.

Amendment VI:

In all criminal prosecutions, the accused shall enjoy the right to a speedy and public trial, by an impartial jury of the State and district wherein the crime shall have been committed, which district shall have been previously ascertained by law, and to be informed of the nature and cause of the accusation; to be confronted with the witnesses against him; to have compulsory process for obtaining witnesses in his favor, and to have the Assistance of Counsel for his defense.

Amendment XIV, Section 1:

All persons born or naturalized in the United States, and subject to the jurisdiction thereof, are citizens of the United States and of the State wherein they reside. No State shall make or enforce any law which shall abridge the privileges or immunities of citizens of the United States; nor shall any State deprive any person of life, liberty, or property, without due process of law; nor deny to any person within its jurisdiction the equal protection of the laws.

Amendment XXI, Section 2:

The transportation or importation into any State, Territory, or possession of the United States for delivery or use therein of intoxicating liquors, in violation of the laws thereof, is hereby prohibited.

APPENDIX C

RESEARCHING COMMUNICATIONS LAW ON WESTLAW®

Analysis

Section 1.   Introduction

Modern Communication Law, Hornbook Student Series, provides a strong base for analyzing even the most complex problem involving communications law. Whether your research requires examination of statutes, case law, expert commentary or other materials, West books and Westlaw are excellent sources of information.

To keep you abreast of current developments, Westlaw provides frequently updated databases. With Westlaw, you have unparalleled legal research resources at your fingertips.

Additional Resources

If you have not previously used Westlaw or have questions not covered in this appendix, see the *Westlaw Reference Manual* or call the West Group Reference Attorneys at 1800REFATTY (18007332889). The West Group Reference Attorneys are trained, licensed attorneys, available 24 hours a day to assist you with your Westlaw search questions.

Section 2.   Westlaw Databases

Each database on Westlaw is assigned an abbreviation called an *identifier*, which you use to access the database. You can find identifiers for all databases in the online Westlaw Directory and in the printed *Westlaw Database Directory*. When you need to know more detailed information about a database, use Scope. Scope contains coverage information, lists of related databases and valuable search tips. To access Scope, click the **Scope** button while in the database.

The following chart lists Westlaw databases that contain information pertaining to communications law. For a complete list of communications law databases, see the online Westlaw Directory or the printed *Westlaw Database Directory*. Because new information is continually being added to Westlaw, you should also check the Welcome to Westlaw window and the Westlaw Directory for new database information.

Selected Westlaw Databases

Database	Identifier	Coverage
Federal Communications— Combined Federal Communications Materials	FCOM–ALL	Varies by source
Federal and State Case Law Combined		
Federal & State Case Law	ALLCASES	Begins with 1945
Federal & State Case Law— Before 1945	ALLCASE–SOLD	17891944
Federal Case Law		
Federal Communications— Cases	FCOM–CS	Begins with 1789
Federal Communications— Supreme Court Cases	FCOM–SCT	Begins with 1790
Federal Communications— Courts of Appeals Cases	FCOM–CTA	Begins with 1891
Federal Communications— District Courts Cases	FCOM–DCT	Begins with 1789
Federal First Amendment— Cases	FCFA–CS	Begins with 1789
Federal First Amendment— Supreme Court Cases	FCFAS–CT	Begins with 1790
Federal First Amendment— Courts of Appeals Cases	FCFA–CTA	Begins with 1891
Federal First Amendment— District Courts Cases	FCFA–DCT	Begins with 1789
State Case Law		
State Case Law	ALLSTATES	Begins with 1945
State Case Law Before 1945	ALLSTATE–SOLD	18211944

Database	Identifier	Coverage
Individual State Case Law	XX–CS (where XX is a state's two-letter postal abbreviation)	Varies by state

Federal Statutes, Regulations and Administrative Materials

Database	Identifier	Coverage
Federal Communications— Code and Regulations	FCOM–CODREG	Varies by source
Federal Communications— U.S. Code Annotated	FCOM–USCA	Current data
Federal Communications— Final, Temporary and Proposed Regulations	FCOM–REG	Varies by source
Federal Communications— Code of Federal Regulations	FCOM–CFR	Current data
Federal Communications— Federal Register	FCOM–FR	Begins with July 1980
Federal Communications— Federal Communications Commission Decisions and Daily Digest	FCOM–ADMIN	Varies by source
Federal Communications— FCC Daily Digest	FCOM–DIGEST	Begins with January 1994
Federal Communications— Federal Communications Commission Decisions	FCOM–FCC	Begins with 1965
FCC Daily Digest	FCCDD	Begins with November 1991
Federal First Amendment— U.S. Code Annotated	FCFA–USCA	Current data
Federal First Amendment— Code of Federal Regulations	FCFA–CFR	Current data
Federal First Amendment— Federal Register	FCFA–FR	Begins with July 1980
Communications Decency Act Documents	CDA–DOC	Begins with February 1996
Legislative History—U.S. Code, 1948 to Present	LH	Begins with 1948
Arnold & Porter Legislative History: Telecommunications Competition and Deregulation Act of 1996	TELECOM–LH	Full history
United States Public Laws	USPL	Current data

Selected Westlaw Databases

Database	Identifier	Coverage

State Statutes and Regulations

Database	Identifier	Coverage
State Statutes—Annotated	ST–ANN–ALL	Varies by state
Individual State Statutes— Annotated	XX–ST–ANN (where XX is a state's two-letter postal abbreviation)	Varies by state
State Administrative Code Multibase	ADC–ALL	Varies by state
Individual State Administrative Codes	XX–ADC (where XX is a state's two-letter postal abbreviation)	Varies by state

Texts, Periodicals and Research Tools

Database	Identifier	Coverage
Texts & Periodicals—All Law Reviews, Texts & Bar Journals	TP–ALL	Varies by publication

Database	Identifier	Coverage
Communications—Law Reviews, Texts & Bar Journals	COM–TP	Varies by publication
First Amendment—Law Reviews, Texts & Bar Journals	CFA–TP	Varies by publication
CommLaw Conspectus	COMLCON	Full coverage begins with 1993 (vol. 1)
Federal Communications Law Journal	FCLJ	Selected coverage begins with 1983 (vol. 35)
Hastings Communications & Entertainment Law Journal (COMM/ENT)	COMENT	Selected coverage begins with 1982 (vol. 5); full coverage begins with 1993 (vol. 16)
Multimedia Law: Forms and Analysis	MULTIMEDLAW	Current through 1995
Rules of the Road for the Information Superhighway: Electronic Communications and the Law	INFOHWY	Current through 1997 pocket part
News and Current Events		
All News	ALLNEWS	Varies by source
Communications News	COMNEWS	Varies by source
Cable TV and New Media Law and Finance	CTVNMLF	Begins with March 1995
Communications Lawyer	COMLAW	Selected coverage begins with 1990 (vol. 8)
Media Law and Policy	MEDIALP	Full coverage begins with 1994 (vol. 3)
Multimedia & Web Strategist	MMEDWST	Begins with October 1995
West Legal Directory™		
West Legal Directory—Communications	WLDCOM	Current data
West Legal Directory—Constitutional	WLDCON	Current data

Section 3. Retrieving a Document with a Citation: Find and Jump

3.1 Find

Find is a Westlaw service that allows you to retrieve a document by entering its citation. Find allows you to retrieve documents from anywhere in Westlaw without accessing or changing databases. Find is available for many documents, including case law (state and federal), the *United States Code Annotated*®, state statutes, administrative materials, and texts and periodicals.

To use Find, simply access the Find service and type the citation. The following list provides some examples:

To Find This Document	Access Find and Type
Near v. State of Minnesota,	51 S.Ct. 625 (1931) **51 sct 625**
In Re PLD Telekom, Inc.,	13 FCC Rcd. 9505 (1998) **13 fccr 9505**
47 U.S.C.A. 605	**47 usca 605**
47 C.F.R. 73.4091	**47 cfr 73.4091**
42 Pa. Cons. Stat. Ann. 5942	**42 pa c s a 5942**
Nev. Rev. Stat. 49.275	**nv st 49.275**

For a complete list of publications that can be retrieved with Find and their abbreviations, consult the Find Publications List. Click the **Pubs List** button after accessing Find.

3.2   Jump

Use Jump markers (> or [f]) to move from one location to another on Westlaw. For example, use Jump markers to go directly from the statute, case or law review article you are viewing to a cited statute, case or article; from a headnote to the corresponding text in the opinion; or from an entry in a statutes index database to the full text of the statute.

Section 4.   Searching with Natural Language: WIN—Westlaw is Natural

Overview: With WIN, you can retrieve documents by simply describing your issue in plain English. If you are a relatively new Westlaw user, Natural Language searching can make it easier for you to retrieve cases that are on point. If you are an experienced Westlaw user, Natural Language gives you a valuable alternative search method.

When you enter a Natural Language description, Westlaw automatically identifies legal phrases, removes common words and generates variations of terms in your description. Westlaw then searches for the concepts in your description. Concepts may include significant terms, phrases, legal citations or topic and key numbers. Westlaw retrieves the 20 documents that most closely match your description, beginning with the document most likely to match.

4.1   Natural Language Search

Access a database, such as Federal CommunicationsCases (FCOMCS). If the Terms and Connectors Query Editor is displayed, click the **Search Type** button and choose **Natural Language**. At the Natural Language Description Editor, type a Natural Language description such as the following:

is the sale of decoders for encrypted cable television signals unlawful

4.2   Next Command

Westlaw displays the 20 documents that most closely match your description, beginning with the document most likely to match. If you want to view additional documents, click your right mouse button and choose **Next 10 Documents** from the pop-up menu, or choose **Next 10 Documents** from the Browse menu.

4.3   Natural Language Browse Commands

Best Mode: To display the best portion (the portion that most closely matches your description) of each document in your search result, click your right mouse button and choose **Next Best** from the pop-up menu or click Best [f].

Standard Browsing Commands: You can also browse your Natural Language search result using standard Westlaw browsing commands, such as citations list, Locate, page mode and term mode. When you browse your Natural Language search result in term mode, the five portions of each document that are most likely to match your description are displayed.

Section 5.   Searching with Terms and Connectors

Overview: With Terms and Connectors searching, you enter a query, which consists of key terms from your issue and connectors specifying the relationship between these terms.

Terms and Connectors searching is useful when you want to retrieve a document for which you know specific details, such as the title or the fact situation. Terms and Connectors searching is also useful when you want to retrieve documents relating to a specific issue. If the Natural Language Description Editor is displayed when you access a database, click the **Search Type** button and choose **Term Search**.

5.1   Terms

Plurals and Possessives: Plurals are automatically retrieved when you enter the singular form of a term. This is true for both regular and irregular plurals (e.g., **child** retrieves *children*). If you enter the plural form of a term, you will not retrieve the singular form.

If you enter the nonpossessive form of a term, Westlaw automatically retrieves the possessive form as well. However, if you enter the possessive form, only the possessive form is retrieved.

Automatic Equivalencies: Some terms have alternative forms or equivalencies; for example, *5* and *five* are equivalent terms. Westlaw automatically retrieves equivalent terms. The *Westlaw Reference Manual* contains a list of equivalent terms.

Compound Words, Abbreviations and Acronyms: When a compound word is one of your search terms, use a hyphen to retrieve all forms of the word. For example, the term **along-side** retrieves *along-side, alongside* and *along side*.

When using an abbreviation or acronym as a search term, place a period after each of the letters to retrieve any of its forms. For example, the term **f.c.c.** retrieves *fcc, f.c.c., f c c* and *f. c. c.* Note: The abbreviation does *not* retrieve *federal communications commission*, so remember to add additional alternative terms to your query such as **"federal communications commission"**.

The Root Expander and the Universal Character: When you use the Terms and Connectors search method, placing the root expander (!) at the end of a root term generates all other terms with that root. For example, adding the ! to the root *encrypt* in the query

encrypt! /5 signal

instructs Westlaw to retrieve such terms as *encrypt, encrypted, encryption* and *encrypting*.

The universal character (*) stands for one character and can be inserted in the middle or at the end of a term. For example, the term

withdr*w

will retrieve *withdraw* and *withdrew*. Adding three asterisks to the root *elect*

elect*

instructs Westlaw to retrieve all forms of the root with up to three additional characters. Terms such as *elected* or *election* are retrieved by this query. However, terms with more than three letters following the root, such as *electronic,* are not retrieved. Plurals are always retrieved, even if more than three letters follow the root.

Phrase Searching: To search for an exact phrase, place it within quotation marks. For example, to search for references to *commercial speech*, type "**commercial speech**". When you are using the Terms and Connectors search method, you should use phrase searching only if you are certain that the terms in the phrase will not appear in any other order.

5.2   Alternative Terms

After selecting the terms for your query, consider which alternative terms are necessary. For example, if you are searching for the term *constitutional*, you might also want to search for the term *unconstitutional*. You should consider both synonyms and antonyms as alternative terms. You can also use the Westlaw thesaurus to add alternative terms to your query.

5.3   Connectors

After selecting terms and alternative terms for your query, use connectors to specify the relationship that should exist between search terms in your retrieved documents. The connectors are described below:

Use:	To retrieve documents with:	Example:
& (and)	both terms	software & copyright
or (space)	either term or both terms	ban! censor!
/p	search terms in the same paragraph	internet /p encrypt!
/s	search terms in the same sentence	actual /s malice
+s	the first search term preceding the second within the same sentence	burden +s prov! proof
/n	search terms within "n" terms of each other (where "n" is a number)	satellite /3 transmi!

Use: + n	To retrieve documents with: the first search term preceding the second by "n" terms (where "n" is a number)	Example: **false + 3 light**
	" 'search terms appearing in the same order as in the quotation marks' **children television act"**	

Use: % (but not)	To exclude documents with: search terms following the YMBOL	Example: **radio /s transmi! % narrow-band**

5.4   Field Restrictions

Overview: Documents in each Westlaw database consist of several segments, or fields. One field may contain the citation, another the title, another the synopsis and so forth. Not all databases contain the same fields. Also depending on the database, fields with the same name may contain different types of information.

To view a list of fields for a specific database and their contents, see Scope for that database. Note that in some databases not every field is available for every document.

To retrieve only those documents containing your search terms in a specific field, restrict your search to that field. To restrict your search to a specific field, type the field name or abbreviation followed by your search terms enclosed in parentheses. For example, to retrieve a case in the Federal First AmendmentSupreme Court Cases database (FCFASCT) entitled *New York Times v. Sullivan,* search for your terms in the title field (ti):

ti("new york times" & sullivan)

The fields discussed below are available in Westlaw databases you might use for researching communications law issues.

Digest and Synopsis Fields: The digest (di) and synopsis (sy) fields, added to case law databases by West's attorney-editors, summarize the main points of a case. The synopsis field contains a brief description of a case. The digest field contains the topic and headnote fields and includes the complete hierarchy of concepts used by West's editors to classify the headnotes to specific West digest topics and key numbers. Restricting your search to the synopsis and digest fields limits your result to cases in which your terms are related to a major issue in the case.

Consider restricting your search to one or both of these fields if

you are searching for common terms or terms with more than one meaning, and you need to narrow your search; or

you cannot narrow your search by using a smaller database.

For example, to retrieve cases that discuss status as a public figure for purposes of defamation actions, access the Federal First AmendmentCases database (FCFACS) and type the following query:

sy,di(defam! /p status /p public private /s figure)

Headnote Field: The headnote field (he) is part of the digest field, but does not contain topic numbers, hierarchical classification information or key numbers. The headnote field contains only a one-sentence summary for each point of law in a case and any supporting citations given by the author of the opinion. A headnote field restriction is useful when you are searching for specific statutory sections or rule numbers. For example, to retrieve headnotes from federal cases that cite 15 U.S.C.A. 1125(a), access the Federal CommunicationsCases database (FCOMCS) and type the following query:

he(15 +5 1125(a))

Topic Field: The topic field (to) is also part of the digest field. It contains hierarchical classification information, including the West digest topic names and numbers and the key numbers. You should restrict search terms to the topic field in a case law database if

a digest field search retrieves too many documents; or

you want to retrieve cases with digest paragraphs classified under more than one topic.

For example, the topic Telecommunications has the topic number 372. To retrieve federal cases that discuss common carrier status in the context of telecommunications, access the Federal CommunicationsCases database (FCOMCS) and type a query like the following:

to(372) /p status /p "common carrier"

To retrieve cases classified under more than one topic and key number, search for your terms in the topic field. For example, to search for cases discussing the balance between freedom of the press and the need for accurate information, which may be classified to Constitutional Law (92), Libel and Slander (237), or Newspapers (274), among other topics, type a query like the following:

to(free! /s press /p accura! inaccura! true truth fals!)

For a complete list of West digest topics and their corresponding topic numbers, access the Key Number service; click the **Key Number Service** button or choose **Key Number Service** from the Services menu.

Note: Slip opinions, cases not reported by West and cases from topical services do not contain the digest, headnote and topic fields.

Prelim and Caption Fields: When searching in a database containing statutes, rules or regulations, restrict your search to the prelim (pr) and caption (ca) fields to retrieve documents in which your terms are important enough to appear in a section name or heading. For example, to retrieve federal regulations regarding airline radio transmissions, access the Federal CommunicationsCode of Federal Regulations database (FCOMCFR) and type the following:

pr,ca(air! & radio)

5.5 Date Restrictions

You can use Westlaw to retrieve documents *decided* or *issued* before, after, or on a specified date, as well as within a range of dates. The following sample queries contain date restrictions:

da(1998) & reporter news! journalist /s privilege

da(aft 1995) & sy,di("freedom of information act" f.o.i.a.)

da(9/26/1997) & shield /5 law statute legislation

You can also search for documents *added to a database* on or after a specified date, as well as within a range of dates. The following sample queries contain added-date restrictions:

ad(aft 1995) & wire-tap! (electronic /5 surveillance)

ad(aft 211998 & bef 2171998) & "electronic mail" e-mail

Section 6. Searching with Topic and Key Number

To retrieve cases that address a specific point of law, use topic and key numbers as your search terms. If you have an on-point case, run a search using the topic and key number from the relevant headnote in an appropriate database to find other cases containing headnotes classified to that topic and key number. For example, to search for federal cases containing headnotes classified under topic 372 (Telecommunications) and key number 461.10 (Radio paging), access the Federal Communica-tionsCases database (FCOMCS) and enter the following query:

372k461.10

For a complete list of West digest topic and key numbers, access the Key Number service: click the **Key Number Service** button or choose **Key Number Service** from the Services menu.

Note: Slip opinions, cases not reported by West and cases from topical services do not contain West topic and key numbers.

Section 7. Verifying Your Research with Citator Services

Overview: A citator service is a tool that helps you ensure that your cases are good law; helps you retrieve cases, legislation or articles that cite a case, rule or statute; and helps you verify that the spelling and format of your citations are correct.

For citations not covered by the citator services, including persuasive secondary authority such as restatements and treatises, use Westlaw as a citator to retrieve cases that cite your authority (see Section 7.3).

7.1   KeyCite

KeyCite is the citation research service from West Group that integrates all case law on Westlaw. KeyCite helps you trace the history of a case, retrieve a list of all cases and selected secondary sources that cite a case, and track legal issues decided in a case.

KeyCite provides both direct and negative indirect history for any case within the scope of its coverage. The History of the Case window displays a case's direct appellate history and its negative indirect history, which consists of cases outside the direct appellate line that may have a negative impact on its precedential value. The history also includes related references, which are opinions involving the same parties and facts but resolving different issues.

In addition to case history, the Citations to the Case window in KeyCite lists all cases on Westlaw and secondary sources, such as law review articles and ALR® annotations, that cite the decision. These citing references are added to KeyCite as soon as they are added to Westlaw. All citing cases on Westlaw are included in KeyCiteeven unpublished opinions.

For citation verification, the KeyCite result provides the case title; parallel citations, including many looseleaf citations; the court of decision; the docket number; and the filing date.

7.2   Shepard's Citations

For case law, Shepard's Citations provides a comprehensive list of cases and other documents that have cited a particular case. Shepard's also includes explanatory analyses to indicate how the citing cases have treated the case, e.g., "followed" or "explained."

For statutes and rules, Shepard's Citations provides a comprehensive list of cases citing a particular statute or rule, as well as information on subsequent legislative action.

7.3   Westlaw As a Citator

Using Westlaw as a citator, you can search for documents citing a specific statute, rule, regulation, agency decision or other authority. For example, to retrieve federal cases citing 47 U.S.C.A. 271(c)(1)(A), access the Federal CommunicationsCases database (FCOMCS) and type a query like the following:

47 /5 271(c)(1)(a)

Section 8.   Researching with WestlawExamples

8.1   Law Review Articles

Recent law review articles are often a good place to begin researching a legal issue because law review articles serve 1) as an excellent introduction to a new topic or review for a stale one, providing terminology to help you formulate a query; 2) as a finding tool for pertinent primary authority, such as rules, statutes and cases; and 3) in some instances, as persuasive secondary authority.

Suppose you need to gain more background information on liability for unauthorized Web page links.

Solution

- To retrieve recent law review articles relevant to your issue, access the CommunicationsLaw Reviews, Texts & Bar Journals database (COMTP). Using the Natural Language search method, enter a description like the following:

  liability for unauthorized web page links

- If you have a citation to an article in a specific publication, use Find to retrieve it. For more information on Find, see Section 3.1 of this appendix. For example, to retrieve the article found at 22 University of Dayton Law Review 547, access Find and type

  22 u dayton l rev 547

- If you know the title of an article but not which journal it appeared in, access the CommunicationsLaw Reviews, Texts & Bar Journals database (COMTP) and search for key terms from the title in the title field. For example, to retrieve the article "Withdrawal of the Reference: Rights, Rules, and Remedies for Unwelcomed WebLinking," type the following Terms and Connectors query:

  ti(remedies & unwelcomed & web-linking)

8.2   Statutes and Regulations

Suppose you need to retrieve federal statutes and any proposed, final or temporary regulations dealing specifically with direct broadcast satellite services.

Solution

- Access the Federal CommunicationsCode and Regulations database (FCOMCODREG). Search for your terms in the prelim and caption fields using the Terms and Connectors search method:

  pr,ca(direct & broadcast & satellite)

- When you know the citation for a specific section of a statute or regulation, use Find to retrieve it. For example, to retrieve 47 U.S.C.A. 335, access Find and type

  47 usca 335

- To look at surrounding statutory sections, use the Table of Contents service. Select a Jump marker in the prelim or caption field. You can also use Documents in Sequence to retrieve the section following 335, even if that following section was not retrieved with your search or Find request. Click the **Docs in Seq** button.

- When you retrieve a statute on Westlaw, it will contain an Update message if legislation amending or repealing it is available online. To display this legislation, select the Jump marker in the Update message.

Because slip copy versions of laws are added to Westlaw before they contain full editorial enhancements, they are not retrieved with Update. To retrieve slip copy versions of laws, access the United States Public Laws database (US-PL) or a states's legislative service database (XX-LEGIS, where XX is the state's two-letter postal abbreviation). Then type **ci(slip)** and descriptive terms, e.g., **ci(slip) & telecommunication.** Slip copy documents are replaced by the editorially enhanced versions within a few working days. Update also does not retrieve legislation that enacts a new statute or covers a topic that will not be incorporated into the statutes. To retrieve this legislation, access US-PL or a legislative service database and enter a query containing terms that describe the new legislation.

8.3 Case Law

Suppose you need to retrieve Pennsylvania case law dealing with the state shield law for journalists.

Solution

- Access the Pennsylvania Cases database (PACS). Type a Natural Language description such as the following:

protection under the journalist shield law

- When you know the citation for a specific case, use Find to retrieve it. (For more information on Find, see Section 3.1 of this appendix.) For example, to retrieve *Davis v. Glanten*, 705 A.2d 879 (Pa. Super. 1997), access Find and type

705 a2d 879

- If you find a topic and key number that is on point, run a search using that topic and key number to retrieve additional cases discussing that point of law. For example, to retrieve cases containing headnotes classified under topic 410 (Witnesses) and key number 196.1 (Journalists), type the following query:

410k196.1

- To retrieve cases written by a particular judge, add a judge field (ju) restriction to your query. For example, to retrieve cases written by Judge Beck that contain headnotes classified under topic 92 (Constitutional Law), type the following query:

ju(beck) & to(92)

8.4 Administrative Decisions

Suppose you need to retrieve any FCC decisions that discuss "trap and trace" devices or pen registers.

Solution

* Access the Federal CommunicationsFederal Communications Commission Decisions database (FCOMFCC). Type a Terms and Connectors query such as the following:

(trap /5 trace) "pen register"

8.5 Citator Services

Suppose one of the cases you retrieve in your case law research is *Infinity Broadcasting Corp. v. Kirkwood*, 965 F. Supp. 553 (S.D.N.Y. 1997). You want to determine whether this case is good law and to find other cases that have cited this case.

Solution

* Use KeyCite to retrieve direct history and negative indirect history for *Infinity Broadcasting Corp. v. Kirkwood*. While viewing the case, click the **KeyCite** button.

* To Shepardize® *Infinity Broadcasting Corp. v. Kirkwood*, click the **Shepard's** button

Table of Cases

C

D

N

Y

Z

*

Table of Statutes

NEW YORK, MCKINNEY'S CIVIL RIGHTS LAW

Sec.	This Work Sec.	Note
50	4.5	4
50	4.5	14
50	4.5	61
50	4.5	63
50	4.6	
50	4.8	7
51	4.3	17
51	4.5	
51	4.5	4
51	4.5	14
51	4.5	20
51	4.5	61
51	4.5	66
51	4.6	
51	4.8	7
79–h	7.5	4
79–h(a)(1)	7.5	16
79–h(a)(6)—(a)(7)	7.5	15
79–h(b)	7.5	29
79–h(b)	7.5	34
79–h(b)	7.11	21
79–h(b)	7.11	30
79–h(c)	7.5	43

NEW YORK, MCKINNEY'S PUBLIC SERVICE LAW

Sec.	This Work Sec.	Note
211—230	13.2	17
215—216	13.2	18

NEW YORK RULES OF COURT

Rule	This Work Sec.	Note
29.1	7.17	91

RULES OF THE CHIEF JUDGE

Rule	This Work Sec.	Note
29.1	8.6	39

RULES OF THE CHIEF ADMINISTRATOR

Rule	This Work Sec.	Note
131.13	7.17	1
131.13	8.6	49

NORTH CAROLINA SUPERIOR AND DISTRICT COURT RULES

Rule	This Work Sec.	Note
15	7.17	91
15	8.6	39

NORTH CAROLINA CODE OF JUDICIAL CONDUCT

Canon	This Work Sec.	Note
3A(7)	7.17	91
3A(7)	8.6	39

NORTH DAKOTA CENTURY CODE

Sec.	This Work Sec.	Note
31–01–06.2	7.5	4
31–01–06.2	7.5	29
31–01–06.2	7.5	57

LOCAL RULES OF THE U.S. DISTRICT COURT FOR THE DISTRICT OF NORTH DAKOTA

Rule	This Work Sec.	Note
21	7.17	91
21	8.6	39

OHIO REVISED CODE

Sec.	This Work Sec.	Note
2739.04	7.5	4
2739.04	7.5	17
2739.04	7.5	25
2739.04	7.5	64
2739.12	7.5	4
2739.12	7.5	25
2739.12	7.5	64
2917.13(B)	7.15	23

OHIO SUPREME COURT RULES

Rule	This Work Sec.	Note
15	7.17	91
15	8.6	39

OHIO COMMON PLEAS COURT RULES

Rule	This Work Sec.	Note
11	7.17	91
11	8.6	39

OHIO MUNICIPAL AND COUNTY COURT RULES

Rule	This Work Sec.	Note
9	7.17	91
9	8.6	39

OHIO CLAIMS COURT LOCAL RULES

Rule	This Work Sec.	Note
18	7.17	91

SOUTH DAKOTA CODIFIED LAWS

Sec.	This Work Sec.	Note
12–18–3	7.16	6

TENNESSEE CODE ANNOTATED

Sec.	This Work Sec.	Note
24–1–208	7.5	4
24–1–208(2)	7.5	39
24–1–208(a)	7.5	18
24–1–208(a)	7.5	29
24–1–208(b)	7.5	53
47–25–1101—47–25–1108	4.5	4
47–25–1101—47–25–1108	4.5	62
47–25–1101—47–25–1108	4.8	8
47–25–1103	4.5	64
47–25–1103	4.5	65
47–25–1103(b)	4.5	41
47–25–1105	4.5	67
47–25–1107	4.5	66

RULES OF THE SUPREME COURT OF TENNESSEE

Rule	This Work Sec.	Note
10	7.17	91
10	7.17	95
10	8.6	39

TENNESSEE CODE OF JUDICIAL CONDUCT

Canon	This Work Sec.	Note
3A(7)	7.17	91
3A(7)	8.6	39
3A(7)(A)(ii)	7.17	95

V.T.C.A., CIVIL PRACTICE AND REMEDIES CODE

Sec.	This Work Sec.	Note
96.001—96.004	5.9	22
96.003	5.9	29

V.T.C.A., PENAL CODE

Sec.	This Work Sec.	Note
42.09	1.5	64

TEXAS RULES OF CIVIL PROCEDURE

Rule	This Work Sec.	Note
18c	7.17	95

TEXAS RULES OF APPELLATE PROCEDURE

Rule	This Work Sec.	Note
21	7.17	95

LOCAL RULES OF UNITED STATES DISTRICT COURT FOR THE WESTERN DISTRICT OF TEXAS

Rule	This Work Sec.	Note
500–2	8.6	10

UTAH CODE ANNOTATED

Sec.	This Work Sec.	Note
45–3–1—45–3–6	4.5	4
45–3–1—45–3–6	4.5	62

VERMONT STATUTES ANNOTATED

Tit.	This Work Sec.	Note
30, §§ 501—508	13.2	16

VERMONT RULES OF CIVIL PROCEDURE

Rule	This Work Sec.	Note
79.2	7.17	91
79.2	8.6	39

VERMONT RULES OF CRIMINAL PROCEDURE

Rule	This Work Sec.	Note
53	7.17	91
53	8.6	39

VERMONT RULES OF APPELLATE PROCEDURE

Rule	This Work Sec.	Note
35	7.17	91
35	8.6	39

VERMONT RULES OF PROBATE PROCEDURE

Rule	This Work Sec.	Note
79.2	7.17	91
79.2	8.6	39

LOCAL RULES FOR THE DISTRICT OF VERMONT

Rule	This Work Sec.	Note
79.2	7.17	91

*

INDEX